Processes of Constitutional Decisionmaking

ASPEN CASEBOOK SERIES

Processes of Constitutional Decisionmaking

Cases and Materials

Eighth Edition

Sanford Levinson
W. St. John Garwood & W. St. John Garwood, Jr.
Centennial Chair in Law
University of Texas Law School

Jack M. Balkin
Knight Professor of Constitutional Law
and the First Amendment
Yale Law School

Akhil Reed Amar
Sterling Professor of Law and Political Science
Yale Law School

Reva B. Siegel
Nicholas deB. Katzenbach Professor of Law
Yale Law School

Cristina M. Rodríguez
Leighton Homer Surbeck Professor of Law
Yale Law School

ASPEN
PUBLISHING

To contact Customer Service, e-mail customer.service@aspenpublishing.com, call 1-800-950-5259, or mail correspondence to:

Aspen Publishing
Attn: Order Department
PO Box 990
Frederick, MD 21705

Printed in the United States of America.

1 2 3 4 5 6 7 8 9 0

ISBN 978-1-5438-3855-8

Library of Congress Cataloging-in-Publication Data

Library of Congress Cataloging-in-Publication Data application is in process.

About Aspen Publishing

Aspen Publishing is a leading provider of educational content and digital learning solutions to law schools in the U.S. and around the world. Aspen provides best-in-class solutions for legal education through authoritative textbooks, written by renowned authors, and breakthrough products such as Connected eBooks, Connected Quizzing, and PracticePerfect.

The Aspen Casebook Series (famously known among law faculty and students as the "red and black" casebooks) encompasses hundreds of highly regarded textbooks in more than eighty disciplines, from large enrollment courses, such as Torts and Contracts to emerging electives such as Sustainability and the Law of Policing. Study aids such as the *Examples & Explanations* and *Glannon Guide* series, both highly popular collections, help law students master complex subject matter.

Major products, programs, and initiatives include:

- **Connected eBooks** are enhanced digital textbooks and study aids that come with a suite of online content and learning tools designed to maximize student success. Designed in collaboration with hundreds of faculty and students, the Connected eBook is a significant leap forward in the legal education learning tools available to students.

- **Connected Quizzing** is an easy-to-use formative assessment tool that tests law students' understanding and provides timely feedback to improve learning outcomes. Delivered through CasebookConnect.com, the learning platform already used by students to access their Aspen casebooks, Connected Quizzing is simple to implement and integrates seamlessly with law school course curricula.

- **PracticePerfect** is a visually engaging, interactive study aid to explain commonly encountered legal doctrines through easy-to-understand animated videos, illustrative examples, and numerous practice questions. Developed by a team of experts, PracticePerfect is the ideal study companion for today's law students.

- The **Aspen Learning Library** enables law schools to provide their students with access to the most popular study aids on the market across all of their courses. Available through an annual subscription, the online library consists of study aids in e-book, audio, and video formats with full text search, note-taking, and highlighting capabilities.

- Aspen's **Digital Bookshelf** is an institutional-level online education bookshelf, consolidating everything students and professors need to ensure success. This program ensures that every student has access to affordable course materials from day one.

- **Leading Edge** is a community centered on thinking differently about legal education and putting those thoughts into actionable strategies. At the core of the program is the Leading Edge Conference, an annual gathering of legal education thought leaders looking to pool ideas and identify promising directions of exploration.

To the memory of Robert McCloskey, a beloved teacher and mentor; to Paul Brest, a valued friend whose invitation to collaborate with him on the second edition of this casebook substantially shaped my future intellectual development; and to the University of Texas Law School, which for a full forty years has been remarkably nurturing in every way—S.L.

To the memory of my parents, Bernard and Bettye Balkin, who gave me their love and an education in the law—J.B.

To my students for their inspiration and to my family—Vinita and Vikram, mom and dad, mummy and poppa, brothers and sisters— for their sustenance—A.R.A.

To Yale, my nephew and my students, in the belief that possibility lives in memory—R.S.

To my teachers and my students—C.M.R.

Summary of Contents

Every casebook involves the construction of a canon—a set of materials and approaches that the editors believe that every student who wishes to master the subject should know. This casebook is no exception. Indeed, we have been particularly conscious of the existing canons of constitutional thought and the kinds of choices that are involved both in the materials presented and in their editing, order, and arrangement. The history of this casebook has been a series of continuing attempts to rethink the existing canon of constitutional law and present a better one. This edition represents our latest views on the subject.

The history of this casebook

The first edition of Processes of Constitutional Decisionmaking, created by Paul Brest, and published in 1975, was born out of personal frustration with the existing methods of teaching constitutional law. Invariably beginning with Marbury v. Madison and related doctrines of judicial review, most casebooks proceeded to examine bodies of substantive doctrine, subject by subject, without much attention to political or historical context. The question of *how* the courts arrived at their decisions continually arose but was not systematically examined. Nor did casebooks explore the role that legislatures, the executive, and other political institutions (for example, political parties and social movements) played in constitutional decisionmaking. The unspoken and repeated message was that the Constitution was largely what the Supreme Court said it was, and if the Supreme Court had not spoken on a particular subject, there was no constitutional law on the question at all.

The first edition, therefore, focused on the methods of constitutional interpretation and decisionmaking that different actors in the system employed and on the processes through which constitutional doctrine was created. Although much has changed in the book's coverage over the years, this basic focus on methods of constitutional interpretation and on the multiple groups and institutions that participate in the creation of constitutional meaning has remained a constant.

The second edition, published in 1983, reflected the lessons learned from teaching the first edition as well as the interests of its new co-editor, Sanford Levinson. As before, the casebook continued its focus on the processes of constitutional change and the role of constitutional interpretations made by nonjudicial actors. However, beginning with the second edition, the book's emphasis became historical. The opening half of the book was (and continues to be) explicitly organized on historical-chronological lines, so that students would confront the legal consciousness of a particular period in the context of multiple constitutional doctrines. Brest retired from active participation in the casebook after the third edition, published in 1992, but the editors have tried to continue his innovative spirit. The fourth edition, published in 2000, consolidated the basic approach of the second and third editions, and added two new authors, Jack Balkin and Akhil Amar.

Reva Siegel joined the casebook for the fifth edition in 2006, and Cristina Rodríguez joined for the present edition.

The organization of the casebook

In this, the eighth edition, we have continued to benefit from classroom experience and from new historical and political science scholarship. Part One of the Casebook, which takes us up to the beginning of the New Deal, is organized chronologically by period. Our primary concern is not the identity of the Chief Justice at a particular point in time (Marshall or Taney) but the succession of *constitutional regimes* in which constitutional law develops. Examples include the early republic of the Federalist (1789-1800) and Jeffersonian (1800-1828) regimes, the Jacksonian regime that leads to the Civil War, and the long regime dominated by the Republican Party that extends from Reconstruction to the New Deal. These chapters examine recurring issues of federalism, property rights, race and sex equality, governmental (and, more particularly, presidential) authority in time of war, and judicial review.

The materials within each of these historical chapters cover different subjects and doctrines but together reflect the constitutional arrangements and political realities that underlie most of the important constitutional questions in a given era. Thus, for example, arguments about state sovereignty and slavery structure much of the jurisprudence of the Jacksonian regime; and we think it is impossible to understand the *Lochner* era's substantive due process decisions apart from its decisions about the commerce power or the taxing and spending powers. Nor can one understand the nineteenth century's treatment of women's rights apart from its understandings about race, or either apart from that era's understanding of federalism and national power.

Part One of the book ends on the brink of the New Deal, which marks the boundary that inaugurates the "modern" period in American constitutional law, as described in the introduction to Part Two.

Chapter 5 continues the casebook's historical periodization, covering questions of government power during the New Deal and Civil Rights regime that lasts roughly from 1934 to 1980. This period, although "modern" in the sense of having very different assumptions than those prevalent in the eighteenth and nineteenth centuries, is no longer "contemporary." The constitutional struggle over the New Deal happened almost 80 years ago. The innovations of the Warren Court, the Civil Rights movement, and the second wave of American feminism in the 1970s seem increasingly distant to most law students; they have become historical artifacts, much like the struggle over the New Deal seemed to the generation that came of age in the 1960s and 1970s. The legal consciousness that underlies much of the Supreme Court's work during this period has slowly given way to new conceptions of federal power, race relations, and civil liberties. The rise of conservative social movements in the 1970s and 1980s, and the dominance of the Republican Party that they helped engender, have had multiple effects in constitutional law.

Ronald Reagan's election in 1980 began a second Republican regime, dominated by conservative social movements, and a correspondingly conservative constitutional jurisprudence, a regime that we are still living in today. This regime has defined our contemporary constitutional world. Whether we are slowly transitioning into a new constitutional regime with a different set of constitutional assumptions will only be known many years after this edition is published.

Chapters 6 through 10 are organized doctrinally. Chapter 6 features sections on contemporary economic regulation, the commerce, taxing, and spending powers, Congressional power under the Civil War amendments, federalism, and separation of powers. It also includes expanded coverage of war and executive power. Chapter 7 covers racial equality and the constitutional treatment of alienage, while Chapter 8 covers sex equality. Chapter 9, entitled, "Liberty, Equality, and Fundamental Rights: The Constitution, the Family, and the Body," covers rights of liberty and equality that concern sexual autonomy, marriage and family formation, intimate association, bodily integrity, and self-defense. Most but not all of these rights are protected by the Fourteenth Amendment and by the Fifth Amendment's Due Process Clause. The chapter also includes a section on constitutional struggles over gun rights and the interpretation of the Second Amendment.

Chapter 10, entitled "The Constitution in the Welfare State," covers affirmative liberties (like education and the rights of the poor), procedural due process, and the problem of conditional subsidies, sometimes called the problem of "unconstitutional conditions." Chapter 10 is organized in this way because we think that it is important for students to understand the welfare state as a central constitutional structure of our era.

Throughout the doctrinal coverage of Chapters 6 through 10 we have structured the casebook with an eye to placing contemporary events in their historical perspective, continually asking the student to compare them to constitutional transformations and upheavals of the past. The doctrinal discussions of race, gender, sexual autonomy, sexual orientation, and gun rights have been thoroughly updated and revised to show how constitutional change occurred in the context of social mobilizations and counter-mobilizations and other aspects of political struggle and contestation. This basic strategy, we hope, will help students to take the longer view of the ebb and flow of American constitutional culture, and to reflect on the key role that social movements and political parties play in shaping that culture.

Our historical approach

We have worked to make the present edition compatible with many different ways of organizing a basic course in constitutional law; nevertheless we retain a strong commitment to a historical approach. As noted above, even in materials that are doctrinally organized, we have tried to highlight the social and political context in which constitutional decisionmaking occurs. A historical approach, we believe, has virtues that are lost in a purely clause-bound approach to constitutional law.

In particular, we think it is important for students to recognize that notions of what constitutes a good or persuasive constitutional argument have changed and will continue to change over time. Arguments that might have seemed perfectly reasonable for well-trained lawyers in one period can seem bizarre or "off-the-wall" in earlier or later periods. Arguments that seem to have been written off for good (like the compact theory of state sovereignty) uncannily reemerge in new guises a century later. Visionary claims of social movements that would be rejected by all right-thinking lawyers of the period become the accepted orthodoxy of later eras. The ideological valence of arguments—as "liberal" or "conservative," moderate or radical—also drifts as arguments are introduced or repeated in new social and legal contexts. Finally, the popularity and persuasiveness of different styles of constitutional argument—for example, textualism or originalism—wax and wane with historical and social change and with concomitant changes in the legal profession.

There is, in short, no transhistorical criterion for "thinking like a constitutional lawyer," other than an abiding faith in the basic constitutional enterprise. There is no better way to demonstrate this, we think, than to let students confront the actual texts produced in different periods and study closely the "common sense" and authoritative legal arguments of the past, witnessing both their strangeness and their resemblance to the constitutional common sense of our own day.

One of the reasons why constitutional argument changes as it does is that the practice of constitutional reasoning is deeply connected to changes in political and social life. Although courts play a central role in the history of constitutional law, other parties play roles equally important in shaping constitutional meaning. Our understandings of the American Constitution would have been very different without Jacksonianism, abolitionism, the Civil War, the feminist movement, the New Deal, the Civil Rights movement, the Religious Right, and other conservative political movements of the modern period. For this reason, we have included not only constitutional arguments from the executive and legislative branches of government, but also constitutional interpretations offered by representatives of important social movements in the country's history, as well as by members of the groups that mobilized against them. And we have repeatedly tried to stress the connections between what occurs in the language of court opinions and the political and social events that surround those decisions.

Finally, we continue to emphasize a historical approach to understand our debt to the past, and to reckon with both our moral successes and our moral failures. From the second edition on, Processes of Constitutional Decisionmaking has contained far more sustained coverage of chattel slavery than any other casebook. We think that, as a doctrinal matter, the question of slavery haunts the whole of antebellum constitutional law and that the legacy of slavery affects the great issues of federalism and equality that came later. But we think it is equally important for law students to confront slavery precisely because everyone now recognizes it to have been a great evil. It was a great evil that was sustained and perpetuated through law and, in particular, through constitutional law as interpreted by the finest legal minds America had to offer. Law students must come to understand how well-trained lawyers acting in good faith could have participated in such a system and rationalized it according to well-accepted modes of legal argument, justifying their work in the name of America's great charter of democracy, liberty, and equality. We think that if they can recognize this use of law in America's constitutional past, they will be better equipped to ask themselves the much more difficult question of whether well-trained lawyers in our own era could be similarly engaged in the rationalization of great injustices in the name of our Constitution, even though there may be great disagreement about what these are. The goal of a historically informed approach is not merely to see the achievements and injustices of the past through our own eyes, but to remind us to consider how our present interpretations of the Constitution might look to future generations.

Constructing the constitutional canon

Our commitment to a historical approach is joined to an equally strong commitment to rethinking the canons of constitutional law—the materials, issues, and problems that law students are exposed to and that law professors write and theorize about. To this end, we have added materials on the Progressive Era amendments, the constitutional controversy surrounding the adoption of paper money, the procedural irregularities surrounding the adoption of the Fourteenth Amendment, America's constitutional treatment of Native Americans, and America's role as a colonial power. We have expanded coverage of the history of the women's movement and the constitutional treatment of women from the antebellum era to the adoption of the Nineteenth Amendment to the struggles over the Equal Rights Amendment and beyond. We think that these additions will give students a richer and fuller vision of constitutional history. They also pose genuine and interesting challenges for constitutional theorists who have neglected important aspects of constitutional interpretation and constitutional decisionmaking because traditional approaches offer much too narrow a view of the relevant materials that must be explained and justified.

If there is one theme that runs through this book, it is that the Supreme Court is not the only interpreter of the Constitution, even if it is surely the most obvious and important one for most lawyers. This view is clearly reflected in our construction of the canon. Throughout the book, we take seriously constitutional decisionmaking by nonjudicial institutions by including materials ranging from resolutions by the Kentucky and Virginia legislatures in the late eighteenth century, to constitutional interpretations by the President and Congress of the United States, to constitutional assertions by social movements, such as the Seneca Falls Declaration of 1848, to constitutional arguments by particular individuals such as senatorial candidates Abraham Lincoln and Stephen Douglas, the noted abolitionist Frederick Douglass, and civil rights pioneer Pauli Murray. Indeed, far from being the only source of constitutional law, the Supreme Court is not even the only judicial source. In this edition we have included more constitutional arguments by lower federal courts, by state supreme courts (often interpreting analogous provisions of state constitutions), and even a few references to the constitutions of other countries.

Among the most important elements of the Constitution are structural features that are rarely litigated, including, among others, bicameralism, equal voting power in the Senate, and the presidential veto. Lawyers pay little attention to them because they are rarely litigated and so little judicial doctrine has developed around them. Nevertheless, these choices are crucial features of constitutional design and the political science literature that studies their consequences is considerable. We have tried to raise a few issues of constitutional design where appropriate, but given the natural focus of a law school casebook, we can do no more than hint at some of the more important questions these provisions raise.

Just as any construction of a constitutional canon involves incorporation and inclusion of some materials, it must also include selection and exclusion of others. As constitutional law has grown in richness and complexity over the years, it has become increasingly difficult to do justice to the field within the pages of a single casebook. Fortunately, new technologies increasingly allow us to escape the limitations of traditional forms of publication. We now offer an appendix of additional materials for several of the chapters, which are noted in the table of contents. These materials, as well as a full e-book version of the casebook, are available at casebookconnect.com. Through this combination of website and traditional text, we hope to create a flexible set of teaching materials that can better respond to future changes in the field.

The organization of any casebook is inevitably ideological, especially in a subject as fraught with ideology as constitutional law. No approach to the study of constitutional law is independent of the instructors' or casebook editors' more general intellectual and political interests. For example, we have already noted the amount of space devoted to the question of slavery, which reflects our view that the question of slavery pervaded American law before the Civil War and that its aftermath set the stage for epic social and constitutional struggles that show no signs of abating to this day. We have also emphasized the role of textual and structural argument in constitutional interpretation, as well as the centrality of social movements and political parties as engines of constitutional change.

The first edition of Processes of Constitutional Decisionmaking explicitly adopted the ideology of the legal process tradition identified with Albert Sacks and Henry Hart, who were especially influential teachers at the Harvard Law School following World War II (and with whom Paul Brest studied during the early 1960s). Hart and Sacks argued that there existed apolitical decisionmaking procedures, adherence to which could provide substantively acceptable and politically legitimate decisions. Although the validity of this hypothesis remains a central concern of this book—for it is a crucial matter about which every student must come to his or her own judgment—the second edition (and its successors) manifested considerable skepticism about the legitimating power of process divorced from larger substantive political values. Nothing that has happened since 1981, when the second edition was prepared, has lessened our skepticism.

The Constitution does not belong to the lawyers, to the politicians, or even to the judges. It belongs to everyone. And the Constitution matters and should matter to everyone, even if arguments about the Constitution are not always phrased in the proper constitutional grammar recognized by legal professionals. Our era, like those before it, is a time of vigorous debate about the central constitutional issues of American life. In this book we have tried to bring out the political and social assumptions of contemporary constitutional discourse and contemporary constitutional decisionmaking. We have tried to show where these assumptions originated and how they have been transformed through time. But, of course, for every assumption that is consciously illuminated, others remain hidden in the shadows. You will get the most out of a course taught from this casebook if you take its agendas seriously while keeping a sharp eye out for its unstated assumptions. For our part, the student we seek is not one who necessarily agrees with us, but one who is willing to engage critically with us and, in the process, to learn and grow.

Acknowledgments

As the Dedication indicates, Sanford Levinson's primary acknowledgments go to Paul Brest and to his university of Texas Law School colleagues over the last four decades. Special mention must be made of unusually supportive deans, including Mark Yudof, the late Michael Sharlot and Bill Powers, Larry Sager, and Ward Farnsworth. It "takes a village" to construct a casebook, including excellent secretaries. Most recently, that has been Trish Do, whose aid in organizing a number of conferences on topics directly relevant to the casebook has been indispensable. Three other persons in this national "village" must also be mentioned: MarkTushnet, many years ago, organized the first "Georgetown schmoozes," a marvelous venue for trying out ideas and listening to what other people are thinking about. Mark Graber picked up the reins from Tushnet, and the "Maryland schmooze" has been equally important over the past twenty-five years or so. (Time flies.) A "Madison schmooze" organized by David Schwartz and Heinz Klug has also become invaluable. Kudos to everyone.

Jack Balkin wishes to thank Bruce Ackerman, Lisa Cardyn, Michael Kavey, Christina Rodríguez, Bill Rubenstein, Teemu Ruskola, Reva Siegel, and Kenji Yoshino for their help and suggestions.

Akhil Amar wishes to thank Bruce Ackerman, Vikram David Amar, Neal Kumar Katyal, and Jed Rubenfeld for their comments and Lisa Berman and Josh Chafetz for their research assistance.

Reva Siegel wishes to thank Jack Balkin, Tessa Bialek, Marisa Doran, Linda Evarts, Cary Franklin, Abigail Horn, Serena Mayeri, Doug NeJaime, Robert Post, Alan Schoenfeld, David Tannenbaum, Ryan Thoreson, Kenji Yoshino, and Nels Ylitello for their help and suggestions.

All of the authors have also benefited from the responses of a number of friends at other institutions. They include, especially, Milner Ball (who pressed the claims of Native Americans to be treated as an important part of the American constitutional narrative), Walter Dellinger (who initially suggested including material from the Lincoln-Douglas debates), Paul Finkelman, Lewis LaRue, Peter Linzer, Doug Ne Jaime, Robert Post, Stephen Siegel, and Kenji Yoshino.

Balkin, J.M., Tradition, Betrayal, and the Politics of Deconstruction. This article appeared in 11 Cardozo L. Rev. 1613 (July/Aug. 1990). Reprinted by permission of the author and Cardozo Law Review.

Balkin, J.M. and Reva B. Siegel, The American Civil Rights Tradition: Anticlassification or Antisubordination?, 58 U. Miami L. Rev. 9, 11-12, 11-14 (2003). Reprinted by permission of the authors.

Black, Charles, The Lawfulness of the Segregation Decisions, 69 Yale L.J. 421 (1960). Copyright © 1959. Reprinted by permission of the Yale Law Journal Company and Fred B. Rothman and Co.

Cross, Frank, The Error of Positive Rights, 48 UCLA L. Rev. 857 (2001). Copyright © 2001 Frank Cross.

Kelly, Alfred, The School Desegregation Case, in Quarrels That Have Shaped the Constitution (John A. Garraty ed.). Copyright © 1987 by Harper & Row, Publishers, Inc. Reprinted by permission of HarperCollins Publishers.

Krieger, Linda, The Content of Our Categories: A Cognitive Bias Approach to Discrimination and Equal Employment Opportunity, 47 Stan. L. Rev. 1161 (1995). Reprinted by permission.

Lawrence, Charles R., III, The Id, the Ego, and Equal Protection: Reckoning with Unconscious Racism, 39 Stan. L. Rev. 317 (1987). Copyright © 1987 by the Board of Trustees of the Leland Stanford Junior University. Reprinted by permission of the Stanford Law Review and Fred B. Rothman and Co.

Levinson, Sanford, The 21st Century Rediscovery of Nullification and Secession in American Political Rhetoric: Frivolousness Incarnate or Serious Arguments to Be Wrestled With?, 67 Ark. L. Rev. 17 (2014), reprinted with revisions in Levinson, ed., Nullification and Secession in Modern Constitutional Thought. Copyright © 2014 by Sanford Levinson.

Michelman, Frank, On Protecting the Poor Through the Fourteenth Amendment, 83 Harv. L. Rev. 7 (1969). Copyright © 1969 Harvard Law Review Association.

Pildes, Richard H., Democracy, Anti-Democracy, and the Canon, 17 Const. Comment. 295, 299-304 (2000). Reprinted by permission of Constitutional Commentary and the author.

Schmidt, Jr., Benno C., Principle and Prejudice: The Supreme Court and Race in the Progressive Era, Part 2: The Peonage Cases, 82 Colum. L. Rev. 646, 699, 705-713 (1982). Reprinted by permission.

Siegel, Reva, Why Equal Protection No Longer Protects: The Evolving Forms of Status- Enforcing State Action, 49 Stan. L. Rev. 111 (1997). Reprinted by permission.

Siegel, Reva, She the People: The Nineteenth Amendment, Sex Equality, Federalism, and the Family, 115 Harv. L. Rev. 947 (2002). Copyright © 2002 Harvard Law Review Association.

Siegel, Reva, Reasoning from the Body: A Historical Perspective on Abortion Regulation and Questions of Equal Protection, 44 Stan. L. Rev. 261 (1992). Reprinted by permission.

Wofford, John, The Blinding Light: The Uses of History in Constitutional Interpretation, 31 U. Chi. L. Rev. 502 (1964). Copyright © 1964 The University of Chicago Law School.

Woodward, C. Vann, The Strange Career of Jim Crow (3d rev. ed. 1974). Copyright © 1974 Oxford University Press.

Editorial Note

Throughout this book, additions to and deletions from quoted material are indicated by brackets and ellipses except that (without notice) citations are modified and eliminated, footnotes are eliminated, and paragraphs are modified to make edited excerpts coherent. Footnote numbers in opinions and other quoted material have been changed to consecutive letters. The authors' own footnotes, including those inserted into quoted material and cases for purposes of editorial comment, are indicated by numbers, running consecutively through each chapter.

THE CONSTITUTION OF THE UNITED STATES

We the People of the United States, in Order to form a more perfect Union, establish Justice, insure domestic Tranquility, provide for the common defense, promote the general Welfare, and secure the Blessings of Liberty to ourselves and our Posterity, do ordain and establish this Constitution for the United States of America.

ARTICLE I

Section 1. All legislative Powers herein granted shall be vested in a Congress of the United States, which shall consist of a Senate and House of Representatives.

Section 2. [1] The House of Representatives shall be composed of Members chosen every second Year by the People of the several States, and the Electors in each State shall have the Qualifications requisite for Electors of the most numerous Branch of the State Legislature.

[2] No Person shall be a Representative who shall not have attained to the Age of twenty five Years, and been seven Years a Citizen of the United States, and who shall not, when elected, be an Inhabitant of that State in which he shall be chosen.

[3] Representatives and direct Taxes shall be apportioned among the several States which may be included within this Union, according to their respective Numbers, which shall be determined by adding to the whole Number of free Persons, including those bound to Service for a Term of Years, and excluding Indians not taxed, three fifths of all other Persons.[1] The actual Enumeration shall be made within three Years after the first Meeting of the Congress of the United States, and within every subsequent Term of ten Years, in such Manner as they shall by Law direct. The Number of Representatives shall not exceed one for every thirty Thousand, but each State shall have at Least one Representative; and until such enumeration shall be made, the State of New Hampshire shall be entitled to chuse three, Massachusetts eight, Rhode-Island and Providence Plantations one, Connecticut five, New-York six, New Jersey four, Pennsylvania eight, Delaware one, Maryland six, Virginia ten, North Carolina five, South Carolina five, and Georgia three.

[4] When vacancies happen in the Representation from any State, the Executive Authority thereof shall issue Writs of Election to fill such Vacancies.

[5] The House of Representatives shall chuse their Speaker and other Officers; and shall have the sole Power of Impeachment.

1. Changed by section 2 of the Fourteenth Amendment.

Section 3. [1] The Senate of the United States shall be composed of two Senators from each State, chosen by the Legislature thereof,[2] for six Years; and each Senator shall have one Vote.

[2] Immediately after they shall be assembled in Consequence of the first Election, they shall be divided as equally as may be into three Classes. The Seats of the Senators of the first Class shall be vacated at the Expiration of the second Year, of the second Class at the Expiration of the fourth Year, and of the third Class at the Expiration of the sixth Year, so that one third may be chosen every second Year; and if Vacancies happen by Resignation, or otherwise, during the Recess of the Legislature of any State, the Executive thereof may make temporary Appointments until the next Meeting of the Legislature, which shall then fill such Vacancies.[3]

[3] No Person shall be a Senator who shall not have attained to the Age of thirty Years, and been nine Years a Citizen of the United States, and who shall not, when elected, be an Inhabitant of that State for which he shall be chosen.

[4] The Vice President of the United States shall be President of the Senate, but shall have no Vote, unless they be equally divided.

[5] The Senate shall chuse their other Officers, and also a President pro tempore, in the Absence of the Vice President, or when he shall exercise the Office of President of the United States.

[6] The Senate shall have the sole Power to try all Impeachments. When sitting for that Purpose, they shall be on Oath or Affirmation. When the President of the United States is tried, the Chief Justice shall preside: And no Person shall be convicted without the Concurrence of two thirds of the Members present.

[7] Judgment in Cases of Impeachment shall not extend further than to removal from Office, and disqualification to hold and enjoy any Office of honor, Trust or Profit under the United States: but the Party convicted shall nevertheless be liable and subject to Indictment, Trial, Judgment and Punishment, according to Law.

Section 4. [1] The Times, Places and Manner of holding Elections for Senators and Representatives, shall be prescribed in each State by the Legislature thereof; but the Congress may at any time by Law make or alter such Regulations, except as to the Places of chusing Senators.

[2] The Congress shall assemble at least once in every Year, and such Meeting shall be on the first Monday in December, unless they shall by Law appoint a different Day.[4]

Section 5. [1] Each House shall be the Judge of the Elections, Returns and Qualifications of its own Members, and a Majority of each shall constitute a Quorum to do Business; but a smaller Number may adjourn from day to day, and may be authorized to compel the Attendance of absent Members, in such Manner, and under such Penalties as each House may provide.

[2] Each House may determine the Rules of its Proceedings, punish its Members for disorderly Behaviour, and, with the Concurrence of two thirds, expel a Member.

---

2. Changed by section 2 of the Seventeenth Amendment.
3. Changed by clause 2 of the Seventeenth Amendment.
4. Changed by section 2 of the Twentieth Amendment.

[3] Each House shall keep a Journal of its Proceedings, and from time to time publish the same, excepting such Parts as may in their Judgment require Secrecy; and the Yeas and Nays of the Members of either House on any question shall, at the Desire of one fifth of those Present, be entered on the Journal.

[4] Neither House, during the Session of Congress, shall, without the Consent of the other, adjourn for more than three days, nor to any other Place than that in which the two Houses shall be sitting.

Section 6. [1] The Senators and Representatives shall receive a Compensation for their Services, to be ascertained by Law, and paid out of the Treasury of the United States. They shall in all Cases, except Treason, Felony and Breach of the Peace, be privileged from Arrest during their Attendance at the Session of their respective Houses, and in going to and returning from the same; and for any Speech or Debate in either House, they shall not be questioned in any other Place.

[2] No Senator or Representative shall, during the Time for which he was elected, be appointed to any civil Office under the Authority of the United States, which shall have been created, or the Emoluments whereof shall have been increased during such time; and no Person holding any Office under the United States, shall be a Member of either House during his Continuance in Office.

Section 7. [1] All Bills for raising Revenue shall originate in the House of Representatives; but the Senate may propose or concur with Amendments as on other Bills.

[2] Every Bill which shall have passed the House of Representatives and the Senate, shall, before it become a Law, be presented to the President of the United States: If he approve he shall sign it, but if not he shall return it, with his Objections to that House in which it shall have originated, who shall enter the Objections at large on their Journal, and proceed to reconsider it. If after such Reconsideration two thirds of that House shall agree to pass the Bill, it shall be sent, together with the Objections, to the other House, by which it shall likewise be reconsidered, and if approved by two thirds of that House, it shall become a Law. But in all such Cases the Votes of both Houses shall be determined by Yeas and Nays, and the Names of the Persons voting for and against the Bill shall be entered on the Journal of each House respectively. If any Bill shall not be returned by the President within ten Days (Sundays excepted) after it shall have been presented to him, the Same shall be a Law, in like Manner as if he had signed it, unless the Congress by their Adjournment prevent its Return, in which Case it shall not be a Law.

[3] Every Order, Resolution, or Vote to which the Concurrence of the Senate and House of Representatives may be necessary (except on a question of Adjournment) shall be presented to the President of the United States; and before the Same shall take Effect, shall be approved by him, or being disapproved by him, shall be repassed by two thirds of the Senate and House of Representatives, according to the Rules and Limitations prescribed in the Case of a Bill.

Section 8. [1] The Congress shall have Power To lay and collect Taxes, Duties, Imposts and Excises, to pay the Debts and provide for the common Defence and general Welfare of the United States; but all Duties, Imposts and Excises shall be uniform throughout the United States;

[2] To borrow Money on the credit of the United States;

[3] To regulate Commerce with foreign Nations, and among the several States, and with the Indian Tribes;

[4] To establish an uniform Rule of Naturalization, and uniform Laws on the subject of Bankruptcies throughout the United States;

[5] To coin Money, regulate the Value thereof, and of foreign Coin, and fix the Standard of Weights and Measures;

[6] To provide for the Punishment of counterfeiting the Securities and current Coin of the United States;

[7] To establish Post Offices and post Roads;

[8] To promote the Progress of Science and useful Arts, by securing for limited Times to Authors and Inventors the exclusive Right to their respective Writings and Discoveries;

[9] To constitute Tribunals inferior to the supreme Court;

[10] To define and punish Piracies and Felonies committed on the high Seas, and Offences against the Law of Nations;

[11] To declare War, grant Letters of Marque and Reprisal, and make Rules concerning Captures on Land and Water;

[12] To raise and support Armies, but no Appropriation of Money to that Use shall be for a longer Term than two Years;

[13] To provide and maintain a Navy;

[14] To make Rules for the Government and Regulation of the land and naval Forces;

[15] To provide for calling forth the Militia to execute the Laws of the Union, suppress Insurrections and repel Invasions;

[16] To provide for organizing, arming, and disciplining, the Militia, and for governing such Part of them as may be employed in the Service of the United States, reserving to the States respectively, the Appointment of the Officers, and the Authority of training the Militia according to the discipline prescribed by Congress;

[17] To exercise exclusive Legislation in all Cases whatsoever, over such District (not exceeding ten Miles square) as may, by Cession of particular States, and the Acceptance of Congress, become the Seat of the Government of the United States, and to exercise like Authority over all Places purchased by the Consent of the Legislature of the State in which the Same shall be, for the Erection of Forts, Magazines, Arsenals, dock-Yards, and other needful Buildings;—And

[18] To make all Laws which shall be necessary and proper for carrying into Execution the foregoing Powers, and all other Powers vested by this Constitution in the Government of the United States, or in any Department or Officer thereof.

Section 9. [1] The Migration or Importation of such Persons as any of the States now existing shall think proper to admit, shall not be prohibited by the Congress prior to the Year one thousand eight hundred and eight, but a Tax or duty may be imposed on such Importation, not exceeding ten dollars for each Person.

[2] The Privilege of the Writ of Habeas Corpus shall not be suspended, unless when in Cases of Rebellion or Invasion the public Safety may require it.

[3] No Bill of Attainder or ex post facto Law shall be passed.

[4] No Capitation, or other direct, Tax shall be laid, unless in Proportion to the Census or enumeration herein before directed to be taken.[5]

[5] No Tax or Duty shall be laid on Articles exported from any State.

5. But see the Sixteenth Amendment.

[6] No Preference shall be given by any Regulation of Commerce or Revenue to the Ports of one State over those of another; nor shall Vessels bound to, or from, one State, be obliged to enter, clear, or pay Duties in another.

[7] No Money shall be drawn from the Treasury, but in Consequence of Appropriations made by Law; and a regular Statement and Account of the Receipts and Expenditures of all public Money shall be published from time to time.

[8] No Title of Nobility shall be granted by the United States: And no Person holding any Office of Profit or Trust under them, shall, without the Consent of the Congress, accept of any present, Emolument, Office, or Title, of any kind whatever, from any King, Prince, or foreign State.

Section 10. [1] No State shall enter into any Treaty, Alliance, or Confederation; grant Letters of Marque and Reprisal; coin Money; emit Bills of Credit; make any Thing but gold and silver Coin a Tender in Payment of Debts; pass any Bill of Attainder, ex post facto Law, or Law impairing the Obligation of Contracts, or grant any Title of Nobility.

[2] No State shall, without the Consent of the Congress, lay any Imposts or Duties on Imports or Exports, except what may be absolutely necessary for executing it's inspection Laws: and the net Produce of all Duties and Imposts, laid by any State on Imports or Exports, shall be for the Use of the Treasury of the United States; and all such Laws shall be subject to the Revision and Controul of the Congress.

[3] No State shall, without the Consent of Congress, lay any Duty of Tonnage, keep Troops, or Ships of War in time of Peace, enter into any Agreement or Compact with another State, or with a foreign Power, or engage in War, unless actually invaded, or in such imminent Danger as will not admit of delay.

ARTICLE II

Section 1. [1] The executive Power shall be vested in a President of the United States of America. He shall hold his Office during the Term of four Years, and, together with the Vice President, chosen for the same Term, be elected, as follows:

[2] Each State shall appoint, in such Manner as the Legislature thereof may direct, a Number of Electors, equal to the whole Number of Senators and Representatives to which the State may be entitled in the Congress: but no Senator or Representative, or Person holding an Office of Trust or Profit under the United States, shall be appointed an Elector.

[3] The Electors shall meet in their respective States, and vote by Ballot for two Persons, of whom one at least shall not be an Inhabitant of the same State with themselves. And they shall make a List of all the Persons voted for, and of the Number of Votes for each; which List they shall sign and certify, and transmit sealed to the Seat of the Government of the United States, directed to the President of the Senate. The President of the Senate shall, in the Presence of the Senate and House of Representatives, open all the Certificates, and the Votes shall then be counted. The Person having the greatest Number of Votes shall be the President, if such Number be a Majority of the whole Number of Electors appointed; and if there be more than one who have such Majority, and have an equal Number of Votes,

then the House of Representatives shall immediately chuse by Ballot one of them for President; and if no Person have a Majority, then from the five highest on the List the said House shall in like Manner chuse the President. But in chusing the President, the Votes shall be taken by States, the Representation from each State having one Vote; A quorum for this purpose shall consist of a Member or Members from two thirds of the States, and a Majority of all the States shall be necessary to a Choice. In every Case, after the Choice of the President, the Person having the greatest Number of Votes of the Electors shall be the Vice President. But if there should remain two or more who have equal Votes, the Senate shall chuse from them by Ballot the Vice President.[6]

[4] The Congress may determine the Time of chusing the Electors, and the Day on which they shall give their Votes; which Day shall be the same throughout the United States.

[5] No Person except a natural born Citizen, or a Citizen of the United States, at the time of the Adoption of this Constitution, shall be eligible to the Office of President; neither shall any Person be eligible to that Office who shall not have attained to the Age of thirty five Years, and been fourteen Years a Resident within the United States.

[6] In Case of the Removal of the President from Office, or of his Death, Resignation, or Inability to discharge the Powers and Duties of the said Office, the Same shall devolve on the Vice President, and the Congress may by Law provide for the Case of Removal, Death, Resignation or Inability, both of the President and Vice President, declaring what Officer shall then act as President, and such Officer shall act accordingly, until the Disability be removed, or a President shall be elected.[7]

[7] The President shall, at stated Times, receive for his Services, a Compensation, which shall neither be increased nor diminished during the Period for which he shall have been elected, and he shall not receive within that Period any other Emolument from the United States, or any of them.

[8] Before he enter on the Execution of his Office, he shall take the following Oath or Affirmation: "I do solemnly swear (or affirm) that I will faithfully execute the Office of President of the United States, and will to the best of my Ability, preserve, protect and defend the Constitution of the United States."

Section 2. [1] The President shall be Commander in Chief of the Army and Navy of the United States, and of the Militia of the several States, when called into the actual Service of the United States; he may require the Opinion, in writing, of the principal Officer in each of the executive Departments, upon any Subject relating to the Duties of their respective Offices, and he shall have Power to grant Reprieves and Pardons for Offences against the United States, except in Cases of Impeachment.

[2] He shall have Power, by and with the Advice and Consent of the Senate, to make Treaties, provided two thirds of the Senators present concur; and he shall nominate, and by and with the Advice and Consent of the Senate, shall appoint Ambassadors, other public Ministers and Consuls, Judges of the supreme Court,

---

6. Superseded by the Twelfth Amendment.
7. Changed by the Twenty-Fifth Amendment.

and all other Officers of the United States, whose Appointments are not herein otherwise provided for, and which shall be established by Law: but the Congress may by Law vest the Appointment of such inferior Officers, as they think proper, in the President alone, in the Courts of Law, or in the Heads of Departments.

[3] The President shall have Power to fill up all Vacancies that may happen during the Recess of the Senate, by granting Commissions which shall expire at the End of their next Session.

Section 3. He shall from time to time give to the Congress Information of the State of the Union, and recommend to their Consideration such Measures as he shall judge necessary and expedient; he may, on extraordinary Occasions, convene both Houses, or either of them, and in Case of Disagreement between them, with Respect to the Time of Adjournment, he may adjourn them to such Time as he shall think proper; he shall receive Ambassadors and other public Ministers; he shall take Care that the Laws be faithfully executed, and shall Commission all the Officers of the United States.

Section 4. The President, Vice President and all civil Officers of the United States, shall be removed from Office on Impeachment for, and Conviction of, Treason, Bribery, or other high Crimes and Misdemeanors.

ARTICLE III

Section 1. The judicial Power of the United States shall be vested in one supreme Court, and in such inferior Courts as the Congress may from time to time ordain and establish. The Judges, both of the supreme and inferior Courts, shall hold their Offices during good Behaviour, and shall, at stated Times, receive for their Services a Compensation, which shall not be diminished during their Continuance in Office.

Section 2. [1] The Judicial Power shall extend to all Cases, in Law and Equity, arising under this Constitution, the Laws of the United States, and Treaties made, or which shall be made, under their Authority;—to all Cases affecting Ambassadors, other public Ministers and Consuls;—to all Cases of admiralty and maritime Jurisdiction;—to Controversies to which the United States shall be a Party;—to Controversies between two or more States;—between a State and Citizens of another State;—between Citizens of different States;—between Citizens of the same State claiming Lands under Grants of different States, and between a State, or the Citizens thereof, and foreign States, Citizens or Subjects.

[2] In all Cases affecting Ambassadors, other public Ministers and Consuls, and those in which a State shall be Party, the supreme Court shall have original Jurisdiction. In all the other Cases before mentioned, the supreme Court shall have appellate Jurisdiction, both as to Law and Fact, with such Exceptions, and under such Regulations as the Congress shall make.

[3] The Trial of all Crimes, except in Cases of Impeachment, shall be by Jury; and such Trial shall be held in the State where the said Crimes shall have been committed; but when not committed within any State, the Trial shall be at such Place or Places as the Congress may by Law have directed.

Section 3. [1] Treason against the United States, shall consist only in levying War against them, or in adhering to their Enemies, giving them Aid and Comfort. No Person shall be convicted of Treason unless on the Testimony of two Witnesses to the same overt Act, or on Confession in open Court.

[2] The Congress shall have Power to declare the Punishment of Treason, but no Attainder of Treason shall work Corruption of Blood, or Forfeiture except during the Life of the Person attainted.

ARTICLE IV

Section 1. Full Faith and Credit shall be given in each State to the public Acts, Records, and judicial Proceedings of every other State. And the Congress may by general Laws prescribe the Manner in which such Acts, Records and Proceedings shall be proved, and the Effect thereof.

Section 2. [1] The Citizens of each State shall be entitled to all Privileges and Immunities of Citizens in the several States.

[2] A Person charged in any State with Treason, Felony, or other Crime, who shall flee from Justice, and be found in another State, shall on Demand of the executive Authority of the State from which he fled, be delivered up, to be removed to the State having Jurisdiction of the Crime.

[3] No Person held to Service or Labour in one State, under the Laws thereof, escaping into another, shall, in Consequence of any Law or Regulation therein, be discharged from such Service or Labour, but shall be delivered up on Claim of the Party to whom such Service or Labour may be due.[8]

Section 3. [1] New States may be admitted by the Congress into this Union; but no new State shall be formed or erected within the Jurisdiction of any other State; nor any State be formed by the Junction of two or more States, or Parts of States, without the Consent of the Legislatures of the States concerned as well as of the Congress.

[2] The Congress shall have Power to dispose of and make all needful Rules and Regulations respecting the Territory or other Property belonging to the United States; and nothing in this Constitution shall be so construed as to Prejudice any Claims of the United States, or of any particular State.

Section 4. The United States shall guarantee to every State in this Union a Republican Form of Government, and shall protect each of them against Invasion; and on Application of the Legislature, or of the Executive (when the Legislature cannot be convened), against domestic Violence.

ARTICLE V

The Congress, whenever two thirds of both Houses shall deem it necessary, shall propose Amendments to this Constitution, or, on the Application of the

8. Superseded by the Thirteenth Amendment.

Legislatures of two thirds of the several States, shall call a Convention for proposing Amendments, which, in either Case, shall be valid to all Intents and Purposes, as Part of this Constitution, when ratified by the Legislatures of three fourths of the several States, or by Conventions in three fourths thereof, as the one or the other Mode of Ratification may be proposed by the Congress; Provided that no Amendment which may be made prior to the Year One thousand eight hundred and eight shall in any Manner affect the first and fourth Clauses in the Ninth Section of the first Article; and that no State, without its Consent, shall be deprived of its equal Suffrage in the Senate.

ARTICLE VI

[1] All Debts contracted and Engagements entered into, before the Adoption of this Constitution, shall be as valid against the United States under this Constitution, as under the Confederation.

[2] This Constitution, and the Laws of the United States which shall be made in Pursuance thereof; and all Treaties made, or which shall be made, under the Authority of the United States, shall be the supreme Law of the Land; and the Judges in every State shall be bound thereby, any Thing in the Constitution or Laws of any State to the Contrary notwithstanding.

[3] The Senators and Representatives before mentioned, and the Members of the several State Legislatures, and all executive and judicial Officers, both of the United States and of the several States, shall be bound by Oath or Affirmation, to support this Constitution; but no religious Test shall ever be required as a Qualification to any Office or public Trust under the United States.

ARTICLE VII

The Ratification of the Conventions of nine States, shall be sufficient for the Establishment of this Constitution between the States so ratifying the Same.[9] Done in Convention by the Unanimous Consent of the States present the Seventeenth Day of September in the Year of our Lord one thousand seven hundred and Eighty seven and of the Independence of the United States of America the Twelfth.

Articles in addition to, and Amendment of the Constitution of the United States of America, proposed by Congress, and ratified by the Legislatures of the several States, Pursuant to the fifth Article of the original Constitution[10]

---

9. The ninth state ratified the Constitution on June 21, 1788. Virginia and New York ratified later in 1788, North Carolina in 1789, and Rhode Island in 1790. George Washington was inaugurated as the first President on April 30, 1789.

10. The Twenty-First Amendment was ratified by state conventions.

AMENDMENT I [1791]

Congress shall make no law respecting an establishment of religion, or prohibiting the free exercise thereof; or abridging the freedom of speech, or of the press; or the right of the people peaceably to assemble, and to petition the Government for a redress of grievances.

AMENDMENT II [1791]

A well regulated Militia, being necessary to the security of a free State, the right of the people to keep and bear Arms, shall not be infringed.

AMENDMENT III [1791]

No Soldier shall, in time of peace be quartered in any house, without the consent of the Owner, nor in time of war, but in a manner to be prescribed by law.

AMENDMENT IV [1791]

The right of the people to be secure in their persons, houses, papers, and effects, against unreasonable searches and seizures, shall not be violated, and no Warrants shall issue, but upon probable cause, supported by Oath or affirmation, and particularly describing the place to be searched, and the persons or things to be seized.

AMENDMENT V [1791]

No person shall be held to answer for a capital, or otherwise infamous crime, unless on a presentment or indictment of a Grand Jury, except in cases arising in the land or naval forces, or in the Militia, when in actual service in time of War or public danger; nor shall any person be subject for the same offence to be twice put in jeopardy of life or limb; nor shall be compelled in any criminal case to be a witness against himself, nor be deprived of life, liberty, or property, without due process of law; nor shall private property be taken for public use, without just compensation.

AMENDMENT VI [1791]

In all criminal prosecutions, the accused shall enjoy the right to a speedy and public trial, by an impartial jury of the State and district wherein the crime shall have been committed, which district shall have been previously ascertained by law, and to be informed of the nature and cause of the accusation; to be confronted with the witnesses against him; to have compulsory process for obtaining witnesses in his favor, and to have the Assistance of Counsel for his defence.

AMENDMENT VII [1791]

In suits at common law, where the value in controversy shall exceed twenty dollars, the right of trial by jury shall be preserved, and no fact tried by a jury, shall be otherwise reexamined in any Court of the United States, than according to the rules of the common law.

AMENDMENT VIII [1791]

Excessive bail shall not be required, nor excessive fines imposed, nor cruel and unusual punishments inflicted.

AMENDMENT IX [1791]

The enumeration in the Constitution, of certain rights, shall not be construed to deny or disparage others retained by the people.

AMENDMENT X [1791]

The powers not delegated to the United States by the Constitution, nor prohibited by it to the States, are reserved to the States respectively, or to the people.

AMENDMENT XI [1798]

The Judicial power of the United States shall not be construed to extend to any suit in law or equity, commenced or prosecuted against one of the United States by Citizens of another State, or by Citizens or Subjects of any Foreign State.

AMENDMENT XII [1804]

The Electors shall meet in their respective states and vote by ballot for President and Vice-President, one of whom, at least, shall not be an inhabitant of the same state with themselves; they shall name in their ballots the person voted for as President, and in distinct ballots the person voted for as Vice-President, and they shall make distinct lists of all persons voted for as President, and of all persons voted for as Vice-President, and of the number of votes for each, which lists they shall sign and certify, and transmit sealed to the seat of the government of the United States, directed to the President of the Senate;—the President of the Senate shall, in the presence of the Senate and House of Representatives, open all the certificates and the votes shall then be counted;—The person having the greatest number of votes for President, shall be the President, if such number be a majority of the whole number of Electors appointed; and if no person have such majority, then from the persons having the highest numbers not exceeding three on the list of those voted for as President, the House of Representatives shall chuse immediately, by ballot, the President. But in chusing the President, the votes shall be taken by states, the representation from each state having one vote; a quorum for this purpose shall consist of a member or members from two-thirds of the states, and a majority of all the states shall be necessary to a choice. [And if the House of Representatives shall not chuse a President whenever the right of choice shall devolve upon them, before the fourth day of March next following, then the Vice-President shall act as President, as in case of the death or other constitutional disability of the President.[11]—The person having the greatest number of votes as Vice-President, shall be the Vice-President, if such number be a majority of the whole number of Electors appointed, and if no person have a majority, then from the two highest numbers on the list, the Senate shall choose the Vice-President; a quorum for the purpose shall consist of two-thirds of the whole number of Senators, and a majority of the whole number shall be necessary to a choice. But no person constitutionally ineligible to the office of President shall be eligible to that of Vice-President of the United States.

AMENDMENT XIII [1865]

Section 1. Neither slavery nor involuntary servitude, except as a punishment for crime whereof the party shall have been duly convicted, shall exist within the United States, or any place subject to their jurisdiction.

Section 2. Congress shall have power to enforce this article by appropriate legislation.

AMENDMENT XIV [1868]

Section 1. All persons born or naturalized in the United States, and subject to the jurisdiction thereof, are citizens of the United States and of the State wherein they reside. No State shall make or enforce any law which shall abridge the privileges or immunities of citizens of the United States; nor shall any State deprive any

11. Superseded by section 3 of the Twentieth Amendment.

person of life, liberty, or property, without due process of law; nor deny to any person within its jurisdiction the equal protection of the laws.

Section 2. Representatives shall be apportioned among the several States according to their respective numbers, counting the whole number of persons in each State, excluding Indians not taxed. But when the right to vote at any election for the choice of electors for President and Vice-President of the United States, Representatives in Congress, the Executive and Judicial officers of a State, or the members of the Legislature thereof, is denied to any of the male inhabitants of such State, being twenty-one years of age, and citizens of the United States, or in any way abridged, except for participation in rebellion, or other crime, the basis of representation therein shall be reduced in the proportion which the number of such male citizens shall bear to the whole number of male citizens twenty-one years of age in such State.

Section 3. No person shall be a Senator or Representative in Congress, or elector of President and Vice-President, or hold any office, civil or military, under the United States, or under any State, who, having previously taken an oath, as a member of Congress, or as an officer of the United States, or as a member of any State legislature, or as an executive or judicial officer of any State, to support the Constitution of the United States, shall have engaged in insurrection or rebellion against the same, or given aid or comfort to the enemies thereof. But Congress may by a vote of two-thirds of each House, remove such disability.

Section 4. The validity of the public debt of the United States, authorized by law, including debts incurred for payment of pensions and bounties for services in suppressing insurrection or rebellion, shall not be questioned. But neither the United States nor any State shall assume or pay any debt or obligation incurred in aid of insurrection or rebellion against the United States, or any claim for the loss or emancipation of any slave; but all such debts, obligations and claims shall be held illegal and void.

Section 5. The Congress shall have the power to enforce, by appropriate legislation, the provisions of this article.

AMENDMENT XV [1870]

Section 1. The right of citizens of the United States to vote shall not be denied or abridged by the United States or by any State on account of race, color, or previous condition of servitude.

Section 2. The Congress shall have the power to enforce this article by appropriate legislation.

AMENDMENT XVI [1913]

The Congress shall have power to lay and collect taxes on incomes, from whatever source derived, without apportionment among the several States, and without regard to any census or enumeration.

AMENDMENT XVII [1913]

[1] The Senate of the United States shall be composed of two Senators from each State, elected by the people thereof, for six years; and each Senator shall have one vote. The electors in each State shall have the qualifications requisite for electors of the most numerous branch of the State legislatures.

[2] When vacancies happen in the representation of any State in the Senate, the executive authority of such State shall issue writs of election to fill such vacancies: *Provided,* That the legislature of any State may empower the executive thereof to make temporary appointments until the people fill the vacancies by election as the legislature may direct.

[3] This amendment shall not be so construed as to affect the election or term of any Senator chosen before it becomes valid as part of the Constitution.

AMENDMENT XVIII [1919]

Section 1. After one year from the ratification of this article the manufacture, sale, or transportation of intoxicating liquors within, the importation thereof into, or the exportation thereof from the United States and all territory subject to the jurisdiction thereof for beverage purposes is hereby prohibited.

Section 2. The Congress and the several States shall have concurrent power to enforce this article by appropriate legislation.

Section 3. This article shall be inoperative unless it shall have been ratified as an amendment to the Constitution by the legislatures of the several States, as provided in the Constitution, within seven years from the date of the submission hereof to the States by the Congress.[12]

AMENDMENT XIX [1920]

[1] The right of citizens of the United States to vote shall not be denied or abridged by the United States or by any State on account of sex.

[2] Congress shall have power to enforce this article by appropriate legislation.

AMENDMENT XX [1933]

Section 1. The terms of the President and the Vice President shall end at noon on the 20th day of January, and the terms of Senators and Representatives at noon on the 3d day of January, of the years in which such terms would have ended if this article had not been ratified; and the terms of their successors shall then begin.

---

12. Repealed by the Twenty-First Amendment.

Section 2. The Congress shall assemble at least once in every year, and such meeting shall begin at noon on the 3d day of January, unless they shall by law appoint a different day.

Section 3. If, at the time fixed for the beginning of the term of the President, the President elect shall have died, the Vice President elect shall become President. If a President shall not have been chosen before the time fixed for the beginning of his term, or if the President elect shall have failed to qualify, then the Vice President elect shall act as President until a President shall have qualified; and the Congress may by law provide for the case wherein neither a President elect nor a Vice President shall have qualified, declaring who shall then act as President, or the manner in which one who is to act shall be selected, and such person shall act accordingly until a President or Vice President shall have qualified.

Section 4. The Congress may by law provide for the case of the death of any of the persons from whom the House of Representatives may chuse a President whenever the right of choice shall have devolved upon them, and for the case of the death of any of the persons from whom the Senate may chuse a Vice President whenever the right of choice shall have devolved upon them.

Section 5. Sections 1 and 2 shall take effect on the 15th day of October following the ratification of this article.

Section 6. This article shall be inoperative unless it shall have been ratified as an amendment to the Constitution by the legislatures of three-fourths of the several States within seven years from the date of its submission.

AMENDMENT XXI [1933]

Section 1. The eighteenth article of amendment to the Constitution of the United States is hereby repealed.

Section 2. The transportation or importation into any State, Territory, or Possession of the United States for delivery or use therein of intoxicating liquors, in violation of the laws thereof, is hereby prohibited.

Section 3. This article shall be inoperative unless it shall have been ratified as an amendment to the Constitution by conventions in the several States, as provided in the Constitution, within seven years from the date of the submission hereof to the States by the Congress.

AMENDMENT XXII [1951]

Section 1. No person shall be elected to the office of the President more than twice, and no person who has held the office of President, or acted as President, for more than two years of a term to which some other person was elected President shall be elected to the office of President more than once. But this Article shall not apply to any person holding the office of President when this Article was proposed by Congress, and shall not prevent any person who may be holding the office of President, or acting as President, during the term within which this Article becomes operative from holding the office of President or acting as President during the remainder of such term.

Section 2. This article shall be inoperative unless it shall have been ratified as an amendment to the Constitution by the legislatures of three-fourths of the several States within seven years from the date of its submission to the States by the Congress.

AMENDMENT XXIII [1961]

Section 1. The District constituting the seat of Government of the United States shall appoint in such manner as Congress may direct: A number of electors of President and Vice President equal to the whole number of Senators and Representatives in Congress to which the District would be entitled if it were a State, but in no event more than the least populous State; they shall be in addition to those appointed by the States, but they shall be considered, for the purposes of the election of President and Vice President, to be electors appointed by a State; and they shall meet in the District and perform such duties as provided by the twelfth article of amendment.

Section 2. The Congress shall have power to enforce this article by appropriate legislation.

AMENDMENT XXIV [1964]

Section 1. The right of citizens of the United States to vote in any primary or other election for President or Vice President, for electors for President or Vice President, or for Senator or Representative in Congress, shall not be denied or abridged by the United States or any State by reason of failure to pay poll tax or other tax.

Section 2. The Congress shall have power to enforce this article by appropriate legislation.

AMENDMENT XXV [1967]

Section 1. In case of the removal of the President from office or of his death or resignation, the Vice President shall become President.

Section 2. Whenever there is a vacancy in the office of the Vice President, the President shall nominate a Vice President who shall take office upon confirmation by a majority vote of both Houses of Congress.

Section 3. Whenever the President transmits to the President pro tempore of the Senate and the Speaker of the House of Representatives his written declaration that he is unable to discharge the powers and duties of his office, and until he transmits to them a written declaration to the contrary, such powers and duties shall be discharged by the Vice President as Acting President.

Section 4. Whenever the Vice President and a majority of either the principal officers of the executive departments or of such other body as Congress may by law provide, transmit to the President pro tempore of the Senate and the Speaker of the House of Representatives their written declaration that the President is unable to discharge the powers and duties of his office, the Vice President shall immediately assume the powers and duties of the office as Acting President.

Thereafter, when the President transmits to the President pro tempore of the Senate and the Speaker of the House of Representatives his written declaration that no inability exists, he shall resume the powers and duties of his office unless the Vice President and a majority of either the principal officers of the executive department or of such other body as Congress may by law provide, transmit within four days to the President pro tempore of the Senate and the Speaker of the House of Representatives their written declaration that the President is unable to discharge the powers and duties of his office. Thereupon Congress shall decide the issue, assembling within forty-eight hours for that purpose if not in session. If the Congress, within twenty-one days after receipt of the latter written declaration, or, if Congress is not in session, within twenty-one days after Congress is required to assemble, determines by two-thirds vote of both Houses that the President is unable to discharge the powers and duties of his office, the Vice President shall continue to discharge the same as Acting President; otherwise, the President shall resume the powers and duties of his office.

AMENDMENT XXVI [1971]

Section 1. The right of citizens of the United States, who are eighteen years of age or older, to vote shall not be denied or abridged by the United States or by any State on account of age.

Section 2. The Congress shall have power to enforce this article by appropriate legislation.

AMENDMENT XXVII [1992][13]

No law, varying the compensation for the services of the Senators and Representatives, shall take effect, until an election of representatives shall have intervened.

13. This amendment was initially proposed in 1789. Whether a 203-year process of ratification calls its validity into question is discussed in Chapter 4, pp. 552-553.

Processes of Constitutional Decisionmaking

PART 1

INTRODUCTION: BACKGROUND TO THE CONSTITUTION[1]

In June 1776, the Continental Congress, meeting in Philadelphia, appointed committees to draft a declaration of independence and to prepare "the form of a confederation to be entered into between these colonies."[2] Within a month, Congress approved the Declaration of Independence of which Thomas Jefferson was the principal drafter. Although Articles of Confederation were submitted to the states in 1777, they did not take formal effect until 1781, when the last state, Maryland, gave its assent.

The Articles called the new nation "The United States of America," but this only generated the question whether the emphasis should be placed on the word "United" or the word "States."[3] Given that the Preamble to the Articles explicitly identified the thirteen states ostensibly joined in "perpetual Union," one writer has suggested that the Articles of Confederation are better conceived as "a treaty among a group of small nations" than a charter for a single nation.[4] Article II emphasized that "[e]ach state retains its sovereignty, freedom, and independence, and every

---

1. For more detailed discussion of many of the issues discussed in this Introduction, see generally Akhil Reed Amar, America's Constitution: A Biography (2005).

2. Quoted in The Formation of the Union (National Archives Pub. No. 70-13), at 34.

3. See Sebastian de Grazia, A Country with No Name: Tales from the Constitution (1997), for a fascinating discussion of the theoretical implications of the name. There were some proposals at the time to rename the new nation "Columbia," but they were resisted in part because any such name would suggest a far more united group of states than many (perhaps most) wished to acknowledge. For exposition of an argument, contrary to that set out in the text above, that the nation in fact preceded the states, see Richard B. Morris, The Forging of the Union Reconsidered: A Historical Refutation of State Sovereignty over Seabeds, 74 Colum. L. Rev. 74 (1974).

4. The Formation of the Union, supra n.2, at 34.

power, jurisdiction, and right, which is not by this Confederation expressly delegated to the United States, in Congress assembled."[5] Each state in the Confederation Congress had one vote, cast by the majority of its delegates (who could number up to seven). The delegates were paid by the states, and, like ambassadors in our own time, they were subject to recall by their respective states should they take positions objectionable to the state legislatures.

Congressional power under the Articles was narrowly limited. There was, for example, no authority to regulate interstate or foreign commerce. The constituent states within the Confederation felt free, both politically and legally, to engage in trade wars with one another. States with good ports, like New York, Rhode Island, and South Carolina, felt free to exploit less advantaged adjoining states, like New Jersey, by charging tariffs from those wishing to use their ports.

Congress had no power to tax the citizenry; it was limited to requisitioning funds from the states themselves, which, as a practical matter, amounted to little more than a request for voluntary donations to the national treasury. Although James Madison had told his fellow members of the Congress in 1783 that requisitions were "sacred & obligatory" upon the States,[6] Hamilton accurately wrote in The Federalist No. 15 that they had been treated by state legislatures as "mere recommendations" that were simply left unpaid. Thus the "Requisition of 1786, the last before the Constitution, 'mandated' payments by the states . . . of $3.8 million, but collected only $663."[7]

Congress had the power to coin money, but states retained the power to issue paper money, which some did with abandon, with inflationary effects. The Articles established neither a national judiciary nor even a genuine executive branch. Congress was authorized to establish such "committees and civil officers as may be necessary for managing the general affairs of the united states [sic] under their direction" and to appoint a "president" of the Congress, who could serve only a single one-year term in any three-year period. In 1781, Congress also established departments of Foreign Affairs, War, Marine, and Treasury, each under a single secretary.

Many Americans felt that the limitations of the Articles helped account for the economic turmoil following the completion of the Revolutionary War in 1783. Concerns about the weakness of the political order led many to call for revisions. The problem, however, was that Article XIII made change extremely difficult: "the Union shall be perpetual; nor shall any alteration at any time hereafter be made in any of [the Articles]; unless such alteration be agreed to in a Congress of the United States, and be afterwards confirmed by the legislatures of *every State*" (emphasis added). In effect, Article XIII gave a single state a veto over any changes. Rhode Island, the second-smallest state—Delaware was the smallest—was often

5. This and other quotations from the Articles are taken from Sources and Documents Illustrating the American Revolution 1764-1788 (Morison ed., 2d ed. 1965), at 178-186.

6. Calvin H. Johnson, Righteous Anger at the Wicked States: The Meaning of the Founders' Constitution 15 (citing Madison, Continental Congress (February 21, 1783), in 25 Journals of the Continental Congress 908).

7. Id. at 1.

blamed for making constitutional reform impossible even though it had less than 2 percent of the total population.

As early as 1783 Alexander Hamilton called for "a General Convention for the purpose of revising and amending the federal Government." James Madison objected, fearing that such a convention would excite "pernicious jealousies" among the states.[8] "[B]y 1785," writes Stanford historian Jack Rakove, Congress's "reputation had fallen so low that any proposal [for amendment] Congress submitted to the states seemed tainted at the source."[9] And, of course, amendment was still likely to be frustrated by the unanimity rule.

"With Congress clearly losing whatever influence it retained, the initiative for reform necessarily shifted to the states."[10] Thus in January 1786, the Virginia assembly adopted a resolution calling for an interstate conference that would, among other things, "take into consideration the trade of the United States; to examine the relative situations and trade of the said States; [and] to consider how far a uniform system in their commercial regulations may be necessary to their common interests and their permanent harmony." Madison supported the resolution.

This led to the Annapolis Conference of September 1786. Twelve delegates from five states met to consider the situation. The practical authority, not to mention legal mandate, of the Annapolis Convention was limited. Its report therefore proposed yet another meeting "to devise such further provisions as shall appear . . . necessary to render the constitution of the Federal Government adequate to the exigencies of the Union."[11] Congress agreed, in February 1787, to authorize a convention "for the *sole and express purpose of revising the Articles of Confederation* and reporting to Congress and the several legislatures such alterations and provisions therein as shall when agreed to in Congress and confirmed by the States render the federal constitution adequate to the exigencies of Government & the preservation of the union."[12] The Convention began meeting in Philadelphia the following May, and it ended up drafting a brand new Constitution.

The delegates had little doubt that they were exceeding the scope of their congressional authorization. Edmund Randolph, the Governor of Virginia—who would later become the first Attorney General of the United States—told the Convention, "There are great seasons when persons with limited powers are justified in exceeding them, and a person would be contemptible not to risk it."[13] His fellow Virginian,

---

8. 9 Papers of James Madison 115-119 (Rutland & Rachal eds., 1975).

9. Jack N. Rakove, Original Meanings: Politics and Ideas in the Making of the Constitution 32 (1996).

10. Id. at 32. A fascinating history of the move toward change can also be found in Bruce Ackerman, 2 We the People: Transformations 32-68 (1998). The most extensive recent history of the move toward constitutional change and the events at the Philadelphia Convention is Michael Klarman, The Framers' Coup: The Making of the United States Constitution (2016).

11. The Formation of the Union, supra n.2, at 50.

12. Id. (emphasis added).

13. 1 Records of the Federal Convention of 1787, at 362 (Farrand ed., 1937) (speech of June 16, 1787).

George Mason, agreed: "In certain seasons of public danger it is commendable to exceed power."[14] So too did New York's Alexander Hamilton: "To rely on & propose any plan not adequate to these exigencies, *merely because it was not clearly within our powers*, would be to sacrifice the means to the end."[15] Hamilton, of course, would, with John Jay and James Madison, under the joint name of "Publius," go on to write the most influential tract in favor of the new Constitution, *The Federalist.* In The Federalist No. 40, Madison defended the Convention's action by writing that the delegates "must have borne in mind, that as the plan to be framed and proposed was to be submitted *to the people themselves* . . . its approbation [would] blot out antecedent errors and irregularities." Throughout American history—and throughout this casebook—we will see similar themes repeated: that the need to meet perceived exigencies or emergencies should prevail over strict fidelity to constitutional norms.

According to the Virginia Plan—which served as a working draft for much of the document—the new federal government would have a far more powerful Congress with a host of new powers, many of which were listed in Article I, §8 of the new Constitution. (Interpreting the scope of those powers will be a major focus of this casebook.) The Virginia Plan also proposed two houses of Congress—unlike the Confederation Congress and the Pennsylvania and Georgia legislatures, which had only a single legislative body. Both houses of the new Congress would be based on the number of free inhabitants in each state. (Not coincidentally, Virginia was then the largest state, narrowly ahead of Pennsylvania.)

Predictably, the Virginia Plan elicited vigorous opposition, especially (though not exclusively) from smaller states that feared being swamped by larger ones. Some of the Southern states feared that if representation was proportional to population, the North might eventually dominate in the Congress, promote its favored economic policies, and threaten the institution of slavery.

Delaware threatened to walk out of the Convention if the Virginia Plan was adopted; Rhode Island did not do so only because that state failed to send delegates to the Convention in the first place. Rhode Island feared that the Convention would try to transform the country in unacceptable ways; it hoped that its veto power over amendment, guaranteed by Article XIII, would be sufficient to stave off such a danger.

After a month of passionate controversy, the Convention agreed on what is now called the Great Compromise: Each state would receive equal representation in the Senate, and Article V provided that "no state, without its consent, shall be deprived of its equal suffrage in the Senate."[16]

---

14. Quoted in Jon Elster, Constitutional Bootstrapping in Philadelphia and Paris, in Constitutionalism, Identity, Difference, and Legitimacy: Theoretical Perspectives 72 (Michel Rosenfeld ed., 1994).

15. 1 Records of the Federal Convention of 1787, at 283 (June 18, 1787) (emphasis added). See also id. at 346 (George Mason).

16. Compare this to the principle of representation in the United Nations General Assembly. The Assembly features equal representation and equal formal voting power by each of its more than 190 members, which range in size from China (1.3 billion people) to Palau (approximately 20,000 residents). With regard to Palau, incidentally, the United States claims responsibility for the defense and foreign policy interests of this 200-island nation.

The distribution of votes in the House, on the other hand, would be (roughly) proportional to population, thus giving greater power to larger states. However, there was an additional compromise. The basis of representation in the House would not be based on the number of free citizens (or even free residents), but, rather the "the whole number of free persons" plus "three-fifths of all other persons" in each state. Everyone understood this formula to refer to slaves. The effect was to give slave states greater representation in the House of Representatives and, equally important, in the Electoral College. For example, in 1790 Virginia's population consisted of approximately 454,983 free persons and 292,627 slaves. The Three-Fifths Clause added the equivalent of 175,576 persons. This significantly increased Virginia's delegation in the House. It also helped ensure the election of Virginia native (and slaveholder) Thomas Jefferson in the 1800 election.

It is worth emphasizing that the South did not support the three-fifths formula because it believed that slaves were worth only three-fifths of a human being. Southern states would have been delighted to count each slave as equivalent to a free person, because that would have increased their representation in the House (and the Electoral College) even more. Slaves would enjoy no political rights, so the effect would be to give free Southerners additional clout in the federal government. Thus the South Carolina delegation at the Convention demanded full representation for slaves.[17] Conversely, Northern states would have liked to exclude slaves entirely from the representation formula, not because they did not believe they were persons, but because Northerners believed that this unfairly increased Southern political power. Representation formulas were tied to those of taxation: Hence complementing the three-fifths compromise on representation was a similar three-fifths compromise in regard to taxation. See Article I, §2, cl. 2. The debate about representation was important because of Congress's new powers. Henceforth it could levy its own taxes and raise revenue without cooperation by state governments, and it could regulate foreign and domestic commerce. Finally, the last clause of Article I, §8 allowed the new Congress "[t]o make all laws which shall be necessary and proper for carrying into execution the foregoing powers, and all other powers vested by this constitution in the government of the United States, or in any department or officer thereof." The scope of these new powers was uncertain, and led to many of the struggles over constitutional interpretation in the pages that follow.

Not only did the Convention go far beyond its congressional mandate, it also jettisoned the unanimity requirement of Article XIII of the old Articles. Article VII of the proposed Constitution simply ignored Article XIII by stating that ratification by *nine* states would be enough to give life to the Constitution. As Madison wrote in The Federalist No. 40, the suggestion that the Convention should simply have proposed amendments to the Articles was refuted by the "the absurdity of subjecting the fate of twelve States to the perverseness or corruption of a thirteenth." Rhode Island's refusal to participate in the Philadelphia Convention in the belief that Article XIII would protect their interests turned out to be a disastrous mistake.[18]

---

17. See Rakove, supra n.9, at 73.

18. Indeed, Rhode Island rejected the proposed Constitution on March 24, 1788, but it made no difference. Because North Carolina did not finally ratify the Constitution until November 21, 1789 (and even then the vote was 194-77), there were only 11 states in the Union when George Washington was inaugurated as the first President of the reordered American polity on April 30, 1789.

Bruce Ackerman describes Article VII's "assertion that nine state 'Conventions' could adequately ratify on behalf of the People [as] plainly an extra-legal assertion of democratic authority."[19] Michael Klarman has labeled Philadelphia as de facto "coup" by national political elites who in fact were fearful of truly "democratic authority."[20] Or one might also conceptualize the events of 1787-1788 as the secession by the ratifying states from the Confederation established by the Articles and the joining of a new polity established by the Constitution.

Many factors contributed to the final approval of the Constitution, of course, but one should not underestimate the importance, at least to supporters of the new Constitution, of perceived military threats to the young nation. James Wilson, for example, told the members of the Pennsylvania Assembly on September 17, 1787, the very day that the Constitution was signed in Philadelphia, that war was "highly probable."[21] A delegate to the Massachusetts ratifying convention told his colleagues that "[w]e are circumscribed with enemies from Maine to Georgia,"[22] with the primary threats being Great Britain, Spain, and American Indian tribes, many of whom had supported the British in the Revolutionary War and were scarcely sympathetic with the territorial expansion of the United States that was already underway.

The threat of war was not only from the outside. Political scientist and historian David Hendrickson emphasizes the importance of the view, derived both from political theorists like Thomas Hobbes and the realities of European political experience, that if the states remained fragmented—perhaps divided into three separate nations comprising, respectively, the New England, mid-Atlantic, and Southern states—they would inevitably end up warring with one another.[23]

---

19. Ackerman, The Storrs Lectures: Discovering the Constitution, 93 Yale L.J. 1013, 1017 n.6 (1984). See also Richard Kay, The Illegality of the Constitution, 4 Const. Comment. 57 (1987). The most vigorous defense of the legality of the procedures by which the Constitution was adopted has been offered by Ackerman's Yale colleague Akhil Reed Amar, who relies on the notion that the Articles were indeed only a "treaty" among the various sovereign states. "By 1787, the Articles had been routinely and flagrantly violated on all sides. And under well-established legal principles in 1787, these material breaches freed each compacting party—each state—to disregard the pact." See Amar, Popular Sovereignty and Constitutional Amendment, in Responding to Imperfection: The Theory and Practice of Constitutional Amendment 92-95 (Sanford Levinson ed., 1995). You might ask yourself if the extent of your esteem for the members of the founding generation depends on their fidelity to existing legal norms. If, at the end of the day, you do not really care who is correct between Ackerman and Amar, does that have implications for your views today about the importance of fidelity to the existing Constitution? Is it more important to be faithful to the law or to respond imaginatively to the "exigencies" of the moment?

20. Michael Klarman, The Framers' Coup: The Making of the United States Constitution (2017). Klarman is less interested in legal controversies surrounding the Convention than he is in the politics and the various interest groups contending for decisionmaking power in Philadelphia.

21. Quoted in Johnson, supra n.6, at 18. See generally Pauline Maier, Ratification: The People Debate the Constitution, 1787-1788 (2010).

22. Id.

23. See David C. Hendrickson, Peace Pact: The Lost World of the American Founding (2003).

Swedish political scientist and historian Max Edling describes the 1787 Constitution as a "revolution in favor of government" and emphasizes the overriding importance of both the taxation and standing army clauses, inasmuch as the two, taken together, allowed the national government to finance and raise professional military defense forces.[24] Some critics of the Constitution were horrified by the prospect of a "standing army." In civic republican political theory, a permanent standing army was an inevitable threat to popular liberty. Instead, free states should rely on citizen militias—that is one explanation for the language of the Second Amendment. However, the exigencies of national defense ultimately prevailed and almost undoubtedly accounted for the narrow margin of victory in several states.

Some Northerners complained about the compromises with slavery manifested in the Constitution.[25] One of the most important has already been mentioned: the "three-fifths" bonus given Southern states with regard both to representation in the House of Representatives and then electing members of the Electoral College who would in turn choose the President. This helped guarantee that until the Civil War, most of the Presidents elected were either friendly to or at least not hostile to the interests of slavery. Moreover, because the President picked members of the federal judiciary, the Supreme Court consistently had a pro-slavery majority before 1861.

Although the words "slave" or "slavery" do not appear in the constitutional text, the interest in protecting slavery accounted for two other provisions. Article I, §9 limited Congress's right to control the "Migration or Importation of such Persons as any of the states now existing shall think proper to admit" until 1808. At that point Congress passed a law prohibiting the importation of slaves into the United States from abroad. (The internal slave trade was not affected.) And Article IV, §2, cl. 3 establishes a duty of states to return any "Person held to Service or Labour in one State, under the Laws thereof," who attempts to escape into another state (one that presumably does not recognize the ownership of one human being by another).

Far more criticism was directed at what was lacking in the original Constitution: the explicit protection of the rights of the citizenry even as the national government was being granted extensive new powers. Indeed, Virginia's George Mason, one of the most respected members of the Philadelphia delegation, refused to sign the Constitution because it lacked what the Virginia Constitution included—a declaration of rights. This became one of the central arguments of those opposing ratification of the Constitution. In the 84th Federalist, Hamilton responded to such calls: "I affirm that the bills of rights . . . are not only unnecessary in the proposed constitution, but would even be dangerous. They would contain various exceptions to powers which are not granted; and on this very account, would afford a colourable pretext to claim more than were granted. For why declare that things shall not

24. Max M. Edling, A Revolution in Favor of Government: Origins of the United States Constitution and the Making of the American State (2003).

25. For citations and discussion, see Amar, America's Constitution, supra n.1, at 87-98.

be done which there is no power to do? Why, for instance, should it be said, that the liberty of the press shall not be restrained, when no power is given by which restrictions may be imposed?"[26]

The principal anti-Federalist response to this argument emphasized the limitations contained in Article I, §9. Why, if the powers of the national government were limited to assigned powers, was it necessary to prohibit Congress from, say, granting titles of nobility? In any event, there was sufficient support for a bill of rights that it became a de facto condition of ratification by many of the delegates. Madison, who had initially agreed with his then-colleague Hamilton on the inefficacy of a formal bill of rights, became the primary architect of the first amendments to the Constitution during the first session of Congress in 1789. Twelve such amendments were proposed, ten of which were ratified in 1791. (One of the two initially nonratified amendments, the original Second Amendment, was deemed to have been ratified in 1992, 203 years after its initial proposal in 1789. The legitimacy of its ratification is considered below at pp. 552-553.)

For many opponents of the Constitution, the lack of a bill of rights was less important than the marked increase in federal power established by the new Constitution. They hoped that a follow-up convention could reconsider some of the decisions made in Philadelphia. Several historians have argued that the Federalists' ultimate agreement to adding a bill of rights was a successful strategy to distract attention from and dampen enthusiasm for a second convention.

NOTE: THE "CONSTITUTION OF CONVERSATION" AND THE "CONSTITUTION OF SETTLEMENT"

Most courses on constitutional law focus on questions of government *powers*, on the one hand, and questions of the *rights* of citizens and other persons on the other. Examples of the former are the powers allocated to the legislature, executive, and judiciary, the subject, respectively, of Articles I, II, and III. Examples of the latter are the rights guaranteed in the Bill of Rights and the three Reconstruction Amendments.

Like most casebooks on constitutional law, much of what you will find in the following pages focuses on powers and rights. The reason for this is simple: The clauses in the Constitution that concern powers and rights have, from the moment of adoption onward, generated the greatest debate and controversy about their

---

26. Hamilton was scarcely unique in making this argument. Probably the most influential version at the time was that of Philadelphia's James Wilson, in an address to the citizens of that city during their consideration of the Constitution, which occurred far earlier than New York's. James Iredell of North Carolina, who with Wilson would be appointed by George Washington to the Supreme Court, told that state's convention that it would be "not only useless, but dangerous, to enumerate a number of rights which are not intended to be given up, because it would be implying, in the strongest manner, that every right not included in the exception might be impaired by the government without usurpation." Speech of July 19, 1788, before the North Carolina ratifying convention, quoted in Dan Farber and Suzanna Sherry, A History of the American Constitution 320 (2d ed. 2005).

proper interpretation. For this reason, in his book Framed: America's 51 Constitutions and the Crisis of Governance (2012), Professor Sanford Levinson refers to these provisions as the "Constitution of Conversation."

This constitutional law casebook is noteworthy in that it looks at the conversation about rights and powers in two distinctive ways. First, it examines the conversation about the Constitution historically. Second, it looks beyond federal courts to consider the positions and arguments of members of Congress, state courts, Presidents, and other members of the executive branch, and members of social movements like Susan B. Anthony and Frederick Douglass.

There is, however, an equally important feature of constitutions. These are the parts of constitutions that are rarely if ever litigated, and that form the basic structures of representative government. They concern issues of constitutional *design* as opposed to constitutional *interpretation.* Levinson calls these features of the Constitution the "Constitution of Settlement." Here are a few examples:

- the decision to have a bicameral Congress rather than a single house (as in the state legislature of Nebraska);
- the allocation of equal voting power in the Senate to each state (the so-called Great Compromise that Madison fervently opposed);
- the creation of a separate executive branch led by a President, who serves a fixed term, who may not be politically allied with majorities in either or both houses of Congress;
- the decision to begin the President's term almost three months after election (four months in the 1787 Constitution);
- the decision to give the President the power to veto laws passed by Congress subject to a difficult-to-achieve two-thirds override vote in both the House and Senate;
- the decision to have different terms of two and six years, respectively, for the Senate and House;
- the grant of exactly two, instead of "an equal number" of senators to each State, which has meant, for example, that the Senate has gained only four new members (with the addition of Hawaii and Alaska in the 1950s) since 1912; and
- the creation of amendment rules in Article V that make it exceedingly difficult to change the Constitution—far more difficult, for example, than almost all state constitutions in the United States and most countries in the world.

The various features of the Constitution of Settlement are crucial to understanding how the American system of government works in practice. They are especially important in understanding the practical ability (or inability) of politicians to govern and thereby maintain political legitimacy. Even if in theory Congress has the *power* to pass certain legislation, the power may mean little if politicians are unable to run the gauntlet of veto points established by the Constitution that make legislation quite difficult. Moreover, the design of institutions may create policy distortions. For example, American agricultural policy and agricultural subsidies are greatly influenced by the fact that the thinly populated states of the Great Plains and upper Midwest have 20 percent of the total vote in the Senate even though they possess only approximately 5 percent of the country's total population. The Electoral College, with its incentive to encourage campaigns that focus on so-called battleground states, means that the political concerns of those states will often play a disproportionate role in the political calculations of Presidents thinking about their prospects for reelection.

It is these "hard-wired" structures that effectively determine the extent to which various policy proposals will pass or be doomed to failure. Professor Frederick Schauer has argued that when it comes to government action, what most Americans truly care about rarely overlaps with the issues normally brought before the United States Supreme Court.[27] The Court has little, if any, connection with decisions about the future of the American economy, America's success (or failure) in various wars and conflicts around the world, global warming, fiscal policy and fiscal discipline, and so on.

Note, however, that by stipulation, these features of the Constitution are not much litigated in the courts. Many of them—consider only the decision to allocate two senators to each state—could not plausibly be altered by arguments about the best interpretation of the Constitution. Rather, if one wishes to change the Constitution of Settlement, the discussion must be about *wisdom* or *design* instead of *meaning* or *interpretation.*

27. See Frederick Schauer, The Supreme Court 2005 Term, Foreword: The Court's Agenda—and the Nation's, 120 Harv. L. Rev. 4 (2006).

Chapter 1

The Bank of the United States: A Case Study

This chapter focuses mainly on one of the first constitutional questions confronted by the new federal government: whether chartering a national bank was within the powers delegated to Congress by Article I. We move from the last decade of the eighteenth century, when the issue came before the legislative and executive branches, through the early decades of the nineteenth century, when it was faced by the Supreme Court and again by different Presidents. Chapter 1 presents some themes that pervade the book, including the strategies of constitutional interpretation and the allocation of decisionmaking authority among the branches of government.

I. EARLY BACKGROUND

"There is nothing in the Constitution about banks and banking, though there might well have been, for the subject was already of both economic and political importance when the Constitution was being written."[1] In 1781, the Continental Congress chartered the Bank of North America. Although there were doubts about Congress's authority under the Articles of Confederation, the bank was justified by its sheer necessity in helping finance the war for independence against Great Britain.[2]

1. Bray Hammond, Banks and Politics in America from the Revolution to the Civil War 103 (1957).

2. Madison initially opposed incorporation of the bank because of "the absence within the Articles of Confederation of any authority, even that of 'inferred necessity,' to create a bank to carry on the war." 3 Papers of James Madison 175 n.16 (1963). When the ordinance of incorporation came to a vote, he cast what he later termed "an acquiescing rather than an affirmative vote." See 4 id. at 19, 21 nn.7, 23 (1965).

At the Philadelphia Convention in 1787, Madison himself proposed that Congress be authorized "to grant charters of incorporation where the interest of the U.S. might require & the legislative provisions of individual States may be incompetent."[3] (At that point in his political career, Madison was a "consolidationist" who supported greatly enhanced powers for a national government.) Rufus King of Massachusetts objected to the proposal on the ground that the "States will be prejudiced and divided into parties by it"; King referred specifically to the concerns of the New York and Philadelphia banking and business communities that Congress might charter a competing banking institution.[4] "Other advocates of the power held back from putting the question to a vote lest it be lost and the record be definitely against it, whereas if not acted on it could be held . . . that the power existed."[5] Gouverneur Morris of Pennsylvania dissuaded his colleague, Robert Morris, from proposing a national bank lest such a provision in the Constitution jeopardize its ratification.[6] The only related proposal brought to a vote—a motion to authorize Congress to charter corporations for the construction of canals—was defeated eight to three.[7] What, if anything, can we infer from this history? On the one hand, it might suggest a rejection of congressional power. On the other, it might also reflect a tactical decision that enhanced national power would be best served by not specifically addressing particular instances. To what extent should these debates matter, given that the deliberations were kept absolutely secret, published for the first time only decades later?

II. THE FIRST BANK OF THE UNITED STATES

In the late eighteenth and early nineteenth centuries, banks served two main functions. First, they were depositories for money. Second, they issued bank notes, on deposits or on other security, which served somewhat the same function as paper money in the absence of a national currency.[8] In December 1790, soon after ratification of the Constitution, Secretary of the Treasury Alexander Hamilton submitted a plan for a national bank to be chartered by Congress and owned jointly by private shareholders and the United States. The bank would strengthen the

---

3. 2 Records of the Federal Convention of 1787, at 615-616 (Farrand ed., 1937) (hereinafter Farrand). No general corporation laws existed in the eighteenth and early nineteenth centuries. Corporate charters, typically giving exclusive rights to quasi-public entities, were tailor-made for the occasion. See Lawrence Friedman, A History of American Law 166-169 (1973).

4. 2 Farrand, supra n.3, at 615-616.

5. Hammond, supra n.1, at 104-105.

6. Id. at 105.

7. 2 Farrand, supra n.3, at 615-616.

8. Article I, §10 prohibits states from coining money or emitting bills of credit. Article I, §8 authorizes Congress to coin money (though not in terms to issue bills of credit). Not until after the Civil War did Congress authorize the issuance of paper money.

national government; it would aid in the collection of taxes and administration of the public finances and could provide loans to the government.[9] The Senate, half of whose 20 members had attended the Philadelphia Convention, unanimously adopted Hamilton's proposal.[10]

A. *The Wilsonian View*

In the House of Representatives, however, a vigorous debate ensued. Most members of the House supported the bill. Several of them invoked the basic purposes of the Constitution listed in the Preamble and general principles of constitutional government. This approach to constitutional interpretation was associated with the founder James Wilson, a member of the Committee of Detail at the Philadelphia Convention and an important defender of the Constitution during ratification.[11] Wilson's theory argued that Americans had formed a national social compact, and the Constitution gave the federal government the powers to achieve the purposes of that compact.[12]

John Laurance argued that "[t]he principles of the government and ends of the constitution . . . were expressed in the preamble, it is established for the common defence and general welfare; the body of that instrument contained provisions the best adapted to the intention of those principles and attainment of those ends. To these ends, principles and provisions Congress was to have . . . a constant eye, and then by the sweeping clause [the Necessary and Proper Clause of Article I, section 8], they were vested with the powers to carry the ends into execution."

Elbridge Gerry explained that the Preamble stated "the great objects for which the constitution was established, and in administering it, we should always keep them in view. And here it is remarkable, that altho' 'common defence and general welfare' are held up in the preamble amongst the primary objects of attention, they are again mentioned in the 8th section of the first article. . . . [I]ndeed common sense dictates the measure; for the security of our property, families, and liberty—of every thing dear to us, depends on our ability to defend them. The means, therefore, for attaining this object, we ought not to omit a year, month, or even a day, if we could avoid it, and we are never provided for defence unless prepared for sudden emergencies."

William Loughton Smith also argued from basic structural principles: "The power to establish a National Bank must reside in Congress—for no individual State can exercise any such power—The right of no particular state is therefore infringed by the institution. . . . [It] is founded on general principles—and will undoubtedly in its operations prove of general utility."

---

9. Hammond, supra n.1, at 114-115.

10. R.K. Moulton, Legislative and Documentary History of the Banks of the United States 13 (1834).

11. Jonathan Gienapp, In Search of Nationhood at the Founding, 89 Fordham L. Rev. 1783 (2021).

12. Id. at 1797-1801.

Fisher Ames pointed both to the Necessary and Proper Clause and the Preamble. The Preamble, he argued, "declares that it is established for the general welfare of the Union; this vested Congress with the authority over all objects of national concern or of a general nature; a National Bank undoubtedly came under this idea, and though not specially mentioned, yet the general design and tendency of the constitution proved more evidently the constitutionality of the system, than its silence in this particular could be construed to express the contrary." Ames noted that the Northwest Ordinance had been established in 1787 by a Confederation Congress with far weaker powers; and that "[t]he government of the western territory was a species of corporation." The authority to set up the western territory, Ames argued, "must of necessity belong to Congress; it could not rest with the individual states. The power here was derived by implication, and was deduced from the reason and necessity of the case."

B. *Madison's View*

[James Madison, who had been elected to the First Congress from Virginia, denounced the bank as beyond Congress's constitutionally delegated authority.[13]

Madison] had entertained this opinion from the date of the Constitution. His impression might, perhaps, be the stronger, because he well recollected that a power to grant charters of incorporation had been proposed in the general convention and rejected.

Is the power of establishing an incorporated Bank among the powers vested by the Constitution in the Legislature of the United States? This is the question to be examined. After some general remarks on the limitations of all political power, he took notice of the peculiar manner in which the Federal Government is limited. It is not a general grant, out of which particular powers are excepted; it is a grant of particular powers only, leaving the general mass in other hands. So it has been understood by its friends and its foes, and so it was to be interpreted.

As preliminaries to the right interpretation, he laid down the following rules:

An interpretation that destroys the very characteristic of the Government cannot be just.

Where the meaning is clear, the consequences, whatever they may be, are to be admitted—where doubtful, it is fairly triable by its consequences.

In controverted cases, the meaning of the parties to the instrument, if to be collected by reasonable evidence, is a proper guide.

Contemporary and concurrent expositions are a reasonable evidence of the meaning of the parties.

In admitting or rejecting a constructive authority, not only the degree of its incidentality to an express authority is to be regarded, but the degree of its importance also; since on this will depend the probability or improbability of its being left to construction.

13. James Madison's Speech to the House of Representatives (1791), in James Madison, Writings 480-490 (Jack Rakove ed., 1999). The text of the speech refers to Madison in the third person because of stylistic practices of the House reporter whose notes are the source of our knowledge of what Madison told his colleagues.

Reviewing the Constitution with an eye to these positions, it was not possible to discover in it the power to incorporate a bank. The only clauses under which such a power could be pretended are either:

1. The power to lay and collect taxes to pay the debts, and provide for the common defence and general welfare; Or,
2. The power to borrow money on the credit of the United States; Or,
3. The power to pass all laws necessary and proper to carry into execution those powers.

The bill did not come within the first power. It laid no taxes to pay the debts, or provide for the general welfare. It laid no tax whatever. It was altogether foreign to the subject.

No argument could be drawn from the terms "common defence" and "general welfare." The power as to these general purposes was limited to acts laying taxes for them; and the general purposes themselves were limited and explained by the particular enumeration subjoined. To understand these terms in any sense, that would justify the power in question, would give the Congress an unlimited power; would render nugatory the enumeration of particular powers; would supercede all the powers reserved to the State Governments. . . .

The case of the Bank established by the former Congress has been cited as a precedent. This was known, he said, to have been the child of necessity. It never could be justified by the regular powers of the articles of Confederation. . . .

The second clause to be examined is that which empowers Congress to borrow money.

Is this bill to borrow money? It does not borrow a shilling. Is there any fair construction by which the bill can be deemed an exercise of the power to borrow money? The obvious meaning of the power to borrow money, is that of accepting it from, and stipulating payment to those who are able and willing to lend. . . .

The third clause is that which gives the power to pass all laws necessary and proper to execute the specified powers.

Whatever meaning this clause may have, none can be admitted, that would give an unlimited discretion to Congress.

Its meaning must, according to the natural and obvious force of the terms and the context, be limited to means necessary to the end, and incident to the nature of the specified powers.

The clause is in fact merely declaratory of what would have resulted by unavoidable implication, as the appropriate, and, as it were, technical means of executing those powers. In this sense it has been explained by the friends of the Constitution, and ratified by the State Conventions.

The essential characteristic of the Government, as composed of limited and enumerated powers, would be destroyed, if instead of direct and incidental means, any means could be used which, in the language of the preamble to the bill, "might be conceived to be conducive to the successful conducting of the finances, or might be conceived to tend to give facility to the obtaining of loans. . . ." If, proceeded he, Congress, by virtue of the power to borrow, can create the means of lending, and, in pursuance of these means, can incorporate a Bank, they may do any thing whatever creative of like means. . . .

If, again, Congress by virtue of the power to borrow money, can create the ability to lend, they may, by virtue of the power to levy money, create the ability to pay it. The ability to pay taxes depends on the general wealth of the society, and this, on the general prosperity of agriculture, manufactures, and commerce. Congress then may give bounties and make regulations on all these objects. . . .

Mark the reasoning on which the validity of the bill depends. To borrow money is made the end, and the accumulation of capitals implied as the means. The accumulation of money is then the end, and the Bank implied as the means. The Bank is then the end, and a charter of incorporation, a monopoly, . . . &c. implied as the means.

If implications, thus remote and thus multiplied, can be linked together, a chain may be formed that will reach every object of legislation, every object within the whole compass of political economy.

The latitude of interpretation required by the bill is condemned by the rule furnished by the Constitution itself.

Congress have power "to regulate the value of money"; yet it is expressly added, not left to be implied, that counterfeiters may be punished.

They have the power "to declare war," to which armies are more incident, than incorporated banks to borrowing; yet the power "to raise and support armies" is expressly added; and to this again, the express power "to make rules and regulations for the government of armies"; a like remark is applicable to the powers as to the navy.

The regulation and calling out of militia are more appurtenant to war than the proposed Bank to borrowing; yet the former is not left to construction.

The very power to borrow money is a less remote implication from the power of war, than an incorporated monopoly Bank from the power of borrowing; yet the power is not left to implication.

It is not pretended that every insertion or omission in the Constitution is the effect of systematic attention. This is not the character of any human work, particularly the work of a body of men. The examples cited, with others that might be added, sufficiently inculcate, nevertheless, a rule of interpretation very different from that on which the bill rests. They condemn the exercise of any power, particularly a great and important power, which is not evidently and necessarily involved in an express power.

It cannot be denied that the power proposed to be exercised is an important power. As a charter of incorporation, the bill creates an artificial person previously not existing in law. It confers important civil rights and attributes, which could not otherwise be claimed. It is, though not precisely similar, at least equivalent, to the naturalization of an alien, by which certain new civil characters are acquired by him. Would Congress have had the power to naturalize, if it had not been expressly given?

He here adverted to a distinction, which he said has not been sufficiently kept in view, between a power necessary and proper for the Government or Union, and a power necessary and proper for executing the enumerated powers.

In the latter case, the powers included in each of the enumerated powers were not expressed, but drawn from the nature of each. In the former, the powers composing the Government were expressly enumerated. This constituted the peculiar nature of the Government, no power, therefore, not enumerated could be inferred from the general nature of Government. Had the power of making treaties, for example, been omitted, however necessary it might have been, the defect could only have been lamented, or supplied by an amendment of the Constitution.

But the proposed Bank could not be called necessary to the Government; at most could be but convenient. Its uses to the Government could be supplied by keeping the taxes a little in advance; by loans from individuals; by other Banks, over which the Government would have equal command; nay greater, as it might grant or refuse to these the privilege (a free and irrevocable gift to the proposed Bank) of using their notes in the federal revenue.

He proceeded next to the contemporary expositions given to the Constitution [in various ratification conventions, which supported the conclusion] that the terms necessary and proper gave no additional powers to those enumerated. . . .

The explanatory declarations and amendment accompanying the ratifications of the several states formed a striking evidence, wearing the same complexion. He referred those who might doubt on the subject, to the several acts of ratification.

The explanatory amendments proposed by Congress themselves, at least, would be good authority with them; all these renunciations of power proceeded on a rule of construction, excluding the latitude now contended for. These explanations were the more to be respected, as they had not only been proposed by Congress, but ratified by nearly three-fourths of the states. [Virginia had not yet ratified the "Bill of Rights."] He read several of the articles proposed, remarking particularly on the [Ninth and Tenth Amendments], the former, as guarding against a latitude of interpretation—the latter, as excluding every source of power not within the constitution itself.

With all this evidence of the sense in which the Constitution was understood and adopted, will it not be said, if the bill should pass, that its adoption was brought about by one set of arguments, and that it is now administered under the influence of another set . . . [?]

It appeared on the whole, he concluded, that the power exercised by the bill was condemned by the silence of the constitution; was condemned by the rule of interpretation arising out of the constitution; was condemned by its tendency to destroy the main characteristic of the constitution; was condemned by the expositions of the friends of the constitution [to] the public; was condemned by the apparent intention of the parties which ratified the constitution; was condemned by the explanatory amendments proposed by Congress themselves to the Constitution; and he hoped it would receive its final condemnation, by the vote of this house.

Madison's view that the new federal government was strictly limited by its enumerated powers was considered novel at the time, and was greeted with considerable skepticism, especially given the Wilsonian premises held by many members of the First Congress.[14] As Richard Primus notes:

> The novelty of Madison's fervent investment in enumerated powers in 1791 helps explain an important but often overlooked feature of the Bank debate: many Members of the First Congress who disagreed with Madison about the constitutionality of the Bank bill did not merely think that Madison had a different view of the Constitution from their own. They doubted that he really believed what he was arguing. In their view, Madison's insistence that the enumeration principle was a centrally important element of the new Constitution transparently contradicted positions he had taken earlier in the First Congress, when other issues of constitutional power were before the House. So in beating the drum for the limiting enumeration this time around, these members of Congress thought, Madison was making an argument of convenience, hoping to use a constitutional smokescreen to defeat a bill he didn't like.

Richard Primus, "The Essential Characteristic": Enumerated Powers and the Bank of the United States, 117 Mich. L. Rev. 415, 423 (2018).

Nevertheless, Madison's arguments for a relatively strict construction of enumerated powers would become more important seven years later—in the debates over the Alien and Sedition Acts—as the First Party System between Federalists and Jeffersonians formed. Once Thomas Jefferson's party took control of the government in 1801, strict construction became the reigning orthodoxy of the nation's dominant party, the Democratic-Republicans. Nevertheless, as we will see, Madison backed off his opposition to a Bank of the United States when he became President himself.[15]

---

14. Akhil Amar argues that Madison's opposition to the new bank stemmed less from constitutional principle and more from his concern that it would shift the center of gravity of power from Virginia to Philadelphia, the nation's financial hub and the government's then provisional capital. He feared that the bank's location in Philadelphia might even cause Congress to rethink its recent decision to locate the nation's capital to Washington D.C. on Virginia's border. Akhil Reed Amar, The Words That Made Us: America's Constitutional Conversation, 1860-1840 358 (2021).

15. Madison, who had a successful political career spanning many decades, turns out, not surprisingly, to have changed his positions a bit over time. There is a substantial literature on what Gordon Wood has called the "Madison Problem"—how consistent he really was over the course of his career. See, e.g., Stanley Elkins & Eric McKitrick, The Age of Federalism 133-161 (1993); Noah Feldman, The Three Lives of James Madison chs. 8-9 (2017) (arguing that Madison shifted fundamentally from a nationalist position to a general skepticism of national power during the 1790s). For defenses of Madison's consistency, see Gordon S. Wood, "Is There a James Madison Problem?", in Revolutionary Characters: What Made the Founders Different 141-172 (2006) (arguing that scholars have overstated changes in Madison's larger views); Jack N. Rakove, The Madisonian Moment, 55 U. Chi. L. Rev. 473, 504 (1988) (arguing that some of Madison's ideas remained constant while others underwent changes ranging from "modest shifts of emphasis" to the acceptance of "radically new positions"). For an overview of Madison's complex thought, see, e.g., Lance Banning, The Sacred Fire of Liberty: James Madison & the Founding of the Federal Republic (1998).

In any case, the House adopted the bill chartering the bank by a vote of 39 to 20. Of the seven Representatives who had attended the Philadelphia Convention, four voted for the measure and three against it. The bill now went to the President, George Washington, for his veto or signature. Washington had presided over the Philadelphia Convention, and although he did not participate directly in the debates, his views were largely nationalist. He asked his cabinet to prepare memoranda on the constitutional questions. Edmund Randolph, the Attorney General, thought the bill unconstitutional, as did Secretary of State Thomas Jefferson. The Secretary of the Treasury, Alexander Hamilton supported the measure.

C. *The Attorney General's Opinion*

Section 35 of the Judiciary Act of 1789, one of the first major pieces of legislation passed by the First Congress, created the office of Attorney General. In addition to having the duty "to prosecute and conduct all suits in the Supreme Court in which the United States shall be concerned," the Attorney General must also "give his advice and opinion upon questions of law when requested by the President of the United States, or when requested by the heads of any of the departments, touching any matters that may concern their departments."[16]

Fulfilling his duty, Randolph informed President Washington why he found the Bank bill unconstitutional: "To be implied in the nature of the federal government would beget a doctrine so indefinite as to grasp every power." Randolph then asked "whether, upon any principle of fair construction, the specified powers of legislation involve the power of granting charters of incorporation?" Randolph rejected use of the Preamble as a source of authority: "To this, it will be here remarked, once for all, that the Preamble if it be operative is a full constitution of itself; and the body of the Constitution is useless; but that it is declarative only of the views of the convention, which they supposed would be best fulfilled by the powers delineated and that such is the legitimate nature of preambles." (Compare Randolph's rejection of the utility of looking to the Preamble with the use made by Jay and Wilson in their opinions in Chisholm v. Georgia, Chapter 2, infra.)

Randolph also rejected using specific powers listed in Article I, §8, including the taxation, borrowing, and commerce powers, as well as the Article IV authority given Congress "to dispose and make all needful Rules and Regulations respecting the Territory or other Property belonging to the United States":

> If the laying and collecting of taxes brings with it every thing which, in the opinion of Congress, may facilitate the payment of taxes; if to borrow money sets political speculation loose, to conceive what may create an ability to lend; if to regulate commerce is to range in the boundless mazes of projects for the apparently best scheme to invite from abroad, or

---

16. See H. Jefferson Powell, The Constitution and the Attorneys General xv (1999). Randolph's entire opinion, excerpts of which are found below, can be found at 3-9.

to diffuse at home, the precious metals; if to dispose of or so to regulate property of the United States, is to incorporate a bank, that stock may be subscribed to it by them, it may without exaggeration be affirmed that a similar construction on every specified federal power, will stretch the arm of Congress into the whole circle of state legislation.

The general qualities of the federal government, independent of the Constitution and the specified powers, being thus insufficient to uphold the incorporation of a bank, we come to the last inquiry, which has been already anticipated, whether it be sanctified by the power to make all laws which shall be necessary and proper for carrying into execution the powers vested by the Constitution. To be necessary is to be incidental, or in other words, may be denominated the natural means of executing a power.

The phrase, "and proper," if it has any meaning, does not enlarge the power of Congress, but rather restricts them. For no power is to be assumed under the general clause, but such as is not only necessary but proper, or perhaps expedient also. But as the friends to the bill ought not to claim any advantage from this clause, so ought not the enemies to it; to quote the clause as having a restricting effect; both ought to consider it among the surplusage which as often proceeds from inattention as caution.

D. *Jefferson's Critique of the Bank*

Jefferson referred to the Philadelphia Convention's rejection of the congressional power to incorporate canals: "[O]ne of the reasons for rejection urged in the debate was, that then they would have a power to erect a bank, which would render the great cities, where there were prejudices and jealousies on the subject, adverse to the reception of the Constitution."[17] Continuing in a more general vein he wrote:[18]

> I consider the foundation of the Constitution as laid on this ground: That "all powers not delegated to the United States, by the Constitution, nor prohibited by it to the States, are reserved to the States or to the people." To take a single step beyond the boundaries thus specially drawn around the powers of Congress is to take possession of a boundless field of power, no longer susceptible of any definition. . . .
>
> It has been urged that a bank will give great facility or convenience in the collection of taxes. Suppose this were true: yet the Constitution allows

17. Since the records of the Convention had not been published, one can well wonder how Jefferson, who had been in Paris during the deliberations in Philadelphia, knew of Madison's unsuccessful proposal.

18. Opinion on the Constitutionality of the Bill for Establishing a National Bank, in 19 Papers of Thomas Jefferson 275, 279-280 (1974).

only the means which are "*necessary*," not those which are merely "convenient" for effecting the enumerated powers. If such a latitude of construction be allowed to this phrase as to give any non-enumerated power, it will go to every one, for there is not one which ingenuity may not torture into a *convenience* in some instance *or other*, to *some one* of so long a list of enumerated powers. It would swallow up all the delegated powers, and reduce the whole to one power, as before observed. Therefore it was that the Constitution restrained them to the *necessary* means, that is to say, to those means without which the grant of power would be nugatory. . . .

E. *Hamilton's Defense*

Alexander Hamilton, Opinion on the Constitutionality of an Act to Establish a Bank[19]

(1791)

. . . [P]rinciples of construction like those espoused by the Secretary of State and the Attorney General would be fatal to the just & indispensable authority of the United States. . . .

[T]his *general principle* is *inherent* in the very *definition* of *Government* and *essential* to every step of the progress to be made by that of the United States; namely—that every power vested in a Government is in its nature *sovereign*, and includes by *force* of the *term*, a right to employ all the *means* requisite, and fairly *applicable* to the attainment of the *ends* of such power; and which are not precluded by restrictions & exceptions specified in the constitution; or not immoral, or not contrary to the essential ends of political society. . . .

This general & indisputable principle puts at once an end to the *abstract* question—Whether the United States have power to *erect a corporation*? that is to say, to give a *legal* or *artificial capacity* to one or more persons, distinct from the natural. For it is unquestionably incident to *sovereign power* to erect corporations, and consequently to *that* of the United States, in *relation to the objects* intrusted to the management of the government. The difference is this: where the authority of the government is general, it can create corporations in *all cases*; where it is confined to certain branches of legislation, it can create corporations only in those cases. . . . It is not denied, that there are *implied*, as well as *express* powers, and that the former are as effectually delegated as the latter. . . .

Then it follows, that as a power of erecting a corporation may as well be *implied* as any other thing; it may as well be employed as an *instrument* or *mean* of carrying into execution any of the specified powers, as any other instrument or mean whatever. The only question must be, in this as in every other case, whether the mean to be employed, or in this instance the corporation to be erected, has a natural relation

19. 8 Papers of Alexander Hamilton 97 (1965).

to any of the acknowledged objects or lawful ends of the government. Thus a corporation may not be erected by congress, for superintending the police of the city of Philadelphia because they are not authorized to *regulate* the *police* of that city; but one may be erected in relation to the collection of the taxes, or to the trade with foreign countries, or to the trade between the States, or with the Indian Tribes, because it is the province of the federal government to regulate those objects & because it is incident to a general *sovereign* or *legislative power* to *regulate* a thing, to employ all the means which relate to its regulation to the *best & greatest advantage*. . . .

[I]t is objected that none but *necessary* & proper means are to be employed, & the Secretary of State maintains, that no means are to be considered as *necessary*, but those without which the grant of the power would be *nugatory*. . . . All the arguments therefore against the constitutionality of the bill derived from the accidental existence of certain State-banks: institutions which *happen* to exist today, & for aught that concerns the government of the United States, may disappear tomorrow, must not only be rejected as fallacious, but must be viewed as demonstrative, that there is a *radical* source of error in the reasoning. . . .

According to both [the grammatical and popular sense of the term], *necessary* often means no more than *needful, requisite, incidental, useful,* or *conducive to.* It is a common mode of expression to say, that it is *necessary* for a government or a person to do this or that thing, when nothing more is intended or understood, than that the interests of the government or person require, or will be promoted, by the doing of this or that thing . . . . The whole turn of the clause containing [the word "necessary"] indicates, that it was the intent of the convention, by that clause to give a liberal latitude to the exercise of the specified powers. . . .

[The alternative] construction would beget endless uncertainty & embarrassment. The cases must be palpable & extreme in which it could be pronounced with certainty, that a measure was absolutely necessary, or one without which the exercise of a given power would be nugatory. There are few measures of any government, which would stand so severe a test. To insist upon it, would be to make the criterion of the exercise of any implied power a *case of extreme necessity*, which is rather a rule to justify the overleaping of the bounds of constitutional authority, than to govern the ordinary exercise of it. . . .

The *degree* in which a measure is necessary, can never be a test of the *legal* right to adopt it. That must ever be a matter of opinion; and can only be a test of expediency. The *relation* between the *measure* and the *end*, between the *nature* of the *mean* employed towards the execution of a power and the object of that power, must be the criterion of constitutionality not the more or less of *necessity* or *utility*.

The practice of the government is against the rule of construction advocated by the Secretary of State. Of this the act concerning light houses, beacons, buoys & public piers, is a decisive example. This doubtless must be referred to the power of regulating trade, and is fairly relative to it. But it cannot be affirmed, that the exercise of that power, in this instance, was strictly necessary; or that the power itself would be *nugatory* without that of regulating establishments of this nature.

This restrictive interpretation of the word *necessary* is also contrary to this sound maxim of construction namely, that the powers contained in a constitution of government, especially those which concern the general administration of the affairs of a country, its finances, trade, defence & ought to be construed liberally, in advancement of the public good. . . .

[T]he doctrine which is contended for . . . does not affirm that the National government is sovereign in all respects, but that it is sovereign to a certain extent: that is, to the extent of the objects of its specified powers.

It leaves therefore a criterion of what is constitutional, and of what is not so. This criterion is the *end* to which the measure relates as a *mean.* If the end be clearly comprehended within any of the specified powers, & if the measure have an obvious relation to that end, and is not forbidden by any particular provision of the constitution—it may safely be deemed to come within the compass of the national authority. . . .

[The ability to charter a corporation] has a relation more or less direct to the power of collecting taxes; to that of borrowing money; to that of regulating trade between the states; and to those of raising, supporting & maintaining fleets & armies. To the two former, the relation may be said to be *immediate.* . . . [I]t is, *clearly,* within the provision which authorizes the making of all *needful* rules & *regulations* concerning the *property* of the United States, as the same has been practiced upon by the Government.

A Bank relates to the collection of taxes in two ways; *indirectly,* by increasing the quantity of circulating medium & quickening circulation, which facilitates the means of paying—*directly,* by creating a *convenient species* of *medium* in which they are to be paid.

The legislative power of borrowing money, & of making all laws necessary & proper for carrying into execution that power, seems obviously competent to the appointment of the organ through which the abilities and wills of individuals may be most efficaciously exerted, for the accommodation of the government by loans. . . .

The institution of a bank has also a natural relation to the regulation of trade between the States: in so far as it is conducive to the creation of a convenient medium of *exchange* between them, and to the keeping up a full circulation by preventing the frequent displacement of the metals in reciprocal remittances, money is the very hinge on which commerce turns. And this does not mean merely gold & silver, many other things have served the purpose with different degrees of utility. Paper has been extensively employed. . . .

[A]s the bill under consideration contemplates the government in the light of a joint proprietor of the stock of the bank, it brings the case within the provision of the clause of the constitution which immediately respects the property of the United States.

DISCUSSION

On February 25, 1791, President Washington signed the act incorporating the Bank of the United States. Whose opinion in these debates do you find most persuasive, and why?

III. THE SECOND BANK

When the bank's 20-year charter lapsed in 1811, Congress refused to renew it. Opposition to the bank came from both Jeffersonian agrarians—though Jefferson himself now publicly supported the bank—and from the private business and banking community who preferred available state-chartered banks. Of the 39 members of Congress who spoke on the issue of renewal, 35 addressed the constitutionality of the bank. Whether because of constitutional doubts or, more likely, because of the strength of antinational forces in Congress, renewal failed by one vote.[20]

Four years later, however, Congress voted to establish the Second Bank of the United States, responding in part to the economic turmoil attached to the War of 1812, as well as to the perceived irresponsible fiscal practices by state banks. The federal government had been seriously inconvenienced by its need to rely on state banks to borrow money and to pay national debts. Although James Madison, now President himself, vetoed the renewal on policy grounds, he explicitly "waiv[ed] the question of the constitutional authority of the Legislature to establish an incorporated bank, as being precluded, in my judgment, by the repeated recognitions under varied circumstances of the validity of such an institution, in acts of the Legislative, Executive, and Judicial branches of the Government, accompanied by indications, in different modes, of a concurrence of the general will of the nation."[21]

Madison did sign a bill chartering the Second Bank of the United States in 1816. This did not necessarily mean, however, that Madison or his party accepted the wide-ranging arguments articulated by Hamilton in 1791. Instead, Eric Lomazoff has argued that the 1816 renewal—which he labels the "Compromise of 1816"—was in effect procured by shifting the primary argument from the "Necessary and Proper Clause," the focus of the original debate in 1791, to the "Coinage Clause" of Article I, which was viewed as significantly less expansive in its implications.[22] (As we will shortly see, John Marshall makes no reference at all to the Coinage Clause in his defense of the bank.)

Lomazoff suggests that by 1816, the function of the bank had become quite different from what it was in 1791. When the First Bank was chartered, there were relatively few state banks. In 1792, for example, there were a total of 12 state banks, with a combined capital of $6.3 million dollars. By 1810, however, there were 102 state banks, with a total capitalization of $56.2 million. This meant, as a practical matter, that the market share of the national bank had decreased from 61 percent in 1792 to only 15.1 percent in 1810.

What remained important about a national bank, Lomazoff argues, is that it could serve a de facto regulatory function by placing limits on the ability of state banks to overheat the economy (and thus risk collapses) by making ill-advised loans. State banks issued notes backed up by specie (gold and silver coins). The Bank of the United States had the ability to redeem state bank notes for specie. Lomazoff argues that the potential threat that the national bank would call in its holdings of state bank notes for specie limited the type and amount of loans state banks could make; this, in turn, helped to reduce the risk of bank failures and

20. Hammond, supra n.1, at 210-222.

21. Quoted in id. at 233. The general story of the renewal is told at 227-233. See also Mark R. Killenbeck, McCulloch v. Maryland: Securing a Nation (2006).

22. See Eric Lomazoff, Reconstructing the National Bank Controversy: Politics and Law in the Early American Republic (2018).

consequent turmoil in the economy. In effect, the Second Bank of the United States began to function as a proto-central bank (the Federal Reserve would not be created until 1913) with responsibilities to monitor the overall supply of currency and, if possible, prevent disruptions to the economy.

Like its predecessor, the Second Bank was by no means a purely governmental agency. Private investors owned 80 percent of the stock and the government owned the remaining 20 percent. Of its 25 directors, 20 were elected by the shareholders, and the President appointed the other 5. The bank did act as the government's primary fiscal agent: The Secretary of the Treasury was required to deposit all public funds in the bank; it was required to keep, transfer, and disburse all government monies given it; and its notes were made legal tender for the payment of government debts. Consider, though, that President Monroe's Secretary of the Treasury Crawford wrote to the new president of the bank in 1819 that "[t]he first duty of the Board [of Directors] is to the stockholders, the second is to the nation."[23] If this is correct, why regard the Bank of the United States as an instrument of the national government at all?

The dispute over the bank was not over, however. A number of states remained intensely hostile and enacted nearly annihilative taxes on the bank, leading to the Court's decision in McCulloch v. Maryland.

IV. JUDICIAL EXAMINATION OF CONGRESS'S AUTHORITY TO CREATE THE BANK

NOTE ON READING AND EDITING CASES

The Supreme Court Justices' opinions in constitutional cases are often very long, and we have necessarily edited most of the cases in this book to focus the issues, to keep the book to a manageable length while covering a variety of issues, and to mitigate tedium. *McCulloch*, however, is unedited.

We suggest that you read Chief Justice Marshall's opinion through once to get a sense of its structure and arguments. Then read it again with a blue pencil (imaginary or real, depending on the projected resale value of this book), trying to omit as much superfluity as you can.

Our own experience as editors is that there is no better way to understand the substance and structure of a person's writing than to edit it. We also hope that you will gain some appreciation of the problems of editing an opinion—not, we hasten to add, so that you will appreciate our hard work, but so you will be skeptical about the relationship between any edited version and the original. Why, after all, do judges write such long opinions if much, if not most, of the language can be excised without any loss to understanding? Moreover, and perhaps paradoxically,

23. Quoted in Richard E. Ellis, Aggressive Nationalism: *McCulloch v. Maryland* and the Foundation of Federal Authority in the Young Republic 106-107 (2007).

it is only by reading an opinion in its entirety that you understand fully what is left out (as well as included) in a judicial opinion. You should note, for example, that Marshall offers no discussion at all of the corporate organization (and loyalties) of the bank. Do you agree that that is utterly irrelevant?

McCulloch v. Maryland

17 U.S. (4 Wheat.) 316 (1819)

[In 1818, the Maryland Assembly enacted a law imposing an annual tax of $15,000 on all banks or branches of banks in the state not chartered by the state legislature. The only bank that fit this description was the Bank of the United States, whose local cashier, J.W. McCulloch, refused to pay the tax. Maryland successfully sued McCulloch in its own courts to recover the statutory penalty for failure to comply with the statute.]

Marshall, C.J.

[The First Question]

[1]¶1 In the case now to be determined, the defendant, a sovereign State, denies the obligation of a law enacted by the legislature of the Union, and the plaintiff, on his part, contests the validity of an act which has been passed by the legislature of that State. The constitution of our country, in its most interesting and vital parts, is to be considered; the conflicting powers of the government of the Union and of its members, as marked in that constitution, are to be discussed; and an opinion given, which may essentially influence the great operation of the government. No tribunal can approach such a question without a deep sense of its importance, and of the awful responsibility involved in its decision. But it must be decided peacefully, or remain a source of hostile legislation, perhaps of hostility of a still more serious nature; and if it is to be so decided, by this tribunal alone can the decision be made. On the Supreme Court of the United States has the constitution of our country devolved this important duty.

¶1. Marshall refers to Maryland as "a sovereign state." What does this mean? *Is* Maryland a sovereign state? Wouldn't a sovereign state have the ability to tax whomever it pleased? Would it have been more accurate to describe Maryland as a "once-sovereign"—i.e., prior to ratifying the Constitution—state? See, however, ¶21 below.

Marshall notes the freighted circumstances surrounding this decision, and that the controversy "must be decided peacefully" lest circumstances lead to "hostility of a still more serious nature" than merely hostile legislation. To what might he be referring?

Marshall suggests in the final sentence in this paragraph that the Constitution has "devolved" upon the Supreme Court "this important duty" to resolve the issue. Marshall supplies no evidence for this assertion. Is there any relevant constitutional text that he might have cited? Even if you think there is, does it devolve any such duty on the Supreme Court "alone"? Do Congress and the President—or for that matter, "We the People"—have any role to play in construing the Constitution's meaning, and, in particular, the proper scope of national power?

[2] The first question made in the cause is, has Congress power to incorporate a bank?

[3] It has been truly said, that this can scarcely be considered as an open question, entirely unprejudiced by the former proceedings of the nation respecting it. The principle now contested was introduced at a very early period of our history, has been recognized by many successive legislatures, and has been acted upon by the judicial department, in cases of peculiar delicacy, as a law of undoubted obligation.

[4][¶4-5] It will not be denied, that a bold and daring usurpation might be resisted, after an acquiescence still longer and more complete than this. But it is conceived that a doubtful question, one on which human reason may pause, and

---

¶4-5. One way of understanding ¶¶4-5 of *McCulloch* is as outlining, on the one hand, those circumstances in which courts (or other constitutional adjudicators) should be *deferential* to the decisions of ordinary political actors and, on the other, those in which courts should be sufficiently *suspicious* of those actors to engage in what contemporary jargon labels as "strict scrutiny" of their decisions. Consider, then, the following sets of oppositions suggested by the argument in these two paragraphs:

"bold and daring usurpation"	scrupulous adherence to what everybody accepts as constitutional duty
clear and unequivocal language	"doubtful question[s]" upon which "human reason might pause"
presence of a "great principle of liberty"	[mere] question of "the respective powers of those who are equally the representatives of the people"
legislation "pass[ed] unobserved"	passed after full debate
political officials are stupid or corrupt	officials are "as pure and as intelligent as this country can boast"

Is it not clear that one generally would support a greater measure of judicial "intervention" in (some combination) of the first column of circumstances than in the second? Similarly, is it not equally clear that there appears to be little justification for such intervention in (some combination) of the second column? The obvious questions are twofold:

1. How does one establish criteria to identify when any given condition is met?

2. How many of the circumstances have to be met to trigger either "strict scrutiny" (and a high probability of judicial invalidation) as against a search only for what contemporary analysts call "minimum rationality" (and a high probability of judicial deference)? Less obvious, but no less important, is the question of judicial capacity to make any of the given inquiries. For example, how precisely do judges (or anyone else) decide how much debate is enough? And how formal must such a debate be? E.g., should formal "hearings" be required of controversial legislation or structured debate in the House and/or Senate, or is it enough if a lot of newspaper editorials are written and legislators with opposing views appear on various talk shows before a vote, without additional debate, in the legislature? Similarly, how does one decide whether a political leader has a "pure" or "intelligent" mind? Think only of our most recent Presidents. Even if we could agree on standards for assessing their purity or intelligence, does that have anything to do with assessing the constitutionality of actions taken under their claims of presidential powers granted by the Constitution? (Should you decide that courts ought not make such inquiries, does that entail that no one else should either?)

the human judgment be suspended, in the decision of which the great principles of liberty are not concerned, but the respective powers of those who are equally the representatives of the people, are to be adjusted; if not put at rest by the practice of the government, ought to receive a considerable impression from that practice. An exposition of the constitution, deliberately established by legislative acts, on the faith of which an immense property has been advanced, ought not to be lightly disregarded.

[5] The power now contested was exercised by the first Congress elected under the present constitution. The bill for incorporating the bank of the United States did not steal upon an unsuspecting legislature, and passed unobserved. Its principle was completely understood, and was opposed with equal zeal and ability. After being resisted, first in the fair and open field of debate, and afterwards in the executive cabinet, with as much persevering talent as any measure has ever experienced, and being supported by arguments which convinced minds as pure and as intelligent as this country can boast, it became a law. The original act was permitted to expire; but a short experience of the embarrassments to which the refusal to revive it exposed the government, convinced those who were most prejudiced against the measure of its necessity, and induced the passage of the present law. It would require no ordinary share of intrepidity to assert that a measure adopted under these circumstances was a bold and plain usurpation, to which the constitution gave no countenance.

[6] These observations belong to the cause; but they are not made under the impression that, were the question entirely new, the law would be found irreconcilable with the constitution.

[7][¶7-11] In discussing this question, the counsel for the State of Maryland have deemed it of some importance, in the construction of the constitution, to consider that instrument not as emanating from the people, but as the act of sovereign and independent States. The powers of the general government, it has been said, are delegated by the States, who alone are truly sovereign; and must be exercised in subordination to the States, who alone possess supreme dominion.

¶7-11. Why might "counsel for the State of Maryland have deemed it of some importance, in the construction of the constitution, to consider that instrument not as emanating from the people, but as the act of sovereign and independent states"? One view, associated with Blackstone, held that sovereignty could rest in only one entity. This, as the anti-Federalists urged during the ratification campaign, posed problems for the proposed constitution, under which two sovereignties operated simultaneously in the same jurisdiction and on the same persons. This view, however, was not universally accepted. See Alison LaCroix, Rhetoric and Reality in Early American Legal History: A Reply to Gordon Wood, 78 U. Chi. L. Rev. 733, 735 (2011). The Federalists responded ingeniously by replacing a theory of "dual sovereignty" of both federal and state governments in favor of a new notion of singular "popular sovereignty," captured most memorably in the first words of the Preamble. See Gordon Wood, The Creation of the American Republic, 1776-1787 ch. 13 (1969).

One can perhaps best understand the placement of these paragraphs early in Marshall's opinion by reference to Professor H. Jefferson Powell's point that a "maxim of political law" during the eighteenth century was that a sovereign can be deprived of any of its powers only by its express consent narrowly construed. Should the states—or the people of the states qua states—be deemed sovereign, the implication of this maxim was that the Constitution

[8] It would be difficult to sustain this proposition. The Convention which framed the constitution was indeed elected by the State legislatures. But the instrument, when it came from their hands, was a mere proposal, without obligation, or pretensions to it. It was reported to the then existing Congress of the United States, with a request that it might "be submitted to a Convention of Delegates, chosen in each State by the people thereof, under the recommendation of its Legislature, for their assent and ratification." This mode of proceeding was adopted; and by the Convention, by Congress, and by the State Legislatures, the instrument was submitted to the people. They acted upon it in the only manner in which they can act safely, effectively, and wisely, on such a subject, by assembling in Convention. It is true, they assembled in their several States—and where else should they have assembled? No political dreamer was ever wild enough to think of breaking down the lines which separate the States, and of compounding the American people into one common mass. Of consequence, when they act, they act in their States. But the measures they adopt do not, on that account, cease to be the measures of the people themselves, or become the measures of the State governments.

---

should be given "the most strict construction that the instrument will bear" in favor of the retention of power by these sovereigns. See Powell, The Original Understanding of Original Intent, 98 Harv. L. Rev. 885, 929-931 (1985) (quoting the Virginia lawyer St. George Tucker). Placement of sovereignty in the national people would still presumably call for "strict construction" against derogation of their rights, but the crucial point is that popular (as opposed to state) sovereignty deprives states of any special claim to having their ostensible rights privileged over the competing claims of the national government.

Marshall appears to offer three models for who was "sovereign": (1) the people of each state, organized in some meaningful way state by state; (2) the state governments; and (3) the people of an undifferentiated whole called the United States. He is surely right that the state legislatures cannot be sovereign (see Article VII), but that, of course, leaves the other two possibilities. If one opts for the first, then would it follow that one should construe the sovereignty of the national government quite narrowly, as suggested above, as against a more capacious construction that might be legitimated by the third possibility? On what basis should one choose between them? Marshall does refer to "the people" in ¶¶7-11, but is this dispositive as to choosing (3) as against (1)? How, for example, does one understand his statement, "No political dreamer was ever wild enough to think of breaking down the lines which separate the States, and of compounding the American people into one common mass. Of consequence, when they act, they act in their States." See Martin S. Flaherty, John Marshall, McCulloch v. Maryland, and "We the People": Revisions in Need of Revising, 43 Wm. & Mary L. Rev. 1339 (2002).

Consider the August 7, 1787, draft of the Constitution, which had the following preamble:

> We the people of the States of New-Hampshire, Massachusetts, Rhode-Island and Providence Plantations [and the other 13 original States] do ordain, declare and establish the following Constitution or the Government of Ourselves and our Posterity.

Recall the preamble to the Articles of Confederation, which similarly mentioned each of the constituent states.

Does it matter that this was changed, for reasons that are wholly unclear, by the Committee on Style? What is the consequence for the "Unionist" argument of Article VII, which sets out the mode of ratification (or of Article V, which sets out the process by which the Constitution is amended)? How does Marshall respond to Maryland's invocation of Article VII? Is the response satisfactory?

[9] From these Conventions the constitution derives its whole authority. The government proceeds directly from the people; is "ordained and established" in the name of the people; and is declared to be ordained, "in order to form a more perfect union, establish justice, ensure domestic tranquility, and secure the blessings of liberty to themselves and to their posterity." The assent of the States, in their sovereign capacity, is implied in calling a Convention, and thus submitting that instrument to the people. But the people were at perfect liberty to accept or reject it; and their act was final. It required not the affirmance, and could not be negatived, by the State governments. The constitution, when thus adopted, was of complete obligation, and bound the State sovereignties.

[10] It has been said, that the people had already surrendered all their powers to the State sovereignties, and had nothing more to give. But, surely, the question whether they may resume and modify the powers granted to government does not remain to be settled in this country. Much more might the legitimacy of the general government be doubted, had it been created by the States. The powers delegated to the State sovereignties were to be exercised by themselves, not by a distinct and independent sovereignty, created by themselves. To the formation of a league, such as was the confederation, the State sovereignties were certainly competent. But when, "in order to form a more perfect union," it was deemed necessary to change this alliance into an effective government, possessing great and sovereign powers, and acting directly on the people, the necessity of referring it to the people, and of deriving its powers directly from them, was felt and acknowledged by all.

[11] The government of the Union, then, (whatever may be the influence of this fact on the case), is, emphatically, and truly, a government of the people. In form and in substance it emanates from them. Its powers are granted by them, and are to be exercised directly on them, and for their benefit.

[12][¶12] This government is acknowledged by all to be one of enumerated powers. The principle, that it can exercise only the powers granted to it, would seem too apparent to have required to be enforced by all those arguments which its enlightened friends, while it was depending before the people, found it necessary to urge. That principle is now universally admitted. But the question respecting the extent of the powers actually granted, is perpetually arising, and will probably continue to arise, as long as our system shall exist.

[13] In discussing these questions, the conflicting powers of the general and State governments must be brought into view, and the supremacy of their respective laws, when they are in opposition, must be settled.

[14] If any one proposition could command the universal assent of mankind, we might expect it would be this—that the government of the Union, though limited in its powers, is supreme within its sphere of action. This would seem to result necessarily from its nature. It is the government of all; its powers are delegated by

---

¶12. This paragraph is often quoted by opponents of what they regard as "overreaching" by the national government. A major question throughout this entire casebook is whether it genuinely restrains someone who shares the "consolidationist" or "nationalist" vision of the Constitution. It is common to describe the Constitution as establishing a national government of "limited and assigned powers." Is it relevant that Marshall in this paragraph refers only to "assigned" powers, though, to be sure, the notion of "limited" powers emerges in ¶¶14, 15, and 38?

all; it represents all, and acts for all. Though any one State may be willing to control its operations, no State is willing to allow others to control them. The nation, on those subjects on which it can act, must necessarily bind its component parts. But this question is not left to mere reason: the people have, in express terms, decided it, by saying, "this constitution, and the laws of the United States, which shall be made in pursuance thereof," "shall be the supreme law of the land," and by requiring that the members of the State legislatures, and the officers of the executive and judicial departments of the States, shall take the oath of fidelity to it.

[15] The government of the United States, then, though limited in its powers, is supreme; and its laws, when made in pursuance of the constitution, form the supreme law of the land, "any thing in the constitution or laws of any State to the contrary notwithstanding."

[16][¶16] Among the enumerated powers, we do not find that of establishing a bank or creating a corporation. But there is no phrase in the instrument which, like the articles of confederation, excludes incidental or implied powers; and which requires that every thing granted shall be expressly and minutely described. Even the 10th amendment, which was framed for the purpose of quieting the excessive jealousies which had been excited, omits the word "expressly," and declares only that the powers "not delegated to the United States, nor prohibited to the States, are reserved to the States or to the people"; thus leaving the question, whether the particular power which may become the subject of contest has been delegated to the one government, or prohibited to the other, to depend on a fair construction of the whole instrument. The men who drew and adopted this amendment had experienced the embarrassments resulting from the insertion of this word in the articles of confederation, and probably omitted it to avoid those embarrassments. A constitution, to contain an accurate detail of all the subdivisions of which its great powers will admit, and of all the means by which they may be carried into execution, would partake of the prolixity of a legal code, and could scarcely be embraced by the human mind. It would probably never be understood by the public. Its nature, therefore, requires, that only its great outlines should be marked, its important objects designated, and the minor ingredients which compose those objects be deduced from the nature of the objects themselves. That this idea was entertained by the framers of the American constitution, is not only to be inferred

---

¶16. Marshall is contrasting the Tenth Amendment with Article II of the Articles of Confederation, which provided: "Each state retains its sovereignty, freedom and independence, and every power, jurisdiction, and right which is not by this confederation expressly delegated to the United States in Congress assembled." Congress was given the opportunity to add the word "expressly" to the proposed text of the Tenth Amendment, but it was rejected. In Marbury v. Madison, 5 U.S. (1 Cranch) 137 (1803), reproduced in Chapter 2 infra, Marshall wrote: "It cannot be presumed that any clause in the constitution is intended to be without effect: and therefore, such a construction is inadmissible, unless the words require it." Does Marshall's construction of the Tenth Amendment give it any effect? Could he properly have read "expressly" into the Tenth Amendment, and, if so, what difference should it make to the outcome of the case?

How does Marshall establish that Article I marks only the "great outlines" of congressional power, and what follows from the proposition? What is the argument based on Article I, §9? Why else might its limitations have been introduced?

from the nature of the instrument, but from the language. Why else were some of the limitations, found in the ninth section of the 1st article, introduced? It is also, in some degree, warranted by their having omitted to use any restrictive term which might prevent its receiving a fair and just interpretation. In considering this question, then, we must never forget, that it is *a constitution* we are expounding.

[17] Although, among the enumerated powers of government, we do not find the word "bank" or "incorporation," we find the great powers to lay and collect taxes; to borrow money; to regulate commerce; to declare and conduct a war; and to raise and support armies and navies. The sword and the purse, all the external relations, and no inconsiderable portion of the industry of the nation, are entrusted to its government. It can never be pretended that these vast powers draw after them others of inferior importance, merely because they are inferior. Such an idea can never be advanced. But it may with great reason be contended, that a government, entrusted with such ample powers, on the due execution of which the happiness and prosperity of the nation so vitally depends, must also be entrusted with ample means for their execution. The power being given, it is the interest of the nation to facilitate its execution. It can never be their interest, and cannot be presumed to have been their intention, to clog and embarrass its execution by withholding the most appropriate means. Throughout this vast republic, from the St. Croix to the Gulf of Mexico, from the Atlantic to the Pacific, revenue is to be collected and expended, armies are to be marched and supported. The exigencies of the nation may require that the treasure raised in the north should be transported to the south, *that* raised in the east conveyed to the west, or that this order should be reversed. Is that construction of the constitution to be preferred which would render these operations difficult, hazardous, and expensive? Can we adopt that construction, (unless the words imperiously require it), which would impute to the framers of that instrument, when granting these powers for the public good, the intention of impeding their exercise by withholding a choice of means? If, indeed, such be the mandate of the constitution, we have only to obey; but that instrument does not profess to enumerate the means by which the powers it confers may be executed; nor does it prohibit the creation of a corporation, if the existence of such a being be essential to the beneficial exercise of those powers. It is, then, the subject of fair inquiry, how far such means may be employed.

[18][¶18-21] It is not denied, that the powers given to the government imply the ordinary means of execution. That, for example, of raising revenue, and applying it to national purposes, is admitted to imply the power of conveying money from place to place, as the exigencies of the nation may require, and of employing the

¶18-21. Counsel for Maryland conceded arguendo that "the powers given to the government imply the ordinary means of execution," but contended that chartering a corporation was extraordinary. In England, only the Crown had the power to incorporate, and in early nineteenth-century America—before the advent of general state corporation laws—charters were regarded as quite special privileges, granted by legislatures on a case-by-case basis. How does Marshall meet Maryland's argument that Congress would have the authority to issue charters only if Article I explicitly granted it? Marshall's response consists in part of the assertion that those who contend that Congress may not employ a particular means in furtherance of an enumerated power have the burden of proof. Is this self-evident? Might one not draw the opposite conclusion from the nature of the federal system and the text of the Tenth Amendment?

usual means of conveyance. But it is denied that the government has its choice of means; or, that it may employ the most convenient means, if, to employ them, it be necessary to erect a corporation.

[19] On what foundation does this argument rest? On this alone: The power of creating a corporation, is one appertaining to sovereignty, and is not expressly conferred on Congress. This is true. But all legislative powers appertain to sovereignty. The original power of giving the law on any subject whatever, is a sovereign power; and if the government of the Union is restrained from creating a corporation, as a means for performing its functions, on the single reason that the creation of a corporation is an act of sovereignty; if the sufficiency of this reason be acknowledged, there would be some difficulty in sustaining the authority of Congress to pass other laws for the accomplishment of the same objects.

[20] The government which has a right to do an act, and has imposed on it the duty of performing that act, must, according to the dictates of reason, be allowed to select the means; and those who contend that it may not select any appropriate means, that one particular mode of effecting the object is excepted, take upon themselves the burden of establishing that exception.

[21] The creation of a corporation, it is said, appertains to sovereignty. This is admitted. But to what portion of sovereignty does it appertain? Does it belong to one more than to another? In America, the powers of sovereignty are divided between the government of the Union, and those of the States. They are each sovereign, with respect to the objects committed to it, and neither sovereign with respect to the objects committed to the other. We cannot comprehend that train of reasoning which would maintain, that the extent of power granted by the people is to be ascertained, not by the nature and terms of the grant, but by its date. Some State constitutions were formed *before*, some *since* that of the United States. We cannot believe that their relation to each other is in any degree dependent upon this circumstance. Their respective powers must, we think, be precisely the same as if they had been formed at the same time. Had they been formed at the same time, and had the people conferred on the general government the power contained in the constitution, and on the States the whole residuum of power, would it have been asserted that the government of the Union was not sovereign with respect to those objects which were entrusted to it, in relation to which its laws were declared to be supreme? If this could not have been asserted, we cannot well comprehend the process of reasoning which maintains, that a power appertaining to sovereignty cannot be connected with that vast portion of it which is granted to the general government, so far as it is calculated to subserve the legitimate objects of that government. The power of creating a corporation, though appertaining to sovereignty, is not, like the power of making war, or levying taxes, or of regulating commerce, a great substantive and independent power, which cannot be implied as incidental to other powers, or used as a means of executing them. It is never the end for which other powers are exercised, but a means by which other objects are accomplished. No contributions are made to charity for the sake of an incorporation, but a corporation is created to administer the charity; no seminary of learning is instituted in order to be incorporated, but the corporate character is conferred to subserve the purposes of education. No city was ever built with the sole object of being incorporated, but is incorporated as affording the best means of being well governed. The power of creating a corporation is never used for its own sake, but for the purpose

of effecting something else. No sufficient reason is, therefore, perceived, why it may not pass as incidental to those powers which are expressly given, if it be a direct mode of executing them.

[22]¶22-26 But the constitution of the United States has not left the right of Congress to employ the necessary means, for the execution of the powers conferred on the government, to general reasoning. To its enumeration of powers is added that of making "all laws which shall be necessary and proper, for carrying into execution the foregoing powers, and all other powers vested by this constitution, in the government of the United States, or in any department thereof."

[23] The counsel for the State of Maryland have urged various arguments, to prove that this clause, though in terms a grant of power, is not so in effect; but is really restrictive of the general right, which might otherwise be implied, of selecting means for executing the enumerated powers.

[24] In support of this proposition, they have found it necessary to contend, that this clause was inserted for the purpose of conferring on Congress the power of making laws. That, without it, doubts might be entertained, whether Congress could exercise its powers in the form of legislation.

[25] But could this be the object for which it was inserted? A government is created by the people, having legislative, executive, and judicial powers. Its legislative powers are vested in a Congress, which is to consist of a Senate and House of Representatives. Each house may determine the rule of its proceedings; and it is declared that every bill which shall have passed both houses, shall, before it becomes a law, be presented to the President of the United States. The 7th section describes the course of proceedings, by which a bill shall become a law; and, then, the 8th section enumerates the powers of Congress. Could it be necessary to say, that a legislature should exercise legislative powers, in the shape of legislation? After allowing each house to prescribe its own course of proceeding, after describing the manner in which a bill should become a law, would it have entered into the mind of a single member of the Convention, that an express power to make laws was necessary to enable the legislature to make them? That a legislature, endowed with legislative powers, can legislate, is a proposition too self-evident to have been questioned.

[26] But the argument on which most reliance is placed, is drawn from the peculiar language of this clause. Congress is not empowered by it to make all laws, which may have relation to the powers conferred on the government, but such only as may be "*necessary and proper*" for carrying them into execution. The word "*necessary*," is considered as controlling the whole sentence, and as limiting the right to pass laws for the execution of the granted powers, to such as are indispensable, and without which the power would be nugatory. That it excludes the choice of means, and leaves to Congress, in each case, that only which is most direct and simple.

¶22-26. Marshall begins by invoking the Necessary and Proper Clause as affirmative support for the exercise of congressional power but immediately turns to defend against Maryland's contention that the clause restricts that power. Marshall deals summarily with the argument that, but for the clause, Article I would not have vested Congress with any legislative authority, and then considers the argument that "necessary" restricts Congress to the "most direct and simple" means of implementing the enumerated powers.

[27]¶27 Is it true, that this is the sense in which the word "necessary" is always used? Does it always import an absolute physical necessity, so strong, that one thing, to which another may be termed necessary, cannot exist without that other? We think it does not. If reference be had to its use, in the common affairs of the world, or in approved authors, we find that it frequently imports no more than that one thing is convenient, or useful, or essential to another. To employ the means necessary to an end, is generally understood as employing any means calculated to produce the end, and not as being confined to those single means, without which the end would be entirely unattainable. Such is the character of human language, that no word conveys to the mind, in all situations, one single definite idea; and nothing is more common than to use words in a figurative sense. Almost all compositions contain words, which, taken in their rigorous sense, would convey a meaning different from that which is obviously intended. It is essential to just construction, that many words which import something excessive, should be understood in a more mitigated sense—in that sense which common usage justifies. The word "necessary" is of this description. It has not a fixed character peculiar to itself. It admits of all degrees of comparison; and is often connected with other words, which increase or diminish the impression the mind receives of the urgency it imports. A thing may be necessary, very necessary, absolutely or indispensably necessary. To no mind would the same idea be conveyed, by these several phrases. This comment on the word is well illustrated, by the passage cited at the bar, from the 10th section of the 1st article of the constitution. It is, we think, impossible to compare the sentence which prohibits a State from laying "imposts, or duties on imports or exports, except what may be *absolutely* necessary for executing its inspection laws," with that which authorizes Congress "to make all laws which shall be necessary and proper for carrying into execution" the powers of the general government, without feeling a conviction that the convention understood itself to change materially the meaning of the word "necessary," by prefixing the word "absolutely." This word, then, like others, is used in various senses; and, in its construction, the subject, the context, the intention of the person using them, are all to be taken into view.

¶27. Note the sources to which Marshall alludes to, though scarcely cites, to support his interpretation of "necessary." Should he have indicated which specific "approved authors" he was drawing on? Should he have turned to dictionaries? Had he looked at Samuel Johnson's Dictionary of the English Language (1755) he would have found the "rigorous" definition: "needful, indispensably requisite"; whereas the first American dictionary, Noah Webster's Compendious Dictionary of the English Language (1806), included "proper." Johnson was writing, of course, more than 30 years before the Philadelphia Convention, Webster almost 20 years afterward. Assuming one is interested in the most likely meaning of "necessary" in 1787, is either of these two dictionaries likely to be a more reliable source?

Incidentally, Marshall's sentence about the "character of human language" is quite similar to Madison's arguments set out in The Federalist No. 37, where he wrote that "no language is so copious as to supply words and phrases for every complex idea, or so correct so not to include many equivocally denoting different ideas." Thus, says Madison, we must adjust to the "unavoidable inaccuracy" of language, which he describes as a "cloudy medium."

[28]¶28-32 Let this be done in the case under consideration. The subject is the execution of those great powers on which the welfare of a nation essentially depends. It must have been the intention of those who gave these powers, to insure, as far as human prudence could insure, their beneficial execution. This could not be done by confiding the choice of means to such narrow limits as not to leave it in the power of Congress to adopt any which might be appropriate, and which were conducive to the end. This provision is made in a constitution intended to endure for ages to come, and, consequently, to be adapted to the various *crises* of human affairs. To have prescribed the means by which government should, in all future time, execute its powers, would have been to change, entirely, the character of the instrument, and give it the properties of a legal code. It would have been an unwise attempt to provide, by immutable rules, for exigencies which, if foreseen at all, must have been seen dimly, and which can be best provided for as they occur. To have declared that the best means shall not be used, but those alone without which the power given would be nugatory, would have been to deprive the legislature of the capacity to avail itself of experience, to exercise its reason, and to accommodate its legislation to circumstances. If we apply this principle of construction to any of the powers of the government, we shall find it so pernicious in its operation that we shall be compelled to discard it. The powers vested in Congress may certainly be carried into execution, without prescribing an oath of office. The power to exact this security for the faithful performance of duty, is not given, nor is it indispensably necessary. The different departments may be established; taxes may be imposed and collected; armies and navies may be raised and maintained; and money may be borrowed, without requiring an oath of office. It might be argued, with as much plausibility as other incidental powers have been assailed, that the Convention was not unmindful of this subject. The oath which might be exacted—that of fidelity to the constitution—is prescribed, and no other can be required. Yet, he would be charged with insanity who should contend, that the legislature might not add to the oath as directed by the constitution, such other oath of office as its wisdom might suggest.

[29] So, with respect to the whole penal code of the United States: whence arises the power to punish in cases not prescribed by the constitution? All admit that the government may, legitimately, punish any violation of its laws; and yet, this is not among the enumerated powers of Congress. The right to enforce the observance of law, by punishing its infraction, might be denied with the more plausibility, because it is expressly given in some cases. Congress is empowered "to provide for the punishment of counterfeiting the securities and current coin of the United States," and "to define and punish piracies and felonies committed on the high seas, and offences against the law of nations." The several powers of Congress may exist, in a very imperfect state to be sure, but they may exist and be carried into execution, although no punishment should be inflicted in cases where the right to punish is not expressly given.

[30] Take, for example, the power "to establish post offices and post roads." This power is executed by the single act of making the establishment. But, from this has been inferred the power and duty of carrying the mail along the post road, from one post office to another. And, from this implied power, has again been

---

¶28-32. To support his "figurative" reading of the word, Marshall looks to the "subject, the context, [and] the intention of the person" using it. What is the argument of ¶28? Does it have any force independent of the counterexamples that follow in ¶¶29-30? Is the argument by counterexample persuasive?

inferred the right to punish those who steal letters from the post office, or rob the mail. It may be said, with some plausibility, that the right to carry the mail, and to punish those who rob it, is not indispensably necessary to the establishment of a post office and post road. This right is indeed essential to the beneficial exercise of the power, but not indispensably necessary to its existence. So, of the punishment of the crimes of stealing or falsifying a record or process of a Court of the United States, or of perjury in such Court. To punish these offences is certainly conducive to the due administration of justice. But courts may exist, and may decide the causes brought before them, though such crimes escape punishment.

[31] The baneful influence of this narrow construction on all the operations of the government, and the absolute impracticability of maintaining it without rendering the government incompetent to its great objects, might be illustrated by numerous examples drawn from the constitution, and from our laws. The good sense of the public has pronounced, without hesitation, that the power of punishment appertains to sovereignty, and may be exercised whenever the sovereign has a right to act, as incidental to his constitutional powers. It is a means for carrying into execution all sovereign powers, and may be used, although not indispensably necessary. It is a right incidental to the power, and conducive to its beneficial exercise.

[32] If this limited construction of the word "necessary" must be abandoned in order to punish, whence is derived the rule which would reinstate it, when the government would carry its powers into execution by means not vindictive in their nature? If the word "necessary" means "needful," "requisite," "essential," "conducive to," in order to let in the power of punishment for the infraction of law; why is it not equally comprehensive when required to authorize the use of means which facilitate the execution of the powers of government without the infliction of punishment?

[33][¶33] In ascertaining the sense in which the word "necessary" is used in this clause of the constitution, we may derive some aid from that with which it is associated. Congress shall have power "to make all laws which shall be necessary and *proper* to carry into execution" the powers of the government. If the word "necessary" was used in that strict and rigorous sense for which the counsel for the State of Maryland contend, it would be an extraordinary departure from the usual course of the human mind, as exhibited in composition, to add a word, the only possible effect of which is to qualify that strict and rigorous meaning; to present to the mind the idea of some choice of means of legislation not strained and compressed within the narrow limits for which gentlemen contend.

[34][¶34-37] But the argument which most conclusively demonstrates the error of the construction contended for by the counsel for the State of Maryland, is founded on the intention of the Convention, as manifested in the whole clause.

¶33. Is Marshall correct that "proper" would be superfluous if "necessary" were read in its rigorous sense? Might "proper" mean "not prohibited by Article I, §9"? Doesn't Marshall's interpretation of "necessary" make "proper" superfluous—at least unless "necessary" is given a somewhat restrictive meaning?

¶34-37. Paragraph 34 seems largely introductory to the perceptive argument of ¶¶35-36 based on the location and phraseology of the clause. But doesn't it suggest an argument in Maryland's favor that Marshall ought to meet: that if Congress would have broad ancillary powers without the clause, and a document should presumptively be read so as to make no clause superfluous, then the Necessary and Proper Clause must be designed to restrict congressional power? Is the response implicit in ¶37 satisfactory?

To waste time and argument in proving that, without it, Congress might carry its powers into execution, would be not much less idle than to hold a lighted taper to the sun. As little can it be required to prove, that in the absence of this clause, Congress would have some choice of means. That it might employ those which, in its judgment, would most advantageously effect the object to be accomplished. That any means adapted to the end, any means which tended directly to the execution of the constitutional powers of the government, were in themselves constitutional. This clause, as construed by the State of Maryland, would abridge, and almost annihilate this useful and necessary right of the legislature to select its means. That this could not be intended, is, we should think, had it not been already controverted, too apparent for controversy. We think so for the following reasons:

[35] 1st. The clause is placed among the powers of Congress, not among the limitations on those powers.

[36] 2nd. Its terms purport to enlarge, not to diminish the powers vested in the government. It purports to be an additional power, not a restriction on those already granted. No reason has been, or can be assigned for thus concealing an intention to narrow the discretion of the national legislature under words which purport to enlarge it. The framers of the constitution wished its adoption, and well knew that it would be endangered by its strength, not by its weakness. Had they been capable of using language which would convey to the eye one idea, and, after deep reflection, impress on the mind another, they would rather have disguised the grant of power, than its limitation. If, then, their intention had been, by this clause, to restrain the free use of means which might otherwise have been implied, that intention would have been inserted in another place, and would have been expressed in terms resembling these. "In carrying into execution the foregoing powers, and all others," &c. "no laws shall be passed but such as are necessary and proper." Had the intention been to make this clause restrictive, it would unquestionably have been so in form as well as in effect.

[37] The result of the most careful and attentive consideration bestowed upon this clause is, that if it does not enlarge, it cannot be construed to restrain the powers of Congress, or to impair the right of the legislature to exercise its best judgment in the selection of measures to carry into execution the constitutional powers of the government. If no other motive for its insertion can be suggested, a sufficient one is found in the desire to remove all doubts respecting the right to legislate on that vast mass of incidental powers which must be involved in the constitution, if that instrument be not a splendid bauble.

[38][¶38] We admit, as all must admit, that the powers of the government are limited, and that its limits are not to be transcended. But we think the sound construction of the constitution must allow to the national legislature that discretion, with respect to the means by which the powers it confers are to be carried into

---

¶38. This is one of the most quoted paragraphs in the American constitutional corpus. Would it be fair to paraphrase it as "Congress can do whatever it wants so long as it does not contravene an express and specific prohibition contained in this text"? Is this consistent with Marshall's acknowledgment in ¶¶14 and 15 that the national government is one of limited and enumerated powers?

execution, which will enable that body to perform the high duties assigned to it, in the manner most beneficial to the people. Let the end be legitimate, let it be within the scope of the constitution, and all means which are appropriate, which are plainly adapted to that end, which are not prohibited, but consist with the letter and spirit of the constitution, are constitutional.

[39] That a corporation must be considered as a means not less usual, not of higher dignity, not more requiring a particular specification than other means, has been sufficiently proved. If we look to the origin of corporations, to the manner in which they have been framed in that government from which we have derived most of our legal principles and ideas, or to the uses to which they have been applied, we find no reason to suppose that a constitution, omitting, and wisely omitting, to enumerate all the means for carrying into execution the great powers vested in government, ought to have specified this. Had it been intended to grant this power as one which should be distinct and independent, to be exercised in any case whatever, it would have found a place among the enumerated powers of the government. But being considered merely as a means, to be employed only for the purpose of carrying into execution the given powers, there could be no motive for particularly mentioning it.

[40] The propriety of this remark would seem to be generally acknowledged by the universal acquiescence in the construction which has been uniformly put on the 3rd section of the 4th article of the constitution. The power to "make all needful rules and regulations respecting the territory or other property belonging to the United States," is not more comprehensive, than the power "to make all laws which shall be necessary and proper for carrying into execution" the powers of the government. Yet all admit the constitutionality of a territorial government, which is a corporate body.

[41] If a corporation may be employed indiscriminately with other means to carry into execution the powers of the government, no particular reason can be assigned for excluding the use of a bank, if required for its fiscal operations. To use one, must be within the discretion of Congress, if it be an appropriate mode of executing the powers of government. That it is a convenient, a useful, and essential instrument in the prosecution of its fiscal operations, is not now a subject of controversy. All those who have been concerned in the administration of our finances, have concurred in representing its importance and necessity; and so strongly have they been felt, that statesmen of the first class, whose previous opinions against it had been confirmed by every circumstance which can fix the human judgment, have yielded those opinions to the exigencies of the nation. Under the confederation, Congress, justifying the measure by its necessity, transcended perhaps its power to obtain the advantage of a bank; and our own legislation attests the universal conviction of the utility of this measure. The time has passed away when it can be necessary to enter into any discussion in order to prove the importance of this instrument, as a means to effect the legitimate objects of the government.

[42][¶42] But, were its necessity less apparent, none can deny its being an appropriate measure; and if it is, the degree of its necessity, as has been very justly

---

¶42. To some extent this paragraph is designed to reassure readers that Congress did not in fact have plenary power. What is a "pretext"? What kinds of inquiry would be necessary to demonstrate its existence?

observed, is to be discussed in another place. Should Congress, in the execution of its powers, adopt measures which are prohibited by the constitution; or should Congress, under the pretext of executing its powers, pass laws for the accomplishment of objects not entrusted to the government; it would become the painful duty of this tribunal, should a case requiring such a decision come before it, to say that such an act was not the law of the land. But where the law is not prohibited, and is really calculated to effect any of the objects entrusted to the government, to undertake here to inquire into the degree of its necessity, would be to pass the line which circumscribes the judicial department, and to tread on legislative ground. This court disclaims all pretensions to such a power.

[43] After this declaration, it can scarcely be necessary to say, that the existence of State banks can have no possible influence on the question. No trace is to be found in the constitution of an intention to create a dependence of the government of the Union on those of the States, for the execution of the great powers assigned to it. Its means are adequate to its ends; and on those means alone was it expected to rely for the accomplishment of its ends. To impose on it the necessity of resorting to means which it cannot control, which another government may furnish or withhold, would render its course precarious, the result of its measures uncertain and create a dependence on other governments, which might disappoint its most important designs, and is incompatible with the language of the constitution. But were it otherwise, the choice of means implies a right to choose a national bank in preference to State banks, and Congress alone can make the election.

[44] After the most deliberate consideration, it is the unanimous and decided opinion of this Court, that the act to incorporate the Bank of the United States is a law made in pursuance of the constitution, and is a part of the supreme law of the land.

[45] The branches, proceeding from the same stock, and being conducive to the complete accomplishment of the object, are equally constitutional. It would have been unwise to locate them in the charter, and it would be unnecessarily inconvenient to employ the legislative power in making those subordinate arrangements. The great duties of the bank are prescribed; those duties require branches; and the bank itself may, we think, be safely trusted with the selection of places where those branches shall be fixed; reserving always to the government the right to require that a branch shall be located where it may be deemed necessary.

A. *The Reaction to* McCulloch

When *McCulloch* was decided in 1819, few persons of stature in the national political community genuinely disputed either the desirability or the constitutionality of the national bank. Yet Marshall's opinion stirred great controversy, for it went far beyond the specifics of the bank, first to portray an eloquent vision of a single nation, governed by a national government possessing broad powers, coupled with a Court willing to offer what could seem like almost complete deference to the decisions reached by Congress. During the months following the decision a number of critical essays appeared in the Richmond *Enquirer*.[24]

---

24. See John Marshall's Defense of the Constitution (Gunther ed., 1969) (hereinafter cited as Gunther).

One author, writing under the pseudonym of Amphictyon, criticized the breadth of Marshall's opinion, especially with respect to the source of the government's power:[25]

> If the powers of the federal government are to be viewed as the grant of the people, without regard to the distinctive features of the states, then it would follow that if a majority of the whole sovereign population of the United States had ratified the constitution, it would immediately have been binding on the minority, although that minority should consist of every individual in one or more states. But we would know that such was not the case. Each state was an independent political society. The constitution was not binding on any state, even the smallest, without its own free and voluntary consent. . . . The respective states then in their sovereign capacity did delegate the federal government its powers, and in so doing were parties to the compact.

The source of the federal government's power had been a matter of controversy at least from the time of the ratification campaigns. In the Virginia ratifying convention, Patrick Henry, a staunch opponent of the new Constitution, demanded why the Preamble to the Constitution said "*We, the people,* instead of *We the States*? States are the characteristics and the soul of a confederation. If the States be not the agents of this compact, it must be one great consolidated government of the people of all States."[26] A delegate responded that no one "but the people have a right to form government,"[27] to which Henry, referring to the fear that a "consolidated government" would ride roughshod over individual liberty, replied that "the principles of this system are extremely pernicious, impolitic, and dangerous."[28] Patrick Henry was expressing a belief, widely held in that and other times, that liberty depended on government by small political units subject to close citizen participation and control.[29] The new Constitution, by contrast, established a national government, having vastly greater powers than the Confederation and the authority over a large and expanding territory.

The most important argument regarding state sovereignty and the relevance thereof to constitutional interpretation was made at the very end of the eighteenth century in the Virginia and Kentucky Resolutions, written by Madison and Jefferson, respectively, that challenged the constitutionality of the Alien and Sedition Acts of 1798.[30] Jefferson had written in the Kentucky Resolution:[31]

---

25. Id. at 56.

26. Quoted in Sources and Documents Illustrating the American Revolution, 1764-1788 and the Formation of the Federal Constitution 309 (Morison ed., 2d ed. 1965).

27. Id. at 315.

28. Id. at 321-322.

29. See Hannah Arendt, On Revolution (1963); Gordon Wood, Creation of the American Republic, 1776-1787 (1969).

30. 1 Stat. 566, 570, 577, 696. See Chapter 2 infra for further discussion of the Acts.

31. The Portable Jefferson 286 (Peterson ed., 1975) (hereinafter Peterson).

> [T]he several states who formed [the Constitution], being sovereign and independent, have the unquestionable right to judge of its infraction, and . . . a nullification, by those sovereignties, of all unauthorized acts done under colour of that instrument, is the rightful remedy.

Amphictyon's essays on *McCulloch* reprinted much of Madison's Virginia Resolution, which similarly asserted that the states were "duty bound to interpose" their authority to arrest the evil of "deliberate, palpable, and dangerous exercise of other powers not granted by the said compact."[32]

Jefferson's response to *McCulloch* can be garnered from an 1820 letter describing the national judiciary as:[33]

> . . . the subtle core of sappers and miners constantly working under ground to undermine the foundations of our confederated fabric. They are construing our Constitution from a coordination of general [i.e., national] and special [i.e., state] government to a general and supreme one alone. This will lay all things at their feet.

Returning to the notion of the Virginia Resolution, Jefferson suggested that the people of two-thirds of the states could, through resolutions of nullification, overrule unconstitutional Supreme Court decisions. Only in this way could the principle be vindicated that the Constitution "is a compact of many independent powers, every single one of which claims an equal right to understand it, and to require its observance."[34] Writing under the name of Hampden in the Richmond *Enquirer*, Spencer Roane, Chief Justice of the Virginia Supreme Court, also responded to *McCulloch*. Among other arguments, he invoked Johnson's Dictionary, "which is believed to be the best in the English language" to show that "necessary" was there defined as "needful" or "indispensably requisite."[35] Roane's arguments drew an admiring letter from Madison, who noted:[36]

> It could not but happen, and was foreseen at the birth of the Constitution, that difficulties and differences of opinion might occasionally arise in expounding terms and phrases necessarily used in such a charter; more especially those which divide legislation between the general and local governments; and that it might require a regular course of practice to liquidate and settle the meaning of some of them. But it was anticipated, I believe, by few, if any, of the friends of the Constitution, that a rule of construction would be introduced as broad and pliant as what has occurred. And those who recollect, and still more, those who shared in what passed in the State conventions, through which the people ratified

---

32. Gunther, supra n.24, at 51. These arguments were later invoked by South Carolina in its efforts to nullify federal laws and in the justification for Southern secession in 1860-1861. See The Nullification Era: A Documentary Record (Freehling ed., 1967).

33. Dumas Malone, 6 Jefferson and His Time 356 (1981) (letter to Thomas Ritchie).

34. Merrill D. Peterson, Thomas Jefferson and the New Nation 994-995 (1970).

35. Gunther, supra n.24, at 133.

36. Letter of September 2, 1819, in 3 Farrand, supra n.3, at 435.

the Constitution, with respect to the extent of the powers vested in Congress, cannot easily be persuaded that the avowal of such a rule would not have prevented its ratification.

Assume that Madison is correct that "shared" understandings in 1787 would have been appalled by the "extent of the powers vested in Congress" according to Marshall. So what? Does that suggest that the doctrinal understanding of congressional power established by Marshall's opinion should be "overruled"? As you will see, *McCulloch* is a truly landmark precedent in American constitutional law, almost certainly cited more often than any other early case.

B. *Marshall's Methods of Constitutional Interpretation*

Within *McCulloch* we can find almost all of the standard forms of constitutional argument that lawyers and judges use today. Philip Bobbitt has popularized the idea of "modalities" of constitutional argument. For purposes of this discussion, we will identify seven of them: (1) appeals to text (and rules for construction of texts), (2) constitutional structure, (3) prudence (or consequences), (4) purpose or intention, (5) judicial precedent, (6) past practice and inter-branch convention, and (7) national ethos and political tradition.[37]

The modalities are invaluable to constitutional argument because they make it easy to analyze problems and construct arguments about constitutional questions. The modalities offer a series of different perspectives on the Constitution. Faced with virtually any question of constitutional law, one can work through the standard forms of argument—what arguments can one make from the constitutional text, what arguments can one make from constitutional structure—and so on through the list. Students should learn to do this until it becomes second nature. Using the modalities allows students to always have something to say about a constitutional question, and to always have several pathways for analysis. More generally, the modalities offer multiple ways to think about what is at stake in a constitutional question; they give lawyers and judges multiple perspectives on how to think about the Constitution and how to formulate and solve constitutional problems.[38]

1. *The text.* Marshall makes arguments from the language of the Tenth Amendment, and from the implications of Article I, §9. But textual arguments include more than just arguments about the meaning of particular words and phrases.

---

37. See generally Philip Bobbitt, Constitutional Fate (1982), an expanded version of Constitutional Fate, 58 Tex. L. Rev. 695 (1980); see also Bobbitt, Constitutional Interpretation (1991). Bobbitt's list, which has been widely adopted, included only six modalities: text, structure, prudence, history, precedent and ethos. For a more expansive catalogue of styles of constitutional argument, see Jack M. Balkin, The New Originalism and the Uses of History, 82 Fordham L. Rev. 641, 659-661 (2013) (listing arguments from text, structure, purpose, consequences, judicial precedent, past practice and inter-branch convention, custom, natural law/natural rights, national ethos, political tradition, and honored authority).

38. See Jack M. Balkin, Arguing About The Constitution: The Topics in Constitutional Interpretation, 33 Const. Comm. 145 (2018).

Notice how Marshall points to the location of the Necessary and Proper Clause among Congress's *powers* in Article I, §8, rather than among the *limitations* of congressional power. In other words, he looks at the location of the Necessary and Proper Clause within the text as a whole, comparing it with other parts of the text.

Marshall also makes the famous statement that "it is *a constitution* we are expounding"? This is an argument about the *kind* of text a constitution is. What does he mean by this? What "constitutes" a "constitution," as distinguished from, say, a statute?

In ¶16 Marshall contrasts the "great outlines" of Article I with "the prolixity of a legal code." (See also Note: Uncertainties of Meaning, below.) In fact, some constitutions are very long and detailed, although the U.S. Constitution is not one of them. What follows from this fact?

2. *Structural argument: The theory and structure of the government established by the Constitution.* Structural arguments ask how a constitution is supposed to operate. In Structure and Relationship in Constitutional Law (1969), a famous book on structural argument, Professor Charles Black, Jr., argues that we should interpret the Constitution using "inference[s] from the structures and relationships created by the constitution." He uses *McCulloch* as an example of how judges make structural arguments. Black points out that "Marshall does not place principal reliance on the [Necessary and Proper] clause as a ground of decision; . . . before he reaches it he has already decided, on the basis of far more general implications, that Congress possesses the power, not expressly named, of establishing a bank and chartering corporations; . . . he addresses himself to the necessary and proper clause only in response to counsel's arguing its *restrictive* force."[39] You will shortly see another powerful use of structural argument in the second part of *McCulloch*, which deals with Maryland's power to tax the bank.

Does it follow from the nature of a federal constitution that the national legislative power should be construed expansively? Or, on the contrary, should one be zealous about limiting national power, lest it in effect swallow up state autonomy? For example, if the Constitution is a treaty like NATO, we should read its powers fairly narrowly to respect the sovereignty of the individual signatory states. But if it is the plan of a national government that represents the American people directly, we should read its provisions flexibly so that it can serve the public good. What features of the Constitution's text and design can one point to decide which characterization is correct? (Note that it might also be the case that neither of these characterizations is correct.)

How does Marshall believe the Constitution is supposed to work? How did Maryland think it should work? These are the classic questions in structural analysis. It is likely that our nation would be very different had Maryland's arguments prevailed. Thus the dispute between Marshall and his critics was about *which* conception of government structure was the right one for the United States.

This puts Marshall's conception of "*a constitution*" in a different light: It is not necessarily a uniquely correct interpretation but rather a desirable vision of the point of the Constitution and of the "national project" of the United States of

39. Charles Black, Structure and Relationship in Constitutional Law 7, 14 (1969).

America. Note that Marshall invokes the Preamble in ¶9 (another example of a textual argument—in this case in aid of a claim about constitutional structure). Recall that Edmund Randolph counseled against reliance on the Preamble for guidance as to constitutional meaning. What are the implications of Marshall's citation to the Preamble?

3. *Prudential argument: What are the likely consequences of a decision?* Where the text is unclear, constitutional interpreters often pay attention to the likely consequences of different interpretations. This practice is so commonplace that people might not even think of it as a distinctive form of argument. For example, in ¶17 Marshall speaks of "[t]he exigencies of the nation" and rejects a "construction of the constitution that would render" the performance of government functions "difficult, hazardous, and expensive." Why should this matter? Should the Constitution always be interpreted to facilitate the performance of governmental functions?

Recall paragraph ¶28, in which Marshall makes a similar comparison and notes that Article I is a provision "made in a constitution intended to endure for ages to come, and, consequently to be adapted to the various *crises* of human affairs." How does this shed light on the best interpretation of the Necessary and Proper Clause? (And how significant is it that it is the word "crises" that is italicized rather than "adapted"?)

You can see from these examples that arguments from consequences and arguments from structure are often connected. Marshall argues that the best structure is one that makes it easy for the federal government to act; Maryland argues that the best structure is the one that gives states the widest leeway to protect their local interests.

Arguments from consequences generally start from the assumption that the text is unclear, and that there is more than one way to read it; hence we should choose the interpretation that produces the best consequences, all other things being equal. If the text is clear, however, we cannot disregard it simply because we dislike the consequences. But the degree of clarity can be contested. If the consequences are very bad, interpreters might strain to conclude that the text is not clear. To what extent is it relevant that Article V makes it unusually difficult to amend the United States Constitution?

Note that there are at least two different types of prudential arguments. The broader category concerns whether a given interpretation—and the doctrine, rule, or result it produces—would have good consequences or bad. The second, narrower category concerns whether allowing *this particular decisionmaker* (e.g., the courts, the executive, the legislature, the states, the federal government) to decide the question in a particular way would have good consequences or bad. In particular, a very familiar question in constitution law is whether having a court decide the question would be a good use of judicial resources, or would tend to serve or undermine the role of the judiciary in protecting legal and constitutional values in the long run.

Judges are often concerned with how their decisions, even if otherwise justified, will play in the political arena. They may be concerned that taking up a controversial question, or offering a broad or ambitious reading of the Constitution, even if correct, will provoke a backlash from the other branches of government or from the public generally, and in the long run this will have worse consequences for the constitutional system than if courts had avoided taking up the issue directly for the moment, deferred to the political branches, or offered a narrow or limited ruling. Prudential considerations sometimes counsel not deciding a case at all, or deciding it only on technical or procedural grounds unrelated to the substantive issues at stake. Alexander Bickel famously called these practices the "passive virtues."[40] Years later Cass Sunstein argued that judges should often be "minimalist"; they should decide constitutional questions as narrowly as possible or should use formulas that leave future questions undecided.[41] As you will see in this course, prudential considerations are never very far away from judicial practice, because constitutional questions often involve some of the most politically heated issues of their time. Are such prudential considerations consistent with the duty of courts to act in a principled fashion? Gerald Gunther famously quipped that Bickel insisted that courts be 100 percent principled 20 percent of the time.[42] On the other hand, is prudence necessary to keep a rule of law system going over time? (We will return to this question in the next chapter in the discussion of Marbury v. Madison.)

The role of institutional prudence in decisionmaking means that there may be a gap between the best interpretation of the Constitution and the most reasonable thing for a particular actor (such as a judge) to do in interpreting the Constitution. To what extent should people in different positions—citizens, legal academics, lower court judges, Supreme Court Justices, members of the executive branch, and individual members of Congress—treat questions of constitutional interpretation differently because of their distinctive roles?

4. *Appeals to purpose or intentions.* Arguments from purpose can appeal to the particular intentions or understandings of specific individuals or groups of individuals. Examples are arguments from legislative history. But often arguments from purpose *attribute* purposes to the text or derive purposes from the text—that is, we reason from the language used and the issues that the language addresses to figure out the likely purposes of a provision.

Recall Marshall's discussion of the purposes of the Tenth Amendment. What kinds of argument about purpose is he making? Is he appealing to subjective intentions or to the purposes of the amendment given its language and placement in the Constitution? In arguing against the First Bank, Jefferson noted that the Philadelphia Convention had rejected a proposal to authorize Congress to charter certain corporations. Marshall does not mention this. This may not be simply because it would not have helped his argument: Judicial references to legislative history were rare and usually frowned on in eighteenth-century Anglo-American jurisprudence. It was much more commonplace to infer purpose from the text. In any event, what importance *should* we place on the purposes or intentions behind the adoption (or rejection) of particular texts? Is Marshall's argument regarding the (limited) scope

---

40. Alexander M. Bickel, The Supreme Court 1960 Term: Foreword: The Passive Virtues, 75 Harv. L. Rev. 40 (1961).

41. Cass R. Sunstein, One Case at a Time: Judicial Minimalism on the Supreme Court (1999).

42. Gerald Gunther, The Subtle Vices of the "Passive Virtues": A Comment on Principle and Expediency in Judicial Review, 64 Colum. L. Rev. 1, 3 (1964).

of the Tenth Amendment enhanced by the knowledge that proposals in both the House of Representatives and the Senate to add the word "expressly" before "delegated" were rejected?[43]

Bobbitt called arguments from intentions "historical" arguments. But it is important to recognize that not all arguments that use history are arguments from purpose or intentions. In fact, one can use history in each modality of constitutional argument; one simply uses it differently.[44]

In *McCulloch*, for example, Marshall uses history in multiple ways. First, he refers to the purposes of the framers of the Philadelphia Convention—which is an argument from purpose or intention. Second, he refers to the history of the adoption of the bank itself under the Washington Administration—which is an argument from past practice. Third, he uses history to show that the failure to have a national bank during the War of 1812 "exposed" the national government to "embarrassments"—which is an argument from consequences.

It is commonplace to associate historical arguments with originalist arguments—that is, arguments about what the Constitution's framers or adopters intended and/or would have understood the Constitution to mean. But the different modalities of argument suggest that history can be useful for many different purposes in interpreting a Constitution.

To be sure, one might use history to discover the purposes or meanings of the adopters of the text. But one might also use history to study how the Constitution functions in practice, the likely consequences of certain interpretations, the growth and development of political traditions, the emergence of conventions of practice, or how later generations understood the nation's constitutional commitments.

Still another way to use history, as we shall see throughout this course, is to argue that we should learn from mistakes or injustices that occurred in the past and that we should interpret the document in the present to avoid making similar errors of judgment. These are arguments from political tradition or ethos.

5. *Past practice and inter-branch convention.* Although Marshall cites no judicial decisions, he nonetheless invokes as precedent the incorporation by Congress in 1791 of the First Bank to support the constitutionality of the 1816 decision to incorporate the Second Bank. And we have seen that Madison justified signing the bill establishing the Second Bank by reference to "repeated recognitions, under varied circumstances, of the validity of such an institution," even though he had denounced the validity of the 1791 incorporation. Why are arguments from past practice relevant to the contemporary meaning of the Constitution? If people have already spent some time thinking about problems, we should defer to their considered judgments. But what if their decisions arose in the context of heated political disagreements or emergencies? In the alternative, one might argue that past practice establishes a convention that should govern later actors. Why should previous Presidents and/or Congresses be able to bind later ones?

---

43. See Neil H. Cogan, ed., The Complete Bill of Rights: The Drafts, Debates, Sources, & Origins 665 (House), 667 (Senate) (1997).

44. On this point, see Jack M. Balkin, The New Originalism and the Uses of History, 82 Fordham L. Rev. 641 (2013).

6. *Judicial precedent. Judicial* precedents, which constitute the lion's share of most law school casebooks, are absent in *McCulloch*; Marshall only discusses previous decisions by *nonjudicial* actors. That is to be expected; very few cases had been decided by the 1810s, and many of Marshall's opinions concern issues of first impression. Generally speaking, as a field of law fills up with judicial precedents, both lawyers and judges rely on them increasingly in their arguments. And, of course, lower courts rely almost exclusively on previous decisions by the Supreme Court and federal circuit courts.

Within the class of judicial precedents, courts might conceivably look not only to their own decisions, but to the decisions of state courts, and, perhaps more controversially, to the decisions of courts in other countries. Precedents from state courts and courts of other nations are not binding on the Supreme Court; at most they may provide persuasive arguments. However, the U.S. Supreme Court, like many other courts in the United States and the United Kingdom, often speaks as if it is bound by its own previous decisions, whether or not they are "persuasive."

Why should the Supreme Court follow its precedents? One reason is that if past judges have thought hard about a problem, later courts should defer to their judgment. But this does not explain why courts should follow precedents that are concededly unwise and unjust. A second reason is fidelity to the rule of law. But common law courts expand, contract, and distinguish precedents all the time, which begs the question of whether it is really the same law that is being applied later on. A third reason is that following precedent lends order and stability to legal argument. Richard Fallon, for example, has written that "a good legal system requires reasonable stability; . . . while decisions that are severely misguided or dysfunctional surely may be overruled, continuity is presumptively desirable with respect to the rest; . . . it would overwhelm the Court and country alike to require the Justices to rethink every constitutional question in every case on the bare, unmediated authority of constitutional text, structure, and original history."[45] But again this is merely a defeasible preference; as Fallon himself notes, courts are willing to sacrifice stability and settlement if there are good enough reasons. Consider one of Justice Holmes's most famous statements, given in a speech on The Path of the Law to the students and faculty of Boston University Law School in 1897: "It is revolting to have no better reason for a rule of law than that so it was laid down in the time of Henry IV. It is still more revolting if the grounds upon which it was laid down have vanished long since, and the rule simply persists from blind imitation of the past." Note as well that there is an important difference between common law precedent and constitutional precedents; while common law precedents can be overturned by statute, constitutional precedents cannot.[46]

7. *National ethos and political tradition.* A seventh kind of constitutional argument looks to the meaning of the American political tradition; it asks whether a

---

45. Richard Fallon, Stare Decisis and the Constitution: An Essay on Constitutional Methodology, 76 N.Y.U. L. Rev. 570, 585 (2001).

46. For theoretical discussions of constitutional precedent, see Michael Gerhardt, The Power of Precedent (2011); Randy J. Kozel, Settled versus Right: A Theory of Precedent (2017).

proposed interpretation is faithful to the meaning or destiny of the country, its deepest commitments, or some important aspect of national character. Bobbitt calls these arguments "ethical," because they concern national ethos. The character of a nation and its commitments sometimes are elucidated by what has happened in the past. Therefore in interpreting the Constitution, people often make arguments about the traditions of the American people and the meaning of the key events in American history. (Examples are appeals to the American Revolution, the Civil War, the New Deal, or the Civil Rights Movement.) Therefore these might be also called arguments from the American political tradition.

When *McCulloch* was decided, the American nation was still relatively new. The only arguments from tradition available concerned the Revolution and, before that, the political traditions of Great Britain. Hence Marshall's arguments about the character of the nation tend to be forward-looking—he asks what kind of nation the United States is and will become. As time goes on, interpreters have many ways of invoking tradition and the meaning of key events in articulating national commitments.

Arguments about national ethos and political tradition are often narrative or historical in character, and are often continuous with the other forms of constitutional argument, particularly arguments from structure, purpose, and past practice. Note that in ¶17 Marshall justifies the need for a flexible constitution on the grounds that "[t]hroughout this vast republic, from the St. Croix to the Gulf of Mexico, from the Atlantic to the Pacific, revenue is to be collected and expended, armies are to be marched and supported. . . . Is that construction of the constitution to be preferred which would render these operations difficult, hazardous, and expensive?" At first this looks like a simple argument about good and bad consequences. But it actually rests on a deeper set of assumptions about the nature of the American nation—as well as its eventual future:[47]

> In Marshall's narrative—one that would be retold countless times under the more familiar name of "Manifest Destiny"—the United States was to become a great country, not only in spirit but also in resources and size; and great countries need constitutions that give them the flexibility to grow and attain their promised greatness.
>
> As Lewis Henry LaRue has pointed out, it is this familiar narrative of America's destiny, as much as anything else, that underpins and justifies the expansive constitutional interpretation of national power in *McCulloch.* The narrative is not everything, but it is surely something. If we told a different story—a Jeffersonian story of a tranquil land of agrarian farmers who hoped to avoid the corruptions of ambition and avarice characteristic of European monarchies, who sought merely to live their lives in peace and harmony in small, close-knit communities—we might well imagine

---

47. J.M. Balkin and Sanford Levinson, The Canons of Constitutional Law, 111 Harv. L. Rev. 963 (1998). For theories of narrative argument in constitutional law, see J.M. Balkin, The Declaration and the Promise of a Democratic Culture, 4 Widener L. Symp. J. 167 (1999); Lewis Henry LaRue, Constitutional Law as Fiction: Narrative in the Rhetoric of Authority (1995).

that it *should* be "difficult, hazardous, and expensive" for the national government to gather revenues, raise armies, sweep across the Continent, and conquer all in its path. If we told a story that opposed the depravity and overreaching of grasping monarchs and their prime ministers to the simple virtues of a self-reliant republican citizenry, we might even more want to nip in the bud any potential mechanisms of national aggrandizement.

8. *Using the modalities.* We have identified seven standard kinds of arguments that lawyers employ in arguing about the Constitution. The list of modalities is by no means closed: We have not mentioned, for example, arguments from natural law and natural rights, which were quite important in the eighteenth and nineteenth centuries. And often there can be more than one way to classify a particular argument. That is as it should be: the study of modalities of argument is not about memorizing a set of rigid formulas but about learning, in practical terms, how to analyze problems and persuade other people about what the Constitution means.

In any case, the seven types of argument detailed above are the ones constitutional lawyers most frequently use. When you face a novel constitutional question, it helps to have them at your fingertips. You will find that simply by working through the modalities and coming up with the best arguments pro and con for each modality, you will learn a great deal about the Constitution, and you will improve your skills as a legal advocate.

NOTE: UNCERTAINTIES OF MEANING

The language of a provision in a written document is often susceptible of more than one meaning; it can be ambiguous, vague, or figurative.[48]

1. Ambiguity

A word or expression is ambiguous if it refers to two or more different concepts. Imagine, for example, that you receive a note suggesting that you meet by "the bank" at noon. Especially if you have just read *McCulloch,* you might immediately think that this refers to a financial services institution, though there might still be confusion as to which among several "banks" is the proposed venue. If, on the other hand, you are an avid angler, "the bank" clearly refers, at least for you, to the local fishing spot, and it would be a clear mistake to go instead to the First National Bank.

Resolving ambiguity normally requires some understanding of the likely purposes of actual speakers or writers. Consider, for example, Article II, §1, cl. 5:

---

48. See generally William Alston, Philosophy of Language, ch. 5 (1964); William Empson, Seven Types of Ambiguity (2d ed. 1947): Willard Van Orman Quine, Word and Object, ch. 4 (1960); I.A. Richards, The Philosophy of Rhetoric (1936); E. Allan Farnsworth, "Meaning" in the Law of Contracts, 76 Yale L.J. 939 (1967); Fredrich Waismann, Analytic-Synthetic V, 13 Analysis 1 (1952).

"No person except a natural born Citizen . . . shall be eligible to the Office of President. . . ." What is the meaning of the phrase in our Constitution, and how do you know? Consider the phrase in its full context: "No person except a natural born Citizen or a Citizen of the United States, at the time of the Adoption of this Constitution, shall be eligible to the Office of President. . . ." Does this help resolve ambiguity, and how?

Terms that appear ambiguous may be given meaning by past practice or by legal stipulation. Consider the case of Texas Senator Ted Cruz, who ran for president in 2016. Cruz was born in Calgary, Canada, to an American mother and a Cuban father. A federal statute treats Cruz as a birthright citizen because his mother, an American citizen, had spent at least five years after her fourteenth birthday within the United States. Can Congress, by statute, settle the question of who is a "natural born" citizen under the meaning of the Constitution? If Congress may not, does this mean that anyone born in Puerto Rico, whose citizenship depends on the 1917 Jones Act, is ineligible to become President? These are, we assure you, not the only examples of gaps and ambiguities to be found in the text of the Constitution.

2. *Vagueness*

Whereas ambiguous meanings tend to differ discretely, as with the two discrete meanings of "bank," vagueness involves marginal indefiniteness in the meaning and application of words, as would be the case if there are multiple financial institutions and there is no a priori reason to think that "bank" refers to one rather than another.[49]

> Thus, "middle-aged" is vague, for it is not clear whether a person aged 40 or a person aged 59 is middle-aged. Of course there are uncontroversial areas of application and nonapplication. At age 5 or 80 one is clearly not middle-aged, and at age 45 one clearly is. [Would this be true even if standard life expectancy increases, as some predict, to 150 years? Even if a 45-year-old in 2015 is clearly "middle-aged," will that necessarily be true of a 45-year-old in 2115?] But on either side of the area of clear application there are indefinitely bounded areas of uncertainty. . . . [T]here is no definite answer to the question, Is a person aged 40 middle-aged? . . . Our inability [to give an answer] is not the result of lack of information about such things as blood pressure and metabolic rate. No additional information would settle the matter, except indirectly by leading us to tighten up the meaning of the word. The indeterminacy is due to an aspect of the meaning of the term rather than to the current state of our knowledge.

Not only abstract concepts but ordinary (nonproper) nouns naming physical objects and intangible things are usually vague—and often incurably so. For many

---

49. William Alston, Vagueness, in 8 Encyclopedia of Philosophy 218 (Edwards ed., 1967).

things are defined by the confluence of a number of attributes (a, b, c, . . . n), and one can never fully describe the combinations of attributes necessary or sufficient for proper application of the noun to particular things:[50]

> Consider the term "lemon," for example. Lemons normally have certain characteristics: a yellow color when ripe, skin of a certain thickness with a waxy texture, ovoid shape, acid taste, a size and hardness that falls within a certain range, and so on. If an object has all these properties, it is definitely a lemon. It might happen that in a particular region of the world, due to atomic fallout, lemon trees started producing fruit of a pinkish color and with a sweet taste, but having all the other characteristics of ordinary lemons. These fruits would doubtless still be lemons: pink lemons or sweet pink lemons. A thing cannot lack all, or even very many, of the typical lemon properties, and still be a lemon; but there is no one property, or group of two or three properties, which an object must have to be properly called a lemon. It must simply have some combination of the cluster or properties which lemons typically have.

Some provisions of the Constitution are quite precise: Article II, §1, cl. 5 requires that the President be at least 35 years old rather than at least "middle-aged," though the term "35 years old" could become ambiguous if there were real dispute about which calendar system to adopt, e.g., lunar or solar, as the metric for determining years of life. Many other provisions are quite vague: What is the "*Commerce* . . . among the several States" that Article I, §8, cl. 3 empowers Congress to regulate? And some provisions, such as the Fourth Amendment's prohibition of "*unreasonable* searches and seizures," seem designedly vague.

3. Nonliteral Usage

Article I, §8, cl. 8 empowers Congress "[t]o promote the Progress of Science and useful Arts, by securing for limited Times to Authors and Inventors the exclusive Right to their respective Writings and Discoveries." Does "writings" include anything besides letters inscribed on a surface? Does it include inscriptions by means other than hand (by printing or photo process), inscriptions of things other than letters (maps, charts, drawings), three-dimensional objects (sculptures, casseroles, automobiles), things not created by humans (driftwood), things not visually perceptible (the contents of phonograph records), ideas (the one-way toll bridge), intangible creations (theater productions, television broadcasts), and systems (computer programs, accounting systems)?[51]

The word "writings" is, to be sure, vague. But the questions posed above do not involve vagueness; they concern whether we should read the language literally.

---

50. George Pitcher, The Philosophy of Wittgenstein 221 (1964) (borrowing an example from Michael Scriven). See also Alston, supra n.49, at 94-95 (1964); Fredrich Waismann, Verifiability, in Logic and Language-First Series (Flew ed., 1952).

51. See generally 1 Melville Nimmer, Copyright §8 (1973).

The Oxford English Dictionary defines the "literal" meaning of a word as its "relatively primary sense . . . as distinguished from any metaphorical or merely suggested meaning." Although true metaphors are rare in legal texts, other kinds of nonliteral, or figurative, usage are very common. An example is a *synecdoche,* where a part stands for a larger whole; or *metonymy,* where something stands for something it is associated with. (For example, people often use "Washington" to stand for the U.S. government, and "White House" to stand for the current presidential administration.) Interpreters are frequently called upon to determine how literally or figuratively to understand a term. Does the Copyright Clause protect only "graphic" works, does it protect only "tangible" works, or does it protect all "expressions of intellectual creation"? It seems obvious that the proper scope of the concept represented by a term depends on the context in which, and the purpose for which, the term is used.

We recur so often to the inherent indeterminacy of language that it is important to emphasize that its indeterminacy is not unlimited; the very concept of "interpretation" implies that the interpreter is not free to stipulate the meanings of the terms he is interpreting. The reason for this is suggested by Wittgenstein's insightful analogy between language and a game. As Gilbert Ryle put it:[52]

> The significance of an expression and the powers or functions in chess of a pawn, a knight or the queen have much in common. To know what the knight can and cannot do, one must know the rules of chess, as well as be familiar with various kinds of chess situations which may arise. . . . Similarly to know what an expression means is to know how it may and may not be employed.

Language is a social practice. Just as a player who stipulates that his knight may move forward one square at a time is not playing chess, someone who stipulates that a word or expression shall mean something without regard to its accepted usage is not engaging in ordinary conversation. The classic example of difficulties that emerge when linguistic conventions are ignored is Humpty Dumpty's attempt to persuade Alice that unbirthdays are better than birthdays:[53]

> "[T]here are three hundred and sixty-four days when you might get unbirthday presents."
>
> "Certainly," said Alice.
>
> "And only *one* for birthday presents, you know. There's glory for you!"
>
> "I don't know what you mean by 'glory,'" Alice said.
>
> Humpty Dumpty smiled contemptuously. "Of course you don't till I tell you. I meant 'there's a nice knock-down argument for you!'"
>
> "But 'glory' doesn't mean 'a nice knock-down argument,'" Alice objected.

52. Gilbert Ryle, The Theory of Meaning, in British Philosophy in the Mid-Century 255 (Mace ed., 1957).

53. Lewis Carroll, Through the Looking Glass, ch. 6 (1865).

> "When *I* use a word," Humpty Dumpty said, in rather a scornful tone, "it means just what I choose it to mean neither more nor less."
>
> "The question is," said Alice, "whether you *can* make words mean so many different things."
>
> "The question is," said Humpty Dumpty, "which is to be master that's all."

As noted earlier, Professor Levinson has distinguished between the Constitutions of "Conversation" and "Settlement." Though the Constitution of Conversation requires wrestling with the many issues of interpretation raised above, the Constitution of Settlement, set out in (mostly) bright-line rules, usually poses fewer interpretive problems. Thus, save for extremely exotic hypotheticals, the date of a newly elected President's inauguration or the number of senators representing Wyoming (or California) is clear (which may be one reason why constitutional law casebooks spend so little time discussing these issues).

V. THE STATES' POWER TO TAX THE BANK OF THE UNITED STATES

Marshall devotes considerable time to demonstrating that Congress had the power to incorporate the Second Bank of the United States. Yet that discussion did not resolve the central issue before the Court: whether it was constitutional for "Maryland, a sovereign state," to use its taxing power in effect to drive the bank out of Maryland. We now return to Marshall's opinion concerning this second question:

McCulloch v. Maryland

[The Second Question]

[46] It being the opinion of the Court, that the act incorporating the bank is constitutional; and that the power of establishing a branch in the State of Maryland might be properly exercised by the bank itself, we proceed to inquire

[47] 2. Whether the State of Maryland may, without violating the constitution, tax that branch?

[48] That the power of taxation is one of vital importance; that it is retained by the States; that it is not abridged by the grant of a similar power to the government of the Union; that it is to be concurrently exercised by the two governments: are truths which have never been denied. But, such is the paramount character of the constitution, that its capacity to withdraw any subject from the action of even this power, is admitted. The States are expressly forbidden to lay any duties on imports or exports, except what may be absolutely necessary for executing their inspection laws. If the obligation of this prohibition must be conceded—if it may restrain a State from the exercise of its taxing power on imports and exports; the same paramount character would seem to restrain, as it certainly may restrain, a State from such other exercise of this power, as is in its nature incompatible with, and repugnant to, the constitutional laws of the Union. A law, absolutely repugnant to another, as entirely repeals that other as if express terms of repeal were used.

[49] On this ground the counsel for the bank place its claim to be exempted from the power of a State to tax its operations. There is no express provision for the case, but the claim has been sustained on a principle which so entirely pervades the constitution, is so intermixed with the materials which compose it, so interwoven with its web, so blended with its texture, as to be incapable of being separated from it, without rending it into shreds.

[50] This great principle is, that the constitution and the laws made in pursuance thereof are supreme; that they control the constitution and laws of the respective States, and cannot be controlled by them. From this, which may be almost termed an axiom, other propositions are deduced as corollaries, on the truth or error of which, and on their application to this case, the cause has been supposed to depend. These are, 1st. That a power to create implies a power to preserve. 2nd. That a power to destroy, if wielded by a different hand, is hostile to, and incompatible with these powers to create and to preserve. 3d. That where this repugnancy exists, that authority which is supreme must control, not yield to that over which it is supreme.

[51] These propositions, as abstract truths, would, perhaps, never be controverted. Their application to this case, however, has been denied; and, both in maintaining the affirmative and the negative, a splendor of eloquence, and strength of argument, seldom, if ever, surpassed, have been displayed.

[52] The power of Congress to create, and of course to continue, the bank, was the subject of the preceding part of this opinion; and is no longer to be considered as questionable.

[53] That the power of taxing it by the States may be exercised so as to destroy it, is too obvious to be denied. But taxation is said to be an absolute power, which acknowledges no other limits than those expressly prescribed in the constitution, and like sovereign power of every other description, is trusted to the discretion of those who use it. But the very terms of this argument admit that the sovereignty of the State, in the article of taxation itself, is subordinate to, and may be controlled by the constitution of the United States. How far it has been controlled by that instrument must be a question of construction. In making this construction, no principle not declared, can be admissible, which would defeat the legitimate operations of a supreme government. It is of the very essence of supremacy to remove all obstacles to its action within its own sphere, and so to modify every power vested in subordinate governments, as to exempt its own operations from their own influence. This effect need not be stated in terms. It is so involved in the declaration of supremacy, so necessarily implied in it, that the expression of it could not make it more certain. We must, therefore, keep it in view while construing the constitution.

[54] The argument on the part of the State of Maryland, is, not that the States may directly resist a law of Congress, but that they may exercise their acknowledged powers upon it, and that the constitution leaves them this right in the confidence that they will not abuse it.

[55] Before we proceed to examine this argument, and to subject it to the test of the constitution, we must be permitted to bestow a few considerations on the nature and extent of this original right of taxation, which is acknowledged to remain with the States. It is admitted that the power of taxing the people and their property is essential to the very existence of government, and may be legitimately

exercised on the objects to which it is applicable, to the utmost extent to which the government may chuse to carry it. The only security against the abuse of this power, is found in the structure of the government itself. In imposing a tax the legislature acts upon its constituents. This is in general a sufficient security against erroneous and oppressive taxation.

[56] The people of a State, therefore, give to their government a right of taxing themselves and their property, and as the exigencies of government cannot be limited, they prescribe no limits to the exercise of this right, resting confidently on the interest of the legislator, and on the influence of the constituents over their representative, to guard them against its abuse. But the means employed by the government of the Union have no such security, nor is the right of a State to tax them sustained by the same theory. Those means are not given by the people of a particular State, not given by the constituents of the legislature, which claim the right to tax them, but by the people of all the States. They are given by all, for the benefit of all—and upon theory, should be subjected to that government only which belongs to all.

[57] It may be objected to this definition, that the power of taxation is not confined to the people and property of a State. It may be exercised upon every object brought within its jurisdiction.

[58] This is true. But to what source do we trace this right? It is obvious, that it is an incident of sovereignty, and is co-extensive with that to which it is an incident. All subjects over which the sovereign power of a State extends, are objects of taxation; but those over which it does not extend, are, upon the soundest principles, exempt from taxation. This proposition may almost be pronounced self-evident.

[59] The sovereignty of a State extends to every thing which exists by its own authority, or is introduced by its permission; but does it extend to those means which are employed by Congress to carry into execution powers conferred on that body by the people of the United States? We think it demonstrable that it does not. Those powers are not given by the people of a single State. They are given by the people of the United States, to a government whose laws, made in pursuance of the constitution, are declared to be supreme. Consequently, the people of a single State cannot confer a sovereignty which will extend over them.

[60] If we measure the power of taxation residing in a State, by the extent of sovereignty which the people of a single State possess, and can confer on its government, we have an intelligible standard, applicable to every case to which the power may be applied. We have a principle which leaves the power of taxing the people and property of a State unimpaired; which leaves to a State the command of all its resources, and which places beyond its reach, all those powers which are conferred by the people of the United States on the government of the Union, and all those means which are given for the purpose of carrying those powers into execution. We have a principle which is safe for the States, and safe for the Union. We are relieved, as we ought to be, from clashing sovereignty; from interfering powers; from a repugnancy between a right in one government to pull down what there is an acknowledged right in another to build up; from the incompatibility of a right in one government to destroy what there is a right in another to preserve. We are not driven to the perplexing inquiry, so unfit for the judicial department, what degree of taxation is the legitimate use, and what degree may amount to the abuse

of the power. The attempt to use it on the means employed by the government of the Union, in pursuance of the constitution, is itself an abuse, because it is the usurpation of a power which the people of a single State cannot give.

[61] We find, then, on just theory, a total failure of this original right to tax the means employed by the government of the Union, for the execution of its powers. The right never existed, and the question whether it has been surrendered, cannot arise.

[62] But, waiving this theory for the present, let us resume the inquiry, whether this power can be exercised by the respective States, consistently with a fair construction of the constitution?

[63] That the power to tax involves the power to destroy; that the power to destroy may defeat and render useless the power to create; that there is a plain repugnance, in conferring on one government a power to control the constitutional measures of another, which other, with respect to those very measures, is declared to be supreme over that which exerts the control, are propositions not to be denied. But all inconsistencies are to be reconciled by the magic of the word CONFIDENCE. Taxation, it is said, does not necessarily and unavoidably destroy. To carry it to the excess of destruction would be an abuse, to presume which, would banish that confidence which is essential to all government.

[64] But is this a case of confidence? Would the people of any one State trust those of another with a power to control the most insignificant operations of their State government? We know they would not. Why, then, should we suppose that the people of any one State should be willing to trust those of another with a power to control the operations of a government to which they have confided their most important and most valuable interests? In the legislature of the Union alone, are all represented. The legislature of the Union alone, therefore, can be trusted by the people with the power of controlling measures which concern all, in the confidence that it will not be abused. This, then, is not a case of confidence, and we must consider it as it really is.

[65] If we apply the principle for which the State of Maryland contends, to the constitution generally, we shall find it capable of changing totally the character of that instrument. We shall find it capable of arresting all the measures of the government, and of prostrating it at the foot of the States. The American people have declared their constitution, and the laws made in pursuance thereof, to be supreme; but this principle would transfer the supremacy, in fact, to the States.

[66] If the States may tax one instrument, employed by the government in the execution of its powers, they may tax any and every other instrument. They may tax the mail; they may tax the mint; they may tax patent rights; they may tax the papers of the custom-house; they may tax judicial process; they may tax all the means employed by the government, to an excess which would defeat all the ends of government. This was not intended by the American people. They did not design to make their government dependent on the States.

[67] Gentlemen say, they do not claim the right to extend State taxation to these objects. They limit their pretensions to property. But on what principle is this distinction made? Those who make it have furnished no reason for it, and the principle for which they contend denies it. They contend that the power of taxation has no other limit than is found in the 10th section of the 1st article of the constitution;

that, with respect to every thing else, the power of the States is supreme, and admits of no control. If this be true, the distinction between property and other subjects to which the power of taxation is applicable, is merely arbitrary, and can never be sustained. This is not all. If the controlling power of the States be established; if their supremacy as to taxation be acknowledged; what is to restrain their exercising this control in any shape they may please to give it? Their sovereignty is not confined to taxation. That is not the only mode in which it might be displayed. The question is, in truth, a question of supremacy; and if the right of the States to tax the means employed by the general government be conceded the declaration that the constitution, and the laws made in pursuance thereof, shall be the supreme law of the land, is empty and unmeaning declamation.

[68] In the course of the argument, the Federalist has been quoted; and the opinions expressed by the authors of that work have been justly supposed to be entitled to great respect in expounding the constitution. No tribute can be paid to them which exceeds their merit; but in applying their opinions to the cases which may arise in the progress of our government, a right to judge of their correctness must be retained; and, to understand the argument, we must examine the proposition it maintains, and the objections against which it is directed. The subject of those numbers, from which passages have been cited, is the unlimited power of taxation which is vested in the general government. The objection to this unlimited power, which the argument seeks to remove, is stated with fullness and clearness. It is, "that an indefinite power of taxation in the latter (the government of the Union) might, and probably would, in time, deprive the former (the government of the States) of the means of providing for their own necessities; and would subject them entirely to the mercy of the national legislature. As the laws of the Union are to become the supreme law of the land; as it is to have power to pass all laws that may be necessary for carrying into execution the authorities with which it is proposed to vest it; the national government might at any time abolish the taxes imposed for State objects, upon the pretence of an interference with its own. It might allege a necessity for doing this, in order to give efficacy to the national revenues; and thus all the resources of taxation might, by degrees, become the subjects of federal monopoly, to the entire exclusion and destruction of the State governments."

[69] The objections to the constitution which are noticed in these numbers, were to the undefined power of the government to tax, not to the incidental privilege of exempting its own measures from State taxation. The consequences apprehended from this undefined power were, that it would absorb all the objects of taxation, "to the exclusion and destruction of the State governments." The arguments of the Federalist are intended to prove the fallacy of these apprehensions; not to prove that the government was incapable of executing any of its powers, without exposing the means it employed to the embarrassments of State taxation. Arguments urged against these objections, and these apprehensions, are to be understood as relating to the points they mean to prove. Had the authors of those excellent essays been asked, whether they contended for that construction of the constitution, which would place within the reach of the States those measures which the government might adopt for the execution of its powers; no man, who has read their instructive pages, will hesitate to admit, that their answer must have been in the negative.

[70] It has also been insisted, that, as the power of taxation in the general and State governments is acknowledged to be concurrent, every argument which would sustain the right of the general government to tax banks chartered by the States, will equally sustain the right of the States to tax banks chartered by the general government.

[71] But the two cases are not on the same reason. The people of all the States have created the general government, and have conferred upon it the general power of taxation. The people of all the States, and the States themselves, are represented in Congress, and, by their representatives, exercise this power. When they tax the chartered institutions of the States, they tax their constituents; and these taxes must be uniform. But, when a State taxes the operations of the government of the United States, it acts upon institutions created, not by their own constituents, but by people over whom they claim no control. It acts upon the measures of a government created by others as well as themselves, for the benefit of others in common with themselves. The difference is that which always exists, and always must exist, between the action of the whole on a part, and the action of a part on the whole—between the laws of a government declared to be supreme, and those of a government which, when in opposition to those laws, is not supreme.

[72] But if the full application of this argument could be admitted, it might bring into question the right of Congress to tax the State banks, and could not prove the right of the States to tax the Bank of the United States.

[73] The Court has bestowed on this subject its most deliberate consideration. The result is a conviction that the States have no power, by taxation or otherwise, to retard, impede, burden, or in any manner control, the operations of the constitutional laws enacted by Congress to carry into execution the powers vested in the general government. This is, we think, the unavoidable consequence of that supremacy which the constitution has declared.

[74] We are unanimously of opinion, that the law passed by the legislature of Maryland, imposing a tax on the Bank of the United States, is unconstitutional and void.

[75] This opinion does not deprive the States of any resources which they originally possessed. It does not extend to a tax paid by the real property of the bank, in common with the other real property within the State, nor to a tax imposed on the interest which the citizens of Maryland may hold in this institution, in common with other property of the same description throughout the State. But this is a tax on the operations of the bank, and is, consequently, a tax on the operation of an instrument employed by the government of the Union to carry its powers into execution. Such a tax must be unconstitutional.

DISCUSSION

1. *Marshall's interpretive strategy.* Outline Marshall's argument in the second part of *McCulloch.* Which of the methods of constitutional interpretation discussed does Marshall employ?

2. *Default rules.* Under Marshall's theory of congressional power announced in the first part of *McCulloch,* Congress could surely have enacted legislation

immunizing the Bank of the United States from the Maryland tax. Why doesn't the Constitution leave the choice to Congress, then?

One might view *McCulloch* as a default rule that prevents states from interfering with federal instrumentalities unless Congress affirmatively permits it. In general, the federal courts have assumed that Congress can waive federal tax immunity and consent to state taxation.[54] If *McCulloch* is a constitutional default rule, what justifies the default, and why should federal courts be authorized to create such a rule? What is their special role in policing intergovernmental relations?

3. *Discrimination.* Is it constitutionally relevant that the Maryland tax by its terms fell only on banks not chartered by the state? Only the Bank of the United States fit that category. Suppose that Maryland passed a tax on *all* banks. Should this have been treated differently? Consider in this context the final paragraph of Marshall's opinion in which he assumes that some taxes would be constitutional. If some of the bank's functions and property, but not others, are constitutionally immune from state taxation, how can one determine which ones are immune?

4. *Questions of degree.* In the first part of the opinion Marshall writes that, if the Court concludes that the bank is "appropriate," then "the degree of its necessity" is to be determined by Congress. If Marshall were a senator or representative, how do you suppose he would approach the question of the bank's "degree of necessity"—as a constitutional question or a political issue? Compare Hamilton's argument for the First Bank, supra. What is the difference between "constitutional" and "political" in this context?

5. *The power to destroy.* Is it true that "the power to tax is the power to destroy," or is this just a "seductive cliche"?[55] Consider Justice Holmes's statement, "Taxes are what we pay for civilized society."[56] Might not both statements be true? Might excessive taxation indeed be destructive, even as the lack of sufficient taxation would threaten the maintenance of "civilized society"?

If so, then who—or what institution—should be charged with deciding whether the line between sufficiency and excess has been crossed? Marshall refers to "the perplexing inquiry, so unfit for the judiciary department, what degree of taxation is the legitimate use, and what degree may amount to the abuse of power." What does he mean by this?

Suppose Marshall is right that judges are not capable of making judgments of degree. Does this justify depriving the states of a legitimate power? Justice Holmes, dissenting in Panhandle Oil Co. v. Knox, 277 U.S. 218, 223 (1928), observed: "In those days it was not recognized as it is today that most of the distinctions of the law are distinctions of degree. If the States had any power it was assumed that they had all power, and that the necessary alternative was to deny it altogether."

---

54. See, e.g., Federal Land Bank Of Wichita v. Kiowa County, 368 U.S. 146, 149 (1961) ("Congress has the power to determine, within the limits of the Constitution, the extent that its instrumentalities shall enjoy immunity from state taxation."); First National Bank of Guthrie Center v. Anderson, 269 U.S. 341, 347 (1926)

55. Graves v. O'Keefe, 306 U.S. 466, 489 (1939) (Frankfurter, J., concurring). See also New York v. United States, 326 U.S. 572, 576 (1946) (Frankfurter, J.) ("rhetorical absolute").

56. Compania General de Tabacos de Filipinas v. Collector of Internal Revenue, 275 U.S. 87, 100 (1927) (dissenting).

Holmes went on to write, "The power to tax is not the power to destroy while this Court sits." Does he mean by this that the Court has a good "legal" conception of the limits of state taxation, or does he merely mean that we can trust courts to exercise sound prudential judgment in deciding when a state goes "too far" in imposing taxes? If this is a prudential judgment, then it argues for treating the rule as merely a constitutional default that Congress can change by consenting to state taxation.

6. *Federal immunities today.* Litigation continues today on the ability of states to tax or to regulate federal instrumentalities. See, e.g., Department of Employment v. United States, 385 U.S. 355 (1966), unanimously holding that the American National Red Cross is an instrumentality of the United States, immune from a state unemployment compensation tax, and that Congress has not waived its immunity. In Jefferson County, Alabama v. Acker, 527 U.S. 423 (1999), the Court considered a suit brought by U.S. federal judges protesting a Jefferson County occupational tax on persons working within the county not otherwise required to pay a license fee under state law. Because the judges hold court within the county, the county attempted to collect the tax. "[T]he judges maintain that they are shielded from payment of the tax by the intergovernmental tax immunity doctrine, while the county urges that the doctrine does not apply unless the tax discriminates against an officeholder because of the source of his pay or compensation." The Court, through Justice Ginsburg, ruled in favor of the county:

> The county's Ordinance lays no "demands directly on the Federal Government," United States v. New Mexico, 455 U.S. 720, 735 (1982); it is, and operates as, a tax on employees' compensation. The Public Salary Tax Act [passed by Congress] allows a State and its taxing authorities to tax the pay federal employees receive "if the taxation does not discriminate against the [federal] employee because of the source of the pay or compensation." 4 U.S.C. §111. We hold that Jefferson County's tax falls within that allowance. . . . In practice, Jefferson County's license tax serves a revenue-raising, not a regulatory, purpose. Jefferson County neither issues licenses to taxpayers, nor in any way regulates them in the performance of their duties based on their status as license taxpayers.

Justices Breyer and O'Connor dissented, largely on the basis of the many exceptions to paying the tax found in the Jefferson County ordinance.

As Justice Ginsburg suggests, states have far less power to *regulate* federal instrumentalities than to levy (nondiscriminatory) taxes against federal officials. A taste of the difficulties provided in regard to state regulation is provided by Johnson v. Maryland, 254 U.S. 51 (1920), which held that, in the absence of any federal regulation on the subject, a Post Office employee driving a government vehicle on official business was not required to possess a state driver's license. Citing *McCulloch,* Justice Holmes wrote:

> It seems to us that the immunity of instruments of the United States from state control in the performance of their duties extends to a requirement that they desist from performance until they satisfy a state officer upon examination that they are competent for a necessary part of them and pay a fee for permission to go on. Such a requirement does not merely touch the Government servants remotely by a general rule of conduct;

> it lays hold of them in their specific attempt to obey orders and requires qualifications in addition to those that the Government has pronounced sufficient. It is the duty of the Department to employ persons competent for their work and that duty it must be presumed has been performed.

Holmes cautioned, however, that "an employee of the United States does not secure a general immunity from state law while acting in the course of his employment" and suggested that "when the United States has not spoken, the subjection to local law would extend to general rules that might affect incidentally the mode of carrying out the employment—as, for instance, a statute or ordinance regulating the mode of turning at the corners of streets." What is the basis for this distinction?

VI. OHIO DISSENTS

Marshall spoke clearly and unequivocally in *McCulloch*: Congress could charter the bank and Maryland could not tax it. So consider the fact that within five years, the Court "was forced, in effect, if not in name, to rehear many of the issues it had tried to settle in *McCulloch*."[57] The explanation is simple: Whatever Marshall might have written, the state of Ohio was not persuaded, and it chose to act according to its own reading of its "sovereign" powers. Like Maryland, it had chosen in 1817 to tax the Bank of the United States, which had a branch in Chillocothe, Ohio. Among the rationales offered for the legitimacy of the tax by its supporters was that the Second Bank "was not merely a government instrument." Thus, as one of them put it, "when we raise the curtain we find [the bank] composed of an association of members, half encircling the globe, . . . where the funds of the stranger, the alien and American, are mingled in one common mass." Thus, argued the committee passing the tax, the Chillocothe branch was "as subject to a tax as any corporate body could be, if acting under the authority of the state."[58]

Theoretical arguments about the status of the bank were replaced, by the time of the 1818 elections in Ohio, by intense public antagonism to the bank, due in part to a downturn in the local economy. The leading legislator described Ohio as being "at the mercy of stockjobbers and Brokers, mostly foreign agents without moral or social feelings of any kind."[59] The legislature passed a bill requiring that each branch of the Second Bank pay a levy of $50,000 to Ohio. "[T]he auditor of Ohio was authorized to appoint someone to forcibly collect the tax from the assets of the bank's branches" should it not otherwise comply with the state's demand.[60]

McCulloch was then decided. It was not received favorably by Ohio's leaders. Governor Brown refused even to call the legislature into special session to discuss the implications of Marshall's decision. Instead, he proclaimed that "Ohio should take a lead in all lawful resistance to any violation of the reserved state sovereignty."

---

57. Ellis, supra n.23, at 143.
58. Id. at 145.
59. Id. at 150.
60. Id. at 151.

It did not matter that that violation issued from a "judicial construction [whose acceptance] would be a death blow to our Union; or to our free government, or both."[61]

The state auditor, one Ralph Osborne, enforced Ohio's law by hiring agents to forcibly enter the Chillocothe branch of the Second Bank. They were described as having acted "in a ruffian-like manner, jumped over the counter, took and held forcible possession of the vault." They then took $120,425 from said vault, which was taken the next day to the state capital in Columbus. Given that this was considerably more than the $50,000 that Ohio claimed, the excess was returned to the Second Bank.[62]

As one might imagine, the Second Bank did not take this lying down, and it promptly sued for an injunction requiring return of the seized monies. In addition to *McCulloch,* it was bolstered by the widespread antagonism to Ohio's precipitate act throughout the East. Ohio's actions were described by some as akin to rebellion or even treason. Telling was an editorial in *Niles Weekly Register,* which had been "an outspoken critic of the constitutionality" of the bank and of Marshall's opinion in *McCulloch.* "It is not for any of the states," wrote Nezekih Niles, "to oppose force to the operation of the law, as settled by the authorities of the United States, however zealous we may be to bring about a different construction of it."[63] Nonetheless, "antibank forces continued to dominate the legislature and governorship."[64]

Interestingly enough, Ohio's demand became in effect that *McCulloch* be re-litigated because of alleged defects in the initial litigation. As one editorial writer put it, "The state of Ohio does not admit that a case between the two parties" in *McCulloch* "is or ought to be *binding on any other party.*"[65] However, even the militantly antibank faction in Ohio stated that it would accept a judicial decision that explicitly considered their own claims as to why Ohio had the right to behave as it did. Thus "[f]rom this point on the dispute between Ohio and the [Second Bank of the United States] was pursued exclusively in legal and constitutional terms."[66] One should not be surprised to discover that Ohio did not prevail.

The litigation raised two important issues. One was procedural: Could Ohio, as a "sovereign state," be sued against its will in a federal court? (The argument was that a suit against Osborne, the auditor who carried out Ohio law, was in fact a suit against the state.) The other issue was substantive: Ohio argued that the Second Bank could not really be viewed as equal to the national government given the degree of private ownership and control of its operations. Interestingly, Ohio did not challenge Congress's right to charter the bank; instead, it disputed that the charter transformed what was essentially a private corporation into the equivalent of the national mint or post office. Public corporations, Ohio's attorney argued,

61. Id. at 152.
62. Id. at 153.
63. Id. at 154.
64. Id. at 155.
65. Id. at 157.
66. Id. at 160.

"are such only as founded by the government for public purpose, where the whole interest belongs also to the government."[67] Ohio presumably could not tax *that* kind of public corporation, but, the state argued, the limitation did not apply in the case of the bank.

In Osborn v. Bank of the United States, 22 U.S. 738 (1824), Marshall rejected all of the state's arguments. After construing the statute incorporating the bank to confer the right to sue in any federal court, Marshall offered a strongly nationalist interpretation of the domain of federal courts, even when a state was involved (but not directly sued) in litigation. He then dismissed Ohio's argument that the bank was not a federal entity. "The bank is not," he proclaimed, "considered as a private corporation, whose principal object is in individual trade and individual profit, but as a public corporation created for public and national purposes." The mixed character of the bank was, in effect, a "necessary and proper" means of achieving the great public objectives that presumably underlay its initial creation.

Although Ohioans remained unpersuaded by Marshall's reasoning in *McCulloch* and *Osborn*, they acquiesced to the Supreme Court's judgment. All monies were returned, and the potential threat to Union abated. Similar results occurred in a somewhat similar, albeit less dramatic, protest against the bank by the state of Georgia, Bank of the United States v. Planters' Bank of Georgia, 22 U.S. (9 Wheat.) 904 (1824).

Marshall's audacious claim that "by this court alone" could the bank's constitutionality be settled appeared to receive empirical support. Indeed, in some ways Ohio's acquiescence in *Osborn* was more impressive, and exemplary of the Court's growing institutional power, than the immediate aftermath of *McCulloch*, where even opponents of the opinion, like Jefferson and Madison, nonetheless expressed no reservations about the particular result.

VII. THE DEMISE OF THE SECOND BANK

One should not think, however, that *Osborn* expressed the last word about the constitutionality of the bank or, for that matter, the institutional authority of the Supreme Court. President Andrew Jackson despised the bank and its private investors. His Whig opposition in Congress, misreading public opinion, decided to recharter the bank in 1832, four years before the 1816 charter would have elapsed. They believed that this would help them in the 1832 elections. In response, Jackson helped make the election a de facto referendum on the bank by vetoing the renewal of the charter—the most important veto in American history up to that time. Jackson accompanied his veto by a message to the Senate that explained not only why he believed the bank was unconstitutional but also addressed the larger question of the allocation of authority to interpret the Constitution.

---

67. Id. at 171.

Andrew Jackson, Veto Message[68]

(July 10, 1832)

The bill "to modify and continue" the act entitled "An act to incorporate the subscribers to the bank of the United States" was presented to me on the 4th July instant. Having considered it with that solemn regard to the principles of the Constitution which the day was calculated to inspire, and come to the conclusion that it ought not to become a law, I herewith return it to the Senate, in which it originated, with my objections. . . .

It is maintained by the advocates of the bank that its constitutionality in all its features ought to be considered as settled by precedent and by the decision of the Supreme Court. To this conclusion I can not assent. Mere precedent is a dangerous source of authority, and should not be regarded as deciding questions of constitutional power except where the acquiescence of the people and the States can be considered as well settled. So far from this being the case on this subject, an argument against the bank might be based on precedent. One Congress, in 1791, decided in favor of a bank; another, in 1811, decided against it. One Congress, in 1815, decided against a bank; another, in 1816, decided in its favor. Prior to the present Congress, therefore, the precedents drawn from that source were equal. If we resort to the States, the expressions of legislative, judicial, and executive opinions against the bank have been probably to those in its favor as 4 to 1. There is nothing in precedent, therefore, which, if its authority were admitted, ought to weigh in favor of the act before me.

If the opinion of the Supreme Court covered the whole ground of this act, it ought not to control the coordinate authorities of this Government. The Congress, the Executive, and the Court must each for itself be guided by its own opinion of the Constitution. Each public officer who takes an oath to support the Constitution swears that he will support it as he understands it, and not as it is understood by others. It is as much the duty of the House of Representatives, of the Senate, and of the President to decide upon the constitutionality of any bill or resolution which may be presented to them for passage or approval as it is of the supreme judges when it may be brought before them for judicial decision. The opinion of the judges has no more authority over Congress than the opinion of Congress has over the judges, and on that point the President is independent of both. The authority of the Supreme Court must not, therefore, be permitted to control the Congress or the Executive when acting in their legislative capacities, but to have only such influence as the force of their reasoning may deserve.

But in the case relied upon the Supreme Court have not decided that all the features of this corporation are compatible with the Constitution. It is true that the court have said that the law incorporating the bank is a constitutional exercise of power by Congress; but taking into view the whole opinion of the court and the reasoning by which they have come to that conclusion, I understand them to have decided that inasmuch as a bank is an appropriate means for carrying into effect

68. 2 Messages and Papers of the Presidents 576-589 (Richardson ed., 1897).

the enumerated powers of the General Government, therefore the law incorporating it is in accordance with that provision of the Constitution which declares that Congress shall have power "to make all laws which shall be necessary and proper for carrying those powers into execution." Having satisfied themselves that the word "necessary" in the Constitution means "needful," "*requisite,*" "*essential,*" "*conducive to,*" and that "a bank" is a convenient, a useful, and essential instrument in the prosecution of the Government's "fiscal operations," they conclude that to "use one must be within the discretion of Congress" and that "the act to incorporate the Bank of the United States is a law made in pursuance of the Constitution"; "but," say they, "*where the law is not prohibited and is really calculated to effect any of the objects intrusted to the Government, to undertake here to inquire into the degree of its necessity would be to pass the line which circumscribes the judicial department and to tread on legislative ground.*"

The principle here affirmed is that the "degree of its necessity," involving all the details of a banking institution, is a question exclusively for legislative consideration. A bank is constitutional, but it is the province of the Legislature to determine whether this or that particular power, privilege, or exemption is "necessary and proper" to enable the bank to discharge its duties to the Government, and from their decision there is no appeal to the courts of justice. Under the decision of the Supreme Court, therefore, it is the exclusive province of Congress and the President to decide whether the particular features of this act are *necessary* and *proper* in order to enable the bank to perform conveniently and efficiently the public duties assigned to it as a fiscal agent, and therefore constitutional, or *unnecessary* and *improper,* and therefore unconstitutional.

Without commenting on the general principle affirmed by the Supreme Court, let us examine the details of this act in accordance with the rule of legislative action which they have laid down. It will be found that many of the powers and privileges conferred on it can not be supposed necessary for the purpose for which it is proposed to be created, and are not, therefore, means necessary to attain the end in view, and consequently not justified by the Constitution. . . .

This act authorizes and encourages transfers of its stock to foreigners and grants them an exemption from all State and national taxation. So far from being "*necessary and proper*" that the bank should possess this power to make it a safe and efficient agent of the Government in its fiscal operations, it is calculated to convert the Bank of the United States into a foreign bank, to impoverish our people in time of peace, to disseminate a foreign influence through every section of the Republic, and in war to endanger our independence. . . .

It is maintained by some that the bank is a means of executing the constitutional power "to coin money and regulate the value thereof." Congress have established a mint to coin money and passed laws to regulate the value thereof. The money so coined, with its value so regulated, and such foreign coins as Congress may adopt are the only currency known to the Constitution. But if they have other power to regulate the currency, it was conferred to be exercised by themselves, and not to be transferred to a corporation. If the bank be established for that purpose, with a charter unalterable without its consent, Congress have parted with their power for a term of years, during which the Constitution is a dead letter. It is neither necessary nor proper to transfer its legislative power to such a bank, and therefore unconstitutional.

By its silence, considered in connection with the decision of the Supreme Court in the case of McCulloch against the State of Maryland, this act takes from the States the power to tax a portion of the banking business carried on within their limits, in subversion of one of the strongest barriers which secured them against Federal encroachments. Banking, like farming, manufacturing, or any other occupation or profession, is *a business*. . . .

Upon the formation of the Constitution the States guarded their taxing power with peculiar jealousy. They surrendered it only as it regards imports and exports. In relation to every other object within their jurisdiction, whether persons, property, business, or professions, it was secured in as ample a manner as it was before possessed. . . .

There is no more appropriate subject of taxation than banks, banking, and bank stocks, and none to which the States ought more pertinaciously to cling.

It can not be *necessary* to the character of the bank as a fiscal agent of the Government that its private business should be exempted from that taxation to which all the State banks are liable, nor can I conceive it "*proper*" that the substantive and most essential powers reserved by the States shall be thus attacked and annihilated as a means of executing the powers delegated to the General Government. . . .

If our power over means is so absolute that the Supreme Court will not call in question the constitutionality of an act of Congress the subject of which "is not prohibited, and is really calculated to effect any of the objects intrusted to the Government," although, as in the case before me, it takes away powers expressly granted to Congress and rights scrupulously reserved to the States, it becomes us to proceed in our legislation with the utmost caution. Though not directly, our own powers and the rights of the States may be indirectly legislated away in the use of means to execute substantive powers. . . . We may not pass an act prohibiting the States to tax the banking business carried on within their limits, but we may, as a means of executing our powers over other objects, place that business in the hands of our agents and then declare it exempt from State taxation in their hands. Thus may our own powers and the rights of the States, which we can not directly curtail or invade, be frittered away and extinguished in the use of means employed by us to execute other powers. That a bank of the United States, competent to all the duties which may be required by the Government, might be so organized as not to infringe on our own delegated powers or the reserved rights of the States I do not entertain a doubt. Had the Executive been called upon to furnish the project of such an institution, the duty would have been cheerfully performed. In the absence of such a call it was obviously proper that he should confine himself to pointing out those prominent features in the act presented which in his opinion make it incompatible with the Constitution and sound policy. . . .

It is to be regretted that the rich and powerful too often bend the acts of government to their selfish purposes. Distinctions in society will always exist under every just government. Equality of talents, of education, or of wealth can not be produced by human institutions. In the full enjoyment of the gifts of Heaven and the fruits of superior industry, economy, and virtue, every man is equally entitled to protection by law; but when the laws undertake to add to these natural and just advantages artificial distinctions, to grant titles, gratuities, and exclusive privileges, to make the rich richer and the potent more powerful, the humble members of society—the farmers, mechanics, and laborers—who have neither the time nor the means of securing like favors to themselves, have a right to complain of the injustice of their Government. There are no necessary evils in government. Its evils exist only in its abuses. If it would confine itself to equal protection, and, as Heaven does its rains, shower its favors alike on the high and the low, the rich and the poor, it would be an unqualified blessing. In the act before me there seems to be a wide and unnecessary departure from these just principles.

Nor is our Government to be maintained or our Union preserved by invasions of the rights and powers of the several States. In thus attempting to make our General Government strong we make it weak. Its true strength consists in leaving individuals and States as much as possible to themselves—in making itself felt, not in its power, but in its beneficence; not in its control, but in its protection; not in binding the States more closely to the center, but leaving each to move unobstructed in its proper orbit.

DISCUSSION

1. Jackson's assertion that even "[i]f the opinion of the Supreme Court covered the whole ground of this act, it ought not to control the coordinate authorities of this Government" presents a fundamental issue of the allocation of constitutional decisionmaking authority among the branches of the national government, to which we return at length in later chapters. Jackson goes on to note that the Supreme Court in *McCulloch* had *not* "decided that all features of this corporation are compatible with the Constitution." He concludes that "it is the exclusive province of Congress and the President to decide whether the particular features of this act are *necessary* and *proper*. . . ." Is this question one of constitutional law, of politics, or both?

2. The history surrounding the adoption of the President's veto power does not shed much light on its scope. Of the early history of its use, Edward Corwin writes:[69]

> [T]he veto power did not escape the early talent of Americans for conjuring up constitutional limitations out of thin air. The veto was solely a self-defensive weapon of the President; it was the means furnished him for carrying out his oath to "preserve, protect and defend the Constitution" and was not validly usable for any other purpose; it did not extend to revenue bills, never having been so employed by the King of England; it did not extend to "insignificant and trivial" matters like private pension bills; it was never intended to give effect merely to presidential desires, but its use must rest on considerations of great weight, and so on and so forth. Although efforts of this sort to forge shackles for the power derived a certain specious plausibility from the rarity of the veto's use in English history, they met with failure from the first. Washington exercised the power twice,

69. Edward Corwin, The President: Office and Powers 279 (quoting Edward Mason, The Veto Power (1891)) (4th ed. 1957).

once on constitutional grounds, once on grounds of expediency. Neither Adams nor Jefferson exercised it at all. Of Madison's six vetoes four urged constitutional objections to the measure involved, two objections of policy. Summing the matter up for the first century under the Constitution, the leading authority on the subject says: "From Jackson's administration to the Civil War vetoes on grounds of expediency became more frequent, but they were still in a decided minority. Since the [Civil] War constitutional arguments in a veto message have been almost unknown." The latter statement applies moreover equally to more recent years, if exception be made for one or two vetoes by Presidents Taft and Coolidge, both of whom had a special penchant for constitutional niceties. . . .

3. Professor Mark Graber has suggested that the Justices appointed to the Court by Jackson and his successor Martin Van Buren, who were drawn from the states-rights-oriented Democratic Party, might well have overruled the broad doctrine enunciated in *McCulloch* had the case ever presented itself.[70] The Court never had such an opportunity, however, because of Jackson's own veto, which was mirrored in later vetoes by various Presidents of legislation passed by Whig-dominated Congresses that rested on an expansive view of national power. Thus, Graber suggests, *McCulloch* survived not so much because it was explicitly reaffirmed by the Court as because the procedures of the American political system, including the presidential veto, sometimes work to preclude given issues from going to the Supreme Court at a particular moment when the Court, whether by affirming or striking down the legislation, could enunciate its own view of the constitutional merits.

Consider in this context the veto provision adopted by the framers of the South African Constitution in 1996. The President can veto an act of parliament by stating his belief that it is unconstitutional, after which it returns to parliament for reconsideration. (The President cannot veto a bill only because of disagreement with its policy.) However, if parliament disagrees with the President's analysis and repasses the act in question, it goes to the South African Constitutional Court, which issues a binding determination as to its constitutionality. If the Court upholds the act, then the President *must* sign it. Is South Africa more faithful to the articulation of judicial power suggested in ¶1 of *McCulloch* than the United States? Which approach offers the better model to a country designing a constitution in the twenty-first century?

4. President Jackson's veto was not overridden, and the bank expired in 1836. But imagine that it *had* been overridden, or that President Jackson had reluctantly signed a bill extending the bank's charter because, for example, it was embedded, as is often the case today, in so-called omnibus legislation treating a wide number of subjects. In the absence of line-item veto authority, which is possessed by most American governors, the President may think it necessary to sign the bill in spite

---

70. Mark Graber, Naked Land Transfers and American Constitutional Development, 53 Vand. L. Rev. 73 (2000).

of its containing unwise or, more to the present point, even unconstitutional (from the President's perspective) aspects as well. At least since the time of Woodrow Wilson's presidency, Presidents have on occasion issued "signing statements" explaining that they regard certain parts of legislation they are signing as unconstitutional and indicating their intention not to comply with the statutory language. See Statement by the State Department (Announcing President Wilson's Refusal to Carry Out the Section of the Jones Merchant Marine Act of June 5, 1920), in 17 A Compilation of the Messages and Papers of the President 8871 (Sept. 24, 1920). Such statements have become quite common since President Eisenhower's tenure in office, especially in regard to bills containing so-called legislative vetoes. The practice became especially controversial during the Administration of George W. Bush, who issued 161 separate signing statements affecting over 1,100 provisions of law in 160 congressional enactments. See, e.g., Charlie Savage, Takeover: The Return of the Imperial Presidency and the Subversion of American Democracy (2007). President Obama continued the practice, though not with the same apparent zeal. As of early 2013, he had issued 21 signing statements affecting 85 specified provisions of various laws.

The most recent consideration of the general issue of a presidential duty to enforce laws about which the President has constitutional doubts is contained in the following Memorandum of Walter Dellinger, Assistant Attorney General in charge of the Office of Legal Counsel, United States Department of Justice, to Abner Mikva, Counsel to the President. Dellinger, who later became acting Solicitor General of the United States, had been professor of law at Duke University, where he taught constitutional law before joining the Clinton Administration.

Walter Dellinger, Presidential Authority to Decline to Execute Unconstitutional Statutes

(November 2, 1994)

Let me start with a general proposition that I believe to be uncontroversial: there are circumstances in which the President may appropriately decline to enforce a statute that he views as unconstitutional.

First, there is significant judicial approval of this proposition. Most notable is the Court's decision in Myers v. United States, 272 U.S. 52 (1926). There the Court sustained the President's view that the statute at issue was unconstitutional without any member of the Court suggesting that the President had acted improperly in refusing to abide by the statute. More recently, in Freytag v. Commissioner, 501 U.S. 868 (1991), all four of the Justices who addressed the issue agreed that the President has "the power to veto encroaching laws . . . or even to disregard them when they are unconstitutional." Id. at 906 (Scalia, J., concurring). . . .

Second, consistent and substantial executive practice also confirms this general proposition. Opinions dating to at least 1860 assert the President's authority to decline to effectuate enactments that the President views as unconstitutional. . . . Moreover, . . . numerous Presidents have provided advance notice of their intention not to enforce specific statutory requirements that they have viewed as unconstitutional, and the Supreme Court has implicitly endorsed this practice. See INS

v. Chadha, 462 U.S. 919, 942 n.13 (1983) (noting that Presidents often sign legislation containing constitutionally objectionable provisions and indicate that they will not comply with those provisions).

While the general proposition that in some situations the President may decline to enforce unconstitutional statutes is unassailable, it does not offer sufficient guidance as to the appropriate course in specific circumstances. . . . I offer the following propositions for your consideration.

1. The President's office and authority are created and bounded by the Constitution; he is required to act within its terms. Put somewhat differently, in serving as the executive created by the Constitution, the President is required to act in accordance with the laws—including the Constitution, which takes precedence over other forms of law. This obligation is reflected in the Take Care Clause and in the President's oath of office.
2. When bills are under consideration by Congress, the executive branch should promptly identify unconstitutional provisions and communicate its concerns to Congress so that the provisions can be corrected. . . .
3. The President should presume that enactments are constitutional. There will be some occasions, however, when a statute appears to conflict with the Constitution. In such cases, the President can and should exercise his independent judgment to determine whether the statute is constitutional. . . . Where possible, the President should construe provisions to avoid constitutional problems.
4. The Supreme Court plays a special role in resolving disputes about the constitutionality of enactments. As a general matter, if the President believes that the Court would sustain a particular provision as constitutional, the President should execute the statute, notwithstanding his own beliefs about the constitutional issue. If, however, the President, exercising his independent judgment, determines both that a provision would violate the Constitution and that it is probable that the Court would agree with him, the President has the authority to decline to execute the same.
5. Where the President's independent constitutional judgment and his determination of the Court's probable decision converge on a conclusion of unconstitutionality, the President must make a decision about whether or not to comply with the provision. That decision is necessarily specific to context, and it should be reached after careful weighing of the effect of compliance with the provision on the constitutional rights of affected individuals and on the executive branch's constitutional authority. Also relevant is the likelihood that compliance or noncompliance will permit judicial resolution of the issue. That is, the President may base his decision to comply (or decline to comply) in part on a desire to afford the Supreme Court an opportunity to review the constitutional judgment of the legislative branch.
6. The President has enhanced responsibility to resist unconstitutional provisions that encroach upon the constitutional powers of the Presidency. Where the President believes that an enactment unconstitutionally limits his powers, he has the authority to defend his office and decline to abide by it, unless he is convinced that the Court would disagree with his

assessment. If the President does not challenge such provisions (i.e., by refusing to execute them), there often will be no occasion for judicial consideration of their constitutionality; a policy of consistent Presidential enforcement of statutes limiting his power thus would deny the Supreme Court the opportunity to review the limitations and thereby would allow for unconstitutional restrictions on the President's authority. Some legislative encroachments on executive authority, however, will not be justiciable or are for other reasons unlikely to be resolved in court. If resolution in the courts is unlikely and the President cannot look to a judicial determination, he must shoulder the responsibility of protecting the constitutional role of the presidency. . . .

7. The fact that a [prior] sitting President signed the statute in question does not change this analysis. The text of the Constitution offers no basis for distinguishing bills based on who signed them; there is no constitutional analogue to the principles of waiver and estoppel. . . . [And it makes no difference if the incumbent President was the one who signed the bill in question.] [T]he President's signing of a bill does not affect his authority to decline to enforce constitutionally objectionable provisions thereof.

In accordance with these propositions, we do not believe that a President is limited to choosing between vetoing, for example, the Defense Appropriations Act [funding the United States armed forces] and executing an unconstitutional provision in it. In our view, the President has the authority to sign legislation containing desirable elements while refusing to execute a constitutionally defective provision. . . .

DISCUSSION

If you accept the legitimacy of Dellinger's basic argument—that the President has the authority (and perhaps the duty) to engage in independent constitutional interpretation, do you agree with his implicit argument that Presidents must always subordinate their own views to those of the Court? Assume that Jackson's veto had been overridden and the rechartering upheld by a Court not yet transformed by Democratic appointments. Would Dellinger have required Jackson to enforce the legislation even if he continued to believe, as argued in the Veto Message, that it was unconstitutional? Would Jackson have any more right to ignore such a decision than did Ohio?

What, incidentally, if the President announces that (s)he will issue a presidential pardon, see Constitution, Article II, §2, to anyone charged with violating a given federal statute that the President believes is unconstitutional? If *that* would not be unconstitutional—can you think of any good arguments why it would be?—then why would it be unconstitutional for the President to refuse to enforce the statute in the first place, even if the Supreme Court would likely uphold it or, to take the strongest example, even if the Supreme Court had in fact already upheld it in an earlier case? Whatever your answers to these questions, you will have the opportunity to reconsider them when you come to the material, infra, concerning Abraham Lincoln's conduct as President during 1861-1865 or President Truman's seizure of the U.S. steel industry during the Korean War in 1951.

Chapter 2

The Constitution in the Early Republic

I. *THE CONSTITUTION DURING THE WASHINGTON ADMINISTRATION*

Many important constitutional decisions were made during the first 12 years of the new Republic brought into being by the ratification of the Constitution in 1788 and, as importantly, the inauguration of George Washington—who remains our only President receiving a unanimous vote of the Electoral College—on April 30, 1789. Among other things, the passage of the Judiciary Act of 1789, which established the basic structure and early powers of the federal judiciary, was an event of constitutive importance. Even so, few important early decisions were made by the United States Supreme Court. Congress and the President were the key decision-makers as to what the Constitution meant, particularly with respect to the scope of their own powers. You have already studied one important such decision: Congress's chartering of the First Bank of the United States. Other early decisions that continue to be of fundamental importance[1] include:

1. *The President's power to remove executive officials.* The "Compromise of 1789" established the understanding that Presidents could dismiss members of the cabinet without congressional approval, even though the Senate had to confirm initial appointments.[2] Although Alexander Hamilton had suggested in The Federalist No. 77 that "[t]he consent of [the Senate] would be necessary to displace as well as to appoint," his co-author of *The Federalist*, James Madison, led a successful fight that gave the President unilateral authority to dismiss certain executive branch officials, a position that prevailed by one vote (cast by Vice President Adams).

---

1. See generally Akhil Reed Amar, America's Unwritten Constitution, ch. 8 (Following Washington's Lead: America's "Georgian" Constitution) (2012).

2. The matter is far more complex than this simple description, and what Congress actually decided in the Decision of 1789 is still debated to this day. See Jonathan Gienapp, The Second Creation: Fixing the American Constitution in the Founding Era 125-163 (2018); Saikrishna Prakash, New Light on the Decision of 1789, 91 Cornell L. Rev. 1021 (2006).

2. *The ban on advisory opinions.* The Supreme Court rejected requests that it in effect issue "advisory opinions" about the constitutional status of proposed legislation by Congress or actions by the executive. Several state supreme courts to this day offer such opinions—including, for example, the Massachusetts Supreme Judicial Court established by the 1780 Massachusetts Constitution drafted by John Adams. Nevertheless, the Justices of the U.S. Supreme Court read the Case and Controversy Clause in Article III to prohibit them. Letter from the Justices of the Supreme Court to George Washington (Aug. 8, 1793), in 6 Documentary History of the Supreme Court of the United States, 1789-1800, app., at 755 (Maeva Marcus et al. eds., 1998).

3. *The President's power over foreign affairs.* The Washington Administration established the President's primary authority to conduct foreign policy, including, for example, recognition of new foreign governments as well as the ability to declare that the United States will be "neutral" with regard to foreign conflicts. Although Congress may also have the right to pass legislation that shapes or affects presidential decisions, President Washington established precedents for the proposition that Presidents need not wait for congressional authorization before acting.

4. *The policy-based veto.* Although, as noted earlier, Washington exercised his Article I veto power only twice, one of those occasions was *not* based on constitutional objections. This precedent would later develop into a general power to veto legislation on policy grounds.

5. *The convention of two presidential terms.* One of George Washington's most important acts was his decision to step down after two terms. As the historian Gordon Wood writes, "The significance of his retirement from the presidency is easy for us to overlook, but his contemporaries knew what it meant."[3] Washington could easily have served until death and established a de facto elective monarchy (something that Hamilton, for example, told the Philadelphia Convention would be highly desirable). "Thus his persistent efforts to retire from the presidency enhanced his moral authority and helped fix the republican character of the Constitution."[4]

Had it been solely up to him, Washington might well have retired after one term, but almost all of his associates believed it was important for him to run for reelection (which he again won unanimously). By "1796 he was so determined to retire that no one could dissuade him, and his voluntary leaving of the office set" an important precedent.[5] Thomas Jefferson, for example, was saying by 1805 that he would not run for a third term, citing Washington's precedent and that "a few more precedents will oppose the obstacle of habit to anyone after a while who shall endeavor to extend his term."[6]

---

3. See Gordon S. Wood, The Greatness of George Washington, Va. Q. Rev., Spring 1992, available at http://www.vqronline.org/articles/1992/spring/wood-greatness-george-washington/.

4. Id.

5. Id.

6. Quoted in Jon Meacham, Thomas Jefferson: The Art of Power 409 (2012).

Ulysses S. Grant toyed with the idea of a third term but never openly sought it, and Theodore Roosevelt ran as a third-party candidate after serving most of two terms. Even so, the formal precedent was maintained until Franklin Roosevelt broke it by successfully running for a third term in 1940 (and then a fourth term in 1944). Nevertheless, argues Wood, "[s]o strong was the sentiment for a two-term limit . . . that the tradition was written into the Constitution in the 22nd amendment in 1951. Washington's action in 1796 was of great significance. That the chief executive of a state should willingly relinquish his office was an object lesson in republicanism at a time when the republican experiment throughout the Atlantic world was very much in doubt."[7]

II. EARLY STRUGGLES OVER STATE AND NATIONAL SOVEREIGNTY: CHISHOLM v. GEORGIA AND THE ELEVENTH AMENDMENT

The question of sovereignty within the American political system—what sovereignty consists in and where it is located—was a major controversy during the founding period; as you will see in this book, echoes of that controversy continue to this day. The first great theorists of sovereignty, Jean Bodin (1530-1596) and Thomas Hobbes (1588-1679), wrote during the transformation of the European continent into independent states claiming a right to be free from intervention by any of their neighbors. One way of defining "sovereignty" is as a right first to rule (without limit) and a concomitant right not to be ruled by others. Although the Convention was dominated by delegates committed to strengthening the national government, making it the effective "sovereign" in terms of actual capacity to govern effectively, they had to contend with a strong minority suspicious of such tendencies. Thus Luther Martin, an active participant from Maryland, noted that "[a]t the separation from the British Empire, the people of America preferred the establishment of themselves into thirteen separate sovereignties instead of incorporating themselves into one."[8]

No one doubted that the new Constitution made significant incursions into the sovereignty of the states. Nevertheless, strong nationalists—which at that point included James Madison—had to make serious compromises. Perhaps most important, Madison had to accept a structural feature that he regarded as thoroughly repugnant—equal representation of all states in the Senate. In addition, the delegates rejected Madison's repeated pleas to give Congress the power to veto any state laws it thought harmful to national interests. Neither the defenders of a strong national government nor the defenders of the prerogatives of the states managed a complete victory coming out of Philadelphia and the state ratification conventions; as a result, the meaning of "sovereignty" within the American political order became (and continues to be) a perennial source of conflict.

---

7. Id.
8. Madison's Notes on the Convention 159.

CHISHOLM v. GEORGIA, 2 U.S. (2 Dall.) 419 (1793): [Alexander Chisholm, a South Carolinian executor of the estate of Robert Farquhar, sued Georgia in the Supreme Court, claiming payment for goods supplied to Georgia by Farquhar during the Revolutionary War. Georgia refused to appear before the Court, claiming a right of "sovereign immunity" against having to do so. Given the language of Article III, which explicitly states that "The Judicial Power shall extend to . . . Controversies . . . between a State and Citizens of another State," four of the five Justices (Justice Iredell dissented) had little trouble in holding that Georgia was indeed liable to suit by private individuals, even though it had not waived sovereign immunity. The notion of "sovereign immunity" developed in Great Britain, which was ruled by monarchs who claimed the mantle of sovereignty. The United States had obviously rejected any such monarchical claims.

Two of the Justices, Chief Justice John Jay, co-author of *The Federalist*, and Justice James Wilson—who was probably second only to Madison in importance at the Philadelphia Convention—wrote especially interesting opinions about the nature of the federal union and popular sovereignty. Justice Iredell dissented, arguing that the states' residual sovereignty meant that they possessed the same common law immunity from suit as enjoyed by the British Crown.]

Jay, C.J.: In determining the sense in which Georgia is a sovereign State, it may be useful to turn our attention to the political situation we were in, prior to the Revolution, and to the political rights which emerged from the Revolution. . . . [T]he people of this country were then subjects of the King of Great Britain, and owed allegiance to him; and all the civil authority then existing or exercised here, flowed from the head of the British Empire. . . .

From the Crown of Great Britain, the sovereignty of their country passed to the people of it. . . . [T]he people . . . continued to consider themselves, in a national point of view, as one people; and they continued without interruption to manage their national concerns. . . . [As proof, Jay quotes the Preamble and its invocation of "We the People of the United States" as the authority by which the new Constitution is "ordained."] Here we see the people acting as sovereigns of the whole country, and, in the language of sovereignty, establishing a Constitution by which it was their will that the State governments should be bound, and to which the State Constitutions should be made to conform. . . .

[A]t the Revolution, the sovereignty devolved on the people, and they are truly the sovereigns of the country, but they are sovereigns without subjects (unless the African slaves among us may be so called), and have none to govern but themselves; the citizens of America are equal as fellow citizens, and as joint tenants in the sovereignty.

[I]n this country there are [no subjects]; . . . for all the citizens being as to civil rights perfectly equal, there is not, in that respect, one citizen inferior to another. It is agreed, that one free citizen may sue another; . . . [and] that one free citizen may sue any number on whom process can be conveniently executed. . . . Can the difference between forty odd thousand [citizens in the City of Philadelphia], and fifty odd thousand [in the state of Delaware] make any distinction as to right? Is it not as easy, and as convenient to the public and parties, to serve a summons on the Governor and Attorney General of Delaware, as on the Mayor or other Officers of the Corporation of Philadelphia? . . . In this land of equal liberty, shall forty odd thousand in one place be compellable to do justice, and yet fifty odd thousand in another place be privileged to do justice only as they may think proper? Such objections would not correspond with the equal rights we claim; with the equality we profess to admire and maintain, and with that popular sovereignty in which every citizen partakes. Grant that the Governor of Delaware holds an office of superior rank to the Mayor of Philadelphia, they are both nevertheless the officers of the people; and however more exalted the one may be than the other, yet in the opinion of those who dislike aristocracy, that circumstance cannot be a good reason for impeding the course of justice.

[Given this logic, Jay then asks whether a citizen should be allowed to sue the United States government, which is just a larger collection of citizens.] [I]n all cases of actions against States or individual citizens, the national courts are supported in all their legal and constitutional proceedings and judgments by the arm of the executive power of the United States; but in cases of actions against the United States, there is no power which the courts can call to their aid. From this distinction, important conclusions are deducible, and they place the case of a State, and the case of the United States, in very different points of view.

I wish the state of society was so far improved, and the science of government advanced to such a degree of perfection, as that the whole nation could, in the peaceable course of law, be compelled to do justice, and be sued by individual citizens. Whether that is, or is not, now the case, ought not to be thus collaterally and incidentally decided: I leave it a question.

WILSON, J.: To the Constitution of the United States, the term SOVEREIGN, is totally unknown. . . . They might have announced themselves "SOVEREIGN" people of the United States. But serenely conscious of the fact, they avoided the ostentatious declaration. . . .

The only reason, I believe, why a free man is bound by human laws is that he binds himself. Upon the same principles upon which he becomes bound by the laws, he becomes amenable to the courts of justice which are formed and authorised by those laws. If one free man, an original sovereign, may do all this, why may not an aggregate of free men, a collection of original sovereigns, do this likewise? If the dignity of each singly is undiminished, the dignity of all jointly must be unimpaired. A state, like a merchant, makes a contract. A dishonest state, like a dishonest merchant, wilfully refuses to discharge it. The latter is amenable to a court of justice. Upon general principles of right, shall the former, when summoned to answer the fair demands of its creditor, be permitted, Proteus-like, to assume a new appearance, and to insult him and justice by declaring "I am a Sovereign state"? Surely not. . . .

In one sense, the term "sovereign" has for its correlative "subject." In this sense, the term can receive no application, for it has no object in the Constitution of the United states. Under that Constitution, there are citizens, but no subjects. . . . As a citizen, I know the government of [Georgia] to be republican; and my short definition of such a government is one constructed on this principle—that the supreme power resides in the body of the people. As a judge of this court, I know, and can decide upon the knowledge that the citizens of Georgia, when they acted upon the large scale of the Union, as a part of the "People of the United States," did not surrender the supreme or sovereign power to that state, but, as to the purposes of the Union, retained it to themselves. As to the purposes of the Union, therefore, Georgia is NOT a sovereign state. . . .

[O]ur national scene opens with the most magnificent object which the nation could present. "The PEOPLE of the United states" are the first personages introduced. Who were those people? They were the citizens of thirteen states, each of which had a separate constitution and government, and all of which were connected together by Articles of Confederation. To the purposes of public strength and felicity, that Confederacy was totally inadequate. A requisition on the several states terminated its legislative authority. Executive or judicial authority it had none. In order therefore to form a more perfect union, to establish justice, to ensure domestic tranquillity, to provide for common defence, and to secure the blessings of liberty, those people, among whom were the people of Georgia, ordained and established the present Constitution. By that Constitution legislative power is vested, executive power is vested, judicial power is vested.

The question now opens fairly to our view, could the people of those states, among whom were those of Georgia, bind those states, and Georgia among the others, by the legislative, executive, and judicial power so vested? If the principles on which I have founded myself are just and true, this question must unavoidably receive an affirmative answer. . . .

The same truth may be deduced from the declared objects [in the Preamble], and the general texture of the Constitution of the United States. One of its declared objects is, to form an union more perfect, than, before that time, had been formed. Before that time, the Union possessed Legislative, but uninforced Legislative power over the States. Nothing could be more natural than to intend that this Legislative power should be enforced by powers Executive and Judicial. Another declared object is, "to establish justice." This points, in a particular manner, to the Judicial authority. And . . . the declaration, "that no State shall pass a law impairing the obligation of contracts"; . . . points, in a particular manner, to the jurisdiction of the Court over the several States. What good purpose could this Constitutional provision secure, if a State might pass a law impairing the obligation of its own contracts; and be amenable, for such a violation of right, to no controuling judiciary power? We have seen, that on the principles of general jurisprudence, a State, for the breach of a contract, may be liable for damages. . . .

But, in my opinion, this doctrine rests not upon the legitimate result of fair and conclusive deduction from the Constitution: It is confirmed, beyond all doubt, by the direct and explicit declaration of the Constitution itself. . . . "The judicial power of the United States shall extend to controversies, between a state and citizens of another State."

Iredell, J., dissenting: "[T]he common law," . . . is the ground-work of the laws in every State in the Union [and is] in force in each State, as it existed in England, (unaltered by any statute) at the time of the first settlement of the country. . . . No other part of the common law of England, it appears to me, can have any reference to this subject, but that part of it which prescribes remedies against the crown. Every State in the Union in every instance where its sovereignty has not been delegated to the United States, I consider to be as completely sovereign, as the United States are in respect to the powers surrendered. The United States are sovereign as to all the powers of Government actually surrendered: Each State in the Union is sovereign as to all the powers reserved. It must necessarily be so, because the United States have no claim to any authority but such as the States have surrendered to them: Of course the part not surrendered must remain as it did before. . . .

[I]n England even in case of a private debt contracted by the King, in his own person, there is no remedy but by petition, which must receive his express sanction, otherwise there can be no proceeding upon it. [Thus, by analogy, a suit against a State depends on the] discretion and good faith of the Legislative body.

NOTE: THE ELEVENTH AMENDMENT

Chisholm generated strong reactions. Georgia, after refusing to appear at all before the Supreme Court lest that concede that it had jurisdiction, went on to pass a bill stating that anyone trying to enforce the decision should "suffer death, without benefit of clergy, by being hanged."[9] Enough other states joined Georgia in its opposition to the Court's decision to make possible the first addition to the Constitution following the first 10 amendments that were part of the initial package of 12 amendments proposed in 1789 and ratified in 1791. The Eleventh Amendment was proposed by Congress on March 4, 1794 and was ratified in February of the following year.

Another important precedent established during this episode was the President's *non*-participation in the constitutional amendment process. In Hollingsworth v. Virginia, 3 U.S. (Dall.) 378 (1798), Justice Chase explained that the President's veto "applies only to the ordinary cases of legislation: He has nothing to do with the proposition, or adoption, of amendments to the Constitution." This makes some sense, given that a veto-proof majority of both houses of Congress is necessary to submit a proposed amendment to the states in the first place. As a result, the President's signature is not necessary for the validity of constitutional amendments. On occasion, Presidents have indicated support for amendments; Abraham Lincoln famously signed the Thirteenth Amendment before sending it to the states for ratification. By contrast, Lincoln's successor, Andrew Johnson, strongly opposed the Fourteenth Amendment and worked hard to defeat it. Nevertheless, the President's approval or disapproval is irrelevant as a constitutional matter because he or she cannot veto a proposed amendment—although the President's support or opposition may be important as a political matter.

The Eleventh Amendment provides that "[t]he Judicial power of the United States shall not be construed to extend to any suit in law or equity, commenced or prosecuted against one of the United States by Citizens of another State, or by Citizens or Subjects of any Foreign State." As the text indicates, it was specifically designed to overrule *Chisholm*. Nevertheless, today the Eleventh Amendment is hardly ever used to ban suits against states by citizens of *other* states. Because of

---

9. James H. Read and Neal Allen, Living, Dead, and Undead: Nullification Past and Present, 1 Am. Pol. Thought 263, 279 (2012), quoting David P. Currie, The Constitution in Congress: The Federalist Period, 1787-1801, at 195-196 (1997).

subsequent interpretations by the Supreme Court, it is primarily used to limit suits against states by citizens of the *same* state.

The justification for this extension is not based on the *text* of the amendment, which seems quite specific in its reference, see, e.g., John Manning, The Eleventh Amendment and the Interpretation of Precise Constitutional Texts, 113 Yale L.J. (2004). Instead, it is based on a different form of interpretation that emphasizes the *structure* of the Union and concomitant rights and powers of the different governments that collectively compose the United States. You have already seen an example of structural argument in the second part of *McCulloch*, where Marshall struck down the Maryland tax because it violated the "texture" of the Constitution rather than any particular provision of the constitutional text.

Consider two possible inferences from the rapid override of *Chisholm* by Congress and the states through their Article V amendment power. The first possibility is that the Court's decision was wrong initially, and the Eleventh Amendment corrected its mistake. If so, then *Chisholm* is entitled to no precedential respect. The second possibility is that the Court's decision was correct, but Congress and the states simply didn't like the outcome. Therefore the Eleventh Amendment really is an "amendment," which changed the 1787 Constitution. How does one choose between these two possibilities? What would explain, for example, four of the five Justices all making the same mistake? What turns on your answer to this question?

III. THE ALIEN AND SEDITION ACTS AND THE KENTUCKY AND VIRGINIA RESOLUTIONS OF 1798

The great constitutional controversy of John Adams's presidency emerged from the country's "quasi-war" with France from 1798 to 1800, and the growing dispute between Federalists and Republicans over foreign policy. In 1798, the Federalist-dominated Congress passed the Alien and Sedition Acts. The constitutionality of each Act was fiercely debated. The debate over the Alien Act concerned whether Congress possessed "inherent" national power to regulate resident aliens in addition to the "enumerated" powers set out in the Constitution. The debate over the Sedition Act concerned not only Congress's power to criminalize sedition, but also the meaning of the Bill of Rights, and, in particular, the scope of the First Amendment.

The constitutional debate over the two Acts did not end with their passage. Kentucky and Virginia passed resolutions asserting the right of states independently to interpret and contest the constitutionality of these Acts, raising crucial questions about the nature of the American Constitution and the scope of state power in the new constitutional order.

A. The Alien Act of 1798

The Alien Act empowered the President to deport "such aliens as he shall judge dangerous to the peace and safety of the United States, or shall have reasonable grounds to suspect are concerned in any treasonable or secret machinations against the Government thereof." The attack on the Act was led by Representative

Albert Gallatin, himself a naturalized citizen born in Switzerland. The New York state legislature had selected Gallatin to be one of the state's two senators, but he was excluded on the ground that he had not fulfilled the constitutional requirement of being nine years a citizen of the United States. (Upon his exclusion, he was promptly elected to the House of Representatives, where, after the retirement of James Madison, he had become the Republican floor leader. He would later gain fame as Jefferson's Secretary of the Treasury.)

Gallatin, committed to Jeffersonian principles of "strict construction," argued that Congress lacked the power to pass the legislation. "The power of regulating alien friends, in every possible case, was understood to be reserved to the States at the time the Constitution was adopted."[10] He did concede, though, that Congress possessed inherent power to restrict the activities of aliens during wartime. Thus he had supported, the previous month, passage of the Alien Enemies Bill, which would apply to male citizens or subjects of a hostile nation upon declaration by the President that war had been declared or an invasion "perpetrated, attempted, or threatened."[11] Indeed, according to Gallatin, the power to pass the Act rested on "a principle which existed prior to the Constitution"[12] and thus, presumably, required no specific authorization in the text. Those affected by the Alien Act, however, came from countries with whom the United States was at peace, whatever the level of tension with France that lay behind the Act. Reference was also made to the fact that Congress *is* assigned the power to provide for "an uniform Rule of Naturalization," the very specification of which, it was argued, supported the proposition that the states retained their power to control immigration per se. That is, even if states had no power to make immigrants U.S. citizens, and therefore members of the common national community, they retained their right to decide whether to welcome immigrants as guests, so to speak, and even to make them citizens of the states themselves, even if not national citizens. (This issue will be treated later in the *Dred Scott* case, infra Chapter 3.)

Consider also Article I, §9: "The Migration or Importation of such Persons as any of the States now existing shall think proper to admit, shall not be prohibited by the Congress prior to the Year one thousand eight hundred and eight, but a Tax or duty may be imposed on such Importation, not exceeding ten dollars for each Person." Does this mean that Congress is completely powerless to deport aliens from non-belligerent states admitted to the United States until 1808, or may it do so for cause? What would be the source of Congress's power in 1798? For that matter, what would be the source of Congress's power to control admission and exclusion of aliens after 1808? (Is the Foreign Commerce Clause relevant here?[13]) Federalist supporters of the Act responded that power to control immigration

---

10. Quoted in Andrew Lenner, Separate Spheres: Republican Constitutionalism in the Federalist Era, 41 Am. J. Legal Hist. 250 (1997). See also Joseph M. Lynch, Negotiating the Constitution: The Earliest Debates over Original Intent, ch. 9 (1999).

11. See David Currie, The Constitution in Congress: The Federalist Period, 1789-1801, at 254-255 (1997).

12. Quoted in Lenner, supra n.10.

13. For an extended discussion of the complex questions involving the sources of federal power to regulate immigration, see Thomas Alexander Aleinkoff, David A. Martin, and Hiroshi Motomura, Immigration and Citizenship: Process and Policy 178-217 (1998).

(and, therefore, to expel suspicious, even if not "enemy" aliens) was inherent in the very conception of being a sovereign state in the international system.

By its own terms, the Alien Act expired on June 25, 1800, and the constitutional arguments made by its supporters did not come before the Supreme Court for almost a century, in Chae Chan Ping v. United States, 130 U.S. 581 (1889), infra Chapter 4, which involved the prohibition of Chinese nationals from entering the United States. As you will see, the Court basically adopted the Federalist argument and relied on the "inherent" power attached to "sovereignty" rather than pointing to any textual assignment of power to Congress. Another important "inherent powers" case is United States v. Curtiss-Wright Export Corp., 299 U.S. 304 (1936). According to Justice Sutherland, "the investment of the federal government with the powers of external sovereignty did not depend upon the affirmative grants of the Constitution. The powers to declare and wage war, to conclude peace, to make treaties, to maintain diplomatic relations with other sovereignties, if they had never been mentioned in the Constitution, would have vested in the federal government as necessary concomitants of nationality. . . ." As to treaties in particular, compare Sutherland's assertion with Madison's speech on the bank. Justice Sutherland's history and metaphysics are open to criticism,[14] but his analysis at least suggests the spirit in which the particular grants of power to Congress and the executive have been amalgamated to create a whole greater than the sum of its parts. One might certainly note, incidentally, that both of these cases involve power of the United States as a member of the wider international system of sovereign states.

B. *The Sedition Act*

The Bill of Rights, though adopted with relatively little fanfare, soon became the focal point of an intense controversy regarding the scope of the First Amendment guaranties of freedom of speech and press. In 1798, the Congress, narrowly divided along Federalist and Republican Party lines, enacted a Sedition Act (that accompanied the Alien Act discussed above).

Section 2 of the Act made it a crime to "write, print, utter or publish . . . any false, scandalous and malicious writing or writings against the government of the United States, or either house of the Congress of the United States, or the President of the United States, with intent to defame [them] . . . or to bring them . . . into contempt or disrepute or to excite against them . . . the hatred of the good people of the United States." Interestingly enough, Section 2 did not mention the Vice President, perhaps because that office was filled, in 1798, by Thomas Jefferson, whom Federalist adherents of the Sedition Act were more than happy to bring

14. See, e.g., Charles Lofgren, United States v. Curtiss-Wright Corporation: An Historical Reassessment, 83 Yale L.J. 1 (1973). See also Madison's argument against the bank, supra.

into disrepute.[15] In any event, the Sedition Act of 1798 was often perceived, both then and by subsequent historians, as a Federalist measure to silence the opposition and keep themselves in power. As Professor Powe notes, "the Federalists identified opposition to their policies with support for France, and their name for the Republicans—the 'internal foe'—expressed their view that the Republican party was a threat to the republic."[16] The leading Republican papers were the targets of prosecutions, and three were forced to cease publication, two permanently. The passage of the Act, and its implementation, sparked fiery debates over the scope of the First Amendment and the proper realms of state and federal power.

1. The Meaning of the First Amendment

The history of the adoption of the First Amendment is sparse. Although there was a broad consensus that the Constitution should guarantee the freedoms of speech and press, few of the new nation's intellectual and political leaders discussed the content and extent of the First Amendment. Freedom of speech and press in 1789 England meant "freedom from prior restraint": Government could no longer censor political material prior to its publication. Once the material was in print, however, its author, printer, and publisher could still be punished for criminal libel, and truth was no defense. Indeed, as the common saying went, "the greater the truth, the greater the libel" and, presumably, the accompanying disillusionment on the part of readers with the political leaders who were the subjects of the "libels." The central question is whether this limited meaning of freedom of the press also held true in the new United States, which had been heavily influenced by its English heritage yet had rebelled against what had come to be seen as tyrannical elements of the British constitutional order.[17]

---

15. 1 Stat. 596 (1798) (expired 1801). Section 1 proscribes combinations or conspiracies with intent to oppose, prevent, or intimidate government laws or operations and that "counsel, advise or attempt to procure any insurrection, riot, unlawful assembly, or combination." Section 3 establishes that defendants can offer the truth of the allegedly libelous material as evidence in their defense. In addition, the Act gave the jury "a right to determine the law and the fact." Section 4 makes the Act law applicable through March 3, 1801, i.e., the last day of the Adams Administration. Libel defendants and freedom of speech advocates had sought the two Section 3 reforms for many years. Under traditional seditious libel laws, courts would not allow the truth of the libel to be proved in court because a true libel was considered more dangerous than a false one. Furthermore, the jury had previously been allowed to decide only the question of whether the defendant had in fact published the libelous material. Judges decided the questions of law: whether the defendant made the remarks with malice and whether they were "of a bad tendency" to sedition.

16. Lucas A. Powe, Jr., The Fourth Estate and the Constitution: Freedom of the Press in America 58 (1991).

17. Seditious libel was the most repressive class of libel, according to Leonard W. Levy, Freedom of Speech and Press in Early American History: Legacy of Suppression 10 (1960). Although difficult to define, "[j]udged by actual prosecutions, the crime consisted of criticizing the government: its form, constitution, officers, laws, symbols, conduct, policies, and so on. In effect, any comment about the government which could be construed to have the bad tendency of lowering it in the public's esteem or of disturbing the peace was seditious libel, subjecting the speaker or writer to criminal prosecution."

2. The Original Understanding

Did the framers of the Bill of Rights intend the First Amendment to do more than protect speech and press from prior restraint? In his 1960 book, Freedom of Speech and Press in Early American History: Legacy of Suppression, Leonard W. Levy argues that they did not. Levy examines legislative proceedings, criminal cases in the courts and legislatures, and writings of political and intellectual leaders in America. He concludes that the evidence shows that none of them advocated any change in the common law of libel as it existed prior to 1798: "Freedom [of speech and press in the colonial period] . . . did not include a right to criticize the legislature."[18] And during the revolutionary period, Levy writes: "No cause was more honored by rhetorical declamation and dishonored in practice than that of freedom of expression . . . from the 1760's through the cessation of hostilities."[19] The states enacted laws punishing criticism of the revolutionary government. Many postrevolutionary state constitutions included no protection for speech or press, and, of course, neither did the Constitution of 1787. In response to criticisms by the anti-Federalists, the Federalists eventually proposed a Bill of Rights, but Levy, argues, there was little discussion of what freedom of speech and press meant: "If definition were unnecessary because of the existence of a tacit and widespread understanding of 'liberty of the press,' only the received or traditional understanding could have been possible. To assume the existence of a general, latitudinarian understanding that veered substantially from the common-law definition is incredible, given the total absence of argumentative analysis of the meaning of the clause on speech and press."[20]

Although many readers accepted Levy's view of the meaning of freedom of speech and the press in eighteenth-century America and his revisionist claim that the First Amendment was not intended to nullify the common law of criminal libel, several commentators have nevertheless chastised Levy for a crabbed reading of his evidence. For example, Merrill Jensen writes:[21]

> The impression given is that there was no freedom anywhere in America, either before or after 1763. But can we assume that the relatively few prosecutions before 1763 silenced all discussion? Did the "rude hand of the law," as Gouverneur Morris called it, touch every man who opposed governmental policies and officeholders? I doubt it. Levy goes on to assert

---

18. Id. at 68.

19. Id. at 63.

20. Id. at 224-225, 233.

21. Merrill Jensen, 75 Harv. L. Rev. 456, 457 (1961). In 1985, Levy published Emergence of a Free Press, an updated version of Legacy of Suppression. Although he modified some of his arguments, he continued to maintain that the framers of the First Amendment cannot be shown to have intended to abolish the common law of seditious libel. For critical reviews, see David Rabban, The Ahistorical Historian: Leonard Levy on Freedom of Expression in Early American History, 37 Stan. L. Rev. 795 (1985); David Anderson, Levy vs. Levy, 84 Mich. L. Rev. 777 (1986).

> flatly that "speech and the press were not free anywhere during the Revolution." He shows that this was correct as a matter of law but pays little attention to practice. No reader of the newspapers of the revolutionary era could accept such a statement. Of course the newspapers and people who supported Great Britain were suppressed when independence drew the line, but any nation, new or old, would do the same thing whatever its laws might be. But the debate among Americans about constitutions, governmental policies, and politicians continued with unabated fervor, and in terms that were libelous by whatever standard one applies. The prosecutions cited give one no idea of what day-to-day journalism was like. . . . Because [Levy] is concerned with seditious libel, and concentrates on the purely legal aspects, he tends to underrate the importance of practice. . . .
>
> Another weakness of the legal approach is that it cannot explain that which is essentially political, where the law was a tool in political battles, not the guiding force. . . . [An] example is Pennsylvania during the Revolution. Levy sees no freedom of expression there because the law did not change. Yet the Pennsylvania newspapers between 1776 and 1789 contain vast amounts of some of the bitterest, most dishonest (and seditious) writing in American political history. Despite the law there was freedom of expression in fact. No governmental institution, political faction, or individual was free from attacks such as few newspapers today would dare to print.

John Cound argues that rather than depicting a legacy of suppression, Levy's evidence actually[22]

> shows the legacy . . . to be one of a continuing and enlarging concern for freedom. If the first amendment is a living and growing idea, as he argues, rather than a fixed statement, its growth began at least a century and a half before 1790. There were those men who, while accepting the doctrine of seditious libel (or at least not openly rejecting it) nonetheless carved out protections for free expression. . . . [I]t seems an oversimplification to say of men who had attacked prosecution after prosecution as groundless and abusive, and who by their own words courted indictment, that "they accepted in substance the Blackstone-Mansfield definition [of freedom of the press]: freedom, under law, from prior restraint," simply because they did not deny the possibility that a government can be libeled.

In 1983, David Anderson, in The Origins of the Press Clause, 30 UCLA L. Rev. 455, reexamined the historical materials and vigorously attacked Levy's thesis, concluding his article as follows:

> Though scholars today may debate whether the press clause has any significance independent of the speech clause, historically there is no doubt that it did. Freedom of the press—not freedom of speech—was the primary concern of the generation that wrote the Declaration of Independence, the Constitution, and the Bill of Rights. Freedom of speech was a

22. John J. Cound, 36 N.Y.U. L. Rev. 253, 256 (1961).

late addition to the pantheon of rights; freedom of the press occupied a central position from the very beginning.

By the time the press clause became part of our Constitution in 1791, it had a considerable legislative history. The revolutionary state constitutions, the ratifying conventions, and the First Congress produced numerous expressions of the idea. These expressions and freedom-of-the-press literature from which they were drawn leave little doubt that press freedom was viewed as being closely related to the experiment of representative self-government. . . . The issue was born of the conflict with England, and its first expressions as a binding principle of law came in the state constitutions drafted contemporaneously with the Declaration of Independence. In these earliest expressions, the relation between freedom of the press and the idea of self-government was explicit. The press was a "bulwark of liberty," "essential to the security of freedom in a state." It had to be protected, not for its own sake, but because it provided a necessary restraint on what the patriots viewed as government's natural tendency toward tyranny and despotism.

In the minds of members of the First Congress, the press clause was part of the new plan of government, no less than if it had been in the original Constitution. To the Anti-Federalists, it was an essential modification of the original Constitution; to the Federalists, it expressed what was already implicit in the Constitution. Their quarrel was only over the necessity of specifically guaranteeing freedom of the press. Neither side doubted its utility. Its value lay, as Professor Blasi says, in "checking the inherent tendency of government officials to abuse the power entrusted to them." Because it plays this role, it is, in Justice Stewart's words, "a structural provision of the Constitution."

That the press clause has a distinct history does not mean, of course, that it must be given a meaning different from the speech clause today, or even that it had a different meaning in 1791. It is possible that checking government power was also the purpose of the speech clause. My own guess, however, is that the latter was more closely related to the incipient notion of individual autonomy that underlay the religion clauses. But in either event, most modern analysis, by focusing on the speech clause, gets the matter upside down. As a means of checking government power, speech was an afterthought, if it was viewed as serving that function at all; the press was expected to be the primary source of restraint.

The legislative history of the press clause has been ignored, largely because it is inconsistent with the conclusions of Leonard Levy, whose work in first amendment history has become the conventional wisdom of our generation. Levy's view is that freedom of the press meant nothing more to the Framers than freedom from prior restraint; the first amendment was not intended to enlarge that common law meaning. . . . If Levy is right, the press could hardly have been expected to occupy any significant structural role. The press would have been at the mercy (except for prior restraints) of most of those whose abuses it was supposed to check.

Levy's thesis is not unassailable. It requires us to accept several remarkable propositions. We must believe that the press clause was directed at what was in America a non-issue—prior restraint—rather

> than at seditious libel, which had been the primary form of restraint on the press during the colonial period. We must believe that the press clauses that were included in nine state constitutions were intended to do nothing more than preserve the English common law. We must believe that the Framers were oblivious to, or hypocritical about, their own sedition in criticizing the government under the Articles of Confederation. We must believe that they did not understand that citizens of representative democracy must be free to criticize government until the Sedition Act taught that lesson a few years later. We must believe that Madison in 1799 misrepresented (or misunderstood) his own views of ten years earlier. . . . A thesis that requires so many suspensions of disbelief ought not be preclusive.

3. The Republican Response

The Sedition Act of 1798 was important not only for its role in delineating the original understandings of the First Amendment, but also because it raised important questions about who had authority to interpret the Constitution. As noted earlier, the Act was vehemently opposed by resolutions adopted by the legislatures of Kentucky and Virginia, which had been written by Jefferson and Madison, respectively. Madison also wrote the Virginia Report of 1800, which elaborated and defended Virginia's position in the face of counter-resolutions by other states.[23] The fifth of the Virginia Resolutions asserted that the Sedition Act was an

> alarming infraction[] of the Constitution, [which] exercises . . . a power not delegated by the Constitution, but on the contrary expressly and positively forbidden by one of the amendments thereto; a power which more than any other ought to produce universal alarm, because it is leveled against that right of freely examining public characters and measures, and of free communication among the people thereon, which has ever been justly deemed the only effectual guardian of every other right.

In the Virginia Report Madison writes:[24]

> In the attempts to vindicate the "Sedition Act," it has been contended . . . [t]hat the "freedom of the press" is to be determined by the meaning of these terms in the common law. . . . The freedom of the press under the common law, is, in the defences of the Sedition Act, made to consist in an exemption from all *previous* restraint on printed publications, by persons authorized to inspect or prohibit them. It appears to the committee, that this idea of the freedom of the press, can never be admitted to be the American idea of it: since a law inflicting penalties on printed publications would have a similar effect with a law authorizing a previous restraint on them. It would seem a mockery to say, that no law should be passed, preventing publications from being made, but that laws might be passed for punishing them in case they should be made.

---

23. See The Virginia Report (J.W. Randolph ed., 1850), available at http://www.constitution.org/rf/vr_1799.htm (hereinafter The Virginia Report).

24. Id.

Perhaps Madison's most important argument against the constitutionality of the Sedition Act under the First Amendment was structural. The freedom of the press in America could not be the same as the English common law restriction against prior restraint of seditious libel because of important differences between the English system of parliamentary democracy and the new American system of popular sovereignty: In England, the people's rights need only be protected from the executive because Parliament has absolute power. In the United States, however, the people retain absolute sovereignty, and the power of *all* the branches of government is limited. "This security of the freedom of the press requires, that it should be exempt, not only from previous restraint by the executive, as in Great Britain, but from legislative restraint also; and this exemption, to be effectual, must be an exemption not only from the previous inspection of licensers, but from the subsequent penalty of laws. The state of the press, therefore, under the common law, cannot . . . be the standard of its freedom in the United States."[25]

The Kentucky Resolutions also declared that the Sedition Act violated the First Amendment. Levy comments: "The reason for the sudden if belated emergence of a sharply articulated body of 'Jeffersonian' thought on freedom of speech and press was the threat that the government of the United States under the Adams administration might attempt to eliminate political criticism, create a one-party press in the country, and by controlling public opinion insure a Federalist victory in the elections of 1800."[26] In any event, Jefferson's and Madison's substantive reading of the freedoms of speech and press laid the foundation for all subsequent interpretations of the First Amendment.

The Kentucky and Virginia Resolutions also argued that the regulation of seditious speech was beyond the limited and enumerated powers of the federal government. The Third Kentucky Resolution provides:

> That . . . no power over the freedom of religion, freedom of speech, or freedom of the press, being delegated to the United States by the Constitution, nor prohibited by it to the states, all lawful powers respecting the same did of right remain, and were reserved to the states, or to the people; that thus was manifested their determination to retain to themselves the right of judging how far the licentiousness of speech and of the press may be abridged without lessening their useful freedom, and how far those abuses which cannot be separated from their use, should be tolerated rather than destroyed; and . . . [a] special provision has been made by one of the amendments to the Constitution, which expressly declares, that "Congress shall make no law respecting an establishment of religion, or prohibiting the free exercise thereof, or abridging the freedom of speech, or of the press," . . . and that libels, falsehoods, and defamations, equally with heresy and false religion, are withheld from the cognizance of federal tribunals: that therefore the [Sedition Act] . . . , which does abridge the freedom of the press, is not law, but is altogether void and of no effect.

---

25. Id.
26. Levy, supra n.17, at 258.

The fourth Virginia Resolution similarly provides:

> That the General Assembly doth also express its deep regret that a spirit has in sundry instances been manifested by the Federal Government, to enlarge its powers by forced constructions of the constitutional charter which defines them; and that indications have appeared of a design to expound certain general phrases . . . , so as to destroy the meaning and effect of the particular enumeration, which necessarily explains and limits the general phrases, and so as to consolidate the States by degrees into one sovereignty, the obvious tendency and inevitable result of which would be to transform the present republican system of the United States into an absolute, or at best, a mixed monarchy.

Note that although opponents of the Sedition Act maintained that the Constitution granted the *federal* government no power over speech or the press, they did not argue that the *states* were deprived of the power to control speech. As we shall see below, the First Amendment's limitations regarding speech were not deemed applicable to the states until 1925.

DISCUSSION

James Madison was initially skeptical of bills of rights. In *The Federalist,* and in correspondence with Thomas Jefferson, Madison had argued that written guarantees of rights like those in a bill of rights were mere "parchment barriers" that might have little effect.[27] Declarations of vague and abstract rights would be easy to manipulate and would offer little protection against a determined majority. The most reliable guarantees of liberty would come from structural features of a constitutional system, such as representative government (instead of direct democracy), separation of powers, checks and balances, and federalism. Madison soon changed his mind and strongly supported a written bill of rights, partly out of conviction, partly out of political expediency (to defeat James Monroe in a contest for the House of Representatives) and partly in order to secure ratification of the new Constitution.

In proposing the Bill of Rights before the First Congress, Madison repeated his earlier concern about parchment barriers, but now ascribed it to others: "It may be thought that all paper barriers against the power of the community are too weak to be worthy of attention. I am sensible they are not so strong as to satisfy gentlemen of every description who have seen and examined thoroughly the texture of such a defence."[28] Despite this objection, Madison argued, written declarations of rights "have a tendency to impress some degree of respect for them, to establish the public opinion in their favor, and rouse the attention of the whole community."[29] These

27. The Federalist No. 48, at 308 (James Madison) (Henry Cabot Lodge ed., 1888); Letter from James Madison to Thomas Jefferson (Oct. 17, 1788), in 5 The Writings of James Madison 269, 272 (Gaillard Hunt ed., 1904) ("Repeated violations of these parchment barriers have been committed by overbearing majorities in every State.").

28. 1 Annals of Cong. 455 (1789).

29. Id.

social and cultural effects "may be one means to control the majority from those acts to which they might be otherwise inclined."[30] Similarly, in his correspondence with Jefferson, Madison noted that stating basic rights in a constitution might have a salutary influence on political culture: "The political truths declared in that solemn manner acquire by degrees the character of fundamental maxims of free Government, and as they become incorporated with the national sentiment, counteract the impulses of interest and passion."[31]

To what extent does the controversy over the Sedition Act vindicate Madison's earlier fear that the First Amendment would prove to be a mere "parchment barrier"? To what extent does it vindicate his later view that the text of the First Amendment would prove to be an important cultural resource that would motivate political action to protect rights through the political process?

C. *The Kentucky and Virginia Resolutions of 1798 and the Doctrine of Nullification*

Apart from their theories of the First Amendment, the enduring importance of the Kentucky and Virginia Resolutions in American political thought (and politics) lies in their theory of what might be called the "metaphysics of Union," quite different from the account of national sovereignty offered in Chisholm v. Georgia by Jay and Wilson.

1. Nullification and Interposition

Both Virginia and Kentucky asserted the authority to declare the Acts unconstitutional. The Kentucky Resolution developed the doctrine of "nullification." It stated:

> That the several states composing the United States of America, are not united on the principle of unlimited submission to their general government; but that by compact, under the style and title of a Constitution for the United States, and of amendments thereto, they constituted a general government for special purposes, delegated to that government certain definite powers, reserving, each state to itself, the residuary mass of right to their own self government; and that whensoever the general government assumes undelegated powers, its acts are unauthoritative, void, and of no force: That to this compact each state acceded as a state, and is an integral party, its co-states forming as to itself, the other party: That the government created by this compact was not made the exclusive or final *judge* of the extent of the powers delegated to itself; since that would have made its discretion, and not the Constitution, the measure of its powers; but that, as in all other cases of compact among parties having no common judge, each party has an equal right to judge for itself, as well of infractions, as of the mode and measure of redress. . . .

30. Id.

31. Letter from James Madison to Thomas Jefferson, supra n.27, at 273.

> That this commonwealth does, therefore, call on its co-states for an expression of their sentiments on the acts concerning aliens, and for the punishment of certain crimes herein before specified, plainly declaring whether these acts are or are not authorized by the Federal compact. And it doubts not that . . . they will view [the general government] as seizing the rights of the states, and consolidating them in the hands of the general government with a power assumed to bind the states, (not merely in cases made federal), but in all cases whatsoever, by laws made, not with their consent, but by others against their consent . . . ; and that the co-states, recurring to their natural right in cases not made federal, will concur in declaring these acts void and of no force, and will each unite with this commonwealth, in requesting their repeal at the next session of Congress.

The final sentence is ambiguous. Can the states themselves invalidate—or "nullify"—the Sedition Act, or can they only urge Congress to repeal it? The Kentucky Resolutions of 1799 clarified Jefferson's position in asserting that "the several states who formed [the Constitution], being sovereign and independent, have the unquestionable right to judge of its infraction and that a nullification, by those sovereignties, of all unauthorized acts done under colour of that instrument, is the rightful remedy."[32]

The Virginia Resolutions address the question in terms of state "interposition":

> That this Assembly doth explicitly and peremptorily declare that it views the powers of the Federal Government as resulting from the compact, to which the States are parties, as limited by the plain sense and intention of the instrument constituting that compact; as no further valid than they are authorized by the grants enumerated in that compact; and that in case of a deliberate, palpable, and dangerous exercise of other powers not granted by the said compact, the States, who are the parties thereto, have the right, and are in duty bound, to interpose for arresting the progress of the evil, and for maintaining within their respective limits, the authorities, rights, and liberties appertaining to them.

Madison's Virginia Report elaborates:[33]

> It appears . . . to be a plain principle, founded in common sense, illustrated by common practice, and essential to the nature of compacts, that, where resort can be had to no tribunal superior to the authority of the parties, the parties themselves must be the rightful judges, in the last resort, whether the bargain made has been pursued or violated. The Constitution of the United States was formed by the sanction of the states given by each in its sovereign capacity. It adds to the stability and dignity, as well as to the authority of the Constitution, that it rests on this legitimate and solid foundation. The states, then, being the parties to the constitutional compact, and in their sovereign capacity, it follows of necessity, that there can be no tribunal above their authority, to decide in the last resort,

32. N.E. Cunningham, Jr., ed., The Early Republic, 1789-1828, at 145-146 (1968).
33. The Virginia Report, supra n.23.

> whether the compact made by them be violated; and, consequently, that, as the parties to it, they must themselves decide, in the last resort, such questions as may be of sufficient magnitude to require their interposition.

To be sure, this ought not be done lightly: "[I]t is evident that the interposition of the parties, in their sovereign capacity, can be called for by occasions only, deeply and essentially affecting the vital principles of their political system."

Madison's concept of "interposition" was ambiguous. At first glance, it might seem identical to Kentucky's theory of "nullification"—the claim that states have the ability to invalidate federal laws on constitutional grounds. Christian Fritz, however, argues that Madison meant that states would interpose their authority to inform the true sovereign—"We the People"—that something had gone amiss and that *they* should do something about it. "[T]he interposer, though public opinion, protests, petitioners, or even the state legislatures as an instrument of the people, focused attention on whether the government was acting in conformity with the people's mandates expressed in their constitutions. A successful interposition occurred when either the government backtracked, conceding that it had overstepped its constitutional boundaries as asserted by the interposition, or when the people in light of the interposition chose to change the constitutional order."[34]

In the Virginia Report, Madison also responds to the objection "that the judicial authority is to be regarded as the sole expositor of the Constitution, in the last resort":[35]

> On this objection it might be observed *first,* that there may be instances of usurped power, which the forms of the Constitution would never draw within the control of the judicial department; *secondly,* that if the decisions of the judiciary be raised above the authority of the sovereign parties to the Constitution, the decision of the other departments, not carried by the forms of the Constitution before the judiciary, must be equally authoritative and final with the decisions of that department. But the proper answer to the objection is, that the resolution of the General Assembly relates to those great and extraordinary cases, in which all the forms of the Constitution may prove ineffectual against infractions dangerous to the essential rights of the parties to it. The resolution supposes that dangerous powers, not delegated, may not only be usurped and executed by the other departments, but that the judicial department also may exercise or sanction dangerous powers beyond the grant of the Constitution; and, consequently, that the ultimate right of the parties to the Constitution, to judge whether the compact has been dangerously violated, must extend to violations by one delegated authority, as well as by another; by the judiciary, as well as by the executive, or the legislature.

---

34. Christian Fritz, American Sovereigns: The People and America's Constitutional Tradition Before the Civil War 193-194 (2008). See also Jonathan Gienapp, How to Maintain a Constitution: The Kentucky and Virginia Resolutions and James Madison's Struggle with the Problem of Constitutional Maintenance, in Sanford Levinson, ed., Nullification and Secession in Modern Constitutional Thought (2016).

35. Id.

> However true, therefore, it may be, that the judicial department, is, in all questions submitted to it by the forms of the Constitution, to decide in the last resort, this resort must necessarily be deemed the last in relation to the authorities of the other departments of the government; not in relation to the rights of the parties to the constitutional compact, from which the judicial, as well as the other departments hold their delegated trusts. On any other hypothesis, the delegation of judicial power would annul the authority delegating it; and the concurrence of this department with the others in usurped powers, might subvert for ever, and beyond the possible reach of any rightful remedy, the very Constitution which all were instituted to preserve.

The North Carolina legislature, though agreeing that the legislation was unconstitutional, refused to support the proposal that states take countermeasures against the federal government. The Rhode Island legislature passed a resolution stating that Article III, §2, of the Constitution places "in the federal courts, exclusively, and in the Supreme Court of the United States, ultimately, the authority of deciding on the constitutionality of any act or law of the Congress of the United States." It further resolved that "this legislature, in their public capacity, do not feel themselves authorized to consider and decide on the constitutionality of the Sedition and Alien laws (so called), yet they are called upon, by the exigency of this occasion to declare that, in their private opinions, these laws are within the powers delegated to Congress, and promotive of the welfare of the United States."[36]

Rhode Island rejected not only the doctrine of nullification, but also the very idea that it had the authority to assess the Act's constitutionality. This may be the earliest suggestion of a strong notion of judicial supremacy regarding constitutional interpretation. Does rejection of the doctrine of nullification necessarily entail "exclusive" authority of assessment in the judiciary (or any other specific institution)? Contrast the view of the Rhode Island legislature with that of Andrew Jackson in his message vetoing the national bank, infra, as well as the discussion following Marbury v. Madison, infra.

States were not necessarily models of consistency, however. Within a decade after the controversy over the Alien and Sedition Acts, Thomas Jefferson, now President of the United States, imposed a draconian embargo on shipment of goods from New England ports to any other country. This was part of his policy of "neutrality" with regard to the continuing warfare in Europe between Great Britain and France and the potential threats to American ships by either of these countries. The New England states were furious, both because they tended to be sympathetic to Great Britain and because it was disastrous for the region's economy. In 1809, the Massachusetts legislature described the embargo as "in many respects, unjust, oppressive and unconstitutional, and not legally binding on the citizens of this state," though it did implore the citizenry to "abstain from forcible resistance" at least until more

36. The responses of Rhode Island, Massachusetts, and Vermont are reprinted in Walter Murphy, James Fleming, and Will Harris, American Constitutional Interpretation 264-265 (1986).

pacific possibilities "shall have been exhausted in vain."[37] Connecticut, too, spoke of its ability to "interpose their protecting shield between the right and liberty of the people, and the assumed power of the General Government,"[38] but it is not clear exactly what such interposition meant (as was the case with Madison's Virginia Report). And Rhode Island, the last state to ratify the Constitution (and the only state not to send representatives to the Philadelphia Convention because of its suspicions of the centralizing sympathies of the Convention's delegates) also passed its own resolution condemning the embargo "in many of its provisions unjust, oppressive, tyrannical and unconstitutional."[39] None of these fulminations, however, generated a genuine "crisis" for the constitutional order (even if some New Englanders did, during the ensuing War of 1812 between the United States and Great Britain, take part in the Hartford Convention that flirted with secession).

2. The Nullification Crisis and the "Tariff of Abominations"

The concept of nullification once again took center stage during the late 1820s and early 1830s. The "Nullification Crisis" during Andrew Jackson's presidency was precipitated when South Carolina attempted to invalidate the 1828 "Tariff of Abominations" and the 1832 Tariff. Among other things, these tariffs served to protect developing Northern industry against British imports; therefore, they significantly impaired the very different economy of the Southern states, which depended on the trade of agricultural goods with Great Britain. Southern States had to pay more for imported goods they did not produce; while reduced exports to America meant that the British might have less money to pay for Southern cotton.

South Carolinians argued that these tariffs were not designed merely as a neutral revenue-raising measure in the public interest, but, instead, violated the requirement that national legislation serve the "general welfare" because they were highly sectional in their distribution of benefits and burdens.[40] The key constitutional theorist of South Carolina's challenge was John C. Calhoun, who served as Vice President both under John Quincy Adams and Andrew Jackson. (He became the first Vice President to resign from office in December 1832, at the height of the Nullification Crisis, after he was elected to be one of South Carolina's senators). On July 26, 1831, Calhoun offered the most fully developed theory of nullification in the "The Fort Hill Address: On the Relations of the States and Federal Government."[41] Adopting the arguments of Jefferson and Madison in the Kentucky and Virginia Resolutions, Calhoun asserted that

37. Quoted in Thomas E. Woods, Jr., Nullification: How to Resist Federal Tyranny in the 21st Century 62-63 (2010). As the title of Woods's book reveals, even today there are those who continue to take extremely seriously the nullificationist arguments articulated especially in the Kentucky Resolutions and then later given fullest form by John C. Calhoun.

38. Id. at 63.

39. Id. at 65.

40. See Keith Whittington, Constitutional Construction: Divided Powers and Constitutional Meaning, ch.3 (on "The Nullification Crisis and the Limits of National Power") (1999).

41. Available at http://oll.libertyfund.org/?option=com_staticxt&staticfile=show.php%3Ftitle= 683&chapter=107120&layout=html&Itemid=27.

The great and leading principle is, that the General Government emanated from the people of several States, forming distinct political communities, and acting in their separate sovereign capacity, and not from all the people forming one aggregate political community; that the Constitution of the United States is, in fact, a compact to which each State is a party, in the character already described; and that The several States, or parties, have a right to judge of its infractions; and in the case of deliberate, palpable, and dangerous exercise of power not delegated, they have the right, in the last resort, to use the language of the Virginia Resolutions, "to interpose for arresting the progress of evil, and for maintaining, within their respective limits, the authorities, rights and liberties appertaining to them." . . . This right of interposition, thus solemnly asserted by the State of Virginia, be it called what it may,—State-right, veto, nullification, or by any other name,—I conceive to be the fundamental principle of our system, resting on facts historically as certain as our own revolution itself, and deductions as simple and demonstrative as that of any political or moral truth whatever; and I firmly believe that on its recognition depends the stability and safety of our political institutions.

. . . So numerous and diversified are the interests of our country, that they could not be fairly represented in a single government, organized so as to give to each great and leading interest, a separate and distinct voice, as in governments to which I have referred. A plan was adopted better suited to our situation, but perfectly novel in its character. The powers of government were divided, not, as heretofore, in reference to classes, but geographically. One General Government was formed for the whole, to which were delegated all the powers supposed to be necessary to regulate the interests common to all the States, leaving others subject to the separate control of the States, being, from their local and peculiar character, such, that they could not be subject to the will of a majority of the whole Union, without the certain hazard of injustice and oppression. It was thus that the interests of the whole were subjected, as they ought to be, to the will of the whole, while the peculiar and local interests were left under the control of the States separately, to whose custody only, they could be safely confided. This distribution of power, settled solemnly by a constitutional compact, to which all the States are parties, constitutes the peculiar character and excellence of our political system. It is truly and emphatically *American, without example or parallel.*

To realize its perfection, we must view the General Government and those of the States as a whole, each in its proper sphere, sovereign and independent; each perfectly adapted to its respective objects; the States acting separately, representing and protecting the local and peculiar interests; and acting jointly through one General Government, with the weight respectively assigned to each by the Constitution, representing and protecting the interest of the whole; and thus perfecting, by an admirable but simple arrangement, the great principle of representation and responsibility, without which no government can be free or just. To preserve this sacred distribution, as originally settled, by coercing each to move in its prescribed orbit, is the great and difficult problem, on the

> solution of which, the duration of our Constitution, of our Union, and, in all probability, our liberty depends. How is this to be effected?
>
> The question is new, when applied to our peculiar political organization, where the separate and conflicting interests of society are represented by distinct, but connected governments; but it is, in reality, an old question under a new form, long since perfectly solved. Whenever separate and dissimilar interests have been separately represented in any government; whenever the sovereign power has been divided in its exercise, the experience and wisdom of ages have devised but one mode by which such political organization can be preserved—the mode adopted in England, and by all governments, ancient and modern, blessed with constitutions deserving to be called free—to give to each co-estate the right to judge of its powers, with a negative or veto on the acts of the others, in order to protect against encroachments, the interests it particularly represents: a principle which all of our constitutions recognize in the distribution of power among their respective departments, as essential to maintain the independence of each; but which, to all who will duly reflect on the subject, must appear far more essential, for the same object, in that great and fundamental distribution of powers between the states and General Government. So essential is the principle, that, to withhold the right from either, where the sovereign power is divided, is, in fact, *to annul the division* itself, and to *consolidate*, in the one left in the exclusive possession of the right, *all* powers of government; for it is not possible to distinguish, practically, between a government having all power, and one having the right to take what powers it pleases.

Calhoun rejected the notion that the federal courts could arbitrate disputes over the nature of federal and state powers. The federal judiciary, he argued, was, like the President and Congress, ultimately responsible to national majorities, "compounded of the majority of the States taken as political bodies, and a majority of the people of the States, estimated in federal numbers. These, united, constitute the real final power which impels and directs the movements of the General Government." The federal courts, therefore, could not be trusted to look out for the interests of individual states:

> The judges are in fact, as truly the judicial representatives of this united majority, as the majority of Congress itself, or the President is its legislative or executive representative; and to confide that power to the Judiciary to determine finally and conclusively what powers are delegated and what reserved, would be in reality, to confide it to the majority, whose agents they are, and by whom they can be controlled in various ways; and of course to subject (against the fundamental principle of our system and all for sound political reasoning) the reserved powers of the States, with all the local and peculiar interests they were intended to protect, to the will of the very majority against which protection was intended. Nor will the tenure by which the judges hold their office, however valuable the provision in many other respects, materially vary the case. Its highest possible effect would be to retard, and not finally to resist, the dominate majority.

So how would "nullification" work in practice? According to Calhoun, it would begin by the declaration by a given state that a federal statute was "null and void." That would not be the last word on the matter. Congress could always propose an amendment explicitly constitutionalizing the act in question or, alternatively, two-thirds of the states could petition for a constitutional convention that could presumably propose a similar legitimizing amendment. Until then, however, the state's declaration would presumably control, at least within its own territory.

The South Carolina legislature declared the Tariffs of 1828 and 1832 unconstitutional and refused to allow collection of federal tariff revenues on imports entering the state. In response, President Jackson pushed through a Force Bill on March 2, 1833, which authorized the President to use force to collect the tariffs. The Crisis ultimately came to an end when Congress passed the Compromise Tariff of 1833, which allowed for the gradual reduction of some tariff rates, and South Carolina agreed to comply. The theory underlying the Crisis, however, remained to be drawn on by later states unhappy with actions of the national government.

DISCUSSION

1. Consider Professor Levinson's comments on some recent proposals in effect to revive the concept of nullification:[42]

> No sane political system would place such power in a single state, or even a small number of states. This fact is quite different, incidentally, from arguing that it is crazy to suggest the need for an alternative to the Supreme Court; this suggestion is just Madison's in 1798. Imagine, for example, that the delegates to Philadelphia had established a "constitutional court," composed of judges appointed by the individual states, which would adjudicate challenges brought by a state to any given federal law, which would, by stipulation, remain in force until final adjudication by the "constitutional court." Indeed, such a proposal for a new "'Court of the Union,'" consisting of fifty state judges, was proposed and debated at the annual meeting of the General Assembly of the States in December 1962.[43] Senator Strom Thurmond of South Carolina introduced the proposal to the Senate in February 1963 as a potential constitutional amendment.[44] One might well regard that proposal as a terrible idea, but it certainly is not "unthinkable" or unresponsive to the concerns expressed by Madison in 1798.[45]

---

42. Adapted from Levinson, The 21st Century Rediscovery of Nullification and Secession in American Political Rhetoric: Frivolousness Incarnate or Serious Arguments to Be Wrestled With?, 67 Ark. L. Rev. 17 (2014), reprinted with revisions in Levinson, ed., Nullification and Secession in Modern Constitutional Thought.

43. William F. Swindler, The Current Challenge to Federalism: The Confederating Proposal, 52 Geo. L.J. 1, 10 (1963).

44. Id. at 11.

45. One might argue that such a proposal describes the European judicial system, where the European courts are very deliberately composed of judges from all of the constituent members. See Leslie Friedman Goldstein: Constituting Federal Sovereignty: The European Union in Comparative Context 45 (2001). In turn, this structure might help explain why even highly controversial decisions of the European courts have met significantly less resistance than was the case within the United States in its first six decades or, arguably, even today. See id. at 14.

It is telling that Thomas Woods, the most active contemporary proponent of nullification—the subtitle of his book describes it as a necessary mode of "resist[ing] federal tyranny"[46]—simply asserts that "[w]e need an institutional structure in which another force in the U.S. [besides the Supreme Court] may say no after the federal government has said yes."[47] Thus, he suggests, "we might consider a second-best alternative [to nullification by a single state] whereby, say, a vote of two-thirds of the states could overturn a federal law."[48] Indeed, this was proposed, under the name of the "Repeal Amendment," by Georgetown law professor Randy Barnett and a number of conservative state officials.[49] After criticism that two-thirds of the states could comprise substantially less than a majority of the American public (given that over half the population currently lives in only ten of the states), Barnett has instead suggested that repeal could be effectuated by the votes of a majority of state legislatives if, at the same time, they included a majority of the population.[50] Is this modified proposal worth serious consideration? What if, instead of state-by-state reconsideration, Barnett instead proposed a national referendum that could overturn offensive federal statutes, modeled after similar referendum options in such states as Maine and Ohio?

2. Bray Hammond once wrote that "the Constitution had not displaced rival principles or reconciled them but had become their dialectical arena."[51] The debate over the compact-of-states theory would reemerge powerfully in 1860-1861, when 11 states argued that they possessed a sovereign right to secede from the Union. Victory on the battlefield by opponents of secession in the North has not in fact settled the argument over how to conceptualize the nature of the American Union. For example, in his first inaugural address, President Ronald Reagan remarked that "all of us need to be reminded that the Federal Government did not create the states; the states created the Federal Government."

The Supreme Court's most recent consideration of these issues occurred in U.S. Term Limits v. Thornton, 514 U.S. 779 (1995). Justice Stevens, writing for the majority, emphasized the "national" character of the United States as part of the rationale for striking down an Arkansas constitutional amendment that would have imposed term limits on candidates for the U.S. Senate and House of Representatives. He quoted, for example, Marshall's insistence that the Constitution was "not given by the people of a particular State, not given by the constituents of the

46. Woods, supra n.37.

47. Id. at 128.

48. Id.

49. See, e.g., Randy E. Barnett, The Case for the Repeal Amendment, 78 Tenn. L. Rev. 813, 816 (2011) (advocating the Repeal Amendment, introduced into Congress, which would give states the power to repeal any federal legislation upon a two-thirds vote).

50. See Randy Barnett, Restoring the Lost Constitution 414-415 (rev. ed. 2014).

51. Bray Hammond, Banks and Politics in America from the Revolution to the Civil War 120 (1957).

legislature, . . . but by the people of all the States." And Justice Kennedy, concurring, stated, "In my view, . . . it is well settled that the *whole people of the United States* asserted their political identity and unity of purpose when they created the federal system" (emphasis added).

However, Justice Thomas, joined by Chief Justice Rehnquist and Justices O'Connor and Scalia, wrote a very sharp dissent describing "the *people of the several States* [as] the only true source of power" (emphasis added):

> The ultimate source of the Constitution's authority is the consent of the people of each individual State, not the consent of the undifferentiated people of the Nation as a whole.
>
> The ratification procedure erected by Article VII makes this point clear. The Constitution took effect once it had been ratified by the people gathered in convention in nine different States. But the Constitution went into effect only "between the States so ratifying the same," Art. VII; it did not bind the people of North Carolina until they had accepted it. . . .

Is Justice Thomas adopting Madison's and Jefferson's arguments in the Kentucky and Virginia Resolutions? In any event, which analysis do you find more persuasive, and why? What, if anything, follows from your answer?

NOTE: JUDICIAL REVIEW BEFORE *MARBURY*: THE SUPREME COURT IN ITS EARLY YEARS

The Supreme Court of the United States was a relatively insignificant institution during the first decade of the new Republic. Presidents Washington and Adams had some difficulty attracting people to serve, and the rate of turnover was high. Three men were appointed Chief Justice during the first 12 years. John Jay resigned after six years to run for governor of New York. (During his tenure he also sailed to England to serve as the principal negotiator of what became known as the Jay Treaty with Great Britain, which, together with his co-authorship of *The Federalist*, remains his primary claim to fame for most historians.) His successor, John Rutledge, had been appointed as an Associate in 1789 but had resigned in 1791, without ever sitting, to go to the more prestigious South Carolina Supreme Court. He was nominated to become Chief Justice of the United States Supreme Court in 1795 but failed to receive Senate confirmation. Thereafter, Oliver Ellsworth was nominated and confirmed in 1796; he served until 1800, when he resigned to accept a diplomatic post in France.

One source of discontent was the onerous duty of "riding circuit," which required each Justice to travel twice a year to sit in the federal circuit court districts. (There were no "circuit courts" in the modern sense; instead, they consisted of district judges sitting together with a Supreme Court Justice as a "circuit court.") The trips were strenuous and time-consuming. In refusing President Adams's offer of reappointment as Chief Justice in 1801, Jay commented that "under a system so defective" the Court would never "obtain the energy, weight and dignity which were essential to its affording due support to the National Government, nor [would it] acquire the public confidence and respect which, as the last resort of the justice of the nation, it should possess."

In any case, one of the most important questions in this early period concerned the power of judicial review—whether federal judges had the power to review the validity of federal legislation or state legislation.[52] (As we will see, these are distinct questions.) The extent to which those who framed and adopted the Constitution assumed or intended that the courts would exercise this power has been the subject of continuing scholarly controversy.

No provision of the Constitution explicitly authorizes the federal judiciary to review the constitutionality of acts of Congress. Moreover, England provided no direct precedent for judicial review. As late as the seventeenth century, the law-making and law-declaring (or judicial) functions of the High Court of Parliament were not sharply differentiated, so that England lacked the concept of separation of powers that underlies the American institution of judicial review. Despite the settled notion that the common law embodied principles of natural or fundamental law and despite Lord Coke's famous dictum in Bonham's Case,[53] the common law courts never assumed the authority to review acts of Parliament. England had no written constitution, and parliamentary supremacy was firmly established at the time of the framing of the first American constitutions. "[I]f the parliament will positively enact a thing to be done which is unreasonable," wrote Blackstone in 1765, "I know of no power in the ordinary forms of the constitution that is vested with authority to control it. . . ."[54]

Some American colonists had invoked principles of natural law or natural rights to contend that the colonial courts should not enforce oppressive English legislation, and that the American Revolution was justified on the basis of a natural right to revolt against oppressive government. But if the received natural law tradition created an atmosphere in which judicial review could flourish, that innovative American institution owed still more to John Locke's Second Treatise of Civil Government (1690). The premise of Locke's social compact was that sovereignty

---

52. See generally Judicial Review and the Supreme Court 1-12 (Levy ed., 1967); Alan Westin, Introduction and Historical Bibliography to Charles Beard, The Supreme Court and the Constitution 1-34, 133-146 (Westin ed., 1962). Compare Charles Beard, The Supreme Court and the Constitution (1912), Raoul Berger, Congress v. The Supreme Court (1969), and Henry Hart, Professor Crosskey and Judicial Review, 67 Harv. L. Rev. 1456 (1954) (book review), with Louis Boudin, Government by Judiciary (1932), Edward Corwin, Court over Constitution: A Study of Judicial Review as an Instrument of Popular Government (1938), and 2 William Crosskey, Politics and the Constitution in the History of the United States (1953).

53. 8 Co. Rep. 107a, 77 Eng. Rep. 638 (1610): "When an Act of Parliament is against common right and reason, or repugnant, or impossible to be performed, the common law will controul it, and adjudge such Act to be void. . . ." See Theodore Plucknett, Bonham's Case and Judicial Review, 40 Harv. L. Rev. 30 (1926); S.E. Thorne, Dr. Bonham's Case, 54 L.Q. Rev. 543 (1938).

54. Blackstone, Commentaries *91. See J.W. Gough, Fundamental Law in English Constitutional History (1955); Charles McIlwain, The High Court of Parliament and Its Supremacy (1910); Edward Corwin, The "Higher Law" Background of American Constitutional Law, 42 Harv. L. Rev. 149, 365 (1928-1929).

did not reside in any agency of government but in "the people" themselves, who (through the American invention of written constitutions) delegated limited authority to those agencies. The legislature was the direct voice of the people, and the early republicans placed a virtually unlimited, populistic faith in the representative branch. But in the years following the Revolutionary War, as state legislatures authorized the issuance of worthless paper money, enacted sweeping debtor relief legislation, and directed oppressive measures against British loyalists, the possibility of legislative abuse—of tyranny of the majority—became increasingly apparent.

One remedy to majority overreaching was bicameralism, which the states adopted in various forms. The other remedy that emerged was judicial review.

If the people were sovereign, and the legislature merely their agent, then (as Hamilton later put it in The Federalist No. 78) "where the will of the legislature declared in its statutes, stands in opposition to that of the people, declared in the constitution, the judges ought to be governed by the latter, rather than the former. They ought to regulate their decisions by the fundamental laws. . . ."[55] Or consider a speech in which James Wilson, second only to Madison in importance at the Philadelphia Convention, told members of the Convention that laws "may be unjust, may be unwise, may be dangerous, may be destructive; and *yet not be so unconstitutional as to justify the judges in refusing to give them effect*" (emphasis added). One might be struck, of course, by how much would *not* be unconstitutional—i.e., "unjust," "unwise," "dangerous," and even "destructive" laws—but Wilson obviously concludes his comment by suggesting that there indeed exist a set of laws "so unconstitutional as to justify the judges in refusing to give them effect."

By 1787, several state courts had asserted the authority to nullify legislative enactments (almost always invoking the fundamental law of the written constitution rather than unwritten natural law). Most of these tentative ventures were met with criticism, however, and some even with threats of discipline and impeachment. Thus it cannot be said that the institution of judicial review was "established" in the states by the time of the Philadelphia Convention.[56] The "intent of the framers" is still the subject of dispute. For present purposes, it suffices to note that the general idea of judicial review was much in the air when the Constitution was framed and ratified. Whether there was a clear consensus that the federal judiciary should review the constitutionality of acts of Congress, there certainly was no consensus that it might not, and, as we will see in a moment, several decisions of the 1790s seem to presuppose the authority to consider the constitutionality of acts

55. See Bernard Bailyn, The Ideological Origins of the American Revolution (1967); Gordon Wood, The Creation of the American Republic, 1776-1787 (1969). There was a long tradition of natural law thinking in Roman Catholicism, inspired by Aristotle and reaching its fullest development in the thought of Thomas Aquinas. The Protestant backgrounds of most British settlers assured that this tradition would be relatively ignored in favor of non-Catholic thinkers like Locke.

56. See William Nelson, Changing Conceptions of Judicial Review: The Evolution of Constitutional Theory in the States, 1790-1860, 120 U. Pa. L. Rev. 1166 (1972). See also Jack Rakove, The Origins of Judicial Review: A Plea for New Contexts, 49 Stan. L. Rev. 1031 (1997).

of Congress (though none of these decisions invalidated any of the laws under consideration). Thus, although *Marbury* met with some criticism, it took no one by surprise. This being said, *how* the federal courts have practiced judicial review has evolved over the course of two centuries of the Constitution's history. Without much fanfare, the early Supreme Court simply assumed that federal courts possessed the power to review the validity of *state* legislation that conflicted with federal treaties and statutes. Professor Currie, for example, points out that in Ware v. Hylton, 3 U.S. (3 Dall.) 199 (1796), "the Court for the first time struck down a state law under the supremacy clause, establishing for all time its power of judicial review of state laws."[57] *Ware* involved a conflict between a Virginia statute providing a defense against creditor claims by alien enemies and the 1783 Treaty of Paris, which provided that creditors on both sides of the Revolutionary War "shall meet with no lawful impediment to the recovery . . . of all bona fide debts heretofore contracted."

The Court also appeared to assume that it had the power to review federal legislation for constitutionality. In Hylton v. United States, 3 U.S. (3 Dall.) 171 (1796), the Court upheld a tax on carriages. Hylton argued that the tax was unconstitutional because it was a "direct tax" under Article I, §2, cl. 3 and Article I, §9, cl. 4. If it were a direct tax, total revenues collected from the tax would have to be apportioned by population from each state; instead the amount of the tax was uniform in each state. The Justices argued that the tax was not direct and therefore did not have to be apportioned by state population. Justice Chase began his opinion by writing that "by the case stated, only one question is submitted to the opinion of this court, whether the law of Congress [at issue] is unconstitutional and void?" After determining that the statute in question was constitutionally unproblematic, Chase concluded by stating that "it is unnecessary, at this time, for me to determine, whether this court, constitutionally possesses the power to declare an act of Congress void, on the ground of its being made contrary to, and in violation of, the Constitution; but if the court have such power, I am free to declare, that I will never exercise it, but in a very clear case." One might think, of course, that Chase had already answered this last question in the affirmative by his very formulation of "the one question . . . submitted to the opinion of the court." All of the other Justices who participated in the decision agreed that the statute was constitutionally legitimate; none challenged the abstract power of the Court to determine otherwise and, presumably, invalidate it. The first instance of such an invalidation came with Marbury v. Madison, infra, but the basic assumption underlying *Marbury* seems to have been relatively well established by 1796.

One might note, incidentally, that the opinions in these cases were "seriatim"; that is, each Justice prepared a separate opinion, as was (and remains) the custom in the United Kingdom. One of Marshall's signal achievements as Chief Justice was to establish a very different practice, by which, ideally (in his view), a single opinion joined in by all the Justices would be published as the "Opinion of the Court."

57. See David Currie, The Constitution in the Supreme Court: The First Hundred Years, 1789-1888, at 41 (1985).

IV. THE ELECTION OF 1800

The 1800 election, won by the Republicans, tested the fledgling political system's ability to accommodate a peaceful transfer of power from the established Federalist Party to a new set of leaders with very different views, whom the old Federalist leadership viewed with the utmost suspicion and even contempt.

Under the system set up by the 1787 Constitution, the President was chosen by electors, who in turn were chosen by state legislatures. The electors named the two individuals they thought most fit to become President. The person who received the most votes and who also obtained a majority of the electors would become President; the runner-up would serve as Vice President.

Electors could vote for at most one candidate from their own state to prevent political pressure to vote for local notables and "favorite sons." The purpose was to force electors to transcend parochialism and reflect dispassionately on who would be the best person to lead the nation.[58]

The members of the founding generation were generally suspicious of, and hostile to, the idea of political parties. They were concerned that loyalty to a party or faction would supplant devotion to the public interest. In The Federalist No. 10, James Madison had explicitly warned against the presence of "factions" in American politics. "By a faction," Madison wrote, "I understand a number of citizens, whether amounting to a majority or minority of the whole, who are united and actuated by some common impulse or of passion, or of interest, adverse to the rights of other citizens, or to the permanent and aggregate interests of the community." The point of Madisonian representative democracy was to select sufficiently virtuous citizens who would focus on only "the permanent and aggregate interests of the community" rather than, say, the strategic interests of their political party. The electors would presumably pick the most virtuous person as President, with the second most admired filling the office of Vice President. George Washington was unanimously viewed as the person most qualified to serve as the first President; indeed, he was the unanimous choice, and his initial cabinet featured widely respected persons who reflected a variety of different views, consisting of Thomas Jefferson, Alexander Hamilton, and Edmund Randolph. (John Adams was the first Vice President.) Washington was also reelected unanimously for a second term.

By the election of 1796, however, Madison's initial vision was in shambles, and two parties had begun to emerge: the Federalists, led by John Adams and Alexander Hamilton, and the Democratic-Republicans, led by Thomas Jefferson. (Madison allied himself with Jefferson.) In the 1796 election Federalist John Adams received 71 electoral votes and became President, while his political opponent, Thomas Jefferson, received 68 electoral votes and became Vice President. Jefferson did not

---

58. See Akhil Reed Amar, America's Constitution: A Biography 167-168 (2005). As to contemporary implications of the "two-state" voting rule, which survives in the Twelfth Amendment that in effect recognized the legitimacy of the American party system, see Sanford Levinson and Ernest A. Young, Who's Afraid of the Twelfth Amendment?, 29 Fla. St. U. L. Rev. 925 (2001) (discussing whether Dick Cheney was in fact a Texan and therefore ineligible to receive the votes of Texas electors if they had also voted for George W. Bush).

become part of the Adams Administration; to the contrary, Adams and Jefferson became ever more bitterly opposed. As noted previously, Jefferson helped to draft the Kentucky Resolutions that opposed the Alien and Sedition Acts, which were passed during the Adams Administration and reflected Federalist political views. Jefferson ran against Adams once again in the 1800 election.

Because the framers of the Constitution did not expect the emergence of national political parties, they assumed that the electors in different parts of the country would often vote for a variety of different candidates, so that none would receive a majority. When that happened, the House of Representatives would choose a President from the list of the top five recipients of electoral votes, with each state having a single vote.

Instead, the election of 1800 turned into a bitter struggle between the two emergent political parties that threatened the political stability of the Union. Consistent with the original constitutional scheme, Democratic-Republican electors not only did not differentiate in their votes between President and Vice President, but also (unlike their Federalist counterparts) did not have the foresight to hold back at least one vote for Thomas Jefferson's de facto running mate, the New Yorker Aaron Burr. This resulted in a tie, with Jefferson and Burr receiving 73 votes each (a majority), whereas Adams received only 65 votes (and his running mate, Charles Cotesworth Pinckney of South Carolina, received 64).[59]

---

59. One of the other anomalies of the election process is that under the Constitution the electoral votes are counted and announced before the Senate by the President of the Senate, whose other job, of course, is Vice President of the United States. This meant that Thomas Jefferson, Vice President in the Adams Administration and Adams's political opponent, got to count the electoral votes for his own election. This was no small boon; Bruce Ackerman and David Fontana have argued that Jefferson played fast and loose with the Georgia electoral votes, which appeared to contain some technical irregularities. See Ackerman and Fontana, Thomas Jefferson Counts Himself into the Presidency, 90 Va. L. Rev. 551 (2004). Had Georgia's four electoral votes not been counted, Jefferson and Burr would have received only 69, one less than the 70 votes required to achieve a majority of the 138 total electoral votes. In that case, the House of Representatives, under the rules of the 1787 Constitution (subsequently altered by the Twelfth Amendment) would have been able to choose among the top five finishers, including John Adams and, perhaps more important, the Federalist de facto vice presidential candidate, Charles Cotesworth Pinckney, who, as a South Carolinian, might well have peeled off a sufficient number of Southern states to make a majority with the Federalist states (the House voted on a one-state/one-vote system). That would have made Pinckney President instead of Jefferson. Jefferson's willingness to overlook the technical irregularities and to count Georgia's votes foreclosed this possibility, and limited the final candidates to only himself and Burr.

Ackerman is highly critical of the 1787 Constitution inasmuch as it proved remarkably dysfunctional in handling the reality of a party system. "Only one thing is clear," he writes. "If America managed to survive its first great crisis, the written constitution wasn't going to save it—to the contrary, it was only making things worse. If there was going to be a successful transition of power, lots more would be required than following the rules laid down by the Founders. Only creative statesmanship had a chance of preventing the constitutional text from unraveling into civil war. The first act of statesmanship involved Thomas Jefferson counting his rivals out of the run-off." Bruce A. Ackerman, The Failure of the Founding Fathers: Jefferson, Marshall, and the Rise of Presidential Democracy 76 (2005).

The shortsightedness of the Jeffersonian electors meant that there was no single winner. The election was thrown into the House of Representatives, where each state delegation received one vote. Because two candidates—Jefferson and Burr—had each received a majority, the House had to choose between them; Adams was out of the race. (See Article II, §1, cl. 3.) Although Jefferson's Republicans had also won control of Congress, that new Congress would not take office until March. Thus the House of Representatives that would resolve the contested presidential election was a "lame-duck" House that was still controlled by a political party, the Federalists, that had just been repudiated in the 1800 election. (The length of the lame-duck session was shortened, and the date of the President's inaugural was moved forward, by the Twentieth Amendment.)

Many Federalists were outraged at the thought of Jefferson becoming President, not least because of his enthusiastic support for the French Revolution. Some so-called irreconcilables were particularly incensed at the fact that Jefferson's margin of victory over Adams was entirely the result of the Constitution's Three-Fifths Clause, which gave Southern states especially an electoral bonus in the House of Representatives and the Electoral College based on their slave populations, even though these slaves had no role in the polity.[60] Many Federalists hoped to engineer an agreement by which the anti-slavery Burr would become President.[61] Burr explicitly disclaimed any part in such an arrangement, although, crucially, he never withdrew and therefore extended the controversy. One obstacle in Burr's path, besides the obvious political fact that he was selected to be Jefferson's Vice President rather than a presidential candidate himself, was the enmity of the Federalist Alexander Hamilton (who would ultimately be killed by Burr in 1804 in the most famous duel in U.S. history).

Because two state delegations were evenly divided (so that their states were not counted), it took 36 ballots until, on February 17, 1801, two of the Federalist "irreconcilables" (one of whom was Delaware's sole representative) gave up the fight and allowed their states to cast their ballots for Jefferson.[62] In the meantime, the two Republican governors of Pennsylvania and Virginia had put their state militias "on alert" in case their party was denied the presidency. One result of the political crisis was the Twelfth Amendment, proposed in 1803 and ratified in 1804.

---

60. See Garry Wills, Negro President: President Jefferson and the Slave Power (2003); Akhil Reed Amar, America's Constitution, supra n.58. Northern states like New York, which still had some 20,000 slaves in 1800, benefitted as well. See Ira Berlin and Leslie Harris, Slavery in New York (2005).

61. Indeed, as Ackerman demonstrates, see The Failure of the Founding Fathers, supra n.59, some Federalists flirted with the idea of passing a "succession in office act" that would in effect have allowed John Marshall, then serving as both Secretary of State and Chief Justice, to become President if the House had been unable to break the tie by the Inauguration Day of March 4, 1801. He persuasively argues that any such attempt would have resulted in civil war.

62. See generally Bernard A. Weisberger, America Afire: Jefferson, Adams, and the Revolutionary Election of 1800 (2000); Joanne B. Freeman, The Election of 1800: A Study in the Logic of Political Change 108 Yale L.J. (1999).

The Twelfth Amendment recognized the emergence of political parties as part of the constitutional system by explicitly holding separate ballots for the candidates for the presidency and vice presidency, so that partisan electors could vote for the "ticket" of their party.

V. EARLY POLITICAL STRUGGLES OVER THE FEDERAL JUDICIARY

Having lost the presidency and Congress to Jefferson and the Republicans, the judiciary was the only remaining source of power, and the Federalists moved to consolidate control over that branch of the national government. The Chief Justiceship was open because of Oliver Ellsworth's resignation in the autumn of 1800. John Jay, the first Chief Justice, whose most important opinion you read in *Chisholm*, had previously resigned in order to become governor of New York. He declined Adams's offer to return to the Supreme Court because of advancing age and the rigors of circuit riding. Adams therefore nominated his Secretary of State, John Marshall. Marshall was quickly confirmed by the lame-duck Federalist Congress, which remained in power until Jefferson's inauguration on March 4, 1801. On February 4, 1801, Marshall assumed the Chief Justiceship, while also retaining his position as secretary of state for the last month of Adams's term. Today this would be viewed as completely unacceptable, but constitutional norms were still evolving in the early Republic. Note that while Article I, §6, cl. 2 of the Constitution explicitly prohibits members of Congress from serving in the executive branch, there is no explicit textual prohibition on simultaneously serving as an executive branch official and a judge.

On February 13, 1801, just three weeks before Inauguration Day and the end of Federalist power, Congress passed the Judiciary Act of 1801. It established a new set of circuit courts (and circuit judges) to complement the federal district and Supreme Court judges. The asserted justification of the 1801 Act was to relieve Supreme Court Justices of the onerous and unpopular duty of riding circuit. Given the timing of the legislation—and the fact that virtually all the new vacancies were filled by Federalists quickly nominated by Adams and confirmed by the lame-duck Senate—Republicans could be excused for believing that the more basic purpose was to entrench Federalist control over the judiciary. A Federalist-controlled judiciary might undermine the new Republican Party by declaring legislation unconstitutional or otherwise making life difficult for the new government. This was, after all, the first time in world history that an existing set of political leaders had been voted out of office by their opponents in a popular election. There was no precedent for a peaceful transfer of power, and such a transition was made all the harder by the fact that political parties—who held fundamentally different views about political issues—had not yet been truly accepted as legitimate.

Jeffersonians—and many subsequent historians—referred to the beneficiaries of the Federalist legislation as "midnight judges," suggesting a foul deed done in darkness. Although the circuit judges had been confirmed, taken their oaths of office, and were beginning to hear cases, the Republicans did not take things lying down. Instead, the now Republican-controlled Congress in effect purged these Federalist judges by repealing the Judiciary Act of 1801; this eliminated the new circuit courts and thus left the circuit judges with no judicial positions to occupy. The Repeal Act was passed on March 8, 1802; seven weeks later, on April 29, Congress passed the Judiciary Act of 1802, which, among other things, reassigned the Supreme Court Justices to their previous role as circuit-riding circuit judges.

The Federalists raised at least two important constitutional objections to the new legislation. The first objection was that it was illegitimate to eliminate the circuit judgeships—after all, Article III, Section 1 states that "[t]he Judges, both of the supreme and inferior Courts, shall hold their Offices during good Behaviour," which has been interpreted as requiring life tenure.[63] The second objection was that it was improper to assign members of the Supreme Court to auxiliary duty as members of "inferior" courts (and to require them to ride circuit to reach these courts).

The Republicans were fully aware that the displaced judges might try to challenge the constitutionality of the Repeal Act before the Federalist-controlled U.S. Supreme Court, so, as part of the Act, the Republicans eliminated the Supreme Court's 1802 term. As a result, the case attacking the Repeal Act, Stuart v. Laird, and the now-famous (and related) case of Marbury v. Madison, were not decided until 1803. The elimination of the 1802 term was a warning shot across the bow that signaled to the Federalist judiciary, including the members of the Supreme Court, that they should quickly adjust to the new political order of things. If they failed to acquiesce in what many historians have termed "the Jeffersonian Revolution," their Republican adversaries might well move to impeach and remove them from office. Because political norms were still being negotiated in the early Republic, it was not entirely clear what constituted an impeachable offense for a federal judge.

Marbury v. Madison should be understood as part of the political struggles over the transition of power from the formerly dominant Federalists to their Jeffersonian successors.[64] Thomas Jefferson ordered Secretary of State James Madison (who had succeeded John Marshall in office) not to deliver a commission of office to William Marbury, appointed by President Adams as a justice of the peace in the District of

---

63. The term "good Behaviour" is a translation of the Latin term of art *quamdiu se bene gesserit,* a type of appointment that historically was opposed to an appointment "at the pleasure" of the appointing agency. The latter kind of appointment meant that the official could be fired at will. In the case of federal judges, the Constitution does not specify a term of years. Therefore "good Behaviour" means that the judge holds office until improper behavior has been demonstrated in an authorized proceeding. For federal judges that proceeding is impeachment. Therefore, the clause is generally read to provide for life tenure until impeachment. Nevertheless, could Congress limit the term of office to, say, 18 years, and assert that the Good Behaviour Clause simply means that the only way judges may be removed before their term expires is by impeachment?

64. There is a copious literature on the political circumstances that generated *Marbury.* In addition to Ackerman, see generally Donald Dewey, Marshall versus Jefferson: The Political Background of Marbury v. Madison (1970); Jean Edward Smith, John Marshall: Defender of a Nation 309-326 (1996); James O'Fallon, *Marbury,* 44 Stan. L. Rev. 219 (1992).

Columbia. Although Adams had signed Marbury's commission, John Marshall, who served as both Secretary of State and Chief Justice until literally the last moment of the Adams Administration, had failed to deliver the commission to Marbury.

Marbury's actual position as justice of the peace was relatively trivial, and unlike Article III judges, his term would have been limited to five years in any instance. Still, he seemed to symbolize Federalist overreaching, and there was a widespread perception that Jefferson would in fact refuse to accept the legitimacy of any decision ordering Madison to deliver the commission.[65] Moreover, Republicans in Congress were already speaking of impeaching Federalist judges on the grounds that they were political partisans rather than impartial jurists. Indeed, the Republican-controlled House of Representatives would vote in 1804 to impeach the Federalist Justice Samuel Chase, although ultimately Chase's prosecutors failed to garner the necessary two-thirds majority in the Senate to convict and remove Chase from office.[66]

In hindsight, the failure to remove Chase signaled that Congress would not use the impeachment power simply to remove political adversaries; thus the episode helped establish a convention of judicial independence.[67] In 1803, however, the degree of judicial independence that would be accepted was not yet clear. The United States was still an infant republic, and judging by the experience of many other developing democracies, there was no guarantee that federal judges would turn out to be very independent at all.

Given the highly charged political atmosphere of the day, the central issue in both Stuart v. Laird and Marbury v. Madison was whether the Court would dare to directly

---

65. See, however, Louise Weinberg, Our *Marbury*, 89 Va. L. Rev. 1235 (2003), for an argument that the likelihood of Jefferson's potential disobedience is exaggerated (and that Marshall therefore assumed that Jefferson would in fact comply with such an order).

66. See, e.g., Keith Whittington, Constitutional Construction 20 (1999).

67. On the rise of "judicial independence," see Scott Douglas Gerber, A Distinct Judicial Power: The Origins of an Independent Judiciary, 1606-1787 (2011). Note, however, that most American judges are state judges, most of whom are either elected or subject to various forms of political accountability after appointment. As Jed Shugerman has argued, the move toward an elected judiciary at the 1846 state constitutional convention in New York was motivated at least in part by a desire to create a judiciary that would be more "independent" from influence by appointing governors or confirming legislators. See Shugerman, The People's Courts: The Rise of Judicial Elections and Judicial Power in America (2012). The complexity of the concept "judicial independence" led Prof. Lewis Kornhauser to write that the "legal debates over adjudication, debates about the design of judicial institutions, and the explanation of the emergence and performance of various judicial institutions would be clearer and progress more rapidly if we abandoned the concept." Quoted in Levinson, Framed: America's 51 Constitutions and the Crisis of Governance 247-248 (2012). Professor Levinson notes, for example, that the method by which federal judges are selected in the United States is scarcely "independent" of a deeply political process, as illustrated by the circumstances of the appointment of John Marshall as Chief Justice and the accompanying "midnight judges" whose tenures in office were the subject of the next two cases. If electing judges seems too "dependent" on the vagaries of public opinion, would we better off if judges appointed their own successors, applying ostensibly "professional" rather than "political" criteria to their selection? This describes, Levinson suggests, the process in Denmark, India, and, until recently, Israel.

challenge the combined weight of executive and congressional authority by carrying out the implications of earlier decisions and actually invalidating a federal statute, thereby potentially provoking a full-scale constitutional crisis. We turn now to the two cases. Although *Marbury* was decided a week earlier, we take up *Stuart* first because in political terms it was in fact the far more important of the two cases at the time.

A. *Stuart v. Laird and the Elimination of the Intermediate Appellate Judiciary*

STUART v. LAIRD 5 U.S. (1 Cranch) 299 (1803): *Stuart* involved a petition by private parties seeking to overturn a ruling by a circuit court in a land dispute. The petitioners argued that the Justices of the Supreme Court held commissions to be Supreme Court Justices, but not circuit judges. Hence they could not return to sit as circuit judges once the positions held by the Federalist circuit judges were abolished. In addition, the petitioners argued, repeal of the circuit judgeships was unconstitutional because according to Article III of the Constitution, once they had received their commissions, the circuit judges had life tenure (and the judicial independence that is the purpose of granting life tenure). Allowing Congress to abolish the courts undermined judicial independence. Finally, the petitioners argued that Congress could not require the Justices to ride circuit in courts of first instance because this would be a major burden on the Justices and would in effect hinder the Court from performing its constitutionally assigned duties.

The lower court decision in *Stuart,* written by Chief Justice Marshall himself, riding circuit, rejected the petitioner's arguments.[68]

Marshall recused himself from sitting on the appeal to the Supreme Court.[69] Justice Paterson wrote the decision for the Supreme Court. He did not

---

68. Marshall acquiesced to the Jeffersonian Repeal Act, in spite of his privately expressed reservations about its constitutionality. Indeed, Bruce Ackerman suggests that Marshall flirted with the idea of a de facto "strike," in which the Supreme Court Justices would simply refuse to ride circuit. After the Republicans abolished the 1802 term of the Supreme Court, however, Marshall and other Federalist judges had to decide what they would do. Ultimately, they followed the new law. See Ackerman, The Failure of the Founding Fathers, supra n. 59, at 164-165. Professor Powe argues that "Marshall knew better" than to believe that the 1802 Act was constitutional, but that he "also knew [the Justices] were in no position to successfully challenge Jefferson." See Lucas A. Powe, The Politics of American Judicial Review: Reflections on the Marshall, Warren, and Rehnquist Courts, 38 Wake Forest L. Rev. 704 (2003).

69. The reasons are unclear. There was certainly no norm that Supreme Court Justices could not sit on appeals from cases they had decided while riding circuit. (It is worth noting that members of federal circuit courts today normally do not recuse themselves when a decision they participated in is appealed to the full court en banc.) It is perhaps even more mysterious why Marshall would recuse himself in Stuart v. Laird but not in Marbury v. Madison, given that Marshall was the Secretary of State whose failure to deliver Marbury's commission in a timely fashion in the first place gave rise to the litigation in *Marbury.* Moreover, as if this did not demonstrate a sufficient conflict of interest, there was a delicate evidentiary question at the heart of *Marbury*: Had his commission in fact been signed? The key witness would have been Marshall himself!

directly address the question whether the abolition of the circuit judgeships violated the life tenure provisions of Article III. Instead he merely held that the transfer of the case from a circuit court established by the now-repealed 1801 Judiciary Act to a reconstructed circuit court staffed by a Supreme Court Justice riding circuit (none other than Marshall himself) posed no constitutional problems: "Congress have constitutional authority to establish from time to time such inferior tribunals as they may think proper; and to transfer a cause from one such tribunal to another. In this last particular, there are no words in the constitution to prohibit or restrain the exercise of legislative power." Patterson then addressed the objection that the members of the Supreme Court did not have authority to ride circuit without specific commissions as circuit judges:

> Another reason for reversal is, that the judges of the supreme court have no right to sit as circuit judges, not being appointed as such, or in other words, that they ought to have distinct commissions for that purpose. To this objection, which is of recent date, it is sufficient to observe, that practice and acquiescence under it for a period of several years, commencing with the organization of the judicial system, afford an irresistible answer, and have indeed fixed the construction. It is a contemporary interpretation of the most forcible nature. This practical exposition is too strong and obstinate to be shaken or controlled. Of course, the question is at rest, and ought not now to be disturbed.

DISCUSSION

1. *Discretion is the better part of valor.* The Court in *Stuart* in effect upheld the constitutionality of the repeal of the Judiciary Act and therefore acquiesced in the Jeffersonian purge of the Federalist circuit judges. That is why *Stuart* was, in 1803, far more important than the now-famous decision in *Marbury*. *Stuart* signifies the complete capitulation by the Supreme Court to the new political reality of Republican hegemony.

Indeed, read in light of Stuart v. Laird, *Marbury* takes on a very different cast. It is often thought to symbolize the independence of the judiciary from politics and its devotion to the rule of law. As you will presently see, however, Marshall's opinion in *Marbury* offers several "imaginative" readings of the Judiciary Act of 1789 and Article III to avoid giving Marbury his commission and upsetting the Republicans, just as Patterson's opinion in *Stuart* dodged the most difficult constitutional questions about judicial independence to uphold the Republicans' elimination of the circuit judgeships created by the Federalist Party. What unites both decisions is that Marshall and his colleagues backed off from a very serious confrontation and were willing to provide the Jeffersonian purge with the blessing of law.

B. Marbury *and Judicial Review of Legislation*

Marbury v. Madison[70]

5 U.S. (1 Cranch) 137 (1803)

[1]¶1 At the last term, viz. December term, 1801, William Marbury [and others] . . . moved the court for a rule to James Madison, Secretary of State of the United States, to show cause why a mandamus should not issue commanding him to cause to be delivered to them respectively their several commissions as justices of the peace in the District of Columbia. This motion was supported by affidavits of the following facts; that notice of this motion had been given to Mr. Madison; that Mr. Adams, the late president of the United States, nominated the applicants to the senate for their advice and consent to be appointed justices of the peace of the district of Columbia; that the senate advised and consented to the appointments; that commissions in due form were signed by the said president appointing them justices, &c. and that the seal of the United States was in due form affixed to the said commissions by the secretary of state; that the applicants have requested Mr. Madison to deliver them their said commissions, who has not complied with that request; and that their said commissions are withheld from them; that the applicants have made application to Mr. Madison as secretary of state of the United States at his office, for information whether the commissions were signed and sealed as aforesaid; that explicit and satisfactory information has not been given in answer to that inquiry, either by the secretary of state or any officer in the department of state; that application has been made to the secretary of the Senate for a certificate of the nomination of the applicants, and of the advice and consent of the senate, who has declined giving such a certificate; whereupon a rule was laid to show cause on the 4th day of this term. . . . Afterwards, on the 24th of February, the following opinion of the court was delivered by the Chief Justice.

---

70. A useful overview of *Marbury* can be found in William Van Alstyne, A Critical Guide to Marbury v. Madison, 1969 Duke L.J. 1. See also Weinberg, supra n.65; Akhil Reed Amar, *Marbury*, Section 13, and the Original Jurisdiction of the Supreme Court, 56 U. Chi. L. Rev. 443 (1989); William Nelson, Marbury v. Madison and the Rise of Judicial Review (2000); Mark Graber and Micahel Perhac, eds., Marbury versus Madison: Documents and Commentary (2002).

¶1. Compare Marshall's statement of the facts with those presented in our own introduction to the case.

It is, incidentally, a considerable understatement to say only that Madison did not supply "explicit and satisfactory information" to the hapless Marbury. He also failed to defend the suit before the Court, which itself may signify what Marshall called in ¶3 the "peculiar delicacy" of the case.

[2]¶2 At the last term on the affidavits then read and filed with the clerk, a rule was granted in this case, requiring the secretary of state to show cause why a mandamus should not issue, directing him to deliver to William Marbury his commission as a justice of the peace for the county of Washington, in the district of Columbia.

[3] No cause has been shown, and the present motion is for a mandamus. The peculiar delicacy of this case, the novelty of some of its circumstances, and the real difficulty attending the points which occur in it, require a complete exposition of the principles, on which the opinion to be given by the court, is founded. . . .

[4]¶4 In the order in which the court has viewed this subject, the following questions have been considered and decided.

¶2. A writ of mandamus is an order issued by a court to a government officer or lower court commanding the performance of a ministerial (i.e., nondiscretionary) duty pertaining to the office.

¶4. In the course of the opinion, the Court holds (first) that on the facts and law Marbury is entitled to the commission; (second) that a judicial remedy will not interfere improperly with the executive's constitutional discretion; and (third) that mandamus is the appropriate remedy; that respondent Madison cannot assert sovereign immunity; that §13 of the Judiciary Act of 1789 authorizes the issuance of mandamus in this case; but that §13 is unconstitutional.

This is an extraordinary way to order the issues. Courts customarily determine initially whether they have jurisdiction to decide the case and only then, if the answer is affirmative, proceed to other issues. See, e.g., Ex parte McCardle, 74 U.S. (7 Wall.) 506, 512, 514 (1869):

> The first question necessarily is that of jurisdiction; for if the act . . . takes away the jurisdiction [of this Court], it is useless, if not improper, to enter into any discussion of other questions. . . . Without jurisdiction the court cannot proceed at all in any cause. Jurisdiction is power to declare the law, and when it ceases to exist, the only function remaining to the court is that of announcing the fact and dismissing the cause.

Professor William Van Alstyne notes that Marshall has been criticized for deciding unnecessary questions in *Marbury*: "If the Court determined that it had no jurisdiction, it would have no occasion to reach the matter of 'peculiar delicacy' [i.e., the amenability of a cabinet officer to suit]. . . . It was therefore improper for Marshall to begin as he did" (supra n.70, at 7). But Van Alstyne comes to Marshall's defense:

> Of at least equal delicacy was the question of the Court's . . . capacity to second guess the constitutionality of acts of Congress. Since the Court might avoid the necessity of confronting the constitutionality of the Judiciary Act by disposing of the case on other grounds (assuming that it were to find Marbury not entitled to his commission), it should seek to do so where possible, as here. . . . Under this view, perhaps Marshall cannot be faulted for postponing consideration of judicial review and the constitutionality of the Judiciary Act until he had first exhausted other possible bases for disposing of the case.

How valid is this defense? Granting that it is desirable to avoid unnecessary constitutional questions, Marshall did not in fact avoid any constitutional question. Is Van Alstyne suggesting that it was important that Marshall demonstrate that he could not avoid the constitutional question? Of course, Marshall nowhere says that he is striving to avoid a constitutional question, and in fact, his opinion ends up discussing a vast number of constitutional questions—and difficult ones at that, see Amar, *Marbury*, supra n.70.

Note Van Alstyne's suggestion that there was "clearly an 'issue' of sorts which preceded any of those touched upon in the opinion. Specifically, it would appear that Marshall should have recused himself in view of his substantial involvement in the background of this controversy" (supra n.70, at 8). See Note, Disqualification of Judges and Justices in the Federal Courts, 86 Harv. L. Rev. 736 (1973).

1st. Has the applicant a right to the commission he demands?

2dly. If he has a right, and that right has been violated, do the laws of his country afford him a remedy?

3dly. If they do afford him a remedy, is it a mandamus issuing from this court?

[5] The first object of inquiry is, 1st. Has the applicant a right to the commission he demands?

[6] His right originates in an act of congress passed in February 1801, concerning the district of Columbia . . . [which] enacts, "that there shall be appointed . . . such number of discreet persons to be justices of the peace as the president of the United States shall, from time to time think expedient, to continue in office for five years."

[7] It appears, from the affidavits, that in compliance with this law, a commission for William Marbury as a justice of peace for the county of Washington, was signed by John Adams, then president of the United States; after which the seal of the United States was affixed to it; but the commission has never reached the person for whom it was made out. . . .

[8] Some point of time must be taken, when the power of the executive over an officer, not removable at his will, must cease. That point of time must be, when the constitutional power of appointment has been exercised. And this power has been exercised, when the last act, required from the person possessing the power has been performed: this last act is the signature of the commission. . . .

[9] The commission being signed, the subsequent duty of the secretary of state is prescribed by law, and not to be guided by the will of the president. He is to affix the seal of the United States to the commission, and is to record it. This is not a proceeding which may be varied, if the judgment of the executive shall suggest one more eligible; but is a precise course accurately marked out by law, and is to be strictly pursued. . . .

[10] It has also occurred as possible, and barely possible, that the transmission of the commission, and the acceptance thereof, might be deemed necessary to complete the right of the plaintiff. The transmission of the commission is a practice, directed by convenience, but not by law. It cannot, therefore, be necessary to constitute the appointment. . . . The appointment is the sole act of the president; the transmission of the commission is the sole act of the officer to whom that duty is assigned, and may be accelerated or retarded by circumstances which can have no influence on the appointment. A commission is transmitted to a person already appointed; not to a person appointed or not, as the letter inclosing the commission should happen to get into the post-office and reach him in safety, or to miscarry. . . .

[11] If the transmission of a commission be not considered as necessary to give validity to an appointment, still less is its acceptance. The appointment is the sole act of the president; the acceptance is the sole act of the officer, and is, in plain common sense, posterior to the appointment. As he may resign, so may he refuse to accept: but neither the one nor the other is capable of rendering the appointment a nonentity. . . .

[12] It is, therefore, decidedly the opinion of the court, that when a commission has been signed by the president, the appointment is made; and that the commission is complete, when the seal of the United States has been affixed to it by the secretary of state.

[13] Where an officer is removable at the will of the executive, the circumstance which completes his appointment is of no concern; because the act is at any

time revocable; and the commission may be arrested, if still in the office. But when the officer is not removable at the will of the executive, the appointment is not revocable, and cannot be annulled: it has conferred legal rights which cannot be resumed. The discretion of the executive is to be exercised, until the appointment has been made. But having once made the appointment, his power over the office is terminated, in all cases where, by law, the officer is not removable by him. The right to the office is then in the person appointed, and he has the absolute unconditional power of accepting or rejecting it.

[14][¶14] Mr. Marbury, then, since his commission was signed by the President and sealed by the secretary of state, was appointed; and as the law creating the office, gave the officer a right to hold for five years, independent of the executive, the appointment was not revocable, but vested in the officer legal rights, which are protected by the laws of his country.

[15] To withhold his commission, therefore, is an act deemed by the court not warranted by law, but violative of a vested legal right.

[16] This brings us to the second inquiry; which is, 2dly. If he has a right, and that right has been violated, do the laws of his country afford him a remedy?

[17] The very essence of civil liberty certainly consists in the right of every individual to claim the protection of the laws whenever he receives an injury. One of the first duties of government is to afford that protection. . . .

[18] The government of the United States has been emphatically termed a government of laws, and not of men. It will certainly cease to deserve this high appellation, if the laws furnish no remedy for the violation of a vested legal right.

[19] If this obloquy is to be cast on the jurisprudence of our country, it must arise from the peculiar character of the case.

[20] It behooves us then to enquire whether there be in its composition any ingredient which shall exempt it from legal investigation, or exclude the injured party from legal redress. . . . Is it in the nature of the transaction? Is the act of delivering or withholding a commission to be considered as a mere political act, belonging to the executive department alone, for the performance of which, entire confidence is placed by our constitution in the supreme executive; and for any misconduct respecting which, the injured individual has no remedy. That there may be such cases is not to be questioned; but that every act of duty, to be performed in any of the great departments of government, constitutes such a case is not to be admitted. [Marshall then discusses and rejects the claim that Madison is entitled to sovereign immunity merely because he is sued in his official capacity as Secretary of State.] It follows then that the question, whether the legality of an act of the head of a department be examinable in a court of justice or not, must always depend on the nature of that act. If some acts be examinable, and others not, there must be some rule of law to guide the court in the exercise of its jurisdiction. In some instances there may be difficulty in applying the rule to particular cases; but there cannot, it is believed, be much difficulty in laying down the rule.

¶14. Marshall's assumption that Congress generally can prevent the President from revoking executive appointments was disapproved in Myers v. United States, 272 U.S. 52 (1926).

[21] By the constitution of the United States, the President is invested with certain important political powers, in the exercise of which he is to use his own discretion, and is accountable only to his country in his political character, and to his own conscience. To aid him in the performance of these duties, he is authorized to appoint certain officers, who act by his authority and in conformity with his orders. In such cases, their acts are his acts; and whatever opinion may be entertained of the manner in which executive discretion may be used, still there exists, and can exist, no power to control that discretion. The subjects are political. They respect the nation, not individual rights, and being entrusted to the executive, the decision of the executive is conclusive. The application of this remark will be perceived by adverting to the act of congress for establishing the department of foreign affairs. This office, as his duties were prescribed by that act, is to conform precisely to the will of the President. He is the mere organ by whom that will is communicated. The acts of such an officer, as an officer, can never be examinable by the courts. But when the legislature proceeds to impose on that officer other duties; when he is directed peremptorily to perform certain acts; when the rights of individuals are dependent on the performance of those acts; he is so far the officer of the law; is amenable to the laws for his conduct; and cannot at his discretion sport away the vested rights of others. The conclusion from this reasoning is, that where the heads of departments are the political or confidential agents of the executive, merely to execute the will of the President, or rather to act in cases in which the executive possesses a constitutional or legal discretion, nothing can be more perfectly clear than that their acts are only politically examinable. But where a specific duty is assigned by law, and individual rights depend upon the performance of that duty, it seems equally clear that the individual who considers himself injured, has a right to resort to the laws of his country for a remedy. . . .

[22] The power of nominating to the senate, and the power of appointing the person nominated, are political powers, to be exercised by the President according to his own discretion. When he has made an appointment, he has exercised his whole power, and his discretion has been completely applied to the case. If, by law, the officer be removable at the will of the President, then a new appointment may be immediately made, and the rights of the officer are terminated. But as a fact which has existed cannot be made never to have existed, the appointment cannot be annihilated; and consequently if the officer is by law not removable at the will of the President; the rights he has acquired are protected by the law, and are not resumeable by the President. They cannot be extinguished by executive authority, and he has the privilege of asserting them in like manner as if they had been derived from any other source.

[23] The question whether a right has vested or not, is, in its nature, judicial, and must be tried by the judicial authority. If, for example, Mr. Marbury had taken the oaths of a magistrate, and proceeded to act as one; in consequence of which a suit had been instituted against him, in which his defence had depended on his being a magistrate; the validity of his appointment must have been determined by judicial authority.

[24] So, if he conceives that, by virtue of his appointment, he has a legal right, either to the commission which has been made out for him, or to a copy of that commission, it is equally a question examinable in a court, and the decision of the

court upon it must depend on the opinion entertained of his appointment. That question has been discussed, and the opinion is, that the latest point of time which can be taken as that at which the appointment was complete, and evidenced, was when, after the signature of the president, the seal of the United States was affixed to the commission.

[25] It is then the opinion of the court, 1st. That by signing the commission of Mr. Marbury, the president of the United States appointed him a justice of peace, for the county of Washington, in the district of Columbia; and that the seal of the United States, affixed thereto by the secretary of state, is conclusive testimony of the verity of the signature, and of the completion of the appointment; and that the appointment conferred on him a legal right to the office for the space of five years.

[26] 2dly. That, having this legal title to the office, he has a consequent right to the commission; a refusal to deliver which, is a plain violation of that right, for which the laws of his country afford him a remedy.

[27] It remains to be inquired whether, 3dly. He is entitled to the remedy for which he applies. This depends on,

1st. The nature of the writ applied for, and,

2dly. The power of this court. . . .

[Marshall discusses the circumstances under which mandamus is appropriate at common law, to conclude:]

[28] This, then, is a plain case for a mandamus, either to deliver the commission, or a copy of it from the record; and it only remains to be inquired, Whether it can issue from this court.

[29][¶29-30] The act to establish the judicial courts of the United States authorizes the supreme court "to issue writs of mandamus, in cases warranted by the

---

¶29-30. The text of §13 of the Judiciary Act of 1789 provides that:

> [T]he Supreme Court shall have exclusive jurisdiction of all controversies of a civil nature, where a state is a party, except between a state and its citizens; and except also between a state and citizens of other states, or aliens, in which latter case it shall have original but not exclusive jurisdiction. And shall have exclusively all such jurisdiction of suits or proceedings against ambassadors, or other public ministers, or their domestics, or domestic servants, as a court of law can have or exercise consistently with the law of nations: and original, but not exclusive jurisdiction of all suits brought by ambassadors, or other public ministers, or in which a consul, or vice consul, shall be a party. And the trial of issues in fact in the Supreme Court, in all actions at law against citizens of the United States, shall be by jury. The Supreme Court shall also have appellate jurisdiction from the circuit courts and courts of the several states, in the cases herein after specially provided for: And shall have power to issue writs of prohibition to the district courts, when proceeding as courts of admiralty and maritime jurisdiction, and writs of mandamus, in cases warranted by the principles and usages of law, to any courts appointed, or persons holding office, under the authority of the United States.

Note that the first portion of §13, following Article III, §2, of the Constitution, grants the Supreme Court original jurisdiction in cases affecting, inter alia, "public ministers." Read in isolation, the term might be thought to include the Secretary of State of the United States, but the context and history of Article III make quite clear that "this refers to diplomatic and consular representatives accredited to the United States by foreign powers. . . ." Ex parte Gruber, 269 U.S. 302 (1925). See also The Federalist No. 81 (Hamilton). Why does Article III put those cases that it does within the Court's original jurisdiction? For the suggestion that the Original Jurisdiction Clause was largely a venue provision linked to issues of geography and litigation convenience, see Amar, *Marbury*, supra n.70.

principles and usages of law, to any courts appointed, or persons holding office, under the authority of the United States."

[30] The secretary of state, being a person holding an office under the authority of the United States, is precisely within the letter of the description; and if this court is not authorized to issue a writ of mandamus to such an officer, it must be because the law is unconstitutional, and therefore absolutely incapable of conferring the authority, and assigning the duties which its words purport to confer and assign.

[31]¶31-41 The constitution vests the whole judicial power of the United States in one supreme court, and such inferior courts as congress shall, from time to time, ordain and establish. This power is expressly extended to all cases arising under the laws of the United States; and consequently, in some form, may be exercised over the present case; because the right claimed is given by a law of the United States.

[32] In the distribution of this power it is declared that "the supreme court shall have original jurisdiction in all cases affecting ambassadors, other public ministers and consuls, and those in which a state shall be a party. In all other cases, the supreme court shall have appellate jurisdiction."

[33] It has been insisted, at the bar, that as the original grant of jurisdiction, to the supreme and inferior courts, is general, and the clause, assigning original jurisdiction to the supreme court, contains no negative or restrictive words; the power remains to the legislature, to assign original jurisdiction to that court in other cases than those specified in the article which has been recited; provided those cases belong to the judicial power of the United States.

[34] If it had been intended to leave it in the discretion of the legislature to apportion the judicial power between the supreme and inferior courts according to the will of that body, it would certainly have been useless to have proceeded further than to have defined the judicial power, and the tribunals in which it should be vested. The subsequent part of the section is mere surplusage, is entirely without meaning, if such is to be the construction. If congress remains at liberty to give this court appellate jurisdiction, where the constitution has declared their jurisdiction shall be original; and original jurisdiction where the constitution has declared it shall be appellate; the distribution of jurisdiction, made in the constitution, is form without substance.

Marshall asserts that §13 grants the Court jurisdiction to issue a writ of mandamus in this case. Is this the most plausible interpretation of §13? Cf. 28 U.S.C. §1651: "Writs: The Supreme Court and all courts established by Act of Congress may issue all writs necessary or appropriate in aid of their respective jurisdictions and agreeable to the usages and principles of law." Should Marshall have been influenced by the fact that many of the same persons who drafted Article III also drafted the Judiciary Act of 1789 and by the canon (long established in England) that ambiguous statutes should be construed, where possible, in a manner consistent with fundamental law (in this case the fundamental written law of the Constitution)?

¶31-41. *Marbury*'s holding that the original jurisdiction of the Supreme Court cannot be enlarged remains the law, but the dictum that Congress cannot confer appellate jurisdiction in the enumerated cases within the Court's original jurisdiction has not been followed. See, e.g., Ames v. Kansas, 111 U.S. 449 (1884).

[35] Affirmative words are often, in their operation, negative of other objects than those affirmed; and in this case, a negative or exclusive sense must be given to them or they have no operation at all.

[36] It cannot be presumed that any clause in the constitution is intended to be without effect; and therefore such a construction is inadmissible, unless the words require it.

[37] If the solicitude of the convention, respecting our peace with foreign powers, induced a provision that the supreme court should take original jurisdiction in cases which might be supposed to affect them; yet the clause would have proceeded no further than to provide for such cases, if no further restriction on the powers of congress had been intended. That they should have appellate jurisdiction in all other cases, with such exceptions as congress might make, is no restriction; unless the words be deemed exclusive of original jurisdiction.

[38] When an instrument organizing fundamentally a judicial system, divides it into one supreme, and so many inferior courts as the legislature may ordain and establish; then enumerates its powers, and proceeds so far to distribute them, as to define the jurisdiction of the supreme court by declaring the cases in which it shall take original jurisdiction, and that in others it shall take appellate jurisdiction; the plain import of the words seems to be, that in one class of cases its jurisdiction is original, and not appellate; in the other it is appellate, and not original. If any other construction would render the clause inoperative, that is an additional reason for rejecting such other construction, and for adhering to their obvious meaning.

[39] To enable this court then to issue a mandamus, it must be shown to be an exercise of appellate jurisdiction, or to be necessary to enable them to exercise appellate jurisdiction.

[40] It has been stated at the bar that the appellate jurisdiction may be exercised in a variety of forms, and that if it be the will of the legislature that a mandamus should be used for that purpose, that will must be obeyed. This is true, yet the jurisdiction must be appellate, not original.

[41] It is the essential criterion of appellate jurisdiction, that it revises and corrects the proceedings in a cause already instituted, and does not create that cause. Although, therefore, a mandamus may be directed to courts, yet to issue such a writ to an officer for the delivery of a paper, is in effect the same as to sustain an original action for that paper, and therefore seems not to belong to appellate, but to original jurisdiction. Neither is it necessary in such a case as this, to enable the court to exercise its appellate jurisdiction.

[42] The authority, therefore, given to the supreme court, by the act establishing the judicial courts of the United States, to issue writs of mandamus to public officers, appears not to be warranted by the constitution; and it becomes necessary to inquire whether a jurisdiction, so conferred, can be exercised.

[43] The question, whether an act, repugnant to the constitution, can become the law of the land, is a question deeply interesting to the United States; but, happily, not of an intricacy proportioned to its interest. It seems only necessary to recognize certain principles, supposed to have been long and well established, to decide it.

[44] That the people have an original right to establish, for their future government, such principles as, in their opinion, shall most conduce to their own happiness, is the basis, on which the whole American fabric has been erected. The

exercise of this original right is a very great exertion; nor can it, nor ought it to be frequently repeated. The principles, therefore, so established, are deemed fundamental. And as the authority, from which they proceed, is supreme, and can seldom act, they are designed to be permanent.

[45] This original and supreme will organizes the government, and assigns, to different departments, their respective powers. It may either stop here; or establish certain limits not to be transcended by those departments.

[46] The government of the United States is of the latter description. The powers of the legislature are defined, and limited; and that those limits may not be mistaken, or forgotten, the constitution is written. To what purpose are powers limited, and to what purpose is that limitation committed to writing, if these limits may, at any time, be passed by those intended to be restrained? The distinction, between a government with limited and unlimited powers, is abolished, if those limits do not confine the persons on whom they are imposed, and if acts prohibited and acts allowed, are of equal obligation. It is a proposition too plain to be contested, that the constitution controls any legislative act repugnant to it; or, that the legislature may alter the constitution by an ordinary act.

[47] Between these alternatives there is no middle ground. The constitution is either a superior, paramount law, unchangeable by ordinary means, or it is on a level with ordinary legislative acts, and like other acts, is alterable when the legislature shall please to alter it.

[48] If the former part of the alternative be true, then a legislative act contrary to the constitution is not law: if the latter part be true, then written constitutions are absurd attempts, on the part of the people, to limit a power, in its own nature illimitable.

[49] Certainly all those who have framed written constitutions contemplate them as forming the fundamental and paramount law of the nation, and consequently the theory of every such government must be, that an act of the legislature, repugnant to the constitution, is void.

[50] This theory is essentially attached to a written constitution, and is consequently to be considered, by this court, as one of the fundamental principles of our society. It is not therefore to be lost sight of in the further consideration of this subject.

[51] [¶51-54]

If an act of the legislature, repugnant to the constitution, is void, does it, notwithstanding its invalidity, bind the courts, and oblige them to give it effect? Or, in other words, though it be not law, does it constitute a rule as operative as if it was a

---

¶51-54. What is Marshall's argument based on the "province and duty of the judicial department"? If one concedes that the Constitution is "law" and that it is paramount to legislative enactments, does it necessarily follow that the judiciary has authority to decide whether a congressional enactment violates the Constitution? Is the Constitution a law, just like other laws that come within a court's purview? Consider Judge Learned Hand's response:

> It is of course true that, when a court decides whether a constitution authorizes a statute, it must first decide what each means, and that, so far, is the kind of duty that courts often exercise, just as they decide conflicts between earlier and later precedents. But if a court, having concluded that a constitution did not authorize the statute, goes on to annul it, its power to

law? This would be to overthrow in fact what was established in theory; and would seem, at first view, an absurdity too gross to be insisted on. It shall, however, receive a more attentive consideration.

[52] It is emphatically the province and duty of the judicial department to say what the law is. Those who apply the rule to particular cases, must of necessity expound and interpret that rule. If two laws conflict with each other, the courts must decide on the operation of each.

[53] So if a law be in opposition to the constitution; if both the law and the constitution apply to a particular case, so that the court must either decide that case conformably to the law, disregarding the constitution; or conformably to the constitution, disregarding the law; the court must determine which of these conflicting rules governs the case. This is of the very essence of judicial duty.

> do so depends upon an authority that is not involved when only statutes or precedents are involved. For a later statute will prevail over an earlier, if they conflict, because a legislature confessedly has authority to change the law as it exists. So too when a court finds two precedents in conflict, it must follow the later one, if that be a decision of a higher court, and it is free to do so if it be one of its own, because, again, confessedly it has authority to change its mind. But when a court declares that a constitution does not authorize a statute, it reviews and reverses an earlier decision of the legislature: and however well based its authority to do so may be, it does not follow from what it does in other instances in which the same question does not arise. . . .

The Bill of Rights 9-10 (1958).

What earlier decision of the legislature does a court review and reverse when it "declares that a constitution does not authorize a statute"? Does Congress implicitly make a constitutional decision with respect to each piece of legislation it enacts?

In appraising Marshall's argument, consider that several European and South American nations have written constitutions as well as courts that perform essentially the same functions as our courts, but that their courts do not adjudge the substantive constitutionality of legislation. Note also that, in nonconstitutional contexts, courts are sometimes required to accept as binding legal and factual determinations by other bodies, even though the courts may believe such determinations to be erroneous. See, e.g., 9 U.S.C. §10; United Steelworkers v. Enterprise Wheel & Car Corp., 363 U.S. 593 (1960).

Compare Marshall's argument with Hamilton's in The Federalist No. 78:

> The interpretation of the laws is the proper and peculiar province of the courts. A constitution is, in fact, and must be regarded by the judges as a fundamental law. It therefore belongs to them to ascertain its meaning, as well as the meaning of any particular act proceeding from the legislative body. If there should happen to be an irreconcilable variance between the two, that which has the superior obligation and validity ought, of course, to be preferred; or, in other words, the Constitution ought to be preferred to the statute, the intention of the people to the intention of their agents. Nor does this conclusion by any means suppose a superiority of the judicial to the legislative power. It only supposes that the power of the people is superior to both; and that where the will of the legislature, declared in its statutes, stands in opposition to that of the people, declared in the Constitution, the judges ought to be governed by the latter rather than the former. They ought to regulate their decisions by the fundamental laws, rather than by those which are not fundamental.

[54] If then the courts are to regard the constitution; and the constitution is superior to any ordinary act of the legislature, the constitution, and not such ordinary act, must govern the case to which they both apply.

[55] Those then who controvert the principle that the constitution is to be considered, in court, as a paramount law, are reduced to the necessity of maintaining that courts must lose their eyes on the constitution, and see only the law.

[56]¶56

This doctrine would subvert the very foundation of all written constitutions. It would declare that an act, which, according to the principles and theory of our government, is entirely void; is yet, in practice, completely obligatory. It would declare, that if the legislature shall do what is expressly forbidden, such act, notwithstanding the express prohibition, is in reality effectual. It would be giving to the legislature a practical and real omnipotence, with the same breath which professes to restrict their powers within narrow limits. It is prescribing limits, and declaring that those limits may be passed at pleasure.

[57]¶57 That it thus reduces to nothing what we have deemed the greatest improvement on political institutions—a written constitution—would of itself be sufficient, in America, where written constitutions have been viewed with so much reverence, for rejecting the construction. But the peculiar expressions of the constitution of the United States furnish additional arguments in favour of its rejection.

¶56. This paragraph implies an argument for judicial review reminiscent of Hamilton's in The Federalist No. 78:

> By a limited Constitution, I understand one which contains certain specified exceptions to the legislative authority; such, for instance, as that it shall pass no bills of attainder, no ex-post-facto laws, and the like. Limitations of this kind can be preserved in practice no other way than through the medium of courts of justice, whose duty it must be to declare all acts contrary to the manifest tenor of the Constitution void. Without this, all the reservations of particular rights or privileges would amount to nothing. . . .
>
> If it be said that the legislative body are themselves the constitutional judges of their own powers, and that the construction they put upon them is conclusive upon the other departments, it may be answered, . . . [i]t is far more rational to suppose, that the courts were designed to be an intermediate body between the people and the legislature, in order, among other things, to keep the latter within the limits assigned to their authority. . . .
>
> [The] independence of judges is . . . requisite to guard the Constitution and the rights of individuals from the effects of those ill humours which the arts of designing men, or the influence of particular conjunctures, sometimes disseminate among the people themselves, and which, though they speedily give place to better information, and more deliberate reflection, have a tendency in the meantime, to occasion dangerous innovations in the government, and serious oppressions of the minor party in the community.

¶57. Here, as in ¶¶49-50, Marshall seeks support for his argument in the fact that ours is a written constitution. Granting that the argument for judicial review would be more difficult to maintain if our Constitution were not written, does the fact that it is written affirmatively support the argument? What purposes, other than providing guidance for the judiciary, can a written constitution serve? In any case, wouldn't you expect the authorization for judicial review, if there were any, to appear in the text of a written constitution?

[58][¶58-61]

The judicial power of the United States is extended to all cases arising under the constitution.

[59] Could it be the intention of those who gave this power, to say that, in using it, the constitution should not be looked into? That a case arising under the constitution should be decided without examining the instrument under which it arises?

[60] This is too extravagant to be maintained.

[61] In some cases then, the constitution must be looked into by the judges. And if they can open it at all, what part of it are they forbidden to read, or to obey?

[62][¶62-68] There are many other parts of the constitution which serve to illustrate this subject.

[63] It is declared that "no tax or duty shall be laid on articles exported from any state." Suppose a duty on the export of cotton, of tobacco, or of flour; and a suit instituted to recover it. Ought judgment to be rendered in such a case? Ought the judges to close their eyes on the constitution, and only see the law?

¶58-61. Marshall here makes an argument based on the text of Article III, §2—"The judicial Power shall extend to all Cases . . . arising under this Constitution. . . ." Outline the necessary steps of the argument, some of which may be only implicit in Marshall's discussion.

Note initially that Article III, §2 is in terms only a grant of jurisdiction. Some jurisdictional provisions—e.g., the Article III provisions relating to admiralty and suits between states—have been held to confer a general lawmaking power. See Hart & Wechsler's The Federal Courts and the Federal System 651-663 (Richard Fallon, Jr. et al. eds., 6th ed. 2009). But jurisdiction does not entail a general lawmaking or law-interpreting authority over all or any issues in the case. For example, in cases coming within the diversity jurisdiction, federal courts must adhere to (even erroneous) state court interpretations of state statutes and constitutions as well as to state judge-made law. See Erie R.R. v. Tompkins, 304 U.S. 64 (1938).

Nonetheless, wouldn't it be pointless to confer federal jurisdiction over "Cases arising under this Constitution" if no issues of constitutional interpretation were open to the courts? But if one concedes this much, does it follow that all issues of constitutional interpretation are open to federal judiciary, and in particular does it follow that issues of the constitutionality of acts of Congress are open? At least two other kinds of cases might arise under the Constitution. First, the argument for federal judicial review of allegedly unconstitutional acts of state legislatures, judges, and officials is very strong, but without the "arising under the Constitution" clause, there would be no federal jurisdiction in many such cases. Second, it might be thought that the courts should consider claims that federal officers have acted unconstitutionally. The colonial experience gave the framers good cause to distrust executive officials; moreover, might not one reasonably conclude that less deference is due the actions of lower-level officers than those of Congress or of the President himself?

(The question posed in the last sentence of ¶61 is the wrong one, isn't it? It is not a matter of what parts of the Constitution the judges may look into, but under what circumstances they may look into it.)

¶62-68. You will not again encounter such easy constitutional issues as these. Does the possibility that Congress might enact blatantly unconstitutional legislation entail or imply judicial authority to hold the legislation unconstitutional? To whom is each of these provisions immediately addressed? To whom is the provision involved in *Marbury* immediately addressed?

[64] The constitution declares that "no bill or attainder of ex post facto law shall be passed."

[65] If, however, such a bill should be passed and a person should be prosecuted under it; must the court condemn to death those victims whom the constitution endeavors to preserve?

[66] "No person," says the constitution, "shall be convicted of treason unless on the testimony of two witnesses to the same overt act, or on confession in open court."

[67] Here the language of the constitution is addressed especially to the courts. It prescribes, directly for them, a rule of evidence not to be departed from. If the legislature should change that rule, and declare one witness, or a confession *out* of court, sufficient for conviction, must the constitutional principle yield to the legislative act?

[68] From these, and many other selections which might be made, it is apparent, that the framers of the constitution contemplated that instrument, as a rule for the government of *courts*, as well as of the legislature.

[69][¶69-71]

¶69-71. Does Marshall's "oath of office" argument prove too much? See Article VI, cl. 3, which requires all state and federal officials to swear or affirm to support the Constitution, and consider this excerpt from Judge Gibson's dissent in Eakin v. Raub, 12 Serg. & Rawle 330 (Pa. 1825), which involved the authority of the Pennsylvania Supreme Court to review the constitutionality of acts of the state legislature. Judge Gibson's opinion refers to and counters almost every one of Marshall's arguments in *Marbury*:

> The oath to support the constitution is not peculiar to the judges, but is taken indiscriminately by every officer of the government and is designed rather as a test of the political principles of the man, than to bind the officer in the discharge of his duty: otherwise, it were difficult to determine, what operation it is to have in the case of a recorder of deeds, for instance, who, in the execution of his office, has nothing to do with the constitution. But granting it to relate to the official conduct of the judge, as well as every other officer, and not to his political principles, still, it must be understood in reference to supporting the constitution, only as far as that may be involved in his official duty, and consequently, if his official duty does not comprehend an inquiry into the authority of the legislature, neither does his oath.
>
> . . . Granting that the object of the oath is to secure a support of the constitution in the discharge of official duty, its terms may be satisfied by restraining it to official duty in the exercise of the ordinary judicial powers. Thus, the constitution may furnish a rule of construction, where a particular interpretation of a law would conflict with some constitutional principle; and such interpretation, where it may, is always to be avoided. But the oath was more probably designed to secure the powers of each of the different branches from being usurped by any of the rest; for instance, to prevent the house of representatives from erecting itself into a court of judicature, or the supreme court from attempting to control the legislature: and in this view, the oath furnishes an argument equally plausible against the right of the judiciary. . . . The official oath, then, relates only to the official conduct of the officer, and does not prove that he ought to stray from the path of his ordinary business, to search for violations of duty in the business of others: nor does it, as supposed, define the powers of the officer.
>
> But do not the judges do a positive act in violation of the constitution, when they give effect to an unconstitutional law? Not if the law has been passed according to the forms established in the constitution. The fallacy of the question is, in supposing that the judiciary adopts the acts of the legislature as its own; whereas, the enactment of a law and the interpretation of it are not concurrent acts, and as the judiciary is not required to concur in the enactment, neither is it in the breach of the constitution which may be the consequence of the enactment; the fault is imputable to the legislature, and on it the responsibility exclusively rests.

Why otherwise does it direct the judges to take an oath to support it? This oath certainly applies, in an especial manner, to their conduct in their official character. How immoral to impose it on them, if they were to be used as the instruments, and the knowing instruments, for violating what they swear to support!

[70] The oath of office, too, imposed by the legislature, is completely demonstrative of the legislative opinion on this subject. It is in these words, "I do solemnly swear that I will administer justice without respect to persons, and do equal right to the poor and to the rich; and that I will faithfully and impartially discharge all the duties incumbent on me as ______, according to the best of my abilities and understanding, agreeably to *the constitution*, and laws of the United States."

[71] Why does a judge swear to discharge his duties agreeably to the constitution of the United States, if that constitution forms no rule for his government? If it is closed upon him, and cannot be inspected by him?

[72] If such be the real state of things, this is worse than solemn mockery. To prescribe, or to take this oath, becomes equally a crime.

[73][¶73-74]

¶73-74. Chief Justice Marshall makes an almost offhand reference to the Supremacy Clause of Article VI of the Constitution. Consider the argument of Herbert Wechsler, Toward Neutral Principles of Constitutional Law, 73 Harv. L. Rev. 1 (1959):

> . . . I must make clear why I believe the power of the courts is grounded in the language of the Constitution and is not a mere interpolation. [He quotes the Supremacy Clause. Wechsler takes issue with the argument of Judge Learned Hand that the Clause means only that, in Hand's language,] "state courts would at times have to decide whether state laws and constitutions, or even a federal statute, were in conflict with the federal constitution" but [Hand denies that this supports the grant of authority to federal courts, including the Supreme Court, to assess the constitutionality of federal legislation].
>
> Are you satisfied, however, to view the supremacy clause in this way, as a grant of jurisdiction to state courts, implying a denial of the power and the duty of all others? This certainly is not its necessary meaning; it may be construed as a mandate to all of officialdom including courts, with a special and emphatic admonition that it binds the judges of the previously independent states. That the latter is the proper reading seems to me persuasive when the other relevant provisions of the Constitution are brought into view.
>
> Article III, section 1 declares that the federal judicial power "shall be vested in one supreme Court, and in such inferior Courts as the Congress may from time to time ordain and establish." This represented, as you know, one of the major compromises of the Constitutional Convention and relegated the establishment vel non of lower federal courts to the discretion of the Congress. None might have been established, with the consequence that, as in other federalisms, judicial work of first instance would all have been remitted to state courts. Article III, section 2 goes on, however, to delineate the scope of the federal judicial power, providing that it "shall extend [inter alia] to all Cases, in Law and Equity, arising under this Constitution . . ." and, further, that the Supreme Court "shall have appellate jurisdiction" in such cases "with such Exceptions, and under such Regulations as the Congress shall make." Surely this means, as section 25 of the Judiciary Act of 1789 took it to mean, that if a state court passes on a constitutional issue, as the supremacy clause provides that it should, its judgment is reviewable, subject to congressional exceptions, by the Supreme Court, in which

It is also not entirely unworthy of observation, that in declaring what shall be the *supreme* law of the land, the *constitution* itself is first mentioned; and not the laws of the United States generally, but those only which shall be made in *pursuance* of the constitution, have that rank.

[74] Thus, the particular phraseology of the constitution of the United States confirms and strengthens the principle, supposed to be essential to all written constitutions, that a law repugnant to the constitution is void; and that *courts*, as well as other departments, are bound by that instrument.

> event that Court must have no less authority and duty to accord priority to constitutional provisions than the court that it reviews. And such state cases might have encompassed every case in which a constitutional issue could possibly arise, since, as I have said, Congress need not and might not have exerted its authority to establish "inferior" federal courts. . . .

If Wechsler is persuasive in arguing that federal judges can properly inquire into any question under the U.S. Constitution that state judges can inquire into, does it also imply that state judges can inquire into the constitutionality of congressional legislation? (Professor Wechsler assumes that it does, but does not explain why.) Note the different way that Article VI treats "laws" and "treaties" and consider Van Alstyne's suggestion that "[t]he phrase 'in pursuance' might also mean merely that only those statutes adopted by Congress after the re-establishment and reconstitution of Congress pursuant to the Constitution itself shall be the supreme law of the land, whereas acts of the earlier Continental Congress constituted merely under the Articles of Confederation, would not necessarily be supreme and binding upon the several states" (supra, at 21).

Assuming that you find the Marshall-Wechsler argument or, for that matter, any other textual argument for judicial review, persuasive, what are the implications with regard to the scope (and therefore, in effect, the frequency) of such review? Recall Justice Chase's conclusion in *Hylton*, that even if the power of judicial review be conceded, "I will never exercise it, but in a very clear case." Was *Marbury* itself such a "clear case"? Presumably, Chase thought it was inasmuch as he joined in Marshall's opinion. What follows, however, if the Constitution is less than clear? Does *Marbury* itself support the proposition that the Court should prefer its own (by definition) debatable reading to one asserted by Congress or the President? Imagine that Marshall's opinion in *Marbury* had been accompanied by a dissenting opinion attacking his interpretation of Article III. Would that mean that Article III is in fact "unclear" or, rather, that the dissenting Justice(s) were inexplicably incompetent in their understanding of the English language?

Consider the approach toward judicial review sketched in Gottfried Dietze, Judicial Review in Europe, 55 Mich. L. Rev. 539, 541 (1957): "European courts have usually tested the formal constitutionality of the laws. This consists of a review of the process of enactment. If it was discovered that the procedural requirements of the constitution had not been complied with, the law in question was declared void. On the other hand, the testing of the content of a legislative act for its 'intrinsic' constitutionality was the exception rather than the rule." Is such an emphasis on procedural requirements a plausible interpretation of the language of "congruence" in Article VI? Note, however, that Europe has become considerably friendlier to substantive judicial review in the half-century since Dietze wrote. See, e.g., Victor Ferreres, Constitutional Courts and Democratic Values: A European Perspective (2009).

[75][¶75]
The rule must be discharged.

DISCUSSION

1. *Marshall's legal analysis.* Marshall's argument that the 1789 Judiciary Act is unconstitutional turns on his construction of the text of the 1789 Act and Article III, §2. See ¶¶29-30, in which Marshall assumes that that §13 expands the Court's original jurisdiction by giving it the power to issue a writ of mandamus against the Secretary of State. See also ¶¶31-41, in which Marshall reads Article III, §2 to mean that Congress cannot enlarge the original jurisdiction of the Supreme Court to cover suits against the Secretary of State (and cannot use the Exceptions and Regulations Clause, which appears at the end of §2, to alter it).

Look closely at the text of §13 (reprinted in the footnote to ¶¶29-30). Many scholars have criticized Marshall for creating a constitutional conflict that could easily have been avoided. First, one might read §13 to say that when courts have *appellate* jurisdiction, they may issue writs of mandamus. Second, one might read §13 to distinguish between *jurisdiction* (the power to hear a case at all) and *remedy* (the power to resolve the case in a particular way). The last part of §13 might say only that *when* the court has lawful jurisdiction, courts may issue writs of mandamus. See Akhil Reed Amar, *Marbury*, Section 13, and the Original Jurisdiction

---

¶75. Consider Robert McCloskey, The American Supreme Court 25-27 (5th ed. 2010):

> The decision is a masterwork of indirection, a brilliant example of Marshall's capacity to sidestep danger while seeming to court it, to advance in one direction while his opponents are looking in another. . . . The danger of a head-on clash with the Jeffersonians was averted by the denial of jurisdiction: but, at the same time, the declaration that the commission was illegally withheld scotched any impression that the Court condoned the administration's behavior. These negative maneuvers were artful achievements in their own right. But the touch of genius is evident when Marshall, not content with having rescued a bad situation, seizes the occasion to set forth the doctrine of judicial review. It is easy for us to see in retrospect that the occasion was golden. The attention of the Republicans was focused on the question of Marbury's commission, and they cared very little how the Court went about justifying a hands-off policy so long as that policy was followed. Moreover, the Court was in a delightful position, so common in its history but so confusing to its critics, of rejecting and assuming power in a single breath, for the Congress had tried here to give the judges an authority they could not constitutionally accept and the judges were high-mindedly refusing. The moment for immortal statement was at hand all right, but only a judge of Marshall's discernment could have recognised it.

McCloskey obviously admires Marshall's political sagacity, which allowed him to avoid the dangerous confrontation with the Jefferson Administration that would have signaled the presence of a full-fledged constitutional crisis and perhaps even threatened the stability of the still very young new political order. McCloskey, a professor of government at Harvard, was not a lawyer and, perhaps, was not "thinking like a lawyer" when praising Marshall. Can (should) a lawyer accept McCloskey's terms of analysis? What if, for example, one agrees with Marshall that Marbury was in fact entitled to his commission but disagrees with him that §13 was unconstitutional? That would mean, of course, that Marbury was entitled to the remedy—the writ of mandamus—that would rectify the wrong done him. Should an honorable judge, in that instance, have failed to give him the remedy, whatever the consequences that might ensue?

of the Supreme Court, 56 U. Chi. L. Rev. 443 (1989). Under either reading, §13 does not attempt to expand the Court's original jurisdiction. Third, and perhaps more controversially, one might read Article III, §2 to allow Congress to adjust the Supreme Court's original jurisdiction.

On the other hand, Marshall might have thought that the text of section 13 really did give the federal courts a free-standing power to supervise federal officials, because the King's Bench in Great Britain, the highest common law court, had a similar power to supervise government officials. See James E. Pfander, *Marbury*, Original Jurisdiction, and the Supreme Court's Supervisory Powers, 101 Colum. L. Rev. 1515, 1523-1549 (2001) (arguing that Marshall's critics have missed this aspect of British law). Thus, Marshall might have believed that Congress intended British practices to carry over to the American Supreme Court. See William Michael Treanor, The Story of Marbury v. Madison: Judicial Autonomy and Political Struggle, in Federal Courts Stories 29-56 (Vicki C. Jackson and Judith Resnik eds., 2010).

Note that only if one reads *both* the Constitution and the statutory text in the ways that Marshall has will a conflict emerge between the statute and the Constitution, and hence, a need to decide whether federal courts may refuse to enforce a federal law that conflicts with the Constitution. Do you think that Marshall made the best interpretation of the statute and the Constitution? Should he have tried to avoid facing the constitutional question if there was a plausible way for him to do so? Did Marshall have good institutional reasons for wanting to address the constitutional question, given the political context in which the case was heard, and Congress's abolition of the Court's 1802 Term?

2. *The power to say "no" and the power to say "yes."* Like Stuart v. Laird, the practical importance of *Marbury* in its own time was the Court's acquiescence (or capitulation) to the newly dominant Jeffersonians. For law professors, however, its importance is that the Supreme Court was willing to invalidate a federal law on constitutional grounds. As previously noted, there was nothing particularly new about the idea that the federal courts could do this; what was new was the Supreme Court actually exerting the power. *Marbury* is the first instance of the Court officially saying "No" to an act of Congress, even if it involved, as McCloskey suggests, a far more important "Yes" to the Republican Party's political dominance—and in Stuart v. Laird, a "Yes" to the 1802 Repeal Act. Perhaps equally important is that *Marbury* also assumed that the Supreme Court had the power to review the legality of the conduct of the executive branch as well as the constitutionality of federal statutes. Much of the work of the federal courts involves review of executive action and administrative decisionmaking.

One reason that we make *McCulloch* the first case that you read in this casebook is that the historical role of the Supreme Court has been far more to legitimize the actions of the national government by saying "Yes" than to invalidate them by saying "No." (The Court's behavior toward state governments, as *McCulloch* itself suggests, has been very different.) Consider whether the Court's ability to legitimate the work of the federal government is in fact enhanced by the theoretical (and practical) possibility that the Court might sometimes say "No."

3. *Judicial review, judicial supremacy, judicial finality, and judicial exclusivity.* Judicial *review* means that a federal court can review statutes (or executive actions) for constitutionality and refuse to enforce them in court proceedings if it finds them

unconstitutional. Judicial *supremacy* means that the federal courts' interpretation of the Constitution is supreme over the other branches. Judicial *finality* means that the federal courts settle the meaning of the Constitution. Judicial *exclusivity* means that the federal courts alone are allowed to say what the Constitution means.

Marbury has meant many different things to different people over the years. As you read the case today, does the notion of judicial review articulated in *Marbury* imply judicial supremacy, judicial finality, or judicial exclusivity? How much power *does Marbury* claim for the judiciary? Does it necessarily stand for the proposition that Supreme Court decisions must be accepted as authoritative by other branches of the national government (judicial supremacy)? Does it mean that the Supreme Court's position on the meaning of the Constitution is final (judicial finality)? Does it mean that the Supreme Court is the only institution that can interpret the Constitution (judicial exclusivity)?

Or does *Marbury* mean something far more modest: that the Court has the duty to pronounce the meaning of the Constitution in the course of resolving specific cases brought by parties before it, and that the parties, in turn, are bound by the Court's judgment in that case, just as they are bound by any judicial resolution? This position would be judicial review, but not necessarily judicial supremacy or exclusivity. The decision would be final as to the parties, but it might not be permanent, because interactions with the states and the other branches of the federal government might eventually lead the Court to change its mind. Which view is closest to what Marshall says in *Marbury*?

Recall Andrew Jackson's Veto Message and his discussion of the precedential force of *McCulloch*, Chapter 1, supra. Was Jackson acting consistently with *Marbury*? Suppose you think that federal courts engage in a "dialogue" or "colloquy" with other political institutions. The very metaphor of "dialogue" presupposes that the Supreme Court might concede that it had been mistaken or that it should defer to the views of other branches on occasion. Recall Marshall's reference in ¶1 of *McCulloch* to the nature and quality of the debate prior to Congress's chartering of the Bank of the United States. Why bother to refer to that debate if Congress is not a worthy partner in the enterprise of constitutional interpretation? In addition, the notion of "dialogue" does not tell us who has the last word, or even if there is a last word.

4. *Departmentalism.* Jackson's Veto Message is an important example of a "departmentalist" view of constitutional interpretation, i.e., the proposition that each branch of the national government—Congress, the executive, and the judiciary—can engage in independent constitutional interpretation. (Walter Dellinger's memorandum, Chapter 1, supra, spells out some of the complexities in determining how the "departments" sort out inevitable conflicts.) Departmentalism is a form of institutionalism—it holds that each branch of the federal government has equal authority to interpret the Constitution. Strictly speaking, it says nothing about the authority of the states or of the general public to interpret the Constitution. (Can you infer anything about the authority of state courts to interpret the Constitution from the Supremacy Clause of Article VI?)

5. *Constitutional protestantism.* Sanford Levinson has defined "constitutional protestantism" as the view that each member of the political community has the duty and the authority to interpret the Constitution for themselves. He draws an analogy to religious Protestantism, which challenged the monopoly of the Catholic

Church on the meaning of Scripture.[71] "When the attempt is made," wrote Martin Luther, "to reprove [Church authorities] out of the Scriptures, they raise the objection that the interpretation of the Scriptures belongs to no one except the pope." But if this were true, asked Luther, "where would be the need or use of the Holy Scriptures?" Luther evoked the classic Protestant notion of the priesthood of all believers: "[I]f we are all priests . . . and all have one faith, one gospel, one sacrament, why should we not also have the power to test and judge what is correct or incorrect in matters of faith"?[72]

Consider in this context Ronald Dworkin's comment that the American version of constitutionalism "does not make the decision of any court conclusive. Sometimes, even after a contrary Supreme Court decision, an individual may still reasonably believe that the law is on his side. . . . A citizen's allegiance is to the law, not to any person's view of what the law is, and he does not behave unfairly so long as he proceeds on his own considered and reasonable view of what the law requires."[73]

6. *Popular constitutionalism.* Popular constitutionalism asserts that the general public, acting through politics, determines and should determine the meaning of the Constitution. Former Stanford Dean Larry D. Kramer has argued that popular constitutionalism was widely accepted at the time of the Constitution's origins:[74] It was widely assumed that popular elections, fought in substantial part over constitutional issues, would be the forum for deliberation about constitutional meaning, and that the elections would in effect settle such controversies. Although some courts in fact claimed powers of judicial review, Kramer argues that "[c]ourts exercising judicial review in the 1790s made no claims of special or exclusive responsibility for interpreting the Constitution. They justified their refusal to enforce laws as a 'political-legal' act on behalf of the people, a responsibility required by their position as the people's faithful agents. Judicial review was a substitute for popular action, a device to maintain popular sovereignty without the need for civil unrest. It was, moreover, a power to be employed cautiously, only when the unconstitutionality of a law was clear beyond doubt. . . ."[75] The ultimate guardian of the Constitution, though, was not the Supreme Court (or even the judiciary in general), but rather an enlightened "public opinion" that took its constitutional duties seriously.

Critics of protestant or popular constitutionalism argue that it invites anarchy. Supporters respond that a single determinative answer imposed by a Supreme Court is inferior to having constitutional meaning resolved through the play of competing political institutions. Nevertheless, is it clear that one is faced with an either/or choice between fixed judicial interpretation and mutable popular interpretation? Throughout this course we will see how the Supreme Court's decisions, over time, have shifted in response to popular mobilizations and political pressures.

---

71. See Sanford Levinson, Constitutional Faith (2d ed. 2011).

72. Martin Luther, Three Treatises, quoted in Levinson, supra, at 24.

73. Ronald Dworkin, Taking Rights Seriously 214-215 (1977).

74. See Larry D. Kramer, The People Themselves: Popular Constitutionalism and Judicial Review (2004).

75. Id. at 99.

That responsiveness, in turn, has helped preserve the Court's legitimacy and its acceptance by the public. Viewed over time, then, the American constitutional order features both strong judicial review *and* robust popular constitutionalism, with the inevitable tension between them a never-ending source of contention that propels the constitutional system onward into history.

7. *Internal and external perspectives.* One can analyze judicial decisions in one of two ways: internally, asking whether the results courts reach make sense based on the logic of the legal arguments that judges offer; or externally, attempting to explain the results in terms of historical, political, social, economic, or other factors. Much of the foregoing analysis of *Stuart* and *Marbury* has been externalist inasmuch as it explains both *Stuart* and *Marbury* by reference to external historical and political factors. By contrast, Louise Weinberg, Our *Marbury*, 89 Va. L. Rev. 1235 (2003), offers the most sustained and legally sophisticated attempt to defend both opinions as motivated entirely by the duty of fidelity to law. You will encounter the alternation between internal and external perspectives repeatedly throughout this course. One view is that these perspectives are inherently in conflict, because the external perspective undermines the distinction between politics and law. Another view asserts, to the contrary, that the external perspective is actually necessary to the rule of law. What makes judicial decisions legitimate (or illegitimate) is the particular way they respond to the social, political, and historical circumstances in which they are decided, even if judges do not always advert to these factors directly.

8. *The United States as a developing democracy.* One way of understanding *Stuart* and *Marbury* is that they exemplify transitions to democracy. Courts in fledgling republics that have only recently thrown off the yoke of colonial domination or dictatorship must accept the influence of political pressures—including threats of impeachment or refusal to comply with judicial decisions—to remain viable until respect for the rule of law and practical judicial independence can be established as an ongoing custom. Americans may like to imagine that their entire history has featured a sturdy tradition of judicial independence that has made it possible for the Supreme Court (and other courts) to invoke the impersonal commands of the law as shields against an overreaching President or Congress. *Marbury* and *Stuart* teach a different lesson. Although judicial independence is an important and desirable value, courts are only *relatively* independent from political struggle, even in non-transitional contexts. One consequence is that, especially in the long run, courts cannot resist the demands of a dominant national political majority. That is merely a positive or descriptive claim. The normative, and far more controversial, claim is that courts should not try to resist the demands of a national political majority. Do you agree? How does this affect your views of *Marbury* and *Stuart*?

9. *Are courts easy to push around?* Consider Alexander Hamilton's defense of life tenure for federal judges in The Federalist No. 78:

> Whoever attentively considers the different departments of power must perceive, that, in a government in which they are separated from each other, the judiciary, from the nature of its functions, will always be the least dangerous to the political rights of the Constitution; because it will be least in a capacity to annoy or injure them. The Executive not only dispenses the honors, but holds the sword of the community. The legislature not only commands the purse, but prescribes the rules by which the

> duties and rights of every citizen are to be regulated. The judiciary, on the contrary, has no influence over either the sword or the purse; no direction either of the strength or of the wealth of the society; and can take no active resolution whatever. It may truly be said to have neither FORCE nor WILL, but merely judgment; and must ultimately depend upon the aid of the executive arm even for the efficacy of its judgments.
>
> This simple view of the matter suggests several important consequences. It proves incontestably, that the judiciary is beyond comparison the weakest of the three departments of power; that it can never attack with success either of the other two; and that all possible care is requisite to enable it to defend itself against their attacks. It equally proves, that though individual oppression may now and then proceed from the courts of justice, the general liberty of the people can never be endangered from that quarter; I mean so long as the judiciary remains truly distinct from both the legislature and the Executive. For I agree, that "there is no liberty, if the power of judging be not separated from the legislative and executive powers." And it proves, in the last place, that as liberty can have nothing to fear from the judiciary alone, but would have every thing to fear from its union with either of the other departments; that as all the effects of such a union must ensue from a dependence of the former on the latter, notwithstanding a nominal and apparent separation; that as, from the natural feebleness of the judiciary, it is in continual jeopardy of being overpowered, awed, or influenced by its co-ordinate branches; and that as nothing can contribute so much to its firmness and independence as permanency in office, this quality may therefore be justly regarded as an indispensable ingredient in its constitution, and, in a great measure, as the citadel of the public justice and the public security.

Do *Stuart* (and *Marbury*) help make Hamilton's case? Consider Hamilton's argument that all that courts have working for them is "judgment," by which he means that courts make reasoned arguments about what the law is. If he is right about this, does this suggest that courts should be particularly scrupulous in paying attention only to the law and not to any "extrinsic" features of the political or social situation in deciding cases, so as to shore up their legitimacy? Or, on the contrary, does it suggest that courts must always speak publicly in terms of rule of law values and what the law requires while simultaneously paying close attention to how far they can push the political branches? Consider Marshall's legal arguments in *Marbury* in this light.

10. *Power politics.* One might argue that Marshall engaged in a power grab by interpreting both the statute and the Constitution in a way that created an easily avoidable constitutional conflict. He then exploited this conflict to justify asserting the power to overturn a congressional law.

But Marshall was not the only actor in the case. Consider Marshall's options given the hostile audience watching him in Congress and the White House. Congress and the President had already asserted their power against the courts, by abolishing the Court's 1802 Term and by eliminating the new circuit judgeships in the 1802 Repeal Act—an act of questionable constitutionality. (See the discussion in Stuart v. Laird.)

Given the hand he was dealt, Marshall defended the authority of the federal courts through the distinctive forms of power that courts have relative to the political branches. His power as a judge consists in bestowing or withholding legitimacy and legality. And he exercised this authority in a way that required no response by the Jeffersonians, and could bear fruit in future years.

11. *Just the facts, ma'am.* Imagine that you were asked to "state the facts" of Stuart v. Laird or of Marbury v. Madison. Are the relevant facts, for example, found (only) within the four corners of a given case, or should an analyst of any given decision be aware of the broader context of the decision, including the general political circumstances of the time? What are the consequences of accepting one or another view of how to ascertain the facts of a case?[76]

C. *Limitations on Judicial Power*

Even though the federal courts have the power of judicial review, their power is also limited in important ways. Our treatment here is brief because each of these topics is covered at great length in casebooks and courses on federal jurisdiction.

1. Jurisdiction Stripping

Article III vests the federal judiciary with "the judicial power of the United States," which includes the power of judicial review. But Article III also recognizes important congressional power to define the shape and scope of the federal judiciary. Lower federal courts need not exist; and in theory, Congress is free to abolish these courts (although it might be obliged to pay the salaries of existing judges). This is the so-called Madisonian Compromise about the federal judiciary reached at the Philadelphia Convention. Textually, note that Article III speaks of "such inferior courts as the Congress *may* from time to time ordain and establish," and that Article I, §8 speaks of the "power" (but not the duty) of Congress to "constitute Tribunals inferior to the supreme Court."

The existence of one "Supreme Court" is mandated by the Constitution, but the Constitution says nothing about the size and shape of that Court. Historically, the size of the Court has varied from between 6 and 10 members, but has been statutorily fixed at 9 for over a century. (Could Congress theoretically expand the Court to encompass 50 or 100 judges, and oblige these judges to hear most of their cases in smaller panels, with larger en banc hearings to deal with certain inter-panel conflicts?) Note also that Congress has power to make "exceptions and regulations" to the Supreme Court's appellate jurisdiction (as noted in *Marbury*).

The largest and most debated questions about congressional power over federal jurisdiction are as follows: To what extent can Congress use its powers to remove various cases entirely from all federal courts? For example, could Congress eliminate lower federal court jurisdiction over abortion cases while simultaneously

---

76. See generally Sanford Levinson and Jack M. Balkin, What Are the Facts of Marbury v. Madison?, 20 Const. Comment. 255 (2004).

"excepting" those cases from the Supreme Court's appellate jurisdiction? This would leave all these issues to be decided in state courts, whose judges typically lack life tenure and some of the other protections enjoyed by Article III judges. Could Congress thus "strip" the jurisdiction of federal courts if its explicit purpose were to undercut the federal judiciary's abortion rulings? If the issue were left to state courts, would such courts continue to be bound by old Supreme Court precedents? Even if not, what, as a practical matter, would prevent these courts from departing from the Supreme Court's prior pronouncements? As a predictive matter, would state courts likely reach the same results as the federal courts would have?

Modern scholars have expressed a range of views, but for simplicity it is useful to consider two main schools of thought. The first school is associated with Professor Henry Hart, who taught at the Harvard Law School in the middle of the twentieth century and whose views were widely influential. According to the Hart school of thought, Congress may indeed use its powers over lower federal courts and over the Supreme Court's appellate jurisdiction so as to leave the last word on certain cases in state courts. But such exceptions, Hart warned, should not go so far as to intrude upon the "essential functions" of the Supreme Court, which Hart did not attempt to define comprehensively.

A competing school of thought builds on the work of Justice Joseph Story. In his landmark opinion in Martin v. Hunter's Lessee, 14 U.S. (1 Wheat.) 304 (1816), and in his famous 1833 treatise, Story stressed the mandatory nature of federal jurisdiction: "The judicial power of the United States *shall* be vested in" the federal judiciary and "*shall* extend to *all* cases, in law and equity, arising under this Constitution, the laws of the United States, and Treaties made, or which shall be made, under their authority. . . ." According to Story, this mandatory language means that although Congress can restrict both lower federal court jurisdiction and the Supreme Court's appellate jurisdiction, Congress may not do both at the same time—at least where federal question cases are concerned. As to these cases, the federal judiciary, and not the state courts, must stand as the last word on the meaning of federal law. Just as Congress may not transfer Article II power to veto federal laws or pardon federal offenses from the President to state governors, so too Congress may not transfer Article III power to resolve finally all federal question cases from the federal judiciary to state courts. Such courts may hear federal question cases in the first instance, but may not stand as the last word: They must be subject to appellate review in some federal court (though not necessarily the Supreme Court). To defend his claim that federal question cases were mandatory whereas diversity suits were not, Story highlighted the fact that in the former category, the Constitution speaks of "*all*" cases, but it does not in the latter. This has come to be known as the "two-tiered" theory of Article III.

For prominent statements by members of the Hart school, see Henry M. Hart, Jr., The Power of Congress to Limit the Jurisdiction of Federal Courts: An Exercise in Dialectic, 66 Harv. L. Rev. 1362 (1953); Paul M. Bator, Congressional Power over the Jurisdiction of the Federal Courts, 27 Vill. L. Rev. 1030 (1982); Martin H. Redish, Constitutional Limitations on Congressional Power to Control Federal Jurisdiction: A Reaction to Professor Sager, 77 Nw. U. L. Rev. 143 (1982); Daniel J. Meltzer, The History and Structure of Article III, 138 U. Pa. L. Rev. 1569 (1990). For scholarship in the mandatory tradition of Justice Story, see Lawrence Gene

Sager, The Supreme Court, 1980 Term—Foreword: Constitutional Limitations on Congress' Authority to Regulate the Jurisdiction of the Federal Courts, 95 Harv. L. Rev. 17 (1981); Robert N. Clinton, A Mandatory View of Federal Court Jurisdiction: A Guided Quest for the Original Understanding of Article III, 132 U. Pa. L. Rev. 741 (1984); Akhil Reed Amar, A Neo-Federalist View of Article III: Separating the Two Tiers of Federal Jurisdiction, 65 B.U. L. Rev. 205 (1985); Akhil Reed Amar, The Two-Tiered Structure of the Judiciary Act of 1789, 138 U. Pa. L. Rev. 1499 (1990).

2. Standing

In the American tradition, litigants who come to court generally must assert their own legal rights, rather than seek to adjudicate and define the rights of others, or the rights of the public as a whole. This basic idea is captured by the doctrine of "standing."

Under the Supreme Court's modern doctrine, standing to bring suit under Article III of the Constitution requires that the plaintiff show three things: First, the plaintiff must have suffered an "injury in fact"—an invasion of a legally protected interest that is (a) concrete and particularized, and (b) actual or imminent, not conjectural or hypothetical. Second, there must be a causal connection between the injury and the conduct complained of; the injury has to be fairly traceable to the challenged action of the defendant, and not the result of the independent action of some third party not before the court. Third, it must be likely, as opposed to merely speculative, that the injury will be redressed by a favorable decision. Lujan v. Defenders of Wildlife, 504 U.S. 555, 560-561 (1992). These three requirements are usually referred to for short as the requirements of (1) injury-in-fact, (2) causation, and (3) redressability.

The Supreme Court justifies its standing doctrine as one way to ensure that it keeps within "the judicial power" under Article III, which is limited to "Cases" and "Controversies." "[T]he Constitution's central mechanism of separation of powers depends largely upon common understanding of what activities are appropriate to legislatures, to executives, and to courts." Id. at 559-560. Standing is one of the doctrines that helps to "identify those disputes which are appropriately resolved through the judicial process," Whitmore v. Arkansas, 495 U.S. 149, 155 (1990).

The three-part test of injury-in-fact, causation, and redressability hides a rather confusing body of case law that has grown up around it. The basic problem is this: Almost anyone who comes to court feels aggrieved in some way—but not all grievances and harms count, legally speaking. The exceedingly spare words of Article III, however, cannot tell us which harms count, when, or for whom—only substantive law can do so, whether that law derives from statutes, or other parts of the Constitution, or common law principles of property, tort, contract, and so on.

For example, is a third party to a contract entitled to come to court to complain that the contract has been breached? This is a question of contract law, not Article III. Are downstream purchasers entitled to come to court to complain about price fixing committed not by their immediate suppliers, but by manufacturers further upstream? This is a question of substantive law under the Sherman Act. Article III can properly demand that plaintiffs must in general assert their own rights—but only substantive law outside Article III can define what the rights are, to whom they attach, against whom they run, and when they vest. At times the Court seems to have recognized as much, and at other times the Court seems to miss this basic point. For good general discussions that nicely clarify the issues at stake, see David P. Currie, Misunderstanding Standing, 1981 Sup. Ct. Rev. 41; William A. Fletcher, The Structure of Standing, 98 Yale L.J. 221 (1988); Cass R. Sunstein, What's Standing After *Lujan*? Of Citizen Suits, "Injuries," and Article III, 91 Mich. L. Rev. 163 (1992).

3. Political Questions

There is often a gap between the best interpretation of the Constitution and what judges enforce in the name of the Constitution. Sometimes, for reasons specific to their role as judges, judges underenforce constitutional norms. Other times, judges may abdicate the field altogether.

There are a variety of reasons justifying abdication, and several of these are lumped together under what has become known as the "political question" doctrine.

The canonical effort to give boundaries to this doctrine took place in Baker v. Carr, 369 U.S. 186 (1962), a case involving a malapportioned state legislature. The defendants claimed that the apportionment issue was unfit for judicial resolution, but the Court disagreed. It identified six circumstances in which a legal issue might be nonjusticiable because it is a political question: (1) where the Constitution makes a textually demonstrable constitutional commitment of the issue to another branch of government; (2) where there is a lack of judicially discoverable and manageable standards for resolving it; (3) where the court would have to make a policy determination of a kind clearly for nonjudicial discretion; (4) where a decision would be disrespectful to coordinate branches of government; (5) where there is an unusual need to treat a political branch's decision as final; and (6) where it is necessary for the federal government to speak with one voice on an issue.

These six factors, in turn, may be conveniently grouped into three sets of reasons for judicial abdication.

The first factor might be called a "jurisdictional" reason for abdication. The argument here is that in a few discrete situations, the Constitution vests judicial, adjudicatory power in another branch of government.

Thus, in the celebrated case of Powell v. McCormack, 395 U.S. 486 (1969), Congressman Adam Clayton Powell sought to challenge the House of Representatives' decision to refuse to seat him in the New York delegation. The House relied on its powers under Article I, §5: "Each House shall be the Judge of the Elections, Returns and Qualifications of its own Members." Chief Justice Warren slightly modified the first prong of the *Baker* test, by asking whether Article I, §5 amounted to a "textually demonstrable commitment of the *adjudicatory* power to determine Powell's qualifications."

The Court ruled that such adjudicatory power, if it existed, extended only to determining whether Congressman Powell met the Constitution's specified qualifications of age, residency, and citizenship. (See Article I, §2, cl. 2.) The Constitution did not give the Congress adjudicatory power to add any new qualifications of its own. (Because the power to adjudicate involves applying a preexisting standard, not making up a new one, legislatively.) Since there was no bona fide dispute about whether Powell met the Constitution's specified qualifications, the Court invalidated the House's effort to exclude Powell. But, the Court noted, in the case of a bona fide dispute about age, for example, each house might well be the final "judge," and Article III courts might be obliged to defer, even if they disagreed with this bona fide judgment. That is because the Constitution explicitly makes each house the "judge" of the qualifications of its own members under Article I, §5.

Factors two and three of the *Baker* test seem to reflect a different idea. Judges deciding cases seek clear doctrinal rules capable of principled exposition. If such rules are unavailable in a given situation, this may counsel judicial abdication—not because there are no constitutional principles at stake, but because they cannot be cleanly implemented in a "judicially manageable" way with proper "legal" tests.

The remaining factors are more prudential; they counsel caution, not because judges need clean lines, but because they are less politically accountable, and are often asked to act after important and hard-to-reverse decisions (like the decision to wage war) have already been made by the other branches.

Recently, in Zivotofsky v. Clinton, 132 S. Ct. 1421, 1427-1428 (*Zivotofsky I*) (2012), the Court maintained that the first two of these six factors are the most important, and it emphasized that the political question doctrine is "a narrow exception to [the] rule" that "the Judiciary has a responsibility to decide cases properly before it, even those it 'would gladly avoid.'"

Two landmark political question cases—one from the beginning of the modern era, and one more recent—may help illustrate the basic ideas at work in the political question doctrine.

In Coleman v. Miller, 307 U.S. 433 (1939), the Justices faced a claim that a constitutional amendment that Congress had proposed 14 years earlier could no longer be ratified by states—too much time had already lapsed, the claim went, and so the amendment proposal should be judicially declared dead. The Justices rejected this argument and labeled the issue a political question for Congress to decide. Writing for himself and two others, Chief Justice Hughes argued that no judicially manageable standards existed—how was a judge to say how much time was too much? For judges to say that 11 years was too long but that 10 years was not would involve awkward line-drawing problems. The obvious counterargument, of course—made by two dissenting Justices—is that judges draw lines every day. Four other Justices agreed that the issue was a nonjusticiable political question, but used more "jurisdictional" language: Article V, they insisted, committed these issues wholly to Congress. But nowhere is there any distinctively judicial language in Article V; if judges may decide whether Congress has acted beyond the scope of its commerce power, why may they not likewise decide whether Congress has acted beyond whatever implicit time limits (if any) Article V imposes? The best argument for the result in *Coleman* is prudential: The amendment in question involved child labor, and grew out of a political effort to reverse the Supreme Court's prior rulings on the question of child labor. In this context, for the Court to step in to kill the amendment would have been rather awkward for reasons of democratic legitimacy—the Court would have been cutting off the people's biggest check on the Court, and doing so in the name of a time-limits idea that was nowhere explicit in Article V. If, however, this is the best theory to explain *Coleman*, it suggests that only those amendments aimed at overturning the judiciary should be seen as political questions. Where other amendments are involved, the willingness of judges to adjudicate constitutional questions (as judges generally do elsewhere) would not raise the specter of judicial self-dealing and self-entrenchment. Indeed, in some cases, quite the opposite is true. Consider, for example, the case of the Twenty-Seventh Amendment, proposed by James Madison in 1789, and ratified by the thirty-eighth state in 1992; this was an amendment designed to restrict congressional self-dealing in setting congressional salaries; to insist that Congress be the sole judge of the constitutional issues here seems to invert the prudential vision that best explains *Coleman*'s result.

Consider also the case of Judge Walter Nixon, who was impeached by the House of Representatives and convicted by the U.S. Senate. When Judge Nixon sought to bring certain legal objections about his Senate trial to court, the Supreme Court unanimously declared the issues involved to be political questions. See Nixon v. United States, 506 U.S. 224 (1993). The Justices diverged in their reasons, but converged in their result, and it is not hard to see why. Constitutional history makes clear that the framers intentionally shifted impeachment from Article III courts to the Senate, so that controversial impeachment issues would be resolved by a sufficiently large and politically accountable body. As a matter of structure and prudence, it would be awkward for judges to try to reinstate, say, an already-ousted President; and where a judge has been removed, there is something constitutionally unseemly about other judges trying to put him back in power (with full pay, of course), thereby nullifying one of the Constitution's main checks on overweening judges. Constitutional text, carefully and holistically construed, confirms all this, and illustrates again the "jurisdictional" variant of the political question doctrine. The notion that an officer who has been impeached and removed may not seek reinstatement in an Article III lawsuit is not some weird exception to judicial review. The officer is fully entitled to judicial review of all relevant issues of fact and law—*but this review occurs in the Senate itself, which sits as a court.* Note the obvious judicial language of Article I, §3, which gives the Senate the sole power to "try" all impeachments, with the power to "convict" and enter "judgment" in "Cases" of impeachment. This repeated judicial language makes clear that the Senate sits as judge and jury, and its rulings of fact and law therefore stand as res judicata in all other tribunals. Intratextual analysis confirms this. When we consult the language of Article III, we see that it exempts "Trial[s]" in "Cases of Impeachment" from the ordinary rules of Article III demanding juries for all crimes. Why? Because "trials" in "cases" of impeachment are to take place and be finally decided in a different court, specified earlier in the document.

D. *Judicial Review in a Democratic Polity*

1. The Countermajoritarian Difficulty

"The root difficulty," wrote Alexander Bickel in perhaps the most influential single book on the role of the Supreme Court published in the twentieth century, "is that judicial review is a counter-majoritarian force in our society":[77]

---

77. Alexander Bickel, The Least Dangerous Branch 16-18 (1962). See also Barry Friedman, The Road to Judicial Supremacy (The History of the Countermajoritarian Difficulty, Part One), 73 N.Y.U. L. Rev. 333 (1998).

> [W]hen the Supreme Court declares unconstitutional a legislative act or the action of an elected executive, it thwarts the will of representatives of the actual people of the here and now; it exercises control, not in behalf of the prevailing majority, but against it. . . . [N]othing in the further complexities and perplexities of the system . . . can alter the essential reality that judicial review is a deviant institution in the American democracy.

Bickel's famous argument that judicial review is "deviant" must be placed in its historical context. It was written following the constitutional struggles over the New Deal, which is described in more detail in Chapter 5. Liberals and progressives who sought to uphold New Deal programs rejected the nineteenth-century view that courts were guardians of the Constitution—and especially guardians of the rights of property. Supporters of the New Deal argued instead that courts should defer to social and economic regulation by the political branches and that courts should respect the judgment of democratically elected institutions.

The New Deal assumption that courts could and would stay out of questions of social and economic regulation, however, became increasingly complicated in the mid-twentieth century as the courts faced new issues of civil rights and civil liberties. The most famous examples are Brown v. Board of Education, the reapportionment cases, and cases involving the First Amendment and other aspects of the Bill of Rights. Indeed, Bickel's own book argued for a balanced approach to judicial review. He believed that courts should preserve their political capital by intervening selectively, but speak only in principled terms when they did intervene.

Many legal scholars following Bickel have offered justifications for the institution of judicial review. Note the extent to which they are functionalist—i.e., focusing on the function of judicial review in American politics—rather than based on the constitutional text or the understandings of the framing generation.

2. Justifications for Judicial Review

What justifies judicial review in a political system like the United States? Consider the following arguments:

a. Supervising Inter- and Intra-governmental Relations

In a federal system with separation of powers, there are many different centers of political power. This is by design. Nevertheless, disputes will inevitably occur between the branches of the federal government, between the federal government and the states, and between individual states or groups of states. Some institution is required to arbitrate these disputes and settle them.[78]

---

78. See Jenna Bednar, William N. Eskridge, Jr., and John Ferejohn, A Political Theory of Federalism, in Constitutional Culture and Democratic Rule 223 (Ferejohn, Rakove & Riley eds., 2001), for an elegant argument that federal systems basically require a strong judicial "umpire," given that both national and state governments have strong incentives to try to renege on the federal "deal" that by definition places limits on both of these governments.

Moreover, the tribal governments of American Indian tribes create yet another system of government relations. See, e.g., Judith Resnik, Dependent Sovereigns: Indian Tribes, States, and Federal Courts, 56 U. Chi. L. Rev. 671 (1989).

The federal courts do not resolve all disputes among the branches; some disputes are considered "political questions." (See the discussion above.) As a practical matter, the power to review state legislation and executive action is probably more important than the ability to review federal legislative and executive action. There is only one federal government, but there are fifty states, and thousands of counties and municipalities. (Invalidation of federal legislation is far more infrequent, and much of the modern federal judiciary's work is the interpretation and application of federal statutes.)

Justice Oliver Wendell Holmes, Jr. famously remarked that "I do not think the United States would come to an end if we lost our power to declare an Act of Congress void. I do think the Union would be imperiled if we could not make that declaration as to the laws of the several states."[79] Similarly, Justice Robert H. Jackson argued that "[T]he power of the Supreme Court to declare acts of the *states* void under the federal Constitution presents an entirely separate issue in our history . . . [and] rests on quite different [and stronger] foundations than does the power to strike down *federal* legislation as unconstitutional."[80]

The power of the federal courts to review the judgments of state courts and the constitutionality of state legislation has not been seriously questioned since Martin v. Hunter's Lessee, 14 U.S. (1 Wheat.) 304 (1816). The Virginia Court of Appeals had refused to obey the Supreme Court's mandate reversing the judgment in a case involving the preemption of state laws by federal treaties. The state court had held unanimously that §25 of the Judiciary Act of 1789, conferring federal appellate jurisdiction, was unconstitutional. The Supreme Court again heard the case and again reversed (though to avoid another conflict, it bypassed the Virginia Court of Appeals and issued its mandate directly to the state trial court).[81] Justice Story noted that "the constitution . . . is crowded with provisions which restrain or annul the sovereignty of the states" and therefore "it is certainly difficult to support the argument that the appellate power over the decisions of state courts is contrary to the genius of our institutions." A contrary holding would be unworkable:

> It is . . . argued, that no great public mischief can result . . . because state judges are bound by an oath to support the constitution of the United States, and must be presumed to be men of learning and integrity. . . . [A]dmitting that the judges of the state courts are, and will be, of as much learning, integrity, and wisdom, as those of the courts of the United States, (which we very cheerfully admit), it does not aid the argument. It is manifest that the constitution has . . . presumed (whether rightly or wrongly we do not inquire) that state attachments, state prejudices, state jealousies, and state interests, might sometimes obstruct, or control, or be supposed to obstruct or control, the regular administration of justice. . . .
>
> This is not all. A motive of another kind, perfectly compatible with the most sincere respect for state tribunals, might induce the grant of appellate power over their decisions. That motive is the importance, and

79. Oliver Wendell Holmes, Jr., Collected Legal Papers 295-296 (1920).

80. Robert H. Jackson, The Struggle for Judicial Supremacy 15 (1941).

81. 1 Charles Warren, The Supreme Court in United States History 450 (1926).

> even necessity of *uniformity* of decisions throughout the whole United States, upon all subjects within the purview of the constitution. Judges of equal learning and integrity, in different states, might differently interpret a statute, or a treaty of the United States, or even the constitution itself: If there were no revising authority to control these jarring and discordant judgments, and harmonize them into uniformity, the laws, the treaties, and the constitution of the United States would be different in different States, and might perhaps, never have precisely the same construction, obligation, or efficacy, in any two states. The public mischiefs that would attend such a state of things would be truly deplorable. . . .

The Court again addressed the constitutionality of §25 in Cohens v. Virginia, 19 U.S. (6 Wheat.) 264 (1821), in which Chief Justice Marshall rejected Virginia's argument that Article III did not confer appellate jurisdiction over state criminal cases. Like Story, Marshall pointed out that the Constitution's design necessarily limited State sovereignty in order to establish an effective working union, and that "[t]he judicial power of every well-constituted government must be co-extensive with the legislative, and must be capable of deciding every judicial question which grows out of the constitution and laws." And like Story, he explained that independent federal review of state judgments was a structural necessity:

> In many States the judges are dependent for office and for salary on the will of the legislature. . . . When we observe the importance which [the Constitution of the United States] attaches to the independence of judges, we are the less inclined to suppose that it can have intended to leave these constitutional questions to tribunals where this independence may not exist, in all cases where a State shall prosecute an individual who claims the protection of an act of Congress. . . .
>
> The mischievous consequences of the construction contended for on the part of Virginia, are also entitled to great consideration. It would prostrate, it has been said, the government and its laws at the feet of every State in the Union. And would not this be its effect? What power of the government could be executed by its own means, in any State disposed to resist its execution by a course of legislation? The laws must be executed by individuals acting within the several States. If these individuals may be exposed to penalties, and if the Courts of the Union cannot correct the judgments by which these penalties may be enforced, the course of the government may be, at any time, arrested by the will of one of its members. Each member will possess a *veto* on the will of the whole. . . .
>
> Let it be admitted, that the cases which have been put are extreme and improbable, yet there are gradations of opposition to the laws, far short of those cases, which might have a baneful influence on the affairs of the nation. Different States may entertain different opinions on the true construction of the constitutional powers of Congress. We know, that at one time, the assumption of the debts contracted by the several States, during the war of our revolution, was deemed unconstitutional by some of them. We know, too, that at other times, certain taxes, imposed by Congress have been pronounced unconstitutional. Other laws have been

> questioned partially, while they were supported by the great majority of the American people. We have no assurance that we shall be less divided than we have been. . . .
>
> These collisions may take place in times of no extraordinary commotion. But a constitution is framed for ages to come, and is designed to approach immortality as nearly as human institutions can approach it. Its course cannot always be tranquil. It is exposed to storms and tempests, and its framers must be unwise statesmen indeed, if they have not provided it, as far as its nature will permit, with the means of self-preservation from the perils it may be destined to encounter. No government ought to be so defective in its organization, as not to contain within itself the means of securing the execution of its own laws against other dangers than those which occur every day. Courts of justice are the means most usually employed; and it is reasonable to expect that a government should repose on its own Courts, rather than on others.

Since these early decisions—and most recently in the wake of Brown v. Board of Education—states have sometimes attempted to thwart the orders and mandates of the federal judiciary. But *Martin* and *Cohens* effectively settled the Supreme Court's authority to revise the judgments of state courts and, in effect, settled the federal judicial power to determine the constitutionality of state laws.

b. Preserving Fundamental Values

Although Bickel argued that judicial review was "countermajoritarian," he also argued that it was necessary to protect fundamental values. Bickel recognized that the justification offered in *Marbury*—based on judicial competence to interpret the written text of the Constitution—was not a good justification for most of the federal judiciary's work. Consider as only one example Marshall's structural argument in the second part of *McCulloch* for an implicit federal immunity to state taxation.

Why should unelected life-tenured federal judges be trusted with preserving fundamental values? Why shouldn't this be left to the political branches? As we will see, political and social movements *have* played a crucial role in articulating the Constitution's values over time. If so, what role are courts supposed to play?

One possibility is that courts play a conserving and conservative role. They try to keep faith with the value choices of the past. They force people into the Article V amendment process if they want to change the Constitution. In fact, as we will see in this book, much constitutional change has occurred outside the official Article V amendment process. Social and political movements arguing in the name of restoring or redeeming fundamental values have changed constitutional understandings. There are so many examples that one would need an entire book—like this one!—to list them.

A second possibility is that judges prevent politics from changing the articulation and application of fundamental values too quickly. If people want to articulate and apply fundamental values differently than they have in the past, courts temporize, giving the public a chance for sober reflection, debate, and deliberation. Political mobilizations for change may not reflect a uniform public will—they may generate countermobilizations that push back. However, if social and political mobilizations, working over a sustained period of time, are able to change public opinion on fundamental questions, the courts will eventually come around and ratify their work. But until then, courts will (and should) resist too much innovation too quickly.

Bickel offered yet another theory: He argued that courts, unlike the political branches, were committed to principled and reasoned elaboration of the Constitution: "[C]ourts have certain capacities for dealing with matters of principle that legislatures and executives do not possess: judges have, or should have, the leisure, the training, and the insulation to follow the ways of the scholar in pursuing the ends of government. . . . Their insulation and the marvelous mystery of time give courts the capacity to appeal to men's better natures, to call forth their aspirations, which may have been forgotten in the moment's hue and cry."[82] Bickel maintained that "the courts . . . are also a great and highly effective educational institution. . . . The Justices in Dean Rostow's phrase, 'are inevitably teachers in a vital national seminar.'" "No other branch of the American government," Bickel maintained, "is nearly so well equipped [as the judiciary] to conduct one. And such a seminar can do a great deal to keep our society from becoming so riven that no court will be able to save it."

Bickel's argument relies on a stylized opposition between principled courts who reason and deliberate, and unprincipled politicians and members of the public who assert their will. Federal courts are the home of reason while ordinary politics is the home of passion and unprincipled compromise. What are the strengths and weaknesses of this account? Consider the metaphor of the "seminar." Is the process of constitutional development a seminar (led by a professor, who assigns the readings, sets the agenda, and leads the discussion), or is it a more democratic and participatory affair?

c. Protecting the Integrity of Democratic Processes

One of the most famous justifications for judicial review begins in a famous footnote: footnote four of the 1938 decision in United States v. Carolene Products Co., discussed in Chapter 5, infra. In the middle of a discussion of why courts should defer to the political process, Justice Harlan F. Stone suggested that the judiciary should nevertheless scrutinize legislation (1) that "restricts those political processes which can ordinarily be expected to bring about repeal of undesirable legislation," or (2) that is based on "prejudice against discrete and insular minorities, which tends seriously to curtail the operation of those political processes ordinarily to be relied upon to protect minorities."

In Democracy and Distrust: A Theory of Judicial Review (1980), John Hart Ely crafted a general theory out of footnote four. The point of judicial review is not to protect fundamental values, but to protect democracy and the democratic political process. In contrast to fundamental rights protection, Ely offered a "participation-oriented, representation-reinforcing" model.[83] When courts protect democracy, they are working with the democratic system rather than counter to it:

---

82. Bickel, supra n.77, at 24-27.

83. John Hart Ely, Democracy and Distrust: A Theory of Judicial Review 87 (1980).

"[U]nlike an approach geared to the judicial imposition of 'fundamental values,' the representation reinforcing orientation . . . is not inconsistent with, but on the contrary is entirely supportive of, the American system of representative democracy. It [is devoted] to policing the mechanisms by which the system seeks to ensure that our elected representatives will actually represent."[84]

Ely argues that democratic "malfunction occurs when the *process* is undeserving of trust"—when "(1) the ins are choking off the channels of political changes to ensure that they will stay in and the outs will stay out, or (2) though no one is actually denied a voice or a vote, representatives beholden to an effective majority are systematically disadvantaging some minority out of simple hostility or a prejudiced refusal to recognize commonalities of interest, and thereby denying that minority the protection afforded other groups by a representative system."[85]

Ely's arguments work best in explaining judicial protection of free speech, voting rights, and some kinds of discrimination against minorities. They work least well in explaining how courts operate in deciding many other kinds of issues that don't concern the integrity of the political process. In fact, Ely's view was that courts should *not* protect other kinds of rights that were not listed in the Constitution's text, including implied fundamental rights to sexual autonomy and family formation. He was also unsure whether courts should use judicial review to limit sex discrimination because women were not a numerical minority. A recurring question is whether protecting "democracy" and "fair process"—which are highly contested terms—inevitably requires courts to engage in precisely the kinds of controversial value decisions that Ely wanted courts to avoid.[86]

3. The Countermajoritarian Difficulty Challenged

There have been two major objections to Bickel's argument. The first is that Bickel deemphasizes the many countermajoritarian features of the political branches, thus making the judiciary seem like far more of an outlier than it really is. The second objection is that Bickel's formulation overlooks the many ways in which the judiciary is either responsive to or coordinates with the political branches, the national political coalition, or popular opinion.

a. The Countermajoritarian Features of the Political Branches

One might wonder whether "countermajoritarian" institutions are all that "deviant" within the American political system. If so, one needs a more complicated argument against judicial review. In his book Our Undemocratic Constitution, Sanford Levinson argues that the American Constitution is rife with undemocratic features, far more undemocratic, in fact, than most of the American state constitutions drafted in the nineteenth century and afterward.[87] Consider only the following features:

---

84. Id. at 102.

85. Id. at 103.

86. On some of the puzzles that follow from a commitment to process protection, see Jack M. Balkin, The Footnote, 83 Nw. L. Rev. 275 (1989).

87. Sanford Levinson, Our Undemocratic Constitution: Where the Constitution Goes Wrong (And How We the People Can Correct It) (pb. ed. 2008). See also Levinson, Framed: America's 51 Constitutions and the Crisis of Governance (2012).

- The malapportionment of the Senate, where Wyoming has equal voting power with California, even though (as of 2017) California has roughly 66 times the population (approximately 39.5 million) as Wyoming (approximately 595,000).
- The rules of the contemporary Senate include the filibuster: Three-fifths of the Senate must vote to cut off debate on any given bill. Although filibusters were rarely invoked throughout much of the nation's history, in the past two decades, since the mid-1990s, the 60-vote requirement has become (and remains) routine for almost all important legislation (except for bills that satisfy the arcane rules regarding "reconciliation"). The Democratic majority in the Senate voted in November 2013 to eliminate the filibuster for most presidential nominations; and in April 2017, the new Republican majority in the Senate extended this change to nominees for the Supreme Court.[88] The availability of the filibuster for most legislation means that 41 senators can—and now routinely do—block legislation backed by a majority of the Senate. In addition, the Senate's practices also allow any single member the right to place a "hold" on presidential nominations and thus prevent the full Senate from exercising its constitutional duty of giving its advice and consent to such nominations.[89]
- The Electoral College, which allows the loser of the plurality vote to win the Presidency. This has happened five times in American history, most recently in 2016. When no candidate gets a majority of the Electoral College (as happened in 1800 and 1824, and came close to occurring in 1948 and 1968) the Constitution requires that the House of Representatives elect the President, with each state delegation receiving one vote. Once again, this rule treats populous states like California and Texas the same as less populous states like Wyoming or Vermont.
- The presidential veto has significant countermajoritarian effects because it allows a single political official to offset majorities of both houses of Congress. It thus converts a bicameral system into the equivalent of a tricameral system. In addition, there is no guarantee that the President has been elected by a majority of the population. For example, in 2000, George

---

88. One cannot, however, assume that a bare majority of the Senate necessarily represents a majority of the American electorate. Given that a majority of the population now lives in only nine states, it is at least theoretically possible, albeit highly unlikely, as an empirical matter, that only 18 senators could represent a majority of the populace. And there have certainly been many instances where a larger minority of senators can be said in fact to represent the popular majority. See, e.g., Benjamin Eidelson, The Majoritarian Filibuster, 122 Yale L.J. 980 (2013).

89. See Philip Shenon, In Protest of Clinton Action, Senator Blocks Nominations, N.Y. Times, June 9, 1999, at A20. As Shenon writes, "Customs that permit a single lawmaker to hold up the workings of the Government might seem undemocratic. But they have a long history in the clubby confines of the Senate." Another veto point that applies to judicial nominations is the "blue slip" rule, by which senators can block judicial nominees from their home states. The current version of the rule, in place since the Trump Administration, applies only to district court judges.

W. Bush lost the popular vote, as did Donald Trump in 2016, and many Presidents who won a plurality of the popular vote have received substantially less than a majority. For example, both Richard Nixon in 1968 and Bill Clinton in 1992 received roughly 43 percent of the popular vote, and both cast significant vetoes blocking congressional legislation. If the President vetoes a bill, two-thirds of *both* houses must vote to override; historically Presidents prevail approximately 95 percent of the time.

- Under the Treaty Clause of Article II, §2, two-thirds of the Senate must concur in a treaty.
- Finally, and perhaps most importantly, Article V imposes significant hurdles for constitutional amendment. Two-thirds of each house of Congress must agree to a proposed constitutional amendment followed by the assent of three-quarters of the states. The latter requirement means, as a practical matter, that proponents of a constitutional amendment must triumph in at least 75 state legislative houses (every state except Nebraska is bicameral, and 38 of the 50 states must agree to a proposed amendment). Opponents of an amendment can prevail simply by gaining one-third plus one of the votes in either the House or the Senate or, if unsuccessful there, by defeating the proposal in only 13 houses in separate states.[90]

b. The "Majoritarian" Aspects of Judicial Review

Bickel's argument starkly contrasts a countermajoritarian judiciary that acts heedless of popular will and a majoritarian political process responsive to the citizenry. However, most political scientists today challenge the premise that judicial review presents a "countermajoritarian difficulty" at all.

Some five years before Bickel's book, Yale political scientist Robert Dahl argued that the Court usually reinforced or worked in conjunction with what political actors wanted, especially over long stretches of time. "The fact is, then, that the policy views dominant on the Court are never for long out of line with the policy views dominant among the lawmaking majorities of the United States. Consequently it would be most unrealistic to suppose that the Court would, for more than a few years at most, stand against any major alternatives sought by a lawmaking majority."[91]

Why is this? Dahl argued that Presidents appointed judges, and the rate of turnover in the federal judiciary kept the judiciary in sync with the views of the national political coalition. Over time, Presidents replaced judges with others more sympathetic to their point of view. Dahl concludes:

---

90. See Sanford Levinson, The Political Implications of Amending Clauses, 12 Const. Comment. 107 (1996). The Equal Rights Amendment (ERA), proposed by Congress in 1972, was ratified by two-thirds of the states, with a majority of the population. Nonetheless, it failed because it did not achieve the approval of the additional states required to bring it up to three-fourths. Assume that the Supreme Court simply interprets the Constitution as including the values instantiated in the ERA. Whatever one would think of that move, could it necessarily be described as "countermajoritarian"? See also Chapter 8.

91. Robert A. Dahl, Decision-Making in a Democracy: The Supreme Court as a National Policy-Maker, 6 J. Pub. L. 279, 294 (1957).

> Except for short-lived transitional periods when the old alliance is disintegrating and the new one is struggling to take control of political institutions, the Supreme Court is inevitably part of the dominant national alliance. As an element in the political leadership of the dominant alliance, the Court of course supports the major policies of the alliance. By itself the Court is almost powerless to affect the course of national policy. . . .
>
> The Supreme Court is not, however, simply an *agent* of the alliance. It is an essential part of the political leadership and possesses some bases of power of its own, the most important of which is the unique legitimacy attributed to its interpretations of the Constitution. This legitimacy the Court jeopardizes if it flagrantly opposes the major policies of the dominant alliance; such a course of action, as we have seen, is one in which the Court will not normally be tempted to engage.
>
> It follows that within the somewhat narrow limits set by the basic policy goals of the dominant alliance, the Court *can* . . . often determine important questions of timing, effectiveness, and subordinate policy. . . .
>
> [T]he Court is least likely to be successful in blocking a determined and persistent lawmaking majority on a major policy and most likely to succeed against a "weak" majority; e.g., a dead one, a transient one, a fragile one, or one weakly united upon a policy of subordinate importance.[92]

Dahl's argument rested on the assumption that there would be regular turnover in the Supreme Court—at the time he wrote, there had been one opening approximately every two years. He also assumed that politics would be governed by a relatively stable national political coalition governed by a dominant political party or a bipartisan coalition.

Both of these assumptions have been put under strain in recent years. First, Supreme Court Justices are living much longer—and staying on the bench far longer—in recent years. Dahl assumed that a President who won two terms would get to appoint about four Justices, but the last two-term Presidents—George W. Bush and Barack Obama—have only received two and three appointment opportunities, respectively. In Obama's case, a Republican-controlled Senate prevented a third appointment by refusing to consider any nominations at all.

This leads to the second difficulty with Dahl's analysis. Since the 1990s, American politics has become increasingly polarized, with many swings in the control of Congress and the Presidency, and many periods of divided government that have led to gridlock. It becomes more difficult to speak of the Court cooperating with a "national political coalition" when no party can maintain control for very long, and when the two parties are so strongly at odds on so many issues, including the kind of issues that judges consider. In this political context, the Supreme Court has a much freer hand to do what it likes, knowing that the Justices will stay on for very long periods of time and that the political branches are too divided to offer much

---

92. Dahl, supra n.91, at 286, 293-294 (the last paragraph is taken from earlier in the article).

resistance. At the same time, the United States Supreme Court has been closely divided between liberal and conservative Justices, so that a change of one or two seats can produce very different legal and political outcomes. As a result, the two parties have pushed hard to secure a working majority on the Supreme Court and the lower federal courts, because this is one area of the federal government in which (ironically, given Bickel's arguments) majorities *can* effectively work their will.

Many scholars in law and political science have offered variations on Dahl's basic insight that judicial review is not countermajoritarian when considered over long stretches of time. Dahl and many political scientists have focused on the relationship between the Supreme Court and the *national political coalition*—which is composed of political officials, party operatives, and other political elites. By contrast, Barry Friedman focuses on the relationship between the Supreme Court and *popular opinion*. He argues that the Supreme Court largely tracks popular opinion over time.[93] Richard Pildes offers a skeptical rebuttal to Friedman and other scholars in "Is the Supreme Court a Majoritarian Institution?," 2010 S. Ct. Rev. 103.

Mark Graber, in The Nonmajoritarian Difficulty: Legislative Deference to the Judiciary, 7 Studies in American Political Development 35 (1993), argues that legislators often prefer to send political "hot potatoes" to the courts rather than pay the political costs of making politically contentious decisions themselves. Examples of such political hot potatoes in the nineteenth century include the expansion of slavery into the territories; examples in the twentieth century include abortion and affirmative action. Graber's argument flips Bickel's assertion that judges are more principled on its head; it is precisely because judges are insulated from elections that they will carry water for politicians and venture where politicians fear to tread. Like most political scientists, Graber is skeptical that the Court has often, if at all, made decisions that it perceived as strongly opposed by the political majority.

Finally, Martin Shapiro offers a different account of why judicial review is not countermajoritarian.[94] Whether or not the Court's policies generally mirror those of the "political branches" of the national government, the political branches are far from the paradigms of democracy our civics textbooks make them out to be. By compensating for defects elsewhere in the system, the Court may actually contribute to the overall representativeness of the government.

NOTE: JUDICIAL "GOOD BEHAVIOR" AND LIFETIME TENURE

One explanation for the Court's "countermajoritarianism" is the long tenure of federal judges. Although early Justices seemed more than willing to depart from the Court for greener pastures (such as John Jay, who wished to become governor of New York), part of the explanation for John Marshall's singular importance is the fact that he remained Chief Justice for a full 34 years following his appointment in 1801.

93. Barry Friedman, The Will of the People: How Public Opinion Has Influenced the Supreme Court and Shaped the Meaning of the Constitution (2009).

94. Martin Shapiro, Freedom of Speech: The Supreme Court and Judicial Review (1966).

Unlike the constitutions of all but one of the American states and most other national constitutions around the world, the United States Constitution adopts neither *term limits* nor *age limits.* By contrast, most state judges in the United States are accountable to the electorate in one way or another; therefore it has been suggested that state judiciaries might suffer from a "majoritarian difficulty," i.e., judges who are too sensitive to the views of the general public. (Are objections to judicial review mitigated by the prospect that judges may be subject to removal by voters?)

"Life tenure" for federal judges is generally thought to follow from Article III, which conditions judicial tenure on maintaining "good Behaviour." This is a legal term of art which means that judges do not serve at the pleasure of the President, like many other federal appointees. Instead, they remain in office until removed for cause through the appropriate legal process for removal. In the case of judges, the Constitution prescribes that the appropriate legal process is impeachment. A rule that judges can only be removed for good cause through impeachment is effectively a rule of life tenure.

By contrast, many modern countries limit the tenure of members of "constitutional courts" (i.e., courts charged with assessing the constitutionality of parliamentary legislation). Term limits are 9 years for Spain, Italy, and the European Court on Human Rights; 10 years for the Czech Republic; and 12 years for South Africa and Germany, although German judges must retire at age of 68. Ireland has no term limit, but judges must retire at age 70.

Why might constitutional designers prefer term or age limits? Conversely, why might constitutional designers prefer tenure for life, which has allowed at least two American Justices, Oliver Wendell Holmes and John Paul Stevens, to serve into their ninetieth years (and, in Stevens's case, for almost 34 years)?

VI. THE LOUISIANA PURCHASE

Marbury was hardly the only important constitutional development of 1803. Arguably the single most important political and constitutional event between the ratification of the Constitution and the outbreak of civil war in 1861 was the purchase of the Louisiana Territory from France in 1803.[95]

An October 1800 treaty between Spain and France returned the territory of Louisiana to France. The agreement had significant implications for the United States because of its effects on control of the Mississippi River and the city of New Orleans. Congress appropriated $2 million, and diplomats were sent to France to negotiate the purchase of New Orleans. Much to their surprise, Napoleon suggested his willingness to sell the entire Territory, and a price of $15 million was agreed upon. Moreover, the treaty of purchase pledged that "the inhabitants of the ceded territory shall be incorporated in the Union of the United States, and

---

95. See generally Everett S. Brown, The Constitutional History of the Louisiana Purchase (1920). See also Jon Kukla, A Wilderness So Immense: The Louisiana Purchase and the Destiny of America (2003); Sanford Levinson and Bartholomew H. Sparrow, eds., The Louisiana Purchase and American Expansion 1803-1898 (2005).

admitted as soon as possible, according to the principles of the Federal Constitution, to the enjoyment of all the rights, advantages, and immunities of citizens of the United States; and in the meantime they shall be maintained and protected in the free enjoyment of their liberty, property, and the religion which they profess."

President Jefferson was a champion of states' rights and a strict construction of national powers under the Constitution (recall the Kentucky Resolutions that he authored only five years earlier). He had significant doubts about whether Congress had the power to add territory to the United States. After all, purchase of new territory was not clearly authorized by the constitutional text; this raised problems given Jefferson's emphasis, clearly set out in his argument against the First Bank of the United States, that the national government was limited to its explicitly assigned powers. Thus he wrote to John Dickinson, a fellow signer of the Declaration of Independence, that "our confederation is certainly confined to the limits established by the revolution. The general government has no powers but such as the constitution has given it; and it has not given it a power of holding foreign territory; and still less of incorporating it into this Union. An amendment of our Constitution seems necessary for this."[96] Jefferson also stressed that adding the Louisiana Territory, which stretched from the Gulf of Mexico to the interior of Montana, would double the size of the United States and fundamentally change the character of the Union. This, he argued, should require explicit ratification by "We the People" through amendment. (Some Federalists, although committed to a strong national government, opposed the purchase on the grounds, among others, that it would serve as a de facto political windfall to slave interests that could readily expand.)

Nevertheless, Jefferson laid the treaty between France and the United States before Congress. Writing to Kentucky Senator Hugh Breckenridge on August 12, 1803, he said:[97]

> This treaty must, of course, be laid before both Houses, because both have important functions to exercise respecting it. They, I presume, will see their duty to their country in ratifying and paying for it, so as to secure a good which would otherwise probably be never again in their power. But I suppose they must then appeal to the nation for an additional article to the Constitution approving and confirming an act which the nation had not previously authorized. The Constitution has made no provision for holding foreign territory, still less for incorporating foreign nations into our Union. The Executive, in seizing the fugitive occurrence which so much advances the good of our country, have done an act beyond the Constitution.

Or, as he told Dickinson immediately after expressing his constitutional doubts, "[i]n the meantime, we must ratify & pay our money, as we have treated, for a thing beyond the constitution, and rely on the nation to sanction an act done for its great good, without its previous authority."[98]

---

96. Quoted in David Meyer, The Constitutional Thought of Thomas Jefferson 246 (1994).

97. Quoted in Downes v. Bidwell, 182 U.S. 244 (1901) (discussed in Chapter 4, infra).

98. Quoted in Meyer, supra n.96, at 247.

One of Jefferson's principal allies, Secretary of the Treasury Gallatin, argued that it would be a "natural construction [of the Constitution] to say that the power of acquiring territory is delegated to the United States by the several provisions which authorize the several branches of government to make war, to make treaties, and to govern the territory of the Union."[99] Nevertheless, Jefferson was apparently not fully convinced. He thus prepared two amendments to the Constitution, the first of which declared that "the province of Louisiana is incorporated with the United States and made part thereof"; and the second of which was couched in somewhat different language, viz.: "Louisiana, as ceded by France to the United States, is made a part of the United States. Its white inhabitants shall be citizens, and stand, as to their rights and obligations, on the same footing as other citizens in analogous situations."

Whatever Jefferson's doubts, he did not press the constitutional point, not least, apparently, because Napoleon began giving signs of pulling back from his agreement, so that time became of the essence. Presented with this possibility, Jefferson wrote one correspondent that "whatever congress shall think it necessary to do, should be done with as little debate as possible, & particularly so far as respects the constitutional difficulty"; to another he emphasized that "the less that is said about the constitutional difficulties, the better."[100] Thus, in October 1803, Jefferson sent the treaty to the Senate, saying that "with the wisdom of Congress it will rest to take those ulterior measures which may be necessary for the immediate occupation and temporary government of the country; for its incorporation into the Union."

Several years later, writing another correspondent about the Purchase, Jefferson said that "[a] strict observance of the written law is doubtless one of the high duties of a good citizen, but it is not the highest. The laws of necessity, of self-preservation, of saving our country when in danger, are of higher obligation. To lose our country by a scrupulous adherence to the written law, would be to lose the law itself, with life, liberty, property and all those who are enjoying them with us; thus absurdly sacrificing the end to the means."

DISCUSSION

1. Many of you have no doubt read the famous (and oft-quoted) statement by Alexis de Tocqueville, "Scarcely any political question arises in the United States that is not resolved, sooner or later, into a judicial question."[101] Although the statement has become a cliché, it is nevertheless mostly false.[102] Had Tocqueville written that "political questions" in the United States often are turned into "legal ones," he would have been on sounder ground, but this still begs the question of how often "legal" questions are actually resolved by courts, instead of by other institutions such as the presidency or Congress or, for that matter, by public opinion.

---

99. Quoted in id. at 246.

100. Quoted in id. at 230.

101. 1 Democracy in America 280 (Vintage Edition 1945, reprinted 1990).

102. Mark A. Graber, Antebellum Perspectives on Free Speech, 10 Wm. & Mary Bill Rts. J. 779, 804-805 (2002).

The intense constitutional debate over the Purchase was settled within the Jefferson Administration and Congress themselves; courts played no role at all. It is true that John Marshall, in American and Ocean Insurance Companies v. Canter, 26 U.S. (1 Pet.) 511 (1828), laconically wrote, without further explanation, that the United States could extend its territory by treaty (or conquest), but no one would seriously regard this as "resolving" the issue rather than, a full quarter-century after the fact, accepting as dispositive the determination of 1803 that expansion was constitutionally legitimate. (Try to imagine for a moment what would have followed from a contrary holding by Marshall, i.e., that the Louisiana Purchase was unconstitutional. Would the United States have had to return the territory to France? Or would the Court have properly said that the Purchase, although unconstitutional, was so much a part of the American fabric that it simply could not be undone?)

2. Jefferson's defense of the Purchase raises a recurrent issue in this casebook: the tension between legal (or constitutional) fidelity and the need to respond to perceived emergencies or other threats to the Republic. Recall, for example, Edmund Randolph's declaration that "[t]here are great seasons when persons with limited powers are justified in exceeding them, and a person would be contemptible not to risk it." How, precisely does one identify the "great seasons" when ignoring ordinary legal constraints is justified? Consider Jefferson's justification for putting aside his constitutional doubts about the Louisiana Purchase. Must one agree, in order to justify Jefferson, that the Purchase involved "necessity," "self-preservation," or "saving our country when in danger"? Indeed, did it meet the criteria of "necessity" that Jefferson put forth in his criticism of chartering the First Bank? Did expanding the reach of American power into Montana have anything at all to do with "self-preservation" or "saving our country when in danger," even if one is willing to use such terms with regard to the port of New Orleans itself? Historian William Freehling has suggested that we would have a better sense of what was involved with the Purchase if we called it "the Midwest Purchase," given that what we today think of as Louisiana was such a relatively small portion of the lands gained by the United States. And, he also argues, the Purchase, far from "saving our country," in fact contributed to its dissolution in 1861 inasmuch as it was the Purchase that put front and center for the next half-century the issue of the expansion of slavery into these newly purchased territories. See Chapter 3, infra.

Did Jefferson behave consistently with his constitutional oath? Does the answer to that question fundamentally affect your view of Jefferson or of the legitimacy of the Louisiana Purchase? Put another way, to what extent do you really care, one way or the other, whether Jefferson obeyed the Constitution? If you don't care, or don't care very much, why do you care about whether contemporary Presidents obey the Constitution today?

NOTE: THE "MARSHALL COURT"

In general, references to the "______ Court," filling in the blank with the name of a Chief Justice, are usually a shorthand for periods of years; they should not be taken to imply either that the Chief Justice was especially influential or that the period differed strikingly from the one that preceded or followed it. The one exception is the Marshall Court, which lasted from 1801 to 1834, in which John Marshall was clearly the dominant figure, particularly during the first two decades of his tenure. Marshall successfully eliminated seriatim opinions and established a tradition—not always followed even then and now completely dissipated—of outward unanimity. What Marshall tried, albeit unsuccessfully, to establish as an operating rule of the Court has in fact been accepted by several countries around the world, which explicitly prohibit dissenting (or concurring) opinions. The Irish Constitution, Article 34.5.5, directs that a decision of the Supreme Court regarding constitutional challenges to legislation "shall be pronounced by such one of the judges of that Court as that Court shall direct, and no other opinion on such question, whether assenting or dissenting, shall be pronounced, nor shall the existence of any such other opinion be disclosed." Similarly, the European Court of Justice (although not the European Court of Human Rights) operates under a rule that "the conclusions reached by the majority of the Judges after final discussion shall determine the decision of the Court," with these conclusions and supporting reasons to be set out in a single impersonal opinion.[103] Even under Marshall, the opinions were scarcely "impersonal," as in the European Court, but, rather, issued under the signature of a specific Justice, to whom authorship of "the Opinion of the Court" may be attributed. It is precisely this latter practice that allows us to speak of "Marshall's [or Story's . . .] view of the Constitution" rather than simply "the Court" of a given era. What is the advantage, if any, of having "signed" rather than completely impersonal opinions?

"Marshall, according to received learning, consciously furthered the political goals of the Federalist Party, first by stretching the Constitution's meaning to increase national power at the expense of state power, and second, by designing constitutional doctrines that protected the upper classes' privileges against the growing democratic onslaught that in 1829 finally placed Andrew Jackson in the White House."[104] There is little doubt that the Marshall Court provided the constitutional foundations for a strong national government and articulated a vision of an unusually powerful national judiciary that would, among other things, take special care to protect property rights against state regulation. But the Marshall Court was not particularly partisan in the modern sense. By the early 1810s the Federalist Party had collapsed following its failure adequately to support the War of 1812 (when some New England "High Federalists" countenanced the thought of secession). Most of the Marshall Court's strongly nationalist decisions were issued, often unanimously, after 1811, when appointees of the Republican Presidents Jefferson and Madison constituted a majority of the Court. Whatever explains those decisions, it cannot plausibly be a desire to enhance the prospects of the Federalist Party against the Republicans.

NOTE: LIMITING THE PRESIDENT'S POWER AS COMMANDER-IN-CHIEF

One theme of *Marbury* is that executive officials are subject to the rule of law as declared by the Supreme Court, even if Marbury ultimately did not receive his commission. It is no small matter, of course, to hold that even the President of the United States is not "above the law" and that federal (or even state) courts could

---

103. See Sanford Levinson, Speaking in the Name of the Law: Some Reflections on Professional Responsibility and Judicial Accountability, 1 U. St. Thomas L.J. 447, 454-463 (2004).

104. William Nelson, The Eighteenth-Century Background of John Marshall's Constitutional Jurisprudence, 76 Mich. L. Rev. 894 (1978).

invalidate presidential actions (in just the same way that they could invalidate congressional attempts to act beyond the legislature's assigned powers).

An early example of this proposition is Marshall's decision only a year after *Marbury* in Little v. Barreme, 6 U.S. (2 Cranch) 170 (1804). In *Little*, U.S. frigates captured the Danish ship Flying Fish, near Hispaniola (now the Dominican Republic). The Danish owners sued Captain Little, who had taken the captured ship to Boston.

The navy had seized the Flying Fish because it was suspected of violating the "non-intercourse act" passed by Congress on February 9, 1799, which prohibited any American ship from going "*to* any port or place within the territory of the French republic, or the dependencies thereof . . . ," including ports of French colonies in the Caribbean (emphasis added). The Act was part of the so-called undeclared or imperfect war between the United States and France, though President Adams devoted much of his own political capital to prevent it from becoming a full-scale war.[105]

Although the Act prohibited ships from traveling *to* France or French possessions, President Adams ordered naval officers "to be vigilant that vessels or cargoes really American, but covered by Danish or other foreign papers, and bound to *or from* French ports, do not escape you" (emphasis added).

Although there was some evidence that the Flying Fish was really American, the district judge in Boston held that the vessel and its cargo were Danish and therefore "neutral property." However, he awarded no damages to the owners because, he held, there was in fact probable cause on the part of Captain Little to suspect that the vessel was indeed American. The circuit court reversed on the grounds that because the Flying Fish was coming from, rather than going to, a French port, it was immune from the Act regardless of whether it was an American vessel.

The Supreme Court, in an opinion written by Marshall, upheld the circuit court and held that Captain Little was liable for damages to the Danish owners.

> It is by no means clear that the president of the United States . . . might not, without any special authority for that purpose . . . have empowered the officers commanding the armed vessels of the United States, to seize . . . American vessels. . . . engaged in this illicit commerce. But . . . the 5th section [of the Act] gives a special authority to seize on the high seas, and limits that authority to the seizure of vessels bound or sailing to a French port[;] the legislature seem to have prescribed that the manner in which this law shall be carried into execution, was to exclude a seizure of any vessel not bound to a French port . . . [Yet i]f only vessels sailing to a French port could be seized on the high seas, that the law would be very often evaded, [and hence] this act of congress appears to have received a different construction from the executive of the United States; a construction much better calculated to give it effect. . . .
>
> These orders given by the executive under the construction of the act of congress made by the department to which its execution was assigned, enjoin the seizure of American vessels sailing from a French port. Is the officer who obeys them liable for damages sustained by this misconstruction of the act, or will his orders excuse him? If his instructions afford him no protection, then the law must take its course, and he must pay such damages as are legally awarded against him. . . .

105. See, e.g., David McCulloch, John Adams 424 (2001).

I confess the first bias of my mind was very strong in favor of the opinion that though the instructions of the executive could not give a right, they might yet excuse from damages . . . [because of the] implicit obedience which military men usually pay to the orders of their superiors, which indeed is indispensably necessary to every military system. . . . I was strongly inclined to think that where, in consequence of orders from the legitimate authority, a vessel is seized with pure intention, the claim of the injured party for damages would be against that government from which the orders proceeded, and would be a proper subject for negotiation. But I have been convinced that I was mistaken. . . . I acquiesce in [the opinion] of my brethren, which is, that the instructions cannot change the nature of the transaction, or legalize an act which without those instructions would have been a plain trespass. . . .

DISCUSSION

1. Would President Adams (and Captain Little) have been on stronger ground had Congress not passed the Non-Intercourse Act in the first place? Under this view, absent congressional action, the President has inherent authority to protect the United States against perceived threats to its vital national interests, but Congress can limit this authority by specifying the President's powers by statute. A second position would be that the President has only the authority granted him by Congress, acting under its powers in Article I, §8. A third position is that the President has inherent authority to protect national security that cannot be altered or limited by Congress. This would mean that the Non-Intercourse Act was unconstitutional to the extent that it limited President Adams. Little v. Barreme rejects this third view of executive power, at least as to the particular executive actions at issue.

2. Suppose that Adams was indifferent to the statutory limitation on his own powers and chose to act as he thought necessary to protect vital American national security interests. (Recall the arguments that would be made only a few years later by Thomas Jefferson concerning the Louisiana Purchase.) Is it fair to hold Captain Little to a duty to know the precise language of the Act and to realize that the President of the United States was acting beyond his constitutional authority? We shall return to this question later in the context first of Abraham Lincoln's conduct as President during the events of 1861-1865 and then of the contemporary "war on terrorism."

VII. THE PROTECTION OF PROPERTY RIGHTS AND THE NATURAL LAW TRADITION

Fletcher v. Peck

10 U.S. (6 Cranch) 87 (1810)

[This case arose out of the notorious Yazoo land-grant scandal. In 1795, a majority of the Georgia legislature had been bribed to convey some 35 million acres of state land to private companies at the bargain price of about 11/2 ¢ per acre. In 1796, the legislature rescinded the grant, but not before large parcels had been sold to Northern investors. A suit on a warranty of title presented the question whether the 1796 rescission could affect the rights of bona fide purchasers not themselves part of the initially fraudulent scheme and, according to Marshall's opinion, without "notice" of it.[106]]

MARSHALL, C.J. . . .

[Subsequent purchasers] were innocent. Yet the legislature of Georgia has involved them in the fate of the first parties to the transaction, and, if the act be valid, has annihilated their rights also. The legislature of Georgia was a party to this transaction; and for a party to pronounce its own deed invalid, whatever cause may be assigned for its invalidity, must be considered as a mere act of power, which must find its vindication in a train of reasoning not often heard in courts of justice. . . .

If a suit be brought to set aside a conveyance obtained by fraud, and the fraud be clearly proved, the conveyance will be set aside, as between the parties; but the rights of third persons, who are purchasers without notice, for a valuable consideration, cannot be disregarded. . . . All titles would be insecure, and the intercourse between man and man would be very seriously obstructed, if this principle be overturned. . . . If the legislature felt itself absolved from those rules of property which are common to all the citizens of the United States, and from those principles of equity which are acknowledged in all our courts, its act is to be supported by its power alone, and the same power may divest any other individual of his lands, if it shall be the will of the legislature so to exert it. . . .

Is the power of the legislature competent to the annihilation of such title, and to a resumption of the property thus held? The principle asserted is, that one

---

106. See C. Peter Magrath, Yazoo—Law and Politics in the New Republic (1966). A vivid sense of the passions underlying the rescission is provided by Senator Albert Beveridge in his classic biography, 4 The Life of John Marshall 562-566 (1919):

> The Legislature further enacted that the "usurped act" and all "records, documents, and deeds" connected with the Yazoo fraud, "shall be expunged from the face and indexes of the books of record of the State, and the enrolled law or usurped act shall then be publicly burnt, in order that no trace of so unconstitutional, vile, and fraudulent a transaction shall remain in the public offices thereof." . . .
>
> A committee, appointed to devise a method for destroying the records, immediately reported that this should be done by cutting out of the books the leaves containing them. As to the enrolled bill containing the "usurped act," an elaborate performance was directed to be held: "A fire shall be made in front of the State House door, and a line formed by the members of both branches around the same. The Secretary of State . . . shall then produce the enrolled bill and usurped act from among the archives of the State and deliver the same to the President of the Senate, who shall examine the same, and shall then deliver the same to the Speaker of the House of Representatives for like examination; and the Speaker shall then deliver them to the Clerk of the House of Representatives, who shall read aloud the title to the same, and shall then deliver them to Messenger of the House, who shall then pronounce—'GOD SAVE THE STATE!! AND LONG PRESERVE HER RIGHTS!! AND MAY EVERY ATTEMPT TO INJURE THEM PERISH AS THESE CORRUPT ACTS NOW DO!!!!'" Every detail of this play was carried out with all theatrical effect. . . . Someone gifted with dramatic genius suggested that the funeral pyre of such unholy legislation should not be lighted by earthly hands, but by fire from Heaven. A sun-glass was produced; Senator Jackson held it above the fagots and the pile was kindled from "the burning rays of the lidless eye of justice.

legislature is competent to repeal any act which a former legislature was competent to pass; and that one legislature cannot abridge the powers of a succeeding legislature. The correctness of this principle, so far as respects general legislation, can never be controverted. But, if an act be done under a law, a succeeding legislature cannot undo it. The past cannot be recalled by the most absolute power. Conveyances have been made, those conveyances have vested legal estates. . . . When, then, a law is in its nature a contract, when absolute rights have vested under that contract, a repeal of the law cannot divest those rights; and the act of annulling them, if legitimate, is rendered so by a power applicable to the case of every individual in the community.

It may well be doubted, whether the nature of society and of government does not prescribe some limits to the legislative power; and if any be prescribed, where are they to be found, if the property of an individual, fairly and honestly acquired, may be seized without compensation? . . . The constitution of the United States declares that no state shall pass any . . . law impairing the obligation of contracts.

Does the case now under consideration come within this prohibitory section of the constitution? In considering this very interesting question, we immediately ask ourselves, what is a contract? Is a grant a contract? A contract is a compact between two or more parties, and is either executory or executed. . . . A contract executed, as well as one which is executory, contains obligations binding on the parties, [including an obligation] not to re-assert [rights possessed prior to the completion of the contract].

Since, then, in fact, a grant [of land] is a contract executed, the obligation of which still continues, and since the constitution uses the general term contract, without distinguishing between those which are executory and those which are executed, it must be construed to comprehend the latter as well as the former. . . .

[The next question is whether the Contract Clause should] be considered as inhibiting the state from impairing the obligation of contracts between two individuals, but as excluding from that inhibition contracts made with itself? The words themselves contain no such distinction. They are general, and are applicable to contracts of every description. If contracts made with the state are to be exempted from their operation, the exception must arise from the character of the contracting party, not from the words which are employed.

Whatever respect might have been felt for the state sovereignties, it is not to be disguised, that the framers of the constitution viewed, with some apprehension, the violent acts which might grow out of the feelings of the moment; and that the people of the United States, in adopting that instrument, have manifested a determination to shield themselves and their property from the effects of those sudden and strong passions to which men are exposed. The restrictions on the legislative power of the states are obviously founded in this sentiment; and the constitution of the United States contains what may be deemed a bill of rights for the people of each state. . . .

It is, then, the unanimous opinion of the court, that, in this case, the estate having passed into the hands of a purchaser for a valuable consideration, without notice, the state of Georgia was restrained, either by general principles which are common to our free institutions, or by the particular provisions of the constitution of the United States, from passing a law whereby the estate of the plaintiff in the premises so purchased could be constitutionally and legally impaired and rendered null and void. . . .

JOHNSON, J.

I do not hesitate to declare, that a state does not possess the power of revoking its own grants. But I do it, on a general principle, on the reason and nature of things; a principle which will impose laws even on the Deity. . . .

When the legislature have once conveyed their interest or property in any subject to the individual, they have lost all control over it; have nothing to act upon; it has passed from them; is vested in the individual; becomes intimately blended with his existence, as essentially so as the blood that circulates through his system. The government may indeed demand of him the one or the other, not because they are not his, but because whatever is his, is his country's. . . .

I have thrown out these ideas, that I may have it distinctly understood, that my opinion on this point is not founded on the provision in the constitution of the United States, relative to laws impairing the obligation of contracts. . . .

I enter with great hesitation upon this question, because it involves a subject of the greatest delicacy and much difficulty. The states and the United States are continually legislating on the subject of contracts, prescribing the mode of authentication, the time within which suits shall be prosecuted for them, in many cases, affecting existing contracts by the laws which they pass, and declaring them to cease or lose their effect for want of compliance, in the parties, with such statutory provisions. All these acts appear to be within the most correct limits of legislative powers, and most beneficially exercised, and certainly could not have been intended to be affected by this constitutional provision; yet where to draw the line, or how to define or limit the words, "obligation of contracts," will be found a subject of extreme difficulty.

DISCUSSION

1. *Language and purpose.* During the depression following the Revolutionary War, many states enacted debtor relief laws, which modified contractual obligations or the procedures available to creditors for enforcing the obligations. The Contract Clause of Article I, §10, was designed to preclude a recurrence of such legislation. See Home Building & Loan Association v. Blaisdell, 290 U.S. 398 (1934) (Sutherland, J., dissenting), Chapter 5, infra. Does a purpose of preventing the state from intervening in the contractual relations between two private individuals necessarily extend to precluding the state from, in effect, rewriting its own contracts should the state legislature believe that the public interest will be served thereby? The answer may depend on the *level of generality* on which the purpose of the clause is conceived. Articulate the purpose of the Contract Clause narrowly enough to foreclose its application to the Georgia statute in *Fletcher.* Now articulate it broadly enough to justify Marshall's interpretation. How can one determine which is the correct level of generality on which to articulate the purpose of the provision?

2. *Judicial inquiry into legislative motivation.* The Court in *Fletcher* was also asked to invalidate the grant because of the Georgia legislature's corruption in enacting the original conveyance. Marshall resisted any such invitation to scrutinize the legislature's motivation:

> It may well be doubted how far the validity of a law depends upon the motives of its framers, and how far the particular inducements, operating on members of the supreme sovereign power of a state, to the formation of a contract by that power, are examinable in a court of justice. If the principle be conceded, that an act of the supreme sovereign power might be declared null by a court, in consequence of the means which procured it, still would there be much difficulty in saying to what extent those means must be applied to produce this effect. Must it be direct corruption, or would interest or undue influence of any kind be sufficient? Must the vitiating cause operate on a majority, or on what number of the members? Would the act be null, whatever might be the wish of the nation, or would its obligation or nullity depend upon the public sentiment?
>
> If the majority of the legislature be corrupted, it may well be doubted, whether it be within the province of the judiciary to control their conduct, and, if less than a majority act from impure motives, the principle by which judicial interference would be regulated, is not clearly discerned.

Marshall avoids a definite conclusion as to the propriety of looking into motivation by declaring that, in any event, "[t]his solemn question cannot be brought . . . collaterally and incidentally before the court, as in this suit between two private parties. It would be indecent, in the extreme, upon a private contract, between two individuals, to enter into an inquiry respecting the corruption of the sovereign power of a state." What, though, of Marshall's basic qualms about looking into legislative motivation? Should a court *ever* be willing to take evidence as to the corrupt background of a bill in deciding whether or not it is constitutional? Is Marshall's argument in *Fletcher* consistent with his later assurance in ¶42 of *McCulloch* that the Court will monitor congressional legislation to make sure that it is genuinely designed to further Congress's powers and not "pretextual"?

3. *Other Contract Clause decisions.* Marshall's expansive interpretation of the Contract Clause continued in Dartmouth College v. Woodward, 17 U.S. (4 Wheat.) 518 (1819), which held that New Hampshire could not unilaterally modify a private institution's charter to place it under public control. Marshall wrote:

> It is more than possible that the preservation of rights of this description was not particularly in the view of the framers of the constitution, when the clause under consideration was introduced into that instrument. It is probable, that interferences of more frequent recurrence, to which the temptation was stronger, and of which the mischief was more extensive, constituted the great motive for imposing this restriction on the State legislatures. But although a particular and a rare case may not, in itself, be of sufficient magnitude to induce a rule, yet it must be governed by the rule, when established, unless some plain and strong reason for excluding it can be given. It is not enough to say, that this particular case was not in the mind of the Convention, when the article was framed, nor of the American people, when it was adopted. It is necessary to go further, and to say that, had this particular case been suggested, the language would have been so varied, as to exclude it, or it would have been made a special exception.

In Sturges v. Crowninshield, 17 U.S. (4 Wheat.) 122 (1819), Marshall also wrote the Court's opinion, holding that a New York bankruptcy law could not operate retroactively to discharge a debt incurred before the law was enacted.

In *Fletcher*, Marshall notes that Article I, §10, besides prohibiting the impairment of the obligation of contracts, prohibits ex post facto laws and bills of attainder. An ex post facto law is a criminal law applied to conduct occurring before its enactment. A bill of attainder is a legislative act finding that specified individuals are guilty of a crime and punishing them for it. Bills of attainder were typically also ex post facto laws. Thus these prohibited legislative measures share the feature that they apply retroactively to defeat settled expectations.

The distinction between retroactive and prospective interference with contractual obligations turned out to be of great significance in Contract Clause doctrine. Concurring in *Dartmouth College*, Justice Story observed that legislative grants might explicitly reserve to the state the power to amend the charters. And in Ogden v. Saunders, 25 U.S. (12 Wheat.) 213 (1827), the Court limited *Sturges* to the retroactive application of bankruptcy laws to preexisting contracts, holding that a statute in existence at the time the contract is made becomes "part of the contract."

In his only dissent in a constitutional case, the Chief Justice, joined by Justices Story and Duvall, argued from principles of natural law and social contract and from the language of the Contract Clause that government could not (in effect) dictate in advance the terms of private contracts to release obligors in the event of their insolvency. Marshall began by pointing to the origins of freedom of contract in natural right: "[I]ndividuals do not derive from government their right to contract, but bring that right with them into society; that obligation is not conferred upon contracts by positive law, but is intrinsic, and is conferred by the act of the parties." Society is not without any powers at all to affect the right to contract; it can control the formalities of contract formation or prohibit specific contracts as violations of public policy. Moreover, Marshall accepted the right of a state to pass laws affecting contract remedies, but he rejected the relevance of that concession by arguing that bankruptcy laws are not merely remedial, because what they do is to turn "obligatory" contracts into de facto "conditional" promises. He feared that "one of the most important features in the Constitution of the United States . . . would lie prostrate, and be construed into an inanimate, inoperative, unmeaning clause." The dissenters read the language of the clause as barring prospective as well as retrospective legislation and viewed *Ogden* as offering a method for returning to the preconstitutional era by which state legislatures felt free to pass allegedly ruinous debtor-relief legislation.

Stephen Siegel points out that a key question lurking behind the bankruptcy issue was the validity of so-called reserve clauses, whereby the legislature put into its grant of corporate charters a proviso "reserving" the right to change their terms.[107]

---

107. Stephen A. Siegel, Understanding the Nineteenth Century Contract Clause, The Role of the Property-Privilege Distinction and "Takings" Clause Jurisprudence, 60 S. Cal. L. Rev. 1 (1986).

"Until the twentieth century, property had a dual signification in Liberal thought. In one sense property denoted, as it still does, all items of wealth. In the other sense property denoted only those valuables whose acquisition was open to all individuals, typically through competition in the free market. Property, in this latter sense, stood in contrast to privilege, which signified wealth that only certain individuals could acquire, usually through designation by affirmative governmental act." Regulation of privilege was far more acceptable than regulation of ordinary property, including contract rights protected by the Contract Clause. It was one thing to allow reservations in charters awarded by the state because such charters were viewed as awarding a privilege to their recipients. It was quite another to allow ordinary contracts to be subject to broad reservations, and in fact no state ever enacted a general "reserve" clause governing private contracts. "[O]ver time," says Siegel, "jurists simply assumed they were unconstitutional."

4. *Appellate review and natural law.* G. Edward White emphasizes the difference in treatment between appeals to the Supreme Court from state court decisions based on §25 of the Judiciary Act of 1789 and appeals from lower federal courts, especially those arising under diversity jurisdiction. He suggests that only in non-§25 cases did the Court feel free to refer to the "general law," including norms of natural law or natural justice, whereas in §25 appeals the Court ostensibly limited itself to constitutional issues and to a far more positivistic, textual conception of the law it was authorized to enforce. White notes that *Fletcher* "was a diversity case, meaning that the Court could draw upon general principles of federal law as well as the Constitution for its sources." Justice Washington later wrote that "no where" in *Fletcher* is it "intimated . . . that a state statute, which divests a vested right, is repugnant to the constitution of the United States." Because *Fletcher* originated in a federal court it was appropriate to refer to general norms of justice; in a §25 case arising from a state court, on the other hand, the Supreme Court could only invalidate the statute where it was "repugnant to the *constitution of the United States.*"[108]

On this analysis, are only those parts of *Fletcher* relying on constitutional text rather than unenumerated norms truly "constitutional"? If so, what is the source of the Court's authority to strike down a state law on non-"constitutional" "general legal" grounds?

NOTE: NATURAL LAW, VESTED RIGHTS, AND THE WRITTEN CONSTITUTION: SOURCES FOR JUDICIAL REVIEW

The reliance in *Fletcher* on "general principles" of law may sound strange, especially coming from Marshall, who seven years earlier had treated judicial review (of congressional legislation) merely as the application of the positive law of the written constitution. This note surveys the concepts of "rights" extant in the late eighteenth and early nineteenth centuries.

---

108. G. Edward White, 3 History of the Supreme Court of the United States: The Marshall Court and Cultural Change, 1815-1835 611, 657-659 (1988).

1. *The Natural Law Tradition in America*[109]

Although its influence has often been exaggerated, the concept of natural or fundamental law—a universal law superior to all man-made laws—pervaded eighteenth-century American intellectual and legal thought. Three features of the English natural law tradition influenced the development of constitutionalism in America. First, the received jurisprudence was that judges did not "make" the common law. Rather, through the "artificial reason of the law," they discovered immutable legal principles, which, together with more specific applications deduced from them, constituted the corpus of the English common law.[110] Second, centuries of revisionist history had transformed the Magna Carta (1215) from a partisan political document to a declaration of the natural rights of Englishmen, and the Petition of Right (1628) and Bill of Rights (1688-1689), as well as the Declaration of Independence (1776), were usually claimed not to establish new principles but to declare preexisting ones. The third source of natural law doctrine was John Locke's Second Treatise on Civil Government (1690). Reasoning deductively from the pregovernmental "state of nature" to the "social compact" formed to improve on that state, Locke derived both the supremacy of the legislature and limitations on its exercise of powers. Of his three basic rights of individuals—"life, liberty, and estate"—the last was most fundamental: Property was an extension of the individual, and the social compact was largely designed to protect whatever distributions of wealth came about through the varying talents and efforts of the members of society.

---

109. See Bernard Bailyn, The Ideological Origins of the American Revolution (1967); Carl Becker, The Declaration of Independence, ch. 2 (1922); J.W. Gough, Fundamental Law in English Constitutional History (1955); Charles Mullett, Fundamental Law and the American Revolution (1933); Gordon Wood, The Creation of the American Republic, 1776-1787 (1969); Benjamin Wright, American Interpretations of Natural Law (1931); Edward Corwin, The "Higher Law" Background of American Constitutional Law, 42 Harv. L. Rev. 149, 365 (1928-1929); Corwin, The Basic Doctrine of American Constitutional Law, 12 Mich. L. Rev. 247 (1914). As noted earlier, a comprehensive study of the "natural law" tradition in the West would surely have to include the Aristotelian influence, particularly on Roman Catholic thought.

110. The quoted phrase is Sir Edward Coke's. James I had claimed that the king was entitled to decide cases, arguing "the law was founded upon reason, and that he and others had reason, as well as the Judges." Coke replied, "[T]rue it was that God had endowed his majesty with excellent science, and great endowments of nature; but his Majesty was not learned in the laws of his realm of England, and causes which concern the life, or inheritance, or goods, or fortunes of his subjects, are not to be decided by natural reason but by the artificial reason and judgment of the law, which law is an act which requires long study and experience, before that a man can attain the cognizance of it. . . ." The king "was greatly offended" at the notion that "he should be under the law, which was treason to affirm." Coke responded, quoting Bracton and invoking fundamental law: "Quod Rex non debet esse sub homine, sed sub Deo et lege" (the King ought to be under no man, but under God and the law). Prohibitions Del Roy, 12 Co. 63, 77 Eng. Rep. 1342 (1609). On the life of Coke, see Katherine Bowen, The Lion and the Throne (1957). See also Gough, supra n.109, ch. 3; David Little, Religion, Order and Law: A Study in Pre-Revolutionary England, ch. 6 (1969).

These elements of the natural law tradition coalesced in the eighteenth-century American view that[111]

> the written constitution [is] . . . a species of social compact, entered into by sovereign individuals in a state of nature. . . . [G]overnmental authority . . . is a trust which, save for the grant of it effected by the written constitution, were non-existent, and private rights, since they precede the constitution, gain nothing of authoritativeness from being enumerated in it, though possibly something of security. These rights are not, in other words, fundamental because they find mention in the written instrument; they find mention there because fundamental. . . . The written constitution is, in short, but a nucleus or core of a much wider region of private rights, which though not reduced to black and white, are as fully entitled to the protection of government as if defined in the minutest detail.

The natural rights of individuals were generally understood to be those that, through judicial "discovery" and the absorption of the Magna Carta, inhered in the common law. As restated in Blackstone's Commentaries 129-139 (1765), the three "absolute rights of individuals" were: "the right of personal security [which] consists in a person's legal and uninterrupted enjoyment of his life, his limbs, his body, his health, and his reputation"; the right of "personal liberty [which] consists in the power of loco-motion, of changing situation, or moving one's person to whatsoever place one's own inclination may direct, without imprisonment or restraint, unless by due course of law"; and "the absolute right, inherent in every Englishman . . . of property: which consists in the free use, enjoyment, and disposal of all his acquisitions, without any control or diminution, save only by the laws of the land."

Perhaps the most audacious invocation of natural law in our history is Justice Johnson's assertion, in his *Fletcher* concurrence, that he bases his invalidation of Georgia's statute "on a general principle, on the reason and nature of things; a principle which will impose laws even on the Deity." Johnson's suggestion that even God, in effect, has a duty to obey what might be termed "general principles of reason" goes back at least to Plato's dialogue *Euthyphro,* where he asks whether propositions of morality are true simply because God (or the gods) command them—which suggests a certain level of arbitrariness in that God presumably has the authority to propound anything at all—or whether there are preexisting principles of morality that bind even God—which paints a picture of God as a kind of "constitutional monarch" who must remain within the bounds of an external law. Similar questions were debated by Christian theologians of the sixteenth and seventeenth centuries.[112] Once again we see the pervasiveness of debates over the meaning of "sovereignty" (and over who possesses sovereignty). Must an earthly sovereign, like the heavenly sovereign, have unlimited powers? What about a popular sovereign? As we saw in several of the *Chisholm* opinions and in Marshall's argument in *McCulloch,* American constitutionalism is premised on the "sovereignty of

---

111. Corwin, The Basic Doctrine of American Constitutional Law, supra n.109, at 247-248.

112. See, e.g., Jean Bethke Elshtain, Sovereignty: God, State, and Self (2008).

the people." One well-known assertion, going back to an eighth-century letter by Alcuin to the Emperor Charlemagne, is that "the voice of the people is the voice of God."[113] Does this mean that popular will as expressed in a constitution should be unlimited? Or, to the contrary, does the fact that constitutional power will be expressed by agents of the people—as opposed to the people themselves—mean that government power *must* be limited in any system of popular sovereignty?

2. *The Judicial Protection of Vested Rights*

The substantive legal issue involved in both *Marbury* and *Fletcher* was the protection of "vested rights." The President was free to appoint or not to appoint Marbury as a justice of the peace. But once Marbury's right to the commission "vested," the government could no more deprive him of it than a seller of real property could take it back after title had vested in the purchaser. The doctrine of vested rights did not encompass all expectations. In his well-known nineteenth-century treatise, Constitutional Limitations, Thomas Cooley explained:[114]

> [A] right cannot be considered a vested right, unless it is something more than such a mere expectation as may be based upon an anticipated continuance of the present general laws: it must have become a title, legal or equitable, to the present or future enjoyment of property, or to the present or future enforcement of a demand, or a legal exemption from a demand, made by another.

The doctrine assumed, in other words, that the basic structure of entitlements was determined by the common law as modified by legislation—that these determined the procedures by which property interests were created and transferred. But once an interest had vested in an individual—once it *belonged* to her—it was immune from government divestment. As Chancellor James Kent wrote in his comprehensive Commentaries on American Law (1826), a statute "affecting and changing vested rights is very generally considered in this country as founded on unconstitutional principles, and consequently inoperative and void."[115] When Kent characterized a law violating vested rights as *unconstitutional* he was not referring to the U.S. Constitution or even to written state constitutions, but rather to what were understood to be *general* constitutional limitations implicit in all free governments—limitations based on natural rights and the nature of the social compact.

The vested rights doctrine developed and flourished primarily in the state courts. It made its first and least equivocal Supreme Court appearance in Calder v. Bull.

113. Alexander Hamilton, speaking to the Constitutional Convention on June 18, 1787, offered the following response to this maxim: "[I]t is not true to fact. The people are turbulent and changing, they seldom judge or determine right." See 1 Records of the Federal Convention of 1787, at 299 (1937).

114. Thomas Cooley, 2 Constitutional Limitations 749 (Carrington ed., 8th ed. 1927).

115. Quoted in id. at 449.

Calder v. Bull

3 U.S. (3 Dall.) 386 (1798)

[A Connecticut probate court had disapproved a will designating the respondents as beneficiaries, thus allowing petitioners to inherit as decedent's heirs at law. The Connecticut legislature passed a resolution setting aside the decree and granting a new hearing, at which the will was approved. To petitioners' claim that the legislative act was an ex post facto law in violation of Article I, §10, the Court responded that the clause was limited to criminal legislation. But Justice Chase, who wrote the most comprehensive of several seriatim opinions, went on to consider whether, apart from this or any other specific provision of the Constitution, a government could deprive a citizen of a vested property right.]

CHASE, J.:

I cannot subscribe to the omnipotence of a state legislature, or that it is absolute and without control; although its authority should not be expressly restrained by the Constitution, or fundamental law, of the State. The people of the United States erected their Constitutions, or forms of government, to establish justice, to promote the general welfare, to secure the blessings of liberty; and to protect their persons and property from violence. The purposes for which men enter into society will determine the nature and terms of the social compact; and as they are the foundation of the legislative power, they will decide what are the proper objects of it. The nature and ends of legislative power will limit the exercise of it. This fundamental principle flows from the very nature of our free Republican governments, that no man should be compelled to do what the laws do not require, nor to refrain from acts which the laws permit. There are acts which the Federal or State Legislature cannot do, without exceeding their authority. There are certain vital principles in our free Republican governments, which will determine and overrule an apparent and flagrant abuse of legislative power; as to authorize manifest injustice by positive law; or to take away that security for personal liberty, or private property, for the protection whereof the government was established. An ACT of the Legislature (for I cannot call it a law) contrary to the great first principles of the social compact, cannot be considered a rightful exercise of legislative authority.

The obligation of a law in governments established on express compact, and on republican principles, must be determined by the nature of the power on which it is founded. A few instances will suffice to explain what I mean. A law that punished a citizen for an innocent action, or, in other words, for an act, which, when done, was in violation of no existing law; a law that destroys, or impairs, the lawful private contracts of citizens; a law that makes a man a judge in his own cause; or a law that takes property from A. and gives it to B. It is against all reason and justice, for a people to intrust a Legislature with such powers; and, therefore, it cannot be presumed that they have done it. The genius, the nature, and the spirit of our State Governments, amount to a prohibition of such acts of legislation; and the general principles of law and reason forbid them.

The Legislature may enjoin, permit, forbid, and punish; they may declare new crimes; and establish rules of conduct for all its citizens in future cases; they may command what is right, and prohibit what is wrong; but they cannot change innocence into guilt; or punish innocence as a crime; or violate the right of an antecedent lawful private contract; or the right of private property. To maintain that our Federal or State Legislature possesses such powers, if they had not been expressly restrained; would, in my opinion, be a political heresy, altogether inadmissible in our free republican governments.

[Applying this theory to the case at bar, Justice Chase found that Connecticut's actions had not deprived the petitioners of a vested property right, since no right vested by the first decree. Chase also pointed out that, as a matter of interpretation, "[i]t is not to be presumed, that the federal or state legislatures will pass laws to deprive citizens of rights vested in them by existing laws; unless for the benefit of the whole community; and on making full satisfaction."]

IREDELL, J.:

[Justice Iredell, in his separate opinion, challenged the basic premise of Chase's inquiry.]

It is true, that some speculative jurists have held, that a legislative act against natural justice must, in itself, be void; but I cannot think that, under such a government, any Court of Justice would possess a power to declare it so. Sir William Blackstone, having put the strong case of an act of Parliament which, should authorize a man to try his own cause, explicitly adds, that even in that case, "there is no court that has power to defeat the intent of the Legislature, when couched in such evident and express words, as leave no doubt whether it was the intent of the Legislature, or no." 1 Bl. Comm. 91.

In order, therefore, to guard against so great an evil, it has been the policy of all the American States, which have, individually, framed their state constitutions since the revolution, and of the people of the United States, when they framed the Federal Constitution, to define with precision the objects of the legislative power, and to restrain its exercise within marked and settled boundaries. If any act of Congress, or of the Legislature of a State, violates those constitutional provisions, it is unquestionably void; though, I admit, that as the authority to declare it void is of a delicate and awful nature, the Court will never resort to that authority, but in a clear and urgent case. If, on the other hand, the Legislature of the Union, or the Legislature of any member of the Union, shall pass a law, within the general scope of their constitutional power, the Court cannot pronounce it to be void, merely because it is, in their judgment, contrary to the principles of natural justice. The ideas of natural justice are regulated by no fixed standard; the ablest and the purest men have differed upon the subject; and all that the Court could properly say, in such an event, would be, that the Legislature, possessed of an equal right of opinion, had passed an act which, in the opinion of the judges, was inconsistent with the abstract principles of natural justice.

DISCUSSION

1. Is Justice Chase making an appeal to what might be termed "transcendent" norms of justice, which by definition would be true in all cultures at all times, or, rather, is he arguing that it is a truth of *our* particular form of polity that the

norms that he identifies are recognized? The first would count as a "natural law" argument. The latter, however, might be better described as what Professor Philip Bobbitt labels as "ethical" argument, by which he means an appeal to the particular ethos of a society, which may, of course, be quite different from that of other societies.[116]

2. Note that Justice Chase could merely be stating a rule of statutory construction: Unless the statutory language is clear, one should not assume that the public has given the legislature power to destroy vested rights (or natural rights), and the legislature should not be presumed to have attempted to violate vested rights (or natural rights). Therefore courts will strain to read statutes in a way that avoids that result. The idea is related to Blackstone's notion of "equitable interpretation," in which a court might depart from the most obvious or plain meaning of a statute in order to avoid violating important rule of law norms. The unresolved question is what Chase believed a court should do if confronted with a clearly drafted statute that clearly violated natural law principles. What difficulties do you see with this approach? Note that modern courts occasionally invoke a "canon of constitutional avoidance" to interpret statutes to avoid declaring them unconstitutional.

3. Justice Iredell seems to view Justice Chase as making a "natural law" argument, about which he states that "[t]he ideas of natural justice are regulated by no fixed standard; the ablest and the purest men have differed upon the subject." He could be interpreted as making two quite different arguments. The first might be termed *ontological*: that is, asking whether transcendent norms of justice really exist in the universe. The second is *epistemological*: Even if one assumes that transcendent moral norms exist, one might doubt whether human beings have adequate means of discerning what they actually are; the reason, according to Iredell, is that the "ablest and the purest men have differed upon the subject." But, of course, it is also true that "the ablest and the purest" judges and scholars have "differed" about many basic issues of constitutional law. Does this prove that there is, for all intents and purposes, no real substance to the entire enterprise that we call constitutional analysis, or only that it is difficult and that very smart (and pure) people of good faith can disagree about important issues? One could, of course, ask similar questions with regard to any discipline, including heated debates among physicists with regard to the status of string theory or among neuropsychologists about the nature of human consciousness. In what ways are good faith disagreements about law different from good faith disagreements about scientific truths? In any event, how important is it that lawyers (and law students) work through such philosophical problems to decide the kinds of questions treated in the Chase and Iredell opinions?

3. The Explicit Federal Constitutional Protection of Rights

The vested rights doctrine aside, judicial protection of individual rights depended mainly on the written provisions of state constitutions and the U.S. Constitution. Article I, §10 prohibited states from passing bills of attainder, ex post facto laws, and laws impairing the obligation of contracts. Article I, §9 applied the first

116. See Philip Bobbitt, Constitutional Interpretation 20-22 (1991).

two prohibitions to the federal government and limited the government's power to suspend the writ of habeas corpus. In 1791, the Constitution was supplemented by a Bill of Rights, which the Court held in Barron v. Baltimore, 32 U.S. (7 Pet.) 243 (1833), applied only to the federal government.[117]

4. *The Ninth Amendment*[118]

The title of Bennett Patterson's 1955 book, The Forgotten Ninth Amendment, accurately captures the status of this provision of the Bill of Rights throughout most of our constitutional history.[119] Nonetheless, if any provision of the U.S. Constitution seems to embody the concept of natural rights, it is the Ninth Amendment: "The enumeration in the Constitution, of certain rights, shall not be construed to deny or disparage others retained by the people." The purpose of the amendment is ambiguous, however. Was it designed to safeguard individual liberties not enumerated in the first eight amendments or only to protect the states against the national government's assumption of powers not delegated by Articles I, II, and III?

Much anti-Federalist opposition to the Constitution in the state conventions focused on the absence of a bill of rights. The Federalist response was that a bill of rights was unnecessary and dangerous—unnecessary because the national government, being one of delegated powers, was not authorized to infringe individual liberties; dangerous because the enumeration would imply the existence of broader powers than were delegated. Recall the critiques of the idea of a written bill of rights offered by Hamilton, James Wilson, and James Iredell, Part One, Introduction, supra.

James Madison had shared the concern that a bill of rights might imply broader federal powers than were granted. Additionally, he wrote to Jefferson,[120] "there is great reason to fear that a positive declaration of some of the most essential rights could not be obtained in the requisite latitude. I am sure that the rights of conscience, in particular, if submitted to public definition would be narrowed much more than they are likely ever to be by an assumed power." Whether because of a change of mind or, as is more likely, a submission to the political demands of his Virginia constituents, Madison became the leading architect of the amendments that would form the Bill of Rights. In presenting to the First Congress the provision that became the Ninth Amendment, Madison explained:[121]

> It has been objected also against a bill of rights, that, by enumerating particular exceptions to the grant of power, it would disparage those rights which were not placed in that enumeration; and it might follow by implication, that those rights which were not singled out, were intended to

---

117. Does anything in the language of the amendments suggest that some of them might be applicable to the states? Compare the First and Seventh Amendments with the others.

118. See generally Randy Barnett, ed., The Rights Retained by the People: The History and Meaning of the Ninth Amendment (2 vols., 1989, 1993).

119. But see Chapter 9, infra.

120. 5 Writings of James Madison 271-272 (Hunt ed., 1904) (letter of Oct. 17, 1788).

121. 1 Annals of Cong. 439 (1789).

> be assigned into the hands of the General Government, and were consequently insecure. This is one of the most plausible arguments I have ever heard urged against the admission of a bill of rights into this system; but, I conceive, that it may be guarded against. I have attempted it, as gentlemen may see by turning to the last clause of the fourth resolution [the Ninth Amendment]. . . .

Professor Kurt Lash has recently argued that the Ninth Amendment was originally understood as an interpretive rule requiring a narrow (perhaps what Marshall would term a "strict" construction) of national power.[122] Noting the concern expressed at many state conventions against possible abuses of national power and the extent to which the proposed bill of rights was a response to such fears, he emphasizes as particularly important several paragraphs toward the conclusion of Madison's speech against the constitutionality of the First Bank, supra Chapter 1. There Madison refers to the "explanatory amendments proposed by Congress," including in this group the Ninth Amendment, which he describes "as guarding against a latitude of interpretation." The Tenth Amendment, Madison says, "exclude[s] every source of power not within the constitution itself."

Madison's argument," writes Professor Lash,[123]

> is easy to follow: The federal government is one of limited enumerated power. All nondelegated powers are reserved to the states. Unduly broad interpretations of these enumerated powers would destroy this principle by allowing the government to invade areas of law reserved to the states. Important powers like those exercised by the Bank Bill are not appropriately derived by implication but require enumeration. The state conventions that ratified the Constitution had been promised that federal power would not receive this kind of latitudinous interpretation, and several states made the adoption of a rule rejecting this kind of interpretation a condition of their ratifying the Constitution. Although implied in the original Constitution, an express rule against latitudinarian constructions found its ultimate expression in the Ninth Amendment.

One might ask, of course, whether this is the most natural reading of the text. That is, Professor Lash is making a historical argument rather than appealing to any "obvious" meaning of the text. Moreover, he himself admits that this original understanding of the Ninth Amendment was quickly "lost" to later interpreters, to be replaced by other views as to its meaning. The very rapidity with which it was lost may suggest that, as with many other (perhaps most, or even all) of the Constitution's provisions, there were in fact different views of its purpose and meaning among those who adopted and ratified it.

Furthermore, any attempt to elucidate the amendment's purposes must deal with some enigmatic data. On the one hand, if the amendment were concerned primarily with safeguarding federalism, it seems to make surplusage of the Tenth

---

122. See Kurt Lash, The Lost Original Meaning of the Ninth Amendment, 83 Tex. L. Rev. 331 (2004).

123. Id. at 393.

Amendment, which speaks explicitly of powers "reserved to the States." Can one plausibly respond that the Ninth Amendment is a rule requiring narrow interpretation of those powers that *are* undoubtedly assigned to the national government, whereas the Tenth Amendment refers to powers that could not even be implied from the assigned power? On the other hand, if the amendment were concerned primarily with safeguarding individual liberties, one might expect to find similar provisions in some of the bills of rights of contemporary state constitutions. There is a further complexity here. In 1791, the Ninth Amendment was unique, but the bills of rights of many nineteenth-century state constitutions paraphrase the amendment.[124]

NOTE: IS CONSTITUTIONAL LAW A COMEDY OR A TRAGEDY?

Fletcher's rhetoric, including its presentation of the Court as a "court of justice," leads the reader to believe that constitutional cases are likely to have "happy endings," in the specific sense that constitutional norms and the norms of justice, whether defined in terms of natural law or of "general principles which are common to our free institutions," will coincide. Is it possible, though, that legal norms, including constitutional ones, may have a more "tragic" dimension, so that the law and norms of justice will be in opposition rather than joined together? Recall that at the Philadelphia Convention James Wilson pointed out a "law may be unjust, may be unwise, may be dangerous, may be destructive; and yet not be so unconstitutional as to justify the judges in refusing to give [it] effect."

The law of chattel slavery forces one to confront the possibility that legal interpretation may sometimes have unhappy endings. Consider Marshall's opinion in a nonconstitutional case, The Antelope, 23 U.S. (10 Wheat.) 66 (1825), which arose in the context of the international trade in slaves. In 1808, Congress prohibited the importation of slaves into the United States. (Could it have constitutionally done so prior to 1808? See Article I, §9, cl. 1 and Article V.) A series of subsequent federal enactments punished persons engaged in the international slave trade, required forfeiture of their ships, and provided that the captives be returned to Africa. The ship Antelope, bearing 280 Africans, most of whom had been seized on the high seas by pirates from slave ships, was apprehended in international waters off the coast of Florida by a U.S. revenue cutter for suspected violation of the slave trade acts.

The vice consuls of Spain and Portugal claimed the Africans as the property of citizens of their countries. They denied that the slaves were ever intended to be introduced to the United States in violation of local law; instead, they claimed, the slaves were being shipped to Brazil or Cuba, where the international slave trade remained perfectly legal. The United States appealed from the circuit courts' decision for the foreign claimants. The issue before the Court was whether the federal statutes applied to forfeit slaves owned by foreign nationals.[125] As Marshall put it, the case was one "in which the sacred rights of liberty and of property come in conflict with each other."

124. See John Ely, Democracy and Distrust 202-204 (1980).

125. The actual facts are considerably more complex. For a rich description of the case and its contents, see John Noonan, Jr., The Antelope: The Ordeal of the Recaptured Africans in the Administrations of James Monroe and John Quincy Adams (1977).

The mood suggested by Marshall's opinion is considerably more somber than in Fletcher v. Peck. He emphasizes that "this court must not yield to feelings which might seduce it from the path of duty, and must obey the mandate of the law." He denounces the slave trade, a traffic "abhorrent . . . to a mind whose original feelings are not blunted by familiarity with the practice," while reminding the reader that "it has[, however,] been sanctioned, in modern times, by the laws of all nations who possess distant colonies, each of whom has engaged in it as a common commercial business, which no other could rightfully interrupt."

Although "the feelings of justice and humanity" have prevailed in several of the American states and in the British parliament to abolish slavery or, at the least, to prohibit the international slave trade, these are, as yet, in effect only local practices, insufficient to change the legal reality of slavery (and the international slave trade) in states that are not so enlightened. Therefore, Marshall argues, it is ultimately irrelevant that slavery (or the slave trade) is "contrary to the law of nature" and "[t]hat every man has a natural right to the fruits of his own labor, is generally admitted," because international law has not yet adopted these principles as general legal norms.

> Throughout Christendom, . . . war is no longer considered, as giving a right to enslave captives. But this triumph of humanity has not been universal. The parties of the modern law of nations do not propagate their principles by force, and Africa has not yet adopted them. Throughout the whole extent of that immense continent, so far as we know its history, it is still the law of nations, that prisoners are slaves. Can those who have themselves renounced this law, be permitted to participate in its effects, by purchasing the beings who are its victims? Whatever might be the answer of a moralist to this question, a jurist must search for its legal solution, in those principles of action which are sanctioned by the usages, the national acts, and the general assent, of that portion of the world of which he considers himself as a part, and to whose law the appeal is made. If we resort to this standard, as the test of international law, the question, as has already been observed, is decided in favor of the legality of the trade. Both Europe and America embarked in it; and for nearly two centuries, it was carried on, without opposition, and without censure. A jurist could not say, that a practice, thus supported, was illegal, and that those engaged in it might be punished, either personally or by deprivation of property. In this commerce thus sanctioned by universal assent, every nation had an equal right to engage. How is this right to be lost? Each may renounce it for its own people; but can this renunciation effect others?
>
> No principle of general law is more universally acknowledged, than the perfect equality of nations. Russia and Geneva have equal rights. It results from this equality, that no one can rightfully impose a rule on another. Each legislates for itself, but its legislation can operate on itself alone. A right, then, which is vested in all, by the consent of all, can be divested only by consent; and this trade, in which all have participated, must remain lawful to those who cannot be induced to relinquish it. As no nation can prescribe a rule for others, none can make a law of nations; and this traffic remains lawful to those whose governments have not forbidden it. If it be consistent with the law of nations, it cannot in itself be piracy. It can be made so only by statute; and the obligation of the statute cannot transcend the legislative power of the state which may enact it.

Thus, said the Court, the United States must recognize the claims of the slave owners to the return of their property that had been illegitimately seized by pirates (and then brought into American waters by the coast guard). "It follows, that a foreign vessel engaged in the African slave-trade, captured on the high seas, in time of peace, by an American cruiser, and brought in for adjudication, would be restored."

DISCUSSION[126]

1. Although The Antelope does not arise under the Constitution, slavery presented the most divisive constitutional issue of the first 70 years of the Republic. Even if The Antelope did not directly affect domestic slavery, Marshall was well aware that anything the Court said about the matter would be critically read within the United States; he might also have been concerned not to antagonize the two foreign nations whose nationals claimed to own the slaves. Are these legitimate reasons for refusing to enforce the purported slaves' natural right to enjoy the "sacred principle" of liberty?

2. In suggesting that some courts may "have carried the principle of suppression further than a deliberate consideration of the subject would justify," Marshall may have been referring to the circuit court decision in United States v. La Jeune Eugenie, 26 F. Cas. 832 (No. 15,551) (C.C. Mass. 1822), in which Justice Story condemned the slave trade as

> repugnant to the great principles of Christian duty, the dictates of natural religion, the obligations of good faith and morality, and the eternal maxims of social justice. When any trade can be truly said to have these ingredients, it is impossible that it can be consistent with any system of law that purports to rest on the authority of reason or revelation. And it is sufficient to stamp any trade as interdicted by public law, when it can be justly affirmed, that it is repugnant to the general principles of justice and humanity.

Note, though, that Story did not dissent in The Antelope. Moreover, Marshall scarcely seems to deny the immorality of slavery. If slavery violates principles of natural law, how could the Court order the return of *any* of the captives seized on The Antelope?

One answer is found in Marshall's own description of the case as a conflict between the "sacred rights of liberty and of property." One might also turn to the distinction between natural and positive law. In 1772, in Somerset's Case, Lord Mansfield ordered discharged from service a slave who had been brought by his Virginia master to England, noting that "the state of slavery is of such a nature, that it is incapable of being introduced on any reasons . . . but only by positive law. . . . It is so odious, that nothing can be suffered to support it but positive law."[127] Marshall's decision in The Antelope is consistent with this view if, as seems likely, he regarded the unwritten but venerable "law of nations" as positive law.

---

126. See generally Robert Cover, Justice Accused: Antislavery and the Judicial Process (1975).

127. Quoted in id. at 6.

Robert Cover writes:[128]

> In a static and simplistic model of law, the judge caught between law and morality has only four choices. He may apply the law against his conscience. He may apply conscience and be faithless to the law. He may resign. Or he may cheat: He may state that the law is not what he believes it to be; and, thus preserve an appearance (to others) of conformity of law and morality. Once we assume a more realistic model of law and of the judicial process, these four positions become only poles setting limits to a complex field of action and motive. For in a dynamic model, law is always becoming. And the judge has a legitimate role in determining what it is that the law will become.

Had you read only Marshall's opinions in *McCulloch* and *Fletcher*, where would you locate him on a continuum between a "static" and "dynamic" conception of law? What if your only acquaintance with Marshall were The Antelope? Where would you wish your own "model judge" to locate herself?

4. Imagine that someone purchases a parrot abroad (say, in Brazil). This is a rare parrot that is regarded by the United States as an "endangered species." (In the alternative, imagine that the United States, influenced by animal rights activists, regards placing these birds in cages for the amusement of their owners as savage and therefore has banned it.) As a consequence, the United States has passed a law banning "bringing into the territory of the United States" any such parrot. The person purchasing the parrot has no connection with the United States. In fact, she is a citizen of a third country, which has no objection to the importation of parrots. She therefore boards an international flight, on a non-U.S. airline, from Brazil to her home country, with parrot in hand (or cage). Alas, the plane is hijacked in midair by a group who demand that it be diverted to the United States. The plane indeed lands in Miami. As the passengers disembark, waiting for the next plane, the parrot's owner is detained and ordered to give up the parrot to U.S. authorities (who will make every effort to return it to the Amazonian forests where parrots thrive). They tell her that she is lucky not to be charged with a criminal violation of the law prohibiting "bringing" parrots into U.S. territory. Needless to say, she is not impressed by this generosity and demands the return of her property. Who do you think should prevail between the United States and the ostensible "owner"? How, if at all, does your answer relate to your response to The Antelope, a case involving human beings (legally) sold into slavery for shipment to other countries where slavery is also legal?

VIII. AMERICAN INDIANS AND THE AMERICAN POLITICAL COMMUNITY

American Indians—Native Americans—were recognized by European settlers as members of distinct tribal entities even as the settlers proceeded to displace them. The U.S. government frequently negotiated with Indian tribes—although

128. Id.

history reveals "numerous accounts of threats, coercion, bribery, and outright fraud by the negotiators for the United States."[129]

Like the issue of slavery, the treatment of Native Americans in American constitutional law also sheds interesting light on the "natural law tradition" underlying the U.S. Constitution as well as the connections (or conflict) between the notions of "courts of law" and "courts of justice" implicit in Fletcher v. Peck and The Antelope. Consider, for example, Chief Justice Marshall's decision in Johnson v. M'Intosh, 21 U.S. 543 (1823), in which he explained why Native Americans lost the right to lands upon their discovery (and conquest) by European states:

> Conquest gives a title which the Courts of the conqueror cannot deny, whatever the private and speculative opinions of individuals may be, respecting the original justice of the claim which has been successfully asserted. The British government, which was then our government, and whose rights have passed to the United States, asserted a title to all the lands occupied by Indians, within the chartered limits of the British colonies. It asserted also a limited sovereignty over them, and the exclusive right of extinguishing the title which occupancy gave to them. These claims have been maintained and established as far west as the river Mississippi, by the sword. The title to a vast portion of the lands we now hold, originates in them. It is not for the Courts of this country to question the validity of this title, or to sustain one which is incompatible with it.
>
> Although we do not mean to engage in the defence of those principles which Europeans have applied to Indian title, they may, we think, find some excuse, if not justification, in the character and habits of the people whose rights have been wrested from them. . . .
>
> However extravagant the pretension of converting the discovery of an inhabited country into conquest may appear; if the principle has been asserted in the first instance, and afterwards sustained; if a country has been acquired and held under it; if the property of the great mass of the community originates in it, it becomes the law of the land, and cannot be questioned. So, too, with respect to the concomitant principle, that the Indian inhabitants are to be considered merely as occupants, to be protected, indeed, while in peace, in the possession of their lands, but to be deemed incapable of transferring the absolute title to others. However this restriction may be opposed to natural right, and to the usages of civilized nations, yet, if it be indispensable to that system under which the country has been settled, and be adapted to the actual condition of the two people, it may, perhaps, be supported by reason, and certainly cannot be rejected by Courts of justice.

---

129. Charles F. Wilkinson and John M. Volkman, Judicial Review of Indian Treaty Abrogation: "As Long as Water Flows or Grass Grows upon the Earth"—How Long a Time Is That?, 63 Cal. L. Rev. 601, 610 (1975). See generally Stuart Banner, How the Indians Lost Their Land: Law and Power on the Frontier (2005).

Is Marshall suggesting that natural justice must yield to rights established by force of arms, or is he suggesting that there is in fact no conflict? What, if anything, does this tell us about the meaning of the natural law tradition?

Indians were not deemed citizens of the new United States. Although the 1790 federal naturalization law restricting admission to free white aliens appeared to foreclose Indian naturalization, several subsequent treaties and statutes contemplated the possibility of Indian citizenship. For example, the Cherokee treaties of 1817 and 1819 included provisions granting land to heads of families "who may wish to become citizens of the United States."[130] It was clear, though, that an Indian who chose to remain a formal member of his tribe could not become a citizen. As James Kettner writes, "the tribes themselves . . . could be considered quasi-sovereign nations, enforcing their own laws and customs and requiring the immediate allegiance of their members."[131] Just as the tension between nation and states, exemplified by *McCulloch*, has remained a pervasive reality in American constitutional law up to the present, so too the relations between Indian tribes and the other units of American government have never been fully resolved. One set of questions involves the power of the national government over Indian tribes. Another concerns whether the states possess any regulatory powers over tribes and their members. One of the earliest judicial decisions involving these relations was Cherokee Nation v. Georgia, 30 U.S. (5 Pet.) 1 (1831). It provoked what Charles Warren, a leading historian of the Supreme Court, termed "the most serious crisis in the history of the Court."[132] At the height of the crisis, former President John Quincy Adams exclaimed that "the Union is in the most imminent danger of dissolution."[133]

Through various treaties with the United States the Cherokees had been allotted approximately four million acres of lands within the territory of Georgia. In 1827, gold was discovered on tribal lands, and the same year the Cherokee Nation declared itself an independent nation and adopted a constitution.[134] The Georgia

---

130. James Kettner, The Development of American Citizenship, 1608-1870, at 292 (1978).

131. Id. at 294. If the United States, as a "sovereign," had the ability to determine who could become a citizen, did the Indian tribes have a similar authority to determine who belonged to their tribes? In United States v. Rogers, 45 U.S. (4 How.) 567 (1846), the Court considered the claim of William Rogers, a white man, that he and Jacob Nicholson had become citizens of the Cherokee Nation. Rogers had killed Nicholson, and he argued that the United States lacked jurisdiction to try him. Although section 25 of the Act of 30 June, 1834 extended "the laws of the United States over the Indian country," a specific proviso excluded punishment for "crimes committed by one Indian against the person or property of another Indian." Chief Justice Taney did not dispute that the tribe had made the two men citizens. Nevertheless, he held that that for purposes of the statute, the tribe's assertion was not dispositive; the status of "Indian" was a racial one rather than a political one. "[W]e think," Taney wrote, "it very clear that a white man who at mature age is adopted in an Indian tribe does not thereby become an Indian. . . . He may by such adoption become entitled to certain privileges in the tribe, and make himself amenable to their laws and usages. Yet he is not an Indian, and the exception is confined to those who by the usages and customs of the Indians are regarded as belonging to their race."

132. Charles Warren, The Supreme Court in American History 189 (1923).

133. A. Beveridge, John Marshall 544 (1919).

134. See White, The Marshall Court and Cultural Change, supra n.108, at 715.

legislature responded by passing "Indian laws" that, among other things, annulled all of the Cherokee "laws, usages, and customs," divided their lands into separate counties under state jurisdiction, and prohibited the Cherokee legislature and courts from meeting. As an assertion of Georgia's sovereignty over the tribe, the state tried and convicted George Tassels for an 1830 homicide he committed on the reservation against another Cherokee. Tassel appealed to the U.S. Supreme Court, which granted a writ of error directing the state to appear. In response, Georgia's governor ordered Tassel's immediate execution.

The Cherokee Nation appealed to the federal government to support its claims against Georgia's abrogation of its treaty rights. President Jackson, who was promoting a policy of Indian removal west of the Mississippi, responded that "the President of the United States has no power to protect them against the laws of Georgia."[135] The Cherokee Nation then attempted to invoke original jurisdiction of the U.S. Supreme Court by describing itself as "a foreign state, not owing allegiance to the United States, nor to any state of this union. . . ."[136] On the merits, the Cherokee Nation claimed that Georgia had violated the Contract Clause, since "treaties . . . are contracts of the highest character and of the most solemn obligation."

The Court rejected the Cherokee Nation's assertion that it was a foreign state and dismissed the claim for lack of jurisdiction. There was no majority opinion. Chief Justice Marshall wrote an opinion for himself and Justice McLean alone. Justices Johnson and Baldwin concurred in the result, but not the reasoning. Justice Thompson dissented, joined by Justice Story, arguing that the actual practice of the United States—through its use of treaties, for example—confirmed that it treated the Cherokees as a separate foreign nation.

Chief Justice Marshall argued that

> [t]hough the Indians are acknowledged to have an unquestionable, and, heretofore, unquestioned right to the lands they occupy, until that right shall be extinguished by a voluntary cession to our government; yet it may well be doubted whether those tribes which reside within the acknowledged boundaries of the United States can, with strict accuracy, be denominated foreign nations. They may, more correctly, perhaps, be denominated domestic dependent nations. They occupy a territory to which we assert a title independent of their will. . . . Meanwhile they are in a state of pupilage. Their relation to the United States resembles that of a ward to his guardian.
>
> They look to our government for protection; rely upon its kindness and its power; appeal to it for relief to their wants; and address the president as their great father. They and their country are considered by foreign nations, as well as by ourselves, as being so completely under the sovereignty and dominion of the United States, that any attempt to acquire their lands, or to form a political connexion with them, would be considered by all as an invasion of our territory, and an act of hostility.

---

135. 30 U.S. (5 Pet.) 8.
136. Id. at 2.

Marshall also pointed to the fact that the Commerce Clause specifically distinguishes the regulation of "commerce with foreign nations, and among the several states, and with the Indian tribes." Finally, Marshall suggested that the case was inappropriate for the judiciary in any event, because it "requires us to control the legislature of Georgia, and to restrain the exertion of its physical force. . . . It savours too much of the exercise of political power to be within the proper province of the judicial department." Justice Johnson concurred:

> With the morality of the case I have no concern; I am called upon to consider it as a legal question. . . .
>
> I think it very clear that the constitution neither speaks of them as states or foreign states, but as just what they were, Indian tribes; an anomaly unknown to the books that treat of states, and which the law of nations would regard as nothing more than wandering hordes, held together only by ties of blood and habit, and having neither laws or government, beyond what is required in a savage state. The distinction is clearly made in that section which vests in Congress power to regulate commerce between the United States with foreign nations and the Indian tribes. . . .

Johnson, however, explained that had the issue been up to him alone, he would have "put my rejection of this notion upon the nature of the claim set up, exclusively."

> I cannot entertain a doubt that it is one of a political character altogether, and wholly unfit for the cognizance of a judicial tribunal. There is no possible view of the subject, that I can perceive, in which a Court of justice can take jurisdiction of the questions made in the bill. . . .
>
> What [do the Cherokee] allegations exhibit but a state of war, and the fact of invasion? . . . [T]he contest is distinctly a contest for empire. It is not a case of meum and tuum in the judicial but in the political sense. Not an appeal to laws but to force. A case in which a sovereign undertakes to assert his right upon his sovereign responsibility; to right himself, and not to appeal to any arbiter but the sword, for the justice of his cause. . . . In the exercise of sovereign right, the sovereign is sole arbiter of his own justice. The penalty or wrong is war and subjugation. . . .
>
> What these people may have a right to claim of the executive power is one thing: whether we are to be the instruments to compel another branch of the government to make good the stipulations of treaties, is a very different question. Courts of justice are properly excluded from all considerations of policy, and therefore are very unfit instruments to control the action of that branch of government; which may often be compelled by the highest considerations of public policy to withhold even the exercise of a positive duty. . . .

DISCUSSION

1. Although there was no majority opinion in *Cherokee Nation,* Marshall's description of Native Americans as "domestic dependent nations" greatly influenced the course of Indian law to the present day.

2. In what ways does the resolution desired by the Cherokees savor more "of the exercise of political power" than the Court's striking down Maryland's tax in *McCulloch* or invalidating Georgia's attempted rescission of the Yazoo land grants in *Fletcher*? Should the Supreme Court generally attempt to avoid accepting jurisdiction when it is foreseeable that a given decision might be met by outright defiance by those to whom it is directed? Professor White noted the widespread perception at the time that "if the Cherokees should win on the jurisdictional issue, and also on the merits, Georgia and the Jackson administration, with the tacit support of Congress, might well decline to endorse the Court's judgment, thereby isolating the Court."[137] Indeed, Georgia symbolized its view that the dispute was entirely a domestic matter by refusing even to appear before the Court to present its opposition to the Cherokees' position.

3. Describe Johnson's mode of analysis. How does it square with his concurrence in Fletcher v. Peck? Can a judge who believes that ascertainable norms of natural justice bind even the Deity, let alone states of the United States, adopt the strict separation between law and morality that is suggested in the first paragraph of opinion? Note that Johnson also suggests that "courts of justice" can say nothing about the exercise of brute force or conquest, or about the exercise of "policy" by the executive branch. How can this be reconciled with his stated views about natural justice?

4. In Worcester v. Georgia, 31 U.S. (6 Pet.) 515 (1832), the Court, with only Justice Baldwin dissenting, held that Georgia's anti-Cherokee laws were unconstitutional. The State had sentenced Worcester to four years' imprisonment for residing within Cherokee lands without procuring a license from Georgia. "The Cherokee nation," Chief Justice Marshall wrote, "is a distinct community, occupying its own territory . . . , in which the laws of Georgia can have no force. . . . The whole intercourse between the United States and this nation, is, by our constitution and laws, vested in the government of the United States." It was this decision that supposedly led to the almost certainly apocryphal remark attributed to President Jackson, "John Marshall has made his decision; now let him enforce it."[138] Even if, as many scholars believe, Jackson did not actually say this, it almost certainly described his attitude. The Supreme Court's decision, however much it seemingly protected the Cherokees from Georgia, did nothing to protect them from the national government of the United States. Led by Jackson, the United States embarked on the policy that forced most Cherokees to march on the "Trail of Tears" to forced relocation in Oklahoma.[139]

IX. WOMEN'S CITIZENSHIP IN THE ANTEBELLUM ERA

The preceding two sections examined the constitutional status of "outsider" or "marginalized" groups in the early Republic: slaves and American Indians. We turn now to a third group: women. In 1776, Abigail Adams had beseeched her husband

137. White, The Marshall Court and Cultural Change, supra n.108, at 723.
138. Leonard Baker, John Marshall: A Life in Law 745 (1974).
139. See John Ehle, Trail of Tears: The Rise and Fall of the Cherokee Nation (1988).

John to "[r]emember the Ladies" while drawing up "the new Code of Laws" for the nascent United States of America.[140] Although unlike slaves or Indians, women were deemed citizens of the United States at the time of the founding, they were nevertheless denied political rights, based on a theory about the relationship between the obligations of political citizenship, economic dependency, and family structure.

At the time of the founding, the franchise was generally restricted to propertied white males on the grounds that people should not be able to vote unless they possessed sufficient independence to exercise the franchise wisely. Dependent individuals included women, children, servants, slaves, apprentices, journeymen, and other propertyless men who labored for others. These individuals were thought to lack independent political judgment (and therefore the capacity to participate in governance) because their vote would likely be controlled by people of property upon whom they depended.[141] This political theory of suffrage and dependency was also connected to a theory about families and family governance. Women, slaves, servants, and apprentices were dependent on, and hence governed by, the male head of a propertied household. The common law regarded relations between husband and wife, parent and child, and master and servant, slave, or apprentice as "domestic relations." The law had special doctrines for each of these status relationships. In general, these relations were hierarchical and reciprocal: The master of the household was obligated to support and represent the interests of his dependents, and they in turn were obligated to serve and obey him as head of the household. Because the master of the house represented the interests of the family as a whole, it was thought appropriate that he alone should have the right to vote.

The common law rules of coverture or marital status spelled out the legal terms of men's governance over women. Husbands had rights to a wife's paid and unpaid labor, and to most property that she brought into the marriage. The wife was obligated to serve and obey her husband, and he was obligated to support and represent her in the legal system. Wives could not sue in the courts or make contracts without their husbands' consent; in turn husbands were legally responsible

---

140. Abigail Adams to John Adams (March 31, 1776), in The Book of Abigail and John: Selected Letters from the Adams Family, 1762-1784, at 120-121 (L.H. Butterfield et al. eds., 1975). Chiding her husband on the very grounds on which the Revolution was fought, Abigail reminded John that "[a]ll men would be tyrants if they could. If particular care and attention is not paid to the Ladies we are determined to foment a Rebelion, and will not hold ourselves bound by any laws in which we have no voice, or Representation." Id. John Adams's jocular reply presages the basic argument that would be made against women's political rights for two centuries: "We [men] dare not exert our power in its full Latitude. We are obliged to go fair, and softly and in Practice you know we are the subjects. We have only the Name of Masters." John Adams to Abigail Adams (April 14, 1776), id. at 122-123.

141. Robert Steinfeld, Property and Suffrage in the Early American Republic, 41 Stan. L. Rev. 335, 340 (1989). In short, persons who were dependent on others economically or in households were deemed unfit to govern because they were subject to the governance of others. Reva B. Siegel, Collective Memory and the Nineteenth Amendment: Reasoning About "the Woman Question" in the Discourse of Sex Discrimination, in History, Memory, and the Law 131-182 (Sarat & Kearns eds., 1999), at 144.

for many aspects of their wives' conduct.[142] The marital status rules simultaneously regulated women's legal rights, the structure of family relations, and social relations between the sexes. These rules were supported by the common law legal fiction of marital unity: The wife's legal identity was merged into the husband's, so that in the eyes of the law, husband and wife were one. As Blackstone put it: "By marriage, the husband and wife are one person in law: that is, the very being or legal existence of the woman is suspended during the marriage, or at least is incorporated and consolidated into that of the husband; under whose wing, protection and cover, she performs everything." 1 William Blackstone, Commentaries 430 (1765).

Restrictions on the franchise were status-based regulations: One's political rights were based on one's position in a larger social structure and social hierarchy. Being able to vote meant that one had a particular status in a family and thus in society; conversely, lacking the right to vote also was correlated with one's subordinate position within a family and in society.

Although these status-based rules seemed at odds with the revolutionary ideology of human liberty and equality, they were justified by a distinction between the public realm of active citizenship and public economic activity and the private realm of domestic relations. Relations between heads of households were relations between free and equal citizens in a public realm; relations between men and women, or between masters and servants, were domestic relations within a private household.[143]

Even so, the theory of coverture faced other theoretical difficulties. As Linda Kerber puts it, "[i]f [a woman] could not make a private contract, how could she enter into the social contract" and become a citizen in the first place?[144] The Supreme Court faced the question of women's political citizenship for the first time in Shanks v. DuPont, 28 U.S. (3 Pet.) 242 (1830). The heirs of Ann Shanks sued to recover lands that had been bequeathed to her. Born in the colonies, Ann Shanks had married a British officer in 1781 during the Revolutionary War, and had moved to England. If Shanks had become a British subject, her heirs could recover under the peace treaty signed with Great Britain.

Justice Story held that a married woman's "political rights" to choose her country of allegiance were not affected by her loss of independent property and contractual rights under the common law rules of coverture. Thus women did not automatically lose the right to American citizenship by marrying aliens. However, because Ann Shanks freely chose to live "voluntarily under British protection," she

---

142. Norma Basch, In the Eyes of the Law: Women, Marriage and Property in Nineteenth-Century New York, 47-55, 70-112 (1982). Although married women could not technically own property in their own right, wealthy families could take advantage of special trust arrangements and equitable devices that gave women limited autonomy over finances. See Susanne Lebsock, Free Women of Petersburg: Status and Culture in a Southern Town, 1784-1860 (1984); Basch, at 70-112 (discussing the equitable separate estate for wives).

143. Christopher Tomlins, Subordination, Authority, Law: Subjects in Labor History, 47 Intl. Labor and Working-Class Historian 56, 74 (1995).

144. Linda K. Kerber, No Constitutional Right to Be Ladies: Women and the Obligations of Citizenship 15 (1998).

was deemed to have chosen British citizenship. *Shanks* was the Supreme Court's first recognition that women had any form of political rights in the face of the common law's theories of marital status.[145]

In the first decades of the nineteenth century, propertyless white males increasingly demanded and obtained suffrage rights.[146] During the same period the first movements for women's rights began, growing out of evangelical movements for temperance and the abolition of slavery.[147]

These early movements for women's rights culminated in the first women's rights convention at Seneca Falls, New York, on July 19 and 20, 1848. The convention issued a Declaration of Sentiments that demanded both suffrage for women and reform of the marital status laws. The Declaration of Sentiments was explicitly based on the language of the Declaration of Independence. It argued that "all men and women are created equal," and substituted for the Declaration's list of grievances against King George a series of examples "of repeated injuries and usurpations on the part of man toward woman, having in direct object the establishment of an absolute tyranny over her." Among these were that:

> He has never permitted her to exercise her inalienable right to the elective franchise.
>
> He has compelled her to submit to laws, in the formation of which she had no voice.
>
> He has withheld from her rights which are given to the most ignorant and degraded men—both natives and foreigners.
>
> Having deprived her of this first right of a citizen, the elective franchise, thereby leaving her without representation in the halls of legislation, he has oppressed her on all sides.
>
> He has made her, if married, in the eye of the law, civilly dead.
>
> He has taken from her all right in property, even to the wages she earns.
>
> He has made her, morally, an irresponsible being, as she can commit many crimes, with impunity, provided they be done in the presence of her husband. In the covenant of marriage, she is compelled to promise obedience to her husband, he becoming, to all intents and purposes, her

---

145. *Shanks* was not the end of the story, however. In 1907, Congress passed a statute that specifically revoked the citizenship of American women who married alien husbands. This statute was upheld in MacKenzie v. Hare, 239 U.S. 299 (1915), on the theory that Congress had the right to treat marriage to a foreigner as equivalent to voluntary expatriation. Justice McKenna explained that the "ancient principle" of the common law that "husband and wife are one" and subject to the husband's "dominance" justified Congress's decision. The Cable Act of 1922, passed in response to *MacKenzie*, preserved citizenship rights for married women if their husbands were from countries whose subjects were eligible for U.S. citizenship. At the time of passage this excluded persons from China and Japan. For a general discussion, see Nancy F. Cott, Marriage and Women's Citizenship in the United States, 1830-1934, 103 Am. Hist. Rev. 1440 (1998).

146. Steinfeld, supra n.141, at 353-360.

147. Eleanor Flexner, Century of Struggle: The Woman's Rights Movement in the United States, 41-52, 181-186 (1959); Ellen Carol Dubois, Feminism and Suffrage: The Emergence of an Independent Women's Movement in America, 1848-1869 (1978).

master—the law giving him power to deprive her of her liberty, and to administer chastisement.

He has so framed the laws of divorce, as to what shall be the proper causes of divorce; in case of separation, to whom the guardianship of the children shall be given, as to be wholly regardless of the happiness of women—the law, in all cases, going upon the false supposition of the supremacy of man, and giving all power into his hands.

After depriving her of all rights as a married woman, if single and the owner of property, he has taxed her to support a government which recognizes her only when her property can be made profitable to it.

He has monopolized nearly all the profitable employments, and from those she is permitted to follow, she receives but a scanty remuneration.

He closes against her all the avenues to wealth and distinction, which he considers most honorable to himself. As a teacher of theology, medicine, or law, she is not known.

He has denied her the facilities for obtaining a thorough education—all colleges being closed against her.

He allows her in Church as well as State, but a subordinate position, claiming Apostolic authority for her exclusion from the ministry, and with some exceptions, from any public participation in the affairs of the Church.

He has created a false public sentiment, by giving to the world a different code of morals for men and women, by which moral delinquencies which exclude women from society, are not only tolerated but deemed of little account in man.

He has usurped the prerogative of Jehovah himself, claiming it as his right to assign for her a sphere of action, when that belongs to her conscience and her God.

He has endeavored, in every way that he could to destroy her confidence in her own powers, to lessen her self-respect, and to make her willing to lead a dependent and abject life.

Now, in view of this entire disfranchisement of one-half the people of this country, their social and religious degradation—in view of the unjust laws above mentioned, and because women do feel themselves aggrieved, oppressed, and fraudulently deprived of their most sacred rights, we insist that they have immediate admission to all the rights and privileges which belong to them as citizens of these United States.

By the 1840s, a few states had already begun to pass "married women's property acts" that allowed married women to own real property acquired before or during marriage. By the 1850s, state legislatures began to pass "earnings statutes" that allowed women to make contracts and gave them property rights in earnings for personal labor other than domestic labor they performed in their homes or labor they performed for family members. However, these statutes preserved the doctrine of marital service, by which men still owned the right to women's labor in the home.[148]

148. See Reva B. Siegel, Home as Work: The First Woman's Rights Claims Concerning Wives' Household Labor, 1850-1880, 103 Yale L.J. 1073 (1994).

The struggle for women's suffrage was less effective. Before the Civil War, many women's rights advocates continued to work within abolitionist organizations, hoping that securing rights for Black people would also result in universal suffrage for men and women. Nevertheless, after the war the Reconstruction Republicans wrote the Fourteenth and Fifteenth Amendments to enfranchise freed men without enfranchising women.[149] They continued to justify this exclusion on the republican theory that linked the rights of political government to family structure and relations of dependence. Society was naturally organized into families whose heads were supposed to speak for them. Women were already indirectly or virtually represented by the male heads of their families—either their husbands or their fathers—who had legal control over them. Moreover, "woman suffrage would destroy the family by introducing discord into marital relations and distracting women from their primary duties as mothers."[150]

DISCUSSION

1. The Seneca Falls Declaration of Sentiments does not invoke a single provision of the antebellum Constitution; instead its language tracks the Declaration of Independence. (Interestingly, however, the Declaration of Sentiments demands "the rights and privileges . . . [of] citizens of the United States," very similar to the language that eventually finds its way into the Fourteenth Amendment.) Note that many of the abolitionists looked to the Declaration as a justification for their ideas about equality under the Constitution, especially because there was no Equal Protection Clause in the Constitution before the Civil War. What considerations make reliance on the Declaration an appropriate or inappropriate form of constitutional argument? Is the Declaration less relevant to constitutional interpretation now because we have an Equal Protection Clause?

2. The Declaration of Sentiments models demands for reform along the lines of the egalitarian republican theory expressed in the Declaration of Independence. That republican theory, however, presumed equality only among heads of households and depended on inequality and even hierarchy within the family unit. The economic and political interests of families, in turn, were identified with the economic and political interests of the men who headed those families. If we took the demands of the early women's rights advocates seriously, what would the egalitarian principles of the Declaration mean for family life? Note that the coverture rules were abolished and suffrage was granted to women by the beginning of the twentieth century. In subsequent chapters, and especially in Chapter 8, we examine whether this has been enough to guarantee women a full measure of constitutional equality.

---

149. Ellen Carol Dubois, Outgrowing the Compact of the Fathers: Equal Rights, Woman Suffrage, and the United States Constitution 1820-1878, 74 J. Am. Hist. 836-852 (1987). See also the discussion of the struggle for woman suffrage in Chapter 4, infra.

150. Siegel, Collective Memory, supra n.141, at 149.

X. REGULATION OF THE INTERSTATE ECONOMY

Gibbons v. Ogden

22 U.S. (9 Wheat.) 1 (1824)

[The New York State Legislature granted Robert Livingston and Robert Fulton the exclusive right to operate steamboats in New York waters for a period of years. Livingston and Fulton assigned to Ogden the exclusive right to operate steamboats between New York City and various places in New Jersey. Ogden brought this action in New York Chancery Court to enjoin Gibbons from operating steamboats between New York and Elizabethtown, New Jersey. Gibbons responded that his boats were licensed pursuant to a 1793 Act of Congress entitled "an act for enrolling and licensing ships and vessels to be employed in the coasting trade and fisheries, and for regulating the same," and that the licenses entitled him to navigate between New York and New Jersey notwithstanding the state-granted monopoly.

The New York courts held for Ogden. The state appellate court held that the federal statute was designed solely "to establish a criterion of *national character*, with a view to enforce the laws which impose *discriminating duties* [favoring] *American* vessels [over] those of foreign countries. The term 'license' seems not be used in the sense . . . [of] a *permit to trade*," because "it is perfectly clear that such a vessel, coasting from one state to another, would have exactly the same right to trade, and the same right of transit, whether she had the coasting license or not. . . . Whether Congress have the power to authorize the coasting trade to be carried on, in vessels propelled by steam, so as to give a *paramount right*, in opposition to the special license given by this state, is a question not yet presented to us. No such act of Congress yet exists. . . ." The Supreme Court reversed.]

MARSHALL, C.J. . . .

As preliminary to the very able discussions of the constitution, which we have heard from the bar, and as having some influence on its construction, reference has been made to the political situation of these states, anterior to its formation. It has been said, that they were sovereign, were completely independent, and were connected with each other only by a league. This is true. But when these allied sovereigns converted their league into a government, when they converted their congress of ambassadors, deputed to deliberate on their common concerns, and to recommend measures of general utility, into a legislature, empowered to enact laws on the most interesting subjects, the whole character in which the states appear, underwent a change, the extent of which must be determined by a fair consideration of the instrument by which that change was effected.

This instrument contains an enumeration of powers expressly granted by the people to their government. It has been said, that these powers ought to be construed strictly. . . . What do gentlemen mean, by a strict construction? If they contend only against that enlarged construction, which would extend words beyond their natural and obvious import, we might question the application of the term, but should not controvert the principle. If they contend for that narrow construction which, in support of some theory not to be found in the constitution, would deny to the government those powers which the words of the grant, as usually understood, import, and which are consistent with the general views and objects of the instrument—for that narrow construction, which would cripple the government, and render it unequal to the objects for which it is declared to be instituted, and to which the powers given, as fairly understood, render it competent—then we cannot perceive the propriety of this strict construction, nor adopt it as the rule by which the constitution is to be expounded. As men, whose intentions require no concealment, generally employ the words which most directly and aptly express the ideas they intend to convey, the enlightened patriots who framed our constitution, and the people who adopted it, must be understood to have employed words in their natural sense, and to have intended what they have said. If, from the imperfection of human language, there should be serious doubts respecting the extent of any given power, it is a well-settled rule, that the objects for which it was given, especially, when those objects are expressed in the instrument itself, should have great influence in the construction. . . . We know of no rule for construing the extent of such powers, other than is given by the language of the instrument which confers them, taken in connection with the purposes for which they were conferred.

The words are, "Congress shall have power to regulate commerce with foreign nations, and among the several states, and with the Indian tribes." The subject to be regulated is commerce; and our constitution being, as was aptly said at the bar, one of enumeration, and not of definition, to ascertain the extent of the power, it becomes necessary to settle the meaning of the word. The counsel for the appellee would limit it to traffic, to buying and selling, or the interchange of commodities, and do not admit that it comprehends navigation. This would restrict a general term, applicable to many objects, to one of its significations. Commerce, undoubtedly, is traffic, but it is something more—it is intercourse. It describes the commercial intercourse between nations, and parts of nations, in all its branches, and is regulated by prescribing rules for carrying on that intercourse. . . .

All America understands, and has uniformly understood, the word "commerce," to comprehend navigation. It was so understood, and must have been so understood, when the constitution was framed. The power over commerce, including navigation, was one of the primary objects for which the people of America adopted their government, and must have been contemplated in forming it. The convention must have used the word in that sense, because all have understood it in that sense; and the attempt to restrict it comes too late. . . .

The word used in the constitution, then comprehends, and has been always understood to comprehend, navigation within its meaning; and a power to regulate navigation, is as expressly granted, as if that term had been added to the word "commerce." To what commerce does this power extend? The constitution informs us, to commerce "with foreign nations, and among the several states, and with the Indian tribes." It has, we believe, been universally admitted, that these words comprehend every species of commercial intercourse between the United States and foreign nations. No sort of trade can be carried on between this country and any other, to which this power does not extend. It has been truly said, that commerce, as the word is used in the constitution, is a unit, every part of which is indicated by the term.

If this be the admitted meaning of the word, in its application to foreign nations, it must carry the same meaning throughout the sentence, and remain a unit, unless there be some plain intelligible cause which alters it. The subject to which the power is next applied, is to commerce, "among the several states." The word "among" means intermingled with. A thing which is among others, is intermingled with them. Commerce among the states, cannot stop at the external boundary line of each state, but may be introduced into the interior. It is not intended to say, that these words comprehend that commerce, which is completely internal, which is carried on between man and man in a state, or between different parts of the same state, and which does not extend to or affect other states. Such a power would be inconvenient, and is certainly unnecessary. Comprehensive as the word "among" is, it may very properly be restricted to that commerce which concerns more states than one. . . . The genius and character of the whole government seem to be, that its action is to be applied to all the external concerns of the nation, and to those internal concerns which affect the states generally; but not to those which are completely within a particular state, which do not affect other states, and with which it is not necessary to interfere, for the purpose of executing some of the general powers of the government. The completely internal commerce of a state, then may be considered as reserved for the state itself.

But in regulating commerce with foreign nations, the power of congress does not stop at the jurisdictional lines of the several states. It would be a very useless power, if it could not pass those lines. The commerce of the United States with foreign nations, is that of the whole United States; every district has a right to participate in it. The deep streams which penetrate our country in every direction, pass through the interior of almost every state in the Union, and furnish the means of exercising this right. If congress has the power to regulate it, that power must be exercised whenever the subject exists. If it exists within the states, if a foreign voyage may commence or terminate at a port within a state, then the power of congress may be exercised within a state.

This principle is, if possible, still more clear, when applied to commerce "among the several states." They either join each other, in which case they are separated by a mathematical line, or they are remote from each other, in which case other states lie between them. What is commerce "among" them; and how is it to be conducted? Can a trading expedition between two adjoining states, commence and terminate outside of each? And if the trading intercourse be between two states remote from each other, must it not commence in one, terminate in the other, and probably pass through a third? Commerce among the states must, of necessity, be commerce with the states. In the regulation of trade with the Indian tribes, the action of the law, especially, when the constitution was made, was chiefly within a state. The power of congress, then, whatever it may be, must be exercised within the territorial jurisdiction of the several states. . . .

We are now arrived at the inquiry—What is this power? It is the power to regulate; that is, to prescribe the rule by which commerce is to be governed. This power, like all others vested in congress, is complete in itself, may be exercised to its utmost extent, and acknowledges no limitations, other than are prescribed in the constitution. These are expressed in plain terms, and do not affect the questions which arise in this case, or which have been discussed at the bar. If, as has always been understood, the sovereignty of congress, though limited to specified objects, is plenary as to those objects, the power over commerce with foreign nations, and among the several states, is vested in congress as absolutely as it would be in a single government, having in its constitution the same restrictions on the exercise of the power as are found in the constitution of the United States. The wisdom and the discretion of congress, their identity with the people, and the influence which their constituents possess at elections, are, in this, as in many other instances, as that, for example, of declaring war, the sole restraints on which they have relied, to secure them from its abuse. They are the restraints on which the people must often rely solely, in all representative governments. The power of congress, then, comprehends navigation, within the limits of every state in the Union; so far as that navigation may be, in any manner, connected with "commerce with foreign nations, or among the several states, or with the Indian tribes." It may, of consequence, pass the jurisdictional line of New York, and act upon the very waters to which the prohibition now under consideration applies.

But it has been urged . . . [that] the states may severally exercise the same power, within their respective jurisdictions. In support of this argument, it is said, that they possessed it as an inseparable attribute of sovereignty, before the formation of the constitution, and still retain it, except so far as they have surrendered it by that instrument; that this principle results from the nature of the government, and is secured by the tenth amendment; that an affirmative grant of power is not exclusive, unless in its own nature it be such that the continued exercise of it by the former possessor is inconsistent with the grant, and that this is not of that description. The appellant, conceding these postulates, except the last, contends, that full power to regulate a particular subject, implies the whole power, and leaves no residuum; that a grant of the whole is incompatible with the existence of a right in another to any part of it. Both parties have appealed to the constitution, to legislative acts, and judicial decisions; and have drawn arguments from all these sources, to support and illustrate the propositions they respectively maintain.

The grant of the power to lay and collect taxes is, like the power to regulate commerce, made in general terms, and has never been understood to interfere with the exercise of the same power by the states; and hence has been drawn an argument which has been applied to the question under consideration. But the two grants are not, it is conceived, similar in their terms or their nature. Although many of the powers formerly exercised by the states, are transferred to the government of the Union, yet the state governments remain, and constitute a most important part of our system.

The power of taxation is indispensable to their existence, and is a power which, in its own nature, is capable of residing in, and being exercised by, different authorities, at the same time. We are accustomed to see it placed, for different purposes, in different hands. Taxation is the simple operation of taking small portions from a perpetually accumulating mass, susceptible of almost infinite division; and a power in one to take what is necessary for certain purposes, is not, in its nature, incompatible with a power in another to take what is necessary for other purposes. Congress is authorized to lay and collect taxes, &c., to pay the debts, and provide for the common defence and general welfare of the United States. This does not interfere with the power of the states to tax for the support of their own governments; nor is the exercise of that power by the states, an exercise of any portion of the power that is granted to the United States. In imposing taxes for state purposes, they are not doing what congress is empowered to do. Congress is not empowered to tax for those purposes which are within the exclusive province of the states. When, then, each government exercises the power of taxation, neither is exercising the power of the other. But when a state proceeds to regulate commerce with foreign nations, or among the several states, it is exercising the very power that is granted to congress, and is doing the very thing which congress is authorized to do. There is no analogy, then, between the power of taxation and the power of regulating commerce.

In discussing the question, whether this power is still in the states, in the case under consideration, we may dismiss from it the inquiry, whether it is surrendered by the mere grant to congress, or is retained until congress shall exercise the power. We may dismiss that inquiry, because it has been exercised, and the regulations which congress deemed it proper to make, are now in full operation. The sole question is, can a state regulate commerce with foreign nations and among the states, while congress is regulating it?

The counsel for the respondent answer this question in the affirmative, and rely very much on the restrictions in the 10th section, as supporting their opinion. They say, very truly, that limitations of a power furnish a strong argument in favor of the existence of that power, and that the section which prohibits the states from laying duties on imports or exports, proves that this power might have been exercised, had it not been expressly forbidden; and, consequently, that any other commercial regulation, not expressly forbidden, to which the original power of the state was competent, may still be made. That this restriction shows the opinion of the convention, that a state might impose duties on exports and imports, if not expressly forbidden, will be conceded; but that it follows, as a consequence, from this concession, that a state may regulate commerce with foreign nations and among the states, cannot be admitted.

We must first determine, whether the act of laying "duties or imposts on imports or exports," is considered in the constitution, as a branch of the taxing power, or of the power to regulate commerce. We think it very clear, that it is considered as a branch of the taxing power. It is so treated in the first clause of the 8th section: "Congress shall have power to lay and collect taxes, duties, imposts and excises"; and before commerce is mentioned, the rule by which the exercise of this power must be governed, is declared. It is, that all duties, imposts and excises shall be uniform. In a separate clause of the enumeration, the power to regulate commerce is given, as being entirely distinct from the right to levy taxes and imposts, and as being a new power, not before conferred. The constitution, then, considers these powers as substantive, and distinct from each other; and so places them in the enumeration it contains. The power of imposing duties on imports is classed with the power to levy taxes, and that seems to be its natural place. But the power to levy taxes could never be considered as abridging the right of the states on that subject; and they might, consequently, have exercised it, by levying duties on imports or exports, had the constitution contained no prohibition on this subject. This prohibition, then, is an exception from the acknowledged power of the states to levy taxes, not from the questionable power to regulate commerce.

But the inspection laws are said to be regulations of commerce, and are certainly recognised in the constitution, as being passed in the exercise of a power remaining with the states. That inspection laws may have a remote and considerable influence on commerce, will not be denied; but that a power to regulate commerce is the source from which the right to pass them is derived, cannot be admitted. The object of inspection laws, is to improve the quality of articles produced by the labor of a country; to fit them for exportation; or, it may be, for domestic use. They act upon the subject, before it becomes an article of foreign commerce, or of commerce among the states, and prepare it for that purpose. They form a portion of that immense mass of legislation, which embraces everything within the territory of a state, not surrendered to the general government; all which can be most advantageously exercised by the states themselves. Inspection laws, quarantine laws, health laws of every description, as well as laws for regulating the internal commerce of a state, and those which respect turnpike roads, ferries, etc., are component parts of this mass.

No direct general power over these objects is granted to congress; and, consequently, they remain subject to state legislation. If the legislative power of the Union can reach them, it must be for national purposes; it must be, where the power is expressly given for a special purpose, or is clearly incidental to some power which is expressly given. It is obvious, that the government of the Union, in the exercise of its express powers, that, for example, of regulating commerce with foreign nations and among the states, may use means that may also be employed by a state, in the exercise of its acknowledged powers; that, for example, of regulating commerce within the state. If congress license vessels to sail from one port to another, in the same state, the act is supposed to be, necessarily, incidental to the power expressly granted to congress, and implies no claim of a direct power to regulate the purely internal commerce of a state, or to act directly on its system of police. So, if a state, in passing laws on subjects acknowledged to be within its control, and with a view to those subjects, shall adopt a measure of the same character with one which congress may adopt, it does not derive its authority from the particular power which has been granted, but from some other, which remains with the state, and may be executed by the same means. All experience shows, that the same measures, or measures scarcely distinguishable from each other, may flow from distinct powers; but this does not prove that the powers themselves are identical. Although the means used in their execution may sometimes approach each other so nearly as to be confounded, there are other situations in which they are sufficiently distinct, to establish their individuality.

In our complex system, presenting the rare and difficult scheme of one general government, whose action extends over the whole, but which possesses only certain enumerated powers; and of numerous state governments, which retain and exercise all powers not delegated to the Union, contests respecting power must arise. Were it even otherwise, the measures taken by the respective governments to execute their acknowledged powers, would often be of the same description, and might, sometimes, interfere. This, however, does not prove that the one is exercising, or has a right to exercise, the powers of the other. . . .

It has been contended by the counsel for the appellant, that, as the word "to regulate" implies in its nature, full power over the thing to be regulated, it excludes, necessarily, the action of all others that would perform the same operation on the same thing. That regulation is designed for the entire result, applying to those parts which remain as they were, as well as to those which are altered. It produces a uniform whole, which is as much disturbed and deranged by changing what the regulating power designs to leave untouched, as that on which it has operated. There is great force in this argument, and the court is not satisfied that it has been refuted.

Since, however, in exercising the power of regulating their own purely internal affairs, whether of trading or police, the states may sometimes enact laws, the validity of which depends on their interfering with, and being contrary to, an act of congress passed in pursuance of the constitution, the court will enter upon the inquiry, whether the laws of New York, as expounded by the highest tribunal of that state, have, in their application to this case, come into collision with an act of congress, and deprived a citizen of a right to which that act entitles him. Should this collision exist, it will be immaterial, whether those laws were passed in virtue of a concurrent power "to regulate commerce with foreign nations and among the several states," or, in virtue of a power to regulate their domestic trade and police. In one case and the other, the acts of New York must yield to the law of congress. . . .

To the court, it seems very clear, that the whole act on the subject of the coasting trade, according to those principles which govern the construction of statutes, implies, unequivocally, an authority to licensed vessels to carry on the coasting trade. . . .

[Marshall goes on to conclude, contrary to the New York courts, that Gibbons's license under the 1793 federal statute entitled him to engage in interstate navigation and trade, notwithstanding Ogden's claims to the exclusive franchise granted by the New York legislature.]

JOHNSON, J.

[Justice William Johnson concurred, adopting the theory only broached by Marshall, i.e., that the power to regulate commerce was exclusively Congress's. During the colonial period, Johnson asserted, "the States had submitted, with murmurs to the commercial restrictions imposed by the parent State." Following independence, they found "themselves in the unlimited possession of those powers over their own commerce, which they had so long been deprived of, and so earnestly coveted, that selfish principle which, well controlled, is so salutary, and which, unrestricted, is so unjust and tyrannical," and consequently began passing a host of "commercial regulations, destructive to the harmony of the States, and fatal to their commercial interests abroad."]

This was the immediate cause that led to the forming of a convention.

The history of the times will, therefore, sustain the opinion, that the grant of power over commerce, if intended to be commensurate with the evils existing, and the purpose of remedying those evils, could be only commensurate with the power of the States over the subject. . . .

The "power to regulate commerce," here meant to be granted, was that power to regulate commerce which previously existed in the States. But what was that power? The States were, unquestionably, supreme; and each possessed that power over commerce, which is acknowledged to reside in every sovereign State. [The] power of a sovereign state over commerce, therefore, amounts to nothing more than a power to limit and restrain it at pleasure. And since the power to prescribe the limits to its freedom, necessarily implies the power to determine what shall remain unrestrained, it follows, that the power must be exclusive; it can reside but in one potentate; and hence, the grant of this power carries with it the whole subject, leaving nothing for the State to act upon. . . .

[With respect to the coasting license ultimately relied on by Marshall to invalidate the New York law,] I cannot overcome the conviction, that if the licensing act was repealed to-morrow, the rights of the appellant to a reversal of the decision complained of, would be as strong. . . .

But the principal objections to these opinions arise, 1st. From the unavoidable action of some of the municipal powers of the States, upon commercial subjects. 2d. From passages in the constitution, which are supposed to imply a concurrent power in the States in regulating commerce.

It is no objection to the existence of distinct, substantive powers, that, in their application, they bear upon the same subject. The same bale of goods, the same cask of provisions, or the same ship, that may be the subject of commercial regulation, may also be the vehicle of disease. And the health laws that require them to be stopped and ventilated, are no more intended as regulations on commerce, than the laws which permit their importation, are intended to inoculate the community with disease. Their different purposes mark the distinction between the powers brought into action; and while frankly exercised, they can produce no serious collision. . . . Inspection laws are of a more equivocal nature, and it is obvious that the constitution has viewed that subject with much solicitude. But so far from sustaining an inference in favour of the power of the States over commerce, I cannot but think that the guarded provisions of the 10th section, on this subject, furnish a strong argument against that inference. It was obvious, that inspection laws must combine municipal with commercial regulations; and, while the power over the subject is yielded to the States, for obvious reasons, an absolute control is given over State legislation on the subject, as far as that legislation may be exercised, so as to affect the commerce of the country. The inferences, to be correctly drawn, from this whole article, appear to me to be altogether in favour of the exclusive grants to Congress of power over commerce, and the reverse of that which the appellee contends for.

[Article 1, §10] negatives the exercise of [the commerce] power to the States, as to the only two objects which could ever tempt them to assume the exercise of that power, to wit, the collection of a revenue from imposts and duties on imports and exports; or from a tonnage duty. As to imposts on imports or exports, such a revenue might have been aimed at directly, by express legislation, or indirectly, in the form of inspection laws; and it became necessary to guard against both. Hence, first, the consent of Congress to such imposts or duties, is made necessary; and as to inspection laws, it is limited to the minimum of expenses. Then, the money so raised shall be paid in to the treasury of the United States, or may be sued for since it is declared to be for their use. And lastly, all such laws may be modified, or repealed, by an act of Congress. It is impossible for a right to be more guarded. . . .

It would be in vain to deny the possibility of a clashing and collision between the measures of the two governments. The line cannot be drawn with sufficient distinctness between the municipal powers of the one, and the commercial powers of the other. . . . Whenever the powers of the respective governments are frankly exercised, with a distinct view to the ends of such powers, they may act upon the same object, or use the same means, and yet the powers be kept perfectly distinct. A resort to the same means, therefore, is no argument to prove the identity of their respective powers. . . .

DISCUSSION

1. *The stakes of the scope of the Commerce Power.* Like *McCulloch,* decided five years earlier, *Gibbons* is an essay on federalism, presenting Marshall's solution to the novel American problem of two sovereigns occupying the same physical space. It has been enormously influential, especially in the post–New Deal world that has accepted an extremely wide scope for congressional regulation under the Commerce Clause. Much of the language in *Gibbons* has been used to justify a broad, pragmatic approach to federal power to regulate the economy in the public interest.

Consider, for example, Marshall's conception of "commerce" as including "the commercial intercourse between nations, and parts of nations, in all its branches," including the regulation of "transportation." Note also Marshall's argument that commerce "among" the states means "commerce which concerns more states than one." Taken to its logical conclusion, this formula would suggest that whenever commercial activity has significant effects in more than one state, it is within Congress's power to regulate. Advocates in the early twentieth century would use these ideas to justify Congress's power to regulate virtually every aspect of commercial life, transportation, and communication. But such readings were a century in the future.

It is important to realize that Congress in fact passed remarkably few laws purporting to regulate interstate commerce prior to the Civil War. State governments were the primary actors regulating the economy in the public interest. For many decades following 1824, the major practical issue before the Court would be less the constitutional legitimacy of congressional enactments than *the power of states* to regulate matters touching on interstate commerce, as in *Gibbons.*

Thus, the political valence of debates over the scope of the commerce power—and over whether both the federal government and the states could regulate interstate commerce—was very different in the early nineteenth century than in the twentieth century and thereafter. Strong nationalists like Marshall read the Commerce Clause broadly (albeit nowhere as broadly as we read it today), and were inclined to hold that the power to regulate interstate commerce lay exclusively in the federal government. But that was not because nationalists advocated regulation. Rather, it was because they preferred open national markets with a minimum of state interference and relatively little regulation other than the (then) modest contributions of the federal government. Advocates of state sovereignty preferred a narrower conception of the federal commerce power so that there would be more space for state regulation, as well as concurrent power by the states and the federal government to regulate interstate commerce.

And hovering over all of this was the question—remarkably unresolved before the Civil War—of the relationship of the federal commerce power to the slavery question. (See the discussion in Groves v. Slaughter, Chapter 3, infra.)

2. *Marshall's binary view.* In Marshall's view, on what theory does the Constitution permit both Congress and the states to levy taxes? Why may not both Congress and the states regulate interstate commerce? How does Marshall respond to Ogden's argument that state inspection (and quarantine) laws are regulations of interstate commerce? Why is it important to Marshall that they *not* be?

3. *The purposes of the commerce power.* Consider the role that the "objects" or "purposes" of constitutional provisions play in Marshall's scheme.

Toward the beginning of the opinion, in discussing interpretation of the commerce power, Marshall refers to "the well-settled rule, that the objects for which [a power] was given . . . should have great influence in the construction." For what purposes was the commerce power given? Consider the following description of proceedings at the Philadelphia Convention.[151]

> The Virginia delegation, led by Washington, Madison, and Randolph, feeling largely responsible for the calling of the Convention, had prepared a series of resolutions as a basis for discussion. The sixth of these resolutions, proposed by Governor Randolph four days after the Convention assembled, read in part as follows:
>
> ". . . that the National Legislature ought to be impowered to enjoy the Legislative Rights vested in Congress by the Confederation & moreover to legislate in all cases to which the separate States are incompetent, or in which the harmony of the United States may be interrupted by the exercise of individual Legislation."
>
> The broad standard thus proposed for the division of power between state and nation was criticized by some of the delegates as being too indefinite, but was approved by the Convention on May 31st by a vote of nine states in favor, none against, one divided. . . .
>
> Shortly afterwards Paterson proposed his New Jersey plan, which included in a very short enumeration of federal powers the provision that Congress could "pass Acts for the regulation of trade & commerce as well with foreign nations as with each other." In the language of James Wilson, subsequently a Supreme Court Justice, in comparing the two plans, under the Virginia Plan "the National Legislature is to make laws in all cases at which the several states are incompetent"; under the New Jersey Plan, "In place of this cong. are to have additional power in a few cases only." The New Jersey Plan was rejected and the Virginia Plan reapproved, on June 19th, by a vote of seven states to three, one being divided.
>
> On July 17th, when Randolph's resolution on the division of powers again came up for debate, Sherman of Connecticut, who alone had opposed the resolution originally, moved that it be amended to add the expression.
>
> "To make laws binding on the people of the United States in all cases which may concern the common interests of the Union; but not to interfere with the Government of the individual States in any matters of internal police which respect the Gov. of such States only, and wherein the general welfare of the U. States is not concerned."
>
> ". . . [This] was defeated, and a motion by [Gunning] Bedford of Delaware to clarify the wording adopted by a vote of eight to two. The resolution then read as follows:

151. Robert Stern, That Commerce Which Concerns More States Than One, 47 Harv. L. Rev. 1335, 1338-1340 (1934).

> "Resolved that the national legislature ought
>
> "1. to possess the legislative rights in Congress by the confederation; and
>
> "2. moreover, to legislate in all cases for the general interests of the Union, and
>
> "3. also in those to which the states are separately incompetent, or
>
> "4. in which the harmony of the United States may be interrupted by the exercise of individual legislation."
>
> With the other resolutions approved by the Convention, this resolution was then sent to the "Com. of detail . . . to . . . report the Constitution." This committee [of Detail] made its report on August 6th, ten days later. It had changed the indefinite language of Resolution VI into an enumeration of the powers of Congress closely resembling Article 1, Section 8 of the Constitution as it was finally adopted. . . .
>
> [T]he Convention did not at any time challenge the radical change made by the committee in the form of the provision for the division of powers between state and nation. It accepted *without discussion* the enumeration of powers made by a committee which had been directed to prepare a constitution based upon the general propositions that the Federal Government was "to legislate in all cases for the general interests of the Union . . . and in those to which the states are separately incompetent." With a few changes and additions, the enumeration by the committee became the present Section 8 of Article I of the Constitution.

Consider Jack Rakove, Original Meanings 178 (1996):

> Though it has been argued that this action [turning the Bedford resolution into an enumeration of powers] marked a crucial, even subversive shift in the deliberations, the fact that it went unchallenged suggests that the committee [of Detail] was only complying with the expectations of the convention. . . . [T]he process that unfolded during its ten days of labor is better explained as an attempt to identify particular areas of governance where there were "general Interests of the Union," where the states were "separately incompetent," or where state legislation could disrupt the national "Harmony."

If Rakove is correct that the Committee of Detail was attempting to give concrete meaning to the Bedford resolution, what rule of construction might courts offer today in construing the scope of federal commerce power? One possibility is that courts should ask whether Congress is attempting to deal with a federal issue, for example, one in which Congress could reasonably conclude that actions within states will have spillover effects in other states, or an issue in which unilateral or conflicting decisions by states would undermine what Congress reasonably believes to be a federal policy. For a development of this theory, see Akhil Reed Amar, America's Constitution: A Biography 107-108 (2005); Jack M. Balkin, Commerce, 109 Mich. L. Rev. 1 (2010); Robert D. Cooter and Neil S. Siegel, Collective Action Federalism: A General Theory of Article I, Section 8, 63 Stan. L. Rev. 115 (2010).

The Framers wrote the Commerce Clause in the context of an agrarian economy in which land transportation was difficult and expensive, without factories and modern mass production techniques, and without substantial national markets in many goods. Once the American economy became deeply interconnected after the development of railroads, telegraphs, and the industrial revolution, the nature of the American economy changed. It became far easier for Congress to point to collective action problems and interstate spillover effects among the states; as a result, its effective powers expanded.

4. *State inspection laws and "pretextual" regulation.* In discussing the allocation of state and national powers under the clause, Marshall writes that inspection, quarantine, and health laws "form a portion of that immense mass of legislation, which embraces everything within the territory of a state, not surrendered to the national government." He comments that "[n]o direct general power over these objects is granted to congress; and, consequently they remain subject to state legislation. If the legislative power of the Union can reach them, it must be for national purposes. . . ."

This suggests that the scope of national power may depend, not only on the *substance* of the regulation, but also on the *purposes* for which the regulation was adopted—on the congruence between the purposes underlying the regulation and the constitutional grant of power. Recall, in this respect, Marshall's discussion of "pretext" in ¶42 of *McCulloch*:

> Should Congress, . . . under the pretext of executing its powers, pass laws for the accomplishment of objects not entrusted to the government; it would become the painful duty of this tribunal, should a case requiring such a decision come before it, to say that such an act was not the law of the land.

Can you think an example of a congressional regulation of interstate commerce that might preempt a state inspection, quarantine, or health law? Can you also think of an example of a congressional regulation of interstate commerce that is simply a "pretext"—i.e., that is not done to accomplish any of the objects entrusted to the national government?

How does one reconcile *McCulloch*'s "pretext" language with Marshall's statements in *Gibbons* about the scope of the commerce power? Marshall says that the "[commerce] power, like all others vested in congress, is complete in itself, may be exercised to its utmost extent, and acknowledges no limitations, other than are prescribed in the constitution," and that "the sovereignty of congress, though limited to specified objects, is plenary as to those objects, [and] the power over commerce . . . among the several states, is vested in congress as absolutely as it would be in a single government"?

Here is how the two ideas might conflict. Suppose, for example, that Congress bans the interstate shipment of lottery tickets, or goods produced through the use of child labor, and suppose opponents of these laws claim that Congress's real purpose was not to regulate interstate commerce but to undermine lotteries or regulate labor conditions within states. We will see this issue arise repeatedly in the late nineteenth and early twentieth centuries. The problem largely goes away after the New Deal; recognizing that a modern economy is thoroughly interconnected, and that most economic activity has interstate effects, courts eventually gave Congress broad discretion to regulate the economy in the national interest.

5. *State regulation of interstate commerce. Gibbons* concerns the federal power to regulate interstate commerce. But may a state regulate interstate commerce in the absence of congressional legislation?

Daniel Webster, who represented Gibbons before the Supreme Court, argued that the Constitution by its own terms completely deprives the states of any powers to regulate interstate commerce: "as the word 'to regulate' implies in its nature, full power over the thing to be regulated, it excludes, necessarily, the action of all others that would perform the same operation on the same thing." Marshall found "great force in this argument," but went on to decide the case on the narrower grounds of statutory preemption. Justice Johnson, however, accepted Webster's argument.

Several years later, in Willson v. Black-Bird Creek Marsh Co., 27 U.S. (2 Pet.) 245 (1829), the Court addressed the constitutionality of state law in the absence of a preemptive federal regulation. The state of Delaware had authorized the plaintiff company to build a dam across a navigable waterway. Defendants, the owners of a sloop licensed and enrolled under the federal act involved in *Gibbons*, broke the plaintiff company's dam. In an action for damages, defendants argued that a state law authorizing construction of the dam conflicted with the Commerce Clause. Chief Justice Marshall wrote:

> [T]he question is to be considered, whether the act incorporating the Black-bird Creek Marsh company is repugnant to the constitution, so far as it authorizes a dam across the creek. The plea states the creek to be navigable, in the nature of a highway, through which the tide ebbs and flows. The act of assembly by which the plaintiffs were authorized to construct their dam, shows plainly that this is one of those many creeks, passing through a deep level marsh, adjoining the Delaware, up which the tide flows for some distance. The value of the property on its banks must be enhanced by excluding the water from the marsh, and the health of the inhabitants probably improved. Measures calculated to produce these objects, provided they do not come into collision with the powers of the general government, are undoubtedly within those which are reserved to the states. But the measure authorized by this act stops a navigable creek, and must be supposed to abridge the rights of those who have been accustomed to use it. But this abridgment, unless it comes in conflict with the constitution or a law of the United States, is an affair between the government of Delaware and its citizens, of which this court can take no cognizance.
>
> The counsel for the plaintiffs in error insist, that it comes in conflict with the power of the United States "to regulate commerce with foreign nations, and among the several states." If congress had passed any act which bore upon the case; any act in execution of the power to regulate commerce, the object of which was to control state legislation over those small navigable creeks into which the tide flows, and which abound throughout the lower country of the middle and southern states; we should feel not much difficulty in saying, that a state law coming to conflict with such act would be void. But congress has passed no such act. The repugnancy of the law of Delaware to the constitution is placed

> entirely on its repugnancy to the power to regulate commerce with foreign nations and among the several states; a power which has not been so exercised as to affect the question. We do not think, that the act empowering the Black-bird Creek Marsh company to place a dam across the creek, can, under all the circumstances of the case, be considered as repugnant to the power to regulate commerce in its dormant state, or as being in conflict with any law passed on the subject.

William Wirt, counsel for the respondent company, characterized the Delaware act as a "health" measure, and described the Black-Bird Creek as "one of those sluggish reptile streams, that do not run but creep, and which, wherever it passes, spreads its venom, and destroys the health of all those who inhabit its marshes." "Can it be asserted," he asked, "that a law authorizing the erection of a dam, and the formation of banks which will draw off the pestilence, and give to those who have before suffered from disease, health and vigor, is unconstitutional?"

Note that Marshall asks whether the dam is "repugnant to the power to regulate commerce in its dormant state." In speaking this way, he is asking what constitutional rule about interstate commerce should apply to state legislation in the absence of Congressional regulation. (This is the commerce power in its "dormant state.") The doctrine of the "Dormant Commerce Clause," as it has developed over two centuries, argues that the federal commerce power is not merely a positive grant of power to the federal government, but also an implied limitation on the power of the states. The judicial doctrines of the Dormant Commerce Clause seek to keep the channels of interstate commerce clear of unjustified state burdens and to prevent states from discriminating in their regulations against outsiders or interstate businesses. The doctrine is, in other words, a constitutional policy of preserving open, integrated, and freely accessible national markets. How do these ideas apply to the facts of Willson v. Black-Bird Creek Marsh Co.?

a. Should it matter what *effects* on interstate commerce the state's action has? How do you suppose the case would have come out if the creek had been a major interstate waterway?

b. Should it matter what the state's *purposes* are? Suppose Wirt had characterized the law not as a health measure, but as a regulation of navigation on the state's waterways, perhaps designed to benefit local businesses. Might the outcome have been different?

Recall Marshall's attraction to the argument in *Gibbons* that the very grant of a power to one government (the United States) precludes "the action of all others that would perform the same operation on the same thing." Is *Black-Bird Creek* consistent with this view?

We have not omitted any part of Marshall's analysis in the *Black-Bird Creek* case. The opinion concludes, elliptically, that "under all the circumstances of the case" the law authorizing erection of the dam does not conflict with the Commerce Clause or with any federal statute. What do you suppose are the relevant "circumstances"? One possible circumstance is that this was a health law as distinguished from a commercial regulation. Do you suppose that this rationale would have sufficed to sustain damming up a major interstate waterway? Another possible "circumstances" of the case might be the belief that the benefits of damming the creek substantially outweighed any impediments to interstate navigation. Does anything in Marshall's opinion in *Black-Bird Creek* suggest this reading? If so, is it consistent with the jurisprudence of *McCulloch* and *Gibbons*?

6. *The Dormant Commerce Clause today*. The modern doctrine of the Dormant Commerce Clause is discussed in Chapter 6, Section III.

NOTE: FEDERAL PREEMPTION

Gibbons v. Ogden holds that a valid congressional regulation of interstate commerce (the 1793 licensing statute) preempts inconsistent state regulations. For that reason, the Court goes on to consider the constitutionality of the underlying federal statute. Chief Justice Marshall assumes that if the 1793 statute is constitutional, it takes precedence over New York's monopoly grant. This is an early version of the doctrine of federal *preemption*. Justice Kennedy summed up the doctrine in the following case:

Arizona v. United States

132 S. Ct. 2492 (2012).

KENNEDY, J:

From the existence of two sovereigns follows the possibility that laws can be in conflict or at cross-purposes. The Supremacy Clause provides a clear rule that federal law "shall be the supreme Law of the Land; and the Judges in every State shall be bound thereby, any Thing in the Constitution or Laws of any State to the Contrary notwithstanding." Art. VI, cl. 2. Under this principle, Congress has the power to preempt state law. There is no doubt that Congress may withdraw specified powers from the States by enacting a statute containing an express preemption provision.

State law must also give way to federal law in at least two other circumstances. First, the States are precluded from regulating conduct in a field that Congress, acting within its proper authority, has determined must be regulated by its exclusive governance. See Gade v. National Solid Wastes Management Assn., 505 U.S. 88, 115 (1992). The intent to displace state law altogether can be inferred from a framework of regulation "so pervasive . . . that Congress left no room for the States to supplement it" or where there is a "federal interest . . . so dominant that the federal system will be assumed to preclude enforcement of state laws on the same subject." Rice v. Santa Fe Elevator Corp., 331 U.S. 218, 230 (1947); see English v. General Elec. Co., 496 U.S. 72, 79 (1990).

Second, state laws are preempted when they conflict with federal law. This includes cases where "compliance with both federal and state regulations is a physical impossibility," Florida Lime & Avocado Growers, Inc. v. Paul, 373 U.S. 132, 142-143 (1963), and those instances where the challenged state law "stands as an obstacle to the accomplishment and execution of the full purposes and objectives of Congress," Hines [v. Davidowitz, 312 U.S. 52, 67 (1941)]; see also Crosby [v.

National Foreign Trade Council, 50 U.S. 363, 373 (2000)] ("What is a sufficient obstacle is a matter of judgment, to be informed by examining the federal statute as a whole and identifying its purpose and intended effects"). In preemption analysis, courts should assume that "the historic police powers of the States" are not superseded "unless that was the clear and manifest purpose of Congress."

[Justice Kennedy went on to hold that three features of an Arizona statute, S.B. 1070, aimed at undocumented aliens, were preempted by federal law. A provision that reinforced federal alien registration requirements was preempted because Congress had occupied the entire field of alien registration. A provision that imposed criminal penalties on undocumented aliens who obtained employment was preempted because the Court determined that Congress sought to impose *both* criminal and civil penalties on employers but *only* civil penalties on employees. Finally, a provision that authorized state and local officials to make warrantless arrests of any person suspected of being an undocumented alien was preempted by a combination of federal laws. Because it is not a crime for a removable alien to remain in the United States, federal law generally limits arrests to those in aid of removal proceedings and generally requires warrants.]

NOTE: LANGUAGE, PURPOSE, AND MEANING[152]

1. Language and Purpose

From the time of Aristotle, it has been recognized that laws articulated in language will inevitably be imperfect and fail of their purposes in some circumstances: "[a]ll law is universal but about some things it is not possible to make a universal statement which shall be correct.[153] Consider James Madison's statement in The Federalist No. 37, in which he responds to critics of the Constitution who complained that its language was insufficiently precise:

> All new laws, though penned with the greatest technical skill, and passed on the fullest and most mature deliberation, are considered as more or less obscure and equivocal, until their meaning be liquidated and ascertained by a series of particular discussions and adjudications. Besides the obscurity arising from the complexity of objects, and the imperfection of the human faculties, the medium through which the conceptions of men are conveyed to each other adds a fresh embarrassment.
>
> The use of words is to express ideas. Perspicuity, therefore, requires not only that the ideas should be distinctly formed, but that they should be expressed by words distinctly and exclusively appropriate to them. But no language is so copious as to supply words and phrases for every complex idea, or so correct as not to include many equivocally denoting different

---

152. See generally Paul Brest, The Misconceived Quest for the Original Understanding, 60 B.U. L. Rev. 204 (1980); Michael Moore, The Semantics of Judging, 54 S. Cal. L. Rev. 151 (1981). See also Frederick Schauer, Playing by the Rules: A Philosophical Examination of Rule-Based Decision Making in Law and in Life (1991).

153. Aristotle, Ethics, Book V, ch. 10, fol. 1137.

> ideas. Hence it must happen that however accurately objects may be discriminated in themselves, and however accurately the discrimination may be considered, the definition of them may be rendered inaccurate by the inaccuracy of the terms in which it is delivered. And this unavoidable inaccuracy must be greater or less, according to the complexity and novelty of the objects defined. When the Almighty himself condescends to address mankind in their own language, his meaning, luminous as it must be, is rendered dim and doubtful by the cloudy medium through which it is communicated.

Madison's argument suggests that sole reliance on the text of the document may sometimes be insufficient to decide legal disputes. Consider in this context a famous passage written by the 16th century English lawyer Edmund Plowden:[154]

> A law of a certain state provides that foreigners scaling the walls of the city shall be capitally punished. But it happened that foreigners innocently passing through the city heard an outcry that enemies had suddenly attacked the city and were making inroads. The foreigners scaled the walls before the citizens, and, defending the city, they saved it. Now, therefore, what of the law? Ought they to die, as the law says? . . .
>
> In order to form a right judgment when the letter of a statute is restrained, and when enlarged, by equity, it is a good way, when you peruse a statute, to suppose that the law-maker is present, and that you have [asked] him the question you want to know touching the equity, then you must give yourself such an answer as you may imagine he would have done, if he had been present. As for example, . . . where the strangers scale the walls, and defend the city, suppose the lawmaker to be present with you, and in your mind put this question to him, shall the strangers be put to death? Then give yourself the same answer which you imagine he, being an upright and reasonable man, would have given, and you will find that he would have said "They shall not be put to death." . . . And therefore when such cases happen which are within the letter, or out of the letter, of a statute, and yet don't directly fall within the plain and natural purport of the letter, but are in some measure to be conceived in a different idea from that in which the text seems to express, it is a good way to give questions and give answers to yourself thereupon, in the same manner as if you were actually conversing with the maker of such laws, and by this means you will easily find out what is the equity of those cases. And if the law-maker would have followed the equity, notwithstanding the words of the law . . . you may safely do the like, for while you do no more than the law-maker would have done, you do not act contrary to the law, but in conformity to it.

To read a provision without regard to its context and likely purposes will yield either unresolvable indeterminacies or plain nonsense. Some judges and scholars have asserted that "[t]he whole aim of construction, as applied to a provision of

---

154. 2 Plowden 459, 466, 467, quoted in Learned Hand, The Bill of Rights 20-22 (1958).

the Constitution, is to discover the meaning, to ascertain and give effect to the intent, of its framers and the people who adopted it."[155] Others maintain that an interpreter should inquire into the "purpose of the provision." For example, Justice Frankfurter wrote:[156]

> You may have observed that I have not yet used the word "intention." All these years I have avoided speaking of the "legislative intent." . . . Legislation has an aim; it seeks to obviate some mischief, to supply an inadequacy, to effect a change of policy, to formulate a plan of government. That aim, that policy is not drawn, like nitrogen, out of the air; it is evidenced in the language of the statute, as read in the light of other external manifestations of purpose. That is what the judge must seek and effectuate, and he ought not to be led off the trail by tests that have overtones of subjective design. We are not concerned with anything subjective. We do not delve into the minds of legislators or their draftsmen, or committee members.

Can the "purpose" of a provision be distinguished from the "intent" of those who drafted or adopted it? Taken *literally*, Justice Frankfurter's statement makes no sense. Things—including statutes and constitutional provisions—do not have "purposes" or "aims"; they do not "seek to obviate" mischiefs. These terms require animate subjects. *Figuratively* speaking, one might describe the "purpose of a provision" tautologously with its language: "[T]he purpose of Article I, §8, cl. 3 is to permit Congress to regulate commerce . . . among the several States." But this seems a fruitless enterprise, and any other figurative reading of the term seems ultimately to refer to the purposes, aims, or seekings—in short the "intent"—of those who framed and adopted the provision.[157]

Nonetheless, Frankfurter's remarks are evocative of a real distinction. The (subjective) aims of those who drafted or adopted a provision can be described on different levels of generality. A rather general description would be: "Their purpose in adopting Article I, §8, cl. 3 was to permit Congress to legislate [in matters of commerce] where the States were separately incompetent." Much more specifically, one might describe the adopters' view of a particular fact situation: "They wanted to prevent the States from imposing tariffs." All other things being equal, a general or vague characterization is likely to describe the aims of more people than a precise or detailed characterization—the target is easier to hit. As one moves from the more specific to the less specific characterization of, or inquiry into, the aims of the framers, one moves from "intent" to "purpose." One can talk about the "purpose of

155. Home Bldg. & Loan Assn. v. Blaisdell, 290 U.S. 398 (1934) (Sutherland, J., dissenting).

156. Felix Frankfurter, Some Reflections on the Reading of Statutes, 1947 Colum. L. Rev. 527, 538-539.

157. The concept of purpose incorporates an element of will. It would simply be a misuse of language to say that a thing's purpose is anything it does or can do, apart from human intention. For example, it is not a purpose of an automobile to pollute, maim, or kill, and only by using a figurative anthropomorphism is it an automobile's purpose to transport passengers.

the provision" simply because it must have been the purpose of (nearly) everyone who voted for the provision and, indeed, understood to be their purpose even by those who voted against it.[158]

These more and less general characterizations of the framers' objectives correlate roughly with different approaches to interpretation. One who inquires into "purpose" may not look much beyond the language of the provision, for the language, when read in the context of the generally understood structure and values of a society, will usually indicate the society's reasons for adopting it. (This suggests why, without being tautologous, many speak anthropomorphically of the "purpose of the provision.") One who inquires into "intent," on the other hand, will examine closely the proceedings and debates that led to the provision's adoption.

The language and purposes of a provision enjoy a symbiotic relationship. The meaning (or application) of a provision is ascertained by examining its language and purposes. The language sets the boundaries of possible meanings and yields the initial—and often the primary—indication of its purposes. At the same time, the purposes of the provision circumscribe the range of its plausible meanings.

2. *Discovering the Adopters' Purposes*[159]

Four sets of proceedings bear directly on the original understanding of the constitutional provisions: the federal Constitutional Convention held in Philadelphia in 1787, the state ratification conventions, congressional proceedings in which amendments were proposed pursuant to Article V, and the state legislative

---

158. On a somewhat related point, can one meaningfully talk about the purpose or intent of those who framed or adopted a provision where there is no evidence that they explicitly considered the particular application of the provision about which their views are sought? Some scholars have suggested a person has no intent whatsoever with respect to a question he did not think about. See, e.g., John Chipman Gray, The Nature and Sources of the Law 172-173 (2d ed. 1921). The contrary view is now generally accepted. See, e.g., Lon Fuller, The Morality of Law 83-87 (1964); Gerald MacCallum, Legislative Intent, 75 Yale L.J. 754 (1966); Henry Hart and Albert Sacks, The Legal Process: Basic Problems in the Making and Application of Law 98 (tent. ed. 1958):

> What is the significance of advertance or inadvertance in the concept of "intention"? Of course, one may "intend" some specific consequences to which he did not consequently advert. If a master tells a servant to "take care of the house" during his absence, he no doubt intends that the servant will do his best to extinguish a fire in the house started by lightning, even though this contingency never actually occurred to him. But does one "intend" everything within the reach of his words which he does not consciously "exclude"? [Wittgenstein writes:] "Someone says to me: 'Show the children a game.' I teach them gaming with dice, and the other says, 'I didn't mean that sort of game.' Must the exclusion of the game with dice have come before his mind when he gave me the order [to make this last statement true]?"

159. See generally Jacobus tenBroek, Admissibility and Use by the United States Supreme Court of Extrinsic Aids in Constitutional Construction, 26 Cal. L. Rev. 287, 437, 664 (1938); 27 Cal. L. Rev. 157, 399 (1939).

proceedings in which they were ratified. Of these, the reports of the secret[160] proceedings of the Philadelphia Convention are probably most often cited and are as problematic as any others. John Wofford writes:[161]

> Max Farrand, in the introduction to his compilation of all accounts of the Convention extant in 1911 [The Records of the Federal Convention of 1787], states that the official journal, apparently containing all motions and votes, was delivered to Washington, then president of the Congress of the Confederation, who in 1796 deposited the papers in the Department of State. There they remained, untouched, until Congress by joint resolution in 1818 ordered them printed. Farrand reports that President Monroe requested his Secretary of State, John Quincy Adams, to take charge of the publication: "The task proved to be a difficult one. The papers were," according to Adams, "no better than the daily minutes from which the regular journal ought to have been, but never was, made out." Adams reports that at his request William Jackson, the secretary of the Convention, called upon him and "looked over the papers, but he had no recollection of them which could remove the difficulties arising from their disorderly state, nor any papers to supply the deficiency of the missing papers." With the expenditure of considerable time and labor, and with the exercise of no little ingenuity, Adams was finally able to collate the whole to his satisfaction. General Bloomfield supplied him with several important documents from the papers of David Brearley; Charles Pinckney sent him a copy of the plan he "believed" to be one he presented to the Convention; Madison furnished the means of completing the records of the last four days. . . . As thus compiled, the Journal, Acts and Proceedings of the Convention . . . which formed the Constitution of the United States was printed in 1819. Adams felt that he there presented a "correct and tolerably clear view of the proceedings of the convention. . . ." Farrand's own judgment, however, is more critical: "As Adams had nothing whatever to guide him in his work of compilation and editing, mistakes were inevitable, and not a few of these were important. . . . With notes so carelessly kept, as were evidently those of the secretary, the Journal cannot be relied upon absolutely. The statement of questions is probably accurate in most cases, but the determination of those questions and in particular the votes upon them should be accepted somewhat tentatively."
>
> Material in addition to the Journal has, of course, been discovered; this enabled Farrand to speak of "mistakes" in the Journal itself. Most important are the notes which Madison made during the proceedings. Madison himself described how he made the notes, and how he then used

160. See Max Farrand, The Framing of the Constitution of the United States 58-59 (1913).

161. Wofford, The Blinding Light: The Uses of History in Constitutional Interpretation, 31 U. Chi. L. Rev. 502, 504-506 (1964). See also Donald Dewey, James Madison Helps Clio Interpret the Constitution, 15 Am. J. Legal Hist. 38 (1971); James Hutson, The Creation of the Constitution: The Integrity of the Documentary Record, 65 Tex. L. Rev. 1 (1986).

> them to reconstruct a more complete account: "I chose a seat in front of the presiding member, with the other members, on my right and left hand. In this favorable position for hearing all that passed I noted in terms legible and in abbreviations and marks intelligible to myself what was read from the Chair or spoken by the members; and losing not a moment unnecessarily between the adjournment and reassembling of the Convention I was enabled to write out my daily notes during the session or within a few finishing days after its close." Madison's notes were not published exactly as he had transcribed them after each session. For after the publication of the official—and inaccurate—Journal, Madison went over his notes and made numerous changes in them. According to Farrand, these emendations "seriously impaired the value of his notes," since many of the Journal's errors were simply duplicated.
>
> By 1911, when Farrand published all of the known records of the Convention, the Journal and Madison's Debates had been supplemented by other (and shorter) records made contemporaneously with the Convention and by statements made later by those who had been present. We know that other records once existed, although Farrand notes that it is "not probable . . . that any such new material would modify to any great extent our conceptions of the Convention's work." In short, we have a picture of the Philadelphia proceedings, the various parts of which are generally consistent with each other. What we do not have, and indeed will never have, is any external check upon completeness of that picture. The conceptions of what occurred at Philadelphia remain, as Farrand put it, "ours."[162]

In her book, Madison's Hand: Revising the Constitutional Convention (2015), Mary Sarah Bilder showed that Madison's notes of the Philadelphia Convention were even less reliable than earlier believed, as Madison continued to revise them over the course of his lifetime. He frequently rewrote his notes, often many years after the Convention, in order to conform with his political positions at the time.

The Court has often discovered the "intent of the framers" in their nonofficial utterances—correspondence, papers, and publications. For example, in Reynolds v. United States, 98 U.S. 145 (1879), in holding that the Free Exercise Clause did not immunize a Mormon from a prosecution for bigamy, the Court cited Thomas

162. Until relatively recently, the main source of proceedings at the state conventions, which also contains material relating to the Philadelphia Convention, had been Debates in the Several State Conventions (Elliott ed., 2d ed. 1836-1845) (five volumes). It is, however, being supplanted by The Documentary History of the Ratification of the Constitution, compiled by historians at the University of Wisconsin. As of 2014, 24 volumes had been published, covering the ratification debates in Pennsylvania, Delaware, New Jersey, Georgia, Connecticut, Massachusetts, Virginia, Rhode Island, and New York. Future volumes will cover North and South Carolina, Maryland, New Hampshire, and Vermont (which joined the Union in 1791). Congressional proceedings are found in the Congressional Globe, later the Congressional Record. State legislative debates are not published in most states, although an official record of actions is kept.

Jefferson's assertion in his letter to the Danbury Baptists that the First Amendment built "a wall of separation between church and state." Chief Justice Waite explained: "Coming as this does from an acknowledged leader of the advocates of the measure, it may be accepted almost as an authoritative declaration of the scope and effect of the amendment. . . ."[163]

What implicit assumptions does Waite make?

Without doubt, the most frequently cited nonofficial source is *The Federalist*, which the Court has typically treated as an authoritative manifestation of the intent of the framers. As Professor Jacobus tenBroek's famously commented,[164] this makes sense only if one treats *The Federalist* as a truly "impartial account of the will of the fathers." But why would one rely on the collective authors to provide such an account?[165]

> The Federalist was composed as an argument on one side of a bitterly controverted question. It was calculated to put the Constitution in the light which would make it most acceptable to the ratifying conventions. It did not even purport to express the intention of the framers. [The Court has rarely paid attention to other writers, with similar experiences,] who were not measurably less capable. Thus, Luther Martin's commentary on the Constitution appears infrequently in the reports, and then generally with disparaging comment. Likewise, the able series of articles written over the name of "Brutus" by Judge Robert Yates. . . . [What explains the difference in citation practices is principally] the not altogether incidental fact that Madison and Hamilton were on the side which turned out to be victorious, and this fact, taken together with their entire careers, has made them great in the eye of posterity—a fact which has given their words a quality of persuasion which has never attached to the utterances of Martin and Yates.[166]

---

163. See also McCollum v. Board of Educ., 333 U.S. 203, 211 (1948). For an excellent criticism of the Court's use of history in construing the religion clauses, see Mark de Wolfe Howe, The Garden and Wilderness (1965).

164. tenBroek, supra n.159, 27 Cal. L. Rev. 157, 162-164 (1939). See also Ray Raphael, Constitutional Myths: What We Get Wrong and How to Get It Right, ch. 6 (2013), which emphasizes the relative unimportance of *The Federalist* at the time of its publication.

165. [Footnote by tenBroek] . . . Hamilton attended the convention only sporadically after the first month. Moreover, John Jay, another of the authors of The Federalist, had not been a delegate to the Constitutional Convention. However, only 5 out of the 85 articles composing The Federalist are attributed to Jay, and these, curiously enough, are almost never cited by the Supreme Court, although this is probably due more to their subject matter than to their authorship.

166. *The Federalist* has also often been touted as a reliable gauge of opinion in the ratifying conventions, on the ground that it was widely published in the states prior to ratification and was the chief means by which the intent of the Convention was transmitted to the states. See, e.g., Legal Tender Cases, 79 U.S. (12 Wall.) 457, 585, 608 (1870). But even if the articles persuaded all who read them, "a considerable number of the conventions in the states had ratified the Constitution while a varying number of The Federalist papers were as yet unpublished. . . ." tenBroek, supra n.159, 27 Cal. L. Rev. at 171.

Is the Court justified in giving more weight to the views of the proponents than of the opponents of the Constitution?

By contrast with later authors, consider John Marshall's treatment of *The Federalist* in *McCulloch.* He was fully aware that The Federalist No. 33 had suggested that conflicts between states and the national government over taxing authority would be handled politically; it did not suggest that courts would resolve the question constitutionally. But that did not stop Marshall from invalidating Maryland's tax.

The Court has also cited the enactments of early Congresses as indicative of the original understanding of constitutional provisions. For example, in Myers v. United States, 272 U.S. 52 (1926), in holding that a statutory provision requiring the Senate's consent for the removal of postmasters unconstitutionally usurped executive power, Chief Justice Taft relied on the debates over, and enactment of, a 1789 law that recognized the President's plenary power to remove his secretary of foreign affairs. Taft argued that the Congress had affirmed the President's exclusive constitutional authority to remove executive appointees, and explained:

> We have devoted much space to this discussion and decision of the question of the Presidential power of removal in the First Congress, not because a Congressional conclusion on a constitutional issue is conclusive, but, first, because of our agreement with the reasons upon which it was avowedly based; second, because this was the decision of the First Congress, on a question of primary importance in the organization of the Government, made within two years after the Constitutional Convention and within a much shorter time after its ratification; and, third, because that Congress numbered among its leaders those who had been members of the Convention.

Interestingly enough, neither the First Congress nor the Court seemed to pay any real attention to Federalist 77, in which Publius (Hamilton) assured his readers that the Senate would have to agree to the removal of executive branch officials, just as it had to confirm them initially.

However, in Martin v. Hunter's Lessee, 14 U.S. (1 Wheat.) 304 (1816), Justice Story concluded his argument that the Supreme Court had appellate jurisdiction over state courts with a reference to the First Congress:

> It is an historical fact, that at the time when the Judiciary Act was submitted to the deliberations of the first congress, composed, as it was, not only of men of great learning and ability, but of men who had acted principal part in framing, supporting, or opposing that constitution, the same exposition was explicitly declared and admitted by the friends and by the opponents of that system.[167]

---

167. Note also that Oliver Ellsworth, who was Chief Justice of the Supreme Court from 1796 to 1800, played a major role in the framing of both Article III and the Judiciary Act of 1789. Michael Kraus, Oliver Ellsworth, in 1 The Justices of the United States Supreme Court 273 (Friedman & Israel eds., 1969).

What assumptions are implicit in these uses of the actions of early Congresses? With respect to the 1789 provision relied on in *Myers*, consider Professor Charles Miller's suggestions that "one reason why the First Congress had exerted little effort on its own behalf was that George Washington was President, and no legislator dared question his wisdom by denying him the right to remove a member of his own cabinet," and that the outcome of Congress's action was largely the result of clever parliamentary maneuvering by James Madison, who managed to divide and conquer two factions, which, for different reasons, believed that the Senate's consent *should* be necessary for presidential removals.[168] Even if he is correct on the specific point, does it hold with regard, say, to §13 of the Judiciary Act, about which there was absolutely no debate in Congress? Should Marshall have deferred to the position of the Congress in *Marbury*? Does his failure to do so stand as a general rejection of the relevance of the First Congress as privileged constitutional interpreter?

XI. THE "GENERAL WELFARE"

A. The Spending Clause and Disaster Relief

Congressional authority under the "General Welfare" Clause was a recurring issue in the early Republic, though, interestingly, there is no judicial opinion directly considering the issue. As one might expect from the debate over the First Bank, members of the Federalist Party, heavily influenced by Hamilton, offered an expansive view of congressional power to spend for the "general welfare." As Professor Currie writes, "[a] fire that devastated the Georgia port city of Savannah presented a spectacular opportunity for Hamilton's disciples, for the idea of aiding the victims had obvious emotional appeal for Southern Representatives, many of whom were ideologically allergic to federal spending. . . . One has the sense that wily Federalists were hoping to slip this one by on sympathy grounds, only to employ it mercilessly as a precedent later on. But the Republicans refused the bait." They insisted that the "general welfare" must be defined in terms of the specific allocations of power in clauses 2-17 rather than a foundation of independent power of Congress.[169] As you will see in Chapter 6, the Supreme Court ultimately accepted the Hamiltonian view and, concomitantly, rejected the more limited Madisonian conception of congressional power.

Even if one accepts a congressional power to spend on behalf of the "general welfare," an independent question is how it is to be defined (and *who* gets to define it). One might wonder exactly why it was in the "general welfare"—i.e., the welfare of Americans living in Massachusetts or Kentucky—to rebuild Savannah, in contrast with what might be termed the "special welfare" of Georgians who might

168. Charles Miller, The Supreme Court and the Uses of History, ch. 4 (1969).

169. See David P. Currie, supra n.57, at 224.

otherwise have had to raise local taxes to pay for reconstructing their principal port city. As Professor Currie writes elsewhere, aiding Savannah "would justify federal relief for local disasters anywhere in the country."[170] Of course, the modern Congress, like its earliest predecessors, does indeed allocate what are often vast amounts of money for "local disasters." Is the justification for this that whatever happens in New Orleans, Miami, or San Diego, does in fact affect all Americans, or, rather, is it that we accept with equanimity the ability of politically influential groups (or cities) to make claims on the public treasury so long as Congress is willing to declare, without more, that it is in the "general welfare" to do so?[171] Similar questions could be raised, of course, about congressional decisions in 1812 to allocate $50,000 of federal funds to relieve the suffering of victims of an earthquake in Caracas, Venezuela; three years later funds were allocated for similar relief of earthquake victims in New Madrid, Missouri.[172]

B. Internal Improvements

The debate over national power crystallized with regard to the passage of legislation funding "internal improvements," including roads and canals. In 1816, for example, then-Representative John C. Calhoun of South Carolina (who would later serve in the Senate and as John Quincy Adams' and Andrew Jackson's Vice President) proposed a bill that would allocate the United States' share of dividends it received from the Bank of the United States to a "fund for constructing roads and canals."[173] Calhoun defended his proposal as a contribution to the "general welfare" of the entire nation:

> The first great object was to perfect the communication from Maine to Louisiana. . . . The next was the connexion of the Lakes with the Hudson River. . . . The next object of chief importance was to connect all the great commercial points on the Atlantic, Philadelphia, Baltimore, Washington, Richmond, Charleston, and Savannah, with the Western States; and finally, to perfect the intercourse between the West and New Orleans.

After much substantial debate, much of it involving constitutional arguments, the House passed the bill by an 86-84 vote; the Senate, after what Professor Currie terms only a "perfunctory" debate (although there, too, senators at least mentioned constitutional issues), agreed with the House by a 20-15 vote. It then went

---

170. David P. Currie, 2 The Constitution in Congress: The Jeffersonians 1803-1827, at 292 (2001).

171. See generally Michele Landis Dauber, Let Me Next Time Be "Tried by Fire": Disaster Relief and the Origins of the American Welfare State, 1789-1874, 92 Nw. U. L. Rev. 967 (1998).

172. See the list of such appropriations in Michele Landis Dauber, The Sympathetic State: Disaster Relief and the Origins of the American Welfare State 60 (2013).

173. See Currie, supra n.170, at 260-267.

to President James Madison for his signature. In 1816, Madison had signed the bill chartering the Second Bank of the United States, arguing that the constitutionality of the bank had been settled by practice. Internal improvements, however, were a different matter, and in literally his last act as President, on March 3, 1817, he vetoed the legislation:

James Madison, Veto Message[174]

(March 3, 1817)

. . . I am constrained by the insuperable difficulty I feel in reconciling the bill with the Constitution of the United States to [veto it]. . . . [I]t does not appear that the power proposed to be exercised by the bill is among the enumerated powers, or that it falls by any just interpretation within the power to make laws necessary and proper for carrying into execution those or other powers vested by the Constitution in the Government of the United States.

"The power to regulate commerce among the several States" can not include such a commerce without a latitude of construction departing from the ordinary import of the terms strengthened by the known inconveniences which doubtless led to the grant of this remedial power to Congress.

To refer the power in question to the clause "to provide for the common defense and general welfare" would be contrary to the established and consistent rules of interpretation, as rendering the special and careful enumeration of powers which follow the clause nugatory and improper. Such a view of the Constitution would have the effect of giving to congress a general power of legislation instead of the defined and limited one hitherto understood to belong to them, the terms "common defense and general welfare" embracing every object and act within the purview of a legislative trust. It would have the effect of subjecting both the Constitution and laws of the several States in all cases not specifically exempted to be superseded by laws of Congress. . . . Such a view of the Constitution, finally, would have the effect of excluding the judicial authority of the United States from its participation in guarding the boundary between legislative powers of the General and State Governments, inasmuch as questions relating to the general welfare, being questions of policy and expediency, are unsusceptible of judicial cognizance and decision.

A restriction of the power "to provide for the common defense and general welfare" to cases which are to be provided for by the expenditure of money would still leave within legislative power of Congress all the great and most important measures of Government, money being the ordinary and necessary means of carrying them into execution.

If a general power to construct roads and canals, and to improve the navigation of water courses, with the train of powers incident thereto, be not possessed by Congress, the assent of the States in the mode provided in the bill can not confer the power. The only cases in which the consent and cession of particular States can extend the power of Congress are those specified and provided for in the Constitution.

---

174. 1 Messages and Papers of the Presidents 584-585 (Richardson ed., 1897).

I am not unaware of the great importance of roads and canals and the improved navigation of water courses, and that a power in the National Legislature to provide for them might be exercised with signal advantage to the general prosperity. But seeing that such a power is not expressly given by the Constitution, and believing that it can not be deduced from any part of it without an inadmissible latitude of construction and a reliance on insufficient precedents; believing also that the permanent success of the Constitution depends on a definite partition of powers between the General and the State Governments, and that no adequate landmarks would be left by the constructive extension of the powers of Congress as proposed in the bill, I have no option but to withhold my signature from it, and to cherishing the hope that its beneficial objects may be attained by a resort for the necessary powers to the same wisdom and virtue in the nation which established the Constitution in its actual form and providently marked out in the instrument itself a safe and practicable mode of improving it as experience might suggest.

Madison's constitutional objections to internal improvements were characteristic of the constitutional philosophy of the Jeffersonian Republican Party, and its successor, Andrew Jackson's Democratic Party. By contrast, "national" Republicans like Calhoun, and later members of the Whig Party, like Daniel Webster, Henry Clay, and Abraham Lincoln, argued that the federal government had the power to make such improvements. The debate over internal improvements was part of the larger debate over "strict" construction of the Constitution during the antebellum era.

Several of Madison's successors, including James Monroe, Andrew Jackson, James K. Polk, and Franklin Pierce joined him in vetoing similar legislation. Thus, in 1854, Franklin Pierce, a Jacksonian Democrat, vetoed a bill awarding public lands to states for the "benefit of indigent insane persons," feeling "compelled to resist the deep sympathies of my own heart in favor of the humane purpose sought to be accomplished and to overcome the reluctance with which I dissent from the conclusions of the two Houses of Congress" because he read the Constitution as not allowing such an act.[175] Democratic resistance continued well after the Civil War: As we will see in Chapter 4, in the 1880s Grover Cleveland—the first Democrat elected to the presidency after Abraham Lincoln—would veto a disaster relief bill to alleviate the problems of drought-stricken Texas farmers.

In 1847, President James K. Polk, also a Jacksonian Democrat, issued a pocket veto of a public improvements bill that would have applied half a million dollars "for the improvement of numerous harbors and rivers lying within the limits and jurisdiction of several of the States of the Union."[176] Polk's veto offers a good summary of the constitutional issues and, just as importantly, the competing constitutional visions of federal power in the antebellum era:

---

175. http://www.presidency.ucsb.edu/ws/?pid=67850.

176. http://www.presidency.ucsb.edu/ws/?pid=67965.

James K. Polk, Veto Message

(December 15, 1847)

[T]he policy of embarking the Federal Government in a general system of internal improvements had its origin but little more than twenty years ago. In a very few years the applications to Congress for appropriations in furtherance of such objects exceeded $200,000,000. In this alarming crisis President Jackson refused to approve and sign the Maysville road bill, the Wabash River bill, and other bills of similar character. His interposition put a check upon the new policy of throwing the cost of local improvements upon the National Treasury, preserved the revenues of the nation for their legitimate objects, by which he was enabled to extinguish the then existing public debt and to present to an admiring world the unprecedented spectacle in modern times of a nation free from debt and advancing to greatness with unequaled strides under a Government which was content to act within its appropriate sphere in protecting the States and individuals in their own chosen career of improvement and of enterprise.

Although the bill under consideration proposes no appropriation for a road or canal, it is not easy to perceive the difference in principle or mischievous tendency between appropriations for making roads and digging canals and appropriations to deepen rivers and improve harbors. All are alike within the limits and jurisdiction of the States, and rivers and harbors alone open an abyss of expenditure sufficient to swallow up the wealth of the nation and load it with a debt which may fetter its energies and tax its industry for ages to come.

[I]t seems impossible, in the nature of the subject, as connected with local representation, that the several objects presented for improvement shall be weighed according to their respective merits and appropriations confined to those whose importance would justify a tax on the whole community to effect their accomplishment. . . .

Already our Confederacy consists of twenty-nine States. . . . In all this vast country, bordering on the Atlantic and Pacific, there are many thousands of bays, inlets, and rivers equally entitled to appropriations for their improvement with the objects embraced in this bill.

We have seen in our States that the interests of individuals or neighborhoods, combining against the general interest, have involved their governments in debts and bankruptcy; and when the system prevailed in the General Government, and was checked by President Jackson, it had begun to be considered the highest merit in a member of Congress to be able to procure appropriations of public money to be expended within his district or State, whatever might be the object. We should be blind to the experience of the past if we did not see abundant evidences that if this system of expenditure is to be indulged in combinations of individual and local interests will be found strong enough to control legislation, absorb the revenues of the country, and plunge the Government into a hopeless indebtedness.

Such a system is subject, moreover, to be perverted to the accomplishment of the worst of political purposes. During the few years it was in full operation, and which immediately preceded the veto of President Jackson of the Maysville road bill, instances were numerous of public men seeking to gain popular favor by holding out to the people interested in particular localities the promise of large disbursements of public money. . . . [T]he people in the vicinity of each were led to believe that their property would be enhanced in value and they themselves be enriched by the large expenditures which they were promised by the advocates of the system should be made from the Federal Treasury in their neighborhood. Whole sections of the country were thus sought to be influenced, and the system was fast becoming one not only of profuse and wasteful expenditure, but a potent political engine.

If the power to improve a harbor be admitted, it is not easy to perceive how the power to deepen every inlet on the ocean or the lakes and make harbors where there are none can be denied. If the power to clear out or deepen the channel of rivers near their mouths be admitted, it is not easy to perceive how the power to improve them to their fountain head and make them navigable to their sources can be denied. Where shall the exercise of the power, if it be assumed, stop? . . . The power to improve harbors and rivers for purposes of navigation, by deepening or clearing out, by dams and sluices, by locking or canalling, must be admitted without any other limitation than the discretion of Congress, or it must be denied altogether. If it be admitted, how broad and how susceptible of enormous abuses is the power thus vested in the General Government! There is not an inlet of the ocean or the Lakes, not a river, creek, or streamlet within the States, which is not brought for this purpose within the power and jurisdiction of the General Government. . . .

Such a system could not be administered with any approach to equality among the several States and sections of the Union. There is no equality among them in the objects of expenditure, and if the funds were distributed according to the merits of those objects some would be enriched at the expense of their neighbors. . . . The true interests of the country would be lost sight of in an annual scramble for the contents of the Treasury, and the Member of Congress who could procure the largest appropriations to be expended in his district would claim the reward of victory from his enriched constituents. The necessary consequence would be sectional discontents and heartburnings, increased taxation, and a national debt never to be extinguished.

. . . The Constitution provides that "no State shall, without the consent of Congress, lay any duty of tonnage." [A duty of tonnage is a fee imposed on a vessel entering, remaining in, or leaving, a port.] With the "consent" of Congress, such duties may be levied, collected, and expended by the States. We are not left in the dark as to the objects of this reservation of power to the States. The subject was fully considered by the Convention that framed the Constitution. It appears in Mr. Madison's report of the proceedings of that body that one object of the reservation was that the States should not be restrained from laying duties of tonnage for the purpose of clearing harbors. Other objects were named in the debates, and among them the support of seamen. . . .

Under this wise system the improvement of harbors and rivers was commenced, or rather continued, from the organization of the Government under the present Constitution. Many acts were passed by the several States levying duties of tonnage, and many were passed by Congress giving their consent to those acts. Such acts have been passed by Massachusetts, Rhode Island, Pennsylvania, Maryland, Virginia, North Carolina, South Carolina, and Georgia, and have been sanctioned by the consent of Congress. . . .

By returning to the early and approved construction of the Constitution and to the practice under it this inequality and injustice will be avoided and at the same time all the really important improvements be made, and, as our experience has proved, be better made and at less cost than they would be by the agency of officers of the United States. . . .

In the proceedings and debates of the General Convention which formed the Constitution and of the State conventions which adopted it nothing is found to countenance the idea that the one intended to propose or the others to concede such a grant of power to the General Government as the building up and maintaining of a system of internal improvements within the States necessarily implies. Whatever the General Government may constitutionally create, it may lawfully protect. If it may make a road upon the soil of the States, it may protect it from destruction or injury by penal laws. So of canals, rivers, and harbors. If it may put a dam in a river, it may protect that dam from removal or injury, in direct opposition to the laws, authorities, and people of the State in which it is situated. If it may deepen a harbor, it may by its own laws protect its agents and contractors from being driven from their work even by the laws and authorities of the State. The power to make a road or canal or to dig up the bottom of a harbor or river implies a right in the soil of the State and a jurisdiction over it, for which it would be impossible to find any warrant.

The States were particularly jealous of conceding to the General Government any right of jurisdiction over their soil, and in the Constitution restricted the exclusive legislation of Congress to such places as might be "purchased with the consent of the States in which the same shall be, for the erection of forts, magazines, dockyards, and other needful buildings." That the United States should be prohibited from purchasing lands within the States without their consent, even for the most essential purposes of national defense, while left at liberty to purchase or seize them for roads, canals, and other improvements of immeasurably less importance, is not to be conceived. . . .

During the [Philadelphia Convention] a motion was made to enlarge the proposed power for "cutting canals" into a power "to grant charters of incorporation when the interest of the United States might require and the legislative provisions of the individual States may be incompetent"; and the reason assigned by Mr. Madison for the proposed enlargement of the power was that it would "secure an easy communication between the States, which the free intercourse now to be opened seemed to call for. The political obstacles being removed, a removal of the natural ones, as far as possible, ought to follow."

The original proposition and all the amendments were rejected, after deliberate discussion, not on the ground, as so much of that discussion as has been preserved indicates, that no direct grant was necessary, but because it was deemed inexpedient to grant it at all. When it is considered that some of the members of the Convention, who afterwards participated in the organization and administration of the Government, advocated and practiced upon a very liberal construction of the Constitution, grasping at many high powers as implied in its various provisions, not one of them, it is believed, at that day claimed the power to make roads and canals, or improve rivers and harbors, or appropriate money for that purpose. Among our early statesmen of the strict-construction class the opinion was universal, when the subject was first broached, that Congress did not possess the power, although some of them thought it desirable.

[Polk quotes the views of Presidents Jefferson, Madison, and Monroe, each of whom argued that Congress lacked constitutional power to create internal improvements.]

No express grant of this power is found in the Constitution. Its advocates have differed among themselves as to the source from which it is derived as an incident. . . . [T]he power to regulate commerce seems now to be chiefly relied upon, especially in reference to the improvement of harbors and rivers. . . . That to "regulate commerce" does not mean to make a road, or dig a canal, or clear out a river, or deepen a harbor would seem to be obvious to the common understanding. To "regulate" admits or affirms the preexistence of the thing to be regulated. In this case it presupposes the existence of commerce, and, of course, the means by which and the channels through which commerce is carried on. It confers no creative power; it only assumes control over that which may have been brought into existence through other agencies, such as State legislation and the industry and enterprise of individuals. If the definition of the word "regulate" is to include the provision of means to carry on commerce, then have Congress not only power to deepen harbors, clear out rivers, dig canals, and make roads, but also to build ships, railroad cars, and other vehicles, all of which are necessary to commerce. There is no middle ground. If the power to regulate can be legitimately construed into a power to create or facilitate, then not only the bays and harbors, but the roads and canals and all the means of transporting merchandise among the several States, are put at the disposition of Congress. . . . If a more extended construction be adopted, it is impossible for the human mind to fix on a limit to the exercise of the power other than the will and discretion of Congress. It sweeps into the vortex of national power and jurisdiction not only harbors and inlets, rivers and little streams, but canals, turnpikes, and railroads—every species of improvement which can facilitate or create trade and intercourse "with foreign nations, and among the several States, and with the Indian tribes."

Should any great object of improvement exist in our widely extended country which can not be ejected by means of tonnage duties levied by the States with the concurrence of Congress, it is safer and wiser to apply to the States in the mode prescribed by the Constitution for an amendment of that instrument whereby the powers of the General Government may be enlarged, with such limitations and restrictions as experience has shown to be proper, than to assume and exercise a power which has not been granted, or which may be regarded as doubtful in the opinion of a large portion of our constituents. This course has been recommended successively by Presidents Jefferson, Madison, Monroe, and Jackson, and I fully concur with them in opinion. If an enlargement of power should be deemed proper, it will unquestionably be granted by the States; if otherwise, it will be withheld; and in either case their decision should be final. In the meantime I deem it proper to add that the investigation of this subject has impressed me more strongly than ever with the solemn conviction that the usefulness and permanency of this Government and the happiness of the millions over whom it spreads its protection will be best promoted by carefully abstaining from the exercise of all powers not dearly granted by the Constitution.

DISCUSSION

1. *Presidential versus judicial interpretation.* Madison's and Polk's veto messages are justified in terms of constitutional fidelity. Congress was unable to override the vetoes, meaning that there would be no judicial resolution of the constitutional question. Would a judicial resolution have been superior to having Presidents make the constitutional decision? Note that if the Whigs had gained the White House and a majority in Congress, previous presidential vetoes would have not prevented them from funding internal improvements. Outside the executive branch, at least, presidential veto statements do not have precedential value like judicial decisions, although it is noteworthy that Polk cites veto statements by his Jeffersonian and Jacksonian predecessors, who agreed with his strict constructionist views.

Unlike most constitutional law casebooks, this one features a number of presidential veto statements because of the statements' constitutional arguments and their contributions to the American constitutional tradition. One would never learn, for example, that the constitutionality of internal improvements was a central bone of contention during the nineteenth century merely by studying decisions of the U.S. Supreme Court.

2. *Internal improvements and the national political process.* What do you make of Polk's argument that the power to expend money on internal improvements would corrupt the political process? The promise of funding for internal improvements in particular states and congressional districts has often been employed to win votes and thereby achieve political compromises. What do you think Polk would say about the political uses of what is sometimes called "pork"? Note that Polk has no problem with Congress allowing states to collect tonnage duties that might be used for internal improvements, but in that case, the money will go to *state treasuries* and *states* will decide how to invest it. Are the problems of political corruption and shady dealing lessened when revenue is collected at the state level and states decide whether or not to engage in various "pork barrel" projects? Will states adequately take national interests into account in their decisions about investments in infrastructure?

Note that Polk also argues that if a power to build internal improvements were granted through the commerce power, it would have no stopping point, and Congress could build and improve almost anything used for commerce and almost every aspect of transportation would fall within its jurisdiction. Was he correct as a matter of constitutional logic? If so, is this a good or a bad result?

3. Given *McCulloch*, do you think that the Marshall Court would have upheld Congress's power to finance "internal improvements"? Although Madison's veto occurred prior to *McCulloch*, later Presidents (like Monroe, Jackson, and Polk) continued to oppose internal improvements on constitutional grounds long after *McCulloch*; and, as we saw in Chapter 1, President Jackson found *McCulloch*'s reasoning irrelevant to his own determination that the Second Bank was unconstitutional. Note, moreover, that the Taney Court might have well have agreed with Jackson and his allies, both on the question of the bank and on internal improvements. In this sense, it was fortunate for advocates of federal power that the issue was never properly presented to the Supreme Court.

Chapter 3

Are We a Nation? The Jacksonian Era to the Civil War, 1835-1865

The first party system of Federalists and Republicans collapsed in the aftermath of the War of 1812, not least because some prominent New England Federalists floated the idea of secession in protest against the policies of President James Madison.[1] A second party system began to emerge after the Era of Good Feelings, a period of supposed consensus under the presidency of James Monroe (who was reelected in 1820 by an electoral vote of 231-1, with the one holdout explaining that George Washington should remain unique in receiving unanimous support). John Randolph, a crusty Virginian, described this show of support as "the unanimity of indifference, and not of approbation," and by 1824 the polity was strikingly divided. One faction, which became the Whig Party, was led by John Quincy Adams, the son of John Adams and Monroe's Secretary of State and the author of the Monroe Doctrine claiming American hegemony over the fate of the Western Hemisphere. Although Adams received both fewer popular and electoral votes than Andrew Jackson—114,023 and 84, respectively, against Jackson's 152,901 popular and 99 electoral votes—the election was thrown into the House of Representatives because two other candidates, Secretary of the Treasury William Crawford of Georgia and Speaker of the House Henry Clay, got enough electoral votes to deprive Jackson of the majority required for election. Although Clay, the fourth-place finisher with 37 electoral votes, could not himself be elected President (because the House of Representatives, under the Twelfth Amendment, must choose among the top three finishers, on a one-state/one-vote basis), he had sufficient influence among his colleagues to be able successfully to throw his support to Adams, who promptly named Clay Secretary of State. South Carolina Representative John C. Calhoun was elected Vice President, having received a clear majority of 181 electoral votes.

Jacksonians promptly began denouncing the "corrupt bargain" that ended the 1824 election and planning for revenge in 1828. A united Democratic Party

1. See, e.g., James Banner, To the Hartford Convention (1970).

was able to elect its ticket of Jackson and Calhoun,[2] although Calhoun would resign the vice presidency as he became increasingly distant from Jackson's nationalist policies (at least relative to South Carolina). The Democrats dominated national politics during the period covered by this chapter, electing Jackson, Martin Van Buren, James Polk, Franklin Pierce, and James Buchanan. The Whig victory of 1840 under the leadership of William Henry Harrison was effectively negated by his death a month after his inauguration and the succession by Vice President John Tyler, a Virginia ex-Democrat, whose principal interest appeared to be strengthening the role of slave states in the Union. (It was Tyler who successfully pressed the annexation of Texas on Congress.) The second Whig to be elected, Zachary Taylor (1848), also died in office, to be succeeded by Millard Fillmore. Not until the triumph of the new Republican Party in 1860, through the election of Abraham Lincoln, would the Democratic hold on the presidency be broken. (No Democrat thereafter would be elected until the 1884 election of Grover Cleveland, although many historians believe that Democrat Samuel Tilden was robbed of the presidency in the disputed election of 1876.)

The period covered by this chapter is often labeled the age of Jacksonian democracy; it featured the emergence of the first mass-based political party and the relaxation on property requirements for the suffrage that took place in the states throughout the 1820s:[3]

> Jacksonian democracy was a national movement in that it opposed disunion and knew no geographical limits. . . . But it was anti-national in rejecting Henry Clay's "American System" [under which Congress would have participated in developing systems of interstate transportation]. That is, the Democrats wanted roads, canals, and (in a few years) railroads to be chartered and aided by the states, but no Federal Government messing into the operations or sharing the expected profits. Jacksonians spoke for the men on the make who resented government grants of special privileges to rival entrepreneurs and who preferred laissez-faire to the positive state. . . . [T]he Jackson men identified themselves with the movement toward more equality. Yet they believed in equality only for white men; they were far less charitable toward the Indian and the Negro than their "aristocratic" foes. Jacksonian Democracy was not "leveling" in the European sense, having no desire to pull down men of wealth to a common plane; but it wanted a fair chance for every man to level up.

Jackson also altered the face of the federal judiciary. He was able to nominate five Justices by 1836, including Marshall's successor as Chief Justice, Roger B.

---

2. See generally Morton Borden, Parties and Politics in the Early Republic, 1789-1815 (1969); Shaw Livermore, Twilight of Federalism: The Disintegration of the Federalist Party, 1815-1830 (1962); Richard McCormick, The Second American Party System: Jacksonian Era (1966).

3. Samuel Eliot Morison, Henry Steele Commager, and William E. Leuchtenberg, The Growth of the American Republic 419-420 (7th ed. 1980). See also Lawrence Friedman, A History of American Law, ch. 3 (1973); Carter Goodrich, Government Promotion of American Canals and Railroads, 1800-1890 (1960).

Taney.[4] A Maryland aristocrat and former Federalist—and the first Roman Catholic to be named to the Supreme Court—Taney had aligned with the Democrats in the 1820s. Jackson first appointed him Attorney General and Secretary of the Treasury. He helped to draft Jackson's Veto Message regarding the bank, supra Chapter 1, including the passage that denied that the constitutional interpretations of the Supreme Court necessarily bound the President. Jackson had nominated Taney to be an Associate Justice in 1835, but the strongly anti-Jackson Senate refused to bring the nomination to a vote. When John Marshall died later that year, Jackson nominated Taney once more, this time to succeed Marshall as Chief Justice. After an eight-month delay, the Senate confirmed Taney as the fifth Chief Justice of the United States.[5] Carl Swisher writes:[6]

> Taney went to the Court with a conviction as to the sanctity of rights of physical and tangible property, and the community rights connected therewith; . . . he distrusted mercantile and banking interests that were strong enough and ruthlessly selfish enough to endanger the interests of stable property and of the community; . . . he had a deep sense of local patriotism for Maryland, which easily extended to the southern states with a similar culture. . . . [A]lthough a firm believer in the Union he was also apparently in greater degree a believer in the rights of states and of what was to become the minority region of the South.

Taney, like five of the seven first Presidents of the United States, was a slaveholder and therefore accepted a view of white superiority that justified racially structured chattel slavery.

In retrospect, the central issue of the antebellum era was whether the United States would survive as a nation. But this begged the very question whether the United States *was* a nation. As the country grew ever larger, it remained unclear whether residents felt bound together in a common enterprise. In the very first chapter of Walden, published in 1854, Henry David Thoreau commented that "[w]e are in great haste to construct a magnetic telegraph from Maine to Texas; but Maine and Texas, it may be, have nothing important to communicate." In fact, many people in New England *did* have a message for people in Texas. They were opposed to the expansion of slavery—Thoreau himself went to jail to protest the Mexican War. (In 1840, William Lloyd Garrison, the leading white abolitionist and editor of *The Liberator*, had burnt the American flag in protest and offered the distinctly radical proposal that the *North* should secede, offering the slogan "No Union with Slaveholders.") Complete abolition of slavery was by no means the majority position in the North, but even many moderate Northerners opposed the expansion of slavery in newly acquired territories.

---

4. Indeed, Whig Presidents made only two appointments, in 1851 and 1853, during the entire period prior to Lincoln's election.

5. At the very least, this should suggest that pitched battles over appointments to the Supreme Court are nothing new in American political life.

6. Carl Swisher, Mr. Chief Justice Taney, in Mr. Justice 38-39 (Dunham & Kurland eds., 1964).

Conversely, as time passed, people in slave states became increasingly concerned that the rest of the nation would interfere with their local institutions, of which the most economically important was chattel slavery. Politicians in the South eventually became convinced that it was impossible to continue political union with those they perceived as anti-slavery zealots (like Abraham Lincoln). Most of this chapter, therefore, will concern, either directly or indirectly, the interplay between constitutional federalism and the existence of chattel slavery as an important part of the economy and culture of many American states (and, therefore, of the United States).

Slavery, however, was not the whole story of this period. This was also a time of burgeoning economic development. Legal historian James Willard Hurst famously referred to the "release of energy" by Americans in settling a geographically expanding country and establishing new businesses. The growing economy demanded, along with institutions like banks, new canals (such as the Erie Canal in New York, one of the principal public works projects in American history), roads, and, by the end of the era, railroads. Although railroads were built by private investors, they depended heavily on the state's exercise of its eminent domain powers to gain rights of way; they also depended on various subsidies and bond issues provided by states and localities who were eager to have railroads run through them. (To this day states and localities offer "tax abatements" to lure attractive industries.) All states, of course, had their own constitutions and courts to interpret them, and suits demanding compensation for takings of property were frequent.[7]

Almost all the relevant litigation on takings, however, concerned issues of state constitutional law.[8] In Barron v. City of Baltimore, 32 U.S. (7 Pet.) 243 (1833), the Supreme Court held that the Just Compensation Clause of the Fifth Amendment—and indeed, the Bill of Rights generally—only limited the national government. Thus, before the Civil War, the only federal constitutional provision that applied to the states *and* that directly concerned economic rights was the Contract Clause. Not surprisingly, it became the most recurrently litigated section of the Constitution in the nineteenth century.[9]

Two of the most noted decisions of the Taney Court were protective of state powers. Charles River Bridge v. Warren Bridge, 36 U.S. (11 Pet.) 420 (1837), was a constitutional challenge to Massachusetts's decision to charter a second bridge (the Warren Bridge) over the Charles River in Boston connecting Boston with Cambridge. The Warren Bridge competed with an earlier bridge, the Charles River Bridge, chartered in 1785. Massachusetts had promised the builders of the Charles River Bridge, in return for their paying the expenses of construction and conveying to Harvard College approximately $650 per year, that they would be able to collect toll revenues ultimately for 70 years. As one might imagine, the first bridge was a great success. Shares that sold for $333 in 1785 were worth over $2,000 by 1814 (roughly three times the earlier value taking inflation into account).

---

7. See Harry Scheiber, The Road to *Munn*: Eminent Domain and the Concept of Public Purpose in State Courts, in Law in American History 329 (Fleming & Bailyn eds., 1971).

8. See Benjamin Wright, The Contract Clause of the Constitution (1931).

9. Id.

Given the increasing traffic across the Charles River into Boston, Massachusetts decided in 1828 to charter a second bridge, literally just yards from the Charles River Bridge; tolls could be charged only until the builders recovered their expenses; thereafter, it would be turned over to the state, which abolished the toll (and therefore, as well, destroyed the value of the former monopoly held by the proprietors of the Charles River Bridge). The question before the Court was whether the state's contract with the proprietors included an implicit promise not to charter a competitor; if so, the second charter, by undermining the value of the first, might violate the Contract Clause.

The Court, in Chief Justice Taney's first major decision, said that there had been no implicit promise, and it established the principle that public franchises should be narrowly construed. Because the petitioner's charter to operate a toll bridge was not in terms exclusive, it would not be read to prevent the state from chartering a bridge nearby, even if, as a practical matter, this wiped out the economic value of the investment based on the original charter. Justice Taney proclaimed that a contrary result would in effect mean that states would be "obliged to stand still" in the face of new developments and needs of the public for effective modes of transportation. Justice Story wrote a bitter dissent, responding to the majority's argument from economic consequences: "I can conceive of no surer play to arrest all public improvements, founded on private capital and enterprise, than to make the outlay of that capital uncertain and questionable, both as to security and as to productiveness. No man will hazard his capital" if, in the case of "success, he has not the slightest security of enjoying the rewards of that success for a single moment."

In West River Bridge Co. v. Dix, 47 U.S. (6 How.) 507 (1848), the Court held that petitioner's franchise did not preclude the state from expropriating its bridge upon payment of compensation: All government grants are implicitly subject to the state's power of eminent domain.

One issue that frequently arose involved the authority of local municipalities within states to issue bonds as a means of attracting new business enterprises. Gelpcke v. Dubuque, 68 U.S. (1 Wall.) 175 (1864), for example, was a diversity action by the holders of municipal bonds issued as part of a railroad promotion. The city defended its nonpayment of the bonds on the ground that issuance of the bonds was beyond its authority under the Iowa Constitution. The city's interpretation of the state constitution was supported by an 1862 Iowa Supreme Court ruling, which had overruled a number of earlier decisions holding that cities must make good on such debts. In *Gelpcke*, the U.S. Supreme Court declined to follow the state supreme court's current interpretation, in spite of its declaration a year earlier that it would follow "the latest settled [state] adjudication" construing a state statute or constitution in Leffingwell v. Warren, 67 U.S. (2 Black) 599 (1863). The Court, however, appeared to be appalled by the substantive injustice of the Iowa court's holding:

> The late case in Iowa, and two other cases of a kindred character in another State, also overruling earlier adjudications, stand out, as far as we are advised, in unenviable solitude and notoriety. However we may regard the late case in Iowa as affecting the future, it can have no effect on the past. "The sound and true rule is, that if the contract, when made, was

valid by the laws of the State as then expounded by all departments of the government, and administered in its courts of justice, its validity and obligation cannot be impaired by any subsequent action of legislation, or decision of its courts altering the construction of the law." The same principle applies where there is a change of judicial decision as to the constitutional power of the Legislature to enact the law. To this rule, thus enlarged, we adhere. It is the law of this court. It rests upon the plainest principles of justice. To hold otherwise would be as unjust as to hold that rights acquired under a statute may be lost by its repeal.

We are not unmindful of the importance of uniformity in the decisions of this court, and those of the highest local courts, giving constructions to the laws and constitutions of their own States. It is the settled rule of this court in such cases, to follow the decisions of the state courts. But there have been heretofore, in the judicial history of this court, as doubtless there will be hereafter, many exceptional cases. We shall never immolate truth, justice, and the law, because a state tribunal has erected the altar and decreed the sacrifice.

Finally, one should take note—especially in light of the Taney Court's generally states' rights stance—of Swift v. Tyson, 41 U.S. (16 Pet.) 1 (1842). There, the Court substantially federalized the subject of commercial law by holding that federal courts should decide commercial litigation with reference to "the general principles and doctrines of commercial jurisprudence" rather than to the "decisions of local tribunals." The substantive issue in *Swift* was whether the owner of a negotiable instrument had acquired it free of the defenses available between the original parties. The action was brought in a federal court in New York, whose state decisions arguably—and against prevailing doctrine—held that the owner was not a holder in due course. In an opinion by Justice Story, the Supreme Court decided to follow the "general" commercial law, which was otherwise. The decision was based on §34 of the Judiciary Act of 1789, also known as the Rules of Decision Act, which provided "that the laws of the several states . . . shall be regarded as the rules of decision . . . in courts of the United States." Story wrote that state judicial decisions were "at most, only evidence of what the laws are, and are not, of themselves, laws."

The decision to reject a peculiar state rule in favor of widely followed commercial practice, rooted in the law merchant—that is, the body of law applying to contracts between merchants—was entirely consistent with the instrumentalist objective of facilitating negotiability (not to mention commonly helping creditors). As Story wrote, "[t]he law respecting negotiable instruments may be truly declared in the language of Cicero . . . to be in great measure, not the law of a single country only, but of the commercial world." Although the state courts remained free to adjudicate disputes based on their own common law doctrines, *Swift* gave rise to an independent body of "federal common law," applied in the increasing number of commercial disputes coming within the federal courts' diversity jurisdiction. Grant Gilmore writes that the decision in *Swift*[10]

10. Grant Gilmore, The Ages of American Law 34 (1977).

was immediately and enthusiastically accepted. No one suggested that it was an unconstitutional usurpation of power by power-crazed judges or that it was a trick played by a wily Federalist judge on his unsuspecting Jacksonian colleagues. No bumper stickers called for Justice Story's impeachment. On the contrary, the doctrine of the general commercial law was warmly welcomed and expansively construed, not only by the lower federal courts but by the state courts as well. For the next half century the Supreme Court of the United States became a great commercial law court.

One way of interpreting *Swift* was a declaration that at least with regard to some important aspects of the economy, we *were* a single nation and that the federal courts would take responsibility for developing a suitable national body of common law sensitive to its needs.

I. INTERSTATE AND FOREIGN COMMERCE AND PERSONAL MOBILITY

Marshall declared in *Gibbons* that he was "tempted" to hold that only Congress could regulate interstate commerce. That would mean that states would be barred from regulating interstate commerce even in the absence of congressional legislation; ultimately Marshall resisted the temptation and held that the New York statute was preempted under the Supremacy Clause by federal legislation. Justice Johnson, however, adopted the more nationalist reading in his concurrence in *Gibbons*. By the end of Jackson's term as President, his appointees constituted a majority of the Court. At least some of the new Justices believed that the Commerce Clause by itself imposed no constraints at all on regulation, and that the states were free to regulate interstate commerce at least in the absence of overriding congressional legislation. The attempt to find a resolution to this debate covered the entire period of Taney's Chief Justiceship.

A. The States' "Police Powers" as a Constraint on the National Commerce Power

New York v. Miln, one of the Taney Court's earliest Commerce Clause decisions, arose out of the rapidly increasing flow of immigrants from Ireland and Northern Europe into the United States. Although national policy encouraged immigration, the Atlantic seaboard states were wary of indigent immigrants. There were no national, or even state, welfare systems at the time. Rather, the poor were a local problem.[11]

11. A 1788 New York statute explicitly enjoined that "[e]very city and town shall support and maintain their own poor." See Friedman, supra n.3, at 187-191.

Mayor of the City of New York v. Miln

36 U.S. (11 Pet.) 102 (1837)

[An 1824 New York State law required the master of a vessel arriving in New York from another country or state to provide a detailed report on "every person brought as a passenger in the ship . . . from any country outside of the United States or from any of the United States, into the port of New York, or into any of the United States, and of all persons landed from the ship, during the voyage at any place, or put on board, or suffered to go on board any other vessel, with intention of proceeding to the city of New York." The law further required the master to post security for the maintenance of immigrants and their children who became wards of the city and to remove any noncitizen whom the mayor deemed likely to become dependent. This was an action to recover $15,000 penalties for violation of the law.]

BARBOUR, J. . . .

It is contended by the counsel for the defendant, that the act in question is a regulation of commerce; that the power to regulate commerce is, by the constitution of the United States, granted to congress; that this power is exclusive, and that consequently, the act is a violation of the constitution of the United States.

On the part of the plaintiff, it is argued, that an affirmative grant of power previously existing in the states to congress, is not exclusive; except, 1st, where it is so expressly declared in terms, by the clause giving the power; or 2d, where a similar power is prohibited to the states; or 3d, where the power in the states would be repugnant to, and incompatible with, a similar power in congress; that this power falls within neither of these predicaments. . . . But [plaintiffs also] deny that it is a regulation of commerce; on the contrary, they assert, that it is a mere regulation of internal police, a power over which is not granted to congress; and which, therefore, as well upon the true construction of the constitution, as by force of the tenth amendment to that instrument, is reserved to, and resides in, the several states.[12]

We shall not enter into any examination of the question, whether the power to regulate commerce, be or be not exclusive of the states, because . . . we are of opinion, that the act is not a regulation of commerce, but of police; and that being thus considered, it was passed in the exercise of a power which rightfully belonged to the states.

That the state of New York possessed power to pass this law, before the adoption of the constitution of the United States, might probably be taken as a truism, without the necessity of proof. But as it may tend to present it in a clearer point of view, we will quote a few passages from a standard writer upon public law, showing the origin and character of this power. Vattel: "The sovereign may forbid the entrance of his territory, either to foreigners in general, or in particular cases, or to certain persons, or for certain particular purposes, according as he may think it

---

12. Lawyers sometimes offer "pleadings in the alternative." Here you see the plaintiff asserting first that the Commerce Clause, correctly interpreted, does not preclude New York from passing this regulation of commerce, and then that the New York legislation ought not be viewed as a regulation of commerce at all.

advantageous to the state." . . . The power then of New York to pass this law having undeniably existed at the formation of the constitution, the simple inquiry is, whether by that instrument it was taken from the states, and granted to congress.

If, as we think, it be a regulation, not of commerce, but police; then it is not taken from the states. To decide this let us examine its purpose, the end to be attained, and the means of its attainment. It is apparent, from the whole scope of the law, that the object of the legislature was, to prevent New York from being burdened by an influx of persons brought thither in ships, either from foreign countries, or from any other of the states; and for that purpose, a report was required of the names, places of birth, &c., of all passengers, that the necessary steps might be taken by the city authorities, to prevent them from becoming chargeable as paupers. Now, we hold, that both the end and the means here used, are within the competency of the states, since a portion of their powers were surrendered to the federal government. Let us see, what powers are left with the states. The Federalist, No. 45, speaking of this subject, says, the powers reserved to the several states, all extend to all the objects, which in the ordinary course of affairs, concern the lives, liberties and properties of the people; and the internal order, improvement and prosperity of the state. And this court, in the case of Gibbons v. Ogden, . . . in speaking of the inspection laws of the states, say, "they form a portion of that immense mass of legislation which embraces everything within the territory of a state, not surrendered to the general government, all which can be most advantageously exercised by the states themselves. Inspection laws, quarantine laws, health laws of every description, as well as laws for regulating the internal commerce of a state, and those which respect turnpike-roads, ferries, &c., are component parts of this mass."

Now, if the act in question be tried by reference to the delineation of power laid down in the preceding quotations, it seems to us, that we are necessarily brought to the conclusion, that it falls within its limits. There is no aspect in which it can be viewed, in which it transcends them. If we look at the place of its operation, we find it to be within the territory, and therefore, within the jurisdiction of New York. If we look at the person on whom it operates, he is found within the same territory and jurisdiction. If we look at the persons for whose benefit it was passed, they are the people of New York, for whose protection and welfare the legislature of that state are authorized and in duty bound to provide. If we turn our attention to the purpose to be attained, it is to secure that very protection, and to provide for that very welfare. If we examine the means by which these ends are proposed to be accomplished, they bear a just, natural and appropriate relation to those ends.

But we are told, that it violates the constitution of the United States, and to prove this, we have been referred to two cases in this court; the first, that of Gibbons v. Ogden, 9 Wheat. 1, and the other that of Brown v. State of Maryland, 12 ibid. 419. . . .

Now, there is not, in this case, one of the circumstances which existed in that of Gibbons v. Ogden, which, in the opinion of the court, rendered it obnoxious to the charge of unconstitutionality. On the contrary, the prominent facts of this case are in striking contrast with those which characterized that. In that case, the theatre on which the law operated was navigable water, over which the court say that the power to regulate commerce extended; in this, it was the territory of New York, over which that state possesses an acknowledged, an undisputed jurisdiction for every purpose of internal regulation; in that, the subject-matter on which it operated, was a vessel claiming the right of navigation; a right which the court say is embraced in the power to regulate commerce; in this, the subjects on which it operates are persons whose rights and whose duties are rightfully prescribed and controlled by the laws of the respective states within whose territorial limits they are found; in that, say the court, the act of a state came into direct collision with an act of the United States; in this, no such collision exists.

Nor is there the least likeness between the facts of this case, and those of Brown v. State of Maryland. . . .[13]

[In *Brown,*] the court did indeed extend the power to regulate commerce, so as to protect the goods imported from a state tax, after they were landed, and were yet in bulk. . . . But how can this apply to persons? They are not the subject of commerce; and not being imported goods, cannot fall within a train of reasoning founded upon the construction of a power given to congress to regulate commerce, and the prohibition to the states from imposing a duty on imported goods. . . .

[The defendant contended that the state law conflicted with and therefore was preempted by federal statutes, enacted in 1799 and 1819, which required the masters of vessels to report on passengers and cargo transported in foreign commerce. Justice Barbour responded that the federal laws were only designed to prevent smuggling, to assure the comfort of passengers, and to "form an accurate

---

13. Brown v. Maryland (1827) held (as Chief Justice Taney later summarized it)

> that an article authorized by a law of Congress to be imported continued to be a part of the foreign commerce of the country while it remained in the hands of the importer for sale, in the original bale, package, or vessel in which it was imported; that the authority given to import necessarily carried with it the right to sell the imported article in the form and shape in which it was imported, and that no State, either by direct assessment or by requiring a license from the importer before he was permitted to sell, could impose any burden upon him or the property imported beyond what the law of Congress had itself imposed; but that when the original package was broken up for use or for retail by the importer, and also when the commodity had passed from his hands into the hands of a purchaser, it ceased to be an import, or a part of foreign commerce, and became subject to the laws of the State, and might be taxed for State purposes, and the sale regulated by the State, like any other property.

Taney, C.J., concurring in the License Cases, 46 U.S. (5 How.) 504 (1847). Taney went on to explain:

> The immense amount of foreign products used and consumed in this country are imported, landed, and offered for sale in a few commercial cities, and a very small portion of them are intended or expected to be used in the States in which they are imported. . . . And where they are in the hands of the importer . . . they may be regarded as merely in transit, on their way to the distant cities, villages, and country for which they are destined, and where they are expected to be used and consumed, and for the supply of which they were in truth imported. And a tax upon them . . . would be hardly more justifiable in principle than a transit duty upon the merchandise when passing through a State. . . . And if a State is permitted to levy it in any form, it will put in the power of a maritime importing State to raise a revenue for the support of its own government from citizens of other States, as certainly and effectively as if the tax was laid openly and without disguise as a duty on imports. Such a power in a State would defeat one of the principal objects of forming and adopting the Constitution. And as it cannot be done directly [see Article I, §10], it could hardly be a just and sound construction of the constitution which would enable a State to accomplish precisely the same thing under another name, and in a different form.

estimate of the increase of population by emigration." In any event,] it is obvious that these laws only affect through the power over navigation, the passengers, whilst on their voyage, and until they shall have landed . . . , and can, with no propriety of language, be said to come into conflict with a law of a state, whose operation only begins when that of the laws of congress ends; whose operation is not even on the same subject. . . .

There is, then, no collision between the law in question, and the acts of congress just commented on; and therefore, if the state law were to be considered as partaking of the nature of a commercial regulation; it would stand the test of the most rigid scrutiny, if tried by the standard laid down in the reasoning of the court, quoted from the case of Gibbons v. Ogden.

But we do not place our opinion on this ground. We choose rather to plant ourselves on what we consider impregnable positions. They are these: That a state has the same undeniable and unlimited jurisdiction over all persons and things, within its territorial limits, as any foreign nation; where that jurisdiction is not surrendered or restrained by the constitution of the United States. That, by virtue of this, it is not only the right, but the bounden and solemn duty of a state, to advance the safety, happiness and prosperity of its people, and to provide for its general welfare, by any and every act of legislation, which it may deem to be conducive to these ends; where the power over the particular subject, or the manner of its exercise is not surrendered or restrained, in the manner just stated. That all those powers which relate to merely municipal legislation, or what may, perhaps, more properly be called internal police, are not thus surrendered or restrained; and that, consequently, in relation to these, the authority of a state is complete, unqualified and exclusive.

We are aware, that it is at all times difficult to define any subject with proper precision and accuracy; if this be so in general, it is emphatically so, in relation to a subject so diversified and multifarious as the one which we are now considering. If we were to attempt it, we would say, that every law came within this description which concerned the welfare of the whole people of a state, or any individual within it . . . and whose operation was within the territorial limits of the state, and upon the persons and things within its jurisdiction.

[T]he section in the act immediately before us [was] obviously passed with a view to prevent [New York's] citizens from being oppressed by the support of multitudes of poor persons, who come from foreign countries, without possessing the means of supporting themselves. There can be no mode in which the power to regulate internal police could be more appropriately exercised. New York, from her particular situation, is, perhaps, more than any other city in the Union, exposed to the evil of thousands of foreign emigrants arriving there, and the consequent danger of her citizens being subjected to a heavy charge in the maintenance of those who are poor. It is the duty of the state to protect its citizens from this evil; they have endeavored to do so, by passing, amongst other things, the section of the law in question. We should, upon principle, say that it had a right to do so.

Let us compare this power with a mass of power, said by this court, in Gibbons v. Ogden, not to be surrendered to the general government. They are inspection laws, quarantine laws, health laws of every description, as well as laws for regulating the internal commerce of a state, &c. . . .

We think, that if the stronger powers, under the necessity of the case, by inspection laws and quarantine laws, to delay the landing of a ship and cargo, which are the subjects of commerce and navigation, and to remove or even to destroy unsound and infectious articles, also the subject of commerce, can be rightfully exercised, then, that it must follow, as a consequence, that powers less strong, such as the one in question, which operates upon no subject either of commerce or navigation, but which operates alone within the limits and jurisdiction of New York, upon a person, at the time, not even engaged in navigation, is still more clearly embraced within the general power of the states to regulate their own internal police, and to take care that no detriment come to the commonwealth. We think it as competent and as necessary for a state to provide precautionary measures against the moral pestilence of paupers, vagabonds, and possibly convicts; as it is to guard against the physical pestilence, which may arise from unsound and infectious articles imported, or from a ship, the crew of which may be laboring under an infectious disease.

THOMPSON, J. . . .

It is not necessary, in this case, to fix any limits upon the legislation of congress and of the states, on this subject; or to say how far congress may, under the power to regulate commerce, control state legislation in this respect. It is enough to say, that whatever the power of congress may be, it has not been exercised so as, in any manner, to conflict with the state law; and if the mere grant of the power to congress does not necessarily imply a prohibition of the states to exercise the power, until congress assumes to exercise it, no objection, on that ground, can arise to this law. Nor is it necessary to decide, definitively, whether the provisions of this law may be considered as at all embraced within the power to regulate commerce. Under either view of the case, the law of New York, so far at least as it is drawn in question in the present suit, is entirely unobjectionable. . . .

The case of Willson v. Blackbird Creek Marsh Company, 2 Pet. 251, is a strong case to show that a power admitted to fall within the power to regulate commerce, may be exercised by the states, until congress assumes the exercise. . . . By the same rule of construction, the law of New York, not coming in conflict with any act of congress, is not void by reason of the dormant power to regulate commerce; even if it should be admitted, that the subject embraced in that law fell within such power. . . .

Whether, therefore, the law of New York, so far as it is drawn in question in this case, be considered as relating purely to the police and internal government of the state, and as part of the system of poor-laws in the city of New York, and in this view belonging exclusively to the legislation of the state; or whether the subject-matter of the law be considered as belonging concurrently to the state and to congress, but never having been exercised by the latter; no constitutional objection can be made to it. . . .

STORY, J., dissenting. . . .

I admit, in the most unhesitating manner, that the states have a right to pass health laws and quarantine laws, and other police laws, not contravening the laws of congress rightfully passed under their constitutional authority. I admit, that they have a right to pass poor-laws, and laws to prevent the introduction of paupers into the state, under the like qualifications. I go further, and admit, that in the exercise of their legitimate authority over any particular subject, the states may generally use the same means which are used by congress, if these means are suitable to the end. But I cannot admit, that the states have authority to enact laws, which act upon subjects beyond their territorial limits, or within those limits and which trench upon the authority of congress in its power to regulate commerce. . . .

It has been argued, that the act of New York is not a regulation of commerce, but is a mere police law upon the subject of paupers; and it has been likened to the cases of health laws, quarantine laws, ballast laws; gunpowder laws, and others of a similar nature. . . . I have already said, that I admit the power of the states to pass such laws, and to use the proper means to effectuate the objects of them; but it is with this reserve, that these means are not exclusively vested in congress. A state cannot make a regulation of commerce, to enforce its health laws, because it is a means withdrawn from its authority. It may be admitted, that it is a means adapted to the end; but it is quite a different question, whether it be a means within the competency of the state jurisdiction. . . .

But how can it be truly said, that the act of New York is not a regulation of commerce? No one can well doubt, that if the same act had been passed by congress, it would have been a regulation of commerce; and in that way, and in that only, would it be a constitutional act of congress. The right of congress to pass such an act has been expressly conceded at the argument. The act of New York purports, on its very face, to regulate the conduct of masters, and owners and passengers, in foreign trade; and in foreign ports and places [by requiring] a report of the passengers taken or landed [there]. . . . I listened with great attention to the argument, to ascertain upon what ground the act of New York was to be maintained not to be a regulation of commerce. I confess, that I was unable to ascertain any, from the reasoning of either of the learned counsel, who spoke for the plaintiff. Their whole argument on this point seemed to me to amount to this: that if it were a regulation of commerce, still it might also be deemed a regulation of police, and a part of the system of poor-laws; and therefore, justifiable as a means to attain the end. In my judgment, for the reasons already suggested, that is not a just consequence, or a legitimate deduction. If the act is a regulation of commerce, and that subject belongs exclusively to congress, it is a means cut off from the range of state sovereignty and state legislation.

And this leads me more distinctly to the consideration of the other point in question; and that is, whether, if the act of New York be a regulation of commerce, it is void and unconstitutional? If the power of congress to regulate commerce be an exclusive power; or if the subject-matter has been constitutionally regulated by congress, so as to exclude all additional or conflicting legislation by the states, then, and in either case, it is clear, that the act of New York is void and unconstitutional. Let us consider the question under these aspects.

It has been argued, that the power of congress to regulate commerce is not exclusive, but concurrent with that of the states. If this were a new question in this court, wholly untouched by doctrine or decision, I should not hesitate to go into a full examination of all the grounds upon which concurrent authority is attempted to be maintained. But in point of fact, the whole argument on this very question . . . was . . . deliberately examined, and deemed inadmissible by the court [in Gibbons v. Ogden]. Mr. Chief Justice Marshall, with his accustomed accuracy and fulness of illustration, reviewed at that time the whole grounds of the controversy; and from that time to the present, the question has been considered (so far as I know) to be at rest. The power given to congress to regulate commerce with foreign nations, and among the states, has been deemed exclusive, from the nature and objects of the power, and the necessary implications growing out of its exercise. Full power to regulate a particular subject, implies the whole power, and leaves no residuum; and a grant of the whole to one, is incompatible with a grant to another of a part. When a state proceeds to regulate commerce with foreign nations, or among the states, it is doing the very thing which congress is authorized to do. And it has been remarked, with great cogency and accuracy, that the regulation of a subject indicates and designates the entire result; applying to those parts which remain as they were, as well as to those parts which are altered. It produces a uniform whole, which is as much disturbed and deranged by changing what the regulating power designs to leave untouched, as that upon which it has operated.

This last suggestion is peculiarly important in the present case; for congress has, by the act of the 2d of March 1819, regulated passenger ships and vessels. Subject to the regulations therein provided, passengers may be brought into the United States from foreign ports. These regulations, being all which congress have chosen to enact, amount, upon the reasoning already stated, to a complete exercise of its power over the whole subject, as well in what is omitted as what is provided for. Unless, then, we are prepared to say, that wherever congress has legislated upon this subject, clearly within its constitutional authority, and made all such regulations, as, in its own judgment and discretion, were deemed expedient; the states may step in and supply all other regulations, which they may deem expedient, as complementary to those of congress, thus subjecting all our trade, commerce and navigation, and intercourse with foreign nations, to the double operations of distinct and independent sovereignties, it seems to me, impossible to maintain the doctrine, that the states have a concurrent jurisdiction with congress on the regulation of commerce, whether congress has or has not legislated upon the subject; a fortiori, when it has legislated.

There is another consideration, which ought not to be overlooked in discussing this subject. It is, that congress, by its legislation, has, in fact, authorized not only the transportation but the introduction of passengers into the country. The act of New York imposes restraints and burdens upon this right of transportation and introduction. It goes even further, and authorizes the removal of passengers, under certain circumstances, out of the state, and at the expense of the master and owner in whose ship they have been introduced; and this, though they are citizens of the United States, and were brought from other states. Now, if this act be constitutional to this extent, it will justify the states in regulating, controlling, and, in effect, interdicting the transportation of passengers from one state to another, in steamboats and packets. They may levy a tax upon all such passengers; they may require bonds from the master, that no such passengers shall become chargeable to the state; they may require such passengers to give bonds, that they shall not become so chargeable; they may authorize the immediate removal of such passengers back to the place from which they came. These would be most burdensome and inconvenient regulations respecting passengers, and would entirely defeat the object of congress in licensing the trade or business. And yet, if the argument which we have heard be well founded, it is a power strictly within the authority of the states, and may be exerted, at the pleasure of all or any of them, to the ruin and, perhaps, annihilation of our passenger navigation. It is no answer to the objection, to say, that the states will have too much wisdom and prudence to exercise the authority to so great an extent. Laws were actually passed, of a retaliatory nature, by the states of New York, New Jersey and Connecticut, during the steamboat controversy, which threatened the safety and security of the Union; and demonstrated the necessity, that the power to regulate commerce among the states should be exclusive in the Union, in order to prevent the most injurious restraints upon it. . . .

[Story then discusses Brown v. State of Maryland and states that its doctrine clearly applies in this case.]

Such is a brief view of the grounds upon which my judgment is, that the act of New York is unconstitutional and void. In this opinion, I have the consolation to know, that I had the entire concurrence, upon the same grounds, of that great constitutional jurist, the late Mr. Chief Justice Marshall. Having heard the former arguments, his deliberate opinion was, that the act of New York was unconstitutional; and that the present case fell directly within the principles established in the case of Gibbons v. Ogden and Brown v. State of Maryland. . . .

DISCUSSION

1. Note well that even Justice Story grants states the right to "to prevent the introduction of paupers into the state." Indeed, in a later decision, Prigg v. Pennsylvania, discussed infra, Story, writing for the majority, stated that "[w]e entertain no doubt whatsoever that the states, in virtue of their general police power, possess full jurisdiction to arrest and restrain runaway slaves, and remove them from their borders, and otherwise to secure themselves against their depredations and evil example, as they certainly may do in cases of idlers, vagabonds, and paupers." Article 4 of the Articles of Confederation, which granted to "the people of each State [a right of] free ingress and regress to and from any other State," explicitly exempted "paupers, vagabonds and fugitives from justice" from the enjoyment of any such right. As Gerald Neuman writes, "[a]lthough the 1787 Constitution omitted this qualification from its Privileges and Immunities Clause, the courts continued to assume that paupers had no right to travel." Indeed, according to Neuman,[14]

> [p]erhaps the most fundamental function of immigration law has been to impede the movement of the poor. In neither the eighteenth century nor the nineteenth century did American law concede the right of the needy to geographic mobility. At the time of independence, the states took with them the heritage of the English poor laws, which made the relief of the poor the responsibility of the local community where they were legally "settled." These laws gave localities various powers to prevent the settlement of persons who might later require support and to "remove" them

---

14. Gerald Neuman, Strangers to the Constitution: Immigrants, Borders, and Fundamental Law 23 (1996).

> to the place where they were legally settled. Accordingly, some of the most important provisions of state immigration law are sprinkled through the state poor laws.

Even if one believes that the Constitution's failure to adopt the language of Article IV limited New York's power to restrict the immigration of paupers who were citizens of other states of the Union, does that necessarily imply an inability to resist the entry of foreign paupers?

2. Justices Thompson and Story seem to address the constitutionality of the New York law in similar terms—do the states have a right to regulate interstate commerce in the absence of relevant national legislation?—though of course they reach different conclusions. Justice Barbour's opinion for the Court has a different focus altogether. After concluding that the law is not preempted by any congressional statutes, he remarks that "we do not place our opinion on this ground. We choose rather to plant ourselves on what we consider impregnable positions," referring to the powers of "internal police" that are not surrendered by the states and with respect to which "the authority of the state is complete, unqualified, and exclusive." What is Barbour's theory? How, if at all, does his concept of the role of these state powers in the federal constitutional scheme differ from Marshall's in *Gibbons*? How does Barbour differentiate the realms of national and state authority?

3. Justice Story's opinion provides the first occasion in this casebook of precedent-based argument in which a judge analyzes a prior case by way of presenting it as the foundation for his own opinion. Reread carefully Story's discussion of Marshall's opinion in *Gibbons*. How accurate is it? Assume that Story's opinion had been the "Opinion of the Court." Would it then count as an authoritative description of *Gibbons*?

4. Extensive discussion of congressional and state authority regarding immigration occurs in the Passenger Cases, 48 U.S. (7 How.) 283 (1849). The Court invalidated New York and Massachusetts laws that imposed a landing fee on alien passengers to pay for the support or medical care of foreign paupers. There was no majority opinion; the majority was divided between those Justices who viewed the regulations as an unconstitutional regulation of foreign commerce and others who struck them down as taxes on imports in violation of Article I, §10.

One should not overestimate the importance of the Passenger Cases. Even the majority scarcely was unsympathetic to state interests. Thus Justice Grier in his seriatim opinion acknowledged "the sacred law of self-defence" as legitimizing the exclusion by states of "lunatics, idiots, criminals, or paupers," as well as a slave state's barring the immigration of free Black people. Indeed, none of the five Justices in the majority can be said to have rejected a substantial quanta of state power over immigration, see Neuman, supra, though they objected to the particular means chosen by Massachusetts and New York in the instant cases. Indeed, as Neuman writes, the Passenger Cases had only limited effect insofar as many states continued to require the posting of bonds, or the payment of a fixed fee in lieu of a bond, to replace the automatic "head tax" struck down by the Supreme Court. It would be a quarter-century before constitutional doctrine developed that placed "exclusive" control in Congress over immigration. See Henderson v. New York, 92 U.S. 259 (1876), and Chy Lung v. Freeman, 92 U.S. 275 (1876). Still, even in 1902, see Morgan's S.S. Co. v. Louisiana Board of Health, 118 U.S. 455, 465-466, the Court emphasized the legitimacy of state "quarantine laws" in regard to immigrants, which had, of course, been endorsed by Marshall in Gibbons v. Ogden, supra.

One must realize that Congress had not passed much legislation affecting immigration by the time the Passenger Cases were decided, so the discussion at that point necessarily involves many "first principles" about the allocation of authority even in the absence of full-scale confrontation between an actual law of Congress and state policy. Chief Justice Taney, perhaps concerned about legislation that Congress might be tempted to adopt, attempted to head off at the pass any notion that Congress was necessarily supreme in regard to all facets of immigration.

Thus, in his own dissent, he denied the existence of any federal power at all over the immigration of persons into the states, which he viewed as a "reserved" power, impervious to limitation by federal treaty or congressional legislation. "[T]he people of the several States" retained the power to expel "from their borders any person, or class or persons, whom it might deem dangerous to its peace, or likely to produce a physical or moral evil among its citizens. . . . [T]he State has the exclusive right to determine, in its sound discretion, whether the danger does or does not exist, free from the control of the general government." The motivation behind Taney's zeal on the point is suggested by his illustration of the danger of the majority's position:

> I cannot believe that it was ever intended to vest in Congress . . . this overwhelming power over the States [of deciding who should or should not be permitted to reside among its citizens]. For [Congress could then grant] the emancipated slaves of the West Indies . . . the absolute right to reside, hire houses, and traffic and trade throughout the Southern States, in spite of any State law to the contrary; inevitably producing the most serious discontent, and ultimately leading to the most painful consequences. . . .

5. *Persons as articles of commerce.* Justice Barbour states that persons "are not the subject of commerce." This is not an accurate statement of current doctrine (and was questionable even at the time). With regard to contemporary doctrine, the Court, in Edwards v. California, 314 U.S. 160 (1941), invalidated a state law attempting to limit the immigration of refugees (who were likely to be "paupers") from the great Dust Bowl of the 1930s in Oklahoma and other states. Although a plurality of four of the Justices would have invalidated it on the basis of the Privileges and Immunities Clause of Article IV, the five-Justice majority rested their decision on the Commerce Clause, holding that California was burdening the national economy because of its restrictive policies. Indeed, Henderson v. New York had earlier based Congress's right to control immigration on the Commerce Clause. (Though recall the debate over the Alien Act, which rooted such powers in an inherent notion of sovereignty. What is the difference between these two arguments? Which is more persuasive?) As Mary Sarah Bilder points out in The Struggle over Immigration: Indentured Servants, Slaves, and Articles of Commerce, 61 Mo. L. Rev. 743 (1996), persons were often treated as items of commerce in the eighteenth and nineteenth centuries. This is clearest, of course, in regard to slaves, who were bought and sold precisely as any other commodity, but she points out that this was true as well in regard to indentured servants, who comprised a very high percentage of the white immigrants to America before the American Revolution. Thus

David Galenson writes that "between half and two-thirds of all white immigrants to the American colonies after the 1630s and before independence came under indenture."[15] "During the term of service," Bilder notes, "indentured servants constituted property: they were assignable under statutory provisions; they could be sold to satisfy a debt; and they passed by descent pursuant to testamentary laws." Indentured servitude as a system of labor basically collapsed after 1819 and had, presumably, vanished by the time that *Miln* was decided.

At the very least, isn't "commerce" any exchange of movable property between willing buyers and sellers, whether the particular "articles of commerce" be widgets, contractually bound workers (consider the modern trade in athletes), or slaves? Why, then, was Barbour so eager to deny persons the status of objects of commerce, particularly given that the "police power" rationale earlier developed in *Gibbons* would have easily offered him a way to justify the New York law even in regard to acknowledged "articles of commerce"? (After all, Marshall explicitly legitimized state quarantine laws that, by definition, block the shipment of goods between states.) One possible answer is that to concede that persons are "articles of commerce" under the Commerce Clause would be to concede as well congressional power to regulate the most important group of such persons, slaves. This, obviously, was a highly volatile suggestion. Thus, Bilder notes, several pro-slavery writers were among the most insistent that slaves were "persons" rather than "articles of commerce," whereas some anti-slavery authors were as eager to define slaves as commodities in order to make slavery subject to regulation by Congress. Once slavery was removed as a topic of constitutional debate by the Thirteenth Amendment, it was easy enough to accept the proposition that persons were indeed "articles of commerce," with whatever powers (for Congress) and limitations (in regard to states) that were attached to such a status.

6. *Elkison v. Deliesseline.* Consider, in the light of *Miln*, the South Carolina Negro Seaman's Act of 1822. That Act, among other things, provided that "any free negroes or persons of color" brought into a South Carolina port by "any vessel" coming "from any other state or foreign port" shall "be seized and confined in gaol until such vessel shall clear out and depart from this state." The vessel's captain was liable for the payment of expenses incurred by the State for the detention; refusal to pay was itself an offense punishable by a fine of not less than $1,000 and imprisonment of not less than two months. Moreover, the persons detained "shall be deemed and taken as absolute slaves, and sold . . ." by the State.

The Act was passed at the time of the Denmark Vesey rebellion, the actual circumstances of which continue to be a highly disputed topic among American historians. Compare, e.g., David Robertson, Denmark Vesey: The Buried History of America's Largest Slave Rebellion and the Man Who Led It (1999), with Michael P. Johnson, Denmark Vesey and His Co-Conspirators, 58 Wm. & Mary Q., 3d Ser., 915-976 (2001). It is uncontroverted that Vesey, with five others, was hanged outside Charleston on July 2, 1822, and that many white South Carolinians, who were in fact a minority of the overall population, most of which consisted of Black slaves, feared that Vesey intended to bring together as many as 9,000 slaves and free Black

15. David Galenson, White Servitude in Colonial America: An Economic Analysis 3-4 (1981).

people who were to march on Charleston, burn the city, and murder the white population.

The terms of the Act were applied to a member of the crew of "the ship Homer, a British ship trading from Liverpool" to Charleston. Justice Johnson, sitting on circuit, described its purpose as "to prohibit ships coming into this port employing colored seamen." He went on to invalidate the Act in Elkison v. Delieseline, 8 F. Cas. 493 (1823), on the ground that it violated the Commerce Clause.

He first generalized what was at issue: "[I]f this state can prohibit Great Britain from employing her colored subjects . . . [or] her subjects of the African race, why not prohibit her from using those of Irish or Scottish nativity? . . ." After pointing out that the Act applied to domestic as well as foreign vessels, he noted that the enforcement of the Act might well encourage retaliation against South Carolina ships by the affected governments.

> [T]he commerce of this city, feeble and sickly, comparatively, as it already is, might be fatally injured. Charleston seamen, Charleston owners, Charleston vessels, might, eo nomine, be excluded from their commerce, or the United States involved in war and confusion. . . . These considerations show its utter incompatibility with the power delegated to congress to regulate commerce with foreign nations and our sister states. . . .
>
> The seaman's offense, therefore, is coming into the state in a ship or vessel; that of the captain consists in bringing him in, and not taking him out of the state, and paying all expenses. Now, according to the laws and treaties of the United States, it was both lawful for this seaman to come into this port, in this vessel, and for the captain to bring him in the capacity of a seaman; and yet these are the very acts for which the state law imposes these heavy penalties. Is there no clashing in this? It is in effect a repeal of the laws of the United States, pro tanto, converting a right into a crime.
>
> . . . [T]he right of the general government to regulate commerce with the sister states and foreign nations is a paramount and exclusive right; and this conclusion we arrive at, whether we examine it with reference to the words of the constitution, or the nature of the grant. . . . In the constitution of the United States, the most wonderful instrument ever drawn by the hand of man, there is a comprehension and precision that is unparalleled. . . . It is true that it contains no prohibition on the states to regulate foreign commerce. Nor was such a prohibition necessary, for the words of the grant sweep away the whole subject, and leave nothing for the states to act upon. Wherever this is the case, there is no prohibitory clause interposed in the constitution. Thus, the states are not prohibited from regulating the value of foreign coins or fixing a standard of weights and measures, for the very words imply a total, unlimited grant. . . .
>
> But to all this the plea of necessity is urged; and of the existence of that necessity we are told the state alone is to judge. Where is this to land us? Is it not asserting the right in each state to throw off the federal constitution at its will and pleasure? . . . But I deny that the state surrendered a single power necessary to its security, against this species of property. What is to prevent their being confined to their ships, if it is dangerous for them to go abroad? This power may be lawfully exercised. To land their cargoes, take in others, and depart, is all that is necessary to ordinary commerce.

> . . . But if the policy of this law was to keep foreign free persons from holding communion with our slaves, it certainly pursues a course altogether inconsistent with its object. . . . [T]he method of disposing of offenders by detaining them here presents the finest facilities in the world for introducing themselves lawfully into the very situation in which they would enjoy the best opportunities of pursuing their designs. Now, if this plea of necessity could avail at all against the constitution and laws of the United States, certainly that law cannot be pronounced necessary which may defeat its own ends; much less when other provisions of unexceptionable legality may be resorted to, which would operate solely to the end proposed, viz., the effectual exclusion of dangerous characters.

This may help explain why Johnson wrote a concurring opinion the next year in *Gibbons* adopting the theory that Marshall was willing only to suggest—that Congress's power to regulate commerce was exclusive, even absent specific legislation.

How do you think that Justice Johnson would have voted in *Miln*? Given the result in *Miln*, how do you think the Supreme Court would have handled the South Carolina statute? Would your answer change had the majority adopted Justice Thompson's view of the concurrent power of a State? Do you think that Justice Story would agree with Justice Johnson's comments about the constitutionality of a more modest statute that simply confined Black seamen to their ships?

7. Lest one believe that *Elkison* had much effect, consider Professor Neuman's observation:[16]

> The *Elkison* case was only the first of the confrontations between Britain and the Southern states over the issue of black seamen. [President John Quincy] Adams sought to calm the British by assuring them that he would try to prevent enforcement of the statute, but that in a federal system he would need time to persuade South Carolina officials. South Carolina, however, definitively rebuffed him. Incidents continued in that and other states, and so, intermittently, did British protests. The treaty issue was particularly difficult because of an ambiguous clause in the commercial treaty making reciprocal liberty of commerce "subject always to the laws and statutes of the two countries, respectively." The U.S. diplomatic stance changed after Andrew Jackson's attorney general took a more expansive view of states' rights and affirmed the states' authority to enact such laws; he also relied in part on the 1803 federal statute forbidding the bringing in of foreign blacks excluded by state laws. The Northern states also continued to protest, but Congress would not act. In 1844 Massachusetts sent agents to South Carolina and Louisiana to institute judicial proceedings to test the constitutionality of the laws, but they were forced to flee under threat of mob violence. Later in that decade, Secretary of State [James Buchanan, who would later become President] instructed the U.S. consul in Jamaica to cooperate in securing compliance with these state laws, and he informed the British that if they insisted that enforcement of the state laws violated the commercial treaty between the two nations, it would become necessary to abrogate the treaty.

---

16. Neuman, supra n.14, at 38-39.

Consider this discussion of *Elkison* in light of the broader context of the debate over "nullification," i.e., the ability of states to declare "null and void" federal statutes or decisions of federal courts, discussed in Chapter 2, supra. Although states never won the official legal right to nullify statutes they disagreed with, they often achieved effective nullification through the "facts on the ground." Thus, Professor Mark Graber explains, "[n]ational political figures rarely made efforts to enforce Supreme Court decisions in the face of local hostility." "[T]he rights of the sailors of color in the South" were often unforced even though "Attorney General William Wirt issued an opinion declaring state prohibitions unconstitutional" (not to mention *Elkison* itself). Nor is this the only such example. "Land claimants in Kentucky received no federal legislative or executive assistance in obtaining actual possession of their judicially granted property rights." So frequently did state officials, "with federal acquiescence," fail to comply with the orders of federal courts "that some recalcitrant states questioned whether any obligation existed to implement federal judicial decisions."[17] Recall in this context Ohio's response to the decision in *McCulloch*, Chapter 1, supra.

B. The Cooley *Accommodation*

Only two years after the hyper-fragmented Passenger Cases, the Court initiated an entirely new approach to analyzing state laws affecting interstate transportation.

Cooley v. Board of Wardens

53 U.S. (12 How.) 299 (1851)

[An 1803 Pennsylvania law required vessels entering and leaving the port of Philadelphia to engage a local pilot to guide them through the harbor. The penalty for noncompliance was one-half the regular fee (for the use of the Society for the Relief of Distressed and Decayed Pilots, their widows and children). This was an action by the Board of Wardens to recover the penalty from the consignee of non-complying vessels engaged in the coastwise trade between New York and Philadelphia. The state courts held for the Board.[18]]

---

17. Mark A. Graber, James Buchanan as Savior? Judicial Power, Political Fragmentation, and the Failed 1831 Repeal of Section 25, 88 Or. L. Rev. 95, 121 (2009).

18. In the course of their opinions, both Justices Curtis and McLean refer to a congressional act of 1789 providing: "That all pilots in the bays, inlets, rivers, harbors, and ports of the United States shall continue to be regulated in conformity with the existing laws of the States, respectively, wherein such pilots may be, or with such laws as the States may respectively hereafter enact for the purpose, until further legislative provision shall be made by Congress." For reasons not of present concern, the Justices did not hold that the challenged Pennsylvania law was authorized by this statute; they therefore treated the state law as if Congress had not legislated on the issue. However, the majority did invoke the federal statute in support of its conclusion that the regulation of pilotage was a local matter, not a national one.

CURTIS, J. . . .

[The laws] rest upon the propriety of securing lives and property exposed to the perils of a dangerous navigation, by taking on board a person peculiarly skilled to encounter or avoid them. . . .

It remains to consider the objection, that it is repugnant to the [Commerce Clause]. That the power to regulate commerce includes the regulation of navigation, we consider settled. And . . . the regulation of the qualifications of pilots, of the modes and times of offering and rendering their services . . . do constitute regulations of navigation, and consequently of commerce, within the just meaning of this clause of the Constitution. . . .

[W]e are brought directly and unavoidably to the consideration of the question, whether the grant of the commercial power to Congress, did per se deprive the States of all power to regulate pilots. . . . [W]hen the nature of a power like this is spoken of, when it is said that the nature of the power requires that it should be exercised exclusively by Congress, it must be intended to refer to the subjects of that power, and to say they are of such a nature as to require exclusive legislation by Congress. Now the power to regulate commerce, embraces a vast field, containing not only many, but exceedingly various subjects, quite unlike in their nature; some imperatively demanding a single uniform rule, operating equally on the commerce of the United States in every port; and some, like the subject now in question, as imperatively demanding that diversity, which alone can meet the local necessities of navigation.

Either absolutely to affirm, or deny that the nature of this power requires exclusive legislation by Congress, is to lose sight of the nature of the subjects of this power, and to assert concerning all of them, what is really applicable but to a part. Whatever subjects of this power are in their nature national, or admit only of one uniform system, or plan of regulation, may justly be said to be of such a nature as to require exclusive legislation by Congress. That this cannot be affirmed of laws for the regulation of pilots and pilotage, is plain. The act of 1789 contains a clear and authoritative declaration by the first Congress, that the nature of this subject is such, that until Congress should find it necessary to exert its power, it should be left to the legislation of the States; that it is local and not national; that it is likely to be the best provided for, not by one system, or plan of regulations, but by as many as the legislative discretion of the several States should deem applicable to the local peculiarities of the ports within their limits. . . . The practice of the States, and of the national government, has been in conformity with this declaration, from the origin of the national government to this time; and the nature of the subject when examined, is such as to leave no doubt of the superior fitness and propriety, not to say the absolute necessity, of different systems of regulation, drawn from local knowledge and experience, and conformed to local wants. How then can we say, that by the mere grant of power to regulate commerce, the States are deprived of all the power to legislate on this subject, because from the nature of the power the legislation of Congress must be exclusive? . . . It is the opinion of a majority of the court that the mere grant to Congress of the power to regulate commerce, did not deprive the States of power to regulate pilots, and that although Congress has legislated on this subject, its legislation manifests an intention . . . not to regulate this subject, but to leave its regulation to the several States. . . .

We have not adverted to the practical consequences of holding that the States possess no power to legislate for the regulation of pilots, though in our apprehension these would be of the most serious importance. For more than sixty years this subject has been acted on by the States. . . .

If the grant of commercial power in the Constitution has deprived the States of all power to legislate for the regulation of pilots, if their laws on this subject are mere usurpations upon the exclusive power of the general government, and utterly void, . . . how are the legislatures of the States to proceed in future, to watch over and amend these laws, as the progressive wants of a growing commerce will require . . . ?

We are of opinion that this State law was enacted by virtue of a power, residing in the State to legislate; that it is not in conflict with any law of Congress; that it does not interfere with any system which Congress has established by making regulations, or by intentionally leaving individuals to their own unrestricted action; that this law is therefore valid, and the judgment of the Supreme Court of Pennsylvania in each case must be affirmed.

McLean, J., dissenting. . . .

It will be found that the principle in this case, if carried out, will deeply affect the commercial prosperity of the country. . . .

Louisiana now imposes a duty upon vessels for mooring in the river opposite the city of New Orleans, which is called a levee tax, and which, on some boats performing weekly trips to that city, amounts to from $3,000 to $4,000 annually. What is there to prevent the thirteen or fourteen states bordering upon the two rivers first named, from regulating navigation on those rivers, although Congress may have regulated the same at some prior period? I speak not of the effect of this doctrine theoretically in this matter, but practically. And if the doctrine be true, how can this court say that such regulations of commerce are invalid? . . .

From this race of legislation between Congress and the states, and between the states, if this principle be maintained, will arise a conflict similar to that which existed before the adoption of the Constitution. . . .

[A dissenting opinion by Justice Daniel is omitted.]

DISCUSSION

1. Justice Curtis's opinion seems to break sharply with both Marshall's and Taney's view of the Commerce Clause. (*Cooley* is rare among Commerce Clause opinions of the period in not even mentioning Gibbons v. Ogden.) Viewed in retrospect, *Cooley* presaged a functional approach to adjudicating state regulations affecting interstate transportation that would become highly influential after 1937. Curtis's approach turned out to be aberrant in its own time, however, and the opinion was widely ignored.

2. How exactly does one define a matter of "local" concern from one that demands a "national" resolution? Consider carefully Justice McLean's example of the "practical" effects of a single boat, traveling down the Mississippi River, becoming subject to a dozen different regulatory regimes, each based on "local" concerns about, say, the safety of the boats. (What if only one state bothered to pass such regulations, while the rest remained indifferent? Would that serve to validate the state regulation?)

NOTE ON CONGRESSIONAL CONSENT

Does the Supreme Court have the "last word" in regard to state regulations affecting interstate commerce? The answer is no. The Wheeling Bridge Cases presented the first situation in which Congress attempted to authorize a state law that the Court had earlier, in the absence of congressional legislation, struck down as an invalid regulation of interstate commerce.[19] The cases arose out of competition between Pennsylvania and Virginia over where the Cumberland Road, one of the major national thoroughfares of the time, would cross the Ohio River. In 1847, the Virginia legislature chartered a corporation to build a bridge across the river in Wheeling (now in West Virginia). In Pennsylvania v. Wheeling & Belmont Bridge Co., 54 U.S. (13 How.) 518 (1852), Pennsylvania sought to enjoin construction of the bridge. By the time the case was heard, the bridge had been built. Justice McLean wrote for the Court, holding that the bridge impermissibly obstructed interstate navigation and ordering it raised to a specified height. (Chief Justice Taney dissented, relying on Willson v. Black-Bird Creek Marsh Co.)

Virginia took its fight to Congress, which attached a rider to a post office appropriation bill by which the bridge was declared to be a lawful structure in its existing position and elevation and was declared to be a post road for the passage of mails. The bill was passed in the face of Pennsylvania's protest against this attempt to "reverse or render inoperative, the solemn adjudication of the Supreme Court."[20] The bridge collapsed in a storm in 1854. Invoking the judgment in the first case, plaintiffs sought to enjoin its rebuilding. In the second Wheeling Bridge case, 59 U.S. (18 How.) 421 (1855), a divided Court sustained the statute and denied the injunction. Justice Nelson wrote:

> So far . . . as this bridge created an obstruction to the free navigation of the river, in view of the previous acts of congress, they are to be regarded as modified by this subsequent legislation; and, although it still may be an obstruction in fact, it is not so in the contemplation of law. . . . The regulation of commerce includes intercourse and navigation, and, of course, the power to determine what shall or shall not be deemed in judgment of law, an obstruction to navigation.

Justice McLean, who had written for the majority in the first case, dissented, asserting that Congress "may . . . declare that no bridge shall be built which shall be an obstruction to the use of a navigable water. And this, it would seem, is as far as the commercial power by congress can be exercised." Since *Wheeling Bridge*, it has been established that Congress can consent to state regulation of interstate commerce that otherwise would be held to run afoul of the Commerce Clause,[21]

---

19. The facts surrounding the case are taken from Carl Swisher, 5 History of the Supreme Court of the United States: The Taney Period, 1836-1864, at 408-420 (1974).

20. Id. at 415. President Franklin Pierce did not veto this bill. Recall that Pierce had raised constitutional objections to a national bill for the relief of insane indigents. On the same Jacksonian principles of limited government, should he have vetoed this bill as well?

21. Cf. Article I, §10, cl. 2: "No State shall, without the Consent of the Congress, lay any Imposts or Duties on Imports or Exports. . . ." This clause does not apply to trade within the United States. Woodruff v. Parham, 75 U.S. (8 Wall.) 123 (1869).

though there is no theoretical account that explains exactly why this is the case. In Prudential Insurance Co. v. Benjamin, 328 U.S. 408 (1946), which sustained Congress's consent to state regulation and taxation of the interstate insurance business after the Court had struck down such regulation as beyond states' authority because of its "interstate character," Justice Rutledge noted that the Court had never invalidated a consent to state regulation of commerce:

> It is true that rationalizations have differed concerning those decisions. . . . But . . . whenever Congress' judgment has been uttered affirmatively to contradict the Court's previously expressed view that specific action taken by the states in Congress' silence was forbidden by the commerce clause, this body has accommodated its previous judgment to Congress' express approval. Some part of this readjustment may be explained in ways acceptable on any theory of the commerce clause and the relations of Congress and the courts toward its functioning. Such explanations, however, hardly go to the root of the matter. For the fact remains that, in these instances, the sustaining of Congress' overriding action has involved something beyond correction of erroneous factual judgment in deference to Congress' presumably better-informed view of the facts, and also beyond giving due deference to its conception of the scope of its powers, when it repudiates, just as when its silence is thought to support, the inference that it has forbidden state action.

"At this point," writes Professor Noel T. Dowling, "it seemed almost as if Mr. Justice Rutledge were leading to a mountain top from which he would point out the 'something beyond' which really went to the root of the matter. But after looking at this point and at that on the broad landscape of his opinion, I was still not sure that my vision had caught the 'something beyond.'"[22]

The short of it is that invalidations of state regulations under the Commerce Clause are less like pure "constitutional" decisions than like decisions holding state laws "preempted" by supervening congressional policy. Only the congressional policy is not—as otherwise it usually is—manifested in any enactment. In an earlier article, Professor Dowling proposed the following doctrine for this area:[23]

> [I]n the absence of affirmative consent a Congressional negative will be presumed in the courts against state action which in its effect upon interstate commerce constitutes an unreasonable interference with national interests, the presumption being rebuttable at the pleasure of Congress. Such a doctrine would free the states from any constitutional disability but at the same time would not give them license to take such action as they see fit irrespective of its effect upon interstate commerce. With respect to such commerce, the question whether the state may act upon it would depend upon the will of Congress expressed in such form as it may choose. State action falling short of such interference would prevail unless and until superseded or otherwise nullified by Congressional action.

---

22. Noel Dowling, Interstate Commerce and State Power—Revised Version, 1947 Colum. L. Rev. 547.

23. Noel Dowling, Interstate Commerce and State Power, 27 Va. L. Rev. 1, 20 (1940).

The reach of the "Dormant Commerce Clause" continues to be controversial. What is the best justification of the division of labor between Court and Congress outlined above, including the fact that Congress may supersede the Court's Dormant Commerce Clause decisions? One possibility is that this arrangement provides a good functional solution to the practical problem of monitoring state legislatures that might be tempted to use their power illegitimately to prefer local as against out-of-state economic interests. But if so, does this mean that Congress should be able to revise or supersede the federal courts' interpretations of other parts of the Constitution as well? If the Dormant Commerce Clause is special, what makes it special?

C. *The Privileges and Immunities of State Citizenship and Personal Mobility Among the States*

The Commerce Clause is not the only part of the Constitution that addresses relationships among the states and limits their sovereignty. The Privileges and Immunities Clause of Article IV, §2, provides: "The citizens of each State shall be entitled to all privileges and immunities of citizens in the several States." Furthermore, the Court has protected individuals' rights to move and resettle among the states, based on its understanding of the structure of federalism and independent of any particular constitutional provision. This section surveys these limitations on state action as they existed in the mid-nineteenth century. Although several of the cases mentioned were decided after the Civil War, they are consistent with the attitudes and doctrines of the Taney Court.

1. The Privileges and Immunities Clause of Article IV

The Privileges and Immunities Clause of Article IV is based on the fourth article of the Articles of Confederation, which provided:

> The better to secure and perpetuate mutual friendship and intercourse among the people of the different States in this Union, the free inhabitants of each of these States, paupers, vagabonds, and fugitives from justice excepted, shall be entitled to all the privileges and immunities of free citizens in the several States; and the people of each State shall have free ingress and regress to and from any other States, and shall enjoy therein all the privileges of trade and commerce, subject to the same duties, impositions, and restrictions as the inhabitants thereof respectively.

The Privileges and Immunities Clause of Article IV does not give a citizen any rights against her own state. Rather, with qualifications, it entitles a citizen of state A, who is present in state B, to the same treatment by state B as B accords its own citizens. As the Court wrote in Paul v. Virginia, 75 U.S. (8 Wall.) 168 (1869),

> It was undoubtedly the object of the clause . . . to place the citizens of each State upon the same footing with citizens of other States, so far as the advantages resulting from citizenship in those States are concerned. It relieves them from the disabilities of alienage in other States; it inhibits

discriminating legislation against them by other States; it gives them the right of free ingress into other States, and egress from them; it insures to them in other States the same freedom possessed by the citizens of those States in the acquisition and enjoyment of property and in the pursuit of happiness; and it secures to them in other States the equal protection of their laws. It has justly been said that no provision in the Constitution has tended so strongly to constitute the citizens of the United States one people as this.

Indeed, without some provision of the kind removing from the citizens of each State the disabilities of alienage in the other States, and giving them equality of privilege with citizens of those States, the Republic would have constituted little more than a league of States. . . .

Does the Privileges and Immunities Clause require that state B accord a citizen of state A every benefit it accords its own citizens? The answer is obviously no. For example, a state may limit the right to vote to its own citizens.

CORFIELD v. CORYELL, F. Cas. No. 3,230 (D. Pa. 1823): [The most elaborate consideration of the reach of the Privileges and Immunities Clause was set out in Justice Bushrod Washington's much-cited circuit court opinion in Corfield v. Coryell, which sustained a New Jersey statute forbidding anyone not "an actual inhabitant and resident" of the state to gather clams and oysters from the state's waters.]

WASHINGTON, J.: The inquiry is, what are the privileges and immunities of citizens in the several states? We feel no hesitation in confining these expressions to those privileges and immunities which are fundamental; which belong of right to the citizens of all free governments[;] and which have, at all times, been enjoyed by the citizens of the several states which compose this Union, from the time of their becoming free, independent, and sovereign.

What these fundamental principles are, it would be more tedious than difficult to enumerate. They may all, however, be comprehended under the following general heads: protection by the government, with the right to acquire and possess property of every kind, and to pursue and obtain happiness and safety, subject, nevertheless, to such restraints as the government may prescribe for the general good of the whole. The right of a citizen of one state to pass through, or to reside in any other state, for purposes of trade, agriculture, professional pursuits, or otherwise; to claim the benefit of the writ of habeas corpus; to institute and maintain actions of any kind in the courts of the state; to take, hold and dispose of property, either real or personal; and an exemption from higher taxes or impositions than are paid by the other citizens of the state; may be mentioned as some of the particular privileges and immunities of citizens, which are clearly embraced by the general description of privileges deemed to be fundamental: to which may be added, the elective franchise, as regulated and established by the laws or constitution of the state in which it is to be exercised.

These, and many others which might be mentioned, are, strictly speaking, privileges and immunities, and the enjoyment of them by the citizens of each state, in every other state, was manifestly calculated (to use the expressions of the preamble of the corresponding provision in the old articles of confederation) "the better to secure and perpetuate mutual friendship and intercourse among the people of the different states of the Union."

But we cannot accede to the proposition which was insisted on by the counsel, that, under this provision of the Constitution, the citizens of the several States are permitted to participate in all the rights which belong exclusively to the citizens of any other particular State, merely upon the ground that they are enjoyed by those citizens; much less, that in regulating the use of the common property of the citizens of such States, the legislature is bound to extend to the citizens of all the other States the same advantages secured to their own citizens.

In *Corfield*, the Court held that fish within the state's waters were the common property of all of the state's citizens, and that it would be "going quite too far to construe the grant of privileges and immunities of citizens, as amounting to a grant of a co-tenancy in the common property of the States, to the citizens of all the other states." (Similar justifications are still offered today to explain why, for example, state universities can prefer state residents to outsiders or even completely disallow any access by nonresidents.) *Paul* held that a state could forbid an out-of-state corporation from doing business in the state because it was not itself a "citizen"; furthermore, incorporation was a special privilege that Virginia was not required to extend to the foreign incorporators. Both of these doctrines have been vitiated by later developments, the most important of which was the Court's acceptance of a corporation as a "person" under the Fourteenth Amendment, Santa Clara v. Southern Pacific Railroad, 118 U.S. 394 (1886).[24]

DISCUSSION

Note carefully Justice Washington's list of fundamental rights in *Coryell.* Is it the list of fundamental liberties you would construct today? Justice Washington includes "the elective franchise" as a fundamental right, and the women's suffrage movement would later use this dictum as support for their argument that women had a constitutional right to vote. See the discussion of the New Departure in Chapter 4, infra. If Justice Washington is correct that the franchise is a privilege and immunity of citizens, does this mean that states must allow noncitizens to vote, or is the right to vote more like the right to gather clams and oysters? Why should that be?

2. Interstate Mobility

CRANDALL v. NEVADA, 73 U.S. (6 Wall.) 35 (1868): The Court struck down a Nevada statute that imposed "a capitation tax of one dollar upon every person leaving the State by any railroad, stage coach, or other vehicle engaged or employed in the business of transporting passengers for hire" and required the carrier to collect the tax from the passengers and turn it over to the state. Crandall, the agent for a stagecoach company, was prosecuted for refusing to pay the tax.

---

24. See Morton Horwitz, The Transformation of American Law 1870-1960: The Crisis of Legal Orthodoxy 66-71 (1992).

Writing for the Court, Justice Miller described the issue as "the right of a State to levy a tax upon persons residing in the State who may wish to get out of it, and upon persons not residing in it who may have occasion to pass through it." He rejected petitioner's argument that the tax violated the prohibition of Article I, §10, against state "Imposts or Duties on Imports or Exports," holding that citizens traveling from one state to another were not imports or exports.

With respect to the claim that the tax violated the Commerce Clause, he first noted that Congress had passed no statute touching on the matter and then relied on Cooley v. Board of Wardens to hold that "[i]nasmuch, therefore, as the tax does not itself institute any regulation of commerce of a national character, or which has a uniform operation over the whole country, it is not easy to maintain [that it violates the Commerce Clause] . . . ," though, in fact, Chief Justice Chase and Justice Clifford rested their own concurring opinions on the Commerce Clause. The majority based invalidation on a quite different ground.

> The people of these United States constitute one nation. They have a government in which all of them are deeply interested. This government has necessarily a capital established by law, where its principal operations are conducted. . . . That government has a right to call to this point any or all of its citizens to aid in its service, as members of the Congress, of the courts, of the executive departments, and to fill all its other offices; and this right cannot be made to depend upon the pleasure of a State over whose territory they must pass to reach the point where these services must be rendered. The government, also, has its offices of secondary importance in all other parts of the country. . . . In all these it demands the services of its citizens, and is entitled to bring them to those points from all quarters of the nation, and no power can exist in a State to obstruct this right that would not enable it to defeat the purposes for which the government was established. . . .
>
> But if the government has these rights on her own account, the citizen also has correlative rights. He has the right to come to the seat of government to assert any claim he may have upon that government, or to transact any business he may have with it. To seek its protection, to share its offices, to engage in administering its functions. He has a right to free access to its sea-ports, through which all the operations of foreign trade and commerce are conducted, to the sub-treasuries, the land offices, the revenue offices, and the courts of justice in the several States, and this right is in its nature independent of the will of any State over whose soil he must pass in the exercise of it.

Miller then cited *McCulloch* for the proposition that it was the very presence of a tax on passage through the state, rather than its actual degree of burdensomeness, that was illegitimate. Moreover, "[i]f one State can do this, so can every other State. And thus one or more States covering the only practicable routes of travel from the east to the west, or from the north to the south, may totally prevent or seriously burden all transportation of passengers from one part of the country to the other. . . ." Miller went on to quote a passage from Taney's opinion in the Passenger Cases:

> Living as we do under a common government, charged with the great concerns of the whole Union, every citizen of the United States from the most remote States or territories, is entitled to free access, not only to the principal departments established at Washington, but also to its judicial tribunals and public offices in every State in the Union. . . . For all the great purposes for which the Federal government was formed we are one people, with one common country. We are all citizens of the United States, and as members of the same community must have the right to pass and repass through every part of it without interruption, as freely as in our own States. And a tax imposed by a State, for entering its territories or harbors, is inconsistent with the rights which belong to citizens of other States as members of the Union, and with the objects which that Union was intended to attain. Such a power in the States could produce nothing but discord and mutual irritation, and they very clearly do not possess it.

DISCUSSION

Note that *Crandall* is an almost unique instance—another is the second part of *McCulloch*—of constitutional interpretation based exclusively on the theory and structure of the federal system without any recourse to the text of the Constitution.[25]

Note also that Justice Miller makes two rather distinct "structural" arguments, which have different implications for the scope of the citizen's right of interstate mobility. One of them refers to what might be termed the "private" interests of the citizen who seeks, for example, to go to a seaport for commercial purposes; the other refers to what might be viewed as the "public" role of the citizen who seeks to participate in government (though, of course, the citizens involved might wish government to support their private interests). Does it matter whether the litigants present themselves in a "private" or "public" role? And is it crucial that the litigants be citizens? Would a resident alien, for example, be unable to challenge the tax in *Crandall*?

Crandall is what might be termed a "right-of-passage" case. Imagine, though, that Crandall wished to *settle* in Nevada rather than merely travel through. Or, further, imagine that Crandall was a convicted felon (in another state), a pauper, a member of a despised political or religious group, or a free person of color? Even if *Crandall* arguably means that every person (or at least every citizen) has a constitutional right to travel freely through a given state on the way to another state, does it also bestow a right to decide to remain in Nevada? (Note that several free states, prior to the Civil War, had prohibited settlement by free Black people.) Would your response change if the person in question were suffering from a communicable disease?

---

25. In United States v. Guest, 383 U.S. 745 (1966), Justice Stewart wrote for the Court, sustaining a federal indictment for conspiracy to interfere with the rights of Black citizens to travel interstate:

> Although the Articles of Confederation provided that "the people of each State shall have free ingress and regress to and from any other State," that right finds no explicit mention in the Constitution. The reason, it has been suggested, is that a right so elementary was conceived from the beginning to be a necessary concomitant of the stronger Union the Constitution created.

II. SLAVERY

In the years after the Louisiana Purchase many slaveholders migrated well northward of present-day Louisiana. Louisiana was uncontroversially admitted to the Union as a slave state in 1812. The next state to be carved out of the vast new territory was Missouri, whose voting inhabitants petitioned in 1819 for admission also as a slave state. This time Congress was enveloped in heated conflict. Anti-slavery Northerners pressed for conditioning Missouri's admission on freeing all slaves born in the state after admission on their twenty-fifth birthday. (This obviously would have had no effect on the existing population, the last slave of whom would presumably not die until the dawn of the twentieth century.) Ultimately, Congress agreed to the Missouri Compromise of 1820, which, among other things, admitted Missouri as a slave state but prohibited slavery in the territories north of latitude 36°30′. To preserve the balance of slave and free states in the Senate, Maine was simultaneously admitted as a new free state. "Angry passions quickly subsided, the sectional alignment dissolved, and politics resumed their delusive tranquility. But a veil had been lifted for the moment, revealing a bloody prospect ahead. 'This monumental question, like a fire bell in the night, awakened and filled me with terror,' wrote Jefferson. 'I considered it at once as the knell of the union.' And J.Q. Adams recorded in his diary: 'I take it for granted that the present question is a mere preamble—a title-page to a great, tragic volume.'"[26] The remainder of this chapter explores the tragic drama predicted by Adams and, among other things, the role played by the U.S. Supreme Court.

A. *The Interstate Slave Trade*

GROVES v. SLAUGHTER, 40 U.S. (15 Pet.) 449 (1841): [A provision of the Mississippi Constitution of 1832, which seemingly forbade importing slaves into the state for sale there, was attacked as an impermissible restriction of interstate commerce. Mississippi was, of course, a slave state, and the provision was almost certainly designed to protect its own slave trade against competition from other states. As Justice Baldwin described the provision in a concurring opinion, it "does not purport to be a regulation of police, for any defined object connected with the internal tranquility of the State, the health, or morals of the people; it is general in its terms; it is aimed at the introduction of slaves as merchandise from other States, not with the intention of excluding diseased, convicted, or insurgent slaves, or such as may be otherwise dangerous to the peace or welfare of the State. Its avowed purpose is to prevent them from being the subjects of intercourse with other States, when introduced for the purpose of sale. . . ."

Justice Thompson's opinion for the Court avoided the issue entirely by construing the state constitution to require the passage of activating legislation.[27]

---

26. Quoted in Morison, Commager, and Leuchtenborg, supra n.3, at 398-399.

27. The provision in question read as follows: "The introduction of slaves into this state as merchandise or for sale shall be prohibited from and after 1 May, 1833. . . ." Although one might doubt that this clause required further action by the Mississippi legislature, the Mississippi Supreme Court had no opportunity to reach the question. *Groves* arose in a Louisiana federal district court as a diversity suit between a Louisiana slavetrader and a Mississippi purchaser; the Louisiana court interpreted the provision as "self-enforcing."

Three concurring Justices carried on a vigorous side debate over the issues that the majority artfully avoided.]

McLean, J., concurring.

[For Justice McLean, an Ohioan and a Marshallian nationalist, the case presented a dilemma. If slaves were an item of commerce, Congress could, if it so chose, prohibit the interstate slave trade by ordinary legislation under the commerce power. But the Marshallian view of congressional exclusivity suggested in *Gibbons* cast doubt on the validity of any state laws regulating the slave trade; it did not distinguish between Mississippi's pro-slavery, protectionist law and Ohio's ban on the slave trade as part of its prohibition of slavery in general. McLean tried to straddle the dilemma. He denied that slaves were an item of commerce: Even "if slaves are considered in some of the States as merchandise, that cannot divest them of the leading and controlling quality of persons by which they are designated in the Constitution." He went on to argue that the states were free to deal with slavery as they wished.]

. . . The power over slavery belongs to the States respectively. It is local in its character, and in its effects; and the transfer or sale of slaves cannot be separated from this power. It is, indeed, an essential part of it.

Each state has a right to protect itself against the avarice and intrusion of the slave dealer; to guard its citizens against the inconveniences and dangers of a slave population.

The right to exercise this power by a State is higher and deeper than the Constitution. The evil involves the prosperity and may endanger the existence of a State. Its power to guard against, or to remedy the evil, rests upon the law of self-preservation; a law vital to every community, and especially to a sovereign State. . . .

Taney, C.J.

[Chief Justice Taney claimed that he addressed the issue only because McLean had raised it, and came to the same conclusion.]

. . . In my judgment the power over this subject is exclusively with the several States . . . and the action of the several States upon this subject, cannot be controlled by Congress, either by virtue of its power to regulate commerce, or by virtue of any other power. . . .

Baldwin, J.

[Justice Baldwin, who like McLean was a nationalist, argued that although a state could abolish slavery entirely, it could not allow slavery and prohibit the slave trade, for slaves were items of commerce and the regulation of interstate commerce lay within the exclusive domain of Congress. In elaborating this position, he made explicit some broader concerns of slavery and federalism.]

. . . As each state has plenary power to legislate on this subject, its laws are the test of what is property; if they recognise slaves as the property of those who hold them, they become the subjects of commerce between the states which so recognise them, and the traffic in them may be regulated by congress, as the traffic in other articles; but no further. Being property, by the law of any state, the owners are protected from any violations of the rights of property by congress, under the fifth amendment of the constitution; these rights do not consist merely in ownership; the right of disposing of property of all kinds, is incident to it, which congress cannot touch. The mode of disposition is regulated by the state of common law; and but for the first clause in the second section of the fourth article of the constitution of the United States, a state might authorize its citizens to deal in slaves, and prohibit it to all others. But that clause secures to the citizens of all the states, "all privileges and immunities of citizens" of any other state, whereby any traffic in slaves or other property, which is lawful to the citizens or settlers of Mississippi, with each other, is equally protected when carried on between them and the citizens of Virginia. Hence, it is apparent, that no state can control this traffic, so long as it may be carried on by its own citizens, within its own limits; as part of its purely internal commerce, any state may regulate it according to its own policy; but when such regulation purports to extend to other states or their citizens, it is limited by the constitution, putting the citizens of all on the same footing as their own. It follows, likewise, that any power of congress over the subject is, as has been well expressed by one of the plaintiffs' counsel, conservative in its character, for the purpose of protecting the property of the citizens of the United States, which is a lawful subject of commerce among the states, from any state law which affects to prohibit its transmission for sale from one state to another, through a third or more states.

Thus, in Ohio, and those states to which the ordinance of 1787 applies, or in those where slaves are not property, not subjects of dealing or traffic among its own citizens, they cannot become so, when brought from other states; their condition is the same as those persons of the same color already in the state; subject in all respects to the provisions of its law, if brought there for the purposes of residence or sale. If, however, the owner of slaves in Maryland, in transporting them to Kentucky or Missouri, should pass through Pennsylvania or Ohio, no law of either state could take away or affect his right of property; nor, if passing from one slave state to another, accident or distress should compel him to touch at any place within a state, where slavery did not exist. Such transit of property, whether of slaves or bales of goods is lawful commerce among the several states, which none can prohibit or regulate, which the constitution protects, and congress may, and ought, to preserve from violation. . . .

But where no object of police is discernible in a state law or constitution, nor any rule of policy, other than that which gives to its own citizens a "privilege," which is denied to citizens of other states, it is wholly different. The direct tendency of all such laws is partial, anti-national, subversive of the harmony which should exist among the states, as well as inconsistent with the most sacred principles of the constitution. . . . For these reasons, my opinion is, that had the contract in question been invalid by the constitution of Mississippi, it would be valid by the constitution of the United States. These reasons are drawn from those principles on which alone this government must be sustained: the leading one of which is, that wherever slavery exists, by the laws of a state, slaves are property in every constitutional sense, and for every purpose, whether as subjects of taxation, as the basis of representation, as articles of commerce, or fugitives from service. To consider them as persons merely, and not property, is, in my settled opinion, the first step towards a state of things to be avoided only by a firm adherence to the fundamental principles of the state and federal governments, in relation to this species of property. If the first step taken be a mistaken one, the successive ones will be fatal to the whole system. I have taken my stand on the only position which, in my judgment, is impregnable; and feel confident in its strength, however it may be assailed in public opinion, here or elsewhere.

NOTE: THE UNITED STATES MAIL AND AMERICAN PLURALISM[28]

In 1792, acting under its Article I powers, Congress passed the Postal Service Act; its goal was to enable individuals located far from one another to remain in communication at what were nominal prices. It was a national program of communications regulations and subsidies designed to promote a united society. By 1830, there were over 100,000 miles of roads connecting the nation, with 6,500 post offices. The Postmaster General was a significant officer; indeed, Justice McLean had served as Andrew Jackson's Postmaster General before being named to the Supreme Court.

Until 1912, the postal service delivered mail on Sunday, which stirred vigorous controversy throughout the nineteenth century. Federal legislation passed in 1810 officially forbade post offices from closing on Sunday, which served, among other things, to stimulate religion-based campaigns to acknowledge the Christian Sabbath by closing the post office. Not all Christians agreed that the government should do so. In 1829, Senator Richard Johnson of Kentucky, the Chair of the Senate Committee on the Post Office and Post Roads, a committed Baptist, a hero of the War of 1812, and later Vice President in the Van Buren Administration, helped to write the "Report on the Transportation of Mails on Sunday," which reaffirmed the secular nature of the Constitution and the concomitant separation of church and state: "Let the national legislature once perform an act which involves the decision of a religious controversy, and it will have passed its legitimate bounds. The precedent will then be established, and the foundation laid for that usurpation of the Divine prerogative in this country, which has been the desolating scourge to the fairest portions of the old world."

Like the Internet today, the postal service could unite far distant members of a family or business partners. But, also like today's Internet, it could also facilitate the spread of allegedly dangerous and alien ideas to places that wished no part of them. Some former slaves who had escaped captivity through the underground railroad, for example, sent taunting letters to their former masters; in addition, "[s]laves who had left the South used the postal service to communicate with loved ones and friends left behind" by sending letters to friendly whites or free Black people, to convey important information to those left behind.[29]

---

28. See generally Isaac Kramnick and R. Laurence Moore, The Godless Constitution: A Moral Defense of the Secular State 131-150 (chapter on Sunday mail delivery) (2005).

29. R.J.M. Blackett, Making Freedom: The Underground Railroad and the Politics of Slavery 14 (2013).

During the 1830s, abolitionists began sending material detailing the iniquity of slavery through the United States mails to leaders of public opinion in the Southern states, who would presumably be persuaded to use their power to end it.[30] In response, several slave states passed laws prohibiting the circulation of anti-slavery publications. Indeed, Clement Eaton states that after 1835 there was "a virtual censorship of the mails crossing the Mason and Dixon line." Although these laws necessarily touched on the powers of federal postal officials and thus raised delicate constitutional problems, they were never litigated, primarily because the federal officials involved were altogether willing to comply with the laws. (Recall that throughout most of the antebellum era, the White House was controlled by Presidents who depended on political coalitions that included slaveholders.)

A legal test of sorts with respect to the freedom of the mails arose in 1857. Mississippi required imprisonment and fine "if any white person circulate or put forth any book, paper, magazine, or pamphlet, containing any sentiment, doctrine, advice, or innuendoes, calculated to produce a disorderly, dangerous, or rebellious disaffection among the colored population." A deputy postmaster in Yazoo City, Mississippi, refused to deliver abolitionist material mailed from Ohio, arguing that its delivery would violate the Mississippi statute inasmuch as the publication in question, the *Cincinnati Gazette*, challenged the practice of chattel slavery. The Postmaster General turned to Attorney General Caleb Cushing for an opinion. Cushing, though from Massachusetts, was an active member of the pro-slavery wing of the Democratic Party that had elected Franklin Pierce and was soon to send James Buchanan of Pennsylvania to the presidency. Cushing issued his opinion on March 2, 1857, just before he left office upon the inauguration of the new President two days later.[31] Federal law prohibits a postmaster from "unlawfully detain[ing]" any mail. The question, therefore, is whether the Yazoo City detention was "lawful." Cushing began by noting:

> [E]ach State has, and must have, jurisdiction as regards the matter of insurrection or treason. To deny this would be to deny to the inhabitants of a State the power of self-preservation. That cannot be denied. In constitutional language, it is a right inalienable and imprescriptible. No political society can effectively cede away the power of self-preservation. If it should undertake to do so, in whatever explicitness of expression, such an act would be null and of no effect. Of course, it does not need to go into the inquiry, whether the law of the State of Mississippi be constitutionally maintainable as a provision of police. It is that, but it is much more. It is a law of self-conservation, in the category of those, which lie at the foundation of all possible forms of human society.
>
> [Given this assumption,] we have the main question very much simplified. It is this: Has a citizen of one of the United States plenary indisputable right to employ the functions and the officers of the Union as the

30. See Clement Eaton, The Freedom-of-Thought Struggle in the Old South, ch. VIII (rev. ed. 1964). All of the quotations in this paragraph are taken from this chapter. See also Michael Kent Curtis, The Curious History of Attempts to Suppress Antislavery Speech, Press, and Petition in 1835-1837, 89 Nw. U. L. Rev. 785 (1995).

31. 8 Opinions of Attorneys General 489.

> means of enabling him to produce insurrection in another of the United States? Can the officers of the Union lawfully lend its functions to the citizens of one of the States for the purpose of promoting insurrection in another State?

It can surely be no surprise, given Cushing's assumption and statement of the question, that the postmaster's failure to deliver the *Gazette* was vindicated:

> [I]n regard to municipal legislation, for the most part, the several United States are foreign each to the other. And the citizens of the State of Mississippi are the only competent judges of how much they may be inconvenienced by the impeded circulation among them of this or that pamphlet or newspaper. That is a question of self-government, which it belongs to them to answer for themselves, not to the citizens of Ohio to answer for them. . . . Moreover, there is here a balance of inconveniences. Insurrections are inconvenient things. It is inconvenient to the people of one State to have their houses burned by means of incendiary missiles projected from behind the secure legal shelter of the boundary line of an adjoining State. If the non-circulation of this or that foreign newspaper in a particular State be an inconvenience to somebody, it is, in the aggregate of all public interests, a much less inconvenience than the occurrence, or even the danger, of insurrection in that State.
>
> It may be unpleasant to some person in Ohio to find that he is not free to promote insurrection in Mississippi. Nevertheless, even at the risk of not accommodating any such perverse taste, each State of the Union has the right to protect itself against domestic violence, and to invoke to that end the friendly co-operation, or at least the neutrality, of the United States.

Cushing did concede that the actual insurrectionary nature of the publication might be a disputable question, so that persons who believed that their rights to have their mail delivered had been violated could challenge the classification in state or federal court, although one might doubt that an all-white Mississippi jury would hesitate to deem anti-slavery materials "insurrectionary." Note the complete absence of any discussion of the First Amendment. With respect to Mississippi's own law, the reason for the omission is doctrinally simple: In the 1833 decision of Barron v. Baltimore, 32 U.S. (7 Pet.) 243, Chief Justice Marshall held, for a unanimous Court, that the Bill of Rights applied only to the national government. Not until 1925 was the Freedom of Speech Clause of the First Amendment made applicable to the states through incorporation in the Fourteenth Amendment. This, however, does not explain the absence of discussion of the First Amendment's application to the national government's refusal to deliver the mail. Is that because Congress could legitimately authorize postmasters to refuse to deliver mail that local authorities legitimately deem an incitement to insurrection? If you disagree with the Attorney General's analysis, is it because it involves a ban on anti-slavery advocacy, or is it because you doubt that these materials could reasonably have caused violence or insurrection in the years immediately before the Civil War? See Chapter 4, infra, for further discussion of the First Amendment and the "clear and present danger" test.

B. *Fugitive Slaves*

Prigg v. Pennsylvania

41 U.S. (16 Pet.) 536 (1842)

[The Fugitive Slave Act of 1793 authorized the owner to seize a fugitive slave and bring him or her before a federal judge or state magistrate, who was required to give a "certificate" to the owner or his agent upon satisfactory proof "that the person so seized or arrested doth, under the laws of the state or territory from which he or she fled, owe service or labor to the person claiming him or her. . . ."

The case arose from the capture in 1837, by Edward Prigg, Nathan Bemis, and others, of Margaret Morgan and her children in Pennsylvania and the subsequent taking of them to Maryland. Southern Pennsylvania was a common refuge for fugitive slaves because of its border with Maryland. Slavecatchers were often sent to recapture fugitives, and they were often less than scrupulous in making sure that those they captured (or kidnapped) were in fact fugitives or, indeed, had ever been slaves at all.

Bemis had succeeded to the Maryland estate of one Ashmore, the owner of Margaret Morgan's parents, who had, says Paul Finkelman, "informally set [them] free" prior to her birth.[32] Margaret was married to Jerry Morgan, a free Black person, and they had, in 1832, moved just across the border to Pennsylvania, where they had several children. "These children were," according to Finkelman, "free under Pennsylvania law and were not subject to the Fugitive Slave Act; they did not fit the constitutional definition of fugitive slaves (persons 'escaping into another' state)." Moreover, inasmuch as the marriage had occurred with the apparent acquiescence of Ashmore, Margaret Morgan might well have been considered to be free herself under either Pennsylvania or Maryland law.

Pennsylvania attorney Thomas Hambly described the circumstances of capture to the U.S. Supreme Court:[33]

> [I]n February, 1837, together with Prigg the defendant and others, [Bemis] came into the State of Pennsylvania and procured a warrant from Thos. Henderson, a justice of the peace, authorising Wm. McCleary, a constable of York County, to arrest and bring before him "the said Margaret and her children." They were seized before any day light, in bed; the mother, father and children put into an open wagon in a cold sleety rain, with scarcely their ordinary clothes on, and conveyed some ten or fifteen miles to Henderson's house. In the mean time Henderson had learned that he had no jurisdiction by the law of Pennsylvania, and he refused when they arrived to adjudicate. It had grown late, was dark and still raining; a consultation was had amongst the captors and it resulted in releasing Jerry Morgan the husband, who was told if he would go back they

32. Paul Finkelman, Sorting out Prigg v. Pennsylvania, 24 Rutgers L.J. 605 (1993).

33. Argument of Mr. Hambly, of York (Pa.), in the Case of Edward Prigg, Lucase & Dever (1842), reprinted in 1 Fugitive Slaves and American Courts: The Pamphlet Literature 121 (Finkelman ed., 1988).

> would meet him in the morning at Esq. Ross's where the mother should be disposed of. He went back, and as soon as he was out of sight, Prigg and Bemis crossed the line into Maryland, with the mother and children, and by the morning light they were sold to a negro trader and in a calaboose ready for shipment to the South.
>
> Such a transaction, of course, aroused the public upon the Pennsylvania side of the line. Pursuit was made, the negroes found, and a complaint laid before the Governor of Pennsylvania of this violation both of territory and law. A demand was made of the executive of Maryland for the guilty parties, but after a long and tedious negociation [sic], the Governor of Maryland refused to surrender them.

Following intense negotiations between Maryland and Pennsylvania, "Maryland sent Prigg to Pennsylvania for trial after Pennsylvania officials agreed that in the event of a conviction he would not be incarcerated . . . until after the United States Supreme Court had ruled on the constitutionality of the relevant state and federal laws."[34] As Hambly informed the Supreme Court, though, "[i]n the meanwhile the mother and children were taken before Judge Archer, of Harford county, adjudged to be slaves and sold." Prigg was convicted under an 1826 Pennsylvania statute expressly designed to prevent self-help in the return of fugitive slaves. The Supreme Court reversed the conviction and held the state law unconstitutional. Justice Story wrote for the Court; six Justices wrote separate opinions, some disagreeing sharply with aspects of the opinion. We excerpt portions of Story's opinion, Taney's opinion concurring in the result, and McLean's dissent.]

STORY, J. . . .

Few questions which have ever come before this court involve more delicate and important considerations; and few upon which the public at large may be presumed to feel a more profound and pervading interest. . . .

Before, however, we proceed to the points more immediately before us, it may be well, in order to clear the case of difficulty, to say, that in the exposition of this part of the constitution, we shall limit ourselves to those considerations which appropriately and exclusively belong to it, without laying down any rules of interpretation of a more general nature. It will, indeed, probably, be found, when we look to the character of the constitution itself, the objects which it seeks to attain, the powers which it confers, the duties which it enjoins, and the rights which it secures, as well as the known historical fact, that many of its provisions were matters of compromise of opposing interests and opinions, that no uniform rule of interpretation can be applied to it, which may not allow, even if it does not positively demand, many modifications, in its actual application to particular clauses. And, perhaps, the safest rule of interpretation, after all, will be found to be to look to the nature and objects of the particular powers, duties and rights, with all the lights and aids of contemporary history; and to give to the words of each just such operation and force, consistent with their legitimate meaning, as may fairly secure and attain the ends proposed.

---

34. Finkelman, supra n.32, at 612.

There are two clauses in the constitution upon the subject of fugitives, which stand in juxtaposition with each other, and have been thought mutually to illustrate each other. They are both contained in the second section of the fourth article, and are in the following words: "A person charged in any state with treason, felony or other crime, who shall flee from justice, and be found in another state, shall, on demand of the executive authority of the state from which he fled, be delivered up, to be removed to the state having jurisdiction of the crime." "No person held to service or labor in one state, under the laws thereof, escaping into another, shall, in consequence of any law or regulation therein, be discharged from such service or labor; but shall be delivered up, on claim of the party to whom such service or labor may be due."

The last clause is that, the true interpretation whereof is directly in judgment before us. Historically, it is well known, that the object of this clause was to secure to the citizens of the slave-holding states the complete right and title of ownership in their slaves, as property, in every state in the Union into which they might escape from the state where they were held in servitude. The full recognition of this right and title was indispensable to the security of this species of property in all the slave-holding states; and, indeed, was so vital to the preservation of their domestic interests and institutions, that it cannot be doubted, that it constituted a fundamental article, without the adoption of which the Union could not have been formed. Its true design was, to guard against the doctrines and principles prevalent in the non-slave-holding states, by preventing them from intermeddling with, or obstructing, or abolishing the rights of the owners of slaves.

By the general Law of nations, no nation is bound to recognise the state of slavery, as to foreign slaves found within its territorial dominions, when it is in opposition to its own policy and institutions, in favor of the subjects of other nations where slavery is recognised. If it does it, it is as a matter of comity, and not as a matter of international right. . . . It is manifest, from this consideration, that if the constitution had not contained this clause, every non-slave-holding state in the Union would have been at liberty to have declared free all runaway slaves coming within its limits, and to have given them entire immunity and protection against the claims of their masters; a course which would have created the most bitter animosities, and engendered perpetual strife between the different states. The clause was, therefore, of the last importance to the safety and security of the southern states, and could not have been surrendered by them, without endangering their whole property in slaves. The clause was accordingly adopted into the constitution, by the unanimous consent of the framers of it; a proof at once of its intrinsic and practical necessity.

How, then, are we to interpret the language of the clause? The true answer is, in such a manner as, consistently with the words, shall fully and completely effectuate the whole objects of it. If, by one mode of interpretation, the right must become shadowy and unsubstantial, and without any remedial power adequate to the end, and by another mode, it will attain its just end and secure its manifest purpose, it would seem, upon principles of reasoning, absolutely irresistible, that the latter ought to prevail. No court of justice can be authorized so to construe any clause of the constitution as to defeat its obvious ends, when another construction, equally accordant with the words and sense thereof, will enforce and protect them.

The clause manifestly contemplates the existence of a positive, unqualified right on the part of the owner of the slave, which no state law or regulation can in any way qualify, regulate, control or restrain. The slave is not to be discharged from service or labor, in consequence of any state law or regulation. Now, certainly, without indulging in any nicety of criticism upon words, it may fairly and reasonably be said, that any state law or state regulation, which interrupts, limits, delays or postpones the right of the owner to the immediate possession of the slave, and the immediate command of his service and labor, operates, pro tanto, a discharge of the slave therefrom. . . . The question [is one] of withholding or controlling the incidents of a positive and absolute right.

. . . Upon this ground, we have not the slightest hesitation in holding, that under and in virtue of the constitution, the owner of a slave is clothed with entire authority, in every state in the Union, to seize and recapture his slave, whenever he can do it, without any breach of the peace or any illegal violence. In this sense, and to this extent, this clause of the constitution may properly be said to execute itself, and to require no aid from legislation, state or national. But the clause of the constitution does not stop here; nor, indeed, consistently with its professed objects, could it do so. Many cases must arise, in which, if the remedy of the owner were confined to the mere right of seizure and recaption, he would be utterly without any adequate redress. He may not be able to lay his hands upon the slave. He may not be able to enforce his rights against persons, who either secrete or conceal, or withhold the slave. He may be restricted by local legislation, as to the mode of proofs of his ownership; as to the courts in which he shall sue, and as to the actions which he may bring; or the process he may use to compel the delivery of the slave. Nay! the local legislation may be utterly inadequate to furnish the appropriate redress . . . ; and this may be innocently as well as designedly done, since every state is perfectly competent, and has the exclusive right, to prescribe the remedies in its own judicial tribunals, to limit the time as well as the mode of redress, and to deny jurisdiction over cases, which its own policy and its own institutions either prohibit or discountenance. If, therefore, the clause of the constitution had stopped at the mere recognition of the right, without providing or contemplating any means by which it might be established and enforced, in cases where it did not execute itself, it is plain, that it would have been, in a great variety of cases, a delusive and empty annunciation. . . .

And this leads us to the consideration of the other part of the clause, which implies at once a guarantee and duty. It says, "but he (the slave) shall be delivered up, on claim of the party to whom such service or labor may be due." Now, we think it exceedingly difficult, if not impracticable, to read this language, and not to feel, that it contemplated some further remedial redress than that which might be administered at the hands of the owner himself. . . . If, indeed, the constitution guarantees the right, and if it requires the delivery upon the claim of the owner (as cannot well be doubted), the natural inference certainly is, that the national government is clothed with the appropriate authority and functions to enforce it. . . . The clause is found in the national constitution, and not in that of any state. It does not point out any state functionaries, or any state action, to carry its provisions into effect. The states cannot, therefore, be compelled to enforce them; and it might well be deemed an unconstitutional exercise of the power of interpretation, to insist, that the states are bound to provide means to carry into effect the duties of the national government, nowhere delegated or intrusted to them by the constitution. On the contrary, the natural, if not the necessary, conclusion is, that the national government, in the absence of all positive provisions to the contrary, is bound, through its own proper departments, legislative, judicial or executive, as the case may require, to carry into effect all the rights and duties imposed upon it by the constitution. . . .

Congress has taken this very view of the power and duty of the national government. As early as the year 1791, the attention of congress was drawn to it (as we shall hereafter more fully see), in consequence of some practical difficulties arising under the other clause, respecting fugitives from justice escaping into other states. The result of their deliberations was the passage of the act of the 12th of February 1793, which [established the right of a slaveowner or his agent to] seize or arrest such fugitive from labor and take him or her before any judge of the circuit or district courts of the United States, residing or being within the state, or before any magistrate of a county, city or town corporate, wherein such seizure or arrest shall be made; and upon proof, to the satisfaction of such judge or magistrate . . . [that the person is in fact a fugitive], to give a certificate thereof to such claimant, his agent or attorney, which shall be sufficient warrant for removing the said fugitive from labor, to the state or territory from which he or she fled. The fourth section provides a penalty against any person, who shall knowingly and willingly obstruct or hinder such claimant, his agent or attorney, in so seizing or arresting such fugitive from labor, or rescue such fugitive from the claimant, or his agent or attorney, when so arrested, or who shall harbor or conceal such fugitive, after notice that he is such; and it also saves to the person claiming such labor or service, his right of action for or on account of such injuries.

In a general sense, this act may be truly said to cover the whole ground of the constitution, . . . because it points out fully all the modes of attaining those objects, which congress, in their discretion, have as yet deemed expedient or proper to meet the exigencies of the constitution. If this be so, then it would seem, upon just principles of construction, that the legislation of congress, if constitutional, must supersede all state legislation upon the same subject; and by necessary implication prohibit it. For, if congress have a constitutional power to regulate a particular subject, and they do actually regulate it in a given manner, and in a certain form, it cannot be, that the state legislatures have a right to interfere, and as it were, by way of compliment to the legislation of congress, to prescribe additional regulations, and what they may deem auxiliary provisions for the same purpose. In such a case, the legislation of congress, in what it does prescribe, manifestly indicates, that it does not intend that there shall be any further legislation to act upon the subject-matter. Its silence as to what it does not do, is as expressive of what its intention is, as the direct provisions made by it. . . . [W]here congress have exercised a power over a particular subject given them by the constitution, it is not competent for state legislation to add to the provisions of congress upon that subject; for that the will of congress upon the whole subject is as clearly established by what it has not declared, as by what it has expressed.

But it has been argued, that the act of congress is unconstitutional, because it does not fall within the scope of any of the enumerated powers of legislation confided to that body; and therefore, it is void. Stripped of its artificial and technical structure, the argument comes to this, that although rights are exclusively secured by, or duties are exclusively imposed upon, the national government, yet, unless the power to enforce these rights or to execute these duties, can be found among the express powers of legislation enumerated in the constitution, they remain without any means of giving them effect by any act of congress; and they must operate solely proprio vigore, however defective may be their operation; nay! even although, in a practical sense, they may become a nullity, from the want of a proper remedy to enforce them, or to provide against their violation. If this be the true interpretation of the constitution, it must, in a great measure, fail to attain many of its avowed and positive objects, as a security of rights, and a recognition of duties. Such a limited construction of the constitution has never yet been adopted as correct, either in theory or practice. No one has ever supposed, that congress could, constitutionally, by its legislation, exercise powers, or enact laws, beyond the powers delegated to it by the constitution. But it has, on various occasions, exercised powers which were necessary and proper as means to carry into effect rights expressly given, and duties expressly enjoined thereby. The end being required, it has been deemed a just and necessary implication, that the means to accomplish it are given also; or, in other words, that the power flows as a necessary means to accomplish the end. . . .

[T]he nature of the provision and the objects to be attained by it, require that it should be controlled by one and the same will, and act uniformly by the same system of regulations throughout the Union. If, then, the states have a right, in the absence of legislation by congress, to act upon the subject, each state is at liberty to prescribe just such regulations as suit its own policy, local convenience and local feelings. The legislation of one state may not only be different from, but utterly repugnant to and incompatible with, that of another. . . .

It is scarcely conceivable, that the slave-holding states would have been satisfied with leaving to the legislation of the non-slave-holding states, a power of regulation, in the absence of that of congress, which would or might practically amount to a power to destroy the rights of the owner. If the argument, therefore, of a concurrent power in the states to act upon the subject-matter, in the absence of legislation by congress, be well founded; then, if congress had never acted at all, or if the act of congress should be repealed, without providing a substitute, there would be a resulting authority in each of the states to regulate the whole subject, at its pleasure, and to dole out its own remedial justice, or withhold it, at its pleasure, and according to its own views of policy and expediency. Surely, such a state of things never could have been intended, under such a solemn guarantee of right and duty. On the other hand, construe the right of legislation as exclusive in congress, and every evil and every danger vanishes. The right and the duty are then co-extensive and uniform in remedy and operation throughout the whole Union. The owner has the same security, and the same remedial justice, and the same exemption from state regulation and control, through however many states he may pass with his fugitive slave in his possession, in transit to his own domicile. . . .

These are some of the reasons, but by no means all, upon which we hold the power of legislation on this subject to be exclusive in congress. To guard, however, against any possible misconstruction of our views, it is proper to state, that we are by no means to be understood, in any manner whatsoever, to doubt or to interfere with the police power belonging to the states, in virtue of their general sovereignty. That police power extends over all subjects within territorial limits of the states, and has never been conceded to the United States. It is wholly distinguishable from the right and duty secured by the provision now under consideration; which is exclusively derived from and secured by the constitution of the United States, and owes its whole efficacy thereto. We entertain no doubt whatsoever, that the states, in virtue of their general police power, possess full jurisdiction to arrest and restrain runaway slaves, and remove them from their borders, and otherwise to secure themselves against their depredations and evil example, as they certainly may do in cases of idlers, vagabonds and paupers. The rights of the owners of fugitive slaves are in no just sense interfered with, or regulated, by such a course; and in many cases, the operations of this police power, although designed generally for other purposes, for protection, safety and peace of the state, may essentially promote and aid the interests of the owners. But such regulations can never be permitted to interfere with, or to obstruct, the just rights of the owner to reclaim his slave, derived from the constitution of the United States, or with the remedies prescribed by congress to aid and enforce the same.

Upon these grounds, we are of opinion, that the act of Pennsylvania upon which this indictment is founded, is unconstitutional and void. It purports to punish as a public offence against that state, the very act of seizing and removing a slave, by his master, which the constitution of the United States was designed to justify and uphold. . . .

Taney, C.J., concurring. . . .

The opinion of the court maintains, that the power over this subject is so exclusively vested in congress, that no state, since the adoption of the constitution, can pass any law in relation to it. In other words, according to the opinion just delivered, the state authorities are prohibited from interfering, for the purpose of protecting the right of the master, and aiding him in the recovery of his property. I think, the states are not prohibited; and that, on the contrary, it is enjoined upon them as a duty, to protect and support the owner, when he is endeavoring to obtain possession of his property found within their respective territories. The language used in the constitution does not, in my judgment, justify the construction given to it by the court. It contains no words prohibiting the several states from passing laws to enforce this right. They are, in express terms, forbidden to make any regulation that shall impair it; but there the prohibition stops. And according to the settled rules of construction for all written instruments, the prohibition being confined to laws injurious to the right, the power to pass laws to support and enforce it, is necessarily implied. And the words of the article which direct that the fugitive "shall be delivered up," seem evidently designed to impose it as a duty upon the people of the several states, to pass laws to carry into execution, in good faith, the compact into which they thus solemnly entered with each other. . . .

[I]t is manifest, from the face of the law, that an effectual remedy was intended to be given, by the act of 1793. It never designed to compel the master to encounter the hazard and expense of taking the fugitive, in all cases, to the distant residence of one of the judges of the courts of the United States; for it authorized him also, to go before any magistrate of the county, city or town corporate wherein the seizure should be made. And congress evidently supposed, that it had provided a tribunal at the place of the arrest, capable of furnishing the master with the evidence of ownership, to protect him more effectually from unlawful interruption.

So far from regarding the state authorities as prohibited from interfering in cases of this description, the congress of that day must have counted upon their cordial co-operation; they legislated with express reference to state support.

McLean, J., dissenting. . . .

In my judgment, there is not the least foundation in the act for the right asserted in the argument, to take the fugitive by force and remove him out of the state.

Such a proceeding can receive no sanction under the act, for it is in express violation of it. The claimant having seized the fugitive, is required by the act, to take him before a federal judge within the state, or a state magistrate within the county, city or town corporate, within which the seizure was made. Now, can there be any pretence, that after the seizure under the statute, the claimant may disregard the other express provision of it, by taking the fugitive, without claim, out of the state? But it is said, the master may seize his slave wherever he finds him, if by doing so, he does not violate the public peace; that the relation of master and slave is not affected by the laws of the state, to which the slave may have fled, and where he is found. . . .

It is admitted, that the rights of the master, so far as regards the services of the slave, are not impaired by this change; but the mode of asserting them, in my opinion, is essentially modified. In the state where the service is due, the master needs no other law than the law of force, to control the action of the slave. But can this law be applied by the master, in a state which makes the act unlawful? . . .

In a state where slavery is allowed, every colored person is presumed to be a slave; and on the same principle, in a non-slave-holding state, every person is presumed to be free, without regard to color. On this principle, the states, both slave-holding and non-slave-holding, legislate. The latter may prohibit, as Pennsylvania has done, under a certain penalty, the forcible removal of a colored person out of the state. . . .

It is very clear, that no power to seize and forcibly remove the slave, without claim, is given by the act of congress. Can it be exercised under the constitution? Congress have legislated on the constitutional power, and have directed the mode in which it shall be executed. The act, it is admitted, covers the whole ground; and that it is constitutional, there seems to be no reason to doubt. Now, under such circumstances, can the provisions of the act be disregarded, and an assumed power set up under the constitution? . . .

I cannot perceive how any one can doubt that the remedy given in the constitution, if, indeed, it give any remedy, without legislation, was designed to be a peaceful one; a remedy sanctioned by judicial authority; a remedy guarded by the forms of law. But the inquiry is reiterated, is not the master entitled to his property? I answer, that he is. His right is guarantied by the constitution, and the most summary means for its enforcement is found in the act of congress; and neither the state nor its citizens can obstruct the prosecution of this right. . . .

The presumption of the state that the colored person is free, may be erroneous in fact; and if so, there can be no difficulty in proving it. But may not the assertion of the master be erroneous also; and if so, how is his act of force to be remedied? The colored person is taken and forcibly conveyed beyond the jurisdiction of the state. This force, not being authorized by the act of congress nor by the constitution, may be prohibited by the state. As the act covers the whole power in the constitution, and carries out, by special enactments, its provisions, we are, in my judgment, bound by the act. We can no more, under such circumstances, administer a remedy under the constitution, in disregard of the act, than we can exercise a commercial or other power in disregard of an act of congress on the same subject. This view respects the rights of the master and the rights of the state; it neither jeopards nor retards the reclamation of the slave; it removes all state action prejudicial to the rights of the master; and recognises in the state a power to guard and protect its own jurisdiction, and the peace of its citizen. . . .

DISCUSSION

1. *Prigg* held that Article IV, §2, cl. 3, was self-executing (i.e., operated of its own force without the need for implementing congressional legislation) and that it authorized a slaveowner to use self-help in capturing a fugitive slave. The Court held that the 1793 Act was constitutional, at least insofar as it authorized federal judges to render fugitive slaves. The Court also intimated that the statute, if not the Constitution, precluded state courts from playing any role whatever in returning fugitive slaves.[35]

Consider Story's analysis of these issues on the merits—especially in the light of McLean's and Taney's criticisms. Can the Court's approval of self-help be reconciled with the Fifth Amendment's requirement that no person shall be "deprived of life, liberty, or property, without due process of law"?

2. Unlike John Marshall, his jurisprudential ally, Joseph Story, never owned or traded slaves. Story came from Boston, a stronghold of the abolitionist movement,

---

35. The Fugitive Slave Clause aside, the current doctrine is that Congress may choose to make federal jurisdiction exclusive or to grant state courts concurrent jurisdiction over any case arising under federal laws or the Constitution. The history and modern doctrine concerning the duty of state courts to entertain actions based on federal statutes is summarized in Testa v. Katt, 330 U.S. 386 (1947). Justice Black wrote:

> Enforcement of federal laws by state courts did not go unchallenged. Violent public controversies existed throughout the first part of the Nineteenth Century until the 1860's concerning the existence of the constitutional supremacy of the Federal Government. During that period there were instances in which this Court and state courts broadly questioned the power and duty of state courts to exercise their jurisdiction to enforce United States civil and penal statutes or the power of the Federal Government to require them to do so. But after the fundamental issues of federal supremacy had been resolved by war, this Court took occasion in 1876 to review the phase of the controversy concerning the relationship of state courts to the Federal Government. . . . It repudiated the assumption that federal laws can be considered by the states as though they were laws emanating from a foreign sovereign. . . . It asserted that the obligation of states to enforce these federal laws is not lessened by reason of the form in which they are cast or the remedy which they provide.

Consider carefully the implications of Justice Black's assertion that "the fundamental issues of federal supremacy [were] resolved by war." We shall have occasion later to examine in depth whether, as a descriptive matter these issues have been fully resolved even now, see Chapters 5 and 6, infra. But there is also the normative-jurisprudential point as to whether legal controversies should be considered capable of resolution by force of arms.

and he often returned to sit as circuit judge. Judicial enforcement of the fugitive slave law was opposed by the abolitionist bar and, especially after *Prigg*, by extra-legal methods as well.[36] As circuit judge, Story had condemned slavery and, in La Jeune Eugenie, 26 F. Cas. 832 (No. 15,551) (C.C.D. Mass. 1822), he had held, in effect, that the slave trade violated the law of nations.

Yet the introductory paragraphs of Justice Story's opinion indicate that he regarded the issues in *Prigg* as extraordinary. In his history of slavery's influence on the Supreme Court's jurisprudence, Paul Finkelman emphasizes both the fervor of Story's nationalism and his belief that the Union was endangered by the dispute over slavery and over states' willingness to enforce the Fugitive Slave Clause (and Law). Paul Finkelman, Supreme Injustice: Slavery in the Nation's Highest Court (2018).

Story's characterization of the historical significance of the Fugitive Slave Clause may have been more a reflection of the political beliefs of 1842 than those of the adopters of the Constitution in 1787. One leading historian, for example, has written that the "clause was not a significant issue in the Convention. Introduced late in the proceedings by a South Carolina delegate, it aroused little debate and received unanimous approval. There is little evidence to support the assertion frequently made in later years that without the clause the Constitution would have failed."[37] Even if this is true, what is its relevance to determining the weight the clause should be given in 1842?

A different perspective is provided by William Story, the Justice's son, who asserted that his father had sought to sabotage enforcement of the fugitive slave law by "leaving the slaveholder to his constitutional remedy of self-help or to recourse to the federal judges—too few and far between to be of practical value."[38] Assume that he is correct in ascribing such motivation to his father. Would it be proper to choose a particular construction of the Constitution because it would sabotage effective enforcement of a legal right—the return of one's fugitive slaves—that one found repugnant?

3. Professor Jamal Greene, referring to the "human tragedy of the decision [as] breathtaking," has written that "Prigg v. Pennsylvania could easily be called the worst Supreme Court decision ever issued":[39]

> The Court's holding was that the Fugitive Slave Clause prohibited states from subjecting slave catchers to a state-sanctioned civil process, except to prevent "breach of the peace, or any illegal violence." Under the logic of the opinion, however, the kidnapping could not itself be outlawed as "illegal violence." Put otherwise, violence against blacks was "legal" violence; "illegal" violence was violence against whites. The decision abided

---

36. See Robert Cover, Justice Accused (1975). See also Albert J. Von Frank, The Trials of Anthony Burns: Freedom and Slavery and Emerson's Boston (1998).

37. Don Fehrenbacher, The Dred Scott Case 25 (1978).

38. Quoted in Cover, supra n.36, at 241. See also Paul Finkelman, Prigg v. Pennsylvania and Northern State Courts: Anti-Slavery Use of a Pro-Slavery Decision, 25 Civil War Hist. 5 (1979).

39. Jamal Greene, The Anticanon, 125 Harv. L. Rev. 379, 428 (2011). See also Sanford Levinson, Is *Dred Scott* Really the Worst Opinion of All Time? Why *Prigg* is Worse than *Dred Scott* (But Is Likely to Stay Out of the "Anti-Canon"), 125 Harv. L. Rev. Forum 23 (2011), available at http://www.harvard lawreview.org/issues/125/december11/forum_768.php.

> the constant threat of enslavement experienced by free brown-skinned Americans in both the North and the South. By constitutionally forbidding states from preventing private violence against blacks, *Prigg* worked a simultaneous assault on due process and on equal protection, the twin pillars of the modern Fourteenth Amendment. . . .

Of course, the Fourteenth Amendment would not be added to the Constitution for another quarter century. Does the result in *Prigg* follow from the fact that in order to form the Union the participants had to accept the legality of slavery, and therefore also had to accept the prerogative of slaveholders to protect their property? Or is *Prigg* indefensible even given the acceptance of slavery?

NOTE: THE RIGHTS OF FREE BLACK PEOPLE BEFORE THE CIVIL WAR

Prigg v. Pennsylvania is a case about slavery, but its facts also suggest the tenuous position of free Black people before the Civil War. The free Black population of the United States grew steadily in the late eighteenth and early nineteenth centuries, as Black people were freed by their masters, purchased their freedom, or escaped slavery and fled to free states and federal territories.

Whites in free states often resented the influx of free Black people into their states, and passed discriminatory legislation designed to restrict Black immigration. In her history of Black civil rights before the Civil War, Kate Masur writes that "From the outset, settlers in the Old Northwest [where slavery could not exist because of the Northwest Ordinance of 1787] adopted laws that imposed special regulations on free African Americans."[40] Ohio's "black laws," for example, required migrants "to register with county officials and post bonds designed to ensure that they would not become dependent on public relief. They barred African Americans from testifying in court cases involving white people, and they allocated funds for the education of white children only.[41] In addition, the Ohio state constitution restricted the right to vote to white men.

Legislatures routinely justified these laws on the grounds that free Black people were more likely to commit crimes, be unable to support themselves and their families, and become a burden on the community. The black laws were modeled on English poor laws. These laws denied rights and refused public support to transients and vagabonds, who were regarded as not part of the community. Thus, the black laws also treated free Black people, even if law abiding and gainfully employed, as not fully members of the community.

Even some white abolitionists treated free Black people as not part of the American community. The American Colonization Society (ACS), founded in Washington in 1816 by a group of elite white men, sought to solve the problem of slavery and a growing free Black population by removing Black people from the United States and resettling them elsewhere, for example, in Africa. Those white abolitionists who supported colonization as a solution assumed that Blacks and

---

40. Kate Masur, Until Justice Be Done: America's First Civil Rights Movement, From the Revolution to Reconstruction 3 (2021).

41. Id.

whites could not live together peaceably as equals in the United States, and therefore Black people should leave.

Antebellum courts saw few problems with the black laws. Courts treated racial distinctions like any other legislative distinction. Costin v. Corporation of Washington, 6 F. Cas. 612 (C.C.D.C. 1821), considered a constitutional challenge to onerous restrictions imposed by the corporation of the city of Washington, D.C., on persons of color. The city required free persons of color to register with the mayor describing their employment, their family, and their means of subsistence; to obtain a surety bond guaranteeing their good behavior; and to obtain certificates from "three respectable white inhabitants" vouching for their "living peaceably," their character, their ability to support themselves. The defendant was fined for living in Washington, D.C., more than thirty days without complying with the statute.

Judge William Cranch construed the regulation to apply only to new residents of the city. He then rejected a constitutional challenge:

> It is said that the constitution [in Article IV, section 2] gives equal rights to all the citizens of the United States, in the several states. But that clause of the constitution does not prohibit any state from denying to some of its citizens some of the political rights enjoyed by others. In all the states certain qualifications are necessary to the right of suffrage; the right to serve on juries, and the right to hold certain offices; and in most of the states the absence of the African color is among those qualifications. Every state has the right to pass laws to preserve the peace and the morals of society; and if there be a class of people more likely than others to disturb the public peace, or corrupt the public morals, and if that class can be clearly designated, it has a right to impose upon that class, such reasonable terms and conditions of residence, as will guard the state from the evils which it has reason to apprehend. A citizen of one state, coming into another state, can claim only those privileges and immunities which belong to citizens of the latter state, in like circumstances. But the present case is like that of a state legislating in regard to its own citizens, and I can see no reason why it may not require security for good behavior from free persons of color, as well as from vagrants, and persons of ill-fame.

(Note the court's assumption that Article IV, section 2 applied in a federal territory.) *Costin* exemplified antebellum understandings: Even assuming that free Black people were citizens (a view that would later be rejected by the Supreme Court in Dred Scott v. Sanford), race was considered an appropriate ground of distinction between citizens in the antebellum period.[42] A state could treat whites and Blacks differently if it thought that the two groups were different in some respect. This authorized legislatures to engage in stereotypical judgments about Black criminality and inferiority. See also State v. Manuel, 20 N.C. 144 (1838), which held that when free persons of color, as opposed to white persons, could not pay criminal fines, the state could hire them out to anyone willing to pay the fine. The Court explained that "[w]hat would be a slight inconvenience to a free negro, might fall upon a white man as intolerable degradation."

---

42. See Mark A. Graber, *Korematsu*'s Ancestors, 74 Ark. L. Rev. __ (forthcoming 2021).

As more and more Black people settled in free states, they began to organize to protest these kinds of laws, arguing that they should have the same rights as white settlers. Black people also opposed colonization, arguing that they were as American as anyone else and had every right to remain in the country where they were born.

In defense of their cause, advocates of Black civil rights pointed to the Declaration of Independence and the Privileges and Immunities Clause of Article IV, section 2. They sought legislative relief because courts were unsympathetic.

Ohio was a key state in the movement for Black civil rights. It had the largest free Black population and the strongest abolitionist movement. It was also the scene of anti-Black riots by whites in Cincinnati in 1829 and 1836. Black mobilization for civil rights eventually led to a coalition with whites that finally achieved the repeal of Ohio's Black Laws in 1849, in a bill that repealed all state laws that "enforce any special disabilities or confer any special privileges on account of color," although it retained the exclusion of Black people from jury service.[43]

As we will see in Chapter 4, citizenship and rights for free Black citizens would not be guaranteed in the North until the passage of the 1866 Civil Rights Act and the Fourteenth Amendment.

C. *Prelude to Secession*

The historian William Freehling has suggested that we might better call the result of Jefferson's 1803 diplomacy the "Midwest Purchase" rather than the "Louisiana Purchase" if we are really to understand its importance for American history, including American constitutional development.[44]

> [I]n the long run, the name "Louisiana Purchase" mischaracterizes an acquisition largely unfit for Louisiana-style institutions. Before the purchase, America stood equally balanced between North and South. Each section controlled eight states. East of the Mississippi River and the purchase, the North figured to pick up five additional states and the South four. Unless slaveholders and slaves could amass in at least a couple of non-Louisiana areas west of the great river, the purchase lands would make Yankees overwhelmingly powerful in the federal government, compared to masters in Louisiana's Deep South latitudes. Or to put it another

---

43. Masur, supra n.40, at 221. Another area of particular concern was the plight of free Black sailors traveling up and down the East Coast of the United States. Southern States passed laws that required Black sailors to reside in jail while their ships docked in Southern ports. These sailors were then often sold as slaves. As we saw earlier in the discussion notes following New York v. Miln, Justice Johnson held in Elkison v. Deliesseline, 8 F. Cas. 493 (1823), that the South Carolina Negro Seaman's Act violated the Commerce Clause. But the case had little practical effect on Southern practices going forward, and Southern states continued to imprison Black sailors. See Masur, supra, at 175-184.

44. See William W. Freehling, The Louisiana Purchase and the Coming of the Civil War, in The Louisiana Purchase and American Expansion 69-82 (Levinson & Sparrow eds., 2005).

way, the diffusion of American folk to the Louisiana Purchase borderlands had the potential to pitch the republic either uncomfortably or disastrously against the slaveholders.

Antagonism between the North and South increased during the years following *Prigg*, exacerbated by the dispute over what in fact would become the most important political (and constitutional) issue of the 1850s—the status of slavery in the territories. By the so-called Compromise of 1850—Freehling suggests that we call it instead "the Armistice of 1850"[45]—California was admitted to the union as a free state, New Mexico and Utah were organized as territories with the issue of slavery being left to future legislation, the slave trade was abolished in the District of Columbia, and a more stringent fugitive slave law was adopted. The Fugitive Slave Act of 1850 provided for the appointment of federal commissioners, who were authorized to issue certificates of removal on the ex parte testimony or affidavits of slaveholders or their agents. Testimony by the alleged slave was excluded and, as if this were not sufficient to bias the outcome, the Act paid the commissioner $10 for issuing the certificate but only $5 if he denied it. Under the juryless procedure established by the Act, 90 percent of the 332 alleged fugitives tried under it were "despatched southwards."[46]

"[A] prosperous black tailor who had resided in Poughkeepsie[, New York] for many years" was seized by slavecatchers and carried back to South Carolina. "In February 1851 agents arrested a black man in southern Indiana, while his horrified wife and children looked on, and returned him to an owner who claimed him as a slave who had run away nineteen years earlier."[47] In 1856, Margaret Garner, who had escaped from Kentucky to Ohio, was about to be captured by a posse; in response, she slit the throat of a daughter and attempted to kill her remaining three children rather than acquiesce in their return to slavery. When Ohio asked permission to try her for manslaughter, a federal judge ordered the Garners returned to their owners, who "promptly sold them down the river to New Orleans. On the way there one of Margaret's other children achieved the emancipation she had sought for him by drowning after a steamboat collision."[48] Such episodes sparked Northern reaction, and Southerners focused on dramatic instances of public opposition in the North, especially in Boston, where armed soldiers had to be called out to control popular demonstrations against the return of fugitives.[49] In Christina, Pennsylvania, an armed struggle left a slaveowner dead, and the national government indicted anti-slavery participants not only for violation of the Fugitive Slave Law, but also for treason![50]

---

45. See William Freehling, The Road to Disunion: Secessionists at Bay, 1776-1854, at 487 (1990).

46. Id. at 536.

47. James M. McPherson, Battle Cry of Freedom: The Civil War Era 80-81 (1988). As it happened, the tailor had his freedom purchased by Black and white friends.

48. Id. at 121.

49. See id. at 119-120 for a description of the tensions in Boston generated by the return of Anthony Burns to slavery.

50. Id. at 84-85.

Legal attacks proved unavailing: Justice McLean, sitting as a circuit court judge in Miller v. McQuerry, 17 F. Cas. 332 (No. 9,583) (C.C.D. Ohio 1853), rejected a challenge to its constitutionality. In Ableman v. Booth, 62 U.S. (21 How.) 506 (1859), in what, for Taney, was a strikingly nationalist opinion, the Chief Justice wrote for the Court sustaining the Act and holding that a Wisconsin state court could not issue a writ of habeas corpus to free a federal prisoner convicted of violating it:

> [N]o State can authorize one of its judges or courts to exercise judicial power, by habeas corpus or otherwise, within the jurisdiction of another and independent Government. And although the State of Wisconsin is sovereign within its territorial limits to a certain extent, yet that sovereignty is limited and restricted by the Constitution of the United States. . . .
>
> The Constitution was not formed merely to guard the State against danger from foreign nations, but mainly to secure union and harmony at home; . . . and to accomplish this purpose, it was felt by the statesmen who framed the Constitution, and by the people who adopted it, that it was necessary that many of the rights of sovereignty which the States possessed should be ceded to the General Government; and that, in the sphere of action assigned to it, it should be supreme, and strong enough to execute its own laws by its own tribunals, without interruption from a State or from State authorities.

The holding concerning the relation between federal and state courts was entirely consistent with the principles of federalism developed in cases such as McCulloch v. Maryland; it remains the law today.

In 1854, the Missouri Compromise was repealed by the Kansas-Nebraska Act. The Nebraska Territory, which lay north of the 36°30′ limit on slavery, was split into two territories, Kansas and Nebraska. Whether slavery would be established in either territory was to be left up to the settlers themselves. The assumption was that the more northern of the two, Nebraska, would become a free state and that Kansas would, therefore, be likely to become a slave state. In fact, the conflict over Kansas settlement and whether the state would eventually become slave or free—which provoked the term "Bleeding Kansas"—was a central issue in the politics of the late 1850s.[51] The repeal of the Missouri Compromise helped to provoke the founding of the Republican Party, one of whose central policies was "free soil," i.e., no further expansion of slavery.

Together with the increasing Northern anger about the enforcement of the Fugitive Slave Act, the Kansas-Nebraska Act "may have been the most important single event pushing the nation toward civil war"[52] insofar as it led to the destruction of the Whig Party, the rise of the Republican Party, and an ultimately fatal split within the Democratic Party. Professor Graber has suggested that one explanation for the destruction of the existing party system and its replacement

---

51. See, e.g., Kenneth Stampp, America in 1857, ch. 6 (1990); James A. Rawley, Race and Politics: "Bleeding Kansas" and the Coming of the Civil War (1979).

52. McPherson, Battle Cry of Freedom, supra n.47, at 121.

by largely regionally based political parties was the Constitution itself.[53] (Recall the discussion in the Introduction on the "Constitution of Settlement"—those aspects of the Constitution that are not usually litigated.) Article I guarantees that members of Congress are elected by state and local constituencies, the House by popular vote and the Senate (until the Seventeenth Amendment) by state legislators. Hence there is little incentive, when campaigning for congressional office, to appear overly solicitous to interests outside those of one's immediate constituents, including the abstract interests of "the nation" when they directly conflict with local interests. Even the President is elected through the Electoral College, which puts a premium on catering to particular "swing" states rather than obtaining a majority of the national electorate. In 1860, Abraham Lincoln, for example, would, with less than 40 percent of the popular vote, receive a healthy majority of the electoral vote, though without any electoral votes from the Southern states, many of whom denied him a place on their ballots. These structural features of the American Constitution accelerated regional division and undermined parties without a strong regional base.

"Bleeding Kansas" got its name in part from the fact that in 1856, John Brown and five of his sons, as part of guerilla warfare against slaveowners, hacked to death five ostensibly pro-slavery settlers on Pottawottamie Creek, near Lawrence. The United States was clearly at risk, and national institutions like Congress and the presidency had become ever increasingly divided on regional lines, seemingly unable to promise any genuine solutions. Only the Supreme Court remained as a plausible "national" body, and many politicians happily turned to the Court as the last best hope for achieving yet one more compromise that would save the Union. It is against this increasingly heated political background that the *Dred Scott* case must be understood. It directly involved the status of nonfugitive slaves in free states and in the territories and the prerepeal legal consequences of the Missouri Compromise. Perhaps more to the point, it involved the legitimacy of the platform of the Republican Party, which was uncompromising in its opposition to further extension of slavery into the territories.

Dred Scott v. Sandford

60 U.S. (19 How.) 393 (1857)

[The basic facts are set out in the introduction to Chief Justice Taney's opinion:]

The plaintiff was a negro [sic] slave, belonging to Dr. Emerson, who was a surgeon in the army of the United States. In the year 1834, he took the plaintiff from the State of Missouri to the military post at Rock Island, in the State of Illinois, and held him there as a slave until the month of April or May, 1836. At the time last mentioned, said Dr. Emerson removed the plaintiff from said military post at Rock Island to the military post at Fort Snelling, situated on the west bank of the Mississippi river, in the Territory known as Upper Louisiana, acquired

53. See Mark Graber, *Dred Scott* and the Problem of Constitutional Evil (2006).

by the United States of France, and situated north of the latitude of thirty-six degrees thirty minutes north, and north of the State of Missouri. Said Dr. Emerson held the plaintiff in slavery at said Fort Snelling, from said last-mentioned date until the year 1838.

In the year 1835, Harriet, who is named in the second count of the plaintiff's declaration, was the negro slave of Major Taliaferro, who belonged to the army of the United States. In that year, 1835, said Major Taliaferro took said Harriet to said Fort Snelling, a military post, situated as hereinbefore stated, and kept her there as a slave until the year 1836, and then sold and delivered her as a slave, at said Fort Snelling, unto the said Dr. Emerson hereinbefore named. Said Dr. Emerson held said Harriet in slavery at said Fort Snelling until the year 1838.

In the year 1836, the plaintiff and Harriet intermarried, at Fort Snelling, with the consent of Dr. Emerson, who then claimed to be their master and owner. Eliza and Lizzie, named in the third count of the plaintiff's declaration, are the fruit of that marriage. Eliza is about fourteen years old, and was born on board the steamboat Gipsey, north of the north line of the State of Missouri, and upon the river Mississippi. Lizzie is about seven years old, and was born in the State of Missouri, at the military post called Jefferson Barracks.

In the year 1838, said Dr. Emerson removed the plaintiff and said Harriet, and their said daughter Eliza, from said Fort Snelling to the State of Missouri, where they have ever since resided.

Before the commencement of this suit, said Dr. Emerson sold and conveyed the plaintiff, and Harriet, Eliza, and Lizzie, to the defendant, as slaves, and the defendant has ever since claimed to hold them, and each of them, as slaves. . . .

Mr. Chief Justice Taney delivered the opinion of the court.

The plaintiff in error, who was also the plaintiff in the court below, was, with his wife and children, held as slaves by the defendant, in the State of Missouri; and he brought this action in the Circuit Court of the United States for that district, to assert the title of himself and his family to freedom.

. . . The defendant pleaded in abatement to the jurisdiction of the court, that the plaintiff was not a citizen of the State of Missouri, as alleged in his declaration, being a negro of African descent, whose ancestors were of pure African blood, and who were brought into this country and sold as slaves. . . .

[A]lthough [the government of the United States] is sovereign and supreme in its appropriate sphere of action, yet it does not possess all the powers which usually belong to the sovereignty of a nation. Certain specified powers, enumerated in the Constitution, have been conferred upon it; and neither the legislative, executive, nor judicial departments of the Government can lawfully exercise any authority beyond the limits marked out by the Constitution. And in regulating the judicial department, the cases in which the courts of the United States shall have jurisdiction are particularly and specifically enumerated and defined; and they are not authorized to take cognizance of any case which does not come within the description therein specified. . . .

[T]he question to be decided is, whether the facts stated in the plea are sufficient to show that the plaintiff is not entitled to sue as a citizen in a court of the United States. . . .

The question is simply this: Can a negro, whose ancestors were imported into this country, and sold as slaves, become a member of the political community formed and brought into existence by the Constitution of the United States, and as such become entitled to all the rights, and privileges, and immunities, guarantied by that instrument to the citizen? One of which rights is the privilege of suing in a court of the United States in the cases specified in the Constitution.

It will be observed, that the plea applies to that class of persons only whose ancestors were negroes of the African race, and imported into this country, and sold and held as slaves. The only matter in issue before the court, therefore, is, whether the descendants of such slaves, when they shall be emancipated, or who are born of parents who had become free before their birth, are citizens of a State, in the sense in which the word citizen is used in the Constitution of the United States. And this being the only matter in dispute on the pleadings, the court must be understood as speaking in this opinion of that class only, that is, of those persons who are the descendants of Africans who were imported into this country, and sold as slaves.

The situation of this population was altogether unlike that of the Indian race. The latter, it is true, formed no part of the colonial communities, and never amalgamated with them in social connections or in government. But although they were uncivilized, they were yet a free and independent people, associated together in nations or tribes, and governed by their own laws. Many of these political communities were situated in territories to which the white race claimed the ultimate right of dominion. But that claim was acknowledged to be subject to the right of the Indians to occupy it as long as they thought proper, and neither the English nor colonial Governments claimed or exercised any dominion over the tribe or nation by whom it was occupied, nor claimed the right to the possession of the territory, until the tribe or nation consented to cede it. These Indian Governments were regarded and treated as foreign Governments, as much so as if an ocean had separated the red man from the white; and their freedom has constantly been acknowledged, from the time of the first emigration to the English colonies to the present day, by the different Governments which succeeded each other. Treaties have been negotiated with them, and their alliance sought for in war; and the people who compose these Indian political communities have always been treated as foreigners not living under our Government. It is true that the course of events has brought the Indian tribes within the limits of the United States under subjection to the white race; and it has been found necessary, for their sake as well as our own, to regard them as in a state of pupilage, and to legislate to a certain extent over them and the territory they occupy. But they may, without doubt, like the subjects of any other foreign Government, be naturalized by the authority of Congress, and become citizens of a State, and of the United States; and if an individual should leave his nation or tribe, and take up his abode among the white population, he would be entitled to all the rights and privileges which would belong to an emigrant from any other foreign people.

We proceed to examine the case as presented by the pleadings.

The words "people of the United States" and "citizens" are synonymous terms, and mean the same thing. They both describe the political body who, according to our republican institutions, form the sovereignty, and who hold the power and conduct the Government through their representatives. They are what we familiarly call the "sovereign people," and every citizen is one of this people, and a constituent member of this sovereignty. The question before us is, whether the class of persons described in the plea in abatement compose a portion of this people, and are constituent members of this sovereignty? We think they are not, and that they are not included, and were not intended to be included, under the word "citizens" in the Constitution, and can therefore claim none of the rights and privileges which that instrument provides for and secures to citizens of the United States. On the contrary, they were at that time considered as a subordinate and inferior class of beings, who had been subjugated by the dominant race, and, whether emancipated or not, yet remained subject to their authority, and had no rights or privileges but such as those who held the power and the Government might choose to grant them.

It is not the province of the court to decide upon the justice or injustice, the policy or impolicy, of these laws. The decision of that question belonged to the political or law-making power; to those who formed the sovereignty and framed the Constitution. The duty of the court is, to interpret the instrument they have framed, with the best lights we can obtain on the subject, and to administer it as we find it, according to its true intent and meaning when it was adopted.

In discussing this question, we must not confound the rights of citizenship which a State may confer within its own limits, and the rights of citizenship as a member of the Union. It does not by any means follow, because he has all the rights and privileges of a citizen of a State, that he must be a citizen of the United States. He may have all of the rights and privileges of the citizen of a State, and yet not be entitled to the rights and privileges of a citizen in any other State. For, previous to the adoption of the Constitution of the United States, every State had the undoubted right to confer on whomsoever it pleased the character of citizen, and to endow him with all its rights. But this character of course was confined to the boundaries of the State, and gave him no rights or privileges in other States beyond those secured to him by the laws of nations and the comity of States. Nor have the several States surrendered the power of conferring these rights and privileges by adopting the Constitution of the United States. Each State may still confer them upon an alien, or any one it thinks proper, or upon any class or description of persons; yet he would not be a citizen in the sense in which that word is used in the Constitution of the United States, nor entitled to sue as such in one of its courts, nor to the privileges and immunities of a citizen in the other States. The rights which he would acquire would be restricted to the State which gave them. The Constitution has conferred on Congress the right to establish an uniform rule of naturalization, and this right is evidently exclusive, and has always been held by this court to be so. Consequently, no State, since the adoption of the Constitution, can by naturalizing an alien invest him with the rights and privileges secured to a citizen of a State under the Federal Government, although, so far as the State alone was concerned, he would undoubtedly be entitled to the rights of a citizen, and clothed with all the rights and immunities which the Constitution and laws of the State attached to that character.

It is very clear, therefore, that no State can, by any act or law of its own, passed since the adoption of the Constitution, introduce a new member into the political community created by the Constitution of the United States. It cannot make him a member of this community by making him a member of its own. And for the same reason it cannot introduce any person, or description of persons, who were not intended to be embraced in this new political family, which the Constitution brought into existence, but were intended to be excluded from it.

The question then arises, whether the provisions of the Constitution, in relation to the personal rights and privileges to which the citizen of a State should be entitled, embraced the negro African race, at that time in this country, or who might afterwards be imported, who had then or should afterwards be made free in any State; and to put it in the power of a single State to make him a citizen of the United States, and end[ow] him with the full rights of citizenship in every other State without their consent? Does the Constitution of the United States act upon him whenever he shall be made free under the laws of a State, and raised there to the rank of a citizen, and immediately clothe him with all the privileges of a citizen in every other State, and in its own courts?

The court think the affirmative of these propositions cannot be maintained. And if it cannot, the plaintiff in error could not be a citizen of the State of Missouri, within the meaning of the Constitution of the United States, and, consequently, was not entitled to sue in its courts.

It is true, every person, and every class and description of persons, who were at the time of the adoption of the Constitution recognized as citizens in the several States, became also citizens of this new political body; but none other; it was formed by them, and for them and their posterity, but for no one else. And the personal rights and privileges guaranteed to citizens of this new sovereignty were intended to embrace those only who were then members of the several State communities, or who should afterwards by birthright or otherwise become members, according to the provisions of the Constitution and the principles on which it was founded. It was the union of those who were at that time members of distinct and separate political communities into one political family, whose power, for certain specified purposes, was to extend over the whole territory of the United States. And it gave to each citizen rights and privileges outside of his State which he did not before possess, and placed him in every other State upon a perfect equality with its own citizens as to rights of person and rights of property; it made him a citizen of the United States.

It becomes necessary, therefore, to determine who were citizens of the several States when the Constitution was adopted. And in order to do this, we must recur to the Governments and institutions of the thirteen colonies, when they separated from Great Britain and formed new sovereignties, and took their places in the family of independent nations. We must inquire who, at that time, were recognized as the people or citizens of a State, whose rights and liberties had been outraged by the English Government; and who declared their independence, and assumed the powers of Government to defend their rights by force of arms.

In the opinion of the court, the legislation and histories of the times, and the language used in the Declaration of Independence, show, that neither the class of persons who had been imported as slaves, nor their descendants, whether they had become free or not, were then acknowledged as a part of the people, nor intended to be included in the general words used in that memorable instrument.

It is difficult at this day to realize the state of public opinion in relation to that unfortunate race, which prevailed in the civilized and enlightened portions of the world at the time of the Declaration of Independence, and when the Constitution of the United States was framed and adopted. But the public history of every European nation displays it in a manner too plain to be mistaken.

They had for more than a century before been regarded as beings of an inferior order, and altogether unfit to associate with the white race, either in social or political relations; and so far inferior, that they had no rights which the white man was bound to respect; and that the negro might justly and lawfully be reduced to slavery for his benefit. He was bought and sold, and treated as an ordinary article of merchandise and traffic, whenever a profit could be made by it. This opinion was at that time fixed and universal in the civilized portion of the white race. It was regarded as an axiom in morals as well as in politics, which no one thought of disputing, or supposed to be open to dispute; and men in every grade and position in society daily and habitually acted upon it in their private pursuits, as well as in matters of public concern, without doubting for a moment the correctness of this opinion.

And in no nation was this opinion more firmly fixed or more uniformly acted upon than by the English Government and English people. They not only seized them on the coast of Africa, and sold them or held them in slavery for their own use; but they took them as ordinary articles of merchandise to every country where they could make a profit on them, and were far more extensively engaged in this commerce than any other nation in the world.

The opinion thus entertained and acted upon in England was naturally impressed upon the colonies they founded on this side of the Atlantic. And, accordingly, a negro of the African race was regarded by them as an article of property, and held, and bought and sold as such, in every one of the thirteen colonies which united in the Declaration of Independence, and afterwards formed the Constitution of the United States. The slaves were more or less numerous in the different colonies, as slave labor was found more or less profitable. But no one seems to have doubted the correctness of the prevailing opinion of the time.

The legislation of the different colonies furnishes positive and indisputable proof of this fact.

It would be tedious, in this opinion, to enumerate the various laws they passed upon this subject. It will be sufficient, as a sample of the legislation which then generally prevailed throughout the British colonies, to give the laws of two of them; one being still a large slaveholding State, and the other the first State in which slavery ceased to exist.

The province of Maryland, in 1717, passed a law declaring "that if any free negro or mulatto intermarry with any white woman, or if any white man shall intermarry with any negro or mulatto woman, such negro or mulatto shall become a slave during life, excepting mulattoes born of white women, who, for such intermarriage, shall only become servants for seven years, to be disposed of as the justices of the county court, where such marriage so happens, shall think fit; to be applied by them towards the support of a public school within the said county. And any white man or white woman who shall intermarry as aforesaid, with any negro or mulatto, such white man or white woman shall become servants during the term of seven years, and shall be disposed of by the justices as aforesaid, and be applied to the uses aforesaid."

The other colonial law to which we refer was passed by Massachusetts in 1705. It is entitled "An act for the better preventing of a spurious and mixed issue," &c.; and it provides . . . "that none of her Majesty's English or Scottish subjects, nor of any other Christian nation, within this province, shall contract matrimony with any negro or mulatto; nor shall any person, duly authorized to solemnize marriage, presume to join any such in marriage, on pain of forfeiting the sum of fifty pounds. . . ."

We give both of these laws in the words used by the respective legislative bodies, because the language in which they are framed, as well as the provisions contained in them, show, too plainly to be misunderstood, the degraded condition of this unhappy race. They were still in force when the Revolution began, and are a faithful index to the state of feeling towards the class of persons of whom they speak, and of the position they occupied throughout the thirteen colonies, in the eyes and thoughts of the men who framed the Declaration of Independence and established the State Constitutions and Governments. They show that a perpetual and impassable barrier was intended to be erected between the white race and the one which they had reduced to slavery, and governed as subjects with absolute and despotic power, and which they then looked upon as so far below them in the scale of created beings, that intermarriages between white persons and negroes or mulattoes were regarded as unnatural and immoral, and punished as crimes, not only in the parties, but in the person who joined them in marriage. And no distinction in this respect was made between the free negro or mulatto and the slave, but this stigma, of the deepest degradation, was fixed upon the whole race. We refer to these historical facts for the purpose of showing the fixed opinions concerning that race, upon which the statesmen of that day spoke and acted. It is necessary to do this, in order to determine whether the general terms used in the Constitution of the United States, as to the rights of man and the rights of the people, was intended to include them, or to give to them or their posterity the benefit of any of its provisions.

The language of the Declaration of Independence is equally conclusive:

It begins by declaring that, "when in the course of human events it becomes necessary for one people to dissolve the political bands which have connected them with another, and to assume among the powers of the earth the separate and equal station to which the laws of nature and nature's God entitle them, a decent respect for the opinions of mankind requires that they should declare the causes which impel them to the separation."

It then proceeds to say: "We hold these truths to be self-evident: that all men are created equal; that they are endowed by their Creator with certain unalienable rights; that among them is life, liberty, and the pursuit of happiness; that to secure these rights, Governments are instituted, deriving their just powers from the consent of the governed."

The general words above quoted would seem to embrace the whole human family, and if they were used in a similar instrument at this day would be so understood. But it is too clear for dispute, that the enslaved African race were not intended to be included, and formed no part of the people who framed and adopted this declaration; for if the language, as understood in that day, would embrace them, the conduct of the distinguished men who framed the Declaration of Independence would have been utterly and flagrantly inconsistent with the principles they asserted; and instead of the sympathy of mankind, to which they so confidently appealed, they would have deserved and received universal rebuke and reprobation.

Yet the men who framed this declaration were great men—high in literary acquirements—high in their sense of honor, and incapable of asserting principles inconsistent with those on which they were acting. They perfectly understood the meaning of the language they used, and how it would be understood by others; and they knew that it would not in any part of the civilized world be supposed to embrace the negro race, which, by common consent, had been excluded from civilized Governments and the family of nations, and doomed to slavery. They spoke and acted according to the then established doctrines and principles, and in the ordinary language of the day, and no one misunderstood them. The unhappy black race were separated from the white by indelible marks, and laws long before established, and were never thought of or spoken of except as property, and when the claims of the owner or the profit of the trader were supposed to need protection.

This state of public opinion had undergone no change when the Constitution was adopted, as is equally evident from its provisions and language.

The brief preamble sets forth by whom it was formed, for what purposes, and for whose benefit and protection. It declares that it is formed by the people of the United States; that is to say, by those who were members of the different political communities in the several States; and its great object is declared to be to secure the blessings of liberty to themselves and their posterity. It speaks in general terms of the people of the United States, and of citizens of the several States, when it is providing for the exercise of the powers granted or the privileges secured to the citizen. It does not define what description of persons are intended to be included under these terms, or who shall be regarded as a citizen and one of the people. It uses them as terms so well understood, that no further description or definition was necessary.

But there are two clauses in the Constitution which point directly and specifically to the negro race as a separate class of persons, and show clearly that they were not regarded as a portion of the people or citizens of the Government then formed.

One of these clauses reserves to each of the thirteen States the right to import slaves until the year 1808, if it thinks proper. And the importation which it thus sanctions was unquestionably of persons of the race of which we are speaking, as the traffic in slaves in the United States had always been confined to them. And by the other provision the States pledge themselves to each other to maintain the right of property of the master, by delivering up to him any slave who may have escaped from his service, and be found within their respective territories. By the first abovementioned clause, therefore, the right to purchase and hold this property is directly sanctioned and authorized for twenty years by the people who framed the Constitution. And by the second, they pledge themselves to maintain and uphold the right of the master in the manner specified, as long as the Government they then formed should endure. And these two provisions show, conclusively, that neither the description of persons therein referred to, nor their descendants, were embraced in any of the other provisions of the Constitution; for certainly these two clauses were not intended to confer on them or their posterity the blessings of liberty, or any of the personal rights so carefully provided for the citizen.

No one of that race had ever migrated to the United States voluntarily; all of them had been brought here as articles of merchandise. The number that had been emancipated at that time were but few in comparison with those held in slavery; and they were identified in the public mind with the race to which they belonged, and regarded as a part of the slave population rather than the free. It is obvious that they were not even in the minds of the framers of the Constitution when they were conferring special rights and privileges upon the citizens of a State in every other part of the Union.

Indeed, when we look to the condition of this race in the several States at the time, it is impossible to believe that these rights and privileges were intended to be extended to them.

It is very true, that in that portion of the Union where the labor of the negro race was found to be unsuited to the climate and unprofitable to the master, but few slaves were held at the time of the Declaration of Independence; and when the Constitution was adopted, it had entirely worn out in one of them, and measures had been taken for its gradual abolition in several others. But this change had not been produced by any change of opinion in relation to this race; but because it was discovered, from experience, that slave labor was unsuited to the climate and productions of these States: for some of the States, where it had ceased or nearly ceased to exist, were actively engaged in the slave trade, procuring cargoes on the coast of Africa, and transporting them for sale to those parts of the Union where their labor was found to be profitable, and suited to the climate and productions. And this traffic was openly carried on, and fortunes accumulated by it, without reproach from the people of the States where they resided. And it can hardly be supposed that, in the States where it was then countenanced in its worst form—that is, in the seizure and transportation—the people could have regarded those who were emancipated as entitled to equal rights with themselves.

And we may here again refer, in support of this proposition, to the plain and unequivocal language of the laws of the several States, some passed after the Declaration of Independence and before the Constitution was adopted, and some since the Government went into operation.

We need not refer, on this point, particularly to the laws of the present slaveholding States. Their statute books are full of provisions in relation to this class, in the same spirit with the Maryland law which we have before quoted. They have continued to treat them as an inferior class, and to subject them to strict police regulations, drawing a broad line of distinction between the citizen and the slave races, and legislating in relation to them upon the same principle which prevailed at the time of the Declaration of Independence. As relates to these States, it is too plain for argument, that they have never been regarded as a part of the people or citizens of the State, nor supposed to possess any political rights which the dominant race might not withhold or grant at their pleasure. And as long ago as 1822, the Court of Appeals of Kentucky decided that free negroes and mulattoes were not citizens within the meaning of the Constitution of the United States; and the correctness of this decision is recognized, and the same doctrine affirmed, in 1 Meigs's Tenn. Reports, 331.

And if we turn to the legislation of the States where slavery had worn out, or measures taken for its speedy abolition, we shall find the same opinions and principles equally fixed and equally acted upon.

Thus, Massachusetts, in 1786, passed a law similar to the colonial one of which we have spoken. The law of 1786, like the law of 1705, forbids the marriage of any white person with any negro, Indian, or mulatto, and inflicts a penalty of fifty pounds upon any one who shall join them in marriage; and declares all such marriage absolutely null and void, and degrades thus the unhappy issue of the marriage by fixing upon it the stain of bastardy. And this mark of degradation was renewed, and again impressed upon the race, in the careful and deliberate preparation of their revised code published in 1836. This code forbids any person from joining in marriage any white person with any Indian, negro, or mulatto, and subjects the party who shall offend in this respect, to imprisonment, not exceeding six months, in the common jail, or to hard labor, and to a fine of not less than fifty nor more than two hundred dollars; and, like the law of 1786, it declares the marriage to be absolutely null and void. It will be seen that the punishment is increased by the code upon the person who shall marry them, by adding imprisonment to a pecuniary penalty.

So, too, in Connecticut. We refer more particularly to the legislation of this State, because it was not only among the first to put an end to slavery within its own territory, but was the first to fix a mark of reprobation upon the African slave trade. . . .

[W]e find that in the same statute passed in 1774, which prohibited the further importation of slaves into the State, there is also a provision by which any negro, Indian, or mulatto servant, who was found wandering out of the town or place to which he belonged, without a written pass such as is therein described, was made liable to be seized by any one, and taken before the next authority to be examined and delivered up to his master—who was required to pay the charge which had accrued thereby. And a subsequent section of the same law provides, that if any free negro shall travel without such pass, and shall be stopped, seized, or taken up, he shall pay all charges arising thereby. And this law was in full operation when the Constitution of the United States was adopted, and was not repealed till 1797. So that up to that time free negroes and mulattoes were associated with servants and slaves in the police regulations established by the laws of the State.

And again, in 1833, Connecticut passed another law, which made it penal to set up or establish any school in that State for the instruction of persons of the African race not inhabitants of the State, or to instruct or teach in any such school or institution, or board or harbor for that purpose, any such person, without the previous consent in writing of the civil authority of the town in which such school or institution might be.

And it appears by the case of Crandall v. The State, reported in 10 Conn. Rep., 340, that upon an information filed against Prudence Crandall for a violation of this law, one of the points raised in the defence was, that the law was a violation of the Constitution of the United States; and that the persons instructed, although of the African race, were citizens of other States, and therefore entitled to the rights and privileges of citizens in the State of Connecticut. But Chief Justice Dagget, before whom the case was tried, held, that persons of that description were not citizens of a State, within the meaning of the word citizen in the Constitution of the United States, and were not therefore entitled to the privileges and immunities of citizens in other States.

The case was carried up to the Supreme Court of Errors of the State, and the question fully argued there. But the case went off upon another point, and no opinion was expressed on this question. . . .

[Discussion of the laws of New Hampshire and Rhode Island is omitted.]

It would be impossible to enumerate and compress in the space usually allotted to an opinion of a court, the various laws, marking the condition of this race, which were passed from time to time after the Revolution, and before and since the adoption of the Constitution of the United States. In addition to those already referred to, it is sufficient to say, that Chancellor Kent, whose accuracy and research no one will question, states in the sixth edition of his Commentaries (published in 1848, 2 vol., 258, note b) that in no part of the country except Maine, did the African race, in point of fact, participate equally with the whites in the exercise of civil and political rights.

The legislation of the States therefore shows, in a manner not to be mistaken, the inferior and subject condition of that race at the time the Constitution was adopted, and long afterwards, throughout the thirteen States by which that instrument was framed; and it is hardly consistent with the respect due to these States, to suppose that they regarded at that time, as fellow-citizens and members of the sovereignty, a class of beings whom they had thus stigmatized; whom, as we are bound, out of respect to the State sovereignties, to assume they had deemed it just and necessary thus to stigmatize, and upon whom they had impressed such deep and enduring marks of inferiority and degradation; or, that when they met in convention to form the Constitution, they looked upon them as a portion of their constituents, or designed to include them in the provisions so carefully inserted for the security and protection of the liberties and rights of their citizens. It cannot be supposed that they intended to secure to them rights, and privileges, and rank, in the new political body throughout the Union, which every one of them denied within the limits of its own dominion. More especially, it cannot be believed that the large slaveholding States regarded them as included in the word citizens, or would have consented to a Constitution which might compel them to receive them in that character from another State. For if they were so received, and entitled to the privileges and immunities of citizens, it would exempt them from the operation of the special laws and from the police regulations which they considered to be necessary for their own safety. It would give to persons of the negro race, who were recognized as citizens in any one State of the Union, the right to enter every other State whenever they pleased, singly or in companies, without pass or passport, and without obstruction, to sojourn there as long as they pleased, to go where they pleased at every hour of the day or night without molestation, unless they committed some violation of law for which a white man would be punished; and it would give them the full liberty of speech in public and in private upon all subjects upon which its own citizens might speak; to hold public meetings upon political affairs, and to keep and carry arms wherever they went. And all of this would be done in the face of the subject race of the same color, both free and slaves, and inevitably producing discontent and insubordination among them, and endangering the peace and safety of the State.

It is impossible, it would seem, to believe that the great men of the slaveholding States, who took so large a share in framing the Constitution of the United States, and exercised so much influence in procuring its adoption, could have been so forgetful or regardless of their own safety and the safety of those who trusted and confided in them.

Besides, this want of foresight and care would have been utterly inconsistent with the caution displayed in providing for the admission of new members into this political family. For, when they gave to the citizens of each State the privileges and immunities of citizens in the several States, they at the same time took from the several States the power of naturalization, and confined that power exclusively to the Federal Government. No State was willing to permit another State to determine who should or should not be admitted as one of its citizens, and entitled to demand equal rights and privileges with their own people, within their own territories. The right of naturalization was therefore, with one accord, surrendered by the States, and confided to the Federal Government. And this power granted to Congress to establish an uniform rule of naturalization is, by the well-understood meaning of the word, confined to persons born in a foreign country, under a foreign Government. It is not a power to raise to the rank of a citizen any one born in the United States, who, from birth or parentage, by the laws of the country, belongs to an inferior and subordinate class. And when we find the States guarding themselves from the indiscreet or improper admission by other States of emigrants from other countries, by giving the power exclusively to Congress, we cannot fail to see that they could never have left with the States a much more important power—that is, the power of transforming into citizens a numerous class of persons, who in that character would be much more dangerous to the peace and safety of a large portion of the Union, than the few foreigners one of the States might improperly naturalize. The Constitution upon its adoption obviously took from the States all power by any subsequent legislation to introduce as a citizen into the political family of the United States any one, no matter where he was born, or what might be his character or condition; and it gave to Congress the power to confer this character upon those only who were born outside of the dominions of the United States. And no law of a State, therefore, passed since the Constitution was adopted, can give any right of citizenship outside of its own territory.

A clause similar to the one in the Constitution, in relation to the rights and immunities of citizens of one State in the other States, was contained in the Articles of Confederation. But there is a difference of language, which is worthy of note. The provision in the Articles of Confederation was, "that the free inhabitants of each of the States, paupers, vagabonds, and fugitives from justice, excepted, should be entitled to all the privileges and immunities of free citizens in the several States."

It will be observed, that under this Confederation, each State had the right to decide for itself, and in its own tribunals, whom it would acknowledge as a free inhabitant of another State. The term free inhabitant, in the generality of its terms, would certainly include one of the African race who had been manumitted. But no example, we think, can be found of his admission to all the privileges of citizenship in any State of the Union after these Articles were formed, and while they continued in force. And, notwithstanding the generality of the words "free inhabitants," it is very clear that, according to their accepted meaning in that day, they did not include the African race, whether free or not: for the fifth section of the ninth article provides that Congress should have the power "to agree upon the number of land forces to be raised, and to make requisitions from each State for its quota in proportion to the number of white inhabitants in such State, which requisition should be binding."

Words could hardly have been used which more strongly mark the line of distinction between the citizen and the subject; the free and the subjugated races. The latter were not even counted when the inhabitants of a State were to be embodied in proportion to its numbers for the general defence. And it cannot for a moment be supposed, that a class of persons thus separated and rejected from those who formed the sovereignty of the States, were yet intended to be included under the words "free inhabitants," in the preceding article, to whom privileges and immunities were so carefully secured in every State.

But although this clause of the Articles of Confederation is the same in principle with that inserted in the Constitution, yet the comprehensive word inhabitant, which might be construed to include an emancipated slave, is omitted; and the privilege is confined to citizens of the State. And this alteration in words would hardly have been made, unless a different meaning was intended to be conveyed, or a possible doubt removed. The just and fair inference is, that as this privilege was about to be placed under the protection of the General Government, and the words expounded by its tribunals, and all power in relation to it taken from the State and its courts, it was deemed prudent to describe with precision and caution the persons to whom this high privilege was given—and the word citizen was on that account substituted for the words free inhabitant. The word citizen excluded, and no doubt intended to exclude, foreigners who had not become citizens of some one of the States when the Constitution was adopted; and also every description of persons who were not fully recognized as citizens in the several States. This, upon any fair construction of the instruments to which we have referred, was evidently the object and purpose of this change of words.

To all this mass of proof we have still to add, that Congress has repeatedly legislated upon the same construction of the Constitution that we have given. Three laws, two of which were passed almost immediately after the Government went into operation, will be abundantly sufficient to show this. The two first are particularly worthy of notice, because many of the men who assisted in framing the Constitution, and took an active part in procuring its adoption, were then in the halls of legislation, and certainly understood what they meant when they used the words "people of the United States" and "citizen" in that well-considered instrument.

The first of these acts is the naturalization law, which was passed at the second session of the first Congress, March 26, 1790, and confines the right of becoming citizens "to aliens being free white persons."

Now, the Constitution does not limit the power of Congress in this respect to white persons. And they may, if they think proper, authorize the naturalization of any one, of any color, who was born under allegiance to another Government. But the language of the law above quoted, shows that citizenship at that time was perfectly understood to be confined to the white race; and that they alone constituted the sovereignty in the Government.

Congress might, as we before said, have authorized the naturalization of Indians, because they were aliens and foreigners. But, in their then untutored and savage state, no one would have thought of admitting them as citizens in a civilized community. And, moreover, the atrocities they had but recently committed, when they were the allies of Great Britain in the Revolutionary war, were yet fresh in the recollection of the people of the United States, and they were even then guarding themselves against the threatened renewal of Indian hostilities. No one supposed then that any Indian would ask for, or was capable of enjoying, the privileges of an American citizen, and the word white was not used with any particular reference to them.

Neither was it used with any reference to the African race imported into or born in this country; because Congress had no power to naturalize them, and therefore there was no necessity for using particular words to exclude them.

It would seem to have been used merely because it followed out the line of division which the Constitution has drawn between the citizen race, who formed and held the Government, and the African race, which they held in subjection and slavery, and governed at their own pleasure.

Another of the early laws of which we have spoken, is the first militia law, which was passed in 1792, at the first session of the second Congress. The language of this law is equally plain and significant with the one just mentioned. It directs that every "free able-bodied white male citizen" shall be enrolled in the militia. The word white is evidently used to exclude the African race, and the word "citizen" to exclude unnaturalized foreigners; the latter forming no part of the sovereignty, owing it no allegiance, and therefore under no obligation to defend it. The African race, however, born in the country, did owe allegiance to the Government, whether they were slave or free; but it is repudiated, and rejected from the duties and obligations of citizenship in marked language.

The third act to which we have alluded is even still more decisive; it was passed as late as 1813 (2 Stat., 809) and it provides: "That from and after the termination of the war in which the United States are now engaged with Great Britain, it shall not be lawful to employ, on board of any public or private vessels of the United States, any person or persons except citizens of the United States, or persons of color, natives of the United States." Here the line of distinction is drawn in express words. Persons of color, in the judgment of Congress, were not included in the word citizens, and they are described as another and different class of persons, and authorized to be employed, if born in the United States. . . .

The conduct of the Executive Department of the Government has been in perfect harmony upon this subject with this course of legislation. The question was brought officially before the late William Wirt, when he was the Attorney General of the United States, in 1821, and he decided that the words "citizens of the United States" were used in the acts of Congress in the same sense as in the Constitution; and that free persons of color were not citizens, within the meaning of the Constitution and laws; and this opinion has been confirmed by that of the late Attorney General, Caleb Cushing, in a recent case, and acted upon by the Secretary of State, who refused to grant passports to them as "citizens of the United States." But it is said that a person may be a citizen, and entitled to that character, although he does not possess all the rights which may belong to other citizens; as, for example, the right to vote, or to hold particular offices; and that yet, when he goes into another State, he is entitled to be recognized there as a citizen, although the State may measure his rights by the rights which it allows to persons of a like character or class resident in the State, and refuse to him the full rights of citizenship.

This argument overlooks the language of the provision in the Constitution of which we are speaking.

Undoubtedly, a person may be a citizen, that is, a member of the community who form the sovereignty, although he exercises no share of the political power, and is incapacitated from holding particular offices. Women and minors, who form a part of the political family, cannot vote; and when a property qualification is required to vote or hold a particular office, those who have not the necessary qualification cannot vote or hold the office, yet they are citizens.

So, too, a person may be entitled to vote by the law of the State, who is not a citizen even of the State itself. And in some of the States of the Union foreigners not naturalized are allowed to vote. And the State may give the right to free negroes and mulattoes, but that does not make them citizens of the State, and still less of the United States. And the provision in the Constitution giving privileges and immunities in other States, does not apply to them.

Neither does it apply to a person who, being the citizen of a State, migrates to another State. For then he becomes subject to the laws of the State in which he lives, and he is no longer a citizen of the State from which he removed. And the State in which he resides may then, unquestionably, determine his status or condition, and place him among the class of persons who are not recognized as citizens, but belong to an inferior and subject race; and may deny him the privileges and immunities enjoyed by its citizens.

But so far as mere rights of person are concerned, the provision in question is confined to citizens of a State who are temporarily in another State without taking up their residence there. It gives them no political rights in the State, as to voting or holding office, or in any other respect. For a citizen of one State has no right to participate in the government of another. But if he ranks as a citizen in the State to which he belongs, within the meaning of the Constitution of the United States, then, whenever he goes into another State, the Constitution clothes him, as to the rights of person, with all the privileges and immunities which belong to citizens of the State. And if persons of the African race are citizens of a State, and of the United States, they would be entitled to all of these privileges and immunities in every State, and the State could not restrict them; for they would hold these privileges and immunities under the paramount authority of the Federal Government, and its courts would be bound to maintain and enforce them, the Constitution and laws of the State to the contrary notwithstanding. And if the States could limit or restrict them, or place the party in an inferior grade, this clause of the Constitution would be unmeaning, and could have no operation; and would give no rights to the citizen when in another State. He would have none but what the State itself chose to allow him. This is evidently not the construction or meaning of the clause in question. It guaranties rights to the citizen, and the State cannot withhold them. And these rights are of a character and would lead to consequences which make it absolutely certain that the African race were not included under the name of citizens of a State, and were not in the contemplation of the framers of the Constitution when these privileges and immunities were provided for the protection of the citizen in other States. . . .

The only two provisions which point to them and include them, treat them as property, and make it the duty of the Government to protect it; no other power, in relation to this race, is to be found in the Constitution; and as it is a Government of special, delegated, powers, no authority beyond these two provisions can be constitutionally exercised. The Government of the United States had no right to interfere for any other purpose but that of protecting the rights of the owner, leaving it altogether with the several States to deal with this race, whether emancipated or not, as each State may think justice, humanity, and the interests and safety of society, require. The States evidently intended to reserve this power exclusively to themselves.

No one, we presume, supposes that any change in public opinion or feeling, in relation to this unfortunate race, in the civilized nations of Europe or in this country, should induce the court to give to the words of the Constitution a more liberal construction in their favor than they were intended to bear when the instrument was framed and adopted. Such an argument would be altogether inadmissible in any tribunal called on to interpret it. If any of its provisions are deemed unjust, there is a mode prescribed in the instrument itself by which it may be amended; but while it remains unaltered, it must be construed now as it was understood at the time of its adoption. It is not only the same in words, but the same in meaning, and delegates the same powers to the Government, and reserves and secures the same rights and privileges to the citizen; and as long as it continues to exist in its present form, it speaks not only in the same words, but with the same meaning and intent with which it spoke when it came from the hands of its framers, and was voted on and adopted by the people of the United States. Any other rule of construction would abrogate the judicial character of this court, and make it the mere reflex of the popular opinion or passion of the day. This court was not created by the Constitution for such purposes. Higher and graver trusts have been confided to it, and it must not falter in the path of duty.

What the construction was at that time, we think can hardly admit of doubt. We have the language of the Declaration of Independence and of the Articles of Confederation, in addition to the plain words of the Constitution itself; we have the legislation of the different States, before, about the time, and since, the Constitution was adopted; we have the legislation of Congress, from the time of its adoption to a recent period; and we have the constant and uniform action of the Executive Department, all concurring together, and leading to the same result. And if anything in relation to the construction of the Constitution can be regarded as settled, it is that which we now give to the word "citizen" and the word "people."

And upon a full and careful consideration of the subject, the court is of opinion, that, upon the facts stated in the plea in abatement, Dred Scott was not a citizen of Missouri within the meaning of the Constitution of the United States, and not entitled as such to sue in its courts. . . .

CURTIS, J., dissenting. . . .

To determine whether any free persons, descended from Africans held in slavery, were citizens of the United States under the Confederation, and consequently at the time of the adoption of the Constitution of the United States, it is only necessary to know whether any such persons were citizens of either of the States under the Confederation, at the time of the adoption of the Constitution.

Of this there can be no doubt. At the time of the ratification of the Articles of Confederation, all free native-born inhabitants of the States of New Hampshire, Massachusetts, New York, New Jersey, and North Carolina, though descended from African slaves, were not only citizens of those States, but such of them as had the other necessary qualifications possessed the franchise of electors, on equal terms with other citizens. . . . [A discussion of state electoral laws is omitted.]

New York, by its Constitution of 1820, required colored persons to have some qualifications as prerequisites for voting, which white persons need not possess. And New Jersey, by its present Constitution, restricts the right to vote to white male citizens. But these changes can have no other effect upon the present inquiry, except to show, that before they were made, no such restrictions existed; and colored in common with white persons, were not only citizens of those States, but entitled to the elective franchise on the same qualifications as white persons, as they now are in New Hampshire and Massachusetts. I shall not enter into an examination of the existing opinions of that period respecting the African race, nor into any discussion concerning the meaning of those who asserted, in the Declaration of Independence, that all men are created equal; that they are endowed by their Creator with certain inalienable rights; that among these are life, liberty, and the pursuit of happiness. My own opinion is, that a calm comparison of these assertions of universal abstract truths, and of their own individual opinions and acts, would not leave these men under any reproach of inconsistency; that the great truths they asserted on that solemn occasion, they were ready and anxious to make effectual, wherever a necessary regard to circumstances, which no statesman can disregard without producing more evil than good, would allow; and that it would not be just to them, nor true in itself, to allege that they intended to say that the Creator of all men had endowed the white race, exclusively, with the great natural rights which the Declaration of Independence asserts. But this is not the place to vindicate their memory. . . .

The fourth of the fundamental articles of the Confederation was as follows: "The free inhabitants of each of these States, paupers, vagabonds, and fugitives from justice, excepted, shall be entitled to all the privileges and immunities of free citizens in the several States." The fact that free persons of color were citizens of some of the several States, and the consequence, that this fourth article of the Confederation would have the effect to confer on such persons the privileges and immunities of general citizenship, were not only known to those who framed and adopted those articles, but the evidence is decisive, that the fourth article was intended to have that effect, and that more restricted language, which would have excluded such persons, was deliberately and purposely rejected.

On the 25th of June, 1778, the Articles of Confederation being under consideration by the Congress, the delegates from South Carolina moved to amend this fourth article, by inserting after the word "free," and before the word "inhabitants," the word "white," so that the privileges and immunities of general citizenship would be secured only to white persons. Two States voted for the amendment, eight States against it, and the vote of one State was divided. The language of the article stood unchanged, and both by its terms of inclusion, "free inhabitants," and the strong implication from its terms of exclusion, "paupers, vagabonds, and fugitives from justice," who alone were excepted, it is clear, that under the Confederation, and at the time of the adoption of the Constitution, free colored persons of African descent might be, and, by reason of their citizenship in certain States, were entitled to the privileges and immunities of general citizenship of the United States.

Did the Constitution of the United States deprive them or their descendants of citizenship?

That Constitution was ordained and established by the people of the United States, through the action, in each State, of those persons who were qualified by its laws to act thereon, in behalf of themselves and all other citizens of that State. In some of the States, as we have seen, colored persons were among those qualified by law to act on this subject. . . . It would be strange, if we were to find in that instrument anything which deprived of their citizenship any part of the people of the United States who were among those by whom it was established. I can find nothing in the Constitution which proprio vigore, deprives of their citizenship any class of persons who were citizens of the United States at the time of its adoption, or who should be native-born citizens of any State after its adoption; nor any power enabling Congress to disfranchise persons born on the soil of any State, and entitled to citizenship of such State by its Constitution and laws. And my opinion is, that, under the Constitution of the United States, every free person born on the soil of a State, who is a citizen of that State by force of its Constitution or laws, is also a citizen of the United States. . . .

It has been . . . objected, that if free colored persons born within a particular State, and made citizens of that State by its Constitution and laws, are thereby made citizens of the United States, then, under the second section of the fourth article of the Constitution, such persons would be entitled to all the privileges and immunities of citizens in the several states; and if so, then colored persons could vote, and be eligible to not only Federal, but offices even in those States whose Constitutions and laws disqualify colored persons from voting or being elected to office.

But this position rests upon an assumption which I deem untenable. Its basis is, that no one can be deemed a citizen of the United States who is not entitled to enjoy all the privileges and franchises which are conferred on any citizen. That this is not true, under the Constitution of the United States, seems to be clear.

. . . So, in all the States, numerous persons, though citizens, cannot vote, or cannot hold office, either on account of their age, or sex, or that want of the necessary legal qualifications. The truth is, that citizenship, under the Constitution of the United States, is not dependent on the possession of any particular political or even of all civil rights; and any attempt so to define it must lead to error. To what citizens the elective franchise shall be confided, is a question to be determined by each State, in accordance with its own views of the necessities or expediencies of its condition. What civil rights shall be enjoyed by its citizens, and whether all shall enjoy the same, or how they may be gained or lost, are to be determined in the same way.

. . . [T]his clause of the Constitution does not confer on the citizens of one State, in all other States, specific and enumerated privileges and immunities. They are entitled to such as belong to citizenship, but not to such as belong to particular citizens attended by other qualifications. . . . It rests with the States themselves so to frame their Constitutions and laws as not to attach a particular privilege or immunity to mere naked citizenship. . . .

It has sometimes been urged that colored persons are shown not to be citizens of the United States by the fact that the naturalization laws apply only to white persons. But whether a person born in the United States be or be not a citizen, cannot depend on laws which refer only to aliens, and do not affect the *status* of persons born in the United States. The utmost effect which can be attributed to them is, to show that Congress has not deemed it expedient generally to apply the rule to colored aliens. That they might do so, if thought fit, is clear. . . .

I do not deem it necessary to review at length the legislation of Congress having more or less bearing on the citizenship of colored persons. It does not seem to me to have any considerable tendency to prove that it has been considered by the legislative department of the Government, that no such persons are citizens of the United States. Undoubtedly they have been debarred from the exercise of particular rights or privileges extended to white persons, but, I believe, always in terms which, by implication, admit they may be citizens. Thus the act of May 17, 1792, for the organization of the militia, directs the enrollment of "every free, able-bodied, white male citizen." An assumption that none but white persons are citizens, would be as inconsistent with the just import of this language, as that all citizens are able-bodied, or males. . . .

DISCUSSION

1. Taney believed that the decision in *Dred Scott* would settle the slavery issue. Instead, the decision became the nation's symbol of the irreconcilable division between North and South.

2. *The regulation of slavery in the federal territories. Dred Scott* is a case of enormous complexity, involving many interlocking issues. Today its most (in)famous holding is the claim that Black people could not be citizens. One might think that the

Court, having found a lack of jurisdiction, might have ended its discussion there. Nevertheless, the majority went on to discuss other substantive issues, including, most importantly, the constitutionality of the Missouri Compromise of 1820. That Act had declared that slavery and involuntary servitude, except as a punishment for crime, were "forever prohibited" in the Louisiana Territory north of the compromise line of 36°30′ north latitude, with the exception of the state of Missouri, which entered the Union as a slave state.

Dred Scott argued that when he and his wife Harriet traveled out of Missouri into the Upper Louisiana Territory, they became free, because slavery could not exist there; hence when they returned to Missouri they became citizens of that state. Scott also argued that he was free because Emerson took him to Rock Island in Illinois, a free state. Taney did not mention a third possible claim: that Eliza, having been born "north of the north line of the State of Missouri" had a legal status different from her father.

Taney disposed of the second claim, concerning the trip to Illinois, on the authority of Strader v. Graham 51 U.S. (10 How.) 82 (1851). Applied to this case, *Strader* held that the law of Missouri, from which the plaintiffs traveled and to which they returned, and not the law of Illinois, determined Dred and Harriet's status. Under Missouri law, a slave regained his status as soon as he returned to Missouri.

Taney's response to Scott's first argument was that the Missouri Compromise was unconstitutional. Taney and the dissenting Justices disagreed about whether the case was governed by the Territory Clause of Article IV, §3, cl. 2, which confers on Congress the power "to dispose of and make all needful rules and regulations respecting the territory or other property belonging to the United States." Taney argued that the clause was irrelevant to the case, because the word "territory" referred only "to the territory which at that time belonged to, or was claimed by, the United States, and was within their boundaries as settled by the treaty with Great Britain," and therefore did not apply to "a territory afterwards acquired from a foreign Government."[54]

Taney argued that although no clause of the Constitution expressly dealt with territories subsequently acquired, the powers of the United States could be inferred from "the provisions and principles of the Constitution, and its distribution of powers."

Taney then argued that when the United States acquired territories, it was bound to give the inhabitants of these territories the same Bill of Rights protections enjoyed by citizens in the states. He argued that the United States could not create colonies where less than full constitutional protections applied.

> There is certainly no power given by the Constitution to the Federal Government to establish or maintain colonies bordering on the United States

---

54. This allowed Taney to explain the fact that the First Congress almost immediately repassed the Northwest Ordinance, passed initially by the Confederation Congress, which, among other things, barred slavery in the Northwest Territories. He argued that the Territory Clause did apply to these lands. They were claimed by various States as part of the treaty with Great Britain and were later ceded to the federal government after the Constitution was ratified. Moreover, Taney insisted, the federal government was merely ratifying the policy of those states by prohibiting slavery. Thus, Taney insisted, "any argument, drawn from precedents, showing the extent of the power which the General Government exercised over slavery in this Territory . . . [was] altogether inapplicable to the case before us."

or at a distance, to be ruled and governed at its own pleasure; nor to enlarge its territorial limits in any way, except by the admission of new States. . . .[55]

The power to expand the territory of the United States by the admission of new States is plainly given; and in the construction of this power by all the departments of the Government, it has been held to authorize the acquisition of territory, not fit for admission at the time, but to be admitted as soon as its population and situation would entitle it to admission. It is acquired to become a State, and not to be held as a colony and governed by Congress with absolute authority; and as the propriety of admitting a new State is committed to the sound discretion of Congress, the power to acquire territory for that purpose, to be held by the United States until it is in a suitable condition to become a State upon an equal footing with the other States, must rest upon the same discretion. It is a question for the political department of the Government, and not the judicial; and whatever the political department of the Government shall recognize as within the limits of the United States, the judicial department is also bound to recognize, and to administer in it the laws of the United States, so far as they apply, and to maintain in the Territory the authority and rights of the Government, and also the personal rights and rights of property of individual citizens, as secured by the Constitution. . . .

[C]itizens of the United States who migrate to a Territory belonging to the people of the United States, cannot be ruled as mere colonists,

---

55. This sentence conceals a profound constitutional issue of its own, manifested in the admission of Texas to the Union in 1844. President Tyler had initially submitted a treaty to the Senate by which Texas, an independent country since its successful revolt against Mexico in 1837, would be annexed to the United States. The treaty was defeated. Although some senators challenged the right of the United States to admit foreign countries to the Union, as distinguished from the purchase of territory from a foreign country, the more substantial basis of opposition was from anti-slavery senators who (correctly) saw the admission of Texas as a boon to what was increasingly being termed the "slavocracy." See generally Frederick Merk, Slavery and the Annexation of Texas (1972). Faced with this defeat, Tyler and other supporters of Texas annexation simply proposed its admission under the Admissions Clause of the Constitution, which requires only a majority vote of each house of Congress, as against the two-thirds of the Senate required by the Treaty Clause. Many opponents denounced the constitutionality of this move, claiming that the Admissions Clause applied only to preexisting territory of the United States and did not allow the direct admission to the Union of a foreign country. Thus Daniel Webster argued that "[w]hen the constitution was formed, it is not probable that either its framers or the people ever looked to the admission of any States into the Union except as then already existed, and such as should be formed out of territories then belonging to the United States." 1 Works of Daniel Webster 355 (1860), quoted in Janice Levering, The Texas Two-Step to Statehood 10 (unpublished paper). In response, proponents of the legislation referred to "the general, unrestricted, unambiguous and unlimited power to admit new States into the Union." Id., quoting Congressman Tibbatts. In March 1845, just before the inauguration of James Polk, a supporter of Texas annexation, Congress voted to admit Texas as a state. Given Taney's general political views, one can surmise that he had no constitutional qualms about the unorthodox process by which Texas came into the Union. For further treatment of the constitutional issues surrounding the Texas annexation, see Mark A. Graber, Settling the West: The Annexation of Texas, the Louisiana Purchase, and Bush v. Gore, in The Louisiana Purchase and American Expansion 1803-1898, at 81-110 (Levinson & Sparrow eds., 2005); David Currie, Texas, in id. at 111-128.

> dependent upon the will of the General Government, and to be governed by any laws it may think proper to impose. . . . Whatever it acquires, it acquires for the benefit of the people of the several States who created it. It is their trustee acting for them, and charged with the duty of promoting the interests of the whole people of the Union in the exercise of the powers specifically granted.
>
> Although Congress has the power to establish territorial governments, the power of Congress over the person or property of a citizen can never be a mere discretionary power under our Constitution and form of Government. The powers of the Government and the rights and privileges of the citizen are regulated and plainly defined by the Constitution itself. And when the Territory becomes a part of the United States, the Federal Government enters into possession in the character impressed upon it by those who created it. It enters upon it with its powers over the citizen strictly defined, and limited by the Constitution, from which it derives its own existence, and by virtue of which alone it continues to exist and act as a Government and sovereignty. It has no power of any kind beyond it; and it cannot, when it enters a Territory of the United States, put off its character, and assume discretionary or despotic powers which the Constitution has denied to it. . . .
>
> For example, no one, we presume, will contend that Congress can make any law in a Territory respecting the establishment of religion, or the free exercise thereof, or abridging the freedom of speech or of the press, or the right of the people of the Territory peaceably to assemble, and to petition the Government for the redress of grievances.
>
> Nor can Congress deny to the people the right to keep and bear arms, nor the right to trial by jury, nor compel any one to be a witness against himself in a criminal proceeding.
>
> These powers, and others, in relation to rights of person, which it is not necessary here to enumerate, are, in express and positive terms, denied to the General Government; and the rights of private property have been guarded with equal care. Thus the rights of property are united with the rights of person, and placed on the same ground by the fifth amendment to the Constitution, which provides that no person shall be deprived of life, liberty, and property, without due process of law. And an act of Congress which deprives a citizen of the United States of his liberty or property, merely because he came himself or brought his property into a particular Territory of the United States, and who had committed no offence against the laws, could hardly be dignified with the name of due process of law. . . .

Taney dismissed the argument that "there is a difference between property in a slave and other property" that would afford the former less protection. To the contrary, he argued,

> [t]he right of property in a slave is distinctly and expressly affirmed in the Constitution. The right to traffic in it, like an ordinary article of merchandise and property, was guarantied to the citizens of the United States, in every State that might desire it, for twenty years. And the Government in express terms is pledged to protect it in all future time, if the slave escapes from his owner. This is done in plain words—too plain to be misunderstood. And no word can be found in the Constitution which gives

Congress a greater power over slave property, or which entitles property of that kind to less protection than property of any other description. The only power conferred is the power coupled with the duty of guarding and protecting the owner in his rights. . . .

Justice Catron concurred:

Congress cannot do indirectly what the Constitution prohibits directly. If the slaveholder is prohibited from going to the Territory with his slaves, who are parts of his family in name and in fact, it will follow that men owning lawful property in their own States, carrying with them the equality of their State to enjoy the common property, may be told, you cannot come here with your slaves, and he will be held out at the border. By this subterfuge, owners of slave property, to the amount of thousand of millions, might be almost as effectually excluded from removing into the Territory of Louisiana north of thirty-six degrees thirty minutes, as if the law declared that owners of slaves, as a class, should be excluded, even if their slaves were left behind.

Just as well might Congress have said to those of the North, you shall not introduce into the territory south of said line your cattle or horses, as the country is already overstocked; nor can you introduce your tools of trade, or machines, as the policy of Congress is to encourage the culture of sugar and cotton south of the line, and so to provide that the Northern people shall manufacture for those of the South, and barter for the staple articles slave labor produces. And thus the Northern farmer and mechanic would be held out, as the slaveholder was for thirty years, by the Missouri restriction.

If Congress could prohibit one species of property, lawful throughout Louisiana when it was acquired, and lawful in the State from whence it was brought, so Congress might exclude any or all property. . . .

[T]he act of 1820, known as the Missouri compromise, violates the most leading feature of the Constitution—a feature on which the Union depends, and which secures to the respective States and their citizens and entire EQUALITY of rights, privileges, and immunities.

Justice McLean, dissenting, argued that the Missouri Compromise was constitutional as a regulation of federal territories prior to their eventual admission as states:

If Congress should deem slaves or free colored persons injurious to the population of a free Territory, as conducing to lessen the value of the public lands, or on any other ground connected with the public interest, they have the power to prohibit them from becoming settlers in it. This can be sustained on the ground of a sound national policy, which is so clearly shown in our history by practical results, that it would seem no considerate individual can question it. And, as regards any unfairness of such a policy to our Southern brethren, as urged in the argument, it is only necessary to say that, with one-fourth of the Federal population of the Union, they have in the slave States a larger extent of fertile territory than is included in the free States; and it is submitted, if masters of slaves be restricted from bringing them into free territory, that the restriction on the free citizens of non-slaveholding States, by bringing slaves into free territory, is four times greater than that complained of by the South. But, not only so; some three or four hundred thousand holders of slaves, by bringing them into free territory, impose a restriction on twenty millions of the free States. The repugnancy to slavery would probably prevent fifty or a hundred freemen from settling in a slave Territory, where one slaveholder would be prevented from settling in a free Territory.

This remark is made in answer to the argument urged, that a prohibition of slavery in the free Territories is inconsistent with the continuance of the Union. Where a Territorial Government is established in a slave Territory, it has uniformly remained in that condition until the people form a State Constitution; the same course where the Territory is free, both parties acting in good faith, would be attended with satisfactory results.

3. *Restrictions on free Black persons in the territories.* Although, as a formal matter, McLean dissented from Taney's rejection of the possibility of Black citizenship—he wrote that "[t]he most general and appropriate definition of the term citizen is 'a freeman.' Being a freeman [Scott] is a citizen within the act of Congress"—he appeared to have an extremely limited notion of what rights citizenship brought within its wake. Note his statement that "[i]f Congress should deem slaves or *free colored persons* injurious to the population of a free Territory, as conducing to lessen the value of the public lands, or on any other ground connected with the public interest, they have the power to prohibit them from becoming settlers in it" (emphasis added). Do you believe that Congress had the power to bar U.S. citizens from settling in a federal territory prior to statehood? What is the relevance of McLean's point that anti-slavery settlers are, in effect, discouraged from settling far more of the actual territories than are slaveowners? Does this mean that slaveholders have a right to settle in at least some of the territory, albeit not all of it?

4. *Restrictions on Black immigration in the states.* Condemnation of slavery as a threat to "free labor" did not mean that whites were particularly sympathetic to Black slaves or to free Black persons. The Indiana constitution of 1851 barred free Black persons from migrating into the state. Black persons already in Indiana, though allowed to remain, were prohibited from voting, serving on juries, or participating in the militia, as well as barred from testifying against whites in court, marrying whites, or attending schools with whites.[56] Similar laws prohibiting Black immigration were passed in Iowa, Illinois, and Oregon, reflecting "the Negrophobia that characterized much of the northern population."[57] Do you think that the Taney Court would have struck down bans on Black immigration and settlement in free states?

5. Dred Scott *and substantive due process.* Taney argues that the Missouri Compromise violates the property rights of citizens under the Due Process Clause of the Fifth Amendment. It is often said that *Dred Scott* is the origin of the Supreme Court's

---

56. James M. McPherson, Ordeal by Fire: The Civil War and Reconstruction 80 (1982).

57. McPherson, Battle Cry of Freedom, supra n.47, at 88. Indeed, as to Oregon, Garrett Epps writes that

> white pioneers were able to prevent black people from settling in Oregon only by the most energetic and determined recourse to legal apartheid. Even before Oregon was a United States territory, its inhabitants formed a provisional government in 1843 and excluded black settlers. In 1850, Congress passed the Donation Land Claim Act, which guaranteed 320 acres to each single white male U.S. citizen homesteading in the Oregon Territory (married white homesteaders received 640 acres). These measures were not of merely theoretical import. An

doctrine of "substantive due process," later invoked in cases like Lochner v. New York and Roe v. Wade. In fact, Taney seems to be invoking a much older doctrine that was recognized at the founding: the idea that the government could not extinguish vested rights of property. See the discussion in Chapter 2, supra, at pp. 160-169. The roots of the idea go back to the Magna Carta, and its reference to "the law of the land," which was generally regarded as equivalent to the formulation "due process of law." See James W. Ely, Jr., The Oxymoron Reconsidered: Myth and Reality in the Origins of Substantive Due Process, 16 Const. Comment. 315 (1999). The basic idea, as it developed in Blackstone and other writers, was that when legislatures took property from A and gave it to B they violated "the law of the land" principle, and hence due process of law. (Recall Justice Chase's view, expressed in Calder v. Bull, that A to B transfers were not "a rightful exercise of authority" and "against all reason and justice.") Indeed, in 1829 in Wilkinson v. Leland, 27 U.S. 627, 658 (1829), Justice Story suggested that principle apparently held whether or not a state had a "law of the land" or Due Process Clause in its constitution: "We know of no case, in which a legislative act to transfer the property of A. to B. without his consent, has ever been held a constitutional exercise of legislative power in any state in the union."

Taney argued that when the federal government applied the Missouri Compromise to Southerners bringing their slaves into free territories, it was taking their property in the slave and giving it to the slave. Hence it destroyed vested rights, which violated the Due Process Clause.

In his dissent, Justice Curtis agreed with Taney that taking vested rights of property violated the Due Process Clause: "This restriction on the legislative power is not peculiar to the Constitution of the United States; it was borrowed from Magna Charta; was brought to America by our ancestors, as part of their inherited liberties, and has existed in all the States, usually in the very words of the great charter." However, Curtis explained, people do not have vested rights in property when they voluntarily enter into jurisdictions that do not recognize that species of property: "[U]nder the power to regulate commerce, Congress could prohibit the importation of slaves; and the exercise of the power was restrained till 1808. A citizen of the United States owns slaves in Cuba, and brings them to the United States, where they are set free by the legislation of Congress. Does this legislation deprive him of his property without due process of law? If so, what becomes of the laws prohibiting the slave trade? If not, how can similar regulation respecting a Territory violate the fifth amendment of the Constitution?" The problem Curtis identifies doesn't arise with estates in land because they are not movable, so they can't cross jurisdictions, but it does apply to chattels that can be moved from place to place.

1850 census noted the presence of at least 54 settlers of African descent, 114 Native Americans or "half-breed," and 38 Native Hawaiians. The total enumerated population was 13,294. The all-white proviso of the Act also rid Oregon of a substantial population of Native Hawaiians, who first came to Oregon country in 1788 as crew members of merchant vessels. Most of the Natives returned to Hawaii after passage of the Act. When Oregonians wrote their first statehood constitution in 1857, they became the first state population to include a constitutional ban on settlement by "free Negroes and mullatoes." Though superseded by the Fourteenth Amendment, the measure was not formally repealed until 1926.

Garrett Epps, To an Unknown God: The Hidden History of Employment Division v. Smith, 30 Ariz. St. L.J. 983, 968-969 n.62 (1999) (citations omitted).

If Taney's vested rights argument is sound, why is the federal government's prohibition on slavery any more confiscatory than that of a state like Illinois through which Dr. Emerson also traveled? Does Taney's argument mean that the federal government is limited with respect to other kinds of property regulations it can enact in the territories? For example, if Congress prohibited bringing into Kansas Territory certain types of drugs (or alcohol) and Dr. Emerson wanted to set up shop as a seller of drugs or a saloon owner, would the federal government be required to permit him to do so under *Dred Scott*? Perhaps Taney meant to say that the right to own slaves was more protected than other forms of property rights subject to regulation. Why might that be so?

6. Taney's opinion included the statement that Congress "could not authorize a territorial government" to do what it itself could not do, i.e., bar slavery in the territories. This, presumably, meant that Senator Stephen Douglas's program of "popular sovereignty," which left the decision up to the settlers themselves in their territorial legislatures, was constitutionally illegitimate, that the only time slavery could be abolished was upon entry to the Union. (Everyone agreed that states had complete autonomy in regard to adoption of slavery, and the "equal footing" doctrine gave new states the same powers enjoyed by Virginia and Massachusetts to make the decision for or against slavery.) Thus, writes James M. McPherson, "[i]t soon dawned on northern Democrats that Taney had aimed to discomfit them as well as the Republicans."[58] Douglas responded, in June 1857, by pointing out that even if a master's right to bring slaves into territories was absolutely protected, nonetheless it remained up to the territorial legislatures to decide, as a practical matter, how much protection to give this right by "appropriate police regulation and local legislation," the absence of which would make the master's formal right "barren and worthless."[59] Douglas's attempt to find a "centrist" position with regard to the issue was unavailing, and his articulation of what became known as the Freeport Doctrine antagonized many pro-slavery Southerners and contributed to the fragmentation within the Democratic Party in the 1860 election that would cost Douglas the presidency.

7. Consider Justice Curtis's reference to Article II and its limitation of eligibility for the presidency to "natural-born citizens." Is this enough to support an inference that anyone born within the United States is automatically a citizen of the United States (and of the state within which he or she is born)? That is, is sentence one of the Fourteenth Amendment, which is viewed as explicitly overruling *Dred Scott*, simply a reversion to a correct understanding of the 1787 Constitution, or does it in fact supply a rule of citizenship that was lacking in the original Constitution?

8. *Dred Scott*, it is safe to say, is the most reviled decision (and Taney's the most reviled opinion) in the history of the Supreme Court. If you share the distaste for them, why? Do you object to the abominable result or to the quality of the legal analysis?

It has become common to ascribe to the *Dred Scott* decision some significant share of the blame for the drift toward war, which would occur four years later. Is this plausible? Why would Southerners have been more, rather than less, inclined toward secession as a result of *Dred Scott*? Republicans, of course, were extremely

58. McPherson, Battle Cry of Freedom, supra n.47, at 177.
59. Quoted in id. at 177-178.

upset to have their party platform declared unconstitutional, but they were already committed to the prohibition of slavery in the territories. Kenneth Stampp suggests that the importance of *Dred Scott* to the onset of the Civil War has been vastly overrated; such events as the struggles in Kansas and John Brown's raids were far more important in convincing Southerners that their only hope lay in secession.[60]

If one objects to Taney's opinion on the grounds that it hastened war, consider that a decision freeing Dred Scott would surely have generated intense opposition by the already secession-prone Southerners, who might not have waited until 1860-1861 to attempt secession. Consider also that the North might not have won a war begun in 1857, especially because of its lack of military preparedness and the fact that its commander-in-chief would have been the feckless James Buchanan rather than Abraham Lincoln. (And Taney's overreaching in *Dred Scott* ultimately led to a war won by the North that freed the slaves.) Is this a good reason to support the result in *Dred Scott*—that it bought the North valuable time? Or is your view that justice, i.e., the repudiation of slavery, should be done (and, indeed, is required by the Constitution) though the heavens (or, at least, the Union) fall?

If you revile the opinion on legal grounds, rather than because of the consequences of the decision, then what are the precise legal errors that you believe Taney makes? Do you, for example, believe that he makes historical errors that vitiate his analysis? Or would you object even if it turned out that he was basically correct in his historical analysis (so that Taney's mistake might be believing himself confined by the original understanding)? Consider Professor Finkelman's statement that "[t]hose who revere the framers and the Constitution can find solace only in the fact that some of the founders in 1776 and 1787 (though probably a minority of both groups) did not intend the results that Taney reached."[61]

Professor Graber has written that most contemporary constitutional theorists today find it necessary to explain why *Dred Scott* was wrongly decided under their favorite theories of constitutional interpretation.[62] In this sense, *Dred Scott* has become an "anticanonical" case, a case that is regularly pointed to as an example of bad constitutional interpretation. Both Graber and Professor Jamal Greene, who has written about the construction of the "anticanon," ask whether the formation of the "anticanon" is driven more by the results than by the quality of the legal reasoning. Graber points out, for example, that, even if Taney's originalist arguments are flawed, the result was entirely defensible given the dominant legal understandings of Taney's day. Moreover, the most notorious holding, that Black people could not be citizens, mustered only two dissents, and the invalidation of the Missouri Compromise, probably more volatile as a political matter, also had the support of a healthy majority of Justices.

---

60. See Stampp, America in 1857, supra n.51, at 108. Recent studies of Brown include Tony Horwitz, Midnight Rising: John Brown and the Raid That Sparked the Civil War (2011), and David S. Reynolds, John Brown, Abolitionist: The Man Who Killed Slavery, Sparked the Civil War, and Seeded Civil Rights (2005).

61. Paul Finkelman, The Constitution and the Intentions of the Framers: The Limits of Historical Analysis, 50 U. Pitt. L. Rev. 349, 395 (1989).

62. Mark A. Graber, Desperately Ducking Slavery: *Dred Scott* and Contemporary Constitutional Theory, 14 Const. Comment. 271 (1997). Professor Graber elaborates his argument in *Dred Scott* and the Problem of Constitutional Evil (2006).

If *Dred Scott* was "rightly decided" as a matter of original understanding, or under the conventional standards of legal analysis of its day, what follows? A very small number of the anti-Federalists opposed ratification of the 1787 Constitution because of their opposition to slavery. Were they right? Should one endorse the noted abolitionist William Lloyd Garrison's denunciation of the Constitution as a "Covenant with Death and Agreement with Hell," a document that no honorable person could agree to or enforce? Garrisonians essentially agreed with slaveowners as to what the Constitution, correctly interpreted, meant with respect to the protection of slavery. They simply drew a different conclusion from this interpretation, which, for Garrison, was summarized in the slogan "No Union with Slaveholders." Frederick Douglass, the leading Black abolitionist of his time, originally agreed with Garrison. Eventually, however, he rejected the conventional interpretation that the Constitution protected slavery, as illustrated in the following speech delivered in 1860, three years after *Dred Scott*. As you read it, compare its analysis, in both mode and result, with those you have read by Story and Taney (among others). Who is most convincing, and why?

Frederick Douglass, The Constitution of the United States: Is It Pro-Slavery or Anti-Slavery?[63]

Speech Delivered in Glasgow, Scotland (March 26, 1860)

[F]irst let me state what is not the question. It is not whether slavery existed in the United States at the time of the adoption of the Constitution; it is not whether slaveholders took part in framing the Constitution; it is not whether those slaveholders, in their hearts, intended to secure certain advantages in that instrument for slavery; it is not whether the American Government has been wielded during seventy-two years in favour of the propagation and permanence of slavery; it is not whether a pro-slavery interpretation has been put upon the Constitution by the American Courts. . . . The real and exact question . . . may be fairly stated thus: 1st, Does the United States Constitution guarantee to any class or description of people . . . the right to enslave, or hold as property, any other class or description of people . . . ? 2nd, Is the dissolution of the union between the slave and free States required by fidelity to the slaves, or by the just demands of conscience? . . .

I . . . deny that the Constitution guarantees the right to hold property in man, and believe that the way to abolish slavery in America is to vote such men into power as will use their powers for the abolition of slavery. . . . I think we had better ascertain what the Constitution itself is . . . I will tell you. It is no vague, indefinite, floating, unsubstantial, ideal something, coloured according to any man's fancy, now a weasel, now a whale, and now nothing. On the contrary, it is a plainly written document, not in Hebrew or Greek, but in English. . . . The American Constitution is a

63. In 2 Life and Writings of Frederick Douglass 467-480 (P. Foner ed., 1950). Douglass was the son of an unknown white man and a part-Indian slave. He spent most of his life in slavery, but was taught how to read and write. Upon his escape, he became a member of the Massachusetts Anti-Slavery Society and became a significant force in the anti-slavery movement, publishing a paper for slaves, and counseling President Lincoln during the Civil War. See William S. McFeely, Frederick Douglass (1995).

written instrument full and complete in itself. No Court in America, no Congress, no President, can add a single word thereto, or take a single word therefrom. . . . [I]t should be borne in mind that the mere text, and only the text, and not any commentaries or creeds written by those who wished to give the text a meaning apart from its plain reading, was adopted as the Constitution of the United States. It should also be borne in mind that the intentions of those who framed the Constitution, be they good or bad, for slavery or against slavery, are to be respected so far, and so far only, as will find those intentions plainly stated in the Constitution. It would be the wildest of absurdities, and lead to endless confusion and mischiefs, if, instead of looking to the written paper itself, for its meaning, it were attempted to make us search it out, in the secret motives, and dishonest intentions, of some of the men who took part in writing it. It was what they said that was adopted by the people, not what they were ashamed or afraid to say, and really omitted to say. Bear in mind, also, and the fact is an important one, that the framers of the Constitution sat with closed doors, and that this was done purposely, that nothing but the result of their labours should be seen, and that result should be judged of by the people free from any of the bias shown in the debates. It should also be borne in mind, and the fact is still more important, that the debates in the convention that framed the Constitution, and by means of which a pro-slavery interpretation is now attempted to be forced upon that instrument, were not published till more than a quarter of a century after the presentation and the adoption of the Constitution.

These debates were purposely kept out of view, in order that the people should adopt, not the secret motives or unexpressed intentions of any body, but the simple text of the paper itself. Those debates form no part of the original agreement. I repeat, the paper itself, and only the paper itself, with its own plainly-written purposes, is the Constitution. It must stand or fall, flourish or fade, on its own individual and self-declared character and objects. Again, where would be the advantage of a written Constitution, if, instead of seeking its meaning in its words, we had to seek them in the secret intentions of individuals who may have had something to do with writing the paper? What will the people of America a hundred years hence care about the intentions of the scriveners who wrote the Constitution? These men are already gone from us, and in the course of nature were expected to go from us. They were for a generation, but the Constitution is for ages. . . . Common sense, and common justice, and sound rules of interpretation all drive us to the words of the law for the meaning of the law. The practice of the Government is dwelt upon with much fervour and eloquence as conclusive to the slaveholding character of the Constitution. . . . But good as this argument is, it is not conclusive. A wise man has said that few people have been found better than their laws, but many have been found worse. To this last rule America is no exception. Her laws are one thing, her practice is another. . . . After all, the fact that men go out of the Constitution to prove it pro-slavery, whether that going out is to the practice of the Government, or to the secret intentions of the writers of the paper, the fact that they do go out is very significant. . . . It is an admission that the thing for which they are looking is not to be found where only it ought to be found, and that is in the Constitution itself. . . .

[B]ecause upon its face [the Constitution does not support a pro-slavery interpretation, my opponent] sums up what he calls the slaveholding provisions of the Constitution[: Article I, §§2, 8, and 9, and Article IV, §2]. It so happens that no such words as "African slave trade," no such words as "slave representation," no such words as "fugitive slaves," no such words as "slave insurrections," are anywhere used in that instrument. [Douglass then reads to his audience the text of these four provisions.] Let us look at them just as they stand, one by one. Let us grant, for sake of the argument, that the first of these provisions, referring to the basis of representation and taxation, does refer to slaves. . . . [G]iving the provisions the very worst construction, what does it amount to? I answer: It is a downright disability laid upon the slaveholding States; one which deprives those States of two-fifths of their natural basis of representation. A black man in a free State is worth just two-fifths more than a black man in a slave State, as a basis of political power under the Constitution. Therefore, instead of encouraging slavery, the Constitution encourages freedom by giving an increase of "two-fifths" of political power to free over slave States. So much for the three-fifths clause; taking it as its worst, it still leans to freedom, not to slavery; for, be it remembered that the Constitution nowhere forbids a coloured man to vote. I come to the next, that which is said guaranteed the continuance of the African slave trade for twenty years. I will also take that for just what my opponent alleges it to have been. . . . [W]hat follows? why, this—that this part of the Constitution, so far as the slave trade is concerned, became a dead letter more than 50 years ago, and now binds no man's conscience for the continuance of any slave trade whatever. . . . But there is still more to be said about this abolition of the slave trade. Men [in 1787], both in England and in America, looked upon the slave trade as the life of slavery. The abolition of the slave trade was supposed to be the certain death of slavery. . . .

American statesmen, in providing for the abolition of the slave trade, thought they were providing for the abolition of slavery. . . . All regarded slavery as an expiring and doomed system, destined to speedily disappear from the country. . . . [T]his very provision, if made to refer to the African slave trade at all, makes the Constitution anti-slavery rather than for slavery, for it says to the slave States, the price you will have to pay for coming into the American Union is, that the slave trade, which you would carry on indefinitely out of the Union, shall be put an end to in twenty years if you come into the Union. . . . [T]he intentions of the framers of the Constitution were good, not bad. . . . I go to the "slave insurrection" clause, though, in truth, there is no such clause. . . . But I will be generous here, as well as elsewhere, and grant that it applies to slave insurrections. Let us suppose that an anti-slavery man is President of the United States (and the day that shall see this the case is not distant) and this very power of suppressing slave insurrection would put an end to slavery. The right to put down an insurrection carries with it the right to determine the means by which it shall be put down. If it should turn out that slavery is a source of insurrection, that there is no security from insurrection while slavery lasts, why, the Constitution would be best obeyed by putting an end to slavery, and an anti-slavery Congress would do that very thing. Thus, you see, the so-called slaveholding provisions of the American Constitution, which a little while ago looked so formidable, are, after all, no defence or guarantee for slavery whatever. But there is one other provision. This is called the "Fugitive Slave Provision." It is called so by those who wish to make it subserve the interest of slavery. . . . But it may be asked—if this clause does not apply to slaves, to whom does it apply?

I answer, that when adopted, it applied to a very large class of persons—namely, redemptioners—persons who had come to America from Holland, from Ireland, and other quarters of the globe . . . and had, for a consideration duly paid, become bound to "serve and labour" for the parties to whom their service and labour was due. It applies to indentured apprentices and others who had become bound for a consideration, under contract duly made, to serve and labour. To such persons this provision applies, and only to such persons. The plain reading of this provision shows that it applies, and that it can only properly and legally apply, to persons "bound to service." Its object plainly is, to secure the fulfillment of contracts for "service and labour." . . . The legal conditions of the slave puts him beyond the operation of this provision. He is not described in it. He is a simple article of property. He does not owe and cannot owe service. He cannot even make a contract. . . . The provision, then, only respects persons who owe service, and they only can owe service who can receive an equivalent and make a bargain. The slave cannot do that, and is therefore exempted from the operation of this fugitive provision. In all matters where laws are taught to be made the means of oppression, cruelty, and wickedness, I am for strict construction. I will concede nothing. It must be shown that it is so nominated in the bond. . . . The very nature of law is opposed to all such wickedness. . . . Law is not merely an arbitrary enactment with regard to justice, reason, or humanity. . . . [Douglass's adversary] laid down some rules of legal interpretation. These rules send us to the history of the law for its meaning. I have no objection to such a course in ordinary cases of doubt. But where human liberty and justice are at stake, the case falls under an entirely different class of rules. There must be something more than history—something more than tradition. The Supreme Court of the United States lays down this rule, and it meets the case exactly—"Where rights are infringed—where the fundamental principles of the law are overthrown—where the general system of the law is departed from, the legislative intention must be expressed with irresistible clearness." The same court says that the language of the law must be construed strictly in favour of justice and liberty. Again, there is another rule of law. It is—Where a law is susceptible of two meanings, the one making it accomplish an innocent purpose, and the other making it accomplish a wicked purpose, we must in all cases adopt that which makes it accomplish an innocent purpose. . . . I only ask you to look at the American Constitution in the light of [these rules of interpretation], and you will see with me that no man is guaranteed a right of property in man, under the provisions of that instrument. If there are two ideas more distinct in their character and essence than another, those ideas are "persons" and "property," "men" and "things." Now, when it is proposed to transform persons into "property" and men into beasts of burden, I demand that the law that contemplates such a purpose shall be expressed with irresistible clearness. The things must not be left to inference, but must be done in plain English. . . .

[Douglass turns to the Preamble of the Constitution, which he quotes.] It has been said that Negroes are not included within the benefits sought under this declaration. This is said by the slaveholders in America . . . but it is not said by the Constitution itself. Its language is "we the people"; not we the white people, not even we the citizens, not we the privileged class, not we the high, not we the low, but we the people; . . . , we the human inhabitants; and, if Negroes are people, they are included in the benefits for which the Constitution of America was ordained and established. . . . I undertake to say, as the conclusion of the whole matter, that the constitutionality of slavery can be made out only by disregarding the plain and common-sense reading of the Constitution itself; by discrediting and casting away as worthless the most beneficent rules of legal interpretation; by ruling the Negro outside of these beneficent rules; by claiming everything for slavery; by denying everything for freedom; by assuming that the Constitution does not mean what it says, and that it says what it does not mean; by disregarding the written Constitution, and interpreting it in the light of a secret understanding. . . . The Constitution declares that no person shall be deprived of life, liberty, or property without due process of law; it secures to every man the right of trial by jury, the privilege of the writ of habeas corpus . . . it secures to every State a republican form of government. Any one of these provisions, in the hands of abolition statesmen, and backed by a right moral sentiment, would put an end to slavery in America. The Constitution forbids the passing of a bill of attainder: that is, a law entailing upon the child the disabilities and hardships imposed upon the parent. Every slave law in America might be repealed on this very ground. . . .

I am, therefore, for drawing the bond of the Union more closely, and bringing the Slave States more completely under the power of the Free States. . . . I have much confidence in the instincts of the slaveholders. They see that the Constitution will afford slavery no protection when it shall cease to be administered by slaveholders. They see, moreover, that if there is once a will in the people of America to abolish slavery, there is no word, no syllable in the Constitution to forbid that result.

DISCUSSION

Douglass's arguments about constitutional interpretation draw on several decades of anti-slavery and abolitionist constitutional arguments by figures such as Joel Tiffany, James Ashley, Alvan Stewart, William Goodell, James Birney, and Lysander Spooner. For a sampling of this tradition, see Randy E. Barnett, Whence Comes Section One?: The Abolitionist Origins of the Fourteenth Amendment, 3 J. Legal Analysis 165 (2011); William M. Wiecek, The Sources of Antislavery Constitutionalism in America, 1760-1848 (1977); Joel Tiffany, A Treatise on the Unconstitutionality of American Slavery: Together with the Powers and Duties of the Federal Government in Relation to That Subject (1849); Lysander Spooner, The Unconstitutionality of Slavery (1845).

Arguments that slavery in the states violated the Constitution or that slavery could be abolished by ordinary statute (much less without compensation to slaveowners) were out of the mainstream throughout the antebellum era. Nevertheless, the Republican Party (and its political predecessors) eventually developed a series of constitutional arguments explaining why the federal government could not permit slavery in federal territories. See Eric Foner, Free Soil, Free Labor, Free Men: The Ideology of the Republican Party Before the Civil War (1970); James Oakes, Freedom National: The Destruction of Slavery in the United States, 1861-1865 (2012).

Although well-trained lawyers like Joseph Story and Roger Taney believed that the constitutionality of slavery was obviously correct, does this mean that Douglass's arguments were necessarily "incorrect"? What exactly does "incorrect" mean in the context of constitutional development? Consider in particular Douglass's last sentence: "[O]nce [there is] a will in the people of America to abolish slavery, there is no word, no syllable in the Constitution to forbid that result." How do changes in political "will" turn previously "off-the-wall" arguments into plausible or even winning arguments?[64]

D. *Judicial Supremacy and* Dred Scott*: The Lincoln-Douglas Debates*

Dred Scott figured centrally in the exchanges between Abraham Lincoln and Stephen Douglas during their campaign for the U.S. Senate in 1858. Lincoln, in his famous "House Divided" speech of June 16, 1858, had denounced the *Dred Scott* decision and, indeed, suggested that it was part of a conspiracy to nationalize slavery. The basis of this fear lay in the facts of a case then before the Taney Court, Lemmon v. The People, 26 Barbour 270 (1857), where Jonathan Lemmon and his wife brought eight slaves into New York as they took one boat from Virginia to New York, where they would catch another boat to New Orleans (on their way ultimately to Texas). Although warned by the ship's captain to leave their slaves on the first boat (where they could presumably be transferred to the second boat) and not to take their slaves into New York, the Lemmons did so while they all waited three days for the next boat to leave. Upon the discovery of the slaves, a New York state court issued a writ of habeas corpus freeing them; Lemmon challenged this on the basis of an alleged federal right to travel from one state to another without risking loss of his property because of the anti-slavery policies of a state through which he was traveling.[65]

On July 9, Douglas attacked Lincoln's views about the validity of *Dred Scott*:[66]

> The right and the province of expounding the Constitution, and construing the law, is vested in the judiciary established by the Constitution. As a lawyer, I feel at liberty to appear before the Court and controvert any principle of law while the question is pending before the tribunal; but when the decision is made, my private opinion, your opinion, all other opinions must yield to the majesty of that authoritative adjudication. . . . What security have you for your property, for your reputation, and for your personal rights, if the courts are not upheld, and their decisions respected when once firmly rendered by the highest tribunal known to the Constitution? . . .
>
> I am opposed to this doctrine of Mr. Lincoln, by which he proposes to take an appeal from the decision of the Supreme Court of the United States, upon this high constitutional question to a Republican caucus

64. On the concepts of "off-the-wall" and "on-the-wall" legal arguments, and how the former frequently change into the latter, see Jack M. Balkin, Constitutional Redemption: Political Faith in an Unjust World 179-183 (2011).

65. The facts and legal significance of *Lemmon* are spelled out in Paul Finkelman, An Imperfect Union: Slavery, Federalism, and Comity 296-312, 329-332 (1981). Recall also Justice Baldwin's opinion in Groves v. Slaughter, which explicitly suggested that there was a constitutional right for slaveowners to travel with their slaves through otherwise free states. *Crandall* was decided after the abolition of slavery. Ask yourself, though, how its doctrine might have applied to a slaveowner in Lemmon's position.

66. The Complete Lincoln-Douglas Debates of 1858, 20 (Paul Angle ed., pub. 1991).

sitting in the country. Yes, or any other caucus or town meeting, whether it be Republican, American, or Democratic. I respect the decisions of that august tribunal; I shall always bow in deference to them.

Lincoln responded on the next day:[67]

I have expressed heretofore, and I now repeat, my opposition to the *Dred Scott* decision, but I should be allowed to state the nature of that opposition. . . . What is fairly implied by the term Judge Douglas has used "resistance to the decision"? I do not resist it. If I wanted to take Dred Scott from his master, I would be interfering with property. . . . But I am doing no such thing as that, but all that I am doing is refusing to obey it as a political rule. If I were in Congress, and a vote should come up on a question whether slavery should be prohibited in a new territory, in spite of that *Dred Scott* decision, I would vote that it should. [Applause; "good for you"; "we hope to see it"; "that's right."]

We will try to reverse that decision. . . . Somebody has to reverse that decision, since it is made, and we mean to reverse it, and we mean to do it peaceably. . . .

Judge Douglas will have it that all hands must take this extraordinary decision, made under . . . extraordinary circumstances, and give their vote in Congress in accordance with it, yield to it and obey it in every possible sense. Circumstances alter cases. Do not gentlemen here remember the case of that same Supreme Court, some twentyfive or thirty years ago, deciding that a national bank was constitutional? . . . The bank charter ran out, and a re-charter was granted by Congress. That re-charter was laid before General Jackson. It was urged upon him, when he denied the constitutionality of the bank, that the Supreme Court had decided that it was constitutional; and that General Jackson then said that the Supreme Court had no right to lay down a rule to govern a co-ordinate branch of the government, the members of which had sworn to support the Constitution—that each member had sworn to support that Constitution as he understood it. I will venture here to say, that I have heard Judge Douglas say that he approved of General Jackson for that act. What has now become of all his tirade about "resistance to the Supreme Court"?

Douglas answered a week later, on July 17, in Springfield:[68]

The court pronounces that law, prohibiting slavery, unconstitutional and void, and Mr. Lincoln is going to pass an act reversing that decision and making it valid. I have never heard before of an appeal being taken from the Supreme Court to the Congress of the United States to reverse its decision. . . .

Mr. Lincoln intimates that there is another mode by which he can reverse the *Dred Scott* decision. How is that? Why, he is going to appeal to the people to elect a President who will appoint judges who will reverse

67. Id. at 36.
68. Id. at 56.

> the *Dred Scott* decision. Well, let us see how that is going to be done. . . . [W]hy, the Republican President is to call up the candidates and catechize them, and ask them, "How will you decide this case if I appoint you judge?" [Shouts of laughter.] . . . Suppose you get a Supreme Court composed of such judges, who have been appointed by a partisan President upon their giving pledges how they would decide a case before it arise, what confidence would you have in such a court? ["None, none."] . . . It is a proposition to make that court the corrupt, unscrupulous tool of a political party. But Mr. Lincoln cannot conscientiously submit, he thinks, to the decision of a court composed of a majority of Democrats. If he cannot, how can he expect us to have confidence in a court composed of a majority of Republicans, selected for the purpose of deciding against the Democracy, and in favor of the Republicans? [Cheers.] The very proposition carries with it the demoralization and degradation destructive of the judicial department of the federal government.
>
> Lincoln responded later that day:[69]
>
> I think, that in respect for judicial authority, my humble history would not suffer in a comparison with that of Judge Douglas. He would have the citizen conform his vote to that decision; the member of Congress, his; the President, his use of the veto power. He would make it a rule of political action for the people and all the departments of the government. I would not. By resisting it as a political rule, I disturb no right of property, create no disorder, excite no mobs.

Lincoln went on to read from an 1820 letter of Thomas Jefferson to a Mr. Jarvis, the author of a publication called the "Republican":[70]

> You seem . . . to consider the judges as the ultimate arbiters of all constitutional questions—a very dangerous doctrine indeed and one which would place us under the despotism of an oligarchy. Our judges see as honest as other men, and not more so. They have, with others, the same passions for party, for power, and the privilege of their corps. . . . [T]heir power is the more dangerous as they are in office for life, and not responsible, as the other functionaries are, to the elective control. The constitution has erected no such single tribunal, knowing that to whatever hands confided, with the corruptions of time and party, its members would become despots. It has more wisely made all the departments co-equal and co-sovereign within themselves.

DISCUSSION

Douglas accuses Lincoln of wishing to "catechize" potential nominees to the Supreme Court in regard to their views about *Dred Scott.* Consider the fact that recent Republican Party platforms call for the appointment of judges "who

---

69. Id. at 77.
70. Id.

recognize the sanctity of human life." In contrast, Presidents Clinton and Obama repeatedly made clear their support for constitutionally protected reproductive rights and, in nominating Judges Ginsburg, Breyer, Sotomayor, and Kagan, picked Justices who are generally thought reliable votes on behalf of maintaining reproductive rights. One presumes that both Democratic and Republican Presidents and their agents have developed methods of assessing the predispositions of their nominees on issues like abortion, affirmative action, and the reach of federal power. Is there anything improper about this?

When the Senate exercises its constitutional duty to "advise and consent" to appointments to the Court, what questions may it ask (and expect answers to) regarding the views of nominees on abortion (or any other issue)? In her confirmation hearings, the first Reagan appointee, Sandra Day O'Connor, refused to answer many questions on *Roe*, saying that she could not[71]

> tell you how I might vote on a particular issue which may come before the Court, or endorse or criticize specific Supreme Court decisions presenting issues which may well come before the Court again. To do so would mean I have prejudged the matter or have morally committed myself to a certain position. Such a statement by me as to how I might resolve a particular issue or what I might do in a future Court action might make it necessary to disqualify myself on the matter.

Does Justice O'Connor's statement imply that it would be equally improper for a nominee to be asked (or answer) questions about the propriety of Justice Marshall's opinions in *McCulloch* and *Gibbons*, which presented an expansive reading of Congress's powers under Article I, the core issue of many contemporary cases involving the scope of national authority under purportedly limited assignment of powers? (Justice Scalia, in his confirmation hearings, refused even to answer questions about Marbury v. Madison, saying that *Marbury* was necessarily implicated in every contemporary case involving judicial review of congressional statutes. Was he justified in doing so?)

Consider the meaning of "prejudgment." If academic appointees to the bench have published vigorous criticism of current judicial doctrines, calling for their overruling at the earliest possible time, should they be expected to answer questions about their writings? If confirmed, should they recuse themselves when those issues come up? Consider a statement by a dissenting Justice indicating hope for future reversal by the Court of its mistaken decision. Does that indicate such "prejudgment" as to require recusal when the issue next comes before the Court?[72]

---

71. Quoted in Sanford Levinson, Should Supreme Court Nominees Have Opinions?, The Nation, Oct. 17, 1981, at 375.

72. See, e.g., the conclusion of Justice O'Connor's dissent in the *Garcia* case, Chapter 6, infra, where, quoting Justice Rehnquist, she indicated that the dissenters' views "will, I am confident, in time again command the support of a majority of this Court."

III. "AND THE WAR CAME":[73] THE PRESIDENT AS COMMANDER-IN-CHIEF AND THE PRESERVATION OF THE UNION[74]

Though defeated in his 1858 bid for the Senate, Lincoln did become President in 1861, elected in 1860 with 39 percent of the popular vote; however, the votes were concentrated such that he would have prevailed in the Electoral College "even if the popular vote of all three of his rivals had been concentrated on one candidate." The problems facing him are suggested by the fact that, while taking every Northern free state except New Jersey, which split its electoral vote, Lincoln "was not on the ballot in the Confederate states, except for Virginia, where he received only 1% of the vote."[75] By the time of his inauguration on March 4, 1861, seven states—South Carolina, Mississippi, Florida, Alabama, Georgia, Louisiana, and Texas—had announced their secession from the Union, and Lincoln was clearly worried, with good reason, that the remaining eight slave states—Maryland, Delaware, Virginia, North Carolina, Tennessee, Kentucky, Arkansas, and Missouri—would follow them into the Confederate States of America.

A. The Debate over Secession

1. President James Buchanan Opposes Both Secession and War

In his final State of the Union message on December 4, 1860, President James Buchanan discussed the movement for secession in the South. He argued that it was caused by "[t]he long-continued and intemperate interference of the Northern people with the question of slavery in the Southern States." Yet Buchanan did not support secession; in fact, he presented powerful arguments against it.

Buchanan pointed out that Lincoln's election "has been effected by a mere plurality, and not a majority of the people." Resort to what Buchanan called "revolutionary resistance" required, he said, "a deliberate, palpable, and dangerous exercise of powers not granted by the Constitution," and he noted that no such exercises had in fact taken place, even if one believed that Lincoln and other Republicans might support such policies. Support, though, was not equivalent to enactment. As a practical matter, Buchanan argued that the Republicans would

---

73. See Abraham Lincoln, Second Inaugural Address, March 4, 1865:

> On the occasion corresponding to this four years ago, all thoughts were anxiously directed to an impending civil war. All dreaded it—all sought to avert it. While the inaugural address was being delivered from this place, devoted altogether to *saving* the Union without war, insurgent agents were in the city seeking to *destroy* it without war—seeking to dissolve the Union, and divide effects, by negotiation. Both parties deprecated war; but one of them would *make* war rather than let the nation survive; and the other would *accept* war rather than let it perish. And the war came.

74. See James G. Randall, Constitutional Problems Under Lincoln (rev. ed. 1964).

75. Mark Neely, The Last Best Hope of Earth: Abraham Lincoln and the Promise of America 59 (1993).

be unsuccessful in realizing their anti-slavery agenda. *Dred Scott* stood as a barrier against the Republican commitment to ban slavery in the territories.

Buchanan argued that secession was unconstitutional. "In order to justify secession as a constitutional remedy" Buchanan wrote, "it must be on the principle that the Federal Government is a mere voluntary association of States, to be dissolved at pleasure by any one of the contracting parties. If this be so, the Confederacy is a rope of sand, to be penetrated and dissolved by the first adverse wave of public opinion in any of the States. . . ." Instead, "the Union was designed to be perpetual." Did this mean that "the people of the States [are] without redress against the tyranny and oppression of the Federal Government?" Not at all. Buchanan cited "the strong and express language in our own Declaration of Independence." But he emphasized that what the Declaration legitimizes is "revolution against an established government, and not a voluntary secession from it by virtue of an inherent constitutional right. . . ."

One might expect Buchanan to issue stern warnings of federal action against illegal secession. However, Buchanan had a restrictive understanding of his powers, even when the law, as he interpreted it, was being flagrantly violated by seceding states. Although the Militia Acts of Congress passed in 1795 and 1807 authorize the President "to call forth the militia and employ the Army and Navy to aid him in" ensuring execution of the laws, this requires that a variety of federal officials in fact be available and capable of performing their institutional roles. Such officials, as a practical matter, were lacking in South Carolina; all the federal officials had resigned. Thus Buchanan claimed the need for "further legislation" that would enable the President (and the country) effectively "to overcome a united opposition in a single State, not to speak of other States who may place themselves in a similar attitude." Without such congressional intervention, Buchanan claimed that he was, in effect, powerless to stop secession.

But Buchanan ultimately relied on more than a legal argument about limited executive power. He argued that "the power to make war against a State is at variance with the whole spirit and intent of the Constitution," where the Union rests on the consent of the governed. Even if war would successfully "preserve the Union," it would be at the price of sundering the fraternity necessary to a true Union. A fratricidal conflict would require the expenditure of both blood and money, generating vast "sufferings and privations of the people during its existence." How would a true Union be reconstructed? "Suppose such a war should result in the conquest of a State; how are we to govern it afterwards? Shall we hold it as a province and govern it by despotic power? . . . The fact is that our Union rests upon public opinion, and can never be cemented by the blood of its citizens shed in civil war. If it can not live in the affections of the people, it must one day perish. Congress possesses many means of preserving it by conciliation, but the sword was not placed in their hand to preserve it by force."

2. South Carolina Justifies Its Secession

Buchanan's pleas to the Southern states to remain in the Union were of no avail. South Carolina formally declared its secession from the Union on December 20, 1860, which was followed four days later by a justification of its position:

Declaration of the Immediate Causes Which Induce and Justify the Secession of South Carolina from the Federal Union[76]

(December 24, 1860)

[The Ordinance begins by quoting the Declaration of Independence and its conclusion that the colonies declaring their independence from Great Britain "are, and of right ought to be, FREE AND INDEPENDENT STATES; and that, as free and independent States, they have full power to levy war, conclude peace, contract alliances, establish commerce, and to do all other acts and things which independent States may of right do." It also quoted the Declaration's general principle that whenever any "form of government becomes destructive of the ends for which it was established, it is the right of the people to alter or abolish it, and to institute a new government."]

In pursuance of this Declaration of Independence, each of the thirteen States proceeded to exercise its separate sovereignty. . . . [I]n 1778, they entered into a League known as the Articles of Confederation, the first Article of which declared "that each State retains its sovereignty, freedom and independence, and every power, jurisdiction and right which is not, by this Confederation, expressly delegated to the United States in Congress assembled."

[The American Revolution concluded with the Treaty of Paris in September 1783, in which Great Britain "acknowledged the independence of each of the separate colonies" by referring to them as "FREE, SOVEREIGN AND INDEPENDENT STATES. . . ."]

Thus were established the two great principles asserted by the Colonies, namely: the right of a State to govern itself; and the right of a people to abolish a Government when it becomes destructive of the ends for which it was instituted. And concurrent with the establishment of these principles, was the fact, that each Colony became and was recognized by the mother Country a FREE, SOVEREIGN AND INDEPENDENT STATE.

[The Ordinance offers a strong version of the "Compact Theory" that views the Constitution as resting on the ratification by "the several sovereign States."]

We hold that the Government thus established is subject to the two great principles asserted in the Declaration of Independence; and we hold further, that the mode of its formation subjects it to a third fundamental principle, namely: the law of compact. We maintain that in every compact between two or more parties, the obligation is mutual; that the failure of one of the contracting parties to perform a material part of the agreement, entirely releases the obligation of the other; and that where no arbiter is provided, each party is remitted to his own judgment to determine the fact of failure, with all its consequences. . . .

[F]ourteen of the States have deliberately refused, for years past, to fulfill their constitutional obligations [to return fugitive slaves with dispatch]. [A]n increasing hostility on the part of the non-slaveholding States to the institution of slavery, has led to a disregard of their obligations. . . . [These States] have enacted

76. http://avalon.law.yale.edu/19th_century/csa_scarsec.asp.

laws which either nullify the Acts of Congress or render useless any attempt to execute them. . . . Thus the constituted compact has been deliberately broken and disregarded by the non-slaveholding States, and the consequence follows that South Carolina is released from her obligation.

The ends for which the Constitution was framed are declared by itself to be "to form a more perfect union, establish justice, insure domestic tranquility, provide for the common defence, promote the general welfare, and secure the blessings of liberty to ourselves and our posterity."

These ends it endeavored to accomplish by a Federal Government, in which each State was recognized as an equal, and had separate control over its own institutions. The right of property in slaves was recognized by giving to free persons distinct political rights, by giving them the right to represent, and burthening them with direct taxes for three-fifths of their slaves; by authorizing the importation of slaves for twenty years; and by stipulating for the rendition of fugitives from labor.

We affirm that these ends for which this Government was instituted have been defeated, and the Government itself has been made destructive of them by the action of the non-slaveholding States. Those States have assume[d] the right of deciding upon the propriety of our domestic institutions; and have denied the rights of property established in fifteen of the States and recognized by the Constitution; they have denounced as sinful the institution of slavery; they have permitted open establishment among them of societies, whose avowed object is to disturb the peace and to eloign the property of the citizens of other States. They have encouraged and assisted thousands of our slaves to leave their homes; and those who remain, have been incited by emissaries, books and pictures to servile insurrection.

[Finally, the Ordinance turns to the baleful consequences of the victory of the Republican Party in the 1860 election:] On the 4th day of March next, this party will take possession of the Government. It has announced that the South shall be excluded from the common territory, that the judicial tribunals shall be made sectional, and that a war must be waged against slavery until it shall cease throughout the United States.

The guaranties of the Constitution will then no longer exist; the equal rights of the States will be lost. The slaveholding States will no longer have the power of self-government, or self-protection, and the Federal Government will have become their enemy. . . .

We, therefore, the People of South Carolina, by our delegates in Convention assembled, appealing to the Supreme Judge of the world for the rectitude of our intentions, have solemnly declared that the Union heretofore existing between this State and the other States of North America, is dissolved, and that the State of South Carolina has resumed her position among the nations of the world, as a separate and independent State; with full power to levy war, conclude peace, contract alliances, establish commerce, and to do all other acts and things which independent States may of right do.

3. Judah Benjamin Defends Secession

Louisiana Senator Judah Benjamin (who would become the first Attorney General of the Confederacy) delivered a passionate farewell address to his colleagues on December 31, 1860.[77] Many of his arguments tracked those made by the South Carolinians, including evocation of the Declaration of Independence. Benjamin also argued that there was a precedent for secession: the transition from the Articles of Confederation to the Constitution itself.

> [Although] . . . the old Articles of Confederacy provided in express terms that they should be perpetual; that they should never be amended or altered without the consent of all the States . . . [nonetheless] nine States of the Confederation seceded from the Confederation, and formed a new Government. They formed it upon the express ground that some of the States had violated their compact. Immediately after, two other States seceded and joined them. They left two alone, Rhode Island and North Carolina; and here is my answer to [Senator Doolittle] from Wisconsin, who asked me the other day, if thirty-three States could expel one, inasmuch as one had the right to leave thirty-three: I point him to the history of our country, to the acts of the fathers, as a full answer upon that subject. After this Government had been organized . . . North Carolina and Rhode Island were still foreign nations, and so treated. . . .

4. Jefferson Davis Takes the Helm of the Confederate States of America

Jefferson Davis, the President of the Confederate States of America—and a former senator from Mississippi—offered yet another response in his inaugural address in Montgomery, Alabama, on February 18, 1861:

> The declared purpose of the compact of Union from which we have withdrawn was "to establish justice, insure domestic tranquility, provide for the common defense, promote the general welfare, and secure the blessings of liberty to ourselves and our posterity"; and when, in the judgment of the sovereign States now composing this Confederacy, it had been perverted from the purposes for which it was ordained, and had ceased to answer the ends for which it was established, a peaceful appeal to the ballot-box declared that so far as they were concerned, the government created by that compact should cease to exist. In this they merely asserted a right which the Declaration of Independence of 1776 had defined to be inalienable; of the time and occasion for its exercise, they, as sovereigns, were the final judges, each for itself. The impartial and enlightened verdict of mankind will vindicate the rectitude of our conduct, and He who knows the hearts of men will judge of the sincerity with which we labored to preserve the Government of our fathers in its spirit. The right solemnly proclaimed at the birth of the States, and which has been affirmed and reaffirmed in the bills of rights of States subsequently admitted into the Union of 1789, undeniably recognize in the people the power to resume the authority delegated for the purposes of government. Thus the sovereign States here represented proceeded to form this Confederacy, and it is by abuse of language that their act has been denominated a revolution. . . .

---

77. The Congressional Globe, Dec. 31, 1860, at 212-217.

5. Lincoln Responds and Acts

March 4, 1861, at long last brought Abraham Lincoln to the White House. In his first inaugural address, Lincoln emphasized his devotion to the Union. He expressed his willingness to address Southern concerns by supporting the so-called Corwin Amendment, strongly supported by outgoing President Buchanan and, in the Senate, by New York Senator William Seward (who would become Lincoln's Secretary of State). The Corwin Amendment was in fact proposed by the Congress and sent to the states for ratification. It stated that "[n]o amendment shall ever be made to the Constitution which will authorize or give to Congress power to abolish or interfere, within any State, with the domestic institutions thereof. . . ." If ratified, ironically, it would have become the Thirteenth Amendment. Lincoln could endorse it precisely because it protected slavery in already existing states, whose legal legitimacy he never challenged. Southern states found it inadequate because it protected slavery *only* in existing states and said nothing about what both sides deemed the truly important issue: the extension of slavery into the territories. Ohio, Maryland, and Illinois ratified the Corwin Amendment, but it was obviously made moot by subsequent developments.

A key argument in Lincoln's first inaugural address was his complete rejection of any theory that would countenance secession:

> I hold, that in contemplation of universal law, and of the Constitution, the Union of these States is perpetual. Perpetuity is implied, if not expressed, in the fundamental law of all national governments. It is safe to assert that no government proper, ever had a provision in its organic law for its own termination. . . .
>
> Again, if the United States be not a government proper, but an association of States in the nature of contract merely, can it, as a contract, be peaceably unmade, by less than all the parties who made it? One party to a contract may violate it—break it, so to speak; but does it not require all to lawfully rescind it?
>
> Descending from these general principles, we find the proposition that, in legal contemplation, the Union is perpetual, confirmed by the history of the Union itself. The Union is much older than the Constitution. It was formed in fact, by the Articles of Association in 1774. It was matured and continued by the Declaration of Independence in 1776. It was further matured and the faith of all the then thirteen States expressly plighted and engaged that it should be perpetual, by the Articles of Confederation in 1778. And finally, in 1787, one of the declared objects for ordaining and establishing the Constitution, was "to form a more perfect union." But if destruction of the Union, by one, or by a part only, of the States, be lawfully possible, the Union is less perfect than before the Constitution, having lost the vital element of perpetuity.
>
> It follows from these views that no State, upon its own mere motion, can lawfully get out of the Union, that resolves and ordinances to that effect are legally void, and that acts of violence, within any State or States, against the authority of the United States, are insurrectionary or revolutionary, according to circumstances.

I therefore consider that, in view of the Constitution and the laws, the Union is unbroken; and, to the extent of my ability, I shall take care, as the Constitution itself expressly enjoins upon me, that the laws of the Union be faithfully executed in all the States.

DISCUSSION

1. What kinds of arguments are presented by Buchanan, South Carolina, Benjamin, Davis, and Lincoln? Who persuades you, and why? What would be the consequences (for a law student or lawyer today) of being persuaded by anyone other than Lincoln?

2. One way of envisioning the American Revolution is as a secession from the British Empire. Consider in this context the remarks to the Senate in 1830 by South Carolina Senator William Smith during a classic debate on the nature of the Union — the legitimacy of South Carolina's attempt to "nullify" what the state termed the "Tariff of Abominations" on the grounds that it exceeded congressional power under the Constitution.[78] Intimations of possible Southern secession arose during the Nullification Crisis and would continue until the Civil War itself.

Senator Smith asserted that there was in fact less cause for secession in 1776 than in 1830. He dismissed as trivial the "three penny tax on tea, which was then merely the beverage of the rich, and a small tax upon stamps." The alleged "Tariff of Abominations," however, was a far more fundamental attack on South Carolina's autonomy, or so Smith argued. Is Smith arguing that the revolution/secession of 1776 was illegitimate? Or, instead, is he arguing that if such a momentous occasion could legitimately be triggered by relatively mild abuses, a fortiori, a rebellion would be justified by far greater incursions on state autonomy?

3. One might think, then, that those who participated in the great events of 1775-1783 would be at least somewhat sympathetic to the theoretical possibility of secession from the new polity framed in Philadelphia should it turn out to be oppressive. There is, however, exceedingly little evidence that this was the case. Professor Akhil Amar, for example, presents powerful evidence that the possibility of secession was explicitly rejected by supporters of the 1787 Constitution (even though, of course, the Constitution was formally silent on the matter). He notes that New York anti-Federalists proposed to ratify the Constitution contingent on the ability of the state to withdraw from the Union if a bill of rights were not added to it by the First Congress. Even though ratification at the Albany Convention was touch and go — ultimately prevailing by a 30-27 vote that would have gone the other way with the switch of only two ratifiers — Federalist supporters rejected the deal and emphasized that the Preamble's commitment to a "more perfect Union"

---

78. William Smith: Speech of Mr. Smith, of South Carolina [February 25, 1830], in Herman Belz, ed., The Webster-Hayne Debate on the Nature of the Constitution: Selected Documents [1830] 331-332, available at http://oll.libertyfund.org/?option=com_staticxt&staticfile=show.php%3Ftitle=1557&chapter=166718&layout=html&Itemid=27.

in effect was the equivalent of the Articles of Confederation's "perpetual Union."[79] And no one at the time seriously asserted the potential dissolubility of the Union.

Even if one agrees with Amar as to the perceptions of the Constitution's ratifiers (and, for that matter, its opponents), is that dispositive as to the arguments made in 1860-1861, modeled on the Declaration of Independence? That is, if one is not an "originalist," committed to interpreting the Constitution as understood by its framers or ratifiers, must one accept their views on secession any more than on any other issue of constitutional meaning?

4. Lincoln asserts that "no government proper, ever had a provision in its organic law for its own termination." Is this an "analytic truth," as in the proposition that there are no married bachelors, or simply an empirical observation, which, however true at the time Lincoln spoke, may have been a function at least in part of the fact that very few countries at the time had written constitutions laying out their "organic law"?

Consider, though, that in the twentieth century Article 70 of the now-defunct Constitution of the Union of Soviet Socialist Republics (USSR) defined the USSR as "an integral, federal, multinational state formed on the principle of socialist federalism as a result of the free self-determination of nations and the voluntary association of equal Soviet Socialist Republics." Article 72 went on to state: "Each Union Republic shall retain the right freely to secede from the USSR." Article 72 later would serve as the basis of several secessionist movements within the republics of the Soviet Union before the dissolution of that country.

Similarly, the contemporary constitution of St. Kitts and Nevis explicitly sets out a procedure by which Nevis could secede. Article 39 of the Federal Democratic Republic of Ethiopia provides that "Every Nation, Nationality and People in Ethiopia has an unconditional right to self-determination, including the right to secession," and sets up a procedure for peaceful secession following a national referendum. The constitution defines a "Nation, Nationality or People" as "a group of people who have or share a large measure of a common culture or similar customs, mutual intelligibility of language, belief in a common or related identities, a common psychological make-up, and who inhabit an identifiable predominantly contiguous territory." Finally, consider that the Canadian Supreme Court, in a decision involving Quebec, suggested that under some circumstances there would be a duty on the part of the national government to recognize a desire of that province to secede.[80] As Professor Wayne Norman has written, the Court "in effect, *read into* the constitution a modest secession clause, even though the constitution itself does not explicitly contemplate secession."[81] Its opinion drew on what the opinion described as "four fundamental and organizing principles of the Constitution . . . , federalism, democracy, constitutionalism and the rule of law, and minority rights."

---

79. See Amar, America's Constitution: A Biography 37-38 (2005). See also Akhil Reed Amar, America's Unwritten Constitution: The Precedents and Principles We Live By 85 (2012) (arguing that the original Constitution emphatically denied state authority to unilaterally secede). Professors Amar and Levinson engage in an extended discussion of this issue in What Do We Talk About When We Talk About the Constitution?, 91 Tex. L. Rev. 1120 (2013).

80. Reference re Secession of Quebec [1998], 2 S.C.R. 217.

81. Wayne Norman, Negotiating Nationalism: Nation-Building, Federalism, and Secession in the Multinational State 200 (2006).

5. Assuming that you in fact admire Lincoln's suppression of the Confederacy, is it because you share the particular views of the Constitution articulated in his inaugural speech or because you support the anti-slavery impulse undergirding Northern opposition to the South that would ultimately be vindicated in the Emancipation Proclamation and the Thirteenth Amendment? What would your view be if the North, convinced that the slavocracy would always remain in political control of the nation, had taken up William Lloyd Garrison's advice and attempted to secede from the South?

6. Several of the Southern states submitted the question of secession to the electorate. In Texas, for example, a referendum held on February 23, 1861, voted 46,129 to 14,697 in favor of the ordinance of secession. Many other states relied on conventions to legitimize their secession. Is there a difference in the legitimacy of secession among these states, or did all behave equally (il)legitimately? As to Texas, consider the following inscription from the memorial to the Southern Confederacy in front of the Texas State Capitol:

> DIED FOR STATE RIGHTS GUARANTEED UNDER THE CONSTITUTION
>
> THE PEOPLE OF THE SOUTH, ANIMATED BY THE SPIRIT OF 1776, TO PRESERVE THEIR RIGHTS, WITHDREW FROM THE FEDERAL COMPACT IN 1861. THE NORTH RESORTED TO COERCION. THE SOUTH, AGAINST OVERWHELMING NUMBERS AND RESOURCES, FOUGHT UNTIL EXHAUSTED.

What is your response to this inscription? Consider these possibilities:

a. It expresses a clearly mistaken view of the 1787 Constitution, and the State of Texas should clearly indicate this.
b. Though it expresses an intellectually defensible—even if not necessarily correct—view of the 1787 Constitution, that view has not prevailed, and the State of Texas should clearly indicate this.
c. The State of Texas should do absolutely nothing and leave it up to viewers to decide for themselves what they think of the inscription.
d. The State of Texas, whatever its decision about the existing inscription, should build a monument to the Union war dead, with an inscription indicating that they fought to vindicate the Constitution of 1787.

Note that none of these possibilities directly addresses the role of slavery in triggering the Civil War. For now, consider this final possibility: The State of Texas should build a memorial to slaves with an inscription that Lincoln's decision to resist the Confederacy, whatever the possible constitutional legitimacy of secession in the abstract, was undoubtedly justified because it overthrew an iniquitous regime of chattel slavery.

7. *The Supreme Court weighs in.* In contrast to Canada, people in the United States did not turn to their Supreme Court to resolve the question of the legality of secession. Indeed, in In re Debs, Chapter 4, infra, the Court wrote that "it would savor somewhat of the puerile and ridiculous to have read a writ of injunction to Lee's army during the late Civil War." Why do you think this is so?

Nevertheless, after the Civil War, the question of the legality of secession did come before the Court.

TEXAS v. WHITE, 7 Wall. 700 (1869): [Texas v. White concerned the legal authority of the secessionist government of Texas to make decisions about U.S. government bonds that had been granted Texas as part of the settlement of the border with New Mexico in the Compromise of 1850. Chief Justice Chase denied the authority of the secessionist government:]

CHASE, C.J.: It is needless to discuss at length the question whether the right of a State to withdraw from the Union for any cause regarded by herself as sufficient is consistent with the Constitution of the United States.

The Union of the States never was a purely artificial and arbitrary relation. It began among the Colonies, and grew out of common origin, mutual sympathies, kindred principles, similar interests, and geographical relations. It was confirmed and strengthened by the necessities of war, and received definite form and character and sanction from the Articles of Confederation. By these, the Union was solemnly declared to "be perpetual." And when these Articles were found to be inadequate to the exigencies of the country, the Constitution was ordained "to form a more perfect Union." It is difficult to convey the idea of indissoluble unity more clearly than by these words. What can be indissoluble if a perpetual Union, made more perfect, is not?

But the perpetuity and indissolubility of the Union by no means implies the loss of distinct and individual existence, or of the right of self-government, by the States. . . . [T]he people of each State compose a State, having its own government, and endowed with all the functions essential to separate and independent existence, and that, "without the States in union, there could be no such political body as the United States." Not only, therefore, can there be no loss of separate and independent autonomy to the States through their union under the Constitution, but it may be not unreasonably said that the preservation of the States, and the maintenance of their governments, are as much within the design and care of the Constitution as the preservation of the Union and the maintenance of the National government. The Constitution, in all its provisions, looks to an indestructible Union composed of indestructible States.

When, therefore, Texas became one of the United States, she entered into an indissoluble relation. All the obligations of perpetual union, and all the guaranties of republican government in the Union, attached at once to the State. The act which consummated her admission into the Union was something more than a compact; it was the incorporation of a new member into the political body. And it was final. The union between Texas and the other States was as complete, as perpetual, and as indissoluble as the union between the original States. There was no place for reconsideration or revocation, except through revolution or through consent of the States. . . .

[Justice Grier dissented, stating, among other things, that "[t]his is to be decided as a *political fact*, not as a *legal fiction*" (emphasis in original). "If I regard the truth of history for the last eight years, I cannot discover the State of Texas as one of these United States."]

To what extent does Texas v. White decide the legality of a future attempt at secession? Is the issue closed, or might it be reopened depending on a change in political circumstances?

NOTE: THE CONFEDERATE CONSTITUTION

The Constitution of the Confederate States of America was written quickly, and used the United States Constitution as its template. Because there was no need to keep post-1789 amendments separate from the main text of the document, the first eight amendments in the Bill of Rights were placed immediately after the other limitations on federal power in Article I, §9. The text of the Ninth and Tenth Amendments were placed in Article VI following, among other things, the Supremacy Clause. However, the texts were altered subtly to emphasize the primacy of the states: Article VI, §5 provided that "[t]he enumeration, in the Constitution, of certain rights shall not be construed to deny or disparage others retained by the people *of the several States*." Article VI, §6 provided that "[t]he powers not delegated to the Confederate States by the Constitution, nor prohibited by it to the States, are reserved to the States, respectively, or to the people *thereof*." The Eleventh Amendment was incorporated into the text of Article III in an interesting way: The judicial power now extended only to suits "between a State and citizens of another State, where the State is plaintiff." Finally, the text of the Twelfth Amendment was incorporated into portions of Article II concerning the Electoral College. Interestingly, the Confederate Constitution contained no explicit guarantee of the right to secede. Nor did it specifically state that free Black people could not be citizens. Some of the most important substantive differences between the U.S. and Confederate Constitutions are listed below:

1. *The Preamble:* The Preamble stated that "We, the people of the Confederate States, each State acting in its sovereign and independent character, in order to form a permanent federal government, establish justice, insure domestic tranquility, and secure the blessings of liberty to ourselves and our posterity invoking the favor and guidance of Almighty God do ordain and establish this Constitution for the Confederate States of America." Note that, in addition to direct invocation of "Almighty God," the phrases "provide for the common defense" and "promote the general welfare" are omitted.

2. *Article I:* Section 1, cl. 2 gave the President a line item veto on individual appropriations "in the same bill." Article I, §2 provided that "no person of foreign birth, not a citizen of the Confederate States, shall be allowed to vote for any officer, civil or political, State or Federal."

Article I, §8, which lists the enumerated powers of Congress, modified the General Welfare and Commerce Clauses in accord with Jacksonian principles against internal improvements. The General Welfare Clause included the proviso that "no bounties shall be granted from the Treasury; nor shall any duties or taxes on importations from foreign nations be laid to promote or foster any branch of industry; and all duties, imposts, and excises shall be uniform throughout the Confederate States." The Commerce Clause stated that "neither this, nor any other clause contained in the Constitution, shall ever be construed to delegate the power to Congress to appropriate money for any internal improvement intended to facilitate commerce; except for the purpose of furnishing lights, beacons, and buoys, and other aids to navigation upon the coasts, and the improvement of harbors and the removing of obstructions in river navigation; in all which cases such duties shall be laid on the navigation facilitated thereby as may be necessary to pay the costs and expenses thereof."

Section 9 included three provisions relating to slavery: Clause 1 provided that "[t]he importation of negroes of the African race from any foreign country other than the slaveholding States or Territories of the United States of America, is hereby forbidden; and Congress is required to pass such laws as shall effectually prevent the same." Clause 2 provided that "Congress shall also have power to prohibit the introduction of slaves from any State not a member of, or Territory not belonging to, this Confederacy." Clause 4 provided that "[n]o bill of attainder, ex post facto law, or law denying or impairing the right of property in negro slaves shall be passed."

Section 9, cl. 9 provided that "Congress shall appropriate no money from the Treasury except by a vote of two-thirds of both Houses, taken by yeas and nays," with a number of exceptions. Clause 20 also provided that "[e]very law, or resolution having the force of law, shall relate to but one subject, and that shall be expressed in the title."

3. *Article II:* Section 1 provided that the President "and the Vice President shall hold their offices for the term of six years; but the President shall not be reeligible."

4. *Article IV:* Section 2 modified the Privileges or Immunities Clause with additional protections for slavery: "The citizens of each State shall be entitled to all the privileges and immunities of citizens in the several States; and shall have the right of transit and sojourn in any State of this Confederacy, with their slaves and other property; and the right of property in said slaves shall not be thereby impaired." The Fugitive Slave Clause of Article IV, §3 was made explicitly about slaves: "No slave or other person held to service or labor in any State or Territory of the Confederate States, under the laws thereof, escaping or lawfully carried into another, shall, in consequence of any law or regulation therein, be discharged from such service or labor; but shall be delivered up on claim of the party to whom such slave belongs, or to whom such service or labor may be due."

Article IV, §3, cl. 3 affirmed the constitutionality of the Louisiana Purchase, while codifying one of the holdings of *Dred Scott*: "The Confederate States may acquire new territory; and Congress shall have power to legislate and provide governments for the inhabitants of all territory belonging to the Confederate States, lying without the limits of the several States; and may permit them, at such times, and in such manner as it may by law provide, to form States to be admitted into the Confederacy. In all such territory the institution of negro slavery, as it now exists in the Confederate States, shall be recognized and protected by Congress and by the Territorial government; and the inhabitants of the several Confederate States and Territories shall have the right to take to such Territory any slaves lawfully held by them in any of the States or Territories of the Confederate States."

5. *Article V:* Section 1 eliminated Congress's role in proposing amendments and instead substituted state conventions: "Upon the demand of any three States, legally assembled in their several conventions, the Congress shall summon a

convention of all the States, to take into consideration such amendments to the Constitution as the said States shall concur in suggesting at the time when the said demand is made." Such amendments would "be ratified by the Legislatures of two-thirds of the several States, or by conventions in two-thirds thereof, as the one or the other mode of ratification may be proposed by the general convention."

DISCUSSION

The Confederate Constitution treated the protection of slavery as an important reason for forming a new constitution. Even so, are there any aspects of the Confederate Constitution that would be desirable in the United States Constitution today?

B. The Authority of the President to Repel Attacks on the Union

Lincoln's first inaugural address was delivered on March 4, 1861. His theoretical argument against the legitimacy of secession did not differ in any substantial respect from that of James Buchanan. What *was* different was Lincoln's conception of his own power to resist secession. Thus, when South Carolina secessionists fired on Fort Sumter on April 12, he quickly acted. On April 15, Lincoln called for a special session of Congress to meet on July 4. Prior to July 4, Lincoln made several important decisions. Some of them, such as calling out the militia, were scarcely controversial, not least because Congress had long since granted the President the authority to respond to attacks on the United States.[82] Others were much more so.

On April 19 and 27, for example, he issued proclamations blockading Confederate ports and authorizing the seizure of ships caught carrying any goods, and not simply war materiel, to them. The foreign shipowners sued, claiming that it was illegal for the President to blockade and seize the ships of neutral countries because there had been no congressional declaration or recognition of a state of war, which did not occur until July 13. Nonetheless, the Supreme Court upheld the Proclamation in a 5-4 decision, with Justice Grier writing for the majority. In the course of addressing whether the blockade and seizure were legal under international law, Grier also explained the President's constitutional authority to use the armed forces to repeal attacks.

Prize Cases

67 U.S. (2 Black) 635 (1863)

GRIER, J.:

The right of prize and capture has its origin in the "jus belli," and is governed and adjudged under the law of nations. To legitimate the capture of a neutral vessel or property on the high seas, a war must exist de facto, and the

82. See, e.g., Stephen I. Vladeck, Note: Emergency Power and the Militia Acts, 114 Yale L.J. 149 (2004).

neutral must have knowledge or notice of the intention of one of the parties belligerent to use this mode of coercion against a port, city, or territory, in possession of the other.

Let us enquire whether, at the time this blockade was instituted, a state of war existed which would justify a resort to these means of subduing the hostile force. . . . As a civil war is never publicly proclaimed, eo nomine, against insurgents, its actual existence is a fact in our domestic history which the Court is bound to notice and to know. The true test of its existence, as found in the writings of the sages of the common law, may be thus summarily stated: "When the regular course of justice is interrupted by revolt, rebellion, or insurrection, so that the Courts of Justice cannot be kept open, civil war exists and hostilities may be prosecuted on the same footing as if those opposing the Government were foreign enemies invading the land."

By the Constitution, Congress alone has the power to declare a national or foreign war. It cannot declare war against a State, or any number of States, by virtue of any clause in the Constitution. The Constitution confers on the President the whole Executive power. He is bound to take care that the laws be faithfully executed. He is Commander-in-Chief of the Army and Navy of the United States, and of the militia of the several States when called into the actual service of the United States. He has no power to initiate or declare a war either against a foreign nation or a domestic State. But by the Acts of Congress of February 28th, 1795, and 3d of March, 1807, he is authorized to call out the militia and use the military and naval forces of the United States in case of invasion by foreign nations, and to suppress insurrection against the government of a State or of the United States.

If a war be made by invasion of a foreign nation, the President is not only authorized but bound to resist force by force. He does not initiate the war, but is bound to accept the challenge without waiting for any special legislative authority. And whether the hostile party be a foreign invader, or States organized in rebellion, it is none the less a war, although the declaration of it be "unilateral." . . .

The President was bound to meet [the Civil War] in the shape it presented itself, without waiting for Congress to baptize it with a name; and no name given to it by him or them could change the fact. . . .

The law of nations is also called the law of nature; it is founded on the common consent as well as the common sense of the world. It contains no such anomalous doctrine as that which this Court are now for the first time desired to pronounce, to wit: That insurgents who have risen in rebellion against their sovereign, expelled her Courts, established a revolutionary government, organized armies, and commenced hostilities, are not enemies because they are traitors; and a war levied on the Government by traitors, in order to dismember and destroy it, is not a war because it is an "insurrection."

Whether the President in fulfilling his duties, as Commander-in-Chief, in suppressing an insurrection, has met with such armed hostile resistance, and a civil war of such alarming proportions as will compel him to accord to them the character of belligerents, is a question to be decided by him, and this court must be governed by the decisions and acts of the Political Department of the government to which this power was intrusted. "He must determine what degree of force the crisis demands." The proclamation of blockade is, itself, official and conclusive evidence to the court that a state of war existed which demanded and authorized a recourse to such a measure, under the circumstances peculiar to the case.

If it were necessary to the technical existence of a war, that it should have a legislative sanction, we find it in almost every act passed at the extraordinary session of the Legislature of 1861, which was wholly employed in enacting laws to enable the Government to prosecute the war with vigor and efficiency. And finally, in 1861, we find Congress . . . passing an act "approving, legalizing, and making valid all the acts, proclamations, and orders of the President, &c., as if they had been issued and done under the previous express authority and direction of the Congress of the United States." Without admitting that such an act was necessary under the circumstances, it is plain that if the President had in any manner assumed powers which it was necessary should have the authority or sanction of Congress, . . . this ratification has operated to perfectly cure the defect. . . .

NELSON, J., dissenting, joined by TANEY, C.J., and CATRON and CLIFFORD, JJ. . . .

In the case of a rebellion or resistance of a portion of the people of a country against the established government, there is no doubt, if in its progress and enlargement the government thus thought to be overthrown sees fit, it may by the competent power recognize or declare the existence of a state of civil war, which will draw after it all the consequences and rights of war between the contending parties. . . . But before this insurrection against the established Government can be dealt with on the footing of a civil war, within the meaning of the law of nations and the Constitution of the United States, and which will draw after it belligerent rights, it must be recognized or declared by the war-making power of the Government. . . .

Now, in one sense, no doubt this is war, and may be a war of the most extensive and threatening dimensions and effects, but it is a statement simply of its existence in a material sense, and has no relevancy or weight when the question is what constitutes war in a legal sense, in the sense of the law of nations, and of the Constitution of the United States. For it must be a war in this sense to attach to it all the consequences that belong to belligerent rights. . . . [T]o constitute a civil war in the sense in which we are speaking, before it can exist, in contemplation of law, it must be recognized or declared by the sovereign power of the State, and which sovereign power by our Constitution is lodged in the Congress of the United States—civil war, therefore, under our system of government, can exist only by an act of Congress, which requires the assent of two of the great departments of the Government, the Executive and Legislative.

. . . But we are asked, what would become of the peace and integrity of the Union in case of an insurrection at home or invasion from abroad if this power could not be exercised by the President in the recess of Congress and until that body could be assembled?

The framers of the Constitution fully comprehended this question, and provided for the contingency. . . . The Constitution declares that Congress shall have power "to provide for calling forth the militia to execute the laws of the Union, suppress insurrections, and repel invasions." Another clause, "that the President shall be Commander-in-chief of the Army and Navy of the United States, and of the militia of the several States when called into the actual service of the United States"; and, again, "He shall take care that the laws shall be faithfully executed." Congress passed laws on this subject in 1792 and 1795.

. . . The 2d section [of the Act of 1795] provides, that when the laws of the United States shall be opposed, or the execution obstructed in any State by combinations too powerful to be suppressed by the course of judicial proceedings, it shall be lawful for the President to call forth the militia of such State, or of any other State or States as may be necessary to suppress such combinations; and by the Act 3 March, 1807 (2 U.S. Laws, 443) it is provided that in case of insurrection or obstruction of the laws, either in the United States or of any State or Territory, where it is lawful for the President to call forth the militia for the purpose of suppressing such insurrection, and causing the laws to be executed, it shall be lawful to employ for the same purpose such part of the land and naval forces of the United States as shall be judged necessary. It will be seen, therefore, that ample provision has been made under the Constitution and laws against any sudden and unexpected disturbance of the public peace from insurrection at home or invasion from abroad. The whole military and naval power of the country is put under the control of the President to meet the emergency. . . .

The Acts of 1795 and 1807 did not, and could not under the Constitution, confer on the President the power of declaring war against a State of this Union, or of deciding that war existed, and upon that ground authorized the capture and confiscation of the property of every citizen of the State whenever it was found on the waters. . . . This great power over the business and property of the citizen is reserved to the legislative department by the express words of the Constitution. It cannot be delegated or surrendered to the Executive. Congress alone can determine whether war exists or should be declared; and until they have acted, no citizen of the State can be punished in his person or property, unless he has committed some offence against a law of Congress passed before the act was committed, which made it a crime, and defined the punishment. . . .

DISCUSSION

1. Note the delay between Lincoln's inauguration and the meeting of Congress on July 4. Why was Congress not in session on Inauguration Day, March 4? (See Article I, §4, cl. 2; Article II, §3. Compare them with the Twentieth Amendment.) Even if Lincoln violated no formal provision of the Constitution in delaying Congress's return until July 4, did he violate its democratic "spirit" by failing to call Congress back into session as soon as was reasonably possible, say May 1 to allow California's representatives sufficient time to make it to Omaha, from where they could then take the train to Washington? (As a matter of fact, the Senate was in session on March 4 to confirm members of Lincoln's cabinet, so presumably even the newly elected Western senators were in Washington then.) Would you think any less of Lincoln if he had called no special session at all and simply waited until Congress convened in December, the date set by the Constitution?

2. Justice Grier mentions the Acts of 1795 and 1807 as providing a basis for Lincoln's actions. Thus, argues Stephen Vladeck, the basis of what is undoubtedly "a broad understanding of the President's war powers with respect to his independent authority to act during crises" is the fact that prior Congresses had delegated, as is their constitutional right, the relevant authority. Thus, he argues, "The Prize Cases, among the most significant" precedents with regard to presidential power "in

the annals of the Supreme Court, turned not on any provision of the Constitution, but on the Militia Acts."[83] If Vladeck is correct in arguing that these early statutes were sufficient to authorize Lincoln's actions, then what precisely is the relevance of the Act of August 6, 1861, by which the members of Congress "hereby approve and in all respects legalize and make valid" the acts done by the President "as if they had been issued and done under the previous express authority and direction of the Congress of the United States"? Is this a kind of congressional "suspenders" provided on top of the "belt" of the earlier legislation, just in case anyone doubts the adequacy of the latter? But if the earlier Acts were, contra Vladeck, insufficient, then would the illegality of Lincoln's proclamation be "cured" by retroactive legitimation? Does this suggest that any violation of separation of powers can in effect be negated if its institutional "victim" acquiesces? Or do ordinary citizens have a stake in the strict maintenance of separation, whatever might be the reaction of political officials occupying the offices in question?

3. What if Congress had passed an act (or joint resolution) specifically repudiating the President's act? (Would the President have had the right to veto any such repudiation? See Article I, §7, cl. 3.) If the earlier acts justified Lincoln, then would Congress's ostensible withdrawal of such authority have any consequence for the actual seizure at issue in the Prize Cases?

Consider in this context the majority's statement that "[t]he President *was bound* to meet [the Civil War] in the shape it presented itself, without waiting for Congress to baptize it with a name; and no name given to it by him or them could change the fact" (emphasis added). Does this suggest a constitutional obligation upon the President, with concomitant constitutionally assigned power, either from the Commander-in-Chief Clause or the oath of office, to do whatever he thought necessary to meet the threat to the Union? Michael Stokes Paulsen[84] argues that so long as the President can plausibly be claiming to defend the overarching constitutional order, he (or in the future she) is authorized by the oath of office itself to disregard any particular part of the Constitution if fidelity to the individual part might, according to the President, threaten the survival of the whole, the constitutional order itself. Paulsen quotes Lincoln: "I felt that measures, otherwise unconstitutional, might become lawful, by becoming indispensable to the preservation of the constitution, through the preservation of the nation."[85] Paulsen fully recognizes that he is defending "dangerous principles,"[86] but, he concludes, "if I am mistaken in all this, so was President Lincoln."[87] Madison might have been cited to the same effect inasmuch as he wrote, in The Federalist No. 41: "It is in vain to oppose constitutional barriers to the impulse of self-preservation. It is worse than in vain; because it plants in the Constitution itself *necessary usurpations of power*, every precedent of which is a germ of unnecessary and multiplied repetitions." (Note that in this sentence, the word "oppose" means "place in opposition to," or "erect," not "argue against.")

---

83. Id. at 179-180.

84. Paulsen, The Constitution of Necessity, 79 Notre Dame L. Rev. 1257 (2004).

85. Id. at 1283 (quoting from letter of April 4, 1864, from Lincoln to United States Senator Albert G. Hodges).

86. Id. at 1296.

87. Id. at 1297.

Should one always read the Constitution as effectively legitimizing whatever a President chooses to do in responding to what the President defines as an "emergency" threatening fundamental interests of national security? Is this the practical meaning of the Court's statement that "[w]hether the President in fulfilling his duties, as Commander-in-Chief, in suppressing an insurrection, has met with such armed hostile resistance, and a civil war of such alarming proportions as will compel him to accord to them the character of belligerents, is a question to be decided by him, and this court must be governed by the decisions and acts of the Political Department of the government to which this power was intrusted." Does this view undermine the concept of a "limited" government, or is it simply the case that the Court has confidence that Presidents will not overreach? (What is the appropriate remedy for overreaching? A suit by private parties against the President for the damage caused them? Impeachment? Loss of the next election?)

One might argue that the notion of "limits" to governmental power in general and executive power in particular rests on a background assumption of political stability, so that governmental (and executive) powers are quite different whenever these background conditions dissolve into instability or "emergency." Such emergencies are sometimes viewed as "states of exception," a term associated especially with the German legal philosopher Carl Schmitt.[88] It was Schmitt, for example, who wrote that "[t]here exists no norm that is applicable to chaos"[89] or, perhaps, even "crisis." There is in fact nothing new about the notion of the "exception" or "emergency." Indeed, political scientist Clinton Rossiter, who published in 1948 a brilliant and disturbing book, Constitutional Dictatorship, noted that the idea goes back at least to ancient Rome, which institutionalized the role of the "dictator" who could safeguard the constitutional order in a time of emergency. Rossiter writes, "No sacrifice is too great for our democracy, least of all the temporary sacrifice of democracy itself."[90]

More recently, the Italian social theorist Giorgio Agamben has written that "the state of exception tends increasingly to appear as the dominant paradigm of government in contemporary politics."[91] If this is true, does it threaten democracy (and the enterprise of constitutional government)?

C. *Lincoln and the Suspension of Habeas Corpus*[92]

On April 27, 1861, President Lincoln issued an order to Commanding General Winfield Scott authorizing him to suspend the writ of habeas corpus. The writ of habeas corpus allows persons who have been deprived of liberty to challenge the legality of their detention in a court. During the period in which the writ is

---

88. Who, as a matter of fact, was the chief academic apologist for Hitler's seizure of power as a means of responding to the ostensible "emergency" facing Weimar Germany.

89. Carl Schmitt, Political Theology: Four Chapters on the Theory of Sovereignty 13 (trans. George Schwab, translating the 1934 German edition) (2005).

90. Clinton Rossiter, Constitutional Dictatorship 314 (1948).

91. Giorgio Agamben, State of Exception 2 (2005).

92. See Carl Swisher, 5 History of the Supreme Court of the United States: The Taney Period 1836-1864, ch. 14 (1974).

suspended, the government can effectively imprison people at will, because the prisoners will have no access to courts to prove that their detention is unlawful.

The Constitution, in §9 of Article I, specifically authorizes the suspension of habeas corpus "when in cases of rebellion or invasion the public safety may require it." The question that Lincoln's action raised was: Who is authorized by the Constitution to make such a determination?

1. Chief Justice Taney on the Exclusive Authority of Congress

As Lincoln prepared for war, Union troops moved through Maryland to gather in Washington, D.C. Maryland was a slave state with cultural sympathies with the South. Many of Maryland's citizens opposed going to war with the South and sought to stay out of the conflict. There was even concern that Maryland might try to secede, cutting off the capital from the rest of the Union.

On April 19, 1861, a pro-Southern mob rioted and attacked Union troops traveling to Washington. On April 29, 1861, the Maryland Legislature voted against secession, but it also protested the presence of Union troops in Maryland. The legislature did not want the federal government to use Maryland as a passageway for any troops that would be used to make war on the South; and it refused to reopen railway lines for that purpose.

On May 25, federal troops arrested John Merryman, a lieutenant in the Maryland Militia, who was accused of participating in the destruction of railroad bridges in order to prevent Union troops from moving through Baltimore.

Merryman was a prominent politician; his father and Chief Justice Taney had attended Dickinson College together. Merryman's lawyer filed a writ of habeas corpus before the Chief Justice, sitting as a circuit judge for the circuit that included Maryland. The writ was addressed to General George Cadwalader.[93]

Taney ordered Cadwalader to appear with Merryman for a hearing, but Cadwalader refused, sending a message that stated that he acted under the authority of President Lincoln's suspension of habeas corpus. Taney then sent a U.S. Marshal to Fort McHenry serve an order on Cadwalader to appear for a contempt hearing, but the Marshall was refused admittance to the fort.

At that point, Taney stated that Merryman's detention was illegal, but issued no order specifying that he be released. Instead, he indicated his intention to write a fuller opinion elaborating his conclusions and to "report them with these proceedings to the President of the United States, and call upon him to perform his constitutional duty to enforce the laws. In other words, to enforce the process of this Court." Taney later produced an extensive opinion, asserting that Merryman's detention was illegal on two grounds:

> 1. The President, under the Constitution and laws of the United States, cannot suspend the privilege of the writ of habeas corpus, nor authorize any military officer to do so.
> 2. A military officer has no right to arrest and detain a person, not subject to the rules and articles of war, for an offence against the laws of the

---

93. By far the most thorough examination is Seth Barrett Tillman, *Ex parte Merryman*: Myth, History, and Scholarship, 224 Mil. L. Rev. 481 (2016).

United States, except in and of the judicial authority and subject to its control—and if the party is arrested by the military, it is the duty of the officer to deliver him over immediately to the civil authority, to be dealt with according to law.

Ex parte Merryman

17 F. Cas. 144 (1861)

I understand that the President not only claims the right to suspend the writ of habeas corpus himself, at his discretion, but to delegate that discretionary power to a military officer, and to leave it to him to determine whether he will or will not obey judicial process that may be served upon him. . . . I certainly listened to [the argument] with some surprise, for I had supposed it to be one of those points of constitutional law upon which there was no difference of opinion, and that it was admitted on all hands, that the privilege of the writ could not be suspended, except by act of congress. . . . [B]elieving, as I do, that the president has exercised a power which he does not possess under the constitution, a proper respect for the high office he fills, requires me to state plainly and fully the grounds of my opinion. . . .

The clause of the constitution, which authorizes the suspension of the privilege of the writ of habeas corpus, is in the 9th section of the first article. This article is devoted to the legislative department of the United States, and has not the slightest reference to the executive department. . . .

It is the second article of the constitution that provides for the organization of the executive department, enumerates the powers conferred on it, and prescribes its duties. And if the high power over the liberty of the citizen now claimed, was intended to be conferred on the president, it would undoubtedly be found in plain words in this article; but here is not a word in it that can furnish the slightest ground to justify the exercise of the power.

. . . The only power, therefore, which the president possesses, where the "life, liberty or property" of a private citizen is concerned, is the power and duty prescribed in the third section of the second article, which requires "that he shall take care that the laws shall be faithfully executed." He is not authorized to execute them himself, or through agents or officers, civil or military, appointed by himself, but he is to take care that they be faithfully carried into execution, as they are expounded and adjudged by the co-ordinate branch of the government to which that duty is assigned by the constitution. It is thus made his duty to come in aid of the judicial authority, if it shall be resisted by a force too strong to be overcome without the assistance of the executive arm; but in exercising this power he acts in subordination to judicial authority, assisting it to execute its process and enforce its judgments.

With such provisions in the constitution, expressed in language too clear to be misunderstood by any one, I can see no ground whatever for supposing that the president, in any emergency, or in any state of things, can authorize the suspension of the privileges of the writ of habeas corpus, except in aid of the judicial power. He certainly does not faithfully execute the laws, if he takes upon himself legislative power, by suspending the writ of habeas corpus, and the judicial power also, by arresting and imprisoning a person without due process of law.

Nor can any argument be drawn from the nature of sovereignty, or the necessity of government, for self-defence in times of tumult and danger. The government of the United States is one of delegated and limited power; it derives its existence and authority altogether from the constitution, and neither of its branches, executive, legislative or judicial, can exercise any of the powers of government beyond those specified and granted; for the tenth article of the amendments to the constitution, in express terms, provides that "the powers not delegated to the United States by the constitution, not prohibited by it to the states, are reserved to the states, respectively, or to the people." . . . The right of the subject to the benefit of the writ of habeas corpus, it must be recollected, was one of the great points in controversy, during the long struggle in England between arbitrary government and free institutions, and must therefore have strongly attracted the attention of the statesmen engaged in framing a new one and, as they supposed, a freer government than the one which they had thrown off by the revolution. From the earliest history of the common law, if a person were imprisoned, no matter by what authority, he had a right to the writ of habeas corpus to bring his case before the king's bench. . . .

[Blackstone writes that] "the happiness of our constitution is, that it is not left to the executive power to determine when the danger of the state is so great as to render [suspension of habeas corpus] expedient. It is the parliament only or legislative power that, whenever it sees proper, can authorize the crown by suspending the habeas corpus for a short and limited time, to imprison suspected persons without giving any reason for so doing." If the president of the United States may suspend the writ, then the constitution of the United States has conferred upon him more regal and absolute power over the liberty of the citizen, than the people of England have thought it safe to entrust to the crown; a power which the queen of England cannot exercise at this day, and which could not have been lawfully exercised by the sovereign even in the reign of Charles the First. . . .

I have exercised all the power which the constitution and laws confer upon me, but that power has been resisted by a force too strong for me to overcome. It is possible that the officer who has incurred this grave responsibility may have misunderstood his instructions, and exceeded the authority intended to be given him; I shall, therefore, order all the proceedings in this case, with my opinion, to be filed and recorded in the circuit court of the United States for the district of Maryland, and direct the clerk to transmit a copy, under seal, to the president of the United States. It will then remain for that high officer, in fulfilment of his constitutional obligation to "take care that the laws be faithfully executed," to determine what measures he will take to cause the civil process of the United States to be respected and enforced.

[Ultimately, the Administration indicted Merryman for treason by a civil grand jury. He was released on bail and never tried.]

2. The President Asserts Executive Authority

Lincoln did not respond directly to Taney, but delivered this message to Congress on July 4:

> Soon after the first call for militia, it was considered a duty to authorize the Commanding General, in proper cases, according to his discretion, to suspend the privilege of the writ of habeas corpus; or, in other words, to

arrest, and detain, without resort to the ordinary processes and forms of law, such individuals as he might deem dangerous to the public safety. This authority has purposely been exercised but very sparingly. Nevertheless, the legality and propriety of what has been done under it, are questioned; and the attention of the country has been called to the proposition that one who is sworn to "take care that the laws be faithfully executed," should not himself violate them. Of course some consideration was given to the questions of power, and propriety, before this matter was acted upon. The whole of the laws which were required to be faithfully executed, were being resisted, and failing of execution, in nearly one-third of the States. Must they be allowed to finally fail of execution, even had it been perfectly clear, that by the use of the means necessary to their execution, some single law, made in such extreme tenderness of the citizen's liberty, that practically, it relieves more of the guilty, than of the innocent, should, to a very limited extent, be violated? To state the question more directly, are all the laws, but one, to go unexecuted, and the government itself go to pieces, lest that one be violated? Even in such a case, would not the official oath be broken, if the government should be overthrown, when it was believed that disregarding the single law, would tend to preserve it? But it was not believed that this question was presented. It was not believed that any law was violated. The provision of the Constitution . . . is equivalent to a provision—is a provision—that such privilege may be suspended when, in cases of rebellion, or invasion, the public safety does require it. It was decided that we have a case of rebellion, and that the public safety does require the qualified suspension of the privilege of the writ which was authorized to be made. Now it is insisted that Congress, and not the Executive, is vested with this power. But the Constitution itself, is silent as to which, or who, is to exercise the power; and as the provision was plainly made for a dangerous emergency, it cannot be believed the framers of the instrument intended, that in every case, the danger should run its course, until Congress could be called together; the very assembling of which might be prevented, as was intended in this case, by the rebellion.

DISCUSSION

1. It is not clear whether Congress's retroactive approval, on August 6, 1861, of "all the acts, proclamations, and orders of the President . . . respecting the army and navy of the United States" included the suspension of the writ of habeas corpus. On March 3, 1863, Congress passed a habeas corpus act providing that "during the present rebellion the President of the United States, whenever, in his judgment, the public safety may require it, is authorized to suspend the privilege of the writ of habeas corpus in any case throughout the United States or any part thereof." Does this congressional authorization affect the power that President Lincoln held prior to its enactment? If so, was his original order suspending habeas corpus unconstitutional? (Some have argued that the suspension was legitimate only so long as Congress was not in session, but that Congress's failure specifically to enact a suspension when it reconvened invalidated further enforcement of the presidential order.)

2. Lincoln is often described as "defying" Ex parte Merryman, but Professor Seth Barrett Tillman suggests that this is incorrect because there was no explicit order. He describes Ex parte Merryman as "effectively an advisory opinion" inasmuch as it simply called on the President to accept Taney's views as to his constitutional duty rather than directly order him to do so.[94] Perhaps one can best describe this as a disagreement between a judge and a President about the limits of executive power. This is no small matter, but it is nevertheless different from outright "defiance" of judicial authority. In his July 4 statement, Lincoln does not argue that he was entitled to ignore an otherwise valid judicial decree, only that he respectfully disagreed with Taney's view that he lacked the general power to suspend habeas corpus without congressional assent. One might compare this with Lincoln's refusal to accept Dred Scott v. Sandford as the law of the land even though he accepted that the case was dispositive as to Dred Scott's legal status.

D. Lincoln: The Great Emancipator

As already noted, Lincoln assumed a moderate stance toward slavery in his Inaugural Address. "I have no purpose, directly or indirectly, to interfere with the institution of slavery in the States where it exists. I believe that I have no lawful right to do so, and I have no inclination to do so." He explicitly reiterated his support of the 1860 Republican platform, which endorsed "the maintenance inviolate of the rights of the States, and especially the right of each State to order and control its own domestic institutions according to its own judgment exclusively." This, of course, helps to explain his support of the Corwin Amendment. However, on January 1, 1863, Lincoln issued the famous Emancipation Proclamation:

> I, Abraham Lincoln, President of the United States, by virtue of the power in me vested as Commander-in-Chief, of the Army and Navy of the United States in time of actual armed rebellion against authority and government of the United States, and as a fit and necessary war measure for suppressing said rebellion, do . . . order and designate as the States and parts of States wherein the people thereof respectively, are this day in rebellion against the United States, the following, to wit: Arkansas, Texas, Louisiana, (except the Parishes of St. Bernard, Plaquemines, Jefferson, St. Johns, St. Charles, St. James[,] Ascension, Assumption, Terrebonne, Lafourche, St. Mary, St. Martin, and Orleans, including the City of New Orleans) [,] Mississippi, Alabama, Florida, Georgia, South-Carolina, North-Carolina, and Virginia, (except the forty-eight counties designated as West Virginia, and also the counties of Berkeley, Accomac, Northampton, Elizabeth-City, York, Princess Ann, and Norfolk, including the cities of Norfolk & Portsmouth[)]; and which excepted parts are, for the present, left precisely as if this proclamation were not issued.
>
> And by virtue of the power, and for the purpose aforesaid, I do order and declare that all persons held as slaves within the designated States . . . are, and henceforward shall be free; and that the Executive

94. Tillman, supra n.93, at 506.

> government of the United States, including the military and naval authorities thereof, will recognize and maintain the freedom of said persons. . . . And upon this act, sincerely believed to be an act of justice, warranted by the Constitution, upon military necessity, I invoke the considerate judgment of mankind, and the gracious favor of Almighty God. . . .

The Emancipation Proclamation is not a general declaration of freedom; consider the care with which certain areas in the rebel states are exempted. Indeed, as late as July of 1864, Lincoln reiterated that he was "unprepared . . . to declare a constitutional competency in Congress to abolish slavery in [the] States," i.e., the loyal slave states of Delaware, Kentucky, Maryland, and Missouri, though he indicated support for legislation that would offer compensation to slaveowners should those states voluntarily agree to abolish slavery at some point in the future.

Instead, Lincoln emphasized the President's power as commander-in-chief to take actions warranted by "military necessity": "As Commander-in-Chief, I suppose I have a right to take any measure which may best subdue the enemy." Beyond this there was the President's duty to preserve the Union: "I felt that measures otherwise unconstitutional might become lawful by becoming indispensable to the preservation of the Constitution through the preservation of the nation."[95]

NOTE: FORMER JUSTICE CURTIS DISSENTS

The Emancipation Proclamation scarcely received universal support, even from the North.[96] Among the most prominent critics was Benjamin R. Curtis, who had vigorously dissented in *Dred Scott* before resigning from the Court shortly thereafter. In September 1862, Lincoln had publicly indicated his intention to issue the Emancipation Proclamation should the South not return to the Union. Curtis responded with an October 1862 pamphlet on "executive power" that expressed strong reservations about a number of Lincoln's actions, including the potential Proclamation.[97] Curtis wrote:

> The persons who are the subjects of this proclamation are held to service by the laws of the respective States in which they reside, enacted by State authority as clear and unquestionable, under our system of government, as any law passed by any State on any subject.
>
> This proclamation, then, by an executive decree, proposes to repeal and annul valid State laws which regulate the domestic relations of their people. . . .
>
> [T]his executive decree holds out this proposed repeal of State laws as a threatened penalty for the continuance of a governing majority of the people of each State, or part of a State, in rebellion against the United States. So that the President hereby assumes to himself the power to denounce it as a punishment against the entire people of a State, that the

96. See, e.g., Louis P. Masur, Lincoln's Hundred Days: The Emancipation Proclamation and the War for the Union (2012).

97. 2 A Memoir of Benjamin Robbins Curtis 306-335 (Benjamin R. Curtis ed., 1879).

95. See Randall, supra n.74, at 351, 358.

valid laws of that State which regulate the domestic condition of its inhabitants shall become null and void, at a certain future date, by reason of the criminal conduct of a governing majority of its people.

This penalty . . . is not to be inflicted on those persons who have been guilty of treason. The freedom of their slaves was already provided for by the act of Congress, recited in a subsequent part of the proclamation.[98]

It is not, therefore, as a punishment of guilty persons that the commander-in-chief decrees the freedom of slaves. It is upon the slaves of loyal persons, or of those who, from their tender years, or other disability, cannot be either disloyal or otherwise, that the proclamation is to operate, if at all; and it is to operate to set them free, in spite of the valid laws of their States. . . .

It has never been doubted that the power to abolish slavery within the States was not delegated to the United States by the Constitution, but was reserved to the States. If the President, as commander-in-chief of the army and navy in time of war, may, by an executive decree, exercise this power to abolish slavery in the States, because he is of opinion that he may thus "best subdue the enemy," what other power, reserved to the States or to the people, may not be exercised by the President, for the same reason that he is of opinion he may thus best subdue the enemy? . . .

Besides, all the powers of the President are executive merely. He cannot make a law. He cannot repeal one. He can only execute the laws. . . .

These conclusions concerning the powers of the President cannot be shaken by the assertion that "rebels have no rights." The assertion itself is not true, in reference either to the seceding States or their people.

It is not true of those States; for the Government of the United States has never admitted, and cannot admit, that as States, they are in rebellion. . . . [T]he Constitution is as much the supreme law of the land in Tennessee to-day, as it was before the void act of secession was attempted by a part of its people. Else the act was effectual, and the State is independent of the Government of the United States, and the war is a war of conquest and subjugation.

Nor is the assertion that "rebels have no rights" applicable to the people of those States. . . . When many millions of people are involved in civil war, humanity, and that public law which in modern times is humane, forbid their treatment as outlaws. And if public law and the Constitution and laws of the United States are now their rules of duty towards us, on what ground shall we deny that public law and the Constitution, and the laws made under it, are also our rules of duty towards them? . . .

---

98. Curtis is referring to the Second Confiscation Act, passed in July 1862, which, in the words of Professor Swisher, was "linked with provisions dealing with the punishment of treason" and applied to the property of all civil and military officers serving under the Confederacy; to the property of any person residing in the North who should assist and give aid and comfort to the rebellion; and to the property of persons "in any state" who, being engaged in the rebellion, did not reestablish their allegiance to the United States within sixty days after a proclamation of warning by the President. Slaves were to be liberated in areas occupied by the armed forces, and the return of fugitive slaves to rebel owners was forbidden.

But, if [it] were conceded that "rebels have no rights," there would still be matter demanding the greatest consideration. For the inquiry which I have invited is not what are their rights, but what are our rights. . . .

It is among the rights of all of us that the executive power should be kept within its prescribed constitutional limits, and should not legislate, by its decrees, upon subjects of transcendent importance to the whole people.

Whether such decrees are wise or unwise, whether their subjects are citizens or not, if they are usurpations of power, our rights are both infringed and endangered. They are infringed, because the power to decide and to act is taken from the people without their consent. They are endangered, because, in a constitutional government, every usurpation of power dangerously disorders the whole framework of the State.

. . . Among all the causes of alarm which now distress the public mind, there are few more terrible . . . than the tendency to lawlessness which is manifesting itself in so many directions. No stronger evidence of this could be afforded than the open declaration of a respectable and widely circulated journal, that "nobody cares" whether a great public act of the President of the United States is in conformity with or is subversive of the supreme law of the land. . . . [O]ur public affairs have become so desperate, and our ability to retrieve them by the use of honest means is so distrusted, and our willingness to use other means so undoubted, that our great public servants may themselves break the fundamental law of the country, and become usurpers of vast powers not intrusted to them, in violation of their solemn oath of office; and "nobody cares."

DISCUSSION

1. Mark E. Neely, Jr., points out that Lincoln's own views on his power to emancipate slaves underwent significant changes during the course of his presidency.[99] Near its beginning, for example, Lincoln wrote a letter, marked "private and confidential," to Illinois Senator Orville H. Browning, who had objected to Lincoln's prompt revocation of an August 30, 1861 order by General John C. Fremont (who had been the Republican candidate for the presidency in 1856) freeing slaves belonging to Missouri rebels. Part of the reason for overruling Fremont was Lincoln's well-merited concern about keeping other slave states, especially Kentucky, in the Union should the war so quickly take on anti-slavery (and not only anti-secession) aims. Lincoln noted as well that Fremont's order went beyond a congressional statute that had been passed on August 6 mandating the confiscation of property, including slaves, "used for insurrectional purposes," which presumably did not cover all property that happened to be owned by those engaged in insurrection. But Lincoln informed Browning that he had constitutional concerns as well:[100]

99. See Mark E. Neely, Jr., The Last Best Hope on Earth, ch. 4 (1993).

100. Letter of September 22, 1861, in Lincoln: Speeches, Letters, Miscellaneous Writings, Presidential Messages and Proclamations 268-269 (Library of America 1989).

> [Fremont's] proclamation . . . is simply "dictatorship." It assumes that the general may do anything he pleases—confiscate the lands and free the slaves of loyal people, as well as of disloyal ones. And going the whole figure I have no doubt would be more popular with some thoughtless people, than that which has been done. But I cannot assume this reckless position; nor allow others to assume it on my responsibility. You speak of it as being the only means of saving the government. On the contrary it is itself the surrender of the government. Can it be pretended that it is any longer the government of the U.S.—any government of Constitution and laws,—wherein a General, or a President, may make permanent rules of property by proclamation.
>
> I do not say Congress might not with propriety pass a law, on the point. . . . I do not say I might not, as a member of Congress, vote for it. What I object to, is, that I as President, shall expressly or impliedly seize and exercise the permanent legislative functions of the government.

By the following May, when General David Hunter issued a similar proclamation in regard to federally controlled areas in South Carolina, Georgia, and Florida, Lincoln revoked it only on the ground that it went well beyond the power of a military officer. However, "I further make known that whether it be competent for me, as Commander-in-Chief of the Army and Navy, to declare the Slaves of any state or states, free, and whether at any time, in any case, it shall have become a necessity indispensable to the maintenance of the government, to exercise such supposed power, are questions which, under my responsibility, I reserve to myself. . . ."[101]

2. In his letter to Browning, Lincoln raises the question of congressional abolition of slavery. Do you agree that Congress could have abolished slavery in the seceding states, by ordinary legislation based on the war power? Could the war powers have justified its abolition in the border states with whom the United States was not at war? Lincoln presumably believed that he was without power to emancipate the slaves even in those parts of the Confederacy that had been brought back under the control of the Union. Would Congress have had any greater power? Congress, incidentally, did not repeal the Fugitive Slave Acts of 1793 and 1850 until June 28, 1864, and they were enforced to permit the recovery of fugitives by loyal slaveowners in Union states until that time.

3. Does the Third Amendment—"No Soldier shall, in time of peace, be quartered in any house, without the consent of the Owner, nor in time of war, but in a manner to be prescribed by law"—throw any light on Emancipation? Imagine Union General Meade's arriving near Gettysburg on June 30, 1863, and simply ordering a loyal Pennsylvania farmer to give up her house for the quartering of Union troops while preparing for the battle that was imminent. Could she have refused, on the basis that Meade offered no documents authorizing him to do so? Would it have sufficed to show a document signed by the President—"I hereby authorize you to quarter troops in any houses that shall be convenient for the

101. Proclamation [of May 19, 1862] Revoking Hunter's Emancipation Order, in id. at 318-319.

purpose"—or would it be necessary for Congress first to have authorized the President to issue such orders? Is it plausible to read the Third Amendment as applying only to the quartering of troops, so that your answer to the last question would be entirely irrelevant to the Emancipation Proclamation, or can the Third Amendment fairly be read as saying that even during time of war, when national existence might be at stake, constitutional norms nonetheless control and that public officials, including Presidents, cannot, in the absence of certain legal formalities, simply do whatever they think advisable in order to achieve their goals?

NOTE: "REVERENCE FOR LAW"

Speaking in 1838, Lincoln declared:[102]

> Let every American, every lover of liberty, every well wisher to his posterity, swear by the blood of the Revolution, never to violate in the least particular, the laws of the country; and never to tolerate their violation by others. As the patriots of seventy-six did to the support of the Declaration of Independence, so to the support of the Constitution and Laws, let every American pledge his life, his property, and his sacred honor; let every man remember that to violate the law, is to trample on the blood of his father, and to tear the character [charter?] of his own, and his children's liberty. Let reverence for the laws, be breathed by every American mother, to the lisping babe, that prattles on her lap—let it be taught in schools, in seminaries, and in colleges; let it be written in Primers, spelling books, and in Almanacs; let it be preached from the pulpit, proclaimed in legislative halls, and enforced in courts of justice. And, in short, let it become the political religion of the nation; and let the old and the young, the rich and poor, the grave and the gay, of all sexes and tongues, and colors and conditions, sacrifice unceasingly upon its altars. . . .
>
> When I so pressingly urge a strict observance of all the laws, let me not be understood that there are no bad laws, nor that grievances may not arise, for the redress of which, no legal provisions have been made. I mean to say no such thing. But I do mean to say, that, although bad laws, if they exist, should be repealed as soon as possible, still while they continue in force, for the sake of example, they should be religiously observed.

Lincoln concluded his impassioned speech by calling for "a reverence for the constitution and laws." As President, Lincoln wrote the following in an 1863 letter to Ohio Democrats upon their passage of a resolution denouncing his policy of military arrests and suspension of habeas corpus:[103]

> You ask, in substance, whether I really claim that I may override all the guarantied rights of individuals, on the plea of conserving the public safety when I may choose to say the public safety requires it. This question, divested of the phraseology calculated to represent me as struggling

---

102. Quoted in The Political Thought of Abraham Lincoln 16-17 (Current ed., 1967).
103. Id. at 262.

> for an arbitrary personal prerogative, is either simply a question who shall decide, or an affirmation that nobody shall decide, what the public safety does require, in cases of Rebellion or Invasion. The constitution contemplates the question as likely to occur for decision, but it does not expressly declare who is to decide it. By necessary implication, when Rebellion or Invasion comes, the decision is to be made, from time to time; and I think the man whom, for the time, the people have, under the constitution, made the commander-in-chief, of their Army and Navy, is the man who holds the power, and bears the responsibility of making it. If he uses the power justly, the same people will probably justify him; if he abuses it, he is in their hand, to be dealt with by all the modes they have reserved to themselves in the constitution.

DISCUSSION

1. Did Lincoln display a "reverence" for the Constitution? Did he comply with the oath of office? The oath states that the President pledges to "preserve, protect and defend the Constitution of the United States." What is meant by "the Constitution" in this oath? Does it refer to (a) specific legal doctrines as currently understood by well-trained lawyers and/or enforced by courts; (b) the President's own views about what the Constitution, rightly interpreted, means; (c) the "spirit" of the Constitution, which might well include a variety of unwritten norms;[104] or (d) a commitment to "constitutionalism" as a broader notion of government that might require, on occasion, indifference to the specifics of a written constitution?[105] Could the President plausibly claim that an oath to defend "the Constitution" allows him to commit acts in emergencies that would be contrary to the Constitution in normal times? Could the President plausibly argue that by acting to preserve the constitutional order he is actually preserving the Constitution?

Compare Lincoln's argument with James Madison's defense, in The Federalist No. 40, of the Philadelphia Convention's exceeding its delegated authority by drafting a new Constitution: "[T]he plan to be framed and proposed was to be submitted to the people themselves" and their "approbation [would] blot out antecedent errors and irregularities." Recall also Thomas Jefferson's willingness to still any of his doubts concerning the constitutionality of the Louisiana Purchase. Do these precedents establish the proposition that Presidents may take constitutionally debatable action on behalf of (what they perceive to be) the public good, leaving it to citizens and the Congress to decide either that the "justice" of their actions legitimates them, or, on the other hand, that they represent a sufficient threat to the constitutional order to merit impeachment?

---

104. See Akhil Reed Amar, America's Unwritten Constitution: The Precedents and Principles We Live By (2012)

105. See, e.g., Walter F. Murphy, Constitutional Democracy: Creating and Maintaining a Just Political Order (2007).

Carl Schmitt referred to Lincoln as "a perfect example" of what Schmitt called the "commissarial dictatorship," that is, a dictatorship entered into ostensibly to save the existing constitutional order.[106] Clinton Rossiter basically agrees: "The eleven weeks between the fall of Sumter and July 4, 1861 constitute the most interesting single episode in the history of constitutional dictatorship. The simple fact that one man was the government of the United States in the most critical period in all its 165 years; and that he acted on no precedent and under no restraint, makes this the paragon of all democratic, constitutional dictatorships." But Rossiter immediately follows this with an all-important caveat: "[I]f Lincoln was a great dictator, he was a greater democrat."[107] Is this a hopelessly self-contradictory sentence, or is it in fact possible to use both "dictator" and "democrat" to describe Lincoln?

Drawing on the conclusion of Justice Curtis's critique of the Proclamation, Professor Levinson has asked, as the title of an article, Was the Emancipation Proclamation Constitutional? Do We/Should We Care What the Answer Is? 2001 U. Ill. L. Rev. 1135. Does your answer turn on whether you believe that Lincoln acted for what we would today regard as a "good" or admirable purpose, that is, freeing the slaves? Would your answer change if a contemporary President, citing Lincoln, violated the Constitution (in your opinion) for what you considered a "bad" or "ignoble" purpose?

2. How do you respond to the following excerpt from a television interview of former President Richard Nixon, forced out of office because of his complicity in the illegal conduct surrounding the so-called Watergate scandals:[108]

Mr. David Frost: what in a sense you're saying is that there are certain situations . . . where the President can decide that it's in the best interests of the nation or something, and do something illegal.

Mr. Nixon: Well, when the President does it, that means that it is not illegal.

Mr. Frost: By definition.

Mr. Nixon: Exactly. If the President, for example, approves something, approves an action because of national security, or, in this case, because of a threat to internal peace and order, of significant magnitude, then the President's decision in that instance is one that enables those who carry it out to carry it out without violating a law. Otherwise they're in an impossible position.

Even if you disagree with Nixon's seeming assertion that the President has sweeping authority to define the law as he sees fit (though always, presumably, for the purpose of safeguarding vital national interests), what of the collateral

---

106. See Agamben, State of Exception, supra n.91, at 20. Schmitt contrasted a "commissarial dictator" with a "transformational" one, who, by definition, is *not* committed to the preservation of the existing constitutional order against those who threatened it. If states of emergency become normalized in contemporary societies, does this distinction start to vanish?

107. Rossiter, supra n.90, at 224.

108. Transcript of Frost-Nixon Interview, N.Y. Times, May 20, 1977, at A16.

proposition that subordinates who obey presidential orders should, in effect, be immunized against charges that they violated law? Should "I was only obeying the clear orders of the President" serve as a conclusive excuse against being criminally sanctioned? (Recall Marshall's opinion in Little v. Barreme, supra, Chapter 2.)

NOTE: THE GETTYSBURG ADDRESS AS CONSTITUTIONAL INTERPRETATION

The Gettysburg Address, delivered by Abraham Lincoln on the occasion of the dedication of the Gettysburg national cemetery on November 19, 1863 (only 20 weeks after the decisive battle conducted there) is probably the best known speech in American history.

The Gettysburg Address

(November 19, 1863)

Four score and seven years ago our fathers brought forth on this continent, a new nation, conceived in Liberty, and dedicated to the proposition that all men are created equal.

Now we are engaged in a great civil war, testing whether that nation, or any nation so conceived and so dedicated, can long endure. We are met on a great battle-field of that war. We have come to dedicate a portion of that field, as a final resting place for those who here gave their lives that that nation might live. It is altogether fitting and proper that we should do this.

But in a larger sense, we cannot dedicate—we cannot consecrate—we cannot hallow—this ground. The brave men, living and dead, who struggled here, have consecrated it, far above our poor power to add or detract. The world will little note, nor long remember what we say here, but it can never forget what they did here. It is for us the living, rather, to be dedicated here to the unfinished work which they who fought here have thus far so nobly advanced. It is rather for us to be here dedicated to the great task remaining before us—that from these honored dead we take increased devotion to that cause for which they gave the last full measure of devotion—that we here highly resolve that these dead shall not have died in vain—that this nation, under God, shall have a new birth of freedom—and that government of the people, by the people, for the people, shall not perish from the earth.

DISCUSSION

1. What are the implications of dating the birth of the United States four score and seven years prior to 1863 (that is, in 1776) instead of three score and fifteen years (that is, 1788, the date of ratification of the Constitution)?

2. To what extent was the unamended Constitution proposed in 1787 and ratified in 1788 (or even the Constitution as amended by the 1791 Bill of Rights) demonstrably "conceived in Liberty, and dedicated to the proposition that all men are created equal"?

3. Presumably, the strongest evidence for Lincoln's proposition (which helps explain the reference to four score and seven years) is the Declaration of Independence. As Gary Wills explains in his book Lincoln at Gettysburg: The Words That

Remade America (1992), Lincoln was one of a number of antebellum thinkers who argued that the Constitution existed to fulfill the principles of the Declaration of Independence. Referring to Proverbs 25:11, which states that "[a] word fitly spoken is like apples of gold in pictures of silver," Lincoln once wrote that the assertion of the principle of liberty for all in the Declaration "was the word, 'fitly spoken' which has proved an 'apple of gold' to us. The Union, and the Constitution, are the picture of silver, subsequently framed around it. The picture was made, not to conceal, or destroy the apple; but to adorn, and preserve it. The picture was made for the apple—not the apple for the picture."[109]

If the picture of silver—the Constitution—was made to frame the apple of gold—the Declaration—should the Declaration in effect be treated as part of the Constitution, so that those charged with interpreting the Constitution, whether Presidents, members of Congress, judges, or ordinary citizens, should draw on (and quote) the Declaration as legal authority?

4. What, precisely, is the "cause" to which the Union soldiers gave their lives? Consider only three possibilities: (a) preserving the Union; (b) eradicating slavery as part of our constitutional fabric; or (c) more ambitiously, securing genuine equality for all persons, Black or white. Which is most congruent with the overall tone of the address? If you believe it is either of the latter possibilities, is this congruent with his first inaugural address or Lincoln's various statements concerning the constitutional propriety of Emancipation?

5. Does a "new birth of freedom" necessarily translate into the fulfillment of the proposition that "all men are created equal"?

6. What is meant by government "of the people," government "by the people," and government "for the people"? Are these three different notions of government, and, if so, could they possibly conflict with one another? (If so, which should take priority?)

E. The Use of Military Tribunals as an Alternative to Trial by Jury

Lambdin P. Milligan and other prominent Democratic critics of the war were arrested by U.S. military officials in Indiana in late 1864; they were charged with planning an armed uprising to seize Union weapons, liberate Confederate prisoners of war, and kidnap the governor of Indiana. Indiana was not a theater of military operations; civil courts were open in which, for example, the defendants might have been charged with treason. However, Indiana had been quite hospitable to "Copperhead" sentiments, and there were reasonable fears that an Indiana jury might be reluctant to convict. The military therefore elected to try Milligan and his co-defendants before a military commission, which found them guilty and sentenced them to hang. They appealed the conviction to the U.S. Circuit Court in Indianapolis; the two judges disagreed and the case therefore was sent on to the Supreme Court. The Court unanimously ruled in favor of Milligan, but split 5-4 on the actual rationale. Indeed, it

109. Abraham Lincoln, Fragment on the Constitution and the Union, in 4 The Collected Works of Abraham Lincoln 169 (Basler ed., 1953).

announced its decision in April 1866, but did not issue its opinions until December. Justice David Davis (who had been Abraham Lincoln's campaign manager in 1860) wrote the opinion for the Court, and Chief Justice Salmon P. Chase (who had been Lincoln's Secretary of the Treasury) wrote the concurring opinion.

Ex parte Milligan

71 U.S. (1 Wall.) 2 (1866)

DAVIS, J. . . .

No graver question was ever considered by this court, nor one which more nearly concerns the rights of the whole people; for it is the birthright of every American citizen when charged with crime, to be tried and punished according to law. . . . The decision of this question does not depend on argument or judicial precedents, numerous and highly illustrative as they are. These precedents inform us of the extent of the struggle to preserve liberty and to relieve those in civil life from military trials. The founders of our government were familiar with the history of that struggle; and secured in a written constitution every right which the people had wrested from power during a contest of ages. . . . These securities for personal liberty thus embodied [in the Bill of Rights and in Article II, §2, which provides that "[t]he Trial of all Crimes, except in Cases of Impeachment, shall be by Jury"], were such as wisdom and experience had demonstrated to be necessary for the protection of those accused of crime. And so strong was the sense of the country of their importance, and so jealous were the people that these rights, highly prized, might be denied them by implication, that when the original Constitution was proposed for adoption it encountered severe opposition; and, but for the belief that it would be so amended as to embrace them, it would never have been ratified. . . .

If, in foreign invasion or civil war, the courts are actually closed, and it is impossible to administer criminal justice according to law, then, on the theatre of active military operations, where war really prevails, there is a necessity to furnish a substitute for the civil authority, thus overthrown, to preserve the safety of the army and society; and as no power is left but the military, it is allowed to govern by martial rule until the laws can have their free course. As necessity creates the rule, so it limits its duration; for, if this government is continued after the courts are reinstated, it is a gross usurpation of power. Martial rule can never exist where the courts are open, and in the proper and unobstructed exercise of their jurisdiction. It is also confined to the locality of actual war. Because, during the late Rebellion it could have been enforced in Virginia, where the national authority was overturned and the courts driven out, it does not follow that it should obtain in Indiana, where that authority was never disputed, and justice was always administered. And so in the case of a foreign invasion, martial rule may become a necessity in one state, when, in another, it would be "mere lawless violence." . . .

But it is said that the jurisdiction is complete under the "laws and usages of war." It can serve no useful purpose to inquire what those laws and usages are, whence they originated, where found, and on whom they operate; they can never be applied to citizens in states which have upheld the authority of the government, and where the courts are open and their process unobstructed. This court has judicial knowledge that in Indiana the Federal authority was always unopposed, and its courts always open to hear criminal accusations and redress grievances; and no usage of war could sanction a military trial there for any offence whatever of a citizen in civil life, in nowise connected with the military service. Congress could grant no such power; and to the honor of our national legislature be it said, it has never been provoked by the state of the country even to attempt its exercise. One of the plainest constitutional provisions was, therefore, infringed when Milligan was tried by a court not ordained and established by Congress, and not composed of judges appointed during good behavior.

[Chief Justice Chase, joined by three other Justices, agreed, in a concurring opinion, that Milligan was entitled to a trial in a civilian court, but for them the central issue was Congress's failure to authorize any deviations from the presumption that Americans were entitled to trial by jury even in time of war. Indeed, the opinion suggests that they read the habeas corpus act of March 3, 1863, which gave the President power to suspend the writ, as affirmatively barring the military trial. Thus, although "[t]he first section authorized the suspension, during the Rebellion, of the writ of habeas corpus throughout the United States by the President[, t]he two next sections *limited this authority* in important respects" (emphasis added).]

CHASE, J., concurring. . . .

We think that Congress had power, though not exercised, to authorize the military commission which was held in Indiana.

Congress has power to raise and support armies; to provide and maintain a navy; to make rules for the government and regulation of the land and naval forces; and to provide for governing such part of the militia as may be in the service of the United States. It is not denied that the power to make rules for the government of the army and navy is a power to provide for trial and punishment by military courts without a jury. It has been so understood and exercised from the adoption of the Constitution to the present time.

Nor, in our judgment, does the fifth, or any other amendment, abridge that power. "Cases arising in the land and naval forces, or in the militia in actual service in time of war or public danger," are expressly excepted from the fifth amendment, "that no person shall be held to answer for a capital or otherwise infamous crime, unless on a presentment or indictment of a grand jury," and it is admitted that the exception applies to the other amendments as well as to the fifth. . . . It is not necessary to attempt any precise definition of the boundaries of [Congress's] power. But may it not be said that government includes protection and defence as well as the regulation of internal administration? And is it impossible to imagine cases in which citizens conspiring or attempting the destruction or great injury of the national forces may be subjected by Congress to military trial and punishment in the just exercise of this undoubted constitutional power? Congress is but the agent of the nation, and does not the security of individuals against the abuse of this, as of every other power, depend on the intelligence and virtue of the people, on their zeal for public and private liberty, upon official responsibility secured by law, and upon the frequency of elections, rather than upon doubtful constructions of legislative powers? . . .

Congress has the power not only to raise and support and govern armies but to declare war. It has, therefore, the power to provide by law for carrying on war. This power necessarily extends to all legislation essential to the prosecution of war with vigor and success. . . . The power to make the necessary laws is in Congress: the power to execute in the President. Both powers imply many subordinate and auxiliary powers. Each includes all authorities essential to its due exercise. But neither can the President, in war more than in peace, intrude upon the proper authority of Congress, nor Congress upon the proper authority of the President. . . . Congress cannot direct the conduct of campaigns, nor can the President, or any commander under him, without the sanction of Congress, institute tribunals for the trial and punishment of offences, either of soldiers or civilians, unless in cases of a controlling necessity, which justifies what it compels, or at least insures acts of indemnity from the justice of the legislature.

We by no means assert that Congress can establish and apply the laws of war where no war has been declared or exists. Where peace exists the laws of peace must prevail. What we do maintain is, that when the nation is involved in war, and some portions of the country are invaded, and all are exposed to invasion, it is within the power of Congress to determine in what states or district such great and imminent public danger exists as justifies the authorization of military tribunals for the trial of crimes and offences against the discipline or security of the army or against the public safety.

In Indiana, for example, at the time of the arrest of Milligan and his co-conspirators, it is established by the papers in the record, that the state was a military district, was the theatre of military operations, had been actually invaded, and was constantly threatened with invasion. It appears, also, that a powerful secret association, composed of citizens and others, existed within the state, under military organization, conspiring against the draft, and plotting insurrection, the liberation of the prisoners of war at various depots, the seizure of the state and national arsenals, armed cooperation with the enemy, and war against the national government.

We cannot doubt that, in such a time of public danger, Congress had power, under the Constitution, to provide for the organization of a military commission, and for trial by that commission of persons engaged in this conspiracy. The fact that the Federal courts were open was regarded by Congress as a sufficient reason for not exercising the power; but that fact could not deprive Congress of the right to exercise it. Those courts might be open and undisturbed in the execution of their functions, and yet wholly incompetent to avert threatened danger, or to punish, with adequate promptitude and certainty, the guilty conspirators.

DISCUSSION

1. The *Milligan* Court takes as a central "fact of this case" that the Civil War was actually over by the time the Supreme Court reached its decision, even if Milligan had been arrested while the war was still going on (though not, at least actively, in Indiana). Would (or should) the Court have been so quick to protect Milligan's rights if the war were still ongoing?[110]

---

110. Gregory P. Downs, After Appomattox: Military Occupation and the Ends of War (2015), argues that a formal state of war did not come to an end with Lee's surrender and that, legally speaking, the war continued at least until 1871. However, after the close of hostilities in 1865, civilian courts were open.

2. *Confiscation of property.* Five years after *Milligan*, in Miller v. United States, 78 U.S. (11 Wall.) 268 (1871), the Court upheld the constitutionality of the Confiscation Acts of 1861 and 1862, which allowed ex parte seizure of property belonging to persons believed to have supported the rebellion. Justice Strong wrote that the confiscation statutes "were not enacted under the municipal power of Congress to legislate for the punishment of crimes against the sovereignty of the United States" but were "an exercise of the war powers of the government," and so "are not affected by the restrictions imposed by the fifth and sixth amendments."

> [T]he power to declare war involves the power to prosecute it by all means and in any manner in which war may be legitimately prosecuted. It therefore includes the right to seize and confiscate all property of an enemy and to dispose of it at the will of the captor. . . . [This right] has no reference whatever to the personal guilt of the owner of confiscated property, and the act of confiscation is not a proceeding against him. The confiscation is not because of crime, but because of the relation of the property to the opposing belligerent, a relation in which it has been brought in consequence of its ownership. It is immaterial to it whether the owner be an alien or a friend, or even a citizen or subject of the power that attempts to appropriate the property. . . . The whole doctrine of confiscation is built upon the foundation that it is an instrument of coercion, which, by depriving an enemy of property within reach of his power, whether within his territory or without it, impairs his ability to resist the confiscating government, while at the same time it furnishes to that government means for carrying on the war. Hence any property which the enemy can use, either by actual appropriation or by the exercise of control over its owner, or which the adherents of the enemy have the power of devoting to the enemy's use, is a proper subject of confiscation.

Compare *Miller* with Ex parte Milligan. Is there an important difference between confiscation of property during time of war and trying persons by military tribunals in places where the courts are open? (Does *Miller*, incidentally, suggest that the Emancipation Proclamation would have been an easy case had it been authorized by Congress?)

3. Does it make a difference, with regard to Chief Justice Chase's analysis, whether Congress overtly *limited* presidential authority to establish military tribunals or simply was silent as to that possibility? In his influential concurrence in Youngstown Sheet and Tube Co. v. Sawyer, 343 U.S. 579 (1952), written some 85 years later, Justice Robert Jackson distinguished (1) assertions of presidential power where Congress affirmatively authorized the action, where "his authority is at its maximum, for it includes all that he possesses in his own right plus all that Congress can delegate"; (2) assertions of presidential power where Congress had been silent on the matter in question where "he can only rely upon his own independent powers"; and (3) assertions of presidential power where Congress has attempted to limit the President's actions. In the third case, Jackson argued, the President's power "is at its lowest ebb, for then he can rely only upon his own constitutional powers minus any constitutional powers of Congress over the matter. Courts can sustain exclusive presidential control in such a case only by disabling the Congress from acting upon the subject." See the discussion of *Youngstown* in Chapter 6, infra.

4. The issues raised by the two opinions in *Milligan* are obviously of far more than historical interest. Do they entail, for example, that (at least) U.S. citizens who are detained within the United States because of suspicions that they are linked with terrorism are entitled to (prompt?) trials in civilian courts (as against military commissions) so long as these courts are "generally open" in the states in which the suspects are detained? Or does any such right depend entirely on whether Congress has authorized the President to forgo such trials to more effectively carry out "the global war against terror"? See Hamdi v. Rumsfeld, 542 U.S. 507 (2004), discussed in Chapter 6, infra.

F. The Legal Tender Cases and the Constitutionality of Paper Money

The Civil War was notable for several innovations, not the least of which was the widespread introduction of paper money as legal tender. The founders were generally hostile to the institution of paper currency. The 1787 Constitution explicitly prohibited states from emitting "bills of credit,"[111] a term generally understood at the time of the Revolution to refer to paper money.[112] During the Revolutionary War, the Continental Congress had issued bills of credit "at an accelerating rate, until by 1780 $100 in paper money was worth only $2.50 in specie. Depreciation continued until in 1781 paper money ceased to circulate as currency—whence the phrase 'not worth a continental.' The states, too issued, paper money, and it too, depreciated, with Virginia currency reaching 0.1 percent of its former value by December 1781."[113]

A provision in the Report on the Committee of Detail at the Philadelphia Convention would have given Congress the power to "borrow money, and emit bills on the credit of the United States." Gouverneur Morris moved to strike the power to emit bills of credit, which passed 9-2. Madison's notes suggest that most of the speakers were strongly opposed to paper money.[114] Although, as Professor

---

111. Article I, §10. The states were also prohibited from coining money. Nevertheless, one should not confuse even clear textual prohibitions with the actual behavior of states. Thus historian Charles Sellers notes that as part of "debtor-relief laws" enacted by Indiana, Illinois, and Missouri, these states also issued "state paper money for the particular benefit of small debtors. To evade the constitutional prohibition against state bills of credit, these state-paper loan offices were usually camouflaged as 'banks' in which the faith and credit of the state governments substituted for a specie capital." The Market Revolution 168 (1991). Not surprisingly, "the judiciary . . . struck down . . . state paper money as patently unconstitutional. By then, however, they had served their emergency purpose. Once shielded through the crisis, chastened small debtors quickly abandoned state paper money." Id. at 164.

112. Kenneth W. Dam, The Legal Tender Cases, 1981 Sup. Ct. Rev. 367, 387.

113. Id. at 383.

114. 2 Farrand, at 310. Madison explained his vote to strike based on his understanding that omitting the language "would not disable the Govt from the use of public notes as far as they could be safe & proper; & would only cut off the pretext for a paper currency and particularly for making the bills a tender either for public and private debts." In other words, Madison believed that the government would be able to "borrow money on the credit of the United States" through sale of interest-bearing bonds and other securities; but it could not issue paper money or make it legal tender. Madison also focused particularly on the use of paper money as legal tender, a distinction that not all of the other framers made. Dam, supra n.112, at 384-387.

Dam writes, "it is difficult to escape the conclusion that the Framers intended to prohibit" paper money,[115] the federal government soon began issuing bills of credit (though not as legal tender), beginning with the War of 1812.[116] This practice continued up to the Civil War, when the constitutionality of paper money became an important issue, in a series of three decisions collectively referred to as the Legal Tender Cases.

The Legal Tender Cases arose out of decisions by Salmon P. Chase, Lincoln's Secretary of the Treasury, about how to finance the Civil War. Chase was a strong believer in hard currency, and as Treasury Secretary he insisted that all government debts be paid in gold specie (coin). Chase had attempted to raise most of the funds through the sale of interest-bearing securities that would bring gold specie to the Treasury. However, his strategy backfired by the end of 1861 when a series of Union defeats led banks to suspend payments of specie. With Union expenses mounting, Chase reluctantly agreed to issue demand notes to pay salaries and suppliers. One could not redeem them in gold or silver but only in bonds that paid 6 percent interest. More important, the Act of February 25, 1862, authorizing the notes included a clause stating that the notes were to be "lawful money and a legal tender in payment of all debts, public and private, within the United States." Because the new notes were green, they became known as "greenbacks." About $431 million was issued by the end of the Civil War, although by 1864 the Treasury was able to finance the war mostly through taxes and bond sales.

By the end of the Civil War, it was generally accepted that the federal government could issue bills of credit. The controversial aspect of the greenbacks was that they were also "legal tender" by law, which meant that creditors had to accept them in payment of debts. Inflationary pressures made gold dollars worth much more than their equivalents in greenbacks. Debtors naturally sought to pay contractual obligations in greenbacks instead of gold coins.

Disputes over Congress's authority to make greenbacks legal tender led to a constitutional challenge. The obvious candidate for congressional power today would be the power "[t]o coin Money [and] regulate Value thereof" in Article I, §8, cl. 5. But it was generally accepted that this clause referred only to the coins—i.e., objects made of metal—and not to paper money.[117] This interpretation was bolstered by the text of the Counterfeiting Clause, Article I, §8, cl. 6, which distinguishes "Securities" from "[the] current Coin of the United States."

HEPBURN v. GRISWOLD, 8 Wall. 603 (1870): [In *Hepburn*, the first of the Legal Tender Cases, the Supreme Court held that Congress lacked the power to make paper money legal tender for debts preexisting the 1862 Act. An opinion for four Justices was written by former Treasury Secretary Salmon P. Chase, who had been appointed Chief Justice in 1864.]

---

115. Dam, supra n.112, at 389.

116. Id. at 389-390.

117. Dam, supra n.112, at 291. However, Robert Natelson has argued that various people in the ratifying debates believed that the new federal government would have the power to "coin" paper money. Robert G. Natelson, Paper Money and The Original Understanding of the Coinage Clause, 31 Harv. J.L. & Pub. Pol. 1017 (2008).

Chase, C.J.:

It has not been maintained in argument, nor, indeed, would any one, however slightly conversant with constitutional law, think of maintaining that there is in the Constitution any express grant of legislative power to make any description of credit currency a legal tender in payment of debts.

We must inquire then whether this can be done in the exercise of an implied power. . . .

[It]t has been maintained in argument that the power to make United States notes a legal tender in payment of all debts is a means appropriate and plainly adapted to the execution of the power to carry on war, of the power to regulate commerce, and of the power to borrow money. . . . [But] [i]t is difficult to say to what express power the authority to make notes a legal tender in payment of pre-existing debts may not be upheld as incidental, upon the principles of this argument. Is there any power which does not involve the use of money? And is there any doubt that Congress may issue and use bills of credit as money in the execution of any power? The power to establish post-offices and post-roads, for example, involves the collection and disbursement of a great revenue. Is not the power to make notes a legal tender as clearly incidental to this power as to the war power?

The argument . . . carries the doctrine of implied powers very far beyond any extent hitherto given to it. It asserts that [whatever] in any degree promotes an end within the scope of a general power, whether, in the correct sense of the word, appropriate or not, may be done in the exercise of an implied power. . . . [Chase argued that the government could have raised sufficient funds to conduct the war by issuing notes backed by government bonds without making them legal tender. Even if there was some advantage to] making the notes a legal tender under new contracts, it by no means follows that any appreciable advantage is gained by compelling creditors to receive them in satisfaction of pre-existing debts. . . .

If [the legal tender requirement] adds nothing to the utility of the notes, it cannot be upheld as a means to the end in furtherance of which the notes are issued. Nor can it, in our judgment, be upheld as such, if, while facilitating in some degree the circulation of the notes, it debases and injures the currency in its proper use to a much greater degree. And these considerations seem to us equally applicable to the powers to regulate commerce and to borrow money. . . .

In the rule stated by Chief Justice Marshall [in *McCulloch*, there is] the limitation that the means [Congress uses] must be not prohibited, but consistent with the letter and spirit of the Constitution.

Among the great cardinal principles of that instrument, no one is more conspicuous or more venerable than the establishment of justice. . . . especially in its relations to [the preservation of the obligations of] contracts. [Although the Contracts Clause applies to the states and not to the federal government,] we think it clear that those who framed and those who adopted the Constitution, intended that the spirit of this prohibition should pervade the entire body of legislation, and that the justice which the Constitution was ordained to establish was not thought by them to be compatible with legislation of an opposite tendency. In other words, we cannot doubt that a law not made in pursuance of an express power, which necessarily and in its direct operation impairs the obligation of contracts, is inconsistent with the spirit of the Constitution.

[Chase argued that the legal tender provision was also inconsistent with the spirit of the Fifth Amendment's Just Compensation Clause, which applied to the federal government.] It does not, in terms, prohibit legislation which appropriates the private property of one class of citizens to the use of another class; but if such property cannot be taken for the benefit of all, without compensation, it is difficult to understand how it can be so taken for the benefit of a part without violating the spirit of the prohibition. . . .

[A]n act which compels all those who hold contracts for the payment of gold and silver money to accept in payment a currency of inferior value deprives such persons of property without due process of law [in violation of the Fifth Amendment] . . . A very large proportion of the property of civilized men exists in the form of contracts. These contracts almost invariably stipulate for the payment of money. . . . [C]ontracts in the United States, prior to the act under consideration, for the payment of money, were contracts to pay the sums specified in gold and silver coin. And it is beyond doubt that the holders of these contracts were and are as fully entitled to the protection of this constitutional provision as the holders of any other description of property.

But it may be said that the holders of no description of property are protected by it from legislation which incidentally only impairs its value. And it may be urged in illustration that the holders of stock in a turnpike, a bridge, or a manufacturing corporation, or an insurance company, or a bank, cannot invoke its protection against legislation which, by authorizing similar works or corporations, reduces its price in the market. But all this does not appear to meet the real difficulty. In the cases mentioned the injury is purely contingent and incidental. In the case we are considering it is direct and inevitable.

If in the cases mentioned the holders of the stock were required by law to convey it on demand to any one who should think fit to offer half its value for it, the analogy would be more obvious. No one probably could be found to contend that an act enforcing the acceptance of fifty or seventy-five acres of land in satisfaction of a contract to convey a hundred would not come within the prohibition against arbitrary privation of property.

We confess ourselves unable to perceive any solid distinction between such an act and an act compelling all citizens to accept, in satisfaction of all contracts for money, half or three-quarters or any other proportion less than the whole of the value actually due, according to their terms. It is difficult to conceive what act would take private property without process of law if such an act would not. . . .

It is not surprising that amid the tumult of the late civil war, and under the influence of apprehensions for the safety of the Republic almost universal, different views, never before entertained by American statesmen or jurists, were adopted by many. The time was not favorable to considerate reflection upon the constitutional limits of legislative or executive authority. If power was assumed from patriotic motives, the assumption found ready justification in patriotic hearts. Many who doubted yielded their doubts; many who did not doubt were silent. Some who were strongly averse to making government notes a legal tender felt themselves constrained to acquiesce in the views of the advocates of the measure. Not a few who then insisted upon its necessity, or acquiesced in that view, have, since the return of peace, and under the influence of the calmer time, reconsidered their conclusions, and now concur in those which we have just announced. These conclusions seem to us to be fully sanctioned by the letter and spirit of the Constitution.

[Justice Grier, writing separately, held as a matter of statutory construction that the Legal Tender Clause of the 1862 Act did not apply to preexisting debts, but agreed that if it were so construed it would be unconstitutional.]

MILLER, J, dissenting, joined by SWAYNE and DAVIS, JJ.:

The legal tender clauses of the statutes under consideration were placed emphatically by those who enacted them, upon their necessity to the further borrowing of money and maintaining the army and navy. It was done reluctantly and with hesitation, and only after the necessity had been demonstrated and had become imperative. . . .

[T]his law was a necessity in the most stringent sense in which that word can be used. But if we adopt the construction of Chief Justice Marshall . . . [c]an it be said that this provision did not conduce towards the purpose of borrowing money, of paying debts, of raising armies, of suppressing insurrection? or that it was not calculated to effect these objects? or that it was not useful and essential to that end? Can it be said that this was not among the choice of means, if not the only means, which were left to Congress to carry on this war for national existence? . . .

The [majority's Fifth Amendment] argument is too vague for my perception, by which the indirect effect of a great public measure, in depreciating the value of lands, stocks, bonds, and other contracts, renders such a law invalid as taking private property for public use, or as depriving the owner of it without due course of law.

A declaration of war with a maritime power would thus be unconstitutional, because the value of every ship abroad is lessened twenty-five or thirty per cent, and those at home almost as much. The abolition of the tariff on iron or sugar would in like manner destroy the furnaces, and sink the capital employed in the manufacture of these articles. Yet no statesman, however warm an advocate of high tariff, has claimed that to abolish such duties would be unconstitutional as taking private property.

If the principle be sound, every successive issue of government bonds during the war was void, because by increasing the public debt it made those already in private hands less valuable.

This whole argument of the injustice of the law . . . and of its opposition to the spirit of the Constitution, is too abstract and intangible for application to courts of justice, and is, above all, dangerous as a ground on which to declare the legislation of Congress void by the decision of a court. It would authorize this court to enforce theoretical views of the genius of the government, or vague notions of the spirit of the Constitution and of abstract justice, by declaring void laws which did not square with those views. It substitutes our ideas of policy for judicial construction, an undefined code of ethics for the Constitution, and a court of justice for the National legislature. . . .

[A]re we . . . to disturb contracts, to declare the law void, because the necessity for its enactment does not appear so strong to us as it did to Congress, or so clear as it was to other courts?

Such is not my idea of the relative functions of the legislative and judicial departments of the government. Where there is a choice of means the selection is with Congress, not the court. If the act to be considered is in any sense essential to the execution of an acknowledged power, the degree of that necessity is for the legislature and not for the court to determine.

The result in *Hepburn* was short-lived. In April 1869, shortly after President Grant took office, the Republican Congress had passed a bill increasing the size of the Supreme Court from eight to nine. Justice Grier, a Democrat, resigned on December 15, 1869, effective on January 31, 1870, giving President Grant two new appointments to the Supreme Court.

On February 7, 1870, the decision in *Hepburn* was announced. (The votes were taken and opinions written prior to Justice Grier's resignation. Consider whether we would today count the vote of a Justice in similar circumstances.) On the same day, President Grant nominated William Strong and Joseph P. Bradley to fill the two vacant Supreme Court seats.[118]

In May 1871, the Court decided Knox v. Lee, 12 Wall. 457 (1871), which held that the 1862 legal tender legislation was constitutional both as to preexisting and subsequent debts. Strong and Bradley joined the three dissenters in *Hepburn* to form a new five-person majority.

Justice Strong's majority opinion argued that the legal tender provisions were justified by the utmost necessity: "The public treasury was nearly empty, and the credit of the government, if not stretched to its utmost tension, had become nearly exhausted."

However, Strong also offered a novel theory of federal power that seemed to go well beyond *McCulloch*:

> [I]t is not indispensable to the existence of any power claimed for the Federal government that it can be found specified in the words of the Constitution, or clearly and directly traceable to some one of the specified powers. Its existence may be deduced fairly from more than one of the substantive powers expressly defined, or from them all combined. It is allowable to group together any number of them and infer from them all that the power claimed has been conferred. Such a treatment of the Constitution is recognized by its own provisions. This is well illustrated in its language respecting the writ of habeas corpus. The power to suspend the privilege of that writ is not expressly given, nor can it be deduced from any one of the particularized grants of power. Yet it is provided that the privileges of the writ shall not be suspended except in certain defined contingencies. This is no express grant of power. It is a restriction. But it shows irresistibly that somewhere in the Constitution power to suspend the privilege of the writ was granted, either by some one or more of the specifications of power, or by them all combined. And, that important powers were understood by the people who adopted the Constitution to have been created by it, powers not enumerated, and not included incidentally in any one of those enumerated, is shown by the amendments [in the Bill of Rights]. . . . They tend plainly to show that, in the judgment

118. Strong and Bradley were actually Grant's second choices. He first tried to nominate Attorney General Ebenezer R. Hoar and former War Secretary Edwin M. Stanton. Although the Senate quickly confirmed Stanton, he died on December 24. The Senate rejected Grant's other nomination on February 3, thus guaranteeing that there would be no Justice Hoar.

> of those who adopted the Constitution, there were powers created by it, neither expressly specified nor deducible from any one specified power, or ancillary to it alone, but which grew out of the aggregate of powers conferred upon the government, or out of the sovereignty instituted. Most of these amendments are denials of power which had not been expressly granted, and which cannot be said to have been necessary and proper for carrying into execution any other powers. Such, for example, is the prohibition of any laws respecting the establishment of religion, prohibiting the free exercise thereof, or abridging the freedom of speech or of the press.

Justice Bradley, concurring, also emphasized the broad powers of the federal government:

> The doctrine so long contended for that the Federal Union was a mere compact of States, and that the States, if they chose, might annul or disregard the acts of the National legislature, or might secede from the Union at their pleasure, and that the General government had no power to coerce them into submission to the Constitution, should be regarded as definitely and forever overthrown. This has been finally effected by the National power, as it had often been before, by overwhelming argument.
>
> The United States is not only a government, but it is a National government, and the only government in this country that has the character of nationality. . . .
>
> Such being the character of the General government, it seems to be a self-evident proposition that it is invested with all those inherent and implied powers which, at the time of adopting the Constitution, were generally considered to belong to every government as such, and as being essential to the exercise of its functions.

In his dissent, Chief Justice Chase explained that while he was Secretary of the Treasury, he was strongly opposed to issuing greenbacks as legal tender, but "thought it indispensably necessary that the authority to issue these notes, should be granted by Congress. The passage of the bill was delayed, if not jeoparded, by the difference of opinion which prevailed on the question of making them a legal tender." That is why, Chase argued, he had told the Ways and Means Committee that the legislation was "necessary." Chase added that "[e]xamination and reflection under more propitious circumstances have satisfied him that this opinion was erroneous, and he does not hesitate to declare it. He would do so, just as unhesitatingly, if his favor to the legal tender clause had been at that time decided, and his opinion as to the constitutionality of the measure clear."[119]

The decision in *Knox* was grounded on the emergency situation facing the Union during the Civil War. The decision was extended a decade later in the last of the Legal Tender Cases, Juilliard v. Greenman, 110 U.S. 421 (1884). After the Civil War, the government attempted to contract the money supply by retiring

---

119. Given this sequence of events, should Chief Justice Chase have recused himself in *Hepburn* and *Knox*? If he had, the constitutionality of the Legal Tender Clause would have been upheld. Should this have made any difference to his decision?

greenbacks from circulation, to fight the inflation caused by the Civil War and allow resumption of specie payments in gold for U.S. currency and bank notes. This policy produced an ongoing conflict over the money supply. In 1878, Congress restricted any further withdrawal of greenbacks and directed the Treasury to keep them permanently in circulation; the Treasury complied by issuing greenbacks in new denominations. When the 1878 Act was challenged in *Juilliard,* the Supreme Court held, 8-1, that Congress could issue legal tender notes in peacetime whether out of necessity or convenience. Justice Gray's majority opinion argued that "the question whether . . . it is . . . wise and expedient to resort to this means, is a political question, to be determined by congress when the question of exigency arises, and not a judicial question, to be afterwards passed upon by the courts."

Justice Field, in dissent, argued that

> [i]f there be anything in the history of the constitution which can be established with moral certainty, it is that the framers of that instrument intended to prohibit the issue of legal-tender notes both by the general government and by the states, and thus prevent interference with the contracts of private parties. . . .
>
> From the decision of the court I see only evil likely to follow. There have been times within the memory of all of us when the legal-tender notes of the United States were not exchangeable for more than one-half of their nominal value. The possibility of such depreciation will always attend paper money. This inborn infirmity no mere legislative declaration can cure. If congress has the power to make the notes a legal tender and to pass as money or its equivalent, why should not a sufficient amount be issued to pay the bonds of the United States as they mature? Why pay interest on the millions of dollars of bonds now due when congress can in one day make the money to pay the principal? And why should there be any restraint upon unlimited appropriations by the government for all imaginary schemes of public improvement, if the printing-press can furnish the money that is needed for them?

DISCUSSION

1. *The Constitution and the money supply.* Put in contemporary terms, Justice Field feared popular control over the money supply, which could not only wreck the economy, but seriously affect the market value of property and contractual rights. During the period from Reconstruction to the New Deal, the struggle between advocates of "hard" and "soft" money was one of the central issues in American political life. The money supply has largely receded from day-to-day political struggle because of the delegation of monetary policy to the Federal Reserve Board. By design, the Board's members are relatively isolated from political accountability; their oversight of national monetary policy is justified by their purportedly superior economic expertise.

Was Justice Field right that control over the currency is too important to be left to ordinary political processes? Was Justice Gray right that this question is inherently political and therefore should be left to whatever devices a democracy creates? In what way is the money supply more or less deserving of protection from popular will than the right to freedom of speech? The right against cruel and unusual punishments? The right to abortion? Does the subsequent creation of the Federal Reserve Board support or undercut Field's argument about the dangers of majority politics?

2. *A quick reversal.* The Legal Tender Cases are famous today for the Court's abrupt reversal from *Hepburn* to *Knox*. Was it appropriate under our constitutional system for President Grant to seek as new Justices persons who would be likely to vote to overturn *Hepburn*, as both Strong and Bradley did? Or should he have appointed them simply on the basis of their presumed professional stature and been content to discover only when *Knox* was issued what their views were on this central issue of the hour? Even if Grant was permitted to select them on the basis of their predicted vote, did Justices Strong and Bradley have any obligation to confound this expectation, as it were, and to respect *Hepburn* as recent precedent, perhaps to safeguard the independence of the Court or dispel any perception among the general populace that constitutional interpretation is indeed simply a function of who happens to be on the Court at a particular time? Does your answer depend on your perception of how bad the consequences of *Hepburn* would have been (either in 1870 or in later years) if the United States had been prevented from making paper money legal tender?

3. *Packing the Court.* The Legal Tender Cases are also noteworthy today because they involved a successful policy of Court reduction and Court packing by the Reconstruction Republicans, which contrasts with FDR's failed attempt to pack the Court, discussed in Chapter 5.

President Grant was able to appoint two new Justices to the Supreme Court because the Reconstruction Congress repeatedly manipulated the size of the Supreme Court. In 1863, Congress increased the number of Justices from nine to ten, which gave Abraham Lincoln an extra appointment. But Justice Catron died in May 1865, leaving only nine Justices.[120] After Lincoln's assassination, Republicans in Congress wanted to prevent Andrew Johnson, a War Democrat, from making any appointments. So in July 1866, Congress effectively shrank the size of the Court by providing that retirements of sitting Justices would not create a vacancy until the total number of Justices was reduced to seven.

After Johnson left office, the Republicans regained the White House and expanded the Court once again. An April 1869 Act not only increased the number of Justices to nine, but also offered salary for life to any Justice who resigned having reached the age of 70 with ten years of service. This provision was specifically aimed at inducing the retirements of Justices Samuel Nelson and Robert Grier, both Northern Democrats. Grier retired at the beginning of 1870, while Nelson retired in 1872.

Were these congressional actions appropriate under our constitutional system? Consider this question in the light of the controversy surrounding President Roosevelt's court-packing plan of 1937.

---

120. Charles Fairman, Reconstruction and Reunion 1864-1868, Part One, 6 History of the Supreme Court of the United States 161 (1971). By an 1863 Act of Congress, the Supreme Court had been increased from nine to ten seats, but Justice Catron died in 1865, leaving only nine Justices.

Suppose that Congress passes a law offering especially generous pensions to Justices over a certain age and years of service in order to induce them to retire. Would your views on such a law depend on whether it was a permanent arrangement or only a one-time "special offer" that expired, say, within a year?[121] What if Congress offered to permanently double the salary (for life) of the Justices who retired?

4. *Post-Civil War visions of federal power.* Justice Strong's and Justice Bradley's broad statements about federal power in Knox v. Lee reflect the political dominance of Republicans in Congress during Reconstruction, the consequences of which will pervade the next chapter. Nevertheless, if their views are taken seriously, doesn't the federal government have general power to do whatever any "sovereign" governments have traditionally done? Note that while Justice Strong engages in the rather implausible fiction that inherent powers always existed and formed the central justification for the Bill of Rights, Justice Bradley grounds his argument on the failed secession of the Southern states. Under his theory, the justification for the federal government's expanded regulatory role would not be the gradual nationalization of commerce, but the reconstruction of the United States as a nation in the aftermath of the Civil War. What, exactly, is wrong with his argument? Do you agree that the correctness or incorrectness of the "compact of states theory" can be settled by war?

---

121. Note that under current rules, federal judges can retire at full pay when their service (of at least 15 years) and age add up to 80. Even so, this possibility does not elicit very many retirements; federal judges and Justices tend to like the authority and influence that come with their jobs.

CHAPTER 4

FROM RECONSTRUCTION TO THE NEW DEAL: 1866-1934

The long period of Republican Party dominance stretching from the end of the Civil War through the New Deal includes Reconstruction, the Gilded Age and the Progressive Era, and encompasses the Chief Justiceships of Salmon Chase (1864-1873), Morrison Waite (1874-1888), Melville Fuller (1888-1910), Edward White (1910-1921), William Taft (1921-1930), and the earlier years of Charles Evans Hughes (1930-1941).

I. THE RECONSTRUCTION CONSTITUTION

A. History of the Adoption of the Reconstruction Amendments[1]

1. The Thirteenth Amendment

On January 31, 1865, the Thirty-Eighth Congress proposed the Thirteenth Amendment—"Neither slavery nor involuntary servitude, except as a punishment for crime whereof the party shall have been duly convicted, shall exist within the United States, or any place subject to their jurisdiction"—ratification of which was completed when Georgia, on December 6, 1865, became the twenty-seventh of the 36 states to give its assent.[2]

---

1. The following materials are based on the following sources: Jack M. Balkin, Living Originalism (2011), Jack M. Balkin, The Reconstruction Power, 85 N.Y.U. L. Rev. 1801 (2010); Akhil Reed Amar, America's Constitution: A Biography (2005); Alex Tsesis, The Thirteenth Amendment and American Freedom: A Legal History (2004); Michael Vorenberg, Final Freedom: The Civil War, the Abolition of Slavery, and the Thirteenth Amendment (2001); Akhil Reed Amar, The Bill of Rights, Creation and Reconstruction (1998); Michael Kent Curtis, No State Shall Abridge: The Fourteenth Amendment and the Bill of Rights (1986); Alexander Bickel, The Original Understanding and the Segregation Decision, 69 Harv. L. Rev. 1 (1955).

2. This sentence is misleadingly simple. See Note: The Unusual Procedural History of the Fourteenth Amendment, infra at pp. 369-378.

Despite the amendment's ban on "slavery" and "involuntary servitude," many of the formerly Confederate states, eight of which had ratified the amendment, adopted so-called Black Codes that were clearly designed to maintain, as much as possible, the subordinated status of the ostensibly freed slaves. The codes[3]

> perpetuated or created many discriminations in the criminal law by applying unequal penalties to Negroes for recognized offenses and by specifying offenses for Negroes only. Laws which prohibited Negroes from keeping weapons or from selling liquor were typical of the latter. Examples of discriminatory penalties were the laws which made it a capital offense for a Negro to rape a white woman, or to assault a white woman with intent to rape. . . . In addition to the discriminations of the criminal laws, post-war black codes hedged in the Negroes with a series of restraints on their business dealings of even the simplest form. Though in many states the Negro could acquire property, Mississippi put sharp limitations on that right.[4] But most restrictive were the provisions concerning contracts for personal service. Many statutes called for specific enforcement of labor contracts against freedmen, with provisions to facilitate capture should a freedman try to escape. Vagrancy laws made it a misdemeanor for a Negro to be without a long-term contract of employment; conviction was followed by a fine, payable by a white man who could then set the criminal to work for him until the benefactor had been completely reimbursed for his generosity.

Section 2 of the Thirteenth Amendment declared that "Congress shall have power to enforce this article by appropriate legislation," and the Black Codes underscored for most members of Congress the necessity for federal legislation if the promise of the amendment was to be achieved. Ultimately, the Congress moved beyond legislation to the proposal of a second "Reconstruction Amendment," the Fourteenth Amendment, proposed by the Thirty-Ninth Congress in June 1866 and declared ratified two years later in July 1868.[5]

---

3. John Frank and Robert Munro, The Original Understanding of "Equal Protection of the Laws," 1972 Wash. U. L.Q. 421, 445-446.

4. As a matter of fact, the Mississippi legislature rejected the amendment on December 4, 1865. This obviously did not prevent its being declared part of the Constitution two days later, when Georgia became the twenty-seventh of the 36 states in the Union to ratify. Many states "ratified" the amendment even after its formal addition to the Constitution, beginning with Oregon on December 8, 1865 and extending to Kentucky's March 18, 1976, ratification (after rejecting it 111 years before on February 24, 1865). Mississippi became the last state to ratify, in a somewhat convoluted manner. In 1995, both houses of the Mississippi legislature voted to ratify the amendment, but notice of such ratification was never sent to the required federal official. So on February 7, 2013, "Secretary of State Delbert Hosemann's office agreed to fix the oversight and file the paperwork, making the ratification official." http://www.huffingtonpost.com/2013/02/18/mississippi-13th-amendment_n_2712289.html.

5. Again, see Note: The Unusual Procedural History of the Fourteenth Amendment, infra at 348-356.

DISCUSSION

1. *What is "slavery"?* Most discussions of the meaning of the Thirteenth Amendment use American chattel slavery as the paradigm and then try to assess the degree to which the challenged practice resembles it. Yet consider that the text says that "[n]either slavery nor involuntary servitude, except as a punishment for crime whereof the party shall have been duly convicted, shall exist within the United States, or any place subject to their jurisdiction." The text presumably refers to *all* forms of slavery, and not only chattel slavery; it also extends its protections to "involuntary servitude," which, presumably, is not the same thing as "slavery." Finally, note that the text appears to permit "slavery or involuntary servitude . . . as a punishment for crime." Is it really possible that we would allow "chattel slavery"—including selling off prisoners at auction—as a punishment for crime today? Or rather does it suggest that some forms of "slavery" or "involuntary servitude" legitimately may be used as forms of criminal punishment, but may not be permitted in any other context?[6]

2. *"Slavery" in the revolutionary period.* As a matter of fact, there was a rich tradition in Anglo-American thought of the seventeenth and eighteenth centuries that considered "slavery" to be synonymous with any systematic practice of illegitimate domination. Bernard Bailyn's magisterial study of pamphlets written during the run-up to the American Revolution, which provided the basis for his deservedly famous Ideological Origins of the American Revolution, emphasized the repeated invocation of "slavery" as the likely fate of the colonists if they submitted to the outrageous claims of their British would-be rulers. "'Slavery,'" he writes, "was a central concept in eighteenth century political discourse. As the absolute political evil, it appears in every statement of political principle, in every discussion of constitutionalism or legal rights, in every exhortation to resistance."[7] As a "political concept," slavery "had a specific meaning that later generations would lose." As an example,

---

6. It is worth nothing that American prisoners have sometimes been treated worse than antebellum slaves. David Oshinsky's important book about the Parchman prison system in Mississippi, "Worse than Slavery": Parchman Farm and the Ordeal of Jim Crow Justice (1996), begins with a series of quotations comparing conditions at Parchman to chattel slavery, and finding the slaves better off. Thus L.G. Shivers, writing in 1930 on A History of the Mississippi Penitentiary, wrote that "[t]he convict's condition [following the Civil War] was much worse than slavery. The life of the slave was valuable to the master, but there was no financial loss . . . if a convict died." (Id., unpaginated.)

The Thirteenth Amendment's exclusion of criminal punishments has also been used to justify chain gangs and other forms of convict labor, especially in the South. See, e.g., the Pulitzer Prize–winning book by Douglas A. Blackmon, Slavery by Another Name: The Re-Enslavement of Black Americans from the Civil War to World War II (2008). Blackmon notes that his book, examining convict labor in Birmingham, Alabama, was inspired by "asking a provocative question: What would be revealed if American corporations were examined through the same sharp lens of historical confrontation as the one then being trained on German corporations that relied on Jewish slave labor during World War II and the Swiss banks that robbed victims of the Holocaust of their fortunes?" Id. at 3.

7. Bernard Bailyn, Ideological Origins of the American Revolution 232 (1967). All quotations below are taken from id. at 232-234.

Bailyn quotes a 1747 newspaper writer who declared that those who are "under the absolute and arbitrary direction of one man are all *slaves*, for he that is obliged to act or not to act according to the arbitrary will and pleasure of a governor, or his director, is as much as *slave* as he who is obliged to act or not according to the arbitrary will and pleasure of a master or his overseer." Interestingly enough, this author wrote that "the slaves of the latter deserve highly to be pitied, the slaves of the former to be held in the utmost contempt." There is obviously a spectrum of slavery, and some varieties may well be worse than others. But, as Bailyn writes, "[t]he degradation of chattel slaves—painfully visible and unambiguously established in law—was *only the final realization of what the loss of freedom could mean everywhere.*"

When American colonists called their condition slavery, therefore, they were not simply engaged in overheated rhetoric. They were repeating what had been taught them as part of their socialization as "free Englishmen." One of the operative principles of the Revolution was the famous motto of "no taxation without representation." Consider John Dickinson's 1768 comment, made in the form of a "letter" from a farmer in Pennsylvania: "*Those* who are *taxed* without their own consent expressed by themselves of their representatives are *slaves. We are taxed* without our consent expressed by ourselves or our representatives. *We* are therefore—SLAVES." Josiah Quincy concluded a 1774 diatribe against the British as follows: "I speak it with grief—I speak it with anguish—Britons are our oppressors. I speak it with alarm—I speak it with indignation—*we are slaves.*" Even John Adams spoke of "the most abject sort of slavery" to refer not to those chattel slaves who still existed in prerevolutionary Massachusetts, but, rather, to the colonists chafing under British mistreatment. The colonial vision that opposed slavery to republican liberty held that slavery meant more than simply being free from compulsion to labor by threats or physical coercion. Rather, the true marker of slavery was that slaves were always potentially subject to domination and to the arbitrary will of another person.[8]

3. *Contemporary interpretations of "slavery" and "involuntary servitude."* Even if the founders had a more capacious sense of slavery in 1787, does this tell us anything about the proper interpretation of "slavery" and "involuntary servitude" in the 1865 Thirteenth Amendment? Does this history permit us to read these terms more broadly today? In answering these questions, consider whether we should make a distinction between power of courts to enforce §1 and Congress's ability to define and prevent "slavery" and the badges and incidents of slavery in §2.

Finally, consider that, unlike their treatment of the Thirteenth Amendment, courts today do not read the text of the Fourteenth Amendment as limited to the precise harms that the amendment was designed to prevent. Why should the two amendments, passed within three years of each other, be interpreted so differently?

2. The Civil Rights Act of 1866

Part of the Thirty-Ninth Congress's response to the Black Codes was the Civil Rights Act of 1866, the first of a series of civil rights bills passed between 1866 and 1875. The bill sought to ensure that free Black people enjoyed the same basic rights

8. See generally Jack M. Balkin and Sanford Levinson, The Dangerous Thirteenth Amendment, 112 Colum. L. Rev. 1459 (2012).

as whites, a goal long sought by the antebellum movement for Black civil rights[9] Debate over the legislation began in January 1866. The final version of §1 of the Civil Rights Act (sometimes called the Civil Rights Bill) provided:

> That all persons born in the United States and not subject to any foreign power, excluding Indians not taxed, are hereby declared to be citizens of the United States; and such citizens, of every race and color, without regard to any previous condition of slavery or involuntary servitude, except as a punishment for crime whereof the party shall have been duly convicted, shall have the same right, in every State and Territory in the United States, to make and enforce contracts, to sue, be parties, and give evidence, to inherit, purchase, lease, sell, hold, and convey real and personal property, and to full and equal benefit of all laws and proceedings for the security of person and property, as is enjoyed by white citizens, and shall be subject to like punishment, pains, and penalties, and to none other, any law, statute, ordinance, regulation, or custom, to the contrary notwithstanding.

The debate over the bill involved two key questions. The first was over a proposed section of the bill, ultimately deleted, which stated that "there shall be no discrimination in civil rights or immunities among the inhabitants of any State or Territory of the United States on account of race, color, or previous condition of slavery." A similar prohibition of "discrimination in civil rights or immunities"—the "civil rights formula"—also had appeared in the Freedman's Bureau Bill[10] of December 1865.

---

9. See Kate Masur, Until Justice Be Done: America's First Civil Rights Movement From The Revolution To Reconstruction xvi, 304-305 (2021).

10. The Freedman's Bureau Bill was designed to implement the Freedman's Bureau, which had been created in March 1865. It authorized the Secretary of War to provide, food, clothing, fuel, shelter, and medical aid to "destitute and suffering refugees and freedmen, their wives and children." Section 7 of the bill provided:

> That whenever in any State or district in which the ordinary course of judicial proceedings has been interrupted by the rebellion, and wherein, in consequence of any State or local law, ordinance, police or other regulation, custom, or prejudice, any of the civil rights or immunities belonging to white persons, including the right to make and enforce contracts, to sue, be parties, and give evidence, to inherit, purchase, lease, sell, hold and convey real and personal property, and to have full and equal benefit of all laws and proceedings for the security of person and estate, including the constitutional right of bearing arms, are refused or denied to negroes, mulattoes, freedmen, refugees, or any other persons, on account of race, color, or any previous condition of slavery or involuntary servitude, or wherein they or any of them are subjected to any other or different punishment, pains, or penalties, for the commission of any act or offence, than are prescribed for white persons committing like acts or offences, it shall be the duty of the President of the United States, through the Commissioner, to extend military protection and jurisdiction over all cases affecting such persons so discriminated against.

The paucity of debate over the formula is probably explained by the bill's geographic limitation. It posed no danger to Northern Democrats and conservative Republicans who, indeed, hoped that they could appease the Radical Republicans by acceding to the measure and avoid a confrontation between President Johnson and the Congress. Their effort failed. Johnson vetoed the bill and the conservatives refused to provide the votes necessary to override the veto.

The bill was vetoed by President Andrew Johnson on February 19, 1866, and never became law. The same formula, "civil rights and immunities," however, reappeared in the first version of the Civil Rights Bill, introduced in the Senate in January 1866.

The debate over this formula was really a proxy for a larger debate over the kinds of rights the bill guaranteed, and thus the kinds of rights that Black people would now enjoy. Did the bill guarantee merely "civil rights"—equal common law rights and equal access to courts; or did it also guarantee equal "political rights" like the right to vote, serve on juries, or hold office; or so-called "social rights" like the right to marry persons of another race, the right to attend integrated public schools, and the right of equal access to integrated facilities? The tripartite distinction between *civil, political,* and *social* equality would prove important in early constructions of the Fourteenth Amendment.

Almost without exception, supporters of the bill asserted that the only rights it secured were those specifically enumerated in §1 and that a broader construction was not intended. For example, Lyman Trumbull (Republican, Illinois), the bill's Senate sponsor, explained that §1 would ensure for Black people "the rights of citizens": "[t]he great fundamental rights set forth in this bill: the right to acquire property, the right to go and come at pleasure, the right to enforce rights in the courts, to make contracts, and to inherit and dispose of property." When James A. McDougall (Democrat, California), fearful that the phrase encompassed suffrage, pressed for a definition of "civil rights," Trumbull responded by quoting the enumeration of rights in §1 and assuring him that there was no reference to "political" rights (i.e., the right to vote). Still, Democrats and conservative Republicans objected vigorously that the phrase "civil rights" might well be construed much more broadly than its sponsors said they intended.

Meanwhile, Edward Cowan, a conservative Republican from Pennsylvania, warned about enforced integration:

> Now, as I understand the meaning and intent of this bill, it is that there shall be no discrimination made between the inhabitants of the several States of this Union, none in any way. In Pennsylvania, for the greater convenience of the people, and for the greater convenience, I may say, of both classes of the people, in certain districts the Legislature has provided schools for colored children, has discriminated as between the two classes of children. We put the African children in this school house, . . . and educate them there as best we can. Is this amendment to the Constitution of the United States abolishing slavery[11] to break up that system which Pennsylvania has adopted for the education of her white and colored children? Are the school directors who carry out that law and who make this distinction between classes of children to be punished for a violation of this statute of the United States? To me it is monstrous.

No one responded to Cowan's point, nor indeed was the issue of segregation ever squarely faced in the debates. And despite objections that its language was too broad, the bill passed in the Senate, 33 to 12.

---

11. Proponents of the Civil Rights Bill argued that it implemented the Thirteenth Amendment.

James F. Wilson (Iowa), a Radical Republican, presented the bill to the House of Representatives with assurances of its limited objectives:

> [Section 1] provides for the equality of citizens of the United States in the enjoyment of "civil rights and immunities." What do these terms mean? Do they mean that in all things civil, social, political, all citizens without distinction of race or color, shall be equal? By no means can they be so construed. Do they mean that all citizens shall vote in the several States? No. . . . Nor do they mean that all citizens shall sit on the juries, or that their children shall attend the same schools. These are not civil rights or immunities. Well, what is the meaning? What are civil rights? I understand civil rights to be simply the absolute rights of individuals, such as—"The right of personal security, the right of personal liberty, and the right to acquire and enjoy property." "Right itself, in civil society, is that which any man is entitled to have, or to do, or to require from others, within the limits of prescribed law." Kent's Commentaries, vol. I, p. 199. . . .
>
> But what of the term "immunities"? . . . It merely secures to citizens of the United States equality in the exemptions of the law. A colored citizen shall not, because he is colored, be subjected to obligations, duties, pains. . . . This is the spirit and scope of the bill, and it goes not one step beyond. . . .

In response to John Bingham's argument that the bill would require much more, Wilson explained: "[T]his bill refers to those rights which belong to men as citizens of the United States and none other; and when [Bingham] talks of setting aside the school laws and jury laws and franchise laws of the States . . . he steps beyond what he must know to be the rule of construction which must apply here, and as a result of which this bill can only relate to matters within the control of Congress." Other Radicals emphasized the narrow scope of the bill. William Windom (Minnesota) believed that the measure did not do enough because it only protected "civil" rights, not "political" rights.

Opponents of the bill stressed the potential breadth of the language, which might include the right to vote, serve on juries, intermarry, and attend public schools. Andrew Jackson Rogers (Democrat, New Jersey) declared: "As a white man is by law authorized to marry a white woman, so does this bill compel the State to grant to the negro the same right of marrying a white woman."

Columbus Delano (moderate Republican, Ohio) feared that the bill would confer "upon the emancipated race the right of being jurors. . . . I presume that the gentleman himself will shrink from the idea of conferring upon this race now, at this particular moment, the right of being jurors, or from so wording this bill as to leave it a serious question and render it debatable hereafter in the courts or elsewhere. . . . [W]e once had in the State of Ohio a law excluding the black population from any participation in the public schools. . . . That law did not of course, place the black population upon an equal footing with the white, and would, therefore, under the terms of this bill be void."

Especially worrisome was the objection that the bill might grant the franchise to freedmen. The leadership finally acceded to an amendment "[t]hat nothing in this act shall be so construed as to affect the laws of any State concerning the right of suffrage," though Wilson still maintained that the amendment "will not change my construction of the bill. I do not believe the term civil rights includes the right of suffrage."

The second major issue of contention was Congress's authority to pass the Civil Rights Bill, including both the grant of citizenship in the first sentence—which overruled *Dred Scott*—and the grant of basic civil rights. Michael Kent Curtis explains that "Republicans believed that the Thirteenth Amendment effectively overruled *Dred Scott* so that Black people were entitled to all rights of citizens."[12] To most Republicans, the opposite of slavery was freedom, and that meant at the very least civil freedom (for some Republicans it meant even more, like the rights to vote and hold public office). Moreover, since Black people had been born in the United States, and were no longer slaves, they were now citizens.

Democrats, by contrast, disputed that freedom meant anything more than the absence of slavery. Michael C. Kerr (Democrat, Indiana) asked:

> Is it slavery or involuntary servitude to forbid a free negro, on account of race or color, to testify against a white man? Is it either to deny to free negroes, on the same account, the privilege of engaging in certain kinds of business . . . such as retailing spiritous liquors? Is it either to deny to children of free negroes or mulattoes on the like account, the privilege of attending the common schools of a State with the children of white men?

This Democratic attack might have been ignored had not other doubts about the bill's constitutionality been expressed by some influential Republicans, including Congressman John Bingham (Ohio), a principal draftsman of the Fourteenth Amendment. Bingham construed the civil rights formula broadly to guarantee political rights like suffrage and jury service; he also believed that the bill would enforce the Bill of Rights against state governments, and he argued that Congress lacked the power to pass such a law.

The bill was recommitted and the civil rights formula struck. In presenting the amended bill to the House, James Wilson stated: "Mr. Speaker, the amendment which has just been read proposes to strike out the general terms relating to civil rights. I do not think it materially changes the bill; but some gentlemen were apprehensive that the words we propose to strike out might give warrant for a latitudinarian construction not intended." Wilson also explained that the amendment made it unnecessary explicitly to exclude the franchise from the bill's coverage. The House and then the Senate passed the amended Civil Rights Act of 1866 and subsequently overrode a presidential veto.[13]

3. The Fourteenth Amendment

Meanwhile, the Joint Committee on Reconstruction, or Committee of Fifteen, was also addressing the problem of racial discrimination. Early in its deliberations over a possible constitutional amendment to supplement the Thirteenth Amendment, the committee rejected the civil rights formula.

---

12. Curtis, No State Shall Abridge, supra n.1, at 48.

13. The text of the Civil Rights Act was reenacted under the authority of §5 of the Fourteenth Amendment in the Enforcement Act of 1870, with the word "person" substituted for the word "citizen." It now appears in 42 U.S.C. §§1981 and 1982.

The committee's first product is sometimes called the "Bingham" amendment, after Representative John Bingham of Ohio, who introduced it in the House. The draft amendment provided: "The Congress shall have power to make all laws which shall be necessary and proper to secure to the citizens of each State all privileges and immunities of citizens in the several States (Art. 4, Sec. 2); and to all persons in the several States equal protection in the rights of life, liberty and property (5th Amendment)."[14]

The language in parenthesis appeared as explanatory material in the Committee of Fifteen's notes, and it shows the origins of the amendment's language.[15] The reference to the Privileges and Immunities Clause of Article IV, §2 is fairly obvious, but the Committee's reference to the Fifth Amendment's Due Process Clause requires a bit more explanation.

Like many nineteenth-century lawyers, the members of the Committee of Fifteen believed that "equal protection" of the laws was simply one aspect of due process of law. Persons living within a state's jurisdiction owed the state allegiance to its laws, while the state in turn owed them the protection of its laws. Due process of law meant that legislatures should respect the separation of powers and not attempt to do what judges did. Nineteenth-century lawyers distinguished between general laws—which were the province of legislatures—and "special" rules directed at particular persons or groups of people—which were the province of judicial determinations. Therefore "due process of law" required that legislatures pass only laws of general application and scope, which did not improperly single out groups of persons for special favor or disfavor.[16] This idea was related to the antebellum objection to "partial" or "class" legislation. As Mark Yudof explains, "[t]he idea that laws should be general and not tainted by considerations of class or caste was widely recognized and accepted before the fourteenth amendment was enacted. It was part-and-parcel of the presumed fairness of governmental processes, of due process of law."[17] It followed that a guarantee of protection of life, liberty, and property under the Due Process Clause also had to be a guarantee of equal protection of the laws.

In the House debates, Bingham argued that his draft amendment imposed no new obligations on the states, but merely allowed Congress to enforce rights (like the rights to jury trial, free speech, and freedom of religion) that states should already have respected. Bingham and many other Republicans believed that,

---

14. Benjamin B. Kendrick, Journal of the Joint Committee of Fifteen on Reconstruction 106 (Columbia University Press, 1914).

15. John Bingham made the same point in explaining the February draft before the House: "The residue of the resolution, as the House will see by a reference to the Constitution, is the language of the second section of the fourth article, and of a portion of the fifth amendment." Cong. Globe, 39th Cong., 1st Sess. 1033 (1866) (statement of Rep. Bingham). For a recent biography of Bingham, see Gerard Magliocca, American Founding Son: John Bingham and the Invention of the Fourteenth Amendment (2013).

16. See Ryan C. Williams, The One and Only Substantive Due Process Clause, 120 Yale L.J. 408, 425, 462-464 (2010).

17. See Mark G. Yudof, Equal Protection, Class Legislation, and Sex Discrimination: One Small Cheer for Mr. Herbert Spencer's "Social Statics," 88 Mich. L. Rev. 1366, 1376 (1990).

despite Barron v. Baltimore, the first eight amendments that we now call the "Bill of Rights" and other enumerated federal constitutional rights applied to the states.[18] The problem, Bingham, argued, was that Congress lacked the power to enforce these rights against states who failed to respect these constitutional guarantees.[19] Hence his proposed amendment created a new enumerated power that specifically authorized Congress to enforce constitutional rights against the states.

Critics raised two basic objections to the draft. First, despite Bingham's assurances that the scope of the amendment was limited, the language seemed to give Congress very broad new powers that, in theory, could displace large parts of existing state legislation. Representative Hale of New York objected that "it is a grant of power in general terms—a grant of the right to legislate for the protection of life, liberty, and property, simply qualified with the condition that it shall be equal legislation."[20]

Second, Representative Giles Hotchkiss of New York objected that although Bingham's draft gave Congress the power to protect equal rights, it said nothing about judicial enforcement. But what if Republicans lost their majority in both houses of Congress? A coalition of Southerners and Northern conservatives might repeal any civil rights legislation and block new protections, leaving Black people defenseless. A new amendment to the Constitution, Hotchkiss argued, "should be a constitutional right that cannot be wrested from any class of citizens, or from the citizens of any State by mere legislation. But this amendment proposes to leave it to the caprice of Congress. . . . Why not provide by an amendment to the Constitution that no State shall discriminate against any class of its citizens; and let that amendment stand as a part of the organic law of the land, subject only to be defeated by another constitutional amendment. We may pass laws here to-day, and the next Congress may wipe them out. Where is your guarantee then?"[21]

Hotchkiss's concerns were prescient. After the Democrats regained control of the House of Representatives in the 1874 election, no new civil rights legislation was passed until 1957.[22] The Reconstruction Republicans assumed that Congress would be the primary actor in civil rights protection; nevertheless, they also realized that

---

18. See Curtis, No State Shall Abridge, supra n.1, at 49-54, 61-63; Amar, The Bill of Rights, supra n.1, at 181-187; Richard L. Aynes, Enforcing the Bill of Rights Against the States: The History and the Future, 18 J. Contemp. Legal Issues 77, 81 (2009). Akhil Amar points out that this view was not limited to Republicans; it was held by many distinguished lawyers and judges before the Civil War. Amar, The Bill of Rights, supra n.1, at 145-162.

19. The Supreme Court had held in Prigg v. Pennsylvania that Congress had the power to enforce the Fugitive Slave Clause of Article IV, §2, but Bingham believed that *Prigg* was wrongly decided. That was one reason why he voted against the Civil Rights Act of 1866.

20. Cong. Globe, 39th Cong., 1st Sess. 1064 (1866); see also id. at 1095 (1866) (Representative Hotchkiss) ("I understand the amendment as now proposed by its terms to authorize Congress to establish uniform laws throughout the United States upon the subject named, the protection of life, liberty, and property.").

21. Cong. Globe, 39th Cong., 1st Sess. 1095 (1866) (statement of Rep. Hotchkiss).

22. The Democrats won control of the House in the 1874 elections. The last Reconstruction-era civil rights bill, the Civil Rights Act of 1875, was passed by a lame-duck session of the Republican-controlled Congress and signed into law on March 1, 1875. 18 Stat. 335 (1875).

once they appointed enough sympathetic judges, judicial review could also be useful to secure their achievements. Thus, during Reconstruction, Congress increased the number of federal judges, expanded federal jurisdiction, and passed a federal removal statute, all designed to give federal courts the ability to supervise states.[23]

These criticisms of the Bingham amendment demonstrated that it lacked sufficient support to move forward. As a result, the draft amendment was tabled in the House and sent back to the Committee of Fifteen for reworking.

The committee reemerged with a proposal after Congress had passed the Civil Rights Act of 1866 over President Johnson's veto. The new amendment was divided into five sections. Section 1 was now self-executing, meaning that courts could enforce it without additional legislation. Congress's own enforcement powers were now placed in a separate §5, with "necessary and proper" replaced by "appropriate," a reference to the test of McCulloch v. Maryland.[24]

Senator Jacob Howard, Speech Introducing the Fourteenth Amendment[25]

Speech delivered in the U.S. Senate (May 23, 1866)

[Senator Jacob Howard of Michigan was a member of the Joint Committee on Reconstruction that drafted the Fourteenth Amendment. He was the floor manager for the amendment in the Senate. In this speech, he introduces the amendment on the floor of the Senate and explains its purposes.]

Mr. Howard. . . . I can only promise to present to the Senate, in a very succinct way, the views and the motives which influenced th[e] committee, so far as I understand those views and motives, in presenting the report which is now before us for consideration, and the ends it aims to accomplish. . . .

The first section . . . relates to the privileges and immunities of citizens of the several States, and to the rights and privileges of all persons, whether citizens or others, under the laws of the United States. It declares that—

> No State shall make or enforce any law which shall abridge the privileges or immunities of citizens of the United States; nor shall any State deprive any person of life, liberty, or property without due process of law; nor deny to any person within its jurisdiction the equal protection of the laws.

---

23. See Howard Gillman, How Political Parties Can Use the Courts to Advance Their Agendas: Federal Courts in the United States, 1875-1891, 96 Am. Pol. Sci. Rev. 511 (2002) (arguing that economic nationalism drove expansion of federal judicial power even more than protection of civil rights).

24. See, e.g., Jack M. Balkin, The Reconstruction Power, supra n.1; Robert J. Kaczorowski, Congress's Power to Enforce Fourteenth Amendment Rights: Lessons from Federal Remedies the Framers Enacted, 42 Harv. J. on Legis. 187, 200-203 (2005); Akhil Reed Amar, Intratextualism, 112 Harv. L. Rev. 747, 822-827 (1999); Michael W. McConnell, Institutions and Interpretation: A Critique of City of Boerne v. Flores, 111 Harv. L. Rev. 153, 178 n.153 (1997).

25. Congressional Globe, 39th Cong., 1st Sess. 2764-2768.

It will be observed that this is a general prohibition upon all the States, as such, from abridging the privileges and immunities of the citizens of the United States. That is its first clause, and I regard it as very important. . . . [It] relates to the privileges and immunities of citizens of the United States as such, and as distinguished from all other persons not citizens of the United States. It is not, perhaps, very easy to define with accuracy what is meant by the expression, "citizen of the United States,"[26] although that expression occurs twice in the Constitution, once in reference to the President of the United States, in which instance it is declared that none but a citizen of the United States shall be President, and again in reference to Senators, who are likewise to be citizens of the United States. Undoubtedly the expression is used in both those instances in the same sense in which it is employed in the amendment now before us. A citizen of the United States is held by the courts to be a person who was born within the limits of the United States and subject to their laws. Before the adoption of the Constitution of the United States, the citizens of each State were, in a qualified sense at least, aliens to one another, for the reason that the several States before that event were regarded by each other as independent Governments, each one possessing a sufficiency of sovereign power to enable it to claim the right of naturalization; and, undoubtedly, each one of them possessed for itself the right of naturalizing foreigners, and each one, also, if it had seen fit so to exercise its sovereign power, might have declared the citizens of every other State to be aliens in reference to itself. With a view to prevent such confusion and disorder, and to put the citizens of the several States on an equality with each other as to all fundamental rights, a clause was introduced in the Constitution declaring that "the citizens of each State shall be entitled to all privileges and immunities of citizens in the several States."

The effect of this clause was to constitute *ipso facto* the citizens of each one of the original States citizens of the United States. And how did they antecedently become citizens of the several States? By birth or by naturalization. They became such in virtue of national law, or rather of natural law which recognizes persons born within the jurisdiction of every country as being subjects or citizens of that country. Such persons were, therefore, citizens of the United States as were born in the country or were made such by naturalization; and the Constitution declares that they are entitled, as citizens, to all the privileges and immunities of citizens in the several States. They are, by constitutional right, entitled to these privileges and immunities, and may assert this right and these privileges and immunities, and ask for their enforcement whenever they go within the limits of the several states of the Union.

I am not aware that the Supreme Court have ever undertaken to define either the nature or extent of the privileges and immunities thus guarantied. . . . But we may gather some intimation of what probably will be the opinion of the judiciary by referring to a case adjudged many years ago in one of the circuit courts of the United States by Judge Washington. . . . It is the case of Corfield vs. Coryell. . . . Judge Washington says:

> "The next question is whether this act infringes that section of the Constitution which declares that 'the citizens of each State shall be entitled to all privileges and immunities of citizens in the several states?'

---

26. Senator Howard delivered this speech before the first sentence, the Citizenship Clause, which defined citizenship, was added to the proposed amendment.

"The inquiry is, what are the privileges and immunities of citizens in the several States? We feel no hesitation in confining these expressions to those privileges and immunities which are in their nature fundamental, which belong of right to the citizens of all free Governments, and which have at all times been enjoyed by the citizens of the several States which compose this Union from the time of their becoming free, independent, and sovereign. What these fundamental principles are it would, perhaps, be more tedious than difficult to enumerate. They may, however, be all comprehended under the following general heads: protection by the Government, the enjoyment of life and liberty, with the right to acquire and possess property of every kind, and to pursue and obtain happiness and safety, subject nevertheless to such restraints as the Government may justly prescribe for the general good of the whole. The right of a citizen of one State to pass through or to reside in any other State, for purposes of trade, agriculture, professional pursuits, or otherwise; to claim the benefit of the writ of *habeas corpus*; to institute and maintain actions of any kind in the courts of the State; to take, hold, and dispose of property, either real personal, and an exemption from higher taxes or impositions than are paid by the other citizens of the State, may be mentioned as some of the particular privileges and immunities of citizens which are clearly embraced by the general description of privileges deemed to be fundamental, to which may be added the elective franchise, as regulated and established by the laws or constitution of the State in which it is to be exercised. These, and many others which might be mentioned, are, strictly speaking, privileges and immunities, and the enjoyment of them by the citizens of each State in every other State was manifestly calculated (to use the expressions of the preamble of the corresponding provision in the old Articles of Confederation) 'the better to secure and perpetuate mutual friendship and intercourse among the people of the different States of the Union.'"

Such is the character of the privileges and immunities spoken of in the second section of the fourth article of the Constitution. To these privileges and immunities, whatever they may be—for they are not and cannot be fully defined in their entire extent and precise nature—to these should be added the personal rights guarantied and secured by the first eight amendments of the Constitution; such as the freedom of speech and of the press; the right of the people peaceably to assemble and petition the Government for a redress of grievances, a right appertaining to each and all the people; the right to keep and to bear arms; the right to be exempted from the quartering of soldiers in a house without the consent of the owner; the right to be exempt from unreasonable searches and seizures, and from any search or seizure except by virtue of a warrant issued upon a formal oath or affidavit; the right of an accused person to be informed of the nature of the accusation against him, and his right to be tried by an impartial jury of the vicinage; and also the right to be secure against excessive bail and against cruel and unusual punishments.

Now, sir, here is a mass of privileges, immunities, and rights, some of them secured by the second section of the fourth article of the Constitution, which I have recited, some by the first eight amendments of the Constitution; and it is a fact well worthy of attention that the course of decision of our courts and the present settled doctrine is, that all these immunities, privileges, rights, thus guarantied by the Constitution or recognized by it, are secured to the citizen solely as a citizen of the United States and as a party in their courts. They do not operate in the slightest degree as a restraint or prohibition upon State legislation. States are not affected by them, and it has been repeatedly held[27] that the restriction contained in the Constitution against the taking of private property for public use without just compensation is not a restriction upon State legislation, but applies only to the legislation of Congress.

Now, sir, there is no power given in the Constitution to enforce and to carry out any of these guarantees. They are not powers granted by the Constitution to Congress, and of course do not come within the sweeping clause of the Constitution authorizing Congress to pass all laws necessary and proper for carrying out the foregoing or granted powers, but they stand simply as a bill of rights in the Constitution, without power on the part of Congress to give them full effect; while at the same time the States are not restrained from violating the principles embraced in them except by their own local constitutions, which may be altered from year to year. The great object of the first section of this amendment is, therefore, to restrain the power of the States and compel them at all times to respect these great fundamental guarantees. . . . This is done by the fifth section of this amendment, which declares that "the Congress shall have power to enforce by appropriate legislation the provisions of this article." Here is a direct affirmative delegation of power to Congress to carry out all the principles of all these guarantees, a power not found in the Constitution.

The last two clauses of the first section of the amendment disable a State from depriving not merely a citizen of the United States, but any person, whoever he may be, of life, liberty, or property without due process of law, or from denying to him the equal protection of the laws of the State. This abolishes all class legislation in the States and does away with the injustice of subjecting one caste of persons to a code not applicable to another. It prohibits the hanging of a black man for a crime for which the white man is not to be hanged. It protects the black man in his fundamental rights as a citizen with the same shield which it throws over the white man. Is it not time, Mr. President, that we extend to the black man, I had almost called it the poor privilege of the equal protection of the law? Ought not the time to be now passed when one measure of justice is to be meted out to a member of one caste while another and a different measure is meted out to the member of another caste, both castes being alike citizens of the United States, both bound to obey the same laws, to sustain the burdens of the same Government, and both equally responsible to justice and to God for the deeds done in the body?

But, sir, the first section of the proposed amendment does not give to either of these classes the right of voting. The right of suffrage is not, in law, one of the privileges or immunities thus secured by the Constitution. It is merely the creature of law. It has always been regarded in this country as the result of positive local law, not regarded as one of those fundamental rights lying at the basis of all society and without which a people cannot exist except as slaves, subject to a despotism.

---

27. This is probably a reference to Barron v. City of Baltimore, 32 U.S. 243 (1833).

As I have already remarked, section one is a restriction upon the States, and does not, of itself, confer any power upon Congress. The power which Congress has, under this amendment, is derived, not from that section, but from the fifth section, which gives it authority to pass laws which are appropriate to the attainment of the great object of the amendment. Look upon the first section, taken in connection with the fifth, as very important. It will, if adopted by the States, forever disable every one of them from passing laws trenching upon those fundamental rights and privileges which pertain to citizens of the United States, and to all persons who may happen to be within their jurisdiction. It establishes equality before the law, and it gives to the humblest, the poorest, the most despised of the race the same rights and the same protection before the law as it gives to the most powerful, the most wealthy, or the most haughty. That, sir, is republican government, as I understand it, and the only one which can claim the praise of a just Government. Without this principle of equal justice to all men and equal protection under the shield of the law, there is no republican government and none that is really worth maintaining.

. . .

[Section 5] gives to Congress power to enforce by appropriate legislation all the provisions of this article of amendment. Without this clause, no power is granted to Congress by the amendment or any one of its sections. It casts upon Congress the responsibility of seeing to it, for the future, that all the sections of the amendment are carried out in good faith, and that no State infringes the rights of persons or property. I look upon this clause as indispensable for the reason that it thus imposes upon Congress this power and this duty. It enables Congress, in case the States shall enact laws in conflict with the principles of the amendment, to correct that legislation by a formal congressional enactment.

DISCUSSION

1. *The Citizenship Clause.* The first sentence of the Fourteenth Amendment, which is similar to the opening sentence of the 1866 Civil Rights Act, overrules *Dred Scott v. Sandford.* It states that anyone born in the United States "and subject to the jurisdiction thereof" is a citizen. It makes state citizenship depend on national citizenship, the reverse of the arrangement before the Civil War. It also guarantees U.S. citizens the right to become the citizen of a state by establishing residence. Before the Civil War, some states in both the North and South had refused to grant free Black people state citizenship and the rights that came with it, and *Dred Scott* made U.S. citizenship legally impossible.

"[S]ubject to the jurisdiction thereof" means subject to the authority of the United States government. This language was designed, by analogy with the traditional rule for natural born subjects in Great Britain, to include all children of noncitizens born in the United States and subject to American law, but to exclude a small number of cases such as "the child of an ambassador or other diplomatic agent of a foreign state, or of an alien enemy in hostile occupation of the place where the child was born." United States v. Wong Kim Ark, 169 U.S. 649, 658 (1898).

Thus (1) children born in slavery before the Thirteenth Amendment; (2) children born of former slaves; and (3) the children of noncitizens all automatically became citizens at birth if the children were born in the United States and were subject to American law. This rule makes the legality of the parents' presence in the United States irrelevant to their children's citizenship. In fact, immigration was barely regulated in 1868, and no one at the time thought in terms of "legal" and "illegal" (or "documented" and "undocumented") immigrants.[28]

2. *The Privileges or Immunities Clause and the Privileges and Immunities Clause.* Senator Howard begins his explanation of the Fourteenth Amendment by pointing to the Privileges and Immunities Clause of Article IV, §2. The standard view of the clause (often called the Comity Clause) was that it was simply an equality provision: It required states to treat citizens from other states the same as it treated its own citizens with respect to certain privileges or immunities. The Supreme Court confirmed this view in Paul v. Virginia, 75 U.S. (8 Wall.) 168 (1869).

Like many Republican thinkers of the time, Howard had a much more substantive view of Article IV, §2. He argued that the Privileges and Immunities Clause in Article IV already bound the states to protect fundamental rights of national citizenship. See Michael Kent Curtis, No State Shall Abridge, supra n.1, at 47-48, 62-91 (1986). In other words, Howard and other Republicans read Article IV's reference to "privileges and immunities of citizens in the several States" to mean "privileges and immunities of citizens of the United States in the several states." Nevertheless, the Republican argument went, there was no method in the antebellum Constitution to enforce these guarantees. Hence the Privileges or Immunities Clause of the new Fourteenth Amendment would establish a clear legal obligation enforceable by the courts; moreover, Congress could also pass enforcing legislation under its §5 powers. Thus it was no accident that what Howard believed to be the central clause in §1 of the Fourteenth Amendment uses the same language as Article IV, §2.

The new Privileges or Immunities Clause had another important effect. Just as states had to treat outsiders equally with their own citizens with respect to certain fundamental rights, so too they would now have to treat their own citizens equally with respect to these rights. Thus the Privileges or Immunities Clause was not only a guarantee of liberty; it was also a guarantee of equality with respect to the basic rights of national citizenship.

As we shall soon see, the Supreme Court quickly robbed the Privileges or Immunities Clause of any importance in the Slaughterhouse Cases and United States v. Cruikshank. As described in later chapters, the Court eventually turned to the Due Process and Equal Protection Clauses to protect fundamental rights.

3. *Incorporation.* According to Senator Howard, the Privileges or Immunities Clause protects the "the personal rights guarantied and secured by the first eight amendments of the Constitution." Thus Howard believed—and represented to the Senate when he introduced the amendment—that the Fourteenth Amendment incorporated the personal rights guarantees of the Bill of Rights. John Bingham, the key drafter of §1, made a similar point in an 1871 speech explaining his motivations. Bingham explained that in Barron v. Baltimore, Chief Justice Marshall had

---

28. See Garrett Epps, The Citizenship Clause: A 'Legislative History', 60 Am. U. L. Rev. 331 (2011); James C. Ho, Defining "American": Birthright Citizenship and the Original Understanding of the 14th Amendment, 9 Green Bag 2d (2006).

argued that if Congress had wished to bind states by constitutional amendments, it should have used language of the form "No state shall." Therefore, Bingham explained, he wrote §1 in precisely this way.[29]

As we will see later on in this casebook, the Supreme Court did not take up this invitation, and the Bill of Rights (or most of it, at any rate) did not become incorporated until the middle of the twentieth century. Moreover, incorporation, when it occurred, came through a creative reading of the Due Process Clause, and not the Privileges or Immunities Clause.

4. *Unenumerated rights.* Note Senator Howard's reliance on Corfield v. Coryell and his remark that the privileges and immunities of citizens of the United States "are not and cannot be fully defined in their entire extent and precise nature." Howard offers a declaratory theory of privileges or immunities. That is, he assumes that these rights are natural rights that preexist the state, and that the Constitution merely declares their existence and makes them enforceable in positive law. How can courts and legislatures determine what those rights are? We will return to this question in Chapter 9. (Recall the debate between Justices Chase and Iredell in Calder v. Bull concerning whether courts could protect natural rights against infringements by state governments. How would the inclusion of the Privileges or Immunities Clause change the terms of that debate?)

5. *Class and caste legislation.* When Howard turns to the Equal Protection and Due Process Clauses, he argues that they serve a different function: "This abolishes all class legislation in the States and does away with the injustice of subjecting one caste of persons to a code not applicable to another." What does the principle against "caste" legislation mean? One possibility suggested by Howard's speech is simple colorblindness. Another is that "caste" legislation is legislation that subordinates one social group to another.

The related notion of "class legislation" involved unjustified singling out a particular group for special burdens or special benefits. Indeed, the expression "equal protection" famously appeared in Andrew Jackson's July 10, 1832 Veto Message, where he stated:

> It is to be regretted that the rich and powerful too often bend the acts of government to their selfish purposes. Distinctions in society will always exist under every just government. Equality of talents, of education, or of wealth can not be produced by human institutions. In the full enjoyment of the gifts of Heaven and the fruits of superior industry, economy, and virtue, every man is equally entitled to protection by law; but when the laws undertake to add to these natural and just advantages artificial distinctions, to grant titles, gratuities, and exclusive privileges, to make the rich richer and the potent more powerful, the humble members of society—the farmers, mechanics, and laborers—who have neither the time nor the means of securing like favors to themselves, have a right to complain of the injustice of their Government. There are no necessary evils in government. Its evils exist only in its abuses. If it would confine itself to

---

29. Barron v. Baltimore, 32 U.S. (7 Pet.) 243, 248-249 (1833); Cong. Globe, 42d Cong., 1st Sess. App. 84 (1871) (statement of Rep. Bingham).

equal protection, and, as Heaven does its rains, shower its favors alike on the high and the low, the rich and the poor, it would be an unqualified blessing.

6. *Voting.* Note that Justice Washington included "the elective franchise, as regulated and established by the laws or constitution of the State in which it is to be exercised" in his list of privileges and immunities. Senator Howard, however, takes pains to insist that voting is not one of the rights guaranteed by the new Fourteenth Amendment. In part, that was because he and other supporters of the amendment did not believe it could pass if Black people were given the right to vote. Hence they settled for the compromise measure of §2, which sought to penalize states that denied Black men the vote. As Howard explained in his discussion of §2:

> Let me not be misunderstood. I do not intend to say, nor do I say, that the proposed amendment, section two, proscribes the colored race. It has nothing to do with that question, as I shall show before I take my seat. I could wish that the elective franchise should be extended equally to the white man and to the black man; and if it were necessary, after full consideration, to restrict what is known as universal suffrage for the purpose of securing this equality, I would go for a restriction; but I deem that impracticable at the present time, and so did the committee.
>
> The colored race are destined to remain among us. They have been in our midst for more than two hundred years; and the idea of the people of the United States ever being able by any measure or measures to which they may resort to expel or expatriate that race from their limits and to settle them in a foreign country, is to me the wildest of all chimeras. The thing can never be done; it is impracticable. For weal or for woe, the destiny of the colored race in this country is wrapped up with our own; they are to remain in our midst, and here spend their years and here bury their fathers and finally repose themselves. We may regret it. It may not be entirely compatible with our taste that they should live in our midst. We cannot help it. Our forefathers introduced them, and their destiny is to continue among us; and the practical question which now presents itself to us is as to the best mode of getting along with them.
>
> The committee were of opinion that the States are not yet prepared to sanction so fundamental a change as would be the concession of the right of suffrage to the colored race. We may as well state it plainly and fairly, so that there shall be no misunderstanding on the subject. It was our opinion that three-fourths of the states of this Union could not be induced to vote to grant the right of suffrage, even in any degree or under any restriction, to the colored race. We may be right in this apprehension or we may be in error. Time will develop the truth; and for one I shall wait with patience the movements of public opinion upon this great and absorbing question. The time may come, I trust it will come, indeed I feel a profound conviction that it is not far distant, when even the people of the States themselves where the colored population is most dense will consent to admit them to the right of suffrage. Sir, the safety and prosperity of those States depend upon it; it is especially for their interest that they

> should not retain in their midst a race of pariahs, so circumstanced as to be obliged to bear the burdens of Government and to obey its laws without any participation in the enactment of the laws.
>
> The second section leaves the right to regulate the elective franchise still with the States, and does not meddle with that right. . . .

As it turned out, the Fifteenth Amendment was ratified four years later in 1870. Does this history mean that the Fourteenth Amendment has no application with respect to voting or the right to hold public office? Or is it that the mechanism for enforcing any right to vote would take place outside the courts? Note that Congress has the power to enforce §2 of the Fourteenth Amendment, which does concern voting rights.

7. *What the Fourteenth Amendment did not say.* The text of §1 of the Fourteenth Amendment does not mention race. This was not an oversight. There were several proposals for banning racial discrimination. For example, on July 22, 1865, Wendell Phillips, one of the most prominent abolitionists, had proposed the following constitutional amendment: "No State shall make any distinction in civil rights and privileges among the naturalized citizens of the United States residing within its limits, or among persons born on its soil of parents permanently resident there, on account of race, color, or descent." On December 5, 1865, Thaddeus Stevens, the leader of the Radical Republicans within the House of Representatives, introduced the following text as a proposed constitutional amendment: "All national and State laws shall be equally applicable to every citizen, and no discrimination shall be made on account of race and color."

Neither text, of course, was adopted, in part, says Andrew Kull, because "moderates" prevailed, and they "would allow those distinctions consistent with 'equal protection.'"[30] As we have seen, moderates did not want a strict rule of colorblindness because it would give Black people the right to vote, and might throw into question laws restricting jury service and banning interracial marriage. To what extent should this affect our interpretation of the Fourteenth Amendment today?

8. *The status of women.* Women's rights arose during Howard's discussion of Black suffrage, since §2 imposed a penalty only for denying the right to vote to males. In defending his position that Black people should have been given the right to vote, Senator Howard quoted Madison for the "vital principle of free government, that those who are to be bound by the laws ought to have a voice in making them." Howard asserted that this principle was "the vital principle of republican government; it is not representation because of taxation." Responding to a question by Senator Sumner, Howard argued that the principle applied to all persons irrespective of color, and "whether they can read or write or not." When asked by Senator Johnson whether this included women, Howard answered:

> Mr. Madison does not say anything about females. . . . I believe Mr. Madison was old enough and wise enough to take it for granted there was such a thing as the law of nature which has a certain influence even in political affairs, and that by that law women and children were not regarded as the

---

30. Andrew Kull, The Color-Blind Constitution, 62ff (1992).

> equals of men. Mr. Madison would not have quibbled about the question of women's voting or of an infant's voting. He lays down a broad democratic principle, that those who are to be bound by the laws ought to have a voice in making them; and everywhere mature manhood is the representative type of the human race.

In the debates over the Fourteenth Amendment, the proponents of the new amendment were careful to avoid claiming that it would invalidate any laws regarding women. Although the framers of the Fourteenth Amendment asserted that women and men were civilly equal, they assumed that existing laws and practices—including coverture—did not deny women equal citizenship. See Cong. Globe, 39th Cong., 1st Sess., at 1089 (Feb. 28, 1866) (remarks of Rep. Bingham) (noting that states would retain ability to regulate married women's ownership of property because property rights were governed by local law while "[t]he rights of life and liberty are theirs [i.e., women's] whatever States may enact"); Cong. Globe, 39th Cong., 1st Sess., at 1064 (1866) (Feb. 27, 1866) (remarks of Rep. Stevens) ("When a distinction is made between two married people or two femmes sole, then it is unequal legislation; but where all of the same class are dealt with in the same way then there is no pretense of inequality."). Responding to Stevens, Representative Hale remarked: "[The] argument seems to me to be more specious than sound. The language of the section gives to *all persons* equal protection. Now if that means you shall extend to one married women the same protection you extend to another, and not the same you extend to unmarried women or men, then by parity of reasoning it will be sufficient if you extend to one negro the same rights you do to another, but not those you extend to a white man. . . . The line of distinction is, I take it, quite as broadly marked between negroes and white men as between married and unmarried women."

What weight should we give these remarks in deciding how the Fourteenth Amendment should apply to questions of sex equality today?

9. *Sections 2, 3, and 4 as strategies of partisan entrenchment.* Contemporary legal analysis focuses almost exclusively on §§1 and 5 of the Fourteenth Amendment and judicial interpretations of the amendment. But most of the congressional debates over the amendment concerned §§2, 3, and 4. The reason is that among other things, the Fourteenth Amendment served as a kind of armistice setting the terms of political reunion with the defeated South. Section 4 extinguished claims for emancipated slaves (an issue unresolved by the Thirteenth Amendment) and ensured that returning Southern Democrats would not attempt to hold the government hostage to repay the Confederacy's war debt or attempt to invalidate the Union debt.

Sections 2 and 3 were designed to create a political regime that would protect Republican values. Professor Mark Graber has argued that, given the experience of *Dred Scott,* Republicans had relatively little confidence in the ability of the judiciary to protect their interests and feared that enlightened legislation would be vulnerable should Democrats ever return to power. They wanted to create structural guarantees that their party's political influence and values would be protected.[31]

---

31. Mark A. Graber, Constructing Constitutional Politics: The Reconstruction Strategy for Protecting Rights (2013), https://digitalcommons.law.umaryland.edu/fac_pubs/1390/.

Graber argues that §§2 and 3 sought to entrench Republican political control to forestall the return of the Southern Democratic political coalition that had dominated American politics prior to Lincoln's election. Because Black people no longer counted as three-fifths of a person, Southern representation in the House would actually increase as a result of the war. The Republicans needed Black suffrage to compete effectively in the South, but in 1866 Republican moderates were unwilling to give Black people the right to vote. Thus §2 provided that although states were not required to allow Black males to vote, their representation in the House and the Electoral College would be proportionately reduced if suffrage was fact denied. The practical effect of §2 was rendered superfluous by state guarantees of Black suffrage in the constitutions of returning Southern states, and by the addition of the Fifteenth Amendment in 1870.

Section 3 tried to limit the limit the power of neo-Confederates by making ineligible to hold any state or national office anyone who had previously served as a federal or state judge or political official (and thus taken an oath to the support the Constitution) and had "engaged in insurrection or rebellion against the same, or given aid or comfort to the enemies thereof." The idea was to disqualify much of the antebellum Southern political class from returning to power. Congress could "remove such disability" by a two-thirds vote. In 1872, Congress removed disabilities for all persons "except Senators and Representatives of the Thirty-sixth and Thirty-seventh Congresses, officers in the judicial, military and naval service of the United States, heads of departments, and foreign ministers of the United States." Ch. 193, 17 Stat. 142. A subsequent act in 1898 provided that "the disability imposed by section 3 . . . incurred heretofore, is hereby removed." Act of June 6, 1898, ch. 389, 30 Stat. 432.

Ultimately, the Republican strategy had only limited success. Democrats regained the House in the 1874 elections and the White House in 1884 and 1892 (they also won the popular vote in the disputed election of 1876 and the election of 1888 but not the Electoral College). Instead, Republicans eventually turned to a different strategy to protect their interests. To bolster their representation in the Senate, they began admitting new states in the West that they believed would reliably vote Republican, while deferring the admission of states that they believed would vote Democratic.

One of the first federal decisions to construe the Fourteenth Amendment concerned a criminal prosecution against the Ku Klux Klan:

UNITED STATES v. HALL, 26 F. Cas. 79 (C.C. Ala 1871): [Hall, a member of the Ku Klux Klan, participated in a Klan raid on a Republican Party meeting in Eutaw, Alabama organized by Black farmers. The Klansmen fired their weapons into the meeting hall, killing two persons and injuring dozens of others. A federal grand jury indicted Hall for conspiring to violate the First Amendment rights of the victims in violation of the Enforcement Act of 1870. The Enforcement Act was passed under Congress's Section 5 powers, and made it a crime to conspire "to injure, oppress, threaten, or intimidate any citizen with intent to prevent or hinder his free exercise and enjoyment of any right or privilege granted or secured to him by the Constitution or laws of the United States." Hall argued that the indictment was defective because the First Amendment was not a privilege or immunity of U.S. citizens under the Fourteenth Amendment.

The case was heard by Judge William B. Woods, sitting as a circuit judge. Woods was a former Union General from Ohio who had settled in Alabama after the war and would later become a Supreme Court Justice. Because this was one of the first cases construing the Fourteenth Amendment, Woods corresponded with Justice Joseph P. Bradley about the interpretation of the new Amendment and incorporated parts of Bradley's reply into his opinion.]

Woods, J.:

[The Fourteenth Amendment] declares that "all persons, born or naturalized in the United States, and subject to the jurisdiction thereof, are citizens of the United States and the state wherein they reside." By the original constitution citizenship in the United States was a consequence of citizenship in a state. By this clause this order of things is reversed. Citizenship in the United States is defined; it is made independent of citizenship in a state, and citizenship in a state is a result of citizenship in the United States. So that a person born or naturalized in the United States, and subject to its jurisdiction, is, without reference to state constitutions or laws, entitled to all the privileges and immunities secured by the constitution of the United States to citizens thereof. . . . .

What are the privileges and immunities of citizens of the United States here referred to? They are undoubtedly those which may be denominated fundamental; which belong of right to the citizens of all free states, and which have at all times been enjoyed by the citizens of the several states which compose this Union from the time of their becoming free, independent and sovereign. Corfield v. Coryell. Among these [are] those which in the constitution are expressly secured to the people, either as against the action of the federal or state governments. Included in these are the right of freedom of speech, and the right peaceably to assemble. . . . [C]ongress is forbidden to impair them by the first amendment, and the states are forbidden to impair them by the fourteenth amendment. . . .

[C]ongress has the power, by appropriate legislation, to protect the fundamental rights of citizens of the United States against unfriendly or insufficient state legislation, for the fourteenth amendment not only prohibits the making or enforcing of laws which shall abridge the privileges of the citizen, but prohibits the states from denying to all persons within its jurisdiction the equal protection of the laws. Denying includes inaction as well as action, and denying the equal protection of the laws includes the omission to protect, as well as the omission to pass laws for protection. The citizen of the United States is entitled to the enforcement of the laws for the protection of his fundamental rights, as well as the enactment of such laws.

Therefore, to guard against the invasion of the citizen's fundamental rights, and to insure their adequate protection, as well against state legislation as state inaction, or incompetency, the amendment gives congress the power to enforce its provisions by appropriate legislation.

And as it would be unseemly for congress to interfere directly with state enactments, and as it cannot compel the activity of state officials, the only appropriate legislation it can make is that which will operate directly on offenders and offenses, and protect the rights which the amendment secures. The extent to which congress shall exercise this power must depend on its discretion in view of the circumstances of each case. If the exercise of it in any case should seem to interfere with the domestic affairs of a state, it must be remembered that it is for the purpose of protecting federal rights, and these must be protected even though it interfere with state laws or the administration of state laws.

We think, therefore, that the right of freedom of speech, and the other rights enumerated in the first eight articles of amendment to the constitution of the United States, are the privileges and immunities of citizens of the United States, that they are secured by the constitution, that congress has the power to protect them by appropriate legislation.

DISCUSSION

1. Woods argues that the Bill of Rights applies to the states through the Privileges or Immunities Clause. In this respect, his initial construction of the Fourteenth Amendment does not differ very much from the views expressed in Jacob Howard's speech introducing the Fourteenth Amendment in the Senate in May 1866.

2. Although, as noted above, Woods had consulted with Justice Bradley in writing the opinion, the Supreme Court would eventually offer a far narrower construction of the Privileges or Immunities Clause and Section 5. The Court rejected incorporation of the First Amendment five years later in United States v. Cruikshank, and Justice Bradley's 1883 opinion in the Civil Rights Cases would adopt a narrow reading of Congress's powers to enforce the Reconstruction Amendments.

NOTE: THE UNUSUAL PROCEDURAL HISTORY OF THE FOURTEENTH AMENDMENT[32]

The preceding materials treat the Fourteenth Amendment as if it were an ordinary Article V amendment. But there was nothing ordinary about the procedures by which the amendment was added to the constitutional text.

Lee's surrender at Appomattox effectively ended the Civil War (though not in a legal sense; see the Note: When Did the Civil War End?, pp. 379-381 infra). Abraham Lincoln was assassinated only three days later. His successor, Andrew Johnson, a Unionist Democrat from Tennessee placed on the ticket with Lincoln as a gesture toward national unity, in effect offered to welcome back the ostensible members of the Confederate States of America if they agreed first to repudiate the legitimacy of secession and then to ratify the Thirteenth Amendment abolishing slavery. (Recall that, according to Lincoln, the Confederate states had never legally left the Union. What, then, did it mean to welcome them back? Recall that the Thirteenth Amendment had

32. Much of the material in this note is drawn from Bruce Ackerman's scholarship on constitutional change during Reconstruction. The initial statements of his thesis can be found in The Storrs Lectures: Discovering the Constitution, 93 Yale L.J. 1013 (1984), and Constitutional Politics/Constitutional Law, 99 Yale L.J. 453 (1989). The thesis is richly elaborated in We the People: Transformations 99-252 (1998) and extensively criticized in John Harrison, The Lawfulness of the Segregation Amendments, 68 U. Chi. L. Rev. 375 (2001), and Amar, America's Constitution, supra n.1, at 364-380.

been proposed on January 31, 1865, before the termination of the war, when none of the Confederate states was represented in Congress. However, Johnson, who believed that the defeated states were still subject to the federal government's war powers, pressured them to ratify the Amendment and accept the end of slavery.

Eight of the operating governments within the states of the defeated Confederacy joined 19 other States that had never left to provide the necessary three-quarters ratification within the then 36-member Union, and on December 18, 1865, William Seward, the Secretary of State, officially proclaimed that the amendment had become part of the Constitution.

However, on December 4, 1865, the Republican majorities in the Thirty-Ninth Congress, which was meeting for the first time since the 1864 elections,[33] exercised their constitutional power—see Article I, §5—to judge the "Qualifications of its own Members" to exclude the men from the former Confederacy who had been elected to sit in the House and Senate. The explanation was simple: If they sat these members, then the legal consequences of the war would be restricted to the addition of the Thirteenth Amendment, *and nothing more.* The Democrats would have more than enough votes to block any proposals for constitutional amendment. Moreover, the Democrats might also have the possible power to block the passage of ordinary legislation, if they could persuade Andrew Johnson to exercise his veto power. This would frustrate the will of the Republican legislative majority and require the same two-thirds majority to pass legislation as was needed to propose constitutional amendments. Beginning in the spring of 1866, Johnson did in fact repeatedly wield his veto pen to oppose important Reconstruction legislation.

Indeed, from the Republican perspective, the future looked even bleaker politically: Before the passage of the Thirteenth Amendment, the South was allowed to count its slaves as only three-fifths of a person for purposes of computing the population base that determined how many representatives in the House each state would receive. Now, because of the Thirteenth Amendment, the Southern states would obtain a significant boost in legally recognized population: All of the former slaves would henceforth count as whole persons, even though the Republicans were quite sure that these new persons would never be allowed to vote. As the result of losing the war, then, the former Confederate states would end up with enhanced power in the House of Representatives and, indirectly, in the Electoral College that elected the President.

In order to prevent this perverse state of affairs—whereby the South was actually politically strengthened by losing the war—the Republican-controlled Congress refused to accept the legitimacy of the Southern representatives and senators who showed up at the Capitol to take their oaths of office. Or, perhaps more to the point, Congress rejected the legitimacy of the white-only electorate that selected the members of the House and of the white-only legislatures that named the senators.

Thus the Fourteenth Amendment was proposed by what Bruce Ackerman calls a "rump" Congress, from which the Democratic opposition from the former Confederate states had been excluded. It did indeed receive two-thirds of the vote of

33. Why this remarkable delay? Again, read Article I, §4, cl. 2. Why do you think that President Johnson did not call Congress into special session immediately after the assassination of his predecessor?

each house of Congress, but only if one chooses to ignore the exclusion of potential opponents. The Fourteenth Amendment received 120 votes in the House and 33 in the Senate. With a full complement of Southern representatives, it would have required 162 votes in the House and 48 in the Senate to gain a two-thirds majority. Ackerman argues that "Southern exclusion . . . was a necessary political condition for the Republicans to gain the two-thirds vote required by Article Five for the proposal of a constitutional amendment."[34] Because Ackerman regards the work of this Congress as a fundamental change in the political order, he compares it to the first constitutional convention in Philadelphia—which he believes also acted with dubious legality. He even calls the Thirty-Ninth Congress a "Convention/Congress."

Of course, gaining two-thirds of each house—no matter how constituted—is not enough to ratify an amendment. The proposed Fourteenth Amendment still needed ratification by 27 states in order to become part of the Constitution. Although eight governments of the former Confederacy voted for the Thirteenth Amendment—presumably on the view that slavery was effectively over anyway—the Fourteenth Amendment presented a number of different issues. It explicitly granting citizenship to Black people and guaranteed them equal civil rights. It also prohibited the assumption of Confederate War debt, imposed conditions on political officeholding by former Confederate leaders, and penalized Southern states for denying Black males the vote. Quite apart from all this, the Fourteenth Amendment was generally understood as changing the balance of power in the American Republic, giving the federal government new and broad powers to oversee states in the name of individual rights. The Southern state legislatures sitting in 1866 were hardly likely to consent to it, and they easily had the votes under Article V to block its ratification at the state level even if Southern representatives were excluded from Congress by the Radical Republicans. Indeed, by the end of 1866, North Carolina, Georgia, Texas, South Carolina, and Louisiana had voted to reject the amendment, to be followed shortly in the new year by Virginia and Mississippi. Moreover, three of the four "border states," i.e., slave states that had remained in the Union—Delaware, Maryland, and Kentucky—rejected the amendment, though Missouri, the fourth, did ratify it.[35] These ten rejections were enough to doom the amendment under the three-quarters rule for ratification set out by Article V.

---

34. Ackerman, Constitutional Politics/Constitutional Law, supra n.32, at 503.

35. The ratification history is unusually complicated, as two other states, New Jersey and Ohio, which had ratified the amendment in 1866 and early 1867, attempted to rescind these ratifications. Although Congress and the Secretary of State chose to count these states as yes votes in mid-July 1867, the issue quickly became moot, thanks to ratifications that came in from Alabama and Georgia, who ratified in mid-July. By July 28, 1868—the date of Seward's formal proclamation that the Fourteenth Amendment "has been adopted"—the amendment's ratification no longer hinged on the results in New Jersey and Ohio. Note that Article V is entirely silent on whether a state, having once ratified an amendment, and before it has been ratified by enough other states to reach the three-fourths requirement, can change its mind. Given that no one would seriously argue that a state, once having voted to reject an amendment could not subsequently change its collective mind and declare its approval, then why should not a state have a prerogative to rescind a ratification that it (or, more accurately, a successor legislature within a state) deems to have been unwise? See generally Michael S. Paulsen, A General Theory of Article V: The Constitutional Lessons of the Twenty-Seventh Amendment, 103 Yale L.J. 677 (1993).

It was this legal reality generated by Article V that triggered what has come to be known as the "congressional" phase of "Reconstruction" (as distinct from "presidential Reconstruction" under Andrew Johnson's leadership). Congress passed the First and Second Reconstruction Acts in March 1867 over President Johnson's veto.[36] The defeated states were occupied by the U.S. military, which meant, among other things, that the state governments of the former Confederacy were effectively dissolved, and the South was put under the authority of military commanders. Federal military and civilian authorities supervised new constitutional conventions that would create new state governments, which were required to accept Black suffrage. The federal military was also to oversee the registration of both white and Black voters. Finally, representatives of the newly constituted state governments were to be allowed admission as members in good standing to the House and Senate only if the state ratified the Fourteenth Amendment, and only after the amendment had gained the support of three-fourths of the states.[37]

President Johnson opposed these policies—on constitutional as well as political grounds—and hoped to use his power as commander-in-chief of the military to stall the conventions that were organized to create the new state governments and ratify the Fourteenth Amendment. In order to do this, he attempted to fire Secretary of War Edwin M. Stanton, in seeming violation of the Tenure in Office Act passed by Congress that had forbidden just such an exercise of executive power by Johnson.[38] The House of Representatives responded by voting a bill of impeachment against Johnson. Johnson's impeachment trial in the Senate began in March 1868. By April, Johnson retreated, in effect recognizing Congress's power to structure the terms of the de facto "peace treaty" between North and South. He nominated a new Secretary of War acceptable to the Congress, and agreed to stop interfering with the ratification process. Johnson was eventually acquitted by one vote.[39] In June 1868, the Congress recognized the legitimacy of the governments

36. Again, it should be emphasized that Johnson's veto would easily have been sustained had the Southern representatives and senators been seated in December 1865.

37. Although all of the former Confederate states did in fact comply with the conditions, it may be worth noting that the three border states did not get around to ratifying the amendment until 1901 (Delaware); 1959 (Maryland); and 1976 (Kentucky). What may be more surprising is that California ratified the amendment only in 1959. See http://www.law.emory.edu/FEDERAL/usconst/amend.html#art-14.

38. Needless to say, there is much controversy over whether Congress has the power so to limit the President's control over who shall serve in his or her cabinet. Most contemporary constitutional lawyers would probably agree with Johnson that the Act was unconstitutional. How important is it to you whether Johnson in fact had a legitimate constitutional argument with regard to the issue over which he was impeached? Consider your earlier response to a similar question with regard to Abraham Lincoln's Emancipation Proclamation. Might Congress have been right to try to remove Johnson from the presidency even if, as a formal matter, he had committed no "high crime and misdemeanor" or, indeed, no "crime" at all?

39. The key vote was cast by Republican Senator Ross of Kansas, and John F. Kennedy selected Ross as one of his subjects in his widely read book Profiles in Courage (1956), which was awarded the Pulitzer Prize in 1957 and which has remained in print since then. Assume for the moment that you believe that the Tenure in Office Act was unconstitutional, so that Johnson committed no "crime" at all in refusing to consider himself bound by it. But assume as

of seven Southern states; by July all seven had ratified the Fourteenth Amendment. (An eighth defeated state, Tennessee, had ratified and been readmitted to Congress the previous year.)

DISCUSSION

1. *The Thirteenth-Fourteenth Amendment paradox.* From the preceding discussion you can see that the Southern states (and state governments) were considered sufficiently legitimate to ratify the Thirteenth Amendment in 1866 but not the Fourteenth Amendment in 1868. (Indeed, Congress refused to seat the Southern representatives two weeks before the official proclamation of the ratification of the Thirteenth Amendment!) Does this fact undermine the legitimacy of either amendment in your view? If so, which one?

Bruce Ackerman, who details the history of this period in his book We The People: Transformations (1998), claims that the Fourteenth Amendment cannot accurately be described as an "Article V" amendment, given the circumstances surrounding its proposal and ratification. Instead, he offers a rich and complex theory that he believes legitimizes the Fourteenth Amendment (and the actions of the Reconstruction Congress) in spite of these procedural defects.

2. *The Guaranty Clause and Black suffrage.* Professor Ackerman's colleague, Akhil Reed Amar, strongly disagrees with Ackerman's suggestion that there is anything improper, from a constitutional perspective, with the proposal and ratification of the Fourteenth Amendment.[40] Amar points out that some congressional Republicans justified their actions by invoking the federal government's Article IV duty to guarantee to each state a "republican form of government." The Civil Rights Act of 1866 had declared the newly freed slaves citizens of the United States. Because postwar Southern governments denied Black people the right to vote or otherwise participate in government, Amar argues, Congress in 1866-1868 took the position that the Southern states were not "republican" and could, therefore, legitimately be denied representation in Congress until their state governments were reformed (or "reconstructed") to achieve "republican" status.[41] Amar also points out that the excluded Southern states had for years repeatedly and flagrantly

---

well that he had not in effect thrown in the towel with regard to his opposition to congressional Reconstruction. Would you still regard it as a "profile in courage" to maintain Johnson in office if it meant the death of the Fourteenth Amendment? Is it relevant to your answer that a new presidential election was coming up in November 1868 (when Ulysses S. Grant, the Union general who had won the War, would be swept into office)? But recall that prior to the Twentieth Amendment, the new President would not be inaugurated until March 4, 1869. Are any of these considerations relevant to deciding whether or not Johnson merited impeachment?

40. See Amar, America's Constitution, supra n.1, at 364-380.

41. Note that Amar is not content to rely simply on Congress's power, under Article I, §5, to "Judge [the] Qualifications of its own Members" except insofar as "judgment" requires presenting good and substantial reasons for the exclusion, which Amar believes were amply present. Consider whether an Article I, §5 "formalist" would have to defend the legitimacy of excluding representatives and senators simply because the majority believed that they had the wrong political views or were from an unpopular racial or ethnic group. See Powell v. McCormack, 395 U.S. 486 (1969).

violated basic rights of free political expression and had shown contempt for basic democratic principles when they took up arms against a duly elected government in 1861. All this, Amar argues, made it sensible for Congress in 1866 to exclude Southern governments from Congress until proper safeguards were in place to ensure future Southern conformity with basic republican principles of free and fair government.

Of course, most (though not all) Northern states also denied African Americans the right to vote. Moreover, millions of female citizens had no participation rights. Quoting leading members of the Reconstruction Congress, Amar responds, first, that the difference in degree between North and South with reference to the actual population of African Americans constituted a difference in kind. Ohio, for example, in disenfranchising Black people, was discriminating against only 2 percent or so of its population. This is, to be sure, regrettable, but it meant that almost all of the (male) population could in fact participate in the enterprise of republican self-government. South Carolina, on the other hand, was a majority Black state, so that disenfranchisement of African Americans in fact meant rule by a minority, the very definition of nonrepublican government.

Women, of course, might make similar arguments about the nonrepublican status of a male-dominated polity. However, Amar notes the widespread belief, however false we may now believe it to be, that women were "virtually represented" by their fathers, brothers, and husbands. To be sure, as we have already seen, strong criticism of such views had been issued at Seneca Falls and would be further amplified in the coming years, ultimately leading to the ratification of the Nineteenth Amendment. In any event, Congress did not believe that the interests of Black people (or more specifically, Black males) would be virtually represented—that is, sympathetically taken into account—by the "unreconstructed" white elites who had attempted to leave the Union in order to preserve chattel slavery. Hence congressional leaders argued that although denial of women's rights to vote did not render Southern governments unrepublican, their denial of the rights of Black males to vote did, and this, Amar claims, justified Congress's decision.

3. Which of these theories do you find more persuasive? *Was* the Fourteenth Amendment properly proposed by Congress and ratified under Article V? If you believe you need more information than we have provided you in these necessarily capsule summaries, what would you like to know and why do you think it would be relevant to your answer?

If you agree with Amar that the Fourteenth Amendment is constitutionally unproblematic, then does its mode of proposal and ratification establish a precedent concerning the meaning of Article V (and Congress's ability to stipulate what counts as a "republican form of government")? Imagine, for example, that you were in Congress in 1979, when the Equal Rights Amendment, proposed by Congress in 1972 and ratified by two-thirds of the 50 states, was languishing because of the inability to get the three further state ratifications necessary to attain the three-quarters required by Article V. Consider whether it would have been legitimate to vote to refuse to seat representatives and senators from the 15 states that had not yet ratified—Alabama, Arizona, Arkansas, Florida, Georgia, Illinois,

Louisiana, Mississippi, Missouri, Nevada, North Carolina, Oklahoma, South Carolina, Utah, and Virginia—on the ground that they had demonstrated themselves to be agents of "patriarchy" and therefore "nonrepublican"? They would, of course, have been allowed to take their seats upon their states' ratification of the ERA. Would this have been constitutional?[42] Could one respond that women in all these anti-ERA states were nevertheless allowed to vote, hold office, serve on juries and in legislatures, and indeed exercise all other political rights on equal terms with men? Or consider a less "extreme" possibility: Could Congress have simply withheld all highway or flood relief funding (or indeed federal funding for all programs) to these states until they ratified the amendment?

4. If you accept neither Ackerman's or Amar's accounts of the legitimacy of the Fourteenth Amendment, what follows? Should we, for example, excise it from the text of the Constitution? If not, then what other theory best justifies its inclusion as part of the U.S. Constitution? Consider the following justifications for the legality of the Fourteenth Amendment:

a. The Southern states tried to leave the Union and therefore forfeited their right to representation in Congress until they were brought back in on proper terms. Note that this account does not explain the acceptance of the state governments for purposes of the Thirteenth Amendment. Also, is it consistent with Lincoln's theory that the Southern states had no right to leave the Union, a theory upon which the war was fought by Lincoln, at least initially? Consider the following refinement of the state-forfeiture theory. There are important differences between being "in the Union" and being a valid state government with full state's rights. For example, federal territories and the national capital were undeniably part of Lincoln's union, but were not entitled to full states' rights, standing outside both the Congress and the Article V amendment process. Could the state-forfeiture theory be sharpened by saying that states that had attempted to secede in effect reverted to the status of federal territories—inside Lincoln's indivisible union but outside Congress and Article V until readmitted on proper terms?

b. The Southern states were in "the grasp of war" until they accepted the North's demands and therefore the North had the right to do whatever it wanted with them. It could count them for Thirteenth Amendment purposes and then change its mind the next day to gain whatever political advantage it thought it could obtain. Hence the Fourteenth Amendment is not an Article V amendment, but an act of raw political and military power that is justified solely on those grounds. (Thus the justification is not, strictly speaking, a legal one but is essentially political.) Does this mean that if the U.S. Congress was willing to call out the troops, they could "legitimately" impose any constitutional change on any segment of the country? What does the word "legitimately" mean here?

---

42. Note that this is not the same thing as asking whether the Supreme Court would properly have issued an injunction requiring the seating of the (alleged) senators and representatives from Utah. Even if the Court would remain silent, it is presumably the duty of all members of Congress (see Article 6) to act in accordance with constitutional norms.

c. The Fourteenth Amendment is so central to our Nation's sense of itself and its guarantees of justice, civil rights, and civil liberties that it must be accepted as legitimate even if there is no textual or procedural justification for it. Would this apply to any amendment that you thought was especially important to the promotion of justice, civil rights, and civil liberties, or just to the Fourteenth Amendment?

d. By the end of the 1870s, or at least by the end of the nineteenth century, so many people accepted the Fourteenth Amendment's legitimacy that no further explanation is needed. At some point, acts of government, even if controversial at the time—and even if we believe that their opponents had the better arguments—become settled and no longer open to discussion or repudiation. Using the debate over the annexation of Texas as an example, Mark Graber has argued that whether a constitutional question remains alive or is regarded as legally "settled" depends on whether the dispute remains alive in the political process, or on the contrary, the losers in the controversy have conceded defeat. See Mark Graber, How the West Was Settled, 38 Tulsa L. Rev. 609 (2003). Consider, though, whether such settlements can ever become "unstuck," if, for example, a mass political movement revives old arguments and begins to elect officials who are committed to overturning the ostensible settlement. Suppose, as was suggested during the massive resistance to Brown v. Board of Education, Southern states should refuse to accept the legitimacy of the Fourteenth Amendment because it was forced on them during Reconstruction. Would they be entitled to engage in interposition or nullification on behalf of their (majority white) citizenry?

Can you think of another way to explain why the Fourteenth Amendment is legally a part of the U.S. Constitution?

5. *Equal suffrage in the Senate.* Note that Article V states that "no State, without its Consent, shall be deprived of its equal Suffrage in the Senate." This appears to suggest that a state could accept diminished representation if it consents; since, however, this would by definition generate unequal suffrage for all of the remaining states (relative to the one that agreed to lose a senator), then one might also interpret Article V as requiring unanimous consent. Is Article V merely a restriction on possible amendments, or is it also a limit on governmental action outside the amendment process? If the latter, did the exclusion of Southern senators violate Article V? If it did, what would constitute an appropriate remedy? Could the affected states sue to enjoin enforcement of the Fourteenth Amendment because it was proposed without their equal representation in the Senate? Could they avoid application of any legislation passed during this period that they did not volunteer to accept diminished representation?

6. *Litigating the Reconstruction Acts: Georgia v. Stanton.* During the period in which the Republican Congress was reconstituting the Southern state governments, the Supreme Court did not rule on the issue of the legality of this process. On April 15, 1867, a month after Congress passed its First Reconstruction Act, the old government of Georgia (supported by President Johnson) sued Secretary of War Edwin M. Stanton, invoking the Court's original jurisdiction. Georgia asked the Court for an injunction against the Republicans' effort to destroy the "existing State of Georgia and to cause to be evicted and substituted in its place . . . another

district and hitherto unknown State, to be called and designated the State of Georgia." By the middle of May, the Supreme Court dismissed Georgia v. Stanton for "want of jurisdiction." The Court argued that the issue was a "political question" not susceptible to judicial review. The case involved "the rights of sovereignty, of political jurisdiction, of government, of corporate existence as a State, with all its constitutional powers and privileges," as opposed to a threatened infringement of "private rights or private property," which would presumably have been justiciable. See Georgia v. Stanton, 73 U.S. 50, 76-77 (1867).

The Court added that it was irrelevant that Georgia claimed that its property (for example, its state capitol building and executive mansion) was also at stake, because the real issue was the destruction of the state's sovereignty. When the question of the legality of Reconstruction did reach the Supreme Court in Ex parte McCardle, involving a claim of individual rights affected by the Reconstruction Acts, Congress removed the Supreme Court's jurisdiction to hear the case in March 1868.

Should the Supreme Court have heard Georgia v. Stanton on its merits? If so, how should it have ruled? How do you think the Reconstruction Congress might have responded to a declaration that the Reconstruction Acts (and, presumably, the process for ratifying the Fourteenth Amendment) were unconstitutional?

7. *The Supreme Court speaks.* Finally, in 1873, in the Slaughterhouse Cases, 83 U.S. (16 Wall.) 36 (1873) (reprinted infra), the Court gave its own account of the provenance of the Thirteenth and Fourteenth Amendments:

> [T]he contests pervading the public mind for many years, between those who desired [slavery's] curtailment and ultimate extinction and those who desired additional safeguards for its security and perpetuation, culminated in the effort, on the part of most of the States in which slavery existed, to separate from the Federal government, and to resist its authority. This constituted the war of the rebellion, and whatever auxiliary causes may have contributed to bring about this war, undoubtedly the overshadowing and efficient cause was African slavery.
>
> In that struggle slavery, as a legalized social relation, perished. . . . But the war being over, those who had succeeded in re-establishing the authority of the Federal government were not content to permit this great act of emancipation to rest on the actual results of the contest or the proclamation of the Executive, both of which might have been questioned in after times, and they determined to place this main and most valuable result in the Constitution of the restored Union as one of its fundamental articles. Hence the thirteenth article of amendment of that instrument. . . .
>
> The process of restoring to their proper relations with the Federal government and with the other States those which had sided with the rebellion, undertaken under the proclamation of President Johnson in 1865, and before the assembling of Congress, developed the fact that, notwithstanding the formal recognition by those States of the abolition of slavery, the condition of the slave race would, without further protection of the Federal government, be almost as bad as it was before. Among the first acts of legislation adopted by several of the States in the legislative bodies which claimed to be in their normal relations with the Federal

> government, were laws which imposed upon the colored race onerous disabilities and burdens, and curtailed their rights in the pursuit of life, liberty, and property to such an extent that their freedom was of little value, while they had lost the protection which they had received from their former owners from motives both of interest and humanity. . . .
>
> These circumstances, whatever of falsehood or misconception may have been mingled with their presentation, forced upon the statesmen who had conducted the Federal government in safety through the crisis of the rebellion, and who supposed that by the thirteenth article of amendment they had secured the result of their labors, the conviction that something more was necessary in the way of constitutional protection to the unfortunate race who had suffered so much. They accordingly passed through Congress the proposition for the fourteenth amendment, and they declined to treat as restored to their full participation in the government of the Union the States which had been in insurrection, until they ratified that article by a formal vote of their legislative bodies.

What theory of the legitimacy of the Thirteenth and Fourteenth Amendments do you think the Court is implying?

4. The Fifteenth Amendment

Through the Reconstruction Acts (see discussion in the previous Note), Congress divided the former Confederate states into military districts and ordered them reorganized into new state governments with universal manhood suffrage. They would be readmitted to the Union when they ratified the Fourteenth Amendment.

The cumulative effect of these decisions was to create a new pro-Republican majority in many of the Southern states, composed of Black males—who were now able to vote under their state constitutions—and their white political allies. These Southern states elected many Republican congressmen and senators for the first time.

In this changed political climate, Black people were not only an important political constituency in the South, but also loyal Republican voters. This made thinkable to Republican moderates and conservatives what had been unthinkable only four years previously—a constitutional amendment giving Black men the right to vote nationwide, which was sent to the states in February 1869 and ratified on February 3, 1870.

The House and Senate passed slightly different versions of the proposed Fifteenth Amendment, each of which would have protected the right of officeholding as well as the right to vote. The Senate version stated that "The right of citizens of the United States to vote and hold office shall not be denied or abridged by the United States, or by any State on account of race, color, or previous condition of servitude." The House version stated that "The right of citizens of the United States to vote and hold office shall not be denied or abridged by any State on account of race, color, nativity, property, creed, or previous condition of servitude."[43]

---

43. See Cong. Globe, 40th Cong. 3d Sess. 1311, 1318 (1869) (Senate version); id. at 1428 (House version).

Unlike the Senate version, the House version did not restrict the national government, and it also prohibited discrimination on the basis of "nativity, property, [or] creed." Note that this version, among other things, would have created a stronger textual case for banning state poll taxes under the Fifteenth Amendment. (Almost a century later, the Twenty-Fourth Amendment banned poll taxes in federal elections, while the Supreme Court held in Harper v. Virginia Board of Elections, 383 U.S. 663 (1966), that poll taxes in state and local elections violated the Fourteenth Amendment.)

When a joint conference committee reconciled the two versions, the Senate version was adopted but the reference to office-holding was dropped.[44] The House quickly accepted the Senate version. The Senate held an extensive debate on whether the omission meant that the right to hold office was not protected or whether it was implied in the right to vote. Without reaching a definite conclusion, senators simply voted for the final version. Political pressures probably played a role: The debate occurred late in the lame-duck session of the Fortieth Congress, and the final Senate vote occurred on February 26, 1869. The March 4 inauguration was only a week away, and the Forty-First Congress would have fewer Republicans. Supporters may have assumed that the conference version was the best they could achieve under the circumstances.[45] Moreover, Congress had previously treated the right to hold office as included within the right to vote when it temporarily reimposed military rule on Georgia for expelling Black state legislators from office.[46] What, if anything, should this history tell us about the meaning of the Fifteenth Amendment today?

NOTE: WHEN DID THE CIVIL WAR END?

One might imagine that the Civil War ended with Lee's surrender at Appomattox Courthouse on April 9, 1865, so that Lincoln's assassination actually occurred after the war was over. General William T. Sherman, famous for his campaign of total war in Georgia and South Carolina, took this view. But that is not how many of the major players in the conflict understood it, at least in constitutional and legal terms.

When war ends matters constitutionally because it changes presumptions about what kinds of power government actors have. Recall that the central question in the Prize Cases was whether a legal state of war existed that allowed President Lincoln unilaterally to impose a blockade on Confederate ports. Lincoln's Emancipation Proclamation was predicated on the commander-in-chief's power to conduct

---

44. Id. at 1563-1564, 1623.

45. See id. at 1626-1627 (statement of Senators Wilson and Morton).

46. See Vikram Amar, Jury Service as Political Participation Akin to Voting, 80 Cornell L. Rev. 203, 228-235 (1995). Virginia, Mississippi, and Texas had still not been readmitted to the Union when the new amendment was proposed, and these three states, along with Georgia, were required to ratify the Fifteenth Amendment (as well as the Fourteenth Amendment, which Georgia had already ratified) as a precondition to representation in Congress. See the discussion of the provenance of the Fourteenth Amendment below.

war. During World War I, and again in World War II, Congress imposed price controls under its war powers.[47] An obvious problem is that if war legally never ends, neither does the war power.[48]

In After Appomattox,[49] Gregory Downs argues that the Civil War lasted until 1871, when the last Southern state was allowed back in Congress, so that, as John Fabian Witt argues, we might well call it "America's Ten Years' War."[50] Certainly, as a juridical matter, the surrender at Appomattox did not end the Civil War. For a lawyer, wars are ended by formal peace treaties or other similar arrangements, not by events on the battlefield.[51] The war against Japan in World War II, for example, did not legally end until a formal treaty was signed in 1951. Until that time, Americans occupied Japan. The American military occupation imposed reforms and structured the terms of the eventual handoff of governance; the Japanese adopted a new democratic constitution in 1947 imposed on them by the Americans.

In like fashion, the Civil War continued legally for some time after hostilities ended, and this fact influenced many of the constitutional arguments during the Reconstruction period. President Andrew Johnson, who resisted much of what the Reconstruction Congress did, nevertheless agreed that a legal state of war continued after Appomattox. Johnson held that the defeated South had to end slavery and ratify the Thirteenth Amendment, and he drew on his powers as a wartime President successfully to put pressure on recalcitrant state governments to do so.

Congress and Johnson differed over whether more was necessary; as we have seen, he opposed Congressional Reconstruction, in which Congress drew on its

---

47. For example, in Woods v. Cloyd W. Miller Co., 333 U.S. 138 (1948), the Supreme Court upheld Title II of the Housing and Rent Act of 1947, which imposed rent controls on housing in "defense rental areas," in this case, parts of Cleveland, Ohio. The purpose of the Act was to respond to rising rents caused by housing shortages during World War II; new residential construction had been limited due to diversion of manpower and materials to the war effort. The Court held that Title II was a valid exercise of the war power of Congress, even though the Act was enacted after the effective date of the presidential proclamation terminating hostilities on December 31, 1946. Justice Douglas explained that "the war power includes the power 'to remedy the evils which have arisen from its rise and progress,' and continues for the duration of that emergency. Whatever may be the consequences when war is officially terminated, the war power does not necessarily end with the cessation of hostilities."

48. In Woods v. Cloyd W. Miller, Justice Douglas addressed the problem: "We recognize the force of the argument that the effects of war under modern conditions may be felt in the economy for years and years, and that, if the war power can be used in days of peace to treat all the wounds which war inflicts on our society, it may not only swallow up all other powers of Congress, but largely obliterate the Ninth and the Tenth Amendments as well. There are no such implications in today's decision. We deal here with the consequences of a housing deficit greatly intensified during the period of hostilities by the war effort. Any power, of course, can be abused. But we cannot assume that Congress is not alert to its constitutional responsibilities. And the question whether the war power has been properly employed in cases such as this is open to judicial inquiry."

49. Gregory P. Downs, After Appomattox: Military Occupation and the Ends of War (2015).

50. John Fabian Witt, back jacket of Downs, supra n.49.

51. See Mary L. Dudziak, War Time: An Idea, Its History, Its Consequences (2013).

own war powers to attempt to bring about genuine regime change in the defeated Confederacy.[52] Not until Georgia's senators were seated in 1871, Downs argued, did Congress cease relying on its war powers. Moreover, during Grant's presidency, Union troops continued to occupy the South to enforce federal law in response to continuing violence and terrorism by vigilante groups such as the Ku Klux Klan. Federal troops remained in the South until they were withdrawn as a result of the Compromise of 1876, discussed infra.

B. The Fourteenth Amendment Limited

The central purpose of the Thirteenth (1865), Fourteenth (1868), and Fifteenth (1870) Amendments—sometimes called the "Civil War" or "Reconstruction" Amendments—was to help provide what Lincoln might have termed "a new birth of freedom" for the recently emancipated slaves. The central question posed to constitutional interpreters of the Fourteenth Amendment was what comprised the rights and freedoms presumably guaranteed. For example, did the Fourteenth Amendment protect the former slaves by preventing only discriminatory treatment of them (and other Black people) relative to the majority white population? Or, instead, did it guarantee to Black people (and to the general population, including non-Blacks) a *substantive* set of rights that were protected against governmental interference? The Court readily decided that the amendment did not protect the political rights of access to the ballot, but this was a different question from what constituted the "civil" rights that all parties to the debate conceded, at least in the abstract, were to be protected by the new constitutional language.

Rogers Smith argues that the Thirteenth and Fourteenth Amendments must be understood in the context of the "free labor" ideology of the Republican Party, with its Lockean insistence "that although the races might not be fully equal in all respects, every human being had a natural right to pursue his trade and reap the fruits of his labor."[53] The first case testing the meaning of "free labor" as a civil right

---

52. One of the great unanswered questions is what Lincoln would have done if he had survived. Lincoln pushed for ratification of the Thirteenth Amendment (as Johnson also did), and he probably would also have resisted ceding power to the Reconstruction Congress. But would he have supported the policies that came to be associated with Congressional Reconstruction, or taken a far milder approach? See Sanford Levinson, The Ten Year War: What If Lincoln Had Not Exited After Four Years?, 51 Tulsa L. Rev. 313 (2016). In his second inaugural address, Lincoln called on all Americans to adopt a policy of "malice toward none and charity toward all," but it is unclear how he would have operationalized this, given the policies of systematic violence and terrorism employed against Black people and Union supporters in the South following the war.

53. Rogers Smith, "One United People": Second-Class Female Citizenship and the American Quest for Community, 1 Yale J.L. & Human. 229, 257 (1989). The classic scholarly treatment of this ideology is Eric Foner, Free Soil, Free Labor, Free Men (1970). See also Eric Foner, Reconstruction: America's Unfinished Revolution 1863-1877, at 228-280 (1988). See also Ronald M. Labbe and Jonathan Lurie, The Slaughterhouse Cases: Regulation, Reconstruction, and the Fourteenth Amendment (2003).

was the Slaughterhouse Cases, where, writes Smith, "New Orleans butchers challenged a monopolistic slaughterhouse charter, granted by the state's North-dominated Reconstruction legislature, which forced them to work at the Crescent City Slaughter-House Company's facilities or give up their trade." In Smith's words, the butchers claimed that by depriving them of the chance to practice their trade outside of the monopoly's facilities, the law "violated the most fundamental right in liberal 'free labor' ideology, the right to labor productively, to pursue their vocation and reap the fruits of their efforts."[54] On behalf of the butchers, former Supreme Court Justice John Campbell argued that the citizenship protected by the Fourteenth Amendment "was based on the liberal commitment to securing fundamental rights against all threats, including any from the states. High among these rights, as 'property of a sacred kind,' was the 'right to labor . . . and to the product of one's faculties.'"[55]

The Slaughterhouse Cases

83 U.S. (16 Wall.) 36 (1873)

[In 1869, Louisiana enacted a statute entitled "An act to protect the health of the city of New Orleans, to locate the stock-landings and slaughter-houses, and to incorporate the Crescent City Live-Stock Landing and Slaughter-House Company." The Act authorized the company to construct a large slaughterhouse, available to any butcher in the city on payment of reasonable compensation, and prohibited the maintenance of any other abattoirs. Its purpose, as described by the Court, was "to remove from the more densely populated part of the city, the noxious slaughter-houses, and large and offensive collections of animals necessarily incident to the slaughtering business of a large city, and to locate them where the convenience, health, and comfort of the people require. . . ."]

Miller, J. . . .

It is not, and cannot be successfully controverted, that it is both the right and the duty of the legislative body—the supreme power of the State or municipality—to prescribe and determine the localities where the business of slaughtering for a great city may be conducted. To do this effectively it is indispensable that all persons who slaughter animals for food shall do it in those places *and nowhere else.*

The statute under consideration . . . does not, as has been asserted, prevent the butcher from doing his own slaughtering. On the contrary, the Slaughter-House Company is required, under a heavy penalty, to permit any person who wishes to do so, to slaughter in their houses; and they are bound to make ample provision for the convenience of all the slaughtering for the entire city. The butcher then is still permitted to slaughter, to prepare, and to sell his own meats; but he is required to slaughter at a specified place and to pay a reasonable compensation for the use of the accommodations furnished him at that place.

---

54. Smith, supra n.53, at 259.
55. Id.

The wisdom of the monopoly granted by the legislature may be open to question, but it is difficult to see a justification for the assertion that the butchers are deprived of the right to labor in their occupation, or the people of their daily service in preparing food, or how this statute, with the duties and guards imposed upon the company, can be said to destroy the business of the butcher, or seriously interfere with its pursuit.

[Moreover, such regulation is traditional.] "Unwholesome trades, slaughter-houses, operations offensive to the senses, the deposit of powder, the application of steam power to propel cars, the building with combustible materials, and the burial of the dead, may all," says Chancellor Kent, "be interdicted by law, in the midst of dense masses of population, on the general and rational principle, that every person ought so to use his property as not to injure his neighbors; and that private interests must be made subservient to the general interests of the community." This is called the police power. . . .

This power is, and must be from its very nature, incapable of any very exact definition or limitation. Upon it depends the security of social order, the life and health of the citizen, the comfort of an existence in a thickly populated community, the enjoyment of private and social life, and the beneficial use of property. "It extends . . . to the protection of the lives, limbs, health, comfort, and quiet of all persons, and the protection of all" property within the State; . . . and persons and property are subjected to all kinds of restraints and burdens in order to secure the general comfort, health, and prosperity of the State. . . .

The regulation of the place and manner of conducting the slaughtering of animals, and the business of butchering within a city, and the inspection of the animals to be killed for meat, and of the meat afterwards, are among the most necessary and frequent exercises of this power. It is not, therefore, needed that we should seek for a comprehensive definition, but rather look for the proper source of its exercise.

. . . The exclusive authority of State legislation over this subject is strikingly illustrated in the case of the City of New York v. Miln. . . .

It cannot be denied that the statute under consideration is aptly framed to remove from the more densely populated part of the city, the noxious slaughter-houses, and large and offensive collections of animals necessarily incident to the slaughtering business of a large city, and to locate them where the convenience, health, and comfort of the people require they shall be located. . . . But it is said that in creating a corporation for this purpose, and conferring upon it exclusive privileges—privileges which it is said constitute a monopoly—the legislature has exceeded its power. If this statute had imposed on the city of New Orleans precisely the same duties, accompanied by the same privileges, which it has on the corporation which it created, it is believed that no question would have been raised as to its constitutionality. In that case the effect on the butchers in pursuit of their occupation and on the public would have been the same as it is now. Why cannot the legislature confer the same powers on another corporation, created for a lawful and useful public object, that it can on the municipal corporation already existing? That wherever a legislature has the right to accomplish a certain result, and that result is best attained by means of a corporation, it has the right to create such a corporation, and to endow it with the powers necessary to effect the desired and lawful purpose, seems hardly to admit of debate. The proposition is ably discussed and affirmed in the case of McCulloch v. The State of Maryland, in relation to the power of Congress to organize the Bank of the United States to aid in the fiscal operations of the government. . . . It may, therefore, be considered as established, that the authority of the legislature of Louisiana to pass the present statute is ample. . . .

The plaintiffs in error . . . allege that the statute is a violation of the Constitution of the United States in these several particulars:

> That it creates an involuntary servitude forbidden by the thirteenth article of amendment;
>
> That it abridges the privileges and immunities of citizens of the United States;
>
> That it denies to the plaintiffs the equal protection of the laws; and,
>
> That it deprives them of their property without due process of law, contrary to the provisions of the first section of the fourteenth article of amendment.
>
> This court is thus called upon for the first time to give construction to these articles. . . .

The most cursory glance at these articles discloses a unity of purpose, when taken in connection with the history of the times, which cannot fail to have an important bearing on any question of doubt concerning their true meaning. . . . [W]e mean the freedom of the slave race, the security and firm establishment of that freedom, and the protection of the newly-made freeman and citizen from the oppressions of those who had formerly exercised unlimited dominion over him. It is true that only the fifteenth amendment, in terms, mentions the negro by speaking of his color and his slavery. But it is just as true that each of the other articles was addressed to the grievances of that race, and designed to remedy them as the fifteenth.

We do not say that no one else but the negro can share in this protection. . . . Undoubtedly while negro slavery alone was in the mind of the Congress which proposed the thirteenth article, it forbids any other kind of slavery, now or hereafter. If Mexican peonage or the Chinese coolie labor system shall develop slavery of the Mexican or Chinese race within our territory, this amendment may safely be trusted to make it void. And so if other rights are assailed by the States which properly and necessarily fall within the protection of these articles, that protection will apply, though the party interested may not be of African descent. But what we do say, and what we wish to be understood, is, that in any fair and just construction of any section or phrase of these amendments, it is necessary to look to the purpose which we have said was the pervading spirit of them all, the evil which they were designed to remedy, and the process of continued addition to the Constitution, until that purpose was supposed to be accomplished, as far as constitutional law can accomplish it. . . . [Justice Miller summarily dismisses appellants' claim based on the Thirteenth Amendment.]

The first section of the fourteenth article . . . opens with a definition of citizenship—not only citizenship of the United States, but citizenship of the States. No such definition was previously found in the Constitution, nor had any attempt been made to define it by act of Congress. . . . But it had been held by this court, in the celebrated *Dred Scott* case, only a few years before the outbreak of the civil war, that a man of African descent, whether a slave or not, was not and could not be a citizen of a State or of the United States. . . . To remove this difficulty primarily, and to establish a clear and comprehensive definition of citizenship which should declare what should constitute citizenship of the United States, and also citizenship of a State, the first clause of the first section was framed.

"All persons born or naturalized in the United States, and subject to the jurisdiction thereof, are citizens of the United States and of the State wherein they reside."

The first observation we have to make on this clause is, that it puts at rest both the questions which we stated to have been the subject of differences of opinion. It declares that persons may be citizens of the United States without regard to their citizenship of a particular State, and it overturns the *Dred Scott* decision by making *all persons* born within the United States and subject to its jurisdiction citizens of the United States. That its main purpose was to establish the citizenship of the negro can admit of no doubt. The phrase, "subject to its jurisdiction" was intended to exclude from its operation children of ministers, consuls, and citizens or subjects of foreign States born within the United States.

. . . [T]he distinction between citizenship of the United States and citizenship of a State is clearly recognized and established. Not only may a man be a citizen of the United States without being a citizen of a State, but an important element is necessary to convert the former into the latter. He must reside within the State to make him a citizen of it, but it is only necessary that he should be born or naturalized in the United States to be a citizen of the Union.

It is quite clear, then, that there is a citizenship of the United States, and a citizenship of a State, which are distinct from each other, and which depend upon different characteristics or circumstances in the individual.

[*Privileges or immunities.*] We think this distinction and its explicit recognition in this amendment of great weight in this argument, because the next paragraph of this same section, which is the one mainly relied on by the plaintiffs in error, speaks only of privileges and immunities of citizens of the United States, and does not speak of those of citizens of the several States. The argument, however, in favor of the plaintiffs rests wholly on the assumption that the citizenship is the same, and the privileges and immunities guaranteed by the clause are the same.

The language is, "No State shall make or enforce any law which shall abridge the privileges or immunities of citizens of *the United States.*" It is a little remarkable, if this clause was intended as a protection to the citizen of a State against the legislative power of his own State, that the word citizen of the State should be left out when it is so carefully used, and used in contradistinction to citizens of the United States, in the very sentence which precedes it. It is too clear for argument that the change in phraseology was adopted understandingly and with a purpose.

Of the privileges and immunities of the citizen of the United States, and of the privileges and immunities of the citizen of the State, and what they respectively are, we will presently consider; but we wish to state here that it is only the former which are placed by this clause under the protection of the Federal Constitution, and that the latter, whatever they may be, are not intended to have any additional protection by this paragraph of the amendment.

If, then, there is a difference between the privileges and immunities belonging to a citizen of the United States as such, and those belonging to the citizen of the State as such the latter must rest for their security and protection where they have heretofore rested; for they are not embraced by this paragraph of the amendment. . . .

The first and the leading case on the [Privileges and Immunities Clause of Article IV] is that of Corfield v. Coryell, decided by Mr. Justice Washington in the Circuit Court for the District of Pennsylvania in 1823. "The inquiry," he says, "is, what are the privileges and immunities of citizens of the several States? We feel no hesitation in confining these expressions to those privileges and immunities which are *fundamental*; which belong of right to the citizens of all free governments, and which have at all times been enjoyed by citizens of the several States which compose this Union, from the time of their becoming free, independent, and sovereign. What these fundamental principles are, it would be more tedious than difficult to enumerate. They may all, however, be comprehended under the following general heads: protection by the government, with the right to acquire and possess property of every kind, and to pursue and obtain happiness and safety, subject, nevertheless, to such restraints as the government may prescribe for the general good of the whole." . . .

In the case of Paul v. Virginia, the court, in expounding this clause of the Constitution, says that "the privileges and immunities secured to citizens of each State in the several States, by the provision in question, are those privileges and immunities which are common to the citizens in the latter States under their constitution and laws by virtue of their being citizens." . . .

Was it the purpose of the fourteenth amendment, by the simple declaration that no State should make or enforce any law which shall abridge the privileges and immunities of *citizens of the United States*, to transfer the security and protection of all the civil rights which we have mentioned, from the States to the Federal government? And where it is declared that Congress shall have the power to enforce that article, was it intended to bring within the power of Congress the entire domain of civil rights heretofore belonging exclusively to the States?

All this and more must follow, if the proposition of the plaintiffs in error be sound. For not only are these rights subject to the control of Congress whenever in its discretion any of them are supposed to be abridged by State legislation, but that body may also pass laws in advance, limiting and restricting the exercise of legislative power by the States, in their most ordinary and usual functions, as in its judgment it may think proper on all such subjects. And still further, such a construction followed by the reversal of the judgments of the Supreme Court of Louisiana in these cases, would constitute this court a perpetual censor upon all legislation of the States, on the civil rights of their own citizens, with authority to nullify such as it did not approve as consistent with those rights, as they existed at the time of the adoption of this amendment. The argument we admit is not always the most conclusive which is drawn from the consequences urged against the adoption of a particular construction of an instrument. But when, as in the case before us, these consequences are so serious, so far-reaching and pervading, so great a departure from the structure and spirit of our institutions; when the effect is to fetter and degrade the State governments by subjecting them to the control of Congress, in the exercise of powers heretofore universally conceded to them of the most ordinary and fundamental character; when in fact it radically changes the whole theory of the relations of the

State and Federal governments to each other and of both these governments to the people; the argument has a force that is irresistible, in the absence of language which expresses such a purpose too clearly to admit of doubt.

We are convinced that no such results were intended by the Congress which proposed these amendments, nor by the legislatures of the States which ratified them.

But lest it should be said that no such privileges and immunities are to be found if those we have been considering are excluded, we venture to suggest some which owe their existence to the Federal government, its National character, its Constitution, or its laws.

One of these is well described in the case of Crandall v. Nevada, 73 U.S. (6 Wall.) 35 (1867). It is said to be the right of the citizen of this great country, protected by implied guarantees of its Constitution, "to come to the seat of government to assert any claim he may have upon that government, to transact any business he may have with it, to seek its protection, to share its offices, to engage in administering its functions. He has the right of free access to its seaports, through which all operations of foreign commerce are conducted, to the subtreasuries, land offices, and courts of justice in the several States." . . .

Another privilege of a citizen of the United States is to demand the care and protection of the Federal government over his life, liberty, and property when on the high seas or within the jurisdiction of a foreign government. Of this there can be no doubt, nor that the right depends upon his character as a citizen of the United States. The right to peaceably assemble and petition for redress of grievances, the privilege of the writ of habeas corpus, are rights of the citizen guaranteed by the Federal Constitution. The right to use the navigable waters of the United States, however they may penetrate the territory of the several States, all rights secured to our citizens by treaties with foreign nations, are dependent upon citizenship of the United States, and not citizenship of a State. One of these privileges is conferred by the very article under consideration. It is that a citizen of the United States can, of his own volition, become a citizen of any State of the Union by a bona fide residence therein, with the same rights as other citizens of that State. To these may be added the rights secured by the thirteenth and fifteenth articles of amendment, and by the other clause of the fourteenth, next to be considered. . . .

[*Due process.*] The argument has not been much pressed in these cases that the defendant's charter deprives the plaintiffs of their property without due process of law, or that it denies to them the equal protection of the law. The first of these paragraphs has been in the Constitution since the adoption of the fifth amendment, as a restraint upon the Federal power. It is also to be found in some form of expression in the constitutions of nearly all the States, as a restraint upon the power of the States. This law, then, has practically been the same as it now is during the existence of the government, except so far as the present amendment may place the restraining power over the States in this matter in the hands of the Federal government.

We are not without judicial interpretation, therefore, both State and National, of the meaning of this clause. And it is sufficient to say that under no construction of that provision that we have ever seen, or any that we deem admissible, can the restraint imposed by the State of Louisiana upon the exercise of their trade by the butchers of New Orleans be held to be a deprivation of property within the meaning of that provision. . . .

[*Equal protection.*] In the light of the history of these amendments, and the pervading purpose of them, . . . it is not difficult to give a meaning to [the Equal Protection] clause. The existence of laws in the States where the newly emancipated negroes resided, which discriminated with gross injustice and hardship against them as a class, was the evil to be remedied by this clause, and by it such laws are forbidden. . . . We doubt very much whether any action of a State not directed by way of discrimination against the negroes as a class, or on account of their race, will ever be held to come within the purview of this provision. It is so clearly a provision for that race and that emergency, that a strong case would be necessary for its application to any other.

FIELD, J., dissenting. . . .

It is contended in justification for the act in question that it was adopted in the interest of the city, to promote its cleanliness and protect its health, and was the legitimate exercise of what is termed the police power of the State. That power undoubtedly extends to all regulations affecting the health, good order, morals, peace, and safety of society, and is exercised on a great variety of subjects, and in almost numberless ways. . . . But under the pretence of prescribing a police regulation the State cannot be permitted to encroach upon any of the just rights of the citizen, which the Constitution intended to secure against abridgment.

In the law in question there are only two provisions which can properly be called police regulations—the one which requires the landing and slaughtering of animals below the city of New Orleans, and the other which requires the inspection of the animals before they are slaughtered. When these requirements are complied with, the sanitary purposes of the act are accomplished. In all other particulars the act is a mere grant to a corporation created by it of special and exclusive privileges by which the health of the city is in no way promoted. It is plain that if the corporation can, without endangering the health of the public, carry on the business of landing, keeping, and slaughtering cattle within a district below the city embracing an area of over a thousand square miles, it would not endanger the public health if other persons were also permitted to carry on the same business within the same district under similar conditions as to the inspection of the animals. . . .

It is also sought to justify the act in question on the same principle that exclusive grants for ferries, bridges, and turnpikes are sanctioned. But it can find no support there. The grant, with exclusive privileges of a right thus appertaining to the government, is a very different thing from a grant, with exclusive privileges, of a right to pursue one of the ordinary trades or callings of life, which is a right appertaining solely to the individual. . . .

The act of Louisiana presents the naked case, unaccompanied by any public considerations, where a right to pursue a lawful and necessary calling, previously enjoyed by every citizen, and in connection with which a thousand persons were daily employed, is taken away and vested exclusively for twenty-five years, for an extensive district and a large population, in a single corporation. . . .

If exclusive privileges of this character can be granted to a corporation of seventeen persons, they may, in the discretion of the legislature, be equally granted to a single individual. If they may be granted for twenty-five years they may be equally granted for a century, and in perpetuity. If they may be granted for the landing and keeping of animals intended for sale or slaughter they may be equally . . . granted for any of the pursuits of human industry, even in its most simple and common forms. Indeed, upon the theory on which the exclusive privileges granted by the act in question are sustained, there is no monopoly, in the most odious form, which may not be upheld.

The question presented is, therefore, one of the gravest importance, not merely to the parties here, but to the whole country. It is nothing less than the question whether the recent amendments to the Federal Constitution protect the citizens of the United States against the deprivation of their common rights by State legislation. In my judgment the fourteenth amendment does afford such protection, and was so intended by the Congress which framed and the States which adopted it. . . .

[Under the] first clause of the fourteenth amendment . . . , [a] citizen of a State is now only a citizen of the United States residing in that State. The fundamental rights, privileges, and immunities which belong to him as a free man and a free citizen, now belong to him as a citizen of the United States, and are not dependent upon his citizenship of any State. . . .

If under the fourth article of the Constitution equality of privileges and immunities is secured between citizens of different States, under the fourteenth amendment the same equality is secured between citizens of the United States.

It will not be pretended that under the fourth article of the Constitution any State could create a monopoly in any known trade or manufacture in favor of her own citizens, or any portion of them, which would exclude an equal participation in the trade or manufacture monopolized by citizens of other States. She could not confer, for example, upon any of her citizens the sole right to manufacture shoes, or boots, or silk, or the sole right to sell those articles in the State so as to exclude non-resident citizens from engaging in a similar manufacture or sale. . . .

Now, what the clause in question does for the protection of citizens of one State against the creation of monopolies in favor of citizens of other States, the fourteenth amendment does for the protection of every citizen of the United States against the creation of any monopoly whatever. The privileges and immunities of citizens of the United States, of every one of them, is secured against abridgment in any form by any State. The fourteenth amendment places them under the guardianship of the National authority. All monopolies in any known trade or manufacture are an invasion of these privileges, for they encroach upon the liberty of citizens to acquire property and pursue happiness. . . .

That amendment was intended to give practical effect to the declaration of 1776 of inalienable rights, rights which are the gift of the Creator, which the law does not confer, but only recognizes. . . .

[The] equality of right, with exemption from all disparaging and partial enactments, in the lawful pursuits of life, throughout the whole country, is the distinguishing privilege of citizens of the United States. To them, everywhere, all pursuits, all professions, all avocations are open without other restrictions than such as are imposed equally upon all others of the same age, sex, and condition. The State may prescribe such regulations for every pursuit and calling of life as will promote the public health, secure the good order and advance the general prosperity of society, but when once prescribed, the pursuit or calling must be free to be followed by every citizen who is within the conditions designated, and will conform to the regulations. This is the fundamental idea upon which our institutions rest, and unless adhered to in the legislation of the country our government will be a republic only in name. The fourteenth amendment, in my judgment, makes it essential to the validity of the legislation of every State that this equality of right should be respected. . . .

I am authorized by the Chief Justice, Mr. Justice Swayne, and Mr. Justice Bradley, to state that they concur with me in this dissenting opinion.

BRADLEY, J., dissenting:

I concur in the opinion which has just been read by Mr. Justice Field. . . .

The people of this country brought with them to its shores the rights of Englishmen; the rights which had been wrested from English sovereigns at various periods of the nation's history. One of these fundamental rights was expressed in these words, found in Magna Carta: "No freeman shall be taken or imprisoned or be dissected of his freehold or liberties or free customs, or be outlawed or exiled, or any otherwise destroyed; nor will we pass upon him or condemn him but by lawful judgment of his peers or by the law of the land." English constitutional writers expound this article as rendering life, liberty, and property inviolable, except by due process of law. This is the very right which the plaintiffs in error claim in this case. . . . Blackstone classifies these fundamental rights under three heads, as the absolute rights of individuals, to wit: the right of personal security, the right of personal liberty, and the right of private property. . . . These are the fundamental rights which can only be taken away by due process of law, and which can only be interfered with, or the enjoyment of which can only be modified, by lawful regulations necessary or proper for the mutual good of all; and these rights, I contend, belong to the citizens of every free government.

For the preservation, exercise, and enjoyment of these rights the individual citizen, as a necessity, must be left free to adopt such calling, profession, or trade as may seem to him most conducive to that end. Without this right he cannot be a freeman. This right to choose one's calling is an essential part of that liberty which it is the object of government to protect; and a calling, when chosen, is a man's property and right. Liberty and property are not protected where these rights are arbitrarily assailed. . . .

The Constitution, it is true, as it stood prior to the recent amendments, specifies, in terms, only a few of the personal privileges and immunities of citizens, but they are very comprehensive in their character. The States were merely prohibited from passing bills of attainder, ex post facto laws, laws impairing the obligation of contracts, and perhaps one or two more. But others of the greatest consequence were enumerated, although they were only secured, in express terms, from invasion by the Federal government; such as the right of habeas corpus, the right of trial by jury, of free exercise of religious worship, the right of free speech and a free press, the right peaceably to assemble for the discussion of public measures, the right to be secure against unreasonable searches and seizures, and above all, and including almost all the rest, the right of *not being deprived of life, liberty, or property, without due process of law.* These, and still others are specified in the original Constitution, or in the early amendments of it, as among the privileges and immunities of citizens of the United States, or, what is still stronger for the force of the argument, the rights of all persons, whether citizens or not. . . .

Admitting . . . that formerly the States were not prohibited from infringing any of the fundamental privileges and immunities of citizens of the United States, except in a few specified cases, that cannot be said now, since the adoption of the fourteenth amendment. In my judgment, it was the intention of the people of this country in adopting that amendment to provide National security against violation by the States of the fundamental rights of the citizen.

. . . [A]ny law which establishes a sheer monopoly, depriving a large class of citizens of the privilege of pursuing a lawful employment, does abridge the privileges of those citizens. . . . [And] [i]n my view, a law which prohibits a large class of citizens from adopting a lawful employment, or from following a lawful employment previously adopted, does deprive them of liberty as well as property, without due process of law. Their right of choice is a portion of their liberty; their occupation is their property. Such a law also deprives those citizens of the equal protection of the laws, contrary to the last clause of the section. . . .

It is futile to argue that none but persons of the African race are intended to be benefited by this amendment. They may have been the primary cause of the amendment, but its language is general, embracing all citizens, and I think it was purposely so expressed.

The mischief to be remedied was not merely slavery and its incidents and consequences; but that spirit of insubordination and disloyalty to the National government which had troubled the country for so many years in some of the States, and that intolerance of free speech and free discussion which often rendered life and property insecure, and led to much unequal legislation. The amendment was an attempt to give voice to the strong National yearning for that time and that condition of things, in which American citizenship should be a sure guaranty of safety, and in which every citizen of the United States might stand erect on every portion of its soil, in the full enjoyment of every right and privilege belonging to a freeman, without fear of violence or molestation.

But great fears are expressed that this construction of the amendment will lead to enactments by Congress interfering with the internal affairs of the States, and establishing therein civil and criminal codes of law for the government of the citizens, and thus abolishing the State governments in everything but name; or else, that it will lead the Federal courts to draw to their cognizance the supervision of State tribunals on every subject of judicial inquiry . . .

In my judgment no such practical inconveniences would arise. Very little, if any, legislation on the part of Congress would be required to carry the amendment into effect. Like the prohibition against passing a law impairing the obligation of a contract, it would execute itself. The point would be regularly raised, in a suit at law, and settled by final reference to the Federal court. As the privileges and immunities protected are only those fundamental ones which belong to every citizen, they would soon become so far defined as to cause but a slight accumulation of business in the Federal courts. Besides, the recognized existence of the law would prevent its frequent violation. But even if the business of the National courts should be increased, Congress could easily supply the remedy by increasing their number and efficiency. The great question is, What is the true construction of the amendment? When once we find that, we shall find the means of giving it effect. The argument from inconvenience ought not to have a very controlling influence in questions of this sort. The National will and National interest are of far greater importance.

In my opinion the judgment of the Supreme Court of Louisiana ought to be reversed.

SWAYNE, J., dissenting:

I concur in the dissent in these cases and in the views expressed by my brethren, Mr. Justice Field and Mr. Justice Bradley. . . . The first eleven amendments to the Constitution were intended to be checks and limitations upon the government which that instrument called into existence. . . . [The thirteenth, fourteenth, and fifteenth] amendments are a new departure, and mark an important epoch in the constitutional history of the country. They trench directly upon the power of the States. . . . Fairly construed these amendments may be said to rise to the dignity of a new Magna Charta. . . .

These amendments are all consequences of the late civil war. The prejudices and apprehension as to the central government which prevailed when the Constitution was adopted were dispelled by the light of experience. The public mind became satisfied that there was less danger of tyranny in the head than of anarchy and tyranny in the members. . . .

The protection provided [by the Fourteenth Amendment] was not intended to be confined to those of any particular race or class, but to embrace equally all races, classes, and conditions of men. It is objected that the power conferred is novel and large. The answer is that the novelty was known and the measure deliberately adopted. The power is beneficent in its nature, and cannot be abused. It is such and should exist in every well-ordered system of polity. . . .

The construction adopted by the majority of my brethren is, in my judgment, much too narrow. It defeats, by a limitation not anticipated, the intent of those by whom the instrument was framed and of those by whom it was adopted. To the extent of that limitation it turns, as it were, what was meant for bread into a stone. By the Constitution, as it stood before the war, ample protection was given against oppression by the Union, but little was given against wrong and oppression by the States. That want was intended to be supplied by this amendment. . . .

DISCUSSION

1. *The political context of* Slaughterhouse. Justice Samuel Miller was an anti-slavery Republican from a small town in Iowa who supported Abraham Lincoln, Reconstruction, and the rights of African Americans. Why, then, did he read the Fourteenth Amendment's Privileges or Immunities Clause so narrowly? The answer has to do with bitter fights over Reconstruction in the South and growing fissures within the Republican Party as the country entered the Gilded Age.[56]

The slaughterhouse law passed by Louisiana's multi-racial Reconstruction legislature was based on a health measure in New York City. For many years New Orleans had been a cesspool of yellow fever and cholera, with butchers throwing carcasses in the river upstream from the town. White elites in New Orleans who used to control the city were furious at the legislature because Black people had

56. See Michael A. Ross, Justice of Shattered Dreams: Samuel Freeman Miller and the Supreme Court during the Civil War Era (2003).

been politically empowered and sought to oppose the legislature in every way possible. They eventually forged an alliance with the unpopular butchers, widely regarded as the cause of repeated epidemics in the city.

The butchers were represented by John Archibald Campbell, a former Supreme Court Justice who had joined the majority in *Dred Scott.* He resigned from the Court in 1861 and eventually became assistant Secretary of War for the Confederacy. After the war, Campbell settled in New Orleans, became a prominent attorney, and brought lawsuits to hamstring Reconstruction and oppose bi-racial governments.

Miller was infuriated that a prominent Confederate was trying to use the new amendments that had been designed to help Black people to undermine Reconstruction legislatures. He believed that Black voting rights were the key to remaking the South. But he was also an old-fashioned federalist who believed that the Reconstruction Amendments did not otherwise fundamentally change the character of the Union. Miller's views in *Slaughterhouse* reflect his beliefs that courts should protect bi-racial Reconstruction governments and that the primary purpose of the new amendments was to protect the civil and political rights of Black people.

Miller also objected to turning the new amendments into a bulwark of economic and property rights. He represented a group of older Republicans who sought to protect small towns and farmers from overreaching by railroads and other businesses. As the Gilded Age progressed, his small-town brand of Republicanism, which opposed using the law to protect bondholders and business interests, fell out of step with the party's general direction. By contrast, the views of the *Slaughterhouse* dissenters eventually proved more hospitable to the Republican Party as it became the party of big business.

2. *The "police power" and general constitutional law.* Notice that before Justice Miller construes the Reconstruction Amendments, he first asks whether the Louisiana statute is within the state's police power. Traditionally, states had the power to protect the health, safety, and welfare of their citizens, but legislation that fell outside the police power—for example, legislation that took real property from A and gave it to B—was constitutionally suspect whether or not it contradicted a specific constitutional provision. (Recall the discussion of Calder v. Bull in Chapter 2, supra.) This idea of a "general constitutional law" continued after the Civil War. See, e.g., Loan Association v. Topeka, 87 U.S. (20 Wall.) 655 (1874) (holding unconstitutional the issuance of municipal bonds, for the benefit of a private ironworks, on the ground that their issuance was not for the public interest and therefore lay beyond the state's taxing power).

Generally speaking, in cases on appeal from state supreme courts, the U.S. Supreme Court would defer to state court judgments that a law was within the state's police power. However, on appeals from lower federal courts, like Loan Association v. Topeka, the Supreme Court would examine the question more closely. See Davidson v. Louisiana, 96 U.S. 97 (1878) (noting that a challenged property tax "may possibly violate some of those principles of general constitutional law, of which we could take jurisdiction if we were sitting in review of a Circuit Court of the United States, as we were in Loan Association v. Topeka"). Because the Slaughterhouse Cases came before the Court on writ of error to the Louisiana Supreme Court, the Supreme Court had little trouble concluding that the statute was an exercise of the state's police power.

3. *The Thirteenth Amendment.* Justice Miller makes short work of the butchers' claim that the monopoly violated the Thirteenth Amendment. The amendment was addressed to "negro slavery," although Miller conceded that the amendment "forbids any other kind of slavery, now or hereafter." On the question of what constitutes "slavery" under the meaning of the Thirteenth Amendment, see the discussion of the history of the Thirteenth Amendment in Section I.A., supra; Jack M. Balkin and Sanford Levinson, The Dangerous Thirteenth Amendment, 112 Colum. L. Rev. 1459 (2012).

The butchers' argument was not that they were being treated like slaves on a Southern plantation. Rather, it was that forcing them to work for a monopoly controlled by a small group of favored businessmen was akin to a feudal servitude. Moreover, it was an "involuntary servitude" because the Louisiana statute forced them, like feudal serfs, to work on a particular piece of land if they wanted to continue to be butchers. They argued that one purpose of the Thirteenth Amendment was to throw off all vestiges of European feudalism.

Justice Field's dissent, while not resolving the Thirteenth Amendment issue, agreed that the comparison to feudalism was apt: "The prohibitions imposed by this act upon butchers and dealers in cattle in these parishes, and the special privileges conferred upon the favored corporation, are similar in principle and as odious in character as the restrictions imposed in the last century upon the peasantry in some parts of France."

Justice Miller dismissed the comparison brusquely, explaining that only servitude to a person was covered by the amendment, not a servitude to land, and that "the obvious purpose was to forbid all shades and conditions of African slavery." Is this a sufficient reply? What is the best answer to the butchers' argument?

4. *"Privileges or immunities of citizens of the United States." Slaugtherhouse* is infamous for its narrow reading of the Privileges or Immunities Clause, which had been designed to be the centerpiece of the new Fourteenth Amendment, and which became virtually a dead letter following the decision. Note that Miller could have decided the case on much narrower grounds. For example, he might have argued that, even if the butchers' right to a livelihood was protected by the Fourteenth Amendment, the Louisiana statute was reasonably designed to protect public health and therefore did not abridge any constitutional rights the butchers might have had. (Compare the way that the Court deals today with economic rights under the Due Process and Equal Protection Clauses).

Instead, Miller argued that the Privileges or Immunities Clause was wholly irrelevant. The butchers needed to look to the states for protection of their economic rights; these were part of their rights as citizens of a state and were quite different from their rights as citizens of the United States.

Why was it important for Justice Miller to distinguish sharply between the rights of national citizenship and the rights of state citizenship? Why could the two sets of rights not overlap to some degree?

Note Miller's concern that a broad interpretation of privileges or immunities would "transfer the security and protection of all the civil rights which we have mentioned, from the States to the Federal government" and that it would "bring within the power of Congress the entire domain of civil rights heretofore belonging exclusively to the States." That is, Miller was concerned that a broad reading of "privileges or immunities" would greatly expand Congress's powers under §5 so that it could regulate virtually every aspect of economic and common law rights in the states. He was worried that a broad reading of the new amendment would seriously undermine federalism. Is Miller's narrow reading of the Privileges or Immunities Clause necessary to prevent this result? How else might one read the Privileges or Immunities Clause to avoid giving Congress the effective equivalent of a national police power over common law and economic rights?

Miller was also worried about expanding the power of the federal judiciary to protect economic rights from state regulation. He argued that a broad reading of the Privileges or Immunities Clause "would constitute this court a perpetual censor upon all legislation of the States, on the civil rights of their own citizens." (Note Justice Bradley's response. Is it convincing?)

To what extent were Miller's fears realized during the *Lochner* era with respect to economic rights? During our own era, with respect to other kinds of rights?

5. *Substantive rights under the Privileges or Immunities Clause.* All of the Justices in *Slaughterhouse* agreed that the Privileges or Immunities Clause protects substantive rights against state abridgement, but they disagreed about what those rights were. Justice Miller argues that the clause protects rights "which owe their existence to the Federal government, its National character, its Constitution, or its laws." His hodgepodge of illustrations is not very illuminating. Some of the examples simply incorporate the Privileges and Immunities Clause of Article IV and other provisions of the Civil War Amendments. Others, such as the right to federal protection "on the high seas or within the jurisdiction of a foreign country," seem beyond a state's ability to infringe. But he also notes the (unenumerated) right to travel recognized in Crandall v. Nevada, the right to become a citizen of a new state to which one traveled, the right to assemble to discuss matters pertaining to the federal government, the right to petition the federal government, and the right of access to federal courts and to other federal agencies, like the federal post office. Some of these rights were important to Black people who settled in free states before the Civil War. But was it likely that these were the central rights that the Reconstruction framers sought to protect against state abridgment?

By contrast, Justice Field asserted broadly that the clause "was intended to give practical effect to the declaration of 1776 of inalienable rights, rights which are gifts of the Creator, which the law does not confer but only recognizes." Justice Bradley asserted that among the rights of citizens are Blackstone's "three absolute rights of individuals," which encompass the "privilege of engaging in any lawful employment for a livelihood." Twenty-four years later, in Allgeyer v. Louisiana, 165 U.S. 578 (1897), the Court would adopt a version of this theory—under the Due Process Clause rather than the Privileges or Immunities Clause—holding that the Fourteenth Amendment protected the right "to live and work where he will; to earn his livelihood by any lawful calling; to pursue any livelihood or avocation; and for that purpose to enter into all contracts which may be proper, necessary, and essential."

Justice Bradley also suggested that the privileges and immunities of citizens of the United States include the guarantees of the first eight amendments to the Constitution. While Justice Miller's opinion is ambiguous on this question (note his references to the rights of petition and assembly), the Court would soon reject the idea in a series of cases beginning with United States v. Cruikshank, 92 U.S. 542 (1876), and leading up to Maxwell v. Dow, 176 U.S. 581 (1900).

6. *"Due process."* The Due Process Clause of the Fourteenth Amendment is identical to the Due Process Clause of the Fifth Amendment. The Fifth Amendment Due Process Clause, as its language implies, was generally understood to guarantee fair process, although it was also designed to protect against special or class legislation and the destruction of vested rights.[57] Shortly before the Civil War, in Murray v. Hoboken Land & Improvement Co., 59 U.S. (18 How.) 272 (1855), Justice Curtis thus described the origin and scope of the Due Process Clause of the Fifth Amendment:

> The words, "due process of law," were undoubtedly intended to convey the same meaning as the words, "by the law of the land," in Magna Carta. Lord Coke, in his commentary on those words says they mean due process of law. The constitutions which had been adopted by the several States before the formation of the federal constitution, following the language of the great charter more closely, generally contained the words, "but by the judgment of his peers, or the law of the land." . . .
>
> The constitution contains no description of those processes which it was intended to allow or forbid. It does not even declare what principles are to be applied to ascertain whether it be due process. It is manifest that it was not left to the legislative power to enact any process which might be devised. The article is a restraint on the legislative as well as on the executive and judicial powers of the government, and cannot be so construed as to leave congress free to make any process "due process of law," by its mere will. To what principles, then, are we to resort to ascertain whether this process, enacted by congress, is due process? To this the answer must be twofold. We must examine the constitution itself, to see whether this process be in conflict with any of its provisions. If not found to be so, we must look to those settled usages and modes of proceeding existing in the common and statute law of England, before the emigration of our ancestors, and which are shown not to have been unsuited to their civil and political condition by having been acted on by them after the settlement of this country.[58]

Plaintiffs in the Slaughterhouse Cases were not attacking an adjudicatory procedure, although they might have been arguing that the slaughterhouse monopoly was class legislation in that it bestowed special advantages on a favored few. (Note Justice Swayne's comment that "[a] more flagrant and indefensible invasion of the rights of many for the benefit of a few has not occurred in the legislative history of the country.")

---

57. See Ryan C. Williams, The One and Only Substantive Due Process Clause, 120 Yale L.J. 408, 425, 462-464 (2010); Mark G. Yudof, Equal Protection, Class Legislation, and Sex Discrimination: One Small Cheer for Mr. Herbert Spencer's "Social Statics," 88 Mich. L. Rev. 1366, 1376 (1990).

58. The Court has not adhered to this static view of procedural due process and has developed an extensive doctrine concerning the procedures—e.g., notice, opportunity to be heard, opportunity to confront adverse witnesses, the impartiality of the tribunal—in various circumstances. See, e.g., Cleveland Board of Education v. Loudermill, 470 U.S. 532 (1985).

Justice Miller quickly dismissed the butchers' due process claims: "[U]nder no construction of that provision that we have ever seen, or any that we deem admissible, can the restraint imposed by the State of Louisiana upon the exercise of their trade by the butchers of New Orleans be held to be a deprivation of property within the meaning of that provision." That did not mean, however, that Miller believed that the Due Process Clause offered no protections for economic rights. Only a year later, in Bartemeyer v. Louisiana, 85 U.S. (18 Wall.) 129 (1874), Miller commented that the application of a state prohibition law to liquor held for sale before the law's enactment would present the "very grave question . . . [w]hether this would be a statute depriving [the owner] of his property without due process of law."

7. *Equal protection of the laws.* Justice Miller argues that the Equal Protection Clause will and should only be used to remedy unjust discrimination against Black people. Is this assumption consistent with the history of the clause? Note Justice Bradley's reply.

8. *Justice Field and Jacksonian egalitarianism.* Justice Field, appointed by Lincoln as a pro-Union Democrat, opposed the state-mandated monopoly in the Slaughterhouse Cases because it established special privileges for a corporation in direct opposition to Jacksonian ideology.[59] Field came out of a tradition that bitterly opposed "class legislation." William Leggett, a Jacksonian writer, commented that "[p]ower and wealth are continually stealing from the many to the few." The rich and powerful are constantly seeking "to monopolize the advantages of the Government, to hedge themselves around with exclusive privileges, and elevate themselves at the expense of the great body of the people."[60]

Although the great fear concerned the rich and the wellborn, Jacksonians did not accept "class legislation" that benefited the poor. Instead, the watchword was an abstract notion of "equal rights," with individuals free to make whatever use of such rights they wished within the economic marketplace.The assumption was that equal rights would adequately protect the poor against depredations by the rich. Justice Field and other laissez faire constitutionalists have been criticized for being insensitive to the opportunities for abuse by the well-off in an economy that increasingly featured dramatic inequalities of wealth. Yet, given their Jacksonian roots, it may well oversimplify to describe them merely as apologists for the rich.

9. *Understanding the war.* It should be obvious that the meaning assigned the Fourteenth Amendment was (and remains) linked with the meaning of the events that brought it into being, i.e., the Civil War and Reconstruction. We have seen an earlier version of the debate with regard to the struggle between Andrew Johnson and his congressional opponents. The *Slaughterhouse* opinions present similarly different narratives of the meaning of the war and its general implications for

---

59. Michael Les Benedict, Laissez-Faire and Liberty: A Re-Evaluation of the Meaning and Origins of Laissez-Faire Constitutionalism, 3 Law & Hist. Rev. 293, 298 (1985) ("[T]he power of government could not legitimately be exercised to benefit one person or group at the expense of others. It was this conviction — not the notion that all government economic activity violated "immutable" economic laws — that lay at the heart of laissez-faire constitutionalism.").

60. Theodore Sedgewick, ed., Political Writings of William Leggett, i, 66-67 (1840), quoted in id. at 319.

American federalism.[61] Consider especially the closing paragraphs of both Justice Bradley's and Justice Swayne's dissenting opinions. How does one decide (and, of course, *who* gets to decide) what is the "real meaning" of such a complex event as the Civil War?

UNITED STATES v. CRUIKSHANK, 92 U.S. 542 (1876): In *Cruikshank*, the Supreme Court relied on the logic of *Slaughterhouse* to dismiss indictments under the 1870 Enforcement Act, which made it a crime to conspire to deny citizens of rights secured by the federal Constitution or laws. *Cruikshank* arose out of the infamous April 1873 Colfax Massacre, one of the most violent episodes of Reconstruction.[62] Following disputed state elections in Louisiana in 1872 that produced parallel governments, whites supporting the Democratic candidate seized the village of Colfax and slaughtered hundreds of innocent Black people who included supporters of the Republican candidate.

The Supreme Court, in an opinion by Chief Justice Waite, held that indictments charging conspiracy to violate Black people's rights to assemble peacefully, petition, and bear arms were insufficient because the Bill of Rights protected citizens only against violations by the federal government, not by the States or by private parties. "The right [of assembly] was not created by the [First] amendment; neither was its continuance guaranteed, except as against congressional interference. For their protection in its enjoyment, therefore, the people must look to the States. The power for that purpose was originally placed there, and it has never been surrendered to the United States."

With respect to the counts charging a conspiracy to violate the right to "bear[] arms for a lawful purpose," the Court explained that "[t]his is not a right granted by the Constitution. Neither is it in any manner dependent upon that instrument for its existence. The second amendment declares that it shall not be infringed; but this, as has been seen, means no more than that it shall not be infringed by Congress. This is one of the amendments that has no other effect than to restrict the powers of the national government."

Indictments charging conspiracy to violate rights to life and liberty failed because these were natural rights properly protected by the States, not rights protected by the federal government: "It is no more the duty of the United States to punish for a conspiracy to falsely imprison or murder within a State, than it would be to punish for false imprisonment or murder itself." Indictments charging conspiracy to violate the right to vote failed because the right to vote was a state right and not a federal right: "[T]he right of suffrage is not a necessary attribute of national citizenship; but that exemption from discrimination in the exercise of that right on account of race, &c., is. The right to vote in the States comes from

61. See especially Pamela Brandwein, Reconstructing Reconstruction: The Supreme Court and the Production of Historical Truth (1999), which analyzes the dramatically different histories of the Fourteenth Amendment.

62. Two recent studies of this important episode are LeeAnna Keith, The Colfax Massacre: The Untold Story of Black Power, White Terror, and the Death of Reconstruction (2008); and Charles Lane, The Day Freedom Died: The Colfax Massacre, the Supreme Court, and the Betrayal of Reconstruction (2008).

the States; but the right of exemption from the prohibited discrimination comes from the United States." Finally, the Court, reading the indictments narrowly, concluded that most of them did not expressly allege racial discrimination and that the two counts that did mention racial animus did not sufficiently specify the rights claimed to be violated.

DISCUSSION

1. Cruikshank *and the Bill of Rights. Cruikshank* is infamous today for crippling federal civil rights enforcement in the South. But it is also notable for making increasingly clear that the Court would not read the Fourteenth Amendment to incorporate the provisions of the Bill of Rights against the states. In this respect, *Cruikshank* was perhaps even more important than *Slaughterhouse* in limiting the scope of the Privileges or Immunities Clause.

2. *United States v. Reese.* In United States v. Reese, 92 U.S. 214 (1875), the Court continued its limitation of Reconstruction-era civil rights laws. It struck down §§3 and 4 of the 1870 Enforcement Act, which prohibited interference with the right to vote. The case involved Louisiana officials who allegedly refused to register Black voters in state elections. The Court noted once again that the right to vote was not a right guaranteed by the federal Constitution but only by the states; hence the Court reasoned that §§3 and 4 were beyond Congress's powers because they did not specifically require a showing of racial discrimination. Justice Hunt disagreed, arguing that "the intention of Congress on this subject is too plain to be discussed. The Fifteenth Amendment had just been adopted, the object of which was to secure to a lately enslaved population protection against violations of their right to vote on account of their color or previous condition."

BRADWELL v. ILLINOIS, 83 U.S. 130 (1873): [This case was decided the same day as *Slaughterhouse*, on April 14, 1873. It also raised a conflict between a free labor interpretation of the Fourteenth Amendment and states' rights views. The Illinois Supreme Court refused Myra Bradwell a license to practice law solely because she was a woman; no one doubted that she otherwise qualified. Her attorney, Republican Senator Matthew Hale Carpenter, cited the rights of the Declaration of Independence as among the "privileges and immunities" protected by the new amendment; among the specific rights protected was that of laboring in one's chosen vocation. "[I]n the pursuit of happiness," said Carpenter, "all avocations, all honors, all positions, are alike open to every one[;] in the protection of these rights all are equal before the law." As Rogers Smith notes, "[b]y resting his case on the liberal right to labor and drawing an analogy between the discrimination against women and the racial oppressions the amendment was universally acknowledged to oppose, Carpenter made a very strong argument. He also faced no opposing counsel."[63] Nonetheless, the Court rebuffed Bradwell's claim, noting the limited scope of the Privileges or Immunities Clause.]

---

63. Smith, supra n.53, at 260.

MILLER, J.: [T]he right to admission to practice in the courts of a State . . . in no sense depends on citizenship of the United States. It has not, as far as we know, ever been made in any State, or in any case, to depend on citizenship at all. Certainly many prominent and distinguished lawyers have been admitted to practice . . . who were not citizens of the United States or of any State. But, on whatever basis this right may be placed, so far as it can have any relation to citizenship at all, it would seem that, as to the courts of a State, it would relate to citizenship of the State, and as to Federal courts, it would relate to citizenship of the United States.

The opinion just delivered in the Slaughter-House Cases renders elaborate argument in the present case unnecessary; for, unless we are wholly and radically mistaken in the principles on which those cases are decided, the right to control and regulate the granting of licenses to practice law in the courts of a State is one of those powers which are not transferred for its protection to the Federal government, and its exercise is in no manner governed or controlled by citizenship of the United States in the party seeking such licensure.

BRADLEY, J., joined by Swayne and Field JJ., concurring: [All three of these Justices had dissented in the Slaughterhouse Cases.] The claim that, under the fourteenth amendment of the Constitution, which declares that no State shall make or enforce any law which shall abridge the privileges and immunities of citizens of the United States, the statute law of Illinois, or the common law prevailing in that State, can no longer be set up as a barrier against the right of females to pursue any lawful employment for a livelihood (the practice of law included), assumes that it is one of the privileges and immunities of women as citizens to engage in any and every profession, occupation, or employment in civil life.

It certainly cannot be affirmed, as an historical fact, that this has ever been established as one of the fundamental privileges and immunities of the sex. On the contrary, the civil law, as well as nature herself, has always recognized a wide difference in the respective spheres and destinies of man and woman. Man is, or should be, woman's protector and defender. The natural and proper timidity and delicacy which belongs to the female sex evidently unfits it for many of the occupations of civil life. The constitution of the family organization, which is founded in the divine ordinance, as well as in the nature of things, indicates the domestic sphere as that which properly belongs to the domain and functions of womanhood. The harmony, not to say identity, of interests and views which belong, or should belong, to the family institution is repugnant to the idea of a woman adopting a distinct and independent career from that of her husband. So firmly fixed was this sentiment in the founders of the common law that it became a maxim of that system of jurisprudence that a woman had no legal existence separate from her husband, who was regarded as her head and representative in the social state; and, notwithstanding some recent modifications of this civil status, many of the special rules of law flowing from and dependent upon this cardinal principle still exist in full force in most States. One of these is, that a married woman is incapable, without her husband's consent, of making contracts which shall be binding on her or him. This very incapacity was one circumstance which the Supreme Court of Illinois deemed important in rendering a married woman incompetent fully to perform the duties and trusts that belong to the office of an attorney and counsellor.

It is true that many women are unmarried and not affected by any of the duties, complications, and incapacities arising out of the married state, but these are exceptions to the general rule. The paramount destiny and mission of woman are to fulfil the noble and benign offices of wife and mother. This is the law of the Creator. And the rules of civil society must be adapted to the general constitution of things, and cannot be based upon exceptional cases.

The humane movements of modern society, which have for their object the multiplication of avenues for woman's advancement, and of occupations adapted to her condition and sex, have my heartiest concurrence. But I am not prepared to say that it is one of her fundamental rights and privileges to be admitted into every office and position, including those which require highly special qualifications and demanding special responsibilities. In the nature of things it is not every citizen of every age, sex, and condition that is qualified for every calling and position. It is the prerogative of the legislator to prescribe regulations founded on nature, reason, and experience for the due admission of qualified persons to professions and callings demanding special skill and confidence. This fairly belongs to the police power of the State; and, in my opinion, in view of the peculiar characteristics, destiny, and mission of woman, it is within the province of the legislature to ordain what offices, positions, and callings shall be filled and discharged by men, and shall receive the benefit of those energies and responsibilities, and that decision and firmness which are presumed to predominate in the sterner sex.

[Chief Justice Chase, who had been one of the leading abolitionist lawyers during the 1850s, "dissented from the judgment of the court, and from all the opinions."]

DISCUSSION

1. *Coverture and equal protection. Bradwell* did not consider the Equal Protection Clause as a possible source of vindication of Bradwell's claims. As Justice Miller suggests in the Slaughterhouse Cases, the Justices believed that the clause was primarily designed to respond to "class legislation" like that directed against Black people; they did not think that the many restrictions on women's right to work outside the home violated this principle. Moreover, the framers of the Fourteenth Amendment did not expect that the Equal Protection Clause, or indeed, the Fourteenth Amendment generally, would alter the common law rules of coverture, under which a woman surrendered almost all of her rights to her husband upon marriage. Thus, Myra Bradwell, as a married woman, might not be able to represent her clients effectively if she could not make binding contracts. But wouldn't this logic suggest that the state could not prevent unmarried women from becoming members of the state bar? Do you find Justice Bradley's response persuasive?

Why do you think that the fourth *Slaughterhouse* dissenter, Chief Justice Chase, dissented in *Bradwell*? (Note that the abolitionist idea of free labor, at least in theory, should apply equally to men and women.)

2. *Separate spheres.* Bradley's opinion in *Bradwell* exemplifies the "separate spheres" ideology of the late nineteenth century, under which social life was divided into two spheres or domains with special gender competences for men and women. According to this ideology, men were self-interested, self-seeking productive

breadwinners who competed in the market, while women were nurturing caretakers centered in the home, who gave men relief from the vicissitudes of market life. The separate spheres ideology reflected changes in economy and society in the nineteenth century that produced new ways of conceptualizing gender relations. The authority-based conception of the household and marriage—in which a husband exercised dominion over his wife—gradually gave way to an affect-based conception, which featured a cult of domesticity that imagined wives willingly submitting to their husbands out of love and altruism. Thus Bradley's opinion explains the exclusion of women from the legal profession not in terms of her husband's authority over her but, rather, her obligations to home and hearth.[64]

NOTE: THE "NEW DEPARTURE" AND WOMEN'S PLACE IN THE CONSTITUTIONAL ORDER

The litigation in *Bradwell* was only one aspect of a far larger debate over women's rights contemporaneous with the passage and early interpretation of the Reconstruction Amendments. Woman suffragists, who had worked hard for the passage of the Thirteenth Amendment and for the extension of new rights to Black people, were bitterly disappointed by §2 of the Fourteenth Amendment. Susan B. Anthony, Elizabeth Cady Stanton, and other leaders of the woman suffrage movement opposed ratification of the Fourteenth Amendment because, as Eric Foner writes, "the second clause for the first time introduced the word 'male' into the Constitution. Alone among suffrage restrictions, those founded on sex would not reduce a state's representation."[65] The movement had hoped that the Constitution would be amended to guarantee the vote to both Black men and to all women. But the National Republican Party opposed woman suffrage, and the abolitionists withdrew their support, fearing an intense struggle over Black voting rights. Consequently, Stanton and Anthony opposed passage of the Fifteenth Amendment because of its "humiliat[ing] rejection of extending suffrage to women."[66]

---

64. On the development of the separate spheres ideology, see, e.g., Linda K. Kerber, Separate Spheres, Female Worlds, Woman's Place: The Rhetoric of Women's History, 75 J. Am. Hist. 9, 21 (1988); Nancy F. Cott, The Bonds of Womanhood: Woman's Sphere in New England, 1780-1835, at 63-100 (1977); see also Reva B. Siegel, The Rule of Love, Wife Beating as Prerogative and Privacy, 105 Yale. L.J. 2117, 2142-2150 (1996).

65. Foner, Reconstruction: America's Unfinished Revolution, supra n.53, at 255.

66. Id. at 447. Stanton and Anthony were upset not only because of the rejection of their efforts at an amendment that included Black people and women but also because they regarded white women as social and cultural superiors of Black men; they were concerned that Black men would be elevated in status and power over them. "While the dominant party have with one hand lifted up TWO MILLION BLACK MEN and crowned them with the honor and dignity of citizenship," Anthony wrote, "with the other they have dethroned FIFTEEN MILLION WHITE WOMEN—their own mothers and sisters, their own wives and daughters—and cast them under the heel of the lowest orders of manhood." Paula Giddings, When and Where I Enter: The Impact of Black Women on Race and Sex in America 66 (1984). The woman suffrage movement split over this issue in 1869, with Stanton and Anthony founding the National Woman Suffrage Association and other suffragists, including Lucy Stone and Antoinette Brown Blackwell founding the American Woman Suffrage

Another 50 years would pass before the Nineteenth Amendment would explicitly bar denial of the suffrage on account of gender.

Whatever their disappointment regarding the language of §2 of the Fourteenth Amendment, shortly after the ratification of the Fourteenth Amendment supporters of the franchise for women embarked on a "new departure" in suffragist constitutional interpretation and argument, based on §1 of the amendment. Francis and Virginia Minor developed the argument that woman suffrage was guaranteed because the right to vote was inextricably tied to the citizenship guaranteed by §1. According to their theory, outlined in resolutions at a St. Louis suffrage convention in October 1869, the Fourteenth Amendment made the privileges and immunities of American citizens "National in character and paramount to all State authority."[67] The St. Louis resolutions cited Corfield v. Coryell for the proposition that the right to vote was a fundamental right.[68]

Although Article I, §2 of the Constitution gave the states power to regulate the qualifications of electors, the states could not violate the principle of equal citizenship by denying the franchise to U.S. citizens.

The Minors' argument also drew on the federal power to naturalize citizens: A naturalized citizen's equal right to vote was guaranteed by federal authority; otherwise a state could make a naturalized citizen a second-class citizen. A fortiori a state could not do this to a natural born citizen. Moreover, if states could deny the franchise to citizens, they could also extend the franchise to noncitizens. This would give noncitizens a higher political status than citizens.[69] Repeatedly, the argument for suffrage claimed that to be disenfranchised was to be lowered in status vis-à-vis other citizens, including Black men.

Association (which supported the Republican Party and passage of the Fifteenth Amendment). The NWSA pushed for a national amendment on woman suffrage, while the AWSA pushed for reform at the state and local level. See Ellen C. Dubois, Feminism and Suffrage: The Emergence of an Independent Women's Movement in American 1848-1869, at 92-161, 164-171, 180-198 (1978).

Note that Black women were often ignored by both supporters and opponents of the Fifteenth Amendment, and found themselves caught between conflicting political goals: On the one hand they feared that without the ballot for Black men, Black people would be increasingly oppressed by whites; on the other hand they feared that if Black men gained the vote they would dominate Black women even more. (For modern analogues to the political dilemmas experienced by Black women in this era, see the discussion of intersectionality in Chapter 8.) Finally, although Black women may have supported the vote for all women, they resented the racism of the white suffragists, which made it difficult to work with them on dignified terms. Despite this, Black women who did participate in the suffrage movement tended to ally themselves with Stanton's and Anthony's wing.

67. Elizabeth Cady Stanton, Susan B. Anthony, and Matilda Joslyn Gage, eds., 2 History of Woman Suffrage 408 (1882).

68. Or as Susan B. Anthony put it:

> Is the right to vote one of the privileges and immunities of citizens? I think the disenfranchised ex-rebels . . . will all agree with me that it is not only one of them, but the one without which all *the others are nothing.*

Id. at 638.

69. Id. at 408-409. Note that some states and territories did, in fact, permit noncitizens to vote, in the expectation that they would eventually apply for citizenship.

The National Woman Suffrage Association adopted the Minors' theory in its political rhetoric. In 1871 and 1872, women attempted to vote in ten states and the District of Columbia. In the most famous demonstration, Susan B. Anthony and 13 other women voted in Rochester, New York in November 1872. The women and the election inspectors who registered them were indicted under provisions of the Ku Klux Klan Act, which had been designed to prevent voting abuses directed against freedmen. The statute made it a crime for any "person to vote without a lawful right to vote or to do any unlawful act to secure a right or opportunity to vote, for himself or any other person."[70]

Anthony argued that she had not violated the statute. In her view, the Fourteenth Amendment automatically gave all citizens, including women and Black people, an equal right to vote. Otherwise, she claimed, the Fourteenth Amendment would have been superfluous, because civil equality was automatically guaranteed by the Thirteenth Amendment and by Article IV, §2.

Moreover, Anthony argued, the Fifteenth Amendment also guaranteed woman suffrage, because it prevented states from denying the vote on account of previous condition of servitude. The marital status laws reduced women to a condition of servitude because they placed women under the dominance of their husbands and denied them the right to own their own labor. Even after married women's property acts, Anthony argued, women were not civil equals without joint ownership of all income produced by the marriage:[71]

> In many of the states there has been special legislation, giving to married women the right to property inherited, or received by bequest, or earned by the pursuit of any avocation outside the home; also, giving her the right to sue and be sued in matters pertaining to such separate property; *but not a single State of this Union has ever secured the wife in the enjoyment of her right to the joint ownership of the joint earnings of the marriage copartnership.* And since, in the nature of things, the vast majority of married women never earn a dollar by work outside their families, nor inherit a dollar from their fathers, it follows that from the day of their marriage to the day of the death of their husbands, not one of them ever has a dollar, except it shall please her husband to let her have it.

In effect, Anthony argued that women still lived under a condition of servitude in violation of the Thirteenth Amendment.

Anthony was tried before Justice Ward Hunt of the U.S. Supreme Court, then sitting on circuit in New York. Justice Hunt, relying on Bradwell v. Illinois, rejected Anthony's constitutional arguments. United States v. Anthony, 24 F. Cas. 829 (N.D.N.Y. 1873) (No. 14,459). Hunt found Anthony guilty as a matter of law, arguing that even if she was mistaken about her right to vote the mistake of law was no defense. He directed the jurors to return a verdict of guilty against her, and refused to allow individual jurors to be polled.

---

70. Act of May 31, 1870, §19, 41 Stat. 140, 144-145 (1870). The Act was designed to prevent Southern whites from casting multiple ballots, thus nullifying the effect of Black votes.

71. 2 History of Woman Suffrage, supra n.67, at 642-644 (emphasis in original).

The next day, Anthony was asked if she had anything to say before sentence was passed. She gave a long speech, continually interrupted by Justice Hunt, who had not expected Anthony to say anything and repeatedly demanded that she sit down and be silent, which she refused to do:

> Your denial of my citizen's right to vote is my denial of my right of consent as one of the governed, my right of representation as one of the taxed, the denial of my right to a jury of my peers as an offender against law, therefore the denial of my sacred rights to life, liberty and property. . . . [S]ince the day of my arrest last November, this is the first time that either myself or any person of my disfranchised class has been allowed a word of defense before judge or jury.
>
> . . . [H]ad your honor submitted my case to the jury, as was clearly your duty, even then I should have had just cause for protest, for not one of those men was my peer. . . .
>
> Even my counsel . . . is my political sovereign. Precisely as no disfranchised person is entitled to sit upon a jury, and no woman is entitled to the franchise, so none but a regularly admitted lawyer is allowed to practice in the courts, and no woman can gain admission to the bar—hence jury, judge, counsel, must all be of the superior class.[72]

The Supreme Court's decision in the Slaughterhouse Cases significantly undermined the suffragist arguments, because it suggested that the Privileges or Immunities Clause had virtually no content. The Supreme Court rejected the suffragist theory of the Fourteenth Amendment a year later.

Minor v. Happersett

82 U.S. 162 (1874)

[In October 1872, Virginia Minor attempted to register to vote in St. Louis. After being refused, she sued for relief, arguing that women possessed a constitutional right to vote. Her case came before the U.S. Supreme Court in May 1873; the state of Missouri, thinking her arguments frivolous, did not even bother to present opposing counsel. The Supreme Court unanimously rejected Minor's arguments in an opinion by Chief Justice Waite, who had replaced Chief Justice Chase, the lone dissenter in Bradwell v. Illinois.]

WAITE, C.J.

There is no doubt that women may be citizens. . . . [I]t did not need [the Fourteenth Amendment] to give them that position. . . .

---

72. Justice Hunt sentenced Anthony to a fine of $100 plus the costs of the prosecution. Anthony stated that she would refuse to pay the fine. Hunt responded that Anthony would not be placed in jail to enforce his order until the fine was paid, in effect freeing her but making an appeal impossible. The other women voters pleaded *nolle prosequi.* The judge found the election inspectors guilty by directed verdict and put them in jail, but they were subsequently pardoned by President Grant. Id. at 689, 691, 695, 715.

Whoever . . . was one of the people of [one of the] States when the Constitution of the United States was adopted, became ipso facto a citizen—a member of the nation created by its adoption. He was one of the persons associating together to form the nation, and was, consequently, one of its original citizens. . . .

[S]ex has never been made one of the elements of citizenship in the United States. In this respect men have never had an advantage over women. The same laws precisely apply to both. The fourteenth amendment did not affect the citizenship of women any more than it did of men. In this particular, therefore, the rights of Mrs. Minor do not depend upon the amendment. . . .

The direct question is, therefore, presented whether all citizens are necessarily voters.

The Constitution does not define the privileges and immunities of citizens. For that definition we must look elsewhere. In this case we need not determine what they are, but only whether suffrage is necessarily one of them.

It certainly is nowhere made so in express terms. . . . The amendment did not add to the privileges and immunities of a citizen. It simply furnished an additional guaranty for the protection of such as he already had. No new voters were necessarily made by it. . . .

[Was] suffrage coextensive with the citizenship of the States at the time of its adoption[?] . . . When the Federal Constitution was adopted, all the States, with the exception of Rhode Island and Connecticut [which operated under charters from the Crown], had constitutions of their own. . . . [I]n no State were all citizens permitted to vote. . . . [The limitation of suffrage to males was explicit in New Hampshire, Massachusetts, New York, and South Carolina. Pennsylvania, Maryland, and North Carolina referred to "freeman" or "freemen," while New Jersey spoke of "all inhabitants" and Georgia of "citizens and inhabitants of the State." All had property qualifications for the vote.]

[I]t cannot for a moment be doubted that if it had been intended to make all citizens of the United States voters, the framers of the Constitution would not have left it to implication. So important a change in the condition of citizenship as it actually existed, if intended, would have been expressly declared.

But if further proof is necessary to show that no such change was intended, it can easily be found both in and out of the Constitution. [Waite quotes the "privileges and immunities" clause of Article IV, §2.] If suffrage is necessarily a part of citizenship, then the citizens of each State must be entitled to vote in the several States precisely as their citizens are. This is more than asserting that they may change their residence and become citizens of the State and thus be voters. It goes to the extent of insisting that while retaining their original citizenship they may vote in any State. This, we think, has never been claimed. [Waite then quotes §2 of the Fourteenth Amendment.] Why this [language], if it was not in the power of the legislature to deny the right of suffrage to some male inhabitants? And if suffrage was necessarily one of the absolute rights of citizenship, why confine the operations of the limitation to male inhabitants? Women and children are, as we have seen, "persons." They are counted in the enumeration upon which the apportionment is to be made, but if they were necessarily voters because of their citizenship unless clearly excluded, why inflict the penalty for the exclusion of males alone? Clearly, no such form of words would have been selected to express the idea here indicated if suffrage was the absolute right of all citizens.

And still again, after the adoption of the fourteenth amendment, it was deemed necessary to adopt the fifteenth. . . . If suffrage was one of [the] privileges and immunities [protected by the Fourteenth Amendment], why amend the Constitution to prevent its being denied on account of race? . . .

It is true that the United States guarantees to every State a republican form of government. . . . All the States had governments when the Constitution was adopted. . . . In all, save perhaps New Jersey, [the right of suffrage] was only bestowed upon men and not upon all of them. Under these circumstances it is certainly now too late to contend that a government is not republican, within the meaning of this guaranty in the Constitution, because women are not made voters. . . .

No new State has ever been admitted to the Union which has conferred the right of suffrage upon women, and this has never been considered a valid objection to her admission. On the contrary, . . . the right of suffrage was withdrawn from women as early as 1807 in the State of New Jersey. . . . Since then the governments of the insurgent States have been reorganized under a requirement that before their representatives could be admitted to seats in Congress they must have adopted new constitutions, republican in form. In no one of these constitutions was suffrage conferred upon women, and yet the States have all been restored to their original position as States in the Union.

Besides this, citizenship has not in all cases been made a condition precedent to the enjoyment of the right of suffrage. Thus, in Missouri, persons of foreign birth, who have declared their intention to become citizens of the United States, may under certain circumstances vote. The same provision is to be found in the constitutions of Alabama, Arkansas, Florida, Georgia, Indiana, Kansas, Minnesota, and Texas.

Certainly, if the courts can consider any question settled, this is one. For nearly ninety years the people have acted upon the idea that the Constitution, when it conferred citizenship, did not necessarily confer the right of suffrage.

DISCUSSION

1. Compare Chief Justice Waite's style of constitutional interpretation in *Minor* with Chief Justice Taney's in *Dred Scott.*

2. Note that the Court offers no normative justification for the exclusion of women. For example, *Minor* does not reiterate the antebellum argument about women necessarily being represented by their husbands. Even as to this argument, which continued to have currency in the general culture, what about those women who chose to remain unmarried? Consider, for example, Abby and Julia Smith, Connecticut sisters who in 1869 refused to pay their taxes because, being denied the right to vote, they were taxed without their representation (one of the principal ideological underpinnings, of course, of the American Revolution in 1776). As Abby Smith asked the Glastonbury, Connecticut town meeting in 1873, "[i]s it any more just to take a woman's property without her consent, than it is to take a man's property without his consent?" Indeed, she concluded by noting that "the robber would have the whole community against him, and he would not be apt to come but once; but from the men of our town we are never safe."[73]

73. Quoted in Linda Kerber, No Constitutional Right to Be Ladies 89 (1998).

3. Would a contrary ruling necessarily have entailed the grant of suffrage to other disfranchised citizens, such as minors? (Every state had an age requirement of 21.) If so, does that imply that Minor properly lost her suit, at least if predicated on the Privileges or Immunities Clause? Or might the right to vote be a "presumptive" privilege, to be restricted only if the state has a very good reason? What constitute good reasons for denying persons the right to vote?

4. Why didn't Minor claim a violation of the Equal Protection Clause? What do the Slaughterhouse Cases have to say about this?

5. As a matter of fact, the modern Supreme Court treats voting as embraced by the Fourteenth Amendment, and Congress has used its legislative powers under the amendment to bar states from depriving persons over 18 years old of the right to vote in federal elections.[74] This development did not occur without dissent: A century after Minor v. Happersett was decided, a second Justice Harlan, the grandson of the Justice Harlan who appears frequently in this chapter, argued vigorously that the history of the Fourteenth Amendment foreclosed its application to voting and that any suffrage complaints arising only under that amendment should be dismissed "for failure to state a claim of federal right."[75] Professor Van Alstyne responded to Justice Harlan's analysis as follows:[76]

> [T]he case can safely be made that there was an original understanding that §1 of the proposed Fourteenth Amendment would not itself immediately invalidate state suffrage laws severely restricting the right to vote. With all of it, however, we cannot safely declare that there was also a clear, uniform understanding that the open-ended phrases of §1—"privileges or immunities of citizens of the United States . . . life, liberty, or property . . . the equal protection of the laws"—would foreclose a different application in the future. . . . The question whether the original understanding was itself intended equally to bind the indefinite future becomes more lively when we note that the Thirty-ninth Congress did not adopt a second alternative: to accomplish specific, narrowly defined ends by producing an equally specific and narrowly defined amendment that, by clear language, could never be applied to suffrage. The failure to pursue that alternative, moreover, could scarcely have been inadvertent.

NOTE: THE FOURTEENTH AMENDMENT, BIRTHRIGHT CITIZENSHIP, AND AMERICAN INDIANS

The first sentence of §1, the Citizenship Clause, overruled *Dred Scott* and established a bright-line rule for determining U.S. citizenship. The "subject to the jurisdiction" language was assumed to include all persons born in the United States and

74. See Oregon v. Mitchell, 400 U.S. 112 (1970).

75. Carrington v. Rash, 380 U.S. 89, 99 (1965).

76. William W. Van Alstyne, The Fourteenth Amendment, the "Right" to Vote, and the Understanding of the Thirty-Ninth Congress, 1965 Sup. Ct. Rev. 52, 72-73. Professor Van Alstyne's argument is based on Alexander Bickel's argument about what the Congress that adopted the Fourteenth Amendment intended with respect to school segregation, supra n.1.

subject to its laws, whether or not their parents were citizens at the time of their birth. It excluded only children born to ambassadors and invading armies.

What about American Indians? An early decision, McKay v. Campbell, 16 F. Cas. 161 (D. Or. 1871), had held that Indians did not fall within the Citizenship Clause because "the Indian tribes within the limits of the United States have always been held to be distinct and independent political communities, retaining the right of self-government, though subject to the protecting power of the United States."

According to this view, Indians were not "subject to the jurisdiction" of the United States, despite the fact that "the protecting power of the United States" left Indians with few, if any rights, that Congress was required to respect. Indeed, in United States v. Kagama, 118 U.S. 375 (1886), the Court held that Congress possessed plenary power over the Indian tribes:

> [The] Indians are within the geographical limits of the United States. The soil and the people within these limits are under the political control of the Government of the United States, or of the States of the Union. There exist within the broad domain of sovereignty but these two. . . . [The] power of the Congress to organize territorial governments, and make laws for their inhabitants, arise not so much from the clause in the Constitution in regard to disposing of and making rules and regulations concerning the Territory and other property of the United States, as from the ownership of the country in which the Territories are, and the rights of exclusive sovereignty which must exist in the National Government, and be found nowhere else. . . .
>
> Indian tribes *are* the wards of the nation. They are communities *dependent* on the United States. Dependent largely for their daily food. Dependent for their political rights. They owe no allegiance to the States, and receive from them no protection. Because of the local ill feeling, the people of the States where they are found are often their deadliest enemies. . . .
>
> The power of the General Government over these remnants of a race once powerful, now weak and diminished in numbers, is necessary to their protection, as well as to the safety of those among whom they dwell. It must exist in that government, because it never has existed anywhere else, because the theatre of its exercise is within the geographical limits of the United States, because it has never been denied, and because it alone can enforce its laws on all the tribe.

Two years earlier, the Court held that Indians born in tribes were not birthright citizens:

ELK v. WILKINS, 112 U.S. 94 (1884): [John Elk, an American Indian, protested the refusal by the voting registrar of Omaha, Nebraska, to accept his claim for registration. Nebraska's constitution granted the right to vote to all males over 21 who were citizens of the United States or "persons of foreign birth who shall have declared their intention to become citizens, conformably to the laws of the United

States on the subject of naturalization, at least thirty days prior to an election." He brought his suit under the Fifteenth Amendment, arguing that he was a citizen and had been prevented from voting on the basis of his race. The Court rejected his argument.]

GREY, J.:

Though the plaintiff alleges that he "had fully and completely surrendered himself to the jurisdiction of the United States," he does not allege that the United States accepted his surrender, or that he has ever been naturalized, or taxed, or in any way recognized or treated as a citizen by the state or by the United States. Nor is it contended by his counsel that there is any statute or treaty that makes him a citizen. The question then is, whether an Indian, born a member of one of the Indian tribes within the United States, is, merely by reason of his birth within the United States, and of his afterwards voluntarily separating himself from his tribe and taking up his residence among white citizens, a citizen of the United States, within the meaning of the first section of the fourteenth amendment of the constitution.

[The conventional legal understanding since the Founding had been that members of Indian tribes] owed immediate allegiance to their several tribes, and were not part of the people of the United States. . . . The alien and dependent condition of the members of the Indian tribes could not be put off at their own will without the action or assent of the United States. They were never deemed citizens of the United States, except under explicit provisions of treaty or statute to that effect, either declaring a certain tribe, or such members of it as chose to remain behind on the removal of the tribe westward, to be citizens, or authorizing individuals of particular tribes to become citizens on application to a court of the United States for naturalization and satisfactory proof of fitness for civilized life. . . .

The main object of the opening sentence of the fourteenth amendment was to settle the question . . . as to the citizenship of free negroes . . . Indians born within the territorial limits of the United States, members of, and owing immediate allegiance to, one of the Indian tribes (an alien though dependent power) although in a geographical sense born in the United States, are no more "born in the United States and subject to the jurisdiction thereof," within the meaning of the first section of the fourteenth amendment, than the children of subjects of any foreign government born within the domain of that government, or the children born within the United States, of ambassadors or other public ministers of foreign nations. This view is confirmed by the second section of the fourteenth amendment, which provides that "representatives shall be apportioned among the several states according to their respective numbers, counting the whole number of persons in each state, excluding Indians not taxed." Slavery having been abolished, and the persons formerly held as slaves made citizens, this clause fixing the apportionment of representatives has abrogated so much of the corresponding clause of the original constitution as counted only three-fifths of such persons. But Indians not taxed are still excluded from the count, for the reason that they are not citizens. Their absolute exclusion from the basis of representation, in which all other persons are now included, is wholly inconsistent with their being considered citizens.

Such Indians, then, not being citizens by birth, can only become citizens in the second way mentioned in the fourteenth amendment, by being "naturalized in the United States," by or under some treaty or statute. . . .

HARLAN, J., joined by WOOD, J., dissenting:

[A]rticle I, [§] 3 . . . requires, in the apportionment of representatives and direct taxes among the several states "according to their respective numbers," the exclusion of "Indians not taxed." This implies that there were, at that time, in the United States, Indians who were taxed; that is, were subject to taxation by the laws of the state of which they were residents. Indians not taxed were those who held tribal relations, and therefore were not subject to the authority of any state, and were subject only to the authority of the United States. . . . The same provision is retained in the fourteenth amendment. . . . Indians in the several states, who are taxed by their laws, are counted in establishing the basis of representation in congress. By the [Civil Rights] act of April 9, 1866, . . . it is provided that "all persons born in the United States, and not subject to any foreign power, excluding Indians not taxed, are hereby declared to be citizens of the United States." This, so far as we are aware, is the first general enactment making persons of the Indian race citizens of the United States. . . .[T]he act of 1866 reached Indians not in tribal relations. . . . Surely every one must admit that an Indian residing in one of the states, and subject to taxation there, became, by force alone of the act of 1866, a citizen of the United States, although he may have been, when born, a member of a tribe. The exclusion of Indians not taxed evinced a purpose to include those subject to taxation in the state of their residence. . . .

At the same session of the congress which passed the act of 1866, the fourteenth amendment was approved and submitted to the states for adoption. Those who sustained the former urged the adoption of the latter, [and there is no evidence in the debates that the framers of the Fourteenth Amendment wished] to abandon the policy inaugurated by the act of 1866. . . . [After the adoption of the Fourteenth Amendment, Congress] enacted statutes providing for the citizenship of Indians [but did so by granting citizenship to whole tribes, because members] could not, while they continued in tribal relations, acquire the citizenship granted by the fourteenth amendment. . . .

[E]very one who participated in the debates, whether for or against the [Fourteenth] amendment, believed that, in the form in which it was approved by congress, it granted, and was intended to grant, national citizenship to every person of the Indian race in this country who was unconnected with any tribe, and who resided, in good faith, outside of Indian reservations and within one of the states or territories of the Union. This fact is, we think, entitled to great weight in determining the meaning and scope of the amendment. . . .

Only in 1924 did Congress pass legislation naturalizing all "Indians born within the territorial limits of the United States" (8 U.S.C. §140(a)(s)).

NOTE: "THE RIDDLE OF HIRAM REVELS"[77]

Hiram Revels was the first African American to serve in the U.S. Senate, having been selected by the (reconstructed) Mississippi legislature to represent that state in 1870. The "riddle" surrounding his status as senator is deceptively simple: Article I, §3 of the Constitution states, "No person shall be a Senator who shall not have attained to the Age of thirty Years, and been nine Years a Citizen of the United States." *Had* Senator Revels been "a Citizen of the United States" since 1861? After all, *Dred Scott* had clearly stated that no slave or descendant of slaves could be a member of the American political community, and it was surely the case that Revels had not been a citizen of Mississippi in 1861 (when the state in fact had attempted to secede from the Union precisely to maintain slavery and the abject domination of Black people). On the other hand, the Fourteenth Amendment states that "[a]ll persons born or naturalized in the United States, and subject to the jurisdiction thereof, are citizens of the United States and of the State wherein they reside." However, the Fourteenth Amendment, designed to overrule *Dred Scott,* was not ratified until 1868. Did it retroactively grant Revels (and all other African Americans born in United States territory) birth citizenship?

Not surprisingly, several Democratic senators challenged Revels's eligibility for the Senate and prevented his taking the oath of office at the same time as the other newly elected senators. (Recall that Albert Gallatin, a Swiss émigré, had been prevented from taking his seat as Pennsylvania's senator because his naturalization had occurred within the relevant nine years. He was quickly elected to the House of Representatives, which has only a seven-year requirement.)

Some of the Democrats attacked the Fourteenth Amendment directly and refused to acknowledge its legitimacy; this would, among other things, leave *Dred Scott* in place. Others accepted the validity of the amendment and the fact that §1 of the amendment was designed to invalidate *Dred Scott,* but denied that it granted Revels citizenship before 1868. Some Republican senators simply denounced *Dred Scott,* in the vivid words of Massachusetts Senator Charles Sumner, as a "putrid corpse . . . a stench in the nostrils . . . to be remembered only as a warning and a shame," suggesting that for them it was *never* legally valid and therefore, presumably, that because Revels would have been recognized as a citizen of the United States had the Court followed the correct understanding of the Constitution, then the Senate should do likewise.

After a three-day debate in the Senate, 48 Republican senators voted to seat him, while 8 Democrats voted against, with 12 Republican senators choosing to be absent from the vote. Thus Revels took the oath of office and served for a year until his term expired in March 1871. Another African-American senator, Blanche Kelso Bruce, also represented Mississippi from 1875 to 1881. In the decades that followed, African Americans were gradually disenfranchised throughout the South. It would be 80 years before the next African-American senator, Edward Brooke of Massachusetts (1967-1979).

---

77. The material in this note is drawn from Richard Primus, The Riddle of Hiram Revels, 119 Harv. L. Rev. 1680 (2006).

DISCUSSION

How would you decide the question of Revels's eligibility to serve in the Senate, given the words of Article I? Note, incidentally, that some members of Congress objected to Texas's joining the Union in 1845 on the grounds that there would be no one eligible to represent the state in the House or the Senate because, after all, Texas had been a Mexican colony or an independent republic prior to joining the Union. One response was that many of Texas's leaders had in fact been American citizens who moved to Texas from other states. (Presumably, they did not lose their American citizenship upon pledging allegiance and serving as public officials in what was, after all, a foreign nation between 1837-1845.) Imagine that Canada fragments and the United States offers admission to British Columbia. Would anyone other than an expatriate U.S. citizen be eligible to represent the new state in the House and Senate for the first seven to nine years? Would all British Columbians born before statehood be ineligible to run for the presidency? Do the decisions to admit Texas (and seat their leaders in the House and Senate) and then to seat Revels serve as precedents for allowing British Columbians to run for office immediately on the province's joining the United States?

C. *Early Application of the Fourteenth Amendment to Race Discrimination*

Strauder v. West Virginia

100 U.S. 303 (1880)

[The petitioner, Taylor Strauder, a Black man, was convicted of murder in state court by a jury from which Black people were excluded by a statute providing: "All white male persons who are twenty-one years of age and who are citizens of this State shall be liable to serve as jurors. . . ." Before the trial, he unsuccessfully sought to remove the case to a federal court[78] and was thereafter unsuccessful in quashing the jury venire and challenging the jury panel. The state supreme court affirmed his conviction. The U.S. Supreme Court reversed.]

STRONG, J. . . .

[The controlling question is whether] by the Constitution and laws of the United States, every citizen of the United States has a right to a trial of an indictment against him by a jury selected and impaneled without discrimination against his race or color, because of race or color. . . .

78. See 28 U.S.C. §1443: "Any of the following civil actions or criminal prosecutions, commenced in a State court may be removed by the defendant to the district court of the United States for the district and division embracing the place wherein it is pending: (1) Against any person who is denied or cannot enforce in the courts of such State a right under any law providing for the equal civil rights of citizens of the United States, or all persons within the jurisdiction thereof. . . ."

It is to be observed that the [question] is not whether a colored man, when an indictment has been preferred against him, has a right to a grand or a petit jury composed in whole or in part of persons of his own race or color, but it is whether, in the composition or selection of jurors by whom he is to be indicted or tried, all persons of his race or color may be excluded by law, solely because of their race or color, so that by no possibility can any colored man sit upon the jury. . . .

[The Fourteenth Amendment] is one of a series of constitutional provisions having a common purpose; namely, securing to a race recently emancipated, a race that through many generations had been held in slavery, all the civil rights that the superior race enjoy. The true spirit and meaning of the amendments, as we said in the SlaughterHouse Cases (16 Wall. 36), cannot be understood without keeping in view the history of the times when they were adopted, and the general objects they plainly sought to accomplish. At the time when they were incorporated into the Constitution, it required little knowledge of human nature to anticipate that those who had long been regarded as an inferior and subject race would, when suddenly raised to the rank of citizenship, be looked upon with jealousy and positive dislike, and that State laws might be enacted or enforced to perpetuate the distinctions that had before existed.

Discriminations against them had been habitual. It was well known that in some States laws making such discriminations then existed, and others might well be expected. The colored race, as a race, was abject and ignorant, and in that condition was unfitted to command the respect of those who had superior intelligence. Their training had left them mere children, and as such they needed the protection which a wise government extends to those who are unable to protect themselves. They especially needed protection against unfriendly action in the States where they were resident. It was in view of these considerations the Fourteenth Amendment was framed and adopted. It was designed to assure to the colored race the enjoyment of all the civil rights that under the law are enjoyed by white persons, and to give to that race the protection of the general government, in that enjoyment, whenever it should be denied by the States. . . .

If this is the spirit and meaning of the amendment, whether it means more or not, it is to be construed liberally, to carry out the purposes of its framers. It ordains . . . that the law in the States shall be the same for the black as for the white; that all persons, whether colored or white, shall stand equal before the laws of the States, and, in regard to the colored race, for whose protection the amendment was primarily designed, that no discrimination shall be made against them by law because of their color. . . . [The amendment guarantees] the right to exemption from unfriendly legislation against them distinctively as colored—exemption from legal discriminations, implying inferiority in civil society, lessening the security of their enjoyment of the rights which others enjoy, and discriminations which are steps towards reducing them to the condition of a subject race.

That the West Virginia statute respecting juries—the statute that controlled the selection of the grand and petit jury in the case of the plaintiff in error—is such a discrimination ought not to be doubted. Nor would it be if the persons excluded by it were white men. If in those States where the colored people constitute a majority of the entire population a law should be enacted excluding all white men from jury service, thus denying to them the privilege of participating equally with the blacks in the administration of justice, we apprehend no one would be heard to claim that it would not be a denial to white men of the equal protection of the laws. Nor if a law should be passed excluding all naturalized Celtic Irishmen, would there be any doubt of its inconsistency with the spirit of the amendment. The very fact that colored people are singled out and expressly denied by a statute all right to participate in the administration of the law, as jurors, because of their color, though they are citizens, and may be in other respects fully qualified, is practically a brand upon them, affixed by the law, an assertion of their inferiority, and a stimulant to that race prejudice which is an impediment to securing to individuals of the race that equal justice which the law aims to secure to all others.

The right to a trial by jury is guaranteed to every citizen of West Virginia by the Constitution of that State, and the constitution of juries is a very essential part of the protection such a mode of trial is intended to secure. The very idea of a jury is a body of men composed of the peers or equals of the person whose rights it is selected or summoned to determine; that is, of his neighbors, fellows, associates, persons having the same legal status in society as that which he holds. . . . It is well known that prejudices often exist against particular classes in the community, which sway the judgment of jurors, and which, therefore, operate in some cases to deny to persons of those classes the full enjoyment of that protection which others enjoy. . . . The framers of the constitutional amendment must have known full well the existence of such prejudice and its likelihood to continue against the manumitted slaves and their race, and that knowledge was doubtless a motive that led to the amendment. By their manumission and citizenship the colored race became entitled to the equal protection of the laws of the States in which they resided; and the apprehension that through prejudice they might be denied that equal protection, that is, that there might be discrimination against them, was the inducement to bestow upon the national government the power to enforce the provision that no State shall deny to them the equal protection of the laws. Without the apprehended existence of prejudice that portion of the amendment would have been unnecessary, and it might have been left to the States to extend equality of protection.

In view of these considerations, . . . how can it be maintained that compelling a colored man to submit to a trial for his life by a jury drawn from a panel from which the State has expressly excluded every man of his race, because of color alone, however well qualified in other respects, is not a denial to him of equal legal protection?

We do not say that within the limits from which it is not excluded by the amendment a State may not prescribe the qualifications of its jurors, and in so doing make discriminations. It may confine the selection to males, to freeholders, to citizens, to persons within certain ages, or to persons having educational qualifications. We do not believe the Fourteenth Amendment was ever intended to prohibit this. Looking at its history, it is clear it had no such purpose. Its aim was against discrimination because of race or color. As we have said more than once, its design was to protect an emancipated race, and to strike down all possible legal discriminations against those who belong to it. . . .[79]

79. Justice Field and Justice Clifford dissented without opinion.

[Justice Field, joined by Justice Clifford, dissented, though their objections were set out in a dissent to a companion case, Ex parte Virginia, 100 U.S. 339 (1880), in which the majority found the Fourteenth Amendment violated by the exclusion by a Virginia judge of Black people from service on juries. The portion of the dissent most relevant to *Strauder* was as follows:]

The fourth clause in the first section of the amendment declares that no State shall "deny to any person within its jurisdiction the equal protection of the laws." . . . [T]he universality of the protection secured necessarily renders . . . untenable [the argument that exclusion from jury service is prohibited]. All persons within the jurisdiction of the State, whether permanent residents or temporary sojourners, whether old or young, male or female, are to be equally protected. Yet no one will contend that equal protection to women, to children, to the aged, to aliens, can only be secured by allowing persons of the class to which they belong to act as jurors in cases affecting their interests. The equality of protection intended does not require that all persons shall be permitted to participate in the government of the State and the administration of its laws, to hold its offices, or be clothed with any public trusts. As already said, the universality of the protection assured repels any such conclusion.

The equality of the protection secured extends only to civil rights as distinguished from those which are political, or arise from the form of the government and its mode of administration. And yet the reach and influence of the amendment are immense. It opens the courts of the country to every one, on the same terms, for the security of his person and property, the prevention and redress of wrongs, and the enforcement of contracts; it assures to every one the same rules of evidence and modes of procedure; it allows no impediments to the acquisition of property and the pursuit of happiness, to which all are not subjected; it suffers no other or greater burdens or charges to be laid upon one than such as are equally borne by others; and in the administration of criminal justice it permits no different or greater punishment to be imposed upon one than such as is prescribed to all for like offences. It secures to all persons their civil rights upon the same terms; but it leaves political rights, or such as arise from the form of government and its administration, as they stood previous to its adoption. It has no more reference to them than it has to social rights and duties, which do not rest upon any positive law, though they are more potential in controlling the intercourse of individuals. In the consideration of questions growing out of these amendments much confusion has arisen from a failure to distinguish between the civil and the political rights of citizens. Civil rights are absolute and personal. Political rights, on the other hand, are conditioned and dependent upon the discretion of the elective or appointing power, whether that be the people acting through the ballot, or one of the departments of their government. The civil rights of the individual are never to be withheld, and may be always judicially enforced. The political rights which he may enjoy, such as holding office and discharging a public trust, are qualified because their possession depends on his fitness, to be adjudged by those whom society has clothed with the elective authority. The Thirteenth and Fourteenth Amendments were designed to secure the civil rights of all persons, of every race, color, and condition; but they left to the States to determine to whom the possession of political powers should be intrusted. This is manifest from the fact that when it was desired to confer political power upon the newly made citizens of the States, as was done by inhibiting the denial to them of the suffrage on account of race, color, or previous condition of servitude, a new amendment was required. . . .

The position that in cases where the rights of colored persons are concerned, justice will not be done to them unless they have a mixed jury, is founded upon the notion that in such cases white persons will not be fair and honest jurors. If this position be correct, there ought not to be any white persons on the jury where the interests of colored persons only are involved. That jury would not be an honest or fair one, of which any of its members should be governed in his judgment by other considerations than the law and the evidence; and that decision would hardly be considered just which should be reached by a sort of compromise, in which the prejudices of one race were set off against the prejudices of the other. To be consistent, those who hold this notion should contend that in cases affecting members of the colored race only, the juries should be composed entirely of colored persons, and that the presiding judge should be of the same race. . . . The jury *de medietate linguoe*, anciently allowed in England for the trial of an alien,[80] was expressly authorized by statute, probably as much because of the difference of language and customs between him and Englishmen, and the greater probability of his defence being more fully understood, as because it would be heard in a more friendly spirit by jurors of his own country and language.

. . . [Ex parte Virginia concerned, among other things, the power of Congress, under §5 of the Fourteenth Amendment, to criminalize the racially discriminatory conduct of the Virginia judge. According to Justice Field, if Congress] can make the exclusion of persons from jury service on account of race or color a criminal offence, it can make their exclusion from office on that account also criminal; and, adopting the doctrine of the district judge in this case [which had found the Virginia judge to have acted in violation of the law], the failure to appoint them to office will be presumptive evidence of their exclusion on that ground. To such a result are we logically led. The legislation of Congress is founded, and is sustained by this court, as it seems to me, upon a theory as to what constitutes the equal protection of the laws, which is purely speculative, not warranted by any experience of the country, and not in accordance with the understanding of the people as to the meaning of those terms since the organization of the government.

DISCUSSION

1. Strauder*'s interpretation of the Fourteenth Amendment.* Justice Strong gives an extended discussion of the purposes behind the Fourteenth Amendment, and offers multiple formulations of its purposes. What does Strong mean when he says that the amendment was designed to prevent "unfriendly" legislation against Black people. Does this mean that "friendly" legislation—i.e., legislation designed to

80. This refers to an English trial procedure that ended only in the nineteenth century by which civil trials involving disputes between, say, English and foreign merchants took place before juries that included foreign members. See Marianne Constable, The Law of the Other: The Mixed Jury and Changing Conceptions of Citizenship, Law and Knowledge (1994).

remedy past discrimination against Black people—is permissible under the Fourteenth Amendment? In the same paragraph, the Court says that the purpose of the amendment was to ensure that "the law in the States shall be the same for the black as for the white." Are these two formulas consistent? Finally, the Court also argues that the Fourteenth Amendment is designed to exempt Black people from "legal discriminations, implying inferiority in civil society . . . [or] which are steps towards reducing them to the condition of a subject race." This is an early version of an "antisubordination" rationale. How is it different from the other formulations? What consequences would it have for classifications that do not imply inferiority and that seek to prevent or counteract racial subordination?

2. *What is the equal protection claim in* Strauder*?* Strauder does not claim that he personally was excluded from jury service. Such a claim might have been brought by Black people excluded from the jury selection process, and would probably be more appropriate under the Fifteenth Amendment, because the right to serve on juries is a political right akin to voting. See generally Vikram David Amar, Jury Service as Political Participation, 80 Cornell L. Rev. 203 (1995). Nor does Justice Strong argue that Strauder is asserting the political rights of Black people who have been excluded. What exactly is the claim that he has been denied equal protection of the laws?

Justice Strong argues that Strauder had been denied equal protection of the law because the West Virginia statute excluding Black people from serving on juries had denied him a fair trial. The idea is that Strauder has a civil right to a fair process for deciding his guilt or innocence (especially when, as here, he faced a capital offense), and under the Equal Protection Clause, he has a right to as fair a process as whites enjoy. When a state interferes with the fairness of the criminal process, it has violated that guarantee of equal protection.

How exactly has the exclusion of Black people from the pool for selecting jurors denied Strauder a fair trial, making it less fair for Black people than for similarly situated whites? Justice Strong does not assert that Strauder is required to have a certain number of Black people on his jury proportionate to the percentage in the local population. Jurors are selected at random from a larger pool, so it is possible that there might be a small number of Black people on the resulting jury, or no Black people at all.

Strong's argument might be that the *process* for picking jurors must be free of racial skewing or racial prejudice. Or his argument might be that the *social meaning* of the exclusion of Black people by statute is the problem, because it "is practically a brand upon them, affixed by the law, an assertion of their inferiority, and a stimulant to that race prejudice which is an impediment to securing to individuals of the race that equal justice which the law aims to secure to all others." Can you think of any additional reasons why exclusion of Black people from the jury pool violates Strauder's right to a fair trial even if Strauder is not guaranteed any particular number of Black people in the actual jury?

Note Justice Strong's assertion that if whites had been excluded in a Black-majority jurisdiction, or Irish people had been excluded, the Fourteenth Amendment would also be violated. Does this tell you what he thinks the problem was with the West Virginia statute? Suppose that Strauder were not Black but Irish and, as before, all Black people were excluded by statute. Would Strauder's conviction violate the Fourteenth Amendment under Justice Strong's theory?

3. *A jury of your peers.* Justice Strong clearly does not think that excluding whole groups of people from jury service denies equal protection of the laws to criminal defendants. The states may "confine the selection to males, to freeholders, to citizens, to persons within certain ages, or to persons having educational qualifications." Why should this be permissible? Doesn't the exclusion of women, for example, suggest women's inferiority in civil society? Today the right to serve on juries is protected both by the Equal Protection Clause, see J.E.B. v. Alabama, 511 U.S. 127 (1994), and by the Sixth Amendment right to trial by jury, which forbids many more kinds of exclusions. See Castaneda v. Partida, 430 U.S. 482 (1977).

Justice Strong argues that the Fourteenth Amendment was designed to guarantee racial equality. Section 1 of the amendment, however, does not mention race. It says "equal protection of the laws." But, not surprisingly, there was not in 1880, nor is there today, general agreement on what equality requires. See, e.g., Douglas Rae et al., Equalities (1981) (suggesting that there are 108 logically coherent notions of "equality"). Whatever the Equal Protection Clause means, it does not mean that states may make no distinctions in how they treat persons subject to their jurisdiction.

In *Strauder*'s concluding paragraph, Justice Strong suggests that property and literacy qualifications are legitimate. Do you agree? What about restricting jury service to citizens? What if a state required proficiency in the English language or, indeed, the ability to see and hear, which would exclude the blind and deaf? Even if you object to these distinctions on grounds of policy, do you think they violate the Constitution? Why or why not?

4. *Civil and political rights.* Justice Field's dissent emphasizes that the Fourteenth Amendment is limited to *civil* rights and, therefore, does not cover *political* rights. As Mark Tushnet notes:[81]

> The lawmakers who discussed equality during Reconstruction accepted midcentury conceptions that distinguished equality with respect to civil rights, to social rights, and to political rights. The core of each conception was also well defined: The core of civil rights included the rights to sue and testify; social rights included the right to select one's associates; voting was the central political right.

The precise contours of these categories were contested, and as Richard Primus explains, "[t]he many political and legal actors who spoke and wrote about rights using these terms did not always employ the categories in the same way."[82] Nevertheless, they provided a general framework for thinking and arguing about the meaning of equality before the law. Consider in this light the following comments by Professor Kaczorowski:[83]

---

81. Tushnet, The Politics of Equality in Constitutional Law, 74 J. Am. Hist. 884 (1987).

82. See Primus, The American Language of Rights 154-156 (1999).

83. Robert Kaczorowski, Revolutionary Constitutionalism in the Era of the Civil War and Reconstruction, 61 N.Y.U. L. Rev. 863, 881-883 (1986). See also Curtis, No State Shall Abridge, supra n.1; Eric Foner, Reconstruction: America's Unfinished Revolution, supra n.53, at 239-261.

> [A]lthough Republicans were virtually unanimous in their support for the protection of the civil rights of blacks, they divided over the question of securing blacks' voting rights. Ultimately, suffrage was intentionally excluded from the rights that the fourteenth amendment and Civil Rights Act of 1866 were to guarantee. The exclusion of suffrage thus helped to reduce political opposition to the measures by neutralizing racist opposition within the Republican party. . . .
>
> The exclusion of suffrage from the framers' definition of civil rights was also dictated by prevailing legal opinion. Legal thinkers defined suffrage as a political privilege to be exercised by competent individuals, not as a natural right of free men. Thus principles of law buttressed political expediency.

As we have seen, Strong's argument characterizes Strauder's claim as one of *civil* rights—that is, a right to a criminal process as fair for Black people as it is for whites. Field, however, makes three objections. First, he argues that the claim has no logical stopping point, and will require that only Black people serve on juries in criminal trials of Black defendants, and indeed, that only Black judges preside. Second, he notes that the argument impugns the impartiality of white jurors because of their race and suggests that they cannot fairly sit in judgment of Black defendants. Finally, he points out that, according to the premises of the argument, adding a mixture of different kinds of people to a jury does not ensure that the jurors will follow the law and the evidence: It simply reaches "a sort of compromise, in which the prejudices of one race were set off against the prejudices of the other." What do you make of Field's objections?

The year 1877 is generally regarded as a watershed in American political history. Under the so-called Compromise of 1877, Southern Democrats abandoned their support for Democrat Samuel J. Tilden, who they claimed had been legally elected President, and supported the seating of Republican Rutherford B. Hayes in exchange, essentially, for the end of Reconstruction. C. Vann Woodward, a leading historian of the postwar South, described the social and political context in which the Court was operating.

C. Vann Woodward, The Strange Career of Jim Crow

6, 69-70 (3d rev. ed. 1974)

The phase that began in 1877 was inaugurated by the withdrawal of federal troops from the South, the abandonment of the Negro as a ward of the nation, the giving up of the attempt to guarantee the freedman his civil and political equality, and the acquiescence of the rest of the country in the South's demand that the whole problem be left to the disposition of the dominant Southern white people. What the new status of the Negro would be was not at once apparent, nor were the Southern white people themselves so united on that subject at first as has been generally assumed. The determination of the Negro's "place" took shape gradually under the influence of economic and political conflicts among divided white people—conflicts that were eventually resolved in part at the expense of the Negro. . . .

The South's adoption of extreme racism was due not so much to a conversion as it was to a relaxation of the opposition. All the elements of fear, jealousy, proscription, hatred, and fanaticism had long been present, as they are present in various degrees of intensity in any society. What enabled them to rise to dominance was not so much cleverness or ingenuity as it was a general weakening and discrediting of the numerous forces that had hitherto kept them in check. The restraining forces included not only Northern liberal opinion in the press, the courts, and the government, but also internal checks imposed by the prestige and influence of the Southern conservatives, as well as by the idealism and zeal of the Southern radicals. What happened toward the end of the century was an almost simultaneous—and sometimes not unrelated—decline in the effectiveness of restraint that had been exercised by all three forces: Northern liberalism, Southern conservatism, and Southern radicalism.

The acquiescence of Northern liberalism in the Compromise of 1877 defined the beginning, but not the ultimate extent, of the liberal retreat on the race issue. The Compromise merely left the freedman to the custody of the conservative Redeemers upon their pledge that they would protect him in his constitutional rights. But as these pledges were forgotten or violated and the South veered toward proscription and extremism, Northern opinion shifted to the right, keeping pace with the South, conceding point after point, so that at no time were the sections very far apart on race policy. The failure of the liberals to resist this trend was due in part to political factors. Since reactionary politicians and their cause were identified with the bloody-shirt issue and the demagogic exploitation of sectional animosities, the liberals naturally felt themselves strongly drawn toward the cause of sectional reconciliation. And since the Negro was the symbol of sectional strife, the liberals joined in deprecating further agitation of his cause and in defending the Southern view of race in its less extreme forms. It was quite common in the eighties and nineties to find in the Nation, Harper's Weekly, the North American Review, or the Atlantic Monthly, Northern liberals and former abolitionists mouthing the shibboleths of white supremacy regarding the Negro's innate inferiority, shiftlessness, and hopeless unfitness for full participation in the white man's civilization. Such expressions doubtless did much to add to the reconciliation of North and South, but they did so at the expense of the Negro. Just as the Negro gained his emancipation and new rights through a falling out between white men, he now stood to lose his rights through the reconciliation of white men.

D. Creation of the State Action Doctrine

The Civil Rights Cases

109 U.S. 3 (1883)

[Section 1 of the Civil Rights Act of 1875 provides: "That all persons within the jurisdiction of the United States shall be entitled to the full and equal enjoyment of the accommodations, advantages, facilities, and privileges of inns, public conveyances on land or water, theatres, and other places of public amusement; subject only to the conditions and limitations established by law, and applicable alike to citizens of every race and color, regardless of any previous condition of servitude." Section 2 makes violation of §1 a misdemeanor and also permits an aggrieved party to recover a civil fine.

These consolidated cases, from California, Kansas, Missouri, New York, and Tennessee, arose out of the exclusion of Black people from inns, theaters, and a railroad on account of their race.]

BRADLEY, J. . . .

[T]he primary and important question in all the cases is the constitutionality of the law . . . [the essence of which is to declare that] . . . colored citizens, whether formerly slaves or not, and citizens of other races, shall have the same accommodations and privileges in all inns, public conveyances, and places of amusement as are enjoyed by white citizens; and vice versa. . . .

Has Congress constitutional power to make such a law? Of course, no one will contend that the power to pass it was contained in the Constitution before the adoption of the last three amendments. The power is sought, first, in the Fourteenth Amendment. . . .

It is State action of a particular character that is prohibited. Individual invasion of individual rights is not the subject-matter of the amendment. It has a deeper and broader scope. It nullifies and makes void all State legislation, and State action of every kind, which impairs the privileges and immunities of citizens of the United States, or which injures them in life, liberty or property without due process of law, or which denies to any of them the equal protection of the laws. [T]he last section of the amendment invests Congress with power to enforce it by appropriate legislation. To enforce what? To enforce the prohibition. To adopt appropriate legislation for correcting the effects of such prohibited State laws and State acts, and thus to render them effectually null, void, and innocuous. This is the legislative power conferred upon Congress, and this is the whole of it. It does not invest Congress with power to legislate upon subjects which are within the domain of State legislation; but to provide modes of relief against State legislation, or State action, of the kind referred to. It does not authorize Congress to create a code of municipal law for the regulation of private rights; but to provide modes of redress against the operation of State laws, and the action of State officers executive or judicial, when these are subversive of the fundamental rights specified in the amendment. Positive rights and privileges are undoubtedly secured by the Fourteenth Amendment; but they are secured by way of prohibition against State laws and State proceedings affecting those rights and privileges, and by power given to Congress to legislate for the purpose of carrying such prohibition into effect: and such legislation must necessarily be predicated upon such supposed State laws or State proceedings, and be directed to the correction of their operation and effect. . . .

An apt illustration of this distinction may be found in some of the provisions of the original Constitution. Take the subject of contracts, for example. The Constitution prohibited the States from passing any law impairing the obligation of contracts. This did not give to Congress power to provide laws for the general enforcement of contracts; nor power to invest the courts of the United States with jurisdiction over contracts, so as to enable parties to sue upon them in those courts. It did, however, give the power to provide remedies by which the impairment of contracts by State legislation might be counteracted and corrected. . . .

And so in the present case, until some State law has been passed, or some State action through its officers or agents has been taken, adverse to the rights of citizens sought to be protected by the Fourteenth Amendment, no legislation of the United States under said amendment, nor any proceeding under such legislation, can be called into activity: for the prohibitions of the amendment are against State laws and acts done under State authority. Of course, legislation may, and should be, provided in advance to meet the exigency when it arises; but it should be adapted to the mischief and wrong which the amendment was intended to provide against; and that is, State laws, or State action of some kind, adverse to the rights of the citizen secured by the amendment. Such legislation cannot properly cover the whole domain of rights appertaining to life, liberty and property, defining them and providing for their vindication. That would be to establish a code of municipal law regulative of all private rights between man and man in society. It would be to make Congress take the place of the State legislatures and to supersede them. It is absurd to affirm that, because the rights of life, liberty and property (which include all civil rights that men have), are by the amendment sought to be protected against invasion on the part of the State without due process of law, Congress may therefore provide due process of law for their vindication in every case; and that, because the denial by a State to any persons, of the equal protection of the laws, is prohibited by the amendment, therefore Congress may establish laws for their equal protection. In fine, the legislation which Congress is authorized to adopt in this behalf is not general legislation upon the rights of the citizen, but corrective legislation, that is, such as may be necessary and proper for counteracting such laws as the States may adopt or enforce, and which, by the amendment, they are prohibited from making or enforcing, or such acts and proceedings as the States may commit or take, and which, by the amendment, they are prohibited from committing or taking. It is not necessary for us to state, if we could, what legislation would be proper for Congress to adopt. It is sufficient for us to examine whether the law in question is of that character.

An inspection of the [1875 Act] shows that it makes no reference whatever to any supposed or apprehended violation of the Fourteenth Amendment on the part of the States. It is not predicated on any such view. It proceeds ex directo to declare that certain acts committed by individuals shall be deemed offenses, and shall be prosecuted and punished by proceedings in the courts of the United States. It does not profess to be corrective of any constitutional wrong committed by the States; it does not make its operation to depend upon any such wrong committed. It applies equally to cases arising in States which have the justest laws respecting the personal rights of citizens, and whose authorities are ever ready to enforce such laws, as to those which arise in States that may have violated the prohibition of the amendment. In other words, it steps into the domain of local jurisprudence, and lays down rules for the conduct of individuals in society towards each other, and imposes sanctions for the enforcement of those rules, without referring in any manner to any supposed action of the State or its authorities.

If this legislation is appropriate for enforcing the prohibitions of the amendment, it is difficult to see where it is to stop. Why may not Congress with equal show of authority enact a code of laws for the enforcement and vindication of all rights of life, liberty, and property? . . . The truth is, that the implication of a power to legislate in this manner is based upon the assumption that if the States are forbidden to legislate or act in a particular way on a particular subject, and power is conferred upon Congress to enforce the prohibition, this gives Congress power to legislate generally upon that subject, and not merely power to provide modes of redress against such State legislation or action. The assumption is certainly unsound. It is repugnant to the Tenth Amendment of the Constitution, which declares that powers not delegated to the United States by the Constitution, nor prohibited by it to the States, are reserved to the States respectively or to the people.

We have not overlooked the fact that the fourth section of the act now under consideration has been held by this court to be constitutional. That section declares "that no citizen, possessing all other qualifications which are or may be prescribed by law, shall be disqualified for service as grand or petit juror in any court of the United States, or of any State, on account of race, color, or previous condition of servitude; and any officer or other person charged with any duty in the selection or summoning of jurors who shall exclude or fail to summon any citizen for the cause aforesaid, shall, on conviction thereof, be deemed guilty of a misdemeanor, and be fined not more than five thousand dollars."

In Ex parte Virginia, 100 U.S. 339, it was held that an indictment against a State officer under this section for excluding persons of color from the jury list is sustainable. But a moment's attention to its terms will show that the section is entirely corrective in its character. Disqualifications for service on juries are only created by the law, and the first part of the section is aimed at certain disqualifying laws, namely, those which make mere race or color a disqualification; and the second clause is directed against those who, assuming to use the authority of the State government, carry into effect such a rule of disqualification. In the Virginia case, the State, through its officer, enforced a rule of disqualification which the law was intended to abrogate and counteract. Whether the statute book of the State actually laid down any such rule of disqualification, or not, the State, through its officer, enforced such a rule: and it is against such State action, through its officers and agents, that the last clause of the section is directed. This aspect of the law was deemed sufficient to divest it of any unconstitutional character, and makes it differ widely from the first and second sections of the same act which we are now considering.

These sections, in the objectionable features before referred to, are different also from the [Civil Rights Act of 1866] re-enacted with some modifications in . . . the Enforcement Act [of 1870, which] declar[es] that all persons within the jurisdiction of the United States shall have the same right in every State and Territory to make and enforce contracts, to sue, be parties, give evidence, and to the full and equal benefit of all laws and proceedings for the security of persons and property as is enjoyed by white citizens, and shall be subject to like punishment, pains, penalties, taxes, licenses and exactions of every kind, and none other, any law, statute, ordinance, regulation or custom to the contrary notwithstanding. [The Civil Rights Act then] proceeds to enact, that any person who, under color of any law, statute, ordinance, regulation or custom, shall subject, or cause to be subjected, any inhabitant of any State or Territory to the deprivation of any rights secured or protected by the preceding section (above quoted), or to different punishment, pains, or penalties, on account of such person being an alien, or by reason of his color or race, than is prescribed for the punishment of citizens, shall be deemed guilty of a misdemeanor, and subject to fine and imprisonment as specified in the act. This law is clearly corrective in its character, intended to counteract and furnish redress against State laws and proceedings, and customs having the force of law, which sanction the wrongful acts specified. . . . The Civil Rights Bill here referred to is analogous in its character to what a law would have been under the original Constitution, declaring that the validity of contracts should not be impaired, and that if any person bound by a contract should refuse to comply with it, under color or pretence that it had been rendered void or invalid by a State law, he should be liable to an action upon it in the courts of the United States, with the addition of a penalty for setting up such an unjust and unconstitutional defence.

. . . [C]ivil rights, such as are guaranteed by the Constitution against State aggression, cannot be impaired by the wrongful acts of individuals, unsupported by State authority in the shape of laws, customs, or judicial or executive proceedings. The wrongful act of an individual, unsupported by any such authority, is simply a private wrong, or a crime of that individual; an invasion of the rights of the injured party, it is true, whether they affect his person, his property, or his reputation; but if not sanctioned in some way by the State, or not done under State authority, his rights remain in full force, and may presumably be vindicated by resort to the laws of the State for redress. An individual cannot deprive a man of his right to vote, to hold property, to buy and sell, to sue in the courts, or to be a witness or a juror; he may, by force or fraud, interfere with the enjoyment of the right in a particular case; he may commit an assault against the person, or commit murder, or use ruffian violence at the polls, or slander the good name of a fellow citizen; but, unless protected in these wrongful acts by some shield of State law or State authority, he cannot destroy or injure the right; he will only render himself amenable to satisfaction or punishment; and amenable therefor to the laws of the State where the wrongful acts are committed. . . .

The law in question without any reference to adverse State legislation on the subject, declares that all persons shall be entitled to equal accommodations and privileges of inns, public conveyances, and places of public amusement, and imposes a penalty upon any individual who shall deny to any citizen such equal accommodations and privileges. This is not corrective legislation; it is primary and direct; it takes immediate and absolute possession of the subject of the right of admission to inns, public conveyances, and places of amusement. It supersedes and displaces State legislation on the same subject, or only allows it permissive force. It ignores such legislation, and assumes that the matter is one that belongs to the domain of national regulation. Whether it would not have been a more effective protection of the rights of citizens to have clothed Congress with plenary power over the whole subject, is not now the question. What we have to decide is, whether such plenary power has been conferred upon Congress by the Fourteenth Amendment; and, in our judgment, it has not.

We have discussed the question presented by the law on the assumption that a right to enjoy equal accommodations and privileges in all inns, public conveyances, and places of public amusement, is one of the essential rights of the citizens which no State can abridge or interfere with. Whether it is such a right, or not, is a different question which, in the view we have taken of the validity of the law on the ground already stated, it is not necessary to examine. . . .

But the power of Congress to adopt direct and primary, as distinguished from corrective legislation, on the subject in hand, is sought, in the second place, from the Thirteenth Amendment, which abolishes slavery. This amendment declares "that neither slavery, nor involuntary servitude, except as a punishment for crime, whereof the party shall have been duly convicted, shall exist within the United States, or any place subject to their jurisdiction"; and it gives Congress power to enforce the amendment by appropriate legislation. . . . [S]uch legislation may be primary and direct in its character; for the amendment is not a mere prohibition of State laws establishing or upholding slavery, but an absolute declaration that slavery or involuntary servitude shall not exist in any part of the United States.

. . . [I]t is assumed, that the power vested in Congress to enforce the article by appropriate legislation, clothes Congress with power to pass all laws necessary and proper for abolishing all badges and incidents of slavery in the United States: and upon this assumption it is claimed, that this is sufficient authority for declaring by law that all persons shall have equal accommodations and privileges in all inns, public conveyances, and places of amusement; the argument being, that the denial of such equal accommodations and privileges is, in itself, a subjection to a species of servitude within the meaning of the amendment. Conceding the major proposition to be true, that Congress has a right to enact all necessary and proper laws for the obliteration and prevention of slavery with all its badges and incidents, is the minor proposition also true, that the denial to any person of admission to the accommodations and privileges of an inn, a public conveyance, or a theatre, does subject that person to any form of servitude, or tend to fasten upon him any badge of slavery? . . .

It may be that by the Black Code (as it was called), in the times when slavery prevailed, the proprietors of inns and public conveyances were forbidden to receive persons of the African race, because it might assist slaves to escape from the control of their masters. This was merely a means of preventing such escapes, and was no part of the servitude itself. A law of that kind could not have any such object now, however justly it might be deemed an invasion of the party's legal right as a citizen, and amenable to the prohibitions of the Fourteenth Amendment.

The long existence of African slavery in this country gave us very distinct notions of what it was, and what were its necessary incidents. Compulsory service of the slave for the benefit of the master, restraint of his movements except by the master's will, disability to hold property, to make contracts, to have a standing in court, to be a witness against a white person, and such like burdens and incapacities, were the inseparable incidents of the institution. Severer punishments for crimes were imposed on the slave than on free persons guilty of the same offences. Congress, as we have seen, by the Civil Rights Bill of 1866, passed in view of the Thirteenth Amendment, before the Fourteenth was adopted, undertook to wipe out these burdens and disabilities, the necessary incidents of slavery, constituting its substance and visible form; and to secure to all citizens of every race and color, and without regard to previous servitude, those fundamental rights which are the essence of civil freedom, namely, the same right to make and enforce contracts, to sue, be parties, give evidence, and to inherit, purchase, lease, sell and convey property, as is enjoyed by white citizens.

Whether this legislation was fully authorized by the Thirteenth Amendment alone, without the support which it afterward received from the Fourteenth Amendment, after the adoption of which it was re-enacted with some additions, it is not necessary to inquire. It is referred to for the purpose of showing that at that time (in 1866) Congress did not assume, under the authority given by the Thirteenth Amendment, to adjust what may be called the social rights of men and races in the community; but only to declare and vindicate those fundamental rights which appertain to the essence of citizenship, and the enjoyment or deprivation of which constitutes the essential distinction between freedom and slavery.

We must not forget that the province and scope of the Thirteenth and Fourteenth amendments are different: the former simply abolished slavery; the latter prohibited the States from abridging the privileges or immunities of citizens of the United States; from depriving them of life, liberty, or property without due process of law, and from denying to any the equal protection of the laws. The amendments are different, and the powers of Congress under them are different. What Congress has power to do under one, it may not have power to do under the other. Under the Thirteenth Amendment, it has only to do with slavery and its incidents. Under the Fourteenth Amendment, it has power to counteract and render nugatory all State laws and proceedings which have the effect to abridge any of the privileges or immunities of citizens of the United States, or to deprive them of life, liberty or property without due process of law, or to deny to any of them the equal protection of the laws. Under the Thirteenth Amendment, the legislation, so far as necessary or proper to eradicate all forms and incidents of slavery and involuntary servitude, may be direct and primary, operating upon the acts of individuals, whether sanctioned by State legislation or not; under the Fourteenth, as we have already shown, it must necessarily be, and can only be, corrective in its character, addressed to counteract and afford relief against State regulations or proceedings.

The only question under the present head, therefore, is, whether the refusal to any persons of the accommodations of an inn, or a public conveyance, or a place of public amusement, by an individual, and without any sanction or support from any State law or regulation, does inflict upon such persons any manner of servitude, or form of slavery, as those terms are understood in this country? Many wrongs may be obnoxious to the prohibitions of the Fourteenth Amendment which are not, in any just sense, incidents or elements of slavery. Such, for example, would be the taking of private property without due process of law; or allowing persons who have committed certain crimes (horse stealing, for example) to be seized and hung by the posse comitatus without regular trial; or denying to any person, or class of persons, the right to pursue any peaceful avocations allowed to others. What is called class legislation would belong to this category, and would be obnoxious to the prohibitions of the Fourteenth Amendment, but would not necessarily be so to the Thirteenth, when not involving the idea of any subjection of one man to another. The Thirteenth Amendment has respect, not to distinctions of race, or class, or color, but to slavery. The Fourteenth Amendment extends its protection to races and classes, and prohibits any State legislation which has the effect of denying to any race or class, or to any individual, the equal protection of the laws.

Now, conceding, for the sake of the argument, that the admission to an inn, a public conveyance, or a place of public amusement, on equal terms with all other citizens, is the right of every man and all classes of men, is it any more than one of those rights which the states by the Fourteenth Amendment are forbidden to deny to any person? And is the Constitution violated until the denial of the right has some State sanction or authority? Can the act of a mere individual, the owner of the inn, the public conveyance or place of amusement, refusing the accommodation, be justly regarded as imposing any badge of slavery or servitude upon the applicant, or only as inflicting an ordinary civil injury, properly cognizable by the laws of the State, and presumably subject to redress by those laws until the contrary appears?

After giving to these questions all the consideration which their importance demands, we are forced to the conclusion that such an act of refusal has nothing to do with slavery or involuntary servitude, and that if it is violative of any right of the party, his redress is to be sought under the laws of the State; or if those laws are adverse to his rights and do not protect him, his remedy will be found in the corrective legislation which Congress has adopted, or may adopt, for counteracting the effect of State laws, or State action, prohibited by the Fourteenth Amendment. It would be running the slavery argument into the ground to make it apply to every act of discrimination which a person may see fit to make as to the guests he will entertain, or as to the people he will take into his coach or cab or car, or admit to his concert or theatre, or deal with in other matters of intercourse or business. Innkeepers and public carriers, by the laws of all the States, so far as we are aware, are bound, to the extent of their facilities, to furnish proper accommodation to all unobjectionable persons who in good faith apply for them. If the laws themselves make any unjust discrimination, amenable to the prohibitions of the Fourteenth Amendment, Congress has full power to afford a remedy under that amendment and in accordance with it.

When a man has emerged from slavery, and by the aid of beneficent legislation has shaken off the inseparable concomitants of that state, there must be some stage in the progress of his elevation when he takes the rank of a mere citizen, and ceases to be the special favorite of the laws, and when his rights as a citizen, or a man, are to be protected in the ordinary modes by which other men's rights are protected. There were thousands of free colored people in this country before the abolition of slavery, enjoying all the essential rights of life, liberty and property the same as white citizens; yet no one, at that time, thought that it was any invasion of his personal status as a freeman because he was not admitted to all the privileges enjoyed by white citizens, or because he was subjected to discriminations in the enjoyment of accommodations in inns, public conveyances and places of amusement. Mere discriminations on account of race or color were not regarded as badges of slavery. . . .

[T]he first and second sections of the act of Congress of March 1st, 1875, entitled "An Act to protect all citizens in their civil and legal rights," are unconstitutional and void. . . .

HARLAN, J., dissenting. . . .

I cannot resist the conclusion that the substance and spirit of the recent amendments of the Constitution have been sacrificed by a subtle and ingenious verbal criticism. . . .

The Thirteenth Amendment, it is conceded, did something more than to prohibit slavery as an *institution*, resting upon distinctions of race, and upheld by positive law. . . . Was it the purpose of the nation simply to destroy the institution, and then remit the race, theretofore held in bondage, to the several States for such protection, in their civil rights, necessarily growing out of freedom, as those States, in their discretion, might choose to provide? Were the States against whose protest the institution was destroyed, to be left free, so far as national interference was concerned, to make or allow discriminations against that race, as such, in the enjoyment of those fundamental rights which by universal concession, inhere in a state of freedom?

That there are burdens and disabilities which constitute badges of slavery and servitude, and that the power to enforce by appropriate legislation the Thirteenth Amendment may be exerted by legislation of a direct and primary character, for the eradication, not simply of the institution, but of its badges and incidents, are propositions which ought to be deemed indisputable. They lie at the foundation of the Civil Rights Act of 1866. . . .

Congress, by the act of 1866, passed in view of the Thirteenth Amendment, before the Fourteenth was adopted, undertook to remove certain burdens and disabilities, the necessary incidents of slavery, and to secure to all citizens of every race and color, and without regard to previous servitude, those fundamental rights which are the essence of civil freedom, namely, the same right to make and enforce contracts, to sue, be parties, give evidence, and to inherit, purchase, lease, sell, and convey property as is enjoyed by white citizens. . . .

I do not contend that the Thirteenth Amendment invests Congress with authority, by legislation, to define and regulate the entire body of the civil rights which citizens enjoy, or may enjoy, in the several States. But I hold that since slavery . . . was the moving or principal cause of the adoption of that amendment, and since that institution rested wholly upon the inferiority, as a race, of those held in bondage, their freedom necessarily involved immunity from, and protection against, all discrimination against them, because of their race, in respect of such civil rights as belong to freemen of other races. Congress, therefore, under its express power to enforce that amendment, by appropriate legislation, may enact laws to protect that people against the deprivation, *because of their race,* of any civil rights granted to other freemen in the same State; and such legislation may be of a direct and primary character, operating upon States, their officers and agents, and, also, upon, at least, such individuals and corporations as exercise public functions and wield power and authority under the State. . . .

It remains now to inquire what are the legal rights of colored persons in respect of the accommodations, privileges and facilities of public conveyances, inns and places of public amusement?

First, as to public conveyances on land and water. . . . In Olcott v. Supervisors, 16 Wall. 678, it was ruled that railroads are public highways, established by authority of the State for the public use; that they are none the less public highways, because controlled and owned by private corporations; that it is a part of the function of government to make and maintain highways for the convenience of the public; that no matter who is the agent, or what is the agency, the function performed is *that of the State*; that although the owners may be private companies, they may be compelled to permit the public to use these works in the manner in which they can be used; that, upon these grounds alone, have the courts sustained the investiture of railroad corporations with the State's right of eminent domain, or the right of municipal corporations, under legislative authority, to assess, levy and collect taxes to aid in the construction of railroads. . . .

Such being the relations these corporations hold to the public, it would seem that the right of a colored person to use an improved public highway, upon the terms accorded to freemen of other races, is as fundamental, in the state of freedom established in this country, as are any of the rights which my brethren concede to be so far fundamental as to be deemed the essence of civil freedom. "Personal liberty consists," says Blackstone, "in the power of locomotion, of changing situation, or removing one's person to whatever places one's own inclination may direct, without restraint, unless by due course of law." But of what value is this right of locomotion, if it may be clogged by such burdens as Congress intended by the act of 1875 to remove? They are burdens which lay at the very foundation of the institution of slavery as it once existed. . . .

Second, as to inns. The same general observations which have been made as to railroads are applicable to inns. . . . In Rex v. Ivens, 7 Carrington & Payne, 213, 32 E.C.L. 495, the court, speaking by Mr. Justice Coleridge, said:

> An indictment lies against an innkeeper who refuses to receive a guest, he having at the time room in his house; and either the price of the guest's entertainment being tendered to him, or such circumstances occurring as will dispense with that tender. This law is founded in good sense. The innkeeper is not to select his guests. He has no right to say to one, you shall come to my inn, and to another you shall not, as every one coming and conducting himself in a proper manner has a right to be received; and for this purpose innkeepers are a sort of public servants, they having in return a kind of privilege of entertaining travellers and supplying them with what they want.

. . . [A] keeper of an inn is in the exercise of a quasi-public employment. The law gives him special privileges and he is charged with certain duties and responsibilities to the public. The public nature of his employment forbids him from discriminating against any person asking admission as a guest on account of the race or color of that person.

Third, as to places of public amusement. . . . [P]laces of public amusement, within the meaning of the act of 1875, are such as are established and maintained under direct license of the law. The authority to establish and maintain them comes from the public. The colored race is a part of that public. The local government granting the license represents them as well as all other races within its jurisdiction. A license from the public to establish a place of public amusement, imports, in law, equality of right, at such places, among all the members of that public. . . .

I am of the opinion that such discrimination practised by corporations and individuals in the exercise of their public or quasi-public functions is a badge of servitude the imposition of which Congress may prevent under its power, by appropriate legislation, to enforce the Thirteenth Amendment; and consequently, without reference to its enlarged power under the Fourteenth Amendment, the act of March 1, 1875, is not, in my judgment, repugnant to the Constitution.

It remains now to consider these cases with reference to the power Congress has possessed since the adoption of the Fourteenth Amendment. Much that has been said as to the power of Congress under the Thirteenth Amendment is applicable to this branch of the discussion, and will not be repeated. . . .

The assumption that this amendment consists wholly of prohibitions upon State laws and State proceedings in hostility to its provisions, is unauthorized by its language. The first clause of the first section—"All persons born or naturalized in the United States, and subject to the jurisdiction thereof, are citizens of the United States, and of the State wherein they reside"—is of a distinctly affirmative character. . . .

The citizenship thus acquired, by [the colored] race, in virtue of an affirmative grant from the nation, may be protected, not alone by the judicial branch of the government, but by congressional legislation of a primary direct character; this, because the power of Congress is not restricted to the enforcement of prohibitions upon State laws or State action. It is, in terms distinct and positive, to enforce "the *provisions* of *this article*" of amendment; not simply those of a prohibitive character, but the provisions—*all* of the provisions—affirmative and prohibitive, of the amendment. . . .

It is, therefore, an essential inquiry what, if any, right, privilege or immunity was given, by the nation, to colored persons when they were made citizens of the State in which they reside. . . . That they became entitled, upon the adoption of the Fourteenth Amendment, "to all privileges and immunities of citizens in the several States," within the meaning of section 2 of article 4 of the Constitution, no one, I suppose, will for a moment question. What are the privileges and immunities to which, by that clause of the Constitution, they became entitled? To this it may be answered, generally, upon the authority of the adjudged cases, that they are those which are fundamental in citizenship in a free republican government, such as are "common to the citizens in the latter States under their constitutions and laws by virtue of their being citizens." . . .

But what was secured to colored citizens of the United States—as between them and their respective States—by the national grant to them of State citizenship? With what rights, privileges, or immunities did this grant invest them? There is one, if there be no other—exemption from race discrimination in respect of any civil right belonging to citizens of the white race in the same State. That, surely, is their constitutional privilege when within the jurisdiction of other States. And such must be their constitutional right, in their own State, unless the recent amendments be splendid baubles, thrown out to delude those who deserved fair and generous treatment at the hands of the nation. Citizenship in this country necessarily imports at least equality of civil rights among citizens of every race in the same State. . . . If the grant to colored citizens of the United States of citizenship in their respective States, imports exemption from race discrimination, in their States, in respect of such civil rights as belong to citizenship, then, to hold that the amendment remits that right to the States for their protection, primarily, and stays the hands of the nation, until it is assailed by State laws or State proceedings, is to adjudge that the amendment, so far from enlarging the powers of Congress—as we have heretofore said it did—not only curtails them, but reverses the policy which the general government has pursued from its very organization. . . .

But if it were conceded that the power of Congress could not be brought into activity until the rights specified in the act of 1875 had been abridged or denied by some State law or State action, I maintain that . . . [t]here has been adverse State Action within the Fourteenth Amendment. . . .

In every material sense applicable to the practical enforcement of the Fourteenth Amendment, railroad corporations, keepers of inns, and managers of places of public amusement are agents or instrumentalities of the State, because they are charged with duties to the public, and are amenable, in respect of their duties and functions, to governmental regulation. It seems to me that . . . a denial, by these instrumentalities of the State, to the citizen, because of his race, of that equality of civil rights secured to him by law, is a denial by the State, within the meaning of the Fourteenth Amendment. If it be not, then that race is left, in respect of the civil rights in question, practically at the mercy of corporations and individuals wielding power under the States. . . .

DISCUSSION

1. *State action and congressional power.* Today the Civil Rights Cases are best known for the Fourteenth Amendment requirement of "state action." But an equally important legacy of the decision is its narrow conception of Congress's power to enforce the Reconstruction Amendments, and, in particular, Congress's power to reach private discrimination under §5 of the Fourteenth Amendment. Despite their name, the Civil Rights Cases significantly limited Congress's ability to protect civil rights through legislation. As we shall see in Chapter 5, when almost a century later Congress once again passed a law banning discrimination in public accommodations—Title II of the Civil Rights Act of 1964—it relied primarily on its power to regulate interstate commerce—a power much expanded as a result of the New Deal—and only secondarily on its powers to enforce the Fourteenth Amendment. (See the discussion in Chapter 5, infra.) The Supreme Court ultimately upheld the Act under the Commerce Clause.

In United States v. Guest, 383 U.S. 745 (1966), six members of the Court took the view that private conspiracies to violate civil rights were within Congress's §5 powers. Whatever precedential value *Guest* had on this question before, it was undermined by United States v. Morrison, 529 U.S. 598 (2000), which struck down a provision of the Violence Against Women Act that allowed suits in federal court against attacks based on the victim's gender. Nevertheless, *Guest* still appears to be good authority for the proposition that Congress may regulate private parties who conspire or "connive" with state officials to abridge constitutional rights. See 383 U.S. at 756-757. And presumably Congress may still reach private conspiracies to interfere with the right to travel, which the Constitution protects from public as well as private interference. Id. at 760. See also Bray v. Alexandria Women's Health Clinic, 506 U.S. 263, 278 (1993).

2. *State neglect.* Private violence against Black people following the end of the Civil War was one of the central concerns of the Reconstruction Congress that led to the Fourteenth Amendment. Although these attacks violated state criminal and civil law, state officials often turned a blind eye to the violence, literally denying Black people the equal protection of the laws. This concern led to theory of "state neglect": When states neglect to protect people within their jurisdiction from private injury, for example, through a custom or practice of nonenforcement, this constitutes state action within the meaning of the Fourteenth Amendment and Congress has the

power to remedy it by legislation.[84] This idea appears in the debates over the 1871 Ku Klux Klan Act,[85] which punished private conspiracies to violate rights. It also appears in the very first judicial construction of §5 by Judge (later Justice) Woods in the 1871 decision in United States v. Hall: "Denying [equal protection] includes inaction as well as action, and denying the equal protection of the laws includes the omission to protect, as well as the omission to pass laws for protection."[86]

Why couldn't the Civil Rights Act of 1875 have been upheld under a theory of state neglect? As Justice Harlan points out, the common law rule was that conveyances, inns, and places of public amusement had to serve everyone. If Black people were denied service in violation of their common law rights, and if state officials refused to protect those rights, then Congress could step in with remedial legislation to secure equal protection of the laws.

Bradley responds that the law is not directed only to state neglect: "It applies equally to cases arising in States which have the justest laws respecting the personal rights of citizens, and whose authorities are ever ready to enforce such laws, as to those which arise in States that may have violated the prohibition of the amendment." A factor that may have weighed heavily with the Court is that the 1875 Act did not protect basic civil rights, but only "social rights" to intermingle with whites on an equal footing. Drawing a contrast to the Civil Rights Act of 1866, which also applied nationwide, Justice Bradley argues that "Congress did not assume [in the Civil Rights Act of 1866] to adjust what may be called the social rights of men and races in the community; but only to declare and vindicate those fundamental rights which appertain to the essence of citizenship, and the enjoyment or deprivation of which constitutes the essential distinction between freedom and slavery." Because the Fourteenth Amendment did not protect social equality between whites and Blacks, it did not give Congress the power to enforce social equality as a remedy for constitutional violations. Justice Harlan, by contrast, believed that equal access to public accommodations was a civil right, a position he would reiterate in Plessy v. Ferguson. Therefore Congress could respond if states refused to enforce this right.

3. Harris *and the Ku Klux Klan Act.* The Court offered an even narrower construction of congressional power under the Reconstruction Amendments in United States v. Harris, 106 U.S. 629 (1883). *Harris* involved prosecutions of a lynch mob in

---

84. See Pamela Brandwein, A Judicial Abandonment of Blacks? Rethinking the "State Action" Cases of the Waite Court, 41 Law & Soc'y Rev. 343, 345-347, 356-357, 363-364 (2007) (discussing different versions of state neglect theory).

85. For example, Representative (later President) James Garfield argued that Congress had the power to pass the Ku Klux Klan Act of 1871 because

> even where the laws are just and equal on their face, yet, by a systematic maladministration of them, or a neglect or refusal to enforce their provisions, a portion of the people are denied equal protection under them. Whenever such a state of facts is clearly made out, I believe the last clause of the first section empowers Congress to step in and provide for doing justice to those persons who are thus denied equal protection.

Cong. Globe, 42d Cong., 1st Sess. App. 153 (1871). Garfield eventually voted for the Klan Act even though the statute did not require proof of state neglect.

86. 26 F. Cas. 79, 81 (C.C.S.D. Ala. 1871) (No. 15,282) (Woods, J.).

Tennessee under the Ku Klux Klan Act, which formed §2 of the Civil Rights Act of 1871. As its name implies, the Ku Klux Klan Act was designed to combat the Klan and other mobs that attempted to frighten or harass Black people and keep them from exercising or enjoying equal civil rights. It created criminal and civil liability "where two or more persons conspire or go in disguise on a highway or on the premises of another for the purpose of depriving any person or class of persons of the equal protection of the laws or of equal privileges and immunities under the laws." In *Harris*, the Court overturned criminal convictions against members of the lynching party on the ground that Congress had no power to reach private conspiracies under §5 of the Fourteenth Amendment. The Klan Act would have seemed to be an excellent candidate for a state neglect theory—in fact, it was designed to remedy state neglect to punish lynching. Nevertheless, the *Harris* Court argued that the Klan Act was defective because it did not specify that the conspiracy was based on a racial motive. This ungenerous reading of the statute seriously undermined the state neglect theory, because even if there was reason to believe that states were turning a blind eye to racially motivated conspiracies, there was no reason to believe that states were not enforcing their criminal laws generally.

Harris only struck down the criminal provisions of the Klan Act. The provisions creating a civil cause of action for private conspiracies—now codified as 42 U.S.C. §1985(3)—were identical in all other respects. They were upheld by the Court in Griffin v. Breckenridge, 403 U.S. 88, 102, 104-107 (1971). Justice Stewart's opinion distinguished *Harris* in two ways. First, it argued that "[t]he language requiring intent to deprive of equal protection, or equal privileges and immunities, means that there must be some racial, or perhaps otherwise class-based, invidiously discriminatory animus behind the conspirators' action." Second, it argued that Congress's authority for the Ku Klux Klan Act stemmed from its powers under §2 of the Thirteenth Amendment as well as its power to protect the federally guaranteed right to travel. The Thirteenth Amendment, unlike parts of the Fourteenth, has no state action requirement.

In Ex parte Yarbrough, 110 U.S. 651 (1884), the Supreme Court upheld Congress's right to reach purely private conspiracies to interfere with the right to vote in federal elections. Justice Miller distinguished *Harris* and other cases construing Congress's §5 powers: "It is quite a different matter when Congress undertakes to protect the citizen in the exercise of rights conferred by the Constitution of the United States essential to the healthy organization of the government itself." Miller's argument was structural: If Congress could not protect citizens from private violence and corruption in exercising their right to vote, the integrity of the government would be threatened. Justice Miller did not identify the specific source of congressional power: He argued that it "is a waste of time to seek for specific sources of the power to pass these laws."

4. *"Running the slavery argument into the ground."* Justice Bradley concedes that Congress has the power to remedy the "badges and incidents of slavery," which may be broader than the practice of slavery itself. This point is still good law today. See Jones v. Alfred H. Mayer Co., 392 U.S. 409 (1968). But Bradley believes that treating discrimination in public accommodations as a relic of slavery would be a *reductio ad absurdum*, because even free Black people were discriminated against before the Civil War.

In private correspondence, Bradley explained that his real concern was enforced social equality between the races: Not only would integrated facilities be "running the slavery argument into the ground," but such a requirement would also impose "slavery" on white people. "Surely," Bradley wrote, "Congress cannot guaranty to the colored people admission to every place of gathering and amusement. To deprive white people of the right of choosing their own company would be to introduce another kind of slavery." The Civil Rights Act of 1866 "has already guarantied to the blacks the right of buying, selling and holding property, and of equal protection of the laws. Are not these the essentials of freedom? Surely a white lady cannot be enforced by Congressional enactment to admit colored persons to her ball or assembly or dinner party." To be sure, "[t]he [Thirteenth A]mendment declares that slavery and involuntary servitude shall be abolished, and that Congress may enforce the enfranchisement of the slaves. Granted: but does freedom of the blacks require the slavery of the whites? [A]nd enforced fellowship would be that."[87]

5. *What are the badges and incidents of slavery?* Construing §2 of the Thirteenth Amendment requires us to confront what precisely constitute the evils of chattel slavery and what would be its "badges and incidents." Does "slavery" consist only in one human being formally possessing the legal right to own another? Or does it apply more broadly to (a) a system of racial oppression—consider the example of the Black Codes; (b) systematic oppression of other groups like Latinos, Asian Americans, religious minorities, and white women, who were never subjected to "officially recognized" forms of chattel slavery; (c) extremely coercive and unfair labor conditions like those experienced in sweatshops or by oppressed agricultural workers; or (d) severe abuses of power or position by private parties, such as child abuse or domestic violence?

One might also distinguish, as the Civil Rights Cases did, between the forms of "slavery" that courts may directly hold illegal under §1 of the Thirteenth Amendment and Congress's power to define and reach a broader class of "badges or incidents of slavery" under §2 of the Thirteenth Amendment. What reasons might there be to give Congress wider latitude to define and punish slavery (or the badges and incidents of slavery) than the courts? What limiting principle would you impose on Congress's powers?

There are significant problems, in fact, in defining the terms "slavery" and "involuntary servitude" for purposes of the Constitution, see the discussion notes to Section III.E, infra, Freedom of Contract and the Problem of "Involuntary Servitude," pp. 505-510. See also Jack M. Balkin and Sanford Levinson, The Dangerous Thirteenth Amendment, 112 Colum. L. Rev. 1459 (2012) (explaining that at the time of the American Revolution the concept of "slavery" was far more capacious than chattel slavery and included not only lack of political representation but subordination to the arbitrary will of another). The concept of slavery is "dangerous" in that the broader the constitutional conception of slavery, the more areas of social life might be called into question—including not only politics and the market, but also power relationships within the family. Put another way, if the language of the Thirteenth Amendment had been interpreted broadly like the language of the Fourteenth Amendment, its reach might be far greater today.

6. *The Citizenship Clause.* In his dissent, Justice Harlan argues that the Civil Rights Act is justified as a means of preventing race discrimination under the

---

87. 7 Charles Fairman, The History of the Supreme Court of the United States: Reconstruction and Reunion, 1864-1888, pt. 2, at 564 (1987).

Thirteenth Amendment, and that public licensees and public accommodations can be treated as state actors for purposes of congressional enforcement under §5. Harlan also argues, however, that Congress has independent authority to enforce the Citizenship Clause. What kinds of legislation might Congress pass to secure equal rights of citizenship? What are the possible limits of this power? See Jack M. Balkin, The Reconstruction Power, 85 N.Y.U. L. Rev. 1801 (2010).

E. Establishment of the "Separate but Equal" Doctrine

Strauder contains language that, taken literally, promises full equality between the races. Yet Justice Strong's opinion also contains uncomfortable references to Blacks' "abject and ignorant" condition, which, he suggests, has left them "unfitted to command the respect of those who had superior intelligence." These remarks reflected widespread assumptions among whites about the inferiority of Black people. Although the Court did not retreat from the specific holding in *Strauder*, many of its subsequent decisions appear more responsive to this assumption of Black inferiority than to the goal of creating a new and more inclusive political community committed to overcoming racial inequality.

Plessy v. Ferguson

163 U.S. 537 (1896)

[A Louisiana statute required railroads carrying passengers within the state to "provide equal but separate accommodations for the white and colored races" and made it a misdemeanor for a passenger to insist on "going into a coach or compartment to which by race he does not belong." The statute gave "officers of . . . passenger trains" the power and the legal obligation "to assign each passenger to the coach or compartment used for the race to which such passenger belongs."

Railroad officers who "insist[ed] on assigning a passenger to a coach or compartment other than the one set aside for the race to which said passenger belongs" were subject to fines and imprisonment. If a passenger refused assignment to any coach or compartment, "said officer shall have power to refuse to carry such passenger on his train, and for such refusal neither he nor the railway company which he represents shall be liable for damages in any of the courts of this State." Finally, the act contained a proviso that exempted racial assignment to "nurses attending children of the other race."

Homer Plessy was an "octoroon," i.e., a person of mixed race "seven-eighths Caucasian and one-eighth African blood." He appeared to be white; "the mixture of colored blood was not discernible in him." Plessy attempted to sit in a coach reserved for whites and was forcibly ejected and imprisoned. The information charging Plessy with violating the statute did not mention whether he was Black or white, and in his own defense "the said Plessy declined and refused, either by pleading or otherwise, to admit that he was in any sense or in any proportion a colored man." After hearing Plessy's challenge to the constitutionality of Louisiana's separate accommodations law, the Supreme Court held that the statute did not violate either the Thirteenth or the Fourteenth Amendments.]

BROWN, J. . . .

The constitutionality of this act is attacked upon the ground that it conflicts both with the Thirteenth Amendment of the Constitution, abolishing slavery, and the Fourteenth Amendment, which prohibits certain restrictive legislation on the part of the States.

That it does not conflict with the Thirteenth Amendment . . . is too clear for argument. Slavery implies involuntary servitude—a state of bondage; the ownership of mankind as a chattel, or at least the control of the labor and services of one man for the benefit of another, and the absence of a legal right to the disposal of his own person, property and services. . . . A statute which implies merely a legal distinction between the white and colored races—a distinction which is founded in the color of the two races, and which must always exist so long as white men are distinguished from the other race by color—has no tendency to destroy the legal equality of the two races, or reestablish a state of involuntary servitude. . . .

The object of the [Fourteenth] [A]mendment was undoubtedly to enforce the absolute equality of the two races before the law, but in the nature of things it could not have been intended to abolish distinctions based upon color, or to enforce social, as distinguished from political equality, or a commingling of the two races upon terms unsatisfactory to either. Laws permitting, and even requiring, their separation in places where they are liable to be brought into contact do not necessarily imply the inferiority of either race to the other, and have been generally, if not universally, recognized as within the competency of the state legislatures in the exercise of their police power. The most common instance of this is connected with the establishment of separate schools for white and colored children, which has been held to be a valid exercise of the legislative power even by courts of States where the political rights of the colored race have been longest and most earnestly enforced. . . . [The Court here cites decisions in states including Massachusetts, New York, Ohio, and California.]

Laws forbidding the intermarriage of the two races may be said in a technical sense to interfere with the freedom of contract, and yet have been universally recognized as within the police power of the State.

The distinction between laws interfering with the political equality of the negro and those requiring the separation of the two races in schools, theatres and railway carriages has been frequently drawn by this court. Thus in Strauder v. West Virginia, 100 U.S. 303, it was held that a law of West Virginia limiting to white male persons, 21 years of age and citizens of the State, the right to sit upon juries, was a discrimination which implied a legal inferiority in civil society, which lessened the security of the right of the colored race, and was a step toward reducing them to a condition of servility. . . .

While we think the enforced separation of the races, as applied to the internal commerce of the State, neither abridges the privileges or immunities of the colored man, deprives him of his property without due process of law, nor denies him the equal protection of the laws, within the meaning of the Fourteenth Amendment, we are not prepared to say that the conductor, in assigning passengers to the coaches according to their race, does not act at his peril, or that the provision of the second section of the act, that denies to the passenger compensation in damages for a refusal to receive him into the coach in which he properly belongs, is a valid exercise of the legislative power. Indeed, we understand it to be conceded by the

State's attorney, that such part of the act as exempts from liability the railway company and its officers is unconstitutional. The power to assign to a particular coach obviously implies the power to determine to which race the passenger belongs, as well as the power to determine who, under the laws of the particular State, is to be deemed a white, and who a colored person. This question, though indicated in the brief of the plaintiff in error, does not properly arise upon the record in this case, since the only issue made is as to the unconstitutionality of the act, so far as it requires the railway to provide separate accommodations, and the conductor to assign passengers according to their race.

It is claimed by the plaintiff in error that, in any mixed community, the reputation of belonging to the dominant race, in this instance the white race, is property, in the same sense that a right of action, or of inheritance, is property. Conceding this to be so, for the purposes of this case, we are unable to see how this statute deprives him of, or in any way affects his right to, such property. If he be a white man and assigned to a colored coach, he may have his action for damages against the company for being deprived of his so called property. Upon the other hand, if he be a colored man and be so assigned, he has been deprived of no property, since he is not lawfully entitled to the reputation of being a white man.

In this connection, it is also suggested by the learned counsel for the plaintiff in error that the same argument that will justify the state legislature in requiring railways to provide separate accommodations for the two races will also authorize them to require separate cars to be provided for people whose hair is of a certain color, or who are aliens, or who belong to certain nationalities, or to enact laws requiring colored people to walk upon one side of the street, and white people upon the other, or requiring white men's houses to be painted white, and colored men's black, or their vehicles or business signs to be of different colors, upon the theory that one side of the street is as good as the other, or that a house or vehicle of one color is as good as one of another color. The reply to all this is that every exercise of the police power must be reasonable, and extend only to such laws as are enacted in good faith for the promotion for the public good, and not for the annoyance or oppression of a particular class. Thus in Yick Wo v. Hopkins, 118 U.S. 356, it was held by this court that a municipal ordinance of the city of San Francisco [that gave municipal authorities arbitrary discretion to permit or refuse to permit the operation of] public laundries . . . without regard to the competency of the persons applying, or the propriety of the places selected for the carrying on the business [was] a covert attempt on the part of the municipality to make an arbitrary and unjust discrimination against the Chinese race.

So far, then, as a conflict with the Fourteenth Amendment is concerned, the case reduces itself to the question whether the statute of Louisiana is a reasonable regulation, and with respect to this there must necessarily be a large discretion on the part of the legislature. In determining the question of reasonableness it is at liberty to act with reference to the established usages, customs and traditions of the people, and with a view to the promotion of their comfort, and the preservation of the public peace and good order. Gauged by this standard, we cannot say that a law which authorizes or even requires the separation of the two races in public conveyances is unreasonable, or . . . obnoxious to the Fourteenth Amendment. . . .

We consider the underlying fallacy of the plaintiff's argument to consist in the assumption that the enforced separation of the two races stamps the colored race with a badge of inferiority. If this be so, it is not by reason of anything found in the act, but solely because the colored race chooses to put that construction upon it. The argument necessarily assumes that if, as has been more than once the case, and is not unlikely to be so again, the colored race should become the dominant power in the state legislature, and should enact a law in precisely similar terms, it would thereby relegate the white race to an inferior position. We imagine that the white race, at least, would not acquiesce in this assumption. The argument also assumes that social prejudices may be overcome by legislation, and that equal rights cannot be secured to the negro except by an enforced commingling of the two races. We cannot accept this proposition. If the two races are to meet upon terms of social equality, it must be the result of natural affinities, a mutual appreciation of each other's merits and a voluntary consent of individuals. As was said by the Court of Appeals of New York in People v. Gallagher, 93 N.Y. 438, 448, "this end can neither be accomplished nor promoted by laws which conflict with the general sentiment of the community upon whom they are designed to operate. When the government, therefore, has secured to each of its citizens equal rights before the law and equal opportunities for improvement and progress, it has accomplished the end for which it was organized and performed all of the functions respecting social advantages with which it is endowed." Legislation is powerless to eradicate racial instincts or to abolish distinctions based upon physical differences, and the attempt to do so can only result in accentuating the difficulties of the present situation. If the civil and political rights of both races be equal one cannot be inferior to the other civilly or politically. If one race be inferior to the other socially, the Constitution of the United States cannot put them upon the same plane.

It is true that the question of the proportion of colored blood necessary to constitute a colored person, as distinguished from a white person, is one upon which there is a difference of opinion in the different States, some holding that any visible admixture of black blood stamps the person as belonging to the colored race (State v. Chavers, 5 Jones, [N.C.] 1, p. 11); others that it depends upon the preponderance of blood (Gray v. State, 4 Ohio, 354; Monroe v. Collins, 17 Ohio St. 665); and still others that the predominance of white blood must only be in the proportion of three fourths. (People v. Dean, 14 Michigan, 406; Jones v. Commonwealth, 80 Virginia, 538.) But these are questions to be determined under the laws of each State and are not properly put in issue in this case. Under the allegations of his petition it may undoubtedly become a question of importance whether, under the laws of Louisiana, the petitioner belongs to the white or colored race.

HARLAN J., dissenting. . . .

By the Louisiana statute . . . [t]he managers of the railroad are not allowed to exercise any discretion in the premises, but are required to assign each passenger to some coach or compartment set apart for the exclusive use of his race. . . . Only "nurses attending children of the other race" are excepted from the operation of the statute. No exception is made of colored attendants travelling with adults. A white man is not permitted to have his colored servant with him in the same coach, even if his condition of health requires the constant, personal assistance of such servant. If a colored maid insists upon riding in the same coach with a white woman whom she has been employed to serve, and who may need her personal attention while travelling, she is subject to be fined or imprisoned for such an exhibition of zeal in the discharge of duty.

[The] State regulates the use of a public highway by citizens of the United States solely upon the basis of race. . . .

In respect of civil rights, common to all citizens, the Constitution of the United States does not, I think, permit any public authority to know the race of those entitled to be protected in the enjoyment of such rights. Every true man has pride of race, and under appropriate circumstances when the rights of others, his equals before the law, are not to be affected, it is his privilege to express such pride and to take such action based upon it as to him seems proper. But I deny that any legislative body or judicial tribunal may have regard to the race of citizens when the civil rights of those citizens are involved. Indeed, such legislation, as that here in question, is inconsistent not only with that equality of rights which pertains to citizenship, National and State, but with the personal liberty enjoyed by every one within the United States.

The Thirteenth Amendment . . . not only struck down the institution of slavery as previously existing in the United States, but it prevents the imposition of any burdens or disabilities that constitute badges of slavery or servitude. It decreed universal civil freedom in this country. This court has so adjudged. [The Thirteenth and Fourteenth Amendments,] if enforced according to their true intent and meaning, will protect all the civil rights that pertain to freedom and citizenship. [The Fifteenth Amendment guaranteed] that no citizen should be denied, on account of his race, the privilege of participating in the political control of his country. . . . These notable additions to the fundamental law were welcomed by the friends of liberty throughout the world. They removed the race line from our governmental systems. At the present term, referring to the previous adjudications [interpreting these amendments], this court declared that "underlying all of those decisions is the principle that the Constitution of the United States, in its present form, forbids, so far as civil and political rights are concerned, discrimination by the General Government or the States against any citizen because of his race. All citizens are equal before the law." Gibson v. Mississippi, 162 U.S. 565.

It was said in argument that the statute of Louisiana does not discriminate against either race, but prescribes a rule applicable alike to white and colored citizens. But this argument does not meet the difficulty. Every one knows that the statute in question had its origin in the purpose, not so much to exclude white persons from railroad cars occupied by blacks, as to exclude colored people from coaches occupied by or assigned to white persons. Railroad corporations of Louisiana did not make discrimination among whites in the matter of accommodation for travellers. The thing to accomplish was, under the guise of giving equal accommodation for whites and blacks, to compel the latter to keep to themselves while travelling in railroad passenger coaches. No one would be so wanting in candor as to assert the contrary. The fundamental objection, therefore, to the statute is that it interferes with the personal freedom of citizens. . . . If a white man and a black man choose to occupy the same public conveyance on a public highway, it is their right to do so, and no government, proceeding alone on grounds of race, can prevent it without infringing the personal liberty of each.

. . . If a State can prescribe, as a rule of civil conduct, that whites and blacks shall not travel as passengers in the same railroad coach, why may it not so regulate the use of the streets of its cities and towns as to compel white citizens to keep on one side of a street and black citizens to keep on the other? Why may it not, upon like grounds, punish whites and blacks who ride together in street cars or in open vehicles on a public road or street? Why may it not require sheriffs to assign whites to one side of a court-room and blacks to the other? And why may it not also prohibit the commingling of the two races in the galleries of legislative halls or in public assemblages convened for the considerations of the political questions of the day? Further, if this statute of Louisiana is consistent with the personal liberty of citizens, why may not the State require the separation in railroad coaches of native and naturalized citizens of the United States, or of Protestants and Roman Catholics?

The answer given at the argument to these questions was that regulations of the kind they suggest would be unreasonable, and could not, therefore, stand before the law. Is it meant that the determination of questions of legislative power depends upon the inquiry whether the statute whose validity is questioned is, in the judgment of the courts, a reasonable one, taking all the circumstances into consideration? A statute may be unreasonable merely because a sound public policy forbade its enactment. But I do not understand that the courts have anything to do with the policy or expediency of legislation. . . .

The white race deems itself to be the dominant race in this country. And so it is, in prestige, in achievements, in education, in wealth and in power. So, I doubt not, it will continue to be for all time, if it remains true to its great heritage and holds fast to the principles of constitutional liberty. But in view of the Constitution, in the eye of the law, there is in this country no superior, dominant, ruling class of citizens. There is no caste here. Our Constitution is color-blind, and neither knows nor tolerates classes among citizens. In respect of civil rights, all citizens are equal before the law. The humblest is the peer of the most powerful. The law regards man as man, and takes no account of his surroundings or of his color when his civil rights as guaranteed by the supreme law of the land are involved.

In my opinion, the judgment this day rendered will, in time, prove to be quite as pernicious as the decision made by this tribunal in the *Dred Scott* case. It was adjudged in that case that the descendants of Africans who were imported into this country and sold as slaves were not included nor intended to be included under the word "citizens" in the Constitution, and could not claim any of the rights and privileges which that instrument provided for and secured to citizens of the United States; that at the time of the adoption of the Constitution they were "considered as a subordinate and inferior class of beings, who had been subjugated by the dominant race, and, whether emancipated or not, yet remained subject to their authority, and had no rights or privileges but such as those who held the power and the government might choose to grant them." 19 How. 393, 404. The recent amendments of the Constitution, it was supposed, had eradicated these principles from our institutions. But it seems that we have yet, in some of the States, a dominant race—a superior class of citizens, which assumes to regulate the enjoyment of civil rights, common to all citizens, upon the basis of race. The present decision, it may well be apprehended, will not only stimulate aggressions, more or less brutal and irritating, upon the admitted rights of colored citizens, but will encourage the belief that it is possible, by means of state enactments, to defeat the beneficent purposes which the people of the United States had in view when they adopted the recent amendments of the Constitution, by one of which the blacks of this country were made citizens of the United States and of the States in which they respectively reside, and whose privileges and immunities, as citizens, the States are forbidden to abridge. Sixty millions of whites are in no danger from the presence here of eight millions of blacks. The destinies of the two races, in this country, are indissolubly linked together, and the interests of both require that the common government of all shall not permit the seeds of race hate to be planted under the sanction of law. What can more certainly arouse race hate, what can more certainly create and perpetuate a feeling of distrust between these races, than state enactments, which, in fact, proceed on the ground that colored citizens are so inferior and degraded that they cannot be allowed to sit in public coaches occupied by white citizens? That, as all will admit, is the real meaning of such legislation as was enacted in Louisiana.

The sure guarantee of the peace and security of each race is the clear, distinct, unconditional recognition by our governments, National and State, of every right that inheres in civil freedom, and of the equality before the law of all citizens of the United States without regard to race. State enactments, regulating the enjoyment of civil rights, upon the basis of race, and cunningly devised to defeat legitimate results of the war, under the pretence of recognizing equality of rights, can have no other result than to render permanent peace impossible, and to keep alive a conflict of races, the continuance of which must do harm to all concerned. This question is not met by the suggestion that social equality cannot exist between the white and black races in this country. That argument, if it can be properly regarded as one, is scarcely worthy of consideration; for social equality no more exists between two races when travelling in a passenger coach or a public highway than when members of the same races sit by each other in a street car or in the jury box, or stand or sit with each other in a political assembly, or when they use in common the streets of a city or town, or when they are in the same room for the purpose of having their names placed on the registry of voters, or when they approach the ballot-box in order to exercise the high privilege of voting.

There is a race so different from our own that we do not permit those belonging to it to become citizens of the United States. Persons belonging to it are, with few exceptions, absolutely excluded from our country. I allude to the Chinese race. But by the statute in question, a Chinaman can ride in the same passenger coach with white citizens of the United States, while citizens of the black race in Louisiana, many of whom, perhaps, risked their lives for the preservation of the Union, who are entitled, by law, to participate in the political control of the State and nation, who are not excluded, by law or by reason of their race, from public stations of any kind, and who have all the legal rights that belong to white citizens, are yet declared to be criminals, liable to imprisonment, if they ride in a public coach occupied by citizens of the white race. It is scarcely just to say that a colored citizen should not object to occupying a public coach assigned to his own race. He does not object, nor, perhaps, would he object to separate coaches for his race, if his rights under the law were recognized. But he objects, and ought never to cease objecting to the proposition, that citizens of the white and black races can be adjudged criminals because they sit, or claim the right to sit, in the same public coach on a public highway.

The arbitrary separation of citizens, on the basis of race, while they are on a public highway, is a badge of servitude wholly inconsistent with the civil freedom and the equality before the law established by the Constitution. It cannot be justified upon any legal grounds.

If evils will result from the commingling of the two races upon public highways established for the benefit of all, they will be infinitely less than those that will surely come from state legislation regulating the enjoyment of civil rights upon the basis of race. We boast of the freedom enjoyed by our people above all other peoples. But it is difficult to reconcile that boast with a state of the law which, practically, puts the brand of servitude and degradation upon a large class of our fellow-citizens, our equals before the law. The thin disguise of "equal" accommodations for passengers in railroad coaches will not mislead any one, nor atone for the wrong this day done.

DISCUSSION

1. *Equality before the law.* In Gibson v. Mississippi, 162 U.S. 565 (1896), decided the same year as *Plessy*, the Court, in a unanimous opinion by Justice Harlan, endorsed "the principle that the constitution of the United States, in its present form, forbids, so far as civil and political rights are concerned, discrimination by the general government, or by the states, against any citizen because of his race. All citizens are equal before the law." Left out of this formula was "social" equality, and as Justice Brown indicates in *Plessy*, the Fourteenth Amendment was not designed to guarantee "social" equality. On the distinction between social and other forms of equality, Professor Tushnet in The Politics of Equality in Constitutional Law, 74 J. Am. Hist. 884 (1987), writes:

> Equality in political and civil rights did not mean, as a legal matter, that blacks could insist on equal treatment in the ordinary course of social life. Whites could refuse to have social contacts with blacks and could exclude blacks from their homes. More significant, the rejection of [social] equality [as a command of the Fourteenth Amendment] was widely believed to imply that segregated education was permissible, as were laws prohibiting racial intermarriage.

2. *Social equality and Pace v. Alabama.* In Pace v. Alabama, 106 U.S. 583 (1883), the Court upheld Alabama's prohibition of interracial marriage and enhanced punishment for interracial adultery or fornication. Justice Field wrote a short, almost perfunctory, opinion for a unanimous Court (which included Justice Harlan) holding that the law was not discriminatory:

> [T]he offense against which [the Alabama law] is aimed cannot be committed without involving the persons of both races in the same punishment. Whatever discrimination is made in the punishment prescribed in the two sections is directed against the offense designated and not against the person of any particular color or race. The punishment of each offending person, whether white or black, is the same.

Given *Pace*, what is surprising about the result in *Plessy*? Justice Harlan's positions in *Pace* and *Plessy* are perhaps best explained by the fact that he believed that questions of marriage and sexual conduct were issues of social equality, which the

Fourteenth Amendment did not guarantee. By contrast, he believed that access to public accommodations—like railroads—raised questions of civil equality. The majority disagreed, treating both issues as questions of social equality. This explanation also helps clarify Harlan's differences with his colleagues in the Civil Rights Cases, which concerned Congress's power to require nondiscrimination in public accommodations.

Harlan's positions in these three cases suggest the inherent tensions in the idea that the Constitution did not guarantee "social equality." That idea, if it made sense at all, was premised on the twin notions of respect for individual privacy and racial symmetry. First, individuals in civil society had the right to make private choices about whom they would associate with, and the state should not interfere with those choices. Second, as long as Blacks and whites were treated symmetrically—so that both races were equally restricted—there was no violation of civil equality.

Plessy shows that these justifications made little sense in the context of Jim Crow laws. Louisiana had not protected individual decisional privacy; rather it had used laws to keep whites and Blacks who might have wanted to associate with each other from doing so. Although the Court argues against the "enforced commingling of the two races," in fact Louisiana had used law to *prevent* certain kinds of private association. Second, the idea of symmetry rang hollow when it was widely understood that the point of separation was not symmetry but the preservation of white supremacy and white sensibilities.

3. Plessy, Pace, *and the original understanding of the Fourteenth Amendment.* As we saw in the discussion of the ratification of the Fourteenth Amendment, Reconstruction Republicans publicly represented that the 1866 Civil Rights Act would not require either that states integrate their public schools or that states permit interracial marriage. They made no public statements suggesting that the Fourteenth Amendment would have a different effect. This policy was politically prudent. Indeed, it is extremely likely that if the public believed that the proposed amendment committed the nation either to racial integration or to the legality of interracial marriage, the amendment could not have gained a two-thirds vote in both houses of Congress or ratification in three-quarters of the state legislatures.

Nevertheless, as we discuss in more detail in Chapter 7 in connection with Brown v. Board of Education, although there was no consensus that the amendment required integration of public facilities, there was also no consensus that it did not. Some congressional Republicans who had supported the amendment believed that it did require states to maintain integrated public schools. See Michael W. McConnell, Originalism and the Desegregation Decisions, 81 Va. L. Rev. 947 (1995). Indeed, some Republicans went further; they argued that laws banning interracial marriage were unconstitutional under the Fourteenth Amendment, preempted under the Civil Rights Act of 1866, or both. Shortly after the ratification of the Fourteenth Amendment, a few state courts staffed by Republican judges held as much, and many states legislatures controlled by Republicans repealed their bans on interracial marriage during the same period. However, once white Democrats regained control of Southern legislatures and judiciaries, state judges quickly reversed course, upholding laws prohibiting interracial marriage. See, e.g., Burns v. State, 48 Ala. 195 (1872) (stating that Alabama's ban on interracial marriage was inconsistent with the 1866 Civil Rights Act), *overruled by* Green v. State, 58

Ala. 190 (1877) (holding that Alabama's law violated neither the Civil Rights Act or the Fourteenth Amendment: "The amendments to the Constitution were evidently designed to secure to citizens, without distinction of race, rights of a civil or political kind only—not such as are merely social, much less those of a purely domestic nature."). See generally David R. Upham, Interracial Marriage and the Original Understanding of the Privileges or Immunities Clause, 42 Hastings Const. L. Q. 213 (2015); Peggy Pascoe, What Comes Naturally: Miscegenation Law and the Making of Race in America (2009); Peter Wallenstein, Tell The Court I Love My Wife: Race, Marriage, and Law: An American History (2002).

Perhaps the most that we can conclude from the history is that *Plessy* and *Pace* were not inconsistent with the understandings of the general public in 1868, or of the persons whose votes were necessary for ratification of the Fourteenth Amendment. Nevertheless, many of the amendment's strongest supporters had far more egalitarian interpretations. If we choose to follow the views of the latter, in what sense are we claiming to be *bound* by "the original understanding" as opposed to simply *honoring* the understandings of those people in the past that we now agree with?

4. Plessy *and the Civil Rights Cases.* It is worth noting how important the Court's earlier decisions limiting congressional power to enforce the Reconstruction Amendments turned out to be. If the Court had upheld the Civil Rights Act of 1875 in the Civil Rights Cases, and had interpreted the Act to require integrated railway cars, *Plessy* would have been a statutory preemption case, and it might well have come out the other way. Similarly, if the Court had not struck down or severely limited the Ku Klux Klan Act and other Reconstruction-era legislation in decisions like United States v. Cruikshank and United States v. Harris, federal officials would have a much broader set of tools available to prosecute lynchings and fight other elements of Jim Crow.

5. *"Physical differences" and the legal construction of racial identity.* Justice Brown argues that "[l]egislation is powerless to eradicate racial instincts or to abolish distinctions based upon physical differences." One wonders what "physical differences" Brown is referring to, since he almost certainly had never laid eyes on Plessy, who was, in the racial language of New Orleans, an "octoroon," meaning that he was one-eighth Black and seven-eighths white.[88] That was enough to make him "Black," because by Louisiana law a "single drop" of "black blood" was enough to earn the label of "blackness." Had Louisiana, for example, adopted a "quarter-blood" rule, requiring at least one Black grandparent, Plessy would have been deemed white. What was the purpose of this statute? The Court refused to inquire into the constitutionality of that definition, considering it a matter of local law. The legal construction of racial identity is still relevant today, in issues including the census, voting and employment discrimination, suspect descriptions, and affirmative action.

6. *Discrimination versus freedom of association.* The Court implicitly contrasts "discrimination" with mere "segregation" and holds that the Constitution prohibits only the former. This view was elaborated by Professor Herbert Wechsler, a distinguished constitutional scholar, in criticizing the Court's 1954 decision in Brown v. Board of Education, Chapter 7, infra:

---

88. See Charles Lofgren, The *Plessy* Case: A Legal-Historical Interpretation 54-55 (1987). Lofgren's is the standard history of this extremely fascinating and complex case.

> For me, assuming equal facilities, the question posed by state-enforced segregation is not one of discrimination at all. Its human and its constitutional dimensions lie entirely elsewhere, in the denial by the state of freedom to associate, a denial that impinges in the same way on any groups or races that may be involved. I think, and I hope not without foundation, that the Southern white also pays heavily for segregation, not only in the sense of guilt that he must carry but also in the benefits he is denied. . . .
>
> But if the freedom of association is denied by segregation, integration forces an association upon those for whom it is unpleasant or repugnant. Is this not the heart of the issue involved, a conflict in human claims of high dimension, not unlike many others that involve the highest freedoms. . . . Given a situation where the state must practically choose between denying the association to those individuals who wish it or imposing it on those who would avoid it, is there a basis in neutral principles for holding that the Constitution demands that the claims for association should prevail?[89]

How would you answer Professor Wechsler's question?

7. *"Reasonableness" and the police power.* The Court states that "every exercise of the police power must be reasonable, and extend only to such laws as are enacted in good faith for the promotion for the public good, and not for the annoyance or oppression of a particular class." The Fourteenth Amendment prohibits class legislation, but the majority did not see Louisiana's law as class legislation, because it reasonably served a valid public purpose and therefore was within the state's police power. What purpose was that?

Presumably, if a race-based law were enacted with an improper motive or were simply a pretext for "annoyance and oppression," the Court would strike it down. Note the similarity to the "pretext" qualification in ¶42 of *McCulloch*, in Chapter 1, supra. Would you trust the Supreme Court in 1896 to determine accurately when racial classifications were "reasonable" and served a public purpose and when they involved the "annoyance and oppression of a particular class"? What about today?

8. *Colorblindness and social inequality.* Justice Harlan's dissent is famous for its statement that "[o]ur Constitution is colorblind." But for Harlan, colorblindness clearly did not mean social equality, as exemplified by his joining the unanimous decision in Pace v. Alabama. Note that Harlan insisted that whites and Blacks were not socially equal even if they sat in the same railway carriage. Thus Harlan suggested that whites could still be socially superior to Black people even if they were equal before the law. What is the source of social inequality for Harlan—private decisionmaking, class position, social meanings, or some combination of the three?

---

89. Herbert Wechsler, Toward Neutral Principles of Constitutional Law, 73 Harv. L. Rev. 1, 34 (1959). Wechsler's famous use of the term "neutral principles" to describe the goals of constitutional adjudication has become the source of an endless debate as to whether it is possible to interpret the Constitution without enforcing politically contestable substantive values.

What did Harlan mean when he suggested that "the white race" would continue to be "the superior race for all time"? Note that in the same paragraph Harlan also insists that "there is no caste" in the United States. What does Harlan mean by "caste," then? Does the law have to directly recognize or classify on the basis of race in order to be complicit in perpetuating a caste system?

9. *Colorblindness and the Chinese.* Justice Harlan has won justified plaudits for his refusal to join his colleagues in legitimating discrimination against African Americans. Consider, however, his comments about the Chinese, "a race so different from our own that we do not permit those belonging to it to become citizens of the United States." Two years after *Plessy*, Justice Harlan joined Chief Justice Fuller in dissenting from the majority in United States v. Wong Kim Ark, 169 U.S. 649 (1898), which held that persons of Chinese descent born in the United States were birthright citizens under the Fourteenth Amendment. Fuller and Harlan vigorously objected, denouncing "the presence within our territory of large numbers of Chinese laborers, of a distinct race and religion, remaining strangers in the land, residing apart by themselves, tenaciously adhering to the customs and usage of their own country, unfamiliar with our institutions and religion, and apparently incapable of assimilating with our people." See generally Gabriel J. Chin, The *Plessy* Myth: Justice Harlan and the Chinese Cases, 82 Iowa L. Rev. 151 (1996). For more extended treatment of anti-Chinese sentiment and resultant legislation, see the Chinese Exclusion Case, infra, pp. 464-470.

You may also recall Taney's reminder in *Dred Scott* that naturalization was limited to "white persons" by the Naturalization Act of 1795; "aliens of African nativity and . . . persons of African descent" were made eligible for citizenship in 1870, but persons of Asian origin remained ineligible to become citizens until 1952. Indeed, the Supreme Court in two cases during the 1920s construed the meaning of "white" as not including one of Japanese descent or of a "high-caste Hindu of full Indian blood." See Takao Ozawa v. United States, 260 U.S. 178 (1922); United States v. Bhagat Singh Thind, 261 U.S. 204 (1923). The Court, however, scarcely came up with a coherent theory of how one determined who was "white" and, therefore, eligible for membership in the American political community. Although *Ozawa* included the passage that "the words 'white persons' are synonymous with the words 'a person of the Caucasian race,'" the Court rejected Thind's claim of eligibility, which had prevailed in the courts below, because of his presentation of evidence that he was the member of a "Caucasian race." Justice Sutherland responded for a unanimous Court:

> The words of familiar speech, which were used by the original framers of the law, were intended to include only the type of man whom they knew as white. The immigration of that day was almost exclusively from the British Isles and Northwestern Europe, whence they and their forebears had come. When they extended the privilege of American citizenship to "any alien being a free white person" it was these immigrants—bone of their bone and flesh of their flesh—and their kind whom they must have had affirmatively in mind. The succeeding years brought immigrants from Eastern, Southern and Middle Europe, among them the Slavs and the dark-eyed, swarthy people of Alpine and Mediterranean stock, and these were received as unquestionably akin to those already here and readily

> amalgamated with them. It was the descendants of these, and other immigrants of like origin, who constituted the white population of the country when [the relevant legislation] was adopted.[90]

10. *"A badge of inferiority."* The Court asserts that nothing intrinsic to the segregation law "stamps the colored race with a badge of inferiority." One possibility is that the distinction between segregation and discrimination rests in part on the social meaning of the separation. Compare, for example, the contemporary social meaning of restrooms segregated by race and by gender. The modern Court would immediately strike down the former; the latter would certainly be upheld (even, one strongly suspects, had the ERA been ratified). What accounts for the distinction?

What does the Court mean when it says "[i]f this be so, it is not by reason of anything found in the act, but solely because the colored race chooses to put that construction upon it"? Suppose that Blacks and whites disagree about the social meaning of racial separation. Whose meaning prevails for purposes of constitutional interpretation? The Court argues that if Black people were the dominant power in the Louisiana legislature (as they had been during Reconstruction), and passed an identical law, whites would not consider themselves as "relegate[d] . . . to an inferior position." Is this true? The Court seems to suggest that whites would still regard themselves as the superior race. Which way should this cut?

The law in *Plessy* was not an isolated enactment; it was part of what became a pervasive scheme of Jim Crow laws, in every Southern and border state, "that extended to churches and schools, to housing and jobs, to eating and drinking . . . to virtually all forms of public transportation, to sports and recreations, to hospitals, orphanages, prisons, and asylums, and ultimately to funeral homes, morgues, and cemeteries."[91] Many of these statutes were passed after 1896. One effect of the *Plessy* decision was to signal to the South that the federal courts would not police Jim Crow policies. (Once again, the Court's earlier decisions in *Cruikshank*, *Harris*, and the Civil Rights Cases proved fateful.)

It is true that the *Plessy* Court conveniently ignored the cultural meaning of state-imposed segregation. But was the problem *simply* one of social meaning, or rather was it a combination of cultural, economic, and political power backed up by state force and private violence?

Suppose you believe that the *Plessy* Court failed to understand the realities of racial segregation, or, more likely, willfully turned a blind eye to them, and thereby made a bad situation worse by blessing Jim Crow policies. One justification for judicial review is that courts should protect the political process, and ensure that minorities and losers in the democratic process are treated fairly. If so, does *Plessy* suggest that courts will not be particularly good at this task, because they will tend to reflect the prejudices and blindnesses of the political majorities that appoint them?

---

90. See generally Ian F. Haney Lopez, White by Law: The Legal Construction of Race (1996). And, as to the assignment of "swarthy" groups to the category of whites, see Matthew Frye Jacobson, Whiteness of a Different Color: European Immigrants and the Alchemy of Race (1998). For further discussion of the complexities of defining racial (and gender) identity, see Chapters 7 and 8, infra.

91. Woodward, The Strange Career of Jim Crow 8 (3rd rev. ed. 1974).

Consider in this context the following comments by Professor Charles Black, who had grown up in Austin, Texas, before going on to teach at the Yale Law School. He had, among other things, worked closely with the NAACP Legal Defense Fund on the litigation in Brown v. Board of Education, Chapter 7 infra, which held "separate but equal" schooling unconstitutional.

Charles Black, the Lawfulness of the Segregation Decisions

69 Yale L.J. 421, 424-427 (1960)

. . . I was raised in the south, in a Texas city where the pattern of segregation was firmly fixed. I am sure it never occurred to anyone, white or colored, to question its meaning. The fiction of "equality" is just about on a level with the fiction of "finding" in the action of trover. I think few candid southerners deny this. Northern people may be misled by the entirely sincere protestations of many southerners that segregation is "better" for the Negroes, is not intended to hurt them. But I think a little probing would demonstrate that what is meant is that it is better for the Negroes to accept a position of inferiority, at least for the indefinite future. . . .

Segregation in the South comes down in apostolic succession from slavery and the *Dred Scott* case. The South fought to keep slavery, and lost. Then it tried the Black Codes, and lost. Then it looked around for something else and found segregation. The movement for segregation was an integral part of the movement to maintain and further "white supremacy." . . . Segregation in the South grew up and is kept going because and only because the white race has wanted it that way. . . . [T]he life of a southern community [is not one] of mutual separation of whites and Negroes, but of one in-group enjoying full normal communal life and one outgroup that is barred from this life and forced into an inferior life of its own. . . . When you are in Leeville and hear someone say "Leeville High," you know he has reference to the white high school; the Negro school will be called something else—Carver High, perhaps, or Lincoln High to our shame. . . .

Segregation is historically and contemporaneously associated in a functioning complex with practices which are indisputably and grossly discriminatory. I have in mind especially the long-continued and still largely effective exclusion of Negroes from voting. . . . [S]egregation is the pattern of law in communities where the extralegal patterns of discrimination against Negroes are the tightest, where Negroes are subjected to the strictest codes of "unwritten law" as to job opportunities, social intercourse, patterns of housing, going to the back door, being called by the first name, saying "Sir," and all the rest of the whole sorry business. . . .

"Separate but equal" facilities are almost never really equal. Sometimes this concerns small things—if the "white" men's room has mixing hot and cold taps, the "colored" men's room will likely have separate taps; it is always the back of the bus for the Negroes; "Lincoln Beach" will rarely if ever be as good as the regular beach. Sometimes it concerns the most vital matter—through the whole history of segregation, colored schools have been so disgracefully inferior to white schools. . . .

Attention is usually focused on these inequalities as things in themselves, correctible by detailed decrees. I am more interested in their very clear character as *evidence* of what segregation means to the people who impose it and to the people who are subjected to it. . . . Further arguments could be piled on top of one another, for we have here to do with the most conspicuous characteristic of a whole regional culture. It is actionable defamation in the South to call a white man a Negro. A small proportion of Negro "blood" puts one in the inferior race for segregation purposes; this is the way in which one deals with a taint, such as a carcinogen in cranberries.

The various items I have mentioned differ in weight; not every one would suffice in itself to establish the character of segregation. Taken together they are of irrefragable strength. The society that has just lost the Negro as a slave, that has just lost out in an attempt to put him under quasi-servile "Codes," the society that views his blood as a contamination and his name as an insult, the society that extralegally imposes on him every humiliating mark of low caste and that until yesterday kept him in line by lynching—this society, careless of his consent, moves by law, first to exclude him from voting, and secondly to cut him off from mixing in the general public life of the community. The Court that refused to see inequality in this cutting off would be making the only kind of law that can be warranted outrageous in advance—law based on self-induced blindness, on flagrant contradiction of known fact.

I have stated all these points shortly because they are matters of common notoriety, matters not so much for judicial notice as for the background knowledge of educated men who live in the world. A court may advise itself of them as it advises itself of the facts that we are a "religious people," that the country is more industrialized than in Jefferson's day, that children are the natural objects of fathers' bounty, that criminal sanctions are commonly thought to deter, that steel is a basic commodity in our economy, that the imputation of unchastity is harmful to a woman. Such judgments, made on such a basis, are in the foundations of all law, decisional as well as statutory; it would be the most unneutral of principles, improvised ad hoc, to require that a court faced with the present problem refuse to note a plain fact about the society of the United States—the fact that the social meaning of segregation is the putting of the Negro in a position of walled-off inferiority—or the other equally plain fact that such treatment is hurtful to human beings. Southern courts, on the basis of just such a judgment, have held that the placing of a white person in a Negro railroad car is an actionable humiliation; must a court pretend not to know that the Negro's situation there is humiliating?

NOTE: THE SPIRIT OF *PLESSY* AND BLACK DISENFRANCHISEMENT

Viewed in terms of the Compromise of 1877, *Strauder* and *Plessy* are not inconsistent with one another. Central to most political compromises is the saving of face. The law struck down in *Strauder*, by its very terms, treated Black people unequally by excluding them from juries. The law upheld in *Plessy* was neutral in appearance, favoring neither Blacks nor whites. The inequality appeared only when one looked behind the words of the statute, and this—though it hardly required much scrutiny—the Court refused to do.

Many of the Court's other decisions from about 1880 to 1930 support C. Vann Woodward's suggestion that "[t]he [C]ourt, like the liberals, was engaged in a bit of reconciliation . . . achieved at the Negro's expense."[92] *Plessy* was reaffirmed in several cases,[93] and in Gong Lum v. Rice, 275 U.S. 78 (1927), it was extended to school segregation. See also Cumming v. Richmond County Bd. of Educ., 175 U.S. 528 (1899) (an opinion written by Justice Harlan, upholding the county's decision, given limited funds, to provide free public education to a high school for whites only); Berea College v. Kentucky, 211 U.S. 45 (1908) (holding that states could require segregation of private schools that were chartered as corporations by the state).

The only major exception to this line of cases involved a restriction on the sale of residential real estate:

BUCHANAN v. WARLEY, 245 U.S. 60 (1917): [In Buchanan v. Warley, a unanimous Court held invalid under the Due Process Clause a Louisville ordinance prohibiting Black persons from residing in a block in which a majority of houses were occupied by whites, and white persons from residing in a block in which a majority of the houses were occupied by Black people. *Buchanan* was a collusive suit by a white seller to compel specific performance of a contract for the purchase of a house by a Black buyer, who ostensibly defended on the ground that the ordinance made the contract illegal.]

Day, J.:

The Fourteenth Amendment and [the Civil Rights Acts of 1866 and 1870] enacted in furtherance of its purpose operate to qualify and entitle a colored man to acquire property without state legislation discriminating against him solely because of color.

[I]n [Plessy v. Ferguson] there was no attempt to deprive persons of color of transportation in the coaches of the public carrier, and the express requirements were for equal though separate accommodations for the white and colored races. . . . [C]lassification of accommodations was permitted upon the basis of equality for both races. . . . [Quoting a Supreme Court of Georgia case, the Court explained a Black person was not] "denied the right to use, control, or dispose of his property, as in this case. . . . 'The effect of the ordinance under consideration was not merely to regulate a business or the like, but was to destroy the right of the individual to acquire, enjoy, and dispose of his property. Being of this character it was void as being opposed to the due process clause of the Constitution.'"

---

92. Id. at 71. For detailed and extensive surveys of the law during this period, see Charles Mangum, The Legal Status of the Negro (1940); Edward Waite, The Negro in the Supreme Court, 30 Minn. L. Rev. 219 (1946).

93. E.g., Chesapeake & O. Ry. v. Kentucky, 179 U.S. 388 (1900); Chiles v. Chesapeake & O. Ry., 218 U.S. 71 (1910); McCabe v. Atchison, T. & S.F.R., 235 U.S. 151 (1914) (in which the Court held, however, that a state could not permit carriers to provide sleeping and dining facilities only for whites). See Hall v. DeCuir, 95 U.S. 485 (1877) (Commerce Clause); Louisville, N.O. & T. Ry. v. Mississippi, 133 U.S. 587 (1890).

That there exists a serious and difficult problem arising from a feeling of race hostility which the law is powerless to control, and to which it must give a measure of consideration, may be freely admitted. But its solution cannot be promoted by depriving citizens of their constitutional rights and privileges. . . .

It is the purpose of [laws restricting the sale of real estate], and, it is frankly avowed it will be their ultimate effect, to require by law, at least in residential districts, the compulsory separation of the races on account of color. Such action is said to be essential to the maintenance of the purity of the races, although it is to be noted in the ordinance under consideration that the employment of colored servants in white families is permitted, and nearby residences of colored persons not coming within the blocks, as defined in the ordinance, are not prohibited. The case presented does not deal with an attempt to prohibit the amalgamation of the races. The right which the ordinance annulled was the civil right of a white man to dispose of his property if he saw fit to do so to a person of color and of a colored person to make such disposition to a white person.

It is urged that this proposed segregation will promote the public peace by preventing race conflicts. Desirable as this is, and important as is the preservation of the public peace, this aim cannot be accomplished by laws or ordinances which deny rights created or protected by the federal Constitution. It is said that such acquisitions by colored persons depreciate property owned in the neighborhood by white persons. But property may be acquired by undesirable white neighbors or put to disagreeable though lawful uses with like results. We think this attempt to prevent the alienation of the property in question to a person of color was not a legitimate exercise of the police power of the state. . . .

DISCUSSION

Although *Buchanan* continues to reflect the distinction between civil and social equality, it takes civil equality seriously. One might explain the result in terms of the supposed uniqueness of real property. It also reflects the *Lochner* era's then-prevailing doctrines of economic due process and freedom of contract.[94]

The spirit of compromise between Northern and Southern whites had mixed effects in other areas of constitutional law. Although *Strauder* had forbidden the statutory exclusion of Black people from juries, exclusion brought about by the discriminatory action of state officials remained pervasive. The Court did intervene in some egregious instances,[95] and its failure to intervene more readily and

94. See, however, Benno C. Schmidt, Principle and Prejudice: The Supreme Court and Race in the Progressive Era, Part 1: The Heyday of Jim Crow, 82 Colum. L. Rev. 444, 498, 523 (1982), for a more generous interpretation of the Supreme Court's motivation in *Buchanan*. David Bernstein places the case within a more general libertarian framework in Philip Sober Controlling Philip Drunk: Buchanan v. Warley in Historical Perspective, 51 Vand. L. Rev. 797 (1998). How much actual impact *Buchanan* had is open to dispute. See, e.g., Michael Klarman, From Jim Crow to Civil Rights: The Supreme Court and the Struggle for Racial Equality 142-146 (2004).

95. E.g., Neal v. Delaware, 103 U.S. 370 (1881); Carter v. Texas, 177 U.S. 442 (1900); Rogers v. Alabama, 192 U.S. 226 (1904). Cf. Yick Wo v. Hopkins, 118 U.S. 356 (1886).

significantly may have been due to difficulties of proof and to a tenable, though narrow, construction of jurisdictional provisions.[96]

NOTE: BLACK DISENFRANCHISEMENT

Perhaps the most important feature of the period in which *Plessy* was decided is the gradual loss of Black voting rights and the effective nullification of the Fifteenth Amendment in the South. The Supreme Court struck down several blatant statutory attempts to circumvent the requirements of the Fifteenth Amendment,[97] but the gradual disfranchisement of Southern Blacks was achieved by a variety of other means, which the Court would not or could not deal with.

The Republican Party had defended Black voting rights from Reconstruction onward, in the hope of building party support in the South. By the time *Plessy* was decided in 1896, however, Republicans recognized that their project had failed: "By the late 1880s, the Republican vote in most southern states was declining significantly, as whites suppressed the black vote and the few remaining white Republicans deserted the party in the midst of rising racial tensions. . . . In 1894, for the first time since black enfranchisement, every one of the twenty-eight southern congressional districts containing a majority black population returned a Democratic representative."[98]

Conversely, the Republican Party made gains in border states, and by 1896, Republicans had secured reliable majorities in many Northern states. As a result, electoral victories in the South (and hence Black voting rights) were far less important to maintaining Republican control of the federal government. Republicans also pushed for the admission of new, sparsely populated states in the West that would help them retain control of the Senate.[99] Courting the interests of whites in the West further disengaged Republicans from the cause of Black voting rights. The party's appeal to border states and the West, together with its support for industrial capitalism changed the party's agenda and the balance of interests in the Republican Party.

As the memory of the Civil War receded, white voters were increasingly uninterested in the suppression of Black votes in the South. Nevertheless, Republicans made one last attempt to protect Black voting rights between 1890 and 1891, in what was called the Lodge bill or the Force bill. In 1888, Republicans won both houses of Congress and the Presidency for the first time since Reconstruction, and it appeared that they might pass a strong voting rights measure to protect Black

---

96. See, e.g., Virginia v. Rives, 100 U.S. 313 (1880), holding that absent a discriminatory statute, a defendant could not remove his trial to federal court by alleging and offering to prove racial exclusion; In re Wood, 140 U.S. 278 (1891), holding that jury exclusion cannot be challenged on habeas corpus; Thomas v. Texas, 212 U.S. 278 (1909), deferring to state court's finding of no discrimination.

97. E.g., Guinn v. United States, 238 U.S. 347 (1915), striking down Oklahoma's "grandfather clause," which exempted from a literacy test all those entitled to vote in 1866 and their lineal descendants.

98. Michael Klarman, The *Plessy* Era, 1998 S. Ct. Rev. 303, 317-318.

99. See Charles Stewart III and Barry R. Weingast, Stacking the Senate, Changing the Nation: Republican Rotten Boroughs, Statehood Politics, and American Political Development, 6 Studies in American Political Development 223 (1992) (describing the political battles for state admission during the last half of the nineteenth century).

people in the South. However, "Republican congressmen proved willing to sacrifice the bill in exchange for legislative action on economic issues deemed to be of greater urgency—namely, the tariff and the currency. The elections bill died of insufficient Republican commitment. In retrospect, it should be seen as the party's last gasp of civil rights ardor for decades to come"[100]

With the Republican Party disengaging from the struggle to protect Black voting rights, Southern states had greater leeway to pursue policies of Black disenfranchisement. Richard Pildes describes the process that eventually swept through the South.

Richard H. Pildes, Democracy, Anti-Democracy, and the Canon

17 Const. Comment. 295, 299-304 (2000)

Black (male) political participation remained extraordinarily high long after federal military forces were withdrawn from the South in 1877. In 1880, two-thirds of adult black men voted in the Presidential election; even in the 1890s, half of black men still voted in key governor's races in Southern states. Black officials also held political offices (around 2,000 in number) at every level in the South, from state Supreme Courts, to the U.S. Senate, down to the county and local level . . . [and] though black officeholding declined sharply by 1880, even that much-reduced number was not again reached until 1972, seven years after the Voting Rights Act. Yet the forces of elite, conservative, white political control, through the organized vehicle of the Democratic Party, slowly recovered political power through a series of increasingly effective tactics: outright violence and intimidation, . . . fraudulent manipulation of ballots; racial gerrymandering of election districts and other dilutive structural devices; and statutory suffrage restrictions that greatly reduced the black and poor-white electorate. . . . This step-by-step process eventually culminated in sufficient white control to produce new constitutional conventions, or suffrage-restricting constitutional amendments through referenda, in every former Confederate state, starting with Mississippi in 1890 and ending with Georgia in 1908. The avowed purpose of these new constitutions was to restore white supremacy, but that was not their only aim. For the Framers of disfranchisement were typically the most conservative, large landowning, wealthy faction of the Democratic Party, who were also seeking to entrench their partisan power and fend off challenges from Republicans, Populists, and other third parties, as well as from the more populist wings of the Democratic Party. While pledging not to disfranchise any whites, they advocated provisions that would remove the less educated, less organized, more impoverished whites from the electorate as well—and that would ensure one-party, Democratic rule, which is precisely what happened from this moment forward through most of the 20th century in the South.

The white-supremacy purposes of these new constitutions were not disguised (though the concomitant aim of reducing populist white political influence was). As expressed by the President of the Alabama Convention whose handiwork Jackson

100. Klarman, The *Plessy* Era, supra n.98, at 318.

Giles would soon challenge, "what is it that we want to do? Why it is within the limits imposed by the Federal Constitution, to establish white supremacy in this State." . . .

The effect of these disenfranchising constitutions throughout the South, combined with statutory suffrage restrictions, was immediate and devastating. In Louisiana, in 1896 there had been 130,334 black voters on the registration rolls and around the same number of white voters (the state's population was about 50 percent white and black); by 1900, two years after the new constitution, registered black voters numbered a mere 5,320. By 1910, 730 registered black voters were left (less than 0.5 percent of eligible black men). In 27 of the state's 60 parishes, not a single black voter was registered any longer; in 9 more parishes, only one black voter was. In South Carolina, black legislators had been the majority in the lower house during Reconstruction; by 1896, the entire state had only 5,500 black voters registered. In Alabama, in 1900 there were 181,471 eligible black voters, but only 3,000 were registered after the new constitutional provisions took effect. In Virginia, there was a 100% drop—in other words, to zero—in estimated black voter turnout between the Presidential elections of 1900 and 1904. North Carolina managed the same complete elimination of black voter turnout over an eight-year period, between the Presidential elections of 1896 and 1904. This was the legal situation Giles sought to challenge in the only way left, through constitutional litigation.

GILES v. HARRIS, 189 U.S. 475 (1903): [Jackson Giles was a Republican Party activist and President of the Colored Men's Suffrage Association; he held a federal patronage job as the janitor in Montgomery, Alabama's federal courthouse. He had registered and voted in Montgomery, Alabama from 1871 to 1901. Giles challenged the systematic denial of African Americans' right to vote to in Alabama. The Court, speaking through Justice Holmes, did not dispute the facts, but refused to grant an injunction on the grounds, among others, that even if the facts were true, the Supreme Court had little practical power to address the problem.]

HOLMES, J.:

The bill imports that the great mass of the white population intends to keep the blacks from voting. To meet such an intent something more than ordering the plaintiff's name to be inscribed upon the lists of 1902 will be needed. If the conspiracy and the intent exist, a name on a piece of paper will not defeat them. Unless we are prepared to supervise the voting in that state by officers of the court, it seems to us that all that the plaintiff could get from equity would be an empty form. Apart from damages to the individual, relief from a great political wrong, if done, as alleged, by the people of a state and the state itself, must be given by them or by the legislative and political department of the government of the United States.

[Justices Brewer, Harlan, and Brown (the author of *Plessy*) dissented.[101]]

---

101. See also Giles v. Teasley, 193 U.S. 146 (1904), denying legal relief arising out of the same disfranchisement scheme.

DISCUSSION

There can be little doubt that the Court averted its eyes from the systematic disenfranchisement of African Americans that was occurring throughout the South around the turn of the century. Should the Court have attempted vigorously to enforce the Fifteenth Amendment even if open defiance of any such efforts might well have been predicted? Is it relevant that, in 1905, neither Congress nor the President might have done very much to come to its aid? (Compare this to 1957, when President Eisenhower sent troops to Little Rock, Arkansas to enforce a judicial desegregation decree.) If the Court is ultimately dependent on popular support and the support of the President and Congress to enforce its decrees, does this mean that *Giles* is correctly decided? We will have occasion later to consider the practical power (and constitutional duty) of the Court to enforce potentially unpopular doctrines in our discussion of Brown v. Board of Education in Chapter 7, infra.

II. CREATING AN "AMERICAN" NATION

A. American Expansionism, Race, Ethnicity, and the Constitution

Downes v. Bidwell is one of the "Insular Cases" litigated following the conquest of Puerto Rico and the Philippines in the Spanish-American War of 1898. Prior expansion had been into territories that, upon settlement, were presumed to be eligible for admission as a state to the United States. Texas presented a special case: It was never a "territory" but an independent country that was admitted to the Union by a majority of each house of Congress in 1844. Opponents of Texas's admission argued that there first had to be an annexation treaty between the United States and Texas, which in turn would have required an (unattainable) support by two-thirds of the senators. However, both Presidents Tyler and Polk, plus a majority of Congress, badly wanted Texas in the Union, which they achieved, however irregularly. By contrast, no such welcoming attitude was applied to Puerto Rico and the Philippines.

DOWNES v. BIDWELL, 182 U.S. 244 (1901): [*Downes* concerned the Uniformity Clause of Article I, §8, cl. 1 of the Constitution, which provides that "all duties, imposts, and excises shall be uniform throughout the United States." Downes was charged duties for oranges shipped to New York from San Juan. The duties were collected under the authority of the Foraker Act of April 12, 1900, which temporarily provided a civil government and sources of revenue for administration of the island of Puerto Rico. Downes sued to recover the duties paid. He argued that Puerto Rico became part of the United States after the ratification of the treaty with Spain that ended the Spanish-American War, so that duty violated the Uniformity Clause.]

Mr. Justice BROWN announced the conclusion and judgment of the Court:

. . . In the case of De Lima v. Bidwell just decided, we held that, upon the ratification of the treaty of peace with Spain, Porto Rico ceased to be a foreign country, and became a territory of the United States. . . . We are now asked to hold that it became a part of the United States within that provision of the Constitution which declares that "all duties, imposts, and excises shall be uniform throughout the United States." Art. 1, §8. . . .

. . . [I]t can nowhere be inferred that the territories were considered a part of the United States. . . . [I]n organizing the territory of Louisiana by act of March 26, 1804, [and] all other territories carved out of this vast inheritance, [Congress] has assumed that the Constitution did not extend to them of its own force, and has in each case made special provision, either that their legislatures shall pass no law inconsistent with the Constitution of the United States, or that the Constitution or laws of the United States shall be the supreme law of such territories. . . . .

[Justice Brown then distinguishes *Dred Scott*, which seemed to reject the power of the United States to establish colonies in which the Constitution did not apply.] Chief Justice [Taney] had already disposed of the case adversely to the plaintiff upon the question of [Dred Scott's right to sue under diversity] jurisdiction. [I]n view of the excited political condition of the country at the time, it is unfortunate that he felt compelled to discuss the question upon the merits . . .

To sustain the judgment in the case under consideration, it by no means becomes necessary to show that none of the articles of the Constitution apply to the island of Porto Rico. There is a clear distinction between such prohibitions as go to the very root of the power of Congress to act at all, irrespective of time of place, and such as are operative only "throughout the United States" or among the several states.

Thus, when the Constitution declares that "no bill of attainder or ex post facto law shall be passed," and that "no title of nobility shall be granted by the United States," it goes to the competency of Congress to pass a bill of that description. Perhaps the same remark may apply to the 1st Amendment, that "Congress shall make no law respecting an establishment of religion, or prohibiting the free exercise thereof; or abridging the freedom of speech, or of the press; or the right of the people to peacefully assemble and to petition the government for a redress of grievances." We do not wish, however, to be understood as expressing an opinion how far the bill of rights contained in the first eight amendments is of general and how far of local application.

. . . Indeed, the practical interpretation put by Congress upon the Constitution has been long continued and uniform to the effect that the Constitution is applicable to territories acquired by purchase or conquest, only when and so far as Congress shall so direct. . . .

We are also of opinion that the power to acquire territory by treaty implies, not only the power to govern such territory, but to prescribe upon what terms the United States will receive its inhabitants, and what their status shall be in what Chief Justice Marshall termed the "American empire." There seems to be no middle ground between this position and the doctrine that if their inhabitants do not become, immediately upon annexation, citizens of the United States, their children thereafter born, whether savages or civilized, are such, and entitled to all the rights, privileges and immunities of citizens. If such be their status, the consequences will be extremely serious. Indeed, it is doubtful if Congress would ever assent to the annexation of territory upon the condition that its inhabitants, however foreign they may be to our habits, traditions, and modes of life, shall become at once citizens of the United States. In all its treaties hitherto the treatymaking power has made special provision for this subject; in the cases of Louisiana and Florida, by stipulating that "the inhabitants shall be incorporated into the Union of the United States and admitted as soon as possible . . . to the enjoyment of all the rights, advantages, and immunities of citizens of the United States"; in the case of Mexico, that they should "be incorporated into the Union, and be admitted at the proper time (to be judged of by the Congress of the United States) to the enjoyment of all the rights of citizens of the United States"; in the case of Alaska, that the inhabitants who remained three years, "with the exception of uncivilized native tribes, shall be admitted to the enjoyment of all the rights," etc.; and in the case of Porto Rico and the Philippines, "that the civil rights and political status of the native inhabitants . . . shall be determined by Congress." In all these cases there is an implied denial of the right of the inhabitants to American citizenship until Congress by further action shall signify its assent thereto. . . .

It is obvious that in the annexation of outlying and distant possessions grave questions will arise from differences of race, habits, laws, and customs of the people, and from differences of soil, climate, and production, which may require action on the part of Congress that would be quite unnecessary in the annexation of contiguous territory inhabited only by people of the same race, or by scattered bodies of native Indians.

We suggest, without intending to decide, that there may be a distinction between certain natural rights enforced in the Constitution by prohibitions against interference with them, and what may be termed artificial or remedial rights which are peculiar to our own system of jurisprudence. Of the former class are the rights to one's own religious opinions and to a public expression of them, or, as sometimes said, to worship God according to the dictates of one's own conscience; the right to personal liberty and individual property; to freedom of speech and of the press; to free access to courts of justice, to due process of law, and to an equal protection of the laws; to immunities from unreasonable searches and seizures, as well as cruel and unusual punishments; and to such other immunities as are indispensable to a free government. Of the latter class are the rights to citizenship, to suffrage, and to the particular methods of procedure pointed out in the Constitution, which are peculiar to Anglo-Saxon jurisprudence, and some of which have already been held by the states to be unnecessary to the proper protection of individuals.

Even if regarded as aliens, [the inhabitants of these islands] are entitled . . . to be protected in life, liberty, and property. . . . We do not desire, however, to anticipate the difficulties which would naturally arise in this connection, but merely to disclaim any intention to hold that the inhabitants of these territories are subject to an unrestrained power on the part of Congress to deal with them upon the theory that they have no rights which it is bound to respect. . . .

. . . If it be once conceded that we are at liberty to acquire foreign territory, a presumption arises that our power with respect to such territories is the same power which other nations have been accustomed to exercise with respect to territories acquired by them. If, in limiting the power which Congress was to exercise within the United States, it was also intended to limit it with regard to such territories as the people of the United States should thereafter acquire, such limitations should have been expressed. . . .

Patriotic and intelligent men may differ widely as to the desireableness of this or that acquisition, but this is solely a political question. [N]o construction of the Constitution should be adopted which would prevent Congress from considering each case upon its merits, unless the language of the instrument imperatively demand it. A false step at this time might be fatal to the development of what Chief Justice Marshall called the American empire. . . .

Mr. Justice WHITE, with whom concurred Mr. Justice SHIRAS and Mr. Justice McKENNA, uniting in the judgment of affirmance: . . .

. . . There is . . . no room in this case to contend that Congress can destroy the liberties of the people of Porto Rico by exercising in their regard powers against freedom and justice which the Constitution has absolutely denied. There can also be no controversy as to the right of Congress to locally govern the island of Porto Rico as its wisdom may decide, and in so doing to accord only such degree of representative government as may be determined on by that body. . . .

The sole and only issue, then, is [this:] Had Porto Rico, at the time of the passage of the act in question, been incorporated into and become an integral part of the United States? . . . [T]he treaty-making power was always deemed to be devoid of authority to incorporate territory into the United States without the assent, express or implied, of Congress. . . . [Drawing on the history of previous territorial acquisitions, White introduces a distinction between "incorporated" and "unincorporated" territory that became dispositive in later cases. He argues that the distinction must exist because of the nature and effect of the treaty power:]

. . . [I]t seems to me impossible to conceive that the treaty-making power by a mere cession can incorporate an alien people into the United States without the express or implied approval of Congress. . . . If the treaty-making power can absolutely, without the consent of Congress, incorporate territory, and if that power may not insert conditions against incorporation, it must follow that the treaty-making power is endowed by the Constitution with the most unlimited right, susceptible of destroying every other provision of the Constitution; that is, it may wreck our institutions. If the proposition be true, then millions of inhabitants of alien territory, if acquired by treaty, can, without the desire or consent of the people of the United States speaking through Congress, be immediately and irrevocably incorporated into the United States, and the whole structure of the government be overthrown. . . .

[T]he provisions of the [Foraker Act] by which the duty here in question was imposed, taken as a whole, seem to me plainly to manifest the intention of Congress that, for the present at least, Porto Rico is not to be incorporated into the United States. . . . [W]hile in an international sense Porto Rico was not a foreign country, since it was subject to the sovereignty of and was owned by the United States, it was foreign to the United States in a domestic sense, because the island had not been incorporated into the United States, but was merely appurtenant thereto as a possession. . . .

[A concurring opinion by Justice Gray is omitted.]

Mr. Chief Justice FULLER, with whom concurred Mr. Justice HARLAN, Mr. Justice BREWER, and Mr. Justice PECKHAM, dissenting:

The 14th Amendment provides that "all persons born or naturalized in the United States, and subject to the jurisdiction thereof, are citizens of the United States and of the state wherein they reside"; and this court naturally held, in the Slaughter-House Cases, that the United States included the District and the territories. . . .

No person is eligible to the office of President unless he has "attained the age of thirty-five years, and been fourteen years a resident within the United States." Clause 5, §1, art. 2. Would a native-born citizen of Massachusetts be ineligible if he had taken up his residence and resided in one of the territories for so many years that he had not resided altogether fourteen years in the states? When voted for he must be a citizen of one of the states (clause 3, §1, art. 2; art. 12), but as to length of time must residence in the territories be counted against him?

The 15th Amendment declares that "the right of citizens of the United States to vote shall not be denied or abridged by the United States or by any state on account of race, color, or previous condition of servitude." Where does that prohibition on the United States especially apply if not in the territories?

The 13th Amendment says that neither slavery nor involuntary servitude "shall exist within the United States or any place subject to their jurisdiction." Clearly this prohibition would have operated in the territories if the concluding words had not been added. The history of the times shows that the addition was made in view of the then condition of the country—the amendment passed the house January 31, 1865—and it is, moreover, otherwise applicable than to the territories. Besides, generally speaking, when words are used simply out of abundant caution, the fact carries little weight.

[N]o satisfactory ground has been suggested for restricting the words "throughout the United States," as qualifying the power to impose duties, to the states, and that conclusion is the more to be avoided when we reflect that it rests, in the last analysis, on the assertion of the possession by Congress of unlimited power over the territories. . . . Much discussion was had at the bar in respect of the citizenship of the inhabitants of Porto Rico, but we are not required to consider that subject at large in these cases. It will be time enough to seek a ford when, if ever, we are brought to the stream. . . .

. . . [T]he contention seems to be that, if an organized and settled province of another sovereignty is acquired by the United States, Congress has the power to keep it, like a disembodied shade, in an intermediate state of ambiguous existence for an indefinite period; and, more than that, that after it has been called from that limbo, commerce with it is absolutely subject to the will of Congress, irrespective of constitutional provisions.

. . . Great stress is thrown upon the word "incorporation," as if possessed of some occult meaning, but I take it that the act under consideration made Porto Rico, whatever its situation before, an organized territory of the United States. [Given that Congress has the power] to impose duties by virtue of clause 1 of §8, how is it that the rule which qualifies the power does not [also] apply . . . ? . . .

The concurring opinion recognizes the fact that Congress, in dealing with the people of new territories or possessions, is bound to respect the fundamental guaranties of life, liberty, and property, but assumes that Congress is not bound, in those territories or possessions, to follow the rules of taxation prescribed by the Constitution. And yet the power to tax involves the power to destroy, and the levy of duties touches all our people in all places under the jurisdiction of the government. The logical result is that Congress may prohibit commerce altogether between the states and territories, and may prescribe one rule of taxation in one territory, and a different rule in another.

That theory assumes that the Constitution created a government empowered to acquire countries throughout the world, to be governed by different rules than those obtaining in the original states and territories, and substitutes for the present system of republican government a system of domination over distant provinces in the exercise of unrestricted power. . . .

[I]t is objected on behalf of the government that the possession of absolute power is essential to the acquisition of vast and distant territories, and that we should regard the situation as it is today, rather than as it was a century ago. "We must look at the situation as comprehending a possibility—I do not say a probability, but a possibility—that the question might be as to the powers of this government in the acquisition of Egypt and the Soudan, or a section of Central Africa, or a spot in the Antarctic Circle, or a section of the Chinese Empire." But it must be remembered that, as Marshall and Story declared, the Constitution was framed for ages to come, and that the sagacious men who framed it were well aware that a mighty future waited on their work. . . .

Mr. Justice Harlan, dissenting: . . .

Whether a particular race will or will not assimilate with our people, and whether they can or cannot with safety to our institutions be brought within the operation of the Constitution, is a matter to be thought of when it is proposed to acquire their territory by treaty. A mistake in the acquisition of territory, although such acquisition seemed at the time to be necessary, cannot be made the ground for violating the Constitution or refusing to give full effect to its provisions. . . . When the acquisition of territory becomes complete, by cession, the Constitution necessarily becomes the supreme law of such new territory, and no power exists in any department of the government to make "concessions" that are inconsistent with its provisions. The authority to make such concessions implies the existence in Congress of power to declare that constitutional provisions may be ignored under special or embarrassing circumstances. No such dispensing power exists in any branch of our government. The Constitution is supreme over every foot of territory, wherever situated, under the jurisdiction of the United States, and its full operation cannot be stayed by any branch of the government in order to meet what some may suppose to be extraordinary emergencies. . . .

We heard much in argument about the "expanding future of our country." It was said that the United States is to become what is called a "world power"; and that if this government intends to keep abreast of the times and be equal to the great destiny that awaits the American people, it must be allowed to exert all the power that other nations are accustomed to exercise. My answer is, that the fathers never intended that the authority and influence of this nation should be exerted otherwise than in accordance with the Constitution. If our government needs more power than is conferred upon it by the Constitution, that instrument provides the mode in which it may be amended and additional power thereby obtained. The People of the United States who ordained the Constitution never supposed that a change could be made in our system of government by mere judicial interpretation.

They never contemplated any such juggling with the words of the Constitution as would authorize the courts to hold that the words "throughout the United States," in the taxing clause of the Constitution, do not embrace a domestic "territory of the United States" having a civil government established by the authority of the United States. . . .

[I]t is . . . said that a new territory, acquired by treaty or conquest, cannot become incorporated into the United States without the consent of Congress. What is meant by such incorporation we are not fully informed, nor are we instructed as to the precise mode in which it is to be accomplished. . . . If Porto Rico, although a territory of the United States, may be treated as if it were not a part of the United States, then New Mexico and Arizona may be treated as not parts of the United States, and subject to such legislation as Congress may choose to enact without any reference to the restrictions imposed by the Constitution. . . .

In my opinion Porto Rico became, at least after the ratification of the treaty with Spain, a part of and subject to the jurisdiction of the United States in respect of all its territory and people, and that Congress could not thereafter impose any duty, impost, or excise with respect to that island and its inhabitants, which departed from the rule of uniformity established by the Constitution.

DISCUSSION

1. Puerto Ricans were granted statutory citizenship by Congress in 1917. Residents of the Philippines, also captured in the 1898 war, never received citizenship. Indeed, given that 1790 naturalization law prohibited the naturalization of nonwhites (modified in 1870 to allow the naturalization of "aliens of African nativity and to persons of African descent"), Filipinos were held ineligible to become American citizens. See In re Lampitoe, 232 F. 382 (S.D.N.Y. 1916). Persons of Chinese descent were made eligible for citizenship in 1943 (when the United States was allied with China during World War II). Only with the passage of the Immigration and Nationality Act of 1952 did Congress adopt as policy that "[t]he right of a person to become a naturalized citizen of the United States shall not be denied or abridged because of race or sex." Note, though, that this does not necessarily apply to discrimination based on "national origin."

2. Did the grant of citizenship to Puerto Ricans automatically serve to "incorporate" Puerto Rico within the United States, as was the case for Alaska when inhabitants of that territory were accorded citizenship, see Rassmussen v. United States, 197 U.S. 516 (1905)? The Court held otherwise in Balzac v. People of Puerto Rico, 258 U.S. 298 (1922), involving the right of Puerto Rican criminal defendants to receive trial by jury. The Court, through Chief Justice Taft, held that there was no such right. The Court should not be quick "to infer, from acts thus easily explained on other grounds, an intention to incorporate in the Union those distant ocean communities of a different origin and language from those of our continental people." From a contemporary perspective, should Taft's opinion be condemned for its failure to accord Puerto Ricans the rights that all other Americans receive in states or "incorporated" territories? Or should it be praised for recognizing that the "American empire" (like America itself) is profoundly multicultural and that the many other legal systems, including the Spanish one under which Puerto Rico

was governed for almost 400 years, reject the Anglo-American emphasis on the jury trial (which, as a matter of fact, has diminished in contemporary Great Britain and the United States)?

3. To this day, Puerto Rico has no vote in the House or Senate, nor does Puerto Rico possess any votes in the Electoral College (unlike the District of Columbia, see the Twenty-Third Amendment). Almost 50 percent of the Puerto Rican population have voted for statehood in nonbinding referenda. Assume that a majority of the population petitions for statehood. Does Congress have a constitutional duty to grant such a petition (even if no Court would order Congress to act thusly in the matter)? What would count as proper reasons for denying it? The fact that most Puerto Ricans speak Spanish? That most are Catholic? That most are non-white? That it is significantly less economically developed than even Mississippi or Arkansas? That admission would "dilute" the voting power now held in the Senate by the 50 states and by the states in the House of Representatives? Is any of these a legitimate reason to deny statehood to Puerto Rico (assuming that a majority of the population of Puerto Rico wish it)? If none of these reasons suffice, can you imagine any others that would?

4. Almost 50 percent of the Puerto Rican population have voted to retain their "commonwealth" status vis-à-vis the United States. Does "commonwealth" represent a genuine constitutional status, or is it simply a label signifying a decision by Congress, exercising its constitutional discretion, to allow Puerto Rico such autonomy and grant Puerto Ricans such "constitutional rights" as it sees fit, subject to reversal whenever Congress and the President (or two-thirds of each house of Congress) believe the American interest demands otherwise? See generally Arnold H. Leibowitz, Defining Status: A Comprehensive Analysis of United States Territorial Relations, ch. 6 (1989); Juan R. Torruella, The Supreme Court and Puerto Rico: The Doctrine of Separate and Unequal (1988).

5. A small percentage of Puerto Ricans favor independence. Assume that the sentiment in favor of independence grows over time. Would the United States be under any constitutional duty to honor this wish for independence, or is it entirely a matter of discretion whether the United States continues to possess Puerto Rico as a colony? Or consider a final possibility, however unlikely it is in practice: Could the United States decide to sell Puerto Rico to another country, in just the way, for example, that Russia sold Alaska to the United States—for $7,200,000, about 2.5 cents per acre, in 1867—and Denmark sold what are now the American Virgin Islands in 1917? Would Puerto Ricans have any constitutional right to object to "deannexation" from the United States by, for example, being sold to, say, Mexico, Brazil, or Spain? See Christina Burnett, The Constitution and Deconstitution of the United States, in The Louisiana Purchase and American Expansion 181 (Levinson & Sparrow eds., 2005).

6. One of the most famous aphorisms in American history is that of "Mr. Dooley" (Finley Peter Dunne): "[N]o matter whether th' Constitution follows th' flag, th' Supreme Court follows th' iliction returns."[102] Dunne, an anti-imperialist, was writing of the Insular Cases and registering his belief that McKinley's smashing

---

102.

victory over William Jennings Bryan in the 1900 presidential election, in which an important issue was the legitimacy of American empire-building, was the primary explanation for the Court's 5-4 decision. Assume for the moment that Dunne was correct. What precisely is wrong with "following the election returns" if the Constitution is indeed unclear and if the people (relatively) clearly endorse one possible interpretation of the Constitution, even if one disagrees with it, over another that one might prefer?

B. *Ethnic Diversity and the Constitution: The Case of Chinese Immigration*

The opinions in the Insular Cases are quite candid with regard to their views about the (in)ability of any and all ethnic groups to become part of the American community. Such discussions were certainly not limited to the context of American expansion into the Pacific or the Caribbean. Recall the discussion earlier in this chapter of the citizenship status of American Indians or Justice Harlan's distinction between African Americans and Chinese immigrants in his famous dissenting opinion in Plessy v. Ferguson. It is, therefore, quite significant that the Court did, in United States v. Wong Kim Ark, 169 U.S. 649 (1898), read sentence one of the Fourteenth Amendment to provide birthright citizenship to children of Chinese immigrants (even though the parents themselves were ineligible for citizenship as a matter of statutory law). However, Chief Justice Fuller dissented, joined by Justice Harlan:

> [T]he fourteenth amendment does not exclude from citizenship by birth children born in the United States of parents permanently located therein, and who might themselves become citizens; nor, on the other hand, does it arbitrarily make citizens of children born in the United States of parents who, according to the will of their native government and of this government, are and must remain aliens.

Perhaps the most notable demonstration of anti-Chinese animus was the passage of so-called Chinese Exclusion Acts that barred the entry of Chinese laborers into the United States.[103] The Acts were challenged and upheld in Chae Chan Ping v. United States, 130 U.S. 581 (1889) (the Chinese Exclusion Case), a case that continues to be of fundamental importance because of its articulation of the federal government's inherent, plenary, and "sovereign" right to control its borders:

CHAE CHAN PING v. UNITED STATES, 130 U.S. 581 (1889): [Chae Chan Ping had lived in San Francisco from 1875 until June 2, 1887, when he returned to his home in China for a visit. He left, in the words of the Court, "having in his possession a certificate, in terms entitling him to return to the United States, bearing date on that day, duly issued to him by the collector of customs of the port of San Francisco. . . ." However, on his return to San Francisco on October 8, 1888,

---

103. See Lucy Salyer, Laws Harsh as Tigers: Chinese Immigrants and the Shaping of Modern Immigration Law (1995); Andrew Gyory, Closing the Gate: Race, Politics, and the Chinese Exclusion Act (1998).

"the collector of the port refused the permit, solely on the ground that under the act of Congress, approved October 1, 1888 [an amendment to the so-called Chinese Exclusion Act of 1882, which had prohibited Chinese laborers from entering the United States], . . . the certificate had been annulled and his right to land abrogated. . . . The captain of the steamship, therefore, detained the appellant on board the steamer." Chae Chan Ping then filed suit in federal court for a writ of habeas corpus on the ground that his detention was illegal. The court rejected his claim and "held as conclusions of law that the appellant was not entitled to enter the United States, and was not unlawfully restrained of his liberty, and ordered that he be remanded to the custody of the master of the steamship from which he had been taken under the writ." He then appealed to the Supreme Court.]

Mr. Justice FIELD delivered the opinion of the court.

The validity of the act is assailed as being in effect an expulsion from the country of Chinese laborers, in violation of existing treaties between the United States and the government of China, and of rights vested in them under the laws of Congress.

[Justice Field then reviews the history of treaties between the United States and the empire of China, beginning in 1844.] Neither the treaty of 1844 nor that of 1858 touched upon the migration and emigration of the citizens and subjects of the two nations, respectively, from one country to the other. But in 1868 a great change in the relations of the two nations was made in that respect. . . . [A key provision of a new treaty that year recognized] "the inherent and inalienable right of man to change his home and allegiance, and also the mutual advantage of the free migration and emigration of their citizens and subjects respectively from the one country to the other for purposes of curiosity, of trade, or as permanent residents." . . .

But notwithstanding these strong expressions of friendship and good will, and the desire they evince for free intercourse, events were transpiring on the Pacific coast which soon dissipated the anticipations indulged as to the benefits to follow the immigration of Chinese to this country. . . . [Subsequent modifications to the 1868 treaty] have been caused by a well-founded apprehension—from the experience of years—that a limitation to the immigration of certain classes from China was essential to the peace of the community on the Pacific coast, and possibly to the preservation of our civilization there. A few words on this point may not be deemed inappropriate here, they being confined to matters of public notoriety, which have frequently been brought to the attention of congress.

The discovery of gold in California in 1848, as is well known, was followed by a large immigration thither from all parts of the world, attracted not only by the hope of gain from the mines, but from the great prices paid for all kinds of labor. The news of the discovery penetrated China, and laborers came from there in great numbers, a few with their own means, but by far the greater number under contract with employers, for whose benefit they worked. These laborers readily secured employment, and, as domestic servants, and in various kinds of outdoor work, proved to be exceedingly useful. For some years little opposition was made to them, except when they sought to work in the mines, but, as their numbers increased, they began to engage in various mechanical pursuits and trades, and thus came in competition with our artisans and mechanics, as well as our laborers in the field.

The competition steadily increased as the laborers came in crowds on each steamer that arrived from China, or Hong Kong, an adjacent English port. They were generally industrious and frugal. Not being accompanied by families, except in rare instances, their expenses were small; and they were content with the simplest fare, such as would not suffice for our laborers and artisans. The competition between them and our people was for this reason altogether in their favor, and the consequent irritation, proportionately deep and bitter, was followed, in many cases, by open conflicts, to the great disturbance of the public peace. The differences of race added greatly to the difficulties of the situation. . . . [T]hey remained strangers in the land, residing apart by themselves, and adhering to the customs and usages of their own country. It seemed impossible for them to assimilate with our people, or to make any change in their habits or modes of living. As they grew in numbers each year the people of the coast saw, or believed they saw, in the facility of immigration, and in the crowded millions of China, where population presses upon the means of subsistence, great danger that at no distant day that portion of our country would be overrun by them, unless prompt action was taken to restrict their immigration. The people there accordingly petitioned earnestly for protective legislation.

In December, 1878, the convention which framed the present constitution of California, being in session, took this subject up, and memorialized congress upon it, setting forth, in substance, that the presence of Chinese laborers had a baneful effect upon the material interests of the state, and upon public morals; that their immigration was in numbers approaching the character of an Oriental invasion, and was a menace to our civilization; that the discontent from this cause was not confined to any political party, or to any class or nationality, but was well nigh universal; that they retained the habits and customs of their own country, and in fact constituted a Chinese settlement within the state, without any interest in our country or its institutions; and praying congress to take measures to prevent their further immigration. This memorial was presented to congress in February, 1879. So urgent and constant were the prayers for relief against existing and anticipated evils, both from the public authorities of the Pacific coast and from private individuals, that congress was impelled to act on the subject. . . . [A new treaty was concluded with China that declared] in its first article that "Whenever, in the opinion of the government of the United States, the coming of Chinese laborers to the United States, or their residence therein, affects or threatens to affect the interests of that country, or to endanger the good order of the said country or of any locality within the territory thereof, the government of China agrees that the government of the United States may regulate, limit, or suspend such coming or residence, but may not absolutely prohibit it. The limitation or suspension shall be reasonable, and shall apply only to Chinese who may go to the United States as laborers, other classes not being included in the limitations. Legislation taken in regard to Chinese laborers will be of such a character only as is necessary to enforce the regulation, limitation, or suspension of immigration, and immigrants shall not be subject to personal maltreatment or abuse." In its second article it declares that "Chinese subjects, whether proceeding to the United States as teachers, students, merchants, or from curiosity, together with their body and household servants, and Chinese laborers who are now in the United States, shall be allowed to go and come of their own free will and accord, and shall be accorded all the rights, privileges, immunities, and exemptions which are accorded to the citizens and subjects of the most favored nation."

. . . On the 6th of May, 1882, an act of congress was approved, to carry this supplementary treaty into effect. [It suspended the immigration of Chinese laborers for ten years, though it also stipulated that the ban] shall not apply to Chinese laborers who were in the United States November 17, 1880. . . . [The collectors of customs at American ports were given the duty of supplying such laborers with] "the proper evidence" of their right to go from and come to the United States. . . . "The certificate herein provided for," says the section, "shall entitle the Chinese laborer to whom the same is issued to return to and reenter the United States upon producing and delivering the same to the collector of customs of the district at which such Chinese laborer shall seek to re-enter."

The enforcement of this act with respect to laborers who were in the United States on November 17, 1880, was attended with great embarrassment, from the suspicious nature, in many instances, of the testimony offered to establish the residence of the parties. . . . To prevent the possibility of the policy of excluding Chinese laborers being evaded, the act of October 1, 1888, the validity of which is the subject of consideration in this case, was passed. . . . [The key provisions provided that] "from and after the passage of this act it shall be unlawful for any Chinese laborer who shall at any time heretofore have been, or who may now or hereafter be, a resident within the United States, and who shall have departed, or shall depart, therefrom, and shall not have returned before the passage of this act, to return to or remain the United States. [Moreover, any certificate of identity previously issued] is hereby declared void and of no effect, and the Chinese laborer claiming admission by virtue thereof shall not be permitted to enter the United States." . . .

Here the objection made is that the act of 1888 impairs a right vested under the treaty of 1880, as a law of the United States, and the statutes of 1882 and of 1884 passed in execution of it. It must be conceded that the act of 1888 is in contravention of express stipulations of the treaty of 1868, and of the supplemental treaty of 1880, but it is not on that account invalid, or to be restricted in its enforcement. The treaties were of no greater legal obligation than the act of congress. By the constitution, laws made in pursuance thereof, and treaties made under the authority of the United States, are both declared to be the supreme law of the land, and no paramount authority is given to one over the other. A treaty, it is true, is in its nature a contract between nations, and is often merely promissory in its character, requiring legislation to carry its stipulations into effect. Such legislation will be open to future repeal or amendment. If the treaty operates by its own force, and relates to a subject within the power of congress, it can be deemed in that particular only the equivalent of a legislative act, to be repealed or modified at the pleasure of congress. In either case the last expression of the sovereign will must control.

The effect of legislation upon conflicting treaty stipulations was elaborately considered in the Head-Money Cases, and it was there adjudged "that, so far as a treaty made by the United States with any foreign nation can become the subject of judicial cognizance in the courts of this country, it is subject to such acts as congress may pass for its enforcement, modification, or repeal." 112 U.S. 580. . . . It will not be presumed that the legislative department of the government will lightly pass laws which are in conflict with the treaties of the country; but that circumstances may arise which would not only justify the government in disregarding their stipulations, but demand in the interests of the country that it should do so, there can be no question. Unexpected events may call for a change in the policy of the country. . . .

The validity of this legislative release from the stipulations of the treaties was, of course, not a matter for judicial cognizance. The question whether our government is justified in disregarding its engagements with another nation is not one for the determination of the courts. . . . [I]f the power mentioned is vested in congress, any reflection upon its motives, or the motives of any of its members in exercising it, would be entirely uncalled for. This court is not a censor of the morals of other departments of the government; it is not invested with any authority to pass judgment upon the motives of their conduct. When once it is established that congress possesses the power to pass an act, our province ends with its construction and its application to cases as they are presented for determination. Congress has the power under the constitution to declare war, and in two instances where the power has been exercised—in the war of 1812 against Great Britain, and in 1846 against Mexico—the propriety and wisdom and justice of its action were vehemently assailed by some of the ablest and best men in the country, but no one doubted the legality of the proceeding, and any imputation by this or any other court of the United States upon the motives of the members of congress who in either case voted for the declaration, would have been justly the cause of animadversion. We do not mean to intimate that the moral aspects of legislative acts may not be proper subjects of consideration. Undoubtedly they may be, at proper times and places, before the public, in the halls of congress, and in all the modes by which the public mind can be influenced. Public opinion thus enlightened, brought to bear upon legislation, will do more than all other causes to prevent abuses; but the province of the courts is to pass upon the validity of laws, not to make them, and, when their validity is established, to declare their meaning and apply their provisions. All else lies beyond their domain.

There being nothing in the treaties between China and the United States to impair the validity of the act of congress of October 1, 1888, was it on any other ground beyond the competency of congress to pass it? If so, it must be because it was not within the power of congress to prohibit Chinese laborers who had at the time departed from the United States, or should subsequently depart, from returning to the United States. Those laborers are not citizens of the United States; they are aliens. That the government of the United States, through the action of the legislative department, can exclude aliens from its territory is a proposition which we do not think open to controversy. Jurisdiction over its own territory to that extent is an incident of every independent nation. It is a part of its independence. If it could not exclude aliens it would be to that extent subject to the control of another power. As said by this court in the case of The Exchange, 7 Cranch 116, 136, speaking by Chief Justice Marshall: "The jurisdiction of the nation within its own territory is necessarily exclusive and absolute. It is susceptible of no limitation not imposed by itself. Any restriction upon it, deriving validity from an external source, would imply a diminution of its sovereignty to the extent of the restriction, and an investment of that sovereignty to the same extent in that power which could impose such restriction. All exceptions, therefore, to the full and complete power of a nation within its own territories, must be traced up to the consent of the nation itself. They can flow from no other legitimate source."

While under our constitution and form of government the great mass of local matters is controlled by local authorities, the United States, in their relation to foreign countries and their subjects or citizens, are one nation, invested with powers which belong to independent nations, the exercise of which can be invoked for the maintenance of its absolute independence and security throughout its entire territory. The powers to declare war, make treaties, suppress insurrection, repel invasion, regulate foreign commerce, secure republican governments to the states, and admit subjects of other nations to citizenship, are all sovereign powers, restricted in their exercise only by the constitution itself and considerations of public policy and justice which control, more or less, the conduct of all civilized nations. As said by this court in the case of Cohens v. Virginia, 6 Wheat. 264, 413, speaking by the same great chief justice: "That the United States form, for many, and for most important purposes, a single nation, has not yet been denied. In war, we are one people. In making peace, we are one people. In all commercial regulations, we are one and the same people. In many other respects, the American people are one; and the government which is alone capable of controlling and managing their interests in all these respects is the government of the Union. It is their government, and in that character they have no other. America has chosen to be in many respects, and to many purposes, a nation; and for all these purposes her government is complete; to all these objects, it is competent. The people have declared that in the exercise of all powers given for these objects it is supreme. It can, then, in effecting these objects, legitimately control all individuals or governments within the American territory. The constitution and laws of a state, so far as they are repugnant to the constitution and laws of the United States, are absolutely void. These states are constituent parts of the United States. They are members of one great empire,—for some purposes sovereign, for some purposes subordinate." . . .

To preserve its independence, and give security against foreign aggression and encroachment, is the highest duty of every nation, and to attain these ends nearly all other considerations are to be subordinated. It matters not in what form such aggression and encroachment come, whether from the foreign nation acting in its national character, or from vast hordes of its people crowding in upon us. The government, possessing the powers which are to be exercised for protection and security, is clothed with authority to determine the occasion on which the powers shall be called forth; and its determinations, so far as the subjects affected are concerned, are necessarily conclusive upon all its departments and officers. If, therefore, the government of the United States, through its legislative department, considers the presence of foreigners of a different race in this country, who will not assimilate with us, to be dangerous to its peace and security, their exclusion is not to be stayed because at the time there are no actual hostilities with the nation of which the foreigners are subjects. The existence of war would render the necessity of the proceeding only more obvious and pressing. The same necessity, in a less pressing degree, may arise when war does not exist, and the same authority which adjudges the necessity in one case must also determine it in the other. In both cases its determination is conclusive upon the judiciary. If the government of the country of which the foreigners excluded are subjects is dissatisfied with this action, it can make complaint to the executive head of our government, or resort to any other measure which, in its judgment, its interests or dignity may demand; and there lies its only remedy. . . .

The power of exclusion of foreigners being an incident of sovereignty belonging to the government of the United States as a part of those sovereign powers delegated by the constitution, the right to its exercise at any time when, in the judgment of the government, the interests of the country require it, cannot be granted away or restrained on behalf of any one. The powers of government are delegated in trust to the United States, and are incapable of transfer to any other parties. They cannot be abandoned or surrendered. Nor can their exercise be hampered, when needed for the public good, by any considerations of private interest. The exercise of these public trusts is not the subject of barter or contract. Whatever license, therefore, Chinese laborers may have obtained, previous to the act of October 1, 1888, to return to the United States after their departure, is held at the will of the government, revocable at any time, at its pleasure. Whether a proper consideration by our government of its previous laws, or a proper respect for the nation whose subjects are affected by its action, ought to have qualified its inhibition, and made it applicable only to persons departing from the country after the passage of the act, are not questions for judicial determination. . . .

During the argument reference was made by counsel to the alien law of June 25, 1798, and to opinions expressed at the time by men of great ability and learning against its constitutionality. We do not attach importance to those opinions in their bearing upon this case. The act vested in the president power to order all such aliens as he should judge dangerous to the peace and safety of the United States, or should have reasonable grounds to suspect were concerned in any treasonable or secret machination against the government, to depart out of the territory of the United States within such time as should be expressed in his order. There were other provisions also distinguishing it from the act under consideration. The act was passed during a period of great political excitement, and it was attacked and defended with great zeal and ability. It is enough, however, to say that it is entirely different from the act before us, and the validity of its provisions was never brought to the test of judicial decision in the courts of the United States.

DISCUSSION

1. Justice Field's opinion is functionally divided into two separate parts. The first concerns the power of the national government in effect to abrogate a treaty, inasmuch as there is no serious question that the legislation violated the terms of the treaty with China. The answer, of course, is that the national government (including, presumably, Congress alone, should it pass legislation over a presidential veto) does indeed have such a power, under the "last in time" rule that, in effect, bars a prior Congress from binding a future one. (The only true way to bind Congress is a constitutional amendment, which does indeed take priority over legislation in a way that a treaty does not.)

Note, though, that the Court writes that "it will not be presumed that the legislative department of the government will lightly pass laws which are in conflict with the treaties of the country. . . ." He may be alluding to the so-called *Charming Betsy* canon of interpretation, derived from John Marshall's opinion in Murray v. Schooner Charming Betsy, 6 U.S. (2 Cranch) 64 (1804). "Under the canon, courts will attempt to construe statutes, when reasonably possible, so that the statutes do not violate international law." See Curtis Bradley and Jack Goldsmith, Congressional Authorization and the War on Terrorism, 118 Harv. L. Rev. 2097 (2005). But this canon does not at all challenge Congress's authority to override international law so long as the meaning of the statute is clear. We shall have occasion later in the course to read about "plain meaning" rules as ways not so much of *limiting* power as *forcing* an open acknowledgment that Congress (presumably, as a practical matter, with presidential support) is in fact intending to renounce the treaty (or, as we shall see, trench on what is a presumptively protected interest of a state within our federal system).

2. It is not enough, though, that Congress has the formal power to override a treaty. In addition, Congress must have the constitutional power to pass the legislation in question. Although Justice Field refers to "those sovereign powers delegated by the constitution" to the national government, one might note that he nowhere quotes any specific text assigning Congress a power to control immigration. He might, for example, have cited Henderson v. New York, 92 U.S. 259 (1876), which held that the Commerce Clause gave Congress exclusive control over immigration to the United States. Instead, he emphasizes control over immigration as a power deriving from the nature of sovereignty itself. Recall a similar discussion in Mayor of New York v. Miln, Chapter 3, though, ironically enough, it arose in the context of the majority's asserting New York's right, as a "sovereign state," to control its borders.

Note the final paragraph of Field's opinion and its allusion to the debate over the constitutionality of the Alien Act in 1798, see Chapter 2, supra. He is fending off the application in the instant case of arguments made, by Albert Gallatin and others, that the Act was beyond Congress's "limited" powers. But recall that defenders of the Act were more than happy to make an argument quite similar to Field's in its reliance on the inherent power of "sovereigns" over aliens. Assuming that the Chinese Exclusion Case is not overruled, do *any* aliens possess a constitutional right not to be summarily deported, upon congressional command, simply because of fears generated by their national origin?

3. Probably the strongest assertion of "inherent sovereign powers" beyond anything assigned in the text is United States v. Curtiss-Wright Export Corp., 299 U.S. 304 (1936). According to Justice Sutherland, "the investment of the federal government with the powers of external sovereignty [i.e., relating to other 'sovereign states' in the international political system] did not depend upon the affirmative grants of the Constitution. The powers to declare and wage war, to conclude peace, to make treaties, to maintain diplomatic relations with other sovereignties, if they had never been mentioned in the Constitution, would have vested in the federal government as necessary concomitants of nationality. . . ." If Justice Sutherland is correct, then is it basically superfluous that the Constitution stipulates the ability of the United States "to declare and wage war . . . [or] to make treaties"? (Recall Madison's argument that leaving out the treaty power would have been a "grave defect" that could not be remedied by interpretation.) Justice Sutherland's history and metaphysics have generated significant criticism,[104] but his analysis reflected the notion, especially prevalent after World War II, that Congress and the executive

---

104. See, e.g., Charles Lofgren, United States v. Curtiss-Wright Corporation: An Historical Reassessment, 83 Yale L.J. 1 (1973).

together have virtually unlimited and plenary powers in the conduct of foreign affairs, despite the familiar claim that the federal government is merely one of limited and enumerated powers.

III. THE RISE OF THE MODERN INDUSTRIAL ORDER AND THE PROTECTION OF ECONOMIC RIGHTS

A. Economic Disorder and Emergency Powers[105]

The decades following the Civil War were times of widespread social protest, stemming from

> the great pace of industrialization and, more particularly, from the swift concentration of economic power in the large corporation. Midwestern and Southern farmers, unable to control their marketing through organization and suffering from a long-term international price decline, complained bitterly of monopolistic rates by railroads, grain elevators, and banks. Factory workers and miners, crowded in slums with insecure status in a rapidly changing economy, periodically rebelled at low wages, long hours, and bad working conditions. Small businessmen, faced with the more efficient, and frequently more ruthless, competition of the large corporation, charged that the continued consolidation of capital was destroying individual opportunity. And many professional and white-collar people, uneasy over the accumulation of great wealth and the growing disparity of rich and poor, feared that the traditional fluidity of American society was fast disappearing. . . . Under the pressure of social discontent, legislators had begun to act in the 1870's and 1880's in regard to railroad and grain elevator rates, labor relations, and other matters affecting large business concerns. In turn, corporation lawyers had been pressing the courts to protect more vigilantly the rights of property against legislative regulation.[106]

This period marked the rise of the movement for organized labor, which, among other things, argued for the right of workers to strike. The year 1877, along with the final withdrawal of federal troops from the South, saw a host of strikes by railroad workers. President Hayes "sent federal troops to Baltimore, St. Louis, Chicago, and Pittsburgh. Pitched battles erupted between strikers and soldiers, with deadly results."[107] Twenty strikers and four soldiers, for example, died in Pittsburgh, while three strikers were killed in Chicago. A decade later, in the Haymarket Affair—or Massacre or

---

105. See generally Sidney Fine, Laissez Faire and the General Welfare State (1956); Richard Hofstadter, Social Darwinism in American Thought (rev. ed. 1955); Arnold Paul, Conservative Crisis and the Rule of Law (1960); Benjamin Twiss, Lawyers and the Constitution: How Laissez Faire Came to the Supreme Court (1942).

106. Paul, supra n.105, at 1-2, 5. But cf. Gabriel Kolko, Railroads and Regulation, 1877-1916 (1965).

107. Peter Irons, A People's History of the Supreme Court 239 (2006).

Riot, depending on one's preferred nomenclature—of 1886, Chicago police attacked a crowd of strikers and a bomb exploded at a rally in Haymarket Square that killed 7 and wounded 59 police officers. "Eight members of anarchist groups that organized the rally were charged with murder and sentenced to death," even though seven of them had not been present and the eighth was delivering a speech when the bomb exploded. Four of them were ultimately hung, one committed suicide, and Illinois Governor John Peter Altgeld pardoned the remaining three because of his belief that the trials were fundamentally flawed. "It is no exaggeration," historian Peter Irons writes, "to describe the battles of workers and employees of the 1870s and 1880s as class warfare, a struggle waged both in the streets and voting booths."[108]

Among the most important labor leaders of the time was Eugene V. Debs, a principal organizer of the American Railway Union. During the economic downturns of the 1890s, the Pullman Palace Car Company (the producer of famous "sleeping cars" that helped to revolutionize travel in America) abruptly cut the wages of their workers, who decided to strike. The strike effectively shut down rail traffic in and out of Chicago, perhaps the major hub of railway transport at the time. President Cleveland responded both by sending in federal troops and seeking an injunction against the strike. Neither of these had been authorized by Congress, which set the stage for the case below.

In re Debs

158 U.S. 564 (1895)

[A federal court issued an injunction against the American Railway Union and its leaders, including Eugene V. Debs, ordering them to end the strike of the Pullman Company and "commanding the defendants 'and all persons combining and conspiring with them'" to cease their interference with the operation of the various railroads. The injunction was not obeyed, and Debs and other union officials were sentenced to jail terms varying from three to six months. The Supreme Court heard their appeal, at which Debs was represented by former United States Senator Lyman Trumbull and Clarence Darrow.

The United States alleged that the 22 railroad companies affected by the strike "were engaged in the business of interstate commerce, and subject to the provisions of [a number of federal laws]. [They annually brought to and from Chicago more than 12 million people, as well as "many millions of tons" of freight. In addition,] each of the roads was under contract to carry, and in fact carrying, the mails of the United States; . . . all were by statute declared post roads of the government; [and] that many were by special acts of congress required, at any and all times, to carry the troops and military forces of the United States, and provisions, munitions, and general supplies therefor. . . . [The bill of complaint] stated at some length the necessity of the continued and uninterrupted running of such interstate railroads for the bringing into the city of Chicago supplies for its citizens and for the carrying on of the varied industries of that city."

---

108. Id. at 240.

The United States accused the American Railway Union of engaging in "a combination and conspiracy to prevent the railroad companies and the receivers, and each of them, from performing their duties as common carriers of interstate commerce. . . . [T]hey had asserted that they could and would tie up, paralyze, and break down any and every of said railway companies and receivers which did not accede to their demands; that, in pursuance of the instructions, commands, and requests of said officers, large numbers of the employees of the railway companies and receivers left their service. . . ."]

Mr. Justice BREWER delivered the opinion of the court.

[W]hile the [national government] is properly styled a government of enumerated powers, yet within the limits of such enumeration it has all the attributes of sovereignty, and, in the exercise of those enumerated powers, acts directly upon the citizen, and not through the intermediate agency of the state. . . . Among the powers expressly given to the national government are the control of interstate commerce and the creation and management of a post-office system for the nation . . .

As, under the constitution, power over interstate commerce and the transportation of the mails is vested in the national government, and congress, by virtue of such grant, has assumed actual and direct control, it follows that the national government may prevent any unlawful and forcible interference therewith. . . . Doubtless, it is within the competency of congress to prescribe by legislation that any interferences with these matters shall be offenses against the United States. . . . But is that the only remedy? . . . By article 3, 2, cl. 3, of the federal constitution, it is provided: "The trial of all crimes except in cases of impeachment shall be by jury; and such trial shall be held in the state where the said crime shall have been committed." If all the inhabitants of a state, or even a great body of them, should combine to obstruct interstate commerce or the transportation of the mails, prosecutions for such offenses had in such a community would be doomed in advance to failure. And if the certainty of such failure was known, and the national government had no other way to enforce the freedom of interstate commerce and the transportation of the mails than by prosecution and punishment for interference therewith, the whole interests of the nation in these respects would be at the absolute mercy of a portion of the inhabitants of that single state.

But there is no such impotency in the national government. The entire strength of the nation may be used to enforce in any part of the land the full and free exercise of all national powers and the security of all rights intrusted by the constitution to its care. The strong arm of the national government may be put forth to brush away all obstructions to the freedom of interstate commerce or the transportation of the mails. If the emergency arises, the army of the nation, and all its militia, are at the service of the nation, to compel obedience to its laws.

[I]s there no other alternative than the use of force on the part of the executive authorities whenever obstructions arise to the freedom of interstate commerce or the transportation of the mails? Is the army the only instrument by which rights of the public can be enforced, and the peace of the nation preserved? . . . The existence of this right of forcible abatement is not inconsistent with, nor does it destroy, the right of appeal, in an orderly way, to the courts for a judicial determination, and an exercise of their powers, by writ of injunction and otherwise, to accomplish the same result. . . .

So, in the case before us, the right to use force does not exclude the right of appeal to the courts for a judicial determination, and for the exercise of all their powers of prevention. Indeed, it is more to the praise than to the blame of the government that, instead of determining for itself questions of right and wrong on the part of these petitioners and their associates, and enforcing that determination by the club of the policeman and the bayonet of the soldier, it submitted all those questions to the peaceful determination of judicial tribunals. . . . [I]t is no sufficient answer to its appeal to one of those courts that it has no pecuniary interest in the matter. The obligations which it is under to promote the interest of all and to prevent the wrongdoing of one, resulting in injury to the general welfare, is often of itself sufficient to give it a standing in court. . . .

Nor is there in this any invasion of the constitutional right of trial by jury. . . . [T]he power of a court to make an order carries with it the equal power to punish for a disobedience of that order, and the inquiry as to the question of disobedience has been, from time immemorial, the special function of the court. . . . [A] court enforcing obedience to its orders by proceedings for contempt is not executing the criminal laws of the land, but only securing to suitors the rights which it has adjudged them entitled to. . . .

[I]t may be true, as suggested, that in the excitement of passion a mob will pay little heed to processes issued from the courts, and it may be, as said by counsel in argument, that it would savor somewhat of the puerile and ridiculous to have read a writ of injunction to Lee's army during the late Civil War. It is doubtless true that inter arma leges silent, and in the throes of rebellion or revolution the processes of civil courts are of little avail, for the power of the courts rests on the general support of the people, and their recognition of the fact that peaceful remedies are the true resort for the correction of wrongs. But does not counsel's argument imply too much? Is it to be assumed that these defendants were conducting a rebellion or inaugurating a revolution, and that they and their associates were thus placing themselves beyond the reach of the civil process of the courts? . . . Whatever any single individual may have thought or planned, the great body of those who were engaged in these transactions contemplated neither rebellion nor revolution, and when in the due order of legal proceedings the question of right and wrong was submitted to the courts, and by them decided, they unhesitatingly yielded to their decisions. . . .

[W]e hold that the government of the United States is one having jurisdiction over every foot of soil within its territory, and acting directly upon each citizen; that, while it is a government of enumerated powers, it has within the limits of those powers all the attributes of sovereignty; that to it is committed power over interstate commerce and the transmission of the mail; that the powers thus conferred upon the national government are not dormant, but have been assumed and put into practical exercise by the legislation of congress; that in the exercise of those powers it is competent for the nation to remove all obstructions upon highways, natural or artificial, to the passage of interstate commerce or the carrying of the mail; that, while it may be competent for the government (through the executive branch and in the use of the entire executive power of the nation) to forcibly remove all such obstructions, it is equally within its competency to appeal to the civil courts for an inquiry and determination as to the existence and character of any alleged obstructions, and if such are found to exist, or threaten to occur, to invoke the powers of those courts to remove or restrain such obstructions. . . .

DISCUSSION

1. Note the Court's insistence that disputes between employers and employees had national repercussions and were therefore within the power of the federal government to regulate, because they interfered with national telecommunications and transportations networks. In re Debs was an early statement of expansive national power, in this case prompted by fear of labor union unrest.

2. Presumably, Congress could have authorized the use of federal troops and the federal judiciary to protect carriage of the mail and the shipment of goods in interstate commerce, by invoking its powers under Article I, §8. What difference should it make that Congress had not done so? Is the power to call out troops and invoke the federal judiciary part of the "executive power" that is assigned to the President in Article II, even though not specified as one of his powers? Note that the Court did not rely on the Militia Acts, but simply assumed that the President had inherent power to break the strike and that the federal courts had power to issue injunctive relief and issue contempt citations without a statutory cause of action. By contrast, in the Pentagon Papers Case, New York Times Co. v. United States, 403 U.S. 713 (1971), the Supreme Court overturned a lower court injunction against *The New York Times*'s publication of the Pentagon Papers detailing early U.S. involvement in the Vietnam War on the ground that Congress had not specifically authorized an injunctive remedy.

3. Strikes involve disputes between a labor force and a management; workers want more in salary than management is willing to pay. Was the Cleveland Administration behaving "neutrally" in sending in troops and seeking injunctive relief (and then defending the jailing of Debs), or was it taking the side of Pullman and other railroads against the American Railway Union? Imagine that the federal government had instead seized the Pullman Palace Car Company and ordered the treasurer of the company to pay the workers the former wage level prior to the unilateral cut announced by the company. The Fifth Amendment clearly recognizes the possibility that the national government might seize private property "for public use," subject to "just compensation." See the analogous problem raised by the Steel Seizure Case, Youngstown Sheet & Tube Co. v. Sawyer, Chapter 6, infra.

B. The Rise of Due Process Protection Against State Economic Regulation

Although the Supreme Court initially resisted using the Fourteenth Amendment to strike down economic regulation in the Slaughterhouse Cases, by 1890 the Court had essentially embraced the theory of the Due Process Clause set out in Justice Bradley's dissent. After the Slaughterhouse Cases, corporations could not expect aid from the Privileges or Immunities Clause of the Fourteenth Amendment. Attention therefore turned to the Due Process Clause. The natural rights tradition clinging to that clause—recall especially Justice Field's dissent and its references to the Declaration of Independence—and the Due Process Clause's inviting references to "property" and "liberty" led corporate lawyers to seize on it.

State courts were the first to respond. Even before the Civil War, New York had protected vested rights under the state constitution's Due Process Clause. In Wynehamer v. New York, 12 N.Y. 378 (1856), Judge Comstock, in one of several seriatim opinions, invoked the Due Process Clause of the New York Constitution to invalidate a law prohibiting the sale of intoxicating liquor on the grounds that it unconstitutionally deprived liquor owners of their property without due process of law.

In Matter of Jacobs, 98 N.Y. 98 (1885), the New York Court of Appeals struck down a statute prohibiting the manufacture of cigars in tenement houses. The court dismissed the ostensible public health (i.e., "police power") rationale of the law to hold that it "interferes with the profitable and free use of his property by the owner or lessee of a tenement house" and "arbitrarily deprives him of his property and of some portion of his personal liberty." In Godcharles v. Wigeman, 113 Pa. 431, 6 A. 354 (1886), the Pennsylvania Supreme Court held "utterly unconstitutional and void" a law requiring mining and manufacturing companies to pay wages in cash (rather than in vouchers redeemable only at the company store):

> An attempt has been made by the legislature to do what, in this country, cannot be done; that is, prevent persons who are sui juris [i.e., persons who possess full legal rights and capacity] from making their own contracts. The Act is an infringement alike of the right of the employer and the employee; more than this, it is an insulting attempt to put the laborer under legislative tutelage, which is not only degrading to his manhood, but *subversive of his rights as a citizen of the United States* (emphasis added).
>
> He may sell labor for what he thinks best, whether money or goods, just as his employer may sell his iron or coal, and any and every law that proposes to prevent him from so doing is an infringement of his constitutional privileges, and consequently vicious and void.

Although not all state courts were so hostile to social legislation and some were avowedly sympathetic, decisions like these became increasingly common.

One important exception to the trend of protecting property and contract rights through the Due Process Clause was liquor regulation. This was due in large part to social mobilization by evangelicals, who wanted to ban the sale of alcohol (and gambling) in their states.[109] Under the logic of Wynehamer v. New

109. See generally John W. Compton, The Evangelical Origins of the Living Constitution (2014).

York, a complete ban on the sale of alcohol—which had long been sold legally in the United States and was not traditionally regarded as an inherently dangerous commodity or a public nuisance—would have violated the Due Process Clause. That is because a complete ban on sales would have destroyed property owners' investments in alcohol and limited their contractual freedom to sell a lawful product to a willing buyer. Nevertheless, in Mugler v. Kansas, 123 U.S. 623 (1887), the Supreme Court, in an opinion by Justice Harlan, held that a total ban on alcohol sales did not violate the Due Process Clause of the Fourteenth Amendment:

> The power which the States have of prohibiting such use by individuals of their property as will be prejudicial to the health, the morals, or the safety of the public is not, and, consistently with the existence and safety of organized society, cannot be, burdened with the condition that the State must compensate such individual owners for pecuniary losses they may sustain by reason of their not being permitted, by a noxious use of their property, to inflict injury upon the community.
>
> The exercise of the police power by the destruction of property which is itself a public nuisance, or the prohibition of its use in a particular way, whereby its value becomes depreciated, is very different from taking property for public use or from depriving a person of his property without due process of law. In the one case, a nuisance only is abated; in the other, unoffending property is taken away from an innocent owner.
>
> It is true, when the defendants in these cases purchased or erected their breweries, the laws of the State did not forbid the manufacture of intoxicating liquors. But the State did not thereby give any assurance, or come under an obligation, that its legislation upon that subject would remain unchanged.

The logic of *Mugler* was in some tension with the theories of economic liberty that would develop in succeeding decades.

The early pressures for federal judicial intervention to protect economic rights came mostly from regulated industries, and the Court first intervened in 1890, not against labor and consumer protection regulation but against railroad rate regulation. The following paragraphs trace the growth of the federal doctrine of what came to be known as "substantive due process"—the protection of substantive liberties under the Due Process Clauses of the Fifth and Fourteenth Amendments.

The first decision, and the "bête noire of laissez faire conservatism,"[110] was Munn v. Illinois, 94 U.S. 113 (1877), which upheld a state law limiting the rates charged by Chicago grain-storage warehouses. Writing for the Court, Chief Justice Waite began by asserting that a state had inherent authority—the "police power"—to regulate "the conduct of its citizens one towards another, and the manner in which each shall use his own property, when such regulation becomes necessary for the public good." He then noted that it was the practice in England, the

110. Paul, supra n.105, at 8.

colonies, and the states "to regulate ferries, common carriers, hackmen, bakers, millers, wharfingers, innkeepers, &c., and in so doing to fix a maximum of charge to be made for services rendered, accommodations furnished, and articles sold," and that the practice was followed in the District of Columbia, which was subject to the Fifth Amendment's Due Process Clause. "From this it is apparent that . . . it was not supposed that statutes regulating the use, or even the price of the use, of private property necessarily deprived an owner of his property without due process of law. Under some circumstances they may, but not under all." This brought the Chief Justice "to inquire as to the principles upon which this power of regulation rests." For the answer, he turned to Lord Chief Justice Hale's seventeenth-century treatise, De Portibus Maris, to conclude that private property may be regulated when it is "affected with a public interest." The criteria for property becoming "clothed with a public interest" are that it is "used in a manner to make it of public consequence, and affects the community at large." The warehouses, which possessed "a virtual monopoly" on the storage of grain bound from the Midwest to national markets, clearly met these criteria.

Finally, the Court refused to hear an argument that the maximum permissible rates were "unreasonable."

> Undoubtedly, in mere private contracts, relating to matters in which the public has no interest, what is reasonable must be ascertained judicially. But this is because the legislature has no control over such a contract. . . . The controlling fact is the power to regulate at all. If that exists, the right to establish the maximum of charge, as one of the means of legislation, is implied. . . . We know that this is a power which may be abused; but that is no argument against its existence. For protection against abuses by legislatures the people must resort to the polls, not to the courts.

Justice Field, joined by Justice Strong, dissented.

The Court reaffirmed *Munn* in the Railroad Commission Cases, 116 U.S. 307 (1886), which upheld state regulation of railroad tariffs (notwithstanding a provision in the railroad's 1884 charter empowering it to set its own charges). Again Chief Justice Waite wrote that the reasonableness of rates was a legislative question. But he went on to caution:

> From what has thus been said, it is not to be inferred that this power of limitation or regulation is itself without limit. This power to regulate is not a power to destroy, and limitation is not the equivalent of confiscation. Under pretence of regulating fares and freights, the State cannot require a railroad corporation to carry persons or property without reward; neither can it do that which in law amounts to a taking of private property for public use without just compensation, or without due process of law.

That same year, in Santa Clara County v. Southern Pacific Railroad, 118 U.S. 394, the Court assumed without discussion that the word "person" in the Due Process Clause of the Fourteenth Amendment encompassed artificial persons, i.e., corporations.[111] The Court explicitly accepted this view two years later in an opinion by Justice Field, Pembina Consolidated Silver Mining Co. v. Pennsylvania, 125 U.S. 181, 188-189 (1888).

Viewed in retrospect, these decisions indicate a gradual weakening of the Court's rejection of substantive due process in the Slaughterhouse Cases. Waite's opinion in *Munn* implied that the Constitution might forbid state regulation of matters that were not "affected with a public interest"; the Railroad Commission Cases explicitly suggested that in extreme cases it might be appropriate for courts to inquire into "reasonableness"; and the Court's definition of "persons" opened the way for direct challenges to regulations by corporations.

Of the Justices who had participated in the Slaughterhouse Cases, only Field, Bradley, and Miller remained on the Court in 1890. That year in the Minnesota Rate Cases, 134 U.S. 418, the Court struck down a statute granting a state railroad commission unreviewable authority to set rates. Justice Blatchford wrote that the reasonableness of rates "is eminently a question for judicial investigation, requiring due process of law for its determination": "If the company is deprived of the power of charging reasonable rates for the use of its property, and such deprivation takes

---

111. On the real and supposed understanding of the framers of the Fourteenth Amendment on this matter, see Howard Graham, Everyman's Constitution, chs. 1-2, 10-12 (1968), which includes Graham's well-known article, The "Conspiracy Theory" of the Fourteenth Amendment, 47 Yale L.J. 371, 48 id. 171 (1938). Corporations were held not to be "citizens" under the Privileges or Immunities Clause. See Paul v. Virginia, 75 U.S. (8 Wall.) 168 (1868); Blake v. McClung, 172 U.S. 239 (1898).

The text of *Santa Clara* does not actually hold that corporations are persons, but the court reporter's headnote, written by J.C. Bancroft Davis, former president of the Newburgh and New York Railway Company, states: "One of the points made and discussed at length in the brief of counsel for defendants in error was that 'corporations are persons within the meaning of the Fourteenth Amendment to the Constitution of the United States.' Before argument, Mr. Chief Justice Waite said: 'The Court does not wish to hear argument on the question whether the provision in the Fourteenth Amendment to the Constitution which forbids a state to deny to any person within its jurisdiction the equal protection of the laws applies to these corporations. We are all of opinion that it does.'"

Before publication on May 26, 1886, Davis wrote to Chief Justice Morrison Waite, to ensure that the headnote reflected the Court's views. Waite replied: "I think your mem. in the California Railroad Tax cases expresses with sufficient accuracy what was said before the argument began. I leave it with you to determine whether anything need be said about it in the report inasmuch as we avoided meeting the constitutional question in the decision." C. Peter Magrath, Morrison R. Waite: The Triumph of Character 224 (1963).

Despite the fact that the Court avoided the question, and the reporter's notes are not part of the Court's opinion and have no legal effect, *Santa Clara* became known as the case that first held that corporations were persons under the Fourteenth Amendment, and the Court began citing it for that proposition in a series of opinions by Justice Field. Pembina Consolidated Silver Mining Co. v. Pennsylvania, 125 U.S. 181, 188-189 (1888); Missouri Pacific Ry. Co. v. Mackey, 127 U.S. 205, 209-210 (1888); Minneapolis & St. Louis Ry. Co. v. Beckwith, 129 U.S. 26, 28 (1889); Charlotte, C. & A. R. Co. v. Gibbes, 142 U.S. 386, 391 (1892). Later cases treated the question as settled. Covington & Lexington Tpk. Road Co. v. Sandford, 164 U.S. 578, 592 (1896); Gulf, Colorado & Santa Fe Ry. Co. v. Ellis, 165 U.S. 150, 154 (1897).

place in the absence of investigation by judicial machinery, it is deprived of the lawful use of its property, and thus, in substance and effect, of the property itself, without due process of law." Justice Bradley, joined by Justices Gray and Lamar, dissented vigorously.

At first glance, the Minnesota Rate Cases seem to build on the tradition of procedural due process to require notice and an opportunity to be heard in the courts before rates could be imposed on the railroads. Such judicializing of administrative rate-making was itself an innovation. But the opinion implied that the judiciary's role was not simply to review the application of legislative criteria to particular cases but to determine—independent of any legislative or administrative criteria—whether the rates established were "reasonable."[112] The broad implications of the decision were not lost on the corporate bar, which rejoiced in it, nor on Justice Bradley, who remarked in dissent with no joy that it "practically overrules Munn v. Illinois."[113]

Within a decade, the Court expanded its inquiries beyond rate regulation to review the substantive validity of legislation of almost every sort. Economic and social theories largely abandoned in the academies and legislative chambers found their last refuge in the judiciary.

C. *The Application of the Bill of Rights to the States*

The Slaughterhouse Cases and United States v. Cruikshank indicated that the Court was reluctant to apply the Bill of Rights to state governments through the Privileges or Immunities Clause. In a third early case, Pumpelly v. Green Bay

---

112. The basic formula was announced eight years later in Smyth v. Ames, 169 U.S. 466 (1898): Rates must yield a fair return upon the present value of the company's assets. For nearly 40 years, the Court was rate-maker and accountant. In FPC v. Natural Gas Pipeline Co., 315 U.S. 575 (1942), the Court noted that "[t]he Constitution does not bind rate-making bodies to the service of any single formula," and in FPC v. Hope Natural Gas Co., 320 U.S. 591 (1944), it expressly repudiated the rule of Smyth v. Ames.

113. Bradley's dissent in *Chicago, Milwaukee & St. Paul* calls for some explanation, since the Court's decision might well be viewed as adopting the position espoused in his dissent in the Slaughterhouse Cases. Bradley's earlier dissent evinces a concern for the plight of small entrepreneurs at the hands of the state-sanctioned monopoly. In a nonconstitutional decision, also written in 1873, he had rejected a railroad's attempt to disclaim common law liability, noting that the carrier and its customer do "not stand on a footing of equality." Railroad Co. v. Lockwood, 84 U.S. (17 Wall.) 357, 379 (1873). From this point of view, there was no inconsistency in upholding legislation constraining "the burdens and charges which those who own [public means of transportation] are authorized to impose upon the public." Bradley argued, moreover, that the Court should accord legislation a presumption of constitutionality:

> I do not mean to say that the legislature, or . . . other legislative agency, may not so act as to deprive parties of their property without due process of law. The Constitution contemplates the possibility of such an invasion of rights. But, acting within their jurisdiction, (as in these cases they have done,) the invasion should be clear and unmistakable to bring the case within that category.

Company, 13 Wall. 166 (1871), Justice Miller wrote for the Court that "though the Constitution of the United States provides that private property shall not be taken for public use without just compensation, it is well settled that this is a limitation on the power of the Federal government, and not on the States." In Walker v. Sauvinet, 92 U.S. 90 (1875), the Court stated sua sponte that the Seventh Amendment right to trial by jury in civil cases did not apply to the states.[114]

In Hurtado v. California, 110 U.S. 516 (1884), the Court held that the Fourteenth Amendment's Due Process Clause did not incorporate the Fifth Amendment right to indictment by grand jury was not required by. (It did not consider the Privileges or Immunities Clause.) Justice Matthews rejected the claim that a long-established legal practice, even one mentioned in the Constitution, was required by due process (as opposed to being merely consistent with it): "[T]o hold that such a characteristic is essential to due process of law, would be to deny every quality of the law but its age, and to render it incapable of progress or improvement. It would be to stamp upon our jurisprudence the unchangeableness attributed to the laws of the Medes and Persians. . . . It is more consonant to the true philosophy of our historical legal institutions to say that the spirit of personal liberty and individual right, which they embodied, was preserved and developed by a progressive growth and wise adaptation to new circumstances and situations of the forms and processes found fit to give, from time to time, new expression and greater effect to modern ideas of self-government."

Justice Harlan was the sole dissenter: "It is difficult . . . to perceive anything in the system of prosecuting human beings for their lives, by information, which suggests that the state which adopts it has entered upon an era of progress and improvement in the law of criminal procedure. . . . Thus, in California nothing stands between the citizen and prosecution for his life except the judgment of a justice of the peace."[115]

Finally, in Maxwell v. Dow, 176 U.S. 581 (1900), the Court squarely considered whether the Fifth Amendment's requirement of grand jury presentment and

---

114. In Spies v. Illinois, 123 U.S. 131 (1887), the Court held that even if the Fifth Amendment self-incrimination and Sixth Amendment jury trial provisions applied to the states through either the Privileges or Immunities or Due Process Clauses, there was no constitutional violation.

115. In Presser v. Illinois, 116 U.S. 252 (1886), Justice Wood followed *Cruikshank* in rejecting claims based on the First and Second Amendments. In O'Neil v. Vermont, 144 U.S. 323 (1892), a dissent by Justice Field, joined by Justice Harlan, argued that the Eighth Amendment's prohibition on cruel and unusual punishments was a privilege or immunity of citizens of the United States (the majority did not reach the issue, arguing that it had not been properly presented on appeal):

> [T]he privileges and immunities of citizens of the United States are such as have their recognition in or guaranty from the constitution of the United States. . . . While, therefore, the 10 amendments, as limitations on power, and, so far as they accomplish their purpose and find their fruition in such limitations, are applicable only to the federal government, and not to the states, yet so far as they declare or recognize the rights of persons they are rights belonging to them as citizens of the United States under the constitution; and the fourteenth amendment, as to all such rights, places a limit upon state power by ordaining that no state shall make or enforce any law which shall abridge them.

the Sixth Amendment's requirement of trial by jury were privileges or immunities of citizenship. An 8-person jury in Utah convicted Maxwell of robbery; Maxwell argued that under Sixth Amendment law, 12 persons were necessary.[116] Utah had also used an information rather than a grand jury indictment.

Justice Rufus Peckham (who also authored Allgeyer v. Louisiana and Lochner v. New York) explained that the question of incorporation had already been settled by the Slaughterhouse Cases. Justice Miller had listed a variety of privileges or immunities of citizens of the United States, but not the criminal procedure guarantees in the Fifth or Sixth Amendments: "A right, such as is claimed here, was not mentioned, and we may suppose it was regarded as pertaining to the state, and not covered by the amendment. . . . [I]f these were such privileges and immunities, they would be among the first that would occur to anyone when enumerating or defining them."

Maxwell pointed to the congressional debates over the adoption of the Fourteenth Amendment to show that Congress had intended to apply the Bill of Rights to the states. Peckham rejected the appeal to legislative history and original intention:

> What speeches were made by other Senators and by Representatives in the House upon this subject is not stated by counsel. . . . [W]hat is said in Congress upon such an occasion may or may not express the views of the majority of those who favor the adoption of the measure. . . . [The meaning] is . . . to be determined by the language actually therein used, and not by the speeches made regarding it. What individual Senators or Representatives may have urged in debate [about] a proposed constitutional amendment, or bill, or resolution, does not furnish a firm ground for its proper construction, nor is it important as explanatory of the grounds upon which the members voted in adopting it.
>
> In the case of a constitutional amendment it is of less materiality than in that of an ordinary bill or resolution. A constitutional amendment must be agreed to, not only by Senators and Representatives, but it must be ratified by the legislatures, or by conventions, in three fourths of the states before such amendment can take effect. The safe way is to read its language in connection with the known condition of affairs out of which the occasion for its adoption may have arisen, and then to construe it, if there be therein any doubtful expressions, in a way, so far as is reasonably possible, to forward the known purpose or object for which the amendment was adopted. This rule could not, of course, be so used as to limit the force and effect of an amendment in a manner which the plain and unambiguous language used therein would not justify or permit.

Justice Harlan dissented:

116. Utah's new constitution required only a jury of eight persons in cases like Maxwell's. Interestingly, in Thompson v. Utah, 170 U.S. 343 (1898), the Court held that a jury of 12 persons was required for crimes committed while Utah was still a federal territory, even for a retrial occurring after Utah became a state. Maxwell's crime occurred after Utah was admitted to the Union in January 1896.

What are the privileges and immunities of "citizens of the United States"? Without attempting to enumerate them, it ought to be deemed safe to say that such privileges and immunities embrace at least those expressly recognized by the Constitution of the United States and placed beyond the power of Congress to take away or impair. . . .

The privileges and immunities specified in the first ten Amendments as belonging to the people of the United States are equally protected by the Constitution. No judicial tribunal has authority to say that some of them may be abridged by the states while others may not be abridged. If a state can take from the citizen charged with crime the right to be tried by a jury of twelve persons, it can, so far as the Constitution of the United States is concerned, take away the remaining privileges and immunities specified in the national Bill of Rights. There is no middle position, unless it be assumed to be one of the functions of the judiciary by an interpretation of the Constitution to mitigate or defeat what its members may deem the erroneous or unwise action of the people in adopting the Fourteenth Amendment.

DISCUSSION

1. *The reinterpretation of the Slaughterhouse Cases.* Justice Peckham based his decision in Maxwell v. Dow on the continuing validity of *Slaughterhouse.* The irony was that three years earlier, in Allgeyer v. Louisiana, also written by Peckham, the Court had effectively overturned *Slaughterhouse*'s central holding. It had adopted the position of the *Slaughterhouse* dissenters that the Fourteenth Amendment protected the right "to live and work where he will; to earn his livelihood by any lawful calling; to pursue any livelihood or avocation; and for that purpose to enter into all contracts which may be proper, necessary, and essential."

As Gerard Magliocca has pointed out, during this period the Court was developing new constitutional protections for freedom of contract and property rights that were in serious tension with—if not inconsistent with—*Slaughterhouse*'s treatment of economic liberty. If *Slaughterhouse* was to remain canonical it had to take on a new meaning: that the Privileges or Immunities Clause did not guarantee the Bill of Rights against the states.[117] As you read through this casebook, you should consider the way that famous cases like *Marbury, McCulloch, Gibbons,* or Brown v. Board of Education take on new meanings as successive generations of Justices employ them for different purposes and reinterpret them to make them consistent with their needs and values.

2. *Twining v. New Jersey and incorporation through the Due Process Clause.* After *Maxwell,* the question of applying the Bill of Rights through the Privileges or Immunities Clause was "no longer open in this court," Twining v. New Jersey, 211 U.S. 78, 98 (1908). *Twining* held that the Fifth Amendment protection against self-incrimination was not a liberty protected by the Due Process Clause, because it was

117. Gerard N. Magliocca, Why Did the Incorporation of the Bill of Rights Fail in the Late Nineteenth Century?, 94 Minn. L. Rev. 102, 138 (2009).

not "a fundamental principle of liberty and justice which inheres in the very idea of free government and is the inalienable right of a citizen of such a government." This early test for incorporation was deliberately restrictive; it rejected Justice Harlan's position that individual rights specifically mentioned in the Constitution automatically applied to the states through the Fourteenth Amendment.

3. *The incorporation of the Just Compensation Clause.* As *Twining* suggests, by the turn of the twentieth century, the debate over the application of the Bill of Rights to the states had shifted to the Due Process Clause—which, not coincidentally, was also the basis of the Court's developing jurisprudence of freedom of contract. Given the Court's developing focus on economic liberty, it is not surprising that the Court's first steps toward incorporation concerned the Fifth Amendment's Just Compensation Clause, which protected property rights. In Chicago, Burlington and Quincy Railroad v. Chicago, 166 U.S. 226 (1897), decided the same month as *Allgeyer*, the Court, in an opinion by Justice Harlan, held that the guarantee of just compensation for takings of private property for public use "was a principle of universal law" and therefore required by due process of law.

By the turn of the century, the U.S. Supreme Court had largely rejected two of the central goals of the Fourteenth Amendment: protecting African Americans from discrimination and securing the basic protections of the Bill of Rights against the states. Instead, the Court developed a Fourteenth Amendment jurisprudence with different aims.

D. The Heyday of Police Power Jurisprudence, 1890-1934

Lochner v. New York

198 U.S. 45 (1905)

[In April 1895, both houses of the New York legislature unanimously passed legislation stating that "[n]o employee shall be required, permitted or suffered to work in a [bakery] more than sixty hours in any one week, or more than ten hours in any one day, unless for the purpose of making a shorter work day on the last day of the week. . . ."[118] Joseph Lochner was convicted of employing a baker in excess of 60 hours in one week.]

PECKHAM, J. . . .

The statute necessarily interferes with the right of contract between the employer and employés, concerning the number of hours in which the latter may labor in the bakery of the employer. The general right to make a contract in relation to his business is part of the liberty of the individual protected by the Fourteenth Amendment of the Federal Constitution. Allgeyer v. Louisiana, 165 U.S. 578

---

118. See Paul Kens, Judicial Power and Reform Politics: The Anatomy of Lochner v. New York 58-59 (1990). Professor Kens notes that the act was amended specifically to state "employee" rather than "person" so as to avoid any inference that a self-employed baker was precluded from working in excess of the hours indicated.

(1897). Under that provision no State can deprive any person of life, liberty or property without due process of law. The right to purchase or to sell labor is part of the liberty protected by this amendment, unless there are circumstances which exclude the right. There are, however, certain powers, existing in the sovereignty of each State in the Union, somewhat vaguely termed police powers, the exact description and limitation of which have not been attempted by the courts. Those powers, broadly stated and without, at present, any attempt at a more specific limitation, relate to the safety, health, morals and general welfare of the public. Both property and liberty are held on such reasonable conditions as may be imposed by the governing power of the State in the exercise of those powers, and with such conditions the Fourteenth Amendment was not designed to interfere.

The State, therefore, has power to prevent the individual from making certain kinds of contracts, and in regard to them the Federal Constitution offers no protection. If the contract be one which the State, in the legitimate exercise of its police power, has the right to prohibit, it is not prevented from prohibiting it by the Fourteenth Amendment. Contracts in violation of a statute, either of the Federal or state government, or a contract to let one's property for immoral purposes, or to do any other unlawful act, could obtain no protection from the Federal Constitution, as coming under the liberty of person or of free contract. Therefore, when the State, by its legislature, in the assumed exercise of its police powers, has passed an act which seriously limits the right to labor or the right of contract in regard to their means of livelihood between persons who are sui juris (both employer and employé), it becomes of great importance to determine which shall prevail—the right of the individual to labor for such time as he may choose, or the right of the State to prevent the individual from laboring or from entering into any contract to labor beyond a certain time prescribed by the State.

This court has recognized the existence and upheld the exercise of the police powers of the States in many cases which might fairly be considered as border ones. . . . [For example, in Holden v. Hardy, 169 U.S. 336 (1898), a] provision in the act of the legislature of Utah was . . . under consideration, the act limiting the employment of workmen in all underground mines or workings . . . [and] in smelting and other institutions for the reduction or refining of ores or metals to eight hours per day. . . . The act was held to be a valid exercise of the police powers of the State. . . . It was held that the kind of employment, mining, smelting, etc., and the character of the employees in such kinds of labor, were such as to make it reasonable and proper for the State to interfere to prevent the employees from being constrained by the rules laid down by the proprietors in regard to labor. . . . There is nothing in Holden v. Hardy which covers the case now before us. . . .

It must, of course, be conceded that there is a limit to the valid exercise of the police power by the State. . . . Otherwise . . . it would be enough to say that any piece of legislation was enacted to conserve the morals, the health or the safety of the people; such legislation would be valid, no matter how absolutely without foundation the claim might be. The claim of the police power would be a mere pretext—become another and delusive name for the supreme sovereignty of the State to be exercised free from constitutional restraint. This is not contended for. In every case that comes before this court, therefore, where legislation of this character is concerned and where the protection of the Federal Constitution is sought, the question necessarily arises: Is this a fair, reasonable and appropriate exercise of the police power of the State, or is it an unreasonable, unnecessary and arbitrary interference with the right of the individual to his personal liberty or to enter into those contracts in relation to labor which may seem to him appropriate or necessary for the support of himself and his family? Of course the liberty of contract relating to labor includes both parties to it. The one has as much right to purchase as the other to sell labor.

This is not a question of substituting the judgment of the court for that of the legislature. If the act be within the power of the State it is valid, although the judgment of the court might be totally opposed to the enactment of such a law. But the question would still remain: Is it within the police power of the State? and that question must be answered by the court.

The question whether this act is valid as a labor law, pure and simple, may be dismissed in a few words. There is no reasonable ground for interfering with the liberty of person or the right of free contract, by determining the hours of labor, in the occupation of a baker. There is no contention that bakers as a class are not equal in intelligence and capacity to men in other trades or manual occupations, or that they are not able to assert their rights and care for themselves without the protecting arm of the State, interfering with their independence of judgment and of action. They are in no sense wards of the State. . . . The law must be upheld, if at all, as a law pertaining to the health of the individual engaged in the occupation of a baker. It does not affect any other portion of the public than those who are engaged in that occupation. Clean and wholesome bread does not depend upon whether the baker works but ten hours per day or only sixty hours a week. . . .

The mere assertion that the subject relates though but in a remote degree to the public health does not necessarily render the enactment valid. The act must have a more direct relation, as a means to an end, and the end itself must be appropriate and legitimate, before an act can be held to be valid which interferes with the general right of an individual to be free in his person and in his power to contract in relation to his own labor. . . .

We think the limit of the police power has been reached and passed in this case. There is, in our judgment, no reasonable foundation for holding this to be necessary or appropriate as a health law. . . .

We think that there can be no fair doubt that the trade of a baker, in and of itself, is not an unhealthy one to that degree which would authorize the legislature to interfere with the right to labor, and with the right of free contract on the part of the individual, either as employer or employé. In looking through statistics regarding all trades and occupations, it may be true that the trade of a baker does not appear to be as healthy as some other trades, and is also vastly more healthy than still others. . . . It might be safely affirmed that almost all occupations more or less affect the health. There must be more than the mere fact of the possible existence of some small amount of unhealthiness to warrant legislative interference with liberty. . . . No trade, no occupation, no mode of earning one's living, could escape this all-pervading power, and the acts of the legislature in limiting the hours of labor in all employments would be valid, although such limitation might seriously cripple the ability of the laborer to support himself and his family. . . .

It is also urged, pursuing the same line of argument, that it is to the interest of the State that its population should be strong and robust, and therefore any legislation which may be said to tend to make people healthy must be valid as health laws, enacted under the police power. If this be a valid argument and a justification for this kind of legislation, it follows that the protection of the Federal Constitution from undue interference with liberty of person and freedom of contract is visionary, wherever the law is sought to be justified as a valid exercise of the police power. Scarcely any law but might find shelter under such assumptions, and conduct, properly so called, as well as contract, would come under the restrictive sway of the legislature. Not only the hours of employés, but the hours of employers, could be regulated, and doctors, lawyers, scientists, all professional men, as well as athletes and artisans, could be forbidden to fatigue their brains and bodies by prolonged hours of exercise, lest the fighting strength of the State be impaired. . . . Statutes of the nature of that under review, limiting the hours in which grown and intelligent men may labor to earn their living, are mere meddlesome interferences with the rights of the individual, and they are not saved from condemnation by the claim that they are passed in the exercise of the police power and upon the subject of the health of the individual whose rights are interfered with, unless there be some fair ground, reasonable in and of itself, to say that there is material danger to the public health or to the health of the employés, if the hours of labor are not curtailed. . . . All that [the State] could properly do has been done by it with regard to the conduct of bakeries, as provided for in the other sections of the act. . . . These several sections provide for the inspection of the premises where the bakery is carried on, with regard to furnishing proper wash-rooms and water-closets, apart from the bake-room, also with regard to providing proper drainage, plumbing and painting. . . . These various sections . . . certainly go to the full extent of providing for the cleanliness and the healthiness, so far as possible, of the quarters in which bakeries are to be conducted. . . .

It was further urged . . . that restricting the hours of labor in the case of bakers was valid because it tended to cleanliness on the part of the workers, as a man was more apt to be cleanly when not overworked, and if cleanly then his "output" was also more likely to be so. . . . In our judgment it is not possible in fact to discover the connection between the number of hours a baker may work in the bakery and the healthful quality of the bread made by the workman. The connection, if any exists, is too shadowy and thin to build any argument for the interference of the legislature. If the man works ten hours a day it is all right, but if ten and a half or eleven his health is in danger and his bread may be unhealthful, and, therefore, he shall not be permitted to do it. This, we think, is unreasonable and entirely arbitrary. When assertions such as we have adverted to become necessary in order to give, if possible, a plausible foundation for the contention that the law is a "health law," it gives rise to at least a suspicion that there was some other motive dominating the legislature than the purpose to subserve the public health or welfare. . . .

It is impossible for us to shut our eyes to the fact that many of the laws of this character, while passed under what is claimed to be the police power for the purpose of protecting the public health or welfare, are, in reality, passed from other motives. We are justified in saying so when, from the character of the law and the subject upon which it legislates, it is apparent that the public health or welfare bears but the most remote relation to the law. The purpose of a statute must be determined from the natural and legal effect of the language employed; and whether it is or is not repugnant to the Constitution of the United States must be determined from the natural effect of such statutes when put into operation, and not from their proclaimed purpose. . . . It seems to us that the real object and purpose were simply to regulate the hours of labor between the master and his employés (all being men, sui juris), in a private business, not dangerous in any degree to morals or in any real and substantial degree, to the health of the employees. Under such circumstances the freedom of master and employés to contract with each other in relation to their employment, and in defining the same, cannot be prohibited or interfered with, without violating the Federal Constitution.

Reversed.

HARLAN, J., joined by WHITE and DAY, JJ., dissenting. . . .

Granting . . . that there is a liberty of contract which cannot be violated even under the sanction of direct legislative enactment, but assuming, as according to settled law we may assume, that such liberty of contract is subject to such regulations as the State may reasonably prescribe for the common good and the wellbeing of society, what are the conditions under which the judiciary may declare such regulations to be in excess of legislative authority and void? Upon this point there is no room for dispute; for, the rule is universal that . . . the power of the courts to review legislative action in respect of a matter affecting the general welfare exists *only* ". . . if a statute purporting to have been enacted to protect the public health, the public morals or the public safety, has no real or substantial relation to those objects, or is, beyond all question, a plain, palpable invasion of rights secured by the fundamental law." . . . If there be doubt as to the validity of the statute, that doubt must therefore be resolved in favor of its validity, and the courts must keep their hands off, leaving the legislature to meet the responsibility for unwise legislation. If the end which the legislature seeks to accomplish be one to which its power extends, and if the means employed to that end, although not the wisest or best, are yet not plainly and palpably unauthorized by law, then the court cannot interfere. In other words, when the validity of a statute is questioned, the burden of proof, so to speak, is upon those who assert it to be unconstitutional.

Let these principles be applied to the present case. . . .

It is plain that this statute was enacted in order to protect the physical wellbeing of those who work in bakery and confectionery establishments. It may be that the statute had its origin, in part, in the belief that employers and employés in such establishments were not upon an equal footing, and that the necessities of the latter often compelled them to submit to such exactions as unduly taxed their strength. Be this as it may, the statute must be taken as expressing the belief of the people of New York that, as a general rule, and in the case of the average man, labor in excess of sixty hours during a week in such establishments may endanger the health of those who thus labor. . . . I find it impossible, in view of common experience, to say that there is here no real or substantial relation between the means employed by the State and the end sought to be accomplished by its legislation. . . .

Professor Hirt in his treatise on the Diseases of the Workers has said: "The labor of the bakers is among the hardest and most laborious imaginable, because it has to be performed under conditions injurious to the health of those engaged in it. It is hard, very hard work, not only because it requires a great deal of physical exertion in an overheated workshop and during unreasonably long hours, but more so because of the erratic demands of the public, compelling the baker to perform the greater part of his work at night, thus depriving him of an opportunity to enjoy the necessary rest and sleep, a fact which is highly injurious to his health." Another writer says: "The constant inhaling of flour dust causes inflammation of the lungs and of the bronchial tubes. The eyes also suffer through this dust, which is responsible for the many cases of running eyes among the bakers. The long hours of toil to which all bakers are subjected produce rheumatism, cramps and swollen legs. The intense heat in the workshops induces the workers to resort to cooling drinks, which together with their habit of exposing the greater part of their bodies to the change in the atmosphere, is another source of a number of diseases of various organs. Nearly all bakers are pale-faced and of more delicate health than the workers of other crafts, which is chiefly due to their hard work and their irregular and unnatural mode of living, whereby the power or resistance against disease is greatly diminished. The average age of a baker is below that of other workmen; they seldom live over their fiftieth year, most of them dying between the ages of forty and fifty. . . ."

We judicially know that the question of the number of hours during which a workman should continuously labor has been, for a long period, and is yet, a subject of serious consideration among civilized peoples, and by those having special knowledge of the laws of health. . . .

I do not stop to consider whether any particular view of this economic question presents the sounder theory. What the precise facts are it may be difficult to say. It is enough for the determination of this case, and it is enough for this court to know, that the question is one about which there is room for debate and for an honest difference of opinion. There are many reasons of a weighty, substantial character, based upon the experience of mankind, in support of the theory that, all things considered, more than ten hours' steady work each day, from week to week, in a bakery or confectionery establishment, may endanger the health, and shorten the lives of the workmen, thereby diminishing their physical and mental capacity to serve the State, and to provide for those dependent upon them.

If such reasons exist that ought to be the end of this case, for the State is not amenable to the judiciary, in respect of its legislative enactments, unless such enactments are plainly, palpably, beyond all questions, inconsistent with the Constitution of the United States.

HOLMES, J., dissenting.

I regret sincerely that I am unable to agree with the judgment in this case, and that I think it my duty to express my dissent.

This case is decided upon an economic theory which a large part of the country does not entertain. If it were a question whether I agreed with that theory, I should desire to study it further and long before making up my mind. But I do not conceive that to be my duty, because I strongly believe that my agreement or disagreement has nothing to do with the right of a majority to embody their opinions in law. It is settled by various decisions of this court that state constitutions and state laws may regulate life in many ways which we as legislators might think as injudicious or if you like as tyrannical as this, and which equally with this interfere with the liberty to contract. Sunday laws and usury laws are ancient examples. A more modern one is the prohibition of lotteries. The liberty of the citizen to do as he likes so long as he does not interfere with the liberty of others to do the same, which has been a shibboleth for some well-known writers, is interfered with by school laws, by the Post Office, by every state or municipal institution which takes his money for purposes thought desirable, whether he likes it or not. The Fourteenth Amendment does not enact Mr. Herbert Spencer's Social Statics. . . .

[A] constitution is not intended to embody a particular economic theory, whether of paternalism and the organic relation of the citizen to the State or of laissez faire. It is made for people of fundamentally differing views, and the accident of our finding certain opinions natural and familiar or novel and even shocking ought not to conclude our judgment upon the question whether statutes embodying them conflict with the Constitution of the United States.

General propositions do not decide concrete cases. The decision will depend on a judgment or intuition more subtle than any articulate major premise. But I think that the proposition just stated, if it is accepted, will carry us far toward the end. Every opinion tends to become a law. I think that the word liberty in the Fourteenth Amendment is perverted when it is held to prevent the natural outcome of a dominant opinion, unless it can be said that a rational and fair man necessarily would admit that the statute proposed would infringe fundamental principles as they have been understood by the traditions of our people and our law. It does not need research to show that no such sweeping condemnation can be passed upon the statute before us. A reasonable man might think it a proper measure on the score of health. Men whom I certainly could not pronounce unreasonable would uphold it as a first instalment of a general regulation of the hours of work. Whether in the latter aspect it would be open to the charge of inequality I think it unnecessary to discuss.

1. The Idea of Police Power Jurisprudence

The period from Allgeyer v. Louisiana in 1897 to West Coast Hotel v. Parrish in 1937 is often called the "*Lochner* era"; during this period the Supreme Court developed a jurisprudence that protected economic liberty under the due process clause.

This jurisprudence is often called "police power jurisprudence" because it concerned the proper scope of the police power of states to regulate health, safety, and welfare in the public interest. The *Lochner* era limited the scope of the police power and the Supreme Court carefully scrutinized legislation (as in *Lochner* itself) which it suspected had a secretly redistributive purpose. Although states were permitted to engage in reasonable attempts to protect health, safety, and welfare, the Court viewed attempts to redistribute income or to rebalance bargaining power between contracting parties as an illegitimate interference with personal liberty. The Court sought to ensure that limitations on individual autonomy were actually justified by the legitimate public purposes of promoting health, safety and welfare rather than being "class legislation" that sought to favor some groups in society (for example, employees) over other groups (for example employers).[119]

As Duncan Kennedy has suggested, the Court during this era viewed individual autonomy and the government police power as two mutually exclusive, non-overlapping domains. Within such a domain, each actor had absolute sovereignty, and the Court conceived its own mission to be the policing of the boundaries between them.[120]

2. The Meanings of "Liberty," "Property," and "Due Process"

The most famous doctrine associated with the *Lochner* era is the theory of liberty of contact. At the beginning of the Court's opinion in *Lochner*, Justice Peckham asserts: "The general right to make a contract in relation to his business is part of the liberty of the individual protected by the Fourteenth Amendment of the Federal Constitution. Allgeyer v. Louisiana. . . . The right to purchase or to sell labor is part of the liberty protected by this amendment, unless there are circumstances which exclude the right." In Allgeyer v. Louisiana, 165 U.S. 578 (1897), Justice Peckham had written for the Court:

> The "liberty" mentioned in [the Fourteenth Amendment] means, not only the right of the citizen to be free from the mere physical restraint of his person, as by incarceration, but the term is deemed to embrace the right of the citizen to be free in the enjoyment of all his faculties; to be free to use them in all lawful ways; to live and work where he will; to earn his livelihood by any lawful calling; to pursue any livelihood or avocation, and for that purpose to enter into all contracts which may be proper, necessary and essential to his carrying out to a successful conclusion the purposes above mentioned.

The Court also associated the constitutional right to make contracts with property rights. In Coppage v. Kansas, 236 U.S. 1 (1915), the Court struck down a statute that prohibited "yellow dog" contracts (contracts forbidding employees to

---

119. See especially the important study by Howard Gillman, The Constitution Besieged: The Rise and Demise of *Lochner* Era Police Powers Jurisprudence (1993).

One can also understand the *Lochner* period as greatly expanding the idea of "general constitutional law," which federal courts had previously been able to invoke only in diversity cases. The jurisprudence of general constitutional law established the legitimate bounds of the legislature's police, taxing, and eminent domain powers, but recognized a broad scope for the police power. See discussion note 1 following The Slaughterhouse Cases, supra; Loan Association v. Topeka, 87 U.S. (20 Wall.) 655 (1874) (holding unconstitutional the issuance of municipal bonds on the ground that their issuance was not for the public interest and therefore lay beyond the state's taxing power). Throughout the Marshall and Taney eras, the core of general constitutional law was the vested rights doctrine; it protected individuals against the retroactive impairment of their property and contract rights. During the *Lochner* era, the Court expanded the scope of general constitutional law and constricted the police power accordingly.

120. Duncan Kennedy, The Rise and Fall of Classical Legal Thought, 1850-1940 (unpublished manuscript, 1975).

join labor unions). The Court wrote: "Included in the right of personal liberty and the *right of private property* . . . is the right to make contracts. . . ." (emphasis added).

Because the Court protected freedom of contract under the Due Process Clause, its doctrines later came to be known as "economic due process," a special case of the doctrine of "substantive due process." The doctrine of substantive due process maintains that the Due Process Clause does more than protect against *improper procedures* that deprive people of life, liberty, or property; it also protects against *substantive infringements* of life, liberty and property quite apart from the procedures the state uses.

The concept of substantive due process evolved from earlier nineteenth century doctrines that protected vested rights and prohibited class legislation. As we have seen, nineteenth century courts sometimes held that laws that imposed special burdens and benefits on particular groups without adequate public justification violated due process because they were special or class legislation. Retroactive infringements of contract or property rights might also violate the vested rights doctrine.

Both of these ideas originated in ideas about process and constitutional structure—namely, that only courts had the power to transfer property rights between persons through judicial decrees and that legislatures should stick to passing laws of general application. Destroying vested rights or enacting class legislation violated separation of powers because legislatures were purporting to assume the powers of courts.

Many of the antecedents of substantive due process built on the prohibition on class legislation, or on the idea that legislatures could not legitimately destroy preexisting vested rights. Wynehamer v. New York, 12 N.Y. 378 (1856), struck down a law banning the sale of intoxicating liquor, which Judge Comstock argued, deprived liquor owners of their property without due process of law and thus destroyed their vested rights. A year later, in Dred Scott v. Sanford, Chief Justice Taney argued that banning slavery in the federal territories violated the Fifth Amendment's Due Process Clause because doing so destroyed vested property rights in slaves whenever slaveholders entered federal territory with their slaves. (See discussion note 5 following Dred Scott in Chapter Four, supra, which discusses some of the problems with Taney's use of this type of argument.).

Abolitionist and anti-slavery thinkers before the Civil War argued that slavery violated due process of law because it arbitrarily took the liberty of slaves and their property in themselves without judicial process.[121] The Republican Party Platform of 1860 invoked the Fifth Amendment's Due Process Clause to deny the authority of Congress, Territorial legislatures, or individuals, to permit or protect slavery in federal territories.[122] These arguments combined concerns about lack of judicial process with the idea that legislatures should not violate the separation of powers through arbitrary or class legislation.

---

121. See, e.g., Randy E. Barnett, Whence Comes Section One? The Abolitionist Origins of the Fourteenth Amendment, 3 J. of Legal Analysis 165, 177-245 (2011) (documenting anti-slavery arguments based on the Fifth Amendment's Due Process Clause).

122. Republican Platform of 1856, reprinted in J.M.H. Frederick, National Party Platforms of The United States 28 (1896). See also Ryan C. Williams, The One and Only Substantive Due Process Clause, 120 Yale L.J. 408, 474-475 (2010).

Section III.B, The Rise of Due Process Protection Against State Economic Regulation After the Civil War, pp. 476-481 supra, described how these antebellum ideas about due process evolved into theories for the protection of business and corporate interests. Many of the key doctrinal innovations were developed in the New York Court of Appeals, where Justice Peckham served before joining the Supreme Court of the United States in 1895.

3. The Scope of the Police Power: Permissible and Impermissible Objectives

The central debate between Justices Peckham and Harlan in *Lochner* concerns whether New York's maximum hour law is within the police power. Why does Peckham think that the maximum hour law is not designed to protect the health, safety, and welfare of bakers or of the general public? Note how he distinguishes Holden v. Hardy, which upheld a maximum hour law for miners. Why are people who work in mines different from people who work in bakeries?[123]

In a famous and influential treatise of the late nineteenth century, Professor Christopher G. Tiedeman argued that the "proper limits" of the police powers are "to compel every one to so use his own property and so conduct himself as not to injure his neighbor or infringe upon his rights."[124] How would one apply this formula in Lochner v. New York? Is the formula circular?

Justice Peckham argues that New York's maximum hour law is not devoted to the protection of health or safety but instead is "a labor law, pure and simple." What does he mean by this? Today people might argue that the maximum hour law is designed to prevent overreaching by employers given that employees lack equal bargaining power. But the *Lochner* era Court did not regard this as a legitimate public purpose. It viewed attempts to alter economic power or redistribute income or wealth through regulation as illegitimate. A good example of the Court's anti-redistributional logic is Coppage v. Kansas, which argued that the Constitution protected a formal equality of contract between employers and employees:

COPPAGE v. KANSAS, 236 U.S. 1 (1915): [A Kansas law forbade employers from making their employees sign "yellow-dog" contracts in which employees promised that they would not join a union. The Supreme Court, in an opinion by Justice Pitney, held that the law violated freedom of contract].

---

123. In Baltimore & Ohio R. Co. v. Interstate Commerce Commission, 221 U.S. 612 (1911), the Court upheld limitations on the hours of railroad employees. Justice Hughes wrote:

> The length of hours of service has a direct relation to the efficiency of the human agencies upon which protection to life and property necessarily depends. . . . In its power suitably to provide for the safety of employees and travelers, Congress was not limited to the enactment of laws relating to mechanical appliances, but it was also competent to consider, and to endeavor to reduce, the dangers incident to the strain of excessive hours of duty on the part of engineers, conductors, train dispatchers, telegraphers, and other persons embraced within the class defined by the act. And in imposing restrictions having reasonable relation to this end there is no interference with liberty of contract as guaranteed by the Constitution.

124. Christopher Tiedeman, A Treatise on the Limitations of Police Power in the United States 8 (1886).

Pitney, J: [Justice Pitney quoted Adair v. United States, 208 U.S. 161 (1908):] "The right of a person to sell his labor upon such terms as he deems proper is, in its essence, the same as the right of the purchaser of labor to prescribe the conditions upon which he will accept such labor from the person offering to sell it. . . . In all such particulars the employer and the employee have equality of right, and any legislation that disturbs that equality is an arbitrary interference with the liberty of contract, which no government can legally justify in a free land."

As to the interest of the employed, it is said . . . to be a matter of common knowledge that "employés, as a rule, are not financially able to be as independent in making contracts for the sale of their labor as are employers in making contracts of purchase thereof." No doubt, wherever the right of private property exists, there must and will be inequalities of fortune; and thus it naturally happens that parties negotiating about a contract are not equally unhampered by circumstances. This applies to all contracts, and not merely to that between employer and employé. Indeed a little reflection will show that wherever the right of private property and the right of free contract co-exist, each party when contracting is inevitably more or less influenced by the question whether he has much property, or little, or none; for the contract is made to the very end that each may gain something that he needs or desires more urgently than that which he proposes to give in exchange. And, since it is self-evident that, unless all things are held in common, some persons must have more property than others, it is from the nature of things impossible to uphold freedom of contract and the right of private property without at the same time recognizing as legitimate those inequalities of fortune that are the necessary result of the exercise of those rights. But the Fourteenth Amendment, in declaring that a State shall not "deprive any person of life, liberty or property without due process of law," gives to each of these an equal sanction; it recognizes "liberty" and "property" as co-existent human rights, and debars the States from any unwarranted interference with either.

And since a State may not strike them down directly it is clear that it may not do so indirectly, as by declaring in effect that the public good requires the removal of those inequalities that are but the normal and inevitable result of their exercise, and then invoking the police power in order to remove the inequalities, without other object in view. The police power is broad, and not easily defined, but it cannot be given the wide scope that is here asserted for it, without in effect nullifying the constitutional guaranty.

We need not refer to the numerous and familiar cases in which this court has held that the power may properly be exercised for preserving the public health, safety, morals, or general welfare, and that such police regulations may reasonably limit the enjoyment of personal liberty, including the right of making contracts. . . . An evident and controlling distinction is this: that in those cases it has been held permissible for the States to adopt regulations fairly deemed necessary to secure some object directly affecting the public welfare, even though the enjoyment of private rights of liberty and property be thereby incidentally hampered; while in that portion of the Kansas statute which is now under consideration—that is to say, aside from coercion, etc.—there is no object or purpose, expressed or implied, that is claimed to have reference to health, safety, morals, or public welfare, beyond the supposed desirability of leveling inequalities of fortune by depriving one who has property of some part of what is characterized as his "financial independence."

In short, an interference with the normal exercise of personal liberty and property rights is the primary object of the statute, and not an incident to the advancement of the general welfare.

The Court nevertheless made exceptions to these principles based on its understandings about the social world.

JACOBSON v. MASSACHUSETTS, 197 U.S. 11(1905): [In *Jacobson*, decided two months before *Lochner*, the Court upheld a compulsory vaccination law, enforced by a five dollar fine, with exemptions for "children who present a certificate, signed by a registered physician, that they are unfit subjects for vaccination." Jacobson asserted that vaccination for smallpox was dangerous and that putting him to the choice of accepting vaccination or paying a fine was an unconstitutional infringement of his liberty. The Court, pointing to the overwhelming consensus of medical experts that smallpox vaccination was safe, rejected the challenge.]

HARLAN, J: [T]he liberty secured by the Constitution of the United States to every person within its jurisdiction does not import an absolute right in each person to be, at all times and in all circumstances, wholly freed from restraint. There are manifold restraints to which every person is necessarily subject for the common good. On any other basis organized society could not exist with safety to its members. Society based on the rule that each one is a law unto himself would soon be confronted with disorder and anarchy. Real liberty for all could not exist under the operation of a principle which recognizes the right of each individual person to use his own, whether in respect of his person or his property, regardless of the injury that may be done to others. . . .

[Defendant pointed to] those of the medical profession who attach little or no value to vaccination as a means of preventing the spread of smallpox, or who think that vaccination causes other diseases of the body. What everybody knows the court must know, and therefore the state court judicially knew, as this court knows, that an opposite theory accords with the common belief, and is maintained by high medical authority. We must assume that, when the statute in question was passed, the legislature of Massachusetts was not unaware of these opposing theories, and was compelled, of necessity, to choose between them. It was not compelled to commit a matter involving the public health and safety to the final decision of a court or jury. It is no part of the function of a court or a jury to determine which one of two modes was likely to be the most effective for the protection of the public against disease. That was for the legislative department to determine in the light of all the information it had or could obtain. . . .

The state legislature proceeded upon the theory which recognized vaccination as at least an effective, if not the best-known, way in which to meet and suppress the evils of a smallpox epidemic that imperiled an entire population. . . . If there is any . . . power in the judiciary to review legislative action in respect of a matter affecting the general welfare, it can only be [according to] the rule that, if a statute purporting to have been enacted to protect the public health, the public morals, or the public safety, has no real or substantial relation to those objects, or is, beyond all question, a plain, palpable invasion of rights secured by the fundamental law, it is the duty of the courts to so adjudge, and thereby give effect to the Constitution. . . .

[I]n view of the methods employed to stamp out the disease of smallpox, [no one] can . . . confidently assert that the means prescribed by the state to that end has no real or substantial relation to the protection of the public health and the public safety. Such an assertion would not be consistent with the experience of this and other countries whose authorities have dealt with the disease of smallpox. . . .

We are not prepared to hold that a minority, residing or remaining in any city or town where smallpox is prevalent, and enjoying the general protection afforded by an organized local government, may thus defy the will of its constituted authorities, acting in good faith for all, under the legislative sanction of the state. If such be the privilege of a minority, then a like privilege would belong to each individual of the community, and the spectacle would be presented of the welfare and safety of an entire population being subordinated to the notions of a single individual who chooses to remain a part of that population. We are unwilling to hold it to be an element in the liberty secured by the Constitution of the United States that one person, or a minority of persons, residing in any community and enjoying the benefits of its local government, should have the power thus to dominate the majority when supported in their action by the authority of the state. . . .

[Justice Peckham (the author of *Lochner*) and Justice Brewer dissented without opinion.]

Another area in which the Court upheld regulation involved women, based on stereotypical understandings of their abilities.

MULLER v. OREGON, 208 U.S. 412 (1908): [*Muller* upheld a statute limiting the workday of women in factories and laundries to ten hours.]

BREWER, J.: That woman's physical structure and the performance of maternal functions place her at a disadvantage in the struggle for subsistence is obvious. This is especially true when the burdens of motherhood are upon her. Even when they are not, by abundant testimony of the medical fraternity continuance for a long time on her feet at work, repeating this from day to day, tends to injurious effects upon the body, and as healthy mothers are essential to vigorous offspring, the physical well-being of woman becomes an object of public interest and care in order to preserve the strength and vigor of the race.

Still again, history discloses the fact that woman has always been dependent upon man. He established his control at the outset by superior physical strength, and this control in various forms, with diminishing intensity, has continued to the present. As minors, though not to the same extent, she has been looked upon in the courts as needing especial care that her rights may be preserved. Education was long denied her, and while now the doors of the school room are opened and her opportunities for acquiring knowledge are great, yet even with that and the consequent increase of capacity for business affairs it is still true that in the struggle for subsistence she is not an equal competitor with her brother. Though limitations upon personal and contractual rights may be removed by legislation, there is that in her disposition and habits of life which will operate against a full assertion of those rights. She will still be where some legislation to protect her seems necessary to secure a real equality of right. Doubtless there are individual exceptions, and there are many respects in which she has an advantage over him; but looking at it from the viewpoint of the effort to maintain an independent position in life, she is not upon an equality. Differentiated by these matters from the other sex, she is properly placed in a class by herself, and legislation designed for her protection may be sustained, even when like legislation is not necessary for men and could not be sustained. It is impossible to close one's eyes to the fact that she still looks to her brother and depends upon him. Even though all restrictions on political, personal and contractual rights were taken away, and she stood, so far as statutes are concerned, upon an absolutely equal plane with him, it would still be true that she is so constituted that she will rest upon and look to him for protection; that her physical structure and a proper discharge of her maternal functions—having in view not merely her own health, but the well-being of the race—justify legislation to protect her from the greed as well as the passion of man. The limitations which this statute places upon her contractual powers, upon her right to agree with her employer as to the time she shall labor, are not imposed solely for her benefit, but also largely for the benefit of all. Many words cannot make this plainer. The two sexes differ in structure of body, in the functions to be performed by each, in the amount of physical strength, in the capacity for long-continued labor, particularly when done standing, the influence of vigorous health upon the future well-being of the race, the self-reliance which enables one to assert full rights, and in the capacity to maintain the struggle for subsistence.

In *Muller*, the Court relied on a 113-page brief filed by future Supreme Court Justice Louis Brandeis and his sister-in-law, Josephine Clara Goldmark, a noted consumer and labor advocate. Their argument in support of Oregon's maximum-hour legislation for women contained only a few pages of legal citations, with the rest consisting of medical and social science testimony about the harms of long working hours on the health, safety, morals, and welfare of women. Although this was not the first such brief, legal briefs that present courts with detailed accounts of social science data and scientific testimony, have come to be called "Brandeis briefs."

4. Burdens of Proof and Questions of Degree

Justice Peckham offers a test to determine whether the New York statute can be upheld as a regulation protecting the health of bakery employees or consumers: "There [must] be some fair ground, reasonable in and of itself, to say that there is a material danger to the public health, or to the health of the employee, if the hours of labor are not curtailed." How does this test differ, theoretically or in application, from Justice Harlan's criterion that the law must "have a real or substantial relation" to the promotion of health? Harlan sets out a number of facts about the health of bakers, to conclude that "there is room for debate and for an honest difference of opinion" whether long hours are injurious.

Peckham does not explicitly deny that there may be. On what basis, then, does the Court strike down the New York statute? Note that Peckham and Harlan apply police power jurisprudence with different burdens of proof and different ways of characterizing the facts before the Court. Harlan is generally willing to give the New York legislature the benefit of the doubt; he cites to treatises that support what he believes to be the legislature's actual purposes. Peckham, by contrast, suspects that the New York legislature may be up to no good (that is, he suspects that it is engaged in a covert attempt at redistribution). He disputes that working in bakeries for long hours is unhealthy either to the bakers or to the people who buy the bread, and he views the ten hour cutoff as arbitrary. He sees nothing special about bakers that prevents them from protecting their own interests through contract. Moreover, he notes that the same arguments for maximum hour laws might be applied to many other professions that the New York legislature does not regulate in the same way. Thus, Peckham emphasizes a lack of fit between the legislature's asserted ends (public health and safety) and the means that it uses to achieve them (regulating the hours of bakers), which suggests to him that it acts out of suspect motives.

Peckham's and Harlan's approaches to the New York statute anticipate modern ideas of different levels of judicial scrutiny. Harlan applies a relatively low level of scrutiny and Peckham applies what we would now call heightened or strict scrutiny.

By contrast, Justice Holmes' dissent operates largely outside of the categories of police power jurisprudence. Why does Holmes think that courts should generally defer to legislatures? What limits, if any, would he place on legislation that violates individual rights?

Holmes' virtual abdication of judicial responsibility in economic legislation would prove highly influential for defenders of the New Deal; his call for judicial restraint in his brief dissent would later be celebrated as a critique of the entire *Lochner* era. Nevertheless, Holmes's general approach looks far less laudable in cases like Giles v. Harris 189 U.S. 475 (1903) (acquiescing in Alabama's disenfranchisement of Black people), and Buck v. Bell, 274 U.S. 200 (1927) (upholding compulsory sterilization).

5. Laissez Faire, Lawyers, and Legal Scholarship

Opponents of nineteenth-century rate and labor regulations typically argued, in the language of traditional conservatism, that the rights of property were insecure in the hands of popularly controlled state legislatures. And they also invoked the laissez faire doctrines of the eighteenth-century economist Adam Smith and the nineteenth-century social Darwinists Herbert Spencer and William Graham Sumner.

Justice Holmes's remark that "The Fourteenth Amendment does not enact Mr. Herbert Spencer's Social Statics" adverted to this history. Holmes' quip is a bit unfair to the Justices in the *Lochner* majority, who were applying police power jurisprudence, not making grand claims about social theory. (In fact, the Justice with the greatest affinity to Social Darwinism on the Court in 1905 was probably Holmes himself.) Nevertheless, like other members of the conservative bar and bench, the *Lochner*-era Justices were influenced by the dominant ideas of their time, which celebrated and justified economic liberty while tending to ignore or blink at the excesses of the First Gilded Age.

Smith is the father of free market theory. In modern and much oversimplified terms, individuals are motivated by self-interest, which leads to competition in the marketplace, which regulates itself so as to produce just the right quantity and quality of goods and services demanded and to allocate them in the most efficient manner.[125] Government plays a legitimate role by providing public goods (e.g., armies and police), regulating monopolies, requiring activities to internalize the external costs they generate (e.g., by preventing or providing damage remedies for "nuisances"), and subsidizing activities (e.g., education) to the extent they produce external benefits. But government-operated enterprises and government intervention in the private sector generally are inefficient and undesirable, and government redistribution of income may subvert incentives and distort the market. Because efficient operation of the market depends on the ability of individuals and firms to transact freely with each other, government constraints on private contracting are especially destructive.

The social Darwinists provided an independent justification for government nonintervention and especially for inequalities of wealth. From the process of natural selection, Herbert Spencer, an Englishman, derived the notion that only the "fittest" ought to survive. His Social Statics (1850) argued against public education, health and safety regulations (except to prevent nuisances), medical licensing, and welfare. Those "sufficiently complete to live . . . *do* live, and it is well that they should live. If they are not sufficiently complete to live, they die, and it is best that they should die." The destitute are "unfit" and "the whole effort of nature is to get rid of such, to clear the world of them, and make room for better."[126] Sumner, a professor of sociology at Yale, brought Spencer's social theory and policy to America with a vengeance:[127] "Let it be understood that we cannot go outside of this alternative: liberty, inequality, survival of the fittest; not-liberty, equality, survival of the unfittest. The former carries society forward and favors all its best members; the latter carries society downwards and favors all its worst members." Laissez faire economics and social Darwinism were in vogue among American intellectuals in the mid-nineteenth century. But opposition to both the pure theories and their social implications began to arise among economists, sociologists, theologians, and statesmen. By the close of the nineteenth century, the notion of the purely negative state was giving way to a different view of the role of government. An advocate of the positive state writes:[128]

> Those who advocated a policy of laissez faire in the years after the Civil War seemingly were conforming to the best traditions of European and American liberalism. . . . Since liberalism originated essentially as a protest

125. "Efficiency" is, today, an economic term of art. An allocation of resources among individuals is efficient (or pareto-optimal) when no alternative distribution could make some individuals better off without making at least one worse off. Conversely, an allocation is inefficient or suboptimal when some individuals could be made better off by a different allocation without making anyone worse off.

126. Herbert Spencer, Social Statics 414-415 (1850).

127. 2 Essays of William Graham Sumner 56 (Keller & Davie eds., 1934).

128. Sidney Fine, Laissez Faire and the General Welfare State 30-32 (1956).

> against an authoritarian order in religion, politics, and economics, it was at the outset a purely negative faith, one aimed at removing the artificial restrictions that blocked human progress. Thus, with respect to government and economics, it became associated with laissez faire and economic freedom. In a complex industrial society, however, if the liberal objectives of individual freedom and equality of opportunity are to be realized it becomes necessary to extend the sphere of social control. The result has been that liberalism, which started out as an essentially negative creed designed to do away with obstructions to individual progress, "has developed as a positive effort to better man's estate by constructive action."
>
> Those who in the industrial order that was emerging in the United States after the Civil War continued to advocate the laissez-faire brand of liberalism tended to establish economic freedom as an end in itself rather than as a means to an end, and were out of harmony with the true spirit of liberalism. They were blind to the compelling necessity for social and economic reform and refused to recognize that some positive action on the part of the state was essential to assure the effective liberty of the individual. Laissez faire in the years after 1865 was the doctrine of the conservatives.

Classical liberalism suited the needs of the corporate bar, and a reactionary spirit pervaded the two most important constitutional law texts of the period—Thomas M. Cooley's A Treatise on the Constitutional Limitations Which Rest upon the Legislative Power of the States of the American Union (1868) and Christopher G. Tiedeman's A Treatise on the Limitations of Police Power in the United States (1886).

The central thesis of both texts was that the regulatory power of the states—the so-called police power—was narrowly circumscribed by fundamental law and written constitutions. The thesis was ahistorical. In the early Republic, when most constitutions had been adopted, the bounds of government regulation had been amorphous and broad. If Locke's theory of the state implied a narrow concept of the public good, Americans (no less than others, and no less than now) picked and chose and often ignored their philosophers. In opposition to Locke, there was Hobbes's expansive notion of the salus populi—the welfare of the people—and a tradition of government regulation going back to the colonies and England. The states had long intervened in the private sector to regulate the prices of labor and commodities and to protect consumers against unhealthy products and fraudulent merchant practices.[129] But Cooley and Tiedeman, with the characteristic dogmatism of treatise writers, asserted that their views were "the law."

Tiedeman argued that the police power could be used only to enforce the maxim "sic utere tuo ut alienum non laedas"—use your own property so as not to injure another's—and to protect public health and morality. He and Cooley

---

129. See Lawrence Friedman, A History of American Law 65-71, 161-163 (1973); Oscar Handlin, Commonwealth: A Study of the Role of Government in the American Economy: Massachusetts, 1774-1861 (rev. ed. 1969); Louis Hartz, Economic Policy and Democratic Thought: Pennsylvania, 1776-1860 (1948).

agreed that "class legislation" (for example, laws aiding an employee against his employer) and legislation interfering with an individual's freedom to make contracts were plainly beyond the scope of legislative power.

6. A Survey of the Court's Work[130]

Between 1890 and 1934, the Supreme Court struck down some 200 statutory and administrative regulations, mostly under the Due Process Clause of the Fourteenth Amendment. The received history tends to exaggerate the Court's activism, however, just as it minimizes the facts that the Court sustained at least as many regulations as it invalidated, that it declined to review many others, and that Holmes and Brandeis—the progressive heroes of the period—did not invariably dissent from substantive due process invalidations or always agree with each other.[131] The Court was considerably more restrained than some of the state supreme courts, and though it certainly never "judged social legislation on the basis of any consistent pattern of ideas which can properly bear the name of an economic theory,"[132] its decisions gain some coherence if one reads them in the context of the ideologies of the times.[133] The Court let stand most laws that appeared to protect the health, safety, or morals of the general public or to prevent consumer deception.

In the area of labor relations, the Court distinguished *Lochner* in sustaining the limitation of women's working hours in Muller v. Oregon, 208 U.S. 412 (1908). But in Adair v. United States, 208 U.S. 161 (1908), and Coppage v. Kansas, 236 U.S. 1 (1915), the Court held that yellow dog contracts could not be outlawed.

After Woodrow Wilson appointed two progressives, Louis Brandeis and John Clarke in 1916, the balance of power on the Court shifted. (Wilson's other appointment, James Clark McReynolds, proved a staunch conservative.) In Bunting v. Oregon, 243 U.S. 426 (1917), the Court completely disregarded *Lochner* and upheld a ten-hour maximum workday for male factory employees. In Wilson v. New, 243 U. S. 332 (1917), the Court upheld the Adamson Act, which established an eight-hour day for interstate railroad employees; it also provided for a temporary guarantee of minimum wages and overtime pay. The Court argued that these regulations were permissible because the railroad industry was "charged with a public interest."

---

130. See generally William Swindler, Court and Constitution in the Twentieth Century: The Old Legality, 1889-1932 (1969); Benjamin Wright, The Growth of American Constitutional Law 153-168 (1942); The Constitution of the United States of America, Analysis and Interpretation 1602-1612, 1643-1709 (Lib. of Cong. rev. ed. 1973). For a sympathetic analysis of the economics of substantive due process, see Richard Posner, Economic Analysis of Law, ch. 19 (1973); cf. Milton Friedman, Capitalism and Freedom (1962); Harold Demsetz, Minorities in the Market Place, 43 N.C. L. Rev. 271 (1965).

131. Note, however, that the practice of writing dissenting opinions was much less common than it is today. Many Justices dissented only if they were strongly opposed to a decision, and, having noted their disagreement in the first decision to establish a doctrine, they often acquiesced in its subsequent applications.

132. Lawrence Friedman, Freedom of Contract and Occupational Licensing, 1890-1910, 53 Cal. L. Rev. 487, 525 (1965).

133. See Howard Gillman, The Constitution Besieged: The Rise and Demise of *Lochner* Era Police Powers Jurisprudence (1993).

Moreover, America's entry into World War I greatly altered the political atmosphere. Laissez-faire ideas gave way to the necessities of war: "The federal government," Robert Post writes, "took control of the operations of the nation's railroads, its telegraphs and telephones, and its shipping industries. It assumed authority to regulate the production and prices of food and fuel. It actively intervened to shape the priorities of the wartime economy. It instituted sharply progressive income taxes. It established national labor policies and agencies. It imposed national prohibition. Nothing like this explosion of federal regulatory power had ever happened before."[134]

But for the contingencies of judicial appointments, the *Lochner* era might have ended at this point. Between 1921 and 1922, however, four Justices retired or died. (For example, Justice John Clarke, a Wilsonian progressive, resigned from the Court in 1922, to work for America's entry into the League of Nations.)

The duty of filling these vacancies fell to Warren Harding, who ran for President in 1920 arguing for a "return to normalcy" following World War I. Harding served as President only a little more than two years—he died in August of 1923, before the discovery of the Teapot Dome Scandal and revelations of widespread corruption in his Administration. But in that brief period he appointed four new Justices to the Court: William Howard Taft (as Chief Justice), George Sutherland, Pierce Butler, and Terry Sanford. These appointments, combined with McReynolds and other holdovers from the White Court, shifted the Supreme Court in a conservative direction once again:[135]

> Having glimpsed the full potential of the regulatory state during World War I, a majority of the Justices of the Taft Court urgently felt the need to establish the principles of a more normal peacetime constitutional order. This meant articulating constitutional limits more sharply and forcefully than the Court had heretofore experienced the need to do. The upshot was a full flowering of the jurisprudence that would eventually launch the Court on its epic course of collision with the New Deal.

The Taft Court struck down various health and safety regulations on the ground that they involved extraordinarily burdensome regulations where less onerous ones would have served substantially as well. E.g., Jay Burns Baking Co. v. Bryan, 264 U.S. 504 (1924) (law requiring precisely standardized weight for bread loaves), and Weaver v. Palmer Bros. Co., 270 U.S. 402 (1926) (law forbidding use of shoddy in quilts).

The Court continued to permit government regulation of rates of railroads and public utilities, while reviewing the rates for reasonableness. More important, however, the Taft Court also narrowed the concept of businesses "affected with a public interest" to restrict the kinds of businesses that were subject to price regulation of any sort. Legislatures could not set maximum charges for the resale of theater tickets, Tyson & Brother v. Banton, 273 U.S. 418 (1927); for services of an

---

134. Robert C. Post, Defending The Lifeworld: Substantive Due Process in the Taft Court Era, 78 B.U. L. Rev. 1489, 1489 (1998).

135. Id. at 1493.

employment agency, Ribnik v. McBride, 277 U.S. 350 (1928); or for the sale of gasoline, Williams v. Standard Oil Co., 278 U.S. 235 (1929). The Court held that these interferences with the free market were unwarranted by monopoly power or any other compelling factor.

One of the most noteworthy decisions of the Taft Court vigorously reasserted the doctrine of economic due process:

ADKINS v. CHILDREN'S HOSPITAL, 261 U.S. 525 (1923): [The Court, in an opinion by Justice Sutherland, invalidated a District of Columbia minimum wage law for women. It distinguished its earlier decision in Muller v. Oregon, 208 U.S. 412 (1908), which upheld a maximum hour law for women.]

SUTHERLAND, J.:

[T]he right to contract about one's affairs is a part of the liberty of the individual protected by [the Due Process] clause, is settled by the decisions of this Court and is no longer open to question. Within this liberty are contracts of employment of labor. In making such contracts, generally speaking, the parties have an equal right to obtain from each other the best terms they can as the result of private bargaining. . . .

There is, of course, no such thing as absolute freedom of contract. It is subject to a great variety of restraints. But freedom of contract is, nevertheless, the general rule, and restraint the exception, and the exercise of legislative authority to abridge it can be justified only by the existence of exceptional circumstances. . . .

In view of the great—not to say revolutionary—changes which have taken place since [Muller v. Oregon], in the contractual, political and civil status of women, culminating in the Nineteenth Amendment [ratified in 1920], it is not unreasonable to say that these differences [between men and women in the enjoyment of civil rights] have now come almost, if not quite, to the vanishing point. . . . [W]hile . . . physical differences must be recognized in appropriate cases, and legislation fixing hours or conditions of work may properly take them into account, we cannot accept the doctrine that women of mature age, sui juris, require or may be subjected to restrictions upon their liberty of contract which could not lawfully be imposed in the case of men under similar circumstances. . . .

The essential characteristics of the statute . . . which differentiate it from the laws fixing hours of labor . . . [is that] the latter . . . deal with incidents of the employment having no necessary effect upon the heart of the contract, that is, the amount of wages to be paid and received. . . . [The Court's previous decisions hold that] the authority to fix hours of labor cannot be exercised except in respect of those occupations where work of long continued duration is detrimental to health. . . . [T]hese decisions afford no real support for any form of law establishing minimum wages.

The feature of this statute which, perhaps more than any other, puts upon it the stamp of invalidity is that it exacts from the employer an arbitrary payment for a purpose and upon a basis having no causal connection with his business, or the contract or the work the employee engages to do. The declared basis . . . is not the value of the service rendered, but the extraneous circumstance that the employee needs to get a prescribed sum of money. to insure her subsistence, health and morals. . . . [T]he fallacy [of this argument] is that it assumes that every employer is bound at all events to furnish it. . . . Certainly the employer, by paying a fair equivalent for the service rendered, though not sufficient to support the employee, has neither caused nor contributed to her poverty. On the contrary, to the extent of what he pays, he has relieved it. . . .

[I]f, in the interest of the public welfare, the police power may be invoked to justify the fixing of a minimum wage, it may, when the public welfare is thought to require it, be invoked to justify a maximum wage. . . . It has been said that legislation of the kind now under review is required in the interest of social justice, for whose ends freedom of contract may lawfully be subjected to restraint. . . . To sustain the individual freedom of action contemplated by the Constitution is not to strike down the common good, but to exalt it, for surely the good of society as a whole cannot be better served than by the preservation against arbitrary restraint of the liberties of its constituent members.

HOLMES, J., dissenting:

I confess that I do not understand the principle on which the power to fix a minimum for the wages of women can be denied by those who admit the power to fix a maximum for their hours of work. . . . The bargain is equally affected whichever half you regulate. Muller v. Oregon, I take it, is as good law today as it was in 1908. It will need more than the Nineteenth Amendment to convince me that there are no differences between men and women, or that legislation cannot take those differences into account. I should not hesitate to take them into account if I thought it necessary to sustain this act. But after Bunting v. Oregon, I had supposed that it was not necessary, and that Lochner v. New York would be allowed a deserved repose.

This statute does not compel anybody to pay anything. It simply forbids employment at rates below those fixed as the minimum requirement of health and right living. It is safe to assume that women will not be employed at even the lowest wages allowed unless they earn them, or unless the employer's business can sustain the burden. In short, the law, in its character and operation, is like hundreds of so-called police laws that have been upheld. . . . The criterion of constitutionality is not whether we believe the law to be for the public good. We certainly cannot be prepared to deny that a reasonable man reasonably might have that belief in view of the legislation of Great Britain, Victoria and a number of the States of this Union.

E. Freedom of Contract and the Problem of "Involuntary Servitude"

In Nothing But Freedom, historian Eric Foner notes that all societies that have ended slavery have struggled over the extent of actual freedom to be enjoyed by the newly emancipated slaves.[136] The title of his book is taken from the comment, by Confederate General Robert V. Richardson, that "[t]he emancipated slaves own nothing, because nothing but freedom has been given to them."[137] Suggestions by Black people and by some of the so-called Radical Reconstructionists that the

136. Eric Foner, Nothing But Freedom: Emancipation and Its Legacy (1983).
137. Id. at 55.

former slaves be given at least "40 acres and a mule" to embark on their new lives were rejected. For example, Horace Greeley, the editor of the *New York Tribune* who was an avid opponent of slavery, dismissed the agitation for confiscation of slaveholders' land and redistribution to former slaves as "either knavery or madness": "People who want farms work for them. The only class we know that takes other people's property because they want it is largely represented in Sing Sing."

Thus Black people in the South were relegated to the market with no resources besides their own labor, which white employers sought to control and exploit. The notorious Black Codes, enacted by many Southern states immediately after the Civil War, established new modes of discipline over the Black labor force. For example, Mississippi required that every January all Black people be able to present written evidence of their employment for the next year, and also empowered all white persons to arrest any Black people who left the service of their employers.[138] The Civil Rights Act of 1866 formally invalidated the Black Codes, but the struggle over control of the labor force continued. Pete Daniel, the leading authority on the history of peonage, explains:[139]

> Lacking land or capital of their own, blacks had little choice but to sign yearly contracts. . . . As military control became less strict in the South, a labor pattern emerged. Most blacks signed annual contracts. Improvident, they took advances on their expected share of the crop. When settlement time came the next fall, the laborers often discovered that their share of the crop did not cover what they owed the supply merchant or the planter. . . . [S]ome planters demanded that workers remain until they had worked out their entire debt, and when planters used indebtedness as an instrument of compulsion, the system became peonage.

Foner and Daniel both indicate that peonage depended on the formal mechanism of contract, supplemented by the use of the criminal law to punish its breach. In 1911, this practice finally came before the Supreme Court, which struck it down, Bailey v. Alabama, 219 U.S. 219. Writing for the Court, Justice Hughes insisted that "[w]e at once dismiss from consideration the fact that the plaintiff in error is a black man. . . . The statute, on its face, makes no racial discrimination, and the record fails to show its existence in fact. No question of a sectional character is presented, and we may view the legislation in the same manner as if it had been enacted in New York or in Idaho." That being said, the majority condemned peonage as well within the "involuntary servitude" banned by the Thirteenth Amendment.

Justice Holmes, joined by Justice Lurton, dissented. The premise "that this case is to be considered and decided in the same way as if it arose in Idaho or New York" for them entailed "that in Alabama it mainly concerns the blacks does not matter." Holmes argued that the case concerned simply the application of an evidentiary presumption, that the failure to comply with an employment contract could be treated as evidence of an intent to defraud at the time the contract was signed.

---

138. To put this in perspective, as late as 1875 English law enforced criminal penalties for breach of contract. Id. at 49, 51.

139. Pete Daniel, The Shadow of Slavery: Peonage in the South 1901-1969, at 19-20 (1972). See also Daniel, The Metamorphosis of Slavery, 1865-1900, 66 J. Am. Hist. 88 (1979).

> The Thirteenth Amendment does not outlaw contracts for labor. . . . If the contract is one that ought not to be made, prohibit it. But if it is a perfectly fair and proper contract, I can see no reason why the State should not throw its weight on the side of performance. . . . I think it a mistake to say that this statute attaches its punishment to the mere breach of a contract to labor. It does not purport to do so; what it purports to punish is fraudulently obtaining money by a false pretense of an intent to keep the written contract in consideration of which the money is advanced. . . . But the import of the statute is supposed to be changed by the provision that a refusal to perform, coupled with a failure to return the money advanced, shall be prima facie evidence of fraudulent intent. I agree that if the statute created a conclusive presumption it might be held to make a disguised change in the substantive law. But it only makes the conduct prima facie evidence, a very different matter. Is it not evidence that a man had a fraudulent intent if he receives an advance upon a contract over night and leaves in the morning? I should have thought that it very plainly was. Of course the statute is in general terms and applies to a departure at any time without excuse or repayment, but that does no harm except on a tacit assumption that this law is not administered as it would be in New York, and that juries will act with prejudice against the laboring man. For prima facie evidence is only evidence, and as such may be held by the jury insufficient to make out guilt. This being so, I take it that a fair jury would acquit, if the only evidence were a departure after eleven months' work, and if it received no color from some special well-known course of events. But the matter well may be left to a jury, because their experience as men of the world may teach them that in certain conditions it is so common for laborers to remain during a part of the season, receiving advances, and then to depart at the period of need in the hope of greater wages at a neighboring plantation, that when a laborer follows that course there is a fair inference of fact that he intended it from the beginning. The Alabama statute, as construed by the state court and as we must take it, merely says, as a court might say, that the prosecution may go to the jury. . . . The right of the State to regulate laws of evidence is admitted, and the statute does not go much beyond the common law.
>
> . . . To sum up, I think that obtaining money by fraud may be made a crime as well as murder or theft; that a false representation, expressed or implied, at the time of making a contract of labor that one intends to perform it and thereby obtaining an advance, may be declared a case of fraudulently obtaining money as well as any other; that if made a crime it may be punished like any other crime, and that an unjustified departure from the promised service without repayment may be declared a sufficient case to go to the jury for their judgment; all without in any way infringing the Thirteenth Amendment or the statutes of the United States.

Several years after *Bailey*, in United States v. Reynolds, 235 U.S. 133 (1914), the Court unanimously struck down Alabama's criminal surety system. The Alabama Code authorized a person to appear as a surety for a defendant convicted of a misdemeanor and pay his fine in exchange for the defendant's entering into an employment contract to repay the surety: The defendant thus avoided imprisonment, but was subject to damages and another conviction if he broke the contract. Of course, the defendant could avoid serving time for breach of the surety contract by entering into a contract with another surety. Reynolds's first labor contract was for 10 months (compared to the 2 months he would have had to spend at hard labor in prison). The second contract bound him for 20 months (compared to less than 4 months of prison labor). As Justice Day described the cycle in his opinion for the Court, "the convict is thus kept chained to an ever-turning wheel of servitude to discharge the obligation which he has incurred to his surety." The criminal surety system was part of a larger scheme designed to provide white employers with cheap Black labor:[140]

> If there is no white man to pay him out, or if his crime is too serious to be paid out, he goes to the chain-gang—and in several states he is thus hired out to private contractors. The private employer then gets him sooner or later. Some of the largest farms in the South are operated by chain-gang labor. The demand for more convicts by white employers is exceedingly strong. . . . The natural tendency . . . is to convict as many Negroes as possible, and to punish the offences charged as severely as possible.

The sureties in *Reynolds* were charged with violating a federal statute, enacted pursuant to the Thirteenth Amendment, that prohibited enforcing "the voluntary or involuntary service or labor of any persons as peons, in liquidation of any debt or obligation." Striking down the Alabama criminal surety system presented a problem for the Court. Benno Schmidt explains:[141]

> The Court was not prepared to cast doubt on the legality of convict leasing, which was also characterized by forced servitude for private masters, often under barbarous conditions. Moreover, there could be nothing wrong with contracts whereby convicts got the money to pay fines and escape imprisonment. Finally, the state's enforcement of the obligations of such contracts by its criminal law undoubtedly increased the opportunities for convicts to make such agreements. . . . But looked at as a whole, with the distorting effects of racism in the system of law enforcement and the history of black forced labor given their due, the Alabama criminal-surety system stood as a major support of involuntary servitude. The Court could not know this, however, or at least it could not claim that it did. The Court had no knowledge about criminal justice system in operation; it had only the indictments . . . before it.

Justice Day approached the problem by noting that the convict had not been rearrested for failing to pay the fine and costs assessed by the State—for the surety had erased that debt. Instead, he had been arrested and convicted for violating his contract with the surety. The Court concluded that forcing the convict to work to repay the debt under the constant threat of another arrest and eventual

---

140. Ray Stannard Baker, Following the Color Line 98 (1964).

141. Benno C. Schmidt, Jr., Principle and Prejudice: The Supreme Court and Race in the Progressive Era, Part 2: The Peonage Cases, 82 Colum. L. Rev. 646, 699 (1982).

imprisonment qualified as involuntary servitude. In a brief concurring opinion, Justice Holmes wrote:

> There seems to me nothing in the Thirteenth Amendment of the Revised Statutes that prevents a State from making a breach of contract, as well a reasonable contract for labor as for other matters, a crime and punishing it as such. But impulsive people with little intelligence or foresight may be expected to lay hold of anything that affords a relief from present pain, even though it will cause greater trouble by and by. The successive contracts, each for a longer term than the last, are the inevitable, and must be taken to have been the contemplated outcome of the Alabama laws. On this ground I am inclined to agree that the statutes in question disclose the attempt to maintain service that the Revised Statutes forbid.[142]

In Principle and Prejudice, Schmidt places *Bailey* and the problem of involuntary servitude within the general context of contract theory:[143]

> Does the *Bailey* decision put forward a plausible constitutional theory, indicating, as both Hughes and Holmes insisted, that the racial aspect of peonage should be ignored? Or should the decision be understood as a doctrinally disguised response to the continuing legacy of forced labor for blacks in the South? Answers to these questions are elusive, but are nonetheless of first importance in appraising the Supreme Court's work during the Progressive era. If *Bailey* is credible in its professions of race-neutrality and its attempt to ground its constitutional doctrine in "the freedom of labor," it belongs where it is virtually never placed by students of constitutional history, in the camp of decisions, such as *Lochner*, *Adair*, and *Coppage*, that based rights and legislative inhibitions on the labor contract, and that made freedom of contract theory the backbone of laissez-faire constitutionalism. *Bailey* is an unsettling presence among these warhorses of substantive due process, both conceptually and as a revelation of

142. In two other cases, the Court declined to strike down government practices challenged under the Thirteenth Amendment. The appellant in Butler v. Perry, 240 U.S. 328 (1916), was convicted under a Florida law that required males between 21 and 45 either to work for six ten-hour days on roads and bridges each year or to avoid the task by providing an able-bodied substitute or paying $3 per day to the county road and bridge fund. Writing for a unanimous Court, Justice McReynolds wrote that the Thirteenth Amendment was not designed to end the ancient tradition of requiring residents to provide labor for road upkeep: "The great purpose in view was liberty under the protection of effective government, not the destruction of the latter by depriving it of essential powers." In the Selective Draft Law Cases, 245 U.S. 366, 390 (1918), the Court upheld the Selective Draft Law of 1917: "[W]e are unable to conceive upon what theory the exaction by government from the citizen of the performance of his supreme and noble duty of contributing to the defense of the rights and honor of the nation . . . can be said to be the imposition of involuntary servitude in violation of the prohibitions of the Thirteenth Amendment."

143. Schmidt, supra n.141, at 702-703, 705-713. See also Schmidt's interesting discussion of the "contradiction between freedom and obligation that lies at the heart of the theory of freedom of contract." Should one's contract voluntarily placing oneself in the position of a slave be enforced?

judicial attitudes. How could a Court devoted to freedom of contract find in the thirteenth amendment a freedom from strict enforcement of contract? To this day, there hovers over the freedom of contract cases the odor of class bias or, at least, benighted indifference to the cruel realities of the laborer's bargaining power in an industrial society. Yet *Bailey*'s protection of workers from airtight enforcement of their labor contracts is a constitutional profession on behalf of free labor that is wholly out of sympathy with the interest of employers in having an effective legal deterrent to breach of labor contracts on farms and plantations, where constancy of labor may be critical in the planting and harvest seasons. As such, it supports the sincerity, if not the realism, of the protestations of worker-interest that mark many of the substantive due process decisions generally thought to be most damaging to the welfare of working people. On the other hand, if *Bailey* is viewed as a result-oriented response to the exploitation of black workers, it marks an instance of vigorous legal realism that sheds light both on the White Court's style of judicial statecraft and on its attitudes toward racial justice.

IV. CONGRESSIONAL REGULATION OF INTERSTATE COMMERCE AND OF THE NATIONAL ECONOMY

A. The Commerce Power

Before the Civil War, the focus of adjudication under the Commerce Clause was the validity of state regulation of commerce when Congress was silent. This continued to be a staple of the Court's docket throughout the nineteenth century and much of the twentieth, and we shall return to doctrines under the "dormant" Commerce Clause in the next chapter. Of more interest in the postwar period, however, is adjudication over the scope of *Congress*'s legislative powers—an issue scarcely confronted by the Court since *McCulloch.*[144] An early case illustrates the application to federal regulation of concepts developed in the state regulation-of-commerce cases of the Marshall and Taney eras. In United States v. DeWitt, 76 U.S. (9 Wall.) 41 (1869), Chief Justice Chase wrote for a unanimous Court, holding that a congressional safety regulation prohibiting the sale of highly combustible illuminating oils lay beyond the congressional power:

> [T]he express grant of power to regulate commerce among the States has always been understood as limited by its terms; and as a virtual denial of any power to interfere with the internal trade and business of the separate States. . . . [The illuminating oil law] is a regulation of police. . . . As a police regulation, relating exclusively to the internal trade of the States, it can only have effect where the legislative authority of Congress excludes,

---

144. Marbury v. Madison and Dred Scott v. Sandford both invalidated congressional statutes, but neither involved the major Article I powers of commerce, taxing, and spending.

territorially, all State legislation, as for example, in the District of Columbia. Within State limits, it can have no constitutional operation.

The law struck down in *DeWitt* was a minor and isolated congressional attempt to use the commerce power to regulate trade. Only toward the end of the nineteenth century, with the Interstate Commerce Act of 1887 and the Sherman Antitrust Act of 1890, did Congress begin to intervene significantly in the burgeoning interstate economy. The Supreme Court's response was mixed and paralleled its reaction to state social and economic legislation in many respects. Almost anything connected with railroads was held to be within Congress's power.[145] For example, in Southern Railway v. United States, 22 U.S. 20 (1911), the Court upheld the Federal Safety Appliance Acts as applied to railroad cars with defective couplers moving solely within a state, noting that railroads are "highways of both interstate and intrastate commerce" and that "whatever brings delay or disaster to one [train], or results in disabling one of its operatives, is calculated to impede the progress and imperil the safety of other trains." On the same theory, the Court sustained congressional regulation of the hours of employees working on the intrastate operations of railroads that also conducted interstate operations. Baltimore & Ohio Railroad Co. v. Interstate Commerce Commission, 221 U.S. 612 (1911). And in the Shreveport Rate case, Houston, E. & W.T. Ry. v. United States, 234 U.S. 342 (1914), the Court held that the Interstate Commerce Commission (ICC) could prohibit railroads from charging lower rates for transportation within Texas than the rates set by the ICC for identical distances between Texas and other states.

Judicial doctrine under the Sherman Act was more complex.[146] In the first decision under the Act, United States v. E.C. Knight Co., 156 U.S. 1 (1895) (the Sugar Trust case), the Court dismissed an action brought under the Sherman Act to set aside the American Sugar Refining Company's acquisition of four other sugar refining companies. Chief Justice Fuller wrote: "It is vital that the independence of the commercial power and of the police power . . . should always be recognized and observed, for while the one furnishes the strongest bond of the union, the other is essential to the preservation of the autonomy of the States." American already produced 65 percent of the sugar refined in the United States, and acquisition of the companies would give it 98 percent of the market. But the power to prevent a monopoly in "manufacture," as distinguished from the "commerce" that follows manufacture, belonged exclusively to the states.

Three doctrinal issues recur throughout the cases of this period. One, suggested by the Sugar Trust case, is whether the particular *subject* of congressional regulation is "interstate commerce" as distinguished from some local activity.

Second, are the *purposes* of a regulation consistent with the purposes for which Congress was delegated the power to regulate interstate commerce? Recall, in this respect, Marshall's "pretext" statement in *McCulloch*: "[S]hould congress, under the pretext of executing its powers, pass laws for the accomplishment of objects not

145. In Railroads and Regulation, 1877-1916 (1965), Gabriel Kolko argues that the railroads welcomed national rate regulation as a means of curbing competition.

146. See Lawrence Friedman, A History of American Law 407-408 (1973); Charles McCurdy, The Knight Sugar Decision of 1895 and the Modernization of American Corporation Law, 1869-1903, 53 Bus. Hist. Rev. 304 (1979).

intrusted to the government, it would become the painful duty of this tribunal to say that such an act was not the law of the land." By way of elaboration on Marshall's point, consider these points: (1) General legislative authority resides in the states. (2) Lawmaking authority is delegated to the national government to achieve certain objectives. (3) There is no justification for exercising authority beyond the scope of the purposes for which it is given.

The last statement may seem to beg the question. Yet this notion is taken for granted and applied widely outside of the area of constitutional law. Consider the consequences if government officials, private trustees, and ordinary individuals—who constantly act under authorization from others—were bound only by the substantive terms of a delegation, not by the purposes for which it was made. Consider, indeed, how often an agent's pursuit of objectives beyond those underlying the delegation is a ground for criticism and even the imposition of civil and criminal penalties. For example, a trustee who administers assets in order to injure the beneficiary or to aid a third party without regard to the beneficiary's interests may be held liable; while another trustee, whose objective conduct is no different but who acted in good faith, may not be chargeable. If the concept of ultra vires action—action outside the scope of authority—is generally concerned with purposes as well as the operative terms of the delegation, should it be different in the case of constitutional delegations of power?

The third recurring issue of the period is whether, independent of the first or second issues, a particular instance of congressional regulation of interstate commerce runs afoul of the reservation of powers to the states recognized by the Tenth Amendment. In *McCulloch*, Marshall asserted that the Tenth Amendment was a tautology. During the period considered in this section, however, the Court treated it as at least the symbol, if not the source, of what Edward Corwin called the doctrine of "dual federalism"—the view that "the coexistence of the states and their powers is itself a limitation upon national power," which restricts Congress's use of the delegated powers to purposes and results that are not reserved to the states.[147]

Champion v. Ames

[The Lottery Case] 188 U.S. 321 (1903)

[An 1895 congressional act prohibited sending lottery tickets through the mails, or from one state to another by any means. Appellants were indicted for conspiring to transport tickets of the Pan-American Lottery Company (based in Asunción, Paraguay) from Texas to California, shipping them by railroad with Wells Fargo Express Co. They challenged the indictment on constitutional grounds.]

Harlan, J. . . .

The appellant insists that the carrying of lottery tickets from one State to another State by an express company engaged in carrying freight and packages from State to State, although such tickets may be contained in a box or package,

147. Edward Corwin, Congress' Power to Prohibit Commerce, 18 Cornell L.Q. 477, 482 (1933) (emphasis omitted).

does not constitute, and cannot by any act of Congress be legally made to constitute, *commerce* among the States within the meaning of the clause of the Constitution. . . .

The Government insists that express companies when engaged, for hire, in the business of transportation from one State to another, are instrumentalities of commerce among the States; that the carrying of lottery tickets from one State to another is commerce which Congress may regulate; and that as a means of executing the power to regulate interstate commerce Congress may make it an offence against the United States to cause lottery tickets to be carried from one State to another.

The questions presented by these opposing contentions are of great moment, and are entitled to receive, as they have received, the most careful consideration.

What is the import of the word "commerce" as used in the Constitution? It is not defined by that instrument. Undoubtedly, the carrying from one State to another by independent carriers of things or commodities that are ordinary subjects of traffic, and which have in themselves a recognized value in money, constitutes interstate commerce. . . .

It was said in argument that lottery tickets are not of any real or substantial value in themselves, and therefore are not subjects of commerce. If that were conceded to be the only legal test as to what are to be deemed subjects of the commerce that may be regulated by Congress, we cannot accept as accurate the broad statement that such tickets are of no value. Upon their face they showed that the lottery company offered a large capital prize, to be paid to the holder of the ticket winning the prize at the drawing advertised to be held at Asunción, Paraguay. . . .

But it is said that the statute in question does not regulate the carrying of lottery tickets from State to State, but by punishing those who cause them to be so carried Congress in effect prohibits such carrying; that in respect of the carrying from one State to another of articles or things that are, in fact, or according to usage in business, the subjects of commerce, the authority given Congress was not to *prohibit*, but only to *regulate*. This view was earnestly pressed at the bar by learned counsel, and must be examined. . . .

In determining whether regulation may not under some circumstances properly take the form or have the effect of prohibition, the nature of the interstate traffic which it was sought by the act of May 2, 1895, to suppress cannot be overlooked. When enacting that statute Congress no doubt shared the views upon the subject of lotteries heretofore expressed by this court. In Phalen v. Virginia, 8 How. 163, 168, after observing that the suppression of nuisances injurious to public health or morality is among the most important duties of Government, this court said: "Experience has shown that the common forms of gambling are comparatively innocuous when placed in contrast with the widespread pestilence of lotteries. The former are confined to a few persons and places, but the latter infests the whole community; it enters every dwelling; it reaches every class; it preys upon the hard earnings of the poor; it plunders the ignorant and simple." In other cases we have adjudged that authority given by legislative enactment to carry on a lottery, although based upon a consideration in money, was not protected by the contract clause of the Constitution; this, for the reason that no State may bargain away its power to protect the public morals, nor excuse its failure to perform a public duty by saying that it had agreed, by legislative enactment, not to do so. Stone v. Mississippi, 101 U.S. 814; Douglas v. Kentucky, 168 U.S. 488.

If a State, when considering legislation for the suppression of lotteries within its own limits, may properly take into view the evils that inhere in the raising of money, in that mode, why may not Congress, invested with the power to regulate commerce among the several States, provide that such commerce shall not be polluted by the carrying of lottery tickets from one State to another? In this connection it must not be forgotten that the power of Congress to regulate commerce among the States is plenary, is complete in itself, and is subject to no limitations except such as may be found in the Constitution. What provision in that instrument can be regarded as limiting the exercise of the power granted? . . .

If it be said that the act of 1895 is inconsistent with the Tenth Amendment, reserving to the States respectively or to the people the powers not delegated to the United States, the answer is that the power to regulate commerce among the States has been expressly delegated to Congress.

Besides, Congress, by that act, does not assume to interfere with traffic or commerce in lottery tickets carried on exclusively within the limits of any State, but has in view only commerce of that kind among the several States. It has not assumed to interfere with the completely internal affairs of any State, and has only legislated in respect of a matter which concerns the people of the United States. As a State may, for the purpose of guarding the morals of its own people, forbid all sales of lottery tickets within its limits, so Congress, for the purpose of guarding the people of the United States against the "widespread pestilence of lotteries" and to protect the commerce which concerns all the States, may prohibit the carrying of lottery tickets from one State to another. In legislating upon the subject of the traffic in lottery tickets, as carried on through interstate commerce, Congress only supplemented the action of those States—perhaps all of them—which, for the protection of the public morals, prohibit the drawing of lotteries, as well as the sale or circulation of lottery tickets, within their respective limits. It said, in effect, that it would not permit the declared policy of the States, which sought to protect their people against the mischiefs of the lottery business, to be overthrown or disregarded by the agency of interstate commerce. We should hesitate long before adjudging that an evil of such appalling character, carried on through interstate commerce, cannot be met and crushed by the only power competent to that end. We say competent to that end, because Congress alone has the power to occupy, by legislation, the whole field of interstate commerce. . . .

FULLER, C.J., joined by Brewer, Shiras, and Peckham, JJ., dissenting. . . .

The power of the State to impose restraints and burdens on persons and property in conservation and promotion of the public health, good order and prosperity is a power originally and always belonging to the States, not surrendered by them to the General Government nor directly restrained by the Constitution of the United States, and essentially exclusive, and the suppression of lotteries as a harmful business falls within this power, commonly called of police. Douglas v. Kentucky, 168 U.S. 488.

It is urged, however, that because Congress is empowered to regulate commerce between the several States, it, therefore, may suppress lotteries by prohibiting the carriage of lottery matter. Congress may indeed make all laws necessary and proper for carrying the powers granted to it into execution, and doubtless an act prohibiting the carriage of lottery matter would be necessary and proper to the execution of a power to suppress lotteries; but that power belongs to the States and not to Congress. To hold that Congress has general police power would be to hold that it may accomplish objects not entrusted to the General Government, and to defeat the operation of the Tenth Amendment. . . .

But apart from the question of bona fides, this act cannot be brought within the power to regulate commerce among the several States, unless lottery tickets are articles of commerce, and, therefore, when carried across state lines, of interstate commerce; or unless the power to regulate interstate commerce includes the absolute and exclusive power to prohibit the transportation of anything or anybody from one State to another. . . .

Is the carriage of lottery tickets from one State to another commercial intercourse? The lottery ticket purports to create contractual relations and to furnish the means of enforcing a contract right.

This is true of insurance policies, and both are contingent in their nature. Yet this court has held that the issuing of fire, marine, and life insurance policies, in one State, and sending them to another, to be there delivered to the insured on payment of premium, is not interstate commerce. Paul v. Virginia, 8 Wall. 168; Hooper v. California, 155 U.S. 648; New York Life Insurance Company v. Cravens, 178 U.S. 389.

In Paul v. Virginia, Mr. Justice Field, in delivering the unanimous opinion of the court, said: "Issuing a policy of insurance is not a transaction of commerce. The policies are simple contracts of indemnity against loss by fire, entered into between the corporations and the assured, for a consideration paid by the latter. These contracts are not articles of commerce in any proper meaning of the word. They are not subjects of trade and barter offered in the market as something having an existence and value independent of the parties to them. They are not commodities to be shipped or forwarded from one State to another, and then put up for sale. They are like other personal contracts between parties which are completed by their signature and the transfer of the consideration. Such contracts are not interstate transactions, though the parties may be domiciled in different States. The policies do not take effect—are not executed contracts—until delivered by the agent in Virginia. They are, then, local transactions, and are governed by the local law. They do not constitute a part of the commerce between the States any more than a contract for the purchase and sale of goods in Virginia by a citizen of New York whilst in Virginia would constitute a portion of such commerce." . . .

If a lottery ticket is not an article of commerce, how can it become so when placed in an envelope or box or other covering, and transported by an express company? To say that the mere carrying of an article which is not an article of commerce in and of itself nevertheless becomes such the moment it is to be transported from one State to another, is to transform a non-commercial article into a commercial one simply because it is transported. I cannot conceive that any such result can properly follow.

It would be to say that everything is an article of commerce the moment it is taken to be transported from place to place, and of interstate commerce if from State to State.

An invitation to dine, or to take a drive, or a note of introduction, all become articles of commerce under the ruling in this case, by being deposited with an express company for transportation. This in effect breaks down all the differences between that which is, and that which is not, an article of commerce, and the necessary consequence is to take from the States all jurisdiction over the subject so far as interstate communication is concerned. It is a long step in the direction of wiping out all traces of state lines, and the creation of a centralized Government. . . .

The Constitution gives no countenance to the theory that Congress is vested with the full powers of the British Parliament, and that, although subject to constitutional limitations, it is the sole judge of their extent and application; and the decisions of this court from the beginning have been to the contrary.

"To what purpose are powers limited, and to what purpose is that limitation committed to writing, if these limits may, at any time, be passed by those intended to be restrained?" asked Marshall, in Marbury v. Madison.

"Should Congress," said the same great magistrate in McCulloch v. Maryland, "under the pretext of executing its powers, pass laws for the accomplishment of objects not entrusted to the Government; it would become the painful duty of this tribunal, should a case requiring such a decision come before it, to say that such an act was not the law of the land."

Does the grant to Congress of the power to regulate interstate commerce impart the absolute power to prohibit it? . . .

The power to prohibit the transportation of diseased animals and infected goods over railroads or on steamboats is an entirely different thing [from the prohibition of lottery tickets], for they would be in themselves injurious to the transaction of interstate commerce, and, moreover, are essentially commercial in their nature. And the exclusion of diseased persons rests on different ground, for nobody would pretend that persons could be kept off the trains because they were going from one State to another to engage in the lottery business. However enticing that business may be, we do not understand these pieces of paper themselves can communicate bad principles by contact. . . .

DISCUSSION

1. *The commerce power versus the "police power."* How do Fuller's and Harlan's views of federal and state powers relate to the views of the Marshall and Taney periods? Would Fuller or Harlan permit a state to prohibit the importation of lottery tickets in the absence of congressional legislation?

How do the Justices' conceptions of the police power relate to their conceptions of the police power in *Lochner*? (Note that Justice Harlan, who dissented in *Lochner*, wrote for the majority in the Lottery case, and that Justice Peckham, who wrote for the Court in *Lochner*, was among the dissenters in the Lottery case.)

2. *"Pretext."* In the penultimate paragraph of his dissent, Fuller quotes Marshall's "pretext" statement in *McCulloch*, implying that the *purposes* underlying the Act are not those for which the commerce power was granted. Why not? Would Fuller's position be stronger if, contrary to the Court's assertion, most states permitted the sale of lottery tickets?

3. *The subject of congressional regulation.* Justice Fuller distinguishes lottery tickets from diseased animals and infected goods, which he says Congress can prohibit from being transported interstate. Consider the possible analogue to his implicit distinction in *Lochner* between occupations that are inherently unhealthy and those that are not.

4. *Evangelical mobilization and the expansion of federal power.* As John Compton has explained, the Court's shift in doctrine in the *Lottery Case* arose in part because of a decades long campaign by evangelical reformers against gambling.[148] Throughout the nineteenth century lotteries had operated through state-granted charters in order to raise funds for public goods and projects. Religious reformers began to press for an end to the practice, arguing that gambling was sinful, addictive, and ruined families. In response, lottery owners argued that state legislatures could not extinguish their charter rights without violating the Contracts Clause. As Justice Harlan notes, the Court held otherwise in Stone v. Mississippi, 101 U.S. 814 (1880) and Douglas v. Kentucky 168 U.S. 488 (1897), explaining that states could not bargain away their police powers to protect health, safety, and welfare. By the 1880s, all states had banned lotteries except Louisiana, where lottery owners had managed to procure a state constitutional provision allowing them to continue their drawings. (The lottery's owners, who were nothing if not resilient, eventually shifted their interstate operations to Florida and held their drawings in Honduras).

The remaining problem was blocking interstate sales. In 1890, Congress banned the use of the federal mails to sell lottery tickets, which the Court upheld under the postal power. Ex parte Rapier, 143 U.S. 110 (1892). The owners of the Louisiana Lottery responded by shipping tickets through private express companies. Anti-lottery activists then pressed for a federal statute, passed in 1895, banning the interstate shipment of lottery tickets generally. This statute, upheld in Champion v. Ames, was justified on what were effectively traditional state police power grounds of promoting health, safety, and welfare. *Champion* thus began to whittle away at the distinction between what states could do through their police powers and what the federal government could do to regulate activities under its commerce power.

Religious reformers were not only concerned about gambling. They also sought to use federal power to ban alcohol and protect traditional morals. As a result, the distinction between the state's police powers and the federal commerce power was further strained in a series of cases in which the Court upheld the power of Congress to ban the transportation of women for purposes of prostitution, Hoke v. United States, 227 U.S. 308 (1913); or for "debauchery" or immoral purposes, even if noncommercial, Caminetti v. United States, 242 U.S. 470 (1917). Similarly, the Court upheld the use of the commerce power to ban the interstate transportation of liquor into dry states. Clark Distilling Co. v. Western Maryland Ry. Co., 242 U.S. 311 (1917). The next target of evangelical (and Progressive) concern was child labor. Bans on child labor, however, affected not the purveyors of vice but the owners of factories. At this point, the Court sought to reestablish a line of demarcation.

Hammer v. Dagenhart

247 U.S. 251 (1918)

DAY, J. . . .

A bill was filed in the United States District Court for the Western District of North Carolina by a father in his own behalf and as next friend of his two minor

148. See John W. Compton, The Evangelical Origins of the Living Constitution (2014).

sons, one under the age of fourteen years and the other between the ages of fourteen and sixteen years, employees in a cotton mill at Charlotte, North Carolina, to enjoin the enforcement of the act of Congress intended to prevent interstate commerce in the products of child labor. . . .

The District Court held the act unconstitutional and entered a decree enjoining its enforcement. This appeal brings the case here. The first section of the act is in the margin.[a]

The controlling question for decision is: Is it within the authority of Congress in regulating commerce among the States to prohibit the transportation in interstate commerce of manufactured goods, the product of a factory in which, within thirty days prior to their removal therefrom, children under the age of fourteen have been employed or permitted to work, or children between the ages of fourteen and sixteen years have been employed or permitted to work more than eight hours in any day, or more than six days in any week, or after the hour of 7 o'clock P.M. or before the hour of 6 o'clock A.M.?

The power essential to the passage of this act, the Government contends, is found in the commerce clause of the Constitution which authorizes Congress to regulate commerce with foreign nations and among the States. . . .

[I]t is insisted that adjudged cases in this court establish the doctrine that the power to regulate given to Congress incidentally includes the authority to prohibit the movement of ordinary commodities and therefore that the subject is not open for discussion. The cases demonstrate the contrary. They rest upon the character of the particular subjects dealt with and the fact that the scope of governmental authority, state or national, possessed over them is such that the authority to prohibit is as to them but the exertion of the power to regulate.

The first of these cases is Champion v. Ames, 188 U.S. 321 (1903), the so-called Lottery case, in which it was held that Congress might pass a law having the effect to keep the channels of commerce free from use in the transportation of tickets used in the promotion of lottery schemes. In Hipolite Egg Co. v. United States, 220 U.S. 45 (1911), this court sustained the power of Congress to pass the Pure Food and Drug Act which prohibited the introduction into the States by means of interstate commerce of impure foods and drugs. In Hoke v. United States, 227 U.S. 308 (1913), this court sustained the constitutionality of the so-called "White Slave Traffic Act" whereby the transportation of a woman in interstate commerce for the purpose of prostitution was forbidden. . . .

---

a. That no producer, manufacturer, or dealer shall ship or deliver for shipment in interstate or foreign commerce any article or commodity the product of any mine or quarry, situated in the United States, in which within thirty days prior to the time of the removal of such product therefrom children under the age of sixteen years have been employed or permitted to work, or any article or commodity the product of any mill, cannery, workshop, factory, or manufacturing establishment, situated in the United States, in which within thirty days prior to the removal of such product therefrom children under the age of fourteen years have been employed or permitted to work, or children between the ages of fourteen years and sixteen years have been employed or permitted to work more than eight hours in any day, or more than six days in any week, or after the hour of seven o'clock postmeridian, or before the hour of six o'clock antemeridian.

In Caminetti v. United States, 242 U.S. 470 (1917), we held that Congress might prohibit the transportation of women in interstate commerce for the purposes of debauchery and kindred purposes. In Clark Distilling Co. v. Western Maryland Ry. Co., 242 U.S. 311 (1917), the power of Congress over the transportation of intoxicating liquors was sustained. . . .

In each of these instances the use of interstate transportation was necessary to the accomplishment of harmful results. In other words, although the power over interstate transportation was to regulate, that could only be accomplished by prohibiting the use of the facilities of interstate commerce to effect the evil intended.

This element is wanting in the present case. The thing intended to be accomplished by this statute is the denial of the facilities of interstate commerce to those manufacturers in the States who employ children within the prohibited ages. The act in its effect does not regulate transportation among the States, but aims to standardize the ages at which children may be employed in mining and manufacturing within the States. The goods shipped are of themselves harmless. The act permits them to be freely shipped after thirty days from the time of their removal from the factory. When offered for shipment, and before transportation begins, the labor of their production is over, and the mere fact that they were intended for interstate commerce transportation does not make their production subject to federal control under the commerce power. . . .

It is further contended that the authority of Congress may be exerted to control interstate commerce in the shipment of child-made goods because of the effect of the circulation of such goods in other States where the evil of this class of labor has been recognized by local legislation, and the right to thus employ child labor has been more rigorously restrained than in the State of production. In other words, that the unfair competition, thus engendered, may be controlled by closing the channels of interstate commerce to manufacturers in those States where the local laws do not meet what Congress deems to be the more just standard of other States.

There is no power vested in Congress to require the States to exercise their police power so as to prevent possible unfair competition. Many causes may cooperate to give one State, by reason of local laws or conditions, an economic advantage over others. The Commerce Clause was not intended to give to Congress a general authority to equalize such conditions. In some of the States laws have been passed fixing minimum wages for women, in others the local law regulates the hours of labor of women in various employments. Business done in such States may be at an economic disadvantage when compared with States which have no such regulations; surely, this fact does not give Congress the power to deny transportation in interstate commerce to those who carry on business where the hours of labor and the rate of compensation for women have not been fixed by a standard in use in other States and approved by Congress.

The grant of power to Congress over the subject of interstate commerce was to enable it to regulate such commerce, and not to give it authority to control the States in their exercise of the police power over local trade and manufacture.

The grant of authority over a purely federal matter was not intended to destroy the local power always existing and carefully reserved to the States in the Tenth Amendment to the Constitution. . . .

The power of the States to regulate their purely internal affairs by such laws as seem wise to the local authority is inherent and has never been surrendered to the general government. To sustain this statute would not be in our judgment a recognition of the lawful exertion of congressional authority over interstate commerce, but would sanction an invasion by the federal power of the control of a matter purely local in its character, and over which no authority has been delegated to Congress in conferring the power to regulate commerce among the States. . . .

In our view the necessary effect of this act is, by means of a prohibition against the movement in interstate commerce of ordinary commercial commodities, to regulate the hours of labor of children in factories and mines within the States, a purely state authority. Thus the act in a twofold sense is repugnant to the Constitution. It not only transcends the authority delegated to Congress over commerce but also exerts a power as to a purely local matter to which the federal authority does not extend. The far reaching result of upholding the act cannot be more plainly indicated than by pointing out that if Congress can thus regulate matters entrusted to local authority by prohibition of the movement of commodities in interstate commerce, all freedom of commerce will be at an end, and the power of the States over local matters may be eliminated and thus our system of government be practically destroyed.

Holmes, J., dissenting.

The single question in this case is whether Congress has power to prohibit the shipment [of certain goods] in interstate or foreign commerce. . . . The objection urged against the power is that the States have exclusive control over their methods of production and that Congress cannot meddle with them, and taking the proposition in the sense of direct intermeddling I agree to it and suppose that no one denies it. But if an act is within the powers specifically conferred upon Congress, it seems to me that it is not made any less constitutional because of the indirect effects that it may have, however obvious it may be that it will have those effects, and that we are not at liberty upon such grounds to hold it void.

The first step in my argument is to make plain what no one is likely to dispute—that the statute in question is within the power expressly given to Congress if considered only as to its immediate effects and that if invalid it is so only upon some collateral ground. The statute confines itself to prohibiting the carriage of certain goods in interstate or foreign commerce. Congress is given power to regulate such commerce in unqualified terms. It would not be argued today that the power to regulate does not include the power to prohibit. Regulation means the prohibition of something, and when interstate commerce is the matter to be regulated I cannot doubt that the regulation may prohibit any part of such commerce that Congress sees fit to forbid. At all events it is established by the Lottery case and others that have followed it that a law is not beyond the regulative power of Congress merely because it prohibits certain transportation out and out. . . . So I repeat that this statute in its immediate operation is clearly within the Congress's constitutional power.

The question then is narrowed to whether the exercise of its otherwise constitutional power by Congress can be pronounced unconstitutional because of its possible reaction upon the conduct of the States in a matter upon which I have admitted that they are free from direct control. I should have thought that matter had been disposed of so fully as to leave no room for doubt. I should have thought that the most conspicuous decisions of this Court had made it clear that the power to regulate commerce and other constitutional powers could not be cut down or qualified by the fact that it might interfere with the carrying out of the domestic policy of any State. . . .

[I]f there is any matter upon which civilized countries have agreed—far more unanimously than they have with regard to intoxicants and some other matters over which this country is now emotionally aroused—it is the evil of premature and excessive child labor. . . .

But I had thought that the propriety of the exercise of a power admitted to exist in some cases was for the consideration of Congress alone and that this Court always had disavowed the right to intrude its judgment upon questions of policy or morals. It is not for this Court to pronounce when prohibition is necessary to regulation if it ever may be necessary—to say that it is permissible as against strong drink but not as against the product of ruined lives.

The act does not meddle with anything belonging to the States. They may regulate their internal affairs and their domestic commerce as they like. But when they seek to send their products across the state line they are no longer within their rights. If there were no Constitution and no Congress their power to cross the line would depend upon their neighbors. Under the Constitution such commerce belongs not to the States but to Congress to regulate. It may carry out its views of public policy whatever indirect effect they may have upon the activities of the States. Instead of being encountered by a prohibitive tariff at her boundaries the State encounters the public policy of the United States which it is for Congress to express. The public policy of the United States is shaped with a view to the benefit of the nation as a whole. If, as has been the case within the memory of men still living, a State should take a different view of the propriety of sustaining a lottery from that which generally prevails, I cannot believe that the fact would require a different decision from that reached in Champion v. Ames. Yet in that case it would be said with quite as much force as in this that Congress was attempting to intermeddle with the State's domestic affairs. The national welfare as understood by Congress may require a different attitude within its sphere from that of some self-seeking State. It seems to me entirely constitutional for Congress to enforce its understanding by all the means at its command. . . .

Mr. Justice McKenna, Mr. Justice Brandeis and Mr. Justice Clarke concur in this opinion.

DISCUSSION

1. The Child Labor Act, by its terms, operated directly upon interstate commerce. In purely formal terms, does the Act differ from the prohibitions of the Federal Lottery Act, the Pure Food and Drug Act, and the White Slave Traffic Act? If not, why was it beyond the commerce power?

Were the *objectives* underlying the Child Labor Act categorically different from those underlying the other Acts? In this respect, did the government overplay its hand by making the "unfair competition" argument? Recall that in the Lottery case the Court thought that perhaps all of the states forbade the sale of lottery tickets. The Court might have made similar assumptions about state policies concerning adulterated food and prostitution. But the very point of the "unfair competition" was that not all states prohibited child labor.[149] If, after the Child Labor case, in the (judicially enforced) silence of Congress, a state had attempted to exclude goods made using child labor, this trade barrier almost surely would have been deemed an impermissible state regulation of interstate commerce. (See Chapter 5, infra.) Equally surely, in the silence of Congress, a state *could* exclude diseased cattle. What is the difference, and does it provide any further insight into the Court's restriction on *Congress's* power in the Child Labor case?

2. *Child labor and the Thirteenth Amendment.* Could Congress have passed either the Child Labor Act or the White Slave Traffic Act (upheld in *Hoke* and *Caminetti*) using its §2 powers to enforce the Thirteenth Amendment? Despite its title, no one in Congress seems to have suggested that an act banning "white slavery" could be justified by Congress's powers to enforce a constitutional amendment banning slavery. Similarly, although some members of Congress overtly compared child labor to slavery (or "peonage," which Congress had regulated under the Thirteenth Amendment), congressmen and senators were either unable or unwilling to connect the dots. Indeed, the House Judiciary Committee refused even to consider a Thirteenth Amendment theory in a bill proposed by Samuel Gompers, president of the American Federation of Labor (who had in some of his writings had spoken out against "wage slavery"), and drafted by a government attorney, James F. Lawson. See Dina Mishra, Child Labor as Involuntary Servitude: The Failure of Congress to Legislate Against Child Labor Pursuant to the Thirteenth Amendment in the Early Twentieth Century, 63 Rutgers L. Rev. 59 (2010). What explains this resistance? Note that to invoke Congress's §2 powers to ban child labor would have cast the charge of slavery—i.e., "illegitimate domination"—against two important features of American life simultaneously: the coercion of the free market on the one hand, and coercion within family relations, on the other.

NOTE: ON "PRISONER'S DILEMMAS" AND CENTRALIZED COORDINATION

Justice Day's opinion for the majority implicitly concedes that there is something "unfair" about state A allowing its industries a competitive advantage against the industries of state B because the former allows a wicked practice. That is, state A's toleration of child labor presumably means that its industries have lower labor costs. Thus, if state B chooses to outlaw child labor, it takes the risk of seeing its products suffer in the marketplace if the higher labor costs imposed on local industries are passed along to consumers; or, perhaps, investors will be discouraged from financing state B's industries because they will be unable to receive the same returns presumably available in the other, less protective, states. Day notes that one of the motivations for the federal child labor law was "that the unfair competition, thus engendered, may be controlled by closing the channels of interstate

149. For an interesting discussion of the facts, politics, and law of child labor, see Stephen Wood, Constitutional Politics in the Progressive Era (1968).

commerce to manufacturers in those States where the local laws do not meet what Congress deems to be the more just standard of other States." For better or worse, though, according to the majority, the Constitution vests no power "in Congress to require the States to exercise their police power so as to prevent possible unfair competition. . . . The Commerce Clause was not intended to give to Congress a general authority to equalize such conditions." If this is an imperfection in the constitutional scheme, the solution, presumably, is to amend the Constitution.

Perhaps state A says that it will consider passing a child labor law if state B goes first. Can state B necessarily trust state A? Can one even be certain that state B, for all of its professed desire to help its children, might not be tempted to maintain child labor if state A went first, given the presumed boon to state B's products?

The situation described may be a classic "prisoner's dilemma," a concept widely used in game theory to describe certain problems of "strategic interaction."[150] The idea is that both parties would be made better off if they could cooperate, but they do not dare because they cannot be sure what the other party will do in response to their unilateral action. As a result, each engages in a strategy that maximizes his or her position on the assumption that the other person will not cooperate.

One response to these kinds of collective action problems, especially as the number of parties rises, is for a central decisionmaker—in this case the federal government—to intervene and force each party to engage in uniform behavior that benefits them all. Under this analysis, North Carolina, the state whose child labor law was the subject of *Hammer*, is a selfish egoist whose decision to allow child labor ends up "forcing" the other states to permit unjust labor practices. If you accept this characterization of the situation, you can perhaps understand why many people thought it so important that Congress have the power to impose a general coordinating rule. On the other hand, one could object that this is not a true prisoner's dilemma, because some states (and some interests within those states) might not agree that a uniform protection of child labor was best for their citizens. Suppose one believed, for example, that most economic regulations, even regulations on child labor, were undesirable infringements on liberty. In that case, a uniform rule would produce the worst possible outcome. If you accept *this* characterization of the situation, can you see why some people thought it important that Congress not have the power to impose a general rule on all of the states?[151] Consider in this context the statement of political scientist Paul Pierson:[152]

---

150. See Douglas G. Baird, Robert H. Gerner, and Randal C. Picker, Game Theory and the Law 31-35 (1995), from which the quoted language and examples are taken. This book is an excellent introduction to a far more complicated subject than can be adequately described in this note.

151. Michael Greve has recently made a sustained argument to this effect: In his view, the Constitution was designed to force states to compete with each other over their business policies. Because capital is mobile, states would (and should) vie with each other to produce business-friendly environments. See Michael Greve, The Upside-Down Constitution (2012). As a result, Greve argues, the government should not provide "solutions" for prisoner's dilemmas. Indeed, doing so actually rewards "cartels" of states who want to use federal regulatory power to stifle their competitors.

152. Paul Pierson, Dismantling the Welfare State? Reagan, Thatcher, and the Politics of Retrenchment 35 (1994).

> The evidence is reasonably clear that federalism constrains welfare state growth. The most important consequence of decentralized institutions is the creation of "fiscal competition" among jurisdictions. Local governments find it difficult to pursue redistributive policies for fear that high taxes will lead business and wealthy individuals to move out while attracting low-income groups who would benefit from generous social programs. Centralized authorities can make such policies uniform throughout a country, limiting the prospects that capital and labor mobility will pose such a dramatic threat to social provision.

It should be clear that a child labor policy, from the perspective of an affected business, is the equivalent of a tax, at least so long as the movement to adult laborers would increase labor costs.

Why do you think North Carolina in 1918 and countries around the world today tolerate child labor and other labor practices barred by American law or otherwise deviate from the kinds of regulatory regimes found in all advanced industrial countries? Imagine that the United States and other developed countries today attempt to outlaw child labor or the 12-hour day in these countries. (You should assume that the prohibition is not accompanied by any financial aid directed at the welfare either of the children or of the parents who are arguably dependent on their children's income or on the marginal gains from working more than eight hours.) Might one view an international prohibition as simply a way by which rich economies protect their industries against the competition of poorer countries that are willing to engage in extraordinary efforts, including child labor, working 12 hours a day, etc., in order, presumably, to benefit future generations?

The collective action issues discussed all too briefly in this note arise in many different contexts. Consider for example, Steward Machine Company v. Davis, described infra in Chapter 5, which upheld the power of Congress under the General Welfare Clause to pass a federal unemployment insurance scheme created by the Social Security Act of 1935. In that opinion, Justice Cardozo described certain "state inaction" in passing unemployment insurance provisions as being generated less by "the lack of sympathetic interest" than by "alarm lest, in laying such a toll upon their industries, they would place themselves in a position of economic disadvantage as compared with neighbors or competitors." He found ample power in Congress to pass national legislation designed to overcome the "fear" that prevented each state from acting in its individual capacity. To what extent, if any, should these kinds of game theoretic analyses play a role in the best interpretation of constitutional provisions? Is this simply another example of how consequences are as important a modality of constitutional interpretation as text, history, or original intention?

NOTE: BINARY OPPOSITIONS AND CONGRESSIONAL ABILITY TO INVOKE ITS POWER UNDER THE COMMERCE CLAUSE

As a result of industrialization and the rise of railroads, telegraphs, and increasingly inexpensive methods of interstate transportation, markets were increasingly national and economic activities increasingly had interstate effects. It therefore became difficult for lawyers and courts to make sense of what activities fell within Congress's powers to regulate the national economy and what activities remained purely "local" and therefore beyond Congress's powers. *Hammer* illustrates how lawyers and judges frequently turned to simple binary oppositions to determine whether Congress had the power to act under the Commerce Clause.

In addition to the distinction between inherently dangerous and harmless goods, the Court mentions another important opposition central to many cases of this period: "manufacture" versus "commerce." As the Court wrote in Kidd v. Pearson, 128 U.S. 1 (1888), "[m]anufacture is transformation—the fashioning of raw materials into a change of form for use. The functions of commerce are different."

In United States v. E.C. Knight Co., 156 U.S. 1 (1895), the Court refused to apply the Sherman Act to a trust that manufactured 95 percent of the sugar sold in the United States. Chief Justice Fuller wrote: "Commerce succeeds to manufacture, and is not part of it. The fact that an article is manufactured for export to another State does not itself make it an article of interstate commerce." He added: "It is vital that the independence of the commercial power and of the police power, and the delimitation between them, however sometimes perplexing, should always be recognized and observed, for while the one furnishes the strongest bond of union, the other is essential to the preservation of the autonomy of the states as required by our dual form of government, and acknowledged evils, however grave and urgent they may appear to be, had better be borne, than the risk be run, in the effort to suppress them, of more serious consequences by resort to expedients of even doubtful constitutionality." Justice Harlan wrote a vigorous lone dissent, copiously citing Marshall's opinions in *McCulloch* and *Gibbons*: "The means employed are the suppression, by legal proceedings, of combinations, conspiracies, and monopolies which, by their inevitable and admitted tendency, improperly restrain trade and commerce among the states. Who can say that such means are not appropriate to attain the end of freeing commercial intercourse among the states from burdens and exactions imposed upon it by combinations which, under principles long recognized in this country, as well as at the common law, are illegal and dangerous to the public welfare? What clause of the Constitution can be referred to which prohibits the means thus prescribed in the act of Congress?"

Harlan's view would ultimately prevail, but not for several decades.

The Court also distinguished on occasion between items in the "flow" of commerce and those not in the flow either because they had not yet entered it or because the flow had come to an end. For example, Swift & Co. v. United States, 196 U.S. 375 (1905), upheld the application of the Sherman Act to the price-fixing practices of stockyard owners. As Justice Sutherland later described this case, "livestock was consigned and delivered to stockyards—not as a place of final destination, but, as . . . 'a throat through which the current flows.'" The pre-1937 Court refused to extend *Swift* beyond its facts. Thus Schechter Poultry Corp. v. United States, 295 U.S. 495 (1935), discussed in Chapter 5, struck down federal regulation of the live poultry industry in New York because "the commodity in question [i.e., chickens], although shipped from another state, had come to rest in the state of its destination, and, as the court pointed out, was no longer in a current or flow of interstate commerce." As you will soon see, all of these categorical distinctions disappeared following the post-1937 transformations of federal power that came with the New Deal.

B. *The Taxing Power*

Shortly after the decision in Hammer v. Dagenhart, Congress enacted the Child Labor Tax Law of 1919, which imposed a 10 percent tax on the net income of any manufacturer employing children below specified ages. The Court struck it down, with only Justice Clarke dissenting.

BAILEY v. DREXEL FURNITURE CO. (The Child Labor Tax Case), 259 U.S. 20 (1922):

TAFT C.J.: Does this law impose a tax with only that incidental restraint and regulation which a tax must inevitably involve? Or does it regulate by the use of the so-called tax as a penalty? . . . If it were an excise on a commodity or other thing of value we might not be permitted under previous decisions of this court to infer solely from its heavy burden that the act intends a prohibition instead of a tax.

But this act is more. It provides a heavy exaction for a departure from a detailed and specified course of conduct in business. That course of business is that employers shall employ in mines and quarries, children of an age greater than sixteen years; in mills and factories, children of an age greater than fourteen years, and shall prevent children of less than sixteen years in mills and factories from working more than eight hours a day or six days in the week.

If an employer departs from this prescribed course of business, he is to pay to the Government one-tenth of his entire net income in the business for a full year. The amount is not to be proportioned in any degree to the extent or frequency of the departures, but is to be paid by the employer in full measure whether he employs five hundred children for a year, or employs only one for a day. Moreover, if he does not know the child is within the named age limit, he is not to pay; that is to say, it is only where he knowingly departs from the prescribed course that payment is to be exacted. Scienter is associated with penalties not with taxes. The employer's factory is to be subject to inspection at any time not only by the taxing officers of the Treasury, the Department normally charged with the collection of taxes, but also by the Secretary of Labor and his subordinates whose normal function is the advancement and protection of the welfare of the workers. In the light of these features of the act, a court must be blind not to see that the so-called tax is imposed to stop the employment of children within the age limits prescribed. Its prohibitory and regulatory effect and purpose are palpable. All others can see and understand this. How can we properly shut our minds to it?

Out of a proper respect for the acts of a coordinate branch of the Government, this court has gone far to sustain taxing acts as such, even though there has been ground for suspecting from the weight of the tax it was intended to destroy its subject. But, in the act before us, the presumption of validity cannot prevail, because the proof of the contrary is found on the very face of its provisions. Grant the validity of this law, and all that Congress would need to do, hereafter, in seeking to take over to its control any one of the great number of subjects of public interest, jurisdiction of which the States have never parted with, and which are reserved to them by the Tenth Amendment, would be to enact a detailed measure of complete regulation of the subject and enforce it by a so-called tax upon departures from it. To give such magic to the word "tax" would be to break down all constitutional limitation of the powers of Congress and completely wipe out the sovereignty of the States.

The difference between a tax and a penalty is sometimes difficult to define and yet the consequences of the distinction in the required method of their collection often are important. Where the sovereign enacting the law has power to impose both tax and penalty the difference between revenue production and mere regulation may be immaterial,[153] but not so when one sovereign can impose a tax only, and the power of regulation rests in another. Taxes are occasionally imposed in the discretion of the legislature on proper subjects with the primary motive of obtaining revenue from them and with the incidental motive of discouraging them by making their continuance onerous. They do not lose their character as taxes because of the incidental motive. But there comes a time in the extension of the penalizing features of the so-called tax when it loses its character as such and becomes a mere penalty with the characteristics of regulation and punishment. Such is the case in the law before us. . . .

The analogy of the *Dagenhart* case is clear. The congressional power over interstate commerce is, within its proper scope, just as complete and unlimited as the congressional power to tax, and the legislative motive in its exercise is just as free from judicial suspicion and inquiry. Yet when Congress threatened to stop interstate commerce in ordinary and necessary commodities, unobjectionable as subjects of transportation, and to deny the same to the people of a State in order to coerce them into compliance with Congress's regulation of state concerns, the court said this was not in fact regulation of interstate commerce, but rather that of State concerns and was invalid. So here the so-called tax is a penalty to coerce people of a State to act as Congress wishes them to act in respect of a matter completely the business of the state government under the Federal Constitution. This case requires as did the *Dagenhart* case the application of the principle announced by Chief Justice Marshall in McCulloch v. Maryland, in [the "pretext" passage, Chapter 1, supra].

Hill v. Wallace, 259 U.S. 44 (1922), decided on the same day as the Child Labor Tax case, held invalid as a regulation of the (local) business of grain trading a tax of 20 cents per bushel on grain future contracts except those made through "boards of trade" designated by the Secretary of Agriculture upon their compliance with detailed regulations specified in the statute. United States v. Constantine, 296 U.S. 287 (1935), struck down a federal excise tax of $1,000 imposed on liquor dealers carrying on business in violation of state or local law; the Court held that the exaction was a penalty rather than a revenue-raising measure.

---

153. Veazie Bank v. Fenno, 75 U.S. (8 Wall.) 533 (1869), is an example. The Court sustained a 10 percent federal tax on personal and state bank notes, apparently designed to deter the use of such notes, commenting:

> Having . . . , in the exercise of undisputed constitutional powers, undertaken to provide a currency for the whole country, it cannot be questioned that Congress may, constitutionally, secure the benefit of it to the people by appropriate legislation. To this end, Congress has denied the quality of legal tender to foreign coins, and has provided by law against the imposition of counterfeit and base coin on the community. To the same end, Congress may restrain, by suitable enactments, the circulation as money of any notes not issued under its own authority. Without this power, indeed, its attempts to secure a sound and uniform currency for the country must be futile.

During the same period, the Court also upheld some federal taxes that appeared to regulate what it viewed as "local" matters. McCray v. United States, 195 U.S. 27 (1904), sustained a law, designed to discourage the sale of margarine that looked like butter, that taxed yellow margarine at 10 cents per pound and white margarine at only 0.25 cents. United States v. Doremus, 249 U.S. 86 (1919), sustained burdensome federal record-keeping requirements on sellers of narcotics, ostensibly designed to enforce a tax on the drugs. In the Child Labor Tax case, Chief Justice Taft distinguished the laws the Court had previously upheld on the ground that, on their face, they were tax rather than regulatory measures. "In neither [*McCray* nor *Veazie Bank*] did the law objected to show on its face as does the law before us the detailed specifications of a regulation of a state concern and business with a heavy exaction to promote the efficacy of such regulation."

C. *The Spending Power*

Recall Madison's veto of an "internal improvements" measure in 1817, Chapter 1, supra, and the fact that many Democratic Presidents throughout the nineteenth century emulated Madison by vetoing similar legislation and thus keeping the issue off the judicial agenda. In 1888, the Court upheld legislation that provided partial federal financing for interstate railroads, California Railroad Cases, 127 U.S. 1 (1888), but Justice Bradley relied on the commerce power rather than the Spending Clause:

> It cannot at the present day be doubted that Congress, under the power to regulate commerce among the several States, as well as to provide for postal accommodations and military exigencies, had authority to pass these laws. . . . Without authority in Congress to establish and maintain such highways and bridges, it would be without authority to regulate one of the most important adjuncts of commerce. [In former times, the] exertion [of this power] was but little called for, as commerce was then mostly conducted by water, and many of our statesman entertained doubts as to the existence of the power to establish ways of communication by land. But since, in consequence of the expansion of the country, the multiplication of its products, and the invention of railroads and locomotion by steam, land transportation has so vastly increased, a sounder consideration of the subject has prevailed and led to the conclusion that Congress has plenary power over the whole subject.

Bradley's argument about congressional power to spend to promote interstate transportation was not perceived as reaching the question of "disaster relief," the constitutionality of which continued to be a recurrent issue before Congress. Precisely because of earlier legislation providing such relief, perhaps most members of Congress believed that the question of constitutionality had essentially been settled. Indeed, Michele Landis Dauber writes that "so clearly constitutional was disaster relief that it actually played a role (a decisive role, it turns out) in the internal improvement debates" that took place in Congress following President Monroe's veto of the internal improvement bill. "A House committee headed by Henry

St. George Tucker investigated and came out in favor of the broad interpretation of the general welfare power based on the precedent of disaster relief."[154] As the Republican Speaker of the House, Joseph Kiefer, put it in 1884, "[t]he General Government has throughout its history selected extraordinary cases for granting relief. Where we shall stop, where the boundary line is, must always rest within the discretion of Congress."[155] Or, as Texas Senator John Reagan told his colleagues during an 1884 debate about relief for the victims of a Mississippi River flood, "we have a long line of precedents which have met the approbation of the most illustrious minds of the past and we know that if we shall do what we are now asked to do we do not violate the Constitution."[156]

There was, however, no unanimity on this point. Recall from Chapter 2, supra, that many Democratic Presidents from Madison to Franklin Pierce vetoed internal improvement legislation on constitutional grounds, and Dauber's own illuminating scholarship reveals that the debate had scarcely been definitively settled during the presidency of Grover Cleveland, the first Democrat to be elected following the Civil War. Interestingly enough, congressional Democrats were less purist than their President. Thus, consider, for example, the following comments in 1884 from Democratic representatives who supported a proposal to allocate $300,000 in aid for the victims of an Ohio River flood. Republicans had gleefully taunted Democratic representatives for contradicting their usual position that the limited powers assigned by the Constitution to Congress included no right to fund, under the General Welfare Clause, disaster relief legislation, which was often described as having nothing to do with the "general welfare" and instead as simply a naked transfer of resources from taxpayers in one part of the country to the lucky recipients of congressional beneficence in another.

Ohio Democrat John Follen responded that "necessity knows neither law nor constitution and never did in this country,"[157] while his colleague Adoniram Warner concurred: "[M]ingled with the appeals that come to us for help are the cries of children and the petitions for women homeless, shelterless, hungry, and in this presence I cannot stop to argue literal construction of the Constitution. I will take the side of mercy and risk it on that." Isaac Jordan, also of Ohio, candidly admitted that he did "not know whether this bill is constitutional or not. We have no time to enter into a discussion of this question. While we would stand here debating it the floods would not abate and the people would perish."

President Cleveland saw matters differently. On February 15, 1887, he vetoed "[a]n act to enable the Commissioner of Agriculture to make a special distribution of seeds in the drought-stricken counties of Texas, and making an appropriation

---

154. Michele Dauber Landis, e-mail to Jack M. Balkin, August 31, 2005.

155. Michele Dauber Landis, The Sympathetic State, 23 Law & Hist. Rev. 387, 404 (2005), quoting the Congressional Record, 67th Cong., 1st Sess., 1884, 15, pt. 3:2294. An expanded version of the argument appears in Michele Dauber Landis, The Sympathetic State: Disaster Reliefs and the Origins of the American Welfare State (2012). See particularly p. 46, Figure 2.1, Table of Disaster Relief Appropriations.

156. Landis, 23 Law & Hist. Rev. at 403, quoting the Congressional Record, 48th Cong., 1st Sess., 1884, 15, pt. 2:1037.

157. All quotations in this paragraph come from Landis, The Sympathetic State, 23 Law & Hist. Rev. at 406, quoting Congressional Record, 48th Cong., 1st Sess., 1884, 15, pt. 2:1033, 1039, 1038.

thereof."[158] Cleveland readily conceded that "there has existed a condition calling for relief" and that the issuance of the new seeds "would serve to avert a continuance or return of an unfortunate blight." Nonetheless, the fact that Congress wished "to indulge a benevolent and charitable sentiment through the appropriation of public funds" did not justify his signing the bill, for

> I can find no warrant for such an appropriation in the Constitution, and I do not believe that the power and duty of the General Government ought to be extended to the relief of individual suffering which is in no manner properly related to the public service [as with veterans, for example] or benefit. A prevalent tendency to disregard the limited mission of [national] power and duty should, I think, be steadfastly resisted, to the end that the lesson should be constantly enforced that though the people support the Government the Government should not support the people.

Indeed, Cleveland argued, "[f]ederal aid in such cases encourages the expectation of paternal care on the part of the Government and weakens the sturdiness of our national character, while it prevents the indulgence among our people of that kindly sentiment and conduct which strengthens the bonds of a common brotherhood."

DISCUSSION

Once again it is important to realize the frequency with which fundamental constitutional issues were debated in Congress and addressed by Presidents in veto messages. The "precedents" on which pro-aid members of Congress relied were prior congressional decisions, not judicial opinions, and President Cleveland in his veto message made no reference to courts. Both President Cleveland and congressmen and senators regarded themselves as fully worthy of making the relevant constitutional determinations.

Consider, however, the possible differences among the arguments they made, particularly those made by the Democratic representatives. One might interpret Representative Follen as making a "first-order" constitutional argument that the Constitution, correctly interpreted, always allows responses to "necessity." (You might consider how many times we have seen arguments from emergency so far in this casebook.) Representatives Warner and Jordan, on the other hand, might be understood as making a "second-order" argument: that *their* duty as representatives is to respond to those who need help, while leaving it up to courts to decide, in due time, whether such legislation is constitutional. Is this a proper conception of the role of a "conscientious legislator"?

Do both Madison and Cleveland provide models of constitutionally "conscientious Presidents"? Madison leaves the reader with little doubt that he believes that the bill represented desirable public policy but was, alas, unconstitutional. Cleveland, by contrast, seems less taken by the policy of the legislation he vetoed because it might encourage victims of disaster in effect to become dependent on public

---

158. 11 Messages and Papers of the Presidents 5142-5143 (Richardson ed., 1897).

welfare, and it might stifle the impulses of others to help out in the belief that there was no need for private charity. Given that Cleveland signed other disaster relief legislation during his presidency, one might choose to read his veto message quite narrowly, referring to the presumptive lack of merits of the particular claims by ostensibly needy Texans, as against a more general rejection of the very idea of congressional authority to redistribute funds to worthier victims of disasters. At the very least, though, it is hard to believe that Cleveland's veto was based on crass political considerations, given the fact that Texas had provided 13 electoral votes in Cleveland's narrow 219-182 electoral vote victory over James G. Blaine in 1884.

Congress (and the White House) remained the primary venues for resolving such arguments, not least because the Supreme Court did not fully address until 1936 the question of Congress's power to spend federal funds in the pursuit of ends not within the enumerated powers of Article I, §8.

D. The Treaty Power

MISSOURI v. HOLLAND, 252 U.S. 416 (1920): [*Holland* involved the constitutionality of the Migratory Bird Treaty Act of July 3, 1918 and subsequent regulations issued by the Secretary of Agriculture, all of which were intended to enforce a 1916 treaty that had been entered into between the United States and Great Britain (in its capacity as the sovereign over Canada, from which the birds in question migrated). Missouri asserted that the statute unconstitutionally interfered with its reserved rights under the Tenth Amendment. The Court disagreed.]

HOLMES, J.: [The treaty] recited that many species of birds in their annual migrations traversed many parts of the United States and of Canada, that they were of great value as a source of food and in destroying insects injurious to vegetation, but were in danger of extermination through lack of adequate protection. It therefore provided for specified closed seasons and protection in other forms, and agreed that the two powers would take or propose to their lawmaking bodies the necessary measures for carrying the treaty out. The above mentioned act . . . prohibited the killing, capturing or selling any of the migratory birds included in the terms of the treaty except as permitted by regulations compatible with those terms, to be made by the Secretary of Agriculture. . . . [T]he question raised is the general one whether the treaty and statute are void as an interference with the rights reserved to the States.

To answer this question it is not enough to refer to the Tenth Amendment, reserving the powers not delegated to the United States, because by Article 2, Section 2, the power to make treaties is delegated expressly, and by Article 6 treaties made under the authority of the United States, along with the Constitution and laws of the United States made in pursuance thereof, are declared the supreme law of the land. If the treaty is valid there can be no dispute about the validity of the statute under Article 1, Section 8, as a necessary and proper means to execute the powers of the Government. The language of the Constitution as to the supremacy of treaties being general, the question before us is narrowed to an inquiry into the ground upon which the present supposed exception is placed.

It is said that a treaty cannot be valid if it infringes the Constitution, that there are limits, therefore, to the treaty-making power, and that one such limit is that what an act of Congress could not do unaided, in derogation of the powers reserved to the States, a treaty cannot do. An earlier act of Congress that attempted by itself and not in pursuance of a treaty to regulate the killing of migratory birds within the States had been held bad in the District Court. United States v. Shauver, 214 Fed. 154; United States v. McCullagh, 221 Fed. 288. Those decisions were supported by arguments that migratory birds were owned by the States in their sovereign capacity for the benefit of their people, and that under cases like Geer v. Connecticut, 161 U.S. 519, this control was one that Congress had no power to displace. The same argument is supposed to apply now with equal force.

Whether the two cases cited were decided rightly or not they cannot be accepted as a test of the treaty power. Acts of Congress are the supreme law of the land only when made in pursuance of the Constitution, while treaties are declared to be so when made under the authority of the United States. It is open to question whether the authority of the United States means more than the formal acts prescribed to make the convention. We do not mean to imply that there are no qualifications to the treaty-making power; but they must be ascertained in a different way. It is obvious that there may be matters of the sharpest exigency for the national well being that an act of Congress could not deal with but that a treaty followed by such an act could, and it is not lightly to be assumed that, in matters requiring national action, "a power which must belong to and somewhere reside in every civilized government" is not to be found. Andrews v. Andrews, 188 U.S. 14. What was said in that case with regard to the powers of the States applies with equal force to the powers of the nation in cases where the States individually are incompetent to act. We are not yet discussing the particular case before us but only are considering the validity of the test proposed. With regard to that we may add that when we are dealing with words that also are a constituent act, like the Constitution of the United States, we must realize that they have called into life a being the development of which could not have been foreseen completely by the most gifted of its begetters. It was enough for them to realize or to hope that they had created an organism; it has taken a century and has cost their successors much sweat and blood to prove that they created a nation. The case before us must be considered in the light of out whole experience and not merely in that of what was said a hundred years ago. The treaty in question does not contravene any prohibitory words to be found in the Constitution. The only question is whether it is forbidden by some invisible radiation from the general terms of the Tenth Amendment. We must consider what this country has become in deciding what that amendment has reserved.

The State as we have intimated founds its claim of exclusive authority upon an assertion of title to migratory birds, an assertion that is embodied in statute. No doubt it is true that as between a State and its inhabitants the State may regulate the killing and sale of such birds, but it does not follow that its authority is exclusive of paramount powers. To put the claim of the State upon title is to lean upon a slender reed. Wild birds are not in the possession of anyone; and possession is the beginning of ownership. The whole foundation of the State's rights is the presence within their jurisdiction of birds that yesterday had not arrived, tomorrow may be in another State and in a week a thousand miles away. If we are to be accurate we cannot put the case of the State upon higher ground than that the treaty deals with creatures that for the moment are within the state borders, that it must be carried out by officers of the United States within the same territory, and that but for the treaty the State would be free to regulate this subject itself.

As most of the laws of the United States are carried out within the States and as many of them deal with matters which in the silence of such laws the State might regulate, such general grounds are not enough to support Missouri's claim. Valid treaties of course "are as binding within the territorial limits of the States as they are elsewhere throughout the dominion of the United States." Baldwin v. Franks, 120 U.S. 678, 683. No doubt the great body of private relations usually fall within the control of the State, but a treaty may override its power. We do not have to invoke the later developments of constitutional law for this proposition; it was recognized as early as Hopkirk v. Bell, 3 Cranch, 454, with regard to statutes of limitation, and even earlier, as to confiscation, in Ware v. Hylton, 3 Dall. 199. It was assumed by Chief Justice Marshall with regard to the escheat of land to the State in Chirac v. Chirac, 2 Wheat. 259, 275 [and other cases]. So as to a limited jurisdiction of foreign consuls within a State. Wildenhus' Case, 120 U.S. 1. Further illustration seems unnecessary, and it only remains to consider the application of established rules to the present case.

Here a national interest of very nearly the first magnitude is involved. It can be protected only by national action in concert with that of another power. The subject matter is only transitorily within the State and has no permanent habitat therein. But for the treaty and the statute there soon might be no birds for any powers to deal with. We see nothing in the Constitution that compels the Government to sit by while a food supply is cut off and the protectors of our forests and our crops are destroyed. It is not sufficient to rely upon the States. The reliance is vain, and were it otherwise, the question is whether the United States is forbidden to act. We are of opinion that the treaty and statute must be upheld.

Only two Justices dissented in *Holland*, without opinion. One might ask, therefore, why a Court so seemingly committed to protecting reserved rights of the states against congressional interference would find Justice Holmes's opinion unexceptionable. One possibility, of course, is that the subject matter of the treaty and congressional statute, migratory birds, is key. How deeply can one credit Missouri's reserved right to regulate geese that might well be transitory visitors to the state on their way from Canada to Texas (or beyond)? Even if one accepted the proposition that Congress could not, by exercising ordinary Article I powers, regulate migratory birds, one might also argue, as Professor Sarah Cleveland suggests, that "a possible interpretation of Holmes is not so much that the treaty power allows the national government to override powers constitutionally reserved to the states as that the treaty power creates a competing interest in the national government, bestowed by the Constitution, which doesn't exist where ordinary legislation is at issue."[159] Query whether the Court must necessarily defer to such a statement of a "competing interest" or whether, as arguably occurred in *Holland*, it can legitimately "balance" the competing weights of the national and state interests.

159. E-mail to Sanford Levinson, July 20, 1999.

A second possibility, though, is that the Court accepted the general proposition that "the President and the Senate together may achieve via the treaty power what Congress and the President cannot do under Article I, section 8 of the Constitution."[160] As G. Edward White has noted, Justice Sutherland, otherwise firmly committed to a limited conception of congressional power, had articulated as early as 1910 a highly expansive notion of national powers in regard to foreign policy; indeed, he would eventually author the *Curtiss-Wright* opinion, Chapter 3, supra, which adopted an "inherent power" view of the subject.[161] The capacity of the United States to enter into any international agreements deemed to serve vital national interests could, therefore, easily come under such an analysis.

There is relatively little case law directly in point, though a plurality opinion did, in 1957, state that a treaty could not "confer power on the Congress, or on any other branch of Government, which is free from the restraints of the Constitution." Reid v. Covert, 354 U.S. 1, 16 (1957). As a practical matter, the issue, though of great theoretical interest, has not spawned significant case law, perhaps because the President and the Senate have been hesitant, on either political or constitutional grounds, to test the limits of their joint power. One reason for such hesitation, no doubt, was the intense and bitter debate that took place in the early 1950s, sparked by a California court's overturning a state law on grounds that it violated the United Nations Charter, Fujii v. State, 217 P.2d 481, aff'd on other grounds, 242 P.2d 617 (1952).

Led by Ohio Senator John Bricker, with the support, among others, of the American Bar Association, repeated attempts were made to amend the Constitution explicitly to restrict the reach of the Treaty Clause. Although the "Bricker Amendment" was ultimately defeated, in part because of opposition by President Eisenhower, the *Reid* dictum, coupled with dictates of political prudence, achieved many of its aims. The fight over the Bricker Amendment had other political consequences. Unlike in many other countries, America's adoption of international human rights treaties has had little influence in shaping American civil rights and civil liberties protections.

See also Bond v. United States, 134 S.Ct. 2077 (2014), discussed in Chapter 6, infra. In *Bond*, the Court narrowly construed a federal statute implementing a chemical weapons treaty that banned the use of toxic chemicals so as not to impinge on state criminal law enforcement. Chief Justice John Roberts explained that "we can insist on a clear indication that Congress meant to reach purely local crimes, before interpreting the statute's expansive language in a way that intrudes on the police power of the States."

Imagine, though, that the statute in Missouri v. Holland had involved child labor and was based on an international treaty, duly submitted by the President and ratified by two-thirds of the Senate, that banned child labor. Could Congress

---

160. Thomas M. Franck and Michael J. Glennon, Foreign Relations and National Security Law 298 (2d ed. 1993). See generally Curtis A. Bradley, The Treaty Power and American Federalism, 97 Mich. L. Rev. 390 (1998), which summarizes much of the extant literature even as he suggests that there are indeed federalism limitations to the scope of the treaty power.

161. G. Edward White, The Transformation of the Constitutional Regime of Foreign Relations, 85 Va. L. Rev. 1, 46-61 (1999).

then have repassed the legislation struck down in *Hammer*? Or consider Article 20 of the International Covenant on Civil and Political Rights: "1. Any propaganda for war shall be prohibited by law. 2. Any advocacy of national, racial, or religious hatred that constitutes incitement to discrimination, hostility or violence shall be prohibited by law." The Senate attached reservations to this provision when it ratified in 1992 (thus indicating that it would not acquiesce).[162] Suppose, however, that the Senate had not done so. Could Congress then have passed a statute enforcing the commitment against hate speech regardless of the potential conflicts with First Amendment doctrine?

E. *The Eleventh Amendment and State Sovereign Immunity*

HANS v. LOUISIANA, 134 U.S. 1 (1890): [Hans was a citizen of Louisiana who sued to recover on bonds issued by the Louisiana legislature on January 24, 1874, which was still one of the "Reconstruction" governments prior to the return of Louisiana to white rule following the Compromise of 1877. An important 1875 law had allowed federal jurisdiction "of all suits of a civil nature, at common law or in equity, . . . arising under the Constitution or laws of the United States, or treaties made, or which shall be made, under their authority."]

Bradley, J.: In the present case, the plaintiff in error contends that he, being a citizen of Louisiana, is not embarrassed by the obstacle of the Eleventh Amendment inasmuch as that Amendment only prohibits suits against a State which are brought by the citizens of another State, or by citizens or subjects of a foreign state. It is true the Amendment does so read, and, if there were no other reason or ground for abating his suit, it might be maintainable; and then we should have this anomalous result, that, in cases arising under the Constitution or laws of the United States, a State may be sued in the federal courts by its own citizens, though it cannot be sued for a like cause of action by the citizens of other States, or of a foreign state; and may be thus sued in the federal courts, although not allowing itself to be sued in its own courts. If this is the necessary consequence of the language of the Constitution and the law, the result is no less startling and unexpected than was the original decision of this Court that . . . a State was liable to be sued by a citizen of another State or of a foreign country. . . .

Looking back from our present standpoint at the decision in Chisholm v. Georgia, we do not greatly wonder at the effect which it had upon the country. Any such power as that of authorizing the federal judiciary to entertain suits by individuals against the States had been expressly disclaimed, and even resented, by the great defenders of the Constitution while it was on its trial before the American people. . . . [Bradley quotes from Federalist No. 81, written by Hamilton, as well as statements at the Virginia ratifying convention by Madison and Marshall.]

---

162. U.S. Senate Resolution of Advice and Consent to Ratification of the International Covenant on Civil and Political Rights, 102d Cong., 2d Sess., 138 Cong. Rec. S 4781-4784 (April 2, 1992).

It seems to us that these views of those great advocates and defenders of the Constitution were most sensible and just, and they apply equally to the present case as to that then under discussion. The letter is appealed to now, as it was then, as a ground for sustaining a suit brought by an individual against a State. The reason against it is as strong in this case as it was in that. It is an attempt to strain the Constitution and the law to a construction never imagined or dreamed of. Can we suppose that, when the Eleventh Amendment was adopted, it was understood to be left open for citizens of a State to sue their own State in the federal courts, while the idea of suits by citizens of other States, or of foreign states, was indignantly repelled? Suppose that Congress, when proposing the Eleventh Amendment, had appended to it a proviso that nothing therein contained should prevent a State from being sued by its own citizens in cases arising under the Constitution or laws of the United States, can we imagine that it would have been adopted by the States? The supposition that it would is almost an absurdity on its face. . . .

HARLAN, J., concurring: I concur with the court in holding that a suit directly against a State by one of its own citizens is not one to which the judicial power of the United States extends, unless the State itself consents to be sued. Upon this ground alone I assent to the judgment. But I cannot give my assent to many things said in the opinion. The comments made upon the decision in Chisholm v. Georgia do not meet my approval. They are not necessary to the determination of the present case. Besides, I am of opinion that the decision in that case was based upon a sound interpretation of the Constitution as that instrument then was.

DISCUSSION

1. *"It is true the Amendment does so read."* If one believes that *Chisholm* was rightly decided, even though the Eleventh Amendment in effect overruled it, and if the text of the Eleventh Amendment is not addressed to suits against states by their own citizens, then what makes *Hans* persuasive? In any event, it continues to be "good law," and accepted by the present Supreme Court, which has significantly extended the principle of state sovereign immunity in a variety of bitterly divided 5-4 decisions. (See Chapter 6, infra, for the details.) Justice Kennedy in particular has emphasized the "dignity" interests of states, which are affronted when they are forced to defend their (mis)conduct in federal court without their consent. Recall Justice Wilson's comments in *Chisholm*. Why does a state's "dignity" outweigh the dignity of citizens of the United States who claim that they were mistreated by the state?

2. *Ex parte Young*. As the Court moved into the *Lochner* era, *Hans* proved a serious stumbling block to litigants who sought to challenge state economic regulations that they believed violated the Fourteenth Amendment. (Recall that *Lochner* itself was an appeal of a criminal conviction and therefore did not raise Eleventh Amendment issues.) In Ex parte Young, 209 U.S. 123 (1908), a complicated lawsuit that arose out of a challenge to Minnesota's system of railroad regulation, the Court created a loophole to allow federal challenges to proceed in civil litigation. Ex parte Young permits civil suits by citizens of a state against the state, provided that (1) the plaintiff names a state official (such as the state Attorney General) charged with enforcing the law rather than the state itself; and (2) the relief sought is injunctive, and does not require the payment of money damages from the state treasury.

Writing for the Court, Justice Peckham, the author of *Lochner*, explained: "[T]he use of the name of the State to enforce an unconstitutional act to the injury of complainants is a proceeding without the authority of and one which does not affect the State in its sovereign or governmental capacity. It is simply an illegal act upon the part of a state official in attempting by the use of the name of the State to enforce a legislative enactment which is void because unconstitutional. If the act which the state Attorney General seeks to enforce be a violation of the Federal Constitution, the officer in proceeding under such enactment comes into conflict with the superior authority of that Constitution, and he is in that case stripped of his official or representative character and is subjected in his person to the consequences of his individual conduct. The State has no power to impart to him any immunity from responsibility to the supreme authority of the United States."

Justice Harlan dissented.

V. "WHEN A NATION IS AT WAR": WORLD WAR I AND THE FIRST AMENDMENT

The federal courts began to develop doctrines applying the First Amendment's Free Speech Clause in response to governmental attempts to suppress opposition to U.S. participation in World War I.[163] The first cases followed Congress's establishment of a military draft in 1917. Emma Goldman, Alexander Berkman, and other prominent radicals were indicted and convicted for conspiring to convince eligible people not to register for the draft.[164]

In June 1917, two months after American entry into the war against Germany, Congress passed an Espionage Act that, among other things, prohibited speech that incited insubordination in the military and naval forces of the United States or that incited people to refuse to serve in the armed forces. The basic framework was established in four cases decided in 1919—Schenck v. United States, 249 U.S. 47 (1919); Sugarman v. United States, 249 U.S. 182 (1919); Frohwerk v. United States, 249 U.S. 204 (1919); and Debs v. United States, 249 U.S. 211 (1919).

In Schenck v. United States, 249 U.S. 47 (1919), Justice Holmes, writing for a unanimous Court, articulated what later came to be known as the "clear and present danger" test. The Court upheld Espionage Act convictions of antiwar advocates who sent circulars to draft-age men, urging them not to join the armed forces:

> It well may be that the prohibition of laws abridging the freedom of speech is not confined to previous restraints, although to prevent them may have been the main purpose. . . . We admit that in many places and in ordinary times the defendants . . . would have been within their constitutional

163. See David M. Rabban, Free Speech in Its Forgotten Years (1997); see also Mark A. Graber, Transforming Free Speech: The Ambiguous Legacy of Civil Libertarianism (1991).

164. Goldman v. United States, 245 U.S. 474 (1918). *Goldman* and companion cases are discussed in David Rabban, The Emergence of Modern First Amendment Doctrine, 50 U. Chi. L. Rev. 1205, 1244-1246 (1984).

> rights. But the character of every act depends upon the circumstances in which it is done. The most stringent protection of free speech would not protect a man in falsely shouting fire in a theatre and causing a panic. . . . The question in every case is whether the words used are used in such circumstances and are of such a nature as to create a clear and present danger that they will bring about the substantive evils that Congress has a right to prevent. It is a question of proximity and degree. When a nation is at war many things that might be said in time of peace are such a hindrance to its effort that their utterance will not be endured so long as men fight and that no Court could regard them as protected by any constitutional right. It seems to be admitted that if an actual obstruction of the recruiting service were proved, liability for words that produced that effect might be enforced. The statute of 1917 in §4 punishes conspiracies to obstruct as well as actual obstruction. If the act, . . . its tendency and the intent with which it is done are the same, we perceive no ground for saying that success alone warrants making the act a crime.

Debs v. United States affirmed the conviction of Eugene V. Debs, the acknowledged leader of American socialism, who had gained over a million votes as the Socialist candidate for the presidency in 1912. Debs was convicted for violating the Espionage Act, based on a speech he delivered in 1918 in Canton, Ohio, expressing his deep opposition to the war. In an opinion that never refers to Debs by name or identifies him as a prominent dissident, Justice Holmes described the speech as follows:

> The main theme of the speech was socialism, its growth, and a prophecy of its ultimate success. With that we have nothing to do, but if a part or the manifest intent of the more general utterances was to encourage those present to obstruct the recruiting service and if in passages such encouragement was directly given, the immunity of the general theme may not be enough to protect the speech. The speaker . . . said that he had to be prudent and might not be able to say all that he thought, thus intimating to his hearers that they might infer that he meant more, but he did say that [people convicted of violating the Espionage Act] were paying the penalty for standing erect and for seeking to pave the way to better conditions for all mankind. Later he . . . said that he was proud of them. He then expressed opposition to Prussian militarism in a way that naturally might have been thought to be intended to include the mode of proceeding in the United States. . . .
>
> The defendant spoke of other cases, and then, after dealing with Russia, said that the master class has always declared the war and the subject class has always fought the battles—that the subject class has had nothing to gain and all to lose, including their lives; that the working class, who furnish the corpses, have never yet had a voice in declaring war and have never yet had a voice in declaring peace. "You have your lives to lose; you certainly ought to have the right to declare war if you consider a war necessary." The defendant next mentioned Rose Pastor Stokes, convicted of attempting to cause insubordination and refusal of duty in the military

> forces of the United States and obstructing the recruiting service. He said that she went out to render her service to the cause in this day of crises, and they sent her to the penitentiary for ten years; that she had said no more than the speaker had said that afternoon; that if she was guilty so was he, and that he would not be cowardly enough to plead his innocence; but that her message that opened the eyes of the people must be suppressed, and so, after a mock trial before a packed jury and a corporation tool on the bench, she was sent to the penitentiary for ten years.
>
> . . . The defendant addressed the jury himself, and while contending that his speech did not warrant the charges said "I have been accused of obstructing the war. I admit it. Gentlemen, I abhor war. I would oppose the war if I stood alone." . . . If [the defendant's speech] was intended [to obstruct recruiting] and if, in all the circumstances, that would be its probable effect, it would not be protected by reason of its being part of a general program and expressions of a general and conscientious belief.

Justice Holmes responded to Debs's constitutional argument by referring to *Schenck*'s clear-and-present-danger test. Holmes concluded that in *Debs* "the jury were most carefully instructed that they could not find the defendant guilty for advocacy of any of his opinions unless the words used had as their natural tendency and reasonably probable effect to obstruct the recruiting service, &c., and unless the defendant had the specific intent to do so in his mind."

Following *Debs*, Holmes changed his views on freedom of speech and wrote a famous dissent, joined by Justice Brandeis, in Abrams v. United States, 250 U.S. 616 (1919). In this dissent he reinterpreted the clear-and-present-danger test as a doctrine that protected free speech.

The Court in *Abrams* affirmed conspiracy convictions under a 1918 amendment to the Act that punished urging curtailment of the production of war material "with the intent . . . to cripple or hinder the United States in the prosecution of the war." Defendants had distributed leaflets that said: "Workers in the ammunition factories, you are producing bullets, bayonets, and cannon to murder not only the Germans, but also your dearest, best, who are in Russia fighting for your freedom. . . . Workers, our reply to [America's] barbaric intervention [to destroy the Bolshevik Revolution] has to be a general strike."

In a dissent joined by Brandeis, Holmes wrote:

> [A]s against dangers peculiar to war, as against others, the principle of the right to free speech is always the same. It is only the present danger of immediate evil or an intent to bring it about that warrants Congress in setting a limit to the expression of opinion where private rights are not concerned. Congress certainly cannot forbid all effort to change the mind of the country. Now nobody can suppose that the surreptitious publishing of a silly leaflet by an unknown man, without more, would present any immediate danger that its opinions would hinder the success of the government arms or have any appreciable tendency to do so. . . .
>
> Persecution for the expression of opinions seems to me perfectly logical. If you have no doubt of your premises or your power and want a certain result with all your heart you naturally express your wishes in

> law and sweep away all opposition. To allow opposition by speech seems to indicate that you think the speech impotent, as when a man says that he has squared the circle, or that you do not care whole heartedly for the result, or that you doubt either your power or your premises. But when men have realized that time has upset many fighting faiths, they may come to believe even more than they believe the very foundations of their own conduct that the ultimate good desired is better reached by free trade in ideas—that the best test of truth is the power of the thought to get itself accepted in the competition of the market, and that truth is the only ground upon which their wishes safely can be carried out. That at any rate is the theory of our Constitution. It is an experiment, as all life is an experiment. Every year if not every day we have to wager our salvation upon some prophecy based upon imperfect knowledge. While that experiment is part of our system I think that we should be eternally vigilant against attempts to check the expression of opinions that we loathe and believe to be fraught with death, unless they so imminently threaten immediate interference with the lawful and pressing purposes of the law that an immediate check is required to save the country.

Holmes also wrote an influential dissent in Gitlow v. New York, 268 U.S. 652 (1925). The Court upheld the conviction of Benjamin Gitlow, a communist (and former state legislator), for violating New York's criminal anarchy law; nevertheless, it also, for the first time, agreed that the First Amendment's protections of free speech applied to the states. The New York law in question prohibited, inter alia, publication of any material that "advocates, advises or teaches the duty, necessity or propriety of overthrowing or overturning organized government by force or violence, . . . or by any unlawful means." Justice Clarke's opinion for the Court emphasized that New York had determined "through its legislative body, that utterances advocating the overthrow of organized government by force, violence and unlawful means, are so inimical to the general welfare and involve such danger of substantive evil that they may be penalized in the exercise of its police power." In *Schenck* and the other Espionage Act cases the government punished speech incidental to a different substantive offense, such as obstruction of recruiting. In *Gitlow*, by contrast, the "legislative body ha[d] determined generally, in the constitutional exercise of its discretion, that utterances of a certain kind involve such danger of substantive evil that they be punished."

Holmes wrote in dissent, joined by Justice Brandeis:

> [I]t is manifest that there was no present danger of an attempt to overthrow the government by force on the part of the admittedly small minority who shared the defendant's views. It is said that this manifesto was more than a theory, that it was an incitement. Every idea is an incitement. It offers itself for belief and if believed it is acted on unless some other belief outweighs it or some failure of energy stifles the movement at its birth. The only difference between the expression of an opinion and an incitement in the narrower sense is the speaker's enthusiasm for the result. Eloquence may set fire to reason. But whatever may be thought of the redundant discourse before us it had no chance of starting a present

conflagration. If in the long run the beliefs expressed in proletarian dictatorship are destined to be accepted by the dominant forces of the community, the only meaning of free speech is that they should be given their chance and have their way.

DISCUSSION

Justices Holmes and Brandeis, who are major architects of the twentieth-century American theory of freedom of speech, never indicated that they had second thoughts about the convictions of Debs and others upheld in the March 1919 cases. What, then, distinguishes *Debs* from the later cases (and the speech-protective theories enunciated in them)?

1. *The status of the speaker.* In *Abrams*, Holmes derides the possibility that the country faced any danger from "the surreptitious publishing of a silly leaflet by an unknown man." Is Debs's very prominence a justification for jailing him for ten years for the crime of opposing service in the armed forces during World War I (the "War to end War")? If not, then why was Abrams to be freed, according to Justice Holmes, from the sentence visited upon Debs?

2. *Imminence of the danger presented.* Although Holmes never elaborated the precise dimensions of "presentness" within the clear-and-present-danger test, he joined in Brandeis's opinion in Whitney v. California, 274 U.S. 652 (1925), which stated:

> There must be reasonable ground to believe that the danger apprehended is imminent. . . . Every denunciation of existing law tends in some measure to increase the probability that there will be a violation of it. . . . But even advocacy of violation, however reprehensible morally, is not a justification for denying free speech where the advocacy falls short of incitement and there is nothing to indicate that the advocacy would be immediately acted on. The wide difference between advocacy and incitement, between preparation and attempt, between assembling and conspiracy, must be borne in mind. . . .
>
> [N]o danger flowing from speech can be deemed clear and present unless the incidence of the evil apprehended is so imminent that it may befall before there is opportunity to full discussion. If there be time to expose through discussion the falsehood and fallacies, to avert the evil by the processes of education, the remedy to be applied is more speech, not enforced silence. Only an emergency can justify repression.

Could Debs possibly be convicted under this version of the clear-and-present-danger test?

3. *Seriousness of the offense.* Justice Brandeis wrote in *Whitney*: "To justify suppression of free speech there must be reasonable ground to fear that *serious evil* will result if free speech is practiced" (emphasis added). Does this mean that advocacy of relatively "unserious evils," such as trespass on private or public property, must be tolerated even when the possibility of action is very high? On the other hand, can the state punish particularly ominous speech even if the probability of harm is very low?

In Dennis v. United States, 241 U.S. 404 (1951), the Supreme Court, although asserting that it was employing Holmes's clear-and-present-danger test, adopted a formula proffered by Judge Learned Hand: "In each case [courts] must ask whether the gravity of the 'evil,' discounted by its improbability, justifies such invasion of free speech as is necessary to avoid the danger." The effect of *Dennis* was that if the legislature believed the potential harm from speech was sufficiently great, the legislature might suppress speech when the harm was highly improbable and might not occur for many years in the future.

Critics of *Dennis*, including the dissenting Justices, Black and Douglas, argued that this test was far too accepting of the suppression of speech: "[T]he judicial inquiry becomes by this formulation as broad and as conjectural as the legislative process itself." Indeed, the concurring opinions by Justices Jackson and Frankfurter, like Justice Clarke's opinion in *Gitlow*, "were pervaded with the idea that the judiciary was unqualified to second-guess Congress about such far-flung judgments and on issues of such magnitude."

Not at all coincidentally, *Dennis* arose during the midst of the Cold War and involved the jailing of top leaders of the Communist Party. No one seriously suggested that there was any immediate likelihood (i.e., "present danger") of overthrowing the constituted form of government (or, indeed, that the leaders were even on the brink of fomenting an attempted revolution). This seemed irrelevant, though, once the even-minimal likelihood was multiplied by the almost infinite gravity of a loss of American liberty. As Robert McCloskey says, the *Dennis* test "simply provided a metaphorical way of explaining why the judiciary felt unable to challenge, on substantive grounds, the congressional will to scotch the Red Menace."[165]

Does this discredit the Hand formula entirely? Is it really plausible that courts should simply ignore the potential seriousness of the threatened harm? Compare speech that has a 40 percent probability of inciting a race riot with speech that has a 40 percent chance of inciting jaywalking. Rigorous adherence to the Holmes-Brandeis formula requires that that the state may act only when probability of harm reaches a very high level of certainty. Otherwise, critics of the Hand formula suggest, decisionmakers, including courts, will be inclined to characterize the cost of potential harm, even if unlikely, as extremely high and therefore justify the suppression of what would otherwise be protected speech.

4. *Institutional competence.* To what extent should courts defer to findings of fact about either danger or probability made by juries (as in *Debs*) or legislatures (as in *Gitlow*)? Is there good reason to believe that judges are more trustworthy guardians of free speech? Does your answer depend on such factors as to how judges reach the bench—most judges in the United States are state judges who are elected or otherwise accountable to the electorate—or their tenure in office? Federal judges are almost unique among American judges (and, for that matter, judges around the world) in having true life tenure, i.e., no term or age limit.

5. *Subsequent developments.* The clear-and-present-danger test was given its modern, and highly speech-protective, formulation in Brandenburg v. Ohio, 395 U.S. 444 (1969). *Brandenburg* reversed the conviction of a Ku Klux Klan leader for violating the Ohio Criminal Syndicalism statute by "advocat[ing] . . . the duty, necessity,

165. Robert McCloskey, The Modern Supreme Court 80 (1972). The quotations in this and the next paragraph are taken from pp. 80-82 of the chapter "The Vinson Court."

or propriety of crime, sabotage, violence, or unlawful methods of terrorism as a means of accomplishing industrial or political reform" and for "voluntarily assembl[ing]" for those purposes. Speaking before a Klan rally, Brandenburg had called for "revengence" against Jews, Black people, and three branches of the national government. In a per curiam opinion, the Court unanimously struck down the Act and Brandenburg's conviction under it, in the process formally overruling *Whitney*'s upholding of the California Criminal Syndicalism Act. The Court wrote:

> [T]he constitutional guarantees of free speech and free press do not permit a State to forbid or proscribe advocacy of the use of force or of law violation except where such advocacy is directed to inciting or producing imminent lawless action and likely to incite or produce such action. . . . "[T]he mere abstract teaching . . . of the moral propriety or even moral necessity for a resort to force and violence, is not the same as preparing a group for violent action and steeling it to such action." A statute which fails to draw this distinction impermissibly . . . sweeps within its condemnation speech which our Constitution has immunized from governmental control. . . . Statutes affecting the right of assembly, like those touching on freedom of speech, must observe the established distinctions between mere advocacy and incitement to imminent lawless action. . . . [The Ohio] statute falls within the condemnation of the First and Fourteenth Amendments.

Does *Brandenberg* protect the kind of speech that Debs gave in Canton? Recall that there he did not directly advocate draft resistance, but merely indicated his strong respect for those who did, as well as his general opposition to the cause for which Americans were being drafted.

NOTE: FURTHER QUESTIONS ON THE CONSTITUTION AND "EMERGENCY POWER" DURING TIME OF WAR

Consider again Justice Holmes's statement in *Schenck*: "When a nation is at war many things that might be said in time of peace are such a hindrance to its effort that their utterance will not be endured so long as men fight and that no Court could regard them as protected by any constitutional right." Is Holmes saying that the guarantee of "freedom of speech" is a principle that might apply differently in different factual contexts? Or is Holmes suggesting that because the public would not stand for the protection of speech like that of Schenck and Debs during a time of war, no court would or should interpret the Constitution to protect them?

Is there anything special about speech that would make it more appropriate to limit the freedoms guaranteed by the First Amendment "when a nation is at war" than other provisions of the Constitution? Consider in this context other wartime cases (including nonjudicial decisions such as the Emancipation Proclamation) that you have read in the course.

Professor Harry Scheiber notes that during World War I Congress delegated vast powers to the President.[166] World War I was obviously not a unique case, and

---

166. Harry Scheiber, Property Rights Versus "Public Necessity": A Perspective on Emergency Powers and the Supreme Court, 28 J. Sup. Ct. Hist. 339, 354-355 (2003).

Presidents have steadily been awarded varieties of new powers by Congress in order to respond to ostensible threats to "national security."

Is there *any* part of the Constitution whose "clear meaning" you would in all circumstances enforce during time of war or time of serious emergency, even if you were persuaded that the costs to the war effort (or the national economy) might be considerable? Or would you simply say that during such periods, the meaning of the constitutional text is not as clear as it might otherwise seem?

Imagine, for example, that Presidents Lincoln or Roosevelt had asked Congress to pass a law suspending the elections of 1864 or 1944 on the ground that the confusion and uncertainty (and the threat to national unity) posed by a presidential election is inappropriate "when a nation is at war." Or imagine instead that a two-term President is an unusually successful commander-in-chief and diplomat-in-chief during a major war, so that a majority of the country expresses support for the idea that she be allowed to run for a third term in violation of the clear text of the Twenty-Second Amendment.

Is it a "self-evident truth" that holding elections at the constitutionally stipulated intervals or limiting Presidents to two terms in office is more fundamental to preserving the American constitutional order than, say, preserving habeas corpus (whose suspension is allowed by the Constitution itself) or preserving the freedoms of speech and press? If the First Amendment can be limited in its reach during time of war or national crisis, why not the structural provisions as well? Should all provisions be equally malleable in times of emergency or should some continue to be strictly, even rigidly, enforced? If the latter, which provisions and why?

Compare American practices with those of the British political system during the period of World War II. Neville Chamberlain, the sitting Prime Minister, was forced to resign his office in 1940, when King George VI named Winston Churchill to replace him. The British had suspended parliamentary elections, which were supposed to be held at least every five years, so that the Parliament that was elected on November 14, 1935, held office until July 1945 (when the British voted Churchill out of office and placed the Labor Party in power). The British practice is that the leader of the winning political party takes over immediately from the previous Prime Minister. Thus Churchill, who was conducting important negotiations with President Truman, who had succeeded Franklin Roosevelt, elected to a fourth term in November 1944, upon Roosevelt's death less than six months later in April 1945, and Soviet dictator Josef Stalin at the Potsdam Conference that began on July 16, 1945, was replaced on July 27 by the new Prime Minister, Clement Attlee.

VI. CONSTITUTIONAL INNOVATION DURING THE PROGRESSIVE PERIOD

Formal change in the Constitution—signified by the addition of new text to the Constitution via the processes of amendment—has tended to occur in spurts. Thus the first ten amendments were added in 1791, and the Thirteenth through Fifteenth Amendments were added between 1865 and 1870. Similarly, the period of the so-called Progressive Era, dating roughly from 1900 to 1920—also saw a burst of constitutional amendment, with the addition of the four new pieces of constitutional text.

A. *The Sixteenth Amendment*

Although proposed by Congress in 1909, the Sixteenth Amendment was not ratified until 1913. It was designed to override Pollock v. Farmers' Loan & Trust Co., 158 U.S. 601 (1895), in which the Court, by a 5-4 vote, had declared unconstitutional the income tax law of 1894, the first such peacetime levy by Congress. The basis of the decision was Article I, §9, cl. 4: "No Capitation, or other direct, Tax shall be laid, unless in Proportion to the Census or Enumeration herein before directed to be taken." A survival of the "requisition" system of taxation that operated during the Articles of Confederation, this in effect would require that the burden of any "direct" tax fall on each state equally in terms of its population. (Recall that the Constitution also included, in Article I, §2, cl. 3, regarding enumeration, a provision that slaves would count as only three-fifths of persons for such purposes.) This meant that if New York had twice the population of North Carolina, then its citizens, in total, should pay to the treasury a sum twice that of the amount paid by North Carolinians. A tax levied on individual incomes would obviously not achieve this result. The Sixteenth Amendment explicitly authorizes Congress "to lay and collect taxes on incomes, from whatever source derived, without apportionment among the several States, and without regard to any census or enumeration." Note carefully the language of the amendment. Would it allow Congress to impose a "value-added tax," similar to those levied in most European countries, a wealth tax, or a national sales tax, unless, of course, one determined that these were "indirect" taxes?

The Court in fact has proved quite willing to describe important taxes as non-direct. Thus, only three years after *Pollock*, the Court found that a tax on trades on the Chicago Board of Trade was an "excise" tax because it was a tax on "use of a facility and not on ownership or sale of property." Nicol v. Ames, 173 U.S. 509, 519 (1898). More striking was a description in 1900 of the estate tax as an "excise" tax because it is not concerned with the ownership of property, but, rather, with the passing of the property at death. Knowlton v. Moore, 178 U.S. 41, 78 (1900). Similarly, a corporate income tax was upheld as an "excise" tax because it was not imposed on the mere ownership of property but upon the carrying on of a business in corporate form. Flint v. Stone Tracey Co., 220 U.S. 107, 150 (1906). By 1929, the Court would summarize the excise tax exemption as allowing "a tax imposed upon a particular use of property or the exercise of single power over property incident to ownership" without apportionment, Bromley v. McCaughn, 280 U.S. 124, 136 (1929) (upholding the gift tax as an excise because it was a tax on a single incident of ownership—the power of giving).

For recent discussion of the "direct tax" conundrum and the continuing vitality, if any, of the constitutional limitation, see Amar, America's Constitution: A Biography, supra n.1, at 405-409; Bruce Ackerman, Taxation and the Constitution, 99 Colum. L. Rev. 1 (1999); Calvin H. Johnson, Apportionment of Direct Taxes: The Foul-up in the Core of the Constitution, 7 Wm. & Mary Bill Rts. J. 1 (1998). One of the major issues treated in these works is the meaning of "direct tax" at the time of the Constitution. How significant do you think such information should be in interpreting the Constitution today?

B. The Seventeenth Amendment

The 1787 Constitution assigned the election of senators to state legislatures. Already by the Jacksonian period there were calls to change the original Constitution in this regard,[167] and, as a practical matter, popular elections played a role in the selection process in many states. (Thus, although the Illinois legislature chose the state's senator, Abraham Lincoln and Stephen A. Douglas conducted their debates in order to influence the electorate to vote for persons of their respective political parties who would, presumably, support their appointment to the Senate.) The House of Representatives first proposed eliminating the role of state legislatures in 1894, and repeated its proposals in 1898, 1900, and 1902. Only in 1911 did the Senate even bring the matter to a vote, and it did not gain the requisite two-thirds support. In 1911, Rep. Victor Berger of Wisconsin introduced a resolution to abolish the Senate. Moreover, a number of state legislatures invoked their Article V right to petition Congress to call a new constitutional convention, which could consider the method of election to the Senate. Thus the Senate finally acquiesced in proposing the amendment in May 1912, and it gained the support of three-quarters of the states less than a year later, when, on April 8, 1913, Connecticut became the thirty-sixth state to ratify the amendment. Two commentators have pronounced the Seventeenth Amendment to be "the most direct alteration in the system of federalism since the Civil War Amendments."[168] You should keep the Seventeenth Amendment in mind when you read more recent cases dealing with federalism, which include, among other things, debates about the extent to which Congress should be trusted to give due weight to what Justice O'Connor has labeled "the legitimate interests of States as States," Garcia v. San Antonio Metropolitan Transit Authority, 469 U.S. 528, 584 (1985) (O'Connor, J., dissenting).

C. The Eighteenth Amendment

The Eighteenth Amendment nationalized the prohibition of alcohol. It represented the culmination of a prohibitionist crusade extending at least back to the 1850s. (Maine was the first state to adopt prohibition, in 1851, and by 1917, 23 states had adopted some form of prohibition, though only 13 were completely dry.) A coalition ranging from members of the Women's Christian Temperance Union to feminists, social reformers, and business labored on behalf of the amendment;[169]

---

167. See the entry on the Seventeenth Amendment in John Vile, Encyclopedia of Constitutional Amendments, Proposed Amendments, and Amending Issues, 1789-1995, at 272 (1996). Further information in the text is taken from this article. See also C.H. Hoebeke, The Road to Mass Democracy: Original Intent and the Seventeenth Amendment (1995); Vikram David Amar, Indirect Effect of Direct Election: A Structural Examination of the Seventeenth Amendment, 49 Vand. L. Rev. 1346 (1996).

168. See Richard Bernstein, with Jerome Agel, Amending America: If We Love the Constitution So Much, Why Do We Keep Trying to Change It? 122 (1993).

169. See, e.g., Robert C. Post, Federalism, Positive Law, and the Emergence of the American Administrative State: Prohibition in the Taft Court Era, 48 Wm. & Mary L. Rev. 1 (2006).

they were assisted by anti-Catholic and anti-immigrant sentiments that identified Catholics and immigrants with alcohol consumption, and by World War I–generated sentiment that identified beer with Germany. The amendment passed Congress in December 1917, and was ratified by the thirty-sixth state in January 1919. One important feature of the Eighteenth Amendment was its bold assertion of national authority. "If the federal government could be given authority over something as personal as alcohol use," Professor David Kyvig writes, "could and should it be given responsibility for other matters as well?"[170]

There is an important connection between the Sixteenth and Eighteenth Amendments. Allowing taxes on income freed the national government from its dependence on import taxes (including those on liquor) or internal excise taxes on whiskey, which, since the beginning of the Union, had served as the major method of collecting federal revenue. (Recall that one of the first disruptive episodes in the new Union was the Whiskey Rebellion in western Pennsylvania, against which President Washington personally took command.) As leaders of the Anti-Saloon League wrote, "[t]he adoption of the Income Tax Amendment . . . furnishes an answer to the revenue problem."[171]

The Eighteenth Amendment also enjoys the distinction of being the only amendment to be formally repealed—via the Twenty-First Amendment, proposed and ratified (by state conventions rather than state legislatures) in 1933 as one of the first acts of the New Deal.

D. The Nineteenth Amendment

The Nineteenth Amendment, ratified in 1920, prohibited discrimination in voting on the basis of sex. Like the Eighteenth Amendment, it represented the fruition of an important social movement that had existed for at least eight decades.[172] (Recall the discussion of the Seneca Falls conference in Chapter 2 and of Minor v. Happersett in this chapter.) As we have seen, opposition to woman suffrage was justified on a number of grounds. First, opponents argued that, by human nature and divine will, women were subordinate to men and therefore unfit to exercise the franchise. Second, because women were economically and legally dependent on men, their interests were appropriately represented by men. This was a version of the republican argument that the family, not the individual, was the basic unit of political representation. Although some women did not have husbands to represent them, they were

170. David Kyvig, Authentic and Explicit Acts: Amending the U.S. Constitution 1776-1995, at 217 (1996).

171. Dan Okrent, Last Call: The Rise and Fall of Prohibition 58 (2010).

172. See generally Eleanor Flexner, Century of Struggle: The Woman's Rights Movement in the United States (rev. ed. 1975); Ellen Carol DuBois, Feminism and Suffrage: The Emergence of an Independent Woman's Movement in America, 1848-1869 (1978). Much of the discussion in this section is drawn from Reva B. Siegel, Collective Memory and the Nineteenth Amendment: Reasoning about "the Woman Question" in the Discourse of Sex Discrimination in History, Memory, and the Law 131-182 (Sarat & Kearns eds., 1999). See also Reva B. Siegel, She the People: The Nineteenth Amendment, Sex Equality, Federalism, and the Family, 115 Harv. L. Rev. 947 (2002).

exceptional because marriage was the appropriate condition of all women. Third, granting the women the vote would weaken this system of family governance, create domestic discord, and draw women away from their duties as wives and mothers.[173]

The suffrage movement not only challenged assumptions about women's abilities, but also the assumptions about political representation, the appropriate structure of the family, and the relationship between the family and the state. Suffragists argued that women's continuing subordination both in the public sphere and within the family demonstrated that men could not and would not represent women's interests fairly. The state should be based on individuals, not households; women should have a direct relationship to the state, independent of their position as wives and mothers.

Radical suffragists argued that the family, rightly conceived, was consistent with woman suffrage. They called for a reform of family structure on more egalitarian lines. Like the anti-suffragists, the radical suffragists believed that there was a deep connection between the subordinate status of women in families and their lack of political and economic rights, but they drew a different conclusion from the fact of this connection. In order to achieve political and economic emancipation for women, one had to dismantle women's inferior status in the family, a status that was enforced and encouraged by law. They argued that the political, economic, and domestic subordination of women were necessarily intertwined:[174]

> Suffragists protested the sex-based restrictions on employment and compensation that impoverished women and drove them into marriage. They deplored women's legally enforced dependency in marriage, particularly property rules that vested in husbands rights to their wives' earnings and to the value of their wives' household labor. They decried law's failure to protect women from physical coercion in marriage, including domestic violence, marital rape and "forced motherhood." They protested double-standards of sexual propriety that punished one sex for conduct in which both were engaged. And they challenged the exclusion of women from juries convened to judge the fate of those in the criminal justice system.

---

173. Siegel, Collective Memory, supra n.172, at 148-149; see also Siegel, She the People, supra n.172, at 980-981:

> The antis' foundational argument was the argument from virtual representation: women did not need the vote because they were already represented in the government by male heads of household. It was this claim of virtual representation that women's demand to vote most directly challenged. Every time woman suffragists invoked American traditions of individualism, "self-government," and "self-representation" in defense of the right to vote—as when during the New Departure suffragists refused to pay taxes without representation—they were challenging a centuries-old conception of the household that gave men authority to represent women in public and private law. Antis answered suffragists' claims for self-government by emphasizing how changing the distribution of the franchise would threaten the unity of the family: granting women the right to vote would introduce domestic discord into the marital relation and distract women from their primary duties as wives and mothers. Like the virtual representation argument, the marital unity argument linked public and private spheres. Examining the constitutional controversy over enfranchising women reveals that it was, from surface to core, an argument about the family.

174. Joan Zimmerman, The Jurisprudence of Equality: The Women's Minimum Wage, the First Equal Rights Amendment, and Adkins v. Children's Hospital, 1905-1923, J. Am. Hist. 178 (1991).

The first major Supreme Court case concerning women's rights after ratification of the Nineteenth Amendment was Adkins v. Children's Hospital, 261 U.S. 525 (1923). *Adkins* involved a District of Columbia law requiring that women (but not men) receive a minimum wage. Justice Sutherland, writing for the Court, struck down the law, arguing that since the adoption of the Nineteenth Amendment, women as well as men were protected by the Court's freedom of contract jurisprudence:

> [T]he ancient inequality of the sexes, otherwise than physical . . . has continued "with diminishing intensity." In view of the great—not to say revolutionary—changes which have taken place since [Muller v. Oregon], in the contractual, political and civil status of women, culminating in the Nineteenth Amendment, it is not unreasonable to say that these differences have now come almost, if not quite, to the vanishing point. . . . [W]hile the physical differences must be recognized in appropriate cases, and legislation fixing hours or conditions of work may properly take them into account, we cannot accept the doctrine that women of mature age, sui juris, require or may be subjected to restrictions upon their liberty of contract which could not lawfully be imposed in the case of men under similar circumstances. To do so would be to ignore all the implications to be drawn from the present day trend of legislation, as well as that of common thought and usage, by which woman is accorded emancipation from that old doctrine that she must be given special protection or be subjected to special restraint in her contractual and civil relationships.

Chief Justice Taft's dissent argued that "[t]he Nineteenth Amendment did not change the physical strength or limitations of women upon which the decision in Muller v. Oregon rests." Justice Holmes's dissent made a similar argument, and added that he believed that *Lochner v. New York* had been effectively overruled in previous cases.

Adkins represents an interesting convergence of suffragist ideas about marital status law with *Lochner*-era laissez faire ideology. Before joining the Supreme Court, Sutherland had been an advisor to Alice Paul of the National Woman's Party on legal issues concerning woman suffrage and on the drafting of a proposed Equal Rights Amendment.[175] Nevertheless, many supporters of women's rights, like Florence Kelley, supported the minimum wage law, and many other forms of protective legislation for women. Kelley believed that suffragists should ally themselves with the sociological jurisprudence of Roscoe Pound and other legal progressives. Indeed, Kelley was one of the authors of the original "Brandeis brief" in Muller v. Oregon. Kelley believed that emphasizing women's maternal functions gave advocates the best chance at reforming working conditions for poor women, because the courts were hostile to arguments about unequal bargaining power and economic inequality.[176]

Alice Paul and the National Woman's Party, on the other hand, argued for an Equal Rights Amendment that would end all discrimination based on sex. Paul eventually came to oppose protective legislation for women. She was attracted to

---

175. Id.
176. Id. at 192-193, 198-199.

the *Lochner* era's notions of formal freedom of contract as a way to eliminate marital status restrictions on women.[177] Kelley rejected this approach. She believed that it was "worse than useless to try to force all women to accept a uniform male standard. . . . Equality under the law for Kelley meant inequality in the workplace in fact."[178] (Whose view of sex equality, Kelley's or Paul's, looks more reasonable in hindsight?)

During the 1920s, a few state and federal courts did read the Nineteenth Amendment broadly as modifying common law marital status rules.[179] Several state supreme courts held that the Nineteenth Amendment's guarantee of political equality for women also gave women the right to hold public office and to serve on juries. (Recall the tripartite distinction between political, civil, and social equality made in debates over ratification of the Fourteenth Amendment, in which voting and jury service were both classified as political rights. And recall the question in *Strauder* about whether the claim was properly based on the Fourteenth Amendment (protecting civil equality) or the Fifteenth Amendment (protecting political equality).) However, many other courts construed the Nineteenth Amendment strictly as affecting only the right to vote.[180] *Adkins* was overruled in 1937; by the 1930s courts had essentially forgotten the Nineteenth Amendment as a constitutional source for women's equality rights. Interestingly, when the Supreme Court began to protect women's equal rights to serve on juries, it relied on the Fourteenth Amendment and not the Nineteenth Amendment.

One of the attributes that links these Progressive Era Amendments is that they have not generated much litigation. Because most lawyers, including legal academics and their students, focus only on those parts of the Constitution that are in fact litigated before courts, these amendments have produced very little in the way of imaginative thought that might use them as the basis of more general argument. Thus when feminists challenged a variety of jury-exclusion rules in the 1960s and 1970s, the basis was the Equal Protection Clause of the Fourteenth Amendment rather than the Nineteenth Amendment. (This, of course, repeated the doctrinal history seen in *Strauder.*) Should these amendments have any continuing importance today? For example, does the Nineteenth Amendment's guarantee of political equality have anything important to tell us about women's civil and social equality?

E. Constitutional Limits on Article V?

One final linkage between the Eighteenth and Nineteenth Amendments is that both generated attacks on the constitutionality of the amendments themselves.

---

177. Id. at 203-204.

178. Id. at 207.

179. See Siegel, Collective Memory, supra n.172, at 158-159; United States v. Hinson, 3 F.2d 200 (1925) (wife responsible for crimes jointly committed with husband); Hollander v. Abrams, 132 A. 224 (N.J. Ch. 1926) (contract for sale of land by wife enforceable even though made without husband's consent).

180. Siegel, Collective Memory, supra n.172, at 161-163; Jennifer K. Brown, Note, The Nineteenth Amendment and Women's Equality, 102 Yale L.J. 2175 (1993).

1. Time Limits

The Eighteenth Amendment was the first in American history to carry with it a time limit—seven years—imposed by a Congress that apparently (and mistakenly) believed that this would serve to hinder its ratification.[181]

The constitutionality of this time limit was challenged in Dillon v. Gloss, 256 U.S. 368 (1921); it was upheld, with Justice Van Devanter stating for a unanimous court that

> We do not find anything in [Article V] which suggests that an amendment once proposed is to be open to ratification for all time, or that ratification in some of the states may be separated from that in others by many years and yet be effective. We do find that which strongly suggests the contrary. First, proposal and ratification are not treated as unrelated acts but as succeeding steps in a single endeavor, the natural inference being that they are not to be widely separated in time. Secondly, it is only when there is deemed to be a necessity therefor that amendments are to be proposed, the reasonable implications being that when proposed they are to be considered and disposed of presently. Thirdly, as ratification is but the expression of the approbation of the people and is to be effective when had in three-fourths of the States, there is a fair implication that it must be sufficiently contemporaneous in that number of States to reflect the will of the people in all sections at relatively the same period, which of course ratification scattered through a long series of years would not do. These considerations and the general spirit of the Article lead to the conclusion expressed by Judge Jameson [citing to Jameson on Constitutional Conventions, 4th ed., §585] "that an alteration of the Constitution proposed today has relation to the sentiment and the felt needs of today, and that, if not ratified early while that sentiment may fairly be supposed to exist, it ought to be regarded as waived, and not again to be voted upon, unless a second time proposed by Congress." That this is the better conclusion becomes even more manifest when what is comprehended in the other view is considered; for,

---

181. Consider the following analysis:

> What §3 of the Eighteenth Amendment did for time, another section of a future amendment could do along other dimensions. For instance, §3 of a hypothetical Twenty-Eighth Amendment proposed in the year 2020 could provide that the amendment would be inoperative unless ratified by four-fifths of the states, rather than a mere three-quarters. Or it could provide that the amendment would be inoperative unless endorsed by the president; or agreed to by supermajorities within individual state legislatures; or unless approved by a national referendum; or unless ratified by states totaling more than 50 percent of the national population. Of course, none of these requirements could formally lower the Article V bar or displace it—that would be pure bootstrap. But by raising the formal bar through a provision specifying when an amendment truly becomes operative, future §3 analogues could, as a practical matter, move America toward a more directly representative system of amendment. If a future §3 required a national referendum vote of approval before the Twenty-Eighth Amendment were to become operative, that fact alone might put pressure on some fence-sitting state legislators to say yes. A yes vote by such a legislature would become less a vote on the proposed Twenty-Eighth's substance, and more a vote to "let the people decide."

Amar, America's Constitution, supra n.1, at 418.

> according to it, four amendments proposed long ago—two in 1789, one in 1810, and one in 1861—are still pending and in a situation where their ratification in some of the States many years since by representatives of generations now largely forgotten may be effectively supplemented in enough more States to make three-fourths by representatives of the present or some future generation. To that view few would be able to subscribe, and in our opinion it is quite untenable. We conclude that the fair inference or implications from Article V is that ratification must be within some reasonable time after the proposal.

Since 1918, many proposed constitutional amendments have carried with them time limits imposed by Congress. The question of the constitutional status of time limits, however, emerged in 1992, with regard to the purported Twenty-Seventh Amendment. Initially the second of 12 amendments proposed in 1789, it prohibits Congress from raising the salaries of its members to take effect before an intervening election.[182] Like the rest of the amendments we now know as the Bill of Rights, the proposal did not have a time limit. Unlike original amendments three through twelve (which today we know as the First through Tenth Amendments), it did not fare well. By 1800, it had gained the ratification of only six states; a seventh state ratified it in 1873. "Rediscovered" in the late 1970s by a student at the University of Texas, it was brought up in many state legislatures. Beginning with Wyoming's ratification on March 3, 1978, it was ratified by 32 states thereafter, with Michigan, on May 7, 1992, becoming the thirty-eighth state to ratify the 1789 proposal. A flurry of newspaper stories brought the amendment, and questions about its status, to public attention. Several leading members of Congress indicated their doubts about the circumstances of "ratification," and it appeared that a legislative debate would ensue.

Some legal commentators, citing *Dillon*, suggested that the amendment had "died" in the 200 years between its first and final ratifications.

At the very least, Yale law professor Paul Gewirtz wrote Illinois Senator Paul Simon that "Congress clearly has the power" to decide "whether ratification has occurred within a reasonable period of time." He cited Coleman v. Miller, 307 U.S. 433 (1939), where Justice Black, writing for a group of four Justices, stated that "Congress has sole and complete control over the amending process," including the power to determine if an amendment "must die unless ratified within a 'reasonable time.'"

In response, Harvard professor Laurence Tribe argued that the plain text of Article V specified that "an amendment 'shall be valid to all Intents and Purposes, as part of this Constitution' when 'ratified' by three-fourths of the states—not that it might face a veto for tardiness."[183] He also suggested that both structural and historical considerations, in addition to raw text, left Congress with nothing to do other than accept the validity of the amendment.

---

182. See Richard B. Bernstein, The Sleeper Wakes: The History and Legacy of the Twenty-Seventh Amendment, 61 Fordham L. Rev. 497 (1992).

183. Laurence Tribe, The 27th Amendment Joins the Constitution, Wall St. J., May 13, 1992, A15.

As it turns out, in the words of the *New York Times*, "Congress . . . rushed to bless the 27th Amendment to the Constitution with near unanimity."[184] Without holding a single day of hearings or engaging in any serious debate, both the House and the Senate on May 20, 1992, pronounced the amendment to be "valid . . . as part of the Constitution of the United States" by votes of 414-3 and 99-0, respectively.[185]

DISCUSSION

Almost everyone has accepted *Dillon*'s view that time limits are legitimate, even if, arguendo, they are not to be inferred absent explicit congressional decision to impose them. See, however, Mason Kalfus, Comment: Why Time Limits on the Ratification of Constitutional Amendments Violate Article V, 66 U. Chi. L. Rev. 437 (1999), which argues that congressionally imposed time limits are unconstitutional insofar as they in effect give Congress too much power to manipulate the amendment process. As to manipulation, note that in 1979 Congress, which had in 1972 proposed the Equal Rights Amendment with a seven-year time limit for ratification, extended the limit for an additional three years. Do you see any constitutional problem with such an extension? (Could a successor Congress, less enamored of a particular proposal than its predecessor, *reduce* a time limit from, say, seven years to four years?)

2. Are There Substantive Limits to Constitutional Amendment?

In addition to these procedural attacks, opponents also attacked the two amendments on the grounds that they invaded the reserved powers of the states. The Court rejected such attacks, in regard to the prohibition amendment, in the National Prohibition Cases, 253 U.S. 350 (1920), and again in Sprague v. United States, 282 U.S. 716 (1931). The former case was argued by Elihu Root, one of the most distinguished lawyers of the era. He told the Court, among other things, that the authors of the Constitution "undoubtedly regarded the power to amend only as authorizing the inclusion of matter of the same general character as the instrument or thing to be amended; as all the constitutions of their day were concerned solely with the distribution and limitation of the powers of government, and not with the direct exercise thereof by the constitution makers themselves, no amendment of the latter sort would have been deemed appropriate or germane by them." Moreover, according to Root, "[t]he so-called Eighteenth Amendment *directly* invades the police powers of the States and *directly* encroaches upon their right of local self-government." To accept its legitimacy would authorize, in effect, "the complete subversion of our dual and federal system of government," at least so long as

---

184. N.Y. Times, May 24, 1992, at 4, 10.

185. As described by a reporter for the *New York Times*, "[c]ongressional leaders' early assertion that the House and the Senate would make the final decision on the validity of the pay-raise amendment had long since faded by the time both houses voted today. The issue had simply dried up in an environment of public anger over Congressional perquisites and pay raises, and as a result today's votes were regarded as entirely political, giving members a chance to be on record as in favor of the amendment." Richard Berke, Congress Backs 27th Amendment, N.Y. Times, May 21, 1992, at A26 (late ed.—final).

two-thirds of each house of Congress and three-quarters of the states assented. The Court unanimously rejected the argument, though, interestingly enough, there was no genuine "opinion" of the Court, only an announcement of the view that the amendment was not constitutionally defective.

A similar rejection met the claim, in Leser v. Garnett, 258 U.S. 130 (1922), that the Nineteenth Amendment, because it fundamentally changed the nature of the electorate in states that had limited suffrage to males, was beyond the scope of Article V. Because the electorate constituted the political community of a state, opponents argued, the Nineteenth Amendment had effectively destroyed the political communities of states that limited suffrage to men and replaced them with new ones.[186] There is an obvious problem in distinguishing the Nineteenth from the Fifteenth Amendment, which eliminated (at least as a formal matter) racial restrictions on the suffrage and added Black people to the electorate in many states. Plaintiffs argued (1) that the Fifteenth Amendment had, in effect, been unanimously assented to by the states, since none had disputed its validity for 45 years; and (2) that the Reconstruction Amendments had effectively constituted a treaty necessary to end the Civil War and prevent its recurrence.

The Supreme Court, speaking through Justice Brandeis, unanimously rejected these arguments:

> This Amendment is in character and phraseology precisely similar to the Fifteenth. For each the same method of adoption was pursued. One cannot be valid and the other invalid. That the Fifteenth is valid, although rejected by six States including Maryland, has been recognized and acted on for half a century. The suggestion that the Fifteenth was incorporated in the Constitution, not in accordance with law, but practically as a war measure which has been validated by acquiescence, cannot be entertained.

Consider whether these cases stand for the proposition that *anything* can be added to (or subtracted from) the Constitution, so long as the proposals gain the assent of two-thirds of each house of Congress and three-quarters of the states, or, on the contrary, whether they should be read as holding only that, as a substantive matter, the granting to the national government of regulatory authority over alcohol or to the collective polity of the expansion, via Article V procedures, of the state electorate, is consistent with the spirit of the Constitution and, for that reason—rather than because of a "plenary power" view of Article V—presents no constitutional problems.

---

186. For a related argument, see George Stewart Brown, The Nineteenth Amendment: The Amending Clause Was Provided for Changing, Limiting, Shifting, or Delegating "Powers of Government." It Was Not Provided for Amending "the People." The 19th Amendment Is Therefore Ultra Vires, 8 Va. L. Rev. 237 (1922). Brown's argument invoked the compact of states theory: "The sovereignty of the People is expressed through the states, which together formed the Union. Acting through the states, the People delegated power to the Federal government, but did not surrender their sovereignty. It follows that Article V can only delegate powers; it cannot alter sovereignty. The Nineteenth Amendment destroyed the sovereignty of the States by altering the qualifications for electors; thus it illegally altered the Sovereignty of the People."

Suppose, for example, that instead of expanding the electorate through amendment, three-quarters of the states voted to contract the electorate by returning to the states the power to disenfranchise Black people or women (or, for that matter, persons under 21; see the Twenty-Sixth Amendment). Could one argue that this amendment would be contrary to the basic structure of constitutional government because it would unfairly cut off part of the People from rights of political governance? How is this argument different from the one rejected in Leser v. Garnett? Is the expansion of the franchise a "one-way ratchet," so that once Black people, women, and persons over 18 have been admitted to We the People, they cannot be excluded? Are *all* expansions of the electorate unproblematic? Suppose that an amendment forced states to give corporations or resident aliens who had filed for citizenship the right to vote. Whatever one thinks of such proposals on the merits, is it clear that future generations could not change their minds and decide to reduce the electorate accordingly? Is the appropriate response to these questions that Article V recognizes no substantive limitations on amendment other than those specifically listed in the text, i.e., that the slave trade cannot be abolished before 1808 and that no state can be deprived equal suffrage in the Senate without its consent? Note that explicit limitations on amendment can be found in the constitutions of other countries. For example, Article 79(3) of the German Basic Law prohibits amendments that would violate "the dignity of man" or destroy the democratic and federal nature of the German Union.[187] Could the German constitutional court properly strike down an amendment allowing chattel slavery because slavery fundamentally violates "the dignity" of all human beings? Note that Article V contains only two explicit substantive limitations on the content of amendments. Does this mean that no others exist and that, as a theoretical matter, the only legal protection against repeal of the Thirteenth Amendment and reinstitution of chattel slavery is the inability of such a proposal to gain the assent of a sufficient number of members of Congress and state legislators?

---

187. See also Walter F. Murphy, Merlin's Memory: The Past and Future Imperfect of the Once and Future Polity, in Responding to Imperfection: The Theory and Practice of Constitutional Amendment (Levinson ed.), 163, 178-180. The Indian Supreme Court, in Golak Nath's Case [1967], A.I.R. 1643, 1670, struck down an amendment of the Indian Constitution as violative of its basic structure. See generally Gary Jeffrey Jacobsohn, Constitutional Identity (2010).

PART 2

CONSTITUTIONAL ADJUDICATION IN THE MODERN WORLD

Having surveyed in Part One a series of interlocking constitutional questions that arose during the first two centuries of constitutional government, we turn in Part Two to the questions that have dominated modern constitutional debate. Some of the questions that we must confront are substantive: For example, what does, or should, "equal protection" or "due process" mean in today's world? Other questions focus more on the constitutional allocation of power (including the power of interpretation) among competing institutions: Who should decide a given substantive issue, courts or legislatures, the states, or the federal government? Yet another set of questions implicates matters of constitutional methodology: Exactly how should faithful interpreters go about the task of interpreting an old Constitution to apply to new issues?

The word "modern" has many meanings. It is sometimes used to mark a division between older traditional practices and newer forms of thought that are consciously posed against them. Or it can be understood as a felt loss of connection to an earlier period of "authentic" tradition, which must be regained at all costs, or which must be consciously reinterpreted or translated in order to become comprehensible and meaningful to us today. See Sanford Levinson and Jack M. Balkin, Law, Music, and Other Performing Arts, 139 U. Pa. L. Rev. 1597 (1991).

In constitutional law, we might understand "modernity" as the moment in which the period of the founding becomes so distant that it begins to seem foreign to us. This leads to at least three possible reactions: (a) we regard ourselves as no longer bound by it, (b) we try to preserve our connection to it through zealous adherence to its concrete manifestations and understandings, or (c) we reject those concrete exemplars and attempt to be true to its spirit through self-conscious historical study, analogy, and reinterpretation.

Constitutional modernity could also refer to a period in which the Supreme Court's role and its relationship to democracy become increasingly problematized. Before the Civil War, the Supreme Court sparingly exercised judicial review to strike down federal statutes. After the Civil War, and in the period leading up to the New Deal, the Supreme Court increasingly begins to strike down both federal and state legislation. Partly as a result, the Supreme Court increasingly becomes understood as an actor in the political system, and the relatively rigid boundaries between law and politics that preserved the Court's legitimacy in earlier times are loosened. Academic critiques of the Court, first by legal progressives and later by legal realists, emphasize the Court's political role and the political character of its doctrinal analysis. They also question the Court's legitimacy as an anti-democratic and anti-majoritarian institution. Particularly in the period after 1937, and especially after the civil rights revolution, the Supreme Court itself begins to problematize its role, and the rhetoric of judicial restraint and the need to avoid unnecessary constitutional decisions becomes ubiquitous in judicial opinions. This modernist anxiety about the practice of judicial review and its relationship to democracy is an element of constitutional modernity that is arguably distinct from the more general problem of constitutional interpretation in a world that has lost an organic connection to tradition.

THE EVOLUTION OF THE BILL OF RIGHTS AND ITS "INCORPORATION" AGAINST THE STATES[1]

Perhaps the most striking feature of modern constitutional jurisprudence is the leading role that the Bill of Rights plays both inside courtrooms and beyond. It was not always so. A separate Bill of Rights was no part of James Madison's careful plan at the Philadelphia Convention of 1787, and the document that emerged from Philadelphia omitted an explicit Bill of Rights. When anti-Federalist skeptics pounced on this omission during ratification debates, Federalists scrambled to defend the document with a jumble of counterarguments. Some Federalists claimed that the entire Constitution was a kind of Bill of Rights; others pointed to the specific rules limiting Congress in Article I, §9 as a functional Bill of Rights; and many also claimed (sometimes contradicting themselves or their allies) that a Bill of Rights would in fact prove useless or even dangerous. Madison himself promised to revisit the issue once the Constitution went into effect. Although he kept his promise, shepherding a set of amendments through the First Congress, many of his colleagues viewed the exercise as a "nauseous" distraction from more important and immediate tasks of nation-building.[2]

Once ratified, the Bill played a remarkably small role during the antebellum era—at least in court. Recall that no federal judge invalidated the Sedition Act of 1798, which in effect made it a federal crime to criticize President John Adams or his allies in Congress. Only once in the entire antebellum era did the Supreme Court use the Bill of Rights to strike down an act of the federal government—in *Dred Scott*'s highly implausible and strikingly casual claim that the Fifth Amendment's Due Process Clause invalidated free-soil laws like the Northwest Ordinance

1. Some of the material presented below borrows from Akhil Reed Amar, The Bill of Rights: Creation and Reconstruction (1998).

2. Letter from James Madison to Richard Peters (Aug. 19, 1789) in 12 The Papers of James Madison 346 (R. Rutland et al. eds., 1979).

and the Missouri Compromise, 60 U.S. (19 How.) 393, 450 (1857). In a review of newspapers published in 1841, Dean Robert Reinstein could not find a single 50th anniversary celebration of the Bill of Rights.[3]

Indeed, the Bill of Rights as conventionally viewed in the antebellum era looked profoundly different from the Bill of Rights as widely understood today. Born in the shadow of a Revolutionary War waged by local governments against an imperial center, the original Bill affirmed various rights against the central government, but none against the states, as the Supreme Court made clear in Barron v. Baltimore, 32 U.S. (7 Pet.) 243 (1833). And the rights that the original Bill did affirm sounded more in localism than libertarianism. (Recall that Madison drafted the Bill, in large part, to ease the anxieties of anti-Federalists.) Congress could not establish a national church, but neither could it disestablish state churches. (Several of the states had government-sponsored churches in the 1780s, and many other "non-establishment" states favored Protestant Christianity in some way or other.) Thus, as originally understood, the First Amendment rule that "Congress shall make no law *respecting* [that is, on the topic of] an establishment of religion" was less anti-establishment than it was pro-states' rights; religious policy would be decided locally, not nationally, in the American equivalent of the European Peace of Augsburg (1555) and Treaty of Westphalia (1648). The Second Amendment celebrated local militias (the heroes of Lexington and Concord), and the Third Amendment likewise reflected uneasiness about a central standing army. Much of the rest of the Bill reinforced the powers of local juries. The Fifth Amendment safeguarded grand juries; the Sixth, criminal petit juries; and the Seventh, civil juries. Beyond these specific clauses, many other parts of the original Bill also championed the role of local and populist juries—who were expected to protect popular publishers in First Amendment cases, hold abusive federal officials liable for unreasonable searches in Fourth Amendment cases, and help assess just compensation against the federal government in Fifth Amendment cases. The only amendment endorsed by every state convention demanding a Bill of Rights during the ratification debates was the Tenth Amendment, which emphatically affirmed states' rights. Madison himself wanted more—a Bill championing countermajoritarian individual rights, and protecting them against states, too—but in the First Congress, he was swimming against the tide. His proposed amendment requiring states to respect speech, press, conscience, and juries passed the House (as the presciently numbered Fourteenth Amendment) but died in a Senate that championed states' rights.

Only after a civil war dramatized the need to limit abusive states would a new Fourteenth Amendment and distinctly modern view of the Bill emerge—a view celebrating individual rights and preventing states from abridging fundamental freedoms. From the 1830s on, anti-slavery crusaders began to develop, contra *Barron*, a "declaratory" interpretation of the Bill of Rights that viewed the Bill not as creating new or merely federalism-based rules applicable only against federal officials, but as affirming and declaring preexisting higher-law norms applicable to all governments, state as well as federal. On this declaratory view, for example, although the

3. Robert J. Reinstein, Completing the Constitution: The Declaration of Independence, Bill of Rights and Fourteenth Amendment, 66 Temp. L. Rev. 361, 365 n.25 (1993).

First Amendment directly regulated "Congress," it also affirmed a preexisting right to free expression; according to *Barron* contrarians, when the amendment referred to "*the* freedom of speech," it thereby implied a preexisting legal freedom. Perhaps this legal freedom of speech could not be enforced against states in federal court, some contrarians conceded. But the First Amendment reference to "the freedom of speech" was itself *evidence* that a true legal right against all governments existed, a right that states were honor-bound to obey even in the absence of a federal enforcement scheme. And what was true of the freedom of speech was also true of the other rights and freedoms explicitly declared in the remainder of the Bill of Rights — the First Amendment freedom of religious exercise, the Fourth Amendment right against unreasonable searches, the Fifth Amendment entitlement to just compensation, and so on. This declaratory theory took shape in a world where many Southern states had enacted extremely repressive laws to prop up slavery — censoring abolitionist speech and press, suppressing anti-slavery preachers, implementing dragnet searches against suspected fugitive slaves and slave sympathizers, imposing savagely cruel punishments on runaway slaves and their allies, and indeed violating virtually every right mentioned in the federal Bill.

With the passage of the Fourteenth Amendment, contrarians sought to write their views into the Constitution itself, and to overrule *Barron*, just as they sought to overrule *Dred Scott*. By proclaiming, in §1 of the Fourteenth Amendment, that "No state shall make or enforce any law which shall abridge the privileges or immunities of citizens of the United States," Reconstruction Republicans tried to make clear that henceforth states would be required by the federal Constitution and by federal courts (and by Congress, too) to obey fundamental rights and freedoms — "privileges" and "immunities" of American "citizens." Where would judges find these freedoms? Among other places, in the federal Bill of Rights itself. Inclusion in the Bill of Rights was strong evidence that a given right — free speech, free exercise, or just compensation, for example — was indeed a fundamental privilege or immunity of all American citizens.[4]

Of course, by seeking to enforce these rights against state governments, Congressman John Bingham and his fellow Reconstructionists were in effect turning

---

4. At this point, an obvious question arises: If the Privileges or Immunities Clause was designed to prevent states from abridging fundamental freedoms and rights such as those spelled out in the federal Bill, why did the Fourteenth Amendment go on to specifically ban states from depriving persons of due process of law? Wasn't due process (a right mentioned in the Fifth Amendment) a "privilege or immunity" already covered? For an answer to this puzzle, see Amar, supra n.1, at 171-174. (Hint: Note that the Privileges or Immunities Clause speaks of the rights of "citizens" whereas the adjoining Due Process Clause sweeps more broadly, including aliens in its protections of all "persons.") Another question is why, if the framers of the Fourteenth Amendment meant to hold states to the Bill of Rights, no more and no less, they didn't say so more directly. Consider the possibility that, strictly speaking, Bingham and company meant both more and less than the first eight amendments as such. See id. at 174-180. On applying the amendment to protect fundamental rights beyond those specified in the Bill itself, consider the views of Justices Murphy and Rutledge, discussed infra n.8. And on the ways in which the Fourteenth Amendment might incorporate something less than the Bill of Rights as such, see infra n.11 (discussing "refined incorporation").

the founders' Bill of Rights on its head. The original Bill had reflected the localism of the American Revolution, whereas Bingham and company were animated by the nationalism of the Civil War. Images of British imperial misbehavior and local heroism had inspired the eighteenth-century Bill of Rights, whereas images of slave state misconduct and national heroism hovered over the Thirty-Ninth Congress that drafted the Fourteenth Amendment. For example, the original First Amendment was worded to emphasize that Congress simply lacked enumerated power to regulate religion or censor speech in the several states. Note how its language—"Congress *shall make no law* . . ."—echoed and inverted the language of the Necessary and Proper Clause: "*Congress shall* have power . . . to *make all laws*. . . ." But Bingham's vision stripped away this original veneer of states' rights, stressing instead that henceforth *states* must not "abridge" (a word borrowed from the First Amendment itself) the freedom of speech or of the press or of religion. What had initially been drafted as an amendment to protect state autonomy in religious matters became, in Bingham's revision, a basis for nationalistic restrictions on states insofar as their policies violated the rights of their citizens to the free and equal exercise of religion.[5]

But as we have already seen, the Court in the 1873 Slaughterhouse Cases strangled the Privileges or Immunities Clause in its crib. (Recall also that Justice Bradley's dissent in that case contained important language recognizing that this key clause was designed to overrule *Barron*.) The Court confirmed that it would not treat the Bill of Rights protections as privileges or immunities of national citizenship applicable to the states in a series of cases from United States v. Cruikshank, 92 U.S. 542 (1876), to Maxwell v. Dow, 176 U.S. 581 (1900). As a result, later generations of judges often turned to the Due Process Clause, using it to accomplish many of the purposes originally intended for the Privileges or Immunities Clause.

The first big step away from *Barron*'s regime came in the 1897 *Chicago Burlington* case, which, like *Barron* itself, involved the norm of just compensation. Using language that nicely tracked the declaratory theory, the Court now held that states were indeed bound by the principle of just compensation laid down in the Fifth Amendment: "The [Fifth Amendment] requirement that property shall not be taken for public use without just compensation is but '*an affirmance* of a great doctrine established by the common law for the protection of private property. It is founded in natural equity, and is laid down by jurists as a principle of universal law.'"[6] Standing alone, this case could be dismissed as a sport—reflecting the special solicitude for property on the turn-of-the-century Court. But over the course of the twentieth century, the Justices made clear that this case did not stand alone. By

5. For general theoretic discussions about how a given text or other sign can come to mean different things in different historical contexts, see Jack M. Balkin, Deconstructive Practice and Legal Theory, 96 Yale L.J. 743 (1987); Jack M. Balkin, Ideological Drift and the Struggle over Meaning, 25 Conn. L. Rev. 869 (1993); Lawrence Lessig, Fidelity in Translation, 71 Tex. L. Rev. 1165 (1993).

6. Chicago, Burlington and Quincy Railroad v. Chicago, 166 U.S. 226, 236 (1897) (emphasis added).

the end of the century, almost all of the rights and freedoms specified in the founders' Bill had come to be applied against state and local governments.

The process began, inauspiciously, in Patterson v. Colorado, 205 U.S. 454 (1907). Writing for the Court, Justice Holmes proclaimed that "even if we were to assume that freedom of speech and freedom of the press were protected from abridgement on the part not only of the United States but also of the states," the newspaper publisher in the case would still lose. (The publisher had published material mocking the justices of the state supreme court. Unamused, the state court—sitting without a jury, proceeding without a specific statute authorizing punishment of nonlitigants, and in effect acting as judges in their own case—held the publisher in contempt and levied a fine on him.) The elder Justice Harlan (who had written the Court's majority opinion in *Chicago Burlington*) dissented, reiterating his view that the Privileges or Immunities Clause encompassed First Amendment (and other Bill of Rights) freedoms, and construing those freedoms far more robustly than had Holmes. By 1925, Holmes's arguendo assumption in *Patterson* had evolved into a stronger assertion, given voice by Justice Sanford writing for the Court in Gitlow v. New York, 268 U.S. 652:

> For present purposes we may and do assume that the freedom of speech and of the Press—which are protected by the First Amendment from abridgement by Congress—are among the fundamental personal rights and "liberties" protected by the due process clause of the Fourteenth Amendment from impairment by the States.

Although Gitlow lost his case, soon thereafter this assumption hardened into a series of holdings invalidating state laws that impermissibly restricted speech, press, and assembly rights. See, e.g., Stromberg v. California, 283 U.S. 359 (1931); Near v. Minnesota, 283 U.S. 697 (1931); De Jonge v. Oregon, 299 U.S. 353 (1937). During this same period, however, the Court also held that other provisions of the federal Bill did not fully apply against states. Writing for the Court in Palko v. Connecticut, 302 U.S. 319 (1937), Justice Cardozo upheld a state law permitting the prosecutor to appeal from a legally erroneous acquittal in a criminal case. Assuming for the sake of argument that an appeal in a comparable federal case would be barred by the Fifth Amendment's Double Jeopardy Clause,[7] Cardozo distinguished between those aspects of the federal Bill that were "of the very essence of a scheme of ordered liberty" and those that were not. Unlike rights of free expression, the right in the case at hand fell into the latter category and should not be imposed on states, Cardozo argued. Applying this framework over the next few years, the

7. Is this an attractive assumption? Why should our criminal justice system allow appellate courts to review and correct a legal error made by the trial judge if and only if that legal error leads to an erroneous conviction as opposed to an erroneous acquittal? If the defendant is entitled to appeal a legal error made against him, why should the prosecutor not have the same entitlement? Note that the issue here is arguably different from, say, rules concerning doubt about factual guilt; although reasonable doubts are to be resolved in defendant's favor, are legal errors the same as factual doubts? For further thoughts, see Akhil Reed Amar, Double Jeopardy Law Made Simple, 106 Yale L.J. 1807 (1997).

Court in Cantwell v. Connecticut, 310 U.S. 296 (1940), and Everson v. Board of Education, 330 U.S. 1 (1947), held that the Fourteenth Amendment made the First Amendment's free exercise and nonestablishment principles, respectively, applicable against states.

The scene was now set for a great debate on the relationship between the founders' Bill of Rights and the Reconstructionists' Fourteenth Amendment. In Adamson v. California, 332 U.S. 46 (1947), Justice Black's dissent put forth his now famous theory of "total incorporation."[8] On this view, the Fourteenth Amendment "incorporated" all the rights and freedoms of the federal Bill and made them applicable against states in precisely the same way as against the federal government. In a separate concurring opinion, Justice Frankfurter vigorously disagreed. On his view, the Reconstruction Amendment required that states obey principles of fundamental fairness and ordered liberty, principles that sometimes might overlap with the Bill of Rights but that bore no necessary logical or evidentiary relation to the Bill as such.[9]

Black may have lost the battle but he eventually won the war. With Frankfurter's retirement in 1962, the anti-incorporation logjam broke, and most of the previously unincorporated provisions of the Bill of Rights came to be applied against the states—though not via Black's theory. Rather, the Court pursued an approach championed by Justice Brennan, called "selective incorporation," by which the Justices purported to play by Frankfurter's ground rules while reaching Black's results. Under this third approach, the Court's analysis could proceed clause by clause, fully incorporating every provision of the Bill deemed "fundamental" without deciding in advance (as Black would have it) whether each and every clause would necessarily pass the test. Methodologically, Brennan's approach seemed to avoid a radical break with existing case law rejecting total incorporation, and even paid lip service to Frankfurter's insistence on fundamental fairness as the touchstone of the Fourteenth Amendment. In practice, however, Brennan's approach held out the possibility of total incorporation through the back door. For him, once a clause in the Bill was deemed "fundamental" it had to be "incorporated" against the states in every aspect, just as Black insisted. And nothing in the logic of selective incorporation precluded the possibility that, when all was said and done, virtually every clause of the Bill would have been deemed fundamental. As things turned out, in

8. Justice Douglas joined Black's dissent, and two other dissenters, Justices Murphy and Rutledge, agreed with Black that the Fourteenth Amendment incorporated the Bill of Rights. Unlike Black, however, Murphy and Rutledge suggested that courts might also use the broad language of the Fourteenth Amendment to protect additional unenumerated rights beyond the Bill of Rights.

9. Note that Frankfurter's test is, in essence, the same test that the Court has often applied generally to so-called substantive due process cases. This similarity should not be surprising once we recall that incorporation of the Bill of Rights was itself viewed by many as a kind of substantive due process, in which judges used the language of the Due Process Clause to protect what were often substantive, nonprocedural rights such as freedom of expression and freedom of religion.

applying this approach, the Warren Court almost always found that a given clause of the Bill did indeed set forth a fundamental right. Today, virtually all the Bill of Rights has come to apply with equal vigor against state and local governments.[10]

The only major exceptions are the Third Amendment (which rarely arises in modern adjudication), the Fifth Amendment grand jury requirement, and the Seventh Amendment's rules regarding civil juries.

The Supreme Court's approach to incorporation has generated a vast amount of academic commentary, some of it quite critical.[11]

---

10. See, e.g., In re Oliver, 333 U.S. 257 (1948) (Sixth Amendment right to public trial); Wolf v. Colorado, 338 U.S. 25 (1949) (Fourth Amendment); Mapp v. Ohio, 367 U.S. 643 (1961) (exclusionary rule); Robinson v. California, 370 U.S. 660 (1962) (Eighth Amendment right against cruel and unusual punishment); Gideon v. Wainwright, 372 U.S. 335 (1963) (Sixth Amendment right to counsel); Malloy v. Hogan, 378 U.S. 1 (1964) (Fifth Amendment right against compelled self-incrimination); Pointer v. Texas, 380 U.S. 400 (1965) (Sixth Amendment right to confront opposing witnesses); Klopfer v. North Carolina, 386 U.S. 213 (1967) (Sixth Amendment right to speedy trial); Washington v. Texas, 388 U.S. 14 (1967) (Sixth Amendment right to compulsory process); Duncan v. Louisiana, 391 U.S. 145 (1968) (Sixth Amendment right to jury trial); Benton v. Maryland, 395 U.S. 784 (1969) (Fifth Amendment right against double jeopardy); Schilb v. Kuebel, 404 U.S. 357 (1971) (Eighth Amendment right against excessive bail) (dictum); McDonald v. City of Chicago, 561 U.S. 3025 (2010) (Second Amendment right to keep and bear arms in the home for purposes of self-defense); Timbs v. Indiana, 139 S. Ct. 682 (2019) (Excessive Fines Clause of the Eighth Amendment); Ramos v. Louisiana, 140 S. Ct. 1390 (2020) (rejecting the result in Apodaca v. Oregon, 406 U.S. 404 (1972) and holding that the Sixth Amendment's requirement of unanimous jury verdicts for serious offenses applies to the states).

11. For famous commentary harshly critical of Justice Black's position, see Charles Fairman, Does the Fourteenth Amendment Incorporate the Bill of Rights?, 2 Stan. L. Rev. 5 (1949). Fairman's scholarship was, in turn, sharply attacked in William Winslow Crosskey, Charles Fairman, "Legislative History," and the Constitutional Limitations on State Authority, 22 U. Chi. L. Rev. 1 (1954); Michael Kent Curtis, No State Shall Abridge: The Fourteenth Amendment and the Bill of Rights (1984); and Richard L. Aynes, On Misreading John Bingham and the Fourteenth Amendment, 103 Yale L.J. 57 (1993). Consider also the following effort to synthesize the three main positions in this modern debate:

> This synthesis, which I shall call "refined incorporation," begins with Black's insight that *all* of the privileges and immunities of citizens recognized in the Bill of Rights became "incorporated" against states by dint of the Fourteenth Amendment. But not all of the provisions of the original Bill of Rights were indeed rights of citizens. Some instead were at least in part rights of states, and as such, awkward to fully incorporate *against* states. Most obvious, of course, is the Tenth Amendment, but other provisions of the first eight amendments resembled the Tenth much more than Justice Black admitted. Thus there is deep wisdom in Justice Brennan's invitation to consider incorporation clause by clause—or more precisely still, right by right—rather than wholesale. But having identified the right unit of analysis, Brennan posed the wrong question: Is a given provision of the original Bill really a *fundamental* right? The right question is whether the provision really guarantees a privilege or immunity of *individual citizens* rather than a right of *states* or the *public* at large. And when we ask this question, clause by clause and right by right, we must be attentive to the possibility, flagged by Frankfurter, that a particular principle in the Bill of Rights may change its shape in the process of absorption into the Fourteenth Amendment. This change can occur for reasons rather different from those that Frankfurter offered. (He, more than Black and Brennan, diverted attention from the right question by his insistence on abstract conceptions of "fundamental fairness" and "ordered liberty" as the sole Fourteenth

This is hardly surprising, given the enormity of the stakes: The process of incorporation has utterly transformed the meaning of the Bill of Rights, and has defined modern constitutional law. Mid-twentieth-century critics of the idea of incorporation—like Justice Frankfurter and the younger Justice Harlan—argued that applying the Bill of Rights against state and local governments would ultimately weaken American liberty. If judges were to use the Bill against states, the argument went, these judges would be tempted to water the Bill down to take account of the considerable diversity of state practice; and then in turn, these judges would hold the federal government to only this watered-down version. But as Justice Black and fellow incorporationists anticipated, extension of the Bill of Rights against the states has, in general, dramatically strengthened the Bill, not weakened it, in both legal doctrine and popular consciousness. Unused muscles atrophy, while those that are regularly put to use grow strong.

In area after area, incorporation enabled judges first to invalidate state and local laws, and then, with this doctrinal base thus built up, to keep Congress in check. The First Amendment is illustrative. Before 1925, when the *Gitlow* Court began in earnest the process of First Amendment incorporation, free speech had *never* prevailed against a repressive statute in the U.S. Supreme Court. Within a few years of incorporation, however, freedom of expression and religion began to win in the High Court in landmark cases involving states, like *Stromberg, Near, De Jonge,* and *Cantwell.* These and other cases began to build up a First Amendment Tradition,[12] in and out of court, and that Tradition could then be used against even federal officials. Not until 1965 did the Supreme Court strike down an act of Congress on First Amendment grounds (in Lamont v. Postmaster General, 381 U.S. 301 (1965)), and when it did so, it relied squarely on doctrine built up in earlier cases involving states. Consider also the flag burning cases of Texas v. Johnson, 491 U.S. 397 (1989), and United States v. Eichman, 496 U.S. 310 (1990). In the first case, the Justices defined the basic First Amendment principles to strike down a *state* statute and then, in the second case, the Court stood its ground on this platform to strike down an act of *Congress.*

The large body of modern legal doctrine concerning the Bill of Rights has rolled out of courtrooms and into the vocabulary and vision of law students, journalists, activists, and ultimately the citizenry at large.[13] But without incorporation, and the steady flow of cases created by state and local laws, the Supreme Court

---

> Amendment litmus tests, and by his disregard of the language and history of the Privileges or Immunities Clause.) Certain alloyed provisions of the original Bill—part citizen right, part state right—may need to undergo refinement and filtration before their citizen-right elements can be absorbed by the Fourteenth Amendment. And other provisions may become less majoritarian and populist, and more libertarian, as they are repackaged in the Fourteenth Amendment as liberal civil rights—"privileges or immunities" of individuals—rather than republican political "right[s] of the people," as in the original Bill.

Amar, supra n.1, at xiv-xv.

12. See generally Harry Kalven, Jr., A Worthy Tradition: Freedom of Speech in America (1988).

13. For an important argument expressing skepticism about the magnitude of impact of Supreme Court decisions generally, see Gerald N. Rosenberg, The Hollow Hope: Can Courts Bring About Social Change? (1991).

would have had far fewer opportunities to be part of the ongoing American conversation about liberty. Perhaps nowhere has the importance of incorporation in shaping American jurisprudence been more evident than in the field of constitutional criminal procedure. The overwhelming majority of criminal cases are prosecuted by state governments under state law; only after the incorporation of the Fourth, Fifth, Sixth, and Eighth Amendments did federal courts develop a robust and highly elaborate—if also highly controversial—jurisprudence of constitutional criminal procedure.[14]

The centrality of race to modern conceptions of civil rights and civil liberties further confirms the significance of Reconstruction. Sometimes the role of the Fourteenth Amendment is explicitly acknowledged—as when the Court in Bolling v. Sharpe, 347 U.S. 497 (1954), read the founders' Fifth Amendment's Due Process Clause in light of the Reconstructionists' Equal Protection Clause. Other times, the influence of the Fourteenth Amendment on the jurisprudence of the Bill of Rights has been almost unconscious, as in the landmark 1964 case of New York Times v. Sullivan, 376 U.S. 254. The facts of this case—involving an all-white local jury from an ex-Confederate state trying to shut down the speech of a Yankee newspaper and a national civil rights movement led by a Black preacher—obviously call to mind images of Reconstruction, but the Court tried to tell a founding story starring Madison and John Peter Zenger rather than a Reconstruction tale touting Bingham and Frederick Douglass.[15] But only the Reconstruction can explain why—contra Zenger—local juries are not always to be trusted to protect free expression.

What are we to make of the fact that our standard legal narrative has often exaggerated the founding and diminished the Reconstruction? Perhaps many of us are guilty of a kind of curiously selective ancestor worship—one that gives too much credit to James Madison and not enough to John Bingham, that celebrates Thomas Jefferson and Patrick Henry but slights Harriet Beecher Stowe and Frederick Douglass. Great as men like James Madison and Thomas Jefferson were, they

14. The corpus of constitutional criminal procedure has swelled so large, as a result of incorporation, that it is now conventional to omit this vast body of material from standard casebooks and courses on constitutional law, relegating these issues to courses and texts on criminal procedure. This casebook follows that convention. For a nice review of earlier (pre-incorporation) constitutional law casebooks that included brief surveys of criminal procedure case law, see Michael Stokes Paulsen, Dirty Harry and the Real Constitution, 64 U. Chi. L. Rev. 1457, 1465-1467 (1997). For general discussions of the current scholarly split between constitutional law and criminal procedure, see Howard W. Gutman, Academic Determinism: The Division of the Bill of Rights, 54 S. Cal. L. Rev. 295 (1981); Jack M. Balkin and Sanford Levinson, The Canons of Constitutional Law, 111 Harv. L. Rev. 963, 1012-1013 (1998). For an effort to bridge this gap, analyzing (and sharply criticizing) current constitutional criminal procedure doctrine from the perspective of standard constitutional law, see Akhil Reed Amar, The Constitution and Criminal Procedure: First Principles (1997).

15. For important discussions of the central role that historical "paradigm cases" do and should play in constitutional adjudication, see Jed Rubenfeld, Reading the Constitution as Spoken, 104 Yale L.J. 1119 (1995); Jed Rubenfeld, Revolution by Judiciary: The Structure of American Constitutional Law (2005).

lived and died as slaveholders, and their Bill of Rights was tainted by its quiet complicity with the original sin of slavery. Even as we celebrate the founders, we must ponder the sobering words of Charles Cotesworth Pinckney in the 1788 South Carolina ratification debates: "Another reason weighed particularly, with the members from this state, against the insertion of a bill of rights. Such bills generally begin with declaring that all men are by nature born free. Now, we should make that declaration with a very bad grace, when a large part of our property consists in men who are actually born slaves."[16]

But the Reconstruction Amendment did begin with an affirmation of the freedom — and citizenship — of all. The midwives of this new birth of freedom were women alongside men, Blacks alongside whites. As twentieth-century judges increasingly came to realize, because of these nineteenth-century men and women, our eighteenth-century Bill of Rights has taken on new life and meaning.

16. 4 Debates on the Adoption of the Federal Constitution 316 (Jonathan Elliot ed., 1836).

CHAPTER 5

THE NEW DEAL AND THE CIVIL RIGHTS ERA

In 1934, the nation was in the midst of an economic depression of unprecedented proportion. Both the national government and the states had adopted emergency measures, designed to palliate or cure. At first, the Supreme Court seemed to acquiesce in these measures—by a margin of one vote. In 1935 and 1936, however, the Court took up battle, striking down a half-dozen regulatory schemes on the ground that they were beyond congressional authority and reasserting its own authority to review the merits of state economic legislation. Then, in 1937, after Franklin Roosevelt's reelection and in the shadow of his proposed plan to "pack" the Court, the Justices again acquiesced, upholding New Deal legislation against both economic due process and federalism-based challenges.

The constitutional struggle over the New Deal eventually led to the creation of a new political and constitutional regime—the New Deal/Civil Rights regime—with a new set of ideas about the purposes of judicial review. The regime culminated in the civil rights mobilizations of the 1960s and the passage of landmark civil rights statutes—the Civil Rights Act of 1964 and the Voting Rights Act of 1965.

This chapter focuses primarily on the questions of economic regulation and congressional power to pass civil rights laws that were debated between 1934 and 1980. The doctrines of equal protection and fundamental rights that emerged during this period are discussed in detail in Chapters 7 through 10.

I. THE DECLINE OF JUDICIAL INTERVENTION AGAINST ECONOMIC REGULATION[1]

A. 1934

By 1934, the country had been mired in the Great Depression for five years. Two decisions presaged the Court's withdrawal from intervention against economic

1. Legal scholars and historians continue to debate exactly how to characterize the significant changes in Supreme Court doctrine between 1934 and 1942. The standard view is that there was a constitutional "revolution" in 1937 in a host of different areas of doctrine. Good examples of this view include Robert McCloskey, The American Supreme Court (1960,

regulation. The first case rejected a substantive due process challenge to a price regulation; the second case involved the Contract Clause.

The appellant in Nebbia v. New York, 291 U.S. 502 (1934), was a storekeeper convicted for selling milk below the minimum retail price of 9¢ a quart fixed by the New York Milk Control Board, an agency established in 1933 pursuant to the recommendation of a legislative committee. The committee attributed the critically depressed state of milk farmers to price cutting among milk distributors and suggested that this destructive competition could be mitigated by, inter alia, setting minimum retail prices. In an opinion by Justice Roberts, the Court upheld the regulation. Stating that "the guaranty of due process . . . demands only that the law shall not be unreasonable, arbitrary, or capricious, and that the means selected shall have a real and substantial relation to the object sought to be attained," he quoted at length from the legislative committee's report to conclude that the regulation "appears not to be unreasonable or arbitrary, or without relation to the purpose to prevent ruthless competition from destroying the wholesale price structure on which the farmer depends for his livelihood, and the community for an assured supply of milk." Justice Roberts then turned to the appellant's contentions, supported by prior decisions of the Court, that price fixing by the legislature was per se unconstitutional except in "businesses affected with a public interest" and that these were limited to franchised public utilities and monopolies. Conceding that the milk industry did not fit this description, Justice Roberts noted that the industry was nonetheless subject to some sorts of regulation in the public interest, and he went on to write:

> [No] constitutional principle bars the state from correcting existing maladjustments by legislation touching prices. . . . The due process clause makes no mention of sales or of prices any more than it speaks of business or contracts or buildings or other incidents of property. . . . It is clear that there is no closed class or category of businesses affected with a public interest. . . . The phrase "affected with a public interest" can, in the nature of things, mean no more than that an industry, for adequate reason, is subject to control for the public good.

---

rev. ed. 1994), at 117ff., and William E. Leuchtenburg, The Supreme Court Reborn: The Constitutional Revolution in the Age of Roosevelt (1995). Barry Cushman offers a revisionist account. Barry Cushman, Rethinking the New Deal Court: The Structure of a Constitutional Revolution (1998). While not denying that a "revolution" occurred, Cushman argues that the changes were far more gradual. They began much earlier, in 1934, with Nebbia v. New York, and were completed with the decisions in United States v. Darby and Wickard v. Filburn in 1941-1942. Another source of controversy is whether there was a "switch" by particular Justices, particularly Owen Roberts and Chief Justice Hughes. Cushman sees their views as relatively consistent and emphasizes instead the consequences of shifts of membership as various Justices retired and were replaced by Roosevelt appointees. For a nice range of other recent interpretations, see generally Richard D. Friedman, Switching Time and Other Thought Experiments: The Hughes Court and Constitutional Transformation, 142 U. Pa. L. Rev. 1891 (1994); 2 Bruce Ackerman, We the People: Transformations 255-382 (1998); Bruce Ackerman, Revolution on a Human Scale, 108 Yale L.J. 2279 (1999); Laura Kalman, Law, Politics, and the New Deal, 108 Yale L.J. 2165 (1999).

Justice McReynolds, joined by Justices Van Devanter, Sutherland, and Butler, dissented: The milk industry was not affected with a public interest. And although "[r]egulation to prevent recognized evils in [any] business has long been upheld as permissible legislative action . . . , fixation of the price at which *A*, engaged in an ordinary business, may sell, in order to enable *B*, a producer, to improve his condition, has not been regarded as within legislative power. This is not regulation, but . . . amounts to the deprivation of the fundamental right which one has to conduct his own affairs honestly and along customary lines." In any case, McReynolds argued, the judiciary had abdicated its responsibility to determine for itself whether the New York law is reasonably related to its goals: "Are federal rights subject to extinction by reports of committees?" Independently evaluating the committee's data, Justice McReynolds concluded that the problem lay in the reduced buying power of consumers, and that because demand was insufficient even at low prices it was unreasonable to believe that "higher charges at stores to impoverished customers when the output is excessive and sale prices by producers are unrestrained, can possibly increase receipts at the farm."

The constitutional jurisprudence of *Lochner*, while not permitting government regulation of wages in the "private" relationship between employer and employee, did allow regulation (albeit judicially supervised) of certain "businesses affected with a public interest," such as railroads. *Nebbia* took an expansive view of this category, but it did not unmistakably signal a clean break with existing doctrine. Neither did the decision in the Minnesota Mortgage Moratorium Case, although it, too, signaled a new flexibility in questions of economic regulation.

Home Building & Loan Association v. Blaisdell

[The Minnesota Mortgage Moratorium Case]
290 U.S. 398 (1934)

[In 1933, the Minnesota legislature enacted the Mortgage Moratorium Law, an emergency measure, which expired in May 1935, granting temporary relief from mortgage foreclosures and execution sales of real estate. At the time, mortgages were not, as they are now, amortized over the length of the contract. Instead, there were usually "balloon" payments at the conclusion of the term. For example, a $10,000 mortgage might require 59 payments of $100 per month, followed by a payment of $4,100 in the sixtieth month. Typically, the bank would agree to "roll over" the mortgage, perhaps at a new interest rate, without requiring the balloon payment, but this obviously presumed a reasonably flourishing economy. The unwillingness of banks to engage in such rollovers during the Depression triggered the moratorium. The particular section involved here authorized a court to extend the period during which a defaulting mortgagor might redeem his property following a foreclosure execution sale. During the period of the extension, the mortgagor was required to pay all or a reasonable part of the reasonable rental value of the property as determined by the court, including taxes, insurance, and mortgage interest. The statute did not reduce mortgage indebtedness or affect the right of a mortgagee to title in fee, or his right to obtain a deficiency judgment, if the mortgagor failed to redeem within the prescribed period.

The Blaisdells' house had been mortgaged to Home Building & Loan. Upon default, the association foreclosed and then purchased the property at the execution sale for approximately two-thirds of its market value. The Blaisdells obtained an extension of the redemption period until May 1935, during which they were required to pay the judicially ascertained fair rental value of $40 per month.

The loan company challenged the Mortgage Moratorium Law on the ground, inter alia, that it violated the Contract Clause, Article I, §10, cl. 1. The Minnesota Supreme Court upheld the law, and the association appealed.]

Hughes, C.J. . . .

In determining whether the provision for this temporary and conditional relief exceeds the power of the State by reason of the clause in the Federal Constitution prohibiting impairment of the obligations of contracts, we must consider the relation of emergency to constitutional power, the historical setting of the contract clause, the development of the jurisprudence of this Court in the construction of that clause, and the principles of construction which we may consider to be established.

Emergency does not create power. Emergency does not increase granted power or remove or diminish the restrictions imposed upon power granted or reserved. The Constitution was adopted in a period of grave emergency. Its grants of power to the Federal Government and its limitations of the power of the States were determined in the light of emergency and they are not altered by emergency. . . .

The constitutional question presented in the light of an emergency is whether the power possessed embraces the particular exercise of it in response to particular conditions. . . . When the provisions of the Constitution, in grant or restriction, are specific, so particularized as not to admit of construction, no question is presented. Thus, emergency would not permit a State to have more than two Senators in the Congress, or permit the election of President by a general popular vote without regard to the number of electors to which the States are respectively entitled, or permit the States to "coin money" or to "make anything but gold and silver coin a tender in payment of debts." But where constitutional grants and limitations of power are set forth in general clauses, which afford a broad outline, the process of construction is essential to fill in the details.

That is true of the contract clause. . . . In the construction of the contract clause, the debates in the Constitutional Convention are of little aid. But the reasons which led to the adoption of that clause, and of the other prohibitions of Section 10 of Article I, are not left in doubt and have frequently been described with eloquent emphasis. The wide-spread distress following the revolutionary period, and the plight of debtors, had called forth in the States an ignoble array of legislative schemes for the defeat of creditors and the invasion of contractual obligations. Legislative interferences had been so numerous and extreme that the confidence essential to prosperous trade had been undermined and the utter destruction of credit was threatened. "The sober people of America" were convinced that some "thorough reform" was needed which would "inspire a general prudence and industry, and give a regular course to the business of society." The Federalist, No. 44. It was necessary to interpose the restraining power of a central authority in order to secure the foundations even of "private faith." . . .

But full recognition of the occasion and general purpose of the clause does not suffice to fix its precise scope. Nor does an examination of the details of prior legislation in the States yield criteria which can be considered controlling. To ascertain the scope of the constitutional prohibition we examine the course of judicial decisions in its application. These put it beyond question that the prohibition is not an absolute one and is not to be read with literal exactness like a mathematical formula. . . .

The obligation of a contract is "the law which binds the parties to perform their agreement." This Court has said that ". . . [n]othing can be more material to the obligation than the means of enforcement. . . . The ideas of validity and remedy are inseparable, and both are parts of the obligation, which is guaranteed by the Constitution against invasion." . . . [But it] "is competent for the States to change the form of the remedy, or to modify it otherwise, as they may see fit, provided no substantial right secured by the contract is thereby impaired. No attempt has been made to fix definitely the line between alterations of the remedy, which are to be deemed legitimate, and those which under the form of modifying the remedy, impair substantial rights. Every case must be determined upon its own circumstances" . . . [and] "[i]n all such cases the question becomes, therefore, one of reasonableness, and of that the legislature is primarily the judge." . . .

The policy of protecting contracts against impairment presupposes the maintenance of a government by virtue of which contractual relations are worth while,—a government which retains adequate authority to secure the peace and good order of society. This principle of harmonizing the constitutional prohibition with the necessary residuum of state power has had progressive recognition in the decisions of this Court. . . .

The legislature cannot "bargain away the public health or the public morals." Thus, the constitutional provision against the impairment of contracts was held not to be violated by an amendment of the state constitution which put an end to a lottery theretofore authorized by the legislature. . . . A similar rule has been applied to the control by the State of the sale of intoxicating liquors. The States retain adequate power to protect the public health against the maintenance of nuisances despite insistence upon existing contracts. Legislation to protect the public safety comes within the same category of reserved power. . . .

The argument is pressed that in the cases we have cited the obligation of contracts was affected only incidentally. This argument proceeds upon a misconception. The question is not whether the legislative action affects contracts incidentally, or directly or indirectly, but whether the legislation is addressed to a legitimate end and the measures taken are reasonable and appropriate to that end. Another argument, which comes more closely to the point, is that the state power may be addressed directly to the prevention of the enforcement of contracts only when these are of a sort which the legislature in its discretion may denounce as being in themselves hostile to public morals, or public health, safety or welfare, or where the prohibition is merely of injurious practices; that interference with the enforcement of other and valid contracts according to appropriate legal procedure, although the interference is temporary and for a public purpose, is not permissible. . . . Undoubtedly, whatever is reserved of state power must be consistent with the fair intent of the constitutional limitation of that power. . . . This principle precludes a construction which would permit the State to adopt as its policy the repudiation of debts or the destruction of contracts or the denial of means to enforce them. But it does not follow that conditions may not arise in which a temporary restraint of enforcement may be consistent with the spirit and purpose of the constitutional provision and thus be found to be within the range of the reserved power of the State to protect the vital interests of the community. . . .

Whatever doubt there may have been that the protective power of the State, its police power, may be exercised—without violating the true intent of the provision of the Federal Constitution—in directly preventing the immediate and literal enforcement of contractual obligations, by a temporary and conditional restraint, where vital public interests would otherwise suffer, was removed by our decisions relating to the enforcement of provisions of leases during a period of scarcity of housing. Marcus Brown Holding Co. v. Feldman, 256 U.S. 170 (1921); Edgar A. Levy Leasing Co. v. Siegel, 258 U.S. 242 (1922). . . . The statutes of New York, declaring that a public emergency existed, directly interfered with the enforcement of covenants for the surrender of the possession of premises on the expiration of leases. Within the City of New York and contiguous counties, the owners of dwellings, including apartment and tenement houses . . . , were wholly deprived until November 1, 1922, of all possessory remedies for the purpose of removing from their premises the tenants or occupants in possession when the laws took effect, . . . providing the tenants or occupants were ready, able and willing to pay a reasonable rent or price for their use and occupation. . . .

It is manifest from this review of our decisions that there has been a growing appreciation of public needs and of the necessity of finding ground for a rational compromise between individual rights and public welfare. The settlement and consequent contraction of the public domain, the pressure of a constantly increasing density of population, the interrelation of the activities of our people and the complexity of our economic interests, have inevitably led to an increased use of the organization of society in order to protect the very bases of individual opportunity. Where, in earlier days, it was thought that only the concerns of individuals or of classes were involved, and that those of the State itself were touched only remotely, it has later been found that the fundamental interests of the State are directly affected; and that the question is no longer merely that of one party to a contract as against another, but of the use of reasonable means to safeguard the economic structure upon which the good of all depends.

It is no answer to say that this public need was not apprehended a century ago, or to insist that what the provision of the Constitution meant to the vision of that day it must mean to the vision of our time. If by the statement that what the Constitution meant at the time of its adoption it means to-day, it is intended to say that the great clauses of the Constitution must be confined to the interpretation which the framers, with the conditions and outlook of their time, would have placed upon them, the statement carries its own refutation. It was to guard against such a narrow conception that Chief Justice Marshall uttered the memorable warning—"We must never forget that it is *a constitution* we are expounding" (McCulloch v. Maryland, 4 Wheat. 316, 407)—"a constitution intended to endure for ages to come, and consequently, to be adapted to the various *crises* of human affairs." When we are dealing with the words of the Constitution, said this Court in Missouri v. Holland,

252 U.S. 416, 433, "we must realize that they have called into life a being the development of which could not have been foreseen completely by the most gifted of its begetters. . . . The case before us must be considered in the light of our whole experience and not merely in that of what was said a hundred years ago."

When we consider the contract clause and the decisions which have expounded it in harmony with the essential reserved power of the States to protect the security of their peoples, we find no warrant for the conclusion that the clause has been warped by these decisions from its proper significance or that the founders of our Government would have interpreted the clause differently had they had occasion to assume that responsibility in the conditions of the later day. The vast body of law which has been developed was unknown to the fathers, but it is believed to have preserved the essential content and the spirit of the Constitution. With a growing recognition of public needs and the relation of individual right to public security, the court has sought to prevent the perversion of the clause through its use as an instrument to throttle the capacity of the States to protect their fundamental interests. This development is a growth from the seeds which the fathers planted. . . .

Applying the criteria established by our decisions we conclude:

1. An emergency existed in Minnesota which furnished a proper occasion for the exercise of the reserved power of the State to protect the vital interests of the community. . . . As the Supreme Court of Minnesota said, the economic emergency which threatened "the loss of homes and lands which furnish those in possession the necessary shelter and means of subsistence" was a "potent cause" for the enactment of the statute.
2. The legislation was addressed to a legitimate end, that is, the legislation was not for the mere advantage of particular individuals but for the protection of a basic interest of society.
3. In view of the nature of the contracts in question—mortgages of unquestionable validity—the relief afforded and justified by the emergency, in order not to contravene the constitutional provision, could only be of a character appropriate to that emergency and could be granted only upon reasonable conditions.
4. The conditions upon which the period of redemption is extended do not appear to be unreasonable. . . . The relief afforded by the statute has regard to the interest of mortgagees as well as to the interest of mortgagors. The legislation seeks to prevent the impending ruin of both by a considerate measure of relief. . . .
5. The legislation is temporary in operation. It is limited to the exigency which called it forth. . . .

We are of the opinion that the Minnesota statute as here applied does not violate the contract clause of the Federal Constitution. Whether the legislation is wise or unwise as a matter of policy is a question with which we are not concerned. . . .

Judgment affirmed.

SUTHERLAND, J., joined by VAN DEVANTER, MCREYNOLDS, and BUTLER, JJ., dissenting. . . . The whole aim of construction, as applied to a provision of the Constitution, is to discover the meaning, to ascertain and give effect to the intent, of its framers and the people who adopted it. The necessities which gave rise to the provision, the controversies which preceded, as well as the conflicts of opinion which were settled by its adoption, are matters to be considered to enable us to arrive at a correct result. The history of the times, the state of things existing when the provision was framed and adopted, should be looked to in order to ascertain the mischief and the remedy. As nearly as possible we should place ourselves in the condition of those who framed and adopted it. . . .

An application of these principles to the question under review removes any doubt, if otherwise there would be any, that the contract impairment clause denies to the several states the power to mitigate hard consequences resulting to debtors from financial or economic exigencies by an impairment of the obligation of contracts of indebtedness. A candid consideration of the history and circumstances which led up to and accompanied the framing and adoption of this clause will demonstrate conclusively that it was framed and adopted with the specific and studied purpose of preventing legislation designed to relieve debtors *especially* in time of financial distress. . . .

Following the Revolution, and prior to the adoption of the Constitution, the American people found themselves in a greatly impoverished condition. Their commerce had been well-nigh annihilated. They were not only without luxuries, but in great degree were destitute of the ordinary comforts and necessities of life. In these circumstances they incurred indebtedness in the purchase of imported goods and otherwise, far beyond their capacity to pay. . . .

In an attempt to meet the situation recourse was had to the legislatures of the several states under the Confederation; and these bodies passed, among other acts, the following: laws providing for the emission of bills of credit and making them legal tender for the payment of debts, and providing also for such payment by the delivery of specific property at a fixed valuation; instalment laws, authorizing payment of overdue obligations at future intervals of time; stay laws and laws temporarily closing access to the courts; and laws discriminating against British creditors. . . .

In the midst of this confused, gloomy, and seriously exigent condition of affairs, the Constitutional Convention of 1787 met at Philadelphia. . . . Shortly prior to the meeting of the Convention, Madison had assailed a bill pending in the Virginia Assembly, proposing the payment of private debts in three annual instalments on the ground that "no legislative principle could vindicate such an interposition of the law in private contracts." . . .

In the plan of government especially urged by Sherman and Ellsworth there was an article proposing that the legislatures of the individual states ought not to possess a right to emit bills of credit, etc., "or in any manner to obstruct or impede the recovery of debts, whereby the interests of foreigners or the citizens of any other state may be affected." And on July 13, 1787, Congress in New York, acutely conscious of the evils engendered by state laws interfering with existing contracts, passed the Northwest Territory Ordinance, which contained the clause: "And, in the just preservation of rights and property, it is understood and declared, that no law ought ever to be made or have force in the said territory, that shall, in any manner whatever, interfere with or affect private contracts, or engagements, bona fide, and without fraud previously formed." It is not surprising, therefore, that, after the Convention had adopted the clauses, no state shall "emit bills of credit," or "make any thing but gold and silver coin a tender in payment of debts," Mr. King moved to add a "prohibition on the states to interfere in private contracts." This was opposed by Gouverneur Morris and Colonel Mason. Colonel Mason thought that this would be carrying the restraint too far; that cases would happen that could not be foreseen where some kind of interference would be essential. This was on August 28. But Mason's view did not prevail, for, on September 14 following, the first clause of Art. I, §10, was altered so as to include the provision, "No state shall . . . pass any . . . law impairing the obligation of contracts," and in that form it was adopted.

Luther Martin, in an address to the Maryland House of Delegates, declared his reasons for voting against the provision. He said that he considered there might be times of such great public calamity and distress as should render it the duty of a government in some measure to interfere by passing laws totally or partially stopping courts of justice, or authorizing the debtor to pay by installments; that such regulations had been found necessary in most or all of the states "to prevent the wealthy creditor and the moneyed man from totally destroying the poor, though industrious debtor. Such times may again arrive." And he was apprehensive of any proposal which took from the respective states the power to give their debtor citizens "a moment's indulgence, however necessary it might be, and however desirous to grant them aid."

On the other hand, Sherman and Ellsworth defended the provision in a letter to the Governor of Connecticut. In the course of the Virginia debates, Randolph declared that the prohibition would be promotive of virtue and justice, and preventive of injustice and fraud; and he pointed out that the reputation of the people had suffered because of frequent interferences by the state legislatures with private contracts. . . .

The provision was strongly defended in The Federalist, both by Hamilton in No. 7 and Madison in No. 44. . . .

Contemporaneous history is replete with evidence of the sharp conflict of opinion with respect to the advisability of adopting the clause. . . .

If it be possible by resort to the testimony of history to put any question of constitutional intent beyond the domain of uncertainty, the foregoing leaves no reasonable ground upon which to base a denial that the clause of the Constitution now under consideration was meant to foreclose state action impairing the obligation of contracts *primarily and especially* in respect of such action aimed at giving relief to debtors *in time of emergency*. And if further proof be required to strengthen what already is inexpugnable, such proof will be found in the previous decisions of this court. . . .

The present exigency is nothing new. From the beginning of our existence as a nation, periods of depression, of industrial failure, of financial distress, of unpaid and unpayable indebtedness, have alternated with years of plenty. . . .

The defense of the Minnesota law is made upon grounds which were discountenanced by the makers of the Constitution and have many times been rejected by this court. That defense should not now succeed because it constitutes an effort to overthrow the constitutional provision by an appeal to facts and circumstances identical with those which brought it into existence. With due regard for the processes of logical thinking, it legitimately cannot be urged that conditions which produced the rule may now be invoked to destroy it. . . .

I quite agree with the opinion of the court that whether the legislation under review is wise or unwise is a matter with which we have nothing to do. Whether it is likely to work well or work ill presents a question entirely irrelevant to the issue. The only legitimate inquiry we can make is whether it is constitutional. If it is not, its virtues, if it have any, cannot save it; if it is, its faults cannot be invoked to accomplish its destruction. If the provisions of the Constitution be not upheld when they pinch as well as when they comfort, they may as well be abandoned. Being unable to reach any other conclusion than that the Minnesota statute infringes the constitutional restriction under review, I have no choice but to say so.

CARDOZO, J. [unpublished concurring opinion] . . .

A hundred years ago when this court decided Bronson v. Kinzie . . . property might be taken without due process of law through the legislation of the states, and the courts of the nation were powerless to give redress, unless indeed they could find that a contract had been broken. Dartmouth College v. Woodward . . . ; Fletcher v. Peck. . . . The judges of those courts had not yet begun to speak of the police power except in an off hand way or in expounding the effect of the commerce clause upon local regulations. The License Cases. . . . Due process in the states was whatever the states ordained. In such circumstances there was jeopardy, or the threat of it, in encroachment, however slight, upon the obligation to adhere to the letter of a contract. Once reject that test, and no other was available, or so it might well have seemed. The states could not be kept within the limits of reason and fair dealing for such restraints were then unknown as curbs upon their power. It was either all or nothing.

The Fourteenth Amendment came, and with it a profound change in the relation between the federal government and the governments of the states. No longer were the states invested with arbitrary power. Their statutes affecting property or liberty were brought within supervision of independent courts and subjected to the rule of reason. The dilemma of "all or nothing" no longer stared us in the face.

Upon the basis of that amendment, a vast body of law unknown to the fathers has been built in treatise and decision. . . . The early cases dealt with the problem as one affecting the conflicting rights and interests of individuals and classes. This was the attitude of the courts up to the Fourteenth Amendment; and the tendency to some extent persisted even later. . . . The rights and interests of the state itself were involved, as it seemed, only indirectly and remotely, if they were thought to be involved at all. We know better in these days, with the passing of the frontier and of the unpeopled spaces of the west. With these and other changes, the welfare of the social organism in any of its parts is bound up more inseparably than ever with the welfare of the whole. A gospel of laissez-faire—of individual initiative—of thrift and industry and sacrifice—may be inadequate in that great society we live in to point the way to salvation, at least for economic life. The state when it acts today by statutes like the one before us is not furthering the selfish good of individuals or classes as ends of ultimate validity. It is furthering its own good by maintaining the economic structure on which the good of all depends. Such at least is its endeavor, however much it miss the mark. The attainment of that end, so august and impersonal, will not be barred and thwarted by the obstruction of a contract set up along the way.

Looking back over the century, one perceives a process of evolution too strong to be set back. The decisions brought together by the Chief Justice [Hughes] show with impressive force how the court in its interpretation of the contract clause has been feeling its way toward a rational compromise between private rights and public welfare. From the beginning it was seen that something must be subtracted from the words of the Constitution in all their literal and stark significance. This was forcefully pointed out by Johnson, J., in Ogden v. Saunders, 12 Wheat. 213, 286. At first refuge was found in the distinction between right and remedy with all its bewildering refinements. Gradually the distinction was perceived to be inadequate. The search was for a broader base, for a division that would separate the lawful and the forbidden by lines more closely in correspondence with the necessities of government. The Fourteenth Amendment was seen to point the way. Contracts were still to be preserved. There was to be no arbitrary destruction of their binding force, nor any arbitrary impairment. There was to be no impairment, even though not arbitrary, except with the limits of fairness, of moderation, and of pressing and emergent need. But a promise exchanged between individuals was not to paralyze the state in its endeavor in times of direful crisis to keep its lifeblood flowing.

To hold this may be inconsistent with things that men said in 1787 when expounding to compatriots the newly written constitution. They did not see the changes in the relation between states and nation or in the play of social forces that lay hidden in the womb of time. It may be inconsistent with things that they believed or took for granted. Their beliefs to be significant must be adjusted to the world they knew. It is not in my judgment inconsistent with what they say today nor with what today they would believe, if they were called upon to interpret "in the light of our whole experience" the constitution that they framed for the needs of an expanding future.

DISCUSSION

1. *Modalities of constitutional interpretation.* Note the rich assortment of methodological moves in *Blaisdell.* The dissenters invoke what they assert to be the obvious original intent of the Contract Clause, as applied to the paradigm case that gave rise to the clause—state relief of debtors in hard times. Cf. Jed Rubenfeld, Revolution by Judiciary (2005) (discussing the importance of historical paradigm cases in constitutional interpretation).

In response, the majority argues that the relevant constitutional text should not be read in the most absolutist way possible—not all modifications of contractual remedies impermissibly "impair" contractual obligations so as to violate the clause. Precedent confirms nonabsolutism, the majority points out. (Consider, for example, a law that prohibits the sale of some new drug; suppose the law has the incidental effect of nullifying preexisting contracts for future sales of this drug. Suppose also that such a law was not purposefully designed so as to redistribute wealth as between buyers and sellers. Is such a law an impermissible "impairment" of "contractual obligation" as such? The *Blaisdell* majority suggests not, in its allusion to the case of "intoxicating liquors.") Perhaps most interesting of all, the majority suggests that the Minnesota law should not be seen as an "ignoble" governmental attempt to redistribute wealth from creditors to debtors. In the extraordinarily severe and indeed unprecedented circumstances of the Great Depression, the Court hints, creditors as a class might be *worse off* if the government were to insist on immediate repayment, which could threaten the collapse of "the economic structure upon which the good of *all* [including, presumably, creditors] depends." The legislation, argues the majority, was "not for the mere advantage of particular individuals but for the protection of a basic interest of society," with due "regard to the interest of mortgagees as well as to the interest of mortgagors. The legislation seeks to prevent the impending ruin of *both*. . . ." On this view, the very breadth of the 1930s economic crisis—implicating not a small group of debtors but the broad swath of society—renders it markedly different from the paradigm case of the 1780s. Note that concern for the general stability of the economic structure is not one that each creditor would necessarily take into account in deciding whether to foreclose—the economic structure might collapse only if all creditors try to foreclose at once, and under these circumstances no single creditor might have a sufficient incentive to exercise restraint. The structure of the problem could thus be analogized to a "race to the bottom" or a "prisoners' dilemma," in which collective action is needed to cure a problem created by the cumulative effect of individually rational actions by individual actors. Note also how this prudential argument intertwines with constitutional text and precedent: A law sincerely designed to help creditors as well as debtors is not a law designed to impermissibly "impair" contractual "obligations." Finally, note the intriguing suggestion of Justice Cardozo that, after the adoption of the Fourteenth Amendment, the language of the Contract Clause need not be read in the same way as it was before. Whereas the "multigenerational synthesis" of the founding and the Reconstruction ultimately led to stricter limits on states in the context of the incorporation of the Bill of Rights, here Cardozo seems to be arguing that it might also appropriately lead to less strictness for states in some contexts.[2]

2. *Law and violence.* Minnesota passed its law (and the Supreme Court considered it) not only within the general context of the Great Depression and its massive economic disruptions, but also within more particular circumstances of social disorder and violence. For example, angry farmers denounced and in some instances forcibly stopped foreclosure of their farms. In Iowa, a local judge who refused to suspend foreclosure proceedings was dragged from a courtroom and had a rope put around his neck before the crowd let him go. The governor of Iowa also declared martial law in six counties and called out the National Guard in order to forestall the perceived threat of rural violence. A New York newspaper editorially

---

2. Consider also the following multigenerational argument: Broad-based economic redistribution, not from person A to person B, but from one broad class (the wealthy) to another broad class (the impoverished) was arguably impermissible at the founding, in light of the spirit of the Contract Clause and the Takings Clause (if the two clauses are read expansively and in tandem). But the Sixteenth Amendment, adopted in 1913, dramatically changed things, making clear that explicitly redistributive economic policies—like an income tax imposed only on the wealthy (a prospect contemplated by many of the proponents of the Sixteenth Amendment)—no longer violated the deep structure of American constitutionalism.

noted that instead of worrying about a merely fantasized threat of a "red revolution" in the cities, Americans should become aware "that actual revolution already exists in the farm belt," provoked by the anguish of "conservatives fighting for the right to hold their homesteads."[3] Do these facts bear on the constitutionality of Minnesota's "moratorium"? If so, why? Because people were suffering?[4] Because judges and legal officials were threatened with violence? To what extent should the social impact of, or popular reaction to, a law influence the determination of its constitutionality? Would your views of, say, Plessy v. Ferguson change if you were persuaded that racially integrated transportation or schools would have been met with a violent response from racists?

3. *Limited emergencies.* The Minnesota statute expired in May 1935, presumably because the legislature naively expected the emergency to be over by then. What if the statute instead had said, "This moratorium shall be in effect until the Governor declares that the emergency no longer exists"? Should that have made a difference in the Court's analysis?

B. 1935-1937

The Court that decided *Nebbia* and *Blaisdell* consisted of three progressives (Stone, Brandeis, and Cardozo), the ultraconservative "four horsemen" (Van Devanter, McReynolds, Sutherland, and Butler), and two swing members (Roberts and Chief Justice Hughes). Roberts wrote *Nebbia* and joined in *Blaisdell*, but "as the New Deal was revealed in all its terrifying dimensions to the conservatives of the nation, he became ready for persuasion. As for the Chief Justice, he was neither clearly liberal nor stubbornly conservative, but he seemed to be much concerned

---

3. See Arthur Schlesinger, The Coming of the New Deal 42-44 (1959).

4. Recall Michele Landis Dauber's argument in The Sympathetic State (2013), that from the earliest times of our constitutional history, the felt need of legislatures to provide relief for "disasters" tested certain conceptions of "limited government." In Minnesota, one state supreme court judge compared "[t]he present nationwide and worldwide business and financial crisis" to a "flood, earthquake, or disturbance," depriving "millions of persons in this nation of their employment and means of earning a living for themselves and their families" and, therefore, generating "widespread want and suffering among our people. . . . " Home Building & Loan Assn v. Blaisdell, 189 Minn. 429, 249 N.W. 336, 340. Generally speaking we do not hold persons responsible for what happens to them as the result of natural disasters; instead we view such persons as victims of outside forces that they could not realistically be expected to have protected themselves against. To be the faultless victim of such a disaster is to make oneself eligible for public sympathy and, more to the point, aid. As Dauber argues, an important part of the argument made by proponents of the mortgage moratorium and, indeed, for much other welfare legislation at the time, was that those who had lost their jobs, and were now threatened with loss of their homes, were not in fact responsible for their fate, which was the result of general structural factors within the economy and society rather than individual weaknesses of character. This dispute about how to characterize those in want continues to play an important part in debates about "welfare" expenditures by the government. Is the attribution of personal responsibility for one's plight relevant to determining the constitutional ability of the state to rectify it?

for the Court's own dignity and was likely sometimes to swing with a conservative majority to avoid the criticism that might follow a 5 to 4 decision. In 1935, therefore, the majority shifted, and for two busy terms the Court waged what is surely the most ambitious dragon-fight in its long and checkered history."[5]

The most significant decisions of these terms struck down recovery measures of the New Deal.[6] They are discussed in Section II, infra. For present purposes, however, the most interesting decision is Morehead v. New York ex rel. Tipaldo, 298 U.S. 587 (1936). The Court invalidated a New York minimum wage law for women on the authority of Adkins v. Children's Hospital, 261 U.S. 525 (1923), which had struck down a District of Columbia minimum wage law. Justice Butler wrote for the five-Justice majority (including Roberts but not Hughes) that "the State is without power by any form of legislation to prohibit, change or nullify contracts between employers and adult women workers as to the amount of wages to be paid."

Morehead was decided in June 1936, toward the close of the term. Following Roosevelt's landslide election in November 1936, he offered his famous "court-packing" plan (discussed in Section II, infra), in which he proposed to add new Justices to the Supreme Court for every Justice over 70 who failed to retire. The plan generated significant opposition, including within Roosevelt's own party. Less than two months later, the Justices reversed field and explicitly overruled *Adkins*.

West Coast Hotel Co. v. Parrish

300 U.S. 379 (1937)

HUGHES, C.J.:

[T]he violation alleged by those attacking minimum wage regulation for women is deprivation of freedom of contract. What is this freedom? The Constitution does not speak of freedom of contract. It speaks of liberty and prohibits the deprivation of liberty without due process of law. In prohibiting that deprivation the Constitution does not recognize an absolute and uncontrollable liberty. Liberty in each of its phases has its history and connotation. But the liberty safeguarded is liberty in a social organization which requires the protection of law against the evils which menace the health, safety, morals and welfare of the people. Liberty under the Constitution is thus necessarily subject to the restraints of due process, and regulation which is reasonable in relation to its subject and is adopted in the interests of the community is due process. . . .

What can be closer to the public interest than the health of women and their protection from unscrupulous and overreaching employers? And if the protection of women is a legitimate end of the exercise of state power, how can it be said that the requirement of the payment of a minimum wage fairly fixed in order to meet the very necessities of existence is not an admissible means to that end? The legislature of the State was clearly entitled to consider the situation of women in

---

5. Robert McCloskey, supra n.1, at 110.

6. See, e.g., Schechter Poultry Corp. v. United States, 295 U.S. 495 (1935); Carter v. Carter Coal Co., 298 U.S. 238 (1936); United States v. Butler, 297 U.S. 1 (1936).

employment, the fact that they are in the class receiving the least pay, and that they are the ready victims of those who would take advantage of their necessitous circumstances. The legislature was entitled to adopt measures to reduce the evils of the "sweating system," the exploiting of workers at wages so low as to be insufficient to meet the bare cost of living, thus making their very helplessness the occasion of a most injurious competition. The legislature had the right to consider that its minimum wage requirements would be an important aid in carrying out its policy of protection. The adoption of similar requirements by many States evidences a deep-seated conviction both as to the presence of the evil and as to the means adapted to check it. Legislative response to that conviction cannot be regarded as arbitrary or capricious, and that is all we have to decide. Even if the wisdom of the policy be regarded as debatable and its effects uncertain, still the legislature is entitled to its judgment.

There is an additional and compelling consideration which recent economic experience has brought into a strong light. The exploitation of a class of workers who are in an unequal position with respect to bargaining power and are thus relatively defenseless against the denial of a living wage is not only detrimental to their health and well being but casts a direct burden for their support upon the community. What these workers lose in wages the taxpayers are called upon to pay. The bare cost of living must be met. We may take judicial notice of the unparalleled demands for relief which arose during the recent period of depression and still continue to an alarming extent despite the degree of economic recovery which has been achieved. It is unnecessary to cite official statistics to establish what is of common knowledge through the length and breadth of the land. While in the instant case no factual brief has been presented, there is no reason to doubt that the State of Washington has encountered the same social problem that is present elsewhere. The community is not bound to provide what is in effect a subsidy for unconscionable employers. The community may direct its law-making power to correct the abuse which springs from their selfish disregard of the public interest. . . .

Our conclusion is that the case of Adkins v. Children's Hospital should be, and it is, overruled.

[Justices Van Devanter, McReynolds, Sutherland, and Butler—the "four horsemen"—dissented, reaffirming their commitment to *Adkins* and *Morehead.*]

West Coast Hotel was soon followed by decisions upholding New Deal legislation under the commerce and spending powers.[7]

Just what brought about this judicial acquiescence remains somewhat obscure. The central figure is Owen Roberts, whose vote made the difference between *Morehead* and *West Coast Hotel.* He also provided the fifth vote in NLRB v. Jones & Laughlin Steel Corp., 301 U.S. 1 (1937), which upheld the National Labor Relations Act.

---

7. E.g., NLRB v. Jones & Laughlin Steel Corp., 301 U.S. 1 (1937); Steward Machine Co. v. Davis, 301 U.S. 548 (1937); see Section II of this chapter, infra.

In popular lore Roberts's change of heart became known as the "switch in time that saved the nine." Nevertheless, there are indications that Roberts had decided to cast his vote to uphold the minimum wage law in *West Coast Hotel* before Roosevelt presented Congress with the court-packing bill.[8] Whatever Roberts's motivation, Roosevelt's court-packing plan ultimately failed, and Supreme Court doctrine ultimately came to chart a new path.

C. *The Modern Doctrine of Economic Due Process*

Nebbia, Blaisdell, and *West Coast Hotel* marked a transformation in thought about the nature and purposes of judicial review. The problem that now faced the Court was to figure out exactly what that transformation meant.

United States v. Carolene Products Co.

304 U.S. 144 (1938)

Mr. Justice STONE delivered the opinion of the Court.

The question for decision is whether the "Filled Milk Act" of Congress of March 4, 1923 . . . which prohibits the shipment in interstate commerce of skimmed milk compounded with any fat or oil other than milk fat, so as to resemble milk or cream, transcends the power of Congress to regulate interstate commerce or infringes the Fifth Amendment.

[The statute contained a declaration by Congress that filled milk—i.e., skimmed milk combined with nondairy fats—"is an adulterated article of food, injurious to the public health, and its sale constitutes a fraud upon the public." The Appellee was indicted for shipping "'Milnut,' a compound of condensed skimmed milk and coconut oil made in imitation or semblance of condensed milk or cream." The Supreme Court first held that Congress had the power to prohibit shipment of adulterated foods in interstate commerce, and then addressed the due process challenge.]

Second. The prohibition of shipment of appellee's product in interstate commerce does not infringe the Fifth Amendment. . . .

[W]e might rest decision wholly on the presumption of constitutionality. But affirmative evidence also sustains the statute. In twenty years evidence has steadily accumulated of the danger to the public health from the general consumption of foods which have been stripped of elements essential to the maintenance of health. The Filled Milk Act was adopted by Congress after committee hearings, in the course of which eminent scientists and health experts testified. An extensive investigation

8. See Felix Frankfurter, Mr. Justice Roberts, 104 U. Pa. L. Rev. 311 (1955). For a rich assortment of views concerning Roberts's apparent "switch in time," see generally the sources cited supra n.1; see also Philip Bobbitt, Constitutional Fate: Theory of the Constitution 27-31, 39-42 (1982); Michael Ariens, A Thrice-Told Tale, or Felix the Cat, 107 Harv. L. Rev. 620 (1994).

was made of the commerce in milk compounds in which vegetable oils have been substituted for natural milk fat, and of the effect upon the public health of the use of such compounds as a food substitute for milk. The conclusions drawn from evidence presented at the hearings were embodied in reports of the House Committee on Agriculture and the Senate Committee on Agriculture and Forestry. Both committees concluded, as the statute itself declares, that the use of filled milk as a substitute for pure milk is generally injurious to health and facilitates fraud on the public.[a]

There is nothing in the Constitution which compels a Legislature, either national or state, to ignore such evidence, nor need it disregard the other evidence which amply supports the conclusions of the Congressional committees that the danger is greatly enhanced where an inferior product, like appellee's, is indistinguishable from a valuable food of almost universal use, thus making fraudulent distribution easy and protection of the consumer difficult.[b]

Here the prohibition of the statute is inoperative unless the product is "in imitation or semblance of milk, cream, or skimmed milk, whether or not condensed." Whether in such circumstance the public would be adequately protected by the prohibition of false labels and false branding imposed by the Pure Food and Drugs Act, or whether it was necessary to go farther and prohibit a substitute food product thought to be injurious to health if used as a substitute when the two are not distinguishable, was a matter for the legislative judgment and not that of courts. . . .

---

a. [footnote 2] The reports may be summarized as follows: There is an extensive commerce in milk compounds made of condensed milk from which the butter fat has been extracted and an equivalent amount of vegetable oil, usually coconut oil, substituted. These compounds resemble milk in taste and appearance and are distributed in packages resembling those in which pure condensed milk is distributed. By reason of the extraction of the natural milk fat the compounded product can be manufactured and sold at a lower cost than pure milk. Butter fat, which constitutes an important part of the food value of pure milk, is rich in vitamins, food elements which are essential to proper nutrition, and are wanting in vegetable oils. The use of filled milk as a dietary substitute for pure milk results, especially in the case of children, in undernourishment, and induces diseases which attend malnutrition. Despite compliance with the branding and labeling requirements of the Pure Food and Drugs Act, there is widespread use of filled milk as a food substitute for pure milk. This is aided by their identical taste and appearance, by the similarity of the containers in which they are sold, by the practice of dealers in offering the inferior product to customers as being as good as or better than pure condensed milk sold at a higher price, by customers' ignorance of the respective food values of the two products, and in many sections of the country by their inability to read the labels placed on the containers. Large amounts of filled milk, much of it shipped and sold in bulk, are purchased by hotels and boarding houses, and by manufactures of food products, such as ice cream, to whose customers labeling restrictions afford no protection.

b. [footnote 3] There is now an extensive literature indicating wide recognition by scientists and dietitians of the great importance to the public health of butter fat and whole milk as the prime source of vitamins, which are essential growth producing and disease preventing elements in the diet.

When the Filled Milk Act was passed, eleven states had rigidly controlled the exploitation of filled milk, or forbidden it altogether. Some thirty-five states have now adopted laws which in terms, or by their operation, prohibit the sale of filled milk.

Appellee raises no valid objection to the present statute by arguing that its prohibition has not been extended to oleomargarine or other butter substitutes in which vegetable fats or oils are substituted for butter fat. The Fifth Amendment has no equal protection clause, and even that of the Fourteenth, applicable only to the states, does not compel their Legislatures to prohibit all like evils, or none. A Legislature may hit at an abuse which it has found, even though it has failed to strike at another.

Third. We may assume for present purposes that no pronouncement of a Legislature can forestall attack upon the constitutionality of the prohibition which it enacts by applying opprobrious epithets to the prohibited act, and that a statute would deny due process which precluded the disproof in judicial proceedings of all facts which would show or tend to show that a statute depriving the suitor of life, liberty, or property had a rational basis.

But such we think is not the purpose or construction of the statutory characterization of filled milk as injurious to health and as a fraud upon the public. There is no need to consider it here as more than a declaration of the legislative findings deemed to support and justify the action taken as a constitutional exertion of the legislative power, aiding informed judicial review, as do the reports of legislative committees, by revealing the rationale of the legislation. Even in the absence of such aids, the existence of facts supporting the legislative judgment is to be presumed, for regulatory legislation affecting ordinary commercial transactions is not to be pronounced unconstitutional unless in the light of the facts made known or generally assumed it is of such a character as to preclude the assumption that it rests upon some rational basis within the knowledge and experience of the legislators.[c]

---

c. [footnote 4] There may be narrower scope for operation of the presumption of constitutionality when legislation appears on its face to be within a specific prohibition of the Constitution, such as those of the first ten Amendments, which are deemed equally specific when held to be embraced within the Fourteenth. See Stromberg v. California, 283 U.S. 359, 369, 370; Lovell v. Griffin, 303 U.S. 444.

It is unnecessary to consider now whether legislation which restricts those political processes which can ordinarily be expected to bring about repeal of undesirable legislation, is to be subjected to more exacting judicial scrutiny under the general prohibitions of the Fourteenth Amendment than are most other types of legislation. On restrictions upon the right to vote, see Nixon v. Herndon, 273 U.S. 536; Nixon v. Condon, 286 U.S. 73; on restraints upon the dissemination of information, see Near v. Minnesota, 283 U.S. 697, 713-714, 718-720, 722; Grosjean v. American Press Co., 297 U.S. 233; Lovell v. Griffin, supra; on interferences with political organizations, see Stromberg v. California, supra, 283 U.S. 359, 369; Fiske v. Kansas, 274 U.S. 380; Whitney v. California, 274 U.S. 357, 377-378; Herndon v. Lowry, 301 U.S. 242; and see Holmes, J., in Gitlow v. New York, 268 U.S. 652, 673; as to prohibition of peaceable assembly, see De Jonge v. Oregon, 299 U.S. 353, 365.

Nor need we enquire whether similar considerations enter into the review of statutes directed at particular religious, Pierce v. Society of Sisters, 268 U.S. 510, or national, Meyer v. Nebraska, 262 U.S. 390; Bartels v. Iowa, 262 U.S. 404; Farrington v. Tokushige, 273 U.S. 284, or racial minorities. Nixon v. Herndon, supra; Nixon v. Condon, supra; whether prejudice against discrete and insular minorities may be a special condition, which tends seriously to curtail the operation of those political processes ordinarily to be relied upon to protect minorities, and which may call for a correspondingly more searching judicial inquiry. Compare McCulloch v. Maryland, 4 Wheat. 316, 428; South Carolina State Highway Department v. Barnwell Bros., 303 U.S. 177, [184] n.2, and cases cited.

The present statutory findings affect appellee no more than the reports of the Congressional committees and since in the absence of the statutory findings they would be presumed, their incorporation in the statute is no more prejudicial than surplusage.

Where the existence of a rational basis for legislation whose constitutionality is attacked depends upon facts beyond the sphere of judicial notice, such facts may properly be made the subject of judicial inquiry, and the constitutionality of a statute predicated upon the existence of a particular state of facts may be challenged by showing to the court that those facts have ceased to exist. Similarly we recognize that the constitutionality of a statute, valid on its face, may be assailed by proof of facts tending to show that the statute as applied to a particular article is without support in reason because the article, although within the prohibited class, is so different from others of the class as to be without the reason for the prohibition, though the effect of such proof depends on the relevant circumstances of each case, as for example the administrative difficulty of excluding the article from the regulated class. But by their very nature such inquiries, where the legislative judgment is drawn in question, must be restricted to the issue whether any state of facts either known or which could reasonably be assumed affords support for it. Here the demurrer challenges the validity of the statute on its face and it is evident from all the considerations presented to Congress, and those of which we may take judicial notice, that the question is at least debatable whether commerce in filled milk should be left unregulated, or in some measure restricted, or wholly prohibited. As that decision was for Congress, neither the finding of a court arrived at by weighing the evidence, nor the verdict of a jury can be substituted for it.

Mr. Justice BLACK concurs in the result and in all of the opinion except the part marked "Third."

[Justice Butler concurred in the result, arguing that the defendant should be permitted to prove at trial that Milnut was not injurious to public health and that its sale was not a fraud on the public, as alleged in the indictment. A statute that excluded products that were demonstrably not injurious to health or calculated to deceive would violate the Fifth Amendment's Due Process Clause. Justice McReynolds dissented. Justices Cardozo and Reed took no part in the consideration or decision of the case.]

DISCUSSION

1. *Common law baselines and economic redistribution. Carolene Products* presents the basic problem of justifying judicial review of legislation after the 1937 transformation in constitutional thought. The use of concepts like the police power or substantive limitations derived from common law categories is essentially discarded. As *West Coast Hotel* recognized, common law rules of contract formation might actually create a "subsidy for unconscionable employers." Nor could regulation of wages and hours be dismissed, as in *Lochner* itself, as an illicit attempt at redistribution. If common law rules themselves could be viewed as a "subsidy," then the distribution of income was partly produced by the choice of legal regime. There was no natural or prepolitical baseline to measure what was redistributional. (Also, recall that the Sixteenth Amendment rather plainly contemplated explicit governmental efforts to reduce economic inequality, see supra n.2.)

Instead, in *West Coast Hotel,* the Court holds that "regulation which is reasonable in relation to its subject and is adopted in the interests of the community is due process." How does the Court establish the criteria of reasonableness and public spiritedness here?

Note the different justifications for upholding the statute in the parts of the opinion marked "Second" and "Third." Do they establish that the legislation is reasonable and in the public interest in the same way? After the discussion in "Third," what exactly does "rational basis" mean?

2. *Interest group pluralism.* One way of justifying the virtual abdication of judicial review in *Carolene Products* is a theory of interest group pluralism. Under this theory, the "public interest" has no real substantive content. It is (and should be) determined largely by whatever majorities happen to want at a given time. The political process allows different groups to form coalitions and to lobby legislators and other government officials to promote their particular interests. The only requirement of due process is that legislators (or those charged with defending the law) be able to explain how serving these goals will also serve the general good. As a result, a court reviewing the statute will strive to put the best face on legislation that may in fact serve a particular interest group.

For example, Professor Geoffrey Miller points out that the legislation at issue in *Carolene Products* was the result of a powerful dairy industry that feared the economic challenge posed by the new purveyors of filled milk. Geoffrey P. Miller, The True Story of *Carolene Products,* 1987 Sup. Ct. Rev. 397. Miller describes the "scientific case against filled milk" as "bogus from the start" (at 420) and argues that the background of *Carolene Products* is best analyzed as "one discrete minority—the nation's dairy farmers and their allies—obtain[ing] legislation harmful to consumers and the public at large" by raising the price of milk (at 428).

Implicit in this interest group theory is that the democratic process is basically fair and that people aggrieved by unjust laws can employ the political process to repeal them. In other words, the pluralist model assumes that no groups persistently exercise inappropriate or unfair degrees of political power in a democracy. Even the Court understood that this assumption was (at least sometimes) unrealistic when it announced its theory of rational basis review in *Carolene Products*; hence it offered a famous caveat in a footnote.

3. *The footnote.* Given the virtual abdication of judicial review of economic legislation implied by the last part of Stone's opinion, why should the Court ever strike down any legislation? Couldn't almost any piece of legislation pass his watered-down test of rationality? Recall that at the same time, Justice Stone and his more liberal colleagues were increasingly trying to protect civil rights and civil liberties like freedom of speech and religion. They saw the rise of fascism in Europe, and were concerned about racial and religious prejudice in the United States. The problem was how to square their desire to protect civil rights and civil liberties with their preference for judicial restraint elsewhere.[9]

Footnote four of the Court's opinion (footnote c in the text) offers a tentative answer to this problem. The first paragraph, inserted at Chief Justice Hughes's request, argues that judicial review is justified by textual commitments in the

9. See Robert Cover, The Origins of Judicial Activism in the Protection of Minorities, 91 Yale L.J. 1287, 1293 (1982).

Constitution, including most prominently the Bill of Rights. Note the reference to incorporation in this paragraph's suggestion that certain portions of the federal Bill "are deemed equally specific [against states] when held to be embraced within the Fourteenth" Amendment (citing, e.g., *Stromberg*). Note also Hughes's effort to distinguish between "specific" provisions of the Bill of Rights and other presumably less specific provisions. Recall Hughes's efforts to draw a similar distinction in *Blaisdell.* But is the language of the Bill of Rights any more "specific" than that of, say, the Contract Clause?

The second and third paragraphs, however, justify judicial review on a different basis, that of protecting democracy. According to this theory:[10]

> The political process works effectively most of the time; representative democracy can generally be trusted to act in the public interest. Nevertheless, in a small, selected group of cases, which can be readily identified, the process malfunctions. In that marginal set of cases the judiciary properly may subject legislation to a higher level of scrutiny, not because it is authorized to impose its value choices upon the majority, but because the process itself is defective, undemocratic, impure. And in the very act of excluding these marginal situations from the norm, the judiciary demonstrates a double fidelity to democracy: First, because it avoids interfering in the normal processes of democratic institutions, and second, because it intervenes in those and only those abnormal cases in which the democratic ideals that justify judicial deference have been disserved.

Hence, footnote four suggested that protecting democracy by protecting democratic civil rights and certain "discrete and insular" minorities could form a new justification for judicial review of legislation. This justification for judicial review, only gestured at in footnote four of *Carolene Products,* was taken up by judges and legal scholars over the course of succeeding decades, and became highly influential in the 1970s and 1980s.[11] The notion that courts should exercise judicial review almost exclusively to protect democracy and guarantee the fairness of legal processes was developed into a general theory of judicial review by John Hart Ely in his influential 1980 book, Democracy and Distrust. For many legal thinkers "footnote four" became symbolic of the general post-1937 approach to judicial review, and spawned an enormous scholarly literature.[12]

---

10. Jack M. Balkin, The Footnote, 83 Nw. U. L. Rev. 275, 298-299 (1989).

11. See, e.g., Owen Fiss, Foreword: The Forms of Justice, 93 Harv. L. Rev. 1, 6 (1979) ("The great and modern charter for ordering the relation between judges and other agencies of government is footnote four of *Carolene Products.*").

12. In addition to Balkin, supra, see Louis Lusky, By What Right? (1975); Bruce A. Ackerman, Beyond *Carolene Products,* 98 Harv. L. Rev. 713 (1985); Milner Ball, Judicial Protection of Powerless Minorities, 59 Iowa L. Rev. 1059 (1974); Lea Brilmayer, *Carolene,* Conflicts and the Fate of the "Insider-Outsider," 134 U. Pa. L. Rev. 1291 (1986); Robert M. Cover, The Origins of Judicial Activism in the Protection of Minorities, 91 Yale L.J. 1287 (1982). The response to Ely's book created its own literature. See, e.g., Laurence Tribe, The Puzzling Persistence of Process-Based Constitutional Theories, 89 Yale L.J. 1063 (1980); Symposium: Judicial Review v. Democracy, 42 Ohio St. L.J. 1 (1981); Douglas Laycock, Taking Constitutions Seriously: A Theory of Judicial Review (Book Review), 59 Tex. L. Rev. 343 (1981).

Nevertheless, this approach is not without its own problems. How does one tell when the democratic process is functioning correctly other than by reference to the substantive results it produces? What makes a minority "discrete and insular" and therefore deserving of protection? Shouldn't courts also protect minorities that are hidden and diffuse and thus unable to form effective lobbies and coalitions?[13] Are there any rights that cannot be justified on the basis of protecting democracy or fair legal process, and if so, are they without constitutional protection (at least in court)?[14] Put another way, are constitutional rights protected only to the extent that one can show some direct connection to democratic malfunction? How thick a conception of democracy are courts entitled to protect?[15] *Carolene Products* assumes that economic questions should be left to the political process. But what if democracy itself is undermined by too great an inequality of wealth, or by the ability of very wealthy individuals and corporations to leverage their wealth to subtly control the political process and hamstring reforms?

Perhaps most importantly, the *Carolene Products* theory of judicial review assumes that judicial review is exceptional because defects in the democratic process are comparatively rare. But if the democratic process is skewed because of previous injustices, inequalities of wealth, social stratification, deep-seated prejudices, gerrymandered districts, self-dealing by politicians, and bureaucratic obstruction, shouldn't more and more situations fall into the world described by the footnote (judicial scrutiny) rather than the world described by the text (judicial deference)? Conversely, if courts simply accept the existing system as basically democratic, won't they indulge in the same fictions about formal liberty and formal equality that characterized the *Lochner* era (although this time to uphold rather than invalidate legislative action)?

4. *Later cases.* Between 1937 and 1941, the Court's composition changed radically. The progressive Justices were succeeded by other progressives,[16] and the old

---

13. Ackerman, supra n.12 (offering the example of sexual orientation minorities).

14. Consider for example, to what extent rights of bodily and sexual autonomy can be justified on the grounds of democracy and fair legal process. Ely famously argued that they could not be. Of course, one might respond that the protection of reproductive rights and sexual autonomy is actually a question of civic equality, which is necessary for democracy. Alternatively, Douglas NeJaime and Reva Siegel argue that judicial protection of sexual autonomy and reproductive rights actually encourages democratic mobilization and participation in democratic politics because it allows groups previously marginalized in democratic politics (or by the criminal law) to organize around rights guarantees. See Douglas NeJaime and Reva Siegel, Answering the *Lochner* Objection: Reexamining Substantive Due Process and the Role of Courts in a Democracy, __ N.Y.U. L. Rev. __ (forthcoming 2021) ("Groups that are marginalized in democratic politics may find that courts provide *alternative fora* with different institutional features that amplify marginalized groups' ability to communicate in democratic politics").

15. See, e.g., Jack M. Balkin, The Constitution of Status, 106 Yale L.J. 2313 (1997) (arguing that the Constitution is ultimately concerned not only with democratic processes but also with a democratic culture, which is opposed to unjust social structures and status hierarchies).

16. Frankfurter replaced Cardozo (1939), who himself had replaced Holmes in 1932; Douglas replaced Brandeis (1939); Stone succeeded Hughes to the Chief Justiceship (1941); Jackson succeeded to Stone's seat as Associate Justice (1941).

conservatives (Van Devanter, McReynolds, Butler, and Sutherland) were replaced by New Dealers.[17] It became increasingly doubtful whether economic regulations had to meet even the minimal requirements suggested by *West Coast Hotel* and *Carolene Products*.

In Olsen v. Nebraska, 313 U.S. 236 (1941), a unanimous Court overruled Ribnik v. McBride, 277 U.S. 350 (1928), to uphold a statute fixing the maximum fee that an employment agency could collect from an employee. Justice Douglas wrote:

> We are not concerned . . . with the wisdom, need, or appropriateness of the legislation. Differences of opinion on that score suggest a choice which "should be left where . . . it was left by the Constitution—to the States and to Congress." There is no necessity for the state to demonstrate before us that evils persist despite the competition which attends the bargaining in this field. In final analysis, the only constitutional prohibitions or restraints which respondents have suggested for the invalidation of this legislation are those notions of public policy embodied in earlier decisions of this Court but which, as Mr. Justice Holmes long admonished, should not be read into the Constitution. Since they do not find expression in the Constitution we cannot give them continuing vitality as standards by which the constitutionality of the economic and social programs of the states is to be determined.

The same year, in United States v. Darby, 312 U.S. 100 (1941), the Court—once again, unanimously—sustained the federal Fair Labor Standards Act of 1938 against a variety of constitutional challenges. With respect to the due process objection to the Act's fixing of maximum hours and minimum wages for men, Justice Stone was content to write for the Court:

> Since our decision in West Coast Hotel Co. v. Parrish, it is no longer open to question that the fixing of a minimum wage is within the legislative power and that the bare fact of its exercise is not a denial of due process under the Fifth more than under the Fourteenth Amendment. Nor is it any longer open to question that it is within the legislative power to fix maximum hours. Similarly the statute is not objectionable because applied alike to both men and women.

In Lincoln Federal Labor Union v. Northwestern Iron & Metal Co., 335 U.S. 525 (1949), a unanimous Court sustained a state prohibition of closed shops. Justice Black noted that the Court had rejected "the *Allgeyer-Lochner-Adair-Coppage* constitutional doctrine" and had returned "to the earlier constitutional principle that states have power to legislate against what are found to be injurious practices in their internal commercial and business affairs, so long as their laws do not run afoul of some specific federal constitutional prohibition." In Day-Brite Lighting, Inc. v. Missouri, 342 U.S. 421 (1952), the Court sustained a law allowing employees

17. Black replaced Van Devanter (1937); Reed replaced Sutherland (1938); Murphy replaced Butler (1940); and Byrnes replaced McReynolds (1941). Roberts, who had abandoned his conservative brethren, remained on the Court until 1945.

four hours' leave with full pay on Election Day. Justice Douglas wrote that the legislature's judgment "may be a debatable one. . . . But if our recent cases mean anything, they leave debatable issues as respects business, economic, and social affairs to legislative decision." Justice Frankfurter concurred in the result without opinion, and Justice Jackson dissented, stating that "[g]etting out the vote is not the business of employers. . . . It is either the voter's own business or the State's business." In Ferguson v. Skrupa, 372 U.S. 726 (1963), which sustained a Kansas statute prohibiting anyone except lawyers from engaging in the business of "debt adjusting,"[18] Justice Black wrote for the Court:

> [T]he Kansas Legislature was free to decide for itself that legislation was needed to deal with the business of debt adjusting. Unquestionably, there are arguments showing that the business of debt adjusting has social utility, but such arguments are properly addressed to the legislature, not to us. We refuse to sit as a "superlegislature to weigh the wisdom of legislation." . . . Whether the legislature takes for its textbook Adam Smith, Herbert Spencer, Lord Keynes, or some other is no concern of ours. The Kansas debt adjusting statute may be wise or unwise. But relief, if any be needed, lies not with us but with the body constituted to pass laws for the State of Kansas.

Justice Harlan concurred in the judgment, citing Williamson v. Lee Optical Co., a case that came to symbolize the Court's deferential approach to economic regulation.

Williamson v. Lee Optical Co.

348 U.S. 483 (1955)

DOUGLAS, J. . . .

This suit was instituted in the District Court to have an Oklahoma law declared unconstitutional and to enjoin state officials from enforcing it for the reason that it allegedly violated various provisions of the Federal Constitution. The matter was heard by a District Court of three judges, as required by 28 U.S.C. §2281. That court held certain provisions of the law unconstitutional. The case is here by appeal.

The District Court held unconstitutional portions of three sections of the Act. First, it held invalid under the Due Process Clause of the Fourteenth Amendment the portions of §2 which make it unlawful for any person not a licensed optometrist or ophthalmologist to fit lenses to a face or to duplicate or replace into frames lenses or other optical appliances, except upon written prescriptive authority of an Oklahoma licensed ophthalmologist or optometrist.

---

18. Debt adjusting is "the making of a contract . . . with a particular debtor whereby the debtor agrees to pay a certain amount of money periodically to the person engaged in the debt adjusting business who shall for a consideration distribute the same among certain specified creditors in accordance with a plan agreed upon."

An ophthalmologist is a duly licensed physician who specializes in the care of the eyes. An optometrist examines eyes for refractive error, recognizes (but does not treat) diseases of the eye, and fills prescriptions for eyeglasses. The optician is an artisan qualified to grind lenses, fill prescriptions, and fit frames.

The effect of §2 is to forbid the optician from fitting or duplicating lenses without a prescription from an ophthalmologist or optometrist. In practical effect, it means that no optician can fit old glasses into new frames or supply a lens, whether it be a new lens or one to duplicate a lost or broken lens, without a prescription. The District Court conceded that it was in the competence of the police power of a State to regulate the examination of the eyes. But it rebelled at the notion that a State could require a prescription from an optometrist or ophthalmologist "to take old lenses and place them in new frames and then fit the completed spectacles to the *face* of the eyeglass wearer." . . . The Court found that through mechanical devices and ordinary skills the optician could take a broken lens or a fragment thereof, measure its power, and reduce it to prescriptive terms. The Court held that "Although on this precise issue of duplication, the legislature in the instant regulation was dealing with a matter of public interest, the particular means chosen are neither reasonably necessary nor reasonably related to the end sought to be achieved." It was, accordingly, the opinion of the court that this provision of the law violated the Due Process Clause by arbitrarily interfering with the optician's right to do business. . . .

The Oklahoma law may exact a needless, wasteful requirement in many cases. But it is for the legislature, not the courts, to balance the advantages and disadvantages of the new requirement. It appears that in many cases the optician can easily supply the new frames or new lenses without reference to the old written prescription. It also appears that many written prescriptions contain no directive data in regard to fitting spectacles to the face. But in some cases the directions contained in the prescription are essential, if the glasses are to be fitted so as to correct the particular defects of vision or alleviate the eye condition. The legislature might have concluded that the frequency of occasions when a prescription is necessary was sufficient to justify this regulation of the fitting of eyeglasses. Likewise, when it is necessary to duplicate a lens, a written prescription may or may not be necessary. But the legislature might have concluded that one was needed often enough to require one in every case. Or the legislature may have concluded that eye examinations were so critical, not only for correction of vision but also for detection of latent ailments or diseases, that every change in frames and every duplication of a lens should be accompanied by a prescription from a medical expert. To be sure, the present law does not require a new examination of the eyes every time the frames are changed or the lenses duplicated. For if the old prescription is on file with the optician, he can go ahead and make the new fitting or duplicate the lenses. But the law need not be in every respect logically consistent with its aims to be constitutional. It is enough that there is an evil at hand for correction, and that it might be thought that the particular legislative measure was a rational way to correct it. . . .

Secondly, the District Court held that it violated the Equal Protection Clause of the Fourteenth Amendment to subject opticians to this regulatory system and to exempt, as §3 of the Act does, all sellers of ready-to-wear glasses. The problem of legislative classification is a perennial one, admitting of no doctrinaire definition. Evils in the same field may be of different dimensions and proportions, requiring different remedies. Or so the legislature may think. Or the reform may take one step at a time, addressing itself to the phase of the problem which seems most acute to the legislative mind. The legislature may select one phase of one field and apply a remedy there, neglecting the others. The prohibition of the Equal Protection Clause goes no further than the invidious discrimination. We cannot say that that point has been reached here. For all this record shows, the ready-to-wear branch of this business may not loom large in Oklahoma or may present problems of regulation distinct from the other branch.

Third, the District Court held unconstitutional, as violative of the Due Process Clause of the Fourteenth Amendment, that portion of §3 which makes it unlawful "to solicit the sale of . . . frames, mountings . . . or any other optical appliances." . . . [R]egulation of the advertising of eyeglass frames was said to intrude "into a mercantile field only casually related to the visual care of the public" and restrict "an activity which in no way can detrimentally affect the people."

An eyeglass frame, considered in isolation, is only a piece of merchandise. But an eyeglass frame is not used in isolation . . . ; it is used with lenses; and lenses, pertaining as they do to the human eye, enter the field of health. Therefore, the legislature might conclude that to regulate one effectively it would have to regulate the other. Or it might conclude that both the sellers of frames and the sellers of lenses were in a business where advertising should be limited or even abolished in the public interest. . . . The advertiser of frames may be using his ads to bring in customers who will buy lenses. If the advertisement of lenses is to be abolished or controlled, the advertising of frames must come under the same restraints; or so the legislature might think. We see no constitutional reason why a State may not treat all who deal with the human eye as members of a profession who should use no merchandising methods for obtaining customers.

Fourth, the District Court held unconstitutional, as violative of the Due Process Clause of the Fourteenth Amendment, the provision of §4 of the Oklahoma Act which reads as follows: "No person, firm, or corporation engaged in the business of retailing merchandise to the general public shall rent space, sublease departments, or otherwise permit any person purporting to do eye examination or visual care to occupy space in such retail store."

It seems to us that this regulation . . . is an attempt to free the profession, to as great an extent as possible, from all taints of commercialism. It certainly might be easy for an optometrist with space in a retail store to be merely a front for the retail establishment. In any case, the opportunity for that nexus may be too great for safety, if the eye doctor is allowed inside the retail store. Moreover, it may be deemed important to effective regulation that the eye doctor be restricted to geographical locations that reduce the temptations of commercialism. Geographical location may be an important consideration in a legislative program which aims to raise the treatment of the human eye to a strictly professional level. We cannot say that the regulation has no rational relation to that objective and therefore is beyond constitutional bounds. . . .

DISCUSSION

1. *"Rationality" analysis: Economic equal protection.* Williamson v. Lee Optical involved challenges not only under the Due Process Clause but also under the Equal Protection Clause. In contrast to the Due Process Clause, the *Lochner* Court had given the Equal Protection Clause little importance outside the context of race. In *Williamson,* the Court treated both clauses as affording essentially the same degree of protection in cases of ordinary social and economic regulation. Whether plaintiffs claimed that a law violated their economic liberties or that the law made arbitrary distinctions, the Court subjected the law to the test of "minimum rationality": The infringement on liberty or the distinctions made had to be "rational." A standard case capturing the post-1937 view of "ordinary" equal protection analysis is Railway Express Agency v. New York, 336 U.S. 106 (1949), which involved a New York City regulation providing that "[n]o person shall operate . . . in or upon any street an advertising vehicle; provided that nothing herein contained shall prevent the putting of business notices upon business delivery vehicles, so long as such vehicles are engaged in the usual business or regular work of the owner and are not used merely or mainly for advertising." The ostensible purpose of this ordinance was to increase traffic safety by limiting potential distractions to drivers. What this meant, practically speaking, was that the Railway Express Agency, which owned hundreds of delivery vans, could not rent space on the side of its delivery vans to businesses wishing to advertise their products. R.E.A. was convicted for violating the ordinance after carrying advertisements for cigarettes, a radio station, and a circus. However, the New York Times Company, which also owned hundreds of delivery trucks, could freely advertise *The New York Times* on the sides of *its* trucks. Without dissent,[19] the Court upheld the ordinance against R.E.A.'s equal protection challenge.

Writing for the Court, Justice Douglas noted R.E.A.'s contention

> that unequal treatment on the basis of such a distinction is not justified by the aim and purpose of the regulation. It is said, for example, that one of appellant's trucks carrying the advertisement of a commercial house would not cause any greater distraction of pedestrians and vehicle drivers than if the commercial house carried the same advertisement on its own truck. . . . It is therefore contended that the classification which the regulation makes has no relation to the traffic problem since a violation turns not on what kind of advertisements are carried on trucks but on whose trucks they are carried.

Justice Douglas, however, described this analysis as "superficial," for he declared that "local authorities may well have concluded that those who advertise their own wares on their trucks do not present the same traffic problem in view of the nature

---

19. Though Justice Rutledge acquiesced in the Court's opinion, "dubitante on the question of equal protection of the laws."

or extent of the advertising which they use. It would take a degree of omniscience which we lack to say that such is not the case." On that assumption, then, the Court "cannot say that the judgment is not an allowable one." The classification at issue relates "to the purpose for which it is made and does not contain the kind of discrimination against which the Equal Protection Clause affords protection."[20]

For a more recent illustration of the modern Court's generally deferential approach to issues of economic regulation, consider Nordlinger v. Hahn, 505 U.S. 1 (1992). The case involved an equal protection challenge to California's well-known initiative, Proposition 13, which generally pegged state property taxes to the initial purchase price, rather than the current market price, of each parcel of real estate. With steeply rising property values, the Proposition 13 regime quickly gave rise to wide property-tax differentials (often more than 10 to 1) for homes of comparable current market value. Writing for himself and seven others, Justice Blackmun upheld this regime, noting that the equal protection standard "is especially deferential in the context of classifications made by complex tax laws." Given this deference, the Court had

> no difficulty in ascertaining at least two rational or reasonable considerations of difference or policy that justify denying petitioner the benefits of her neighbors' lower assessments. [These neighbors had houses of comparable current market value, but had bought them many years earlier, at much lower prices.] First, the State has a legitimate interest in local neighborhood preservation, continuity, and stability. The State therefore legitimately can decide to structure its tax system to discourage rapid turnover in ownership of homes and businesses, for example, in order to inhibit displacement of lower income families by the forces of gentrification or of established, "mom-and-pop" businesses by newer chain operations. By permitting older owners to pay progressively less in taxes than new owners of comparable property, the . . . assessment scheme rationally furthers this interest.

---

20. Is *Railway Express* still good law? At the time it was decided, the Supreme Court did not treat garden-variety commercial advertising as "speech" whose regulation triggered heightened (more-than-rational-basis) scrutiny under the First Amendment. In Greater New Orleans Broadcasting Association, Inc. v. United States, 527 U.S. 173 (1999), the Court unanimously struck down a federal statute regulating casino advertising. Some casino advertisers were covered by the statute and other casino advertisers were not. The overall pattern of exclusion and inclusion struck the Court as so "pierced by exemptions and inconsistencies" as to violate the First Amendment freedom of speech. Inexplicably, *Railway Express* went unmentioned in the opinion.

Has the Supreme Court begun to turn the First Amendment into a font for a new, *Lochner*-like jurisprudence protecting the rights of corporations and other propertied folk? For an early argument (as of 1990) that this might be so, see Jack M. Balkin, Some Realism About Pluralism: Legal Realist Approaches to the First Amendment, 1990 Duke L.J. 375. The law in *Greater New Orleans* may well have been a patchwork. But was it truly invidious? Was there any true First Amendment threat, such as incumbent-entrenchment or political debate-skewing, afoot? Consider the argument of Judge Linde, infra, that a law should not be declared unconstitutional simply because judges find it to be a crazy quilt (consider, for example, the tax code), but only if judges can find an affirmatively impermissible government purpose at work.

> Second, the State legitimately can conclude that a new owner at the time of acquiring his property does not have the same reliance interest warranting protection against higher taxes as does an existing owner. The State may deny a new owner at the point of purchase the right to "lock in" to the same assessed value as is enjoyed by an existing owner of comparable property, because an existing owner rationally may be thought to have vested expectations in his property or home that are more deserving of protection than the anticipatory expectations of a new owner at the point of purchase. A new owner has full information about the scope of future tax liability before acquiring the property, and if he thinks the future tax burden is too demanding, he can decide not to complete the purchase at all. By contrast, the existing owner, already saddled with his purchase, does not have the option of deciding not to buy his home if taxes become prohibitively high. To meet his tax obligations, he might be forced to sell his home or to divert his income away from the purchase of food, clothing, and other necessities. In short, the State may decide that it is worse to have owned and lost, than never to have owned at all.[21]

Justice Stevens dissented, arguing that the law was "arbitrary and unreasonable" and "irrational" in treating new owners so differently from old owners.[22]

2. *Gunther's Foreword.* In a famous article, Gerald Gunther argued that in reviewing economic legislation for rationality, the Court should be "less willing to supply justifying rationales by exercising its imagination." Gerald Gunther, Foreword, In Search of Evolving Doctrine on a Changing Court: A Model for a Newer Equal Protection, 86 Harv. L. Rev. 1 (1972). Rather, rationality review should require a statement of the state's purposes as gleaned from some "authoritative state source," including legislative history, or even from "a state court or state attorney general's description of [the legislation's] purpose." Do you agree?

With respect to judicial use of legislative history, note that many states do not regularly publish the reports of legislative committees and debates within the legislatures. Would Gunther's proposal mean, then, that states *must* begin publishing legislative records in order to provide evidence of the purposes underlying their handiwork? With respect to statements by a state attorney general, why wouldn't a lawyer representing the state posit *all* plausible legitimate objectives that might sustain a challenged law, even if no one suggested them in a committee report or in the legislature?

---

21. Is failure to get something you want but do not yet have ever different from losing something you already have? For a quick and accessible discussion of the concepts of "loss aversion" and the "endowment effect" and some of their possible implications for law, see Cass R. Sunstein, The Future of Law and Economics: Looking Forward: Behavioral Analysis of Law, 64 U. Chi. L. Rev. 1175, 1179-1181 (1997).

22. Suppose that California instead imposed no tax at all on homes as such, but simply imposed a very large tax on the purchase of a home, to be paid by the buyer upon purchase. Would Justice Stevens find this tax unconstitutional? Note that this tax in some ways treats new buyers even worse than did Proposition 13: They are forced to pay in one lump sum, rather than over the years, whereas old homeowners who simply keep their homes are not taxed at all.

3. *Legislative errors: Railroad Retirement Board v. Fritz.* Contra Gunther's suggestion, existing doctrine typically treats the actual purposes behind economic legislation as largely irrelevant to its constitutionality, as long as some hypothetical purpose exists that satisfies the requirements of minimum rationality. Nevertheless, should the Court inquire into whether members of the legislature were hoodwinked by lobbyists or misunderstood the terms of legislation they were voting on? Do the arguments for judicial deference to popular will make sense when the people's representatives do not know what they are voting for? If a court discovers that legislators were misled, should it strike down the law and "remand" the statute so that the legislature can properly reconsider the matter? Or does this solution place too great a demand on busy legislators?

In United States Railroad Retirement Board v. Fritz, 449 U.S. 166 (1980), the Court upheld a provision of the Railroad Retirement Act of 1974, which reorganized the pension system to save money. Under the Act, employees would continue to be able to receive Railroad Retirement and Social Security benefits plus an additional "windfall" or "dual" benefit if they worked at least one day, or "retained a current connection with" a railroad in 1974. The Bill, in essence, guaranteed that these benefits would be preserved for current employees but not for persons who were no longer in the railroad industry, even if their length of service and employment histories were identical in all other respects. Justice Brennan, in dissent, argued that the Bill was drafted by railroad management and labor representatives who did not represent the interests of former employees, and did not inform legislators that they were preserving benefits for current employees by reducing those for former employees. Indeed, Justice Brennan argued,

> the Joint Committee negotiators and Railroad Retirement Board members who testified at congressional hearings perpetuated the inaccurate impression that all retirees with earned vested dual benefits under prior law would retain their benefits unchanged. . . . Most striking is the following colloquy between Representative Dingell and Mr. Dempsey:
>
> "*Mr. Dingell:* Who is going to be adversely affected? Somebody has to get it in the neck on this. Who is going to be that lucky fellow?
>
> *Mr. Dempsey:* Well, I don't think so really. I think this is the situation in which everyone wins. Let me explain. . . .
>
> *Mr. Dingell:* Mr. Dempsey, I see some sleight of hand here but I don't see how it is happening. I applaud it but I would like to understand it. My problem is that you are going to go to a realistic system that is going to cost less but pay more in benefits. Now if you have accomplished this, I suggest we should put you in charge of the social security system."

Justice Rehnquist's majority opinion responded:

> [W]e disagree with the District Court's conclusion that Congress was unaware of what it accomplished or that it was misled by the groups that appeared before it. If this test were applied literally to every member of any legislature that ever voted on a law, there would be very few laws which would survive it. The language of the statute is clear, and we have historically assumed that Congress intended what it enacted. To be sure, appellees lost a political battle in which they had a strong interest, but this is neither the first nor the last time that such a result will occur in the legislative forum.

Justice Rehnquist then added, in a footnote:

> The Constitution presumes that, absent some reason to infer antipathy, even improvident decisions will eventually be rectified by the democratic processes and that judicial intervention is generally unwarranted, no matter how unwisely we may think a political branch has acted. Vance v. Bradley, 440 U.S. 93, 97 (1979).

4. *The constitutional basis for economic due process and equal protection.* It should be obvious that the Fourteenth Amendment does not and should not prohibit all "discrimination" as such, at least if "discrimination" simply means "distinctions among individuals or classes of individuals." The major business of any legislative body is deciding who or what should receive certain benefits or bear certain burdens. (For example, murder laws impose certain "burdens" on murderers and in that sense "discriminate" against the activity of murder.) Indeed, can you think of *any* laws that apply universally to all persons, things, or activities—that is, that do not classify at all?

If all laws in some sense discriminate, it is also true that all laws are in another sense perfectly rational and perfectly tailored. Every law tautologically accomplishes the precise result of the law itself. A regulation that limits emissions from blue cars and only blue cars might seem irrational if we focus only on the goal of emissions reduction, but the law perfectly accomplishes the objective of "reducing emissions from blue cars." To hold a law "irrational," it seems, judges must refuse to credit at least part of the law's tautological objective.[23] This refusal is easiest to defend when judges can point to something in the Constitution that renders a certain objective or purpose *itself* unconstitutional. For example, a law that limited only the emissions of cars owned by Black people might very well fit the joint purposes of reducing pollution and of disfavoring African-Americans—but the second purpose is *itself* a clear violation of the Fourteenth Amendment, read in light of its history. (Recall that the paradigm historical case of unequal protection, in the minds of the Reconstruction Congress, involved the infamous Black Codes that sought to stigmatize Black people and treat them unequally.)

But are laws designed to favor one industry over another constitutionally similar to laws targeting Black people for abuse? Consider how easily the laws challenged in *Railway Express Agency* and *Williamson* could have been upheld on the simple grounds that they promoted certain industries—newspapers and optometrists, respectively—favored by the regulations. Note Judge Hans Linde's comment on *Williamson*: "If Oklahoma had said that it gave independent optometrists a monopoly on fitting eyeglass frames in order to assure them the financial ability to render their other professional services at prices people could afford, there should be no need to demonstrate any health risks from having frames fitted by opticians in drug stores." On Linde's view, "[l]aws are not unconstitutional merely because they are shown to be useless" but only if they contravene "a constitutional criterion found elsewhere in the Constitution than in the due process clause itself." Hans Linde, Without "Due Process": Unconstitutional Law in Oregon, 49 Or. L. Rev. 125, 174, 177 n.154 (1970).

---

23. See Note, Legislative Purpose, Rationality, and Equal Protection, 82 Yale L.J. 123 (1972).

Linde's views, however, are in tension with Smith v. Cahoon, 283 U.S. 553 (1931), where Chief Justice Hughes, writing for a unanimous Court, invalidated a Florida statute that required commercial carriers to post liability bonds to indemnify persons injured through the carriers' negligence. Exempted from this requirement were carriers engaged exclusively in transporting farm, fish, and seafood products. Note the date of *Smith.* Is the case still good law today? Should it be? The Court called the statute "wholly arbitrary" so far as it "was designed to safeguard the public with respect to the use of the highways." But why wasn't the statute wholly nonarbitrary in accomplishing the *joint* purposes of highway safety and seafood subsidy? And what, precisely, is unconstitutional about government subsidies (even indirect ones) for seafood?

5. Lochner*'s legacy?* Consider the argument that judges and legislators "make" law in different ways. Whereas judges craft common law rules with an eye toward precedent and past practice, using techniques of analogic reasoning ("treating like cases alike") and detailed reason-giving, legislatures are authorized to make new rules, with sometimes arbitrary or at least artificial boundaries. These laws are legitimated by distinctive characteristics of the *legislative* process—democratic accountability rather than judicial reasoning. When judges require that legislators must make laws with the same kind of "rationality" characteristic of judicial opinions, the judiciary in effect subordinates legislative lawmaking to judicial lawmaking. In doing so, are judges engaging in a kind of *Lochner* jurisprudence, impermissibly privileging the common law process over the legislative process?

D. Modern Contract Clause Doctrine [Online]

E. Modern Takings Clause Doctrine[24] [Online]

II. THE CREATION OF THE NEW DEAL SETTLEMENT AND THE RELAXATION OF JUDICIAL CONSTRAINTS ON CONGRESSIONAL POWER

A. 1935-1936—The Supreme Court Confronts Roosevelt over Federal Power

The Great Depression, which began following the 1929 stock market crash, had devastating effects on the world economy, and the economy of the United States. At one point the unemployment rate rose to 25%. As the economy collapsed and incomes shrank, people could not pay their debts, putting banks under severe

---

24. See generally Joseph L. Sax, Takings and the Police Power, 74 Yale L.J. 36, 37 (1964); Frank Michelman, Property, Utility and Fairness: Comments on the Ethical Foundations of "Just Compensation Law," 80 Harv. L. Rev. 1165 (1967); Bruce Ackerman, Private Property and the Constitution (1977); Richard Epstein, Takings: Private Property and the Power of Eminent Domain (1985); Jed Rubenfeld, Usings, 102 Yale L.J. 1077 (1993).

strain. Many failed. When Franklin Roosevelt assumed the presidency in March 1932, he quickly declared a bank holiday to prevent runs on banks that would have had a crushing effect. Roosevelt's early response to the Great Depression was experimental, producing the fabled "100 days" in which Congress quickly passed many different laws, including the Glass-Steagall Act, the Homeowners Refinancing Act, the Agricultural Adjustment Act, the Securities Act of 1933, the Tennessee Valley Authority Act, and the National Industrial Recovery Act (NIRA). These early New Deal statutes and presidential orders formed part of what is now called the "First New Deal."

In three key cases between 1935 and 1936, the Supreme Court struck down several of the key recovery measures of the First New Deal, including the Agricultural Adjustment Act, the Bituminous Coal Act of 1935, and the National Industrial Recovery Act.

SCHECHTER POULTRY CORP. v. UNITED STATES, 295 U.S. 495 (1935): [The National Industrial Recovery Act was the centerpiece of Roosevelt's First New Deal. It sought to stabilize the economy by coopting businesses and trade associations to create codes of fair dealing and wage and price controls for various industries. The NIRA also gave workers the right to bargain collectively and form unions. In essence, the NIRA proposed that capital and labor work together in the public interest to restore the economy. The NIRA has often been described as an attempt to implement the political philosophy of "corporatism": The state organizes society into groups; these groups, in turn, are expected to work together with the state and with each other to generate durable settlements that reduce group conflict, promote social harmony, and serve the public interest.

The National Recovery Administration (NRA) created by the NIRA oversaw the creation of business codes that regulated various industries. *Schechter* involved a "Live Poultry Code" that had been established as "a code for fair competition for the live poultry industry of the metropolitan area in and about the City of New York." The Schechter family operated a kosher slaughterhouse accused of violating the poultry codes; the Schecters complained that the codes interfered with how they worked with local rabbis to obtain a kosher certification. Because the government charged the Schechters with selling sick chickens, the litigation became known as the "Sick Chicken Case."

The Supreme Court unanimously held that the federal government lacked power under the Commerce Clause to regulate wages and hours in New York poultry slaughterhouses that obtained almost all their live poultry from out of state but sold only to New York retailers.]

Hughes, C.J.:

In determining how far the federal government may go in controlling intrastate transactions upon the ground that they "affect" interstate commerce, there is a necessary and well-established distinction between direct and indirect effects. The precise line can be drawn only as individual cases arise, but the distinction is clear in principle. Direct effects are illustrated by the railroad cases we have cited, as, e.g., the effect of failure to use prescribed safety appliances on railroads which are the highways of both interstate and intrastate commerce, injury to an employee engaged in interstate transportation by the negligence of an employee engaged in an intrastate movement, the fixing of rates for intrastate transportation which unjustly discriminate against interstate commerce. But where the effect of intrastate transactions upon interstate commerce is merely indirect, such transactions remain within the domain of state power. If the commerce clause were construed to reach all enterprises and transactions which could be said to have an indirect effect upon interstate commerce, the federal authority would embrace practically all the activities of the people, and the authority of the state over its domestic concerns would exist only by sufferance of the federal government. . . .

The persons employed in slaughtering and selling in local trade are not employed in interstate commerce. Their hours and wages have no direct relation to interstate commerce. The question of how many hours these employees should work and what they should be paid differs in no essential respect from similar questions in other local businesses which handle commodities brought into a state and there dealt in as a part of its internal commerce.

[T]he government argues that hours and wages affect prices; that slaughterhouse men sell at a small margin above operating costs; that labor represents 50 to 60 per cent. of these costs; that a slaughterhouse operator paying lower wages or reducing his cost by exacting long hours of work translates his saving into lower prices; that this results in demands for a cheaper grade of goods: and that the cutting of prices brings about a demoralization of the price structure. Similar conditions may be adduced in relation to other businesses. The argument of the government proves too much. If the federal government may determine the wages and hours of employees in the internal commerce of a state, because of their relation to cost and prices and their indirect effect upon interstate commerce, it would seem that a similar control might be exerted over other elements of cost, also affecting prices, such as the number of employees, rents, advertising, methods of doing business, etc. All the processes of production and distribution that enter into cost could likewise be controlled. If the cost of doing an intrastate business is in itself the permitted object of federal control, the extent of the regulation of cost would be a question of discretion and not of power.

CARDOZO, J., concurring, joined by STONE, J.:

I find no authority in that grant for the regulation of wages and hours of labor in the intrastate transactions that make up the defendants' business. . . . There is a view of causation that would obliterate the distinction between what is national and what is local in the activities of commerce. Motion at the outer rim is communicated perceptibly, though minutely, to recording instruments at the center. A society such as ours "is an elastic medium which transmits all tremors throughout its territory; the only question is of their size." Per Learned Hand, J., in the court below. The law is not indifferent to considerations of degree. Activities local in their immediacy do not become interstate and national because of distant repercussions. What is near and what is distant may at times be uncertain. There is no penumbra of uncertainty obscuring judgment here. To find immediacy or directness here is to find it almost everywhere. If centripetal forces are to be isolated to the exclusion of the forces that oppose and counteract them, there will be an end to our federal system.

CARTER v. CARTER COAL CO., 298 U.S. 238 (1936): [The Bituminous Coal Act of 1935, another example of legislation in the First New Deal, was designed to stabilize the coal industry. It sought to prevent unfair competitive practices by setting wage and price controls, and to promote labor peace by legalizing collective bargaining between labor unions and management.

The Act imposed a 15 percent excise tax on the sale of coal by a mining company. Ninety percent of tax would be abated if the company accepted a code formulated by the National Bituminous Coal Commission.

Part II of the code (the price-fixing provisions) imposed minimum prices for the sale of coal. Part III of the code (the labor provisions) gave mining employees the right to organize and bargain collectively, and imposed minimum wage and maximum hour requirements determined by an administrative board.

The Supreme Court, citing the Child Labor Tax Case, held that the 15 percent excise tax could not be justified under Congress's power to tax, because it "is not imposed for [the purpose of raising] revenue but exacted as a penalty to compel compliance with the regulatory provisions of the act." It then asked whether Congress could pass the tax under the Commerce Clause. It concluded that the labor provisions of Part III were beyond Congress's Commerce power. Justice Sutherland wrote the majority opinion, joined by Justices McReynolds, Van Devanter, Butler, and Roberts.]

SUTHERLAND, J.:

[T]he proposition, often advanced and as often discredited, that the power of the federal government inherently extends to purposes affecting the Nation as a whole with which the states severally cannot deal or cannot adequately deal, and the related notion that Congress, entirely apart from those powers delegated by the Constitution, may enact laws to promote the general welfare, have never been accepted but always definitely rejected by this court. . . . In the Framers Convention, the proposal to confer a general power akin to that just discussed was included in Mr. Randolph's resolutions, the sixth of which, among other things, declared that the National Legislature ought to enjoy the legislative rights vested in Congress by the Confederation, and "moreover to legislate in all cases to which the separate States are incompetent, or in which the harmony of the United States may be interrupted by the exercise of individual Legislation." The convention, however, declined to confer upon Congress power in such general terms; instead of which it carefully limited the powers which it thought wise to intrust to Congress by specifying them, thereby denying all others not granted expressly or by necessary implication. It made no grant of authority to Congress to legislate substantively for the general welfare, United States v. Butler, and no such authority exists, save as the general welfare may be promoted by the exercise of the powers which are granted.

There are many subjects in respect of which the several states have not legislated in harmony with one another, and in which their varying laws and the failure of some of them to act at all have resulted in injurious confusion and embarrassment. The state laws with respect to marriage and divorce present a case in point; and the great necessity of national legislation on that subject has been from time to time vigorously urged. Other pertinent examples are laws with respect to negotiable instruments, desertion and nonsupport, certain phases of state taxation, and others which we do not pause to mention. In many of these fields of legislation, the necessity of bringing the applicable rules of law into general harmonious relation has been so great that a Commission on Uniform State Laws, composed of commissioners from every state in the Union, has for many years been industriously and successfully working to that end by preparing and securing the passage by the several states of uniform laws. If there be an easier and constitutional way to these desirable results through congressional action, it thus far has escaped discovery. . . .

Every journey to a forbidden end begins with the first step; and the danger of such a step by the federal government in the direction of taking over the powers of the states is that the end of the journey may find the states so despoiled of their powers, or—what may amount to the same thing—so relieved of the responsibilities which possession of the powers necessarily enjoins, as to reduce them to little more than geographical subdivisions of the national domain. It is safe to say that if, when the Constitution was under consideration, it had been thought that any such danger lurked behind its plain words, it would never have been ratified. . . .

As used in the Constitution, the word "commerce" is the equivalent of the phrase "intercourse for the purposes of trade," and includes transportation, purchase, sale, and exchange of commodities between the citizens of the different states. And the power to regulate commerce embraces the instruments by which commerce is carried on. . . .

The distinction between manufacture and commerce was discussed in Kidd v. Pearson, 128 U.S. 1 (1888) [holding that Iowa did not violate the dormant Commerce Clause when it prohibited the manufacturing of alcoholic beverages in Iowa, even if the product was sold in other states]. . . . Chief Justice Fuller, speaking for this court in United States v. E.C. Knight Co., said: . . . "Commerce succeeds to manufacture, and is not a part of it. . . . The fact that an article is manufactured for export to another state does not of itself make it an article of interstate commerce, and the intent of the manufacturer does not determine the time when the article or product passes from the control of the state and belongs to commerce. . . ."

That commodities produced or manufactured within a state are intended to be sold or transported outside the state does not render their production or manufacture subject to federal regulation under the commerce clause. . . .

We have seen that the word "commerce" is the equivalent of the phrase "intercourse for the purposes of trade." Plainly, the incidents leading up to and culminating in the mining of coal do not constitute such intercourse. The employment of men, the fixing of their wages, hours of labor, and working conditions, the bargaining in respect of these things—whether carried on separately or collectively—each and all constitute intercourse for the purposes of production, not of trade. The latter is a thing apart from the relation of employer and employee, which in all producing occupations is purely local in character. Extraction of coal from the mine is the aim and the completed result of local activities. Commerce in the coal mined is not brought into being by force of these activities, but by negotiations, agreements and circumstances entirely apart from production. Mining brings the subject-matter of commerce into existence. Commerce disposes of it. . . .

[N]one of [the] essential antecedents of production constitutes a transaction in or forms any part of interstate commerce. Schechter Poultry Corp. v. United States. Everything which moves in interstate commerce has had a local origin. Without local production somewhere, interstate commerce, as now carried on, would practically disappear. Nevertheless, the local character of mining, of manufacturing, and of crop growing is a fact, and remains a fact, whatever may be done with the products.

[Cases like] Swift & Company v. United States, 196 U.S. 375 [which upheld the constitutionality of antitrust regulation of the Chicago slaughterhouses] . . . rest upon the circumstance that the acts in question constituted direct interferences with the "flow" of commerce among the states. In the Swift Case, live stock was consigned and delivered to stockyards—not as a place of final destination, but, as the court said in Stafford v. Wallace, 258 U.S. 495, 516, "a throat through which the current flows." The sales which ensued merely changed the private interest in the subject of the current without interfering with its continuity. It was nowhere suggested in these cases that the interstate commerce power extended to the growth or production of the things [like raising cattle] which, after production, entered the flow [of commerce]. . . .

The restricted field covered by the Swift and kindred cases is illustrated by the Schechter Case. There the commodity in question, although shipped from another state, had come to rest in the state of its destination, and, as the court pointed out, was no longer in a current or flow of interstate commerce. The Swift doctrine was rejected as inapposite. In the Schechter Case the flow had ceased. Here it had not begun. The difference is not one of substance. The applicable principle is the same.

But section 1 (the Preamble) of the [Bituminous Coal] act now under review declares that all production and distribution of bituminous coal "bear upon and directly affect its interstate commerce"; and that regulation thereof is imperative for the protection of such commerce. The contention of the government is that the labor provisions of the act may be sustained in that view.

That the production of every commodity intended for interstate sale and transportation has some effect upon interstate commerce may be, if it has not already been, freely granted; and we are brought to the final and decisive inquiry, whether here that effect is direct, as the "Preamble" recites, or indirect. The distinction is not formal, but substantial in the highest degree, as we pointed out in the Schechter Case[:] "If the commerce clause were construed . . . to reach all enterprises and transactions which could be said to have an indirect effect upon interstate commerce, the federal authority would embrace practically all the activities of the people, and the authority of the state over its domestic concerns would exist only by sufferance of the federal government. . . . [T]he distinction between direct and indirect effects of intrastate transactions upon interstate commerce must be recognized as a fundamental one, essential to the maintenance of our constitutional system."

Whether the effect of a given activity or condition is direct or indirect is not always easy to determine. The word "direct" implies that the activity or condition invoked or blamed shall operate proximately—not mediately, remotely, or collaterally—to produce the effect. It connotes the absence of an efficient intervening agency or condition. And the extent of the effect bears no logical relation to its character. The distinction between a direct and an indirect effect turns, not upon the magnitude of either the cause or the effect, but entirely upon the manner in which the effect has been brought about. If the production by one man of a single ton of coal intended for interstate sale and shipment, and actually so sold and shipped, affects interstate commerce indirectly, the effect does not become direct by multiplying the tonnage, or increasing the number of men employed, or adding to the expense or complexities of the business, or by all combined. It is quite true that rules of law are sometimes qualified by considerations of degree, as the government argues. But the matter of degree has no bearing upon the question here, since that question is not—What is the *extent* of the local activity or condition, or the extent of the effect produced upon interstate commerce? but—What is the *relation* between the activity or condition and the effect?

Much stress is put upon the evils which come from the struggle between employers and employees over the matter of wages, working conditions, the right of collective bargaining, etc., and the resulting strikes, curtailment, and irregularity of production and effect on prices; and it is insisted that interstate commerce is *greatly* affected thereby. But, in addition to what has just been said, the conclusive answer is that the evils are all local evils over which the federal government has no legislative control. The relation of employer and employee is a local relation. At common law, it is one of the domestic relations. The wages are paid for the doing of local work. Working conditions are obviously local conditions. The employees are not engaged in or about commerce, but exclusively in producing a commodity. And the controversies and evils, which it is the object of the act to regulate and minimize, are local controversies and evils affecting local work undertaken to accomplish that local result. Such effect as they may have upon commerce, however extensive it may be, is secondary and indirect. An increase in the greatness of the effect adds to its importance. It does not alter its character. . . .

[In addition to holding that the labor provisions of Part III were beyond Congress's powers, the Court also held that the Act violated the Fifth Amendment because it "delegates the power to fix maximum hours of labor to a part of the producers and the miners." It then held that the price-fixing provisions of Part II were not severable because they were dependent on the labor provisions of Part III; it therefore struck down the entire Act.

Chief Justice Hughes concurred in part and dissented in part. Justice Cardozo dissented, joined by Justices Brandeis and Stone. He concluded that the price-fixing provisions of Part II were within Congress's commerce power, and that it was premature to consider the labor provisions of Part III, which were severable from the price-fixing provisions.]

DISCUSSION

1. *Labor as a "domestic" relation.* Note Justice Sutherland's claim in *Carter* that "[t]he relation of employer and employee is a local relation. At common law, it is one of the domestic relations." If labor and capital are mobile, why would these relations be inherently local?

2. *Direct and indirect effects.* Do *Carter* and *Schechter* make clear the nature of the direct-indirect criterion? *Carter* explains that directness is not the same as the size of an effect. Even if an effect on commerce is enormous, it might still not be direct. What is the basis of the distinction? How would the Court have treated the rules fixing prices for the sale of coal? Note that both the distinction between commerce and manufacture and the economic critique of the distinction can be traced to Marshall's views in Gibbons v. Ogden. Both the manufacturing/commerce distinction and the later distinction between direct and indirect effects were mediating

doctrines designed to paper over internal tensions and to articulate an intelligible difference between what was local and what was national. The problem in the 1930s was that doctrines that might have made some practical sense in 1820 were placed under enormous strain by a very different economic reality.

3. *The nondelegation doctrine.* In addition to striking down the National Industrial Recovery Act under the Commerce Clause, the Court in *Schechter Poultry* also held that the Act created an unlawful delegation of legislative power to the President and private industry to create business codes:

> Section 3 of the Recovery Act . . . is without precedent. It supplies no standards for any trade, industry, or activity. It does not undertake to prescribe rules of conduct to be applied to particular states of fact determined by appropriate administrative procedure. Instead of prescribing rules of conduct, it authorizes the making of codes to prescribe them. For that legislative undertaking, section 3 sets up no standards, aside from the statement of the general aims of rehabilitation, correction, and expansion described in section 1. In view of the scope of that broad declaration and of the nature of the few restrictions that are imposed, the discretion of the President in approving or prescribing codes, and thus enacting laws for the government of trade and industry throughout the country, is virtually unfettered. We think that the code-making authority thus conferred is an unconstitutional delegation of legislative power.

Concurring, Justice Cardozo famously described the Act's broad grant of power to the President and private industry to achieve fairness and to improve business conditions, taken to its logical conclusion, as "delegation running riot." The nondelegation doctrine announced in *Schechter* and Panama Refining v. Ryan, 293 U.S. 388 (1935)—striking down another part of the National Industrial Recovery Act that gave the President the power to prevent interstate shipment of petroleum in excess of certain quotas—was largely abandoned within a decade, as the country came to terms with the administrative state. See, e.g., Yakus v. United States, 321 U.S. 414 (1944) (upholding broad delegation of rulemaking power to the Office of Price Administration under the Emergency Price Control Act of 1942). In 1946, Congress passed the Administrative Procedure Act to impose judicial review on administrative agencies. The details are beyond the scope of this course, but are covered in courses on Administrative Law.

UNITED STATES v. BUTLER, 297 U.S. 1 (1936): [The Agricultural Adjustment Act of 1933 authorized the Secretary of Agriculture to spend federal funds in return for agreements by farmers to reduce their productive acreage—and thus, presumably, raise the prices of the crops being produced. The Court held that the Act was an invasion of the "reserved power" of the states and beyond Congress's spending power. Justice Roberts's majority opinion was joined by Chief Justice Hughes and Justices McReynolds, Sutherland, Van Devanter, and Butler.]

ROBERTS, J.: [T]here should be no misunderstanding as to the function of this court in such a case. It is sometimes said that the court assumes a power to overrule or control the action of the people's representatives. This is a misconception.

The Constitution is the supreme law of the land ordained and established by the people. All legislation must conform to the principles it lays down. When an act of Congress is appropriately challenged in the courts as not conforming to the constitutional mandate the judicial branch of the Government has only one duty,—to lay the article of the Constitution which is invoked beside the statute which is challenged and to decide whether the latter squares with the former. All the court does, or can do, is to announce its considered judgment upon the question. The only power it has, if such it may be called, is the power of judgment. This court neither approves nor condemns any legislative policy. Its delicate and difficult office is to ascertain and declare whether the legislation is in accordance with, or in contravention of, the provisions of the Constitution; and, having done that, its duty ends.

. . . Since the foundation of the Nation sharp differences of opinion have persisted as to the true interpretation of the ["General Welfare" Clause]. Madison asserted it amounted to no more than a reference to the other powers enumerated in the subsequent clauses of the same section; that, as the United States is a government of limited and enumerated powers, the grant of power to tax and spend for the general national welfare must be confined to the enumerated legislative fields committed to the Congress. In this view the phrase is mere tautology, for taxation and appropriation are or may be necessary incidents of the exercise of any of the enumerated legislative powers. Hamilton, on the other hand, maintained the clause confers a power separate and distinct from those later enumerated, is not restricted in meaning by the grant of them, and Congress consequently has a substantive power to tax and to appropriate, limited only by the requirement that it shall be exercised to provide for the general welfare of the United States. Each contention has had the support of those whose views are entitled to weight.

This court has noticed the question, but has never found it necessary to decide which is the true construction. Mr. Justice Story, in his Commentaries, espouses the Hamiltonian position. We shall not review the writings of public men and commentators or discuss the legislative practice. Study of all these leads us to conclude that the reading advocated by Mr. Justice Story is the correct one. While, therefore, the power to tax is not unlimited, its confines are set in the clause which confers it, and not in those of §8 which bestow and define the legislative powers of the Congress. It results that the power of Congress to authorize expenditure of public moneys for public purposes is not limited by the direct grants of legislative power found in the Constitution.

But the adoption of the broader construction leaves the power to spend subject to limitations. . . . Hamilton, in his well known Report on Manufactures, states that the purpose must be "general, and not local." . . .

We are not now required to ascertain the scope of the phrase "general welfare of the United States" or to determine whether an appropriation in aid of agriculture falls within it. Wholly apart from that question, another principle embedded in our Constitution prohibits the enforcement of the Agricultural Adjustment Act. The act invades the reserved rights of the states. It is a statutory plan to regulate and control agricultural production, a matter beyond the powers delegated to the federal government. The tax, the appropriation of the funds raised, and the direction for their disbursement, are but parts of the plan. They are but means to an unconstitutional end.

From the accepted doctrine that the United States is a government of delegated powers, it follows that those not expressly granted, or reasonably to be implied from such as are conferred, are reserved to the states or to the people. To forestall any suggestion to the contrary, the Tenth Amendment was adopted. The same proposition, otherwise stated, is that powers not granted are prohibited. None to regulate agricultural production is given, and therefore legislation by Congress for that purpose is forbidden.

It is an established principle that the attainment of a prohibited end may not be accomplished under the pretext of the exertion of powers which are granted [quoting Marshall's "pretext" statement in *McCulloch*]. . . .

[The Child Labor Tax Case and similar] decisions demonstrate that Congress could not, under the pretext of raising revenue, lay a tax on processors who refuse to pay a certain price for cotton, and exempt those who agree so to do, with the purpose of benefiting producers.

If the taxing power may not be used as the instrument to enforce a regulation of matters of state concern with respect to which the Congress has no authority to interfere, may it, as in the present case, be employed to raise the money necessary to purchase a compliance which the Congress is powerless to command? The Government asserts that whatever might be said against the validity of the plan if compulsory, it is constitutionally sound because the end is accomplished by voluntary cooperation. There are two sufficient answers to the contention. The regulation is not in fact voluntary. The farmer, of course, may refuse to comply, but the price of such refusal is the loss of benefits. The amount offered is intended to be sufficient to exert pressure on him to agree to the proposed regulation. The power to confer or withhold unlimited benefits is the power to coerce or destroy. If the cotton grower elects not to accept the benefits, he will receive less for his crops; those who receive payments will be able to undersell him. The result may well be financial ruin. The coercive purpose and intent of the statute is not obscured by the fact that it has not been perfectly successful. . . .

But if the plan were one for purely voluntary cooperation it would stand no better so far as federal power is concerned. At best it is a scheme for purchasing with federal funds submission to federal regulation of a subject reserved to the states. . . . The Congress cannot invade state jurisdiction to compel individual action; no more can it purchase such action. . . . It does not help to declare that local conditions throughout the nation have created a situation of national concern; for this is but to say that whenever there is a widespread similarity of local conditions, Congress may ignore constitutional limitations upon its own powers and usurp those reserved to the states. If, in lieu of compulsory regulation of subjects within the states' reserved jurisdiction, which is prohibited, the Congress could invoke the taxing and spending power as a means to accomplish the same end, clause 1 of §8 of Article I would become the instrument for total subversion of the governmental powers reserved to the individual states. . . .

STONE, J., joined by BRANDEIS and CARDOZO, JJ., dissenting.

The present stress of widely held and strongly expressed differences of opinion of the wisdom of the Agricultural Adjustment Act makes it important, in the interest of clear thinking and sound result, to emphasize at the outset certain propositions which should have controlling influence in determining the validity of the Act. They are:

1. The power of courts to declare a statute unconstitutional is subject to two guiding principles of decision which ought never to be absent from judicial

consciousness. One is that courts are concerned only with the power to enact statutes, not with their wisdom. The other is that while unconstitutional exercise of power by the executive and legislative branches of the government is subject to judicial restraint, the only check upon our own exercise of power is our own sense of self-restraint. For the removal of unwise laws from the statute books appeal lies not to the courts but to the ballot and to the processes of democratic government.

2. The constitutional power of Congress to levy an excise tax upon the processing of agricultural products is not questioned. The present levy is held invalid, not for any want of power in Congress to lay such a tax to defray public expenditures, including those for the general welfare, but because the use to which its proceeds are put is disapproved. . . .

[Federal expenditures] would fail of their purpose and thus lose their constitutional sanction if the terms of payment were not such that by their influence on the action of the recipients the permitted end would be attained. The power of Congress to spend is inseparable from persuasion to action over which Congress has no legislative control. . . .

The spending power of Congress is in addition to the legislative power and not subordinate to it. This independent grant of the power of the purse, and its very nature, involving in its exercise the duty to insure expenditure within the granted power, presuppose freedom of selection among divers ends and aims, and the capacity to impose such conditions as will render the choice effective. It is a contradiction in terms to say that there is power to spend for the national welfare, while rejecting any power to impose conditions reasonably adapted to the attainment of the end which alone would justify the expenditure. . . .

A tortured construction of the Constitution is not to be justified by recourse to extreme examples of reckless congressional spending which might occur if courts could not prevent—expenditures which, even if they could be thought to effect any national purpose, would be possible only by action of a legislature lost to all sense of public responsibility. Such suppositions are addressed to the mind accustomed to believe that it is the business of courts to sit in judgment on the wisdom of legislative action. Courts are not the only agency of government that must be assumed to have capacity to govern. Congress and the courts both unhappily may falter or be mistaken in the performance of their constitutional duty. But interpretation of our great charter of government which proceeds on any assumption that the responsibility for the preservation of our institutions is the exclusive concern of any one of the three branches of government, or that it alone can save them from destruction is far more likely, in the long run, "to obliterate the constituent members" of "an indestructible union of indestructible states" than the frank recognition that language, even of a constitution, may mean what it says: that the power to tax and spend includes the power to relieve a nationwide economic maladjustment by conditional gifts of money.

DISCUSSION

Until United States v. Butler, the Supreme Court had not fully addressed Congress's power to spend federal funds in the pursuit of ends not within the enumerated powers of Article I, §8. As we have seen, before that, the political branches engaged in most of the constitutional debates about the scope of the spending power.

Even though it invalidated the Agricultural Adjustment Act, *Butler* remains important today because it explicitly rejected Madison's (and many of his successors') views of the spending power, and adopted the Hamiltonian view that Congress's powers to "provide" for the general welfare are independent of its other powers. Thus, although *Butler* dealt a serious blow to the Roosevelt Administration's attempts to deal with the Great Depression, it laid the foundations for the regulatory and welfare state that emerged later on in the twentieth century.

The unpopularity of the NIRA and the *Schechter* decision led Roosevelt to switch political strategies for combatting the Great Depression. He abandoned the corporatist approach—delegating economic regulation to businesses and labor unions—and instead focused on social welfare legislation and labor regulation. This latter approach is the Second New Deal, exemplified by the Fair Labor Standards Act and the Social Security Act. The Second New Deal also featured the creation of the Works Progress Administration, the Rural Electrification Act, and the Public Utility Holding Company Act of 1935, which broke up utility holding companies.[25]

As fate would have it, most of the legislation the Supreme Court struck down—the NIRA, the Bituminous Coal Act, and the Agricultural Adjustment Act—came from the earlier, corporatist period of the First New Deal. But one should not assume that the Court was motivated either by populism or by a desire to promote social welfare programs. Rather, the Court was defending the old order of constitutional understandings that characterized the *Lochner* period.

Nevertheless, the effect of the Court's work in invalidating these elements of the First New Deal was that the parts of the New Deal that survived had a different character and would henceforth carry a different political meaning. Most of what eventually remained standing were the social welfare programs of the Second New Deal. The constitutional struggle between the Court and the political branches thus produced the New Deal as we know it today.

All of this, however, lay in the future. In 1936, even after its change in political strategy, the Roosevelt Administration worried that the Supreme Court would leave standing very little of its legislative agenda to deal with the Great Depression. A majority of the Court seemed to have turned decisively against the Administration's programs. Perhaps more worrisome, constitutional challenges to a new spate of laws—the Fair Labor Standards Act, the National Labor Relations Act, and the Social Security Act—loomed in the coming months.

The Administration's concerns were only heightened by the Court's decision in Morehead v. New York ex rel. Tipaldo, 298 U.S. 587 (1936), which seemed to signal a retreat from Nebbia v. New York, and an apparent reaffirmation of the Court's substantive due process/liberty of contract jurisprudence.

Roosevelt was reelected in November by overwhelming margins; in early February 1937, "with characteristic indirection, [he] presented Congress with a judiciary

---

25. See, e.g., Paul Conklin, The New Deal (1967); Ellis Hawley, The New Deal and the Problem of Monopoly (1966).

plan that purported to cope with the supposed problem of overcrowded federal court dockets. It would have enabled him to appoint a new judge to supplement any judge over seventy who failed to retire (retirement could not of course be made compulsory, for the Constitution protects judicial tenure 'during good behavior'). The significant fact was that the plan would permit the President to appoint six new Supreme Court Justices, and thus to insure approval of the New Deal program. It was, as it was called, a 'court-packing plan.' . . . And it was offered by a President who had just received an overwhelming popular vote of confidence and who had not yet been denied in Congress any of his important demands. Even the five or six judges who had provoked this threat must have slept rather uneasily for a few months."[26]

Roosevelt defended his plan in a nationally broadcast radio address:

Franklin D. Roosevelt, "Fireside Chat"[27]

(March 9, 1937)

The American people have learned from the depression. For in the last three national elections an overwhelming majority of them voted a mandate that the Congress and the President begin the task of providing . . . protection [from the depression]—not after long years of debate, but now.

The Courts, however, have cast doubts on the ability of the elected Congress to protect us against catastrophe by meeting squarely our modern social and economic conditions. . . . Last Thursday I described the American form of Government as a three horse team provided by the Constitution to the American people so that their field might be plowed. The three horses are, of course, the three branches of government—the Congress, the Executive and the Courts. Two of the horses are pulling in unison today; the third is not. . . . It is the American people themselves who are in the driver's seat. It is the American people themselves who want the furrow plowed. It is the American people themselves who expect the third horse to pull in unison with the other two.

I hope that you have re-read the Constitution of the United States in these past few weeks. Like the Bible, it ought to be read again and again.

It is an easy document to understand when you remember that it was called into being because the Articles of Confederation under which the original thirteen States tried to operate after the Revolution showed the need of a National Government with power enough to handle national problems. In its Preamble, the Constitution states that it was intended to form a more perfect Union and promote the general welfare; and the powers given to the Congress to carry out those purposes can be best described by saying that they were all the powers needed to meet each and every problem which then had a national character and which could not be met by merely local action.

---

26. McCloskey, supra n.1, at 113. See also William Leuchtenburg, The Origins of Franklin D. Roosevelt's "Court-Packing" Plan, 1966 Sup. Ct. Rev. 347.

27. From Gerhard Peters and John T. Woolley, The American Presidency Project. http://www.presidency.ucsb.edu/ws/?pid=15381.

But the framers went further. Having in mind that in succeeding generations many other problems then undreamed of would become national problems, they gave to the Congress the ample broad powers "to levy taxes . . . and provide for the common defense and general welfare of the United States."

That, my friends, is what I honestly believe to have been the clear and underlying purpose of the patriots who wrote a Federal Constitution to create a National Government with national power, intended as they said, "to form a more perfect union for ourselves and our posterity."

For nearly twenty years there was no conflict between the Congress and the Court. Then Congress passed a statute which, in 1803, the Court said violated an express provision of the Constitution. The Court claimed the power to declare it unconstitutional and did so declare it. But a little later[28] the Court itself admitted that it was an extraordinary power to exercise and through Mr. Justice Washington laid down this limitation upon it: "It is but a decent respect due to the wisdom, the integrity and the patriotism of the legislative body, by which any law is passed, to presume in favor of its validity until its violation of the Constitution is proved beyond all reasonable doubt."

But since the rise of the modern movement for social and economic progress through legislation, the Court has more and more often and more and more boldly asserted a power to veto laws passed by the Congress and State Legislatures in complete disregard of this original limitation.

In the last four years the sound rule of giving statutes the benefit of all reasonable doubt has been cast aside. The Court has been acting not as a judicial body, but as a policy-making body.

When the Congress has sought to stabilize national agriculture, to improve the conditions of labor, to safeguard business against unfair competition, to protect our national resources, and in many other ways, to serve our clearly national needs, the majority of the Court has been assuming the power to pass on the wisdom of these Acts of the Congress—and to approve or disapprove the public policy written into these laws.

The Court in addition to the proper use of its judicial functions has improperly set itself up as a third House of the Congress—a super-legislature, as one of the justices has called it—reading into the Constitution words and implications which are not there, and which were never intended to be there.

We have, therefore, reached the point as a Nation where we must take action to save the Constitution from the Court and the Court from itself. We must find a way to take an appeal from the Supreme Court to the Constitution itself. We want a Supreme Court which will do justice under the Constitution—not over it. In our Courts we want a government of laws and not of men.

I want—as all Americans want—an independent judiciary as proposed by the framers of the Constitution. That means a Supreme Court that will enforce the Constitution as written—that will refuse to amend the Constitution by the arbitrary exercise of judicial power—amendment by judicial say-so. It does not mean a judiciary so independent that it can deny the existence of facts universally recognized. . . .

28. This is a reference to Ogden v. Saunders, 25 U.S. 213, 270 (1827).

When I commenced to review the situation with the problem squarely before me, I came by a process of elimination to the conclusion that, short of amendments, the only method which was clearly constitutional, and would at the same time carry out other much needed reforms, was to infuse new blood into all our Courts. We must have men worthy and equipped to carry out impartial justice. But, at the same time, we must have Judges who will bring to the Courts a present-day sense of the Constitution—Judges who will retain in the Courts the judicial functions of a court, and reject the legislative powers which the courts have today assumed.

In forty-five out of the forty-eight States of the Union, Judges are chosen not for life but for a period of years. In many States Judges must retire at the age of seventy. Congress has provided financial security by offering life pensions at full pay for Federal Judges on all Courts who are willing to retire at seventy. . . .

What is my proposal? It is simply this: whenever a Judge or Justice of any Federal Court has reached the age of seventy and does not avail himself of the opportunity to retire on a pension, a new member shall be appointed by the President then in office, with the approval, as required by the Constitution, of the Senate of the United States.

That plan has two chief purposes. By bringing into the judicial system a steady and continuing stream of new and younger blood, I hope, first, to make the administration of all Federal justice speedier and, therefore, less costly; secondly, to bring to the decision of social and economic problems younger men who have had personal experience and contact with modern facts and circumstances under which average men have to live and work. This plan will save our national Constitution from hardening of the judicial arteries. . . .

Those opposing this plan have sought to arouse prejudice and fear by crying that I am seeking to "pack" the Supreme Court. . . . If by that phrase "packing the Court" it is charged that I wish to place on the bench spineless puppets who would disregard the law and would decide specific cases as I wished them to be decided, I make this answer: that no President fit for his office would appoint, and no Senate of honorable men fit for their office would confirm, that kind of appointees to the Supreme Court.

But if by that phrase the charge is made that I would appoint and the Senate would confirm Justices worthy to sit beside present members of the Court who understand those modern conditions, that I will appoint Justices who will not undertake to override the judgment of the Congress on legislative policy, that I will appoint Justices who will act as Justices and not as legislators—if the appointment of such Justices can be called "packing the Courts," then I say that I and with me the vast majority of the American people favor doing just that thing—now.

Is it a dangerous precedent for the Congress to change the number of the Justices? The Congress has always had, and will have, that power. The number of Justices has been changed several times before, in the Administrations of John Adams and Thomas Jefferson—both signers of the Declaration of Independence—Andrew Jackson, Abraham Lincoln and Ulysses S. Grant.

I suggest only the addition of Justices to the bench in accordance with a clearly defined principle relating to a clearly defined age limit. Fundamentally, if in the future, America cannot trust the Congress it elects to refrain from abuse of our Constitutional usages, democracy will have failed far beyond the importance to it of any kind of precedent concerning the Judiciary. . . .

Until my first term practically every President of the United States had appointed at least one member of the Supreme Court. President Taft appointed five members and named a Chief Justice; President Wilson, three; President Harding, four, including a Chief Justice; President Coolidge, one; President Hoover, three, including a Chief Justice.

Such a succession of appointments should have provided a Court well-balanced as to age. But chance and the disinclination of individuals to leave the Supreme bench have now given us a Court in which five Justices will be over seventy-five years of age before next June and one over seventy. Thus a sound public policy has been defeated.

I now propose that we establish by law an assurance against any such ill-balanced Court in the future. I propose that hereafter, when a Judge reaches the age of seventy, a new and younger Judge shall be added to the Court automatically. In this way I propose to enforce a sound public policy by law instead of leaving the composition of our Federal Courts, including the highest, to be determined by chance or the personal decision of individuals. . . . Our difficulty with the Court today rises not from the Court as an institution but from human beings within it. But we cannot yield our constitutional destiny to the personal judgment of a few men who, being fearful of the future, would deny us the necessary means of dealing with the present.

This plan of mine is no attack on the Court; it seeks to restore the Court to its rightful and historic place in our system of Constitutional Government and to have it resume its high task of building anew on the Constitution "a system of living law." The Court itself can best undo what the Court has done. . . .

[Roosevelt explains why new constitutional amendments will be unavailing:] There are many types of amendment proposed. Each one is radically different from the other. There is no substantial group within the Congress or outside it who are agreed on any single amendment.

It would take months or years to get substantial agreement upon the type and language of an amendment. It would take months and years thereafter to get a two-thirds majority in favor of that amendment in both Houses of the Congress.

Then would come the long course of ratification by three-fourths of all the States. No amendment which any powerful economic interests or the leaders of any powerful political party have had reason to oppose has ever been ratified within anything like a reasonable time. And thirteen States which contain only five percent of the voting population can block ratification even though the thirty-five States with ninety-five percent of the population are in favor of it. . . . Even if an amendment were passed, and even if in the years to come it were to be ratified, its meaning would depend upon the kind of Justices who would be sitting on the Supreme Court bench. An amendment, like the rest of the Constitution, is what the Justices say it is rather than what its framers or you might hope it is. . . .

DISCUSSION

1. What is Roosevelt's theory of federal power? Why does he think that the text of the Constitution supports his views? Do you agree that his account of constitutional purposes is more faithful to the framers' design than that of the Court in cases like *Carter Coal*?

2. *The presumption of constitutionality.* What is Roosevelt's theory of judicial review? Note Roosevelt's quotation of Justice Bushrod Washington that when a law is passed, courts should "presume in favor of its validity until its violation of the Constitution is proved beyond all reasonable doubt." Does this describe the actual practice of the federal courts in the country's first century and a half?

3. What does Roosevelt mean by his statement that "[w]e must find a way to take an appeal from the Supreme Court to the Constitution itself"? Roosevelt compares the three branches of government to a three-horse team, with the American people in the driver's seat. Why does Roosevelt think that the federal courts should be responsive to popular will, or have a duty to work with the other two branches?

4. *New amendments or new constitutional interpretations?* Roosevelt argues that a quest for an Article V amendment to overturn the Court's decisions would be fruitless. What are the reasons he gives?

Note that between 1913 and 1933, Congress had ratified six new amendments and had repealed the Eighteenth Amendment. What features of the political situation in 1937 were different, in Roosevelt's view? Note also that an amendment giving Congress the power to regulate child labor had been sent to the states in 1924 and was still awaiting ratification at the time Roosevelt spoke (the amendment is technically still under consideration today, having been ratified by 28 states as of 1937).

Instead, Roosevelt argues that the only way to ensure that the Constitution is properly interpreted over time is to regularly rotate the composition of the courts to bring in "new blood." Do you agree?

5. *The proper size of the Supreme Court.* The United States Constitution, unlike many state constitutions and other national constitutions, is completely silent on the size of the Supreme Court. The initial number of Justices was six; this had the interesting consequence that a decision by a majority was also a decision by a two-thirds majority. The number of Justices fluctuated during the Court's first century from five to ten, though it has stabilized at nine since 1871. Akhil Amar has queried whether the number nine had in effect become part of America's "unwritten Constitution," so that Roosevelt committed not only a political, but also a constitutional faux pas in his proposal to increase the number of Justices. Akhil Reed Amar, America's Unwritten Constitution 353-356 (2012). Does the failure of Roosevelt's proposal solidify the constitutional status of a nine-member Court? Do you believe it would be proper to increase or diminish the size of the Court in the future?

Within weeks after Roosevelt gave his court-packing speech, on March 29, 1937, the Court decided West Coast Hotel v. Parrish, discussed in Section I, supra. A similar change was afoot in the Court's federalism decisions.

NLRB v. JONES & LAUGHLIN STEEL CORP., 301 U.S. 1 (1937): [NLRB v. Jones & Laughlin, argued after Roosevelt announced his court-packing plan, and decided on April 12, 1937, was a watershed case, although it purported to maintain continuity with the past. At issue was the National Labor Relations Act of 1935, which prohibits employers "from engaging in any unfair labor practice affecting commerce." The Act defines "commerce" as "trade, traffic, commerce, transportation, or communication among the several States," and defines "affecting commerce" as "in commerce, or burdening or obstructing commerce or the free flow of commerce, or having led or tending to lead to a labor dispute burdening or obstructing commerce or the free flow of commerce." Respondent was charged with interfering with the rights of employees to organize and bargain collectively in its Aliquippa, Pennsylvania, steel manufacturing plant. As the Court noted, the respondent corporation with its 19 subsidiaries was a "completely integrated [multistate] enterprise, owning and operating ore, coal and limestone properties, lake and river transportation facilities and terminal railroads. . . ."

This made especially appealing the government's argument that the manufacturing process, though not itself commerce, was in the "stream" or "flow" of commerce. Cf. Stafford v. Wallace, 258 U.S. 495 (1922). But the Court refused to restrict its analysis to this metaphor.]

HUGHES, C.J.:

Although activities may be intrastate in character when separately considered, if they have such a close and substantial relation to interstate commerce that their control is essential or appropriate to protect that commerce from burdens and obstructions, Congress cannot be denied the power to exercise that control. Undoubtedly, the scope of this power must be considered in light of our dual system of government and may not be extended so as to embrace effects upon interstate commerce so indirect and remote that to embrace them, in view of our complex society, would effectively obliterate the distinction between what is national and what is local and create a completely centralized government. The question is necessarily one of degree. . . .

It is thus apparent that the fact that the employees here concerned were engaged in production is not determinative. The question remains as to the effect upon interstate commerce of the labor practice involved. In the *Schechter* case we found that the effect there was so remote as to be beyond the federal power. To find "immediacy or directness" there was to find it "almost everywhere," a result inconsistent with the maintenance of our federal system. . . .

[T]he stoppage of [respondent's manufacturing] operations by industrial strife would have a most serious effect upon interstate commerce. In view of respondent's far-flung activities, it is idle to say that the effect would be indirect or remote. It is obvious that it would be immediate and might be catastrophic.

DISCUSSION

In NLRB v. Friedman-Harry Marks Clothing Co., 301 U.S. 58 (1937), decided on the same day as *Jones & Laughlin*, the Court upheld the NLRA as applied to a small Virginia clothing manufacturer, most of whose materials came from, and most of whose finished products were marketed in, other states. In a brief opinion, the Court cited *Jones & Laughlin* and referred to the size, importance, and interstate character of the clothing industry and the interstate impact of a strike. Justice McReynolds, joined by Justices Van Devanter, Sutherland, and Butler, dissented from both Labor Relations Act decisions, arguing that any "effect on interstate commerce by the discharge of the employees shown there would be indirect and remote in the highest degree."

Together *Jones & Laughlin* and *West Coast Hotel* marked the beginning of the end of Roosevelt's confrontation with the Court. Ironically, Roosevelt's court-packing plan failed to gain Congress's approval and cost him an enormous amount of political capital, ultimately undermining his ability to move his domestic agenda. His political capital was further damaged by his failed attempt to "purge" a number of Southern conservative Democrats in the 1938 elections by supporting their more liberal challengers in Democratic primaries.

Nevertheless, in the spring of 1937, Justice Van Devanter retired. He was replaced by Senator Hugo Black of Alabama—a fervent defender of the New Deal. Black's appointment, and those that followed within a few years, gave Roosevelt a firm majority on the Court that would uphold New Deal legislation and state economic regulation.

Jones & Laughlin and *West Coast Hotel* were soon followed by decisions upholding New Deal legislation under the commerce and spending powers. The Court upheld the National Labor Relations Act in NLRB v. Jones & Laughlin Steel Corp., 301 U.S. 1 (1937); it upheld the Social Security Act in Steward Machine Co. v. Davis, 301 U.S. 548 (1937), and Helvering v. Davis, 301 U.S. 619 (1937). Just as the Court forged a new path in its treatment of economic rights after 1937, it also reshaped its federalism doctrines in a wide range of areas, including the commerce, taxing and spending powers.

Justice Black was sworn in on August 19, 1937. The next month, Roosevelt took a victory lap in his battle with the Court in a speech celebrating the 150th Anniversary of the Constitution, explaining his views about constitutional interpretation:

Franklin D. Roosevelt, Address on Constitution Day, Washington, D.C.[29]

(September 17, 1937)

The Constitution of the United States was a layman's document, not a lawyer's contract. . . . Madison, most responsible for it, was not a lawyer; nor was Washington or Franklin, whose sense of the give-and-take of life had kept the Convention together.

This great layman's document was a charter of general principles, completely different from the "whereases" and the "parties of the first part" and the fine print which lawyers put into leases and insurance policies and installment agreements.

When the Framers were dealing with what they rightly considered eternal verities, unchangeable by time and circumstance, they used specific language. In no uncertain terms, for instance, they forbade titles of nobility, the suspension of habeas corpus and the withdrawal of money from the Treasury except after appropriation by law. With almost equal definiteness they detailed the Bill of Rights.

But when they considered the fundamental powers of the new national government they used generality, implication and statement of mere objectives, as intentional phrases which flexible statesmanship of the future, within the Constitution,

29. From Gerhard Peters and John T. Woolley, The American Presidency Project, http://www.presidency.ucsb.edu/ws/?pid=15459.

could adapt to time and circumstance. For instance, the framers used broad and general language capable of meeting evolution and change when they referred to commerce between the States, the taxing power and the general welfare.

Even the Supreme Court was treated with that purposeful lack of specification. . . . Clearly a majority of the delegates believed that the relation of the Court to the Congress and the Executive, like the other subjects treated in general terms, would work itself out by evolution and change over the years.

But for one hundred and fifty years we have had an unending struggle between those who would preserve this original broad concept of the Constitution as a layman's instrument of government and those who would shrivel the Constitution into a lawyer's contract. . . . In this constant struggle the lawyers of no political party, mine or any other, have had a consistent or unblemished record. But the lay rank and file of political parties has had a consistent record. . . . They have considered as most sacred the concrete welfare of the generation of the day. And with laymen's common sense of what government is for, they have demanded that all three branches be efficient, that all three be interdependent as well as independent, and that all three work together to meet the living generation's expectations of government.

[W]henever legalistic interpretation has clashed with contemporary sense on great questions of broad national policy, ultimately the people and the Congress have had their way. But that word "ultimately" covers a terrible cost.

It cost a Civil War to gain recognition of the constitutional power of the Congress to legislate for the territories. It cost twenty years of taxation on those least able to pay to recognize the constitutional power of the Congress to levy taxes on those most able to pay. It cost twenty years of exploitation of women's labor to recognize the constitutional power of the States to pass minimum wage laws for their protection. It has cost twenty years already—and no one knows how many more are to come—to obtain a constitutional interpretation that will let the Nation regulate the shipment in national commerce of goods sweated from the labor of little children.

We know it takes time to adjust government to the needs of society. But modern history proves that reforms too long delayed or denied have jeopardized peace, undermined democracy and swept away civil and religious liberties. . . .

You will find no justification in any of the language of the Constitution for delay in the reforms which the mass of the American people now demand. Yet nearly every attempt to meet those demands for social and economic betterment has been jeopardized or actually forbidden by those who have sought to read into the Constitution language which the framers refused to write into the Constitution. . . . [T]he government of the United States refuses to forget that the Bill of Rights was put into the Constitution not only to protect minorities against intolerance of majorities, but to protect majorities against the enthronement of minorities.

Nothing would so surely destroy the substance of what the Bill of Rights protects than its perversion to prevent social progress. The surest protection of the individual and of minorities is that fundamental tolerance and feeling for fair play which the Bill of Rights assumes. But tolerance and fair play would disappear here as it has in some other lands if the great mass of people were denied confidence in their justice, their security and their self-respect. Desperate people in other lands surrendered their liberties when freedom came merely to mean humiliation and starvation. The crisis of 1933 should make us understand that.

On this solemn anniversary I ask that the American people rejoice in the wisdom of their Constitution. . . . I ask that they have faith in its ultimate capacity to work out the problems of democracy, but that they justify that faith by making it work now rather than twenty years from now. I ask that they give their fealty to the Constitution itself and not to its misinterpreters. I ask that they exalt the glorious simplicity of its purposes, rather than a century of complicated legalism. . . . So we revere it, not because it is old but because it is ever new, not in the worship of its past alone but in the faith of the living who keep it young, now and in the years to come.

DISCUSSION

1. What theory of constitutional interpretation does Roosevelt offer in his Constitution Day address and his March 1937 fireside chat?

2. Do you agree with Roosevelt that certain parts of the Constitution's language were designed to be adaptable to changing conditions? Note Roosevelt's argument that some provisions of the Constitution were deliberately made relatively general or relatively specific, and therefore should be interpreted accordingly: While the specific and concrete provisions offer little interpretive discretion to future generations, the more abstract and general provisions delegate to later generations the duty to interpret them according to contemporary understandings and needs. For a modern version of this argument, see Jack M. Balkin, Living Originalism (2011).

Do you agree with Roosevelt that the language in the Bill of Rights is significantly more "definit[e]" than the language describing Congress's powers? Putting that issue to one side, what are the similarities and differences between Roosevelt's approach to constitutional interpretation and John Marshall's? What about Fredrick Douglass's?

3. What does Roosevelt mean by his famous claim that the Constitution is a layman's document rather than a lawyer's contract? In particular, what does that assertion mean for the lawyers and judges who will inevitably have to interpret it in litigation or in court decisions?

B. The Emergence of Modern Commerce Clause Doctrine

In 1938, Congress passed a second Agricultural Adjustment Act, premised on the commerce rather than the spending power. The Act included congressional findings that excess production moving in interstate commerce caused disorderly marketing, and the Act imposed penalties for marketing farm commodities in excess of quotas set by the Secretary of Agriculture. Justice Roberts, who had written the Court's opinion in *Butler* striking down the 1933 Act, supra Chapter 4, wrote for the Court in Mulford v. Smith, 307 U.S. 38 (1939), sustaining the 1938 Act as applied to tobacco warehousemen penalized for marketing excessive tobacco. Justices Butler and McReynolds dissented.

If it was unlikely that the old Court would have held for the government in *Mulford,* there could be no doubt that United States v. Darby, 312 U.S. 100 (1941), and Wickard v. Filburn, 317 U.S. 111 (1942), marked a new era for the Commerce Clause.

United States v. Darby

312 U.S. 100 (1941)

[Sections 6 and 7 of the Fair Labor Standards Act of 1938 prescribed minimum wage and maximum hours for employees engaged in the production of goods related to interstate commerce as described in the opinion below. Appellee, a Georgia lumber manufacturer, was indicted for violating the Act. The government appealed from the district court's judgment quashing the indictment.]

STONE, J. . . .

THE PROHIBITION OF SHIPMENT OF THE PROSCRIBED GOODS IN INTERSTATE COMMERCE

Section 15(a)(1) prohibits, and the indictment charges, the shipment in interstate commerce, of goods produced for interstate commerce by employees whose wages and hours of employment do not conform to the requirements of the Act. Since this section is not violated unless the commodity shipped has been produced under labor conditions prohibited by §6 and §7, the only question arising under the commerce clause with respect to such shipments is whether Congress has the constitutional power to prohibit them.

While manufacture is not of itself interstate commerce, the shipment of manufactured goods interstate is such commerce and the prohibition of such shipment by Congress is indubitably a regulation of the commerce. . . .

But it is said that . . . while the prohibition is nominally a regulation of the commerce its motive or purpose is regulation of wages and hours of persons engaged in manufacture, the control of which has been reserved to the states and upon which Georgia and some of the States of destination have placed no restriction; that the effect of the present statute is not to exclude the proscribed articles from interstate commerce in aid of state regulation . . . but instead, under the guise of a regulation of interstate commerce, it undertakes to regulate wages and hours within the state contrary to the policy of the state which has elected to leave them unregulated.

The power of Congress over interstate commerce "is complete in itself, may be exercised to its utmost extent, and acknowledges no limitations other than are prescribed in the Constitution." Gibbons v. Ogden. That power can neither be enlarged nor diminished by the exercise or non-exercise of state power. . . .

Such regulation is not a forbidden invasion of state power merely because either its motive or its consequence is to restrict the use of articles of commerce within the states of destination; and is not prohibited unless by other Constitutional provisions. It is no objection to the assertion of the power to regulate interstate commerce that its exercise is attended by the same incidents which attend the exercise of the police power of the states.

The motive and purpose of the present regulation are plainly to make effective the Congressional conception of public policy that interstate commerce should not be made the instrument of competition in the distribution of goods produced under substandard labor conditions, which competition is injurious to the commerce and to the states from and to which the commerce flows. The motive and purpose of a regulation of interstate commerce are matters for the legislative judgment upon the exercise of which the Constitution places no restriction and over which the courts are given no control. . . . [W]e conclude that the prohibition of the shipment interstate of goods produced under the forbidden substandard labor conditions is within the constitutional authority of Congress. . . .

Hammer v. Dagenhart has not been followed. The distinction on which the decision was rested that Congressional power to prohibit interstate commerce is limited to articles which in themselves have some harmful or deleterious property—a distinction which was novel when made and unsupported by any provision of the Constitution—has long since been abandoned. The thesis of the opinion that the motive of the prohibition or its effect to control in some measure the use or production within the states of the article thus excluded from the commerce can operate to deprive the regulation of its constitutional authority has long since ceased to have force. And finally we have declared "The authority of the federal government over interstate commerce does not differ in extent or character from that retained by the states over intrastate commerce."

The conclusion is inescapable that Hammer v. Dagenhart was a departure from the principles which prevailed in the interpretation of the commerce clause. . . . It should be and now is overruled.

VALIDITY OF THE WAGE AND HOUR REQUIREMENTS

Section 15(a)(2) and §§6 and 7 require employers to conform to the wage and hour provisions with respect to all employees engaged in the production of goods for interstate commerce. As appellee's employees are not alleged to be "engaged in interstate commerce" the validity of the prohibition turns on the question whether the employment, under other than the prescribed labor standards, of employees engaged in the production of goods for interstate commerce is so related to the commerce and so affects it as to be within the reach of the power of Congress to regulate it.

. . . As the Government seeks to apply the statute in the indictment, and as the court below construed the phrase "produced for interstate commerce," it embraces at least the case where an employer engaged, as is appellee, in the manufacture and shipment of goods in filling orders of extrastate customers, manufactures his product with the intent or expectation that according to the normal course of his business all or some part of it will be selected for shipment to those customers.

. . . The obvious purpose of the Act was not only to prevent the interstate transportation of the proscribed product, but to stop the initial step toward transportation, production with the purpose of so transporting it. Congress was not unaware that most manufacturing businesses shipping their product in interstate commerce make it in their shops without reference to its ultimate destination and then after manufacture select some of it for shipment interstate and some intrastate according to the daily demands of their business, and that it would be practically impossible, without disrupting manufacturing businesses, to restrict the prohibited kind of production to the particular pieces of lumber, cloth, furniture or the like which later move in interstate rather than intrastate commerce. . . .

There remains the question whether such restriction on the production of goods for commerce is a permissible exercise of the commerce power. The power of Congress over interstate commerce is not confined to the regulation of commerce among the states. It extends to those activities intrastate which so affect interstate commerce or the exercise of the power of Congress over it as to make regulation of them appropriate means to the attainment of a legitimate end, the exercise of the granted power of Congress to regulate interstate commerce. . . .

Congress, having by the present Act adopted the policy of excluding from interstate commerce all goods produced for the commerce which do not conform to the specified labor standards, it may choose the means reasonably adapted to the attainment of the permitted end, even though they involve control of intrastate activities. . . .

We think also that §15(a)(2), now under consideration, is sustainable independently of §15(a)(1), which prohibits shipment or transportation of the proscribed goods. As we have said the evils aimed at by the Act are the spread of substandard labor conditions through the use of the facilities of interstate commerce for competition by the goods so produced with those produced under the prescribed or better labor conditions; and the consequent dislocation of the commerce itself caused by the impairment or destruction of local businesses by competition made effective through interstate commerce. The Act is thus directed at the suppression of a method or kind of competition in interstate commerce which it has in effect condemned as "unfair." . . .

The means adopted by §15(a)(2) for the protection of interstate commerce by the suppression of the production of the condemned goods for interstate commerce is so related to the commerce and so affects it as to be within the reach of the commerce power. . . . So far as Carter v. Carter Coal Co. is inconsistent with this conclusion, its doctrine is limited in principle by . . . decisions under the Sherman Act and the National Labor Relations Act. . . .

Our conclusion is unaffected by the Tenth Amendment which provides: "The powers not delegated to the United States by the Constitution, nor prohibited by it to the States, are reserved to the States respectively, or to the people." The amendment states but a truism that all is retained which has not been surrendered. There is nothing in the history of its adoption to suggest that it was more than declaratory of the relationship between the national and state governments as it had been established by the Constitution before the amendment or that its purpose was other than to allay fears that the new national government might seek to exercise powers not granted, and that the states might not be able to exercise fully their reserved powers. . . .

Reversed.

WICKARD v. FILBURN, 317 U.S. 111 (1942): [Wickard, the Secretary of Agriculture sought to penalize an Ohio farmer, Roscoe Filburn, for growing wheat in excess of his allotment under the Agricultural Adjustment Act of 1938. Although Filburn's 239-bushel surplus was intended wholly for consumption on his farm and not for sale, it was deemed "available for marketing" within the Act. The district court enjoined enforcement. The Supreme Court unanimously reversed.]

JACKSON, J.:

Whether the subject of the regulation in question was "production," "consumption," or "marketing" is . . . not material for purposes of deciding the question of federal power before us. That an activity is of local character . . . might help in determining whether in the absence of Congressional action it would be permissible for the state to exert its power on the subject matter, even though in so doing it to some degree affected interstate commerce. But even if appellee's activity be local and though it may not be regarded as commerce, it may still, whatever its nature, be reached by Congress if it exerts a substantial economic effect on interstate commerce, and this irrespective of whether such effect is what might at some earlier time have been defined as "direct" or "indirect." . . .

The wheat industry has been a problem industry for some years. . . . The decline in the export trade has left a large surplus in production which, in connection with an abnormally large supply of wheat and other grains in recent years, caused congestion in a number of markets. . . .

The maintenance by government regulation of a price for wheat undoubtedly can be accomplished as effectively by sustaining or increasing the demand as by limiting the supply. The effect of the statute before us is to restrict the amount which may be produced for market and the extent as well to which one may forestall resort to the market by producing to meet his own needs. That appellee's own contribution to the demand for wheat may be trivial by itself is not enough to remove him from the scope of federal regulation where, as here, his contribution, taken together with that of many others similarly situated, is far from trivial.

It is well established by decision of this Court that the power to regulate commerce includes the power to regulate the prices at which commodities in that commerce are dealt in and practices affecting such prices. One of the primary purposes of the Act in question was to increase the market price of wheat, and to that end to limit the volume thereof that could affect the market. It can hardly be denied that a factor of such volume and variability as home-consumed wheat would have a substantial influence on price and market conditions. This may arise because being in marketable condition such wheat overhangs the market and, if induced by rising prices, tends to flow into the market and check price increases. But if we assume that it is never marketed, it supplies a need of the man who grew it which would otherwise be reflected by purchases in the open market. Homegrown wheat in this sense competes with wheat in commerce. The stimulation of commerce is a use of the regulatory function quite as definitely as prohibitions or restrictions thereon. This record leaves us in no doubt that Congress may properly have considered that wheat consumed on the farm where grown, if wholly outside the scheme of regulation, would have a substantial effect in defeating and obstructing its purpose to stimulate trade therein at increased prices.

DISCUSSION

1. *(Almost) no constitutional limits, or (almost) no judicial review? Darby* and *Wickard* represent a retreat from the federal courts' earlier attempts to come up with judicially administrable rules that would distinguish national from purely local subjects of regulation; they announce that courts will henceforth will defer to Congress's judgment on these questions. Some constitutional norms may be real—and in principle binding on political actors, who also take oaths of office to support the Constitution—but not fully enforceable in court because of various court-specific institutional constraints. For example, in implementing the Constitution, courts

must follow strict rules of evidence, often aim for clear doctrinal rules capable of principled judicial exposition and easy application in lower courts, and sometimes face constraints in their practical capacity to unsettle legislative faits accomplis. Where a judicial ruling upholding a governmental practice rests on particular court-specific limits, are other branches especially obliged to carefully consider the constitutional norms that judges are underenforcing? Recall that President Jackson thought so in responding to *McCulloch*. See generally Paul Brest, The Conscientious Legislator's Guide to Constitutional Interpretation, 27 Stan. L. Rev. 585 (1975); Lawrence G. Sager, Fair Measure: The Status of Underenforced Constitutional Norms, 91 Harv. L. Rev. (1978).

2. *Interstate economic competition*. Taken together, the unanimous holdings in *Darby* and *Wickard* might seem to recognize that Congress enjoys sweeping—virtually unbounded?—power to regulate a national economy under the Commerce Clause. But recall that both cases concerned regulation that was arguably economic in purpose, aimed at influencing prices and quantities of economic goods and services. Recall also the obvious concern about interstate competition on the surface of *Darby*. The problem was that any state seeking to require minimum wages for all in-state workers risked having this policy undercut by sister states. If State A required its employers to pay X dollars an hour, sister State B could set its minimum wage at a lower level, and cost-conscious employers might flee State A and set up shop in B instead. Indeed, goods manufactured in State B could then be sold at lower prices even in State A itself. Under such conditions, State A might find it hard to maintain its desired minimum wage policy as a practical political matter. Note that under judicial doctrine crafted under the Commerce Clause, State A could not simply ban the sale of any good manufactured by low-wage labor in sister states; nor was it clear that A could impose some kind of offsetting tariff, which could have been seen as an impermissible effort to regulate employment relations beyond its borders. Thus, it is theoretically possible that almost every state preferred to have a minimum wage law set at X dollars an hour—but only if all sister states adopted the same policy. In such a scenario, only through collective action in Congress could the great majority of states implement their preferred policies: If each state acted on its own without any coordination with other states, a kind of "race to the bottom" might ensue. If Congress were somehow barred from acting, and states individually were in effect limited in their ability to make their desired regulations stick, then the upshot would be that *no one* could effectively regulate minimum wages. The Commerce Clause—designed merely to apportion power between Congress and the states—would have had the strong substantive effect of requiring laissez faire. Consider again, in this light, *Darby*'s language that "interstate commerce should not be made the instrument of competition in the distribution of goods produced under substandard labor conditions" and that "the spread of substandard labor conditions [via] interstate commerce" created by "competition" between low-wage and high-wage products was an "evil" that Congress could properly seek to eradicate.

Consider also the history of the specification of federal powers in the Philadelphia Convention of 1787. An early draft resolution provided "that the National Legislature ought to be impowered to . . . legislate in all cases to which the separate States are incompetent, or in which the harmony of the United States may be interrupted by the exercise of individual Legislation." This general resolution later gave way to the specific enumerations of congressional power in Article I, §8, including the Interstate Commerce Clause. In the ratification debates, the influential framer James Wilson declared that "[w]hatever object of government is confined, in its operation and effects, within the bounds of a particular state, should be considered as belonging to the government of that state; whatever object of government extends, in its operation or effects, beyond the bounds of a particular state, should be considered as belonging to the United States." On a broad structural view, when regulations in one state could have strong "spillover" effects in other states (what economists call positive or negative "externalities"), Congress should have power to "harmonize" relations between states, which are individually "incompetent" to internalize the full effects of their respective regulations. Cf. *McCulloch*, supra Chapter 1. Wasn't *Darby* a case of true interstate externalities? How about *Wickard*?

NOTE: ON CONSTITUTIONAL REVOLUTION

Most constitutional scholars agree that something important happened to American constitutional law in the years between 1937 and 1942, because it is widely acknowledged that key doctrines changed rather quickly in a wide range of areas. Scholars disagree about whether it counts as a revolution or a return to (or deviation from) correct constitutional understandings. They also disagree about why (or whether) it was legitimate. As a result, the New Deal has become a standard example for theorizing the grounds of legitimate constitutional change.

Bruce Ackerman's theory of "constitutional moments" argues that at significant periods in history the American people amend the Constitution outside of Article V. See Bruce Ackerman, We the People: Foundations (1991); Bruce Ackerman, We the People: Transformations (1998). In Ackerman's model, one or more branches of government, led by an ascendant social movement party that claims a mandate for revolutionary change, is opposed by a branch that resists change. The conflict between the branches leads to a major constitutional crisis that is resolved when the defenders of the old order concede defeat, leading to a new constitutional regime. As we saw in Chapter 4, Ackerman argues that Reconstruction involved a constitutional moment: Congressional Republicans claimed a mandate for change, opposed by President Johnson. He eventually capitulated under threat of impeachment.

While Congress took the lead during Reconstruction (due to Lincoln's assassination), the President took the lead during the New Deal. At first, when FDR pushed for new laws inconsistent with existing judicial understandings of federal power and economic due process, the Supreme Court struck down this legislation, producing a constitutional crisis. Ackerman argues that this led to a period of special deliberation about the country's future, and set the stage for a "triggering election," in which the American people decided whether or not to support a constitutional transformation. This election, Ackerman argues, was the 1936 election, which Roosevelt and the Democrats won by a decisive margin. Although the Democrats considered amending Article V during this period, the constitutional crisis gave way in 1937 when the Supreme Court capitulated to Roosevelt's constitutional views in *West Coast Hotel* and NLRB v. Jones & Laughlin. Roosevelt then used a series of "transformative appointments" to produce a Court friendly to his constitutional principles. The Justices decided a series of cases (including *Darby* and *Wickard*) that, in Ackerman's view, effectively amended the Constitution. The opposition Republican Party capitulated to this transformation by 1940 and accepted the legitimacy of the New Deal, leading to a constitutional solution to the crisis and the beginning of what Ackerman calls America's "Third Republic." (The "Second Republic" begins with Reconstruction.)

Jack Balkin and Sanford Levinson argue that constitutional law changes through "partisan entrenchment" in the judiciary. See Jack M. Balkin and Sanford Levinson, Understanding the Constitutional Revolution, 87 Va. L. Rev. 1045 (2001). Because of the President's appointments power, the party that controls the White House can appoint new jurists to the federal courts who share roughly similar views on matters that are particularly important to the party. Stocking the judiciary with jurists of roughly similar ideological views can produce, over time, significant changes in constitutional doctrine:

> When enough like minded judges are appointed to the federal judiciary, they begin to change constitutional understandings and constitutional doctrine. If more people are appointed in a relatively short period of time, the changes will occur more quickly. Constitutional revolutions are the cumulative result of successful partisan entrenchment when the entrenching party has a relatively coherent political ideology or can pick up sufficient ideological allies from the appointees of other parties. Thus, the Warren Court is the culmination of years of Democratic appointments to the Supreme Court, assisted by a few key liberal Republicans.

Not all Presidents have engaged in strategies of partisan entrenchment; sometimes Presidents merely seek to reward political favors or curry favor with particular constituencies. Moreover, when the President lacks support in the Senate, he usually must appoint more moderate candidates. Nevertheless, Presidents who seek deliberately to change constitutional doctrine through the appointments process often succeed. Because President Roosevelt and the Democrats kept winning elections between 1932 and 1948, they were able to stock the courts with judges who supported the New Deal. These judges believed in broad federal power and judicial restraint in social and economic legislation, and they changed constitutional doctrine accordingly. By 1942, the Democrats had made eight consecutive appointments to the Supreme Court, all committed New Dealers. It is hardly surprising that this changed constitutional doctrine as well as more basic constitutional understandings about what sorts of arguments were plausible and implausible.

Ackerman's theory and Balkin and Levinson's differ in several respects. Ackerman views constitutional moments as the epitome of democratic self-governance; they are self-conscious transformations of the grounds of constitutionalism by We the People over a relatively short period of time. Balkin and Levinson argue that constitutional change can occur slowly and may involve gradual retrenchment as well as dramatic transformation. Such change is "roughly but imperfectly democratic" because the courts respond over the long run to changes in the governing political coalition.

According to Ackerman, if the conditions for a constitutional moment are met, they establish new standards of legitimacy and correctness. By contrast, the theory of partisan entrenchment guarantees neither legitimate nor correct interpretations of the Constitution. It describes constitutional change but does not necessarily justify it. For example, the Compromise of 1877 led to a new political coalition that appointed Justices who used the Fourteenth Amendment to protect railroad and business interests rather than the interests of African Americans. Because this coalition kept returning to power, it eventually produced *Plessy* and *Lochner*, just as the Democrats' control of the White House before the Civil War produced a Court that decided *Dred Scott*. Thus, while Ackerman argues that the New Deal is just as binding as an Article V amendment until the next constitutional moment, Balkin and Levinson argue that the continued survival of the New Deal settlement is best explained by the needs of the dominant political coalition. If that coalition changes sufficiently over time—for example, because of the influence of new social movements—the constitutional doctrines of the New Deal could be cut back or even altered substantially.

As you ponder the material in this chapter, ask yourself whether either theory, or both, captures what happened in constitutional law during the twentieth and early twenty-first centuries. Do you think the New Deal transformation in due process and federalism doctrine was a legitimate transformation? Why or why not?

C. *The Taxing and Spending Power*

The post-1937 taxing and spending power cases are not significantly different in tone or outcome from some earlier decisions, such as McCray v. United States, 195 U.S. 27 (1904). Nevertheless, following the New Deal, the Court interpreted the Child Labor Tax Case, Bailey v. Drexel Furniture Company, narrowly.

In Sonzinsky v. United States, 300 U.S. 506 (1937), the Court unanimously upheld a law requiring persons dealing in certain firearms (e.g., machine guns with silencers, sawed-off shotguns and rifles) to register with the collector of internal revenue and pay a $200 annual tax. Another provision imposed a $200 tax on each transfer of such firearms. Petitioner argued that the Act was not designed to raise revenue but to prohibit transfer of the weapons.

Justice Stone, writing for the majority, explained that "[e]very tax is in some measure regulatory. To some extent it interposes an economic impediment to the activity taxed as compared with others not taxed. But a tax is not any the less a tax because it has a regulatory effect; and it has long been established that an Act of Congress which on its face purports to be an exercise of the taxing power is not any the less so because the tax is burdensome or tends to restrict or suppress the things taxed." Justice Stone pointed out that "the annual tax of $200 is productive of some revenue," and that ended the matter. "Inquiry into the hidden motives which may move Congress to exercise a power constitutionally conferred upon it is beyond the competency of courts." The Supreme Court would not infer a pretextual purpose to Congress from "the measure of the regulatory effect of a tax."

The Court took a similarly deferential view in United States v. Kahriger, 345 U.S. 22 (1953), where it upheld a federal provision that required persons engaged in the business of accepting wagers to pay a $50 occupational tax and register with the collector of internal revenues. Appellee argued that the tax was only a pretext for penalizing intrastate gambling and thus infringed "the police power which is reserved to the states."

Justice Reed, writing for the majority, rejected the argument: "[A] federal excise tax does not cease to be valid merely because it discourages or deters the activities taxed. Nor is the tax invalid because the revenue obtained is negligible. . . . As with [other] excise taxes which we have held to be valid, the instant tax has a regulatory effect. But regardless of its regulatory effect, the wagering tax produces revenue."

Justice Reed added that "[i]t is axiomatic that the power of Congress to tax is extensive and sometimes falls with crushing effect on businesses deemed unessential or inimical to the public welfare, or where, as in dealings with narcotics, the collection of the tax also is difficult." Responding to *McCulloch*'s language about pretext, he noted that "[w]here federal legislation has rested on other congressional powers, such as the Necessary and Proper Clause or the Commerce Clause, this Court has generally sustained the statutes, despite their effect on matters ordinarily considered state concern. . . . It is hard to understand why the power to tax should raise more doubts . . . than other federal powers."

Justice Jackson concurred, but expressed concerns that the tax compelled taxpayers to incriminate themselves. Justice Black, joined by Justice Douglas, dissented solely on the ground that the Act compelled self-incrimination in violation of the Fifth Amendment. Justice Frankfurter dissented on federalism grounds.

The major post-1937 challenge to Congress's taxing and spending power involved the unemployment compensation scheme created by the Social Security Act of 1935.

STEWARD MACHINE COMPANY v. DAVIS, 301 U.S. 548 (1937): [Congress had imposed a tax on employers, based on their employees' wages. The proceeds went into the United States Treasury (as do internal revenue collections generally) and were not earmarked for any purpose. The tax was then used to create an incentive for states to create an unemployment compensation system that would be administered by the United States Treasury. A credit of up to 90 percent of the federal tax was allowed to the extent the employer contributed to a state unemployment fund that met detailed requirements specified in the Act and was approved by the Social Security Board. Contributions to the state fund were to be turned over immediately to the Treasury, which would invest, administer, and disburse them.]

CARDOZO, J. . . . The excise is not void as involving the coercion of the States in contravention of the Tenth Amendment or of restrictions implicit in our federal form of government. [Justice Cardozo recounted the unprecedented numbers of unemployed caused by the Great Depression:] [T]he states were unable to give the requisite relief. The problem had become national in area and dimensions. There was need of help from the nation if the people were not to starve. . . . Many [states] held back through alarm lest, in laying such a toll upon their industries, they would place themselves in a position of economic disadvantage as compared with neighbors or competitors. Two consequences ensued. One was that the freedom of a state to contribute its fair share to the solution of a national problem was paralyzed by fear. The other was that in so far as there was failure by the states to contribute relief according to the measure of their capacity, a disproportionate burden, and a mountainous one, was laid upon the resources of the Government of the nation.

The Social Security Act is an attempt to find a method by which all these public agencies may work together to a common end. . . .

Who then is coerced through the operation of this statute? Not the taxpayer. He pays in fulfillment of the mandate of the local legislature. Not the state. . . . For all that appears she is satisfied with her choice, and would be sorely disappointed if it were now to be annulled. . . . [E]very rebate from a tax when conditioned upon conduct is in some measure a temptation. But to hold that . . . temptation is equivalent to coercion is to plunge the law in endless difficulties. . . . Nothing in the case suggests the exertion of a power akin to undue influence, if we assume that such a concept can ever be applied with fitness to the relations between state and nation. . . . We cannot say that [Alabama] was acting, not of her unfettered will, but under the strain of a persuasion equivalent to undue influence, when she chose to have relief administered under laws of her own making, by agents of her own selection, instead of under federal laws, administered by federal officers, with all the ensuing evils, at least to many minds, of federal patronage and power. . . .

In ruling as we do, we leave many questions open. We do not say that a tax is valid, when imposed by act of Congress, if it is laid upon the condition that a state may escape its operation through the adoption of a statute unrelated in subject matter to activities fairly within the scope of national policy and power. No such question is before us. . . .

In a companion case, Helvering v. Davis, 301 U.S. 619 (1937), with only Justices McReynolds and Butler dissenting, the Court upheld the old-age benefit provisions of the Social Security Act:

> The problem is plainly national in area and dimensions. Moreover, laws of the separate states cannot deal with it effectively. . . . State and local governments are often lacking in the resources that are necessary to finance an adequate program of security for the aged. . . . Apart from the failure of resources, states and local governments are at times reluctant to increase so heavily the burden of taxation to be borne by their residents for fear of placing themselves in a position of economic disadvantage as compared with neighbors or competitors. . . . A system of old age pensions has special dangers of its own, if put in force in one state and rejected in another. The existence of such a system is a bait to the needy and dependent elsewhere, encouraging them to migrate and seek a haven of repose. Only a power that is national can serve the interests of all.
>
> Whether wisdom or unwisdom resides in the scheme of benefits set forth in Title II, it is not for us to say. The answer to such inquiries must come from Congress, not the courts. Our concern here as often is with power, not with wisdom. Counsel for respondent has recalled to us the virtues of self-reliance and frugality. There is a possibility, he says, that aid from a paternal government may sap those sturdy virtues and breed a race

of weaklings. If Massachusetts so believes and shapes her laws in that conviction, must her breed of sons be changed, he asks, because some other philosophy of government finds favor in the halls of Congress? But the answer is not doubtful. One might ask with equal reason whether the system of protective tariffs is to be set aside at will in one state or another whenever local policy prefers the rule of laissez faire. The issue is a closed one. It was fought out long ago. When money is spent to promote the general welfare, the concept of welfare or the opposite is shaped by Congress, not the states. So the concept be not arbitrary, the locality must yield. Constitution, art. 6, par. 2.

DISCUSSION

1. *Interstate competition and the "general welfare."* Unlike the commerce power, Congress's Article I power to tax and spend is not, by its terms, limited to distinctly interstate problems, although the Constitution does speak of taxing and spending on behalf of "the general welfare." But wasn't there an obvious interstate — that is, federal — problem that gave rise to federal legislation in *Steward* and *Helvering*? Each state on its own might hesitate to adopt strong unemployment policies, financed by taxes on employers. Such policies might cause employers to move to sister states, and might also attract unemployed workers from other states, causing the state to become an unemployment-benefit "magnet." A similar concern might prevent a state from offering a generous old-age pension. Even if virtually every state preferred high benefits, each might end up "racing to the bottom" in the absence of some mechanism of coordination. Could an interstate compact among states, under Article I, §10, have solved the problem? (Remember that such a compact would have required congressional approval.) What if a handful of states try to "hold out" in the multistate bargaining process? For an important plea for greater use of interstate compacts as an instrument of "intermediate federalism," see David L. Shapiro, Federalism: A Dialogue 126-137 (1995).

III. NATIONAL POWER IN THE CIVIL RIGHTS ERA

A. The 1960s Civil Rights Legislation: Commerce Power or Reconstruction Power?

1. The Civil Rights Movement and the Civil Rights Act of 1964

The Civil Rights Movement of the late 1950s and early 1960s transformed American politics, and led to our nation's second Reconstruction. Although the exact origins of the movement are still debated among historians, one plausible starting point is the 1953 bus boycott in Baton Rouge, Louisiana, which protested segregated seating on buses. Brown v. Board of Education, decided the next year (and discussed in Chapter 7), then placed the issue of school desegregation on the national agenda. The Baton Rouge boycott inspired the more famous boycott in Montgomery, Alabama in 1955-1956. The arrest of Rosa Parks for disorderly conduct in December 1955 led to plans for a city-wide boycott of segregated buses and to the emergence of a then-obscure Montgomery pastor named Martin Luther King, Jr. Eventually, the Supreme Court summarily affirmed a lower federal court decision holding that Alabama's and Montgomery's bus segregation laws were unconstitutional in Browder v. Gayle, 142 F. Supp. 707 (M.D. Ala. 1956), *aff'd*, 352 U.S. 903 (1956).

A group of college students in Greensboro, North Carolina in 1961 initiated "sit-ins" at a local Woolworth's lunch-counter to protest the segregationist practices of that national chain. They were quickly emulated all over the South, at lunch-counters, movie houses, and other places of "public accommodation." A spate of litigation defended the protesters and challenged the segregationist practices—much of it handled by the NAACP Legal Defense Fund, Inc. (the "Inc. Fund"), led by Thurgood Marshall. In addition, there were ever-increasing public demonstrations, often led by Dr. King and the Southern Christian Leadership Conference, as well as the newly organized (and more radical) Student Non-Violent Coordinating Committee, not to mention a variety of other groups and leaders. The "Freedom Riders," many of them members of the Congress for Racial Equality, rode interstate buses into Alabama and Mississippi in 1961. They were met with systematic violence, much of it supported by state and local police and officials determined to preserve segregation. Nevertheless, at the national political level, relatively little happened; President John F. Kennedy depended on then-powerful Southern Democrats in both the House and Senate[30]—almost all of them avid supporters of segregation—to support his legislative agenda. As a result, Kennedy was at best a tepid supporter of civil rights during this period.

Matters changed after demonstrations in Birmingham, Alabama in April and May 1963. King, for example, was arrested and jailed, which led to his now-famous "Letter from a Birmingham Jail" setting out the case for immediate action and rejecting the call for "patience" on the part of African Americans faced with daily humiliations.[31] "We have waited for more than 340 years for our constitutional and God-given rights," King wrote.

> The nations of Asia and Africa are moving with jetlike speed toward gaining political independence, but we stiff creep at horse-and-buggy pace toward gaining a cup of coffee at a lunch counter. Perhaps it is easy for those who have never felt the stinging darts of segregation to say, "Wait." But when you have seen vicious mobs lynch your mothers and fathers at will and drown your sisters and brothers at whim; when you have seen hate-filled policemen curse, kick and even kill your black brothers and sisters; when you see the vast majority of your twenty million Negro brothers smothering in an airtight cage of poverty in the midst of an affluent society; when you suddenly find your tongue twisted and your speech

30. On the importance of these Southern Democrats to the ruling Democratic Party coalition, see Ira Katznelson, Fear Itself: The New Deal and the Origins of Our Time (2013).

31. Martin Luther King, Jr., Letter from a Birmingham Jail, April 16, 1963, at http://mlk-kpp01.stanford.edu/index.php/encyclopedia/documentsentry/annotated_letter_from_birmingham/.

> stammering as you seek to explain to your six-year-old daughter why she can't go to the public amusement park that has just been advertised on television, and see tears welling up in her eyes when she is told that Funtown is closed to colored children, and see ominous clouds of inferiority beginning to form in her little mental sky, and see her beginning to distort her personality by developing an unconscious bitterness toward white people; when you have to concoct an answer for a five-year-old son who is asking: "Daddy, why do white people treat colored people so mean?"; when you take a cross-country drive and find it necessary to sleep night after night in the uncomfortable corners of your automobile because no motel will accept you; when you are humiliated day in and day out by nagging signs reading "white" and "colored"; when your first name becomes "nigger," your middle name becomes "boy" (however old you are) and your last name becomes "John," and your wife and mother are never given the respected title "Mrs."; when you are harried by day and haunted by night by the fact that you are a Negro, living constantly at tiptoe stance, never quite knowing what to expect next, and are plagued with inner fears and outer resentments; when you go forever fighting a degenerating sense of "nobodiness"—then you will understand why we find it difficult to wait.

Birmingham was then wracked by renewed demonstrations, including a "Children's March." Over 3,000 children, some of them as young as nine years old, braved the wrath of Birmingham police under the direction of Police Commissioner Eugene "Bull" Connor and fire-hoses that he ordered directed at the children.[32] Children were arrested and jailed for many days. Television clips of this brutality, plus Alabama Governor George C. Wallace's attempt to resist a court order that would desegregate the University of Alabama, led to an important Civil Rights Address by President Kennedy on June 11, 1963, in which he argued for a new federal civil rights bill:[33]

> Difficulties over segregation and discrimination exist in every city, in every State of the Union, producing in many cities a rising tide of discontent that threatens the public safety. Nor is this a partisan issue. In a time of domestic crisis men of good will and generosity should be able to unite regardless of party or politics. This is not even a legal or legislative issue alone. It is better to settle these matters in the courts than on the streets, and new laws are needed at every level, but law alone cannot make men see right.
>
> We are confronted primarily with a moral issue. It is as old as the scriptures and is as clear as the American Constitution.
>
> The heart of the question is whether all Americans are to be afforded equal rights and equal opportunities, whether we are going to treat our

---

32. See, e.g., Cynthia Levinson, We've Got a Job: The 1963 Birmingham Children's March (2012).

33. The American Presidency Project, at http://www.presidency.ucsb.edu/ws/?pid=9271.

> fellow Americans as we want to be treated. If an American, because his skin is dark, cannot eat lunch in a restaurant open to the public, if he cannot send his children to the best public school available, if he cannot vote for the public officials who represent him, if, in short, he cannot enjoy the full and free life which all of us want, then who among us would be content to have the color of his skin changed and stand in his place? Who among us would then be content with the counsels of patience and delay?
>
> One hundred years of delay have passed since President Lincoln freed the slaves, yet their heirs, their grandsons, are not fully free. They are not yet freed from the bonds of injustice. They are not yet freed from social and economic oppression. And this Nation, for all its hopes and all its boasts, will not be fully free until all its citizens are free.
>
> . . . The fires of frustration and discord are burning in every city, North and South, where legal remedies are not at hand. Redress is sought in the streets, in demonstrations, parades, and protests which create tensions and threaten violence and threaten lives.
>
> We face, therefore, a moral crisis as a country and as a people. It cannot be met by repressive police action. It cannot be left to increased demonstrations in the streets. It cannot be quieted by token moves or talk. It is a time to act in the Congress, in your State and local legislative body and, above all, in all of our daily lives.

On August 28, 1963, the March on Washington for Jobs and Freedom culminated in a rally at the Lincoln Memorial. Martin Luther King, Jr. addressed the need for a civil rights bill during his famous "I Have A Dream" speech, arguing for, among other things, equality in public accommodations, criminal justice, employment, and voting rights:[34]

> There are those who are asking the devotees of civil rights, "When will you be satisfied?" We can never be satisfied as long as the Negro is the victim of the unspeakable horrors of police brutality. We can never be satisfied as long as our bodies, heavy with the fatigue of travel, cannot gain lodging in the motels of the highways and the hotels of the cities. We cannot be satisfied as long as the Negro's basic mobility is from a smaller ghetto to a larger one. We can never be satisfied as long as our children are stripped of their selfhood and robbed of their dignity by signs stating: "for whites only." We cannot be satisfied as long as a Negro in Mississippi cannot vote and a Negro in New York believes he has nothing for which to vote. No, no, we are not satisfied, and we will not be satisfied until "justice rolls down like waters, and righteousness like a mighty stream."

Kennedy's civil rights proposal soon stalled in Congress. Kennedy's assassination in November 1963 gave his successor, Lyndon B. Johnson, an opportunity to push through a civil rights bill, which became the Civil Rights Act of 1964. Passage

---

34. "I Have a Dream," Address delivered at the March on Washington for Jobs and Freedom, Martin Luther King, Jr. Papers Project, http://mlk-kpp01.stanford.edu/kingweb/publications/speeches/address_at_march_on_washington.pdf.

required overcoming the longest filibuster in American history, led by Georgia Senator Richard B. Russell. Among the most important speeches were those delivered by Democratic Minnesota Senator Hubert H. Humphrey (who would later be chosen by Johnson as his running mate for the 1964 election) and Illinois Republican Senator (and minority leader) Everett McKinley Dirksen.

Before beginning his three-and-a-half-hour speech, Humphrey opened a copy of the Bible and read aloud from Matthew 7:12: "'Therefore all things whatsoever ye would that men should do to you, do ye even so to them, for this is the law and the prophets.' . . . It is to fulfill this great admonition — this is what we are trying to do in this bill."[35] Humphrey argued that the central purpose of the new bill was freedom from humiliation.[36] Humphrey compared two books on the logistics of travel in America, one of them for families travelling with their dogs, the other for African Americans travelling to (and in) the South. "In Augusta, Ga., for example," Humphrey noted, "there are five hotels and motels that will take dogs, and only one where a Negro can go with confidence." Humphrey told his colleagues that if whites — and at that time *all* members of the Senate were white — "were to experience the humiliation and insult which awaits Negro Americans in thousands and thousands of such places, we, too, would be quick to protest." Humphrey's co-floor manager, the California Republican Thomas Kuchel, immediately followed up with a speech emphasizing the "urgency" of ending the "humiliating forms of discrimination" confronting Black Americans. President Johnson, a Texan, added his own voice by noting that "[w]e cannot deny to a group of our own people," he argued, "the essential elements of human dignity which a majority of our citizens claim for ourselves."

After many days of debate, it was still uncertain whether supporters could obtain the then-required two-thirds majority of the Senate to invoke "cloture," and bring the filibuster to an end. Dirksen delivered a famous speech that helped to procure the key final votes. Quoting Victor Hugo, Dirksen stated that "'*Stronger than all the armies is an idea whose time has come.*' The time has come for equality of opportunity in sharing in government, in education, and in employment. It will not be stayed or denied. It is here."[37]

> Since the act of 1875 on public accommodations and the Supreme Court decision of 1883 [*The Civil Rights Cases*] which struck it down, America has changed. The population then was 45 million. Today it is 190 million. In the Pledge of Allegiance to the Flag we intone, "One nation, under God." And so it is. It is an integrated nation. Air, rail, and highway transportation

---

35. The quotations in this paragraph are taken from Clay Risen, The Bill of the Century 191ff (2014).

36. Bruce A. Ackerman, We the People, Part Three: The Civil Rights Revolution (2014), a constitutional history of the period, argues that the anti-humiliation principle was the central focus of the Civil Rights Revolution.

37. See United States Congress, Senate, Congressional Record, 88th Cong. 2nd Sess., pp. 13319-13320, available at http://www.senate.gov/artandhistory/history/resources/pdf/DirksenCivilRights.pdf.

make it so. A common language makes it so. A tax pattern which applies equally to white and nonwhite makes it so. Literacy makes it so. The mobility provided by eighty million autos makes it so. The accommodations laws in thirty-four states and the District of Columbia makes it so. The fair employment practice laws in thirty states make it so. Yes, our land has changed since the Supreme Court decision of 1883. . . .

America grows. America changes. And on the civil rights issue we must rise with the occasion. That calls for cloture and for the enactment of a civil rights bill.

. . . [A]nother reason [is] our covenant with the people. For many years, each political party has given major consideration to a civil rights plank in its platform. . . . Were these pledges so much campaign stuff or did we mean it? Were these promises on civil rights but idle words for vote-getting purposes or were they a covenant meant to be kept? If all this was mere pretense, let us confess the sin of hypocrisy now and vow not to delude the people again. . . . To those who have charged me with doing a disservice to my party because of my interest in the enactment of a good civil rights bill—and there have been a good many who have made that charge—I can only say that our party found its faith in the Declaration of Independence in which a great Democrat, Jefferson by name, wrote the flaming words: *We hold these truths to be self-evident that all men are created equal.*

. . . There is another reason why we dare not temporize with the issue which is before us. It is essentially moral in character. It must be resolved. It will not go away. Its time has come. Nor is it the first time in our history that an issue with moral connotations and implications has swept away the resistance, the fulminations, the legalistic speeches, the ardent but dubious arguments, the lamentations and the thought patterns of an earlier generation and pushed forward to fruition. . . . [Dirksen offered various examples, including the abolition of child labor and the protection of women's suffrage under the Nineteenth Amendment.] These are but some of the things touching closely the affairs of the people which were met with stout resistance, with shrill and strident cries of radicalism, with strained legalisms, with anguished entreaties that the foundations of the Republic were being rocked. But an inexorable moral force which operates in the domain of human affairs swept these efforts aside and today they are accepted as parts of the social, economic and political fabric of America.

. . . Today is . . . the one hundredth anniversary of the nomination of Abraham Lincoln for a second term for the presidency on the Republican ticket. Two documents became the blueprints for his life and his conduct. The first was the Declaration of Independence which proclaimed the doctrine that all men are created equal. The second was the Constitution, the preamble to which began with the words: *We, the people . . . do ordain and establish this Constitution for the United States of America.* These were the articles of his superb and unquenchable faith. Nowhere and at no time did he more nobly reaffirm that faith than at Gettysburg 101 years ago when he spoke of "a new nation, conceived in liberty and dedicated to the proposition that all men are created equal." It is to take us further down that road that a bill is pending before us. We have a duty to get that job done. . . . I trust we shall not fail in that duty. . . .

DISCUSSION

1. *Constitutional arguments by politicians and by courts.* It is worth comparing the rhetoric of Senators Humphrey and Dirksen with that of the Supreme Court decisions upholding the Civil Rights Act, which appear infra. Humphrey invokes the Gospel of St. Matthew as stating the central purpose of the law; Dirksen invokes the Declaration, the Preamble to the Constitution, and the Gettysburg Address as justification for its passage.

Generally speaking, federal courts do not rely on the Declaration, the Preamble, or the Gettysburg Address as either binding or persuasive authority for constitutional arguments. Should they? What is the difference between permissible constitutional arguments by politicians in legislative debates and the constitutional arguments offered by courts in published opinions?

Consider Senator Humphrey's use of the Gospel of Matthew. As the centrality of Rev. Martin Luther King, Jr. to the Civil Rights Movement suggests, it is impossible to understand the passage of the Civil Rights Act without paying attention to the key role played by religion. Thus Clay Risen writes in his history of the Civil Rights Act, "Of all the forces and personalities that coalesced around the bill, perhaps none was more critical to its passage than the network of religious organizations and their array of adherents."[38] Would religious materials be a proper source of *legal or constitutional* insight (as opposed to moral insight) for a court deciding on the constitutionality of the Civil Rights Act? Could they be cited in an opinion in the same way that Humphrey does? If not, then what explains the difference between your expectations about courts and your expectations about Presidents, senators, and public officials like Humphrey?

2. *"An idea whose time has come."* Senator Dirksen dismissively contrasts "legalistic speeches" and "strained legalisms" that delay the resolution of important moral questions with the presence of "an inexorable moral force which operates in the domain of human affairs." How does Dirksen know that "the time has come" for a civil rights bill? Dirksen's opponents, such as Senator Barry Goldwater, argued that the Civil Rights Act was beyond Congress's powers and seriously interfered with individual liberty. Suppose that Dirksen conceded that earlier in the nation's history such a bill would not have been constitutional. What has changed in the interim to alter the correct interpretation of the Constitution? Put another way, what theory undergirds Dirksen's account of living constitutionalism?

2. Congressional Power to Pass the Civil Rights Bill

When Congress considered prohibiting race discrimination in employment, hotels, restaurants, and the like in the early 1960s, it faced a choice. Should it rely on its commerce powers, or should it rely instead on its explicit authority under §2 of the Thirteenth Amendment and §5 of the Fourteenth Amendment to "enforce" the provisions of these amendments?

Relying on Congress's Reconstruction powers would require the Supreme Court to confront and overrule (at least large chunks of) its 1883 decision in the Civil Rights Cases, supra Chapter 4. In the Civil Rights Cases, the Court had severely

38. Clay Risen, The Bill of the Century 195 (2014).

limited Congress's ability to enforce the Reconstruction Amendments by prohibiting private racial discrimination. In contrast, the constitutional struggle over the New Deal had given Congress broad powers to regulate private activity through regulating interstate commerce. Using those powers seemed like the path of least (judicial) resistance, because it went with the grain of recent cases like *Darby* and *Wickard* rather than against the grain of the Civil Rights Cases.

Lawyers in the Kennedy and Johnson Justice Departments were far more attracted by the Commerce Clause approach, and Attorney General Robert Kennedy's testimony before congressional committees emphasized the costs to the economy of racial discrimination. But there were problems with this approach, too. In his June 5, 1963 letter to the Department of Justice, Professor Gerald Gunther argued that the real issues underlying the proposed civil rights law had rather little to do with economic concerns, or with interstate externalities:[39]

> The proposed end run by way of the commerce clause seems to me ill-advised in every respect. . . . I know of course that the commerce power is a temptingly broad one. But surely responsible statutory drafting should have a firmer basis than, for example, some of the loose talk in recent newspaper articles about the widely accepted, unrestricted availability of the commerce clause to achieve social ends. Some qualifications seem in order. Thus, most of the obviously "social" laws, as with lottery and prostitution legislation, have their immediate impact on the interstate movement and rest on the power to prohibit that movement. Most "social" laws are not directly aimed at intrastate affairs, are not attempts to regulate internal activities as such. Where immediate regulations of intrastate conduct have been imposed, a demonstrable economic effect on interstate commerce, business, trade has normally been required. That kind of showing has been made, for example, with regard to the control of "local" affairs in the labor relations and agricultural production fields. The commerce clause "hook" has been put to some rather strained uses in the past, I know; but the substantive content of the commerce clause would have to be drained beyond any point yet reached to justify the simplistic argument that all intrastate activity may be subjected to any kind of national regulation merely because some formal crossing of an interstate boundary once took place, without regard to the relationship between the aim of the regulation and interstate trade. The aim of the proposed anti-discrimination legislation, I take it, is quite unrelated to any concern with national commerce in any substantive sense. It would, I think, pervert the meaning and purpose of the commerce clause to invoke it as the basis for this legislation.
>
> . . . I would much prefer to see the Government channel its resources of ingenuity and advocacy into the development of a viable interpretation of the Fourteenth Amendment, the provision with a natural linkage to the race problem. That would seem to me a considerably less demeaning task than the construction of an artificial commercial facade.

---

39. Quoted in Gerald Gunther, Constitutional Law 203 (10th ed. 1980).

In the Senate Committee hearings that ensued, a variety of views were expressed.[40] Senator Thurmond argued that earlier congressional legislation under the Commerce Clause involved efforts "to regulate economic affairs of life" whereas the pending civil rights Bill was designed to "regulate moral and social affairs." Attorney General Kennedy countered that discrimination itself "is having a very adverse effect on our economy." Assistant Attorney General Burke Marshall elaborated:

> Discrimination burdens Negro interstate travelers and therefore inhibits interstate travel. It artificially restricts the market available for interstate goods and services. . . . It inhibits the holding of conventions and meetings in segregated cities. . . . And it restricts business enterprises in their choice of location for offices and plants, thus preventing the most effective allocation of national resources.

Senator Cooper declared:

> If there is a right of equal use of accommodations held out to the public, it is a right of citizenship and a constitutional right under the 14th amendment. It has nothing to do with whether a business is in interstate commerce or whether discrimination against individuals places a burden on commerce. It does not depend upon the commerce clause and cannot be limited by that clause. . . .

Senator Pastore sounded a similar theme:

> I believe in this bill, because I believe in the dignity of man, not because it impedes our commerce. I don't think any man has a right to say to another man, You can't eat in my restaurant because you have dark skin; no matter how clean you are, you can't eat in my restaurant. That deprives a man of his full stature as an American citizen. That shocks me. That hurts me. And that is the reason why I want to vote for this law. . . . [W]hat we are talking about is a moral issue . . . [and] that morality, it seems to me, comes under the 14th amendment.

In response, Marshall cautioned that "I think it would be a mistake to rely solely on the 14th amendment . . . [because the Bill then] might not be held constitutional. I think it would be a disservice to pass a bill that was later thrown out by the Supreme Court."

In the end, Congress chose to place primary emphasis on its commerce power in enacting Title II of the Civil Rights Act of 1964, which prohibited discrimination and segregation in various places of "public accommodation" (such as hotels, restaurants, movie theaters, and sports arenas) "if [their] operations affect commerce." The statute went on to specify the "affect commerce" trigger with greater precision—for example, hotels containing more than five rooms, and restaurants offering to serve interstate travelers or where a "substantial portion" of the food served "has moved in commerce." The statute gave rise to two test cases, decided

40. For more extended excerpts than the items quoted here, see id. at 199-203.

the same day, challenging Congress's power to pass the Civil Rights Act. In each case, the Supreme Court unanimously upheld the statute, with Justice Clark writing for the Court.

HEART OF ATLANTA MOTEL v. UNITED STATES, 379 U.S. 241 (1964): *Heart of Atlanta* involved a challenge to Title II brought by an Atlanta, Georgia, motel with 216 rooms. The motel, the Court noted, stood readily accessible to interstate highways, advertised in various national media, and served a clientele 75 percent of which came from out of state. The Court held that the Commerce Clause gave Congress "ample power" on the facts of the case at hand, and declined to consider other possible sources of congressional power. Justice Clark pointed to testimony before Congress suggesting that "millions of people of all races travel[] from State to State; that Negroes in particular have been the subject of discrimination in transient accommodations, having to travel great distances to secure the same; that often they have been unable to obtain accommodations and have had to call upon friends to put them up overnight; and that these conditions had become so acute as to require the listing of available lodging for Negroes in a special guidebook which was itself 'dramatic testimony to the difficulties' Negroes encounter in travel."

The Court also noted a variety of prior congressional laws regulating, inter alia, white slavery, gambling, deceptive sales practices, securities fraud, drug misbranding, wages and hours, labor unions, crop control, and discrimination against shippers. In Clark's words:

> That Congress was legislating against moral wrongs in many of these areas rendered its enactments no less valid. In framing Title II of this Act Congress was also dealing with what it considered a moral problem. But that fact does not detract from the overwhelming evidence of the disruptive effect that racial discrimination has had on commercial intercourse. It was this burden which empowered Congress to enact appropriate legislation, and, given this basis for the exercise of its power, Congress was not restricted by the fact that the particular obstruction to interstate commerce with which it was dealing was also deemed a moral and social wrong.

KATZENBACH v. McCLUNG, 379 U.S. 294 (1964): [This case involved Ollie's Barbecue, a family-owned restaurant in Birmingham, Alabama, with a seating capacity of 220 customers located on a state highway 11 blocks from an interstate highway. Of the approximately $150,000 worth of food procured by the restaurant in the preceding year, almost half consisted of meat bought from a local supplier who had in turn procured it from outside the state.]

CLARK, J.:

[The testimony before Congress] is replete with . . . the burdens placed on interstate commerce by racial discrimination in restaurants. A comparison of per capita spending by Negroes in restaurants, theaters, and like establishments indicated less spending, after discounting income differences, in areas where discrimination is widely practiced. This condition, which was especially aggravated in the South, was attributed in the testimony of the Under Secretary of Commerce to racial segregation. This diminutive spending springing from a refusal to serve

Negroes and their total loss as customers has, regardless of the absence of direct evidence, a close connection to interstate commerce. The fewer customers a restaurant enjoys the less food it sells and consequently the less it buys. In addition, the Attorney General testified that this type of discrimination imposed "an artificial restriction on the market" and interfered with the flow of merchandise. In addition, there were many references to discriminatory situations causing wide unrest and having a depressant effect on general business conditions in the respective communities. . . . Likewise, it was said, that discrimination deterred professional, as well as skilled, people from moving into areas where such practices occurred and thereby caused industry to be reluctant to establish there.

We believe that this testimony afforded ample basis for the conclusion that established restaurants in such areas sold less interstate goods because of the discrimination, that interstate travel was obstructed directly by it, that business in general suffered and that many new businesses refrained from establishing there as a result of it. Hence the District Court was in error in concluding that there was no connection between discrimination and the movement of interstate commerce. The court's conclusion that such a connection is outside "common experience" flies in the face of stubborn fact. It goes without saying that, viewed in isolation, the volume of food purchased by Ollie's Barbecue from sources supplied from out of state was insignificant when compared with the total foodstuffs moving in commerce. But, as our late Brother Jackson said for the Court in Wickard v. Filburn, 317 U.S. 111 (1942): "That appellee's own contribution to the demand for wheat may be trivial by itself is not enough to remove him from scope of federal regulation where, as here, his contribution, taken together with that of many other similarly situated, is far from trivial." . . .

. . . Of course, the mere fact that Congress has said when a particular activity shall be deemed to affect commerce does not preclude further examination by this Court. But where we find that the legislators, in light of the facts and testimony before them, have a rational basis for finding a chosen regulatory scheme necessary to the protection of commerce, our investigation is at an end.

Justices Black, Douglas, and Goldberg each wrote a concurring opinion applicable to both *Heart of Atlanta* and *McClung*. All agreed that Title II could be sustained under the commerce power. Justices Black and Goldberg both implied that Congress also had power to prohibit discrimination in privately owned places of public accommodation under §5 of the Fourteenth Amendment.

Justice Douglas went further:

> I would prefer to rest on the assertion of legislative power contained in section 5 of the Fourteenth Amendment which states: "The Congress shall have power to enforce, by appropriate legislation, the provisions of this article"—a power which the Court concedes was exercised at least in part in this Act.
>
> A decision based on the Fourteenth Amendment would have a more settling effect, making unnecessary litigation over whether a particular restaurant or inn is within the commerce definitions of the Act or whether

a particular customer is an interstate traveler. Under my construction, the Act would apply to all customers in all the enumerated places of public accommodation. And that construction would put an end to all obstructionist strategies and finally close one door on a bitter chapter in American history.

How important was unanimity in these cases? Had Congress relied squarely and solely on its power to "enforce" the Thirteenth and Fourteenth Amendments, what were the odds that the 1964 Court would have upheld a federal law regulating the behavior of arguably "private" entities such as family-owned restaurants? Would the Court likely have been unanimous?[41]

How should a constitutionally conscientious member of Congress respond if he or she thinks that Congress *does* have broad Reconstruction power authority, but also believes that at least several Justices, and perhaps a majority, might disagree? For more discussion of the modern Supreme Court's understanding of Congress's Reconstruction powers, see Chapter 6.

DISCUSSION

1. *Later Commerce Clause cases.* Consider also Daniel v. Paul, 395 U.S. 298 (1969), and Perez v. United States, 402 U.S. 146 (1971). In *Daniel,* the Court applied Title II to the Lake Nixon Club, "a 232-acre amusement area with swimming, boating, sun bathing, picknicking, miniature golf, and dancing facilities and a snack bar," located near Little Rock, Arkansas. Under §201(c)(4), an entire establishment is covered by the Act if any covered facility "is physically located within its premises." The Court found that the snack bar was covered both because it offered to serve interstate travelers and because it served food that had moved in interstate commerce. Although the club advertised only in local media, these included a magazine distributed to guests at Little Rock hotels and restaurants. Justice Brennan

---

41. During the years immediately preceding enactment of the Civil Rights Act of 1964, many Black civil rights protesters were convicted in state courts for criminal trespass when they refused to leave places of public accommodation after being denied service because of their race. In several of these cases, the Supreme Court strained to find ways to overturn the trespass convictions without overturning the Civil Rights Cases. See Christopher W. Schmidt, The Sit-Ins and the State Action Doctrine, 18 Wm. & Mary Bill Rts. J. 767 (2010).

In Hamm v. City of Rock Hill, 379 U.S. 306 (1964), the Court construed Title II to abate all pending sit-in convictions, assuming without discussion that the commerce power authorized retroactive application of the Act. In dissent, Justices Black, Harlan, Stewart, and White criticized the Court's interpretation of the Act. Justices Black and Harlan also asserted that the interpretation presented constitutional difficulties, the latter noting that "the legislative record is barren of any evidence showing that giving effect to *past* state trespass convictions would result in placing any burden on *present* interstate commerce. Such evidence, at the very least, would be a prerequisite to the validity of any purported exercise of the Commerce power in this regard." Are these constitutional doubts well founded? Would there have been comparable doubts had Congress tried to rely more prominently on its Reconstruction powers?

wrote that "it would be unrealistic to assume that none of the 100,000 patrons actually served by the Club each season was an interstate traveler." Additionally, the snack bar served "a limited fare—hotdogs and hamburgers on buns, soft drinks, and milk. The District Court took judicial notice of the fact that the 'principal ingredients going into the bread were produced and processed in other States' and that 'certain ingredients [of the soft drinks] were probably obtained from out-of-State sources.' . . . Thus, at the very least, three of the four food items sold at the snack bar contain ingredients originating outside of the State. There can be no serious doubt that a 'substantial portion of the food' served at the snack bar has moved in interstate commerce."

Justice Black dissented. He objected to the Court's speculative assumptions of fact and concluded that the Act could not be applied to "this country people's recreation center, lying in what may be, so far as we know, a little 'sleepy hollow' between Arkansas hills miles away from any interstate highway. This would be stretching the Commerce Clause so as to give the Federal Government complete control over every little remote country place of recreation in every nook and cranny of every precinct and county in every one of the 50 states." Justice Black believed that application of the Act to the Lake Nixon Club could have been sustained under §5 of the Fourteenth Amendment but noted that, with respect to establishments of this sort, Congress had "tied the Act and limited its protection" to the commerce power.

The petitioner in *Perez* lent money to one Miranda and exacted increasingly large payments from him under threats of injuring him and his family. All of the events took place within New York State. The Court affirmed petitioner's conviction under the Federal Consumer Credit Protection Act for engaging in "extortionate credit transactions." Justice Douglas noted that the testimony before congressional committees supported the Act's findings that "[o]rganized crime is interstate and international in character. . . . A substantial part of the income of organized crime is generated by extortionate credit transactions. . . . Extortionate credit transactions are carried on to a substantial extent in interstate and foreign commerce and through the means and instrumentalities of such commerce. Even where extortionate credit transactions are purely intrastate in character, they nevertheless directly affect interstate and foreign commerce." To petitioner's argument that there was no evidence that his conduct had any interstate ramifications, Justice Douglas responded (citing *Darby* and *McClung*):

> Petitioner is clearly *a member of the class* which engages in extortionate credit transactions as defined by Congress. . . . Where the *class of activities* is regulated and that *class* is within the reach of federal power, the courts have no power "to excise as trivial, individual instances" of the class.

Only Justice Stewart dissented:

> [U]nder the statute before us a man can be convicted without any proof of interstate movement, of the use of the facilities of interstate commerce, or of facts showing that his conduct affected interstate commerce. I think the Framers of the Constitution never intended that the National Government might define as a crime and prosecute such wholly local activity through the enactment of federal criminal laws.

> In order to sustain this law we would, in my view, have to be able at the least to say that Congress could rationally have concluded that loan sharking is an activity with interstate attributes that distinguish it in some substantial respect from other local crime. But it is not enough to say that loan sharking is a national problem, for all crime is a national problem. It is not enough to say that some loan sharking has interstate characteristics, for any crime may have an interstate setting. And the circumstance that loan sharking has an adverse impact on interstate business is not a distinguishing attribute, for interstate business suffers from almost all criminal activity, be it shoplifting or violence in the streets.
>
> Because I am unable to discern any rational distinction between loan sharking and other local crime, I cannot escape the conclusion that this statute was beyond the power of Congress to enact. The definition and prosecution of local, intrastate crime are reserved to the States under the Ninth and Tenth Amendments.

2. *National problems versus federal (interstate) problems.* Consider the possibility that Justice Stewart's dissent in *Perez* was right in saying that Congress, before legislating, must do more than identify a "national" problem—that is, a problem that might exist everywhere. On this view, Congress should also identify a *federal* problem—a problem *between* the states, created by positive or negative "spillover effects" between states, or by the incapacity of individual states to deal with problems on their own. On one hand, imagine a crime that occurs everywhere, but whose effects are wholly localized, and felt within the state of the crime. In this situation, why shouldn't individual states be trusted to handle the problem? In other words, what reason exists for federal intervention on top (or instead) of state lawmaking? On the other hand, imagine a crime that either has important effects outside the crime state, or that has other important interstate features. Here, the argument against the permissibility of federal involvement seems much weaker. And on the facts of *Perez*, weren't there important federal (that is, interstate) features of the problem? Loansharking is typically not done by discrete local thugs, each acting alone. Rather, it often involves interstate networks of criminals—*organized* crime that is organized in part to exploit the limits of each state's power in a federal system. Acting alone, for example, no single state has plenary and unilateral authority to pursue investigations of coconspirators hiding out in sister states. On this view, *Perez* was indeed an easy case, involving both economic harms and interstate dimensions.

B. The Reconstruction Power in the Civil Rights Era

Between 1875 and 1957, Congress passed no major civil rights measures. And as we have seen, Congress chose to rely primarily on its Interstate Commerce Clause powers in adopting the Civil Rights Act of 1964. But over the following decades, several important cases reached the Court concerning the scope of Congress's powers under the Thirteenth, Fourteenth, and Fifteenth Amendments. The issues raised by these cases are myriad and intricate; many are considered at length in casebooks on civil rights and voting rights. For present purposes, our chief focus is on the interplay of congressional and judicial power to interpret and enforce the provisions of the Reconstruction Amendments.

These amendments are self-executing: The first section of each amendment prohibits certain practices even in the absence of implementing legislation. But each of the amendments also provides (with minor stylistic variation) that "Congress shall have the power to enforce this article by appropriate legislation."[42] What, precisely, does this mean? When Congress seeks to outlaw a given state law or private practice as violative of Congress's understanding of the Reconstruction Amendments, what should courts do if they have not yet ruled on the law or practice in question or, indeed, have *upheld* its constitutionality?

We have already seen one instance in which Congress may overrule a judicial decision. Since the *Wheeling Bridge* decision (1855), supra Chapter 3, Congress has had the final say about whether a state regulation of interstate commerce is impermissibly burdensome. However, the logic of the Commerce Clause arguably differs sharply from that of the Reconstruction Amendments. The Commerce Clause is in terms *solely* a grant of legislative power to Congress; its self-executing aspect had to be inferred and was, indeed, disputed well into the nineteenth century (and Justices Scalia and Thomas have revived the dispute in our own time; see Chapter 6, infra). When Congress legislates under the Commerce Clause, it need not concern itself with the constitutionality of any state statutes that the proposed law will affect or preempt; Congress must determine only that the proposed law is within its delegated powers and does not contravene any constitutional limitations.[43] Is the same true of congressional power under the Reconstruction Amendments, or does Congress have the power to prohibit only antecedently *unconstitutional* laws and practices? Also, note that Congress enjoys authority under the Commerce Clause to bless commerce-obstructing state laws and practices that would otherwise be declared unconstitutional by federal courts. Should Congress enjoy similar authority to undo (as opposed to add to) judicial declarations of rights under the Reconstruction Amendments?

Consider also congressional power to counter a judicial decision that a given *federal* law or practice passes constitutional muster. For example, wasn't Congress free to repeal the Sedition Act of 1798 even after federal courts had upheld the law? To repeal it even if the repeal were motivated by a belief that the courts had erred and that the Act was indeed unconstitutional? (Recall that, as events actually unfolded, Congress allowed the repressive Act to expire, and President Jefferson—who thought the Act unconstitutional—pardoned those who had already been convicted.) Does Congress's power to overrule the judiciary in a Sedition Act situation suggest that Congress should likewise be allowed to overrule judicial action that underprotects individual rights against the states? Or is there a decisive difference

---

42. This is also true of the Nineteenth, Twenty-Fourth, and Twenty-Sixth Amendments.

43. A typical example is the Federal Surface Mining Control and Reclamation Act of 1977, upheld in Hodel v. Virginia Surface Mining and Reclamation Assn., Inc., 452 U.S. 264 (1981), as a valid exercise of Congress's power under the Commerce Clause. The Act displaced a number of state regulations of strip mining, but Congress had no need to find, or even to inquire into the possibility, that these laws were "unconstitutional." It was enough that Congress found them hindrances to an effective national policy regarding strip mining.

between a Congress that limits *its own* powers beyond what the judiciary demands (as in the Sedition Act hypothetical), and a Congress that seeks to wield affirmative authority to limit *state laws or private practices* in the name of Reconstruction values of liberty, equality, and citizenship?

A good deal of congressional legislation under the Civil War Amendments is essentially procedural, designed narrowly to implement and enforce judicially declared rights. For example, 42 U.S.C. §1983, which is regularly invoked in civil rights litigation, does not purport to invalidate any state practices that a court has not independently held unconstitutional; rather, it is merely a device allowing aggrieved persons to come to court and present their claims. By contrast, the Voting Rights Act of 1965 invalidated state practices that no court had, or has to this day, declared per se unconstitutional. The passage of that Act led to an important debate in American politics about the purposes of the Reconstruction Amendments, and of the Constitution itself.

NOTE: THE VOTING RIGHTS ACT OF 1965

Given the difficulty of passing the Civil Rights Act of 1964, many observers assumed that it would be the last such bill for a while; instead, within a year it was succeeded by the Voting Rights Act of 1965, one of the most transformative pieces of legislation in our nation's history.

There are many explanations for the remarkably rapid shift from a focus on public accommodations and employment to voting rights, but one is the emphasis placed on voting rights by the Civil Rights Movement itself. Direct action—such as "sit-ins," the Children's March, and the August 1963 March on Washington—played an important role in creating the context within which the Civil Rights Act of 1964 was passed. Marches for voting rights helped generate support for the Voting Rights Act. President Johnson also made clear that he viewed civil rights as a fundamental commitment of his presidency.

On March 7, 1965, "Bloody Sunday," over 500 Black and white protesters attempted to cross the Edmund Pettus Bridge at the beginning of a march for voting rights. The march was planned to proceed from Selma, Alabama to the state capital of Montgomery. The marchers were met by remarkable violence led by Dallas County Sheriff Jim Clark; much of that violence was captured on national television. John Lewis, then a leader of the Student Non-Violent Coordinating Committee and later (because of the Voting Rights Act) a member of Congress representing Atlanta, had his skull split open. A white minister, James Reeb, was killed.

A second march began on March 9, but protesters were turned back by police. A third march was then planned, and the marchers sought court protection. Federal District Judge Frank M. Johnson[44] wrote that "[t]he law is clear that the right to petition one's government for the redress of grievances may be exercised in large

44. Johnson was one of the subjects of Jack Peltason's 58 Lonely Men: Southern Federal Judges and School Desegregation (1961), detailing the courage and travails of federal judges called upon to enforce civil rights in the South against the opposition of local whites—often under threats of personal violence.

groups . . . , and these rights may be exercised by marching, even along public highways."[45] Approximately 3,200 marchers crossed the Edmund Pettus Bridge on March 21, and by the time they reached Montgomery on March 25, after marching about 12 miles a day and sleeping in fields, they numbered about 25,000.

During the midst of the controversy, on March 15, 1965, President Johnson made a famous evening address before a joint session of Congress that was covered by all of the major television networks.

Lyndon B. Johnson, Special Message to the Congress: The American Promise

(March 15, 1965)[46]

I speak tonight for the dignity of man and the destiny of Democracy. I urge every member of both parties, Americans of all religions and of all colors, from every section of this country, to join me in that cause.

At times, history and fate meet at a single time in a single place to shape a turning point in man's unending search for freedom. So it was at Lexington and Concord. So it was a century ago at Appomattox. So it was last week in Selma, Alabama. There, long suffering men and women peacefully protested the denial of their rights as Americans. Many of them were brutally assaulted. One good man—a man of God—was killed.

There is no cause for pride in what has happened in Selma. There is no cause for self-satisfaction in the long denial of equal rights of millions of Americans. But there is cause for hope and for faith in our Democracy in what is happening here tonight. For the cries of pain and the hymns and protests of oppressed people have summoned into convocation all the majesty of this great government—the government of the greatest nation on earth. Our mission is at once the oldest and the most basic of this country—to right wrong, to do justice, to serve man. In our time we have come to live with the moments of great crises. Our lives have been marked with debate about great issues, issues of war and peace, issues of prosperity and depression.

But rarely in any time does an issue lay bare the secret heart of America itself. Rarely are we met with a challenge, not to our growth or abundance, or our welfare or our security, but rather to the values and the purposes and the meaning of our beloved nation. The issue of equal rights for American Negroes is such an issue. And should we defeat every enemy, and should we double our wealth and conquer the stars, and still be unequal to this issue, then we will have failed as a people and as a nation. For, with a country as with a person, "what is a man profited if he shall gain the whole world, and lose his own soul?"

---

45. Williams v. Wallace, 240 F. Supp. 100, 106 (M.D. Ala. 1960).

46. The American Presidency Project, at http://www.presidency.ucsb.edu/ws/?pid=26805; LBJ Presidential Library, http://www.lbjlib.utexas.edu/johnson/archives.hom/speeches.hom/650315.asp.

There is no Negro problem. There is no Southern problem. There is no Northern problem. There is only an American problem.

And we are met here tonight as Americans—not as Democrats or Republicans; we're met here as Americans to solve that problem. This was the first nation in the history of the world to be founded with a purpose.

The great phrases of that purpose still sound in every American heart, North and South: "All men are created equal." "Government by consent of the governed." "Give me liberty or give me death." And those are not just clever words, and those are not just empty theories. In their name Americans have fought and died for two centuries and tonight around the world they stand there as guardians of our liberty risking their lives. Those words are promised to every citizen that he shall share in the dignity of man. This dignity cannot be found in a man's possessions. It cannot be found in his power or in his position. It really rests on his right to be treated as a man equal in opportunity to all others. It says that he shall share in freedom. He shall choose his leaders, educate his children, provide for his family according to his ability and his merits as a human being.

To apply any other test, to deny a man his hopes because of his color or race or his religion or the place of his birth is not only to do injustice, it is to deny Americans and to dishonor the dead who gave their lives for American freedom. Our fathers believed that if this noble view of the rights of man was to flourish it must be rooted in democracy. This most basic right of all was the right to choose your own leaders. The history of this country in large measure is the history of expansion of the right to all of our people.

Many of the issues of civil rights are very complex and most difficult. But about this there can and should be no argument: every American citizen must have an equal right to vote. There is no reason which can excuse the denial of that right. There is no duty which weighs more heavily on us than the duty we have to insure that right. Yet the harsh fact is that in many places in this country men and women are kept from voting simply because they are Negroes.

Every device of which human ingenuity is capable, has been used to deny this right. The Negro citizen may go to register only to be told that the day is wrong, or the hour is late, or the official in charge is absent. And if he persists and, if he manages to present himself to the registrar, he may be disqualified because he did not spell out his middle name, or because he abbreviated a word on the application. And if he manages to fill out an application, he is given a test. The registrar is the sole judge of whether he passes this test. He may be asked to recite the entire Constitution, or explain the most complex provisions of state law.

And even a college degree cannot be used to prove that he can read and write. For the fact is that the only way to pass these barriers is to show a white skin. Experience has clearly shown that the existing process of law cannot overcome systematic and ingenious discrimination. No law that we now have on the books, and I have helped to put three of them there, can insure the right to vote when local officials are determined to deny it. In such a case, our duty must be clear to all of us. The Constitution says that no person shall be kept from voting because of his race or his color.

We have all sworn an oath before God to support and to defend that Constitution. We must now act in obedience to that oath. Wednesday, I will send to Congress a law designed to eliminate illegal barriers to the right to vote. . . .

This bill will establish a simple, uniform standard which cannot be used, however ingenious the effort, to flout our Constitution. It will provide for citizens to be registered by officials of the United States Government, if the state officials refuse to register them. It will eliminate tedious, unnecessary lawsuits which delay the right to vote. Finally, this legislation will insure that properly registered individuals are not prohibited from voting. . . .

But experience has plainly shown that this is the only path to carry out the command of the Constitution. To those who seek to avoid action by their national government in their home communities, who want to and who seek to maintain purely local control over elections, the answer is simple: open your polling places to all your people. Allow men and women to register and vote whatever the color of their skin. Extend the rights of citizenship to every citizen of this land. There is no Constitutional issue here. The command of the Constitution is plain. There is no moral issue. It is wrong—deadly wrong—to deny any of your fellow Americans the right to vote in this country.

There is no issue of state's rights or national rights. There is only the struggle for human rights. I have not the slightest doubt what will be your answer. But the last time a President sent a civil rights bill to the Congress it contained a provision to protect voting rights in Federal elections. That civil rights bill was passed after eight long months of debate. And when that bill came to my desk from the Congress for signature, the heart of the voting provision had been eliminated.

This time, on this issue, there must be no delay, or no hesitation, or no compromise with our purpose. We cannot, we must not, refuse to protect the right of every American to vote in every election that he may desire to participate in.

And we ought not, and we cannot, and we must not wait another eight months before we get a bill. We have already waited 100 years and more and the time for waiting is gone. So I ask you to join me in working long hours and nights and weekends, if necessary, to pass this bill. And I don't make that request lightly, for, from the window where I sit, with the problems of our country, I recognize that from outside this chamber is the outraged conscience of a nation, the grave concern of many nations and the harsh judgment of history on our acts.

But even if we pass this bill the battle will not be over. What happened in Selma is part of a far larger movement which reaches into every section and state of America. It is the effort of American Negroes to secure for themselves the full blessings of American life. Their cause must be our cause too. Because it's not just Negroes, but really it's all of us, who must overcome the crippling legacy of bigotry and injustice.

And we shall overcome.

As a man whose roots go deeply into Southern soil, I know how agonizing racial feelings are. I know how difficult it is to reshape the attitudes and the structure of our society. But a century has passed—more than 100 years—since the Negro was freed. And he is not fully free tonight. It was more than 100 years ago that Abraham Lincoln—a great President of another party—signed the Emancipation Proclamation. But emancipation is a proclamation and not a fact.

A century has passed—more than 100 years—since equality was promised, and yet the Negro is not equal. A century has passed since the day of promise, and the promise is unkept. The time of justice has now come, and I tell you that I believe sincerely that no force can hold it back. It is right in the eyes of man and God that it should come, and when it does, I think that day will brighten the lives of every American. For Negroes are not the only victims. How many white children have gone uneducated? How many white families have lived in stark poverty? How many white lives have been scarred by fear, because we wasted energy and our substance to maintain the barriers of hatred and terror?

And so I say to all of you here and to all in the nation tonight that those who appeal to you to hold on to the past do so at the cost of denying you your future. . . .

DISCUSSION

1. *Constitutional interpretation.* Johnson's speech, although clearly not in the form of a legal brief, nevertheless purports to interpret the deep meaning of the American Constitution. Note, in addition to his references to Matthew 16:26 and Patrick Henry's call for revolution, Johnson's use of the Declaration of Independence. This is not the first time in this casebook that we have seen the Declaration invoked as the key to the meaning of the American Constitution. Is the Declaration actually part of the Constitution, or is it merely a helpful (or perhaps indispensable) guide to its proper interpretation? See Akhil Reed Amar, America's Unwritten Constitution (2012); Charles L. Black, A New Birth of Freedom (1997).

2. *Overcoming.* Quoting the civil rights song of the 1960s, Johnson says that "we shall overcome." What precisely must be "overcome"? Is it custom, tradition, local government, or features of the Constitution itself? Is the tradition of racial injustice in the United States, and the use of state sovereignty and limited government to enforce that tradition, a *deviation* from the true meaning of the American experiment in democratic self-government? Or is it rather a *feature* of the American constitutional tradition that Johnson believes must now be "alter[ed] or abolish[ed]," to quote the words of the Declaration? (Compare the contrasting views of Frederick Douglass and William Lloyd Garrison about the relationship between the antebellum Constitution and slavery).

Note that, like the 1964 Civil Rights Act, the 1965 Voting Rights Act was criticized as inconsistent with federalism and limited federal power. The new act intervened significantly into one of the most central functions of state and local governments—holding elections. The Act also treated some states—particularly those in the former Confederacy—differently from those in other parts of the country. (We will see this objection resurface almost 50 years later, in 2013, in Shelby County v. Holder, Chapter 6, infra. In *Shelby County*, the Roberts Court struck down part of the Act under the principle of "equal sovereignty" of the states.)

Does Johnson's argument mean that older constitutional understandings of limited federal power—and concomitant protections for state's rights—must be "overcome" and replaced by new understandings more congruent with the Declaration's claim of equality and the Preamble's call to "establish justice"? Why, precisely, *should* the Constitution's limitations on federal power and its checks and balances be altered to match changing notions of what is just and unjust? What is Johnson's answer to this question?

3. *The equal right to vote.* Johnson states that "every American citizen must have an equal right to vote" and that although "[m]any of the issues of civil rights are

very complex and most difficult . . . about this [one] there can and should be no argument. . . . There is no reason which can excuse the denial of that right."

Is Johnson merely making a point about *racial* equality, or is he making the much broader claim that "*every* American citizen must have an *equal* right to vote"? If so, what is the basis of this assertion? One possibility might be a narrative argument: Consider his claim that "The history of this country in large measure is the history of expansion of the right to all of our people." What is the normative force of that story? How does the Declaration, which speaks of the equality of *persons*—including aliens, who ordinarily do not have the right to vote—support Johnson's argument, which is about the equality of *citizens* to vote?

If there is a general right to vote implied in the Constitution, what limits on the franchise (e.g., residency, mental competency) should still be permitted? In Harper v. Virginia Board of Elections, 383 U.S. 663 (1966) (discussed in Chapter 10 infra), the Court held that the right to vote is a "fundamental interest" protected by the Equal Protection Clause. *Harper* was a challenge to poll taxes in state elections. The text of the recently adopted Twenty-Fourth Amendment (ratified in January 1964) had banned poll taxes only in *federal* elections; nevertheless, in *Harper* the Court argued that imposing poll taxes in *state* elections violated the Equal Protection Clause.

In Oregon v. Mitchell, 400 U.S. 112 (1970), discussed infra, the Court held that Congress did not have the power to prevent age discrimination in voting by statute. In response, the Twenty-Sixth Amendment was adopted in 1971. It provides that no person 18 or older may be denied the right to vote on the basis of age.

Following its passage, the Voting Rights Act was soon challenged in federal court. In the two cases set out below, the Supreme Court sustained provisions of the Act that banned the use of various literacy tests, even though only a few years earlier the Court had unanimously upheld a literacy test against constitutional attack in Lassiter v. Northampton Board of Elections, 360 U.S. 45 (1959).

South Carolina v. Katzenbach

383 U.S. 301 (1966)

WARREN, C.J.

The Voting Rights Act was designed by Congress to banish the blight of racial discrimination in voting, which has infected the electoral process in part of our country for nearly a century. The Act creates stringent new remedies for voting discrimination where it persists on a pervasive scale, and in addition the statute strengthens existing remedies for pockets of voting discrimination elsewhere in the country. . . .

I

Two points emerge vividly from the voluminous legislative history of the Act contained in the committee hearings and floor debates. First: Congress felt itself confronted by an insidious and pervasive evil which had been perpetuated in certain parts of our country through unremitting and ingenious defiance of the Constitution. Second: Congress concluded that the unsuccessful remedies which it had prescribed in the past would have to be replaced by sterner and more elaborate measures in order to satisfy the clear commands of the Fifteenth Amendment. . . .

[B]eginning in 1890, the States of Alabama, Georgia, Louisiana, Mississippi, North Carolina, South Carolina, and Virginia enacted tests still in use which were specifically designed to prevent Negroes from voting. Typically, they made the ability to read and write a registration qualification and also required completion of a registration form. These laws were based on the fact that as of 1890 in each of the named States, more than two-thirds of the adult Negroes were illiterate while less than one-quarter of the adult whites were unable to read or write. At the same time, alternate tests were prescribed in all of the named States to assure that white illiterates would not be deprived of the franchise. These included grandfather clauses, property qualifications, "good character" tests, and the requirement that registrants "understand" or "interpret" certain matter.

The course of subsequent Fifteenth Amendment litigation in this Court demonstrates the variety and persistence of these and similar institutions designed to deprive Negroes of the right to vote. Grandfather clauses were invalidated in Guinn v. United States, 238 U.S. 347, and Myers v. Anderson, 238 U.S. 368. Procedural hurdles were struck down in Lane v. Wilson, 307 U.S. 268. The white primary was outlawed in Smith v. Allwright, 321 U.S. 649, and Terry v. Adams, 345 U.S. 461. Improper challenges were nullified in United States v. Thomas, 362 U.S. 58. Racial gerrymandering was forbidden by Gomillion v. Lightfoot, 364 U.S. 339. Finally, discriminatory application of voting tests was condemned in Schnell v. Davis, 336 U.S. 933; Alabama v. United States, 371 U.S. 37; and Louisiana v. United States, 380 U.S. 145.

According to the evidence in recent Justice Department voting suits, the latter stratagem is now the principal method used to bar Negroes from the polls. Discriminatory administration of voting qualifications has been found in all eight Alabama cases, in all nine Louisiana cases, and in all nine Mississippi cases which have gone to final judgment. Moreover, in almost all of these cases, the courts have held that the discrimination was pursuant to a widespread "pattern or practice." White applicants for registration have often been excused altogether from the literacy and understanding tests or have been given easy versions, have received extensive help from voting officials, and have been registered despite serious errors in their answers. Negroes, on the other hand, have typically been required to pass difficult versions of all the tests, without any outside assistance and without the slightest error. The good-morals requirement is so vague and subjective that it has constituted an open invitation to abuse at the hands of voting officials. Negroes obliged to obtain vouchers from registered voters have found it virtually impossible to comply in areas where almost no Negroes are on the rolls.

In recent years, Congress has repeatedly tried to cope with the problem by facilitating case-by-case litigation against voting discrimination. . . . Despite the earnest efforts of the Justice Department and of many federal judges, these new laws have done little to cure the problem of voting discrimination. . . .

The previous legislation has proved ineffective for a number of reasons. Voting suits are unusually onerous to prepare, sometimes requiring as many as 6,000 man-hours spent combing through registration records in preparation for trial. Litigation has been exceedingly slow, in part because of the ample opportunities for delay afforded voting officials and others involved in the proceedings. Even when favorable decisions have finally been obtained, some of the States affected have merely switched to discriminatory devices not covered by the federal decrees or have enacted difficult new tests designed to prolong the existing disparity between white and Negro registration. Alternatively, certain local officials have defied and evaded court orders or have simply closed their registration offices to freeze the voting rolls. . . .

II

The Voting Rights Act of 1965 reflects Congress' firm intention to rid the country of racial discrimination in voting. The heart of the Act is a complex scheme of stringent remedies aimed at areas where voting discrimination has been most flagrant. Section 4(a)-(d) lays down a formula defining the States and political subdivisions to which these new remedies apply.

The first of the remedies . . . is the suspension of literacy tests and similar voting qualifications for a period of five years from the last occurrence of substantial voting discrimination. Section 5 prescribes a second remedy, the suspension of all new voting regulations pending review by federal authorities to determine whether their use would perpetuate voting discrimination. The third remedy . . . is the assignment of federal examiners on certification by the Attorney General to list qualified applicants who are thereafter entitled to vote in all elections. . . .

Coverage Formula

The remedial sections of the Act assailed by South Carolina automatically apply to any State, or to any separate political subdivision such as a county or parish, for which [certain specific] findings have been made [concerning low voting registration or voting participation, and the use of certain specified voting tests susceptible to discriminatory application].

Statutory coverage of a State or political subdivision under §4(b) is terminated if the area obtains a declaratory judgment from the District Court for the District of Columbia, determining that tests and devices have not been used during the preceding five years to abridge the franchise on racial grounds. . . .

Suspension of Tests

In a State or political subdivision covered by §4(b) of the Act, no person may be denied the right to vote in any election because of his failure to comply with a "test or device." On account of this provision, South Carolina is temporarily barred from enforcing [its literacy test]. . . .

III

. . . [T]he basic question presented by the case [is]: Has Congress exercised its powers under the Fifteenth Amendment in an appropriate manner with relation to the States? . . .

Section 1 of the Fifteenth Amendment . . . has always been treated as self-executing and has repeatedly been construed, without further legislative specification, to invalidate state voting qualifications or procedures which are discriminatory on their face or in practice.

South Carolina contends that the cases cited above are precedents only for the authority of the judiciary to strike down state statutes and procedures—that to allow an exercise of this authority by Congress would be to rob the courts of their rightful constitutional role. On the contrary, §2 of the Fifteenth Amendment expressly declares that "Congress shall have power to enforce this article by appropriate legislation." By adding this authorization, the framers indicated that Congress was to be chiefly responsible for implementing the rights created in §1. "It is the power of Congress which has been enlarged. Congress is authorized to *enforce* the prohibitions by appropriate legislation. Some legislation is contemplated to make the [Civil War] amendments fully effective." Ex parte Virginia, 100 U.S. 339, 345. Accordingly, in addition to the courts, Congress has full remedial powers to effectuate the constitutional prohibition against racial discrimination in voting.

Congress has repeatedly exercised these powers in the past, and its enactments have repeatedly been upheld. . . . The basic test to be applied in a case involving §2 of the Fifteenth Amendment is the same as in all cases concerning the express powers of Congress with relation to the reserved powers of the States. Chief Justice Marshall laid down the classic formulation, 50 years before the Fifteenth Amendment was ratified: "Let the end be legitimate, let it be within the scope of the constitution, and all means which are appropriate, which are plainly adapted to that end, which are not prohibited, but consist with the letter and spirit of the constitution, are constitutional." *McCulloch.* The Court has subsequently echoed his language in describing each of the Civil War Amendments. . . .

We therefore reject South Carolina's argument that Congress may appropriately do no more than to forbid violations of the Fifteenth Amendment in general terms—that the task of fashioning specific remedies or of applying them to particular localities must necessarily be left entirely to the courts. Congress is not circumscribed by any such artificial rules under §2 of the Fifteenth Amendment.

IV

Congress exercised its authority under the Fifteenth Amendment in an inventive manner when it enacted the Voting Rights Act of 1965. . . . Congress had found that case-by-case litigation was inadequate to combat widespread and persistent discrimination in voting, because of the inordinate amount of time and energy required to overcome the obstructionist tactics invariably encountered in these lawsuits. After enduring nearly a century of systematic resistance of the Fifteenth Amendment, Congress might well decide to shift the advantage of time and inertia from the perpetrators of the evil to its victims. . . .

The Act intentionally confines these remedies to a small number of States and political subdivisions which in most instances were familiar to Congress by name. This, too, was a permissible method of dealing with the problem. Congress had learned that substantial voting discrimination presently occurs in certain sections of the country, and it knew no way of accurately forecasting whether the evil might spread elsewhere in the future. In acceptable legislative fashion, Congress chose to limit its attention to the geographic areas where immediate action seemed necessary. . . .

Suspension of Tests

We now arrive at consideration of the specific remedies prescribed by the Act for areas included within the coverage formula. South Carolina assails the temporary suspension of existing voting qualifications, reciting the rule laid down by

Lassiter v. Northampton County Bd. of Elections, 360 U.S. 45 (1959), that literacy tests and related devices are not in themselves contrary to the Fifteenth Amendment. In that very case, however, the Court went on to say, "Of course a literacy test, fair on its face, may be employed to perpetuate that discrimination which the Fifteenth Amendment was designed to uproot." The record shows that in most of the States covered by the Act, including South Carolina, various tests and devices have been instituted with the purpose of disenfranchising Negroes, have been framed in such a way as to facilitate this aim, and have been administered in a discriminatory fashion for many years. Under these circumstances, the Fifteenth Amendment has clearly been violated.

BLACK, J., concurring and dissenting.

I agree with substantially all of the Court's opinion sustaining the power of Congress under §2 of the Fifteenth Amendment to suspend state literacy tests and similar voting qualifications and to authorize the Attorney General to secure the appointment of federal examiners to register qualified voters in various sections of the country. . . .

I dissent from its holding that every part of §5 of the Act is constitutional. . . . Section 5 [provides] that a State covered by §4(b) can in no way amend its constitution or laws relating to voting without first trying to persuade the Attorney General of the United States or the Federal District Court for the District of Columbia that the new proposed laws do not have the purpose and will not have the effect of denying the right to vote to citizens on account of their race or color.

. . . Section 5, by providing that some of the States cannot pass state laws or adopt state constitutional amendments without first being compelled to beg federal authorities to approve their policies, so distorts our constitutional structure of government as to render any distinction drawn in the Constitution between state and federal power almost meaningless.

Katzenbach v. Morgan

384 U.S. 641 (1966)

BRENNAN, J.

These cases concern the constitutionality of §4(e) of the Voting Rights Act of 1965. [It] provides that no person who has successfully completed the sixth primary grade in a public school in, or a private school accredited by, the Commonwealth of Puerto Rico in which the language of instruction was other than English shall be denied the right to vote in any election because of his inability to read or write English.

Appellees, registered voters in New York City, brought this suit to challenge the constitutionality of §4(e) insofar as it pro tanto prohibits the enforcement of the election laws of New York requiring an ability to read and write English as a condition of voting. . . .

The Attorney General of the State of New York argues that . . . §4(e) cannot be sustained as appropriate legislation to enforce the Equal Protection Clause unless the judiciary decides—even with the guidance of a congressional judgment—that the application of the English literacy requirement prohibited by §4(e) is forbidden by the Equal Protection Clause itself. We disagree. Neither the language nor history of §5 supports such a construction. As was said with regard to §5 in Ex parte Virginia, "It is the power of Congress which has been enlarged. Congress is authorized to *enforce* the prohibitions by appropriate legislation. Some legislation is contemplated to make the amendments fully effective." A construction of §5 that would require a judicial determination that the enforcement of the state law precluded by Congress violated the Amendment, as a condition of sustaining the congressional enactment, would depreciate both congressional resourcefulness and congressional responsibility for implementing the Amendment. It would confine the legislative power in this context to the insignificant role of abrogating only those state laws that the judicial branch was prepared to adjudge unconstitutional. . . .

Thus our task in this case is not to determine whether the New York English literacy requirement as applied to deny the right to vote to a person who successfully completed the sixth grade in a Puerto Rican school violates the Equal Protection Clause. Accordingly, our decision in Lassiter v. Northampton Election Bd. sustaining the North Carolina English literacy requirement as not in all circumstances prohibited by the first sections of the Fourteenth and Fifteenth Amendments, is inapposite. *Lassiter* did not present the question before us here: Without regard to whether the judiciary would find that the Equal Protection Clause itself nullifies New York's English literacy requirement as so applied, could Congress prohibit the enforcement of the state law by legislating under §5 of the Fourteenth Amendment? In answering this question, our task is limited to determining whether such legislation is, as required by §5, appropriate legislation to enforce the Equal Protection Clause.

By including §5 the draftsmen sought to grant to Congress, by a specific provision applicable to the Fourteenth Amendment, the same broad powers expressed in the Necessary and Proper Clause. . . . Correctly viewed, §5 is a positive grant of legislative power authorizing Congress to exercise its discretion in determining whether and what legislation is needed to secure the guarantees of the Fourteenth Amendment.

We therefore proceed to the consideration whether §4(e) is "appropriate legislation" to enforce the Equal Protection Clause, that is, under the *McCulloch* standard, whether §4(e) may be regarded as an enactment to enforce the Equal Protection Clause, whether it is "plainly adapted to that end" and whether it is not prohibited by but is consistent with "the letter and spirit of the constitution."[a]

There can be no doubt that §4(e) may be regarded as an enactment to enforce the Equal Protection Clause. . . . More specifically, §4(e) may be viewed as

---

a. Contrary to the suggestion of the dissent, §5 does not grant Congress power to exercise discretion in the other direction and to enact "statutes so as in effect to dilute equal protection and due process decisions of this Court." We emphasize that Congress' power under §5 is limited to adopting measures to enforce the guarantees of the Amendment: §5 grants Congress no power to restrict, abrogate, or dilute these guarantees. Thus, for example, an enactment authorizing the States to establish racially segregated systems of education would not be—as required by §5—a measure "to enforce" the Equal Protection Clause since that clause of its own force prohibits such state laws.

a measure to secure for the Puerto Rican community residing in New York nondiscriminatory treatment by government—both in the imposition of voting qualifications and the provision or administration of governmental services, such as public schools, public housing and law enforcement.

Section 4(e) [is] "plainly adapted" to furthering these aims of the Equal Protection Clause. The practical effect of §4(e) is to prohibit New York from denying the right to vote to large segments of its Puerto Rican community. Congress has thus prohibited the State from denying to that community the right that is "preservative of all rights." This enhanced political power will be helpful in gaining nondiscriminatory treatment in public services for the entire Puerto Rican community.[b] Section 4(e) thereby enables the Puerto Rican minority better to obtain "perfect equality of civil rights and the equal protection of the laws."

It was well within congressional authority to say that this need of the Puerto Rican minority for the vote warranted federal intrusion upon any state interests served by the English literacy requirement. It was for Congress, as the branch that made this judgment, to assess and weigh the various conflicting considerations—the risk or pervasiveness of the discrimination in governmental services, the effectiveness of eliminating the state restriction on the right to vote as a means of dealing with the evil, the adequacy or availability of alternative remedies, and the nature and significance of the state interests that would be affected by the nullification of the English literacy requirement as applied to residents who have successfully completed the sixth grade in a Puerto Rican school. It is not for us to review the congressional resolution of these factors. It is enough that we be able to perceive a basis upon which the Congress might resolve the conflict as it did. There plainly was such a basis to support §4(e) in the application in question in this case. Any contrary conclusion would require us to be blind to the realities familiar to the legislators.

The result is no different if we confine our inquiry to the question whether §4(e) was merely legislation aimed at the elimination of an invidious discrimination in establishing voter qualifications.

We are told that New York's English literacy requirement originated in the desire to provide an incentive for non-English speaking immigrants to learn the English language and in order to assure the intelligent exercise of the franchise. Yet Congress might well have questioned, in light of the many exemptions provided,[c]

---

b. Cf. James Everard's Breweries v. Day, 265 U.S. 545 (1924), which held that, under the enforcement clause of the Eighteenth Amendment, Congress could prohibit the prescription of intoxicating malt liquor for medicinal purposes even though the Amendment itself only prohibited the manufacture and sale of intoxicating liquors for beverage purposes. Cf. also the settled principle applied in the Shreveport Case . . . and expressed in United States v. Darby, 312 U.S. 100, 118, that the power of Congress to regulate interstate commerce "extends to those activities intrastate which so affect interstate commerce or the exercise of the power of Congress over it as to make regulation of them appropriate means to the attainment of a legitimate end. . . ."

c. The principal exemption complained of is that for persons who had been eligible to vote before January 1, 1922.

and some evidence suggesting that prejudice played a prominent role,[d] whether these were actually the interests being served. Congress might have also questioned whether denial of a right deemed so precious and fundamental in our society was a necessary or appropriate means of encouraging persons to learn English, or of furthering the goal of an intelligent exercise of the franchise. Finally, Congress might well have concluded that as a means of furthering the intelligent exercise of the franchise, an ability to read or understand Spanish is as effective as ability to read English for those to whom Spanish-language newspapers and Spanish-language radio and television programs are available to inform them of election issues and governmental affairs. Since Congress undertook to legislate so as to preclude the enforcement of the state law, and did so in the context of a general appraisal of literacy requirements for voting, see South Carolina v. Katzenbach, supra, to which it brought a specially informed legislative competence, it was Congress' prerogative to weigh these competing considerations. . . .

There remains the question whether the congressional remedies adopted in §4(e) constitute means which are not prohibited by, but are consistent "with the letter and spirit of the constitution." [A]ppellees contend that §4(e) fails in this regard [because it] works an invidious discrimination in violation of the Fifth Amendment[.] [Section 4(e)] prohibit[s] the enforcement of the English literacy requirement only for those educated in American-flag schools (schools located within United States jurisdiction) in which the language of instruction was other than English, and not for those educated in schools beyond the territorial limits of the United States in which the language of instruction was also other than English. This is not a complaint that Congress, in enacting §4(e), has unconstitutionally denied or diluted anyone's right to vote but rather that Congress violated the Constitution by not extending the relief effected in §4(e) to those educated in non-American-flag schools. . . .

Section 4(e) does not restrict or deny the franchise but in effect extends the franchise to persons who otherwise would be denied it by state law. . . . We need only decide whether the challenged limitation on the relief effected in §4(e) was permissible. In deciding that question, that principle that calls for the closest scrutiny of distinctions in laws *denying* fundamental rights is inapplicable; for the distinction challenged by appellees is presented only as a limitation on a reform measure aimed at eliminating an existing barrier to the exercise of the franchise. Rather, in deciding the constitutional propriety of the limitations in such a reform measure we are guided by the familiar principles that . . . "reform may take one step at a time, addressing itself to the phase of the problem which seems most acute to the legislative mind," Williamson v. Lee Optical Co.

---

d. This evidence consists in part of statements made in the Constitutional Convention first considering the English literacy requirement, such as the following made by the sponsor of the measure: "More precious even than the forms of government are the mental qualities of our race. While those stand unimpaired, all is safe. They are exposed to a single danger, and that is that by constantly changing our voting citizenship through the wholesale, but valuable and necessary infusion of Southern and Eastern European races. . . . The danger has begun. . . . We should check it." . . .

. . . In the context of the case before us, the congressional choice to limit the relief effected in §4(e) may, for example, reflect Congress' greater familiarity with the quality of instruction in American-flag schools, a recognition of the unique historic relationship between the Congress and the Commonwealth of Puerto Rico, an awareness of the Federal Government's acceptance of the desirability of the use of Spanish as the language of instruction in Commonwealth schools, and the fact that Congress has fostered policies encouraging migration from the Commonwealth to the States. . . . We hold . . . that the limitation on relief effected in §4(e) does not constitute a forbidden discrimination since these factors might well have been the basis for the decision of Congress to go "no farther than it did."

[Cardona v. Power, 384 U.S. 672 (1966), decided on the same day as *Morgan*, overturned the New York Court of Appeals, which had sustained the English literacy requirement against the challenge of appellant, a resident of New York educated in Puerto Rico, who did not, however, allege that she had completed sixth grade (as required by §4(e) of the Voting Rights Act). The Supreme Court vacated the judgment and remanded the case to allow the state court to determine whether appellant was covered by §4(e), and, alternatively, whether "in light of this federal enactment, those applications of the New York English literacy requirement not in terms prohibited by §4(e) have continuing validity."

Justice Harlan dissented in both cases, arguing that the New York literacy requirement challenged in *Cardona* was constitutional and that §4(e) of the Voting Rights Act challenged in *Morgan* was unconstitutional.]

HARLAN, J., joined by STEWART, J., dissenting.

I. THE *CARDONA* CASE

I believe the same interests recounted in *Lassiter* indubitably point toward upholding the rationality of the New York voting test. It is true that the issue here is not so simply drawn between literacy per se and illiteracy. Appellant alleges that she is literate in Spanish, and that she studied American history and government in United States Spanish-speaking schools in Puerto Rico. . . .

Although to be sure there is a difference between a totally illiterate person and one who is literate in a foreign tongue, I do not believe that this added factor vitiates the constitutionality of the New York statute. Accepting appellant's allegations as true, it is nevertheless also true that the range of material available to a resident of New York literate only in Spanish is much more limited than what is available to an English-speaking resident, that the business of national, state, and local government is conducted in English, and that propositions, amendments, and offices for which candidates are running listed on the ballot are likewise in English. It is also true that most candidates, certainly those campaigning on a national or statewide level, make their speeches in English. New York may justifiably want its voters to be able to understand candidates directly, rather than through possibly imprecise translations or summaries reported in a limited number of Spanish news media. . . . Given the State's legitimate concern with promoting and safeguarding the intelligent use of the ballot, and given also New York's long experience with the process of integrating non-English-speaking residents into the mainstream of

American life, I do not see how it can be said that this qualification for suffrage is unconstitutional. I would uphold the validity of the New York statute, unless the federal statute prevents that result, the question to which I now turn.

II. THE *MORGAN* CASES . . .

The pivotal question in [these cases] is what effect the added factor of a congressional enactment has on the straight equal protection argument dealt with above. The Court declares that since §5 of the Fourteenth Amendment gives to the Congress power to "enforce" the prohibitions of the Amendment by "appropriate" legislation, the test for judicial review of any congressional determination in this area is simply one of rationality; that is, in effect, was Congress acting rationally in declaring that the New York statute is irrational? . . . I believe the Court has confused the issue of how much enforcement power Congress possesses under §5 with the distinct issue of what questions are appropriate for congressional determination and what questions are essentially judicial in nature.

When [judicially] recognized state violations of federal constitutional standards have occurred, Congress is of course empowered by §5 to take appropriate remedial measures to redress and prevent the wrongs. . . .

Section 4(e), however, presents a significantly different type of congressional enactment. The question here is not whether the statute is appropriate remedial legislation to cure an established violation of a constitutional command, but whether there has in fact been an infringement of that constitutional command, that is, whether a particular state practice or, as here, a statute is so arbitrary or irrational as to offend the command of the Equal Protection Clause of the Fourteenth Amendment. That question is one for the judicial branch ultimately to determine. Were the rule otherwise, Congress would be able to qualify this Court's constitutional decisions under the Fourteenth and Fifteenth Amendments, let alone those under other provisions of the Constitution, by resorting to congressional power under the Necessary and Proper Clause. In view of this Court's holding in *Lassiter*, that an English literacy test is a permissible exercise of state supervision over its franchise, I do not think it is open to Congress to limit the effect of that decision as it has undertaken to do by §4(e). In effect the Court reads §5 of the Fourteenth Amendment as giving Congress the power to define the *substantive* scope of the Amendment. If that indeed be the true reach of §5, then I do not see why Congress should not be able as well to exercise its §5 "discretion" by enacting statutes so as in effect to dilute equal protection and due process decisions of this Court. In all such cases there is room for reasonable men to differ as to whether or not a denial of equal protection or due process has occurred, and the final decision is one of judgment. Until today this judgment has always been one for the judiciary to resolve.

I do not mean to suggest in what has been said that a legislative judgment of the type incorporated in §4(e) is without any force whatsoever. Decisions on questions of equal protection and due process are based not on abstract logic, but on empirical foundations. To the extent "legislative facts" are relevant to a judicial determination, Congress is well equipped to investigate them, and such determinations are of course entitled to due respect. In South Carolina v. Katzenbach such legislative findings were made to show that racial discrimination in voting was actually occurring. Similarly, in Heart of Atlanta Motel, Inc. v. United States, 379 U.S. 241, and Katzenbach

v. McClung, 379 U.S. 294, this Court upheld Title II of the Civil Rights Act of 1964 under the Commerce Clause. There again the congressional determination that racial discrimination in a clearly defined group of public accommodations did effectively impede interstate commerce was based on "voluminous testimony," which had been put before the Congress and in the context of which it passed remedial legislation.

But no such factual data provide a legislative record supporting §4(e) by way of showing that Spanish-speaking citizens are fully as capable of making informed decisions in a New York election as are English-speaking citizens. Nor was there any showing whatever to support the Court's alternative argument that §4(e) should be viewed as but a remedial measure designed to cure or assure against unconstitutional discrimination of other varieties, e.g., in "public schools, public housing and law enforcement," to which Puerto Rican minorities might be subject in such communities as New York. . . .

At least in the area of primary state concern a state statute that passes constitutional muster under the judicial standard of rationality should not be permitted to be set at naught by a mere contrary congressional pronouncement unsupported by a legislative record justifying that conclusion. . . .

DISCUSSION

1. *Later voting cases.* The Voting Rights Act Amendments of 1970 suspended for a period of five years the use of literacy tests in any federal, state, or local election anywhere in the United States. In Oregon v. Mitchell, 400 U.S. 112 (1970), although the Court divided on all other aspects of the 1970 Amendments (as discussed below), it unanimously sustained this provision.

In 1975, Congress further extended the Voting Rights Act by making permanent the nationwide ban of literacy and similar tests based in part on a congressional finding that voting discrimination against citizens of language minorities is "pervasive and national in scope."

The Court revisited voting rights issues in City of Mobile v. Bolden, 446 U.S. 55 (1980), and City of Rome v. United States, 446 U.S. 156 (1980), decided on the same day.

Mobile was a challenge to the city's "commission" form of government under the Fourteenth and Fifteenth Amendments. The Court held that §1 of the Fourteenth and Fifteenth Amendments prohibited only *intentional* discrimination. Justice Stewart wrote for a plurality including Chief Justice Burger and Justices Powell and Rehnquist. Justice Stevens concurred in the judgment. Justices White, Brennan, and Marshall wrote dissenting opinions.[47]

---

47. Congress has essentially attempted to overturn *Mobile* by passing a 1982 amendment to the Voting Rights Act that eliminates the intent requirement and substitutes a "totality of circumstances" test by which the courts should measure the "opportunity" of "members of a class of citizens protected by [the Act] . . . to participate in the political process and to elect representatives of their choice." In a series of cases, the Court has enforced this statutory amendment, "assuming but never directly addressing its constitutionality." Bush v. Vera, 517 U.S. 952 (O'Connor, J., concurring) (1996). "Meanwhile, lower courts have unanimously affirmed its constitutionality." Id. Can you see why?

Rome involved the Voting Rights Act of 1965. Under the Act, when covered jurisdictions try to change their voting practices, they must be approved in advance ("precleared") by the Attorney General or the United States District Court for the District of Columbia, on a finding that the practice "does not have the purpose and *will not have the effect* of denying or abridging the right to vote on account of race or color" (emphasis added). Section 4(a) of the Act permits a covered jurisdiction to "bail out" of this requirement by proving that it has not used a voting test or device discriminatorily for the preceding 17 years. The city of Rome, Georgia, sought to make changes in its voting practices. The district court found that the city had no discriminatory purpose, but that the changes would have a discriminatory effect on the city's Black residents.

The Supreme Court, in an opinion by Justice Marshall, held that only the state, and not a subdivision, may invoke §4(a) of the Act. It also reaffirmed Congress's power to require preclearance of covered jurisdictions. Justice Marshall explained that South Carolina v. Katzenbach "makes clear that Congress may, under the authority of §2 of the Fifteenth Amendment, prohibit state action that, though in itself not violative of §1, perpetuates the effects of past discrimination." These prohibitions are valid so long as they are "'appropriate,' as that term is defined in McCulloch v. Maryland" to attack racial discrimination. "[T]he Act's ban on electoral changes that are discriminatory in effect is an appropriate method of promoting the purposes of the Fifteenth Amendment, even if it is assumed that §1 of the Amendment prohibits only intentional discrimination in voting. Congress could rationally have concluded that, because electoral changes by jurisdictions with a demonstrable history of intentional racial discrimination in voting create the risk of purposeful discrimination, it was proper to prohibit changes that have a discriminatory impact."[48] Justices Powell, Rehnquist, and Stewart dissented.

2. McCulloch *and the scope of Reconstruction power.* Note the prominent allusions to *McCulloch* in the *Katzenbach* cases and their progeny. If *McCulloch* lays down the proper test by which judges should measure congressional action under the Reconstruction Amendments, wouldn't this mean that Congress's power is broad indeed? Recall that prior to the Civil War, the Court had never once invalidated an act of Congress on *McCulloch* grounds; nor had the Court done so between 1937 and 1966, when the *Katzenbach* cases were decided. For arguments that the Reconstruction Congress drafted the language of the Enforcement Clauses with *McCulloch*'s sweeping vision of congressional power in mind, see Steven A. Engel, Note, The *McCulloch* Theory of the Fourteenth Amendment: *City of Boerne v. Flores* and the Original Understanding of Section 5, 109 Yale L.J. 115 (1999); Akhil Reed Amar, Intratextualism, 112 Harv. L. Rev. 747, 825-826 (1999). Consider in this regard the Reconstruction Amendments' explicit textual echo of *McCulloch*'s famous passage: "Let the end be legitimate . . . and all means which are *appropriate* . . . are constitutional" (emphasis added).

---

48. The city invoked National League of Cities v. Usery, 426 U.S. 833 (1976), discussed in Chapter 6, infra, to argue that Congress could not interfere with the structure of state institutions. Marshall responded that "principles of federalism that might otherwise be an obstacle to congressional authority are necessarily overridden by the power to enforce the Civil War Amendments 'by appropriate legislation.'"

3. *The nature of congressional power: Remedial, or substantive, or fact-finding, or what?* Justice Brennan supports §4(e) of the Voting Rights Act of 1965 under two alternative theories: (1) as a provision to secure nondiscriminatory treatment of Puerto Ricans in the provision of public services; and (2) as the embodiment of a congressional judgment that disfranchising the persons covered by §4(e) is itself an unconstitutional discrimination. Under the first theory, Congress does not engage in independent constitutional interpretation but only implements a judicial interpretation of the Equal Protection Clause. Established judicial doctrine holds that discrimination in the provision of public services based on the recipients' ethnic origin violates the Fourteenth Amendment. Congress has merely made the factual determinations (a) that New York is discriminating in this fashion and (b) that enfranchising Puerto Ricans will tend to ameliorate such discrimination.

Under the alternative theory, Congress makes a substantive constitutional decision not previously or subsequently made by the Court. On this view, although the Court had held in the *Lassiter* case that literacy tests were not in themselves unconstitutional, Congress was properly entitled to hold a different substantive interpretation of the constitutional right at stake. Such a determination is not simply one of fact; it encompasses a choice of values of the sort involved in most adjudication under the Fourteenth Amendment. Read expansively, the second theory authorizes Congress to create novel Fourteenth Amendment doctrine, not only in the Court's silence, but even in the face of judicial doctrine.

4. *Brennan's ratchet.* Note one important limit on Congress's power, as expounded by the Court in Katzenbach v. Morgan: In footnote 10 of the opinion (footnote a in the preceding excerpt), Justice Brennan insists that Congress has power only to add to the Court's bans on states, not to subtract from them. Is this "ratchet" view of the Reconstruction power normatively attractive? What is its constitutional basis? What happens when conflicting constitutional rights and interests press up against each other? (For example, would congressionally blessed affirmative action for Black people ever violate the constitutional rights of non-Blacks? See infra, Chapter 7.) Also, consider the argument that even if Congress enjoys "power" under the Reconstruction Amendments, it remains bound by the affirmative limits set forth in places like the Bill of Rights. (Note that the Fifth Amendment, which limits Congress, has been construed to require Congress to abide by principles of "equal protection," see, e.g., Bolling v. Sharpe, 347 U.S. 497 (1954), infra, Chapter 7.)

5. *Reconstruction power through the eyes of the conscientious Congress member.* If Congress is authorized to determine that a state practice is intrinsically unconstitutional, what criteria should it employ? Is *McCulloch*'s description of the scope of congressional powers—"Let the end be legitimate," etc.—relevant to this question? What, if any, deference should Congress accord the supposed judgment of a state legislature that its practice promotes desirable or important objectives? If certain federal statutes are premised on the intrinsic unconstitutionality of the invalidated state practice, should Congress be as free to repeal these as any other laws, or do they have a precedential force akin to the Court's constitutional decisions?

6. *Mapping the middle ground: Jones v. Mayer and Oregon v. Mitchell.* In a pair of cases marking the transition from the Warren Court to the Burger Court, the Justices at first reaffirmed that Congress's Reconstruction power was sweeping and then held that the power was not plenary.

JONES v. ALFRED H. MAYER CO., 392 U.S. 409 (1968): [In *Jones*, the Justices confronted a Reconstruction-era statute, 42 U.S.C. §1982, that originally derived from Congress's famous Civil Rights Act of 1866, see Chapter 4, supra. Over the dissent of Justice Harlan (joined by Justice White), the Court construed the statute to prohibit certain forms of private race discrimination in real estate. In perhaps its most expansive recognition of congressional Reconstruction power, the Court upheld Congress's authority to pass such a law under §2 of the Thirteenth Amendment (an issue the dissenters did not reach). It bears emphasis that Congress's law, as construed by the Court, went far beyond what any previous Court had said (or any future Court would likely say) about what §1 of the Thirteenth Amendment independently prohibited: Section 1 prohibits "slavery and involuntary servitude," and it would be hard to say that a private person's mere refusal to enter into economic dealings with Black people—perhaps in a state where slavery had never existed—amounts to "slavery" or "involuntary servitude" as such. Rather, the *Jones* Court explicitly recognized that Congress's power under §2 went well beyond what judges could plausibly prohibit under §1. Justice Stewart wrote for the Court, joined by six of his colleagues.]

STEWART, J.

[T]he fact that §1982 operates upon the unofficial acts of private individuals, whether or not sanctioned by state law, presents no constitutional problem. If Congress has power under the Thirteenth Amendment to eradicate conditions that prevent Negroes from buying and renting property because of their race or color, then no federal statute calculated to achieve that objective can be thought to exceed the constitutional power of Congress simply because it reaches beyond state action to regulate the conduct of private individuals. The constitutional question in this case, therefore, comes to this: Does the authority of Congress to enforce the Thirteenth Amendment "by appropriate legislation" include the power to eliminate all racial barriers to the acquisition of real and personal property? We think the answer to that question is plainly yes.

"By its own unaided force and effect," the Thirteenth Amendment "abolished slavery, and established universal freedom." Whether or not the Amendment itself did any more than that—a question not involved in this case—it is at least clear that the Enabling Clause of that Amendment empowered Congress to do much more. For that clause clothed "Congress with power to pass all laws necessary and proper for abolishing all badges and incidents of slavery in the United States."

Those who opposed passage of the Civil Rights Act of 1866 argued in effect that the Thirteenth Amendment merely authorized Congress to dissolve the legal bond by which the Negro slave was held to his master. Yet many had earlier opposed the Thirteenth Amendment on the very ground that it would give Congress virtually unlimited power to enact laws for the protection of Negroes in every State. And the majority leaders in Congress—who were, after all, the authors of the Thirteenth Amendment—had no doubt that its Enabling Clause contemplated the sort of positive legislation that was embodied in the 1866 Civil Rights Act. Their chief spokesman, Senator Trumbull of Illinois, the Chairman of the Judiciary Committee, had brought the Thirteenth Amendment to the floor of the Senate in 1864. In defending the constitutionality of the 1866 Act, he argued that, if the narrower construction of the Enabling Clause were correct, then

> "the trumpet of freedom that we have been blowing throughout the land has given an 'uncertain sound,' and the promised freedom is a delusion. Such was not the intention of Congress, which proposed the constitutional amendment, nor is such the fair meaning of the amendment itself. . . . I have no doubt that under this provision . . . we may destroy all these discriminations in civil rights against the black man; and if we cannot, our constitutional amendment amounts to nothing. It was for that purpose that the second clause of that amendment was adopted, which says that Congress shall have authority, by appropriate legislation, to carry into effect the article prohibiting slavery. Who is to decide what that appropriate legislation is to be? The Congress of the United States; and it is for Congress to adopt such appropriate legislation as it may think proper, so that it be a means to accomplish the end."

Surely Senator Trumbull was right. Surely Congress has the power under the Thirteenth Amendment rationally to determine what are the badges and the incidents of slavery, and the authority to translate that determination into effective legislation. Nor can we say that the determination Congress has made is an irrational one. For this Court recognized long ago that, whatever else they may have encompassed, the badges and incidents of slavery—its "burdens and disabilities"—included restraints upon "those fundamental rights which are the essence of civil freedom, namely, the same right . . . to inherit, purchase, lease, sell and convey property, as is enjoyed by white citizens."[a] Just as the Black Codes, enacted after the Civil War to restrict the free exercise of those rights, were substitutes for the slave system, so the exclusion of Negroes from white communities became a substitute for the Black Codes. And when racial discrimination herds men into ghettos and makes their ability to buy property turn on the color of their skin, then it too is a relic of slavery.

---

a. The Court did conclude in the Civil Rights Cases that "the act of . . . the owner of the inn, the public conveyance or place of amusement, refusing . . . accommodation" cannot be "justly regarded as imposing any badge of slavery or servitude upon the applicant." "It would be running the slavery argument into the ground," the Court thought, "to make it apply to every act of discrimination which a person may see fit to make as to the guests he will entertain, or as to the people he will take into his coach or cab or car, or admit to his concert or theatre, or deal with in other matters of intercourse or business." Mr. Justice Harlan dissented, expressing the view that "such discrimination practised by corporations and individuals in the exercise of their public or quasi-public functions is a badge of servitude the imposition of which Congress may prevent under its power, by appropriate legislation, to enforce the Thirteenth Amendment." Whatever the present validity of the position taken by the majority on that issue—a question rendered largely academic by Title II of the Civil Rights Act of 1964 (see Heart of Atlanta Motel v. United States; Katzenbach v. McClung)—we note that the entire Court agreed upon at least one proposition: The Thirteenth Amendment authorizes Congress not only to outlaw all forms of slavery and involuntary servitude but also to eradicate the last vestiges and incidents of a society half slave and half free, by securing to all citizens, of every race and color, "the same right to make and enforce contracts, to sue, be parties, give evidence, and to inherit, purchase, lease, sell and convey property, as is enjoyed by white citizens."

Negro citizens, North and South, who saw in the Thirteenth Amendment a promise of freedom—freedom to "go and come at pleasure" and to "buy and sell when they please"—would be left with "a mere paper guarantee" if Congress were powerless to assure that a dollar in the hands of a Negro will purchase the same thing as a dollar in the hands of a white man. At the very least, the freedom that Congress is empowered to secure under the Thirteenth Amendment includes the freedom to buy whatever a white man can buy, the right to live wherever a white man can live. If Congress cannot say that being a free man means at least this much, then the Thirteenth Amendment made a promise the Nation cannot keep.

Representative Wilson of Iowa was the floor manager in the House for the Civil Rights Act of 1866. In urging that Congress had ample authority to pass the pending Bill, he recalled the celebrated words of Chief Justice Marshall in McCulloch v. Maryland:

> "Let the end be legitimate, let it be within the scope of the constitution, and all means which are appropriate, which are plainly adapted to that end, which are not prohibited, but consist with the letter and spirit of the constitution, are constitutional."

"The end is legitimate," the Congressman said, "because it is defined by the Constitution itself. The end is the maintenance of freedom. . . . A man who enjoys the civil rights mentioned in this bill cannot be reduced to slavery. . . . This settles the appropriateness of this measure, and that settles its constitutionality."

We agree.

In retrospect, *Jones* marks the high tide of judicial recognition of Congress's Reconstruction power. *Jones* was decided in the shadow of the assassination of Dr. Martin Luther King, Jr., and before the election of President Richard Nixon, who waged a campaign that sought to appeal to White Southern voters.[49]

---

49. Aren't Justice Stewart's expansive views of congressional power in *Jones* in some tension with his votes in earlier cases like *Morgan* and later cases like *Mitchell* and *Rome*? Stewart's *Jones* opinion was criticized in a June 20, 1968 editorial in *The Wall Street Journal*, and the Justice, remarkably, wrote a letter to the editor defending his opinion. In pertinent part, it read as follows:

> The Supreme Court held (1) that this law [i.e., §1982] means what it says, and (2) that Congress had constitutional power to pass it. You say this made the Court a "legislature." What would the Court have been if it had held (1) that the law does not mean what it says, or (2) that Congress did not have power to pass it?
>
> I add only that Congress, having enacted 42 U.S.C. 1982, remains free to amend it at any time.

The Wall Street Journal, July 3, 1968, at 6.

For scholarly commentary critical of the Court's statutory exegesis in *Jones*, see Gerhard Casper, *Jones v. Mayer*: Clio, Bemused and Confused Muse, 1968 Sup. Ct. Rev. 89; Earl M. Maltz, Civil Rights, the Constitution, and Congress 1863-1869, at 70-78 (1990).

By 1970, two key members of the Warren Court—Chief Justice Earl Warren himself, and Justice Abe Fortas—were gone, replaced by Nixon appointees Warren Burger and Harry Blackmun, respectively.

OREGON v. MITCHELL, 400 U.S. 112 (1970): A badly splintered Court decided that Congress went too far in attempting to confer voting rights upon young adults. Under the Voting Rights Act Amendments of 1970, Congress sought to ban the denial of suffrage on account of age, to anyone 18 years or older.

The ban applied to both state and federal elections, and was accompanied by an explicit congressional finding that the rule in place in most states, setting the voting cut-off at age 21, "(1) denies and abridges the inherent constitutional rights of citizens eighteen years of age . . . to vote—a particularly unfair treatment of such citizens in view of the national defense responsibilities imposed upon such citizens; (2) has the effect of denying to citizens eighteen years of age . . . the due process and equal protection of laws . . . ; and (3) does not bear a reasonable relationship to any compelling State interest."

Five Justices ruled that this law went beyond the Reconstruction powers vested in Congress, but these five failed to coalesce around a single opinion on this key point. Four Justices (Douglas, Brennan, White, and Marshall) voted to uphold the law in its entirety while four other Justices (Chief Justice Burger, and Justices Harlan, Stewart, and Blackmun) voted to strike down the law as applied to both state and federal elections. In the middle stood Justice Black, who ruled that Congress did have power, under Article I, §4, to give young adults the right to vote in *federal* elections, but lacked authority, under the Reconstruction Amendments, to mandate this rule for *state* elections: "Above all else, the framers of the Civil War Amendments intended to deny to the States the power to discriminate against persons on account of their race." Distinguishing away the *Katzenbach* cases, Black argued that Congress's efforts to protect young adults were not designed to remedy or prevent racial discrimination.

Justice Douglas argued that under the test of *McCulloch*, securing "[e]quality of voting by all who are deemed mature enough to vote is certainly consistent 'with the letter and spirit of the constitution.' . . . [E]lection inequalities created by state laws and based on factors other than race may violate the Equal Protection Clause. . . . The reach of §5 to 'enforce' equal protection by eliminating election inequalities would seem quite broad. Certainly there is not a word of limitation in §5 which would restrict its applicability to matters of race alone."

Justice Brennan, joined by Justices Marshall and White, argued that "there is [a] serious question whether a statute granting the franchise to citizens 21 and over while denying it to those between the ages of 18 and 21 could . . . withstand present scrutiny under the Equal Protection Clause. Regardless of the answer to this question, however, it is clear to us that proper regard for the special function of Congress in making determinations of legislative fact compels this Court to respect those determinations unless they are contradicted by evidence far stronger than anything that has been adduced in these cases."

"[A]lthough equal protection requires that all persons 'under like circumstances and conditions' be treated alike, such a formulation merely raises, but does not answer the question whether a legislative classification has resulted in different treatment of persons who are in fact 'under like circumstances and conditions.'"

"When a state legislative classification is subjected to judicial challenge as violating the Equal Protection Clause, it comes before the courts cloaked by the presumption that the legislature has . . . acted within constitutional limitations. . . . But, as we have consistently held, this limitation on judicial review of state legislative classifications is a limitation stemming, not from the Fourteenth Amendment itself, but from the nature of judicial review. It is simply a 'salutary principle of judicial decision,' . . . Courts, therefore, will overturn a legislative determination of a factual question only if the legislature's finding is so clearly wrong that it may be characterized as 'arbitrary,' 'irrational,' or 'unreasonable.'"

"Limitations stemming from the nature of the judicial process, however, have no application to Congress. . . . [Congress may] pursuant to its [Section 5] power, undertake an investigation in order to determine whether the factual basis necessary to support a state legislative discrimination actually exists. . . . Section 5 empowers Congress to make its own determination on the matter. See Katzenbach v. Morgan. It should hardly be necessary to add that if the asserted factual basis necessary to support a given state discrimination does not exist, §5 of the Fourteenth Amendment vests Congress with power to remove the discrimination by appropriate means."

Justice Stewart, in an opinion joined by Chief Justice Burger and Justice Blackmun, argued that "Katzenbach v. Morgan does not hold that Congress has the power to determine what are and what are not 'compelling state interests' for equal protection purposes. . . . The Court's opinion made clear that Congress could impose on the States a remedy for the denial of equal protection that elaborated upon the direct command of the Constitution, and that it could override state laws on the ground that they were in fact used as instruments of invidious discrimination even though a court in an individual lawsuit might not have reached that factual conclusion. [In this case] [t]he state laws that [§302 of the Act] invalidates do not invidiously discriminate against any discrete and insular minority."

Writing only for himself, Justice Harlan attacked the very idea that the Fourteenth Amendment addressed issues of voting discrimination. Such "political rights" were intended to be untouched by §1 of that amendment: "[T]he very fact that constitutional amendments were deemed necessary to bring about federal abolition of state restrictions on voting by reason of race (Amdt. XV), sex (Amdt. XIX), and, even with respect to federal elections, the failure to pay state poll taxes (Amdt. XXIV), is itself forceful evidence of the common understanding in 1869, 1919, and 1962, respectively, that the Fourteenth Amendment did not empower Congress to legislate in these respects."[50]

---

50. Note that the logic of Justice Harlan's dissent calls into question not merely Congress's power to cure restrictive state voting rules, but also the Court's power to do the same. Under a long line of cases, epitomized by the one-person, one-vote ruling in Reynolds v. Sims, 377 U.S. 533 (1964), the Court had invoked—and indeed, continues to invoke—the Fourteenth Amendment to strike down all sorts of voting discriminations. Are all these cases wrongly decided? Or merely wrongly labeled, assuming that Harlan's history is correct, and seen as decisive? Might Congress and federal courts have justified their efforts to democratize state voting rules by appealing not to the Fourteenth Amendment, but to the Republican Guarantee Clause of Article IV—whose text and history suggest that it is centrally concerned with the allocation of political rights within states? For a general discussion, see Akhil Reed Amar, The Central Meaning of Republican Government: Popular Sovereignty, Majority Rule, and the Denominator Problem, 65 U. Colo. L. Rev. 749 (1994).

Before leaving *Mitchell*, it is worthwhile to note the larger political backdrop against which the case was decided. In 1970, the United States was in the middle of a long, bloody, and highly controversial war in Vietnam, sending hundreds of thousands of young adults to fight far from home. Under these conditions, there was a strong fairness argument that those who were being asked or made to fight and die should be allowed to vote on whether and how the war should continue.[51]

Were some of the Justices too quick to dismiss the "fanciful" idea that in 1970, young adults subject to the draft were especially vulnerable to a certain kind of discrimination at the hands of their elders? That, if given the vote, young adults might make a decisive political difference? In the wake of *Mitchell*, Congress proposed, and the states in 1971 ratified, the Twenty-Sixth Amendment, whose opening section reads as follows: "The right of citizens of the United States, who are eighteen years of age or older, to vote shall not be denied or abridged by the United States or by any State on account of age." *Mitchell* thus stands as one of only four cases—alongside Chisholm v. Georgia, 2 U.S. (2 Dall.) 419 (1793) (overruled by the Eleventh Amendment); Dred Scott v. Sandford, 60 U.S. (19 How.) 393 (1857) (overruled by the Fourteenth Amendment); and Pollock v. Farmers' Loan & Trust Co., 157 U.S. 429, modified on rehearing, 158 U.S. 601 (1895) (overruled by the Sixteenth Amendment)—to be overruled by an explicit constitutional amendment.

---

51. Cf. Amar, supra n.50, at 771-772:

> [Under classical Republican Theory, roughly] speaking, those who voted equally should be equally armed, and those who bore arms militarily should vote. Over and over, and across the centuries, we can see this Republican Theory inscribed in the text of our Constitution. The Second Amendment's two clauses equated the "well regulated militia" with "the People"—the same people who in the Preamble "ordain[ed] and establish[ed] this Constitution." . . . Section Two of the Fourteenth Amendment defined a state's presumptive electorate as "male inhabitants of [a] State, *being twenty-one years of age*, and citizens"—roughly speaking, the same group that constituted the state's general militia. The Fifteenth Amendment entitled Black men to vote long before women of all races became eligible, in part because Black men had borne arms for their country and provided the Union the margin of victory. When it became clear that wars had ceased to be highly structured, ritualized competitions between armies of men, but instead pitted entire societies and economies against each other, women won the vote under the Nineteenth Amendment. Indeed, Woodrow Wilson and other politicians explicitly endorsed women's suffrage in recognition of women's role as economic soldiers in the war effort against Germany. And more recently, the Twenty-Sixth Amendment extended the vote to young adults on the theory that if they were old enough to bear arms in Vietnam, they were old enough to vote on the wisdom of that war, and on all else.
>
> The same Republican linkage emerges if we focus on the Constitution as an act—as an embodied ordaining and establishing—rather than as a mere text. In various states, it appears that militiamen who had borne arms for the Revolution were part of "the People" who elected delegates to specially-called ratifying conventions, regardless of whether these militiamen met the property qualifications for voting for ordinary state legislatures.

For more discussion of these linkages, see generally Akhil Reed Amar, The Bill of Rights: Creation and Reconstruction 48-49, 216-218, 258 (1998).

Chapter 6

Federalism, Separation of Powers, and National Security in the Modern Era

Ronald Reagan's election in 1980 changed the tenor of American politics, emboldened new conservative social movements, and made the Republican Party the dominant party in American politics. These developments had important effects in many different areas of American constitutional law. In this chapter, however, we focus on the development of the structural features of the Constitution in the modern era. Although most of these developments occurred after 1980, a few, such as those involving presidential power, date back to the 1960s and 1970s. We also discuss the contemporary understanding of war powers that emerged with the creation of the National Security State following World War II and further developed following the September 11, 2001 terrorist attacks.

I. JUDICIAL CONSTRAINTS ON CONGRESSIONAL POWER

A. The Rehnquist and Roberts Courts: Finding Limits on Federal Power

In 1987, Justice William Rehnquist became Chief Justice William Rehnquist, per the nomination of President Ronald Reagan and the confirmation of the Senate. Both the President[1] and the new Chief Justice shared a belief in the

1. Recall that Reagan was a state governor for eight years. In his First Inaugural Address, he declared: "It is my intention to curb the size and influence of the Federal

importance of state governments in a federal system—a belief also shared by several other Justices appointed by President Reagan and his successor, George H.W. Bush. But can this belief in the importance of state governments and insistence that the federal government remain a government of *limited* powers be translated into workable judicial doctrine? If so, how? Keep these questions in mind as you confront the major Rehnquist Court cases on federalism and enumerated power, discussed next.

---

establishment and to demand recognition of the distinction between the powers granted to the Federal Government and those reserved to the States or to the people. All of us need to be reminded that the Federal Government did not create the States; the States created the Federal Government." In 1987, President Reagan issued Executive Order 12,612, 3 C.F.R. 252 (1987):

> Sec. 2. Fundamental Federalism Principles. In formulating and implementing policies that have federalism implications, Executive departments and agencies shall be guided by the following fundamental federalism principles
>
> (a) Federalism is rooted in the knowledge that our political liberties are best assured by limiting the size and scope of the national government.
>
> (b) The people of the States created the national government when they delegated to it those enumerated governmental powers relating to matters beyond the competence of the individual States. All other sovereign powers, save those expressly prohibited the States by the Constitution, are reserved to the States or to the people.
>
> (c) The constitutional relationship among sovereign governments, State and national, is formalized in and protected by the Tenth Amendment to the Constitution.
>
> (d) The people of the States are free, subject only to restrictions in the Constitution itself or in constitutionally authorized Acts of Congress, to define the moral, political, and legal character of their lives.
>
> (e) In most areas of governmental concern, the States uniquely possess the constitutional authority, the resources, and the competence to discern the sentiments of the people and to govern accordingly. In Thomas Jefferson's words, the States are "the most competent administrations for our domestic concerns and the surest bulwarks against antirepublican tendencies."
>
> (f) The nature of our constitutional system encourages a healthy diversity in the public policies adopted by the people of the several States according to their own conditions, needs, and desires. In the search for enlightened public policy, individual States and communities are free to experiment with a variety of approaches to public issues.
>
> (g) Acts of the national government—whether legislative, executive, or judicial in nature—that exceed the enumerated powers of that government under the Constitution violate the principle of federalism established by the Framers.
>
> (h) Policies of the national government should recognize the responsibility of—and should encourage opportunities for—individuals, families, neighborhoods, local governments, and private associations to achieve their personal, social, and economic objectives through cooperative effort.
>
> (i) In the absence of clear constitutional or statutory authority, the presumption of sovereignty should rest with the individual States. Uncertainties regarding the legitimate authority of the national government should be resolved against regulation at the national level.

For the subsequent fate of this order under the Clinton Administration, see Executive Order 13,083, 3 C.F.R. 146 (1998); Executive Order 13,095, 3 C.F.R. 202 (1998).

1. The Commerce Power

United States v. Lopez

514 U.S. 549 (1995)

[After respondent, then a twelfth-grade student, carried a concealed handgun into his high school, he was charged with violating the Gun-Free School Zones Act of 1990, which forbids "any individual knowingly to possess a firearm at a place that [he] knows . . . is a school zone," 18 U.S.C. §922(q)(1)(A). He challenged the Act as beyond the scope of congressional power under the Commerce Clause.]

REHNQUIST, C.J. . . .

We start with first principles. The Constitution creates a Federal Government of enumerated powers. See Art. I, §8. As James Madison wrote, "the powers delegated by the proposed Constitution to the federal government are few and defined. Those which are to remain in the State governments are numerous and indefinite." The Federalist No. 45. This constitutionally mandated division of authority "was adopted by the Framers to ensure protection of our fundamental liberties." Gregory v. Ashcroft, 501 U.S. 452, 458 (1991). "Just as the separation and independence of the coordinate branches of the Federal Government serve to prevent the accumulation of excessive power in any one branch, a healthy balance of power between the States and the Federal Government will reduce the risk of tyranny and abuse from either front." . . .

[Prior to the New Deal, the Court held] that certain categories of activity such as "production," "manufacturing," and "mining" were within the province of state governments, and thus were beyond the power of Congress under the Commerce Clause. . . .

Jones & Laughlin Steel, Darby, and *Wickard* ushered in an era of Commerce Clause jurisprudence that greatly expanded the previously defined authority of Congress under that Clause. In part, this was a recognition of the great changes that had occurred in the way business was carried on in this country. Enterprises that had once been local or at most regional in nature had become national in scope. But the doctrinal change also reflected a view that earlier Commerce Clause cases artificially had constrained the authority of Congress to regulate interstate commerce.

But even these modern-era precedents which have expanded congressional power under the Commerce Clause confirm that this power is subject to outer limits. . . .

[W]e have identified three broad categories of activity that Congress may regulate under its commerce power. First, Congress may regulate the use of the channels of interstate commerce. See, e.g., *Darby*; *Heart of Atlanta Motel* ("[T]he authority of Congress to keep the channels of interstate commerce free from immoral and injurious uses has been frequently sustained, and is no longer open to question."). Second, Congress is empowered to regulate and protect the instrumentalities of interstate commerce, or persons or things in interstate commerce, even though the threat may come only from intrastate activities. See, e.g., Shreveport Rate Cases, 234 U.S. 342 (1914); Southern R. Co. v. United States, 222 U.S. 20 (1911) (upholding amendments to Safety Appliance Act as applied to vehicles used in intrastate commerce); Perez [v. United States, 402 U.S. 146,] 150 [(1971)] ("[F]or example, the destruction of an aircraft, or . . . thefts from interstate shipments"). Finally, Congress' commerce authority includes the power to regulate those activities having a substantial relation to interstate commerce, *Jones & Laughlin Steel*, i.e., those activities that substantially affect interstate commerce.

Within this final category, admittedly, our case law has not been clear whether an activity must "affect" or "substantially affect" interstate commerce in order to be within Congress's power to regulate it under the Commerce Clause. We conclude, consistent with the great weight of our case law, that the proper test requires an analysis of whether the regulated activity "substantially affects" interstate commerce.

We now turn to consider the power of Congress, in the light of this framework, to enact §922(q). The first two categories of authority may be quickly disposed of: §922(q) is not a regulation of the use of the channels of interstate commerce, nor is it an attempt to prohibit the interstate transportation of a commodity through the channels of commerce; nor can §922(q) be justified as a regulation by which Congress has sought to protect an instrumentality of interstate commerce or a thing in interstate commerce. Thus, if §922(q) is to be sustained, it must be under the third category as a regulation of an activity that substantially affects interstate commerce. First, we have upheld a wide variety of congressional Acts regulating intrastate economic activity where we have concluded that the activity substantially affected interstate commerce. Examples include the regulation of intrastate coal mining, intrastate extortionate credit transactions, *Perez*, restaurants utilizing substantial interstate supplies, *McClung*, inns and hotels catering to interstate guests, *Heart of Atlanta Motel*, and production and consumption of homegrown wheat, *Wickard*. These examples are by no means exhaustive, but the pattern is clear. Where economic activity substantially affects interstate commerce, legislation regulating that activity will be sustained.

Even *Wickard*, which is perhaps the most far reaching example of Commerce Clause authority over intrastate activity, involved economic activity in a way that the possession of a gun in a school zone does not. . . .

Section 922(q) is a criminal statute that by its terms has nothing to do with "commerce" or any sort of economic enterprise, however broadly one might define those terms.[a] Section 922(q) is not an essential part of a larger regulation of economic activity, in which the regulatory scheme could be undercut unless the intrastate activity were regulated. It cannot, therefore, be sustained under our cases upholding regulations of activities that arise out of or are connected with a

---

a. Under our federal system, the "'States possess primary authority for defining and enforcing the criminal law.'" When Congress criminalizes conduct already denounced as criminal by the States, it effects a "'change in the sensitive relation between federal and state criminal jurisdiction.'" . . . [S]ee also Statement of President George Bush on Signing the Crime Control Act of 1990, 26 Weekly Comp. of Pres. Doc. 1944, 1945 (Nov. 29, 1990) ("Most egregiously, section [922(q)] inappropriately overrides legitimate State firearms laws with a new and unnecessary Federal law. The policies reflected in these provisions could legitimately be adopted by the States, but they should not be imposed upon the States by the Congress").

commercial transaction, which viewed in the aggregate, substantially affects interstate commerce.

Second, §922(q) contains no jurisdictional element which would ensure, through case-by-case inquiry, that the firearm possession in question affects interstate commerce. . . . Although as part of our independent evaluation of constitutionality under the Commerce Clause we of course consider legislative findings, and indeed even congressional committee findings, regarding effect on interstate commerce, the Government concedes that "neither the statute nor its legislative history contain[s] express congressional findings regarding the effects upon interstate commerce of gun possession in a school zone." We agree with the Government that Congress normally is not required to make formal findings as to the substantial burdens that an activity has on interstate commerce. But to the extent that congressional findings would enable us to evaluate the legislative judgment that the activity in question substantially affected interstate commerce, even though no such substantial effect was visible to the naked eye, they are lacking here. . . .

The Government's essential contention, in fine, is that we may determine here that §922(q) is valid because possession of a firearm in a local school zone does indeed substantially affect interstate commerce. The Government argues that possession of a firearm in a school zone may result in violent crime and that violent crime can be expected to affect the functioning of the national economy in two ways. First, the costs of violent crime are substantial, and, through the mechanism of insurance, those costs are spread throughout the population. Second, violent crime reduces the willingness of individuals to travel to areas within the country that are perceived to be unsafe. Cf. *Heart of Atlanta Motel.* The Government also argues that the presence of guns in schools poses a substantial threat to the educational process by threatening the learning environment. A handicapped educational process, in turn, will result in a less productive citizenry. That, in turn, would have an adverse effect on the Nation's economic well-being. As a result, the Government argues that Congress could rationally have concluded that §922(q) substantially affects interstate commerce.

We pause to consider the implications of the Government's arguments. The Government admits, under its "costs of crime" reasoning, that Congress could regulate not only all violent crime, but all activities that might lead to violent crime, regardless of how tenuously they relate to interstate commerce. Similarly, under the Government's "national productivity" reasoning, Congress could regulate any activity that it found was related to the economic productivity of individual citizens: family law (including marriage, divorce, and child custody), for example. Under the theories that the Government presents in support of §922(q), it is difficult to perceive any limitation on federal power, even in areas such as criminal law enforcement or education where States historically have been sovereign. Thus, if we were to accept the Government's arguments, we are hard pressed to posit any activity by an individual that Congress is without power to regulate.

Although Justice Breyer argues that acceptance of the Government's rationales would not authorize a general federal police power, he is unable to identify any activity that the States may regulate but Congress may not. . . .

Justice Breyer focuses, for the most part, on the threat that firearm possession in and near schools poses to the educational process and the potential economic consequences flowing from that threat. Specifically, the dissent reasons that (1) gun-related violence is a serious problem; (2) that problem, in turn, has an adverse effect on classroom learning; and (3) that adverse effect on classroom learning, in turn, represents a substantial threat to trade and commerce. This analysis would be equally applicable, if not more so, to subjects such as family law and direct regulation of education.

For instance, if Congress can, pursuant to its Commerce Clause power, regulate activities that adversely affect the learning environment, then, a fortiori, it also can regulate the educational process directly. Congress could determine that a school's curriculum has a "significant" effect on the extent of classroom learning. As a result, Congress could mandate a federal curriculum for local elementary and secondary schools because what is taught in local schools has a significant "effect on classroom learning," and that, in turn, has a substantial effect on interstate commerce.

Justice Breyer rejects our reading of precedent and argues that "Congress . . . could rationally conclude that schools fall on the commercial side of the line." Again, Justice Breyer's rationale lacks any real limits because, depending on the level of generality, any activity can be looked upon as commercial. Under the dissent's rationale, Congress could just as easily look at child rearing as "falling on the commercial side of the line" because it provides a "valuable service—namely, to equip [children] with the skills they need to survive in life and, more specifically, in the workplace." We do not doubt that Congress has authority under the Commerce Clause to regulate numerous commercial activities that substantially affect interstate commerce and also affect the educational process. That authority, though broad, does not include the authority to regulate each and every aspect of local schools. . . .

These are not precise formulations, and in the nature of things they cannot be. But we think they point the way to a correct decision of this case. The possession of a gun in a local school zone is in no sense an economic activity that might, through repetition elsewhere, substantially affect any sort of interstate commerce. Respondent was a local student at a local school; there is no indication that he had recently moved in interstate commerce, and there is no requirement that his possession of the firearm have any concrete tie to interstate commerce.

To uphold the Government's contentions here, we would have to pile inference upon inference in a manner that would bid fair to convert congressional authority under the Commerce Clause to a general police power of the sort retained by the States. Admittedly, some of our prior cases have taken long steps down that road, giving great deference to congressional action. The broad language in these opinions has suggested the possibility of additional expansion, but we decline here to proceed any further. To do so would require us to conclude that the Constitution's enumeration of powers does not presuppose something not enumerated, and that there never will be a distinction between what is truly national and what is truly local, cf. *Jones & Laughlin Steel.* This we are unwilling to do.

Justice KENNEDY, with whom Justice O'CONNOR joins, concurring.

The history of the judicial struggle to interpret the Commerce Clause during the transition from the economic system the Founders knew to the single, national market still emergent in our own era counsels great restraint before the Court determines that the Clause is insufficient to support an exercise of the national power.

That history gives me some pause about today's decision, but I join the Court's opinion with these observations on what I conceive to be its necessary though limited holding. . . . [Cases such as *Darby*, *Wickard*,] . . . Heart of Atlanta Motel, Inc. v. United States, Katzenbach v. McClung, and Perez v. United States . . . are within the fair ambit of the Court's practical conception of commercial regulation and are not called in question by our decision today.

. . . [F]ederalism was the unique contribution of the Framers to political science and political theory. See Friendly, Federalism: A Foreword, 86 Yale L.J. 1019 (1977); G. Wood, The Creation of the American Republic, 1776-1787, pp. 524-532, 564 (1969). Though on the surface the idea may seem counter-intuitive, it was the insight of the Framers that freedom was enhanced by the creation of two governments, not one. "In the compound republic of America, the power surrendered by the people is first divided between two distinct governments, and then the portion allotted to each subdivided among distinct and separate departments. Hence a double security arises to the rights of the people. The different governments will control each other, at the same time that each will be controlled by itself." The Federalist No. 51. See also Gregory v. Ashcroft, New York v. United States. . . .

The theory that two governments accord more liberty than one requires for its realization two distinct and discernable lines of political accountability: one between the citizens and the Federal Government; the second between the citizens and the States. If, as Madison expected, the Federal and State Governments are to control each other, see The Federalist No. 51, and hold each other in check by competing for the affections of the people, see The Federalist No. 46, those citizens must have some means of knowing which of the two governments to hold accountable for the failure to perform a given function. "Federalism serves to assign political responsibility, not to obscure it." Were the Federal Government to take over the regulation of entire areas of traditional state concern, areas having nothing to do with the regulation of commercial activities, the boundaries between the spheres of federal and state authority would blur and political responsibility would become illusory. Cf. New York v. United States. . . .

Whatever the judicial role, it is axiomatic that Congress does have substantial discretion and control over the federal balance. . . . At the same time, the absence of structural mechanisms to require [federal] officials to undertake this principled task [of balancing federal and state power], and the momentary political convenience often attendant upon their failure to do so, argue against a complete renunciation of the judicial role. . . .

[I]t is well established that education is a traditional concern of the States. . . . While it is doubtful that any State, or indeed any reasonable person, would argue that it is wise policy to allow students to carry guns on school premises, considerable disagreement exists about how best to accomplish that goal. In this circumstance, the theory and utility of our federalism are revealed, for the States may perform their role as laboratories for experimentation to devise various solutions where the best solution is far from clear.

If a State or municipality determines that harsh criminal sanctions are necessary and wise to deter students from carrying guns on school premises, the reserved powers of the States are sufficient to enact those measures. Indeed, over 40 States already have criminal laws outlawing the possession of firearms on or near school grounds. . . .

The statute now before us forecloses the States from experimenting and exercising their own judgment in an area to which States lay claim by right of history and expertise, and it does so by regulating an activity beyond the realm of commerce in the ordinary and usual sense of that term. The tendency of this statute to displace state regulation in areas of traditional state concern is evident from its territorial operation. There are over 100,000 elementary and secondary schools in the United States. Each of these now has an invisible federal zone extending 1,000 feet beyond the (often irregular) boundaries of the school property. In some communities no doubt it would be difficult to navigate without infringing on those zones. . . . Absent a stronger connection or identification with commercial concerns that are central to the Commerce Clause, that interference contradicts the federal balance the Framers designed and that this Court is obliged to enforce.

Justice Thomas, concurring. . . .

Although I join the majority, I write separately to observe that our case law has drifted far from the original understanding of the Commerce Clause. In a future case, we ought to temper our Commerce Clause jurisprudence in a manner that both makes sense of our more recent case law and is more faithful to the original understanding of that Clause. . . .

I

At the time the original Constitution was ratified, "commerce" consisted of selling, buying, and bartering, as well as transporting for these purposes. See 1 S. Johnson, A Dictionary of the English Language 361 (4th ed. 1773) (defining commerce as "Intercour[s]e; exchange of one thing for another; interchange of any thing; trade; traffick"); N. Bailey, An Universal Etymological English Dictionary (26th ed. 1789) ("trade or traffic"); T. Sheridan, A Complete Dictionary of the English Language (6th ed. 1796) ("Exchange of one thing for another; trade, traffick"). This understanding finds support in the etymology of the word, which literally means "with merchandise." See 3 Oxford English Dictionary 552 (2d ed. 1989) (com—"with"; merci—"merchandise"). In fact, when Federalists and Anti-Federalists discussed the Commerce Clause during the ratification period, they often used trade (in its selling/bartering sense) and commerce interchangeably. See The Federalist No. 4 (J. Jay) (asserting that countries will cultivate our friendship when our "trade" is prudently regulated by Federal Government); id., No. 7 (A. Hamilton) (discussing "competitions of commerce" between States resulting from state "regulations of trade"); id., No. 40 (J. Madison) (asserting that it was an "acknowledged object of the Convention . . . that the regulation of trade should be submitted to the general government"); Lee, Letters of a Federal Farmer No. 5, in Pamphlets on the Constitution of the United States 319 (P. Ford ed. 1888); Smith, An Address to the People of the State of New York, in id., at 107.

As one would expect, the term "commerce" was used in contradistinction to productive activities such as manufacturing and agriculture. Alexander Hamilton, for example, repeatedly treated commerce, agriculture, and manufacturing as three separate endeavors. See, e.g., The Federalist No. 36 (referring to "agriculture, commerce, manufactures"); id., No. 21 (distinguishing commerce, arts, and industry); id., No. 12 (asserting that commerce and agriculture have shared interests). The same distinctions were made in the state ratification conventions. See, e.g., 2 Debates in the Several State Conventions on the Adoption of the Federal Constitution 57 (J. Elliot ed. 1836) (T. Dawes at Massachusetts convention); id., at 336 (M. Smith at New York convention).

Moreover, interjecting a modern sense of commerce into the Constitution generates significant textual and structural problems. For example, one cannot replace "commerce" with a different type of enterprise, such as manufacturing. When a manufacturer produces a car, assembly cannot take place "with a foreign nation" or "with the Indian Tribes." Parts may come from different States or other nations and hence may have been in the flow of commerce at one time, but manufacturing takes place at a discrete site. Agriculture and manufacturing involve the production of goods; commerce encompasses traffic in such articles.

The Port Preference Clause also suggests that the term "commerce" denoted sale and/or transport rather than business generally. According to that Clause, "no Preference shall be given by any Regulation of Commerce or Revenue to the Ports of one State over those of another." U.S. Const., Art. I, §9, cl. 6. Although it is possible to conceive of regulations of manufacturing or farming that prefer one port over another, the more natural reading is that the Clause prohibits Congress from using its commerce power to channel commerce through certain favored ports.

The Constitution not only uses the word "commerce" in a narrower sense than our case law might suggest, it also does not support the proposition that Congress has authority over all activities that "substantially affect" interstate commerce. The Commerce Clause does not state that Congress may "regulate matters that substantially affect commerce with foreign Nations, and among the several States, and with the Indian Tribes." In contrast, the Constitution itself temporarily prohibited amendments that would "affect" Congress' lack of authority to prohibit or restrict the slave trade or to enact unproportioned direct taxation. Art. V. Clearly, the Framers could have drafted a Constitution that contained a "substantially affects interstate commerce" Clause had that been their objective.

In addition to its powers under the Commerce Clause, Congress has the authority to enact such laws as are "necessary and proper" to carry into execution its power to regulate commerce among the several States. U.S. Const., Art. I, §8, cl. 18. But on this Court's understanding of congressional power under these two Clauses, many of Congress' other enumerated powers under Art. I, §8, are wholly superfluous. After all, if Congress may regulate all matters that substantially affect commerce, there is no need for the Constitution to specify that Congress may enact bankruptcy laws, cl. 4, or coin money and fix the standard of weights and measures, cl. 5, or punish counterfeiters of United States coin and securities, cl. 6. Likewise, Congress would not need the separate authority to establish post offices and post roads, cl. 7, or to grant patents and copyrights, cl. 8, or to "punish Piracies and Felonies committed on the high Seas," cl. 10. It might not even need the power to raise and support an Army and Navy, cls. 12 and 13, for fewer people would engage in commercial shipping if they thought that a foreign power could expropriate their property with ease. Indeed, if Congress could regulate matters that substantially affect interstate commerce, there would have been no need to specify that Congress can regulate international trade and commerce with the Indians. As the Framers surely understood, these other branches of trade substantially affect interstate commerce.

Put simply, much if not all of Art. I, §8 (including portions of the Commerce Clause itself), would be surplusage if Congress had been given authority over matters that substantially affect interstate commerce. An interpretation of cl. 3 that makes the rest of §8 superfluous simply cannot be correct. Yet this Court's Commerce Clause jurisprudence has endorsed just such an interpretation: The power we have accorded Congress has swallowed Art. I, §8.[a] . . .

Our construction of the scope of congressional authority has the additional problem of coming close to turning the Tenth Amendment on its head. Our case law could be read to reserve to the United States all powers not expressly prohibited by the Constitution. Taken together, these fundamental textual problems should, at the very least, convince us that the "substantial effects" test should be reexamined. . . .

III

B

I am aware of no cases prior to the New Deal that characterized the power flowing from the Commerce Clause as sweepingly as does our substantial effects test. My review of the case law indicates that the substantial effects test is but an innovation of the 20th century. . . .

These cases all establish a simple point: From the time of the ratification of the Constitution to the mid-1930s, it was widely understood that the Constitution granted Congress only limited powers, notwithstanding the Commerce Clause. Moreover, there was no question that activities wholly separated from business, such as gun possession, were beyond the reach of the commerce power. If anything, the "wrong turn" was the Court's dramatic departure in the 1930s from a century and a half of precedent. . . .

V

This extended discussion of the original understanding and our first century and a half of case law does not necessarily require a wholesale abandonment of our more recent opinions.[b] It simply reveals that our substantial effects test is far removed from both the Constitution and from our early case law and that the Court's opinion should not be viewed as "radical" or another "wrong turn" that must be corrected in the future. The analysis also suggests that we ought to temper our Commerce Clause jurisprudence. . . .

---

a. There are other powers granted to Congress outside of Art. I, §8, that may become wholly superfluous as well due to our distortion of the Commerce Clause. For instance, Congress has plenary power over the District of Columbia and the territories. See U.S. Const., Art. I, §8, cl. 17, and Art. IV, §3, cl. 2. The grant of comprehensive legislative power over certain areas of the Nation, when read in conjunction with the rest of the Constitution, further confirms that Congress was not ceded plenary authority over the whole Nation.

b. Although I might be willing to return to the original understanding, I recognize that many believe that it is too late in the day to undertake a fundamental reexamination of the past 60 years. Consideration of stare decisis and reliance interests may convince us that we cannot wipe the slate clean.

At an appropriate juncture, I think we must modify our Commerce Clause jurisprudence. Today, it is easy enough to say that the Clause certainly does not empower Congress to ban gun possession within 1,000 feet of a school.

Justice STEVENS, dissenting.

The welfare of our future "Commerce with foreign Nations, and among the several States," U.S. Const., Art. I, §8, cl. 3, is vitally dependent on the character of the education of our children. I therefore agree entirely with Justice Breyer's explanation of why Congress has ample power to prohibit the possession of firearms in or near schools—just as it may protect the school environment from harms posed by controlled substances such as asbestos or alcohol. I also agree with Justice Souter's exposition of the radical character of the Court's holding and its kinship with the discredited, pre-Depression version of substantive due process. Cf. Dolan v. City of Tigard, 512 U.S. 374, 405-411 (1994) (Stevens, J., dissenting). I believe, however, that the Court's extraordinary decision merits this additional comment.

Guns are both articles of commerce and articles that can be used to restrain commerce. Their possession is the consequence, either directly or indirectly, of commercial activity. In my judgment, Congress' power to regulate commerce in firearms includes the power to prohibit possession of guns at any location because of their potentially harmful use; it necessarily follows that Congress may also prohibit their possession in particular markets. The market for the possession of handguns by school-age children is, distressingly, substantial. Whether or not the national interest in eliminating that market would have justified federal legislation in 1789, it surely does today.

Justice SOUTER, dissenting.

. . . The distinction between what is patently commercial and what is not looks much like the old [*Lochner*-era] distinction between what directly affects commerce and what touches it only indirectly. And the act of calibrating the level of deference by drawing a line between what is patently commercial and what is less purely so will probably resemble the process of deciding how much interference with contractual freedom was fatal. Thus, it seems fair to ask whether the step taken by the Court today does anything but portend a return to the untenable jurisprudence from which the Court extricated itself almost 60 years ago. The answer is not reassuring. . . .

The Court observes that the Gun-Free School Zones Act operates in two areas traditionally subject to legislation by the States, education and enforcement of criminal law. The suggestion is either that a connection between commerce and these subjects is remote, or that the commerce power is simply weaker when it touches subjects on which the States have historically been the primary legislators. Neither suggestion is tenable. As for remoteness, it may or may not be wise for the National Government to deal with education, but Justice Breyer has surely demonstrated that the commercial prospects of an illiterate State or Nation are not rosy, and no argument should be needed to show that hijacking interstate shipments of cigarettes can affect commerce substantially, even though the States have traditionally prosecuted robbery. And as for the notion that the commerce power diminishes the closer it gets to customary state concerns, that idea has been flatly rejected, and not long ago. The commerce power, we have often observed, is plenary. . . .

Nor is there any contrary authority in the reasoning of our cases imposing clear statement rules in some instances of legislation that would significantly alter the state-national balance. . . .

There remain questions about legislative findings. The Court of Appeals expressed the view, that the result in this case might well have been different if Congress had made explicit findings that guns in schools have a substantial effect on interstate commerce, and the Court today does not repudiate that position. . . . Might a court aided by such findings have subjected this legislation to less exacting scrutiny (or, put another way, should a court have deferred to such findings if Congress had made them)? The answer to either question must be no, although as a general matter findings are important and to be hoped for in the difficult cases. . . . If, indeed, the Court were to make the existence of explicit congressional findings dispositive in some close or difficult cases something other than rationality review would be afoot. The resulting congressional obligation to justify its policy choices on the merits would imply either a judicial authority to review the justification (and, hence, the wisdom) of those choices, or authority to require Congress to act with some high degree of deliberateness, of which express findings would be evidence. But review for congressional wisdom would just be the old judicial pretension discredited and abandoned in 1937, and review for deliberateness would be as patently unconstitutional as an Act of Congress mandating long opinions from this Court. . . .

[This does not mean] that findings are pointless. They may, in fact, have great value in telling courts what to look for, in establishing at least one frame of reference for review, and in citing to factual authority. . . . But . . . as long as rational [basis] is the touchstone, . . . I would not allow for the possibility, as the Court's opinion may, that the addition of congressional findings could in principle have affected the fate of the statute here.

Because Justice Breyer's opinion demonstrates beyond any doubt that the Act in question passes the rationality review that the Court continues to espouse, today's decision may be seen as only a misstep, its reasoning and its suggestions not quite in gear with the prevailing standard, but hardly an epochal case. I would not argue otherwise, but I would raise a caveat. Not every epochal case has come in epochal trappings. *Jones & Laughlin* did not reject the direct-indirect standard in so many words; it just said the relation of the regulated subject matter to commerce was direct enough. But we know what happened.

Justice BREYER, with whom Justice STEVENS, Justice SOUTER, and Justice GINSBURG join, dissenting.

In my view, the statute falls well within the scope of the commerce power as this Court has understood that power over the last half century.

I

In reaching this conclusion, I apply three basic principles of Commerce Clause interpretation. First, the power to "regulate Commerce . . . among the several States" encompasses the power to regulate local activities insofar as they significantly affect interstate commerce. See, e.g. Gibbons v. Ogden; Wickard v. Filburn. . . .

Second, in determining whether a local activity will likely have a significant effect upon interstate commerce, a court must consider, not the effect of an individual act (a single instance of gun possession), but rather the cumulative effect of all similar instances (i.e., the effect of all guns possessed in or near schools). See, e.g., *Wickard*. . . .

Third, the Constitution requires us to judge the connection between a regulated activity and interstate commerce, not directly, but at one remove. Courts must give Congress a degree of leeway in determining the existence of a significant factual connection between the regulated activity and interstate commerce—both because the Constitution delegates the commerce power directly to Congress and because the determination requires an empirical judgment of a kind that a legislature is more likely than a court to make with accuracy. The traditional words "rational basis" capture this leeway. Thus, the specific question before us, as the Court recognizes, is not whether the "regulated activity sufficiently affected interstate commerce," but, rather, whether Congress could have had "a rational basis" for so concluding.

I recognize that we must judge this matter independently. "Simply because Congress may conclude that a particular activity substantially affects interstate commerce does not necessarily make it so." And, I also recognize that Congress did not write specific "interstate commerce" findings into the law under which Lopez was convicted. Nonetheless, as I have already noted, the matter that we review independently (i.e., whether there is a "rational basis") already has considerable leeway built into it. And, the absence of findings, at most, deprives a statute of the benefit of some extra leeway. This extra deference, in principle, might change the result in a close case, though, in practice, it has not made a critical legal difference. See, e.g., Katzenbach v. McClung (noting that "no formal findings were made, which of course are not necessary"); *Perez*. . . .

II

Applying these principles to the case at hand, we must ask whether Congress could have had a rational basis for finding a significant (or substantial) connection between gun-related school violence and interstate commerce. Or, to put the question in the language of the explicit finding that Congress made when it amended this law in 1994: Could Congress rationally have found that "violent crime in school zones," through its effect on the "quality of education," significantly (or substantially) affects "interstate" or "foreign commerce"? As long as one views the commerce connection, not as a "technical legal conception," but as "a practical one," Swift & Co. v. United States, 196 U.S. 375, 398 (1905) (Holmes, J.), the answer to this question must be yes. Numerous reports and studies—generated both inside and outside government—make clear that Congress could reasonably have found the empirical connection that its law, implicitly or explicitly, asserts. [At this point, Justice Breyer directs the reader to the Appendix to his opinion, which spans more than a dozen pages in U.S. Reports and cites more than 150 relevant articles and studies—"Congressional Materials," "Other Federal Government Materials," and "Other Readily Available Materials"—to support the connection.]

For one thing, reports, hearings, and other readily available literature make clear that the problem of guns in and around schools is widespread and extremely serious. These materials report, for example, that four percent of American high school students (and six percent of inner-city high school students) carry a gun to school at least occasionally; that 12 percent of urban high school students have had guns fired at them; that 20 percent of those students have been threatened with guns; and that, in any 6-month period, several hundred thousand schoolchildren are victims of violent crimes in or near their schools. And, they report that this widespread violence in schools throughout the Nation significantly interferes with the quality of education in those schools. Based on reports such as these, Congress obviously could have thought that guns and learning are mutually exclusive. Congress could therefore have found a substantial educational problem—teachers unable to teach, students unable to learn—and concluded that guns near schools contribute substantially to the size and scope of that problem.

Having found that guns in schools significantly undermine the quality of education in our Nation's classrooms, Congress could also have found, given the effect of education upon interstate and foreign commerce, that gun-related violence in and around schools is a commercial, as well as a human, problem. Education, although far more than a matter of economics, has long been inextricably intertwined with the Nation's economy. When this Nation began, most workers received their education in the workplace, typically (like Benjamin Franklin) as apprentices. As late as the 1920s, many workers still received general education directly from their employers—from large corporations, such as General Electric, Ford, and Goodyear, which created schools within their firms to help both the worker and the firm. (Throughout most of the 19th century fewer than one percent of all Americans received secondary education through attending a high school.) As public school enrollment grew in the early 20th century, the need for industry to teach basic educational skills diminished. But, the direct economic link between basic education and industrial productivity remained. Scholars estimate that nearly a quarter of America's economic growth in the early years of this century is traceable directly to increased schooling; that investment in "human capital" (through spending on education) exceeded investment in "physical capital" by a ratio of almost two to one; and that the economic returns to this investment in education exceeded the returns to conventional capital investment.

In recent years the link between secondary education and business has strengthened, becoming both more direct and more important. Scholars on the subject report that technological changes and innovations in management techniques have altered the nature of the workplace so that more jobs now demand greater educational skills. There is evidence that "service, manufacturing or construction jobs are being displaced by technology that requires a better-educated worker or, more likely, are being exported overseas," that "workers with truly few skills by the year 2000 will find that only one job out of ten will remain," and that

> "over the long haul the best way to encourage the growth of high-wage jobs is to upgrade the skills of the work force. . . . Better-trained workers become more productive workers, enabling a company to become more competitive and expand."

Increasing global competition also has made primary and secondary education economically more important. The portion of the American economy attributable to international trade nearly tripled between 1950 and 1980, and more than 70 percent of American-made goods now compete with imports. Yet, lagging worker productivity has contributed to negative trade balances and to real hourly compensation that has fallen below wages in 10 other industrialized nations. At least some significant part of this serious productivity problem is attributable to students who emerge from classrooms without the reading or mathematical skills necessary to compete with their European or Asian counterparts, and, presumably, to high school dropout rates of 20 to 25 percent (up to 50 percent in inner cities). Indeed, Congress has said, when writing other statutes, that "functionally or technologically illiterate" Americans in the work force "erode" our economic "standing in the international marketplace," and that "our Nation is . . . paying the price of scientific and technological illiteracy, with our productivity declining, our industrial base ailing, and our global competitiveness dwindling."

Finally, there is evidence that, today more than ever, many firms base their location decisions upon the presence, or absence, of a work force with a basic education. Scholars on the subject report, for example, that today, "high speed communication and transportation make it possible to produce most products and services anywhere in the world," that "modern machinery and production methods can therefore be combined with low wage workers to drive costs down," that managers can perform "back office functions anywhere in the world now," and say that if they "can't get enough skilled workers here" they will "move the skilled jobs out of the country," with the consequence that "rich countries need better education and retraining, to reduce the supply of unskilled workers and to equip them with the skills they require for tomorrow's jobs." In light of this increased importance of education to individual firms, it is no surprise that half of the Nation's manufacturers have become involved with setting standards and shaping curricula for local schools, that 88 percent think this kind of involvement is important, that more than 20 States have recently passed educational reforms to attract new business, and that business magazines have begun to rank cities according to the quality of their schools.

The economic links I have just sketched seem fairly obvious. Why then is it not equally obvious, in light of those links, that a widespread, serious, and substantial physical threat to teaching and learning also substantially threatens the commerce to which that teaching and learning is inextricably tied? That is to say, guns in the hands of six percent of inner-city high school students and gun-related violence throughout a city's schools must threaten the trade and commerce that those schools support. The only question, then, is whether the latter threat is (to use the majority's terminology) "substantial." The evidence of (1) the extent of the gun-related violence problem, (2) the extent of the resulting negative effect on classroom learning, and (3) the extent of the consequent negative commercial effects, see supra, when taken together, indicate a threat to trade and commerce that is "substantial." At the very least, Congress could rationally have concluded that the links are "substantial."

Specifically, Congress could have found that gun-related violence near the classroom poses a serious economic threat (1) to consequently inadequately educated workers who must endure low paying jobs, and (2) to communities and businesses that might (in today's "information society") otherwise gain, from a well-educated work force, an important commercial advantage of a kind that location near a railhead or harbor provided in the past. Congress might also have found these threats to be no different in kind from other threats that this Court has found within the commerce power, such as the threat that loan sharking poses to the "funds" of "numerous localities," *Perez*, and that unfair labor practices pose to instrumentalities of commerce. As I have pointed out, Congress has written that "the occurrence of violent crime in school zones" has brought about a "decline in the quality of education" that "has an adverse impact on interstate commerce and the foreign commerce of the United States." 18 U.S.C. §922(q)(1)(F), (G). The violence-related facts, the educational facts, and the economic facts, taken together, make this conclusion rational. And, because under our case law, the sufficiency of the constitutionally necessary Commerce Clause link between a crime of violence and interstate commerce turns simply upon size or degree, those same facts make the statute constitutional.

To hold this statute constitutional is not to "obliterate" the "distinction between what is national and what is local"; nor is it to hold that the Commerce Clause permits the Federal Government to "regulate any activity that it found was related to the economic productivity of individual citizens," to regulate "marriage, divorce, and child custody," or to regulate any and all aspects of education. First, this statute is aimed at curbing a particularly acute threat to the educational process—the possession (and use) of life-threatening firearms in, or near, the classroom. The empirical evidence that I have discussed above unmistakably documents the special way in which guns and education are incompatible. . . . [T]he immediacy of the connection between education and the national economic well-being is documented by scholars and accepted by society at large in a way and to a degree that may not hold true for other social institutions. It must surely be the rare case, then, that a statute strikes at conduct that (when considered in the abstract) seems so removed from commerce, but which (practically speaking) has so significant an impact upon commerce.

In sum, a holding that the particular statute before us falls within the commerce power would not expand the scope of that Clause. Rather, it simply would apply pre-existing law to changing economic circumstances. It would recognize that, in today's economic world, gun-related violence near the classroom makes a significant difference to our economic, as well as our social, well-being. In accordance with well-accepted precedent, such a holding would permit Congress "to act in terms of economic . . . realities," would interpret the commerce power as "an affirmative power commensurate with the national needs," and would acknowledge that the "commerce clause does not operate so as to render the nation powerless to defend itself against economic forces that Congress decrees inimical or destructive of the national economy."

III

The majority's holding—that §922 falls outside the scope of the Commerce Clause—creates three serious legal problems. First, the majority's holding runs contrary to modern Supreme Court cases that have upheld congressional actions despite connections to interstate or foreign commerce that are less significant than the effect of school violence. . . .

The second legal problem the Court creates comes from its apparent belief that it can reconcile its holding with earlier cases by making a critical distinction between "commercial" and noncommercial "transaction[s]." That is to say, the

Court believes the Constitution would distinguish between two local activities, each of which has an identical effect upon interstate commerce, if one, but not the other, is "commercial" in nature. As a general matter, this approach fails to heed this Court's earlier warning not to turn "questions of the power of Congress" upon "formula[s]" that would give "controlling force to nomenclature such as 'production' and 'indirect' and foreclose consideration of the actual effects of the activity in question upon interstate commerce." *Wickard.* See also United States v. Darby (overturning the Court's distinction between "production" and "commerce" in the child labor case, Hammer v. Dagenhart); Swift & Co. v. United States, 196 U.S. at 398 (Holmes, J.) ("Commerce among the States is not a technical legal conception, but a practical one, drawn from the course of business"). . . .

More importantly, if a distinction between commercial and noncommercial activities is to be made, this is not the case in which to make it. . . . Schools that teach reading, writing, mathematics, and related basic skills serve both social and commercial purposes, and one cannot easily separate the one from the other. American industry itself has been, and is again, involved in teaching. . . .

In 1990, the year Congress enacted the statute before us, primary and secondary schools spent $230 billion — that is, nearly a quarter of a trillion dollars — which accounts for a significant portion of our $5.5 trillion gross domestic product for that year. The business of schooling requires expenditure of these funds on student transportation, food and custodial services, books, and teachers' salaries. These expenditures enable schools to provide a valuable service — namely, to equip students with the skills they need to survive in life and, more specifically, in the workplace. Certainly, Congress has often analyzed school expenditure as if it were a commercial investment, closely analyzing whether schools are efficient, whether they justify the significant resources they spend, and whether they can be restructured to achieve greater returns. Why could Congress, for Commerce Clause purposes, not consider schools as roughly analogous to commercial investments from which the Nation derives the benefit of an educated work force?

The third legal problem created by the Court's holding is that it threatens legal uncertainty in an area of law that, until this case, seemed reasonably well settled. . . .

DISCUSSION

1. *How broadly does* Lopez *sweep?* Does *Lopez* betoken a dramatic rollback of congressional power under the Commerce Clause, or merely a disinclination to extend expansive cases like *Wickard* and *McClung* any further? Note the differences of tone and emphasis between, for example, Justice Thomas on the one hand, and Justices Kennedy and O'Connor on the other. For a careful and comprehensive analysis of the breadth of *Lopez*, suggesting the modesty of its reach, see Deborah Jones Merritt, Commerce!, 94 Mich. L. Rev. 674 (1995).

2. *Judicial review as a remand to Congress?* If Congress were to revisit and reenact the identical statute in the aftermath of *Lopez*, but this time with more careful and explicit findings attempting to identify the link between the law and bona fide issues of interstate commerce (in a manner akin to Justice Breyer's dissent), might

the new law pass Supreme Court muster? The majority opinion does not rule this out—and Justice Kennedy's concurrence (joined by Justice O'Connor) contains some intriguing language about the possibility that Congress might "revise its law to demonstrate its commercial character." Also, note Justice Kennedy's concluding paragraph calling for "a stronger connection *or identification* with commercial concerns" (emphasis added). Why should the same law pass muster merely because Congress chants some magic words in a "findings" section that do not change the substantive command of the statute?

One possible answer is that "findings" after a Supreme Court invalidation would represent an explicit acknowledgment by Congress that it carefully deliberated on the specific federalism implications that concerned the Court. If, for court-specific reasons—such as the difficulty of drawing workable doctrinal lines, and the felt need to defer to legislative judgments about complicated empirical realities—judges systemically underenforce the limits on Congress's Commerce Clause powers, perhaps the Court might try to enforce federalism values more indirectly, by simply encouraging Congress to pay special attention to these concerns in drafting legislation. Legislative findings thus might serve a purpose akin to the purpose served by a clear-statement rule, cf. Gregory v. Ashcroft, infra, Section II.

Of course, the Court might also believe that, were Congress to focus more closely on federalism issues, federal lawmakers would likely modify federal intervention to better accommodate state interests. The law in *Lopez* was cleverly tailored to fit "political" concerns of federalism. Congresspersons from urban districts tended to support the law more than did those from rural districts, and the law reflected this differential support by drawing a 1,000-foot-wide buffer zone around each school. Such zones left wide areas of rural districts untouched, but virtually blanketed urban areas like Manhattan. But was the law equally well tailored to fit "legal" concerns of federalism? Recall Justice Kennedy's reminder that state and local laws addressing guns and/or schools exist in most jurisdictions. How did the federal act mesh with these laws? For example, how did federal law apply to a homeowner living next to a schoolyard who lawfully buys a gun under state law, and then proceeds to drive home with it? Under one section of the federal statute, such a person would apparently be exempt if his state licensed guns, and he had a license, but would (at least arguably) be a federal felon if his state did not even require gun licenses. See 18 U.S.C. §922(q)(2)(B)(ii). Does this make sense? For specific discussion, see Merritt, supra, at 693. For outstanding general analysis of the myriad ways in which state and federal law interact, see Henry Hart, The Relations Between State and Federal Law, 54 Colum. L. Rev. 489 (1954); Paul Mishkin, The Variousness of "Federal Law": Competence and Discretion in the Choice of National and State Rules for Decision, 105 U. Pa. L. Rev. 797 (1957).

As things turned out, Congress did revisit the issue of guns in schools in the wake of *Lopez*. In late 1996, Congress enacted a new version of §922, with explicit findings, and with a narrower sweep. Under the new version, it is "unlawful for any individual knowingly to possess a firearm that has moved in or that otherwise affects interstate or foreign commerce at a place that the individual knows, or has reasonable cause to believe, is a school zone." Pub. L. No. 104-208, §657, 110 Stat. 3009 (1996). Is this change enough to satisfy the Court's concerns? Should it be enough?[2] Note also that before the *Lopez* case was decided, but after Mr. Lopez's gun crime had occurred, Congress in a 1994 statute did make findings about the link between school gun violence and commerce. The government in *Lopez* chose not to rely on these findings. Why? (Might the Ex Post Facto Clause be relevant here?)

3. *Modalities of interpretation.* Different Justices often approach constitutional law with distinctive methodological emphases. Justice Thomas, for example, pays great attention to constitutional text and history in *Lopez.* Particularly noteworthy is his effort to construe the words of the Commerce Clause in light of a different constitutional clause using the word "commerce" (and also a clause using the word "affect"). For more discussion of this "intratextual" technique, see the discussion following City of Boerne v. Flores, infra. By contrast, Justice Souter places primary reliance on the lessons of New Deal case law; whereas Justice Breyer sounds repeated prudential notes in his plea that Commerce Clause doctrine must be practical. Recall Professor Bobbitt's extremely insightful catalogue and analysis of various modes of constitutional interpretation; see Philip Bobbitt, Constitutional Fate: Theory of the Constitution (1980).

4. *A structural middle approach?* Consider a structural approach to *Lopez* that tries to steer a middle course between the majority and the dissenters. On this view, each state should be trusted to regulate affairs whose effects are felt within its geographic limits, but Congress may step in to deal with interstate spillovers—where actions in one state have real effects in other states. This was the view of federal power explicitly put forth by framer (and soon-to-be Justice) James Wilson in the Pennsylvania ratifying debates of 1788. On a Wilsonian reading, "Commerce" should be understood not merely to mean "economic" affairs, as Justice Thomas would have it, but virtually any "dealings" or "transactions."

While structurally inspired, this noneconomic reading of "commerce" also finds some important textual support in the Oxford English Dictionary (OED), and makes good sense of early federal practice. Bolingbroke's famous mid-eighteenth-century tract, *The Idea of a Patriot King*, spoke of the "free and easy commerce of social life" and other founding-era texts cited in the OED referred to "domestic animals which have the greatest Commerce with mankind" and "our Lord's commerce with his disciples." Structurally, the broader reading would seem to make better sense of the framers' general goals by enabling Congress to regulate all interactions (and altercations) with foreign nations and Indian tribes—interactions that, if improperly handled by a single state acting on its own, might lead to needless wars or otherwise compromise the interests of sister states. Draft language at Philadelphia had in fact empowered Congress "to regulate affairs with the Indians," but the word "affairs" dropped out when the delegates opted to fold the Indian clause into the general interstate and international "commerce" provision. Without a broad reading of "commerce" in this clause, it is not entirely clear whence the federal government would derive its needed power to deal with noneconomic international incidents—or for that matter to address the entire range of vexing

2. Lower courts have upheld the amended version as satisfying *Lopez*'s requirement of a jurisdictional predicate. See United States v. Dorsey, 418 F.3d 1038, 1046 (9th Cir. 2005); United States v. Danks, 221 F.3d 1037, 1038-1039 (8th Cir. 1999).

nonmercantile interactions and altercations that might arise among states.[3] Notably, the First Congress did in fact enact a statute regulating noneconomic interactions and altercations—"intercourse"—with Indians. See An Act to Regulate Trade and Intercourse with the Indian Tribes, July 22, 1790, 1 Stat. 137. Section 5 of this Act dealt with crimes—whether economic or not—committed by Americans on Indian lands. Wasn't this early statute obviously grounded in the Commerce Clause, and doesn't it suggest the good sense of construing "commerce" in this clause to mean "intercourse" more generally?[4]

The key distinction, on this view, is between intrastate and interstate transactions—between "national" problems everywhere, and "federal" problems affecting relations between ("among," in the words of the clause) states. For example, even if burning homegrown logs in home fireplaces is not particularly "commercial" in Justice Thomas's view, Congress should be allowed to regulate the air pollution it creates if (and only if) other states are affected—say, because the wind blows the pollution into adjoining states. Similarly, if a private person hunting on his own estate seeks to kill an endangered species that regularly migrates across state lines, or that has DNA that might help scientists in other states cure human diseases, this is an easy case for federal involvement, even if our hunter is killing for sport, not profit.

But what exactly was the interstate problem in *Lopez*? Why wouldn't each state obviously have a strong interest in protecting its children from gun violence? Indeed, if, as Justice Breyer argues, high-wage employers seek to locate in areas with strong schools, wouldn't each state have a good incentive to protect kids in schools? As a "practical" matter—to use Justice Breyer's approach—wasn't the federal law largely grandstanding, given that the vast majority of local crimes are prosecuted by state governments and not the feds?

Would this middle approach lend itself to principled doctrinal exposition and enforcement in courts? If not, does it nonetheless set out a workable distinction for a constitutionally conscientious Congressperson?

5. *Narrow versus broad time-framing.* Note that whether we find effects in sister states may often depend on how narrowly or broadly we frame the issue, temporally. If we consider effects over long periods of time, then we will often find them radiating out over broad stretches of space. But guns in schools seems a rather easy case for narrow time-framing—the harm is so graphic and immediate in time that the main effects are felt locally in space. Contrast the issue of school violence with the issue of school curriculum. The *Lopez* majority seemed very skeptical of the notion that Congress should have power to "mandate a federal curriculum for local elementary and secondary schools"—but consider the following broadly framed "federal" argument for a congressionally defined curriculum: Economic growth

---

3. It might be countered that federal authority to regulate all truly international issues, whether or not economic, derives not from the Commerce Clause but from general structural principles of national sovereignty. Cf. United States v. Curtiss-Wright Export Corp., 299 U.S. 304 (1936). But if it is permissible to range beyond strict textual enumeration in the international domain, à la *Curtiss-Wright,* why not in the interstate domain? If sound structural principles support federal power in the former, why not in the latter as well?

4. Some of the material in this paragraph is borrowed from Akhil Reed Amar, America's Constitution: A Biography (2005).

depends on the ability of workers to move easily from state to state, within a single firm, or switching firms. But moving across states is harder when each state has a different curriculum—a common set of curricular standards makes it easier for parents to relocate with minimal disruption to their children's education. Without federal coordination, no state acting individually has sufficient incentive to develop a nationwide standard. Also, each state might underinvest in its primary education, on the rational assumption that it will not fully internalize the long-term benefits of a good educational system, or suffer the long-term harms of a bad one; people move across states over the course of their lifetime, and the benefits of a good primary education in State A largely redound to sister states. On this view, Congress might indeed have a legitimate role in setting minimum standards for states, or "bribing" states, through conditional funding statutes, to spend more on education than they might otherwise. Note how these arguments for federal intervention seek to identify genuine "transactions" across state lines—movement of employee/parents, or of former students—but these interstate effects are most visible when we expand the temporal frame of analysis. Compare, in this regard, the broader time frame implicit in Justice Breyer's approach. (But does such a broad time frame intuitively work when the harm involved is so immediate and urgent—like blood in schools?) For general discussions of narrow versus broad temporal framing in other areas of law, see Mark Kelman, Interpretive Construction in the Substantive Criminal Law, 33 Stan. L. Rev. 591 (1981); Jack M. Balkin, The Rhetoric of Responsibility, 76 Va. L. Rev. 197 (1990).

6. *Maintaining fidelity to the founding in a changed world.* Suppose the founders believed two things: (1) The federal government should be allowed to regulate all truly interstate issues; and (2) state governments would nonetheless retain regulatory control over myriad and important topics. These two beliefs could coexist in a world where most transactions did not affect sister states. But suppose that as a result of dramatic improvements in communication, transportation, and scientific knowledge over the next two centuries, many more of the transactions that occur today do genuinely involve interstate effects—movement of pollution molecules across state lines, economic impacts in sister states, interstate migration of persons, interstate shipment of goods, and so on. If so, the two beliefs of the founders cannot coexist today. But which of the two should be abandoned? The *Lopez* majority seems more willing to sacrifice the first principle; the Breyer dissent, the second. For more discussion, see Jack M. Balkin, Constitutional Interpretation and the Problem of History, 63 N.Y.U. L. Rev. 911 (1988); Lawrence Lessig, Translating Federalism: United States v. Lopez, 1995 Sup. Ct. Rev. 125.

7. *Litigating* Lopez*: United States v. Morrison.* In United States v. Morrison, 529 U.S. 598 (2000), Chief Justice Rehnquist spoke for the same five-person majority as in *Lopez*, and once again held that a congressional statute exceeded the proper scope of the Commerce Clause. The particular provision at issue, §13981 of the Violence Against Women Act of 1994 (VAWA), vested victims of gender-motivated violence with a federal civil cause of action against their assailants. In the case before the Court, Christy Brzonkala, a student enrolled at Virginia Polytechnic Institute, brought a federal suit against two members of the varsity football team, who, she alleged, had pinned her down and repeatedly raped her within 30 minutes of meeting her. The Court treated the case as squarely governed by *Lopez*:

> Gender-motivated crimes of violence are not, in any sense of the phrase, economic activity. While we need not adopt a categorical rule against aggregating the effects of any noneconomic activity in order to decide these cases, thus far in our Nation's history our cases have upheld Commerce Clause regulation of intrastate activity only where that activity is economic in nature. [Moreover,] [l]ike the Gun-Free School Zones Act at issue in *Lopez,* [VAWA] contains no jurisdictional element establishing that the federal cause of action is in pursuance of Congress' power to regulate interstate commerce. . . . We accordingly reject the argument that Congress may regulate noneconomic, violent criminal conduct based solely on that conduct's aggregate effect on interstate commerce.

Violence against women, said the majority, was not *commercial* in nature (in an economic sense). Nor had Congress added a jurisdictional element that would establish its *interstate* character.

How should we analyze *Morrison* from the standpoint of interstate spillovers? Violence against women is a huge problem everywhere. Does that make it a *federal* problem—i.e., a problem that occurs "among" or between the states—as opposed to a national problem?

Could Congress reasonably have concluded that violence against women has interstate spillover effects that make it a federal problem? In *Morrison* (unlike in *Lopez*) Congress had made legislative findings about the effects of gender-motivated violence on interstate commerce when it enacted VAWA. In particular, Congress found that gender-motivated violence affects interstate commerce "by deterring potential victims from traveling interstate, from engaging in employment in interstate business, and from transacting with business, and in places involved in interstate commerce; . . . by diminishing national productivity, increasing medical and other costs, and decreasing the supply of and the demand for interstate products." H.R. Conf. Rep. No. 103-711, at 385.

Are these findings sufficient to make an interstate spillover argument along the lines of *Heart of Atlanta Motel* and Katzenbach v. McClung? Recall that Congress found that discrimination against Black people in public accommodations led to less interstate travel and less consumption of goods and services in and from states that practiced racial discrimination. Are the interstate effects of gender-motivated violence on women's decisions to travel and conduct business interstate sufficiently similar?

Note that even if you think that the interstate effects *are* sufficiently similar and sufficiently substantial, they would not have been enough for the *Morrison* Court. Why? Because of the Court's new distinction between economic and noneconomic activity. After *Lopez,* it does not matter whether we can demonstrate interstate spillover effects from violence against women, if the activity that Congress aims at is not itself "economic." This distinction allowed the *Morrison* Court to distinguish *Heart of Atlanta Motel* and Katzenbach v. McClung. In those cases, the activity regulated was the decision to sell or not to sell goods and services to Black people—clearly an economic activity.[5]

---

5. Under *Lopez,* Congress might protect women-owned *businesses* from gender-motivated violence, but that is because Congress is preventing disruption to the channels and facilities of interstate commerce.

In his dissent, Justice Souter complained that "the legislative record [of interstate effects] here is far more voluminous than the record compiled by Congress and found sufficient in two prior cases upholding Title II of the Civil Rights Act of 1964 against Commerce Clause challenges." But Congress's findings were made in a pre-*Lopez* world; they did not take into account the Court's distinction between economic and noneconomic activity and therefore they were not sufficient, in the eyes of the *Morrison* majority:

> The reasoning that petitioners advance seeks to follow the but-for causal chain from the initial occurrence of violent crime (the suppression of which has always been the prime object of the States' police power) to every attenuated effect upon interstate commerce. If accepted, petitioners' reasoning would allow Congress to regulate any crime as long as the nationwide, aggregated impact of that crime has substantial effects on employment, production, transit, or consumption. Indeed, if Congress may regulate gender-motivated violence, it would be able to regulate murder or any other type of violence since gender-motivated violence, as a subset of all violent crime, is certain to have lesser economic impacts than the larger class of which it is a part.

Chief Justice Rehnquist also argued that upholding VAWA would be problematic because doing so would allow Congress to intrude on traditional state functions like family law: "Petitioners' reasoning, moreover, will not limit Congress to regulating violence but may, as we suggested in *Lopez*, be applied equally as well to family law and other areas of traditional state regulation since the aggregate effect of marriage, divorce, and childrearing on the national economy is undoubtedly significant."

Is it true that family law has traditionally been an exclusively local concern in American law and politics? Cf. Jill Elaine Hasday, Federalism and the Family Reconstructed, 45 UCLA L. Rev. 1297 (1998) (pointing out that the federal government has been heavily involved in regulating domestic relations since Reconstruction); Kristin A. Collins, Federalism's Fallacy: The Early Tradition of Federal Family Law and the Invention of States' Rights, 26 Cardozo L. Rev. 1761, 1767 (2005); Ann Laquer Estin, Federalism and Child Support, 5 Va. J. Soc. Pol'y & L. 541, 541-542 (1998) (noting broad reach of federal regulation in tax, pension, and bankruptcy statutes, as well as federal rules regarding child support, custody jurisdiction, and federal welfare policy).

In any case, whether an activity is traditionally regulated by states is orthogonal to whether it has spillover effects in different jurisdictions or whether a federal solution may be valuable to harmonize inconsistent approaches. See the discussion of education in a national economy in discussion note 5, supra. Note, moreover, that as the economy changes, a traditional focus of state regulation like labor or manufacturing may come to have increasing varieties and degrees of interstate spillover effects. Can you think of areas of family and social welfare policy that might have such spillover effects?

VAWA supporters also tried to uphold §13981 as a valid exercise of congressional power to enforce the Fourteenth Amendment, but the *Morrison* majority also rejected this §5 argument. This part of the case is discussed later in this Chapter.

8. *Adding a jurisdictional element: Scarborough v. United States.* In *Lopez*, Chief Justice Rehnquist noted that the Gun Free School Zones Act "contains no jurisdictional element which would ensure, through case-by-case inquiry, that the firearm possession in question affects interstate commerce." Similarly, in *Morrison*, the Court reiterated that "[s]uch a jurisdictional element may establish that the enactment is in pursuance of Congress' regulation of interstate commerce." As noted above, in 1996, Congress passed a new version of the Gun Free School Zones Act which made it "unlawful for any individual knowingly to possess a firearm that has moved in or that otherwise affects interstate or foreign commerce" in a school zone. Does this mean that Congress can get around the limitations of *Lopez* and *Morrison* simply by adding jurisdictional language?

In Scarborough v. United States, 431 U.S. 563, 575 (1977), the Court interpreted a federal statute that imposed criminal penalties on any felon who "who receives, possesses, or transports in commerce or affecting commerce . . . any firearm." The Court stated that "we see no indication that Congress intended to require any more than the minimal nexus that the firearm have been, at some time, in interstate commerce." (Cf. United States v. Bass, 404 U.S. 336 (1971), in which the Court interpreted a felon possession statute to require a nexus to to interstate commerce.)

Although it did not reach the constitutional question, the *Scarborough* Court seemed to assume that Congress could constitutionally regulate the possession of firearms solely because they had previously moved across state lines. Thus, *Scarborough* seems to recognize an additional method for Congressional regulation under the Commerce Clause.

Lower courts have sought to reconcile *Scarborough* with *Lopez* and *Morrison*. For the most part, they have concluded that adding a jurisdictional requirement satisfies the Constitution to the extent that the requirement tends to show that there is a nexus between what Congress wishes to regulate and one of the three categories of permissible objects of Commerce Clause regulation outlined in *Lopez* and *Morrison*: (1) regulation of the channels of interstate commerce; (2) regulation of instrumentalities of (or persons or things in) interstate commerce; or (3) regulation of activities substantially affecting interstate commerce.

It is fairly easy to show a nexus to interstate commerce (1) when Congress makes it a crime to cross state lines to perform a certain act; (2) when Congress makes it a crime to use facilities of interstate commerce (for example, telephones, or the internet) to perform an act; (3) when Congress makes it a crime to attack or injure persons or businesses engaged in interstate commerce; or (4) when Congress makes it a crime to interfere with persons traveling or communicating (or persons attempting to travel or communicate) using channels, facilities or instrumentalities of interstate commerce. The nexus is more attenuated when Congress regulates mere possession of things that have, at some point in their history, moved in interstate commerce or been offered for sale in interstate commerce.

In most cases, lower courts have found that the jurisdictional element provides a sufficient nexus to interstate commerce; in a few other cases courts have simply concluded that, notwithstanding *Lopez* and *Morrison*, *Scarborough* applies. See, e.g., United States v. Patton, 451 F.3d 615 (10th Cir. 2006) (collecting cases, and noting tension with *Lopez* and *Morrison*, but concluding that *Scarborough* is still good law).

In United States v. Alderman, 565 F.3d 641 (9th Cir. 2009), the Ninth Circuit, voting 2-1, upheld a federal law that made it a crime for a felon to possess body armor that had been "sold or offered for sale in interstate commerce." 18 U.S.C. §§931, 921(a)(35). The Ninth Circuit doubted that there was much connection between mere possession of body armor and any of the three *Lopez* categories. Nevertheless, it found the case indistinguishable from *Scarborough*; therefore it concluded that there was a sufficient nexus to interstate commerce, at least until the Supreme Court instructed otherwise.

Justice Thomas dissented from the denial of the grant of certiorari, joined by Justice Scalia. Alderman v. United States, 562 U.S. 1163 (2011) ("the lower courts' reading of *Scarborough*, by trumping the *Lopez* framework, could very well remove any limit on the commerce power. The Ninth Circuit's interpretation of *Scarborough* seems to permit Congress to regulate or ban possession of any item that has ever been offered for sale or crossed state lines."). At some point, the Supreme Court will resolve the issue, but the Court may have taken its time because so many federal criminal laws rely on a jurisdictional predicate.

Consider *Scarborough* from a structural perspective. A jurisdictional element should suffice to bring a regulation within Congress's Commerce Power when the jurisdictional limitation shows that Congress is responding to a federal problem, that is, one that has spillover effects between states or creates collective action problems among the states.

A different approach would insist that *Scarborough* is required by the Constitution's text. Anything that crosses state lines is within Congress's power to regulate, because things that move interstate involve "commerce among the several states," no matter how long ago the crossing might have occurred. The basic idea is that if Congress has the power to regulate anything that crosses into the United States from a foreign country, then it must have power to regulate anything that crosses state lines. Do you agree?

How would you add a jurisdictional predicate to the civil rights remedy struck down in *Morrison*? Would the addition of such a jurisdictional hook make it more likely that regulating gender-motivated violence responds to a federal problem or is otherwise within Congress's powers?

9. *Litigating* Lopez*: Gonzales v. Raich.* In Gonzales v. Raich, 545 U.S. 1 (2005), the four *Lopez* dissenters, joined by Justices Kennedy and Scalia, voted to uphold congressional laws criminalizing marijuana possession even when these federal laws prohibited local cultivation and use of marijuana for medical reasons pursuant to a valid California statute that decriminalized the matter for state law purposes. Angel Raich, who suffered from a variety of serious medical conditions and was using marijuana as prescribed by a board-certified physician to control her excruciating pain, sought a declaratory judgment that federal drug laws could not properly be applied against her. She alleged that the marijuana that she used had never been bought or sold and had never crossed a state line.

In an opinion authored by Justice Stevens and joined by Justices Kennedy, Souter, Ginsburg, and Breyer, the Court rejected the challenge to Congress's power. The majority distinguished *Lopez* and *Morrison* on the grounds that they involved regulation of noneconomic activity:

> Unlike those at issue in *Lopez* and *Morrison*, the activities regulated by the CSA [Controlled Substances Act] are quintessentially economic. "Economics" refers to "the production, distribution, and consumption of commodities." Webster's Third New International Dictionary 720 (1966). The CSA is a statute that regulates the production, distribution, and consumption of commodities for which there is an established, and lucrative, interstate market. Prohibiting the intrastate possession or manufacture of an article of commerce is a rational (and commonly utilized) means of regulating commerce in that product. Such prohibitions include specific decisions requiring that a drug be withdrawn from the market as a result of the failure to comply with regulatory requirements as well as decisions excluding Schedule I drugs entirely from the market. Because the CSA is a statute that directly regulates economic, commercial activity, our opinion in *Morrison* casts no doubt on its constitutionality.[6]

At the same time, the Court reaffirmed its commitment to Wickard v. Filburn, and held that *Raich* fell on the *Wickard* side of the line. Just as the farmer's individual consumption of wheat in *Wickard*, when combined with other comparably situated farmers' consumption, could affect prices and outputs in a genuinely interstate wheat market, so Raich's use could not be hermetically sealed off from the larger—and truly interstate—issue of the marijuana market.

Both wheat and marijuana were "fungible" commodities, the Court observed; and in Raich's case the federal government had legitimate reasons to fear that some marijuana earmarked for Raich and others under the California Compassionate Use Act might be diverted into illegal uses. The majority also expressed concern that some lax physicians might face market pressure to overprescribe medical marijuana. In one footnote, the majority drew attention to the fact that "patients residing in the cities of Oakland and Santa Cruz and in the counties of Sonoma and Tehama are permitted to possess 3 pounds of processed marijuana"—an amount "yield[ing] roughly 3,000 joints or cigarettes." According to the majority, the "likelihood that all . . . production will promptly terminate when patients recover or will precisely match the patients' medical needs during their convalescence seems remote; whereas the danger that excesses will satisfy some of the admittedly enormous demand for recreational use seems obvious. . . . [N]o small number of unscrupulous people will make use of the California exemptions to serve their commercial ends whenever it is feasible to do so."

Raich argued, nevertheless, that the state's legalization of marijuana for medical use when prescribed by a licensed physician created a distinct category that included only noneconomic intrastate activity; this justified a carve-out from federal regulatory authority. The Court rejected the idea: "[L]imiting the activity to marijuana possession and cultivation 'in accordance with state law' cannot serve to place respondents' activities beyond congressional reach. The Supremacy Clause unambiguously provides that if there is any conflict between federal and state law, federal law shall prevail. . . . Just as state acquiescence to federal regulation cannot

---

6. Do you accept the Court's definition of "economic" activity? Note once more that defining what is "economic" and what is not becomes unnecessary if one focuses instead on what is federal and interstate.

expand the bounds of the Commerce Clause, so too state action cannot circumscribe Congress' plenary commerce power."

Concurring in the judgment, Justice Scalia seconded the majority's point that "[d]rugs like marijuana are fungible commodities [and] marijuana that is grown at home and possessed for personal use is never more than an instant from the interstate market—and this is so whether or not the possession is for medicinal use or lawful use under the laws of a particular State." Justice Scalia also stressed that insofar as Congress sought to regulate issues that were not themselves interstate commerce, but that were instead intrastate and noncommercial (in an economic sense), such regulation was nonetheless permissible if the regulatory overhang was a necessary (in a *McCulloch* sense) adjunct to a valid, nonpretextual interstate regulatory program:

> [W]here Congress has the authority to enact a regulation of interstate commerce, "it possesses every power needed to make that regulation effective." . . . The regulation of an intrastate activity may be essential to a comprehensive regulation of interstate commerce even though the intrastate activity does not itself "substantially affect" interstate commerce. Moreover, as . . . *Lopez* . . . suggests, Congress may regulate even noneconomic local activity if that regulation is a necessary part of a more general regulation of interstate commerce. The relevant question is simply whether the means chosen are "reasonably adapted" to the attainment of a legitimate end under the commerce power.

In advancing this idea, Justice Scalia relied not on the Commerce Clause in isolation, but on this clause in tandem with the Necessary and Proper Clause. Citing *McCulloch,* Justice Scalia argued that the latter clause "empowers Congress to enact laws in the effectuation of its enumerated powers that are not within its authority to enact in isolation." Whether or not you agree with this principle of federal power, recall from Chapter 1 that *McCulloch* did not argue that the Necessary and Proper Clause added extra authority; rather Chief Justice Marshall placed primary reliance on his expansive understandings of the various enumerated powers individually and collectively.

Dissenting on behalf of herself, the Chief Justice, and Justice Thomas, Justice O'Connor argued that no proven problem of diversion existed, and that "California's Compassionate Use Act and similar state legislation may well isolate activities relating to medical marijuana from the illicit market." But why must the federal government run the risk in the absence of proof positive either way? And if John Marshall was right to insist in *McCulloch* that Congress did not need to rely on state banks and could choose to establish its own bank, why must the modern Congress rely on state drug enforcement programs?

Justice O'Connor complained that on the majority view in *Raich,* very little was left of *Lopez* itself. For example, a future Congress might well impose special criminal penalties on guns near schools if such penalties were linked to a larger congressional ban on *all* guns. Ironically, by *expanding* the scope of federal criminal regulation of firearms—by displacing *even more* state law with a *far broader* federal gun policy—Congress apparently could do the very thing that the *Lopez* Court, in the name of states' rights, tried to prevent Congress from doing.

There is indeed an irony here, but wasn't this irony built into *Lopez* itself? Recall that in *Lopez*, the Court pointedly observed that "Section 922(q) is not an essential part of a larger regulation of economic activity, in which the regulatory scheme could be undercut unless the intrastate activity were regulated." (For those structuralists who prefer to focus less on the economic-noneconomic distinction, clarity would be improved by substituting the word "interstate" for the word "economic" in this passage.) Note also that in other federalism contexts, the Court, when limiting Congress, has at times suggested that Congress might find other ways of skinning the cat, while dissenters have stressed that these other ways might ironically be less respectful of states' rights. For example, although Congress may not *require* state legislatures to enact laws, Congress apparently may *bribe* them to do so under the Spending Clause, see New York v. United States, 505 U.S. 144 (1992), discussed infra in Section II.B. (Could Congress have bribed states into enacting and enforcing state-law versions of the Gun-Free School Zones Act or the VAWA?) And although Congress is not always allowed to impose liability on private parties in response to state misconduct, it may have broader power to hold the states themselves liable in such situations, according to the *Morrison* Court majority. But, as Justice Breyer pointed out in his *Morrison* dissent, federal liability imposed directly on states might be seen as *less* friendly to states' rights than the cooperative federalism system of private liability embodied in VAWA, which gave state governments incentives to work with the federal government, rather than litigate against it, in combating violence against women. Also, because Congress is prevented from commandeering state executives, it may find itself obliged to create larger federal bureaucracies displacing state structures altogether, see Printz v. United States, 521 U.S. 898 (1997), also discussed infra in Section II.B.

In light of the various ways in which Congress may detour around the *Lopez* line, is this case largely symbolic? (If so, is *Lopez* any different from many other doctrinal lines in modern constitutional law?) Is the symbol at issue in *Lopez*—the reminder that even today, our federal system remains, in principle, a system of limited federal powers—one worthy of judicial affirmation? Is the judicial game of finding the relatively rare case in which Congress has overstepped worth the candle?[7]

On the other hand, hasn't the Court drawn the line in a rather sensible place? In areas where there truly are interstate (indeed, international) markets or law-evading enterprises organized on an interstate (or international) scale so as to defy or evade successful regulation by individual states, congressional power has been strongly affirmed in cases such as *Perez* and *Raich*. And in situations where no real interstate spillovers or interstate organizations exist—*Lopez* and *Morrison*—congressional power has been clipped. And, thus far at least, the Court has not sought to limit Congress from regulating truly interstate but less obviously economic issues, involving endangered species, pollution molecules, and the like.

---

7. If there is a reasonable dispute about whether Congress has acted within its commerce power, why shouldn't the Court defer to Congress's judgment? Or is the point that since *Lopez* represents such an exceptional set of circumstances, it really doesn't matter much what rules courts settle on as long as they abide by the basic terms of the New Deal settlement?

10. *Reaffirming* Raich: *Taylor v. United States.* The Court followed *Raich* in Taylor v. United States, 136 S. Ct. 2074 (2016). Petitioner Taylor was convicted under the Hobbs Act, which makes it a crime for a person to affect commerce, or to attempt to do so, by robbery. 18 U.S.C. §1951(a). The Act defines "commerce" broadly as interstate commerce "and all other commerce over which the United States has jurisdiction." §1951(b)(3). Taylor was part of a gang that broke into two homes in an unsuccessful search for marijuana. Taylor appealed his conviction on the ground that the government had to prove that the marijuana was part of interstate commerce; he contended that the marijuana was locally grown.

Justice Alito, writing for six Justices, upheld Taylor's conviction. He argued that in order to satisfy the Act's element of affecting (or attempting to affect) commerce, the government simply needed to prove that Taylor attempted to rob marijuana dealers of their drugs and drug money. His opinion reaffirmed the reasoning of *Raich*: "[T]he activity at issue, the sale of marijuana, is unquestionably an economic activity. It is, to be sure, a form of business that is illegal under federal law and the laws of most States. But there can be no question that marijuana trafficking is a moneymaking endeavor—and a potentially lucrative one at that."

Justice Alito explained that in *Raich* "[t]he Court reaffirmed Congress' power to regulate purely local activities that are part of an economic 'class of activities' that have a substantial effect on interstate commerce. The production, possession, and distribution of controlled substances constitute a 'class of activities' that in the aggregate substantially affect interstate commerce, and therefore, the Court held, Congress possesses the authority to regulate (and to criminalize) the production, possession, and distribution of controlled substances even when those activities occur entirely within the boundaries of a single State. Any other outcome, we warned, would leave a gaping enforcement hole in Congress's regulatory scheme." Because "the market for marijuana, including its intrastate aspects, is 'commerce over which the United States has jurisdiction,' . . . a robber who affects or attempts to affect even the intrastate sale of marijuana grown within the State affects or attempts to affect commerce over which the United States has jurisdiction." Justice Alito concluded: "Our holding today is limited to cases in which the defendant targets drug dealers for the purpose of stealing drugs or drug proceeds. We do not resolve what the Government must prove to establish Hobbs Act robbery where some other type of business or victim is targeted."

Justice Thomas dissented, arguing that the Hobbs Act should apply only to robberies that actually affected interstate commerce, such as "those that affect the channels of interstate commerce or instrumentalities of interstate commerce. A robbery that forces an interstate freeway to shut down thus may form the basis for a valid Hobbs Act conviction. So too might a robbery of a truckdriver who is in the course of transporting commercial goods across state lines. But if the Government cannot prove that a robbery in a State affected interstate commerce, then the robbery is not punishable under the Hobbs Act. Sweeping in robberies that do not affect interstate commerce comes too close to conferring on Congress a general police power over the Nation."

One of the Roberts Court's first major Commerce Clause decisions raised once again the federal government's power to solve an interstate problem—in this case, the provision of health care.

National Federation of Independent Business v. Sebelius

[The Health Care Case]
567 U.S. 519 (2012)

[In March 2010, Congress enacted the Patient Protection and Affordable Care Act in order to increase the number of Americans covered by health insurance and decrease the cost of health care. Twenty-six states, several individuals, and the National Federation of Independent Business challenged two key provisions of the Act as unconstitutional, and argued that, because the Affordable Care Act lacked a severability clause, the entire Act should be declared unconstitutional.

One part of the Court's opinion considered the constitutionality of the individual mandate, which requires most Americans to maintain "minimum essential" health insurance coverage or make a "[s]hared responsibility payment" to the government. In 2016, for example, the payment is 2.5 percent of an individual's household income, but no less than $695 and no more than the average yearly premium for insurance that covers 60 percent of the cost of ten specified services (for example, prescription drugs and hospitalization). 26 U.S.C. §5000A. Individuals are exempted if they have qualifying health insurance through their employer or otherwise, receive health care through Medicare or Medicaid, are below the poverty line, live outside the country, serve in the military, are dependents, or have a religious objection. (The other challenged provision—the expansion of the federal Medicaid program that provides medical coverage for the poor—is discussed infra.)

Five Justices—Chief Justice Roberts and the four joint dissenters—held that the mandate was beyond Congress's powers under the Commerce Clause and Necessary and Proper Clause. However, the Chief Justice and four other Justices held that the mandate was a constitutional exercise of Congress's power to tax. That portion of the opinion appears infra in the discussion of the taxing power.]

Chief Justice ROBERTS announced the judgment of the Court.

According to the Government, the health care market is characterized by a significant cost-shifting problem. Everyone will eventually need health care at a time and to an extent they cannot predict, but if they do not have insurance, they often will not be able to pay for it. Because state and federal laws nonetheless require hospitals to provide a certain degree of care to individuals without regard to their ability to pay, hospitals end up receiving compensation for only a portion of the services they provide. To recoup the losses, hospitals pass on the cost to insurers through higher rates, and insurers, in turn, pass on the cost to policy holders in the form of higher premiums. Congress estimated that the cost of uncompensated care raises family health insurance premiums, on average, by over $1,000 per year.

In the Affordable Care Act, Congress addressed the problem of those who cannot obtain insurance coverage because of preexisting conditions or other health issues. It did so through the Act's "guaranteed-issue" and "community rating" provisions. These provisions together prohibit insurance companies from denying coverage to those with such conditions or charging unhealthy individuals higher premiums than healthy individuals.

The guaranteed-issue and community-rating reforms do not, however, address the issue of healthy individuals who choose not to purchase insurance to cover potential health care needs. In fact, the reforms sharply exacerbate that problem, by providing an incentive for individuals to delay purchasing health insurance until they become sick, relying on the promise of guaranteed and affordable coverage. The reforms also threaten to impose massive new costs on insurers, who are required to accept unhealthy individuals but prohibited from charging them rates necessary to pay for their coverage. This will lead insurers to significantly increase premiums on everyone.

The individual mandate was Congress's solution to these problems. By requiring that individuals purchase health insurance, the mandate prevents cost-shifting by those who would otherwise go without it. In addition, the mandate forces into the insurance risk pool more healthy individuals, whose premiums on average will be higher than their health care expenses. This allows insurers to subsidize the costs of covering the unhealthy individuals the reforms require them to accept. The Government claims that Congress has power under the Commerce and Necessary and Proper Clauses to enact this solution.

The Government contends that the individual mandate is within Congress's power because the failure to purchase insurance "has a substantial and deleterious effect on interstate commerce" by creating the cost-shifting problem. . . . [But] Congress has never attempted to rely on that power to compel individuals not engaged in commerce to purchase an unwanted product. Legislative novelty is not necessarily fatal; there is a first time for everything. But sometimes "the most telling indication of [a] severe constitutional problem . . . is the lack of historical precedent" for Congress's action. . . . The examples of other congressional mandates cited by Justice Ginsburg . . . are not to the contrary. Each of those mandates—to report for jury duty, to register for the draft, to purchase firearms in anticipation of militia service, to exchange gold currency for paper currency, and to file a tax return—are based on constitutional provisions other than the Commerce Clause. [relocated footnote—Eds.]

The Constitution grants Congress the power to "*regulate* Commerce." Art. I, §8, cl. 3 (emphasis added). The power to *regulate* commerce presupposes the existence of commercial activity to be regulated. If the power to "regulate" something included the power to create it, many of the provisions in the Constitution would be superfluous. For example, the Constitution gives Congress the power to "coin Money," in addition to the power to "regulate the Value thereof." *Id.*, cl. 5. And it gives Congress the power to "raise and support Armies" and to "provide and maintain a Navy," in addition to the power to "make Rules for the Government and Regulation of the land and naval Forces." *Id.*, cls. 12-14. If the power to regulate the armed forces or the value of money included the power to bring the subject of the regulation into existence, the specific grant of such powers would have been unnecessary. The language of the Constitution reflects the natural understanding that the power to regulate assumes there is already something to be regulated. . . .

Our precedent also reflects this understanding. As expansive as our cases construing the scope of the commerce power have been, they all have one thing in common: They uniformly describe the power as reaching "activity." It is nearly impossible to avoid the word when quoting them. . . .

The individual mandate . . . does not regulate existing commercial activity. It instead compels individuals to *become* active in commerce by purchasing a product, on the ground that their failure to do so affects interstate commerce. Construing the Commerce Clause to permit Congress to regulate individuals precisely *because* they are doing nothing would open a new and potentially vast domain to congressional authority. . . . Allowing Congress to justify federal regulation by pointing to the effect of inaction on commerce would bring countless decisions an individual could *potentially* make within the scope of federal regulation, and . . . empower Congress to make those decisions for him. . . .

Indeed, the Government's logic would justify a mandatory purchase to solve almost any problem. . . . [M]any Americans do not eat a balanced diet. . . . [This] increases health care costs, to a greater extent than the failure of the uninsured to purchase insurance. Those increased costs are borne in part by other Americans who must pay more, just as the uninsured shift costs to the insured. Congress addressed the insurance problem by ordering everyone to buy insurance. Under the Government's theory, Congress could address the diet problem by ordering everyone to buy vegetables. . . .

Congress already enjoys vast power to regulate much of what we do. Accepting the Government's theory would give Congress the same license to regulate what we do not do, fundamentally changing the relation between the citizen and the Federal Government.

To an economist, perhaps, there is no difference between activity and inactivity; both have measurable economic effects on commerce. But the distinction between doing something and doing nothing would not have been lost on the Framers, who were "practical statesmen," not metaphysical philosophers. . . .

The Government . . . argues that because sickness and injury are unpredictable but unavoidable, "the uninsured as a class are active in the market for health care, which they regularly seek and obtain." The individual mandate "merely regulates how individuals finance and pay for that active participation—requiring that they do so through insurance, rather than through attempted self-insurance with the back-stop of shifting costs to others."

[T]he phrase "active in the market for health care" . . . has no constitutional significance. An individual who bought a car two years ago and may buy another in the future is not "active in the car market" in any pertinent sense. . . . The mandate primarily affects healthy, often young adults who are less likely to need significant health care and have other priorities for spending their money. It is precisely because these individuals, as an actuarial class, incur relatively low health care costs that the mandate helps counter the effect of forcing insurance companies to cover others who impose greater costs than their premiums are allowed to reflect. If the individual mandate is targeted at a class, it is a class whose commercial inactivity rather than activity is its defining feature.

The Government, however, claims that this does not matter. The Government regards it as sufficient to trigger Congress's authority that almost all those who are uninsured will, at some unknown point in the future, engage in a health care transaction. Asserting that "[t]here is no temporal limitation in the Commerce Clause," the Government argues that because "[e]veryone subject to this regulation is in or will be in the health care market," they can be "regulated in advance."

The proposition that Congress may dictate the conduct of an individual today because of prophesied future activity finds no support in our precedent. We have said that Congress can anticipate the *effects* on commerce of an economic activity. But we have never permitted Congress to anticipate that activity itself in order to regulate individuals not currently engaged in commerce. Each one of our cases . . . involved preexisting economic activity. . . . Everyone will likely participate in the markets for food, clothing, transportation, shelter, or energy; that does not authorize Congress to direct them to purchase particular products in those or other markets today. The Commerce Clause is not a general license to regulate an individual from cradle to grave, simply because he will predictably engage in particular transactions. Any police power to regulate individuals as such, as opposed to their activities, remains vested in the States.

The Government argues that the individual mandate can be sustained as a sort of exception to this rule, because health insurance is a unique product. According to the Government, upholding the individual mandate would not justify mandatory purchases of items such as cars or broccoli because, as the Government puts it, "[h]ealth insurance is not purchased for its own sake like a car or broccoli; it is a means of financing healthcare consumption and covering universal risks." But cars and broccoli are no more purchased for their "own sake" than health insurance. They are purchased to cover the need for transportation and food. . . .

The Government next contends that Congress has the power under the Necessary and Proper Clause to enact the individual mandate because the mandate is an "integral part of a comprehensive scheme of economic regulation"—the guaranteed-issue and community-rating insurance reforms. . . . Although the Clause gives Congress authority to "legislate on that vast mass of incidental powers which must be involved in the constitution," it does not license the exercise of any "great substantive and independent power[s]" beyond those specifically enumerated. Instead, the Clause is "'merely a declaration, for the removal of all uncertainty, that the means of carrying into execution those [powers] otherwise granted are included in the grant.'" . . . [L]aws that undermine the structure of government established by the Constitution. . . . are not "consist[ent] with the letter and spirit of the constitution," *McCulloch*, are not "*proper* [means] for carrying into Execution" Congress's enumerated powers. Rather, they are, "in the words of The Federalist, 'merely acts of usurpation' which 'deserve to be treated as such.'" . . .

Each of our prior cases upholding laws under that Clause involved exercises of authority derivative of, and in service to, a granted power. For example, we have upheld provisions permitting continued confinement of those *already in federal custody* when they could not be safely released, *Comstock*; criminalizing bribes involving organizations *receiving federal funds*, Sabri v. United States, 541 U.S. 600 (2004); and tolling state statutes of limitations while cases are *pending in federal court*, Jinks v. Richland County, 538 U.S. 456 (2003). The individual mandate, by contrast, vests Congress with the extraordinary ability to create the necessary predicate to the exercise of an enumerated power.

This is in no way an authority that is "narrow in scope," or "incidental" to the exercise of the commerce power. Rather, such a conception of the Necessary and Proper Clause would work a substantial expansion of federal authority. No longer would Congress be limited to regulating under the Commerce Clause those who by some preexisting activity bring themselves within the sphere of federal regulation. Instead, Congress could reach beyond the natural limit of its authority and draw within its regulatory scope those who otherwise would be outside of it. Even if the individual mandate is "necessary" to the Act's insurance reforms, such an expansion of federal power is not a "proper" means for making those reforms effective.

[I]n [Gonzales v.] Raich . . . Congress's attempt to regulate the interstate market for marijuana would therefore have been substantially undercut if it could not also regulate intrastate possession and consumption. Accordingly, we recognized that "Congress was acting well within its authority" under the Necessary and Proper Clause even though its "regulation ensnare[d] some purely intrastate activity." *Raich* thus did not involve the exercise of any "great substantive and independent power," *McCulloch,* of the sort at issue here. Instead, it concerned only the constitutionality of "individual *applications* of a concededly valid statutory scheme." *Raich* (emphasis added).

Just as the individual mandate cannot be sustained as a law regulating the substantial effects of the failure to purchase health insurance, neither can it be upheld as a "necessary and proper" component of the insurance reforms. The commerce power thus does not authorize the mandate.

Justice GINSBURG, with whom Justice SOTOMAYOR joins, and with whom Justice BREYER and Justice KAGAN join as to Parts I, II, III, and IV, concurring in part, concurring in the judgment in part, and dissenting in part.

The large number of individuals without health insurance, Congress found, heavily burdens the national health-care market. . . . [M]edical-care providers deliver significant amounts of care to the uninsured for which the providers receive no payment. In 2008, for example, hospitals, physicians, and other health-care professionals received no compensation for $43 billion worth of the $116 billion in care they administered to those without insurance.

Health-care providers . . . pass[] along the cost of uncompensated care to . . . the government and private insurance companies. In response, private insurers increase their premiums, shifting the cost of the elevated bills from providers onto those who carry insurance. . . . Those with health insurance subsidize the medical care of those without it. As economists would describe what happens, the uninsured "free ride" on those who pay for health insurance. . . . [B]ecause any uninsured person may need medical care at any moment and because health-care companies must account for that risk, every uninsured person impacts the market price of medical care and medical insurance.

The failure of individuals to acquire insurance has other deleterious effects on the health-care market. Because those without insurance generally lack access to preventative care, they do not receive treatment for conditions—like hypertension and diabetes—that can be successfully and affordably treated if diagnosed early on. When sickness finally drives the uninsured to seek care, once treatable conditions have escalated into grave health problems, requiring more costly and extensive intervention. The extra time and resources providers spend serving the uninsured lessens the providers' ability to care for those who do have insurance.

States cannot resolve the problem of the uninsured on their own. Like Social Security benefits, a universal health-care system, if adopted by an individual State, would be "bait to the needy and dependent elsewhere, encouraging them to migrate and seek a haven of repose." Helvering v. Davis. An influx of unhealthy individuals into a State with universal health care would result in increased spending on medical services. To cover the increased costs, a State would have to raise taxes, and private health-insurance companies would have to increase premiums. Higher taxes and increased insurance costs would, in turn, encourage businesses and healthy individuals to leave the State.

States that undertake health-care reforms on their own thus risk "placing themselves in a position of economic disadvantage as compared with neighbors or competitors." . . . "[O]ut-of-state residents continue to seek and receive millions of dollars in uncompensated care in Massachusetts hospitals, limiting the State's efforts to improve its health care system through the elimination of uncompensated care." Facing that risk, individual States are unlikely to take the initiative in addressing the problem of the uninsured, even though solving that problem is in all States' best interests. Congress' intervention was needed to overcome this collective action impasse. . . .

The Commerce Clause, it is widely acknowledged, "was the Framers' response to the central problem that gave rise to the Constitution itself." Under the Articles of Confederation, the Constitution's precursor, the regulation of commerce was left to the States. This scheme proved unworkable, because the individual States, understandably focused on their own economic interests, often failed to take actions critical to the success of the Nation as a whole.

What was needed was a "national Government . . . armed with a positive & compleat authority in all cases where uniform measures are necessary." See Letter from James Madison to Edmund Randolph (Apr. 8, 1787), in 9 Papers of James Madison 368, 370 (R. Rutland ed. 1975). The Framers' solution was the Commerce Clause, which, as they perceived it, granted Congress the authority to enact economic legislation "in all Cases for the general Interests of the Union, and also in those Cases to which the States are separately incompetent." 2 Records of the Federal Convention of 1787, pp. 131-132, ¶ 8 (M. Farrand rev. 1966). . . .

Beyond dispute, Congress had a rational basis for concluding that the uninsured, as a class, substantially affect interstate commerce. Those without insurance consume billions of dollars of health-care products and services each year. Those goods are produced, sold, and delivered largely by national and regional companies who routinely transact business across state lines. The uninsured also cross state lines to receive care. Some have medical emergencies while away from home. Others, when sick, go to a neighboring State that provides better care for those who have not prepaid for care.

Not only do those without insurance consume a large amount of health care each year; critically, as earlier explained, their inability to pay for a significant portion of that consumption drives up market prices, foists costs on other consumers, and reduces market efficiency and stability. Given these far reaching effects on interstate commerce, the decision to forgo insurance is hardly inconsequential or equivalent to "doing nothing," . . . ; it is, instead, an economic decision Congress has the authority to address under the Commerce Clause.

The minimum coverage provision, furthermore, bears a "reasonable connection" to Congress' goal of protecting the health-care market from the disruption caused by individuals who fail to obtain insurance. By requiring those who do not carry insurance to pay a toll, the minimum coverage provision gives individuals a strong incentive to insure. This incentive, Congress had good reason to believe, would reduce the number of uninsured and, correspondingly, mitigate the adverse impact the uninsured have on the national health-care market. . . .

[E]veryone will, at some point, consume health-care products and services. Thus, if The Chief Justice is correct that an insurance-purchase requirement can be applied only to those who "actively" consume health care, the minimum coverage provision fits the bill.

The Chief Justice does not dispute that all U.S. residents participate in the market for health services over the course of their lives. But, The Chief Justice insists, the uninsured cannot be considered active in the market for health care, because "[t]he proximity and degree of connection between the [uninsured today] and [their] subsequent commercial activity is too lacking."

This argument has multiple flaws. First, more than 60% of those without insurance visit a hospital or doctor's office each year. Nearly 90% will within five years. An uninsured's consumption of health care is thus quite proximate: It is virtually certain to occur in the next five years and more likely than not to occur this year.

Equally evident, Congress has no way of separating those uninsured individuals who will need emergency medical care today (surely their consumption of medical care is sufficiently imminent) from those who will not need medical services for years to come. No one knows when an emergency will occur, yet emergencies involving the uninsured arise daily. To capture individuals who unexpectedly will obtain medical care in the very near future, then, Congress needed to include individuals who will not go to a doctor anytime soon. Congress, our decisions instruct, has authority to cast its net that wide.

Second, it is Congress' role, not the Court's, to delineate the boundaries of the market the Legislature seeks to regulate. The Chief Justice defines the health-care market as including only those transactions that will occur either in the next instant or within some (unspecified) proximity to the next instant. But Congress could reasonably have viewed the market from a long-term perspective, encompassing all transactions virtually certain to occur over the next decade, not just those occurring here and now. . . . An individual "is not 'active in the car market,'" The Chief Justice observes, simply because he or she may someday buy a car. The analogy is inapt. The inevitable yet unpredictable need for medical care and the guarantee that emergency care will be provided when required are conditions nonexistent in other markets. . . . Although an individual *might* buy a car or a crown of broccoli one day, there is no certainty she will ever do so. And if she eventually wants a car or has a craving for broccoli, she will be obliged to pay at the counter before receiving the vehicle or nourishment. She will get no free ride or food, at the expense of another consumer forced to pay an inflated price. Upholding the minimum coverage provision on the ground that all are participants or will be participants in the health-care market would therefore carry no implication that Congress may justify under the Commerce Clause a mandate to buy other products and services.

Nor is it accurate to say that the minimum coverage provision "compel[s] individuals . . . to purchase an unwanted product," or "suite of products." If unwanted today, medical service secured by insurance may be desperately needed tomorrow. Virtually everyone, I reiterate, consumes health care at some point in his or her life. Health insurance is a means of paying for this care, nothing more. In requiring individuals to obtain insurance, Congress is therefore not mandating the purchase of a discrete, unwanted product. Rather, Congress is merely defining the terms on which individuals pay for an interstate good they consume: Persons subject to the mandate must now pay for medical care in advance (instead of at the point of service) and through insurance (instead of out of pocket). Establishing payment terms for goods in or affecting interstate commerce is quintessential economic regulation well within Congress' domain. . . .

At bottom, The Chief Justice's and the joint dissenters' "view that an individual cannot be subject to Commerce Clause regulation absent voluntary, affirmative acts that enter him or her into, or affect, the interstate market expresses a concern for individual liberty that [is] more redolent of Due Process Clause arguments." Plaintiffs have abandoned any argument pinned to substantive due process, however, and now concede that the provisions here at issue do not offend the Due Process Clause.

[The concern that without the activity/inactivity distinction] the commerce power would otherwise know no limits . . . is unfounded. . . . [T]he unique attributes of the health-care market render everyone active in that market and give rise to a significant free-riding problem that does not occur in other markets. . . .

Congress would remain unable to regulate noneconomic conduct that has only an attenuated effect on interstate commerce and is traditionally left to state law. See *Lopez*; *Morrison*. . . . [But] [a]n individual's decision to self-insure . . . is an economic act with the requisite connection to interstate commerce. . . . Other provisions of the Constitution also check congressional overreaching. A mandate to purchase a particular product would be unconstitutional if, for example, the edict impermissibly abridged the freedom of speech, interfered with the free exercise of religion, or infringed on a liberty interest protected by the Due Process Clause.

Supplementing these legal restraints is a formidable check on congressional power: the democratic process. As the controversy surrounding the passage of the Affordable Care Act attests, purchase mandates are likely to engender political resistance. This prospect is borne out by the behavior of state legislators. Despite their possession of unquestioned authority to impose mandates, state governments have rarely done so.

When contemplated in its extreme, almost any power looks dangerous. The commerce power, hypothetically, would enable Congress to prohibit the purchase and home production of all meat, fish, and dairy goods, effectively compelling Americans to eat only vegetables. Yet no one would offer the "hypothetical and unreal possibilit[y]" of a vegetarian state as a credible reason to deny Congress the authority ever to ban the possession and sale of goods. The Chief Justice accepts just such specious logic when he cites the broccoli horrible as a reason to deny Congress the power to pass the individual mandate. . . .

[As to the Necessary and Proper Clause,] . . . the Chief Justice [does not] . . . explain *why* the power to direct either the purchase of health insurance or, alternatively, the payment of a penalty collectible as a tax is more far-reaching than other implied powers this Court has found meet under the Necessary and Proper Clause. These powers include the power to enact criminal laws; the power to imprison, including civil imprisonment, see, *e.g.*, *Comstock*; and the power to create a national bank, see *McCulloch*. . . . [H]ow is a judge to decide, when ruling on the constitutionality of a federal statute, whether Congress employed an "independent power," or merely a "derivative" one, [w]hether the power used is "substantive," or just "incidental"? The instruction the Chief Justice, in effect, provides lower courts: You will know it when you see it.

[T]he minimum coverage provision, along with other provisions of the ACA, addresses the very sort of interstate problem that made the commerce power essential in our federal system. The crisis created by the large number of U.S. residents who lack health insurance is one of national dimension that States are "separately incompetent" to handle. Far from trampling on States' sovereignty, the ACA attempts a federal solution for the very reason that the States, acting separately, cannot meet the need.

. . . [T]he joint dissenters contend that the minimum coverage provision is not necessary and proper because it was not the "only . . . way" Congress could have made the guaranteed-issue and community rating reforms work. . . . [But] "we long ago rejected the view that the Necessary and Proper Clause demands that an Act of Congress be '*absolutely* necessary' to the exercise of an enumerated power." Rather, the statutory provision at issue need only be "conducive" and "[reasonably] adapted" to the goal Congress seeks to achieve. *McCulloch.*

Justice Scalia, Justice Kennedy, Justice Thomas, and Justice Alito, dissenting.

[I]f [the individual mandate] "regulates" anything, it is the *failure* to maintain minimum essential coverage. . . . But that failure—that abstention from commerce—is not "Commerce." To be sure, *purchasing* insurance *is* "Commerce"; but one does not regulate commerce that does not exist by compelling its existence. . . . We do not doubt that the buying and selling of health insurance contracts is commerce generally subject to federal regulation. But when Congress provides that (nearly) all citizens must buy an insurance contract, it goes beyond "adjust[ing] by rule or method," or "direct[ing] according to rule," it directs the creation of commerce. . . .

Raich is no precedent for what Congress has done here. That case's prohibition of growing (cf. *Wickard*), and of possession (cf. innumerable federal statutes) did not represent the expansion of the federal power to direct into a broad new field. The mandating of economic activity does, and since it is a field so limitless that it converts the Commerce Clause into a general authority to direct the economy, that mandating is not "consist[ent] with the letter and spirit of the constitution." McCulloch v. Maryland.

Moreover, . . . [t]he Court's opinion in *Raich* pointed out that the growing and possession prohibitions were the only practicable way of enabling the prohibition of interstate traffic in marijuana to be effectively enforced. [But] [t]here are many ways other than this unprecedented Individual Mandate by which the regulatory scheme's goals of reducing insurance premiums and ensuring the profitability of insurers could be achieved. For instance, those who did not purchase insurance could be subjected to a surcharge when they do enter the health insurance system. Or they could be denied a full income tax credit given to those who do purchase the insurance.

The Government was invited, at oral argument, to suggest what federal controls over private conduct (other than those explicitly prohibited by the Bill of Rights or other constitutional controls) could *not* be justified as necessary and proper for the carrying out of a general regulatory scheme. It was unable to name any. . . .

[T]he main objection many have to the Mandate is that they have no intention of purchasing most or even any of such goods or services and thus no need to buy insurance for those purchases. The Government responds that the health-care market involves "essentially universal participation[.]" [This is] not true. It is true enough that everyone consumes "health care," if the term is taken to include the purchase of a bottle of aspirin. But the health care "market" that is the object of the Individual Mandate not only includes but principally consists of goods and services that the young people primarily affected by the Mandate *do not purchase*. They are quite simply not participants in that market, and cannot be made so (and thereby subjected to regulation) by the simple device of defining participants to include all those who will, later in their lifetime, probably purchase the goods or services covered by the mandated insurance. Such a definition of market participants is unprecedented, and were it to be a premise for the exercise of national power, it would have no principled limits.

[T]he Government [argues] that Congress . . . has purported to regulate "economic and financial decision[s] to forego [*sic*] health insurance coverage and [to] attempt to self-insure," since those decisions have "a substantial and deleterious effect on interstate commerce[.]" But . . . the decision to forgo participation in an interstate market is not itself commercial activity (or indeed any activity at all) within Congress' power to regulate. It is true that, at the end of the day, it is inevitable that each American will affect commerce and become a part of it, even if not by choice. But if every person comes within the Commerce Clause power of Congress to regulate by the simple reason that he will one day engage in commerce, the idea of a limited Government power is at an end. . . .

The dissent treats the Constitution as though it is an enumeration of those problems that the Federal Government can address. . . . The Constitution is not that. It enumerates not federally soluble *problems*, but federally available *powers*. The Federal Government can address whatever problems it wants but can bring to their solution only those powers that the Constitution confers, among which is the power to regulate commerce. None of our cases say anything else. Article I contains no whatever-it-takes-to-solve-a-national-problem power. . . .

Justice THOMAS, dissenting.

I adhere to my view that "the very notion of a 'substantial effects' test under the Commerce Clause is inconsistent with the original understanding of Congress' powers and with this Court's early Commerce Clause cases." As I have explained, the Court's continued use of that test "has encouraged the Federal Government to persist in its view that the Commerce Clause has virtually no limits." The Government's unprecedented claim in this suit that it may regulate not only economic activity but also *inactivity* that substantially affects interstate commerce is a case in point.

DISCUSSION

1. *The effect of the Commerce Clause holding.* Five Justices argue that Congress cannot reach "inactivity" under the Commerce Clause, even abetted by the Necessary and Proper Clause. Assuming that this is holding and not dicta, the practical effect is likely to be limited—first, because federal purchase mandates have been

relatively rare, and second, because the Court upheld the mandate anyway under Congress's power to tax. If Congress ever passes a new purchase mandate in the future, it can simply use the Taxing power (as in the ACA itself). Nothing in Chief Justice Roberts's opinion suggests that Congress could not tax people who don't buy broccoli. The central restraint on Congress is political—such a bill would be very unpopular. (Ironically, Congress *does* require the public to buy broccoli and many other foods, albeit indirectly—through agricultural subsidies.)

2. *The Health Care Case and the Constitution outside the courts.* The Health Care Case offers an excellent example of how constitutional ideas in politics eventually influence judicial decisions. The debate over the Affordable Care Act in 2009 and 2010 was extremely contentious, with opponents arguing that the Act would involve a government takeover of health care, and former vice presidential candidate Sarah Palin (among others) darkly warning about "death panels" hidden in the Act. The individual mandate had originally been a Republican idea, developed at the Heritage Foundation as a conservative alternative to the Clinton health care proposal in the 1990s. However, after President Obama and the Democrats made it a key element of their proposal, congressional Republicans began to oppose it, first on policy grounds, and later, on constitutional grounds. The Act passed along party lines in March 2010. Several lawsuits were quickly filed around the country, targeting the individual mandate and the Medicaid expansion. The hope was that if either or both of these elements were struck down, the courts might invalidate the entire Act. In fact, this was the conclusion of the four Justices in the joint dissent: "[T]he Act before us here exceeds federal power both in mandating the purchase of health insurance and in denying nonconsenting States all Medicaid funding. These parts of the Act are central to its design and operation, and all the Act's other provisions would not have been enacted without them. In our view it must follow that the entire statute is inoperative."

When the litigation began, most constitutional scholars, relying on existing precedents, believed that the odds that either provision would be held unconstitutional were fairly small. Nevertheless, the rise of the Tea Party and the Republican landslide of 2010 gave hope to mandate opponents. The unconstitutionality of the mandate became virtually the official position of the Republican Party, which put its considerable resources behind promoting constitutional arguments against the mandate, not only in the courts but also in the public sphere. As a result, constitutional arguments against the mandate quickly moved from "off the wall" to "on the wall," and, by the conclusion of the oral arguments at the Supreme Court in March 2012, many observers expected that the individual mandate would be held unconstitutional. For a discussion of the role of different actors in altering public understandings of the challenge, see Jack M. Balkin, From Off the Wall to On the Wall: How the Mandate Challenge Went Mainstream, Atlantic, June 4, 2012, at http://www.theatlantic.com/national/archive/2012/06/from-off-the-wall-to-on-thewall-how-the-mandate-challenge-went-mainstream/258040/.

What do these events tell us about the relationship between political change and constitutional change? Can you think of other examples in the cases we have studied in which powerful political mobilizations changed the plausibility of constitutional arguments? What are the similarities to and differences from the health care litigation?

3. *The Commerce Clause and individual liberty*. Mandate opponents argued that it was unprecedented for the government to force individuals to purchase goods and services from private parties. If the mandate was upheld, Congress could force individuals to do all sorts of things, thus undermining personal liberty, and working a fundamental change in the relationship between the federal government and its citizens. See Randy E. Barnett, Commandeering the People: Why the Individual Health Insurance Mandate Is Unconstitutional, 5 N.Y.U. J.L. & Liberty 581 (2010). Although the arguments against the mandate technically concerned the limits to Congress's commerce power (and the Necessary and Proper Clause), they sounded in notions of individual liberty, including, in particular, economic liberty. Constitutional arguments against purchase mandates couched in terms of economic liberty, however, would doom both federal mandates and state mandates, like that in the Massachusetts plan promoted by Governor Mitt Romney, President Obama's opponent in the 2012 election.

In the post–New Deal era, mandate opponents were unlikely to argue for protecting freedom of contract as a matter of substantive due process. (And nothing in Chief Justice Roberts's opinion or the joint dissent would prevent *states* from imposing mandates identical to the ACA's.) Nevertheless, the idea of protecting economic liberty through limitations on federal power has a long history in debates in American constitutional law. Can you think of examples?

4. *The activity/inactivity distinction*. Both Roberts and the joint dissent argue that Congress can regulate activities under the Commerce Clause (and Necessary and Proper Clause), but not inactivity. If Congress could regulate inactivity, they argue, there would be no limit to the federal government's powers. However, such limits already exist, for example, in *Lopez* and *Morrison*. Is the activity/inactivity distinction necessary to preserve the rule of *Lopez* and *Morrison* or the principle that the federal government is one of limited and enumerated powers? Why? Does the distinction promote federalism, individual freedom, or both?

The activity/inactivity distinction is related to the act/omission distinction. Lawyers are sometimes able to manipulate this distinction by expanding or contracting the relevant time frame or by redescribing events in different ways. See Mark Kelman, Interpretive Construction in the Substantive Criminal Law, 33 Stan. L. Rev. 591 (1981); Jack M. Balkin, The Rhetoric of Responsibility, 76 Va. L. Rev. 197 (1990).

Is the activity/inactivity distinction subject to manipulation in the same way? For example, people may be active or inactive in commerce depending on how broadly we describe the market in which they participate (health care, health insurance, purchase of over-the-counter remedies, etc.) and depending on how broadly we consider the relevant time frame (day, month, year, decade, lifetime). We could describe people as "not insuring" or as "voluntarily exposing themselves to risks that will have to be subsidized by others." Another example: At the time Title II of the Civil Rights Act was passed in 1964, the proprietor of the Heart of Atlanta Motel was engaged in a kind of inaction because he refused to serve Black people—and the law required him to do so. On the other hand, the owner was operating a hotel that served white people. In Wickard v. Filburn, Justice Jackson described Filburn's conduct both as activity and inactivity: "The effect of the statute before us is to restrict the amount which may be produced for market and the extent, as well, to which one may forestall resort to the market by producing to meet his own needs."

That is, the problem that Congress sought to address was that Filburn was failing to purchase wheat in the market. Mark Tushnet, The "Activity-Inactivity" Distinction, Balkinization, Dec. 13, 2010, at http://balkin.blogspot.com/2010/12/activity-inactivity-distinction.html.

Are there administrable ways for courts to fix the relevant description of events, the relevant market, and the relevant time frame in order to decide how to apply the activity/inactivity distinction? Can judges just rely on "common sense"? In her opinion in the Health Care Case, Justice Ginsburg argued that it was obvious that almost everyone was engaged in the health care market, or soon would be; therefore requiring the purchase of health insurance was simply a way of regulating how people pay for commercial transactions in which they will inevitably engage. The joint dissent argued that this description of the situation was too broad—because it would suggest that since everyone is in the food market, or soon will be, they can be required to purchase broccoli—and that the relevant market was the market for health insurance. Is there a correct answer to this question?

5. *Workarounds.* Could Congress get around the activity/inactivity distinction by requiring that everyone who purchases more than $500 of health care related products or services in a calendar year must henceforth be subject to an insurance mandate or pay a $500 yearly penalty? Could Congress require that everyone who buys more than $500 worth of food in a given year must henceforth purchase $500 of broccoli each year or be subject to a $500 penalty?

Could Congress require purchase of health insurance if a person has ever been previously covered by health insurance? Has ever visited an emergency room and received subsidized treatment? Has ever crossed state lines in order to receive medical care? Has ever received medical care in more than one state? (Would such requirements be constitutional if applied retroactively? What if they were only applied prospectively?)

Opponents of the individual mandate have proposed a six-month waiting period to purchase health insurance for those who have not purchased insurance by a certain date or who have let their health insurance coverage lapse. Such a waiting period rule encourages people to purchase insurance before they become sick and thus deters free riding. After *Sebelius,* does Congress have the power under the Commerce Clause to impose a waiting period requirement for those who are not currently in the health insurance market? If so, is it because the waiting period requirement is not a mandate but merely an incentive to act? (Wasn't that also true of the ACA mandate, which created an incentive in the form of a tax?) Or is it because the waiting period requirement is a prohibition on activity rather than a requirement to act? Which is a greater imposition on individual liberty, being required to purchase health insurance or being refused the right to buy health insurance for six months if you or your family becomes sick? What conception of liberty is at stake in your answer?

6. *Necessary but not proper?* Chief Justice Roberts and the joint dissent argue that the mandate was not necessary and proper to make the guaranteed issue and community ratings rules effective. Roberts claimed that even if the mandate was "necessary," it was not "proper." He argued that the mandate would "undermine the structure of government established by the Constitution" and was "not consist[ent] with the letter and spirit of the constitution." It would involve a "great

substantive and independent power," and work "a substantial expansion of federal authority." How should judges apply these ideas in future cases? Did the vast expansion of Commerce Clause authority in *Darby* and *Wickard* (already) violate this test? Compare Roberts's arguments with those of the Court in United States v. Comstock, 560 U.S. 126 (2010), discussed infra, in which the Court upheld the creation of a system of federal civil confinement designed to deal with the problem created by persons released from a federal prison system, which in turn was created to deal with the problem of punishing persons who violated federal crimes, which in turn were created to further Congress's exercise of its various powers, including the powers created by the Necessary and Proper Clause. If the civil commitment scheme is not the assumption of a "great substantive and independent power," or "a substantial expansion of federal authority," why is the individual mandate?

Note that Roberts assumes that the statute challenged in *Wickard* is "proper." If so, is Roberts's argument just another way of saying that Congress cannot reach inactivity through the Necessary and Proper Clause if it cannot reach it through the Commerce Clause? To what extent is this consistent with the logic of *McCulloch*? With logic of *Comstock*?

The joint dissent reached the same conclusion a little differently. It argued that the mandate is not necessary and proper for two reasons. First, *Raich* involved a situation of true necessity, whereas in this case there were other ways to achieve the goals of the ACA other than using a mandate. (Is this consistent with *McCulloch*?) Second, the joint dissent argued that mandates greatly expand federal power into new fields. If mandates are necessary and proper to realize the statute's goals, there are no limits to federal power, and that cannot be proper. Again, does this assume that *Lopez* and *Morrison* would become effectively irrelevant?

Is it clear that there is no limiting principle that would allow the mandate but not give the federal government unlimited regulatory power? For example, what if the Court had held that only mandates to exchange money for goods or services—that is, to engage in commerce—were permitted under the Commerce Clause and Necessary and Proper Clause, but no other mandates? (Thus, a mandate to eat broccoli or to exercise once a day would not fall within the commerce power, even when assisted by the Necessary and Proper Clause, even if it would be otherwise helpful to Congress's regulatory goals.) Is *this* distinction significantly less administrable than the activity/inactivity distinction?

UNITED STATES v. COMSTOCK, 560 U.S. 126 (2010): By a 7-2 vote, the Supreme Court upheld a federal civil commitment statute as within Congress's powers under the Necessary and Proper Clause without reaching any questions of its constitutionality under the Bill of Rights. 18 U.S.C. §4248 allows a district court to order the civil commitment of a mentally ill, sexually dangerous federal prisoner beyond the date he would otherwise be released. The statute authorizes the federal government to request civil commitment if neither the State of a prisoner's domicile nor the State in which the prisoner was tried will assume the responsibility for the prisoner's "custody, care, and treatment." §4248(d). The individual must (1) currently be "in the custody of the [Federal] Bureau of Prisons"; (2) have previously "engaged or attempted to engage in sexually violent conduct or child molestation"; (3) currently "suffer from a serious mental illness, abnormality, or disorder"; and (4) "as a result of" that mental illness, abnormality, or disorder be "sexually dangerous to others," in that "he would have serious difficulty in refraining from sexually violent conduct or child molestation if released." §§4247(a)(5)-(6).

Justice Breyer's majority opinion explained that "in determining whether the Necessary and Proper Clause grants Congress the legislative authority to enact a particular federal statute, we look to see whether the statute constitutes a means that is rationally related to the implementation of a constitutionally enumerated power. Sabri v. United States, 541 U.S. 600 (2004) (using term 'means-ends rationality' to describe the necessary relationship)."

"Neither Congress' power to criminalize conduct, nor its power to imprison individuals who engage in that conduct, nor its power to enact laws governing prisons and prisoners, is explicitly mentioned in the Constitution. But Congress nonetheless possesses broad authority to do each of those things" by the "authority granted by the Necessary and Proper Clause."

Justice Breyer pointed out that "Congress has long been involved in the delivery of mental health care to federal prisoners, and has long provided for their civil commitment." In the 1940s, for example, Congress amended its civil commitment regime to take account of mentally ill and mentally incompetent prisoners whose terms have expired, responding to concerns that long sentences of prisoners might sever their connection to any state so that no state would be willing to assume responsibility for them upon release. It was reasonable for Congress to extend its system to mentally ill sexually dangerous prisoners because "the Federal Government is the custodian of its prisoners" and "[a]s federal custodian, it has the constitutional power to act in order to protect nearby (and other) communities from the danger federal prisoners may pose." Section 4248 did not violate state sovereignty protected by the Tenth Amendment because "[t]he powers delegated to the United States by the Constitution include those specifically enumerated powers listed in Article I along with the implementation authority granted by the Necessary and Proper Clause. Virtually by definition, these powers are not powers that the Constitution reserved to the States."

Nor did §4248 "invade state sovereignty or otherwise improperly limit the scope of powers that remain with the States. . . . To the contrary, it requires *accommodation* of state interests: The Attorney General must inform the State in which the federal prisoner 'is domiciled or was tried' that he is detaining someone with respect to whom those States may wish to assert their authority, and he must encourage those States to assume custody of the individual. He must also immediately 'release' that person 'to the appropriate official of' either State 'if such State will assume [such] responsibility.' And either State has the right, at any time, to assert its authority over the individual, which will prompt the individual's immediate transfer to State custody."

Finally, Justice Breyer rejected respondents' argument "that, when legislating pursuant to the Necessary and Proper Clause, Congress' authority can be no more than one step removed from a specifically enumerated power. . . . [E]ven the dissent acknowledges that Congress has the implied power to criminalize any conduct that might interfere with the exercise of an enumerated power, and also the additional power to imprison people who violate those (inferentially authorized) laws, and the additional power to provide for the safe and reasonable management of those prisons, and the additional power to regulate the prisoners' behavior even after their release."

Justice Kennedy concurred in the judgment, arguing that the proper test is not the highly deferential minimum rationality test of Williamson v. Lee Optical. "Rather, under the Necessary and Proper Clause, application of a rational basis test should be at least as exacting as it has been in the Commerce Clause cases, if not more so." Commerce Clause precedents like United States v. Lopez, Justice Kennedy argued, "require a tangible link to commerce, not a mere conceivable rational relation, as in *Lee Optical*." They require "a demonstrated link in fact, based on empirical demonstration." Moreover, Justice Kennedy argued, "[i]t is of fundamental importance to consider whether essential attributes of state sovereignty are compromised by the assertion of federal power under the Necessary and Proper Clause; if so, that is a factor suggesting that the power is not one properly within the reach of federal power."

Justice Alito also concurred in the judgment, although stating "I am concerned about the breadth of the Court's language, and the ambiguity of the standard that the Court applies." Nevertheless, "[m]ost federal criminal statutes rest upon a congressional judgment that, in order to execute one or more of the powers conferred on Congress, it is necessary and proper to criminalize certain conduct, and in order to do that it is obviously necessary and proper to provide for the operation of a federal criminal justice system and a federal prison system. . . . Just as it is necessary and proper for Congress to provide for the apprehension of escaped federal prisoners, it is necessary and proper for Congress to provide for the civil commitment of dangerous federal prisoners who would otherwise escape civil commitment as a result of federal imprisonment."

"Some years ago, a distinguished study group created by the Judicial Conference of the United States found that, in a disturbing number of cases, no State was willing to assume the financial burden of providing for the civil commitment of federal prisoners who, if left at large after the completion of their sentences, would present a danger to any communities in which they chose to live or visit. These federal prisoners, having been held for years in a federal prison, often had few ties to any State; it was a matter of speculation where they would choose to go upon release; and accordingly no State was enthusiastic about volunteering to shoulder the burden of civil commitment. . . . This is not a case in which it is merely possible for a court to think of a rational basis on which Congress might have perceived an attenuated link between the powers underlying the federal criminal statutes and the challenged civil commitment provision. Here, there is a substantial link to Congress' constitutional powers."

Justice Thomas, joined by Justice Scalia, dissented: "[T]he power to care for the mentally ill and, where necessary, the power to protect the community from the dangerous tendencies of some mentally ill persons, are among the numerous powers that remain with the States. . . . Section 4248 closely resembles the involuntary civil-commitment laws that States have enacted under their *parens patriae* and general police powers. Indeed, it is clear, on the face of the Act and in the Government's arguments urging its constitutionality, that §4248 is aimed at protecting society from acts of sexual violence, not toward carrying into Execution any enumerated power or powers of the Federal Government."

"[P]rotecting society from violent sexual offenders is certainly an important end. . . . But the Constitution does not vest in Congress the authority to protect society from every bad act that might befall it. In my view, this should decide the question. Section 4248 runs afoul of our settled understanding of Congress' power under the Necessary and Proper Clause. Congress may act under that Clause only when its legislation 'carr[ies] into Execution one of the Federal Government's enumerated powers.' Section 4248 does not execute *any* enumerated power. Section 4248 is therefore unconstitutional. . . ."

"The absence of a constitutional delegation of general police power to Congress does not leave citizens vulnerable to the harms Congress seeks to regulate in §4248 because, as recent legislation indicates, the States have the capacity to address the threat that sexual offenders pose. . . . States plainly have the constitutional authority to take charge of a federal prisoner released within their jurisdiction. In addition, the assumption that a State knowingly would fail to exercise that authority is, in my view, implausible. . . . [N]either the Court nor the concurrences argue that a State has the power to refuse such a person domicile within its borders. Thus, they appear to assume that, in the absence of 18 U.S.C. §4248, a State would take no action when informed by the BOP [Bureau of Prisons] that a sexually dangerous federal prisoner was about to be released within its jurisdiction. In light of the plethora of state laws enacted in recent decades to protect communities from sex offenders, the likelihood of such an occurrence seems quite remote. But even in the event a State made such a decision, the Constitution assigns the responsibility for that decision, and its consequences, to the state government alone."

In a portion of the dissent not joined by Justice Scalia, Justice Thomas added: "The Necessary and Proper Clause does not provide Congress with authority to enact any law simply because it furthers *other laws* Congress has enacted in the exercise of its incidental authority; the Clause plainly requires a showing that every federal statute 'carr[ies] into Execution' one or more of the Federal Government's *enumerated* powers. . . . Federal laws that criminalize conduct that interferes with enumerated powers, establish prisons for those who engage in that conduct, and set rules for the care and treatment of prisoners awaiting trial or serving a criminal sentence satisfy this test because each helps to 'carr[y] into Execution' the enumerated powers that justify a criminal defendant's arrest or conviction. For example, Congress' enumerated power '[t]o establish Post Offices and post Roads,' Art. I, §8, cl. 7, would lack force or practical effect if Congress lacked the authority to enact criminal laws 'to punish those who steal letters from the post office, or rob the mail.' Similarly, that enumerated power would be compromised if there were no prisons to hold persons who violate those laws, or if those prisons were so poorly managed that prisoners could escape or demand their release on the grounds that the conditions of their confinement violate their constitutional rights, at least as we have defined them. Civil detention under §4248, on the other hand, lacks any such connection to an enumerated power."

DISCUSSION

1. *Comstock* is based on a familiar justification for federal power: a collective action problem among the states, in this case what is sometimes called a NIMBY ("not in my back yard") problem. Once a known mentally ill sexual predator is released into a state's custody, the state is under enormous pressure to institute

its own civil commitment proceedings, at which point the state will be stuck with the costs of taking care of the former prisoner, possibly indefinitely. Therefore no state has an incentive to ask for custody; each hopes that some other state will foot the bill. As Justice Alito puts it, "[t]he statute recognizes that, in many cases, no State will assume the heavy financial burden of civilly committing a dangerous federal prisoner who, as a result of lengthy federal incarceration, no longer has any substantial ties to any State." Most states would be happier if the federal government simply solved this problem for them (using federal tax money), and that is why 29 states as amici curiae argued for the constitutionality of the statute. Justices Thomas and Scalia counter that if the federal government simply releases a prisoner into some state's custody, that state will have ample incentives to assume responsibility. This solves the collective action problem a different way, by giving the federal government the power to choose which state will have to bear the costs of long-term care and custody. Is this solution more or less respectful of state interests?

2. In its arguments before the Supreme Court, the government declined to base Congress's authority for the civil commitment scheme on the Commerce Clause, relying instead on the Necessary and Proper Clause. Why do you think the government made this choice? Was it correct to do so in light of *Lopez* and *Morrison*?

Consider possible theories under the commerce power: (1) the civil commitment system is "part of a broader regulatory scheme" under *Raich* that would be otherwise undermined; (2) the civil commitment scheme regulates the consumption and travel activities of former federal prisoners; and (3) the civil commitment scheme is a reasonable means of preventing states from attempting to dump dangerous former prisoners on other states. Do you think the Court would accept any of these theories, or any other theories under the commerce power?

3. *Subsequent case: United States v. Kebodeaux.* In United States v. Kebodeaux, 570 U.S. 387 (2013), the Supreme Court considered Congress's powers to apply the Sex Offender Registration and Notification Act (SORNA), which requires federal sex offenders to register in the states where they live, study, and work, to a discharged member of the Air Force who had previously been required to register as a sex offender under a predecessor statute, the Wetterling Act. The Court decided, 7-2, that SORNA was within Congress's powers under the Military Regulations Clause and the Necessary and Proper Clause.

Justice Breyer, writing for five Justices, noted that Congress did not apply SORNA to a person who had been "unconditionally released" and who lacked "any . . . special relationship with the federal government." Instead, Kebodeaux was "already subject to [constitutionally valid] federal registration requirements that were themselves a valid exercise of federal power under the Military Regulations Clause."

"Here, under the authority granted to it by the Military Regulation and Necessary and Proper Clauses, Congress could promulgate the Uniform Code of Military Justice. It could specify that the sex offense of which Kebodeaux was convicted was a military crime under that Code. It could punish that crime through imprisonment and by placing conditions upon Kebodeaux's release. And it could make the civil registration requirement at issue here a consequence of Kebodeaux's offense and conviction. This civil requirement, while not a specific condition of Kebodeaux's release, was in place at the time Kebodeaux committed his offense, and was a consequence of his violation of federal law."

Chief Justice Roberts concurred in the judgment, explaining that he disagreed with Justice Breyer's decision "to discuss the general public safety benefits of the registration requirement." To Chief Justice Roberts, this sounded too much like a suggestion that there is a "federal police power," which "does not exist."

Such a power could not be inferred from the Necessary and Proper Clause because it was not "proper." "Chief Justice Marshall was emphatic that no 'great substantive and independent power' can be 'implied as incidental to other powers, or used as a means of executing them.' [*McCulloch*]. . . . It is difficult to imagine a clearer example of such a 'great substantive and independent power' than the power to 'help protect the public . . . and alleviate public safety concerns.' . . . I find it implausible to suppose—and impossible to support—that the Framers intended to confer such authority by implication rather than expression. A power of that magnitude vested in the Federal Government is not 'consist[ent] with the letter and spirit of the constitution,' *McCulloch,* and thus not a 'proper [means] for carrying into Execution' the enumerated powers of the Federal Government."

Consider Chief Justice Roberts's remarks about the Necessary and Proper Clause in the light of his opinion in NFIB v. Sebelius, supra. There Chief Justice Roberts argued that an individual mandate to purchase health insurance, even if "necessary," was not "proper" because it assumed a "great substantive and independent power" to compel people to enter into commercial transactions.

Justice Alito also concurred in the judgment. Justices Scalia and Thomas dissented.

2. The Taxing Power

National Federation of Independent Business v. Sebelius

[The Health Care Case]
567 U.S. 519 (2012)

[The 2010 Patient Protection and Affordable Care Act's individual mandate requires most Americans to maintain "minimum essential" health insurance coverage or make a "[s]hared responsibility payment" to the government. In 2016, for example, the payment is 2.5 percent of an individual's household income, but no less than $695 and no more than the average yearly premium for insurance that covers 60 percent of the cost of ten specified services (for example, prescription drugs and hospitalization). 26 U.S.C. §5000A. Individuals are exempted if they have qualifying health insurance through their employer or otherwise, receive health care through Medicare or Medicaid, are below the poverty line, live outside the country, serve in the military, are dependents, or have a religious objection.

The Act provides that this "penalty" will be paid by the "taxpayer" to the Internal Revenue Service with "a taxpayer's return," and "shall be assessed and collected in the same manner" as tax penalties, such as the penalty for claiming too large an income tax refund. The Act, however, bars the IRS from using several of its normal enforcement tools, such as criminal prosecutions and levies. And some individuals who are subject to the mandate are nonetheless exempt from the penalty—for example, those with income below a certain threshold and members of Indian tribes.]

Chief Justice ROBERTS announced the judgment of the Court and delivered the opinion of the Court with respect to Part[] III-C, . . . and an opinion with respect to Part[] III-B.

III

B

. . . Because the Commerce Clause does not support the individual mandate, it is necessary to turn to the Government's second argument: that the mandate may be upheld as within Congress's enumerated power to "lay and collect Taxes." Art. I, §8, cl. 1.

The Government's tax power argument asks us to view the statute differently than we did in considering its commerce power theory. In making its Commerce Clause argument, the Government defended the mandate as a regulation requiring individuals to purchase health insurance. The Government does not claim that the taxing power allows Congress to issue such a command. Instead, the Government asks us to read the mandate not as ordering individuals to buy insurance, but rather as imposing a tax on those who do not buy that product.

The text of a statute can sometimes have more than one possible meaning. To take a familiar example, a law that reads "no vehicles in the park" might, or might not, ban bicycles in the park. And it is well established that if a statute has two possible meanings, one of which violates the Constitution, courts should adopt the meaning that does not do so. Justice Story said that 180 years ago: "No court ought, unless the terms of an act rendered it unavoidable, to give a construction to it which should involve a violation, however unintentional, of the constitution." Justice Holmes made the same point a century later: "[T]he rule is settled that as between two possible interpretations of a statute, by one of which it would be unconstitutional and by the other valid, our plain duty is to adopt that which will save the Act."

The most straightforward reading of the mandate is that it commands individuals to purchase insurance. After all, it states that individuals "shall" maintain health insurance. 26 U.S.C. §5000A(a). . . . Under our precedent, it is therefore necessary to ask whether the Government's alternative reading of the statute—that it only imposes a tax on those without insurance—is a reasonable one.

Under the mandate, if an individual does not maintain health insurance, the only consequence is that he must make an additional payment to the IRS when he pays his taxes. See §5000A(b). That, according to the Government, means the mandate can be regarded as establishing a condition—not owning health insurance—that triggers a tax—the required payment to the IRS. Under that theory, the mandate is not a legal command to buy insurance. Rather, it makes going without insurance just another thing the Government taxes, like buying gasoline or earning income. And if the mandate is in effect just a tax hike on certain taxpayers who do not have health insurance, it may be within Congress's constitutional power to tax.

The question is not whether that is the most natural interpretation of the mandate, but only whether it is a "fairly possible" one. As we have explained, "every reasonable construction must be resorted to, in order to save a statute from unconstitutionality." The Government asks us to interpret the mandate as imposing a tax, if it would otherwise violate the Constitution. Granting the Act the full measure of deference owed to federal statutes, it can be so read, for the reasons set forth below.

C

The exaction the Affordable Care Act imposes on those without health insurance looks like a tax in many respects. The "[s]hared responsibility payment," as the statute entitles it, is paid into the Treasury by "taxpayer[s]" when they file their tax returns. 26 U.S.C. §5000A(b). It does not apply to individuals who do not pay federal income taxes because their household income is less than the filing threshold in the Internal Revenue Code. For taxpayers who do owe the payment, its amount is determined by such familiar factors as taxable income, number of dependents, and joint filing status. The requirement to pay is found in the Internal Revenue Code and enforced by the IRS, which—as we previously explained—must assess and collect it "in the same manner as taxes." This process yields the essential feature of any tax: it produces at least some revenue for the Government. United States v. Kahriger, 345 U.S. 22 (1953). Indeed, the payment is expected to raise about $4 billion per year by 2017. . . .

Our cases confirm this functional approach. For example, in [Bailey v.] Drexel Furniture [(The Child Labor Tax Case)], we focused on three practical characteristics of the so-called tax on employing child laborers that convinced us the "tax" was actually a penalty. First, the tax imposed an exceedingly heavy burden—10 percent of a company's net income—on those who employed children, no matter how small their infraction. Second, it imposed that exaction only on those who knowingly employed underage laborers. Such scienter requirements are typical of punitive statutes, because Congress often wishes to punish only those who intentionally break the law. Third, this "tax" was enforced in part by the Department of Labor, an agency responsible for punishing violations of labor laws, not collecting revenue. *Drexel Furniture*; see also, *e.g.*, [Department of Revenue of Montana v.] Kurth Ranch, [511 U.S. 767 (1994)] (considering, *inter alia*, the amount of the exaction, and the fact that it was imposed for violation of a separate criminal law); *Constantine* (same).

The same analysis here suggests that the shared responsibility payment may for constitutional purposes be considered a tax, not a penalty: First, for most Americans the amount due will be far less than the price of insurance, and, by statute, it can never be more. It may often be a reasonable financial decision to make the payment rather than purchase insurance, unlike the "prohibitory" financial punishment in *Drexel Furniture*. Second, the individual mandate contains no scienter requirement. Third, the payment is collected solely by the IRS through the normal means of taxation—except that the Service is *not* allowed to use those means most suggestive of a punitive sanction, such as criminal prosecution. The reasons the Court in *Drexel Furniture* held that what was called a "tax" there was a penalty support the conclusion that what is called a "penalty" here may be viewed as a tax.[a]

None of this is to say that the payment is not intended to affect individual conduct. Although the payment will raise considerable revenue, it is plainly designed to expand health insurance coverage. But taxes that seek to influence conduct are nothing new. Some of our earliest federal taxes sought to deter the purchase of imported manufactured goods in order to foster the growth of domestic industry. Today, federal and state taxes can compose more than half the retail price of cigarettes, not just to raise more money, but to encourage people to quit smoking. And we have upheld such obviously regulatory measures as taxes on selling marijuana and sawed-off shotguns. Indeed, "[e]very tax is in some measure regulatory. To some extent it interposes an economic impediment to the activity taxed as compared with others not taxed." Sonzinsky [v. United States, 300 U.S. 506 (1937)]. That §5000A seeks to shape decisions about whether to buy health insurance does not mean that it cannot be a valid exercise of the taxing power.

In distinguishing penalties from taxes, this Court has explained that "if the concept of penalty means anything, it means punishment for an unlawful act or omission." . . . While the individual mandate clearly aims to induce the purchase of health insurance, it need not be read to declare that failing to do so is unlawful. Neither the Act nor any other law attaches negative legal consequences to not buying health insurance, beyond requiring a payment to the IRS. The Government agrees with that reading, confirming that if someone chooses to pay rather than obtain health insurance, they have fully complied with the law.

Indeed, it is estimated [by the Congressional Budget Office] that four million people each year will choose to pay the IRS rather than buy insurance. We would expect Congress to be troubled by that prospect if such conduct were unlawful. That Congress apparently regards such extensive failure to comply with the mandate as tolerable suggests that Congress did not think it was creating four million outlaws. It suggests instead that the shared responsibility payment merely imposes a tax citizens may lawfully choose to pay in lieu of buying health insurance.

The plaintiffs contend that Congress's choice of language—stating that individuals "shall" obtain insurance or pay a "penalty"—requires reading §5000A as punishing unlawful conduct, even if that interpretation would render the law unconstitutional. We have rejected a similar argument before. In New York v. United States we . . . [interpreted statutory] "[p]enalties for failure to comply" [with requirements to dispose of low-level radioactive waste as] impos[ing] only "a series of incentives" for the State to take responsibility for its waste. We then sustained the charge paid to the Federal Government as an exercise of the taxing power. We see no insurmountable obstacle to a similar approach here.

The joint dissenters argue that we cannot uphold §5000A as a tax because Congress did not "frame" it as such. In effect, they contend that even if the Constitution

---

a. We do not suggest that any exaction lacking a scienter requirement and enforced by the IRS is within the taxing power. Congress could not, for example, expand its authority to impose criminal fines by creating strict liability offenses enforced by the IRS rather than the FBI. But the fact that the exaction here is paid like a tax, to the agency that collects taxes—rather than, for example, exacted by Department of Labor inspectors after ferreting out willful malfeasance—suggests that this exaction may be viewed as a tax.

permits Congress to do exactly what we interpret this statute to do, the law must be struck down because Congress used the wrong labels. An example may help illustrate why labels should not control here. Suppose Congress enacted a statute providing that every taxpayer who owns a house without energy efficient windows must pay $50 to the IRS. The amount due is adjusted based on factors such as taxable income and joint filing status, and is paid along with the taxpayer's income tax return. Those whose income is below the filing threshold need not pay. The required payment is not called a "tax," a "penalty," or anything else. No one would doubt that this law imposed a tax, and was within Congress's power to tax. That conclusion should not change simply because Congress used the word "penalty" to describe the payment. . . .

Our precedent demonstrates that Congress had the power to impose the exaction in §5000A under the taxing power, and that §5000A need not be read to do more than impose a tax. That is sufficient to sustain it. The "question of the constitutionality of action taken by Congress does not depend on recitals of the power which it undertakes to exercise." Woods v. Cloyd W. Miller Co., 333 U.S. 138 (1948).

Even if the taxing power enables Congress to impose a tax on not obtaining health insurance, any tax must still comply with other requirements in the Constitution. Plaintiffs argue that the shared responsibility payment does not do so, citing Article I, §9, clause 4. That clause provides: "No Capitation, or other direct, Tax shall be laid, unless in Proportion to the Census or Enumeration herein before directed to be taken." This requirement means that any "direct Tax" must be apportioned so that each State pays in proportion to its population. According to the plaintiffs, if the individual mandate imposes a tax, it is a direct tax, and it is unconstitutional because Congress made no effort to apportion it among the States.

Even when the Direct Tax Clause was written it was unclear what else, other than a capitation (also known as a "head tax" or a "poll tax"), might be a direct tax. See Springer v. United States, 102 U.S. 586 (1881). Soon after the framing, Congress passed a tax on ownership of carriages, over James Madison's objection that it was an unapportioned direct tax. This Court upheld the tax, in part reasoning that apportioning such a tax would make little sense, because it would have required taxing carriage owners at dramatically different rates depending on how many carriages were in their home State. See Hylton v. United States, 3 Dall. 171 (1796) (opinion of Chase, J.). The Court was unanimous, and those Justices who wrote opinions either directly asserted or strongly suggested that only two forms of taxation were direct: capitations and land taxes. See *id.*, at 175; *id.*, at 177 (opinion of Paterson, J.); *id.*, at 183 (opinion of Iredell, J.).

That narrow view of what a direct tax might be persisted for a century. In 1880, for example, we explained that "*direct taxes*, within the meaning of the Constitution, are only capitation taxes, as expressed in that instrument, and taxes on real estate." *Springer*. In 1895, we expanded our interpretation to include taxes on personal property and income from personal property, in the course of striking down aspects of the federal income tax. Pollock v. Farmers' Loan & Trust Co., 158 U.S. 601 (1895). That result was overturned by the Sixteenth Amendment, although we continued to consider taxes on personal property to be direct taxes. See Eisner v. Macomber, 252 U.S. 189 (1920).

A tax on going without health insurance does not fall within any recognized category of direct tax. It is not a capitation. Capitations are taxes paid by every person, "without regard to property, profession, or *any other circumstance.*" *Hylton, supra,* at 175 (opinion of Chase, J.) (emphasis altered). The whole point of the shared responsibility payment is that it is triggered by specific circumstances—earning a certain amount of income but not obtaining health insurance. The payment is also plainly not a tax on the ownership of land or personal property. The shared responsibility payment is thus not a direct tax that must be apportioned among the several States.

There may, however, be a more fundamental objection to a tax on those who lack health insurance. Even if only a tax, the payment under §5000A(b) remains a burden that the Federal Government imposes for an omission, not an act. If it is troubling to interpret the Commerce Clause as authorizing Congress to regulate those who abstain from commerce, perhaps it should be similarly troubling to permit Congress to impose a tax for not doing something.

Three considerations allay this concern. First, and most importantly, it is abundantly clear the Constitution does not guarantee that individuals may avoid taxation through inactivity. A capitation, after all, is a tax that everyone must pay simply for existing, and capitations are expressly contemplated by the Constitution. The Court today holds that our Constitution protects us from federal regulation under the Commerce Clause so long as we abstain from the regulated activity. But from its creation, the Constitution has made no such promise with respect to taxes. See Letter from Benjamin Franklin to M. Le Roy (Nov. 13, 1789) ("Our new Constitution is now established . . . but in this world nothing can be said to be certain, except death and taxes").

Whether the mandate can be upheld under the Commerce Clause is a question about the scope of federal authority. Its answer depends on whether Congress can exercise what all acknowledge to be the novel course of directing individuals to purchase insurance. Congress's use of the Taxing Clause to encourage buying something is, by contrast, not new. Tax incentives already promote, for example, purchasing homes and professional educations. Sustaining the mandate as a tax depends only on whether Congress *has* properly exercised its taxing power to encourage purchasing health insurance, not whether it *can.* Upholding the individual mandate under the Taxing Clause thus does not recognize any new federal power. It determines that Congress has used an existing one.

Second, Congress's ability to use its taxing power to influence conduct is not without limits. A few of our cases policed these limits aggressively, invalidating punitive exactions obviously designed to regulate behavior otherwise regarded at the time as beyond federal authority. See, *e.g.,* United States v. Butler, 297 U.S. 1 (1936); [Bailey v.] Drexel Furniture. More often and more recently we have declined to closely examine the regulatory motive or effect of revenue-raising measures. See *Kahriger* (collecting cases). We have nonetheless maintained that "'there comes a time in the extension of the penalizing features of the so-called tax when it loses its character as such and becomes a mere penalty with the characteristics of regulation and punishment.'" *Kurth Ranch* (quoting *Drexel Furniture*).

We have already explained that the shared responsibility payment's practical characteristics pass muster as a tax under our narrowest interpretations of the taxing power. Because the tax at hand is within even those strict limits, we need not here decide the precise point at which an exaction becomes so punitive that the taxing power does not authorize it. It remains true, however, that the "'power to tax is not the power to destroy while this Court sits.'" Oklahoma Tax Comm'n v. Texas Co., 336 U.S. 342 (1949) (quoting Panhandle Oil Co. v. Mississippi ex rel. Knox, 277 U.S. 218 (1928) (Holmes, J., dissenting)).

Third, although the breadth of Congress's power to tax is greater than its power to regulate commerce, the taxing power does not give Congress the same degree of control over individual behavior. Once we recognize that Congress may regulate a particular decision under the Commerce Clause, the Federal Government can bring its full weight to bear. Congress may simply command individuals to do as it directs. An individual who disobeys may be subjected to criminal sanctions. Those sanctions can include not only fines and imprisonment, but all the attendant consequences of being branded a criminal: deprivation of otherwise protected civil rights, such as the right to bear arms or vote in elections; loss of employment opportunities; social stigma; and severe disabilities in other controversies, such as custody or immigration disputes.

By contrast, Congress's authority under the taxing power is limited to requiring an individual to pay money into the Federal Treasury, no more. If a tax is properly paid, the Government has no power to compel or punish individuals subject to it. We do not make light of the severe burden that taxation—especially taxation motivated by a regulatory purpose—can impose. But imposition of a tax nonetheless leaves an individual with a lawful choice to do or not do a certain act, so long as he is willing to pay a tax levied on that choice.[b]

The Affordable Care Act's requirement that certain individuals pay a financial penalty for not obtaining health insurance may reasonably be characterized as a tax. Because the Constitution permits such a tax, it is not our role to forbid it, or to pass upon its wisdom or fairness. . . .

The judgment of the Court of Appeals for the Eleventh Circuit is affirmed in part and reversed in part.

It is so ordered.

[Justices Scalia, Kennedy, Thomas, and Alito dissented jointly. They argued that the statute could not fairly be read as a tax as opposed to a mandate, and therefore they did not reach the question whether it was a constitutional exercise of the taxing power. They also argued that the question of whether the tax was a direct tax, which would violate Article I, §9, cl. 4, had not been adequately briefed or argued.]

DISCUSSION

1. *Tax or penalty?* The text of individual mandate, 26 U.S.C. §5000A, currently appears in Title 26 of the U.S. Code—Internal Revenue Code, in Subtitle

---

b. Of course, individuals do not have a lawful choice not to pay a tax due, and may sometimes face prosecution for failing to do so (although not for declining to make the shared responsibility payment, see 26 U.S.C. §5000A(g)(2)). But that does not show that the tax restricts the lawful choice whether to undertake or forgo the activity on which the tax is predicated. Those subject to the individual mandate may lawfully forgo health insurance and pay higher taxes, or buy health insurance and pay lower taxes. The only thing they may not lawfully do is not buy health insurance and not pay the resulting tax.

D: Miscellaneous Excise Taxes. As Chief Justice Roberts notes, the text of the statute refers repeatedly to the "taxpayer" and the "taxpayer's return." It also says that "[a]n applicable individual shall for each month beginning after 2013 ensure that the individual, and any dependent of the individual who is an applicable individual, is covered under minimum essential coverage for such month." Roberts reads the statute in context as a tax, because failure to meet this requirement has no other legal consequences than the levying of a tax.[8] (In 2017, Congress set the amount of the tax as zero beginning in 2019, effectively repealing the individual mandate.)

2. *The scope of the taxing power.* What are the limits of the taxing power after the Health Care Case? Roberts points to four features that distinguish a lawful tax from an unlawful penalty: First, "for most Americans the amount due will be far less than the price of insurance, and, by statute, it can never be more." This means "that [i]t may often be a reasonable financial decision to make the payment rather than purchase insurance, unlike the 'prohibitory' financial punishment in *Drexel Furniture*." Second, the tax was not structured like a criminal penalty—for example, it did not have a scienter requirement. Third, the tax was administered and collected by the IRS like other taxes. Fourth, failure to purchase insurance was not treated as an unlawful act, and there were no adverse consequences other than having to pay the tax. Which of these criteria is the most important?

Note that the upshot of Roberts's argument is that a constitutional tax creates *incentives* rather than *mandates* for behavior; that is, it always preserves the option to pay the tax, which is not so high that it effectively compels or coerces compliance with the government's preferred regulatory outcome. For a discussion of the constitutional limits on the tax power, see Robert D. Cooter & Neil Siegel, Not the Power to Destroy: An Effects Theory of the Tax Power, 98 Va. L. Rev. 1195 (2012).

Roberts could also have added a fifth criterion: The tax did not burden a fundamental right. Thus, a tax on people who refuse to attend church weekly would violate the Free Exercise Clause (and the Establishment Clause); a tax on people who refuse to eat broccoli might violate the Due Process Clause. Are all taxes that affect the exercise of fundamental rights unconstitutional? The federal income tax sometimes taxes married couples filing jointly more than two people filing separately. Is this constitutional?

3. *Using taxes rather than mandates.* The effect of Roberts's argument is that if Congress wishes to impose mandates on people who are not already engaged in an activity that could be regulated by the Commerce Clause, it must use the taxing power instead, always giving people the option to pay the tax. Are there structural reasons to prefer taxes to mandates in these circumstances? Does the doctrine promote federalism? Regardless of whether it promotes federalism, does it promote individual liberty?

4. *Two versions of the avoidance canon.* Given that Chief Justice Roberts believed that the individual mandate was already a constitutional tax, why was it necessary for him to reach the merits of the Commerce Clause argument and hold the mandate beyond Congress's Commerce power?

---

8. See Marsha Coyle, The Roberts Court: The Struggle for the Constitution 321-322 (2013) (describing discussions between Acting Solicitor General Neal Katyal and Akhil Amar about how to structure the tax argument to win the vote of Chief Justice Roberts); Akhil Reed Amar, The Lawfulness of Health-Care Reform, SSRN, at http://papers.ssrn.com/sol3/papers.cfm?abstract_id=1856506 (offering multiple versions of the tax argument).

Roberts defended his approach by arguing that "the statute reads more naturally as a command to buy insurance than as a tax, and I would uphold it as a command if the Constitution allowed it. It is only because the Commerce Clause does not authorize such a command that it is necessary to reach the taxing power question. And it is only because we have a duty to construe a statute to save it, if fairly possible, that §5000A can be interpreted as a tax. Without deciding the Commerce Clause question, I would find no basis to adopt such a saving construction."

Roberts is advocating an older version of the "avoidance" canon—in essence, he is saying that a court may adopt an interpretation that is plausible but not the most natural reading only if the court believes that a statute *would* be unconstitutional if given its most natural interpretation. This means that it must first pass on the constitutionality of the most natural interpretation before it can consider alternative readings.

The modern avoidance canon is different—it maintains that out of respect for co-ordinate branches of government and in order to promote judicial restraint, courts should avoid holding statutes unconstitutional when reasonably possible. Therefore courts should adopt readings fairly supported by the statute's language in order to allow the court to avoid deciding a difficult constitutional question. Thus, in her opinion concurring in part and dissenting in part, Justice Ginsburg objects that "I see no reason to undertake a Commerce Clause analysis that is not outcome determinative."

Note that Roberts's version of the avoidance canon depends on his being able to say that although the tax interpretation is "fairly possible," it is not the most "natural" reading. The modern version of the avoidance canon does not require this.

5. *Holding or dicta?* Parts III-A and III-B of Chief Justice Roberts's opinion (which no other Justices join) purport to hold that Congress may not enact the individual mandate under the Commerce Clause, even assisted by the Necessary and Proper Clause. Is this holding merely dicta?

In Marks v. United States, 430 U.S. 188, 193 (1977), the Court explained its test for determining the holding of a case when there is no majority opinion on a particular issue: "When a fragmented Court decides a case and no single rationale explaining the result enjoys the assent of five Justices, the holding of the Court may be viewed as that position taken by those Members who concurred in the judgments on the narrowest grounds."

The problem here is that the four Justices who agree with Roberts on limiting the Commerce Clause and the Necessary and Proper Clause do not concur in the judgment; they dissent. The joint dissenters make arguments similar to and even more restrictive than Roberts's arguments, but they do not agree with the judgment of the Court and they do not join Part III of Roberts's opinion. Instead, they merely criticize his holding on the tax power.

Note, interestingly, that Part III-C of his opinion, joined by five Justices, notes in passing that "[t]he Court today holds that our Constitution protects us from federal regulation under the Commerce Clause so long as we abstain from the regulated activity." Even if you believe that Roberts's arguments (other than the tax power holding) are either dicta or a plurality opinion, do you expect that lower federal courts will treat them as law, given that lower courts know that five Justices now support doctrines that limit federal powers? How *should* lower courts interpret these opinions?

6. The ACA's opponents try one more time: California v. Texas. In 2017, as part of a tax reform bill, Congress changed §5000A(a)'s monetary penalty for failing to purchase health insurance to $0, effectively nullifying the penalty. Subsequently, the State of Texas (along with over a dozen states and two individuals) brought suit against federal officials, seeking to strike down the entire ACA on the grounds that because the mandate no longer raised any revenue, it could no longer be justified as an exercise of Congress's taxing power. They sought a declaration that (1) the individual mandate was unconstitutional, (2) a finding that the rest of the Act is not severable from the mandate, and (3) an injunction against enforcement of the rest of the Act. Petitioner California and other States intervened to defend the Act's constitutionality.

In California v. Texas, 141 S. Ct. 2104 (2021), The Supreme Court, in a 7-2 opinion by Justice Breyer, held that none of the plaintiffs had standing to challenge §5000A(a). Although the individual plaintiffs argued that the language of the individual mandate "commands them to buy health insurance . . . the statutory provision . . . has no means of enforcement. With the penalty zeroed out, the IRS can no longer seek a penalty from those who fail to comply. . . . Because of this, there is no possible Government action that is causally connected to the plaintiffs' injury—the costs of purchasing health insurance." The state plaintiffs also lacked standing: They complained about the added costs of implementing other ACA programs, not the individual mandate, and they did not assert that the other programs were unconstitutional.

Justice Alito, joined by Justice Gorsuch, dissented: "I would hold that the States have demonstrated standing to seek relief from the ACA provisions that burden them and that they claim are inseparable from the individual mandate." Reaching the merits, Justice Alito concluded that "the individual mandate exceeds the scope of Congress's enumerated legislative powers." Then, relying on the joint dissent in *Sibelius* (which he had joined), he argued that the rest of the ACA was not severable from the individual mandate, and therefore should be declared unconstitutional as well.

Wouldn't the fact that Congress had kept the rest of the ACA in place and zeroed out the mandate in 2017 suggest that Congress believed that the mandate was severable from the rest of the ACA? No, Alito argued: "[T]he 2017 Act cannot plausibly be viewed as the manifestation of a congressional intent to preserve the ACA in altered form. The 2017 Act would not have passed the House without the votes of the Members who had voted to scrap the ACA just a few months earlier, and the repeal of the tax or penalty, which they obviously found particularly offensive, was their fallback option. They eliminated the tax or penalty and left the chips to fall as they might. Thus, under the reasoning of the *NFIB* dissent, the provisions burdening the States are inseverable from the individual mandate."

3. The Spending Power

In South Dakota v. Dole, 483 U.S. 203 (1987), Chief Justice Rehnquist wrote for the Court to uphold a congressional statute that directed the Secretary of Transportation to withhold from a state a percentage of federal highway funds it would otherwise be entitled to should the state permit the purchase or public possession of alcohol by a person under 21. South Dakota, which allowed 19-year-olds to purchase beer, argued that the statute was unconstitutional under the Twenty-First Amendment, which the Court had earlier found "grants the State virtually complete control over whether to permit importation or sale of liquor and how to structure the liquor distribution system." California Retail Liquor Dealers Assn. v. Midcal Aluminum, Inc., 445 U.S. 97, 110 (1980). South Dakota asserted that it would therefore be unconstitutional for Congress to pass a national drinking-age law and that indirect control through the withholding of federal funds was also unconstitutional.

On behalf of himself and six other Justices, Chief Justice Rehnquist wrote that "we need not decide . . . [whether the Twenty-First Amendment] would prohibit an attempt by Congress to legislate directly a national minimum drinking age. Here, Congress has acted indirectly under its spending power to encourage uniformity in the State's drinking ages. . . . [W]e find this legislative effort within constitutional bounds even if Congress may not regulate drinking ages directly." Citing a number of cases going back to United States v. Butler, 297 U.S. 1 (1936), supra Chapter 5, the Court stated that "objectives not thought to be within Article I's 'enumerated legislative fields,' may nevertheless be attained through the use of the spending power and the conditional grant of federal funds." To be sure, Congress's power under the spending power is not unlimited: "First, the exercise of the spending power must be in pursuit of 'the general welfare,'" though Congress is entitled to considerable deference in regard to judgments about what constitutes such welfare. "Second, we have required that if Congress desires to condition the States' receipt of federal funds, it 'must do so unambiguously . . . , enabl[ing] the States to exercise their choice knowingly, cognizant of the consequences of their participation.' Third, our cases have suggested (without significant elaboration) that conditions on federal grants might be illegitimate if they are unrelated 'to the federal interest in particular national projects or programs.' . . . Finally, we have noted that other constitutional provisions may provide an independent bar to the conditional grant of federal funds." The statute met the first three requirements:

> Congress found that the differing drinking ages in the States created particular incentives for young persons to combine their desire to drink with their ability to drive, and that this interstate problem required a national solution. The means it chose to address this dangerous situation were reasonably calculated to advance the general welfare. The conditions upon which States receive the funds, moreover, could not be more clearly stated by Congress. . . . Indeed, the condition imposed by Congress is directly related to one of the main purposes for which highway funds are expended—safe interstate travel. This goal of the interstate highway system had been frustrated by varying drinking ages among the States. A presidential commission appointed to study alcohol-related accidents and fatalities on the Nation's highways concluded that the lack of uniformity in the States' drinking ages created "an incentive to drink and drive" because "young persons commut[e] to border States where the drinking age is lower." By enacting, Congress conditioned the receipt of federal funds in a way reasonably calculated to address this particular impediment to a purpose for which the funds are expended.

The fourth question was "whether the Twenty-first Amendment constitutes an 'independent constitutional bar' to the conditional grant of federal funds." Citing Oklahoma v. Civil Service Comm'n, and Steward Machine Co. v. Davis, the Court described "the language in our earlier opinions" as standing "for the unexceptionable proposition that the power may not be used to induce the States to engage in activities that would themselves be unconstitutional. Thus, for example, a grant of federal funds conditioned on invidiously discriminatory state action or the infliction of cruel and unusual punishment" would be unconstitutional. Here, though, the policy being pressed upon South Dakota—the raising of the minimum drinking age—would violate no one's constitutional rights. The Court also noted that South Dakota would lose only 5 percent of its allotted funds for its failure to follow federal policy. This "mild encouragement" by Congress did not approach the point "at which 'pressure turns into compulsion.'" *Davis.*

Justice O'Connor dissented, arguing that "the Court's application of the requirement that the condition imposed be reasonably related to the purpose for which the funds are expended, is cursory and unconvincing."

> The Court reasons that Congress wishes that the roads it builds may be used safely, that drunk drivers threaten highway safety, and that young people are more likely to drive while under the influence of alcohol under existing law than would be the case if there were a uniform national drinking age of 21. It hardly needs saying, however, that if the purpose is to deter drunken driving, it is far too over- and under-inclusive. It is over-inclusive because it stops teenagers from drinking even when they are not about to drive on interstate highways. It is under-inclusive because teenagers pose only a small part of the drunken driving problem in this Nation.

Thus she found too "attenuated" the linkage between the national interest and the particular conditions imposed. To allow the statute to operate in this case in effect allowed Congress to

> regulate almost any area of a State's social, political, or economic life on the theory that use of the interstate transportation system is somehow enhanced. If, for example, the United States were to condition highway moneys upon moving the state capital, I suppose it might argue that interstate transportation is facilitated by locating local governments in places easily accessible to interstate highways—or, conversely, that highways might become overburdened if they had to carry traffic to and from the state capital. In my mind, such a relationship is hardly more attenuated than the one which the Court finds supports §158.

Justice O'Connor cited *Butler* for the distinction between spending and regulation. There Justice Roberts noted "[t]here is an obvious difference between a statute stating the conditions upon which moneys shall be expended and one effective only upon assumption of a contractual obligation to submit to a regulation which otherwise could not be enforced." According to Justice O'Connor, "the *Butler* Court saw the Agricultural Adjustment Act for what it was—an exercise of regulatory, not spending, power. The error in *Butler* was not the Court's conclusion that the Act was essentially regulatory, but rather its crabbed view of the extent of Congress' regulatory power under the Commerce Clause."

Justice Brennan also dissented, on the ground "that regulation of the minimum age of purchasers of liquor falls squarely within the ambit of those powers reserved to the States by the Twenty-first Amendment. Since States possess this constitutional power, Congress can not condition a federal grant in a manner that abridges this right."

National Federation of Independent Business v. Sebelius

[The Health Care Case]
567 U.S. 519 (2012)

[In addition to creating an individual mandate to purchase health insurance, discussed infra, the 2010 Patient Protection and Affordable Care Act also expanded Medicaid to increase the number of poor persons receiving health care. The preexisting Medicaid program offers federal funding to states to assist pregnant women, children, needy families, the blind, the elderly, and the disabled in obtaining medical care. The Affordable Care Act expands the scope of the Medicaid program and increases the number of individuals the states must cover. For example, the Act requires state programs to provide Medicaid coverage by 2014 to adults with incomes up to 133 percent of the federal poverty level. Many states before the Act cover adults with children only if their income is considerably lower and do not cover childless adults at all. The Act increases federal funding to cover the states' costs in expanding Medicaid coverage. Until 2016, the federal government covered 100 percent of the new costs, thereafter reducing gradually to 90 percent. (The percentages that the federal government covers under the existing Medicaid plan vary by state between 50 to 83 percent.) If a state does not comply with the Act's new coverage requirements, it may lose not only the federal funding for those requirements but also all of its federal Medicaid funds. Twenty-six states challenged this condition, arguing that it was beyond Congress's powers under the General Welfare Clause.]

Chief Justice Roberts announced the judgment of the Court and delivered [an] opinion with respect to Part IV, in which Justice Breyer and Justice Kagan join.

IV

A

The States . . . contend that the Medicaid expansion exceeds Congress's authority under the Spending Clause. They claim that Congress is coercing the States to adopt the changes it wants by threatening to withhold all of a State's Medicaid grants, unless the State accepts the new expanded funding and complies with the conditions that come with it. This, they argue, violates the basic principle that the "Federal Government may not compel the States to enact or administer a federal regulatory program."

There is no doubt that the Act dramatically increases state obligations under Medicaid. The current Medicaid program requires States to cover only certain discrete categories of needy individuals—pregnant women, children, needy families, the blind, the elderly, and the disabled. There is no mandatory coverage for most childless adults, and the States typically do not offer any such coverage. The States also enjoy considerable flexibility with respect to the coverage levels for parents of needy families. On average States cover only those unemployed parents who make less than 37 percent of the federal poverty level, and only those employed parents who make less than 63 percent of the poverty line.

The Medicaid provisions of the Affordable Care Act, in contrast, require States to expand their Medicaid programs by 2014 to cover *all* individuals under the age of 65 with incomes below 133 percent of the federal poverty line. The Act also establishes a new "[e]ssential health benefits" package, which States must provide to all new Medicaid recipients—a level sufficient to satisfy a recipient's obligations under the individual mandate. The Affordable Care Act provides that the Federal Government will pay 100 percent of the costs of covering these newly eligible individuals through 2016. In the following years, the federal payment level gradually decreases, to a minimum of 90 percent. In light of the expansion in coverage mandated by the Act, the Federal Government estimates that its Medicaid spending will increase by approximately $100 billion per year, nearly 40 percent above current levels.

The Spending Clause grants Congress the power "to pay the Debts and provide for the . . . general Welfare of the United States." U.S. Const., Art. I, §8, cl. 1. We have long recognized that Congress may use this power to grant federal funds to the States, and may condition such a grant upon the States' "taking certain actions that Congress could not require them to take." Such measures "encourage a State to regulate in a particular way, [and] influenc[e] a State's policy choices." *New York.* The conditions imposed by Congress ensure that the funds are used by the States to "provide for the . . . general Welfare" in the manner Congress intended.

At the same time, our cases have recognized limits on Congress's power under the Spending Clause to secure state compliance with federal objectives. . . . "We have repeatedly characterized . . . Spending Clause legislation as 'much in the nature of a *contract*.'" Barnes v. Gorman, 536 U.S. 181 (2002) (quoting Pennhurst State School and Hospital v. Halderman, 451 U.S. 1 (1981)). The legitimacy of Congress's exercise of the spending power "thus rests on whether the State voluntarily and knowingly accepts the terms of the 'contract.'" *Pennhurst.* Respecting this limitation is critical to ensuring that Spending Clause legislation does not undermine the status of the States as independent sovereigns in our federal system. That system "rests on what might at first seem a counterintuitive insight, that 'freedom is enhanced by the creation of two governments, not one.'" For this reason, "the Constitution has never been understood to confer upon Congress the ability to require the States to govern according to Congress' instructions." *New York.* Otherwise the two-government system established by the Framers would give way to a system that vests power in one central government, and individual liberty would suffer.

That insight has led this Court to strike down federal legislation that commandeers a State's legislative or administrative apparatus for federal purposes. See, *e.g., Printz*; *New York.* It has also led us to scrutinize Spending Clause legislation to ensure that Congress is not using financial inducements to exert a "power akin to undue influence." Steward Machine Co. v. Davis, 301 U.S. 548 (1937). Congress may use its spending power to create incentives for States to act in accordance with federal policies. But when "pressure turns into compulsion," *ibid.*, the legislation runs contrary to our system of federalism. "[T]he Constitution simply does not give

Congress the authority to require the States to regulate." *New York*. That is true whether Congress directly commands a State to regulate or indirectly coerces a State to adopt a federal regulatory system as its own.

Permitting the Federal Government to force the States to implement a federal program would threaten the political accountability key to our federal system. "[W]here the Federal Government directs the States to regulate, it may be state officials who will bear the brunt of public disapproval, while the federal officials who devised the regulatory program may remain insulated from the electoral ramifications of their decision." [*New York*.] Spending Clause programs do not pose this danger when a State has a legitimate choice whether to accept the federal conditions in exchange for federal funds. In such a situation, state officials can fairly be held politically accountable for choosing to accept or refuse the federal offer. But when the State has no choice, the Federal Government can achieve its objectives without accountability, just as in *New York* and *Printz*. Indeed, this danger is heightened when Congress acts under the Spending Clause, because Congress can use that power to implement federal policy it could not impose directly under its enumerated powers.

We addressed such concerns in *Steward Machine*. That case involved a federal tax on employers that was abated if the businesses paid into a state unemployment plan that met certain federally specified conditions. An employer sued, alleging that the tax was impermissibly "driv[ing] the state legislatures under the whip of economic pressure into the enactment of unemployment compensation laws at the bidding of the central government." We acknowledged the danger that the Federal Government might employ its taxing power to exert a "power akin to undue influence" upon the States. But we observed that Congress adopted the challenged tax and abatement program to channel money to the States that would otherwise have gone into the Federal Treasury for use in providing national unemployment services. Congress was willing to direct businesses to instead pay the money into state programs only on the condition that the money be used for the same purposes. Predicating tax abatement on a State's adoption of a particular type of unemployment legislation was therefore a means to "safeguard [the Federal Government's] own treasury." We held that "[i]n such circumstances, if in no others, inducement or persuasion does not go beyond the bounds of power."

In rejecting the argument that the federal law was a "weapon[ ] of coercion, destroying or impairing the autonomy of the states," the Court noted that there was no reason to suppose that the State in that case acted other than through "her unfettered will." Indeed, the State itself did "not offer a suggestion that in passing the unemployment law she was affected by duress."

As our decision in *Steward Machine* confirms, Congress may attach appropriate conditions to federal taxing and spending programs to preserve its control over the use of federal funds. In the typical case we look to the States to defend their prerogatives by adopting "the simple expedient of not yielding" to federal blandishments when they do not want to embrace the federal policies as their own. The States are separate and independent sovereigns. Sometimes they have to act like it.

The States, however, argue that the Medicaid expansion is far from the typical case. They object that Congress has "crossed the line distinguishing encouragement from coercion," *New York*, in the way it has structured the funding: Instead of simply refusing to grant the new funds to States that will not accept the new conditions, Congress has also threatened to withhold those States' existing Medicaid funds. The States claim that this threat serves no purpose other than to force unwilling States to sign up for the dramatic expansion in health care coverage effected by the Act.

Given the nature of the threat and the programs at issue here, we must agree. We have upheld Congress's authority to condition the receipt of funds on the States' complying with restrictions on the use of those funds, because that is the means by which Congress ensures that the funds are spent according to its view of the "general Welfare." Conditions that do not here govern the use of the funds, however, cannot be justified on that basis. When, for example, such conditions take the form of threats to terminate other significant independent grants, the conditions are properly viewed as a means of pressuring the States to accept policy changes.

In South Dakota v. Dole, we considered a challenge to a federal law that threatened to withhold five percent of a State's federal highway funds if the State did not raise its drinking age to 21. The Court found that the condition was "directly related to one of the main purposes for which highway funds are expended—safe interstate travel." At the same time, the condition was not a restriction on how the highway funds—set aside for specific highway improvement and maintenance efforts—were to be used.

We accordingly asked whether "the financial inducement offered by Congress" was "so coercive as to pass the point at which 'pressure turns into compulsion.'" By "financial inducement" the Court meant the threat of losing five percent of highway funds; no new money was offered to the States to raise their drinking ages. We found that the inducement was not impermissibly coercive, because Congress was offering only "relatively mild encouragement to the States." We observed that "all South Dakota would lose if she adheres to her chosen course as to a suitable minimum drinking age is 5%" of her highway funds. In fact, the federal funds at stake constituted less than half of one percent of South Dakota's budget at the time. In consequence, "we conclude[d] that [the] encouragement to state action [was] a valid use of the spending power." Whether to accept the drinking age change "remain[ed] the prerogative of the States not merely in theory but in fact."

In this case, the financial "inducement" Congress has chosen is much more than "relatively mild encouragement"—it is a gun to the head. . . . A State that opts out of the Affordable Care Act's expansion in health care coverage thus stands to lose not merely "a relatively small percentage" of its existing Medicaid funding, but *all* of it. Medicaid spending accounts for over 20 percent of the average State's total budget, with federal funds covering 50 to 83 percent of those costs. The Federal Government estimates that it will pay out approximately $3.3 trillion between 2010 and 2019 in order to cover the costs of *pre* expansion Medicaid. In addition, the States have developed intricate statutory and administrative regimes over the course of many decades to implement their objectives under existing Medicaid. It is easy to see how the *Dole* Court could conclude that the threatened loss of less than half of one percent of South Dakota's budget left that State with a "prerogative" to reject Congress's desired policy, "not merely in theory but in fact." The threatened loss of over 10 percent of a State's overall budget, in contrast, is economic dragooning that leaves the States with no real option but to acquiesce in the

Medicaid expansion.[a] Justice Ginsburg claims that *Dole* is distinguishable because here "Congress has not threatened to withhold funds earmarked for any other program." But that begs the question: The States contend that the expansion is in reality a new program and that Congress is forcing them to accept it by threatening the funds for the existing Medicaid program. We cannot agree that existing Medicaid and the expansion dictated by the Affordable Care Act are all one program simply because "Congress styled" them as such. If the expansion is not properly viewed as a modification of the existing Medicaid program, Congress's decision to so title it is irrelevant.[b]

Here, the Government claims that the Medicaid expansion is properly viewed merely as a modification of the existing program because the States agreed that Congress could change the terms of Medicaid when they signed on in the first place. The Government observes that the Social Security Act, which includes the original Medicaid provisions, contains a clause expressly reserving "[t]he right to alter, amend, or repeal any provision" of that statute. 42 U.S.C. §1304. So it does. But "if Congress intends to impose a condition on the grant of federal moneys, it must do so unambiguously." *Pennhurst.* A State confronted with statutory language reserving the right to "alter" or "amend" the pertinent provisions of the Social Security Act might reasonably assume that Congress was entitled to make adjustments to the Medicaid program as it developed. Congress has in fact done so, sometimes conditioning only the new funding, other times both old and new.

The Medicaid expansion, however, accomplishes a shift in kind, not merely degree. The original program was designed to cover medical services for four particular categories of the needy: the disabled, the blind, the elderly, and needy families with dependent children. Previous amendments to Medicaid eligibility merely altered and expanded the boundaries of these categories. Under the Affordable Care Act, Medicaid is transformed into a program to meet the health care needs of the entire nonelderly population with income below 133 percent of the poverty level. It is no longer a program to care for the neediest among us, but rather an

---

a. Justice Ginsburg observes that state Medicaid spending will increase by only 0.8 percent after the expansion. That not only ignores increased state administrative expenses, but also assumes that the Federal Government will continue to fund the expansion at the current statutorily specified levels. It is not unheard of, however, for the Federal Government to increase requirements in such a manner as to impose unfunded mandates on the States. More importantly, the size of the new financial burden imposed on a State is irrelevant in analyzing whether the State has been coerced into accepting that burden. "Your money or your life" is a coercive proposition, whether you have a single dollar in your pocket or $500.

b. Nor, of course, can the number of pages the amendment occupies, or the extent to which the change preserves and works within the existing program, be dispositive. Take, for example, the following hypothetical amendment: "All of a State's citizens are now eligible for Medicaid." That change would take up a single line and would not alter any "operational aspect[ ] of the program" beyond the eligibility requirements. Yet it could hardly be argued that such an amendment was a permissible modification of Medicaid, rather than an attempt to foist an entirely new health care system upon the States.

element of a comprehensive national plan to provide universal health insurance coverage.[c]

Indeed, the manner in which the expansion is structured indicates that while Congress may have styled the expansion a mere alteration of existing Medicaid, it recognized it was enlisting the States in a new health care program. Congress created a separate funding provision to cover the costs of providing services to any person made newly eligible by the expansion. While Congress pays 50 to 83 percent of the costs of covering individuals currently enrolled in Medicaid, once the expansion is fully implemented Congress will pay 90 percent of the costs for newly eligible persons. The conditions on use of the different funds are also distinct. Congress mandated that newly eligible persons receive a level of coverage that is less comprehensive than the traditional Medicaid benefit package.

As we have explained, "[t]hough Congress' power to legislate under the spending power is broad, it does not include surprising participating States with postacceptance or 'retroactive' conditions." *Pennhurst*. A State could hardly anticipate that Congress's reservation of the right to "alter" or "amend" the Medicaid program included the power to transform it so dramatically.

Justice Ginsburg claims that in fact this expansion is no different from the previous changes to Medicaid, such that "a State would be hard put to complain that it lacked fair notice." But the prior change she discusses—presumably the most dramatic alteration she could find—does not come close to working the transformation the expansion accomplishes. She highlights an amendment requiring States to cover pregnant women and increasing the number of eligible children. But this modification can hardly be described as a major change in a program that—from its inception—provided health care for "families with dependent children." Previous Medicaid amendments simply do not fall into the same category as the one at stake here.

The Court in *Steward Machine* did not attempt to "fix the outermost line" where persuasion gives way to coercion. The Court found it "[e]nough for present purposes that wherever the line may be, this statute is within it." We have no need to fix a line either. It is enough for today that wherever that line may be, this statute is surely beyond it. Congress may not simply "conscript state [agencies] into the national bureaucratic army," and that is what it is attempting to do with the Medicaid expansion.

B

Nothing in our opinion precludes Congress from offering funds under the Affordable Care Act to expand the availability of health care, and requiring that

---

c. Justice Ginsburg suggests that the States can have no objection to the Medicaid expansion, because "Congress could have repealed Medicaid [and,] [t]hereafter, . . . could have enacted Medicaid II, a new program combining the pre-2010 coverage with the expanded coverage required by the ACA." But it would certainly not be that easy. Practical constraints would plainly inhibit, if not preclude, the Federal Government from repealing the existing program and putting every feature of Medicaid on the table for political reconsideration. Such a massive undertaking would hardly be "ritualistic." The same is true of Justice Ginsburg's suggestion that Congress could establish Medicaid as an exclusively federal program.

States accepting such funds comply with the conditions on their use. What Congress is not free to do is to penalize States that choose not to participate in that new program by taking away their existing Medicaid funding. Section 1396c [of the Medicaid Act] gives the Secretary of Health and Human Services the authority to do just that. It allows her to withhold *all* "further [Medicaid] payments . . . to the State" if she determines that the State is out of compliance with any Medicaid requirement, including those contained in the expansion. In light of the Court's holding [that §1396c is unconstitutional when applied to withdraw existing Medicaid funds from States that decline to comply with the expansion], the Secretary cannot apply §1396c to withdraw existing Medicaid funds for failure to comply with the requirements set out in the expansion.

That fully remedies the constitutional violation we have identified. . . . Today's holding does not affect the continued application of §1396c to the existing Medicaid program. Nor does it affect the Secretary's ability to withdraw funds provided under the Affordable Care Act if a State that has chosen to participate in the expansion fails to comply with the requirements of that Act.

The Court today limits the financial pressure the Secretary may apply to induce States to accept the terms of the Medicaid expansion. As a practical matter, that means States may now choose to reject the expansion; that is the whole point. . . .

We have no way of knowing how many States will accept the terms of the expansion, but we do not believe Congress would have wanted the whole Act to fall, simply because some may choose not to participate. The other reforms Congress enacted, after all, will remain "fully operative as a law," and will still function in a way "consistent with Congress' basic objectives in enacting the statute[.]" Confident that Congress would not have intended anything different, we conclude that the rest of the Act need not fall in light of our constitutional holding.

Justice GINSBURG, with whom Justice SOTOMAYOR joins, . . . dissenting in part. . . .

V

[T]he spending power conferred by the Constitution, the Court has never doubted, permits Congress to define the contours of programs financed with federal funds. And to expand coverage, Congress could have recalled the existing legislation, and replaced it with a new law making Medicaid as embracive of the poor as Congress chose.

The question posed by the 2010 Medicaid expansion, then, is essentially this: To cover a notably larger population, must Congress take the repeal/reenact route, or may it achieve the same result by amending existing law? The answer should be that Congress may expand by amendment the classes of needy persons entitled to Medicaid benefits. A ritualistic requirement that Congress repeal and reenact spending legislation in order to enlarge the population served by a federally funded program would advance no constitutional principle and would scarcely serve the interests of federalism. To the contrary, such a requirement would rigidify Congress' efforts to empower States by partnering with them in the implementation of federal programs. . . .

Medicaid, as amended by the ACA, . . . is not two spending programs; it is a single program with a constant aim—to enable poor persons to receive basic health care when they need it. Given past expansions, plus express statutory warning that Congress may change the requirements participating States must meet, there can be no tenable claim that the ACA fails for lack of notice. Moreover, States have no entitlement to receive any Medicaid funds; they enjoy only the opportunity to accept funds on Congress' terms. Future Congresses are not bound by their predecessors' dispositions; they have authority to spend federal revenue as they see fit. The Federal Government, therefore, is not, as The Chief Justice charges, threatening States with the loss of "existing" funds from one spending program in order to induce them to opt into another program. Congress is simply requiring States to do what States have long been required to do to receive Medicaid funding: comply with the conditions Congress prescribes for participation.

A majority of the Court, however, buys the argument that prospective withholding of funds formerly available exceeds Congress' spending power. Given that holding, I entirely agree with The Chief Justice as to the appropriate remedy. It is to bar the withholding found impermissible—not, as the joint dissenters would have it, to scrap the expansion altogether. The dissenters' view that the ACA must fall in its entirety is a radical departure from the Court's normal course. When a constitutional infirmity mars a statute, the Court ordinarily removes the infirmity. It undertakes a salvage operation; it does not demolish the legislation. See, *e.g.*, Brockett v. Spokane Arcades, Inc., 472 U.S. 491 (1985) (Court's normal course is to declare a statute invalid "to the extent that it reaches too far, but otherwise [to leave the statute] intact"). That course is plainly in order where, as in this case, Congress has expressly instructed courts to leave untouched every provision not found invalid. See 42 U.S.C. §1303. Because The Chief Justice finds the withholding—not the granting—of federal funds incompatible with the Spending Clause, Congress' extension of Medicaid remains available to any State that affirms its willingness to participate.

. . .

The Chief Justice correctly notes that the reimbursement rate for participating States is different regarding individuals who became Medicaid-eligible through the ACA. But the rate differs only in its generosity to participating States. Under pre-ACA Medicaid, the Federal Government pays up to 83% of the costs of coverage for current enrollees. Even if one agreed that a change of as little as 7 percentage points carries constitutional significance, is it not passing strange to suggest that the purported incursion on state sovereignty might have been averted, or at least mitigated, had Congress offered States *less* money to carry out the same obligations?

Consider also that Congress could have repealed Medicaid. Thereafter, Congress could have enacted Medicaid II, a new program combining the pre-2010 coverage with the expanded coverage required by the ACA. By what right does a court stop Congress from building up without first tearing down?

The Chief Justice finds the Medicaid expansion vulnerable because it took participating States by surprise. . . . If I understand his point correctly, it was incumbent on Congress, in 1965, to warn the States clearly of the size and shape potential changes to Medicaid might take. . . . [Yet] from the start, the Medicaid Act put States on notice that the program could be changed: "The right to alter, amend, or repeal any provision of [Medicaid]," the statute has read since 1965, "is hereby reserved to the Congress." . . . The Chief Justice insists that the most recent expansion, in contrast to its predecessors, "accomplishes a shift in kind, not merely degree." But why was Medicaid altered only in degree, not in kind, when [between 1988 and 1990] Congress required States to cover millions of children and pregnant women? In short, given [the language of the Medicaid statute], and the enlargement of Medicaid in the years since 1965, a State would be hard put to complain that it lacked fair notice when, in 2010, Congress altered Medicaid to embrace a larger portion of the Nation's poor.

[W]hen future Spending Clause challenges arrive, as they likely will in the wake of today's decision, how will litigants and judges assess whether "a State has a legitimate choice whether to accept the federal conditions in exchange for federal funds"? Are courts to measure the number of dollars the Federal Government might withhold for noncompliance? The portion of the State's budget at stake? And which State's—or States'—budget is determinative: the lead plaintiff, all challenging States (26 in this case, many with quite different fiscal situations), or some national median? Does it matter that Florida, unlike most States, imposes no state income tax, and therefore might be able to replace foregone federal funds with new state revenue?[a] Or that the coercion state officials in fact fear is punishment at the ballot box for turning down a politically popular federal grant?

The coercion inquiry, therefore, appears to involve political judgments that defy judicial calculation. . . . At bottom, my colleagues' position is that the States' reliance on federal funds limits Congress' authority to alter its spending programs. This gets things backwards: Congress, not the States, is tasked with spending federal money in service of the general welfare. And each successive Congress is empowered to appropriate funds as it sees fit. When the 110th Congress reached a conclusion about Medicaid funds that differed from its predecessors' view, it abridged no State's right to "existing," or "pre-existing," funds. For, in fact, there are no such funds. There is only money States *anticipate* receiving from future Congresses.

[T]he Court does not strike down any provision of the ACA. It prohibits only the "application" of the Secretary's authority to withhold Medicaid funds from States that decline to conform their Medicaid plans to the ACA's requirements. Thus the ACA's authorization of funds to finance the expansion remains intact, and the Secretary's authority to withhold funds for reasons other than noncompliance with the expansion remains unaffected. . . . The Chief Justice is undoubtedly

a. Federal taxation of a State's citizens, according to the joint dissenters, may diminish a State's ability to raise new revenue. This, in turn, could limit a State's capacity to replace a federal program with an "equivalent" state-funded analog. But it cannot be true that "the amount of the federal taxes extracted from the taxpayers of a State to pay for the program in question is relevant in determining whether there is impermissible coercion." When the United States Government taxes United States citizens, it taxes them "in their individual capacities" as "the people of America"—not as residents of a particular State. . . . A State therefore has no claim on the money its residents pay in federal taxes, and federal "spending programs need not help people in all states in the same measure." In 2004, for example, New Jersey received 55 cents in federal spending for every dollar its residents paid to the Federal Government in taxes, while Mississippi received $1.77 per tax dollar paid. Thus no constitutional problem was created when Arizona declined for 16 years to participate in Medicaid, even though its residents' tax dollars financed Medicaid programs in every other State.

right to conclude that Congress may offer States funds "to expand the availability of health care, and requir[e] that States accepting such funds comply with the conditions on their use." I therefore concur in the judgment with respect to Part IV-B of The Chief Justice's opinion. . . .

Justice SCALIA, Justice KENNEDY, Justice THOMAS, and Justice ALITO, dissenting. . . .

IV

D

[I]f States really have no choice other than to accept the package, the offer is coercive, and the conditions cannot be sustained under the spending power. And as our decision in South Dakota v. Dole makes clear, theoretical voluntariness is not enough. . . .

The Federal Government suggests that it is sufficient if States are "free, *as a matter of law*, to turn down" federal funds. According to the Federal Government, neither the amount of the offered federal funds nor the amount of the federal taxes extracted from the taxpayers of a State to pay for the program in question is relevant in determining whether there is impermissible coercion.

This argument ignores reality. When a heavy federal tax is levied to support a federal program that offers large grants to the States, States may, as a practical matter, be unable to refuse to participate in the federal program and to substitute a state alternative. Even if a State believes that the federal program is ineffective and inefficient, withdrawal would likely force the State to impose a huge tax increase on its residents, and this new state tax would come on top of the federal taxes already paid by residents to support subsidies to participating States.[a]

Acceptance of the Federal Government's interpretation of the anticoercion rule would permit Congress to dictate policy in areas traditionally governed primarily at the state or local level. Suppose, for example, that Congress enacted legislation offering each State a grant equal to the State's entire annual expenditures for primary and secondary education. Suppose also that this funding came with conditions governing such things as school curriculum, the hiring and tenure of teachers, the drawing of school districts, the length and hours of the school day, the school calendar, a dress code for students, and rules for student discipline. *As a matter of law*, a State could turn down that offer, but if it did so, its residents would not only be required to pay the federal taxes needed to support this expensive new program, but they would also be forced to pay an equivalent amount in state taxes. And if the State gave in to the federal law, the State and its subdivisions would surrender their traditional authority in the field of education. Asked at oral argument

---

a. Justice Ginsburg argues that "[a] State . . . has no claim on the money its residents pay in federal taxes." This is true as a formal matter. "When the United States Government taxes United States citizens, it taxes them 'in their individual capacities' as 'the people of America'—not as residents of a particular State." But unless Justice Ginsburg thinks that there is no limit to the amount of money that can be squeezed out of taxpayers, heavy federal taxation diminishes the practical ability of States to collect their own taxes.

whether such a law would be allowed under the spending power, the Solicitor General responded that it would.

E

[I]n structuring the ACA, Congress unambiguously signaled its belief that every State would have no real choice but to go along with the Medicaid Expansion. If the anticoercion rule does not apply in this case, then there is no such rule. . . . [M]edicaid has long been the largest federal program of grants to the States. In 2010, the Federal Government directed more than $552 billion in federal funds to the States. *This amount equals nearly 22% of all state expenditures combined.*

The Court of Appeals concluded that the States failed to establish coercion in this case in part because the "states have the power to tax and raise revenue, and therefore can create and fund programs of their own if they do not like Congress's terms." But the sheer size of this federal spending program in relation to state expenditures means that a State would be very hard pressed to compensate for the loss of federal funds by cutting other spending or raising additional revenue. [For example,] if Arizona lost federal Medicaid funding, the State would have to commit an additional 33% of all its state expenditures to fund an equivalent state program along the lines of pre-expansion Medicaid. This means that the State would have to allocate 45% of its annual expenditures for that one purpose.

The States are far less reliant on federal funding for any other program. After Medicaid, the next biggest federal funding item is aid to support elementary and secondary education, which amounts to 12.8% of total federal outlays to the States, and equals only 6.6% of all state expenditures combined. . . . [T]he offer that the ACA makes to the States—go along with a dramatic expansion of Medicaid or potentially lose all federal Medicaid funding—is quite unlike anything that we have seen in a prior spending-power case. In South Dakota v. Dole, the total amount that the States would have lost if every single State had refused to comply with the 21-year-old drinking age was approximately $614.7 million—or about 0.19% of all state expenditures combined. South Dakota stood to lose, at most, funding that amounted to less than 1% of its annual state expenditures. Under the ACA, by contrast, the Federal Government has threatened to withhold 42.3% of all federal outlays to the states, or approximately $233 billion. South Dakota stands to lose federal funding equaling 28.9% of its annual state expenditures. Withholding $614.7 million, equaling only 0.19% of all state expenditures combined, is aptly characterized as "relatively mild encouragement," but threatening to withhold $233 billion, equaling 21.86% of all state expenditures combined, is a different matter. . . .

If Congress had thought that States might actually refuse to go along with the expansion of Medicaid, Congress would surely have devised a backup scheme so that the most vulnerable groups in our society, those previously eligible for Medicaid, would not be left out in the cold. But nowhere in the over 900-page Act is such a scheme to be found. . . . The Federal Government does not dispute the inference that Congress anticipated 100% state participation, but it argues that this assumption was based on the fact that ACA's offer was an "exceedingly generous" gift. . . . [But] [i]f that offer is "exceedingly generous," as the Federal Government maintains, why have more than half the States brought this lawsuit, contending that the offer is coercive? And why did Congress find it necessary to threaten that any State refusing to accept this "exceedingly generous" gift would risk losing all Medicaid funds? Congress could have made just the *new* funding provided under the ACA contingent on acceptance of the terms of the Medicaid Expansion. Congress took such an approach in some earlier amendments to Medicaid, separating new coverage requirements and funding from the rest of the program so that only new funding was conditioned on new eligibility extensions. See, *e.g.*, Social Security Amendments of 1972, 86 Stat. 1465.

Congress' decision to do otherwise here reflects its understanding that the ACA offer is not an "exceedingly generous" gift that no State in its right mind would decline. Instead, acceptance of the offer will impose very substantial costs on participating States. . . . [A]fter 2019 the Federal Government will cover only 90% of the costs associated with the Expansion, with state spending projected to increase by at least $20 billion by 2020 as a consequence. . . . [T]he Federal Government [may later] change funding terms and reduce the percentage of funds it will cover. This would leave the States to bear an increasingly large percentage of the bill. Finally, after 2015, the States will have to pick up the tab for 50% of all administrative costs associated with implementing the new program, costs that could approach $12 billion between fiscal years 2014 and 2020.

In sum, it is perfectly clear from the goal and structure of the ACA that the offer of the Medicaid Expansion was one that Congress understood no State could refuse. The Medicaid Expansion therefore exceeds Congress' spending power and cannot be implemented.

[The joint dissent concluded that simply making the Medicaid expansion optional would be inconsistent with the design of the statute; it would rewrite the statute and therefore was not an appropriate remedy. "The Court regards its strained statutory interpretation as judicial modesty. It is not. It amounts instead to a vast judicial overreaching." Therefore the entire Medicaid expansion—including the option for states to participate—must be struck down. Moreover, because both the Medicaid expansion and the individual mandate were unconstitutional, the rest of the ACA would not operate in the manner that Congress intended. Therefore the entire ACA must be struck down.]

DISCUSSION

1. *The spending power after NFIB v. Sebelius.* Note carefully the differences between Chief Justice Roberts's account of the spending power (joined by Justices Breyer and Kagan) and that of the joint dissent.

The joint dissent argues that because the size of the threatened withdrawal of federal funding is so great, the Medicaid expansion is an offer the states cannot refuse, and therefore it is coercive. This might suggest that the federal government may not impose new conditions on (and thus threaten to withdraw funding from) *any* program that has become a sufficiently large percentage of a state's budget. Does the joint dissent's test allow the federal government to abolish existing programs that constitute a significant proportion of a state's budget?

The joint dissenters also argue that if the federal government offers the states participation in a sufficiently large social welfare program, states may not be able to refuse and so the offer is coercive. First, the federal tax dollars paid by a state's citizens that the state forgoes will be given to the poor in other states. Second, the state will have to raise additional state taxes to provide comparable services. Does this mean that it was unconstitutional for Congress to offer the states Medicaid in the first place? Does it mean that there is a limit on how much money the federal government can offer to the states with conditions attached?

Roberts's argument is different. He distinguishes between two situations. In the first, Congress places conditions on funds it gives to states for a particular program. For example, Congress gives highway funds to states in exchange for states' promise that the roads will be built with certain types of materials and will have certain types of safety signs. These conditions, Roberts argues, are perfectly appropriate because they help ensure that Congress's distribution of money serves the general welfare, as required by the text of the General Welfare Clause.

The second situation is when Congress asks states to do something or else it will withdraw funds from an *unrelated* or *independent* program. Imagine, for example, that Congress requires states to spend highway funds on extra roadway signs; but if a state refuses, Congress will withdraw not only its highway funding but also all of its educational grants to the state. In this situation, Roberts argues, we must inquire into whether there is undue coercion.

In South Dakota v. Dole, for example, federal highway funding was made conditional on raising a state's drinking age. *Dole* held that the condition had to be—and was—germane to the purposes for which the funds were offered, in this case, highway safety. Nevertheless, Roberts pointed out, the condition did not concern how states should use the highway funds themselves.

In this sort of situation, when "conditions take the form of threats to terminate other significant independent grants," Roberts argues, courts must inquire whether the bargain is unduly coercive. In *Dole*, the amount of money that the state would lose was very small: about 5 percent of South Dakota's highway funds, and less than half of 1 percent of South Dakota's budget. Therefore, the Court concluded that the bargain was not coercive. In the case of the Medicaid extension, by contrast, "Medicaid spending accounts for over 20 percent of the average State's total budget, with federal funds covering 50 to 83 percent of those costs." Therefore, Roberts concludes, this bargain, which threatens to withdraw at least 10 percent of a state's budget, is coercive. (Note in particular Roberts's statement that although one half of 1 percent would not be coercive, 10 percent would be "dragooning".)

There is an obvious rejoinder: In this case, Congress is not threatening to terminate *another* program. Its conditions are all conditions on states' use of Medicaid funds. The ACA simply expands Medicaid, and all the federal government has done is add new conditions. That is permissible because Congress had reserved the right to add new conditions to Medicaid by statute, and the states agreed to that bargain. In particular, Congress might argue, providing medical care for a larger number of poor people—including working families—may save both the federal government and the states money in the long run, by keeping adults and children from falling into poverty in the first place, ensuring healthier pregnancies, and reducing the number of disabled persons.

Roberts responds that if the changes to an existing program are sufficiently drastic, they are changes in kind rather than degree, and the resulting program is a "new" and independent program. In essence, Roberts says, Congress is threatening to withdraw funding from Old Medicaid if the states do not agree to participate in

New Medicaid. It is true that Congress reserved the right to add new conditions to Medicaid in its original agreement with the states. However, "[a] State could hardly anticipate that Congress's reservation of the right to 'alter' or 'amend' the Medicaid program included the power to transform it so dramatically." Because there is no fair warning, courts should treat the new conditions as part of a new program separate from Old Medicaid. Therefore, we must ask whether the amount that Congress threatens to withdraw from the older program is so great as to be coercive.

How would this test apply to other federal statutes, for example, federal civil rights laws? Title IX of the Education Amendments of 1972 and Title VI of the Civil Rights Act of 1964 impose conditions on federal grants of funds to states and local governments and require nondiscrimination on the basis of sex, race, and other categories. The Civil Rights Restoration Act of 1988, 42 U.S.C. §2000d4a, states that state agencies, school districts, and municipalities that receive federal funds must comply with these laws in all areas of their operations, not merely in the particular program or activity that has received federal funding. If Congress amended its civil rights laws to prohibit sexual orientation discrimination in entities that receive federal funds, could states refuse to accept the new conditions on the grounds that Congress had created an unexpected "new" program? On the grounds that they had become dependent on federal funding for many decades and could not realistically refuse any new conditions?

2. *More workarounds.* How easy will it be for Congress to work around Roberts's new test? For example, could Congress simply abolish Medicaid and create a new program in its place and invite the states to participate? Could Congress stipulate that a state may participate in Medicaid for only a year at a time and then must reapply each year to a new program in order to receive funding?

Congress can, if it wishes, simply convert Medicaid into a fully federal program like Medicare. But then it would have to increase the number of federal employees in order to administer the program. Are there good reasons for the federal government to ask states to administer federal-state cooperative programs like Medicaid? How does Roberts's new test affect the federal government's incentives?

4. The Treaty Power

BOND v. UNITED STATES, 572 U.S. 844 (2014): In 1997 the United States ratified the international Convention on the Prohibition of the Development, Production, Stockpiling, and Use of Chemical Weapons and on Their Destruction. The treaty is not self-executing, and in order to implement it, Congress enacted the Chemical Weapons Convention Implementation Act of 1998. The statute forbids any person knowingly to "possess[ ] or use . . . any chemical weapon," defined as "[a] toxic chemical" not used for "[a]ny peaceful purpose related to an industrial, agricultural, research, medical, or pharmaceutical activity or other activity."

Petitioner Bond discovered that her husband had an affair with her best friend, Myrlinda Haynes. Seeking revenge, she spread two toxic chemicals on Haynes's car, mailbox, and door knob, hoping that Haynes would develop an uncomfortable rash. Haynes suffered a minor chemical burn that she treated by rinsing with water; otherwise Bond's attempt at revenge was entirely unsuccessful. Federal prosecutors charged Bond with violating the Implementation Act, and Bond challenged the Act on the grounds that it was beyond Congress's powers.

Chief Justice Roberts, writing for six Justices, held that it was unnecessary to reach the constitutional question. Invoking the clear statement rule of Gregory v. Ashcroft and United States v. Bass, 404 U.S. 336 (1971), the Court held that the Implementation Act did not reach Bond's conduct: "[I]t is appropriate to refer to basic principles of federalism embodied in the Constitution to resolve ambiguity in a federal statute. In this case, the ambiguity derives from the improbably broad reach of the [term] 'chemical weapon' . . . ; the deeply serious consequences of adopting such a boundless reading; and the lack of any apparent need to do so in light of the context from which the statute arose—a treaty about chemical warfare and terrorism. [W]e can insist on a clear indication that Congress meant to reach purely local crimes, before interpreting the statute's expansive language in a way that intrudes on the police power of the States." Roberts explained that "[T]he chemicals in this case are not of the sort that an ordinary person would associate with instruments of chemical warfare." Accordingly, the Act should not be "transform[ed] . . . from one whose core concerns are acts of war, assassination, and terrorism into a massive federal anti-poisoning regime that reaches the simplest of assaults."

Justice Scalia, joined by Justices Thomas, concurred in the judgment. He argued that the Court should reach the constitutional question and limit Congress's powers. He denied that the Necessary and Proper Clause gives Congress the power "to enact laws for carrying into execution 'Treaties,' even treaties that do not execute themselves, such as the Chemical Weapons Convention." The Necessary and Proper Clause, Scalia, explained, gives Congress the power to "[t]o make all Laws which shall be necessary and proper for carrying into Execution the foregoing Powers and all other Powers vested by this Constitution in the Government of the United States, or in any Department or Officer thereof." But the Treaty Power of Article II only gives the President and the Senate the power "to make Treaties," not to enforce them: "[A] power to help the President *make* treaties is not a power to *implement* treaties already made."

Justice Thomas, joined by Justices Scalia and Alito, also concurred in the judgment. He argued that "the Treaty Power can be used to arrange intercourse with other nations, but not to regulate purely domestic affairs. . . . [T]he Treaty Power is limited to matters of international intercourse. Even if a treaty may reach some local matters, it still *must* relate to intercourse with other nations." Thomas argued that the Court's central precedent construing the Treaty Power, Missouri v. Holland [see Chapter 4, Section IV.D] was correct on its facts, although he disagreed with its broad statement of congressional power. "[T]he treaty at issue addressed migratory birds that were 'only transitorily within the State and ha[d] no permanent habitat therein.' . . . As such, the birds were naturally a matter of international intercourse because they were creatures in international transit." Thomas added, "I acknowledge that the distinction between matters of international intercourse and matters of purely domestic regulation may not be obvious in all cases. But this Court has long recognized that the Treaty Power is limited, and hypothetical difficulties in line-drawing are no reason to ignore a constitutional limit on federal power. . . ."

Justice Alito also concurred in the judgment: "I believe that the treaty power is limited to agreements that address matters of legitimate international concern. . . . [T]he heart of the Convention clearly represents a valid exercise of the treaty power. But insofar as the Convention may be read to obligate the United States to enact domestic legislation criminalizing conduct of the sort at issue in this case, which typically is the sort of conduct regulated by the States, the Convention exceeds the scope of the treaty power."

DISCUSSION

1. *An unclear statement?* The *Bond* litigation, which encompassed many years, and two separate Supreme Court decisions, was organized as a full-throated attack on Missouri v. Holland's statement that "If the treaty is valid there can be no dispute about the validity of the statute under Article 1, Section 8, as a necessary and proper means to execute the powers of the Government." The concern of *Holland*'s critics is that this might allow an end-run around constitutional limits on federal power. The majority chose not to address that question. Instead, its clear statement rule allows federal courts to impose federalism limitations on legislation that implements treaties through statutory construction.

If a majority of the Justices were unwilling to impose limits on the Treaty Power in this case, it is hard to think of a situation in which the current Court would be tempted. Nevertheless, Justice Thomas lays a marker for future litigation, perhaps hoping that new appointments will change the Court's mind.

Note that one irony of the Court's clear statement rule is that the actual scope of the Implementation Act has now become less clear. Future litigation will have to determine whether a particular chemical is "of the sort that an ordinary person would associate with instruments of chemical warfare" or whether a toxic chemical is used in ways related to "war, assassination, and terrorism." The Court notes later in the opinion that dumping chemicals in a city's water supply might be prohibited by the statute even if the chemicals are not the sort used in chemical warfare. Does terrorism have to be motivated by purely political goals? Should the statute reach a case in which a person poisons the city's water supply because his girlfriend had recently broken up with him?

2. *"Purely domestic affairs."* Justice Thomas argues that the Treaty Power should be limited to questions of international concern or "international intercourse," but should not reach matters of purely domestic concern. The problem is making sense of this distinction in the modern world. Today countries are interested in reaching agreements on a wide variety of questions ranging from human rights to the environment, public health, terrorism and kidnapping. That is because many seemingly "domestic" concerns have spillover effects internationally, and vice-versa.

Both Justice Scalia and Thomas are concerned about the expanding scope of treaties, which, in Scalia's words, have "sought to regulate states' treatment of their own citizens, or even 'the activities of individuals and private entities.'" One important reason for this is the growth of international human rights discourse. Human rights claims often seek to regulate the way that nation states treat their own citizens or people living within their borders. The litigation in *Bond* occurred against the background of a larger political debate over whether international law in general, and human rights treaties in particular, unduly interfere with American sovereignty. Note that while a federalism objection seeks to limit federal power, an objection based on sovereignty is an assertion of national power. How are the two concerns connected?

American foreign policy has long been concerned with the treatment and well-being of people in other countries for economic, diplomatic and security reasons, as well as for "purely" humanitarian reasons. Human rights problems often become economic, military, and strategic problems, and vice-versa. If America is concerned with how other countries treat people living within their borders, why should other countries not be equally interested in how Americans treat people living within the United States? Justice Thomas "acknowledge[s] that the distinction between matters of international intercourse and matters of purely domestic regulation may not be obvious in all cases." Can you think of a plausible way to draw this line?

3. *What is the scope of the Treaty Power?* A central purpose of the new national government created by the 1787 Constitution was to enable to the national government to deal effectively with foreign affairs. That meant that the federal government had to have the power to make credible commitments to foreign powers in order to promote the interests of the Union as a whole. If the federal government "wrote checks that could not be cashed," other countries would be less likely to deal with it cooperatively and peacefully. This basic structural insight suggests that (with a few exceptions to be noted presently) as long as another country is genuinely interested in bargaining over a particular subject matter, it is a proper concern of the Treaty Power.

It follows that sham treaties would not be constitutional. Imagine that the United States agrees with the government of Kuwait that each country will ban the possession of guns near schools, that Kuwait has no other interest in the question, and that the federal government wants to get around the *Lopez* decision. Such a sham treaty would not be within the Treaty Power. (The question remains, of course, how one would prove that such a treaty was a sham.)

Note that this analysis derives the scope of the power to make and implement treaties from the structural need to solve collective action problems in a federal union of states. The basic principle is that federal powers arise from federal problems. But even federal powers that solve such collective action problems are limited in two ways. First, the federal government is always limited by individual rights protections in the Bill of Rights and other parts of the Constitution. See Reid v. Covert, 357 U.S. 1 (1957) (plurality opinion). If so, treaties can't bargain away constitutional rights any more than Congress can rescind these rights through the Commerce Clause. Second, to the extent that states as states enjoy certain intergovernmental immunities (see the discussion of New York v. United States), those immunities would also seem to limit treaties just as they limit the other powers of Congress. So (for example) the United States could not agree to a treaty that required a state to move its capital to a port city to make trade with another nation easier. See Coyle v. Oklahoma, 221 U.S. 559 (1911).

In the Virginia Ratifying Convention, James Madison suggested a further limit on the Treaty Power: "I do not conceive that power is given to the President and Senate to dismember the empire, or to alienate any great, essential right." 3 Elliot 514 (June 18, 1788). Read literally, that would mean that the United States could never give up any portion of its territory through a treaty. That would make little sense given the historical practice of nations; in fact, the United States has settled disputes with other countries (most notably Great Britain) by surrendering claims to disputed territories or by adjusting boundaries. In fact, to settle a war, the United States would presumably be permitted to give up the entire state of Alaska to Russia, although it would not have the power to agree to move Alaska's capital from Juneau to Anchorage!

4. *The treaty power and the foreign and Indian commerce power.* Quite apart from the treaty power, it is worth noting that among its enumerated powers, Congress already has the power "[t]o regulate commerce [that is, intercourse and exchanges] with foreign nations, . . . and with the Indian tribes." A statute genuinely designed to facilitate relations or exchanges with a foreign nation (or an Indian tribe) is already within Congress's enumerated powers even in the absence of a foreign treaty. See Akhil Amar, America's Constitution: A Biography 107 & n.17 (2005); Jack M. Balkin, Living Originalism 155-159 (2011).

5. *Necessary and proper to make but not to execute treaties?* Is Justice Scalia's distinction between the power to make and the power to execute treaties plausible? Does the constitutional text require it? Note that the President's ability to make treaties with other countries in the future may be affected by whether the United States can make credible commitments to execute and enforce its treaties. What is Scalia's best response to this argument? There is also a certain degree of tension between Scalia's argument and *McCulloch*: Chief Justice Marshall argued that implied powers inevitably accompany the enumerated powers. Why isn't the power to enforce or execute treaties an implied power that naturally accompanies the power to make treaties?

6. *The power to implement treaties.* Justice Alito concedes that the Chemical Weapons Convention is a legitimate subject of treaty making. At that point, why doesn't the logic of *McCulloch* and Gonzales v. Raich come into play? In Commerce Clause jurisprudence, Congress has the power to reach purely local activities if it believes that doing so is necessary to effectuate a larger interstate regulatory scheme. Why doesn't it follow, then, that Congress has the power to reach domestic activities as part of a larger international regulatory scheme? At the same time, just as in the Commerce Clause area, the Court's new clear statement rule in *Bond* allows the federal judiciary to interpret statutes sympathetically and narrowly to avoid unnecessary interference in local concerns.

5. The Reconstruction Power

Recall that, in the half-century between 1937 and 1987, the Court had repeatedly upheld various exercises of congressional power under the Thirteenth, Fourteenth, and Fifteenth Amendments. Only once had the Justices held that Congress had exceeded its Reconstruction power—by a 5-4 vote—in a case (Oregon v. Mitchell) that failed to generate a majority opinion and that was quickly overturned by a constitutional amendment. On the other hand, the precise basis for sweeping congressional power under the Reconstruction clauses was not entirely clear. Was the power simply remedial, or dependent on superior fact-finding or line-drawing capacities of Congress, or was it something broader still? When the Court had upheld (or would uphold) a given state practice, could Congress invoke the Reconstruction Amendments to strike down the practice on the simple theory that the Court was wrong—that, properly understood, the Reconstruction Amendments condemned the practice in question? Such sweeping authority might seem to threaten both the Rehnquist Court's resurgent theory of states' rights, and a strong version of judicial supremacy. How would the Court react? The answer came in 1997.

City of Boerne v. Flores

521 U.S. 507 (1997)

KENNEDY, J.

A decision by local zoning authorities to deny a church a building permit was challenged under the Religious Freedom Restoration Act of 1993 (RFRA), 107 Stat. 1488, 42 U.S.C. §2000bb et seq. The case calls into question the authority of Congress to enact RFRA. We conclude the statute exceeds Congress' power. . . .

II

Congress enacted RFRA in direct response to the Court's decision in Employment Div., Dept. of Human Resources of Ore. v. Smith, 494 U.S. 872 (1990). There we considered a Free Exercise Clause claim brought by members of the Native American Church who were denied unemployment benefits when they lost their jobs because they had used peyote. Their practice was to ingest peyote for sacramental purposes, and they challenged an Oregon statute of general applicability which made use of the drug criminal. [Distinguishing away earlier cases, the *Smith* Court held that, absent special circumstances, the Free Exercise Clause was not violated by a facially neutral and secular law, drafted without legislative animus, that had the effect (but not the intent) of interfering with a given religious practice. In particular, the *Smith* Court] declined to apply the balancing test set forth in Sherbert v. Verner, 374 U.S. 398 (1963), under which we would have asked whether Oregon's prohibition substantially burdened a religious practice and, if it did, whether the burden was justified by a compelling government interest. . . .

Four Members of the [*Smith*] Court disagreed. They argued the law placed a substantial burden on the Native American Church members so that it could be upheld only if the law served a compelling state interest and was narrowly tailored to achieve that end. Justice O'Connor concluded Oregon had satisfied the test, while Justice Blackmun, joined by Justice Brennan and Justice Marshall, could see no compelling interest justifying the law's application to the members.

These points of constitutional interpretation were debated by Members of Congress in hearings and floor debates. Many criticized the Court's reasoning, and this disagreement resulted in the passage of RFRA. Congress announced: "(1) The framers of the Constitution, recognizing free exercise of religion as an unalienable right, secured its protection in the First Amendment to the Constitution; (2) laws 'neutral' toward religion may burden religious exercise as surely as laws intended to interfere with religious exercise; (3) governments should not substantially burden religious exercise without compelling justification; (4) in Employment Division v. Smith, the Supreme Court virtually eliminated the requirement that the government justify burdens on religious exercise imposed by laws neutral toward religion; and (5) the compelling interest test as set forth in prior Federal court rulings is a workable test for striking sensible balances between religious liberty and competing prior governmental interests." 42 U.S.C. §2000bb(a).

The Act's stated purposes are:

> "(1) to restore the compelling interest test as set forth in Sherbert v. Verner and Wisconsin v. Yoder, 406 U.S. 205 (1972) and to guarantee its application in all cases where free exercise of religion is substantially burdened; and
>
> "(2) to provide a claim or defense to persons whose religious exercise is substantially burdened by government." §2000bb(b).

RFRA prohibits "government" from "substantially burdening" a person's exercise of religion even if the burden results from a rule of general applicability unless the government can demonstrate the burden "(1) is in furtherance of . . . a compelling governmental interest; and (2) is the least restrictive means of furthering that compelling governmental interest." §2000bb-1. The Act's mandate applies to any "branch, department, agency, instrumentality, and official (or other person acting under color of law) of the United States," as well as to any "State, or . . . subdivision of a State." §2000bb-2(1). . . .

III

A

Under our Constitution, the Federal Government is one of enumerated powers. *McCulloch*; see also The Federalist No. 45. The judicial authority to determine the constitutionality of laws, in cases and controversies, is based on the premise that the "powers of the legislature are defined and limited; and that those limits may not be mistaken, or forgotten, the constitution is written." Marbury v. Madison.

Congress relied on its Fourteenth Amendment enforcement power in enacting the most far reaching and substantial of RFRA's provisions, those which impose its requirements on the States. . . .

The parties disagree over whether RFRA is a proper exercise of Congress' §5 power "to enforce" by "appropriate legislation" the constitutional guarantee that no State shall deprive any person of "life, liberty, or property, without due process of law" nor deny any person "equal protection of the laws."

In defense of the Act respondent contends, with support from the United States as amicus, that RFRA is permissible enforcement legislation. Congress, it is said, is only protecting by legislation one of the liberties guaranteed by the Fourteenth Amendment's Due Process Clause, the free exercise of religion, beyond what is necessary under *Smith*. It is said the congressional decision to dispense with proof of deliberate or overt discrimination and instead concentrate on a law's effects accords with the settled understanding that §5 includes the power to enact legislation designed to prevent as well as remedy constitutional violations. It is further contended that Congress' §5 power is not limited to remedial or preventive legislation. All must acknowledge that §5 is "a positive grant of legislative power" to Congress, Katzenbach v. Morgan. . . .

Legislation which deters or remedies constitutional violations can fall within the sweep of Congress' enforcement power even if in the process it prohibits conduct which is not itself unconstitutional and intrudes into "legislative spheres of autonomy previously reserved to the States." For example, the Court upheld a suspension of literacy tests and similar voting requirements under Congress' parallel power to enforce the provisions of the Fifteenth Amendment as a measure to combat racial discrimination in voting, South Carolina v. Katzenbach, despite the facial constitutionality of the tests under Lassiter v. Northampton County Bd. of Elections. We have also concluded that other measures protecting voting rights are within Congress' power to enforce the Fourteenth and Fifteenth Amendments, despite the burdens those measures placed on the States. South Carolina v. Katzenbach (upholding several provisions of the Voting Rights Act of 1965); Katzenbach v. Morgan (upholding ban on literacy tests that prohibited certain people schooled in Puerto Rico from voting); Oregon v. Mitchell (upholding 5-year nationwide ban on literacy tests and similar voting requirements for registering to vote); City of Rome v. United States (upholding 7-year extension of the Voting Rights Act's requirement that certain jurisdictions preclear any change to a "standard, practice, or procedure with respect to voting").

It is also true, however, that "as broad as the congressional enforcement power is, it is not unlimited." Oregon v. Mitchell (opinion of Black, J.). In assessing the breadth of §5's enforcement power, we begin with its text. Congress has been given the power "to enforce" the "provisions of this article." We agree with respondent, of course, that Congress can enact legislation under §5 enforcing the constitutional right to the free exercise of religion. The "provisions of this article," to which §5 refers, include the Due Process Clause of the Fourteenth Amendment. Congress' power to enforce the Free Exercise Clause follows from our holding in Cantwell v. Connecticut, 310 U.S. 296, 303 (1940), that the "fundamental concept of liberty embodied in [the Fourteenth Amendment's Due Process Clause] embraces the liberties guaranteed by the First Amendment."

Congress' power under §5, however, extends only to "enforcing" the provisions of the Fourteenth Amendment. The Court has described this power as "remedial." The design of the Amendment and the text of §5 are inconsistent with the suggestion that Congress has the power to decree the substance of the Fourteenth Amendment's restrictions on the States. Legislation which alters the meaning of the Free Exercise Clause cannot be said to be enforcing the Clause. Congress does not enforce a constitutional right by changing what the right is. It has been given the power "to enforce," not the power to determine what constitutes a constitutional violation. Were it not so, what Congress would be enforcing would no longer be, in any meaningful sense, the "provisions of [the Fourteenth Amendment]."

While the line between measures that remedy or prevent unconstitutional actions and measures that make a substantive change in the governing law is not easy to discern, and Congress must have wide latitude in determining where it lies, the distinction exists and must be observed. There must be a congruence and proportionality between the injury to be prevented or remedied and the means adopted to that end. Lacking such a connection, legislation may become substantive in operation and effect. History and our case law support drawing the distinction, one apparent from the text of the Amendment.

1[9]

The Fourteenth Amendment's history confirms the remedial, rather than substantive, nature of the Enforcement Clause. The Joint Committee on Reconstruction of the 39th Congress began drafting what would become the Fourteenth Amendment in January 1866. The objections to the Committee's first draft of the Amendment, and the rejection of the draft, have a direct bearing on the central issue of defining Congress' enforcement power. In February, Republican Representative John Bingham of Ohio reported the following draft amendment to the House of Representatives on behalf of the Joint Committee:

> "The Congress shall have power to make all laws which shall be necessary and proper to secure to the citizens of each State all privileges and immunities of citizens in the several States, and to all persons in the several States equal protection in the rights of life, liberty, and property." Cong. Globe, 39th Cong., 1st Sess., 1034 (1866).

The proposal encountered immediate opposition, which continued through three days of debate. Members of Congress from across the political spectrum criticized the Amendment, and the criticisms had a common theme: The proposed Amendment gave Congress too much legislative power at the expense of the existing constitutional structure. Democrats and conservative Republicans argued that the proposed Amendment would give Congress a power to intrude into traditional areas of state responsibility, a power inconsistent with the federal design central to the Constitution. Typifying these views, Republican Representative Robert Hale of New York labeled the Amendment "an utter departure from every principle ever dreamed of by the men who framed our Constitution," and warned that under it "all State legislation, in its codes of civil and criminal jurisprudence and procedures . . . may be overridden, may be repealed or abolished, and the law of Congress established instead." Senator William Stewart of Nevada likewise stated the Amendment would permit "Congress to legislate fully upon all subjects affecting life, liberty, and property," such that "there would not be much left for the State Legislatures," and would thereby "work an entire change in our form of government." . . . Some radicals . . . also objected that giving Congress primary responsibility for enforcing legal equality would place power in the hands of changing congressional majorities.

As a result of these objections having been expressed from so many different quarters, the House voted to table the proposal until April . . . [and] the Joint Committee began drafting a new article of Amendment, which it reported to Congress on April 30, 1866.

Section 1 of the new draft Amendment imposed self-executing limits on the States. Section 5 prescribed that "the Congress shall have power to enforce, by appropriate legislation, the provisions of this article." Under the revised Amendment, Congress' power was no longer plenary but remedial. Congress was granted the power to make the substantive constitutional prohibitions against the States effective. Representative Bingham said the new draft would give Congress "the

9. Note that Justice Scalia, who joined the rest of the Court's opinion, did not join this section discussing the history of the Fourteenth Amendment.

power . . . to protect by national law the privileges and immunities of all the citizens of the Republic . . . whenever the same shall be abridged or denied by the unconstitutional acts of any State." Representative Stevens described the new draft Amendment as "allowing Congress to correct the unjust legislation of the States." See also statement of Sen. Howard (§5 "enables Congress, in case the States shall enact laws in conflict with the principles of the amendment, to correct that legislation by a formal congressional enactment"). The revised Amendment proposal did not raise the concerns expressed earlier regarding broad congressional power to prescribe uniform national laws with respect to life, liberty, and property. After revisions not relevant here, the new measure passed both Houses and was ratified in July 1868 as the Fourteenth Amendment. . . .

The design of the Fourteenth Amendment has proved significant also in maintaining the traditional separation of powers between Congress and the Judiciary. The first eight Amendments to the Constitution set forth self-executing prohibitions on governmental action, and this Court has had primary authority to interpret those prohibitions. The Bingham draft, some thought, departed from that tradition by vesting in Congress primary power to interpret and elaborate on the meaning of the new Amendment through legislation. Under it, "Congress, and not the courts, was to judge whether or not any of the privileges or immunities were not secured to citizens in the several States." While this separation of powers aspect did not occasion the widespread resistance which was caused by the proposal's threat to the federal balance, it nonetheless attracted the attention of various Members. As enacted, the Fourteenth Amendment confers substantive rights against the States which, like the provisions of the Bill of Rights, are self-executing. The power to interpret the Constitution in a case or controversy remains in the Judiciary.

2

The remedial and preventive nature of Congress' enforcement power, and the limitation inherent in the power, were confirmed in our earliest cases on the Fourteenth Amendment. In the Civil Rights Cases, 109 U.S. 3 (1883), the Court invalidated sections of the Civil Rights Act of 1875 which prescribed criminal penalties for denying to any person "the full enjoyment of" public accommodations and conveyances, on the grounds that it exceeded Congress' power by seeking to regulate private conduct. The Enforcement Clause, the Court said, did not authorize Congress to pass "general legislation upon the rights of the citizen, but corrective legislation; that is, such as may be necessary and proper for counteracting such laws as the States may adopt or enforce, and which, by the amendment, they are prohibited from making or enforcing. . . ." The power to "legislate generally upon" life, liberty, and property, as opposed to the "power to provide modes of redress" against offensive state action, was "repugnant" to the Constitution. . . . Although the specific holdings of these early cases might have been superseded or modified, see, e.g., Heart of Atlanta Motel, Inc. v. United States, their treatment of Congress' §5 power as corrective or preventive, not definitional, has not been questioned. . . .

3

Any suggestion that Congress has a substantive, non-remedial power under the Fourteenth Amendment is not supported by our case law. In Oregon v. Mitchell, a majority of the Court concluded Congress had exceeded its enforcement powers by enacting legislation lowering the minimum age of voters from 21 to 18 in state and local elections. The five Members of the Court who reached this conclusion explained that the legislation intruded into an area reserved by the *Constitution to the States*. . . .

There is language in our opinion in Katzenbach v. Morgan which could be interpreted as acknowledging a power in Congress to enact legislation that expands the rights contained in §1 of the Fourteenth Amendment. This is not a necessary interpretation, however, or even the best one. . . . The Court perceived a factual basis on which Congress could have concluded that New York's literacy requirement "constituted an invidious discrimination in violation of the Equal Protection Clause." [The Court's] rationales for upholding §4(e) rested on unconstitutional discrimination by New York and Congress' reasonable attempt to combat it. As Justice Stewart explained in Oregon v. Mitchell, interpreting *Morgan* to give Congress the power to interpret the Constitution "would require an enormous extension of that decision's rationale." If Congress could define its own powers by altering the Fourteenth Amendment's meaning, no longer would the Constitution be "superior paramount law, unchangeable by ordinary means." It would be "on a level with ordinary legislative acts, and, like other acts, . . . alterable when the legislature shall please to alter it." Marbury v. Madison. Under this approach, it is difficult to conceive of a principle that would limit congressional power. Shifting legislative majorities could change the Constitution and effectively circumvent the difficult and detailed amendment process contained in Article V.

B

Respondent contends that RFRA is a proper exercise of Congress' remedial or preventive power. The Act, it is said, is a reasonable means of protecting the free exercise of religion as defined by *Smith*. It prevents and remedies laws which are enacted with the unconstitutional object of targeting religious beliefs and practices. To avoid the difficulty of proving such violations, it is said, Congress can simply invalidate any law which imposes a substantial burden on a religious practice unless it is justified by a compelling interest and is the least restrictive means of accomplishing that interest. If Congress can prohibit laws with discriminatory effects in order to prevent racial discrimination in violation of the Equal Protection Clause, then it can do the same, respondent argues, to promote religious liberty.

While preventive rules are sometimes appropriate remedial measures, there must be a congruence between the means used and the ends to be achieved. The appropriateness of remedial measures must be considered in light of the evil presented. Strong measures appropriate to address one harm may be an unwarranted response to another, lesser one. A comparison between RFRA and the Voting Rights Act is instructive. In contrast to the record which confronted Congress and the judiciary in the voting rights cases, RFRA's legislative record lacks examples of modern instances of generally applicable laws passed because of religious bigotry. The history of persecution in this country detailed in the hearings mentions no episodes occurring in the past 40 years. . . . Rather, the emphasis of the hearings was on laws of general applicability which place incidental burdens on religion. Much of the discussion centered upon anecdotal evidence of autopsies performed on Jewish individuals and Hmong immigrants in violation of their religious beliefs, and on zoning regulations and historic preservation laws (like the one at issue here), which as an incident of their normal operation, have adverse effects on churches and synagogues. It is difficult to maintain that they are examples of legislation enacted or enforced due to animus or hostility to the burdened religious practices or that they indicate some widespread pattern of religious discrimination in this country. Congress' concern was with the incidental burdens imposed, not the object or purpose of the legislation. This lack of support in the legislative record, however, is not RFRA's most serious shortcoming. . . .

Regardless of the state of the legislative record, RFRA cannot be considered remedial, preventive legislation, if those terms are to have any meaning. RFRA is so out of proportion to a supposed remedial or preventive object that it cannot be understood as responsive to, or designed to prevent, unconstitutional behavior. It appears, instead, to attempt a substantive change in constitutional protections. Preventive measures prohibiting certain types of laws may be appropriate when there is reason to believe that many of the laws affected by the congressional enactment have a significant likelihood of being unconstitutional. . . .

RFRA is not so confined. Sweeping coverage ensures its intrusion at every level of government, displacing laws and prohibiting official actions of almost every description and regardless of subject matter. RFRA's restrictions apply to every agency and official of the Federal, State, and local Governments. RFRA applies to all federal and state law, statutory or otherwise, whether adopted before or after its enactment. RFRA has no termination date or termination mechanism. Any law is subject to challenge at any time by any individual who alleges a substantial burden on his or her free exercise of religion.

The reach and scope of RFRA distinguish it from other measures passed under Congress' enforcement power, even in the area of voting rights. In South Carolina v. Katzenbach, the challenged provisions were confined to those regions of the country where voting discrimination had been most flagrant, and affected a discrete class of state laws, i.e., state voting laws. Furthermore, to ensure that the reach of the Voting Rights Act was limited to those cases in which constitutional violations were most likely (in order to reduce the possibility of overbreadth), the coverage under the Act would terminate "at the behest of States and political subdivisions in which the danger of substantial voting discrimination has not materialized during the preceding five years." The provisions restricting and banning literacy tests, upheld in Katzenbach v. Morgan, and Oregon v. Mitchell, attacked a particular type of voting qualification, one with a long history as a "notorious means to deny and abridge voting rights on racial grounds." In *City of Rome,* the Court rejected a challenge to the constitutionality of a Voting Rights Act provision which required certain jurisdictions to submit changes in electoral practices to the Department of Justice for preimplementation review. The requirement was placed only on jurisdictions with a history of intentional racial discrimination in voting. Like the provisions at issue in South Carolina v. Katzenbach, this provision permitted a covered jurisdiction to avoid preclearance requirements under certain conditions and, moreover, lapsed in seven years. This is not to say, of course, that §5 legislation requires termination dates, geographic restrictions, or egregious predicates. Where, however, a congressional enactment pervasively prohibits constitutional state action in an effort to remedy or to prevent unconstitutional state action, limitations of this kind tend to ensure Congress' means are proportionate to ends legitimate under §5.

The stringent test RFRA demands of state laws reflects a lack of proportionality or congruence between the means adopted and the legitimate end to be achieved. If an objector can show a substantial burden on his free exercise, the State must demonstrate a compelling governmental interest and show that the law is the least restrictive means of furthering its interest. Claims that a law substantially burdens someone's exercise of religion will often be difficult to contest. Requiring a State to demonstrate a compelling interest and show that it has adopted the least restrictive means of achieving that interest is the most demanding test known to constitutional law. If "'compelling interest' really means what it says . . . many laws will not meet the test. . . . [The test] would open the prospect of constitutionally required religious exemptions from civic obligations of almost every conceivable kind." Laws valid under *Smith* would fall under RFRA without regard to whether they had the object of stifling or punishing free exercise. We make these observations not to reargue the position of the majority in *Smith* but to illustrate the substantive alteration of its holding attempted by RFRA. Even assuming RFRA would be interpreted in effect to mandate some lesser test, say one equivalent to intermediate scrutiny, the statute nevertheless would require searching judicial scrutiny of state law with the attendant likelihood of invalidation. This is a considerable congressional intrusion into the States' traditional prerogatives and general authority to regulate for the health and welfare of their citizens.

The substantial costs RFRA exacts, both in practical terms of imposing a heavy litigation burden on the States and in terms of curtailing their traditional general regulatory power, far exceed any pattern or practice of unconstitutional conduct under the Free Exercise Clause as interpreted in *Smith*. Simply put, RFRA is not designed to identify and counteract state laws likely to be unconstitutional because of their treatment of religion. In most cases, the state laws to which RFRA applies are not ones which will have been motivated by religious bigotry. If a state law disproportionately burdened a particular class of religious observers, this circumstance might be evidence of an impermissible legislative motive. Cf. Washington v. Davis, 426 U.S. 229 (1976). RFRA's substantial burden test, however, is not even a discriminatory effects or disparate impact test. It is a reality of the modern regulatory state that numerous state laws, such as the zoning regulations at issue here, impose a substantial burden on a large class of individuals. When the exercise of religion has been burdened in an incidental way by a law of general application, it does not follow that the persons affected have been burdened any more than other citizens, let alone burdened because of their religious beliefs. . . .

When Congress acts within its sphere of power and responsibilities, it has not just the right but the duty to make its own informed judgment on the meaning and force of the Constitution. This has been clear from the early days of the Republic. In 1789, when a Member of the House of Representatives objected to a debate on the constitutionality of legislation based on the theory that "it would be officious" to consider the constitutionality of a measure that did not affect the House, James Madison explained that "it is incontrovertibly of as much importance to this branch of the Government as to any other, that the constitution should be preserved entire. It is our duty." Were it otherwise, we would not afford Congress the presumption of validity its enactments now enjoy.

Our national experience teaches that the Constitution is preserved best when each part of the government respects both the Constitution and the proper actions and determinations of the other branches. When the Court has interpreted the Constitution, it has acted within the province of the Judicial Branch, which embraces the duty to say what the law is. Marbury v. Madison. When the political branches of the Government act against the background of a judicial interpretation of the Constitution already issued, it must be understood that in later cases and controversies the Court will treat its precedents with the respect due them under settled principles, including stare decisis, and contrary expectations must be disappointed. RFRA was designed to control cases and controversies, such as the one before us; but as the provisions of the federal statute here invoked are beyond congressional authority, it is this Court's precedent, not RFRA, which must control. . . . Broad as the power of Congress is under the Enforcement Clause of the Fourteenth Amendment, RFRA contradicts vital principles necessary to maintain separation of powers and the federal balance.

STEVENS, J., concurring.

In my opinion, [RFRA] is a "law respecting an establishment of religion" that violates the First Amendment to the Constitution. . . .

If the historic landmark on the hill in Boerne happened to be a museum or an art gallery owned by an atheist, it would not be eligible for an exemption from the city ordinances that forbid an enlargement of the structure. Because the landmark is owned by the Catholic Church, it is claimed that RFRA gives its owner a federal statutory entitlement to an exemption from a generally applicable, neutral civil law. Whether the Church would actually prevail under the statute or not, the statute has provided the Church with a legal weapon that no atheist or agnostic can obtain. This governmental preference for religion, as opposed to irreligion, is forbidden by the First Amendment.

[The concurring opinion of Scalia, J., joined by Stevens, J., defending the correctness of *Smith*, is omitted.]

O'CONNOR, J., dissenting, joined in part by BREYER, J. . . .

I remain of the view that *Smith* was wrongly decided, and I would use this case to reexamine the Court's holding there. Therefore, I would direct the parties to brief the question whether *Smith* represents the correct understanding of the Free Exercise Clause and set the case for reargument. If the Court were to correct the misinterpretation of the Free Exercise Clause set forth in *Smith*, it would simultaneously put our First Amendment jurisprudence back on course and allay the legitimate concerns of a majority in Congress who believed that *Smith* improperly restricted religious liberty. We would then be in a position to review RFRA in light of a proper interpretation of the Free Exercise Clause.

I

I agree with much of the reasoning set forth in Part III-A of the Court's opinion. Indeed, if I agreed with the Court's standard in *Smith*, I would join the opinion. As the Court's careful and thorough historical analysis shows, Congress lacks the "power to decree the substance of the Fourteenth Amendment's restrictions on the

States." Rather, its power under §5 of the Fourteenth Amendment extends only to enforcing the Amendment's provisions. In short, Congress lacks the ability independently to define or expand the scope of constitutional rights by statute. Accordingly, whether Congress has exceeded its §5 powers turns on whether there is a "congruence and proportionality between the injury to be prevented or remedied and the means adopted to that end." This recognition does not, of course, in any way diminish Congress' obligation to draw its own conclusions regarding the Constitution's meaning. Congress, no less than this Court, is called upon to consider the requirements of the Constitution and to act in accordance with its dictates. But when it enacts legislation in furtherance of its delegated powers, Congress must make its judgments consistent with this Court's exposition of the Constitution and with the limits placed on its legislative authority by provisions such as the Fourteenth Amendment.

The Court's analysis of whether RFRA is a constitutional exercise of Congress' §5 power, set forth in Part III-B of its opinion, is premised on the assumption that *Smith* correctly interprets the Free Exercise Clause. This is an assumption that I do not accept. I continue to believe that *Smith* adopted an improper standard for deciding free exercise claims. In *Smith*, five Members of this Court—without briefing or argument on the issue—interpreted the Free Exercise Clause to permit the government to prohibit, without justification, conduct mandated by an individual's religious beliefs, so long as the prohibition is generally applicable. Contrary to the Court's holding in that case, however, the Free Exercise Clause is not simply an antidiscrimination principle that protects only against those laws that single out religious practice for unfavorable treatment. Rather, the Clause is best understood as an affirmative guarantee of the right to participate in religious practices and conduct without impermissible governmental interference, even when such conduct conflicts with a neutral, generally applicable law. Before *Smith*, our free exercise cases were generally in keeping with this idea: where a law substantially burdened religiously motivated conduct—regardless whether it was specifically targeted at religion or applied generally—we required government to justify that law with a compelling state interest and to use means narrowly tailored to achieve that interest.

The Court's rejection of this principle in *Smith* is supported neither by precedent nor . . . by history. The decision has harmed religious liberty. For example, a Federal District Court, in reliance on *Smith*, ruled that the Free Exercise Clause was not implicated where Hmong natives objected on religious grounds to their son's autopsy, conducted pursuant to a generally applicable state law. The Court of Appeals for the Eighth Circuit held that application of a city's zoning laws to prevent a church from conducting services in an area zoned for commercial uses raised no free exercise concerns, even though the city permitted secular not-for-profit organizations in that area. . . .

Stare decisis concerns should not prevent us from revisiting our holding in *Smith*. "Stare decisis is a principle of policy and not a mechanical formula of adherence to the latest decision, however recent and questionable, when such adherence involves collision with a prior doctrine more embracing in its scope, intrinsically sounder, and verified by experience." This principle is particularly true in constitutional cases, where—as this case so plainly illustrates—"correction through legislative action is practically impossible." . . .

Accordingly, I believe that we should reexamine our holding in *Smith*, and do so in this very case. In its place, I would return to a rule that requires government to justify any substantial burden on religiously motivated conduct by a compelling state interest and to impose that burden only by means narrowly tailored to achieve that interest. . . .

SOUTER, J., dissenting.

To decide whether the Fourteenth Amendment gives Congress sufficient power to enact the Religious Freedom Restoration Act, the Court measures the legislation against the free-exercise standard of *Smith*. . . . I have serious doubts about the precedential value of the *Smith* rule and its entitlement to adherence. . . . [T]his case should be set down for reargument permitting plenary reexamination of the issue. Since the Court declines to follow that course, our free-exercise law remains marked by an "intolerable tension," and the constitutionality of the Act of Congress to enforce the free-exercise right cannot now be soundly decided. I would therefore dismiss the writ of certiorari as improvidently granted, and I accordingly dissent from the Court's disposition of this case.

BREYER, J., dissenting.

I agree with Justice O'Connor that the Court should direct the parties to brief the question whether *Smith* was correctly decided, and set this case for reargument. I do not, however, find it necessary to consider the question whether, assuming *Smith* is correct, §5 of the Fourteenth Amendment would authorize Congress to enact the legislation before us. . . .

DISCUSSION

1. *Challenging the Court's account.* None of the Justices squarely took issue with the majority's analysis of congressional power under §5 (although Justices Breyer and Souter did not reach the question). But consider the following counterarguments.

The textual counterargument: The Court says that whenever Congress goes beyond the Court's interpretation of the substantive rights conferred by §1 of the Fourteenth Amendment, Congress thereby ceases to "enforce" §1. Congress has the power only to "enforce" the true meaning of §1, not to add to it. But a pro-Congress critic might see this assertion as perfectly circular and question-begging. Congress believes it is not *adding to* the meaning of free exercise. Rather (on this view), *Smith* wrongly subtracted from the meaning and Congress is merely restoring it, *enforcing* its true meaning. Why—textually—does the Court's view of *Smith*'s rightness trump Congress's view of its wrongness? At this point, the question becomes in part, who decides the true meaning of §1? To a textualist, isn't it relevant that the Fourteenth Amendment explicitly speaks of *Congress* as enforcer? Perhaps Congress is not the *exclusive* enforcer; but doesn't the text signal a very important role for Congress, above and beyond the Court (which of course is not textually mentioned in §5)?

The "intratextual" and doctrinal counterargument: "Intratextualism" is a technique of parsing the words of a contested clause in light of other clauses of the

Constitution that use similar or identical words. Recall, for example, Chief Justice Marshall's efforts in *McCulloch* to parse the Article I, §8 words "necessary and proper" in light of the Article I, §10 words "absolutely necessary"; and Justice Thomas's efforts in *Lopez* to construe the word "commerce" in the Commerce Clause in light of the word "commerce" in the port preference clause. Akhil Reed Amar has criticized *Boerne* for failing to pay heed to this technique:[10]

> [T]he words of Section 5 do not stand alone. They are part of a single coherent Constitution and must be read alongside the rest of the document. And when they are, a strong—perhaps devastating—objection to Justice Kennedy's overly confident assertions arises, an objection that he does not see because he is reading with blinkers on. Here are the words of Section 2 of the Thirteenth Amendment: "Congress shall have power to enforce this article by appropriate legislation." These words are *in pari materia* with the words of Section 5 of the Fourteenth Amendment. A very powerful intratextual presumption arises that these two parallel clauses must be interpreted in parallel fashion. What's sauce for one should be sauce for the other. But Section 2 of the Thirteenth Amendment has not been read simply to allow Congress to remedy violations of Section 1 (of the Thirteenth). Acting under Section 2, Congress has passed broad substantive legislation ranging far beyond the self-executing rights under Section 1 (as defined by the Supreme Court). No court ever said, or ever would say, that when private person A refuses to deal commercially with private person B because B is black, this refusal is "slavery" or "involuntary servitude" within the meaning of Section 1 of the Thirteenth Amendment. And yet the Court in the famous case of Jones v. Alfred Mayer Co. upheld congressional laws banning this refusal under its Section 2 enforcement power.
>
> The *Boerne* Court says that once Congress goes beyond remedial enforcement of the Fourteenth Amendment Section 1, Congress would no longer be enforcing the Amendment "in any meaningful sense." If this is so for the Fourteenth, why not for the Thirteenth, too? Or to be more blunt, as this is *not* true for the Thirteenth, why is it so for the Fourteenth? The *Boerne* Court offers no answer to the obvious inconsistency here—it never even sees the issue. It is reading Section 5 of the Fourteenth and does not even see Section 2 of the Thirteenth.

Amar proceeds to argue that, just as Congress has substantive power under the Thirteenth Amendment to define "badges and incidents" of slavery that go beyond judicial definitions of slavery under §1 (of the Thirteenth), so Congress under the Fourteenth Amendment should have substantive, and not merely remedial, power to define "badges and incidents" of freedom and citizenship that go beyond judicial interpretations of rights under §1 (of the Fourteenth).

The structural counterargument: To support its view that only the Court can ultimately determine the true meaning of §1 rights (which Congress may then remedially enforce under §5), the *Boerne* majority wraps itself in *Marbury*. But

10. Akhil Reed Amar, Intratextualism, 112 Harv. L. Rev. 747, at 822-823 (1999).

isn't this too quick? If more-than-remedial congressional power in *Boerne* would have violated *Marbury*, why didn't more-than-remedial congressional power in *Jones v. Alfred Mayer*? Even under *Marbury*, other branches of the federal government are sometimes allowed to have a broader view of a constitutional right, and to make that broader view stick. For example, courts upheld the Sedition Act of 1798, but President Jefferson deemed the Act unconstitutional and pardoned all concerned. Surely Congress could also have repealed this Act, and done so on the simple theory that the courts were wrong? Likewise, in RFRA—putting aside Establishment Clause concerns (as did the *Boerne* majority)—Congress was free to impose an effects test on *federal* practices burdening religion—and to do so simply because it thought *Smith* wrong. And individual state legislatures were likewise free to provide similar protections in their respective states. None of this threatens *Marbury*, rightly understood; judicial review sets a floor of rights-protection, not a ceiling. If so, what is wrong with saying that although Congress cannot generally bless a state practice that the Court has held unconstitutional under §1, Congress can *add to* the list of "privileges" and "immunities" that states shall not abridge? (Note that Madison at the Philadelphia Convention sought to vest Congress with a general right to veto state practices that Congress thought violated the Constitution. Madison also believed in federal judicial review over states. Is there anything contradictory about holding states to both federal judicial and federal legislative review, with states generally held to whichever standard is higher?) These arguments return us, in a way, to Brennan's ratchet, see Katzenbach v. Morgan, Chapter 5. On this view, even though Congress should have very broad power under the Fourteenth Amendment to outlaw state practices that violate *Congress's* understanding of Reconstruction values of liberty, equality, and citizenship, this broad power does not exempt Congress from compliance with affirmative limits on its powers such as those set out in the first nine amendments. Congress may not generally bless a state law that denies Fourteenth Amendment due process (as defined by the Court) in part because Congress *itself* may not violate Fifth Amendment due process (as defined by the Court). Of course, tricky issues arise when conflicting constitutional rights bump up against each other—for example, when overly broad protections of the rights of Black people might be seen as violating the rights of non-Blacks in the context of affirmative action, or when overly broad protections of free exercise run afoul of Establishment Clause principles. But the Court opinion in *Boerne* did not rely on the Establishment Clause; only Justice Stevens did.

The historical counterargument: Several scholars have sharply criticized the *Boerne* Court's historical account, including Michael McConnell,[11] Mark Graber,[12] Jack Balkin,[13] and Akhil Reed Amar.

11. Michael W. McConnell, Institutions and Interpretation: A Critique of City of Boerne v. Flores, 111 Harv. L. Rev. 153, 182 (1997)

12. Mark A. Graber, The Constitution as a Whole: A Partial Political Science Perspective, 33 U. Rich. L. Rev. 343 (1999).

13. Jack M. Balkin, The Reconstruction Power, 85 N.Y.U L. Rev. 1801 (2010).

Akhil Reed Amar, Intratextualism

112 Harv. L. Rev. 747 (1999)

[T]he framers of the Fourteenth Amendment itself—the Thirty-Ninth Congress—had a broad view of Section 2 of the Thirteenth Amendment. We know this because they adopted the Civil Rights Act of 1866, which swept far beyond merely prohibiting slavery and involuntary servitude, and the basis for their action was Section 2 of the Thirteenth Amendment. At the very moment that they were proposing another "enforcement" clause in the Fourteenth Amendment, they were speaking loud and clear about what the parallel enforcement clause of the Thirteenth Amendment meant.[a] And they said it meant more than mere remedial legislation.

This noteworthy fact about the Thirty-Ninth Congress—which, again, Justice Kennedy never notices because he never sees the freight train coming—seems much stronger than the facts about that Congress that he does mention. He stresses the fact that lawmakers rejected an early draft of the Fourteenth Amendment that in effect would have given Congress plenary legislative power. But there is a large gap between plenary power on one extreme and only remedial power on the other. To reject the former is not to affirm the latter—as is clear if we spend just an instant thinking about Section 2 of the Thirteenth Amendment, under which Congress has less than plenary and more than remedial power. In the Thirteenth Amendment this middle ground is captured by the concept of "badges and incidents" of slavery, which Section 1 does not abolish of its own force, but which can be abolished by Congress under Section 2.

[There are] comparable middle-ground possibilities for the Fourteenth Amendment. . . . [For example,] Congress could have power to define rights that in good faith it considers truly fundamental and basic, and these rights, once defined—"badges and incidents of freedom and citizenship"—would thereafter be enforceable, even against states, as "privileges" and "immunities" of American "citizens." . . .

The legislative history that *Boerne* invokes supports my middle-ground positions. The early draft of the Fourteenth Amendment, which was rejected because it in effect conferred plenary power on Congress, read as follows:

> The Congress shall have power to make all laws which shall be necessary and proper to secure to the citizens of each State all privileges and immunities of citizens in the several States, and to all persons in the several States equal protection in the rights of life, liberty, and property.

---

a. Admittedly, Representative John Bingham, the father of Section 1 of the Fourteenth Amendment, did not share his colleagues' broad view of Section 2 of the Thirteenth. (Or if he did, he thought that even under a broad view, encompassing substantive and not merely remedial enforcement, Section 2 was still not broad enough to support the wide-ranging Civil Rights Bill.) But on this issue Bingham was outvoted by two-thirds of his colleagues, who overrode President Johnson's veto—the same two-thirds necessary to pass the Fourteenth Amendment on to the states.

The objection to this draft was twofold: Congress would have power to legislate even in the absence of any state misconduct and even on private parties (the state action issue), and would have power over virtually everything, because everything implicates life, liberty, and property. But note how the middle ground I am proposing avoids both problems. First, it accepts the state action doctrine—Congress can legislate rights against states, not private persons. Second, it further limits Congress's power by focusing on privileges and immunities of citizens, not life, liberty, and property. Life, liberty, and property encompass almost everything, but the privileges and immunities of citizens that I am highlighting include only things that are in a real and sincere sense deemed truly fundamental.

The rejected draft is also noteworthy for its intratextual echo of the Article I, Section 8, Necessary and Proper Clause. This clause was associated with broad congressional power in *McCulloch*. It might be thought that the abandonment of this language in the final version of Section 5 signaled a retreat from a broad view of congressional enforcement authority. On the contrary, the framers saw the Enforcement Clause phrase "appropriate legislation" as equivalent to the Article I, Section 8 phrase "proper laws." Ordinary dictionaries confirm the obvious etymological link between "proper" and "appropriate." And in one of *McCulloch*'s most famous passages, Marshall cemented this etymological linkage in words that the Thirty-Ninth Congress knew and relied on: "Let the end be legitimate, let it be within the scope of the constitution, and all means which are *appropriate*, which are plainly adapted to that end, which are not prohibited, but consist with the letter and spirit of the constitution, are constitutional."[b] Only a couple of years after the Fourteenth Amendment became part of our supreme law, the Supreme Court itself quoted this famous passage in full and then declared that "it must be taken then as finally settled, so far as judicial decisions can settle anything, that the words" of the Necessary and Proper Clause were "equivalent" to the word "appropriate." [Hepburn v. Griswold, 75 U. S. 603, 615 (1870).] And here is what the Court said in the 1880s, in language prominently relied on in *Jones*, about the Enforcement Clause of the Thirteenth Amendment: "[It] clothes Congress with power to pass all laws necessary and proper for abolishing all badges and incidents of slavery in the United States. . . ." [The Civil Rights Cases, 109 U.S. 3, 20 (1883)].

Overly exuberant statements of judicial supremacy are in vogue these days, but it is ironic to read all this back into the Fourteenth Amendment, in which Congress (the good guys) drafted emphatic constitutional language to repudiate the arrogant *Dred Scott* Court (the bad guys). Congress did not insist on being the only interpreter of fundamental rights. It was aware that it might one day fall into

---

b. Emphasis added. For clear evidence that the 39th Congress had these key words from McCulloch in mind when they drafted the Fourteenth Amendment, see Cong. Globe, 39th Cong., 1st Sess. 1118 (1866) (remarks of Rep. James Wilson). Wilson was the House sponsor of the Civil Rights Act of 1866, which he defended under Section 2 of the Thirteenth Amendment. Doubts about the sufficiency of this basis for congressional power eventually helped lead to congressional adoption of the Fourteenth Amendment, which was (among other things) designed to provide a rock-solid foundation for the Act. In this passage, Wilson defended the pending civil rights bill by quoting verbatim Section 2 of the Thirteenth Amendment and then explicitly linking its wording to the key words from *McCulloch* (which Wilson also quoted verbatim).

the wrong hands, and so it created a self-executing Section 1 that courts could enforce on their own. But courts can also at times fall into the wrong hands, as the Thirty-Ninth Congress well knew. Thus the most sensible reading of the Fourteenth Amendment would involve both courts and Congress in the task of protecting truly fundamental rights against states, with states generally held to whichever standard was stricter—more protective of fundamental freedoms—in any given instance.

Whereas the Warren Court, as we have seen, never once struck down a congressional statute that had been enacted pursuant to Congress's power to "enforce" the Reconstruction Amendments, and the Burger Court did so only once (in the splintered 1970 case of Oregon v. Mitchell), such invalidations became a trademark of the Rehnquist Court.

UNITED STATES v. MORRISON, 529 U.S. 598 (2000) (The VAWA Case): [*Morrison* was a constitutional challenge to §13981 of the Violence Against Women Act of 1994, which empowered a victim of gender-based violence to bring suit for damages in federal court against the perpetrator of this violence. A young woman brought suit against two young men who, she claimed, had raped and brutalized her. The two men defended on the ground that VAWA was unconstitutional, and the United States intervened to defend the statute's constitutionality. Chief Justice Rehnquist, writing for a majority of five (including Justices O'Connor, Kennedy, Scalia, and Thomas), ruled that §13981 exceeded the proper scope of congressional authority under the Commerce Clause. The Court then considered whether VAWA was a constitutional exercise of Congress's §5 powers.]

Rehnquist, C.J.:

Petitioners [assert] that there is pervasive bias in various state justice systems against victims of gender-motivated violence. This assertion is supported by a voluminous congressional record. Specifically, Congress received evidence that many participants in state justice systems are perpetuating an array of erroneous stereotypes and assumptions. Congress concluded that these discriminatory stereotypes often result in insufficient investigation and prosecution of gender-motivated crime, inappropriate focus on the behavior and credibility of the victims of that crime, and unacceptably lenient punishments for those who are actually convicted of gender-motivated violence. Petitioners contend that this bias denies victims of gender-motivated violence the equal protection of the laws and that Congress therefore acted appropriately in enacting a private civil remedy against the perpetrators of gender-motivated violence to both remedy the States' bias and deter future instances of discrimination in the state courts. . . .

However, the language and purpose of the Fourteenth Amendment place certain limitations on the manner in which Congress may attack discriminatory conduct. These limitations are necessary to prevent the Fourteenth Amendment from obliterating the Framers' carefully crafted balance of power between the States and the National Government. . . . Foremost among these limitations is the time-honored principle that the Fourteenth Amendment, by its very terms, prohibits only state action. . . . [In] United States v. Harris, 106 U.S. 629 (1883), . . . the Court [struck down] §2 of the Civil Rights Act of 1871 [the Ku Klux Klan Act] . . . [which] punish[ed] "private persons" for "conspiring to deprive any one of the equal protection of the laws enacted by the State." . . . [In] the *Civil Rights Cases*[, 109 U.S. 3 (1883)], we held that the public accommodation provisions of the Civil Rights Act of 1875, which applied to purely private conduct, were beyond the scope of the §5 enforcement power. [See also] United States v. Cruikshank, 92 U.S. 542, 554 (1876) ("The fourteenth amendment prohibits a state from depriving any person of life, liberty, or property, without due process of law; but this adds nothing to the rights of one citizen as against another. It simply furnishes an additional guaranty against any encroachment by the States upon the fundamental rights which belong to every citizen as a member of society").

The force of the doctrine of *stare decisis* behind these decisions stems not only from the length of time they have been on the books, but also from the insight attributable to the Members of the Court at that time. Every Member had been appointed by President Lincoln, Grant, Hayes, Garfield, or Arthur—and each of their judicial appointees obviously had intimate knowledge and familiarity with the events surrounding the adoption of the Fourteenth Amendment. . . .

Petitioners alternatively argue that, unlike the situation in the *Civil Rights Cases*, here there has been gender-based disparate treatment by state authorities, whereas in those cases there was no indication of such state action. [But] the Congresses that enacted the Civil Rights Acts of 1871 and 1875 had a purpose similar to that of Congress in enacting §13981: There were state laws on the books bespeaking equality of treatment, but in the administration of these laws there was discrimination against newly freed slaves. The statement of Representative Garfield in the House . . . [is] representative: "[T]he chief complaint is not that the laws of the State are unequal, but that even where the laws are just and equal on their face, yet, by a systematic maladministration of them, or a neglect or refusal to enforce their provisions, a portion of the people are denied equal protection under them." Cong. Globe, 42d Cong., 1st Sess., App. 153 (1871) (statement of Rep. Garfield). . . .

But even if that distinction were valid, we do not believe it would save §13981's civil remedy. For the remedy is simply not "corrective in its character, adapted to counteract and redress the operation of such prohibited [s]tate laws or proceedings of [s]tate officers." Civil Rights Cases; [City of Boerne v.] Flores. Section 13981 is not aimed at proscribing discrimination by officials which the Fourteenth Amendment might not itself proscribe; it is directed not at any State or state actor, but at individuals who have committed criminal acts motivated by gender bias. . . . The section is, therefore, unlike any of the §5 remedies that we have previously upheld [in] Katzenbach v. Morgan . . . [and] South Carolina v. Katzenbach. . . .

Section 13981 is also different from these previously upheld remedies in that it applies uniformly throughout the Nation. Congress' findings indicate that the problem of discrimination against the victims of gender-motivated crimes does not exist in all States, or even most States. By contrast, the §5 remedy upheld in Katzenbach v. Morgan, was directed only to the State where the evil found by Congress existed, and in South Carolina v. Katzenbach, supra, the remedy was directed only to those States in which Congress found that there had been discrimination. . . .

Breyer, J., dissenting:

[I]n United States v. Harris and the Civil Rights Cases, the Court held that §5 does not authorize Congress to use the Fourteenth Amendment as a source of power to remedy the conduct of *private persons*. . . . The Federal Government's argument, however, is that Congress used §5 to remedy the actions of *state actors*, namely, those States which, through discriminatory design or the discriminatory conduct of their officials, failed to provide adequate (or any) state remedies for women injured by gender-motivated violence—a failure that the States, and Congress, documented in depth.

Neither *Harris* nor the *Civil Rights Cases* considered this kind of claim. The Court in *Harris* specifically said that it treated the federal laws in question as "directed *exclusively* against the action of private persons, without reference to the laws of the State, or their administration by her officers." See also *Civil Rights Cases* (observing that the statute did "not profess to be corrective of any constitutional wrong committed by the States" and that it established "rules for the conduct of individuals in society towards each other, . . . without referring in any manner to any supposed action of the State or its authorities").

The Court responds directly to the relevant "state actor" claim by finding that the present law lacks "'congruence and proportionality'" to the state discrimination that it purports to remedy . . . because the law, unlike federal laws prohibiting literacy tests for voting, imposing voting rights requirements, or punishing state officials who intentionally discriminated in jury selection, . . . is not "directed . . . at any State or state actor."

But why can Congress not provide a remedy against private actors? Those private actors, of course, did not themselves violate the Constitution. But this Court has held that Congress at least sometimes can enact remedial "[l]egislation . . . [that] prohibits conduct which is not itself unconstitutional." *Flores*; Katzenbach v. Morgan; South Carolina v. Katzenbach. The statutory remedy does not in any sense purport to "determine what constitutes a constitutional violation." It intrudes little upon either States or private parties. It may lead state actors to improve their own remedial systems, primarily through example. It restricts private actors only by imposing liability for private conduct that is, in the main, already forbidden by state law. Why is the remedy "disproportionate"? And given the relation between remedy and violation—the creation of a federal remedy to substitute for constitutionally inadequate state remedies—where is the lack of "congruence"?

The majority adds that Congress found that the problem of inadequacy of state remedies "does not exist in all States, or even most States." But Congress had before it the task force reports of at least 21 States documenting constitutional violations. And it made its own findings about pervasive gender-based stereotypes hampering many state legal systems, sometimes unconstitutionally so. The record nowhere reveals a congressional finding that the problem "does not exist" elsewhere. Why can Congress not take the evidence before it as evidence of a national problem? This Court has not previously held that Congress must document the existence of a problem in every State prior to proposing a national solution. . . . Despite my doubts about the majority's §5 reasoning, I need not, and do not, answer the §5 question, which I would leave for more thorough analysis if necessary on another occasion. Rather, in my view, the Commerce Clause provides an adequate basis for the statute before us. . . .

DISCUSSION

1. *Helping states rather than hurting them.* No member of the Rehnquist Court strongly challenged the Chief Justice's account of the Fourteenth Amendment. Two of the four dissenters, Justices Souter and Ginsburg, limited themselves to the Commerce Clause; Justice Breyer, joined by Justice Stevens, expressed "doubts about the majority's section 5 reasoning" but did not reach a firm conclusion.

Even so, Breyer adverts to a larger and important point: VAWA was specifically designed to help state and local governments deal with domestic violence and sexual assault. In addition to the civil rights remedy, VAWA distributed over $1.6 billion in funds to states and local governments for rape prevention and education programs, victim services programs, improved security in public transit, the construction and maintenance of battered women's shelters, and funding for additional law enforcement to assist with prosecution of cases of violence against women. If Congress had authorized a direct civil remedy for damages against states and localities, it would be draining this money from state and local coffers. Worse yet, it would be allowing private individuals to impugn state and local officials at the very moment when it was trying to work with them. On the other hand, a civil remedy against private tortfeasors would allow local officials to cooperate with victims of sexual assault and domestic violence without fear that they would be blamed for failing to protect them through the criminal justice system. Thus, aiming the remedy at private parties was, if anything, more respectful to state prerogatives.

2. *What part of "equal protection of the laws" don't you understand?* A more basic objection to *Morrison* is that it fails to take seriously the history of the Fourteenth Amendment and what the Reconstruction framers meant to achieve in giving Congress the power to enforce "equal protection of the laws" and basic guarantees of equal citizenship.

Following the Civil War, "whites in the South terrorized blacks and white unionists; victims were murdered, raped and lynched; their property was stolen and their houses were burned. All of these acts violated state tort or criminal law, but state and local officials in the South turned a blind eye to this violence."[14] The report of the Joint Committee on Reconstruction, which drafted and proposed the Fourteenth Amendment, described in great detail horrific examples of private violence against Black people—as well as violence against whites who supported their interests. The central problem was that states had abdicated their responsibilities to secure equal protection of the laws in the most basic sense. The Joint Committee's report identified giving Congress the power to stop private violence as a central justification for the new amendment.[15] In fact, there was far more of a focus on violence in the Joint Committee's Report than even on the Black Codes.[16]

Protecting Black people from private violence due to state neglect was as important and central a purpose for the new amendment as abolishing the Black

---

14. Jack M. Balkin, The Reconstruction Power, 85 N.Y.U L. Rev. 1801, 1846 (2010).

15. Report of the Joint Committee on Reconstruction (1866).

16. Laurent B. Frantz, Congressional Power to Enforce the Fourteenth Amendment Against Private Acts, 73 Yale L.J. 1353, 1354 & nn.10-13 (1964) (collecting examples in report of discriminatory legislation and private violence).

Codes.[17] Therefore, "[a] reasonable construction of the enforcement clause of the Fourteenth Amendment must at least give Congress the power to prevent lynchings and private violence directed at people when states will not afford the victims the equal protection of the laws."[18]

There is an obvious analogy to gender-motivated violence, Akhil Amar argues: "[R]ather than dwelling on commerce clause issues far removed from women's equality, the *Morrison* dissenters would have done better to begin with the Fourteenth Amendment's citizenship clause, and to explain how gender-motivated violence against women can pose a threat to equal citizenship in a manner analogous (though not identical) to the ways that other power structures have threatened the equal citizenship of blacks."[19] According to the Citizenship Clause, all Americans are "born" free and equal citizens. One sensible interpretation of this sentence, then, is that no American should be treated as a second-class citizen because of his or her birth status—because, say, he was born Black or she was born female. "[I]n the case of both race and sex, the dissenters could have argued, Congress may properly act to dismantle what it plausibly perceives to be large social structures creating and sustaining conditions of unequal citizenship, in which some citizens are systematically disrespected or mistreated on the basis of birth status."

State action arises from neglect in enforcing the laws equally, and, as Justice Breyer notes, Congress made extensive and detailed findings of how state tort and criminal law systems had let women down and treated their claims of violence inadequately or even dismissively. But there is also state action in a deeper, more historical sense: "[G]overnment has created marriage laws leaving women's property and bodies largely at the mercy of men; and has erected unjustified obstacles to rape prosecution. Through such laws, government has historically invested men with an improper sense of entitlement over women's bodies. . . . To vindicate the vision of the Fourteenth Amendment (read through the prism of the Nineteenth), Congress may pass expressive laws affirming women's equal status and citizenship so as to make clear to all that women have rights that men are bound to respect."[20]

3. *Picking your framers.* Chief Justice Rehnquist duly notes the state neglect argument; he even quotes Representative (later President) James Garfield's explanation of why Congress had the power to secure equal protection of the laws against private violence in the Ku Klux Klan Act. But Rehnquist responds that the Klan Act and the 1875 Civil Rights Act were unconstitutional, relying on the work of the 1883 Supreme Court that decided *Harris* and the *Civil Rights Cases.* The 1883 Court, he explains, was stocked with people who surely must have understood the Fourteenth Amendment's original meaning.

The problem is that the 1883 Court spoke after the Compromise of 1876, which ended Reconstruction, withdrew the federal troops that secured Black civil rights, and remitted Black people to white-controlled governments. It reflected not the vision of the Reconstruction framers but a very different sensibility. One might

17. Balkin, The Reconstruction Power, supra n.13.

18. Id.

19. Akhil Reed Amar, The Supreme Court 1999 Term—Foreword: The Document and the Doctrine, 114 Harv. L. Rev. 26 (2000).

20. Id.

think that the actual Reconstruction Congress had a far better understanding of Congress's powers under the Fourteenth Amendment. As Akhil Amar points out:[21]

> Many of the Congressmen supporting [the Klan Act and the 1875 Civil Rights Act] had been leading architects of the Fourteenth Amendment itself. Why doesn't Chief Justice Rehnquist focus our attention on the views of *these* men—crusaders for racial justice like John Bingham and Charles Sumner? And what about the first Justice Harlan? After all, he dissented in the *Civil Rights Cases*, arguing that Congress had broad *Prigg*-ish power to address even certain private conduct, and that the Citizenship Clause of the Fourteenth Amendment had no state action requirement. This is the same Harlan who later dissented in *Plessy*. If he was right in *Plessy*, perhaps he was right here? Or to put the point differently, isn't Chief Justice Rehnquist's effort to rehabilitate the *Civil Rights Cases* rather like trying to revive *Plessy* itself? Indeed, many commentators in the 1960s believed that the Warren Court had impliedly overruled the *Civil Rights Cases* in Jones v. Alfred Mayer, much as it had earlier overruled *Plessy* itself *sub silentio* in *Brown*.[22]

In fact, the earliest federal judicial construction of Section 5 would be that of Judge Woods in United States v. Hall, 26 F. Cas. 79 (C.C. Ala 1871), discussed in Chapter 4:

> [T]he fourteenth amendment . . . prohibits the states from denying . . . the equal protection of the laws. Denying includes inaction as well as action, and denying the equal protection of the laws includes the omission to protect, as well as the omission to pass laws for protection. . . . Therefore, to guard against the invasion of the citizen's fundamental rights, and to insure their adequate protection, as well against state legislation as state inaction, or incompetency, the amendment gives congress the power to enforce its provisions by appropriate legislation.
>
> And as it would be unseemly for congress to interfere directly with state enactments, and as it cannot compel the activity of state officials, the only appropriate legislation it can make is that which will operate directly on offenders and offenses, and protect the rights which the amendment secures. The extent to which congress shall exercise this power must depend on its discretion in view of the circumstances of each case. If the exercise of it in any case should seem to interfere with the domestic affairs of a state, it must be remembered that it is for the purpose of protecting federal rights, and these must be protected even though it interfere with state laws or the administration of state laws.

---

21. Id.

22. Three years after *Jones*, the Supreme Court also undermined United States v. Harris. Griffin v. Breckenridge, 403 U.S. 88, 104-105 (1971), upheld the civil provisions of the 1871 Klan Act (which were identical to the criminal provisions struck down in *Harris*) as an exercise of Congress's powers under §2 of the Thirteenth Amendment.

Suppose that the Court adopted Judge Wood's account of the original meaning of Section 5. How should it have decided *Morrison*?

In *Boerne* and *Morrison*, the Rehnquist Court held that Congress simply lacked power to regulate certain issues. In another, more technical line of cases, the Court has upheld congressional regulatory power, but only under the Commerce Clause and not under the Reconstruction Amendments. Ordinarily, very little might turn on the precise source of congressional power once such power is conceded to exist. But in one corner of law, the precise source does matter. It concerns the Court's (rather convoluted) doctrine of sovereign immunity under the Eleventh Amendment, which (as currently interpreted by the Court) prevents courts from awarding money damages in suits against nonconsenting state governments (See the note on State Sovereign Immunity, Section II.B, infra).

In Fitzpatrick v. Bitzer, 447 U.S. 445 (1976), the Court explained that the Eleventh Amendment might prevent plaintiffs from recovering damages against state governments when Congress regulates states under its Commerce power. But the Eleventh Amendment is no obstacle when plaintiffs sue under statutes passed under Congress's powers to enforce the Reconstruction Amendments: "When Congress acts pursuant to [section] 5, not only is it exercising legislative authority that is plenary within the terms of the constitutional grant, it is exercising that authority under one section of a constitutional Amendment whose other sections by their own terms embody limitations on state authority."

The upshot is that the more the Court limited Congress's powers using *Boerne*'s "congruence and proportionality test," the more it would limit damage suits in civil rights cases brought against state governments. This had important consequences in the decisions that followed.

Board of Trustees of the University of Alabama v. Garrett

531 U.S. 356 (2001)

Rehnquist, C.J.:

We decide here whether employees of the State of Alabama may recover money damages by reason of the State's failure to comply with the provisions of Title I of the Americans with Disabilities Act of 1990 (ADA or Act). We hold that such suits are barred by the Eleventh Amendment. . . .

In Fitzpatrick v. Bitzer . . . we held that "the Eleventh Amendment, and the principle of state sovereignty which it embodies, are necessarily limited by the enforcement provisions of §5 of the Fourteenth Amendment." As a result, we concluded, Congress may subject nonconsenting States to suit in federal court when it does so pursuant to a valid exercise of its §5 power. . . . Accordingly, the ADA can apply to the States only to the extent that the statute is appropriate §5 legislation. . . .

City of Boerne . . . confirmed . . . the long-settled principle that it is the responsibility of this Court, not Congress, to define the substance of constitutional guarantees. Accordingly, §5 legislation reaching beyond the scope of §1's actual guarantees must exhibit "congruence and proportionality between the injury to be prevented or remedied and the means adopted to that end." . . .

In Cleburne v. Cleburne Living Center, Inc., 473 U.S. 432 (1985), we [held that legislation that discriminates on the basis of mental disability] . . . incurs only the minimum "rational-basis" review applicable to general social and economic legislation [and] we explained that . . . "it would be difficult to find a principled way to distinguish a variety of other groups who have perhaps immutable disabilities setting them off from others, who cannot themselves mandate the desired legislative responses, and who can claim some degree of prejudice from at least part of the public at large." . . . Thus, the result of *Cleburne* is that States are not required by the Fourteenth Amendment to make special accommodations for the disabled, so long as their actions towards such individuals are rational. They could quite hard headedly—and perhaps hardheartedly—hold to job-qualification requirements which do not make allowance for the disabled. If special accommodations for the disabled are to be required, they have to come from positive law and not through the Equal Protection Clause. . . .

. . . The legislative record of the ADA . . . simply fails to show that Congress did in fact identify a pattern of irrational state discrimination in employment against the disabled.

Respondents contend that the inquiry as to unconstitutional discrimination should extend not only to States themselves, but to units of local governments, such as cities and counties, . . . but the Eleventh Amendment does not extend its immunity to units of local government. . . . Congress made a general finding in the ADA that "historically, society has tended to isolate and segregate individuals with disabilities, and, despite some improvements, such forms of discrimination against individuals with disabilities continue to be a serious and pervasive social problem." The record assembled by Congress includes many instances to support such a finding. But the great majority of these incidents do not deal with the activities of States.

Respondents in their brief cite half a dozen examples from the record that did involve States. . . . Several of these incidents undoubtedly evidence an unwillingness on the part of state officials to make the sort of accommodations for the disabled required by the ADA. Whether they were irrational under our decision in *Cleburne* is more debatable. . . . [T]hese incidents taken together fall far short of even suggesting the pattern of unconstitutional discrimination on which §5 legislation must be based. . . .

Justice Breyer maintains that Congress applied Title I of the ADA to the States in response to a host of incidents representing unconstitutional state discrimination in employment against persons with disabilities. A close review of the relevant materials, however, [shows that they] consist[] not of legislative findings, but of unexamined, anecdotal accounts of "adverse, disparate treatment by state officials" . . . [which] often does not amount to a constitutional violation where rational-basis scrutiny applies. . . . [T]he House and Senate committee reports on the ADA [conclude only that] "Discrimination still persists in such critical areas as *employment in the private sector*, public accommodations, public services, transportation, and telecommunications." . . . Congress' failure to mention States in its legislative findings addressing discrimination in employment reflects that body's judgment that no pattern of unconstitutional state action had been documented.

[Moreover,] the rights and remedies created by the ADA against the States would raise the same sort of concerns as to congruence and proportionality as were found in *City of Boerne*. For example, whereas it would be entirely rational (and therefore constitutional) for a state employer to conserve scarce financial resources by hiring employees who are able to use existing facilities, the ADA requires employers to "mak[e] existing facilities used by employees readily accessible to and usable by individuals with disabilities." . . . [T]he accommodation duty far exceeds what is constitutionally required. . . . The ADA also forbids "utilizing standards, criteria, or methods of administration" that disparately impact the disabled, without regard to whether such conduct has a rational basis. . . .

Congressional enactment of the ADA represents its judgment that there should be a "comprehensive national mandate for the elimination of discrimination against individuals with disabilities." Congress is the final authority as to desirable public policy, but in order to authorize private individuals to recover money damages against the States, there must be a pattern of discrimination by the States which violates the Fourteenth Amendment, and the remedy imposed by Congress must be congruent and proportional to the targeted violation. . . . [T]o uphold the Act's application to the States would allow Congress to rewrite the Fourteenth Amendment law laid down by this Court in *Cleburne.*

[A concurring opinion by Justice Kennedy, joined by Justice O'Connor, is omitted.]

BREYER, J., joined by STEVENS, SOUTER, and GINSBURG, JJ., dissenting.

. . . Congress compiled a vast legislative record documenting "'massive, society-wide discrimination'" against persons with disabilities. . . . [And] Congress created a special task force to assess the need for comprehensive legislation. That task force held hearings in every State, attended by more than 30,000 people, including thousands who had experienced discrimination first hand. . . .

The powerful evidence of discriminatory treatment throughout society in general, including discrimination by private persons and local governments, implicates state governments as well, for state agencies form part of that same larger society. There is no particular reason to believe that they are immune from the "stereotypic assumptions" and pattern of "purposeful unequal treatment" that Congress found prevalent. The Court claims that it "make[s] no sense" to take into consideration constitutional violations committed by local governments. But the substantive obligation that the Equal Protection Clause creates applies to state and local governmental entities alike. . . . Local governments often work closely with, and under the supervision of, state officials, and in general, state and local government employers are similarly situated. . . . In any event, there is no need to rest solely upon evidence of discrimination by local governments or general societal discrimination. There are roughly 300 examples of discrimination by state governments themselves in the legislative record. . . .

[T]hose who presented instances of discrimination rarely provided additional, independent evidence sufficient to prove in court that, in each instance, the discrimination they suffered lacked justification from a judicial standpoint. . . . But a legislature is not a court of law. And Congress, unlike courts, must, and does, routinely draw general conclusions—for example, of likely motive or of likely relationship to legitimate need—from anecdotal and opinion-based evidence of this kind, particularly when the evidence lacks strong refutation. . . . In reviewing §5 legislation, we have never required the sort of extensive investigation of each piece of evidence that the Court appears to contemplate. . . . Nor has the Court traditionally required Congress to make findings as to state discrimination, or to break down the record evidence, category by category. . . .

Regardless, Congress expressly found substantial unjustified discrimination against persons with disabilities. . . . Moreover, it found that such discrimination typically reflects "stereotypic assumptions" or "purposeful unequal treatment" . . . . In making these findings, Congress followed our decision in *Cleburne*, which established that . . . discrimination that rests solely upon "negative attitude[s]," "fea[r]," or "irrational prejudice," [against the disabled violates the Fourteenth Amendment.] . . .

The evidence in the legislative record bears out Congress' finding that the adverse treatment of persons with disabilities was often arbitrary or invidious in this sense, and thus unjustified. . . . [It includes] hundreds of examples of discrimination by state and local governments. . . . Congress could have reasonably believed that these examples represented signs of a widespread problem of unconstitutional discrimination.

The Court's failure to find sufficient evidentiary support may well rest upon its decision to hold Congress to a strict, judicially created evidentiary standard. . . . [But] "[l]imitations stemming from the nature of the judicial process . . . have no application to Congress." Rational-basis review—with its presumptions favoring constitutionality—is "a paradigm of *judicial* restraint." And the Congress of the United States is not a lower court. . . .

There is simply no reason to require Congress, seeking to determine facts relevant to the exercise of its §5 authority, to adopt rules or presumptions that reflect a court's institutional limitations. Unlike courts, Congress can readily gather facts from across the Nation, assess the magnitude of a problem, and more easily find an appropriate remedy. . . . Unlike courts, Congress directly reflects public attitudes and beliefs, enabling Congress better to understand where, and to what extent, refusals to accommodate a disability amount to behavior that is callous or unreasonable to the point of lacking constitutional justification. Unlike judges, Members of Congress can directly obtain information from constituents who have first-hand experience with discrimination and related issues.

Moreover, unlike judges, Members of Congress are elected. When the Court has applied the majority's burden of proof rule, it has explained that we, *i.e.*, the courts, do not "'sit as a superlegislature to judge the wisdom or desirability of legislative policy determinations.'" To apply a rule designed to restrict courts as if it restricted Congress' legislative power is to stand the underlying principle—a principle of judicial restraint—on its head. But without the use of this burden of proof rule or some other unusually stringent standard of review, it is difficult to see how the Court can find the legislative record here inadequate. Read with a reasonably favorable eye, the record indicates that state governments subjected those with disabilities to seriously adverse, disparate treatment. . . .

The Court argues in the alternative that the statute's damage remedy is not "congruent" with and "proportional" to the equal protection problem that Congress found. . . . The Court suggests that the Act's "reasonable accommodation" requirement, "far excee[d] what is constitutionally required." But we have upheld disparate impact standards [in §5 remedies] in contexts where they were not "constitutionally required."

And what is wrong with a remedy that, in response to unreasonable employer behavior, requires an employer to make accommodations that are reasonable? Of course, what is "reasonable" in the statutory sense and what is "unreasonable" in the constitutional sense might differ. In other words, the requirement may exceed what is necessary to avoid a constitutional violation. But it is just that power—the power to require more than the minimum—that §5 grants to Congress, as this Court has repeatedly confirmed. . . . "Congress' §5 power is not confined to the enactment of legislation that merely parrots the precise wording of the Fourteenth Amendment." Rather, Congress can prohibit a "somewhat broader swath of conduct, including that which is not itself forbidden by the Amendment's text"). . . .

I recognize nonetheless that this statute imposes a burden upon States in that it removes their Eleventh Amendment protection from suit, thereby subjecting them to potential monetary liability. Rules for interpreting §5 that would provide States with special protection, however, run counter to the very object of the Fourteenth Amendment. . . . [T]he Civil War Amendments . . . were "specifically designed as an expansion of federal power and an intrusion on state sovereignty." And, ironically, the greater the obstacle the Eleventh Amendment poses to . . . the decentralized remedy of private damage actions . . . the more Congress, seeking to cure important national problems . . . will have to rely on more uniform remedies, such as federal standards and court injunctions, which are sometimes draconian and typically more intrusive. . . .

DISCUSSION

1. Prior to *Garrett*, the Supreme Court had also held that Congress could not allow money damage awards when states violated the Age Discrimination in Employment Act (ADEA) because the ADEA was not a valid exercise of §5 power. Kimel v. Florida Board of Regents, 528 U.S. 62 (2000). That is because the Court has held that discrimination on the basis of age, like discrimination based on disability, is subject only to rational basis review.

2. *Section 5 strict scrutiny.* The Rehnquist Court does not treat Congress's findings in the post-*Boerne* cases in the same way that the Warren Court treated Congress's findings in cases like South Carolina v. Katzenbach and Katzenbach v. Morgan. What explains the difference? One possibility is that the latter cases deal with race discrimination, to which the Court applies strict scrutiny. But see Shelby County v. Holder, infra.

3. *Privileges or immunities of national citizenship?* Consider the following argument: When a state violates a valid federal law enacted under the Commerce Clause (or any other Article I power, for that matter), the state thereby violates the Supremacy Clause. And under even the crabbed interpretation of the Fourteenth Amendment furnished by the Court in the 1873 Slaughterhouse Cases, supra Chapter 4, the "privileges" and "immunities" of citizenship include rights "which owe their existence to the Federal government, its National character, its Constitution, *or its laws.*" (Recall that the dissenters believed that the Fourteenth Amendment did more than reenact the Supremacy Clause, but even they thought it did at least this much.)

As a matter of logic, then, it would seem that:

(1) Whenever Congress has passed a valid law creating individual rights and a state violates that valid federal law, the state has thereby abridged a "privilege or immunity" of citizenship, in violation of §1 of the Fourteenth Amendment.
(2) Such a violation authorizes Congress to remedy and enforce the §1 right via §5 statute.
(3) A clearly worded congressional statute expressly enacted pursuant to the Fourteenth Amendment, explicitly aimed at states, and holding them liable for their violations of valid federal law, would be a properly "congruent" and "proportional" congressional act of enforcement.

The Court, however, has not viewed the matter this way. See Florida Prepaid Postsecondary Education Expense Board v. College Savings Bank, 527 U.S. 627 (1999); College Savings Bank v. Florida Prepaid Postsecondary Expense Board, 527 U.S. 666 (1999).

Like *Kimel* and *Garrett,* each of these §5 cases featured the same 5-4 line-up of Justices as did *Morrison* and *Lopez.*

4. *Findings of fact.* Should §5 power depend on whether Congress can point to a clear pattern of state misbehavior, as most of these cases seem to suggest? The *Kimel* Court stressed that states had not generally engaged in invidious age discrimination. And in *Morrison,* Chief Justice Rehnquist argued that "the problem of discrimination against the victims of gender-motivated crimes does not exist in all States, or even most States." But which way does that cut? The very fact that most states do not practice such discrimination means that a federal law banning it does not interfere very much with states' rights. Moreover, broad state compliance with an antidiscrimination norm may in fact be evidence that such a norm is indeed fundamental in modern society.[23] Just as the Court often looks to state practice in determining fundamental rights under §1, why shouldn't Congress be allowed to do so in enacting laws under §5? And shouldn't the fact that states generally refrain from engaging in a given dubious practice be grounds for allowing Congress to proclaim a Fourteenth Amendment right—a privilege or immunity of citizenship—against the practice in question?

5. *The reach of* Boerne*:* Hibbs *and* Lane. In two post-*Garrett* cases, the Court has found that two other federal laws are properly founded on §5 power.

In Nevada Department of Human Resources v. Hibbs, 538 U.S. 721 (2003), the Court upheld the application of the Family and Medical Leave Act (FMLA) to state governments as a valid exercise of §5 power. Under the FMLA, state employees, whether male or female, were guaranteed 12 weeks of annual leave to care for seriously ill family members. The Act aimed to ease the plight of working women, via a gender-neutral statute. (If only wives, mothers, and daughters were eligible for family leave, employers might be less enthusiastic about hiring women in the

23. Indeed, as we shall see in Chapter 9, the Court sometimes justifies the creation of fundamental rights (or the expansion of existing ones) based on whether there is an emerging consensus that the right is fundamental, and it looks to the trend in state legislatures as evidence.

first place; thus the Act applied to all workers, male and female, thereby challenging previous stereotypes—stereotypes that had been reinforced by previous state action—that family care was the unique obligation of women workers.) Joined by Justice O'Connor and the four dissenters in *Morrison,* Chief Justice Rehnquist, writing for the Court, deemed this statute a valid §5 enactment. (For more analysis of *Hibbs,* see infra, Chapter 8.)

In Tennessee v. Lane, 541 U.S. 509 (2004), the four *Morrison* dissenters, led by Justice Stevens, combined with Justice O'Connor to uphold under §5 a portion of the ADA that regulated access to public buildings and governmental programs. The case at hand involved a wheelchair-bound paraplegic summoned to answer criminal charges on the second floor of a county courthouse that had no elevator. At his first appearance he crawled up two flights of stairs; the next time, he refused to crawl or be carried, and was subsequently jailed for failure to appear. Justice Stevens held that as applied to public facilities like courthouses, the ADA did more than protect against disability discrimination; it also "enforce[s] a variety of other basic constitutional guarantees, infringements of which are subject to more searching judicial review," including the due process right to access to courts and to fair hearings and the Sixth Amendment's right to confront witnesses.

In both *Hibbs* and *Lane,* the Court argued that Congress could pass prophylactic measures that reached more broadly than conduct that the Court viewed as unconstitutional. There are two kinds of prophylactic measures. The first reaches a broad range of conduct in order to alleviate problems of proof. The second reaches a broad range of conduct in order to prevent constitutional violations from happening in the first place. The FMLA, for example, obviates problems of proving that a particular employer's leave policies were based on stereotypical views about men and women; in addition, by creating a uniform national right, it nips such tendencies in the bud.

Why, we might wonder, did the Court in *Hibbs* and *Lane* deem congressional action sufficiently "congruent" and "proportionate" to pass muster? Perhaps the cases at hand were seen as closer to Fourteenth Amendment values that the Court itself had recognized in previous cases—involving the rights of women to be free from gender stereotyping and discrimination, and the fundamental right of citizens to have adequate access to courts, legislatures, and other governmental operations. But of course *Morrison* also involved gender discrimination, yet the Court gave Congress much less deference in that case. Can you explain the pattern of cases? Note that only one Justice—O'Connor—was a member of the majority in each of these cases.

6. Boerne *in the Roberts Court—The FMLA revisited.* The Roberts Court refused to expand *Hibbs* and *Lane* further in Coleman v. Court of Appeals of Maryland, 566 U.S. 30 (2012). Another part of the Family and Medical Leave Act entitles an employee to take up to 12 workweeks of unpaid leave per year for the employee's own serious health condition when the condition interferes with the employee's ability to perform at work.

Justice Kennedy, in a plurality opinion joined by Chief Justice Roberts, Justice Alito, and Justice Thomas, held that *Hibbs* did not apply to these "self-care provisions" of the FMLA, and therefore Congress lacked the power under §5 of the Fourteenth Amendment to abrogate the states' immunity from damage lawsuits when state employers unlawfully refused to grant self-care leaves to their employees:

"Without widespread evidence of sex discrimination or sex stereotyping in the administration of sick leave, it is apparent that the congressional purpose in enacting the self-care provision is unrelated to these supposed wrongs. The legislative history of the self-care provision reveals a concern for the economic burdens on the employee and the employee's family resulting from illness-related job loss and a concern for discrimination on the basis of illness, not sex."

Justice Thomas concurred, adding that he believed *Hibbs* was wrongly decided. Justice Scalia concurred in the judgment, arguing that the Court should abandon its "congruence and proportionality" test: "I would limit Congress's §5 power to the regulation of conduct that *itself* violates the Fourteenth Amendment. Failing to grant state employees leave for the purpose of self-care—or any other purpose, for that matter—does not come close."

Justice Ginsburg, joined by Justice Breyer, Justice Sotomayor, and Justice Kagan, dissented. Justice Ginsburg argued that the "self-care" provisions were also designed to prevent sex discrimination: Arguing that discrimination against pregnant women should be considered a form of sex discrimination, Justice Ginsburg explained that "[t]he self-care provision responds to . . . evidence [of discrimination against pregnant women] by requiring employers to allow leave for 'ongoing pregnancy, miscarriages, . . . the need for prenatal care, childbirth, and recovery from childbirth.'" Justice Ginsburg quoted congressional reports explaining that it was better to require employers to provide self-care leave for *both* men and women—instead of providing leave only following pregnancy or due to pregnancy-related illness—because this would remove employers' incentives to discriminate against pregnant women and women of child-bearing age. Because a guarantee of self-care leave for both men and women alleviated employer incentives toward pregnancy discrimination, and because it was without pay and therefore not too burdensome to employers, Justice Ginsburg concluded that it was congruent and proportional to Congress's evidence of pregnancy discrimination in employment.

Even if pregnancy discrimination did not count as sex discrimination, Ginsburg argued, Congress understood that "[r]equiring States to provide gender-neutral parental and family-care leave alone [without self-care leave] . . . would promote precisely the type of workplace discrimination Congress sought to reduce. The 'pervasive sex-role stereotype that caring for family members is women's work,' [Congress believed,] led employers to regard required parental and family-care leave as a woman's benefit" that few men would use. "Congress therefore had good reason to conclude that the self-care provision—which men no doubt would use—would counter employers' impressions that the FMLA would otherwise install female leave. Providing for self-care would thus reduce employers' corresponding incentive to discriminate against women in hiring and promotion."

Shelby County, Alabama v. Holder

570 U.S. 529 (2013)

[Section 5 of the Voting Rights Act of 1965 requires that covered jurisdictions—which are listed in §4(b) of the Act—must preclear any changes to their voting systems with the Department of Justice (or with a three-judge district court in Washington) to ensure that they do not "ha[ve] the purpose nor . . . the effect of denying or abridging the right to vote on account of race or color." 42 U.S.C. §1973c(a). Jurisdictions listed in §4(b)'s coverage formula were originally determined by a test of those states that had used a forbidden test or device in November 1964, and had less than 50 percent voter registration or turnout in the 1964 presidential election. Today covered jurisdictions include most of the South, Arizona, and Alaska, along with various counties and townships throughout the United States.

Congress reauthorized the Act for 5 years in 1970, for 7 years in 1975, and for 25 years in 1982. The coverage formula, based on the use of voting-eligibility tests and the rate of registration and turnout among all voters, remained the same, but the measurements were based on 1968 and eventually 1972 levels. In 2006, Congress extended the Voting Rights Act for 25 more years. Once again it maintained the existing coverage formula, keeping 1972 as the baseline date for measuring which jurisdictions would be subject to preclearance requirements.

In 2009, the Supreme Court considered a challenge to the constitutionality of §5 of the Voting Rights Act from a Texas municipal utility district. In Northwest Austin Municipal Util. Dist. No. One v. Holder, 557 U.S. 193 (2009), the Court stated that "[t]he Act's preclearance requirements and its coverage formula raise serious constitutional questions under either [the] test" of City of Boerne v. Flores or South Carolina v. Katzenbach, but avoided the constitutional question by interpreting the statute to exclude the district from the Act's coverage.

Shelby County, as a political subdivision of Alabama, is a covered jurisdiction under §4(b). It brought a new challenge to the VRA, arguing that §4(b), the VRA's coverage formula, and §5, the preclearance requirement, are facially unconstitutional and asked for a permanent injunction against their enforcement.]

Chief Justice Roberts delivered the opinion of the Court.

. . .

II

In *Northwest Austin,* we stated that "the Act imposes current burdens and must be justified by current needs." And we concluded that "a departure from the fundamental principle of equal sovereignty requires a showing that a statute's disparate geographic coverage is sufficiently related to the problem that it targets." These basic principles guide our review of the question before us.

A

[T]he Federal Government does not . . . have a general right to review and veto state enactments before they go into effect. A proposal to grant such authority to "negative" state laws was considered at the Constitutional Convention, but rejected in favor of allowing state laws to take effect, subject to later challenge under the Supremacy Clause.

Outside the strictures of the Supremacy Clause, States retain broad autonomy in structuring their governments and pursuing legislative objectives. Indeed, the Constitution provides that all powers not specifically granted to the Federal Government are reserved to the States or citizens. Amdt. 10. This "allocation of powers in our federal system preserves the integrity, dignity, and residual sovereignty of the States." But the federal balance "is not just an end in itself: Rather, federalism secures to citizens the liberties that derive from the diffusion of sovereign power."

More specifically, "'the Framers of the Constitution intended the States to keep for themselves, as provided in the Tenth Amendment, the power to regulate elections.'" Gregory v. Ashcroft, 501 U.S. 452 (1991). Of course, the Federal Government retains significant control over federal elections. For instance, the Constitution authorizes Congress to establish the time and manner for electing Senators and Representatives. Art. I, §4, cl. 1. But States have "broad powers to determine the conditions under which the right of suffrage may be exercised." And "[e]ach State has the power to prescribe the qualifications of its officers and the manner in which they shall be chosen." Boyd v. Nebraska ex rel. Thayer, 143 U.S. 135 (1892). . . .

Not only do States retain sovereignty under the Constitution, there is also a "fundamental principle of *equal* sovereignty" among the States. *Northwest Austin.* Over a hundred years ago, this Court explained that our Nation "was and is a union of States, equal in power, dignity and authority." Coyle v. Smith, 221 U.S. 559 (1911). Indeed, "the constitutional equality of the States is essential to the harmonious operation of the scheme upon which the Republic was organized." *Coyle* concerned the admission of new States, and *Katzenbach* rejected the notion that the principle operated as a *bar* on differential treatment outside that context. At the same time, as we made clear in *Northwest Austin*, the fundamental principle of equal sovereignty remains highly pertinent in assessing subsequent disparate treatment of States.

The Voting Rights Act sharply departs from these basic principles. It suspends "*all* changes to state election law—however innocuous—until they have been precleared by federal authorities in Washington, D.C." States must beseech the Federal Government for permission to implement laws that they would otherwise have the right to enact and execute on their own, subject of course to any injunction in a §2 action. The Attorney General has 60 days to object to a preclearance request, longer if he requests more information. If a State seeks preclearance from a three-judge court, the process can take years.

And despite the tradition of equal sovereignty, the Act applies to only nine States (and several additional counties). While one State waits months or years and expends funds to implement a validly enacted law, its neighbor can typically put the same law into effect immediately, through the normal legislative process. Even if a noncovered jurisdiction is sued, there are important differences between those proceedings and preclearance proceedings; the preclearance proceeding "not only switches the burden of proof to the supplicant jurisdiction, but also applies substantive standards quite different from those governing the rest of the nation."

All this explains why, when we first upheld the Act in 1966, we described it as "stringent" and "potent." *Katzenbach.* We recognized that it "may have been an uncommon exercise of congressional power," but concluded that "legislative measures not otherwise appropriate" could be justified by "exceptional conditions." We have since noted that the Act "authorizes federal intrusion into sensitive areas of state and local policymaking," and represents an "extraordinary departure from the traditional course of relations between the States and the Federal Government." As we reiterated in *Northwest Austin*, the Act constitutes "extraordinary legislation otherwise unfamiliar to our federal system."

B

In 1966, we found these departures from the basic features of our system of government justified. The "blight of racial discrimination in voting" had "infected the electoral process in parts of our country for nearly a century." *Katzenbach.* Several States had enacted a variety of requirements and tests "specifically designed to prevent" African-Americans from voting. Case-by-case litigation had proved inadequate to prevent such racial discrimination in voting, in part because States "merely switched to discriminatory devices not covered by the federal decrees," "enacted difficult new tests," or simply "defied and evaded court orders." Shortly before enactment of the Voting Rights Act, only 19.4 percent of African-Americans of voting age were registered to vote in Alabama, only 31.8 percent in Louisiana, and only 6.4 percent in Mississippi. Those figures were roughly 50 percentage points or more below the figures for whites.

In short, we concluded that "[u]nder the compulsion of these unique circumstances, Congress responded in a permissibly decisive manner." We also noted then and have emphasized since that this extraordinary legislation was intended to be temporary, set to expire after five years.

At the time, the coverage formula—the means of linking the exercise of the unprecedented authority with the problem that warranted it—made sense. We found that "Congress chose to limit its attention to the geographic areas where immediate action seemed necessary." The areas where Congress found "evidence of actual voting discrimination" shared two characteristics: "the use of tests and devices for voter registration, and a voting rate in the 1964 presidential election at least 12 points below the national average." We explained that "[t]ests and devices are relevant to voting discrimination because of their long history as a tool for perpetrating the evil; a low voting rate is pertinent for the obvious reason that widespread disenfranchisement must inevitably affect the number of actual voters." We therefore concluded that "the coverage formula [was] rational in both practice and theory." It accurately reflected those jurisdictions uniquely characterized by voting discrimination "on a pervasive scale," linking coverage to the devices used to effectuate discrimination and to the resulting disenfranchisement. The formula ensured that the "stringent remedies [were] aimed at areas where voting discrimination ha[d] been most flagrant."

C

Nearly 50 years later, things have changed dramatically. Shelby County contends that the preclearance requirement, even without regard to its disparate coverage, is now unconstitutional. Its arguments have a good deal of force. In the covered jurisdictions, "[v]oter turnout and registration rates now approach parity. Blatantly discriminatory evasions of federal decrees are rare. And minority candidates hold office at unprecedented levels." The tests and devices that blocked access to the ballot have been forbidden nationwide for over 40 years.

Those conclusions are not ours alone. Congress said the same when it reauthorized the Act in 2006, writing that "[s]ignificant progress has been made in eliminating first generation barriers experienced by minority voters, including increased numbers of registered minority voters, minority voter turnout, and minority representation in Congress, State legislatures, and local elected offices." The House Report elaborated that "the number of African-Americans who are registered and who turn out to cast ballots has increased significantly over the last 40 years, particularly since 1982," and noted that "[i]n some circumstances, minorities register to vote and cast ballots at levels that surpass those of white voters." That Report also explained that there have been "significant increases in the number of African-Americans serving in elected offices"; more specifically, there has been approximately a 1,000 percent increase since 1965 in the number of African-American elected officials in the six States originally covered by the Voting Rights Act.

[Justice Roberts cites statistics showing that the gap between white and Black registration has largely been closed between 1965 and 2004 in the six originally covered states, and that in two states, Georgia and Mississippi, a very slightly higher number of Black people of voting age are now registered than whites.]

[C]ensus Bureau data from the most recent election indicate that African-American voter turnout exceeded white voter turnout in five of the six States originally covered by §5, with a gap in the sixth State of less than one-half of one percent. The preclearance statistics are also illuminating. In the first decade after enactment of §5, the Attorney General objected to 14.2 percent of proposed voting changes. In the last decade before reenactment, the Attorney General objected to a mere 0.16 percent.

There is no doubt that these improvements are in large part *because of* the Voting Rights Act. The Act has proved immensely successful at redressing racial discrimination and integrating the voting process. During the "Freedom Summer" of 1964, in Philadelphia, Mississippi, three men were murdered while working in the area to register African-American voters. On "Bloody Sunday" in 1965, in Selma, Alabama, police beat and used tear gas against hundreds marching in support of African-American enfranchisement. Today both of those towns are governed by African-American mayors. Problems remain in these States and others, but there is no denying that, due to the Voting Rights Act, our Nation has made great strides.

Yet the Act has not eased the restrictions in §5 or narrowed the scope of the coverage formula in §4(b) along the way. Those extraordinary and unprecedented features were reauthorized—as if nothing had changed. In fact, the Act's unusual remedies have grown even stronger. When Congress reauthorized the Act in 2006, it did so for another 25 years on top of the previous 40—a far cry from the initial five-year period. Congress also expanded the prohibitions in §5. We had previously interpreted §5 to prohibit only those redistricting plans that would have the purpose or effect of worsening the position of minority groups. In 2006, Congress amended §5 to prohibit laws that could have favored such groups but did not do so because of a discriminatory purpose, see 42 U.S.C. §1973c(c), even though we had stated that such broadening of §5 coverage would "exacerbate the substantial federalism costs that the preclearance procedure already exacts, perhaps to the extent of raising concerns about §5's constitutionality," Reno v. Bossier Parish School Bd., 528 U.S. 320 (2000) (*Bossier II*). In addition, Congress expanded §5 to prohibit any voting law "that has the purpose of or will have the effect of diminishing the ability of any citizens of the United States," on account of race, color, or language minority status, "to elect their preferred candidates of choice." §1973c(b). In light of those two amendments, the bar that covered jurisdictions must clear has been raised even as the conditions justifying that requirement have dramatically improved.

We have also previously highlighted the concern that "the preclearance requirements in one State [might] be unconstitutional in another." *Northwest Austin.* See Georgia v. Ashcroft, 539 U.S., at 491 (Kennedy, J., concurring) ("considerations of race that would doom a redistricting plan under the Fourteenth Amendment or §2 [of the Voting Rights Act] seem to be what save it under §5"). Nothing has happened since to alleviate this troubling concern about the current application of §5.

Respondents do not deny that there have been improvements on the ground, but argue that much of this can be attributed to the deterrent effect of §5, which dissuades covered jurisdictions from engaging in discrimination that they would resume should §5 be struck down. Under this theory, however, §5 would be effectively immune from scrutiny; no matter how "clean" the record of covered jurisdictions, the argument could always be made that it was deterrence that accounted for the good behavior.

The provisions of §5 apply only to those jurisdictions singled out by §4. We now consider whether that coverage formula is constitutional in light of current conditions.

III

A

When upholding the constitutionality of the coverage formula in 1966, we concluded that it was "rational in both practice and theory." *Katzenbach.* The formula looked to cause (discriminatory tests) and effect (low voter registration and turnout), and tailored the remedy (preclearance) to those jurisdictions exhibiting both.

By 2009, however, we concluded that the "coverage formula raise[d] serious constitutional questions." *Northwest Austin.* As we explained, a statute's "current burdens" must be justified by "current needs," and any "disparate geographic coverage" must be "sufficiently related to the problem that it targets." The coverage formula met that test in 1965, but no longer does so.

Coverage today is based on decades-old data and eradicated practices. The formula captures States by reference to literacy tests and low voter registration and turnout in the 1960s and early 1970s. But such tests have been banned nationwide for over 40 years. And voter registration and turnout numbers in the covered States have risen dramatically in the years since. Racial disparity in those numbers was compelling evidence justifying the preclearance remedy and the coverage formula. There is no longer such a disparity.

In 1965, the States could be divided into two groups: those with a recent history of voting tests and low voter registration and turnout, and those without those characteristics. Congress based its coverage formula on that distinction. Today the Nation is no longer divided along those lines, yet the Voting Rights Act continues to treat it as if it were.

B

The Government's defense of the formula is limited. First, the Government contends that the formula is "reverse-engineered": Congress identified the jurisdictions to be covered and *then* came up with criteria to describe them. Under that reasoning, there need not be any logical relationship between the criteria in the formula and the reason for coverage; all that is necessary is that the formula happen to capture the jurisdictions Congress wanted to single out.

The Government suggests that *Katzenbach* sanctioned such an approach, but the analysis in *Katzenbach* was quite different. *Katzenbach* reasoned that the coverage formula was rational because the "formula . . . was relevant to the problem": "Tests and devices are relevant to voting discrimination because of their long history as a tool for perpetrating the evil; a low voting rate is pertinent for the obvious reason that widespread disenfranchisement must inevitably affect the number of actual voters."

Here, by contrast, the Government's reverse engineering argument does not even attempt to demonstrate the continued relevance of the formula to the problem it targets. And in the context of a decision as significant as this one—subjecting a disfavored subset of States to "extraordinary legislation otherwise unfamiliar to our federal system"—that failure to establish even relevance is fatal.

The Government falls back to the argument that because the formula was relevant in 1965, its continued use is permissible so long as any discrimination remains in the States Congress identified back then—regardless of how that discrimination compares to discrimination in States unburdened by coverage. This argument does not look to "current political conditions," but instead relies on a comparison between the States in 1965. That comparison reflected the different histories of the North and South. It was in the South that slavery was upheld by law until uprooted by the Civil War, that the reign of Jim Crow denied African-Americans the most basic freedoms, and that state and local governments worked tirelessly to disenfranchise citizens on the basis of race. The Court invoked that history—rightly so—in sustaining the disparate coverage of the Voting Rights Act in 1966. See *Katzenbach* ("The constitutional propriety of the Voting Rights Act of 1965 must be judged with reference to the historical experience which it reflects.").

But history did not end in 1965. By the time the Act was reauthorized in 2006, there had been 40 more years of it. In assessing the "current need[]" for a preclearance system that treats States differently from one another today, that history cannot be ignored. During that time, largely because of the Voting Rights Act, voting tests were abolished, disparities in voter registration and turnout due to race were erased, and African-Americans attained political office in record numbers. And yet the coverage formula that Congress reauthorized in 2006 ignores these developments, keeping the focus on decades-old data relevant to decades-old problems, rather than current data reflecting current needs.

The Fifteenth Amendment commands that the right to vote shall not be denied or abridged on account of race or color, and it gives Congress the power to enforce that command. The Amendment is not designed to punish for the past; its purpose is to ensure a better future. To serve that purpose, Congress—if it is to divide the States—must identify those jurisdictions to be singled out on a basis that makes sense in light of current conditions. It cannot rely simply on the past. We made that clear in *Northwest Austin,* and we make it clear again today.

C

In defending the coverage formula, the Government, the intervenors, and the dissent also rely heavily on data from the record that they claim justify disparate coverage. Congress compiled thousands of pages of evidence before reauthorizing the Voting Rights Act. . . . Regardless of how to look at the record, however, no one can fairly say that it shows anything approaching the "pervasive," "flagrant," "widespread," and "rampant" discrimination that faced Congress in 1965, and that clearly distinguished the covered jurisdictions from the rest of the Nation at that time.

But a more fundamental problem remains: Congress did not use the record it compiled to shape a coverage formula grounded in current conditions. It instead reenacted a formula based on 40-year-old facts having no logical relation to the present day. The dissent relies on "second-generation barriers," which are not impediments to the casting of ballots, but rather electoral arrangements that affect the weight of minority votes. That does not cure the problem. Viewing the preclearance requirements as targeting such efforts simply highlights the irrationality of continued reliance on the §4 coverage formula, which is based on voting tests and access to the ballot, not vote dilution. We cannot pretend that we are reviewing an updated statute, or try our hand at updating the statute ourselves, based on the new record compiled by Congress. Contrary to the dissent's contention, we are not ignoring the record; we are simply recognizing that it played no role in shaping the statutory formula before us today.

The dissent also turns to the record to argue that, in light of voting discrimination in Shelby County, the county cannot complain about the provisions that subject it to preclearance. But that is like saying that a driver pulled over pursuant to a policy of stopping all redheads cannot complain about that policy, if it turns out his license has expired. Shelby County's claim is that the coverage formula here is unconstitutional in all its applications, because of how it selects the jurisdictions subjected to preclearance. The county was selected based on that formula, and may challenge it in court.

D

The dissent proceeds from a flawed premise. It quotes the famous sentence from McCulloch v. Maryland: "Let the end be legitimate, let it be within the scope of the constitution, and *all means which are appropriate, which are plainly adapted to that end,* which are not prohibited, but consist with the letter and spirit of the constitution, are constitutional." But this case is about a part of the sentence that the dissent does not emphasize—the part that asks whether a legislative means is "consist[ent] with the letter and spirit of the constitution." The dissent states that "[i]t cannot tenably be maintained" that this is an issue with regard to the Voting Rights Act, but four years ago, in an opinion joined by two of today's dissenters, the Court expressly stated that "[t]he Act's preclearance requirement and its coverage formula raise serious constitutional questions." *Northwest Austin.* The dissent does not explain how those "serious constitutional questions" became untenable in four short years. . . .

In other ways as well, the dissent analyzes the question presented as if our decision in *Northwest Austin* never happened. For example, the dissent refuses to consider the principle of equal sovereignty, despite *Northwest Austin*'s emphasis on its significance. *Northwest Austin* also emphasized the "dramatic" progress since 1965, but the dissent describes current levels of discrimination as "flagrant," "widespread," and "pervasive." Despite the fact that *Northwest Austin* requires an Act's "disparate geographic coverage" to be "sufficiently related" to its targeted problems, the dissent maintains that an Act's limited coverage actually eases Congress's burdens, and suggests that a fortuitous relationship should suffice. Although *Northwest Austin* stated definitively that "current burdens" must be justified by "current needs," the dissent argues that the coverage formula can be justified by history, and that the required showing can be weaker on reenactment than when the law was first passed.

There is no valid reason to insulate the coverage formula from review merely because it was previously enacted 40 years ago. If Congress had started from scratch in 2006, it plainly could not have enacted the present coverage formula. It would have been irrational for Congress to distinguish between States in such a fundamental way based on 40-year-old data, when today's statistics tell an entirely different story. And it would have been irrational to base coverage on the use of voting tests 40 years ago, when such tests have been illegal since that time. But that is exactly what Congress has done.

* * *

Striking down an Act of Congress "is the gravest and most delicate duty that this Court is called on to perform." We do not do so lightly. That is why, in 2009, we took care to avoid ruling on the constitutionality of the Voting Rights Act when asked to do so, and instead resolved the case then before us on statutory grounds. But in issuing that decision, we expressed our broader concerns about the constitutionality of the Act. Congress could have updated the coverage formula at that time, but did not do so. Its failure to act leaves us today with no choice but to declare §4(b) unconstitutional. The formula in that section can no longer be used as a basis for subjecting jurisdictions to preclearance.

Our decision in no way affects the permanent, nationwide ban on racial discrimination in voting found in §2. We issue no holding on §5 itself, only on the coverage formula. Congress may draft another formula based on current conditions. Such a formula is an initial prerequisite to a determination that exceptional conditions still exist justifying such an "extraordinary departure from the traditional course of relations between the States and the Federal Government." Our country has changed, and while any racial discrimination in voting is too much, Congress must ensure that the legislation it passes to remedy that problem speaks to current conditions.

The judgment of the Court of Appeals is reversed.

It is so ordered.

Justice THOMAS, concurring.

I join the Court's opinion in full but write separately to explain that I would find §5 of the Voting Rights Act unconstitutional as well. The Court's opinion sets forth the reasons. . . . While the Court claims to "issue no holding on §5 itself," its own opinion compellingly demonstrates that Congress has failed to justify "'current burdens'" with a record demonstrating "'current needs.'" By leaving the inevitable conclusion unstated, the Court needlessly prolongs the demise of that provision. For the reasons stated in the Court's opinion, I would find §5 unconstitutional.

Justice GINSBURG, with whom Justice BREYER, Justice SOTOMAYOR, and Justice KAGAN join, dissenting.

In the Court's view, the very success of §5 of the Voting Rights Act demands its dormancy. Congress was of another mind. Recognizing that large progress has been made, Congress determined, based on a voluminous record, that the scourge of discrimination was not yet extirpated. The question this case presents is who decides whether, as currently operative, §5 remains justifiable, this Court, or a Congress charged with the obligation to enforce the post-Civil War Amendments "by appropriate legislation." [The Court purports to declare unconstitutional only the coverage formula set out in §4(b). But without that formula, §5 is immobilized. Relocated footnote.—EDS.]

With overwhelming support in both Houses, Congress concluded that, for two prime reasons, §5 should continue in force, unabated. First, continuance would facilitate completion of the impressive gains thus far made; and second, continuance would guard against backsliding. Those assessments were well within Congress' province to make and should elicit this Court's unstinting approbation.

I

[The Court acknowledges that] "voting discrimination still exists; no one doubts that." But the Court today terminates the remedy that proved to be best suited to block that discrimination. The Voting Rights Act of 1965 (VRA) has worked to combat voting discrimination where other remedies had been tried and failed. Particularly effective is the VRA's requirement of federal preclearance for all changes to voting laws in the regions of the country with the most aggravated records of rank discrimination against minority voting rights.

A century after the Fourteenth and Fifteenth Amendments guaranteed citizens the right to vote free of discrimination on the basis of race, the "blight of racial discrimination in voting" continued to "infec[t] the electoral process in parts of our country." Early attempts to cope with this vile infection resembled battling the Hydra. Whenever one form of voting discrimination was identified and prohibited, others sprang up in its place. This Court repeatedly encountered the remarkable "variety and persistence" of laws disenfranchising minority citizens. . . .

During this era, the Court recognized that discrimination against minority voters was a quintessentially political problem requiring a political solution. As Justice Holmes explained: If "the great mass of the white population intends to keep the blacks from voting," "relief from [that] great political wrong, if done, as alleged, by the people of a State and the State itself, must be given by them or by the legislative and political department of the government of the United States." Giles v. Harris, 189 U.S. 475 (1903). . . .

[T]he Voting Rights Act became one of the most consequential, efficacious, and amply justified exercises of federal legislative power in our Nation's history. Requiring federal preclearance of changes in voting laws in the covered jurisdictions—those States and localities where opposition to the Constitution's commands were most virulent—the VRA provided a fit solution for minority voters as well as for States. . . .

Although the VRA wrought dramatic changes in the realization of minority voting rights, the Act, to date, surely has not eliminated all vestiges of discrimination against the exercise of the franchise by minority citizens. Jurisdictions covered by the preclearance requirement continued to submit, in large numbers, proposed changes to voting laws that the Attorney General declined to approve, auguring that barriers to minority voting would quickly resurface were the preclearance remedy eliminated. Congress also found that as "registration and voting of minority citizens increas[ed], other measures may be resorted to which would dilute increasing minority voting strength." Efforts to reduce the impact of minority votes, in contrast to direct attempts to block access to the ballot, are aptly described as "second-generation barriers" to minority voting.

Second-generation barriers come in various forms. One of the blockages is racial gerrymandering, the redrawing of legislative districts in an "effort to segregate the races for purposes of voting." Another is adoption of a system of at-large voting in lieu of district-by-district voting in a city with a sizable black minority. By switching to at-large voting, the overall majority could control the election of each city council member, effectively eliminating the potency of the minority's votes. A similar effect could be achieved if the city engaged in discriminatory annexation by incorporating majority-white areas into city limits, thereby decreasing the effect of VRA-occasioned increases in black voting. Whatever the device employed, this Court has long recognized that vote dilution, when adopted with a discriminatory purpose, cuts down the right to vote as certainly as denial of access to the ballot. See also H.R. Rep. No. 109-478, p. 6 (2006) (although "[d]iscrimination today is more subtle than the visible methods used in 1965," "the effect and results are the same, namely a diminishing of the minority community's ability to fully participate in the electoral process and to elect their preferred candidates").

In response to evidence of these substituted barriers, Congress reauthorized the VRA for five years in 1970, for seven years in 1975, and for 25 years in 1982. Each time, this Court upheld the reauthorization as a valid exercise of congressional power. As the 1982 reauthorization approached its 2007 expiration date, Congress again considered whether the VRA's preclearance mechanism remained an appropriate response to the problem of voting discrimination in covered jurisdictions.

Congress did not take this task lightly. Quite the opposite. The 109th Congress that took responsibility for the renewal started early and conscientiously. . . .

In the long course of the legislative process, Congress "amassed a sizable record." *Northwest Austin* (describing the "extensive record" supporting Congress' determination that "serious and widespread intentional discrimination persisted in covered jurisdictions"). The House and Senate Judiciary Committees held 21 hearings, heard from scores of witnesses, received a number of investigative reports and other written documentation of continuing discrimination in covered jurisdictions. In all, the legislative record Congress compiled filled more than 15,000 pages. The compilation presents countless "examples of flagrant racial discrimination" since the last reauthorization; Congress also brought to light systematic evidence that "intentional racial discrimination in voting remains so serious and widespread in covered jurisdictions that section 5 preclearance is still needed."

After considering the full legislative record, Congress made the following findings: The VRA has directly caused significant progress in eliminating first-generation barriers to ballot access, leading to a marked increase in minority voter registration and turnout and the number of minority elected officials. 2006 Reauthorization §2(b)(1). Fannie Lou Hamer, Rosa Parks, and Coretta Scott King Voting Rights Act Reauthorization and Amendments Act of 2006 (hereinafter 2006 Reauthorization) §2(b)(1). But despite this progress, "second generation barriers constructed to prevent minority voters from fully participating in the electoral process" continued to exist, as well as racially polarized voting in the covered jurisdictions, which increased the political vulnerability of racial and language minorities in those jurisdictions. §§2(b)(2)-(3). Extensive "[e]vidence of continued discrimination," Congress concluded, "clearly show[ed] the continued need for Federal oversight" in covered jurisdictions. §§2(b)(4)-(5). The overall record demonstrated to the federal lawmakers that, "without the continuation of the Voting Rights Act of 1965 protections, racial and language minority citizens will be deprived of the opportunity to exercise their right to vote, or will have their votes diluted, undermining the significant gains made by minorities in the last 40 years." §2(b)(9).

Based on these findings, Congress reauthorized preclearance for another 25 years, while also undertaking to reconsider the extension after 15 years to ensure that the provision was still necessary and effective. 42 U.S.C. §1973b(a)(7), (8) (2006 ed., Supp. V). The question before the Court is whether Congress had the authority under the Constitution to act as it did.

II

In answering this question, the Court does not write on a clean slate. It is well established that Congress' judgment regarding exercise of its power to enforce the Fourteenth and Fifteenth Amendments warrants substantial deference. The VRA addresses the combination of race discrimination and the right to vote, which is "preservative of all rights." When confronting the most constitutionally invidious form of discrimination, and the most fundamental right in our democratic system, Congress' power to act is at its height.

The basis for this deference is firmly rooted in both constitutional text and precedent. The Fifteenth Amendment, which targets precisely and only racial discrimination in voting rights, states that, in this domain, "Congress shall have power to enforce this article by appropriate legislation."[a] In choosing this language, the Amendment's framers invoked Chief Justice Marshall's formulation of the scope of

a. The Constitution uses the words "right to vote" in five separate places: the Fourteenth, Fifteenth, Nineteenth, Twenty-Fourth, and Twenty-Sixth Amendments. Each of these Amendments contains the same broad empowerment of Congress to enact "appropriate legislation" to enforce the protected right. The implication is unmistakable: Under our constitutional structure, Congress holds the lead rein in making the right to vote equally real for all U.S. citizens. These Amendments are in line with the special role assigned to Congress in protecting the integrity of the democratic process in federal elections. U.S. Const., Art. I, §4 ("[T]he Congress may at any time by Law make or alter" regulations concerning the "Times, Places and Manner of holding Elections for Senators and Representatives."); Arizona v. Inter Tribal Council of Ariz., Inc.

Congress' powers under the Necessary and Proper Clause: "Let the end be legitimate, let it be within the scope of the constitution, and *all means which are appropriate, which are plainly adapted to that end*, which are not prohibited, but consist with the letter and spirit of the constitution, are constitutional." McCulloch v. Maryland (emphasis added).

It cannot tenably be maintained that the VRA, an Act of Congress adopted to shield the right to vote from racial discrimination, is inconsistent with the letter or spirit of the Fifteenth Amendment, or any provision of the Constitution read in light of the Civil War Amendments. Nowhere in today's opinion, or in *Northwest Austin*, is there clear recognition of the transformative effect the Fifteenth Amendment aimed to achieve. Notably, "the Founders' first successful amendment told Congress that it could 'make no law' over a certain domain"; in contrast, the Civil War Amendments used "language [that] authorized transformative new federal statutes to uproot all vestiges of unfreedom and inequality" and provided "sweeping enforcement powers . . . to enact 'appropriate' legislation targeting state abuses." A. Amar, America's Constitution: A Biography 361, 363, 399 (2005). See also McConnell, Institutions and Interpretation: A Critique of City of Boerne v. Flores, 111 Harv. L. Rev. 153, 182 (1997) (quoting Civil War–era framer that "the remedy for the violation of the fourteenth and fifteenth amendments was expressly not left to the courts. The remedy was legislative.").

The stated purpose of the Civil War Amendments was to arm Congress with the power and authority to protect all persons within the Nation from violations of their rights by the States. In exercising that power, then, Congress may use "all means which are appropriate, which are plainly adapted" to the constitutional ends declared by these Amendments. *McCulloch.* So when Congress acts to enforce the right to vote free from racial discrimination, we ask not whether Congress has chosen the means most wise, but whether Congress has rationally selected means appropriate to a legitimate end. "It is not for us to review the congressional resolution of [the need for its chosen remedy]. It is enough that we be able to perceive a basis upon which the Congress might resolve the conflict as it did." Katzenbach v. Morgan.

Until today, in considering the constitutionality of the VRA, the Court has accorded Congress the full measure of respect its judgments in this domain should garner. South Carolina v. Katzenbach supplies the standard of review: "As against the reserved powers of the States, Congress may use any rational means to effectuate the constitutional prohibition of racial discrimination in voting." Faced with subsequent reauthorizations of the VRA, the Court has reaffirmed this standard. *E.g., City of Rome.* Today's Court does not purport to alter settled precedent establishing that the dispositive question is whether Congress has employed "rational means."

For three reasons, legislation *re*-authorizing an existing statute is especially likely to satisfy the minimal requirements of the rational-basis test. First, when reauthorization is at issue, Congress has already assembled a legislative record justifying the initial legislation. Congress is entitled to consider that preexisting record as well as the record before it at the time of the vote on reauthorization. This is especially true where, as here, the Court has repeatedly affirmed the statute's constitutionality and Congress has adhered to the very model the Court has upheld.

Second, the very fact that reauthorization is necessary arises because Congress has built a temporal limitation into the Act. It has pledged to review, after a span of years (first 15, then 25) and in light of contemporary evidence, the continued need for the VRA.

Third, a reviewing court should expect the record supporting reauthorization to be less stark than the record originally made. Demand for a record of violations equivalent to the one earlier made would expose Congress to a catch-22. If the statute was working, there would be less evidence of discrimination, so opponents might argue that Congress should not be allowed to renew the statute. In contrast, if the statute was not working, there would be plenty of evidence of discrimination, but scant reason to renew a failed regulatory regime.

This is not to suggest that congressional power in this area is limitless. It is this Court's responsibility to ensure that Congress has used appropriate means. The question meet for judicial review is whether the chosen means are "adapted to carry out the objects the amendments have in view." Ex parte Virginia, 100 U.S. 339 (1880). The Court's role, then, is not to substitute its judgment for that of Congress, but to determine whether the legislative record sufficed to show that "Congress could rationally have determined that [its chosen] provisions were appropriate methods." *City of Rome.*

In summary, the Constitution vests broad power in Congress to protect the right to vote, and in particular to combat racial discrimination in voting. This Court has repeatedly reaffirmed Congress' prerogative to use any rational means in exercise of its power in this area. And both precedent and logic dictate that the rational-means test should be easier to satisfy, and the burden on the statute's challenger should be higher, when what is at issue is the reauthorization of a remedy that the Court has previously affirmed, and that Congress found, from contemporary evidence, to be working to advance the legislature's legitimate objective.

III

The 2006 reauthorization of the Voting Rights Act fully satisfies the standard stated in *McCulloch*: Congress may choose any means "appropriate" and "plainly adapted to" a legitimate constitutional end. As we shall see, it is implausible to suggest otherwise.

A

I begin with the evidence on which Congress based its decision to continue the preclearance remedy. The surest way to evaluate whether that remedy remains in order is to see if preclearance is still effectively preventing discriminatory changes to voting laws. On that score, the record before Congress [in 2006] was huge. In fact, Congress found there were *more* DOJ objections between 1982 and 2004 (626) than there were between 1965 and the 1982 reauthorization (490).

All told, between 1982 and 2006, DOJ objections blocked over 700 voting changes based on a determination that the changes were discriminatory. Congress found that the majority of DOJ objections included findings of discriminatory intent, and that the changes blocked by preclearance were "calculated decisions to keep minority voters from fully participating in the political process." On top of that, over the same time period the DOJ and private plaintiffs succeeded in more than 100 actions to enforce the §5 preclearance requirements.

In addition to blocking proposed voting changes through preclearance, DOJ may request more information from a jurisdiction proposing a change. In turn, the jurisdiction may modify or withdraw the proposed change. The number of such modifications or withdrawals provides an indication of how many discriminatory proposals are deterred without need for formal objection. Congress received evidence that more than 800 proposed changes were altered or withdrawn since the last reauthorization in 1982.[b] Congress also received empirical studies finding that DOJ's requests for more information had a significant effect on the degree to which covered jurisdictions "compl[ied] with their obligatio[n]" to protect minority voting rights.

Congress also received evidence that litigation under §2 of the VRA was an inadequate substitute for preclearance in the covered jurisdictions. Litigation occurs only after the fact, when the illegal voting scheme has already been put in place and individuals have been elected pursuant to it, thereby gaining the advantages of incumbency. An illegal scheme might be in place for several election cycles before a §2 plaintiff can gather sufficient evidence to challenge it. And litigation places a heavy financial burden on minority voters. Congress also received evidence that preclearance lessened the litigation burden on covered jurisdictions themselves, because the preclearance process is far less costly than defending against a §2 claim, and clearance by DOJ substantially reduces the likelihood that a §2 claim will be mounted.

The number of discriminatory changes blocked or deterred by the preclearance requirement suggests that the state of voting rights in the covered jurisdictions would have been significantly different absent this remedy. Surveying the type of changes stopped by the preclearance procedure conveys a sense of the extent to which §5 continues to protect minority voting rights.

[Justice Ginsburg offers multiple examples of attempted changes to electoral systems that would have harmed minority voting rights that were blocked by the pre-2006 VRA.]

These examples, and scores more like them, fill the pages of the legislative record, [and] Congress further received evidence indicating that formal requests of the kind set out above represented only the tip of the iceberg. There was what one commentator described as an "avalanche of case studies of voting rights violations in the covered jurisdictions," ranging from "outright intimidation and violence against minority voters" to "more subtle forms of voting rights deprivations."

True, conditions in the South have impressively improved since passage of the Voting Rights Act. Congress noted this improvement and found that the VRA was

---

b. This number includes only changes actually proposed. Congress also received evidence that many covered jurisdictions engaged in an "informal consultation process" with DOJ before formally submitting a proposal, so that the deterrent effect of preclearance was far broader than the formal submissions alone suggest. All agree that an unsupported assertion about "deterrence" would not be sufficient to justify keeping a remedy in place in perpetuity. But it was certainly reasonable for Congress to consider the testimony of witnesses who had worked with officials in covered jurisdictions and observed a real-world deterrent effect.

the driving force behind it. But Congress also found that voting discrimination had evolved into subtler second-generation barriers, and that eliminating preclearance would risk loss of the gains that had been made. . . .

B

I turn next to the evidence on which Congress based its decision to reauthorize the coverage formula in §4(b). Because Congress did not alter the coverage formula, the same jurisdictions previously subject to preclearance continue to be covered by this remedy. The evidence just described, of preclearance's continuing efficacy in blocking constitutional violations in the covered jurisdictions, itself grounded Congress' conclusion that the remedy should be retained for those jurisdictions.

There is no question, moreover, that the covered jurisdictions have a unique history of problems with racial discrimination in voting. Consideration of this long history, still in living memory, was altogether appropriate. . . . Congress was especially mindful of the need to reinforce the gains already made and to prevent backsliding.

Of particular importance, even after 40 years and thousands of discriminatory changes blocked by preclearance, conditions in the covered jurisdictions demonstrated that the formula was still justified by "current needs." *Northwest Austin.*

Congress learned of these conditions through a report, known as the Katz study, that looked at §2 suits between 1982 and 2004. Because the private right of action authorized by §2 of the VRA applies nationwide, a comparison of §2 lawsuits in covered and noncovered jurisdictions provides an appropriate yardstick for measuring differences between covered and noncovered jurisdictions. If differences in the risk of voting discrimination between covered and noncovered jurisdictions had disappeared, one would expect that the rate of successful §2 lawsuits would be roughly the same in both areas.[c] The study's findings, however, indicated that racial discrimination in voting remains "concentrated in the jurisdictions singled out for preclearance." *Northwest Austin.*

Although covered jurisdictions account for less than 25 percent of the country's population, the Katz study revealed that they accounted for 56 percent of successful §2 litigation since 1982. Controlling for population, there were nearly *four* times as many successful §2 cases in covered jurisdictions as there were in noncovered jurisdictions. The Katz study further found that §2 lawsuits are more likely to succeed when they are filed in covered jurisdictions than in noncovered jurisdictions. From these findings—ignored by the Court—Congress reasonably concluded that the coverage formula continues to identify the jurisdictions of greatest concern.

The evidence before Congress, furthermore, indicated that voting in the covered jurisdictions was more racially polarized than elsewhere in the country. While racially polarized voting alone does not signal a constitutional violation, it is a factor

---

c. Because preclearance occurs only in covered jurisdictions and can be expected to stop the most obviously objectionable measures, one would expect a lower rate of successful §2 lawsuits in those jurisdictions if the risk of voting discrimination there were the same as elsewhere in the country.

that increases the vulnerability of racial minorities to discriminatory changes in voting law. The reason is twofold. First, racial polarization means that racial minorities are at risk of being systematically outvoted and having their interests underrepresented in legislatures. Second, "when political preferences fall along racial lines, the natural inclinations of incumbents and ruling parties to entrench themselves have predictable racial effects. Under circumstances of severe racial polarization, efforts to gain political advantage translate into race-specific disadvantages."

In other words, a governing political coalition has an incentive to prevent changes in the existing balance of voting power. When voting is racially polarized, efforts by the ruling party to pursue that incentive "will inevitably discriminate against a racial group." Just as buildings in California have a greater need to be earthquake-proofed, places where there is greater racial polarization in voting have a greater need for prophylactic measures to prevent purposeful race discrimination. . . .

Congress might have been charged with rigidity had it afforded covered jurisdictions no way out or ignored jurisdictions that needed superintendence. Congress, however, responded to this concern. Critical components of the congressional design are the statutory provisions allowing jurisdictions to "bail out" of preclearance, and for court-ordered "bail ins." The VRA permits a jurisdiction to bail out by showing that it has complied with the Act for ten years, and has engaged in efforts to eliminate intimidation and harassment of voters. [Section 3] also authorizes a court to subject a noncovered jurisdiction to federal preclearance upon finding that violations of the Fourteenth and Fifteenth Amendments have occurred there.

Congress was satisfied that the VRA's bailout mechanism provided an effective means of adjusting the VRA's coverage over time. Nearly 200 jurisdictions have successfully bailed out of the preclearance requirement, and DOJ has consented to every bailout application filed by an eligible jurisdiction since the current bailout procedure became effective in 1984. The bail-in mechanism has also worked. Several jurisdictions have been subject to federal preclearance by court orders, including the States of New Mexico and Arkansas.

This experience exposes the inaccuracy of the Court's portrayal of the Act as static, unchanged since 1965. Congress designed the VRA to be a dynamic statute, capable of adjusting to changing conditions. True, many covered jurisdictions have not been able to bail out due to recent acts of noncompliance with the VRA, but that truth reinforces the congressional judgment that these jurisdictions were rightfully subject to preclearance, and ought to remain under that regime.

IV

Congress approached the 2006 reauthorization of the VRA with great care and seriousness. The same cannot be said of the Court's opinion today. The Court makes no genuine attempt to engage with the massive legislative record that Congress assembled. Instead, it relies on increases in voter registration and turnout as if that were the whole story. Without even identifying a standard of review, the Court dismissively brushes off arguments based on "data from the record," and declines to enter the "debat[e about] what [the] record shows." One would expect more from an opinion striking at the heart of the Nation's signal piece of civil-rights legislation.

A

Shelby County launched a purely facial challenge to the VRA's 2006 reauthorization. "A facial challenge to a legislative Act," the Court has other times said, "is, of course, the most difficult challenge to mount successfully, since the challenger must establish that no set of circumstances exists under which the Act would be valid." United States v. Salerno, 481 U.S. 739 (1987). . . . Yet the Court's opinion in this case contains not a word explaining why Congress lacks the power to subject to preclearance the particular plaintiff that initiated this lawsuit—Shelby County, Alabama. The reason for the Court's silence is apparent, for as applied to Shelby County, the VRA's preclearance requirement is hardly contestable. . . . Between 1982 and 2005, Alabama had one of the highest rates of successful §2 suits, second only to its VRA-covered neighbor Mississippi. In other words, even while subject to the restraining effect of §5, Alabama was found to have "deni[ed] or abridge[d]" voting rights "on account of race or color" more frequently than nearly all other States in the Union. . . . Alabama's sorry history of §2 violations alone provides sufficient justification for Congress' determination in 2006 that the State should remain subject to §5's preclearance requirement. [Justice Ginsburg cited multiple examples of recent voting discrimination in Alabama and of "the persistence of racial discrimination in state politics."]

These recent episodes forcefully demonstrate that §5's preclearance requirement is constitutional as applied to Alabama and its political subdivisions. And under our case law, that conclusion should suffice to resolve this case. . . .

The VRA's . . . severability provision states: "If any provision of [this Act] or the application thereof to any person or circumstances is held invalid, the remainder of [the Act] and the application of the provision to other persons not similarly situated or to other circumstances shall not be affected thereby." 42 U.S.C. §1973p. . . . In other words, even if the VRA could not constitutionally be applied to certain States—*e.g.*, Arizona and Alaska—§1973p calls for those unconstitutional applications to be severed, leaving the Act in place for jurisdictions as to which its application does not transgress constitutional limits.

B

The Court stops any application of §5 by holding that §4(b)'s coverage formula is unconstitutional. It pins this result, in large measure, to "the fundamental principle of equal sovereignty." In *Katzenbach*, however, the Court held, in no uncertain terms, that the principle "*applies only to the terms upon which States are admitted to the Union*, and not to the remedies for local evils which have subsequently appeared." (emphasis added).

Katzenbach, the Court acknowledges, "rejected the notion that the [equal sovereignty] principle operate[s] as a bar on differential treatment outside [the] context [of the admission of new States]." . . . In today's decision, the Court ratchets up what was pure dictum in *Northwest Austin*, attributing breadth to the equal sovereignty principle in flat contradiction of *Katzenbach*. The Court does so with nary an explanation of why it finds *Katzenbach* wrong, let alone any discussion of whether *stare decisis* nonetheless counsels adherence to *Katzenbach*'s ruling on the limited "significance" of the equal sovereignty principle.

Today's unprecedented extension of the equal sovereignty principle outside its proper domain—the admission of new States—is capable of much mischief. Federal statutes that treat States disparately are hardly novelties. See, *e.g.*, 28 U.S.C. §3704 (no State may operate or permit a sports-related gambling scheme, unless that State conducted such a scheme "at any time during the period beginning January 1, 1976, and ending August 31, 1990"); 26 U.S.C. §142(*l*) (EPA required to locate green building project in a State meeting specified population criteria); 42 U.S.C. §3796bb (at least 50 percent of rural drug enforcement assistance funding must be allocated to States with "a population density of fifty-two or fewer persons per square mile or a State in which the largest county has fewer than one hundred and fifty thousand people, based on the decennial census of 1990 through fiscal year 1997"); §§13925, 13971 (similar population criteria for funding to combat rural domestic violence); §10136 (specifying rules applicable to Nevada's Yucca Mountain nuclear waste site, and providing that "[n]o State, other than the State of Nevada, may receive financial assistance under this subsection after December 22, 1987"). Do such provisions remain safe given the Court's expansion of equal sovereignty's sway?

Of gravest concern, Congress relied on our pathmarking *Katzenbach* decision in each reauthorization of the VRA. It had every reason to believe that the Act's limited geographical scope would weigh in favor of, not against, the Act's constitutionality. See, *e.g.*, United States v. Morrison, 529 U.S. 598 (2000) (confining preclearance regime to States with a record of discrimination bolstered the VRA's constitutionality). Congress could hardly have foreseen that the VRA's limited geographic reach would render the Act constitutionally suspect.

In the Court's conception, it appears, defenders of the VRA could not prevail upon showing what the record overwhelmingly bears out, *i.e.*, that there is a need for continuing the preclearance regime in covered States. In addition, the defenders would have to disprove the existence of a comparable need elsewhere. I am aware of no precedent for imposing such a double burden on defenders of legislation.

C

The Court has time and again declined to upset legislation of this genre unless there was no or almost no evidence of unconstitutional action by States. See, *e.g.*, City of Boerne v. Flores, 521 U.S. 507 (1997). . . . Given a record replete with examples of denial or abridgment of a paramount federal right, the Court should have left the matter where it belongs: in Congress' bailiwick.

Instead, the Court strikes §4(b)'s coverage provision because, in its view, the provision is not based on "current conditions." [Yet] [v]olumes of evidence supported Congress' determination that the prospect of retrogression was real. Throwing out preclearance when it has worked and is continuing to work to stop discriminatory changes is like throwing away your umbrella in a rainstorm because you are not getting wet.

But, the Court insists, the coverage formula is no good; it is based on "decades-old data and eradicated practices." Even if the legislative record shows, as engaging with it would reveal, that the formula accurately identifies the jurisdictions with the worst conditions of voting discrimination, that is of no moment, as the Court sees it. Congress, the Court decrees, must "star[t] from scratch." I do not see why that should be so. . . .

By [2006], the [coverage] formula had been in effect for many years, and *all* of the jurisdictions covered by it were "familiar to Congress by name." The question before Congress: Was there still a sufficient basis to support continued application of the preclearance remedy in each of those already-identified places? There was at that point no chance that the formula might inadvertently sweep in new areas that were not the subject of congressional findings. And Congress could determine from the record whether the jurisdictions captured by the coverage formula still belonged under the preclearance regime. If they did, there was no need to alter the formula. That is why the Court, in addressing prior reauthorizations of the VRA, did not question the continuing "relevance" of the formula.

Consider once again the components of the record before Congress in 2006. The coverage provision identified a known list of places with an undisputed history of serious problems with racial discrimination in voting. Recent evidence relating to Alabama and its counties was there for all to see. Multiple Supreme Court decisions had upheld the coverage provision, most recently in 1999. There was extensive evidence that, due to the preclearance mechanism, conditions in the covered jurisdictions had notably improved. And there was evidence that preclearance was still having a substantial real-world effect, having stopped hundreds of discriminatory voting changes in the covered jurisdictions since the last reauthorization. In addition, there was evidence that racial polarization in voting was higher in covered jurisdictions than elsewhere, increasing the vulnerability of minority citizens in those jurisdictions. And countless witnesses, reports, and case studies documented continuing problems with voting discrimination in those jurisdictions. In light of this record, Congress had more than a reasonable basis to conclude that the existing coverage formula was not out of sync with conditions on the ground in covered areas. And certainly Shelby County was no candidate for release through the mechanism Congress provided.

The Court holds §4(b) invalid on the ground that it is "irrational to base coverage on the use of voting tests 40 years ago, when such tests have been illegal since that time." But the Court disregards what Congress set about to do in enacting the VRA. That extraordinary legislation scarcely stopped at the particular tests and devices that happened to exist in 1965. The grand aim of the Act is to secure to all in our polity equal citizenship stature, a voice in our democracy undiluted by race. As the record for the 2006 reauthorization makes abundantly clear, second-generation barriers to minority voting rights have emerged in the covered jurisdictions as attempted *substitutes* for the first-generation barriers that originally triggered preclearance in those jurisdictions.

The sad irony of today's decision lies in its utter failure to grasp why the VRA has proven effective. The Court appears to believe that the VRA's success in eliminating the specific devices extant in 1965 means that preclearance is no longer needed. With that belief, and the argument derived from it, history repeats itself. The same assumption—that the problem could be solved when particular methods of voting discrimination are identified and eliminated—was indulged and proved wrong repeatedly prior to the VRA's enactment. Unlike prior statutes, which singled out particular tests or devices, the VRA is grounded in Congress' recognition of the "variety and persistence" of measures designed to impair minority voting rights.

Katzenbach. In truth, the evolution of voting discrimination into more subtle second-generation barriers is powerful evidence that a remedy as effective as preclearance remains vital to protect minority voting rights and prevent backsliding. . . .

It was the judgment of Congress that "40 years has not been a sufficient amount of time to eliminate the vestiges of discrimination following nearly 100 years of disregard for the dictates of the 15th amendment and to ensure that the right of all citizens to vote is protected as guaranteed by the Constitution." 2006 Reauthorization §2(b)(7), 120 Stat. 577. That determination of the body empowered to enforce the Civil War Amendments "by appropriate legislation" merits this Court's utmost respect. In my judgment, the Court errs egregiously by overriding Congress' decision.

* * *

For the reasons stated, I would affirm the judgment of the Court of Appeals.

DISCUSSION

1. *A new doctrine? Shelby County* promised to resolve the question whether the "congruence and proportionality" standard of *Boerne* would also apply to the Voting Rights Act, or whether the Court would retain the test of reasonableness in *McCulloch* used in the civil rights era cases of South Carolina v. Katzenbach, Katzenbach v. Morgan, and Oregon v. Mitchell.

Shelby County ducks that question completely. Instead, it creates a new doctrine of equal sovereignty: "[A] departure from the fundamental principle of equal sovereignty requires a showing that a statute's disparate geographic coverage is sufficiently related to the problem that it targets." Because "the Act imposes current burdens" it "must be justified by current needs."

As Justice Ginsburg points out, the equal sovereignty doctrine was mostly concerned with questions of state admission, and even in this context it was honored in the breach as much as the observance. It had never been applied to Fourteenth Amendment §5 or Fifteenth Amendment §2 legislation in the past; and South Carolina v. Katzenbach said the principle was not germane. The idea of "equal sovereignty" was offered as dicta in *Northwest Austin,* joined by eight Justices. In the hands of Chief Justice Roberts, however, it has now been elevated into a powerful new doctrine by five Justices in *Shelby County.*

2. *Equal sovereignty versus the Reconstruction paradigm.* One reason why the doctrine of equal sovereignty seems puzzling in this context concerns the history of Reconstruction itself. Congress, then acting under the authority of the Guarantee Clause, divided Southern states into military districts, supervised them as wards of the Union, and restored them to full status only after they had given Black people the right to vote and ratified the Fourteenth Amendment. The paradigm case that led to the Reconstruction Amendments involved treating states differently based on the history of how they had treated Black people. See Akhil Reed Amar, The Lawfulness of Section 5—and Thus of Section 5, 126 Harv. L. Rev. Forum 109, 110 (2013) ("In short, any serious constitutional analysis of the special preclearance system of the Voting Rights Act must come to grips with the special preclearance

system that generated the Fourteenth Amendment itself in the 1860s."). Are the two situations distinguishable? Could Congress have passed the VRA under the Guarantee Clause today? If so, do you believe the Supreme Court would have used the equal sovereignty principle to limit Congress's powers under that clause as well?

Underlying the Justices' arguments about congressional power and federalism are contrasting understandings of the meaning and consequence of the Civil War and Reconstruction. While the majority looks to founding-era conceptions of state sovereignty, the dissent emphasizes, as Justice Ginsburg puts it, "the transformative effect the Fifteenth Amendment aimed to achieve," and the responsibilities given to Congress to enforce equal rights and monitor violations of these rights by sometimes unwilling state governments.

3. *Equal sovereignty as heightened scrutiny?* What level of scrutiny is implicit in the new "equal sovereignty" doctrine? It seems to be clearly more than *McCulloch* and *Katzenbach*, which used tests either of reasonableness or rationality.

In fact, the new test seems to be even more stringent than the congruence and proportionality test of *Boerne* itself. *Boerne* went out of its way not to disturb the civil rights era cases. Later cases like *Hibbs* and Tennessee v. Lane suggested that Congress is on strongest ground when it attempts to support constitutional guarantees against suspect classifications or violations of fundamental rights that the Court has already recognized. This is especially so when Congress makes detailed findings of fact of previous violations of constitutional rights.

The VRA concerned *both* suspect classifications (race, ethnicity, and nationality) and a fundamental right (the right to vote). It also featured an ample record of voting rights violations and factual findings. All this, however, turned out to be insufficient under the new doctrine of "equal sovereignty."

4. *Current conditions.* Chief Justice Roberts argues that the Voting Rights Act is unconstitutional because it does not respond to "current conditions." However, as Justice Ginsburg points out, the statute includes self-updating provisions. It allows jurisdictions that have demonstrated that they no longer discriminate to "bail out"; it also allows the Department of Justice to ask courts to find that jurisdictions that have discriminated should be "bailed in." (See the discussion in discussion note 9, infra.) These remedies, moreover, are not merely hypothetical; they have actually been employed to change the coverage formula over time. Chief Justice Roberts's opinion does not respond to this point. Should it be sufficient to meet the majority's concerns?

5. *The Court's treatment of congressional findings of fact.* Justice Ginsburg spends considerable time walking us through Congress's findings of bad behavior by covered jurisdictions and she emphasizes Congress's thoroughness and conscientiousness in compiling the record. Chief Justice Roberts, by contrast, emphasizes that Black registrations in covered jurisdictions are now at parity with noncovered jurisdictions and that "no one can fairly say that [the record] shows anything approaching the 'pervasive,' 'flagrant,' 'widespread,' and 'rampant' discrimination that faced Congress in 1965, and that clearly distinguished the covered jurisdictions from the rest of the Nation at that time." Justice Ginsburg notes that Congress believed that it needed to address second-generation denials of voting rights; Chief Justice Roberts regards these as an inadequate justification for maintaining the current coverage formula. How respectful is the majority of congressional judgments? How respectful should it be?

Is the problem the size of the congressional record or simply the length of years the coverage formula has been in effect without substantial change? Assuming that Congress was determined to maintain the current coverage formula, is there any record that the majority would have accepted?

6. *The reach of the equal sovereignty doctrine.* How far does the new "equal sovereignty" doctrine extend? Justice Ginsburg's dissent points out a number of federal programs that treat states differently. Also consider the interaction of the "equal sovereignty" principle with the General Welfare Clause: Many social welfare programs, including, for example, Medicaid reimbursements, vary by state. Different states get very different amounts of funding in various federal programs, largely as a result of logrolling and the political strength of small-state senators. Does the new doctrine reach these programs?

Another possibility is that the "equal sovereignty" doctrine was created in order to resolve this particular case—to strike down §4 of the Voting Rights Act—and that it will rarely be invoked again outside of the civil rights context. In that case, it is merely an artifact of the Court's inability to cobble together five votes for an interpretation of the *Boerne* standard.

7. *The VRA as a "racial entitlement."* The majority appeared to be suspicious of Congress's decision to maintain the old coverage formula. At oral argument, Justice Scalia was particularly suspicious of the fact that the VRA was reauthorized for 25 years by overwhelming margins. "I think it is . . . very likely attributable, to a . . . perpetuation of racial entitlement. . . . Whenever a society adopts racial entitlements, it is very difficult to get out of them through the normal political processes. I don't think there is anything to be gained by any Senator to vote against continuation of this act. And I am fairly confident it will be reenacted in perpetuity unless—unless a court can say it does not comport with the Constitution. . . . Even the name of it is wonderful: The Voting Rights Act. Who is going to vote against that in the future?" Shelby County v. Holder, Oral Arg. Trans. 47-48.

What does Justice Scalia mean by "racial entitlement" in this context? Isn't Justice Scalia right that it was very difficult for most politicians to vote against the extension of the Voting Rights Act, one of the crown jewels of the civil rights movement? Once the Court strikes down the coverage formula, however, it changes the status quo and political expectations. It now becomes easier for Congresspersons and senators to resist passing a new version of the VRA on the grounds that the Court has declared parts of the old version unconstitutional. Which way should this cut? Is the Court's attempt to shake up political understandings a good thing or a bad thing?

8. *Changing the coverage formula is hard to do.* One reason why Congress has maintained basically the same coverage formula for decades is that it was quite difficult for Congress to agree on a new one. Many legislators did not want their states added to the covered jurisdictions, and some were opposed to the idea of preclearance in general. Most of the new jurisdictions that would be added were Republican strongholds, which raised partisan hackles.

The *Boerne* test, which most legislators thought would apply to any constitutional challenge of the 2006 re-extension, created additional problems. Congress had to guess how the courts would apply *Boerne* to a law like the Voting Rights Act, which was prophylactic, had already been in operation for years, and applied only to certain parts of the country. How could Congress show congruence and proportionality in a law that is already in place? What record of discrimination would be sufficient? The difficulty was that virtually any theory one might come up with could be employed by a critic to prove the opposite conclusion.

For example, one might think evidence of voting rights violations in covered jurisdictions would be helpful in showing why the Act was congruent and proportional. On the other hand, if the Act was working well, there might be relatively few voting rights violations in the covered jurisdictions. That evidence, in turn, could mean either that the Act was necessary or that it was superfluous. And if the voting rights violations continued, that might suggest that the law wasn't working very well.

Moreover, one had to take into account the fact that the law reached only some parts of the country. Again, Congress didn't know what the courts would end up requiring under *Boerne*. Courts might require a showing that covered jurisdictions were more likely to violate voting rights than noncovered jurisdictions. But if there wasn't a significant discrepancy, or noncovered jurisdictions actually had more voting rights violations, it might mean either that the Act was working well (because it prevented violations in covered jurisdictions) or that it was unnecessary. As a result, Professor Nathaniel Persily explains:[24]

> Supporters of reauthorization decided that the safest course of action was to stick with the coverage formula that the Supreme Court had previously upheld. Despite the recognized need to extend coverage to the newest generation of voting rights violators, constitutional and political constraints prevented any alteration of the statute's geographic reach. . . . [A]ny change in the coverage formula [created] an additional gamble on the ability of Congress to predict what types of evidence the Court would find important. . . . [Therefore] [t]he new Act [did not try] to capture all of the worst voting rights violators, but rather an effort to capture some of them and to preserve historic gains where they had been made. [S]upporters of the Act sought to develop an evidentiary record for the principal purpose of explaining why the covered jurisdictions should remain covered, rather than justifying the coverage of certain jurisdictions but not others.

Political incentives also help explain why the Voting Rights Act's reauthorizations have been for increasingly longer periods. A 25-year reauthorization, unlike the original 5-year reauthorization in 1965, allows politicians to kick the can down the road and not have to take up very messy questions. Twenty-five years is longer than the careers of most national politicians and covers two to three reapportionment cycles. In addition, many politicians have adjusted to the status quo, just as they did to the reapportionment doctrines that began with Reynolds v. Sims. Many politicians may conclude that it is better to live with the current coverage formula than risk a new status quo that might undermine their interests.

Finally, the Voting Rights Act creates cross-cutting alliances between the two major political parties. The Act gives incentives for Republicans to pack as many Democratic-leaning voters as possible into districts virtually guaranteed to elect

---

24. Nathaniel Persily, The Promise and Pitfalls of the New Voting Rights Act, 117 Yale L.J. 174, 193-195 (2007).

minority representatives. This allows Republicans to create a relatively larger number of districts dominated by conservative, white, and rural voters who are likely to elect Republicans to office. The status quo thus appeals to some conservative Republicans who would otherwise oppose elements of the Act, as well as to Democrats who want to maximize minority representation, especially in the South.

9. *Remedies after* Shelby County. Many political observers are skeptical that the current Congress, which is ideologically polarized, can come up with a new coverage formula. If the VRA actually serves the status quo, won't politicians of both parties have an interest in coming up with something that approximates it? On the other hand, once the status quo is dissolved, the effect of doing nothing changes, and so too does the calculus of interests. Collective action problems may result in inertia, even if the previous system was somewhat more desirable for many politicians.

Note, however, that lawsuits under §2 of the Voting Rights Act are still available to protect minority voting rights, although they are expensive and time-consuming and lack the advantages that made preclearance such an effective remedy. In addition, §3(c) of the Voting Rights Act allows a court in a successful voting rights lawsuit involving a noncovered jurisdiction to impose preclearance requirements on that jurisdiction for a specified period of time. Section 3(c) thus allows voting rights litigation to temporarily create a new set of covered jurisdictions. In addition, Professor Joey Fishkin has argued that Congress could achieve many of the aims of the previous version of §5 by amending §3 so that "Section 5 coverage commence[s] automatically in any jurisdiction that a court determines has violated Section 2. Coverage should last ten years (to cover a redistricting cycle) and should include other jurisdictions physically within the covered jurisdiction." See Joey Fishkin, The Way Forward After Shelby County, Balkinization, June 25, 2013, at http://balkin.blogspot.com/2013/06/the-way-forward-after-shelby-county.html.

Under *Shelby County*'s new doctrine of equal sovereignty, is §3(c) constitutional because it involves a court order premised on a previous violation of law as opposed to congressional findings of voting rights violations under §5?

10. *The Elections Clause.* Another possible source of congressional power to protect voting rights is the Elections Clause of Article I, §4, cl. 1: "The Times, Places and Manner of holding Elections for Senators and Representatives, shall be prescribed in each State by the Legislature thereof; but the Congress may at any time by Law make or alter such Regulations, except as to the places of chusing Senators." Although the Elections Clause does not concern election of state officers, states normally hold elections for both state and federal offices on the same day so in practice federal regulations will set the norm.

In Arizona v. Inter Tribal Council of Arizona, 570 U.S. 1 (2013), the Supreme Court held, 7-2, that Arizona's requirement that voters seeking to register provide documentary evidence of citizenship was preempted by the National Voter Registration Act of 1993. The NVRA prescribes a federal registration form that requires that a registrant aver that he or she is a citizen, but does not require documentary evidence of citizenship.

Justice Scalia's majority opinion explained that under the Elections Clause Congress had plenary power to displace state law with respect to how federal elections would be conducted, but it did not give Congress the power to impose different voter qualifications than the states: "[T]he Elections Clause empowers

Congress to regulate *how* federal elections are held, but not *who* may vote in them." This statement is inconsistent with the judgment of Oregon v. Mitchell, which held that Congress could, by statute, give 18-year-olds the right to vote in federal elections. Justice Scalia explained, however, that although a majority of Justices agreed that Congress could pass such a law, four relied on Congress's powers under §5 of the Fourteenth Amendment, and only Justice Black relied on the Elections Clause.

Could Congress have passed—or could it reenact—§4 of the Voting Rights Act under the Elections Clause? Note that under the Elections Clause, Congress could not require preclearance of changes in voting rules affecting only state and local government offices—and a very large number of preclearance issues concern elections for state and local officials. In addition, Congress could not require preclearance of changes in voter eligibility rules, only changes in the way that states proved eligibility to register or vote, the kinds of voting machines used, the number and location of polling places, the hours and days available for polling, and so on. For example, Congress could probably not require preclearance of voting rules that disenfranchise felons, but it might be able to regulate how states purge voter rolls of suspected felons and noncitizens.

In *Inter Tribal Council of Arizona*, Justice Scalia stated that Congress's power over the "Times, Places and Manner" of congressional elections "is paramount, and may be exercised at any time, and to any extent which it deems expedient; and so far as it is exercised, and no farther, the regulations effected supersede those of the State which are inconsistent therewith" (quoting Ex parte Siebold, 100 U.S. 371, 392 (1880)). How would *Shelby County*'s new "equal sovereignty" principle interact with this test?

BRNOVICH v. DEMOCRATIC NATIONAL COMMITTEE, 2021 WL 2690267. [The Supreme Court further limited the reach of the Voting Rights Act of 1965 in a 6-3 decision written by Justice Alito.

Following the Supreme Court's 2013 decision in *Shelby County*, Section 2 of the Voting Rights Act remained as the Act's primary vehicle for protecting voting rights. Section 2(a) provides that: "No voting qualification or prerequisite to voting or standard, practice, or procedure shall be imposed or applied by any State or political subdivision in a manner which results in a denial or abridgement of the right of any citizen of the United States to vote on account of race or color." 52 U.S.C. §10301(a). Section 2(b) provides that "[a] violation of subsection (a) is established if, based on the totality of circumstances, it is shown that the political processes leading to nomination or election in the State or political subdivision are not equally open to participation by members of [a given race] in that [those] members have less opportunity than other members of the electorate to participate in the political process and to elect representatives of their choice." §10301(b).

In Mobile v. Bolden, 446 U.S. 55 (1980), the Supreme Court interpreted an earlier version of the Voting Rights Act to require plaintiffs to show purposeful discrimination. In response, Congress passed the 1982 Amendments, which sought to reject the intent test and substitute a test of fair equal opportunity to vote, focusing on the "results" of a state voting practice. Thornburg v. Gingles 478 U.S. 30, 35 (1986). *Gingles* developed a multi-factor test to determine whether a state had violated equal opportunity to vote.

Gingles involved redistricting schemes that diluted the votes of minority voters. In *Brnovich,* the Court considered Section 2's application to regulations of the time, place, and manner of voting, such as regulation of where and how long polls are open, when voters can register, rules for absentee ballots, and voter identification laws. These and related voting rules have been major grounds of contention since the Supreme Court held in Crawford v. Marion County Election Board, 553 U.S. 181 (2008), that voter identification requirements did not violate the Fifteenth Amendment.]

Alito, J.:

[T]he core of §2(b) is the requirement that voting be "equally open." The statute's reference to equal "opportunity" may stretch that concept to some degree to include consideration of a person's ability to use the means that are equally open. But equal openness remains the touchstone. . . .

[B]ecause voting necessarily requires some effort and compliance with some rules, the concept of a voting system that is "equally open" and that furnishes an equal "opportunity" to cast a ballot must tolerate the "usual burdens of voting." Mere inconvenience cannot be enough to demonstrate a violation of §2. . . . [T]he degree to which a voting rule departs from what was standard practice when §2 was amended in 1982 is a relevant consideration. Because every voting rule imposes a burden of some sort, it is useful to have benchmarks with which the burdens imposed by a challenged rule can be compared. The burdens associated with the rules in widespread use when §2 was adopted are therefore useful. . . . We doubt that Congress intended to uproot facially neutral time, place, and manner regulations that have a long pedigree or are in widespread use in the United States. . . .

To the extent that minority and non-minority groups differ with respect to employment, wealth, and education, even neutral regulations, no matter how crafted, may well result in some predictable disparities in rates of voting and noncompliance with voting rules. But the mere fact there is some disparity in impact does not necessarily mean that a system is not equally open or that it does not give everyone an equal opportunity to vote. The size of any disparity matters.

[T]he strength of the state interests served by a challenged voting rule is also an important factor that must be taken into account. As noted, every voting rule imposes a burden of some sort, and therefore, in determining "based on the totality of circumstances" whether a rule goes too far, it is important to consider the reason for the rule. Rules that are supported by strong state interests are less likely to violate § 2. One strong and entirely legitimate state interest is the prevention of fraud. Fraud can affect the outcome of a close election, and fraudulent votes dilute the right of citizens to cast ballots that carry appropriate weight. Fraud can also undermine public confidence in the fairness of elections and the perceived legitimacy of the announced outcome. . . .

We also do not find the disparate-impact model employed in Title VII and Fair Housing Act cases useful here. . . . For example, we think it inappropriate to read §2 to impose a strict "necessity requirement" that would force States to demonstrate that their legitimate interests can be accomplished only by means of the voting regulations in question. . . . [This] would have the effect of invalidating a great many neutral voting regulations with long pedigrees that are reasonable means of pursuing legitimate interests. It would also transfer much of the authority to regulate election procedures from the States to the federal courts . . .

Even if the plaintiffs had shown a disparate burden caused by [Arizona's law], the State's justifications [of preventing election fraud] would suffice to avoid §2 liability. "A State indisputably has a compelling interest in preserving the integrity of its election process." . . .

The dissent, by contrast, would rewrite the text of §2 and make it turn almost entirely on just one circumstance—disparate impact. That is a radical project . . . §2 does not deprive the States of their authority to establish non-discriminatory voting rules, and that is precisely what the dissent's radical interpretation would mean in practice. The dissent is correct that the Voting Rights Act exemplifies our country's commitment to democracy, but there is nothing democratic about the dissent's attempt to bring about a wholesale transfer of the authority to set voting rules from the States to the federal courts.

[Justice Gorsuch, joined by Justice Thomas, concurred, noting that the Court had not decided whether voting rights plaintiffs even had an implied cause of action to sue under §2.]

KAGAN, J., joined by BREYER and SOTOMAYOR, JJ., dissenting:

Today, the Court undermines Section 2 and the right it provides. The majority fears that the statute Congress wrote is too "radical"—that it will invalidate too many state voting laws. So the majority writes its own set of rules, limiting Section 2 from multiple directions. Wherever it can, the majority gives a cramped reading to broad language. And then it uses that reading to uphold two election laws from Arizona that discriminate against minority voters. . . . What is tragic here is that the Court has (yet again) rewritten—in order to weaken—a statute that stands as a monument to America's greatness, and protects against its basest impulses. What is tragic is that the Court has damaged a statute designed to bring about "the end of discrimination in voting." . . .

The rashness of [*Shelby County*] soon became evident. Once Section 5's strictures came off, States and localities put in place new restrictive voting laws, with foreseeably adverse effects on minority voters. On the very day Shelby County issued, Texas announced that it would implement a strict voter-identification requirement that had failed to clear Section 5. Other States—Alabama, Virginia, Mississippi—fell like dominoes, adopting measures similarly vulnerable to preclearance review. The North Carolina Legislature, starting work the day after *Shelby County*, enacted a sweeping election bill eliminating same-day registration, forbidding out-of-precinct voting, and reducing early voting, including souls-to-the-polls Sundays. . . . States and localities redistricted—drawing new boundary lines or replacing neighborhood-based seats with at-large seats—in ways guaranteed to reduce minority representation. And jurisdictions closed polling places in mostly minority areas, enhancing an already pronounced problem.

And that was just the first wave of post–*Shelby County* laws. In recent months, State after State has taken up or enacted legislation erecting new barriers to voting. Those laws shorten the time polls are open, both on Election Day and before. They impose new prerequisites to voting by mail, and shorten the windows to apply for and return mail ballots. They make it harder to register to vote, and easier to purge voters from the rolls. Two laws even ban handing out food or water to voters standing in line.

Some of those restrictions may be lawful under the Voting Rights Act. But chances are that some have the kind of impact the Act was designed to prevent—that they make the political process less open to minority voters than to others.

So the Court decides this Voting Rights Act case at a perilous moment for the Nation's commitment to equal citizenship. It decides this case in an era of voting-rights retrenchment—when too many States and localities are restricting access to voting in ways that will predictably deprive members of minority groups of equal access to the ballot box. . . . Congress never meant for Section 2 to bear all of the weight of the Act's commitments. That provision looks to courts, not to the Executive Branch, to restrain discriminatory voting practices. And litigation is an after-the-fact remedy, incapable of providing relief until an election—usually, more than one election—has come and gone. So Section 2 was supposed to be a back-up, for all its sweep and power. But after *Shelby County*, the vitality of Section 2—a "permanent, nationwide ban on racial discrimination in voting"—matters more than ever. For after *Shelby County*, Section 2 is what voters have left. . . .

The oddest part of the majority's analysis is the idea that 'what was standard practice when § 2 was amended in 1982 is a relevant consideration.' The 1982 state of the world is no part of the Section 2 test. An election rule prevalent at that time may make voting harder for minority than for white citizens; Section 2 then covers such a rule, as it covers any other. And contrary to the majority's unsupported speculation, Congress 'intended' exactly that. Section 2 was meant to disrupt the status quo, not to preserve it—to eradicate then-current discriminatory practices, not to set them in amber. . . .

Throughout American history, election officials have asserted anti-fraud interests in using voter suppression laws. Poll taxes, the classic mechanism to keep black people from voting, were often justified as "preserv[ing] the purity of the ballot box [and] facilitat[ing] honest elections." A raft of election regulations—including "elaborate registration procedures" and "early poll closings"—similarly excluded white immigrants (Irish, Italians, and so on) from the polls on the ground of "prevent[ing] fraud and corruption." . . . States have always found it natural to wrap discriminatory policies in election-integrity garb.

Congress enacted Section 2 to prevent those maneuvers from working. It knew that States and localities had over time enacted measure after measure imposing discriminatory voting burdens. And it knew that governments were proficient in justifying those measures on non-racial grounds. So Congress called a halt. It enacted a statute that would strike down all unnecessary laws, including facially neutral ones, that result in members of a racial group having unequal access to the political process.

But the majority is out of sympathy with that measure. The majority thinks a statute that would remove those laws is . . . too "radical" to stomach. The majority objects to an excessive "transfer of the authority to set voting rules from the States to the federal courts." It even sees that transfer as "[un]democratic." But . . . history makes clear the incongruity, in interpreting this statute, of the majority's paean to state authority—and conversely, its denigration of federal responsibility for ensuring non-discriminatory voting rules. The Voting Rights Act was meant to replace state and local election rules that needlessly make voting harder for members of one race than for others. The text of the Act perfectly reflects that objective. The "democratic" principle it upholds is not one of States' rights as against federal courts. The democratic principle it upholds is the right of every American, of every race, to have equal access to the ballot box. The majority today undermines that principle as it refuses to apply the terms of the statute. By declaring some racially discriminatory burdens inconsequential, and by refusing to subject asserted state interests to serious means-end scrutiny, the majority enables voting discrimination.

II. AFFIRMATIVE LIMITS ON CONGRESSIONAL REGULATIONS OF STATE GOVERNMENTS

Even if enumerated congressional power exists, under the Commerce Clause, or the Reconstruction power, or elsewhere, various rights cut across these powers, and further constrain Congress. For example, even where there is a clear connection to interstate commerce, Congress may not pass laws that abridge free expression, or freedom of religion, or due process. A law barring private interstate employers from discriminating against employees on the basis of their political viewpoints might be generally permissible, but could such a law be applied to, say, a national political-opinion magazine (like *The New Republic* or *The Weekly Standard*) deciding whom to hire as a columnist? In such a case, the First Amendment cuts across the commerce power, limiting what would otherwise be permissible.

Do state governments have a similar claim to certain kinds of affirmative exemptions from federal laws otherwise within the commerce power? If so, exactly where does this claim to affirmative exemptions come from?

A. From the Hughes Court to the Burger Court: Practically No Limits?

In the half-century between the New Deal and the Rehnquist Court, state claims for affirmative exemptions did not fare particularly well with the Justices. For example, in United States v. California, 297 U.S. 175 (1936), the Court unanimously upheld a fine against a railroad wholly owned by the state for a violation of the Federal Safety Appliance Act. In the wake of United States v. California, states were held subject to a variety of federal labor laws enacted pursuant to the commerce power. See, e.g., California v. Taylor, 353 U.S. 553 (1957) (Railway Labor Act); Parden v. Terminal Railway, 377 U.S. 184 (1964) (Federal Employers' Liability Act), overruled on other grounds; College Savings Bank v. Florida Prepaid Postsecondary Education Expense Board, 527 U.S. 666 (1999).

In 1961, Congress extended the Fair Labor Standards Act of 1938 to every employee "employed in an enterprise engaged in commerce or in the production of goods for commerce." In 1966, the Act was further extended to the employees of hospitals, elementary and secondary schools, and institutions of higher education, including those owned and operated by states. In Maryland v. Wirtz, 392 U.S. 183 (1968), the Court upheld the Act as amended.

In 1974, Congress extended the minimum wage and maximum hour regulations to almost all state and municipal employees. In National League of Cities v.

Usery, 426 U.S. 833 (1976), in only the second decision since the 1930s to strike down an act of Congress on federalism grounds—Oregon v. Mitchell was the first—the Court overruled Maryland v. Wirtz, by a 5-4 vote.

National League of Cities v. Usery

426 U.S. 833 (1976)

Rehnquist, J.:

This Court has never doubted that there are limits upon the power of Congress to override state sovereignty, even when exercising its otherwise plenary powers to tax or to regulate commerce which are conferred by Art. I of the Constitution. . . . In Fry v. United States, 421 U.S. 542 (1975), the Court recognized that an express declaration of this limitation is found in the Tenth Amendment: . . . "The Amendment expressly declares the constitutional policy that Congress may not exercise power in a fashion that impairs the States' integrity or their ability to function effectively in a federal system." . . . It is one thing to recognize the authority of Congress to enact laws regulating individual businesses. . . . It is quite another to uphold a similar exercise of congressional authority directed, not to private citizens, but to the States as States. We have repeatedly recognized that there are attributes of sovereignty attaching to every state government which may not be impaired by Congress, not because Congress may lack an affirmative grant of legislative authority to reach the matter, but because the Constitution prohibits it from exercising the authority in that manner. . . . Coyle v. Oklahoma, 221 U.S. 559 (1911). . . .

One undoubted attribute of state sovereignty is the States' power to determine the wages which shall be paid to those whom they employ in order to carry out their governmental functions, what hours those persons will work, and what compensation will be provided where these employees may be called upon to work overtime. . . .

[The new amendments will] significantly alter or displace the States' abilities to structure employer-employee relationships in such areas as fire prevention, police protection, sanitation, public health, and parks and recreation. . . . Indeed, it is functions such as these which governments are created to provide, services such as these which the States have traditionally afforded their citizens. If Congress may withdraw from the States the authority to make those fundamental employment decisions upon which their systems for performance of these functions must rest, we think there would be little left of the States' "separate and independent existence." Thus, . . . Congress has sought to wield its power in a fashion that would impair the States' "ability to function effectively in a federal system." . . . We hold that insofar as the challenged amendments operate to directly displace the States' freedom to structure integral operations in areas of traditional governmental functions, they are not within the authority granted Congress by Art. I, §8, cl. 3. *Wirtz* must be overruled.

Brennan, J., with Marshall and White, JJ. dissenting:

[N]othing in the Tenth Amendment constitutes a limitation on congressional exercise of powers delegated by the Constitution to Congress. . . . My Brethren boldly assert that the decision as to wages and hours is an "undoubted attribute of state sovereignty," and then never say why. . . . The portent of such a sweeping holding is so ominous for our constitutional jurisprudence as to leave one incredulous.

STEVENS, J., dissenting:

The Court holds that the Federal Government may not interfere with a sovereign State's inherent right to pay a substandard wage to the janitor at the state capitol. The principle on which the holding rests is difficult to perceive. The Federal Government may, I believe, require the State to act impartially when it hires or fires the janitor, to withhold taxes from his paycheck, to observe safety regulations when he is performing his job, to forbid him from burning too much soft coal in the capitol furnace, from dumping untreated refuse in an adjacent waterway, from overloading a state-owned garbage truck, or from driving either the truck or the governor's limousine over 55 miles an hour. Even though these and many other activities of the capitol janitor are activities of the State qua State, I have no doubt that they are subject to federal regulation.

The Court attempted to apply *National League of Cities* in a series of cases, but was unable to find another example in which the legal principle applied. Hodel v. Virginia Surface Mining & Recl. Assn., 452 U.S. 264 (1981); United Transportation Union v. Long Island R. Co., 455 U.S. 678 (1982); FERC v. Mississippi, 456 U.S. 742 (1982); EEOC v. Wyoming, 460 U.S. 226 (1983). Less than a decade later, the Court revisited the issue, and overruled *National League of Cities.* Once again, the vote was 5-4. Justice Blackmun, who had voted with the majority in *National League of Cities,* now joined its four dissenters to proclaim the Court's adventure a mistake.

Garcia v. San Antonio Metropolitan Transit Authority

469 U.S. 528 (1985)

[The Department of Labor determined that a San Antonio mass-transit system did not fall under the rule set forth in *National League of Cities,* and thus was required to abide by federal minimum wage laws. The Court took the opportunity to reconsider *National League of Cities.*]

BLACKMUN, J.

[T]he attempt to draw the boundaries of state regulatory immunity in terms of "traditional governmental function" is not only unworkable but is also inconsistent with established principles of federalism and, indeed, with those very federalism principles on which *National League of Cities* purported to rest. That case, accordingly, is overruled. . . . Any rule of state immunity that looks to the "traditional," "integral," or "necessary" nature of governmental functions inevitably invites an unelected federal judiciary to make decisions about which state policies it favors and which ones it dislikes. . . .

We therefore now reject, as unsound in principle and unworkable in practice, a rule of state immunity from federal regulation that turns on a judicial appraisal of whether a particular governmental function is "integral" or "traditional." . . .

. . . [W]e look for the States' "residuary and inviolable sovereignty," The Federalist No. 39, (J. Madison), in the shape of the constitutional scheme rather than in predetermined notions of sovereign power . . . [T]he principal means chosen by the Framers to ensure the role of the States in the federal system lies in the structure of the Federal Government itself. . . . The Framers thus gave the States a role in the selection both of the Executive and the Legislative Branches of the Federal Government. The States were vested with indirect influence over the House of Representatives and the Presidency by their control of electoral qualifications and their role in Presidential elections. U.S. Const., Art. I, §2, and Art. II, §1. They were given more direct influence in the Senate, where each State received equal representation and each Senator was to be selected by the legislature of his State. Art. I, §3. The significance attached to the States' equal representation in the Senate is underscored by the prohibition of any constitutional amendment divesting a State of equal representation without the State's consent. Art. V. . . . In short, the Framers chose to rely on a federal system in which special restraints on federal power over the States inhered principally in the workings of the National Government itself, rather than in discrete limitations on the objects of federal authority. State sovereign interests, then, are more properly protected by procedural safeguards inherent in the structure of the federal system than by judicially created limitations on federal power. . . .

We realize that changes in the structure of the Federal Government have taken place since 1789, not the least of which has been the substitution of popular election of Senators by the adoption of the Seventeenth Amendment in 1913, and that these changes may work to alter the influence of the States in the federal political process. Nonetheless, against this background, we are convinced that the fundamental limitation that the constitutional scheme imposes on the Commerce Clause to protect the "States as States" is one of process rather than one of result. Any substantive restraint on the exercise of Commerce Clause powers must find its justification in the procedural nature of this basic limitation, and it must be tailored to compensate for possible failings in the national political process rather than to dictate a "sacred province of state autonomy." . . .

[W]e perceive nothing in the overtime and minimum-wage requirements of the FLSA, as applied to SAMTA, that is destructive of state sovereignty or violative of any constitutional provision. SAMTA faces nothing more than the same minimum-wage and overtime obligations that hundreds of thousands of other employers, public as well as private, have to meet. . . .

The political process ensures that laws that unduly burden the States will not be promulgated. In the factual setting of these cases the internal safeguards of the political process have performed as intended. These cases do not require us to identify or define what affirmative limits the constitutional structure might impose on federal action affecting the States under the Commerce Clause. See Coyle v. Oklahoma, 221 U.S. 559 (1911).

. . . *National League of Cities* . . . attempted to articulate affirmative limits on the Commerce Clause power in terms of core governmental functions and fundamental attributes of state sovereignty. But the model of democratic decisionmaking the Court there identified underestimated, in our view, the solicitude of the national political process for the continued vitality of the States. Attempts by other courts since then to draw guidance from this model have proved it both impracticable and doctrinally barren. In sum, in *National League of Cities* the Court tried to repair what did not need repair. . . .

Justice POWELL, with whom THE CHIEF JUSTICE, Justice REHNQUIST, and Justice O'CONNOR join, dissenting.

. . . Today's opinion does not explain how the States' role in the electoral process guarantees that particular exercises of the Commerce Clause power will not infringe on residual state sovereignty. Members of Congress are elected from the various States, but once in office they are Members of the Federal Government. Although the States participate in the Electoral College, this is hardly a reason to view the President as a representative of the States' interest against federal encroachment. We noted recently "[the] hydraulic pressure inherent within each of the separate Branches to exceed the outer limits of its power. . . ." INS v. Chadha, 462 U.S. 919 (1983). The Court offers no reason to think that this pressure will not operate when Congress seeks to invoke its powers under the Commerce Clause, notwithstanding the electoral role of the States.

The Court apparently thinks that the States' success at obtaining federal funds for various projects and exemptions from the obligations of some federal statutes is indicative of the "effectiveness of the federal political process in preserving the States' interests. . . ." The fact that Congress generally does not transgress constitutional limits on its power to reach state activities does not make judicial review any less necessary to rectify the cases in which it does do so. The States' role in our system of government is a matter of constitutional law, not of legislative grace. . . . More troubling than the logical infirmities in the Court's reasoning is the result of its holding, i.e., that federal political officials, invoking the Commerce Clause, are the sole judges of the limits of their own power. . . .

. . . The Framers believed that the separate sphere of sovereignty reserved to the States would ensure that the States would serve as an effective "counterpoise" to the power of the Federal Government. The States would serve this essential role because they would attract and retain the loyalty of their citizens. . . . Like Hamilton, Madison saw the States' involvement in the everyday concerns of the people as the source of their citizens' loyalty.

Thus, the harm to the States that results from federal overreaching under the Commerce Clause is not simply a matter of dollars and cents. Nor is it a matter of the wisdom or folly of certain policy choices. Rather, by usurping functions traditionally performed by the States, federal overreaching under the Commerce Clause undermines the constitutionally mandated balance of power between the States and the Federal Government, a balance designed to protect our fundamental liberties. . . .

. . . In *National League of Cities,* we spoke of fire prevention, police protection, sanitation, and public health as "typical of [the services] performed by state and local governments in discharging their dual functions of administering the public law and furnishing public services." Not only are these activities remote from any normal concept of interstate commerce, they are also activities that epitomize the concerns of local, democratic self-government. In emphasizing the need to protect traditional governmental functions, we identified the kinds of activities engaged in by state and local governments that affect the everyday lives of citizens. These are services that people are in a position to understand and evaluate, and in a democracy, have the right to oversee. . . .

The Court maintains that the standard approved in *National League of Cities* "disserves principles of democratic self-governance." In reaching this conclusion, the Court looks myopically only to persons elected to positions in the federal government. It disregards entirely the far more effective role of democratic self-government at the state and local levels. . . . [M]embers of the immense federal bureaucracy are not elected, know less about the services traditionally rendered by States and localities, and are inevitably less responsive to recipients of such services, than are state legislatures, city councils, boards of supervisors, and state and local commissions, boards, and agencies. It is at these state and local levels—not in Washington as the Court so mistakenly thinks—that "democratic self-government" is best exemplified. . . .

Justice REHNQUIST, dissenting. . . .

[Doctrinal details aside, *National League of Cities* recognized a basic] principle that will, I am confident, in time again command the support of a majority of this Court.

Justice O'CONNOR, with whom Justice POWELL and Justice REHNQUIST join, dissenting. . . .

The central issue of federalism, of course, is whether any realm is left open to the States by the Constitution—whether any area remains in which a State may act free of federal interference. . . . Just as surely as the Framers envisioned a National Government capable of solving national problems, they also envisioned a republic whose vitality was assured by the diffusion of power not only among the branches of the Federal Government, but also between the Federal Government and the States. In the 18th century these intentions did not conflict because technology had not yet converted every local problem into a national one. A conflict has now emerged, and the Court today retreats rather than reconcile the Constitution's dual concerns for federalism and an effective commerce power. . . .

[R]ecent changes in the workings of Congress, such as the direct election of Senators and the expanded influence of national interest groups, become relevant. These changes may well have lessened the weight Congress gives to the legitimate interests of States as States. As a result, there is now a real risk that Congress will gradually erase the diffusion of power between State and Nation on which the Framers based their faith in the efficiency and vitality of our Republic. . . .

The *spirit* of the Tenth Amendment, . . . is that the States will retain their integrity in a system in which the laws of the United States are nevertheless supreme. . . . For example, Congress might rationally conclude that the location a State chooses for its capital may affect interstate commerce, but the Court has suggested that Congress would nevertheless be barred from dictating that location because such an exercise of a delegated power would undermine the state sovereignty inherent in the Tenth Amendment. Coyle v. Oklahoma, 221 U.S. 559, 565 (1911). . . .

. . . This principle requires the Court to enforce affirmative limits on federal regulation of the States to complement the judicially crafted expansion of the interstate commerce power. . . .

The last two decades have seen an unprecedented growth of federal regulatory activity, as the majority itself acknowledges. . . . For example, recently the Federal Government has, with this Court's blessing, undertaken to tell the States the age at which they can retire their law enforcement officers, and the regulatory standards, procedures, and even the agenda which their utilities commissions must consider and follow. The political process has not protected against these encroachments on state activities, even though they directly impinge on a State's ability to make and enforce its laws. With the abandonment of *National League of Cities,* all that stands between the remaining essentials of state sovereignty and Congress is the latter's underdeveloped capacity for self-restraint. . . .

DISCUSSION

1. *The basis of* National League of Cities*: Text or structure?* Justice Rehnquist's decision in *National League of Cities* is typically described by scholars and lawyers as based on the Tenth Amendment. But is it? The Tenth Amendment is only mentioned in a single passage, introducing and quoting a prior case. Professor H. Jefferson Powell has argued that *National League of Cities* is written as a structural, not a textual, opinion: Even the invocation of the amendment itself avoids careful examination of its language, and instead treats it as exemplifying the broader *structural* idea that state governments play a special role in the Constitution and do not exist merely at the sufferance of Congress. According to Powell, "The Tenth Amendment is 'an express declaration' of the state sovereignty limitation, not its source." Jeff Powell, The Compleat Jeffersonian: Justice Rehnquist and Federalism, 91 Yale L.J. 1317, 1329 (1982). Can you see why Justice Rehnquist might prefer not to build his argument on the rock of the Tenth's text? Recall that he seeks to deploy the amendment as the source of an affirmative exemption, akin to the Sixth Amendment and the Fifth Amendment Due Process Clause. But the Fifth and Sixth Amendments, by their grammar and syntax, "cut across" Congress's enumerated powers: Even where Congress is plainly regulating, say, interstate commerce, these amendments have bite. By contrast, the grammar of the Tenth Amendment seems to define states' rights residually—these rights merely mark the absence of enumerated power, rather than cutting across it. To see the point another way, recall that *National League of Cities* does not challenge Congress's power to apply its minimum wage, as a general matter, to private employers. But if exemption from minimum wage laws is a textual right of states under the Tenth, why isn't a similar exemption a textual right of private employers? Note that the amendment's text speaks of rights reserved to both "the states" and "the people" in its last clause.

2. *The* Coyle *problem.* Justice Blackmun's *Garcia* opinion declines to specify "what affirmative limits the constitutional structure might impose on federal action affecting the States under the Commerce Clause. See Coyle v. Oklahoma, 221 U.S. 559 (1911)." If Congress tried to dictate to a state the location of its state capital, or the length of its governor's term of office, would the *Garcia* Court uphold such a law as long as it was plausibly linked to, say, the Commerce Clause? If not, then how and where should the line be drawn between these hypotheticals and the facts of *Garcia*? For example, is it relevant that these hypothetical laws seek to single out "states qua states," regulating them in a manner very different from

typical regulations of private enterprise? That these regulations seek to restructure the political organization of a state? (If you think these or other distinctions are relevant, why? What is the theory of federalism, and of its values, that makes such distinctions relevant?) As you confront the Rehnquist Court cases, infra, consider whether the laws at issue in these cases are closer to the law in *Garcia* or closer to the state-capital issue flagged by *Coyle.* For an important and influential argument that congressional laws seeking to dictate state political structures raise special concerns and call for special judicial scrutiny, see Deborah Jones Merritt, The Guarantee Clause and State Autonomy: Federalism for a Third Century, 88 Colum. L. Rev. 1 (1988). Cf. id. at 56-57 (distinguishing between permissible federal wage regulations of state firefighters—who do not exercise "legislative, executive, or judicial" functions—and more suspect federal efforts to regulate the state's employment of police, legislators, and judges).

3. *The political safeguards of federalism and the composition of the Supreme Court.* Building on the analysis offered by James Madison in The Federalist Nos. 45 and 46, Professor Herbert Wechsler argued in a famous and influential article that[25]

> the national political process in the United States—and especially the role of the states in the composition and selection of the central government—is intrinsically well-adapted to retarding or restraining new intrusions by the center on the domain of the states. Far from a national authority that is expansionist by nature, the inherent tendency in our system is precisely the reverse, necessitating the widest support before intrusive measures of importance can receive significant consideration, reacting readily to opposition grounded in resistance within the states.

Some of the political safeguards invoked by Professor Wechsler, such as the equal representation of states in the Senate, remain intact. Others, including the extent of state control over the federal election process, have been limited by subsequent judicial decisions, congressional legislation, and constitutional amendments requiring the apportionment of congressional districts on a "one person, one vote" basis, the elimination of poll taxes and literacy tests, limitations on durational residency and other state-law requirements for voting, and the enfranchisement of citizens over 18.

Professor Larry Kramer argues that several of the particular safeguards invoked by Professor Wechsler, such as equal state representation in the Senate, are implausible as safeguards of state institutions, as distinguished from protecting the political interests of people who live in small states. See Larry D. Kramer, Putting the Politics Back into the Political Safeguards of Federalism, 100 Colum. L. Rev. 215 (2000). Such institutions arguably were protected prior to the Seventeenth Amendment when state legislatures chose senators, but there is no reason to believe that the mass electorate that now chooses senators would be particularly interested in safeguarding state institutions if they believed, politically, that national institutions could do a better job of achieving their political goals. Still, Kramer argues, there are political

25. Herbert Wechsler, The Political Safegaurds of Federalism: The Role of the States in the Composition and Selection of the National Government, 54 Colum. L. Rev. 543, 557-558 (1954).

safeguards, though they rest in something not highlighted by Wechsler: the operation of the highly decentralized system of American political parties, by which figures on the national political stage must constantly forge political alliances with state and local officials. And Kramer is, if anything, even more skeptical than Wechsler about the useful role of the Court in monitoring the relationship between Congress and the states. Thus, he writes, "I think the Justices have little idea what they are doing when they intrude . . . [:] no clear picture how their decisions affect governmental operations beyond the particular statutes they invalidate, no hint whether they have made government better or worse." One reason for this bleak view may be the fact that extremely few members of the current Court have had significant experience as actual participants in either state or national government. There are, for example, no former governors, senators, cabinet officials, or, indeed, Presidents, on the current Court. Compare, e.g., those Courts that included former governors Charles Evans Hughes or Earl Warren, former senators George Sutherland or Hugo Black, former cabinet officials John Marshall, Roger Taney, Charles Evans Hughes again, Robert Jackson, or, finally, former President William Howard Taft. Is significant political experience a desideratum in Supreme Court appointees?

4. *Federalism and separation of powers.* To what extent are federalism and separation of powers similar? For example, if you believe that the federal judiciary should generally defer to federal laws that arguably offend states' rights, because states are represented in the political process, then should the same be true of federal laws that arguably offend the rights of the President or of Congress? (Both, after all, are likewise represented.) Conversely, if these separation of powers cases are generally justiciable, should the same be true of federalism cases? If not, why not?

5. *The meaning of* Marbury. Justice Powell argues that the sort of extreme deference championed by the *Garcia* majority violates the principle of Marbury v. Madison. But does *Marbury* do anything more than affirm the right and the power of federal judges to refuse to enforce a law in their own courtrooms, once they are fully persuaded that the law is unconstitutional? Does *Marbury*, for example, bar the courts from opting to indulge a strong presumption of constitutionality prior to reaching the conclusion that a given law is indeed unconstitutional? Does *Marbury* require the Court to fashion doctrinal rules imposing substantive limits on Congress even where the Court believes that (a) Congress is well structured to respect the constitutional rights in question and that (b) courts are ill structured to implement the relevant constitutional norms in a doctrinally sound way, with sufficiently manageable judicial standards and "principled" doctrinal rules? If *Marbury* really means that deference is never proper, is *Marbury* inconsistent with some of the language of McCulloch v. Maryland? Compare Justice Powell's invocation of *Marbury* with Justice Kennedy's (and other Justices') invocation of *Marbury* in Reconstruction power cases like *City of Boerne*; also, be on the lookout for citations to *Marbury* in some of the modern separation of powers cases, infra, Sections IV and V.

B. The Rehnquist Court: Finding Affirmative Limits

William Rehnquist's 1976 *National League of Cities* opinion reflected a deep belief in the importance of states' rights, and a willingness to deploy federal judicial power in support of these rights. But over the next decade, the Court never used the *National League of Cities* doctrine—or any other states' rights doctrine, for that matter—to invalidate congressional action. And as we have seen, the *Garcia* Court seemed to lay *National League of Cities* to rest in 1985. Two years later, President Reagan nominated, and the Senate confirmed, Justice Rehnquist to sit as Chief Justice. Would the new Chief Justice be able to lead his Court back toward his vision of federalism? If so, how would issues of stare decisis affect the Court's path back? Note that *Garcia* explicitly overruled *National League of Cities*, which in turn had explicitly overruled Maryland v. Wirtz. Note also that Justices Rehnquist and O'Connor expressed their hope that *Garcia* would be overcome (if not overruled) at some later date.[26] Keep an eye on issues of stare decisis as you read the following federalism cases, handed down by the Rehnquist Court. To what extent do these cases manage to "move" the law while maintaining fidelity to cases like *Garcia*? Some related questions to keep in mind: To what extent are the movements in case law a product of (a) a different set of issues reaching the Court, (b) new facts emerging, (c) a changed political landscape, (d) gravitational pulls exerted by developments in legal doctrine outside federalism, (e) new Justices joining the Court, and (f) simple changes of heart? What other factors may also be at work?

In South Carolina v. Baker, 485 U.S. 505 (1988), South Carolina challenged the constitutionality of §310(b)(1) of the Tax Equity and Fiscal Responsibility Act of 1982 (TEFRA), which eliminated the exemption from federal income tax of interest earned on nonregistered bonds issued by states and local municipalities. The exemption was maintained for registered bonds, whose ownership is recorded on a central list. Both private and public bonds were affected, because Congress determined that nonregistered "bearer bonds" lent themselves to tax avoidance and to use in illegal activities. The State claimed that the regulation of its bonds violated the Tenth Amendment.[27] As a result of TEFRA, states now issue only registered bonds, because the sale of nonregistered bonds would require the payment of substantially higher interest rates in order to overcome the loss of the tax exemption.

The Court upheld the provision. Justice Brennan, writing for the majority, treated the statute as a functional prohibition of nonregistered bonds. He found the Tenth Amendment claim foreclosed by *Garcia*, which he described as holding that the limits of Congress's authority to regulate state activities "are structural—not substantive—i.e., that States must find their protection from congressional regulation through the national political process, not through judicially defined spheres of unregulatable state activity." South Carolina claimed that §310(b)(1) was "imposed by the vote of an uninformed Congress relying on incomplete information." Justice Brennan countered that South Carolina presented no evidence of such "extraordinary defects in the national political process" as to justify judicial intervention. "Where, as here, the national political *process* did not operate in a defective manner, the Tenth Amendment is not implicated." Chief Justice Rehnquist and Justice Scalia, concurring in separate opinions, rejected

26. What do these developments suggest about the importance of precedent in constitutional decisionmaking? Recall Justice Scalia's comments concerning stare decisis in Chapter 1, supra.

27. South Carolina also claimed that the tax violated the doctrine of intergovernmental tax immunity. See Collector v. Day, 78 U.S. (11 Wall.) 113 (1871); Pollock v. Farmers' Loan & Trust Co., 157 U.S. 429 (1895).

Justice Brennan's reading of *Garcia.* Justice Scalia described that case "as explicitly disclaiming the proposition attributed to it," and quoted, with emphasis, the following sentence from *Garcia*: "These cases do not require us to identify or define what affirmative limits *the constitutional structure* might impose on federal action affecting the States under the Commerce Clause." He went on to say, "I agree only that that structure does not prohibit what the Federal Government has done here." Chief Justice Rehnquist argued that South Carolina would lose even under *National League of Cities* because the facts showed that the provision had no practical impact on state borrowing practices since tax exemption (and thus lower interest rates) was still available for registered bonds:

> This well-supported conclusion that Section 310(b)(1) has had a *de minimis* impact on the States should end, rather than begin, the Court's constitutional inquiry. Even the more expansive conception of the Tenth Amendment espoused in *National League of Cities* recognized that only congressional action that "operate[s] to directly displace the States' freedom to structure integral operations in areas of traditional governmental functions" runs afoul of the authority granted Congress. The Special Master determined that no such displacement has occurred through the implementation of the TEFRA requirements; I see no need to go further, as the majority does, to discuss the possibility of defects in the national political process that spawned TEFRA.

Justice O'Connor dissented. Three years later, however, it would be Justice O'Connor who spoke for the majority in an important federalism case that presaged many of the Court's future federalism doctrines.

Gregory v. Ashcroft

501 U.S. 452 (1991)

[The Missouri Constitution provides that "all judges other than municipal judges shall retire at the age of seventy years." In 1974, Congress extended the substantive provisions of the federal Age Discrimination in Employment Act of 1967 (ADEA) to include the states as employers. Pub. L. 93-259, §28(a), 88 Stat. 74, 29 U.S.C. §630(b)(2).

At the same time, Congress amended the definition of "employee" to exclude all elected and most high-ranking government officials. Under the Act, as amended, "[t]he term 'employee' means an individual employed by any employer except that the term 'employee' shall not include any person elected to public office in any State or political subdivision of any State by the qualified voters thereof, or any person chosen by such officer to be on such officer's personal staff, or an appointee on the policymaking level or an immediate adviser with respect to the exercise of the constitutional or legal powers of the office." 29 U.S.C. §630(f).

Two state judges subject to Missouri's mandatory retirement rule challenged it as in violation of the federal ADEA. Governor Ashcroft of Missouri defended the retirement rule on federalism grounds; he also argued on statutory grounds that the §630(f) exclusion of certain public officials also excludes judges, like petitioners, who are appointed to office by the Governor and are then subject to retention election.

The Supreme Court, in an opinion by Justice O'Connor, held that Missouri's retirement provision did not violate the ADEA. While noting that the Court was not questioning its recent decision in *Garcia*, she nevertheless argued that the proper interpretation of the statute should be guided by principles of federalism and respect for state sovereignty.]

O'CONNOR, J.:

As every schoolchild learns, our Constitution establishes a system of dual sovereignty between the States and the Federal Government. This Court also has recognized this fundamental principle. In Tafflin v. Levitt, 493 U.S. 455 (1990), "we beg[a]n with the axiom that, under our federal system, the States possess sovereignty concurrent with that of the Federal Government, subject only to limitations imposed by the Supremacy Clause." Over 120 years ago, the Court described the constitutional scheme of dual sovereigns:

> "'The people of each State compose a State, having its own government, and endowed with all the functions essential to separate and independent existence.' . . . 'Without the States in union, there could be no such political body as the United States.' Not only, therefore, can there be no loss of separate and independent autonomy to the States, through their union under the Constitution, but it may be not unreasonably said that the preservation of the States, and the maintenance of their governments, are as much within the design and care of the Constitution as the preservation of the Union and the maintenance of the National government. The Constitution, in all its provisions, looks to an indestructible Union, composed of indestructible States." Texas v. White. . . .

This federalist structure of joint sovereigns preserves to the people numerous advantages. It assures a decentralized government that will be more sensitive to the diverse needs of a heterogenous society; it increases opportunity for citizen involvement in democratic processes; it allows for more innovation and experimentation in government; and it makes government more responsive by putting the States in competition for a mobile citizenry. See generally McConnell, Federalism: Evaluating the Founders' Design, 54 U. Chi. L. Rev. 1484, 1491-1511 (1987); Merritt, The Guarantee Clause and State Autonomy: Federalism for a Third Century, 88 Colum. L. Rev. 1, 3-10 (1988).

Perhaps the principal benefit of the federalist system is a check on abuses of government power. "The 'constitutionally mandated balance of power' between the States and the Federal Government was adopted by the Framers to ensure the protection of 'our fundamental liberties.'" Just as the separation and independence of the coordinate branches of the Federal Government serve to prevent the accumulation of excessive power in any one branch, a healthy balance of power between the States and the Federal Government will reduce the risk of tyranny and abuse from either front. Alexander Hamilton explained to the people of New York, perhaps optimistically, that the new federalist system would suppress completely "the attempts of the government to establish a tyranny":

> "In a confederacy the people, without exaggeration, may be said to be entirely the masters of their own fate. Power being almost always the rival of power, the general government will at all times stand ready to check the usurpations of the state governments, and these will have the same disposition towards the general government. The people, by throwing themselves into either scale, will infallibly make it preponderate. If their rights are invaded by either, they can make use of the other as the instrument of redress." The Federalist No. 28.

James Madison made much the same point:

> "In a single republic, all the power surrendered by the people is submitted to the administration of a single government; and the usurpations are guarded against by a division of the government into distinct and separate departments. In the compound republic of America, the power surrendered by the people is first divided between two distinct governments, and then the portion allotted to each subdivided among distinct and separate departments. Hence a double security arises to the rights of the people. The different governments will control each other, at the same time that each will be controlled by itself." [The Federalist] No. 51.

One fairly can dispute whether our federalist system has been quite as successful in checking government abuse as Hamilton promised, but there is no doubt about the design. If this "double security" is to be effective, there must be a proper balance between the States and the Federal Government. These twin powers will act as mutual restraints only if both are credible. In the tension between federal and state power lies the promise of liberty.

The Federal Government holds a decided advantage in this delicate balance: the Supremacy Clause. As long as it is acting within the powers granted it under the Constitution, Congress may impose its will on the States. Congress may legislate in areas traditionally regulated by the States. This is an extraordinary power in a federalist system. It is a power that we must assume Congress does not exercise lightly.

The present case concerns a state constitutional provision through which the people of Missouri establish a qualification for those who sit as their judges. This provision goes beyond an area traditionally regulated by the States; it is a decision of the most fundamental sort for a sovereign entity. Through the structure of its government, and the character of those who exercise government authority, a State defines itself as a sovereign. "It is obviously essential to the independence of the States, and to their peace and tranquility, that their power to prescribe the qualifications of their own officers . . . should be exclusive, and free from external interference, except so far as plainly provided by the Constitution of the United States."

Congressional interference with this decision of the people of Missouri, defining their constitutional officers, would upset the usual constitutional balance of federal and state powers. For this reason, "it is incumbent upon the federal courts to be certain of Congress' intent before finding that federal law overrides" this balance. We explained recently: "If Congress intends to alter the 'usual constitutional balance between the States and the Federal Government,' it must make its intention to do so 'unmistakably clear in the language of the statute.'" . . . This plain statement rule is nothing more than an acknowledgement that the States retain substantial sovereign powers under our constitutional scheme, powers with which Congress does not readily interfere. . . .

In light of the ADEA's clear exclusion of most important public officials, it is at least ambiguous whether Congress intended that appointed judges nonetheless be included. In the face of such ambiguity, we will not attribute to Congress an intent to intrude on state governmental functions regardless of whether Congress acted pursuant to its Commerce Clause powers or §5 of the Fourteenth Amendment.

[Justice White, joined by Justice Stevens, concurred in part, dissented in part, and concurred in the judgment. Justice Blackmun, joined by Justice Marshall, dissented.]

DISCUSSION

1. *Clear-statement rules and constitutional doubts.* In addition to promoting the political safeguards of federalism, *Gregory*'s clear-statement rule has a second virtue, according to the Court: It enables the Justices to avoid the hard constitutional question that would be presented if the law were to be read as applicable to state judges. This use of clear-statement rules follows in the tradition of Justice Brandeis's famous concurrence in Ashwander v. T.V.A., 297 U.S. 288 (1936), cataloguing a variety of techniques for avoiding unnecessary constitutional decisions. In England, where judges have historically lacked the direct power of judicial review, clear-statement rules have long been used to ensure that certain privileged practices are not lightly overridden by Parliament. For a thoughtful discussion of the Court's use of clear-statement rules to protect certain legal interests, see William N. Eskridge, Jr. and Philip P. Frickey, Quasi-Constitutional Law: Clear Statement Rules as Constitutional Lawmaking, 45 Vand. L. Rev. 593 (1992). When such rules are announced by the Court in advance, and applied prospectively, they may make it harder to accomplish certain legislative results—it may be difficult in some instances to round up votes for "Simon Says" language in the legislature—but the rules of the game in Congress are clear. However, when rules of construction apply to laws passed before such rules were announced, they may effect a kind of "bait and switch" in which lawmakers think that one set of words will suffice to accomplish purpose X, only to learn later that they needed to speak more clearly. On the other hand, clear-statement rules are arguably more deferential than standard judicial review: The Justices are not (or at least, not yet) saying that Congress may not do X—only that if it seeks to do so, it must speak very clearly.

2. *Federalism and liberty.* Federalism serves multiple purposes, according to the *Gregory* majority. But the Court identifies liberty-protection as "perhaps the principal benefit." Analogizing federalism to separation of powers, and quoting at length from The Federalist Nos. 28 and 51, the Court claims that "a healthy balance of power between the States and the Federal government will reduce the risk of tyranny and abuse from either front." Do you agree? Do the facts of *Gregory* implicate liberty in any direct way? (Even if not, does the *Gregory* rule, in your view, in any way impede liberty?) For prominent statements of liberty-protection as a key virtue of federalism, with emphasis on the seldom-quoted but important language of The Federalist No. 28, see Martin Diamond, The Federalist's View of Federalism, in Essays in Federalism 21 (1961); Laurence H. Tribe, American Constitutional Law 3 n.6 (1978); Akhil

Reed Amar, Of Sovereignty and Federalism, 96 Yale L.J. 1425, 1492-1520 (1987). For other more general elaborations of the theme of "vertical" checks and balances between state and federal officials in order to disperse power and limit government abuse, see Robert F. Nagel, Federalism as a Fundamental Value: National League of Cities in Perspective, 1981 Sup. Ct. Rev. 81; Andrzej Rapaczynski, From Sovereignty to Process: The Jurisprudence of Federalism After *Garcia*, 1985 Sup. Ct. Rev. 341; Michael W. McConnell, Federalism: Evaluating the Founders' Design, 54 U. Chi. L. Rev. 1484 (1987); Merritt, Merritt, The Guarantee Clause and State Autonomy: Federalism for a Third Century, 88 Colum. L. Rev. 1 (1988).

With *Gregory* on the books—affirming the constitutional importance of states while pledging allegiance to *Garcia*—the Rehnquist Court quickly found another case pitting congressional power against states' rights. But this time, the issue went beyond clear-statement rules. In the 1992 case reprinted below, the Court—for only the second time in a half-century (putting aside the overruled *National League of Cities* case)—struck down a federal statute in the name of states' rights. As in *Gregory*, Justice O'Connor spoke for the Court, seeking to steer around *Garcia* rather than sink it. As in *Gregory*, the remaining members of the *Garcia* majority (now down to three) sharply dissented.

New York v. United States

505 U.S. 144 (1992)

[Faced with a looming shortage of disposal sites for low level radioactive waste in 31 states, Congress enacted the Low Level Radioactive Waste Policy Amendments Act of 1985. The Act is designed to get states, either by themselves or in "regional compacts" with other states, to come up with policies for the disposal of radioactive waste generated within their borders. The Act has three provisions designed to give states incentives to comply.

First, the Act creates monetary incentives for states to develop waste disposal sites. The Act authorizes States with radioactive disposal sites to impose a surcharge on radioactive waste received from other States. The Secretary of Energy then collects a portion of this surcharge and places it in an escrow account. When States achieve a series of milestones in developing waste disposal sites, they receive portions of the fund.

Second, the Act creates incentives for states to develop waste disposal sites by restricting access to existing sites. It authorizes States with radioactive waste disposal sites and regional compacts gradually to increase the cost of access to their disposal sites, and eventually to deny access altogether to radioactive waste generated in states that do not meet federal deadlines.

The third incentive is the "take title" provision. If a state or regional compact fails to provide for the disposal of all internally generated waste by a particular date, the state or regional compact must, upon the request of the waste's generator or owner, take title to and possession of the radioactive waste. It will also become liable for all damages suffered by the generator or owner as a result of the state's failure to promptly take possession.

In the seven years following the Act, Congress approved nine regional compacts, encompassing 42 of the states. New York's residents generate a relatively large share of the nation's low level radioactive waste. Instead of joining a regional compact, New York enacted legislation that provided for the siting and financing of a disposal facility in New York. The state identified five potential sites, three in Allegany County and two in Cortland County, but residents opposed the state's choice of location.

The State of New York and the two counties then sued the United States, arguing that the Act was inconsistent with the Tenth Amendment. The States of Washington, Nevada, and South Carolina intervened as defendants.]

O'CONNOR, J.:

II

A

The Tenth Amendment . . . restrains the power of Congress, but this limit is not derived from the text of the Tenth Amendment itself, which . . . is essentially a tautology. Instead, the Tenth Amendment confirms that the power of the Federal Government is subject to limits that may, in a given instance, reserve power to the States. . . . Most of our recent cases interpreting the Tenth Amendment have concerned the authority of Congress to subject state governments to generally applicable laws. The Court's jurisprudence in this area has traveled an unsteady path. See *Wirtz*; *National League of Cities*; *Garcia*. This litigation presents no occasion to apply or revisit the holdings of any of these cases, as this is not a case in which Congress has subjected a State to the same legislation applicable to private parties.

This litigation instead concerns the circumstances under which Congress may use the States as implements of regulation; that is, whether Congress may direct or otherwise motivate the States to regulate in a particular field or a particular way. . . .

1

As an initial matter, Congress may not simply "commandeer the legislative processes of the States by directly compelling them to enact and enforce a federal regulatory program." Hodel v. Virginia Surface Mining & Reclamation Assn., Inc., 452 U.S. 264, 288 (1981). In *Hodel*, the Court upheld the Surface Mining Control and Reclamation Act of 1977 precisely because it did not "commandeer" the States into regulating mining. The Court found that "the States are not compelled to enforce the steep-slope standards, to expend any state funds, or to participate in the federal regulatory program in any manner whatsoever. If a State does not wish to submit a proposed permanent program that complies with the Act and implementing regulations, the full regulatory burden will be borne by the Federal Government."

The Court reached the same conclusion the following year in FERC v. Mississippi. . . . We observed that "this Court never has sanctioned explicitly a federal command to the States to promulgate and enforce laws and regulations.". . .

These statements in *FERC* and *Hodel* were not innovations. While Congress has substantial powers to govern the Nation directly, including in areas of intimate concern to the States, the Constitution has never been understood to confer upon

Congress the ability to require the States to govern according to Congress' instructions. See Coyle v. Smith, 221 U.S. 559 (1911). . . .

Indeed, the question whether the Constitution should permit Congress to employ state governments as regulatory agencies was a topic of lively debate among the Framers. Under the Articles of Confederation, Congress lacked the authority in most respects to govern the people directly. In practice, Congress "could not directly tax or legislate upon individuals; it had no explicit 'legislative' or 'governmental' power to make binding 'law' enforceable as such." Amar, Of Sovereignty and Federalism, 96 Yale L.J. 1425, 1447 (1987).

The inadequacy of this governmental structure was responsible in part for the Constitutional Convention. . . . The Convention generated a great number of proposals for the structure of the new Government, but two quickly took center stage. Under the Virginia Plan, as first introduced by Edmund Randolph, Congress would exercise legislative authority directly upon individuals, without employing the States as intermediaries. Under the New Jersey Plan, as first introduced by William Paterson, Congress would continue to require the approval of the States before legislating, as it had under the Articles of Confederation. . . . One frequently expressed objection to the New Jersey Plan was that it might require the Federal Government to coerce the States into implementing legislation. . . . There are but two modes, by which the end of a General Government can be attained: the 1st is by coercion as proposed by Mr. Paterson's plan[, the 2nd] by real legislation as proposed by the other plan. Coercion [is] impracticable, expensive, cruel to individuals. . . . We must resort therefore to a national Legislation over individuals." Madison echoed this view: "The practicability of making laws, with coercive sanctions, for the States as political bodies, had been exploded on all hands." . . .

In the end, the Convention opted for a Constitution in which Congress would exercise its legislative authority directly over individuals rather than over States; for a variety of reasons, it rejected the New Jersey Plan in favor of the Virginia Plan. This choice was made clear to the subsequent state ratifying conventions. Oliver Ellsworth, a member of the Connecticut delegation in Philadelphia, explained the distinction to his State's convention: "This Constitution does not attempt to coerce sovereign bodies, states, in their political capacity. . . . But this legal coercion singles out the . . . individual." Charles Pinckney, another delegate at the Constitutional Convention, emphasized to the South Carolina House of Representatives that in Philadelphia "the necessity of having a government which should at once operate upon the people, and not upon the states, was conceived to be indispensable by every delegation present." Rufus King, one of Massachusetts' delegates, returned home to support ratification by recalling the Commonwealth's unhappy experience under the Articles of Confederation and arguing: "Laws, to be effective, therefore, must not be laid on states, but upon individuals." At New York's convention, Hamilton (another delegate in Philadelphia) exclaimed: "But can we believe that one state will ever suffer itself to be used as an instrument of coercion? The thing is a dream; it is impossible. Then we are brought to this dilemma—either a federal standing army is to enforce the requisitions, or the federal treasury is left without supplies, and the government without support. What, sir, is the cure for this great evil? Nothing, but to enable the national laws to operate on individuals, in the same manner as those of the states do." At North Carolina's convention, Samuel Spencer recognized that "all the laws of the Confederation were binding on the states in their political capacities, . . . but now the thing is entirely different. The laws of Congress will be binding on individuals." In providing for a stronger central government, therefore, the Framers explicitly chose a Constitution that confers upon Congress the power to regulate individuals, not States. . . .

2

This is not to say that Congress lacks the ability to encourage a State to regulate in a particular way, or that Congress may not hold out incentives to the States as a method of influencing a State's policy choices. Our cases have identified a variety of methods, short of outright coercion, by which Congress may urge a State to adopt a legislative program consistent with federal interests. Two of these methods are of particular relevance here.

First, under Congress' spending power, "Congress may attach conditions on the receipt of federal funds." South Dakota v. Dole. Such conditions must (among other requirements) bear some relationship to the purpose of the federal spending; otherwise, of course, the spending power could render academic the Constitution's other grants and limits of federal authority. Where the recipient of federal funds is a State, as is not unusual today, the conditions attached to the funds by Congress may influence a State's legislative choices. . . .

Second, where Congress has the authority to regulate private activity under the Commerce Clause, we have recognized Congress' power to offer States the choice of regulating that activity according to federal standards or having state law preempted by federal regulation. This arrangement, which has been termed "a program of cooperative federalism," is replicated in numerous federal statutory schemes. These include the Clean Water Act, the Occupational Safety and Health Act of 1970, the Resource Conservation and Recovery Act of 1976, and the Alaska National Interest Lands Conservation Act.

By either of these methods, as by any other permissible method of encouraging a State to conform to federal policy choices, the residents of the State retain the ultimate decision as to whether or not the State will comply. If a State's citizens view federal policy as sufficiently contrary to local interests, they may elect to decline a federal grant. If state residents would prefer their government to devote its attention and resources to problems other than those deemed important by Congress, they may choose to have the Federal Government rather than the State bear the expense of a federally mandated regulatory program, and they may continue to supplement that program to the extent state law is not pre-empted. Where Congress encourages state regulation rather than compelling it, state governments remain responsive to the local electorate's preferences; state officials remain accountable to the people.

By contrast, where the Federal Government compels States to regulate, the accountability of both state and federal officials is diminished. If the citizens of New York, for example, do not consider that making provision for the disposal of radioactive waste is in their best interest, they may elect state officials who share their view. That view can always be pre-empted under the Supremacy Clause if it is contrary to the national view, but in such a case it is the Federal Government that makes the decision in full view of the public, and it will be federal officials that suffer the consequences if the decision turns out to be detrimental or unpopular. But where the Federal Government directs the States to regulate, it may be state officials who will bear the brunt of public disapproval, while the federal officials who devised the regulatory program may remain insulated from the electoral ramifications of their decision. Accountability is thus diminished when, due to federal coercion, elected state officials cannot regulate in accordance with the views of the local electorate in matters not pre-empted by federal regulation. See Merritt, 88 Colum. L. Rev. at 61-62.

III

A

[Justice O'Connor held that the Act's use of monetary incentives was constitutional.] Congress has authorized States with disposal sites to impose a surcharge on radioactive waste received from other States. [T]he Secretary of Energy collects a portion of this surcharge and places the money in an escrow account. . . . States achieving a series of milestones receive portions of this fund.

[Authorizing the surcharge is] an unexceptionable exercise of Congress' power to authorize the States to burden interstate commerce. While the Commerce Clause has long been understood to limit the States' ability to discriminate against interstate commerce, that limit may be lifted, as it has been here, by an expression of the "unambiguous intent" of Congress. Whether or not the States would be permitted to burden the interstate transport of low level radioactive waste in the absence of Congress' approval, the States can clearly do so with Congress' approval, which is what the Act gives them. [And] the Secretary's collection of a percentage of the surcharge, is no more than a federal tax on interstate commerce, which petitioners do not claim to be an invalid exercise of either Congress' commerce or taxing power. [Finally, refunding the money if a State achieves certain milestones] is a conditional exercise of Congress' authority under the Spending Clause. . . . See generally South Dakota v. Dole. The expenditure is for the general welfare; the States are required to use the money they receive for the purpose of assuring the safe disposal of radioactive waste. The conditions imposed are unambiguous . . . [and] reasonably related to the purpose of the expenditure; both the conditions and the payments embody Congress' efforts to address the pressing problem of radioactive waste disposal. . . .

B

[Justice O'Connor held that the Act's access incentives were constitutional.] Where federal regulation of private activity is within the scope of the Commerce Clause, we have recognized the ability of Congress to offer states the choice of regulating that activity according to federal standards or having state law pre-empted by federal regulation. See *Hodel*; *FERC*. . . . [The Act's access incentives present a choice for States that do not join a regional compact and do not have their own radioactive waste disposal sites:] States may either regulate the disposal of radioactive waste according to federal standards by attaining local or regional self-sufficiency, or their residents who produce radioactive waste will be subject to federal regulation authorizing sited States and regions to deny access to their disposal sites. The affected

States are not compelled by Congress to regulate, because any burden caused by a State's refusal to regulate will fall on those who generate waste and find no outlet for its disposal, rather than on the State as a sovereign. A State whose citizens do not wish it to attain the Act's milestones may devote its attention and its resources to issues its citizens deem more worthy; the choice remains at all times with the residents of the State, not with Congress. The State need not expend any funds, or participate in any federal program, if local residents do not view such expenditures or participation as worthwhile. Nor must the State abandon the field if it does not accede to federal direction; the State may continue to regulate the generation and disposal of radioactive waste in any manner its citizens see fit. . . .

C

The take title provision is of a different character. [If States do not] regulat[e] pursuant to Congress' direction, [they have] the option of taking title to and possession of the low level radioactive waste generated within their borders and becoming liable for all damages waste generators suffer as a result of the States' failure to do so promptly. In this provision, Congress has crossed the line distinguishing encouragement from coercion. . . .

Because an instruction to state governments to take title to waste, standing alone, would be beyond the authority of Congress, and because a direct order to regulate, standing alone, would also be beyond the authority of Congress, it follows that Congress lacks the power to offer the States a choice between the two. . . . Either way, "the Act commandeers the legislative processes of the States by directly compelling them to enact and enforce a federal regulatory program," an outcome that has never been understood to lie within the authority conferred upon Congress by the Constitution. . . .

The take title provision appears to be unique. No other federal statute has been cited which offers a state government no option other than that of implementing legislation enacted by Congress. Whether one views the take title provision as lying outside Congress' enumerated powers, or as infringing upon the core of state sovereignty reserved by the Tenth Amendment, the provision is inconsistent with the federal structure of our Government established by the Constitution.

IV

A

[T]he United States argues that the Constitution's prohibition of congressional directives to state governments can be overcome where the federal interest is sufficiently important to justify state submission. . . . [But no] matter how powerful the federal interest involved, the Constitution simply does not give Congress the authority to require the States to regulate. The Constitution instead gives Congress the authority to regulate matters directly and to pre-empt contrary state regulation. Where a federal interest is sufficiently strong to cause Congress to legislate, it must do so directly; it may not conscript state governments as its agents.

Second, the United States argues that the Constitution does, in some circumstances, permit federal directives to state governments. . . . Federal statutes enforceable in state courts do, in a sense, direct state judges to enforce them, but this sort of federal "direction" of state judges is mandated by the text of the Supremacy Clause. No comparable constitutional provision authorizes Congress to command state legislatures to legislate. Additional cases cited by the United States discuss the power of federal courts to order state officials to comply with federal law. Again, however, the text of the Constitution plainly confers this authority on the federal courts, the "judicial Power" of which "shall extend to all Cases, in Law and Equity, arising under this Constitution, [and] the Laws of the United States . . . ; [and] to Controversies between two or more States; [and] between a State and Citizens of another State." U.S. Const., Art. III, §2. The Constitution contains no analogous grant of authority to Congress. Moreover, the Supremacy Clause makes federal law paramount over the contrary positions of state officials; the power of federal courts to enforce federal law thus presupposes some authority to order state officials to comply. . . .

B

[It is no objection that] public officials representing the State of New York lent their support to the Act's enactment. . . . Respondents note that the Act embodies a bargain among the sited and unsited States, a compromise to which New York was a willing participant and from which New York has reaped much benefit. Respondents then pose what appears at first to be a troubling question: How can a federal statute be found an unconstitutional infringement of state sovereignty when state officials consented to the statute's enactment?

The answer follows from an understanding of the fundamental purpose served by our Government's federal structure. The Constitution does not protect the sovereignty of States for the benefit of the States or state governments as abstract political entities, or even for the benefit of the public officials governing the States. To the contrary, the Constitution divides authority between federal and state governments for the protection of individuals. State sovereignty is not just an end in itself: "Rather, federalism secures to citizens the liberties that derive from the diffusion of sovereign power. . . . Just as the separation and independence of the coordinate branches of the Federal Government serve to prevent the accumulation of excessive power in any one branch, a healthy balance of power between the States and the Federal Government will reduce the risk of tyranny and abuse from either front." Gregory v. Ashcroft. See The Federalist No. 51.

Where Congress exceeds its authority relative to the States, therefore, the departure from the constitutional plan cannot be ratified by the "consent" of state officials. An analogy to the separation of powers among the branches of the Federal Government clarifies this point. The Constitution's division of power among the three branches is violated where one branch invades the territory of another, whether or not the encroached-upon branch approves the encroachment. In Buckley v. Valeo, 424 U.S. 1 (1976), for instance, the Court held that Congress had infringed the President's appointment power, despite the fact that the President himself had manifested his consent to the statute that caused the infringement by signing it into law. . . . In INS v. Chadha, 462 U.S. 919 (1983), we held that the legislative veto violated the constitutional requirement that legislation be presented to the President, despite Presidents' approval of hundreds of statutes containing a legislative veto provision. The constitutional authority of Congress cannot be expanded by the "consent" of the governmental unit whose domain is thereby narrowed, whether that unit is the Executive Branch or the States.

State officials thus cannot consent to the enlargement of the powers of Congress beyond those enumerated in the Constitution. Indeed, the facts of these cases raise the possibility that powerful incentives might lead both federal and state officials to view departures from the federal structure to be in their personal interests. Most citizens recognize the need for radioactive waste disposal sites, but few want sites near their homes. As a result, while it would be well within the authority of either federal or state officials to choose where the disposal sites will be, it is likely to be in the political interest of each individual official to avoid being held accountable to the voters for the choice of location. If a federal official is faced with the alternatives of choosing a location or directing the States to do it, the official may well prefer the latter, as a means of shifting responsibility for the eventual decision. If a state official is faced with the same set of alternatives—choosing a location or having Congress direct the choice of a location—the state official may also prefer the latter, as it may permit the avoidance of personal responsibility. The interests of public officials thus may not coincide with the Constitution's intergovernmental allocation of authority. Where state officials purport to submit to the direction of Congress in this manner, federalism is hardly being advanced.

Nor does the State's prior support for the Act estop it from asserting the Act's unconstitutionality. While New York has received the benefit of the Act in the form of a few more years of access to disposal sites in other States, New York has never joined a regional radioactive waste compact. Any estoppel implications that might flow from membership in a compact thus do not concern us here. The fact that the Act, like much federal legislation, embodies a compromise among the States does not elevate the Act (or the antecedent discussions among representatives of the States) to the status of an interstate agreement requiring Congress' approval under the Compact Clause. That a party collaborated with others in seeking legislation has never been understood to estop the party from challenging that legislation in subsequent litigation.

V

Petitioners also contend that the Act is inconsistent with the Constitution's Guarantee Clause, which directs the United States to "guarantee to every State in this Union a Republican Form of Government." U.S. Const., Art. IV, §4. . . . In most of the cases in which the Court has been asked to apply the Clause, the Court has found the claims presented to be nonjusticiable under the "political question" doctrine. . . . Luther v. Borden, 48 U.S. (7 How.) 1 (1849). . . . Even if we assume that petitioners' claim is justiciable, neither the monetary incentives provided by the Act nor the possibility that a State's waste producers may find themselves excluded from the disposal sites of another State can reasonably be said to deny any State a republican form of government. . . .

VI

[T]he take title provision may be severed without doing violence to the rest of the Act. The Act is still operative and it still serves Congress' objective of encouraging the States to attain local or regional self-sufficiency in the disposal of low level radioactive waste. It still includes two incentives that coax the States along this road. A State whose radioactive waste generators are unable to gain access to disposal sites in other States may encounter considerable internal pressure to provide for the disposal of waste, even without the prospect of taking title. The sited regional compacts need not accept New York's waste after the 7-year transition period expires, so any burden caused by New York's failure to secure a disposal site will not be borne by the residents of other States. . . .

VII

[T]he Federal Government may not compel the States to enact or administer a federal regulatory program. The Constitution permits both the Federal Government and the States to enact legislation regarding the disposal of low level radioactive waste. The Constitution enables the Federal Government to pre-empt state regulation contrary to federal interests, and it permits the Federal Government to hold out incentives to the States as a means of encouraging them to adopt suggested regulatory schemes. It does not, however, authorize Congress simply to direct the States to provide for the disposal of the radioactive waste generated within their borders. . . .

Justice WHITE, with whom Justice BLACKMUN and Justice STEVENS join, concurring in part and dissenting in part. . . . I can only join Parts III-A and III-B, and I respectfully dissent from the rest of [the Court's] opinion. . . .

. . . The Low-Level Radioactive Waste Policy Act of 1980 (1980 Act), and its amendatory 1985 Act, resulted from the efforts of state leaders to achieve a state-based set of remedies to the waste problem. They sought not federal pre-emption or intervention, but rather congressional sanction of interstate compromises they had reached. . . . [T]he 1985 Act was very much the product of cooperative federalism, in which the States bargained among themselves to achieve compromises for Congress to sanction. . . .

New York's actions subsequent to enactment of the 1980 and 1985 Acts fairly indicate its approval of the interstate agreement process embodied in those laws within the meaning of Art. I, §10, cl. 3, of the Constitution, which provides that "no State shall, without the Consent of Congress, . . . enter into any Agreement or Compact with another State." . . . As it was undertaking . . . initial steps to honor the interstate compromise embodied in the 1985 Act, New York continued to take full advantage of the import concession made by the sited States, by exporting its low-level radioactive waste for the full 7-year extension period provided in the 1985 Act. By gaining these benefits and complying with certain of the 1985 Act's deadlines, therefore, New York fairly evidenced its acceptance of the federal-state arrangement—including the take title provision.

Although unlike the 42 States that compose the nine existing and approved regional compacts, New York has never formalized its assent to the 1980 and 1985 statutes, our cases support the view that New York's actions signify assent to a constitutional interstate "agreement" for purposes of Art. I, §10, cl. 3. . . . In my view, New York acted in a manner to signify its assent to the 1985 Act's take title provision as part of the elaborate compromise reached among the States.

The State should be estopped from asserting the unconstitutionality of a provision that seeks merely to ensure that, after deriving substantial advantages from the 1985 Act, New York in fact must live up to its bargain by establishing an in-state low-level radioactive waste facility or assuming liability for its failure to act. . . .

[T]o say, as the Court does, that the incursion on state sovereignty "cannot be ratified by the 'consent' of state officials," is flatly wrong. In a case involving a congressional ratification statute to an interstate compact, the Court upheld a provision that Tennessee and Missouri had waived their immunity from suit. Over their objection, the Court held that "the States who are parties to the compact by accepting it and acting under it assume the conditions that Congress under the Constitution attached." In so holding, the Court determined that a State may be found to have waived a fundamental aspect of its sovereignty—the right to be immune from suit—in the formation of an interstate compact even when in subsequent litigation it expressly denied its waiver. . . .

The Court announces that it has no occasion to revisit such decisions as *Garcia* because "this is not a case in which Congress has subjected a State to the same legislation applicable to private parties." . . . The Court's distinction between a federal statute's regulation of States and private parties for general purposes, as opposed to a regulation solely on the activities of States, is unsupported by our recent Tenth Amendment cases. In no case has the Court rested its holding on such a distinction. . . .

[I]n *Garcia*, we stated the proper inquiry: "We are convinced that the fundamental limitation that the constitutional scheme imposes on the Commerce Clause to protect the 'States as States' is one of process rather than one of result. Any substantive restraint on the exercise of Commerce Clause powers must find its justification in the procedural nature of this basic limitation, and it must be tailored to compensate for possible failings in the national political process rather than to dictate a 'sacred province of state autonomy.'" Where it addresses this aspect of respondents' argument, the Court tacitly concedes that a failing of the political process cannot be shown in these cases because it refuses to rebut the unassailable arguments that the States were well able to look after themselves in the legislative process that culminated in the 1985 Act's passage. Indeed, New York acknowledges that its "congressional delegation participated in the drafting and enactment of both the 1980 and the 1985 Acts." The Court rejects this process-based argument by resorting to generalities and platitudes about the purpose of federalism being to protect individual rights.

Ultimately, I suppose, the entire structure of our federal constitutional government can be traced to an interest in establishing checks and balances to prevent the exercise of tyranny against individuals. But these fears seem extremely far distant to me in a situation such as this. We face a crisis of national proportions in the disposal of low-level radioactive waste, and Congress has acceded to the wishes of the States by permitting local decisionmaking rather than imposing a solution from Washington. New York itself participated and supported passage of this legislation at both the gubernatorial and federal representative levels, and then enacted state laws specifically to comply with the deadlines and timetables agreed upon by the States in the 1985 Act. For me, the Court's civics lecture has a decidedly hollow ring at a time when action, rather than rhetoric, is needed to solve a national problem.

[T]hough I disagree with the Court's conclusion that the take title provision is unconstitutional, I do not read its opinion to preclude Congress from adopting a similar measure through its powers under the Spending or Commerce Clauses. The Court makes clear that its objection is to the alleged "commandeering" quality of the take title provision. As its discussion of the surcharge and rebate incentives reveals, the spending power offers a means of enacting a take title provision under the Court's standards. Congress could, in other words, condition the payment of funds on the State's willingness to take title if it has not already provided a waste disposal facility. . . .

Similarly, should a State fail to establish a waste disposal facility by the appointed deadline (. . . January 1, 1996), Congress has the power pursuant to the Commerce Clause to regulate directly the producers of the waste. Thus, as I read it, Congress could amend the statute to say that if a State fails to meet the January 1, 1996, deadline for achieving a means of waste disposal, and has not taken title to the waste, no low-level radioactive waste may be shipped out of the State of New York.

Justice STEVENS, concurring in part and dissenting in part.

Under the Articles of Confederation, the Federal Government had the power to issue commands to the States. Because that indirect exercise of federal power proved ineffective, the Framers of the Constitution empowered the Federal Government to exercise legislative authority directly over individuals within the States, even though that direct authority constituted a greater intrusion on state sovereignty. Nothing in that history suggests that the Federal Government may not also impose its will upon the several States as it did under the Articles. The Constitution enhanced, rather than diminished, the power of the Federal Government.

The notion that Congress does not have the power to issue "a simple command to state governments to implement legislation enacted by Congress," is incorrect and unsound. There is no such limitation in the Constitution. The Tenth Amendment surely does not impose any limit on Congress' exercise of the powers delegated to it by Article I. Nor does the structure of the constitutional order or the values of federalism mandate such a formal rule. To the contrary, the Federal Government directs state governments in many realms. The Government regulates state-operated railroads, state school systems, state prisons, state elections, and a host of other state functions. Similarly, there can be no doubt that, in time of war, Congress could either draft soldiers itself or command the States to supply their quotas of troops. I see no reason why Congress may not also command the States to enforce federal water and air quality standards or federal standards for the disposition of low-level radioactive wastes.

The Constitution gives this Court the power to resolve controversies between the States. Long before Congress enacted pollution-control legislation, this Court crafted a body of "interstate common law" to govern disputes between States involving interstate waters. In such contexts, we have not hesitated to direct States to undertake specific actions. For example, we have "imposed on States an affirmative duty to take reasonable steps to conserve and augment the water supply of an interstate stream." Thus, we unquestionably have the power to command an upstream State that is polluting the waters of a downstream State to adopt appropriate regulations to implement a federal statutory command.

With respect to the problem presented by the cases at hand, if litigation should develop between States that have joined a compact, we would surely have the power to grant relief in the form of specific enforcement of the take title provision. Indeed, even if the statute had never been passed, if one State's radioactive waste created a nuisance that harmed its neighbors, it seems clear that we would have had the power to command the offending State to take remedial action. If this Court has such authority, surely Congress has similar authority. . . .

DISCUSSION

1. *Congress versus court as overseer of states.* Justice Stevens emphasizes the power of federal courts to issue affirmative orders to states, and suggests that Congress should enjoy comparable power. Justice White, in a footnote, also points to the Reconstruction Amendments as an important source of congressional authority over state governments. These arguments, however, do not persuade the majority in *New York*. Is there a similarity between the vision in *New York* and the vision later articulated in *City of Boerne v. Flores*, in which the Court claimed for itself a privileged role vis à vis Congress in overseeing states?

2. *Accountability or autonomy?* The *New York* majority claims that its rule will promote political accountability—the electorate will know which government to blame for which problem. But doesn't the nature of our constitutional system—with an elaborate separation of powers at the federal level, overlaid by federalism, and a written Constitution—inherently lend itself to certain kinds of confusion? At the federal level, the President blames Congress; Congress blames the President; and both blame the Court for ruling certain policies off the table, or for misconstruing or rewriting legislation. (Note how the Court in *New York* almost literally "rewrote" the congressional statute at issue, eliminating one clause but enforcing the rest.) What's more, actual policies as experienced by citizens are an intricate mix of state and federal action, with both sets of governments claiming credit when things go well, and pointing fingers at each other when they don't. If clear lines of political accountability were the chief goal, might we be better off with a pure parliamentary system concentrating all power in a single government that is more clearly responsible for whatever happens on its watch?

The chief problem with such a concentrated system, however, is that it fails to sufficiently disperse power and "check" a possibly abusive regime. And so perhaps a better argument for the *New York* rule is simply this: State governments are designed to be constitutionally independent from the federal government in certain ways, in part so that they may stand as competing political power centers and rallying points for opponents of the central regime. Congress may not treat state legislatures as its puppets; such legislatures are supposed to be autonomous watchdogs, not wholly subservient lapdogs. If Congress could tell a state that it must pass certain bills, then Congress could in principle control the entire agenda of a state legislature, leaving it with no independence or time to devise its own agenda as a counterweight to Congress's. No single congressional mandate is likely to occupy a state legislature's entire docket, of course, but the cleanest and most judicially manageable line is simply to prevent all affirmative commandeering. By its nature, "the power to commandeer is the power to destroy," cf. *McCulloch*, and thus should be nipped in the bud. (The power of Congress to displace or preempt state legislatures does not pose an identical threat; each legislature would remain free to define its own agenda, and could, for example, devote its entire term to laying out in detail why Congress was misguided, and what state citizens should do to demonstrate their opposition.) On this state-autonomy view, state legislatures should remain free to define their own agendas, just as should, say, the Democratic Party, the Sierra Club, the *New York Times*, and the Catholic Church. Note that when Congress first threatened free speech, with the infamous Sedition Act of 1798, state legislatures in Virginia and Kentucky mobilized opposition and engaged in legislative free speech, via the Virginia and Kentucky Resolves—in a manner that obviously reenacted the role that colonial governments had played a generation earlier in response to Parliamentary abuses. For more discussion of the link between "freedom of speech" and legislative "speech and debate" and more discussion of these Resolves as exemplifying how federalism can support liberty, see Akhil Reed Amar, The Bill of Rights: Creation and Reconstruction (1998); Akhil Reed Amar, Of Sovereignty and Federalism, 96 Yale L.J. 1425, 1492-1503 (1987).

3. *Bribing versus commandeering*. The *New York* Court says that states may be "bribed" into legislating, via conditional funding statutes, but not commandeered via direct coercion. If the main idea is accountability, isn't bribery more troubling because it is so indirect and insidious? In the case of outright coercion, isn't it *easier* for the state government to say, "Don't blame us—the feds *made* us do it"? Does the autonomy/competing-power-center rationale better explain why federal "bribery" is permissible?

4. *The NIMBY problem*. If there was a special accountability problem on the facts of the *New York* case, was it created by commandeering, or by something else? Consider the general accountability concern raised by certain specific siting decisions. We all need a site to dump our waste, but each of us says, "Not In My Back Yard!" As a result, politicians want to mandate that a site be found, but want to avoid personally picking the particular site; once the site is picked, neighboring residents may turn into intense single-issue voters targeting their ire at the decisionmaker who chose the site. (The rest of us are happy to be spared, but much less focused and intense; our diffuse support for the decisionmaker may not politically offset the more focused hostility.) In NIMBY situations, can you see why politicians might choose particularly intricate and opaque procedures to blur responsibility for particular siting decisions? Would governmental compensation aimed at the adversely affected neighborhood—even if not strictly dictated by Takings Clause principles—be appropriate to "spread the cost"? Note that such compensation raises hard questions about who should get how much—and also requires higher taxes for the rest of us.

5. *Serious federal impairment?* Justice White seems to claim both that the Court's actions seriously impede Congress's ability to solve a national crisis, and that Congress can evade the *New York* rule rather easily. Which is it? Can't Congress rather easily "contract around" the case by bribing states, or by directly regulating (for example, by barring any shipment of waste across state lines, thus forcing New Yorkers to find a place for their own waste)—or simply by allowing the other sanctions in the 1985 Act to kick in and put strong pressure on the State of New York? Recall that the Court does not strike down the law in toto, only one piece of it. Was

this piece particularly important? Did this piece (as opposed to the other provisions of the Act) in fact reflect the specific input of state governments?

6. *The Guarantee Clause.* Justice O'Connor also treads carefully in her treatment of the Article IV republican government Guarantee Clause. To have relied on the clause would have been doctrinally abrupt, given its generally low profile in modern Supreme Court case law. In the text, history, and structure of the Constitution itself, however, the clause is anything but peripheral. And unlike the grammar of the Tenth Amendment, which seems to protect states' rights residually, the Guarantee Clause offers a plausible textual basis for protecting states' rights in an affirmative fashion, akin to the modern Bill of Rights, cutting across federal enumerated power. Note how Justice O'Connor begins the process of "rehabilitating" the clause as important and justiciable, without actually relying on it.

7. *Congress, the Court, states, and the "dormant" Commerce Clause.* In the absence of congressional legislation, a state law that generally required private trash sites to accept only trash generated within the state would face tough sledding in federal court as a highly suspect "discrimination" against sister states, see City of Philadelphia v. New Jersey, 437 U.S. 617 (1978). But as the *New York* majority makes clear, Congress can authorize this kind of state "discrimination" under its own Commerce Clause power. For a quick summary of the modern contours of, and debate about, "Dormant" Commerce Clause doctrine, see infra, Section III.

8. *Commandeering versus preemption.* In Murphy v. National Collegiate Athletic Association, 138 S. Ct. 1461 (2018), the Court considered a challenge to the Professional and Amateur Sports Protection Act (PASPA). PASPA made it unlawful for a State or its subdivisions "to sponsor, operate, advertise, promote, license, or authorize by law or compact . . . a lottery, sweepstakes, or other betting, gambling, or wagering scheme based . . . on" competitive sporting events, and for "a person to sponsor, operate, advertise, or promote" those same gambling schemes if done "pursuant to the law or compact of a governmental entity." PASPA grandfathered existing forms of sports gambling in four States. New Jersey sought to decriminalize sports gambling in Atlantic City. The NCAA, which was one of a number of organizations authorized to sue to enforce PASPA's provisions, sued to stop it.

The Supreme Court, in an opinion by Justice Alito, held that "prohibiting state authorization of sports gambling . . . violates the anticommandeering rule" of New York v. United States. PASPA "unequivocally dictates what a state legislature may and may not do. . . . It is as if federal officers were installed in state legislative chambers and were armed with the authority to stop legislators from voting on any offending proposals. A more direct affront to state sovereignty is not easy to imagine." Alito argued that "prohibiting a State from enacting new laws" is just as unconstitutional as requiring states to pass laws. "It was a matter of happenstance that the laws challenged in *New York* and *Printz* commanded 'affirmative' action as opposed to imposing a prohibition. The basic principle—that Congress cannot issue direct orders to state legislatures—applies in either event."

This argument, however, required the Court to distinguish PASPA from a federal law banning sports gambling, which would preempt state laws to the contrary. Justice Alito argued that in preemption cases, Congress regulates individuals, not states: "Our cases have identified three different types of preemption—'conflict,' 'express,' and 'field'—but all of them work in the same way: Congress enacts a law that imposes restrictions or confers rights on private actors; a state law confers rights or imposes restrictions that conflict with the federal law; and therefore the federal law takes precedence and the state law is preempted."

The problem, however, is that federal statutes that preempt states often are couched in terms of prohibitions on states. Justice Alito gave as an example the Airline Deregulation Act of 1978, which provided that "no State or political subdivision thereof . . . shall enact or enforce any law, rule, regulation, standard, or other provision having the force and effect of law relating to rates, routes, or services of any [covered] air carrier." Although "[t]his language might appear to operate directly on the States," Alito argued, "it is a mistake to be confused by the way in which a preemption provision is phrased. . . . [I]t is clear that this provision operates just like any other federal law with preemptive effect. It confers on private entities (i.e., covered carriers) a federal right to engage in certain conduct subject only to certain (federal) constraints. . . . In sum, regardless of the language sometimes used by Congress and this Court, every form of preemption is based on a federal law that regulates the conduct of private actors, not the States."

How plausible is this distinction? If the issue is the regulation of private actors, what is the practical difference between PAPSA and a federal law that makes sports gambling unlawful except in four states? The Court explained that "PASPA does not make sports gambling itself a federal crime. Instead, it allows the Attorney General, as well as professional and amateur sports organizations, to bring civil actions to enjoin violations." Why should the method of enforcement matter?

9. *Founding history.* The *New York* Court claims that its anticommandeering rule finds strong support in the history of the founding. Justice Stevens disputes this, and Justice White dismisses it as "window dressing." Note that many of the historical sources relied upon by the Court suggest that it is simply impossible or impractical for the federal government to coerce a state government as such—or at least, to coerce a state government to perform an affirmative task. Is this true today? In any event, why would the matter be any different if a recalcitrant state refused to do what it had promised after receiving federal funds (or after entering into a properly blessed interstate compact)? Does the Court's history support its doctrinal rule distinguishing between permissible federal "encouragement" via conditional funding, and impermissible federal "coercion"? Consider the following historical study written shortly after New York v. United States was decided:

Saikrishna Bangalore Prakash, Field Office Federalism

79 Va. L. Rev. 1957 (1993)

[Based on constitutional text, history, and structure, Prakash argued that Congress should not be allowed to compel state legislatures to pass laws, but should be allowed to mandate that state executive and judicial officers affirmatively enforce federal laws.]

[In the words of Hamilton's Federalist No. 16, the federal government] "must stand in need of no intermediate legislations; but must itself be empowered to employ the arm of the ordinary magistrate to execute its own resolutions." . . .

Why the distinction between the state magistracy and state legislatures? Ellsworth's views on the question are illustrative. "I am for coercion by law—that coercion which acts only upon delinquent individuals. This Constitution does not attempt to coerce sovereign bodies, states, in their political capacity." First, as Ellsworth notes, state legislatures ("sovereign bodies") wielded whatever sovereignty the state government possessed. The legislatures represented the people of the state and acted according to their interests. Outsiders who tried to force these institutions to obey (like the Continental Congress) were simply not going to be heeded.

Second, state legislatures exercised legislative will and discretion. They determined what laws should be passed and which legislation was better left unenacted. Because they exercised will, they could not be made to comply mechanically with federal requisitions. State legislatures, then, embodied the states "in their political capacity."

Third, the multimember character of state legislatures made coercion of legislatures difficult. Who would be held accountable for failure to satisfy a requisition, the whole legislative body or only those who had opposed fulfilling the congressional requisition? Where the national government's authority was "confined to the collective bodies of the communities that compose it, every breach of the laws must involve a state of war." Hence, the Constitution abandoned coercion of multimember "sovereign bodies."

Finally, the Founding Generation relinquished requisitioning state legislatures because in practice the system simply had failed to deliver. State legislatures repeatedly ignored Articles [of Confederation] requisitions. In such a system, requisitions were really only supplications, as even opponents of the Constitution understood. Short of a civil war, state legislatures could not be forced to comply. As Ellsworth insisted, "no coercion is applicable to such legislative bodies, but that of an armed force." Better to abandon the phantom authority altogether.

The magistracy, however, were perceived differently. They did not exercise state sovereignty; they were not "sovereign bodies." Rather they were the servants of the legislature; the servants of the laws of the land. Nor did they exercise legislative will; they were not the embodiment of a state's "political capacity" that Ellsworth discussed. Instead they mechanically enforced the laws of the land. For these reasons they could not pick and choose which laws to enforce and, thus, could not discriminate against federal law. Moreover, coercion could more easily be applied against the magistracy. Execution and adjudication normally took place through the agency of a single person. Delinquent individual executive or judicial officers could be held accountable for maladministration of the laws in a manner that state legislators could not be held responsible for failure to heed congressional attempts at commandeering. Finally, the Founding Generation considered commandeering state executives and judges more efficacious under the Articles than the misguided attempts to commandeer state legislatures. State executives and courts could not defy federal authority as easily as state legislatures had. . . .

. . . *New York*'s "commandeering" dividing line ought to be shifted. Justice O'Connor admits that the federal government may commandeer state courts. . . . [S]tate executives are really more like state judges than state legislators. State executives and judges must administer the laws of the land, even if those laws emanate from Congress. Similarly, Justice Stevens is quite correct in noting that the federal government may commandeer state executives and courts. He merely falters in not recognizing the peculiar nature of state legislatures and the failed commandeering attempts under the Articles. Whether or not we perceive state legislatures as fundamentally different from the state magistracy, the Constitution so views them.

In essence, Prakash argued that *New York* was right on its facts, but overbroad in its language. In 1997, however, the Court rejected Prakash's effort to split the difference between the *New York* majority and its dissenters; by a 5-4 vote in the *Printz* case, excerpted next, the Court applied the *New York* rule to strike down a law that "commandeered" state executive power.

Printz v. United States

521 U.S. 898 (1997)

[The 1993 Brady Handgun Violence Prevention Act, Pub. L. No. 103-159, 107 Stat. 1536, 18 U.S.C. §922(s)(2), required the Attorney General to establish a national system for instantly checking prospective handgun purchasers' backgrounds. As an interim measure, prior to the establishment of this national instant background check system, the Act required the "chief law enforcement officer" (CLEO) of each local jurisdiction to conduct background checks on prospective handgun purchasers. Two Western sheriffs challenged these interim provisions as violative of the *New York* principle.]

SCALIA, J. . . .

II

. . . The petitioners here object to being pressed into federal service, and contend that congressional action compelling state officers to execute federal laws is unconstitutional. Because there is no constitutional text speaking to this precise question, the answer to the CLEOs' challenge must be sought in historical understanding and practice, in the structure of the Constitution, and in the jurisprudence of this Court. . . .

Petitioners contend that compelled enlistment of state executive officers for the administration of federal programs is, until very recent years at least, unprecedented. The Government contends, to the contrary, that "the earliest Congresses enacted statutes that required the participation of state officials in the implementation of federal laws." The Government's contention demands our careful consideration, since early congressional enactments "provide 'contemporaneous and weighty evidence' of the Constitution's meaning." . . . Conversely if, as petitioners contend, earlier Congresses avoided use of this highly attractive power, we would have reason to believe that the power was thought not to exist. . . .

These early laws establish, at most, that the Constitution was originally understood to permit imposition of an obligation on state *judges* to enforce federal prescriptions, insofar as those prescriptions related to matters appropriate for the judicial power. That assumption was perhaps implicit in one of the provisions of the

Constitution, and was explicit in another. In accord with the so-called Madisonian Compromise, Article III, §1, established only a Supreme Court, and made the creation of lower federal courts optional with the Congress—even though it was obvious that the Supreme Court alone could not hear all federal cases throughout the United States. And the Supremacy Clause, Art. VI, cl. 2, announced that "the Laws of the United States . . . shall be the supreme Law of the Land; and the Judges in every State shall be bound thereby." It is understandable why courts should have been viewed distinctively in this regard; unlike legislatures and executives, they applied the law of other sovereigns all the time. The principle underlying so-called "transitory" causes of action was that laws which operated elsewhere created obligations in justice that courts of the forum state would enforce. The Constitution itself, in the Full Faith and Credit Clause, Art. IV, §1, generally required such enforcement with respect to obligations arising in other States.

For these reasons, we do not think the early statutes imposing obligations on state courts imply a power of Congress to impress the state executive into its service. Indeed, it can be argued that the numerousness of these statutes, contrasted with the utter lack of statutes imposing obligations on the States' executive (notwithstanding the attractiveness of that course to Congress), suggests an assumed absence of such power. The only early federal law the Government has brought to our attention that imposed duties on state executive officers is the Extradition Act of 1793, which required the "executive authority" of a State to cause the arrest and delivery of a fugitive from justice upon the request of the executive authority of the State from which the fugitive had fled. That was in direct implementation, however, of the Extradition Clause of the Constitution itself, see Art. IV, §2. . . .

[T]he Government also appeals to other sources we have usually regarded as indicative of the original understanding of the Constitution. It points to portions of The Federalist which reply to criticisms that Congress's power to tax will produce two sets of revenue officers. . . . "Publius" responded that Congress will probably "make use of the State officers and State regulations, for collecting" federal taxes, The Federalist No. 36, and predicted that "the eventual collection [of internal revenue] under the immediate authority of the Union, will generally be made by the officers, and according to the rules, appointed by the several States," id., No. 45. The Government also invokes the Federalist's more general observations that the Constitution would "enable the [national] government to employ the ordinary magistracy of each [State] in the execution of its laws," id., No. 27, and that it was "extremely probable that in other instances, particularly in the organization of the judicial power, the officers of the States will be clothed in the correspondent authority of the Union," id., No. 45. But none of these statements necessarily implies—what is the critical point here—that Congress could impose these responsibilities *without the consent of the States.* They appear to rest on the natural assumption that the States would consent to allowing their officials to assist the Federal Government. . . .

To complete the historical record, we must note that there is not only an absence of executive-commandeering statutes in the early Congresses, but there is an absence of them in our later history as well, at least until very recent years. . . .

The Government points to a number of federal statutes enacted within the past few decades that require the participation of state or local officials in implementing federal regulatory schemes. Some of these are connected to federal funding measures, and can perhaps be more accurately described as conditions upon the grant of federal funding than as mandates to the States; others, which require only the provision of information to the Federal Government, do not involve the precise issue before us here, which is the forced participation of the States' executive in the actual administration of a federal program. . . . Even assuming they represent assertion of the very same congressional power challenged here, they are of such recent vintage that they are no more probative than the statute before us of a constitutional tradition that lends meaning to the text. Their persuasive force is far outweighed by almost two centuries of apparent congressional avoidance of the practice. Compare INS v. Chadha, 462 U.S. 919 (1983), in which the legislative veto, though enshrined in perhaps hundreds of federal statutes, most of which were enacted in the 1970s and the earliest of which was enacted in 1932, was nonetheless held unconstitutional.

III

The constitutional practice we have examined above tends to negate the existence of the congressional power asserted here, but is not conclusive. We turn next to consideration of the structure of the Constitution. . . .

A

It is incontestible that the Constitution established a system of "dual sovereignty." Gregory v. Ashcroft. Although the States surrendered many of their powers to the new Federal Government, they retained "a residuary and inviolable sovereignty," The Federalist No. 39. This is reflected throughout the Constitution's text, including (to mention only a few examples) the prohibition on any involuntary reduction or combination of a State's territory, Art. IV, §3; the Judicial Power Clause, Art. III, §2, and the Privileges and Immunities Clause, Art. IV, §2, which speak of the "Citizens" of the States; the amendment provision, Article V, which requires the votes of three-fourths of the States to amend the Constitution; and the Guarantee Clause, Art. IV, §4, which "presupposes the continued existence of the states and . . . those means and instrumentalities which are the creation of their sovereign and reserved rights." Residual state sovereignty was also implicit, of course, in the Constitution's conferral upon Congress of not all governmental powers, but only discrete, enumerated ones, which implication was rendered express by the Tenth Amendment[]. . . .[a]

. . . We have set forth the historical record in more detail elsewhere, see New York v. United States, and need not repeat it here. It suffices to repeat the conclusion: "The Framers explicitly chose a Constitution that confers upon Congress the

---

a. [The dissent] falsely presumes that the Tenth Amendment is the exclusive textual source of protection for principles of federalism. Our system of dual sovereignty is reflected in numerous constitutional provisions, and not only those, like the Tenth Amendment, that speak to the point explicitly. It is not at all unusual for our resolution of a significant constitutional question to rest upon reasonable implications. See, e.g., Myers v. United States, 272 U.S. 52 (1926) (finding by implication from Art. II, §§1, 2, that the President has the exclusive power to remove executive officers). [Footnote relocated by editors.]

power to regulate individuals, not States."[b] The great innovation of this design was that "our citizens would have two political capacities, one state and one federal, each protected from incursion by the other." . . .[c]

This separation of the two spheres is one of the Constitution's structural protections of liberty. "Just as the separation and independence of the coordinate branches of the Federal Government serve to prevent the accumulation of excessive power in any one branch, a healthy balance of power between the States and the Federal Government will reduce the risk of tyranny and abuse from either front." *Gregory*; . . . The Federalist No. 51; See also The Federalist No. 28. The power of the Federal Government would be augmented immeasurably if it were able to impress into its service—and at no cost to itself—the police officers of the 50 States.

B

[F]ederal control of state officers would . . . also have an effect upon . . . the separation and equilibration of powers between the three branches of the Federal Government itself. The Constitution does not leave to speculation who is to administer the laws enacted by Congress; the President, it says, "shall take Care that the Laws be faithfully executed." . . . The Brady Act effectively transfers this responsibility to thousands of CLEOs in the 50 States, who are left to implement the program without meaningful Presidential control (if indeed meaningful Presidential control is possible without the power to appoint and remove). The insistence of the

---

b. The dissent, reiterating Justice Stevens' dissent in New York, maintains that the Constitution merely augmented the pre-existing power under the Articles to issue commands to the States with the additional power to make demands directly on individuals. That argument, however, was squarely rejected by the Court in New York, and with good reason. Many of Congress's powers under Art. I, §8, were copied almost verbatim from the Articles of Confederation, indicating quite clearly that "where the Constitution intends that our Congress enjoy a power once vested in the Continental Congress, it specifically grants it." Prakash, Field Office Federalism, 79 Va. L. Rev. 1957, 1972 (1993).

c. Justice Breyer's dissent would have us consider the benefits that other countries, and the European Union, believe they have derived from federal systems that are different from ours. We think such comparative analysis inappropriate to the task of interpreting a constitution, though it was of course quite relevant to the task of writing one. The Framers were familiar with many federal systems, from classical antiquity down to their own time; they are discussed in Nos. 18-20 of The Federalist. Some were (for the purpose here under discussion) quite similar to the modern "federal" systems that Justice Breyer favors. Madison's and Hamilton's opinion of such systems could not be clearer. Federalist No. 20, after an extended critique of the system of government established by the Union of Utrecht for the United Netherlands, concludes:

> "I make no apology for having dwelt so long on the contemplation of these federal precedents. Experience is the oracle of truth; and where its responses are unequivocal, they ought to be conclusive and sacred. The important truth, which it unequivocally pronounces in the present case, is that a sovereignty over sovereigns, a government over governments, a legislation for communities, as contradistinguished from individuals, as it is a solecism in theory, so in practice it is subversive of the order and ends of civil polity. . . ."

Antifederalists, on the other hand, pointed specifically to Switzerland—and its then-400 years of success as a "confederate republic"—as proof that the proposed Constitution and its federal structure was unnecessary. The fact is that our federalism is not Europe's. . . .

Framers upon unity in the Federal Executive—to insure both vigor and accountability—is well known. See The Federalist No. 70; see also Calabresi & Prakash, The President's Power to Execute the Laws, 104 Yale L.J. 541 (1994). That unity would be shattered, and the power of the President would be subject to reduction, if Congress could act as effectively without the President as with him, by simply requiring state officers to execute its laws. . . .[d]

IV

Finally, and most conclusively in the present litigation, we turn to the prior jurisprudence of this Court. Federal commandeering of state governments is such a novel phenomenon that this Court's first experience with it did not occur until the 1970s. . . .

When we were at last confronted squarely with a federal statute that unambiguously required the States to enact or administer a federal regulatory program, our decision should have come as no surprise. . . . "The Federal Government," we held, "may not compel the States to enact or administer a federal regulatory program." *New York.*

The Government contends that *New York* is distinguishable on the following ground: . . . "The constitutional line is crossed only when Congress compels the States to make law in their sovereign capacities." . . .

The Government . . . maintains that requiring state officers to perform discrete, ministerial tasks specified by Congress does not violate the principle of *New York* because it does not diminish the accountability of state or federal officials. This argument fails even on its own terms. By forcing state governments to absorb the financial burden of implementing a federal regulatory program, Members of Congress can take credit for "solving" problems without having to ask their constituents to pay for the solutions with higher federal taxes. And even when the States are not forced to absorb the costs of implementing a federal program, they are still put in the position of taking the blame for its burdensomeness and for its defects. See Merritt, Three Faces of Federalism: Finding a Formula for the Future, 47 Vand. L. Rev. 1563, 1580, n.65 (1994). Under the present law, for example, it will be the CLEO and not some federal official who stands between the gun purchaser and immediate possession of his gun. And it will likely be the CLEO, not some federal official, who will be blamed for any error (even one in the designated federal database) that causes a purchaser to be mistakenly rejected. . . .

V

. . . We held in *New York* that Congress cannot compel the States to enact or enforce a federal regulatory program. Today we hold that Congress cannot circumvent that prohibition by conscripting the State's officers directly. The Federal Government may neither issue directives requiring the States to address particular

---

d. [C]ontrol by the unitary Federal Executive is also sacrificed when States voluntarily administer federal programs, but the condition of voluntary state participation significantly reduces the ability of Congress to use this device as a means of reducing the power of the Presidency.

problems, nor command the States' officers, or those of their political subdivisions, to administer or enforce a federal regulatory program. It matters not whether policymaking is involved, and no case-by-case weighing of the burdens or benefits is necessary; such commands are fundamentally incompatible with our constitutional system of dual sovereignty. . . .

O'CONNOR, J., concurring. . . .

Our holding, of course, does not spell the end of the objectives of the Brady Act. States and chief law enforcement officers may voluntarily continue to participate in the federal program. Moreover, the directives to the States are merely interim provisions scheduled to terminate November 30, 1998. Congress is also free to amend the interim program to provide for its continuance on a contractual basis with the States if it wishes, as it does with a number of other federal programs. See, e.g., 23 U.S.C. §402 (conditioning States' receipt of federal funds for highway safety program on compliance with federal requirements).

In addition, the Court appropriately refrains from deciding whether other purely ministerial reporting requirements imposed by Congress on state and local authorities pursuant to its Commerce Clause powers are similarly invalid. See, e.g., 42 U.S.C. §5779(a) (requiring state and local law enforcement agencies to report cases of missing children to the Department of Justice). . . .

THOMAS, J., concurring.

In my "revisionist" view, the Federal Government's authority under the Commerce Clause . . . does not extend to the regulation of wholly intrastate, point-of-sale transactions. See *Lopez* (concurring opinion). Absent the underlying authority to regulate the intrastate transfer of firearms, Congress surely lacks the corollary power to impress state law enforcement officers into administering and enforcing such regulations. . . .

Even if we construe Congress' authority to regulate interstate commerce to encompass those intrastate transactions that "substantially affect" interstate commerce, I question whether Congress can regulate the particular transactions at issue here. . . . The Second Amendment . . . appears to contain an express limitation on the government's authority. . . . This Court has not had recent occasion to consider the nature of the substantive right safeguarded by the Second Amendment. If, however, the Second Amendment is read to confer a personal right to "keep and bear arms," a colorable argument exists that the Federal Government's regulatory scheme, at least as it pertains to the purely intrastate sale or possession of firearms, runs afoul of that Amendment's protections.[a] As the parties did not raise this argument, however, we need not consider it here. Perhaps, at some future date, this Court will have the opportunity to determine whether Justice Story was

---

a. [Footnote by Justice Thomas] Marshaling an impressive array of historical evidence, a growing body of scholarly commentary indicates that the "right to keep and bear arms" is, as the Amendment's text suggests, a personal right. Other scholars, however, argue that the Second Amendment does not secure a personal right to keep or to bear arms. Although somewhat overlooked in our jurisprudence, the Amendment has certainly engendered considerable academic, as well as public, debate.

correct when he wrote that the right to bear arms "has justly been considered, as the palladium of the liberties of a republic." . . .

Justice STEVENS, with whom Justice SOUTER, Justice GINSBURG, and Justice BREYER join, dissenting.

When Congress exercises the powers delegated to it by the Constitution, it may impose affirmative obligations on executive and judicial officers of state and local governments as well as ordinary citizens. . . .

These cases do not implicate the more difficult questions associated with congressional coercion of state legislatures addressed in *New York.*

I

The text of the Constitution provides a sufficient basis for a correct disposition of this case.

Article I, §8, grants the Congress the power to regulate commerce among the States. . . . [T]hat provision adequately supports the regulation of commerce in handguns effected by the Brady Act. . . .

Unlike the First Amendment, which prohibits the enactment of a category of laws that would otherwise be authorized by Article I, the Tenth Amendment imposes no restriction on the exercise of delegated powers. . . . The Amendment confirms the principle that the powers of the Federal Government are limited to those affirmatively granted by the Constitution, but it does not purport to limit the scope or the effectiveness of the exercise of powers that are delegated to Congress. Thus, the Amendment provides no support for a rule that immunizes local officials from obligations that might be imposed on ordinary citizens.[a] Indeed, it would be more reasonable to infer that federal law may impose greater duties on state officials than on private citizens because another provision of the Constitution requires that "all executive and judicial Officers, both of the United States and of the several States, shall be bound by Oath or Affirmation, to support this Constitution." U.S. Const., Art. VI, cl. 3. . . .

The reasoning in our unanimous opinion explaining why state tribunals with ordinary jurisdiction over tort litigation can be required to hear cases arising under the Federal Employers' Liability Act applies equally to local law enforcement officers whose ordinary duties parallel the modest obligations imposed by the Brady Act:

> The suggestion that the act of Congress is not in harmony with the policy of the State, and therefore that the courts of the State are free to decline jurisdiction, is quite inadmissible, because it presupposes what in legal contemplation does not exist. When Congress, in the exertion of the power confided to it by the Constitution, adopted that act, it spoke for

---

a. [Footnote by Justice Stevens] Recognizing the force of the argument, the Court suggests that this reasoning is in error because—even if it is responsive to the submission that the Tenth Amendment roots the principle set forth by the majority today—it does not answer the possibility that the Court's holding can be rooted in a "principle of state sovereignty" mentioned nowhere in the constitutional text. As a ground for invalidating important federal legislation, this argument is remarkably weak.

> all the people and all the States, and thereby established a policy for all. That policy is as much the policy of Connecticut as if the act had emanated from its own legislature, and should be respected accordingly in the courts of the State. . . .

There is not a clause, sentence, or paragraph in the entire text of the Constitution of the United States that supports the proposition that a local police officer can ignore a command contained in a statute enacted by Congress pursuant to an express delegation of power enumerated in Article I.

II

Under the Articles of Confederation the National Government had the power to issue commands to the several sovereign states, but it had no authority to govern individuals directly. Thus, it raised an army and financed its operations by issuing requisitions to the constituent members of the Confederacy, rather than by creating federal agencies to draft soldiers or to impose taxes.

That method of governing proved to be unacceptable, not because it demeaned the sovereign character of the several States, but rather because it was cumbersome and inefficient. Indeed, a confederation that allows each of its members to determine the ways and means of complying with an overriding requisition is obviously more deferential to state sovereignty concerns than a national government that uses its own agents to impose its will directly on the citizenry. The basic change in the character of the government that the Framers conceived was designed to enhance the power of the national government, not to provide some new, unmentioned immunity for state officers. . . .

Indeed, the historical materials strongly suggest that the Founders intended to enhance the capacity of the federal government by empowering it—as a part of the new authority to make demands directly on individual citizens—to act through local officials. Hamilton made clear that the new Constitution, "by extending the authority of the federal head to the individual citizens of the several States, will enable the government to employ the ordinary magistracy of each, in the execution of its laws." The Federalist No. 27. Hamilton's meaning was unambiguous; the federal government was to have the power to demand that local officials implement national policy programs. As he went on to explain: "It is easy to perceive that this will tend to destroy, in the common apprehension, all distinction between the sources from which [the state and federal governments] might proceed; and will give the federal government the same advantage for securing a due obedience to its authority which is enjoyed by the government of each State." . . .

More specifically, during the debates concerning the ratification of the Constitution, it was assumed that state agents would act as tax collectors for the federal government. Opponents of the Constitution had repeatedly expressed fears that the new federal government's ability to impose taxes directly on the citizenry would result in an overbearing presence of federal tax collectors in the States. Federalists rejoined that this problem would not arise because, as Hamilton explained, "the United States . . . will make use of the State officers and State regulations for collecting" certain taxes. Id., No. 36. Similarly, Madison made clear that the new central government's power to raise taxes directly from the citizenry would "not be resorted to, except for supplemental purposes of revenue . . . and that the eventual collection, under the immediate authority of the Union, will generally be made by the officers . . . appointed by the several States." Id., No. 45. . . .

The Court assumes that the imposition of such essentially executive duties on state judges and their clerks sheds no light on the question whether executive officials might have an immunity from federal obligations. . . . As one scholar has noted, "two centuries ago, state and local judges and associated judicial personnel performed many of the functions today performed by executive officers, including such varied tasks as laying city streets and ensuring the seaworthiness of vessels." Caminker, State Sovereignty and Subordinacy: May Congress Commandeer State Officers to Implement Federal Law?, 95 Colum. L. Rev. 1001, 1045, n.176 (1995). . . . The majority's insistence that this evidence of federal enlistment of state officials to serve executive functions is irrelevant simply because the assistance of "judges" was at issue rests on empty formalistic reasoning of the highest order.

The Court's evaluation of the historical evidence, furthermore, fails to acknowledge the important difference between policy decisions that may have been influenced by respect for state sovereignty concerns, and decisions that are compelled by the Constitution.[b]

The Court concludes its review of the historical materials with a reference to the fact that our decision in INS v. Chadha invalidated a large number of statutes enacted in the 1970s, implying that recent enactments by Congress that are similar to the Brady Act are not entitled to any presumption of validity. But in *Chadha,* unlike this case, our decision rested on the Constitution's express bicameralism and presentment requirements, not on judicial inferences drawn from a silent text and a historical record that surely favors the congressional understanding. . . .

III

The Court's "structural" arguments are not sufficient. . . . The fact that the Framers intended to preserve the sovereignty of the several States simply does not speak to the question whether individual state employees may be required to perform federal obligations, such as registering young adults for the draft, creating state emergency response commissions designed to manage the release of hazardous substances, collecting and reporting data on underground storage tanks that may pose an environmental hazard, and reporting traffic fatalities and missing children to a federal agency.

As we explained in *Garcia*: "The principal means chosen by the Framers to ensure the role of the States in the federal system lies in the structure of the Federal Government itself. It is no novelty to observe that the composition of the Federal Government was designed in large part to protect the States from overreaching by Congress." Given the fact that the Members of Congress are elected by the people of the several States, with each State receiving an equivalent number of Senators in order to ensure that even the smallest States have a powerful voice in the

---

b. Indeed, an entirely appropriate concern for the prerogatives of state government readily explains Congress' sparing use of this otherwise "highly attractive" power. Congress' discretion, contrary to the majority's suggestion, indicates not that the power does not exist, but rather that the interests of the States are more than sufficiently protected by their participation in the National Government.

legislature, it is quite unrealistic to assume that they will ignore the sovereignty concerns of their constituents. It is far more reasonable to presume that their decisions to impose modest burdens on state officials from time to time reflect a considered judgment that the people in each of the States will benefit therefrom.[c] . . .

[U]nelected judges are better off leaving the protection of federalism to the political process in all but the most extraordinary circumstances.

Perversely, the majority's rule seems more likely to damage than to preserve the safeguards against tyranny provided by the existence of vital state governments. By limiting the ability of the Federal Government to enlist state officials in the implementation of its programs, the Court creates incentives for the National Government to aggrandize itself. In the name of State's rights, the majority would have the Federal Government create vast national bureaucracies to implement its policies. This is exactly the sort of thing that the early Federalists promised would not occur, in part as a result of the National Government's ability to rely on the magistracy of the states. See, e.g., The Federalist No. 36 (Hamilton); id., No. 45 (Madison). . . .

These cases do not involve any mandate to state legislatures to enact new rules. When legislative action, or even administrative rule-making, is at issue, it may be appropriate for Congress either to pre-empt the State's lawmaking power and fashion the federal rule itself, or to respect the State's power to fashion its own rules. But this case, unlike any precedent in which the Court has held that Congress exceeded its powers, merely involves the imposition of modest duties on individual officers. The Court seems to accept the fact that Congress could require private persons, such as hospital executives or school administrators, to provide arms merchants with relevant information about a prospective purchaser's fitness to own a weapon; indeed, the Court does not disturb the conclusion that flows directly from our prior holdings that the burden on police officers would be permissible if a similar burden were also imposed on private parties with access to relevant data. See *New York*; *Garcia*. A structural problem that vanishes when the statute affects private individuals as well as public officials is not much of a structural problem. . . .

IV

Finally, the Court advises us that the "prior jurisprudence of this Court" is the most conclusive support for its position. . . .

The majority relies upon dictum in *New York* to the effect that "the Federal Government may not compel the States to enact *or administer* a federal regulatory

---

c. The majority also makes the more general claim that requiring state officials to carry out federal policy causes states to "take the blame" for failed programs. . . . The problem is of little real consequence . . . because to the extent that a particular action proves politically unpopular, we may be confident that elected officials charged with implementing it will be quite clear to their constituents where the source of the misfortune lies. . . . Moreover, we can be sure that CLEOs will inform disgruntled constituents who have been denied permission to purchase a handgun about the origins of the Brady Act requirements. The Court's suggestion that voters will be confused over who is to "blame" for the statute reflects a gross lack of confidence in the electorate that is at war with the basic assumptions underlying any democratic government.

program" (emphasis added). But that language was wholly unnecessary to the decision of the case. It is, of course, beyond dispute that we are not bound by the dicta of our prior opinions. . . .

Importantly, the majority either misconstrues or ignores three cases that are more directly on point. In *FERC*, we upheld a federal statute requiring state utilities commissions, inter alia, to take the affirmative step of considering federal energy standards in a manner complying with federally specified notice and comment procedures, and to report back to Congress. . . .

Similarly, in Puerto Rico v. Branstad, 483 U.S. 219 (1987), we overruled our earlier decision in Kentucky v. Dennison, 65 U.S. 66 (1861), and held that the Extradition Act of 1793 permitted the Commonwealth of Puerto Rico to seek extradition of a fugitive from its laws without constitutional barrier. The Extradition Act, as the majority properly concedes, plainly imposes duties on state executive officers. . . .[d]

Finally, the majority provides an incomplete explanation of our decision in Testa v. Katt, 330 U.S. 386 (1947), and demeans its importance. In that case the Court unanimously held that state courts of appropriate jurisdiction must occupy themselves adjudicating claims brought by private litigants under the federal Emergency Price Control Act of 1942, regardless of how otherwise crowded their dockets might be with state law matters. . . . The notion that the Framers would have had no reluctance to "press state judges into federal service" against their will but would have regarded the imposition of a similar—indeed, far lesser—burden on town constables as an intolerable affront to principles of state sovereignty, can only be considered perverse. If such a distinction had been contemplated by the learned and articulate men who fashioned the basic structure of our government, surely some of them would have said so.

The provision of the Brady Act that crosses the Court's newly defined constitutional threshold is more comparable to a statute requiring local police officers to report the identity of missing children to the Crime Control Center of the Department of Justice than to an offensive federal command to a sovereign state. If Congress believes that such a statute will benefit the people of the Nation, and serve the interests of cooperative federalism better than an enlarged federal bureaucracy, we should respect both its policy judgment and its appraisal of its constitutional power.

---

d. Moreover, Branstad unequivocally rejected an important premise that resonates throughout the majority opinion: namely, that because the States retain their sovereignty in areas that are unregulated by federal law, notions of comity rather than constitutional power govern any direction by the National Government to state executive or judicial officers. That construct was the product of the ill-starred opinion of Chief Justice Taney in Kentucky v. Dennison, announced at a time when "the practical power of the Federal Government [was] at its lowest ebb." As we explained:

> "If it seemed clear to the Court in 1861, facing the looming shadow of a Civil War, that 'the Federal Government, under the Constitution, has no power to impose on a State officer, as such, any duty whatever, and compel him to perform it,' basic constitutional principles now point as clearly the other way."
>
> "Kentucky v. Dennison is the product of another time. The conception of the relation between the States and the Federal Government there announced is fundamentally incompatible with more than a century of constitutional development. Yet this decision has stood while the world of which it was a part has passed away. We conclude that it may stand no longer."

Justice SOUTER, dissenting. . . .

In deciding these cases, which I have found closer than I had anticipated, it is The Federalist that finally determines my position. I believe that the most straightforward reading of No. 27 is authority for the Government's position here, and that this reading is both supported by No. 44 and consistent with Nos. 36 and 45. . . .

. . . To be sure, it does not follow that any conceivable requirement may be imposed on any state official. I continue to agree, for example, that Congress may not require a state legislature to enact a regulatory scheme and that *New York* was rightly decided (even though I now believe its dicta went too far toward immunizing state administration as well as state enactment of such a scheme from congressional mandate); after all, the essence of legislative power, within the limits of legislative jurisdiction, is a discretion not subject to command. . . .

. . . I recognize that my reading of The Federalist runs counter to the view of Justice Field, who stated explicitly in United States v. Jones, 109 U.S. 513 (1883), that the early examples of state execution of federal law could not have been required against a State's will. But that statement, too, was dictum, and as against dictum even from Justice Field, Madison and Hamilton prevail. [Also,] I do not read any of The Federalist material as requiring the conclusion that Congress could require administrative support without an obligation to pay fair value for it. The quotation from No. 36, for example, describes the United States as paying. If, therefore, my views were prevailing in these cases, I would remand for development and consideration of petitioners' points, that they have no budget provision for work required under the Act and are liable for unauthorized expenditures.

Justice BREYER, with whom Justice STEVENS joins, dissenting.

[T]he United States is not the only nation that seeks to reconcile the practical need for a central authority with the democratic virtues of more local control. At least some other countries, facing the same basic problem, have found that local control is better maintained through application of a principle that is the direct opposite of the principle the majority derives from the silence of our Constitution. The federal systems of Switzerland, Germany, and the European Union, for example, all provide that constituent states, not federal bureaucracies, will themselves implement many of the laws, rules, regulations, or decrees enacted by the central "federal" body. They do so in part because they believe that such a system interferes less, not more, with the independent authority of the "state," member nation, or other subsidiary government, and helps to safeguard individual liberty as well.

Of course, we are interpreting our own Constitution, not those of other nations, and there may be relevant political and structural differences between their systems and our own. Cf. The Federalist No. 20 (rejecting certain aspects of European federalism). But their experience may nonetheless cast an empirical light on the consequences of different solutions to a common legal problem—in this case the problem of reconciling central authority with the need to preserve the liberty-enhancing autonomy of a smaller constituent governmental entity. And that experience here offers empirical confirmation of the implied answer to a question Justice Stevens asks: Why, or how, would what the majority sees as a constitutional alternative—the creation of a new federal gun-law bureaucracy, or the expansion of an existing federal bureaucracy—better promote either state sovereignty or individual liberty?

As comparative experience suggests, there is no need to interpret the Constitution as containing an absolute principle—forbidding the assignment of virtually any federal duty to any state official. Nor is there a need to read the Brady Act as permitting the Federal Government to overwhelm a state civil service. The statute uses the words "reasonable effort,"—words that easily can encompass the considerations of, say, time or cost, necessary to avoid any such result.

Regardless, as Justice Stevens points out, the Constitution itself is silent on the matter. Precedent supports the Government's position here. . . . Thus, there is neither need nor reason to find in the Constitution an absolute principle, the inflexibility of which poses a surprising and technical obstacle to the enactment of a law that Congress believed necessary to solve an important national problem.

DISCUSSION

1. *Methodological musical chairs?* Justice Scalia is often described as a textualist, but his *Printz* opinion candidly stresses other modes of interpretation—doctrine, structure, and history. Conversely, Justice Stevens—who, for example, has strongly supported the less-than-textual opinion in Roe v. Wade, places particular emphasis on text, and sounds eerily like critics of *Roe* when he suggests that "unelected" judges should defer to the political process. And Justice Souter, celebrated for his especially strong belief in precedent, in this case finds original intent more compelling than various judicial "dicta." What, if anything, do you make of all this?

2. Printz *and* Prigg. Note that Justice Story's opinion in Prigg v. Pennsylvania, 41 U.S. (16 Pet.) 536 (1842), supra Chapter 3, presaged the rule laid down in *Printz* when it declared that the Constitution's Fugitive Slave Clause

> does not point to any state functionaries, or any state action, to carry its provisions into effect. The states cannot, therefore be compelled to enforce them; and it might well be deemed an unconstitutional exercise of the power of interpretation [of the Fugitive Slave Act of 1793], to insist, that states are bound to provide means to carry into effect the duties of the national government.

Prigg went unmentioned in *Printz*. Why? For a fascinating historical analysis of the "nationalistic" roots of the *Printz* rule in the eighteenth and nineteenth centuries—with nationalists like Story using various antecedents of the rule to force the federal government to rely on its own officers—see Roderick M. Hills, Jr., The Political Economy of Cooperative Federalism: Why State Autonomy Makes Sense and "Dual Sovereignty" Doesn't, 96 Mich. L. Rev. 813 (1998).

3. *Commandeering and the Coase theorem.* Professor Hills suggests that *Printz* might be defensible on a "Coasean" rationale. States have something unique and valuable to the federal government: functioning administrative systems that can be used to enforce federal policies. The *Printz* rule, Hills argues, does not prevent Congress from deploying such systems—especially when it is cheaper to use an existing state apparatus than to create a new federal one. Rather, *Printz* simply requires the federal government to "bid" for state services, just as it typically acquires other useful things (employees, pencils, buildings, and so on) by paying for them. The *Printz* rule, according to Hills, merely establishes a firm baseline entitlement as a

starting point for Coasean bargaining. Without this secure baseline, the feds could simply grab rather than bribe, leaving states overly vulnerable, Hills argues. But is the baseline of states very secure, even with *Printz* on the books, given all the other ways that the federal government may affect states (via preemption threats, the federal taxing power, and broad power to withhold money from uncooperative states)? Without a vast and perhaps unworkable increase in judicial monitoring of all these other federal levers, isn't it easy enough for Congress to undermine the *Printz* baseline by using all its other powers—for example, by eliminating the current block grants given to states, and then promising to restore them only to those states willing to be cooperative?

4. *Commandeering versus "using."* Note, in this connection, Justice Souter's suggestion that Congress has a kind of eminent domain right to demand state executive enforcement, so long as the feds pay "fair value" for services rendered. Is the basic idea of *Printz* and *New York* that Congress may prohibit state action, but may not affirmatively "use" state governments without compensation? If this is indeed the basic idea, does it have a strong functional logic, or is it simply a kind of constitutional etiquette, a rule of politesse reflecting respect for the special "dignity" of states?

5. *The unitary executive.* Doesn't Justice Scalia's emphasis on the unitary federal executive prove too much? If compelling state sheriffs to enforce the Brady Act violates some right of the President to control all law enforcement, then why isn't this right equally violated when sheriffs *voluntarily choose* to enforce the Brady Act? On Scalia's theory, is the unitary executive also violated when private persons help enforce federal laws—for example, by bringing suits for damages to enforce the Sherman Act, or federal civil rights laws?

6. *Comparative constitutional law.* Consider the exchange between Justices Scalia and Breyer about European federalism. American lawyers, judges, politicians, and law professors have tended to focus much more attention on, for example, the lessons of American history than on the lessons to be drawn from the experiences of other countries around the world. Is this focus justified? Are recent developments around the world—the rise of many new democratic and federal states, the increasing availability of English-language versions of foreign legal materials, the globalization effect of the Internet, and so on—likely to make comparative analysis more important in the future?

NOTE: STATE SOVEREIGN IMMUNITY

After *Printz*, the federal government cannot oblige state legislatures or state executives to enforce federal laws, but can generally oblige state judiciaries to enforce federal laws; see Testa v. Katt, 330 U.S. 386 (1947). This differential treatment of the three branches of state government narrowed somewhat in Alden v. Maine, 527 U.S. 706 (1999). Featuring the same 5-4 lineup as *Printz* (with Justice Kennedy writing for the five and Justice Souter for the four), the Court held that a Maine state court could not be obliged to hear damage suits brought against the state of Maine itself, even if the state had indeed violated a valid federal law. The case involved the same statute as at issue in the 1976 *National League of Cities* case, the Fair Labor Standards Act, prescribing minimum wages for state as well as private employees. Recall that *National League of Cities* invalidated the Act as applied to state employees performing traditional state functions, and that *National League of Cities* was in turn overruled in the 1985 *Garcia* case, with dissenting Justices Rehnquist and O'Connor vowing to continue the fight. In *Alden*, unlike *National League of Cities*, the majority was emphatic that the FLSA was a proper federal law that did constitutionally bind state employers. But, said the Court, if the state violated the law, it could not be obliged to entertain a private suit for damages at the behest of the wronged employee. (Suits brought by the U.S. government might be different, said the Court; and so were suits brought under laws enacted pursuant to the Reconstruction power, cf. Fitzpatrick v. Bitzer, 427 U.S. 445 (1976), and injunctive suits brought to force future compliance as opposed to damage suits brought to remedy past violations; cf. Ex parte Young, 209 U.S. 123 (1908), discussed below.)

In the earlier *Seminole Tribe* case (discussed below), the Court had in effect barred private employees from bringing FLSA damage suits in federal district court. Thus, the combination of *Seminole Tribe* and *Alden* drove a wedge between right and remedy: The federal law applied to Alden and vested him with rights as a private citizen, but no court was open to provide him a full private remedy for its violation.

According to the Court, "[t]he generation that designed and adopted our federal system considered immunity from private suits central to sovereign dignity." This immunity derived not from the text of the Eleventh Amendment (discussed below) "but from the structure of the original Constitution." Immunity in one's own court—even immunity to violate a necessary and proper law and get away with it, without making the rights-holder whole—was, said the Court, part of the "dignity" and "respect" owed states as "members of the federation." In language reminiscent of *New York* and *Printz*, the Court declared:

> A power to press a State's own courts into federal service to coerce the other branches of the State . . . is the power first to turn the State against itself and ultimately to commandeer the entire political machinery of the State against its will and at the behest of individuals. Such plenary federal control of state governmental processes denigrates the separate sovereignty of the States. . . .
>
> Underlying constitutional form are considerations of great substance. Private suits against nonconsenting States—especially suits for money damages—may threaten the financial integrity of the States. It is indisputable that, at the time of the founding, many of the States could have been forced into insolvency but for their immunity from private suits for money damages. Even today, an unlimited congressional power to authorize suits in state court to levy upon the treasuries of the States for compensatory damages, attorney's fees, and even punitive damages could create staggering burdens, giving Congress a power and a leverage over the States that is not contemplated by our constitutional design. The potential national power would pose a severe and notorious danger to the States and their resources. . . .
>
> When Congress legislates in matters affecting the States, it may not treat these sovereign entities as mere prefectures or corporations. Congress must accord States the esteem due to them as joint participants in a federal system, one beginning with the premise of sovereignty in both the

central Government and the separate States. Congress has ample means to ensure compliance with valid federal laws, but it must respect the sovereignty of the States.

In sharp dissent, Justice Souter argued that the majority's appeals to "sovereign dignity" were "thoroughly anomalous":

> It would be hard to imagine anything more inimical to the republican conception, which rests on the understanding of its citizens precisely that the government is not above them, but of them, its actions being governed by law just like their own. . . . Furthermore, the very idea of dignity ought also to imply that the State should be subject to, and not outside of, the law. . . .
>
> It is equally puzzling to hear the Court say that "federal power to authorize private suits for money damages would place unwarranted strain on the States' ability to govern in accordance with the will of their citizens." So long as the citizens' will, expressed through state legislation, does not violate valid federal law, the strain will not be felt; and to the extent that state action does violate federal law, the will of the citizens of the United States already trumps that of the citizens of the State: the strain then is not only expected, but necessarily intended. . . .
>
> [T]he Court abandons a principle . . . close[] to the hearts of the Framers: that where there is a right, there must be a remedy. Lord Chief Justice Holt could state this as an unquestioned proposition already in 1702. . . . Blackstone considered it "a general and indisputable rule, that where there is a legal right, there is also a legal remedy, by suit or action at law, whenever that right is invaded." The generation of the Framers thought the principle so crucial that several States put it into their constitutions. And when Chief Justice Marshall asked about *Marbury*, "If he has a right, and that right has been violated, do the laws of his country afford him a remedy?," the question was rhetorical, and the answer clear:
>
> > "The very essence of civil liberty certainly consists in the right of every individual to claim the protection of the laws, whenever he receives an injury. One of the first duties of government is to afford that protection. In Great Britain the king himself is sued in the respectful form of a petition, and he never fails to comply with the judgment of his court."
>
> Yet today the Court has no qualms about saying frankly that the federal right to damages afforded by Congress under the FLSA cannot create a concomitant private remedy. The right was "made for the benefit of" petitioners; they have been "hindered by another of that benefit"; but despite what has long been understood as the "necessary consequence of law," they have no action. It will not do for the Court to respond that a remedy was never available where the right in question was against the sovereign. A State is not the sovereign when a federal claim is pressed against it, and even the English sovereign opened itself to recovery and, unlike Maine, provided the remedy to complement the right. To the Americans of the founding generation it would have been clear (as it was to Chief Justice Marshall) that if the King would do right, the democratically chosen

Government of the United States could do no less. The Chief Justice's contemporaries might well have reacted to the Court's decision today in the words spoken by Edmund Randolph when responding to the objection to jurisdiction in *Chisholm*: "[The Framers] must have viewed human rights in their essence, not in their mere form."

DISCUSSION

1. *Federalism, liberty, and remedies*. Both the majority and dissenting opinions raise deep questions. Recall that the main purpose of federalism, according to the Rehnquist Court, is to protect liberty. We might ask the majority: How is liberty protected when valid rights go unremedied? Are governments truly "sovereign" in America when they violate the law? When a state violates a federal law, doesn't it also violate due process *of law*? If so, why does Congress lack Reconstruction power to insist that states must remedy their own violations of law and make victims whole? And we might ask the dissenters: If, in America, the people, and not governments, are truly sovereign; if the Constitution and laws limit the government, and mark the boundaries of proper governmental power and "sovereignty"; and if every right deserves a full judicial remedy, then why should the *federal* government ever be allowed to invoke sovereign immunity to defeat a valid claim for recovery when that government has violated the limits imposed on it in the Constitution by the Sovereign People? Note that the dissenters did not challenge the idea of federal sovereign immunity for constitutional torts; and the majority explicitly founded its decision on the idea that state governments were entitled to "reciprocal" dignity.

Consider the argument that sovereign immunity—state or federal—has no proper place in a Constitution based on popular sovereignty, and that each government should have reciprocity not in shielding itself when it violates the Constitution, but in empowering citizens to gain full remedies when the *other* government has violated the Constitution. On this view, the federal government should be recognized as having broad power to provide Americans with remedies—including remedies against the states themselves—when states have violated the Constitution and valid federal laws. The "reciprocal" counterpart of this federal power is not the "sovereign" immunity of states when states are lawless; but the rightful authority of states to empower citizens to pursue remedies against the federal government when the feds have violated the Constitution. (For example, state property law helps give a citizen "standing" to sue when the federal government has taken his property without due process, in violation of the Fifth Amendment; and state tort law helps provide a remedy when federal officials violate a citizen's Fourth Amendment rights through an improper search or seizure of his person or property.) Akhil Reed Amar has argued this sort of remedial competition between state and federal government enlists federalism in support of liberty, vindicating the language of The Federalist Nos. 28 and 51 that the Rehnquist Court has identified as the foundation of its federalism jurisprudence. He associates this view of federalism with §1983 of Title 42 of the U.S. Code—a general remedial statute adopted by Congress during Reconstruction providing for remedies against lawless state actors—and with "converse-1983" laws that he says states should adopt to help remedy constitutional torts committed by federal officials. For elaboration, see Amar,

Of Sovereignty and Federalism, 96 Yale L.J. 1425 (1987); Akhil Reed Amar, Using State Law to Protect Federal Constitutional Rights: Some Questions and Answers About Converse-1983, 64 U. Colo. L. Rev. 159 (1993); Akhil Reed Amar, Five Views of Federalism: "Converse-1983" in Context, 47 Vand. L. Rev. 1229 (1994).

2. *The modern Eleventh Amendment debate.* The Rehnquist Court's treatment of the Tenth Amendment is usefully examined alongside its Eleventh Amendment case law. Recall that the amendment was adopted in the 1790s to reverse the Court's decision in Chisholm v. Georgia, 2 U.S. (2 Dall.) 419 (1793). In *Chisholm*—perhaps the biggest case to reach the pre-Marshall Court—the Justices construed language of Article III conferring federal jurisdiction over certain categories of lawsuits based not on the legal subject matter of the suits (e.g., the presence of a federal question or an admiralty law issue), but merely on the diverse-party alignments they presented: "Controversies . . . between a State and Citizens of another State" and "Controversies . . . between a State . . . and foreign . . . Citizens or Subjects." The *Chisholm* suit was brought in assumpsit by a South Carolina citizen against the state of Georgia, to recover for the state's breach of a war-supplies contract. Georgia claimed that federal courts could not hear the case—the relevant diversity language of Article III, it argued, applied only to lawsuits where states were plaintiffs against out-of-staters, not involuntary defendants. The Supreme Court disagreed, and went on to suggest that Georgia should be held liable for its breach—even though both Georgia and South Carolina law would have allowed the state to escape liability for mere breach of contract. (At common law, contracts with states were not legally enforceable.) No federal law violation was alleged in *Chisholm*—it is important to note that the plaintiff did not claim that Georgia's conduct had violated the Contract Clause or any other federal norm.

To modern observers, the Court's ruling in *Chisholm* thus seems to violate important federalism principles later clarified in the famous case of Erie R.R. v. Tomkins, 304 U.S. 64 (1938): In a mere diversity lawsuit raising no question of federal law, federal courts should generally apply state law rather than fashioning their own "general federal common law." The Eleventh Amendment's response to *Chisholm* was drafted in extremely narrow terms: "The judicial power of the United States shall not be construed to extend to any suit in law or equity, commenced or prosecuted against one of the United States by Citizens of another State, or by Citizens or subjects of any Foreign State."

Many leading scholars today believe that this language simply repealed part of the above-quoted language of Article III, which had conferred a species of diversity jurisdiction even in cases involving no claim of federal right. But, the modern "diversity school" insists, the amendment left untouched plenary federal jurisdiction in federal question and admiralty cases, and of course said nothing about suits brought by a citizen against his own state. On this view, even after the amendment, federal judicial power to enforce federal law remained co-extensive with the reach of federal law itself. For representative statements of this "diversity school," see William A. Fletcher, A Historical Interpretation of the Eleventh Amendment: A Narrow Construction of an Affirmative Grant of Jurisdiction Rather Than a Prohibition Against Jurisdiction, 35 Stan. L. Rev. 1033 (1983); John J. Gibbons, The Eleventh Amendment and State Sovereign Immunity: A Reinterpretation, 83 Colum. L. Rev. 1889 (1983); Akhil Reed Amar, Of Sovereignty and Federalism, 96 Yale L.J. 1425 (1987); Vicki C. Jackson, The Supreme Court, the Eleventh Amendment, and State Sovereign Immunity, 98 Yale L.J. 1 (1988).

This, however, has not been the Court's view. In Louisiana v. Jumel, 107 U.S. 711 (1883), the Court held that the amendment barred a lower federal court from hearing a constitutional ("federal question") claim brought against Louisiana by a citizen of a sister state. Several years later, in Hans v. Louisiana, 134 U.S. 1 (1890), the Court held that federal question suits brought by Louisiana citizens against the state should likewise be barred. (Otherwise, the Court reasoned, federal courts would be discriminating against out-of-staters like Jumel.) *Hans* also contained broad language about state sovereign immunity; and this language threatened to undermine legitimate interests in enforcing federal law against lawless states. This threat was blunted to an important extent by the Court's landmark decision in Ex parte Young, 209 U.S. 123 (1908), which in effect allowed citizens to sue states for prospective injunctive relief by suing a state official, rather than the state itself. Nevertheless, damage suits brought against states (or against state officials in their official capacity, where the recovery sought would come directly from the state treasury) continued to be ousted from federal court under the (il)logic of *Hans*. See, e.g., Edelman v. Jordan, 415 U.S. 651 (1974).

Modern Supreme Court case law concerning the Eleventh Amendment and the intertwined issue of state sovereign immunity is a tangled web of intricate and highly controversial case law. These issues are covered in painstaking detail in casebooks on federal jurisdiction, and so here we shall simply offer a quick overview of recent developments. On at least two occasions, the "diversity school" reading of the amendment has commanded four votes, see, e.g., Atascadero State Hosp. v. Scanlon, 473 U.S. 234 (1985) (Brennan, J., dissenting, joined by Marshall, Blackmun, and Stevens, JJ.); Seminole Tribe of Florida v. Florida, 517 U.S. 44 (1996) (Souter, J., dissenting, joined by Stevens, Ginsburg, and Breyer, JJ.). The Court has permitted Congress to "abrogate" the amendment, and subject states to damage lawsuits in federal court, if Congress is acting pursuant to its powers under the Reconstruction Amendments, see Fitzpatrick v. Bitzer, 427 U.S. 445 (1976).

In Pennsylvania v. Union Gas Co., 491 U.S. 1 (1989), the Court upheld Congress's power to similarly abrogate the Eleventh Amendment via a statute enacted under the commerce power, but *Union Gas* did not generate a single opinion for the five Justices who adhered to this result. In the 1996 *Seminole Tribe* case, a sharply divided Court overruled *Union Gas*, in an opinion authored by Chief Justice Rehnquist. *Seminole* raised many important questions, and several were answered the day that *Alden* came down. Could a citizen barred by *Seminole* from bringing his federal damages suit in federal court instead demand that state courts open their doors? No, said *Alden*. Would *Fitzpatrick* be read broadly, enabling Congress to use its Reconstruction power to pry open court doors on behalf of federal rights-holders? No, said the Court in Florida Prepaid Postsecondary Education Expense Board v. College Savings Bank, 527 U.S. 627 (1999), in an opinion per Chief Justice Rehnquist decided the same day as *Alden*, and featuring the same 5-4 vote, with Justice Stevens writing for the four in dissent.[28] (Note the link between *Florida*, constricting Congress's Reconstruction power, and City of Boerne v. Flores, discussed in

28. See also Allen v. Cooper, 140 S. Ct. 994 (2020) (applying *Florida Prepaid* to hold that Congress lacked authority to abrogate the states' sovereign immunity from copyright infringement suits in the Copyright Remedy Clarification Act of 1990).

Section I.A, supra.) Could states that continued to engage in interstate commercial activities after these activities had been regulated by Congress be deemed to have waived their sovereign immunity? No, said the Court in a third case decided the same day, and featuring the same line-up, with Justice Scalia writing for the five and Justice Breyer writing for the four. Note that this case—like *Seminole*—required the Court to explicitly overrule a prior precedent. See College Savings Bank v. Florida Prepaid Postsecondary Expense Board, 527 U.S. 666 (1999), overruling Parden v. Terminal Ry. of Alabama Docks Dept., 377 U.S. 184 (1964). The dissenters in these cases gave clear notice that they did not consider the matter settled. Thus Justice Souter closed his *Alden* dissent with the following words:

> The Court has swung back and forth with regrettable disruption on the enforceability of the FLSA against the States, but if the present majority had a defensible position one could at least accept its decision with an expectation of stability ahead. As it is, any such expectation would be naive. The resemblance of today's state sovereign immunity to the *Lochner* era's industrial due process is striking. The Court began this century by imputing immutable constitutional status to a conception of economic self-reliance that was never true to industrial life and grew insistently fictional with the years, and the Court has chosen to close the century by conferring like status on a conception of state sovereign immunity that is true neither to history nor to the structure of the Constitution. I expect the Court's late essay into immunity doctrine will prove the equal of its earlier experiment in laissez-faire, the one being as unrealistic as the other, as indefensible, and probably as fleeting.[29]

NOTE: COOPERATIVE (AND UNCOOPERATIVE) FEDERALISM

Standard debates about federalism, as exemplified by cases like *Garcia, Printz*, and *Lopez*, revolve around the scope of state regulatory immunity and the limits of federal regulatory power. But the actual development of governance since the New Deal has changed federal-state relations in ways that do not map onto these debates particularly well.

The standard model assumes that centralization of power best serves national interests, while decentralization and devolution benefit the states and local interests. As national governance has become more complicated, however, it has also become clear that decentralization and devolution of power may also serve national interests. Conversely, states and local governments may actually increase their influence and power by structuring national policy debates and participating in national regulatory programs.

---

29. Important questions still remain to be decided. For example, may the United States government formally join a lawsuit brought by a private citizen like Alden, and thereby pry open court doors, on the theory that state sovereign immunity cannot be invoked in a lawsuit against the federal government itself? See Jonathan R. Siegel, The Hidden Source of Congress's Power to Abrogate State Sovereign Immunity, 73 Tex. L. Rev. 539 (1995) (discussing *qui tam* actions).

The "new nationalism" refers to the body of scholarship that describes these phenomena.[30] This work focuses on the ways that decentralization shapes the national political process and the ways that state power shapes the implementation of federal programs.

1. *How decentralization drives the national political process.* Many if not most policy and constitutional questions—including health care, immigration, voting rights, same-sex marriage, drug policy, education, and privacy—start in debates in state and local governments.[31] Different decisionmakers will reach different answers and compromises. Multiple jurisdictions for politics allow more sites in which politics can occur, which, in turn, shapes national debates.[32] In this way, the development of rights depends on federal structure; federal structure, in turn, generates friction and controversy that engenders the political development of rights.[33]

Moreover, federalism continually produces oppositional politics that counteracts federal initiatives. American party politics operates countercyclically: When one party dominates national politics, the other party often gains in state and local governments that want to serve as a counterweight to Washington, D.C. Finally, Heather Gerken argues that multiple jurisdictions allow groups to "dissent by deciding."[34] Political minorities at the national level are never shut out of politics as long as they can exert influence or possess majority control in state or local governments.

2. *The role of state power in the implementation of national programs.* As the federal government has grown, it has relied increasingly on state and local governments to implement its programs, ranging from social insurance programs (Medicaid, Obamacare) to educational policy (No Child Left Behind, Common Core) to criminal law enforcement (enforcement of marijuana and other drug laws).[35] Conversely, states have signed up to implement these programs because the alternative is not to have a say in regulation at all.[36]

One irony of modern constitutional law is that as the formal power of the federal government increased following the New Deal and the civil rights revolution,

---

30. See, e.g., Heather K. Gerken, Federalism as the New Nationalism: An Overview, 123 Yale L.J. 1889 (2013).

31. Heather K. Gerken, Windsor's Mad Genius: The Interlocking Gears of Rights and Structure, 95 B.U. L. Rev. 587 (2015); Heather K. Gerken, The Loyal Opposition, 123 Yale L.J. 1958 (2014).

32. See, e.g., Cristina M. Rodriguez, Federalism and National Consensus 4 (Oct. 2014) (unpublished manuscript); Jessica Bulman-Pozen, Partisan Federalism, 127 Harv. L. Rev. 1077 (2014); Jessica Bulman-Pozen, From Sovereignty and Process to Administration and Politics: The Afterlife of American Federalism, 123 Yale L.J. 1920 (2014).

33. Heather K. Gerken, Windsor's Mad Genius: The Interlocking Gears of Rights and Structure, supra n.31.

34. Heather K. Gerken, Dissenting by Deciding, 57 Stan. L. Rev. 1745 (2005).

35. See, e.g., Abbe R. Gluck, Intrastatutory Federalism and Statutory Interpretation: State Implementation of Federal Law in Health Reform and Beyond, 121 Yale L.J. 534 (2011).

36. Abbe R. Gluck, Nationalism as the New Federalism (and Federalism as the New Nationalism): A Complementary Account (and Some Challenges) to the Nationalist School, 59 St. Louis U. L.J. 1045 (2015).

the practical power of the states in enforcing federal programs also increased in tandem. After setting up new programs, the federal government often relies on state and local governments to implement them, or it engages in continuous interaction with analogous state programs in order to coordinate efforts. Taken together, these practices create what is sometimes called "cooperative federalism."

In cooperative federalism, states and local governments willingly participate in federal initiatives. Yet because of the federal structure of politics, state and local governments are not simply loyal operatives of the federal government. Quite the contrary: They have independent bases of political power, and their own set of constituents to which they must answer. Their constituencies may differ in important ways from national constituencies. Hence when they work with the federal government, they always serve two masters, not one.

3. *Uncooperative federalism.* Heather Gerken and Jessica Bulman-Pozen point out that this dual loyalty may lead to the phenomenon of "uncooperative federalism."[37] States and local governments can resist, modify, or even partially nullify federal programs they do not like, because these federal programs cannot function without state and local implementation and cooperation. In this way, states and local governments can defend the values of local majorities in the construction and implementation of federal policies.

Even when state and local officials cooperate rather than obstruct federal programs, they exercise what Gerken calls "the power of the servant."[38] The federal government needs states and local governments as agents to implement its programs, but it cannot completely monitor or control what these agents do. Moreover, because these agents enjoy independent sources of political power, the federal government often negotiates and compromises with state and local officials as much as it gives orders to them.

4. *How state power affects the separation of powers.* Depending on the nature of the program, both Congress and the executive may benefit from state and local governments' ability to shape implementation. For example, members of Congress may object to the way that the executive is implementing congressional statutes through administrative regulation. State and local actors can check executive aggrandizement and support Congress by pushing back at regulations, shaping how programs are implemented, and promoting compromises with federal officials.[39]

Conversely, states and local governments can empower the President. Congressional statutes often give the President the power to waive or modify certain features of programs—such as federal welfare laws, the Affordable Care Act, Medicaid, or No Child Left Behind—by making deals with the states about how they will implement them.[40] The result is that the President can reform or modify programs

37. Jessica Bulman-Pozen and Heather K. Gerken, Uncooperative Federalism, 118 Yale L.J. 1256 (2009).

38. Heather K. Gerken, Of Sovereigns and Servants, 115 Yale L.J. 2633 (2006).

39. Jessica Bulman-Pozen, Federalism as a Safeguard of the Separation of Powers, 112 Colum. L. Rev. 459 (2012).

40. See generally David J. Barron and Todd D. Rakoff, In Defense of Big Waiver, 113 Colum. L. Rev. 265 (2013); Sam Bagenstos, Federalism by Waiver After the Health Care Case, in The Health Care Case: The Supreme Court's Decision and Its Implications 227 (Nathan Persily et al. eds., 2013).

by striking deals with state and local regulators with results that could never have been achieved if the President attempted to pass the reforms through a polarized and dysfunctional Congress.[41] In fact, the use of waivers in federal programs is one of the most important methods of presidential lawmaking in a politically polarized system. At the same time, the President can justify the waivers on the grounds that their use respects federalism and the value of using the states as laboratories for policy experimentation.

As a result, state and local officials are players in the national separation of powers. They can tilt toward one branch or the other depending on their constituents' needs, and they can shift their alliances as new issues arise.

5. *Criminal law enforcement.* The federal government can work with states in other ways. For example, although the federal government has extensive criminal laws on the books, it simply lacks the resources to enforce all of them. Therefore it has developed policies of cooperation with state law enforcement agencies. This approach has facilitated the decriminalization of marijuana use in some states.

The federal government has stated that its interest in prosecution is limited to what it regards as serious matters—like preventing the distribution of marijuana to minors, the diversion of revenues to cartels or criminal enterprises, and the use of violence in the cultivation and distribution of marijuana.[42] Conversely, it has stated that it is not interested in prosecuting minor possession offenses, leaving them to state and local officials to address under state law. It has also declined to assert that state laws are preempted by federal law. This relationship between state and federal law enforcement, in turn, has allowed states to effectively decriminalize marijuana possession and use within their borders.[43] And the federal government gets something out of the deal. It allows federal officials to experiment with different policies of decriminalization in different jurisdictions, which, given the likely political and legal response, it would never have been able to implement on its own.[44]

6. *The political safeguards of federalism, revisited.* Stepping back and looking at our current system of governance, we get the following picture: The federal government, through its New Deal powers of taxing, spending, and commerce, can regulate virtually any area of social life. Yet states, far from being crowded out by the expansion of federal power, have been ushered in as essential participants. Even so, the role of the states has changed considerably from the assumptions of the founding. States no longer have clear spaces of unencumbered regulatory power. Instead, their power comes from the fact that the federal government, no matter how great its powers may be in theory, cannot actually enforce its power everywhere. As a result, the federal government leaves a great deal of regulation to the states. And even where the federal government does regulate, states exercise considerable

---

41. Jessica Bulman-Pozen, Executive Federalism, 102 Va. L. Rev. 953 (2016).

42. See, e.g., Memorandum from James M. Cole, Deputy Attorney Gen., to U.S. Attorneys, Guidance Regarding Marijuana Enforcement 2 (Aug. 29, 2013), available at http://www.justice.gov/iso/opa/resources/3052013829132756857467.pdf.

43. Robert A. Mikos, On the Limits of Supremacy: Medical Marijuana and the States' Overlooked Power to Legalize Federal Crime, 62 Vand. L. Rev. 1421 (2009).

44. See Cristina M. Rodriguez, Negotiating Conflict Through Federalism: Institutional and Popular Perspectives, 123 Yale L.J. 2094 (2014).

influence over how federal law actually operates (or does not operate) through implementation, negotiation, and resistance.

This picture requires us to rethink the debate over the political safeguards of federalism discussed in cases like *Garcia*.[45] The debate has usually been organized around whether states are adequately protected because they are represented in the political process, for example, in the Senate. If states are adequately protected, judicial enforcement of federalism guarantees is unnecessary, but if states are not adequately protected, courts should step in. Defenders of national power have contended that states are generally adequately protected by the national political process, while defenders of state power have usually objected that these protections are illusory because of the way that national politics and national political parties have developed.

Cooperative federalism and related phenomena suggest a different account of how the national political process protects the interests of states, and, indirectly, the particular constituencies that states represent. States are protected politically because federal officials need to work with them and negotiate with them.[46] As a result, states can strike deals that secure their constituents different implementations of federal policies. Through their bargaining power and influence, different states can achieve a diversity of policy outcomes. This, in turn, serves many of the traditional goals of federalism, including experimentation, mutual learning, competition, and choice. Indeed, not only are states protected in this way, but so too are substate units like cities and counties, who are crucial partners in many different kinds of federal programs in areas ranging from health and educational policy to criminal enforcement, social services, and immigration.

7. *Sovereigns and stakeholders.* This revised account of the political safeguards of federalism asserts that states and local governments are protected not as *sovereigns* (for, after all, cities and counties are not sovereigns) but as *stakeholders*, whose participation is crucial for the practical success of federal programs. We might even call this the *stakeholder model of federalism.* Instead of viewing the states as independent sovereigns in a federal system, we should think of states as indispensable stakeholders in the direction and implementation of federal policy.

8. *Institutional realism.* The new nationalist model argues that federalism debates should focus on the political world we are actually living in, rather than on an idealized world of federal-state relations that no longer exists. As the cases in this casebook suggest, throughout most of the nation's history, the historical debate over federalism has been waged in terms of whether it is a good idea for courts to guarantee states distinct spheres of regulatory control or enforce limitations on federal power to protect state autonomy. The goal of protecting state power, in turn, is to support individual liberty and act as a check on federal encroachment. (See discussion note 3 to Gregory v. Ashcroft, supra.)

The basic terms of dispute have become increasingly irrelevant following the New Deal. Even the Rehnquist and Roberts Courts' federalism doctrines have altered the New Deal settlement only at the margins. There is very little that the

---

45. Heather K. Gerken, Federalism and Nationalism: Time for a Détente?, 59 Wash. U. L. Rev. 997 (2015).

46. Erin Ryan, Federalism and the Tug of War Within (2012).

federal government cannot do through its combination of powers if it possesses the political will to act. For example, in *Sebelius*, the federal government was able to pass the individual mandate through the taxing power, and Chief Justice Roberts acknowledged that by structuring the Affordable Care Act differently, the government could also have required the states to adopt the Medicaid expansion.

9. *Protecting states as stakeholders*. What are the doctrinal consequences of the new nationalism? Does it change how courts should decide federalism cases?

The model of cooperative federalism suggests that the best way to protect states may not be to carve out spheres of regulatory immunity or limited federal power. Rather, it is to accept the broad scope of federal power but give states bargaining leverage. States protect the interests of their citizens—their political base—through their influence and participation in federal governance. They exercise political power through their ability to implement (or not implement) federal programs and to structure the terms in which federal power will be exercised.

If, for example, you regard marijuana legalization as a victory for individual liberty, the victory has not come from judicial limits on the federal commerce power. (The Supreme Court upheld federal power to regulate marijuana in *Raich* and again this Term in *Taylor*.) Rather, the achievement is due to the fact that the federal government relies on the states for the enforcement of drug laws. This gives states bargaining leverage to push the federal government to experiment with different ways of organizing drug enforcement.

However, states can only exercise this role of protecting their citizens if they have (1) "skin in the game"—that is, a stake in federal governance—and (2) some form of bargaining leverage. It follows that the most important federalism doctrines might be those that give states both a stake *and* leverage in federal governance. If states increasingly protect their citizens and exercise their power as stakeholders, the courts assist them best when they protect their role as stakeholders.

How might this be accomplished? First, courts can adopt rules that require—or at least give incentives—for the federal government to bargain with states in regulatory initiatives rather than simply commanding states' obedience. Doing so puts friction into the system of federal power in order to encourage the federal government to negotiate and work with states. This might provide an additional justification for the anticommandeering principle recognized in *Printz*[47] or the Court's construction of the spending power in NFIB v. Sebelius.[48] How would one write the majority opinions in these cases from a new nationalist perspective?

Note, however, that the consequence of this approach in *Sebelius* is that the federal government has to get the states to agree to expand Medicaid. It may not succeed. Some states will refuse for political and ideological reasons, with the result that many poor people, especially in red states, will not get Medicaid for many years, if at all. If you oppose the Medicaid expansion, that presents no problems. It is a genuine problem, however, if you support the federal government's expansion of medical care for the poor. Are the advantages of this model of federalism worth the costs?

---

47. Roderick M. Hills, Jr., The Political Economy of Cooperative Federalism: Why State Autonomy Makes Sense and "Dual Sovereignty" Doesn't, 96 Mich. L. Rev. 813 (1998).

48. Heather K. Gerken, Federalism and Nationalism: Time for a Détente?, supra n.45.

On the other hand, are court-enforced limits on federal power actually necessary to give the states leverage in implementing federal programs? Suppose that NFIB v. Sebelius had gone the other way and the federal government was allowed to impose its Medicaid expansion on all of the states. Wouldn't recalcitrant states still have "the power of the servant" because they would implement the Medicaid expansion in their own way?

The difference between the two scenarios is that in the first scenario, poor people don't get Medicaid at all in some red states, while in the second, poor people in these states get Medicaid in the manner that state opponents of Obamacare prefer. Which result in NFIB v. Sebelius is more consistent with the premises of the new nationalism? If both results are consistent, what advice does the model give to judges?

A second way for courts to implement the new nationalist model is to use clear statement rules rather than imposing simple limits on federal power. Clear statement rules do not prevent the federal government from acting; rather they require clear statements from Congress before federal power can be exercised in certain ways. Two examples are Gregory v. Ashcroft and Bond v. United States, supra. Clear statement rules require additional political capital to achieve certain goals. Therefore, they may indirectly enhance the role of states as stakeholders in federal policy.

If one adopted the new nationalist approach, would any of the cases you have read so far come out differently? Or is the primary value of this approach to give a different set of perspectives on how and when to empower states in their political relationships with the federal government?

III. INTERSTATE FEDERALISM AND THE NATIONAL ECONOMY

Federalism has at least two important dimensions—vertical and horizontal. Vertically, federalism focuses on the relation between state governments and the federal government. Horizontally, the focus is on the relationships between sister states. These two dimensions are of course importantly related, especially given that horizontal relations are often policed vertically, by Congress and federal courts. Also, recall the language in paragraph 64 of *McCulloch*, supra Chapter 1, recasting the vertical conflict between the Bank of the United States and the state of Maryland as a horizontal conflict; in taxing a federal instrumentality that all states had helped pay for, Maryland was in effect taxing her sister states, Marshall argued. (Note also how Justice White tries to make a similar argument in his dissent in New York v. United States, though the majority plainly disagrees.) Having considered in detail various aspects of vertical federalism in the modern era, we now quickly survey two aspects of horizontal federalism: "dormant" Commerce Clause doctrine, and interstate privileges and immunities under Article IV. The briskness of this quick tour is not meant to suggest the unimportance of these issues, especially in a modern, mobile, interconnected economy. But judicial doctrine under the dormant Commerce Clause is often highly fact-specific; and of course subject to easy overruling by Congress, which is free both to ban what courts have blessed, and to bless what courts have banned. Also, issues under the "dormant" Commerce Clause may at times be closely connected to statutory questions of implied congressional preemption of certain state regulatory efforts; many of these issues are best studied in courses on legislation, administrative law, and regulated industries. So too, doctrine under the Article IV Privileges and Immunities Clause is covered in greater detail in courses and casebooks on conflicts of law. Those readers looking for more extensive analysis are also directed to the third edition of this casebook, which covers these issues at considerably greater length.

A. *Dormant Commerce Clause*

The so-called Dormant Commerce Clause, a term coined by Chief Justice Marshall in his opinion in Willson v. Black-Bird Creek Marsh Co., 27 U.S. (2 Pet.) 245 (1829), supra Chapter 2, was developed by the Court to restrain states from enforcing laws that burdened interstate commerce. The textual foundations of dormant Commerce Clause doctrine, however, are shaky: The Commerce Clause empowers Congress to regulate commerce "among the several states," but does not explicitly grant power to federal courts to invalidate state laws in the absence of congressional action. From this "great silence," H.P. Hood & Sons, Inc. v. Du Mond, 336 U.S. 525 (1949), the Court has inferred that absent congressional action, states have a "residuum of power" to regulate local affairs, even if their actions affect interstate commerce, provided that their regulation does not impermissibly "trespass upon national interests." Great Atl. & Pac. Tea Co. v. Cottrell, 424 U.S. 366, 373 (1976). The textual embarrassments of dormant Commerce Clause doctrine have led some—most prominently Justices Scalia and Thomas—to call for extreme judicial restraint in this domain. See, e.g., Tyler Pipe Indus. Inc. v. Washington State Dept. of Revenue, 483 U.S. 232 (1987), and Bendix Autolite Corp. v. Midwesco Enters., 486 U.S. 888 (1988) (Scalia, J., dissenting) (calling on the Court to rein in its balancing approach, and concentrate merely on state laws that facially discriminate against out-of-state interests); Camps Newfound/Owatonna, Inc. v. Town of Harrison, 520 U.S. 564 (1997) (Thomas, J., dissenting) (offering a sharp critique of existing doctrine, and pointing to the Article I, §10 Imports-Exports Clause as the proper focus of judicial attention). On the other hand, there is an obvious structural need for some federal institution to regularly monitor parochial, protectionistic, burdensome, and/or mutually inconsistent state regulations that threaten an integrated national economy. Congress may not be well suited to be the first line of defense against the myriad and fact-specific threats to this economy posed by an almost infinite number of possible state and local laws; and so even if Justices Scalia and Thomas were to persuade their colleagues to leave the field, it seems likely that Congress would pass a broad and loosely worded framework statute inviting the courts back in to keep doing pretty much what they have been doing. Put another way, Congress today legislates against the backdrop of default rules generated by the Court's dormant Commerce Clause doctrine, and appears by its actions and inactions over many decades to have rather forcefully embraced the federal judiciary as its partner in keeping states under control in the economic domain.[49]

1. Burdensome Laws: The Development of a Balancing Test

Early twentieth-century dormant Commerce Clause cases—many of them involving state regulations of transportation—routinely attempted to distinguish between "direct" and "indirect" burdens on commerce. But led by Justice Stone in the 1930s and 1940s, the Court began to move away from this sharp dichotomy toward a more candid and nuanced balancing of state interests against national goals. See, e.g., South Carolina State Highway Dept. v. Barnwell Brothers, 303 U.S. 177 (1938) (Stone, J.), and South Pacific Co. v. Arizona, 325 U.S. 761 (1945) (Stone, C.J.), both of which are discussed below.

The direct-indirect approach was explicitly rejected by the Court in Pike v. Bruce Church Inc., 397 U.S. 137 (1970). The case involved an Arizona statute requiring that all cantaloupes grown in Arizona and offered for sale be packed in Arizona before shipment for sale out of state. The statute was challenged by Bruce Church, which wanted to ship uncrated cantaloupes to nearby facilities in Blythe, California, for packing and processing. The stipulated facts indicated that it would cost the company about $200,000 to build a packing facility within Arizona. In his majority opinion, Justice Stewart put forth the following "general rule":

> Where the statute regulates evenhandedly to effectuate a legitimate local public interest, and its effects on interstate commerce are only incidental, it will be upheld unless the burden imposed in such commerce is clearly excessive in relation to the putative local benefits. If a legitimate

---

49. Because the Dormant Commerce Clause provides a default rule of federal-state relations, the modern Supreme Court has recognized that Congress has the power to authorize state regulations that courts would otherwise have struck down in the absence of Congressional action—for example, because the state regulations burden or discriminate against interstate commerce. See, e.g., Prudential Ins. Co. v. Benjamin, 328 U.S. 408, 434 (1946); Southern Pacific Co. v. Arizona, 325 U.S. 761, 769 (1945) (Congress may "permit the states to regulate the commerce in a manner which would otherwise not be permissible"). The Court, however will not assume that Congress has done so unless Congress clearly expresses such an intention. South-Central Timber Development, Inc. v. Wunnicke, 467 U.S. 82, 91-92 (1984) ("for a state regulation to be removed from the reach of the dormant Commerce Clause, congressional intent must be unmistakably clear").

The standard justification for this rule is that Congress decides national policy about interstate commerce, and if Congress wants to choose a different approach, the courts will defer. See Prudential Ins. Co. v. Benjamin, supra at 434. ("Congress may keep the way open, confine it broadly or closely, or close it entirely, subject only to the restrictions placed upon its authority by other constitutional provisions and the requirement that it shall not invade the domains of action reserved exclusively for the states.") Congress has occasionally exercised this special power. In the McCarran-Ferguson Act, ch. 20, 59 Stat. 33 (1945) (codified at 15 U.S.C. §§1011-1015), for example, Congress has authorized states to regulate insurance companies in ways that favor in-state insurers.

This feature of the doctrine makes the Dormant Commerce Clause unique in American constitutional law. Congress cannot, for example, waive the states' obligations to respect the First Amendment or the Equal Protection Clause.

> local purpose is found, then the question becomes one of degree. And the extent of the burden that will be tolerated will of course depend on the nature of the local interest involved, and on whether it could be promoted as well with a lesser impact on interstate activities.

Applying this test, Justice Stewart invalidated the Arizona statute, finding Arizona's interest in protecting the reputation of its produce "minimal" when placed against the requirement that the packer "build and operate an unneeded $200,000 packing plant in the state."

The *Pike* test was refined in Hughes v. Oklahoma, 441 U.S. 322 (1979), which struck down an Oklahoma statute that prohibited minnows procured in Oklahoma waters from being transported outside the state. The *Hughes* decision developed the *Pike* rule into a three-pronged test. The Court considered (1) whether the challenged statute regulates evenhandedly with only "incidental" effects on interstate commerce, or instead discriminates against interstate commerce either on its face or in practical effect; (2) whether the statute serves a legitimate local purpose; and if so, (3) whether alternative means could promote this local purpose as effectively without discriminating against interstate commerce. Thus, like the Court's analysis in *Pike*, the *Hughes* test balanced the state's interest in promulgating a statute against the burden that the statute imposes on interstate commerce.

One particularly interesting strand of balancing cases concerns state regulations of transportation—regulations of the size and specifications of trucks traveling along highways, for example. On the one hand, the Court has recognized a state's strong safety interests in controlling its own streets and thoroughfares. On the other hand, the Court has been sensitive to the need for each state to bear its share of supporting a national transportation network that can be threatened by unnecessary or conflicting local laws. Compare, e.g., South Carolina State Highway Dept. v. Barnwell Brothers, 303 U.S. 177 (1938) (upholding a state law regulating truck size in a nondiscriminatory way, whose burdens fell largely on intrastate shippers, and whose specifics plausibly served legitimate interests in safety and road conservation), with South Pacific Co. v. Arizona, 325 U.S. 761 (1945) (striking down a state law regulating train size that had dubious safety benefits, that interfered with the "national uniformity . . . practically indispensable to the operation of an efficient and economical national railway system," and whose burdens fell on train traffic that was more than 90 percent interstate), and with Bibb v. Navajo Freight Lines, Inc., 359 U.S. 520 (1959) (invalidating a state law regulating truck mudflaps differently from—and in part inconsistently with—the mudflap regulations of sister states).

2. Facially Discriminatory Laws: The "Per Se Invalidity" Test

In cases where state law overtly discriminates against out-of-state economic interests in a fashion akin to a tariff, quota, or outright embargo, the Supreme Court has routinely abandoned the balancing approach in favor of a "virtually per se rule of invalidity." For example, in City of Philadelphia v. New Jersey, 437 U.S. 617 (1978), the Court invalidated a 1973 New Jersey statute that prohibited the importation of most solid or liquid waste originating outside the borders of the state. Although New Jersey argued that it enacted the law to protect the state's environment while additional landfills and alternative disposal methods were being developed, the Court concluded that "whatever New Jersey's ultimate purpose, it may not be accomplished by discriminating against articles of commerce coming from outside the State unless there is some reason, apart from their origin, to treat them differently." The state, said Justice Stewart for the Court, could not achieve the legitimate goals of conservation of landfill facilities by "the illegitimate means of isolating the State from the national economy. . . . [T]here is no basis to distinguish out-of-state waste from domestic waste. If the one is inherently harmful, so is the other. Yet New Jersey has banned the former while leaving its landfill sites open to the latter." Thus, the mere invocation of an allegedly benign purpose did not save a facially discriminatory statute: "[T]he evil of protectionism can reside in legislative means as well as legislative ends." For more recent cases reaffirming this approach, see Chemical Waste Management, Inc. v. Hunt, 504 U.S. 334 (1992), Fort Gratiot Sanitary Landfill, Inc. v. Michigan Department of Natural Resources, 504 U.S. 353 (1992), and Oregon Waste Systems, Inc. v. Department of Environmental Quality of the State of Oregon, 511 U.S. 93 (1994), all of which invalidated efforts to discriminate against out-of-state garbage. Recall, in this regard, that Congress remains free to bless overt state discriminations, cf. New York v. United States, supra.

3. The Market Participant Exception

In Hughes v. Alexandria Scrap Corp., 426 U.S. 794 (1976)—handed down the same day as *National League of Cities*—the Court addressed for the first time "the question whether, when a state enters the market as purchaser for end use of items in interstate commerce, it may [restrict] its trade to its own citizens or businesses within the state." Upholding a Maryland statute that would otherwise have been declared per se invalid under the *Philadelphia* test, the Court applied the market participant test to determine whether the challenged state activity was the type of action with which the Commerce Clause was concerned, or instead, merely "market participation" by the state and thus beyond the reach of the clause.

The statutes considered in *Alexandria Scrap* were designed by Maryland to remove abandoned autos from state highways by paying a bounty to licensed scrap processors for the destruction of cars formerly titled in the state. The Maryland legislature, however, imposed stricter documentation requirements for out-of-state firms, thus producing a "precipitate decline" in the number of abandoned cars delivered to out-of-state processors. In upholding Maryland's program, Justice Powell's opinion for the Court concluded that not "every action by a state that has the effect of reducing in some manner the flow of goods in interstate commerce is potentially an impermissible burden." Although the Court recognized that the effect of the program was to reduce the movement of junked cars interstate, it ruled that discriminating between in-state processors and out-of-state processors in the purchase of cars was not "the kind of action with which the Commerce Clause is concerned." Thus, in articulating this new test, the Court emphasized the form, not the effect, of the state's activity.

The Court more fully articulated the market participant test in Reeves, Inc. v. Stake, 447 U.S. 429 (1980). For 50 years, South Dakota's state-owned cement plant had sold cement to both in-state and out-of-state buyers. In 1978, however, production problems and a nationwide cement shortage led the state to supply all in-state customers first and to distribute the remaining volume on a first-come, first-served basis. The majority, per Justice Blackmun, upheld South Dakota's policy, arguing that because "the Commerce Clause responds principally to state taxes and regulatory measures," the state is exempt when acting in its proprietary capacity. For a more recent case applying and refining this exception, see White v. Massachusetts Council of Construction Employers, 460 U.S. 204 (1983), upholding an order by the mayor of Boston requiring all construction projects paid for by the city to hire at least half of their workers from the ranks of city residents.

4. General Theories of Dormant Commerce

Scholars have vigorously debated the purpose and justification for judicial intervention under the dormant Commerce Clause. Proponents of the free trade theory claim that the doctrine promotes the national interest in free trade between the states, arguing that the Commerce Clause demands that state boundaries not be used to inhibit the flow of goods. Professor Maltz, for example, claims that the United States depends upon the "free location" principle, which permits individuals to freely engage in commerce in any state. See Earl M. Maltz, How Much Regulation Is Too Much—An Examination of Commerce Clause Jurisprudence, 50 Geo. Wash. L. Rev. 47 (1981). Thus, Maltz asserts that courts may intervene when a state discriminates against out-of-state producers, and contends that the free trade model necessitates judicial balancing where state regulations affect interstate trade. Consistent with this emphasis, the Court has also referred to the free trade principle to support its Dormant Commerce Clause decisions. See, e.g., H.P. Hood & Sons, Inc. v. Du Mond, 336 U.S. 525, 539 (1949).

On the other hand, scholars adopting a value-oriented approach have argued that the Commerce Clause protects "national unity." Professor Regan, for example, makes a structural argument on behalf of the "political viability of the union itself" to justify the invocation of the dormant Commerce Clause. On his view, the doctrine should target state laws with a "protectionist purpose"—that is, laws that "seek[] only a transfer of wealth from foreigners to their local competitors, which is an improper goal for a state in the context of federal union." Donald H. Regan, The Supreme Court and State Protectionism: Making Sense of the Dormant Commerce Clause, 84 Mich. L. Rev. 1091 (1986).

Others have offered a process-based justification for the dormant Commerce Clause. In an approach that parallels his famous footnote 4 in *Carolene Products,* Justice Stone argued against legislation that benefits individuals within the state at the expense of those outside its borders. As he stated, "when the regulation is of such a character that its burden falls principally upon those without the state, legislative action is not likely to be subjected to those political restraints which are normally exerted on legislation where it affects adversely some interests within the state." South Carolina State Highway Dept. v. Barnwell Bros., 303 U.S. 177, 185 n.2 (1938). Is this process approach attractive? If so, can it account for the doctrine—for example, the market participant exception? Or should that exception be understood as an accommodation of a competing principle, which values the expressive autonomy of states—their "consumer sovereignty," so to speak—when they act in a nonregulatory capacity? The state's ability to hoard resources for locals is a major issue in the modern welfare state, to be examined at much greater length in Chapter 9.

B. *Interstate Privileges and Immunities*

Recall that Article IV requires each state to accord citizens of sister states various "privileges and immunities." The essence of this clause, which has its roots in similar language in the Articles of Confederation, is that a state may not treat fellow Americans from sister states simply as outsiders or foreigners; rather, in many important ways, each state must evenhandedly extend the benefit of its laws to all Americans within its boundaries. For example, a state may not selectively close the doors of its courtrooms to citizens from other states; and must likewise respect the right of fellow Americans to buy real property, make contracts, open businesses, worship, speak, and exercise many other civil rights, on equal terms with state citizens.

Also recall that in Minor v. Happersett, 88 U.S. 162 (1874), supra Chapter 4, the Court made clear that Article IV had important limits. It did not, said the Court, require state A to let visitors from other states vote in state A's elections, for example. "Political rights" such as voting, jury service, state officeholding, and militia service apparently fall outside the scope of the civil rights—the "privileges" and "immunities" of "citizens"—embraced by the clause. Two years later, McCready v. Virginia, 94 U.S. 391 (1876), held that the clause did not prohibit Virginia from granting its citizens the exclusive privilege of planting oysters in the state's tidal waters. Chief Justice Waite wrote that the state—and thus, its citizenry—owns these waters, and that the planting of oysters in them "is, in fact, a property right, and not a mere privilege or immunity of citizenship. . . . [T]he citizens of one State are not invested by [the Privileges and Immunities] clause of the Constitution with any interest in the common property of the citizens of another State."

In Toomer v. Witsell, 334 U.S. 385 (1948), however, Chief Justice Vinson wrote that this "whole ownership theory . . . is now generally regarded as but a fiction expressive in legal shorthand of the importance to its people that a State have power to preserve and regulate the exploitation of an important resource." His opinion went on to hold that the Privileges and Immunities Clause safeguards the right of one state to do business in another state "on terms of substantial equality with the citizens of that State" and struck down a South Carolina law that imposed a discriminatory license fee on nonresidents shrimping in the state's territorial waters. Justice Frankfurter, joined by Justice Jackson, concurred in judgment, but thought that "it is not conceivable that the framers of the Constitution meant to obliterate all special relations between a State and its citizens." Consider also Pennsylvania v. West Virginia, 262 U.S. 553 (1923), in which the Court invalidated a West Virginia requirement that all domestic needs for natural gas be satisfied before any gas could be transported outside the state. Justice Holmes, joined by Justice Brandeis, dissented, arguing "that the Constitution does not prohibit a state from securing a reasonable preference for its own inhabitants in the enjoyment of its products even when the effect of its law is to keep property within its boundaries that otherwise would have passed outside."

In Baldwin v. Montana Fish and Game Commission, 436 U.S. 371 (1978), Justice Blackmun, for a 6-3 Court, held that "only with respect to those 'privileges' and 'immunities' bearing upon the vitality of the Nation as a single entity must the State treat all citizens, resident and nonresident, equally." The Court thus upheld a Montana hunting licensing scheme that charged nonresidents significantly more than residents, noting that "equality in access to Montana elk is not basic to the maintenance or well-being of the Union." *Toomer* was distinguished as a case involving "commercial" licenses and thus equality of business opportunities, as opposed to recreational hunting. Justice Brennan, in a dissent joined by Justices White and Marshall, argued that such a reading rendered the Privileges and Immunities Clause "impotent."

The same year, in Hicklin v. Orbeck, 437 U.S. 518 (1978), the Court unanimously struck down an Alaska statute requiring that Alaska residents be preferred to nonresidents for jobs connected with oil and gas pipelines. Assuming, arguendo, that a state could constitutionally deal with its unemployment problem by requiring private employers to discriminate against nonresidents if the nonresidents were the unique source of the problem, Justice Brennan noted that Alaska's unemployment resulted from indigenous factors such as its residents' lack of education and training, rather than from an influx of job-seekers as such. Moreover, the statutory preference extended to all Alaskans, not just the unemployed.

The 1985 case of Supreme Court of New Hampshire v. Piper, 470 U.S. 274, involved a challenge to the New Hampshire Supreme Court's Rule 42, which made residency in the state a requirement for admittance to the New Hampshire bar. Plaintiff Kathryn Piper had passed the New Hampshire state bar examination, but wanted to continue to reside in Lower Waterford, Vermont—about 400 yards from the New Hampshire border. Justice Powell, for an eight-Justice majority, held that the opportunity to practice law is a "fundamental right." According to the Court:

> The Clause does not preclude discrimination against nonresidents where: (i) there is a substantial reason for the difference in treatment; and (ii) the discrimination practiced against nonresidents bears a substantial relationship to the State's objective. In deciding whether the discrimination bears a close or substantial relationship to the State's objective, the Court has considered the availability of less restrictive means.

Noting that the state met neither of these criteria, the Court struck down the law. Justice Rehnquist dissented, writing that "conclusory second-guessing of difficult legislative decisions, such as the Court resorts to today, is not an attractive way for federal courts to engage in judicial review." The Court later relied on *Piper* to strike down similar residency requirements in Supreme Court of Virginia v. Friedman, 487 U.S. 59 (1988), and Virgin Islands Bar Association v. Thorsten, 489 U.S. 546 (1989).

For a thoughtful general framework of analysis for assessing various issues of horizontal federalism, see Douglas Laycock, Equal Citizens of Equal and Territorial States: The Constitutional Foundations of Choice of Law, 92 Colum. L. Rev. 249 (1992). See also infra, Chapter 9, discussing related issues of interstate federalism under the "right to travel" rubric.

IV. THE EXECUTIVE POWER OF THE UNITED STATES

Alongside federalism, separation of powers stands as a central structural feature of the American Constitution. Much of the material we have already reviewed in this chapter can be understood as implicating both themes, involving the three-way interplay between the Court, the Congress, and states. In this interplay, the federal executive branch has often been hidden from view—although the careful reader will have glimpsed the important roles of Franklin Roosevelt, Richard Nixon, and Ronald Reagan, among others, in the story thus far.

It is now time to bring the American President center stage, and consider in more detail some of the extraordinary powers of this office, and some important limits on those powers. Although we shall consider these powers seriatim, recall that all of them are, by the first sentence of Article II, vested in a single person: the President. Try to see how these powers might interact and overlap in specific contexts. For example, note that the same person has important war powers as Commander-in-Chief, treaty negotiator, appointer and receiver of ambassadors, and more general head of state; and also important controls over domestic prosecutions, via the pardon power and the power to appoint the Attorney General. Are there synergies across these powers? Note that in this respect the President is rather different from state governors, who are not central figures in wars and foreign affairs, and who typically lack power under their respective state constitutions over their state attorneys general.[50]

A. The (Non)Prosecution Power

One overarching theme of this casebook is that many important constitutional decisions occur outside of the judiciary. Even within the judiciary, not all major decisions are made by the Supreme Court. Recall, for example, that various lower federal courts in the 1790s addressed the constitutionality of the 1798 Sedition Act, but that the issue never reached the Supreme Court, and was eventually mooted by the victory of Jefferson and the Republicans in the election of 1800. President Jefferson pardoned all those convicted, and the new Congress allowed the Act to expire. Thus the lower courts; the President (both Adams and Jefferson); the Congress (both in 1798 and after 1800); the state legislatures (two of which issued famous Resolutions against the Act in 1798, most of which elected senators in 1800, and all of which helped pick the President in 1800); and the electorate—all these actors played more direct roles in the constitutional drama than did the Supreme Court itself.

In the mid-1960s, many vital questions of constitutional law were being decided by the Warren Court; but Congress and the President were also in the

---

50. For important overall assessments of presidential power, see Steven G. Calabresi and Kevin H. Rhodes, The Structural Constitution: Unitary Executive, Plural Judiciary, 105 Harv. L. Rev. 1153 (1992); Steven G. Calabresi and Saikrishna B. Prakash, The President's Power to Execute the Laws, 104 Yale L.J. 541 (1994); Steven G. Calabresi, Some Normative Arguments for the Unitary Executive, 48 Ark. L. Rev. 23 (1995). For a more recent essay inspired by the impressive work of Professor Calabresi, see Akhil Reed Amar, Some Opinions on the Opinions Clause, 82 Va. L. Rev. 647 (1996).

thick of things, adopting landmark civil rights laws and pursuing important strategies of civil rights enforcement. Another lead actor in the great national drama was the U.S. Court of Appeals for the (old) Fifth Circuit, spanning the deep South from Florida to Texas. It was this court that had primary responsibility for enforcing the Second Reconstruction coming out of Washington, D.C. See generally Jack Bass, Unlikely Heroes (1981). The next case comes from that court and that era. The facts of the case are gripping, but they fully appear only at the end of the last opinion, per Judge Wisdom. No peeking.

United States v. Cox

342 F.2d 167, cert. denied sub nom. Cox v. Hauberg, 381 U.S. 935 (1965)

JONES, Circuit Judge.

On October 22, 1964, an order of the United States District Court for the Southern District of Mississippi, signed by Harold Cox, a judge of that Court, was entered. The order, with caption and formal closing omitted, is as follows:

> "THE GRAND JURY, duly elected, impaneled and organized, for the Southern District of Mississippi, reconvened on order of the Court at 9:00 A.M., October 21, 1964, in Court Room Number 2 in Jackson, Mississippi, for the general dispatch of its business. . . . On the morning of October 22, 1964, the grand jury, through its foreman, made known to the Court in open court that they had requested Robert E. Hauberg, United States Attorney, to prepare certain indictments which they desired to bring against some of the persons under consideration and about which they had heard testimony, and the United States Attorney refused to draft or sign any such indictments on instructions of the Acting Attorney General of the United States; whereupon the Court ordered and directed said United States Attorney to draft such true bills or no bills as the grand jury may have duly voted and desired to report and to sign such instruments as required by law under penalty of contempt. The United States Attorney was afforded one hour within which to decide as to whether or not he would abide by the instructions and order of the Court in such respect. At the end of such time, the Court re-convened and the United States Attorney was specifically asked in open court as to whether or not he intended to conform with the order and direction of the Court in said respects whereupon the United States Attorney answered that he respectfully declined to do so on instructions from Nicholas deB. Katzenbach, Acting Attorney General. He was thereupon duly adjudged by the Court to be in civil contempt of the Court. . . .
>
> "WHEREFORE, IT IS ORDERED AND ADJUDGED by the Court that Robert E. Hauberg, United States Attorney, is guilty of civil contempt of this Court and in the presence of the Court for his said refusal to obey its said order and he is ordered into custody of the United States Marshal to be confined by him in the Hinds County, Mississippi, jail, there to remain until he purges himself of this contempt by agreeing to conform to said order by performing his official duty for the grand jury as requested. . . .

> "IT IS FURTHER ORDERED by the Court that a citation issue to Nicholas deB. Katzenbach, Acting Attorney General of the United States, directing him to appear before this Court and show cause why he should not be adjudged guilty of contempt of this Court for his instructions and directions to the United States Attorney to disregard and disobey the orders of this Court in the respects stated. . . ."

The United States Attorney, Robert E. Hauberg, and the Acting Attorney General, Nicholas deB. Katzenbach, have appealed from the order. . . . The facts recited in the order are uncontroverted. No further facts are essential to a decision of the issues before this Court. Although the issues here presented arose, in part at least, as an incident of a civil rights matter, no civil rights questions are involved in the rather broad inquiry which we are called upon to make.

The constitutional requirement of an indictment or presentment as a predicate to a prosecution for capital or infamous crimes has for its primary purpose the protection of the individual from jeopardy except on a finding of probable cause by a group of his fellow citizens, and is designed to afford a safeguard against oppressive actions of the prosecutor or a court. The constitutional provision is not to be read as conferring on or preserving to the grand jury, as such, any rights or prerogatives. The constitutional provision is, as has been said, for the benefit of the accused. . . .

Traditionally, the Attorney for the United States had the power to enter a nolle prosequi of a criminal charge at any time after indictment and before trial, and this he could have done without the approval of the court or the consent of the accused. . . .

It is now provided by the Federal Rules of Criminal Procedure that the Attorney General or the United States Attorney may by leave of court file a dismissal of an indictment. Rule 48(a) Fed. Rules Crim. Proc. 18 U.S.C.A. In the absence of the Rule, leave of court would not have been required. The purpose of the Rule is to prevent harassment of a defendant by charging, dismissing and re-charging without placing a defendant in jeopardy. Rule 7 . . . provides that "[the indictment] shall be signed by the attorney for the government."

The judicial power of the United States is vested in the federal courts, and extends to prosecutions for violations of the criminal laws of the United States. The executive power is vested in the President of the United States, who is required to take care that the laws be faithfully executed. The Attorney General is the hand of the President in taking care that the laws of the United States in legal proceedings and in the prosecution of offenses, be faithfully executed. The role of the grand jury is restricted to a finding as to whether or not there is probable cause to believe that an offense has been committed. The discretionary power of the attorney for the United States in determining whether a prosecution shall be commenced or maintained may well depend upon matters of policy wholly apart from any question of probable cause. Although as a member of the bar, the attorney for the United States is an officer of the court, he is nevertheless an executive official of the Government, and it is as an officer of the executive department that he exercises a discretion as to whether or not there shall be a prosecution in a particular case. It follows, as an incident of the constitutional separation of powers, that the courts are not to interfere with the free exercise of the discretionary powers of the attorneys of the United States in their control over criminal prosecutions. The provision of Rule 7, requiring the signing of the indictment by the attorney for the Government, is a recognition of the power of Government counsel to permit or not to permit the bringing of an indictment. If the attorney refuses to sign, as he has the discretionary power of doing, we conclude that there is no valid indictment. It is not to be supposed that the signature of counsel is merely an attestation of the act of the grand jury. The signature of the foreman performs that function. . . . Rather, we think, the requirement of the signature is for the purpose of evidencing the joinder of the attorney for the United States with the grand jury in instituting a criminal proceeding in the court. Without the signature there can be no criminal proceeding brought upon an indictment.

If it were not for the discretionary power given to the United States Attorney to prevent an indictment by withholding his signature, there might be doubt as to the constitutionality of the requirement of Rule 48 for leave of court for a dismissal of a pending prosecution.

Because, as we conclude, the signature of the Government attorney is necessary to the validity of the indictment and the affixing or withholding of the signature is a matter of executive discretion which cannot be coerced or reviewed by the courts, the contempt order must be reversed. . . .

Judges Tuttle, Jones, Brown and Wisdom join in the conclusion that the signature of the United States Attorney is essential to the validity of an indictment. Judge Brown, as appears in his separate opinion, is of the view that the United States Attorney is required, upon the request of the grand jury, to draft forms of indictments in accordance with its desires. The order before us for review is in the conjunctive; it requires the United States Attorney to prepare and sign. A majority of the court, having decided that the direction to sign is erroneous, the order on appeal will be reversed. . . .

RIVES, GEWIN and Griffen B. BELL, Circuit Judges (concurring in part and dissenting part):

[T]he basic issue before this Court is whether the controlling discretion as to the institution of a felony prosecution rests with the Attorney General or with the grand jury. The majority opinion would ignore the broad inquisitorial powers of the grand jury, and limit the constitutional requirement of Amendment V to the benefit of the accused.

We agree with Professor Orfield that:

> "The grand jury serves two great functions. One is to bring to trial persons accused of crime upon just grounds. The other is to protect persons against unfounded or malicious prosecutions by insuring that no criminal proceeding will be undertaken without a disinterested determination of probable guilt. The inquisitorial function has been called the more important. . . ."

A federal grand jury has the unquestioned right to inquire into any matter within the jurisdiction involving violations of law and to return an indictment if it finds a reasonable probability that a crime has been committed. This it may do at the instance of the court, the District Attorney, the Attorney General or on its own initiative, from evidence it may gather or from knowledge of its members. . . .

The finding and return of the indictment are the acts of the grand jury. When United States Attorney prepares and signs an indictment, he does not adopt, approve, or vouch for the charge, nor does he institute a criminal prosecution. . . . The United States Attorney cannot, except in an advisory capacity, inquire into the merits of whether indictments should be found and returned in particular cases being considered by the grand jury. Only the grand jurors themselves have that power. It would be grossly wrong for it to be usurped. . . .

. . . The signature of the United States Attorney is a mere authentication that the indictment is the act of the grand jury. . . .

The Attorney General insists that the prosecution of offenses against the United States is an executive function of the Attorney General deraigned from the executive power vested in the President to "take care that the laws be faithfully executed." The short answer is that one of the most fundamental and important of the laws so to be faithfully executed is the clear and explicit provision of the Fifth Amendment to the Constitution that "No person shall be held to answer for a capital, or otherwise infamous crime, unless on a presentment or indictment of a Grand Jury."

Moreover, in point of law and reality, the plenary inquisitorial power of the grand jury does not impinge in the slightest upon the executive function of the Attorney General to prosecute or not to prosecute offenses against the United States, for as soon as the indictment is returned, "The Attorney General or the United States Attorney may by leave of court file a dismissal. . . ." Rule 48(a), F. R. Crim. P. . . .

The grand jury may be permitted to function in its traditional sphere, while at the same time enforcing the separation of powers doctrine as between the executive and judicial branches of the government. This can best be done, indeed, it is mandatory, by requiring the United States Attorney to assist the grand jury in preparing indictments which they wish to consider or return, and by requiring the United States Attorney to sign any indictment that is to be returned. Then, once the indictment is returned, the Attorney General or the United States Attorney can refuse to go forward. That refusal will, of course, be in open court and not in the secret confines of the grand jury room. To permit the district court to compel the United States Attorney to proceed beyond this point would invest prosecutorial power in the judiciary, power which under the Constitution is reserved to the executive branch of the government. It may be that the court, in the interest of justice, may require a showing of good faith, and a statement of some rational basis for dismissal. In the unlikely event of bad faith or irrational action, not here present, it may be that the court could appoint counsel to prosecute the case. In brief, the court may have the same inherent power to administer justice to the government as it does to the defendant. That question is not now before us and may never arise. Except for a very limited discretion, however, the court's power to withhold leave to dismiss an indictment is solely for the protection of the defendant. . . .

We agree that proper enforcement of the law does not require that indictments should be returned in every case where probable cause exists. Public policy may in some instances require that a case not be prosecuted. Such consideration of public policy may be submitted to and acted on by the grand jury. . . . In the few cases in which the United States Attorney is unable to persuade the grand jury and the Attorney General disagrees with its action, his recourse is not to prevent the grand jury from finding and returning an effective indictment, but to file a dismissal of the indictment under Rule 48(a), F. R. Crim. P. . . . [The executive decision to forgo prosecution should not be made] in the shadows of secrecy, with the Attorney General not being required to disclose his reasons. How much better is the constitutional system by which the grand jury can find and return an effective indictment upon which a prosecution for crime is instituted. At that point the power of the grand jury ceases. It is effectively checked and overbalanced by the power of the Attorney General, recognized in Rule 48(a), to move for a dismissal of the indictment. The court may then require such a motion to be heard in open court. Instead of a prevention in the shadows of secrecy, there would be a dismissal in a formal, public judicial proceeding. . . .

John R. Brown, Circuit Judge (concurring specially):

Mine is a middle course. I agree with the opinion written by Judge Jones that the District Attorney may not be compelled to sign the formal indictment which the Grand Jury has voted to return. . . . But I do not agree that the District Attorney may ignore the efforts of the Grand Jury to the point of declining to prepare in proper legal form the indictment they have voted to return. On the contrary, I am of the view that the Court may properly compel the District Attorney to act as legal scrivener to the Grand Jury. The Court may, therefore, order the District Attorney to prepare the indictment in legal form [but not to sign it]. . . .

Responsibility for determining whether a prosecution is to be commenced or maintained must be clearly fixed. The power not to initiate is indeed awesome. But it has to reside somewhere. And the more clearly pinpointed it is, the more the public interest is served through the focus of relentless publicity upon that decision. It may not, with safety, be left to a body whose great virtue is the combination of anonymity, transitory authority, and political unresponsibility.

All must be aware now that there are times when the interests of the nation require that a prosecution be foregone. These instances will most often be in the area of state secrets and national security. With stakes so high, the safety of our country, and hence the security of the world, ought not to be imperiled by leaving the important decision to a body having no definitive political responsibility. And it is hardly realistic to suggest, as do the dissenters, that these factors may be evaluated by the Grand Jury. What will be the source of their information? How extensive will it be? How close will a Grand Jury session approach a presidential cabinet meeting? How will essential government secrets be kept when disclosed to persons none of whom as Grand Jurors will have been subjected to customary security clearance checks?

And even in less sensitive areas, the practical operation of the prosecutorial function makes imperative the need for executive determination. The familiar example is the deliberate choice between those to be prosecuted and those who, often equally guilty, are named as co-conspirators but not as defendants, or others not named who are used as star government witnesses. And in other situations, of which the instant case may well be typical, the executive's purpose to effectuate specific policies thought to be of major importance would be frustrated or encumbered were a Grand Jury given the sole prerogative of determining when a prosecution is to be effectively commenced. . . .

Finally, it seems to me incongruous to assert, as do the dissenters, that the signing of the indictment is a ministerial act having no function other than one of authentication. . . . I do not see why an indictment formally signed by the foreman and reported in a solemn open court proceeding as the act of the Grand Jury needs "authentication." And I am at a complete loss to understand how the District Attorney—excluded as he is from the Grand Jury while it is voting,—can "authenticate" from hearsay, or why his imprimatur is any better or different than that which would come from other Grand Jurors, each of whom can be polled by the Judge, not as to his vote, but whether a majority did vote to return the true bill. . . .

The fact is that the signature of the District Attorney has much more awesome consequence. Without a doubt that signature, together with that of the Grand Jury's foreman, is a formal, effective initiation of a prosecution. . . . With it, the whole prosecution has been started. And what was previously an unfettered discretionary right on the part of the executive not to initiate prosecution has now been set in motion and can be stopped only on the executive taking affirmative action for dismissal with all of the uncertainties which F. R. Crim. P. 48(a) generates.

But while I am firm that signature is a vital and significant act which reflects the exercise of an executive discretion to initiate prosecution—a thing here lacking—I am equally positive that the District Attorney has the duty to prepare the indictment when requested to do so by the Grand Jury. . . .

To me the thing seems this simple: the Grand Jury is charged to report. It determines what it is to report. It determines the form in which it reports. Once it determines that what it wants to report is to be in the form of a true bill indictment, it obviously needs legal help. . . . Although, as the Court holds, the "indictment" thus returned would be ineffective without the signature of the District Attorney, reporting its conclusion in traditional legal form would do two things. First, it would clearly reflect the conscientious conclusion of the Grand Jury itself. And, second, it would, at the same time, sharply reveal the difference of view as between the Grand Jury and the prosecuting attorney.

This leads to the second important reason. The powers of the Executive are so awesome in determining those whom it will not prosecute, that where there is a difference between the Grand Jury and the Executive, this determination and the resulting conflict of views should be revealed in open court. With great power comes great responsibility. Disclosure of this difference of view and the resulting impasse would subject this decision of the Executive to the scrutiny of an informed electorate. The issue would be clearly drawn and the responsibility, both legally and in the public mind, plainly fixed. There would not be the sort of thing reflected in this record in which only in the loosest way could the public see what it was the Grand Jury purposed to do and what the Executive declined to help it to do. . . .

By following this middle course we preserve fully the rightful independence of the Grand Jury in its inquisitorial role and the time-proved wisdom of the separation of powers which commits determination (and responsibility) to the Executive. . . .

Wisdom, Circuit Judge (concurring specially): . . .

The dissenters show judicial craftsmanship of the highest order in writing persuasively about "the traditional sphere" of the grand jury while not turning up one case holding that a court may compel a prosecutor to prepare and sign a bill of indictment requested by a grand jury. Not one case in all the years between 1166 and 1965! I submit that the result reached in the dissent is the product of a misunderstanding of the historical meaning of "presentment and indictment," a failure to give effect to the difference between the sword and the shield of the grand jury, and an abstract approach that disregards the factual setting in which the issue is presented.

Nothing in the position of any of the judges in the majority "ignores" or tends to diminish the purely inquisitorial role of the federal grand jury. But when that role goes beyond inquiry and report and becomes accusatorial, no aura of traditional or constitutional sanctity surrounds the grand jury. The Grand Jury earned its place in the Bill of Rights by its shield, not by its sword.

I

The Fifth Amendment requires the grand jury's "presentment or indictment" as a prerequisite to trial for a "capital, or otherwise infamous crime." This language provides no aid and comfort to the notion that either the grand jury or the court has the power to compel prosecution once the grand jury has exercised its accusatorial function. . . .

Historians usually trace the English grand jury back to the Assize of Clarendon issued by Henry II in 1166, based not on Anglo-Saxon antecedents but on Norman-French inquests. . . .

From its beginning until its abolition by Parliament in 1933, the English common law presenting jury could act on its own knowledge, or on the information of others, or on the Crown's written bill of indictment. But only when this bill was preferred to the grand jury by the Crown and endorsed as a "true bill" was the accusation known as an indictment. This was the accepted usage when the Fifth Amendment was adopted. Blackstone explained:

> "A presentment, generally taken, is a very comprehensive term; including not only presentments properly so called, but also inquisitions of office, and indictments by a grand jury. A presentment, properly speaking, is the notice taken by a grand jury of any offence from their own knowledge or observation, without any bill of indictment laid before them at the suit of the king. . . . An indictment is a written accusation of one or more persons of a crime or misdemeanor, preferred to, and presented upon oath by, a grand jury. . . . When the grand jury have heard the evidence, if they think it a groundless accusation, they used formerly to endorse on the back of the bill, 'ignoramus'; or, we know nothing of it; intimating, that though the facts might possibly be true, that truth did not appear to them: but now, they assert in English, more absolutely, 'not a true bill'; or (which is the better way) 'not found'; and then the party is discharged without farther answer. . . . If they are satisfied of the truth of the accusation, they then endorse upon it, 'a true bill,' antiently, 'billa vera.' The indictment is then said to be found, and the party stands indicted."

The Fifth Amendment, therefore, does not offer a grand jury a choice between presentment or indictment. Unless there is a bill of indictment preferred to the grand jury at the instance of the Government, there can be no indictment. It is entirely in the hands of the Government whether to submit an accusation to the grand jury leading to presentment in the form of an indictment and serving as the initial pleading in a criminal prosecution. . . .

Presentment is a natural corollary to the grand jury's inquisitorial power, either for an inquisition of office or for a prosecutory purpose. Its use here would not accomplish its prosecutory purpose, because the Attorney General still could decline to submit a bill of indictment to the grand jury. On the other hand, in this case a presentment in open court with an appropriate minute entry would meet many of the objections to the government's position raised in the dissenting opinion and Judge Brown's opinion. . . . This use of presentment would be in accord with the established procedure in the common law and with the original understanding of the framers. . . .

In sum, there is nothing in my view or in that of the other judges in the majority that would, as the dissenting judges assert, authorize Government counsel to "radically reduce the powers of the grand jury." The grand jury never had a plenary power to indict. It had a limited power to indict—after accusation by the Crown or the Government in the form of a bill of indictment preferred to the grand jury. . . .

The decision of the majority does not affect the inquisitorial power of the grand jury. No one questions the jury's plenary power to inquire, to summon and interrogate witnesses, and to present either findings and a report or an accusation in open court by presentment.

Finally, the decision does not affect the power of the grand jury to shield suspected law violators. By refusing to indict, the grand jury has the unchallengeable power to defend the innocent from government oppression by unjust prosecution. And it has the equally unchallengeable power to shield the guilty, should the whims of the jurors or their conscious or subconscious response to community pressures induce twelve or more jurors to give sanctuary to the guilty.

II

Because recognition of the grand jury's shield-like function is lodged in the Bill of Rights, the bedrock of basic rights, it is fair to say that national policy favors a liberal construction of the power of the grand jury to protect the individual against official tyranny. No such policy favors the grand jury in its accusatorial role. Accordingly, we look for and should expect to find a check on its unjust accusations similar to the grand jury's check on the government's unjust accusations.

[T]he framers wove a web of checks and balances designed to prevent abuse of power, regardless of the age, origin, and character of the institution. . . . [T]he power of the executive not to prosecute, and therefore not to take steps necessarily leading to prosecution, is the appropriate curb on a grand jury in keeping with the constitutional theory of checks and balances. Such a check is especially necessary, if there is any question of the grand jury's and the district court's being in agreement; if they differ, of course the district court may dismiss the grand jury. The need is rendered more acute if there is a possibility that community hostility against the suspected offenders, individually or as a race, may jeopardize justice before the petit jury. In short, if we give the same meaning to "presentment or indictment" that Madison and others gave to these terms when Madison introduced the Bill of Rights in the First Congress, the grand jury provision in the Bill of Rights cuts both ways: it prevents harassment and intimidation and oppression through unjust prosecution—by the Grand Jury or by the Government.

III

The prosecution of offenses against the United States is an executive function within the exclusive prerogative of the Attorney General. . . . That official, the chief law-enforcement officer of the Federal Government is "the hand of the president in taking care that the laws of the United States in protection of the interests of the United States in legal proceedings and in the prosecution of offenses be faithfully executed." . . .

"The district attorney has absolute control over criminal prosecutions, and can dismiss or refuse to prosecute, any of them at his discretion. The responsibility is wholly his." The determination of whether and when to prosecute "is a matter of policy for the prosecuting officer and not for the determination of the courts." As another court has stated it:

> All of these considerations point up the wisdom of vesting broad discretion in the United States Attorney. The federal courts are powerless to interfere with his discretionary power. The Court cannot compel him to prosecute a complaint, or even an indictment, whatever his reasons for not acting. The remedy for any dereliction of his duty lies, not with the courts, but, with the executive branch of our government and ultimately with the people.[a]

. . . Thus, "courts generally refuse to order the prosecutor to initiate a prosecution on the ground that it is a discretionary act which may not be compelled by mandamus." . . . Rule 7(c), requiring that the indictment be signed by the United States Attorney, preserves the prosecutor's traditional discretion as to whether to initiate prosecution.

The reason for vesting discretion to prosecute in the Executive, acting through the Attorney General is two-fold. First, in the interests of justice and the orderly, efficient administration of the law, some person or agency should be able to prevent an unjust prosecution. The freedom of the petit jury to bring in a verdict of not guilty and the progressive development of the law in the direction of making more meaningful the guarantees of an accused person's constitutional rights give considerable protection to the individual before and after trial. They do not protect against a baseless prosecution. This is a harassment to the accused and an expensive strain on the machinery of justice. The appropriate repository for authority to prevent a baseless prosecution is the chief law-enforcement officer whose duty, unlike the grand jury's duty, is to collect evidence on both sides of a case.

Second, when, within the context of law-enforcement, national policy is involved, because of national security, conduct of foreign policy, or a conflict

---

a. In the hearing on the confirmation of Attorney General Jackson as Associate Justice of the Supreme Court, the nomination was attacked because of Jackson's failure to prosecute Drew Pearson and Robert S. Allen for criminal libel on Senator Tydings. Jackson had taken the position that it was the policy of the Department of Justice to avoid the criminal libel laws when the courts were open to the injured party in civil proceedings, and that prosecutions of this character would tend to impair freedom of the press. Republican Senator (now Mr. Justice) Burton stated:

> "The prosecuting attorney, being charged, as he is charged, with the great responsibility of deciding under the laws of the United States, the laws under which he is serving, whether a case should be prosecuted, owes a duty to himself, his community, and the Constitution to decide whether the case should be prosecuted. . . . In my judgment the Attorney General was within his rights when he declined to prosecute, and in stating the grounds as he did state them under the circumstances."

between two branches of government, the appropriate branch to decide the matter is the executive branch. The executive is charged with carrying out national policy on law-enforcement and, generally speaking, is informed on more levels than the more specialized judicial and legislative branches. In such a situation, a decision not to prosecute is analogous to the exercise of executive privilege. The executive's absolute and exclusive discretion to prosecute may be rationalized as an illustration of the doctrine of separation of powers, but it would have evolved without the doctrine and exists in countries that do not purport to accept this doctrine. . . .

IV

This brings me to the facts. They demonstrate, better than abstract principles or legal dicta, the imperative necessity that the United States, through its Attorney General, have uncontrollable discretion to prosecute.

The crucial fact here is that Goff and Kendrick, two Negroes, testified in a suit by the United States against the Registrar of Clarke County, Mississippi, and the State of Mississippi, to enforce the voting rights of Negroes under the Fourteenth Amendment and the Civil Rights Act.

Goff and Kendrick testified that some seven years earlier at Stonewall, Mississippi, the registrar had refused to register them or give them application forms. They said that they had seen white persons registering, one of whom was a B. Floyd Jones. Ramsey, the registrar, testified that Jones had not registered at that time or place, but had registered the year before in Enterprise, Mississippi. He testified also that he had never discriminated against Negro applicants for registration.[b] Jones testified that he was near the registration table in Stonewall in 1955, had talked with the registrar, and had shaken hands with him. The presiding judge, Judge W. Harold Cox, stated from the bench that Goff and Kendrick should be "bound over to await the action of the grand jury for perjury."[c]

---

b. Judge Cox found "as a fact from the evidence that negro citizens have been discriminated against by the registrar," although he found also that there was "no pattern or practice of discrimination." In its original opinion in the Ramsey case this Court noted the "testimony which witness by witness convicts Ramsey of palpable discrimination." In his opinion Judge Rives noted that "This case reveals gross and flagrant denials of the rights of Negro citizens to vote." And on rehearing, this Court ruled that the finding that "there was no pattern or practice in the discrimination by the Registrar" was "clearly erroneous." No one has suggested that Mr. Ramsey may have been guilty of perjury.

c. When counsel for the State, Mr. Riddell, completed Mr. Ramsey's direct examination, and before his cross-examination, respondent Judge W. Harold Cox, who was presiding, stated:

> "I want to hear from the government about why this Court shouldn't require this Negro Reverend W.G. Goff and his companion Kendrick to show cause why they shouldn't be bound over to await the action of the grand jury for perjury. I want to hear from you on that.
>
> "I think they ought to be put under about a $3,000.00 bond each to await the action of a grand jury. Unless I change my mind that is going to be the order. 'BY MR. STERN (Government counsel): I will be happy to reconcile their testimony.' 'BY THE COURT: I just want these Negroes to know that they can't come into this Court and swear to something as important as that was and is and get by with it. I don't care who brings them here.' 'BY MR. STERN: understand.' 'BY THE COURT: Yes sir. And I mean that for whites alike, but I am talking about the case at hand. I just don't intend to put up with perjury. . . .'"

In January 1963 attorneys of the Department of Justice requested the Federal Bureau of Investigation to investigate the possible perjury. The FBI completed a full investigation in March 1963 and referred the matter to the Department's Criminal Division. In June 1963 the Criminal Division advised the local United States Attorney, Mr. Hauberg, that the matter presented "no basis for a perjury prosecution." Mr. Hauberg informed Judge Cox of the Department's decision. Judge Cox stated that in his view the matter was clearly one for the grand jury and that he would be inclined, if necessary, to appoint an outside attorney to present the matter to the grand jury. (I find no authority for a federal judge to displace the United States Attorney by appointing a special prosecutor.) On receiving this information, the Criminal Division again reviewed its files and concluded that the charge of perjury could not be sustained. General Katzenbach, then Deputy Attorney General, after reviewing the files, concurred in the Criminal Division's decision. In September 1963 General Katzenbach called on Judge Cox as a courtesy to explain why the Department had arrived at the conclusion that no perjury was involved. Judge Cox, unconvinced, requested the United States Attorney to present to the grand jury the Goff and Kendrick cases, which he regarded as cases of "palpable perjury."

In October 1963 Goff and Kendrick were arrested, jailed for two days, and placed on a $3,000 bond for violations of State law for falsely testifying in federal court. After their indictment by a state grand jury, the Department of Justice filed suit against the State District Attorney, seeking to enjoin the state prosecution on the grounds that: (1) the States have no authority to prosecute for alleged perjury committed while testifying in a federal court; (2) the purpose and effect of the State's prosecution was to threaten and intimidate Goff and Kendrick and to inhibit them and other Negroes from registering to vote. The district court (per Mize, J.) ruled in favor of the United States. . . .

Against the backdrop of Mississippi versus the Nation in the field of civil rights, we have a heated but bona fide difference of opinion between Judge Cox and the Attorney General as to whether two Negroes, Goff and Kendrick, should be prosecuted for perjury. Taking a narrow view of the case, we would be justified in holding that the Attorney General's implied powers, by analogy to the express powers of Rule 48(a), give him discretion to prosecute. Here there was a bona fide, reasonable exercise of discretion made after a full investigation and long consideration of the case—both sides of the case, not just the evidence tending to show guilt. If the grand jury is dissatisfied with that administrative decision, it may exercise its inquisitorial power and make a presentment in open court. It could be said, that is all there is to the case. But there is more to the case.

This Court, along with everyone else, knows that Goff and Kendrick, if prosecuted, run the risk of being tried in a climate of community hostility. They run the risk of a punishment that may not fit the crime. The Registrar, who provoked the original litigation, runs no risk, notwithstanding the fact that the district court, in effect, found that Ramsay did not tell the truth on the witness stand. In these circumstances, the very least demands of justice require that the discretion to prosecute be lodged with a person or agency insulated from local prejudices and parochial pressures. This is not the hard case that makes bad law. . . . This case is unusual only for the clarity with which the facts, speaking for themselves, illuminate the imperative necessity in American Federalism that the discretion to prosecute be lodged in the Attorney General of United States.

The decision not to prosecute represents the exercise of a discretion analogous to the exercise of executive privilege. As a matter of law, the Attorney General has concluded that there is not sufficient evidence to prove perjury. As a matter of fact, the Attorney General has concluded that trial for perjury would have the effect of inhibiting not only Goff and Kendrick but other Negroes in Mississippi from registering to vote. There is a conflict, therefore, between society's interest in law enforcement (diluted in this case by the Attorney General's conclusion that the evidence does not support the charge of guilt) and the national policy, set forth in the Constitution and the Civil Rights Acts, of outlawing racial discrimination. It is unthinkable that resolution of this important conflict affecting the whole Nation should lie with a majority of twenty-three members of a jury chosen from the Southern District of Mississippi. The nature of American Federalism, looking to the a differences between the Constitution and the Articles of Confederation, requires that the power to resolve this question lies in the unfettered discretion of the President of a United States or his deputy for law enforcement, the Attorney General. . . .

DISCUSSION

1. *Just the facts, ma'am.* Ordinarily, judicial opinions open with the facts. Yet Judge Jones's plurality opinion offers a rather thin rendition of the facts; and Judge Wisdom puts the facts at the end of his opinion. What accounts for this? It is important to understand that every narrative of facts in an opinion or brief or other legal document is unavoidably selective; lawyers and judges must decide which of the infinite number of real-world facts are legally relevant to the case at hand—and to do this (or at least, to do this well), they must obviously have a legal theory that explains why some facts are relevant and others are not. Which, if any, of the facts at the end of Judge Wisdom's opinion, do you think were legally relevant? (Would your legal view of the case be different if a multiracial grand jury were seeking to indict a white lynch mob, and a white supremacist Attorney General were balking?)

2. *Construing statutes in the shadow of constitutional principles.* Note the intricate interplay between issues of statutory construction under Rules 7 and 48, and issues of constitutional principle under Articles II and III and the Fifth Amendment. A good deal of American-style "judicial review" occurs not when judges wheel out the Constitution to strike down a law, but when they invoke it more subtly to inflect their readings of statutes, regulations, ordinances, rules, and the like.

3. *Jury service and voting.* Note that the grand jury in *Cox* was doubtless all white; very few Black people served on Mississippi juries in 1965 because very few Black people were permitted to vote in that state at that time. Of course, this vicious cycle of jury exclusion and voting was precisely what civil rights activists and the Attorney General were trying to break by proving, for example, the voting rights violations of Mississippi registrars.

4. *The Cold War imperative.* How important were issues of foreign policy in shaping the President's response to domestic issues of race policy and prosecution policy? Consider the arguments of Professors Dudziak and Bell that these

issues were tightly intertwined. America in the 1950s and 1960s was locked in a global struggle against Communism, with Asia, Africa, Central America, and South America as major ideological battlegrounds. To win this war, America needed to win the hearts and minds of "colored" persons around the globe, but the mistreatment of Black people in places like Mississippi — gleefully publicized by America's enemies — threatened to undermine America's efforts abroad. Even Presidents unmoved by considerations of justice had to pay attention, Dudziak and Bell argue. See Mary L. Dudziak, Desegregation as a Cold War Imperative, 41 Stan. L. Rev. 61 (1988); Mary L. Dudziak, The Little Rock Crisis and Foreign Affairs: Race, Resistance, and the Image of American Democracy, 70 S. Cal. L. Rev. 1641 (1997); Derrick A. Bell, Jr., Brown v. Board of Education and the Interest-Convergence Dilemma, 93 Harv. L. Rev. 518 (1980); see also Michael J. Klarman, *Brown,* Racial Change, and the Civil Rights Movement, 80 Va. L. Rev. 7 (1994). See also the discussion of *Brown* and the Cold War in Chapter 7.

5. *Prosecutions, presentments, publicity, and pardons.* Although the executive is often said to have the power of "prosecutorial" discretion, the power is better described as one of "nonprosecutorial" discretion — the discretionary and plenary power *not* to prosecute. This is the power upheld by *Cox*— the courts may not compel or mandamus a prosecution, and neither may a grand jury. Conversely, the President's power to affirmatively prosecute can rather easily be thwarted by grand juries and courts; the former may simply refuse to agree to an indictment, and the latter may always throw the case out.

Of course, plenary power not to prosecute is capable of great abuse. But does *Cox* persuade you of some of the reasons why the power should exist — why not all crimes can or should be prosecuted, and why complete power to say no should reside in the executive branch? Note how all the judges propose *publicity* as the main check on this power — though at different stages of the game. Judge Wisdom points to the power of publicity early on — the grand jury's power to make known that it thinks something stinks, via a public presentment or report. For historical background on this key presentment power, see Akhil Reed Amar, The Bill of Rights: Creation and Reconstruction 19, 84-87 (1998). For a fascinating discussion of a grand jury's efforts to publicize perceived wrongdoing in Rocky Flats, Colorado, and a more general modern-day analysis of the presentment power, see Renee B. Lettow, Note, Reviving Federal Grand Jury Presentments, 103 Yale L.J. 1333 (1994). Judge Brown picks a slightly different mechanism of publicity, in his decision that the prosecutor must help the grand jury draft the document it seeks to publicize. The dissenters opt for a later point — in open court after the (forcibly signed) indictment has been filed. And note that even if judges were to somehow invoke Rule 48 to prevent the prosecutor from dismissing the indictment at that point, the President himself always retains the power to say no — decisively — via the pardon power vested in him by Article II. The exercise of this power of course is highly visible, satisfying the functional need to focus responsibility for controversial or dubious exercises of the power of nonprosecution. Recall that a presidential pardon may issue well before any trial or conviction, as Hamilton pointed out in The Federalist No. 69 — and as the more famous facts surrounding our next case should remind us.

United States v. Nixon, President of the United States

418 U.S. 683 (1974)

BURGER, C.J. . . .

On March 1, 1974, a grand jury of the United States District Court for the District of Columbia returned an indictment charging seven named individuals[a] with various offenses, including conspiracy to defraud the United States and to obstruct justice. Although he was not designated as such in the indictment, the grand jury named the President, among others, as an unindicted coconspirator.[b] On April 18, 1974, upon motion of the Special Prosecutor, see n.[c], infra, a subpoena duces tecum was issued . . . to the President by the United States District Court and made returnable on May 2, 1974. This subpoena required the production, in advance of the September 9 trial date, of certain tapes, memoranda, papers, transcripts, or other writings relating to certain precisely identified meetings [in the Oval Office] between the President and others. . . . On April 30, the President publicly released edited transcripts of 43 conversations; portions of 20 conversations subject to subpoena in the present case were included. On May 1, 1974, the President's counsel filed a "special appearance" and a motion to quash the subpoena [on the ground that the subpoenaed materials were within his executive privilege against disclosure of confidential communications]. . . .

II. JUSTICIABILITY

In the District Court, the President's counsel argued that the court lacked jurisdiction to issue the subpoena because the matter was an intra-branch dispute between a subordinate and superior officer of the Executive Branch and hence not subject to judicial resolution. That argument has been renewed in this Court with emphasis on the contention that the dispute does not present a "case" or "controversy" which can be adjudicated in the federal courts. The President's counsel argues that the federal courts should not intrude into areas committed to the other branches of Government. He views the present dispute as essentially a "jurisdictional" dispute within the Executive Branch which he analogizes to a dispute between two congressional committees. Since the Executive Branch has exclusive authority and absolute discretion to decide whether to prosecute a case, Confiscation Cases, 7 Wall. 454 (1869); United States v. Cox, it is contended that a President's decision is final in determining what evidence is to be used in a given criminal case. Although his counsel concedes that the President has delegated certain specific

---

a. The seven defendants were John N. Mitchell, H.R. Haldeman, John D. Ehrlichman, Charles W. Colson, Robert C. Mardian, Kenneth W. Parkinson, and Gordon Strachan. Each had occupied either a position of responsibility on the White House staff or a position with the Committee for the Re-election of the President. [John Mitchell, for example, had served as Richard Nixon's Attorney General—EDS.]

b. The cross-petition . . . raised the issue whether the grand jury acted within its authority in naming the President as an unindicted coconspirator. [W]e find resolution of this issue unnecessary to resolution of the question whether the claim of privilege is to prevail . . . [footnote relocated by editors].

powers to the Special Prosecutor, he has not "waived nor delegated to the Special Prosecutor the President's duty to claim privilege as to all materials . . . which fall within the President's inherent authority to refuse to disclose to any executive officer." The Special Prosecutor's demand for the items therefore presents, in the view of the President's counsel, a political question under Baker v. Carr, 369 U.S. 186 (1962), since it involves a "textually demonstrable" grant of power under Art. II. . . .

Our starting point is the nature of the proceeding for which the evidence is sought—here a pending criminal prosecution. It is a judicial proceeding in a federal court alleging violation of federal laws and is brought in the name of the United States as sovereign. Under the authority of Art. II, §2, Congress has vested in the Attorney General the power to conduct the criminal litigation of the United States Government. It has also vested in him the power to appoint subordinate officers to assist him in the discharge of his duties. Acting pursuant to those statutes, the Attorney General has delegated the authority to represent the United States in these particular matters to a Special Prosecutor with unique authority and tenure.[c]

The regulation gives the Special Prosecutor explicit power to contest the invocation of executive privilege in the process of seeking evidence deemed relevant to the performance of these specially delegated duties.[d] So long as this regulation is extant it has the force of law. In United States *ex rel.* Accardi v. Shaughnessy, 347 U.S. 260 (1954), regulations of the Attorney General delegated certain of his discretionary powers to the Board of Immigration Appeals and required that Board to exercise its own discretion on appeals in deportation cases. The Court held that so long as the Attorney General's regulations remained operative, he denied himself the authority to exercise the discretion delegated to the Board even though the original authority was his and he could reassert it by amending the regulations. . . .

Here, as in *Accardi*, it is theoretically possible for the Attorney General to amend or revoke the regulation defining the Special Prosecutor's authority. But he has not done so.[e] So long as this regulation remains in force the Executive Branch

---

c. The regulation issued by the Attorney General pursuant to his statutory authority, vests in the Special Prosecutor plenary authority to control the course of investigations and litigation related to "all offenses arising out of the 1972 Presidential Election . . . , allegations involving the President, members of the White House staff, or Presidential appointees . . ." In particular, the Special Prosecutor was given full authority, inter alia, "to contest the assertion of 'Executive Privilege.' . . ." The regulation then goes on to provide:

> ". . . In accordance with assurances given by the President to the Attorney General that the President will not exercise his Constitutional powers to effect the discharge of the Special Prosecutor or to limit the independence that he is hereby given, the Special Prosecutor will not be removed from his duties except for extraordinary improprieties on his part and without the President's first consulting the Majority and the Minority Leaders and Chairmen and ranking Minority Members of the Judiciary Committees of the Senate and House of Representatives and ascertaining that their consensus is in accord with his proposed action."

d. That this was the understanding of Acting Attorney General Robert Bork, the author of the regulation establishing the independence of the Special Prosecutor, is shown by his testimony before the Senate Judiciary Committee. . . . Acting Attorney General Bork gave similar assurances to the House Subcommittee on Criminal Justice. . . . At his confirmation hearings, Attorney General William Saxbe testified that he shared Acting Attorney General Bork's views concerning the Special Prosecutor's authority to test any claim of executive privilege in the courts.

is bound by it, and indeed the United States as the sovereign composed of the three branches is bound to respect and to enforce it. Moreover, the delegation of authority to the Special Prosecutor in this case is not an ordinary delegation by the Attorney General to a subordinate officer: with the authorization of the President, the Acting Attorney General provided in the regulation that the Special Prosecutor was not to be removed without the "consensus" of eight designated leaders of Congress. n.[c], supra. . . .

IV. THE CLAIM OF PRIVILEGE

A

[W]e turn to the claim that the subpoena should be quashed because it demands "confidential conversations between a President and his close advisors that it would be inconsistent with the public interest to produce." The first contention is a broad claim that the separation of powers doctrine precludes judicial review of a President's claim of privilege. The second contention is that if he does not prevail on the claim of absolute privilege, the court should hold as a matter of constitutional law that the privilege prevails over the subpoena duces tecum.

In the performance of assigned constitutional duties each branch of the Government must initially interpret the Constitution, and the interpretation of its powers by any branch is due great respect from the others. The President's counsel, as we have noted, reads the Constitution as providing an absolute privilege of confidentiality for all Presidential communications. Many decisions of this Court, however, have unequivocally reaffirmed the holding of Marbury v. Madison, that "[it] is emphatically the province and duty of the judicial department to say what the law is." No holding of the Court has defined the scope of judicial power specifically relating to the enforcement of a subpoena for confidential Presidential communications for use in a criminal prosecution, but other exercises of power by the Executive Branch and the Legislative Branch have been found invalid as in conflict with the Constitution. Powell v. McCormack, Youngstown Sheet & Tube Co. v. Sawyer. . . .

. . . "Deciding whether a matter has in any measure been committed by the Constitution to another branch of government, or whether the action of that branch exceeds whatever authority has been committed, is itself a delicate exercise in constitutional interpretation, and is a responsibility of this Court as ultimate interpreter of the Constitution."

Notwithstanding the deference each branch must accord the others, the "judicial Power of the United States" vested in the federal courts by Art. III, §1, of the Constitution can no more be shared with the Executive Branch than the Chief Executive, for example, can share with the Judiciary the veto power, or the Congress share with the Judiciary the power to override a Presidential veto. Any other conclusion would be contrary to the basic concept of separation of powers and the checks and balances that flow from the scheme of a tripartite government. We

---

e. At his confirmation hearings, Attorney General William Saxbe testified that he agreed with the regulation adopted by Acting Attorney General Bork and would not remove the Special Prosecutor except for "gross impropriety." There is no contention here that the Special Prosecutor is guilty of any such impropriety.

therefore reaffirm that it is the province and duty of this Court "to say what the law is" with respect to the claim of privilege presented in this case. *Marbury.*

B

In support of his claim of absolute privilege, the President's counsel urges two grounds, one of which is common to all governments and one of which is peculiar to our system of separation of powers. The first ground is the valid need for protection of communications between high Government officials and those who advise and assist them in the performance of their manifold duties; the importance of this confidentiality is too plain to require further discussion. Human experience teaches that those who expect public dissemination of their remarks may well temper candor with a concern for appearances and for their own interests to the detriment of the decisionmaking process.[f] Whatever the nature of the privilege of confidentiality of Presidential communications in the exercise of Art. II powers, the privilege can be said to derive from the supremacy of each branch within its own assigned area of constitutional duties. Certain powers and privileges flow from the nature of enumerated powers;[g] the protection of the confidentiality of Presidential communications has similar constitutional underpinnings.

The second ground asserted by the President's counsel in support of the claim of absolute privilege rests on the doctrine of separation of powers. Here it is argued that the independence of the Executive Branch within its own sphere, insulates a President from a judicial subpoena in an ongoing criminal prosecution, and thereby protects confidential Presidential communications.

However, neither the doctrine of separation of powers, nor the need for confidentiality of high-level communications, without more, can sustain an absolute, unqualified Presidential privilege of immunity from judicial process under all circumstances. The President's need for complete candor and objectivity from advisers calls for great deference from the courts. However, when the privilege depends solely on the broad, undifferentiated claim of public interest in the confidentiality of such conversations, a confrontation with other values arises. Absent a claim of need to protect military, diplomatic, or sensitive national security secrets, we find it difficult to accept the argument that even the very important interest in confidentiality of Presidential communications is significantly diminished by production of such material for in camera inspection with all the protection that a district court will be obliged to provide.

---

f. There is nothing novel about governmental confidentiality. The meetings of the Constitutional Convention in 1787 were conducted in complete privacy. Moreover, all records of those meetings were sealed for more than 30 years after the Convention. Most of the Framers acknowledged that without secrecy no constitution of the kind that was developed could have been written.

g. The Special Prosecutor argues that there is no provision in the Constitution for a Presidential privilege as to the President's communications corresponding to the privilege of Members of Congress under the Speech or Debate Clause. But the silence of the Constitution on this score is not dispositive. "The rule of constitutional interpretation announced in *McCulloch*, that that which was reasonably appropriate and relevant to the exercise of a granted power was to be considered as accompanying the grant, has been so universally applied that it suffices merely to state it."

The impediment that an absolute, unqualified privilege would place in the way of the primary constitutional duty of the Judicial Branch to do justice in criminal prosecutions would plainly conflict with the function of the courts under Art. III. . . .

C

Since we conclude that the legitimate needs of the judicial process may outweigh Presidential privilege, it is necessary to resolve those competing interests in a manner that preserves the essential functions of each branch. The right and indeed the duty to resolve that question does not free the Judiciary from according high respect to the representations made on behalf of the President. United States v. Burr, 25 F. Cas. 187, 190, 191-192 (No. 14,694) (CC Va. 1807).

The expectation of a President to the confidentiality of his conversations and correspondence, like the claim of confidentiality of judicial deliberations, for example, has all the values to which we accord deference for the privacy of all citizens and, added to those values, is the necessity for protection of the public interest in candid, objective, and even blunt or harsh opinions in Presidential decisionmaking. A President and those who assist him must be free to explore alternatives in the process of shaping policies and making decisions and to do so in a way many would be unwilling to express except privately. These are the considerations justifying a presumptive privilege for Presidential communications. The privilege is fundamental to the operation of Government and inextricably rooted in the separation of powers under the Constitution. . . . We agree with Mr. Chief Justice Marshall's observation, therefore, that "[in] no case of this kind would a court be required to proceed against the president as against an ordinary individual." United States v. Burr.

But this presumptive privilege must be considered in light of our historic commitment to the rule of law. This is nowhere more profoundly manifest than in our view that "the twofold aim [of criminal justice] is that guilt shall not escape or innocence suffer." . . . The ends of criminal justice would be defeated if judgments were to be founded on a partial or speculative presentation of the facts. The very integrity of the judicial system and public confidence in the system depend on full disclosure of all the facts, within the framework of the rules of evidence. To ensure that justice is done, it is imperative to the function of courts that compulsory process be available for the production of evidence needed either by the prosecution or by the defense.

Only recently the Court restated the ancient proposition of law, albeit in the context of a grand jury inquiry rather than a trial, "that 'the public . . . has a right to every man's evidence,' except for those persons protected by a constitutional, common-law, or statutory privilege." The privileges referred to by the Court are designed to protect weighty and legitimate competing interests. Thus, the Fifth Amendment to the Constitution provides that no man "shall be compelled in any criminal case to be a witness against himself." And, generally, an attorney or a priest may not be required to disclose what has been revealed in professional confidence. These and other interests are recognized in law by privileges against forced disclosure, established in the Constitution, by statute, or at common law. Whatever their origins, these exceptions to the demand for every man's evidence are not lightly created nor expansively construed, for they are in derogation of the search for truth. In this case the President . . . does not place his claim of privilege on the ground they are military or diplomatic secrets. As to these areas of Art. II duties the courts have traditionally shown the utmost deference to Presidential responsibilities. In C. & S. Air Lines v. Waterman S.S. Corp., 333 U.S. 103, 111 (1948), dealing with Presidential authority involving foreign policy considerations, the Court said:

> "The President, both as Commander-in-Chief and as the Nation's organ for foreign affairs, has available intelligence services whose reports are not and ought not to be published to the world. It would be intolerable that courts, without the relevant information, should review and perhaps nullify actions of the Executive taken on information properly held secret."

In United States v. Reynolds, 345 U.S. 1 (1953), dealing with a claimant's demand for evidence in a Tort Claims Act case against the Government, the Court said:

> "It may be possible to satisfy the court, from all the circumstances of the case, that there is a reasonable danger that compulsion of the evidence will expose military matters which, in the interest of national security, should not be divulged. When this is the case, the occasion for the privilege is appropriate, and the court should not jeopardize the security which the privilege is meant to protect by insisting upon an examination of the evidence, even by the judge alone, in chambers."

No case of the Court, however, has extended this high degree of deference to a President's generalized interest in confidentiality. Nowhere in the Constitution, as we have noted earlier, is there any explicit reference to a privilege of confidentiality, yet to the extent this interest relates to the effective discharge of a President's powers, it is constitutionally based.

The right to the production of all evidence at a criminal trial similarly has constitutional dimensions. The Sixth Amendment explicitly confers upon every defendant in a criminal trial the right "to be confronted with the witnesses against him" and "to have compulsory process for obtaining witnesses in his favor." Moreover, the Fifth Amendment also guarantees that no person shall be deprived of liberty without due process of law. It is the manifest duty of the courts to vindicate those guarantees, and to accomplish that it is essential that all relevant and admissible evidence be produced.

In this case we must weigh the importance of the general privilege of confidentiality of Presidential communications in performance of the President's responsibilities against the inroads of such a privilege on the fair administration of criminal justice. The interest in preserving confidentiality is weighty indeed and entitled to great respect. However, we cannot conclude that advisers will be moved to temper the candor of their remarks by the infrequent occasions of disclosure because of the possibility that such conversations will be called for in the context of a criminal prosecution.

On the other hand, the allowance of the privilege to withhold evidence that is demonstrably relevant in a criminal trial would cut deeply into the guarantee of due process of law and gravely impair the basic function of the courts. . . . Without access to specific facts a criminal prosecution may be totally frustrated. The President's broad interest in confidentiality of communications will not be vitiated by disclosure of a limited number of conversations preliminarily shown to have some bearing on the pending criminal cases.

We conclude that when the ground for asserting privilege as to subpoenaed materials sought for use in a criminal trial is based only on the generalized interest in confidentiality, it cannot prevail over the fundamental demands of due process of law in the fair administration of criminal justice. The generalized assertion of privilege must yield to the demonstrated, specific need for evidence in a pending criminal trial. . . .

We now turn to the important question of the District Court's responsibilities in conducting the in camera examination of Presidential materials or communications delivered under the compulsion of the subpoena duces tecum.

E

. . . Statements that meet the test of admissibility and relevance must be isolated; all other material must be excised. . . . It is elementary that in camera inspection of evidence is always a procedure calling for scrupulous protection against any release or publication of material not found by the court, at that stage, probably admissible in evidence and relevant to the issues of the trial for which it is sought. That being true of an ordinary situation, it is obvious that the District Court has a very heavy responsibility to see to it that Presidential conversations, which are either not relevant or not admissible, are accorded that high degree of respect due the President of the United States. Mr. Chief Justice Marshall, sitting as a trial judge in the *Burr* case, supra, was extraordinarily careful to point out that "[in] no case of this kind would a court be required to proceed against the president as against an ordinary individual."

. . . The need for confidentiality even as to idle conversations with associates in which casual reference might be made concerning political leaders within the country or foreign statesmen is too obvious to call for further treatment. We have no doubt that the District Judge will at all times accord to Presidential records that high degree of deference suggested in United States v. Burr, supra, and will discharge his responsibility to see to it that until released to the Special Prosecutor no in camera material is revealed to anyone. This burden applies with even greater force to excised material; once the decision is made to excise, the material is restored to its privileged status and should be returned under seal to its lawful custodian.

Mr. Justice REHNQUIST took no part in the consideration or decision of these cases.

DISCUSSION

1. *Article II hierarchy and justiciability.* The Court in passing analogizes the dispute between Richard Nixon and Leon Jaworski to one between two congressional committees, but wasn't it more akin to a dispute between the Senate and a staffer, or the Court and a law clerk? Constitutionally, Nixon was *chief* executive, and the special prosecutor was an executive-branch *inferior* officer, who had been handpicked by the Attorney General, who in turn had been handpicked by the President.

Moreover, Nixon had been elected by the nation, whereas Jaworski and his predecessor Archibald Cox had not even been confirmed by the Senate. Why does the Court downplay this obvious hierarchy? Given that Jaworski was nothing more than Nixon's subordinate, wouldn't a more accurate case caption have been Nixon (inferior) v. Nixon (real)? If so, how was this dispute justiciable? If Jaworski wanted the tapes disclosed for good executive-branch reasons (the need to prosecute criminals) and Nixon wanted the tapes kept secret for good executive-branch reasons (the need for Oval Office confidentiality), why shouldn't the *chief* executive ordinarily and obviously have the last word on this dispute about executive-branch policy?

2. *Presentments, publicity, politics, and prosecutions.* The Court's answer leans heavily on the fact that the Nixon Administration had lawfully delegated certain powers to the Special Prosecutor. But the Court also concedes that the Nixon Administration is free simply to rescind the regulation unilaterally—and *then,* Nixon could tell Jaworski what to do or where to go. Thus, the Court admits that at the end of the day, Nixon does legally have the last word—but only if he first (through his Attorney General) rescinds the regulation. Why are the Justices insisting that Nixon jump through two hoops? Why isn't it enough that in their very courtroom, the President was clearly saying that he disagreed with his inferior about the proper discharge of executive-branch business?

The best answer is one the Court never states forthrightly: Richard Nixon was a crook, using the Oval Office as the hub of an ongoing criminal conspiracy to obstruct justice, and the Court already had evidence under seal that proved this. If Nixon wanted to fire or countermand Jaworksi, he would not get a finger of support from the Justices; he would have to do it himself (twice) at high noon on Main Street, for all to see. There is an obvious connection here to the publicity idea of *Cox*; in effect, the Court is forcing Nixon to attempt his whitewash in broad daylight. Politically, of course, this put Nixon in an impossible position, after he and his Administration had assured the people, the press, and the Congress that he would not fire Jaworski the way he had fired Archibald Cox, in the notorious "Saturday Night Massacre." Note how the Court subtly relies on these representations in its opinion. Note also how the grand jury, by naming Nixon as an "unindicted" coconspirator, in effect issued a kind of presentment, which (when leaked) had precisely the publicity effect predicted by Judge Wisdom in *Cox*.

3. *Pardon me?* Putting aside rescission of the regulation, are there any other ways in which Richard Nixon could, à la Coase, have somehow "contracted around" the result in the Tapes Case? Note that even after the Justices' decision, Nixon in theory retained the power to pardon Mitchell, Haldeman, Erlichman, et al. Had he done so, the pending criminal lawsuits against these defendants would have evaporated, and so too would the specific subpoenas these lawsuits had generated. Of course, such high-visibility pardons would doubtless have immediately led to a complete collapse of Nixon's political base. Impeachment proceedings—already well underway when the Justices sat—would surely have accelerated, and Congress in these proceedings would have demanded the tapes, and treated any refusal to hand them over as *itself* an impeachable offense. (Note that the Constitution explicitly denies the President the power to pardon in a case of impeachment.) These theoretical possibilities remind us that the legal decision in the Supreme Court was nested in a broader political and constitutional context in which the President retained certain formal legal powers that, politically, were unavailable to him.

Instead of pardoning or rescinding, Nixon chose to comply with the Court's order, and when the tapes came out, they quickly led to Nixon's resignation. Soon thereafter, newly installed President Gerald Ford issued a full (and highly visible) pardon to Nixon; but Ford paid a heavy political price—many believe that this cost him the election against Jimmy Carter in 1976.

4. *The legislative veto problem.* Chief Justice Burger claims that the regulation vesting Jaworski with various powers has "the force of law." But as a law, it seems constitutionally suspect, vesting certain congressional barons with a legislative veto over an inherently executive decision—whether to fire a wholly executive-branch official. As President Washington and Congressman Madison helped establish early on, in one of the most important constitutional settlements of the early Republic, the President alone decides whom to fire within the executive branch; Congress members can jawbone, but cannot legally obstruct any purely executive-branch removal. To be sure, later political disputes muddied the waters—Andrew Johnson in 1868 was impeached by the House and nearly convicted by the Senate when he fired the Secretary of War without Senate approval. But early in the twentieth century, the Court emphatically endorsed President Washington's view in the landmark case of Myers v. United States, 272 U.S. 52 (1926). Authored by Chief Justice (and former President and Yale Law professor) William Howard Taft, *Myers* stood as a towering precedent in 1974, when *Nixon* was decided. If anything, *Myers*'s condemnation of legislative vetoes stands even taller today, in light of INS v. Chadha, 462 U.S. 919 (1983), Bowsher v. Synar, 478 U.S. 714 (1986), and Morrison v. Olson 487 U.S. 654 (1988), discussed infra, all of which reiterated its teaching on this point. Consider also what the *Nixon* Court itself says only a few pages after treating this regulation as "law":

> [T]he "judicial Power of the United States" vested in the federal courts by Art. III, §1, of the Constitution can no more be shared with the Executive Branch than the Chief Executive, for example, can share with the Judiciary the veto power, or the Congress share with the Judiciary the power to override a Presidential veto. Any other conclusion would be contrary to the basic concept of separation of powers. . . .

How, it might be asked, is it any different if the President seeks as a matter of law to share the removal power with Congress?

If the Nixon regulation could not properly count as "law" in a courtroom, what function did it serve? A political scientist would probably see this regulation as a read-my-lips political promise designed for public consumption more than judicial doctrine; through this "regulation," Nixon was precommitting himself politically, credibly guaranteeing that if he later violated this promise he would pay a huge political penalty.

5. *The meaning of* Marbury. Does *Marbury* stand for the proposition that the Supreme Court is "the ultimate interpreter of the Constitution"? If so, where does Chief Justice Marshall say that? If not, where does the modern Court get this idea? (Note that this specific phrase itself makes its first appearance in *U.S. Reports* in 1962.) Does *Marbury* mean that the Constitution should never be read as decisively committing certain issues to the political branches? Does *Marbury* mean that other branches must defer to the Court even if they have a more expansive vision of the constitutional right in question? For example, suppose that a newspaper reporter, subpoenaed to provide information given to her by a confidential source, refuses

to comply, claiming that she has a reporter's privilege under the First Amendment. If the Supreme Court were to reject her argument, would *Marbury* mean that the President *must* allow his subordinates to prosecute her, even if he agrees with her position? Cf. Judge Wisdom's opinion in *Cox*, supra, at note a (discussing nonprosecution policy of Attorney General Robert Jackson). Would *Marbury* prevent the President from pardoning her? (Recall once again that President Jefferson pardoned those convicted of violating the 1798 Sedition Act.) If the President in these cases may permissibly have a broader view of the constitutional right—and make that broader view stick—why not in *Nixon*? Why, in other words, is a broader view of the confidentiality privilege under Article II any different than a broader view of the confidentiality privilege under Amendment I? Because Nixon is in effect playing two roles—privilege claimant and President—in a way that makes us especially wary of self-dealing? Because we know that Nixon was a crook, trying to use the privilege to cover up his own wrongdoing?

Is the Court's overblown rhetoric about its own role perhaps a reflection of fear that the President might try to defy a Court order, making the Justices look impotent or plunging the country into a genuine crisis? Might this also account for the Court's unanimity? For a provocative discussion, see Michael Stokes Paulsen, Nixon Now: The Courts and the Presidency After Twenty-Five Years, 83 Minn. L. Rev. 1337 (1999).

6. *The irrelevance of* Burr *and the Bill of Rights.* In United States v. Burr, an 1807 lower court case decided by John Marshall riding circuit, Marshall had subpoenaed various documents from President Jefferson. In *Nixon*, Chief Justice Burger repeatedly insists that Marshall's subpoena was indistinguishable from the one sought by Jaworski. But isn't the distinction obvious, especially to anyone who has read *Cox*? In *Burr*, a criminal defendant (former Vice President Aaron Burr) sought to subpoena evidence to prove his innocence, whereas in *Nixon*, the "government" (i.e., Jaworski) sought to subpoena evidence to prove the guilt of various criminal defendants. Fundamental issues of due process and fairness were at stake in *Burr*: The government cannot prosecute a man while suppressing evidence of his innocence. See, e.g., Brady v. Maryland, 373 U.S. 83 (1963) (discussing the general duty of prosecutors to disclose exculpatory evidence upon request). Had Jefferson resisted the subpoena—on the perfectly legitimate ground that the evidence sought was too confidential to be disclosed—Marshall would never have tried to coerce the President to surrender the stuff. Instead, the great judge would simply have dismissed the prosecution, and released the defendant. The Constitution and laws nowhere demanded that Burr *must* be prosecuted; they merely required that *if* prosecuted, he be given exculpatory evidence. *Burr* thus respected the President's right to decide the executive-branch policy question at hand: It was left wholly up to Jefferson to choose which was more important to him—getting Burr convicted, or keeping confidential communications secret.

But in *Nixon*, Chief Justice Burger turns *Burr* upside down, insisting that due process demands that all possible evidence of the criminal defendants' guilt *must* be produced, even if both the defendants and the President prefer otherwise. This view finds no support in the text or history of the Due Process Clause, which protects a "person" from unfair government prosecution (as in *Burr*), but says nothing about any government right or duty to prosecute every possible defendant using every possible scrap of evidence. Indeed, Burger's views here reflect a reading of due process never seen before nor since in *U.S. Reports*. (Recall the *Cox* court's reminder that the Fifth Amendment is a shield of the defendant.) Burger also oddly invokes the Sixth Amendment, which pointedly speaks of the rights of "the accused" to produce exculpatory evidence but, once again, says nothing about any government right or duty to produce all inculpatory evidence. Indeed, at times Burger seems to imply that any rule limiting prosecutors' ability to procure "all relevant and admissible evidence" is constitutionally suspect. Does he really mean to cast doubt on a great range of traditional evidentiary privileges—attorney-client, priest-penitent, doctor-patient, husband-wife, and so on? Would Congress be barred, after the Tapes Case, from passing a statute defining a broader executive privilege than the Court was prepared to recognize? (Doubtless this broader privilege would interfere with truth-seeking in some judicial cases—but isn't that true of all privileges?)

7. *The structural basis for executive privilege. Nixon* does purport to recognize a limited privilege for confidential Oval Office conversations, but says this executive privilege should be balanced against the judicial need for evidence. In this balance, the need for confidentiality is ordinarily outweighed (absent national security concerns) if the evidence sought for a judicial proceeding is specific, admissible, and relevant. But isn't this a rather puny privilege, on balance? After all, *anyone* can resist a subpoena that is overbroad or irrelevant. Thus, on Burger's logic, essential and wholly proper (but politically sensitive) conversations in the Oval Office are entitled to less legal protection than conversations between spouses or between attorneys and clients.

For example, suppose the President is considering whether to appoint Jane Doe to some high post. This is a key part of his job, as specified by the Constitution's Article II Appointments Clause. Aides brief the President on possible dirt on Doe, her friends, and family, reporting both facts and rumors. This information might bear on Doe's fitness and also might come up in the press or in a Senate confirmation. For the President to do the job the Constitution assigns him, it is necessary and proper—indeed imperative—that he receive this confidential information. But the Tapes Case, if we take its due-process, truth-over-privilege logic seriously, suggests that any county prosecutor in a state criminal case, or any plaintiff in a civil case, could subpoena this conversation in a lawsuit designed to embarrass Doe and/or the President. If so, aides will hesitate to tell the President what he needs to know to do his job. Are we back to Mississippi trumping the nation, as Judge Wisdom worried?

Admittedly, the Constitution does not create executive privilege in so many words. But it does create a system of federalism and separation of powers. And so the best argument for executive privilege is structural, and runs something like this: As a matter of federalism, state and local prosecutors should not be allowed to disrupt the proper performance of national executive functions. Cf. *McCulloch*; see also Charles L. Black, Jr., Structure and Relationship in Constitutional Law (1969). As a matter of separation of powers, each branch must have some internal space—a separate house, if you will—to ponder its delicate business free from the intermeddling of other branches. Senators must be free to talk candidly and confidentially amongst themselves and with staff in cloakrooms; judges must enjoy comparable freedom in superconfidential judicial conferences, and in conversations with law clerks; jurors in the jury room ordinarily deliberate together with absolute secrecy to promote candor; and the same basic principle holds true for the presidency and the Oval Office. This principle was explicitly affirmed by the Supreme Court in no less a case than Marbury v. Madison. When Attorney General Levi Lincoln hesitated to answer certain questions about what President Jefferson had confided to him, feeling "himself bound to maintain the rights of the executive," the *Marbury* Court reassured him that "if he thought that any thing was communicated to him in confidence he was not bound to disclose it." Why does Burger omit all mention of *this* (highly relevant, it seems) part of *Marbury*?

8. *Just the facts, ma'am (again).* If the foregoing analysis is accepted, the Nixon Tapes Case reached the right result, but with sloppily overbroad reasoning that failed to identify some of the important—and limiting—facts in the case at hand. Here is what the Court could have said—but did not, quite:

> "The executive power vested in the President by the sweeping words of Article II includes the general right to decide who shall be criminally prosecuted, and how, and also the right to keep confidential good-faith conversations with executive-branch aides about proper executive-branch policy. But, like other privileges in our law, executive privilege has limits and exceptions. Under the well-established crime-fraud exception, attorneys cannot invoke lawyer-client privilege when independent evidence confirms that they are trying to shield from view ongoing criminal misconduct and obstruction of justice. Likewise, the presumptive privilege shielding conversations among jurors yields when there is independent evidence that a juror has been bribed and is using the jury room itself to obstruct justice. Similarly, conversations by executive officials planning ongoing crimes are not protected by Article II. The conversations sought by Jaworski are conversations among persons designated by the grand jury as co-conspirators—including Nixon himself, though the President was not indicted (and perhaps could not be constitutionally indicted). The evidence under seal already in the Court's possession provides strong and independent confirmation of this conspiracy. And the conversations sought by Jaworski are not merely evidence of the conspiracy—they are the conspiracy itself. (The essence of a 'conspiracy,' of course, is an agreement among persons effected by words.) Under these unusual circumstances, executive privilege yields."

Chief Justice Burger instead wrote a sweeping opinion that had the virtue of not attacking Richard Nixon personally—and not highlighting certain indelicate facts—but, perhaps, the vice of making little sense when honestly applied to honest Presidents.

Trump v. Vance

140 S. Ct. 2412 (2020)

Chief Justice ROBERTS delivered the opinion of the Court.

In our judicial system, "the public has a right to every man's evidence." Since the earliest days of the Republic, "every man" has included the President of the United States. Beginning with Jefferson and carrying on through Clinton, Presidents have uniformly testified or produced documents in criminal proceedings when called upon by federal courts. This case involves—so far as we and the parties can tell—the first *state* criminal subpoena directed to a President. The President contends that the subpoena is unenforceable. We granted certiorari to decide whether Article II and the Supremacy Clause categorically preclude, or require a heightened standard for, the issuance of a state criminal subpoena to a sitting President.

I

In the summer of 2018, the New York County District Attorney's Office opened an investigation into what it opaquely describes as "business transactions involving multiple individuals whose conduct may have violated state law." A year later, the office—acting on behalf of a grand jury—served a subpoena *duces tecum* (essentially a request to produce evidence) on Mazars USA, LLP, the personal accounting firm of President Donald J. Trump. The subpoena directed Mazars to produce financial records relating to the President and business organizations affiliated with him, including "[t]ax returns and related schedules," from "2011 to the present."

The President, acting in his personal capacity, sued the district attorney and Mazars in Federal District Court to enjoin enforcement of the subpoena. He argued that, under Article II and the Supremacy Clause, a sitting President enjoys absolute immunity from state criminal process. He asked the court to issue a "declaratory judgment that the subpoena is invalid and unenforceable while the President is in office" and to permanently enjoin the district attorney "from taking any action to enforce the subpoena." Mazars, concluding that the dispute was between the President and the district attorney, took no position on the legal issues raised by the President. . . . [The District Court and the Second Circuit rejected the President's request for an injunction.] We granted certiorari.

II

In the summer of 1807, all eyes were on Richmond, Virginia. Aaron Burr, the former Vice President, was on trial for treason. Fallen from political grace after his fatal duel with Alexander Hamilton, and with a murder charge pending in New Jersey, Burr followed the path of many down-and-out Americans of his day—he headed West in search of new opportunity. But Burr was a man with outsized ambitions. Together with General James Wilkinson, the Governor of the Louisiana Territory, he hatched a plan to establish a new territory in Mexico, then controlled by Spain. Both men anticipated that war between the United States and Spain was imminent, and when it broke out they intended to invade Spanish territory at the head of a private army.

But while Burr was rallying allies to his cause, tensions with Spain eased and rumors began to swirl that Burr was conspiring to detach States by the Allegheny Mountains from the Union. Wary of being exposed as the principal co-conspirator, Wilkinson took steps to ensure that any blame would fall on Burr. He sent a series of letters to President Jefferson accusing Burr of plotting to attack New Orleans and revolutionize the Louisiana Territory.

Jefferson, who despised his former running mate Burr for trying to steal the 1800 presidential election from him, was predisposed to credit Wilkinson's version of events. The President sent a special message to Congress identifying Burr as the "prime mover" in a plot "against the peace and safety of the Union." According to Jefferson, Burr contemplated either the "severance of the Union" or an attack on Spanish territory. Jefferson acknowledged that his sources contained a "mixture of rumors, conjectures, and suspicions" but, citing Wilkinson's letters, he assured Congress that Burr's guilt was "beyond question."

The trial that followed was "the greatest spectacle in the short history of the republic," complete with a Founder-studded cast. People flocked to Richmond to watch, massing in tents and covered wagons along the banks of the James River, nearly doubling the town's population of 5,000. Burr's defense team included Edmund Randolph and Luther Martin, both former delegates at the Constitutional Convention and renowned advocates. Chief Justice John Marshall, who had recently squared off with the Jefferson administration in *Marbury v. Madison,* 1 Cranch 137 (1803), presided as Circuit Justice for Virginia. Meanwhile Jefferson, intent on conviction, orchestrated the prosecution from afar, dedicating Cabinet meetings to the case, peppering the prosecutors with directions, and spending nearly $100,000 from the Treasury on the five-month proceedings.

In the lead-up to trial, Burr, taking aim at his accusers, moved for a subpoena *duces tecum* directed at Jefferson. The draft subpoena required the President to produce an October 21, 1806 letter from Wilkinson and accompanying documents, which Jefferson had referenced in his message to Congress. The prosecution opposed the request, arguing that a President could not be subjected to such a subpoena and that the letter might contain state secrets. Following four days of argument, Marshall announced his ruling to a packed chamber.

The President, Marshall declared, does not "stand exempt from the general provisions of the constitution" or, in particular, the Sixth Amendment's guarantee that those accused have compulsory process for obtaining witnesses for their defense. *United States v. Burr,* 25 F. Cas. 30, 33-34 (No. 14,692d) (CC Va. 1807). At common law the "single reservation" to the duty to testify in response to a subpoena was "the case of the king," whose "dignity" was seen as "incompatible" with appearing "under the process of the court." But, as Marshall explained, a king is born to power and can "do no wrong." The President, by contrast, is "of the people" and subject to the law. According to Marshall, the sole argument for exempting the President from testimonial obligations was that his "duties as chief magistrate demand his whole time for national objects." But, in Marshall's assessment, those demands were "not unremitting." And should the President's duties preclude his attendance at a particular time and place, a court could work that out upon return of the subpoena.

Marshall also rejected the prosecution's argument that the President was immune from a subpoena *duces tecum* because executive papers might contain state secrets. "A subpoena duces tecum," he said, "may issue to any person to whom an ordinary subpoena may issue." As he explained, no "fair construction" of the Constitution supported the conclusion that the right "to compel the attendance of witnesses[ ] does not extend" to requiring those witnesses to "bring[ ] with them such papers as may be material in the defence." And, as a matter of basic fairness, permitting such information to be withheld would "tarnish the reputation of the court." As for "the propriety of introducing any papers," that would "depend on the character of the paper, not on the character of the person who holds it." Marshall acknowledged that the papers sought by Burr could contain information "the disclosure of which would endanger the public safety," but stated that, again, such concerns would have "due consideration" upon the return of the subpoena.

While the arguments unfolded, Jefferson, who had received word of the motion, wrote to the prosecutor indicating that he would—subject to the prerogative to decide which executive communications should be withheld—"furnish on all occasions, whatever the purposes of justice may require." His "personal attendance," however, was out of the question, for it "would leave the nation without" the "sole branch which the constitution requires to be always in function."

Before Burr received the subpoenaed documents, Marshall rejected the prosecution's core legal theory for treason and Burr was accordingly acquitted. Jefferson, however, was not done. Committed to salvaging a conviction, he directed the prosecutors to proceed with a misdemeanor (yes, misdemeanor) charge for inciting war against Spain. Burr then renewed his request for Wilkinson's October 21 letter, which he later received a copy of, and subpoenaed a second letter, dated November 12, 1806, which the prosecutor claimed was privileged. Acknowledging that the President may withhold information to protect public safety, Marshall instructed that Jefferson should "state the particular reasons" for withholding the letter. *United States v. Burr*, 25 F. Cas. 187, 192 (No. 14,694) (CC Va. 1807). The court, paying "all proper respect" to those reasons, would then decide whether to compel disclosure. But that decision was averted when the misdemeanor trial was cut short after it became clear that the prosecution lacked the evidence to convict.

In the two centuries since the Burr trial, successive Presidents have accepted Marshall's ruling that the Chief Executive is subject to subpoena. In 1818, President Monroe received a subpoena to testify in a court-martial against one of his appointees. His Attorney General, William Wirt—who had served as a prosecutor during Burr's trial—advised Monroe that, per Marshall's ruling, a subpoena to testify may "be properly awarded to the President." Monroe offered to sit for a deposition and ultimately submitted answers to written interrogatories.

Following Monroe's lead, his successors have uniformly agreed to testify when called in criminal proceedings, provided they could do so at a time and place of their choosing. In 1875, President Grant submitted to a three-hour deposition in the criminal prosecution of a political appointee embroiled in a network of tax-evading whiskey distillers. A century later, President Ford's attempted assassin subpoenaed him to testify in her defense. See *United States v. Fromme*, 405 F. Supp. 578 (ED Cal. 1975). Ford obliged—from a safe distance—in the first videotaped deposition of a President. President Carter testified via the same means in the trial of two local officials who, while Carter was Governor of Georgia, had offered to contribute to his campaign in exchange for advance warning of any state gambling raids. Two years later, Carter gave videotaped testimony to a federal grand jury investigating whether a fugitive financier had entreated the White House to quash his extradition proceedings. President Clinton testified three times, twice via deposition pursuant to subpoenas in federal criminal trials of associates implicated during the Whitewater investigation, and once by video for a grand jury investigating possible perjury.

The bookend to Marshall's ruling came in 1974 when the question he never had to decide—whether to compel the disclosure of official communications over the objection of the President—came to a head. That spring, the Special Prosecutor appointed to investigate the break-in of the Democratic National Committee Headquarters at the Watergate complex filed an indictment charging seven defendants associated with President Nixon and naming Nixon as an unindicted co-conspirator. As the case moved toward trial, the Special Prosecutor secured a subpoena *duces tecum* directing Nixon to produce, among other things, tape recordings of Oval Office meetings. Nixon moved to quash the subpoena, claiming that the Constitution provides an absolute privilege of confidentiality to all presidential communications. This Court rejected that argument in *United States v. Nixon*, 418 U.S. 683 (1974), a decision we later described as "unequivocally and emphatically endors[ing] Marshall's" holding that Presidents are subject to subpoena. *Clinton v. Jones*, 520 U.S. 681, 704 (1997).

The *Nixon* Court readily acknowledged the importance of preserving the confidentiality of communications "between high Government officials and those who advise and assist them." . . . But, like Marshall two centuries prior, the Court recognized the countervailing interests at stake. Invoking the common law maxim that "the public has a right to every man's evidence," the Court observed that the public interest in fair and accurate judicial proceedings is at its height in the criminal setting, where our common commitment to justice demands that "guilt shall not escape" nor "innocence suffer." Because these dual aims would be "defeated if judgments" were "founded on a partial or speculative presentation of the facts," the *Nixon* Court recognized that it was "imperative" that "compulsory process be available for the production of evidence needed either by the prosecution or the defense."

The Court thus concluded that the President's "generalized assertion of privilege must yield to the demonstrated, specific need for evidence in a pending criminal trial." Two weeks later, President Nixon dutifully released the tapes.

III

The history surveyed above all involved *federal* criminal proceedings. Here we are confronted for the first time with a subpoena issued to the President by a local grand jury operating under the supervision of a *state* court. . . . While the subpoena was directed to the President's accounting firm, the parties agree that the papers at issue belong to the President and that Mazars is merely the custodian. Thus, for purposes of immunity, it is functionally a subpoena issued to the President. [relocated footnote—Eds.]

[The] President. . . . argues that the Supremacy Clause gives a sitting President absolute immunity from state criminal subpoenas because compliance with those subpoenas would categorically impair a President's performance of his Article II functions. The Solicitor General . . . urges us to resolve this case by holding that a state grand jury subpoena for a sitting President's personal records must, at the very least, "satisfy a heightened standard of need," which the Solicitor General contends was not met here.

A

. . .

Marshall's ruling in *Burr*, entrenched by 200 years of practice and our decision in *Nixon*, confirms that *federal* criminal subpoenas do not "rise to the level of constitutionally forbidden impairment of the Executive's ability to perform its constitutionally mandated functions." *Clinton*. But the President, joined in part by the Solicitor General, argues that *state* criminal subpoenas pose a unique threat of impairment and thus demand greater protection. To be clear, the President does not contend here that *this* subpoena, in particular, is impermissibly burdensome. Instead he makes a *categorical* argument about the burdens generally associated with state criminal subpoenas, focusing on three: diversion, stigma, and harassment. . . .

1

The President's primary contention, which the Solicitor General supports, is that complying with state criminal subpoenas would necessarily divert the Chief Executive from his duties. . . . He grounds that concern in *Nixon v. Fitzgerald*, which recognized a President's "absolute immunity from damages liability predicated on his official acts." . . . [W]e expressly rejected immunity based on distraction alone 15 years later in *Clinton v. Jones* . . . [when] President Clinton argued that the risk of being "distracted by the need to participate in litigation" entitled a sitting President to absolute immunity from civil liability, not just for official acts, as in *Fitzgerald*, but for private conduct as well. We disagreed with that rationale, explaining that the "dominant concern" in *Fitzgerald* was not mere distraction but the distortion of the Executive's "decisionmaking process" with respect to official acts that would stem from "worry as to the possibility of damages." The Court recognized that Presidents constantly face myriad demands on their attention, "some private, some political, and some as a result of official duty." But, the Court concluded, "[w]hile such distractions may be vexing to those subjected to them, they do not ordinarily implicate constitutional . . . concerns."

The same is true of criminal subpoenas. Just as a "properly managed" civil suit is generally "unlikely to occupy any substantial amount of" a President's time or attention, two centuries of experience confirm that a properly tailored criminal subpoena will not normally hamper the performance of the President's constitutional duties. If anything, we expect that in the mine run of cases, where a President is subpoenaed during a proceeding targeting someone else, as Jefferson was, the burden on a President will ordinarily be lighter than the burden of defending against a civil suit.

The President, however, believes the district attorney is investigating him and his businesses. In such a situation, he contends, the "toll that criminal process . . . exacts from the President is even heavier" than the distraction at issue in *Fitzgerald* and *Clinton*, because "criminal litigation" poses unique burdens on the President's time and will generate a "considerable if not overwhelming degree of mental preoccupation."

But the President is not seeking immunity from the diversion occasioned by the prospect of future criminal *liability*. Instead he concedes—consistent with the position of the Department of Justice—that state grand juries are free to investigate a sitting President with an eye toward charging him after the completion of his term. . . . The President's objection therefore must be limited to the *additional* distraction caused by the subpoena itself. But that argument runs up against the 200 years of precedent establishing that Presidents, and their official communications, are subject to judicial process, see *Burr*, even when the President is under investigation, see *Nixon*.

2

The President next claims that the stigma of being subpoenaed will undermine his leadership at home and abroad. Notably, the Solicitor General does not endorse this argument, perhaps because we have twice denied absolute immunity claims by Presidents in cases involving allegations of serious misconduct. See *Clinton*; *Nixon*. But even if a tarnished reputation were a cognizable impairment, there is nothing inherently stigmatizing about a President performing "the citizen's normal duty of . . . furnishing information relevant" to a criminal investigation. *Branzburg v. Hayes*, 408 U.S. 665, 691 (1972). Nor can we accept that the risk of association with persons or activities under criminal investigation can absolve a President of such an important public duty. Prior Presidents have weathered these associations in federal cases, and there is no reason to think any attendant notoriety is necessarily greater in state court proceedings.

To be sure, the consequences for a President's public standing will likely increase if he is the one under investigation. But, again, the President concedes that such investigations are permitted under Article II and the Supremacy Clause, and receipt of a subpoena would not seem to categorically magnify the harm to the President's reputation.

Additionally, while the current suit has cast the Mazars subpoena into the spotlight, longstanding rules of grand jury secrecy aim to prevent the very stigma the President anticipates. . . . [T]hose who make unauthorized disclosures regarding a grand jury subpoena do so at their peril. See, *e.g.*, N.Y. Penal Law Ann. § 215.70 (West 2010) (designating unlawful grand jury disclosure as a felony).

3

Finally, the President and the Solicitor General warn that subjecting Presidents to state criminal subpoenas will make them "easily identifiable target[s]" for harassment. *Fitzgerald*. But we rejected a nearly identical argument in *Clinton*, where then-President Clinton argued that permitting civil liability for unofficial acts would "generate a large volume of politically motivated harassing and frivolous litigation." The President and the Solicitor General nevertheless argue that state criminal subpoenas pose a heightened risk and could undermine the President's ability to "deal fearlessly and impartially" with the States. They caution that, while federal prosecutors are accountable to and removable by the President, the 2,300 district attorneys in this country are responsive to local constituencies, local interests, and local prejudices, and might "use criminal process to register their dissatisfaction with" the President. What is more, we are told, the state courts supervising local grand juries may not exhibit the same respect that federal courts show to the President as a coordinate branch of Government.

We recognize, as does the district attorney, that harassing subpoenas could, under certain circumstances, threaten the independence or effectiveness of the

Executive. Even so, in *Clinton* we found that the risk of harassment was not "serious" because federal courts have the tools to deter and, where necessary, dismiss vexatious civil suits. And, while we cannot ignore the possibility that state prosecutors may have political motivations, here again the law already seeks to protect against the predicted abuse.

First, grand juries are prohibited from engaging in "arbitrary fishing expeditions" and initiating investigations "out of malice or an intent to harass." . . . These protections, as the district attorney himself puts it, "apply with special force to a President, in light of the office's unique position as the head of the Executive Branch." And, in the event of such harassment, a President would be entitled to the protection of federal courts. The policy against federal interference in state criminal proceedings, while strong, allows "intervention in those cases where the District Court properly finds that the state proceeding is motivated by a desire to harass or is conducted in bad faith." *Huffman v. Pursue, Ltd.*, 420 U.S. 592, 611 (1975).

Second, contrary to Justice Alito's characterization, our holding does not allow States to "run roughshod over the functioning of [the Executive B]ranch." The Supremacy Clause prohibits state judges and prosecutors from interfering with a President's official duties. See, *e.g.*, *Tennessee v. Davis*, 100 U.S. 257, 263 (1880) ("No State government can . . . obstruct [the] authorized officers" of the Federal Government.). Any effort to manipulate a President's policy decisions or to "retaliat[e]" against a President for official acts through issuance of a subpoena, would thus be an unconstitutional attempt to "influence" a superior sovereign "exempt" from such obstacles, see *McCulloch*. We generally "assume[ ] that state courts and prosecutors will observe constitutional limitations." *Dombrowski v. Pfister*, 380 U.S. 479, 484 (1965). Failing that, federal law allows a President to challenge any allegedly unconstitutional influence in a federal forum, as the President has done here. . . .

Given these safeguards and the Court's precedents, we cannot conclude that absolute immunity is necessary or appropriate under Article II or the Supremacy Clause. Our dissenting colleagues agree. Justice Thomas reaches the same conclusion based on the original understanding of the Constitution reflected in Marshall's decision in *Burr*. And Justice Alito, also persuaded by *Burr*, "agree[s]" that "not all" state criminal subpoenas for a President's records "should be barred." On that point the Court is unanimous.

B

We next consider whether a state grand jury subpoena seeking a President's private papers must satisfy a heightened need standard. The Solicitor General would require a threshold showing that the evidence sought is "critical" for "specific charging decisions" and that the subpoena is a "last resort," meaning the evidence is "not available from any other source" and is needed "now, rather than at the end of the President's term." . . .

We disagree, for three reasons. First, such a heightened standard would extend protection designed for official documents to the President's private papers. As the Solicitor General and Justice Alito acknowledge, their proposed test is derived from executive privilege cases that trace back to *Burr*. There, Marshall explained that if Jefferson invoked presidential privilege over executive communications, the court would not "proceed against the president as against an ordinary individual" but would instead require an affidavit from the defense that "would clearly show the paper to be essential to the justice of the case." *Burr*. The Solicitor General and Justice Alito would have us apply a similar standard to a President's personal papers. But this argument does not account for the relevant passage from *Burr*: "If there be a paper in the possession of the executive, which is *not of an official nature*, he must stand, as respects that paper, in nearly the same situation with any other individual" (emphasis added). And it is only "nearly"—and not "entirely"—because the President retains the right to assert privilege over documents that, while ostensibly private, "partake of the character of an official paper."

Second, neither the Solicitor General nor Justice Alito has established that heightened protection against state subpoenas is necessary for the Executive to fulfill his Article II functions. Beyond the risk of harassment, which we addressed above, the only justification they offer for the heightened standard is protecting Presidents from "unwarranted burdens." In effect, they argue that even if federal subpoenas to a President are warranted whenever evidence is material, state subpoenas are warranted "only when [the] evidence is essential." But that double standard has no basis in law. For if the state subpoena is not issued to manipulate, the documents themselves are not protected, and the Executive is not impaired, then nothing in Article II or the Supremacy Clause supports holding state subpoenas to a higher standard than their federal counterparts.

Finally, in the absence of a need to protect the Executive, the public interest in fair and effective law enforcement cuts in favor of comprehensive access to evidence. Requiring a state grand jury to meet a heightened standard of need would hobble the grand jury's ability to acquire "all information that might possibly bear on its investigation." And, even assuming the evidence withheld under that standard were preserved until the conclusion of a President's term, in the interim the State would be deprived of investigative leads that the evidence might yield, allowing memories to fade and documents to disappear. This could frustrate the identification, investigation, and indictment of third parties (for whom applicable statutes of limitations might lapse). More troubling, it could prejudice the innocent by depriving the grand jury of *exculpatory* evidence.

Rejecting a heightened need standard does not leave Presidents with "no real protection." To start, a President may avail himself of the same protections available to every other citizen. These include the right to challenge the subpoena on any grounds permitted by state law, which usually include bad faith and undue burden or breadth. . . . And, as in federal court, "[t]he high respect that is owed to the office of the Chief Executive . . . should inform the conduct of the entire proceeding, including the timing and scope of discovery." *Clinton*. . . .

Furthermore, although the Constitution does not entitle the Executive to absolute immunity or a heightened standard, he is not "relegate[d]" only to the challenges available to private citizens. A President can raise subpoena-specific constitutional challenges, in either a state or federal forum. As previously noted, he can challenge the subpoena as an attempt to influence the performance of his official duties, in violation of the Supremacy Clause. This avenue protects against local political machinations "interposed as an obstacle to the effective operation of a federal constitutional power."

In addition, the Executive can—as the district attorney concedes—argue that compliance with a particular subpoena would impede his constitutional duties. . . .

As a result, "once the President sets forth and explains a conflict between judicial proceeding and public duties," or shows that an order or subpoena would "significantly interfere with his efforts to carry out" those duties, "the matter changes." At that point, a court should use its inherent authority to quash or modify the subpoena, if necessary to ensure that such "interference with the President's duties would not occur." . . .

The daylight between our opinion and Justice Thomas's "dissent" is not as great as that label might suggest. We agree that Presidents are neither absolutely immune from state criminal subpoenas nor insulated by a heightened need standard. We agree that Presidents may challenge specific subpoenas as impeding their Article II functions. And, although we affirm while Justice Thomas would vacate, we agree that this case will be remanded to the District Court. [relocated footnote—EDS.]

* * *

Two hundred years ago, a great jurist of our Court established that no citizen, not even the President, is categorically above the common duty to produce evidence when called upon in a criminal proceeding. We reaffirm that principle today and hold that the President is neither absolutely immune from state criminal subpoenas seeking his private papers nor entitled to a heightened standard of need. . . . The arguments presented here and in the Court of Appeals were limited to absolute immunity and heightened need. The Court of Appeals, however, has directed that the case be returned to the District Court, where the President may raise further arguments as appropriate.

We affirm the judgment of the Court of Appeals and remand the case for further proceedings consistent with this opinion.

It is so ordered.

Justice KAVANAUGH, with whom Justice GORSUCH joins, concurring in the judgment.

The Court today unanimously concludes that a President does not possess absolute immunity from a state criminal subpoena, but also unanimously agrees that this case should be remanded to the District Court, where the President may raise constitutional and legal objections to the subpoena as appropriate. I agree with those two conclusions. . . .

The longstanding precedent that has applied to federal criminal subpoenas for official, privileged Executive Branch information is *United States v. Nixon*, 418 U.S. 683 (1974). That landmark case requires that a prosecutor establish a "demonstrated, specific need" for the President's information. . . . [This] is a tried-and-true test that accommodates both the interests of the criminal process and the Article II interests of the Presidency. . . .

A state criminal subpoena to a President raises Article II and Supremacy Clause issues because of the potential for a state prosecutor to use the criminal process and issue subpoenas in a way that interferes with the President's duties, through harassment or diversion. Cf. *Nixon v. Fitzgerald*, 457 U.S. 731, 751-753 (1982). . . .

Because this case again entails a clash between the interests of the criminal process and the Article II interests of the Presidency, I would apply the longstanding

Nixon "demonstrated, specific need" standard to this case. The majority opinion does not apply the *Nixon* standard. . . . That said, the majority opinion appropriately takes account of some important concerns that also animate *Nixon* and the Constitution's balance of powers. The majority opinion explains that a state prosecutor may not issue a subpoena for a President's personal information out of bad faith, malice, or an intent to harass a President; as a result of prosecutorial impropriety; to seek information that is not relevant to an investigation; that is overly broad or unduly burdensome; to manipulate, influence, or retaliate against a President's official acts or policy decisions; or in a way that would impede, conflict with, or interfere with a President's official duties. All nine Members of the Court agree, moreover, that a President may raise objections to a state criminal subpoena not just in state court but also in federal court. . . . In the end, much may depend on how the majority opinion's various standards are applied in future years and decades. It will take future cases to determine precisely how much difference exists between (i) the various standards articulated by the majority opinion, (ii) the overarching *Nixon* "demonstrated, specific need" standard that I would adopt, and (iii) Justice Thomas's and Justice Alito's other proposed standards. In any event, in my view, lower courts in cases of this sort involving a President will almost invariably have to begin by delving into why the State wants the information; why and how much the State needs the information, including whether the State could obtain the information elsewhere; and whether compliance with the subpoena would unduly burden or interfere with a President's official duties. . . .

Justice THOMAS, dissenting.

. . . I agree with the majority that the President is not entitled to absolute immunity from *issuance* of the subpoena. But he may be entitled to relief against its *enforcement.* I therefore agree with the President that the proper course is to vacate and remand. If the President can show that "his duties as chief magistrate demand his whole time for national objects," *United States v. Burr,* 25 F. Cas. 30, 34 (No. 14,692d) (CC Va. 1807) (Marshall, C. J.), he is entitled to relief from enforcement of the subpoena. . . .

The text of the Constitution explicitly addresses the privileges of some federal officials, but it does not afford the President absolute immunity. Members of Congress are "privileged from Arrest during their Attendance at the Session of their respective Houses, and in going to and returning from the same," except for "Treason, Felony and Breach of the Peace." Art. I, § 6, cl. 1. The Constitution further specifies that, "for any Speech or Debate in either House, they shall not be questioned in any other Place." *Ibid.* By contrast, the text of the Constitution contains no explicit grant of absolute immunity from legal process for the President. As a Federalist essayist noted during ratification, the President's "person is not so much protected as that of a member of the House of Representatives" because he is subject to the issuance of judicial process "like any other man in the ordinary course of law." An American Citizen I (Sept. 26, 1787), in 2 Documentary History of the Ratification of the Constitution 141 (M. Jansen ed. 1976) (emphasis deleted). . . .

In addition to contesting the issuance of the subpoena, the President also seeks injunctive and declaratory relief against its enforcement. The majority recognizes that the President can seek relief from enforcement, but it does not vacate and remand for the lower courts to address this question. I would do so and instruct them to apply the standard articulated by Chief Justice Marshall in *Burr*: If the President is unable to comply because of his official duties, then he is entitled to injunctive and declaratory relief. . . . Chief Justice Marshall set out the pertinent standard: To avoid enforcement of the subpoena, the President must "sho[w]" that "his duties as chief magistrate demand his whole time for national objects." . . .

Although *Burr* involved a federal subpoena, the same principle applies to a state subpoena. The ability of the President to discharge his duties until his term expires or he is removed from office by the Senate is "integral to the structure of the Constitution." . . . Accordingly, a federal court may provide injunctive and declaratory relief to stay enforcement of a state subpoena when the President meets the *Burr* standard. . . .

The President and the Solicitor General argue that the grand jury must make a showing of heightened need. I agree with the majority's decision not to adopt this standard, but for different reasons. The constitutional question in this case is whether the President is able to perform the duties of his office, whereas a heightened need standard addresses a logically independent issue. Under a heightened-need standard, a grand jury with only the usual need for particular information would be refused it when the President is perfectly able to comply, while a grand jury with a heightened need would be entitled to it even if compliance would place undue obligations on the President. This result makes little sense and lacks any basis in the original understanding of the Constitution. I would leave questions of the grand jury's need to state law. [relocated footnote—Eds.]. . .

I would vacate and remand to allow the District Court to determine whether enforcement of this subpoena should be enjoined because the President's "duties as chief magistrate demand his whole time for national objects." Accordingly, I respectfully dissent.

Justice Alito, dissenting.

This case is almost certain to be portrayed as a case about the current President and the current political situation, but the case has a much deeper significance. While the decision will of course have a direct effect on President Trump, what the Court holds today will also affect all future Presidents—which is to say, it will affect the Presidency, and that is a matter of great and lasting importance to the Nation.

The event that precipitated this case is unprecedented. Respondent Vance, an elected state prosecutor, launched a criminal investigation of a sitting President and obtained a grand jury subpoena for his records. The specific question before us—whether the subpoena may be enforced—cannot be answered adequately without considering the broader question that frames it: whether the Constitution imposes restrictions on a State's deployment of its criminal law enforcement powers against a sitting President. If the Constitution sets no such limits, then a local prosecutor may prosecute a sitting President. And if that is allowed, it follows *a fortiori* that the subpoena at issue can be enforced. On the other hand, if the Constitution does not permit a State to prosecute a sitting President, the next logical question is whether the Constitution restrains any other prosecutorial or investigative weapons. . . .

[B]ecause "[t]he President is the only person who alone composes a branch of government . . . , there is not always a clear line between his personal and official affairs." *Trump v. Mazars USA, LLP.* As a result, the law's treatment of the person who serves as President can have an important effect on the institution, and the institution of the Presidency plays an indispensable role in our constitutional system. . . .

"Constitutionally speaking, the President never sleeps. The President must be ready, at a moment's notice, to do whatever it takes to preserve, protect, and defend the Constitution and the American people." Amar & Katyal, Executive Privileges and Immunities: The Nixon and Clinton Cases, 108 Harv. L. Rev. 701, 713 (1995). Without a President who is able at all times to carry out the responsibilities of the office, our constitutional system could not operate, and the country would be at risk. . . .

The second structural feature is the relationship between the Federal Government and the States. . . . The Constitution permitted the States to retain many of the sovereign powers that they previously possessed, but it gave the Federal Government powers that were deemed essential for the Nation's well-being and, indeed, its survival. And it provided for the Federal Government to be independent of and, within its allotted sphere, supreme over the States. Art. VI, cl. 2. Accordingly, a State may not block or interfere with the lawful work of the National Government. . . .

[T]wo centuries of case law prohibit the States from taxing, regulating, or otherwise interfering with the lawful work of federal agencies, instrumentalities, and officers. The Court premised these cases on the principle that "the activities of the Federal Government are free from regulation by any State. No other adjustment of competing enactments or legal principles is possible." *Mayo v. United States,* 319 U.S. 441, 445 (1943) (footnote omitted). . . .

In *McCulloch,* Maryland's sovereign taxing power had to yield, and in a similar way, a State's sovereign power to enforce its criminal laws must accommodate the indispensable role that the Constitution assigns to the Presidency. This must be the rule with respect to a state prosecution of a sitting President. Both the structure of the Government established by the Constitution and the Constitution's provisions on the impeachment and removal of a President make it clear that the prosecution of a sitting President is out of the question. It has been aptly said that the President is the "sole indispensable man in government," and subjecting a sitting President to criminal prosecution would severely hamper his ability to carry out the vital responsibilities that the Constitution puts in his hands. . . .

The constitutional provisions on impeachment provide further support for the rule that a President may not be prosecuted while in office. . . . After providing that the judgment cannot impose any punishment beyond removal from the Presidency and disqualification from holding any other federal office, the Constitution states that "the Party convicted shall nevertheless be liable and subject to Indictment, Trial, Judgment, and Punishment, according to Law." Art. I, § 3, cl. 7. The plain implication is that criminal prosecution, like removal from the Presidency and disqualification from other offices, is a consequence that can come about only after the Senate's judgment, not during or prior to the Senate trial. . . .

While the prosecution of a sitting President provides the most dramatic example of a clash between the indispensable work of the Presidency and a State's exercise of its criminal law enforcement powers, other examples are easy to imagine. Suppose state officers obtained and sought to execute a search warrant for a sitting President's private quarters in the White House. Suppose a state court authorized surveillance of a telephone that a sitting President was known to use. Or suppose that a sitting President was subpoenaed to testify before a state grand jury and, as is generally the rule, no Presidential aides, even those carrying the so-called "nuclear football," were permitted to enter the grand jury room. What these examples illustrate is a principle that this Court has recognized: legal proceedings involving a sitting President must take the responsibilities and demands of the office into account. See *Clinton v. Jones*, 520 U.S. 681, 707 (1997).

It is not enough to recite sayings like "no man is above the law" and "the public has a right to every man's evidence." These sayings are true—and important—but they beg the question, . . . the nature of the office demands in some instances that the application of laws be adjusted at least until the person's term in office ends.

I now come to the specific investigative weapon at issue in the case before us—a subpoena for a sitting President's records. This weapon is less intrusive in an immediate sense than those mentioned above. Since the records are held by, and the subpoena was issued to, a third party, compliance would not require much work on the President's part. And after all, this is just one subpoena.

But . . . [i]f we say that a subpoena to a third party is insufficient to undermine a President's performance of his duties, what about a subpoena served on the President himself? Surely in that case, the President could turn over the work of gathering the requested documents to attorneys or others recruited to perform the task. And if one subpoena is permitted, what about two? Or three? Or ten? Drawing a line based on such factors would involve the same sort of "perplexing inquiry, so unfit for the judicial department" that Marshall rejected in *McCulloch*.

The Court faced a similar issue when it considered whether a President can be sued for an allegedly unlawful act committed in the performance of official duties. See *Nixon v. Fitzgerald*, 457 U.S. 731 (1982). We did not ask whether the particular suit before us would have interfered with the carrying out of Presidential duties. (It could not have had that effect because President Nixon had already left office.)

Instead, we adopted a rule for all such suits, and we should take a similar approach here. The rule should take into account both the effect of subpoenas on the functioning of the Presidency and the risk that they will be used for harassment.

I turn first to the question of the effect of a state grand jury subpoena for a President's records. When the issuance of such a subpoena is part of an investigation that regards the President as a "target" or "subject," the subpoena can easily impair a President's "energetic performance of [his] constitutional duties." Few individuals will simply brush off an indication that they may be within a prosecutor's crosshairs. Few will put the matter out of their minds and go about their work unaffected. For many, the prospect of prosecution will be the first and last thing on their minds every day.

Respondent asserts that his office has never characterized President Trump as a "target" of the investigation, but by the same token, respondent has never said that the President is not a "target." [relocated footnote—Eds.]

We have come to expect our Presidents to shoulder burdens that very few people could bear, but it is unrealistic to think that the prospect of possible criminal prosecution will not interfere with the performance of the duties of the office. . . .

There are more than 2,300 local prosecutors and district attorneys in the country. Many local prosecutors are elected, and many prosecutors have ambitions for higher elected office. . . . If a sitting President is intensely unpopular in a particular district—and that is a common condition—targeting the President may be an alluring and effective electoral strategy. But it is a strategy that would undermine our constitutional structure. . . .

In light of the above, a subpoena like the one now before us should not be enforced unless it meets a test that takes into account the need to prevent interference with a President's discharge of the responsibilities of the office. . . . [T]he point is that we should not treat this subpoena like an ordinary grand jury subpoena and should not relegate a President to the meager defenses that are available when an ordinary grand jury subpoena is challenged. But that, at bottom, is the effect of the Court's decision.

The Presidency deserves greater protection. Thus, in a case like this one, a prosecutor should be required (1) to provide at least a general description of the possible offenses that are under investigation, (2) to outline how the subpoenaed records relate to those offenses, and (3) to explain why it is important that the records be produced and why it is necessary for production to occur while the President is still in office. . . .

In the present case, the district attorney made a brief proffer, but important questions were left hanging. It would not be unduly burdensome to insist on answers before enforcing the subpoena.

One obvious question concerns the scope of the subpoena. The subpoena issued by the grand jury is largely a copy of the subpoenas issued by Committees of the House of Representatives, and it would be quite a coincidence if the records relevant to an investigation of possible violations of New York criminal law just so happened to be almost identical to the records thought by congressional Committees to be useful in considering federal legislation. It is therefore appropriate to ask the district attorney to explain the need for the various items that the subpoena covers.

The district attorney should also explain why it is important that the information in question be obtained from the President's records rather than another source. And the district attorney should set out why he finds it necessary that the records be produced now as opposed to when the President leaves office. At argument, respondent's counsel told us that his office's concern is the expiration of the statute of limitations, but there are potential solutions to that problem. Even if New York law does not automatically suspend the statute of limitations for prosecuting a President until he leaves office, it may be possible to eliminate the problem by waiver. And if the prosecutor's statute-of-limitations concerns relate to parties other than the President, he should be required to spell that out.

There may be other good reasons why immediate enforcement is important, such as the risk that evidence or important leads will be lost, but if a prosecutor believes that immediate enforcement is needed for such a reason, the prosecutor should be required to provide a reasonably specific explanation why that is so and why alternative means, such as measures to preserve evidence and prevent spoliation, would not suffice. . . .

Unlike this rule, which would not undermine any legitimate state interests, the opinion of the Court provides no real protection for the Presidency. The Court discounts the risk of harassment and assumes that state prosecutors will observe constitutional limitations, and I also assume that the great majority of state prosecutors will carry out their responsibilities responsibly. But for the reasons noted, there is a very real risk that some will not. . . . For all practical purposes, the Court's decision places a sitting President in the same unenviable position as any other person whose records are subpoenaed by a grand jury. . . .

The Court's decision threatens to impair the functioning of the Presidency and provides no real protection against the use of the subpoena power by the Nation's 2,300+ local prosecutors. Respect for the structure of Government created by the Constitution demands greater protection for an institution that is vital to the Nation's safety and well-being.

I therefore respectfully dissent.

DISCUSSION

1. *Running out the clock.* Throughout his candidacy for President, and his term in office, Donald Trump resisted providing access to his tax returns. The reasons why remain mysterious, but his conduct—so different from other modern presidential candidates—repeatedly generated suspicions among his political opponents that he had something to hide.

Even though the Supreme Court announced that the President was not immune from state subpoenas, the Court sent the case back to the New York courts with instructions to consider any subpoena-specific challenges Trump might have. That means that litigation over the grand jury subpoena would continue until well after the 2020 elections. The practical effect of *Trump v. Vance*, therefore, is that Trump was able to run for President twice without ever having to reveal what was in his tax returns. To this extent, and despite the Court's rebuke of his claims of absolute immunity, the case was a short-term win for President Trump. But it will have long-term repercussions for Trump, and for future Presidents.

2. *Federalism and unpopular Presidents.* In one sense, *Vance* follows straightforwardly from the logic of *United States v. Nixon.* The two most important differences are, first, that the material being requested was not subject to executive privilege—which made the prosecutor's claim even stronger. The second difference, however, is that *Nixon* did not involve a state criminal prosecution. As Justices Alito and Thomas note, there are many state and local prosecutors who might want to make trouble for a President who is unpopular in their part of the country.

How much should this matter? Presidents Bush and Obama were very unpopular in different parts of the country, and yet neither faced a state grand jury subpoena. On the other hand, President Clinton did have to testify before a federal grand jury, but that is because he was caught lying in a deposition in the Paula Jones sexual harassment case.

Is Trump's situation *sui generis* because there was long-standing concern about his illegal activities before he became President, and Americans are very unlikely to elect such a person again? Or, in our highly polarized age, does *Vance* mean that, from now on, every President will be under criminal investigation by some local or state prosecutor?

3. *The* Nixon *standard.* Justices Kavanaugh and Gorsuch argue that even though the material is not privileged, the New York prosecutor should have to meet the "demonstrated, specific need" standard of *United States v. Nixon.* This would

help deter ambitious and politically motivated prosecutors from fishing expeditions. How difficult would it be for the prosecutor to meet that standard? To what extent does that question turn on whether the President himself is actually a target of the investigation?

NOTE: CONGRESSIONAL OVERSIGHT

How broadly does executive privilege extend when Congress is engaged in oversight of the executive branch? May the President refuse to provide documents to Congress, and prohibit members of the executive branch from testifying before Congress? These issues came to a head in the third year of Donald Trump's presidency, when Democrats gained control of the House of Representatives. Under the previous Republican majority, there was relatively little oversight or investigation into President Trump's many scandals. Democrats signaled that they were ready to make up for lost time. They began to issue multiple requests for documents and testimony. President Trump offered a characteristically aggressive response: "'We're fighting all the subpoenas,' Mr. Trump told reporters outside the White House. 'These aren't, like, impartial people. The Democrats are trying to win [the] 2020 [election].' "[51]

Thus began a series of controversies in which House Democrats requested material and testimony, and the White House refused. We can divide the controversies into two basic sets of issues.

1. *Assertions of executive privilege and categorical "immunity" with respect to Administration documents and the testimony of Administration officials.* President Trump repeatedly asserted executive privilege with respect to document requests from Congress. He also repeatedly refused to allow current and former Administration officials to testify before Congress. Executive privilege allows the President to prevent senior advisors who work with and advise him every day from disclosing their conversations and interactions with him. In order to protect that privilege, the executive branch has historically asserted testimonial immunity with respect to the President's close advisors who regularly meet with and advise him. Moreover, it has also asserted this immunity with respect to former officials. These claims of testimonial immunity have been executive branch positions in both Democratic and Republican Administrations.

However, the President does not have effective control over former officials, and it is up to them to decide whether to testify, and, if so, whether to assert the privilege (or a form of "immunity" from testimony).[52] They may do so out of their loyalty to the President for whom they served, in order to protect the institution of the Presidency, because of their ethical obligations as attorneys, or for other political or personal reasons.

---

51. Charlie Savage, Trump Vows Stonewall of 'All' House Subpoenas, Setting Up Fight Over Powers, N.Y. Times, April 24, 2019, https://www.nytimes.com/2019/04/24/us/politics/donald-trump-subpoenas.html.

52. See Marty Lederman, What Is a Private Citizen to Do (When Caught in the Middle of an Interbranch Dispute)?, Balkinization, July 11, 2007, https://balkin.blogspot.com/2007/07/whatis-private-citizen-to-do-when.html.

The only judicial decision squarely on point rejects the Executive branch's position on testimonial immunity. In Comm. on Judiciary, U.S. House of Representatives v. Miers, 558 F. Supp. 2d 53, 100-02 (D.D.C. 2008), the district court rejected absolute immunity for former senior presidential advisors. The case involved Harriet Miers, who at that time was a former White House Counsel to President George W. Bush. The district court agreed that immunity might be appropriate in cases "where national security or foreign affairs form the basis for the Executive's assertion of privilege." Senior advisors could also "assert executive privilege in response to any specific questions posed by the Committee." The district court, however, rejected a general immunity from having to testify:

> There are powerful reasons supporting the rejection of absolute immunity as asserted by the Executive here. If the Court held otherwise, the presumptive presidential privilege could be transformed into an absolute privilege and Congress's legitimate interest in inquiry could be easily thwarted. . . . [I]f the Executive's absolute immunity argument were to prevail, Congress could be left with no recourse to obtain information that is plainly not subject to any colorable claim of executive privilege. . . . Clear precedent and persuasive policy reasons confirm that the Executive cannot be the judge of its own privilege. . . . Ms. Miers is not excused from compliance with the Committee's subpoena by virtue of a claim of executive privilege that may ultimately be made. Instead, she must appear before the Committee to provide testimony, and invoke executive privilege where appropriate.

The executive branch has not accepted the *Miers* decision as a correct statement of the law.[53]

President Trump also asserted the privilege beyond the smaller circle of senior advisors who interact with and advise the President every day.[54] In addition, the Trump Administration asserted a prophylactic claim of executive privilege with respect to large classes of documents.[55]

Beyond the central precedent of *United States v. Nixon*, which held that executive privilege must yield to "the fundamental demands of due process of law in the fair administration of justice," there is very little case law on the scope of executive privilege. (See *Miers, supra.*) A large number of opinions have been produced not by the courts but by the Justice Department's Office of Legal Counsel, and

53. A decision by Judge Katani Brown Jackson also rejected testimonial immunity in Comm. on the Judiciary, U.S. House of Representatives v. McGahn, 415 F. Supp. 3d 148, 214-215 (D.D.C. 2019), but that opinion was vacated by the D.C. Circuit on standing grounds.

54. See, e.g., Jacqueline Thomsen, White House sought to assert executive privilege in Kobach interview on census citizenship question, Cummings says, The Hill, June 7, 2019, https://thehill.com/regulation/court-battles/447510-white-house-sought-to-assert-executive-privilege-in-kobach-interview; Ryan Goodman & John T. Nelson, Annie Donaldson Is Not the President's "Alter Ego," Just Security, June 24, 2019, https://www.justsecurity.org/64681/annie-donaldson-is-not-the-presidents-alter-ego/.

55. See Jonathan Shaub, The Prophylactic Executive Privilege, Lawfare, June 14, 2019, https://www.lawfareblog.com/prophylactic-executive-privilege.

therefore are understandably sympathetic to the position of the President. Whatever one thinks the actual scope of executive privilege should be, the President has institutional incentives to claim a far broader privilege in conflicts with Congress and the courts.

One reason for the lack of case law is the practical problem of enforcement. Congress can issue a subpoena for documents or testimony. But if the President asserts executive privilege, Congress's options are limited.

First, Congress can vote (or threaten to vote) government officials in contempt for failing to appear, or for refusing to produce requested documents. For example, a Republican-controlled House held Attorney General Eric Holder in criminal and civil contempt in 2012 in a dispute over document production in the House's investigation of the Fast and Furious scandal involving the Bureau of Alcohol, Tobacco, and Firearms. The contempt citation, however, was practically ineffective: The document production issues were not resolved until the spring of 2019, long after President Obama left office.

That is because Congress has few ways of enforcing its orders. Congress has inherent powers to enforce its orders through contempt proceedings, arrest, and imprisonment, but it has chosen not to use them for close to a century. See McGrain v. Daugherty, 273 U.S. 135 (1927) (upholding Congress's power to arrest and detain a witness in a Congressional investigation of antitrust policy); Anderson v. Dunn, 19 U.S. (6 Wheat.) 204 (1821) (holding that Congress has the power to punish for contempt). Because Congress does not use its own contempt powers, Congress has to rely on criminal or civil proceedings.

Criminal proceedings require Congress to refer a matter to a U.S. Attorney. But the U.S. Attorney works for the Justice Department, which is part of the executive branch. The usual policy of the Justice Department is to refuse to bring criminal contempt proceedings against a member of the executive branch who is relying upon a claim of privilege or immunity that the President and DOJ have approved. For example, after the House held Attorney General Eric Holder in contempt in 2012, the Justice Department refused to prosecute.

That leaves civil proceedings. Congress can go to federal court to enforce its orders, but court proceedings generally take a great deal of time—sometimes many years. By the time the appeals process is exhausted, the Administration may be out of office—or Congress held by a different party.

As a result, most disputes over executive privilege are resolved by negotiations between the two branches, which usually come to some sort of accommodation. Because Congress and the President regularly need to cooperate on many topics and at many levels, there are reasons for each to accommodate the other. Each also has its own balance of considerations. The executive branch has to balance concerns about bad publicity (i.e., that it is hiding something illegal or embarrassing), and about the possibility of congressional payback in other contexts, against the executive branch's interests in protecting the confidentiality of its operations over the long run. Conversely, Congress has to balance its desire for information against its own concerns about bad publicity, as well as the possibility that negotiations will break down and Congress must go to the courts and face a protracted struggle.

In the Trump Administration, the executive branch had somewhat fewer incentives for cooperation than usual, because there was very little that Trump wanted from a Democratic House and he had little to gain politically from cooperating with House Democrats. Accordingly, President Trump made fairly broad assertions of privilege and attempted to delay resolution of disputes with Congress, cooperating only when necessary. By acting intransigently on multiple fronts, he was able to put off Congress indefinitely. Even if many of his claims of executive privilege and testimonial immunity were overblown, they simply added to Congress's work in having to deal with them.

To be sure, Congress can always threaten to impeach the President for his refusals. It can also begin impeachment proceedings and use them to investigate the President. There is a plausible argument that executive privilege must yield, or that its scope is far narrower, when Congress is investigating articles of impeachment. Otherwise, the President would truly be beyond investigation and accountability.

As a matter of fact, the House of Representatives did impeach Donald Trump in December 2019 (and then again as he was leaving office in January 2021). One of the two counts in the first Trump impeachment was for obstructing Congress in its investigations of the President. But the result of Trump's first impeachment showed how hollow the threat of impeachment actually was against a determined President. President Trump was quickly acquitted by a Senate controlled by members of his own party. President Trump knew that no matter how uncooperative he was, he could not be removed as long as he had 41 votes in the Senate; moreover, he could use the very fact that he was impeached to show his supporters that he was being unfairly treated by the other party. Under these conditions, why should Trump have cooperated?

Following Trump's first impeachment, Congress's options to obtain compliance for oversight requests became quite limited. For example, the House could have tried to leverage things that the President wanted or needed from House Democrats. But the Republican Party controlled the Senate, and the House had no control over executive branch appointments and judgeships.

Although disputes and bargaining between the branches have been commonplace. President Trump's blanket assertion that he would fight *all* congressional requests for documents and testimony was unprecedented in American history. What role should norms and conventions play in characterizing what is happening? In restraining the political branches?[56] What should the other participants do if one of the participants refuses to accept their understanding of the existing norms? If you think that Trump did breach existing norms and conventions, will his norm-breaking have any long-term effects, or do you predict that things will snap back to normal?

2. *Documents from third parties and third-party witnesses unconnected to the Administration.* Congress has also sought documents from third parties who are not former senior advisors to the President. Executive privilege generally does not apply in these cases. Nevertheless, the Trump Administration sought to block Congress from reviewing them. This litigation eventually reached the Supreme Court in the spring of 2020.

---

56. On the role of norms in executive branch practice, see Daphna Renan, Presidential Norms and Article II, 131 Harv. L. Rev. 2187 (2018). On the role of norms more generally in sustaining the rule of law, see Tara Leigh Grove, The Origins (and Fragility) of Judicial Independence, 71 Vand. L. Rev. 465 (2018).

Trump v. Mazars USA, LLP

140 S. Ct. 2019 (2020)

Chief Justice ROBERTS delivered the opinion of the Court.

Over the course of five days in April 2019, three committees of the U.S. House of Representatives issued four subpoenas seeking information about the finances of President Donald J. Trump, his children, and affiliated businesses. We have held that the House has authority under the Constitution to issue subpoenas to assist it in carrying out its legislative responsibilities. . . .

[The House Committee on Financial Services issued a subpoena to Deutsche Bank seeking any document related to account activity, due diligence, foreign transactions, business statements, debt schedules, statements of net worth, tax returns, and suspicious activity identified by Deutsche Bank. It issued a second subpoena to Capital One for similar information. The Permanent Select Committee on Intelligence issued a subpoena to Deutsche Bank that mirrored the subpoena issued by the Financial Services Committee. And the House Committee on Oversight and Reform issued a subpoena to the President's personal accounting firm, Mazars USA, LLP, demanding information related to the President and several affiliated businesses. Although each of the committees sought overlapping sets of financial documents, each supplied different justifications for the requests, explaining that the information would help guide legislative reform in areas ranging from money laundering and terrorism to foreign involvement in U.S. elections.]

The House asserts that the financial information sought here—encompassing a decade's worth of transactions by the President and his family—will help guide legislative reform in areas ranging from money laundering and terrorism to foreign involvement in U.S. elections. The President contends that the House lacked a valid legislative aim and instead sought these records to harass him, expose personal matters, and conduct law enforcement activities beyond its authority. The question presented is whether the subpoenas exceed the authority of the House under the Constitution. . . .

II

[H]istorically, disputes over congressional demands for presidential documents have not ended up in court. Instead, they have been hashed out in the "hurly-burly, the give-and-take of the political process between the legislative and the executive."

That practice began with George Washington and the early Congress. In 1792, a House committee requested Executive Branch documents pertaining to General St. Clair's campaign against the Indians in the Northwest Territory, which had concluded in an utter rout of federal forces when they were caught by surprise near the present-day border between Ohio and Indiana. See T. Taylor, Grand Inquest: The Story of Congressional Investigations 19-23 (1955). Since this was the first such request from Congress, President Washington called a Cabinet meeting, wishing to take care that his response "be rightly conducted" because it could "become a precedent."

The meeting, attended by the likes of Alexander Hamilton, Thomas Jefferson, Edmund Randolph, and Henry Knox, ended with the Cabinet of "one mind": The

House had authority to "institute inquiries" and "call for papers" but the President could "exercise a discretion" over disclosures, "communicat[ing] such papers as the public good would permit" and "refus[ing]" the rest. President Washington then dispatched Jefferson to speak to individual congressmen and "bring them by persuasion into the right channel." The discussions were apparently fruitful, as the House later narrowed its request and the documents were supplied without recourse to the courts. See 3 Annals of Cong. 536 (1792).

Jefferson, once he became President, followed Washington's precedent. . . . Ever since, congressional demands for the President's information have been resolved by the political branches without involving this Court. . . . Congress and the President maintained this tradition of negotiation and compromise—without the involvement of this Court—until the present dispute. Indeed, from President Washington until now, we have never considered a dispute over a congressional subpoena for the President's records. And, according to the parties, the appellate courts have addressed such a subpoena only once, when a Senate committee subpoenaed President Nixon during the Watergate scandal. *Senate Select Committee on Presidential Campaign Activities v. Nixon*, 498 F.2d 725 (CADC 1974) (en banc). In that case, the court refused to enforce the subpoena, and the Senate did not seek review by this Court. . . .

This dispute therefore represents a significant departure from historical practice. Although the parties agree that this particular controversy is justiciable, we recognize that it is the first of its kind to reach this Court; that disputes of this sort can raise important issues concerning relations between the branches; that related disputes involving congressional efforts to seek official Executive Branch information recur on a regular basis, including in the context of deeply partisan controversy; and that Congress and the Executive have nonetheless managed for over two centuries to resolve such disputes among themselves without the benefit of guidance from us. Such longstanding practice " 'is a consideration of great weight' " in cases concerning "the allocation of power between [the] two elected branches of Government," and it imposes on us a duty of care to ensure that we not needlessly disturb "the compromises and working arrangements that [those] branches . . . themselves have reached." *NLRB v. Noel Canning*, 573 U.S. 513, 524-526 (2014). . . .

Congress has no enumerated constitutional power to conduct investigations or issue subpoenas, but we have held that each House has power "to secure needed information" in order to legislate. *McGrain v. Daugherty*, 273 U.S. 135, 161 (1927). This "power of inquiry—with process to enforce it—is an essential and appropriate auxiliary to the legislative function." Without information, Congress would be shooting in the dark, unable to legislate "wisely or effectively." The congressional power to obtain information is "broad" and "indispensable." *Watkins v. United States*, 354 U.S. 178, 187, 215 (1957). It encompasses inquiries into the administration of existing laws, studies of proposed laws, and "surveys of defects in our social, economic or political system for the purpose of enabling the Congress to remedy them."

Because this power is "justified solely as an adjunct to the legislative process," it is subject to several limitations. Most importantly, a congressional subpoena is valid only if it is "related to, and in furtherance of, a legitimate task of the Congress." The subpoena must serve a "valid legislative purpose," *Quinn v. United States*,

349 U.S. 155, 161 (1955); it must "concern[ ] a subject on which legislation 'could be had,' " *Eastland v. United States Servicemen's Fund,* 421 U.S. 491, 506 (1975) (quoting *McGrain*).

Furthermore, Congress may not issue a subpoena for the purpose of "law enforcement," because "those powers are assigned under our Constitution to the Executive and the Judiciary." *Quinn.* Thus Congress may not use subpoenas to "try" someone "before [a] committee for any crime or wrongdoing." *McGrain.* Congress has no " 'general' power to inquire into private affairs and compel disclosures," and "there is no congressional power to expose for the sake of exposure," *Watkins.* "Investigations conducted solely for the personal aggrandizement of the investigators or to 'punish' those investigated are indefensible."

Finally, recipients of legislative subpoenas retain their constitutional rights throughout the course of an investigation. And recipients have long been understood to retain common law and constitutional privileges with respect to certain materials, such as attorney-client communications and governmental communications protected by executive privilege.

The President contends, as does the Solicitor General appearing on behalf of the United States, that the usual rules for congressional subpoenas do not govern here because the President's papers are at issue. They argue for a more demanding standard based in large part on cases involving the Nixon tapes—recordings of conversations between President Nixon and close advisers discussing the break-in at the Democratic National Committee's headquarters at the Watergate complex. The tapes were subpoenaed by a Senate committee and the Special Prosecutor investigating the break-in, prompting President Nixon to invoke executive privilege and leading to two cases addressing the showing necessary to require the President to comply with the subpoenas. See *Nixon*; *Senate Select Committee.* . . .

Quoting *Nixon,* the President asserts that the House must establish a "demonstrated, specific need" for the financial information, just as the Watergate special prosecutor was required to do in order to obtain the tapes. And drawing on *Senate Select Committee*—the D. C. Circuit case refusing to enforce the Senate subpoena for the tapes—the President and the Solicitor General argue that the House must show that the financial information is "demonstrably critical" to its legislative purpose.

We disagree that these demanding standards apply here. Unlike the cases before us, *Nixon* and *Senate Select Committee* involved Oval Office communications over which the President asserted executive privilege. That privilege safeguards the public interest in candid, confidential deliberations within the Executive Branch; it is "fundamental to the operation of Government." *Nixon.* As a result, information subject to executive privilege deserves "the greatest protection consistent with the fair administration of justice." We decline to transplant that protection root and branch to cases involving nonprivileged, private information, which by definition does not implicate sensitive Executive Branch deliberations.

The standards proposed by the President and the Solicitor General—if applied outside the context of privileged information—would risk seriously impeding Congress in carrying out its responsibilities. The President and the Solicitor General would apply the same exacting standards to *all* subpoenas for the President's information, without recognizing distinctions between privileged and nonprivileged information, between official and personal information, or between various legislative objectives. Such a categorical approach would represent a significant departure from the longstanding way of doing business between the branches, giving short shrift to Congress's important interests in conducting inquiries to obtain the information it needs to legislate effectively. . . .

Legislative inquiries might involve the President in appropriate cases; as noted, Congress's responsibilities extend to "every affair of government." *Ibid.* (internal quotation marks omitted). Because the President's approach does not take adequate account of these significant congressional interests, we do not adopt it.

The House meanwhile would have us ignore that these suits involve the President. Invoking our precedents concerning investigations that did not target the President's papers, the House urges us to uphold its subpoenas because they "relate[ ] to a valid legislative purpose" or "concern[ ] a subject on which legislation could be had." That approach is appropriate, the House argues, because the cases before us are not "momentous separation-of-powers disputes." . . .

The House's approach fails to take adequate account of the significant separation of powers issues raised by congressional subpoenas for the President's information. Congress and the President have an ongoing institutional relationship as the "opposite and rival" political branches established by the Constitution. As a result, congressional subpoenas directed at the President differ markedly from congressional subpoenas we have previously reviewed, and they bear little resemblance to criminal subpoenas issued to the President in the course of a specific investigation. Unlike those subpoenas, congressional subpoenas for the President's information unavoidably pit the political branches against one another.

Far from accounting for separation of powers concerns, the House's approach aggravates them by leaving essentially no limits on the congressional power to subpoena the President's personal records. Any personal paper possessed by a President could potentially "relate to" a conceivable subject of legislation, for Congress has broad legislative powers that touch a vast number of subjects. The President's financial records could relate to economic reform, medical records to health reform, school transcripts to education reform, and so on. . . . Without limits on its subpoena powers, Congress could "exert an imperious controul" over the Executive Branch and aggrandize itself at the President's expense, just as the Framers feared. The Federalist No. 71 (A. Hamilton); No. 48 (J. Madison); *Bowsher v. Synar*, 478 U.S. 714, 721-722, 727 (1986). And a limitless subpoena power would transform the "established practice" of the political branches. *Noel Canning*. Instead of negotiating over information requests, Congress could simply walk away from the bargaining table and compel compliance in court.

The House and the courts below suggest that these separation of powers concerns are not fully implicated by the particular subpoenas here, but we disagree. We would have to be "blind" not to see what "[a]ll others can see and understand": that the subpoenas do not represent a run-of-the-mill legislative effort but rather a clash between rival branches of government over records of intense political interest for all involved.

The interbranch conflict here does not vanish simply because the subpoenas seek personal papers or because the President sued in his personal capacity. The President is the only person who alone composes a branch of government. As a result, there is not always a clear line between his personal and official affairs. "The interest of the man" is often "connected with the constitutional rights of the place." The Federalist No. 51. Given the close connection between the Office of the President and its occupant, congressional demands for the President's papers can implicate the relationship between the branches regardless whether those papers are personal or official. Either way, a demand may aim to harass the President or render him "complaisan[t] to the humors of the Legislature." [The Federalist] No. 71. In fact, a subpoena for personal papers may pose a heightened risk of such impermissible purposes, precisely because of the documents' personal nature and their less evident connection to a legislative task. No one can say that the controversy here is less significant to the relationship between the branches simply because it involves personal papers. Quite the opposite. That appears to be what makes the matter of such great consequence to the President and Congress.

In addition, separation of powers concerns are no less palpable here simply because the subpoenas were issued to third parties. Congressional demands for the President's information present an interbranch conflict no matter where the information is held—it is, after all, the President's information. Were it otherwise, Congress could sidestep constitutional requirements any time a President's information is entrusted to a third party—as occurs with rapidly increasing frequency. Indeed, Congress could declare open season on the President's information held by schools, archives, internet service providers, e-mail clients, and financial institutions. The Constitution does not tolerate such ready evasion; it "deals with substance, not shadows." *Cummings v. Missouri*, 4 Wall. 277, 325 (1867).

Congressional subpoenas for the President's personal information implicate weighty concerns regarding the separation of powers. Neither side, however, identifies an approach that accounts for these concerns. . . . A balanced approach is necessary, one that takes a "considerable impression" from "the practice of the government," *McCulloch* v. *Maryland*, and "resist[s]" the "pressure inherent within each of the separate Branches to exceed the outer limits of its power," *INS v. Chadha*, 462 U.S. 919, 951 (1983). We therefore conclude that, in assessing whether a subpoena directed at the President's personal information is "related to, and in furtherance of, a legitimate task of the Congress," courts must perform a careful analysis that takes adequate account of the separation of powers principles at stake, including both the significant legislative interests of Congress and the "unique position" of the President, *Clinton*. . . .

First, courts should carefully assess whether the asserted legislative purpose warrants the significant step of involving the President and his papers. " '[O]ccasion[s] for constitutional confrontation between the two branches' should be avoided whenever possible." Congress may not rely on the President's information if other sources could reasonably provide Congress the information it needs in light of its particular legislative objective. The President's unique constitutional position means that Congress may not look to him as a "case study" for general legislation.

Unlike in criminal proceedings, where "[t]he very integrity of the judicial system" would be undermined without "full disclosure of all the facts," *Nixon*, efforts to craft legislation involve predictive policy judgments that are "not hamper[ed] . . . in quite the same way" when every scrap of potentially relevant evidence is not available. . . .

Second, to narrow the scope of possible conflict between the branches, courts should insist on a subpoena no broader than reasonably necessary to support Congress's legislative objective. The specificity of the subpoena's request "serves as an important safeguard against unnecessary intrusion into the operation of the Office of the President."

Third, courts should be attentive to the nature of the evidence offered by Congress to establish that a subpoena advances a valid legislative purpose. The more detailed and substantial the evidence of Congress's legislative purpose, the better. That is particularly true when Congress contemplates legislation that raises sensitive constitutional issues, such as legislation concerning the Presidency. . . .

Fourth, courts should be careful to assess the burdens imposed on the President by a subpoena. We have held that burdens on the President's time and attention stemming from judicial process and litigation, without more, generally do not cross constitutional lines. See *Vance*; *Clinton*. But burdens imposed by a congressional subpoena should be carefully scrutinized, for they stem from a rival political branch that has an ongoing relationship with the President and incentives to use subpoenas for institutional advantage.

Other considerations may be pertinent as well; one case every two centuries does not afford enough experience for an exhaustive list.

When Congress seeks information "needed for intelligent legislative action," it "unquestionably" remains "the duty of *all* citizens to cooperate." Congressional subpoenas for information from the President, however, implicate special concerns regarding the separation of powers. The courts below did not take adequate account of those concerns. The judgments of the Courts of Appeals for the D.C. Circuit and the Second Circuit are vacated, and the cases are remanded for further proceedings consistent with this opinion.

It is so ordered.

Justice THOMAS, dissenting.

. . . I would hold that Congress has no power to issue a legislative subpoena for private, nonofficial documents—whether they belong to the President or not. Congress may be able to obtain these documents as part of an investigation of the President, but to do so, it must proceed under the impeachment power. Accordingly, I would reverse the judgments of the Courts of Appeals. . . .

The scope of [Congress's] implied powers is very limited. The Constitution does not sweep in powers "of inferior importance, merely because they are inferior." *McCulloch*. . . . At the time of the founding, the power to subpoena private, nonofficial documents was not included by necessary implication in any of Congress' legislative powers. This understanding persisted for decades and is consistent with the Court's first decision addressing legislative subpoenas, *Kilbourn v. Thompson*, 103 U.S. 168 (1881). The test that this Court created in *McGrain v. Daugherty*, 273 U.S. 135 (1927), and the majority's variation on that standard today, are without support as applied to private, nonofficial documents. . . . I express no opinion about the constitutionality of legislative subpoenas for other kinds of evidence. [relocated footnote—EDS.]

The Committees argue that Congress wields the same investigatory powers that the British Parliament did at the time of the founding. But this claim overlooks one of the fundamental differences between our Government and the British Government: Parliament was supreme. Congress is not. . . . [I]n a system in which Congress is not supreme, the individual protections in the Bill of Rights, such as the prohibition on unreasonable searches and seizures, meaningfully constrain Congress' power to compel documents from private citizens. . . .

The subpoenas in these cases also cannot be justified based on the practices of 18th-century American legislatures. . . . [N]one of the examples from 18th-century colonial and state history support a power to issue a legislative subpoena for private, nonofficial documents.

Given that Congress has no exact precursor in England or colonial America, founding-era congressional practice is especially informative about the scope of implied legislative powers. Thus, it is highly probative that no founding-era Congress issued a subpoena for private, nonofficial documents. . . . Congress began issuing them by the end of the 1830s. However, the practice remained controversial in Congress and this Court throughout the first century of the Republic. . . .

When this Court first addressed a legislative subpoena, it refused to uphold it. After casting doubt on legislative subpoenas generally, the Court in *Kilbourn v. Thompson*, held that the subpoena at issue was unlawful because it sought to investigate private conduct. . . . The Court did not reach a conclusion on the . . . theory that a legislative subpoena power was necessary for Congress to carry out its legislative duties. But it observed that, based on British judicial opinions, not "much aid [is] given to the doctrine, that this power exists as one necessary to enable either House of Congress to exercise successfully their function of legislation." . . .

The Court instead based its decision on the fact that the subpoena at issue "ma[de] inquiry into the private affairs of the citizen." Such a power, the Court reasoned, "is judicial and not legislative," and "no judicial power is vested in the Congress or either branch of it, save in the cases" of punishing Members, compelling Members' attendance, judging elections and qualifications, and impeachment and trial. . . .

Nearly half a century later, in *McGrain v. Daugherty*, the Court reached the question reserved in *Kilbourn*—whether Congress has the power to issue legislative subpoenas. It rejected *Kilbourn*'s reasoning and upheld the power to issue legislative subpoenas as long as they were relevant to a legislative power. Although *McGrain* involved oral testimony, the Court has since extended this test to subpoenas for private documents. The Committees rely on *McGrain*, but this line of cases misunderstands both the original meaning of Article I and the historical practice underlying it. . . .

The opinion in *McGrain* lacks any foundation in text or history with respect to subpoenas for private, nonofficial documents. It fails to recognize that Congress, unlike Parliament, is not supreme. It does not cite any specific precedent for issuing legislative subpoenas for private documents from 18th-century colonial or state practice. And it identifies no founding-era legislative subpoenas for private documents.

Since *McGrain*, the Court has pared back Congress' authority to compel testimony and documents. It has held that certain convictions of witnesses for contempt of Congress violated the Fifth Amendment. See *Watkins v. United States*, 354 U.S. 178 (1957) (Due Process Clause); *Quinn v. United States*, 349 U.S. 155 (1955) (Self-Incrimination Clause); see also *Barenblatt v. United States*, 360 U.S. 109, 153-154 (1959) (Black, J., dissenting). It has also affirmed the reversal of a conviction on the ground that the Committee lacked authority to issue the subpoena. See *United States v. Rumely*, 345 U.S. 41 (1953). And today, it creates a new four-part, nonexhaustive test for cases involving the President. Rather than continue our trend of trying to compensate for *McGrain*, I would simply decline to apply it in these cases because it is readily apparent that the Committees have no constitutional authority to subpoena private, nonofficial documents. . . .

If the Committees wish to investigate alleged wrongdoing by the President and obtain documents from him, the Constitution provides Congress with a special mechanism for doing so: impeachment. . . . I express no view on whether there are any limitations on the impeachment power that would prevent the House from subpoenaing the documents at issue. [relocated footnote—Eds.]

Justice Alito, dissenting.

Justice Thomas makes a valuable argument about the constitutionality of congressional subpoenas for a President's personal documents. In these cases, however, I would assume for the sake of argument that such subpoenas are not categorically barred. Nevertheless, legislative subpoenas for a President's personal documents are inherently suspicious. Such documents are seldom of any special value in considering potential legislation, and subpoenas for such documents can easily be used for improper non-legislative purposes. Accordingly, courts must be very sensitive to separation of powers issues when they are asked to approve the enforcement of such subpoenas.

In many cases, disputes about subpoenas for Presidential documents are fought without judicial involvement. If Congress attempts to obtain such documents by subpoenaing a President directly, those two heavyweight institutions can use their considerable weapons to settle the matter. But when Congress issues such a subpoena to a third party, Congress must surely appreciate that the Judiciary may be pulled into the dispute, and Congress should not expect that the courts will allow the subpoena to be enforced without seriously examining its legitimacy.

Whenever such a subpoena comes before a court, Congress should be required to make more than a perfunctory showing that it is seeking the documents for a legitimate legislative purpose and not for the purpose of exposing supposed Presidential wrongdoing. The House can inquire about possible Presidential wrongdoing pursuant to its impeachment power, but the Committees do not defend these subpoenas as ancillary to that power.

Instead, they claim that the subpoenas were issued to gather information that is relevant to legislative issues, but there is disturbing evidence of an improper law enforcement purpose. In addition, the sheer volume of documents sought calls out for explanation.

The Court recognizes that the decisions below did not give adequate consideration to separation of powers concerns. Therefore, after setting out a non-exhaustive list of considerations for the lower courts to take into account, the Court vacates the judgments of the Courts of Appeals and sends the cases back for reconsideration. I agree that the lower courts erred and that these cases must be remanded, but I do not think that the considerations outlined by the Court can be properly satisfied unless the House is required to show more than it has put forward to date.

Specifically, the House should provide a description of the type of legislation being considered, and while great specificity is not necessary, the description should be sufficient to permit a court to assess whether the particular records sought are of any special importance. The House should also spell out its constitutional authority to enact the type of legislation that it is contemplating, and it should justify the scope of the subpoenas in relation to the articulated legislative needs. In addition, it should explain why the subpoenaed information, as opposed to information available from other sources, is needed. Unless the House is required to make a showing along these lines, I would hold that enforcement of the subpoenas cannot be ordered. Because I find the terms of the Court's remand inadequate, I must respectfully dissent.

DISCUSSION

1. *Catch me if you can.* As in Trump v. Vance, the result in Trump v. Mazars allowed President Trump to run out the clock on congressional investigations into his finances prior to the 2020 election.

2. *Why can't we all just get along?* The Court notes that it has never been asked to pass on a subpoena like this before, and that is because the political branches usually negotiate the issue. But one reason why Congress negotiates the issue is because, as discussed earlier, Congress has few practical alternatives. Recourse to the courts takes time, and therefore normally favors the party that wants to delay, which is usually the President.

Mazars does little to disturb this arrangement. Its new four-part test is complicated, highly fact-specific, and requires a balancing of interests. Therefore, it can't easily be applied in a clear-cut fashion by lower courts. For that reason, it will, if anything, protract litigation rather than speed it up. In essence, the Supreme Court is saying to Congress and the President: We are annoyed that things got this far. Work things out on your own next time, because if you don't, and come back to the courts, the resolution is going to take a very long time, because the criteria we have just announced are very fact-specific.

Of course, the way the Court has resolved the controversy means that if succeeding presidents are as intransigent as President Trump proved to be, they too will have little to fear from the courts. They will usually be able to run out the clock, as he has done in this case. And that means that Congress will have to find other forms of leverage.

3. *Mixed results for Congress.* There are still other reasons to think that *Mazars* is not a major victory for congressional oversight. When the litigation began, the baseline was *Watkins*, which held that courts would generally defer to Congress. It is true that the Court rejected President Trump's most aggressive claims. But the four-factor test moves things away from deference to Congress and toward greater protection for the President. In addition, the Justice Department (and the OLC) now get to develop the Court's new four-factor test in litigation. They will do what they can to push the doctrinal development of the *Mazars* test in the direction of presidential power, and in the long run, they may well succeed.

4. *Using the President as a "case study."* Before *Mazars*, it was generally recognized that Congress's ability to investigate had to relate to potential legislation it might pass. But in practice, this was not much of a limitation. Congress can pass laws on virtually any subject. (What it cannot do through the commerce power, for example, it can do through the spending power, and so on.) Moreover, because Congress has the power, under Article V, to propose new constitutional amendments, it

can presumably hold hearings for the purpose of considering a new amendment to the Constitution that would increase its existing powers.

In *Mazars*, the Court makes clear that "Congress may not rely on the President's information if other sources could reasonably provide Congress the information it needs in light of its particular legislative objective. The President's unique constitutional position means that Congress may not look to him as a 'case study' for general legislation." So, if Congress wants to investigate international money laundering, it can't use President Trump's financial records from Mazars and Deutsche Bank as a convenient way to study the more general problem.

Suppose that Congress suspects that the President himself has engaged in illegal money laundering, which puts him a compromising position with respect to a foreign power. After *Mazars*, how should it articulate the purposes of its investigation? Must it declare that it is considering impeaching the President, or can it stop short of that?

5. *Presidential harassment.* The Court is clearly worried about the possibility that Congress will harass the President with investigations to score political points. But in Trump v. Vance, the Court does not seem particularly worried that state and local prosecutors—a far larger number of independent actors—will use the criminal process to harass the President. What explains the difference between the two situations?

6. *Litigation about the President's tax returns. Mazars* does not resolve all of the disputes between the President and Congress. One example concerns the President's tax returns.

In defiance of long-standing political conventions, President Trump famously refused to disclose his tax returns during the 2016 campaign, offering various excuses for why he was not yet able to do so. After the election, he announced that he would not release them. His refusal to make his tax returns public infuriated his political opponents, who sought various ways to discover what was in them.

Federal law treats federal tax returns as confidential, and the Treasury Department generally may not disclose them to the public or to other parties. 26 U.S.C. §§ 6103(a), 7213(a). However, there are exceptions for authorized disclosures. One such disclosure appears in 26 U.S.C. §6103(f)(1), which provides that "Upon written request from the chairman of the Committee on Ways and Means of the House of Representatives, the chairman of the Committee on Finance of the Senate, or the chairman of the Joint Committee on Taxation, the Secretary [of the Treasury] shall furnish such committee with any return or return information specified in such request, except that any return or return information which can be associated with, or otherwise identify, directly or indirectly, a particular taxpayer shall be furnished to such committee only when sitting in closed executive session unless such taxpayer otherwise consents in writing to such disclosure." Subsection (f)(4)(A) authorizes the House Ways and Means Committee and the Senate Finance Committee—unlike other committees—to share such information with the full House or Senate, thereby effectively making it public.

On April 3, 2019, the Chairman of the House Committee on Ways and Means, Representative Richard Neal, requested the last six years of President Trump's individual tax returns, and those of eight associated business entities, as well as the audit histories and work papers associated with each return. Chairman Neal explained the reason for his request as follows:

> Consistent with its authority, the Committee is considering legislative proposals and conducting oversight related to our Federal tax laws, including, but not limited to, the extent to which the IRS audits and enforces the Federal tax laws against a President. Under the Internal Revenue Manual, individual income tax returns of a President are subject to mandatory examination, but this practice is IRS policy and not codified in the Federal tax laws. It is necessary for the Committee to determine the scope of any such examination and whether it includes a review of underlying business activities required to be reported on the individual income tax return.

Treasury Secretary Steven Mnuchin refused to release the returns, and on June 13, 2019, the Office of Legal Counsel issued an opinion supporting his position.[57] The OLC opinion argued that the request "was pretextual and that its true aim was to make the President's tax returns public, which is not a legitimate legislative purpose." The OLC claimed that the real reasons for the request are to discover and expose to the public Trump's potential financial conflicts of interest and ties to foreign nations, and, in particular, to assess what "the Russians have on Donald Trump politically, personally, [and] financially" and to "help the American people better understand the extent of Trump's financial ties to Putin's Russia" (quoting House members).

Following the 2020 election, the House of Representatives brought suit to enforce its subpoena. How should a court decide the case after *Mazars*? Does the existence of a federal statute make any difference to *Mazars*' four-factor test?

On June 16, 2021, after President Biden and a new Congress took office, Chairman Neal sent the Treasury Department a new written request. It sought the same categories of information, but for tax years 2015 through 2020. Neal's request reiterated that the Committee's principal interest was "the extent to which the IRS audits and enforces the Federal tax laws against a President." But it added that the Committee was also interested in whether "former President Trump's tax returns could reveal hidden business entanglements raising tax law and other issues, including conflicts of interest, affecting proper execution of the former President's responsibilities," and that "[a]n independent examination might also show foreign financial influences on former President Trump that could inform relevant congressional legislation."

On July 30, 2021, the Biden OLC issued a new opinion.[58] It disagreed with the previous OLC opinion and concluded that the Treasury Secretary should provide the tax returns as required by federal statute:

> The 2019 Opinion went astray . . . in suggesting that the Executive Branch should closely scrutinize the Committee's stated justifications for its requests in a manner that failed to accord the respect and deference

---

57. Congressional Committee's Request for the President's Tax Returns Under 26 U.S.C. § 6103(f), Office of Legal Counsel (June 13, 2019), https://www.justice.gov/olc/file/1173756/download.

58. Ways and Means Committee's Request for the Former President's Tax Returns and Related Tax Information Pursuant to 26 U.S.C. § 6103(f)(1), 45 Op. O.L.C. __ (July 30, 2021), https://s3.documentcloud.org/documents/21030541/olc-opinion-on-ways-and-means-committees-request-for-trump-tax-returns.pdf.

due a coordinate branch of government. The 2019 Opinion also failed to give due weight to the fact that the Committee was acting pursuant to a carefully crafted statute that reflects a judgment by the political branches, going back nearly a century, that the congressional tax committees should have special access to tax information given their roles in overseeing the national tax system. Particularly in light of this special statutory authority, Treasury should conclude that a facially valid tax committee request lacks a legitimate legislative purpose only in exceptional circumstances.

Applying the proper degree of deference due the Committee, we believe that there is ample basis to conclude that its June 2021 Request for former President Trump's tax information would further the Committee's principal stated objective of assessing the IRS's presidential audit program—a plainly legitimate area for congressional inquiry and possible legislation. The Chairman's additional stated objectives for reviewing that tax information are also legitimate, and the Committee has authority to seek the records for those reasons as well. Even if some individual members of Congress hope to see information from the former President's tax returns disclosed on the public record merely "for the sake of exposure," Trump v. Mazars USA, LLP, 140 S. Ct. 2019, 2032 (2020) (internal quotation marks omitted), that would not invalidate the legitimate objectives that the Committee's receipt of the information in question could serve.

B. The Appointment Power

Although Archibald Cox and Leon Jaworski proved fiercely independent during the Watergate scandal, the structure of a system in which "watchdogs" were formally picked by the very Administration they were supposed to watch rankled some sensibilities. In retrospect, we might question whether the system was indeed broken, and needed fixing. After all, the constitutional machinery had worked rather well in Watergate. Cox and Jaworski were independent because nothing less would satisfy a Congress armed with powers of oversight, appropriations, and impeachment, and a press and opposition party armed with the First Amendment. To be sure, politics rather than law framed whether an outside prosecutor would be named, who he would be, how he would operate, and when (if ever) he would be removed. But part of the genius of the Constitution was to establish competing power centers and trust their natural incentives and mutual jealousies to keep the system in balance. And if more formal institutions were necessary, perhaps they could have been built within the Congress itself, through the development of a professionalized and bipartisan staff specially charged with White House oversight. But instead, reformers in the wake of Watergate sought to bolster the power of judges and to strengthen the hand of special prosecutors by rendering them more formally independent of the White House. Under the provisions of the so-called Ethics in Government Act of 1978, the Attorney General was authorized to bring certain preliminary investigations of high governmental officials and insiders to the attention of a special panel of three federal judges picked by the Chief Justice. These judges, in turn, were supposed to appoint a special prosecutor to continue the investigation. When the Act reached the courts in the mid-1980s, critics such as Justice Scalia warned, in sharp language, that the Act flouted basic principles of separation of powers and fundamental fairness. Supporters of the Act deemed these criticisms overwrought. As you ponder the next set of materials with the benefit of hindsight, ask yourself who had more constitutional foresight.

Morrison v. Olson

487 U.S. 654 (1988)

[Theodore B. Olson, a former Assistant Attorney General, and two other Justice Department lawyers refused to obey subpoenas issued by an independent counsel appointed under the Ethics in Government Act of 1978. Under the Act's provisions, the Special Division—a special court created by the Act—appoints the independent counsel, sets the scope of the counsel's investigations, and authorizes the counsel to prosecute any violations of federal law. In this case, the independent counsel was investigating the three lawyers for giving false or misleading testimony to Congress and for withholding documents from Congress. Olson argued that the subpoenas were invalid because the Independent Counsel Act was unconstitutional.

In the D.C. Court of Appeals, the majority ruled that an independent counsel is not an "inferior Officer" of the United States for purposes of the Appointments Clause. Accordingly, the court found the Act invalid because it does not provide for the independent counsel to be nominated by the President and confirmed by the Senate, as the Clause requires for "principal" officers. The majority also argued that the Act violated the Appointments Clause insofar as it empowered a court of law to appoint an "inferior" officer who performs core executive functions; the Act's delegation of various powers to the Special Division violated the limitations of Article III; and the Act's restrictions on the Attorney General's power to remove an independent counsel violated the separation of powers. Finally, the court held that the Act interfered with the Executive Branch's prerogative to "take care that the Laws be faithfully executed," Art. II, 3. On appeal, the Supreme Court reversed.]

Chief Justice Rehnquist delivered the opinion of the Court. . . .

III

. . .

The parties do not dispute that "[t]he Constitution for purposes of appointment . . . divides all its officers into two classes." As we stated in Buckley v. Valeo, 424 U.S. 1, 132 (1976): "Principal officers are selected by the President with the advice and consent of the Senate. Inferior officers Congress may allow to be appointed by the President alone, by the heads of departments, or by the Judiciary." The initial question is, accordingly, whether appellant is an "inferior" or a "principal" officer. If she is the latter, as the Court of Appeals concluded, then the Act is in violation of the Appointments Clause.

The line between "inferior" and "principal" officers is one that is far from clear, and the Framers provided little guidance into where it should be drawn. We need not attempt here to decide exactly where the line falls between the two types of officers, because in our view appellant clearly falls on the "inferior officer" side of that line. Several factors lead to this conclusion.

First, appellant is subject to removal by a higher Executive Branch official. Although appellant may not be "subordinate" to the Attorney General (and the President) insofar as she possesses a degree of independent discretion to exercise the powers delegated to her under the Act, the fact that she can be removed by the Attorney General indicates that she is to some degree "inferior" in rank and authority. Second, appellant is empowered by the Act to perform only certain, limited duties. . . . Admittedly, the Act delegates to appellant "full power and independent authority to exercise all investigative and prosecutorial functions and powers of the Department of Justice," but this grant of authority does not include any authority to formulate policy for the Government or the Executive Branch, nor does it give appellant any administrative duties outside of those necessary to operate her office. The Act specifically provides that in policy matters appellant is to comply to the extent possible with the policies of the Department.

Third, appellant's office is limited in jurisdiction. Not only is the Act itself restricted in applicability to certain federal officials suspected of certain serious federal crimes, but an independent counsel can only act within the scope of the jurisdiction that has been granted by the Special Division[—the special court created by the Independent Counsel Act which selects the independent counsel—] pursuant to a request by the Attorney General. Finally, appellant's office is limited in tenure. There is concededly no time limit on the appointment of a particular counsel. Nonetheless, the office of independent counsel is "temporary" in the sense that an independent counsel is appointed essentially to accomplish a single task, and when that task is over the office is terminated, either by the counsel herself or by action of the Special Division. Unlike other prosecutors, appellant has no ongoing responsibilities that extend beyond the accomplishment of the mission that she was appointed for and authorized by the Special Division to undertake. In our view, these factors relating to the "ideas of tenure, duration . . . and duties" of the independent counsel, are sufficient to establish that appellant is an "inferior" officer in the constitutional sense. . . .

This does not, however, end our inquiry under the Appointments Clause. Appellees argue that even if appellant is an "inferior" officer, the Clause . . . does not contemplate congressional authorization of "interbranch appointments," in which an officer of one branch is appointed by officers of another branch. The relevant language of the Appointments Clause is worth repeating. It reads: ". . . but the Congress may by Law vest the Appointment of such inferior Officers, as they think proper, in the President alone, in the courts of Law, or in the Heads of Departments." On its face, the language of this "excepting clause" admits of no limitation on interbranch appointments. Indeed, the inclusion of "as they think proper" seems clearly to give Congress significant discretion to determine whether it is "proper" to vest the appointment of, for example, executive officials in the "courts of Law." . . .

We also note that the history of the Clause provides no support for appellees' position. . . . [In the Philadelphia Convention,] there was little or no debate on the question whether the Clause empowers Congress to provide for interbranch appointments, and there is nothing to suggest that the Framers intended to prevent Congress from having that power.

We do not mean to say that Congress' power to provide for interbranch appointments of "inferior officers" is unlimited. In addition to separation-of-powers concerns, which would arise if such provisions for appointment had the potential to impair the constitutional functions assigned to one of the branches, [Court precedent] suggests that Congress' decision to vest the appointment power in the courts would be improper if there was some "incongruity" between the functions normally performed by the courts and the performance of their duty to appoint. In this case, however, we do not think it impermissible for Congress to vest the power to appoint independent counsel in a specially created federal court. We thus disagree with the Court of Appeals' conclusion that there is an inherent incongruity about a court having the power to appoint prosecutorial officers.[a] . . . Lower courts have also upheld interim judicial appointments of United States Attorneys, and Congress itself has vested the power to make these interim appointments in the district courts.[b] Congress, of course, was concerned when it created the office of independent counsel with the conflicts of interest that could arise in situations when the Executive Branch is called upon to investigate its own high-ranking officers. If it were to remove the appointing authority from the Executive Branch, the most logical place to put it was in the Judicial Branch. In the light of the Act's provision making the judges of the Special Division ineligible to participate in any matters relating to an independent counsel they have appointed, we do not think that appointment of the independent counsel by the court runs afoul of the constitutional limitation on "incongruous" interbranch appointments.

IV

Appellees next contend that the powers vested in the Special Division by the Act conflict with Article III of the Constitution. We have long recognized that by the express provision of Article III, the judicial power of the United States is limited to "Cases" and "Controversies." As a general rule, we have broadly stated that "executive or administrative duties of a nonjudicial nature may not be imposed on judges holding office under Art. III of the Constitution." The purpose of this limitation is to help ensure the independence of the Judicial Branch and to prevent the Judiciary from encroaching into areas reserved for the other branches. . . .

. . . In our view, Congress' power under the Clause to vest the "Appointment" of inferior officers in the courts may, in certain circumstances, allow Congress to give the courts some discretion in defining the nature and scope of the appointed official's authority. Particularly when, as here, Congress creates a temporary "office" the nature and duties of which will by necessity vary with the factual circumstances giving rise to the need for an appointment in the first place, it may vest the power

a. Indeed, in light of judicial experience with prosecutors in criminal cases, it could be said that courts are especially well qualified to appoint prosecutors. This is not a case in which judges are given power to appoint an officer in an area in which they have no special knowledge or expertise, as in, for example, a statute authorizing the courts to appoint officials in the Department of Agriculture or the Federal Energy Regulatory Commission.

b. We note also the longstanding judicial practice of appointing defense attorneys for individuals who are unable to afford representation, notwithstanding the possibility that the appointed attorney may appear in court before the judge who appointed him.

to define the scope of the office in the court as an incident to the appointment of the officer pursuant to the Appointments Clause. This said, we do not think that Congress may give the Division unlimited discretion to determine the independent counsel's jurisdiction. In order for the Division's definition of the counsel's jurisdiction to be truly "incidental" to its power to appoint, the jurisdiction that the court decides upon must be demonstrably related to the factual circumstances that gave rise to the Attorney General's investigation and request for the appointment of the independent counsel in the particular case.

The Act also vests in the Special Division various powers and duties in relation to the independent counsel that, because they do not involve appointing the counsel or defining his or her jurisdiction, cannot be said to derive from the Division's Appointments Clause authority. . . .

. . . Some of these allegedly "supervisory" powers conferred on the court are passive: the Division merely "receives" reports from the counsel or the Attorney General, it is not entitled to act on them or to specifically approve or disapprove of their contents. Other provisions of the Act do require the court to exercise some judgment and discretion, but the powers granted by these provisions are themselves essentially ministerial. The Act simply does not give the Division the power to "supervise" the independent counsel in the exercise of his or her investigative or prosecutorial authority. And, the functions that the Special Division is empowered to perform are not inherently "Executive." . . .

V

. . . Two Terms ago we [held in] Bowsher v. Synar, 478 U.S. 714, 730 (1986), . . . that "Congress cannot reserve for itself the power of removal of an officer charged with the execution of the laws except by impeachment." A primary antecedent for this ruling was our 1926 decision in Myers v. United States, 272 U.S. 52. *Myers* had considered the propriety of a federal statute by which certain postmasters of the United States could be removed by the President only "by and with the advice and consent of the Senate." There too, Congress' attempt to involve itself in the removal of an executive official was found to be sufficient grounds to render the statute invalid. . . .

Unlike both *Bowsher* and *Myers,* this case does not involve an attempt by Congress itself to gain a role in the removal of executive officials other than its established powers of impeachment and conviction. The Act instead puts the removal power squarely in the hands of the Executive Branch; an independent counsel may be removed from office, "only by the personal action of the Attorney General, and only for good cause." There is no requirement of congressional approval of the Attorney General's removal decision, though the decision is subject to judicial review. In our view, the removal provisions of the Act make this case more analogous to Humphrey's Executor v. United States, 295 U.S. 602 (1935), and Wiener v. United States, 357 U.S. 349 (1958), than to *Myers* or *Bowsher.* . . .

Appellees contend that *Humphrey's Executor* and *Wiener* are distinguishable from this case because they did not involve officials who performed a "core executive function." They argue that our decision in *Humphrey's Executor* rests on a distinction between "purely executive" officials and officials who exercise "quasi-legislative" and "quasi-judicial" powers. In their view, when a "purely executive" official is involved, the governing precedent is *Myers*, not *Humphrey's Executor*. And, under *Myers*, the President must have absolute discretion to discharge "purely" executive officials at will.

We undoubtedly did rely on the terms "quasi-legislative" and "quasi-judicial" to distinguish the officials involved in *Humphrey's Executor* and *Wiener* from those in *Myers*, but our present considered view is that the determination of whether the Constitution allows Congress to impose a "good cause"-type restriction on the President's power to remove an official cannot be made to turn on whether or not that official is classified as "purely executive." The analysis contained in our removal cases is designed not to define rigid categories of those officials who may or may not be removed at will by the President, but to ensure that Congress does not interfere with the President's exercise of the "executive power" and his constitutionally appointed duty to "take care that the laws be faithfully executed" under Article II. . . .

. . . There is no real dispute that the functions performed by the independent counsel are "executive" in the sense that they are law enforcement functions that typically have been undertaken by officials within the Executive Branch. As we noted above, however, the independent counsel is an inferior officer under the Appointments Clause, with limited jurisdiction and tenure and lacking policymaking or significant administrative authority. Although the counsel exercises no small amount of discretion and judgment in deciding how to carry out his or her duties under the Act, we simply do not see how the President's need to control the exercise of that discretion is so central to the functioning of the Executive Branch as to require as a matter of constitutional law that the counsel be terminable at will by the President.

Nor do we think that the "good cause" removal provision at issue here impermissibly burdens the President's power to control or supervise the independent counsel, as an executive official, in the execution of his or her duties under the Act. This is not a case in which the power to remove an executive official has been completely stripped from the President, thus providing no means for the President to ensure the "faithful execution" of the laws. Rather, because the independent counsel may be terminated for "good cause," the Executive, through the Attorney General, retains ample authority to assure that the counsel is competently performing his or her statutory responsibilities in a manner that comports with the provisions of the Act. . . .[c]

B

The final question to be addressed is whether the Act, taken as a whole, violates the principle of separation of powers by unduly interfering with the role of the Executive Branch. . . .

We observe first that this case does not involve an attempt by Congress to increase its own powers at the expense of the Executive Branch. Unlike some of our previous cases, most recently Bowsher v. Synar, this case simply does not pose

---

c. Indeed, during the hearings on the 1982 amendments to the Act, [Associate Attorney General Giuliani] testified that the "good cause" standard contained in the amendments "would make the special prosecutor no more independent than officers of the many so-called independent agencies in the executive branch."

a "dange[r] of congressional usurpation of Executive Branch functions." See also INS v. Chadha, 462 U.S. 919, 958 (1983). Indeed, with the exception of the power of impeachment—which applies to all officers of the United States—Congress retained for itself no powers of control or supervision over an independent counsel. The Act does empower certain Members of Congress to request the Attorney General to apply for the appointment of an independent counsel, but the Attorney General has no duty to comply with the request, although he must respond within a certain time limit. Other than that, Congress' role under the Act is limited to receiving reports or other information and oversight of the independent counsel's activities, functions that we have recognized generally as being incidental to the legislative function of Congress.

Similarly, we do not think that the Act works any judicial usurpation of properly executive functions. . . . [T]he Special Division has no power to appoint an independent counsel sua sponte; it may only do so upon the specific request of the Attorney General, and the courts are specifically prevented from reviewing the Attorney General's decision not to seek appointment. In addition, once the court has appointed a counsel and defined his or her jurisdiction, it has no power to supervise or control the activities of the counsel. As we pointed out in our discussion of the Special Division in relation to Article III, the various powers delegated by the statute to the Division are not supervisory or administrative, nor are they functions that the Constitution requires be performed by officials within the Executive Branch. . . . It is undeniable that the Act reduces the amount of control or supervision that the Attorney General and, through him, the President exercises over the investigation and prosecution of a certain class of alleged criminal activity. The Attorney General is not allowed to appoint the individual of his choice; he does not determine the counsel's jurisdiction; and his power to remove a counsel is limited. Nonetheless, the Act does give the Attorney General several means of supervising or controlling the prosecutorial powers that may be wielded by an independent counsel. Most importantly, the Attorney General retains the power to remove the counsel for "good cause," a power that we have already concluded provides the Executive with substantial ability to ensure that the laws are "faithfully executed" by an independent counsel. No independent counsel may be appointed without a specific request by the Attorney General, and the Attorney General's decision not to request appointment if he finds "no reasonable grounds to believe that further investigation is warranted" is committed to his unreviewable discretion. The Act thus gives the Executive a degree of control over the power to initiate an investigation by the independent counsel. In addition, the jurisdiction of the independent counsel is defined with reference to the facts submitted by the Attorney General, and once a counsel is appointed, the Act requires that the counsel abide by Justice Department policy unless it is not "possible" to do so. Notwithstanding the fact that the counsel is to some degree "independent" and free from executive supervision to a greater extent than other federal prosecutors, in our view these features of the Act give the Executive Branch sufficient control over the independent counsel to ensure that the President is able to perform his constitutionally assigned duties. . . .

Justice Scalia, dissenting.

It is the proud boast of our democracy that we have "a government of laws and not of men." Many Americans are familiar with that phrase; not many know its derivation. It comes from Part the First, Article XXX, of the Massachusetts Constitution of 1780, which reads in full as follows:

> "In the government of this Commonwealth, the legislative department shall never exercise the executive and judicial powers, or either of them: The executive shall never exercise the legislative and judicial powers, or either of them: The judicial shall never exercise the legislative and executive powers, or either of them: to the end it may be a government of laws and not of men."

The Framers of the Federal Constitution similarly viewed the principle of separation of powers as the absolutely central guarantee of a just Government. In No. 47 of The Federalist, Madison wrote that "[n]o political truth is certainly of greater intrinsic value, or is stamped with the authority of more enlightened patrons of liberty." The Federalist No. 47. Without a secure structure of separated powers, our Bill of Rights would be worthless, as are the bills of rights of many nations of the world that have adopted, or even improved upon, the mere words of ours. . . .

II

. . . Article II, §1, cl. 1, of the Constitution provides: "The executive Power shall be vested in a President of the United States."

As I described at the outset of this opinion, this does not mean *some of* the executive power, but *all of* the executive power. It seems to me, therefore, that the decision of the Court of Appeals invalidating the present statute must be upheld on fundamental separation-of-powers principles if the following two questions are answered affirmatively: (1) Is the conduct of a criminal prosecution (and of an investigation to decide whether to prosecute) the exercise of purely executive power? (2) Does the statute deprive the President of the United States of exclusive control over the exercise of that power? Surprising to say, the Court appears to concede an affirmative answer to both questions, but seeks to avoid the inevitable conclusion that since the statute vests some purely executive power in a person who is not the President of the United States it is void.

[As to the first question, g]overnmental investigation and prosecution of crimes is a quintessentially executive function. As for the second question, whether the statute before us deprives the President of exclusive control over that quintessentially executive activity: The Court does not, and could not possibly, assert that it does not. That is indeed the whole object of the statute. Instead, the Court points out that the President, through his Attorney General, has at least *some* control. That concession is alone enough to invalidate the statute, but I cannot refrain from pointing out that the Court greatly exaggerates the extent of that "some" Presidential control. "Most importan[t]" among these controls, the Court asserts, is the Attorney General's "power to remove the counsel for 'good cause.'" This is somewhat like referring to shackles as an effective means of locomotion. . . .

. . . Finally, the Court points out that the Act directs the independent counsel to abide by general Justice Department policy, except when not "possible." The exception alone shows this to be an empty promise. Even without that, however, one would be hard put to come up with many investigative or prosecutorial "policies" (other than those imposed by the Constitution or by Congress through law) that are absolute. Almost all investigative and prosecutorial decisions—including the ultimate decision whether, after a technical violation of the law has been found, prosecution is warranted—involve the balancing of innumerable legal and practical considerations. Indeed, even political considerations (in the nonpartisan sense) must be considered, as exemplified by the recent decision of an independent counsel to subpoena the former Ambassador of Canada, producing considerable tension in our relations with that country. Another preeminently political decision is whether getting a conviction in a particular case is worth the disclosure of national security information that would be necessary. The Justice Department and our intelligence agencies are often in disagreement on this point, and the Justice Department does not always win. The present Act even goes so far as specifically to take the resolution of that dispute away from the President and give it to the independent counsel. In sum, the balancing of various legal, practical, and political considerations, none of which is absolute, is the very essence of prosecutorial discretion. To take this away is to remove the core of the prosecutorial function, and not merely "some" Presidential control.

As I have said, however, it is ultimately irrelevant *how much* the statute reduces Presidential control. . . . It is not for us to determine, and we have never presumed to determine, how much of the purely executive powers of government must be within the full control of the President. The Constitution prescribes that they *all* are. . . .

Is it unthinkable that the President should have such exclusive power, even when alleged crimes by him or his close associates are at issue? No more so than that Congress should have the exclusive power of legislation, even when what is at issue is its own exemption from the burdens of certain laws. No more so than that this Court should have the exclusive power to pronounce the final decision on justiciable cases and controversies, even those pertaining to the constitutionality of a statute reducing the salaries of the Justices. A system of separate and coordinate powers necessarily involves an acceptance of exclusive power that can theoretically be abused. . . . While the separation of powers may prevent us from righting every wrong, it does so in order to ensure that we do not lose liberty. The checks against any branch's abuse of its exclusive powers are twofold: First, retaliation by one of the other branch's use of its exclusive powers: Congress, for example, can impeach the executive who willfully fails to enforce the laws; the executive can decline to prosecute under unconstitutional statutes; and the courts can dismiss malicious prosecutions. Second, and ultimately, there is the political check that the people will replace those in the political branches . . . who are guilty of abuse. Political pressures produced special prosecutors—for Teapot Dome and for Watergate, for example—long before this statute created the independent counsel.

The Court has, nonetheless, replaced the clear constitutional prescription that the executive power belongs to the President with a "balancing test." What are the standards to determine how the balance is to be struck, that is, how much removal of Presidential power is too much? . . .

In my view, moreover, even as an ad hoc, standardless judgment the Court's conclusion must be wrong. . . .

[I]n the 10 years since the institution of the independent counsel was established by law, there have been nine highly publicized investigations, a source of constant political damage to two administrations. That they could not remotely be described as merely the application of "normal" investigatory and prosecutory standards is demonstrated by . . . the following facts: Congress appropriates approximately $50 million annually for general legal activities, salaries, and expenses of the Criminal Division of the Department of Justice. This money is used to support "[f]ederal appellate activity," "[o]rganized crime prosecution," "[p]ublic integrity" and "[f]raud" matters, "[n]arcotic & dangerous drug prosecution," "[i]nternal security," "[g]eneral litigation and legal advice," "special investigations," "[p]rosecution support," "[o]rganized crime drug enforcement," and "[m]anagement & administration." By comparison, between May 1986 and August 1987, four independent counsel (not all of whom were operating for that entire period of time) spent almost $5 million (one-tenth of the amount annually appropriated to the entire Criminal Division), spending almost $1 million in the month of August 1987 alone. . . .

III

[T]he Court does not attempt to "decide exactly" what establishes the line between principal and "inferior" officers, but is confident that, whatever the line may be, appellant "clearly falls on the 'inferior officer' side" of it. The Court gives three reasons: First, she "is subject to removal by a higher Executive Branch official," namely, the Attorney General. Second, she is "empowered by the Act to perform only certain, limited duties." Third, her office is "limited in jurisdiction" and "limited in tenure."

The first of these lends no support to the view that appellant is an inferior officer. Appellant is removable only for "good cause" or physical or mental incapacity. By contrast, most (if not all) principal officers in the Executive Branch may be removed by the President at will. I fail to see how the fact that appellant is more difficult to remove than most principal officers helps to establish that she is an inferior officer. And I do not see how it could possibly make any difference to her superior or inferior status that the President's limited power to remove her must be exercised through the Attorney General. If she were removable at will by the Attorney General, then she would be subordinate to him and thus properly designated as inferior; but the Court essentially admits that she is not subordinate. If it were common usage to refer to someone as "inferior" who is subject to removal for cause by another, then one would say that the President is "inferior" to Congress.

The second reason offered by the Court—that appellant performs only certain, limited duties—may be relevant to whether she is an inferior officer, but it mischaracterizes the extent of her powers. As the Court states: "Admittedly, the Act delegates to appellant [the] 'full power and independent authority to exercise all investigative and prosecutorial functions and powers of the Department of Justice.'" Moreover, in addition to this general grant of power she is given a broad range of specifically enumerated powers, including a power not even the Attorney General possesses: to "contes[t] in court . . . any claim of privilege or attempt to withhold evidence on grounds of national security." Once all of this is "admitted," it seems to me impossible to maintain that appellant's authority is so "limited" as to render her an inferior officer. . . .

The final set of reasons given by the Court for why the independent counsel clearly is an inferior officer emphasizes the limited nature of her jurisdiction and tenure. Taking the latter first, I find nothing unusually limited about the independent counsel's tenure. To the contrary, unlike most high ranking Executive Branch officials, she continues to serve until she (or the Special Division) decides that her work is substantially completed. This particular independent prosecutor has already served more than two years, which is at least as long as many Cabinet officials. As to the scope of her jurisdiction, there can be no doubt that is small (though far from unimportant). But within it she exercises more than the full power of the Attorney General. The Ambassador to Luxembourg is not anything less than a principal officer, simply because Luxembourg is small. And the federal judge who sits in a small district is not for that reason "inferior in rank and authority." . . .

More fundamentally, however, it is not clear from the Court's opinion why the factors it discusses—even if applied correctly to the facts of this case—are determinative of the question of inferior officer status. . . . I think it preferable to look to the text of the Constitution and the division of power that it establishes. These demonstrate, I think, that the independent counsel is not an inferior officer because she is not *subordinate* to any officer in the Executive Branch (indeed, not even to the President). Dictionaries in use at the time of the Constitutional Convention gave the word "inferiour" two meanings which it still bears today: (1) "[l]ower in place, . . . station, . . . rank of life, . . . value or excellency," and (2) "[s]ubordinate." S. Johnson, Dictionary of the English Language (6th ed. 1785). In a document dealing with the structure (the constitution) of a government, one would naturally expect the word to bear the latter meaning—indeed, in such a context it would be unpardonably careless to use the word unless a relationship of subordination was intended. If what was meant was merely "lower in station or rank," one would use instead a term such as "lesser officers." At the only other point in the Constitution at which the word "inferior" appears, it plainly connotes a relationship of subordination. Article III vests the judicial power of the United States in "one supreme Court, and in such *inferior* Courts as the Congress may from time to time ordain and establish." U.S. Const., Art. III, §1 (emphasis added). In Federalist No. 81, Hamilton pauses to describe the "inferior" courts authorized by Article III as inferior in the sense that they are "subordinate" to the Supreme Court.

That "inferior" means "subordinate" is also consistent with what little we know about the evolution of the Appointments Clause. As originally reported to the Committee on Style, the Appointments Clause provided no "exception" from the standard manner of appointment (President with the advice and consent of the Senate) for inferior officers. On September 15, 1787, the last day of the Convention before the proposed Constitution was signed, in the midst of a host of minor changes that were being considered, Gouverneur Morris moved to add the exceptions clause. No great debate ensued; the only disagreement was over whether it was necessary at all. Nobody thought that it was a fundamental change, excluding from the President's appointment power and the Senate's confirmation power a category of officers who might function on their own, outside the supervision of those appointed in the more cumbersome fashion. And it is significant that in the very brief discussion Madison mentions (as in apparent contrast to the "inferior officers" covered by the provision) "Superior Officers." Of course one is not a "superior officer" without some supervisory responsibility, just as, I suggest, one is not an "inferior officer" within the meaning of the provision under discussion unless one is subject to supervision by a "superior officer." It is perfectly obvious, therefore, both from the relative brevity of the discussion this addition received, and from the content of that discussion, that it was intended merely to make clear (what Madison thought already was clear) that those officers appointed by the President with Senate approval could on their own appoint their subordinates, who would, of course, by chain of command still be under the direct control of the President.

This interpretation is, moreover, consistent with our admittedly sketchy precedent in this area. . . . [I]in United States v. Nixon, we noted that the Attorney General's appointment of the Watergate Special Prosecutor was made pursuant to the Attorney General's "power to appoint subordinate officers to assist him in the discharge of his duties.". . . We explicitly stated that the Special Prosecutor was a "subordinate office[r]," because, in the end, the President or the Attorney General could have removed him at any time, if by no other means than amending or revoking the regulation defining his authority. . . .

To be sure, it is not a *sufficient* condition for "inferior" officer status that one be subordinate to a principal officer. . . . Even an officer who is subordinate to a department head can be a principal officer. . . . But it is surely a *necessary* condition for inferior officer status that the officer be subordinate to another officer.

The independent counsel is not even subordinate to the President. The Court essentially admits as much. . . .

IV

. . . Before the present decision it was established . . . (1) that the President's power to remove principal officers who exercise purely executive powers could not be restricted, see *Myers*, and (2) that his power to remove inferior officers who exercise purely executive powers, and whose appointment Congress had removed from the usual procedure of Presidential appointment with Senate consent, could be restricted, at least where the appointment had been made by an officer of the Executive Branch, see ibid.; United States v. Perkins, 116 U.S. 483, 485 (1886).[a]

The Court could have resolved the removal power issue in this case by simply relying upon its erroneous conclusion that the independent counsel was an inferior officer, and then extending our holding that the removal of inferior officers appointed by the Executive can be restricted, to a new holding that even the removal of inferior officers appointed by the courts can be restricted. That would in my view be a considerable and unjustified extension, giving the Executive full discretion in neither the selection nor the removal of a purely executive officer. The course the Court has chosen, however, is even worse.

Since our 1935 decision in Humphrey's Executor v. United States, 295 U.S. 602—which was considered by many at the time the product of an activist, anti-New Deal Court bent on reducing the power of President Franklin Roosevelt—it

---

a. [T]he President must have control over all exercises of the executive power. That requires that he have plenary power to remove principal officers such as the independent counsel, but it does not require that he have plenary power to remove inferior officers. Since the latter are, as I have described, subordinate to, i.e., subject to the supervision of, principal officers who (being removable at will) have the President's complete confidence, it is enough—at least if they have been appointed by the President or by a principal officer—that they be removable for cause, which would include, of course, the failure to accept supervision. . . .

has been established that the line of permissible restriction upon removal of principal officers lies at the point at which the powers exercised by those officers are no longer purely executive. Thus, removal restrictions have been generally regarded as lawful for so-called "independent regulatory agencies," such as the Federal Trade Commission, the Interstate Commerce Commission, and the Consumer Product Safety Commission, which engage substantially in what has been called the "quasi-legislative activity" of rulemaking, and for members of Article I courts, such as the Court of Military Appeals, who engage in the "quasi-judicial" function of adjudication. . . . Today, however, *Humphrey's Executor* is swept into the dustbin of repudiated constitutional principles. "[O]ur present considered view," the Court says, "is that the determination of whether the Constitution allows Congress to impose a 'good cause'-type restriction on the President's power to remove an official cannot be made to turn on whether or not that official is classified as 'purely executive.'" . . .

. . . "[O]ur present considered view" is simply that any executive officer's removal can be restricted, so long as the President remains "able to accomplish his constitutional role." There are now no lines. If the removal of a prosecutor, the virtual embodiment of the power to "take care that the laws be faithfully executed," can be restricted, what officer's removal cannot? This is an open invitation for Congress to experiment. What about a special Assistant Secretary of State, with responsibility for one very narrow area of foreign policy, who would not only have to be confirmed by the Senate but could also be removed only pursuant to certain carefully designed restrictions? Could this possibly render the President "[un]able to accomplish his constitutional role"? Or a special Assistant Secretary of Defense for Procurement? The possibilities are endless. . . .

V

The purpose of the separation and equilibration of powers in general, and of the unitary Executive in particular, was not merely to assure effective government but to preserve individual freedom. Those who hold or have held offices covered by the Ethics in Government Act are entitled to that protection as much as the rest of us, and I conclude my discussion by considering the effect of the Act upon the fairness of the process they receive.

Only someone who has worked in the field of law enforcement can fully appreciate the vast power and the immense discretion that are placed in the hands of a prosecutor with respect to the objects of his investigation. Justice Robert Jackson, when he was Attorney General under President Franklin Roosevelt, described it in a memorable speech to United States Attorneys, as follows:

> ". . . One of the greatest difficulties of the position of prosecutor is that he must pick his cases, because no prosecutor can even investigate all of the cases in which he receives complaints. If the Department of Justice were to make even a pretense of reaching every probable violation of federal law, ten times its present staff will be inadequate. We know that no local police force can strictly enforce the traffic laws, or it would arrest half the driving population on any given morning. What every prosecutor is practically required to do is to select the cases for prosecution and to select those in which the offense is the most flagrant, the public harm the greatest, and the proof the most certain.

> "If the prosecutor is obliged to choose his case, it follows that he can choose his defendants. Therein is the most dangerous power of the prosecutor: that he will pick people that he thinks he should get, rather than cases that need to be prosecuted. With the law books filled with a great assortment of crimes, a prosecutor stands a fair chance of finding at least a technical violation of some act on the part of almost anyone. In such a case, it is not a question of discovering the commission of a crime and then looking for the man who has committed it, it is a question of picking the man and then searching the law books, or putting investigators to work, to pin some offense on him. It is in this realm — in which the prosecutor picks some person whom he dislikes or desires to embarrass, or selects some group of unpopular persons and then looks for an offense, that the greatest danger of abuse of prosecuting power lies. It is here that law enforcement becomes personal, and the real crime becomes that of being unpopular with the predominant or governing group, being attached to the wrong political views, or being personally obnoxious to or in the way of the prosecutor himself."

Under our system of government, the primary check against prosecutorial abuse is a political one. The prosecutors who exercise this awesome discretion are selected and can be removed by a President, whom the people have trusted enough to elect. Moreover, when crimes are not investigated and prosecuted fairly, nonselectively, with a reasonable sense of proportion, the President pays the cost in political damage to his administration. . . . That result, of course, was precisely what the Founders had in mind when they provided that all executive powers would be exercised by a single Chief Executive. As Hamilton put it, "[t]he ingredients which constitute safety in the republican sense are a due dependence on the people, and a due responsibility." Federalist No. 70. The President is directly dependent on the people, and since there is only one President, he is responsible. The people know whom to blame, whereas "one of the weightiest objections to a plurality in the executive . . . is that it tends to conceal faults and destroy responsibility."

That is the system of justice the rest of us are entitled to, but what of that select class consisting of present or former high-level Executive Branch officials? . . . An independent counsel is selected, and the scope of his or her authority prescribed, by a panel of judges. What if they are politically partisan, as judges have been known to be, and select a prosecutor antagonistic to the administration, or even to the particular individual who has been selected for this special treatment? There is no remedy for that, not even a political one. Judges, after all, have life tenure, and appointing a surefire enthusiastic prosecutor could hardly be considered an impeachable offense. So if there is anything wrong with the selection, there is effectively no one to blame. The independent counsel thus selected proceeds to assemble a staff. . . . [I]n the nature of things this has to be done by finding lawyers who are willing to lay aside their current careers for an indeterminate amount of time, to take on a job that has no prospect of permanence and little prospect for promotion. One thing is certain, however: it involves investigating and perhaps prosecuting a particular individual. Can one imagine a less equitable manner of fulfilling the executive responsibility to investigate and prosecute? What would be the reaction if, in an area not covered by this statute, the Justice Department posted a public notice inviting applicants to assist in an investigation and possible prosecution of a certain prominent person? Does this not invite what Justice Jackson described as "picking the man and then searching the law books, or putting investigators to work, to pin some offense on him"? To be sure, the investigation must relate to the area of criminal offense specified by the life-tenured judges. But that has often been (and nothing prevents it from being) very broad—and should the independent counsel or his or her staff come up with something beyond that scope, nothing prevents him or her from asking the judges to expand his or her authority or, if that does not work, referring it to the Attorney General, whereupon the whole process would recommence and, if there was "reasonable basis to believe" that further investigation was warranted, that new offense would be referred to the Special Division, which would in all likelihood assign it to the same independent counsel. It seems to me not conducive to fairness. But even if it were entirely evident that unfairness was in fact the result—the judges hostile to the administration, the independent counsel an old foe of the President, the staff refugees from the recently defeated administration—*there would be no one accountable to the public to whom the blame could be assigned.*

. . . It is true, of course, that a similar list of horribles could be attributed to an ordinary Justice Department prosecution—a vindictive prosecutor, an antagonistic staff, etc. But the difference is the difference that the Founders envisioned when they established a single Chief Executive accountable to the people: the blame can be assigned to someone who can be punished.

. . . It is . . . an additional advantage of the unitary Executive that it can achieve a more uniform application of the law. Perhaps that is not always achieved, but the mechanism to achieve it is there. The mini-Executive that is the independent counsel, however, operating in an area where so little is law and so much is discretion, is intentionally cut off from the unifying influence of the Justice Department, and from the perspective that multiple responsibilities provide. What would normally be regarded as a technical violation (there are no rules defining such things), may in his or her small world assume the proportions of an indictable offense. What would normally be regarded as an investigation that has reached the level of pursuing such picayune matters that it should be concluded, may to him or her be an investigation that ought to go on for another year. How frightening it must be to have your own independent counsel and staff appointed, with nothing else to do but to investigate you until investigation is no longer worthwhile—with whether it is worthwhile not depending upon what such judgments usually hinge on, competing responsibilities. And to have that counsel and staff decide, with no basis for comparison, whether what you have done is bad enough, willful enough, and provable enough, to warrant an indictment. How admirable the constitutional system that provides the means to avoid such a distortion. And how unfortunate the judicial decision that has permitted it. . . .

[Justice Kennedy did not participate in this case.]

DISCUSSION

1. *The facts of Morrison v. Olson.* Morrison v. Olson arose out of a 1982 battle between President Reagan and the Democratic-controlled House of Representatives

over the disclosure of documents that concerned how effectively the Reagan Administration was enforcing the Superfund Law, an environmental law. The Reagan EPA was beset by scandals and Democrats accused the Administration of attempting to undermine the environmental laws. President Reagan directed the Administrator of the EPA, Anne Gorsuch Burford, to assert executive privilege and withhold the requested documents from Congress. In response, the House voted to hold Burford in contempt, after which both she and the Administration filed a lawsuit against the House. In March 1983, the administration agreed to give the relevant House Subcommittees limited access to the documents, and Burford resigned.

The House, however, was not satisfied, and continued its investigations into the Justice Department's role in withholding the documents. On March 10, 1983, a day after Burford's resignation, Theodore Olson, then head of the Office of Legal Counsel, testified before a House Subcommittee. In 1985, the majority members of the Judiciary Committee published a report on their investigations, suggesting that Olson had given false and misleading testimony to the Subcommittee, and that two other Justice Department colleagues, Edward Schmults and Carol Dinkins, had wrongfully withheld documents and misled Congress, obstructing its investigation. The Chairman of the Judiciary Committee requested an independent counsel to investigate the allegations against the three Justice Department officials. Olson refused to cooperate with the independent counsel's investigation on the ground that the Independent Counsel Act was unconstitutional, leading to the litigation that became Morrison v. Olson.

Theodore Olson would later argue Bush v. Gore on behalf of the George W. Bush presidential campaign and serve as Solicitor General of the United States in the Bush Administration. In 2017, Anne Gorsuch Burford's son, Neil Gorsuch, was appointed to the Supreme Court to fill the seat of the recently deceased Justice Antonin Scalia, who wrote the dissent in Morrison v. Olson.

2. *Construing statutes in the shadow of constitutional principles.* Section 592 of the independent counsel statute provided that "[t]he Attorney General shall apply to the division of the court for the appointment of an independent counsel if . . . the Attorney General, upon completion of a preliminary investigation under this chapter, determines that there are reasonable grounds to believe that further investigation is warranted." If read with the emphasis on the word *shall*, this provision would seem to impose a strict legal duty on the Attorney General to trigger the judicial appointment of an independent counsel even in cases where the AG would prefer otherwise as a matter of policy. But the *Morrison* majority, in an oft-overlooked passage, essentially defanged this provision. Implicitly placing the emphasis not on the word *shall* but on the notion that it is the *Attorney General* who must decide that there are truly *reasonable* grounds for deciding that further investigation is truly *warranted*, the *Morrison* Court reads this provision to give the AG "unreviewable discretion" to not trigger the appointment. This reading helps make the statute more constitutionally palatable to majority. Note the similarity to the *Cox* court's reading of Rule 7, and the *Nixon* Court's reminder that the regulation empowering the special prosecutor may be rescinded by executive branch; in all three contexts, the gravitational pull of constitutional principles under Article II appears to inflect the reading of nonconstitutional texts.

3. *Recasting precedents.* Precedent counts for a great deal in modern constitutional adjudications, but precedent can be read in different ways. Note the *Morrison*

majority's effort to recast the *Myers* and *Humphrey's Executor* precedents. If read at face value, these cases distinguish between officials who exercise purely executive power on the one hand, and those who wield quasi-legislative or quasi-judicial power on the other. The *Morrison* majority, however reads these cases not for what they said but for what they did; the more relevant distinction, the *Morrison* Court announces (in retrospect), is that Congress tried to participate in the removal process in *Myers* (via a legislative veto on presidential removal), but not in *Humphrey's Executor*. Regardless of what you think about the use of the technique in *Morrison,* note that judicial rewriting of old precedents—explaining why earlier decisions were right on their facts but wrong in some of their language—is an important part of the modern judicial craft, allowing case law to evolve while maintaining links to the past.

4. *The meaning of "inferiority."* Did the *Morrison* majority play fast and loose with the word "inferior"? Can one truly be both "inferior" and "independent" at the same time? Note that the Court emphasizes that the special division should not be understood as the independent counsel's supervisor—lest judges become superprosecutors of sorts. But if the three judges are not Morrison's supervisor, who is? Can there be an "inferior" officer without a corresponding "superior" officer? Following Justice Scalia's lead, let us consider the possible light that "intratextualism"—construing one clause of the Constitution in light of similarly worded clauses—might shed on the meaning of the word "inferior." Note that Article I, §8 speaks of "tribunals *inferior to* the *Supreme* Court." Here, it seems, there is a clear hierarchical chain of command—"inferior" tribunals must follow the commands of their superior, the Supreme Court. (This helps explain why such tribunals are bound by High Court precedent, see Evan H. Caminker, Why Must Inferior Courts Obey Superior Court Precedents?, 46 Stan. L. Rev. 817, 828-837 (1994).) Does the same word—"inferior"—mean the same thing in the Appointments Clause context, namely, that an "inferior" officer must be subordinate to his "superior," the relevant appointing authority (whether court or department head or President)?

A considerable amount of historical evidence suggests so. The language permitting unilateral appointment of inferior officers emerged on the last day of the Philadelphia Convention, and with little debate—facts suggesting that it was viewed as a minor housekeeping measure to spare the Senate's time. (The only other recorded discussion of inferior officers occurred a week earlier and strongly supports this interpretation: Recall that Rufus King stated that he "did not suppose it was meant that all the minute officers were to be appointed by the Senate, or any other original source, but by the higher officers *of the departments to which they belong*.") Allowing major officers to pick their own assistants keeps faith with this housekeeping reading. But authorizing judges to appoint prosecutors—or diplomats or colonels, for that matter—seems very different. Had the delegates understood that the clause could be so applied, we would expect to find considerably more discussion.

In keeping with the housekeeping reading, the First Congress in one of its earliest statutes vested the Secretary of the Department of Foreign Affairs with the power to appoint and supervise *his own assistant*: "There shall be in the said department, an inferior officer, to be appointed by the said principal officer, and to be employed therein as he shall deem proper. . . ." Soon thereafter, Congress used similar language in allowing the Secretary of War to appoint and monitor his own assistant. In his landmark 1833 treatise on the Constitution, Joseph Story wrote that:[59]

> The courts of the Union possess the narrow prerogative of appointing *their own* clerk, and reporter. . . . The heads of department are, in like manner, generally entitled to the appointment of the clerks in their *respective* offices. . . . [And] the postmaster general . . . is invested with the sole and exclusive authority to appoint, and remove all *deputy* post-masters.

Six years after the publication of Story's 1833 treatise, the Supreme Court expounded the Appointments Clause as follows in Ex parte Hennen, 38 U.S. (13 Pet.) 230 (1839):

> The appointing power here designated . . . was no doubt intended to be exercised by the department of the government to which the officer to be appointed most appropriately belonged. The appointment of *clerks of Courts* properly belongs to the *Courts* of law; and that a clerk is one of the inferior officers contemplated by this provision in the Constitution cannot be questioned. Congress, in the exercise of the power here given, by the act of the 24th of September, 1789, establishing the judicial Courts of the United States . . . , declare that the Supreme Court, and the District Courts shall have power to appoint clerks of their *respective* Courts; and that the clerk for each District Court shall be clerk also of the Circuit Court in such district.

The basic structural idea at play in the appointments context was accountability: When an inferior officer misbehaved, the polity would know whom to blame—the appointing authority responsible for choosing and monitoring the inferior. See, e.g., The Federalist No. 70, at 428 (Alexander Hamilton) (Clinton Rossiter ed., 1961) ("Scandalous appointments to important offices have been made [in New York by a governor acting behind closed doors with his council]. . . . When inquiry has been made, the blame has been laid by the governor on the members of the council, who, on their part, have charged it upon his nomination; while the people remain altogether at a loss to determine by whose influence their interests have been committed to hands so unqualified and so manifestly improper."); see also The Federalist No. 76, at 455 (Alexander Hamilton) ("The sole and undivided [appointment] responsibility of one man will naturally beget a livelier sense of duty and a more exact regard to reputation."); The Federalist No. 77, at 461 (Alexander Hamilton) ("The blame of a bad nomination would fall upon the President singly and absolutely."). One can summarize the structural arguments this way: An inferior officer must not only be below a superior on the organization chart, but must also be inferior *to* the superior. There must be a relationship of hierarchy or a chain of command. This hierarchy can manifest in different ways. The superior officer is the person who is vested with the power

59. Joseph Story, Commentaries on the Constitution of the United States 1530, at 387 (Boston, Hilliard, Gray & Co. 1833) (emphasis added).

to hire the inferior officer who works under them, who has the power to supervise the inferior, who has the power to countermand the inferior, and, in some cases, to fire the inferior. The point of this hierarchy is that if the inferior officer errs or proves incompetent or corrupt, the public knows who to blame. Note that lower-level employees in the executive branch may have civil service protections, and they may be hired by people in the executive branch other than their direct supervisors. But they are still inferior officers if their superiors can supervise and countermand their actions.

In the context of Article III, lower court judges are not appointed by higher court judges, and all of them have life tenure. But the higher court judges have the power to supervise lower court judges and reverse their decisions.

5. *The judicial role.* In the D.C. Circuit decision below, In Re Sealed Case, 838 F.2d 476 (1988), rev'd sub nom. Morrison v. Olson, 487 U.S. 654 (1988), Judge Silberman argued that the independent counsel statute also violated the separation of powers:

> . . . [I]t must be incongruous if an officer of one branch is authorized to appoint an officer of another branch who is assigned a duty central to the constitutional role of that other branch. . . . [Otherwise,] a court could be empowered to appoint all officers subordinate to a department head. If, for example, two-thirds of the House and Senate—a sufficient number to override a veto—disagreed strongly with the President's agricultural policy, Congress could place in a particular court, perceived as more in agreement with Congress' policy views, the authority to appoint all Department of Agriculture officers subordinate to the Secretary. That device would neatly prevent the President from implementing his own agricultural policy. Or . . . Congress could employ the same technique to prevent the President from exercising effective control over either the State or Defense Department. It is difficult to see, if the independent counsel is correct concerning inter-branch appointments, why Congress could not delegate to a particular court—perhaps by a definition that fitted only one district judge—the appointment of all Executive Branch officers (save department heads).
>
> [A]ssume that Congress has lost confidence in the President's policy implicating only one subject matter within a department's jurisdiction—perhaps U.S. policy towards Latin America, or arms control negotiations, or the Executive Branch's presentation of cases to the Supreme Court. Under the independent counsel's view, Congress [could require] that a particular court appoint the officials responsible for implementing those policies. And as with the Act before us, Congress could forbid any other Executive Branch official to interfere with the special appointee's jurisdiction. [In the alternative, if] Congress . . . was dissatisfied with the trend of federal judicial decisions, [it] might place authority to appoint all inferior judicial officers including Justices' and judges' clerks in one department head (perhaps the Attorney General), thereby hoping to influence opinions or at least to obstruct the perceived undesirable trend.

The independent counsel statute was criticized (especially by Judge Silberman) not only as impermissibly intruding upon the executive branch, but also for distorting the proper role of the judicial branch. Akhil Amar has argued that[60]

> [p]rosecutors wield *executive* power, whereas judges should exercise only *judicial* power. Asking judges to pick prosecutors is like asking them to appoint generals or name ambassadors. . . . [C]onsider how unwise the statute is, sucking judges into partisan politics. Judges decide law in open court. But no *law* can say who should be the prosecutor in any given case — that's a question of policy, personality, and politics. To decide this question, judges will need to act like politicos, talking secretly to politicians to figure out who will be an acceptable candidate to all sides. Judges may well pick a fellow judge lacking prosecutorial experience, who in turn may well make many rookie mistakes. (Sound familiar?) And judges in the nature of things can't properly supervise prosecutors without [impermissibly turning themselves] into superprosecutors.

Consider also the argument that judges will not be good at picking prosecutors because they have limited information about past prosecutorial performance. Whereas the Attorney General has relatively complete information about the track record of federal prosecutors (including information about cases not brought because of the sound exercise of discretion), judges generally do not and should not have access to this treasure trove of intraexecutive intelligence, implicating various out-of-court activities that lie beyond the proper province of judicial supervision. Finally, consider the special awkwardness of judicial involvement when independent counsels are formally involved in the impeachment process — which the framers generally sought to take away from ordinary judges. Did the 1978 Congress and the *Morrison* Justices give these judicial-role issues enough attention?

6. *Bargaining in the shadow of the Court.* One of the main lessons of the Coase theorem is that legal rules often establish a baseline, or default rule, against which further bargaining among interested parties may take place. Baseline starting points matter, but these starting points need not be ending points. In *Morrison*, even if Justice Scalia's view had prevailed, note that members of Congress could have used their oversight, appropriations, publicity, and impeachment powers to put a great deal of pressure on the Attorney General and President to initiate prosecutions that the Administration might prefer not to initiate. (Oversight in Congress could even be given to a "blue ribbon" commission of outside investigators who enjoyed especially strong credibility in the press and public.) Conversely, even after the *Morrison* case, recall that the President could have effectively and unilaterally "reversed" the Court simply by pardoning Mr. Olson, thus "removing" Ms. Morrison de facto by giving her no one to prosecute. Anyone who today doubts this presidential power should recall that in December 1992, President George Bush pardoned Caspar Weinberger, thereby effectively putting the Iran-Contra independent counsel Lawrence Walsh out of business. Indeed, just as Presidents nowadays deploy their veto power proactively — waving their veto pens in the air early on and announcing what

---

60. Akhil Reed Amar, Should We Ditch the Independent Prosecutor Law?, Slate (http://www.slate.com), Feb. 16-19, 1999.

bills will and will not get past their desk—a truly skillful chief executive could wield the pardon broadsword as a surgical scalpel by explaining the facts of life to an independent counsel (publicly or privately): Unless she does X and Y and refrains from Z, the President will be obliged to pardon. Granted, all this may make the President look bad politically—and so we return once again to the critical issues of publicity highlighted by the *Cox* and *Nixon* cases.

7. *From Independent Counsels to Special Counsels.* Upon expiration of the Independent Counsel Act in 1999, the Department of Justice issued regulations for Special Counsels appointed by the Attorney General. 28 CFR §600.1-10. The relevant regulations provide that "The Attorney General, or in cases in which the Attorney General is recused, the Acting Attorney General, will appoint a Special Counsel when he or she determines that criminal investigation of a person or matter is warranted and (a) That investigation or prosecution of that person or matter by a United States Attorney's Office or litigating Division of the Department of Justice would present a conflict of interest for the Department or other extraordinary circumstances; and (b) That under the circumstances, it would be in the public interest to appoint an outside Special Counsel to assume responsibility for the matter." §600.1.

According to §600.7(b), "[t]he Special Counsel shall not be subject to the day-to-day supervision of any official of the Department. However, the Attorney General may request that the Special Counsel provide an explanation for any investigative or prosecutorial step, and may after review conclude that the action is so inappropriate or unwarranted under established Departmental practices that it should not be pursued. In conducting that review, the Attorney General will give great weight to the views of the Special Counsel. If the Attorney General concludes that a proposed action by a Special Counsel should not be pursued, the Attorney General shall notify Congress. . . ."

Section §600.7(d) provides that "[t]he Special Counsel may be disciplined or removed from office only by the personal action of the Attorney General. The Attorney General may remove a Special Counsel for misconduct, dereliction of duty, incapacity, conflict of interest, or for other good cause, including violation of Departmental policies. The Attorney General shall inform the Special Counsel in writing of the specific reason for his or her removal."

Do these regulations cure the constitutional difficulties that Justice Scalia's dissent identified with the Independent Counsel Act?

8. *Is* Morrison *good law today?* Consider, finally, another important presidential power at work in the independent counsel story—the presidential power to nominate Justices, subject of course to Senate confirmation. Only three of the Justices who voted with the majority in *Morrison* were still on the Court in 1999. Does the *Morrison* vision still command the allegiance of a Court majority? What, if anything, do you make of the following case?

Edmond v. United States

520 U.S. 651 (1997)

Justice SCALIA delivered the opinion of the Court.

We must determine in this case whether Congress has authorized the Secretary of Transportation to appoint civilian members of the Coast Guard Court of

Criminal Appeals, and if so, whether this authorization is constitutional under the Appointments Clause of Article II. . . .

III

. . . As we recognized in Buckley v. Valeo, 424 U.S. 1 (1976), the Appointments Clause of Article II is more than a matter of "etiquette or protocol"; it is among the significant structural safeguards of the constitutional scheme. By vesting the President with the exclusive power to select the principal (noninferior) officers of the United States, the Appointments Clause prevents congressional encroachment upon the Executive and Judicial Branches. This disposition was also designed to assure a higher quality of appointments: the Framers anticipated that the President would be less vulnerable to interest-group pressure and personal favoritism than would a collective body. "The sole and undivided responsibility of one man will naturally beget a livelier sense of duty, and a more exact regard to reputation." The Federalist No. 76. The President's power to select principal officers of the United States was not left unguarded, however, as Article II further requires the "Advice and Consent of the Senate." This serves both to curb executive abuses of the appointment power, and "to promote a judicious choice of [persons] for filling the offices of the union," The Federalist No. 76. By requiring the joint participation of the President and the Senate, the Appointments Clause was designed to ensure public accountability for both the making of a bad appointment and the rejection of a good one. Hamilton observed:

> "The blame of a bad nomination would fall upon the president singly and absolutely. The censure of rejecting a good one would lie entirely at the door of the senate; aggravated by the consideration of their having counteracted the good intentions of the executive. If an ill appointment should be made, the executive for nominating, and the senate for approving, would participate, though in different degrees, in the opprobrium and disgrace." Id., No. 77.

The prescribed manner of appointment for principal officers is also the default manner of appointment for inferior officers. "But," the Appointments Clause continues, "the Congress may by Law vest the Appointment of such inferior Officers, as they think proper, in the President alone, in the Courts of Law, or in the Heads of Departments." This provision, sometimes referred to as the "Excepting Clause," was added to the proposed Constitution on the last day of the Grand Convention, with little discussion. As one of our early opinions suggests, its obvious purpose is administrative convenience—but that convenience was deemed to outweigh the benefits of the more cumbersome procedure only with respect to the appointment of "inferior Officers." Section 323(a), which confers appointment power upon the Secretary of Transportation, can constitutionally be applied to the appointment of Court of Criminal Appeals judges only if those judges are "inferior Officers."

Our cases have not set forth an exclusive criterion for distinguishing between principal and inferior officers for Appointment Clause purposes. Among the offices that we have found to be inferior are that of a district court clerk, an election supervisor, a vice-consul charged temporarily with the duties of the consul, and a "United States commissioner" in district court proceedings. Most recently, in Morrison v.

Olson, we held that the independent counsel created by provisions of the Ethics in Government Act of 1978, was an inferior officer. In reaching that conclusion, we relied on several factors: that the independent counsel was subject to removal by a higher officer (the Attorney General), that she performed only limited duties, that her jurisdiction was narrow, and that her tenure was limited.

Petitioners are quite correct that the last two of these conclusions do not hold with regard to the office of military judge at issue here. It is not "limited in tenure," as that phrase was used in *Morrison* to describe "appointment essentially to accomplish a single task [at the end of which] the office is terminated." Nor are military judges "limited in jurisdiction," as used in *Morrison* to refer to the fact that an independent counsel may investigate and prosecute only those individuals, and for only those crimes, that are within the scope of jurisdiction granted by the special three-judge appointing panel. However, *Morrison* did not purport to set forth a definitive test for whether an office is "inferior" under the Appointments Clause. . . .

To support principal-officer status, petitioners emphasize the importance of the responsibilities that Court of Criminal Appeals judges bear. . . . We do not dispute that military appellate judges are charged with exercising significant authority on behalf of the United States. This, however, is also true of offices that we have held were "inferior" within the meaning of the Appointments Clause. Generally speaking, the term "inferior officer" connotes a relationship with some higher ranking officer or officers below the President: whether one is an "inferior" officer depends on whether he has a superior. It is not enough that other officers may be identified who formally maintain a higher rank, or possess responsibilities of a greater magnitude. If that were the intention, the Constitution might have used the phrase "lesser officer." Rather, in the context of a clause designed to preserve political accountability relative to important government assignments, we think it evident that "inferior officers" are officers whose work is directed and supervised at some level by others who were appointed by presidential nomination with the advice and consent of the Senate.

This understanding of the Appointments Clause conforms with the views of the first Congress. On July 27, 1789, Congress established the first executive department, the Department of Foreign Affairs. In so doing, it expressly designated the Secretary of the Department as a "principal officer," and his subordinate, the Chief Clerk of the Department, as an "inferior officer." . . . Congress used similar language in establishing the Department of War, repeatedly referring to the Secretary of that department as a "principal officer," and the chief clerk, who would be "employed" within the Department as the Secretary "shall deem proper," as an "inferior officer."

Supervision of the work of Court of Criminal Appeals judges is divided between the Judge Advocate General (who in the Coast Guard is subordinate to the Secretary of Transportation) and the Court of Appeals for the Armed Forces. The Judge Advocate General exercises administrative oversight over the Court of Criminal Appeals. He is charged with the responsibility to "prescribe uniform rules of procedure" for the court, and must "meet periodically [with other Judge Advocates General] to formulate policies and procedure in regard to review of court-martial cases." It is conceded by the parties that the Judge Advocate General may also remove a Court of Criminal Appeals judge from his judicial assignment without cause. The power to remove officers, we have recognized, is a powerful tool for control. *Bowsher*; *Myers*.

. . . What is significant is that the judges of the Court of Criminal Appeals have no power to render a final decision on behalf of the United States unless permitted to do so by other executive officers. . . .

We conclude that 49 U.S.C. §323(a) authorizes the Secretary of Transportation to appoint judges of the Coast Guard Court of Criminal Appeals; and that such appointment is in conformity with the Appointments Clause of the Constitution, since those judges are "inferior Officers" within the meaning of that provision, by reason of the supervision over their work exercised by the General Counsel of the Department of Transportation in his capacity as Judge Advocate General and the Court of Appeals for the Armed Forces. The judicial appointments at issue in this case are therefore valid.

Justice SOUTER, concurring in part and concurring in the judgment. . . .

The Court states that "generally speaking, the term 'inferior officer' connotes a relationship [of supervision and direction] with some higher ranking officer or officers below the President; whether one is an 'inferior' officer depends on whether he has a superior." The Court goes on to show that administrative supervision of these judges by the Judge Advocate General of the Coast Guard, combined with his power to control them by removal from a case, establishes that the intermediate appellate judges here have the necessary superior. With this conclusion I agree, but unlike the Court I am not prepared to decide on that basis alone that these judges are inferior officers.

Because the term "inferior officer" implies an official superior, one who has no superior is not an inferior officer. This unexceptionable maxim will in some instances be dispositive of status. . . .

It does not follow, however, that if one is subject to some supervision and control, one is an inferior officer. Having a superior officer is necessary for inferior officer status, but not sufficient to establish it. See, e.g., *Morrison* (Scalia, J., dissenting). Accordingly, in *Morrison*, the Court's determination that the independent counsel was "to some degree 'inferior'" to the Attorney General did not end the enquiry. The Court went on to weigh the duties, jurisdiction, and tenure associated with the office before concluding that the independent counsel was an inferior officer. Thus, under *Morrison*, the Solicitor General of the United States, for example, may well be a principal officer, despite his statutory "inferiority" to the Attorney General. . . .

DISCUSSION

1. *Further reading*. For thoughtful discussion of *Morrison*'s status after *Edmond*, see Nick Bravin, Note, Is Morrison v. Olson Still Good Law? The Court's New Appointments Clause Jurisprudence, 98 Colum. L. Rev. 1103, 1117-1120 (1998).

2. *Subsequent case: Free Enterprise Fund v. PCAOB*. In Free Enterprise Fund v. Public Company Accounting Oversight Board, 561 U.S. 477 (2010), the Court distinguished *Humphrey's Executor* and *Morrison* and held that Congress could not insulate an inferior officer from removal by a principal officer if the principal officer could not be removed by the President.

At issue was the Public Company Accounting Oversight Board (PCAOB), created as part of a series of accounting reforms in the Sarbanes-Oxley Act of 2002, which responded to corporate scandals in the early 2000s. The PCAOB is composed of five members appointed by the Securities and Exchange Commission. While the SEC has oversight of the Board, it cannot remove Board members at will, but only "for good cause shown," and in accordance with specified procedures. For purposes of the litigation the parties agreed that the Board is part of the government for constitutional purposes, that its members are "Officers of the United States," and that the SEC Commissioners cannot be removed by the President except for "inefficiency, neglect of duty, or malfeasance in office" [quoting *Humphrey's Executor*].

The Supreme Court, in a 5-4 decision written by Chief Justice Roberts, explained that "we have previously upheld limited restrictions on the President's removal power. In those cases, however, only one level of protected tenure separated the President from an officer exercising executive power. It was the President—or a subordinate he could remove at will—who decided whether the officer's conduct merited removal under the good-cause standard."

By contrast, the Act creating the PCAOB "does something quite different. It not only protects Board members from removal except for good cause, but withdraws from the President any decision on whether that good cause exists. That decision is vested instead in other tenured officers—the Commissioners—none of whom is subject to the President's direct control. The result is a Board that is not accountable to the President, and a President who is not responsible for the Board."

This arrangement, Chief Justice Roberts explained, "is contrary to Article II's vesting of the executive power in the President. Without the ability to oversee the Board, or to attribute the Board's failings to those whom he can oversee, the President is no longer the judge of the Board's conduct. He is not the one who decides whether Board members are abusing their offices or neglecting their duties. He can neither ensure that the laws are faithfully executed, nor be held responsible for a Board member's breach of faith. This violates the basic principle that the President 'cannot delegate ultimate responsibility or the active obligation to supervise that goes with it,' because Article II 'makes a single President responsible for the actions of the Executive Branch.'"

"[I]f Congress can shelter the bureaucracy behind two layers of good-cause tenure, why not a third? . . . The officers of such an agency—safely encased within a Matryoshka doll of tenure protections—would be immune from Presidential oversight, even as they exercised power in the people's name. . . . [B]y granting the Board executive power without the Executive's oversight, this Act subverts the President's ability to ensure that the laws are faithfully executed—as well as the public's ability to pass judgment on his efforts. The Act's restrictions are incompatible with the Constitution's separation of powers."

Justice Breyer, joined by Justices Stevens, Ginsburg, and Sotomayor, dissented, arguing that the majority's ban on dual insulation did not achieve its stated goal of ensuring presidential accountability: "[S]o long as the President is legitimately foreclosed from removing the Commissioners except for cause (as the majority assumes), nullifying the Commission's power to remove Board members only for cause will not resolve the problem the Court has identified: The President will still be 'powerless to intervene' by removing the Board members if the Commission reasonably decides not to do so. . . . [T]he Court fails to show why two layers of 'for cause' protection—Layer One insulating the Commissioners from the President, and Layer Two insulating the Board from the Commissioners—impose any more serious limitation upon the President's powers than one layer."

Justice Breyer also argued that "because the Court's 'double for-cause' rule applies to all appointees who are 'inferior officer[s],'" and because that term is so vague and undefined, the majority's decision threatened to "sweep[] hundreds, perhaps thousands of high level government officials within the scope of the Court's holding, putting their job security and their administrative actions and decisions constitutionally at risk."

In response, the Court emphasized the limited scope of its holding: "[M]any civil servants within independent agencies would not qualify as 'Officers of the United States,' who [like members of the Board] 'exercis[e] significant authority pursuant to the laws of the United States.' . . . We do not decide the status of other Government employees, nor do we decide whether 'lesser functionaries subordinate to officers of the United States' must be subject to the same sort of control as those who exercise 'significant authority pursuant to the laws.' . . . Nothing in our opinion . . . should be read to cast doubt on the use of what is colloquially known as the civil service system within independent agencies." The Court also added in a footnote: "[F]or similar reasons, our holding also does not address that subset of independent agency employees who serve as administrative law judges. Whether administrative law judges are necessarily 'Officers of the United States' is disputed. And unlike members of the Board, many administrative law judges of course perform adjudicative rather than enforcement or policymaking functions, or possess purely recommendatory powers."

Finally, the Court explained, the opinion did not "increase the President's authority to remove military officers. Without expressing any view whatever on the scope of that authority, it is enough to note that we see little analogy between our Nation's armed services and the Public Company Accounting Oversight Board. Military officers are broadly subject to Presidential control through the chain of command and through the President's powers as Commander in Chief. The President and his subordinates may also convene boards of inquiry or courts-martial to hear claims of misconduct or poor performance by those officers. Here, by contrast, the President has no authority to initiate a Board member's removal for cause. . . ."

United States v. Arthrex, Inc.

141 S. Ct. 1970 (2021)

[The Patent Trial and Appeal Board (PTAB), an executive tribunal within the Patent and Trademark Office (PTO), reviews the validity of patents previously issued by the PTO. In an adversarial process called inter partes review, members of the PTAB reconsider whether existing patents satisfy the novelty and nonobviousness requirements for inventions. The Board is largely composed of Administrative Patent Judges (APJs) appointed by the Secretary of Commerce. The Board has the final word within the executive branch on the validity of a challenged patent. Billions of dollars can turn on a Board decision.

Petitioners challenged the constitutionality, under the Appointments Clause of the Constitution, of allowing APJs to issue decisions on behalf of the executive branch.]

ROBERTS, C.J.:

Congress provided that APJs would be appointed as inferior officers, by the Secretary of Commerce as head of a department. The question presented is whether the nature of their responsibilities is consistent with their method of appointment. . . .

The starting point for each party's analysis is our opinion in *Edmond* [*v. United States*, 520 U.S. 651 (1997)]. There we explained that "[w]hether one is an 'inferior' officer depends on whether he has a superior" other than the President. An inferior officer must be "directed and supervised at some level by others who were appointed by Presidential nomination with the advice and consent of the Senate.". . .

[T]he PTO Director possesses powers of "administrative oversight." The Director fixes the rate of pay for APJs, controls the decision whether to institute inter partes review, and selects the APJs to reconsider the validity of the patent. The Director also promulgates regulations governing inter partes review, issues prospective guidance on patentability issues, and designates past PTAB decisions as "precedential" for future panels. He is the boss, except when it comes to the one thing that makes the APJs officers exercising "significant authority" in the first place—their power to issue decisions on patentability. In contrast to the scheme approved by Edmond, no principal officer at any level within the Executive Branch "direct[s] and supervise[s]" the work of APJs in that regard.

What was "significant" to the outcome [in *Edmond*]—review by a superior executive officer—is absent here: APJs have the "power to render a final decision on behalf of the United States" without any such review by their nominal superior or any other principal officer in the Executive Branch. The only possibility of review is a petition for rehearing, but Congress unambiguously specified that "[o]nly the Patent and Trial Appeal Board may grant rehearings." §6(c). . . .

This "diffusion of power carries with it a diffusion of accountability." *Free Enterprise Fund*. . . . The Government and Smith & Nephew assemble a catalog of steps the Director might take to affect the decisionmaking process of the PTAB, despite his lack of any statutory authority to review its decisions. . . . If all else fails, the Government says, the Director can intervene in the rehearing process to reverse Board decisions. . . . [H]e could "stack" the original panel to rehear the case with additional APJs assumed to be more amenable to his preferences[, or] he could assemble an entirely new panel consisting of himself and two other officers appointed by the Secretary—in practice, the Commissioner for Patents and the APJ presently designated as Chief Judge—to decide whether to overturn a decision and reach a different outcome binding on future panels. The Government insists that the Director, by handpicking (and, if necessary, re-picking) Board members, can indirectly influence the course of inter partes review.

That is not the solution. It is the problem. The Government proposes (and the dissents embrace) a roadmap for the Director to evade a statutory prohibition on review without having him take responsibility for the ultimate decision. Even if the Director succeeds in procuring his preferred outcome, such machinations blur the lines of accountability demanded by the Appointments Clause. The parties are left with neither an impartial decision by a panel of experts nor a transparent decision for which a politically accountable officer must take responsibility. And the public can only wonder "on whom the blame or the punishment of a pernicious measure, or series of pernicious measures ought really to fall." The Federalist No. 70, at 476 (A. Hamilton). . . .

Given the insulation of PTAB decisions from any executive review, the President can neither oversee the PTAB himself nor "attribute the Board's failings to those whom he can oversee." *Free Enterprise Fund.* APJs accordingly exercise power that conflicts with the design of the Appointments Clause "to preserve political accountability." *Edmond.*

[The Chief Justice, in a part of the opinion joined only by Justices Alito, Kavanaugh, and Barrett, concluded that in order for the statutory review system to be constitutional, the PTO Director must have the power to "review final PTAB decisions and, upon review, . . . issue decisions himself on behalf of the Board."] [T]he appropriate remedy is a remand to the Acting Director for him to decide whether to rehear the petition filed by Smith & Nephew. Although the APJs' appointment by the Secretary allowed them to lawfully adjudicate the petition in the first instance, they lacked the power under the Constitution to finally resolve the matter within the Executive Branch. Under these circumstances, a limited remand to the Director provides an adequate opportunity for review by a principal officer. Because the source of the constitutional violation is the restraint on the review authority of the Director, rather than the appointment of APJs by the Secretary, Arthrex is not entitled to a hearing before a new panel of APJs. . . .

[Justice Gorsuch concurred on the merits but dissented on the remedy. He argued that the Court should not have attempted to repair the unconstitutional statutory scheme of review. "Asking what a past Congress would have done if confronted with a contingency it never addressed calls for raw speculation. Speculation that, under traditional principles of judicial remedies, statutory interpretation, and the separation of powers, a court of law has no authority to undertake." Instead, he "would . . . identify[] the constitutional violation, explain[] our reasoning, and 'set[] aside' the PTAB decision in this case."]

BREYER, J., joined by SOTOMAYOR and KAGAN, JJ., concurring in part and dissenting in part:

[Justice Breyer argued that given the plurality's holding of unconstitutionality, its remedial solution was sensible and therefore concurred in the remedy. But he dissented from the Court's holding that the statutory scheme was unconstitutional.]

[T]he Court should interpret the Appointments Clause as granting Congress a degree of leeway to establish and empower federal offices. Neither that Clause nor anything else in the Constitution describes the degree of control that a superior officer must exercise over the decisions of an inferior officer. To the contrary, the Constitution says only that "Congress may by Law vest the Appointment of such inferior Officers, as they think proper, . . . in the Heads of Departments." Art. II, § 2, cl. 2. The words "by Law . . . as they think proper" strongly suggest that Congress has considerable freedom to determine the nature of an inferior officer's job, and that courts ought to respect that judgment. . . .

[O]ur Appointments Clause precedents . . . require only that an inferior officer be "directed and supervised at some level," *Edmond.* . . . Even were I to assume, with the majority, that the Director must have power to "control" the APJs, the statutes grant the Director considerable control . . . of decisions insofar as they determine policy. The Director cannot rehear and decide an individual case on his own; but Congress had good reason for seeking independent Board determinations in those cases—cases that will apply, not create, Director-controlled policy. . . ."

[T]he Court, when deciding cases such as these, should conduct a functional examination of the offices and duties in question rather than a formalist, judicial-rules-based approach. In advocating for a "functional approach," I mean an approach that would take account of, and place weight on, why Congress enacted a particular statutory limitation. It would also consider the practical consequences that are likely to follow from Congress' chosen scheme.

[A] functional approach, which considers purposes and consequences, undermines the Court's result. Most agencies (and courts for that matter) have the power to reconsider an earlier decision, changing the initial result if appropriate. Congress believed that the PTO should have that same power and accordingly created procedures for reconsidering issued patents. Congress also believed it important to strengthen the reconsideration power with procedural safeguards. . . . Given the technical nature of patents, the need for expertise, and the importance of avoiding political interference, Congress chose to grant the APJs a degree of independence. These considerations set forth a reasonable legislative objective sufficient to justify the restriction upon the Director's authority that Congress imposed. And, as Justice Thomas thoroughly explains, there is no reason to believe this scheme will prevent the Director from exercising policy control over the APJs or will break the chain of accountability that is needed to hold the President responsible for bad nominations.

More broadly, I see the Court's decision as one part of a larger shift in our separation-of-powers jurisprudence [toward formalism]. . . . I continue to believe that a more functional approach to constitutional interpretation in this area is superior. . . . The nature of the PTAB calls for technically correct adjudicatory decisions. . . . [T]hat fact calls for greater, not less, independence from those potentially influenced by political factors. The Court's decision prevents Congress from establishing a patent scheme consistent with that idea.

But there are further reasons for a functional approach that extend beyond the bounds of patent adjudication. First, the Executive Branch has many different constituent bodies, many different bureaus, many different agencies, many different tasks, many different kinds of employees. Administration comes in many different shapes and sizes. Appreciating this variety is especially important in the context of administrative adjudication, which typically demands decisionmaking (at least where policy made by others is simply applied) that is free of political influence. Are the President and Congress, through judicial insistence upon certain mechanisms for removal or review, to be denied the ability to create independent adjudicators?

Second, the Constitution is not a detailed tax code, and for good reason. The Nation's desires and needs change, sometimes over long periods of time. In the 19th century the Judiciary may not have foreseen the changes that produced the New Deal, along with its accompanying changes in the nature of the tasks that Government was expected to perform. We may not now easily foresee just what kinds of tasks present or future technological changes will call for. The Founders wrote a Constitution that they believed was flexible enough to respond to new needs as those needs developed and changed over the course of decades or centuries. At the same time, they designed a Constitution that would protect certain basic principles. A principle that prevents Congress from affording inferior level adjudicators some decisionmaking independence was not among them.

Finally, the Executive Branch and Congress are more likely than are judges to understand how to implement the tasks that Congress has written into legislation. That understanding encompasses the nature of different mechanisms of bureaucratic control that may apply to the many thousands of administrators who will carry out those tasks. And it includes an awareness of the reasonable limits that can be placed on supervisors to ensure that those working under them enjoy a degree of freedom sufficient to carry out their responsibilities. Considered as a group, unelected judges have little, if any, experience related to this kind of a problem.

This is not to say that the Constitution grants Congress free rein. But in this area of the law a functional approach, when compared with the highly detailed judicial-rules-based approach reflected in the Court's decision, is more likely to prevent inappropriate judicial interference. It embodies, at least to a degree, the philosopher's advice: "Whereof one cannot speak, thereof one must be silent."

THOMAS, J., dissenting:

[J]ust who are these "principal" officers that Congress unsuccessfully sought to smuggle into the Executive Branch without Senate confirmation? About 250 administrative patent judges who sit at the bottom of an organizational chart, nestled under at least two levels of authority. Neither our precedent nor the original understanding of the Appointments Clause requires Senate confirmation of officers inferior to not one, but *two* officers below the President. . . .

There can be no dispute that administrative patent judges are, in fact, inferior: They are lower in rank to at least two different officers. . . . [T]he Director and Secretary are also functionally superior because they supervise and direct the work administrative patent judges perform. . . .

Unlike the Judge Advocate General and CAAF in *Edmond*, the Director *may* influence individual proceedings. The Director decides in the first instance whether to institute, refuse to institute, or de-institute particular reviews, a decision that is "final and nonappealable." If the Director institutes review, he then may select which administrative patent judges will hear the challenge. § 6(c). Alternatively, he can avoid assigning any administrative patent judge to a specific dispute and instead designate himself, his Deputy Director, and the Commissioner of Patents. In addition, the Director decides which of the thousands of decisions issued each year bind other panels as precedent. No statute bars the Director from taking an active role to ensure the Board's decisions conform to his policy direction.

But, that is not all. If the administrative patent judges "(somehow) reach a result he does not like, the Director can add more members to the panel—including himself—and order the case reheard.". . .

[I]nstead of finding it persuasive that administrative patent judges seem to be inferior officers—"an understanding consistent with their appointment"—the majority suggests most of *Edmond* is superfluous: All that matters is whether the Director has the statutory authority to individually reverse Board decisions. . . . [But] there is no precedential basis (or historical support) for boiling down "inferior-officer" status to the way Congress structured a particular agency's process for reviewing decisions. . . .

Perhaps the better way to understand the Court's opinion today is as creating a new form of intrabranch separation-of-powers law. . . . It never expressly tells us whether administrative patent judges are inferior officers or principal. And the Court never tells us whether the appointment process complies with the Constitution. The closest the Court comes is to say that "the source of the constitutional violation" is not "the appointment of [administrative patent judges] by the Secretary." Under our precedent and the Constitution's text, that should resolve the suit. If the appointment process for administrative patent judges—appointment by the Secretary—does not violate the Constitution, then administrative patent judges must be inferior officers. See Art. II, § 2, cl. 2. And if administrative patent judges are inferior officers and have been properly appointed as such, then the Appointments Clause challenge fails. After all, the Constitution provides that "Congress may by Law vest the Appointment of . . . inferior Officers . . . in the Heads of Departments." Ibid.

The majority's new Appointments Clause doctrine, though, has nothing to do with the validity of an officer's appointment. Instead, it polices the dispersion of executive power among officers. Echoing our doctrine that Congress may not mix duties and powers from different branches into one actor, the Court finds that the constitutional problem here is that Congress has given a specific power—the authority to finally adjudicate inter partes review disputes—to one type of executive officer that the Constitution gives to another. . . . That analysis is doubly flawed. . . . Nowhere does the Constitution acknowledge any such thing as "inferior-officer power" or "principal-officer power." And it certainly does not distinguish between these sorts of powers in the Appointments Clause.

And even if it did, early patent dispute schemes establish that the power exercised by the administrative patent judges here does not belong exclusively to principal officers. Nonprincipal officers could—and did—render final decisions in specific patent disputes, not subject to any appeal to a superior executive officer. . . .

More broadly, interpreting the Appointments Clause to bar any nonprincipal officer from taking "final" action poses serious line-drawing problems. The majority assures that not every decision by an inferior officer must be reviewable by a superior officer. But this sparks more questions than it answers. Can a line prosecutor offer a plea deal without sign off from a principal officer? If faced with a life-threatening scenario, can an FBI agent use deadly force to subdue a suspect? Or if an inferior officer temporarily fills a vacant office tasked with making final decisions, do those decisions violate the Appointments Clause? And are courts around the country supposed to sort through lists of each officer's (or employee's) duties, categorize each one as principal or inferior, and then excise any that look problematic? . . .

Although the parties raise only an Appointments Clause challenge and the plurality concedes that there is no appointment defect, the Court appears to suggest that the real issue is that this scheme violates the Vesting Clause. According to the majority, the PTAB's review process inverts the executive "chain of command," allowing administrative patent judges to wield "unchecked . . . executive power" and to "dictat[e]" what the Director must do. . . .

[E]ven if the chain of command were broken, Senate confirmation of an administrative patent judge would offer no fix. As Madison explained, the Senate's role in appointments is an exception to the vesting of executive power in the President; it gives another branch a say in the hiring of executive officials. 1 Annals of Cong. 463 (1789). An Article II Vesting Clause problem cannot be remedied by stripping away even more power from the Executive.

[F]inally, historical practice establishes that the vesting of executive power in the President did not require that every patent decision be appealable to a principal officer. . . .

[T]he Court never directly says that any law or action violates the Vesting Clause. The Court simply criticizes as overly formalistic the notion that both Clauses do exactly what their names suggest: The Appointments Clause governs only appointments; the Vesting Clause deals just with the vesting of executive power in the President. I would not be so quick to stare deeply into the penumbras of the Clauses to identify new structural limitations. . . .

Seila Law LLC v. Consumer Financial Protection Bureau

140 S. Ct. 2183 (2020)

[In 2010, Congress created the Consumer Financial Protection Bureau (CFPB) as an independent financial regulator within the Federal Reserve System to enforce consumer protection laws with respect to financial products and ensure that markets for consumer financial products and services are fair, transparent, and competitive. Congress placed the CFPB under the leadership of a single Director, appointed by the President with the advice and consent of the Senate. The Director serves for a term of five years, during which the President may remove the Director from office only for "inefficiency, neglect of duty, or malfeasance in office." After the CFPB began an investigation of Seila Law for consumer protection violations, the firm refused an agency order to produce documents for the investigation, arguing that the agency structure violated the separation of powers.]

Chief Justice Roberts delivered the opinion of the Court with respect to Part . . . III.

III

We hold that the CFPB's leadership by a single individual removable only for inefficiency, neglect, or malfeasance violates the separation of powers.

A

Article II provides that "[t]he executive Power shall be vested in a President," who must "take Care that the Laws be faithfully executed." Art. II, §1, cl. 1; *id.*, §3. The entire "executive Power" belongs to the President alone. But because it would be "impossib[le]" for "one man" to "perform all the great business of the State," the Constitution assumes that lesser executive officers will "assist the supreme

Magistrate in discharging the duties of his trust." 30 Writings of George Washington 334 (J. Fitzpatrick ed. 1939).

These lesser officers must remain accountable to the President, whose authority they wield. As Madison explained, "[I]f any power whatsoever is in its nature Executive, it is the power of appointing, overseeing, and controlling those who execute the laws." 1 Annals of Cong. 463 (1789). That power, in turn, generally includes the ability to remove executive officials, for it is "only the authority that can remove" such officials that they "must fear and, in the performance of [their] functions, obey." *Bowsher* [*v. Synar*, 478 U.S. 714, 726 (1986)].

The President's removal power has long been confirmed by history and precedent. It "was discussed extensively in Congress when the first executive departments were created" in 1789. "The view that 'prevailed, as most consonant to the text of the Constitution' and 'to the requisite responsibility and harmony in the Executive Department,' was that the executive power included a power to oversee executive officers through removal." (quoting Letter from James Madison to Thomas Jefferson (June 30, 1789), 16 Documentary History of the First Federal Congress 893 (2004)). The First Congress's recognition of the President's removal power in 1789 "provides contemporaneous and weighty evidence of the Constitution's meaning," and has long been the "settled and well understood construction of the Constitution."

The Court recognized the President's prerogative to remove executive officials in *Myers v. United States*, 272 U.S. 52 (1926). Chief Justice Taft . . . concluded that Article II "grants to the President" the "general administrative control of those executing the laws, including the power of appointment *and removal* of executive officers." (emphasis added). Just as the President's "selection of administrative officers is essential to the execution of the laws by him, so must be his power of removing those for whom he cannot continue to be responsible." "[T]o hold otherwise," the Court reasoned, "would make it impossible for the President . . . to take care that the laws be faithfully executed."

We recently reiterated the President's general removal power in *Free Enterprise Fund* [which held that Congress could not insulate an official] by *two* layers of for-cause removal protection. . . . *Free Enterprise Fund* left in place two exceptions to the President's unrestricted removal power. First, in *Humphrey's Executor* [*v. United States*, 295 U.S. 602 (1935)], decided less than a decade after *Myers*, the Court upheld a statute that protected the Commissioners of the FTC from removal except for "inefficiency, neglect of duty, or malfeasance in office." . . . [T]he Court limited its holding "to officers of the kind here under consideration." . . . Rightly or wrongly, the Court viewed the FTC (as it existed in 1935) as exercising "no part of the executive power." Instead, it was "an administrative body" that performed "specified duties as a legislative or as a judicial aid." It acted "as a legislative agency" in "making investigations and reports" to Congress and "as an agency of the judiciary" in making recommendations to courts as a master in chancery. "To the extent that [the FTC] exercise[d] any executive *function*[,] as distinguished from executive *power* in the constitutional sense," it did so only in the discharge of its "quasi-legislative or quasi-judicial powers." (emphasis added).

As we observed in *Morrison v. Olson*, 487 U.S. 654 (1988), "[I]t is hard to dispute that the powers of the FTC at the time of *Humphrey's Executor* would at the present time be considered 'executive,' at least to some degree.". . . [relocated footnote—Eds.]

[*Humphrey's Executor*] identified several organizational features that helped explain its characterization of the FTC as non-executive. Composed of five members—no more than three from the same political party—the Board was designed to be "non-partisan" and to "act with entire impartiality."

The FTC's duties were "neither political nor executive," but instead called for "the trained judgment of a body of experts" "informed by experience." And the Commissioners' staggered, seven-year terms enabled the agency to accumulate technical expertise and avoid a "complete change" in leadership "at any one time."

In short, *Humphrey's Executor* permitted Congress to give for-cause removal protections to a multimember body of experts, balanced along partisan lines, that performed legislative and judicial functions and was said not to exercise any executive power. Consistent with that understanding, the Court later applied "[t]he philosophy of *Humphrey's Executor*" to uphold for-cause removal protections for the members of the War Claims Commission—a three-member "adjudicatory body" tasked with resolving claims for compensation arising from World War II. *Wiener v. United States*, 357 U.S. 349, 356 (1958). . . .

We have recognized a second exception for *inferior* officers in two cases, *United States v. Perkins* and *Morrison v. Olson*. Article II distinguishes between two kinds of officers—principal officers (who must be appointed by the President with the advice and consent of the Senate) and inferior officers (whose appointment Congress may vest in the President, courts, or heads of Departments). § 2, cl. 2. While "[o]ur cases have not set forth an exclusive criterion for distinguishing between principal and inferior officers," we have in the past examined factors such as the nature, scope, and duration of an officer's duties. *Edmond v. United States*, 520 U.S. 651, 661 (1997). More recently, we have focused on whether the officer's work is "directed and supervised" by a principal officer. *Id.* [relocated footnote—Eds.]. . .

In *Perkins*, we upheld tenure protections for a naval cadet-engineer. And, in *Morrison*, we upheld a provision granting good-cause tenure protection to an independent counsel appointed to investigate and prosecute particular alleged crimes by high-ranking Government officials. Backing away from the reliance in *Humphrey's Executor* on the concepts of "quasi-legislative" and "quasi-judicial" power, we viewed the ultimate question as whether a removal restriction is of "such a nature that [it] impede[s] the President's ability to perform his constitutional duty." Although the independent counsel was a single person and performed "law enforcement functions that typically have been undertaken by officials within the Executive Branch," we concluded that the removal protections did not unduly interfere with the functioning of the Executive Branch because "the independent counsel [was] an inferior officer under the Appointments Clause, with limited jurisdiction and tenure and lacking policymaking or significant administrative authority."

These two exceptions—one for multimember expert agencies that do not wield substantial executive power, and one for inferior officers with limited duties and no policymaking or administrative authority—"represent what up to now have been the outermost constitutional limits of permissible congressional restrictions on the President's removal power."

B

Neither *Humphrey's Executor* nor *Morrison* resolves whether the CFPB Director's insulation from removal is constitutional. Start with *Humphrey's Executor*. Unlike the New Deal–era FTC upheld there, the CFPB is led by a single Director who cannot be described as a "body of experts" and cannot be considered "non-partisan" in the same sense as a group of officials drawn from both sides of the aisle. Moreover, while the staggered terms of the FTC Commissioners prevented complete turnovers in agency leadership and guaranteed that there would always be some Commissioners who had accrued significant expertise, the CFPB's single-Director structure and five-year term guarantee abrupt shifts in agency leadership and with it the loss of accumulated expertise.

[I]nstead of making reports and recommendations to Congress, as the 1935 FTC did, the [CFPB] Director possesses the authority to promulgate binding rules fleshing out 19 federal statutes, including a broad prohibition on unfair and deceptive practices in a major segment of the U.S. economy. And instead of submitting recommended dispositions to an Article III court, the Director may unilaterally issue final decisions awarding legal and equitable relief in administrative adjudications. Finally, the Director's enforcement authority includes the power to seek daunting monetary penalties against private parties on behalf of the United States in federal court—a quintessentially executive power not considered in *Humphrey's Executor*.

The logic of *Morrison* also does not apply. Everyone agrees the CFPB Director is not an inferior officer, and her duties are far from limited. Unlike the independent counsel, who lacked policymaking or administrative authority, the Director has the sole responsibility to administer 19 separate consumer-protection statutes that cover everything from credit cards and car payments to mortgages and student loans. It is true that the independent counsel in *Morrison* was empowered to initiate criminal investigations and prosecutions, and in that respect wielded core executive power. But that power, while significant, was trained inward to high-ranking Governmental actors identified by others, and was confined to a specified matter in which the Department of Justice had a potential conflict of interest. By contrast, the CFPB Director has the authority to bring the coercive power of the state to bear on millions of private citizens and businesses, imposing even billion-dollar penalties through administrative adjudications and civil actions.

In light of these differences, the constitutionality of the CFPB Director's insulation from removal cannot be settled by *Humphrey's Executor* or *Morrison* alone.

C

The question instead is whether to extend those precedents to the "new situation" before us, namely an independent agency led by a single Director and vested with significant executive power. We decline to do so. Such an agency has no basis in history and no place in our constitutional structure.

[A]n agency with a structure like that of the CFPB is almost wholly unprecedented. After years of litigating the agency's constitutionality, the Courts of Appeals, parties, and *amici* have identified "only a handful of isolated" incidents in which Congress has provided good-cause tenure to principal officers who wield power alone rather than as members of a board or commission. . . .

[T]he Social Security Administration (SSA) has been run by a single Administrator since 1994. [But t]hat example, too, is comparatively recent and controversial. . . . In addition, unlike the CFPB, the SSA lacks the authority to bring enforcement actions against private parties. Its role is largely limited to adjudicating claims for Social Security benefits.

The only remaining example is the Federal Housing Finance Agency (FHFA), created in 2008 to assume responsibility for Fannie Mae and Freddie Mac. That agency is essentially a companion of the CFPB, established in response to the same financial crisis. It regulates primarily Government-sponsored enterprises, not purely private actors. And its single-Director structure is a source of ongoing controversy. . . .

With the exception of the one-year blip for the Comptroller of the Currency [during the Civil War], these isolated examples are modern and contested. And they do not involve regulatory or enforcement authority remotely comparable to that exercised by the CFPB. The CFPB's single-Director structure is an innovation with no foothold in history or tradition. . . . The dissent categorizes the CFPB as one of many "financial regulators" that have historically enjoyed some insulation from the President. But even assuming financial institutions like the Second Bank and the Federal Reserve can claim a special historical status, the CFPB is in an entirely different league. It acts as a mini legislature, prosecutor, and court, responsible for creating substantive rules for a wide swath of industries, prosecuting violations, and levying knee-buckling penalties against private citizens. And, of course, it is the only agency of its kind run by a single Director. [relocated footnote—EDS.]

In addition to being a historical anomaly, the CFPB's single-Director configuration is incompatible with our constitutional structure. Aside from the sole exception of the Presidency, that structure scrupulously avoids concentrating power in the hands of any single individual.

"The Framers recognized that, in the long term, structural protections against abuse of power were critical to preserving liberty." *Bowsher.* Their solution to governmental power and its perils was simple: divide it. To prevent the "gradual concentration" of power in the same hands, they enabled "[a]mbition . . . to counteract ambition" at every turn. The Federalist No. 51 (J. Madison). At the highest level, they "split the atom of sovereignty" itself into one Federal Government and the States. They then divided the "powers of the new Federal Government into three defined categories, Legislative, Executive, and Judicial." *Chadha.*

They did not stop there. Most prominently, the Framers bifurcated the federal legislative power into two Chambers: the House of Representatives and the Senate, each composed of multiple Members and Senators. Art. I, §§2, 3.

The Executive Branch is a stark departure from all this division. The Framers viewed the legislative power as a special threat to individual liberty, so they divided that power to ensure that "differences of opinion" and the "jarrings of parties" would "promote deliberation and circumspection" and "check excesses in the majority." See The Federalist No. 70 (A. Hamilton); see also *id.*, No. 51. By contrast, the Framers thought it necessary to secure the authority of the Executive so that he could carry out his unique responsibilities. See *id.*, No. 70. As Madison put it, while "the weight of the legislative authority requires that it should be . . . divided, the weakness of the executive may require, on the other hand, that it should be fortified." *Id.*, No. 51.

The Framers deemed an energetic executive essential to "the protection of the community against foreign attacks," "the steady administration of the laws," "the protection of property," and "the security of liberty." *Id.*, No. 70. Accordingly, they chose not to bog the Executive down with the "habitual feebleness and dilatoriness" that comes with a "diversity of views and opinions." *Id.* Instead, they gave the Executive the "[d]ecision, activity, secrecy, and dispatch" that "characterise the proceedings of one man." *Id.*

To justify and check *that* authority—unique in our constitutional structure—the Framers made the President the most democratic and politically accountable official in Government. Only the President (along with the Vice President) is elected by the entire Nation. And the President's political accountability is enhanced by the solitary nature of the Executive Branch, which provides "a single object for the jealousy and watchfulness of the people." *Id.* The President "cannot delegate ultimate responsibility or the active obligation to supervise that goes with it," because Article II "makes a single President responsible for the actions of the Executive Branch."

The resulting constitutional strategy is straightforward: divide power everywhere except for the Presidency, and render the President directly accountable to the people through regular elections. In that scheme, individual executive officials will still wield significant authority, but that authority remains subject to the ongoing supervision and control of the elected President. Through the President's oversight, "the chain of dependence [is] preserved," so that "the lowest officers, the middle grade, and the highest" all "depend, as they ought, on the President, and the President on the community." 1 Annals of Cong. 499 (J. Madison).

The CFPB's single-Director structure contravenes this carefully calibrated system by vesting significant governmental power in the hands of a single individual accountable to no one. The Director is neither elected by the people nor meaningfully controlled (through the threat of removal) by someone who is. The Director does not even depend on Congress for annual appropriations. . . . Yet the Director may *unilaterally*, without meaningful supervision, issue final regulations, oversee adjudications, set enforcement priorities, initiate prosecutions, and determine what penalties to impose on private parties. With no colleagues to persuade, and no boss or electorate looking over her shoulder, the Director may dictate and enforce policy for a vital segment of the economy affecting millions of Americans.

The CFPB Director's insulation from removal by an accountable President is enough to render the agency's structure unconstitutional. But several other features of the CFPB combine to make the Director's removal protection even more problematic. In addition to lacking the most direct method of presidential control—removal at will—the agency's unique structure also forecloses certain indirect methods of Presidential control.

Because the CFPB is headed by a single Director with a five-year term, some Presidents may not have any opportunity to shape its leadership and thereby influence its activities. A President elected in 2020 would likely not appoint a CFPB Director until 2023, and a President elected in 2028 may *never* appoint one. That means an unlucky President might get elected on a consumer-protection platform and enter office only to find herself saddled with a holdover Director from a competing political party who is dead set *against* that agenda. To make matters worse, the agency's single-Director structure means the President will not have the opportunity to appoint any other leaders—such as a chair or fellow members of a Commission or Board—who can serve as a check on the Director's authority and help bring the agency in line with the President's preferred policies.

The CFPB's receipt of funds outside the appropriations process further aggravates the agency's threat to Presidential control. The President normally has the opportunity to recommend or veto spending bills that affect the operation of administrative agencies. And, for the past century, the President has annually submitted a proposed budget to Congress for approval. Presidents frequently use these budgetary tools "to influence the policies of independent agencies." But no similar opportunity exists for the President to influence the CFPB Director. Instead, the Director receives over $500 million per year to fund the agency's chosen priorities. And the Director receives that money from the Federal Reserve, which is itself funded outside of the annual appropriations process. This financial freedom makes it even more likely that the agency will "slip from the Executive's control, and thus from that of the people." . . .

Amicus . . . questions the textual basis for the removal power and highlights statements from Madison, Hamilton, and Chief Justice Marshall expressing "heterodox" views on the subject. But those concerns are misplaced. It is true that "there is no 'removal clause' in the Constitution," but neither is there a "separation of powers clause" or a "federalism clause." These foundational doctrines are instead evident from the Constitution's vesting of certain powers in certain bodies. As we have explained many times before, the President's removal power stems from Article II's vesting of the "executive Power" in the President. . . .

[T]ext, first principles, the First Congress's decision in 1789, *Myers*, and *Free Enterprise Fund* all establish that the President's removal power is the rule, not the exception. While we do not revisit *Humphrey's Executor* or any other precedent today, we decline to elevate it into a freestanding invitation for Congress to impose additional restrictions on the President's removal authority. . . .

[T]he dissent would endorse whatever "the times demand, so long as the President retains the ability to carry out his constitutional functions." But that amorphous test provides no real limiting principle. . . . [relocated footnote—Eds.]

Finally, *amicus* contends that if we identify a constitutional problem with the CFPB's structure, we should avoid it by broadly construing the statutory grounds for removing the CFPB Director from office. The Dodd-Frank Act provides that the Director may be removed for "inefficiency, neglect of duty, or malfeasance in office." In *amicus*' view, that language could be interpreted to reserve substantial discretion to the President. . . .

Constitutional avoidance is not a license to rewrite Congress's work to say whatever the Constitution needs it to say in a given situation. Without a proffered interpretation that is rooted in the statutory text and structure, and would avoid the constitutional violation we have identified, we take Congress at its word that it meant to impose a meaningful restriction on the President's removal authority. . . .

IV

Having concluded that the CFPB's leadership by a single independent Director violates the separation of powers, we now turn to the appropriate remedy. . . . The only constitutional defect we have identified in the CFPB's structure is the

Director's insulation from removal. If the Director were removable at will by the President, the constitutional violation would disappear. . . . The provisions of the Dodd-Frank Act bearing on the CFPB's structure and duties remain fully operative without the offending tenure restriction. Those provisions are capable of functioning independently, and there is nothing in the text or history of the Dodd-Frank Act that demonstrates Congress would have preferred *no* CFPB to a CFPB supervised by the President. Quite the opposite. Unlike the Sarbanes-Oxley Act at issue in *Free Enterprise Fund*, the Dodd-Frank Act contains an express severability clause. There is no need to wonder what Congress would have wanted if "any provision of this Act" is "held to be unconstitutional" because it has told us: "the remainder of this Act" should "not be affected." . . .

Congress [may have] preferred an independent CFPB to a dependent one; but . . . the critical question [is] whether Congress would have preferred a dependent CFPB to *no agency at all.* That is the only question we have the authority to decide, and the answer seems clear. . . .

* * *

In our constitutional system, the executive power belongs to the President, and that power generally includes the ability to supervise and remove the agents who wield executive power in his stead. While we have previously upheld limits on the President's removal authority in certain contexts, we decline to do so when it comes to principal officers who, acting alone, wield significant executive power. The Constitution requires that such officials remain dependent on the President, who in turn is accountable to the people. . . .

Justice THOMAS, with whom Justice GORSUCH joins, concurring in part and dissenting in part.

[B]ecause the Court takes a step in the right direction by limiting *Humphrey's Executor* to "multimember expert agencies that *do not wield substantial executive power,*" I join Parts I, II, and III of its opinion. I respectfully dissent from the Court's severability analysis, however, because I do not believe that we should address severability in this case.

The decision in *Humphrey's Executor* poses a direct threat to our constitutional structure and, as a result, the liberty of the American people. The Court concludes that it is not strictly necessary for us to overrule that decision. But with today's decision, the Court has repudiated almost every aspect of *Humphrey's Executor.* In a future case, I would repudiate what is left of this erroneous precedent. . . .

Despite the defined structural limitations of the Constitution and the clear vesting of executive power in the President, Congress has increasingly shifted executive power to a *de facto* fourth branch of Government—independent agencies. These agencies wield considerable executive power without Presidential oversight. They are led by officers who are insulated from the President by removal restrictions, "reduc[ing] the Chief Magistrate to [the role of] cajoler-in-chief." But "[t]he people do not vote for the Officers of the United States. They instead look to the President to guide the assistants or deputies subject to his superintendence." Because independent agencies wield substantial power with no accountability to either the President or the people, they "pose a significant threat to individual liberty and to the constitutional system of separation of powers and checks and balances." . . . Our tolerance of independent agencies in *Humphrey's Executor* is an unfortunate example of the Court's failure to apply the Constitution as written. That decision has paved the way for an ever-expanding encroachment on the power of the Executive, contrary to our constitutional design. . . .

Humphrey's Executor relies on one key premise: the notion that there is a category of "quasi-legislative" and "quasi-judicial" power that is not exercised by Congress or the Judiciary, but that is also not part of "the executive power vested by the Constitution in the President." . . . The problem is that the Court's premise was entirely wrong. The Constitution does not permit the creation of officers exercising "quasi-legislative" and "quasi-judicial powers" in "quasi-legislative" and "quasi-judicial agencies." No such powers or agencies exist. Congress lacks the authority to delegate its legislative power, *Whitman v. American Trucking Assns., Inc.*, 531 U.S. 457, 472 (2001), and it cannot authorize the use of judicial power by officers acting outside of the bounds of Article III, *Stern v. Marshall*, 564 U.S. 462, 484 (2011). Nor can Congress create agencies that straddle multiple branches of Government. The Constitution sets out three branches of Government and provides each with a different form of power—legislative, executive, and judicial. Free-floating agencies simply do not comport with this constitutional structure. "[A]gencies have been called quasi-legislative, quasi-executive or quasi-judicial, as the occasion required, in order to validate their functions within the separation-of-powers scheme of the Constitution." But "[t]he mere retreat to the qualifying 'quasi' is implicit with confession that all recognized classifications have broken down, and 'quasi' is a smooth cover which we draw over our confusion as we might use a counterpane to conceal a disordered bed." . . .

Continued reliance on *Humphrey's Executor* to justify the existence of independent agencies creates a serious, ongoing threat to our Government's design. Leaving these unconstitutional agencies in place does not enhance this Court's legitimacy; it subverts political accountability and threatens individual liberty. . . . We simply cannot compromise when it comes to our Government's structure. Today, the Court does enough to resolve this case, but in the future, we should reconsider *Humphrey's Executor in toto*. And I hope that we will have the will to do so. . . .

While I think that the Court correctly resolves the merits of the constitutional question, I do not agree with its decision to sever the removal restriction. . . . Given my concerns about our modern severability doctrine and the fact that severability makes no difference to the dispute before us, I would resolve this case by simply denying the CFPB's petition to enforce the civil investigative demand.

Justice KAGAN, with whom Justice GINSBURG, Justice BREYER, and Justice SOTOMAYOR join, concurring in the judgment with respect to severability and dissenting in part.

Throughout the Nation's history, this Court has left most decisions about how to structure the Executive Branch to Congress and the President, acting through legislation they both agree to. In particular, the Court has commonly allowed those two branches to create zones of administrative independence by limiting the President's power to remove agency heads. The Federal Reserve Board. The Federal Trade Commission (FTC). The National Labor Relations Board. Statute after statute establishing such entities instructs the President that he may not discharge their directors except for cause — most often phrased as inefficiency, neglect of duty, or malfeasance in office. Those statutes, whose language the Court has repeatedly approved, provide the model for the removal restriction before us today. If precedent were any guide, that provision would have survived its encounter with this Court—and so would the intended independence of the Consumer Financial Protection Bureau (CFPB).

Our Constitution and history demand that result. The text of the Constitution allows these common for-cause removal limits. Nothing in it speaks of removal. And it grants Congress authority to organize all the institutions of American governance, provided only that those arrangements allow the President to perform his own constitutionally assigned duties. Still more, the Framers' choice to give the political branches wide discretion over administrative offices has played out through American history in ways that have settled the constitutional meaning. From the first, Congress debated and enacted measures to create spheres of administration — especially of financial affairs — detached from direct presidential control. As the years passed, and governance became ever more complicated, Congress continued to adopt and adapt such measures — confident it had latitude to do so under a Constitution meant to "endure for ages to come." *McCulloch v. Maryland*, 4 Wheat. 316, 415 (1819) (approving the Second Bank of the United States). Not every innovation in governance — not every experiment in administrative independence — has proved successful. And debates about the prudence of limiting the President's control over regulatory agencies, including through his removal power, have never abated. But the Constitution — both as originally drafted and as practiced — mostly leaves disagreements about administrative structure to Congress and the President, who have the knowledge and experience needed to address them. Within broad bounds, it keeps the courts — who do not — out of the picture.

The Court today fails to respect its proper role. It recognizes that this Court has approved limits on the President's removal power over heads of agencies much like the CFPB. Agencies possessing similar powers, agencies charged with similar missions, agencies created for similar reasons. The majority's explanation is that the heads of those agencies fall within an "exception" — one for multimember bodies and another for inferior officers — to a "general rule" of unrestricted presidential removal power. And the majority says the CFPB Director does not. That account, though, is wrong in every respect. The majority's general rule does not exist. Its exceptions, likewise, are made up for the occasion — gerrymandered so the CFPB falls outside them. And the distinction doing most of the majority's work — between multimember bodies and single directors — does not respond to the constitutional values at stake. If a removal provision violates the separation of powers, it is because the measure so deprives the President of control over an official as to impede his own constitutional functions. But with or without a for-cause removal provision, the President has at least as much control over an individual as over a commission — and possibly more. That means the constitutional concern is, if anything, ameliorated when the agency has a single head. Unwittingly, the majority shows why courts should stay their hand in these matters. . . .

In second-guessing the political branches, the majority second-guesses as well the wisdom of the Framers and the judgment of history. It writes in rules to the

Constitution that the drafters knew well enough not to put there. It repudiates the lessons of American experience, from the 18th century to the present day. And it commits the Nation to a static version of governance, incapable of responding to new conditions and challenges. Congress and the President established the CFPB to address financial practices that had brought on a devastating recession, and could do so again. Today's decision wipes out a feature of that agency its creators thought fundamental to its mission—a measure of independence from political pressure. I respectfully dissent.

I

The text of the Constitution, the history of the country, the precedents of this Court, and the need for sound and adaptable governance—all stand against the majority's opinion. They point not to the majority's "general rule" of "unrestricted removal power" with two grudgingly applied "exceptions." Rather, they bestow discretion on the legislature to structure administrative institutions as the times demand, so long as the President retains the ability to carry out his constitutional duties. And most relevant here, they give Congress wide leeway to limit the President's removal power in the interest of enhancing independence from politics in regulatory bodies like the CFPB.

What does the Constitution say about the separation of powers—and particularly about the President's removal authority? (Spoiler alert: about the latter, nothing at all.) . . .

[T]he separation of powers is, by design, neither rigid nor complete. . . . [A]s James Madison stated, the creation of distinct branches "did not mean that these departments ought to have no partial agency in, or no controul over the acts of each other." The Federalist No. 47 (emphasis deleted). To the contrary, Madison explained, the drafters of the Constitution—like those of then-existing state constitutions—opted against keeping the branches of government "absolutely separate and distinct." Or as Justice Story reiterated a half-century later: "[W]hen we speak of a separation of the three great departments of government," it is "not meant to affirm, that they must be kept wholly and entirely separate." 2 J. Story, Commentaries on the Constitution of the United States §524, p. 8 (1833). Instead, the branches have—as they must for the whole arrangement to work—"common link[s] of connexion [and] dependence."

One way the Constitution reflects that vision is by giving Congress broad authority to establish and organize the Executive Branch. Article II presumes the existence of "Officer[s]" in "executive Departments." §2, cl. 1. But it does not, as you might think from reading the majority opinion, give the President authority to decide what kinds of officers—in what departments, with what responsibilities—the Executive Branch requires. Instead, Article I's Necessary and Proper Clause puts those decisions in the legislature's hands. Congress has the power "[t]o make all Laws which shall be necessary and proper for carrying into Execution" not just its own enumerated powers but also "all other Powers vested by this Constitution in the Government of the United States, or in any Department or Officer thereof." §8, cl. 18. Similarly, the Appointments Clause reflects Congress's central role in structuring the Executive Branch. Yes, the President can appoint principal officers, but only as the legislature "shall . . . establish[ ] by Law" (and of course subject to the Senate's advice and consent). Art. II, §2, cl. 2. And Congress has plenary power to decide not only what inferior officers will exist but also who (the President or a head of department) will appoint them. So as Madison told the first Congress, the legislature gets to "create[ ] the office, define[ ] the powers, [and] limit[ ] its duration." 1 Annals of Cong. 582 (1789). The President, as to the construction of his own branch of government, can only try to work his will through the legislative process. . . .

The majority relies for its contrary vision on Article II's Vesting Clause, but the provision can't carry all that weight. Or as Chief Justice Rehnquist wrote of a similar claim in *Morrison v. Olson*, 487 U.S. 654 (1988), "extrapolat[ing]" an unrestricted removal power from such "general constitutional language"—which says only that "[t]he executive Power shall be vested in a President"—is "more than the text will bear." Dean John Manning has well explained why, even were it not obvious from the Clause's "open-ended language." Separation of Powers as Ordinary Interpretation, 124 Harv. L. Rev. 1939, 1971 (2011). The Necessary and Proper Clause, he writes, makes it impossible to "establish a constitutional violation simply by showing that Congress has constrained the way '[t]he executive Power' is implemented"; that is exactly what the Clause gives Congress the power to do. Only "a *specific* historical understanding" can bar Congress from enacting a given constraint. And nothing of that sort broadly prevents Congress from limiting the President's removal power. . . .

Nor can the Take Care Clause come to the majority's rescue. That Clause cannot properly serve as a "placeholder for broad judicial judgments" about presidential control. To begin with, the provision—"he shall take Care that the Laws be faithfully executed"—speaks of duty, not power. Art. II, §3. . . .

History no better serves the majority's cause. As Madison wrote, "a regular course of practice" can "liquidate & settle the meaning of" disputed or indeterminate constitutional provisions. The majority lays claim to that kind of record, asserting that its muscular view of "[t]he President's removal power has long been confirmed by history." But that is not so. The early history—including the fabled Decision of 1789—shows mostly debate and division about removal authority. And when a "settle[ment of] meaning" at last occurred, it was not on the majority's terms. Instead, it supports wide latitude for Congress to create spheres of administrative independence. . . .

Delegates to the Constitutional Convention never discussed whether or to what extent the President would have power to remove executive officials. As a result, the Framers advocating ratification had no single view of the matter. . . . [In] the Decision of 1789, . . . Congress addressed the removal power while considering the bill creating the Department of Foreign Affairs. . . . The best [historical account] is that the First Congress was "deeply divided" on the President's removal power, and "never squarely addressed" the central issue here. The congressional debates revealed three main positions. Some shared Hamilton's Federalist No. 77 view: The Constitution required Senate consent for removal. At the opposite extreme, others claimed that the Constitution gave absolute removal power to the President. And a third faction maintained that the Constitution placed Congress in the driver's seat: The legislature could regulate, if it so chose, the President's authority to remove. In the end, Congress passed a bill saying nothing about removal, leaving the President free to fire the Secretary of Foreign Affairs at will. But the only one of the three views definitively rejected was Hamilton's theory of necessary Senate consent. As even strong proponents of executive power have shown, Congress never "endorse[d] the view that [it] lacked authority to modify" the President's removal authority when it wished to. The summer of 1789 thus ended without resolution of the critical question: Was the removal power "beyond the reach of congressional regulation?" . . .

At the same time, the First Congress gave officials handling financial affairs—as compared to diplomatic and military ones—some independence from the President. . . . Congress . . . deemed the Comptroller of the Treasury's settlements of public accounts "final and conclusive." That decision, preventing presidential overrides, marked the Comptroller as exercising independent judgment. True enough, no statute shielded the Comptroller from discharge. But even James Madison, who at this point opposed most removal limits, told Congress that "there may be strong reasons why an officer of this kind should not hold his office at the pleasure" of the Secretary or President. At the least, as Professor Prakash writes, "Madison maintained that Congress had the [constitutional] authority to modify [the Comptroller's] tenure."

Contrary to the majority's view, then, the founding era closed without any agreement that Congress lacked the power to curb the President's removal authority. And as it kept that question open, Congress took the first steps—which would launch a tradition—of distinguishing financial regulators from diplomatic and military officers. The latter mainly helped the President carry out his own constitutional duties in foreign relations and war. The former chiefly carried out statutory duties, fulfilling functions Congress had assigned to their offices. In addressing the new Nation's finances, Congress had begun to use its powers under the Necessary and Proper Clause to design effective administrative institutions. And that included taking steps to insulate certain officers from political influence. . . .

As the decades and centuries passed, those efforts picked up steam. Confronting new economic, technological, and social conditions, Congress—and often the President—saw new needs for pockets of independence within the federal bureaucracy. And that was especially so, again, when it came to financial regulation. . . . Enacted under the Necessary and Proper Clause, those measures —creating some of the Nation's most enduring institutions—themselves helped settle the extent of Congress's power. "[A] regular course of practice," to use Madison's phrase, has "liquidate[d]" constitutional meaning about the permissibility of independent agencies.

Take first Congress's decision in 1816 to create the Second Bank of the United States—"the first truly independent agency in the republic's history." Of the twenty-five directors who led the Bank, the President could appoint and remove only five. Yet the Bank had a greater impact on the Nation than any but a few institutions, regulating the Nation's money supply in ways anticipating what the Federal Reserve does today. . . . [B]y the early 19th century, Congress established a body wielding enormous financial power mostly outside the President's dominion. . . .

In response to wartime economic pressures, President Lincoln (not known for his modest view of executive power) asked Congress to establish an office called the Comptroller of the Currency. The statute he signed made the Comptroller removable only with the Senate's consent. . . . A year later, Congress amended the statute to permit removal by the President alone, but only upon "reasons to be communicated by him to the Senate." . . .

And then, nearly a century and a half ago, the floodgates opened. In 1887, the growing power of the railroads over the American economy led Congress to create the Interstate Commerce Commission. Under that legislation, the President could remove the five Commissioners only "for inefficiency, neglect of duty, or malfeasance in office"—the same standard Congress applied to the CFPB Director. More—many more—for-cause removal provisions followed. In 1913, Congress gave the Governors of the Federal Reserve Board for-cause protection to ensure the agency would resist political pressure and promote economic stability. The next year, Congress provided similar protection to the FTC in the interest of ensuring "a continuous policy" "free from the effect" of "changing [White House] incumbency." The Federal Deposit Insurance Corporation (FDIC), the Securities and Exchange Commission (SEC), the Commodity Futures Trading Commission. In the financial realm, "independent agencies have remained the bedrock of the institutional framework governing U.S. markets." By one count, across all subject matter areas, 48 agencies have heads (and below them hundreds more inferior officials) removable only for cause. So year by year by year, the broad sweep of history has spoken to the constitutional question before us: Independent agencies are everywhere.

What is more, the Court's precedents before today have accepted the role of independent agencies in our governmental system. To be sure, the line of our decisions has not run altogether straight. But we have repeatedly upheld provisions that prevent the President from firing regulatory officials except for such matters as neglect or malfeasance. In those decisions, we sounded a caution, insisting that Congress could not impede through removal restrictions the President's performance of his own constitutional duties. (So, to take the clearest example, Congress could not curb the President's power to remove his close military or diplomatic advisers.) But within that broad limit, this Court held, Congress could protect from at-will removal the officials it deemed to need some independence from political pressures. Nowhere do those precedents suggest what the majority announces today: that the President has an "unrestricted removal power" subject to two bounded exceptions.

The majority grounds its new approach in *Myers*, ignoring the way this Court has cabined that decision. *Myers*, the majority tells us, found an unrestrained removal power "essential to the [President's] execution of the laws." What the majority does not say is that within a decade the Court abandoned that view (much as later scholars rejected Taft's one-sided history). In *Humphrey's Executor* v. *United States*, 295 U.S. 602 (1935), the Court unceremoniously—and unanimously—confined *Myers* to its facts. "[T]he narrow point actually decided" there, *Humphrey's* stated, was that the President could "remove a postmaster of the first class, without the advice and consent of the Senate." Nothing else in Chief Justice Taft's prolix opinion "c[a]me within the rule of *stare decisis*." (Indeed, the Court went on, everything in *Myers* "out of harmony" with *Humphrey's* was expressly "disapproved.") Half a century later, the Court was more generous. Two decisions read *Myers* as standing for the principle that Congress's own "participation in the removal of executive officers is unconstitutional." *Bowsher v. Synar*, 478 U.S. 714, 725 (1986); see *Morrison*. *Bowsher* made clear that *Myers* had nothing to say about Congress's power to enact a provision merely "limit[ing] the President's powers of removal" through a for-cause provision. That issue, the Court stated, was "not presented" in "the *Myers* case." Instead, the relevant cite was *Humphrey's*.

And *Humphrey's* found constitutional a statute identical to the one here, providing that the President could remove FTC Commissioners for "inefficiency, neglect of duty, or malfeasance in office." The *Humphrey's* Court, as the majority notes, relied in substantial part on what kind of work the Commissioners performed. (By contrast, nothing in the decision turned—as the majority suggests—on any of the agency's organizational features.) According to *Humphrey's*, the Commissioners' primary work was to "carry into effect legislative policies"—"filling in and administering the details embodied by [a statute's] general standard." In addition, the Court noted, the Commissioners recommended dispositions in court cases, much as a special master does. Given those "quasi-legislative" and "quasi-judicial"—as opposed to "purely executive"—functions, Congress could limit the President's removal authority. Or said another way, Congress could give the FTC some "independen[ce from] executive control."

The majority is quite right that today we view *all* the activities of administrative agencies as exercises of "the 'executive Power.' " But we well understand, just as the *Humphrey's* Court did, that those activities may "take 'legislative' and 'judicial' forms." The classic examples are agency rulemakings and adjudications, endemic in agencies like the FTC and CFPB. In any event, the Court would soon make clear that Congress can also constrain the President's removal authority over officials performing even the most "executive" of functions. [relocated footnote—Eds.]. . .

Even *Free Enterprise Fund*, in which the Court recently held a removal provision invalid, operated within the framework of this precedent—and in so doing, left in place a removal provision just like the one here. . . . Members of an accounting board were protected from removal by SEC Commissioners, who in turn were protected from removal by the President. The Court found that the two-layer structure deprived the President of "adequate control" over the Board members. . . . The Court observed that it did not "take issue with for-cause limitations in general"—which *do* enable the President to determine whether good cause for discharge exists (because, say, an official has violated the law). And the Court's solution to the constitutional problem it saw was merely to strike one level of insulation, making the Board removable by the SEC at will. That remedy left the SEC's own for-cause protection in place. The President could thus remove Commissioners for malfeasance or neglect, but not for policy disagreements.

[F]or almost a century, this Court has made clear that Congress has broad discretion to enact for-cause protections in pursuit of good governance. . . . The deferential approach this Court has taken gives Congress the flexibility it needs to craft administrative agencies. Diverse problems of government demand diverse solutions. They call for varied measures and mixtures of democratic accountability and technical expertise, energy and efficiency. Sometimes, the arguments push toward tight presidential control of agencies. The President's engagement, some people say, can disrupt bureaucratic stagnation, counter industry capture, and make agencies more responsive to public interests. See, well, Kagan, Presidential Administration, 114 Harv. L. Rev. 2245, 2331-2346 (2001). At other times, the arguments favor greater independence from presidential involvement. Insulation from political pressure helps ensure impartial adjudications. It places technical issues in the hands of those most capable of addressing them. It promotes continuity, and prevents short-term electoral interests from distorting policy. (Consider, for example, how the Federal Reserve's independence stops a President trying to win a second term from manipulating interest rates.) Of course, the right balance between presidential control and independence is often uncertain, contested, and value-laden. No mathematical formula governs institutional design; trade-offs are endemic to the enterprise. But that is precisely why the issue is one for the political branches to debate—and then debate again as times change. And it's why courts should stay (mostly) out of the way. Rather than impose rigid rules like the majority's, they should let Congress and the President figure out what blend of independence and political control will best enable an agency to perform its intended functions. . . .

II

[T]he CFPB emerged out of disaster. The collapse of the subprime mortgage market "precipitat[ed] a financial crisis that wiped out over $10 trillion in American household wealth and cost millions of Americans their jobs, their retirements, and their homes." In that moment of economic ruin, the President proposed and Congress enacted legislation to address the causes of the collapse and prevent a recurrence. An important part of that statute created an agency to protect consumers from exploitative financial practices. The agency would take over enforcement of almost 20 existing federal laws. And it would administer a new prohibition on "unfair, deceptive, or abusive act[s] or practice[s]" in the consumer-finance sector.

No one had a doubt that the new agency should be independent. As explained already, Congress has historically given—with this Court's permission—a measure of independence to financial regulators like the Federal Reserve Board and the FTC. And agencies of that kind had administered most of the legislation whose enforcement the new statute transferred to the CFPB. The law thus included an ordinary for-cause provision—once again, that the President could fire the CFPB's Director only for "inefficiency, neglect of duty, or malfeasance in office." That standard would allow the President to discharge the Director for a failure to "faithfully execute[ ]" the law, as well as for basic incompetence. But it would not permit removal for policy differences. . . .

The CFPB Director exercises the same powers, and receives the same removal protections, as the heads of other, constitutionally permissible independent agencies [such as the FTC, the SEC, and the Federal Reserve Board]. How could it be that this opinion is a dissent?. . . .

The majority focuses on one (it says sufficient) reason: The CFPB Director is singular, not plural. . . . [But] *Humphrey's* and later precedents give no support to the majority's view that the number of people at the apex of an agency matters to the constitutional issue. . . . [And t]he CFPB's single-director structure has a fair bit of precedent behind it. . . . Still more important, novelty is not the test of constitutionality when it comes to structuring agencies. See *Mistretta v. United States*, 488 U.S. 361, 385 (1989) ("[M]ere anomaly or innovation" does not violate the separation of powers). Congress regulates in that sphere under the Necessary and Proper Clause, not (as the majority seems to think) a Rinse and Repeat Clause. The Framers understood that new times would often require new measures, and exigencies often demand innovation. See *McCulloch*. In line with that belief, the history of the administrative sphere—its rules, its practices, its institutions—is replete with experiment and change. Indeed, each of the agencies the majority says now fits within its "exceptions" was once new; there is, as the saying goes, "a first time for everything." So even if the CFPB differs from its forebears in having a single director, that departure is not itself "telling" of a "constitutional problem." In deciding what *this* moment demanded, Congress had no obligation to make a carbon copy of a design from a bygone era.

And Congress's choice to put a single director, rather than a multimember commission, at the CFPB's head violates no principle of separation of powers. The purported constitutional problem here is that an official has "slip[ped] from the Executive's control" and "supervision"—that he has become unaccountable to the President. So to make sense on the majority's own terms, the distinction between singular and plural agency heads must rest on a theory about why the former more easily "slip" from the President's grasp. But the majority has nothing to offer. In fact, the opposite is more likely to be true: To the extent that such matters are measurable, individuals are easier than groups to supervise. . . .

[T]he majority's distinction cuts the opposite way: More powerful control mechanisms are needed (if anything) for commissions. Holding everything else equal, those are the agencies more likely to "slip from the Executive's control." Just consider your everyday experience: It's easier to get one person to do what you want than a gaggle. So too, you know exactly whom to blame when an individual—but not when a group—does a job badly. The same is true in bureaucracies. A multimember structure reduces accountability to the President because it's harder for him to oversee, to influence—or to remove, if necessary—a group of five or more commissioners than a single director. Indeed, that is *why* Congress so often resorts to hydra-headed agencies. "[M]ultiple membership," an influential Senate Report concluded, is "a buffer against Presidential control" (especially when combined, as it often is, with partisan-balance requirements). Senate Committee on Governmental Affairs, Study on Federal Regulation, S. Doc. No. 95-91, vol. 5, p. 75 (1977). So, for example, Congress constructed the Federal Reserve as it did because it is "easier to protect a board from political control than to protect a single appointed official." R. Cushman, The Independent Regulatory Commissions 153 (1941). It is hard to know why Congress did not take the same tack when creating the CFPB. But its choice brought the agency only closer to the President—more exposed to his view, more subject to his sway. In short, the majority gets the matter backward: Where presidential control is the object, better to have one than many. . . .

III

Recall again how this dispute got started. In the midst of the Great Recession, Congress and the President came together to create an agency with an important mission. It would protect consumers from the reckless financial practices that had caused the then-ongoing economic collapse. Not only Congress but also the President thought that the new agency, to fulfill its mandate, needed a measure of independence. So the two political branches, acting together, gave the CFPB Director the same job protection that innumerable other agency heads possess. All in all, those branches must have thought, they had done a good day's work. Relying on their experience and knowledge of administration, they had built an agency in the way best suited to carry out its functions. They had protected the public from financial chicanery and crisis. They had governed.

And now consider how the dispute ends—with five unelected judges rejecting the result of that democratic process. The outcome today will not shut down the CFPB: A different majority of this Court, including all those who join this opinion, believes that *if* the agency's removal provision is unconstitutional, it should be severed. But the majority on constitutionality jettisons a measure Congress and the President viewed as integral to the way the agency should operate. The majority does so even though the Constitution grants to Congress, acting with the President's approval, the authority to create and shape administrative bodies. And even though those branches, as compared to courts, have far greater understanding of political control mechanisms and agency design.

Nothing in the Constitution requires that outcome; to the contrary. "While the Constitution diffuses power the better to secure liberty, it also contemplates that practice will integrate the dispersed powers into a workable government." *Youngstown Sheet & Tube Co. v. Sawyer*, 343 U.S. 579, 635 (1952) (Jackson, J., concurring). The Framers took pains to craft a document that would allow the structures of governance to change, as times and needs change. The Constitution says only a few words about administration. As Chief Justice Marshall wrote: Rather than prescribing "immutable rules," it enables Congress to choose "the means by which government should, in all future time, execute its powers." *McCulloch.* It authorizes Congress to meet new exigencies with new devices. So Article II does not generally prohibit independent agencies. Nor do any supposed structural principles. Nor do any odors wafting from the document. Save for when those agencies impede the President's performance of his own constitutional duties, the matter is left up to Congress. . . .

The Constitution does not distinguish between single-director and multimember independent agencies. It instructs Congress, not this Court, to decide on agency design. Because this Court ignores that sensible—indeed, that obvious—division of tasks, I respectfully dissent.

DISCUSSION

1. Seila Law *and the "unitary executive."* Behind the debate between Chief Justice Roberts, Justice Thomas, and Justice Kagan is a longer debate over the theory of the "unitary executive." The theory of a "unitary executive" emerged in the conservative movement during the 1970s, and was further articulated in the decades that followed. Stephen Skowronek, The Conservative Insurgency and Presidential Power: A Developmental Perspective on the Unitary Executive, 122 Harv. L. Rev. 2070 (2009). The theory was originally developed in the context of the Nixon, Ford, and Reagan Administrations, when a Republican President faced a liberal Democratic Congress and a bureaucracy and civil service developed during the New Deal/Civil Rights regime.

The unitary executive theory made sense given the goals of the conservative movement. The point was to make the conservative insurgency more effective by allowing the President to get control of the bureaucracy, and to resist congressional interference with the President's exercise of powers, both in domestic and foreign affairs.

Of course, if the tables were turned, and Congress were controlled by Republicans and the White House by Democrats, the unitary executive might sometimes assist liberal causes. But conservative insurgents realized that their real opponent was government bureaucracies and the growing activist state. Because bureaucracies tend over time to increase regulation, it is better to get control over them. Analogous considerations applied to foreign policy: Presidents of both parties like to exercise their foreign policy powers without congressional interference, so it is better to give them a freer hand. Thus, for a political movement that sought to dismantle regulation and promote a muscular approach to foreign policy, empowering the presidency at the expense of the bureaucracy and Congress seemed like a good bet.

Conservative lawyers in the Reagan Justice Department, many of whom became distinguished lawyers and scholars, grounded the theory of the unitary executive in the initial grant in Article II, section 1, that "[t]he executive power shall be vested in a President of the United States of America." They argued that this vesting clause demanded a unitary executive. As Chief Justice Roberts, who served as a young lawyer in the Reagan Justice Department, puts it in *Seila Law*, "The entire 'executive Power' belongs to the President alone," and "lesser officers must remain accountable to the President, whose authority they wield."

The idea that the executive is "unitary" is sometimes associated with three ideas, two of which are closely connected, and the third of which is quite different:

The first idea is that because the executive is unitary, the President must have complete and exclusive power over the choice of people who work under him and who exercise any part of "the executive power of the United States." Under the text of the Constitution, the President does not have complete power to *hire*. See Art. II, §2 (noting Senate's role in advice and consent, and Congress's role in the appointment of inferior officers). So the unitary executive theory has focused instead on the power to *fire* officials. But this idea has never been fully realized in practice: Congress has provided tenure protection for civil servants, for-cause protections for inferior officers, and similar protections for members of multi-member "independent" federal agencies. The issue in *Seila Law* was whether to extend these practices to a regulatory agency with a single head.

The second, closely related idea is the President's complete power to *direct* executive officials. Taken literally, this would mean that the President has complete power to direct executive officials in all of their functions, including those that Congress has assigned to those officials—and perhaps even that the President could countermand those decisions or perform them himself.

This, too, has never been the way the federal bureaucracy has been run, especially given the vast growth of the federal bureaucracy in the twentieth century. In fact, the idea was rejected early on. Attorney General William Wirt explained in the first of a series of opinions that where Congress has clearly indicated that an officer's decision is to be final and conclusive within the Executive branch, the President may not review the "correctness" of the officer's judgment, let alone execute the authority himself. The President and Accounting Offices, 1 Op. Att'y Gen. 624, 625-629 (1823). The idea has also not been realized in "independent" federal agencies, versions of which have existed since the First Bank of the United States.

A third idea, which is sometimes confusingly associated with the "unitary executive," but is logically distinct, is that the President has broad inherent powers that Congress may not interfere with. This idea of inherent executive power became especially important during the George W. Bush Administration, when Administration lawyers argued that, because the President was "Commander in Chief of the Army and Navy of the United States," he had the unilateral power to use military force overseas; he could engage in foreign surveillance practices without congressional authorization; and, in general, he was subject only to very limited congressional oversight in foreign affairs. If Congress wanted to check the Executive, the proper way to do it was to threaten to withhold funding, using the spending powers granted to Congress under Article I, section 8.

A broad theory of inherent executive power has also never been fully realized in practice. Congress can shape the structure of federal offices and the duties of federal officers; under *Youngstown* it has concurrent authority with the President to regulate in a wide range of situations, including in foreign policy. Outside of a small number of areas in which the Constitution gives complete authority to the President, see, e.g., *Zivitofsky* (presidential power to recognize foreign governments), Congress may limit or direct the exercise of executive authority.

Although it may not seem obvious at first, the idea that Congress may not interfere with executive branch functions is actually in some tension with the first two ideas, which concern presidential control over the federal bureaucracy. As the federal government grew larger and larger, more and more of the people who actually governed were part of the executive branch and the President grew more and more powerful. If the President had complete control over all of these people, *and* could avoid substantial congressional control and oversight, the president would become increasingly like a dictator. This would be inconsistent with the constitutional idea that branches were separated but with checks and balances, so that no branch could be a law unto itself.

Put another way, the founders thought that Congress, and not the President, would be the most dangerous branch. They probably did not expect that the President would eventually become the most powerful actor in the constitutional system and have at his command an enormous federal bureaucracy and huge military forces that could be stationed or dispatched around the globe. But the rise of the administrative state and America's status as world superpower undermined those assumptions. The greater the President's powers grew in the twentieth century, the more he needed checking by the other branches. Justice Thomas's concurrence argues that checks on the President's power undermine individual liberty. But it is at least as plausible to argue that an unconstrained president is a threat to liberty.

We see this tension in Chief Justice Roberts's account. He notes that the framers wanted to separate and check power and avoid the concentration of power in any part of the government. But he treats the presidency as an exception: "Aside from the sole exception of the Presidency, that structure scrupulously avoids concentrating power in the hands of any single individual." Later he says that " 'The Framers recognized that, in the long term, structural protections against abuse of power were critical to preserving liberty.' . . . Their solution to governmental power and its perils was simple: divide it. . . . The Executive Branch is a stark departure from all this division."

2. *Independent agencies: normal, exceptional, or unconstitutional?* Faced with a history of independent agencies and a large federal bureaucracy that the President cannot dismiss at will, Roberts attempts to describe these practices as exceptional, preserving the ones that currently exist but not extending them.

He explains that the basic principle of the unitary executive does not apply to inferior officers "with limited duties and no policymaking or administrative authority." They may have tenure or for-cause protections. This is how he explains the independent counsel statute upheld in *Morrison v. Olson.*

Second, Roberts argues that there is an exception for "a multimember body of experts, balanced along partisan lines, that performed legislative and judicial functions and was said not to exercise any executive power." (citing *Humphrey's Executor v. United States,* 295 U.S. 602 (1935).) Of course, as Roberts concedes, the idea that independent federal agencies do not actually exercise executive power makes little sense today. Taken literally, this exception would not be much of an exception at all, because most of today's independent agencies wouldn't fit within it. (Justice Thomas emphasizes this point.)

Roberts notes the problem but does not really resolve it. He says only that there is an exception for "multimember expert agencies that do not wield substantial executive power." He then argues that deviations from any of the current exceptions are presumptively unconstitutional. New innovations are suspect. (The question Roberts leaves hanging is whether *existing* independent agencies, which may wield "substantial executive power," are also unconstitutional, as Justice Thomas contends.)

Justice Kagan, by contrast, sees for-cause protections and independent federal agencies as perfectly normal, rather than exceptional. Citing *McCulloch v. Maryland,* she argues that the Constitution was designed to allow Congress to experiment with different ways of solving problems of governance, and that the President does not have immunity from these experiments. Of course, this principle, taken too far, would swallow up the presidency. So, she argues that there are limits where legislation would "impede . . . the President's performance of his own constitutional duties," so that, "to take the clearest example, Congress could not curb the President's power to remove his close military or diplomatic advisers."

Justice Thomas, who is far more of a revolutionary than the Chief Justice, wants to take the unitary executive theory to its logical conclusion. What Justice Kagan calls normal, and Chief Justice Roberts calls exceptional, is simply unconstitutional. Thomas speaks of the continued presence of independent agencies as "a serious, ongoing threat to our Government's design. Leaving these unconstitutional agencies in place does not enhance this Court's legitimacy; it subverts political accountability and threatens individual liberty. . . . We simply cannot compromise when it comes to our Government's structure." It is not a surprise, then, that Thomas believes the courts have no power to sever the for-cause provision and that the entire CFPB should be eliminated.

Because of Roberts's deliberate ambiguity, as noted above, Thomas's position on independent agencies has not yet been definitively ruled out. The question is whether there are five votes for it.

3. *What's at stake? Political accountability versus non-partisan expertise.* Why the Justices care so much about the structure of the CFPB may be mystifying at first. It is not immediately clear what values are at stake. Chief Justice Roberts sums up the

issue this way: "the expansion of [the federal] bureaucracy into new territories the Framers could scarcely have imagined only sharpens our duty to ensure that the Executive Branch is overseen by a President accountable to the people." The idea is that the people who exercise governance—who make decisions that affect our lives—should be accountable through elections. Since members of the bureaucracy are not elected, they need to be controlled by an official who is elected. So, if members of the bureaucracy perform badly or prove to be corrupt, the public can pressure the President, who can fire them or order them to shape up.

This model of political accountability faces two difficulties. First, it may not be a very realistic account of how the public actually holds bureaucrats accountable. A second term President faces very few electoral pressures. A first term President is unlikely to be thrown out of office because of a particular policy decision by the head of an agency. Most decisions by the bureaucracy pass unnoticed by the public, although they matter greatly to particular businesses. In many contexts, the accountability argument seems fairly weak.

A better argument for political accountability would be the old political saw that "personnel is politics." Elect a conservative Republican to the presidency, and you can more or less be assured that conservative Republicans will be carrying out the government's agenda. Conversely, if officials stray from the party's agenda, the President will be more likely to get rid of them.

That explanation makes more sense from the perspective of the conservative movement that pushed for the theory of the unitary executive in the first place. Presidential ability to hire and fire helps guarantee that officials subject to dismissal will be ideologically consistent with the White House. It does not, however, guarantee that they will be competent or not be corrupt.

This kind of accountability also seems orthogonal to the question of "liberty" emphasized by Justice Thomas. The President's ability to control subordinates to effectuate the President's ideological program may increase or decrease liberty, depending on the President's policy preferences and ideology (Some Presidents, for example, may want more regulation of financial institutions to protect consumers, while others may want to deregulate). Similarly, the ability of the public to hold presidents accountable for the actions of their subordinates may increase liberty, or it may have precisely the opposite effect. Presidents Trump and Obama, for example, both were responsive to the public (or at least, the part of the public that voted for them) but both had very different accounts of the kinds of liberty they wanted executive branch officials to protect and how best to protect them.

A second problem is that not all governing problems respond well to this kind of political accountability. Some kinds of government decisions are best insulated from everyday electoral politics, and certainly from the executive's desire to settle scores. Justice Kagan gives the example of the Federal Reserve: "the Federal Reserve's independence stops a President trying to win a second term from manipulating interest rates." Throughout the nineteenth century, monetary policy was a hot political question shaped by partisan politics. This encouraged short-term political thinking that sometimes led to panics and economic disasters. The creation of a central bank was designed to put the control of the money supply—and interest rates—in the hands of experts relatively isolated from day-to-day political pressure. (Although the Federal Reserve Board was created in 1913, the restrictions on presidential removal at will were added to the statute in 1935 during the New Deal.)

Once you see the problem, it becomes ubiquitous. We don't want the President to use the FBI and the Justice Department to protect the President's friends and punish the President's enemies. We want the prosecutorial power to reflect the larger policy concerns of an Administration, but not fine-grained political determinations and score settling. (This was a recurrent problem in the Trump Administration: The President cast aside post-Watergate norms that restrained the political and self-dealing uses of prosecutorial power.)[61] We want the military to serve the foreign policy aims of successive Presidents, and not become the ideological arm of the party in power. We want the Post Office just to deliver the mail, and so on.

Political accountability and non-partisan expertise must be balanced, and the right balance might be different in different contexts and subject matters. Chief Justice Roberts argues that multiple-member independent agencies give presidents of different parties a chance to shape the direction of these agencies without dominating them, so it strikes a good balance. By contrast, "[b]ecause the CFPB is headed by a single Director with a five-year term, some Presidents may not have any opportunity to shape its leadership and thereby influence its activities." Does Roberts's logic allow for fully non-partisan commissions, as employed in some states?

4. *Five heads are better than one?* Even if we grant Justice Kagan's argument that for-cause provisions and independent federal agencies are perfectly consistent with the separation of powers, it does not follow that Congress made the right choice in designing the CFPB. Why might Congress have chosen an agency with a single head rather than multiple heads? What are the problems both for political accountability and for non-partisan expertise with a single head? Suppose that a multi-member body would have been a better design choice on both counts. Justice Kagan's argument is that the choice is Congress's call, and not the Supreme Court's.

Does this follow from *McCulloch*, or does the argument prove too much? Why shouldn't the Court subject Congress's design choices to some measure of scrutiny, requiring that Congress justify its reasons, rather than simply defer (Kagan) or ask whether the design is exactly the same as previous designs (Roberts)?

5. *Two's company, but one's a crowd?* Justice Thomas would argue that a multi-member agency is no more constitutional than a single-member agency. Justice Kagan would turn this logic around and argue that a single-member agency is no more unconstitutional than a multi-member agency. If one director is unconstitutional, how many extra directors does it take to make the CFPB constitutional? Would two be enough? Would three? If so, why? Chief Justice Roberts avoids the issue by getting rid of the for-cause provision. How would you resolve the question he avoided?

6. *A third way?* Akhil Amar argues that the history of the executive branch provides a middle way between Justice Kagan's and Justice Thomas's positions:

---

61. See, e.g., Katie Benner, Charlie Savage, Sharon LaFraniere and Ben Protess, After Stone Case, Prosecutors Say They Fear Pressure From Trump, N.Y. Times, Feb. 12, 2020, https://www.nytimes.com/2020/02/12/us/politics/justice-department-roger-stone-sentencing.html ("numerous legal scholars say that Mr. Trump has shredded norms that kept presidents in check for decades, undermining public trust in federal law enforcement and creating at least the perception that criminal cases are now subject to political influence from the White House.").

> Viewed through the prism of practice, the Constitution allows independent agencies to be created when three factors converge: first, when an executive entity is best headed up by a committee rather than by a single officer; second, when it makes sense to create continuity-enhancing fixed-tenure offices embodying technical expertise or nonpartisanship in a specific policy domain; and third, when an executive agency does not routinely interfere with specific constitutional grants of personal presidential authority, such as the powers to command the military, to personally monitor all cabinet heads, to pardon criminals, to parley with foreign leaders, to make appointments, to define an overall national agenda, and, more generally, to superintend the entire executive branch.

Akhil Reed Amar, America's Unwritten Constitution: The Precedents and Principles We Live By 385 (2012).

Amar argues that the constitutional text, which says nothing about removal (outside of impeachment), does not require that the commissioners who lead multimember independent agencies be treated exactly like the heads of departments. Requiring that independent agency commissioners be removable only for cause also does not "contravene the Decision of 1789, which only addressed departments akin to the State Department, the War Department, and the Treasury Department—departments with single heads."

Practice, Amar argues, offers the best justification for treating agencies run by multi-member commissions differently from cabinet heads and single member heads of agencies. History shows that with where an independent federal agency is run by a committee, the limitation on presidential power is relatively modest:

> Although the powers vested in independent agencies and the limited removability of these agency officials do constrain presidents, virtually all modern presidents have accepted these constraints. By contrast, many presidents have loudly objected to improvisations such as the legislative veto or the 1978-style independent counsel. Those improvisations weakened presidents vis-à-vis Congress and courts, whereas limitations on the removal of independent-agency officials have merely reshuffled power among presidents over time. Although President A may not remove at will all the officials he inherits on his first day in office, his successor, President B, will likewise be unable to remove at will all the officials that A manages to appoint during his tenure. Each president thus gets his fair share of presidential power, albeit with a time lag.
>
> Put a different way, independent agencies do not involve any legislative vetoes in removals; nor do they give judges nonjudicial power to appoint executive officials. . . . [L]aws establishing independent agencies do not vest members of other branches with any executive power whatsoever. Rather, these laws, in keeping with the necessary-and proper clause, merely allocate authority within the executive branch between the president and his subordinates. . . .
>
> [M]odern presidents confront a qualitatively different supervisory situation from the one faced by George Washington, who stood atop a federal bureaucracy of infinitesimal size, by modern standards. In the end, the simple fact that modern presidents themselves have embraced

> independent agencies furnishes a strong reason for the rest of us to make room for these agencies as we ponder the laconic language of Article II.

Amar, supra, at 385-386.

7. *The unitary executive in the states.* It is worth noting that most state constitutions have nothing like a unitary executive. For example, fewer than 10 percent of the 50 states allow their governors to appoint the state attorney general. Most elect the attorney general (along with several other state officials) —which solves the political accountability problem in a different way. (In fact, the attorney general and the governor can, in theory, be from different political parties.) On the other hand, the Tennessee Supreme Court picks the state's Attorney General for an eight-year term, which tends to insulate that official from direct political control. Many states also have bipartisan or nonpartisan commissions for different purposes, including legislative redistricting. Should the federal system adopt innovations in design from the states? Which ones?

8. *The reach of* Seila Law*: Collins v. Yellen.* In Collins v. Yellen, 141 S. Ct. 1761 (2021), the Supreme Court applied *Seila Law* to the Federal Housing Finance Agency (FHFA). FHFA was created in 2008 as an independent fedreal agency tasked with regulating Fannie Mae and Freddie Mac—two of the Nation's leading sources of mortgage financing—and, if necessary, stepping in as their conservator or receiver. At the head of the Agency, Congress installed a single Director, removable by the President only for cause.

The Court, in an opinion by Justice Alito, argued that this arrangement was unconstitutional under *Seila Law.* It did not matter that FHFA was a far less powerful agency than the Consumer Financial Protection Bureau involved in *Seila Law*: "the nature and breadth of an agency's authority is not dispositive in determining whether Congress may limit the President's power to remove its head. . . . The removal power helps the President maintain a degree of control over the subordinates he needs to carry out his duties as the head of the Executive Branch, and it works to ensure that these subordinates serve the people effectively and in accordance with the policies that the people presumably elected the President to promote. . . . [B]ecause the President, unlike agency officials, is elected, this control is essential to subject Executive Branch actions to a degree of electoral accountability."

It also did not matter that FHFA regulated Government-sponsored agencies rather than private actors: "[T]he President's removal power serves important purposes regardless of whether the agency in question affects ordinary Americans by directly regulating them or by taking actions that have a profound but indirect effect on their lives."

Finally, it did not matter that the for-cause requirement was fairly weak, so that FHFA's director could be dismissed whenever a Director "disobey[ed] a lawful [Presidential] order," including one about the Agency's policy discretion. "[T]he Constitution prohibits even 'modest restrictions' on the President's power to remove the head of an agency with a single top officer. The President must be able to remove not just officers who disobey his commands but also those he finds 'negligent and inefficient,' those who exercise their discretion in a way that is not 'intelligen[t] or wis[e],' those who have 'different views of policy,' those who come 'from a competing political party who is dead set against [the President's] agenda,' and those in whom he has simply lost confidence." Since even a weak "for cause" provision "does not mean the same thing as 'at will,' . . . the removal restriction in the Recovery Act violates the separation of powers."

Justice Sotomayor, joined, by Justice Breyer, concurring in part and dissenting in part, noted that *Seila Law* had limited its holding to single-director agencies "wield[ing] significant executive power." In doing so, "*Seila Law* expressly distinguished the Federal Housing Finance Agency (FHFA), another independent Agency headed by a single Director, on the ground that the FHFA does not possess 'regulatory or enforcement authority remotely comparable to that exercised by the CFPB.' . . . Moreover, the Court found it significant that, unlike the CFPB, the FHFA 'regulates primarily Government- sponsored enterprises, not purely private actors.'" In addition, "[t]he FHFA also draws on a long tradition of independence enjoyed by financial regulators, including the Comptroller of the Treasury, the Second Bank of the United States, the Federal Reserve Board, the Securities and Exchange Commission, the Commodity Futures Trading Commission, and the Federal Deposit Insurance Corporation. The public has long accepted (indeed, expected) that financial regulators will best perform their duties if separated from the political exigencies and pressures of the present moment." Because "the FHFA does not wield significant executive power, the executive power it does wield is exercised over Government affiliates, and its independence is supported by historical tradition[,] . . . [a]ll considerations weigh in favor of recognizing Congress' power to make the FHFA Director removable only for cause."

9. *The reach of Collins v. Yellen.* Following the decision in Collins v. Yellen, President Biden fired Social Security Commissioner Andrew Saul, a Trump appointee, after Saul refused to submit his resignation. The White House argued that Saul, among other things, had "undermined and politicized Social Security disability benefits, . . . reduced due process protections for benefits appeals hearings, and taken other actions that run contrary to the mission of the agency and the President's policy agenda." In 1994, Congress changed the Social Security Administration (SSA) from a component of the Department of Health and Human Services into an independent federal agency. It provided that the agency would be led by a single Commissioner, who may be removed only for neglect of duty or malfeasance in office. See 42 U.S.C. §902(a)(3). The Office of Legal Counsel produced a memo applying *Collins* and *Seila Law*: "We believe that the best reading of those decisions compels the conclusion that the statutory restriction on removing the Commissioner is unconstitutional. Therefore, the President may remove the Commissioner at will." See Constitutionality of the Commissioner of Social Security's Tenure Protection, 45 Op. O.L.C. __ (July 8, 2021), https://www.justice.gov/olc/file/1410736/download.

NATIONAL LABOR RELATIONS BOARD v. NOEL CANNING, 573 U.S. 513 (2014): The National Labor Relations Board consists of five members, appointed by the President. The Board requires a quorum of three members in order to make its decisions. See 29 U.S.C. §153(b).

By 2008, the terms of three of the five members had expired and President George W. Bush and the Senate were unable to agree on new appointments. As a result, the Board had only two active members. The two-member board continued to issue opinions and orders, which the Supreme Court declared illegal in New Process Steel, L.P. v. NLRB, 560 U.S. 674, 687-688 (2010) (holding that in the absence of a lawfully appointed quorum, the Board cannot exercise its powers). President Barack Obama nominated three new members to the Board to fill the expired terms; but Senate Republicans filibustered the appointments.

Ordinarily the President must obtain "the Advice and Consent of the Senate" before appointing an "Office[r] of the United States." U.S. Const., Art. II, §2, cl. 2. However, there is an exception for "recess appointments." The Constitution gives the President the power "to fill up all Vacancies that may happen during the Recess of the Senate, by granting Commissions which shall expire at the End of their next Session." Art. II, §2, cl. 3.

To enable the Board to continue operations, President Obama made two recess appointments to the NLRB in March 2010. These appointments expired at the end of 2011, at which point the NLRB once again lacked a quorum to do business.

To prevent Obama from making any new recess appointments to the NLRB, the House of Representatives, which was now controlled by Republicans as a result of the 2010 elections, refused to adjourn and refused to allow the Senate to adjourn. According to Art. I, §5, cl. 4, "Neither House, during the Session of Congress, shall, without the Consent of the other, adjourn for more than three days." As a result, from December 17, 2011 to January 20, 2012, the Senate held a series of *pro forma* meetings on Tuesdays and Fridays at which no business was conducted. (Sundays do not count as legislative days.) During this period, the second session of the 112th Congress officially began on January 3, 2012.

In response, President Obama argued that despite the *pro forma* sessions, the Senate was actually in recess. He appointed three people he had previously nominated to the NLRB through recess appointments on January 4, 2012, the day after the second session of the Senate officially began, although the Senate did not resume its ordinary business until January 20th, 2012.

On February 8, 2012, the Board found that Noel Canning, a Pepsi-Cola distributor, had engaged in an unfair labor practice in violation of the National Labor Relations Act because it had unlawfully refused to execute a collective bargaining agreement with a labor union. On appeal, Noel Canning argued that the Board's orders were void because the new board members were not legally appointed and therefore the Board lacked a quorum to do business.

1a. *Inter-session and intra-session recesses.* Noel Canning argued that "the Recess of the Senate" applied only to "inter-session" recesses that occur between the formal sessions of the House and Senate. These end when the House or Senate passes a resolution adjourning "*sine die*," *i.e.*, without specifying a date to return (in which case Congress reconvenes when the next formal session is scheduled to begin). Both the Senate and House also take other breaks in the middle of formal sessions. The Senate and House take an "intra-session" recess by passing a resolution stating that it will adjourn to a fixed date. Noel Canning argued that "the Recess of the Senate" did not include these "intra-session" breaks. Because President Obama made his appointments on January 4th, after the second session began, his appointments did not fall within the scope of the Recess Appointments Clause.

Justice Breyer, writing for five Justices, disagreed. "[T]he word 'the' frequently (but not always) indicates 'a particular thing.' But the word can also refer 'to a term used generically or universally.' The Constitution, for example, directs the Senate to choose a President *pro tempore* 'in *the* Absence of the Vice-President.' Art. I, §3, cl.

5 (emphasis added). And the Federalist Papers refer to the chief magistrate of an ancient Achaean league who 'administered the government in *the* recess of the Senate.' The Federalist No. 18, at 113 (J. Madison) (emphasis added). . . . The constitutional text is thus ambiguous. And we believe the Clause's purpose demands the broader interpretation. The Clause gives the President authority to make appointments during 'the recess of the Senate' so that the President can ensure the continued functioning of the Federal Government when the Senate is away. The Senate is equally away during both an inter-session and an intra-session recess."

Justice Breyer then turned to historical practice, which, he claimed, "offers strong support for the broad interpretation." Congress generally took no intra-session breaks before the Civil War. But "[i]n 1867 and 1868, Congress for the first time took substantial, nonholiday intra-session breaks, and President Andrew Johnson made dozens of recess appointments. . . . In all, between the founding and the Great Depression, Congress took substantial intra-session breaks (other than holiday breaks) in four years: 1867, 1868, 1921, and 1929. And in each of those years the President made intra-session recess appointments."

Moreover, "[s]ince 1929, and particularly since the end of World War II, Congress has shortened its inter-session breaks as it has taken longer and more frequent intra-session breaks; Presidents have correspondingly made more intra-session recess appointments. Indeed, if we include military appointments, Presidents have made thousands of intra-session recess appointments."

The Senate, Justice Breyer, explained, has acquiesced in this practice: "Since Presidents began making intra-session recess appointments, individual Senators have taken differing views about the proper definition of 'the recess.' But neither the Senate considered as a body nor its committees, despite opportunities to express opposition to the practice of intra-session recess appointments, has done so."

1b. *How long an intra-session recess is sufficient?* Justice Breyer next turned to the question of "how long a recess must be in order to fall within the Clause. Is a break of a week, or a day, or an hour too short to count as a 'recess'? The Clause itself does not say." The Court "agree[d] with the Solicitor General that a 3-day recess would be too short. . . . The Adjournments Clause reflects the fact that a 3-day break is not a significant interruption of legislative business. . . . A Senate recess that is so short that it does not require the consent of the House is not long enough to trigger the President's recess-appointment power." At the same time, "we have not found a single example of a recess appointment made during an intra-session recess that was shorter than 10 days. . . . There are a few historical examples of recess appointments made during inter-session recesses shorter than 10 days [but] we regard these few scattered examples as anomalies." The Court therefore concluded that, "in light of historical practice, . . . a recess of more than 3 days but less than 10 days is presumptively too short to fall within the Clause," while leaving open "the possibility that some very unusual circumstance—a national catastrophe, for instance, that renders the Senate unavailable but calls for an urgent response—could demand the exercise of the recess-appointment power during a shorter break."

2. *Which vacancies can the President fill with a recess appointment?* Noel Canning's second argument was that the phrase "vacancies that may happen during the recess of the Senate," Art. II, §2, cl. 3, applies only to vacancies that first *occurred* when the Senate was in recess. Because the NLRB vacancies began while the Senate was in session, President Obama could not later use a recess appointment to fill them when

the Senate was in recess. Justice Breyer rejected this argument as well; he explained that the phrase also applies "to vacancies that initially occur before a recess and continue to exist during the recess." Justice Breyer "concede[d] that the most natural meaning of 'happens'" to a modern ear "is that the vacancy 'happens' when it initially occurs." But, he argued, the phrase is ambiguous. Thomas Jefferson once wrote that the Clause is "certainly susceptible of [two] constructions." It "may mean 'vacancies that may happen to be' or 'may happen to fall'" during a recess.

Breyer noted particularly Attorney General William Wirt's advice to President Monroe in 1823. Wirt explained that the broader interpretation is "most accordant with" the Constitution's "reason and spirit" and that a narrower interpretation would frustrate the purpose of the Clause: "Put the case of a vacancy occurring in an office, held in a distant part of the country, on the last day of the Senate's session. Before the vacancy is made known to the President, the Senate rises. The office may be an important one; the vacancy may paralyze a whole line of action in some essential branch of our internal police; the public interests may imperiously demand that it shall be immediately filled. But the vacancy happened to occur during the session of the Senate; and if the President's power is to be limited to such vacancies only as happen to occur during the recess of the Senate, the vacancy in the case put must continue, however ruinous the consequences may be to the public." 1 Op. Atty. Gen. 631, 632 (1823).

Once again Breyer looked to historical practice to confirm his interpretation: "The tradition of applying the Clause to pre-recess vacancies dates at least to President James Madison. . . . Nearly every subsequent Attorney General to consider the question throughout the Nation's history has thought the same. Indeed, as early as 1862, Attorney General Bates advised President Lincoln that his power to fill pre-recess vacancies was 'settled . . . as far . . . as a constitutional question can be settled,' and a century later Acting Attorney General Walsh gave President Eisenhower the same advice 'without any doubt.' . . . [W]e have enough information to believe that the Presidents since Madison have made many recess appointments filling vacancies that initially occurred prior to a recess, [and] [n]o one disputes that every President since James Buchanan has made recess appointments to pre-existing vacancies. [Given the data available to us,] we think it is a fair inference that a large proportion of the recess appointments in the history of the Nation have filled pre-existing vacancies."

To be sure, Breyer explained, "there was some sporadic disagreement [in the Senate] with the broad interpretation. [In] 1863 the Senate Judiciary Committee disagreed with the broad interpretation." The Senate also passed the Pay Act, which provided that "no money shall be paid . . . as a salary, to any person appointed during the recess of the Senate, to fill a vacancy . . . which . . . existed while the Senate was in session." But by 1905 "the Senate [had] subsequently abandoned its hostility," and "in 1940 Congress amended the Pay Act to authorize salary payments (with some exceptions) [in cases] where . . . a vacancy . . . did not initially occur during a recess but happened to exist during that recess. By paying salaries to this kind of recess appointee, the 1940 Senate (and later Senates) in effect supported the President's interpretation of the Clause." Given a consistent interpretation by the executive branch since Madison's presidency, and the fact that "[t]he Senate as a body has not countered this practice for nearly three-quarters of a century, perhaps longer, . . . we are reluctant to upset this traditional practice where doing so would seriously shrink the authority that Presidents have believed existed and have exercised for so long."

3. *Can the President disregard the* pro forma *sessions as a sham?* Noel Canning's third argument was that the Senate was not in recess because of the *pro forma* sessions, while the Solicitor General argued that they were a sham and that the President could disregard them because the Senate conducted no business until January 20th.

This time the Court agreed with Noel Canning: "We hold that, for purposes of the Recess Appointments Clause, the Senate is in session when it says it is, provided that, under its own rules, it retains the capacity to transact Senate business." Justice Breyer noted that "the Constitution explicitly empowers the Senate to "determine the Rules of its Proceedings." Art. I, §5, cl. 2, and that the Court's precedents have given the Senate broad authority to decide how and when to conduct its business, citing Marshall Field & Co. v. Clark, 143 U.S. 649 (1892); United States v. Ballin, 144 U.S. 1 (1892). The Court nevertheless cautioned that "deference to the Senate cannot be absolute. When the Senate is without the *capacity* to act, under its own rules, it is not in session even if it so declares." But in this case, "the Senate *has* enacted legislation during *pro forma* sessions even when it has said that no business will be transacted. Indeed, the Senate passed a bill by unanimous consent [extending cuts in the payroll tax] during the second *pro forma* session after its December 17 adjournment. And that bill quickly became law. Pub. L. 112-78, 125 Stat. 1280."

Justice Scalia, joined by Chief Justice Roberts and by Justices Thomas and Alito, concurred in the judgment. Justice Scalia agreed with Noel Canning that the President can only make recess appointments during an inter-session recess, and then only when the vacancy occurred while the Senate was between sessions. He argued that the "plain meaning" of the text was unambiguous. He also read historical practice quite differently than Justice Breyer, arguing that there was no consensus on the part of executive-branch officials or acquiescence by the Senate. Finally, he argued that even if these had existed, the Court should not defer to intra-branch conventions in the face of the text's plain meaning.

> The Constitution's core, government-structuring provisions are no less critical to preserving liberty than are the later adopted provisions of the Bill of Rights. . . . Those structural provisions reflect the founding generation's deep conviction that "checks and balances were the foundation of a structure of government that would protect liberty." [Our] decisions all rest on the bedrock principle that "the constitutional structure of our Government" is designed first and foremost not to look after the interests of the respective branches, but to "protec[t] individual liberty."
>
> [T]his Court does not defer to the other branches' resolution of . . . controversies [about the Constitution's government-structuring provisions]; . . . our role is in no way "lessened" because it might be said that "the two political branches are adjusting their own powers between themselves." Since the separation of powers exists for the protection of individual liberty, its vitality "does not depend" on "whether 'the encroached-upon branch approves the encroachment.'" Rather, policing the "enduring structure" of constitutional government when the political branches fail to do so is "one of the most vital functions of this Court." . . . [A] self-aggrandizing practice adopted by one branch well

after the founding, often challenged, and never before blessed by this Court—in other words, the sort of practice on which the majority relies in this case—does not relieve us of our duty to interpret the Constitution in light of its text, structure, and original understanding.

DISCUSSION

1. *The political context. Noel Canning* arose in the context of recent political struggles between the President and Congress that, in turn, reflected increasing political polarization and dysfunction in Washington. As the country's politics polarized at the close of the twentieth century, an unwritten norm emerged that all significant action in the Senate required 60 votes. This allowed senators of the party opposite the President to block many executive appointments that previously would not have been filibustered.

Perhaps unsurprisingly, increasing polarization led to increasing use of recess appointments. Modern practice allowed Presidents to make intra-session appointments when the Senate was adjourned for a significant period of time. When the Democrats regained control of the Senate in 2007, they sought to prevent President George W. Bush from using recess appointments to appoint figures they considered objectionable by conducting *pro forma* sessions when most members of Congress were not in town. Although President Bush's legal advisors did not regard the strategy as constitutionally effective, he did not challenge it during the remainder of his presidency.

Once Barack Obama became President, Republicans engaged in a selective strategy of frustrating his appointments to key agencies, including the NLRB and the new Consumer Financial Protection Bureau created as part of the Dodd-Frank financial services reforms. Republicans used holds and filibusters to prevent appointments while the Senate was in session. This left the possibility of recess appointments, and Obama made one such appointment to the NLRB during a recess in July 2009 after the Republicans had filibustered the nomination. Although the Republicans did not control the Senate, after the 2010 elections, they did control the House. House Republicans refused to consent to an adjournment in order to keep the Senate in session and prevent President Obama from making recess appointments.

Unlike President Bush, President Obama decided to test the legality of the Senate's new practices. If he did not act, the NLRB would soon lack enough members to constitute a quorum, which would effectively disable it. Republicans, who often opposed the Board's enforcement of labor regulations, did not regard this as a major disadvantage. Republicans also served notice that they would not confirm anyone to head the Consumer Financial Protection Bureau, regardless of qualifications, unless the President agreed to turn the Bureau into a multimember commission and make other changes to Dodd-Frank. Dodd-Frank only allows the CFPB to exercise some of its powers once an agency head is successfully appointed. By preventing an appointment, Republicans would, in effect, cripple the agency and limit its ability to engage in enforcement and rulemaking. These political maneuvers set the stage for the legal battle in *Noel Canning*.

In July 2013, Senate Democrats threatened to alter the Senate's filibuster rules for executive nominations by simple majority vote—the "nuclear option." (Senate Republicans had threatened a similar strategy in 2005 when the Democrats had filibustered several George W. Bush circuit court appointments.) In response, Senate Republicans agreed to allow confirmation of several nominees, including to the NLRB and the Consumer Financial Protection Bureau. Then on November 21, 2013, the Senate voted 52-48 to eliminate the use of the filibuster against all executive-branch nominees and judicial nominees other than to the Supreme Court. On the constitutional issues, see Akhil Reed Amar, America's Unwritten Constitution: The Precedents and Principles We Live By 356-369 (2012). As noted below, the change in Senate rules greatly lessens the need for Presidents to turn to recess appointments, at least when the President's party controls the Senate.

2. *Separation of powers or separation of parties?* Although *Noel Canning* was litigated as a case about separation of powers between the executive and legislative branches, the more important constitutional check in today's world is that of party. After all, if both the House and Senate had been controlled by Democrats, there would have been no constitutional conflict with President Obama.

One effect of *Noel Canning* is that the Court has legitimated the current strategy of using *pro forma* Senate sessions to prevent recess appointments. Hence if the party opposing the President controls the Senate, it can effectively prevent all recess appointments by refusing to adjourn.

It might also seem that if the opposition party controls the House, the House can prevent recess appointments—as it did in this case—by refusing to adjourn, thus forcing the Senate to engage in *pro forma* sessions. That may not be the end of the story, however. In 2012, Senate Majority Leader Harry Reid, a Democrat, went along with House Speaker John Boehner's gambit to keep both chambers open over the holidays. But suppose that the Senate Majority Leader informs the President by letter, signed by all of the members of the majority party, that the *pro forma* sessions demanded by the House are actually a sham and that no business will be conducted? Justice Breyer's opinion argues that the Court should defer to the Senate's own judgment about its operations. What result? (Is it clear that a third party like Noel Canning would have standing to assert a constitutional claim if the Senate maintains that it is in recess? Would the House have standing? See Raines v. Byrd, 521 U.S. 811 (1997).)[62]

There is an additional wild card: Art. II, §3 states that "[I]n Case of Disagreement between [the Houses], with Respect to the Time of Adjournment, [the President] may adjourn them to such Time as he shall think proper." Could the President, holding such a letter from the Majority Leader, announce that the two Houses are in disagreement, adjourn Congress temporarily, and make a series of recess appointments? Would this be consistent with the purposes of the Advice and Consent requirements of Art. II, §2, cl. 2? Would the question of

---

62. For a more detailed discussion, see Akhil Reed Amar and Timothy Noah, How to Resolve the Recess Appointment Crisis: An Elegant Legal Solution, The New Republic, January 6, 2012, at http://www.newrepublic.com/article/politics/99285/how-resolve-the-recess-appointment-crisis-elegant-legal-solution.

disagreement between the Houses, or of the President's powers to adjourn Congress, be justiciable?

Although quite interesting, many of these questions may never arise in practice for a simple reason. Once the Senate changed its filibuster rules for appointments, the House's leverage was greatly reduced. A disciplined Senate of the same party as the President will normally make it unnecessary for the President to resort to recess appointments in most cases. The ordinary process of advice and consent will be available to make all the appointments the President needs when the Senate is in session. (Obviously the President will have trouble appointing people that even senators in the President's *own* party oppose.)

If the President's party controls the Senate, and supports the President's nominees, then the only way to prevent presidential appointments is if the opposition party in the Senate is willing to bring the business of the Senate to a halt through means other than filibusters. And that may lead the Senate majority to change the rules once again.

3. *The role of subsequent practice.* Note that Justice Breyer's opinion turns to the history of subsequent practice because he asserts that the text is ambiguous. Indeed, one of the great themes of his opinion is that "'[l]ong settled and established practice is a consideration of great weight in a proper interpretation of constitutional provisions' regulating the relationship between Congress and the President. . . . [T]his Court has treated practice as an important interpretive factor even when the nature or longevity of that practice is subject to dispute, and even when that practice began after the founding era."

Justice Scalia strongly disagrees that the text is at all ambiguous. If the majority and dissent disagree, does that mean that the text really is ambiguous? If the text *is* unambiguous, do you believe that subsequent practice can legitimately change the text's practical meaning? (Note that one's conclusions about ambiguity are not made in the abstract. They may be affected by one's views about the purpose of the provision, its relationship to other parts of the Constitution, the legitimacy of subsequent practice, and so on. See the discussion of Attorney General Wirt's argument in note 6, infra.)

4. *Evolving constitutional norms or adverse possession?* Justice Breyer views the relevant history as evolving toward a settled set of conventions concerning when Presidents may use the recess appointments power. Justice Scalia, by contrast, argues that there are no settled conventions; there is only an executive power grab that members of the Senate have protested from time to time, both in public statements and in legislation like the 1863 Pay Act. He points out that the Senate, because it is a multi-member body, has a much harder time protesting presidential usurpation, and making its objections stick. Therefore courts should be especially alert to the possibility of presidential overreaching.

Because inter-branch conventions often arise out of the push and pull of everyday politics, how do we tell which account of the history is correct? Is this just a form of "winners's history" or is there a more or less apolitical or objective way to decide the question?

Justice Scalia also argues that even if a settled convention had developed, it cannot change the meaning of the Constitution. An earlier Congress cannot constitutionally give away the power of future Congresses. Note that the Office of Legal Counsel generally takes the same view of executive power—an earlier President cannot bind all future Presidents by surrendering executive power. Recall Acting Solicitor General Walter Dellinger's memo on presidential authority to decline to execute unconstitutional statutes in Chapter 1, in which he points out that "there is no constitutional analogue to the principles of waiver and estoppel." Yet even if both branches deny that previous waivers or adjustments bind their successors, shifts in inter-branch relations nevertheless do develop over time. What the best explanation of this? Should we say that inter-branch conventions continue to exist for so long as both sides find them convenient? If so, why should judges enforce those conventions?

Finally, Justice Scalia points out that the Court did not defer to settled conventions in INS v. Chadha, even though Congress had placed legislative vetoes in provisions for half a century. Yet there are important differences between the practices of recess appointments and of the legislative veto. The practice of recess appointments begins in James Madison's presidency, not the middle of the twentieth century. In addition, while every President from Woodrow Wilson forward disputed the constitutionality of legislative veto until the Supreme Court held it unconstitutional, the Senate eventually acquiesced to recess appointments.

5. *The interpretive status of inter-branch conventions.* Even if the history unambiguously demonstrates settled practice, why *should* subsequent practice between Congress and the President settle constitutional meaning, either between the branches themselves, or in judicial constructions of the Constitution? To what extent are the reasons similar to or different from the reason why judges attempt to respect prior judicial precedents? Following precedent is sometimes justified on grounds of (1) rule of law values—treating like cases alike and avoiding the appearance of political decisionmaking; (2) the fact that the public and other branches of government rely on precedents as stable law; and (3) judicial humility in the face of a reasonable judgment by past actors. Which of these reasons apply to inter-branch conventions?

Note that there is a difference between Congress and the President accepting a course of conduct as a practical matter and judges writing that course of conduct into constitutional doctrine. Conventions may change over time, but judicial doctrine fixes them into place at a particular moment in time. To avoid that result, courts could treat inter-branch conventions as nonjusticiable, but that is hard to do when private parties' interests—like those of Noel Canning and the labor union—are at stake.

6. *William Wirt's argument—purposivism versus plain meaning.* Note carefully Attorney General Wirt's argument—which Justice Breyer quotes—for why Presidents must be able to make recess appointments even if the vacancy originally occurs while the Senate is in session. Wirt's view is that you cannot understand whether a constitutional provision is ambiguous until you understand its purposes and how it works in conjunction with other features of the constitutional system. Breyer, adopting Wirt's purposive approach to interpretation, rejects a "plain meaning" reading of the text in favor of a pragmatic reading.

Note that Wirt's concern is not simply one of presidential convenience. If an executive-branch position is important, and a replacement is urgent, the President could, in theory, call the Senate back into session to consider a new appointment. See Art. II, §3. But the senators may not *want* to have to travel back to Washington for a special session to consider a single appointment. In some cases, allowing the President to make recess appointments may serve the Senate's interests as well as the President's.

7. *Using framework statutes to prevent gaming the system.* Justice Breyer points out that under Wirt's reading, Presidents might be able to game the system by waiting until the Senate leaves town to make recess appointments. But these appointments will be temporary, and if the appointee wants eventual confirmation, Presidents have incentives not to anger the senators by tricking them. That is why many if not most recess appointments have been relatively noncontroversial. (Breyer gives several examples in his opinion: "President Franklin Roosevelt . . . commissioned Dwight Eisenhower as a permanent Major General during an intra-session recess; President Truman made Dean Acheson Under Secretary of State; and President George H.W. Bush reappointed Alan Greenspan as Chairman of the Federal Reserve Board.")

Moreover, Congress can pass legislation to encourage good-faith presidential behavior. The 1940 Pay Act—still on the books—is a useful example of how this might be done. If a vacancy arises less than 30 days before the end of a session, the President may make a recess appointment and the appointee will be compensated as usual. But if the appointment is made more than 30 days before the end of the session, the appointee will receive no pay until the Senate confirms, at which point pay will be awarded retroactively.

Note the logic behind such a framework statute: The Senate designs the rules so that the President's use of recess appointments furthers the Senate's own interests. In the last 30 days of a session, the Senate may not want its agenda sidetracked by presidential appointments. (Similarly, senators may not want to be called back for a special session when they are back home meeting their constituents and raising money.) The Pay Act allows the President to make short-term appointments in these cases. But if a vacancy occurs earlier, the rules are different. Recess appointees should not expect to be paid if the President appoints someone particularly unpalatable or controversial.

8. *Separation of powers and liberty.* While Justice Breyer emphasizes that courts should construe the Constitution so that government can function, Justice Scalia argues that the point of separation of powers is to hinder government efficiency in certain ways in the interests of liberty. What kind of liberty is Scalia concerned with? Sometimes it is obvious how separation of powers promotes liberty: Allowing the same actor to be both prosecutor, judge, and jury would be quite dangerous. But what is the liberty interest that is protected by a narrow reading of the Recess Appointments Clause?

In *Noel Canning* itself, the effect of banning recess appointments would be to prevent the National Labor Relations Board from enforcing the country's labor laws. This certainly furthers the liberty of Noel Canning, which refused to execute a collective bargaining agreement and was charged with an unfair labor practice by the Board. But it also might undermine the practical liberty of the union and its members, who rely on collective bargaining rights to protect themselves. Similarly, until the Senate rules were changed in November 2013, Republicans refused to allow any appointments to the Consumer Financial Protection Bureau, in part because they thought that the Bureau was a bad idea. Moreover, they believed that without a change in its organization, the Bureau would likely adopt consumer protection regulations that they thought were unfair to banks and other financial institutions. Such regulations might impinge on the liberty of some actors in society. But they might also provide valuable rights to others, for example, citizens who are harmed by predatory lending practices.

Under this account, limits on presidential appointments protect the sort of liberty that is realized through government *inaction* or *nonenforcement* of the laws. They do not protect the kinds of liberty—or security—that depend on government action or enforcement of the laws. (Compare the arguments connecting federalism to liberty.)

What about the appointment of judges? Is liberty enhanced when there are not enough judges to vindicate the constitutional rights of individuals? Note, however, that there is a different concern about allowing recess appointments for federal judges. If federal judges—who would ordinarily enjoy life tenure—are appointed for a one-year term, they are effectively on "probation" and they may be tempted to decide cases to increase their chances of Senate confirmation. While it might be a good idea for recess appointees in the *executive branch* to work harmoniously with senators so as to ensure later confirmation, we should expect more independence from federal *judges*.

9. *Separation of powers and government integrity*. The example of judges suggests a different rationale for how checks and balances might protect liberty. The point is not ensuring liberty through government *inaction* but rather liberty through government *integrity*. Without checks on the President's appointment powers, Presidents may appoint cronies and corrupt people to office. These people may turn out to be incompetent or dishonest. Sometimes they will do nothing when they should act, but other times they will act badly or stupidly, or based on improper motives. The argument for checks and balances to preserve government integrity protects all kinds of liberties, not simply those that might follow from government inaction.

Why might congressional Republicans have believed that President Obama should not be trusted to have a free hand in his appointments to the NLRB? To the IRS? To the CIA? Should senators be allowed to refuse to confirm *anyone* to a certain office, regardless of their honesty and qualifications?

C. *The Veto Power*

As we have seen, the President has rather broad powers to execute the laws—encompassing the power to decline criminal prosecution, the power to pardon, the power to make all appointments of principal officers (and, indeed, of inferior officers unless Congress by law properly specifies otherwise), the power to remove cabinet officers and many other high-level executive officers at will, and the power to set policies for his administration. We have also seen important limits on these powers. But the President is not simply chief executive; he is also a vital part of the legislative process, via the veto power. The combination of law-execution power and veto power is a powerful one, as the next case illustrates.

Immigration and Naturalization Service v. Chadha

462 U.S. 919 (1983)

Chief Justice BURGER delivered the opinion of the Court.

I

[The INS began deportation proceedings against Jagdish Chadha, a Kenya citizen holding a British passport whose nonimmigrant student visa had expired. In response, Chadha sought to remain in the United States under a provision allowing the Attorney General, in his discretion and acting through the Immigration and Naturalization Service, to suspend deportation in cases where an alien had been continuously resident in America for at least seven years and where "deportation would, in the opinion of the Attorney General, result in extreme hardship." §244(a)(1) of the Act, 8 U.S.C. §1254(a)(1). After finding that such hardship existed in Chadha's case, the INS suspended his deportation, and a report of the suspension was transmitted to Congress, per §244(c)(1) of the Act. Under §244(c)(2) of the Act, 8 U.S.C. §1254(c)(2), Congress then had the power to veto the Attorney General's determination that Chadha should not be deported:

> "if . . . , prior to the close of the session of the Congress next following the session at which a case is reported, either the Senate or the House of Representatives passes a resolution stating in substance that it does not favor the suspension of such deportation, the Attorney General shall thereupon deport such alien or authorize the alien's voluntary departure at his own expense under the order of deportation in the manner provided by law. If, within the time above specified, neither the Senate nor the House of Representatives shall pass such a resolution, the Attorney General shall cancel deportation proceedings."]

. . . Representative Eilberg, Chairman of the Judiciary Subcommittee on Immigration, Citizenship, and International Law, introduced a resolution opposing "the granting of permanent residence in the United States to [six] aliens," including Chadha. . . . The resolution had not been printed and was not made available to other Members of the House prior to or at the time it was voted on. So far as the record before us shows, the House consideration of the resolution was based on Representative Eilberg's statement from the floor that

> "[it] was the feeling of the committee, after reviewing 340 cases, that the aliens contained in the resolution [Chadha and five others] did not meet these statutory requirements, particularly as it relates to hardship; and it is the opinion of the committee that their deportation should not be suspended."

The resolution was passed without debate or recorded vote. Since the House action was pursuant to §244(c)(2), the resolution was not treated as an Art. I legislative act; it was not submitted to the Senate or presented to the President for his action.

After the House veto of the Attorney General's decision to allow Chadha to remain in the United States, the Immigration Judge reopened the deportation proceedings to implement the House order deporting Chadha. Chadha moved to terminate the proceedings on the ground that §244(c)(2) is unconstitutional. The Immigration Judge held that he had no authority to rule on the constitutional validity of §244(c)(2). On November 8, 1976, Chadha was ordered deported pursuant to the House action.

Chadha appealed the deportation order to the Board of Immigration Appeals, again contending that §244(c)(2) is unconstitutional. The Board held that it had "no power to declare unconstitutional an act of Congress" and Chadha's appeal was dismissed.

. . . Chadha filed a petition for review of the deportation order in the United States Court of Appeals for the Ninth Circuit. The Immigration and Naturalization Service agreed with Chadha's position before the Court of Appeals and joined him in arguing that §244(c)(2) is unconstitutional. In light of the importance of the question, the Court of Appeals invited both the Senate and the House of Representatives to file briefs amici curiae.

After full briefing and oral argument, the Court of Appeals held that the House was without constitutional authority to order Chadha's deportation; accordingly it directed the Attorney General "to cease and desist from taking any steps to deport this alien based upon the resolution enacted by the House of Representatives." The essence of its holding was that §244(c)(2) violates the constitutional doctrine of separation of powers.

II

Before we address the important question of the constitutionality of the one-House veto provision of §244(c)(2), we first consider several challenges to the authority of this Court to resolve the issue raised. . . .

Severability

Congress . . . contends that the provision for the one-House veto in §244(c)(2) cannot be severed from §244. Congress argues that if the provision for the one-House veto is held unconstitutional, all of §244 must fall. If §244 in its entirety is violative of the Constitution, it follows that the Attorney General has no authority to suspend Chadha's deportation under §244(a)(1) and Chadha would be deported. From this, Congress argues that Chadha lacks standing to challenge the constitutionality of the one-House veto provision because he could receive no relief even if his constitutional challenge proves successful.

Only recently this Court reaffirmed that the invalid portions of a statute are to be severed "[unless] it is evident that the Legislature would not have enacted those provisions which are within its power, independently of that which is not." Here, however, we need not embark on that elusive inquiry since Congress itself has provided the answer to the question of severability in §406 of the Immigration and Nationality Act, note following 8 U.S.C. §1101, which provides:

> "If any particular provision of this Act, or the application thereof to any person or circumstance, is held invalid, the remainder of the Act and the application of such provision to other persons or circumstances shall not be affected thereby."

This language is unambiguous and gives rise to a presumption that Congress did not intend the validity of the Act as a whole, or of any part of the Act, to depend upon whether the veto clause of §244(c)(2) was invalid. The one-House veto provision in §244(c)(2) is clearly a "particular provision" of the Act as that language is used in the severability clause. Congress clearly intended "the remainder of the Act" to stand if "any particular provision" were held invalid. Congress could not have more plainly authorized the presumption that the provision for a one-House veto in §244(c)(2) is severable from the remainder of §244 and the Act of which it is a part.

The presumption as to the severability of the one-House veto provision in §244(c)(2) is supported by the legislative history of §244. That section and its precursors supplanted the long-established pattern of dealing with deportations like Chadha's on a case-by-case basis through private bills. Although it may be that Congress was reluctant to delegate final authority over cancellation of deportations, such reluctance is not sufficient to overcome the presumption of severability raised by §406.

The Immigration Act of 1924 required the Secretary of Labor to deport any alien who entered or remained in the United States unlawfully. The only means by which a deportable alien could lawfully remain in the United States was to have his status altered by a private bill enacted by both Houses and presented to the President pursuant to the procedures set out in Art. I, §7, of the Constitution. These private bills were found intolerabl[y time-consuming] by Congress. . . .

The proposal to permit one House of Congress to veto the Attorney General's suspension of an alien's deportation was incorporated in the Immigration and Nationality Act of 1952. Plainly, Congress' desire to retain a veto in this area cannot be considered in isolation but must be viewed in the context of Congress' irritation with the burden of private immigration bills. This legislative history is not sufficient to rebut the presumption of severability raised by §406 because there is insufficient evidence that Congress would have continued to subject itself to the onerous burdens of private bills had it known that §244(c)(2) would be held unconstitutional.

A provision is further presumed severable if what remains after severance "is fully operative as a law." There can be no doubt that §244 is "fully operative" and workable administrative machinery without the veto provision in §244(c)(2). Entirely independent of the one-House veto, the administrative process enacted by Congress authorizes the Attorney General to suspend an alien's deportation under §244(a). Congress' oversight of the exercise of this delegated authority is preserved since all such suspensions will continue to be reported to it under §244(c)(1). Absent the passage of a bill to the contrary,[a] deportation proceedings

---

a. Without the provision for one-House veto, Congress would presumably retain the power, during the time allotted in §244(c)(2), to enact a law, in accordance with the requirements of Art. I of the Constitution, mandating a particular alien's deportation, unless, of course, other constitutional principles place substantive limitations on such action. Cf. Attorney General Jackson's attack on H.R. 9766, 76th Cong., 3d Sess. (1940), a bill to require the Attorney General to deport an individual alien. The Attorney General called the bill "an historical departure from an unbroken American practice and tradition. It would be the first time that an act of Congress singled out a named individual for deportation." S. Rep. No. 2031, 76th Cong., 3d Sess., pt. 1, p. 9 (1940) (reprinting Jackson's letter of June 18, 1940). See n.[d] infra.

will be canceled when the period specified in §244(c)(2) has expired. Clearly, §244 survives as a workable administrative mechanism without the one-House veto. . . .

Jurisdiction

. . . Although the Attorney General was satisfied that the House action was invalid and that it should not have any effect on his decision to suspend deportation, he appropriately let the controversy take its course through the courts. . . .

Case or Controversy

It is also contended that this is not a genuine controversy but "a friendly, nonadversary, proceeding," upon which the Court should not pass. This argument rests on the fact that Chadha and the INS take the same position on the constitutionality of the one-House veto. But it would be a curious result if, in the administration of justice, a person could be denied access to the courts because the Attorney General of the United States agreed with the legal arguments asserted by the individual. A case or controversy is presented by these cases. First, from the time of Congress' formal intervention, the concrete adverseness is beyond doubt. Congress is . . . a proper party to defend the constitutionality of §244(c)(2). . . . Second, . . . the INS's agreement with Chadha's position does not alter the fact that the INS would have deported Chadha absent the Court of Appeals judgment. . . .

Political Question

It is also argued that these cases present a nonjusticiable political question. . . .

. . . No policy underlying the political question doctrine suggests that Congress or the Executive, or both acting in concert and in compliance with Art. I, can decide the constitutionality of a statute; that is a decision for the courts.[b] . . .

---

b. The suggestion is made that §244(c)(2) is somehow immunized from constitutional scrutiny because the Act containing §244(c)(2) was passed by Congress and approved by the President. *Marbury* resolved that question. The assent of the Executive to a bill which contains a provision contrary to the Constitution does not shield it from judicial review. See *National League of Cities*; *Buckley*; *Myers*. In any event, 11 Presidents, from Mr. Wilson through Mr. Reagan, who have been presented with this issue have gone on record at some point to challenge congressional vetoes as unconstitutional. . . . Furthermore, it is not uncommon for Presidents to approve legislation containing parts which are objectionable on constitutional grounds. For example, after President Roosevelt signed the Lend-Lease Act of 1941, Attorney General [and later Justice] Jackson released a memorandum explaining the President's view that the provision allowing the Act's authorization to be terminated by concurrent resolution was unconstitutional. Jackson, A Presidential Legal Opinion, 66 Harv. L. Rev. 1353 (1953).

III

A

We turn now to the question whether action of one House of Congress under §244(c)(2) violates strictures of the Constitution. . . .

Explicit and unambiguous provisions of the Constitution prescribe and define the respective functions of the Congress and of the Executive in the legislative process. Since the precise terms of those familiar provisions are critical to the resolution of these cases, we set them out verbatim. Article I provides:

> "All legislative Powers herein granted shall be vested in a Congress of the United States, which shall consist of a Senate and House of Representatives." Art. I, §1.
>
> "Every Bill which shall have passed the House of Representatives and the Senate, shall, before it becomes a law, be presented to the President of the United States. . . ." Art. I, §7, cl. 2.
>
> "Every Order, Resolution, or Vote to which the Concurrence of the Senate and House of Representatives may be necessary (except on a question of Adjournment) shall be presented to the President of the United States; and before the Same shall take Effect, shall be approved by him, or being disapproved by him, shall be repassed by two thirds of the Senate and House of Representatives, according to the Rules and Limitations prescribed in the Case of a Bill." Art. I, §7, cl. 3.

These provisions of Art. I are integral parts of the constitutional design for the separation of powers. We have recently noted that "[the] principle of separation of powers was not simply an abstract generalization in the minds of the Framers: it was woven into the document that they drafted in Philadelphia in the summer of 1787." Just as we relied on the textual provision of Art. II, §2, cl. 2, to vindicate the principle of separation of powers in *Buckley*, we see that the purposes underlying the Presentment Clauses, Art. I, §7, cls. 2, 3, and the bicameral requirement of Art. I, §1, and §7, cl. 2, guide our resolution of the important question presented in these cases. The very structure of the Articles delegating and separating powers under Arts. I, II, and III exemplifies the concept of separation of powers, and we now turn to Art. I.

THE PRESENTMENT CLAUSES

The records of the Constitutional Convention reveal that the requirement that all legislation be presented to the President before becoming law was uniformly accepted by the Framers. Presentment to the President and the Presidential veto were considered so imperative that the draftsmen took special pains to assure that these requirements could not be circumvented. During the final debate on Art. I, §7, cl. 2, James Madison expressed concern that it might easily be evaded by the simple expedient of calling a proposed law a "resolution" or "vote" rather than a "bill." As a consequence, Art. I, §7, cl. 3 was added.

The decision to provide the President with a limited and qualified power to nullify proposed legislation by veto was based on the profound conviction of the

Framers that the powers conferred on Congress were the powers to be most carefully circumscribed. It is beyond doubt that lawmaking was a power to be shared by both Houses and the President. In The Federalist No. 73, Hamilton focused on the President's role in making laws:

> "If even no propensity had ever discovered itself in the legislative body to invade the rights of the Executive, the rules of just reasoning and theoretic propriety would of themselves teach us that the one ought not to be left to the mercy of the other, but ought to possess a constitutional and effectual power of self-defence."

See also The Federalist No. 51. . . .

The President's role in the lawmaking process also reflects the Framers' careful efforts to check whatever propensity a particular Congress might have to enact oppressive, improvident, or ill-considered measures. The President's veto role in the legislative process was described later during public debate on ratification:

> "It establishes a salutary check upon the legislative body, calculated to guard the community against the effects of faction, precipitancy, or of any impulse unfriendly to the public good, which may happen to influence a majority of that body.
>
> ". . . The primary inducement to conferring the power in question upon the Executive is, to enable him to defend himself; the secondary one is to increase the chances in favor of the community against the passing of bad laws, through haste, inadvertence, or design." The Federalist No. 73.

See also The Pocket Veto Case, 279 U.S. 655, 678 (1929); *Myers*. The Court also has observed that the Presentment Clauses serve the important purpose of assuring that a "national" perspective is grafted on the legislative process:

> "The President is a representative of the people just as the members of the Senate and of the House are, and it may be, at some times, on some subjects, that the President elected by all the people is rather more representative of them all than are the members of either body of the Legislature whose constituencies are local and not countrywide. . . ." *Myers*.

Bicameralism

The bicameral requirement of Art. I, §§1, 7, was of scarcely less concern to the Framers than was the Presidential veto and indeed the two concepts are interdependent. By providing that no law could take effect without the concurrence of the prescribed majority of the Members of both Houses, the Framers reemphasized their belief, already remarked upon in connection with the Presentment Clauses, that legislation should not be enacted unless it has been carefully and fully considered by the Nation's elected officials. . . .

. . . Madison [pointed] up the need to divide and disperse power in order to protect liberty:

> "In republican government, the legislative authority necessarily predominates. The remedy for this inconveniency is to divide the legislature into

> different branches; and to render them, by different modes of election and different principles of action, as little connected with each other as the nature of their common functions and their common dependence on the society will admit." The Federalist No. 51. . . .

We see therefore that the Framers were acutely conscious that the bicameral requirement and the Presentment Clauses would serve essential constitutional functions. The President's participation in the legislative process was to protect the Executive Branch from Congress and to protect the whole people from improvident laws. The division of the Congress into two distinctive bodies assures that the legislative power would be exercised only after opportunity for full study and debate in separate settings. The President's unilateral veto power, in turn, was limited by the power of two-thirds of both Houses of Congress to overrule a veto thereby precluding final arbitrary action of one person. It emerges clearly that the prescription for legislative action in Art. I, §§1, 7, represents the Framers' decision that the legislative power of the Federal Government be exercised in accord with a single, finely wrought and exhaustively considered, procedure.

IV

The Constitution sought to divide the delegated powers of the new Federal Government into three defined categories, Legislative, Executive, and Judicial, to assure, as nearly as possible, that each branch of government would confine itself to its assigned responsibility. The hydraulic pressure inherent within each of the separate Branches to exceed the outer limits of its power, even to accomplish desirable objectives, must be resisted. Although not "hermetically" sealed from one another, the powers delegated to the three Branches are functionally identifiable. When any Branch acts, it is presumptively exercising the power the Constitution has delegated to it. When the Executive acts, he presumptively acts in an executive or administrative capacity as defined in Art. II. And when, as here, one House of Congress purports to act, it is presumptively acting within its assigned sphere. . . .

Examination of the action taken here by one House pursuant to §244(c)(2) reveals that it was essentially legislative in purpose and effect. In purporting to exercise power defined in Art. I, §8, cl. 4, to "establish an uniform Rule of Naturalization," the House took action that had the purpose and effect of altering the legal rights, duties, and relations of persons, including the Attorney General, Executive Branch officials and Chadha, all outside the Legislative Branch. Section 244(c)(2) purports to authorize one House of Congress to require the Attorney General to deport an individual alien whose deportation otherwise would be canceled under §244. The one-House veto operated in these cases to overrule the Attorney General and mandate Chadha's deportation; absent the House action, Chadha would remain in the United States. Congress has acted and its action has altered Chadha's status.

The legislative character of the one-House veto in these cases is confirmed by the character of the congressional action it supplants. Neither the House of Representatives nor the Senate contends that, absent the veto provision in §244(c)(2), either of them, or both of them acting together, could effectively require the Attorney General to deport an alien once the Attorney General, in the exercise of legislatively delegated authority,[c] had determined the alien should remain in the United States. Without the challenged provision in §244(c)(2), this could have been achieved, if at all, only by legislation requiring deportation.[d] Similarly, a veto by one House of Congress under §244(c)(2) cannot be justified as an attempt at amending the standards set out in §244(a)(1), or as a repeal of §244 as applied to Chadha. Amendment and repeal of statutes, no less than enactment, must conform with Art. I.

The nature of the decision implemented by the one-House veto in these cases further manifests its legislative character. After long experience with the clumsy, time-consuming private bill procedure, Congress made a deliberate choice to delegate to the Executive Branch, and specifically to the Attorney General, the authority to allow deportable aliens to remain in this country in certain specified circumstances. It is not disputed that this choice to delegate authority is precisely the kind of decision that can be implemented only in accordance with the procedures set out in Art. I. Disagreement with the Attorney General's decision on Chadha's deportation—that is, Congress' decision to deport Chadha—no less than Congress' original choice to delegate to the Attorney General the authority to make that decision, involves determinations of policy that Congress can implement in only one way; bicameral passage followed by presentment to the President. Congress must abide by its delegation of authority until that delegation is legislatively altered or revoked.[e]

Finally, we see that when the Framers intended to authorize either House of Congress to act alone and outside of its prescribed bicameral legislative role, they narrowly and precisely defined the procedure for such action. There are four provisions in the Constitution, explicit and unambiguous, by which one House may act alone with the unreviewable force of law, not subject to the President's veto:

(a) The House of Representatives alone was given the power to initiate impeachments. Art. I, §2, cl. 5;
(b) The Senate alone was given the power to conduct trials following impeachment on charges initiated by the House and to convict following trial. Art. I, §3, cl. 6;
(c) The Senate alone was given final unreviewable power to approve or to disapprove Presidential appointments. Art. II, §2, cl. 2;
(d) The Senate alone was given unreviewable power to ratify treaties negotiated by the President. Art. II, §2, cl. 2.

---

c. Congress protests that affirming the Court of Appeals in these cases will sanction "lawmaking by the Attorney General. . . . Why is the Attorney General exempt from submitting his proposed changes in the law to the full bicameral process?" . . . When the Attorney General performs his duties pursuant to §244, he does not exercise "legislative" power. . . .

d. We express no opinion as to whether such legislation would violate any constitutional provision. See n.[a], supra.

e. This does not mean that Congress is required to capitulate to "the accretion of policy control by forces outside its chambers." The Constitution provides Congress with abundant means to oversee and control its administrative creatures. Beyond the obvious fact that Congress ultimately controls administrative agencies in the legislation that creates them, other means of control, such as durational limits on authorizations and formal reporting requirements, lie well within Congress' constitutional power.

Clearly, when the Draftsmen sought to confer special powers on one House, independent of the other House, or of the President, they did so in explicit, unambiguous terms.[f] These carefully defined exceptions from presentment and bicameralism underscore the difference between the legislative functions of Congress and other unilateral but important and binding one-House acts provided for in the Constitution. These exceptions are narrow, explicit, and separately justified; none of them authorize the action challenged here. On the contrary, they provide further support for the conclusion that congressional authority is not to be implied and for the conclusion that the veto provided for in §244(c)(2) is not authorized by the constitutional design of the powers of the Legislative Branch.

Since it is clear that the action by the House under §244(c)(2) was not within any of the express constitutional exceptions authorizing one House to act alone, and equally clear that it was an exercise of legislative power, that action was subject to the standards prescribed in Art. I. The bicameral requirement, the Presentment Clauses, the President's veto, and Congress' power to override a veto were intended to erect enduring checks on each Branch and to protect the people from the improvident exercise of power by mandating certain prescribed steps. To preserve those checks, and maintain the separation of powers, the carefully defined limits on the power of each Branch must not be eroded. To accomplish what has been attempted by one House of Congress in this case requires action in conformity with the express procedures of the Constitution's prescription for legislative action: passage by a majority of both Houses and presentment to the President. . . .

Justice Powell, concurring in the judgment.

The Court's decision, based on the Presentment Clauses, apparently will invalidate every use of the legislative veto. The breadth of this holding gives one pause. Congress has included the veto in literally hundreds of statutes, dating back to the 1930s. Congress clearly views this procedure as essential to controlling the

---

f. An exception from the Presentment Clauses was ratified in Hollingsworth v. Virginia, 3 Dall. 378 (1798). There the Court held Presidential approval was unnecessary for a proposed constitutional amendment which had passed both Houses of Congress by the requisite two-thirds majority. See U.S. Const., Art. V. One might also include another "exception" to the rule that congressional action having the force of law be subject to the bicameral requirement and the Presentment Clauses. Each House has the power to act alone in determining specified internal matters. Art. I, §7, cls. 2, 3, and §5, cl. 2. However, this "exception" only empowers Congress to bind itself and is noteworthy only insofar as it further indicates the Framers' intent that Congress not act in any legally binding manner outside a closely circumscribed legislative arena, except in specific and enumerated instances. Although the bicameral check was not provided for in any of these provisions for independent congressional action, precautionary alternative checks are evident. For example, Art. II, §2, requires that two-thirds of the Senators present concur in the Senate's consent to a treaty, rather than the simple majority required for passage of legislation. Similarly, the Framers adopted an alternative protection, in the stead of Presidential veto and bicameralism, by requiring the concurrence of two-thirds of the Senators present for a conviction of impeachment. Art. I, §3. We also note that the Court's holding in *Hollingsworth*, supra, that a resolution proposing an amendment to the Constitution need not be presented to the President, is subject to two alternative protections. First, a constitutional amendment must command the votes of two-thirds of each House. Second, three-fourths of the states must ratify any amendment.

delegation of power to administrative agencies.[a] One reasonably may disagree with Congress' assessment of the veto's utility, but the respect due its judgment as a coordinate branch of Government cautions that our holding should be no more extensive than necessary to decide these cases. In my view, the cases may be decided on a narrower ground. When Congress finds that a particular person does not satisfy the statutory criteria for permanent residence in this country it has assumed a judicial function in violation of the principle of separation of powers. Accordingly, I concur only in the judgment.

I

A

The Framers perceived that "[the] accumulation of all powers legislative, executive and judiciary in the same hands, whether of one, a few or many, and whether hereditary, self appointed, or elective, may justly be pronounced the very definition of tyranny." The Federalist No. 47. Theirs was not a baseless fear. . . .

One abuse that was prevalent during the Confederation was the exercise of judicial power by the state legislatures. The Framers were well acquainted with the danger of subjecting the determination of the rights of one person to the "tyranny of shifting majorities." . . .

It was to prevent the recurrence of such abuses that the Framers vested the executive, legislative, and judicial powers in separate branches. Their concern that a legislature should not be able unilaterally to impose a substantial deprivation on one person was expressed not only in this general allocation of power, but also in more specific provisions, such as the Bill of Attainder Clause, Art. I, §9, cl. 3. As the Court recognized in United States v. Brown, 381 U.S. 437, 442 (1965), "the Bill of Attainder Clause was intended not as a narrow, technical . . . prohibition, but rather as an implementation of the separation of powers, a general safeguard against legislative exercise of the judicial function, or more simply—trial by legislature." This Clause, and the separation-of-powers doctrine generally, reflect the Framers' concern that trial by a legislature lacks the safeguards necessary to prevent the abuse of power. . . .

II

. . . On its face, the House's action appears clearly adjudicatory. The House did not enact a general rule; rather it made its own determination that six specific persons did not comply with certain statutory criteria. It thus undertook the type of decision that traditionally has been left to other branches. Even if the House did not make a de novo determination, but simply reviewed the Immigration and

---

a. [T]he legislative veto has been included in a wide variety of statutes, ranging from bills for executive reorganization to the War Powers Resolution. Whether the veto complies with the Presentment Clauses may well turn on the particular context in which it is exercised, and I would be hesitant to conclude that every veto is unconstitutional on the basis of the unusual example presented by this litigation.

Naturalization Service's findings, it still assumed a function ordinarily entrusted to the federal courts.[b]

The impropriety of the House's assumption of this function is confirmed by the fact that its action raises the very danger the Framers sought to avoid—the exercise of unchecked power. In deciding whether Chadha deserves to be deported, Congress is not subject to any internal constraints that prevent it from arbitrarily depriving him of the right to remain in this country.[c] Unlike the judiciary or an administrative agency,[d] Congress is not bound by established substantive rules. Nor is it subject to the procedural safeguards, such as the right to counsel and a hearing before an impartial tribunal, that are present when a court or an agency adjudicates individual rights. The only effective constraint on Congress' power is political, but Congress is most accountable politically when it prescribes rules of general applicability. When it decides rights of specific persons, those rights are subject to "the tyranny of a shifting majority."

Chief Justice Marshall observed: "It is the peculiar province of the legislature to prescribe general rules for the government of society; the application of those rules to individuals in society would seem to be the duty of other departments." Fletcher v. Peck, 6 Cranch 87, 136 (1810). In my view, when Congress undertook to apply its rules to Chadha, it exceeded the scope of its constitutionally prescribed authority. I would not reach the broader question whether legislative vetoes are invalid under the Presentment Clauses.

Justice WHITE, dissenting.

Today the Court not only invalidates §244(c)(2) of the Immigration and Nationality Act, but also sounds the death knell for nearly 200 other statutory provisions in which Congress has reserved a "legislative veto." . . .

The prominence of the legislative veto mechanism in our contemporary political system and its importance to Congress can hardly be overstated. It has become a central means by which Congress secures the accountability of executive and independent agencies. Without the legislative veto, Congress is faced with a Hobson's choice: either to refrain from delegating the necessary authority, leaving itself with a hopeless task of writing laws with the requisite specificity to cover endless special circumstances across the entire policy landscape, or in the alternative, to abdicate

---

b. Although the parallel is not entirely complete, the effect on Chadha's personal rights would not have been different in principle had he been acquitted of a federal crime and thereafter found by one House of Congress to have been guilty.

c. When Congress grants particular individuals relief or benefits under its spending power, the danger of oppressive action that the separation of powers was designed to avoid is not implicated. Similarly, Congress may authorize the admission of individual aliens by special Acts, but it does not follow that Congress unilaterally may make a judgment that a particular alien has no legal right to remain in this country. As Attorney General [and later Justice] Robert Jackson remarked, such a practice "would be an historical departure from an unbroken American practice and tradition."

d. We have recognized that independent regulatory agencies and departments of the Executive Branch often exercise authority that is "judicial in nature." This function, however, forms part of the agencies' execution of public law and is subject to the procedural safeguards, including judicial review, provided by the Administrative Procedure Act.

its law-making function to the Executive Branch and independent agencies. To choose the former leaves major national problems unresolved; to opt for the latter risks unaccountable policymaking by those not elected to fill that role. Accordingly, over the past five decades, the legislative veto has been placed in nearly 200 statutes. The device is known in every field of governmental concern: reorganization, budgets, foreign affairs, war powers, and regulation of trade, safety, energy, the environment, and the economy.

I

. . . During the 1970s the legislative veto was important in resolving a series of major constitutional disputes between the President and Congress over claims of the President to broad impoundment, war, and national emergency powers. The key provision of the War Powers Resolution, 50 U.S.C. §1544(c), authorizes the termination by concurrent resolution of the use of armed forces in hostilities. A similar measure resolved the problem posed by Presidential claims of inherent power to impound appropriations. Congressional Budget and Impoundment Control Act of 1974, 31 U.S.C. §1403. . . . Although the War Powers Resolution was enacted over President Nixon's veto, the Impoundment Control Act was enacted with the President's approval. These statutes were followed by others resolving similar problems. . . .

. . . Perhaps there are other means of accommodation and accountability, but the increasing reliance of Congress upon the legislative veto suggests that the alternatives to which Congress must now turn are not entirely satisfactory. . . .

II

[O]ur task should be to determine whether the legislative veto is consistent with the purposes of Art. I and the principles of separation of powers which are reflected in that Article and throughout the Constitution. We should not find the lack of a specific constitutional authorization for the legislative veto surprising, and I would not infer disapproval of the mechanism from its absence. From the summer of 1787 to the present the Government of the United States has become an endeavor far beyond the contemplation of the Framers. Only within the last half-century has the complexity and size of the Federal Government's responsibilities grown so greatly that the Congress must rely on the legislative veto as the most effective if not the only means to insure its role as the Nation's lawmaker. But the wisdom of the Framers was to anticipate that the Nation would grow and new problems of governance would require different solutions. Accordingly, our Federal Government was intentionally chartered with the flexibility to respond to contemporary needs without losing sight of fundamental democratic principles. . . .

III

The power to exercise a legislative veto is not the power to write new law without bicameral approval or Presidential consideration. The veto must be authorized by statute and may only negative what an Executive department or independent agency has proposed. . . .

A

[T]he historical background of the Presentment Clause itself . . . reveals only that the Framers were concerned with limiting the methods for enacting new legislation. The Framers were aware of the experience in Pennsylvania where the legislature had evaded the requirements attached to the passing of legislation by the use of "resolves," and the criticisms directed at this practice by the Council of Censors. There is no record that the Convention contemplated, let alone intended, that these Art. I requirements would someday be invoked to restrain the scope of congressional authority pursuant to duly enacted law. . . .

B

. . . The Court's holding today that all legislative-type action must be enacted through the lawmaking process ignores that legislative authority is routinely delegated to the Executive Branch, to the independent regulatory agencies, and to private individuals and groups.

"The rise of administrative bodies probably has been the most significant legal trend of the last century. . . . They have become a veritable fourth branch of the Government, which has deranged our three-branch legal theories. . . ."

Theoretically, agencies and officials were asked only to "fill up the details," and the rule was that "Congress cannot delegate any part of its legislative power except under the limitation of a prescribed standard." Chief Justice Taft elaborated the standard in J.W. Hampton & Co. v. United States, 276 U.S. 394, 409 (1928): "If Congress shall lay down by legislative act an intelligible principle to which the person or body authorized to fix such rates is directed to conform, such legislative action is not a forbidden delegation of legislative power." In practice, however, restrictions on the scope of the power that could be delegated diminished and all but disappeared. In only two instances did the Court find an unconstitutional delegation. Panama Refining Co. v. Ryan, 293 U.S. 388 (1935); A.L.A. Schechter Poultry Corp. v. United States, 295 U.S. 495 (1935). In other cases, the "intelligible principle" through which agencies have attained enormous control over the economic affairs of the country was held to include such formulations as "just and reasonable," "public interest," "public convenience, interest, or necessity," and "unfair methods of competition."

[F]or present purposes, these cases establish that by virtue of congressional delegation, legislative power can be exercised by independent agencies and Executive departments without the passage of new legislation. For some time, the sheer amount of law—the substantive rules that regulate private conduct and direct the operation of government—made by the agencies has far outnumbered the lawmaking engaged in by Congress through the traditional process. There is no question but that agency rulemaking is lawmaking in any functional or realistic sense of the term. . . .

If Congress may delegate lawmaking power to independent and Executive agencies, it is most difficult to understand Art. I as prohibiting Congress from also reserving a check on legislative power for itself. Absent the veto, the agencies receiving delegations of legislative or quasi-legislative power may issue regulations having the force of law without bicameral approval and without the President's signature. It is thus not apparent why the reservation of a veto over the exercise of that legislative power must be subject to a more exacting test. In both cases, it is enough that the initial statutory authorizations comply with the Art. I requirements.

[T]he Court's decision today suggests that Congress may place a "veto" power over suspensions of deportation in . . . the hands of an independent agency, but is forbidden to reserve such authority for itself. Perhaps this odd result could be justified on other constitutional grounds, such as the separation of powers, but certainly it cannot be defended as consistent with the Court's view of the Art. I presentment and bicameralism commands.[a]

. . . If the effective functioning of a complex modern government requires the delegation of vast authority which, by virtue of its breadth, is legislative or "quasi-legislative" in character, I cannot accept that Art. I—which is, after all, the source of the nondelegation doctrine—should forbid Congress to qualify that grant with a legislative veto.

C

The Court also takes no account of perhaps the most relevant consideration: However resolutions of disapproval under §244(c)(2) are formally characterized, in reality, a departure from the status quo occurs only upon the concurrence of opinion among the House, Senate, and President. Reservations of legislative authority to be exercised by Congress should be upheld if the exercise of such reserved authority is consistent with the distribution of and limits upon legislative power that Art. I provides.

1

. . . The history of the Immigration and Nationality Act makes clear that §244(c)(2) did not alter the division of actual authority between Congress and the Executive. At all times, whether through private bills, or through affirmative concurrent resolutions, or through the present one-House veto, a permanent change in a deportable alien's status could be accomplished only with the agreement of the Attorney General, the House, and the Senate.

2

The central concern of the presentment and bicameralism requirements of Art. I is that when a departure from the legal status quo is undertaken, it is done with the approval of the President and both Houses of Congress—or, in the event of a Presidential veto, a two-thirds majority in both Houses. This interest is fully satisfied by the operation of §244(c)(2). The President's approval is found in the Attorney General's action in recommending to Congress that the deportation order for a given alien be suspended. The House and the Senate indicate their approval of the Executive's action by not passing a resolution of disapproval within

a. As the Court acknowledges, the "provisions of Art. I are integral parts of the constitutional design for the separation of powers." But these separation-of-powers concerns are that legislative power be exercised by Congress, executive power by the President, and judicial power by the Courts. A scheme which allows delegation of legislative power to the President and the departments under his control, but forbids a check on its exercise by Congress itself obviously denigrates the separation-of-powers concerns underlying Art. I. . . .

the statutory period. Thus, a change in the legal status quo—the deportability of the alien—is consummated only with the approval of each of the three relevant actors. The disagreement of any one of the three maintains the alien's pre-existing status: the Executive may choose not to recommend suspension; the House and Senate may each veto the recommendation. The effect on the rights and obligations of the affected individuals and upon the legislative system is precisely the same as if a private bill were introduced but failed to receive the necessary approval. "The President and the two Houses enjoy exactly the same say in what the law is to be as would have been true for each without the presence of the one-House veto, and nothing in the law is changed absent the concurrence of the President and a majority in each House."

Thus understood, §244(c)(2) fully effectuates the purposes of the bicameralism and presentment requirements. . . .

[I]t may be asserted that Chadha's status before legislative disapproval is one of nondeportation and that the exercise of the veto, unlike the failure of a private bill, works a change in the status quo. This position plainly ignores the statutory language. At no place in §244 has Congress delegated to the Attorney General any final power to determine which aliens shall be allowed to remain in the United States. Congress has retained the ultimate power to pass on such changes in deportable status. By its own terms, §244(a) states that whatever power the Attorney General has been delegated to suspend deportation and adjust status is to be exercisable only "[as] hereinafter prescribed in this section." Subsection (c) is part of that section. A grant of "suspension" does not cancel the alien's deportation or adjust the alien's status to that of a permanent resident alien. A suspension order is merely a "deferment of deportation," which can mature into a cancellation of deportation and adjustment of status only upon the approval of Congress—by way of silence—under §244(c)(2). Only then does the statute authorize the Attorney General to "cancel deportation proceedings," and "record the alien's lawful admission for permanent residence. . . ." The Immigration and Naturalization Service's action, on behalf of the Attorney General, "cannot become effective without ratification by Congress." Until that ratification occurs, the Executive's action is simply a recommendation that Congress finalize the suspension—in itself, it works no legal change.[b]

---

b. I agree with Justice Rehnquist that Congress did not intend the one-House veto provision of §244(c)(2) to be severable. Although the general rule is that the presence of a saving clause creates a presumption of divisibility, I read the saving clause contained in §406 of the Immigration and Nationality Act as primarily pertaining to the severability of major parts of the Act from one another, not the divisibility of different provisions within a single section. Surely, Congress would want the naturalization provisions of the Act to be severable from the deportation sections. But this does not support preserving §244 without the legislative veto any more than a saving provision would justify preserving immigration authority without quota limits.

More relevant is the fact that for 40 years Congress has insisted on retaining a voice on individual suspension cases—it has frequently rejected bills which would place final authority in the Executive Branch. It is clear that Congress believed its retention crucial. Given this history, the Court's rewriting of the Act flouts the will of Congress. [Footnote relocated.—Eds.]

IV

. . . The Attorney General's suspension of deportation is equivalent to a proposal for legislation. The nature of the Attorney General's role as recommendatory is not altered because §244 provides for congressional action through disapproval rather than by ratification. In comparison to private bills, which must be initiated in the Congress and which allow a Presidential veto to be overridden by a two-thirds majority in both Houses of Congress, §244 augments rather than reduces the Executive Branch's authority. So understood, congressional review does not undermine, as the Court of Appeals thought, the "weight and dignity" that attends the decisions of the Executive Branch. . . .

I do not suggest that all legislative vetoes are necessarily consistent with separation- of-powers principles. A legislative check on an inherently executive function, for example, that of initiating prosecutions, poses an entirely different question. But the legislative veto device here—and in many other settings—is far from an instance of legislative tyranny over the Executive. It is a necessary check on the unavoidably expanding power of the agencies, both Executive and independent, as they engage in exercising authority delegated by Congress.

V

Today's decision strikes down in one fell swoop provisions in more laws enacted by Congress than the Court has cumulatively invalidated in its history. . . . I must dissent.

Justice REHNQUIST, with whom Justice WHITE joins, dissenting.

A severability clause creates a presumption that Congress intended the valid portion of the statute to remain in force when one part is found to be invalid. A severability clause does not, however, conclusively resolve the issue. "[The] determination, in the end, is reached by" asking "[what] was the intent of the lawmakers," and "will rarely turn on the presence or absence of such a clause." Because I believe that Congress did not intend the one-House veto provision of §244(c)(2) to be severable, I dissent.

Section 244(c)(2) is an exception to the general rule that an alien's deportation shall be suspended when the Attorney General finds that statutory criteria are met. It is severable only if Congress would have intended to permit the Attorney General to suspend deportations without it. This Court has held several times over the years that exceptions such as this are not severable because

> "by rejecting the exceptions intended by the legislature . . . the statute is made to enact what confessedly the legislature never meant. It confers upon the statute a positive operation beyond the legislative intent, and beyond what anyone can say it would have enacted in view of the illegality of the exceptions."

By severing §244(c)(2), the Court permits suspension of deportation in a class of cases where Congress never stated that suspension was appropriate. I do not believe we should expand the statute in this way without some clear indication that Congress intended such an expansion. . . .

The Court finds that the legislative history of §244 shows that Congress intended §244(c)(2) to be severable because Congress wanted to relieve itself of the burden of private bills. But the history elucidated by the Court shows that Congress was unwilling to give the Executive Branch permission to suspend deportation on its own. Over the years, Congress consistently rejected requests from the Executive for complete discretion in this area. Congress always insisted on retaining ultimate control, whether by concurrent resolution, as in the 1948 Act, or by one-House veto, as in the present Act. Congress has never indicated that it would be willing to permit suspensions of deportation unless it could retain some sort of veto.

It is doubtless true that Congress has the power to provide for suspensions of deportation without a one-House veto. But the Court has failed to identify any evidence that Congress intended to exercise that power. On the contrary, Congress' continued insistence on retaining control of the suspension process indicates that it has never been disposed to give the Executive Branch a free hand. By severing §244(c)(2) the Court has "confounded" Congress' "intention. . . ."

DISCUSSION

1. *Executive review.* The Constitution is law, and executive officials take an oath to uphold it. Why, then, were the executive officials in this case prepared to do something they considered both unconstitutional (and hence, illegal) and unjust unless they got a permission slip from the judiciary? Remember, the Attorney General believes that the legislative veto provision is both unconstitutional and severable. Why then does the *Chadha* Court say that the AG acted "appropriately" when he took initial steps to carry out the House's action by deporting Chadha? Wouldn't it have been more "appropriate" to simply refuse to give any effect to the House's unconstitutional action? (If the House had resolved that Chadha's head be chopped off, or had issued some other obviously unconstitutional edict or attainder, shouldn't the AG simply ignore the House?) Of course, if the AG's refusal to deport were challenged in court, he must be prepared to defend this refusal, by pointing out that his actions were indeed lawful—he was following the Constitution rather than the unconstitutional statute, just as the Supremacy Clause commands. And if the Supreme Court were to disagree with his position—and mandamus Chadha's deportation—then presumably the AG at that point would comply, having received definitive judicial guidance that he had somehow misconstrued the Constitution. But why shouldn't his default position in the absence of such a Court order be that he will follow the Constitution, not the statute, if the two conflict? Why, in other words, should the burden be on the rather helpless Chadha to come to court, rather than, say, on Congress (which is in general more able to shoulder the burdens of litigation, and in this case constitutionally culpable, under the AG's good faith understanding of the Constitution)?

One possible answer is that if the AG were to ignore the House legislative veto, it is unclear that the House or anyone else in fact had "standing" to challenge him. But if so, is this the AG's fault, or Congress's problem? And whence the premise that all constitutional issues must reach the Court in order to be properly decided? For a rich discussion of the occasions on which the executive branch should follow its best understanding of the Constitution unless and until courts order otherwise, see Frank H. Easterbrook, Presidential Review, 40 Case W. Res. L. Rev. 905 (1990).

2. *Presidential waiver?* If the President signs a bill into law, why doesn't he thereby waive his right to challenge it as a violation of presidential prerogatives? Consider the following possible answers: (a) The statute may be unconstitutional in only a small and severable particular, and he should not be obliged to veto the entire bill because of one minor glitch that can be judicially excised later. (b) The President when he signs might deem the provision constitutional but later on he might in good faith and after careful reflection change his mind, as he has a right to do. (c) The unconstitutionality of a provision may become clear only after the President has in good faith tried to implement it, and has come to perceive a constitutional difficulty not visible on the face of the provision. (d) The President who signs should not be allowed to sign away the right of his successors in office to object. (e) The right at stake is not really the President's but the people's, and thus he is not allowed to give away what is not really his. Do you agree with any of these answers? Are there other answers? For a thoughtful argument that the President has a duty to veto a bill in case (a), rather than simply sign it and later challenge it, see Michael B. Rappaport, The President's Veto and the Constitution, 87 Nw. U. L. Rev. 735 (1993). Among other things, Professor Rappaport argues that vetoes give Congress a clear choice whether it prefers no statute at all instead of a statute stripped of the offensive clause. By contrast, when Presidents sign bills and then get judges to "rewrite" them by excising the unconstitutional clause, important values of bicameralism are slighted, Professor Rappaport argues.

3. *Formalism versus realism.* Compare Chief Justice Burger's style of analysis with that of Justice White. Critics of the majority opinion find it overly "formalistic" and wooden. Conversely, critics of the White dissent see it as insufficiently attentive to rules and principles laid down by the words and architecture of the Constitution itself. Does Justice Powell offer an alternative to both?

4. *Formal proofs and functional precepts.* Consider the following two "formal" proofs of *Chadha*'s rightness. Proof #1: The federal government has only three kinds of power—legislative, executive, and judicial (as laid down in the first three Articles and confirmed by the Tenth Amendment). Hence the legislative veto must fit into one of these three boxes. If it is an exercise of legislative power, it requires bicameralism and presentment. If, conversely, it is an exercise of executive or judicial power, it may not be carried out by the Congress, which is not given such powers (outside a few carefully specified contexts). Either way, the legislative veto fails. QED. Proof #2: In voting against Jagdish Chadha, Congress was doing one of two things—either applying the "hardship" standard specified in the earlier statute, or laying down a new "hardship" standard. If the first, this effort to apply a prior law to a later and specific fact situation is an impermissible effort to wield judicial power (cf. Powell). If the second, this effort to adopt a new legislative standard requires bicameralism and presentment (cf. Burger). Either way, the legislative veto fails. QED. Do you find these "formal" proofs persuasive or clarifying?

If not, perhaps it is because without more, these organizational chart arguments fail to offer up a sufficiently rich functional account of *why* the different powers of government are indeed separated—of the values and vision informing the framers' design. Perhaps the best structural defense of *Chadha* would go something like this: The separation of powers is designed to encourage legislators to draft standards generally and prospectively, behind a kind of veil of ignorance: All persons who henceforth do X shall be deported unless Y and Z. Once this general legislative rule is in place, the executive branch must carry it out, and if the executive has misapplied the rule, legally aggrieved persons (those with "standing") can come to court to complain. The executive and judicial powers are mighty, because they operate on named, known individuals—they decide whether Jagdish Chadha the man wins or loses. But these branches do not get to make up the general rules applicable against Chadha—these have already been specified in advance by the legislature. And although the legislative power is also mighty, the rules laid down should be general and prospective, giving all individuals clear notice of how to avoid deportation, applying evenhandedly to all persons in the future, and setting forth the principles of law to be followed by the other branches. Thus the rule of law is suitably impersonal: No group of officials can harm Chadha simply because they don't like him as a person.

But this system is frustrated when legislatures pass rules that are no rules at all. In principle, the legislature may not "delegate" lawmaking power, as such, giving the executive branch complete carte blanche to do whatever it likes. But no law can specify everything in advance, and so as a practical matter it is hard for courts after the fact to come up with clean doctrinal tests distinguishing between those laws that in effect delegate *lawmaking* power on the one hand and those laws on the other hand that simply create permissible zones of *executive* discretion, suitably bounded by statutory rules and policies established by the legislature itself. A Depression-era statute that said "anything that President Roosevelt henceforth decrees to improve the economy shall be law" would seem to go too far—and the Court in a pair of 1935 cases did indeed strike down overly broad delegations of power. (In light of contemporaneous events in Italy and Germany, the Court was doubtless concerned about government by dictators or corporate councils; and once Congress has given up sweeping power to the President, it is hard to get it back—the President may simply veto all repeal efforts, and so Congress must muster two-thirds majorities in each house to override.) But short of such extreme cases, it is hard to say when a given law gives too much discretion, and imposes too little constraint. Because this "how much" question is judicially unmanageable we are left with a genuine but judicially underenforced constitutional principle against delegated lawmaking. But the "who" question is more manageable than the "how much" question. Congress is more likely to legislate mush with no rules if it gets to control law application *itself*. It is less likely to draft overbroad laws with little guidance if *someone else other than Congress* will get to exercise all the discretion that the law creates. And so judges can enforce the nondelegation principle more cleanly by saying to Congress, "you may not delegate enforcement discretion to yourselves; whatever discretion you create will be wielded by someone else, with no formal veto on your part—so draft as carefully as you can!" If, however, this is the best structural account undergirding *Chadha*, it calls into serious question the Court's treatment of the severability issue, see discussion note 7, infra.

5. *Fast-track legislation and other congressional responses.* The legislative veto was designed in part as a substitute for the cumbersome private bill system. (Note also that private bills seem to be in tension with the equality, impersonality, and rule-of-law vision sketched out in discussion note 4, supra; are laws singling persons out for special benefits different from laws singling persons out for special burdens?) But

the cumbersome nature of the private bills is simply a function of internal House rules and practices about agendas and debates—and these can easily be changed by Congress itself. Thus, after *Chadha*, Congress could come very close to replicating the legislative veto with the following system. First, the AG is authorized by law only to postpone deportation for, say, one year—after that, she must deport in all cases, even those of hardship. Second, where the AG finds hardship, she shall propose to Congress a private waiver for the alien in question. Third, such waiver/private bill proposals must come before Congress, and must be voted on by each house within the year. Such proposals shall be unamendable and nondebatable, and must appear on a priority legislative calendar. (All of these rules can be implemented by each house under internal House rules pursuant to Article I, §5.) In such a system, deportation will occur if either branch says no—the private bill will fail. (In effect, each branch will be able to veto a permanent suspension of deportation.) But if both branches say yes, then presumably the President will sign into law the private waiver bill that his own AG has proposed, and the deportation will be permanently suspended. For a clever discussion of how such "fast-track" legislation can accomplish virtually everything that the legislative veto tried to accomplish, but without violating any constitutional rule, see the Thomas F. Ryan Lecture delivered by then-Judge (now Justice) Stephen G. Breyer, The Legislative Veto After *Chadha*, 72 Geo. L.J. 785 (1984).

Consider also Louis Fisher's statement that "[n]otwithstanding the mandate in *Chadha*, Congress continued to add legislative vetoes to bills"—he says that there have been more than 200 such bills—"and Presidents Reagan and Bush [and, presumably, Clinton] continued to sign them into law," even though the accompanying signing statements included such language, as in one by President Bush, that the provisions "constitute legislative vetoes similar to those declared unconstitutional by the Supreme Court in INS v. Chadha. Accordingly, I will treat them as having no legal force or effect in this or any other legislation in which they appear." Fisher comments, though, that "[a]lthough the President may treat committee vetoes as having no legal force or effect, agencies have a different attitude" inasmuch as "[t]hey have to live with their review committees, year after year, and have a much greater incentive to make accommodations and stick by them." See Louis Fisher, The Legislative Veto: Invalidated, It Survives, 56 Law & Contemp. Probs. 273, 288 (1993).

It may also be the case, in the language of economics, that the legislative veto is an easily substitutable political commodity. Consider the following analysis:[63]

> Also surviving *Chadha* are other mechanisms for legislative influence over agency actions: (a) hearings and informal pressure by congressional oversight committees, as well as publicity generated by legislator criticisms; (b) refusal by Congress to appropriate monies to wayward agencies, or to appropriate funds subject to substantive conditions (e.g., that the money will not be spent to carry out specified rules or policies); and (c) informal pressure by appropriations subcommittees and language in their committee reports earmarking funds for certain projects or policies and not for others.

---

63. Daniel A. Farber, William N. Eskridge, Jr., and Philip P. Frickey, Constitutional Law: Themes for the Constitution's Third Century 974 (2d ed. 1998).

See also Jessica Korn, The Power of Separation: American Constitutionalism and the Myth of the Legislative Veto (1996), which argues that these mechanisms are in fact more effective than the legislative veto in molding agency action to accord with congressional desires. Thus, Korn says, "the legislative veto shortcut was inconsequential to congressional control of the policymaking process because of the extensive set of powers in the Constitution already available to members of Congress" (p. 13). And, as Professor Tribe notes, "even a sweeping interpretation [of *Chadha*] contains nothing that would prevent Congress from enacting 'report and wait' provisions . . . mandating that rule changes proposed pursuant to delegated authority shall not take effect as law until after the legislative session in which they have been reported to Congress by the Attorney General." Such provisions give Congress "an orderly opportunity to pass regular, otherwise valid legislation [presented to the President] denying legal effect to exercises of delegated authority with which it disagrees." Laurence H. Tribe, 1 American Constitutional Law 150-151 (3d ed. 2000).

6. *White's dissent.* The easy availability of the fast-track option tends to undercut one of White's arguments in dissent, namely, that the legislative veto is an indispensable tool in the modern world. It remains to consider three other arguments he advances. First, he stresses that the law creating the legislative veto in the first place itself satisfied bicameralism and presentment. Should that be enough to sustain the legislative veto? What if the initial law said, "everything that FDR henceforth decrees shall be law, with the same force as if it had been decreed by Congress"? What if the law gave this decree power not to FDR, but to Bill Gates, or to the Speaker of the House, or to the 435 members of Congress acting without the President? White's second argument is that if Congress can lawfully delegate its legislative power, it should be allowed to condition that delegation; and that if Congress can properly delegate broad power to the executive branch, it should likewise be allowed to delegate such broad power to itself. Does discussion note 4 satisfactorily answer this argument? If not, does the Court have a better answer? White's third argument is that the statute really does respect bicameralism and presentment if we see the baseline as Chadha-out rather than Chadha-in. If the legal status quo is that Chadha is "out" and must be deported, then this baseline is altered only when both houses (by not vetoing) and the executive (by proposing suspension via the AG) agree that he should be allowed to stay "in." It is a clever argument, but would it persuade a strict adherent to constitutional form? Note that in cases of 50-50 ties, the results are not identical; and in White's world, the executive's "signature" comes before Congress has acted and through the hand of the AG, rather than at the end and through the hand of the President, per Article I, §7. But doesn't this argument bear on severability? Isn't the statute best construed as establishing a baseline of Chadha-out rather than Chadha-in? If so, and if the legislative veto is technically and formally unconstitutional, why isn't the proper judicial response to strike down *both* the AG's suspension power and the legislative veto condition on that power, thus returning us to a Chadha-out baseline? As Justice Rehnquist argues, weren't the two provisions—suspension power and legislative veto of that power—inextricably intertwined, with the second as an indispensable condition of the first?

7. *Severability.* The Court majority argues otherwise, but its reasoning seems suspect. First, it points to a general severability clause and says that Congress "could

not have more plainly authorized" severability. But the severability clause was not specific to §244; it was a boilerplate general clause inserted in the context of a very large statute with many sections, and the Court points to no evidence whatsoever that the clause was drafted with the legislative veto provision in mind in particular. Put another way, the severability clause cannot tell us which words, phrases, and sentences should be understood as a single provision, such that if part of the provision falls, the rest should as well since the parts were designed as mutual conditions. There is strong reason to doubt that Congress intended to give the executive total control to suspend; and if the suspension clause is struck down along with the offending legislative veto, we are back to the basic "Chadha-out" baseline created by the statute; and Breyeresque fast-track schemes can easily solve the legislative time-consumption problem that had bedeviled the earlier private bill system.

So far the argument has been couched in terms of the intent of the original legislature—striking down both suspension and veto reaches, a result much closer to what the statute did than striking down the legislative veto alone. But given that what the real-life legislators actually wanted to do was unconstitutional—as the Court holds—one might wonder whether the only question is what these people actually would have wanted or did intend. A different approach, less backward-looking, would ask whether the constitutional principles that justify invalidating the legislative veto in the first place bear on the severability question. Cf. Evan H. Caminker, Note, A Norm-Based Remedial Model for Underinclusive Statutes, 95 Yale L.J. 1185 (1986). Are the constitutional values that condemn legislative vetoes indifferent on the severability question? Not really. If the best structural argument for *Chadha*'s result is the structural vision set out supra discussion note 4, then this vision encourages Congress to be as specific as possible, and indeed tries to give Congress incentives to avoid broad delegation by warning Congress *in advance* that it may not delegate to itself. Arguably, the majority undercuts all this when it rewrites the law to give the executive branch unfettered discretion to suspend—discretion that Congress never knowingly gave up.

A final approach to severability would understand that, whichever way the Court decides the severability question, that decision might be mistaken, and the political branches should be allowed to "contract around" it, à la Coase. If the Court strikes down both executive suspension and legislative veto, Congress would be free to give the executive suspension power free of strings—and with its eyes open about what it is giving up. Congress would also be free to pass a fast-track private bill allowing Chadha in. But once the Court severs the legislative veto while preserving executive suspension power, the game-theoretic dynamic is different. First, if the baseline is Chadha-in, it is far from clear that the political branches may agree to send him out—such a private bill penalizing Jagdish Chadha by name would raise serious attainder issues. And if Congress is more concerned about the more general problem of executive suspension power without strings or guidelines, any effort to add such guidelines or to remove this power will likely be vetoed by the President himself, as a diminution of his existing and unfettered power (courtesy of the Court's rewrite of the original statute). Thus, the "transactions costs" of "contracting around" a mistaken Court-defined baseline are not symmetric; in the event of any doubt at all about severability, perhaps the issue should be resolved in a way that is easier to correct. This approach, too, argues against the Court's decision to expand executive suspension power while trimming away the legislative veto.

The Court seemed to think that if the legislative veto provision were not severable, Chadha would lack standing. This is doubtful. Severability is better understood as a remedial question arising *after* a person with standing has proved unconstitutionality. If the statute is not severable, this might mean simply that Chadha *loses* the relief he seeks—just as a person bringing an action for damages against a police officer might succeed in proving that the officer acted unlawfully, but lose in the end because the officer's actions were nevertheless performed in good faith, such that no damages lie as a matter of remedy law. It would not, however, mean that Chadha was the wrong person to bring the suit, or that somehow his rights were not at stake in the litigation. Nor is it likely that the Court's severability ruling was necessary to avoid unfairness to Jagdish Chadha, the man. As the Court noted in a passage not included in the preceding case excerpt, Chadha was eligible to stay in America on grounds other than the AG's actions under §244.

8. *The War Powers Act.* Although the severability issue might seem a minor wrinkle in *Chadha,* in some contexts it is anything but. For example, the War Powers Act of 1973, discussed in more detail infra, authorizes the President to engage in certain military actions, and then conditions this authorization upon a legislative veto. If this statute is now unconstitutional under *Chadha,* it may be quite important whether the specific legislative grant of power survives, as severable from the conditions on that power embodied in the legislative veto provision.

9. *From the legislative veto to the line item veto.* Fulfilling a promise made as part of the "Contract with America" that helped sweep the Republican Party into the leadership of the House of Representatives in 1994 for the first time in a half-century, Congress enacted—and the President signed into law—the Line Item Veto Act of 1996 (LIVA), regulating the budget process. The Act had many intricacies; for simplicity, imagine a budget consisting of three separate appropriations. Line 1 says that X shall be spent on guns; line 2 that Y shall be spent on butter; and line 3 that Z shall be spent on pork. LIVA sought to regulate the budget process as follows: After the President signs this budget bill into law, he has five days to trim spending. If he decides that any single line of the budget is wasteful, he can in effect cancel the line and spend zero instead of X, Y, or Z. If Congress disagrees, it can then pass a "disapproval bill," which in turn must be presented to the President. If such a disapproval bill becomes law, with the President's signature or over his veto, the President must spend the amount specified in the bill and his earlier cancellation in effect becomes null and void.

In Clinton v. City of New York, 524 U.S. 417 (1998), the Court, by a 6-3 vote, struck LIVA down. The majority opinion, per Justice Stevens, argued that LIVA was unconstitutional because the President was in effect vetoing individual lines in a bill rather than the bill as a whole, because he was in effect repealing a duly enacted law without securing a new law supported by majorities in both houses, and because he was in effect rewriting the law rather than enforcing it. If any of these characterizations were in fact true, LIVA must indeed fall, so long as *Chadha* stands. (Can you see why?) But the *Clinton* dissenters—Justices Breyer and Scalia joined by Justice O'Connor—argued with great force and verve that the majority's characterizations precisely missed the point. They claimed that despite the rather outlandish label of "line item veto"—a label that, they suggested, simply confused analysis and befuddled the Court majority—LIVA was in fact quite traditional and constitutionally benign. Suppose, they argued, that the law explicitly said the following: "The President may choose to spend X or nothing on guns, Y or nothing on butter, and Z or nothing on pork. And he must make his decisions within five days of signing the budget." Here it is plain that the President, in trimming spending, is not vetoing a line but rather exercising the discretion given him by the statute as a whole. He is not repealing the budget unilaterally but implementing the blueprint drafted by Congress. He is not rewriting the law but faithfully executing it according to its literal terms. LIVA used different words, but meant the same thing, as this hypothetical statute, which seemed clearly constitutional to the dissenters.

The dissenters admitted that their hypothetical law vested the President with considerable discretion—but, they pointed out, no more than countless statutes enacted ever since the First Congress. Many spending laws over the last two centuries have told the President that he could spend up to X on a given project. LIVA in fact was far stricter than these traditional spending bills: It said the President who wants to spend nothing rather than X, Y, or Z must decide quickly and must report his reasons. This clean and open decision made the President visibly accountable to the American electorate.

In addition to this analysis, we might add the following important points: If Congress for any reason decided that LIVA gave up too much, Congress was free to undo the damage any time it liked simply by proposing a budget that includes the words "LIVA shall not apply to this bill [or to parts A, B, and C thereof]." If Congress were to pass a law that said the President could spend whatever he wants, with no maximum, *then* we might well have a problem—quite literally a blank check that Congress could not easily retract. (Every time it tried, the President would veto, and Congress would need two-thirds in each house to override.) But the prospect that the President might spend less than the Congress has authorized does not raise symmetric dangers of a monarch run amok: Like kings of old, the President will eventually have to return to the legislature for more money to run his government, and when he does legislators can make him dance their tune (or at least compromise).

In *Clinton*'s aftermath, lawmakers who seek to reinstate LIVA's effects have two main options. First, they can explicitly write budget laws along the lines of the dissenters' hypothetical statute. Second, they can enact each budget line as a separate bill. Given that budgets now contain thousands of lines, this approach would need to be implemented by internal House rules under Article I, §5, allowing a legislator to push a button once on a megabudget and have that vote electronically counted as a vote for each line as its own bill (unless the legislator specifies otherwise). Can you see the analogy between this push-button rule and the fast-track device described by then-Judge Breyer as a proper response to *Chadha*?

In rejecting LIVA, the *Clinton* Court seemed to catch the whiff of an Imperial Presidency in the air, but might we also catch of a trace of congressional imperialism? According to the statute, the President was allowed to trim lines only if he signed the budget into law. If, however, he vetoed the budget and it became law via congressional override, he apparently lost his trimming power. Thus, perhaps the real problem with LIVA was that Congress was in effect bribing the President into surrendering his veto pen. In the budgetary context, the bribe made a difference because not all lines were subject to cancellation under LIVA's technical rules; and so a President could not simply sign a budget bill he actually opposed and then undo all the damage five days later. More generally, if Congress can sneak this little kicker into all other laws—formally vesting the President with extra power only if he abdicates the veto—then the careful constitutional balance between the two branches may be slyly undone.

The obvious counterargument is that legislators play tit for tat all the time. If the President vetoes bill A, Congress will refuse to pass bill B. But to a constitutional formalist—and the majority in *City of New York* was nothing if not formalist—there is a world of difference between informal political understandings and formal legal commands. Formally, shouldn't any given law mean the same thing whether or not it contains the President's signature? Similarly, a law should formally mean the same thing whether Senator X voted for it or against it. Clever pork-packers should not be allowed to draft a budget bill that explicitly authorizes federal money for a given state if and only if the senators from that state vote for the bill. Such a bill could create a situation where all senators are in effect bribed and coerced into voting yes—lest their state lose out on its fair share of the pork—even though virtually everyone thinks the overall bill is bad. By now, readers of this casebook should recognize this as a classic "prisoner's dilemma"—individual senators acting rationally end up with a collectively irrational result. One of the main advantages of the presidential veto is that it can be used by a truly national representative—the President—to protect the whole against the parts. And so we should not lightly allow Congress to undercut the veto formally. If, indeed, this was the true danger lurking in LIVA, no one on the Court noticed. For a thoughtful discussion, see Michael B. Rappaport, Veto Burdens and the Line Item Veto Act, 91 Nw. U. L. Rev. 771 (1997).

D. *The Power of the Sword*

1. Emergency Power During Wartime

Fewer than five years after the cessation of World War II, the United States became involved in the conflict between South Korea (supported by the United Nations) and North Korea. Following President Truman's decision to cross the 38th parallel and move toward the northern border of North Korea, the People's Republic of China entered the fray. (The war thereafter bogged down, and finally ended in 1953 with an armistice that maintained the division of Korea into two countries, one allied with the West, the other with the Communist bloc.) In April 1952, following months of efforts at mediation between the United Steelworkers of America and the management of the country's major steel producers, the union announced its intention to begin a nationwide strike on April 9.

The Taft-Hartley Act, passed in 1947, allowed the President to seek (through a court order) an 80-day "cooling off" period to temporarily stop or prevent a strike that would "imperil or threaten to imperil the national health or safety." Instead of invoking Taft-Hartley, however, President Truman ordered the Secretary of the Treasury, John Sawyer, to seize the steel mills and to operate them in the name of the United States. He claimed that uninterrupted production of steel was vital to the successful prosecution of the Korean War. Truman notified Congress of his action; Congress took no action. The affected companies immediately filed suit claiming that the seizure violated the Constitution. The executive order that they challenged read as follows:

Executive Order

Directing the Secretary of Commerce to Take Possession of and Operate the Plants and Facilities of Certain Steel Companies

WHEREAS on December 16, 1950, I proclaimed the existence of a national emergency which requires that the military, naval, air, and civilian defenses of this country be strengthened as speedily as possible to the end that we may be able to repel any and all threats against our national security and to fulfill our responsibilities in the efforts being made throughout the United Nations and otherwise to bring about a lasting peace; and

WHEREAS American fighting men and fighting men of other nations of the United Nations are now engaged in deadly combat with the forces of aggression in Korea, and forces of the United States are stationed elsewhere overseas for the purpose of participating in the defense of the Atlantic Community against aggression; and

WHEREAS the weapons and other materials needed by our armed forces and by those joined with us in the defense of the free world are produced to a great extent in this country, and steel is an indispensable component of substantially all of such weapons and materials; and

WHEREAS steel is likewise indispensable to the carrying out of programs of the Atomic Energy Commission of vital importance to our defense efforts; and

WHEREAS a continuing and uninterrupted supply of steel is also indispensable to the maintenance of the economy of the United States, upon which our military strength depends; and

WHEREAS a controversy has arisen between certain companies in the United States producing and fabricating steel and the elements thereof and certain of their workers represented by the United Steel Workers of America, CIO, regarding terms and conditions of employment; and

WHEREAS the controversy has not been settled through the processes of collective bargaining or through the efforts of the Government, including those of the Wage Stabilization Board, to which the controversy was referred on December 22, 1951, pursuant to Executive Order No. 10233, and a strike has been called for 12:01 A.M., April 9, 1952; and

WHEREAS a work stoppage would immediately jeopardize and imperil our national defense and the defense of those joined with us in resisting aggression, and would add to the continuing danger of our soldiers, sailors, and airmen engaged in combat in the field; and

WHEREAS in order to assure the continued availability of steel and steel products during the existing emergency, it is necessary that the United States take possession of and operate the plants, facilities, and other property of the said companies as hereinafter provided:

NOW, THEREFORE, by virtue of the authority vested in me by the Constitution and laws of the United States, and as President of the United States and Commander in Chief of the armed forces of the United States, it is hereby ordered as follows:

1. The Secretary of Commerce is hereby authorized and directed to take possession of all or such of the plants, facilities, and other property of the companies named in the list attached hereto, or any part thereof, as he may deem necessary in the interests of national defense; and to operate or

to arrange for the operation thereof and to do all things necessary for, or incidental to, such operation.

2. In carrying out this order the Secretary of Commerce may act through or with the aid of such public or private instrumentalities or persons as he may designate; and all Federal agencies shall cooperate with the Secretary of Commerce to the fullest extent possible in carrying out the purposes of this order.
3. The Secretary of Commerce shall determine and prescribe terms and conditions of employment under which the plants, facilities, and other properties possession of which is taken pursuant to this order shall be operated. The Secretary of Commerce shall recognize the rights of workers to bargain collectively through representatives of their own choosing and to engage in concerted activities for the purpose of collective bargaining, adjustment of grievances, or other mutual aid or protection, provided that such activities do not interfere with the operation of such plants, facilities, and other properties.
4. Except so far as the Secretary of Commerce shall otherwise provide from time to time, the managements of the plants, facilities, and other properties possession of which is taken pursuant to this order shall continue their functions, including the collection and disbursement of funds in the usual and ordinary course of business in the names of their respective companies and by means of any instrumentalities used by such companies.
5. Except so far as the Secretary of Commerce may otherwise direct, existing rights and obligations of such companies shall remain in full force and effect, and there may be made, in due course, payments of dividends on stock, and of principal, interest, sinking funds, and all other distributions upon bonds, debentures, and other obligations, and expenditures may be made for other ordinary corporate or business purposes.
6. Whenever in the judgment of the Secretary of Commerce further possession and operation by him of any plant, facility, or other property is no longer necessary or expedient in the interest of national defense, and the Secretary has reason to believe that effective future operation is assured, he shall return the possession and operation of such plant, facility, or other property to the company in possession and control thereof at the time possession was taken under this order.
7. The Secretary of Commerce is authorized to prescribe and issue such regulations and orders not inconsistent herewith as he may deem necessary or desirable for carrying out the purposes of this order; and he may delegate and authorize subdelegation of such of his functions under this order as he may deem desirable.

Harry S. Truman. The White House, April 8, 1952.

At the trial before the District Court, Assistant Attorney General Baldridge, representing the United States, made the following claims about the power of the President:[64]

---

64. For a historical overview of the case, see Maeva Marcus, Truman and the Steel Seizure Case: The Limits of Presidential Power (1994).

The Court: So you contend the Executive has unlimited power in time of an emergency?

Mr. Baldridge: He has the power to take such action as is necessary to meet the emergency.

The Court: If the emergency is great, it is unlimited, is it?

Mr. Baldridge: I suppose if you carry it to its logical conclusion, that is true. But I do want to point out that there are two limitations on the Executive power. One is the ballot box and the other is impeachment. . . .

The Court: Let me put a case to you. . . . Supposing the President should declare that the public interest required the seizure of your home and directed an agent to seize it and to dispossess you: Do you think or do you contend that the court could not restrain that act because the President had declared an emergency and because he had directed an agent to carry out his will?

Mr. Baldridge: I would rather, Your Honor, not answer a case in that extremity. We are dealing here with a situation involving a grave national emergency . . . that requires the exercise of rather unusual powers in these particular circumstances. I do not believe any President would exercise such unusual power unless, in his opinion, there was a grave and an extreme national emergency existing. . . .

The Court: [I]s it not . . . your view that the powers of the Government are limited by and enumerated in the Constitution of the United States?

Mr. Baldridge: That is true, Your Honor, with respect to legislative powers.

The Court: But it is not true, you say, as to the Executive?

Mr. Baldridge: No. Section 1, of Article II of the Constitution . . . reposes all of the executive power in the Chief Executive. . . . In so far as the Executive is concerned, all executive power is vested in the President. In so far as legislative powers are concerned, the Congress has only those powers that are specifically delegated to it, plus the implied power to carry out the powers specifically enumerated.

The Court: So, when the sovereign people adopted the Constitution, it enumerated the powers set up in the Constitution but limited the powers of the Congress and limited the powers of the judiciary, but it did not limit the powers of the Executive. Is that what you say?

Mr. Baldridge: That is the way we read Article II of the Constitution. . . . It is our position that the President is accountable only to the country, and that the decisions of the President are conclusive. . . . [H]aving a broad grant of power[,] the executive, particularly in times of national emergency, can meet whatever situation endangers the national safety of the country. . . . I want to say that we had an emergency situation here. Somebody had to deal with it. The legislative

> [route, i.e., asking Congress for specific authority to seize the mills] was too slow. As of April 8th, midnight, the Taft-Hartley [route] was too slow. In either event, there would have been an indefinite stoppage of steel production. Are we to say, then, that there is no power in Government any place to meet as serious a situation as this, when it confronts the security of this nation? . . . I just say that as of midnight on April 8th this seizure procedure appeared to be the only effective way to avoid a strike and to avoid a cessation for an indefinite period of production of steel necessary to national security and national defense.

District Judge Pine ("the Court" in this colloquy) enjoined the seizure. The Court of Appeals for the District of Columbia stayed the order, and the Supreme Court immediately granted certiorari. Justice Black wrote for five Justices (two of whom had been appointed by President Truman) affirming issuance of the injunction; a sixth Justice (Clark) concurred in the judgment but did not join Black's opinion for the Court. Each of the Justices who did join Black's opinion also wrote separately. Chief Justice Vinson dissented, joined by Justices Reed and Minton.

Youngstown Sheet & Tube Co. v. Sawyer

343 U.S. 579 (1952)

Mr. Justice Black delivered the opinion of the Court. . . .

In the latter part of 1951, a dispute arose between the steel companies and their employees over terms and conditions that should be included in new collective bargaining agreements. Long-continued conferences failed to resolve the dispute. On December 18, 1951, the employees' representative, United Steelworkers of America, C.I.O., gave notice of an intention to strike when the existing bargaining agreements expired on December 31. The Federal Mediation and Conciliation Service then intervened in an effort to get labor and management to agree. This failing, the President on December 22, 1951, referred the dispute to the Federal Wage Stabilization Board to investigate and make recommendations for fair and equitable terms of settlement. The Board's report resulted in no settlement. On April 4, 1952, the Union gave notice of a nation-wide strike called to begin at 12:01 A.M. April 9. The indispensability of steel as a component of substantially all weapons and other war materials led the President to believe that the proposed work stoppage would immediately jeopardize our national defense and that governmental seizure of the steel mills was necessary in order to assure the continued availability of steel. Reciting these considerations for this action, the President, a few hours before the strike was to begin, issued Executive Order 10340. . . .

II

The President's power, if any, to issue the order must stem either from an act of Congress or from the Constitution itself. There is no statute that expressly authorizes the President to take possession of property as he did here. Nor is there any act of Congress to which our attention has been directed from which such a power can fairly be implied. Indeed, we do not understand the Government to rely on statutory authorization for this seizure. . . .

Moreover, the use of the seizure technique to solve labor disputes in order to prevent work stoppages was not only unauthorized by any congressional enactment; prior to this controversy, Congress had refused to adopt that method of settling labor disputes [in the Taft-Hartley Act of 1947, because] it was thought that the technique of seizure, like that of compulsory arbitration, would interfere with the process of collective bargaining. Consequently, the plan Congress adopted in that Act did not provide for seizure under any circumstances. Instead, the plan sought to bring about settlements by use of the customary devices of mediation, conciliation, investigation by boards of inquiry, and public reports. In some instances temporary injunctions were authorized to provide cooling-off periods. All this failing, unions were left free to strike after a secret vote by employees as to whether they wished to accept their employers' final settlement offer.

It is clear that if the President had authority to issue the order he did, it must be found in some provision of the Constitution. And it is not claimed that express constitutional language grants this power to the President. The contention is that presidential power should be implied from the aggregate of his powers under the Constitution. Particular reliance is placed on provisions in Article II which say that "The executive Power shall be vested in a President . . ."; that "he shall take Care that the Laws be faithfully executed"; and that he "shall be Commander in Chief of the Army and Navy of the United States."

The order cannot properly be sustained as an exercise of the President's military power as Commander in Chief of the Armed Forces. The Government attempts to do so by citing a number of cases upholding broad powers in military commanders engaged in day-to-day fighting in a theater of war. Such cases need not concern us here. Even though "theater of war" be an expanding concept, we cannot with faithfulness to our constitutional system hold that the Commander in Chief of the Armed Forces has the ultimate power as such to take possession of private property in order to keep labor disputes from stopping production. This is a job for the Nation's lawmakers, not for its military authorities.

Nor can the seizure order be sustained because of the several constitutional provisions that grant executive power to the President. In the framework of our Constitution, the President's power to see that the laws are faithfully executed refutes the idea that he is to be a lawmaker. The Constitution limits his functions in the lawmaking process to the recommending of laws he thinks wise and the vetoing of laws he thinks bad. And the Constitution is neither silent nor equivocal about who shall make laws which the President is to execute. The first section of the first article says that "All legislative Powers herein granted shall be vested in a Congress of the United States. . . ."

The President's order does not direct that a congressional policy be executed in a manner prescribed by Congress—it directs that a presidential policy be executed in a manner prescribed by the President. The preamble of the order itself, like that of many statutes, sets out reasons why the President believes certain policies should be adopted, proclaims these policies as rules of conduct to be followed, and again, like a statute, authorizes a government official to promulgate additional rules and regulations consistent with the policy proclaimed and needed to carry that policy into execution. The power of Congress to adopt such public policies as those proclaimed by the order is beyond question. It can authorize the taking of private property for public use. It can make laws regulating the relationships between employers and employees, prescribing rules designed to settle labor disputes, and fixing wages and working conditions in certain fields of our economy. The Constitution does not subject this lawmaking power of Congress to presidential or military supervision or control.

It is said that other Presidents without congressional authority have taken possession of private business enterprises in order to settle labor disputes. But even if this be true, Congress has not thereby lost its exclusive constitutional authority to make laws necessary and proper to carry out the powers vested by the Constitution "in the Government of the United States, or any Department or Officer thereof."

The Founders of this Nation entrusted the lawmaking power to the Congress alone in both good and bad times. It would do no good to recall the historical events, the fears of power and the hopes for freedom that lay behind their choice. Such a review would but confirm our holding that this seizure order cannot stand. . . .

Mr. Justice FRANKFURTER, concurring.[a]

[W]ith the utmost unwillingness, with every desire to avoid judicial inquiry into the powers and duties of the other two branches of the government, I cannot escape consideration of the legality of Executive Order No. 10340.

. . . It is . . . incumbent upon this Court to avoid putting fetters upon the future by needless pronouncements today. . . .

The issue before us can be met, and therefore should be, without attempting to define the President's powers comprehensively. . . .

. . . We must therefore put to one side consideration of what powers the President would have had if there had been no legislation whatever bearing on the authority asserted by the seizure, or if the seizure had been only for a short, explicitly temporary period, to be terminated automatically unless Congressional approval were given. These and other questions, like or unlike, are not now here. I would exceed my authority were I to say anything about them. . . .

In adopting the provisions which it did, by the Labor Management Relations [Taft-Hartley] Act of 1947, for dealing with a "national emergency" arising out of a breakdown in peaceful industrial relations, Congress was very familiar with Governmental seizure as a protective measure. On a balance of considerations, Congress chose not to lodge this power in the President. It chose not to make available in advance a remedy to which both industry and labor were fiercely hostile. . . .

In any event, nothing can be plainer than that Congress made a conscious choice of policy in a field full of perplexity and peculiarly within legislative responsibility for choice. In formulating legislation for dealing with industrial conflicts,

---

a. In an oddly located paragraph following Justice Black's opinion of the Court, and separate from his own formal concurrence, Justice Frankfurter also offered the following words:

> Although the considerations relevant to the legal enforcement of the principle of separation of powers seem to me more complicated and flexible than may appear from what Mr. Justice Black has written, I join his opinion because I thoroughly agree with the application of the principle to the circumstances of this case. Even though such differences in attitude toward this principle may be merely differences in emphasis and nuance, they can hardly be reflected by a single opinion for the Court. Individual expression of views in reaching a common result is therefore important.

Congress could not more clearly and emphatically have withheld authority than it did in 1947. . . .

It cannot be contended that the President would have had power to issue this order had Congress explicitly negated such authority in formal legislation. Congress has expressed its will to withhold this power from the President as though it had said so in so many words. . . . It would be not merely infelicitous draftsmanship but almost offensive gaucherie to write such a restriction upon the President's power in terms into a statute rather than to have it authoritatively expounded, as it was, by controlling legislative history.

By the Labor Management Relations Act of 1947, Congress said to the President, "You may not seize. Please report to us and ask for seizure power if you think it is needed in a specific situation."

. . . Absence of authority in the President to deal with a crisis does not imply want of power in the Government. Conversely the fact that power exists in the Government does not vest it in the President. The need for new legislation does not enact it. Nor does it repeal or amend existing law. . . .

To be sure, the content of the three authorities of government is not to be derived from an abstract analysis. The areas are partly interacting, not wholly disjointed. The Constitution is a framework for government. Therefore the way the framework has consistently operated fairly establishes that it has operated according to its true nature. Deeply embedded traditional ways of conducting government cannot supplant the Constitution or legislation, but they give meaning to the words of a text or supply them. It is an inadmissibly narrow conception of American constitutional law to confine it to the words of the Constitution and to disregard the gloss which life has written upon them. In short, a systematic, unbroken, executive practice, long pursued to the knowledge of the Congress and never before questioned, engaged in by Presidents who have also sworn to uphold the Constitution, making as it were such exercise of power part of the structure of our government, may be treated as a gloss on "executive Power" vested in the President by §1 of Art. II. . . .

. . . No [firmly established] practice can be vouched for executive seizure of property at a time when this country was not at war, in the only constitutional way in which it can be at war. It would pursue the irrelevant to reopen the controversy over the constitutionality of some acts of Lincoln during the Civil War. Suffice it to say that he seized railroads in territory where armed hostilities had already interrupted the movement of troops to the beleaguered Capital, and his order was ratified by the Congress. . . .

Down to the World War II period, then, the record is barren of instances comparable to the one before us. Of twelve seizures by President Roosevelt prior to the enactment of the War Labor Disputes Act in June, 1943, three were sanctioned by existing law, and six others were effected after Congress, on December 8, 1941, had declared the existence of a state of war. In this case, reliance on the powers that flow from declared war has been commendably disclaimed by the Solicitor General. . . .

Mr. Justice Douglas, concurring.

There can be no doubt that the emergency which caused the President to seize these steel plants was one that bore heavily on the country. But the emergency did not create power; it merely marked an occasion when power should be exercised. And the fact that it was necessary that measures be taken to keep steel in production does not mean that the President, rather than the Congress, had the constitutional authority to act. The Congress, as well as the President, is trustee of the national welfare. The President can act more quickly than the Congress. The President with the armed services at his disposal can move with force as well as with speed. All executive power—from the reign of ancient kings to the rule of modern dictators—has the outward appearance of efficiency.

Legislative power, by contrast, is slower to exercise. There must be delay while the ponderous machinery of committees, hearings, and debates is put into motion. That takes time; and while the Congress slowly moves into action, the emergency may take its toll in wages, consumer goods, war production, the standard of living of the people, and perhaps even lives. Legislative action may indeed often be cumbersome, time-consuming, and apparently inefficient. But as Mr. Justice Brandeis stated in his dissent in Myers v. United States:

> "The doctrine of the separation of powers was adopted by the Convention of 1787, not to promote efficiency but to preclude the exercise of arbitrary power. The purpose was, not to avoid friction, but, by means of the inevitable friction incident to the distribution of the governmental powers among three departments, to save the people from autocracy."

. . . A determination that sanctions should be applied, that the hand of the law should be placed upon the parties, and that the force of the courts should be directed against them, is an exercise of legislative power. In some nations that power is entrusted to the executive branch as a matter of course or in case of emergencies. We chose another course. We chose to place the legislative power of the Federal Government in the Congress. The language of the Constitution is not ambiguous or qualified. It places not some legislative power in the Congress; Article I, Section 1 says "All legislative Powers herein granted shall be vested in a Congress of the United States, which shall consist of a Senate and House of Representatives."

The legislative nature of the action taken by the President seems to me to be clear. . . . The command of the Fifth Amendment is that no "private property be taken for public use, without just compensation." That constitutional requirement has an important bearing on the present case.

The President has no power to raise revenues. That power is in the Congress by Article I, Section 8 of the Constitution. The President might seize and the Congress by subsequent action might ratify the seizure. But until and unless Congress acted, no condemnation would be lawful. The branch of government that has the power to pay compensation for a seizure is the only one able to authorize a seizure or make lawful one that the President has effected. That seems to me to be the necessary result of the condemnation provision in the Fifth Amendment. It squares with the theory of checks and balances expounded by Mr. Justice Black in the opinion of the Court in which I join.

If we sanctioned the present exercise of power by the President, we would be expanding Article II of the Constitution and rewriting it to suit the political conveniences of the present emergency. Article II which vests the "executive Power" in the President defines that power with particularity. Article II, Section 2 makes the Chief Executive the Commander in Chief of the Army and Navy. But our history and tradition rebel at the thought that the grant of military power carries with it authority over civilian affairs. Article II, Section 3 provides that the President shall "from time to time give to the Congress Information of the State of the Union, and recommend to their Consideration such Measures as he shall judge necessary and expedient." The power to recommend legislation, granted to the President, serves only to emphasize that it is his function to recommend and that it is the function of the Congress to legislate. Article II, Section 3 also provides that the President "shall take Care that the Laws be faithfully executed." But . . . the power to execute the laws starts and ends with the laws Congress has enacted.

The great office of President is not a weak and powerless one. The President represents the people and is their spokesman in domestic and foreign affairs. The office is respected more than any other in the land. It gives a position of leadership that is unique. . . .

Mr. Justice JACKSON, concurring in the judgment and opinion of the Court.

That comprehensive and undefined presidential powers hold both practical advantages and grave dangers for the country will impress anyone who has served as legal adviser to a President in time of transition and public anxiety. [Justice Jackson had, before being named to the Supreme Court, served as Solicitor General and Attorney General under President Roosevelt.] While an interval of detached reflection may temper teachings of that experience, they probably are a more realistic influence on my views than the conventional materials of judicial decision which seem unduly to accentuate doctrine and legal fiction. . . .

A judge, like an executive adviser, may be surprised at the poverty of really useful and unambiguous authority applicable to concrete problems of executive power as they actually present themselves. Just what our forefathers did envision, or would have envisioned had they foreseen modern conditions, must be divined from materials almost as enigmatic as the dreams Joseph was called upon to interpret for Pharaoh. A century and a half of partisan debate and scholarly speculation yields no net result but only supplies more or less apt quotations from respected sources on each side of any question. . . . And court decisions are indecisive because of the judicial practice of dealing with the largest questions in the most narrow way.

The actual art of governing under our Constitution does not and cannot conform to judicial definitions of the power of any of its branches based on isolated clauses or even single Articles torn from context. While the Constitution diffuses power the better to secure liberty, it also contemplates that practice will integrate the dispersed powers into a workable government. It enjoins upon its branches separateness but interdependence, autonomy but reciprocity. Presidential powers are not fixed but fluctuate, depending upon their disjunction or conjunction with those of Congress. We may well begin by a somewhat over-simplified grouping of practical situations in which a President may doubt, or others may challenge, his powers, and by distinguishing roughly the legal consequences of this factor of relativity.

1. When the President acts pursuant to an express or implied authorization of Congress, his authority is at its maximum, for it includes all that he possesses in his own right plus all that Congress can delegate. In these circumstances, and in these only, may he be said (for what it may be worth) to personify the federal sovereignty. If his act is held unconstitutional

under these circumstances, it usually means that the Federal Government as an undivided whole lacks power. A seizure executed by the President pursuant to an Act of Congress would be supported by the strongest of presumptions and the widest latitude of judicial interpretation, and the burden of persuasion would rest heavily upon any who might attack it.

2. When the President acts in absence of either a congressional grant or denial of authority, he can only rely upon his own independent powers, but there is a zone of twilight in which he and Congress may have concurrent authority, or in which its distribution is uncertain. Therefore, congressional inertia, indifference or quiescence may sometimes, at least as a practical matter, enable, if not invite, measures on independent presidential responsibility. In this area, any actual test of power is likely to depend on the imperatives of events and contemporary imponderables rather than on abstract theories of law.
3. When the President takes measures incompatible with the expressed or implied will of Congress, his power is at its lowest ebb, for then he can rely only upon his own constitutional powers minus any constitutional powers of Congress over the matter. Courts can sustain exclusive presidential control in such a case only by disabling the Congress from acting upon the subject. Presidential claim to a power at once so conclusive and preclusive must be scrutinized with caution, for what is at stake is the equilibrium established by our constitutional system.

Into which of these classifications does this executive seizure of the steel industry fit? It is eliminated from the first by admission, for it is conceded that no congressional authorization exists for this seizure. That takes away also the support of the many precedents and declarations which were made in relation, and must be confined, to this category.

Can it then be defended under flexible tests available to the second category? It seems clearly eliminated from that class because Congress has not left seizure of private property an open field but has covered it by three statutory policies inconsistent with this seizure[, including the provisions of the Taft-Hartley Act]. None of these were invoked. In choosing a different and inconsistent way of his own, the President cannot claim that it is necessitated or invited by failure of Congress to legislate upon the occasions, grounds and methods for seizure of industrial properties.

This leaves the current seizure to be justified only by the severe tests under the third grouping, where it can be supported only by any remainder of executive power after subtraction of such powers as Congress may have over the subject. In short, we can sustain the President only by holding that seizure of such strike-bound industries is within his domain and beyond control by Congress. Thus, this Court's first review of such seizures occurs under circumstances which leave presidential power most vulnerable to attack and in the least favorable of possible constitutional postures.

. . . Nothing in our Constitution is plainer than that declaration of a war is entrusted only to Congress. Of course, a state of war may in fact exist without a formal declaration. But no doctrine that the Court could promulgate would seem to me more sinister and alarming than that a President whose conduct of foreign affairs is so largely uncontrolled, and often even is unknown, can vastly enlarge his mastery over the internal affairs of the country by his own commitment of the Nation's armed forces to some foreign venture. . . .

There are indications that the Constitution did not contemplate that the title Commander in Chief of the Army and Navy will constitute him also Commander in Chief of the country, its industries and its inhabitants. He has no monopoly of "war powers," whatever they are. While Congress cannot deprive the President of the command of the army and navy, only Congress can provide him an army or navy to command. It is also empowered to make rules for the "Government and Regulation of land and naval Forces," by which it may to some unknown extent impinge upon even command functions.

That military powers of the Commander in Chief were not to supersede representative government of internal affairs seems obvious from the Constitution and from elementary American history. Time out of mind, and even now in many parts of the world, a military commander can seize private housing to shelter his troops. Not so, however, in the United States, for the Third Amendment says, "No Soldier shall, in time of peace be quartered in any house, without the consent of the Owner, nor in time of war, but in a manner to be prescribed by law." Thus, even in war time, his seizure of needed military housing must be authorized by Congress. It also was expressly left to Congress to "provide for calling forth the Militia to execute the Laws of the Union, suppress Insurrections and repel Invasions. . . ." Such a limitation on the command power, written at a time when the militia rather than a standing army was contemplated as the military weapon of the Republic, underscores the Constitution's policy that Congress, not the Executive, should control utilization of the war power as an instrument of domestic policy. Congress, fulfilling that function, has authorized the President to use the army to enforce certain civil rights. On the other hand, Congress has forbidden him to use the army for the purpose of executing general laws except when expressly authorized by the Constitution or by Act of Congress. . . .

We should not use this occasion to circumscribe, much less to contract, the lawful role of the President as Commander in Chief. I should indulge the widest latitude of interpretation to sustain his exclusive function to command the instruments of national force, at least when turned against the outside world for the security of our society. But, when it is turned inward, not because of rebellion but because of a lawful economic struggle between industry and labor, it should have no such indulgence. His command power is not such an absolute as might be implied from that office in a militaristic system but is subject to limitations consistent with a constitutional Republic whose law and policy-making branch is a representative Congress. The purpose of lodging dual titles in one man was to insure that the civilian would control the military, not to enable the military to subordinate the presidential office. . . .

. . . The claim of inherent and unrestricted presidential powers has long been a persuasive dialectical weapon in political controversy. While it is not surprising that counsel should grasp support from such unadjudicated claims of power, a judge cannot accept self-serving press statements of the attorney for one of the interested parties as authority in answering a constitutional question, even if the advocate was himself. [Justice Jackson here is referring to the Government's citation of his own opinion, written while Attorney General, upholding broad executive power on behalf of President Roosevelt.] . . .

The appeal, however, that we declare the existence of inherent powers ex necessitate to meet an emergency asks us to do what many think would be wise, although it is something the forefathers omitted. They knew what emergencies were, knew the pressures they engender for authoritative action, knew, too, how they afford a ready pretext for usurpation. We may also suspect that they suspected that emergency powers would tend to kindle emergencies. Aside from suspension of the privilege of the writ of habeas corpus in time of rebellion or invasion, when the public safety may require it, they made no express provision for exercise of extraordinary authority because of a crisis. I do not think we rightfully may so amend their work, and, if we could, I am not convinced it would be wise to do so, although many modern nations have forthrightly recognized that war and economic crises may upset the normal balance between liberty and authority. Their experience with emergency powers may not be irrelevant to the argument here that we should say that the Executive, of his own volition, can invest himself with undefined emergency powers.

Germany, after the First World War, framed the Weimar Constitution, designed to secure her liberties in the Western tradition. However, the President of the Republic, without concurrence of the Reichstag, was empowered temporarily to suspend any or all individual rights if public safety and order were seriously disturbed or endangered. This proved a temptation to every government, whatever its shade of opinion, and in 13 years suspension of rights was invoked on more than 250 occasions. Finally, Hitler persuaded President Von Hindenberg to suspend all such rights, and they were never restored. . . .

Executive power has the advantage of concentration in a single head in whose choice the whole Nation has a part, making him the focus of public hopes and expectations. In drama, magnitude and finality his decisions so far overshadow any others that almost alone he fills the public eye and ear. No other personality in public life can begin to compete with him in access to the public mind through modern methods of communications. By his prestige as head of state and his influence upon public opinion he exerts a leverage upon those who are supposed to check and balance his power which often cancels their effectiveness.

Moreover, rise of the party system has made a significant extraconstitutional supplement to real executive power. No appraisal of his necessities is realistic which overlooks that he heads a political system as well as a legal system. Party loyalties and interests, sometimes more binding than law, extend his effective control into branches of government other than his own and he often may win, as a political leader, what he cannot command under the Constitution. Indeed, Woodrow Wilson, commenting on the President as leader both of his party and of the Nation, observed, "If he rightly interpret the national thought and boldly insist upon it, he is irresistible. . . . His office is anything he has the sagacity and force to make it." I cannot be brought to believe that this country will suffer if the Court refuses further to aggrandize the presidential office, already so potent and so relatively immune from judicial review, at the expense of Congress. . . .

Mr. Justice Burton, concurring in both the opinion and judgment of the Court.

[T]his emergency [is different] from one in which Congress takes no action and outlines no governmental policy. In the case before us, Congress authorized a procedure which the President declined to follow. . . .

. . . The present situation is not comparable to that of an imminent invasion or threatened attack. We do not face the issue of what might be the President's constitutional power to meet such catastrophic situations. Nor is it claimed that the current seizure is in the nature of a military command addressed by the President, as Commander-in-Chief, to a mobilized nation waging, or imminently threatened with, total war.

The controlling fact here is that Congress, within its constitutionally delegated power, has prescribed for the President specific procedures, exclusive of seizure, for his use in meeting the present type of emergency. Congress has reserved to itself the right to determine where and when to authorize the seizure of property in meeting such an emergency. Under these circumstances, the President's order of April 8 invaded the jurisdiction of Congress. It violated the essence of the principle of the separation of governmental powers. Accordingly, the injunction against its effectiveness should be sustained.

Mr. Justice CLARK, concurring in the judgment of the Court. . . .

I conclude that where Congress has laid down specific procedures to deal with the type of crisis confronting the President, he must follow those procedures in meeting the crisis; but that in the absence of such action by Congress, the President's independent power to act depends upon the gravity of the situation confronting the nation. I cannot sustain the seizure in question because here, . . . Congress had prescribed methods to be followed by the President in meeting the emergency at hand.

. . . [T]he Government made no effort to comply with the procedures established by the Selective Service Act of 1948, a statute which expressly authorizes seizures when producers fail to supply necessary defense materiel.[a]

Mr. Chief Justice VINSON, with whom Mr. Justice REED and Mr. Justice MINTON join, dissenting. . . . Some members of the Court are of the view that the President is without power to act in time of crisis in the absence of express statutory authorization. Other members of the Court affirm on the basis of their reading of certain statutes. . . .

I

Those who suggest that this is a case involving extraordinary powers should be mindful that these are extraordinary times. A world not yet recovered from the devastation of World War II has been forced to face the threat of another and more terrifying global conflict.

Accepting in full measure its responsibility in the world community, the United States was instrumental in securing adoption of the United Nations Charter,

---

a. The Government has offered no explanation, in the record, the briefs, or the oral argument, as to why it could not have made both a literal and timely compliance with the provisions of that Act. . . .

approved by the Senate by a vote of 89 to 2. The first purpose of the United Nations is to "maintain international peace and security, and to that end: to take effective collective measures for the prevention and removal of threats to the peace, and for the suppression of acts of aggression or other breaches of the peace. . . ." In 1950, when the United Nations called upon member nations "to render every assistance" to repel aggression in Korea, the United States furnished its vigorous support. For almost two full years, our armed forces have been fighting in Korea, suffering casualties of over 108,000 men. Hostilities have not abated. The "determination of the United Nations to continue its action in Korea to meet the aggression" has been reaffirmed. Congressional support of the action in Korea has been manifested by provisions for increased military manpower and equipment and for economic stabilization, as hereinafter described.

Further efforts to protect the free world from aggression are found in the congressional enactments of the Truman Plan for assistance to Greece and Turkey and the Marshall Plan for economic aid needed to build up the strength of our friends in Western Europe. In 1949, the Senate approved the North Atlantic Treaty under which each member nation agrees that an armed attack against one is an armed attack against all. Congress immediately implemented the North Atlantic Treaty by authorizing military assistance to nations dedicated to the principles of mutual security under the United Nations Charter. The concept of mutual security recently has been extended by treaty to friends in the Pacific. . . .

Congress also directed the President to build up our own defenses. Congress, recognizing the "grim fact . . . that the United States is now engaged in a struggle for survival" and that "it is imperative that we now take those necessary steps to make our strength equal to the peril of the hour," granted authority to draft men into the armed forces. As a result, we now have over 3,500,000 men in our armed forces. . . . The President has the duty to execute the foregoing legislative programs. Their successful execution depends upon continued production of steel and stabilized prices for steel.

II

. . . The steel mills were seized for a public use. . . .

Admitting that the Government could seize the mills, plaintiffs claim that the implied power of eminent domain can be exercised only under an Act of Congress; under no circumstances, they say, can that power be exercised by the President unless he can point to an express provision in enabling legislation. . . .

Under this view, the President is left powerless at the very moment when the need for action may be most pressing and when no one, other than he, is immediately capable of action. Under this view, he is left powerless because a power not expressly given to Congress is nevertheless found to rest exclusively with Congress.

III

A review of executive action demonstrates that our Presidents have on many occasions exhibited the leadership contemplated by the Framers when they made the President Commander in Chief, and imposed upon him the trust to "take Care that the Laws be faithfully executed." With or without explicit statutory authorization, Presidents have at such times dealt with national emergencies by acting promptly and resolutely to enforce legislative programs, at least to save those programs until Congress could act. Congress and the courts have responded to such executive initiative with consistent approval.

Our first President displayed at once the leadership contemplated by the Framers. . . . When international disputes engendered by the French revolution threatened to involve this country in war, and while congressional policy remained uncertain, Washington issued his Proclamation of Neutrality. Hamilton, whose defense of the Proclamation has endured the test of time, invoked the argument that the Executive has the duty to do that which will preserve peace until Congress acts and, in addition, pointed to the need for keeping the Nation informed of the requirements of existing laws and treaties as part of the faithful execution of the laws. . . .

Jefferson's initiative in the Louisiana Purchase, the Monroe Doctrine, and Jackson's removal of Government deposits from the Bank of the United States further serve to demonstrate by deed what the Framers described by word when they vested the whole of the executive power in the President. . . .

Without declaration of war, President Lincoln took energetic action with the outbreak of the War Between the States. He summoned troops and paid them out of the Treasury without appropriation therefor. He proclaimed a naval blockade of the Confederacy and seized ships violating that blockade. Congress, far from denying the validity of these acts, gave them express approval. The most striking action of President Lincoln was the Emancipation Proclamation, issued in aid of the successful prosecution of the War Between the States, but wholly without statutory authority.

In an action furnishing a most apt precedent for this case, President Lincoln without statutory authority directed the seizure of rail and telegraph lines leading to Washington. Many months later, Congress recognized and confirmed the power of the President to seize railroads and telegraph lines and provided criminal penalties for interference with Government operation. This Act did not confer on the President any additional powers of seizure. Congress plainly rejected the view that the President's acts had been without legal sanction until ratified by the legislature. Sponsors of the bill declared that its purpose was only to confirm the power which the President already possessed. Opponents insisted a statute authorizing seizure was unnecessary and might even be construed as limiting existing Presidential powers. . . .

IV

. . . The President reported to Congress the morning after the seizure that he acted because a work stoppage in steel production would immediately imperil the safety of the Nation by preventing execution of the legislative programs for procurement of military equipment. And, while a shutdown could be averted by granting the price concessions requested by plaintiffs, granting such concessions would disrupt the price stabilization program also enacted by Congress. Rather than fail to execute either legislative program, the President acted to execute both.

Much of the argument in this case has been directed at straw men. We do not now have before us the case of a President acting solely on the basis of his own notions of the public welfare. Nor is there any question of unlimited executive power in this case. The President himself closed the door to any such claim when he sent his Message to Congress stating his purpose to abide by any action of Congress, whether approving or disapproving his seizure action. Here, the President immediately made sure that Congress was fully informed of the temporary action he had taken only to preserve the legislative programs from destruction until Congress could act.

The absence of a specific statute authorizing seizure of the steel mills as a mode of executing the laws—both the military procurement program and the anti-inflation program—has not until today been thought to prevent the President from executing the laws. Unlike an administrative commission confined to the enforcement of the statute under which it was created, or the head of a department when administering a particular statute, the President is a constitutional officer charged with taking care that a "mass of legislation" be executed. Flexibility as to mode of execution to meet critical situations is a matter of practical necessity. . . .

There is no statute prohibiting seizure as a method of enforcing legislative programs. Congress has in no wise indicated that its legislation is not to be executed by the taking of private property (subject of course to the payment of just compensation) if its legislation cannot otherwise be executed. Indeed, the Universal Military Training and Service Act authorizes the seizure of any plant that fails to fill a Government contract or the properties of any steel producer that fails to allocate steel as directed for defense production. And the Defense Production Act authorizes the President to requisition equipment and condemn real property needed without delay in the defense effort. Where Congress authorizes seizure in instances not necessarily crucial to the defense program, it can hardly be said to have disclosed an intention to prohibit seizures where essential to the execution of that legislative program.

Whatever the extent of Presidential power on more tranquil occasions, and whatever the right of the President to execute legislative programs as he sees fit without reporting the mode of execution to Congress, the single Presidential purpose disclosed on this record is to faithfully execute the laws by acting in an emergency to maintain the status quo, thereby preventing collapse of the legislative programs until Congress could act. The President's action served the same purposes as a judicial stay entered to maintain the status quo in order to preserve the jurisdiction of a court. In his Message to Congress immediately following the seizure, the President explained the necessity of his action in executing the military procurement and anti-inflation legislative programs and expressed his desire to cooperate with any legislative proposals approving, regulating or rejecting the seizure of the steel mills. Consequently, there is no evidence whatever of any Presidential purpose to defy Congress or act in any way inconsistent with the legislative will.

. . . There is no cause to fear Executive tyranny so long as the laws of Congress are being faithfully executed. Certainly there is no basis for fear of dictatorship when the Executive acts, as he did in this case, only to save the situation until Congress could act.

V

Plaintiffs place their primary emphasis on the Labor Management Relations Act of 1947, hereinafter referred to as the Taft-Hartley Act, but do not contend that that Act contains any provision prohibiting seizure. . . .

Plaintiffs admit that the emergency procedures of Taft-Hartley are not mandatory. Nevertheless, plaintiffs apparently argue that, since Congress did provide the 80-day injunction method for dealing with emergency strikes, the President cannot claim that an emergency exists until the procedures of Taft-Hartley have been exhausted. This argument was not the basis of the District Court's opinion and, whatever merit the argument might have had following the enactment of Taft-Hartley, it loses all force when viewed in light of the statutory pattern confronting the President in this case.

. . . Faced with immediate national peril through stoppage in steel production on the one hand and faced with destruction of the wage and price legislative programs on the other, the President took temporary possession of the steel mills as the only course open to him consistent with his duty to take care that the laws be faithfully executed.

. . . The President's action has thus far been effective, not in settling the dispute, but in saving the various legislative programs at stake from destruction until Congress could act in the matter.

VI

The diversity of views expressed in the six opinions of the majority, the lack of reference to authoritative precedent, the repeated reliance upon prior dissenting opinions, the complete disregard of the uncontroverted facts showing the gravity of the emergency and the temporary nature of the taking all serve to demonstrate how far afield one must go to affirm the order of the District Court.

. . . Faced with the duty of executing the defense programs which Congress had enacted and the disastrous effects that any stoppage in steel production would have on those programs, the President acted to preserve those programs by seizing the steel mills. There is no question that the possession was other than temporary in character and subject to congressional direction—either approving, disapproving or regulating the manner in which the mills were to be administered and returned to the owners. The President immediately informed Congress of his action and clearly stated his intention to abide by the legislative will. . . .

DISCUSSION

1. *Just the facts, ma'am (again).* Note the different factual narratives offered in the different opinions. Those in the majority see this as a case about strikes and industrial peace—about unions and the domestic economy far from a theater of war. They stress one statute in particular—the Taft-Hartley Act, which gives the President no express power to act as he did in a domestic labor dispute. The dissenters frame a much broader narrative; there are many statutes and treaties at play, a mass of laws, and the President must do his best to carry out the spirit of all these laws. Most important this is a case about war and death—about global commitments and American soldiers at war and their need for steel. These different accounts of the legally relevant facts should remind you that legal arguments are embedded in larger narrative frameworks and visions. See generally Jack M. Balkin and Sanford Levinson, The Canons of Constitutional Law, 111 Harv. L. Rev. 963, 987-991 (1998); Jack M. Balkin, Cultural Software: A Theory of Ideology, Chapter 9

(1998); Jack M. Balkin, A Night in the Topics: The Reason of Legal Rhetoric and the Rhetoric of Legal Reason, in Law's Stories: Narrative and Rhetoric in the Law 211 (Peter Brooks & Paul Gewirtz eds., 1996); L.H. LaRue, Constitutional Law as Fiction: Narrative in the Rhetoric of Authority (1995).

2. *Why didn't Truman use the Taft-Hartley Act?* Note that instead of seizing the steel mills, President Truman could have sought an injunction to stop a labor strike, a course of action available to him under the 1947 Taft-Hartley Act. See Maeva Marcus, Truman and the Steel Seizure Case: The Limits of Presidential Power 77-78 (1994).

Nevertheless, Truman rejected the use of Taft-Hartley to resolve the crisis for several reasons. First, Truman had long been a supporter of (and supported by) organized labor; the Taft-Hartley Act was strongly opposed by labor and in fact had been passed over Truman's veto. Second, Truman believed that seeking a labor injunction was unfair to workers because it would freeze their wages in place and give management little incentive to bargain, thus in effect taking management's side over labor's. Third, Truman argued that the Taft-Hartley procedure did not allow an immediate injunction, and that invoking it would only delay the ultimate resolution of the dispute between labor and management. See Harry S. Truman, Special Message to the Congress on the Steel Strike, June 10th, 1952, The American Presidency Project, at http://www.presidency.ucsb.edu/ws/index.php?pid=14152.

As Neal Devins and Louis Fisher explain, "[a]gainst this backdrop, Truman had a hard time convincing the nation that the steel seizure represented a national emergency instead of a labor dispute. . . . *Time* magazine accused Truman of acting 'primarily as a politician, not as a President. . . . Politician Harry Truman was obviously operating on the axiom of political arithmetic that there are more votes in Big Labor than in Big Steel.' And the *Nation* argued that 'a just settlement of a labor dispute' is not enough to excuse the president's 'arbitrary exercise of executive power.'" Neal Devins and Louis Fisher, The Steel Seizure Case: One of a Kind?, 19 Const. Comment. 63, 67 (2002) (citing Marcus at 89-90).

In addition, by this point in his presidency Truman was a very unpopular President, in large part due to the deeply unpopular Korean War, which Truman had used to justify the seizure in the first place. Truman had sent troops into Korea without a formal declaration of war. Although the public initially supported his action, Truman took much of the blame as the war dragged on. Devins and Fisher speculate that "[h]ad the nation supported Truman and his war, there would have been no public outcry following the seizure and, consequently, the courts would not have been pressured to check a runaway President. For example, had Truman seized the steel mills in 1950 (when the public stood behind his Korean initiative), the Supreme Court might well have looked for a way to avoid ruling against the president." Id. at 74. Do you agree?

3. *Constitutional modalities.* Professor Philip Bobbitt has characterized Justice Black's method of constitutional interpretation as paradigmatically "textual," based on the notion that the Constitution's commands can be derived directly from the plain meaning of the text. Bobbitt contrasts this to a "prudential argument," which he defines as "constitutional argument actuated by the political and economic circumstances surrounding the decision. Thus, prudentialists generally hold that in times of national emergency even the plainest of constitutional limitations can be ignored" if it is in the public interest to do so. Philip Bobbitt, Constitutional Fate:

Theory of the Constitution 25, 61 (1982). Note, for example, that the majority opinion says that postfounding historical practice is irrelevant, whereas many of the other Justices in their separate opinions devote considerable attention to such practice.

4. *Counting noses.* The methodological tension between Black's opinion for the Court, and the concurring opinions of Justices Frankfurter, Jackson, and Burton tracks an important substantive tension. If the statute books are simply silent—neither authorizing nor prohibiting a given presidential act—the Black opinion for the Court seems to say that the President loses. The seizure of the steel mills is a kind of "legislative act" and Congress has "exclusive constitutional authority" in this situation. The case at hand is one where the President has acted "without [affirmative] congressional authority." Justice Douglas seems to agree with all this, but do the three others who "join" Black's opinion? Don't they all say that if the statute books were merely silent, the issue would be importantly different than the case at hand?

Why do you suppose that these Justices signed on to an opinion where they seem to disagree in important respects both with its interpretive methodology and its substantive logic? In order to present a more united front against the chief executive? (Note that all five votes are essential to generate a majority opinion.) But exactly what does a majority opinion mean if separate concurrences undercut its logic? Which should a faithful lower court judge follow—what the Court says in its majority opinion, or what the individual Justices say in their concurrences? How should today's Court view the "holding" of *Youngstown*? Note that many people consider Justice Jackson's opinion to be as important as—if not more important than—Justice Black's majority opinion.

You might wonder why Justice Black was assigned to write the opinion for the Court, given that his views were apparently not those of the Court's center. Assignments are made by the Chief Justice, or, if the Chief is in dissent (as was the case in *Youngstown*), by the senior Justice voting with the majority—in this case, Justice Black.

5. *Formal versus informal wars.* Both Justice Frankfurter and Justice Jackson indicate a reluctance to define the Korean "enterprise" as a "war" despite the engagement of American troops. Assume that Congress had formally declared war on Korea. Would the seizure then have been constitutionally proper?

6. *Legal ethics: Robert Jackson's two hats.* Note Justice Robert Jackson's response to invocations of arguments made earlier by Attorney General Robert Jackson. The distinction here is the one between an advocate and a judge. What do you think of this distinction? When, if ever, should a judge or Justice recuse himself because of earlier statements he may have made as an advocate?

Professor Levinson has argued that Justice Jackson's concurrence is the greatest single opinion in the history of the Supreme Court. See Sanford Levinson, The Rhetoric of the Judicial Opinion, in Law's Stories: Narrative and Rhetoric in the Law 187, 202-204 (Peter Brooks & Paul Gewirtz eds., 1996). Yet, of course, it gained only one vote, Justice Jackson's. One explanation is that among the most powerful features of the opinion are precisely Jackson's own self-references to his service in the Roosevelt Administration and, indeed, his authorship, as Attorney General, of an opinion justifying a very expansive reading of presidential power. Had he excised these references, might other Justices have been more willing to sign on to his famous delineation of the possible relationships between President and Congress? Would it have been worth it, though? Is Justice Jackson's self-reference mere self-indulgence or does it cast a powerful light on the way that Justices ought to think, so that American constitutional law would be far poorer had those paragraphs not appeared in the United States Reports?

7. *The sounds of legislative silence.* Note that the dissenters do not necessarily disagree with the *constitutional* logic of Justices Frankfurter, Jackson, Burton, and Clark. The dissenters do not argue that President Truman may lawfully ignore a congressional prohibition on the facts of this case. Rather, they deny that the Taft-Hartley law is such a prohibition. It is, on their reading, merely silent. Note how much of a difference it makes how this silence is construed—whether the default rule of interpretation is one that allows everything not explicitly prohibited, or one that prohibits everything not explicitly allowed, or something in between. The size and shape of Justice Jackson's category 2—the "twilight zone" where statutes are silent—will depend on a prior statutory interpretation that the statute is indeed silent, rather than impliedly authorizing (category 1) or impliedly prohibiting (category 3) presidential action.

Note that given the interplay of issues, it is possible that five Justices believe that the statutes are indeed simply silent, rather than prohibitory; and that seven Justices believe that in case of mere silence, the President wins; but that nevertheless, these two Court majorities do not "add up" to a victory for the President. Imagine that Justices Black and Douglas agree with the dissenters that the statutes are merely silent. Nevertheless, Black and Douglas also think—as a matter of constitutional law rather than statutory interpretation—that the President loses in cases of mere silence. The other seven Justices may well disagree with Black and Douglas on this constitutional point, but on the statutory question, four of these seven (Frankfurter, Jackson, Clark, and Burton) read the statute as an implied prohibition, thus taking the facts of the case outside category 2 into category 3.

Now turn away from what Congress did before the seizure to what it must do afterwards. Over and over, the dissenters suggest that the President has acted—in a manner like a temporary restraining order—simply to preserve the status quo so that Congress has a chance to act. This was Lincoln's theory in the Civil War—he acted unilaterally, and then asked Congress to bless his actions by passing a statute authorizing them retroactively. Had he not acted, he argued, the war would have been lost immediately, and Congress would have lost any real chance to thwart secession. Is Truman's position similar? Did he concede that he needed an affirmative law to bless his actions? Put another way, would his seizure at some point lapse or sunset, if Congress, having had time to act, chose to do nothing or stalemated? Or was he simply saying that if Congress passes a statute disagreeing with him, he will abide by such a statute?

The difference here is between needing a majority of both houses (in order to pass a blessing enactment), or simply needing a third plus one in either house (in order to fend off a veto override, if Congress tries to pass a statute disagreeing with the President). Consider the words of the President in his message to Congress the day after the seizure: "It may be that the Congress will deem some other course to be wiser . . . that is a matter for the Congress to determine. It may be, on the other hand, that the Congress will wish to pass legislation establishing specific terms and conditions with reference to the operation of the steel mills by the Government.

Sound legislation of this character might be very desirable. On the basis of the facts that are known to me at this time, I do not believe that immediate congressional action is essential; but I would, of course, be glad to cooperate in developing any legislative proposals which the Congress may wish to consider. If the Congress does not deem it necessary to act at this time, I shall continue to do all that is within my power to keep the steel industry operating and at the same time make every effort to bring about a settlement of the dispute so the mills can be returned to their private owners as soon as possible." Consider also the letter Truman sent to the President of the Senate, 12 days later (during which Congress had taken no action): "The Congress can, if it wishes, reject the course of action I have followed in this matter." See Charles L. Black, Jr., Some Thought on the Veto, 40 Law & Contemp. Probs. 87 (1976).

8. *The judicial role.* Consider the *institutional* role of the Supreme Court in adjudicating conflicts between the Congress and the President over military policy. Does, say, a judicial injunction against the commitment of troops seem less tenable than other areas involving judicial invalidation of political acts?

9. *Subsequent history: The* Dames & Moore *case.* In Dames & Moore v. Regan, 453 U.S. 654 (1981), the Court considered the constitutionality of executive orders under which President Carter, in an agreement with Iran for the release of over 400 American hostages, "nullified attachments and liens on Iranian assets in the United States, directed that these assets be transferred to Iran, and suspended claims against Iran that may be presented to an International Claims Tribunal." Following his inauguration, President Reagan "ratified" the orders.

Dames & Moore had sued the government of Iran, an Iranian agency, and several Iranian banks for services performed under a contract. A federal district court attached the property of several defendants in order to secure any judgment that might be entered against them. The Court subsequently found in favor of Dames & Moore, which then attempted to execute the judgment by having the attached property sold. Prior to sale, however, the district court stayed execution of its judgment and "ordered that all prejudgment attachments obtained against the Iranian defendants be vacated and that further proceedings against the bank defendants be stayed in light of the Executive Orders." Dames & Moore complained that the orders were unconstitutional. The Supreme Court granted a writ of certiorari.

Justice Rehnquist, writing for a unanimous Court on the point at issue, emphasized that "we attempt to lay down no general 'guidelines' covering other situations not involved here, and attempt to confine the opinion only to the very questions necessary to decision of the case." The Court noted that "the President's action in nullifying the attachments and ordering the transfer of the assets was taken pursuant to specific congressional authorization." As to "the President's authority to suspend claims pending in American courts," there was no such statutory authorization, though statutory provisions are nonetheless "highly relevant in the looser sense of indicating congressional acceptance of a broad scope for executive action in circumstances such as those presented in this case." Justice Rehnquist also noted "a history of congressional acquiescence in conduct of the sort engaged in by the President" and went on to pronounce as "[c]rucial to our decision today . . . the conclusion that Congress has implicitly approved the practice of claim settlement by executive agreement."

NOTE: THE POWER TO WAGE WAR

Congress has not formally declared war on an enemy since 1941. Yet the United States has been involved in recurrent military hostilities since the end of World War II, including the Korean, Vietnamese, Iraqi, and Serbian conflicts. Although in none of these did Congress invoke its Article I power "to declare war," it has often purported to approve military action; consider, for example, the 1964 Gulf of Tonkin Resolution authorizing the President to engage in retaliation for alleged attacks on American military forces in Vietnam, which served as the legal underpinning for the subsequent buildup of American forces. In addition, there have been numerous "minor" military actions, in areas of the world ranging from Lebanon to the Dominican Republic and Grenada. There has been recurrent debate about the constitutional legitimacy of these military actions.

1. The Constitutional Issues

Consider three positions. One position is that Presidents can use military force at their complete discretion whenever they like. The Declare War Clause is irrelevant to this decision; it means only that Congress has power to declare that war exists for purposes of international law. (In addition, under the General Welfare Clause, Congress also has the power to appropriate or refuse to appropriate funds for military actions.)

A second view would maintain that "declare war" in Article I, §8 means "make war" or "engage in war" and hence whenever the President uses military force he must obtain congressional consent. This position must make an exception for serious emergencies but would otherwise restrict most presidential uses of armed forces abroad. In addition, Congress could give the President continuing advance authorization for emergencies; an example of such a statute is the early Militia Acts discussed in the Prize Cases.

A third position is closer to actual practice since World War II. It holds that the President, even without prior congressional authorization, has discretion to use military force in furtherance of American interests in at least two situations: The first are comparatively "minor" actions of brief duration and involving limited military intervention. The second are emergency situations where important American interests are at stake and there is no time for Congress to deliberate and approve military action in advance. In other cases, Congress must offer some kind of authorization of military force, which may or may not also include a formal declaration of war. Under this third reading, some (but not all) military actions constitute "war" within the meaning of the Declare War Clause and therefore require congressional authorization, even if they do not require a formal declaration of war for purposes of international law and no such declaration ever occurs.

This textual argument creates its own difficulties. The Constitution also uses the term "war" in Article I, §10, which provides that "[n]o state shall, without the consent of Congress, . . . engage in a war, unless actually invaded, or in such imminent danger as will not admit of delay." Does this mean that the President must obtain congressional approval in all cases in which a state would have to obtain congressional approval to engage in "war"?

The answer is almost certainly no. Quite apart from the differences between "declare war" and "engage in a war," there are important structural differences between these two provisions. Article I, §10 is designed to prevent the states, as much as possible, from interfering with (and causing problems for) a single national foreign policy. By contrast, the President generally takes the lead in shaping American foreign policy, and strategic use of military force may be an important element in conducting an effective foreign policy. Thus, the balance of powers between the President and Congress is designed to ensure *democratic accountability* for significant military interventions rather than to prevent meddlesome states from creating foreign policy crises. Hence, the question of "war" for purposes of Article I, §10, concerns state interventions that might interfere with a unitary U.S. foreign and military policy, while the question of "war" for purposes of the Declare War Clause concerns those interventions that, for reasons of democratic accountability, both President and Congress should have to commit to.

The debates on these questions in the 1787 Philadelphia Convention are particularly sparse. The original text gave Congress the power to "make war." The following discussion ensued on August 17 (spellings as in the original):

> "To make war"
>
> Mr Pinkney opposed the vesting this power in the Legislature. Its proceedings were too slow. It wd. meet but once a year. The Hs. of Reps. would be too numerous for such deliberations. The Senate would be the best depositary, being more acquainted with foreign affairs, and most capable of proper resolutions. If the States are equally represented in Senate, so as to give no advantage to large States, the power will notwithstanding be safe, as the small have their all at stake in such cases as well as the large States. It would be singular for one authority to make war, and another peace.
>
> Mr Butler. The Objections agst the Legislature lie in a great degree agst the Senate. He was for vesting the power in the President, who will have all the requisite qualities, and will not make war but when the Nation will support it.
>
> Mr. Madison and Mr Gerry moved to insert "declare," striking out "make" war; leaving to the Executive the power to repel sudden attacks.
>
> Mr Sharman thought it stood very well. The Executive shd. be able to repel and not to commence war. "Make" better than "declare" the latter narrowing the power too much.
>
> Mr Gerry never expected to hear in a republic a motion to empower the Executive alone to declare war.
>
> Mr. Elseworth. there is a material difference between the cases of making war, and making peace. It shd. be more easy to get out of war, than into it. War also is a simple and overt declaration. peace attended with intricate & secret negociations.
>
> Mr. Mason was agst giving the power of war to the Executive, because not safely to be trusted with it; or to the Senate, because not so constructed as to be entitled to it. He was for clogging rather than facilitating war; but for facilitating peace. He preferred "declare" to "make."
>
> On the Motion to insert declare—in place of Make, it was agreed to.

2. The Statutory Issues: The War Powers Resolution

In the aftermath of the Vietnam War, Congress passed, over President Nixon's veto, the War Powers Resolution of 1973. Its central purpose was to increase Congress's role in decisionmaking regarding the commitment of American troops. Section 4(a) of the WPR requires the President to submit a report to Congress within 48 hours of the introduction of American troops, in the absence of a declaration of war,

> (1) into hostilities or into situations where imminent involvement in hostilities is clearly indicated by the circumstances;
> (2) into the territory, airspace or waters of a foreign nation, while equipped for combat, except for deployments which relate solely to supply, replacement, repair, or training of such forces; or
> (3) in numbers which substantially enlarge United States Armed Forces equipped for combat already located in a foreign country.

Submission of such a report triggers a 60-day decisionmaking period. Section 5(b) provides that at the end of that period, "the President shall terminate any use of United States Armed forces" reported on "unless the Congress (1) has declared war or has enacted a specific authorization for such use of United States Armed Forces, (2) has extended by law such sixty-day period, or (3) is physically unable to meet as a result of an armed attack upon the United States." This 60-day period can also be extended by 30 additional days should the President notify Congress "that unavoidable military necessity respecting the safety of United States Armed Forces requires the continued use of such armed forces in the course of bringing about a prompt removal of such forces."

Section 5(c) provides that, notwithstanding these requirements, whenever "United States Armed Forces are engaged in hostilities outside the territory of the United States, its possessions and territories without a declaration of war or specific statutory authorization, such forces shall be removed by the President if the Congress so directs by concurrent resolution."

The War Powers Act has been the topic of major constitutional debate, in large measure because of the specific process chosen for invocation of congressional power. Under §5(c), the President is given no opportunity to veto a concurrent resolution directing immediate withdrawal. Every President since Nixon has argued that this aspect of the Act is unconstitutional. Congress has not yet attempted to use the War Powers Act to limit presidential action. Dramatic examples of the practical irrelevance of the Act involved President Reagan's and Bush's commitments of American military forces to the Persian Gulf. Congressional majorities self-consciously avoided invoking the Act, over the heated protest of several legislators. Imagine that Congress, over the President's objections, passed a law directing the removal of American troops from a particular theater of involvement. Would the statute be constitutional?

Although most Administrations have taken the position that Congress may not end presidential involvement through a joint resolution that is not subject to a presidential veto, this constitutional objection does not apply to the rest of the War Powers Resolution. For example, the Obama Administration, relying on a 1980 Office of Legal Counsel opinion, has assumed that the 60-day requirement of the

War Powers Act in §5(b) is constitutional. See Presidential Power to Use the Armed Forces Abroad Without Statutory Authorization, 4A Op. O.L.C. 185, 196 (1980).

How would you analyze the 60-day requirement under *Youngstown*? Note that the President might well argue that §5(b), like the early Militia Acts, should be construed as a standing authorization for the President to take military action for up to 60 days. But see WPA §8(d)(2): "Nothing in this joint resolution . . . shall be construed as granting any authority to the President with respect to the introduction of United States Armed Forces into hostilities or into situations wherein involvement in hostilities is clearly indicated by the circumstances which authority he would not have had in the absence of this joint resolution." As discussed below, even if §5(b) is constitutional, Congress has fairly limited ways to enforce the 60-day limit.

3. Standing and Justiciability

Even if a military intervention goes beyond presidential power or violates the War Powers Resolution, it is not clear that these issues can be challenged in court. In Raines v. Byrd, 521 U.S. 811 (1997), the Supreme Court held that individual Congresspersons and senators did not have standing as legislators to challenge the constitutionality of a line item veto bill. In Campbell v. Clinton, 203 F.3d 19, 21 (D.C. Cir. 2000), cert. denied, 531 U.S. 815 (2000), which relied on Raines v. Byrd, the D.C. Circuit rejected the standing of Congresspersons to challenge President Clinton's intervention in Kosovo. (Note that, even if one gets past the standing question, one must also show that the constitutional and statutory questions are not political questions. Assuming that the constitutional question involves a political question, why would the application of a statute like the War Powers Resolution be nonjusticiable?)

4. Political Remedies and Collective Action Problems

Even if members of Congress lack standing to challenge a President's decision to use military force, that does not mean that there is no constitutional or legal remedy. As the Court noted in *Raines*, the most likely remedy comes from the political process. Congress can attempt to pass legislation over the President's veto requiring that the President end the intervention. Congress can refuse to appropriate funding for the intervention, and it can refuse to allow existing funds to be used for the intervention. And, of course, if all else fails, Congress can threaten to impeach the President or threaten to hold up other legislation that the President wants passed.

It may not even be necessary for Congress to pass new legislation to have an effect. Pressure exercised through resolutions by one house or a joint resolution by both houses may strongly signal to Presidents that the country is not behind them or, that they are in violation of the law, and that they should end the intervention quickly. Congress can also use public debates and hearings to shape public opinion against an intervention, although usually not as effectively as the President can.

Nevertheless, political remedies face political obstacles. Congress as a whole has incentives to sit on its hands and wait to see whether a military mission is successful or not. That is because Congress as a whole is composed of individual Congresspersons and senators, who have various incentives to avoid responsibility. Congresspersons and senators, especially those who may consider running for President someday, do not want to guess wrong about military operations. If a candidate takes a strong stand against a military action that goes well, this will be used against the candidate later. Conversely, as Hillary Clinton discovered in the 2008 presidential campaign, supporting a war that later becomes unpopular can undermine a candidate's political support.

As a result of these pressures, Congress may adopt a position of what we might call belligerent acquiescence: While individual members denounce the Administration, measures designed either to approve or to hinder a presidential intervention are difficult to pass.

A further complicating factor is that in military interventions the United States often works in concert with international organizations like the North Atlantic Treaty Organization (NATO). The United States has sometimes turned to its allies in NATO, for example, when it is unlikely that the United Nations will take effective action or action that is consistent with U.S. interests.

Quite apart from Congress's tendencies toward inertia, Congress has incentives not to undermine such international organizations because their effectiveness serves the long-term interests of the United States. Thus, if Congress believes that defunding a particular intervention would destroy NATO's future credibility, or the credibility of the United States within NATO, it may do nothing.

These considerations help explain why Congress decided to create the decisional structure of the War Powers Resolution. If Congress does nothing, the President must end an intervention after 60 days. Does this shifting of the default rule better serve American interests?

Since the passage of the War Powers Act, Congress has authorized major operations in the Gulf and Iraq wars. Other military operations since 1973 have, for the most part, either been relatively brief (so that they fall within the 60-day period) or relatively inconsequential. The most interesting contrary example before the 2011 Libya intervention (discussed infra) was President Clinton's decision to bomb Kosovo in 1999. The Kosovo intervention was also performed in conjunction with NATO, and it was also justified largely on humanitarian grounds. Ultimately, the Clinton Administration argued that Congress had retroactively authorized the intervention because of a subsequent appropriations measure. The Kosovo example shows why Congress is in a difficult situation: If Congress funds an ongoing mission to maintain the credibility of the United States or NATO, or to avoid a military disaster, the President may use this as evidence of implicit congressional approval.

Note, however, that many members of Congress might want to have it both ways. They might want to assert that the President has gone beyond the 60-day limit and is acting illegally, but they might not want to force the President to end an intervention that has already begun. As a result, Congress does nothing, or, as in the Kosovo case, provides appropriations. Does this mean that the 60-day clock is a bad idea? Would another model make more sense?

5. Humanitarian Intervention: The Libya Crisis

In mid-February 2011, a popular uprising began against the autocratic government of Colonel Muammar Qaddafi of Libya, which led to a civil war. The Libyan government was reported to have bombed and strafed protesters and deliberately targeted civilians. On March 12, the Arab League called for a no-fly zone in Libya, and on March 17, the United Nations Security Council adopted Resolution 1973, which imposed a no-fly zone and called for the use of military force to protect civilians. In response, on March 19, the United States along with its NATO allies launched airstrikes against Libyan targets to enforce Resolution 1973. President Obama provided a report to Congress on March 21, stating that no ground troops would be deployed.

Sometime around April 4, NATO took over leadership in maintaining the no-fly zone in Libya, and the United States adopted a supporting role. According to the Obama Administration, the United States provided surveillance and refueling for allied warplanes. The United States continued to fire missiles from unmanned drones; it also engaged in a relatively small percentage of manned air missions (approximately 10 percent) in proportion to the manned air missions by NATO forces.

Treating the March 21, 2011 report as the starting date of the introduction of American forces into hostilities, the War Power Resolution's 60-day clock would have run out on May 20, 2011, and the 30-day extension to withdraw forces would have run out around June 18. The intervention continued, however, and as noted below, the Obama Administration took the position that the clock was tolled when it handed leadership off to NATO.

Fighting in Libya ended in October 2011 following the death of Muammar Qaddafi. Congress debated but ultimately never authorized the Libya operation. In June 2011, the House of Representatives passed two resolutions. The first protested the operation and stated that "[t]he President shall not deploy, establish, or maintain the presence of units and members of the United States Armed Forces on the ground in Libya unless the purpose of the presence is to rescue a member of the Armed Forces from imminent danger." The second, added to an appropriations bill funding military construction and the Department of Veterans Affairs, stated that none of the money in the bill could be spent "in contravention of the War Powers Act." The Senate never passed a similar resolution, and congressional interest in the controversy lapsed following the end of the operation.

On June 15, the Obama Administration provided an explanation to Congress. It argued that the President had constitutional authority to begin the Libya operation without congressional approval "[g]iven the important U.S. interests served by U.S. military operations in Libya and the limited nature, scope and duration of the anticipated actions."[65] President Obama was not responding to an attack on American soil, to threats of danger to Americans living abroad, to threats to American property, or to an attack on American allies. Instead, the President intervened in Libya in order to avoid a humanitarian disaster. By imposing a no-fly zone, NATO sought to limit Qaddafi's forces and weaken his military power so that he could not threaten or harm innocent civilians.

At a press conference on March 18, President Obama argued that the intervention promoted important American interests:[66]

> Now, here is why this matters to us. Left unchecked, we have every reason to believe that Qaddafi would commit atrocities against his people. Many thousands could die. A humanitarian crisis would ensue. The entire

65. United States Activities in Libya, June 15, 2011, at http://www.foreignpolicy.com/files/fp_uploaded_documents/110615_United_States_Activities_in_Libya_-_6_15_11.pdf.

66. Remarks by the President on the Situation in Libya (Mar. 18, 2011), at http://www.whitehouse.gov/the-press-office/2011/03/18/remarks-president-situation-libya.

> region could be destabilized, endangering many of our allies and partners. The calls of the Libyan people for help would go unanswered. The democratic values that we stand for would be overrun. Moreover, the words of the international community would be rendered hollow.

Are these interests sufficient to justify presidential military intervention without congressional authorization? When the President uses force for humanitarian reasons rather than to protect American citizens, troops, or material interests, is there a greater reason to require congressional authorization, either before or immediately after the intervention begins?[67]

In an April 2011 OLC opinion, the Administration also argued that supporting the United Nations Security Council's "credibility and effectiveness" was another national interest. Is this sufficient justification under the circumstances? Couldn't the President almost always justify humanitarian intervention on these grounds if the Administration is working in concert with NATO or other international organizations?

6. Technological Change and the Constitution

Consider how changes in the technology of warfare might alter the constitutional and statutory issues discussed above. America's use of air power and drone technology in the Libya intervention limited potential American casualties. Accordingly, the Obama Administration, in an OLC opinion, argued that the Libya intervention was not a "war" that required congressional authorization because the operation was limited in three ways. First, the operation was limited to airpower, and did not use ground troops. Airpower limits the number and degree of casualties that can be inflicted on American soldiers; compared to airpower, the use of ground troops makes withdrawal difficult and hence tends to restrict Congress's options once the operation begins. Second, the Administration argued that the use of airpower was connected to the limited goals of the Libya intervention. These were (1) enforcing the no-fly zone and (2) preventing humanitarian disaster; conquest of territory was not a goal. Third, the Administration argued that the bombing would not prepare the way for a later ground invasion, which reduced the risk that the intervention would result in a sustained commitment.[68]

---

67. Note that the need to work with other countries and international organizations greatly complicates the President's ability to request permission from Congress in a timely fashion:

> Why didn't Obama ask Congress—then in session—to authorize air power in late February or early March, well before the crisis climaxed? Partly because the situation was delicate, tactically and diplomatically. Obama did not want the world to think the United States was trigger happy, and any congressional resolution that occurred before an international consensus crystallized might have made it far more difficult to persuade the world of America's benign intentions. Only after an alliance of Arab and world leaders requested America's help would a congressional resolution have been appropriate—and by then massacres seemed imminent. Thus, even when Congress is able to act quickly, it is not always able to act at just the right moment, internationally.

Akhil Reed Amar, Bomb Away, Mr. President, Slate, June 29, 2011, at http://www.slate.com/articles/news_and_politics/jurisprudence/2011/06/bomb_away_mr_president.single.html.

68. Authority to Use Military Force in Libya, April 1, 2011, at http://www.justice.gov/olc/2011/authority-military-usein-libya.pdf.

What do you make of these arguments? Why does the fact that America uses a technology that (mostly) shields troops from harm mean that "war" is not occurring and that Congress need not approve the action? Akhil Amar argues that—from the standpoint of both the Constitution and the War Powers Resolution—the risk of harm to American soldiers should matter:[69]

> [T]he Constitution distinguishes between armies and navies, and regulates armies more strictly. (For example, army appropriations must be re-voted every two years; not so for navy appropriations.) This distinction exists because the Framers believed that armies posed a greater threat to American lives and liberty than did navies. Today, the air power is likewise less of a threat to American lives and limbs. . . . Because the Libya mission poses little threat to Americans, one of the central purposes of the War Powers Resolution—to prevent Vietnam-style risks to Americans unless America's elected legislators have specifically approved these risks—is not implicated.

Does this mean that Presidents can use any amount of long-range missiles, unmanned drones, and various forms of military robotics without engaging in "war"? Even if American troops face no immediate threat of reprisal, does this mean that no reprisals will be forthcoming, especially in the form of terrorist attacks and other forms of asymmetrical warfare?

Indeed, one might worry that the development of long-distance technologies that are likely to risk harm only to people who are not Americans might mean that ordinary democratic processes are no longer sufficient to check presidential ambitions or presidential adventurism. Because Americans will not return home in body bags, the President will feel freer to employ these technologies and intervene militarily in other parts of the world. Could this change in technology create some of the same problems that originally led the framers to require consultation with Congress before the country goes to war?

The Administration also argued that the Libya operation was in full compliance with the War Powers Resolution because the 60-day clock stopped in early April, when American forces took what was largely a supporting role to NATO operations. In terms of the language of §4(a)(1) of the WPR, the Obama Administration argued that "United States Armed Forces" were no longer "introduced . . . into hostilities or into situations where imminent involvement in hostilities is clearly indicated by the circumstances."

Testifying before Congress, State Department Legal Advisor Harold Koh argued that "the operative term 'hostilities,' is an ambiguous standard" that must be developed case by case through inter-branch dialogue in light of changing circumstances that the drafters could not have foreseen. However, as a general matter, "the Executive Branch understands the term 'to mean a situation in which units of the U.S. armed forces are actively engaged in exchanges of fire with opposing units of hostile forces.'"[70] Following the handoff to NATO, U.S. military activities did not

69. Amar, Bomb Away, Mr. President, supra n.67.

70. Testimony by Legal Adviser Harold Hongju Koh, U.S. Department of State, on Libya and War Powers Before the Senate Foreign Relations Committee, June 28, 2011, at http://foreign.senate.gov/imo/media/doc/Koh_Testimony.pdf.

"involve active exchanges of fire with hostile forces," and members of the U.S. military were not "involved in significant armed confrontations or sustained confrontations of any kind with hostile forces. . . . American strikes have been confined, on an as-needed basis, to the suppression of enemy air defenses to enforce the no-fly zone, and to limited strikes by Predator unmanned aerial vehicles against discrete targets in support of the civilian protection mission; since the handoff to NATO, the total number of U.S. munitions dropped has been a tiny fraction of the number dropped in Kosovo."

Why does the switch to unmanned drones increase the chances that "hostilities" have ended? One possible reason is that "hostilities" require more or less continuous exchanges of fire between combatants. As long as unmanned drones are doing most of the killing, and American troops are not being fired at, or only being attacked intermittently, there are no hostilities. The use of drones, moreover, means that American involvement can be ended easily, unlike the use of ground troops.

This statutory argument, however, recapitulates the constitutional issues discussed above: The fact that an aggressor is not vulnerable does not mean that there are no hostilities occurring. Such a reading would give Presidents incentives to use remote-control weapons and make increased investments in missiles, unmanned drones, and robotics in order to get around the 60-day limitation.

The War Powers Resolution was drafted in light of the experience of the Vietnam War: A large commitment of ground troops that was difficult to extricate once operations had begun. Yet military technology and military strategy have changed in the interim. How should we interpret the War Powers Resolution in interventions that primarily involve long-distance warfare like drones or robotics? Consider the possibility that the War Powers Resolution, designed for Vietnam-style conflicts, is technologically outmoded and must be redrafted to take into account these changed realities.

Consider, for example, the problem of cyberattacks, where belligerents seek to use the Internet to destroy infrastructural capacities, or in the alternative, seek to exploit computers (and the resources these computers control) in other countries. Do cyberattacks count as "hostilities" under the WPR? How should the WPR be redrafted to account for them?

7. Congressional Authorizations in the War on Terror and the War in Iraq

As noted previously, Congress has generally avoided declarations of war in recent years, instead relying on resolutions authorizing the use of military force. These authorizations usually contain language exempting the President from particular features of the War Powers Act by stating that in Congress's view he has satisfied the Act's requirements. The American response to the September 11, 2001 attacks and the war in Iraq are two examples of recent congressional practice.

On September 18, 2001, Congress passed a resolution authorizing "the President . . . to use all necessary and appropriate force against those nations, organizations, or persons he determines planned, authorized, committed, or aided the terrorist attacks that occurred on September 11, 2001, or harbored such organizations or persons, in order to prevent any future acts of international terrorism against the United States by such nations, organizations or persons." Authorization for Use of Military Force, §2(a), 115 Stat. 224 (2001). Section 2(b) of the resolution "declares that this section is intended to constitute specific statutory authorization within the meaning of section 5(b) of the War Powers Resolution," thus in effect waiving the 60-day limit for presidential use of the armed forces, but added that "[n]othing in this resolution supercedes any requirement of the War Powers Resolution." Does this mean that Congress may, by a subsequent joint resolution, remove its authorization and order an end to the President's use of military force?

On October 16, 2002, Congress gave President Bush authority "to use the Armed Forces of the United States as he determines to be necessary and appropriate in order to (1) defend the national security of the United States against the continuing threat posed by Iraq; and (2) enforce all relevant United Nations Security Council resolutions regarding Iraq." Authorization for the Use of Military Force Against Iraq Resolution of 2002, 116 Stat. 1498 (2002). Like the previous resolution, §3(c)(1) of the October 16 resolution "is intended to constitute specific statutory authorization within the meaning of section 5(b) of the War Powers Resolution."

2. Executive Detention

Hamdi v. Rumsfeld

542 U.S. 507 (2004)

Justice O'Connor announced the judgment of the Court and delivered an opinion, in which The Chief Justice, Justice Kennedy, and Justice Breyer join.

At this difficult time in our Nation's history, we are called upon to consider the legality of the Government's detention of a United States citizen on United States soil as an "enemy combatant" and to address the process that is constitutionally owed to one who seeks to challenge his classification as such. The United States Court of Appeals for the Fourth Circuit held that petitioner's detention was legally authorized and that he was entitled to no further opportunity to challenge his enemy-combatant label. We now vacate and remand. We hold that although Congress authorized the detention of combatants in the narrow circumstances alleged here, due process demands that a citizen held in the United States as an enemy combatant be given a meaningful opportunity to contest the factual basis for that detention before a neutral decisionmaker.

I

On September 11, 2001, the al Qaeda terrorist network used hijacked commercial airliners to attack prominent targets in the United States. Approximately 3,000 people were killed in those attacks. One week later, [on September 18, 2001,] in response to these "acts of treacherous violence," Congress passed a resolution authorizing the President to "use all necessary and appropriate force against those nations, organizations, or persons he determines planned, authorized, committed, or aided the terrorist attacks" or "harbored such organizations or persons, in order to prevent any future acts of international terrorism against the United States by such nations, organizations or persons." Authorization for Use of Military Force ("the AUMF"), 115 Stat. 224. Soon thereafter, the President ordered United States Armed Forces to Afghanistan, with a mission to subdue al Qaeda and quell the Taliban regime that was known to support it.

This case arises out of the detention of a man whom the Government alleges took up arms with the Taliban during this conflict. His name is Yaser Esam Hamdi. Born an American citizen in Louisiana in 1980, Hamdi moved with his family to Saudi Arabia as a child. By 2001, the parties agree, he resided in Afghanistan. At some point that year, he was seized by members of the Northern Alliance, a coalition of military groups opposed to the Taliban government, and eventually was turned over to the United States military. The Government asserts that it initially detained and interrogated Hamdi in Afghanistan before transferring him to the United States Naval Base in Guantanamo Bay in January 2002. In April 2002, upon learning that Hamdi is an American citizen, authorities transferred him to a naval brig in Norfolk, Virginia, where he remained until a recent transfer to a brig in Charleston, South Carolina. The Government contends that Hamdi is an "enemy combatant," and that this status justifies holding him in the United States indefinitely—without formal charges or proceedings—unless and until it makes the determination that access to counsel or further process is warranted.

In June 2002, Hamdi's father, Esam Fouad Hamdi, filed the present petition for a writ of habeas corpus under 28 U.S.C. §2241 in the Eastern District of Virginia, naming as petitioners his son and himself as next friend. The elder Hamdi alleges in the petition that he has had no contact with his son since the Government took custody of him in 2001, and that the Government has held his son "without access to legal counsel or notice of any charges pending against him." . . . Although his habeas petition provides no details with regard to the factual circumstances surrounding his son's capture and detention, Hamdi's father has asserted in documents found elsewhere in the record that his son went to Afghanistan to do "relief work," and that he had been in that country less than two months before September 11, 2001, and could not have received military training. The 20-year-old was traveling on his own for the first time, his father says, and "[b]ecause of his lack of experience, he was trapped in Afghanistan once that military campaign began." . . .

[T]he Government filed a response and a motion to dismiss the petition, [attaching] a declaration from one Michael Mobbs (hereinafter "Mobbs Declaration"), who identified himself as Special Advisor to the Under Secretary of Defense for Policy. Mobbs indicated that in this position, he has been "substantially involved with matters related to the detention of enemy combatants in the current war against the al Qaeda terrorists and those who support and harbor them (including the Taliban)." He expressed his "familiar[ity]" with Department of Defense and United States military policies and procedures applicable to the detention, control, and transfer of al Qaeda and Taliban personnel, and declared that "[b]ased upon my review of relevant records and reports, I am also familiar with the facts and circumstances related to the capture of . . . Hamdi and his detention by U.S. military forces." Ibid. Mobbs then set forth what remains the sole evidentiary support that the Government has provided to the courts for Hamdi's detention. The declaration states that Hamdi "traveled to Afghanistan" in July or August 2001, and that he thereafter "affiliated with a Taliban military unit and received weapons training." It asserts that Hamdi "remained with his Taliban unit following the attacks of September 11" and that, during the time when Northern Alliance forces were "engaged in battle with the Taliban," "Hamdi's Taliban unit surrendered" to those forces, after which he "surrender[ed] his Kalishnikov assault rifle" to them. The Mobbs Declaration also states that, because al Qaeda and the Taliban "were and are hostile forces engaged in armed conflict with the armed forces of the United States," "individuals associated with" those groups "were and continue to be enemy combatants." Mobbs states that Hamdi was labeled an enemy combatant "[b]ased upon his interviews and in light of his association with the Taliban." According to the declaration, a series of "U.S. military screening team[s]" determined that Hamdi met "the criteria for enemy combatants," and "a subsequent interview of Hamdi has confirmed that he surrendered and gave his firearm to Northern Alliance forces, which supports his classification as an enemy combatant." . . .

Concluding that the factual averments in the Mobbs Declaration, "if accurate," provided a sufficient basis upon which to conclude that the President had constitutionally detained Hamdi pursuant to the President's war powers, [the Fourth Circuit Court of Appeals] ordered the habeas petition dismissed. . . . We now vacate the judgment below and remand.

II

The threshold question before us is whether the Executive has the authority to detain citizens who qualify as "enemy combatants." There is some debate as to the proper scope of this term, and the Government has never provided any court with the full criteria that it uses in classifying individuals as such. It has made clear, however, that, for purposes of this case, the "enemy combatant" that it is seeking to detain is an individual who, it alleges, was "'part of or supporting forces hostile to the United States or coalition partners'" in Afghanistan and who "'engaged in an armed conflict against the United States'" there. We therefore answer only the narrow question before us: whether the detention of citizens falling within that definition is authorized.

The Government maintains that no explicit congressional authorization is required, because the Executive possesses plenary authority to detain pursuant to Article II of the Constitution. We do not reach the question whether Article II provides such authority, however, because we agree with the Government's alternative position, that Congress has in fact authorized Hamdi's detention, through the AUMF.

[Hamdi argues] that his detention is forbidden by [the Non-Detention Act,] 18 U.S.C. §4001(a). Section 4001(a) states that "[n]o citizen shall be imprisoned or otherwise detained by the United States except pursuant to an Act of Congress." Congress passed §4001(a) in 1971 as part of a bill to repeal the Emergency Detention Act of 1950, 50 U.S.C. §811 et seq., which provided procedures for executive detention, during times of emergency, of individuals deemed likely to engage in espionage or sabotage. Congress was particularly concerned about the possibility that the Act could be used to reprise the Japanese internment camps of World War II. The Government . . . argues [first] that §4001(a) . . . applies only to "the control of civilian prisons and related detentions," not to military detentions. Second, it maintains that §4001(a) is satisfied, because Hamdi is being detained "pursuant to an Act of Congress"—the AUMF. [W]e conclude that the AUMF is explicit congressional authorization for the detention of individuals in the narrow category we describe (assuming, without deciding, that such authorization is required), and that the AUMF satisfied §4001(a)'s requirement that a detention be "pursuant to an Act of Congress" (assuming, without deciding, that §4001(a) applies to military detentions).

The AUMF authorizes the President to use "all necessary and appropriate force" against "nations, organizations, or persons" associated with the September 11, 2001, terrorist attacks. 115 Stat. 224. There can be no doubt that individuals who fought against the United States in Afghanistan as part of the Taliban, an organization known to have supported the al Qaeda terrorist network responsible for those attacks, are individuals Congress sought to target in passing the AUMF. We conclude that detention of individuals falling into the limited category we are considering, for the duration of the particular conflict in which they were captured, is so fundamental and accepted an incident to war as to be an exercise of the "necessary and appropriate force" Congress has authorized the President to use.

The capture and detention of lawful combatants and the capture, detention, and trial of unlawful combatants, by "universal agreement and practice," are "important incident[s] of war." The purpose of detention is to prevent captured individuals from returning to the field of battle and taking up arms once again. Naqvi, Doubtful Prisoner-of-War Status, 84 Int'l Rev. Red Cross 571, 572 (2002) ("[C]aptivity in war is 'neither revenge, nor punishment, but solely protective custody, the only purpose of which is to prevent the prisoners of war from further participation in the war'").

There is no bar to this Nation's holding one of its own citizens as an enemy combatant. In [Ex parte] Quirin, [317 U.S. 1, 25 (1942),] one of the detainees, Haupt, alleged that he was a naturalized United States citizen. We held that "[c]itizens who associate themselves with the military arm of the enemy government, and with its aid, guidance and direction enter this country bent on hostile acts, are enemy belligerents within the meaning of . . . the law of war." While Haupt was tried for violations of the law of war, nothing in *Quirin* suggests that his citizenship would have precluded his mere detention for the duration of the relevant hostilities. Nor can we see any reason for drawing such a line here. A citizen, no less than an alien, can be "part of or supporting forces hostile to the United States or coalition partners" and "engaged in an armed conflict against the United States"; such a citizen, if released, would pose the same threat of returning to the front during the ongoing conflict.

In light of these principles, it is of no moment that the AUMF does not use specific language of detention. Because detention to prevent a combatant's return to the battlefield is a fundamental incident of waging war, in permitting the use of "necessary and appropriate force," Congress has clearly and unmistakably authorized detention in the narrow circumstances considered here.

Hamdi objects, nevertheless, that Congress has not authorized the *indefinite* detention to which he is now subject. The Government responds that "the detention of enemy combatants during World War II was just as 'indefinite' while that war was being fought." We take Hamdi's objection to be not to the lack of certainty regarding the date on which the conflict will end, but to the substantial prospect of perpetual detention. We recognize that the national security underpinnings of the "war on terror," although crucially important, are broad and malleable. As the Government concedes, "given its unconventional nature, the current conflict is unlikely to end with a formal cease-fire agreement." The prospect Hamdi raises is therefore not far-fetched. If the Government does not consider this unconventional war won for two generations, and if it maintains during that time that Hamdi might, if released, rejoin forces fighting against the United States, then the position it has taken throughout the litigation of this case suggests that Hamdi's detention could last for the rest of his life.

It is a clearly established principle of the law of war that detention may last no longer than active hostilities. See Article 118 of the Geneva Convention (III) Relative to the Treatment of Prisoners of War, Aug. 12, 1949, [1955] 6 U.S.T. 3316, 3406, T.I.A.S. No. 3364 ("Prisoners of war shall be released and repatriated without delay after the cessation of active hostilities"). See also Article 20 of the Hague Convention (II) on Laws and Customs of War on Land, July 29, 1899, 32 Stat. 1817 (as soon as possible after "conclusion of peace"); Hague Convention (IV), supra, Oct. 18, 1907, 36 Stat. 2301 ("conclusion of peace" (Art. 20)); Geneva Convention, supra, July 27, 1929, 47 Stat. 2055 (repatriation should be accomplished with the least possible delay after conclusion of peace (Art. 75)).

Hamdi contends that the AUMF does not authorize indefinite or perpetual detention. Certainly, we agree that indefinite detention for the purpose of interrogation is not authorized. Further, we understand Congress' grant of authority for the use of "necessary and appropriate force" to include the authority to detain for the duration of the relevant conflict, and our understanding is based on longstanding law-of-war principles. If the practical circumstances of a given conflict are entirely unlike those of the conflicts that informed the development of the law of war, that understanding may unravel. But that is not the situation we face as of this date. Active combat operations against Taliban fighters apparently are ongoing in Afghanistan. The United States may detain, for the duration of these hostilities, individuals legitimately determined to be Taliban combatants who "engaged in an armed conflict against the United States." If the record establishes that United States troops are still involved in active combat in Afghanistan, those detentions are part of the exercise of "necessary and appropriate force," and therefore are authorized by the AUMF.

Ex parte Milligan does not undermine our holding about the Government's authority to seize enemy combatants, as we define that term today. In that case, the Court made repeated reference to the fact that its inquiry into whether the military tribunal had jurisdiction to try and punish Milligan turned in large part on the fact that Milligan was not a prisoner of war, but a resident of Indiana arrested while at home there. That fact was central to its conclusion. Had Milligan been captured while he was assisting Confederate soldiers by carrying a rifle against Union troops on a Confederate battlefield, the holding of the Court might well have been different. The Court's repeated explanations that Milligan was not a prisoner of war suggest that had these different circumstances been present he could have been detained under military authority for the duration of the conflict, whether or not he was a citizen.[a]

[T]he Court in Ex parte Quirin dismissed the language of *Milligan* that the petitioners had suggested prevented them from being subject to military process. . . . Justice Scalia [argues] that the military does not have authority to try an

a. Here the basis asserted for detention by the military is that Hamdi was carrying a weapon against American troops on a foreign battlefield; that is, that he was an enemy combatant. The legal category of enemy combatant has not been elaborated upon in great detail. The permissible bounds of the category will be defined by the lower courts as subsequent cases are presented to them.

American citizen accused of spying against his country during wartime; [but] *Quirin* makes undeniably clear that this is not the law today. Haupt . . . was accused of being a spy. The Court in *Quirin* found him "subject to trial and punishment by [a] military tribunal[ ]" for those acts, and held that his citizenship did not change this result. . . .

Justice Scalia [distinguishes] *Quirin*, . . . because "[i]n *Quirin* it was uncontested that the petitioners were members of enemy forces," while Hamdi challenges his classification as an enemy combatant. But [for] Justice Scalia . . . the only options are congressional suspension of the writ of habeas corpus or prosecution for treason or some other crime. He does not explain how his historical analysis supports . . . a third option—detention under some other process after concession of enemy-combatant status—or why a concession [that one is an enemy combatant] should carry any different effect than proof of enemy-combatant status in a proceeding that comports with due process. To be clear, our opinion only finds legislative authority to detain under the AUMF once it is sufficiently clear that the individual is, in fact, an enemy combatant; whether that is established by concession or by some other process that verifies this fact with sufficient certainty seems beside the point.

Further, Justice Scalia largely ignores the context of this case: a United States citizen captured in a *foreign* combat zone. . . . Because Justice Scalia finds the fact of battlefield capture irrelevant, his distinction based on the fact that the petitioner "conceded" enemy combatant status is beside the point. Justice Scalia can point to no case or other authority for the proposition that those captured on a foreign battlefield (whether detained there or in U.S. territory) cannot be detained outside the criminal process.

Moreover, Justice Scalia presumably would come to a different result if Hamdi had been kept in Afghanistan or even Guantanamo Bay. This creates a perverse incentive. Military authorities faced with the stark choice of submitting to the full-blown criminal process or releasing a suspected enemy combatant captured on the battlefield will simply keep citizen-detainees abroad. Indeed, the Government transferred Hamdi from Guantanamo Bay to the United States naval brig only after it learned that he might be an American citizen. It is not at all clear why that should make a determinative constitutional difference.

III

Even in cases in which the detention of enemy combatants is legally authorized, there remains the question of what process is constitutionally due to a citizen who disputes his enemy-combatant status. . . .

[The Government argues] that further factual exploration is unwarranted and inappropriate in light of the extraordinary constitutional interests at stake. Under the Government's most extreme rendition of this argument, "[r]espect for separation of powers and the limited institutional capabilities of courts in matters of military decision-making in connection with an ongoing conflict" ought to eliminate entirely any individual process, restricting the courts to investigating only whether legal authorization exists for the broader detention scheme. At most, the Government argues, courts should review its determination that a citizen is an enemy combatant under a very deferential "some evidence" standard. Under this review, a court would assume the accuracy of the Government's articulated basis for Hamdi's detention, as set forth in the Mobbs Declaration, and assess only whether that articulated basis was a legitimate one. In response, Hamdi emphasizes that this Court consistently has recognized that an individual challenging his detention may not be held at the will of the Executive without recourse to some proceeding before a neutral tribunal to determine whether the Executive's asserted justifications for that detention have basis in fact and warrant in law. . . . The District Court, agreeing with Hamdi, apparently believed that the appropriate process would approach the process that accompanies a criminal trial. It therefore disapproved of the hearsay nature of the Mobbs Declaration and anticipated quite extensive discovery of various military affairs. Anything less, it concluded, would not be "meaningful judicial review."

Both of these positions highlight legitimate concerns. And both emphasize the tension that often exists between the autonomy that the Government asserts is necessary in order to pursue effectively a particular goal and the process that a citizen contends he is due before he is deprived of a constitutional right. The ordinary mechanism that we use for balancing such serious competing interests, and for determining the procedures that are necessary to ensure that a citizen is not "deprived of life, liberty, or property, without due process of law," is the test that we articulated in Mathews v. Eldridge, 424 U.S. 319 (1976). *Mathews* dictates that the process due in any given instance is determined by weighing "the private interest that will be affected by the official action" against the Government's asserted interest, "including the function involved" and the burdens the Government would face in providing greater process. The *Mathews* calculus then contemplates a judicious balancing of these concerns, through an analysis of "the risk of an erroneous deprivation" of the private interest if the process were reduced and the "probable value, if any, of additional or substitute safeguards." . . .

Striking the proper constitutional balance here is of great importance to the Nation during this period of ongoing combat. But it is equally vital that our calculus not give short shrift to the values that this country holds dear or to the privilege that is American citizenship. It is during our most challenging and uncertain moments that our Nation's commitment to due process is most severely tested; and it is in those times that we must preserve our commitment at home to the principles for which we fight abroad.

With due recognition of these competing concerns, we believe that neither the process proposed by the Government nor the process apparently envisioned by the District Court below strikes the proper constitutional balance when a United States citizen is detained in the United States as an enemy combatant. . . . We therefore hold that a citizen-detainee seeking to challenge his classification as an enemy combatant must receive notice of the factual basis for his classification, and a fair opportunity to rebut the Government's factual assertions before a neutral decisionmaker. . . . At the same time, the exigencies of the circumstances may demand that, aside from these core elements, enemy combatant proceedings may be tailored to alleviate their uncommon potential to burden the Executive at a time of ongoing military conflict. Hearsay, for example, may need to be accepted as the most reliable available evidence from the Government in such a proceeding. Likewise, the Constitution would not be offended by a presumption in favor of the Government's evidence, so long as that presumption remained a rebuttable one and fair opportunity for rebuttal were provided. Thus, once the Government puts forth credible evidence that the habeas petitioner meets the enemy-combatant criteria, the onus could shift to the petitioner to rebut that evidence with more persuasive evidence that he falls outside the criteria. A burden-shifting scheme of this sort would meet the goal of ensuring that the errant tourist, embedded journalist, or local aid worker has a chance to prove military error while giving due regard to the Executive once it has put forth meaningful support for its conclusion that the detainee is in fact an enemy combatant. . . .

We think it unlikely that this basic process will have the dire impact on the central functions of warmaking that the Government forecasts. The parties agree that initial captures on the battlefield need not receive the process we have discussed here; that process is due only when the determination is made to *continue* to hold those who have been seized. . . . While we accord the greatest respect and consideration to the judgments of military authorities in matters relating to the actual prosecution of a war, and recognize that the scope of that discretion necessarily is wide, it does not infringe on the core role of the military for the courts to exercise their own time-honored and constitutionally mandated roles of reviewing and resolving claims like those presented here. . . .

D

In so holding, we necessarily reject the Government's assertion that separation of powers principles mandate a heavily circumscribed role for the courts in such circumstances. Indeed, the position that the courts must forgo any examination of the individual case and focus exclusively on the legality of the broader detention scheme cannot be mandated by any reasonable view of separation of powers, as this approach serves only to *condense* power into a single branch of government. We have long since made clear that a state of war is not a blank check for the President when it comes to the rights of the Nation's citizens. [*Youngstown*]. Whatever power the United States Constitution envisions for the Executive in its exchanges with other nations or with enemy organizations in times of conflict, it most assuredly envisions a role for all three branches when individual liberties are at stake. Likewise, we have made clear that, unless Congress acts to suspend it, the Great Writ of habeas corpus allows the Judicial Branch to play a necessary role in maintaining this delicate balance of governance, serving as an important judicial check on the Executive's discretion in the realm of detentions. Thus, while we do not question that our due process assessment must pay keen attention to the particular burdens faced by the Executive in the context of military action, it would turn our system of checks and balances on its head to suggest that a citizen could not make his way to court with a challenge to the factual basis for his detention by his government, simply because the Executive opposes making available such a challenge. Absent suspension of the writ by Congress, a citizen detained as an enemy combatant is entitled to this process.

Because we conclude that due process demands some system for a citizen detainee to refute his classification, the proposed "some evidence" standard is inadequate. Any process in which the Executive's factual assertions go wholly unchallenged or are simply presumed correct without any opportunity for the alleged combatant to demonstrate otherwise falls constitutionally short. [T]he "some evidence" standard in the past . . . primarily has been employed by courts in examining an administrative record developed after an adversarial proceeding—one with process at least of the sort that we today hold is constitutionally mandated in the citizen enemy-combatant setting. This standard therefore is ill suited to the situation in which a habeas petitioner has received no prior proceedings before any tribunal and had no prior opportunity to rebut the Executive's factual assertions before a neutral decisionmaker.

Today we are faced only with such a case. Aside from unspecified "screening" processes, and military interrogations in which the Government suggests Hamdi could have contested his classification, Hamdi has received no process. An interrogation by one's captor, however effective an intelligence-gathering tool, hardly constitutes a constitutionally adequate factfinding before a neutral decisionmaker. Compare Brief for Respondents 42-43 (discussing the "secure interrogation environment," and noting that military interrogations require a controlled "interrogation dynamic" and "a relationship of trust and dependency" and are "a critical source" of "timely and effective intelligence") with Concrete Pipe [& Products of Cal., Inc. v. Construction Laborers Pension Trust for Southern Cal.], 508 U.S. 602, 617-618 (1993) ("one is entitled as a matter of due process of law to an adjudicator who is not in a situation which would offer a possible temptation to the average man as a judge . . . which might lead him not to hold the balance nice, clear and true" that even purportedly fair adjudicators "are disqualified by their interest in the controversy to be decided is, of course, the general rule"). Plainly, the "process" Hamdi has received is not that to which he is entitled under the Due Process Clause.

There remains the possibility that the standards we have articulated could be met by an appropriately authorized and properly constituted military tribunal. Indeed, it is notable that military regulations already provide for such process in related instances, dictating that tribunals be made available to determine the status of enemy detainees who assert prisoner-of-war status under the Geneva Convention. In the absence of such process, however, a court that receives a petition for a writ of habeas corpus from an alleged enemy combatant must itself ensure that the minimum requirements of due process are achieved. . . . We anticipate that a District Court would proceed with the caution that we have indicated is necessary in this setting, engaging in a factfinding process that is both prudent and incremental. We have no reason to doubt that courts faced with these sensitive matters will pay proper heed both to the matters of national security that might arise in an individual case and to the constitutional limitations safeguarding essential liberties that remain vibrant even in times of security concerns.

IV

Hamdi asks us to hold that the Fourth Circuit also erred by denying him immediate access to counsel upon his detention and by disposing of the case without permitting him to meet with an attorney. Since our grant of certiorari in this case, Hamdi has been appointed counsel, with whom he has met for consultation purposes on several occasions, and with whom he is now being granted unmonitored meetings. He unquestionably has the right to access to counsel in connection with the proceedings on remand. No further consideration of this issue is necessary at this stage of the case.

The judgment of the United States Court of Appeals for the Fourth Circuit is vacated, and the case is remanded for further proceedings.

Justice SOUTER, with whom Justice GINSBURG joins, concurring in part, dissenting in part, and concurring in the judgment.

The plurality rejects [the government's position] on the exercise of habeas jurisdiction and so far I agree with its opinion. The plurality does, however, accept the Government's position that if Hamdi's designation as an enemy combatant is correct, his detention (at least as to some period) is authorized by an Act of Congress as required by [the Non-Detention Act, 18 U.S.C. §4001(a)], that is, by the Authorization for Use of Military Force, 115 Stat. 224 (hereinafter Force Resolution). Here, I disagree and respectfully dissent. The Government has failed to demonstrate that the Force Resolution authorizes the detention complained of here even on the facts the Government claims. If the Government raises nothing further than the record now shows, the Non-Detention Act entitles Hamdi to be released. . . .

II

The threshold issue is how broadly or narrowly to read the Non-Detention Act [18 U.S.C. §4001(a)], the tone of which is severe: "No citizen shall be imprisoned or otherwise detained by the United States except pursuant to an Act of Congress." Should the severity of the Act be relieved when the Government's stated factual justification for incommunicado detention is a war on terrorism, so that the Government may be said to act "pursuant" to congressional terms that fall short of explicit authority to imprison individuals? With one possible though important qualification, the answer has to be no. . . . The fact that Congress intended to guard against a repetition of the World War II internments when it repealed [an earlier Cold War statute that authorized the Attorney General in emergencies to detain anyone reasonably thought likely to engage in espionage or sabotage] and gave us §4001(a) provides a powerful reason to think that §4001(a) was meant to require clear congressional authorization before any citizen can be placed in a cell. . . . [T]he internments of the 1940's were accomplished by Executive action . . . Congress . . . intended to preclude reliance on vague congressional authority . . . for detention or imprisonment at the discretion of the Executive.

[Moreover], when Congress passed §4001(a) it was acting in light of an interpretive regime that subjected enactments limiting liberty in wartime to the requirement of a clear statement and it presumably intended §4001(a) to be read accordingly. . . . Ex parte Endo, [323 U.S. 283 (1944)] . . . decided the same day as *Korematsu* . . . set out this principle for scrutinizing wartime statutes in derogation of customary liberty: "In interpreting a wartime measure we must assume that [its] purpose was to allow for the greatest possible accommodation between . . . liberties and the exigencies of war. We must assume, when asked to find implied powers in a grant of legislative or executive authority, that the law makers intended to place no greater restraint on the citizen than was clearly and unmistakably indicated by the language they used." . . .

[T]he defining character of American constitutional government is its constant tension between security and liberty, serving both by partial helpings of each. In a government of separated powers, deciding finally on what is a reasonable degree of guaranteed liberty whether in peace or war (or some condition in between) is not well entrusted to the Executive Branch of Government, whose particular responsibility is to maintain security. For reasons of inescapable human nature, the branch of the Government asked to counter a serious threat is not the branch on which to rest the Nation's entire reliance in striking the balance between the will to win and the cost in liberty on the way to victory; the responsibility for security will naturally amplify the claim that security legitimately raises. A reasonable balance is more likely to be reached on the judgment of a different branch, just as Madison said in remarking that "the constant aim is to divide and arrange the several offices in such a manner as that each may be a check on the other—that the private interest of every individual may be a sentinel over the public rights." The Federalist No. 51. Hence the need for an assessment by Congress before citizens are subject to lockup, and likewise the need for a clearly expressed congressional resolution of the competing claims.

III

Under this principle of reading §4001(a) robustly to require a clear statement of authorization to detain, none of the Government's arguments suffices to justify Hamdi's detention.

[Justice Souter argues that the legislative history of §4001(a) shows that it was not limited to detentions for domestic crimes but was intended to apply to wartime military detentions justified on grounds of national security.]

[T]he Force Resolution was adopted one week after the attacks of September 11, 2001; it naturally speaks with some generality, but its focus is clear, and that is on the use of military power. . . . [I]t never so much as uses the word detention, and . . . Congress [has already provided a] well-stocked statutory arsenal of defined criminal offenses covering the gamut of actions that a citizen sympathetic to terrorists might commit. . . .

C

[Justice Souter notes that the government could argue that §4001(a) is satisfied because Hamdi's detention is consistent with the laws of war concerning detention of people captured on the battlefield. But the argument fails because the government is not actually acting in a way that is consistent with the laws of war.] By holding [Hamdi] incommunicado, . . . the Government obviously has not been treating him as a prisoner of war [consistent with the Third Geneva Convention], and in fact the Government claims that no Taliban detainee is entitled to prisoner of war status. This treatment appears to be a violation of the Geneva Convention provision that even in cases of doubt, captives are entitled to be treated as prisoners of war "until such time as their status has been determined by a competent tribunal.". . . [At the very least,] the Government has not made out its claim that in detaining Hamdi . . . , it is acting in accord with the laws of war authorized to be applied against citizens by the Force Resolution. . . .

D

[I]t is instructive to recall Justice Jackson's observation that the President is not Commander in Chief of the country, only of the military. Youngstown Sheet & Tube Co. v. Sawyer, 343 U.S. 579, 643-644 (1952) (concurring opinion); see also id., at 637-638 (Presidential authority is "at its lowest ebb" where the President acts contrary to congressional will). There may be room for one qualification to Justice Jackson's statement, however: in a moment of genuine emergency, when the Government must act with no time for deliberation, the Executive may be able to detain a citizen if there is reason to fear he is an imminent threat to the safety of the Nation and its people (though I doubt there is any want of statutory authority). This case, however, does not present that question, because an emergency power of necessity must at least be limited by the emergency; Hamdi has been locked up for over two years. . . .

IV

Because I find Hamdi's detention forbidden by §4001(a) and unauthorized by the Force Resolution, I would not reach any questions of what process he may be due in litigating disputed issues in a proceeding under the habeas statute or prior to the habeas enquiry itself. . . . Since this disposition does not command a majority of the Court, however, the need to give practical effect to the conclusions of eight members of the Court rejecting the Government's position calls for me to join with the plurality in ordering remand on terms closest to those I would impose. . . .

Justice SCALIA, with whom Justice STEVENS joins, dissenting.

Where the Government accuses a citizen of waging war against it, our constitutional tradition has been to prosecute him in federal court for treason or some other crime. Where the exigencies of war prevent that, the Constitution's Suspension Clause, Art. I, §9, cl. 2, allows Congress to relax the usual protections temporarily. Absent suspension, however, the Executive's assertion of military exigency has not been thought sufficient to permit detention without charge. No one contends that the congressional Authorization for Use of Military Force, on which the Government relies to justify its actions here, is an implementation of the Suspension Clause. Accordingly, I would reverse the decision below. . . .

Several limitations give my views in this matter a relatively narrow compass. They apply only to citizens, accused of being enemy combatants, who are detained within the territorial jurisdiction of a federal court. This is not likely to be a numerous group; currently we know of only two, Hamdi and Jose Padilla. Where the citizen is captured outside and held outside the United States, the constitutional requirements may be different. Moreover, even within the United States, the accused citizen-enemy combatant may lawfully be detained once prosecution is in progress or in contemplation. The Government has been notably successful in securing conviction, and hence long-term custody or execution, of those who have waged war against the state.

I frankly do not know whether these tools are sufficient to meet the Government's security needs, including the need to obtain intelligence through interrogation. It is far beyond my competence, or the Court's competence, to determine that. But it is not beyond Congress's. If the situation demands it, the Executive can ask Congress to authorize suspension of the writ—which can be made subject to whatever conditions Congress deems appropriate, including even the procedural novelties invented by the plurality today. To be sure, suspension is limited by the Constitution to cases of rebellion or invasion. But whether the attacks of September 11, 2001, constitute an "invasion," and whether those attacks still justify suspension several years later, are questions for Congress rather than this Court. If civil rights are to be curtailed during wartime, it must be done openly and democratically, as the Constitution requires, rather than by silent erosion through an opinion of this Court. . . .

Many think it not only inevitable but entirely proper that liberty give way to security in times of national crisis—that, at the extremes of military exigency, inter arma silent leges. Whatever the general merits of the view that war silences law or modulates its voice, that view has no place in the interpretation and application of a Constitution designed precisely to confront war and, in a manner that accords with democratic principles, to accommodate it. Because the Court has proceeded to meet the current emergency in a manner the Constitution does not envision, I respectfully dissent.

Justice THOMAS, dissenting.

The Executive Branch, acting pursuant to the powers vested in the President by the Constitution and with explicit congressional approval, has determined that Yaser Hamdi is an enemy combatant and should be detained. This detention falls squarely within the Federal Government's war powers, and we lack the expertise and capacity to second-guess that decision. As such, petitioners' habeas challenge should fail, and there is no reason to remand the case. The plurality reaches a contrary conclusion by failing adequately to consider basic principles of the constitutional structure as it relates to national security and foreign affairs and by using the balancing scheme of Mathews v. Eldridge, 424 U.S. 319 (1976). I do not think that the Federal Government's war powers can be balanced away by this Court. Arguably, Congress could provide for additional procedural protections, but until it does, we have no right to insist upon them. But even if I were to agree with the general approach the plurality takes, I could not accept the particulars. The plurality utterly fails to account for the Government's compelling interests and for our own institutional inability to weigh competing concerns correctly. I respectfully dissent.

I

[B]ecause the Founders understood that they could not foresee the myriad potential threats to national security that might later arise, they chose to create a Federal Government that necessarily possesses sufficient power to handle any threat to the security of the Nation. . . . The Founders intended that the President have primary responsibility—along with the necessary power—to protect the national security and to conduct the Nation's foreign relations. They did so principally because the structural advantages of a unitary Executive are essential in these domains. "Energy in the executive is a leading character in the definition of good government. It is essential to the protection of the community against foreign attacks." The Federalist No. 70 (A. Hamilton). The principle "ingredien[t]" for "energy in the executive" is "unity." This is because "[d]ecision, activity, secrecy, and dispatch will generally characterise the proceedings of one man, in a much more eminent degree, than the proceedings of any greater number."

These structural advantages are most important in the national-security and foreign-affairs contexts. "Of all the cares or concerns of government, the direction of war most peculiarly demands those qualities which distinguish the exercise of power by a single hand." The Federalist No. 74 (A. Hamilton). Also for these reasons, John Marshall explained that "[t]he President is the sole organ of the nation in its external relations, and its sole representative with foreign nations." 10 Annals of Cong. 613 (1800). To this end, the Constitution vests in the President "[t]he executive Power," Art. II, §1, provides that he "shall be Commander in Chief of the" armed forces, §2, and places in him the power to recognize foreign governments, §3.

This Court has long recognized these features and has accordingly held that the President has *constitutional* authority to protect the national security and that this authority carries with it broad discretion. . . . With respect to foreign affairs as well, the Court has recognized the President's independent authority and need to be free from interference. See, e.g., United States v. Curtiss-Wright Export Corp., 299 U.S. 304, 320 (1936) (explaining that the President "has his confidential sources of information. He has his agents in the form of diplomatic, consular and other officials. Secrecy in respect of information gathered by them may be highly necessary, and the premature disclosure of it productive of harmful results").

Congress, to be sure, has a substantial and essential role in both foreign affairs and national security. But it is crucial to recognize that *judicial* interference in these domains destroys the purpose of vesting primary responsibility in a unitary Executive. . . . [W]ith respect to certain decisions relating to national security and foreign affairs, the courts simply lack the relevant information and expertise to second-guess determinations made by the President based on information properly withheld. [Moreover,] even if the courts could compel the Executive to produce the necessary information, such decisions are simply not amenable to judicial determination because "[t]hey are delicate, complex, and involve large elements of prophecy."

. . .

I acknowledge that the question whether Hamdi's executive detention is lawful is a question properly resolved by the Judicial Branch, though the question comes to the Court with the strongest presumptions in favor of the Government. The plurality agrees that Hamdi's detention is lawful if he is an enemy combatant. But the question whether Hamdi is actually an enemy combatant is "of a kind for which the Judiciary has neither aptitude, facilities nor responsibility and which has long been held to belong in the domain of political power not subject to judicial intrusion or inquiry." That is, although it is appropriate for the Court to determine the judicial question whether the President has the asserted authority, we lack the information and expertise to question whether Hamdi is actually an enemy combatant, a question the resolution of which is committed to other branches.

II

. . . Although the President very well may have inherent authority to detain those arrayed against our troops, I agree with the plurality that we need not decide that question because Congress has authorized the President to do so [through the AUMF]. . . . The plurality, however, qualifies its recognition of the President's authority to detain enemy combatants in the war on terrorism [relying on the Geneva Conventions and the law of war]. But I do not believe that we may diminish the Federal Government's war powers by reference to a treaty and certainly not to a treaty that does not apply. . . .

III

I agree with the plurality that the Federal Government has power to detain those that the Executive Branch determines to be enemy combatants. But I do not think that the plurality has adequately explained the breadth of the President's authority to detain enemy combatants, an authority that includes making virtually conclusive factual findings. In my view, the structural considerations discussed above, as recognized in our precedent, demonstrate that we lack the capacity and responsibility to second-guess this determination. . . .

In this context, due process requires nothing more than a good-faith executive determination. . . . [A]n executive, acting pursuant to statutory and constitutional authority may, consistent with the Due Process Clause, unilaterally decide to detain an individual if the executive deems this necessary for the public safety *even if he is mistaken*. . . . The Government's asserted authority to detain an individual that the President has determined to be an enemy combatant, at least while hostilities continue, comports with the Due Process Clause. . . . [T]he Executive's decision that a detention is necessary to protect the public need not and should not be subjected to judicial second-guessing. Indeed, at least in the context of enemy-combatant determinations, this would defeat the unity, secrecy, and dispatch that the Founders believed to be so important to the warmaking function. . . .

Justice Scalia apparently does not disagree that the Federal Government has all power necessary to protect the Nation. If criminal processes do not suffice, however, Justice Scalia would require Congress to suspend the writ. But the fact that the writ may not be suspended "unless when in Cases of Rebellion or Invasion the public Safety may require it," Art. I, §9, cl. 2, poses two related problems. First, this condition might not obtain here or during many other emergencies during which this detention authority might be necessary. Congress would then have to choose between acting unconstitutionally and depriving the President of the tools he needs to protect the Nation. Second, I do not see how suspension would make constitutional otherwise unconstitutional detentions ordered by the President. It simply removes a remedy. Justice Scalia's position might therefore require one or both of the political branches to act unconstitutionally in order to protect the Nation. But the power to protect the Nation must be the power to do so lawfully. . . .

IV

. . . At issue here is the . . . interest of the security of the Nation. The Government seeks to further that interest by detaining an enemy soldier not only to prevent him from rejoining the ongoing fight [but also] to gather critical intelligence regarding the intentions and capabilities of our adversaries, a function that the Government avers has become all the more important in the war on terrorism.

Additional process, the Government explains, will destroy the intelligence gathering function. It also does seem quite likely that, under the process envisioned by the plurality, various military officials will have to take time to litigate this matter. And though the plurality does not say so, a meaningful ability to challenge the Government's factual allegations will probably require the Government to divulge highly classified information to the purported enemy combatant, who might then upon release return to the fight armed with our most closely held secrets.

Ultimately, the plurality's dismissive treatment of the Government's asserted interests arises from its apparent belief that enemy-combatant determinations are not part of "the actual prosecution of a war," or one of the "central functions of warmaking." This seems wrong: Taking *and holding* enemy combatants is a quintessential aspect of the prosecution of war. Moreover, this highlights serious difficulties in applying the plurality's balancing approach here. First, in the war context, we know neither the strength of the Government's interests nor the costs of imposing additional process.

Second, it is at least difficult to explain why the result should be different for other military operations that the plurality would ostensibly recognize as "central functions of warmaking." . . . Because a decision to bomb a particular target might extinguish *life* interests, the plurality's analysis seems to require notice to potential targets. To take one more example, in November 2002, a Central Intelligence Agency (CIA) Predator drone fired a Hellfire missile at a vehicle in Yemen carrying an al Qaeda leader, a citizen of the United States, and four others. It is not clear whether the CIA knew that an American was in the vehicle. But the plurality's due process would seem to require notice and opportunity to respond here as well. . . .

For these reasons, I would affirm the judgment of the Court of Appeals.

DISCUSSION

1. *The aftermath of* Hamdi. Following the decision in *Hamdi*, the government decided not to give Hamdi a hearing to determine his status. Instead, it announced that it believed that Hamdi no longer posed a threat to the United States or had any intelligence value, and released Hamdi to Saudi Arabia in October 2004, after holding him without charges for almost three years. In return Hamdi agreed to renounce terrorism, surrender his U.S. citizenship, and not to visit Afghanistan, Iraq, Israel, Pakistan, or Syria. Finally, he agreed not to sue the United States over his captivity.[71] What reasons might the government have had to continue to hold Hamdi and litigate its right to detain him indefinitely even if it believed that Hamdi had no intelligence value and did not constitute a threat?

2. *Construing the scope of congressional authorization.* Where deviations from normal legal procedures are justified on grounds of war and national security, the Court is more likely to defer to the President when it believes that Congress approves; conversely, it is more likely to seek to check the President only when

---

71. USA Today, Hamdi Returns to Saudi Arabia, http://usatoday30.usatoday.com/news/world/2004-10-11-hamdi_x.htm?POE=NEWISVA (last visited July 7, 2014); Findlaw, Yaser Esam Hamdi v. Donald Rumsfeld: Settlement Agreement, http://news.findlaw.com/hdocs/docs/hamdi/91704stlagrmnt.html (last visited Nov. 8, 2005).

he acts unilaterally or in the face of congressional disapproval.[72] This means that courts often play their most significant role in determining the existence and scope of congressional approval. By finding or refusing to find such approval, or by construing the scope of congressional approval broadly or narrowly, courts can limit and channel presidential ambitions without directly denying the existence of executive power.

Hamdi, Justice O'Connor avoids deciding whether the President may detain enemy combatants on his own authority as Commander-in-Chief; instead she argues that Congress has approved some detentions and then construes that approval narrowly. The plurality's narrow definition of "enemy combatant" limits the political and legal legitimacy of the President's actions if he seeks to detain people on the basis of a broader definition. Of course, the President can always go to Congress to seek a broader authorization. But if he does so, he will be acting many years after the September 11 attacks, when passions have cooled and Congress may provide greater oversight. Thus, by construing the terms of consent between the two branches and then deferring to that constructed agreement, the Court creates a space of power for itself.

Do you agree with the plurality's assertion that the language of the AUMF is sufficiently clear to authorize the President to detain enemy combatants, under the laws of war, for the purposes of incapacitation? Should a clearer statement be required where detention of citizens is at stake?

According to Justice Scalia, the President may only detain citizens as enemy combatants if Congress suspends the writ of habeas corpus. Otherwise, the government must use the normal resources of the criminal justice system. None of the Justices believed that the AUMF suspended the writ. Why? If the AUMF is not clear enough to suspend the writ of habeas corpus, why does it provide a sufficiently clear authorization to detain citizens as enemy combatants, especially if this will also deny citizens Bill of Rights protections?

3. *Who is an enemy combatant?* The *Hamdi* plurality defines the term "enemy combatant" narrowly to include "an individual who . . . was part of or supporting forces hostile to the United States or coalition partners in Afghanistan and who engaged in an armed conflict against the United States there" (internal quotation marks omitted). May the President hold citizen detainees who do not fit this definition?

Consider for example, the example of Jose Padilla, a U.S. citizen who had converted to Islam and taken the name Abdullah al Muhajir. Padilla was arrested at O'Hare Airport on May 8, 2002, after returning from Pakistan. He was detained under a material witness warrant issued by a federal district court in New York. On June 9, 2002, he was declared an enemy combatant and placed in a military brig in South Carolina for three and a half years. Originally, the Justice Department claimed that Padilla was an al Qaeda operative who was planning to explode a "dirty bomb"—a conventional bomb that would spread radioactive material—in an

72. See Samuel Issacharoff and Richard Pildes, Between Civil Libertarianism and Executive Unilateralism: An Institutional Process Approach to Rights During Wartime, in The Constitution in Wartime: Beyond Alarmism and Complacency 161-197 (Mark Tushnet ed., 2005), for a more developed version of this argument, with abundant historical examples.

American city. Two years later, the Justice Department stated that it believed that Padilla was planning to leak natural gas into apartment buildings and blow them up.

The *Hamdi* plurality suggests that capture on the battlefield in a foreign country is an important factor in its decision. It distinguishes Ex parte Milligan on the grounds that "Milligan was not a prisoner of war, but a resident of Indiana arrested while at home there. . . . Had Milligan been captured while he was assisting Confederate soldiers by carrying a rifle against Union troops on a Confederate battlefield, the holding of the Court might well have been different." How does the plurality's reasoning apply to the War on Terror, in which operatives and spies may not be apprehended on anything remotely resembling a "battlefield"?

In Rumsfeld v. Padilla, 542 U.S. 426 (2004), the Supreme Court held, 5-4, without reaching the merits, that Padilla should have filed his habeas petition in the District Court for the Southern District of South Carolina, rather than in New York, where he had originally been detained as a material witness. Justice Stevens, joined by Justices Souter, Ginsburg, and Breyer, dissented, arguing that the federal court in New York had jurisdiction to hear Padilla's claims and that his detention was illegal. Ultimately, the Bush Administration decided to avoid a Supreme Court opinion on the President's ability to detain Padilla as an enemy combatant, and it moved Padilla to the criminal justice system in January 2006. A federal jury convicted him of conspiracy to murder persons overseas and of providing material support to terrorists overseas. He was never indicted or convicted for the acts for which he was originally detained.

In December 2011, Congress passed and President Obama signed into law the National Defense Authorization Act for Fiscal Year 2012 (NDAA). Section 1021 gives congressional authorization for indefinite military detention "pending disposition under the laws of war." It defined a "covered person" subject to detention as "(1) A person who planned, authorized, committed, or aided the terrorist attacks that occurred on September 11, 2001, or harbored those responsible for those attacks" or "(2) A person who was a part of or substantially supported al-Qaeda, the Taliban, or associated forces that are engaged in hostilities against the United States or its coalition partners, including any person who has committed a belligerent act or has directly supported such hostilities in aid of such enemy forces." At the same time, it stated that "[n]othing in this section is intended to limit or expand the authority of the President or the scope of the Authorization for Use of Military Force" and that "Nothing in this section shall be construed to affect existing law or authorities relating to the detention of United States citizens, lawful resident aliens of the United States, or any other persons who are captured or arrested in the United States."

4. *Detention for purposes of interrogation.* The *Hamdi* plurality argues that the President is justified in detaining citizens according to the laws of war in order to prevent the captured person from returning to the battlefield. What if the purpose of detention is not incapacitation but to facilitate interrogation?

The government's admitted purpose in holding Jose Padilla, for example, was primarily to obtain information from him. In fact, the government initially opposed allowing Padilla to meet with an attorney because it "could set back by months the government's efforts to bring psychological pressure to bear upon Padilla in an effort to interrogate him, and could compromise the government's interrogation techniques." Padilla ex rel. Newman v. Rumsfeld, 243 F. Supp. 2d 42,

46 (S.D.N.Y. 2003). According to a January 9, 2003 declaration of Vice Admiral Lowell E. Jacoby, Director of the Defense Intelligence Agency, successful interrogation "is largely dependent upon creating an atmosphere of dependency and trust between the subject and the interrogator." It may take "months, or even years," to "obtain valuable intelligence from a subject." "Any insertion of counsel into the subject-interrogator relationship, for example—even if only for a limited duration or for a specific purpose—can undo months of work and may permanently shut down the interrogation process." Id. at 50.

If someone like Padilla is held primarily for the purposes of interrogation, is his detention authorized under the AUMF? The plurality says that "indefinite detention for the purpose of interrogation is not authorized." What about detention for five years? Could the government insist that a citizen's detention is justified for purposes of both interrogation and incapacitation?

5. *Indefinite detention.* The *Hamdi* plurality holds that Hamdi may only be detained "for the duration of the relevant conflict," in this case the war in Afghanistan. What about a citizen, like Padilla, who is accused of being an al Qaeda operative? The War on Terror has no definite endpoint. If the purpose for detention is incapacitation, does this mean that someone like Padilla could, in theory, be held for the rest of his life? Given that the purpose of attacking Afghanistan was to eliminate al Qaeda, why can't the government insist that Hamdi is part of the War on Terror as well?

6. *The unitary executive and judicial review.* Justice Thomas's dissent assumes that "Congress . . . has a substantial and essential role in both foreign affairs and national security. But it is crucial to recognize that *judicial* interference in these domains destroys the purpose of vesting primary responsibility in a unitary Executive" (emphasis in original). Thomas argues that the courts lack the necessary expertise to determine whether citizens like Hamdi are enemy combatants. If so, then is the President's decision that a citizen is an enemy combatant effectively unreviewable? Does Thomas's logic apply equally to citizens apprehended in the United States? Would Thomas's position permit indefinite detention of citizens for purposes of interrogation, without rights to a hearing or a right to counsel?

7. *Guantanamo Bay and the detention of noncitizens.* Following the September 11, 2001 attacks, the United States arrested persons from many different countries suspected of fighting on behalf of the Taliban in Afghanistan, working for al Qaeda, or working for various other terrorist organizations. Many of these persons were detained at the U.S. Naval Base in Guantanamo Bay, Cuba. The United States occupies Guantanamo Bay under a lease and treaty recognizing Cuba's ultimate sovereignty, but which gives the United States complete jurisdiction and control for so long as it does not abandon the leased areas. An estimated 775 detainees have been held at Guantanamo at some point since 9/11. Other detainees, including those believed to be top members of al Qaeda, were placed in secret locations around the world operated by the CIA. The Administration's acknowledged purpose for placing detainees at Guantanamo Bay and in other undisclosed locations was to avoid falling under the supervision of American courts. The detainees have been interrogated but most have not been charged with any crime. Over time, the United States has sought to release the Guantanamo detainees to their home countries. As of July 2021, approximately 39 detainees still remain.

In Rasul v. Bush, 542 U.S. 466 (2004), the Supreme Court, in a 5-4 decision written by Justice Stevens, held that the Guantanamo detainees had the right to bring habeas petitions to challenge the legality of their detention. *Rasul* was premised on an interpretation of the scope of the federal habeas statute. In response, Congress passed §§1005(e) and (h) of the Detainee Treatment Act of 2005 (also known as the Graham-Levin amendment), which withdrew habeas jurisdiction for petitions filed by aliens detained "by the Department of Defense at Guantanamo Bay, Cuba" and "any other action against the United States or its agents relating to any aspect of the detention" of aliens there. In Hamdan v. Rumsfeld, discussed infra, the Supreme Court evaded these jurisdictional limitations by holding that they did not apply retroactively to cases already on appeal.

3. Military Tribunals

On November 13, 2001, President Bush issued an executive order authorizing the creation of military tribunals to try persons suspected of terrorist activities arising out of the September 11 attacks on the United States. Detention, Treatment, and Trial of Certain Non-Citizens in the War Against Terrorism, 66 Fed. Reg. 57,833 (Nov. 13, 2001). A person was subject to detention and to trial by a military tribunal if the President determined that there was reason to believe that the individual is or was a member of the al Qaeda terrorist organization, "has engaged in, aided or abetted, or conspired to commit, acts of international terrorism, or acts in preparation therefore, that have caused, threaten to cause, or have as their aim to cause, injury to or adverse effects on the United States, its citizens, national security, foreign policy, or economy," or has harbored such a person. The order provided for conviction and sentencing upon a two-thirds vote of the members of the commission present at the time of voting. (Subsequent Department of Defense regulations issued in March 2002 made clear that a unanimous verdict would be required for a death sentence but not for noncapital offenses.) Review of the decision rested solely in the President or in military officials that he or the Secretary of Defense designated. The Order stated that defendants "shall not be privileged to seek any remedy or maintain any proceeding, directly or indirectly, or to have any such remedy or proceeding sought on the individual's behalf, in (i) any court of the United States, or any State thereof, (ii) any court of any foreign nation, or (iii) any international tribunal."

Traditional rules of criminal procedure and evidence that apply in ordinary criminal courts were relaxed and evidence that would ordinarily be excluded from a criminal trial (or a military court-martial) could be admitted as long as it would "have probative value to a reasonable person." There was no requirement of grand jury presentment or indictment. Finally, the military tribunals could be held in secret. The presiding officer could exclude the accused and defense counsel from parts of the proceedings and the accused did not have the right to examine all of the evidence against him.

In Hamdan v. Rumsfeld, 548 U.S. 557 (2006), the Supreme Court held 5-3 that the system of military commissions was illegal, and violated the Uniform Code of Military Justice (UCMJ) and the Geneva Conventions. Justice Stevens's majority opinion analyzed the legality of the commissions in terms of congressional authorization. It was unnecessary to decide whether the President could create military commissions without congressional approval, because Congress had approved the creation of military commissions in Article 21 of the UCMJ. Given Congress's previous action in passing the UCMJ, the Court would treat Congress's authorization as the basis of the President's power. In a footnote, Justice Stevens explained: "Whether or not the President has independent power, absent congressional authorization, to convene military commissions, he may not disregard limitations that Congress has, in proper exercise of its own war powers, placed on his powers. See Youngstown Sheet & Tube Co. v. Sawyer, 343 U.S. 579, 637 (1952) (Jackson, J., concurring). The Government does not argue otherwise."

Justice Stevens argued that "there is nothing in the text or legislative history of the AUMF even hinting that Congress intended to expand or alter the authorization set forth in Article 21 of the UCMJ. . . . Together, the UCMJ, the AUMF, and the [2005 Detainee Treatment Act] at most acknowledge a general Presidential authority to convene military commissions in circumstances where justified under the 'Constitution and laws,' including the law of war." For this reason, Justice Stevens, concluded, the military commission convened to try Hamdan was illegal because its procedures differed from—and were less protective than—those authorized under the UCMJ and Common Article 3 of the Geneva Conventions.

"Article 36 [of the UCMJ] places two restrictions on the President's power to promulgate rules of procedure for courts-martial and military commissions alike. First, no procedural rule he adopts may be 'contrary to or inconsistent with' the UCMJ—however practical it may seem. Second, the rules adopted must be 'uniform insofar as practicable.' That is, the rules applied to military commissions must be the same as those applied to courts-martial unless such uniformity proves impracticable." Justice Stevens argued that "[n]othing in the record before us demonstrates that it would be impracticable to apply court-martial rules in this case. [T]he only reason offered in support of that determination is the danger posed by international terrorism. Without for one moment underestimating that danger, it is not evident to us why it should require, in the case of Hamdan's trial, any variance from the rules that govern courts-martial."

"Common Article 3 [of the Geneva Conventions] . . . requires that Hamdan be tried by a 'regularly constituted court affording all the judicial guarantees which are recognized as indispensable by civilized peoples' . . . [and] [t]he regular military courts in our system are the courts-martial established by congressional statutes."

Justice Alito, joined by Justice Scalia and Justice Thomas (in part), dissented. Chief Justice Roberts, who had participated on the D.C. Circuit panel below before he was confirmed to the Supreme Court, did not participate.

Hamdan is another example of how judicial construction of congressional authorization shapes the constitutional powers of the President; although the decision is nominally statutory, it has strongly constitutional overtones. *Hamdan* required a new congressional authorization (as interpreted by the Court) in order to create a new set of military commissions that differed from the requirements of the UCMJ and the Geneva Conventions (as the Court interpreted them). It did not prevent special military commissions for Guantanamo detainees, but by striking down the existing commissions it required Congress to publicly state (1) that it no longer wanted to abide by the principle of uniformity announced in the UCMJ, (2) that it no longer would require that military commissions abide by the laws of war as the Court had interpreted them, or (3) that Congress no longer considered the Geneva Conventions binding on the United States. (The third possibility was politically infeasible.)

In response to *Hamdan*, Congress passed the Military Commissions Act of 2006. The MCA established a new set of military commissions with special rules of evidence and procedure less protective than those in the UMCJ for the purpose of trying "alien unlawful enemy combatants." Responding to the Court's holding that the previous commissions violated the Geneva Conventions, the MCA declared that the new commissions complied with the Geneva Conventions, and prohibited defendants before such commissions from "invok[ing] the Geneva Conventions as a source of rights." It also stated that "no person may invoke the Geneva Conventions as a source of legal rights in habeas corpus or civil actions against the United States, current or former officers, employees, agents, military personnel, in any U.S. or state court." Several of the MCA's evidentiary and procedural provisions were subsequently modified in the Military Commissions Act of 2009.

What constitutional values are served by requiring Congress (and the President) to make such choices publicly? Given the result, was the Court's intervention an exercise in futility? An act of legitimation? What are the costs of courts intervening in this way?

4. Habeas Corpus for the Guantanamo Detainees

As noted above, Congress responded to *Hamdi* with the Detainee Treatment Act of 2005 in order to prevent Guantanamo detainees from raising habeas challenges in the federal courts. The Court was only able to hear *Hamdan* because the majority interpreted the Detainee Treatment Act to permit a limited set of habeas appeals. Section 7 of the Military Commissions Act of 2006 responded to that interpretation, shutting the door the Court had opened. Section 7(a) of the MCA eliminated habeas corpus jurisdiction to hear habeas petitions by aliens that the President had designated as enemy combatants.

Article I, §9, cl. 2, provides that "[t]he Privilege of the Writ of Habeas Corpus shall not be suspended, unless when in Cases of Rebellion or Invasion the public Safety may require it." The Bush Administration argued that the Suspension Clause was not violated. Habeas did not extend to the Guantanamo detainees, or, if it did, that the Administration and Congress had provided an effective alternative to habeas.

Following *Hamdi*, the Secretary of Defense set up Combatant Status Review Tribunals to review claims that detainees were being held unlawfully. Under the Detainee Treatment Act of 2005, detainees could appeal these determinations of their status as enemy combatants only to the D.C. Circuit, which was limited to whether the status determination was consistent with the "standards and procedures" set forth by the Secretary of Defense, and whether those standards and procedures were "consistent with the Constitution and laws of the United States." Similarly, the MCA provided that the D.C. Circuit had exclusive jurisdiction to hear appeals from the new military tribunals, limited to "matters of law" and to whether the decision was consistent with "the standards and practices" in the MCA, and, "to the extent applicable, the Constitution and laws of the United States."

BOUMEDIENE v. BUSH, 553 U.S. 723 (2008): [In *Boumediene,* the Court, in a 5-4 decision, held that the Suspension Clause applied to detainees held at Guantanamo Bay, that Congress had not declared that it was suspending the writ of habeas corpus, and that §7 of the MCA was an inadequate substitute for habeas corpus and therefore illegal.]

KENNEDY, J.:

[T]he Government says the Suspension Clause affords petitioners no rights because the United States does not claim sovereignty over the place of detention. [We] do not question the Government's position that Cuba, not the United States, maintains sovereignty, in the legal and technical sense of the term, over Guantanamo Bay. [But] it is not altogether uncommon for a territory to be under the de jure sovereignty of one nation, while under the plenary control, or practical sovereignty, of another. . . .

The Government's formal sovereignty-based test raises troubling separation-of-powers concerns as well. . . . The United States has maintained complete and uninterrupted control of the bay for over 100 years. . . . Yet the Government's view is that the Constitution [has] had no effect there, at least as to noncitizens, because the United States disclaimed sovereignty in the formal sense of the term. The necessary implication of the argument is that by surrendering formal sovereignty over any unincorporated territory to a third party, while at the same time entering into a lease that grants total control over the territory back to the United States, it would be possible for the political branches to govern without legal constraint.

Our basic charter cannot be contracted away like this. . . . [T]o hold the political branches have the power to switch the Constitution on or off at will . . . would permit a striking anomaly in our tripartite system of government, leading to a regime in which Congress and the President, not this Court, say "what the law is." Marbury v. Madison, 1 Cranch 137 (1803).

These concerns have particular bearing upon the Suspension Clause question in the cases now before us, for the writ of habeas corpus is itself an indispensable mechanism for monitoring the separation of powers. The test for determining the scope of this provision must not be subject to manipulation by those whose power it is designed to restrain. . . .

We hold that Art. I, §9, cl. 2, of the Constitution has full effect at Guantanamo Bay. If the privilege of habeas corpus is to be denied to the detainees now before us, Congress must act in accordance with the requirements of the Suspension Clause. The MCA does not purport to be a formal suspension of the writ; and the Government, in its submissions to us, has not argued that it is. Petitioners, therefore, are entitled to the privilege of habeas corpus to challenge the legality of their detention. . . .

Petitioners identify what they see as myriad deficiencies in the CSRTs. The most relevant for our purposes are the constraints upon the detainee's ability to rebut the factual basis for the Government's assertion that he is an enemy combatant. [T]he detainee has limited means to find or present evidence to challenge the Government's case against him. He does not have the assistance of counsel and may not be aware of the most critical allegations that the Government relied upon to order his detention. See App. to Pet. for Cert. in No. 06-1196, at 156, F(8) (noting that the detainee can access only the "unclassified portion of the Government

Information"). The detainee can confront witnesses that testify during the CSRT proceedings. But given that there are in effect no limits on the admission of hearsay evidence—the only requirement is that the tribunal deem the evidence "relevant and helpful,"—the detainee's opportunity to question witnesses is likely to be more theoretical than real. . . .

[A]lthough we make no judgment as to whether the CSRTs, as currently constituted, satisfy due process standards, we agree with petitioners that, even when all the parties involved in this process act with diligence and in good faith, there is considerable risk of error in the tribunal's findings of fact. . . . And given that the consequence of error may be detention of persons for the duration of hostilities that may last a generation or more, this is a risk too significant to ignore.

For the writ of habeas corpus, or its substitute, to function as an effective and proper remedy in this context, the court that conducts the habeas proceeding must have the means to correct errors that occurred during the CSRT proceedings. This includes some authority to assess the sufficiency of the Government's evidence against the detainee. It also must have the authority to admit and consider relevant exculpatory evidence that was not introduced during the earlier proceeding. . . .

Chief Justice Roberts dissented, joined by Justices Scalia, Thomas, and Alito: "This statutory scheme provides the combatants held at Guantanamo greater procedural protections than have ever been afforded alleged enemy detainees—whether citizens or aliens—in our national history. So who has won? Not the detainees. The Court's analysis leaves them with only the prospect of further litigation to determine the content of their new habeas right, followed by further litigation to resolve their particular cases, followed by further litigation before the D.C. Circuit—where they could have started had they invoked the DTA procedure."

Justice Scalia also wrote a dissenting opinion, joined by Chief Justice Roberts, Justice Thomas, and Justice Alito: "Today, for the first time in our Nation's history, the Court confers a constitutional right to habeas corpus on alien enemies detained abroad by our military forces in the course of an ongoing war. . . . The game of bait-and-switch that today's opinion plays upon the Nation's Commander in Chief will make the war harder on us. It will almost certainly cause more Americans to be killed."

DISCUSSION

1. *A tug of war. Boumediene* is the third in a series of cases (along with Rasul v. Bush and *Hamdan*) involving the Court's jurisdiction to hear appeals from the Guantanamo detainees, restricting what the President could do and inviting the President and Congress to respond if they liked. Congress and the President have done so repeatedly. In response to *Rasul,* Congress passed the Detainee Treatment Act of 2005 to keep the federal courts from hearing habeas petitions from Guantanamo detainees. In response, in *Hamdan,* the Court construed the DTA to allow it to hear habeas petitions in the cases before it and then held that the President's military commissions were illegal. Then, in response to *Hamdan,* the President and Congress passed the Military Commissions Act of 2006, reinstating the commissions. Section 7 of the MCA once again sought to eliminate habeas and federal question jurisdiction for the Guantanamo detainees. In *Boumediene,* the Court

struck down §7, making clear that the Suspension Clause applies to detainees held at Guantanamo Bay. In theory, the President and Congress could respond once again by officially suspending the writ of habeas corpus, but it is very unlikely that they will so do.

In one sense, the sequence of cases from Hamdi v. Rumsfeld to *Rasul* to *Hamdan* to *Boumediene* is remarkable: They are among a very small number of decisions in which the Supreme Court rejects a claim made by the President in wartime, *Youngstown* being the most obvious example.

In *Youngstown,* the Court believed that Congress had not gone along with the President's decision to seize the steel mills. Hence, it treated the case as falling into "box three" of Justice Jackson's theory, where the President's power was at its lowest ebb. Similarly, in *Hamdi* and *Hamdan,* the Court construed Congress as giving its authority (under the AUMF and the UCMJ) for some presidential actions but not for others. And in *Rasul* and *Hamdan,* it artfully read jurisdictional provisions to give it permission to hear the cases before it.

In *Boumediene,* by contrast, the President and Congress explicitly agreed to strip jurisdiction in habeas cases. Why then isn't this a case in "box one" of *Youngstown* where the full war powers of the national government are being asserted, and why didn't the Court defer?

One answer might be the political situation in the country: an unpopular war in Iraq coupled with continuing reports of torture and abuse at Guantanamo Bay, Abu Ghraib, Bagram, and the CIA "black sites." *Youngstown* was decided in 1952 when President Truman was weakened by the Korean War and had lost much of his popularity. Given President Bush's record-setting levels of unpopularity, and the fact that the Democrats took control of Congress following the 2006 elections (after the passage of the Military Commissions Act), the Court risked very little by refusing to defer to the President. Is it particularly inappropriate for courts to intervene in matters of war when Presidents are politically weakened; or on the contrary, is it only when Presidents are weakened politically that courts feel able to insist that Presidents abide by constitutional guarantees?

A second possible reason why the Court intervened in *Boumediene* is that the majority no longer believed that the separation of powers between Congress and the White House acted as a realistic check on the President, especially when one party controlled the political branches. As Justice Jackson explained in *Youngstown*: "[The] rise of the party system has made a significant extraconstitutional supplement to real executive power. No appraisal of his necessities is realistic which overlooks that he heads a political system as well as a legal system. Party loyalties and interests, sometimes more binding than law, extend his effective control into branches of government other than his own and he often may win, as a political leader, what he cannot command under the Constitution." In this context, note that members of Congress might have been unwilling to cross a President of their own party but perfectly happy to let the courts take the political heat. Senator Arlen Specter, head of the Senate Judiciary Committee, denounced the Military Commissions Act for unconstitutionally suspending habeas corpus but voted for it anyway, presumably hoping that the courts would strike it down. See Charles Babington and Jonathan Weisman, Senate Approves Detainee Bill Backed by Bush: Constitutional Challenges Predicted, Wash. Post, Sept. 29, 2006 at A01, available at http://www.washingtonpost.com/wp-dyn/content/article/2006/09/28

/AR2006092800824.html (quoting Specter as supporting the bill because "the court will clean it up"). Does this mean that courts *should* be less deferential to national security laws passed under periods of one-party rule?

A third possible explanation of *Boumediene* was that the MCA was not simply a dispute about the relative powers of Congress vis-à-vis the President, but involved an attempt to strip the Court of its own jurisdiction. Hence the Court was far more likely to be protective of its own turf and far more willing to push back at the President. This, however, begs the question of what the Court's power should have been. According to Justice Scalia and the dissenters, the Court had no authority to hear the cases in the first place, so it lost nothing by the passage of §7.

2. *You've come a long way, baby.* Justice Kennedy, without a trace of irony, cites to Marbury v. Madison as a justification for the Court's jurisdiction to hear these cases and subject the actions of the political branches to the rule of law. In *Marbury*, the Supreme Court went out of its way to hold that it did not have jurisdiction to hear Marbury's case in order to avoid provoking a confrontation with a Republican President and Congress. (And in Stuart v. Laird, decided a week later, the Court meekly refused to stand up to the Republicans' elimination of circuit judgeships despite the Constitution's guarantee of life tenure.) Clearly, the Court feels it is more powerful today than it was in Jefferson's time. Is it fair to say that *Boumediene* could only have occurred in a world after Cooper v. Aaron and Bush v. Gore?

3. *Could Congress respond by suspending the writ?* In theory, at least, Congress and the President could respond by repassing §7 of the MCA with a clear statement that they intended to suspend the writ of habeas corpus under Article I, §9. However, as noted above, it is very unlikely that the current Congress would do this.

Suspensions under the Habeas Corpus Clause are permitted only if the United States is currently in a state of rebellion or invasion, and the public safety requires suspension. Is this test satisfied under current conditions? Note that §7 of the MCA is permanent legislation that is not limited to a temporary state of emergency—it has no sunset provision, and it applies to detainees captured and held anywhere in the world.

One argument for the constitutionality of a suspension would be that the judgment whether these tests have been satisfied and a state of emergency exists rests solely with Congress and is a political question that cannot be reviewed by the courts. So if Congress declares that the United States is under an emergency of indefinite or even permanent duration, the Court should defer to its decision. Does this prove too much?

4. *What did* Boumediene *achieve? The role of the D.C. Circuit.* Following its decisions in *Hamdi, Hamdan,* and *Boumediene,* the Supreme Court has largely delegated the task of developing the law of executive detention to the District of Columbia Circuit Court of Appeals. In a series of decisions following *Boumediene,* the D.C. Circuit has mostly interpreted the Supreme Court's decisions in favor of executive power and against the claims of detainees. Concurring in Esmail v. Obama, 639 F.3d 1075 (D.C. Cir. 2011), Judge Laurence Silberman reflected on "the unusual incentives and disincentives that bear on judges on the D.C. Circuit courts—particularly the Court of Appeals—charged with deciding these detainee habeas cases." He criticized the Supreme Court and argued that his colleagues should always err on the side of denying habeas petitions brought by Guantanamo inmates.

Comparing these cases to "the typical criminal case," Judge Silberman explained that "[w]hen we are dealing with detainees, candor obliges me to admit that one can not help but be conscious of the infinitely greater downside risk to our country, and its people, of an order releasing a detainee who is likely to return to terrorism." In fact, he maintained, "I doubt any of my colleagues will vote to grant a petition [for habeas corpus] if he or she believes that it is somewhat likely that the petitioner is an al Qaeda adherent or an active supporter . . . [although] I, like my colleagues, certainly would release a petitioner against whom the government could not muster even 'some evidence.'" Yet "if it turns out that regardless of our decisions the executive branch does not release winning petitioners because no other country will accept them and they will not be released into the United States, then the whole process leads to virtual advisory opinions. It becomes a charade prompted by the Supreme Court's defiant—if only theoretical—assertion of judicial supremacy, see *Boumediene*, sustained by posturing on the part of the Justice Department, and providing litigation exercise for the detainee bar."

What do you make of Judge Silberman's remarkably candid opinion? Given that the D.C. Circuit has been given the responsibility for developing the law of executive detention, do its members have good reason to read the Supreme Court's decisions as narrowly as possible in favor of the executive and, in some cases, even beyond what the executive itself asks for?

On one reading, the cases from *Hamdi* through *Boumediene* have defended rule of law values against an overreaching executive in a time of national emergency, although they have not necessarily done very much in the way of protecting civil liberties. On another reading, these cases have been an unwarranted and meddlesome interference with the President's attempt to secure the safety of the nation in a rapidly changing political and military context. And on still another reading, these cases have been neither a victory for the rule of law nor a significant interference with the President's ability to innovate. Rather, the effect of these cases has been to legitimate the construction of a new system of preventive detention outside the criminal process in which persons suspected of terrorism or material assistance to terrorism can be maintained indefinitely with little chance that federal courts will ever release them. Which reading strikes you as most plausible?

5. Torture and Presidential Power

As noted previously in connection with Hamdi v. Rumsfeld, although the official justification for detention has been incapacitation, the actual practice of the United States in detaining terrorist suspects has been interrogation for the purpose of gathering intelligence. Prisoner abuse scandals at Abu Ghraib prison in Iraq and previous reports of prisoner abuse at Guantanamo Bay, Cuba led to investigations about government policy for prisoner interrogations after September 11, and about whether government officials permitted or engaged in torture and cruel, inhuman, and degrading treatment of prisoners for intelligence-gathering purposes. These investigations revealed that the Bush Administration had been deliberating about the permissible bounds of prisoner interrogation for some time.

In order to fulfill its treaty obligations under the U.N. Convention Against Torture and Other Cruel, Inhuman or Degrading Treatment or Punishment, Congress has prohibited torture overseas. Section 2340A makes it illegal for anyone "outside the United States [to] commit[] or attempt[] to commit torture." Section 2340 defines torture as "an act committed by a person acting under the color of law specifically intended to inflict severe physical or mental pain or suffering (other than pain or suffering incidental to lawful sanctions) upon another person within his custody or physical control." Congress created the overseas ban on torture in §2340A because it assumed that torture performed by public officials in the United States was already prohibited by the Due Process Clause and the Eighth Amendment's prohibition on cruel and unusual punishments.

On August 1, 2002, the Office of Legal Counsel (OLC) produced a memo entitled "Re: Standards of Conduct for Interrogation under 18 U.S.C. 2340-2340A," for Alberto R. Gonzales, counsel to President Bush.[73] The OLC memo was written at the request of the CIA, which had been conducting interrogations of top-level al Qaeda operatives held in undisclosed locations outside the United States. The CIA sought greater authority to conduct more aggressive interrogations of prisoners than had been permitted prior to the September 11, 2001 attacks on the United States.

The OLC memo discussed to what extent the Administration and members of the armed forces were legally bound by U.S. and international law prohibiting torture and prisoner abuse. The memorandum was signed by Jay S. Bybee, then head of OLC, who later became a judge on the Ninth U.S. Circuit Court of Appeals.

Another memorandum, dated March 6, 2003, was authored by a Department of Defense working group that had been convened by Defense Secretary Donald H. Rumsfeld to come up with new interrogation guidelines for detainees at Guantanamo Bay, Cuba. This memo incorporated significant parts of the legal theories offered in the OLC memo.[74]

The OLC and Defense Department concluded that prohibitions on what constituted "torture" under §2340A and the U.N. Convention could be read quite narrowly. Hence the United States could engage in "a wide array of acts that constitute cruel, inhuman, or degrading treatment or punishment [and that] do not amount to torture."[75] It concluded that a coercive procedure could not be considered torture under §2340A unless it caused pain equivalent to that accompanying "serious physical injury, such as organ failure, impairment of bodily function or even death."[76]

Second, the OLC and Defense Department memos asserted that congressional statutes and international laws against torture could not in any case constitutionally bind the President. The OLC memo explained:[77]

> Even if an interrogation method were arguably to violate Section 2340A, the statute would be unconstitutional if it impermissibly encroached on

---

73. See Memorandum from Jay S. Bybee, U.S. Dept. of Justice, to Alberto R. Gonzales, Counsel to the President (Aug. 1, 2002), available at http://www.washingtonpost.com/wp-srv/nation/documents/dojinterrogationmemo20020801.pdf.

74. See Working Group, Report on the Detainee Interrogations in the Global War on Terrorism (2003), available at http://en.wikisource.org/wiki/Working_Group_Report_on_Detainee_Interrogations (last visited July 2, 2014).

75. Id. at 31.

76. Id. at 13.

77. Id. at 31, 33-36, 39.

the President's constitutional power to conduct a military campaign. As Commander-in-Chief, the President has the constitutional authority to order interrogations of enemy combatants to gain intelligence information concerning the military plans of the enemy. The commands of the Commander-in-Chief power are especially pronounced in the middle of a war when the country has already suffered a direct attack. In such a case, the information gained from interrogations may prevent future attacks by foreign enemies. Any effort to apply Section 2340A in a manner that interferes with the President's direction of such core war matters as the detention and interrogation of enemy combatants thus would be unconstitutional.

. . . [T]he President enjoys complete discretion in the exercise of his Commander-in-Chief authority and in conducting operations against hostile forces. . . . That authority is at its height in the middle of a war. . . . [W]ithout a clear statement otherwise, we will not read a criminal statute as infringing on the President's authority in these areas. . . .

[S]ection 2340A must be construed as not applying to interrogations undertaken pursuant to his Commander-in-Chief authority. . . . Congress lacks authority under Article I to set the terms and conditions under which the President may exercise his authority as Commander-in-Chief to control the conduct of operations during a war. . . . Congress may no more regulate the President's ability to detain and interrogate enemy combatants than it may regulate his ability to direct troop movements on the battlefield. . . .

[Even if Congress enacted §2340A] with full knowledge and consideration of the President's Commander-in-Chief power, and . . . intended to restrict his discretion in the interrogation of enemy combatants, . . . we conclude that the Department of Justice could not enforce Section 2340A against federal officials acting pursuant to the President's constitutional authority to wage a military campaign.

. . . Any effort by Congress to regulate the interrogation of enemy combatants would violate the Constitution's sole vesting of the Commander-in-Chief authority in the President. There can be little doubt that intelligence operations, such as the detention and interrogation of enemy combatants and leaders, are both necessary and proper for the effective conduct of a military campaign. Indeed, such operations may be of more importance in a war with an international terrorist organization than one with the conventional armed forces of a nation-state, due to the former's emphasis on secret operations and surprise attacks against civilians. It may be the case that only successful interrogations can provide the information necessary to prevent the success of covert terrorist attacks upon the United States and its citizens. Congress can no more interfere with the President's conduct of the interrogation of enemy combatants than it can dictate strategic or tactical decisions on the battlefield. Just as statutes that order the President to conduct warfare in a certain manner or for specific goals would be unconstitutional, so too are laws that seek to prevent a President from gaining the intelligence he believes necessary to prevent attacks on the United States.

After the OLC and Department of Defense memos became public, the Bush Administration disowned them and instructed the Justice Department to prepare new legal opinions that construed the definition of torture somewhat more broadly. These new legal opinions, however, did not disavow the constitutional theory of presidential power offered in the OLC and Department of Defense memos.

On December 30, 2005, Congress passed the Detainee Treatment Act. Section 1003 of the Act provided that "[n]o individual in the custody or under the physical control of the United States Government, regardless of nationality or physical location, shall be subject to cruel, inhuman, or degrading treatment or punishment." "[C]ruel, inhuman, or degrading treatment or punishment" was defined as "the cruel, unusual, and inhumane treatment or punishment prohibited by the Fifth, Eighth, and Fourteenth Amendments to the Constitution of the United States, as defined in the United States Reservations, Declarations and Understandings to the United Nations Convention Against Torture and Other Forms of Cruel, Inhuman or Degrading Treatment or Punishment done at New York, December 10, 1984." If, according to the OLC memo, §2340A could not bind the President, why should the prohibitions in the Detainee Treatment Act?

Upon taking office, President Barack Obama issued an executive order repealing previous executive orders concerning CIA interrogations and henceforth limiting interrogation methods to those listed in the Army Field Manual. Executive Order 13491—Ensuring Lawful Interrogations (Jan. 22, 2009). The Obama Administration ultimately concluded that it would not bring any criminal prosecutions for torture or abuse in prisoner interrogations.

DISCUSSION

1. *Maximum power, twilight zone, or lowest ebb?* According to the OLC memo, may Congress ever pass laws limiting what the President might seek to do as Commander-in-Chief? The OLC memo does not mention *Youngstown*. Is it consistent with that decision? Consider the following arguments:

(a) The OLC's memo is inconsistent with *Youngstown*. When the President attempts to do what Congress has specifically forbidden him to do, his power is at its lowest ebb. He lacks inherent authority to violate both congressional law and international agreements prohibiting torture.

(b) The OLC's memo is completely consistent with *Youngstown*. Even though Congress has attempted to limit the President's authority to authorize torture, this does not place the President's power at its lowest ebb. Congress's attempt is ineffective because Congress does not have concurrent power with the President to regulate detention and interrogation of enemy combatants.

Is it clear from the constitutional text that Congress has no authority to regulate the interrogation or detention of prisoners captured by the military and held in custody by the military or the CIA? Consider Congress's powers in Article I, §8, cl. 10 ("To define and punish piracies and felonies committed on the high seas, and offences against the law of nations"), cl. 11 ("To declare war, grant letters of marque and reprisal, and make rules concerning captures on land and water"), and cl. 14 ("To make rules for the government and regulation of the land and naval forces"). How should those powers be reconciled with the President's power as Commander-in-Chief? Could the President argue that Congress has some power to regulate interrogations by the military but not by the CIA?

How does the OLC memo's account of the Commander-in-Chief power interact with the President's Article II duty to take care that the laws be faithfully executed? Could the President respond that there is no conflict, because the President has no duty to abide by laws that cannot constitutionally be applied to him in any case?

2. *Just following orders.* The Department of Defense memo of March 6, 2003 argues that people who engaged in torture at the direction of the executive may not be prosecuted for war crimes because they were following the orders of a superior. Following orders is usually not a defense under both American and international law if the subordinate knows or has reason to know that the order is unlawful. The memo interprets this doctrine to mean that "the defense of superior orders will generally be available for U.S. Armed Forces personnel engaged in exceptional interrogations except where the conduct goes so far as to be patently unlawful." Consider the following argument: The OLC and Department of Defense memos take the position that actions ordered by the President under his authority as Commander-in-Chief are presumptively lawful, and that statutes and international laws to the contrary must be construed as inapplicable to him. If the President orders a subordinate to torture someone, the subordinate may presume that this order does not violate any existing law when the law is properly construed so as to avoid a constitutional conflict. Hence the presidential order is not "patently unlawful" and the subordinate is insulated from liability for war crimes.

Section 1004 of the Detainee Treatment Act of 2005 created a good faith defense in civil actions or criminal prosecutions brought against interrogators of "aliens who the President or his designees have determined are believed to be engaged in or associated with international terrorist activity that poses a serious, continuing threat to the United States, its interests, or its allies." If the interrogation practices in question "were officially authorized and determined to be lawful at the time that they were conducted," then "it shall be a defense that such officer, employee, member of the Armed Forces, or other agent did not know that the practices were unlawful and a person of ordinary sense and understanding would not know the practices were unlawful. Good faith reliance on advice of counsel should be an important factor, among others, to consider in assessing whether a person of ordinary sense and understanding would have known the practices to be unlawful."

3. *Nixon and Lincoln redux.* Compare the OLC memo's theory of the presidency with the views of Lincoln and Nixon about presidential power discussed in Chapter 3, supra. Which view does the OLC memo most resemble?

6. Targeted Killings

In his dissent in *Hamdi*, Justice Thomas noted that instead of detaining a person on the battlefield, the President could simply order an unmanned drone to execute the person. In fact, the Obama Administration has increasingly employed drone attacks to target persons it believes are al Qaeda operatives, including

American citizens. Does the Constitution limit the President's ability to order such attacks?

In answering this question, first consider the question of presidential power under *Youngstown* and *Hamdi.* Does the AUMF authorize targeted killings according to its terms, or impliedly because such attacks are consistent with the laws of war? Next, consider whether targeted killings are consistent with the Bill of Rights. *Hamdi* interprets the Fifth Amendment to require due process when citizens suspected of being terrorists are detained. What does due process mean in the context of targeted killings using drones?

Consider the case of Anwar al-Awlaki, an American citizen born in New Mexico, who was placed on the Obama Administration's secret "kill list" and was eventually killed by a drone operated by the CIA in Yemen in September 2011. American officials speaking without attribution argued that a drone attack on al-Awlaki was appropriate because he was an influential cleric who became a leader of al Qaeda in the Arabian Peninsula, and he was suspected of instructing Umar Farouk Abdulmutallab, the so-called underwear bomber, to blow up a plane flying over Detroit in 2009, as well as inspiring other home-grown American terrorists.[78] Al-Awlaki, however, was never changed with a crime, and these allegations were never proved in court. Another drone strike in October killed a group of people including al-Awlaki's 16-year-old son, Abdulrahman al-Awlaki, who was born in Colorado.

Because the drone program had been run by the CIA, the Obama Administration did not officially acknowledge the existence of the program, or the authorization of strikes against American citizens, despite the fact that the events were widely reported in the press. However, on May 23, 2013, President Obama acknowledged the program in a speech before the National Defense University in Washington, D.C.

The same day, the Administration produced a memo explaining its policies on the use of lethal force against persons it believes to be terrorists or in league with terrorist organizations:[79]

> The policy of the United States is not to use lethal force when it is feasible to capture a terrorist suspect. . . . Lethal force will not be proposed or pursued as punishment or as a substitute for prosecuting a terrorist suspect in a civilian court or a military commission. Lethal force will be used only to prevent or stop attacks against U.S. persons, and even then, only when capture is not feasible and no other reasonable alternatives exist to address the threat effectively. In particular, lethal force will be used outside areas of active hostilities only when the following preconditions are met:
>
> *First,* there must be a legal basis for using lethal force, whether it is against a senior operational leader of a terrorist organization or the forces that organization is using or intends to use to conduct terrorist attacks.

---

78. Carrie Johnson, Holder Spells Out Why Drones Target U.S. Citizens, NPR, Mar. 6, 2012, at http://www.npr.org/2012/03/06/148000630/holder-gives-rationale-for-drone-strikes-on-citizens.

79. U.S. Policy Standards and Procedures for the Use of Force in Counterterrorism Operations Outside the United States and Areas of Active Hostilities, May 23, 2013, at http://www.whitehouse.gov/sites/default/files/uploads/2013.05.23_fact_sheet_on_ppg.pdf.

> *Second*, the United States will use lethal force only against a target that poses a continuing, imminent threat to U.S. persons. It is simply not the case that all terrorists pose a continuing, imminent threat to U.S. persons; if a terrorist does not pose such a threat, the United States will not use lethal force.
>
> *Third*, the following criteria must be met before lethal action may be taken:
>
> 1) Near certainty that the terrorist target is present;
> 2) Near certainty that non-combatants will not be injured or killed;
> 3) An assessment that capture is not feasible at the time of the operation;
> 4) An assessment that the relevant governmental authorities in the country where action is contemplated cannot or will not effectively address the threat to U.S. persons; and
> 5) An assessment that no other reasonable alternatives exist to effectively address the threat to U.S. persons. Finally, whenever the United States uses force in foreign territories, international legal principles, including respect for sovereignty and the law of armed conflict, impose important constraints on the ability of the United States to act unilaterally—and on the way in which the United States can use force. The United States respects national sovereignty and international law.

Central to the Obama Administration's argument is that there must be "a continuing, imminent threat to U.S. persons." However, a DOJ White Paper leaked to the press in February 2013 suggested that the Administration defines "imminence" in a special way:[80]

> [T]he condition that an operational leader present an "imminent" threat of violent attack against the United States does not require the United States to have clear evidence that a specific attack on U.S. persons and interests will take place in the immediate future. . . . The threat posed by al-Qa'ida and its associated forces demands a broader concept of imminence in judging when a person continually planning terror attacks presents an imminent threat. . . . [I]mminence must incorporate considerations of the relevant window of opportunity, the possibility of reducing collateral damage to civilians, and the likelihood of heading off future disastrous attacks on Americans. . . . [A] high level official could conclude, for example, that an individual poses an "imminent threat" of violent attack against the United States where he is an operational leader of al-Qa'ida or an associated force and is personally and continually involved in planning terrorist attacks against the United States. Moreover, where the al-Qa'ida member in question has recently been involved in activities posing an imminent threat of violent attack against the United States, and there is no evidence that he has renounced or abandoned such activities,

---

80. Department of Justice White Paper, Lawfulness of Lethal Operation Directed Against a U.S. Citizen Who Is a Senior Operational Leader of Al-Qaida or an Associated Force, pp. 7-8, at http://msnbcmedia.msn.com/i/msnbc/sections/news/020413_DOJ_White_Paper.pdf.

> that member's involvement in al-Qa'ida's continuing terrorist campaign against the United States would support the conclusion that the member poses an imminent threat.

In a May 23, 2013 letter from Attorney General Eric Holder to Senate Judiciary Chairman Senator Patrick Leahy, the Attorney General explained that Anwar al-Awlaki posed an imminent threat because of his past plots against the United States and because "information that remains classified to protect sensitive sources and methods evidences al-Aulaqi's involvement in the planning of numerous other plots against U.S. and Western interests and makes clear he was continuing to plot attacks when he was killed."[81]

When the concept of imminence is understood in this way, do you believe that the Administration's criteria are consistent with the Fifth Amendment's Due Process Clause? Should the President be required to seek permission from a court akin to a warrant before the President may order a targeted killing? Such proceedings would likely have to be held ex parte and in secret. Is this the sort of activity that is appropriate for judicial oversight?

Another model of analysis argues that a judicial hearing is not necessary because the correct analogy is to the police shooting a fleeing criminal suspect whom the police reasonably believe poses a danger to others. No hearings are involved in such cases; the police officer simply acts based on his or her best judgment in order to protect the public safety. This analogy views the Fifth Amendment as irrelevant, and instead looks to the Fourth Amendment, which protects the security of the person against unreasonable searches and seizures. (The shooting is a "seizure" of the suspect's person.)

In Tennessee v. Garner, 471 U.S. 1 (1985), the Court considered the constitutional limits on the use of deadly force against a suspect fleeing from the police. The Court conceptualized the question as whether there was a "seizure" of a person under the Fourth Amendment, and if so, whether the seizure was reasonable under the circumstances. The Court held that "[t]he use of deadly force to prevent the escape of all felony suspects, whatever the circumstances, is constitutionally unreasonable. It is not better that all felony suspects die than that they escape. Where the suspect poses no immediate threat to the officer and no threat to others, the harm resulting from failing to apprehend him does not justify the use of deadly force to do so. . . . [But] [w]here the officer has probable cause to believe that the suspect poses a threat of serious physical harm, either to the officer or to others, it is not constitutionally unreasonable to prevent escape by using deadly force." How would you apply *Garner* to targeted killings? What role does imminent harm play in the determination?

7. Diplomatic Recognition

ZIVOTOFSKY v. KERRY (*Zivotofsky II*), 576 U.S. 1059 (2015): [Menachem Binyamin Zivotofsky was born in 2002 to United States citizens living in Jerusalem. In December 2002, Zivotofsky's mother visited the American Embassy in Tel Aviv to

---

81. See also Letter from Attorney General Holder to Senator Leahy, May 22, 2013, at p. 3, at http://www.justice.gov/slideshow/AG-letter-5-22-13.pdf.

request both a passport and a consular report of birth abroad for her son. (A consular report of birth is used to establish U.S. citizenship for children of American parents born abroad.) Zivotofsky's mother asked that his place of birth be listed as "Jerusalem, Israel." §214(d) of the Foreign Relations Authorization Act (FRAA), states for "purposes of the registration of birth, certification of nationality, or issuance of a passport of a United States citizen born in the city of Jerusalem, the Secretary shall, upon the request of the citizen or the citizen's legal guardian, record the place of birth as Israel." The Embassy officials refused to list Zivotofsky's place of birth as "Israel" on his passport, citing the executive branch's longstanding position that the United States does not recognize any country as having sovereignty over Jerusalem. Zivotofsky's parents brought suit on his behalf in federal court, seeking to enforce §214(d). In Zivotofsky v. Clinton, 566 U.S. 189 (2012) (*Zivotofsky I*), the Supreme Court held that this issue was not a political question. During the litigation, Zivotofsky focused on the passport claim and waived any argument that his consular report of birth abroad should be treated differently than his passport. The Court therefore considered only the passport arguments, although Justice Thomas's separate opinion treated the passport and consular reports as presenting distinct legal issues.]

KENNEDY, J.:

[W]hen "the President takes measures incompatible with the expressed or implied will of Congress . . . he can rely only upon his own constitutional powers minus any constitutional powers of Congress over the matter." *Youngstown.* (Jackson, J., concurring). To succeed in this third category, the President's asserted power must be both "exclusive" and "conclusive" on the issue.

[T]he Secretary contends that §214(d) infringes on the President's exclusive recognition power by "requiring the President to contradict his recognition position regarding Jerusalem in official communications with foreign sovereigns." . . . [T]he Secretary acknowledges the President's power is "at its lowest ebb." Because the President's refusal to implement §214(d) falls into Justice Jackson's third category, his claim must be "scrutinized with caution," and he may rely solely on powers the Constitution grants to him alone. . . .

Recognition is a "formal acknowledgement" that a particular "entity possesses the qualifications for statehood" or "that a particular regime is the effective government of a state." It may also involve the determination of a state's territorial bounds. . . . The Secretary asserts that the President exercises the recognition power based on the Reception Clause, which directs that the President "shall receive Ambassadors and other public Ministers." Art. II, §3. . . . At the time of the founding . . . receiving an ambassador was tantamount to recognizing the sovereignty of the sending state. . . . It is a logical and proper inference, then, that a Clause directing the President alone to receive ambassadors would be understood to acknowledge his power to recognize other nations. . . . The inference . . . is further supported by his additional Article II powers. . . . In addition to receiving an ambassador, recognition may occur on "the conclusion of a bilateral treaty," or the "formal initiation of diplomatic relations," including the dispatch of an ambassador. The President has the sole power to negotiate treaties, see United States v. Curtiss-Wright Export Corp., 299 U.S. 304 (1936), and the Senate may not conclude or ratify a treaty without Presidential action. The President, too, nominates the Nation's ambassadors and dispatches other diplomatic agents. Congress may not send an ambassador without his involvement. Beyond that, the President himself has the power to open diplomatic channels simply by engaging in direct diplomacy with foreign heads of state and their ministers. The Constitution thus assigns the President means to effect recognition on his own initiative. Congress, by contrast, has no constitutional power that would enable it to initiate diplomatic relations with a foreign nation. Because these specific Clauses confer the recognition power on the President, the Court need not consider whether or to what extent the Vesting Clause, which provides that the "executive Power" shall be vested in the President, provides further support for the President's action here. Art. II, §1, cl. 1.

The text and structure of the Constitution grant the President the power to recognize foreign nations and governments. The question then becomes whether that power is exclusive. The various ways in which the President may unilaterally effect recognition—and the lack of any similar power vested in Congress—suggest that it is. So, too, do functional considerations. Put simply, the Nation must have a single policy regarding which governments are legitimate in the eyes of the United States and which are not. Foreign countries need to know, before entering into diplomatic relations or commerce with the United States, whether their ambassadors will be received; whether their officials will be immune from suit in federal court; and whether they may initiate lawsuits here to vindicate their rights. These assurances cannot be equivocal.

Recognition is a topic on which the Nation must "'speak . . . with one voice.'" That voice must be the President's. Between the two political branches, only the Executive has the characteristic of unity at all times. And with unity comes the ability to exercise, to a greater degree, "[d]ecision, activity, secrecy, and dispatch." The Federalist No. 70 (A. Hamilton). The President is capable, in ways Congress is not, of engaging in the delicate and often secret diplomatic contacts that may lead to a decision on recognition. See, *e.g.*, United States v. Pink, 315 U.S. 203 (1942). He is also better positioned to take the decisive, unequivocal action necessary to recognize other states at international law. These qualities explain why the Framers listed the traditional avenues of recognition—receiving ambassadors, making treaties, and sending ambassadors—as among the President's Article II powers.

[T]he President since the founding has exercised this unilateral power to recognize new states—and the Court has endorsed the practice. See Banco Nacional de Cuba v. Sabbatino, 376 U.S. 398 (1964); *Pink*; Williams v. Suffolk Ins. Co., 13 Pet. 415 (1839). Texts and treatises on international law treat the President's word as the final word on recognition. See, *e.g.*, Restatement (Third) of Foreign Relations Law §204, at 89 ("Under the Constitution of the United States the President has exclusive authority to recognize or not to recognize a foreign state or government"). . . .

The Secretary now urges the Court to define the executive power over foreign relations in even broader terms. He contends that under the Court's precedent the President has "exclusive authority to conduct diplomatic relations," along with "the bulk of foreign-affairs powers." In support of his submission that the President has broad, undefined powers over foreign affairs, the Secretary quotes United States v. Curtiss-Wright Export Corp., which described the President as "the sole organ of the federal government in the field of international relations." This Court declines to acknowledge that unbounded power. . . . The *Curtiss-Wright* case does not extend so far as the Secretary suggests. In *Curtiss-Wright*, the Court considered whether a congressional delegation of power to the President was constitutional. Congress had passed a joint resolution giving the President the discretion to prohibit arms sales to certain militant powers in South America. The resolution provided criminal penalties for violation of those orders. The Court held that the delegation was constitutional, reasoning that Congress may grant the President substantial authority and discretion in the field of foreign affairs. . . .

[*Curtiss-Wright*] dealt with congressionally authorized action, not a unilateral Presidential determination [and] did not hold that the President is free from Congress' lawmaking power in the field of international relations. . . . The Executive is not free from the ordinary controls and checks of Congress merely because foreign affairs are at issue. See, *e.g.*, Medellín v. Texas, 552 U.S. 491 (2008); *Youngstown*; Little v. Barreme, 2 Cranch 170 (1804). It is not for the President alone to determine the whole content of the Nation's foreign policy.

That said, judicial precedent and historical practice teach that it is for the President alone to make the specific decision of what foreign power he will recognize as legitimate, both for the Nation as a whole and for the purpose of making his own position clear within the context of recognition in discussions and negotiations with foreign nations. Recognition is an act with immediate and powerful significance for international relations, so the President's position must be clear. Congress cannot require him to contradict his own statement regarding a determination of formal recognition. . . .

In separation-of-powers cases this Court has often "put significant weight upon historical practice." NLRB v. Noel Canning. Here, history is not all on one side, but on balance it provides strong support for the conclusion that the recognition power is the President's alone. . . . From the first Administration forward, the President has claimed unilateral authority to recognize foreign sovereigns. For the most part, Congress has acquiesced in the Executive's exercise of the recognition power. On occasion, the President has chosen, as may often be prudent, to consult and coordinate with Congress. As Judge Tatel noted in this case, however, "the most striking thing" about the history of recognition "is what is absent from it: a situation like this one," where Congress has enacted a statute contrary to the President's formal and considered statement concerning recognition.

[S]ection 214(d) . . . requires the President, through the Secretary, to identify citizens born in Jerusalem who so request as being born in Israel. But . . . [a]s a matter of United States policy, neither Israel nor any other country is acknowledged as having sovereignty over Jerusalem. In this way, §214(d) "directly contradicts" the "carefully calibrated and longstanding Executive branch policy of neutrality toward Jerusalem."

If the power over recognition is to mean anything, it must mean that the President not only makes the initial, formal recognition determination but also that he may maintain that determination in his and his agent's statements. . . . Under international law, recognition may be effected by "written or oral declaration of the recognizing state." In addition an act of recognition must "leave no doubt as to the intention to grant it." Thus, if Congress could alter the President's statements on matters of recognition or force him to contradict them, Congress in effect would exercise the recognition power.

As Justice Jackson wrote in *Youngstown*, when a Presidential power is "exclusive," it "disabl[es] the Congress from acting upon the subject." Here, the subject is quite narrow: The Executive's exclusive power extends no further than his formal recognition determination. But as to that determination, Congress may not enact a law that directly contradicts it. This is not to say Congress may not express its disagreement with the President in myriad ways. For example, it may enact an embargo, decline to confirm an ambassador, or even declare war. But none of these acts would alter the President's recognition decision.

If Congress may not pass a law, speaking in its own voice, that effects formal recognition, then it follows that it may not force the President himself to contradict his earlier statement. That congressional command would not only prevent the Nation from speaking with one voice but also prevent the Executive itself from doing so in conducting foreign relations. . . .

The flaw in §214(d) is further underscored by the undoubted fact that the purpose of the statute was to infringe on the recognition power—a power the Court now holds is the sole prerogative of the President. The statute is titled "United States Policy with Respect to Jerusalem as the Capital of Israel." The House Conference Report proclaimed that §214 "contains four provisions related to the recognition of Jerusalem as Israel's capital." And, indeed, observers interpreted §214 as altering United States policy regarding Jerusalem—which led to protests across the region. From the face of §214, from the legislative history, and from its reception, it is clear that Congress wanted to express its displeasure with the President's policy by, among other things, commanding the Executive to contradict his own, earlier stated position on Jerusalem. This Congress may not do.

Breyer, J., concurring: I continue to believe that this case presents a political question inappropriate for judicial resolution. . . . But because precedent precludes resolving this case on political question grounds, I join the Court's opinion.

Thomas, J., concurring in the judgment in part and dissenting in part: [S]ection 214(d) [is unconstitutional] insofar as it directs the President, contrary to his wishes, to list "Israel" as the place of birth of Jerusalem-born citizens on their passports. The President has long regulated passports under his residual foreign affairs power, and this portion of §214(d) does not fall within any of Congress' enumerated powers. By contrast, §214(d) poses no such problem insofar as it regulates consular reports of birth abroad. Unlike passports, these reports were developed to effectuate the naturalization laws, and they continue to serve the role of identifying persons who need not be naturalized to obtain U.S. citizenship. The regulation of these reports does not fall within the President's foreign affairs powers, but within Congress' enumerated powers under the Naturalization and Necessary and Proper Clauses.

Roberts, C.J., joined by Alito, J., dissenting:

Today's decision is a first: Never before has this Court accepted a President's direct defiance of an Act of Congress in the field of foreign affairs. We have instead stressed that the President's power reaches "its lowest ebb" when he contravenes the express will of Congress, "for what is at stake is the equilibrium established by our constitutional system." Youngstown Sheet & Tube Co. v. Sawyer (Jackson, J., concurring). . . . [T]he Executive may disregard "the expressed or implied will of Congress" only if the Constitution grants him a power "at once so conclusive and preclusive" as to "disabl[e] the Congress from acting upon the subject." *Youngstown* (Jackson, J., concurring). . . . For our first 225 years, no President prevailed when contradicting a statute in the field of foreign affairs. See Medellín v. Texas, 552 U.S. 491 (2008); Hamdan v. Rumsfeld, 548 U.S. 557 (2006); *Youngstown* (majority opinion); Little v. Barreme, 2 Cranch 170 (1804).

[T]he majority places great weight on the Reception Clause, which directs that the Executive "shall receive Ambassadors and other public Ministers." Art. II, §3. But that provision, framed as an obligation rather than an authorization, appears alongside the *duties* imposed on the President by Article II, Section 3, not the *powers* granted to him by Article II, Section 2. . . . [A]t the time of the founding, "there was no reason to view the reception clause as a source of discretionary authority for the president." . . . The President does have power to make treaties and appoint ambassadors. Art. II, §2. But those authorities are *shared* with Congress, so they hardly support an inference that the recognition power is *exclusive.*

[A]s for history, the majority admits that it too points in both directions. Some Presidents have claimed an exclusive recognition power, but others have expressed uncertainty about whether such preclusive authority exists. Those in the skeptical camp include Andrew Jackson and Abraham Lincoln, leaders not generally known for their cramped conceptions of Presidential power. Congress has also asserted its authority over recognition determinations at numerous points in history. The majority therefore falls short of demonstrating that "Congress has accepted" the President's exclusive recognition power. . . . In sum, although the President has authority over recognition, I am not convinced that the Constitution provides the "conclusive and preclusive" power required to justify defiance of an express legislative mandate. *Youngstown* (Jackson, J., concurring). . . .

But even if the President does have exclusive recognition power, he still cannot prevail in this case, because the statute at issue *does not implicate recognition.* [Section] 214(d) simply gives an American citizen born in Jerusalem the option to designate his place of birth as Israel "[f]or purposes of" passports and other documents. The State Department itself has explained that "identification"—not recognition—"is the principal reason that U.S. passports require 'place of birth.'" Congress has not disputed the Executive's assurances that §214(d) does not alter the longstanding United States position on Jerusalem. And the annals of diplomatic history record no examples of official recognition accomplished via optional passport designation. . . . At most, the majority worries that there may be a *perceived* contradiction based on a *mistaken* understanding of the effect of §214(d), insisting that some "observers interpreted §214 as altering United States policy regarding Jerusalem." To afford controlling weight to such impressions, however, is essentially to subject a duly enacted statute to an international heckler's veto.

Moreover, expanding the President's purportedly exclusive recognition power to include authority to avoid potential misunderstandings of legislative enactments proves far too much. Congress could validly exercise its enumerated powers in countless ways that would create more severe perceived contradictions with Presidential recognition decisions than does §214(d). If, for example, the President recognized a particular country in opposition to Congress's wishes, Congress could declare war or impose a trade embargo on that country. A neutral observer might well conclude that these legislative actions had, to put it mildly, created a perceived contradiction with the President's recognition decision. And yet each of them would undoubtedly be constitutional. So too would statements by nonlegislative actors that might be seen to contradict the President's recognition positions, such as the declaration in [the 2012 Democratic] political party platform that "Jerusalem is and will remain the capital of Israel."

Ultimately, the only power that could support the President's position is the one the majority purports to reject: the "exclusive authority to conduct diplomatic relations." [A]s the majority rightly acknowledges, *Curtiss-Wright* did not involve a claim that the Executive could contravene a statute; it held only that he could act pursuant to a legislative delegation. The expansive language in *Curtiss-Wright* casting the President as the "sole organ" of the Nation in foreign affairs certainly has attraction for members of the Executive Branch. . . . But our precedents have never accepted such a sweeping understanding of executive power. See *Hamdan*; *Dames & Moore*; *Youngstown* (majority opinion); *id.* (Jackson, J., concurring); cf. Little [v. Barreme]. . . .

SCALIA, J., joined by THE CHIEF JUSTICE and ALITO, J., dissenting:

[§214(d) is based in] Congress's power to "establish an uniform Rule of Naturalization," Art. I, §8, cl. 4, [which] enables it to grant American citizenship to someone born abroad. The naturalization power also enables Congress to furnish the people it makes citizens with papers verifying their citizenship—say a consular report of birth abroad (which certifies citizenship of an American born outside the United States) or a passport (which certifies citizenship for purposes of international travel). As the Necessary and Proper Clause confirms, every congressional power "carries with it all those incidental powers which are necessary to its complete and effectual execution." Cohens v. Virginia, 6 Wheat. 264 (1821). Even on a miserly understanding of Congress's incidental authority, Congress may make grants of citizenship "effectual" by providing for the issuance of certificates authenticating them.

One would think that if Congress may grant Zivotofsky a passport and a birth report, it may also require these papers to record his birthplace as "Israel." The birthplace specification promotes the document's citizenship-authenticating function by identifying the bearer, distinguishing people with similar names but different birthplaces from each other, helping authorities uncover identity fraud, and facilitating retrieval of the Government's citizenship records. To be sure, recording Zivotofsky's birthplace as "Jerusalem" rather than "Israel" would fulfill these objectives, but when faced with alternative ways to carry its powers into execution, Congress has the "discretion" to choose the one it deems "most beneficial to the people." McCulloch v. Maryland. It thus has the right to decide that recording birthplaces as "Israel" makes for better foreign policy. Or that regardless of international politics, a passport or birth report should respect its bearer's conscientious belief that Jerusalem belongs to Israel. . . .

I agree that the Constitution *empowers* the President to extend recognition on behalf of the United States, but I find it a much harder question whether it makes that power exclusive. The Court tells us that "the weight of historical evidence" supports exclusive executive authority over "the formal determination of recognition." But even with its attention confined to formal recognition, the Court is forced to admit that "history is not all on one side." . . .

[In any case,] §214(d) has nothing to do with recognition. Section 214(d) does not require the Secretary to make a formal declaration about Israel's sovereignty over Jerusalem. And nobody suggests that international custom infers acceptance of sovereignty from the birthplace designation on a passport or birth report, as it does from bilateral treaties or exchanges of ambassadors. Recognition would preclude the United States (as a matter of international law) from later contesting Israeli sovereignty over Jerusalem. But making a notation in a passport or birth report does not encumber the Republic with any international obligations. It leaves the Nation free (so far as international law is concerned) to change its mind in the future. That would be true even if the statute required *all* passports to list "Israel." But in fact it requires only those passports to list "Israel" for which the citizen (or his guardian) *requests* "Israel"; all the rest, under the Secretary's policy, list "Jerusalem." It is utterly impossible for this deference to private requests to constitute an act that unequivocally manifests an intention to grant recognition. . . .

The best indication that §214(d) does not concern recognition comes from the State Department's policies concerning Taiwan. According to the Solicitor General, the United States "acknowledges the Chinese position" that Taiwan is a part of China, but "does not take a position" of its own on that issue. Even so, the State Department has for a long time recorded the birthplace of a citizen born in Taiwan as "China." It indeed *insisted* on doing so until Congress passed a law (on which §214(d) was modeled) giving citizens the option to have their birthplaces recorded as "Taiwan." The Solicitor General explains that the designation "China" "involves a geographic description, not an assertion that Taiwan is . . . part of sovereign China." Quite so. Section 214(d) likewise calls for nothing beyond a "geographic description"; it does not require the Executive even to assert, never mind formally recognize, that Jerusalem is a part of sovereign Israel. Since birthplace specifications in citizenship documents are matters within Congress's control, Congress may treat Jerusalem as a part of Israel when regulating the recording of birthplaces, even if the President does not do so when extending recognition. . . . [Section 214(d)] displays symbolic support for Israel's territorial claim. That symbolism may have tremendous significance as a matter of international diplomacy, but it makes no difference as a matter of constitutional law.

Even if the Constitution gives the President sole power to extend recognition, it does not give him sole power to make all decisions relating to foreign disputes over sovereignty. To the contrary, a fair reading of Article I allows Congress to decide for itself how its laws should handle these controversies. Read naturally, power to "regulate Commerce with foreign Nations," §8, cl. 3, includes power to regulate imports from Gibraltar as British goods or as Spanish goods. Read naturally, power to "regulate the Value . . . of foreign Coin," §8, cl. 5, includes power to honor (or not) currency issued by Taiwan. And so on for the other enumerated powers. . . . The Taiwan Relations Act of 1979 grants Taiwan capacity to sue and be sued, even though the United States does not recognize it as a state. 22 U.S.C. §3303(b)(7). Section 214(d) continues in the same tradition.

The Constitution likewise does not give the President exclusive power to determine which claims to statehood and territory "are legitimate in the eyes of the United States." Congress may express its own views about these matters by declaring war, restricting trade, denying foreign aid, and much else besides. . . . History does not even support an exclusive Presidential power to make what the Court calls "formal statements" about "the legitimacy of a state or government and its territorial bounds." For a long time, the Houses of Congress have made formal statements announcing their own positions on these issues, again without provoking constitutional objections. A recent resolution expressed the House of Representatives' "strong support for the legitimate, democratically-elected Government of Lebanon" and condemned an "illegitimate" and "unjustifiable" insurrection by "the terrorist group Hizballah." H. Res. 1194, 110th Cong., 2d Sess., 1, 4 (2008). An earlier enactment declared "the sense of the Congress that . . . Tibet . . . is an occupied country under the established principles of international law" and that "Tibet's true representatives are the Dalai Lama and the Tibetan Government in exile." §355, 105 Stat. 713 (1991). After Texas won independence from Mexico, the Senate resolved that "the State of Texas having established and maintained an independent Government, . . . it is expedient and proper . . . that the independent political existence of the said State be acknowledged by the Government of the United States." Cong. Globe, 24th Cong., 2d Sess., 83 (1837).

In the final analysis, the Constitution may well deny Congress power to recognize—the power to make an international commitment accepting a foreign entity as a state, a regime as its government, a place as a part of its territory, and so on. But whatever else §214(d) may do, it plainly does not make (or require the President to make) a commitment accepting Israel's sovereignty over Jerusalem. . . . To the extent doubts linger about whether the United States recognizes Israel's sovereignty over Jerusalem, §214(d) leaves the President free to dispel them by issuing a disclaimer of intent to recognize. A disclaimer always suffices to prevent an act from effecting recognition. Restatement (Second) of Foreign Relations Law of the United States §104(1) (1962). Recall that an earlier law grants citizens born in Taiwan the right to have their birthplaces recorded as "Taiwan." The State Department has complied with the law, but states in its Foreign Affairs Manual: "The United States does not officially recognize Taiwan as a 'state' or 'country,' although passport issuing officers may enter 'Taiwan' as a place of birth." Nothing stops a similar disclaimer here. . . .

DISCUSSION

1. *How much does* Zivotofsky *increase executive power over foreign affairs?* In his dissent, Chief Justice Roberts emphasizes that *Zivotofsky* is a rare case: The Court upholds presidential power in the face of a contrary legislative decision by Congress. This is "box three" of Jackson's *Youngstown* framework, in which the President's power is "at its lowest ebb."

But the power upheld in *Zivotofsky* is not all that extensive. It is the power to formally acknowledge on behalf of the nation that a particular political "entity possesses the qualifications for statehood" or "that a particular regime is the effective government of a state." The President's power of recognition also extends to recognizing the "territorial bounds" of the state. This includes the power to assert which government has sovereign authority over a particular piece of territory, or, as in the case of Jerusalem, the power to avoid taking any official position on the question at all. Six Justices held that this power is exclusive with the President, while the dissenters—the Chief Justice and Justices Scalia and Alito—assume that the President can make these determinations in the absence of a decision by Congress.

Yet the majority opinion goes out of its way to emphasize that, outside of the recognition power, Congress is a full partner in foreign affairs. Eight Justices agree that Congress can substantially undermine the President's decisions on foreign affairs—for example, by refusing to pass laws, withholding appropriations, failing to appoint an ambassador, imposing trade sanctions, or enacting other regulations of foreign commerce at odds with the President's wishes. (Justice Thomas's opinion does not address this issue.) And all of the Justices except Justice Thomas agree that, outside of the recognition authority, the President must obey laws passed by Congress in the field of international relations.

The majority also goes out of its way to rebuff the Secretary of State's assertion that "the President has 'exclusive authority to conduct diplomatic relations,' along with 'the bulk of foreign-affairs powers.'" It reinterprets *Curtiss-Wright*, the standard cite of advocates of executive power in foreign affairs: "*Curtiss-Wright* did not hold that the President is free from Congress' lawmaking power in the field of international relations. . . . It is not for the President alone to determine the whole content of the Nation's foreign policy." Thus, although it supported presidential authority in a narrow class of cases, *Zivotofsky* contains far more language limiting executive power.

2. *Has Congress acquiesced? Two kinds of acquiescence.* The majority, reasoning from inter-branch convention, argues that "[t]he weight of historical evidence indicates Congress has accepted that the power to recognize foreign states and governments and their territorial bounds is exclusive to the Presidency." But there are two ways that a branch might acquiesce to the decisions of another branch. First, Congress might agree with the President's *particular decision on the merits*, or it might defer to the President's particular judgment for prudential reasons. In the same way, the President might defer to Congress on the merits or for prudential reasons. The majority gives examples in which Presidents Jackson and Lincoln deferred to Congress's judgments about recognition. In the alternative, a branch might acquiesce in the other branch's *right to decide* the matter *in general*. How do we tell which kind of acquiescence has occurred? The mere fact that Congress has generally gone along with the President does not mean that it has surrendered its powers completely; after all, the majority does not believe that Jackson's and Lincoln's examples show that the President acquiesced to congressional power over recognition.

Is the case for congressional acquiescence weaker or stronger than the case for congressional acquiescence in NLRB v. Noel Canning? On the general problem of how to interpret inter-branch conventions and acquiescence, see Curtis A. Bradley and Neil S. Siegel, After Recess: Historical Practice, Textual Ambiguity, and Constitutional Adverse Possession, 2014 Sup. Ct. Rev. 1 (2014).

3. *A narrower holding?* The strongest argument for the result in the case does not come from the history of inter-branch conventions or judicial precedents. It is structural. Successful conduct of international relations requires that the U.S. government have the ability to make clear commitments to other nations. (See the discussion of the Treaty Power in Bond v. United States.) Hence, Congress may not muddy the waters by making the President or his employees contradict his previous statements about recognition. But does the law in *Zivotofsky* actually do this? None of the Justices argued that the law in question formally contradicted the President's recognition determination. At most the law forces the President's agents to

contradict his determination by issuing passports that say "Israel." Therefore, Marty Lederman suggests that the Court might easily have adopted a narrower holding. Whatever Congress's power to regulate foreign policy, "when its views contradict the President's, Congress does not have the power to control the Executive's conduct of *diplomacy*, that is, of deciding what to say to foreign officials. Or, even narrower than that, the Court could have held that Congress at a minimum cannot compel the President to *contradict* himself when engaged in diplomatic activity."[82]

4. *Two visions of the "unitary executive."* Two different theories of executive power are sometimes called the theory of the "unitary executive." The first theory concerns executive power to direct subordinates. Subject to congressional statutes that organize the executive branch and create its departments, the President decides how to run the executive branch and deploy executive power. The executive is "unitary" because all executive power rests in the President and in the President's agents, whom the President (ultimately) directs. (See the discussion in Morrison v. Olson and Seila Law v. Consumer Financial Protection Bureau in Section IVB, supra.) Lederman's approach is fully consistent with this model—Congress may not force the President's employees to take a different position on recognition than their boss.

A second theory that is sometimes called the theory of the "unitary executive" is associated with scholars like Professor John Yoo and with the George W. Bush Administration. This theory holds that when the President exercises express or implied executive powers granted under Article II, Congress may not interfere with those powers, and laws to the contrary are unconstitutional. Justice Thomas's opinion is closest to this model. Yet, as we have seen, the other eight Justices reject it.

5. *Speaking with one voice?* Justice Kennedy argues that "[r]ecognition is a topic on which the Nation must "'speak . . . with one voice'" and that "[t]hat voice must be the President's." Why? Kennedy offers standard arguments about the characteristic features of executive power: the President's ability to exercise "[d]ecision, activity, secrecy, and dispatch." The Federalist No. 70 (A. Hamilton). But this argument might simultaneously prove both too little and too much. It might prove too little if Congress deliberates and makes a firm determination about recognition that is inconsistent with the President's, for example, by overriding a presidential veto. In that case, it's not clear why the President's greater energy and dispatch matter all that much. The question would be definitively settled, and the nation would speak with a single voice—Congress's, as embodied in federal law.

The argument might prove too much because the same logic would seem to apply equally to a wide range of other foreign policy issues beyond formal recognition. In all of those areas, however, *Zivotofsky* holds that Congress has a say, and can even work to undermine the President's carefully planned foreign policy. In virtually every other area of foreign affairs, one could also point to the importance of "one voice," and emphasize the President's superior ability to work with "decision, activity, secrecy, and dispatch." If those arguments don't win in all of the

---

82. Marty Lederman, Thoughts on *Zivotofsky*, Part Five: Why Did the Majority Choose to Decide Whether the President's "Recognition" Power is Exclusive?, Just Security, June 13, 2015, at http://justsecurity.org/23825/thoughts-zivotofsky-part-five-majority-choose-decide-presidents-recognition-power-exclusive/.

other contexts of foreign policy, why should they win only in the context of formal statements of recognition? On the other hand, if *Zivotofsky* is just a case that tells Congress that it can't force Presidents to talk out of both sides of their mouth in conducting diplomatic relations — or direct the President's subordinates to disagree with their boss on questions of diplomacy — these problems are greatly reduced, if not eliminated.

E. *Presidential Privileges and Immunities*

The Constitution specifies certain courtroom immunities for members of Congress in Article I, §6: Federal lawmakers enjoy permanent immunity from any lawsuit based on their "speech or debate" in Congress, and enjoy temporary immunity from civil arrest while the legislature is in session. (At the founding, certain civil lawsuits could be initiated by seizing or arresting the person of the defendant; without the protection of the Arrest Clause, a single civil plaintiff — whose legal claims might ultimately prove baseless in court and who in fact might be politically motivated — might have been able to prevent a lawmaker from representing his constituents while the Congress was in session.) The Constitution, however, is silent on what if any litigation immunities are appropriate for other government officials, including the President.

This silence, however, has not meant that other officers enjoy no courtroom immunities. Rather, it has meant that such immunities are typically derived from structural considerations. For example, although the Vice President is, strictly speaking, not covered by the text of the Speech or Debate Clause, it would be structurally anomalous to allow him to be sued for a speech he made in the Senate as its presiding officer. Likewise, it would be strange if a President could be sued for allegedly libelous statements made in the State of the Union message — or in a press conference defending his legislative agenda, for that matter. (Suppose, for example, the President were to attack cigarette companies or gun manufacturers or the HMO industry.) In 1896, the Court made clear in Spalding v. Vilas, 161 U.S. 483, that judges were likewise privileged from lawsuits for any statements that they make in their courtrooms or judicial opinions. See also n.[g] in United States v. Nixon, supra, rejecting the idea that the only proper constitutional immunities are those specified in Article I, §6.

What litigation immunities are structurally sound for the President? Or to recast the point textually, what immunities are properly interpreted as being implicit in the "executive power of the United States" vested in the President by the opening sentence of Article II? In a pair of cases in the last three decades, the Supreme Court has attempted to answer these questions. In the first case, Nixon v. Fitzgerald, 457 U.S. 731 (1982), the Court held that ex-President Nixon could not be sued for allegedly having violated the plaintiff's First Amendment rights while acting as President. Nixon, said the Court, was absolutely immune for all conduct arising out of his official duties as President. In the second lawsuit, Clinton v. Jones, 520 U.S. 681 (1997), the Court held that sitting President Clinton could be sued in federal court for allegedly having violated plaintiff's civil rights while acting as the governor of Arkansas. Clinton, said the Court, had no immunity (at least in federal court) for private actions that did not arise out of any presidential conduct.

The *Fitzgerald* case was decided by a 5-4 vote, with Justice Powell writing for the Court, joined by Chief Justice Burger and Justices Rehnquist, Stevens, and O'Connor. Justice White wrote the main dissent, joined by Justices Brennan, Marshall, and Blackmun. Ernest Fitzgerald was a whistleblower who alleged that President Nixon had fired him in retaliation for his testimony before Congress about military cost overruns. Fitzgerald claimed that the firing violated his First Amendment rights, and sought damages. The Court assumed arguendo that Nixon had indeed violated the Constitution, but said it didn't matter—such damage lawsuits might chill presidential behavior, and so they should be barred (unless, perhaps, Congress plainly provided otherwise).

The result in *Fitzgerald* can be questioned. If the President did indeed violate the Constitution, wouldn't "chilling" such violations be a good thing? If the concern is that many frivolous suits would be filed, couldn't this problem have been addressed by a rule that required losing plaintiffs to compensate the defendant? (Such a rule would help weed out weak claims without barring strong ones.) If the fear is that some unconstitutional conduct might nevertheless have been carried out in good faith, and for sound policy reasons, wouldn't this be an argument for allowing the plaintiff to get a full remedy, but indemnifying the ex-President with public funds? There is an analogy here to the Takings Clause doctrine—if the rest of us benefit from the way the President used Fitzgerald, why shouldn't we all bear the loss rather than singling him out for an unfair burden? Shouldn't we strive for a system in which every constitutional right has a proper remedy?

With the *Fitzgerald* case on the books, Paula Corbin Jones brought suit against President Bill Clinton. She alleged that Clinton had sexually harassed her and violated her civil rights before he became President. Clinton sought a ruling that the lawsuit must be delayed until he left the presidency. Before the case was decided, many leading scholars argued that Clinton's claims were much weaker than Nixon's: Nixon, after all, sought immunity for official acts as President, whereas Clinton was seeking immunity for obviously private conduct. Other scholars, including two of the editors of this casebook, signed a brief arguing that Clinton's claims were in fact stronger than Nixon's. Nixon sought permanent immunity in a way that withheld all remedy from Fitzgerald, and denied him his day in court; Clinton, by contrast, sought merely to postpone the lawsuit, not preclude it—sought only temporary immunity, not permanent immunity. Although the *Fitzgerald* case involved underlying conduct that touched on the presidency, at the time of the lawsuit Nixon was simply a private citizen, and so litigation would not disrupt him from doing what he was elected to do. Conversely, Clinton was being sued while in office, and—these scholars argued—litigation might well prove disruptive. Putting aside the specific facts of the case, the structural argument was that one person should not be allowed to commandeer the President's time, divert him from his agenda, and thus undo the votes of millions—or at least, should not be allowed to do this without explaining why the lawsuit could not have been brought before the Clinton presidency, or could not wait for the end of the Clinton presidency. Note that the argument here bears a self-conscious structural similarity to Arrest Clause immunity for legislators under Article I, §6: While "in session" an elected lawmaker should be allowed to do the people's business, and disruptive private lawsuits should be put on hold until the end of the session.

The Supreme Court, by a 9-0 vote, ruled against Clinton. Justice Stevens wrote for the Court, and Justice Breyer concurred in the judgment only. Dismissing the concern about possible disruption, the Court declared that "if properly managed by the District Court, [the case] appears to us highly unlikely to occupy any substantial amount of [the President's] time." Justice Breyer expressed doubts on this score, and also pointed out that the historical evidence from the founding era supported the President's claim far more than the majority had admitted. In many ways, his opinion sounded more like a dissent, until its closing paragraphs. (Is it possible that, as in the Nixon Tapes Case, the symbolism of unanimity was important to the Justices?) Perhaps most important for our purposes in studying the interactive processes of constitutional decisionmaking, it should be emphasized that both *Fitzgerald* and *Jones* noted that Congress by law might well have the power to deviate from the baseline laid down by the Court. In *Fitzgerald*, the Justices noted that the plaintiff had sued directly under the Constitution, and could point to no specific congressional statute that authorized his suit against the President. Accordingly, "we need not address directly the immunity question as it would arise if Congress expressly had created a damages action against the President." (Note the connection here to Justice Jackson's *Youngstown* categories, which distinguished between congressional silence and explicit congressional statutes seeking to bolster or limit the President.) In *Jones*, the Justices were blunt: "If Congress deems it appropriate to afford the President stronger protection, it may respond with appropriate legislation." If you were a constitutionally conscientious member of Congress, would you support legislation to alter the judicial baselines set by *Fitzgerald* and *Jones*? Why or why not? Are you able to take into account certain features of the problem that would have been inappropriate or difficult for judges to consider?

At least one large and interesting question about presidential immunity remains open after *Jones*: May a sitting President be criminally prosecuted outside of an impeachment court? If so, how and by whom? The *Jones* Court pointedly did not reach this question, distinguishing the case at hand from "the question whether a court may compel the attendance of the President at any specific time or place." Note that in *Jones*, the President needn't have appeared in court; indeed, he could have simply paid a default judgment. In a typical criminal case, by contrast, defendants may be physically obliged—with leg irons, if need be—to stand trial. Also, unlike a mere civil suit, a criminal conviction and imprisonment could effect a de facto removal from office. And if a President were to be incarcerated upon conviction, and later won on appeal, how could we give back to him (and those that voted for him) the lost days of his presidency? This special problem does not arise in civil suits like *Jones*. We should also note that although the *Jones* Court thought that very little historical evidence supported presidential immunity from civil suit in federal court, there is a great deal of historical evidence supporting the notion that a sitting President may not be forced to stand trial in an ordinary criminal court against his will. (For a quick summary of this historical evidence, see this casebook's supplemental website materials on presidential impeachment at http://jackbalkin.yale.edu/sites/default/files/files/impeachmentmaterials1.pdf.) Moreover, in a civil case, there is never a "plaintiff-standing" problem. *Anyone* can bring a civil suit. But who can bring a criminal suit against a sitting President, and in whose name? For all these reasons, it would be a mistake to read *Jones* as having decided the question of whether a sitting President can be forced to stand trial in a criminal case.

(Note also that the *Jones* Court pointedly avoided ruling on whether a civil plaintiff could sue the President in *state* court presided over by a *state* judge.)

Akhil Amar and Brian Kalt have argued, based on structural grounds, that a sitting President is constitutionally immune from ordinary state or federal criminal prosecution, but that he or she can be prosecuted after leaving office. Akhil Reed Amar and Brian C. Kalt, The Presidential Privilege Against Prosecution, 2 Nexus 11 (1997). In testimony before the U.S. Senate, Amar summarized their argument as follows:

> [A] sitting President claiming the full privileges of his office may only be criminally tried by this Court, the Senate, sitting in impeachment, and can be criminally tried elsewhere only after he has left office.
>
> [The] basic constitutional argument is . . . structural . . . sounding in both separation of powers and federalism. Other impeachable officers—Vice Presidents, cabinet officers, judges and justices—may be indicted while in office. *But the Presidency is constitutionally unique—in the President the entirety of the power of a branch of government is vested. . . .*
>
> [Consider] the following hypothetical, which implicates federalism as well as separation of powers: Could some clever state or county prosecutor in Charleston, South Carolina have indicted Abraham Lincoln in March 1861, and ordered him to stand trial in Charleston? If so, there might well be no United States today bringing us all together. I believe that the Constitution gave Lincoln immunity in this situation—so long as he was in office. The President is elected by the whole nation, and no one part of the nation should have the power to undo a decision of the whole.[a] This is the kind of structural argument exemplified by Marshall's classic opinion in McCulloch v. Maryland.
>
> What is true of a state criminal prosecution is also true of a federal criminal prosecution. Here too, we cannot let a part undo the whole. Any one federal grand jury or federal petit jury will come from one city—be it Charleston or Little Rock or the District of Columbia. The President is elected by the entire nation, and should be judged by the entire nation. His true grand jury is the House, his true petit jury is the Senate, and the true indictment that he is subject to is called an impeachment. What's more, any effort to indict him by an independent counsel would also violate the Constitution's Article II Appointments Clause. . . . [Independent] Counsel [Kenneth] Starr is, constitutionally speaking, an "inferior" officer. He was never, as counsel, confirmed by this body, the Senate of the United States. Were he to claim the power to indict a sitting President, it would be impossible to argue with a straight face that he is simply some

---

a. The Lincoln hypothetical helps make clear that: (1) innocent Presidents may be targeted by political opponents; (2) local decision-makers cannot always be trusted to decide the fate of a sitting President; and (3) the cost to the nation of allowing open season on Presidents can be extraordinary. In particular, Vice Presidents are not always perfect substitutes. (Pop Quiz: Name Lincoln's Vice President in 1861. Hint: the answer is obscure, and it is not Andrew Johnson, whose efforts to replace Lincoln four years later raised serious problems in their own right.)

> "inferior" officer. He would breaking with the historical and traditional approach of the Justice Department—and even if you think he would be right, you cannot say he would truly be *inferior.* He would be claiming for himself the power to imprison the Chief Executive Officer. This power is awesome—it is anything but an "inferior" power that can be vested in an "inferior" officer. This issue of course did not arise in the 1988 Supreme Court case, Morrison v. Olson, since the President in that case was not a target. (And remember, Richard Nixon was only named an *unindicted* coconspirator.) Since *Morrison,* the Court has been even more strict in insisting that the word "inferior" be taken seriously in the Appointments Clause, as evidenced by the 1997 case, Edmond v. United States. Any indictment of the President by Counsel Starr would in my view violate the teaching of *Edmond.*
>
> [O]f course no man is above the law. Once out of office, an ex-President may be tried just like anyone else—and that day of reckoning can of course be speeded up if the House and the Senate decide to impeach and remove. Moreover, since a sitting President's immunity sounds in personal jurisdiction, it may well be waivable, and if so, political pressure may be brought upon a President to consent to be tried.[b] The question is not whether a President is accountable to law and to the country—but *how, when,* and *by whom.*

F. Presidential Selection

In light of the momentous powers and privileges of the President, the mode by which he is chosen is hugely significant. This too is a constitutional decision of sorts, with the American people deciding via constitutional processes who our constitutional President shall be. But issues of presidential selection and succession are typically slighted in casebooks written by law professors, who tend to focus more on those parts of the Constitution that are regularly litigated in the Supreme Court. And so the study of presidential selection and succession is largely today the province of political scientists more than of constitutional law professors in law schools.

Perhaps the biggest question is whether the Electoral College makes sense in modern America. Here is what the fourth edition of this casebook—written before the election of 2000—had to say about the matter:

> Admittedly, the electoral college was a brilliant 18th-century device to solve 18th-century problems. The Framers emphatically did not want a President dependent on the legislature, so they rejected a parliamentary model in which the legislature would pick its own leader as prime minister and chief executive officer. How, then, to pick the President? The

b. Thus, there may be a difference between indicting a sitting President against his will, and forcing him to stand trial against his will. The former may be permissible even if the latter is not (bracketing for the moment the serious appointments clause objections to independent counsels).

visionary James Wilson proposed direct national popular election, but the scheme was deemed unworkable for three reasons. First, very few candidates would have truly continental reputations among ordinary citizens; ordinary folk across the vast continent would not have enough good information to choose intelligently among national figures. Second, a populist Presidency was seen as dangerous—inviting demagoguery and possibly dictatorship as one man claimed to embody the Voice of the American People. Third, national election would upset a careful balance of power among states. Since the South didn't let blacks vote, southern voices would count less in a direct national election. A state could increase its clout by recklessly extending its franchise—for example, if (heaven forbid!) a state let women vote, it could double its weight in a direct national election. Under the electoral college system, by contrast, a state could get a fixed number of electoral votes whether its franchise was broad or narrow—indeed, whether or not it let ordinary voters pick electors.

But do these arguments work today? Improvements in communications technology, and the rise of political parties, make possible direct election and a populist Presidency—de facto, that is our scheme today. Blacks and women are no longer selectively disenfranchised, and states no longer play key roles in defining the electorate or in deciding whether to give the voters a direct voice in choosing electors. Direct national election would encourage states to encourage voters to vote on Election Day; but today, this hardly seems a strong reason to *oppose* direct election. Ingenious, indirect, sophisticated arguments made on behalf of the electoral college by clever theorists these days are legion—but almost all seem make-weight. If the scheme is so good, why doesn't any U.S. state, or any foreign nation, copy it? A low plurality winner in a three- or four-way race is possible even with the electoral college; and could be avoided in a direct national election by single transferable voting (with voters listing their 2nd and 3rd choices on the ballot, in effect combining the "first heat" and "run off" elections into a single transaction).

The only two real arguments against abolition of the electoral college sound in federalism and inertia. Only federalism can explain why we should use an electoral college to pick presidents but not governors. But it's hard to see what the federalism argument is, *today*. Should the specter of the national government administering a national election give us the cold sweats? A razor-thin popular vote margin might occasion a national recount, but states now manage recounts all the time, and new technology will make counting and recounting much easier in the future. (And today, a razor-thin electoral college margin may require recounts in a number of closely contested states even if there is a clear national popular winner.) Inertial, Burkean, arguments take two forms. First, the argument goes, a change in presidential selection rules would radically change the game in ways hard to foresee: Candidates wouldn't care about winning states—only votes—and campaign strategies might change dramatically and for the worse. But it's hard to see why. Given that, historically, the electoral college leader has also tended to be the popular vote leader, the strategy for winning shouldn't change dramatically if we switch from one measure to the other. This sets up the second inertial point: The dreaded specter of a clear popular loser becoming the electoral college winner hasn't materialized since Rutherford B. Hayes (1876) and Benjamin Harrison (1888) last century—"Why worry?" But that's what someone might say after three trigger pulls in Russian Roulette. One day, we will end up with a clear Loser President—clear beyond any quibbles about uncertain ballots.[74] And the question is, will this Loser/Winner be seen as legitimate at home and abroad? If our modern national democratic ethos, when focused on the thing, would balk at a byzantine system that defies the people's choice on election day, true Burkean theory would seem to argue against the electoral college. If We the People would amend the Constitution after the Loser President materializes, why are we now just waiting for the inevitable accident to happen?[75]

To what extent do the elections of 2000 and 2016 confirm or contradict the foregoing analysis? On the election of 2000, see also this casebook's supplemental website materials on the remarkable case of Bush v. Gore, 531 U.S. 98 (2000), at http://jackbalkin.yale.edu/sites/default/files/files/bushvgore.pdf.

The National Popular Vote Initiative seeks to reform the Electoral College through an interstate compact. Under the plan, state legislatures enact laws that assign their electoral votes to the candidate who receives a majority of the popular vote. The compact is made effective when states with a majority of the nation's electoral votes join the agreement. As of July 2014, 11 states with 161 electoral votes—approximately 30 percent of the nation's electoral votes—had joined the compact. For a discussion of the constitutional issues, see Akhil Reed Amar, America's Unwritten Constitution 457-461 (2012); Vikram David Amar, Response: The Case for Reforming Presidential Elections by Subconstitutional Means: The Electoral College, the National Popular Vote Compact, and Congressional Power, 100 Geo. L.J. 237 (2011).

---

74. In the 1988 election, for example, George Bush beat Michael Dukakis by more than 7 million votes. But if fewer than 600,000 voters in certain key states had switched sides, Dukakis would have won in the Electoral College, though Bush would still have trounced him in the popular vote, 52 percent to 46 percent. See 19 America Votes 9 (Richard M. Scammon & Alice V. McGillivray eds., 1991).

75. Other possible constitutional accidents waiting to happen involve presidential succession. Is democratic legitimacy well served when the people vote for President A and end up, because of death or disability, with Vice President B, representing very different policies? (Examples include William Henry Harrison and John Tyler, Abraham Lincoln and Andrew Johnson, James Garfield and Chester A. Arthur, and William McKinley and Theodore Roosevelt.) Also, what kind of legitimacy would there have been if the people in 1996 elected Democrats Bill Clinton and Al Gore, but ended up (as a result of a hypothetical double death in 1997) with Republican Newt Gingrich? (The current presidential succession statute specifies the Speaker of the House as third in line.) For suggestions that the process of vice presidential selection and the laws dealing with presidential succession should be rethought, see Ruth C. Silva, Presidential Succession (1951); Richard D. Friedman, Some Modest Proposals on the Vice-Presidency, 86 Mich. L. Rev. 1703 (1988); Akhil Reed Amar and Vik Amar, President Quayle?, 78 Va. L. Rev. 913 (1992); Akhil Reed Amar and Vikram David Amar, Is the Presidential Succession Law Constitutional?, 48 Stan. L. Rev. 113 (1995).

A recurrent issue in discussions of the Electoral College is the problem of "faithless electors," who vote for someone other than the presidential or vice-presidential candidate of the party that selected them for its slate of electors. Most States also compel electors to pledge in advance to support the nominee of that party. This Court upheld such a pledge requirement in Ray v. Blair, 343 U.S. 214, 228 (1952) rejecting the argument that the Constitution "demands absolute freedom for the elector to vote his own choice." In Chiafalo v. Washington, 140 S. Ct. 2316 (2020), the Supreme Court held that states may also penalize an elector for breaking his pledge and voting for someone other than the presidential candidate who won his State's popular vote. Justice Kagan, speaking for seven Justices, found this power in Article II, section 1, which provides that "[e]ach State shall appoint, in such Manner as the Legislature thereof may direct, a Number of Electors."

> Article II, §1's appointments power gives the States far-reaching authority over presidential electors, absent some other constitutional constraint. . . . This Court has described that clause as "conveying the broadest power of determination" over who becomes an elector. McPherson v. Blacker, 146 U.S. 1, 27 (1892). And the power to appoint an elector (in any manner) includes power to condition his appointment—that is, to say what the elector must do for the appointment to take effect. A State can require, for example, that an elector live in the State or qualify as a regular voter during the relevant time period. Or more substantively, a State can insist (as *Ray* allowed) that the elector pledge to cast his Electoral College ballot for his party's presidential nominee, thus tracking the State's popular vote. Or—so long as nothing else in the Constitution poses an obstacle—a State can add, as Washington did, an associated condition of appointment: It can demand that the elector actually live up to his pledge, on pain of penalty. Which is to say that the State's appointment power, barring some outside constraint, enables the enforcement of a pledge like Washington's.

Justice Thomas, joined by Justice Gorsuch, agreed that state penalties were constitutional, but argued that the power does not derive from Article II, section 1. Rather, "When the Constitution is silent, authority resides with the States or the people. This allocation of power is both embodied in the structure of our Constitution and expressly required by the Tenth Amendment."

NOTE: THE EMOLUMENTS CLAUSES [ONLINE]

NOTE: PRESIDENTIAL IMPEACHMENT [ONLINE]

CHAPTER 7

RACE AND THE EQUAL PROTECTION CLAUSE

This chapter focuses on the meaning of the Equal Protection Clause of the Fourteenth Amendment—"No state shall . . . deny to any person within its jurisdiction the equal protection of the laws"—with respect to racial equality. We begin with the school desegregation case, Brown v. Board of Education, which ushers in the modern conception of the Equal Protection Clause, and trace the story of the constitutional battles over school segregation that followed in the wake of *Brown*. The rest of the chapter considers contemporary issues of racial discrimination.

I. BROWN v. BOARD OF EDUCATION AND THE CONSTITUTIONAL STRUGGLE OVER DESEGREGATION

A. Background to the School Desegregation Case

Like most previous wars, World War II was in fact good for African Americans insofar as the pressing needs of the military and of war industry provided jobs and a new measure of economic and political independence, especially in the great cities of the North and Midwest. New waves of migration brought Black people from the Jim Crow South to the North, which further increased the voting power of the Northern urban areas. African Americans had unprecedented access to jobs, higher wages, and union membership. Alfred Kelly continues the story of the years prior to *Brown.*[1]

> [In addition to the changing domestic, economic, and political conditions,] the equalitarian ideology of American war propaganda, which presented the United States as a champion of democracy engaged in a death struggle with the German racists, created in the minds and hearts of most white persons a new and intense awareness of the shocking contrast between the country's too comfortable image of itself and the cold realities of American racial segregation. Both pragmatic propaganda interests

1. Alfred Kelly, The School Desegregation Case, Quarrels That Have Shaped the Constitution 243, 247-249, 253 (John Garraty ed., 1964). See also Michael Klarman, From Jim Crow to Civil Rights: The Supreme Court and the Struggle for Racial Equality 288-289 (2004).

and the new idealism demanded certain steps for the Negro's further integration, both in society and in the war effort.

Some of this crisis-imposed, wartime integration took place on an official level: in a series of executive orders, the Roosevelt administration expanded the employment of Negroes in the federal bureaucracy, wrote "no discrimination" clauses into war contracts, established in 1941 a Fair Employment Practices Commission, and even took a few hesitant steps toward racial integration in the armed forces. Meantime, in 1939, Attorney General Frank Murphy, already something of a radical idealist on the integration and Negro civil rights questions, had established a Civil Rights Division in the Department of Justice, which in turn undertook what was to prove to be a generation-long legal quest for new federal guarantees against lynching and new safeguards for Negro voting rights. Congress, also, bestirred itself. The Soldiers Vote Act of 1942 abolished the poll tax as a prerequisite for voting by members of the armed services, while the so-called La Follette Civil Liberties Committee began its own investigation into the lynching problem.

It was inevitable that the Negro's new nationalized political power, his enhanced economic position, and the vast improvement in ideological climate in the country presently would spill over into the courts, to produce a new series of decisions reflecting the altered position of the Negro in America. The dynamics of this process are hardly very mysterious. Several of the Roosevelt appointees to the Court after 1937 were practical politicians whom the exigencies of the New Deal had intensely aware of the "political power shift" implicit in the Negro's new party role. Hugo Black, Robert Jackson, Frank Murphy, and Wiley Rutledge all fell into this category. Or, like Felix Frankfurter and William O. Douglas, the new appointees were legal academicians who reflected the equalitarian idealism of the liberal university communities of the North. . . .

It needs only to be added here that the succession of justices appointed to the Court after the war—Fred M. Vinson, Harold Burton, Sherman Minton, and Tom Clark—while they tended generally to be more conservative than New Deal era justices, nonetheless had been trained in the hard practical school of politics and shared to the full an awareness of the altered position of the Negro in American society. Earl Warren, the mild-mannered middle-of-the-road Republican who came to the chief justiceship in 1953, epitomized as no one else could have this new politico-judicial understanding. The Negro's altered role was no mere matter of New Deal radical idealism. It was a point of view which had been thoroughly absorbed by the working politicians of both parties.

It is hardly open to question, then, that this flow of Democratic and Republican appointees to the High Court after 1937 would in no great length of time have produced something of a constitutional revolution in the Negro's status. But this process, inevitable as it may well have been, was vastly accelerated by the legal assault on segregation first launched in the late 1930's by a powerful and dedicated Negro interest group, the National Association for the Advancement of Colored People. The desegregation campaign commenced about 1935 by the NAACP got under way very slowly, but it continued without interruption and with growing success for the next generation.[2] It was a campaign which would make the NAACP the "cutting edge" of all the complex social and political forces that were at work to produce a desegregated America.

[The NAACP's postwar school desegregation began with] . . . a series of suits to force the admission of Negroes to Southern graduate professional schools, above all state university law schools. Several major considerations led NAACP officials to adopt this scheme. First, most Southern states did not even attempt to maintain a facade of equality in professional educational facilities for Negroes, so that their classic "separate but equal" defense, the Association hoped, would prove to be inapplicable. Second, NAACP lawyers believed that if the Southern states countered this strategy by trying to provide genuinely equal facilities for Negroes in graduate education, the effort would prove to be both awesomely expensive and impossible of actual achievement. . . .

The NAACP lawyers were also deliberately exploiting a peculiarity of Southern racial sentiment. The South . . . regarded racial mixing in graduate and professional education as far less invidious than in primary and secondary schools or even in collegiate education. As a consequence, they hoped, Southern officials might be expected to resist graduate school integration with less emotional conviction than would be the case for lower-level schools. As [Thurgood] Marshall, with characteristic humor, later put the matter: "Those racial supremacy boys somehow think that little kids of six or seven are going to get funny ideas about sex and marriage just from going to school together, but for some equally funny reason youngsters in law school aren't supposed to feel that way. We didn't get it but we decided that if that was what the South believed, then the best thing for the moment was to go along."

NOTE: *BROWN* AND THE COLD WAR

As the preceding excerpt suggests, courts always operate within a larger political, social, and cultural context. Consider Michael Klarman's list of "underlying forces that made *Brown* a realistic judicial possibility in 1954": "World War II, the ideological revulsion against Nazi fascism, the Cold War imperative, the growing political empowerment of northern blacks, the increasing economic and social integration of the nation, and changing southern racial attitudes."[3] One should

---

2. Thus Missouri ex rel. Gaines v. Canada, 305 U.S. 337 (1938), held that Missouri did not provide equal protection by paying the tuition for Black students at out-of-state law schools while denying them admission to the state school. Chief Justice Hughes wrote that petitioner was entitled to "facilities [within the state] substantially equal to those which the State there afforded for persons of the white race" and that in the absence of such facilities he must be admitted to the one state school. Justice McReynolds, joined by Justice Butler, dissented, arguing that the state had made a "fair effort" to solve a difficult problem and that its solution was "far from [an] unmistakable disregard of [petitioner's] rights."

3. Michael J. Klarman, *Brown*, Racial Change, and the Civil Rights Movement, 80 Va. L. Rev. 7, 14 (1994).

also not underestimate the impact of President Truman's decision to desegregate the armed forces over the marked opposition of the Joint Chiefs of Staff.[4]

Derrick Bell has argued for what he calls the "interest convergence" thesis—that Black progress only occurs when the interests of whites converge with those of Blacks. Derrick Bell, Brown v. Board of Education and the Interest-Convergence Dilemma, 93 Harv. L. Rev. 518 (1980). Thus Bell suggested that *Brown* was made possible by the changes in the interests of white elites following the Cold War. Mary Dudziak amply supports Bell's thesis in her study Desegregation as a Cold War Imperative, 41 Stan. L. Rev. 61 (1988), which focuses on foreign policy events leading up to the decision in *Brown*. Dudziak shows how the domestic issue of desegregation was framed in part by the larger context of international criticism. In his now-classic study, An American Dilemma: The Negro Problem and Modern Democracy (1944), Swedish sociologist Gunnar Myrdal had directed the world's attention to the divergence between America's professed democratic ideals and the second-class status of its Black citizens. Myrdal issued the following challenge: "America, for all its international prestige, power, and future security, needs to demonstrate to the world that American Negroes can be satisfactorily integrated into its democracy." Not surprisingly, after the onset of the Cold War, Myrdal's generally "well-intentioned" criticisms were put to distinctly ideological uses by East Bloc governments.

This international situation provided a strategic advantage to American opponents of segregation. In 1946, the National Negro Congress petitioned the U.N. for "relief from oppression," and in 1947, the NAACP submitted A Statement on the Denial of Human Rights to Minorities in the Case of Citizens of Negro Descent in the United States of America and an Appeal to the United Nations for Redress.[5] Although the U.N. took no action on the charges, they were publicized widely overseas. In 1951, the Civil Rights Congress filed a petition under the United Nations Convention on the Prevention and Punishment of the Crime of Genocide, charging the U.S. government with Black genocide.[6]

---

4. Exec. Order No. 9,981, 13 Fed. Reg. 4,313 (1948). Indeed, Truman's Democratic Party split over its strong civil rights platform at the 1948 Convention. Truman nevertheless was able to win reelection. The Truman Administration also urged the Court to overturn *Plessy* in 1950. See William Berman, The Politics of Civil Rights in the Truman Administration 55, 68, 118 (1970). What explains Truman's rather courageous record on civil rights? Alonzo Hamby writes:

> No historian can precisely define Truman's motivation on so complex and emotional an issue; it was probably not entirely clear even to Truman. It seems fair to say that he really believed in the principles of equal rights and equal opportunity. But it is also just to observe that he was well aware of the importance of the black vote. It is reasonable to assume that he acted in part out of a sense of self-interest but more important that he interpreted his self-interest in a fashion both astute and morally enlightened.

Alonzo Hamby, Liberalism and Its Challengers: FDR to Reagan 66-67 (1985).

5. Gerald N. Rosenberg, The Hollow Hope: Can Courts Bring About Social Change? 163 (1991).

6. Mary L. Dudziak, Desegregation as a Cold War Imperative, 41 Stan. L. Rev. 61, 96 (1988). This thesis is further elaborated in Mary Dudziak, Cold War Civil Rights: Race in the Image of American Democracy (2000).

Given these significant embarrassments, desegregation became a matter of direct concern to the State Department. In its amicus brief in *Brown*, the Department of Justice emphasized how segregation interfered with the country's foreign policy: "Racial discrimination furnishes grist for the Communist propaganda mills, and it raises doubts even among friendly nations as to the intensity of our devotion to the democratic faith."[7] In support, the brief quoted Secretary of State Dean Acheson at length, including his statement that school desegregation in particular had been[8]

> singled out for hostile foreign comment in the United Nations and elsewhere. Other peoples cannot understand how such a practice can exist in a country which professes to be a staunch supporter of freedom, justice, and democracy. . . . [R]acial discrimination in the United States remains a source of constant embarrassment to this Government in the day-to-day conduct of its foreign relations; and it jeopardizes the effective maintenance of our moral leadership of the free and democratic nations of the world.

Dudziak argues that when *Brown* finally came, part of its political utility lay in the fact that it[9]

> laundered the principles of democracy in the eyes of the world. The decision announced that racial segregation and American constitutional rights were inconsistent with each other. After *Brown*, the State Department could blame racism on the Klan and the crazies. They could argue that the American Constitution provided for effective social change. And, most importantly, they could point to the *Brown* decision as evidence that racism was at odds with the principles of American democracy. This foreign policy angle, this Cold War imperative, was one of the critical factors driving the federal government's postwar civil rights efforts.

For whatever combination of international and domestic reasons, the NAACP's legal strategy in its fight against segregation was ultimately successful.[10] A unanimous Court reaffirmed *Gaines* in Sipuel v. University of Oklahoma Board of Regents, 332 U.S. 631 (1948). (Justices McReynolds and Butler had resigned in the interim and been replaced by Justices Rutledge and Murphy.) The Court held that petitioner had a constitutional right to an equal education and could not be denied entrance to a state law school solely because of her race. However, on remand, a trial court gave the state the option of establishing a separate Black law school, and the Supreme Court, in Fisher v. Hurst, 333 U.S. 147 (1948), refused to order the state to desegregate its law school.

Two years later, however, in Sweatt v. Painter, 339 U.S. 629 (1950), the Court held that a hastily established law school for Black law students did not and probably could not provide an education equal to that offered by the University of Texas Law School. Chief Justice Vinson wrote for the Court:

---

7. Dudziak, Desegregation as a Cold War Imperative, supra at 110-111.

8. Id. at 111-112.

9. Id. at 118-119.

10. See Mark Tushnet, The NAACP's Legal Strategy Against Segregated Education, 1925-1950 (1987).

> In terms of number of the faculty, variety of courses and opportunity for specialization, size of the student body, scope of the library, availability of law review and similar activities, the University of Texas Law School is superior. What is more important, the University of Texas Law School possesses to a far greater degree those qualities which are incapable of objective measurement but which make for greatness in a law school. Such qualities, to name but a few, include reputation of the faculty, experience of the administration, position and influence of the alumni, standing in the community, traditions and prestige. . . .
>
> The law school, the proving ground for legal learning and practice, cannot be effective in isolation from the individuals and institutions with which the law interacts. . . . The law school to which Texas is willing to admit petitioner excludes from its student body members of the racial groups which number 85% of the population of the State and include most of the lawyers, witnesses, jurors, judges and other officials with whom petitioner will inevitably be dealing when he becomes a member of the Texas Bar.

McLaurin v. Oklahoma State Regents, 339 U.S. 637 (1950), decided the same day as *Sweatt*, held that petitioner, having been admitted to the state university to pursue a graduate program not offered at the state's school for Black people, could not be required to sit in separate sections of the classroom, library, and cafeteria. Chief Justice Vinson again wrote for a unanimous Court, stating that the "restrictions impair and inhibit [petitioner's] ability to study, to engage in discussions and exchange views with other students, and, in general, to learn his profession." To the argument that petitioner might still be set apart by his fellow students, Vinson responded:

> [T]here is a vast difference—a Constitutional difference—between restrictions imposed by the state which prohibit the intellectual commingling of students, and the refusal of individuals to commingle where the state presents no such bar. . . . The removal of the state restrictions will not necessarily abate individual and group predilections, prejudices and choices. But at the very least, the state will not be depriving appellant of the opportunity to secure acceptance by his fellow students on his own merits.

In 1952, the NAACP presented the Court with the issue of segregation in elementary and secondary public schools. Brown v. Board of Education, 347 U.S. 483 (1954), and its four companion cases were first argued during the 1952 term of the Supreme Court. Toward the close of the term, on June 8, 1953, the Court set the cases for reargument. A principal reason, it has been suggested, is because the Court was badly split as to the outcome of the case. Before the reargument, Chief Justice Vinson died on September 8, 1953 and was replaced by the Governor of California, Earl Warren.[11] Felix Frankfurter is said to have confided to a clerk that this was "the first indication that I have ever had that there is a God."[12]

---

11. The Senate confirmed Warren's appointment on March 1, 1954, two months before *Brown* was decided, but President Eisenhower had given Warren a recess appointment on September 30, 1953. See Article II, §2, cl. 3 ("The President shall have the power to fill up all vacancies that may happen during the recess of the Senate, by granting commissions, which shall expire at the end of their next session."). Consider whether this sequence of events could have occurred today.

12. Bernard Schwarz, Super Chief 72 (1983).

The Court requested counsel "[i]n their briefs and on oral argument . . . to discuss particularly the following questions . . .":

1. What evidence is there that the Congress which submitted and the State legislatures and conventions which ratified the Fourteenth Amendment contemplated or did not contemplate, understood or did not understand, that it would abolish segregation in the public schools?
2. If neither the Congress in submitting nor the States in ratifying the Fourteenth Amendment understood that compliance with it would require the immediate abolition of segregation in public schools, was it nevertheless the understanding of the framers of the Amendment
   (a) that future Congresses might, in the exercise of their power under Section 5 of the Amendment, abolish such segregation, or
   (b) that it would be within the judicial power, in light of future conditions, to construe the Amendment as abolishing segregation of its own force?
3. On the assumption that the answers to questions 2(a) and (b) do not dispose of the issue, is it within the judicial power, in construing the Amendment, to abolish segregation in public schools?

The parties in *Brown* responded to the Court's questions on the original understanding with lengthy historical briefs.[13] See Chapter 4 for a summary of the historical evidence.

B. The School Desegregation Case

Brown v. Board of Education of Topeka, Kansas[14]

347 U.S. 483 (1954)

WARREN, C.J.

These cases come to us from the States of Kansas, South Carolina, Virginia, and Delaware. They are premised on different facts and different local conditions, but a common legal question justifies their consideration together in this consolidated opinion.

In each of the cases, minors of the Negro race, through their legal representatives, seek the aid of the courts in obtaining admission to the public schools of their community on a nonsegregated basis. In each instance, they had been denied admission to schools attended by white children under laws requiring or permitting segregation according to race. This segregation was alleged to deprive the plaintiffs of the equal protection of the laws under the Fourteenth Amendment. In each of

---

13. The petitioners in *Brown* commissioned various historians, including Howard J. Graham, Alfred H. Kelly, C. Vann Woodward, John Hope Franklin, and Horace Bond, to prepare monographs for their use. See generally Kelly, supra n.1.

14. *Brown* is actually a joinder of four separate cases, as the Court notes in its first sentence. A fifth case, from the District of Columbia, was decided separately as Bolling v. Sharpe, 347 U.S. 497 (1954).

the cases other than the Delaware case, a three-judge federal district court denied relief to the plaintiffs on the so-called "separate but equal" doctrine announced by this Court in Plessy v. Ferguson, 163 U.S. 537. Under the doctrine, equality of treatment is accorded when the races are provided substantially equal facilities, even though these facilities be separate. In the Delaware case, the Supreme Court of Delaware adhered to that doctrine, but ordered that the plaintiffs be admitted to the white schools because of their superiority to the Negro schools.

The plaintiffs contend that segregated public schools are not "equal" and cannot be made "equal," and that hence they are deprived of the equal protection of the laws. Because of the obvious importance of the question presented, the Court took jurisdiction. Argument was heard in the 1952 Term, and reargument was heard this Term on certain questions propounded by the Court.

Reargument was largely devoted to the circumstances surrounding the adoption of the Fourteenth Amendment in 1868. It covered exhaustively consideration of the Amendment in Congress, ratification by the states, then existing practices in racial segregation, and the views of proponents and opponents of the Amendment. This discussion and our own investigation convince us that, although these sources cast some light, it is not enough to resolve the problem with which we are faced. At best, they are inconclusive. The most avid proponents of the post-War Amendments undoubtedly intended them to remove all legal distinctions among "all persons born or naturalized in the United States." Their opponents, just as certainly, were antagonistic to both the letter and the spirit of the Amendments and wished them to have the most limited effect. What others in Congress and the state legislatures had in mind cannot be determined with any degree of certainty.

An additional reason for the inconclusive nature of the Amendment's history, with respect to segregated schools, is the status of public education at that time. In the South, the movement toward free common schools, supported by general taxation, had not yet taken hold. Education of white children was largely in the hands of private groups. Education of Negroes was almost nonexistent, and practically all of the race were illiterate. In fact, any education of Negroes was forbidden by law in some states. Today, in contrast, many Negroes have achieved outstanding success in the arts and sciences as well as in the business and professional world. It is true that public school education at the time of the Amendment had advanced further in the North, but the effect of the Amendment on Northern States was generally ignored in the congressional debates. Even in the North, the conditions of public education did not approximate those existing today. The curriculum was usually rudimentary; ungraded schools were common in rural areas; the school term was but three months a year in many states; and compulsory school attendance was virtually unknown. As a consequence, it is not surprising that there should be so little in the history of the Fourteenth Amendment relating to its intended effect on public education.

In the first cases in this Court construing the Fourteenth Amendment, decided shortly after its adoption, the Court interpreted it as proscribing all state-imposed discriminations against the Negro race. The doctrine of "separate but equal" did not make its appearance in this Court until 1896 in the case of Plessy v. Ferguson, supra, involving not education but transportation. American courts have since labored with the doctrine for over half a century. In this Court, there have been six cases involving the "separate but equal" doctrine in the field of public education.

In Cumming v. County Board of Education, 175 U.S. 528, and Gong Lum v. Rice, 275 U.S. 78, the validity of the doctrine itself was not challenged. In more recent cases, all on the graduate school level, inequality was found in that specific benefits enjoyed by white students were denied to Negro students of the same educational qualifications. Missouri ex rel. Gaines v. Canada, 305 U.S. 337; Sipuel v. Oklahoma, 332 U.S. 631; Sweatt v. Painter, 339 U.S. 629; McLaurin v. Oklahoma State Regents, 339 U.S. 637. In none of these cases was it necessary to re-examine the doctrine to grant relief to the Negro plaintiff. And in Sweatt v. Painter, supra, the Court expressly reserved decision on the question whether Plessy v. Ferguson should be held inapplicable to public education.

In the instant cases, that question is directly presented. Here, unlike Sweatt v. Painter, there are findings below that the Negro and white schools involved have been equalized, or are being equalized, with respect to buildings, curricula, qualifications and salaries of teachers, and other "tangible" factors. Our decision, therefore, cannot turn on merely a comparison of these tangible factors in the Negro and white schools involved in each of the cases. We must look instead to the effect of segregation itself on public education.

In approaching this problem, we cannot turn the clock back to 1868 when the Amendment was adopted, or even to 1896 when Plessy v. Ferguson was written. We must consider public education in the light of its full development and its present place in American life throughout the Nation. Only in this way can it be determined if segregation in public schools deprives these plaintiffs of the equal protection of the laws.

Today, education is perhaps the most important function of state and local governments. Compulsory school attendance laws and the great expenditures for education both demonstrate our recognition of the importance of education to our democratic society. It is required in the performance of our most basic public responsibilities, even service in the armed forces. It is the very foundation of good citizenship. Today it is a principal instrument in awakening the child to cultural values, in preparing him for later professional training, and in helping him to adjust normally to his environment. In these days, it is doubtful that any child may reasonably be expected to succeed in life if he is denied the opportunity of an education. Such an opportunity, where the state has undertaken to provide it, is a right which must be made available to all on equal terms.

We come then to the question presented: Does segregation of children in public schools solely on the basis of race, even though the physical facilities and other "tangible" factors may be equal, deprive the children of the minority group of equal educational opportunities? We believe that it does.

In Sweatt v. Painter, supra, in finding that a segregated law school for Negroes could not provide them equal educational opportunities, this Court relied in large part on "those qualities which are incapable of objective measurement but which make for greatness in a law school." In McLaurin v. Oklahoma State Regents, supra, the Court, in requiring that a Negro admitted to a white graduate school be treated like all other students, again resorted to intangible considerations: ". . . his ability to study, to engage in discussions and exchange views with other students, and, in general, to learn his profession." Such considerations apply with added force to children in grade and high schools. To separate them from others of similar age and qualifications solely because of their race generates a feeling of inferiority as to their status in the community that may affect their hearts and minds in a way unlikely ever to be undone. The effect of this separation on their educational opportunities was well stated by a finding in the Kansas case by a court which nevertheless felt compelled to rule against the Negro plaintiffs:

> Segregation of white and colored children in public schools has a detrimental effect upon the colored children. The impact is greater when it has the sanction of the law; for the policy of separating the races is usually interpreted as denoting the inferiority of the negro group. A sense of inferiority affects the motivation of a child to learn. Segregation with the sanction of law, therefore, has a tendency to [retard] the educational and mental development of negro children and to deprive them of some of the benefits they would receive in a racial[ly] integrated school system.

Whatever may have been the extent of psychological knowledge at the time of Plessy v. Ferguson, this finding is amply supported by modern authority. Any language in Plessy v. Ferguson contrary to this finding is rejected.

We conclude that in the field of public education the doctrine of "separate but equal" has no place. Separate educational facilities are inherently unequal. Therefore, we hold that the plaintiffs and others similarly situated for whom the actions have been brought are, by reason of the segregation complained of, deprived of the equal protection of the laws guaranteed by the Fourteenth Amendment. This disposition makes unnecessary any discussion whether such segregation also violates the Due Process Clause of the Fourteenth Amendment.

Because these are class actions, because of the wide applicability of this decision, and because of the great variety of local conditions, the formulation of decrees in these cases presents problems of considerable complexity. On reargument, the consideration of appropriate relief was necessarily subordinated to the primary question—the constitutionality of segregation in public education. We have now announced that such segregation is a denial of the equal protection of the laws. In order that we may have the full assistance of the parties in formulating decrees, the cases will be restored to the docket, and the parties are requested to present further argument on Questions 4 and 5 previously propounded by the Court for the reargument this Term.

The Attorney General of the United States is again invited to participate. The Attorneys General of the states requiring or permitting segregation in public education will also be permitted to appear as amici curiae upon request to do so by September 15, 1954, and submission of briefs by October 1, 1954.

It is so ordered.

BOLLING v. SHARPE, 347 U.S. 497 (1954): [In Bolling v. Sharpe, decided the same day as *Brown*, the Supreme Court unanimously held segregation of the public schools in the District of Columbia unconstitutional under the Fifth Amendment's Due Process Clause.]

WARREN, C.J.:

[T]he Fifth Amendment, which is applicable in the District of Columbia, does not contain an equal protection clause as does the Fourteenth Amendment which applies only to the states. But the concepts of equal protection and due process, both stemming from our American ideal of fairness, are not mutually exclusive.

The "equal protection of the laws" is a more explicit safeguard of prohibited unfairness than "due process of law," and, therefore, we do not imply that the two are always interchangeable phrases. But, as this Court has recognized, discrimination may be so unjustifiable as to be violative of due process.

Classifications based solely upon race must be scrutinized with particular care, since they are contrary to our traditions and hence constitutionally suspect. As long ago as 1896, this Court declared the principle "that the Constitution of the United States, in its present form, forbids, so far as civil and political rights are concerned, discrimination by the General Government, or by the States, against any citizen because of his race." And in Buchanan v. Warley, 245 U.S. 60, the Court held that a statute which limited the right of a property owner to convey his property to a person of another race was, as an unreasonable discrimination, a denial of due process of law.

Although the Court has not assumed to define "liberty" with any great precision, that term is not confined to mere freedom from bodily restraint. Liberty under law extends to the full range of conduct which the individual is free to pursue, and it cannot be restricted except for a proper governmental objective. Segregation in public education is not reasonably related to any proper governmental objective, and thus it imposes on Negro children of the District of Columbia a burden that constitutes an arbitrary deprivation of their liberty in violation of the Due Process Clause.

In view of our decision that the Constitution prohibits the states from maintaining racially segregated public schools, it would be unthinkable that the same Constitution would impose a lesser duty on the Federal Government. We hold that racial segregation in the public schools of the District of Columbia is a denial of the due process of law guaranteed by the Fifth Amendment to the Constitution.

DISCUSSION

1. *The role of history in* Brown. The Justices asked for reargument on the Framers' understanding about whether racial segregation of public schools violated the Fourteenth Amendment. Ultimately, the Justices decided that the history was "inconclusive." (See Note: *Brown* and the Original Understanding, infra.) Yet this is not the only way that history mattered to the Justices in *Brown.* Chief Justice Warren looks at events that occurred after the ratification of the Fourteenth Amendment. He points out that universal public education was a novelty at the time of the adoption of the Fourteenth Amendment, but by 1954 education was central to democratic citizenship. By 1954, he claims, "the opportunity of an education, . . . where the state has undertaken to provide it, is a right which must be made available to all on equal terms."

Why does Warren point to the changed status of education in American life? Is he arguing that the principles underlying the Fourteenth Amendment must be interpreted differently as social conditions change? Is there more than one way to interpret the Constitution's text in light of changed circumstances? If so, how do judges decide which is the best response?

2. *Who counts?* To what extent should the principles of the Framers matter, given that Black people—and many other Americans—lacked political power to influence the adoption of the Fourteenth Amendment?

3. Brown *and the constitutional canon.* There are at least two different kinds of history that matter to constitutional interpretation. The first is the history of making or adopting constitutional provisions. The second is the history of living under a constitution and debating the meaning of its provisions. As we have seen, *Brown* was preceded by 80 years of struggles over the meaning of the Reconstruction Amendments, and the opinion was highly controversial in its own day. Yet within a decade after the Court's decision, *Brown* had become a venerated icon. It had come to stand for the very idea of equality in the United States, and became the touchstone of debates over equal protection. Arguments about the Fourteenth Amendment today are often phrased in terms of claims about *Brown.* As you read the materials in this chapter, ask yourself how *Brown* became the standard for determining the proper meaning of the Equal Protection Clause.

4. *What is the principle behind* Brown*? Anticlassification and antisubordination.* What theory of equality underlies the decision in *Brown*? Consider two different principles against racial discrimination. The first is that the Constitution is opposed to the maintenance of racial caste, second-class citizenship, or the subordination of any group by law. The second is that the Constitution is colorblind and protects individuals from racial classifications. Call the first formulation the *antisubordination* principle and the second the *anticlassification* principle. Although these two principles reach identical results in many cases—state-enforced segregation of public schools being one of them—they tend to produce different results in many others. Two important contemporary examples in which the principles diverge are (1) affirmative action policies and (2) practices that do not facially classify on the basis of race but nevertheless have a foreseeably adverse impact on minority groups.

At the time *Brown* was decided, people may not have even discerned antisubordination and anticlassification as two separate principles.[15]

There is language in *Brown* and in *Bolling* that might reflect either principle. For example, Warren's opinion in *Brown* states that "[t]o separate [black schoolchildren] from others of similar age and qualifications solely because of their race generates a feeling of inferiority as to their status in the community that may affect

---

15. See Reva B. Siegel, Equality Talk: Antisubordination and Anticlassification Values in Constitutional Struggles over *Brown,* 117 Harv. L. Rev. 1470, 1476 (2004).

Nor was the conflict between these two principles apparent during the opening years of the civil rights movement. Much of Martin Luther King Jr.'s rhetoric, for example, combines both elements. In his famous "I Have a Dream" speech, delivered at the Lincoln Memorial on August 28, 1963, King spoke of his dream that his "four little children will one day live in a nation where they will not be judged by the color of their skin but by content of their character." Yet King's speech is also about the maintenance of social inferiority. That injustice is not redeemed simply by the elimination of formal barriers: "We cannot be satisfied as long as a colored person in Mississippi cannot vote and a colored person in New York believes he has nothing for which to vote." In King's view, even if New York did not practice Jim Crow, it did not follow that there were no problems of racial inequality there. King was concerned with much more than formal equality before the law: The official title of the March on Washington was The March for Jobs and Freedom.

their hearts and minds in a way unlikely ever to be undone." Warren also quotes the district court opinion in *Brown* that "[s]egregation of white and colored children in public schools has a detrimental effect upon the colored children. The impact is greater when it has the sanction of the law; for the policy of separating the races is usually interpreted as denoting the inferiority of the negro group." *Bolling,* unlike *Brown,* actually refers to racial classifications, but its rationale is that if segregation in the states is unconstitutional, it would be unthinkable if it were not also unconstitutional in the District of Columbia. In a series of per curiam decisions immediately following *Brown* (see the discussion infra), the Court simply struck down segregated state facilities without giving any explanation at all.

5. Suppose that a town has significant residential racial segregation. Consider three cases:

a. In the first case, the school board designates Black and white schools and directs students to attend schools associated with each student's race.

b. In the second case, the school board draws attendance zones to create "neighborhood" schools; as a result, most Blacks and most whites go to separate schools and the schools are racially identifiable. The school board's purpose (although not publicly stated) in adopting the neighborhood school policy is to separate the races.

c. In the third case, the school board draws attendance zones to create "neighborhood" schools; as a result, most Blacks and most whites go to separate schools and the schools are racially identifiable. The school board's stated purpose is to allow students to attend schools close to their homes, even though it is foreseeable—and understood by the school board—that this will substantially separate students by race.

All three cases involve state action by the school board. What are the harms in these three cases? Are these harms the same or different in the three cases? Do any or all of these cases violate the principle of *Brown*? If so, why?

6. *"Green follows white."* Although today we think of the NAACP's strategy as an attack on segregation, much of Thurgood Marshall's early work actually employed the "separate but equal" doctrine of *Plessy* to equalize facilities for Blacks and whites. Marshall gradually decided to push for the goal of desegregation rather than equalization before his victory in Sweatt v. Painter in 1950, "but even toward the end of the 1940s he was willing to devote resources to equalization suits."[16] Ultimately, the NAACP chose desegregation because it believed that white majorities would not adequately fund schools for Black children unless white children were also learning in them. This was the idea that "green follows white."

Not all Black people were convinced that integration was the right answer: Many feared that the end of segregation would threaten the jobs of African-American professionals and particularly African-American schoolteachers; others feared that whites would resist desegregation with violence. Although Marshall was committed to desegregation and the integrative ideal, he repeatedly had to convince his constituents that desegregation was the best direction for Black children.[17]

16. Mark Tushnet, Making Civil Rights Law: Thurgood Marshall and the Supreme Court, 1936-1961, at 151 (1994).

17. Id. at 152.

Consider the debates within different parts of the Black community immediately following World War II. What would be the arguments for and against prioritizing the integration of public elementary and secondary schools over other ways of challenging Jim Crow and racial subordination in the United States?[18]

NOTE: A "DISSENT" FROM *BROWN*

Brown v. Board of Education has no dissenting opinion. However, in 1956, virtually all of the senators and congressmen in the Deep South signed the "Southern Manifesto" arguing that the Court's decision was not only incorrect but an abuse of power:

> DECLARATION OF CONSTITUTIONAL PRINCIPLES[19]
>
> [The Southern Manifesto]
>
> . . . We regard the decisions of the Supreme Court in the school cases as a clear abuse of judicial power. It climaxes a trend in the Federal Judiciary undertaking to legislate, in derogation of the authority of Congress, and to encroach upon the reserved rights of the States and the people.
>
> The original Constitution does not mention education. Neither does the 14th Amendment nor any other amendment. The debates preceding the submission of the 14th Amendment clearly show that there was no intent that it should affect the system of education maintained by the States.
>
> The very Congress which proposed the amendment subsequently provided for segregated schools in the District of Columbia.
>
> When the amendment was adopted in 1868, there were 37 States of the Union. . . . Every one of the 26 States that had any substantial racial differences among its people, either approved the operation of segregated schools already in existence or subsequently established such schools by action of the same lawmaking body which considered the 14th Amendment.
>
> [T]he doctrine of separate but equal schools . . . began in the North, not in the South, and it was followed not only in Massachusetts, but in Connecticut, New York, Illinois, Indiana, Michigan, Minnesota, New Jersey, Ohio, Pennsylvania and other northern states. . . .
>
> Plessy v. Ferguson . . . has been followed in many other cases. [T]he Supreme Court . . . unanimously declared in 1927 in Lum v. Rice that the "separate but equal" principle is "within the discretion of the State in regulating its public schools and does not conflict with the 14th Amendment."
>
> This interpretation, restated time and again, became a part of the life of the people of many of the States and confirmed their habits, traditions,

---

18. For a history of the debates within the Black community in Atlanta during the civil rights era, see Tomiko Brown-Nagin, Courage to Dissent: Atlanta and the Long History of the Civil Rights Movement (2011). See also Derrick Bell's imaginary dissent from *Brown* in What Brown v. Board of Education Should Have Said 185-200 (Jack M. Balkin ed., 2001).

19. Excerpted from 102 Cong. Rec. H3948, 4004 (Mar. 12, 1956).

and way of life. It is founded on elemental humanity and commonsense, for parents should not be deprived by Government of the right to direct the lives and education of their own children.

Though there has been no constitutional amendment or act of Congress changing this established legal principle almost a century old, the Supreme Court of the United States, with no legal basis for such action, undertook to exercise their naked judicial power and substituted their personal political and social ideas for the established law of the land.

This unwarranted exercise of power by the Court, contrary to the Constitution, is creating chaos and confusion in the States principally affected. It is destroying the amicable relations between the white and Negro races that have been created through 90 years of patient effort by the good people of both races. It has planted hatred and suspicion where there has been heretofore friendship and understanding.

Without regard to the consent of the governed, outside mediators are threatening immediate and revolutionary changes in our public schools systems. If done, this is certain to destroy the system of public education in some of the States. . . .

We decry the Supreme Court's encroachment on the rights reserved to the States and to the people, contrary to established law, and to the Constitution.

We commend the motives of those States which have declared the intention to resist forced integration by any lawful means.

We appeal to the States and people who are not directly affected by these decisions to consider the constitutional principles involved against the time when they too, on issues vital to them may be the victims of judicial encroachment.

Even though we constitute a minority in the present Congress, we have full faith that a majority of the American people believe in the dual system of government which has enabled us to achieve our greatness and will in time demand that the reserved rights of the States and of the people be made secure against judicial usurpation.

We pledge ourselves to use all lawful means to bring about a reversal of this decision which is contrary to the Constitution and to prevent the use of force in its implementation.

In this trying period, as we all seek to right this wrong, we appeal to our people not to be provoked by the agitators and troublemakers invading our States and to scrupulously refrain from disorder and lawless acts.

DISCUSSION

1. The Southern Manifesto offers a competing interpretation of the Constitution. It argues for (1) judicial restraint, (2) adherence to long existing precedents, both judicial and nonjudicial, (3) fidelity to the original understanding, and (4) respect for structural principles of federalism. All four of these factors, it claims, point in the same direction—upholding the right of individual states to decide for themselves

whether or not to segregate their public schools. Hence it concludes that the Court had abandoned sound rule of law principles and substituted its own political judgment, and that its decision was illegitimate. What, precisely, is wrong with this argument?

2. The Southern Manifesto is a prime example of constitutional interpretation outside the courts, in this case by national political leaders who acted in concert with a growing countermobilization that sought to resist an unpopular Supreme Court decision.[20] Compare this example of constitutional interpretation by non-judicial actors with others you have studied so far. Are all such examples of popular constitutionalism equally legitimate? If some are less legitimate than others, is there a way of demarcating them independent of "winner's history" or one's own sense of whether they comport with the best interpretation of the Constitution?

3. The Southern Manifesto is not the only possible way one might dissent from the decision in *Brown*. Derrick Bell argues that the Court might have reaffirmed *Plessy* but enforced it strictly to require genuine equality between Black and white schools. Bell's reinterpretation of *Plessy* would also have required the courts to order that states commit sufficient resources to make all schools measure up to national norms of educational quality. Finally, he would have insisted that Black parents have representation on school boards that affected their children's education. Derrick Bell, "Dissenting," *in* What Brown v. Board of Education Should Have Said 185-200 (Jack M. Balkin ed., 2001). Would such a remedy have been possible in 1954? Would the results have been better than what actually happened in the 50 years following *Brown*?

NOTE: *BROWN* AND THE ORIGINAL UNDERSTANDING

In its order for reargument in *Brown* the Supreme Court asked the parties to address what the framers and ratifiers of the Fourteenth Amendment "contemplated or did not contemplate, understood or did not understand" about the Fourteenth Amendment's application to school segregation. This unusual order can be explained by the context of the decision: The Warren Court was contemplating overturning an 80-year-old precedent, Plessy v. Ferguson. Some of the Justices may have hoped that if it could be shown that the framers of the amendment wanted to forbid segregated public schools, the Court could justify its opinion as a return to origins rather than as a revolutionary innovation. Today, few people in public life assert that *Brown*'s legitimacy depends on its consistency with the framers' intentions. At the time, however, as the Court considered breaking with *Plessy*, it considered this question.

Ultimately, the Court found the history of the framers intentions' "inconclusive"—in Chief Justice Warren's words. Professor Alexander Bickel, then a clerk for Justice Frankfurter, did an exhaustive study of the legislative history, later published as Alexander Bickel, The Original Understanding and the Segregation Decision, 69 Harv. L. Rev. 1 (1955). Bickel's study noted the debate over the 1866 Civil Rights

---

20. See generally George Lewis, The White South and the Red Menace: Segregationists, Anticommunism and Massive Resistance, 1945-1965 (2004); Massive Resistance: Southern Opposition to the Second Reconstruction (Clive Webb ed., 2005).

Act discussed in Chapter 4, supra. Supporters of the civil rights act insisted that it would guarantee only civil equality, not political or social equality, and would not give Black people the right to vote, secure a right to racial intermarriage, or disturb segregated schools. Bickel thus concluded that "section 1 of the fourteenth amendment, like section 1 of the Civil Rights Act of 1866, carried out the relatively narrow objectives of [Republican] Moderates, and hence, as originally understood, was meant to apply neither to jury service, nor suffrage, nor antimiscegenation statutes, nor segregation."[21]

Although Bickel focused on the congressional debates, the story was much the same in the states, whose ratification was necessary to make the Fourteenth Amendment law. At the time of the adoption of the Fourteenth Amendment, most states segregated their public schools by law. Before the war only Massachusetts required integrated public schools, joined by Rhode Island, Connecticut, and Michigan after the Civil War. A few Northern states near the Canadian border, with tiny Black populations, were silent on the question, and implicitly permitted integrated schools, while a few Midwestern states completely excluded Black people from public education. In the South, segregation of public schools was virtually universal; the only notable exception was an attempt at integration in Reconstruction-era New Orleans, an experiment that was eventually crushed by white resistance. See Michael J. Klarman, The *Plessy* Era, 1998 Sup. Ct. Rev. 303, 339-340. Although "[m]ost northern states formally abolished school segregation in the 1870s or 1880s . . . segregation remained prevalent in regions of those states where the largest percentage of the black population resided. Moreover, by the 1890s, accelerating black migration northward resulted in the resegregation of schools in some localities that had formerly enjoyed integration." Id. at 341.

Bickel concluded that "an explicit provision going further than the Civil Rights Act could not have been carried in the 39th Congress." Nevertheless, he suggested that the very openness of the Fourteenth Amendment's language might reflect a "compromise permitting [Moderates and Radicals] to go to the country with language that they could, where necessary, defend against damaging alarms raised by the opposition, but that at the same time was sufficiently elastic to permit reasonable future advances."[22] Vague language allowed "the Moderates [to] consolidate[] the victory they had achieved in the Civil Rights Act debate. They could go forth and honestly defend themselves against charges that on the day after ratification Negroes were going to become white men's 'social equals,' marry their daughters, vote in their elections, sit on their juries, and attend schools with their children."[23] Radicals, in turn, could later press for further measures. "[N]o specific purpose going beyond the coverage of the Civil Rights Act is suggested; rather an awareness on the part of these framers that it was *a constitution* they were writing, which led to a choice of language capable of growth."[24]

Forty years later, in Originalism and the Desegregation Decisions, 81 Va. L. Rev. 947 (1995), Michael McConnell challenged the received view that *Brown* is

---

21. Alexander Bickel, The Original Understanding and the Segregation Decision, 69 Harv. L. Rev. 1, 58 (1955).

22. Id. at 61.

23. Id. at 62.

24. Id. at 63.

inconsistent with the original understanding of the framers and ratifiers of the Fourteenth Amendment. McConnell points to congressional debates following ratification—in particular, the debates over what became the Civil Rights Act of 1875. "While the Thirty-ninth Congress concentrated on passing the Amendment—a context in which avoidance or obfuscation of controversial issues is often the best strategy—later Congresses were forced to determine what it meant, in the context of the most difficult questions of the day." After a detailed analysis of the postratification debates, McConnell concludes:[25]

> Between 1870 and 1875, both houses of Congress voted repeatedly, by large margins, in favor of legislation premised on the theory that de jure segregation of public schools is unconstitutional. The desegregation bills never became law because, for procedural reasons, a two-thirds majority of the House of Representatives was required for final passage. Even so, the Reconstruction Congress passed legislation prohibiting segregation of inns, theaters, railroads, and other common carriers, and rejected legislation that would have countenanced segregated education on a separate-but-equal basis.

According to McConnell, the beliefs of the congressmen he analyzes, many of whom were in the Congress that proposed the Amendment in 1866, are significant in much the same way that the views of the First Congress have been accorded special authority in the interpretation of the 1787 Constitution. One can discover the original understanding, he argues, by looking both at what was said before a new constitutional enactment and what was said immediately afterward.

DISCUSSION

1. Before an Article V amendment is ratified, supporters are likely to argue that its effects will be relatively modest to gain as much support as possible. Thus, before ratification, Bickel explains, moderates received assurances that the new amendment would not require that "Negroes were going to become white men's 'social equals,' marry their daughters, vote in their elections, sit on their juries, and attend schools with their children." After the amendment is ratified, however, its supporters are free to argue that its scope is more ambitious, because it is already law. McConnell points to evidence of these broader interpretations. Given the reasons why original understandings should guide interpretation, which set of representations of the original understanding should be controlling? Note, moreover, that by 1870, the Fifteenth Amendment had enfranchised Black voters, creating a potentially important new constituency for Republicans, and so congressional Republicans had additional incentives to interpret the Fourteenth Amendment broadly. If we are trying to determine the understandings of the persons who framed the amendment before its ratification, to what extent should any of this matter?

---

25. McConnell, Originalism and the Desegregation Decisions, 81 Va. L. Rev. 947, 1140 (1995).

2. Note that McConnell's argument focuses on the intentions of congressmen rather than the understandings of the ratifiers of the Fourteenth Amendment, or general public opinion or public understandings about the constitutionality of school segregation. He concedes that[26]

> school desegregation was deeply unpopular among whites, in both North and South, and school segregation was very commonly practiced. In ordinary times, this might be dispositive, or nearly so. Constitutional amendments generally reflect, rather than contradict, popular opinion. But these were not ordinary times. This was a time when a political minority, armed with the prestige of victory in the Civil War and with military control over the political apparatus of the rebel states, imposed constitutional change on the Nation as the price of reunion, with little regard for popular opinion.

McConnell points out that this result should hardly be objectionable, given that the Fifteenth Amendment was passed under similar circumstances:[27]

> [T]he evidence of popular opinion and actual practice on this issue is virtually the same as that regarding school desegregation: enfranchisement of black citizens was wildly unpopular, had been rejected overwhelmingly by popular referenda in numerous states, was repudiated by the Republican platform in 1868, and had been adopted in actual practice only by a small handful of states. . . . It should be obvious that there were great disjunctions between legal enactments, popular opinion, and actual practice at this time. I do not pretend to have a theory explaining why the political system diverged so sharply from popular opinion, other than to suspect that in the aftermath of a Civil War, the political victors considered entrenchment of their principles more important than pleasing constituents. Whatever the explanation, constitutional interpreters would make a serious mistake if they assumed that popular opinion and actual practice during this period were an accurate indication of legal meaning. As we know from examples of unambiguous provisions of law, like the Fifteenth Amendment, this was not always the case. That is why I have focused here on the legal dimension of the debate over school segregation, the actual arguments made by opponents and proponents regarding the meaning of the new amendment. That, it seems to me, is a more reliable guide to legal meaning than either popular opinion or actual practice.

Given the requirements of Article V, does McConnell adequately justify why the understandings of the ratifiers and the views of the general populace should be ignored? On what basis does his claim about original meaning rest?

Does the analogy to the Fifteenth Amendment succeed? After all, if the Fifteenth Amendment is "unambiguous," the Fourteenth is surely not. Does the fact that Congress effectively forced the Fourteenth Amendment on unwilling states

26. Michael McConnell, The Originalist Justification for *Brown*: A Reply to Professor Klarman, 81 Va. L. Rev. 1937, 1940 (1995).

27. Id. at 1940-1941.

prove that only its meaning should apply, or does it prove rather that the states gave it a much less generous interpretation?

3. Two-thirds of each house must vote for a proposed amendment, and the school desegregation bill never actually passed Congress. Yet, as McConnell notes, "[o]pposition to the school desegregation bill commanded somewhat more than one third of the members of each house of Congress" and because of procedural rules this effectively prevented passage of the bill.[28] However, McConnell argues, "this overstates the degree of support for the interpretation of the Fourteenth Amendment that was advocated by the segregationists, because '[s]ome part—unquantifiable but substantial—of the opposition to the schools bill was based on admittedly nonconstitutional arguments, which should not be taken into consideration in assessing the dominant understanding of the constitutional provision.'"[29] Such "nonconstitutional arguments" might presumably include prudential considerations about whom the bill would most likely benefit, which party might stand to benefit most from passage or defeat, or even opposition based on outright racial prejudice. Why do these arguments play no role in determining the meaning of the amendment, especially if they could have been offered against passage of the amendment in the first place?

4. Even if these objections are placed to one side, does McConnell's argument successfully avoid the basic problem of originalism in racial questions—that the original understanding behind the Fourteenth Amendment was consistent with racist attitudes toward Black people and permitted many different forms of racial inequality? Consider Michael Klarman's rejoinder:[30]

> Even McConnell's originalist defense of *Brown* does not enable him to justify Court decisions such as Strauder v. West Virginia and Loving v. Virginia [which struck down laws criminalizing interracial marriage]. McConnell accepts the conventional view that the Framers of the Fourteenth Amendment distinguished civil from political and social rights, and barred racial discrimination only with regard to the former. Jury service, like voting, was plainly deemed at the time to constitute a political right and interracial marriage a social one. Must an originalist like McConnell thus believe that the Constitution even today permits the state to bar racial minorities from jury service and to forbid interracial marriage? Likewise, McConnell's originalist interpretation of the Fourteenth Amendment would apparently permit the state to draw racial distinctions in all areas of life not qualifying as civil rights—e.g., access to public golf courses, swimming pools, etc. Thus even if McConnell has saved *Brown* for originalists, much else of consequence has eluded his grasp.

5. While acknowledging that the Fourteenth Amendment, "as originally understood, was [not] meant to apply . . . to . . . school segregation,"[31] Bickel

---

28. Id. at 1947-1948.

29. Id. at 1948.

30. Michael Klarman, *Brown*, Originalism, and Constitutional Theory: A Response to Professor McConnell, 81 Va. L. Rev. 1881, 1919-1920 (1995).

31. Bickel, The Original Understanding and the Segregation Decision, supra n.21, at 58.

nevertheless argues that the broad and vague language of the Fourteenth Amendment can be understood as a sort of "agreement to disagree" between Moderates and Radicals. It left open the possibility that the language might be applied more expansively in the future. Under this account, the original understanding of the Fourteenth Amendment implicitly delegated to others the task of working out its practical meaning in the future. If Bickel is correct, why should *that* understanding—rather than the concrete understandings of the framers and ratifiers—be binding on us today?

6. *The problem of Bolling v. Sharpe.* Whatever one's views about *Brown,* it is hard to argue that Bolling v. Sharpe is consistent with the original understanding or intentions of the framers of the Fifth Amendment. In 1791, most Black people were held in slavery. McConnell argues that *Bolling* cannot be squared with the original meaning of the Fifth Amendment, and therefore that "[t]he suggestion that the Due Process Clause of the Fifth Amendment prohibits segregation of public facilities is without foundation." Michael McConnell, "Concurring in the Judgment," in What Brown v. Board of Education Should Have Said 166 (Jack M. Balkin ed., 2001). Nevertheless, McConnell argues, the Supreme Court should have held that, because Congress had not specifically authorized segregation, the District of Columbia School Board acted beyond its legal authority in segregating the schools, even though they had been segregated for many, many years. See id. at 168. McConnell's point is that using a clear statement rule would have put pressure on Congress to acquiesce in the desegregation of the schools in 1954. Do you think this would have been a satisfactory solution?

7. *Equal protection and the federal government.* Are there any historical arguments for applying equality norms to the federal government? Consider the following theories:

(a) *A permissible gloss on due process of law.* As noted in Chapter 4, by the time the Fourteenth Amendment was enacted, it was widely accepted that due process of law included the ideas of equality before the law, and that laws should be general and impartial, and that there should be no class legislation. In fact, the Fourteenth Amendment's Equal Protection Clause was modeled on a widely accepted construction of the Fifth Amendment's Due Process Clause.[32] As Akhil Amar puts it, "for the framers and ratifiers of the Fourteenth Amendment, the words of its Equal Protection Clause were not expressing a different idea than the words of the Due Process Clause but were elaborating the same idea: the Equal Protection Clause was in part a clarifying gloss on the due process idea."[33] If so, then reading both the Fifth Amendment's and Fourteenth Amendment's Due Process Clauses to protect equality should be a permissible construction today, even if does not follow from the original understanding of the Fifth Amendment.

(b) *The Citizenship Clause.* The Fourteenth Amendment's Citizenship Clause provides that "[a]ll persons born or naturalized in the United States, and subject to the jurisdiction thereof, are citizens of the United States and of the State wherein they reside." This clause applies to both the states and the federal government. The

32. Jack M. Balkin, Living Originalism 251 (2011).

33. Akhil Reed Amar, Intratextualism, 112 Harv. L. Rev. 747, 772 (1999).

guarantee of citizenship means a guarantee of *equal* citizenship—there could be no first- and second-class citizens—and hence guarantees equality before the law.[34]

Note that although these two theories explain why equality norms might apply to the federal government today, they do not show by themselves that the result in *Bolling* was correct as a matter of original understanding. Even if the Reconstruction framers believed that the federal government had to treat Black people equally before the law, a further question is whether they believed that all federal facilities—including schools—had to be desegregated.

8. *Per curiam decisions following* Brown *and* Bolling. Chief Justice Warren's opinion in Brown v. Board of Education did not analyze the segregation of school children in terms of either forbidden racial classifications or strict scrutiny. Instead, *Brown* emphasized that racially segregated schools harmed children by causing powerful feelings of "inferiority as to their status in the community." *Brown* addressed the harmful consequences of separating school children in a specific institutional context.

The Court soon made it clear enough that *Brown*'s holding was not so limited. In a series of unsigned per curiam opinions, the Court extended *Brown* beyond the context of education. It enjoined segregation in state-run parks, golf courses, beaches, bathhouses, and bus systems, without explaining the principle on which the decisions rested.[35] These per curiam decisions enlarged *Brown*'s prohibition on racial segregation, while deferring explosive questions about *Brown*'s reach.

At the time, some explained the per curiam decisions as demonstrating that the Court was implicitly importing doctrines prohibiting racial classification into the Fourteenth Amendment context. Yet it was clear that the Court was not acting on the assumption that all state action that classified on the basis of race was unconstitutional.

In the same period in which the Court decided the per curiam cases, it refused to decide a challenge to Virginia's antimiscegenation law in Naim v. Naim, as discussed in Section II below.[36] Contemporaries understood that the Court was

---

34. For a discussion of the history of the Citizenship Clause showing its connections to equality, see Ryan C. Williams, Originalism and the Other Desegregation Decision, 99 Va. L. Rev. 493, 501 (2013) ("The Citizenship Clause was adopted against a longstanding political and legal tradition that closely associated the status of 'citizenship' with the entitlement to legal equality."); Jack M. Balkin, The Reconstruction Power, 85 N.Y.U. L. Rev. 1801, 1819-1820 (explaining that "[t]he constitutional declaration of citizenship was simultaneously a grant of the rights of citizenship" and therefore gave Congress power to enforce equality before the law).

35. See New Orleans City Park Improvement Assn. v. Detiege, 358 U.S. 54, 54 (1958) (mem.) (per curiam), *aff'g* 252 F. Supp. 2d 122 (5th Cir. 1958) (public parks and golf courses); Gayle v. Browder, 352 U.S. 903, 903 (1956) (mem.) (per curiam), *aff'g* 142 F. Supp. 707 (M.D. Ala. 1956) (intrastate buses); Holmes v. City of Atlanta, 350 U.S. 879, 879 (1955) (mem.) (per curiam), vacating and remanding 223 F.2d 93 (5th Cir. 1955) (municipal golf courses); Mayor and City Council of Baltimore City v. Dawson, 350 U.S. 877, 877 (1955) (mem.) (per curiam), *aff'g* 220 F.2d 386 (4th Cir. 1955) (public beaches and bathhouses); Muir v. Louisville Park Theatrical Ass'n, 347 U.S. 971, 971 (1954) (mem.) (per curiam), vacating and remanding 202 F.2d 275 (6th Cir. 1953) (municipal recreational facilities). For a more extensive list of the Court's per curiam desegregation decisions, see 2 Thomas I. Emerson et al., Political and Civil Rights in the United States 1249 (student ed. 1967).

36. See Naim v. Naim, 350 U.S. 891, 891 (1955) (mem.) (per curiam) (vacating judgment), remanded to 90 S.E.2d 849 (Va.) (reinstating judgment), motion to recall mandate denied per curiam, 350 U.S. 985 (1956) (mem.) (dismissing for want of a properly presented federal question).

proceeding incrementally and by indirection, so as not to inflame resistance to its authority further. The Court seems to have been especially concerned not to address questions about the constitutionality of antimiscegenation laws too soon after *Brown*, when Southerners were denouncing *Brown* itself as a dangerous first step in a "social program for amalgamation of the two races."

C. Brown's *Legacy, Fulfilled or Betrayed? Four Decades of School Desegregation*

1. *Brown II* and "All Deliberate Speed"

BROWN v. BOARD OF EDUCATION (*BROWN II*), 349 U.S. 294 (1955): [The Court's opinion in *Brown I* concluded by setting the cases for reargument on the question of appropriate relief. Chief Justice Warren again wrote for a unanimous Court, setting out guidelines for implementation.]

WARREN, C.J.: Full implementation of [the principle announced in *Brown I*] may require solution of varied local school problems. School authorities have the primary responsibility for elucidating, assessing, and solving these problems; courts will have to consider whether the action of school authorities constitutes good faith implementation of the governing constitutional principles. Because of their proximity to local conditions and the possible need for further hearings, the courts which originally heard these cases can best perform this judicial appraisal. Accordingly, we believe it appropriate to remand the cases to those courts.

In fashioning and effectuating the decrees, the courts will be guided by equitable principles. Traditionally, equity has been characterized by a practical flexibility in shaping its remedies and by a facility for adjusting and reconciling public and private needs. These cases call for the exercise of these traditional attributes of equity power. At stake is the personal interest of the plaintiffs in admission to public schools as soon as practicable on a nondiscriminatory basis. To effectuate this interest may call for elimination of a variety of obstacles in making the transition to school systems operated in accordance with the constitutional principles set forth in our May 17, 1954, decision. Courts of equity may properly take into account the public interest in the elimination of such obstacles in a systematic and effective manner. But it should go without saying that the vitality of these constitutional principles cannot be allowed to yield simply because of disagreement with them.

While giving weight to these public and private considerations, the courts will require that the defendants make a prompt and reasonable start toward full compliance with our May 17, 1954, ruling. Once such a start has been made, the courts may find that additional time is necessary to carry out the ruling in an effective manner. The burden rests upon the defendants to establish that such time is necessary in the public interest and is consistent with good faith compliance at the earliest practicable date. To that end, the courts may consider problems related to administration, arising from the physical condition of the school plant, the school transportation system, personnel, revision of school districts and attendance areas into compact units to achieve a system of determining admission to the public schools on a nonracial basis, and revision of local laws and regulations which may be necessary in solving the foregoing problems. They will also consider the adequacy of any plans the defendants may propose to meet these problems and to effectuate a transition to a racially nondiscriminatory school system. During this period of transition, the courts will retain jurisdiction of these cases.

The . . . cases are remanded to the District Courts to take such proceedings and enter such orders and decrees consistent with this opinion as are necessary and proper to admit to public schools on a racially nondiscriminatory basis with all deliberate speed the parties to these cases.

The effect of *Brown I* and *Brown II* was that the right to be free from segregation was severed from the remedy. As a result, none of the students in the Deep South benefited directly from the cases that they brought. Should the Court have decreed the immediate admission to "white schools" of the named plaintiffs?

Ironically, the separation of right from remedy in *Brown II* presaged the history of desegregation litigation, which focused on how to structure remedies in the face of open and hidden resistance, the widely varying circumstances in which segregation occurred, and the constantly changing demographics of the country. By the century's end, *Brown* stood as an icon of American constitutional law, revered by all as a statement of the country's most abiding principles. Yet large numbers of schools in the United States are largely segregated by race.

2. "Massive Resistance" to School Desegregation

Although the District of Columbia and some school districts in the border states began to desegregate their schools almost immediately, the South responded to *Brown* with a barrage of measures designed to preserve and entrench segregation. This inaugurated the era of "massive resistance" to Southern desegregation. As noted previously, virtually all of the congressmen and senators from the Deep South signed a "Southern Manifesto" claiming that *Brown* was illegitimate and asserting the right of states to ignore the decision.[37] Georgia redesigned its state flag to reincorporate elements of the Confederate battle flag as a symbol of resistance to the opinion. State legislatures adopted resolutions of "nullification" and "interposition," which declared that the Court's decisions were without effect. Southern states enacted statutes mandating school segregation, ordering state and local officials to take all measures within their authority to preserve segregation, terminating state funds for racially mixed schools, placing the public schools directly under the authority of the governor or state board of education with plenary power to close them, providing tuition grants to enable pupils to attend private schools, and repealing compulsory attendance laws.[38] Most of these schemes were struck down by lower federal courts. The Supreme Court remained largely silent during this period. However, in Cooper v. Aaron, 358 U.S. 1 (1958), it ordered Little Rock, Arkansas, to proceed with school desegregation in the face of state-inspired

37. See 102 Cong. Rec. H3948, 4004 (Mar. 12, 1956).

38. See Note, Interposition vs. Judicial Power—A Study of Ultimate Authority in Constitutional Questions, 1 Race Rel. L. Rep. 465 (1956); Robert McKay; "With All Deliberate Speed"—A Study of School Desegregation, 31 N.Y.U. L. Rev. 911, 1017-1049 (1956); McKay, "With All Deliberate Speed": Legislative Reaction and Judicial Development 1956-1957, 43 Va. L. Rev. 1205, 1216-1228 (1957).

opposition, violence, and disorder; and in Griffin v. Prince Edward County School Board, 377 U.S. 218 (1964), the Court ordered a county school system reopened after it had been closed for five years to avoid desegregation.

Southern districts had traditionally assigned pupils to the schools nearest their homes, employing dual, overlapping attendance zones for the Black and white schools. Because of the contiguity of Black and white neighborhoods in many Southern communities, it would have been relatively simple to consolidate the dual zones into unitary ones producing substantial desegregation. However, some white pupils would be sent to the formerly Black schools, which apart from their social status were inferior in every traditional measure of school quality. For these reasons, unitary zoning was not common.

The most popular school desegregation scheme was freedom of choice, under which each child could opt to attend either a formerly white or Black school. By the late 1960s, freedom of choice was prevalent. It seldom yielded much desegregation. White students rarely chose to attend Black identified schools, while Black students were reluctant to attend white identified schools because of fears of harassment and violent retaliation from whites. Harassment, threats, and retaliatory violence were rarely prevented or punished by school or other government officials, and thus many Black parents and their children were reluctant to assert their rights.[39]

Ten years after *Brown*, less than 1 percent of Black children in the Deep South attended schools with whites. Not only were the court-approved desegregation plans inadequate, but school districts did not desegregate voluntarily, so that each one had to be sued in a separate action. Almost all school litigation in the South was conducted by the NAACP Legal Defense and Educational Fund, Inc., a private organization whose small central staff, aided by handfuls of local cooperating attorneys, obviously could not take on each of the thousand-odd districts.[40] Delay was on the defendants' side. Many judges were hostile to *Brown* and to the plaintiffs and attorneys seeking to implement it; many other judges were subjected to strong pressures from the communities in which they lived.[41] Moreover, school desegregation cases, unlike most other litigation, never ended.

3. The Political Branches Respond: 1964-1968

By this point, however, the political climate of the country had changed. Lyndon Johnson's landslide victory in the 1964 election energized the political branches to do something about civil rights. In 1964, Congress enacted the first

---

39. See U.S. Commission on Civil Rights, Survey of School Desegregation in the Southern and Border States, 1965-66, at 51-52 (1966). See also the commission's report, Southern School Desegregation, 1966-67, at 88 (1967).

40. The Legal Defense Fund began as the legal arm of the NAACP, but in 1939 it became an independent organization. During the early years following *Brown*, the Supreme Court also thwarted attempts of several states to harass or oust the NAACP and others seeking to implement *Brown*. See NAACP v. Alabama, 357 U.S. 449 (1958); NAACP v. Button, 371 U.S. 415 (1963).

41. Southern Justice 165-227 (Friedman ed., 1965); J.W. Peltason, Fifty-Eight Lonely Men (1961); United States Commission on Civil Rights, Federal Enforcement of School Desegregation 48-54 (1969); Note, Judicial Performance in the Fifth Circuit, 73 Yale L.J. 90 (1963).

comprehensive civil rights act since Reconstruction. Titles IV and IX of the Civil Rights Act of 1964 authorized the attorney general to initiate and intervene in school desegregation suits. More important, Title VI prohibited discrimination in programs receiving federal financial assistance and required each department responsible for federally funded programs to issue regulations to achieve this end. Congress appropriated $2.4 billion under the Elementary and Secondary Education Act of 1965, much of it for school districts having "educationally disadvantaged" children. Once Congress began subsidizing state and local education in earnest, it had leverage independent of the courts to enforce *Brown*.

Nonetheless, in 1968, more than three-quarters of all Black children in the South still attended the "formerly" Black schools—which remained all-Black—and the formerly white schools were still clearly identifiable as white, though some of them were now sprinkled with handfuls of Black children who had the courage and stamina to choose them. A major difficulty was that the initial version of the guidelines issued by the Department of Health, Education and Welfare (HEW) to implement Title VI accepted freedom-of-choice plans. School districts argued that, absent improper coercion, a well-designed freedom-of-choice plan succeeded by definition: The Constitution required no more than that Black and white children have the option to attend schools with children of the other race. Support for this position was typically sought in the offhand remark of the district court in Briggs v. Elliott, 132 F. Supp. 776, 777 (E.D.S.C. 1955), one of the cases consolidated with *Brown*, that "[t]he Constitution . . . does not require integration. It merely forbids [segregation]."

Nevertheless, HEW began to update its guidelines to require that schools demonstrate that increasing percentages of Black students were attending formerly white schools in order to retain federal funding. These guidelines began to make a difference. In United States v. Jefferson County Bd. of Education, 372 F.2d 836 (5th Cir. 1966), *aff'd en banc*, 380 F.2d 385 (5th Cir. 1967), the Fifth Circuit Court of Appeals argued that courts should give "great weight" to the HEW's percentage guidelines "in determining whether school desegregation plans meet the standards of *Brown* and other decisions of the Supreme Court," noting that "*[t]he courts acting alone have failed*." (emphasis in original).

4. The Supreme Court Reasserts Itself

Finally, in 1968, the Supreme Court intervened. It explained what school officials had to do to make formally segregated school districts in the South unitary. In Green v. New Kent County School Board, 391 U.S. 430 (1968), the Court held unanimously that freedom-of-choice plans were constitutionally inadequate when their effect was to perpetuate racially identified schools. The goal of desegregation plans should be "[t]he transition to a unitary, nonracial system of public education." "The [School] Board," Justice Brennan explained, "must be required to formulate a new plan and in light of other courses which appear open to the Board, such as zoning, fashion steps which promise realistically to convert promptly to a system without a 'white' school and a 'Negro' school, but just schools."

Green is, in many ways, the most important of the Supreme Court's school desegregation cases after *Brown* itself. To a large extent, the history of school desegregation can be understood in terms of the acceptance or rejection of *Green*'s focus on racially identifiable schools.

From one perspective, *Green* was a logical extension of *Brown*. Racially identifiable "Black" and "white" schools tend to perpetuate the racial subordination of Blacks. "Black" identified schools inevitably receive less money and less attention from a majority white political process, and white parents avoid them. As long as schools are racially identified, Black people will never achieve equality of opportunity. From another perspective, *Green* was an unwarranted extension of *Brown*: *Brown* is simply a rule about school assignment policies, which cannot be on the basis of race. If schools become racially identified as "Black" or "white" through a combination of demographic shifts, economic changes, and other "private choices," the Constitution is not thereby offended. The dialectic between these two positions shaped much of the debate that followed.

After *Green*, most Southern districts moved to geographic zoning. In many rural areas and smaller cities where large-scale residential segregation was not pervasive, this produced considerable desegregation. However, it also produced "white flight" from districts with high percentages of Black students to other areas or to private schools. In Monroe v. Board of Commissioners, 391 U.S. 450 (1968), the Court alluded to the problem by quoting *Brown II*: "[T]he vitality of these constitutional principles cannot be allowed to yield simply because of disagreement with them."[42]

5. *Swann* and Metropolitan Segregation in the South

In Swann v. Charlotte-Mecklenburg Board of Education, 402 U.S. 1 (1971), the Court approved broad equitable discretion for federal district courts in fashioning school desegregation remedies, including busing "as one tool of school desegregation" in order to achieve racial balance. *Swann* also upheld the limited use of racial goals in remedial orders, but cautioned that "[t]he constitutional command to desegregate schools does not mean that every school in every community must always reflect the racial composition of the school system as a whole." Thus, "the existence of some small number of one-race, or virtually one-race, schools within a district is not in and of itself the mark of a system that still practices segregation by law."

The Court also stressed the limits of judicial intervention. The goal of desegregation was achieving a unitary school district, and no more: "At some point, these

---

42. During this same period the Court faced the problem of governmental aid to private segregated schools that arose as a result of school desegregation. In Norwood v. Harrison, 413 U.S. 455 (1973), the Court held that Mississippi could not lend textbooks to students attending private segregated schools pursuant to a longstanding program of providing free textbooks to all public and private school students. Chief Justice Burger pointed out that "[t]his Court has consistently affirmed decisions enjoining state tuition grants to students attending racially discriminatory private schools. A textbook lending program is not legally distinguishable from the forms of state assistance foreclosed by the prior cases. . . . Racial discrimination in state-operated schools is barred by the Constitution and '[i]t is also axiomatic that a state may not induce, encourage or promote private persons to accomplish what it is constitutionally forbidden to accomplish.'"

school authorities and others like them should have achieved full compliance with this Court's decision in *Brown*. The system would then be 'unitary' in the sense required by our decision in *Green*." The Court noted that demographic changes would inevitably alter existing residential patterns and therefore school populations: "Neither school authorities nor district courts are constitutionally required to make year-by-year adjustments of the racial composition of student bodies once the affirmative duty to desegregate has been accomplished and racial discrimination through official action is eliminated from the system. This does not mean that federal courts are without power to deal with future problems; but in the absence of a showing that either the school authorities or some other agency of the State has deliberately attempted to fix or alter demographic patterns to affect the racial composition of the schools, further intervention by a district court should not be necessary."

6. School Segregation in the North—The Court Confronts the De Jure/De Facto Distinction

Swann gave the federal courts considerable discretion to combat Southern opposition to desegregation. Armed with this power, federal judges used result-oriented remedies to circumvent the constant subterfuges of politicians and school boards. However, as the South began to integrate after 1968, Northern schools still remained largely segregated, leading to charges of unfairness by Southern politicians who felt that the federal courts were singling them out.

Northern segregation was often the result of what was described as "de facto" rather than "de jure" segregation. The segregation of Northern schools was usually not the result of direct state mandates concerning pupil assignments or otherwise expressly written into law. Instead racially discriminatory practices by Northern states—including zoning and administrative decisionmaking—coupled with residential segregation and general societal discrimination had produced school districts with populations segregated by race. This segregation was called "de facto" even though it might have been partly the result of deliberate acts of public and private discrimination independent of school assignment policies. Moreover, if a school board adopted a particular assignment plan—for example, a neighborhood school policy—knowing that it would result in segregated schools, the resulting segregation would still be called de facto unless it could be shown that the school board was covertly using race as a decisionmaking factor. The distinction between de facto and de jure discrimination remained unsettled throughout the 1970s.[43]

By the time the Court began to turn to Northern segregation, the political climate had also begun to change. Although the Supreme Court had approved the use of busing in *Swann*, the idea of busing school children to achieve desegregation was

---

43. Until the 1973 decision in Keyes v. School District No. 1, Denver, Colorado, 413 U.S. 189 (1973), discussed infra, the Supreme Court did not treat purpose to desegregate as determinative, especially with respect to the Southern desegregation lawsuits. In Wright v. City of Emporia, 407 U.S. 451 (1972), the City of Emporia, Virginia had been part of a larger county-wide school district. In response to a county-wide desegregation order, the city decided to carve out a new Emporia-only desegregated school district. This had the effect of separating several white-identified schools in the City of Emporia from Black-identified

politically unpopular, particularly in the North. Moreover, the course of Southern integration was shaped by the growth of Southern cities and suburbs, as well as a decline of the percentage of whites in urban school districts, both of which made the problems of combating Southern segregation increasingly resemble those of the North.

Both Richard Nixon and George Wallace played on the unpopularity of busing in the 1968 election. A key element of Nixon's "Southern strategy" to break up the old Democratic New Deal coalition of labor, minorities, Northern liberals, and Southern Democrats was his strong and repeated acceptance of *Brown* combined with an equally strong opposition to compulsory busing of students. In this way Nixon sought to position himself as a defender of civil rights while repeatedly signaling to Southern whites that he would be far more sympathetic to their concerns than liberal Democrats.[44]

Congress also responded to the unpopularity of busing. The Education Amendments of 1972 included a provision that prohibited the use of federal funds for transportation of students to achieve racial balance. (These amendments had mostly symbolic effect because courts later interpreted them to apply only to busing designed to remedy de facto segregation. See Drummond v. Acree, 409 U.S. 1228 (1972) (Justice Powell in Chambers).)

Perhaps equally important, President Nixon was able to appoint four new Justices to the Supreme Court. Until 1971, the Supreme Court's opinions on school desegregation had been unanimous, in part to show a united front against possible Southern intransigence, and the opinions had dealt for the most part with the problems of desegregation in Southern and border states. Chief Justice Burger, a Nixon appointee, continued this tradition of unanimity in his 1971 opinion in *Swann*. With the appointment of Justices Rehnquist and Powell the same year, however, that tradition ended. Rehnquist was highly critical of the Court's approach, and Powell, a former member of the Richmond school board and the Virginia State Board of Education, had his own views about the nature and methods of Northern and Southern desegregation.

The Court's first important statement on Northern segregation came in Keyes v. School District No. 1, Denver, Colorado, 413 U.S. 189 (1973). Denver's school system

---

schools in the county. The city argued its purposes were benign—to promote equality education for its children—and not to avoid the desegregation order.

The Court held, 5-4, that this plan was unconstitutional, with all four Nixon appointees in dissent. Justice Stewart's majority opinion argued that the city's actual purpose was irrelevant. "'[I]f the establishment of an Emporia school district is not enjoined, the black students in the county will watch as nearly one-half the total number of white students in the county abandon the county schools for a substantially whiter system.' The message of this action, coming when it did, cannot have escaped the Negro children in the county. As we noted in *Brown I*: 'To separate [Negro school children] from others of similar age and qualifications solely because of their race generates a feeling of inferiority as to their status in the community that may affect their hearts and minds in a way unlikely ever to be undone.' We think that, under the circumstances, the District Court could rationally have concluded that the same adverse psychological effect was likely to result from Emporia's withdrawal of its children from the Greensville County system."

44. On Nixon's political and legal strategy, see Gareth Davies, Richard Nixon and the Desegregation of Southern Schools, 19 J. Pol. Hist. 368 (2007).

was highly segregated with respect to whites, Blacks, and Latinos, but the Denver school system had never been segregated by the mandate of any state law. Plaintiffs claimed that the schools nonetheless were de jure segregated as the result of the school board's race-conscious manipulation of attendance zones and selection of school sites.

Justice Brennan's majority opinion accepted that the central distinction between "de jure segregation and so-called de facto segregation . . . is *purpose* or *intent* to segregate." Brennan therefore used presumptions and burdens of proof to reach de facto segregation, arguing that "a finding of intentionally segregative school board actions in a meaningful portion of a school system, . . . creates a presumption that other segregated schooling within the system is not adventitious. It establishes . . . a prima facie case of unlawful segregative design on the part of school authorities, and shifts to those authorities the burden of proving that other segregated schools within the system are not also the result of intentionally segregative actions." Brennan held that "[w]here school authorities have been found to have practiced purposeful segregation . . . in a meaningful or significant segment of a school system, . . . it is both fair and reasonable to require that the school authorities bear the burden of showing that their actions as to other segregated schools within the system were not also motivated by segregative intent."

Justice Powell, concurring in part and dissenting in part, argued that "we should abandon [the de jure/de facto] distinction which long since has outlived its time, and formulate constitutional principles of national rather than merely regional application." Powell argued that "the familiar root cause of segregated schools in *all* the biracial metropolitan areas of our country is essentially the same: one of segregated residential and migratory patterns" creating segregative effects in school attendance that were "often perpetuated and rarely ameliorated by action of public school authorities. This is a national, not a southern, phenomenon. And it is largely unrelated to whether a particular State had or did not have segregative school laws."

Proof of intent to segregate should not be necessary, Powell argued. Instead, Powell argued that "where segregated public schools exist within a school district to a substantial degree, there is a prima facie case that the duly constituted public authorities (I will usually refer to them collectively as the 'school board') are sufficiently responsible to warrant imposing upon them a nationally applicable burden to demonstrate they nevertheless are operating a genuinely integrated school system." The Equal Protection Clause required that "once the State has assumed responsibility for education, local school boards will operate *integrated school systems* within their respective districts," which might include some one-race schools. Powell argued, however, that the Constitution did not require busing to achieve racial balance in schools: "A *constitutional requirement* of extensive student transportation solely to achieve integration . . . is . . . likely to divert attention and resources from the foremost goal of any school system: the best quality education for all pupils. The Equal Protection Clause . . . does not require that school authorities undertake widespread student transportation solely for the sake of maximizing integration."[45]

45. Justice Rehnquist dissented, arguing that *Brown* did not justify the "drastic extension" in *Green*. Ensuring "that the assignment of a child to a particular school is not made to depend on his race" does not "require that school boards affirmatively undertake to achieve racial mixing in schools where such mixing is not achieved in sufficient degree by neutrally drawn boundary lines."

Keyes is notable for the apparent "deal" that Justice Powell, the conservative Democrat from Richmond, Virginia, offered the liberal majority headed by Justice Brennan. Powell offered to eliminate the de jure/de facto distinction, which, as a practical matter, would make it much easier to establish that school systems were in violation of the Fourteenth Amendment by operating systems with "racially identifiable" schools. But in return, liberals would have to agree to rein in the use of busing as a remedy. This would leave many urban school districts practically segregated, especially as whites were leaving for new suburban areas in both the North and the South. Justice Brennan rejected Powell's offer, preferring to maintain the requirement that plaintiffs must show intent to maintain a segregated school system, buttressed by various presumptions and burden of proof rules. At the time, Justice Brennan did not assume a strong dichotomy between purpose and effect, because, for example, purpose might be demonstrated by the foreseeable effects of state decisionmaking, a path that a number of courts of appeals followed in enforcing *Keyes*. Brennan's decision to reject Powell's approach had fateful consequences, not only for the school cases, but for equal protection doctrine generally.

7. The Turning Point—Inter-District Relief

By the mid-1970s, President Nixon's appointments, as well as the changing political mood of the country, began to have an effect. In August 1974, as part of the Education Amendments of 1974, Pub. L. No. 93-380, 88 Stat. 484 (1974), Congress passed the Equal Education Opportunities Act, 20 U.S.C. §1714, which among other things prohibited "any court, department or agency of the United States [from ordering] transportation of any student to a school other than the school closest or next closest to his place of residence which provides the appropriate grade level and type education for such student." Although because of subsequent court interpretations the legislation had no practical effect, it symbolized increasing national opposition to busing and school desegregation remedies. By now majorities in both Houses of Congress as well as the Nixon Administration had lined up against the use of busing to achieve racial balance.

The crucial turning point in the history of desegregation efforts was the Detroit metropolitan school litigation. The City of Detroit was predominantly Black and the suburbs predominantly white, and the crucial question was to what extent courts could issue desegregation orders that included multiple school districts, thus combining central cities and suburbs in one metropolitan plan. Such orders, if permitted, would reduce the incentives for white flight. Quite apart from integrative effects, they might pool resources between richer and poorer school districts.

The Court considered these issues in Milliken v. Bradley, 418 U.S. 717 (1974), decided in July 1974 while Congress was debating the Equal Education Opportunities Act that purported to limit busing. For the first time since *Brown I*, the Supreme Court overturned a district court's desegregation decree for going too far in redressing segregation. President Nixon's four Supreme Court appointees, joined by Justice Stewart, formed the five-person majority.

Chief Justice Burger's majority opinion emphasized the importance of local control over school districts. He noted that although the Detroit school system and state officials had pursued policies to segregate white and Black students, there was no evidence that the suburban school districts had attempted to segregate their students by race. He explained that "the scope of the remedy is determined by the nature and extent of the constitutional violation. Before the boundaries of separate and autonomous school districts may be set aside by consolidating the separate units for remedial purposes or by imposing a cross-district remedy, it must first be shown . . . that racially discriminatory acts of the state or local school districts, or of a single school district have been a substantial cause of inter-district segregation." If, for example, "racially discriminatory acts of one or more school districts caused racial segregation in an adjacent district, or . . . district lines have been deliberately drawn on the basis of race," an inter-district remedy might be permissible. "Conversely, without an inter-district violation and inter-district effect, there is no constitutional wrong calling for an inter-district remedy."

Because the majority found no substantial evidence that the suburban districts had been segregated because of racially discriminatory decisions in the Detroit school system, courts could not combine them in a single remedy. The fact that state officials helped maintain a dual school system in Detroit did not change the result: "Disparate treatment of white and Negro students occurred within the Detroit school system, and not elsewhere, and on this record the remedy must be limited to that system. The constitutional right of the Negro respondents residing in Detroit is to attend a unitary school system in that district. Unless petitioners drew the district lines in a discriminatory fashion, or arranged for white students residing in the Detroit District to attend schools in [the suburbs], they were under no constitutional duty to make provisions for Negro students to do so."[46]

Justice White's dissent, joined by Douglas, Brennan, and Marshall, JJ., emphasized that the key actor was the State of Michigan, which controlled local school districts, and whose agencies had participated in the intentional segregation of the public schools. Just as the federal courts had the power to ignore local boundary lines in legislative reapportionment cases, "the configuration of local governmental units [should not be] immune from alteration when necessary to redress constitutional violations" in desegregation suits. The Court "does not question the District Court's findings that any feasible Detroit-only plan would leave many schools 75 to 90 percent black and that the district would become progressively more black as whites left the city. Neither does the Court suggest that including the suburbs in a desegregation plan would be impractical or infeasible because of educational considerations, because of the number of children requiring transportation, or because of the length of their rides. . . . Apparently, no matter how much less burdensome or more effective and efficient in many respects, such as transportation, the metropolitan plan might be, the school district line may not be crossed."

Justice Marshall's dissent added: "The State's creation, through de jure acts of segregation, of a growing core of all-Negro schools inevitably acted as a magnet to attract Negroes to the areas served by such schools and to deter them from settling

---

46. Chief Justice Burger distinguished the Court's earlier decisions in Wright v. Emporia, 407 U.S. 451 (1972), and United States v. Scotland Neck Bd. of Educ., 407 U.S. 484 (1972), where the Court forbade carving new (largely white) school districts from existing de jure segregated districts in the process of dismantling dual school systems. Although the evident purpose of the secessions was to create segregated enclaves, the Court in the 1972 decisions relied solely on the effects and characterized the lower courts' inquiry into purpose as fruitless and irrelevant.

either in other areas of the city or in the suburbs. By the same token, the growing core of all-Negro schools inevitably helped drive whites to other areas of the city or to the suburbs. . . . The State must . . . bear part of the blame for the white flight to the suburbs. . . . Allowing that flight to the suburbs to succeed, the Court today allows the State to profit from its own wrong and to perpetuate for years to come the separation of the races it achieved in the past by purposeful state action." Limiting the remedy to Detroit, Marshall argued, "does not promise to achieve actual desegregation at all," and would maintain racially identifiable schools in violation of *Swann*: "Under a Detroit-only decree, Detroit's schools will clearly remain racially identifiable in comparison with neighboring schools in the metropolitan community. Schools with 65% and more Negro students will stand in sharp and obvious contrast to schools in neighboring districts with less than 2% Negro enrollment. Negro students will continue to perceive their schools as segregated educational facilities and this perception will only be increased when whites react to a Detroit-only decree by fleeing to the suburbs to avoid integration. School district lines, however innocently drawn, will surely be perceived as fences to separate the races when, under a Detroit-only decree, white parents withdraw their children from the Detroit city schools and move to the suburbs in order to continue them in all-white schools. The message of this action will not escape the Negro children in the city of Detroit. See Wright [v. City of Emporia, 407 U.S. 451, 466 (1972)]. It will be of scant significance to Negro children who have for years been confined by de jure acts of segregation to a growing core of all-Negro schools surrounded by a ring of all-white schools that the new dividing line between the races is the school district boundary. . . ."

On remand, the district court was faced with the task of integrating a school district that was approximately 70 percent Black. It decided instead on a plan of educational reform, remedial education, magnet schools, counseling, and career guidance. On appeal, the Supreme Court affirmed. Milliken v. Bradley, 433 U.S. 267 (1977) (*Milliken II*). The Court argued that remedies for segregation were not limited to pupil reassignment, and that the court might order the state to expend funds for remedial education designed to put Black students roughly in the position they would have been but for the original constitutional violation. See also Missouri v. Jenkins, 495 U.S. 33 (1990) (*Jenkins I*) (upholding power of district court to order a local government body to raise taxes to finance a magnet school program, but reversing for abuse of discretion on the facts of the case).

8. An Era of Retrenchment

Following Ronald Reagan's election in 1980, the Justice Department continued prosecuting school desegregation suits. However, new, more conservative appointees began to replace the judges and Justices who had decided the key desegregation cases of the 1960s and 1970s. New conservative judges appointed by Presidents Reagan and George H.W. Bush, perhaps even more than the four Justices appointed by President Nixon, sought to withdraw federal courts from public school litigation. The Supreme Court strongly signaled to district courts that they should declare remaining districts under federal court order unitary whether or not desegregation efforts had been completely achieved; and that district courts should not attempt to counteract the effects of resegregation caused by demographic changes. See Pasadena City Board of Education v. Spangler, 427 U.S. 424 (1976) (holding that the school board need not continue to reassign students on the basis of race to compensate for demographic changes); Board of Education of Oklahoma City v. Dowell, 498 U.S. 111 237 (1991) (a desegregation degree should be dissolved following "a finding by the District Court that the Oklahoma City School District was being operated in compliance with the commands of the Equal Protection Clause of the Fourteenth Amendment, and that it was unlikely that the Board would return to its former ways"); Freeman v. Pitts, 503 U.S. 467 (1992) ("federal courts have the authority to relinquish supervision and control of school districts in incremental stages, before full compliance has been achieved in every area of school operations"). In *Freeman*, Justice Kennedy's opinion emphasized the limited nature of federal relief for resegregation when there was no finding of ongoing constitutional violations by the state:

> Where resegregation is a product not of state action but of private choices, it does not have constitutional implications. It is beyond the authority and beyond the practical ability of the federal courts to try to counteract these kinds of continuous and massive demographic shifts. To attempt such results would require ongoing and never-ending supervision by the courts of school districts simply because they were once *de jure* segregated. . . . As the *de jure* violation becomes more remote in time and these demographic changes intervene, it becomes less likely that a current racial imbalance in a school district is a vestige of the prior *de jure* system. The causal link between current conditions and the prior violation is even more attenuated if the school district has demonstrated its good faith.

MISSOURI v. JENKINS, 515 U.S. 70 (1995) (*JENKINS II*): [In *Jenkins II*, the Supreme Court returned to the long-running desegregation lawsuit involving the Kansas City Metropolitan School District (KCMSD). In 1985, after years of litigation in the district and circuit courts, the district court ordered an extensive capital improvements program for KCMSD schools and required the state to institute a "magnet plan" providing for the establishment of several magnet schools. The dual goal of the court's remedial orders was to attract white students back into public schools and to provide minority students an educational experience of the quality they would have received absent the effects of segregation. To this end, the district judge ordered across-the-board salary increases for teachers and staff, aimed at improving educational quality and attracting white suburban students. It also ordered continued state funding for the magnet schools so long as student achievement scores remained below national norms. In a 5-4 decision by Justice Rehnquist, the Supreme Court held that the goal of attracting white students from outside the KCMSD was not permissible within an intra-district remedy under *Milliken II*.

Justice Thomas concurred, arguing that *Brown* required only an end to intentional segregation, but did not require that Blacks and whites attend the same schools:]

THOMAS, J., concurring:

It never ceases to amaze me that the courts are so willing to assume that anything that is predominantly black must be inferior. Instead of focusing on remedying the harm done to those black schoolchildren injured by segregation, the

District Court here sought to convert the Kansas City, Missouri, School District (KCMSD) into a "magnet district" that would reverse the "white flight" caused by desegregation. . . . [T]he court has read our cases to support the theory that black students suffer an unspecified psychological harm from segregation that retards their mental and educational development. This approach not only relies upon questionable social science research rather than constitutional principle, but it also rests on an assumption of black inferiority. [W]e have permitted the federal courts to exercise virtually unlimited equitable powers to remedy this alleged constitutional violation[,] . . . trampl[ing] upon principles of federalism and the separation of powers and [freeing] courts to pursue other agendas unrelated to the narrow purpose of precisely remedying a constitutional harm.

The mere fact that a school is black does not mean that it is the product of a constitutional violation. . . . "The differentiating factor between de jure segregation and so-called de facto segregation . . . is purpose or intent to segregate." . . . [T]he existence of one-race schools is not by itself an indication that the State is practicing segregation. The continuing "racial isolation" of schools after de jure segregation has ended may well reflect voluntary housing choices or other private decisions. Here, for instance, the demography of the entire KCMSD has changed considerably since 1954. Though blacks accounted for only 18.9% of KCMSD's enrollment in 1954, by 1983-1984 the school district was 67.7% black. That certain schools are overwhelmingly black in a district that is now more than two-thirds black is hardly a sure sign of intentional state action. . . .

In effect, the court found that racial imbalances constituted an ongoing constitutional violation that continued to inflict harm on black students. This position appears to rest upon the idea that any school that is black is inferior, and that blacks cannot succeed without the benefit of the company of whites. . . . *Brown I* did not say that "racially isolated" schools were inherently inferior; the harm that it identified was tied purely to de jure segregation, not de facto segregation. Indeed, *Brown I* itself did not need to rely upon any psychological or social-science research in order to announce the simple, yet fundamental, truth that the government cannot discriminate among its citizens on the basis of race. . . .

Segregation was not unconstitutional because it might have caused psychological feelings of inferiority. Public school systems that separated blacks and provided them with superior educational resources—making blacks "feel" superior to whites sent to lesser schools—would violate the Fourteenth Amendment, whether or not the white students felt stigmatized, just as do school systems in which the positions of the races are reversed. Psychological injury or benefit is irrelevant to the question whether state actors have engaged in intentional discrimination—the critical inquiry for ascertaining violations of the Equal Protection Clause. The judiciary is fully competent to make independent determinations concerning the existence of state action without the unnecessary and misleading assistance of the social sciences.

Regardless of the relative quality of the schools, segregation violated the Constitution because the State classified students based on their race. Of course, segregation additionally harmed black students by relegating them to schools with substandard facilities and resources. But neutral policies, such as local school assignments, do not offend the Constitution when individual private choices concerning work or residence produce schools with high black populations. The

Constitution does not prevent individuals from choosing to live together, to work together, or to send their children to school together, so long as the State does not interfere with their choices on the basis of race.

Given that desegregation has not produced the predicted leaps forward in black educational achievement, there is no reason to think that black students cannot learn as well when surrounded by members of their own race as when they are in an integrated environment. Indeed, it may very well be that what has been true for historically black colleges is true for black middle and high schools. Despite their origins in "the shameful history of state-enforced segregation," these institutions can be "both a source of pride to blacks who have attended them and a source of hope to black families who want the benefits of . . . learning for their children." Because of their "distinctive histories and traditions," black schools can function as the center and symbol of black communities, and provide examples of independent black leadership, success, and achievement. . . .

"Racial isolation" itself is not a harm; only state-enforced segregation is. After all, if separation itself is a harm, and if integration therefore is the only way that blacks can receive a proper education, then there must be something inferior about blacks. Under this theory, segregation injures blacks because blacks, when left on their own, cannot achieve. To my way of thinking, that conclusion is the result of a jurisprudence based upon a theory of black inferiority.

This misconception has drawn the courts away from the important goal in desegregation. The point of the Equal Protection Clause is not to enforce strict race-mixing, but to ensure that blacks and whites are treated equally by the State without regard to their skin color. The lower courts should not be swayed by the easy answers of social science, nor should they accept the findings, and the assumptions, of sociology and psychology at the price of constitutional principle.

DISCUSSION

1. What possible remedies are available to a district court judge in a case like *Jenkins*? What is accomplished, for example, by taking steps to ensure that the remaining white students in the KCMSD are spread relatively evenly among majority Black schools? Wouldn't more good be done by making sure that the schools are safe and relatively effective places to learn? One way of understanding the district court's "magnet schools" remedy was to use the law of desegregation to improve the quality of education within the district in the face of white voters who had largely abandoned the public schools. However, in *Jenkins* the Court insisted that improving the quality of the schools was not the purpose of the Equal Protection Clause. Note in this context that the Court had previously held in San Antonio Independent School District v. Rodriguez, 411 U.S. 1 (1973), that education is not a fundamental right and that states are not required to guarantee equality in educational quality or educational expenditures.[47] Is *Brown* a case about racial classification, a case about educational opportunity, or both? Note that, taken together, *Milliken I* and *Rodriguez* effectively acquiesce in white abandonment of largely Black

47. This doctrine is covered in more detail in Chapter 10, infra.

and Hispanic inner cities, because there is no right to integration that would create incentives for equal educational funding between city and suburban schools and, after *Rodriguez*, there is no federal constitutional right to equal educational opportunity.

2. Due to demographic changes, many urban public school districts are "disproportionately" minority. In practical terms, does *Jenkins* signal the acceptance of "separate but equal" as long as there is no evidence of continuing segregative intent by school districts? Do you agree with Justice Thomas that this result is acceptable? Given Justice Thomas's position, what constitutional remedies, if any, do minority communities have if they believe that state and local governments are paying insufficient attention to their concerns and are failing to guarantee equal educational opportunity for their children?

3. Fordice *and higher education*. The federal courts have also applied *Brown II* to the desegregation of colleges and universities. The leading case is United States v. Fordice, 505 U.S. 717 (1992). As Justice White's majority opinion explained, "a state university system is quite different in very relevant respects from primary and secondary schools. Unlike attendance at the lower level schools, a student's decision to seek higher education has been a matter of choice. The State historically has not assigned university students to a particular institution. Moreover, like public universities throughout the country, Mississippi's institutions of higher learning are not fungible — they have been designated to perform certain missions. Students who qualify for admission enjoy a range of choices of which institution to attend." Nevertheless, the Court held that "the adoption and implementation of race-neutral policies alone" is not sufficient "to demonstrate that the State has completely abandoned its prior dual system. . . . If the State perpetuates policies and practices traceable to its prior system that continue to have segregative effects — whether by influencing student enrollment decisions or by fostering segregation in other facets of the university system — and such policies are without sound educational justification and can be practicably eliminated, the State has not satisfied its burden of proving that it has dismantled its prior system."

Justice Thomas concurred, arguing in particular that states should be permitted to maintain historically Black colleges and universities as long as they remain "open to all on a race-neutral basis, but with established traditions and programs that might disproportionately appeal to one race or another." Thomas pointed out that "these institutions have succeeded in part because of their distinctive histories and traditions; for many, historically black colleges have become 'a symbol of the highest attainments of black culture.'" Does Thomas's argument require him to acknowledge an asymmetry in the position and the permissible treatment of whites and Blacks? May Mississippi have "traditionally white" colleges with established traditions and programs designed to appeal disproportionately to white students?

Twelve years after *Jenkins II*, the Supreme Court once again considered the constitutionality of school assignment policies. This time, however, the question was not what remedies federal courts could order. Rather, the question was whether local school boards could voluntarily employ race-conscious pupil assignment policies in order to promote racial integration, in situations where courts had either not found a previous constitutional violation or school districts had been declared unitary under the guidelines established in Freeman v. Pitts. In Parents Involved in Community Schools v. Seattle School District No. 1, 551 U.S. 701 (2007), the Court struck down voluntary integration plans in Seattle and Louisville. Chief Justice Roberts's plurality opinion argued that these plans were nothing more than attempts at "racial balancing" and were prohibited by the Equal Protection Clause.

Parents Involved is a watershed in the Court's understanding of the constitutional value of racial integration. In the 1950s and 1960s, the Supreme Court encouraged voluntary integration by school boards, because so many state officials were resisting integration and because the courts were simply unable to police all of the local school boards around the country. By 2007, the Supreme Court had taken the position that voluntary integration efforts by local officials were prohibited by the Constitution because they involved racial classifications. The Court's reasoning rests on the interpretation of its affirmative action decisions, and therefore the case is discussed later on in this chapter in the context of those decisions.

II. THE ANTIDISCRIMINATION PRINCIPLE AND THE "SUSPECT CLASSIFICATION" STANDARD

The opinion in *Brown* emphasized the particular harms to young children caused by segregation in the classroom. But to what forms of racial segregation did *Brown* apply, and in what institutional contexts? To de jure racial segregation in public education only? To all racially segregative practices that inflicted like harm on African Americans? To all racially segregative practices involving state action? Did *Brown* itself hold the answers to these questions, or was further consideration of the Equal Protection Clause required? In the years following *Brown*, heated debates over the justifications for the decision evolved into equally fervent disputes about the decision's reach and proper application.

A. The Origins of the Suspect Classification Doctrine

1. The Japanese Internment Case

KOREMATSU v. UNITED STATES, 323 U.S. 214 (1944): [Full American participation in World War II began on December 7, 1941, after the devastating Japanese attack on Pearl Harbor, which destroyed much of the American naval fleet. In the aftermath, latent anti-Japanese prejudice burst forth, with suspicions being expressed about the loyalty of *all* persons of Japanese descent, whether resident aliens or American citizens. Calls were made for the removal of such persons from their homes in the Western states. The Attorney General of California at the time, Earl Warren, supported such proposals, stating that "[e]very alien Japanese should be considered in the light of a potential fifth column."[48] (Although Warren apparently had reservations about applying such terms to Japanese-Americans, he registered no public complaint about the blanket policies that were adopted.) After a bitter battle within the executive branch, President Roosevelt on February 19, 1942 signed Executive Order 9066 directing the War Department (now known as the Department of Defense) to "prescribe military areas . . . from which any and all persons may be excluded, and with respect to which the right of any person to enter, remain in, or leave shall be subject to whatever restrictions the Commander might impose." Attorney General Francis Biddle protested that the order was "ill-advised, unnecessary, and unnecessarily cruel," to which the President responded, "[T]his must be a military decision."[49]

On March 21, 1942, Congress passed a statute making it a criminal offense for anyone to "enter, remain in, leave, or commit any act in any military area or military zone . . . contrary to the restrictions applicable to any such area or zone." Shortly thereafter, General DeWitt, Military Commander of the Western Defense Command, ordered a curfew of all persons of Japanese ancestry on the West Coast, including both Japanese resident aliens and Japanese-American citizens. The Supreme Court later upheld this order in Hirabayashi v. United States, 320 U.S. 81 (1943).

On May 3, General DeWitt issued Civilian Exclusion Order No. 34, which stated that, by noon on May 9, all persons of Japanese ancestry were to be removed from Military Area No. 1 to detention camps. The detention camps were chosen over simply requiring resettlement outside of the forbidden area in part because "many states in the nation's interior made it clear that Japanese migration eastward spelled trouble."[50] The governor of Wyoming publicly stated that "[t]here would be Japs hanging from every pine tree" if his state became their destination. Similarly, the Idaho attorney general, stating that "[w]e want to keep this a white man's country," urged that "all Japanese should be put in concentration camps."[51] It was against this background that Fred Korematsu, a native-born Fourteenth Amendment birthright citizen convicted of disobeying the Order by remaining in his home, challenged its constitutionality.[52] By a vote of 6 to 3, the Court upheld Korematsu's conviction for violating the exclusion order.]

BLACK, J., delivered the opinion of the Court:

It should be noted, to begin with, that all legal restrictions which curtail the civil rights of a single racial group are immediately suspect. That is not to say that all such restrictions are unconstitutional. It is to say that courts must subject them to the most rigid scrutiny. Pressing public necessity may sometimes justify the existence of such restrictions; racial antagonism never can. . . .

---

48. Quoted in Ed Cray, Chief Justice: A Biography of Earl Warren 118 (1997). Although toward the end of his life, Warren told a former law clerk that he regretted his actions, "the stiff-necked Warren resisted any public acknowledgment of responsibility." See id. at 520.

49. Quoted in David Kennedy, Freedom from Fear: The American People in Depression and War, 1929-1945, at 753 (1999).

50. Id.

51. Quoted in id.

52. See Peter Irons, Justice at War (1983), for a complete review of the Japanese exclusion litigation.

In the light of the principles we announced in the *Hirabayashi* case, we are unable to conclude that it was beyond the war power of Congress and the Executive to exclude those of Japanese ancestry from the West Coast war area at the time they did. True, exclusion from the area in which one's home is located is a far greater deprivation than constant confinement to the home from 8 P.M. to 6 A.M. Nothing short of apprehension by the proper military authorities of the gravest imminent danger to the public safety can constitutionally justify either. . . . The military authorities, charged with the primary responsibility of defending our shores, concluded that curfew provided inadequate protection and ordered exclusion. . . .

Here, as in the *Hirabayashi* case, "we cannot reject as unfounded the judgment of the military authorities and Congress that there were disloyal members of that population, whose number and strength could not be precisely and quickly ascertained. We cannot say that the war-making branches of the Government did not have ground for believing that in a critical hour such persons could not readily be isolated and separately dealt with, and constituted a menace to the national defense and safety, which demanded that prompt and adequate measures be taken against it."

Like curfew, exclusion of those of Japanese origin was deemed necessary because of the presence of an unascertained number of disloyal members of the group, most of whom we have no doubt were loyal to this country. It was because we could not reject the finding of the military authorities that it was impossible to bring about an immediate segregation of the disloyal from the loyal that we sustained the validity of the curfew order as applying to the whole group. In the instant case, temporary exclusion of the entire group was rested by the military on the same ground. The judgment that exclusion of the whole group was for the same reason a military imperative answers the contention that the exclusion was in the nature of group punishment based on antagonism to those of Japanese origin. That there were members of the group who retained loyalties to Japan has been confirmed by investigations made subsequent to the exclusion. Approximately five thousand American citizens of Japanese ancestry refused to swear unqualified allegiance to the United States and to renounce allegiance to the Japanese Emperor, and several thousand evacuees requested repatriation to Japan.

We uphold the exclusion order as of the time it was made and when the petitioner violated it. . . . Since the petitioner has not been convicted of failing to report or to remain in an assembly or relocation center, we cannot in this case determine the validity of those separate provisions of the order. It is sufficient here for us to pass upon the order which petitioner violated. . . .

It is said that we are dealing here with the case of imprisonment of a citizen in a concentration camp solely because of his ancestry, without evidence or inquiry concerning his loyalty and good disposition towards the United States. Our task would be simple, our duty clear, were this a case involving the imprisonment of a loyal citizen in a concentration camp because of racial prejudice. Regardless of the true nature of the assembly and relocation centers—and we deem it unjustifiable to call them concentration camps with all the ugly connotations that term implies—we are dealing specifically with nothing but an exclusion order. To cast this case into outlines or racial prejudice, without reference to the real military dangers which were presented, merely confuses the issue. Korematsu was not excluded from the Military Area because of hostility to him or his race. He *was* excluded because we are at war with the Japanese Empire, because the properly constituted military authorities feared an invasion of our West Coast and felt constrained to take proper security measures, because they decided that the military urgency of the situation demanded that all citizens of Japanese ancestry be segregated from the West Coast temporarily, and finally, because Congress, reposing its confidence in this time of war in our military leaders—as inevitably it must—determined that they should have the power to do just this. There was evidence of disloyalty on the part of some, the military authorities considered that the need for action was great, and time was short. We cannot—by availing ourselves of the calm perspective of hindsight—now say that at that time these actions were unjustified.

FRANKFURTER, J., concurring.

[T]he war power of the Government is "the power to wage war successfully." Therefore, the validity of action under the war power must be judged wholly in the context of war. . . . To recognize that military orders are "reasonably expedient military precautions" in time of war and yet to deny them constitutional legitimacy makes of the Constitution an instrument of dialectic subtleties not reasonably to be attributed to the hard-headed Framers, of whom a majority had actual participation in war. . . . [This] does not carry with it approval of that which Congress and the Executive did. That is their business, not ours.

[A dissenting opinion by Justice Roberts is omitted.]

MURPHY, J., dissenting.

[T]he exclusion order necessarily must rely for its reasonableness upon the assumption that all persons of Japanese ancestry may have a dangerous tendency to commit sabotage and espionage and to aid our Japanese enemy in other ways. . . . [T]his forced exclusion was the result in good measure of this erroneous assumption of racial guilt rather than bona fide military necessity. . . . [T]he Commanding General's Final Report on the evacuation from the Pacific Coast area . . . refers to all individuals of Japanese descent as "subversive," as belonging to "an enemy race" whose "racial strains are undiluted," and as constituting "over 112,000 potential enemies . . . at large today" along the Pacific Coast. . . . [N]o reliable evidence is cited to show that such individuals were generally disloyal, or had generally so conducted themselves in this area as to constitute a special menace to defense installations or war industries, or had otherwise by their behavior furnished reasonable ground for their exclusion as a group. . . . The main reasons relied upon by those responsible for the forced evacuation . . . appear to be largely an accumulation of much of the misinformation, half-truths and insinuations that for years have been directed against Japanese Americans by people with racial and economic prejudices—the same people who have been among the foremost advocates of the evacuation. . . .

[T]o infer that examples of individual disloyalty prove group disloyalty and justify discriminatory action against the entire group is to deny that under our system of law individual guilt is the sole basis for deprivation of rights. Moreover, this inference, which is at the very heart of the evacuation orders, has been used in support of the abhorrent and despicable treatment of minority groups by the dictatorial tyrannies which this nation is now pledged to destroy.

No adequate reason is given for the failure to treat these Japanese Americans on an individual basis by holding investigations and hearings to separate the loyal from the disloyal, as was done in the case of persons of German and Italian ancestry. It is asserted merely that the loyalties of this group "were unknown and time was of the essence." Yet nearly four months elapsed after Pearl Harbor before the first exclusion order was issued; nearly eight months went by until the last order was issued; and the last of these "subversive" persons was not actually removed until almost eleven months had elapsed. [N]ot one person of Japanese ancestry was accused or convicted of espionage or sabotage after Pearl Harbor while they were still free, a fact which is some evidence of the loyalty of the vast majority of these individuals and of the effectiveness of the established methods of combatting these evils. It seems incredible that under these circumstances it would have been impossible to hold loyalty hearings for the mere 112,000 persons involved—or at least for the 70,000 American citizens—especially when a large part of this number represented children and elderly men and women. Any inconvenience that may have accompanied an attempt to conform to procedural due process cannot be said to justify violations of constitutional rights of individuals.

I dissent, therefore, from this legalization of racism. Racial discrimination in any form and in any degree has no justifiable part whatever in our democratic way of life. . . . All residents of this nation are kin in some way by blood or culture to a foreign land. Yet they are primarily and necessarily a part of the new and distinct civilization of the United States. They must accordingly be treated at all times as the heirs of the American experiment and as entitled to all the rights and freedoms guaranteed by the Constitution.

JACKSON, J., dissenting.

Korematsu was born on our soil, of parents born in Japan. The Constitution makes him a citizen of the United States by nativity and a citizen of California by residence. No claim is made that he is not loyal to this country. There is no suggestion that apart from the matter involved here he is not law-abiding and well disposed. Korematsu, however, has been convicted of an act not commonly a crime. It consists merely of being present in the state whereof he is a citizen, near the place where he was born, and where all his life he has lived. . . .

[C]ourts can never have any real alternative to accepting the mere declaration of the authority that issued the order that it was reasonably necessary from a military viewpoint. A military order, however unconstitutional, is not apt to last longer than the military emergency. . . . But once a judicial opinion rationalizes such an order to show that it conforms to the Constitution, or rather rationalizes the Constitution to show that the Constitution sanctions such an order, the Court for all time has validated the principle of racial discrimination in criminal procedure and of transplanting American citizens. The principle then lies about like a loaded weapon ready for the hand of any authority that can bring forward a plausible claim of an urgent need. . . . I should hold that a civil court cannot be made to enforce an order which violates constitutional limitations even if it is a reasonable exercise of military authority. The courts can exercise only the judicial power, can apply only law, and must abide by the Constitution, or they cease to be civil courts and become instruments of military policy. . . . I do not suggest that the courts should have attempted to interfere with the Army in carrying out its task. But I do not think they may be asked to execute a military order that has no place in law under the Constitution. I would reverse the judgment and discharge the prisoner.

DISCUSSION

1. *Courts in times of emergency.* From the perspective of a half-century of distance—and even, probably, from the perspective of 1944, when *Korematsu* was decided—it is easy enough to agree with Justice Murphy's denunciation of the policy. By that time, the fears that Pearl Harbor presaged attacks on the United States itself had been left behind, and the Battle of Midway had signaled to most military analysts that a Japanese defeat was inevitable. Moreover, it was altogether clear by that time that the fears of a Japanese "fifth column" were totally and completely groundless. Indeed, not a single Japanese resident alien or Japanese-American U.S. citizen committed any espionage during the entire period of the war. In addition, "some three thousand [Japanese-Americans] were recruited into the 442nd Regimental Combat Team, an all Japanese (segregated) unit that distinguished itself fighting in Italy."[53] (Why do you think the so-called Nisei Regiment was sent to Italy rather than to the Pacific Theater? Would it have been legitimate to adopt a policy by which persons with German surnames or with relatives living in Germany were sent to the Pacific Theater?) Finally, we know, because of historian Peter Irons, that the government was aware, by the time of the argument before the Supreme Court, that General DeWitt's fear of Japanese-Americans was wholly unfounded, but failed to inform the Court of this fact.[54] Indeed, a San Francisco federal district court in 1984 reversed Fred Korematsu's conviction on the basis of evidence brought forth by Irons.

Suppose, however, that *Korematsu* had been heard in May 1942—only six months after Pearl Harbor—instead of 1944. What should the Court have done then? Consider Justice Jackson's dissent, which argues that courts should simply refuse to enforce military orders because doing so would set a precedent. Would this have been realistically possible in the wake of the Pearl Harbor attack? Addressing a group of students at the University of Hawaii in February 2014, Justice Antonin Scalia remarked: "Well of course *Korematsu* was wrong. . . . And I think we have repudiated in a later case. But you are kidding yourself if you think the same thing will not happen again. . . . I would not be surprised to see it happen again, in time of war. It's no justification, but it is the reality." Elias Isquith, Antonin Scalia Says Japanese Internment Could Happen Again, Salon, Feb. 4, 2014, at http://www.salon.com/2014/02/04/antonin_scalia_says_japanese_internment_could_happen_again/.

2. *Strict scrutiny.* One irony of *Korematsu* is that—although the decision has been widely criticized in hindsight—the case offered an early version of the strict scrutiny standard: "[A]ll legal restrictions which curtail the civil rights of a single racial group are immediately suspect [and] courts must subject them to the

---

53. Kennedy, Freedom from Fear, supra n.49, at 255.

54. See Irons, Justice at War, supra n.52. Korematsu v. United States, 584 F. Supp. 1406 (N.D. Cal. 1984). In 1988, Congress passed a measure formally apologizing to the Japanese-American community for the measures adopted under Executive Order 9066 and awarding each detention survivor $20,000. See generally Peter Irons, ed., Justice Delayed: The Record of the Japanese-American Internment Cases (1989), which details the re-litigation in the 1980s of several of the most important cases of the 1940s.

most rigid scrutiny." Chief Justice Warren's opinion in Bolling v. Sharpe cited both *Korematsu* and *Hirabayashi* for the proposition that "[c]lassifications based solely upon race must be scrutinized with particular care, since they are contrary to our traditions and hence constitutionally suspect." In *Korematsu* and *Hirabayashi*, as in *Bolling*, the issue was not racial discrimination by state government but discrimination by the federal government. However, as we shall see, Chief Justice Warren also cited *Korematsu* and *Hirabayashi* as authority in Loving v. Virginia, infra.

3. *Discrimination against Asian Americans and the Black/white paradigm.* In Chapters 2 and 4, we noted the variety of forms of discrimination that were visited on Asians residing in the United States (recall, for example, the Chinese Exclusion Cases). Neil Gotanda argues that *Korematsu* demonstrates one of the distinctive features of discrimination against Asian Americans (as well as Hispanics) that tends to differentiate it from discrimination against Black people. Gotanda is among a growing number of scholars who have rejected the "black/white paradigm" for understanding race relations in the United States: "One of the critical features of legal treatment of other non-whites has been the inclusion of a notion of 'foreignness' in considering their racial identity and legal status." According to Gotanda, the specific forms of discrimination that Asian Americans, Hispanic Americans, Arab Americans, and other non-Black minorities suffer cannot be understood without taking into account "the persistence of the view that even American-born non-whites were somehow 'foreign.' This undeserved stigma became, and may remain, an unarticulated basis for the legal treatment of these groups, leading to unfair and often shocking consequences."[55]

Gotanda argues that "any assertion or demonstration of traditional culture [by Asian Americans] is a potential reaffirmation of foreign and therefore un-American conduct."[56] By contrast, distinctively Black cultural assertions (for example, modes of dress and behavior, the use of Black dialect or slang) are not generally regarded as un-American, although they may sometimes be stigmatized by whites as inferior or threatening.

Recall Justice Harlan's dissent in Plessy v. Ferguson, in which he notes that the Chinese are "a race so different from our own that we do not permit those belonging to it to become citizens of the United States." Hence Harlan decries the unfairness that "a Chinaman can ride in the same passenger coach with white citizens of the United States" while Black people, "who have all the legal rights that belong to white citizens," cannot.[57] Harlan's dissent is notable for its rhetorical strategy of playing one minority group off against another. Black people "really are" Americans, while the Chinese, no matter how long they may have resided in the country, are foreigners.

The flip side of Harlan's rhetorical strategy of playing off Asians (in this case Chinese) against Blacks is to play Blacks off against Asians, i.e., to argue that Black

55. Neil Gotanda, Other Non-Whites in American Legal History: A Review of Justice at War, 85 Colum. L. Rev. 1186, 1188 (1985).

56. Neil Gotanda, Asian American Rights and the "Miss Saigon Syndrome," in Asian Americans and the Supreme Court: A Documentary History 1087, 1097 (Hyung-chan Kim ed., 1992).

57. Plessy v. Ferguson, 163 U.S. 537, 561 (1896).

people should not receive special advantages that Asians do not. This produces the second distinctive way in which Asian Americans are stereotyped, not as devious and inscrutable foreigners, but as upstanding immigrant members of society, the so-called model minority. As Frank Wu explains:[58]

> This ubiquitous superminority image has suggested that Asian Americans achieve economic success and gain societal acceptance through conservative values and hard work. . . . The image is a myth because Asian Americans have not achieved economic success except in a superficial sense. Comparing equally educated individuals, whites earn more money than Asian Americans. Qualifications count less than race, in a pattern of regular discrimination, not so-called "reverse" discrimination. The discrimination which Asian Americans in fact face can be reinforced by the exaggerations of the myth. This reinforcement occurs, for example, when non-Asian Americans believe that Asian Americans should be subjected to maximum quotas in college admissions because they have done too well and represent unfair competition. Everyone should know that the model minority myth is deployed in ways that expose the insincerity of its goodwill. The myth is used to denigrate other racial minorities. It is used to ask African Americans, rhetorically, "Well, the Asian Americans succeeded; why can't you?" As the original New York Times article introducing the image put it, Asian Americans stand in contrast to "problem minorities."

Note that the "model minority" stereotype works in two directions: It reinforces the notion that Black people are responsible for their poor socioeconomic status, and it makes poverty among Asian Americans and discrimination against them relatively invisible because Asian Americans are simply assumed to be more successful than Black Americans. You should consider this dual effect of stereotypes about Asian Americans when we turn to the materials on race-conscious affirmative action.

OYAMA v. CALIFORNIA, 332 U.S. 633 (1948): California's Alien Land Laws prohibited ownership of agricultural land by persons ineligible to become U.S. citizens. In the 1930s, Kajiro Oyama, a Japanese citizen, purchased two parcels of land as a gift for his minor son Fred, who was a birthright citizen. When the family was sent to Utah during World War II, California attempted to sell the land, arguing that Kajiro's purchases were not real gifts for his son but attempts to evade the Alien Land Laws.

The Supreme Court ruled that California had treated similar purchases by non-Japanese parents for their children differently. Therefore it violated Fred Oyama's rights under the Equal Protection Clause. Chief Justice Vinson's majority opinion did not pass on the constitutionality of the Alien Land Law or Kajiro Oyama's rights.

58. Frank H. Wu, Changing America: Three Arguments About Asian Americans and the Law, 45 Am. U. L. Rev. 811, 814 (1996). Wu argues that the model minority myth exposes the hollowness of the colorblind Constitution: "Ironically, when Asian Americans are used to attack affirmative action, the case for evaluating the merit of individuals focuses on the supposed success of a racial group." Id. at 816.

Justice Black (the author of *Korematsu*) and Justice Douglas concurred. They argued that the Alien Land Laws were unconstitutional, because they were designed to discriminate against aliens of Japanese ancestry: "If there is any one purpose of the Fourteenth Amendment that is wholly outside the realm of doubt, it is that the Amendment was designed to bar States from denying to some groups, on account of their race or color, any rights, privileges, and opportunities accorded to other groups. I would now overrule the previous decisions of this Court that sustained state land laws which discriminate against people of Japanese origin residing in this country. " Justice Murphy, joined by Justice Rutledge, also concurred: "The Alien Land Law . . . was designed to effectuate a purely racial discrimination, to prohibit a Japanese alien from owning or using agricultural land solely because he is a Japanese alien. It is rooted deeply in racial, economic and social antagonisms." Justices Reed, Burton, and Jackson dissented. The California Supreme Court subsequently held the Alien Land Laws unconstitutional in 1952, and the California legislature repealed them in 1956.

DISCUSSION

What explains Justice Black's different opinions in *Korematsu* and *Oyama*? The fact that *Korematsu* involved an emergency and *Oyama* did not? The fact that *Korematsu* involved the federal War Power and *Oyama* was a state economic regulation? Still another possible reason is the effect of World War II itself: By 1948, the United States was committed to a regime of international human rights. Justice Black argued that "[The Alien Land] law stands as an obstacle to the free accomplishment of our policy in the international field. . . . [W]e have recently pledged ourselves to cooperate with the United Nations to 'promote * * * universal respect for, and observance of, human rights and fundamental freedoms for all without distinction as to race, sex, language, or religion.' How can this nation be faithful to this international pledge if state laws which bar land ownership and occupancy by aliens on account of race are permitted to be enforced?"

2. The Court Strikes Down Antimiscegenation Statutes

Shortly after *Brown*, plaintiffs challenged Virginia's ban on interracial marriage. The Virginia Supreme Court upheld the ban; the Supreme Court vacated and remanded for further proceedings, ostensibly to further develop the evidentiary record, at which point the Virginia Supreme Court simply reinstated its previous decision.[59] The Supreme Court, fearful of directly addressing the question of interracial marriage so soon after its decision in *Brown*, refused to decide whether *Brown* applied to Virginia's ban on interracial marriage; instead, in Naim v. Naim, 350 U.S. 985 (1956), it dismissed the appeal from Virginia's Supreme Court as improvidently granted, leaving the status quo in place.

---

59. See Naim v. Naim, 350 U.S. 891, 891 (1955) (mem.) (per curiam) (vacating judgment), *remanded to* 90 S.E.2d 849 (Va.) (reinstating judgment), *motion to recall mandate denied per curiam*, 350 U.S. 985 (1956) (mem.) (dismissing for want of a properly presented federal question).

However, by 1964, the political situation had changed considerably. The Civil Rights Act was signed on July 2, 1964; in November, Lyndon Johnson was elected by a landslide. That December, in McLaughlin v. Florida, 379 U.S. 184 (1964), the Court invalidated a statute that punished interracial cohabitation more severely than cohabitation by persons of the same race. In so doing, the Court repudiated Pace v. Alabama, 106 U.S. 583 (1883), a Reconstruction-era decision that upheld an Alabama statute that punished interracial cohabitation or fornication more severely than intraracial fornication (see Chapter 4). Justice White argued that "*Pace* represents a limited view of the Equal Protection Clause which has not withstood analysis in the subsequent decisions of this Court":

> Judicial inquiry under the Equal Protection Clause . . . does not end with a showing of equal application among the members of the class defined by the legislation. The courts must reach and determine the question whether the classifications drawn in a statute are reasonable in light of its purpose—in this case, whether there is an arbitrary or invidious discrimination between those classes covered by Florida's cohabitation law and those excluded. That question is what *Pace* ignored and what must be faced here.
>
> Normally, the widest discretion is allowed the legislative judgment in determining whether to attack some, rather than all, of the manifestations of the evil aimed at; and normally that judgment is given the benefit of every conceivable circumstance which might suffice to characterize the classification as reasonable rather than arbitrary and invidious. But we deal here with a classification based upon the race of the participants, which must be viewed in light of the historical fact that the central purpose of the Fourteenth Amendment was to eliminate racial discrimination emanating from official sources in the States. This strong policy renders racial classifications "constitutionally suspect," Bolling v. Sharpe, and subject to the "most rigid scrutiny," Korematsu v. United States, 323 U.S. 214; and "in most circumstances irrelevant" to any constitutionally acceptable legislative purpose, Hirabayashi v. United States, 320 U.S. 81. Thus it is that racial classifications have been held invalid in a variety of contexts. See, e.g., Virginia Board of Elections v. Hamm, 379 U.S. 19 (designation of race in voting and property records); Anderson v. Martin, 375 U.S. 399 (designation of race on nomination papers and ballots); Watson v. City of Memphis, 373 U.S. 526 (segregation in public parks and playgrounds); Brown v. Board of Education, 349 U.S. 294 (segregation in public schools). . . .
>
> There is involved here an exercise of the state police power which trenches upon the constitutionally protected freedom from invidious official discrimination based on race. Such a law, even though enacted pursuant to a valid state interest, bears a heavy burden of justification . . . and will be upheld only if it is necessary, and not merely rationally related, to the accomplishment of a permissible state policy.

Three years later, the Supreme Court finally took up the constitutionality of Virginia's law.

Loving v. Virginia

338 U.S. 1 (1967)

Mr. Chief Justice WARREN delivered the opinion of the Court.

This case presents a constitutional question never addressed by this Court: whether a statutory scheme adopted by the State of Virginia to prevent marriages between persons solely on the basis of racial classifications violates the Equal Protection and Due Process Clauses of the Fourteenth Amendment. For reasons which seem to us to reflect the central meaning of those constitutional commands, we conclude that these statutes cannot stand consistently with the Fourteenth Amendment.

In June 1958, two residents of Virginia, Mildred Jeter, a Negro woman, and Richard Loving, a white man, were married in the District of Columbia pursuant to its laws. Shortly after their marriage, the Lovings returned to Virginia and established their marital abode in Caroline County. [A] grand jury [indicted] the Lovings [for] violating Virginia's ban on interracial marriages. On January 6, 1959, the Lovings pleaded guilty to the charge and were sentenced to one year in jail; however, the trial judge suspended the sentence for a period of 25 years on the condition that the Lovings leave the State and not return to Virginia together for 25 years. He stated in an opinion that:

> Almighty God created the races white, black, yellow, malay and red, and he placed them on separate continents. And but for the interference with his arrangement there would be no cause for such marriages. The fact that he separated the races shows that he did not intend for the races to mix.

[The Supreme Court of Appeals of Virginia upheld the constitutionality of the anti-miscegenation statutes and affirmed the Lovings' convictions.]

The two statutes under which appellants were convicted and sentenced are part of a comprehensive statutory scheme aimed at prohibiting and punishing interracial marriages. The Lovings were convicted of violating §20-58 of the Virginia Code:

> Leaving State to evade law.—If any white person and colored person shall go out of this State, for the purpose of being married, and with the intention of returning, and be married out of it, and afterwards return to and reside in it, cohabiting as man and wife, they shall be punished as provided in §20-59, and the marriage shall be governed by the same law as if it had been solemnized in this State. The fact of their cohabitation here as man and wife shall be evidence of their marriage.

Section 20-59, which defines the penalty for miscegenation, provides:

> Punishment for marriage.—If any white person intermarry with a colored person, or any colored person intermarry with a white person, he shall be guilty of a felony and shall be punished by confinement in the penitentiary for not less than one nor more than five years.

Other central provisions in the Virginia statutory scheme are §20-57, which automatically voids all marriages between "a white person and a colored person" without any judicial proceeding, and §§20-54 and 1-14 which, respectively, define "white persons" and "colored persons and Indians" for purposes of the statutory prohibitions. The Lovings have never disputed in the course of this litigation that Mrs. Loving is a "colored person" or that Mr. Loving is a "white person" within the meanings given those terms by the Virginia statutes.

Virginia is now one of 16 States which prohibit and punish marriages on the basis of racial classifications. Penalties for miscegenation arose as an incident to slavery and have been common in Virginia since the colonial period. The present statutory scheme dates from the adoption of the Racial Integrity Act of 1924, passed during the period of extreme nativism which followed the end of the First World War. The central features of this Act, and current Virginia law, are the absolute prohibition of a "white person" marrying other than another "white person," a prohibition against issuing marriage licenses until the issuing official is satisfied that the applicants' statements as to their race are correct, certificates of "racial composition" to be kept by both local and state registrars, and the carrying forward of earlier prohibitions against racial intermarriage.

In upholding the constitutionality of these provisions in the decision below, the Supreme Court of Appeals of Virginia referred to its 1955 decision in Naim v. Naim, 197 Va. 80, 87 S.E.2d 749, as stating the reasons supporting the validity of these laws. In *Naim*, the state court concluded that the State's legitimate purposes were "to preserve the racial integrity of its citizens," and to prevent "the corruption of blood," "a mongrel breed of citizens," and "the obliteration of racial pride," obviously an endorsement of the doctrine of White Supremacy. The court also reasoned that marriage has traditionally been subject to state regulation without federal intervention, and, consequently, the regulation of marriage should be left to exclusive state control by the Tenth Amendment.

While the state court is no doubt correct in asserting that marriage is a social relation subject to the State's police power, the State does not contend in its argument before this Court that its powers to regulate marriage are unlimited notwithstanding the commands of the Fourteenth Amendment. . . . Instead, the State argues that the meaning of the Equal Protection Clause, as illuminated by the statements of the Framers, is only that state penal laws containing an interracial element as part of the definition of the offense must apply equally to whites and Negroes in the sense that members of each race are punished to the same degree. Thus, the State contends that, because its miscegenation statutes punish equally both the white and the Negro participants in an interracial marriage, these statutes, despite their reliance on racial classifications do not constitute an invidious discrimination based upon race. The second argument advanced by the State assumes the validity of its equal application theory. The argument is that, if the Equal Protection Clause does not outlaw miscegenation statutes because of their reliance on racial classifications, the question of constitutionality would thus become whether there was any rational basis for a State to treat interracial marriages differently from other marriages. On this question, the State argues, the scientific evidence is substantially in doubt and, consequently, this Court should defer to the wisdom of the state legislature in adopting its policy of discouraging interracial marriages.

Because we reject the notion that the mere "equal application" of a statute containing racial classifications is enough to remove the classifications from the Fourteenth Amendment's proscription of all invidious racial discriminations, we do not accept the State's contention that these statutes should be upheld if there is any possible basis for concluding that they serve a rational purpose. [In] cases involving distinctions not drawn according to race, the Court has merely asked whether there is any rational foundation for the discriminations, and has deferred to the wisdom of the state legislatures. In the case at bar, however, we deal with statutes containing racial classifications, and the fact of equal application does not immunize the statute from the very heavy burden of justification which the Fourteenth Amendment has traditionally required of state statutes drawn according to race.

The State argues that statements in the Thirty-ninth Congress about the time of the passage of the Fourteenth Amendment indicate that the Framers did not intend the Amendment to make unconstitutional state miscegenation laws. Many of the statements alluded to by the State concern the debates over the Freedmen's Bureau Bill, which President Johnson vetoed, and the Civil Rights Act of 1866 enacted over his veto. While these statements have some relevance to the intention of Congress in submitting the Fourteenth Amendment, it must be understood that they pertained to the passage of specific statutes and not to the broader, organic purpose of a constitutional amendment. As for the various statements directly concerning the Fourteenth Amendment, we have said in connection with a related problem, that although these historical sources "cast some light" they are not sufficient to resolve the problem. . . . We have rejected the proposition that the debates in the Thirty-ninth Congress or in the state legislatures which ratified the Fourteenth Amendment supported the theory advanced by the State, that the requirement of equal protection of the laws is satisfied by penal laws defining offenses based on racial classifications so long as white and Negro participants in the offense were similarly punished. McLaughlin v. State of Florida, 379 U.S. 184 (1964).

The State finds support for its "equal application" theory in the decision of the Court in Pace v. State of Alabama, 106 U.S. 583 (1883). In that case, the Court upheld a conviction under an Alabama statute forbidding adultery or fornication between a white person and a Negro which imposed a greater penalty than that of a statute proscribing similar conduct by members of the same race. The Court reasoned that the statute could not be said to discriminate against Negroes because the punishment for each participant in the offense was the same. However, as recently as the 1964 Term, in rejecting the reasoning of that case, we stated "*Pace* represents a limited view of the Equal Protection Clause which has not withstood analysis in the subsequent decisions of this Court." *McLaughlin.* As we there demonstrated, the Equal Protection Clause requires the consideration of whether the classifications drawn by any statute constitute an arbitrary and invidious discrimination. The clear and central purpose of the Fourteenth Amendment was to eliminate all official state sources of invidious racial discrimination in the States.

There can be no question but that Virginia's miscegenation statutes rest solely upon distinctions drawn according to race. The statutes proscribe generally accepted conduct if engaged in by members of different races. Over the years, this Court has consistently repudiated "(d)istinctions between citizens solely because of their ancestry" as being "odious to a free people whose institutions are founded upon the doctrine of equality." Hirabayashi v. United States, 320 U.S. 81, 100

(1943). At the very least, the Equal Protection Clause demands that racial classifications, especially suspect in criminal statutes, be subjected to the "most rigid scrutiny," Korematsu v. United States, 323 U.S. 214, 216 (1944), and, if they are ever to be upheld, they must be shown to be necessary to the accomplishment of some permissible state objective, independent of the racial discrimination which it was the object of the Fourteenth Amendment to eliminate. Indeed, two members of this Court have already stated that they "cannot conceive of a valid legislative purpose . . . which makes the color of a person's skin the test of whether his conduct is a criminal offense." (Stewart, J., joined by Douglas, J., concurring).

There is patently no legitimate overriding purpose independent of invidious racial discrimination which justifies this classification. The fact that Virginia prohibits only interracial marriages involving white persons demonstrates that the racial classifications must stand on their own justification, as measures designed to maintain White Supremacy. We have consistently denied the constitutionality of measures which restrict the rights of citizens on account of race. There can be no doubt that restricting the freedom to marry solely because of racial classifications violates the central meaning of the Equal Protection Clause.

These statutes also deprive the Lovings of liberty without due process of law in violation of the Due Process Clause of the Fourteenth Amendment. The freedom to marry has long been recognized as one of the vital personal rights essential to the orderly pursuit of happiness by free men.

Marriage is one of the "basic civil rights of man," fundamental to our very existence and survival. To deny this fundamental freedom on so unsupportable a basis as the racial classifications embodied in these statutes, classifications so directly subversive of the principle of equality at the heart of the Fourteenth Amendment, is surely to deprive all the State's citizens of liberty without due process of law. The Fourteenth Amendment requires that the freedom of choice to marry not be restricted by invidious racial discriminations. Under our Constitution, the freedom to marry or not marry, a person of another race resides with the individual and cannot be infringed by the State.

Mr. Justice STEWART, concurring.

I have previously expressed the belief that "it is simply not possible for a state law to be valid under our Constitution which makes the criminality of an act depend upon the race of the actor." *McLaughlin.* Because I adhere to that belief, I concur in the judgment of the Court.

DISCUSSION

1. *Anticlassification versus antisubordination.* The Court in *Loving* objected to the statute both on the grounds that it involved an invidious racial classification and on the grounds that the bar on racial intermarriage promoted white supremacy. Similarly, *Brown* described the wrong of segregated public education as inflicting injuries of racial differentiation and racial subordination: "To separate [children] from others of similar age and qualifications solely because of their race generates a feeling of inferiority as to their status in the community that may affect their hearts and minds in a way unlikely ever to be undone."

In later years, people pointed to the language in these cases and asserted that they stood for two competing principles that seemed to resolve the disputes facing the Court quite differently. According to the *anticlassification* principle, the Constitution prohibited racial classifications. According to the *antisubordination* principle, the Constitution enjoined practices of racial subordination.

The anticlassification approach argues that the harm of inequality stems from classifying persons according to race, a practice that is assumed by its nature to be invidious. An antisubordination approach argues that the harm of inequality arises from unjust forms of social hierarchy or social subordination. While the first approach looks to whether a statute or other government action involves a facial classification (or is secretly intended to classify), the second approach looks to the impact of state action in fostering or reproducing an unjust social structure.

Anticlassification and antisubordination understandings developed together; it was only in disputes over *Brown*'s enforcement that advocates began to speak of anticlassification and antisubordination as distinct and competing principles with different practical applications. In fact, in the years immediately before and after *Brown* these frameworks were understood as interconnected, and contemporaries discussed *Brown* as vindicating values that today we associate with the antisubordination approach. See Reva B. Siegel, Equality Talk: Antisubordination and Anticlassification Values in Constitutional Struggles over *Brown*, 117 Harv. L. Rev. 1470, 1478-1480, 1500, 1534 (2004).

2. *The stakes of the choice between anticlassification and antisubordination approaches to equality.* Jack Balkin and Reva Siegel explain:[60]

> The idea of distinguishing between anticlassification and antisubordination principles arose at a critical juncture in American race history . . . when American law had discredited the most prominent and overtly discriminatory practices enforcing racial segregation. At this juncture in the struggle over disestablishing Jim Crow, the Court faced important questions about the constitutionality of two kinds of practices: practices that employed racial criteria to integrate formerly segregated institutions and practices that preserved the racial segregation of institutions through formally neutral rules that made no overt reference to race. The stakes were high. Depending on how the Court dealt with the legality of affirmative action and the legitimacy of facially neutral practices with a disparate impact on racial minorities, the Constitution would either rationalize or destabilize the practices that sustained the racial stratification of American society now that the most overt forms of segregation were abolished.
>
> The questions facing the Court put at issue the very meaning of *Brown* and the civil rights movement. If the Court read *Brown* as invalidating segregation on the ground that it violated an anticlassification principle, then facially neutral practices with disparate impact on racial minorities would be presumptively constitutional, while affirmative action

60. Jack M. Balkin and Reva B. Siegel, The American Civil Rights Tradition: Anticlassification or Antisubordination?, 58 U. Miami L. Rev. 9, 11-12 (2003).

> would not. On the other hand, if the Court read *Brown* as invalidating segregation on the ground that it violated an antisubordination principle, then affirmative action would be presumptively constitutional, while facially neutral practices with a disparate impact on minorities would not.

For one of the most influential statements of the antisubordination approach in the 1970s, see Owen Fiss, Groups and the Equal Protection Clause, 5 Phil. & Pub. Aff. 107 (1976).

3. *Status enforcing legislation.* Under the antisubordination approach, the goal of equality law is to combat unjust forms of *social stratification*—that is, forms of group inequality that occur over many different areas of social life and that tend to persist over time. Consider Jack M. Balkin, The Constitution of Status, 106 Yale L.J. 2313, 2323-2324 (1997):

> In many societies, *status hierarchies* emerge between groups with distinctive identities or styles of life. The most obvious example of a status hierarchy is a system of social caste; but status hierarchies can be much less rigid and even quite fluid. . . . [A] status hierarchy is sustained by a system of social meanings in which one group receives relatively positive associations and another correspondingly negative associations. As a result, their identities are not freestanding: The identity of one is defined in part by its relationship to the identity of the other, and a change in the meanings attributed to one will affect not only its own social identity, but the identity of the other group. In a hierarchy with many status groups, there can be many different ways of differentiating the various groups and their respective lifestyles, and hence the system of social meanings (and the results of changes in social meanings) can be quite complex.
>
> There is no necessary limitation on what characteristics can serve to distinguish status groups in a status hierarchy. They can be mutable or immutable, physical or ideological, matters of behavior or matters of appearance. The most familiar ones in the United States are organized along lines of race, sex, religion, immigrant status, and ethnicity. Conversely, not every distinguishing trait or characteristic corresponds to a status group in a status hierarchy. The number of traits that might be used to distinguish human beings is limitless, but the organization of a status hierarchy is a result of a particular history of social stratification and subordination. The question is not whether identifying traits exist that might distinguish people, but whether society has organized itself into a system of super- and subordination based on those traits. The issue is social stratification based on traits, not the nature of the traits themselves.
>
> Thus, what constitutional lawyers call "immutability" is neither a necessary nor a sufficient criterion for a status group. The question is whether the trait can be endowed with sufficient cultural meaning to support a system of social stratification. Religious identity can serve this function even though religions proselytize and gain new converts. The point is not what the trait is, but what it can be made to mean in opposition to other traits.
>
> Obviously, a system of subordination cannot be stable if it is too easy to exit from the criteria of subordinate status. That is why biological traits

> can be such useful markers of cultural differentiation. The advantage of immutability lies in its guarantee of stability—it helps ensure that social hierarchy can be reproduced effectively. Yet a trait does not have to be biologically based for group membership to be relatively stable over time.
>
> Conversely, even biological traits like skin color can allow for the exit of one's children (through miscegenation), and hence so-called immutable criteria like race may have to be buttressed or even constituted by legal or cultural rules. Thus the Jim Crow regime featured cultural and legal prohibitions on interracial marriage (if not interracial sex) and elaborate rules of hypodescent [for example, the rule that one drop of black blood makes one black] to define who was white and black given the inevitability of racial mixing.

How did the antimiscegenation legislation in *Loving* help enforce the higher racial status of whites? One important purpose, as Balkin notes, is to help maintain notions of who is Black and who is white, as well as who was a member of one's family and who was not.

During slavery, slaves were often forbidden to marry. White masters had sexual access to Black women, producing illegitimate children whose status was determined by that of their mother. Hence it was essential to use marriage law to separate one's family from one's slaves, and one's relations from one's property, especially given that slavery was also regarded as a "domestic" institution. See Dorothy Roberts, The Genetic Tie, 62 U. Chi. L. Rev. 209 (1995). Conversely, because under the slave system, status traveled with the mother, it was vital to keep white women from sexual access by Black men. The purity of white identity (with its accompanying rights and privileges) and the degraded status of Black identity were preserved through rules of marriage and descent.

Under the system of Jim Crow that replaced chattel slavery, it was still important to preserve white racial identity and distinguish it from Black identity, as well as to constrain Black male and white female sexuality. Although the Fourteenth Amendment granted civil equality to Black people, it did not grant "social equality," i.e., equal social status. The civil/political/social distinction transformed the status regime that had existed during slavery and granted Black people a larger degree of freedom and equality than they had enjoyed previously. However, it still preserved the status hierarchy of whites over Blacks, and the social inequality of the two races. Social equality was symbolized by all forms of social intermingling, ranging from attendance at dinner parties to membership in clubs, to the schools one's children attended; however, sexual and marriage partners were perhaps the most central aspects of social equality because rules about sex, marriage, and descent were central to preserving racial identity. Thus, Emily Van Tassel notes that "'Social Equality' became virtually synonymous with interracial marriage in the late nineteenth century, and was used as a slogan against all manner of rights-access by blacks in much the same way as the term 'white supremacy.'"[61] In State v. Scott, 39 Ga. 321, 326-327 (1869), while upholding a conviction for miscegenation, the court explained:

---

61. Emily Field Van Tassel, "Only the Law Would Rule Between Us": Antimiscegenation, the Moral Economy of Dependency, and the Debate over Rights After the Civil War, 70 Chi.-Kent L. Rev. 873 (1995).

> Before the laws, the Code of Georgia makes all citizens equal, without regard to race or color. But it does not create, nor does any law of the State attempt to enforce, moral or social equality between the different races or citizens of the State. Such equality does not in fact exist, and never can. The God of nature made it otherwise, and no human law can produce it, and no human tribunal can enforce it. There are gradations and classes throughout the universe. From the tallest arch angel in Heaven down to the meanest reptile on earth, moral and social inequalities exist, and must continue to exist through all eternity.
>
> . . . The fortunes of war have compelled us to yield to the freedmen the legal rights above mentioned, but we have neither authorized nor enacted the marriage relation between the races, nor have we enacted laws or placed it in the power of the Legislature hereafter to make laws, regulating the social *status*, so as to compel our people to meet the colored race on terms of social equality. . . . Indeed, the most absolute and despotic governments do not attempt to regulate social *status* by fixed laws, or to enforce social equality among races or classes without their consent.

Note that in State v. Scott the court insisted that Black people enjoyed full legal equality in the state of Georgia, but that legal equality could coexist with social inequality. In other words, the court believed that a realm of private behavior and interaction in which whites held greater social status than Blacks was entirely consistent with the equality of the two races before the law. Is this combination of legal equality and social inequality merely an aspect of a Jim Crow regime that made many racial classifications, or could it still be true today, when classifications based on race are for the most part illegal? Does a racial status hierarchy need racial classifications to reproduce itself, or can it do so through facially neutral legal rules?

These questions raise once again the distinction between anticlassification and antisubordination approaches—between a theory of equality that looks to the presence or absence of racial classifications (or the intent to classify by race), and a theory that looks to the social meanings of being Black and white, and to the institutions and justifications that preserve social stratification and status hierarchy. As noted earlier, both of these notions of equality are present to some degree in *Loving*.

According to the anticlassification principle, the goal of equality is to avoid racial classifications; law is complicit in inequality to the extent that it makes such classifications. According to the antisubordination principle, the goal of equality is to dismantle social structures that can use law in many different ways besides direct racial classification; law is complicit in inequality to the extent that it contains status-enforcing rules or doctrines. Anticlassification theory asks law to eschew racial classification, so that law can exist outside the system of racial hierarchy and regulate it. Antisubordination theory sees law as inevitably caught up in the system of racial hierarchy and racial meanings, even (and especially) when it tries to regulate them; the question for antisubordination theory is how law can best help to dismantle a system of which law is inevitably a part.

4. *To what extent are the anticlassification and antisubordination principles really in conflict?* Anticlassification and antisubordination approaches overlap and are

interdependent. As we will see in the materials that follow, what counts as an impermissible racial classification is not always clear-cut. Courts must make policy decisions about whether to count a challenged practice as a "classification" that is "on the basis of" "race"; in different situations, each of these key terms can become contestable. Often antisubordination values play a crucial role in deciding what violates the anticlassification principle. In fact, as Jack Balkin and Reva Siegel have pointed out[62]

> the anticlassification principle cannot by itself decide many important issues of antidiscrimination law. A decision maker must adopt additional criteria in order to apply the principle so that it can decide concrete cases. These implementing criteria cannot be derived from the anticlassification principle itself; as a result, many different legal regimes could be consistent with the anticlassification imperative. Courts must make a variety of implementing decisions in order to apply the anticlassification principle; and . . . they do not make such implementing decisions in any consistent manner. [This] suggests that the discourse of anticlassification conceals other values that do much of the work in determining which practices antidiscrimination law enjoins. . . .
>
> Sometimes . . . courts have implemented the anticlassification principle in a fashion that preserves status relations. But often, and particularly as the civil rights agenda expands, the judiciary has applied the anticlassification principle in ways that dismantle status relations. [A]pplication of the anticlassification principle shifts over time in response to social contestation. As social protest delegitimates certain practices, courts are often moved, consciously or unconsciously, by perceptions of status harm to find violations of the anticlassification principle where they saw none before. Considered from this historical vantage point, American civil rights jurisprudence vindicates both anticlassification and antisubordination commitments.

5. *The strict scrutiny test. Loving* is the modern origin of the "strict scrutiny" doctrine for racial classifications under the Equal Protection Clause (note that Brown v. Board of Education does not use the language of scrutiny at all). In *Loving*, the Court speaks of the test as whether the law in question is "necessary to the accomplishment of some permissible state objective, independent of the racial discrimination which it was the object of the Fourteenth Amendment to eliminate." Today, the Court describes the strict scrutiny test as whether the law in question is "narrowly tailored to achieve a compelling governmental interest." What are the differences between these two formulations?

6. *What justifies strict scrutiny for racial classifications?* In *Loving*, Chief Justice Warren does not spend much time explaining why classifications based on race deserve strict scrutiny; instead he quotes *Hirabayashi*—which upheld race-based curfews—for the proposition that distinctions based on race are "odious to a free people whose institutions are founded upon the doctrine of equality." What reasons might there be for treating distinctions based on race differently from other

---

62. Balkin and Siegel, The American Civil Rights Tradition, supra n.60, at 11-14.

kinds of distinctions that receive only rational basis scrutiny? Consider the following possibilities:[63]

(1) Racial classifications are likely to reflect a defect in the political process, demonstrating that some races are unfairly shut out of the political process, or are unable to form part of effective governing coalitions because of irrational prejudice;
(2) Racial classifications involve distinctions based on immutable characteristics that ordinarily have no relationship to merit or to legitimate government interests;
(3) Racial classifications are likely to reflect the view that some races are morally or behaviorally superior (or inferior) to others; or reflect dubious race-based stereotypes that prevent individuals from being judged on their own merits;
(4) Racial classifications are likely to involve "selective sympathy and indifference": "the unconscious failure to extend to a minority the same recognition of humanity, and hence the same sympathy and care, given as a matter of course to one's own group";[64]
(5) Racial classifications are likely to involve restrictions or disadvantages that dominant majorities would not impose on themselves, thus violating a principle of reciprocity;
(6) Racial classifications are likely to enforce a system of cumulative disadvantages, in which racial groups are disfavored or disadvantaged in many different spheres of life, perpetuating and entrenching inequalities in multiple dimensions: wealth, employment opportunities, access to housing, social capital, and health;
(7) Racial classifications impose especially great harms on individuals by humiliating them, denying them equal dignity and the right to be considered as individuals;
(8) Racial classifications are likely to exacerbate group-based politics and legitimate the notion that people are entitled to seek special treatment or spoils for members of their own racial or ethnic group; and
(9) Racial classifications are likely to breed resentment by disfavored groups, undermine political and social solidarity among citizens, and generate the sense that the legal and political system is skewed or illegitimate.

---

63. See Paul Brest, Foreword: In Defense of the Antidiscrimination Principle, 90 Harv. L. Rev. 1, 6-11 (1976); John Hart Ely, Democracy and Distrust: A Theory of Judicial Review (1980); Peter J. Rubin, Reconnecting Doctrine and Purpose: A Comprehensive Approach to Strict Scrutiny After *Adarand* and *Shaw*, 149 U. Pa. L. Rev. 1 (2000); Reva B. Siegel, Antibalkanization: An Emerging Ground of Decision in Race Equality Cases, 120 Yale L.J. 1278 (2011).

64. See Brest, Foreword: In Defense of the Antidiscrimination Principle, supra n.63, at 7-8.

How many of these justifications are connected to the antisubordination principle? Which ones concern fairness of process? Which concern harms to individuals? Which concern harms to society as a whole or to political legitimacy?

Do these justifications adequately distinguish racial classifications from other kinds of legal classifications that may rest on stereotypes, reflect status competition or selective sympathy and indifference, exacerbate social divisions, or perpetuate cumulative disadvantages?

7. *Immutability as a justification for strict scrutiny.* Is immutability sufficient to distinguish racial classifications? Consider Jack Balkin's analysis of the immutability argument:[65]

> Discrimination against blacks . . . is not unjust simply because race is an immutable characteristic. Focusing on immutability per se confuses biological with sociological considerations. It confuses the physical existence of the trait with what the trait means in a social system. Racial discrimination is wrong because of the historical creation of a status hierarchy organized around the meaning of skin color. The question to ask is not whether a trait is immutable, but whether there has been a history of using the trait to create a system of social meanings, or define a social hierarchy, that helps dominate and oppress people. Any conclusions about the importance of immutability already presuppose a view about background social structure.
>
> Indeed, a focus on immutability makes sense only as long as we recognize its relationship to social structure. Social hierarchies often assign differential social meanings to immutable traits because they make exit from low status more difficult. But not all immutable characteristics are or have been the basis for unjust social hierarchies, and not all unjust social hierarchies are founded on immutable characteristics.
>
> Religion is not an immutable trait—many religions are always looking for new converts—but status-based discrimination against religious groups is surely also unjust. Defenders of the immutability criterion can point to the Religion Clauses as an independent justification for protection of religious minorities; but this puts the cart before the horse. The Religion Clauses exist in part because the Framers recognized that religious intolerance was an evil long before they recognized that racial intolerance was.
>
> The importance of immutability as a criterion of judgment is also sometimes defended on the grounds that immutable characteristics—for example, race—are morally irrelevant. But this argument, too, really depends on a view about the justness of a particular status hierarchy. When status distinctions are internalized in a culture, status hierarchies make traits morally relevant. They become signs of positive and negative associations. They become permissible proxies for inferences about character, honesty, ability, and judgment. Such traits are morally irrelevant only to persons not in the grip of that particular hierarchy. In the aristocracy of pre-Revolutionary America, for example, high birth was

65. Balkin, The Constitution of Status, at 2365-2367.

viewed as correlating with many other positive attributes—honesty, sagacity, learning, and good manners—and society was organized to make these positive associations a self-fulfilling prophecy. Generations of whites thought blacks naturally inferior; succeeding generations who learned not to make biological arguments have nevertheless continued to regard blacks as culturally inferior—as displaying negative qualities of sloth, violence, and licentiousness. A characteristic becomes "morally irrelevant" precisely when we understand the status hierarchy it is based on to be unjust. Only then do we become embarrassed to use the trait as a signifier of, or a proxy for, positive or negative associations. Our objection to the moral relevance of the characteristic is really our objection to the system of social meanings and the hierarchy of social status that uses this trait as a criterion for judgment. The real issue is whether society has created an unjust status hierarchy organized around a particular trait or set of traits, whether those traits are immutable, or—like religion—voluntarily chosen or instilled through socialization.

B. The Reach of the Suspect Classification Doctrine

Does the strict scrutiny rule of Loving v. Virginia apply to all government classifications based on race? Consider the following contexts and ask how well the various justifications for strict scrutiny apply to them. We address race-conscious affirmative action in Section F, infra; but it is worth noting that in several of these examples, the debate over affirmative action is very much on the minds of legal decisionmakers.

1. Racial Segregation in Prisons

JOHNSON v. CALIFORNIA, 543 U.S. 499 (2005): The California Department of Corrections (CDC) had a policy of placing all new male prisoners and all male prisoners transferred from other state facilities in double cells in reception centers for up to 60 days upon their arrival. During that time they were assigned cellmates based on their race; cellmate assignments were further subdivided within each racial group. Japanese-Americans were housed separately from Chinese-Americans, and northern California Hispanics were separated from southern California Hispanics. The rest of the state prison facilities—including dining areas, yards, and cells—were fully integrated. After the 60-day period prisoners were allowed to choose their own cellmates. The CDC defended the policy as necessary to prevent violence by racial gangs; it argued that the Court should review its judgment, not under strict scrutiny but under the more deferential standard of Turner v. Safley, 482 U.S. 78 (1987). *Turner* involved a challenge to restrictions on inmate marriages and correspondence between inmates under the Due Process Clause and the First Amendment. It held that where prisoners allege that prison regulations violate their fundamental rights, deference to prison administrators counsels a relaxed standard; courts should ask only whether the regulation was "reasonably related" to "legitimate penological interests," with no inquiry into less restrictive alternatives.

The Supreme Court, in an opinion by Justice O'Connor, held that the CDC policy was subject to strict scrutiny and remanded for further proceedings to determine whether the policy could satisfy that standard: "The need for strict scrutiny is no less important here, where prison officials cite racial violence as the reason for their policy. . . . Indeed, by insisting that inmates be housed only with other inmates of the same race, it is possible that prison officials will breed further hostility among prisoners and reinforce racial and ethnic divisions. By perpetuating the notion that race matters most, racial segregation of inmates 'may exacerbate the very patterns of [violence that it is] said to counteract.'" Justice O'Connor rejected the *Turner* standard because "[t]he right not to be discriminated against based on one's race . . . is not a right that need necessarily be compromised for the sake of proper prison administration." Moreover, the *Turner* standard "would allow prison officials to use race-based policies even when there are race-neutral means to accomplish the same goal, and even when the race-based policy does not in practice advance that goal. . . . [And under *Turner*] there is no obvious limit to permissible segregation in prisons. It is not readily apparent why, if segregation in reception centers is justified, segregation in the dining halls, yards, and general housing areas is not also permissible. Any of these areas could be the potential site of racial violence."

Chief Justice Rehnquist did not participate in the case.

Justice Ginsburg, joined by Justices Souter and Breyer, concurred, noting that "the same standard of review ought not control judicial inspection of every official race classification. . . . 'Actions designed to burden groups long denied full citizenship stature are not sensibly ranked with measures taken to hasten the day when entrenched discrimination and its aftereffects have been extirpated.' There is no pretense here, however, that the California Department of Corrections (CDC) installed its segregation policy to 'correct inequalities.'" Justice Stevens dissented on the grounds that the CDC policy would not pass muster under either the strict scrutiny standard or the more relaxed *Turner* standard.

Justice Thomas dissented, joined by Justice Scalia. He argued that the relaxed *Turner* standard, and not strict scrutiny, should apply to racial classifications in prisons. "The Constitution has always demanded less within the prison walls." Justice Thomas emphasized that racial violence in prisons was a serious problem that prison officials and not courts were best suited to address. The need for deference to prison officials justified application of the *Turner* test: "[T]wo Terms ago, in upholding the University of Michigan Law School's affirmative-action program, [in Grutter v. Bollinger], this Court deferred to the judgment by the law school's faculty and administrators on their need for diversity in the student body. Deference would seem all the more warranted in the prison context, for whatever the Court knows of administering educational institutions, it knows much less about administering penal ones. The potential consequences of second-guessing the judgments of prison administrators are also much more severe."

2. Family Formation

a. Child Custody Decisions Following Divorce

In Palmore v. Sidoti, 466 U.S. 429 (1984), the Supreme Court unanimously invalidated "a judgment of a state court divesting a natural mother of the custody of her infant child because of her remarriage to a person of a different race" on the grounds that this would be in the best interests of the child. When Linda and Anthony Sidoti, both white, divorced in May 1980, the Florida court awarded custody of their three-year-old daughter to the mother. In September 1981, Anthony petitioned for a modification of that judgment on the ground, among others, that Linda was living with an African-American man (whom she had married by the time of the hearing). Although the court specifically found that Linda remained a fit parent and that her husband was "respectable," it awarded custody to Anthony. The court apparently took into account a counselor's conclusion that Linda "has chosen for herself and for her child, a lifestyle unacceptable to her father *and to society* (emphasis supplied by the Supreme Court)." The Florida court added: "[D]espite the strides that have been made in bettering relations between the races in this country, it is inevitable that Melanie will, if allowed to remain in her present situation and attain[] school age and thus [become] more vulnerable to peer pressures, suffer from the social stigmatization that is sure to come."

Chief Justice Burger observed that "it is clear that the outcome would have been different had petitioner married a Caucasian male of similar respectability," and that "the action of the Florida court must be tested by 'the most exacting scrutiny.'" Chief Justice Burger explained: "There is a risk that a child living with a step-parent of a different race may be subject to a variety of pressures and stresses not present if the child were living with parents of the same racial or ethnic origin. The question, however, is whether the reality of private biases and the possible injury they might inflict are permissible considerations for removal of an infant child from the custody of its natural mother. We have little difficulty concluding that they are not. The Constitution cannot control such prejudices but neither can it tolerate them. Private biases may be outside the reach of the law, but the law cannot, directly or indirectly, give them effect."

b. Race-Matching Policies in Adoption

Palmore v. Sidoti involved a decision about which parent in a previously existing family (divided by divorce) would receive custody of a child. Does the same reasoning apply to adoption, in which a child is placed in a new family?

Many adoption agencies seek to "match" children to their prospective adoptive parents on the basis of religion (almost always based on the biological mother), race and ethnic background (e.g., Italian, Polish, "Mediterranean"), and physical appearance (height, hair and eye color). Is a conscious attempt by a state adoption agency to achieve a racial "match" in child placement constitutional? Compare James S. Bowen, Cultural Convergences and Divergences: The Nexus Between Putative Afro-American Family Values and the Best Interests of the Child, 26 J. Fam. L. 487 (1987-1988) (arguing that "[a] Black child must be raised as a Black child," and "[g]iven a situation of equipoise between two possible adoptive families, race may be a determinative factor in deciding the placement of a Black child in contemporary American society"), with Elizabeth Bartholet, Where Do Black Children Belong? The Politics of Race-Matching in Adoption, 139 U. Pa. L. Rev. 1163, 1223 (1991) (arguing that race-matching policies "conflict with the basic law of the land on race discrimination," and harm children by significantly hindering transracial adoptions even in cases in which in-race placement is not an option).

Suppose that instead of directly promoting race-matching, a state adoption agency simply classifies children by race, asks prospective parents what race of child they would prefer, and attempts to honor the prospective parents' choice? Could this be justified on the grounds that adoptive children are better off if they are placed consistent with the preferences of prospective parents? Professor Richard Banks calls this practice "facilitative accommodation," and argues that it violates the Equal Protection Clause as much as deliberate race-matching by the state: "[Facilitating] [a]doptive parents' racial preferences dramatically diminish[es] the pool of potential parents available to black children relative to that available to white children. The pool of parents available to black children is also of lower average quality than that available to white children, in part because many of those whites who adopt black children do so because they are considered by agencies to be among the least desirable parents for white children. The severity of the social inequality produced by adoptive parents' preferences is made starkly clear by a fact too often accepted as inevitable, albeit lamentable, rather than as a predictable outcome of our own preference-promoting policies: Black children are simply worth less than white children."[66]

The controversy over transracial adoptions is reflected by the passage of 42 U.S.C. §1996b, titled "Interethnic adoption," which provides that:

> A person or government that is involved in adoption or foster care placements may not — (A) deny to any individual the opportunity to become an adoptive or a foster parent, on the basis of the race, color, or national origin of the individual, or of the child, involved; or (B) delay or deny the placement of a child for adoption or into foster care, on the basis of the race, color, or national origin of the adoptive or foster parent, or the child, involved.

Compare this with 25 U.S.C. §1915, dealing with "Placement of Indian children," which requires that:

> In any adoptive placement of an Indian child under State law, a preference shall be given, in the absence of good cause to the contrary, to a placement with (1) a member of the child's extended family; (2) other members of the Indian child's tribe; or (3) other Indian families.

A recurring feature of courses on American Indian law is that there is a considerable tension between the standard equal protection doctrine involving racial and ethnic classification and the specialized doctrines of law that deal with American Indians. For now, it is enough to ask you to compare the two federal laws and to ask yourself which you prefer and why. Note, incidentally, that 42 U.S.C. §1996b does not, at least on its face, extend to prohibiting a state agency from responding to potential adopters' own preferences as to race. Should it have?

On the tensions between "standard" equal protection doctrine and family law, see generally Katie R. Eyer, Constitutional Colorblindness and the Family, 162 U. Pa. L. Rev. 537 (2014).

---

66. R. Richard Banks, The Color of Desire: Fulfilling Adoptive Parents' Racial Preferences Through Discriminatory State Action, 107 Yale L.J. 875, 881 (1998).

3. Government Collection and Use of Racial Data

Is *Loving* consistent with federal census practices that identify or classify citizens by race or ethnicity? Since 1790, the census has asked persons for their race. The 2000 Census, for example, featured several questions about racial and ethnic identity. The short form of the census questionnaire asks whether a person is of Spanish, Hispanic, or Latino heritage. It asks a person's race and directs the person to check off a box with the following choices: (1) white; (2) Black, African American, or Negro; (3) American Indian or Alaska native, with space to provide the name of the enrolled or principal tribe; (4) Asian Indian; (5) Chinese; (6) Filipino; (7) other Asian, with a space to print the race; (8) Japanese; (9) Korean; (10) Vietnamese; (11) Native Hawaiian; (12) Guamanian or Chamorro; (13) Samoan; (14) Other Pacific Islander, and a space to print in the race; or (15) "Some other race," with a space in which the person is to print the name of the race. Each member of a household is asked a similar question, thus allowing the government to know which members of which races are living with each other. In addition, the census also asks how each person in the household is related to the others. A question concerning the relationships that persons who live in a single household have to each other has been included in the census since 1880.

A long form of the census questionnaire, given to a selected percentage of households, asks additionally for a person's "ancestry or ethnic origin," giving as examples "Italian, Jamaican, African American, Cambodian, Cape Verdean, Norwegian, Dominican, French Canadian, Haitian, Korean, Lebanese, Polish, Nigerian, Mexican, Taiwanese, Ukranian, etc." It asks whether a person speaks a language other than English at home, what that language is, and how well the person speaks English, giving choices from "very well" to "not at all." A question concerning the language spoken at home was on the census form from 1890 through 1940, and reappeared on the census forms from 1960 through the 1990 census. Finally, the long form asks where a person was born, when the person first entered the United States, and whether the person is a citizen of the United States.

In Morales v. Daley, 116 F. Supp. 2d 801 (S.D. Tex. 2000), plaintiffs objected that asking about their racial and ethnic identities violated their right to the equal protection component of the Due Process Clause of the Fifth Amendment and enabled the government to make race-based decisions; they argued that collecting data about racial identity could easily be abused, offering the example of Japanese internment during World War II. The government defended its questions on the grounds that collecting information about race and ethnicity was "needed to assess racial disparities in health and environmental risks," was "required by states to meet legislative redistricting requirements by knowing the racial makeup of the voting age population" and was "required to enforce provisions under the Civil Rights Act which prohibits discrimination based upon race, sex, religion and national origin."

The district court rejected the plaintiff's arguments: "Plaintiffs' position is based upon a misunderstanding of the distinction between collecting demographic data so that the government may have the information it believes at a given time it needs in order to govern, and governmental use of suspect classifications without a compelling interest. . . . The issue is whether requiring a person to self-classify racially or ethnically, knowing to what use such classifications have been put in the past, can violate the due process implications of the Fifth Amendment. This court holds that such self-classifications do not."

In Anderson v. Martin, 375 U.S. 399 (1964), the Court unanimously invalidated a Louisiana statute requiring that the ballots in all elections designate the race of the candidates. The Court rejected the state's argument that the requirement was nondiscriminatory since the labeling provision applied equally to Black and white candidates. Justice Clark wrote: "[B]y directing the citizen's attention to the single consideration of race or color, the State indicates that a candidate's race or color is an important—perhaps paramount—consideration in the citizen's choice, which may decisively influence the citizen to cast his ballot along racial lines. . . . The vice lies . . . in the placing of the power of the State behind a racial classification that induces racial prejudice at the polls." However, the same year, in Tancil v. Wools, 379 U.S. 19 (1964), the Court summarily affirmed the judgment of a three-judge district court invalidating Virginia laws that required officials to keep voting and property-owner records on a racially segregated basis, but sustaining a law that required that every divorce decree recite the race of the spouses.

Why are divorce decrees and census questionnaires different from voting and property owner records? Is *Loving* consistent with the state practice of identifying persons (or their parents) by race on birth certificates, drivers' licenses, and other official documents?

DISCUSSION

1. Why exactly does the Court in *Morales* reject the plaintiff's claims? Is "self-classification" not racial classification within the meaning of *Loving*? Does government use of racial self-description eliminate state action, or does it simply change the government's role in generating racial identity or information? Recall Justice Harlan's claim in his dissent in *Plessy*: "In respect of civil rights, common to all citizens, the constitution of the United States does not, I think, permit any public authority to know the race of those entitled to be protected in the enjoyment of such rights. . . . Our constitution is color-blind, and neither knows nor tolerates classes among citizens." Why *should* the government be permitted to "know" the race of its citizens? If you think that this sort of "knowledge" is permissible, then what is the ban on racial classification about?

Section 709(c) of the Civil Rights Act of 1964 requires that employers "make and keep" records of their employment decisions and provide reports to the Equal Employment Opportunity Commission. These records often include the race, sex, and ethnicity of employees and applicants, and are used by the government and civil rights attorneys to demonstrate violations of civil rights laws and by courts to fashion remedies. In like fashion, §402 of the Act requires a biannual survey to determine educational opportunity by race. Does collecting information necessary to comply with the Civil Rights Act violate the Equal Protection Clause?

Reva Siegel notes that "[t]he civil rights movement's stance on racial designations and data collection seems to have shifted with the uses to which such information was put. . . . The NAACP's caution was no doubt due to the ways in which Southerners were using . . . data [on crime and illegitimate births] to construct new rationalizations for racial exclusion that would survive in the post-*Brown* world."

However, "as racial designation and data collection became an integral part of the enforcement of civil rights legislation, the movement's stance on the practice changed accordingly."[67]

Consider in this light the proposed (but ultimately unsuccessful) California Racial Privacy Initiative, which would have prohibited the state government from collecting data that classified individuals by race, ethnicity, or national origin in "the operation of public education, public contracting or public employment" and would have raised high procedural hurdles to collecting information about race, ethnicity, or national origin in other state programs. Interestingly, police officers were exempted from the prohibition against classifying individuals by race, and "[n]either the governor, the legislature nor any statewide agency shall require law enforcement officers to maintain records that track individuals on the basis of said classifications, nor shall the governor, the legislature or any statewide agency withhold funding to law enforcement agencies on the basis of the failure to maintain such records." What was the purpose of these exemptions?

2. *Failure to count minorities.* With *Morales* compare City of New York v. United States Department of Commerce, 34 F.3d 1114 (2d Cir. 1994), holding that the Census Bureau's decision to adopt methods that systematically undercounted minorities was subject to review "under the more traditional standard applicable to an equal protection claim that a fundamental right has been denied on the basis of race or ethnicity." If the collection of racial data by itself does not raise strict scrutiny, why does systematic undercounting of minorities?

In Prieto v. Stans, 321 F. Supp. 420, 423 (N.D. Cal. 1970), plaintiffs argued that Congress's failure to include Mexican-Americans as a separate census category would lead to significant undercounting and thus fewer educational and other resources would be directed to the Mexican-American community. The Court rejected a claim of unconstitutional discrimination, noting "the patent inability of the Bureau to account with 100% accuracy for every one of the myriad groups and subgroups in America. If there is 'discrimination' here it is of the non-legal variety which must of necessity occur whenever any categorization is made which impliedly excludes other possible categories. Because we are satisfied that the plaintiffs will be counted and their rights safeguarded, we cannot say that the failure to specifically provide for a Mexican-American category on the census forms approaches discrimination considered to be invidious and hence unlawful by the courts of this land." Are *City of New York* and *Prieto* consistent?

NOTE: FOUR CONCEPTS OF "RACE": STATUS-BASED, FORMAL, HISTORICAL, AND CULTURAL

The word "race" is ubiquitous in constitutional law, but the term has many different uses. Neil Gotanda has identified at least four different senses of the word in the Supreme Court's opinions, which reflect wider cultural and political uses: "status-race, formal-race, historical-race, and culture-race."[68]

---

67. Reva B. Siegel, Equality Talk, supra n.15, at 1516 n.158.

68. Neil Gotanda, A Critique of "Our Constitution Is Color-Blind," 44 Stan. L. Rev. 1, 3-4 (1994).

"Status race is the traditional notion of race as an indicator of social status." This is the way of talking about race that justified white supremacy: to be white is to have higher status and to be Black (or of any other race) is to have lower status.

A formal conception of race, by contrast, identifies race according to "socially constructed formal categories . . . under which black and white are seen as neutral, apolitical descriptions, reflecting merely 'skin color' or country of ancestral origin." A person has a particular race because of his or her skin color, parents' race, or country of origin. Formal race can also be defined legally through other devices, for example, a person's ancestry combined with a legal rule that defines race. For example, in Plessy v. Ferguson, Homer Plessy was Black according to Louisiana law because some of his ancestors were legally defined as Black. The key feature of formal race, Gotanda explains, is that it is defined as "unrelated to ability, disadvantage, or moral culpability. Moreover, formal-race categories are unconnected to social attributes such as culture, education, wealth, or language." Formal conceptions of race became popular as a rhetorical response to the status race talk that justified white supremacy and Jim Crow. Because status race talk stereotypes Black people as having undesirable characteristics simply by virtue of being Black, formal race discourse developed in part as a denial of the stereotype. It treats race as conceptually distinct from every social attribute or attitude, so that race has no necessary cultural implications, whether good or bad. One is invoking a conception of formal race when one decries stereotyping and says things like "just because a person is black (or white) doesn't mean that they are. . . ." Obviously, talking in terms of formal race is deeply connected to the discourse of colorblindness.

Historical race, by contrast, "does assign substance to racial categories." Historical race refers to the history of past and continuing racial subordination. The meaning of "race," and the consequences of using racial classification is understood in terms of its historical uses and abuses. When courts apply "strict scrutiny" to racial classifications because of the past history of disadvantaging people by race, they are treating race as a *historical* category. By contrast, when courts justify strict scrutiny because race has no connection to talent or ability, they are treating race as a *formal* category.

Finally, race as culture (culture-race) focuses on aspects of culture associated with a race. On this understanding, race is more than a site of injury or inequality. A cultural conception of "blackness" may associate being "black" with "African-American culture, community, and consciousness." African-American "[c]ulture," explains Gotanda, "refers to broadly shared beliefs and social practices; [the African-American] community refers to both the physical and spiritual senses of the term; and African-American consciousness refers to Black Nationalist and other traditions of self-awareness and to action based on that self-awareness." Culture-race is the concept used when Blackness is associated with the idea of cultural diversity.

Note that while a formal conception of race treats race as a category that applies equally to all (or almost all) of its members, race as culture-race refers to traits, behaviors, attitudes, and beliefs that some but not all members of the group share, and in varying degrees. Thus, one can be "black" in a formal sense (as defined by skin color or descent) but not "black" in a cultural sense.

Throughout these materials it will be important to notice when courts and other government actors shift from one use of the term "race" to another. For example, when courts argue that it is demeaning to assume that Black people think alike because of their race, or that race is morally irrelevant to government decisionmaking, they are invoking a formal notion of race. However, when courts argue that it is permissible for police officers to consider race in developing drug courier profiles, or when they argue that Blackness is a proxy for a distinctive life experience, they are invoking a notion of culture-race. When courts argue that racial distinctions are odious because they cause interracial hostility and stigmatize minorities, they are invoking a notion of historical-race. When people argue that the death penalty is unfair because it punishes Blacks who kill whites more than whites who kill Blacks, they are implicitly criticizing a notion of racial status, i.e., that white lives are worth more than Black lives.

When plaintiffs argue that a certain government policy or business practice is discriminatory because it disproportionately harms Blacks more than whites, they are probably employing either a cultural or a historical conception of race, because not all members of the group are equally affected. When defendants respond that for this very reason the policy or practice does not discriminate on the basis of race, they are probably employing a formal conception of race.

Note that people can invoke more than one sense of the word simultaneously: For example, an advocate of educational affirmative action who says that colleges should try to admit more Black students because they bring distinctive life experiences to college campuses can be referring to race both as culture and as the product of a history of subordination.

Consider these categories in light of the cases we have just studied about the reach of suspect classification doctrine. What notion of race is implicit in Justice O'Connor's argument against temporary segregation of prisoners in Johnson v. California? In Chief Justice Burger's opinion in Palmore v. Sidoti? In the arguments for and against accommodating racial preferences in adoption? In the census cases?

In American politics, both conservatives and liberals opportunistically invoke different conceptions of race to support their views about desegregation, affirmative action, crime, welfare policy, and other issues. The same is true of courts as well. Often when a majority opinion employs one conception of race, the dissent will employ another; each may shift uses from paragraph to paragraph and from sentence to sentence. You should learn to be aware of the subtle (and not-so-subtle) shifts in the meaning of "race" in legal and policy arguments. This will help you understand what is at stake in debates over race.

C. *When Is a Decision Made "on the Basis of" Race?*

The most obvious form of race-dependent decision is a statute, like the jury-exclusion law struck down in Strauder v. West Virginia, that by its very terms classifies people by race. Laws segregating the races or prohibiting interracial cohabitation purport to treat the races formally equally but still classify on the basis of race. With the demise of the distinction between civil and social equality, however, courts today hold that these distinctions violate the antidiscrimination principle.

This section considers situations in which a government decision does not formally mention race as a basis for the decision. Employers, for example, may deny someone a job because of his or her race while explaining the decision entirely on other grounds. Legislation may adversely affect racial minorities although the statute does not employ overt racial classifications.

To what extent does the antidiscrimination principle reach these decisions? The Supreme Court's doctrines have changed widely over the years. As the materials show, the way the Court has reasoned about the question has varied with social and political changes in the country.

Inevitably, the question whether a decision is "on account of race" is not just a question of psychology, any more than the issue of mens rea or intention is in criminal or tort law. Ultimately, the question is one of social theory and social policy—under what conditions and for what reasons will we say that a decision is "on account of race" or "because of race"?

1. Early Cases

As we have seen, one purpose of the Fourteenth Amendment was to prevent "class" or "caste" legislation. Such legislation did not always involve formal classification. The central question was whether a group had been unjustifiably singled out for special burdens. For example, the Court held early on that laws that do not overtly classify on the basis of race may nonetheless violate the Fourteenth Amendment if they are administered in a race-dependent manner:

YICK WO v. HOPKINS, 118 U.S. 356 (1886): [The San Francisco Board of Supervisors, which had authority to issue permits to operate laundries in wooden buildings, had granted permits to none of 200 Chinese applicants and to all but one of about 80 Caucasian applicants. The Court reversed petitioners' convictions for operating laundries without permits.]

MATTHEWS, J.:

[T]he facts shown establish an administration directed so exclusively against a particular class of persons as to warrant and require the conclusion, that, whatever may have been the intent of the ordinances as adopted, they are applied by the public authorities charged with their administration, and thus representing the State itself, with a mind so unequal and oppressive as to amount to a practical denial by the State of that equal protection of the laws which is secured to the petitioners, as to all other persons, by the broad and benign provisions of the Fourteenth Amendment to the Constitution of the United States. Though the law itself be fair on its face and impartial in appearance, yet if it is applied and administered by public authority with an evil eye and an unequal hand, so as practically to make unjust and illegal discriminations between persons in similar circumstances, material to their rights, the denial of equal justice is still within the prohibition of the Constitution. . . .

The present cases, as shown by the facts disclosed in the record, are within this class. It appears that both petitioners have complied with every requisite, deemed by the law or by the public officers charged with its administration, necessary for the protection of neighboring property from fire, or as a precaution against injury to the public health. No reason whatever, except the will of the supervisors, is assigned why they should not be permitted to carry on, in the accustomed manner, their harmless and useful occupation, on which they depend for a livelihood. And while this consent of the supervisors is withheld from them and from two hundred others who have also petitioned, all of whom happen to be Chinese subjects, eighty others, not Chinese subjects, are permitted to carry on the same business under similar conditions. The fact of this discrimination is admitted. No reason for it is shown, and the conclusion cannot be resisted, that no reason for it exists except hostility to the race and nationality to which the petitioners belong, and which in the eye of the law is not justified.

Similarly, a law might be class legislation even if the text of the law did not single out a group by name, if evidence and surrounding context showed that the law had an inappropriate purpose.

HO AH KOW v. NUNAN, 12 F. CAS. 252 (NO. 6546) (C.C.D. CAL. 1879): [A San Francisco ordinance required that every male imprisoned in the county jail have his hair "cut or clipped to a uniform length of one inch from the scalp thereof." Justice Field, sitting on circuit, argued that the legislation was unconstitutional class legislation.]

FIELD, Circuit Justice:

The complaint avers that it is the custom of Chinamen to shave the hair from the front of the head and to wear the remainder of it braided into a queue; that the deprivation of the queue is regarded by them as a mark of disgrace, and is attended, according to their religious faith, with misfortune and suffering after death; that the defendant knew of this custom and religious faith of the Chinese, and knew also that the plaintiff venerated the custom and held the faith; yet, in disregard of his rights, inflicted the injury complained of. . . .

The [policy] was not intended and cannot be maintained as a measure of discipline or as a sanitary regulation. The act by itself has no tendency to promote discipline, and can only be a measure of health in exceptional cases. Had the ordinance contemplated a mere sanitary regulation it would have been limited to such cases and made applicable to females as well as to males, and to persons awaiting trial as well as to persons under conviction. . . . It is special legislation on the part of the supervisors against a class of persons who, under the constitution and laws of the United States, are entitled to the equal protection of the laws. The ordinance was intended only for the Chinese in San Francisco. This was avowed by the supervisors on its passage, and was so understood by every one. The ordinance is known in the community as the "Queue Ordinance," being so designated from its purpose to reach the queues of the Chinese, and it is not enforced against any other persons. The reason advanced for its adoption, and now urged for its continuance, is, that only the dread of the loss of his queue will induce a Chinaman to pay his fine. . . .

The class character of this legislation is none the less manifest because of the general terms in which it is expressed. The statements of supervisors in debate on the passage of the ordinance cannot, it is true, be resorted to for the purpose of explaining the meaning of the terms used; but they can be resorted to for the purpose of ascertaining the general object of the legislation proposed, and the mischiefs sought to be remedied. Besides, we cannot shut our eyes to matters of public notoriety and general cognizance. When we take our seats on the bench we are not struck with blindness, and forbidden to know as judges what we see as men; and where an ordinance, though general in its terms, only operates upon a special race, sect or class, it being universally understood that it is to be enforced only against that race, sect or class, we may justly conclude that it was the intention of the body adopting it that it should only have such operation, and treat it accordingly. We may take notice of the limitation given to the general terms of an ordinance by its practical construction as a fact in its history, as we do in some cases that a law has practically become obsolete. If this were not so, the most important provisions of the constitution, intended for the security of personal rights, would, by the general terms of an enactment, often be evaded and practically annulled. The complaint in this case shows that the ordinance acts with special severity upon Chinese prisoners, inflicting upon them suffering altogether disproportionate to what would be endured by other prisoners if enforced against them. Upon the Chinese prisoners its enforcement operates as "a cruel and unusual punishment."

Many illustrations might be given where ordinances, general in their terms, would operate only upon a special class, or upon a class, with exceptional severity, and thus incur the odium and be subject to the legal objection of intended hostile legislation against them. We have, for instance, in our community a large number of Jews. . . . Now, if they should in some quarter of the city overcrowd their dwellings and thus become amenable, like the Chinese, to the act concerning lodging-houses and sleeping apartments, an ordinance of the supervisors requiring that all prisoners confined in the county jail should be fed on pork would be seen by every one to be leveled at them; and, notwithstanding its general terms, would be regarded as a special law in its purpose and operation.

In Guinn v. United States, 238 U.S. 347 (1915), the Oklahoma Constitution was amended to require literacy tests for voting but exempted anyone descended from a person entitled to vote on January 1, 1866 or a person "who at that time resided in some foreign nation." Although the law did not formally discriminate on the basis of race, the Supreme Court held that the law violated the Fifteenth Amendment, arguing that there was no plausible reason for the exemption other than to disenfranchise Black voters: "[W]e are unable to discover how, unless the prohibitions of the 15th Amendment were considered, the slightest reason was afforded for basing the classification upon a period of time prior to the 15th Amendment. Certainly it cannot be said that there was any peculiar necromancy in the time named which engendered attributes affecting the qualification to vote which would not exist at another and different period unless the 15th Amendment was in view."

In Gomillion v. Lightfoot, 364 U.S. 339 (1960), the Alabama legislature changed the boundaries of the city of Tuskegee from a square to what Justice Frankfurter described as "an uncouth twenty-eight-sided figure"; the effect was to remove all but a handful of Black voters, but not a single white voter, from the city limits. The Court struck down the law, finding these facts "tantamount for all practical purposes to a mathematical demonstration that the legislature is solely concerned with segregating white and colored voters by fencing Negro citizens out of town."

2. Brown v. Board of Education and Desegregation

Brown I and *Brown II* required formerly segregated schools to desegregate. As noted earlier, many Southern school districts responded with plans that offered students "freedom of choice"; these programs had almost no integrative effect because Black children were often afraid to go to all-white schools, while white parents usually refused to send their children to formerly all-Black schools. In Green v. County Sch. Bd. of New Kent County, supra, the Supreme Court held that states had an affirmative obligation to dismantle racially identifiable schools. Faced with continual resistance to integration, the Court inevitably focused on the practical effects of government decisions to decide whether local governments had violated the Fourteenth Amendment. See Green v. County Sch. Bd. of New Kent County, Va., 391 U.S. 430, 437-439 (1968) ("The obligation of the district courts, as it always has been, is to assess the effectiveness of a proposed plan in achieving desegregation."); Wright v. Council of City of Emporia, 407 U.S. 451 (1971) ("[A]n inquiry into the 'dominant' motivation of school authorities is as irrelevant as it is fruitless. The mandate of *Brown II* was to desegregate schools, and we have said that '[t]he measure of any desegregation plan is its effectiveness.'").

Similarly, the Court looked to effects when assessing formally race-neutral means of slowing or avoiding desegregation. In Griffin v. Prince Edward County School Board, 377 U.S. 218 (1964), the school board closed down the school system after a court had ordered that it be desegregated. The Supreme Court ordered it reopened, stating:

> [T]he record in the present case could not be clearer that Prince Edward's public schools were closed and private schools operated in their place with state and county assistance, for one reason and one reason only: to ensure . . . that white and colored children in Prince Edward County would not, under any circumstances, go to the same school. Whatever nonracial grounds might support a State's allowing a county to abandon public schools, the object must be a constitutional one, and grounds of race and opposition to desegregation do not qualify as constitutional.[69]

---

69. On the other hand, in Palmer v. Thompson, 403 U.S. 217 (1971), plaintiffs challenged a decision by the city council of Jackson, Mississippi to close the city's public swimming pools following a federal court order to desegregate them in 1962. The district court found that the closing was justified to preserve peace and order and because the pools could not be operated economically on an integrated basis, and held that the city's action did not deny Black citizens equal protection of the laws. The Supreme Court affirmed in a 5-4 decision. It distinguished *Griffin* on the grounds that in *Griffin* the state had not only closed the schools but set up "a thinly disguised 'private' school system actually planned and carried out by the State and the county to maintain segregated education with public funds." If "Jackson attempts to run segregated public pools either directly or indirectly, or participates in a subterfuge whereby pools are nominally run by 'private parties' but actually by the city, relief will be available in the federal courts."

Responding to plaintiff's argument that the closing was racially motivated, Justice Black's opinion stated that "no case in this Court has held that a legislative act may violate equal protection solely because of the motivations of the men who voted for it." He also argued that "it is extremely difficult for a court to ascertain the motivation, or collection of different motivations, that lie behind a legislative enactment.. . . . It is difficult or impossible for any court to determine the 'sole' or 'dominant' motivation behind the choices of a group of legislators. Furthermore, there is an element of futility in a judicial attempt to invalidate

3. The Interplay Between the Fourteenth Amendment and the Civil Rights Acts

In light of *Brown, Green,* and subsequent cases, by the early 1970s, many judges and lawyers assumed that the Equal Protection Clause required state and local governments to act in ways that avoided entrenching racial segregation. They argued that the Constitution prohibited state action that had a racially disparate impact that was not justified by a sufficiently weighty public purpose. The Supreme Court's construction of the 1964 Civil Rights Act and other civil rights laws was especially influential, and led many courts and commentators to assume that the constitutional standard for equal protection was either identical to or similar to the statutory standard.

GRIGGS v. DUKE POWER CO., 401 U.S. 424 (1971): [*Griggs* construed Title VII of the Civil Rights Act of 1964 to prohibit an employer from requiring high school diplomas of job applicants and subjecting them to a general intelligence test, where the effect was to disadvantage Black applicants and where the criteria had not been demonstrated to predict job performance. Duke Power had openly discriminated before the effective date of Title VII; after the effective date of Title VII, the company dropped race from its job descriptions and required a standardized test and high school degree for new hires or transfers, but did not require current employees to meet these new standards for employment. Specifically, prior to 1965, the company expressly limited Black employees to serving in one of its five departments—the labor department, whose positions all paid less than the lowest paid positions in the other four departments. In 1965, in order to qualify for a transfer from the labor department to the higher paying departments, all employees were required to have a high school degree, or if they lacked that, to have passed two standardized tests. New employees seeking placement outside the labor department needed to have graduated and passed the two exams.

Chief Justice Burger wrote for a unanimous Court:]

BURGER, C.J.:

The objective of Congress in the enactment of Title VII . . . was to achieve equality of employment opportunities and remove barriers that have operated in the past to favor an identifiable group of white employees over other employees. Under the Act, practices, procedures, or tests neutral on their face, and even neutral in terms of intent, cannot be maintained if they operate to "freeze" the status quo of prior discriminatory employment practices. The Court of Appeals' opinion,

---

a law because of the bad motives of its supporters. If the law is struck down for this reason, rather than because of its facial content or effect, it would presumably be valid as soon as the legislature or relevant governing body repassed it for different reasons."

Shortly after *Palmer,* in Lemon v. Kurtzman, 403 U.S. 602 (1971), a case involving the Establishment Clause, a unanimous Court reaffirmed that legislation subsidizing church-related schools requires close judicial scrutiny of the statute's purpose. Five years later, in Washington v. Davis, 426 U.S. 229 (1976), discussed infra, Justice White wrote: "To the extent that *Palmer* suggests a generally applicable proposition that legislative purpose is irrelevant in constitutional adjudication, our prior cases . . . are to the contrary."

and the partial dissent, agreed that, on the record in the present case, "whites register far better on the Company's alternative requirements" than Negroes. This consequence would appear to be directly traceable to race. Basic intelligence must have the means of articulation to manifest itself fairly in a testing process. Because they are Negroes, petitioners have long received inferior education in segregated schools. . . . Congress did not intend by Title VII, however, to guarantee a job to every person regardless of qualifications. . . . Discriminatory preference for any group, minority or majority, is precisely and only what Congress has proscribed. What is required by Congress is the removal of artificial, arbitrary, and unnecessary barriers to employment when the barriers operate invidiously to discriminate on the basis of racial or other impermissible classification.

Congress has now provided that tests or criteria for employment or promotion may not provide equality of opportunity merely in the sense of the fabled offer of milk to the stork and the fox.[70] On the contrary, Congress has now required that the posture and condition of the job-seeker be taken into account. It has—to resort again to the fable—provided that the vessel in which the milk is proffered be one all seekers can use. The Act proscribes not only overt discrimination but also practices that are fair in form, but discriminatory in operation. The touchstone is business necessity. If an employment practice which operates to exclude Negroes cannot be shown to be related to job performance, the practice is prohibited.

On the record before us, neither the high school completion requirement nor the general intelligence test is shown to bear a demonstrable relationship to successful performance of the jobs for which it was used. Both were adopted, as the Court of Appeals noted, without meaningful study of their relationship to job performance ability. . . . The evidence . . . shows that employees who have not completed high school or taken the tests have continued to perform satisfactorily and make progress in departments for which the high school and test criteria are now used. The promotion record of present employees who would not be able to meet the new criteria thus suggests the possibility that the requirements may not be needed for the limited purpose of preserving the avowed policy of advancement within the Company. . . .

The Court of Appeals held that the Company had adopted the diploma and test requirements without any "intention to discriminate against Negro employees." We do not suggest that either the District Court or the Court of Appeals erred in examining the employer's intent; but good intent or absence of discriminatory intent does not redeem employment procedures or testing mechanisms that operate as "built-in headwinds" for minority groups and are unrelated to measuring job capability. . . . Congress directed the thrust of the Act to the consequences of employment practices, not simply the motivation. More than that, Congress has placed on the employer the burden of showing that any given requirement must have manifest relationship to the employment in question.

---

70. The Court is referring to one of Aesop's fables, The Fox and the Stork. The fox served the stork a drink in a shallow dish, which was useless to the stork because of its long beak; the stork retaliated by serving the fox with a tall narrow jar, which was useless to the fox.

DISCUSSION

1. *How disparate impact works.* Under Title VII, plaintiffs can challenge facially neutral employment actions with a disparate impact on one of the Act's protected classes. Once the plaintiff shows that some employment practice causes a disparate impact on minorities or women, the burden shifts to the employer to show that the challenged practice is justified by business necessity. If the employer makes such a showing, the practice is lawful, unless the challenging party can show that the employer has alternative ways to meet its business needs with lesser exclusionary impact. Courts do not require employers to adopt alternatives that are less effective or more expensive.

2. *Rationales for disparate impact liability.* Why impose disparate impact liability? Disparate impact liability is commonly understood to redress at least three kinds of discrimination that are common in societies that have recently repudiated centuries-old traditions of discrimination.

The first is covert intentional discrimination. Once a society adopts laws prohibiting discrimination, discrimination may simply go underground.[71] When discrimination is hidden, it is hard to prove. Disparate impact tests probe facially neutral practices to ensure their enforcement does not mask covert intentional discrimination.

The second is implicit or unconscious bias. Discrimination does not end suddenly; it fades slowly. Even after a society repudiates a system of formal hierarchy, social scientists have shown that traditional norms continue to shape judgments in ways that may not be perceptible even to the decisionmaker herself. Disparate impact tests probe facially neutral practices to ensure their enforcement does not reflect implicit bias or unconscious discrimination.[72]

The third form of bias is sometimes termed structural discrimination. An employer acting without bias may adopt a standard that has a disparate impact on groups because the standard selects for traits whose allocation has been shaped by past discrimination, whether practiced by the employer or by others with whom the employer is in close dealings.[73] Disparate impact tests probe facially neutral

---

71. For example, in *Griggs*, the employer had openly discriminated against Blacks prior to the effective date of Title VII, expressly limiting Black employees to serving in the labor department, whose positions paid less than the lowest-paid positions in all its other departments. See *Griggs*, 401 U.S. at 426.

72. See, e.g., Watson v. Fort Worth Bank & Trust, 487 U.S. 977, 990 (1988) (plurality opinion) (explaining that disparate impact liability is important because "even if one assumed that [intentional] discrimination can be adequately policed through disparate treatment analysis, the problem of subconscious stereotypes and prejudices would remain").

73. Cf. Michael Selmi, Was the Disparate Impact Theory a Mistake?, 53 UCLA L. Rev. 701, 715 (2006) ("[T]he disparate impact theory was not seen initially as a broad alternative concept of discrimination, but rather, the cause of action originated to deal with specific issues involving past intentional discrimination."); see also Richard A. Primus, Equal Protection and Disparate Impact: Round Three, 117 Harv. L. Rev. 493, 538 (2003) (Title VII's disparate impact doctrine "aims to redress self-perpetuating patterns of racial hierarchy inherited from a time of de jure discrimination."); Steven L. Willborn, The Disparate Impact Model of Discrimination: Theory and Limits, 34 Am. U. L. Rev. 799, 808-811 (1984) (identifying one rationale for disparate impact as preventing the perpetuation of past intentional discrimination and critiquing it).

practices to ensure their enforcement does not unnecessarily perpetuate the effects of past intentional discrimination.

Where disparate impact liability is used to ensure that job requirements are in fact job related—i.e., that requirements reflect the functional needs of the job, rather than hidden intentional discrimination, unconscious discrimination, or the legacy of past discrimination—disparate impact promotes equal opportunity. This is the Court's assumption in Griggs v. Duke Power Co.

3. *"Because of race."* Note that the language of Title VII specifically prohibits discrimination "because of . . . race." What story does the Court tell to explain why the testing requirement is "because of race"? Is the explanatory story the Court tells solely one about disproportionate impact? Or is it a story about the present effects of past unequal treatment? Why does the Court mention the history of education in North Carolina? What does the Court mean by "the posture and condition of the job seeker," or by "employment procedures or testing mechanisms that operate as 'built-in headwinds' for minority groups"?

4. *Anticlassification and antisubordination.* Consider the justifications for disparate impact discussed above. Which are most like the anticlassification approach? Which are most like the antisubordination approach?

5. *Conceptions of "race."* When the Court says that the discrimination in *Griggs* is "because of race," what conception of "race" is it using? The Court appears to be invoking a historical or cultural conception of race rather than a formal conception. It looks to how race has historically been used for purposes of subordination, rather than treating race as simply an accident of skin color. On the other hand, the business necessity justification assumes that practices that have adverse effects on minorities but are justified by business needs are not based on race. Is this the same or a different understanding of "race"?[74]

6. The disparate impact test of *Griggs* was codified in the Civil Rights Act of 1991, which requires an employer to "demonstrate that the challenged practice is job-related for the position in question and consistent with business necessity."[75] In order to establish a prima facie case, complainants must specify the particular practices alleged to have a disparate impact.

During the early 1970s, and especially in the wake of *Griggs*, many lower federal courts held that government decisions that inflicted disproportionately harmful effects on minorities violated the Equal Protection Clause unless the government

---

74. Note that if the challenged business practice is judged to be a matter of business necessity, the decision is not because of "race" as a matter of law, even though it disproportionately burdens Blacks. Is that because there could be no causal story one could offer about how Blacks historically were denied certain opportunities that led to the present disproportionate impact? Or is it because at this point the law refuses to treat such effects as being "because of" race? Consider the extent to which notions like "causation" and "intention" act as gatekeepers for permitting and withholding liability in antidiscrimination law, just as they do in tort law and criminal law.

75. Civil Rights Act of 1991, §105(a), 42 U.S.C. §2000e-2(k)(1)(A)(i) (2006).

could show a sufficiently important interest that justified the regulation.[76] Similarly, lower courts applied the disparate impact test of *Griggs* in public employment cases brought under the Equal Protection Clause.[77] Congress extended Title VII to state and local governments in the Equal Employment Opportunity Act of 1972, but many courts assumed that the tests under Title VII and the Constitution were the same. As the First Circuit explained, "[w]e cannot conceive that the words of the Fourteenth Amendment, as it has been applied in racial cases, demand anything less." Castro v. Beecher, 459 F.2d 725, 732-733 (1st Cir. 1972).

In this period, courts also regularly looked to foreseeable effects in finding unconstitutional purposes. Keyes v. School District No. 1, 413 U.S. 189 (1973), was the Court's first school desegregation decision outside the South. The Court held that "the differentiating factor between de jure segregation and so-called de facto segregation . . . is purpose or intent to segregate." Many courts finding segregation under *Keyes* inferred unlawful purpose from the foreseeable consequences of a school board's actions. Segregative effects raised an inference of segregative purposes, shifting the burden of explanation to the school board.[78]

4. The Court Separates the Fourteenth Amendment from the Civil Rights Acts

As we have seen, the federal courts began to shift course in the 1970s due in part to Richard Nixon's judicial appointments, and increasing popular opposition to the Warren and Burger Courts' desegregation decisions. In Lau v. Nichols, 414 U.S. 563 (1974), the Court signaled a new approach to equal protection: It began to separate the question of what the Constitution required from what statutes or administrative regulations required. *Lau* struck down a San Francisco educational

---

76. See, e.g., Metro. Hous. Dev. Corp. v. Vill. of Arlington Heights, 517 F.2d 409, 413 (7th Cir. 1975), *rev'd*, 429 U.S. 252 (1977) ("Regardless of the Village Board's motivation, if this alleged discriminatory effect exists, the decision violates the Equal Protection Clause unless the Village can justify it by showing a compelling interest."); Baker v. Columbus Mun. Separate Sch. Dist., 462 F.2d 1112, 1114 (5th Cir. 1972) ("Whenever the effect of a law or policy produces such a racial distortion it is subject to strict scrutiny. . . . In order to withstand an equal protection attack it must be justified by an overriding purpose independent of its racial effects.").

77. Castro v. Beecher, 459 F.2d 725, 732 (1st Cir. 1972) ("The public employer must, we think, in order to justify the use of a means of selection shown to have a racially disproportionate impact, demonstrate that the means is in fact substantially related to job performance."). In Washington v. Davis, the Court cited five decisions of courts of appeals following this approach.

78. See United States v. Texas Education Agency, 532 F.2d 380, 388 (5th Cir. 1976) (*Keyes* "incorporat[es] in school segregation law the ordinary rule of tort law that a person intends the natural and foreseeable consequences of his actions"); United States v. School Dist. of Omaha, 521 F.2d 530, 535-536 (8th Cir. 1975) ("a presumption of segregative intent arises once it is established that school authorities have engaged in acts or omissions, the natural, probable and foreseeable consequence of which is to bring about or maintain segregation"); Morgan v. Kerrigan, 509 F.2d 580 (1st Cir. 1974) ("the foreseeable racial impact of such decisions [places on defendants] the burden of proving the absence of segregative intent").

policy that required students who only spoke Chinese to attend classes taught in English without any supplementary English language instruction or bilingual education programs. But the Court rested its decision not on the Constitution but on enforcement guidelines adopted under Title VI of the 1964 Civil Rights Act.

In 1976, the Supreme Court limited equal protection doctrine by making explicit the distinction between what the Equal Protection Clause requires and what equality obligations Congress may require by statute. In Washington v. Davis, the Court held that *Griggs*'s "disparate impact" standard was not required by the Fourteenth Amendment.

Washington v. Davis

426 U.S. 229 (1976)

[Respondents, who were Black, had applied to become police officers in the District of Columbia. There applications were rejected because they had failed a written personnel test ("Test 21," developed and widely used by the Civil Service Commission). They sued to invalidate the test on the ground that it was racially discriminatory in violation of the Fifth Amendment. (At the time respondents filed suit, Title VII of the Civil Rights Act of 1964 did not cover municipal employees.) The Court of Appeals invalidated the test solely on the ground that it disproportionately excluded minorities and that petitioners had not proved that it related to job performance. In effect, the Court of Appeals incorporated into the Fifth and (by implication) the Fourteenth Amendments the Supreme Court's interpretation of Title VII in *Griggs*. The Supreme Court reversed.]

WHITE, J. . . .

Because the Court of Appeals erroneously applied the legal standards applicable to Title VII cases in resolving the constitutional issue before it, we reverse its judgment in respondents' favor. . . .

As the Court of Appeals understood Title VII, employees or applicants proceeding under it need not concern themselves with the employer's possibly discriminatory purpose but instead may focus solely on the racially differential impact of the challenged hiring or promotion practices. This is not the constitutional rule. We have never held that the constitutional standard for adjudicating claims of invidious racial discrimination is identical to the standards applicable under Title VII, and we decline to do so today.

The central purpose of the Equal Protection Clause of the Fourteenth Amendment is the prevention of official conduct discriminating on the basis of race. It is also true that the Due Process Clause of the Fifth Amendment contains an equal protection component prohibiting the United States from invidiously discriminating between individuals or groups. But our cases have not embraced the proposition that a law or other official act, without regard to whether it reflects a racially discriminatory purpose, is unconstitutional *solely* because it has a racially disproportionate impact.

Almost 100 years ago, Strauder v. West Virginia, 100 U.S. 303 (1880), established that the exclusion of Negroes from grand and petit juries in criminal proceedings violated the Equal Protection Clause, but the fact that a particular jury or a series of juries does not statistically reflect the racial composition of the community does not in itself make out an invidious discrimination forbidden by the Clause. . . .

The school desegregation cases have also adhered to the basic equal protection principle that the invidious quality of a law claimed to be racially discriminatory must ultimately be traced to a racially discriminatory purpose. That there are both predominantly black and predominantly white schools in a community is not alone violative of the Equal Protection Clause. The essential element of de jure segregation is "a current condition of segregation resulting from intentional state action." Keyes v. School Dist. No. 1, 413 U.S. 189, 205 (1973). "The differentiating factor between de jure segregation and so-called de facto segregation . . . is *purpose* or *intent* to segregate." Id. The Court has also recently rejected allegations of racial discrimination based solely on the statistically disproportionate racial impact of various provisions of the Social Security Act because "[t]he acceptance of appellants' constitutional theory would render suspect each difference in treatment among the grant classes, however lacking in racial motivation and however otherwise rational the treatment might be." Jefferson v. Hackney, 406 U.S. 535, 548 (1972). . . .

This is not to say that the necessary discriminatory racial purpose must be express or appear on the face of the statute, or that a law's disproportionate impact is irrelevant in cases involving Constitution-based claims of racial discrimination. A statute, otherwise neutral on its face, must not be applied so as invidiously to discriminate on the basis of race. Yick Wo v. Hopkins, 118 U.S. 356 (1886). It is also clear from the cases dealing with racial discrimination in the selection of juries that the systematic exclusion of Negroes is itself such an "unequal application of the law . . . as to show intentional discrimination." Akins v. Texas. A prima facie case of discriminatory purpose may be proved as well by the absence of Negroes on a particular jury combined with the failure of the jury commissioners to be informed of eligible Negro jurors in a community or with racially non-neutral selection procedures. With a prima facie case made out, "the burden of proof shifts to the State to rebut the presumption of unconstitutional action by showing that permissible racially neutral selection criteria and procedures have produced the monochromatic result."

Necessarily, an invidious discriminatory purpose may often be inferred from the totality of the relevant facts, including the fact, if it is true, that the law bears more heavily on one race than another. It is also not infrequently true that the discriminatory impact—in the jury cases for example, the total or seriously disproportionate exclusion of Negroes from jury venires—may for all practical purposes demonstrate unconstitutionality because in various circumstances the discrimination is very difficult to explain on nonracial grounds. Nevertheless, we have not held that a law, neutral on its face and serving ends otherwise within the power of government to pursue, is invalid under the Equal Protection Clause simply because it may affect a greater proportion of one race than of another. Disproportionate impact is not irrelevant, but it is not the sole touchstone of an invidious racial discrimination forbidden by the Constitution. Standing alone, it does not trigger the rule, McLaughlin v. Florida, 379 U.S. 184 (1964), that racial classifications are to be subjected to the strictest scrutiny and are justifiable only by the weightiest of considerations.

There are some indications to the contrary in our cases. In Palmer v. Thompson, 403 U.S. 217 (1971), the city of Jackson, Miss., following a court decree to this effect, desegregated all of its public facilities save five swimming pools which had been operated by the city and which, following the decree, were closed by ordinance pursuant to a determination by the city council that closure was necessary to preserve peace and order and that integrated pools could not be economically operated. Accepting the finding that the pools were closed to avoid violence and economic loss, this Court rejected the argument that the abandonment of this service was inconsistent with the outstanding desegregation decree and that the otherwise seemingly permissible ends served by the ordinance could be impeached by demonstrating that racially invidious motivations had prompted the city council's action. The holding was that the city was not overtly or covertly operating segregated pools and was extending identical treatment to both whites and Negroes. The opinion warned against grounding decision on legislative purpose or motivation, thereby lending support for the proposition that the operative effect of the law rather than its purpose is the paramount factor. But the holding of the case was that the legitimate purposes of the ordinance—to preserve peace and avoid deficits—were not open to impeachment by evidence that the councilmen were actually motivated by racial considerations. Whatever dicta the opinion may contain, the decision did not involve, much less invalidate, a statute or ordinance having neutral purposes but disproportionate racial consequences.[a]

Wright v. Council of City of Emporia, 407 U.S. 451 (1972), also indicates that in proper circumstances, the racial impact of a law, rather than its discriminatory purpose, is the critical factor. That case involved the division of a school district. The issue was whether the division was consistent with an outstanding order of a federal court to desegregate the dual school system found to have existed in the area. The constitutional predicate for the District Court's invalidation of the divided district was "the enforcement until 1969 of racial segregation in a public school system of which Emporia had always been a part." There was thus no need to find "an independent constitutional violation." Ibid. Citing Palmer v. Thompson, we agreed with the District Court that the division of the district had the effect of interfering with the federal decree and should be set aside.

That neither *Palmer* nor *Wright* was understood to have changed the prevailing rule is apparent from Keyes v. School Dist. No. 1, supra, where the principal issue in litigation was whether and to what extent there had been purposeful discrimination resulting in a partially or wholly segregated school system. . . .

Both before and after Palmer v. Thompson, however, various Courts of Appeals have held in several contexts, including public employment, that the substantially disproportionate racial impact of a statute or official practice standing alone and without regard to discriminatory purpose, suffices to prove racial discrimination violating the Equal Protection Clause absent some justification going substantially beyond what would be necessary to validate most other legislative classifications. The cases impressively demonstrate that there is another side to the issue; but, with

a. To the extent that Palmer suggests a generally applicable proposition that legislative purpose is irrelevant in constitutional adjudication, our prior cases—as indicated in the text—are to the contrary. . . .

all due respect, to the extent that those cases rested on or expressed the view that proof of discriminatory racial purpose is unnecessary in making out an equal protection violation, we are in disagreement.

As an initial matter, we have difficulty understanding how a law establishing a racially neutral qualification for employment is nevertheless racially discriminatory and denies "any person . . . equal protection of the laws" simply because a greater proportion of Negroes fail to qualify than members of other racial or ethnic groups. Had respondents, along with all others who had failed Test 21, whether white or black, brought an action claiming that the test denied each of them equal protection of the laws as compared with those who had passed with high enough scores to qualify them as police recruits, it is most unlikely that their challenge would have been sustained. Test 21, which is administered generally to prospective Government employees, concededly seeks to ascertain whether those who take it have acquired a particular level of verbal skill; and it is untenable that the Constitution prevents the Government from seeking modestly to upgrade the communicative abilities of its employees rather than to be satisfied with some lower level of competence, particularly where the job requires special ability to communicate orally and in writing. Respondents, as Negroes, could no more successfully claim that the test denied them equal protection than could white applicants who also failed. The conclusion would not be different in the face of proof that more Negroes than whites had been disqualified by Test 21. That other Negroes also failed to score well would, alone, not demonstrate that respondents individually were being denied equal protection of the laws by the application of an otherwise valid qualifying test being administered to prospective police recruits.

Nor on the facts of the case before us would the disproportionate impact of Test 21 warrant the conclusion that it is a purposeful device to discriminate against Negroes and hence an infringement of the constitutional rights of respondents as well as other black applicants. . . .

Under Title VII, Congress provided that when hiring and promotion practices disqualifying substantially disproportionate numbers of blacks are challenged, discriminatory purpose need not be proved, and that it is an insufficient response to demonstrate some rational basis for the challenged practices. It is necessary, in addition, that they be "validated" in terms of job performance in any one of several ways, perhaps by ascertaining the minimum skill, ability or potential necessary for the position at issue and determining whether the qualifying tests are appropriate for the selection of qualified applicants for the job in question. However this process proceeds, it involves a more probing judicial review of, and less deference to, the seemingly reasonable acts of administrators and executives than is appropriate under the Constitution where special racial impact, without discriminatory purpose, is claimed. We are not disposed to adopt this more rigorous standard for the purposes of applying the Fifth and the Fourteenth Amendments in cases such as this.

A rule that a statute designed to serve neutral ends is nevertheless invalid, absent compelling justification, if in practice it benefits or burdens one race more than another would be far-reaching and would raise serious questions about, and perhaps invalidate, a whole range of tax, welfare, public service, regulatory, and licensing statutes that may be more burdensome to the poor and to the average black than to more affluent whites.

Given that rule, such consequences would perhaps be likely to follow. However, in our view, extension of the rule beyond those areas where it is already applicable by reason of statute, such as in the field of public employment, should await legislative prescription. . . .

STEVENS, J., concurring.

While I agree with the Court's disposition of this case, I add these comments on the constitutional issue. . . .

The requirement of purposeful discrimination is a common thread running through the cases summarized [by the Court]. . . . Frequently the most probative evidence of intent will be objective evidence of what actually happened rather than evidence describing the subjective state of mind of the actor. For normally the actor is presumed to have intended the natural consequences of his deeds. This is particularly true in the case of governmental action which is frequently the product of compromise of collective decisionmaking, and of mixed motivation. It is unrealistic, on the one hand, to require the victim of alleged discrimination to uncover the actual subjective intent of the decisionmaker or, conversely, to invalidate otherwise legitimate action simply because an improper motive affected the deliberation of a participant in the decisional process. A law conscripting clerics should not be invalidated because an atheist voted for it.

My point in making this observation is to suggest that the line between discriminatory purpose and discriminatory impact is not nearly as bright, and perhaps not quite as critical, as the reader of the Court's opinion might assume. I agree, of course, that a constitutional issue does not arise every time some disproportionate impact is shown. On the other hand, when the disproportion is as dramatic as in Gomillion v. Lightfoot, 364 U.S. 339, or Yick Wo v. Hopkins, 1 18 U.S. 356, it really does not matter whether the standard is phrased in terms of purpose or effect. Therefore, although I accept the statement of the general rule in the Court's opinion, I am not yet prepared to indicate how that standard should be applied in the many cases which have formulated the governing standard in different language. . . .

There are two reasons why I am convinced that the challenge to Test 21 is insufficient. First, the test serves the neutral and legitimate purpose of requiring all applicants to meet a uniform minimum standard of literacy. Reading ability is manifestly relevant to the police function, there is no evidence that the required passing grade was set at an arbitrarily high level, and there is sufficient disparity among high schools and high school graduates to justify the use of a separate uniform test. Second, the same test is used throughout the federal service. The applicants for employment in the District of Columbia Police Department represent such a small fraction of the total number of persons who have taken the test that their experience is of minimal probative value in assessing the neutrality of the test itself. That evidence, without more, is not sufficient to overcome the presumption that a test which is this widely used by the Federal Government is in fact neutral in its effect as well as its "purpose" as that term is used in constitutional adjudication. . . .

[Justices Brennan and Marshall dissented on grounds unrelated to the constitutional issue of racially disproportionate impact.]

VILLAGE OF ARLINGTON HEIGHTS v. METROPOLITAN HOUSING DEVELOPMENT CORP., 429 U.S. 252 (1977): In *Arlington Heights*, the Court considered a challenge to the city's refusal to rezone a 15-acre parcel from single-family to multiple-family classification. Using federal financial assistance, MHDC planned to build 190 clustered townhouse units for low- and moderate-income tenants. The Court, in an opinion by Justice Powell, reversed the Court of Appeals, which had found the "ultimate effect" of the decision was racially discriminatory. The Court reaffirmed the rule of Washington v. Davis that mere showing of discriminatory effect was not sufficient; plaintiffs had to show that intent to discriminate was a "motivating factor," even if it was not the sole, dominant, or primary factor. It offered a list of factors for courts to use to determine whether governmental decisions were racially motivated. These included (1) the impact of the official action, including whether "a clear pattern, unexplainable on grounds other than race, emerges from the effect of state action even when the governing legislation appears neutral on its face" (although the Court cautioned that such situations would be "rare"); (2) "the historical background of the decision . . . particularly if it reveals a series of official actions taken for invidious purposes"; (3) "[t]he specific sequence of events leading up the challenged decision"; (4) "[d]epartures from the normal procedural sequence"; (5) "[s]ubstantive departures [where] the factors usually considered important by the decisionmaker strongly favor a decision contrary to the one reached"; and (6) "[t]he legislative or administrative history . . . especially where there are contemporary statements by members of the decisionmaking body, minutes of its meetings, or reports."

The Court explained in a footnote that even proof that a decision "was motivated in part by a racially discriminatory purpose" did not necessarily result in its invalidation. Such proof would "have shifted to the Village the burden of establishing that the same decision would have resulted even had the impermissible purpose not been considered. . . . See Mt. Healthy City School Dist. Bd. of Education v. Doyle, 429 U.S. 274 (1977)." The Court then independently reviewed the evidence and concluded that although

> [t]he impact of the Village's decision does arguably bear more heavily on racial minorities . . . there is little about the sequence of events leading up to the decision that would spark suspicion. . . . The rezoning request progressed according to the usual procedures. . . . The statements by the Plan Commission and Village Board members, as reflected in the official minutes, focused almost exclusively on the zoning aspects of the MHDC petition, and the zoning factors on which they relied are not novel criteria in the Village's rezoning decisions. . . . In sum, . . . [r]espondents simply failed to carry their burden of proving that discriminatory purpose was a motivating factor in the Village's decision.

PERSONNEL ADMINISTRATOR OF MASSACHUSETTS v. FEENEY, 442 U.S. 256 (1979): In a sex discrimination case, the Court glossed *Davis*'s requirement of discriminatory purpose by sharply distinguishing between unconstitutional intention and the foreseeable effects of government action.

Feeney involved a challenge to a Massachusetts statute that provided a civil service preference for veterans; a preference that effectively excluded most women from the upper levels of civil service employment in the State of Massachusetts. At the time, only 1.8 percent of Massachusetts veterans were women. The plaintiff argued that the Massachusetts legislature could easily have foreseen this effect, given that federal law excluded most women from military service during the relevant period. Justice Stewart, writing for the majority, argued that the foreseeable impact of the statute was not sufficient to prove discriminatory purpose under the Equal Protection Clause:

"Most laws classify, and many affect certain groups unevenly, even though the law itself treats them no differently from all other members of the class described by the law. When the basic classification is rationally based, uneven effects upon particular groups within a class are ordinarily of no constitutional concern. The calculus of effects, the manner in which a particular law reverberates in a society, is a legislative and not a judicial responsibility. . . .

"The cases of Washington v. Davis, supra, and Arlington Heights v. Metropolitan Housing Dev. Corp., recognize that when a neutral law has a disparate impact upon a group that has historically been the victim of discrimination, an unconstitutional purpose may still be at work. But those cases signaled no departure from the settled rule that the Fourteenth Amendment guarantees equal laws, not equal results. . . .

"'Discriminatory purpose' . . . implies more than intent as volition or intent as awareness of consequences. It implies that the decisionmaker, in this case a state legislature, selected or reaffirmed a particular course of action at least in part 'because of,' not merely 'in spite of,' its adverse effects upon an identifiable group. Yet nothing in the record demonstrates that this preference for veterans was originally devised or subsequently re-enacted because it would accomplish the collateral goal of keeping women in a stereotypic and predefined place in the Massachusetts Civil Service. To the contrary, the statutory history shows that the benefit of the preference was consistently offered to 'any person' who was a veteran."

The Court quickly applied the new rule of *Feeney* to the desegregation context,[79] and, as we will see later on in this chapter, to equal protection challenges to the death penalty.[80]

DISCUSSION

1. *Judicial retreat?* In the years between *Loving* and *Feeney*, federal courts often scrutinized facially neutral state policies. Sometimes they asked whether policies

---

79. See Columbus v. Penick, 443 U.S. 449, 464-465 (1979) ("[D]isparate impact and foreseeable consequences, without more, do not establish a constitutional violation. Nevertheless, the District Court correctly noted that actions having foreseeable and anticipated disparate impact are relevant evidence to prove the ultimate fact, forbidden purpose. . . . See Personnel Administrator of Massachusetts v. Feeney, 442 U.S. 256, 279 n.25 (1979)."); Dayton v. Brinkman, 443 U.S. 526, 537 n.9 (1979) ("We have never held that as a general proposition the foreseeability of segregative consequences makes out a prima facie case of purposeful racial discrimination and shifts the burden of producing evidence to the defendants if they are to escape judgment; and even more clearly there is no warrant in our cases for holding that such foreseeability routinely shifts the burden of persuasion to the defendants.").

80. See McCleskey v. Kemp, 481 U.S. 279, 298 (1987) ("For this claim to prevail, McCleskey would have to prove that the Georgia Legislature enacted or maintained the death penalty statute because of an anticipated racially discriminatory effect.").

with a disparate racial impact were warranted by compelling public purposes; at other times, they probed policies with foreseeable adverse racial impact for evidence of illicit purpose. Foreseeable adverse racial impact continued to play a significant role in proving discriminatory purpose, even after *Davis.*

After *Feeney*, federal courts began to understand their role differently. To limit the role of federal courts in reviewing decisions of representative government, the Supreme Court began to distinguish more strongly between government intention and the foreseeable consequences of government policies, and to require a showing of specific intent to harm, which made it much harder for minority plaintiffs to prove that their constitutional rights had been violated. By adopting this narrow view of discriminatory purpose, federal courts retreated, leaving contested questions of racial equality to political actors. So long as government did not explicitly classify on the basis of race, as *Feeney* explained, "[t]he calculus of effects, the manner in which a particular law reverberates in a society, is a legislative and not a judicial responsibility."[81]

The distinction between what the Constitution *permitted* and what it *required* served federalism values because it gave local officials control over the scope and extent of integration efforts. It also served separation of powers values because it left to Congress and the political branches decisions about how much effort to invest in promoting racial equality or racial integration. In the approach to equal protection favored by the Burger Court, courts would protect only a core of equality norms and leave to the political branches responsibility for resolving most contentious questions about race relations. See Reva B. Siegel, The Supreme Court Term October 2012—Foreword: Equality Divided, 127 Harv. L. Rev. 1, 9-23 (2013).

One argument for the *Davis/Feeney* model is judicial restraint. Requiring proof of specific intent to harm respects democracy by not second-guessing political actors who must weigh many different factors and please many different constituencies. It keeps judges from moving too far ahead of what majorities want in promoting racial equality and dismantling existing structures of social stratification. The *Davis/Feeney* model also refrains from ascribing unconstitutional motivations unless there is very clear evidence of a deliberate desire to harm minorities. Absent this sort of evidence, the court applies rational basis scrutiny to laws that have a disproportionate impact, as explained in *Carolene Products* and Williamson v. Lee Optical.

But *Carolene Products* also suggested that "prejudice against discrete and insular minorities may be a special condition, which tends seriously to curtail the operation of those political processes ordinarily to be relied upon to protect minorities,

---

81. Similarly, the Court explained in Swann v. Charlotte-Mecklenburg Bd. of Educ., 402 U.S. 1, 16 (1971), that local government officials had wide discretion to address de facto segregation:

> School authorities are traditionally charged with broad power to formulate and implement educational policy and might well conclude, for example, that in order to prepare students to live in a pluralistic society each school should have a prescribed ratio of Negro to white students reflecting the proportion for the district as a whole. To do this as an educational policy is within the broad discretionary powers of school authorities; absent a finding of a constitutional violation, however, that would not be within the authority of a federal court.

and which may call for a correspondingly more searching judicial inquiry." Sometimes political majorities may not care much about the harmful effects of their policies on minority groups. Moreover, politicians may deliberately play to racial resentments in promoting legislation that, on its face, does not mention race. If one goal of judicial review is to protect against failures in the democratic process, what should the doctrine look like?

For a reading of *Davis* emphasizing that the decision left open proof of intent by reasoning from context rather than demanding proof of the mental state of government actors, see Ian Haney-López, Intentional Blindness, 87 N.Y.U. L. Rev. 1779, 1806-1808 (2012). In this wide-ranging history of the Supreme Court's intent doctrine, Professor Haney-López describes the Court's shifting, after *Davis*, from context- to motive-based views of intent. He argues that the Burger Court's subsequent demand for proof of "malicious intent" was allied to the rise of colorblindness in the affirmative action cases, or what he terms "intentional blindness." See id. at 1786.

2. *Which version of intent does the Constitution require? Feeney* reinterprets *Davis* to require a showing of specific intent to harm. But the term "intent" has many different meanings in different parts of the law. For example, in intentional tort, intent merely means the intention to perform the act that violates a legally protected interest. Tort law also often assumes that tortfeasors intend the foreseeable consequences of their actions; thus a person who fires a bullet at a person at close range is assumed to have intended to strike that person. The Model Penal Code notes at least five different types of intention: purposefully (with a purpose to produce a certain result), knowingly (acting knowing that a certain result will occur), recklessly (acting without concern for consequences), negligently (failing to take due care to prevent a result), and liability without fault. Model Penal Code §2.02(1) (1962). Why should the Equal Protection Clause require the most stringent test of intention—specific purpose to harm members of a group? Why shouldn't acting with full knowledge of the consequences to a disadvantaged group be sufficient? Should knowledge of consequences be at least sufficient to raise a rebuttable presumption that an act is illegal? Why should tort law provide plaintiffs more protection than the Equal Protection Clause provides African Americans or women?

3. *Intent to harm versus stereotypical thinking. Feeney* argues that invidious intention requires a purpose to act "'because of,' not merely 'in spite of,' its adverse effects upon an identifiable group." But this does not capture many different kinds of discrimination, even overt discrimination. For example, employers might refuse to hire minorities or women not because they wish to harm them but because of stereotypical beliefs about their abilities, attitudes, behavior, priorities, or work ethic. A zoning commission's desire to exclude might rest on the belief that minorities will undermine property values and increase crime. A legislature might place an environmentally hazardous site in a minority neighborhood not out of a desire to harm minorities but because legislators believe that minorities will object less strenuously or effectively. Can one interpret *Davis* and *Feeney* to include these cases?

4. *Implicit bias.* There is rich evidence of the role that implicit associations play in ordinary decisionmaking. See https://implicit.harvard.edu/implicit. Why have courts not adapted the discriminatory purpose standard to take account of this understanding of human cognition? Are there other institutional contexts in which

we might incorporate this knowledge? Is the implicit bias model an appropriate one for courts to employ in the design of liability standards? See Jerry Kang and Kristin Lane, Seeing Through Colorblindness: Implicit Bias and the Law, 58 UCLA L. Rev. 465 (2010).

5. *Tilting toward anticlassification.* In *Feeney*, Justice Stewart observed that "[t]he calculus of effects, the manner in which a particular law reverberates in a society, is a legislative and not a judicial responsibility." In doing so, he rejects the equal protection law of the previous decades, in which, as we have seen, courts often scrutinized policies lacking express racial classifications but having foreseeable adverse impact on racial minorities. Courts often looked to purpose and impact together as interrelated ways of probing the legitimacy of state action. In adopting a standard of proof—malice—that is often hard to prove, *Feeney* made it harder for plaintiffs to challenge facially neutral laws with adverse effects on minorities. In this respect, *Feeney* moved doctrine toward an anticlassification approach and away from an antisubordination approach to equality.

6. Davis *and* Feeney*: Preservation through transformation.* Reva Siegel argues that the *Davis/Feeney* discriminatory purpose doctrine limits the reach of the Equal Protection Clause in much the same way that the nineteenth-century distinction between political, civil, and social equality did.[82]

> The ways in which the legal system enforces social stratification are various and evolve over time. Efforts to reform a status regime bring about changes in its rule structure and justificatory rhetoric—a dynamic I have elsewhere called "preservation-through-transformation." In short, status-enforcing state action evolves in form as it is contested.
>
> The civil-political-social rights distinction . . . offered a framework within which white Americans could disestablish slavery, guarantee the emancipated slaves equality at law, and yet continue to justify policies and practices that perpetuated the racial stratification of American society. . . .
>
> Just as the interpretation of equal protection offered in *Plessy* emerged from the Court's efforts to disestablish slavery, the interpretation of equal protection we inherit today emerged from the Court's efforts to disestablish segregation. . . .
>
> The governing equal protection framework identifies race- and gender-conscious remedies as pernicious "discrimination," while deflecting attention from the many ways that the state continues to regulate the social status of minorities and women, thereby constructing discrimination against minorities and women as a practice of the (distant) past. The social position of minorities and women thus appears to be a legacy of past discrimination—or the product of culture, choice, and ability—while the state's continuing role in shaping the life prospects of minorities and women disappears from view. . . .

---

82. Reva Siegel, Why Equal Protection No Longer Protects: The Evolving Forms of Status-Enforcing State Action, 49 Stan. L. Rev. 1111, 1113, 1129, 1143-1146 (1997).

It is not difficult for us to imagine alternatives to the current constitutional framework. Since the early 1970s, the disparate impact doctrines of Title VII have illustrated what a different equal protection framework might look like—one in which courts scrutinized the impact of governmental practices, rather than the mental state of governmental decisionmakers.

Suppose that the Court had decided *Davis* differently, and that, in some or all regulatory contexts, doctrines of heightened scrutiny now constrained the government from adopting facially neutral policies that significantly contributed to the race and gender stratification of American society; in those contexts where disparate impact analysis applied, the government would have to justify its policies, and show that it lacked feasible, less discriminatory means for achieving its objectives. Suppose, further, that courts reviewing the justifications for such facially neutral policies were as concerned with the government's duty to govern impartially as they are now concerned with judges' obligations of deference. Such an equal protection framework would not bar all policies that perpetuated race or gender stratification; but it would alter the nature of public conversation about such policies. In such a world, state actors would be required to acknowledge and justify their role in perpetuating forms of race and gender stratification. In a world where governmental actors were regularly called upon to justify the racial and gender consequences of their policy choices, the government's role in perpetuating race and gender inequality would be far more visible than it now is. In such a world, equal protection litigation might move the nation closer to disestablishing historic patterns of race and gender stratification than current constitutional doctrines now do.

Thus, if our legal culture supplies reasons for adopting the prevailing interpretation of equal protection, it also supplies resources for imagining an alternative interpretation of equal protection. In much the same way, the legal culture of nineteenth-century America supplied reasons for adopting *Plessy*'s interpretation of equal protection, as well as the resources for imagining the interpretation of equal protection that Justice Harlan proposed. In matters of constitutional interpretation, no less than in other spheres of life, the nation makes choices for which it can be held morally accountable. We now regularly condemn the interpretive choices the nation made during the Reconstruction era, but how are we to evaluate our own?

Today, government rarely classifies by race or gender, but it conducts a "war on drugs," regulates education and residential zoning, responds to "sexual assault" and "domestic violence," and makes policy concerning "child care," "family leave," "child support," and the "welfare" of "single-headed house holds" in ways that often perpetuate, or aggravate, historic patterns of race and gender inequality. We might construe equal protection guarantees to require heightened scrutiny of the justifications for the design and administration of some or all of these facially neutral

> policies, yet we do not. As we condemn the ways in which past generations of Americans interpreted the meaning of equal protection, we might also consider how future generations of Americans will judge our own.

Note that under federal law developers are required to prepare "environmental impact statements." Is there any reason to think that racial minorities deserve less reasoned consideration under the Equal Protection Clause?

7. Griggs *versus* Davis. One possible reason why the Court held that disproportionate impact stated a claim in *Griggs* and not in *Davis* is that Title VII is limited in scope to employment, while the Fourteenth Amendment covers discrimination of every possible sort. The Court may have believed that *Griggs* was good employment policy when interpreting a statute; but it might also have thought that a general disparate impact principle applied to many different areas of government policy would have been undesirable, unpredictable, or uncontainable.

Nevertheless, could the Court have plausibly limited a Fourteenth Amendment disproportionate-impact principle to particular subject areas of discrimination? Note that in jury selection cases, the Court has adopted a different standard. See Castaneda v. Partida, 430 U.S. 482, 494-495 (1977) ("Once the defendant has shown substantial underrepresentation of his group [in the grand jury pool], he has made out a prima facie case of discriminatory purpose, and the burden then shifts to the State to rebut that case.").

8. *"But-for" motivation.* In Hunter v. Underwood, 471 U.S. 222 (1985), the Court struck down a provision of the Alabama Constitution that disenfranchised persons convicted of certain enumerated felonies and misdemeanors, including "any . . . crime involving moral turpitude." Appellees, one of whom was Black and the other white, were disenfranchised after being convicted of presenting worthless checks. The lower court found that, although the provision was neutral on its face, it had a racially discriminatory impact on Black people. Justice Rehnquist, writing for a unanimous Court, stated that the proper inquiry was whether the provision was adopted with a discriminatory purpose and that "[o]nce racial discrimination is shown to have been a 'substantial' or 'motivating' factor behind enactment of the law, the burden shifts to the law's defenders to demonstrate that the law would have been enacted without this factor." After reviewing the circumstances of its adoption in 1901, the Court found that racial animus "was a motivating factor for the provision, and that [it] would not have been adopted . . . in the absence of the racially discriminatory motivation." In response to evidence that the provision was also motivated by a desire to disenfranchise poor whites, the Court held that "an additional purpose to discriminate against poor whites would not render nugatory the purpose to discriminate against all blacks, and it is beyond peradventure that the latter was a 'but-for' motivation for the enactment of [the provision]." The Court concluded: "Without deciding whether [the provision] would be valid if enacted today without any impermissible motivation, we simply observe that its original enactment was motivated by a desire to discriminate against blacks on account of race and the section continues to this day to have that effect. As such, it violates equal protection under *Arlington Heights.*"

NOTE: COMMENTARIES ON THE INTENT STANDARD

Linda Hamilton Krieger argues that the *Davis/Feeney* framework for proving discriminatory purpose does not take account of scientific theories of human cognition.[83]

> [It] is a central premise of social cognition theory . . . that cognitive structures and processes involved in categorization and information processing can in and of themselves result in stereotyping and other forms of biased intergroup judgment previously attributed to motivational processes. The social cognition approach to discrimination [makes] three claims[:]
>
> [First,] stereotyping . . . is nothing special. It is simply a form of categorization, similar in structure and function to the categorization of natural objects. According to this view, stereotypes, like other categorical structures, are cognitive mechanisms that all people, not just "prejudiced" ones, use to simplify the task of perceiving, processing, and retaining information about people in memory. They are central, and indeed essential to normal cognitive functioning.
>
> [Second,] once in place, stereotypes bias intergroup judgment and decisionmaking. According to this view, stereotypes operate as "person prototypes" or "social schemas." As such, they function as implicit theories, biasing in predictable ways the perception, interpretation, encoding, retention, and recall of information about other people. These biases are cognitive rather than motivational. They operate absent intent to favor or disfavor members of a particular social group. And, perhaps most significant for present purposes, they bias a decisionmaker's judgment long before the "moment of decision," as a decisionmaker attends to relevant data and interprets, encodes, stores, and retrieves it from memory. These biases "sneak up on" the decisionmaker, distorting bit by bit the data upon which his decision is eventually based.
>
> [Third,] [s]tereotypes, when they function as implicit prototypes or schemas, operate beyond the reach of decisionmaker self-awareness. Empirical evidence indicates that people's access to their own cognitive processes is in fact poor. Accordingly, cognitive bias may well be both unintentional and unconscious. . . .
>
> Viewed through the lens of social cognition theory, [the law] construes the role of motivation in intergroup discrimination precisely backwards. [C]ognitive biases in social judgment operate automatically and must be controlled, if at all, through subsequent "mental correction." Intergroup discrimination, or at least that variant which results from cognitive sources of bias, is automatic. It does not result from a motive or intent to discriminate; it is an unwelcome byproduct of otherwise adaptive cognitive processes. But, like many unwanted byproducts, it can be controlled. . . .

83. Linda Hamilton Krieger, The Content of Our Categories: A Cognitive Bias Approach to Discrimination and Equal Employment Opportunity, 47 Stan. L. Rev. 1161 (1995).

> [W]e should expect that a self-professed "colorblind" decisionmaker will fall prey to the various sources of cognitive bias we have examined. For even if this decisionmaker's conscious inferential process is colorblind, the categorical structures through which he collects, sorts, and recalls information are not. In a culture in which race, gender, and ethnicity are salient, even the well-intentioned will inexorably categorize along racial, gender, and ethnic lines. And once these categorical structures are in place, they can be expected to distort social perception and judgment. . . .
>
> [P]eople cannot be admonished out of categorical divisions so long as those divisions help them explain and function in their natural or social environment. And so long as people categorize along lines of race, gender, or ethnicity, we can expect the resulting categorization-related distortions in social perception and judgment to bias intergroup decisionmaking. . . .
>
> To establish liability for . . . discrimination, a . . . plaintiff [should] simply be required to prove that his group status played a role in causing the employer's action or decision. Causation would no longer be equated with intentionality. The critical inquiry would be whether the applicant or employee's group status "made a difference" in the employer's action, not whether the decisionmaker intended that it make a difference.

Charles Lawrence, on the other hand, argues that courts should use the cultural meaning of social practices as a proxy for unconscious racism.[84]

> [T]his article proposes a new test to trigger judicial recognition of race-based behavior. It posits a connection between unconscious racism and the existence of cultural symbols that have racial meaning. It suggests that the "cultural meaning" of an allegedly racially discriminatory act is the best available analogue for, and evidence of, a collective unconscious that we cannot observe directly. This test would thus evaluate governmental conduct to determine whether it conveys a symbolic message to which the culture attaches racial significance. A finding that the culture thinks of an allegedly discriminatory governmental action in racial terms would also constitute a finding regarding the beliefs and motivations of the governmental actors: The actors are themselves part of the culture and presumably could not have acted without being influenced by racial considerations, even if they are unaware of their racist beliefs. Therefore, the court would apply strict scrutiny.

As an example, Lawrence discusses City of Memphis v. Greene, 451 U.S. 100 (1981), in which Black plaintiffs unsuccessfully challenged the construction of a wall between white and Black communities in Memphis. Lawrence notes that there were plenty of reasons to be suspicious of this result.

> The closing was effected by the erection of a barrier at the point of separation between the black and white neighborhoods. It was a unique step,

84. Charles R. Lawrence III, The Id, the Ego, and Equal Protection: Reckoning with Unconscious Racism, 39 Stan. L. Rev. 317, 319-326, 357-358 (1987).

> not part of a uniform city planning effort, taken at the request of white property owners who expressed concern about excess traffic and danger to children. One person soliciting signatures for a petition in favor of the street closing had referred to the traffic as "undesirable traffic."
>
> The Court refused to probe beneath the surface of the residents' expressed purposes, asserting that, because the plaintiffs had sued the mayor and city council, it is the latter's motivation that must be ascertained. The Court similarly refused to hold that the history of resistance to desegregation in Memphis, the fact that the white neighborhood in question developed as a result of pre–World War II segregation, and evidence of present racial animus required the district court to find that the city council's action was racially motivated, since there was no showing that "the residents of Hein Park would have welcomed the heavy flow of transient traffic through their neighborhood if the drivers had been predominantly white."

Under Lawrence's preferred approach, the city's action

> would have a cultural meaning growing out of a long history of whites' need to separate themselves from blacks as a symbol of their superiority. Individual members of the city council might well have been unaware that their continuing need to maintain their superiority over blacks, or their failure to empathize with how construction of the wall would make blacks feel, influenced their decision. But if one were to ask even the most self-deluded among them what the residents of Memphis would take the existence of the wall to mean, the obvious answer would be difficult to avoid. If one told the story leading to the wall's construction while omitting one vital fact—the race of those whose vehicular traffic the barrier excluded—and then asked Memphis citizens to describe the residents of the community claiming injury, few, if any, would not guess that they were black.
>
> The current racial meanings of governmental actions are strong evidence that the process defects of group vilification and misapprehension of costs and benefits have occurred whether or not the decisionmakers were conscious that race played a part in their decisionmaking. Moreover, actions that have racial meaning within the culture are also those actions that carry a stigma for which we should have special concern. . . .
>
> [T]he intent doctrine's focus on the narrowest and most unrealistic understanding of individual fault has also engendered much of the resistance to and resentment of affirmative action programs and other race-conscious remedies for past and continuing discrimination. If there can be no discrimination without an identifiable criminal, then "innocent" individuals will resent the burden of remedying an injury for which the law says they are not responsible. Understanding the cultural source of our racism obviates the need for fault, as traditionally conceived, without denying our collective responsibility for racism's eradication. We cannot be individually blamed for unconsciously harboring attitudes that are inescapable in a culture permeated with racism. And without the necessity for blame, our resistance to accepting the need and responsibility for remedy will be lessened.

DISCUSSION

1. Both Professors Krieger and Lawrence assume that if defendants are not charged with intentional bias against minorities, they will be less upset and defensive about charges of discrimination. Do you think this is true? Wouldn't Professor Lawrence agree that losing a discrimination suit has a distinctive "cultural meaning" as well, especially since most people have no idea what the actual content of legal doctrines are?

Putting these questions aside, are accusations of racism the only things at stake in employment discrimination or zoning cases, or are there distributive and material consequences as well? Consider, for example, whether tort defendants are happier with a system of strict liability, which requires no showing of fault and under which plaintiffs presumably can prove liability more easily.

2. Professor Krieger argues that plaintiffs must show that their "group status played a role in causing the employer's action or decision." But if Krieger is correct that racial and gender categorizations are ubiquitous and even helpful in getting about the world, won't it always be the case that cognitive framing played some role?

3. If Professors Krieger and Lawrence are correct, what kinds of expert testimony would or should be required to succeed in a discrimination lawsuit? Does Professor Krieger's theory require the use of cognitive psychologists in Title VII and Fourteenth Amendment cases?

Under Professor Lawrence's theory, is it enough to rely on judges to take judicial notice of the cultural meaning of racially disproportionate practices? If judges are also victims of unconscious racism, won't they deny these meanings to themselves? Does this mean that courts (or the parties) should hire cultural anthropologists to explain what a practice means culturally? Suppose that whites and Blacks tend to disagree about the cultural meaning of a particular practice. For example, suppose that a large majority of Black people insist that the closing of the street in Memphis is about race, while a large majority of whites insist it is about lowering crime and preserving peace and quiet, or that it is about keeping out poor people with loud and raucous habits. Whose view about social meaning should prevail?

4. Consider the fact that in American political life people often understand that certain issues are "about race" or are racially salient even though they can also be plausibly asserted not to be racial issues. Examples are debates about education, zoning, immigration, welfare, and crime. Because overt appeals to race are considered inappropriate today, particularly by whites, over the years many white politicians have learned to speak in "code" that invokes notions of race and racial salience without explicitly mentioning race, and in ways that can also be plausibly denied. To what extent should the law recognize these facts? Are there institutional reasons why courts might refuse to base equal protection doctrine on the understanding of race discrimination that Krieger and Lawrence believe the law should recognize?

5. Something like Professor Lawrence's theory has been adopted, surprisingly, in a somewhat different area of constitutional law: the Establishment Clause. Under the Establishment Clause, government is not permitted to endorse religion over nonreligion or endorse one religion over another. See County of Allegheny

v. American Civil Liberties Union, 492 U.S. 573 (1989). Questions of endorsement arise in many situations ranging from state-sponsored prayers to the display of nativity scenes. Justice O'Connor has been the primary exponent of the "no-endorsement" theory over the years. Just as Lawrence argues that the government violates the Equal Protection Clause when it sends a message of cultural inferiority to racial minorities, O'Connor argues that the government violates the Establishment Clause when its actions have the purpose or effect of endorsing religion or nonreligion to a reasonable observer. Endorsement violates the Establishment Clause because the government may not make people's religious beliefs or their membership in a particular religious group determinative of their political standing in the community. See Wallace v. Jaffree, 472 U.S. 38, 69-70 (1985) (O'Connor, J., concurring). When government action has the purpose or effect of endorsing religion, it sends a message to some members of the community that they are favored insiders; and it sends a message to others who adhere to different beliefs that they are disfavored outsiders, "not full members of the political community." Lynch v. Donnelly, 465 U.S. 668, 688 (1984) (O'Connor, J., concurring). Justice O'Connor's endorsement test is, in effect, a test of the cultural meaning of a contested government practice.

Note that Justice O'Connor refers to both the purpose and the effect of government action. Thus, it does not matter whether a large crucifix on the top of (say) a state's Supreme Court building was designed to endorse Christianity or make non-Christians feel like less than equal citizens. What matters is that it has that effect. As a result, O'Connor's test requires that the cultural meaning be "reasonable" to avoid the problem of unreasonable or hypersensitive plaintiffs. The test is what a "reasonable observer" familiar with the history of the practice would understand the practice to mean. In *Lynch* itself, Justice O'Connor held that the display of a nativity scene, featuring the baby Jesus, Mary, and Joseph, and accompanied by a Christmas tree and various seasonal characters, was not an endorsement of Christianity. Does this mean that non-Christians who disagree with her conclusion are "unreasonable"? Is the judgment of favoritism, as Justice Brown said of segregated facilities in Plessy v. Ferguson, solely "because [non-Christians] choose to put that construction upon it"?

Can you think of any reason why the Court has adopted something like a "cultural meaning test" in religion cases but has not done so in race cases? Put another way, why shouldn't Washington v. Davis apply in Establishment Clause cases, so that the government should be able to place crosses in government buildings unless plaintiffs prove that it specifically sought to endorse Christianity? Conversely, if you think that racism is a much more serious problem in the United States than endorsement of mainstream Christianity, why shouldn't it be easier to prove racial discrimination than religious endorsement?

Suppose that the courts adopted Professor Lawrence's test, and asked whether a "reasonable observer" would see a particular practice as racially motivated. Does the decision in *Lynch* give you any suggestion of how easy it would be to get the kinds of people who are appointed to the federal judiciary to see the racial and cultural meanings that Lawrence sees?

6. *Skepticism about proving invidious intention.* Professors Krieger and Lawrence argue that because the test of invidious intention relies on bad psychology, it does not go far enough. Justice Scalia, dissenting in an Establishment Clause case,

Edwards v. Aguillard, 482 U.S. 578 (1987), has argued in the opposite direction. Because inquiries into legislative intention make little sense, Scalia argues, the Court should not inquire into intention at all. *Edwards* concerned the constitutionality of a Louisiana statute requiring that "creation science" be taught in classes where evolution is presented as a possible explanation for the origin of life. The Supreme Court struck down the statute under a doctrine that invalidated a law if its purpose was "to endorse or disapprove of religion." Justice Scalia argues that

> discerning the subjective motivation of those enacting the statute is, to be honest, almost always an impossible task. . . . [A] particular legislator need not have voted for the Act either because he wanted to foster religion or because he wanted to improve education. He may have thought the bill would provide jobs for his district, or may have wanted to make amends with a faction of his party he had alienated on another vote, or he may have been a close friend of the bill's sponsor, or he may have been repaying a favor he owed the Majority Leader, or he may have hoped the Governor would appreciate his vote and make a fundraising appearance for him, or he may have been seeking favorable publicity, or he may have been reluctant to hurt the feelings of a loyal staff member who worked on the bill, or he may have been settling an old score with a legislator who opposed the bill, or he may have been mad at his wife who opposed the bill, or he may have been intoxicated and utterly *un*motivated when the vote was called, or he may have accidentally voted "yes" instead of "no," or, of course, he may have had (and very likely did have) a combination of some of the above reasons and many other motivations. To look for *the sole purpose* of even a single legislator is probably to look for something that does not exist. . . .
>
> [W]here ought we to look for the individual legislator's purpose? We cannot of course assume that every member present . . . agreed with the motivation expressed in a particular legislator's pre-enactment floor or committee statement. . . . Can we assume, then, that they all agree with the motivation expressed in the staff-prepared committee reports they might have read . . . ? Should we consider post-enactment floor statements? Or post-enactment testimony from legislators, obtained expressly for the lawsuit? Should we consider media reports on the realities of the legislative bargaining? All of these sources, of course are eminently manipulable. . . .
>
> [And] we must still confront the question . . . how *many* of them must have the invalidating intent. If a state senate approves a bill by vote of 26 to 25, and only one of the 26 intended solely to advance religion [or exhibit racial prejudice], is the law unconstitutional? What if 13 of the 26 had that intent? . . . Or is it possible that the intent of the bill's sponsor is alone enough to invalidate it—on a theory, perhaps that even though everyone else's intent was pure, what they produced was the fruit of a forbidden tree?
>
> Because there are no good answers to these questions, this court has recognized . . . that determining the subjective intent of legislators is a perilous enterprise. . . . Given the many hazards in assuming the subjective intent of governmental decisionmakers, the [duty to ascertain purpose] is

defensible, I think, only if the text of the Establishment Clause demands it. That is surely not the case.

How would Scalia's arguments apply to equal protection doctrine? Does the text of the Equal Protection Clause require an inquiry into subjective motivations of lawmakers? If not, should the clause prohibit only those laws that, on their face, discriminate on the basis of race? Scalia argues that it may be possible to determine the "'objective purpose' of a statute (i.e., the public good at which its provisions appear to be directed)" from its text or from its preamble. Is it likely that many laws will have the "objective purpose" of harming minorities?

5. The Future of Disparate Impact Legislation

The 1970s settlement limited what courts could do under the Constitution to protect minorities and women from laws disproportionately burdening them, but allowed the political branches to go much further than courts would or could. Beginning in the 1980s, however, a more conservative Court began to chip away at disparate impact law. In Wards Cove Packing v. Atonio, 490 U.S. 642 (1989), the Court made it more difficult for plaintiffs to prove disparate impact claims. This decision was reversed by the Civil Rights Restoration Act of 1991, which reinstated the *Griggs* framework. See discussion note 1 following *Griggs*, supra. In Alexander v. Sandoval, 532 U.S. 275 (2001), the Court, in an opinion by Justice Scalia, held that Title VI did not provide a private right of action to enforce disparate impact rules created by administrative agencies, which, in effect, closed the door on future disparate impact suits modeled on Lau v. Nichols. More recently, the Court decided a Title VII case avoiding a constitutional challenge to disparate impact liability; Justice Scalia, concurring, suggested that disparate impact rules may be constitutionally suspect.

RICCI v. DeSTEFANO, 557 U.S. 557 (2009): Title VII of the 1964 Civil Rights Act makes it unlawful for an employer "to discriminate against any individual with respect to his compensation, terms, conditions, or privileges of employment, because of such individual's race, color, religion, sex, or national origin." 42 U.S.C. §2000e-2(a)(1). It prohibits both disparate treatment discrimination and disparate impact discrimination.

Disparate treatment discrimination occurs when an employer has treated a particular person less favorably than others because of a protected trait. A disparate-treatment plaintiff must establish that the defendant had a discriminatory intent or motive for taking a job-related action. Disparate impact discrimination occurs when an employer uses a particular employment practice that causes a disparate impact on the basis of race, color, religion, sex, or national origin. 42 U.S.C. §2000e-2(k)(1)(A)(i). The employer may defend by demonstrating that the practice is job related for the position in question and consistent with business necessity. If the employer meets that burden, a plaintiff may still succeed by showing that the employer refuses to adopt an available alternative employment practice that has less disparate impact and serves the employer's legitimate needs. §§2000e-2(k)(1)(A)(ii) and (C).

The City of New Haven, Connecticut used a combination of written and oral tests to identify firefighters for promotion to vacant lieutenant and captain positions. Under these tests, white candidates significantly outperformed minority candidates. Under the rules for filling vacancies, only white candidates would be immediately promoted to lieutenant; of the nine candidates who would be immediately promoted to captain, seven were white and two were Hispanic. No African-American candidates would be immediately promoted to either position. A rancorous public debate ensued, with different groups arguing about whether the tests were fair or biased. Those claiming bias argued that the tests had a discriminatory impact on racial minorities and threatened a disparate impact lawsuit if the city made promotions based on the tests. Those claiming the tests were fair and neutral threatened a disparate treatment lawsuit if the city, relying on the statistical racial disparity, ignored the test results and denied promotions to the candidates who had performed well.

The city ultimately threw out the examination results. Seventeen white firefighters and one Hispanic firefighter who passed the exams sued the city on a disparate treatment theory, arguing that throwing out the test results treated them less favorably than other employees because of race. They also alleged a violation of the Equal Protection Clause. The city argued in defense that if it had certified the test results, it could have faced Title VII liability for adopting a practice that had a disparate impact on minority firefighters. The district court granted summary judgment for the defendants, and the Second Circuit affirmed.

The Supreme Court reversed, in an opinion by Justice Kennedy. Justice Kennedy emphasized the injustice of throwing out the results of an exam that the city had already administered to candidates competing for promotion in good faith. "The City's actions would violate the disparate-treatment prohibition of Title VII absent some valid defense. All the evidence demonstrates that the City chose not to certify the examination results because of the statistical disparity based on race—*i.e.*, how minority candidates had performed when compared to white candidates. . . . Whatever the City's ultimate aim—however well intentioned or benevolent it might have seemed—the City made its employment decision because of race. The City rejected the test results solely because the higher scoring candidates were white."

The Court then considered when "the purpose to avoid disparate-impact liability excuses what otherwise would be prohibited disparate-treatment discrimination." . . . Justice Kennedy observed: "Title VII does not prohibit an employer from considering, before administering a test or practice, how to design that test or practice in order to provide a fair opportunity for all individuals, regardless of their race. And when, during the test-design stage, an employer invites comments to ensure the test is fair, that process can provide a common ground for open discussions toward that end." The issue in this case, however, was whether it was legal to invalidate the test results after the test had already been given. "We hold only that, under Title VII, before an employer can engage in intentional discrimination for the asserted purpose of avoiding or remedying an unintentional disparate impact, the employer must have a strong basis in evidence to believe it will be subject to disparate-impact liability if it fails to take the race-conscious, discriminatory action." (Justice Kennedy derived the "strong basis in evidence" test from the Court's affirmative action cases construing the Equal Protection Clause.)

The Court held that the City of New Haven could not meet the "strong basis in evidence" standard, and therefore violated Title VII. It therefore did not reach the question whether New Haven's actions also violated the Equal Protection Clause, or "whether a legitimate fear of disparate impact is ever sufficient to justify discriminatory treatment under the Constitution."

Justice Ginsburg, joined by Justices Stevens, Souter, and Breyer, dissented. She strongly disagreed with the majority's assumption that "[w]hen an employer changes an employment practice in an effort to comply with Title VII's disparate-impact provision . . . it acts 'because of race.'" Justice Ginsburg argued that "Title VII's disparate-treatment and disparate-impact proscriptions must be read as complementary" rather than in conflict, as the majority did, because Title VII's purpose is to encourage voluntary compliance to desegregate workplaces. "[E]mployers who reject . . . criteria [that operate to the disadvantage of minorities] due to reasonable doubts about their reliability can hardly be held to have engaged in discrimination 'because of' race. . . . I would therefore hold that an employer who jettisons a selection device when its disproportionate racial impact becomes apparent does not violate Title VII's disparate-treatment bar automatically or at all, subject to this key condition: The employer must have good cause to believe the device would not withstand examination for business necessity."

Justice Ginsburg pointed to New Haven's choice of a 60/40 ratio for written and oral parts of the examination as particularly vulnerable to criticism. The weighting toward written questions was not necessary to effective job performance, because "the oral component, more so than the written component, addressed the sort of 'real-life scenarios' fire officers encounter on the job." In addition, many municipalities prefer assessment tests that simulate actual work conditions.

Even so, the majority's new "strong basis in evidence" standard, she argued, would make efforts at voluntary compliance more difficult, would encourage "costly disparate treatment litigation," and was tantamount to a demand that the employer establish that it has violated the law.

Justice Alito, concurring, agreed with the majority's "strong basis in evidence" test and also agreed that New Haven could not meet that standard. He argued that no matter which test was used, summary judgment for the city was inappropriate if "professed concern about disparate-impact litigation was simply a pretext" for intentional racial discrimination. Justice Alito argued that there was evidence that "the City's real reason was illegitimate, namely, the desire to placate a politically important racial constituency," in this case African Americans, who were essential to the mayor's political viability.

Justice Ginsburg responded: "The real issue . . . is not whether the mayor and his staff were politically motivated; it is whether their attempt to score political points was legitimate (i.e., nondiscriminatory). Were they seeking to exclude white firefighters from promotion (unlikely, as a fair test would undoubtedly result in the addition of white firefighters to the officer ranks), or did they realize, at least belatedly, that their tests could be toppled in a disparate-impact suit? In the latter case, there is no disparate-treatment violation. Justice Alito, I recognize, would disagree."

Justice Scalia, concurring, argued that the case raised the larger issue of whether disparate impact liability was constitutional in the first place. The present case asked "[w]hether . . . Title VII's disparate-treatment provisions forbid 'remedial' race-based actions when a disparate-impact violation would *not* otherwise result." But the real problem, Justice Scalia explained, is that Title VII "not only permits but affirmatively *requires* [race-based] actions when a disparate-impact violation *would* otherwise result."

"But if the Federal Government is prohibited from discriminating on the basis of race, then surely it is also prohibited from enacting laws mandating that third parties—e.g., employers, whether private, State, or municipal—discriminate on the basis of race. As the facts of these cases illustrate, Title VII's disparate-impact provisions place a racial thumb on the scales, often requiring employers to evaluate the racial outcomes of their policies, and to make decisions based on (because of) those racial outcomes. That type of racial decisionmaking is, as the Court explains, discriminatory. See Personnel Administrator of Mass. v. Feeney, 442 U.S. 256 (1979)."

"To be sure, the disparate-impact laws do not mandate imposition of quotas, but it is not clear why that should provide a safe harbor. Would a private employer not be guilty of unlawful discrimination if he refrained from establishing a racial hiring quota but intentionally designed his hiring practices to achieve the same end? Surely he would. Intentional discrimination is still occurring, just one step up the chain. Government compulsion of such design would therefore seemingly violate equal protection principles. Nor would it matter that Title VII requires consideration of race on a wholesale, rather than retail, level. . . . And of course the purportedly benign motive for the disparate-impact provisions cannot save the statute. See Adarand Constructors, Inc. v. Pena, 515 U.S. 200 (1995)."

"It might be possible to defend the law by framing it as simply an evidentiary tool used to identify genuine, intentional discrimination—to 'smoke out,' as it were, disparate treatment. . . . But arguably the disparate-impact provisions sweep too broadly to be fairly characterized in such a fashion—since they fail to provide an affirmative defense for good-faith (i.e., nonracially motivated) conduct, or perhaps even for good faith plus hiring standards that are entirely reasonable. . . . It is one thing to free plaintiffs from proving an employer's illicit intent, but quite another to preclude the employer from proving that its motives were pure and its actions reasonable."

"The Court's resolution of these cases makes it unnecessary to resolve these matters today. But the war between disparate impact and equal protection will be waged sooner or later, and it behooves us to begin thinking about how—and on what terms—to make peace between them."

DISCUSSION

Although *Ricci* is specifically decided on nonconstitutional grounds, the Justices clearly have constitutional issues in mind. These concern what is a racial classification and what is an improper discriminatory purpose.

1. *When is a decision "because of" or "based on" race?* Allied to the debate over intention is the question of what we mean by a decision "based on" race. The majority in *Ricci* assumes that New Haven's decision to change the employment test was "based on" race because the city was concerned that using the test might result in its hiring no African-American officers. At other points in its opinion, however, the majority suggests that the city violated the law, not because it was concerned with the potential exclusionary impact of the test, but because it publicly adopted the

test and then publicly invalidated the test for race-related reasons, changing course in ways that invited reliance and stimulated racial resentments.

If government decisionmakers recognize that one of several possible methods of meeting the government needs will have a foreseeable adverse impact on minorities and, consequently, decide to meet the government's needs in some other way, is that change of course an unlawful decision "because of" race? Consider Justice Kennedy's concurring opinion in *Parents Involved*:

> School boards may pursue the goal of bringing together students of diverse backgrounds and races through other means, including strategic site selection of new schools; drawing attendance zones with general recognition of the demographics of neighborhoods; allocating resources for special programs; recruiting students and faculty in a targeted fashion; and tracking enrollments, performance, and other statistics by race. These mechanisms are race conscious but do not lead to different treatment based on a classification that tells each student he or she is to be defined by race, so it is unlikely any of them would demand strict scrutiny to be found permissible. . . . Executive and legislative branches, which for generations now have considered these types of policies and procedures, should be permitted to employ them with candor and with confidence that a constitutional violation does not occur whenever a decisionmaker considers the impact a given approach might have on students of different races. Assigning to each student a personal designation according to a crude system of individual racial classifications is quite a different matter; and the legal analysis changes accordingly.

Parents Involved, 551 U.S. at 789 (Kennedy, J., concurring).

Is the choice of the employment test in *Ricci* more like the strategic site selection of a new school—or instead more like the consideration of the race of individual applicants for school admission that the Court rejected in *Parents Involved*? If the city may consider how changing the site of a school will affect its likely racial composition, why may it not consider how changing an employment test will affect the likely racial composition of the pool from which it may select officers for its fire department? (Suppose, for example, that the city learns from various experts that a test that emphasizes oral presentations and assessments of on-the-job skills will likely result in improved achievement by minority applicants.) May it consider this information before selecting an employment test? If the City may consider this information before selecting a test, can the City follow the same reasoning and change the test *after* applicants have already taken it? What makes the second scenario more problematic? Put another way, is the motive or mental state of the decisionmaker crucial, or is the crucial factor the perceptions—and likely resentment—of the public? Is there any principled basis on which appearance could or should matter in deciding whether a policy decision is impermissibly race-based? Should the law take racial resentment into consideration? When and why? Are such considerations ever relevant to equal protection doctrine? Ought they be?

2. *What is discriminatory purpose?* The 1970s settlement in *Davis* and *Feeney* allowed government policies with a disparate racial impact on racial minorities—even if entirely known or foreseeable—unless plaintiffs could show

intentional discrimination. To prove intentional discrimination, minority plaintiffs would have to show that "the decisionmaker [must have] selected or reaffirmed a particular course of action at least in part 'because of,' not merely 'in spite of,' its adverse effects upon an identifiable group."

In *Ricci*, however, and in disparate impact situations more generally, an employer's decision to take steps to prevent disparate impact on minorities primarily burdens whites. Justice Scalia assumes that deliberately choosing employment practices to prevent disparate impact on minorities would violate *Feeney*. Is this correct? Why isn't the employer's decision "in spite of" the effects on whites? Perhaps more to the point, since the state action in this case is the federal government's, why isn't the federal government's purpose the integration of workforces rather than a desire to harm members of the white majority?

Suppose one applied Scalia's interpretation of Washington v. Davis and *Feeney* to previous constitutional challenges of legislation that had disparate impacts on African Americans, Latinos, and women. Would the cases come out differently?

Perhaps Scalia's argument is that disparate impact is constitutionally troublesome because it requires employers to consider the racial effects of their actions. If so, why wouldn't this concern make unconstitutional any federal policies that encourage voluntary compliance with workplace integration? Note that Scalia's argument in *Ricci* recapitulates in the employment context the debate between the Justices in *Parents Involved* about whether voluntary attempts to integrate schools are a forbidden form of racial balancing.

Note also the issue of symmetry between deliberate integration and segregation implicit in Scalia's argument: Scalia assumes that federal attempts to get employers to integrate workforces (through threats of disparate impact liability) are just as constitutionally objectionable as federal efforts to encourage the maintenance of segregated workforces because both "requir[e] employers to evaluate the racial outcomes of their policies, and to make decisions based on (because of) those racial outcomes." Should the Constitution treat these two purposes differently?

Justice Alito's concurrence focuses on the statutory question of forbidden purpose in Title VII. He assumes that scrapping the firefighter's test to please a powerful African-American constituency is an illegitimate form of racial discrimination. But if so, does this mean that making political decisions with predictable disparate impacts on minorities in order to please white voters also makes a decision illegitimate?

Suppose that a state decides to offer admission to any person who graduates in the top 10 percent of their high school class to the state university, regardless of their test scores or cumulative grade point average, with the purpose of increasing minority enrollments. Suppose also that the state adopts this policy in order to please minority voters while simultaneously avoiding political opposition by white parents who are opposed to race-based affirmative action. Assuming that the state has limited slots available, the foreseeable effect is that fewer whites will be admitted to the university. Is this a racially motivated decision under *Feeney*?

3. *The reach of* Ricci. While Justice Scalia suggests that disparate impact liability doctrine is constitutionally suspect on its face, Justice Kennedy's majority opinion is less clear. He explains that "Title VII does not prohibit an employer from considering, before administering a test or practice, how to design that test or practice in

order to provide a fair opportunity for all individuals, regardless of their race. And when, during the test-design stage, an employer invites comments to ensure the test is fair, that process can provide a common ground for open discussions toward that end." Are these actions not decisions made on the basis of race? If retesting is on the basis of race, and these are not, what triggers the "strong basis in evidence test"? One possibility is that *Ricci* equates "on the basis of race" with overt or public considerations of race that disrupt conventional expectations. If so, how is the case like or unlike other decisions about race by the Roberts and Rehnquist Courts?

D. Race and the Criminal Justice System

Among the most important consequences of the intent standard of *Davis* and *Feeney* are its consequences for constitutional challenges to racial disparities in the administration of the criminal justice system.

1. The War on Drugs and the Powder Cocaine/Crack Cocaine Distinction

UNITED STATES v. CLARY, 4 F.3D 709 (8TH CIR. 1994): [Defendant brought an equal protection challenge to the federal sentencing guidelines for the crime of possession of cocaine with intent to distribute. 21 U.S.C §841(b)(1)(A)(iii) provides for a ten-year minimum sentence for persons found possessing 50 grams or more of cocaine base. A similar ten-year minimum is imposed for those possessing over 5,000 grams of powder cocaine. The Sentencing Commission adopted the 100 to 1 ratio in U.S.S.G. §2D1.1. Clary argued that the 100 to 1 ratio discriminated against African Americans.]

John R. Gibson, Senior Circuit Judge:

The [district] court outlined the events leading up to passage of the crack statute. The court cited several news articles submitted by members of Congress for publication in the Congressional Record which portrayed crack dealers as unemployed, gang-affiliated, gun-toting, young black males. Legislators, the court reasoned, used these media accounts as informational support for the statute. The district court also pointed to perceived procedural irregularities surrounding Congress' approval of the crack sentencing provisions. For instance, few hearings were held in the House on the enhanced penalties for crack. While many Senators called for a more measured response, the Senate committee conducted a single morning hearing. Finally, although the penalties were originally set at 50 to 1, they were arbitrarily doubled.

The district court also observed that 98.2 percent of defendants convicted of crack cocaine charges in the Eastern District of Missouri between the years 1988 and 1992 were African American. Nationally, 92.6 percent of those convicted of crack cocaine charges were African American, as opposed to 4.7 percent who were white. With respect to powder cocaine, the percentages were largely reversed. The court found that this statistical evidence demonstrated both the disparate impact of the 100 to 1 ratio and the probability that "the subliminal influence of unconscious racism had permeated federal prosecution throughout the nation."

While the government directed the court to evidence that Congress considered crack to be more dangerous because of its potency, addictiveness, affordability and prevalence, the court found evidence in the record contradicting many of the legislators' beliefs. In particular, the court questioned Congress' conclusion that crack was 100 times more potent or dangerous than powder cocaine, referring to testimony that there is no reliable medical evidence that crack cocaine is more addictive than powder cocaine. In light of these factors, the court found the punishment of crack at 100 times greater than powder cocaine to be a "frenzied, irrational response." The court repeatedly stressed that "cocaine is cocaine." . . .

[In] past decisions by this court [we found] that Congress clearly had rational motives for creating the distinction between crack and powder cocaine. Among the reasons were "the potency of the drug, the ease with which drug dealers can carry and conceal it, the highly addictive nature of the drug, and the violence which often accompanies trade in it." [We also] squarely reject[ed] the argument that crack cocaine sentences disparately impact on African Americans. [Under] Personnel Administrator of Massachusetts v. Feeney, 442 U.S. 256 (1979), . . . even if a neutral law has a disproportionate adverse impact on a racial minority, it is unconstitutional only if that effect can be traced to a discriminatory purpose. Discriminatory purpose "implies that the decisionmaker, in this case [Congress], selected or reaffirmed a particular course of action at least in part 'because of' not merely 'in spite of,' its adverse effects upon an identifiable group." [T]here was no evidence that Congress or the Sentencing Commission had a racially discriminatory motive when it crafted the Guidelines with extended sentences for crack cocaine felonies.

[At congressional hearings on crack cocaine,] Dr. Robert Byck, Professor of Psychiatry and Pharmacology at Yale University, . . . contrasted inhaling crack vapor to packing a nose with cocaine powder (the most common form of using cocaine powder). Byck stated that crack is more dangerous than cocaine powder because as a person breathes crack vapor, an almost unlimited amount of the drug can enter the body. "Moreover, the speed of the material going to the brain is very rapid." He also commented on the marketability of crack cocaine, stating that "here suddenly, we have cocaine available in a little package, in unit dosage, available at a price that kids can pay initially." . . .

This case undoubtedly presents the most complete record on this issue to come before this court. Nevertheless, we are satisfied that both the record before the district court and the district court's findings fall short of establishing that Congress acted with a discriminatory purpose in enacting the statute, and that Congress selected or reaffirmed a particular course of action "at least in part 'because of,' not merely 'in spite of' its adverse effects upon an identifiable group." While impact is an important starting point, *Arlington Heights* made clear that impact alone is not determinative absent a pattern as stark as that in Gomillion v. Lightfoot, 364 U.S. 339 (1960), or Yick Wo v. Hopkins, 118 U.S. 356 (1886).

We . . . question the district court's reliance on "unconscious racism." The court reasoned that a focus on purposeful discrimination will not show more subtle and deeply-buried forms of racism. The court's reasoning, however, simply does not address the question whether Congress acted with a discriminatory purpose. Similar failings affect the court's statement that although intent per se may not have entered into Congress' enactment of the crack statutes, Congress' failure to account for a substantial and foreseeable disparate impact on African Americans nonetheless violates the spirit and letter of equal protection.

We also question the court's reliance on media-created stereotypes of crack dealers and its conclusion that this information "undoubtedly served as the touchstone that influenced racial perceptions held by legislators and the public as related to the 'crack epidemic.'" Although the placement of newspaper and magazine articles in the Congressional Record indicates that this information may have affected at least some legislators, these articles hardly demonstrate that the stereotypical images "undoubtedly" influenced the legislators' racial perceptions. It is too long a leap from newspaper and magazine articles to an inference that Congress enacted the crack statute because of its adverse effect on African American males, instead of the stated purpose of responding to the serious impact of a rapidly-developing and particularly-dangerous form of drug use. Similarly, the evidence of the haste with which Congress acted and the action it took is as easily explained by the seriousness of the perceived problem as by racial animus. . . .

Other testimony before the district court demonstrates the particular lack of support for the court's conclusion about Congress' motivation in passing the statute. . . . Eric E. Sterling, [who was] Counsel to the Subcommittee of Criminal Justice of the House of Representatives at the time the statutes in question were passed . . . stated that the members of Congress did not have racial animus, but rather "racial consciousness," an awareness that the "problem in the inner cities . . . was about to explode into the white part of the country." Sterling believed that Congress wanted the penalties to be applied wherever crack was being trafficked, although Congress was aware that crack was used primarily by minorities. He further described the seriousness of the problem as reported by the popular press, and stated his view that the creation and promulgation of the law was based on "crass political interest." His opinion was that the motivating factor for the legislation was a perception that crack cocaine posed a unique and unprecedented problem for American narcotics enforcement. . . .

For the most part, the other witnesses that testified before the district court were medical witnesses, several of whom contested the medical information before the Senate that showed differences between crack and powder cocaine. Scientific disagreement with testimony in congressional hearings, offered at a later time and after additional research, simply does not establish discriminatory purpose, or for that matter, a lack of scientific support for Congress' action.

We reverse and remand to the district court for resentencing consistent with this opinion.

DISCUSSION

1. Given that the political debate over crack cocaine was clearly racially coded, and that legislators played on this association for "crass political interest," why does it raise no problems under the Fourteenth Amendment?

2. Is it relevant that some leading African-American members of Congress, such as Charles Rangel, who represented Harlem in New York City for many years, did not object to the powder cocaine–crack cocaine distinction, and that 11 of the 21 Black members of the House of Representatives voted for the 1986 legislation

that created the 100 to 1 crack-powder differential? One reason for their voting behavior, suggested by Randall Kennedy in his book Race, Crime, and the Law 370-380 (1996), is that Black crack cocaine dealers have as their primary victims other members of the Black community. Kennedy calls on persons interested in the health and safety of urban African Americans to sympathize and empathize more with the potential victims of crack cocaine dealers and less with the dealers themselves.[85] While stopping short of endorsing the sentencing differential himself, Kennedy argues that it is entirely rational for non-drug-using, law-abiding Black people to support extraordinary measures of punishment against those who are perceived as special threats to their own community. A fortiori, he insists, the sentencing differential cannot be racist or a violation of equal protection: "Even if these policies are misguided," Kennedy argues, "being mistaken is different from being racist, and the difference is one that greatly matters."[86]

3. Given that the House of Representatives has 435 voting members, does the fact that 11 out of 21 Black members of Congress supported the sentencing differential, or that different elements in the Black community might have different views on the bill necessarily insulate the measure from equal protection scrutiny? Suppose that white representatives voted for the bill due to racialized stereotypes and fears of Black drug dealers invading white suburban neighborhoods, and that Black congressmen in inner-city districts were happy to go along because they believed that getting tough on crack cocaine would help their voting constituents more than it would hurt them. Should the test be whether the bill actually works to the benefit of a minority group in the long run (always difficult to prove), or what the bill meant to the people who voted for it? Does the fact that Charles Rangel voted for the bill primarily to help his constituents, the vast majority of whom are racial and ethnic minorities, pose any problems from the standpoint of the Equal Protection Clause? How exactly is Black support for the bill germane to the questions that courts must consider under the Equal Protection Clause?

Suppose that courts reject an equal protection challenge to the sentencing guidelines using *Feeney*. Does that judgment resolve all equal protection concerns that members of the legislative or executive branches might have about the guidelines?

4. In August 2010, President Obama signed a new law that changed the sentencing disparity from 100 to 1 to 18 to 1. See PBS Newshour, New Drug Law Narrows Crack, Powder Cocaine Sentencing Gap, http://www.pbs.org/newshour/bb/law/july-dec10/sentencing_08-03.html. By 2010, reform had become uncontroversial: The bill passed unanimously in the Senate and by a voice vote in the House. Does this legislative solution cure any equal protection problems that might have existed?

---

85. See also Kate Stith, The Government Interest in Criminal Law: Whose Interest Is It, Anyway?, in Public Values in Constitutional Law 137, 158 (Stephen E. Gottlieb ed., 1993).

86. For a response disputing Kennedy's argument, see David Cole, The Paradox of Race and Crime: A Comment on Randall Kennedy's "Politics of Distinction," 83 Geo. L.J. 2547 (1995). Cole emphasizes the costs to the Black community of large numbers of Blacks being incarcerated for long sentences as a result of the crack-powder distinction coupled with existing patterns of law enforcement that operate to the disadvantage of Blacks.

2. Administering Death

McCleskey v. Kemp

481 U.S. 279 (1987)

POWELL, J. delivered the opinion of the Court.

This case presents the question whether a complex statistical study that indicates a risk that racial considerations enter into capital sentencing determinations proves that petitioner McCleskey's capital sentence is unconstitutional under the . . . Fourteenth Amendment.

I

[Warren McCleskey, an African American, was convicted of killing a white police officer while committing an armed robbery. The jury that convicted him also held a separate penalty hearing following conviction. Georgia law allows the imposition of the death penalty only if the jury finds beyond reasonable doubt that the murder was accompanied by "aggravating circumstances." Two such circumstances, both found by McCleskey's jury, are the commission of the murder during the course of an armed robbery and the victim's being a peace officer engaged in the performance of his duties. The jury sentenced McCleskey to death.

McCleskey challenged the sentence on the ground that the Georgia capital sentencing process was administered in a racially discriminatory manner. His principal evidence was a complex statistical study performed by three researchers, the chief of whom was David Baldus of the University of Iowa.]

The Baldus study is actually two sophisticated statistical studies that examine over 2,000 murder cases that occurred in Georgia during the 1970s. The raw numbers collected by Professor Baldus indicate that defendants charged with killing white persons received the death penalty in 11% of the cases, but defendants charged with killing blacks received the death penalty in only 1% of the cases. The raw numbers also indicate a reverse racial disparity according to the race of the defendant: 4% of the black defendants received the death penalty, as opposed to 7% of the white defendants.

Baldus also divided the cases according to the combination of the race of the defendant and the race of the victim. He found that the death penalty was assessed in 22% of the cases involving black defendants and white victims; 8% of the cases involving white defendants and white victims; 1% of the cases involving black defendants and black victims; and 3% of the cases involving white defendants and black victims.

Similarly, Baldus found that prosecutors sought the death penalty in 70% of the cases involving black defendants and white victims; 32% of the cases involving white defendants and white victims; 15% of the cases involving black defendants and black victims; and 19% of the cases involving white defendants and black victims.

Baldus subjected his data to an extensive analysis, taking account of 230 variables that could have explained the disparities on nonracial grounds. One of his models concludes that, even after taking account of 39 nonracial variables, defendants charged with killing white victims were 4.3 times as likely to receive a death sentence as defendants charged with killing blacks. According to this model, black defendants were 1.1 times as likely to receive a death sentence as other defendants. Thus, the Baldus study indicates that black defendants, such as McCleskey, who kill white victims have the greatest likelihood of receiving the death penalty. . . .

II

McCleskey's first claim is that the Georgia capital punishment statute violates the Equal Protection Clause of the Fourteenth Amendment. . . . As a black defendant who killed a white victim, McCleskey claims that the Baldus study demonstrates that he was discriminated against because of his race and because of the race of his victim. . . . We agree with the Court of Appeals, and every other court that has considered such a challenge, that this claim must fail.

A

. . . [T]o prevail under the Equal Protection Clause, McCleskey must prove that the decisionmakers in his case acted with discriminatory purpose. He offers no evidence specific to his own case that would support an inference that racial considerations played a part in his sentence. Instead, he relies wholly on the Baldus study. . . .

The Court has accepted statistics as proof of intent to discriminate in certain limited contexts. First, this Court has accepted statistical disparities as proof of an equal protection violation in the selection of the jury venire in a particular district. . . . Second, this Court has accepted statistics in the form of multiple regression analyses to prove statutory violations under Title VII.

But the nature of the capital sentencing decision, and the relationship of the statistics to that decision, are fundamentally different from the corresponding elements in the venire-selection or Title VII cases. Most importantly, each particular decision to impose the death penalty is made by a petit jury selected from a properly constituted venire. Each jury is unique in its composition, and the Constitution requires that its decision rest on consideration of innumerable factors that vary according to the characteristics of the individual defendant and the facts of the particular capital offense. Thus, the application of an inference drawn from the general statistics to a specific decision in a trial and sentencing simply is not comparable to the application of an inference drawn from general statistics to a specific venire-selection or Title VII case. In those cases, the statistics relate to fewer entities, and fewer variables are relevant to the challenged decisions.

Another important difference between the cases in which we have accepted statistics as proof of discriminatory intent and this case is that, in the venire-selection and Title VII contexts, the decisionmaker has an opportunity to explain the statistical disparity. Here, the State has no practical opportunity to rebut the Baldus study. "[C]ontrolling considerations of . . . public policy" dictate that jurors "cannot be called . . . to testify to the motives and influences that led to their verdict." Similarly, the policy considerations behind a prosecutor's traditionally "wide discretion" suggest the impropriety of our requiring prosecutors to defend their decisions to seek death penalties, "often years after they were made." Moreover, absent far stronger proof, it is unnecessary to seek such a rebuttal, because a legitimate and unchallenged explanation for the decision is apparent from the record:

McCleskey committed an act for which the United States Constitution and Georgia laws permit imposition of the death penalty.

Finally, McCleskey's statistical proffer must be viewed in the context of his challenge. McCleskey challenges decisions at the heart of the State's criminal justice system. . . . Implementation of [the criminal law] necessarily requires discretionary judgments. Because discretion is essential to the criminal justice process, we would demand exceptionally clear proof before we would infer that the discretion has been abused. . . . Accordingly, we hold that the Baldus study is clearly insufficient to support an inference that any of the decisionmakers in McCleskey's case acted with discriminatory purpose.

B

McCleskey also suggests that the Baldus study proves that the State as a whole has acted with a discriminatory purpose. He appears to argue that the State has violated the Equal Protection Clause by adopting the capital punishment statute and allowing it to remain in force despite its allegedly discriminatory application. But "'[d]iscriminatory purpose' . . . implies more than intent as volition or intent as awareness of consequences. It implies that the decisionmaker, in this case a state legislature, selected or reaffirmed a particular course of action at least in part 'because of,' not merely 'in spite of,' its adverse effects upon an identifiable group." For this claim to prevail, McCleskey would have to prove that the Georgia Legislature enacted or maintained the death penalty statute because of an anticipated racially discriminatory effect. [There is no evidence supporting such a proposition.]

Nor has McCleskey demonstrated that the legislature maintains the capital punishment statute because of the racially disproportionate impact suggested by the Baldus study. . . . Accordingly, we reject McCleskey's equal protection claims. . . .

IV

. . . [McCleskey] further contends that the Georgia capital punishment system is arbitrary and capricious in application, and therefore his sentence is excessive, because racial considerations may influence capital sentencing decisions in Georgia. . . . Even Professor Baldus does not contend that his statistics prove that race enters into any capital sentencing decisions or that race was a factor in McCleskey's particular case. Statistics at most may show only a likelihood that a particular factor entered into some decisions. There is, of course, some risk of racial prejudice influencing a jury's decision in a criminal case. . . . The question "is at what point that risk becomes constitutionally unacceptable." McCleskey asks us to accept the likelihood allegedly shown by the Baldus study as the constitutional measure of an unacceptable risk of racial prejudice influencing capital sentencing decisions. This we decline to do. . . .

The capital sentencing decision requires the individual jurors to focus their collective judgment on the unique characteristics of a particular criminal defendant. It is not surprising that such collective judgments often are difficult to explain. But the inherent lack of predictability of jury decisions does not justify their condemnation. On the contrary, it is the jury's function to make the difficult and uniquely human judgments that defy codification and that "buil[d] discretion, equity, and flexibility into a legal system." H. Kalven & H. Zeisel, The American Jury 498 (1966).

McCleskey's argument that the Constitution condemns the discretion allowed decisionmakers in the Georgia capital sentencing system is antithetical to the fundamental role of discretion in our criminal justice system. . . . [A] capital-punishment system that did not allow for discretionary acts of leniency "would be totally alien to our notions of criminal justice."

At most, the Baldus study indicates a discrepancy that appears to correlate with race. Apparent disparities in sentencing are an inevitable part of our criminal justice system. . . . Where the discretion that is fundamental to our criminal process is involved, we decline to assume that what is unexplained is invidious. In light of the safeguards designed to minimize racial bias in the process, the fundamental value of jury trial in our criminal justice system, and the benefits that discretion provides to criminal defendants, we hold that the Baldus study does not demonstrate a constitutionally significant risk of racial bias affecting the Georgia capital-sentencing process.

V

. . . [I]f we accepted McCleskey's claim that racial bias has impermissibly tainted the capital sentencing decision, we could soon be faced with similar claims as to other types of penalty. Moreover, the claim that his sentence rests on the irrelevant factor of race easily could be extended to apply to claims based on unexplained discrepancies that correlate to membership in other minority groups, and even to gender. . . . Also, there is no logical reason that such a claim need be limited to racial or sexual bias. If arbitrary and capricious punishment is the touchstone under the Eighth Amendment, such a claim could—at least in theory—be based upon any arbitrary variable, such as the defendant's facial characteristics, or the physical attractiveness of the defendant or the victim, that some statistical study indicates may be influential in jury decisionmaking. As these examples illustrate, there is no limiting principle to the type of challenge brought by McCleskey. The Constitution does not require that a State eliminate any demonstrable disparity that correlates with a potentially irrelevant factor in order to operate a criminal justice system that includes capital punishment. As we have stated specifically in the context of capital punishment, the Constitution does not "plac[e] totally unrealistic conditions on its use." . . . McCleskey's arguments are best presented to [l]egislatures [who are] are better qualified to weigh and "evaluate the results of statistical studies in terms of their own local conditions and with a flexibility of approach that is not available to the courts[.]" Capital punishment is now the law in more than two-thirds of our States. It is the ultimate duty of courts to determine on a case-by-case basis whether these laws are applied consistently with the Constitution. Despite McCleskey's wide-ranging arguments that basically challenge the validity of capital punishment in our multiracial society, the only question before us is whether in his case, the law of Georgia was properly applied. We agree with the District Court and the Court of Appeals for the Eleventh Circuit that this was carefully and correctly done in this case.

Brennan, J., joined by Marshall, Blackmun, and Stevens, JJ., dissenting. [Justice Brennan focused primarily on the Eighth Amendment. Parts of his opinion were relevant to the equal protection claim as well:]

At some point in this case, Warren McCleskey doubtless asked his lawyer whether a jury was likely to sentence him to die. A candid reply to this question would have been disturbing. First, counsel would have to tell McCleskey that few of the details of the crime or of McCleskey's past criminal conduct were more important than the fact that his victim was white. . . . The story could be told in a variety of ways, but McCleskey could not fail to grasp its essential narrative line: there was a significant chance that race would play a prominent role in determining if he lived or died. . . .

The statistical evidence in this case . . . relentlessly documents the risk that McCleskey's sentence was influenced by racial considerations. This evidence shows that there is a better than even chance in Georgia that race will influence the decision to impose the death penalty: a majority of defendants in white-victim crimes would not have been sentenced to die if their victims had been black. . . .

Evaluation of McCleskey's evidence cannot rest solely on the numbers themselves. We must also ask whether the conclusion suggested by those numbers is consonant with our understanding of history and human experience. Georgia's legacy of a race-conscious criminal justice system, as well as this Court's own recognition of the persistent danger that racial attitudes may affect criminal proceedings, indicate that McCleskey's claim is not a fanciful product of mere statistical artifact. . . .

The ongoing influence of history is acknowledged, as the majority observes, by our "'unceasing efforts' to eradicate racial prejudice from our criminal justice system." These efforts, however, signify not the elimination of the problem but its persistence. Our cases reflect a realization of the myriad of opportunities for racial considerations to influence criminal proceedings: in the exercise of peremptory challenges; in the selection of the grand jury; in the selection of the petit jury; in the exercise of prosecutorial discretion; in the conduct of argument; and in the conscious or unconscious bias of jurors. . . .

. . . Warren McCleskey's evidence confronts us with the subtle and persistent influence of the past. His message is a disturbing one to a society that has formally repudiated racism, and a frustrating one to a Nation accustomed to regarding its destiny as the product of its own will. Nonetheless, we ignore him at our peril, for we remain imprisoned by the past as long as we deny its influence in the present.

Blackmun, J., joined by Marshall, Stevens, and Brennan, JJ., dissenting.

[T]he Court . . . ignore[s] a significant element of [McCleskey's] claim . . . [the role of the prosecutor,] the quintessential state actor in a criminal proceeding. . . . I concentrate on the decisions within the prosecutor's office through which the State decided to seek the death penalty and, in particular, the point at which the State proceeded to the penalty phase after conviction. This is the step at which the evidence of the effect of the racial factors was especially strong, but is ignored by the Court.

[A] criminal defendant . . . may establish a prima facie case of purposeful discrimination "by showing that the totality of the relevant facts gives rise to an inference of discriminatory purpose." Once the defendant establishes a prima facie case, the burden shifts to the prosecution to rebut that case. . . .

McCleskey produced evidence concerning the role of racial factors at the various steps in the decisionmaking process, focusing on the prosecutor's decision as to which cases merit the death sentence. McCleskey established that the race of the victim is an especially significant factor at the point where the defendant has been convicted of murder and the prosecutor must choose whether to proceed to the penalty phase of the trial and create the possibility that a death sentence may be imposed or to accept the imposition of a sentence of life imprisonment. McCleskey demonstrated this effect at both the statewide level and in Fulton County where he was tried and sentenced. The statewide statistics indicated that black defendant/white victim cases advanced to the penalty trial at nearly five times the rate of the black defendant/black victim cases (70% vs. 15%), and over three times the rate of white defendant/black victim cases (70% vs. 19%). . . .

McCleskey [also] showed that the process by which the State decided to seek a death penalty in his case and to pursue that sentence throughout the prosecution was susceptible to abuse. . . . [A]t every stage of a prosecution, the Assistant District Attorney exercised much discretion. . . . [And] McCleskey presented evidence of the history of prior discrimination in the Georgia system. . . . [McCleskey's] showing is of sufficient magnitude that, absent evidence to the contrary, one must conclude that racial factors entered into the decisionmaking process that yielded McCleskey's death sentence. . . . [The state] must demonstrate that legitimate racially neutral criteria and procedures yielded this racially skewed result. . . .

The Court's statement that the decision to impose death is made by the petit jury . . . disregards the fact that the prosecutor screens the cases throughout the pretrial proceedings and decides to seek the death penalty and to pursue a capital case to the penalty phase where a death sentence can be imposed. McCleskey's claim in this regard lends itself to analysis under the framework we apply in assessing challenges to other prosecutorial actions. See Batson v. Kentucky, 476 U.S. 79 (1986). It is appropriate to judge claims of racially discriminatory prosecutorial selection of cases according to ordinary equal protection standards.

One of the final concerns discussed by the Court may be the most disturbing aspect of its opinion. Granting relief to McCleskey in this case, it is said, could lead to further constitutional challenges. That, of course, is no reason to deny McCleskey his rights under the Equal Protection Clause. If a grant of relief to him were to lead to a closer examination of the effects of racial considerations throughout the criminal-justice system, the system, and hence society, might benefit. . . .

[A dissenting opinion by Justice Stevens, joined by Justice Blackmun, is omitted.]

DISCUSSION

1. Note that even successful equal protection challenges always lend themselves to at least two formally adequate remedies. Assuming that A at the outset is treated better than B, the remedy could be either to give B what A now gets or to reduce A's benefits to the level of B's. What should the remedy have been if McCleskey's claim of unequal treatment had been upheld? However you might treat the case of the particular complainant, Warren McCleskey (who was ultimately

executed by Georgia in 1991), what more general changes in Georgia's death penalty process might have emerged from a victory by McCleskey?

2. The lawyers pressing McCleskey's claim were associated with the NAACP Legal Defense Fund, which is strongly opposed to capital punishment. They would surely have sought an overall reduction in the use of the death penalty. But consider the following comment by Randall Kennedy:[87]

> My critique of McCleskey v. Kemp does not proceed from abolitionist premises. Rather, it seeks to delineate a response to race-of-the-victim disparities that vindicate the claims of racial justice—with or without capital punishment. I am more concerned with the plight of black communities whose welfare is slighted by criminal justice systems that respond more forcefully to the killing of whites than the killing of blacks than I am concerned with the plight of murderers, black or white. McCleskey understandably portrayed the case in a defendant-oriented fashion. I portray the case, by contrast, in a community-oriented fashion. I conceptualize *McCleskey* as an instance of racial inequality in the provision of public goods. Whereas other cases have involved the racially unequal provision of street lights, sidewalks and sewers, *McCleskey* involves racial inequality in the provision of a peculiar sort of public good—capital sentencing.

3. Suspect Descriptions

BROWN v. CITY OF ONEONTA, 221 F.3D 329 (2D CIR. 1999): Police responded to a call from a 77-year-old woman who reported that someone broke into her house shortly before 2:00 A.M. and attacked her. She was unable to identify her assailant's face, but said that he was wielding a knife; that he was a Black man, based on her view of his hand and forearm; and that he was young, because of the speed with which he crossed her room. She also told the police that, as they struggled, the suspect had cut himself on the hand with the knife. A police canine unit tracked the assailant's scent from the scene of the crime toward a nearby college campus, the State University of New York College at Oneonta (SUCO), but lost the trail after several hundred yards. Fewer than 300 Black people live in the town of Oneonta, and just 2 percent of the students at SUCO are Black.

The police immediately contacted SUCO and requested a list of its Black male students. An official at SUCO supplied the list, and the police attempted to locate and question every Black male student at SUCO. This endeavor produced no suspects. Then, over a period of several days, the police conducted a "sweep" of Oneonta, stopping and questioning non-white persons on the streets and inspecting their hands for cuts. More than 200 persons were questioned during that period, but no suspect was apprehended. Several people whose names appeared on the SUCO list and those who were approached and questioned by the police sued the city and the local police department, arguing that the roundup was impermissible racial profiling in violation of the Equal Protection Clause.

---

87. McCleskey v. Kemp: Race, Capital Punishment, and the Supreme Court, 101 Harv. L. Rev. 1388, 1394 (1988).

The Second Circuit rejected this claim on a motion for summary judgment:

> [Plaintiffs] were not questioned solely on the basis of their race. They were questioned on the altogether legitimate basis of a physical description given by the victim of a crime. Defendants' policy was race-neutral on its face; their policy was to investigate crimes by interviewing the victim, getting a description of the assailant, and seeking out persons who matched that description. This description contained not only race, but also gender and age, as well as the possibility of a cut on the hand. In acting on the description provided by the victim of the assault—a description that included race as one of several elements—defendants did not engage in a suspect racial classification that would draw strict scrutiny. The description, which originated not with the state but with the victim, was a legitimate classification within which potential suspects might be found. . . .
>
> [A]ttempting to question every person fitting a general description . . . may well have a disparate impact on small minority groups in towns such as Oneonta. If there are few black residents who fit the general description, for example, it would be more useful for the police to use race to find a black suspect than a white one. It may also be practicable for law enforcement to attempt to contact every black person who was a young male, but quite impossible to contact every such white person. If a community were primarily black with very few white residents and the search were for a young white male, the impact would be reversed. The Equal Protection Clause, however, has long been interpreted to extend to governmental action that has a disparate impact on a minority group only when that action was undertaken with discriminatory intent. Without additional evidence of discriminatory animus, the disparate impact of an investigation such as the one in this case is insufficient to sustain an equal protection claim. . . . [Plaintiffs] allege that at least one woman, Sheryl Champen, was stopped by law enforcement officials during their sweep of Oneonta. This allegation is significant because it may indicate that defendants considered race more strongly than other parts of the victim's description. However, this single incident, to the extent that it was related to the investigation, is not sufficient in our view to support an equal protection claim under the circumstances of this case.

DISCUSSION

1. When police gather information about a crime, and ask about the racial identity of a suspect, is this a racial classification? What if they merely record racial data that witnesses supply? In *Oneonta*, the Second Circuit argued that strict scrutiny should not apply because the suspect description originated with a private party and not the state. Why should this make a difference, given that the state credited the description and decided to engage in the sweeps? Does reliance on nonstate sources eliminate state action? The risk of error or of stereotyping? The role of the state in the construction of racial categories? How, if at all, does your analysis of

whether the use of race in the census is a racial classification help you answer the question of whether the use of race in a suspect description is a racial classification?

2. Suppose that the police conduct a search for a suspect relying on racial elements of a suspect description. Is the search a racial classification? What if police discard other elements of the suspect description and rely largely if not exclusively on the racial elements of the suspect description? What if they rely only on race and gender (e.g., they search only for a Black man)?

3. The Second Circuit also argued that strict scrutiny should not apply because the suspect description was not solely based on race. Should the characterization of a practice as a racial classification that is subject to strict scrutiny depend on whether the state relies solely on race or uses race only as one of several factors? Note that the Supreme Court has applied strict scrutiny in affirmative action cases like *Croson* and *Adarand*, even though government contracts are awarded on the basis of a combination of factors of which race is only one. Similarly, strict scrutiny applies to affirmative action in education even though admissions committees consider many factors other than race in assessing qualifications. Why should government contractors and universities engaged in affirmative action be treated with greater scrutiny than the police in *Oneonta*?

4. What would be the consequence of holding that the police sweep was "on the basis of race" and subject to strict scrutiny? Would this unduly hamper police investigative practices? Or would it serve as an important and necessary check on police abuses? Note that in determining whether government practices are race-based state action, courts employ a binary approach rather than a continuum; practices either are, or are not, racial classifications subject to scrutiny. Consider the possibility that the characterization "racial classification" is at least in part normative rather than positive. Intuitions that race-related practices are benign or legitimate determine whether they are characterized as racial classifications subject to strict scrutiny. Thus, the legal category of what counts as "race-based" decisionmaking, like the categories of "causation" and "intent" in criminal law and tort law, is flexible and shaped by policy considerations that may or may not be overtly acknowledged. In *Oneonta*, for example, the Second Circuit probably considered the police practices involved legitimate and wished to leave police officers considerable discretion in the future. But suppose one was concerned that police practices might be illicit or racially biased. What should the proper test be? For a discussion of possible theories of the case, see the opinions in the denial of rehearing en banc, Brown v. City of Oneonta, 235 F.3d 769 (2d Cir. 2000).

5. For two recent district court decisions finding that consideration of race in suspect apprehension violates equal protection, see Melendres v. Arpaio, 2013 WL 2297173 (D. Ariz. May 24, 2013); Floyd v. City of New York, 2013 U.S. Dist. LEXIS 113271 (S.D.N.Y. Aug. 12, 2013).

NOTE: RACIAL PROFILING AND THE EQUAL PROTECTION CLAUSE

Numerous statistical studies comparing the percentage of minority motorists stopped and searched in comparison to the percentage of white motorists similarly treated strongly suggest that police throughout the United States use traffic violations as a pretext for stopping and searching motor vehicles driven by minorities.[88] This phenomenon, sometimes called "racial profiling," is often colloquially referred to as the "offense" of "driving while black." In 1995, the Maryland Police Department entered into a consent decree promising to end traffic stops on Interstate 95 based on race, but the practice apparently continues.[89] Similar studies in New Jersey and other states confirm the basic trend.[90]

The Fourth Amendment protects people from unreasonable searches and seizures. Nevertheless, the Supreme Court has held that the subjective motivations of a police officer who stops an automobile are irrelevant to the legality of the stop. The only question is whether the officer had probable cause to believe that a violation of law had occurred. In Whren v. United States, 517 U.S. 806 (1996), defendants argued that because police can almost always find an excuse to stop a car for a traffic violation, police will be "tempt[ed] to use traffic stops as a means of investigating other law violations, as to which no probable cause or even articulable suspicion exists," and to stop motorists based on "impermissible factors, such as the race of the car's occupants." They argued that the Fourth Amendment test for traffic stops should not be "whether probable cause existed to justify the stop; but rather, whether a police officer, acting reasonably, would have made the stop for the reason given." The Court in a unanimous opinion by Justice Scalia, rejected this test.

> [Our previous] cases foreclose any argument that the constitutional reasonableness of traffic stops depends on the actual motivations of the individual officers involved. We of course agree with petitioners that the Constitution prohibits selective enforcement of the law based on considerations such as race. But the constitutional basis for objecting to intentionally discriminatory application of laws is the Equal Protection Clause, not the Fourth Amendment. Subjective intentions play no role in ordinary, probable-cause Fourth Amendment analysis.

---

88. See Jennifer A. Larrabee, "DWB (Driving While Black)" and Equal Protection: The Realities of an Unconstitutional Police Practice, 6 J.L. & Pol'y 291 (1997); Angela J. Davis, Race, Cops and Traffic Stops, 51 U. Miami L. Rev. 425, 441 (1997).

89. See Paul W. Valentine, Maryland Settles Lawsuit over Racial Profiles; Police Allegedly Targeted Minorities for Searches, Wash. Post, Jan. 5, 1995, at B1; Michael Schneider, State Police I-95 Drug Unit Found to Search Black Motorists Four Times More Often Than White: Analysis Raises Questions About Trooper Procedures, Baltimore Sun, May 23, 1996, at 2B.

90. For example:

> In New Jersey, 75% of drivers stopped for investigation on portions of the New Jersey Turnpike are African-Americans and Latinos, yet this group only makes up 13.5% of the annual drivers on the Turnpike. Minority drivers traveling through the suburbs of Texas' major cities are twice as likely to receive tickets for traffic violations than are white drivers. On portions of Interstate 95 in Maryland, 71% of the motorists stopped and searched in the first nine months of 1995 were African-Americans. In one Florida county, 62% of the drivers stopped were minorities, and on an interstate in Colorado, 190 of 200 stops "targeted minorities." These statistics clearly indicate that minorities are disproportionately being stopped by police. The inference to be drawn from this is that police are using race as a factor in deciding whom to stop for traffic violations.

Larrabee, "DWB (Driving While Black)" and Equal Protection, supra n.88, at 297-298.

In United States v. Armstrong, 517 U.S. 456 (1996), the Supreme Court stated that in order to prove a selective prosecution claim under the Equal Protection Clause, the claimant

> must demonstrate that the . . . prosecutorial policy "had a discriminatory effect and that it was motivated by a discriminatory purpose." To establish a discriminatory effect in a race case, the claimant must show that similarly situated individuals of a different race were not prosecuted.

To establish the right to discovery in a selective prosecution case a criminal defendant must "produce some evidence that similarly situated defendants of other races could have been prosecuted, but were not."

In the context of racial profiling, does this mean that it is not enough to show that Black people were disproportionately stopped for traffic violations, but that the plaintiff must also show that whites who violated the traffic laws were not stopped? Most statistics on traffic stops describe the racial distribution for persons who were stopped, but not the percentages for those who violated the traffic laws but were not stopped.[91]

Does this mean that existing statistics alone cannot succeed in a racial profiling case under the Equal Protection Clause? Or should courts treat cases of selective prosecution differently from the case of selective traffic stops? Note that in *Armstrong* the Supreme Court specifically reserved judgment on the question "whether a defendant must satisfy the similarly situated requirement in a case 'involving direct admissions by [prosecutors] of discriminatory purpose.'" How likely are police officers to admit that they stop motorists on the basis of their race?

Does racial profiling of persons of Arab or Middle Eastern descent in the wake of 9/11 present different constitutional problems than racial profiling of Black people and Latinos? Consider the following contrasting claims:

1. The events of 9/11 should have no effect on the constitutional analysis of the issues because racial profiling is unconstitutional in any case. It is not as effective a law enforcement tool as people think, it is likely to be abused, it associates group membership with criminality (or reinforces existing associations), and it helps further the subordination of social groups on the basis of their race or ethnicity. What has happened to Black people and Latinos in the past will now be visited

---

91. In *Armstrong*, the Supreme Court specifically rejected the view

> that a defendant may establish a colorable basis for discriminatory effect without evidence that the Government has failed to prosecute others who are similarly situated to the defendant. . . . The Court of Appeals reached [this] decision in part because it started "with the presumption that people of all races commit all types of crimes—not with the premise that any type of crime is the exclusive province of any particular racial or ethnic group." It cited no authority for this proposition, which seems contradicted by the most recent statistics of the United States Sentencing Commission. Those statistics show: More than 90% of the persons sentenced in 1994 for crack cocaine trafficking were black; 93.4% of convicted LSD dealers were white; and 91% of those convicted for pornography or prostitution were white. Presumptions at war with presumably reliable statistics have no proper place in the analysis of this issue.

Is there reason to believe that Blacks and other minorities commit traffic offenses more often than whites?

upon on people of Middle Eastern descent and people with Muslim names. Officials and the general public will be unlikely to understand the differences between different ethnic groups and religions. For example, police officers may harass male members of the Sikh religion who wear turbans even though they are not Muslims and come from countries having no connection to the events of 9/11. Moreover, by focusing attention on people who are of Middle Eastern descent, racial profiling tends to direct attention away from whites like Timothy McVeigh or John Walker Lindh. Even though the Oklahoma City bombing was one of the most serious terrorist incidents in American history, it is unlikely that police officers will begin to profile young disaffected white veterans.

2. Racial profiling is an effective constitutional tool of law enforcement whose rationality has been confirmed by the events of the September 11, 2001 terrorist attacks. In this context, consider the remarks made by the political satirist (and later Senator) Al Franken at the National Press Club in Washington, DC on February 28, 2002:[92]

> I don't understand the reluctance to profile young Arab men. . . . The way I look at it is if it had been 19 Jewish comedians on September 11th who had done that, . . . and I'm in line to get on the plane, and they go, "Mr. Franken, we need to talk to you—you are a Jewish comedian." I'd say, "Thank you—please check my butt," you know—(laughter)—"and while you're at it, will you check Mr. Seinfeld's?" . . . I have been traveling a lot, and I do meet young Arab men who say, "Yeah, you know, sure—I feel better." So I don't understand why a 30-year-old mother with two kids in a stroller [is] put through the kind of delays, and people who sort of fit—I hate to say it—the profile of a hijacker aren't necessarily randomly pulled over. And that may be controversial, but I think it's kind of common sense.

3. The case of racial profiling against Black people and Latinos differs in important respects from the post-9/11 racial profiling that might be used against persons of Arab and Middle Eastern nationality or descent, because:

(a) The offenses and harms that racial profiling might be used for are much more serious and pose a much greater threat to the country. The use or sale of illegal drugs is simply not in the same category as acts of terrorism.

(b) The way race is constructed is different in the two cases. Post-9/11 racial profiling constructs those profiled as a dangerous foreign other. Racial profiling robs Arab Americans of their American identity and reinforces the idea that to be American is to be white. How is this different from the construction of Latino or Asian racial identity? Assuming that such racial profiling is importantly different from the racial profiling used against African Americans, how should it affect the constitutional analysis?

Conversely, because foreignness is at issue, racial profiling allows (for example) Arab Americans to demonstrate their patriotism and loyalty by voluntarily

---

92. See https://www.upi.com/The-world-according-to-Al-Franken/10731015281876/ (last visited November 8, 2017).

submitting to inspections, which distinguishes their situation from that of African Americans, who do not symbolically establish their law-abidingness by allowing their cars to be searched by police officers. Even if this suggested difference is plausible, how should it affect the constitutional question?

(c) Racial profiling on the basis of Arab and Middle Eastern descent is different because it necessarily presents two different situations constitutionally: It is based on country of origin as well as race. Some people who will be adversely affected by the profiling will be American citizens, but many others will be aliens. As discussed infra, although distinctions based on alienage by state officials are often subject to strict scrutiny, distinctions based on alienage by federal officials are subject only to a test of rationality. Is this significantly different from the problem involved in the Japanese internment cases? Does this mean that racial profiling by state officials should be viewed with greater concern than profiling by federal officials?

For a discussion of some of the constitutional and policy issues of profiling, see Bernard Harcourt, Rethinking Racial Profiling: A Critique of the Economics, Civil Liberties, and Constitutional Literature, and of Criminal Profiling More Generally, 71 U. Chi. L. Rev. 1275 (2004); Richard Banks, Beyond Profiling: Race, Policing and the Drug War, 56 Stan. L. Rev. 571 (2003); Albert W. Alschuler, Racial Profiling and the Constitution, 2002 U. Chi. Legal F. 163 (2002); Leti Volpp, The Citizen and the Terrorist, 49 UCLA L. Rev. 1575 (2002).

E. "Preferential" Treatment for Racial Minorities

1. The Central Issues

Since the end of the Second Reconstruction, legislatures rarely make overt racial classifications that burden minority groups. Instead, modern cases generally involve nonminority plaintiffs—usually whites—challenging programs designed to assist minorities, often called "affirmative action" programs.[93] This is not accidental. As we have seen, cases like *Davis* and *Feeney* made it harder for minorities to bring successful equal protection challenges to facially neutral state action that adversely affected them. In the meantime, mobilization against affirmative action programs that might benefit minorities brought a new series of cases (and Justices) to the Supreme Court. The result has been a significant shift in the docket and decisions of the Supreme Court in equal protection law. Earlier cases like *Brown* and *Loving*

---

93. The term "affirmative action," which now refers to explicit racial classifications, was first used in a series of executive orders by Presidents Kennedy and Johnson designed to eliminate the effects of past racial discrimination. On the history of affirmative action, see, e.g., Carl E. Brody, Jr., A Historical Review of Affirmative Action and the Interpretation of Its Legislative Intent by the Supreme Court, 29 Akron L. Rev. 291 (1996); James E. Jones, Jr., The Origins of Affirmative Action, 21 U.C. Davis L. Rev. 383 (1988); Robert J. Weiss, "We Want Jobs": A History of Affirmative Action (1997).

concerned protection of minorities. By the end of the 1970s, the Supreme Court's cases primarily involved members of majority groups who sought to use the Equal Protection Clause to challenge affirmative action policies and civil rights initiatives.

These cases led to long-running debates between the Justices about the role of the courts and the proper interpretation of the Equal Protection Clause. Some Justices—like William Brennan and Thurgood Marshall—believed that there was an important difference between laws and programs that harmed minority groups and affirmative action policies that sought to help them. These Justices believed that strict scrutiny should be reserved for the former kinds of cases, while courts should apply intermediate scrutiny to the latter case to prevent unfairness to majority groups. Other Justices, like Antonin Scalia, believed that all affirmative action programs were per se unconstitutional.

A growing group of Justices, led by Lewis Powell, Sandra Day O'Connor, and Anthony Kennedy, argued for strict scrutiny in both kinds of cases, while actually developing a new form of "strict scrutiny" for affirmative action programs that was importantly different from the kind of judicial scrutiny we saw in Loving v. Virginia.

This new form of strict scrutiny nominally applied to all racial classifications. In fact, however, it allowed certain forms of affirmative action policies (especially in education) while seriously limiting or restricting all other forms. This new kind of strict scrutiny was no longer fatal in fact, especially in education cases. Rather, strict scrutiny gave conditional permission to affirmative action programs, if they met certain restrictions on justifications and form. In particular, governments could not adopt affirmative action programs in order to remedy past societal discrimination. The Court worked to strictly control the shape, reach, and duration of affirmative action programs in order to reduce the resentments they might occasion.

The rationale for this new form of strict scrutiny of affirmative action programs evolved over time: from overt concern about protecting innocent whites, to concern about protecting minorities from stigma, to a more generalized concern about protecting society as a whole from the conflict and divisiveness caused by debates over affirmative action.[94]

Four basic questions reappear in the cases that follow.

First, what standard of scrutiny should apply? Is the standard of review the same for classifications that burden minorities and classifications designed to assist them? After considerable debate, the Supreme Court eventually held that strict scrutiny should apply.

Second, assuming that strict scrutiny applies, is the *application* of the standard symmetrical? Does "strict scrutiny" mean the same thing for policies designed to assist minorities as it does for Jim Crow policies that attempted to preserve white supremacy and that were outlawed during the Second Reconstruction? Or should courts be more respectful of the judgments of legislatures and educational officials in affirmative action programs? On this issue, the Supreme Court has been more equivocal, sometimes applying a version of strict scrutiny that is considerably less

---

94. For an account distinguishing the anticlassification, antisubordination, and antibalkanization perspectives in the Court's affirmative action decisions, see Reva B. Siegel, From Colorblindness to Antibalkanization: An Emerging Ground of Decision in Race Equality Cases, 120 Yale L.J. 1278 (2011).

stringent and more deferential to government actors than if Jim Crow laws were involved.

Third, assuming that strict scrutiny applies, what purposes are sufficiently "compelling" to satisfy strict scrutiny? From the 1970s through the 1990s, the Supreme Court rejected a host of goals offered by legislatures as not sufficiently compelling. The most important of the goals the Court rejected was the goal of remedying past societal discrimination. (Ironically, the original purpose of affirmative action, as announced in the Johnson and Kennedy Administrations, was to remedy past societal discrimination.[95])

Fourth, once again assuming that strict scrutiny applies, what policies are sufficiently narrowly tailored to survive strict scrutiny? What kinds of tests does narrow tailoring require, and what values do they serve? Here again, the Court has offered a variety of answers, depending on whether the regulatory context is government contracting, elementary and secondary education, or higher education.

As you read the cases in this chapter, ask yourself how the Court's doctrines reflect changing popular debates from the end of the Second Reconstruction until today.

2. The Early Cases

The Supreme Court had few opportunities to consider "benign" racial classifications until the Second Reconstruction, in part because the most common racial classifications until the 1970s were Jim Crow and anti-Asian policies.

The Court first addressed these issues in United States v. Montgomery County Board of Education, 395 U.S. 225 (1969), and Swann v. Charlotte-Mecklenburg Board of Education, 402 U.S. 1 (1971), where it cautiously approved of the race-conscious assignment of teachers and pupils to remedy deeply entrenched patterns of state-mandated segregation. In DeFunis v. Odegaard, 416 U.S. 312 (1974), petitioner, who had been denied admission to the University of Washington Law School, challenged the school's preferential admissions program, claiming a violation of equal protection, but the Court held the controversy moot because the petitioner, who had been ordered admitted by a lower court, was nearing graduation.

Four years later, in University of California Regents v. Bakke, 438 U.S. 265 (1978), the Court finally considered the constitutionality of state affirmative action programs.

REGENTS OF THE UNIVERSITY OF CALIFORNIA v. BAKKE, 438 U.S. 265 (1978): The University of California at Davis Medical School instituted a special affirmative action program in 1973 and 1974 that set aside 16 seats out of 100 for "economically and/or educationally disadvantaged" applicants and members of a "minority

---

95. As President Johnson explained in a famous speech on June 4, 1965 at Howard University: "You do not wipe away the scars of centuries by saying: 'now, you are free to go where you want, do as you desire, and choose the leaders you please.' You do not take a man who for years has been hobbled by chains, liberate him, bring him to the starting line of a race, saying, 'you are free to compete with all the others,' and still justly believe you have been completely fair. . . . This is the next and more profound stage of the battle for civil rights. We seek not just freedom but opportunity—not just legal equity but human ability—not just equality as a right and a theory, but equality as a fact and as a result."

group," which included African-Americans, Chicanos, Asians, and American Indians. In 1974, the special program was reserved only for minority students. Candidates whose undergraduate GPA fell below 2.5 were automatically rejected from the regular program but not the special program. Special admissions candidates were not rated against general applicants, but could be rejected for failure to meet certain requirements. Alan Bakke, a white male whose application was considered under the general admissions program, was denied admission in 1973 and 1974. In both years, applicants were admitted under the special program with "significantly lower" scores than Bakke. Bakke sued the university, arguing that its policy violated both the Equal Protection Clause of the Fourteenth Amendment and Title VI of the Civil Rights Act of 1964, which provides that "No person in the United States shall, on the ground of race, color, or national origin, be excluded from participation in, be denied the benefits of, or be subjected to discrimination under any program or activity receiving Federal financial assistance." The Medical School admitted that it could not prove that Bakke would not have been admitted in the absence of the special program.

Justice Powell, in a judgment concurred in by Chief Justice Burger, and Justices Stewart, Rehnquist, and Stevens, affirmed the Supreme Court of California's judgment that Davis's "special admissions program [is] unlawful and . . . that [Bakke] be admitted to the Medical School." In a judgment concurred in by Justices Brennan, White, Marshall, and Blackmun, Justice Powell also overturned the California Supreme Court's "judgment enjoining petitioner from according any consideration to race in its admissions process." There was no majority opinion, but Justice Powell's separate opinion was for many years widely viewed as stating the law.

Justice Powell argued that strict scrutiny applied because the right to equal protection was an individual right; therefore it "cannot mean one thing when applied to one individual and something else when applied to a person of another color. If both are not accorded the same protection, then it is not equal." He also rejected the argument that strict scrutiny should not apply "because white males, such as respondent, are not a 'discrete and insular minority' requiring extraordinary protection from the majoritarian political process." Although Powell conceded that the Fourteenth Amendment was originally concerned with the promotion of freedom and equality for Black people, "it was no longer possible to peg the guarantees of the Fourteenth Amendment to the struggle for equality of one racial minority" because "the United States had become a Nation of minorities[,] [e]ach [of which] had to struggle—and to some extent struggles still—to overcome the prejudices not of a monolithic majority, but of a 'majority' composed of various minority groups of whom it was said—perhaps unfairly in many cases—that a shared characteristic was a willingness to disadvantage other groups."

Powell rejected a "two-class theory," arguing that

> the difficulties entailed in varying the level of judicial review according to a perceived "preferred" status of a particular racial or ethnic minority are intractable [because] the concepts of "majority" and "minority" necessarily reflect temporary arrangements and political judgments. . . . [T]he white "majority" itself is composed of various minority groups, most of which can lay claim to a history of prior discrimination at the hands of the State and private individuals. Not all of these groups can receive preferential

> treatment and corresponding judicial tolerance of distinctions drawn in terms of race and nationality, for then the only "majority" left would be a new minority of white Anglo-Saxon Protestants. There is no principled basis for deciding which groups would merit "heightened judicial solicitude" and which would not. Courts would be asked to evaluate the extent of the prejudice and consequent harm suffered by various minority groups. Those whose societal injury is thought to exceed some arbitrary level of tolerability then would be entitled to preferential classifications at the expense of individuals belonging to other groups. Those classifications would be free from exacting judicial scrutiny. As these preferences began to have their desired effect, and the consequences of past discrimination were undone, new judicial rankings would be necessary. The kind of variable sociological and political analysis necessary to produce such rankings simply does not lie within the judicial competence—even if they otherwise were politically feasible and socially desirable.

Justice Powell argued that preferences may not always be benign, that "preferential programs may only reinforce common stereotypes holding that certain groups are unable to achieve success without special protection based on a factor having no relationship to individual worth," and that "there is a measure of inequity in forcing innocent persons in respondent's position to bear the burdens of redressing grievances not of their making."

Powell next asked what interests were sufficiently compelling to meet the standard of strict scrutiny. Davis argued that it could engage in affirmative action to "counter[] the effects of societal discrimination." Powell conceded that "[t]he State certainly has a legitimate and substantial interest in ameliorating, or eliminating where feasible, the disabling effects of identified discrimination." However, Powell distinguished between "redress[ing] the wrongs worked by specific instances of racial discrimination" and "remedying of the effects of 'societal discrimination,' an amorphous concept of injury that may be ageless in its reach into the past." "We have never approved a classification that aids persons perceived as members of relatively victimized groups at the expense of other innocent individuals in the absence of judicial, legislative, or administrative findings of constitutional or statutory violations." The Regents had not made findings about specific acts of past discrimination, nor were they the proper body to do so, because their "broad mission is education, not the formulation of any legislative policy or the adjudication of particular claims of illegality."

By contrast, Justice Powell agreed that "the attainment of a diverse student body . . . clearly is a constitutionally permissible goal for an institution of higher education. Academic freedom, though not a specifically enumerated constitutional right, long has been viewed as a special concern of the First Amendment. The freedom of a university to make its own judgments as to education includes the selection of its student body." "[T]he right to select those students who will contribute the most to the 'robust exchange of ideas,' . . . invokes a countervailing constitutional interest, that of the First Amendment." Powell concluded that diversity is "of paramount importance" to the University's mission; hence it is "compelling in the context of a university's admissions program."

However, setting aside a specified number of seats was not an appropriate means to achieve the goal of diversity. Powell pointed to Harvard College's admissions program as proof that "assignment of a fixed number of places to a minority group is not a necessary means toward [educational diversity]." In Harvard's program "race or ethnic background may be deemed a 'plus' in a particular applicant's file, yet it does not insulate the individual from comparison with all other candidates for the available seats." It "consider[s] all pertinent elements of diversity in light of the particular qualifications of each applicant," and "treats each applicant as an individual in the admissions process. The applicant who loses out on the last available seat to another candidate receiving a 'plus' on the basis of ethnic background will not have been foreclosed from all consideration for that seat simply because he was not the right color or had the wrong surname. It would mean only that his combined qualifications, which may have included similar nonobjective factors, did not outweigh those of the other applicant."

Justice Brennan, joined by Justices White, Marshall, and Blackmun, dissented. They argued that the strict scrutiny normally accorded racial classifications was inappropriate. Whites as a group lacked the "traditional indicia of suspectness: the class is not saddled with such disabilities, or subjected to such a history of purposeful unequal treatment, or relegated to such a position of political powerlessness as to command extraordinary protection from the majoritarian political process." They argued that "racial classifications designed to further remedial purposes 'must serve important governmental objectives and must be substantially related to achievement of those objectives.'" Some degree of scrutiny is necessary because "the line between honest and thoughtful appraisal of the effects of past discrimination and paternalistic stereotyping is not so clear. . . . State programs designed ostensibly to ameliorate the effects of past racial discrimination obviously create the same hazard of stigma, since they may promote racial separatism and reinforce the views of those who believe that members of racial minorities are inherently incapable of succeeding on their own." Moreover, "the most 'discrete and insular' of whites [may] be called upon to bear the immediate, direct costs of benign discrimination. . . . [B]ecause of the significant risk that racial classifications established for ostensibly benign purposes can be misused, causing effects not unlike those created by invidious classifications," rational basis review is inappropriate. "Instead, to justify such a classification an important and articulated purpose for its use must be shown. In addition, any statute must be stricken that stigmatizes any group or that singles out those least well represented in the political process to bear the brunt of a benign program."

Requiring "a judicial determination of a constitutional or statutory violation as a predicate for race-conscious remedial actions would be self-defeating," and "would severely undermine efforts to achieve voluntary compliance with the requirements of law." Brennan concluded that "a state government may adopt race-conscious programs if the purpose of such programs is to remove the disparate racial impact its actions might otherwise have and if there is reason to believe that the disparate impact is itself the product of past discrimination, whether its own or that of society at large."

Brennan argued that the Harvard plan touted by Powell was not more constitutionally palatable than Davis's set aside: One still had to decide the degree of preference, and it will result in the exclusion of some white candidates. "Furthermore, the extent of the preference inevitably depends on how many minority applicants the particular school is seeking to admit in any particular year. It may be that the Harvard plan is more acceptable to the public than is the Davis 'quota.' . . . But there is no basis for preferring a particular preference program simply because in achieving the same goals that the Davis Medical School is pursuing, it proceeds in a manner that is not immediately apparent to the public."

Justice Marshall, dissenting, argued that:

> In light of the sorry history of discrimination and its devastating impact on the lives of Negroes, bringing the Negro into the mainstream of American life should be a state interest of the highest order. . . . While I applaud the judgment of the Court that a university may consider race in its admissions process, it is more than a little ironic that, after several hundred years of class-based discrimination against Negroes, the Court is unwilling to hold that a class-based remedy for that discrimination is permissible. [T]oday's judgment ignores the fact that for several hundred years Negroes have been discriminated against, not as individuals, but rather solely because of the color of their skins. It is unnecessary in 20th-century America to have individual Negroes demonstrate that they have been victims of racial discrimination; the racism of our society has been so pervasive that none, regardless of wealth or position, has managed to escape its impact. The experience of Negroes in America has been different in kind, not just in degree, from that of other ethnic groups. It is not merely the history of slavery alone but also that a whole people were marked as inferior by the law. And that mark has endured. The dream of America as the great melting pot has not been realized for the Negro; because of his skin color he never even made it into the pot. . . .
>
> [H]ad the Court been willing in 1896, in Plessy v. Ferguson, to hold that the Equal Protection Clause forbids differences in treatment based on race, we would not be faced with this dilemma in 1978. [F]or 58 years, from *Plessy* to Brown v. Board of Education, ours was a Nation where, *by law*, an individual could be given "special" treatment based on the color of his skin.
>
> It is because of a legacy of unequal treatment that we now must permit the institutions of this society to give consideration to race in making decisions about who will hold the positions of influence, affluence, and prestige in America. For far too long, the doors to those positions have been shut to Negroes. If we are ever to become a fully integrated society, one in which the color of a person's skin will not determine the opportunities available to him or her, we must be willing to take steps to open those doors. I do not believe that anyone can truly look into America's past and still find that a remedy for the effects of that past is impermissible. . . .
>
> I fear that we have come full circle. After the Civil War our Government started several "affirmative action" programs. This Court in the Civil Rights Cases and Plessy v. Ferguson destroyed the movement toward complete equality. For almost a century no action was taken, and this nonaction was with the tacit approval of the courts. Then we had Brown v. Board of Education and the Civil Rights Acts of Congress, followed by numerous

affirmative-action programs. *Now*, we have this Court again stepping in, this time to stop affirmative-action programs of the type used by the University of California.

Justice Blackmun also dissented:

> It is somewhat ironic to have us so deeply disturbed over [a race-conscious program when] institutions of higher learning, albeit more on the undergraduate than the graduate level, have given conceded preferences up to a point to those possessed of athletic skills, to the children of alumni, to the affluent who may bestow their largess on the institutions, and to those having connections with celebrities, the famous, and the powerful. Programs of admission to institutions of higher learning are basically a responsibility for academicians and for administrators and the specialists they employ. The judiciary, in contrast, is ill-equipped and poorly trained for this. The administration and management of educational institutions are beyond the competence of judges and are within the special competence of educators, provided always that the educators perform within legal and constitutional bounds. For me, therefore, interference by the judiciary must be the rare exception and not the rule.

Justice Stevens, joined by Chief Justice Burger and Justices Stewart and Rehnquist, concurred in the judgment in part and dissented in part. They argued that Davis's program violated Title VI and they did not reach the constitutional issues.

3. Affirmative Action from *Bakke* to *Croson*

Between *Bakke* and Justice Powell's retirement in 1987, the Court decided a number of cases involving affirmative action. Several of these cases involved Title VII, while others involved affirmative action programs under the Equal Protection Clause. See United Steelworkers v. Weber, 443 U.S. 193 (1979) (upholding a private employer's voluntary affirmative action plan under Title VII of the Civil Rights Act of 1964); Johnson v. Transportation Agency, 480 U.S. 616 (1987) (upholding a voluntary affirmative action program benefiting women on the ground that under Title VII preferential hiring programs require only showing of a "manifest imbalance" between the percentage of minorities employed and the percentage of minorities in the population, rather than the stricter equal protection standard of a "firm" basis in the evidence); Sheet Metal Workers v. EEOC, 478 U.S. 421 (1986) (upholding "narrowly tailored" affirmative action program imposed upon a union found to have engaged in illegal discrimination under Title VII and later found in contempt for failing to fulfill the court's earlier remedial order); Firefighters v. Cleveland, 478 U.S. 501 (1986) (holding that Title VII permitted a consent decree that benefited minorities who were not victims of defendant's previous discrimination).

In Fullilove v. Klutznick, 448 U.S. 448 (1980), the Court upheld the "minority business enterprise" (MBE) provision of the Public Works Employment Act of 1977, which required that 10 percent of federal funds granted for local public works projects must be used to procure services or supplies from businesses owned by minority group members. Congress included the MBE program because difficulties confronting minority contractors—such as lack of working capital, inability to meet bonding requirements, and unfamiliarity with bidding opportunities and procedures—were often the results of past discrimination. The regulations allowed waiver of the 10 percent requirement on a showing that it could not reasonably be met.

Chief Justice Burger announced the judgment of the Court in a plurality opinion sustaining the statute in an opinion joined by Justices White and Powell. Chief Justice Burger found the MBE program was within Congress's powers under §5 of the Fourteenth Amendment. Although "the Act recites no preambulary 'findings' on the subject," "we are satisfied that Congress had abundant historical basis from which it could conclude that traditional procurement practices, when applied to minority businesses, could perpetuate the effects of prior discrimination." Without articulating the standard of judicial review being applied, Burger characterized the injury to the complainant as "relatively light" and wrote that "[w]hen effectuating a limited and properly tailored remedy to cure the effects of prior discrimination such a 'sharing of the burden' by innocent parties is not impermissible."

Justice Powell concurred, arguing that Congress's competence to make findings of unlawful discrimination was "beyond question," and that the legislative history "demonstrates that Congress reasonably concluded that private and governmental discrimination had contributed to the negligible percentage of public contracts awarded minority contractors." The government interest in redressing this discrimination was "compelling." "Congress' choice of remedy should be upheld . . . if the means selected are equitable and reasonably necessary to the redress of identifiable discrimination." Although the legislative history of the MBE was sparse, Powell argued that "[Congress acquires] information and expertise . . . in the consideration and enactment of earlier legislation. After Congress has legislated repeatedly in an area of national concern, its Members gain experience that may reduce the need for fresh hearings or prolonged debate when Congress again considers action in that area. . . . [W]e properly may examine the total contemporary record of congressional action dealing with the problems of racial discrimination against minority business enterprises."

Justice Marshall, joined by Justices Brennan and Blackmun, concurred in the judgment on the basis of their separate opinion (with Justice White) in *Bakke*. Justice Stewart, joined by Justice Rehnquist, dissented on the ground that "[u]nder our Constitution, the government may never act to the detriment of a person solely because of that person's race, whether or not the person is a member of a racial minority." Justice Stevens also dissented, arguing that the statute was not narrowly tailored as a remedy for past discrimination. He also pointed out that affirmative action programs create uncomfortable problems of defining who qualifies as a racial minority who might receive a preference:

> Why were these six racial classifications, and no others, included in the preferred class? Why are aliens excluded from the preference although they are not otherwise ineligible for public contracts? What percentage of Oriental blood or what degree of Spanish-speaking skill is required for membership in the preferred class? How does the legacy of slavery and the history of discrimination against the descendants of its victims support

a preference for Spanish-speaking citizens who may be directly competing with black citizens in some overpopulated communities? Why is a preference given only to owners of business enterprises and why is that preference unaccompanied by any requirement concerning the employment of disadvantaged persons? Is the preference limited to a subclass of persons who can prove that they are subject to a special disability caused by part discrimination, as the Court's opinion indicates? Or is every member of the racial class entitled to a preference as the statutory language seems plainly to indicate? Are businesses formed just to take advantage of the preference eligible?

In Wygant v. Jackson Board of Education, 476 U.S. 267 (1986), the Court rejected a local school district's affirmative action plan that would lay off nonminority teachers first in order to preserve "the current percentage of minority personnel employed at the time of the layoff." Justice Powell's plurality opinion applied strict scrutiny and held that "alleviat[ing] the effects of societal discrimination" and providing "minority faculty role models" were not compelling state purposes. Powell argued that "[t]he Court has insisted upon some showing of prior discrimination by the governmental unit involved before allowing limited use of racial classifications in order to remedy such discrimination. . . . [B]efore it embarks on an affirmative action program, [a public employer must have] convincing evidence that remedial action is warranted[,] sufficient evidence to justify the conclusion that there has been prior discrimination." The trial court had made no "factual determination that the employer had a strong basis in evidence for its conclusion that remedial action was necessary."

In addition, "the layoff provision was not a legally appropriate means of achieving even a compelling purpose" because of "the burden that a preferential layoff scheme imposes on innocent parties. In cases involving valid hiring goals, the burden to be borne by innocent individuals is diffused to a considerable extent among society generally. Though hiring goals may burden some innocent individuals, they simply do not impose the same kind of injury that layoffs impose. Denial of a future employment opportunity is not as intrusive as loss of an existing job. . . . Layoffs disrupt these settled expectations in a way that general hiring goals do not." Justice Marshall, joined by Justices Brennan and Blackmun, dissented, arguing that the layoff provisions were necessary to preserve integration of the public schools because seniority provisions in the union contract meant that minority teachers, who were the last hired, would be the first fired. "[L]ack of some layoff protection would have crippled the efforts to recruit minority applicants. Adjustment of the layoff hierarchy under these circumstances was a necessary corollary of an affirmative action hiring policy."

4. Affirmative Action in the Rehnquist Court

Ronald Reagan's bids for the presidency in 1980 and 1984 sought to attract former Democrats by focusing on "social issues" including busing, quota systems, and affirmative action. Once in office, Reagan sought to change civil rights law and enforcement. A top priority of the Reagan Justice Department was to establish a new definition of "discrimination" that would focus on the law's unfairness to whites.[96] In 1987, Justice Powell, who had written the controlling opinion in *Bakke*, and joined the plurality in *Fullilove*, retired. President Reagan's nomination of Judge Robert Bork to replace Justice Powell failed to win Senate confirmation, and his second nominee, Judge Douglas Ginsburg, withdrew due to allegations that he had smoked marijuana. Reagan's third nominee, Justice Anthony Kennedy, was confirmed. 1987 is in many respects a watershed year, reflecting the beginning of a new conservative majority, which was bolstered by the replacement of Justice Marshall by Justice Thomas in 1991. We have already seen the effect of this majority in cases involving federalism. Another of its most important effects was in the area of affirmative action.

City of Richmond v. J.A. Croson Co.

488 U.S. 469 (1989)

Justice O'CONNOR announced the judgment of the Court and delivered the opinion of the Court with respect to Parts I, III-B, and IV, an opinion with respect to Part II, in which Chief Justice REHNQUIST and Justice WHITE joined, and an opinion with respect to Parts III-A and V, in which Justice KENNEDY also joined.

I

[The Richmond City Council adopted a Minority Business Utilization Plan based on the one upheld in Fullilove v. Klutznick that required prime contractors on city construction projects to subcontract at least 30 percent of the dollar amount of the contract to one or more Minority Business Enterprises (MBEs). The City Council also adopted *Fullilove*'s definition of MBEs: "[a] business at least fifty-one (51) percent of which is owned and controlled . . . by minority group members." "Minority group members" were defined as "[c]itizens of the United States who are Blacks, Spanish speaking, Orientals, Indians, Eskimos, or Aleuts." There was no geographic limit to the Plan; an otherwise qualified MBE from anywhere in the United States could avail itself of the 30 percent set-aside. The Plan expired on June 30, 1988, and was in effect for approximately five years. A provision, formulated by a city administrative agency, permitted waiver of the requirement only where it could be shown that "sufficient, relevant, qualified [MBEs] . . . are unavailable or unwilling to participate in the contract to enable meeting the 30% MBE goal."

The Plan was adopted by the Richmond City Council after a public hearing. Seven members of the public spoke to the merits of the ordinance: five were in opposition, two in favor. Proponents of the set-aside provision relied on a study that indicated that, while the general population of Richmond was 50 percent Black, only .67 percent of the city's prime construction contracts had been awarded to minority businesses in the five-year period from 1978 to 1983. It was also established that a variety of contractors' associations, whose representatives appeared

96. Reva B. Siegel, The Supreme Court Term October 2012—Foreword: Equality Divided, 127 Harv. L. Rev. 1, 32-34 (2013).

in opposition to the ordinance, had virtually no minority businesses within their membership. There was no direct evidence of race discrimination on the part of the city in letting contracts or any evidence that the city's prime contractors had discriminated against minority-owned subcontractors.]

II

[Justice O'Connor distinguished *Fullilove* on the ground that] Congress, unlike any State or political subdivision, has a specific constitutional mandate to enforce the dictates of the Fourteenth Amendment. . . . The power to "enforce" may at times also include the power to define situations which Congress determines threaten principles of equality and to adopt prophylactic rules to deal with those situations. . . .

That Congress may identify and redress the effects of society-wide discrimination does not mean that, a fortiori, the State and their political subdivisions are free to decide that such remedies are appropriate. Section 1 of the Fourteenth Amendment is an explicit constraint on state power, and the States must undertake any remedial efforts in accordance with that provision. To hold otherwise would be to cede control over the content of the Equal Protection Clause to the 50 state legislatures and their myriad political subdivisions. . . . We believe that such a result would be contrary to the intentions of the Framers of the Fourteenth Amendment, who desired to place clear limits on the State's use of race as a criterion for legislative action, and to have the federal courts enforce those limitations. . . .

It would seem equally clear, however, that a state or local subdivision (if delegated the authority from the State) has the authority to eradicate the effects of private discrimination within its own legislative jurisdiction. . . . *Wygant*['s statement that there must be "some showing of prior discrimination by the governmental unit involved" concerned] a race-based layoff program affecting [the state's] own work force. . . . As a matter of state law, the city of Richmond has legislative authority over its procurement policies, and can use its spending powers to remedy private discrimination, if it identifies that discrimination with the particularity required by the Fourteenth Amendment. . . . Thus, if the city could show that it had essentially become a "passive participant" in a system of racial exclusion practiced by elements of the local construction industry, we think it clear that the city could take affirmative steps to dismantle such a system. It is beyond dispute that any public entity, state or federal, has a compelling interest in assuring that public dollars, drawn from the tax contributions of all citizens, do not serve to finance the evil of private prejudice.

III

A

[T]he "rights created by the first section of the Fourteenth Amendment are, by its terms, guaranteed to the individual. The rights established are personal rights." The Richmond Plan denies certain citizens the opportunity to compete for a fixed percentage of public contracts based solely upon their race. To whatever racial group these citizens belong, their "personal rights" to be treated with equal dignity and respect are implicated by a rigid rule erecting race as the sole criterion in an aspect of public decisionmaking.

Absent searching judicial inquiry into the justification for such race-based measures, there is simply no way of determining what classifications are "benign" or "remedial" and what classifications are in fact motivated by illegitimate notions of racial inferiority or simple racial politics. . . . Classifications based on race carry a danger of stigmatic harm. Unless they are strictly reserved for remedial settings, they may in fact promote notions of racial inferiority and lead to a politics of racial hostility. We thus reaffirm the view expressed by the plurality in *Wygant* that the standard of review under the Equal Protection Clause is not dependent on the race of those burdened or benefited by a particular classification. [We] agree[] with the view expressed by Justice Powell in *Bakke,* that "[t]he guarantee of equal protection cannot mean one thing when applied to one individual and something else when applied to a person of another color." . . .

Even were we to accept a reading of the guarantee of equal protection under which the level of scrutiny varies according to the ability of different groups to defend their interests in the representative process, heightened scrutiny would still be appropriate in the circumstances of this case. One of the central arguments for applying a less exacting standard to "benign" racial classifications is that such measures essentially involve a choice made by dominant racial groups to disadvantage themselves. If one aspect of the judiciary's role under the Equal Protection Clause is to protect "discrete and insular minorities" from majoritarian prejudice or indifference, some maintain that these concerns are not implicated when the "white majority" places burdens upon itself. See J. Ely, Democracy and Distrust 170 (1980).

In this case, blacks comprise approximately 50% of the population of the city of Richmond. Five of the nine seats on the City Council are held by blacks. The concern that a political majority will more easily act to the disadvantage of a minority based on unwarranted assumptions or incomplete facts would seem to militate for, not against, the application of heightened judicial scrutiny in this case.

B

Like the "role model" theory employed in *Wygant,* a generalized assertion that there has been past discrimination in an entire industry provides no guidance for a legislative body to determine the precise scope of the injury it seeks to remedy. It "has no logical stopping point." *Wygant.* "Relief" for such an ill-defined wrong could extend until the percentage of public contracts awarded to MBEs in Richmond mirrored the percentage of minorities in the population as a whole.

Appellant argues that it is attempting to remedy various forms of past discrimination that are alleged to be responsible for the small number of minority businesses in the local contracting industry. Among these the city cites the exclusion of blacks from skilled construction trade unions and training programs. This past discrimination has prevented them "from following the traditional path from laborer to entrepreneur." The city also lists a host of nonracial factors which would seem to face a member of any racial group attempting to establish a new business enterprise, such as deficiencies in working capital, inability to meet bonding requirements, unfamiliarity with bidding procedures, and disability caused by an inadequate track record.

While there is no doubt that the sorry history of both private and public discrimination in this country has contributed to a lack of opportunities for black entrepreneurs, this observation, standing alone, cannot justify a rigid racial quota in the awarding of public contracts in Richmond, Virginia. Like the claim that discrimination in primary and secondary schooling justifies a rigid racial preference in medical school admissions, an amorphous claim that there has been past discrimination in a particular industry cannot justify the use of an unyielding racial quota. . . .

Defining these sorts of injuries as "identified discrimination" would give local governments license to create a patchwork of racial preferences based on statistical generalizations about any particular field of endeavor. . . . The 30% quota cannot in any realistic sense be tied to any injury suffered by anyone. The District Court relied upon five predicate "facts" in reaching its conclusion that there was an adequate basis for the 30% quota: (1) the ordinance declares itself to be remedial; (2) several proponents of the measure stated their views that there had been past discrimination in the construction industry; (3) minority businesses received .67% of prime contracts from the city while minorities constituted 50% of the city's population; (4) there were very few minority contractors in local and state contractors' associations; and (5) in 1977, Congress made a determination that the effects of past discrimination had stifled minority participation in the construction industry nationally.

None of these "findings," singly or together, provide the city of Richmond with a "strong basis in evidence for its conclusion that remedial action was necessary." There is nothing approaching a prima facie case of a constitutional or statutory violation by anyone in the Richmond construction industry.

The District Court accorded great weight to the fact that the city council designated the Plan as "remedial." But the mere recitation of a "benign" or legitimate purpose for a racial classification, is entitled to little or no weight. . . .

Reliance on the disparity between the number of prime contracts awarded to minority firms and the minority population of the city of Richmond is similarly misplaced. . . .

In the employment context, we have recognized that for certain entry level positions or positions requiring minimal training, statistical comparisons of the racial composition of an employer's workforce to the racial composition of the relevant population may be probative of a pattern of discrimination. But where special qualifications are necessary, the relevant statistical pool for purposes of demonstrating discriminatory exclusion must be the number of minorities qualified to undertake the particular task.

In this case, the city does not even know how many MBEs in the relevant market are qualified to undertake prime or subcontracting work in public construction projects. Nor does the city know what percentage of total city construction dollars minority firms now receive as subcontractors on prime contracts let by the city.

To a large extent, the set-aside of subcontracting dollars seems to rest on the unsupported assumption that white prime contractors simply will not hire minority firms. . . . Without any information on minority participation in subcontracting, it is quite simply impossible to evaluate overall minority representation in the city's construction expenditures.

The city and the District Court also relied on evidence that MBE membership in local contractors' associations was extremely low. Again, standing alone this evidence is not probative of any discrimination in the local construction industry. There are numerous explanations for this dearth of minority participation, including past societal discrimination in education and economic opportunities as well as both black and white career and entrepreneurial choices. . . . The mere fact that black membership in these trade organizations is low, standing alone, cannot establish a prima facie case of discrimination.

For low minority membership in these associations to be relevant, the city would have to link it to the number of local MBEs eligible for membership. If the statistical disparity between eligible MBEs and MBE membership were great enough, an inference of discriminatory exclusion could arise. In such a case, the city would have a compelling interest in preventing its tax dollars from assisting these organizations in maintaining a racially segregated construction market.

Finally, the city and the District Court relied on Congress' finding in connection with the set-aside approved in *Fullilove* that there had been nationwide discrimination in the construction industry. The probative value of these findings for demonstrating the existence of discrimination in Richmond is extremely limited. . . .

In sum, none of the evidence presented by the city points to any identified discrimination in the Richmond construction industry. We, therefore, hold that the city has failed to demonstrate a compelling interest in apportioning public contracting opportunities on the basis of race. . . .

The foregoing analysis applies only to the inclusion of blacks within the Richmond set-aside program. There is absolutely no evidence of past discrimination against Spanish-speaking, Oriental, Indian, Eskimo, or Aleut persons in any aspect of the Richmond construction industry. . . . The random inclusion of racial groups that, as a practical matter, may never have suffered from discrimination in the construction industry in Richmond, suggests that perhaps the city's purpose was not in fact to remedy past discrimination. . . .

IV

As noted by the court below, it is almost impossible to assess whether the Richmond Plan is narrowly tailored to remedy prior discrimination since it is not linked to identified discrimination in any way. We limit ourselves to two observations in this regard.

First, there does not appear to have been any consideration of the use of race-neutral means to increase minority business participation in city contracting. Many of the barriers to minority participation in the construction industry relied upon by the city to justify a racial classification appear to be race neutral. If MBEs disproportionately lack capital or cannot meet bonding requirements, a race-neutral program of city financing for small firms would, a fortiori, lead to greater minority participation. The principal opinion in *Fullilove* found that Congress had carefully examined and rejected race-neutral alternatives before enacting the MBE set-aside. There is no evidence in this record that the Richmond City Council has considered any alternatives to a race-based quota.

Second, the 30% quota cannot be said to be narrowly tailored to any goal, except perhaps outright racial balancing. It rests upon the "completely unrealistic" assumption that minorities will choose a particular trade in lockstep proportion to their representation in the local population. . . .

Even in the absence of evidence of discrimination, the city has at its disposal a whole array of race-neutral devices to increase the accessibility of city contracting opportunities to small entrepreneurs of all races. Simplification of bidding procedures, relaxation of bonding requirements, and training and financial aid for disadvantaged entrepreneurs of all races would open the public contracting market to all those who have suffered the effects of past societal discrimination or neglect. . . . Business as usual should not mean business pursuant to the unthinking exclusion of certain members of our society from its rewards.

In the case at hand, . . . it is simply impossible to say that the city has demonstrated "a strong basis in evidence for its conclusion that remedial action was necessary." *Wygant.*

Proper findings in this regard are necessary to define both the scope of the injury and the extent of the remedy necessary to cure its effects. Such findings also serve to assure all citizens that the deviation from the norm of equal treatment of all racial and ethnic groups is a temporary matter, a measure taken in the service of the goal of equality itself. Absent such findings, there is a danger that a racial classification is merely the product of unthinking stereotypes or a form of racial politics. . . . Because the city of Richmond has failed to identify the need for remedial action in the awarding of its public construction contracts, its treatment of its citizens on a racial basis violates the dictates of the Equal Protection Clause. Accordingly, the judgment of the Court of Appeals for the Fourth Circuit is affirmed.

[Justice Stevens and Justice Kennedy issued individual opinions concurring in part and concurring in the judgment.]

SCALIA, J., concurring in the judgment.

I agree with much of the Court's opinion, and, in particular, with its conclusion that strict scrutiny must be applied to all governmental classification by race, whether or not its asserted purpose is "remedial" or "benign." I do not agree, however, with the Court's dicta suggesting that, despite the Fourteenth Amendment, state and local governments may in some circumstances discriminate on the basis of race in order (in a broad sense) "to ameliorate the effects of past discrimination." The benign purpose of compensating for social disadvantages, whether they have been acquired by reason of prior discrimination or otherwise, can no more be pursued by the illegitimate means of racial discrimination than can other assertedly benign purposes we have repeatedly rejected. The difficulty of overcoming the effects of past discrimination is as nothing compared with the difficulty of eradicating from our society the source of those effects, which is the tendency—fatal to a nation such as ours—to classify and judge men and women on the basis of their country of origin or the color of their skin. A solution to the first problem that aggravates the second is no solution at all. . . .

We have in some contexts approved the use of racial classifications by the Federal Government to remedy the effects of past discrimination. I do not believe that we must or should extend those holdings to the States. . . .

A sound distinction between federal and state (or local) action based on race rests not only upon the substance of the Civil War Amendments, but upon social reality and governmental theory. . . . The struggle for racial justice has historically been a struggle by the national society against oppression in the individual States. And the struggle retains that character in modern times. . . . What the record shows, in other words, is that racial discrimination against any group finds a more ready expression at the state and local than at the federal level. To the children of the Founding Fathers, this should come as no surprise. An acute awareness of the heightened danger of oppression from political factions in small, rather than large, political units dates to the very beginning of our national history. . . .

Richmond [enacted] a set-aside clearly and directly beneficial to the dominant political group, which happens also to be the dominant racial group. The same thing has no doubt happened before in other cities (though the racial basis of the preference has rarely been made textually explicit)—and blacks have often been on the receiving end of the injustice. Where injustice is the game, however, turnabout is not fair play.

In my view there is only one circumstance in which the States may act by race to "undo the effects of past discrimination": where that is necessary to eliminate their own maintenance of a system of unlawful racial classification. . . .

A State can, of course, act "to undo the effects of past discrimination" in many permissible ways that do not involve classification by race. . . . And, of course, a State may "undo the effects of past discrimination" in the sense of giving the identified victim of state discrimination that which it wrongfully denied him. . . . That is worlds apart from the system here, in which those to be disadvantaged are identified solely by race.

I agree with the Court's dictum that a fundamental distinction must be drawn between the effects of "societal" discrimination and the effects of "identified" discrimination, and that the situation would be different if Richmond's plan were "tailored" to identify those particular bidders who "suffered from the effects of past discrimination by the city or prime contractors." In my view, however, the reason that would make a difference is not, as the Court states, that it would justify race-conscious action, but rather that it would enable race-neutral remediation. . . . In other words, far from justifying racial classification, identification of actual victims of discrimination makes it less supportable than ever, because more obviously unneeded. . . .

It is plainly true that in our society blacks have suffered discrimination immeasurably greater than any directed at other racial groups. But those who believe that racial preferences can help to "even the score" display, and reinforce, a manner of thinking by race that was the source of the injustice and that will, if it endures within our society, be the source of more injustice still. . . . Racial preferences appear to "even the score" (in some small degree) only if one embraces the proposition that our society is appropriately viewed as divided into races, making it right that an injustice rendered in the past to a black man should be compensated for by discriminating against a white. Nothing is worth that embrace. Since blacks have been disproportionately disadvantaged by racial discrimination, any race-neutral remedial program aimed at the disadvantaged as such will have a disproportionately beneficial impact on blacks. Only such a program, and not one that operates on the basis of race, is in accord with the letter and the spirit of our Constitution.

Since I believe that the appellee here had a constitutional right to have its bid succeed or fail under a decisionmaking process uninfected with racial bias, I concur in the judgment of the Court.

MARSHALL, J., with whom Justice BRENNAN and Justice BLACKMUN join, dissenting.

It is a welcome symbol of racial progress when the former capital of the Confederacy acts forthrightly to confront the effects of racial discrimination in its midst. . . . A majority of this Court holds today, however, that the Equal Protection Clause of the Fourteenth Amendment blocks Richmond's initiative. The essence of the majority's position is that Richmond has failed to catalogue adequate findings to prove that past discrimination has impeded minorities from joining or participating fully in Richmond's construction contracting industry. I find deep irony in second-guessing Richmond's judgment on this point. As much as any municipality in the United States, Richmond knows what racial discrimination is; a century of decisions by this and other federal courts has richly documented the city's disgraceful history of public and private racial discrimination. In any event, the Richmond City Council has supported its determination that minorities have been wrongly excluded from local construction contracting. Its proof includes statistics showing that minority-owned businesses have received virtually no city contracting dollars and rarely if ever belonged to area trade associations; testimony by municipal officials that discrimination has been widespread in the local construction industry; and the same exhaustive and widely publicized federal studies relied on in *Fullilove*, studies which showed that pervasive discrimination in the Nation's tight-knit construction industry had operated to exclude minorities from public contracting. These are precisely the types of statistical and testimonial evidence which, until today, this Court had credited in cases approving of race-conscious measures designed to remedy past discrimination.

More fundamentally, today's decision marks a deliberate and giant step backward in this Court's affirmative action jurisprudence. Cynical of one municipality's attempt to redress the effects of past racial discrimination in a particular industry, the majority launches a grapeshot attack on race-conscious remedies in general. The majority's unnecessary pronouncements will inevitably discourage or prevent governmental entities, particularly States and localities, from acting to rectify the scourge of past discrimination. This is the harsh reality of the majority's decision, but it is not the Constitution's command.

I

[T]he majority downplays the fact that the City Council had before it a rich trove of evidence that discrimination in the Nation's construction industry had seriously impaired the competitive position of businesses owned or controlled by members of minority groups. . . . The majority's refusal to recognize that Richmond has proven itself no exception to the dismaying pattern of national exclusion which Congress so painstakingly identified infects its entire analysis of this case. . . . The congressional program upheld in *Fullilove* was based upon an array of congressional and agency studies which documented the powerful influence of racially exclusionary practices in the business world. [A]s of 1977, there was "abundant evidence" in the public domain "that minority businesses ha[d] been denied effective participation in public contracting opportunities by procurement practices that perpetuated the effects of prior discrimination." Significantly, this evidence demonstrated that discrimination had prevented existing or nascent minority-owned businesses from obtaining not only federal contracting assignments, but state and local ones as well. . . .

The City Council's members also heard . . . testimony from city official as to the exclusionary history of the local construction industry. As the District Court noted, not a single person who testified before the City Council denied that discrimination in Richmond's construction industry had been widespread. So long as one views Richmond's local evidence of discrimination against the backdrop of systematic nationwide racial discrimination which Congress had so painstakingly identified in this very industry, this case is readily resolved.

II

. . . My view has long been that race-conscious classifications designed to further remedial goals "must serve important governmental objectives and must be substantially related to achievement of those objectives" in order to withstand constitutional scrutiny. . . . Richmond has two powerful interests in setting aside a portion of public contracting funds for minority-owned enterprises. The first is the city's interest in eradicating the effects of past racial discrimination. It is far too late in the day to doubt that remedying such discrimination is a compelling, let alone an important, interest. . . .

Richmond has a second compelling interest in setting aside, where possible, a portion of its contracting dollars. That interest is the prospective one of preventing the city's own spending decisions from reinforcing and perpetuating the exclusionary effects of past discrimination. . . .

The majority is wrong to trivialize the continuing impact of government acceptance or use of private institutions or structures once wrought by discrimination. When government channels all its contracting funds to a white-dominated community of established contractors whose racial homogeneity is the product of private discrimination, it does more than place its imprimatur on the practices which forged and which continue to define that community. It also provides a measurable boost to those economic entities that have thrived within it, while denying important economic benefits to those entities which, but for prior discrimination, might well be better qualified to receive valuable government contracts. In my view, the interest in ensuring that the government does not reflect and reinforce prior private discrimination in dispensing public contracts is every bit as strong as the interest in eliminating private discrimination—an interest which this Court has repeatedly deemed compelling. . . . Cities like Richmond may not be constitutionally required to adopt set-aside plans. But there can be no doubt that when Richmond acted affirmatively to stem the perpetuation of patterns of discrimination through its own decisionmaking, it served an interest of the highest order.

2

The remaining question with respect to the "governmental interest" prong of equal protection analysis is whether Richmond has proffered satisfactory proof of past racial discrimination to support its twin interests in remediation and in governmental nonperpetuation. . . . The city's local evidence confirmed that Richmond's construction industry did not deviate from this pernicious national pattern. The fact that just .67% of public construction expenditures over the previous five years had gone to minority-owned prime contractors, despite the city's racially mixed population, strongly suggest that construction contracting in the area was rife with "present economic inequities." To the extent this enormous disparity did not itself demonstrate that discrimination had occurred, the descriptive testimony of Richmond's elected and appointed leaders drew the necessary link between the pitifully small presence of minorities in construction contracting and past exclusionary practices. That no one who testified challenged this depiction of widespread racial discrimination in area construction contracting lent significant weight to these accounts. The fact that area trade associations had virtually no minority members dramatized the extent of present inequities and suggested the lasting power of past discriminatory systems. In sum, to suggest that the facts on which Richmond has relied do not provide a sound basis for its finding of past racial discrimination simply blinks credibility. . . .

[W]here the issue is not present discrimination but rather whether past discrimination has resulted in the continuing exclusion of minorities from an historically tight-knit industry, a contrast between population and work force is entirely appropriate to help gauge the degree of the exclusion. . . . This contrast is especially illuminating in cases like this, where a main avenue of introduction into the work force—here, membership in the trade associations whose members presumably train apprentices and help them procure subcontracting assignments—is itself grossly dominated by nonminorities. . . .

B

In my judgment, Richmond's set-aside plan also comports with the second prong of the equal protection inquiry, for it is substantially related to the interests it seeks to serve in remedying past discrimination and in ensuring that municipal contract procurement does not perpetuate that discrimination. . . . Like the federal provision [upheld in *Fullilove*], Richmond's is limited to five years in duration and was not renewed when it came up for reconsideration in 1988. Like the federal provision, Richmond's contains a waiver provision freeing from its subcontracting requirements those nonminority firms that demonstrate that they cannot comply with its provisions. Like the federal provision, Richmond's has a minimal impact on innocent third parties. While the measure affects 30% of public contracting dollars, that translates to only 3% of overall Richmond area contracting. Finally, like the federal provision, Richmond's does not interfere with any vested right of a contractor to a particular contract; instead it operates entirely prospectively. . . .

[T]he majority's suggestion that Richmond should have first undertaken such race-neutral measures as a program of city financing for small firms ignores the fact that such measures, while theoretically appealing, have been discredited by Congress as ineffectual in eradicating the effects of past discrimination in this very industry. . . .

As for Richmond's 30% target, the majority states that this figure "cannot be said to be narrowly tailored to any goal, except perhaps outright racial balancing."

The majority ignores two important facts. First, the set-aside measure affects only 3% of overall city contracting; thus, any imprecision in tailoring has far less impact than the majority suggests. But more important, the majority ignores the fact that Richmond's 30% figure was patterned directly on the *Fullilove* precedent. Congress' 10% figure fell "roughly halfway between the present percentage of minority contractors and the percentage of minority group members in the Nation." The Richmond City Council's 30% figure similarly falls roughly halfway between the present percentage of Richmond-based minority contractors (almost zero) and the percentage of minorities in Richmond (50%).

III

[T]oday, for the first time, a majority of this Court has adopted strict scrutiny as its standard of Equal Protection Clause review of race-conscious remedial measures. This is an unwelcome development. A profound difference separates governmental actions that themselves are racist, and governmental actions that seek to remedy the effects of prior racism or to prevent neutral governmental activity from perpetuating the effects of such racism.

Racial classifications "drawn on the presumption that one race is inferior to another or because they put the weight of government behind racial hatred and separatism" warrant the strictest judicial scrutiny because of the very irrelevance of these rationales. By contrast, racial classifications drawn for the purpose of remedying the effects of discrimination that itself was race-based have a highly pertinent basis: the tragic and indelible fact that discrimination against blacks and other racial minorities in this Nation has pervaded our Nation's history and continues to scar our society. . . .

In concluding that remedial classifications warrant no different standard of review under the Constitution than the most brute and repugnant forms of state sponsored racism, a majority of this Court signals that it regards racial discrimination as largely a phenomenon of the past, and that government bodies need no longer preoccupy themselves with rectifying racial injustice. I, however, do not believe this Nation is anywhere close to eradicating racial discrimination or its vestiges. In constitutionalizing its wishful thinking, the majority today does a grave disservice not only to those victims of past and present racial discrimination in this Nation whom government has sought to assist, but also to this Court's long tradition of approaching issues of race with the utmost sensitivity.

B

[The majority emphasizes that] blacks in Richmond are a "dominant racial grou[p]" in the city[,] . . . that "blacks comprise approximately 50% of the population of the city of Richmond" and that "[f]ive of the nine seats on the City Council are held by blacks."

[But] [i]t cannot seriously be suggested that nonminorities in Richmond have any "history of purposeful unequal treatment." Nor is there any indication that they have any of the disabilities that have characteristically afflicted those groups this Court has deemed suspect. Indeed, the numerical and political dominance of nonminorities within the State of Virginia and the Nation as a whole provide an enormous political check against the "simple racial politics" at the municipal level which the majority fears. If the majority really believes that groups like Richmond's nonminorities, which comprise approximately half the population but which are outnumbered even marginally in political fora, are deserving of suspect class status for these reasons alone, this Court's decisions denying suspect status to women and to persons with below-average incomes stand on extremely shaky ground. . . .

[Justice Blackmun wrote a brief dissent supporting Justice Marshall's opinion.]

DISCUSSION

1. *The (apparent) triumph of strict scrutiny and the anticlassification principle.* President Reagan's appointments of Justices O'Connor, Scalia, and Kennedy provided the crucial fifth vote to declare that strict scrutiny would apply in affirmative action cases. Justices O'Connor and Kennedy agree with Justice Powell's position in *Bakke* that classifications that burden majority and minority groups should be equally subject to strict scrutiny, while Justice Scalia argued that race-conscious remedies should be limited to the actual victims of discrimination, meaning that affirmative action policies would almost always be unconstitutional. Justices Brennan, Marshall, White, and Blackmun argued that a lower standard of intermediate scrutiny should apply to benign racial classifications.

On one view, *Croson* represents the triumph of the anticlassification principle over the antisubordination principle. For the first time, strict scrutiny would sharply limit the forms of race-conscious remedial action that governments could adopt. Yet Justice Scalia's position did not prevail, and after *Croson*, affirmative action remains constitutional so long as government satisfies the required constitutional predicates. In this sense, the doctrine of strict scrutiny set forth in *Croson* still allows benign racial classifications in sharply constrained circumstances (for example, in order to prevent the state from becoming a passive participant in private discrimination). Insofar as it continues to permit affirmative action, it is still responsive to antisubordination concerns.

2. Croson *and* Fullilove. In Fullilove v. Klutznick, the Court deferred to Congress's judgments and findings concerning past discrimination in the national construction industry and held that Congress's affirmative action remedy was appropriately tailored give those findings. The City of Richmond based its program on the program upheld in *Fullilove.* Nevertheless, the majority in *Croson* distinguished *Fullilove* by asserting (among other things) that Congress has unique remedial powers under §5 of the Fourteenth Amendment that the states do not possess. This distinction proved not to be lasting, as the Court subsequently held in Adarand Constructors v. Pena that strict scrutiny applies both to the states and the federal government. Adopting strict scrutiny in *Adarand* suggested that the Court's new conservative majority was unlikely to defer to findings of fact about private discrimination by either the states or the federal government.

3. Croson *and the fate of* Carolene Products. The theory of judicial review introduced in *Carolene Products* argues that heightened scrutiny should apply to legislation that burdens "discrete and insular minorities." It follows that legislation that burdens a group that is not a discrete and insular minority, like whites, should receive the usual presumption of constitutionality because the dispreferred can rely on the ordinary processes of democracy to repeal unwise or unfair legislation. For

this reason, for many years, the Court's liberals argued that an intermediate scrutiny approach was appropriate in cases involving benign race-based classifications.

In *Croson*, the Court rejected such an approach, over Justice Marshall's strong protest. Although Justice O'Connor points to the fact that Black people constitute a majority of the City of Richmond and control the Richmond City Council, there is no evidence that her opinion would have reached a different conclusion if whites were a majority and, indeed, had controlled all of the Council seats. Indeed, even if the white citizens of Richmond had unanimously agreed to the plan in a referendum, it would have still been subjected to strict scrutiny. Note that, in any case, the other groups benefited by the affirmative action plan—in particular Hispanics—did not constitute a majority in Richmond, yet the Court did not try to sever these parts of the plan from the portion that benefited African Americans. Should it have?

4. *Why are there so few Black contractors in Richmond?* Contrast the narratives told by the majority and the dissent about how Black people came to have such low representation in the construction industry in Richmond. What kinds of causal assumptions do the two sides make?

Justice O'Connor argues that "the 30% quota" chosen by the Richmond City Council "cannot be said to be narrowly tailored to any goal, except perhaps outright racial balancing. It rests upon the 'completely unrealistic' assumption that minorities will choose a particular trade in lockstep proportion to their representation in the local population." Why, precisely, does O'Connor think that, absent discrimination, minorities would not choose a particular trade in roughly the same proportion as the general population?

One theory would be that some social groups simply have cultural preferences for certain types of occupations rather than others. Thus, we might find very few Jews going into the pork sausage industry. Is there any reason to think that African Americans have a special distaste for the contracting industry? Note that similar arguments have often been offered to explain why women stay out of certain professions, like contracting. Is this "lack of interest" phenomenon based purely on private preferences that are unrelated to societal discrimination? See Vicki Schultz, Telling Stories About Women and Work: Judicial Interpretations of Sex Segregation in the Workplace in Title VII Cases Raising the Lack of Interest Argument, 103 Harv. L. Rev. 1750 (1990).

A second reason to expect disparities in representation would be that some social groups gravitate toward certain occupations in random patterns due to the effects of immigration. Thus, if one Korean family opens a grocery store, members of their family and friends who emigrate from Korea subsequently might work for them, learn skills, and eventually open their own grocery store. As a result, without any form of social discrimination at work, more Koreans will end up working in grocery stores, than say, tobacco shops or diners. Given that most African Americans did not immigrate into this country recently, is this an adequate explanation for their lack of representation in the construction industry?

A third explanation is that some social groups are harder working and more energetic than others, adapt themselves better to majority expectations, and therefore are better represented in the most remunerative occupations. For example, the higher representation of Jews in professions like law and medicine is sometimes explained in this way. However, to offer this sort of explanation means that one must also believe that other social groups have, by comparison, less of these desirable traits and that explains why they do worse. Consider Morris Abram:

> Because groups—black, white, Hispanic, male, and female—do not necessarily have the same distribution of, among other characteristics, skills, interest, motivation, and age, a fair shake system may not produce proportional representation across occupations and professions, and certainly not at any given time. This uneven distribution, however, is not necessarily the result of discrimination. Thomas Sowell has shown through comparative studies of ethnic group performance that discrimination alone cannot explain these ethnic groups' varying levels of achievement. Groups such as the Japanese, Chinese and West Indian blacks have fared very well in American society despite racial bias against these groups.[97]

Consider whether this is an explanation the Court would be likely to offer for the lack of Black participation in the Richmond construction industry. Is it in tension with the colorblind assumption that government agencies (in this case, federal courts) should not presume that skin color makes a difference in how people are likely to behave?

Note once again that this sort of explanation of Black underrepresentation in the construction industry involves what Professor Gotanda calls a cultural conception of race rather than the formal notion of race that lies at the heart of the colorblindness principle. Opponents of affirmative action generally reject a cultural conception of race when it is argued that Black people add special diversity in education; it is said to involve invidious stereotyping to assume that the way one thinks or behaves is strongly correlated with the color of one's skin. If so, why should one accept a cultural account as an explanation of Black underrepresentation here? Is it fair to invoke a formal account of race to combat arguments for affirmative action based on diversity and invoke a cultural account of race to combat arguments for affirmative action based on the need to remedy past discrimination? See Reva B. Siegel, The Racial Rhetorics of Colorblind Affirmative Action, in Representing Affirmative Action (Robert Post ed., 1998). On the other hand, should it be permissible to invoke cultural notions of race to justify diversity-based affirmative action and formal accounts of race to justify remedial affirmative action?

Even if this kind of cultural explanation could be offered to explain Black underrepresentation in the Richmond construction industry, is it unrelated to societal discrimination? Can Abram's account explain why so few contractors were Black in a city that was 50 percent Black, and why only .67 percent of the city's

---

97. Morris B. Abram, Affirmative Action: Fair Shakers and Social Engineers, 99 Harv. L. Rev. 1312, 1315-1316 (1986). See also Charles Murray, What It Means to Be a Libertarian: A Personal Interpretation 85-86 (1997) ("[A] system that . . . judg[ed] each case perfectly on its merits[] would produce drastically different proportions of men and women hired by police forces, blacks and whites put in jail, or Jews and gentiles admitted to elite law schools"); Nathan Glazer, Affirmative Discrimination: Ethnic Inequality and Public Policy 62-63 (1975) (distribution of jobs among minority groups is best explained by differences in educational qualifications, regional variables, and difficult to qualify factors "such as taste, or, if you will, culture").

prime construction contracts were awarded to minority businesses in the five-year period from 1978 to 1983? Even if one thought that the private preferences and tastes of Black people played a significant role in steering them away from construction jobs in addition to the effects of private discrimination, is the 30 percent figure chosen by the Richmond City Council in a 50 percent Black population entirely unreasonable?

5. *Strict scrutiny and racial group similarity and difference.* The above analysis suggests that the Court's strict scrutiny doctrine is premised on a skepticism that underrepresentation or stratification is actually caused by public or private racial discrimination. Instead, underrepresentation or stratification is more likely the result of cultural factors. The irony, then, is that the Court's colorblindness theory, which justifies strict scrutiny, is premised on assumptions about racial difference.

6. *Colorblindness versus "social engineering."* Justice O'Connor's rejection of the 30 percent figure as "outright racial balancing" suggests that she believes either that racial stratification and racial segregation of labor markets will occur naturally, without much private racial discrimination, or that even if private racial discrimination plays a significant role, there is nothing that government can do to prevent such racial stratification and racial segregation. Attempting to achieve more equal representation of Black people in the construction industry would be mere "social engineering" that would not eradicate racism but merely stoke the fires of racial resentment. Compare this analysis to Justice Brown's comment in *Plessy* that "[l]egislation is powerless to eradicate racial instincts or to abolish distinctions based upon physical differences, and the attempt to do so can only result in accentuating the difficulties of the present situation." Could one fairly summarize O'Connor's argument as substituting the word "cultural" for the word "physical"?

7. Metro Broadcasting: *Diversity as a justification for affirmative action. Croson* held that strict scrutiny applied to racial classifications by states and local governments but distinguished classifications by the federal government because of Congress's §5 powers to enforce the Fourteenth Amendment. In Metro Broadcasting v. FCC, 497 U.S. 547 (1990), the Court, by a 5-4 margin, upheld two of the Federal Communications Commission's minority preference policies, which gave preferences for minority owned businesses in obtaining new broadcasting licenses. Justice Brennan's majority opinion, following *Fullilove,* applied intermediate scrutiny. Analogizing the case to *Bakke,* Justice Brennan wrote that "[j]ust as a 'diverse student body' contributing to a 'robust exchange of ideas' is a 'constitutionally permissible goal' on which a race-conscious university admissions program may be predicated, the diversity of views and information on the airwaves serves important First Amendment values." Justice O'Connor's dissent argued that at most *Fullilove* held that Congress's §5 powers allowed it to pass special kinds of remedial legislation, not applicable in this case. Justice Kennedy's dissent compared the majority's opinion to the Court's use of a reasonableness standard in Plessy v. Ferguson.

Following *Metro Broadcasting,* Justices Brennan and Marshall left the Court, and were replaced by Justices Souter and Thomas, respectively. Although the appointment of Justice Souter to replace Justice Brennan did not change the balance of power on the Court on affirmative action, Justice Marshall's replacement by Justice Thomas did.

ADARAND CONSTRUCTORS v. PENA, 515 U.S. 200 (1995): [Section 8(a) of the Small Business Act awarded compensation to prime contractors doing business with the federal government if they hired subcontractors certified as small businesses controlled by "socially and economically disadvantaged individuals." These are presumed by law to include "Black Americans, Hispanic Americans, Native Americans, Asian Pacific Americans, and other minorities, or any other individual found to be disadvantaged by the [Small Business] Administration pursuant to Section 8(a) of the Small Business Act." Adarand, which had submitted the low bid for a federal highway construction project in Colorado, challenged the award of a subcontract to the Gonzales Construction Company. The Court, by a vote of 5-4, overruled *Metro Broadcasting.*]

O'CONNOR, J.:

[T]he Court's cases through *Croson* had established three general propositions with respect to governmental racial classifications. First, skepticism: "Any preference based on racial or ethnic criteria must necessarily receive a most searching examination." Second, consistency: "The standard of review under the Equal Protection Clause is not dependent on the race of those burdened or benefited by a particular classification." And third, congruence: "Equal protection analysis in the Fifth Amendment area is the same as that under the Fourteenth Amendment." Taken together, these three propositions lead to the conclusion that any person, of whatever race, has the right to demand that any governmental actor subject to the Constitution justify any racial classification subjecting that person to unequal treatment under the strictest judicial scrutiny. . . .

[T]he Fifth and Fourteenth Amendments to the Constitution protect persons, not groups. It follows from that principle that all governmental action based on race—a group classification long recognized as "in most circumstances irrelevant and therefore prohibited"—should be subjected to detailed judicial inquiry to ensure that the personal right to equal protection of the laws has not been infringed. . . . Accordingly, we hold today that all racial classifications, imposed by whatever federal, state, or local governmental actor, must be analyzed by a reviewing court under strict scrutiny. In other words, such classifications are constitutional only if they are narrowly tailored measures that further compel governmental interests. . . .

Finally, we wish to dispel the notion that strict scrutiny is "strict in theory, but fatal in fact." The unhappy persistence of both the practice and the lingering effects of racial discrimination against minority groups in this country is an unfortunate reality, and government is not disqualified from acting in response to it. As recently as 1987, for example, every Justice of this Court agreed that the Alabama Department of Public Safety's "pervasive, systematic, and obstinate discriminatory conduct" justified a narrowly tailored race-based remedy. When race-based action is necessary to further a compelling interest, such action is within constitutional constraints if it satisfies the "narrow tailoring" test this Court has set out in previous cases. . . .

SCALIA, J., concurring in part and concurring in the judgment:

I join the opinion of the Court . . . except insofar as it may be inconsistent with the following: In my view, government can never have a "compelling interest" in discriminating on the basis of race in order to "make up" for past racial discrimination in the opposite direction. Individuals who have been wronged by unlawful racial discrimination should be made whole; but under our Constitution there can be no such thing as either a creditor or a debtor race. That concept is alien to the Constitution's focus upon the individual. . . . To pursue the concept of racial entitlement—even for the most admirable and benign of purposes—is to reinforce and preserve for future mischief the way of thinking that produced race slavery, race privilege and race hatred. In the eyes of government, we are just one race here. It is American.

THOMAS, J., concurring in part and concurring in the judgment:

I believe that there is a "moral [and] constitutional equivalence" between laws designed to subjugate a race and those that distribute benefits on the basis of race in order to foster some current notion of equality. Government cannot make us equal; it can only recognize, respect, and protect us as equal before the law. . . . As far as the Constitution is concerned, it is irrelevant whether a government's racial classifications are drawn by those who wish to oppress a race or by those who have a sincere desire to help those thought to be disadvantaged. There can be no doubt that the paternalism that appears to lie at the heart of this program is at war with the principle of inherent equality that underlies and infuses our Constitution. . . . In my mind, government-sponsored racial discrimination based on benign prejudice is just as noxious as discrimination inspired by malicious prejudice. In each instance, it is racial discrimination, plain and simple.

STEVENS, J., with whom GINSBURG, J., joins, dissenting:

. . . There is no moral or constitutional equivalence between a policy that is designed to perpetuate a caste system and one that seeks to eradicate racial subordination. Invidious discrimination is an engine of oppression, subjugating a disfavored group to enhance or maintain the power of the majority. Remedial race-based preferences reflect the opposite impulse: a desire to foster equality in society. . . . The consistency that the Court espouses would disregard the difference between a "No Trespassing" sign and a welcome mat. It would treat a Dixiecrat Senator's decision to vote against Thurgood Marshall's confirmation in order to keep African Americans off the Supreme Court as on a par with President Johnson's evaluation of his nominee's race as a positive factor. It would equate a law that made black citizens ineligible for military service with a program aimed at recruiting black soldiers. An attempt by the majority to exclude members of a minority race from a regulated market is fundamentally different from a subsidy that enables a relatively small group of newcomers to enter that market. . . .

[T]oday's lecture about "consistency" will produce the anomalous result that the Government can more easily enact affirmative-action programs to remedy discrimination against women than it can enact affirmative-action programs to remedy discrimination against African Americans—even though the primary purpose of the Equal Protection Clause was to end discrimination against the former slaves. When a court becomes preoccupied with abstract standards, it risks sacrificing common sense at the altar of formal consistency.

As a matter of constitutional and democratic principle, a decision by representatives of the majority to discriminate against the members of a minority race is fundamentally different from those same representatives' decision to impose incidental costs on the majority of their constituents in order to provide a benefit to a disadvantaged minority. . . .

[Justice Souter, joined by Justice Ginsburg and Justice Breyer, and Justice Ginsburg, joined by Justice Breyer, also dissented.]

NOTE: ORIGINALISM AND AFFIRMATIVE ACTION

Justice Thomas and the late Justice Scalia have been strong supporters of a jurisprudence of original meaning, which, in their version, looks to the meanings, understandings, and practices of the adopting generation. In the Court's affirmative action cases, however, they did not attempt to discern whether the framers and adopters of the Fourteenth Amendment would have regarded race-conscious affirmative action programs as unconstitutional, and whether the idea of a "colorblind" Constitution has any basis in the original meaning or original understanding of the Civil War Amendments. In fact, only a nonoriginalist, Justice Thurgood Marshall, writing in *Bakke*, sought to investigate the original understanding of the Reconstruction framers; he concluded that the history supported the constitutionality of affirmative action programs.[98]

Reviewing the history of the period suggests some of the complicated problems that arise from applying originalist methods to contemporary problems, and the difficulties that inevitably occur in trying to discern the present constitutional consequences of original meanings, understandings, and practices.

1. *Was federal Reconstruction legislation race-conscious or race-neutral?* Eric Schnapper writes:

> From the closing days of the Civil War until the end of civilian Reconstruction some five years later, Congress adopted a series of social welfare programs whose benefits were expressly limited to blacks. These programs were generally open to all blacks, not only to recently freed slaves, and were adopted over repeatedly expressed objections that such racially exclusive measures were unfair to whites. The race-conscious Reconstruction programs were enacted concurrently with the fourteenth amendment and were supported by the same legislators who favored the constitutional guarantee of equal protection. This history strongly suggests that the framers of the amendment could not have intended it generally to prohibit affirmative action for blacks or other disadvantaged groups.

---

98. Regents of the Univ. of Cal v. Bakke, 438 U.S. 265, 397-398 (1978) (separate opinion of Marshall, J.). See also *Croson*, 488 U.S. at 559-561 (Marshall, J., dissenting) ("[N]othing in the Amendments themselves, or in our long history of interpreting or applying those momentous charters, suggests that States, exercising their police power, are in any way constitutionally inhibited from working alongside the Federal Government in the fight against discrimination and its effects.").

Eric Schnapper, Affirmative Action and the Legislative History of the Fourteenth Amendment, 71 Va. L. Rev. 753, 754, 760-761 (1985). Schnapper emphasizes in particular the 1865 and 1866 Freedmen's Bureau Acts.

Paul Moreno has responded that all "Freedmen's Bureau and civil rights acts from 1865 onwards" granted benefits and special treatment to "refugees and freedmen," a facially race-neutral classification that also included white refugees of the Civil War. Paul Moreno, Racial Classifications and Reconstruction Legislation, 61 J. S. Hist. 271, 277-278 (1995). Although Schnapper contends that the inclusion of white refugees "was not a significant impetus in the adoption of the [1865] Act," Moreno insists that "the inclusion of white refugees was crucial to the adoption of the act." Schnapper points out that in practice, the benefits of the 1865 Act went overwhelmingly to Black people, and that "[f]reedmen were the only beneficiaries of programs such as education, labor regulation, Bureau farms, land distribution, adjustments of real estate disputes, [and] supervision of the civil and criminal justice systems through the freedmen's courts." This suggests that the inclusion of white refugees was primarily a fig leaf designed to mollify Democrats and more conservative Republicans. This also tends to support both Schnapper's view that the Act was race-conscious in intention and Moreno's view that the price of passage was that it be formally race-neutral.

Stephen Siegel objects to Moreno's arguments on another ground: He points out that the reference to "freedmen" and to "previous condition of servitude" in the Freedmen's Acts (and other Reconstruction-era legislation) was clearly a racial category. He points out that "[i]n post-bellum America, race, color, and 'previous condition of servitude' were fully interchangeable" particularly because Southern legislatures used the category of "previous condition of servitude" as a means of subordinating Black people. Stephen A. Siegel, The Federal Government's Power to Enact Color-Conscious Laws: An Originalist Inquiry, 92 Nw. U. L. Rev. 477, 560 (1998). Hence, in Siegel's view, statutes that gave benefits to "freedmen and refugees" would still be color-conscious even if some refugees were white.

Siegel points out that not only the Freedmen's Acts but many other pieces of legislation specifically granted benefits to people based on their previous condition of servitude. For example, prior to the 1865 Freedmen's Act, Congress had created a bank for "persons heretofore held in slavery in the United States, or their descendants," Act of March 3, 1865, ch. 92, 13 Stat. 510. Moreno argues that Reconstruction legislation designed to benefit former slaves was not color-conscious, but was only designed to remedy actual victims of race discrimination, a form of remedial relief that modern-day opponents of affirmative action are happy to accept. To demonstrate this, Moreno points to the fact that the phrase "and other persons of African descent" was struck from the bill. How does one explain the retention of the words "or their descendants"?

Similar problems occur in discerning the meaning of the 1866 Freedmen's Bureau Act, which extended the 1865 Act. Schnapper argues that while the 1866 Act was also formally race-neutral in its application to "freedmen and refugees," much opposition was based on the grounds that its benefits went exclusively to Black people and that the law in effect made a racial distinction. "Congressman

Taylor most forcefully expressed this argument, in language that bears an uncanny resemblance to modern objections to affirmative action programs":[99]

> This, sir, is what I call class legislation—legislation for a particular class of the blacks to the exclusion of all whites. . . . I warn the gentlemen in their zeal to elevate and ameliorate the condition of the freedmen not to allow this bill to pass regardless of the great principle, equality before the law. . . . Many persons in our community have been proclaiming equality before the law so long, taking their text from the institution of slavery . . . it would be well to stop and consider whether or not by passing this bill in its present shape we shall not overleap the mark and land on the other side, and before we are aware of it, not have the freedmen equal before the law, but superior.

Proponents of the 1866 bill responded to these arguments by insisting that the bill was race-neutral, and emphasized the Bureau's provision of goods to white refugees, but opponents insisted that this was a sham.[100] President Johnson vetoed the first version of the 1866 bill, but Congress passed a new bill that overrode his veto. This version extended the Bureau for two years, for the benefit of "all loyal refugees and freedmen," but also directed the Bureau to provide educational facilities for freedmen until the states "made provision for the education of their citizens without distinction of color." Is the latter provision race-conscious? Note that it was in the interests of supporters of the Freedmen's Bureau Act to insist that the Act was race-neutral even if their intention was primarily to benefit Black people, and it was in the interests of their opponents to argue that the Act was in effect special favoritism for Black people, even if some whites were actually benefited. Given this political background, what consequences should any of this have for the question of race-conscious affirmative action programs today?

2. *Was federal Reconstruction legislation at all relevant to the meaning of the Fourteenth Amendment?* A different objection to Schnapper's arguments is that congressional action is irrelevant to the meaning of the Fourteenth Amendment, because the federal government was not bound by the Fourteenth Amendment. However, this argument proves too much for originalist opponents of affirmative action, since it completely undermines *Adarand* as a matter of original understanding, not to mention Bolling v. Sharpe. (Recall the earlier discussion of *Bolling*'s consistency with original meaning.)

In fact, an originalist might argue that the Equal Protection Clause is not the relevant provision. The Citizenship Clause (which applies to both the federal government and the states) and the Privileges or Immunities Clause (which guarantees Privileges or Immunities of national citizenship), are the relevant provisions. Under the Citizenship Clause, the United States must respect the equal citizenship status of all citizens. The Privileges or Immunities Clause provides that U.S. citizenship

99. Schnapper, at 763-764.

100. Despite these accusations by opponents of the Freedmen's Act of 1866, Moreno points out that assistance to white refugees in terms of food, fuel, and clothing was quite substantial, especially "in the areas that had been most loyal to the Union, especially in the border states and the high country." Moreno, at 287.

comes with privileges and immunities, which include equality in civil rights. If the states cannot abridge the privileges and immunities of national citizenship, then a fortiori neither can the national government. Hence, if the states may not treat Blacks and whites unequally with respect to civil rights, neither can the federal government.[101] Under this interpretation, what power, if any, would Congress have to pursue race-conscious affirmative action under §5 of the Fourteenth Amendment?

Stephen Siegel rejects this argument from implication: "The exclusion of the national government from the [Privileges or Immunities Clause] seems quite deliberate. Reconstruction era constitution makers knew how to bind both the states and the federal government when they thought it appropriate."[102]

As a result, he concludes that "nothing in the Founding era Constitution limits federal power to enact race-based classifications" and that "although the Reconstruction Amendments constrain federal power over certain subjects, such as slavery, citizenship and voting, they still leave the national government with extensive power to enact race-based laws."[103] Do you agree?

3. *Was federal Reconstruction legislation about civil equality or social equality?* Jed Rubenfeld argues that the best evidence of the original understanding is not the Freedman's Bureau Acts, but other congressional legislation:[104]

> In July 1866, the Thirty-Ninth Congress—the selfsame Congress that had just framed the Fourteenth Amendment—passed a statute appropriating money for . . . "the relief of destitute colored women and children." In 1867, the Fortieth Congress—the same body that was driving the Fourteenth Amendment down the throat of the bloody South—passed a statute providing money for . . . the destitute "colored" persons in the nation's capital. Year after year in the Civil War period—before, during, and after ratification of the Fourteenth Amendment—Congress made special appropriations and adopted special procedures for awarding bounty and prize money to the "colored" soldiers and sailors of the Union Army.
>
> These statutes are not like the well-known Freedmen's Bureau Acts of the same period, directing benefits to blacks but using classifications that were formally race-neutral. On the contrary, these statutes expressly refer to color in the allotment of federal benefits. Nor are these statutes buried in archives deep within the Library of Congress. They are, if not

---

101. See Akhil Reed Amar, The Bill of Rights: Creation and Reconstruction 281-283 (1998); Akhil Reed Amar, Constitutional Rights in a Federal System: Rethinking Incorporation and Reverse Incorporation, in Benchmarks: Great Constitutional Controversies in the Supreme Court 71 (Terry Eastland ed., 1995); Mark A. Graber, A Constitutional Conspiracy Unmasked, Why "No State" Does Not Mean "No State," 10 Const. Comment. 87 (1993).

102. Stephen A. Siegel, The Federal Government's Power to Enact Color-Conscious Laws: An Originalist Inquiry, 92 Nw. U. L. Rev. 477, 571 (1998). Siegel points to the Thirteenth and Fifteenth Amendments as examples.

103. Id. at 481-482.

104. Jed Rubenfeld, Affirmative Action, 107 Yale L.J. 427, 430-432 (1997) (citing Act of July 28, 1866, ch. 296, 14 Stat. 310, 317; Resolution of Mar. 16, 1867, No. 4, 15 Stat. 20). See also Siegel, The Federal Government's Power to Enact Color-Conscious Laws, supra n.102, at 560-562 (offering additional examples).

well-known, at least knowable by anyone who takes three minutes with the United States Statutes at Large (look up "colored" in the indexes for more). What do they prove? Only that those who profess fealty to the "original understanding," who abhor judicial "activism," or who hold that the legal practices at the time of enactment "say what they say" and dictate future interpretation, cannot categorically condemn color-based distribution of governmental benefits as they do.

Is this a compelling argument that race-conscious affirmative action was acceptable to the framers of the Fourteenth Amendment? Recall that the Thirty-Ninth Congress was wary about granting Black people full equality. They made a distinction between civil, political, and social equality.[105] Thus, one response to Rubenfeld's argument is that the framers accepted race-conscious relief that concerned social matters like education and welfare, but not questions of civil equality like the making of contracts. This distinction flowed from the fact that they expected Black people to be socially and politically unequal and only civilly equal.

How does this translate into contemporary terms? One view would be that affirmative action in education is permissible but not affirmative action in government contracting. Another view would be that education and forms of government assistance are so central to equal opportunity in today's world that the distinction between civil and social equality has completely eroded; hence no affirmative action programs are permissible. Of course, this leads back to the general problem of the appropriate way of interpreting the original understanding. One could argue in precisely the opposite direction—that the framers' repeated use of affirmative action in social matters means that affirmative action in contracting is now permissible given that the civil/social distinction has been exploded.

Whatever one's view on these questions, the historical record also tends to undermine several features of current doctrine that limit affirmative action programs. The framers of the Fourteenth Amendment offered welfare relief to indigent Black people whether or not they were the victims of discrimination, or, at the very least, without requiring any showing of previous discrimination. In almost every case the body (Congress) that created the race-conscious program was not the governmental unit that had previously discriminated against the recipients of the program. Nor did Congress make detailed findings of its previous discriminatory acts against Black people. This suggests that the current Court's rejection of programs that remedy general societal discrimination is unsupported by the original understanding. Also inconsistent with the original understanding is the current Court's requirement that only the governmental unit that previously discriminated against minorities may engage in race-conscious remedies, and then only to alleviate the effects of its (well-documented) past discrimination.

4. *Did the framers of the Fourteenth Amendment subscribe to a "colorblind" theory?* One might argue that the framers' desire for complete civil equality between Blacks and whites should be expanded into a general prohibition on any race-conscious

---

105. Note that this distinction concerned the meaning of the Privileges or Immunities Clause. Recall that prior to the *Slaughterhouse Cases*, the Privileges or Immunities Clause, and not the Equal Protection Clause, was understood to be the primary guarantor of Black equality.

relief because the deepest meaning of the Fourteenth Amendment is the principle of colorblindness. Yet it is not at all clear that the framers of the Fourteenth Amendment believed in a colorblindness principle, although it was repeatedly pressed on them by more radical thinkers like Thaddeus Stevens and the abolitionist Wendell Phillips.[106] Indeed, the evidence is quite to the contrary. Colorblindness was at most accepted in the area of civil rights, not political rights or social rights. Andrew Kull writes that the framers chose to speak of "privileges or immunities" and "equal protection" rather than colorblindness because they were worried that a colorblindness rule would give Blacks the vote: "[T]he evidence shows that an open-ended promise of equality was added to the Constitution because to its moderate proponents it meant less, not more, than the rule of nondiscrimination that was the rejected radical alternative."[107] How, then, should an originalist interpret the constitutional text? If the political/civil/social distinction was important to the framers and adopters of the Fourteenth Amendment, why should it not be for modern-day originalists?

"With Justice Harlan's dissenting opinion in *Plessy*," Kull writes, "the color-blind Constitution became one of the available meanings of the Fourteenth Amendment."[108] But even here the meaning of colorblindness is morally ambiguous. Like the framers of the Fourteenth Amendment, Justice Harlan believed that nothing in the colorblindness principle guaranteed full social equality for Black people; to Harlan colorblindness was perfectly consistent with Blacks remaining social inferiors to whites "for all time." What does social inequality mean today, and what is its relationship to colorblindness in contemporary law and politics?

5. The Court Reaffirms *Bakke*

Following *Croson* and *Adarand*, a key question was whether the Court would revisit its previous decision in *Bakke*. A year after *Adarand*, in Hopwood v. State of Texas, 78 F.3d 932 (5th Cir. 1996), the Fifth Circuit held that "Justice Powell's argument in *Bakke* garnered only his own vote and has never represented the view of a majority of the Court in *Bakke* or any other case." It read *Adarand* as holding that the only compelling justification that the Supreme Court had recognized for affirmative action was remedying past discrimination and that "non-remedial state interests will never justify racial classifications." It concluded that "the use of ethnic diversity simply to achieve racial heterogeneity, even as part of the consideration of a number of factors, is unconstitutional"; and barred the University of Texas Law School from using race in its admissions decisions. The Supreme Court did not grant certiorari in *Hopwood*; instead, it considered a pair of challenges to the admissions policies at the Law School and the undergraduate program at the University of Michigan.

---

106. Stevens's proposal for the Fourteenth Amendment (which was essentially the same as Phillips's) was introduced on December 5, 1866, and was explicitly based on the abolitionist demand for colorblindness: "All national and State laws shall be equally applicable to every citizen, and no discrimination shall be made on account of race and color." Cong. Globe, 39th Cong., 1st Sess. 10 (1865).

107. Andrew Kull, The Color-Blind Constitution 69 (1992).

108. Id. at 118.

Grutter v. Bollinger

539 U.S. 306 (2003)

Justice O'CONNOR delivered the opinion of the Court.

This case requires us to decide whether the use of race as a factor in student admissions by the University of Michigan Law School (Law School) is unlawful.

I

A

[Michigan's admissions] policy requires admissions officials to evaluate each applicant based on all the information available in the file, including a personal statement, letters of recommendation, and an essay describing the ways in which the applicant will contribute to the life and diversity of the Law School. . . . [A]dmissions officials must consider the applicant's undergraduate grade[s] and Law School Admissions Test (LSAT) score; [however] even the highest possible score does not guarantee admission to the Law School. Nor does a low score automatically disqualify an applicant. Rather, . . . admissions officials [must] look beyond grades and test scores to . . . [s]o-called "soft variables" such as "the enthusiasm of recommenders, the quality of the undergraduate institution, the quality of the applicant's essay, and the areas and difficulty of undergraduate course selection."

The policy aspires to "achieve that diversity which has the potential to enrich everyone's education and thus make a law school class stronger than the sum of its parts." [It] . . . recognizes "many possible bases for diversity admissions" [but] reaffirm[s] the Law School's longstanding commitment to "one particular type of diversity," that is, "racial and ethnic diversity with special reference to the inclusion of students from groups which have been historically discriminated against, like African-Americans, Hispanics and Native Americans, who without this commitment might not be represented in our student body in meaningful numbers." By enrolling a "'critical mass' of [underrepresented] minority students," the Law School seeks to "ensur[e] their ability to make unique contributions to the character of the Law School." . . .

B

[Petitioner Barbara Grutter is a white Michigan resident who applied to the Law School in 1996 with a 3.8 grade point average and 161 LSAT score. The Law School initially placed petitioner on a waiting list, but subsequently rejected her application. She sued the University of Michigan, the Law School, and various university officials arguing that their admissions policy violated the Fourteenth Amendment and Title VI of the Civil Rights Act of 1964, which requires recipients of federal funds not to discriminate on the basis of race. She alleged that her application was rejected because the Law School uses race as a "predominant" factor, giving applicants who belong to certain minority groups "a significantly greater chance of admission than students with similar credentials from disfavored racial groups."]

During the 15-day bench trial, the parties introduced extensive evidence concerning the Law School's use of race in the admissions process. Dennis Shields, Director of Admissions when petitioner applied to the Law School, testified that he did not direct his staff to admit a particular percentage or number of minority students, but rather to consider an applicant's race along with all other factors. . . . [A]t the height of the admissions season, he would frequently consult the so-called "daily reports" that kept track of the racial and ethnic composition of the class (along with other information such as residency status and gender) . . . to ensure that a critical mass of underrepresented minority students would be reached. . . . Shields stressed, however, that he did not seek to admit any particular number or percentage of underrepresented minority students.

Erica Munzel, who succeeded Shields as Director of Admissions, testified that "'critical mass'" means "'meaningful numbers'" or "'meaningful representation,'" . . . a number that encourages underrepresented minority students to participate in the classroom and not feel isolated. Munzel stated there is no number, percentage, or range of numbers or percentages that constitute critical mass. . . . The current Dean of the Law School, Jeffrey Lehman . . . indicated that critical mass means numbers such that underrepresented minority students do not feel isolated or like spokespersons for their race. . . . [P]rofessor Richard Lempert, who chaired the faculty committee that drafted the 1992 policy . . . explained that [the point of the focus on historically discriminated against groups was not] to remedy past discrimination, but rather to include students who may bring to the Law School a perspective different from that of members of groups which have not been the victims of such discrimination. . . . [O]ther groups, such as Asians and Jews, have experienced discrimination, but . . . were not mentioned in the policy because individuals who are members of those groups were already being admitted to the Law School in significant numbers. Kent Syverud . . . a professor at the Law School when the 1992 admissions policy was adopted . . . [testified] that when a critical mass of underrepresented minority students is present, racial stereotypes lose their force because nonminority students learn there is no "minority viewpoint" but rather a variety of viewpoints among minority students.

[R]elying on data obtained from the Law School, petitioner's expert, Dr. Kinley Larntz, generated and analyzed "admissions grids" for the years in question (1995-2000). . . . He concluded that membership in certain minority groups "is an extremely strong factor in the decision for acceptance," and that applicants from these minority groups "are given an extremely large allowance for admission" as compared to applicants who are members of nonfavored groups. Dr. Larntz conceded, however, that race is not the predominant factor in the Law School's admissions calculus.

Dr. Stephen Raudenbush, the Law School's expert, [testified that] a race-blind admissions system would have a "'very dramatic,'" negative effect on underrepresented minority admissions. He testified that in 2000, 35 percent of underrepresented minority applicants were admitted [and] predicted that if race were not considered, only 10 percent of those applicants would have been admitted. [U]nderrepresented minority students would have comprised 4 percent of the entering class in 2000 instead of the actual figure of 14.5 percent.

II

A

. . . Since this Court's splintered decision in *Bakke*, Justice Powell's opinion announcing the judgment of the Court has served as the touchstone for constitutional analysis of race-conscious admissions policies. Public and private universities across the Nation have modeled their own admissions programs on Justice Powell's views on permissible race-conscious policies. . . . In Justice Powell's view, when governmental decisions "touch upon an individual's race or ethnic background, he is entitled to a judicial determination that the burden he is asked to bear on that basis is precisely tailored to serve a compelling governmental interest." . . .

[J]ustice Powell rejected [as compelling] an interest in "reducing the historic deficit of traditionally disfavored minorities in medical schools and in the medical profession" as an unlawful interest in racial balancing. . . . Justice Powell [also] rejected an interest in remedying societal discrimination because such measures would risk placing unnecessary burdens on innocent third parties "who bear no responsibility for whatever harm the beneficiaries of the special admissions program are thought to have suffered." [Finally], Justice Powell rejected an interest in "increasing the number of physicians who will practice in communities currently underserved," concluding that even if such an interest could be compelling in some circumstances the program under review was not "geared to promote that goal."

Justice Powell approved the university's use of race to further only one interest: "the attainment of a diverse student body." With the important proviso that "constitutional limitations protecting individual rights may not be disregarded," Justice Powell grounded his analysis in the academic freedom that "long has been viewed as a special concern of the First Amendment." Justice Powell emphasized that nothing less than the "'nation's future depends upon leaders trained through wide exposure' to the ideas and mores of students as diverse as this Nation of many peoples." In seeking the "right to select those students who will contribute the most to the 'robust exchange of ideas,'" a university seeks "to achieve a goal that is of paramount importance in the fulfillment of its mission." Both "tradition and experience lend support to the view that the contribution of diversity is substantial."

Justice Powell was, however, careful to emphasize that in his view race "is only one element in a range of factors a university properly may consider in attaining the goal of a heterogeneous student body." For Justice Powell, "[i]t is not an interest in simple ethnic diversity, in which a specified percentage of the student body is in effect guaranteed to be members of selected ethnic groups," that can justify the use of race. Rather, "[t]he diversity that furthers a compelling state interest encompasses a far broader array of qualifications and characteristics of which racial or ethnic origin is but a single though important element." . . . [F]or the reasons set out below, today we endorse Justice Powell's view that student body diversity is a compelling state interest that can justify the use of race in university admissions.

B

We have held that all racial classifications imposed by government "must be analyzed by a reviewing court under strict scrutiny." This means that such classifications are constitutional only if they are narrowly tailored to further compelling governmental interests. . . . Strict scrutiny is not "strict in theory, but fatal in fact." *Adarand.* Although all governmental uses of race are subject to strict scrutiny, not all are invalidated by it. . . . When race-based action is necessary to further a compelling governmental interest, such action does not violate the constitutional guarantee of equal protection so long as the narrow-tailoring requirement is also satisfied. . . . Not every decision influenced by race is equally objectionable and strict scrutiny is designed to provide a framework for carefully examining the importance and the sincerity of the reasons advanced by the governmental decisionmaker for the use of race in that particular context.

III

A

[B]efore this Court, as they have throughout this litigation, respondents assert only one justification for their use of race in the admissions process: obtaining "the educational benefits that flow from a diverse student body." In other words, the Law School asks us to recognize, in the context of higher education, a compelling state interest in student body diversity.

We first wish to dispel the notion that the Law School's argument has been foreclosed, either expressly or implicitly, by our affirmative-action cases decided since *Bakke.* . . . [W]e have never held that the only governmental use of race that can survive strict scrutiny is remedying past discrimination. . . . Today, we hold that the Law School has a compelling interest in attaining a diverse student body.

The Law School's educational judgment that such diversity is essential to its educational mission is one to which we defer. The Law School's assessment that diversity will, in fact, yield educational benefits is substantiated by respondents and their *amici.* Our scrutiny of the interest asserted by the Law School is no less strict for taking into account complex educational judgments in an area that lies primarily within the expertise of the university. Our holding today is in keeping with our tradition of giving a degree of deference to a university's academic decisions, within constitutionally prescribed limits.

We have long recognized that, given the important purpose of public education and the expansive freedoms of speech and thought associated with the university environment, universities occupy a special niche in our constitutional tradition. In announcing the principle of student body diversity as a compelling state interest, Justice Powell invoked our cases recognizing a constitutional dimension, grounded in the First Amendment, of educational autonomy: "The freedom of a university to make its own judgments as to education includes the selection of its student body." From this premise, Justice Powell reasoned that by claiming "the right to select those students who will contribute the most to the 'robust exchange of ideas,'" a university "seek[s] to achieve a goal that is of paramount importance in the fulfillment of its mission." Our conclusion that the Law School has a compelling interest in a diverse student body is informed by our view that attaining a diverse student body is at the heart of the Law School's proper institutional mission, and that "good faith" on the part of a university is "presumed" absent "a showing to the contrary."

As part of its goal of "assembling a class that is both exceptionally academically qualified and broadly diverse," the Law School seeks to "enroll a 'critical mass' of minority students." The Law School's interest is not simply "to assure within its student body some specified percentage of a particular group merely because of its race or ethnic origin." *Bakke* (opinion of Powell, J.). That would amount to outright racial balancing, which is patently unconstitutional. Rather, the Law School's concept of critical mass is defined by reference to the educational benefits that diversity is designed to produce.

These benefits are substantial. As the District Court emphasized, the Law School's admissions policy promotes "cross-racial understanding," helps to break down racial stereotypes, and "enables [students] to better understand persons of different races." These benefits are "important and laudable," because "classroom discussion is livelier, more spirited, and simply more enlightening and interesting" when the students have "the greatest possible variety of backgrounds."

The Law School's claim of a compelling interest is further bolstered by its *amici*, who point to the educational benefits that flow from student body diversity. In addition to the expert studies and reports entered into evidence at trial, numerous studies show that student body diversity promotes learning outcomes, and "better prepares students for an increasingly diverse workforce and society, and better prepares them as professionals."

These benefits are not theoretical but real, as major American businesses have made clear that the skills needed in today's increasingly global marketplace can only be developed through exposure to widely diverse people, cultures, ideas, and viewpoints. Brief for 3M et al. as *Amici Curiae* 5; Brief for General Motors Corp. as *Amicus Curiae* 3-4. What is more, high-ranking retired officers and civilian leaders of the United States military assert that, "[b]ased on [their] decades of experience," a "highly qualified, racially diverse officer corps . . . is essential to the military's ability to fulfill its principle mission to provide national security." Brief for Julius W. Becton, Jr. et al. as *Amici Curiae* 27. The primary sources for the Nation's officer corps are the service academies and the Reserve Officers Training Corps (ROTC), the latter comprising students already admitted to participating colleges and universities. At present, "the military cannot achieve an officer corps that is *both* highly qualified *and* racially diverse unless the service academies and the ROTC used limited race-conscious recruiting and admissions policies." Ibid. (emphasis in original). To fulfill its mission, the military "must be selective in admissions for training and education for the officer corps, *and* it must train and educate a highly qualified, racially diverse officer corps in a racially diverse setting." Id., at 29 (emphasis in original). We agree that "[i]t requires only a small step from this analysis to conclude that our country's other most selective institutions must remain both diverse and selective." Ibid.

We have repeatedly acknowledged the overriding importance of preparing students for work and citizenship, describing education as pivotal to "sustaining our political and cultural heritage" with a fundamental role in maintaining the fabric of society. This Court has long recognized that "education . . . is the very foundation of good citizenship." Brown v. Board of Education. For this reason, the diffusion of knowledge and opportunity through public institutions of higher education must be accessible to all individuals regardless of race or ethnicity. The United States, as *amicus curiae*, affirms that "[e]nsuring that public institutions are open and available to all segments of American society, including people of all races and ethnicities, represents a paramount government objective." And, "[n]owhere is the importance of such openness more acute than in the context of higher education." Effective participation by members of all racial and ethnic groups in the civic life of our Nation is essential if the dream of one Nation, indivisible, is to be realized.

Moreover, universities, and in particular, law schools, represent the training ground for a large number of our Nation's leaders. Sweatt v. Painter (describing law school as a "proving ground for legal learning and practice"). Individuals with law degrees occupy roughly half the state governorships, more than half the seats in the United States Senate, and more than a third of the seats in the United States House of Representatives. The pattern is even more striking when it comes to highly selective law schools. A handful of these schools accounts for 25 of the 100 United States Senators, 74 United States Courts of Appeals judges, and nearly 200 of the more than 600 United States District Court judges.

In order to cultivate a set of leaders with legitimacy in the eyes of the citizenry, it is necessary that the path to leadership be visibly open to talented and qualified individuals of every race and ethnicity. All members of our heterogeneous society must have confidence in the openness and integrity of the educational institutions that provide this training. As we have recognized, law schools "cannot be effective in isolation from the individuals and institutions with which the law interacts." See Sweatt v. Painter. Access to legal education (and thus the legal profession) must be inclusive of talented and qualified individuals of every race and ethnicity, so that all members of our heterogeneous society may participate in the educational institutions that provide the training and education necessary to succeed in America.

The Law School does not premise its need for critical mass on "any belief that minority students always (or even consistently) express some characteristic minority viewpoint on any issue." To the contrary, diminishing the force of such stereotypes is both a crucial part of the Law School's mission, and one that it cannot accomplish with only token numbers of minority students. Just as growing up in a particular region or having particular professional experiences is likely to affect an individual's views, so too is one's own, unique experience of being a racial minority in a society, like our own, in which race unfortunately still matters. The Law School has determined, based on its experience and expertise, that a "critical mass" of underrepresented minorities is necessary to further its compelling interest in securing the educational benefits of a diverse student body.

B

. . . To be narrowly tailored, a race-conscious admissions program cannot use a quota system — it cannot "insulat[e] each category of applicants with certain desired qualifications from competition with all other applicants." *Bakke* (opinion of Powell, J.). Instead, a university may consider race or ethnicity only as a "'plus' in a particular applicant's file," without "insulat[ing] the individual from comparison with all other candidates for the available seats." In other words, an admissions program must be "flexible enough to consider all pertinent elements of diversity in light of the particular qualifications of each applicant, and to place them on the same footing for consideration, although not necessarily according them the same weight."

We find that the Law School's admissions program bears the hallmarks of a narrowly tailored plan. As Justice Powell made clear in *Bakke*, truly individualized consideration demands that race be used in a flexible, nonmechanical way. It follows from this mandate that universities cannot establish quotas for members of certain racial groups or put members of those groups on separate admissions tracks. Nor can universities insulate applicants who belong to certain racial or ethnic groups from the competition for admission. Universities can, however, consider race or ethnicity more flexibly as a "plus" factor in the context of individualized consideration of each and every applicant.

We are satisfied that the Law School's admissions program, like the Harvard plan described by Justice Powell, does not operate as a quota. Properly understood, a "quota" is a program in which a certain fixed number or proportion of opportunities are "reserved exclusively for certain minority groups." Quotas "'impose a fixed number or percentage which must be attained, or which cannot be exceeded,'" and "insulate the individual from comparison with all other candidates for the available seats." In contrast, "a permissible goal . . . require[s] only a good-faith effort . . . to come within a range demarcated by the goal itself," and permits consideration of race as a "plus" factor in any given case while still ensuring that each candidate "compete[s] with all other qualified applicants."

Justice Powell's distinction between the medical school's rigid 16-seat quota and Harvard's flexible use of race as a "plus" factor is instructive. Harvard certainly had minimum *goals* for minority enrollment, even if it had no specific number firmly in mind. See *Bakke* (opinion of Powell, J.) ("10 or 20 black students could not begin to bring to their classmates and to each other the variety of points of view, backgrounds and experiences of blacks in the United States"). What is more, Justice Powell flatly rejected the argument that Harvard's program was "the functional equivalent of a quota" merely because it had some "'plus'" for race, or gave greater "weight" to race than to some other factors, in order to achieve student body diversity.

The Law School's goal of attaining a critical mass of underrepresented minority students does not transform its program into a quota. As the Harvard plan described by Justice Powell recognized, there is of course "some relationship between numbers and achieving the benefits to be derived from a diverse student body, and between numbers and providing a reasonable environment for those students admitted." "[S]ome attention to numbers," without more, does not transform a flexible admissions system into a rigid quota. Nor, as Justice Kennedy posits, does the Law School's consultation of the "daily reports," which keep track of the racial and ethnic composition of the class (as well as of residency and gender), "suggest[ ] there was no further attempt at individual review save for race itself" during the final stages of the admissions process. To the contrary, the Law School's admissions officers testified without contradiction that they never gave race any more or less weight based on the information contained in these reports. Moreover, as Justice Kennedy concedes, between 1993 and 2000, the number of African-American, Latino, and Native-American students in each class at the Law School varied from 13.5 to 20.1 percent, a range inconsistent with a quota. . . .

That a race-conscious admissions program does not operate as a quota does not, by itself, satisfy the requirement of individualized consideration. When using race as a "plus" factor in university admissions, a university's admissions program must remain flexible enough to ensure that each applicant is evaluated as an individual and not in a way that makes an applicant's race or ethnicity the defining feature of his or her application. The importance of this individualized consideration in the context of a race-conscious admissions program is paramount. See *Bakke* (opinion of Powell, J.) (identifying the "denial . . . of th[e] right to individualized consideration" as the "principal evil" of the medical school's admissions program).

Here, the Law School engages in a highly individualized, holistic review of each applicant's file, giving serious consideration to all the ways an applicant might contribute to a diverse educational environment. The Law School affords this individualized consideration to applicants of all races. There is no policy, either *de jure* or *de facto,* of automatic acceptance or rejection based on any single "soft" variable. Unlike the program at issue in Gratz v. Bollinger, *ante,* the Law School awards no mechanical, predetermined diversity "bonuses" based on race or ethnicity. . . .

We also find that, like the Harvard plan Justice Powell referenced in *Bakke,* the Law School's race-conscious admissions program adequately ensures that all factors that may contribute to student body diversity are meaningfully considered alongside race in admissions decisions. With respect to the use of race itself, all underrepresented minority students admitted by the Law School have been deemed qualified. By virtue of our Nation's struggle with racial inequality, such students are both likely to have experiences of particular importance to the Law School's mission, and less likely to be admitted in meaningful numbers on criteria that ignore those experiences.

The Law School does not, however, limit in any way the broad range of qualities and experiences that may be considered valuable contributions to student body diversity. To the contrary, the 1992 policy makes clear "[t]here are many possible bases for diversity admissions," and provides examples of admittees who have lived or traveled widely abroad, are fluent in several languages, have overcome personal adversity and family hardship, have exceptional records of extensive community service, and have had successful careers in other fields. The Law School seriously considers each "applicant's promise of making a notable contribution to the class by way of a particular strength, attainment, or characteristic—e.g., an unusual intellectual achievement, employment experience, nonacademic performance, or personal background."

What is more, the Law School actually gives substantial weight to diversity factors besides race. The Law School frequently accepts nonminority applicants with grades and test scores lower than underrepresented minority applicants (and other nonminority applicants) who are rejected. . . . Justice Kennedy speculates that "race is likely outcome determinative for many members of minority groups" who do not fall within the upper range of LSAT scores and grades. But the same could be said of the Harvard plan discussed approvingly by Justice Powell in *Bakke,* and indeed of any plan that uses race as one of many factors.

Petitioner and the United States argue that the Law School's plan is not narrowly tailored because race-neutral means exist to obtain the educational benefits of student body diversity that the Law School seeks. We disagree. Narrow tailoring does not require exhaustion of every conceivable race-neutral alternative. Nor does it require a university to choose between maintaining a reputation for excellence or fulfilling a commitment to provide educational opportunities to members of all racial groups. Narrow tailoring does, however, require serious, good faith consideration of workable race-neutral alternatives that will achieve the diversity the university seeks.

We agree with the Court of Appeals that the Law School sufficiently considered workable race-neutral alternatives. The District Court took the Law School to task for failing to consider race-neutral alternatives such as "using a lottery system" or "decreasing the emphasis for all applicants on undergraduate GPA and LSAT scores." But these alternatives would require a dramatic sacrifice of diversity, the academic quality of all admitted students, or both.

The Law School's current admissions program considers race as one factor among many, in an effort to assemble a student body that is diverse in ways broader than race. Because a lottery would make that kind of nuanced judgment impossible, it would effectively sacrifice all other educational values, not to mention every other kind of diversity. So too with the suggestion that the Law School simply lower admissions standards for all students, a drastic remedy that would require the Law School to become a much different institution and sacrifice a vital component of its educational mission. The United States advocates "percentage plans," recently adopted by public undergraduate institutions in Texas, Florida, and California to guarantee admission to all students above a certain class-rank threshold in every high school in the State. The United States does not, however, explain how such plans could work for graduate and professional schools. Moreover, even assuming such plans are race-neutral, they may preclude the university from conducting the individualized assessments necessary to assemble a student body that is not just racially diverse, but diverse along all the qualities valued by the university. . . .

We are mindful, however, that "[a] core purpose of the Fourteenth Amendment was to do away with all governmentally imposed discrimination based on race." Accordingly, race-conscious admissions policies must be limited in time. . . .

In the context of higher education, the durational requirement can be met by sunset provisions in race-conscious admissions policies and periodic reviews to determine whether racial preferences are still necessary to achieve student body diversity. Universities in California, Florida, and Washington State, where racial preferences in admissions are prohibited by state law, are currently engaged in experimenting with a wide variety of alternative approaches. Universities in other States can and should draw on the most promising aspects of these race-neutral alternatives as they develop.

The requirement that all race-conscious admissions programs have a termination point "assure[s] all citizens that the deviation from the norm of equal treatment of all racial and ethnic groups is a temporary matter, a measure taken in the service of the goal of equality itself." *Croson* (plurality opinion).

We take the Law School at its word that it would "like nothing better than to find a race-neutral admissions formula" and will terminate its race-conscious admissions program as soon as practicable. It has been 25 years since Justice Powell first approved the use of race to further an interest in student body diversity in the context of public higher education. Since that time, the number of minority applicants with high grades and test scores has indeed increased. We expect that 25 years from now, the use of racial preferences will no longer be necessary to further the interest approved today. . . .

[A concurring opinion by Justice Ginsburg, joined by Justice Breyer, is omitted.]

Chief Justice REHNQUIST, with whom Justice SCALIA, Justice KENNEDY, and Justice THOMAS join, dissenting.

. . . I do not believe . . . that the University of Michigan Law School's (Law School) means are narrowly tailored to the interest it asserts. The Law School claims it must take the steps it does to achieve a "'critical mass'" of underrepresented minority students. But its actual program bears no relation to this asserted goal. Stripped of its "critical mass" veil, the Law School's program is revealed as a naked effort to achieve racial balancing. . . .

In practice, the Law School's program bears little or no relation to its asserted goal of achieving "critical mass." Respondents explain that the Law School seeks to accumulate a "critical mass" of *each* underrepresented minority group. But the record demonstrates that the Law School's admissions practices with respect to these groups differ dramatically and cannot be defended under any consistent use of the term "critical mass."

From 1995 through 2000, the Law School admitted between 1,130 and 1,310 students. Of those, between 13 and 19 were Native American, between 91 and 108 were African-Americans, and between 47 and 56 were Hispanic. If the Law School is admitting between 91 and 108 African-Americans in order to achieve "critical mass," thereby preventing African-American students from feeling "isolated or like spokespersons for their race," one would think that a number of the same order of magnitude would be necessary to accomplish the same purpose for Hispanics and Native Americans. Similarly, even if all of the Native American applicants admitted in a given year matriculate, which the record demonstrates is not at all the case, how can this possibly constitute a "critical mass" of Native Americans in a class of over 350 students? In order for this pattern of admission to be consistent with the Law School's explanation of "critical mass," one would have to believe that the objectives of "critical mass" offered by respondents are achieved with only half the number of Hispanics and one-sixth the number of Native Americans as compared to African-Americans. [Chief Justice Rehnquist notes statistics suggesting that it was considerably easier for African Americans with particular combinations of GPA and LSAT scores to be admitted than Hispanics.] . . . These statistics have a significant bearing on petitioner's case. Respondents have *never* offered any race-specific arguments explaining why significantly more individuals from one underrepresented minority group are needed in order to achieve "critical mass" or further student body diversity. They certainly have not explained why Hispanics, who they have said are among "the groups most isolated by racial barriers in our country," should have their admission capped out in this manner. True, petitioner is neither Hispanic nor Native American. But the Law School's disparate admissions practices with respect to these minority groups demonstrate that its alleged goal of "critical mass" is simply a sham. . . .

Only when the "critical mass" label is discarded does a likely explanation for these numbers emerge. . . . [T]he correlation between the percentage of the Law School's pool of applicants who are members of the three minority groups and the percentage of the admitted applicants who are members of these same groups is far too precise to be dismissed as merely the result of the school paying "some attention to [the] numbers." [F]rom 1995 through 2000 the percentage of admitted applicants who were members of these minority groups closely tracked the percentage of individuals in the school's applicant pool who were from the same groups. . . .

Not only do respondents fail to explain this phenomenon, they attempt to obscure it. ("The Law School's minority enrollment percentages . . . diverged from the percentages in the applicant pool by as much as 17.7% from 1995-2000."). But the divergence between the percentages of underrepresented minorities in the applicant pool and in the *enrolled* classes is not the only relevant comparison. In fact, it may not be the most relevant comparison. The Law School cannot precisely control which of its admitted applicants decide to attend the university. But it can and, as the numbers demonstrate, clearly does employ racial preferences in extending offers of admission. Indeed, the ostensibly flexible nature of the Law School's admissions program that the Court finds appealing, appears to be, in practice, a carefully managed program designed to ensure proportionate representation of applicants from selected minority groups. [T]his is precisely the type of racial balancing that the Court itself calls "patently unconstitutional."

Justice KENNEDY, dissenting.

The Court confuses deference to a university's definition of its educational objective with deference to the implementation of this goal. In the context of university admissions the objective of racial diversity can be accepted based on empirical data known to us, but deference is not to be given with respect to the methods by which it is pursued. . . .

[T]he Law School has the burden of proving, in conformance with the standard of strict scrutiny, that it did not utilize race in an unconstitutional way. At the very least, the constancy of admitted minority students and the close correlation between the racial breakdown of admitted minorities and the composition of the applicant pool, discussed by The Chief Justice, require the Law School either to produce a convincing explanation or to show it has taken adequate steps to ensure individual assessment. The Law School does neither.

The obvious tension between the pursuit of critical mass and the requirement of individual review increased by the end of the admissions season. Most of the decisions where race may decide the outcome are made during this period. The admissions officers consulted the daily reports which indicated the composition of the incoming class along racial lines. . . . [This] suggests there was no further attempt at individual review save for race itself. The admissions officers could use the reports to recalibrate the plus factor given to race depending on how close they were to achieving the Law School's goal of critical mass. The bonus factor of race would then become divorced from individual review; it would be premised instead on the numerical objective set by the Law School. . . .

There is no constitutional objection to the goal of considering race as one modest factor among many others to achieve diversity, but an educational institution must ensure, through sufficient procedures, that each applicant receives individual consideration and that race does not become a predominant factor in the admissions decisionmaking. . . .

Constant and rigorous judicial review forces the law school faculties to undertake their responsibilities as state employees in this most sensitive of areas with utmost fidelity to the mandate of the Constitution. Dean Allan Stillwagon, who directed the Law School's Office of Admissions from 1979 to 1990, explained the difficulties he encountered in defining racial groups entitled to benefit under the School's affirmative action policy. He testified that faculty members were "breathtakingly cynical" in deciding who would qualify as a member of underrepresented minorities. An example he offered was faculty debate as to whether Cubans should be counted as Hispanics: One professor objected on the grounds that Cubans were Republicans. Many academics at other law schools who are "affirmative action's more forthright defenders readily concede that diversity is merely the current rationale of convenience for a policy that they prefer to justify on other grounds." Peter H. Schuck, Affirmative Action: Past, Present, and Future, 20 Yale L. & Pol'y Rev. 1, 34 (2002) (citing Levinson, Diversity, 2 U. Pa. J. Const. L. 573, 577-578 (2000); Rubenfeld, Affirmative Action, 107 Yale L.J. 427, 471 (1997)). . . .

If universities are given the latitude to administer programs that are tantamount to quotas, they will have few incentives to make the existing minority admissions schemes transparent and protective of individual review. The unhappy consequence will be to perpetuate the hostilities that proper consideration of race is designed to avoid. . . . Other programs do exist which will be more effective in bringing about the harmony and mutual respect among all citizens that our constitutional tradition has always sought. They, and not the program under review here, should be the model, even if the Court defaults by not demanding it.

Justice SCALIA, with whom Justice THOMAS joins, concurring in part and dissenting in part.

[As] [t]he Chief Justice . . . demonstrates, the University of Michigan Law School's mystical "critical mass" justification . . . [is] a sham to cover a scheme of racially proportionate admissions.

I also join Parts I through VII of Justice Thomas's opinion. I find particularly unanswerable his central point: that the allegedly "compelling state interest" at issue here is not the incremental "educational benefit" that emanates from the fabled "critical mass" of minority students, but rather Michigan's interest in maintaining a "prestige" law school whose normal admissions standards disproportionately exclude blacks and other minorities. If that is a compelling state interest, everything is.

I add the following: The "educational benefit" that the University of Michigan seeks to achieve by racial discrimination consists, according to the Court, of "'cross-racial understanding,'" and "'better prepar[ation of] students for an increasingly diverse workforce and society,'" all of which is necessary not only for work, but also for good "citizenship." This is not, of course, an "educational benefit" on which students will be graded on their Law School transcript (Works and Plays Well with Others: B+) or tested by the bar examiners (Q: Describe in 500 words or less your cross-racial understanding). For it is a lesson of life rather than law. . . . If properly considered an "educational benefit" at all, it is surely not one that is either uniquely relevant to law school or uniquely "teachable" in a formal educational setting. *And therefore:* If it is appropriate for the University of Michigan Law School to use racial discrimination for the purpose of putting together a "critical mass" that will convey generic lessons in socialization and good citizenship, surely it is no less appropriate—indeed, *particularly* appropriate—for the civil service system of the State of Michigan to do so. . . . And surely private employers cannot be criticized—indeed, should be praised—if they also "teach" good citizenship to their adult employees through a patriotic, all-American system of racial discrimination in hiring. The nonminority individuals who are deprived of a legal education, a civil service job, or any job at all by reason of their skin color will surely understand.

Unlike a clear constitutional holding that racial preferences in state educational institutions are impermissible, or even a clear anticonstitutional holding that racial preferences in state educational institutions are OK, today's *Grutter-Gratz* split double header seems perversely designed to prolong the controversy and the litigation. . . . Some future lawsuits . . . may focus on whether, in the particular setting at issue, any educational benefits flow from racial diversity. . . . Still other suits may challenge the bona fides of the institution's expressed commitment to the educational benefits of diversity that immunize the discriminatory scheme in *Grutter.* (Tempting targets, one would suppose, will be those universities that talk the talk of multiculturalism and racial diversity in the courts but walk the walk of tribalism and racial segregation on their campuses—through minority-only student organizations, separate minority housing opportunities, separate minority student centers, even separate minority-only graduation ceremonies.) And still other suits may claim that the institution's racial preferences have gone below or above the mystical *Grutter*-approved "critical mass." Finally, litigation can be expected on behalf of minority groups intentionally short changed in the institution's composition of its generic minority "critical mass." I do not look forward to any of these cases. The Constitution proscribes government discrimination on the basis of race, and state-provided education is no exception.

Justice THOMAS, with whom Justice SCALIA joins as to Parts I-VII, concurring in part and dissenting in part.

. . . The majority upholds the Law School's racial discrimination not by interpreting the people's Constitution, but by responding to a faddish slogan of the cognoscenti. Nevertheless, I concur in part in the Court's opinion. First, I agree with the Court insofar as its decision, which approves of only one racial classification, confirms that further use of race in admissions remains unlawful. Second, I agree with the Court's holding that racial discrimination in higher education admissions will be illegal in 25 years. I respectfully dissent from the remainder of the Court's opinion and the judgment, however, because I believe that the Law School's current use of race violates the Equal Protection Clause and that the Constitution means the same thing today as it will in 300 months.

I

[T]he Constitution abhors classifications based on race, not only because those classifications can harm favored races or are based on illegitimate motives, but also because every time the government places citizens on racial registers and makes race relevant to the provision of burdens or benefits, it demeans us all. . . .

II

[T]he Law School maintains that it wishes to obtain "educational benefits that flow from student body diversity."[a]. . . [T]he Law School . . . apparently believes that only a racially mixed student body can lead to the educational benefits it seeks. How, then, is the Law School's interest in these allegedly unique educational "benefits" *not* simply the forbidden interest in "racial balancing," that the majority expressly rejects? . . .

One must . . . consider the Law School's refusal to entertain changes to its current admissions system that might produce the same educational benefits. The Law School adamantly disclaims any race-neutral alternative that would reduce "academic selectivity," which would in turn "require the Law School to become a very different institution, and to sacrifice a core part of its educational mission." In other words, the Law School seeks to improve marginally the education it offers without sacrificing too much of its exclusivity and elite status. . . . Unless each constituent part of this state interest is of pressing public necessity, the Law School's use of race is unconstitutional. I find each of them to fall far short of this standard.

III . . .

B

Under the proper standard, there is no pressing public necessity in maintaining a public law school at all and, it follows, certainly not an elite law school. Likewise, marginal improvements in legal education do not qualify as a compelling state interest.

1

While legal education at a public university may be good policy or otherwise laudable, it is obviously not a pressing public necessity when the correct legal standard is applied. Additionally, circumstantial evidence as to whether a state activity is of pressing public necessity can be obtained by asking whether all States feel compelled to engage in that activity. [T]he absence of a public, American Bar Association (ABA) accredited, law school in Alaska, Delaware, Massachusetts, New Hampshire, and Rhode Island provides further evidence that Michigan's maintenance of the Law School does not constitute a compelling state interest.

---

a. "[D]iversity," for all of its devotees, is more a fashionable catchphrase than it is a useful term, especially when something as serious as racial discrimination is at issue. Because the Equal Protection Clause renders the color of one's skin constitutionally irrelevant to the Law School's mission, I refer to the Law School's interest as an "aesthetic." That is, the Law School wants to have a certain appearance, from the shape of the desks and tables in its classrooms to the color of the students sitting at them. I also use the term "aesthetic" because I believe it underlines the ineffectiveness of racially discriminatory admissions in actually helping those who are truly underprivileged. [T]he Law School's racial discrimination does nothing for those too poor or uneducated to participate in elite higher education and therefore presents only an illusory solution to the challenges facing our Nation. [Relocated footnote.—Eds.]

2

. . . Michigan has no compelling interest in having a law school at all, much less an *elite* one. Still, even assuming that a State may, under appropriate circumstances, demonstrate a cognizable interest in having an elite law school, Michigan has failed to do so here. . . .

The only interests that can satisfy the Equal Protection Clause's demands are those found within a State's jurisdiction. The only cognizable state interests vindicated by operating a public law school are, therefore, the education of that State's citizens and the training of that State's lawyers.

The Law School today, however, does precious little training of those attorneys who will serve the citizens of Michigan. [L]ess than 16% of the Law School's graduating class elects to stay in Michigan after law school. . . . It does not take a social scientist to conclude that it is precisely the Law School's status as an elite institution that causes it to be a waystation for the rest of the country's lawyers, rather than a training ground for those who will remain in Michigan. The Law School's decision to be an elite institution does little to advance the welfare of the people of Michigan or any cognizable interest of the State of Michigan. . . .

IV

The interest in remaining elite and exclusive that the majority thinks so obviously critical requires the use of admissions "standards" that, in turn, create the Law School's "need" to discriminate on the basis of race. . . . The Court never explicitly holds that the Law School's desire to retain the status quo in "academic selectivity" is itself a compelling state interest. Therefore, the Law School should be forced to choose between its classroom aesthetic and its exclusionary admissions system—it cannot have it both ways.

With the adoption of different admissions methods, such as accepting all students who meet minimum qualifications, the Law School could achieve its vision of the racially aesthetic student body without the use of racial discrimination. . . .

B

1

The Court's deference to the Law School's conclusion that its racial experimentation leads to educational benefits will, if adhered to, have serious collateral consequences. The Court relies heavily on social science evidence to justify its deference. The Court never acknowledges, however, the growing evidence that racial (and other sorts) of heterogeneity actually impairs learning among black students. [Justice Thomas cites studies that show that "black students attending HBCs [Historically Black Colleges] report higher academic achievement than those attending predominantly white colleges," that "black students experience superior cognitive development at Historically Black Colleges" and that "even among blacks, 'a substantial diversity moderates the cognitive effects of attending an HBC.'"] . . .

The majority grants deference to the Law School's "assessment that diversity will, in fact, yield educational benefits[.]" It follows, therefore, that an HBC's assessment that racial homogeneity will yield educational benefits would similarly be given deference. An HBC's rejection of white applicants in order to maintain racial homogeneity seems permissible, therefore, under the majority's view of the Equal

Protection Clause. Contained within today's majority opinion is the seed of a new constitutional justification for a concept I thought long and rightly rejected—racial segregation. . . .

C

. . . The sky has not fallen at Boalt Hall at the University of California, Berkeley, for example. Prior to Proposition 209's adoption of Cal. Const., Art. 1, §31(a), which bars the State from "grant[ing] preferential treatment . . . on the basis of race . . . in the operation of . . . public education," Boalt Hall enrolled 20 blacks and 28 Hispanics in its first-year class for 1996. In 2002, without deploying express racial discrimination in admissions, Boalt's entering class enrolled 14 blacks and 36 Hispanics. Total underrepresented minority student enrollment at Boalt Hall now exceeds 1996 levels. Apparently the Law School cannot be counted on to be as resourceful. The Court is willfully blind to the very real experience in California and elsewhere, which raises the inference that institutions with "reputation[s] for excellence," rivaling the Law School's have satisfied their sense of mission without resorting to prohibited racial discrimination.

V

Putting aside the absence of any legal support for the majority's reflexive deference, there is much to be said for the view that the use of tests and other measures to "predict" academic performance is a poor substitute for a system that gives every applicant a chance to prove he can succeed in the study of law. The rallying cry that in the absence of racial discrimination in admissions there would be a true meritocracy ignores the fact that the entire process is poisoned by numerous exceptions to "merit." For example, in the national debate on racial discrimination in higher education admissions, much has been made of the fact that elite institutions utilize a so-called "legacy" preference to give the children of alumni an advantage in admissions. This, and other, exceptions to a "true" meritocracy give the lie to protestations that merit admissions are in fact the order of the day at the Nation's universities. The Equal Protection Clause does not, however, prohibit the use of unseemly legacy preferences or many other kinds of arbitrary admissions procedures. What the Equal Protection Clause does prohibit are classifications made on the basis of race. So while legacy preferences can stand under the Constitution, racial discrimination cannot. I will not twist the Constitution to invalidate legacy preferences or otherwise impose my vision of higher education admissions on the Nation. The majority should similarly stay its impulse to validate faddish racial discrimination the Constitution clearly forbids.

In any event, there is nothing ancient, honorable, or constitutionally protected about "selective" admissions. The University of Michigan should be well aware that alternative methods have historically been used for the admission of students, for it brought to this country the German certificate system in the late-19th century. Under this system, a secondary school was certified by a university so that any graduate who completed the course offered by the school was offered admission to the university. The certification regime supplemented, and later virtually replaced (at least in the Midwest), the prior regime of rigorous subject-matter entrance examinations. The facially race-neutral "percent plans" now used in Texas, California, and Florida, are in many ways the descendents of the certificate system.

Certification was replaced by selective admissions in the beginning of the 20th century, as universities sought to exercise more control over the composition of their student bodies. Since its inception, selective admissions has been the vehicle for racial, ethnic, and religious tinkering and experimentation by university administrators. The initial driving force for the relocation of the selective function from the high school to the universities was the same desire to select racial winners and losers that the Law School exhibits today. Columbia, Harvard, and others infamously determined that they had "too many" Jews, just as today the Law School argues it would have "too many" whites if it could not discriminate in its admissions process.

Columbia employed intelligence tests precisely because Jewish applicants, who were predominantly immigrants, scored worse on such tests. Thus, Columbia could claim (falsely) that "'[w]e have not eliminated boys because they were Jews and do not propose to do so. We have honestly attempted to eliminate the lowest grade of applicant [through the use of intelligence testing] and it turns out that a good many of the low grade men are New York City Jews.'" In other words, the tests were adopted with full knowledge of their disparate impact.

Similarly no modern law school can claim ignorance of the poor performance of blacks, relatively speaking, on the Law School Admissions Test (LSAT). Nevertheless, law schools continue to use the test and then attempt to "correct" for black underperformance by using racial discrimination in admissions so as to obtain their aesthetic student body. The Law School's continued adherence to measures it knows produce racially skewed results is not entitled to deference by this Court. The Law School itself admits that the test is imperfect, as it must, given that it regularly admits students who score at or below 150 (the national median) on the test. . . .

Having decided to use the LSAT, the Law School must accept the constitutional burdens that come with this decision. The Law School may freely continue to employ the LSAT and other allegedly merit-based standards in whatever fashion it likes. What the Equal Protection Clause forbids, but the Court today allows, is the use of these standards hand-in-hand with racial discrimination. An infinite variety of admissions methods are available to the Law School. Considering all of the radical thinking that has historically occurred at this country's universities, the Law School's intractable approach toward admissions is striking. . . .

VI

The absence of any articulated legal principle supporting the majority's principal holding suggests another rationale. I believe what lies beneath the Court's decision today are the benighted notions that one can tell when racial discrimination benefits (rather than hurts) minority groups, and that racial discrimination is necessary to remedy general societal ills. This Court's precedents supposedly settled both issues, but clearly the majority still cannot commit to the principle that racial classifications are per se harmful and that almost no amount of benefit in the eye of the beholder can justify such classifications. . . .

I must contest the notion that the Law School's discrimination benefits those admitted as a result of it. The Court spends considerable time discussing the impressive display of *amicus* support for the Law School in this case from all corners of society. But nowhere in any of the filings in this Court is any evidence that the purported "beneficiaries" of this racial discrimination prove themselves by performing at (or even near) the same level as those students who receive no preferences. . . . The Law School seeks only a facade—it is sufficient that the class looks right, even if it does not perform right.

The Law School tantalizes unprepared students with the promise of a University of Michigan degree and all of the opportunities that it offers. These overmatched students take the bait, only to find that they cannot succeed in the cauldron of competition. And this mismatch crisis is not restricted to elite institutions. Indeed, to cover the tracks of the aestheticists, this cruel farce of racial discrimination must continue—in selection for the Michigan Law Review, and in hiring at law firms and for judicial clerkships—until the "beneficiaries" are no longer tolerated. While these students may graduate with law degrees, there is no evidence that they have received a qualitatively better legal education (or become better lawyers) than if they had gone to a less "elite" law school for which they were better prepared. And the aestheticists will never address the real problems facing "underrepresented minorities,"[b] instead continuing their social experiments on other people's children.

Beyond the harm the Law School's racial discrimination visits upon its test subjects, no social science has disproved the notion that this discrimination "engender[s] attitudes of superiority or, alternatively, provoke[s] resentment among those who believe that they have been wronged by the government's use of race." "These programs stamp minorities with a badge of inferiority and may cause them to develop dependencies or to adopt an attitude that they are 'entitled' to preferences."

It is uncontested that each year, the Law School admits a handful of blacks who would be admitted in the absence of racial discrimination. Who can differentiate between those who belong and those who do not? The majority of blacks are admitted to the Law School because of discrimination, and because of this policy all are tarred as undeserving. . . . When blacks take positions in the highest places of government, industry, or academia, it is an open question today whether their skin color played a part in their advancement. The question itself is the stigma. . . .

The Court . . . holds that racial discrimination in admissions should be given another 25 years before it is deemed no longer narrowly tailored to the Law School's fabricated compelling state interest. While I agree that in 25 years the practices of the Law School will be illegal, they are, for the reasons I have given, illegal now. The majority does not and cannot rest its time limitation on any evidence that the gap in credentials between black and white students is shrinking or will be gone in that timeframe. In recent years there has been virtually no change, for example, in the proportion of law school applicants with LSAT scores of 165 and higher who are black. In 1993 blacks constituted 1.1% of law school applicants in that score range, though they represented 11.1% of all applicants. In 2000 the comparable

---

b. For example, there is no recognition by the Law School in this case that even with their racial discrimination in place, black men are "underrepresented" at the Law School. See ABA-LSAC Guide 426 (reporting that the Law School has 46 black women and 28 black men). Why does the Law School not also discriminate in favor of black men over black women, given this underrepresentation? The answer is, again, that all the Law School cares about is its own image among know-it-all elites, not solving real problems like the crisis of black male underperformance.

numbers were 1.0% and 11.3%. No one can seriously contend, and the Court does not, that the racial gap in academic credentials will disappear in 25 years. Nor is the Court's holding that racial discrimination will be unconstitutional in 25 years made contingent on the gap closing in that time.

Indeed, the very existence of racial discrimination of the type practiced by the Law School may impede the narrowing of the LSAT testing gap. An applicant's LSAT score can improve dramatically with preparation, but such preparation is a cost, and there must be sufficient benefits attached to an improved score to justify additional study. . . .

I therefore can understand the imposition of a 25-year time limit only as a holding that the deference the Court pays to the Law School's educational judgments and refusal to change its admissions policies will itself expire. At that point these policies will clearly have failed to "eliminat[e] the [perceived] need for any racial or ethnic" discrimination because the academic credentials gap will still be there. . . .

GRATZ v. BOLLINGER, 539 U.S. 244 (2003): [This was a companion case to *Grutter*; it challenged the University of Michigan's undergraduate affirmative action program. The university ranked applications according to a 150-point scale. Based on the index score, the following decisions would usually be made: 100-150 (admit); 95-99 (admit or postpone); 90-94 (postpone or admit); 75-89 (delay or postpone); 74 and below (delay or reject). The Office of Undergraduate Admissions (OUA) assigned points based on a number of factors, including high school grades, standardized test scores, high school quality, curriculum strength, geography, alumni relationships, and leadership. An applicant automatically received a bonus of 20 points of the 100 needed to guarantee admission if he or she possessed any one of the following "miscellaneous" factors: membership in an underrepresented racial or ethnic minority group (which included African Americans, Hispanics, and Native Americans); attendance at a predominantly minority or disadvantaged high school; or recruitment for athletics. In addition, Michigan residents receive 10 points, and children of alumni receive 4. Admissions counselors may assign an outstanding essay up to 3 points and may award up to 5 points for an applicant's personal achievement, leadership, or public service.

In addition, admissions counselors could "flag" applications for further review by an Admissions Review Committee (ARC) after determining that an applicant (1) was academically prepared to succeed at the university, (2) had achieved a minimum selection index score, and (3) possessed a quality or characteristic important to the university's composition of its freshman class, such as high class rank, unique life experiences, challenges, circumstances, interests or talents, socioeconomic disadvantage, and underrepresented race, ethnicity, or geography. The ARC reviewed "flagged" applications individually and decided whether to admit, defer, or deny the applicant.

Chief Justice Rehnquist wrote the majority opinion. On the basis of *Grutter*, he rejected petitioner's claims that "racial classifications [may only be used] to remedy identified discrimination," and that "diversity [could not be a compelling interest] for employing racial preferences." However, he held that the undergraduate admissions plan was not narrowly tailored to achieve a compelling interest in diversity:]

Rehnquist, C.J.:

Justice Powell's opinion in *Bakke* emphasized the importance of considering each particular applicant as an individual, assessing all of the qualities that individual possesses, and in turn, evaluating that individual's ability to contribute to the unique setting of higher education. . . .

The current [admissions] policy does not provide such individualized consideration. The [College's] policy automatically distributes 20 points to every single applicant from an "underrepresented minority" group, as defined by the University. The only consideration that accompanies this distribution of points is a factual review of an application to determine whether an individual is a member of one of these minority groups. Moreover, unlike Justice Powell's example, where the race of a "particular black applicant" could be considered without being decisive, the [College's] automatic distribution of 20 points has the effect of making "the factor of race . . . decisive" for virtually every minimally qualified underrepresented minority applicant. . . .

Respondents emphasize the fact that the [College] has created the possibility of an applicant's file being flagged for individualized consideration by the ARC. . . . But the fact that the "review committee can look at the applications individually and ignore the points," once an application is flagged, is of little comfort under our strict scrutiny analysis. The record does not reveal precisely how many applications are flagged for this individualized consideration, but it is undisputed that such consideration is the exception and not the rule in the . . . admissions program. Additionally, this individualized review is only provided *after* admissions counselors automatically distribute the University's version of a "plus" that makes race a decisive factor for virtually every minimally qualified underrepresented minority applicant.

Respondents contend that "[t]he volume of applications and the presentation of applicant information make it impractical for [the College] to use the . . . admissions system" upheld by the Court today in *Grutter*. But the fact that the implementation of a program capable of providing individualized consideration might present administrative challenges does not render constitutional an otherwise problematic system.

O'Connor, J., concurring:

Although the Office of Undergraduate Admissions does assign 20 points to some "soft" variables other than race, the points available for other diversity contributions, such as leadership and service, personal achievement, and geographic diversity, are capped at much lower levels. Even the most outstanding national high school leader could never receive more than five points for his or her accomplishments—a mere quarter of the points automatically assigned to an underrepresented minority solely based on the fact of his or her race. Of course, as Justice Powell made clear in *Bakke*, a university need not "necessarily accor[d]" all diversity factors "the same weight," and the "weight attributed to a particular quality may vary from year to year depending on the 'mix' both of the student body and the applicants for the incoming class." But the selection index, by setting up automatic, predetermined point allocations for the soft variables, ensures that the diversity contributions of applicants cannot be individually assessed. This policy stands in sharp contrast to the law school's admissions plan, which enables admissions officers to make nuanced judgments with respect to the contributions each applicant is likely to make to the diversity of the incoming class.

[Justice Thomas concurred, adding that "I would hold that a State's use of racial discrimination in higher education admissions is categorically prohibited by the Equal Protection Clause." Justice Breyer concurred in the judgment but noted that he "agree[d] with Justice Ginsburg that, in implementing the Constitution's equality instruction, government decisionmakers may properly distinguish between policies of inclusion and exclusion, for the former are more likely to prove consistent with the basic constitutional obligation that the law respect each individual equally."

Justice Stevens, joined by Justice Souter, dissented on the ground that the plaintiffs lacked standing to raise their claims because, in contrast to plaintiff in *Grutter*, they "had already enrolled at other schools before they filed their class-action complaint in this case."

Justice Souter also dissented separately on the merits (Justice Ginsburg joined this portion of his opinion).]

SOUTER, J., dissenting:

Grutter reaffirms the permissibility of individualized consideration of race to achieve a diversity of students, at least where race is not assigned a preordained value in all cases. On the other hand, Justice Powell's opinion in [*Bakke*] rules out a racial quota or set-aside, in which race is the sole fact of eligibility for certain places in a class. [T]he freshman admissions system . . . is closer to what *Grutter* approves than to what *Bakke* condemns. . . .

The record does not describe a system with a quota like the one struck down in *Bakke*, which "insulate[d]" all nonminority candidates from competition from certain seats. The *Bakke* plan "focused *solely* on ethnic diversity" and effectively told nonminority applicants that "[n]o matter how strong their qualifications, quantitative and extracurricular, including their own potential for contribution to educational diversity, they are never afforded the chance to compete with applicants from the preferred groups for the [set-aside] special admissions seats."

The plan here, in contrast, lets all applicants compete for all places and values an applicant's offering for any place not only on grounds of race, but on grades, test scores, strength of high school, quality of course of study, residence, alumni relationships, leadership, personal character, socioeconomic disadvantage, athletic ability, and quality of a personal essay. A nonminority applicant who scores highly in these other categories can readily garner a selection index exceeding that of a minority applicant who gets the 20-point bonus. . . .

[I]n contrast to the college's forthrightness in saying just what plus factor it gives for membership in an underrepresented minority, it is worth considering the character of one alternative thrown up as preferable, because supposedly not based on race. Drawing on admissions systems used at public universities in California, Florida, and Texas, the United States contends that Michigan could get student diversity in satisfaction of its compelling interest by guaranteeing admission to a fixed percentage of the top students from each high school in Michigan.

While there is nothing unconstitutional about such a practice, it nonetheless suffers from a serious disadvantage. It is the disadvantage of deliberate obfuscation. The "percentage plans" are just as race conscious as the point scheme (and fairly so), but they get their racially diverse results without saying directly what they are doing or why they are doing it. In contrast, Michigan states its purpose directly and, if this were a doubtful case for me, I would be tempted to give Michigan an extra point of its own for its frankness. Equal protection cannot become an exercise in which the winners are the ones who hide the ball. . . .

GINSBURG, J., dissenting, joined by SOUTER, J.:

The stain of generations of racial oppression is still visible in our society, and the determination to hasten its removal remains vital. One can reasonably anticipate, therefore, that colleges and universities will seek to maintain their minority enrollment—and the networks and opportunities thereby opened to minority graduates—whether or not they can do so in full candor through adoption of affirmative action plans of the kind here at issue. Without recourse to such plans, institutions of higher education may resort to camouflage. For example, schools may encourage applicants to write of their cultural traditions in the essays they submit, or to indicate whether English is their second language. Seeking to improve their chances for admission, applicants may highlight the minority group associations to which they belong, or the Hispanic surnames of their mothers or grandparents. In turn, teachers' recommendations may emphasize who a student is as much as what he or she has accomplished. If honesty is the best policy, surely Michigan's accurately described, fully disclosed College affirmative action program is preferable to achieving similar numbers through winks, nods, and disguises.

DISCUSSION

1. *What is "diversity"?* Since *Bakke*, the only compelling interest the Court has recognized for race-conscious affirmative action in admissions has been diversity. Remedying past societal discrimination, promoting distributive justice among competing groups in the present, and providing role models have all been held to be not compelling governmental interests. Hence all justifications universities offered for their affirmative action policies had to be phrased in terms of promoting diversity. Not surprisingly, the word has taken on multiple and occasionally conflicting connotations.

Consider four different types of diversity: The first is ideological diversity, which is concerned with ensuring a mix of students with different beliefs (including but not limited to beliefs about politics and religion). The second is experiential diversity, which is concerned with ensuring a mix of students who have had different backgrounds and experiences (applicants who are poor or rich, have gone parachuting, have worked in relief agencies in the Third World, are former soldiers, battled childhood traumas or diseases, etc.). The third is diversity of talents, which is concerned with ensuring a mix of students with different talents and abilities (athletes, cello players, actors, etc.). The fourth type of diversity is demographic diversity, which is concerned with ensuring a mix of students from different ethnic, social, and religious groups.

Note that these forms of diversity may overlap, but they may also point in quite different directions. For example, admitting a conservative pro-life white female who plays the flute may add to ideological diversity and diversity of talents, but it may not necessarily promote demographic diversity. Admitting an additional African-American student may promote demographic or experiential diversity, but it may not promote either demographic or experiential diversity as much as adding a student from Malaysia or Kazakhstan. What kinds of diversity is the University of Michigan interested in? Which types of diversity does the critical mass policy involved in *Grutter* best promote? The use of points in *Gratz*?

Now consider the reasons that Justice O'Connor gives in *Grutter* for why diversity is important. First, diversity promotes mutual understanding between students of different races. Second, it better prepares students for life in an increasingly diverse and multicultural society. Third, diversity fosters "the diffusion of knowledge and opportunity through public institutions of higher education . . . to all individuals regardless of race or ethnicity." It promotes participation in elite institutions (and thus eventual placement in elite positions) by all racial and ethnic groups in the United States, which in turn helps secure the "[e]ffective participation by members of all racial and ethnic groups in the civic life of our Nation." Fourth, diversity enhances the legitimacy of society's leaders in the eyes of the citizenry, because to ensure legitimacy "it is necessary that the path to leadership be visibly open to talented and qualified individuals of every race and ethnicity."

Given the explanations Justice O'Connor offers for why diversity is a compelling state interest, which forms of diversity—ideological, experiential, talent-based, or demographic—are most closely connected to those reasons? Which are least closely connected?

2. *Diversity, distributive justice, and social solidarity.* Note Justice O'Connor's third argument for why diversity is a compelling state interest—diversity helps ensure a fair distribution of elite opportunities (including opportunities within the legal profession) among racial and ethnic groups in American society. This might be a backward-looking argument for remedying past societal discrimination and existing social stratification. If so, does *Grutter* sneak in through the back door considerations of distributive fairness that were excluded at the beginning of the Court's affirmative action jurisprudence? Is this argument consistent with Justice Powell's claim that racial balancing is not a legitimate goal of affirmative action and that remedying past societal discrimination is not a compelling state interest?

On the other hand, O'Connor's concern for diversity might be a forward-looking argument for ensuring a measure of distributive fairness among existing racial and ethnic groups in order to promote their mutual trust, integration, and cooperation. From this perspective, gross inequality threatens social bonds; diversity helps forge connections between different social groups and thereby promotes the cohesion and solidarity of society as a whole.

What should we make of Justice O'Connor's fourth argument, that diversity promotes legitimacy? Is the "legitimacy" she is talking about merely sociological—that in order for society to function properly America must seem to be fair, whether it is or not? Or is the argument one of moral legitimacy—that in order for its leaders to deserve the citizenry's respect, America must provide a fair share of opportunities in elite institutions to the various social, racial, and ethnic groups in American society? For an account of how the use of "diversity" shifts and expands in the transition from *Bakke* to *Grutter*, see Robert C. Post, Foreword: Fashioning the Legal Constitution: Culture, Courts, and Law, 117 Harv. L. Rev. 4, 60-64 (2003).

3. *The antibalkanization principle?* For decades, the Supreme Court has sharply divided in equal protection race discrimination cases. Some Justices would take a predominantly anticlassification approach and declare affirmative action unconstitutional, while others argue for an antisubordination approach and would defer in proper situations to race-conscious government programs. Nevertheless, the swing Justices in these cases—like Justices Powell, O'Connor, and Kennedy—have applied scrutiny in a third way. Reva Siegel points out that several of their opinions applying strict scrutiny—including *Grutter*—appear to be based on a concern with preventing social division and building social cohesion:

> [There is] a third perspective on equal protection in the opinions of swing Justices who have voted to uphold and to restrict race conscious remedies because of concern about social divisiveness which, they believe, both extreme racial stratification and unconstrained racial remedies can engender. . . . [This is] the antibalkanization perspective. . . . Because Justices reasoning from an antibalkanization perspective [such as Justices Lewis Powell, Sandra Day O'Connor, and Anthony Kennedy] understand that pervasive racial stratification can leave some groups feeling like outsiders or nonparticipants, [these] Justices permit and sometimes encourage government to act in ways that promote racial integration (a form of equality realized through social cohesion). [But because they also] understand that interventions promoting racial integration can become a locus of racial conflict, they insist that race-conscious interventions undertaken for compelling public-regarding purposes must nonetheless anticipate and endeavor to ameliorate race-conscious resentments. . . .
>
> . . . Moderates have employed strict scrutiny, not to bar all race-conscious efforts to integrate, but rather to impose a particular social form on government's race-conscious efforts to integrate: to insist that when government engages in a race-conscious act in support of integration, government interacts with the public in ways that emphasize commonality among citizens and minimize the appearance of racial partiality. . . . In *Bakke*, Justice Powell emphasized commonality when he rejected remedial justifications for educational affirmative action in favor of racial "diversity" and when he imposed conditions on affirmative action, such as the requirements that schools consider all applicants together and consider every applicant as an individual. Justice O'Connor followed this example, leading the Court to impose constraints on affirmative action in *Gratz* and *Grutter* designed to diminish the salience of race in the administration of the programs. . . .

Reva B. Siegel, From Colorblindness to Antibalkanization: An Emerging Ground of Decision in Race Equality Cases, 120 Yale L.J. 1278 (2011).

4. *Did the Court apply strict scrutiny in* Grutter? Note Justice O'Connor's statement that the Court will defer to "[t]he Law School's educational judgment that . . . diversity is essential to its educational mission" because of "complex educational judgments in an area that lies primarily within the expertise of the university."

Is deference to the judgments of an institution accused of racial discrimination characteristic of strict scrutiny? If not, then perhaps the Court is not applying strict scrutiny, even though it insists that it is. Similarly, do you believe that the Court would give Michigan the same degree of deference if the university announced that educational considerations made it necessary to increase enrollments of white students? If not, then perhaps the reason why the Court gives university officials the benefit of the doubt is because it thinks that Michigan's decisionmaking process is more benign than invidious. A different degree of scrutiny applies to policies designed to assist minorities as opposed to policies that discriminate against them. Both of these positions, of course, are inconsistent with the Court's opinions in *Adarand* and *Croson,* not to mention language in *Grutter* itself. Does this mean that Justice Marshall's and Justice Brennan's positions in *Bakke* have effectively won out in educational affirmative action, although the Court is unwilling to say so?

5. *Is "critical mass" a form of racial balancing?* Does Justice O'Connor have any good response to the dissenters' charge that a critical mass of African Americans should be of the same size as a critical mass of Latinos or Native Americans, and hence Michigan cannot justify admitting different percentages of each group? If the goal of affirmative action is to give major demographic groups in American society a fair share of opportunities at elite institutions, Michigan's admissions decisions would make some sense. Michigan might wish to ensure that Black people, Latinos, and Native Americans were represented in the entering class in rough proportion to the number of applications received. On the other hand, Michigan might conclude that because Asian Americans will likely be fairly well represented in the entering class, there is no need to give them any admissions preference. Nevertheless, what, if anything, does this justification for affirmative action in education have to do with achieving a "critical mass" of minorities, or with the various forms of diversity described above?

6. *Diversity or elite status but not both.* Do you agree with Justice Thomas's claim that for purposes of the Equal Protection Clause, the University of Michigan Law School cannot properly assert an interest in producing elites who will practice law outside the state? Thomas points out that if Michigan wants diversity, it can simply reduce entrance requirements and surrender its elite status. If the purpose of affirmative action is to provide a fair share of elite opportunities to all races and all segments of society, it would be particularly important for Michigan to remain an elite institution, for the surest path to elite positions in society is through elite educational institutions. Note, however, that this response to Justice Thomas would require the Court to admit that affirmative action is about issues of distributive justice rather than simply about a question of academic freedom.

7. *The cost of "individualized determinations."* Will all schools be equally able to adhere to the rules set forth in *Grutter* and *Gratz*? Compare very selective institutions that receive 15,000 applications to fill a class of 1,500 with large state universities that receive many times that number of applications in a single year. Will the latter institutions be able to provide individualized determinations of each and every file? Do the Court's decisions in *Grutter* and *Gratz* mean that schools cannot use computer programs to weed out or sort applications based on a set of factors assigned a particular weight, like grade point average, standardized test scores, alumni relations, athletic recruitment, and the like? Do the Court's decisions mean that race cannot be one of those factors in a computer program? Or do the decisions mean that at some point in the process, every file must be read by a human being and judged according to the totality of its characteristics before a decision is made to accept or reject an applicant for admission?

8. *Racial classifications, again.* Are all race-conscious decisions by universities equally subject to strict scrutiny? Suppose that the University of Michigan does not use race in admissions, but it makes extra efforts to encourage minority students to apply to the University of Michigan and to attend if they are accepted. It does not make the same efforts for white students. Is this policy a racial classification subject to strict scrutiny?

6. The Roberts Court Interprets *Brown* in Light of Affirmative Action

Parents Involved In Community Schools v. Seattle School District No. 1

551 U.S. 701 (2007)

Chief Justice ROBERTS announced the judgment of the Court, and delivered the opinion of the Court with respect to Parts I, II, III-A, and III-C, and an opinion with respect to Parts III-B and IV, in which Justices SCALIA, THOMAS, and ALITO join.

[The Seattle School District No. 1 and Jefferson County Public Schools in Louisville voluntarily adopted plans to promote racial diversity. Seattle has never been subject to court-ordered desegregation for operating segregated schools, but adopted its plan to correct for the effects of racially identifiable housing patterns on school assignments.

Seattle allocated slots in oversubscribed high schools by using tiebreakers. The first selects for students who have a sibling enrolled at the chosen school. The second selects for students whose race will help balance the oversubscribed school. Approximately 41 percent of enrolled students in the district's public schools are white; 59 percent are non-white. If an oversubscribed school is not within 10 percentage points of the district's overall white/non-white racial balance, the tiebreaker selects for the student who would bring the school closer into balance. The third tiebreaker selects for students who are closest in geographic proximity to the oversubscribed school.

The Louisville school district had been subject to a court-ordered desegregation decree since 1975. It was dissolved in 2000 when the district was declared unitary, having eliminated "[t]o the greatest extent practicable" the vestiges of its prior policy of segregation.

In 2001, after the decree was dissolved, Jefferson County adopted its voluntary student assignment plan. Schools that are not magnet schools must maintain a minimum Black enrollment of 15 percent, and a maximum Black enrollment of 50 percent. Approximately 34 percent of the district's 97,000 students are Black; most of the remaining 66 percent are white.

Parents of kindergartners, first-graders, and students new to the district may select first and second choices among schools within their geographical area for initial assignment. Students are assigned based on available space, but once a school has reached less than 15 percent or more than 50 percent Black, it will take only students who will keep the racial balance within these guidelines. Students initially assigned may also transfer to other schools in the district, subject to availability of space and the same requirements of racial balance. Petitioner Crystal Meredith, who sought to transfer her son Joshua for kindergarten from a school ten miles away to one a mile away was refused because she was told it would adversely impact the racial balance of the school to which he had been assigned.]

. . .

III

A

It is well established that when the government distributes burdens or benefits on the basis of individual racial classifications, that action is reviewed under strict scrutiny. In order to satisfy this searching standard of review, the school districts must demonstrate that the use of individual racial classifications in the assignment plans here under review is "narrowly tailored" to achieve a "compelling" government interest.

[O]ur prior cases, in evaluating the use of racial classifications in the school context, have recognized two interests that qualify as compelling. The first is the compelling interest of remedying the effects of past intentional discrimination. Yet the Seattle public schools have not shown that they were ever segregated by law, and were not subject to court-ordered desegregation decrees. The Jefferson County public schools were previously segregated by law [but] [i]n 2000, the District Court that entered that decree dissolved it, finding that Jefferson County had "eliminated the vestiges associated with the former policy of segregation and its pernicious effects," and thus had achieved "unitary" status. . . . We have emphasized that the harm being remedied by mandatory desegregation plans is the harm that is traceable to segregation, and that "the Constitution is not violated by racial imbalance in the schools, without more." Milliken v. Bradley. Once Jefferson County achieved unitary status, it had remedied the constitutional wrong that allowed race-based assignments. Any continued use of race must be justified on some other basis.

The second government interest we have recognized as compelling for purposes of strict scrutiny is the interest in diversity in higher education upheld in Grutter [v. Bollinger, 539 U.S. 306, 326 (2003)]. . . . The diversity interest was not focused on race alone but encompassed "all factors that may contribute to student body diversity" [including] "admittees who have lived or traveled widely abroad, are fluent in several languages, have overcome personal adversity and family hardship, have exceptional records of extensive community service, and have had successful careers in other fields." . . . [T]he admissions program at issue [in *Grutter*] focused on each applicant as an individual, and not simply as a member of a particular racial group. The classification of applicants by race upheld in *Grutter* was only as part of a "highly individualized, holistic review." As the Court explained, "[t]he importance of this individualized consideration in the context of a race-conscious admissions program is paramount." The point of the narrow tailoring analysis in which the *Grutter* Court engaged was to ensure that the use of racial classifications was indeed part of a broader assessment of diversity, and not simply an effort to achieve racial balance, which the Court explained would be "patently unconstitutional."

In the present cases, by contrast, race is not considered as part of a broader effort to achieve "exposure to widely diverse people, cultures, ideas, and viewpoints"; race, for some students, is determinative standing alone. The districts argue that other factors, such as student preferences, affect assignment decisions under their plans, but under each plan when race comes into play, it is decisive by itself. . . . Even when it comes to race, the plans here employ only a limited notion of diversity, viewing race exclusively in white/nonwhite terms in Seattle and black/"other" terms in Jefferson County. The Seattle "Board Statement Reaffirming Diversity Rationale" speaks of the "inherent educational value" in "[p]roviding students the opportunity to attend schools with diverse student enrollment." But under the Seattle plan, a school with 50 percent Asian-American students and 50 percent white students but no African-American, Native American, or Latino students would qualify as balanced, while a school with 30 percent Asian-American, 25 percent African-American, 25 percent Latino, and 20 percent white students would not. It is hard to understand how a plan that could allow these results can be viewed as being concerned with achieving enrollment that is "'broadly diverse,'" *Grutter.*

. . . In upholding the admissions plan in *Grutter,* [moreover] . . . this Court relied upon considerations unique to institutions of higher education, noting that in light of "the expansive freedoms of speech and thought associated with the university environment, universities occupy a special niche in our constitutional tradition." . . . The present cases are not governed by *Grutter.*

B

Perhaps recognizing that reliance on *Grutter* cannot sustain their plans, both school districts assert additional interests. . . . Seattle contends that its use of race helps to reduce racial concentration in schools and to ensure that racially concentrated housing patterns do not prevent nonwhite students from having access to the most desirable schools. Jefferson County has articulated a similar goal, phrasing its interest in terms of educating its students "in a racially integrated environment." Each school district argues that educational and broader socialization benefits flow from a racially diverse learning environment, and each contends that because the diversity they seek is racial diversity—not the broader diversity at issue in *Grutter*—it makes sense to promote that interest directly by relying on race alone.

The parties and their *amici* dispute whether racial diversity in schools in fact has a marked impact on test scores and other objective yardsticks or achieves intangible socialization benefits. The debate is not one we need to resolve, however, because it is clear that the racial classifications employed by the districts are not narrowly tailored to the goal of achieving the educational and social benefits asserted to flow from racial diversity. In design and operation, the plans are directed only to racial balance, pure and simple, an objective this Court has repeatedly condemned as illegitimate.

The plans are tied to each district's specific racial demographics, rather than to any pedagogic concept of the level of diversity needed to obtain the asserted educational benefits. . . . [T]he racial demographics in each district—whatever they happen to be—drive the required "diversity" numbers. The plans here are not tailored to achieving a degree of diversity necessary to realize the asserted educational benefits; instead the plans are tailored, in the words of Seattle's Manager of Enrollment Planning, Technical Support, and Demographics, to "the goal established by the school board of attaining a level of diversity within the schools that approximates the district's overall demographics." . . .

Jefferson County's expert referred to the importance of having "at least 20 percent" minority group representation for the group "to be visible enough to make a difference," and noted that "small isolated minority groups in a school are not likely to have a strong effect on the overall school." The Jefferson County plan, however, is based on a goal of replicating at each school "an African-American enrollment equivalent to the average district-wide African American enrollment." . . .

This working backward to achieve a particular type of racial balance, rather than working forward from some demonstration of the level of diversity that provides the purported benefits, is a fatal flaw under our existing precedent. We have many times over reaffirmed that "[r]acial balance is not to be achieved for its own sake." *Grutter* itself reiterated that "outright racial balancing" is "patently unconstitutional."

Accepting racial balancing as a compelling state interest would justify the imposition of racial proportionality throughout American society, contrary to our repeated recognition that "[a]t the heart of the Constitution's guarantee of equal protection lies the simple command that the Government must treat citizens as individuals, not as simply components of a racial, religious, sexual or national class." Miller v. Johnson, 515 U.S. 900, 911 (1995). Allowing racial balancing as a compelling end in itself would "effectively assur[e] that race will always be relevant in American life, and that the 'ultimate goal' of 'eliminating entirely from governmental decisionmaking such irrelevant factors as a human being's race' will never be achieved." *Croson*. . . . The validity of our concern that racial balancing has "no logical stopping point," *Croson*, is demonstrated here by the degree to which the districts tie their racial guidelines to their demographics. As the districts' demographics shift, so too will their definition of racial diversity.

[I]n Seattle the plans are defended as necessary to address the consequences of racially identifiable housing patterns. [But] remedying past societal discrimination does not justify race-conscious government action. See, e.g., Shaw v. Hunt, 517 U.S. 899, 909-910 (1996) ("[A]n effort to alleviate the effects of societal discrimination is not a compelling interest"); *Croson*.

The principle that racial balancing is not permitted is one of substance, not semantics. Racial balancing is not transformed from "patently unconstitutional" to a compelling state interest simply by relabeling it "racial diversity." While the school districts use various verbal formulations to describe the interest they seek to promote—racial diversity, avoidance of racial isolation, racial integration—they offer no definition of the interest that suggests it differs from racial balance.

Jefferson County phrases its interest as "racial integration," but integration certainly does not require the sort of racial proportionality reflected in its plan. Even in the context of mandatory desegregation, we have stressed that racial proportionality is not required, . . . and here Jefferson County has already been found to have eliminated the vestiges of its prior segregated school system.

The en banc Ninth Circuit declared that "when a racially diverse school system is the goal (or racial concentration or isolation is the problem), there is no more effective means than a consideration of race to achieve the solution." [T]his conclusory argument cannot sustain the plans. . . . To the extent the objective is sufficient diversity so that students see fellow students as individuals rather than solely as members of a racial group, using means that treat students solely as members of a racial group is fundamentally at cross-purposes with that end.

C

The districts assert, as they must, that the way in which they have employed individual racial classifications is necessary to achieve their stated ends. The minimal effect these classifications have on student assignments, however, suggests that other means would be effective. Seattle's racial tiebreaker results, in the end, only in shifting a small number of students between schools. . . . Similarly, Jefferson County's use of racial classifications has only a minimal effect on the assignment of students. . . . While we do not suggest that *greater* use of race would be preferable, the minimal impact of the districts' racial classifications on school enrollment casts doubt on the necessity of using racial classifications. . . .

The districts have also failed to show that they considered methods other than explicit racial classifications to achieve their stated goals. Narrow tailoring requires "serious, good faith consideration of workable race-neutral alternatives," *Grutter*, and yet in Seattle several alternative assignment plans—many of which would not have used express racial classifications—were rejected with little or no consideration. Jefferson County has failed to present any evidence that it considered alternatives, even though the district already claims that its goals are achieved primarily through means other than the racial classifications.

IV

. . . Justice Breyer seeks to justify the plans at issue under our precedents recognizing the compelling interest in remedying past intentional discrimination. . . . The distinction between segregation by state action and racial imbalance caused by other factors has been central to our jurisprudence in this area for generations. The dissent elides this distinction between *de jure* and *de facto* segregation, casually intimates that Seattle's school attendance patterns reflect illegal segregation, and fails to credit the judicial determination—under the most rigorous standard—that Jefferson County had eliminated the vestiges of prior segregation. The dissent thus alters in fundamental ways not only the facts presented here but the established law. . . .

Justice Breyer's dissent next relies heavily on dicta from Swann v. Charlotte Mecklenburg Bd. of Ed. [But] *Swann* addresses only a possible state objective; it says nothing of the permissible *means*—race conscious or otherwise—that a school district might employ to achieve that objective. The reason for this omission is clear enough, since the case did not involve any voluntary means adopted by a school district. . . .

. . . Justice Breyer's dissent candidly dismisses the significance of this Court's repeated *holdings* that all racial classifications must be reviewed under strict scrutiny, arguing that a different standard of review should be applied because the districts use race for beneficent rather than malicious purposes. . . . Justice Breyer . . . relies on the good intentions and motives of the school districts, stating that he has found "no case that . . . repudiated this constitutional asymmetry between that which seeks to *exclude* and that which seeks to *include* members of minority races." We have found many. Our cases clearly reject the argument that motives affect the strict scrutiny analysis. See Johnson [v. California]; *Adarand*; *Croson*.

This argument that different rules should govern racial classifications designed to include rather than exclude is not new; it has been repeatedly pressed in the past, and has been repeatedly rejected. . . .

Justice Breyer also suggests that other means for achieving greater racial diversity in schools are necessarily unconstitutional if the racial classifications at issue in these cases cannot survive strict scrutiny. These other means—e.g., where to construct new schools, how to allocate resources among schools, and which academic offerings to provide to attract students to certain schools—implicate different considerations than the explicit racial classifications at issue in these cases, and we express no opinion on their validity—not even in dicta. Rather, we employ the familiar and well-established analytic approach of strict scrutiny to evaluate the plans at issue today, an approach that in no way warrants the dissent's cataclysmic concerns. Under that approach, the school districts have not carried their burden of showing that the ends they seek justify the particular extreme means they have chosen—classifying individual students on the basis of their race and discriminating among them on that basis. . . .

If the need for the racial classifications embraced by the school districts is unclear, even on the districts' own terms, the costs are undeniable. "[D]istinctions between citizens solely because of their ancestry are by their very nature odious to a free people whose institutions are founded upon the doctrine of equality." *Adarand.* Government action dividing us by race is inherently suspect because such classifications promote "notions of racial inferiority and lead to a politics of racial hostility," *Croson,* "reinforce the belief, held by too many for too much of our history, that individuals should be judged by the color of their skin," Shaw v. Reno, 509 U.S. 630, 657 (1993), and "endorse race-based reasoning and the conception of a Nation divided into racial blocs, thus contributing to an escalation of racial hostility and conflict." As the Court explained in Rice v. Cayetano, 528 U.S. 495, 517 (2000), "[o]ne of the principal reasons race is treated as a forbidden classification is that it demeans the dignity and worth of a person to be judged by ancestry instead of by his or her own merit and essential qualities."

All this is true enough in the contexts in which these statements were made—government contracting, voting districts, allocation of broadcast licenses, and electing state officers—but when it comes to using race to assign children to schools, history will be heard. In Brown v. Board of Education, 347 U.S. 483 (1954) (*Brown I*), we held that segregation deprived black children of equal educational opportunities regardless of whether school facilities and other tangible factors were equal, because government classification and separation on grounds of race themselves denoted inferiority. It was not the inequality of the facilities but the fact of legally separating children on the basis of race on which the Court relied to find a constitutional violation in 1954. See *id.*, at 494 ("'The impact [of segregation] is greater when it has the sanction of the law'"). The next Term, we accordingly stated that "full compliance" with *Brown I* required school districts "to achieve a system of determining admission to the public schools *on a nonracial basis.*" *Brown II* (emphasis added).

The parties and their *amici* debate which side is more faithful to the heritage of *Brown,* but the position of the plaintiffs in *Brown* was spelled out in their brief and could not have been clearer: "[T]he Fourteenth Amendment prevents states from according differential treatment to American children on the basis of their color or race." What do the racial classifications at issue here do, if not accord differential treatment on the basis of race? As counsel who appeared before this Court for the plaintiffs in *Brown* put it: "We have one fundamental contention which we will seek to develop in the course of this argument, and that contention is that no State has any authority under the equal-protection clause of the Fourteenth Amendment to use race as a factor in affording educational opportunities among its citizens." There is no ambiguity in that statement. And it was that position that prevailed in this Court, which emphasized in its remedial opinion that what was "[a]t stake is the personal interest of the plaintiffs in admission to public schools as soon as practicable *on a non-discriminatory basis*," and what was required was "determining admission to the public schools *on a nonracial basis*." *Brown II* (emphasis added). What do the racial classifications do in these cases, if not determine admission to a public school on a racial basis? Before *Brown*, schoolchildren were told where they could and could not go to school based on the color of their skin. The school districts in these cases have not carried the heavy burden of demonstrating that we should allow this once again—even for very different reasons. For schools that never segregated on the basis of race, such as Seattle, or that have removed the vestiges of past segregation, such as Jefferson County, the way "to achieve a system of determining admission to the public schools on a nonracial basis," *Brown II*, is to stop assigning students on a racial basis. The way to stop discrimination on the basis of race is to stop discriminating on the basis of race. . . .

Justice THOMAS, concurring.

[C]ontrary to the dissent's arguments, resegregation is not occurring in Seattle or Louisville; these school boards have no present interest in remedying past segregation; and these race-based student assignment programs do not serve any compelling state interest. Accordingly, the plans are unconstitutional. Disfavoring a color-blind interpretation of the Constitution, the dissent would give school boards a free hand to make decisions on the basis of race—an approach reminiscent of that advocated by the segregationists in Brown v. Board of Education. This approach is just as wrong today as it was a half-century ago. The Constitution and our cases require us to be much more demanding before permitting local school boards to make decisions based on race.

I

[R]acial imbalance is not segregation, and the mere incantation of terms like resegregation and remediation cannot make up the difference. [I]n the context of public schooling, segregation is the deliberate operation of a school system to "carry out a governmental policy to separate pupils in schools solely on the basis of race." *Swann*. . . . Racial imbalance is the failure of a school district's individual schools to match or approximate the demographic makeup of the student population at large. Racial imbalance is not segregation.[a] Although presently observed racial imbalance might result from past *de jure* segregation, racial imbalance can also result from any number of innocent private decisions, including voluntary housing choices. Because racial imbalance is not inevitably linked to unconstitutional segregation, it is not unconstitutional in and of itself.

Although there is arguably a danger of racial imbalance in schools in Seattle and Louisville, there is no danger of resegregation. No one contends that Seattle

---

a. The dissent refers repeatedly and reverently to "'integration.'" However, outside of the context of remediation for past de jure segregation, "integration" is simply racial balancing. Therefore, the school districts' attempts to further "integrate" are properly thought of as little more than attempts to achieve a particular racial balance.

has established or that Louisville has reestablished a dual school system that separates students on the basis of race. The statistics cited [by Justice Breyer] [a]t most . . . show a national trend toward classroom racial imbalance. However, racial imbalance without intentional state action to separate the races does not amount to segregation. To raise the specter of resegregation to defend these programs is to ignore the meaning of the word and the nature of the cases before us.[b] . . .

This Court has carved out a narrow exception to [the] general rule [forbidding the use of race] for cases in which a school district has a "history of maintaining two sets of schools in a single school system deliberately operated to carry out a governmental policy to separate pupils in schools solely on the basis of race." In such cases, race-based remedial measures are sometimes required.[c] But without a history of state enforced racial separation, a school district has no affirmative legal obligation to take race-based remedial measures to eliminate segregation and its vestiges.

Neither of the programs before us today is compelled as a remedial measure, and no one makes such a claim. . . .

[T]he dissent conflates the concepts of segregation and racial imbalance. . . . [T]he further we get from the era of state-sponsored racial separation, the less likely it is that racial imbalance has a traceable connection to any prior segregation. [Moreover,] a school cannot "remedy" racial imbalance in the same way that it can remedy segregation. Remediation of past *de jure* segregation is a one-time process involving the redress of a discrete legal injury inflicted by an identified entity. At some point, the discrete injury will be remedied, and the school district will be declared unitary. Unlike *de jure* segregation, there is no ultimate remedy for racial imbalance. Individual schools will fall in and out of balance in the natural course, and the appropriate balance itself will shift with a school district's changing demographics. Thus, racial balancing will have to take place on an indefinite basis—a continuous process with no identifiable culpable party and no discernable end

---

b. The dissent's assertion that these plans are necessary for the school districts to maintain their "hard-won gains" reveals its conflation of segregation and racial imbalance. For the dissent's purposes, the relevant hard-won gains are the present racial compositions in the individual schools in Seattle and Louisville. However, the actual hard-won gain in these cases is the elimination of the vestiges of the system of state-enforced racial separation that once existed in Louisville. To equate the achievement of a certain statistical mix in several schools with the elimination of the system of systematic de jure segregation trivializes the latter accomplishment. Nothing but an interest in classroom aesthetics and a hypersensitivity to elite sensibilities justifies the school districts' racial balancing programs. But "the principle of inherent equality that underlies and infuses our Constitution" required the disestablishment of de jure segregation. Assessed in any objective manner, there is no comparison between the two.

c. [T]he remedies this Court authorized lower courts to compel in early desegregation cases like *Green* and *Swann* were exceptional. Sustained resistance to *Brown* prompted the Court to authorize extraordinary race-conscious remedial measures (like compelled racial mixing) to turn the Constitution's dictate to desegregate into reality. Even if these measures were appropriate as remedies in the face of widespread resistance to *Brown*'s mandate, they are not forever insulated from constitutional scrutiny. Rather, "such powers should have been temporary and used only to overcome the widespread resistance to the dictates of the Constitution."

point. In part for those reasons, the Court has never permitted outright racial balancing solely for the purpose of achieving a particular racial balance.

II

Lacking a cognizable interest in remediation, neither of these plans can survive strict scrutiny because neither plan serves a genuinely compelling state interest. The dissent avoids reaching that conclusion by unquestioningly accepting the assertions of selected social scientists while completely ignoring the fact that those assertions are the subject of fervent debate. . . .

[T]he constitutional problems with government race-based decisionmaking are not diminished in the slightest by the presence or absence of an intent to oppress any race or by the real or asserted well-meaning motives for the race-based decisionmaking. *Adarand.* Purportedly benign race-based decisionmaking suffers the same constitutional infirmity as invidious race-based decisionmaking. *Id.*, at 240 (Thomas, J., concurring in part and concurring in judgment) ("As far as the Constitution is concerned, it is irrelevant whether a government's racial classifications are drawn by those who wish to oppress a race or by those who have a sincere desire to help those thought to be disadvantaged").

Even supposing it mattered to the constitutional analysis, the race-based student assignment programs before us are not as benign as the dissent believes. [E]very time the government uses racial criteria to "bring the races together," someone gets excluded, and the person excluded suffers an injury solely because of his or her race. The petitioner in the Louisville case received a letter from the school board informing her that her *kindergartner* would not be allowed to attend the school of petitioner's choosing because of the child's race. Doubtless, hundreds of letters like this went out from both school boards every year these race-based assignment plans were in operation. This type of exclusion, solely on the basis of race, is precisely the sort of government action that pits the races against one another, exacerbates racial tension, and "provoke[s] resentment among those who believe that they have been wronged by the government's use of race." . . .

[T]he school boards have no interest in remedying the sundry consequences of prior segregation unrelated to schooling, such as "housing patterns, employment practices, economic conditions, and social attitudes." General claims that past school segregation affected such varied societal trends are "too amorphous a basis for imposing a racially classified remedy," because "[i]t is sheer speculation" how decades-past segregation in the school system might have affected these trends. Consequently, school boards seeking to remedy those societal problems with race-based measures in schools today would have no way to gauge the proper scope of the remedy. Indeed, remedial measures geared toward such broad and unrelated societal ills have "'no logical stopping point,'" and threaten to become "ageless in their reach into the past, and timeless in their ability to affect the future."

[T]he dissent argues that the interest in integration has an educational element. The dissent asserts that racially balanced schools improve educational outcomes for black children. In support, the dissent unquestioningly cites certain social science research to support propositions that are hotly disputed among social scientists. In reality, it is far from apparent that coerced racial mixing has any educational benefits, much less that integration is necessary to black achievement.

Scholars have differing opinions as to whether educational benefits arise from racial balancing. Some have concluded that black students receive genuine educational benefits. Others have been more circumspect. And some have concluded that there are no demonstrable educational benefits. The *amicus* briefs in the cases before us mirror this divergence of opinion.

[A]dd to the inconclusive social science the fact of black achievement in "racially isolated" environments. . . . Even after *Brown*, some schools with predominantly black enrollments have achieved outstanding educational results. There is also evidence that black students attending historically black colleges achieve better academic results than those attending predominantly white colleges.

The Seattle school board itself must believe that racial mixing is not necessary to black achievement. Seattle operates a K-8 "African-American Academy," which has a "nonwhite" enrollment of 99%. That school was founded in 1990 as part of the school board's effort to "increase academic achievement." According to the school's most recent annual report, "[a]cademic excellence" is its "primary goal." This racially imbalanced environment has reportedly produced test scores "higher across all grade levels in reading, writing and math." Contrary to what the dissent would have predicted, the children in Seattle's African-American Academy have shown gains when placed in a "highly segregated" environment.

Given this tenuous relationship between forced racial mixing and improved educational results for black children, the dissent cannot plausibly maintain that an educational element supports the integration interest, let alone makes it compelling. . . .

Perhaps recognizing as much, the dissent argues that the social science evidence is "strong enough to permit a democratically elected school board reasonably to determine that this interest is a compelling one." This assertion is inexplicable. It is not up to the school boards—the very government entities whose race-based practices we must strictly scrutinize—to determine what interests qualify as compelling under the Fourteenth Amendment to the United States Constitution. Rather, this Court must assess independently the nature of the interest asserted and the evidence to support it in order to determine whether it qualifies as compelling under our precedents. . . . The dissent's proposed test—whether sufficient social science evidence supports a government unit's conclusion that the interest it asserts is compelling . . . would leave our equal-protection jurisprudence at the mercy of elected government officials evaluating the evanescent views of a handful of social scientists. To adopt the dissent's deferential approach would be to abdicate our constitutional responsibilities.[d]

[T]he dissent argues that the racial balancing in these plans is not an end in itself but is instead intended to "teac[h] children to engage in the kind of

---

d. The dissent accuses me of "feel[ing] confident that, to end invidious discrimination, one must end *all* governmental use of race-conscious criteria" and chastises me for not deferring to democratically elected majorities. Regardless of what Justice Breyer's goals might be, this Court does not sit to "create a society that includes all Americans" or to solve the problems of "troubled inner-city schooling." We are not social engineers. The United States Constitution dictates that local governments cannot make decisions on the basis of race. Consequently, regardless of the perceived negative effects of racial imbalance, I will not defer to legislative majorities where the Constitution forbids it.

cooperation among Americans of all races that is necessary to make a land of three hundred million people one Nation." . . . [I]f governments may constitutionally use racial balancing to achieve these aspirational ends in schools, they may use racial balancing to achieve similar goals at every level—from state-sponsored 4-H clubs, to the state civil service. Moreover, . . . it will always be important for students to learn cooperation among the races. If this interest justifies race-conscious measures today, then logically it will justify race-conscious measures forever. . . .

[T]he dissent points to data that indicate that "black and white students in desegregated schools are less racially prejudiced than those in segregated schools." By the dissent's account, improvements in racial attitudes depend upon the increased contact between black and white students thought to occur in more racially balanced schools. There is no guarantee, however, that students of different races in the same school will actually spend time with one another. Schools frequently group students by academic ability as an aid to efficient instruction, but such groupings often result in classrooms with high concentrations of one race or another. In addition to classroom separation, students of different races within the same school may separate themselves socially. Therefore, even supposing interracial contact leads directly to improvements in racial attitudes and race relations, a program that assigns students of different races to the same schools might not capture those benefits. Simply putting students together under the same roof does not necessarily mean that the students will learn together or even interact.

Furthermore, it is unclear whether increased interracial contact improves racial attitudes and relations. . . . Some studies have even found that a deterioration in racial attitudes seems to result from racial mixing in schools. . . . As I explained in *Grutter*, only "those measures the State must take to provide a bulwark against anarchy . . . or to prevent violence" and "a government's effort to remedy past discrimination for which it is responsible" constitute compelling interests. Neither of the parties has argued—nor could they—that race-based student assignment is necessary to provide a bulwark against anarchy or to prevent violence. . . .

III

Most of the dissent's criticisms of today's result can be traced to its rejection of the color-blind Constitution. The dissent attempts to marginalize the notion of a color-blind Constitution by consigning it to me and Members of today's plurality.[e] But

---

It should escape no one that behind Justice Breyer's veil of judicial modesty hides an inflated role for the Federal Judiciary. The dissent's approach confers on judges the power to say what sorts of discrimination are benign and which are invidious. Having made that determination (based on no objective measure that I can detect), a judge following the dissent's approach will set the level of scrutiny to achieve the desired result. Only then must the judge defer to a democratic majority. In my view, to defer to one's preferred result is not to defer at all.

e. I have no quarrel with the proposition that the Fourteenth Amendment sought to bring former slaves into American society as full members. [But] the color-blind Constitution does not bar the government from taking measures to remedy past state-sponsored discrimination—indeed, it requires that such measures be taken in certain circumstances. Race-based government measures during the 1860's and 1870's to remedy *state-enforced slavery* were therefore not inconsistent with the color-blind Constitution.

I am quite comfortable in the company I keep. My view of the Constitution is Justice Harlan's view in *Plessy*: "Our Constitution is color blind, and neither knows nor tolerates classes among citizens." Plessy v. Ferguson (dissenting opinion). And my view was the rallying cry for the lawyers who litigated *Brown*. See, e.g., Brief for Appellants in Brown v. Board of Education, O.T. 1953, Nos. 1, 2, and 4 p. 65 ("That the Constitution is color blind is our dedicated belief"); Brief for Appellants in Brown v. Board of Education, O.T. 1952, No. 1, p. 5 ("The Fourteenth Amendment precludes a state from imposing distinctions or classifications based upon race and color alone").

The dissent appears to pin its interpretation of the Equal Protection Clause to current societal practice and expectations, deference to local officials, likely practical consequences, and reliance on previous statements from this and other courts. Such a view was ascendant in this Court's jurisprudence for several decades. It first appeared in *Plessy*, where the Court asked whether a state law providing for segregated railway cars was "a reasonable regulation." The Court deferred to local authorities in making its determination, noting that in inquiring into reasonableness "there must necessarily be a large discretion on the part of the legislature." The Court likewise paid heed to societal practices, local expectations, and practical consequences by looking to "the established usages, customs and traditions of the people, and with a view to the promotion of their comfort, and the preservation of the public peace and good order." . . .

The segregationists in *Brown* embraced the arguments the Court endorsed in *Plessy*. Though *Brown* decisively rejected those arguments, today's dissent replicates them to a distressing extent. Thus, the dissent argues that "[e]ach plan embodies the results of local experience and community consultation." Similarly, the segregationists made repeated appeals to societal practice and expectation. The dissent argues that "weight [must be given] to a local school board's knowledge, expertise, and concerns," and with equal vigor, the segregationists argued for deference to local authorities. The dissent argues that today's decision "threatens to substitute for present calm a disruptive round of race-related litigation," and claims that today's decision "risks serious harm to the law and for the Nation." The segregationists also relied upon the likely practical consequences of ending the state-imposed system of racial separation. . . .

The similarities between the dissent's arguments and the segregationists' arguments do not stop there. Like the dissent, the segregationists repeatedly cautioned the Court to consider practicalities and not to embrace too theoretical a view of the Fourteenth Amendment. And just as the dissent argues that the need for these programs will lessen over time, the segregationists claimed that reliance on segregation was lessening and might eventually end.

What was wrong in 1954 cannot be right today.[f] . . . None of the considerations trumpeted by the dissent is relevant to the constitutionality of the school boards' race based plans because no contextual detail—or collection of contextual details,

---

f. It is no answer to say that these cases can be distinguished from *Brown* because *Brown* involved invidious racial classifications whereas the racial classifications here are benign. How does one tell when a racial classification is invidious? The segregationists in *Brown* argued that their racial classifications were benign, not invidious. It is the height of arrogance for Members of this Court to assert blindly that their motives are better than others.

can "provide refuge from the principle that under our Constitution, the government may not make distinctions on the basis of race."

In place of the color-blind Constitution, the dissent would permit measures to keep the races together and proscribe measures to keep the races apart.[g] Although no such distinction is apparent in the Fourteenth Amendment, the dissent would constitutionalize today's faddish social theories that embrace that distinction. The Constitution is not that malleable. Even if current social theories favor classroom racial engineering as necessary to "solve the problems at hand," the Constitution enshrines principles independent of social theories. . . . Indeed, if our history has taught us anything, it has taught us to beware of elites bearing racial theories. . . . Can we really be sure that the racial theories that motivated *Dred Scott* and *Plessy* are a relic of the past or that future theories will be nothing but beneficent and progressive? That is a gamble I am unwilling to take, and it is one the Constitution does not allow.

Justice KENNEDY, concurring in part and concurring in the judgment.

[I] join Parts III-A and III-C for reasons provided below. My views do not allow me to join the balance of the opinion by The Chief Justice, which seems to me to be inconsistent in both its approach and its implications with the history, meaning, and reach of the Equal Protection Clause. Justice Breyer's dissenting opinion, on the other hand, rests on what in my respectful submission is a misuse and mistaken interpretation of our precedents. This leads it to advance propositions that, in my view, are both erroneous and in fundamental conflict with basic equal protection principles. As a consequence, this separate opinion is necessary to set forth my conclusions in the two cases before the Court.

I

[T]he dissent finds that the school districts have identified a compelling interest in increasing diversity, including for the purpose of avoiding racial isolation. The plurality, by contrast, does not acknowledge that the school districts have identified a compelling interest here. For this reason, among others, I do not join Parts III-B and IV. Diversity, depending on its meaning and definition, is a compelling educational goal a school district may pursue.

[T]he inquiry into less restrictive alternatives demanded by the narrow tailoring analysis requires in many cases a thorough understanding of how a plan works. The government bears the burden of justifying its use of individual racial classifications. As part of that burden it must establish, in detail, how decisions based on an individual student's race are made in a challenged governmental program. The Jefferson County Board of Education fails to meet this threshold mandate. . . .

---

g. The dissent does not face the complicated questions attending its proposed standard. For example, where does the dissent's principle stop? Can the government force racial mixing against the will of those being mixed? Can the government force black families to relocate to white neighborhoods in the name of bringing the races together? What about historically black colleges, which have "established traditions and programs that might disproportionately appeal to one race or another"? The dissent does not and cannot answer these questions because the contours of the distinction it propounds rest entirely in the eye of the beholder.

Jefferson County in its briefing has explained how and when it employs these classifications only in terms so broad and imprecise that they cannot withstand strict scrutiny. While it acknowledges that racial classifications are used to make certain assignment decisions, it fails to make clear, for example, who makes the decisions; what if any oversight is employed; the precise circumstances in which an assignment decision will or will not be made on the basis of race; or how it is determined which of two similarly situated children will be subjected to a given race-based decision.

[J]efferson County fails to make clear to this Court—even in the limited respects implicated by Joshua's initial assignment and transfer denial—whether in fact it relies on racial classifications in a manner narrowly tailored to the interest in question, rather than in the far-reaching, inconsistent, and ad hoc manner that a less forgiving reading of the record would suggest. When a court subjects governmental action to strict scrutiny, it cannot construe ambiguities in favor of the State.

As for the Seattle case, the school district has gone further in describing the methods and criteria used to determine assignment decisions on the basis of individual racial classifications. The district, nevertheless, has failed to make an adequate showing in at least one respect. It has failed to explain why, in a district composed of a diversity of races, with fewer than half of the students classified as "white," it has employed the crude racial categories of "white" and "non-white" as the basis for its assignment decisions.

The district has identified its purposes as follows: "(1) to promote the educational benefits of diverse school enrollments; (2) to reduce the potentially harmful effects of racial isolation by allowing students the opportunity to opt out of racially isolated schools; and (3) to make sure that racially segregated housing patterns did not prevent non-white students from having equitable access to the most popular over-subscribed schools." Yet the school district does not explain how, in the context of its diverse student population, a blunt distinction between "white" and "non-white" furthers these goals. As the Court explains, "a school with 50 percent Asian-American students and 50 percent white students but no African-American, Native-American, or Latino students would qualify as balanced, while a school with 30 percent Asian-American, 25 percent African-American, 25 percent Latino, and 20 percent white students would not." Far from being narrowly tailored to its purposes, this system threatens to defeat its own ends, and the school district has provided no convincing explanation for its design. Other problems are evident in Seattle's system, but there is no need to address them now. As the district fails to account for the classification system it has chosen, despite what appears to be its ill fit, Seattle has not shown its plan to be narrowly tailored to achieve its own ends; and thus it fails to pass strict scrutiny.

II

[P]arts of the opinion by The Chief Justice imply an all-too-unyielding insistence that race cannot be a factor in instances when, in my view, it may be taken into account. The plurality opinion is too dismissive of the legitimate interest government has in ensuring all people have equal opportunity regardless of their race. The plurality's postulate that "[t]he way to stop discrimination on the basis of race is to stop discriminating on the basis of race," is not sufficient to decide these cases. Fifty years of experience since Brown v. Board of Education, should teach us that the problem before us defies so easy a solution. School districts can seek to reach *Brown*'s objective of equal educational opportunity. The plurality opinion is at least open to the interpretation that the Constitution requires school districts to ignore the problem of *de facto* resegregation in schooling. I cannot endorse that conclusion. To the extent the plurality opinion suggests the Constitution mandates that state and local school authorities must accept the status quo of racial isolation in schools, it is, in my view, profoundly mistaken.

The statement by Justice Harlan that "[o]ur Constitution is color-blind" was most certainly justified in the context of his dissent in Plessy v. Ferguson, 163 U.S. 537, 559 (1896). [A]s an aspiration, Justice Harlan's axiom must command our assent. In the real world, it is regrettable to say, it cannot be a universal constitutional principle.

In the administration of public schools by the state and local authorities it is permissible to consider the racial makeup of schools and to adopt general policies to encourage a diverse student body, one aspect of which is its racial composition. If school authorities are concerned that the student-body compositions of certain schools interfere with the objective of offering an equal educational opportunity to all of their students, they are free to devise race conscious measures to address the problem in a general way and without treating each student in different fashion solely on the basis of a systematic, individual typing by race.

School boards may pursue the goal of bringing together students of diverse backgrounds and races through other means, including strategic site selection of new schools; drawing attendance zones with general recognition of the demographics of neighborhoods; allocating resources for special programs; recruiting students and faculty in a targeted fashion; and tracking enrollments, performance, and other statistics by race. These mechanisms are race conscious but do not lead to different treatment based on a classification that tells each student he or she is to be defined by race, so it is unlikely any of them would demand strict scrutiny to be found permissible. Executive and legislative branches, which for generations now have considered these types of policies and procedures, should be permitted to employ them with candor and with confidence that a constitutional violation does not occur whenever a decisionmaker considers the impact a given approach might have on students of different races. Assigning to each student a personal designation according to a crude system of individual racial classifications is quite a different matter; and the legal analysis changes accordingly.

Each respondent has asserted that its assignment of individual students by race is permissible because there is no other way to avoid racial isolation in the school districts. Yet, as explained, each has failed to provide the support necessary for that proposition. And individual racial classifications employed in this manner may be considered legitimate only if they are a last resort to achieve a compelling interest.

In the cases before us it is noteworthy that the number of students whose assignment depends on express racial classifications is limited. I join Part III-C of the Court's opinion because I agree that in the context of these plans, the small number of assignments affected suggests that the schools could have achieved their stated ends through different means. These include the facially race-neutral means set forth above or, if necessary, a more nuanced, individual evaluation of school needs and student characteristics that might include race as a component. The latter approach would be informed by *Grutter*, though of course the criteria relevant to student placement would differ based on the age of the students, the needs of the parents, and the role of the schools.

III

The dissent rests on the assumptions that these sweeping race-based classifications of persons are permitted by existing precedents; that its confident endorsement of race categories for each child in a large segment of the community presents no danger to individual freedom in other, prospective realms of governmental regulation; and that the racial classifications used here cause no hurt or anger of the type the Constitution prevents. Each of these premises is, in my respectful view, incorrect. [I]n his critique of that analysis, I am in many respects in agreement with The Chief Justice. The conclusions he has set forth in Part III-A of the Court's opinion are correct, in my view, because the compelling interests implicated in the cases before us are distinct from the interests the Court has recognized in remedying the effects of past intentional discrimination and in increasing diversity in higher education. As the Court notes, we recognized the compelling nature of the interest in remedying past intentional discrimination in Freeman v. Pitts, 503 U.S. 467, 494 (1992), and of the interest in diversity in higher education in *Grutter.* At the same time, these compelling interests, in my view, do help inform the present inquiry. And to the extent the plurality opinion can be interpreted to foreclose consideration of these interests, I disagree with that reasoning.

[T]he general conclusions upon which [the dissent] relies have no principled limit and would result in the broad acceptance of governmental racial classifications in areas far afield from schooling. The dissent's permissive strict scrutiny (which bears more than a passing resemblance to rational-basis review) could invite widespread governmental deployment of racial classifications. There is every reason to think that, if the dissent's rationale were accepted, Congress, assuming an otherwise proper exercise of its spending authority or commerce power, could mandate either the Seattle or the Jefferson County plans nationwide. There seems to be no principled rule, moreover, to limit the dissent's rationale to the context of public schools. The dissent emphasizes local control, the unique history of school desegregation, and the fact that these plans make less use of race than prior plans, but these factors seem more rhetorical than integral to the analytical structure of the opinion.

[In] *Grutter*... the Court sustained a system that, it found, was flexible enough to take into account "all pertinent elements of diversity," and considered race as only one factor among many, *id.*, at 340. Seattle's plan, by contrast, relies upon a mechanical formula that has denied hundreds of students their preferred schools on the basis of three rigid criteria: placement of siblings, distance from schools, and race. If those students were considered for a whole range of their talents and school needs with race as just one consideration, *Grutter* would have some application. That, though, is not the case. . . .

B

[O]ur [school desegregation] cases [have] recognized a fundamental difference between those school districts that had engaged in *de jure* segregation and those whose segregation was the result of other factors. School districts that had engaged in *de jure* segregation had an affirmative constitutional duty to desegregate; those that were *de facto* segregated did not. The distinctions between *de jure* and *de facto* segregation extended to the remedies available to governmental units in addition to the courts. For example, in Wygant v. Jackson Bd. of Ed., 476 U.S. 267, 274 (1986), the plurality noted: "This Court never has held that societal discrimination alone is sufficient to justify a racial classification. Rather, the Court has insisted upon some showing of prior discrimination by the governmental unit involved before allowing limited use of racial classifications in order to remedy such discrimination." The Court's decision in *Croson* reinforced the difference between the remedies available to redress *de facto* and *de jure* discrimination [by rejecting the] "claim that past societal discrimination alone can serve as the basis for rigid racial preferences." . . .

From the standpoint of the victim, it is true, an injury stemming from racial prejudice can hurt as much when the demeaning treatment based on race identity stems from bias masked deep within the social order as when it is imposed by law. The distinction between government and private action, furthermore, can be amorphous both as a historical matter and as a matter of present-day finding of fact. Laws arise from a culture and vice versa. Neither can assign to the other all responsibility for persisting injustices.

Yet, like so many other legal categories that can overlap in some instances, the constitutional distinction between *de jure* and *de facto* segregation has been thought to be an important one. It must be conceded its primary function in school cases was to delimit the powers of the Judiciary in the fashioning of remedies. See, e.g., *Milliken*. The distinction ought not to be altogether disregarded, however, when we come to that most sensitive of all racial issues, an attempt by the government to treat whole classes of persons differently based on the government's systematic classification of each individual by race. There, too, the distinction serves as a limit on the exercise of a power that reaches to the very verge of constitutional authority. Reduction of an individual to an assigned racial identity for differential treatment is among the most pernicious actions our government can undertake. The allocation of governmental burdens and benefits, contentious under any circumstances, is even more divisive when allocations are made on the basis of individual racial classifications.

Notwithstanding these concerns, allocation of benefits and burdens through individual racial classifications was found sometimes permissible in the context of remedies for *de jure* wrong. Where there has been *de jure* segregation, there is a cognizable legal wrong, and the courts and legislatures have broad power to remedy it. The remedy, though, was limited in time and limited to the wrong. The Court has allowed school districts to remedy their prior *de jure* segregation by classifying individual students based on their race. The limitation of this power to instances where there has been *de jure* segregation serves to confine the nature, extent, and duration of governmental reliance on individual racial classifications.

The cases here were argued upon the assumption, and come to us on the premise, that the discrimination in question did not result from *de jure* actions. And when *de facto* discrimination is at issue our tradition has been that the remedial rules are different. The State must seek alternatives to the classification and differential treatment of individuals by race, at least absent some extraordinary showing not present here.

C

[One might object:] If it is legitimate for school authorities to work to avoid racial isolation in their schools, must they do so only by indirection and general policies? Does the Constitution mandate this inefficient result? Why may the authorities not recognize the problem in candid fashion and solve it altogether through resort to direct assignments based on student racial classifications? . . .

The argument ignores the dangers presented by individual classifications, dangers that are not as pressing when the same ends are achieved by more indirect means. When the government classifies an individual by race, it must first define what it means to be of a race. Who exactly is white and who is nonwhite? To be forced to live under a state-mandated racial label is inconsistent with the dignity of individuals in our society. And it is a label that an individual is powerless to change. Governmental classifications that command people to march in different directions based on racial typologies can cause a new divisiveness. The practice can lead to corrosive discourse, where race serves not as an element of our diverse heritage but instead as a bargaining chip in the political process. On the other hand race-conscious measures that do not rely on differential treatment based on individual classifications present these problems to a lesser degree. . . .

This Nation has a moral and ethical obligation to fulfill its historic commitment to creating an integrated society that ensures equal opportunity for all of its children. A compelling interest exists in avoiding racial isolation, an interest that a school district, in its discretion and expertise, may choose to pursue. Likewise, a district may consider it a compelling interest to achieve a diverse student population. Race may be one component of that diversity, but other demographic factors, plus special talents and needs, should also be considered. What the government is not permitted to do, absent a showing of necessity not made here, is to classify every student on the basis of race and to assign each of them to schools based on that classification. Crude measures of this sort threaten to reduce children to racial chits valued and traded according to one school's supply and another's demand.

[A] sense of stigma may already become the fate of those separated out by circumstances beyond their immediate control. But . . . [e]ven so, measures other than differential treatment based on racial typing of individuals first must be exhausted.

The decision today should not prevent school districts from continuing the important work of bringing together students of different racial, ethnic, and economic backgrounds. Due to a variety of factors—some influenced by government, some not—neighborhoods in our communities do not reflect the diversity of our Nation as a whole. Those entrusted with directing our public schools can bring to bear the creativity of experts, parents, administrators, and other concerned citizens to find a way to achieve the compelling interests they face without resorting to widespread governmental allocation of benefits and burdens on the basis of racial classifications.

With this explanation I concur in the judgment of the Court.

Justice Stevens, dissenting.

. . . There is a cruel irony in The Chief Justice's reliance on our decision in Brown v. Board of Education. The first sentence in the concluding paragraph of his opinion states: "Before *Brown*, schoolchildren were told where they could and could not go to school based on the color of their skin." . . . The Chief Justice fails to note that it was only black schoolchildren who were so ordered; indeed, the history books do not tell stories of white children struggling to attend black schools. In this and other ways, The Chief Justice rewrites the history of one of this Court's most important decisions. . . .

[I]f we look at cases decided during the interim between *Brown* and *Adarand*, we can see how a rigid adherence to tiers of scrutiny obscures *Brown*'s clear message. Perhaps the best example is provided by our approval of the decision of the Supreme Judicial Court of Massachusetts in 1967 upholding a state statute mandating racial integration in that State's school system. See School Comm. of Boston v. Board of Education, 352 Mass. 693, 227 N.E.2d 729. Rejecting arguments comparable to those that the plurality accepts today, that court noted: "It would be the height of irony if the racial imbalance act, enacted as it was with the laudable purpose of achieving equal educational opportunities, should, by prescribing school pupil allocations based on race, founder on unsuspected shoals in the Fourteenth Amendment." . . . Our ruling on the merits [on appeal] simply stated that the appeal was "dismissed for want of a substantial federal question." School Comm. of Boston v. Board of Education, 389 U.S. 572 (1968) (per curiam). That decision not only expressed our appraisal of the merits of the appeal, but it constitutes a precedent that the Court overrules today. The subsequent statements by the unanimous Court in Swann v. Charlotte-Mecklenburg Bd. of Ed., 402 U.S. 1 (1971), by then Justice Rehnquist in chambers in Bustop, Inc. v. Los Angeles Bd. of Ed., 439 U.S. 1380 (1978), and by the host of state court decisions cited by Justice Breyer, were fully consistent with that disposition. Unlike today's decision, they were also entirely loyal to *Brown*.

The Court has changed significantly since it decided *School Comm. of Boston* in 1968. It was then more faithful to *Brown* and more respectful of our precedent than it is today. It is my firm conviction that no Member of the Court that I joined in 1975 would have agreed with today's decision.

Justice BREYER, with whom Justice STEVENS, Justice SOUTER, and Justice GINSBURG join, dissenting.

[I]n dozens of . . . cases [following *Brown*], this Court told school districts previously segregated by law what they must do at a minimum to comply with *Brown*'s constitutional holding. The measures required by those cases often included race-conscious practices, such as mandatory busing and race based restrictions on voluntary transfers.

Beyond those minimum requirements, the Court left much of the determination of how to achieve integration to the judgment of local communities. . . . As a result, different districts—some acting under court decree, some acting in order to avoid threatened lawsuits, some seeking to comply with federal administrative orders, some acting purely voluntarily, some acting after federal courts had dissolved earlier orders—adopted, modified, and experimented with hosts of different kinds of plans, including race-conscious plans, all with a similar objective: greater racial integration of public schools. The techniques that different districts have employed range "from voluntary transfer programs to mandatory reassignment." . . .

Overall these efforts brought about considerable racial integration. More recently, however, progress has stalled. Between 1968 and 1980, the number of black children attending a school where minority children constituted more than half of the school fell from 77% to 63% in the Nation (from 81% to 57% in the South) but then reversed direction by the year 2000, rising from 63% to 72% in the Nation (from 57% to 69% in the South). Similarly, between 1968 and 1980, the number of black children attending schools that were more than 90% minority fell from 64% to 33% in the Nation (from 78% to 23% in the South), but that too reversed direction, rising by the year 2000 from 33% to 37% in the Nation (from 23% to 31% in the South). As of 2002, almost 2.4 million students, or over 5% of all public school enrollment, attended schools with a white population of less than 1%. Of these, 2.3 million were black and Latino students, and only 72,000 were white. Today, more than one in six black children attend a school that is 99-100% minority. In light of the evident risk of a return to school systems that are in fact (though not in law) resegregated, many school districts have felt a need to maintain or to extend their integration efforts.

The upshot is that myriad school districts operating in myriad circumstances have devised myriad plans, often with race-conscious elements, all for the sake of eradicating earlier school segregation, bringing about integration, or preventing retrogression. Seattle and Louisville are two such districts, and the histories of their present plans set forth typical school integration stories.

[T]he distinction between *de jure* segregation (caused by school systems) and *de facto* segregation (caused, e.g., by housing patterns or generalized societal discrimination) is meaningless in the present context, thereby dooming the plurality's endeavor to find support for its views in that distinction. [R]eal-world efforts to substitute racially diverse for racially segregated schools (however caused) are complex, to the point where the Constitution cannot plausibly be interpreted to rule out categorically all local efforts to use means that are "conscious" of the race of individuals.

In both Seattle and Louisville, the local school districts began with schools that were highly segregated in fact. In both cities plaintiffs filed lawsuits claiming unconstitutional segregation. In Louisville, a federal district court found that school segregation reflected pre-*Brown* state laws separating the races. In Seattle, the plaintiffs alleged that school segregation unconstitutionally reflected not only generalized societal discrimination and residential housing patterns, but also *school board policies and actions* that had helped to create, maintain, and aggravate racial segregation. In Louisville, a federal court entered a remedial decree. In Seattle, the parties settled after the school district pledged to undertake a desegregation plan. In both cities, the school boards adopted plans designed to achieve integration by bringing about more racially diverse schools. In each city the school board modified its plan several times in light of, for example, hostility to busing, the threat of resegregation, and the desirability of introducing greater student choice. And in each city, the school boards' plans have evolved over time in ways that progressively *diminish* the plans' use of explicit race-conscious criteria. . . .

Both [Louisville and Seattle] faced problems that reflected initial periods of severe racial segregation, followed by such remedial efforts as busing, followed by evidence of resegregation, followed by a need to end busing and encourage the return of, e.g., suburban students through increased student choice. When formulating the plans under review, both districts drew upon their considerable experience with earlier plans, having revised their policies periodically in light of that experience. Both districts rethought their methods over time and explored a wide range of other means, including nonrace-conscious policies. Both districts also considered elaborate studies and consulted widely within their communities.

Both districts sought greater racial integration for educational and democratic, as well as for remedial, reasons. Both sought to achieve these objectives while preserving their commitment to other educational goals, e.g., districtwide commitment to high-quality public schools, increased pupil assignment to neighborhood schools, diminished use of busing, greater student choice, reduced risk of white flight, and so forth. Consequently, the present plans expand student choice; they limit the burdens (including busing) that earlier plans had imposed upon students and their families; and they use race-conscious criteria in limited and gradually diminishing ways. In particular, they use race-conscious criteria only to mark the outer bounds of broad population-related ranges.

The histories also make clear the futility of looking simply to whether earlier school segregation was *de jure* or *de facto* in order to draw firm lines separating the constitutionally permissible from the constitutionally forbidden use of "race-conscious" criteria. . . .

A court finding of *de jure* segregation cannot be the crucial variable. After all, a number of school districts in the South that the Government or private plaintiffs challenged as segregated *by law* voluntarily desegregated their schools *without a court order*—just as Seattle did. . . . Moreover, Louisville's history makes clear that a community under a court order to desegregate might submit a race-conscious remedial plan *before* the court dissolved the order, but with every intention of following that plan even *after* dissolution. How could such a plan be lawful the day before dissolution but then become unlawful the very next day? On what legal ground can the majority rest its contrary view?

Are courts really to treat as merely *de facto* segregated those school districts that avoided a federal order by voluntarily complying with *Brown*'s requirements? This Court has previously done just the opposite, permitting a race conscious remedy without any kind of court decree. Because the Constitution emphatically does not forbid the use of race-conscious measures by districts in the South that voluntarily desegregated their schools, on what basis does the plurality claim that the law forbids Seattle to do the same?

The histories also indicate the complexity of the tasks and the practical difficulties that local school boards face when they seek to achieve greater racial integration. The boards work in communities where demographic patterns change, where they must meet traditional learning goals, where they must attract and retain effective teachers, where they should (and will) take account of parents' views and maintain *their* commitment to public school education, where they must adapt to court intervention, where they must encourage voluntary student and parent action—where they will find that their own good faith, their knowledge, and their understanding of local circumstances are always necessary but often insufficient to solve the problems at hand. . . .

II

. . .

A longstanding and unbroken line of legal authority tells us that the Equal Protection Clause permits local school boards to use race-conscious criteria to achieve positive race-related goals, even when the Constitution does not compel it. [In] Swann [v. Charlotte-Mecklenburg Bd. of Ed., 402 U.S. 1, 16 (1971)], Chief Justice Burger, on behalf of a unanimous Court in a case of exceptional importance, wrote:

> School authorities are traditionally charged with broad power to formulate and implement educational policy and might well conclude, for example, that in order to prepare students to live in a pluralistic society each school should have a prescribed ratio of Negro to white students reflecting the proportion for the district as a whole. To do this as an educational policy is within the broad discretionary powers of school authorities.

The statement was not a technical holding in the case. But the Court set forth in *Swann* a basic principle of constitutional law—a principle of law that has found "wide acceptance in the legal culture." . . .

Lower state and federal courts had considered the matter settled and uncontroversial even before this Court decided *Swann*. . . . *Swann* was not a sharp or unexpected departure from prior rulings; it reflected a consensus that had already emerged among state and lower federal courts. . . . Numerous state and federal courts explicitly relied upon *Swann*'s guidance for decades to follow. . . . Courts are not alone in accepting as constitutionally valid the legal principle that *Swann* enunciated—i.e., that the government may voluntarily adopt race-conscious measures to improve conditions of race even when it is not under a constitutional obligation to do so. That principle has been accepted by every branch of government and is rooted in the history of the Equal Protection Clause itself. Thus, Congress has enacted numerous race-conscious statutes that illustrate that principle or rely upon its validity. See, e.g., 20 U.S.C. §6311(b)(2)(C)(v) (No Child Left Behind Act); §1067 *et seq.* (authorizing aid to minority institutions).

In fact, without being exhaustive, I have counted 51 federal statutes that use racial classifications. I have counted well over 100 state statutes that similarly employ racial classifications. Presidential administrations for the past half-century have used and supported various race-conscious measures. And during the same time, hundreds of local school districts have adopted student assignment plans that use race-conscious criteria.

That *Swann*'s legal statement should find such broad acceptance is not surprising. For *Swann* is predicated upon a well-established legal view of the Fourteenth Amendment. That view understands the basic objective of those who wrote the Equal Protection Clause as forbidding practices that lead to racial exclusion. The Amendment sought to bring into American society as full members those whom the Nation had previously held in slavery.

There is reason to believe that those who drafted an Amendment with this basic purpose in mind would have understood the legal and practical difference between the use of race-conscious criteria in defiance of that purpose, namely to keep the races apart, and the use of race-conscious criteria to further that purpose, namely to bring the races together. Although the Constitution almost always forbids the former, it is significantly more lenient in respect to the latter.

Sometimes Members of this Court have disagreed about the degree of leniency that the Clause affords to programs designed to include. But I can find no case in which this Court has followed Justice Thomas' "colorblind" approach. And I have found no case that otherwise repudiated this constitutional asymmetry between that which seeks to *exclude* and that which seeks to *include* members of minority races. . . .

[N]o case—not *Adarand, Gratz, Grutter,* or any other—has ever held that the test of "strict scrutiny" means that all racial classifications—no matter whether they seek to include or exclude—must in practice be treated the same. . . . [In] *Adarand,* [t]he Court made clear that "[s]trict scrutiny does not trea[t] dissimilar race-based decisions as though they were equally objectionable." It added that the fact that a law "treats [a person] unequally because of his or her race . . . says nothing about the ultimate validity of any particular law." And the Court, . . . sought to "*dispel the notion* that strict scrutiny" is as likely to condemn *inclusive* uses of "race-conscious" criteria as it is to invalidate *exclusionary* uses. That is, it is *not* in all circumstances "'strict in theory, but fatal in fact.'" . . . The Court's holding in *Grutter* demonstrates that the Court meant what it said, for the Court upheld an elite law school's race conscious admissions program.

The upshot is that the cases to which the plurality refers, though all applying strict scrutiny, do not treat exclusive and inclusive uses the same. Rather, they apply the strict scrutiny test in a manner that is "fatal in fact" only to racial classifications that harmfully *exclude*; they apply the test in a manner that is *not* fatal in fact to racial classifications that seek to *include*. . . .

Governmental use of race-based criteria can arise in the context of, for example, census forms, research expenditures for diseases, assignments of police officers patrolling predominantly minority-race neighborhoods, efforts to desegregate racially segregated schools, policies that favor minorities when distributing goods or services in short supply, actions that create majority minority electoral districts, peremptory strikes that remove potential jurors on the basis of race, and others. Given the significant differences among these contexts, it would be surprising if the law required an identically strict legal test for evaluating the constitutionality of race-based criteria as to each of them.

Here, the context is one in which school districts seek to advance or to maintain racial integration in primary and secondary schools. It is a context, as *Swann* makes clear, where history has required special administrative remedies. And it is a context in which the school boards' plans simply set race-conscious limits at the outer boundaries of a broad range.

This context is *not* a context that involves the use of race to decide who will receive goods or services that are normally distributed on the basis of merit and which are in short supply. It is not one in which race-conscious limits stigmatize or exclude; the limits at issue do not pit the races against each other or otherwise significantly exacerbate racial tensions. They do not impose burdens unfairly upon members of one race alone but instead seek benefits for members of all races alike. The context here is one of racial limits that seek, not to keep the races apart, but to bring them together. . . .

I believe that the law requires application here of a standard of review that is not "strict" in the traditional sense of that word. . . . Nonetheless, in light of *Grutter* and other precedents, . . . I shall apply the version of strict scrutiny that those cases embody. . . .

III

[T]he principal interest advanced in these cases [is] an interest in promoting or preserving greater racial "integration" of public schools. By this term, I mean the school districts' interest in eliminating school-by-school racial isolation and increasing the degree to which racial mixture characterizes each of the district's schools and each individual student's public school experience.

[This] interest . . . possesses three essential elements. First, there is a historical and remedial element: an interest in setting right the consequences of prior conditions of segregation. . . .

Second, there is an educational element: an interest in overcoming the adverse educational effects produced by and associated with highly segregated schools. Studies suggest that children taken from those schools and placed in integrated settings often show positive academic gains. Other studies reach different conclusions. But the evidence supporting an educational interest in racially integrated schools is well established and strong enough to permit a democratically elected school board reasonably to determine that this interest is a compelling one. . . .

Third, there is a democratic element: an interest in producing an educational environment that reflects the "pluralistic society" in which our children will live. It is an interest in helping our children learn to work and play together with children of different racial backgrounds. It is an interest in teaching children to engage in the kind of cooperation among Americans of all races that is necessary to make a land of three hundred million people one Nation.

Again, data support this insight. There are again studies that offer contrary conclusions. Again, however, the evidence supporting a democratic interest in racially integrated schools is firmly established and sufficiently strong to permit a school board to determine, as this Court has itself often found, that this interest is compelling.

For example, one study documented that "black and white students in desegregated schools are less racially prejudiced than those in segregated schools," and that "interracial contact in desegregated schools leads to an increase in interracial sociability and friendship." Other studies have found that both black and white students who attend integrated schools are more likely to work in desegregated companies after graduation than students who attended racially isolated schools. Further research has shown that the desegregation of schools can help bring adult communities together by reducing segregated housing. Cities that have implemented successful school desegregation plans have witnessed increased interracial contact and neighborhoods that tend to become less racially segregated. These effects not only reinforce the prior gains of integrated primary and secondary education; they also foresee a time when there is less need to use race-conscious criteria.

. . . The compelling interest at issue here, then, includes an effort to eradicate the remnants, not of general "societal discrimination," but of primary and secondary school segregation; it includes an effort to create school environments that provide better educational opportunities for all children; it includes an effort to help create citizens better prepared to know, to understand, and to work with people of all races and backgrounds, thereby furthering the kind of democratic government our Constitution foresees. If an educational interest that combines these three elements is not "compelling," what is?

[In addition], remedial interests [do not] vanish the day after a federal court declares that a district is "unitary." . . . "Past wrongs to the black race, wrongs committed by the State and in its name, are a stubborn fact of history. And stubborn facts of history linger and persist." I do not understand why this Court's cases, which rest the significance of a "unitary" finding in part upon the wisdom and desirability of returning schools to local control, should deprive those local officials of legal *permission* to use means they once found necessary to combat persisting injustices.

For his part, Justice Thomas faults my citation of various studies supporting the view that school districts can find compelling educational and civic interests in integrating their public schools. He is entitled of course to his own opinion as to which studies he finds convincing. . . . [But] [i]f we are to insist upon unanimity in the social science literature before finding a compelling interest, we might never find one. I believe only that the Constitution allows democratically elected school boards to make up their own minds as to how best to include people of all races in one America.

. . .

I next ask whether the plans before us are "narrowly tailored" to achieve these "compelling" objectives. . . . Several factors, taken together, . . . lead me to conclude that the boards' use of race-conscious criteria in these plans passes even the strictest "tailoring" test.

First, the race-conscious criteria at issue only help set the outer bounds of *broad* ranges. They constitute but one part of plans that depend primarily upon other, nonracial elements. To use race in this way is not to set a forbidden "quota."

In fact, the defining feature of both plans is greater emphasis upon student choice. In Seattle, for example, in more than 80% of all cases, that choice alone determines which high schools Seattle's ninth graders will attend. After ninth grade, students can decide voluntarily to transfer to a preferred district high school (without any consideration of race-conscious criteria). *Choice*, therefore, is the "predominant factor" in these plans. *Race* is not. . . .

Second, broad-range limits on voluntary school choice plans are less burdensome, and hence more narrowly tailored, than other race-conscious restrictions this Court has previously approved. See, e.g., *Swann*. Indeed, the plans before us are *more narrowly tailored* than the race-conscious admission plans that this Court approved in *Grutter*. Here, race becomes a factor only in a fraction of students' non-merit-based assignments — not in large numbers of students' merit-based applications. Moreover, the effect of applying race conscious criteria here affects potentially disadvantaged students *less severely*, not more severely, than the criteria at issue in *Grutter*. Disappointed students are not rejected from a State's flagship graduate program; they simply attend a different one of the district's many public schools, which in aspiration and in fact are substantially equal. And, in Seattle, the disadvantaged student loses at most one year at the high school of his choice. . . .

Third, the manner in which the school boards developed these plans itself reflects "narrow tailoring." Each plan was devised to overcome a history of segregated public schools. Each plan embodies the results of local experience and community consultation. Each plan is the product of a process that has sought to enhance student choice, while diminishing the need for mandatory busing. And each plan's use of race-conscious elements is *diminished* compared to the use of race in preceding integration plans.

The school boards' widespread consultation, their experimentation with numerous other plans, indeed, the 40-year history [of their attempts at desegregation], make clear that plans that are less explicitly race-based are unlikely to achieve the board's "compelling" objectives. The history of each school system reveals highly segregated schools, followed by remedial plans that involved forced busing, followed by efforts to attract or retain students through the use of plans that abandoned busing and replaced it with greater student choice. Both cities once tried to achieve more integrated schools by relying solely upon measures such as redrawn district boundaries, new school building construction, and unrestricted voluntary transfers. In neither city did these prior attempts prove sufficient to achieve the city's integration goals.

Moreover, giving some degree of weight to a local school board's knowledge, expertise, and concerns in these particular matters is not inconsistent with rigorous judicial scrutiny. It simply recognizes that judges are not well suited to act as school administrators. Indeed, in the context of school desegregation, this Court has repeatedly stressed the importance of acknowledging that local school boards better understand their own communities and have a better knowledge of what in practice will best meet the educational needs of their pupils. . . .

[Justice Kennedy asks:] Why does Seattle's plan group Asian-Americans, Hispanic-Americans, Native-Americans, and African-Americans together, treating all as similar minorities? The majority suggests that Seattle's classification system could permit a school to be labeled "diverse" with a 50% Asian American and 50% white student body, and no African-American students, Hispanic students, or students of other ethnicity.

The 50/50 hypothetical has no support in the record here; it is conjured from the imagination. In fact, Seattle apparently began to treat these different minority groups alike in response to the federal Emergency School Aid Act's requirement that it do so. Moreover, maintaining this federally mandated system of classification makes sense insofar as Seattle's experience indicates that the relevant circumstances in respect to each of these different minority groups are roughly similar, e.g., in terms of residential patterns, and call for roughly similar responses. This is confirmed by the fact that Seattle has been able to achieve a desirable degree of diversity without the *greater* emphasis on race that drawing fine lines among minority groups would require. . . . [T]he plurality cannot object that the constitutional defect is the individualized use of race and simultaneously object that not enough account of individuals' race has been taken. . . .

V

[C]onsider the effect of the plurality's views on the parties before us and on similar school districts throughout the Nation. . . . The districts' past and current plans are not unique. They resemble other plans, promulgated by hundreds of local school boards, which have attempted a variety of desegregation methods that have evolved over time in light of experience. . . .

[A]t a minimum, the plurality's views would threaten a surge of race-based litigation. Hundreds of state and federal statutes and regulations use racial classifications for educational or other purposes. In many such instances, the contentious force of legal challenges to these classifications, meritorious or not, would displace earlier calm.

[D]e facto resegregation is on the rise. It is reasonable to conclude that such resegregation can create serious educational, social, and civic problems. Given the conditions in which school boards work to set policy, they may need all of the means presently at their disposal to combat those problems. Yet the plurality would deprive them of at least one tool that some districts now consider vital—the limited use of broad race-conscious student population ranges.

I use the words "may need" here deliberately. The plurality, or at least those who follow Justice Thomas' "'color-blind'" approach, may feel confident that, to end invidious discrimination, one must end *all* governmental use of race conscious criteria including those with inclusive objectives. By way of contrast, I do not claim to know how best to stop harmful discrimination; how best to create a society that includes all Americans; how best to overcome our serious problems of increasing *de facto* segregation, troubled inner city schooling, and poverty correlated with race. But, as a judge, I do know that the Constitution does not authorize judges to dictate solutions to these problems. Rather, the Constitution creates a democratic political system through which the people themselves must together find answers. And it is for them to debate how best to educate the Nation's children and how best to administer America's schools to achieve that aim. The Court should leave them to their work. And it is for them to decide, to quote the plurality's slogan, whether the best "way to stop discrimination on the basis of race is to stop discriminating on the basis of race." That is why the Equal Protection Clause outlaws invidious discrimination, but does not similarly forbid all use of race-conscious criteria. . . .

VI

[T]he plurality cites in support those who argued in *Brown* against segregation, and Justice Thomas likens the approach that I have taken to that of segregation's defenders. But segregation policies did not simply tell schoolchildren "where they could and could not go to school based on the color of their skin"; they perpetuated a caste system rooted in the institutions of slavery and 80 years of legalized subordination. The lesson of history is not that efforts to continue racial segregation are constitutionally indistinguishable from efforts to achieve racial integration. Indeed, it is a cruel distortion of history to compare Topeka, Kansas, in the 1950's to Louisville and Seattle in the modern day—to equate the plight of Linda Brown (who was ordered to attend a Jim Crow school) to the circumstances of Joshua McDonald (whose request to transfer to a school closer to home was initially declined). This is not to deny that there is a cost in applying "a state-mandated racial label." But that cost does not approach, in degree or in kind, the terrible harms of slavery, the resulting caste system, and 80 years of legal racial segregation.

[N]ot everyone welcomed this Court's decision in *Brown*. Three years after that decision was handed down, the Governor of Arkansas ordered state militia to block the doors of a white schoolhouse so that black children could not enter. The President of the United States dispatched the 101st Airborne Division to Little Rock, Arkansas, and federal troops were needed to enforce a desegregation decree. See Cooper v. Aaron, 358 U.S. 1 (1958). Today, almost 50 years later, attitudes toward race in this Nation have changed dramatically. Many parents, white and black alike, want their children to attend schools with children of different races. Indeed, the very school districts that once spurned integration now strive for it. The long history of their efforts reveals the complexities and difficulties they have faced. And in light of those challenges, they have asked us not to take from their hands the instruments they have used to rid their schools of racial segregation, instruments that they believe are needed to overcome the problems of cities divided by race and poverty. The plurality would decline their modest request.

The plurality is wrong to do so. The last half-century has witnessed great strides toward racial equality, but we have not yet realized the promise of *Brown*. To invalidate the plans under review is to threaten the promise of *Brown*. The plurality's position, I fear, would break that promise. This is a decision that the Court and the Nation will come to regret.

DISCUSSION

1. *Fighting over the legacy of* Brown. All the Justices claim to be faithful to the memory and the principles of Brown v. Board of Education. The case contains 91 separate references to the *Brown* litigation. But the Justices have very different ideas of what *Brown* meant.[109] The plurality argues that *Brown* stood for colorblindness in student assignment policies and strict scrutiny for racial classifications by the state. The dissent argues that *Brown* stood for the principles of racial integration and antisubordination.

Justice Thomas tries to show that the arguments of the dissenters are the same as those of the defenders of segregation and massive resistance. On the other hand, Justice Thomas's own arguments have much in common with segregationist critics of *Brown*. Thomas is deeply skeptical of elite and social science arguments that integration is good for children—or that racial isolation is bad. He finds little advantage to racial mixing, assumes that different races will self-segregate socially, and suggests that predominantly Black schools may be better for Black children.

During the 1960s and 1970s, proponents of racial integration often looked to federal courts to enforce *Brown* against recalcitrant state school boards; their opponents sought to promote states' rights, localism, and deference to the expertise of local school boards. In *Parents Involved*, the plurality wants federal courts to carefully supervise school districts so that they do not violate the Equal Protection Clause in their quest for racial integration, which the plurality refers to as "racial balancing." Conversely, the dissent, which supports the school boards' attempts at integration, wants to defer to their expertise and knowledge of local conditions. During the 1960s and 1970s, opponents of student assignment policies

109. Indeed, at one point Chief Justice Roberts remarks that a key issue the case is "which side is more faithful to the heritage of *Brown*." *Parents Involved*, 551 U.S. at 747.

accused federal courts of judicial activism, elitism, and "social engineering" when they second-guessed local school boards in the name of the Constitution. In *Parents Involved*, Justice Thomas accuses the Seattle and Louisville school boards of elitism and social engineering in pursuing racial integration and insists that federal courts must stop them in the name of the Constitution.

2. *De jure and de facto.* The plurality opinion regards school districts that voluntarily desegregated without court order as never having any constitutional obligation to desegregate. And it regards school districts that federal courts declared unitary as being legally pristine—in the same position as districts that were never segregated. As a result, it treats race-conscious plans by districts in Seattle and Louisville not as attempts to continue and adjust remedial plans but as illegal attempts at racial balancing. These are not the understandings that governed equal protection law in the decades immediately after *Brown.*

At the time *Brown* was decided, segregation was rampant in both North and South. The Court appreciated that desegregation required voluntary efforts to integrate. After *Brown*, federal courts faced the task of desegregating the nation's schools, and often encountered a hostile reception from local school boards. Federal courts could not enjoin every school board in the country, and they could not long succeed against school boards determined to resist them. Any realistic attempt at integration required substantial compliance and cooperation by local school boards. As a result, courts encouraged and welcomed voluntary plans for integration, as the language in *Swann* (whether dicta or not) itself suggests: "School authorities are traditionally charged with broad power to formulate and implement educational policy and might well conclude, for example, that in order to prepare students to live in a pluralistic society each school should have a prescribed ratio of Negro to white students reflecting the proportion for the district as a whole. To do this as an educational policy is within the broad discretionary powers of school authorities."

The political context of the 1960s and 1970s meant that courts would look favorably on school boards that chose to integrate without a court order as well as school boards that worked with courts to produce integration plans and maintained them over time without court supervision.

Sometimes, as in Louisville, school boards resisted and litigation resulted. Courts might want to declare districts unitary and turn over the task of desegregation to school districts if they believed they had come to act in good faith and were willing to take the political heat for integration. Thus, declaring a district unitary *did not* necessarily mean that segregation had been completely eliminated and desegregation plans were no longer needed. Rather, declaring a distinct unitary mean that desegregation plans would continue under the supervision and adjustment of the local school board as opposed to a federal court.

As the Supreme Court became more conservative in the 1990s, it sought to accelerate this process and trust school boards more and more. In cases like Board of Education of Oklahoma City v. Dowell and Freeman v. Pitts, the Supreme Court strongly signaled to the lower courts that they should end federal court supervision and declare districts unitary as soon as possible. In Freeman v. Pitts, the Court held that federal courts could declare districts unitary even before full compliance had occurred, as long as school districts had made "a good faith commitment to the entirety of a desegregation plan."

3. *Desegregation, not integration.* Following *Brown,* critics who wanted to limit the force of the opinion argued that it required only desegregation, not integration. Section III-B of the plurality opinion (which Justice Kennedy does not join) suggests that "racial balancing" is not a compelling interest. What is racial balancing? Is *any* concern with results or numbers whatsoever unconstitutional? How does the plurality explain the difference between "racial balancing" and racial integration? Is racial integration a legitimate interest for the plurality?

4. *Justice Kennedy's concurrence.* Because his vote is necessary to make a majority, Justice Kennedy's limiting concurrence will no doubt be the focus of much future litigation. Like Justice Powell's *Bakke* opinion, it may determine what *Parents Involved* actually means in practice.

Two points about Kennedy's approach are worth noting at the outset. First, contrary to the plurality, Justice Kennedy argues that increasing diversity and avoiding racial isolation can be compelling state interests that might even justify race-based state action if narrowly tailored. Second, Kennedy argues that school districts may take facially race-neutral but race-conscious measures to combat de facto resegregation and bring students of different backgrounds together.

Kennedy primarily objects to student assignment policies that use the race of an individual student as the controlling factor in determining where that individual student goes to school. Thus, Kennedy distinguishes between two kinds of race-conscious policies.

a. The first type of policy considers the race of an individual student in deciding where the student goes to school. Any such policy, Kennedy argues, is subject to strict scrutiny.

To survive strict scrutiny, the school district must show that other policies that do not assign individual students to schools based on their race will not be as effective. Kennedy believes that, in this case, the minimal effects of race-based assignment policies show that they were unnecessary and therefore not narrowly tailored. Does this mean that if race-based assignment policies produced far more significant effects than facially race-neutral alternatives that they would be narrowly tailored? Kennedy also objects to the use of a binary white/non-white divide in racial assignment policies. Does this mean that if school districts used more racial categories their plans would be narrowly tailored?

Kennedy also suggests that student assignment policies that use the race of individual students to determine where the student will be placed must involve, at a minimum, multifactor individualized considerations roughly akin to the sort approved in *Grutter.*

Requiring multifactor individualized considerations of individual students would convert student assignment policies into something more like individual applications to colleges. Individualized considerations would be costly and thus far less likely to be employed by large school districts. Note that Kennedy also objected to the Louisville plan because the criteria it used were not sufficiently transparent. Ironically, *Grutter* is premised on the notion that decisions using multifactor individualized considerations will be less transparent and therefore less overtly based on race.

b. A second type of race-conscious policy does not assign individual students to schools on the basis of their race. Rather, it uses facially race-neutral criteria for race-conscious reasons. Examples would be decisions about where to place new schools, where to draw attendance zones, and student assignment criteria based on poverty and socioeconomic status. Kennedy suggests that "it is unlikely that any of [these policies] would demand strict scrutiny to be found permissible." Does that mean that narrow tailoring requirements would not apply? Would rational basis apply?

Note that Chief Justice Roberts's plurality opinion specifically avoids stating its views about the constitutionality of such race-conscious policies. But if the avowed purpose of these policies is to assign percentages of students to different schools because of their race, wouldn't this be an attempt at "racial balancing" according to the Justices in the plurality?

How do *Davis* and *Feeney* apply to race-conscious policies—like school siting decisions and redrawing of attendance zones? Are such policies subject to strict scrutiny under *Davis* because they are motivated by a conscious intention to discriminate on the basis of race? Are they permissible under *Feeney*, because they are not employed out of a desire to harm whites?

Kennedy's approach seems to view benign race-conscious *purpose* that uses race-neutral *means* as outside of strict scrutiny. Given the plurality's views about motive in Part IV, can the Justices in the plurality adopt the same approach?

FISHER v. UNIVERSITY OF TEXAS AT AUSTIN [*FISHER II*] 136 S. Ct. 2198 (2016): In *Fisher II*, the Court applied *Grutter* to Texas's hybrid system for undergraduate admissions. Approximately three quarters of the freshman class were admitted as a result of the State's Top Ten Percent Law, which awards admission to Texas flagship schools to students who graduate from a Texas high school in the top 10 percent of their class. The remaining 25 percent of the student body was admitted through a holistic admissions process which considered race as one factor. Petitioner Abigail Fisher, who had not graduated in the top ten percent of her high school class, argued that the holistic system was unnecessary and not narrowly tailored because the Ten Percent Plan already constituted a race-neutral alternative that would admit some minority students.

The Court, in a 4-3 opinion by Justice Kennedy, upheld Texas's program. Building on *Grutter*, he stated that "the decision to pursue 'the educational benefits that flow from student body diversity' . . . is, in substantial measure, an academic judgment to which some, but not complete, judicial deference is proper." However, in determining whether the University's use of race is narrowly tailored, the school bears the "burden of demonstrating that 'available' and 'workable' 'race-neutral alternatives' do not suffice."

Justice Kennedy warned that "[a] university's goals cannot be elusory or amorphous—they must be sufficiently measurable to permit judicial scrutiny of the policies adopted to reach them." In this case, however, "[t]he record reveals that . . . the University articulated concrete and precise goals . . . : the destruction of stereotypes, the 'promot[ion of] cross-racial understanding,' 'the preparation of a student body "for an increasingly diverse workforce and society," and the 'cultivat[ion of] a set of leaders with legitimacy in the eyes of the citizenry.'" All of these "objectives, as a general matter, mirror the 'compelling interest' this Court has approved in its prior cases." In addition, the University offered a "'reasoned, principled explanation' for its decision" through conducting a year-long study that showed that its race-neutral policies did not meet its educational goals. Moreover, "[t]he fact that race consciousness played a role in only a small portion of admissions decisions should be a hallmark of narrow tailoring, not evidence of unconstitutionality."

The Court cautioned that universities had a continuing obligation to ensure that their admissions programs were constitutional: "The University must continue to use [its] data to scrutinize the fairness of its admissions program [and] to assess whether changing demographics have undermined the need for a race-conscious policy. . . . The Court's affirmance of the University's admissions policy today does not necessarily mean the University may rely on that same policy without refinement."

Justice Thomas dissented, arguing that "'a State's use of race in higher education admissions decisions is categorically prohibited by the Equal Protection Clause.' . . . I would overrule *Grutter.* "

Justice Alito, joined by Chief Justice Roberts and Justice Thomas, also dissented: "When it adopted its race-based plan, UT said that the plan was needed to promote classroom diversity. It pointed to a study showing that African-American, Hispanic, and Asian-American students were underrepresented in many classes. But UT has never shown that its race-conscious plan actually ameliorates this situation. . . . [A]lthough UT's records should permit it to determine without much difficulty whether holistic admittees are any more likely than students admitted through the Top Ten Percent Law, to enroll in the classes lacking racial or ethnic diversity, UT either has not crunched those numbers or has not revealed what they show. Nor has UT explained why the underrepresentation of Asian-American students in many classes justifies its plan, which discriminates *against* those students."

DISCUSSION

1. *Continuing obligations.* Does *Fisher II* make state universities vulnerable to periodic suits from opponents of affirmative action? If you were serving as university counsel, what practical steps would you advise the university to take to discharge its "ongoing obligation to engage in constant deliberation and continued reflection regarding its admissions policies"?

2. *The Constitutionality of the Ten Percent Plan.* When the Fisher litigation first arrived at the Court in *Fisher I,* 570 U.S. 297 (2013), Justice Ginsburg noted in her dissent that it was misleading to call the Texas Ten Percent Plan race-neutral, because it is transparently motivated by a purpose to increase minority enrollments. It makes use of the fact of significant residential (and thus high school) segregation in Texas. If the Ten Percent Plan has a race-conscious purpose, why is it constitutional? Does it violate *Davis* or *Feeney*? One might argue that the Ten Percent Plan does not violate *Davis* or *Feeney* because the plan was adopted not *because* it harmed any racial or ethnic group, but *in spite of* any such harm. In particular, supporters might argue that the purpose of the Ten Percent Plan is to reward excellence and acknowledge student efforts in all of Texas's high schools. Should this matter?[110]

---

110. For a discussion, in the years before *Fisher,* of some of the constitutional issues, see Richard Primus, Equal Protection and Disparate Impact: Round Three, 117 Harv. L. Rev. 493, 540-564 (2003); Kim Forde-Mazrui, The Constitutional Implications of Race-Neutral Affirmative Action, 88 Geo. L.J. 2331 (2000).

Although *Fisher II* does not view the Ten Percent Plan as sufficient by itself to produce educational diversity, it nevertheless assumes that it is constitutional. This suggests that a majority of the Court is willing to recognize a difference between benign and invidious race-consciousness in the creation of facially race-neutral programs and statutes (i.e., programs that do not overtly make racial classifications). The Court also seems to be willing to allow governments to use facially race-neutral means to achieve greater representation of minorities in colleges and universities. In these programs, governments may act to promote diversity and equal opportunity. The same distinction appears in Justice Kennedy's limiting concurrence in *Parents Involved.*

3. *Critical mass.* Justice Alito's dissent reiterates Chief Justice Rehnquist's critique in *Grutter* of "critical mass" as a justification for diversity. Alito argues that using race-conscious affirmative action to achieve a critical mass of minorities is a disguised form of racial balancing designed to make Texas's admissions roughly reflect the demographics of the state.

Suppose the Court acknowledged that state universities are trying to achieve a rough relationship between the percentage of particular minorities of college age in their state and the number of minority applicants they accept, but that this practice is nevertheless legitimate, building on Justice O'Connor's arguments in *Grutter* that educational institutions must "cultivate a set of leaders with legitimacy in the eyes of the citizenry." Would such candor be appropriate? If the Court wanted to adopt this approach, how would it have to change its affirmative action doctrines?

4. *Discrimination against Asian-Americans.* Justice Alito's dissent does not object, as previous Justices have, that affirmative action programs unfairly discriminate against whites, that they will stir up white resentment against minorities, or that they harm the minorities they purport to help. Instead, he argues that affirmative action programs discriminate against another minority, Asian-Americans. This criticism recalls arguments in the early years of affirmative action that race-conscious admissions policies were unfair to another minority, Jews, because they were reminiscent of quotas that had previously limited the admission of Jews to elite institutions. Should affirmative action programs be permitted to increase enrollments for some minority groups, but not for others? How does your answer connect to the diversity rationale? To Justice O'Connor's arguments in *Grutter* about legitimacy in the eyes of the citizenry?

NOTE: RACIAL REDISTRICTING AND THE EQUAL PROTECTION CLAUSE

In Baker v. Carr, 389 U.S. 186 (1962), the Supreme Court held for the first time that issues involving the fairness of drawing state legislative districts were "justiciable," i.e., appropriate for judicial resolution; two years later, in Reynolds v. Sims, 377 U.S. 533 (1964), the Court adopted the "one-person-one-vote standard" as the test for assessing the constitutional adequacy of such districts under the Equal Protection Clause.

The attempt to draw boundary lines to maximize particular political outcomes is often called "gerrymandering." Beginning in 1993, the Supreme Court, in a series of 5-4 decisions, held that redistricting designed to increase the electoral representation of Black people through the creation of districts where minorities constituted a majority of voters was subject to scrutiny under the Equal Protection Clause. The key case was Shaw v. Reno, 509 U.S. 630 (1993), holding that "redistricting legislation that is so extremely irregular on its face that it rationally can be viewed only as an effort to segregate the races for purposes of voting, without regard for traditional districting principles and without sufficiently compelling justification" stated a claim under the Equal Protection Clause.

The rationale of *Shaw* was clarified in succeeding cases. In Miller v. Johnson, 515 U.S. 900 (1995), Justice Kennedy explained that the plaintiff's burden is to show

> either through circumstantial evidence of a district's shape and demographics or more direct evidence going to legislative purpose, that race was the predominant factor motivating the legislature's decision to place a significant number of voters within or without a particular district. To make this showing, a plaintiff must prove that the legislature subordinated traditional race-neutral districting principles, including but not limited to compactness, contiguity, respect for political subdivisions or communities defined by actual shared interests, to racial considerations. Where these or other race-neutral considerations are the basis for redistricting legislation, and are not subordinated to race, a state can "defeat a claim that a district has been gerrymandered on racial lines."

However, in Hunt v. Cromartie, 526 U.S. 541 (1999), the Court, in an opinion by Justice Thomas, noted that

> [o]ur prior decisions have made clear that a jurisdiction may engage in constitutional political gerrymandering, even if it so happens that the most loyal Democrats happen to be black Democrats and even if the State were conscious of that fact. Evidence that blacks constitute even a supermajority in one congressional district while amounting to less than a plurality in a neighboring district will not, by itself, suffice to prove that a jurisdiction was motivated by race in drawing its district lines when the evidence also shows a high correlation between race and party preference.

F. Citizenship and Alienage Under the Equal Protection Clause

1. The Early Interplay of Race and Alienage

The 1787 Constitution gave Congress power to regulate naturalization, and, by implication, immigration, although historically there has been some debate over the precise source of Congress's powers to control immigration. In Chapter 1, for example, we noted the debates about congressional power to pass the Alien Act of 1798. In our discussion of Mayor of the City of New York v. Miln in Chapter 3, we noted cases such as Henderson v. New York, 92 U.S. 259 (1876), that suggested that the federal authority over immigration lay in the commerce power. Finally, in the Chinese Exclusion Cases discussed in Chapter 4, we noted the rise of the modern plenary power doctrine.

Throughout the nineteenth century, issues of citizenship were intertwined with those of race, even though the two concepts were nominally distinct. Naturalization was limited to "white persons" by the Naturalization Act of 1795, although "aliens of African nativity and . . . persons of African descent" were made eligible for citizenship in 1870. (There were, however, extremely few immigrants from Africa who took advantage of this formal change in American immigration law.)

The national reaction to Chinese immigration also mixed issues of race and alienage. Passage of the Chinese Exclusion Act in 1882, upheld in the Chinese Exclusion Case, 130 U.S. 581 (1889), and Fong Yue Ting v. United States, 149 U.S. 698 (1893), tied together issues of race and national origin. Chinese, like other Asians, could not become U.S. citizens; as Justice Harlan pointed out in his dissent in Plessy v. Ferguson, the Chinese were "a race so different from our own that we do not permit those belonging to it to become citizens of the United States. Persons belonging to it are, with few exceptions, absolutely excluded from our country." As noted in Chapter 4, during the 1920s the Supreme Court had to construe the meaning of the word "white" to decide that a person of Japanese descent or of a "high-caste Hindu of full Indian blood" could not become citizens. Takao Ozawa v. United States, 260 U.S. 178 (1922); United States v. Bhagat Singh Thind, 261 U.S. 204 (1923). Persons of Asian descent remained ineligible to become citizens until 1952 (save for immigrants from our wartime ally China, who were made eligible for citizenship in 1943).

Nevertheless, the Citizenship Clause of the Fourteenth Amendment cross cut the racial features of immigration policy, and in United States v. Wong Kim Ark, 169 U.S. 649 (1898), the Court held that persons of Chinese descent born in the United States were birthright citizens under the Fourteenth Amendment.

Moreover, despite the federal government's power to exclude aliens from the United States, even on the basis of race, the Court nonetheless did impose some limits on *state* power with regard to discrimination against aliens. In Yick Wo v. Hopkins, 118 U.S. 356 (1886), the Court struck down the patently discriminatory application of a city ordinance regulating laundry facilities operated by Chinese immigrants. The Court explained: "The Fourteenth Amendment to the Constitution is not confined to the protection of citizens. . . . [Its] provisions are universal in their application, to all persons within the territorial jurisdiction, without regard to any differences of race, of color, or of nationality; and the equal protection of the laws is a pledge of the protection of equal laws."

Despite *Yick Wo*, aliens continued to confront facially discriminatory federal and state statutes that placed varying restrictions on noncitizens. Anti-alien laws, particularly in the employment area, were commonplace and, when challenged, usually upheld by state and federal courts. See, e.g., Ohio ex rel. Clarke v. Deckebach, 274 U.S. 392 (1927) (statute prohibiting aliens from operating pool halls upheld); Crane v. New York, 239 U.S. 195 (1915) (public works contracts); Patsone v. Pennsylvania, 232 U.S. 138 (1914) (hunting); Trageser v. Gray, 73 Md. 250, 20 A. 905 (1890) (selling liquor). But see Juniata Limestone Co. v. Fagley, 187 Pa. 193, 40 A. 977 (1898) (state tax on aliens' wages invalidated). Many statutes were upheld by the courts under a "public interest" rationale that a state, in its capacity as guardian, had the exclusive authority to limit the use of its public resources and funds solely to its citizens. But many more statutes were upheld on the ground that a state could regulate aliens pursuant to its police powers in order to protect the health, safety, welfare, and morals of the citizens of the community. See, e.g., Miller v. Niagara Falls, 207 A.D. 798, 202 N.Y.S. 549 (4th Dist. 1924) (upholding ordinance prohibiting aliens from selling soft drinks because of the danger of soft drinks to the welfare of the community); Commonwealth v. Hana, 195 Mass. 262, 81 N.E. 149 (1907) (peddler's license denied to aliens because of the opportunity to cheat customers).

The public interest doctrine was limited slightly by the Supreme Court in Truax v. Raich, 239 U.S. 33 (1915), which invalidated an Arizona statute forbidding private businesses consisting of more than five persons from having work forces comprised of more than 20 percent aliens. The Court noted that "[t]he discrimination defined by the act does not pertain to the regulation or distribution of the public domain, or of the common property or resources of the people of the state, the enjoyment of which may be limited to its citizens as against both aliens and the citizens of other states." The state's police power "to promote the health, safety, morals, and welfare of those within its jurisdiction . . . does not go so far as to make it possible for the state to deny to lawful inhabitants, because of their race or nationality, the ordinary means of earning a livelihood. It requires no argument to show that the right to work for a living in the common occupations of the community is of the very essence of the personal freedom and opportunity that it was the purpose of the Amendment to secure. If this could be refused solely upon the ground of race or nationality, the prohibition of the denial to any person of the equal protection of the laws would be a barren form of words. . . . The discrimination against aliens in the wide range of employments to which the act relates is made an end in itself."

The Court added that the law could not be viewed as a reasonable classification because it interfered with the federal government's power to control immigration: "The authority to control immigration — to admit or exclude aliens — is vested solely in the Federal Government. The assertion of an authority to deny to aliens the opportunity of earning a livelihood when lawfully admitted to the State would be tantamount to the assertion of the right to deny them entrance and abode, for in ordinary cases they cannot live where they cannot work. And, if such a policy were permissible, the practical result would be that those lawfully admitted to the country under the authority of the acts of Congress, instead of enjoying in a substantial sense and in their full scope the privileges conferred by the admission, would be segregated in such of the States as chose to offer hospitality."

The Court concluded that "[n]o special public interest with respect to any particular business is shown that could possibly be deemed to support the enactment, for, as we have said, it relates to every sort. The discrimination is against aliens as such in competition with citizens in the described range of enterprises, and in our opinion it clearly falls under the condemnation of the fundamental law." One might, of course, analyze *Truax* within the context of the general sympathy shown by the Court of that era to a relatively unregulated private economic market. Although the case certainly protected the interests of job-seeking aliens, it just as certainly protected the interests of employers who might well have supported an expansion of the labor pool because of the pressure this would place on applicants to work for lower wages than might otherwise have been the case.

In Takahashi v. Fish & Game Commission, 334 U.S. 410 (1948), the Court considered a California law that denied fishing licenses to aliens ineligible for citizenship. The Court rejected California's contention that the statute was justified by the state's special public interest in conserving the supply of fish in its jurisdictional waters, which, it claimed, were the common property of the citizens of the state.

> The Federal Government has broad constitutional powers in determining what aliens shall be admitted to the United States, the period they may remain, regulation of their conduct before naturalization, and the terms and conditions of their naturalization. Under the Constitution the states are granted no such powers; they can neither add to nor take from the conditions lawfully imposed by Congress upon admission, naturalization and residence of aliens in the United States or the several states. State laws which impose discriminatory burdens upon the entrance or residence of aliens lawfully within the United States conflict with this constitutionally derived federal power to regulate immigration, and have accordingly been held invalid. . . . The Fourteenth Amendment and the laws adopted under its authority thus embody a general policy that all persons lawfully in this country shall abide "in any state" on an equality of legal privileges with all citizens under non-discriminatory laws.

The Court rejected "the state's claim that it has power to single out and ban its lawful alien inhabitants, and particularly certain racial and color groups within this class of inhabitants, from following a vocation simply because Congress has put some such groups in special classifications in exercise of its broad and wholly distinguishable powers over immigration and naturalization."

The Court stated that it was "unnecessary to resolve the controversy concerning the underlying racial motives that prompted enactment of the legislation." However, Justice Murphy's concurrence, joined by Justice Rutledge, argued that the statute was "the direct outgrowth of antagonism toward persons of Japanese ancestry" and therefore violated the Equal Protection Clause.

Although the public interest doctrine was undermined in *Takahashi*, it was not fully rejected until 1971, four years after the Supreme Court held in *Loving* that racial classifications were subject to strict scrutiny.

2. Regulation of Aliens by State Governments

Graham v. Richardson[111]

403 U.S. 365 (1971)

Blackmun, J., delivered the opinion of the Court. . . .

The issue here is whether the Equal Protection Clause of the Fourteenth Amendment prevents a State from conditioning welfare benefits either (a) upon the beneficiary's possession of United States citizenship, or (b) if the beneficiary is an alien, upon his having resided in this country for a specified number of years.

111. Together with Sailer v. Leger, on appeal from the United States District Court for the Eastern District of Pennsylvania.

I

[Arizona required citizenship or 15 years of residence in the United States in order to receive welfare benefits. Appellee Richardson had emigrated from Mexico in 1956 and resided in Arizona from that time. At the time of the litigation, she was "permanently and totally disabled," but was ineligible for benefits because she had retained Mexican citizenship and had not lived in Arizona the requisite length of time. A Pennsylvania statute limited welfare only to citizens.]

II

. . . It has long been settled . . . that the term "person" [in the Fourteenth Amendment] encompasses lawfully admitted resident aliens as well as citizens of the United States and entitles both citizens and aliens to the equal protection of the laws of the State in which they reside. . . .

Under traditional equal protection principles, a State retains broad discretion to classify as long as its classification has a reasonable basis. . . . But the Court's decisions have established that classifications based on alienage, like those based on nationality or race, are inherently suspect and subject to close judicial scrutiny. Aliens as a class are a prime example of a "discrete and insular" minority (see U.S. v. Carolene Products Co., 304 U.S. 144, 152-53, n.4 (1938)) for whom such heightened judicial solicitude is appropriate. . . .

Arizona and Pennsylvania seek to justify their restrictions on the eligibility of aliens for public assistance solely on the basis of a State's "special public interest" in favoring its own citizens over aliens in the distribution of limited resources such as welfare benefits. It is true that this Court on occasion has upheld state statutes that treat citizens and noncitizens differently, the ground for distinction having been that such laws were necessary to protect special interests of the State or its citizens. Thus, in Truax v. Raich, 239 U.S. 33 (1915), the Court, in striking down an Arizona statute restricting the employment of aliens, emphasized that "[t]he discrimination defined by the act does not pertain to the regulation or distribution of the public domain, or of the common property or resources of the people of the State, the enjoyment of which may be limited to its citizens as against both aliens and the citizens of other States." And in Crane v. New York, 239 U.S. 195 (1915), the Court [upheld] a New York statute prohibiting the employment of aliens on public works projects. The New York court's opinion contained [then Justice of the New York Court of Appeals Cardozo's] well known observation:

> To disqualify aliens is discrimination indeed, but not arbitrary discrimination, for the principle of exclusion is the restriction of the resources of the state to the advancement and profit of the members of the state. Ungenerous and unwise such discrimination may be. It is not for that reason unlawful. . . . The state in determining what use shall be made of its own moneys, may legitimately consult the welfare of its own citizens rather than that of aliens. Whatever is a privilege rather than a right, may be made dependent on citizenship. In its war against poverty, the state is not required to dedicate its own resources to citizens and aliens alike.

Whatever may be the contemporary vitality of the special public-interest doctrine . . . , we conclude that a State's desire to preserve limited welfare benefits for its own citizens is inadequate to justify Pennsylvania's making noncitizens ineligible for public assistance, and Arizona's restricting benefits to citizens and longtime resident aliens. First, the special public interest doctrine was heavily grounded on the notion that "[w]hatever is a privilege, rather than a right, may be made dependent upon citizenship." But this Court now has rejected the concept that constitutional rights turn upon whether a governmental benefit is characterized as a "right" or as a "privilege." Second, as the Court recognized in Shapiro v. Thompson [which struck down a law withholding welfare benefits from newly arrived persons], ". . . [t]he saving of welfare costs cannot justify an otherwise invidious classification." Since an alien as well as a citizen is a "person" for equal protection purposes, a concern for fiscal integrity is [not a] compelling justification for the questioned classification in these cases. . . .

We agree with the three-judge court in the Pennsylvania case that the

> justification of limiting expenses is particularly inappropriate and unreasonable when the discriminated class consists of aliens. Aliens like citizens pay taxes and may be called into the armed forces. . . . [A]liens may live within a state for many years, work in the state and contribute to the economic growth of the state.

There can be no "special public interest" in tax revenues to which aliens have contributed on an equal basis with the residents of the State.

Accordingly, we hold that a state statute that denies welfare benefits to resident aliens and one that denies them to aliens who have not resided in the United States for a specified number of years violate the Equal Protection Clause.

III

An additional reason why the state statutes at issue in these cases do not withstand constitutional scrutiny emerges from the area of federal-state relations. The National Government has "broad constitutional powers in determining what aliens shall be admitted to the United States, the period they may remain, regulation of their conduct before naturalization, and the terms and conditions of their naturalization." Pursuant to that power, Congress has provided . . . that "[a]liens who are paupers, professional beggars, or vagrants" or aliens who "are likely at any time to become public charges" shall be excluded from admission into the United States and that any alien lawfully admitted shall be deported who "has within five years after entry become a public charge from causes not affirmatively shown to have arisen after entry." . . . But Congress has not seen fit to impose any burden or restriction on aliens who become indigent after their entry into the United States. . . .

State laws that restrict the eligibility of aliens for welfare benefits merely because of their alienage conflict with these overriding national policies in an area constitutionally entrusted to the Federal Government. . . .

Congress has broadly declared as federal policy that lawfully admitted resident aliens who become public charges for causes arising after their entry are not subject to deportation, and that as long as they are here they are entitled to the full and equal benefit of all state laws for the security of persons and property. The state statutes at issue in the instant cases impose auxiliary burdens upon the entrance of residence of aliens who suffer the distress, after entry, of economic dependency on public assistance. . . .

[Justice Blackmun goes on to quote from a passage of *Truax* considering the consequence of allowing states to limit the opportunities of aliens for employment:]

> [I]f such a policy were permissible, the practical result would be that those lawfully admitted to the country under the authority of the acts of Congress, instead of enjoying in a substantial sense and in their full scope the privileges conferred by the admission, would be segregated in such of the States as chose to offer hospitality.

The same is true here, for in the ordinary case, an alien, becoming indigent and unable to work, will be unable to live where, because of discriminatory denial of public assistance, he cannot "secure the necessities of life, including food, clothing and shelter." State alien residency requirements that either deny welfare benefits to noncitizens or condition them on longtime residency, equate with the assertion of a right, inconsistent with federal policy, to deny entrance and abode. Since such laws encroach upon exclusive federal power, they are constitutionally impermissible.

Bernal v. Fainter

467 U.S. 216 (1984)

Marshall, J., delivered the opinion of the Court.

The question posed by this case is whether a statute of the State of Texas violates the Equal Protection Clause of the Fourteenth Amendment . . . by denying aliens the opportunity to become notaries public. . . .

I

[Bernal], a native of Mexico, is a resident alien who has lived in the United States since 1961. He works as a paralegal for Texas Rural Legal Aid, Inc., helping migrant farmworkers on employment and civil rights matters. In order to administer oaths to these workers and to notarize their statements for use in civil litigation, [he] applied in 1978 to become a notary public. . . . The Texas Secretary of State denied [Bernal's] application because he failed to satisfy the statutory requirement that a notary public be a citizen of the United States. . . .

II

As a general matter, a state law that discriminates on the basis of alienage can be sustained only if it can withstand strict judicial scrutiny. In order to withstand strict scrutiny, the law must advance a compelling state interest by the least restrictive means available. Applying this principle, we have invalidated an array of state statutes that denied aliens the right to pursue various occupations. In Sugarman v. Dougall, 413 U.S. 634 (1973), we struck down a state statute barring aliens from employment in permanent positions in the competitive class of the state civil service. In In re Griffith, 413 U.S. 717 (1973), we nullified a state law excluding aliens from eligibility for membership in the State Bar. And in Examining Board v. Flores de Otero, 426 U.S. 572 (1976), we voided a state law that excluded aliens from the practice of civil engineering.

We have, however, developed a narrow exception to the rule that discrimination based on alienage triggers strict scrutiny. This exception has been labeled the "political function" exception and applies to laws that exclude aliens from positions intimately related to the process of democratic self-governance. The contours of the "political function" exception are outlined by our prior decisions. In Foley v. Connelie, 435 U.S. 291 (1978), we held that a State may require police to be citizens because, in performing a fundamental obligation of government, police "are clothed with authority to exercise an almost infinite variety of discretionary powers" often involving the most sensitive areas of daily life. In Ambach v. Norwick, 441 U.S. 68 (1979), we held that a State may bar aliens who have not declared their intent to become citizens from teaching in the public schools because teachers, like police, possess a high degree of responsibility and discretion in the fulfillment of a basic governmental obligation. They have direct, day-to-day contact with students, exercise unsupervised discretion over them, act as role models, and influence their students about the government and the political process. Finally, in Cabell v. Chavez-Salido, 454 U.S. 432 (1982), we held that a State may bar aliens from positions as probation officers because they, like police and teachers, routinely exercise discretionary power, involving a basic governmental function, that places them in a position of direct authority over other individuals.

The rationale behind the political-function exception is that within broad boundaries a State may establish its own form of government and limit the right to govern to those who are full-fledged members of the political community. Some public positions are so closely bound with the formulation and implementation of self-government that the State is permitted to exclude from those positions persons outside the political community, hence, persons who have not become part of the process of democratic self-determination.

> The exclusion of aliens from basic governmental processes is not a deficiency in the democratic system but a necessary consequence of the community's process of political self-definition. Self-government, whether direct or through representatives, begins by defining the scope of the community of the governed and thus of the governors as well: Aliens are by definition those outside of this community.

We have therefore lowered our standard of review when evaluating the validity of exclusions that entrust only to citizens important elective and nonelective positions whose operations "go to the heart of representative government." . . .

To determine whether a restriction based on alienage fits within the narrow political-function exception, we devised in *Cabell* a two-part test.

> First, the specificity of the classification will be examined: a classification that is substantially overinclusive or underinclusive tends to undercut the governmental claim that the classification serves legitimate political ends. . . . Second, even if the classification is sufficiently tailored, it may be applied in the particular case only to "persons holding state elective or

important nonelective executive, legislative, and judicial positions," those officials who "participate directly in the formulation, execution, or review of broad public policy" and hence "perform functions that go to the heart of representative government."

III

[Does the Texas statute satisfy the *Cabell* test? It applies only to appointment as a notary public and therefore] does not indiscriminately sweep within its ambit a wide range of offices and occupations but specifies only one particular post with respect to which the State asserts a right to exclude aliens. Clearly, then, the statute is not overinclusive. . . . Less clear is whether [it] is fatally underinclusive. Texas does not require court reporters to be United States citizens even though they perform some of the same services as notaries. Nor does Texas require that its Secretary of State be a citizen, even though he holds the highest appointive position in the State and performs many important functions, including the supervision of the licensing of all notaries public. We need not decide this issue, however, because of our decision with respect to the second prong of the *Cabell* test.

. . . [T]he State emphasizes that notaries are designated as public officers by the Texas Constitution. . . . This Court, however, has never deemed the source of a position—whether it derives from a State's statute or its Constitution—as the dispositive factor in determining whether a State may entrust the position only to citizens. Rather, this Court has always looked to the actual function of the position as the dispositive factor. The focus of our inquiry has been whether a position was such that the officeholder would necessarily exercise broad discretionary power over the formulation or execution of public policies importantly affecting the citizen population—power of the sort that a self-governing community could properly entrust only to full-fledged members of that community. . . .

The State maintains that even if the actual function of a post is the touchstone of a proper analysis, Texas notaries public should still be classified among those positions from which aliens can properly be excluded because the duties of Texas notaries entail the performance of functions sufficiently consequential to be deemed "political." The Court of Appeals ably articulated this argument:

> With the power to acknowledge instruments such as wills and deeds and leases and mortgages; to take out-of-court depositions; to administer oaths; and the discretion to refuse to perform any of the foregoing acts, notaries public in Texas are involved in countless matters of importance to the day-to-day functioning of state government. The Texas political community depends upon the notary public to insure that those persons executing documents are accurately identified, to refuse to certify any identification that is false or uncertain, and to insist that oaths are properly and accurately administered. Land titles and property succession depend upon the care and integrity of the notary public, as well as the familiarity of the notary with the community, to verify the authenticity of the execution of the documents.

We recognize the critical need for a notary's duties to be carried out correctly and with integrity. But a notary's duties, important as they are, hardly implicate responsibilities that go to the heart of representative government. Rather, these duties are essentially clerical and ministerial. In contrast to state troopers, notaries do not routinely exercise the State's monopoly of legitimate coercive force. Nor do notaries routinely exercise the wide discretion typically enjoyed by public school teachers when they present materials that educate youth respecting the information and values necessary for the maintenance of a democratic political system. To be sure, considerable damage could result from the negligent or dishonest performance of a notary's duties. But the same could be said for the duties performed by cashiers, building inspectors, the janitors who clean up the offices of public officials, and numerous other categories of personnel upon whom we depend for careful, honest service. What distinguishes such personnel from those to whom the political-function exception is properly applied is that the latter are invested either with policymaking responsibility or broad discretion in the execution of public policy that requires the routine exercise of authority over individuals. Neither of these characteristics pertains to the functions performed by Texas notaries.

The inappropriateness of applying the political-function exception to Texas notaries is further underlined by our decision in In re Griffiths, in which we subjected to strict scrutiny a Connecticut statute that prohibited noncitizens from becoming members of the State Bar. Along with the usual power and privileges accorded to members of the bar, Connecticut gave to members of its Bar additional authority that encompasses the very duties performed by Texas notaries—authority to "sign writs and subpoenas, take recognizances, administer oaths and take depositions and acknowledgements of deeds." In striking down Connecticut's citizenship requirement, we concluded that "[i]t in no way denigrates a lawyer's high responsibilities to observe that [these duties] hardly involve matters of state policy or acts of such unique responsibility as to entrust them only to citizens." If it is improper to apply the political-function exception to a citizenship requirement in a state bar, it would be anomalous to apply the exception to the citizenship requirement that governs eligibility to become a Texas notary. We conclude, then, that the "political function" exception is inapplicable . . . and that the statute is therefore subject to strict judicial scrutiny.

IV

To satisfy strict scrutiny, the State must show that [the statute] furthers a compelling state interest by the least restrictive means available. Respondents maintain that [the statute] serves "its legitimate concern that notaries be reasonably familiar with state law and institutions" and "that notaries may be called upon years later to testify to acts they have performed." However, both of these asserted justifications utterly fail to meet the stringent requirements of strict scrutiny. There is nothing in the record that indicates that resident aliens, as a class, are so incapable of familiarizing themselves with Texas law as to justify the State's absolute and classwide exclusion. . . . Furthermore, if the State's concern with ensuring a notary's familiarity with state law were truly "compelling," one would expect the State to give some sort of test actually measuring a person's familiarity with the law. The State, however, administers no such test. . . . Similarly inadequate is the State's purported interest in ensuring the later availability of notaries' testimony. This justification fails because the State fails to advance a factual showing that the unavailability of notaries' testimony presents a real, as opposed to a merely speculative, problem to the State. Without a factual underpinning, the State's asserted interest lacks the weight we have required of interests properly denominated as compelling.

Rehnquist, J., dissenting.

I dissent for the reasons stated in my dissenting opinion in Sugarman v. Dougall, 413 U.S. 634, 649 (1973). [In *Sugarman,* which prohibited aliens from certain civil service positions, and its companion case, In re Griffiths, which involved a prohibition on aliens becoming members of the State Bar, Justice Rehnquist wrote:]

The Court . . . holds that an alien is not really different from a citizen, and that any legislative classification on the basis of alienage is "inherently suspect."[112] The Fourteenth Amendment, the Equal Protection Clause of which the Court interprets as invalidating the state legislation here involved, contains no language concerning "inherently suspect classifications," or, for that matter, merely "suspect classifications." The principal purpose of those who drafted and adopted the Amendment was to prohibit the States from invidiously discriminating by reason of race, Slaughter-House Cases, and, because of this plainly manifested intent, classifications based on race have rightly been held "suspect" under the Amendment. But there is no language used in the Amendment, or any historical evidence as to the intent of the Framers, which would suggest to the slightest degree that it was intended to render alienage a "suspect" classification, that it was designed in any way to protect "discrete and insular minorities" other than racial minorities, or that it would in any way justify the result reached by the Court. . . .

I

The Court, by holding . . . that a citizen-alien classification is "suspect" in the eyes of our Constitution, fails to mention, let alone rationalize, the fact that the Constitution itself recognizes a basic difference between citizens and aliens. That distinction is constitutionally important in no less than 11 instances in a political document noted for its brevity. . . .

Not only do the numerous classifications on the basis of citizenship that are set forth in the Constitution cut against both the analysis used and the results reached by the Court in these cases; the very Amendment which the Court reads to prohibit classifications based on citizenship establishes the very distinction which the Court now condemns as "suspect." . . . In constitutionally defining who is a citizen of the United States, Congress [in proposing the Fourteenth Amendment] obviously thought it was doing something, and something important. Citizenship meant something, a status in and relationship with a society which is continuing and more basic than mere presence or residence. . . .

Decisions of this Court holding that an alien is a "person" within the meaning of the Fourteenth Amendment are simply irrelevant to the question of whether

---

112. Elsewhere in the opinion, Rehnquist wrote that what "would most disturb native-born citizens and especially naturalized citizens who have worked diligently to learn about our history, mores, and political institutions and who have successfully completed the rigorous process of naturalization, is the intimation, if not statement, that they are really not any different from aliens."

that Amendment prohibits legislative classifications based upon this particular status. . . .

[T]he Court now relies in part on the decisions in Truax v. Raich, 239 U.S. 33 (1915), and Takahashi v. Fish Comm's, 334 U.S. 410 (1948). In *Truax*, the Court invalidated a state statute which prohibited employers of more than five persons from employing more than 20% noncitizens. The law was applicable to all citizens. In holding that the law was invalid . . . , the Court . . . noted that "it should be added that the act is not limited to persons who are engaged in public work or receive the benefit of public moneys." . . .

Takahashi involved a statute which prohibited aliens "ineligible for citizenship" under federal law from receiving commercial fishing licenses. . . . Two features of that law should be noted. First, the statutory classification was not one involving citizens and aliens; it classified citizens and those resident aliens eligible for citizenship into one group, and resident aliens ineligible for citizenship into another. No reason for discriminating among resident aliens is apparent. Second, and most important, is the fact that, although the Court properly refused to inquire into the legislative motive, the overwhelming effect of the law was to bar resident aliens of Japanese ancestry from procuring fishing licenses. [United States law at the time prohibited persons of Japanese ancestry from becoming naturalized citizens.] The Court was not blind to this fact, or to history. The state statute that classifies aliens on the basis of country of origin is much more likely to classify on the basis of race, and thus conflict with the core purpose of the Equal Protection Clause, than a statute that, as here, merely distinguishes between alienage as such and citizenship as such. . . .

[Justice Rehnquist then turns to Graham v. Richardson, supra. He focuses on the Court's reliance on footnote 4 of United States v. Carolene Products Co.]

The mere recitation of the words "insular and discrete minority" is hardly a constitutional reason for prohibiting state legislative classifications such as are involved here. . . .

Our society, consisting of over 200 million individuals of multitudinous origins, customs, tongues, beliefs, and cultures is, to say the least, diverse. It would hardly take extraordinary ingenuity for a lawyer to find "insular and discrete" minorities at every turn in the road. Yet, unless the Court can precisely define and constitutionally justify both the terms and analysis it uses, these decisions today stand for the proposition that the Court can choose a "minority" it "feels" deserves "solicitude" and thereafter prohibit the States from classifying that "minority" differently from the "majority." I cannot find, and the Court does not cite, any constitutional authority for such a "ward of the Court" approach to equal protection.

The only other apparent rationale for the invocation of the "suspect classification" approach in these cases is that alienage is a "status," and the Court does not feel it "appropriate" to classify on that basis. This rationale would appear to be similar to that utilized in Weber v. Aetna Casualty & Surety Co., 406 U.S. 164 (1972) [, in which the Court, with Justice Rehnquist dissenting, indicated that classifications based on the "illegitimacy" of a child would be subject to special scrutiny]. . . . But there is a marked difference between a status or condition such as illegitimacy, national origin, or race, which cannot be altered by an individual and the "status" of the appellant. There is nothing in the record indicating that their status as aliens cannot be changed by their affirmative acts.

II

These statutes do not classify on the basis of country of origin; the distinctions are not between native Americans and "foreigners," but between citizens and aliens. The process of naturalization was specifically designed by Congress to require a foreign national to demonstrate that he or she is familiar with the history, traditions, and institutions of our society in a way that a native-born citizen would learn from formal education and basic social contact. Congress specifically provided that an alien seeking citizenship status must demonstrate "an understanding of the English language" and "a knowledge and understanding of the fundamentals of the history, and of the principles and form of government, of the United States." The purpose was to make the alien establish that he or she understood, and could be integrated into, our social system. . . .

I do not believe that it is irrational for [states to require civil servants] to be citizens, either natural born or naturalized. The proliferation of public administration that our society has witnessed in recent years, as a result of the regulation of conduct and the dispensation of services and funds, has vested a great deal of de facto decisionmaking or policymaking authority in the hands of employees who would not be considered the textbook equivalent of policymakers of the legislative or "top" administrative variety. Nevertheless, as far as the private individual who must seek approval or services is concerned, many of these "low level" civil servants are in fact policymakers. Goldberg v. Kelly implicitly recognized that those who apply facts to individual cases are as much "governors" as those who write the laws or regulations the "low-level" administrator must "apply." Since policymaking for a political community is not necessarily the exclusive preserve of the legislators, judges, and "top" administrators, it is not irrational for New York to provide that only citizens should be admitted to the competitive civil service.

But the justification of efficient government is an even more convincing rationale. Native-born citizens can be expected to be familiar with the social and political institutions of our society; with the society and political mores that affect how we react and interact with other citizens. Naturalized citizens have also demonstrated their willingness to adjust to our patterns of living and attitudes, and have demonstrated a basic understanding of our institutions, system of government, history, and traditions. It is not irrational to assume that aliens as a class are not familiar with how we as individuals treat others and how we expect "government" to treat us. An alien who grew up in a country in which political mores do not reject bribery or self-dealing to the same extent that our culture does; in which an imperious bureaucracy historically adopted a complacent or contemptuous attitude toward those it was supposed to serve; in which fewer if any checks existed on administrative abuses; in which "low-level" civil servants serve at the will of their superiors—could rationally be thought not to be able to deal with the public and with citizen civil servants with the same rapport that one familiar with our political and social mores would, or to approach his duties with the attitude that such positions exist for service, not personal sinecures of either the civil servant or his or her superior. . . .

Connecticut's requirement of citizenship [for lawyers] reflects its judgment that something more than technical skills are needed to be a lawyer under our system. I do not believe it is irrational for a State that makes that judgment to require that lawyers have an understanding of the American political and social experience, whether gained from growing up in this country, as in the case of a native-born citizen, or from the naturalization process, as in the case of a foreign-born citizen. I suppose the Connecticut Bar Examining Committee could itself administer tests in American history, government, and sociology, but the State did not choose to go this route. Instead, it chose to operate on the assumption that citizens as a class might reasonably be thought to have a significantly greater degree of understanding of our experience than would aliens. . . .

DISCUSSION

1. *Community and alienage.* It seems clear that a state can deny the right to vote to resident aliens. But why? One assumes that what justifies the denial of the most "fundamental" of all interests in a democratic polity is that aliens are not members of the political community and are, therefore, not entitled to help shape the community's decisions even if they clearly have strong interests in the electoral outcomes.[113] But what constitutes citizens as a political "community" (rather than simply a collection of persons who happen to share the common legal category of citizenship)? What is it that joins in political fellowship a group of citizens of the United States composed of a Jehovah's Witness from Maine, a Vietnamese refugee living in Houston, and a member of the Ku Klux Klan?

In this context, examine Justice Rehnquist's assumptions about the consequences of growing up in the United States or preparing for naturalization. How plausible are they, and how would you prove or disprove their validity? (Who ought to have the burden of coming forth with relevant evidence?) Does the persuasiveness of Justice Rehnquist's dissent ultimately turn on these assumptions?

2. *Equal protection or preemption.* Note the difference between Parts II and III of the Court's opinion in Graham v. Richardson. Does it matter which theory one chooses to explain the state's inability to discriminate against aliens? Which of these parts proves determinative in *Bernal,* and does it matter?

In Toll v. Moreno, 458 U.S. 1 (1982), the Court, through Justice Brennan, emphasized "the preeminent role of the Federal Government with respect to the regulation of aliens within our borders" while striking down a Maryland statute imposing special costs on aliens attending the state university. The Court quoted a passage from *Takahashi* stating that "[u]nder the Constitution the states . . . can neither add to nor take from the conditions lawfully imposed by Congress upon admission, naturalization and residence of aliens in the United States or the several states." And Justice Brennan went on to acknowledge in a footnote that several "commentators have noted . . . that many of the Court's decisions concerning alienage classifications . . . are better explained in preemption than equal protection

113. See Sanford Levinson, Suffrage and Community: Who Should Vote?, 1989 Fla. L. Rev. 545.

terms."[114] If one were to adopt such a focus, the operative rule might be something like this: When Congress adopts legislation resulting in the permanent residence of an alien, a state cannot interfere with the national policy by setting up barriers to the resident alien's ability to flourish in the United States unless those barriers can survive strict scrutiny.

3. *Illegal aliens and education.* In Plyler v. Doe, 457 U.S. 202 (1982), discussed at greater length in Chapter 9, the Supreme Court held that Texas could not prohibit children of illegal aliens from enrolling in Texas public schools. Justice Brennan, writing for a 5-4 majority, rejected Texas's argument that illegal aliens were not "persons within its jurisdiction" and therefore exempt from the requirements of the Equal Protection Clause:

> The Fourteenth Amendment provides that "No State shall . . . deprive any person of life, liberty or property, without due process of law; nor deny to *any person within its jurisdiction* the equal protection of the laws." [Emphasis added.] Appellants argue at the outset that undocumented aliens, because of their immigration status, are not "persons within the jurisdiction" of the State of Texas, and that they therefore have no right to the equal protection of Texas law. We reject this argument. Whatever his status under the immigration laws, an alien is surely a "person" in any ordinary sense of that term. Aliens, even aliens whose presence in this country is unlawful, have long been recognized as "persons" guaranteed due process of law by the Fifth and Fourteenth Amendments. Shaughnessy v. Mezei, 345 U.S. 206, 212 (1953); Wong Wing v. United States, 163 U.S. 228, 238 (1986). Indeed, we have clearly held that the Fifth Amendment protects aliens whose presence in this country is unlawful from invidious discrimination by the Federal Government. Mathews v. Diaz, 426 U.S. 67, 77 (1976). . . .
>
> There is simply no support for appellants' suggestion that "due process" is somehow of greater stature than "equal protection" and therefore available to a larger class of persons. To the contrary, each aspect of the Fourteenth Amendment reflects an elementary limitation on state power. To permit a State to employ the phrase "within its jurisdiction" in order to identify subclasses of persons whom it would define as beyond its jurisdiction, thereby relieving itself of the obligation to assure that its laws are designed and applied equally to those persons, would undermine the principal purpose for which the Equal Protection Clause was incorporated in the Fourteenth Amendment. The Equal Protection Clause was intended to work nothing less than the abolition of all caste and invidious class based legislation. That objective is fundamentally at odds with the power the State asserts here to classify persons subject to its laws as nonetheless excepted from its protection.
>
> Although the congressional debate concerning §1 of the Fourteenth Amendment was limited, that debate clearly confirms the understanding

---

114. See Note, The Equal Treatment of Aliens: Preemption as Equal Protection, 31 Stan. L. Rev. 1069 (1979); Note, State Burdens on Resident Aliens: A New Preemption Analysis, 89 Yale L.J. 940 (1980).

that the phrase "within its jurisdiction" was intended in a broad sense to offer the guarantee of equal protection to all within a State's boundaries, and to all upon whom the State would impose the obligations of its laws. Indeed, it appears from those debates that Congress, by using the phrase "person within its jurisdiction," sought expressly to ensure that the equal protection of the laws was provided to the alien population. Representative Bingham reported to the House the draft resolution of the Joint Committee of Fifteen on Reconstruction (H.R. 63) that was to become the Fourteenth Amendment. Cong. Globe, 39th Cong., 1st Sess. 1033 (1866). Two days later, Bingham posed the following question in support of the resolution: "Is it not essential to the unity of the Government and the unity of the people that all persons, whether citizens or strangers, within this land, shall have equal protection in every State in this Union in the rights of life and liberty and property?" Senator Howard, also a member of the Joint Committee of Fifteen, and the floor manager of the Amendment in the Senate, was no less explicit about the broad objectives of the Amendment, and the intention to make its provisions applicable to all who "may happen to be" within the jurisdiction of a State: "The last two clauses of the first section of the amendment disable a State from depriving not merely a citizen of the United States, but *any person, whoever he may be,* of life, liberty, or property without due process of law, or from denying to him the equal protection of the laws of the State. This abolishes all class legislation in the States, and does away with the injustice of subjecting one caste of persons to a code not applicable to another. . . . It will, if adopted by the States, forever disable every one of them from passing laws trenching upon those fundamental rights and privileges which pertain to citizens of the United States, *and to all persons who may happen to be within their jurisdiction.*" Cong. Globe, 39th Cong., 1st Sess. 2766 (1866) (emphasis added).

Use of the phrase "within its jurisdiction" thus does not detract from, but rather confirms the understanding that the protection of the Fourteenth Amendment extends to anyone, citizen or stranger, who is subject to the laws of a State, and reaches into every corner of a State's territory. That a person's initial entry into a State or into the United States, was unlawful, and that he may for that reason be expelled, cannot negate the simple fact of his presence within the State's territorial perimeter. Given such presence, he is subject to the full range of obligations imposed by the State's civil and criminal laws. And until he leaves the jurisdiction—either voluntarily or involuntarily in accordance with the Constitution and the laws of the United States—he is entitled to the equal protection of the laws that a State may choose to establish. . . .

Justice Brennan concluded that although children of illegal immigrants were not a suspect class and although education was not a fundamental right, Texas's law failed the test of rationality because the state failed to show that its policy furthered a "substantial state interest." Texas's policy, Justice Brennan argued, "imposes a lifetime hardship on a discrete class of children not accountable for their disabling status. The stigma of illiteracy will mark them for the rest of their lives. By denying these children a basic education, we deny them the ability to live within the structure of our civic institutions, and foreclose any realistic possibility that they will contribute in even the smallest way to the progress of our Nation. In determining the rationality of [Texas's policy], we may appropriately take into account its costs to the Nation and to the innocent children who are its victims."

Chief Justice Burger, joined by Justices White, Rehnquist, and O'Connor, dissented, noting that the Texas's law involved neither a suspect class nor a fundamental right, and therefore need only pass the test of "a rational relation to a legitimate state purpose." "[I]t is simply not 'irrational' for a State to conclude that it does not have the same responsibility to provide benefits for persons whose very presence in the State and this country is illegal as it does to provide for those persons lawfully present."

3. Regulation of Resident Aliens by the Federal Government

The Constitution gives Congress the right to control naturalization, and gives the federal government the power to regulate foreign affairs. Thus, the preemption arguments that apply to state regulation do not apply to the federal government. Does the equal protection component of the Due Process Clause of the Fifth Amendment, first adverted to in Bolling v. Sharpe, restrict the federal government in the same way that the Fourteenth Amendment restricts the states?

The Court considered Congress's power over lawfully admitted aliens in Mathews v. Diaz, 426 U.S. 67 (1976), and Hampton v. Mow Sun Wong, 426 U.S. 88 (1976). In *Mathews,* a unanimous Court upheld a congressional limitation on the participation of aliens in federal Medicare programs to aliens who had both been admitted as permanent residents and had been continuously resident in the United States for five years. Writing for the Court, Justice Stevens noted that "[i]n the exercise of its broad power over naturalization and immigration, Congress regularly makes rules that would be unacceptable if applied to citizens."

Justice Stevens wrote: "It is obvious that Congress has no constitutional duty to provide all aliens with the welfare benefits provided to citizens." The only question was whether the classifications were reasonable; the Court held that they were. Distinguishing *Graham,* the Court emphasized the difference between states and Congress:

> Insofar as state welfare policy is concerned, there is little, if any, basis for treating persons who are citizens of another State differently from persons who are citizens of another country. Both groups are noncitizens as far as the State's interests in administering its welfare programs are concerned. Thus, a division by a State of the category of persons who are not citizens of that State into subcategories of United States citizens and aliens has no apparent justification, whereas, a comparable classification by the Federal Government is a routine and normally legitimate part of its business. Furthermore, whereas the Constitution inhibits every State's power to restrict travel across its own borders, Congress is explicitly empowered to exercise that type of control across the borders of the United States.
>
> . . . [I]t is not "political hypocrisy" to recognize that the Fourteenth Amendment's limits on state powers are substantially different from the

constitutional provisions applicable to the federal power over immigration and naturalization.

In *Hampton*, Justice Stevens wrote for a five-Justice majority to invalidate a United States Civil Service Commission regulation that barred resident aliens from competing for positions in the federal civil service. The Court rested the decision on pure due process grounds, explicitly declining to hold that the regulation violated the equal protection component of the Fifth Amendment. Justice Stevens emphasized the far-reaching consequences of the prohibition and the facts that it had not been directly ordered by either Congress or the President nor had its merits been fully considered by the Commission. The Court acknowledged "that overriding national interests may provide a justification for a citizenship requirement in the federal service even though an identical requirement may not be enforced by a State," but denied that "the federal power over aliens is so plenary that any agent of the National Government may arbitrarily subject all resident aliens to different substantive rules from those applied to citizens."

> The rule enforced by the Commission has its impact on an identifiable class of persons who, entirely apart from the rule itself, are already subject to disadvantages not shared by the remainder of the community. Aliens are not entitled to vote and . . . are often handicapped by a lack of familiarity with our language and customs. The added disadvantage resulting from the enforcement of the rule—ineligibility for employment in a major sector of the economy, is of sufficient significance to be characterized as a deprivation of an interest in liberty. Indeed, we deal with a rule which deprives a discrete class of persons of an interest in liberty on a wholesale basis. By reason of the Fifth Amendment, such a deprivation must be accompanied by due process.

Following the decision in *Hampton*, President Ford issued an executive order making citizenship a condition for federal employment. The order has not subsequently been reviewed by the Supreme Court. Consider, though, Professor Tribe's suggestion that the Fifth Amendment's equal protection component "would invalidate even congressional or presidential discrimination against resident aliens as such where no substantial justification could be shown."[115]

DISCUSSION

1. *The reach of Mathews v. Diaz.* Does *Mathews* hold that all federal discriminations against aliens are subject only to rational basis review? Consider the following arguments for a narrower theory. Which, if any, do you think would be workable?

(a) Federal classifications that discriminate against persons who are not resident aliens, for example, immigrants who are not yet resident aliens, persons on student visas, or other visitors who have come to the country temporarily, should be treated differently from those classifications that discriminate against resident

115. See Laurence Tribe, American Constitutional Law 1546 n.12 (1988).

aliens. The latter discriminations should be subject to strict scrutiny. See Gerald M. Rosberg, The Protection of Aliens from Discriminatory Treatment by the National Government, 1977 Sup. Ct. Rev. 275, 335. Note that this rule would have afforded little protection to, for example, nonresident aliens and aliens on student visas who were rounded up on suspicion of terrorist activities following the September 11, 2001 attacks on the United States.

(b) Application of judicial scrutiny should depend on the purposes for the classification. "When a categorical preference for American citizens cannot be justified in terms of immigration and naturalization policy or as an adjunct to our international bargaining posture, the basis for relaxing the scrutiny otherwise applicable to discrimination against aliens as a class" should not apply. Neal Katyal and Laurence Tribe, Waging War, Deciding Guilt: Trying the Military Tribunals, 111 Yale L.J. 1259, 1300-1301 (2002). What sorts of restrictions on aliens could not be justified in terms of immigration and naturalization policy, or in terms of the conduct of foreign policy?

(c) Federal classifications that are motivated by racial prejudice should not be insulated from judicial scrutiny; hence courts must inquire whether a particular federal classification against aliens is motivated by racial stereotyping or racial prejudice. Is this theory consistent with the Chinese Exclusion Case (Chae Chan Ping v. United States) that gave Congress plenary power to exclude "foreigners of a different race"? Would this rule prohibit the government from having different quotas for admission of aliens from different countries?

(d) Federal classifications that affect fundamental rights like those in the federal Bill of Rights, as well as rights of marriage and procreation, should be subject to strict scrutiny, whether they apply to immigrants, visitors, or resident aliens. Cf. David Cole, Enemy Aliens, 54 Stan. L. Rev. 953 (2002) (arguing that "distinctions between citizens and aliens do not generally justify differential application of First Amendment speech and association rights or Fifth Amendment due process protections"). Under this theory, could Congress expel aliens who advocate violence against the United States if it could not punish citizens who do so? Could it have different rules for admitting family members (including spouses) of citizens and resident aliens?

In Zadvydas v. Davis, 533 U.S. 678 (2001), the Court held that an alien ordered removed from the country because of his criminal record but whom no country was willing to accept could not be kept in custody indefinitely. The Court interpreted the relevant statute to authorize only temporary detention pending removal in order to avoid constitutional problems under the Due Process Clause. Justice Breyer wrote for a 5-4 majority:

> A statute permitting indefinite detention of an alien would raise a serious constitutional problem. The Fifth Amendment's Due Process Clause forbids the Government to "deprive" any "person . . . of . . . liberty . . . without due process of law." Freedom from imprisonment—from government custody, detention, or other forms of physical restraint—lies at the heart of the liberty that Clause protects. And this Court has said that government detention violates that Clause unless the detention is ordered in a criminal proceeding with adequate procedural protections, or, in certain special and "narrow" non-punitive "circumstances," where a special

> justification, such as harm-threatening mental illness, outweighs the "individual's constitutionally protected interest in avoiding physical restraint." Kansas v. Hendricks, 521 U.S. 346 (1997). . . .
>
> It is well established that certain constitutional protections available to persons inside the United States are unavailable to aliens outside of our geographic borders. But once an alien enters the country, the legal circumstance changes, for the Due Process Clause applies to all "persons" within the United States, including aliens, whether their presence here is lawful, unlawful, temporary, or permanent. Indeed, this Court has held that the Due Process Clause protects an alien subject to a final order of deportation, though the nature of that protection may vary depending upon status and circumstance.

Justices Scalia, Thomas, Kennedy, and Chief Justice Rehnquist dissented.

How much constitutional protection does *Zadvydas* offer? Note that the Court did not dispute that aliens may be subject to quite different procedures than citizens without running afoul of the Due Process Clause. Moreover, the Court noted that although preventive detention was not authorized in this case, it did not have before it a situation involving "terrorism or other special circumstances where special arguments might be made for forms of preventive detention and for heightened deference to the judgments of the political branches with respect to matters of national security."

Zadvydas, as noted, dealt with readily deportable aliens who did not, however, have a country willing to accept them. Consider, however, Auguste v. Ridge, 395 F.3d 123 (3d Cir. 2005), involving the deportation of a felon from Haiti. The country was willing to accept Auguste, but it has a policy of placing such persons in jail for a period of time in order to discourage a return to criminal ways by those returning to Haiti under such circumstances. Although the Third Circuit found that the conditions of Haitian jails approached "slave ships" in their severity, it held, nonetheless, that since the conditions did not meet the strict definition of "torture" adopted by the Court, Auguste had no right not to be returned to his home country.

2. *Congressional authorization.* May Congress authorize states to discriminate against aliens? In Graham v. Richardson, the Court considered Arizona's suggestion that its 15-year durational residency requirement for aliens was authorized by federal law. The Court rejected Arizona's construction of the relevant federal statutes and then went on to say:

> But if [the statutes] were to be read so as to authorize discriminatory treatment of aliens at the option of the States, [that would present] serious constitutional questions. Although the Federal Government admittedly has broad constitutional power to determine what aliens shall be admitted to the United States, the period they may remain, and the terms and conditions of their naturalization, Congress does not have the power to authorize the individual States to violate the Equal Protection Clause. Under Art. I, §8, cl. 4, of the Constitution, Congress' power is to "establish a uniform Rule of Naturalization." A congressional enactment construed so as to permit state legislatures to adopt divergent laws on the subject

of citizenship requirements for federally supported welfare programs would appear to contravene this explicit constitutional requirement of uniformity.

Is the Court's advisory construction of the "uniformity" provision persuasive? So long as all immigrants are equally liable to the decisions of the states wherein they happen to reside, wouldn't the "uniformity" provision be satisfied?

Consider in this context §411 of the Personal Responsibility and Work Opportunity Reconciliation Act of 1996, which explicitly made ineligible "for any State or local public benefit" anyone who is an illegal immigrant to the United States. Note well that this does not simply grant states discretion to decide whether to extend such persons welfare benefits, but appears to require that states not offer any such benefits, presumably as part of the national policy to discourage illegal immigration. Does §411 present any constitutional difficulties? There are, however, some limited exceptions, such as "[a]ssistance for health care items and service that are necessary for the treatment of an emergency medical condition of the alien involved and are not related to an organ transplant process" and "short-term, non-cash, in-kind emergency disaster relief," and "[p]ublic health assistance for immunizations with respect to immunizable diseases and for testing and treatment of symptoms of communicable diseases." Are these exceptions constitutionally required or matters of legislative grace?

Even if the 1996 law were not part of the legal horizon, one might well wonder about the status of *Plyler*, given the changes in membership on the Court since 1982. None of the Justices who decided the case are still on the Court today.

So consider the constitutional status of a law like Proposition 187, passed by the voters of California in 1994 via the initiative and referendum process. It provided that "A person shall not receive any public social services to which he or she may be otherwise entitled," or "receive any health care services from a publicly-funded health care facility, to which he or she is otherwise entitled, until the legal status of that person has been verified" as a U.S. citizen, a lawfully admitted permanent resident alien, or "[a]n alien lawfully admitted for a temporary period of time." Section 187 also prohibited access to public schools (including elementary, secondary, and university public educational institutions) to any person who is not a citizen, permanent resident, or "otherwise authorized under federal law to be present in the United States."

Is Proposition 187 constitutional, in whole or in part? Does your answer depend on whether this question is asked as of 1995, i.e., before the passage of the 1996 "welfare reform" act, or afterward? See League of United Latin American Citizens v. Wilson, 997 F. Supp. 1244 (C.D. Cal. 1997).

TRUMP v. HAWAII, 138 S. CT. 2392 (2018) [Online]

CHAPTER 8

SEX EQUALITY

The previous chapter considered how the Court has interpreted the Equal Protection Clause to speak to questions of race inequality during the last half-century. Given the history of the Fourteenth Amendment, this presents perhaps the most straightforward application of the clause. But the Equal Protection Clause is not restricted to questions of race discrimination. The Fourteenth Amendment announces its guarantees in general language, declaring that no state shall "deny to any person within its jurisdiction the equal protection of the laws." After deciding *Brown* and associated doctrines of race discrimination, in the 1970s the Court began to interpret the clause to speak to other forms of inequality—especially to questions of sex discrimination.

The sex discrimination cases present fundamental questions concerning constitutional change. For nearly a century after ratification of the Fourteenth Amendment, the Court invalidated no law under the Equal Protection Clause on the ground that it discriminated between the sexes. Then, during the 1970s, the Court began to interpret the clause as prohibiting many state laws that distributed rights and obligations by sex. The chapter examines the justifications the Court offered for this new body of equal protection law and explores its practical reach. How did the Court decide what forms of state action, in addition to race-based state action, would require extraordinary justification (more than minimum rationality) under the Equal Protection Clause? And once it decided closely to scrutinize sex-based state action, how did the Court determine which forms of sex-based regulation warranted invalidation? When does sex discrimination law diverge from the Court's racial discrimination precedents? In what areas might this body of law still be evolving?

What do the equal protection sex discrimination cases teach about the dynamics of constitutional change? How might the sex discrimination cases serve as precedent governing the claims of other groups seeking suspect class status under the Equal Protection Clause?

I. THE SEX EQUALITY CLAIMS UNDER THE FOURTEENTH AMENDMENT: SOCIAL MOVEMENTS AND CONSTITUTIONAL CHANGE

A. The Fourteenth Amendment's First Century

Before the Civil War, many committed to the cause of abolishing slavery were also committed to the cause of women's rights. After the Civil War, woman suffrage advocates helped petition for the Reconstruction Amendments. Once the amendments were ratified, the suffrage movement made claims on them, asserting that the Fourteenth Amendment embodied a commitment to protect human rights that was broad enough to emancipate women. Yet, as we saw in Chapter 4, the Court was not receptive to equality claims that the suffrage movement advanced under the newly ratified Fourteenth Amendment. In this period—and for much of the ensuing century—the Court viewed state action that discriminated between the sexes as rationally reflecting differences in the social roles of men and women. It rejected Myra Bradwell's claim that an Illinois law denying women the right to practice law violated the Fourteenth Amendment. Justice Bradley's concurrence in Bradwell v. Illinois, 83 U.S. (16 Wall.) 130, 141 (1873), has since become notorious:

> [T]he civil law, as well as nature herself, has always recognized a wide difference in the respective spheres and destinies of man and woman. . . . The constitution of the family organization, which is founded in the divine ordinance, as well as in the nature of things, indicates the domestic sphere as that which properly belongs to the domain and functions of womanhood. . . . The paramount destiny and mission of woman are to fulfill the noble and benign offices of wife and mother. This is the law of the Creator.

Justice Bradley rested his interpretation of the Fourteenth Amendment on understandings about family structure—on the common law of marital status and the ideology of "separate spheres." Given that "a married woman is incapable, without her husband's consent, of making contracts which shall be binding on her or him," Justice Bradley reasoned, the Illinois Supreme Court was perfectly justified in its concerns that Mrs. Bradwell could not adequately represent her clients. This restriction on women's participation in professional life was wholly intelligible within the prevailing "separate spheres" ideology, which held that women were specially suited for the work of family maintenance, while men were destined for the world of public affairs.

Women's efforts to secure protection for the right to vote on the same terms as men fared no better under the Fourteenth Amendment than did the claim to practice law. As Chapter 4 recounts, in the aftermath of the Civil War, when leaders of the suffrage movement failed to persuade the Thirty-Ninth Congress to enfranchise women, Frances Minor and others called for a "New Departure under the Fourteenth Amendment," in which hundreds of women began to assert a constitutional right to vote. The Court rejected women's claim to vote under the Fourteenth Amendment in Minor v. Happersett, 88 U.S. (21 Wall.) 162 (1875). The Court acknowledged that women were citizens of the United States, but nonetheless held without dissent that the right to vote was not a privilege or immunity of United States citizenship.

After the Court rejected women's suffrage claims under the Fourteenth Amendment, the movement began its quest for a constitutional amendment that would recognize that women were entitled to vote on the same terms as men. Over the next several decades, the movement struggled to win recognition of this equal citizenship claim and to refute opponents of woman suffrage who argued that differences in family roles justified different citizenship roles for men and women.[1]

---

1. For an account of the debate over marriage, citizenship, and suffrage in the campaign, see Reva B. Siegel, She the People: The Nineteenth Amendment, Sex Equality, Federalism, and the Family, 115 Harv. L. Rev. 947 (2002).

In 1920, the movement finally secured ratification of the Nineteenth Amendment, which prohibited states from limiting suffrage on grounds of sex.

Initially, at least, ratification of the woman suffrage amendment influenced the Court's interpretation of the Fourteenth Amendment. One of the most prominent examples involved protective labor laws. By the early twentieth century, the Court had adopted a sex-differentiated framework for enforcing liberty of contract under the Fourteenth Amendment; it ruled in Muller v. Oregon, 208 U.S. 412, 422-423 (1908), that states might regulate women's employment in ways *Lochner* barred the regulation of men's employment because

> [t]he two sexes differ in structure of body, in the functions to be performed by each, in the amount of physical strength, in the capacity for long continued labor, particularly when done standing, the influence of vigorous health upon the future well-being of the race, the self-reliance which enables one to assert full rights, and in the capacity to maintain the struggle for subsistence. This difference justifies a difference in legislation. . . .

After ratification of the Nineteenth Amendment, the Court retreated from this sex-differentiated framework for determining whether protective labor legislation violated liberty of contract. In Adkins v. Children's Hospital, 261 U.S. 525 (1923), the Court ruled that a minimum wage law for women violated liberty of contract.[2] Justice Sutherland's opinion in *Adkins* pointed to changes in women's status, particularly those embodied in the Nineteenth Amendment, as a reason for distinguishing *Muller*; and, the *Adkins* Court interpreted the Nineteenth Amendment as embodying a norm of equal citizenship that had implications, outside the context of voting, for the interpretation of the Fourteenth Amendment.[3] (See Note on Nineteenth Amendment, infra.)

But the Court did not continue to develop this synthetic interpretation of the Fourteenth and Nineteenth Amendments. By the end of the 1920s, courts had limited the Nineteenth Amendment's importance to the question of voting, and by 1937, as Chapter 5 recounts, the Court overruled *Adkins*'s freedom-of-contract doctrine as an outmoded relic of *Lochner*-era jurisprudence.[4] Whatever promise *Adkins* may have held for the equal treatment of women in the workplace was repudiated in Goesaert v. Cleary, 335 U.S. 464 (1948), which applied the minimum rationality standard to sustain a Michigan statute forbidding a woman to work as a bartender unless she was the "wife or daughter of the male owner" of the establishment. "Beguiling as the subject is," Justice Frankfurter's majority opinion stated, "it need

---

2. Many in the women's movement supported protective labor legislation, even in sex-based form, and so were wary of the Court's decision in *Adkins*. For more on the debate in the women's movement over protective labor legislation, see Joan G. Zimmerman, The Jurisprudence of Equality: The Women's Minimum Wage, the First Equal Rights Amendment, and *Adkins v. Children's Hospital*, 1905-1923, 78 J. Am. Hist. 188 (1991).

3. See Siegel, She the People, supra n.1, at 1012-1019, which argues that the Court in *Adkins* recognized the Nineteenth Amendment as embodying a sex equality norm that extended beyond the voting booth.

4. You will recall from Chapter 5 that *West Coast Hotel* (1937) employed an extremely deferential form of review to uphold a minimum wage law that treated women differently than men.

not detain us long." After noting the "historic calling" of "the alewife, sprightly and ribald," Frankfurter explained that "[t]he Fourteenth Amendment did not tear history up by the roots." In his view,

> Michigan could, beyond question, forbid all women from working behind a bar. This is so despite the vast changes in the social and legal position of women. The fact that women may now have achieved the virtues that men have long claimed as their prerogatives and now indulge in vices that men have long practiced, does not preclude the States from drawing a sharp line between the sexes, certainly in such matters as the regulation of the liquor traffic. See the Twenty-First Amendment. . . . The Constitution does not require legislatures to reflect sociological insight, or shifting social standards, any more than it requires them to keep abreast of the latest scientific standards.

Noting that Michigan did allow some women to tend bar, Frankfurter wrote that "while Michigan may deny to all women opportunities for bartending, Michigan cannot play favorites among women without rhyme or reason." Sufficient rhyme and reason, however, was found in Michigan's presumed assumption that "the oversight assured through ownership of a bar by a barmaid's husband or father minimizes hazards that may confront a barmaid without such protecting oversight. This Court is certainly not in a position to gainsay such belief by the Michigan legislature." Because "the line they have drawn is not without a basis in reason, we cannot give ear to the suggestion that the real impulse behind this legislation was an unchivalrous desire of male bartenders to try to monopolize the calling."

A similar view of gender relations appears in Hoyt v. Florida, 368 U.S. 57 (1961), which upheld a law that included women on jury lists only when women requested it. Even though the law produced virtually all-male juries, the Court sustained the sex-based exemption against equal protection challenge, reasoning that "a woman is still regarded as the center of home and family life."[5]

Like *Bradwell* and *Muller, Hoyt* interpreted the Fourteenth Amendment through the lens of the family, reasoning that women's citizenship was expressed in different activities and arenas than men's.[6]

B. Movement Roots of Modern Sex Discrimination Law

For a century, the Court had looked to the family in defining women's rights under the Fourteenth Amendment. But change was in the air. A decade after *Hoyt,* the Court unanimously rejected this line of reasoning in Reed v. Reed, 404 U.S. 71, 76 (1971), a case in which the Court purported to apply only the minimal rationality standard, yet held that an Idaho law that preferred men over women as estate

---

5. *Hoyt* was overruled by Taylor v. Louisiana, 419 U.S. 522 (1975), which held that a criminal defendant was deprived of his Sixth Amendment right to a jury composed of a cross-section of the community by a practice of automatically exempting women from jury duty unless they had filed a declaration of their desire to serve. See also Duren v. Missouri, 439 U.S. 357 (1979).

6. For an account of *Hoyt* that analyzes the role of privileges for women in a legal order that systematically accorded women less authority than men, see Linda K. Kerber, No Constitutional Right to Be Ladies: Women and the Obligations of Citizenship 124-220 (1998).

administrators made "the very kind of arbitrary legislative choice forbidden by the Equal Protection Clause of the Fourteenth Amendment." The announcement represented a startling shift in the Court's interpretation of the amendment. For the first time in history, the Court used the Equal Protection Clause to invalidate a statute on the grounds that it discriminated against women, characterizing as "arbitrary" the kind of legislative distinction its previous cases had repeatedly characterized as reasonable. What accounts for this fundamental shift in constitutional understanding?

The Court's decision in *Reed* reflected years of concerted advocacy by a newly mobilizing women's movement, as veterans of the suffrage movement in the National Woman's Party were joined by women in the labor and civil rights movements who were inspired by the civil rights revolution of the 1960s. An early and crucial site of mobilization was President Kennedy's Commission on the Status of Women, which, beginning in 1961, brought together feminists from across the country and enabled them to develop strategies for coordinated action. The seeds of constitutional change first took root in the executive branch and over the decade spread to the legislature and then finally to the courts.

Women involved with the President's Commission assisted in the passage of two laws—the Equal Pay Act of 1963 and Title VII of the Civil Rights Act of 1964—that committed the federal government to enforcing sex equality principles. The Equal Pay Act required employers to provide male and female employees equal pay for equal work.[7] Given the extreme sex segregation of the labor force in the 1960s, the Act affected only a small number of women—those who were performing the same jobs as men. The Act did not address sex discrimination in hiring and promotion, the largest barriers to equal opportunity in employment. However, the hearings in the executive and legislative branches that led to passage of the Act gave visibility to the inequalities women faced in the labor force, and publicly acknowledged the value of their labor in the market, as well as the home. In this way the Equal Pay Act created foundations for the more far-reaching antidiscrimination regime that began in 1964 with the passage of Title VII of the Civil Rights Act.[8]

Debates over Title VII focused on race discrimination in employment. "Sex" was added to the list of impermissible grounds for discrimination by a Southern legislator known for his opposition to civil rights. Supporters of women's rights nevertheless rallied behind the amendment and secured its inclusion in the 1964 Civil Rights Act.[9] Initially, the federal government did little to enforce the provision.

7. Equal Pay Act of 1963, Pub. L. No. 88-38, 77 Stat. 56 (codified as amended at 29 U.S.C. §206(d) (2000)).

8. For more on the Commission and the Equal Pay Act, see Cynthia Harrison, On Account of Sex: The Politics of Women's Issues, 1945-1968, 89-105 (1988); Leila J. Rupp and Verta Taylor, Survival in the Doldrums: The American Women's Rights Movement, 1945 to the 1960s, 174-176 (1987); Mary Becker, The Sixties Shift to Formal Equality and the Courts: An Argument for Pragmatism and Politics, 40 Wm. & Mary L. Rev. 209 (1998).

9. For an account of the debates surrounding the enactment and early enforcement of the sex discrimination provisions of Title VII, see Cary Franklin, Inventing the "Traditional Concept" of Sex Discrimination, 125 Harv. L. Rev. 1307 (2012); see also Jo Freeman, How "Sex" Got into Title VII: Persistent Opportunism as a Maker of Public Policy, 9 Law & Ineq. 163 (1991). Congress expressed clear and unequivocal commitment to enforcing the sex equality provisions of the 1964 Civil Rights Act in 1972. See infra.

The National Organization for Women (NOW) was formed to pressure an Equal Employment Opportunity Commission (EEOC) more interested in racial justice than sex equality to enforce the prohibition on sex discrimination in the workplace. The struggle to secure enforcement of the new federal employment discrimination statute helped mobilize women around issues of workplace equality and forged bonds of commonality between the women's movement and the civil rights movement. Inclusion of sex in the Title VII framework suggested a new approach to questions of sex equality under the Fourteenth Amendment, demonstrating similarities in the dynamics of race and sex discrimination that, to this point in time, had eluded the courts.

The race-sex analogy was not new. The woman suffrage movement often invoked it in constitutional arguments over the shape of Reconstruction—but the political salience and appeal of the analogy waned with the repudiation of the New Departure, the demise of Reconstruction, and the spread of Jim Crow. The appeal and power of the race-sex analogy depended on contexts in which it was deployed. In the 1960s, the women's movement gave the analogy new life, as the movement sought to persuade courts and legislatures that women were entitled to the kinds of rights then accorded racial minorities.[10]

A path-breaking advocate of the race-sex analogy in this period was Pauli Murray, an African-American lawyer in the civil rights and women's rights movements, who played an important role in forging modern understandings of discrimination. As a young lawyer, Murray contributed to the NAACP's litigation strategy in Brown v. Board of Education, and in 1961, she was appointed to the President's Commission on the Status of Women. While serving on the commission and studying at Yale Law School (where she was the first African American to earn a J.S.D.), Murray authored a series of papers outlining a legal strategy for challenging sex discriminatory state action that drew on the litigation strategies and constitutional arguments of the civil rights movement. These arguments were first published in an article co-authored with Mary Eastwood after passage of Title VII entitled "Jane Crow and the Law."[11]

Murray argued that the legal victories of the civil rights movement could be replicated for the women's rights cause by persuading courts that sexism and racism were analogous and often overlapping forms of discrimination. To explain why discriminating by sex was wrong—at a time when courts viewed sex-based state action as rationally reflecting differences in the family roles of men and women—Murray employed the concept of the "stereotype" that the civil rights

---

10. See Serena Mayeri, "A Common Fate of Discrimination": Race-Gender Analogies in Legal and Historical Perspective, 110 Yale L.J. 1045 (2001). See generally Serena Mayeri, Reasoning from Race: Feminism, Law, and the Civil Rights Revolution (2011).

11. Pauli Murray and Mary O. Eastwood, Jane Crow and the Law: Sex Discrimination and Title VII, 34 Geo. Wash. L. Rev. 232 (1965). For more on Murray's views on the intersection of sex and race, see Alice Kessler-Harris, In Pursuit of Equity: Women, Men, and the Quest for Economic Citizenship in 20th-Century America 226-234 (2001); Serena Mayeri, Constitutional Choices: Legal Feminism and the Historical Dynamics of Change, 92 Cal. L. Rev. 755 (2004).

movement was then using to challenge the dynamics of ethnic and racial prejudice. By the 1960s, the civil rights movement had established that racial stereotyping "results in a partial blindness to the actual qualities of individuals, and consequently is a persistent and prolific breeding ground for irrational treatment of them."[12] Murray employed the stereotyping concept to challenge sex distinctions that were then commonly thought rationally to reflect physical differences between men and women. She argued that gender stereotypes, like racial and ethnic stereotypes, were insensitive to differences among individuals within a group, and engendered similar harms:[13]

> Stereotypes function to rationalize discriminatory attitudes and practices toward an identifiable group. When they are ascribed to groups on the basis of observable permanent biological characteristics such as race and sex, they resist change stubbornly. Sexual stereotypes have undergirded laws and customs which treat *all* women as a single class and make distinctions based upon the sole factor of their sex. They disregard the fact that women vary as individuals in their body structure, physical strength, intellectual and emotional capacities, aspirations and expectations, just as men do.

Murray had an opportunity to test arguments drawing on concepts of stereotyping and the race-sex analogy during the mid-1960s in White v. Crook, a suit brought by the American Civil Liberties Union (ACLU) challenging the exclusion of Black people and women from an Alabama jury that acquitted white defendants accused of murdering two civil rights workers. The three-judge panel that heard White v. Crook accepted the ACLU's claim that the de facto exclusion of Black people from jury service violated the Fourteenth Amendment. Declaring that its function was "to apply the Constitution as a living document to the legal cases and controversies of contemporary society," the district court also ruled that the de jure exclusion of women from jury service was arbitrary and so violated equal protection, even if the legislative history of the Fourteenth Amendment and case law applying the Equal Protection Clause had never been so construed.[14] Although the court ordered different remedies for the exclusion of Black people and women from jury service, its decision in White v. Crook vindicated Murray's belief in the race-sex analogy as a basis for making sex equality claims on the Fourteenth Amendment.[15]

The race-sex analogy was constitutionally elaborated by Ruth Bader Ginsburg, a young law professor and women's rights advocate chosen by the ACLU to write the appellant's Supreme Court brief in Reed v. Reed—the 1971 case in which the Court first invalidated a statute as violating the Equal Protection Clause because

---

12. Louis Lusky, The Stereotype: Hard Core of Racism, 13 Buff. L. Rev. 450 (1963-1964).

13. Pauli Murray, The Negro Woman's Stake in the Equal Rights Amendment, 6 Harv. C.R.-C.L. L. Rev. 253, 255 (1971).

14. White v. Crook, 251 F. Supp. 401, 408 (M.D. Ala. 1966).

15. For more on White v. Crook, see Kerber, No Constitutional Right to Be Ladies, supra n.6, at 197-199.

it discriminated on the basis of sex. Ginsburg's brief argued that under the Fourteenth Amendment[16]

> is presumptively impermissible to distinguish on the basis of congenital and unalterable biological traits of birth over which the individual has no control and for which he or she should not be penalized. Such conditions include not only race, a matter clearly within the "suspect classification" doctrine, but include as well the sex of the individual.

Ginsburg's brief in *Reed* urged the Court to take the unprecedented step of invalidating a sex-discriminatory statute by demonstrating how sex discrimination resembled the forms of race discrimination the Court had already invalidated under the Equal Protection Clause. The brief repeatedly emphasized the injustice of discrimination based on traits that were "immutable" and "highly visible," arguing that "American women have been stigmatized historically as an inferior class" and "lack political power to remedy the discriminatory treatment they are accorded in the law and in society generally." Because "legislators have found it easy to draw gross, stereotypical distinctions" on the basis of the sex characteristic, it was necessary for the Court to subject sex-based legislation to a particularly searching form of inquiry under the Fourteenth Amendment.[17]

Yet to persuade the Court to treat sex distinctions like race distinctions, women's advocates had to do more than assert the analogy: They had to demonstrate how laws enforcing traditional family roles injured women. The race-gender analogy was only persuasive to the extent that the movement could demonstrate that women's exclusion from certain forms of civic life was neither an inevitable nor a benign incident of their traditional roles as wives and mothers. This was the message of NOW, which was founded in 1966 at a meeting of the state commissions on the status of women.[18] Formed in an effort to pressure the EEOC to enforce Title VII's ban on sex discrimination, NOW's Statement of Purpose contained a broad declaration that women were entitled to participate in all of the core activities of citizenship on the same terms as men. Coauthored by Betty Friedan and Pauli Murray, NOW's Statement invited Americans to reimagine the social organization of the family so that it would no longer constitute an impediment to women's participation in public life:[19]

> WE BELIEVE that this nation has a capacity at least as great as other nations, to innovate new social institutions which will enable women to enjoy true equality of opportunity and responsibility in society, without conflict with their responsibilities as mothers and homemakers. . . . We do

---

16. Brief for Appellant, Reed v. Reed, 404 U.S. 71 (1971).

17. For more on Ginsburg's legal strategy in *Reed*, see Amy Leigh Campbell, Raising the Bar: Ruth Bader Ginsburg and the ACLU Women's Rights Project, 11 Tex. J. Women & L. 157 (2002); Ruth Cowan, Women's Rights Through Litigation, 8 Colum. Hum. Rts. L. Rev. 373 (1976).

18. For more on the founding of NOW, see Betty Friedan, It Changed My Life 91-232 (1976); Harrison, On Account of Sex, supra n.8, at 192-209.

19. Nat'l Org. for Women, Statement of Purpose (1966), reprinted in Feminist Chronicles, 1953-1993, at 159, 161-162 (Toni Carabillo et al. eds., 1993).

> not accept the traditional assumption that a woman has to choose between marriage and motherhood, on the one hand, and serious participation in industry or the professions on the other. We question the present expectation that all normal women will retire from job or profession for 10 or 15 years, to devote their full time to raising children, only to reenter the job market at a relatively minor level. . . . Above all, we reject the assumption that these problems are the unique responsibility of each individual women [sic], rather than a basic social dilemma which society must solve. True equality of opportunity and freedom of choice for women requires such practical, and possible innovations as a nationwide network of child-care center[s], which will make it unnecessary for women to retire completely from society until their children are grown, and national programs to provide retraining for women who have chosen to care for their own children full-time.

NOW's manifesto tied a claim of right to a claim about social structure: Vindicating women's right to equality with men required transforming the social organization of the family.

The movement made the organization of the family the centerpiece of its inaugural demonstrations. On August 26, 1970, NOW held a "Women's Strike For Equality" on the fiftieth anniversary of the ratification of the Nineteenth Amendment. The one-day strike was staged in 40 cities across the nation to publicize the movement's three core demands: Women sought access to abortion, publicly supported child-care, and equal opportunity in jobs and education.[20] The movement was arguing that equal opportunity required transformation of the conditions in which women bore and raised children.

By staging the strike on the fiftieth anniversary of the Nineteenth Amendment's ratification, NOW located its demands in a constitutional framework. In an era when the Court had not yet recognized sex discrimination claims under the Fourteenth Amendment or accorded constitutional protections to the abortion right, the strikers invoked the Nineteenth Amendment to assert that women had a constitutional right to equal citizenship with men. Their demands called attention to the fact that a half-century after the Nineteenth Amendment's ratification, the right to vote had not proven adequate to make women equal citizens with men, and that more was required.

By the late 1960s, those in the women's movement who sought constitutional change via amendment joined ranks with those who sought change through litigation, and the movement adopted a "dual strategy" for constitutional reform, seeking a more expansive interpretation of the Fourteenth Amendment and the

---

20. For more on the strike, see Shirley Bernard, The Women's Strike: August 26, 1970 (Ph.D. thesis, Union Graduate School of Experimenting Colleges and Universities-Antioch College 1975); Jo Freeman, The Politics of Women's Liberation: A Case Study of an Emerging Social Movement and Its Relation to the Policy Process 84-85 (1975); Ruth Rosen, The World Split Open: How the Modern Women's Movement Changed America 92-93 (2001); and Robert C. Post and Reva B. Siegel, Legislative Constitutionalism and Section Five Power: Policentric Interpretation of the Family and Medical Leave Act, 112 Yale L.J. 1943, 1988-2004 (2003).

enactment of an Equal Rights Amendment.[21] The success of the dual strategy and the growing power of the women's movement in the early 1970s engaged the attention of the Ninety-Second Congress. The Congress responded to NOW's constitutional claims by enacting an unprecedented number of federal protections for women's rights. In 1972, it passed, and sent to the states for ratification, the Equal Rights Amendment, and, that same year, applied Title VII to the states, in legislation that emphasized the urgency of combating sex discrimination in employment. Congress also enacted Title IX, which prohibited sex discrimination in all educational programs receiving federal funds, passed legislation prohibiting sex discrimination in public- and private-sector transactions, and enacted child-care legislation plainly responsive to movement demands for reforms that would alleviate conflicts between work and family.[22]

As Congress enacted legislation that recognized women as equal citizens, the Court responded. Indeed, when the Court took the first steps toward declaring sex a "suspect" classification under the Equal Protection Clause in the early 1970s, it was to this burst of lawmaking that a plurality of the Court pointed.

Frontiero v. Richardson

411 U.S. 677 (1973)

BRENNAN, J., joined by DOUGLAS, WHITE, and MARSHALL, JJ.

[In an effort to attract career personnel through reenlistment, Congress established a scheme for the provision of fringe benefits to members of the uniformed services on a competitive basis with business and industry. A member of the uniformed services with dependents was entitled to an increased "basic allowance for quarters" and a member's dependents were provided comprehensive medical and dental care, under 37 U.S.C. §§401, 403, and 10 U.S.C. §§1072, 1076.] Under these statutes, a serviceman may claim his wife as a "dependent" without regard to whether she is in fact dependent upon him for any part of her support. A servicewoman, on the other hand, may not claim her husband as a "dependent" under these programs unless he is in fact dependent upon her for over one-half of his support. . . .

I

[A]ppellant Sharron Frontiero, a lieutenant in the United States Air Force, sought increased quarters allowances, and housing and medical benefits for her husband, appellant Joseph Frontiero, on the ground that he was her "dependent." Although such benefits would automatically have been granted with respect to the wife of a male member of the uniformed services, appellant's application was denied because she failed to demonstrate that her husband was dependent on her

21. See Mayeri, Constitutional Choices, supra n.11, at 784-792.

22. For a more detailed account of these legislative innovations, see Freeman, The Politics of Women's Liberation, supra, at 202-204; Post and Siegel, Legislative Constitutionalism, supra n.20, at 1995-1996.

for more than one-half of his support. Appellants then commenced this suit, contending that, by making this distinction, the statutes unreasonably discriminate on the basis of sex in violation of the Due Process Clause of the Fifth Amendment.[a]

In essence, appellants asserted that the discriminatory impact of the statutes is twofold: first, as a procedural matter, a female member is required to demonstrate her spouse's dependency, while no such burden is imposed upon male members; and second, as a substantive matter, a male member who does not provide more than one-half of his wife's support receives benefits, while a similarly situated female member is denied such benefits. Appellants therefore sought a permanent injunction against the continued enforcement of these statutes and an order directing the appellees to provide Lieutenant Frontiero with the same housing and medical benefits that a similarly situated male member would receive.

Although the legislative history of these statutes sheds virtually no light on the purposes underlying the differential treatment accorded male and female members, a majority of the three-judge District Court surmised that Congress might reasonably have concluded that, since the husband in our society is generally the "bread-winner" in the family—and the wife typically the "dependent" partner—"it would be more economical to require married female members claiming husbands to prove actual dependency than to extend the presumption of dependency to such members." Indeed, given the fact that approximately 99% of all members of the uniformed services are male, the District Court speculated that such differential treatment might conceivably lead to a "considerable saving of administrative expense and manpower."

II

At the outset, appellants contend that classifications based upon sex, like classifications based upon race, alienage, and national origin, are inherently suspect and must therefore be subjected to close judicial scrutiny. We agree and, indeed, find at least implicit support for such an approach in our unanimous decision only last Term in Reed v. Reed, 404 U.S. 71 (1971).

In *Reed*, the Court considered the constitutionality of an Idaho statute providing that, when two individuals are otherwise equally entitled to appointment as administrator of an estate, the male applicant must be preferred to the female. Appellant, the mother of the deceased, and appellee, the father, filed competing petitions for appointment as administrator of their son's estate. Since the parties, as parents of the deceased, were members of the same entitlement class, the statutory preference was invoked and the father's petition was therefore granted. Appellant claimed that this statute, by giving a mandatory preference to males over females without regard to their individual qualifications, violated the Equal Protection Clause of the Fourteenth Amendment.

The Court noted that the Idaho statute "provides that different treatment be accorded to the applicants on the basis of their sex; it thus establishes a classification subject to scrutiny under the Equal Protection Clause." Under "traditional"

---

a. "[W]hile the Fifth Amendment contains no equal protection clause, it does forbid discrimination that is 'so unjustifiable as to be violative of due process.'" Schneider v. Rusk, 377 U.S. 163, 168 (1964).

equal protection analysis, a legislative classification must be sustained unless it is "patently arbitrary" and bears no rational relationship to a legitimate governmental interest.

In an effort to meet this standard, appellee contended that the statutory scheme was a reasonable measure designed to reduce the workload on probate courts by eliminating one class of contests. Moreover, the appellee argued that the mandatory preference for male applicants was in itself reasonable since "men [are] as a rule more conversant with business affairs than . . . women." Indeed, appellee maintained that "it is a matter of common knowledge, that women still are not engaged in politics, the professions, business or industry to the extent that men are." And the Idaho Supreme Court, in upholding the constitutionality of this statute, suggested that the Idaho Legislature might reasonably have "concluded that in general men are better qualified to act as an administrator than are women."

Despite these contentions, however, the Court held the statutory preference for male applicants unconstitutional. In reaching this result, the Court implicitly rejected appellee's apparently rational explanation of the statutory scheme, and concluded that, by ignoring the individual qualifications of particular applicants, the challenged statute provided "dissimilar treatment for men and women who are . . . similarly situated."

The Court therefore held that, even though the State's interest in achieving administrative efficiency "is not without some legitimacy," "[t]o give a mandatory preference, to members of either sex over members of the other, merely to accomplish the elimination of hearings on the merits, is to make the very kind of arbitrary legislative choice forbidden by the [Constitution]. . . ." This departure from "traditional" rational-basis analysis with respect to sex-based classifications is clearly justified.

There can be no doubt that our Nation has had a long and unfortunate history of sex discrimination.[b] Traditionally, such discrimination was rationalized by an attitude of "romantic paternalism" which, in practical effect, put women, not on a pedestal, but in a cage. Indeed, this paternalistic attitude became so firmly rooted in our national consciousness that, 100 years ago, a distinguished Member of this Court was able to proclaim:

> Man is, or should be, woman's protector and defender. The natural and proper timidity and delicacy which belongs to the female sex evidently unfits it for many of the occupations of civil life. The constitution of the family organization, which is founded in the divine ordinance, as well as in the nature of things, indicates the domestic sphere as that which properly belongs to the domain and functions of womanhood. The harmony, not to say identity, of interests and views which belong, or should belong, to the family institution is repugnant to the idea of a woman adopting a distinct and independent career from that of her husband. . . .

---

b. Indeed, the position of women in this country at its inception is reflected in the view expressed by Thomas Jefferson that women should be neither seen nor heard in society's decisionmaking councils.

> The paramount destiny and mission of woman are to fulfill the noble and benign offices of wife and mother. This is the law of the Creator. Bradwell v. [Illinois, 83 U.S. (16 Wall.)] 130, 141 (1873) (Bradley, J., concurring).

As a result of notions such as these, our statute books gradually became laden with gross, stereotyped distinctions between the sexes and, indeed, throughout much of the 19th century the position of women in our society was, in many respects, comparable to that of Black people under the pre–Civil War slave codes. Neither slaves nor women could hold office, serve on juries, or bring suit in their own names, and married women traditionally were denied the legal capacity to hold or convey property or to serve as legal guardians of their own children. And although Black people were guaranteed the right to vote in 1870, women were denied even that right—which is itself "preservative of other basic civil and political rights"—until adoption of the Nineteenth Amendment half a century later.

It is true, of course, that the position of women in America has improved markedly in recent decades. Nevertheless, it can hardly be doubted that, in part because of the high visibility of the sex characteristic, women still face pervasive although at times more subtle, discrimination in our educational institutions, in the job market and, perhaps most conspicuously, in the political arena.[c]

Moreover, since sex, like race and national origin, is an immutable characteristic determined solely by the accident of birth, the imposition of special disabilities upon the members of a particular sex because of their sex would seem to violate "the basic concept of our system that legal burdens should bear some relationship to individual responsibility. . . ." And what differentiates sex from such non-suspect statuses as intelligence or physical disability, and aligns it with the recognized suspect criteria, is that the sex characteristic frequently bears no relation to ability to perform or contribute to society. As a result, statutory distinctions between the sexes often have the effect of invidiously relegating the entire class of females to inferior legal status without regard to the actual capabilities of its individual members.

We might also note that, over the past decade, Congress has itself manifested an increasing sensitivity to sex-based classifications. In Tit. VII of the Civil Rights Act of 1964, for example, Congress expressly declared that no employer, labor union, or other organization subject to the provisions of the Act shall discriminate against any individual on the basis of "race, color, religion, *sex*, or national origin." Similarly, the Equal Pay Act of 1963 provides that no employer covered by the Act "shall discriminate . . . between employees on the basis of *sex*," and §1 of the Equal Rights Amendment, passed by Congress on March 22, 1972, and submitted to the legislatures of the States for ratification, declares that "[e]quality of rights under the law shall not be denied or abridged by the United States or by any State on account of

---

c. It is true, of course, that when viewed in the abstract, women do not constitute a small and powerless minority. Nevertheless, in part because of past discrimination, women are vastly underrepresented in this Nation's decisionmaking councils. There has never been a female President, nor a female member of this Court. Not a single woman presently sits in the U.S. Senate, and only 14 women hold seats in the House of Representatives. And, as appellants point out, this underrepresentation is present throughout all levels of our State and Federal Government.

sex." Thus, Congress itself has concluded that classifications based upon sex are inherently invidious, and this conclusion of a coequal branch of Government is not without significance to the question presently under consideration.

With these considerations in mind, we can only conclude that classifications based upon sex, like classifications based upon race, alienage, or national origin, are inherently suspect, and must therefore be subjected to strict judicial scrutiny. Applying the analysis mandated by that stricter standard of review, it is clear that the statutory scheme now before us is constitutionally invalid.

III

The sole basis of the classification established in the challenged statutes is the sex of the individuals involved. . . . [T]he statutes operate so as to deny benefits to a female member, such as appellant Sharron Frontiero, who provides less than one-half of her spouse's support, while at the same time granting such benefits to a male member who likewise provides less than one-half of his spouse's support. Thus, to this extent at least, it may fairly be said that these statutes command "dissimilar treatment for men and women who are . . . similarly situated." Reed v. Reed.

Moreover, the Government concedes that the differential treatment accorded men and women under these statutes serves no purpose other than mere "administrative convenience." In essence, the Government maintains that, as an empirical matter, wives in our society frequently are dependent upon their husbands, while husbands rarely are dependent upon their wives. Thus, the Government argues that Congress might reasonably have concluded that it would be both cheaper and easier simply conclusively to presume that wives of male members are financially dependent upon their husbands, while burdening female members with the task of establishing dependency in fact.[d]

The Government offers no concrete evidence, however, tending to support its view that such differential treatment in fact saves the Government any money. In order to satisfy the demands of strict judicial scrutiny, the Government must demonstrate, for example, that it is actually cheaper to grant increased benefits with respect to *all* male members, than it is to determine which male members are in fact entitled to such benefits and to grant increased benefits only to those members whose wives actually meet the dependency requirement. Here, however, there is substantial evidence that, if put to the test, many of the wives of male members would fail to qualify for benefits. And in light of the fact that the dependency determination with respect to the husbands of female members is presently made solely on the basis of affidavits, rather than through the more costly hearing process, the Government's explanation of the statutory scheme is, to say the least, questionable.

In any case, our prior decisions make clear that, although efficacious administration of governmental programs is not without some importance, "the Constitution recognizes higher values than speed and efficiency." And when we enter the

---

d. It should be noted that these statutes are not in any sense designed to rectify the effects of past discrimination against women. On the contrary, these statutes seize upon a group of women who have historically suffered discrimination in employment, and rely on the effects of this past discrimination as a justification for heaping on additional economic disadvantages.

realm of "strict judicial scrutiny," there can be no doubt that "administrative convenience" is not a shibboleth, the mere recitation of which dictates constitutionality. On the contrary, any statutory scheme which draws a sharp line between the sexes, *solely* for the purpose of achieving administrative convenience, necessarily commands "dissimilar treatment for men and women who are . . . similarly situated," and therefore involves the "very kind of arbitrary legislative choice forbidden by the [Constitution]. . . ." We therefore conclude that, by according differential treatment to male and female members of the uniformed services for the sole purpose of achieving administrative convenience, the challenged statutes violate the Due Process Clause of the Fifth Amendment insofar as they require a female member to prove the dependency of her husband.[e]

Reversed.

Mr. Justice STEWART concurs in the judgment, agreeing that the statutes before us work an invidious discrimination in violation of the Constitution. Reed v. Reed, 404 U.S. 71.

POWELL, J., joined by BURGER, C.J., and BLACKMUN, J., concurring.

I agree that the challenged statutes constitute an unconstitutional discrimination against servicewomen in violation of the Due Process Clause of the Fifth Amendment, but I cannot join the opinion of Mr. Justice Brennan, which would hold that all classifications based upon sex, "like classifications based upon race, alienage, and national origin," are "inherently suspect and must therefore be subjected to close judicial scrutiny." It is unnecessary for the Court in this case to characterize sex as a suspect classification, with all of the far-reaching implications of such a holding. Reed v. Reed, 404 U.S. 71 (1971), which abundantly supports our decision today, did not add sex to the narrowly limited group of classifications which are inherently suspect. In my view, we can and should decide this case on the authority of *Reed* and reserve for the future any expansion of its rationale. There is another, and I find compelling, reason for deferring a general categorizing of sex classifications invoking the strictest test of judicial scrutiny. The Equal Rights Amendment, which if adopted will resolve the substance of this precise question, has been approved by the Congress and submitted for ratification by the States. If this Amendment is duly adopted, it will represent the will of the people accomplished in the manner prescribed by the Constitution. By acting prematurely and unnecessarily, as I view it, the Court has assumed a decisional responsibility at the very time when state legislatures, functioning within the traditional democratic process, are debating the proposed Amendment. It seems to me that this reaching out to pre-empt by judicial action a major political decision which is currently in process of resolution does not reflect appropriate respect for duly prescribed legislative processes.

There are times when this Court, under our system, cannot avoid a constitutional decision on issues which normally should be resolved by the elected

e. As noted earlier, the basic purpose of these statutes was to provide fringe benefits to members of the uniformed services in order to establish a compensation pattern which would attract career personnel through reenlistment. Our conclusion in no wise invalidates the statutory schemes except insofar as they require a female member to prove the dependency of her spouse.

representatives of the people. But democratic institutions are weakened, and confidence in the restraint of the Court is impaired, when we appear unnecessarily to decide sensitive issues of broad social and political importance at the very time they are under consideration within the prescribed constitutional processes.

REHNQUIST, J., dissents for the reasons stated by Judge Rives in his opinion for the District Court, Frontiero v. Laird, 341 F. Supp. 201 (1972).

DISCUSSION

1. *Stereotyping*: *Frontiero* is a pay discrimination case involving a practice, prevalent before enactment of the Equal Pay Act, of paying men and women different wages for the same work. In *Frontiero*, the government justified its decision to pay valuable dependent benefits to all male soldiers, but only to some female soldiers, by invoking what was then the most commonplace rationale for such discriminatory compensation practices. The government argued that men should receive more pay than women because most men needed to support their families, whereas most women did not.

How did the compensation scheme at issue in *Frontiero* reflect stereotyping? Was the government reasoning on the basis of faulty generalizations? If not, were there other forms of cognitive error that made the compensation policy constitutionally offensive? Is the belief that men often support their wives, while wives generally do not support their husbands, a form of prejudice? Does it denigrate women, or men? Does the *Frontiero* opinion suggest that it is wrong for government to support traditional family roles? Only in certain contexts? If so, why in this case? How is the policy struck down in *Frontiero* like or unlike the kinds of race-based state action invalidated in the cases you read in Chapter 7?

2. *Individuals versus groups*: Is the *Frontiero* opinion concerned about governmental practices that injure individuals, or groups? Can these concerns be disentangled? What difference does it make to emphasize one or the other? How might it bear on the way the Court evaluates the sex discrimination claims of men?

3. *Extending heightened scrutiny to other groups?* Justice Brennan's plurality opinion argues that the case for extending heightened scrutiny to sex discrimination depends on identifying similarities between race and sex discrimination. How should courts decide what other kinds of discrimination—in addition to sex discrimination—are sufficiently "like" race discrimination to warrant heightened equal protection scrutiny? What features of race discrimination are salient for purposes of this inquiry?

A February 2011 letter from Attorney General Eric Holder to congressional leaders regarding the Defense of Marriage Act (DOMA) explains the Department of Justice's position that heightened scrutiny applies to laws classifying on the basis of sexual orientation. Holder describes the relevant inquiry:[23]

---

23. Letter from Eric H. Holder, Jr., Attorney Gen. of the U.S., to Rep. John A. Boehner, Speaker, U.S. House of Representatives (Feb. 23, 2011) (footnotes and citations omitted), available at http://www.justice.gov/opa/pr/2011/February/11-ag-223.html. For more discussion of the use of the race analogy framework and factors in determining whether to apply heightened scrutiny to sexual orientation discrimination, see Chapter 9, infra.

> [The Supreme Court has] rendered a number of decisions that set forth the criteria that should inform this and any other judgment as to whether heightened scrutiny applies: (1) whether the group in question has suffered a history of discrimination; (2) whether individuals "exhibit obvious, immutable, or distinguishing characteristics that define them as a discrete group"; (3) whether the group is a minority or is politically powerless; and (4) whether the characteristics distinguishing the group have little relation to legitimate policy objectives or to an individual's "ability to perform or contribute to society." . . .

Consider the criteria described above. To what other groups might the race analogy extend? Do classifications made on the basis of sexual orientation warrant heightened scrutiny? (See Chapter 9, infra.) Classifications based on disability? (See the discussion in Section V, infra.) What other groups can you identify that are enough "like race" that heightened scrutiny is required?

4. Why might the case for heightened scrutiny depend on the extent to which challenged discrimination resembles race discrimination? Is the race analogy relevant as a matter of original understanding? Or does it simply supply a framework for evaluating unfairness? Perhaps it offers an easily administrable heuristic to settle disputes about the interpretation of an open-ended (or implicit) guarantee such as the equality guarantee of the Fifth and Fourteenth Amendments. What other constitutional values does the analogy vindicate? Does it limit judicial decisionmaking in the service of democratic self-determination? Federalism? Might some other analytical framework better vindicate the relevant constitutional values?

5. What significance did debates over ratification of the ERA have for the Court in *Frontiero?* Justice Powell argued that one Congress sent the ERA to the states for ratification, courts should have deferred to the political process in deciding sex discrimination cases. By contrast, Justice Brennan and the plurality interpreted Congress's action as a reason to apply strict scrutiny. Was it possible for the Justices not to listen to the ongoing debate? Was it their duty to listen? Perhaps equally important, how should they have listened, and what should they have drawn from the debates over the ERA?

Drawing on *Frontiero*'s text and conference notes, Serena Mayeri offers this account of how the ERA campaign influenced the Justices' deliberation in the case:[24]

> Brennan's plurality opinion in *Frontiero* suggests that the ERA's pendency moved at least four justices to the view that, as Brennan put it in a memorandum to Powell, "the 'suspect' approach is the proper one and . . . further . . . now is the time, and this is the case, to make that clear." . . . Freely admitting that the ERA's prospects for ratification were dim, Brennan couldn't "see that we gain anything by awaiting what is at best an uncertain outcome." . . . Decisive congressional action on the subjcct was enough for Justice Byron White, too. He wrote to his colleagues during the *Frontiero* deliberations: "I would think that sex is a suspect classification, if for

24. Mayeri, Constitutional Choices, supra n.11, at 827-828.

> no other reason than the fact that Congress has submitted a constitutional amendment making sex discrimination unconstitutional." . . . White went on to declare that he "would remain of the same view whether the amendment is adopted or not." . . . The language of the *Frontiero* plurality opinion is likewise unambiguous on this point, making clear that the Court's newfound recognition of a "long and unfortunate history of sex discrimination" was indebted to unprecedented, tangible congressional support of an antidiscrimination principle. It also seems likely that the backdrop of legislative solicitude for women's rights influenced the justices who went along with the result in *Frontiero* without endorsing strict scrutiny. Absent the women's movement's renaissance and its legislative manifestations, it is hard to imagine Justices Burger, Blackmun, Stewart, and Powell spontaneously responding to feminist lawyers' arguments.

Which approach to the constitutional question in *Frontiero* was correct? The position adopted by the plurality opinion Justice Brennan authored? Or the concurring opinion Justice Powell authored? Or was there yet some other approach that the Court should have adopted?

6. As you think about these questions, consider whether the Court is best understood as a countermajoritarian body, or whether instead the Court acts in response to popular social movements. If the Supreme Court and the federal courts decide to follow changing social and political trends, they may obviate the need for Article V amendments. This happened during the New Deal, for example. Considerable talk of Article V solutions to the crisis over federal power dried up as a result of the Court's post-1937 jurisprudence.[25] Because it is so difficult to pass Article V amendments, taking even a little wind out of the sails of proponents may be enough to kill an amendment, particularly when the amendment is controversial, as the ERA surely was.

If this theory about the interplay between Supreme Court decisionmaking and Article V amendment is correct, what does this say about the Court's appropriate role in interpreting the Constitution? Should courts exercise judicial restraint and preserve existing understandings of the Constitution, leaving it to mobilized citizens to amend the Constitution? Or, on the contrary, should courts interpret the Constitution in response to the claims of social movements with demonstrated broad and deep support from the American public, whether or not these movements garner the supermajority support required for an Article V amendment?

Judicial review is often described as countermajoritarian. Consider the fact that the ERA was in fact approved by a significant majority of the states representing a significant majority of the population. Does it make sense to criticize Brennan's position in *Frontiero* as "countermajoritarian" if its doctrine was, arguably, approved by legislative majorities at both the federal and state levels and failed to become part of the formal text only because of the strikingly countermajoritarian procedures of Article V?

---

25. Bruce Ackerman, 2 We The People: Transformations 315, 334-335 (1998).

NOTE: REASONING FROM RACE IN *FRONTIERO* AND BEYOND

As we have seen, the modern women's movement built its case in part by framing an analogy between race and sex discrimination, a strategy to which judges responded. In *Frontiero*, for example, Justice Brennan wrote: "[T]hroughout much of the 19th century the position of women in our society was, in many respects, comparable to that of blacks under the pre-Civil War slave codes." Serena Mayeri has described the power of such analogies: "They can inspire empathy and understanding of harms previously unrecognized, and they may be desirable, if not necessary, in an adjudicative system based upon fidelity to precedent."[26] Indeed, the first instinct of many judges, lawyers, commentators, and students in addressing the constitutionality of sex discrimination is to treat race discrimination as a point of comparison and to inquire to what extent gender classifications share the characteristics that call racial classifications into disfavor. Courts use two overlapping strategies to consider the applicability of the race analogy: (a) by recalling the rationales for treating racial classifications as suspect and asking whether they apply to gender classifications, and (b) by identifying the features of race that make it seem special and asking whether gender shares these features.

One question to face at the outset is whether this comparison of rationales and traits focuses on the right questions. If we want to understand the similarities and differences between racial and sexual inequality, we may have to look past particular traits considered in isolation, and toward the social structures, institutions, sets of social meanings, and accepted justifications that have traditionally been used to subordinate Black people on the one hand and women on the other. There are important differences between the forms of racial and sexual inequality. Whereas strategies for subordination of Black people emphasize separation and degradation, subordination of women has been achieved largely through expectations about family life and role differentiation. Moreover, because of romantic love and family connections, men often express paternalistic attitudes toward women rather than overt disdain and contempt. Although it was common during the Jim Crow era to argue that Black people were biologically inferior to whites, this argument has gone out of fashion and is generally understood to be invidious and racist. On the other hand, it is quite commonplace to hear biological justifications for sex-differentiated roles and for separate facilities for women. To what extent is the invocation of biological differences appropriate and to what extent does it disguise or misrepresent social structures that subordinate women to men? As you read this chapter, consider how the race analogy might help make visible the injuries of sex inequality and in what ways it might efface them. In what ways might it hamper recognition of one group's distinctive experience of inequality to compare their experience to that of another group?

The race-sex analogy has also been criticized for obscuring the distinctive ways in which women of color experience discrimination on the basis of race *and* sex. Individuals have multiple, simultaneous affiliations; intersectionality is the name sometimes given to the special problems that arise from the crosscutting nature

26. Mayeri, "A Common Fate of Discrimination," supra n.10, at 1046. See generally Mayeri, Reasoning from Race, supra n.10.

of identity. Serena Mayeri has suggested that "by stressing the parallel, rather than the intersectional, synthetic, and overlapping, aspects of various forms of inequality" the race-sex analogy "can obscure the experiences of individuals and groups who suffer discrimination among multiple axes."[27] The race-sex analogy may imply that men are the primary victims of race discrimination and white women are the primary victims of sex discrimination. As described earlier, however, the analogy emerged in the 1960s in large part due to the efforts of Pauli Murray, who sought to address the unique problems of intersectionality. Murray realized that without a complementary sex equality movement, progress toward racial equality would only benefit Black men.[28] She noted that "dual victimization" created many disadvantages for Black women and explained: "Because these disadvantages are not wholly attributable to racial status, they cannot be remedied by policies directed solely against racial discrimination."[29] Further, Murray envisioned the race-sex analogy as an opportunity to highlight the distinct experiences of African-American women with respect to sex equality. She explained that Black women experienced sexism differently than white women, with "neither the advantages of the idealizations of 'womanhood' and 'motherhood' which are part of American mythology, nor the 'protections' extended to women. . . ."[30] Murray advocated for women's rights litigation under the Fourteenth Amendment in part as a means by which to link the civil rights and women's rights movements at a time when the pro-ERA movement was using racist appeals in an attempt to win support from Southern segregationist legislators.[31] The race-sex analogy in that era connected the anti-racist and anti-feminist movements as never before.[32] As you read this chapter, consider whether strategies to combat sex discrimination might address or obscure intersectionality.

NOTE: THE EQUAL RIGHTS AMENDMENT

Between 1923 and 1972, resolutions proposing an equal rights amendment were introduced in every term of Congress. In 1972, Congress proposed the following amendment for ratification by state legislatures:

> Section 1. Equality of rights under the law shall not be denied or abridged by the United States or by any State on account of sex.
>
> Section 2. The Congress shall have the power to enforce, by appropriate legislation, the provisions of this article.

In submitting the ERA to the states for ratification, Congress was responding to the women's movement, whose arguments and activities in the 1960s and early 1970s are described in the opening pages of this chapter. At the point that Congress submitted the amendment to the states for ratification, the ERA seemed

---

27. Id. at 1049.

28. Id. at 1063.

29. Murray, The Negro Woman's Stake in the Equal Rights Amendment, supra n.13, at 256.

30. Id. at 254.

31. Mayeri, Constitutional Choices, supra n.11, at 764.

32. Mayeri, "A Common Fate of Discrimination," supra n.10, at 1070-1072.

to have broad-based social support. The House of Representatives voted 354-23 in favor of the amendment; the Senate, in turn, overwhelmingly endorsed it by a vote of 84-8 on March 22, 1972. Hawaii unanimously approved the amendment that very day, 25 minutes after learning of the Senate's vote. Delaware, Nebraska, and New Hampshire followed suit the next day, with Idaho and Iowa joining these states on March 24. By early 1973, 30 of the 38 states needed to ratify had endorsed the amendment, most of them unanimously or by lopsided votes.[33]

Thereafter, however, a vigorous anti-ERA movement successfully blocked approval in most of the remaining states, so that by 1977 only 35 states had endorsed the amendment. By the initial expiration date of the ERA, March 22, 1979, 35 states had ratified the amendment, just three short of the requirement for passage. However, four of those states voted to rescind their ratification. After a heated debate, Congress rejected these states' desires and voted to extend the ratification period for three additional years to 1982. Despite the extension, the ERA failed to garner approval in any more states. The proposed amendment expired on June 30, 1982.[34]

The movement to block the constitutional amendment was led by Phyllis Schlafly, who founded STOP ERA in 1972. The group was the best organized and most prominent of a number of anti-ERA organizations, many of which were women-led and predominantly female, including American Women Already Well Endowed (AWARE), Scratch Women's Lib, and Happiness of Womenhood (HOW). Schlafly and her allies viewed claims for equal citizenship advanced by the women's movement as threatening traditional households, diminishing the status and security of those women who cared for family members while depending on male breadwinners. In an essay entitled "What's Wrong with 'Equal Rights' for Women," Schlafly denounced ERA supporters:[35]

> They view the home as a prison, and the wife and mother as a slave. To these women's libbers, marriage means dirty dishes and dirty laundry. . . .
>
> Women's lib is a total assault on the role of the American woman as wife and mother, and on the family as the basic unit of society.
>
> Women's libbers are promoting free sex instead of the "slavery" of marriage. They are promoting Federal "day-care centers" for babies instead of homes. They are promoting abortions instead of families.

Schlafly mobilized opposition to the ERA by suggesting it threatened fundamental changes in gender arrangements. She imputed to the ERA power to effectuate social change of a kind that ERA supporters insisted was beyond the amendment's ambit.[36] At various points Schlafly or her supporters suggested that, as a result of the ERA, private schools would have to be coed; all sports, including contact sports, would be coed; there would be government-funded abortions

---

33. See Jane J. Mansbridge, Why We Lost the ERA 12-13 (1986); Janet K. Boles, The Politics of the Equal Rights Amendment 2-3, tbl. 1.1 (1979).

34. Mansbridge, Why We Lost the ERA, supra, at 13. The following states failed to ratify the ERA: Alabama, Arizona, Arkansas, Florida, Georgia, Illinois, Louisiana, Mississippi, Missouri, Nevada, North Carolina, Oklahoma, South Carolina, Utah, and Virginia. Boles, The Politics of the Equal Rights Amendment, supra, at 3, tbl. 1.1.

35. Quoted in Mansbridge, Why We Lost the ERA, supra n.33, at 104.

36. Id. at 110-115.

and homosexual school teachers; women would be forced into combat; men would refuse to support their wives; the government would take away a woman's right to her home and support of her children; and the government would legalize homosexual marriages and adoption by homosexuals.[37]

The themes Schlafly sounded were voiced by critics in positions of government authority, as well. In 1970, when William Rehnquist was Assistant Attorney General, he wrote a memo to President Nixon's special consultant Leonard Garment advising Garment of the ERA supporters' "doctrinaire insistence upon rigid equality between men and women":[38]

> I cannot help thinking that there is also present somewhere within this movement a virtually fanatical desire to obscure not only legal differentiation between men and women, but insofar as possible, physical distinctions between the sexes. I think there are overtones of dislike and distaste for the traditional difference between men and women in the family unit, and in some cases very probably a complete rejection of the woman's traditionally different role in this regard.

The ERA gathered renewed interest during the 2010s. In 2008, a Facebook page dedicated to support for the ERA began discussing sexist responses to Hillary Clinton's candidacy for the Democratic nomination for President in 2008 and protesting the Supreme Court's pay equity decision in Lilly Ledbetter v. Goodyear Tire & Rubber Co., 550 U.S. 618 (2007).[39] After Donald Trump became President, prompting a national Women's March in January 2017, focus on the ERA's ratification intensified.[40] Shortly thereafter, in March 2017, Nevada's Legislature ratified the 1972 proposal. Illinois followed in 2018, and on January 15, 2020, Virginia voted to ratify the ERA, bringing the total to 38 states who, at one point or another, have ratified the ERA since 1972. However, 5 states had rescinded their ratifications in the 1970s: Nebraska (1973), Tennessee (1974), Idaho (1977), Kentucky (1978),

---

37. See, e.g., ERA and Homosexual "Marriages," Phyllis Schlafly Rep. (Eagle Forum, Alton, Ill.), Sept. 1974, at §2; E.R.A. Means Abortion and Population Shrinkage, Phyllis Schlafly Rep., Dec. 1974, at §2; Will E.R.A. Make Child-Care the State's Job?, Phyllis Schlafly Rep., Nov. 1975, at §2; The Family and the Future of America, Phyllis Schlafly Rep., Oct. 1978, at §2; The International Human Rights Treaties, Phyllis Schlafly Rep., Dec. 1979, at §1; Phyllis Schlafly, The Power of the Positive Woman (1977). See also Jane De Hart-Mathews and Donald Mathews, The Cultural Politics of the ERA's Defeat, in Rights of Passage: The Past and Future of the ERA 44, 48-51 (Joan Hoff-Wilson ed., 1986) (discussing anxieties about the ERA undermining traditional womanhood and blurring sex roles in areas such as the military, sex crimes, abortion, integrated restrooms, homosexuality, and the family).

38. Memorandum from William Rehnquist, Assistant Attorney General, to Leonard Garment, Special Counsel to the President, reprinted in Rehnquist, ERA Would Threaten Family Unit, Legal Times, Sept. 15, 1986, at 4.

39. For the ERA Facebook page, see https://www.facebook.com/ERAusa/.

40. For a short history of the recent mobilization, see Dahlia Lithwick, The ERA Is Back: The '70s-era constitutional amendment could be the perfect remedy for the #MeToo era, Slate, Apr. 23, 2018, https://slate.com/news-and-politics/2018/04/the-equal-rights-amendment-could-be-the-perfect-remedy-for-the-metoo-era.html; The Equal Rights Amendment: Unfinished Business for the Constitution, http://www.equalrightsamendment.org/; Jessica Newirth, Equal Means Equal: Why the Time for an Equal Rights Amendment Is Now (2015).

and South Dakota (1979).[41] This raises the question of whether Virginia's ratification counts as the 38th state needed to ratify.[42]

The day after Virginia ratified, the National Archives announced that it would not take any action to certify the ERA as part of the Constitution. It stated that it would follow the advice of the Department of Justice's Office of Legal Counsel (OLC), which had issued a memo arguing that it was too late for states to ratify the amendment because the deadline had passed.[43]

On February 13, 2020, the House of Representatives voted to lift the ratification deadline by a vote of 232-183.[44]

Virginia filed suit in federal district court, asserting that the Constitution had been amended because the deadline in the joint resolution supporting the ERA as initially sent to the states was outside Congress's Article V powers. The state asked the court to order the archivist to publish the amendment.[45]

What is the legal effect of these events? Has the Constitution been amended?

DISCUSSION

1. *Failure or Success?* The ERA was not ratified in the 1970s or the 1980s, but did it fail? David Strauss calls the ERA the "leading recent example of [the] . . . rejected, yet ultimately triumphant" constitutional amendment:[46]

> Today, it is difficult to identify any respect in which constitutional law is different from what it would have been if the ERA had been adopted. For the last quarter-century, the Supreme Court has acted as if the Constitution contains a provision forbidding discrimination on the basis of gender. The Court requires an "exceedingly persuasive" justification for gender classifications, and it invalidates gender classifications that rest on what it considers "'archaic and overbroad' generalization[s]," such as the

---

41. Thomas H. Neale, Cong. Res. Serv., The Proposed Equal Rights Amendment: Contemporary Ratification Issues, (December 29, 2019), https://crsreports.congress.gov/product/pdf/R/R42979/19.

42. See Rachel Frank, Previewing the ERA Debates, Balkinization, https://balkin.blogspot.com/2018/06/previewing-era-debates.html, on which this discussion note is based.

43. Office of Legal Counsel, Ratification of the Equal Rights Amendment (Jan. 6, 2020), https://www.justice.gov/olc/file/1235176/download; US Archives confirms it won't take steps to certify ERA, Associated Press, Jan. 28, 2020, https://apnews.com/0b1f3d4cb590caab15e35d24c9997fd8.

44. H.J. Res. 79 (Feb. 13, 2020), https://www.congress.gov/bill/116th-congress/house-joint-resolution/79/text.

45. For a discussion of the issues in the lawsuit, see Julie Suk, Who Decides the Future of the Equal Rights Amendment?, Take Care, July 6, 2020, https://takecareblog.com/blog/who-decides-the-future-of-the-equal-rights-amendment.

46. David A. Strauss, The Irrelevance of Constitutional Amendments, 114 Harv. L. Rev. 1457, 1476-1477 (2001). Other commentators have offered similar interpretations of the ERA's defeat. See, e.g., Robert C. Post, The Supreme Court, 2002 Term—Foreword: Fashioning the Legal Constitution: Culture, Courts, and the Law, 117 Harv. L. Rev. 4, 55-56 (2003).

view that women are less likely than men to work outside the home. The Court does treat gender-based classifications differently from race-based classifications—the latter being the paradigmatic form of discrimination forbidden by the Fourteenth Amendment—but it has justified the difference not on the ground that the ERA was rejected, but rather on the ground that the two forms of classification sometimes operate differently.

Strauss argues that the amendment process is "irrelevant" because the Constitution is best understood on the model of the common law, a body of law elaborated by judicial interpretation that does not depend on the content of the text. Others disagree, pointing out that the Constitution's embodiment *as* a text that can be debated and amended makes the Constitution the object of mobilization, which in turn helps ensure that interpretations by legal professionals remain informed by evolving popular understandings.[47] William N. Eskridge, Jr., observes that "[t]he power of the women's movement was such that the Court felt impelled in the 1970s to rule unconstitutional most invidious sex discriminations."[48]

On this account, the ERA succeeded in changing the Constitution's interpretation by provoking popular debate about the meaning of equal citizenship. Citizens who believed the Court was wrong to uphold sex discriminatory laws moved to amend the Constitution. The possibility of amending the Constitution to recognize women's equal citizenship prompted social mobilization, countermobilization, and energetic debate about the meaning of equality in the family, the military, and other institutions—a debate in which proponents and opponents of the ERA were ultimately obliged to address each other's arguments in an effort to persuade the public. The Article V framework thus served a crucial constitutional function even if it failed to produce changes in the Constitution's text: It channeled popular debate over constitutional values and ensured that judicial interpretation of the Constitution was tutored by evolving public understanding of the Constitution's meaning.[49]

2. *The ERA's influence on the Supreme Court.* Attending to the interplay of interpretive and amending processes makes salient not only the ways in which the Court responded to the views of the ERA's supporters, but also the ways that the Court responded to the views of the ERA's opponents. As you read the cases in this chapter, especially cases like *Geduldig*, *Feeney*, and *Rostker*, infra, consider how the Court may have construed the Constitution's equal protection guarantees in response to views expressed by the ERA's opponents concerning the enduring significance of sex differentiation, in matters of family life and of war. Chapter 9 describes the influence of the ERA's opponents on the Court's due process jurisprudence.

As we begin to explore the relationship of the ERA campaign and the law of equal protection and due process, it becomes more difficult to characterize this

---

47. See Reva B. Siegel, Text in Contest: Gender and the Constitution from a Social Movement Perspective, 150 U. Pa. L. Rev. 297 (2001).

48. William N. Eskridge, Jr., Channeling: Identity-Based Social Movements and Public Law, 150 U. Pa. L. Rev. 419, 502 (2001).

49. See Reva B. Siegel, Constitutional Culture, Social Movement Conflict and Constitutional Change: The Case of the De Facto ERA, 94 Cal. L. Rev. 1323 (2006).

chapter of Article V history. Can we say that the Court decisively adopted the views of groups mobilized for, or against, constitutional change—or did it speak for Americans torn between them?

3. *The ERA's reemergence in the 2020s: the role of time limits.* The renewed interest in the ERA in the twenty-first century raises a host of constitutional questions. Can states disregard time limits set by Congress? One might distinguish between time limits which appear in the actual text of the proposal (call these textual time limits) and time limits which appear only in the congressional resolution that sends the proposed amendment to the states (call these proposal time limits). Amendments 18 and 20-22 have textual time limits; later amendments (with the notable exception of the Twenty-Seventh, to be discussed shortly) have included time limits in the congressional proposal. One might argue, as Nevada legislators did in 2017, that while states cannot ratify a proposed amendment which, by its own terms, expires on a certain date, they need not be bound by time limits that appear only in the congressional proposal that accompanies the text.[50]

Article V specifies that "[t]he Congress, whenever two thirds of both houses shall deem it necessary, *shall propose amendments* to this Constitution." Such proposals "shall be valid to all intents and purposes, as part of this Constitution, when ratified by the legislatures of three fourths of the several states, or by conventions in three fourths thereof, *as the one or the other mode of ratification may be proposed by the Congress.*"

Defenders of congressional prerogatives might argue that this language gives Congress complete power to decide both the nature of the proposal and the conditions under which ratification becomes effective. Defenders of state prerogatives might respond that the language does no such thing: Congress merely has the power to decide whether ratifications will be by state legislatures or by state conventions; hence, it may not impose additional conditions. For this reason, the 1982 extension was completely unnecessary, and its expiration was irrelevant.

In Dillon v. Gloss, 256 U.S. 368 (1921), the Supreme Court held that Congress had the power to impose time limits on a proposed amendment to the Constitution, and that seven years was a reasonable requirement. (*Dillon* involved the Eighteenth Amendment, which included time limits in the text of the amendment itself). Conversely, the Supreme Court held in Coleman v. Miller, 307 U.S. 433 (1939), that if Congress chooses not to add time limits, proposals remain alive indefinitely. The Court argued that the question of whether ratification is timely is a political question, left to Congress's judgment. *Coleman* involved a proposed Child Labor Amendment (which would have given Congress the power to pass laws regulating child labor); both the Child Labor Amendment and the Nineteenth Amendment contained no time limits, unlike Amendments 18 and 20-26.

Note that if one accepts that Congress gets to make decisions about ratification, it might also follow that Congress has the power to extend the deadline if it

50. Colin Dwyer & Carrie Kaufman, Nevada Ratifies The Equal Rights Amendment . . . 35 Years After The Deadline, Morning Edition, National Public Radio, March 21, 2017, https://www.npr.org/sections/thetwo-way/2017/03/21/520962541/nevada-on-cusp-of-ratifying-equal-rights-amendment-35-years-after-deadline.

chooses. That would mean that the 1982 extension was valid. But what if a state (such as Nevada and Illinois) ratifies after the extension has expired? Again, there are several possibilities. The ratifications after 1982 might be invalid. Or Congress may accept these ratifications as valid retroactively, if it passes a new joint resolution promulgating the ratification of the new amendment. (Query: Would such a promulgating resolution require a two-thirds vote of both houses or only a simple majority? Note that the text of Article V says nothing about Congress's role in promulgation. From a structural perspective, does it make better sense to hold a promulgating resolution to the supermajority standards of an Article V proposing resolution, or to ordinary majority standards?)

4. *Contemporaneous ratification: The problem of transgenerational amendments.* Behind these debates are larger questions about the purposes behind Article V.

One might argue that too much time has passed for the ERA to be ratified. Congressional amendments should reflect the will of a supermajority of Americans, which must be expressed within a bounded period of time — perhaps seven years (as *Dillon* suggested), or within a single generation.

On the other hand, consider the Twenty-Seventh Amendment, which was the second of the original 12 proposed by Congress in 1789. The third through twelfth proposals became Amendments 1 through 10, what we now call the Bill of Rights. The Madison Amendment, as it is sometimes called, was finally ratified in 1992, and became Amendment 27. The 200 years between proposal and ratification of the Twenty-Seventh Amendment are many times longer than the 40-some years that have elapsed since the ERA was sent to the states in 1972.

5. *Concurrent ratification: The problem of rescissions.* A different objection is that five states have rescinded their ratifications. That means that ratification requires six more states, not just one. The argument for this view is that a valid amendment to the Constitution requires the *concurrent* agreement of three quarters of the states, even if all of the states ratify at different points in time. The agreement of the states is not concurrent if one of the states withdraws consent before the finish line is reached.

On the other hand, the text of Article V only mentions ratifications, not rescissions. There is also some institutional precedent for not counting recessions. Congress refused to accept rescissions of the Fourteenth and Nineteenth Amendments (although it is not clear that counting the rescissions would have brought the total under three quarters of the states, see the discussion of the ratification of the Fourteenth Amendment in Chapter 4). The Attorneys General of the states that attempted to rescind the ERA expressed doubts about whether they were effective. Aside from text and precedent, are there good structural arguments for not counting rescissions? If a state may change its mind and vote for an amendment during the ratification process, why shouldn't it be able to change its mind and vote against?

6. *Promulgation: The problem of who decides and announces ratification.* The text of Article V does not make clear who decides when and whether an amendment has properly been ratified. One theory is that as soon as three quarters of the state legislatures ratify, the amendment is part of the Constitution. But this begs the question of what to do if there is a dispute about whether the requirements have

been met. (Suppose that a state tries to rescind, or there is a dispute about whether both houses of a state legislature properly voted on the proposal.) *Coleman* seems to suggest that the issue is a political question that is left to Congress. If so, then Congress can resolve any disputes — and bestow a much needed dose of political legitimacy — by passing a joint resolution promulgating a new amendment.

The Twenty-Seventh Amendment offers an interesting example. After Michigan ratified the Twenty-Seventh Amendment in May 1992, the United States Archivist proclaimed that a new amendment had been added to the Constitution, operating on the advice of the Department of Justice, which took the position that contemporaneous ratification and congressional approval were both unnecessary. Congress, however, passed a joint resolution two days later proclaiming that the Twenty-Seventh Amendment was now (i.e., when Congress spoke) a valid part of the Constitution. Because of popular upset about a financial scandal involving the House bank, both the President and Congress were eager to pronounce the Twenty-Seventh Amendment ratified: This showed that they were responding to public outcry about government corruption. As a result, the case of the Twenty-Seventh Amendment did not provide a clear example of who would decide if there was disagreement between the political branches.

Whatever the answer to this question, congressional promulgation has an additional advantage: It bestows legitimacy on the ratification process, and may help silence concerns about whether the process was consistent with constitutional norms. The ERA presents a case in which the ratification process has been protracted, but the constitutional norm at issue has grown in authority and interpretive significance in the intervening decades. Even so, opponents might raise objections; hence, congressional promulgation might help quiet concerns about the legitimacy of the ratification process. Thus, although congressional ratification may not be necessary legally, it may be important politically. (How might this affect your views about the proper voting rules for promulgation, as discussed in note 1, supra?) Suppose that Congress passed a joint resolution promulgating the ERA, and a plaintiff brought suit under the amendment. How, if at all, would or should congressional promulgation influence federal courts' judgment about whether the amendment was properly part of the Constitution?

7. *Interpretation: What would a new amendment mean?* Suppose that three quarters of the states— however you count them — ratify the proposed ERA and Congress passes a joint resolution of promulgation. How should courts interpret the new amendment? Should they look to what people in the 1970s thought about what the ERA would do, or should they look to what people *today* think about what the ERA would do? Or are both of these irrelevant to its proper construction? Think about previous debates about originalism in this casebook. Note that originalist arguments presuppose a bounded period of time that fixes original meaning or original understanding. But what if this assumption is lacking? Can originalism operate under these conditions?

Suppose that Congress prepares a legislative report accompanying its joint resolution offering its views about what the new amendment means. Should courts follow the views of this report? Suppose, for example, that the report says that the new amendment has nothing whatsoever to do with gay rights, or transgender rights. Should courts take this as binding or as very persuasive?

Suppose a judge concluded that (1) the long ratification history of the ERA supplied evidence of many deliberative agents operating in many times and places and espousing many different views; and (2) Congress lacked power to create a ratification history and a definitive meaning for the amendment as part of the promulgation process. How should the judge interpret the amendment?

8. *The difference an ERA makes — short term and long term effects.* What constitutional protections would an Equal Rights Amendment provide in addition to those already provided by the equality guarantees of the Fifth and Fourteenth Amendments? (Eagle Forum, through which Phyllis Schlafly led opposition to the ERA since its introduction in the 1970s, has complied a top ten list.[51])

Look at the text of the proposed ERA and consider its likely effects. Is there any reason why a judge who does not think that gay rights or transgender rights are protected by the Constitution would change his or her mind after the ratification of the ERA? What about a judge who believes that the Constitution should be interpreted in light of the contested and evolving views of the American people? Put another way, what difference will this particular piece of constitutional text make?

In what areas of law — if any — do you think adding an ERA to existing equal protection case law would be likely to make the most difference? Is the current Supreme Court likely to share this view?

Consider what laws Congress might enact under section two of the ERA, which provides that "The Congress shall have the power to enforce, by appropriate legislation, the provisions of this article." Given existing interpretations of the Commerce Clause and section five of the Fourteenth Amendment, what new kinds of legislation might the ERA's section two enable Congress to enact? Would the state action requirement announced in the *Civil Rights Cases* apply to Section two legislation enforcing the new amendment? Would the *Boerne* rule of congruence and proportionality?

Even if you think that the text would probably not change any current judge's mind, how might it affect political mobilization around constitutional norms? Put another way, what do you think a ratified ERA in 2018 would do — either now or in the future — in American politics, or in American constitutional law? What effect might the new text have in a generation?

NOTE: THE NINETEENTH AMENDMENT

The Fourteenth Amendment emerged in *Frontiero* as the primary constitutional locus of sex equality claims, displacing the Nineteenth Amendment. Nonetheless, the Nineteenth Amendment remains an important constitutional basis

---

51. Eagle Forum, Top ten cases that prove the Equal Rights Amendment would have been a disaster, http://eagleforum.org/era/2002/top-ten.shtml (listing *Rostker v. Goldberg, Harris v. McRae, Baehr v. Lewin, Ohio v. Akron Ctr. For Reproductive Health, Bob Jones University v. United States, United States v. Morrison, Boy Scouts of America v. Dale, Personnel Adm'r of Massachusetts v. Feeney, Parham v. Hughes, and Miller v. Albright*).

for women's equality claims, supporting both textual and historical forms of argument. Both the text and the history of the Nineteenth Amendment are concerned with issues of sex and citizenship. The debates over the Nineteenth Amendment teach that the family has historically played a central role in regulating women's citizenship.

The amendment's opponents claimed that women did not need to vote because the men in their families adequately represented them and considered women's interests as they cast their votes. Opponents further argued that women's enfranchisement would destroy the family, displacing women from their separate sphere within the home, introducing domestic discord into the marital relationship, and distracting women from their duties as wives and mothers. See Reva B. Siegel, She the People: The Nineteenth Amendment, Sex Equality, Federalism, and the Family, 115 Harv. L. Rev. 947 (2002).

Suffragists challenged the theory of "virtual representation," the traditional understanding of the household in which men had the authority to represent women. Over the decades, suffragists brought their own questions about the family to the debate:[52]

> To counter the argument that women could rely on men to represent them and to demonstrate why women needed the vote, suffragists provided a detailed indictment of male privilege in the family and elsewhere. Suffragists protested the sex-based restrictions on employment and compensation that impoverished women and drove them into marriage. They challenged women's legally enforced dependency in marriage, particularly property rules that vested in the husband a right to his wife's earnings and to the value of his wife's household labor. They denounced the law's failure to protect women from physical coercion in marriage, including domestic violence, marital rape, and "forced motherhood." Suffragists objected to conventions that held men and women to inconsistent standards of sexual propriety, and they protested women's exclusion from juries, especially in cases involving women accused of committing crimes. . . . At the same time that suffragists challenged traditional conceptions of the family, they undertook to show how enfranchising women would not harm the family and could well strengthen and support it. The vision of family life that suffragists defended was not, of course, that of the common law: the movement was seeking to reform the common law of marital status at the same time it sought the vote. The two initiatives sprang from a common vision. The suffrage movement was exploring new, more egalitarian conceptions of the family that contemplated a far more prominent role for women in the nation's economic and political institutions.
>
> The multi-generational debate over woman suffrage was a debate about the family. The Nineteenth Amendment thus has the potential to be read broadly — not simply as a rule governing voting — but as an amendment that repudiated women's subordination through the

52. Siegel, She the People, supra n.1, at 992-993.

> family and recognized women's equality as citizens. Indeed, in the 1920s immediately after the amendment's adoption, there were signs that courts, including the United States Supreme Court, viewed the amendment as having broad normative implications. In Adkins v. Children's Hospital, the Supreme Court pointed to changes "in the contractual, political and civil status of women, culminating in the Nineteenth Amendment" to strike down a minimum wage law that applied only to women. Adkins v. Children's Hosp., 261 U.S. 525, 553 (1923). The *Adkins* Court noted "the present day trend of legislation, as well as that of common thought and usage, by which woman is accorded emancipation from that old doctrine that she must be given special protection nor be subjected to special restraint in her contractual and civil relationships."

The "old doctrine" to which the Court referred was the common law of marital status that restricted the legal capacity of wives. The *Adkins* decision thus illustrates an understanding of the Nineteenth Amendment as fundamentally changing women's status as citizens, with implications for constitutional interpretation beyond suffrage, across diverse bodies of law. But the Court soon overruled *Adkins* (a *Lochner*-era decision), and within a short time after the Nineteenth Amendment's ratification, courts had begun to read the amendment as applying primarily to voting.

The prevailing judicial interpretation of the amendment is a narrow one: The Nineteenth Amendment is viewed as a rule concerning voting that has no normative significance on women's citizenship or equality beyond the franchise. One could instead draw upon movement and legislative history leading to the Nineteenth Amendment's ratification, by reading the Nineteenth Amendment synthetically with the Fourteenth Amendment, as jointly supplying a constitutional basis for women's equality. Reading the Fourteenth Amendment's Equal Protection Clause in light of the Nineteenth Amendment and its history demonstrates that "a core meaning of equal citizenship for women is freedom from subordination in and through the family."[53] See also Reva B. Siegel, The Nineteenth Amendment and the Democratization of the Family, 129 Yale L.J.F. 450 (2020).

---

53 Siegel, She the People, supra n.1, at 953. For commentators advocating such a synthetic approach within very different interpretive frameworks, see Akhil Reed Amar, The Supreme Court, 1999 Term—Foreword: The Document and the Doctrine, 114 Harv. L. Rev. 26, 51-53 (2000); Michael C. Dorf, Equal Protection Incorporation, 88 Va. L. Rev. 951, 980-981 (2002); Vicki C. Jackson, Holistic Interpretation: Fitzpatrick v. Bitzer and Our Bifurcated Constitution, 53 Stan. L. Rev. 1259, 1290-1291 (2001); Reva B. Siegel, She the People: The Nineteenth Amendment, Sex Equality, Federalism and the Family, 115 Harv. L. Rev. 947, 976-977, 1040-1044 (2002). For a suggestion that the collective memory of women's disfranchisement and of its constitutional rectification through the Nineteenth Amendment bears on the interpretation of the Fourteenth Amendment, see Justice Ginsburg's opinion for the Court in United States v. Virginia, infra.

II. WHAT DOES INTERMEDIATE SCRUTINY PROHIBIT?

A. Intermediate Scrutiny, Sex Stereotyping, and Laws Enforcing Breadwinner/Caregiver Roles

Equal protection doctrine concerning sex-based state action has its own distinctive form, whose outlines can only partly be understood by considering constitutional law prohibiting race discrimination. In the early 1970s, advocates argued that the similarities between race and sex discrimination were sufficiently compelling that the Court should review sex-based state action in the same strict scrutiny framework that it used to review race-based state action; they persuaded a plurality of the Court in *Frontiero*, but never secured a majority. Instead, as the remainder of this chapter explores, in 1976 the Court adopted an "intermediate scrutiny" framework of review that bars many, but not all, forms of sex-based state action.

In the years after its decisions in *Reed* and *Frontiero*, the Court did not immediately settle on a standard for reviewing sex-based classifications. Notably, in this early period, the Court instinctively moved to separate review of pregnancy-related regulation from other sex discrimination cases. Recall the plurality's observation in *Frontiero* that "what differentiates sex from such non-suspect statuses as intelligence or physical disability, and aligns it with the recognized suspect criteria, is that the sex characteristic frequently bears no relation to ability to perform or contribute to society. As a result, statutory distinctions between the sexes often have the effect of invidiously relegating the entire class of females to inferior legal status without regard to the actual capabilities of its individual members." *Frontiero*, supra. Does the race-sex analogy provide a framework for determining when regulation directed at pregnant women is suspect?

In the years before *Frontiero*, feminist lawyers brought equal protection cases that demonstrated how sex stereotyping shaped the regulation of pregnant women. In a brief challenging an Air Force policy that required women in the service who became pregnant to abort the pregnancy or resign (while allowing new fathers to continue to serve), Ginsburg sought "to persuade the Court that the Fourteenth Amendment precluded the state from discriminating in ways that reinforced traditional conceptions of women's sex and family roles."[54] In cases involving restrictions on pregnant women, movement lawyers argued that state action reinforcing sex-role stereotypes violated the Constitution's equal protection guarantee.[55]

But the Court did not follow the movement's lead. Instead, one year after protecting the abortion right in Roe v. Wade, the Court announced in Geduldig v. Aiello, infra, that discrimination on the basis of pregnancy is not necessarily discrimination on the basis of sex within the meaning of *Reed* and *Frontiero*. The Court thus separated the new body of equal protection law regulating sex-based state action from the emerging constitutional jurisprudence of abortion. (Discussion

---

54. Cary Franklin, The Anti-Stereotyping Principle in Constitutional Sex Discrimination Law, 85 N.Y.U. L. Rev. 83, 127 (2010).

55. Neil S. Siegel and Reva B. Siegel, Pregnancy and Sex Role Stereotyping: From *Struck* to *Carhart*, 70 Ohio St. L.J. 1095 (2009).

of pregnancy discrimination appears later in this chapter, and Chapter 9, infra, addresses constitutional doctrines protecting reproductive liberties.)

The new "intermediate scrutiny" standard: Shortly after adopting a seemingly deferential approach in reviewing the regulation of pregnancy, a majority of the Court settled on an "intermediate" standard for reviewing sex-based state action in Craig v. Boren, 429 U.S. 190 (1976). The framework the Court adopted in *Craig* makes sex-based state action presumptively unconstitutional. For the government to employ sex classifications, the government must carry the burden of showing that its use of sex-based criteria is "substantially related" to the achievement of "important governmental objectives." The standard adopted in *Craig* parallels the strict scrutiny framework, which requires the government to defend race-based state action as "necessary" to achieve a "compelling government interest." The Court never explained the reasons for the difference in its scrutiny of race- and sex-based state action. It never explained whether the different standard of review reflects (1) judgments about the original understanding of the Fourteenth Amendment, (2) concerns about intervening in then-pending debates over the ERA's ratification, or (3) instead might reflect differences in the structure of sex and race discrimination (e.g., the numerosity of the protected class or belief in the functional significance and benign character of certain practices of sex differentiation).

In *Craig*, a young man argued that an Oklahoma law that allowed girls aged 18-21, but not boys of the same age, to purchase "near-beer" violated equal protection. (In *Craig* and many of the ensuing 1970s cases, the Court employed the same standard of review to evaluate men's and women's sex discrimination claims.) The Court upheld his claim, reasoning that that state's evidence of sex differences in drunk driving rates was insufficient to justify its sex-based regulatory scheme. *Craig* highlighted the Court's concern about the application of group-based generalizations to individuals, with Justice Brennan noting that "proving broad sociological propositions by statistics is a dubious business, and one that inevitably is in tension with the normative philosophy that underlies the Equal Protection Clause."

Under rational basis review, the Court commonly allows government to allocate benefits and burdens to groups on the basis of generalizations about them. *Craig*'s claim that state action predicated on generalizations is "in tension with the normative philosophy that underlies the Equal Protection Clause" implicitly aligned intermediate scrutiny of sex-based state action with equal protection doctrines concerning race discrimination.

But, in elaborating the new intermediate scrutiny standard, the *Craig* opinion did not explicitly invoke the race analogy as the plurality opinion in *Frontiero* did. The Court instead discussed the dangers of a particular kind of generalization about differences between the sexes. *Craig* warned against sex-based state action premised on "increasingly outdated misconceptions concerning the role of females in the home rather than in the 'marketplace and world of ideas,'" noting that such laws had been "rejected as loose-fitting characterizations incapable of supporting state statutory schemes that were premised on their accuracy." *Craig*, 429 U.S. at 198-199.

In the 1970s, regulatory programs still commonly discriminated between men and women in allocating burdens and benefits, and such discrimination was justified as rationally reflecting differences in family roles. Government programs were premised on the male breadwinner/female caregiver model: the supposition that men were wage earners who supported their families, while women contributed to the family through nurturing and homemaking activities as dependents of male wage earners. Federal social security and welfare law and state family law reflected the same assumptions about sex-role differentiation that informed market practices of explicit sex-based wage discrimination invalidated by the Equal Pay Act and Title VII.

In a series of equal protection cases decided under the Fifth and Fourteenth Amendments in the 1970s, the Court struck down sex-based laws premised on the male breadwinner/female caregiver model. For example, in Weinberger v. Wiesenfeld, 420 U.S. 636 (1975), the Court invalidated the "mother's insurance benefit" provision of the Social Security Act, 42 U.S.C. §402(g), which provided benefits to widows (but not widowers) having minor children in their care. Writing for the majority, Justice Brennan identified the provision as reflecting an "archaic and overbroad generalization not tolerated under the Constitution . . . namely, that male workers' earnings are vital to the support of their families, while the earnings of female wage earners do not significantly contribute to their families' support." *Weinberger,* 420 U.S. at 643 (citations and internal punctuation omitted). The law was unconstitutional both as it presumed women's wages were not necessary for family support and as it denied women wage earners the ability to provide for their family's support that was granted to similarly situated male workers. In this way, the sex-based regulatory regime helped validate and entrench the very social assumptions on which it was premised. In Califano v. Goldfarb, 430 U.S. 199 (1977), the Court struck down another Social Security provision under which a widow was entitled to survivors' benefits based on her deceased husband's coverage regardless of dependency, but only a widower who received at least half of his support from his deceased wife was entitled to benefits. Justice Brennan wrote for a plurality of the Court:

> The only conceivable justification for writing the presumption of wives' dependency into the statute is the assumption, not verified by the Government . . . but based simply on "archaic and overbroad" generalizations, that it would save the Government time, money, and effort simply to pay benefits to all widows, rather than to require proof of dependency of both sexes. We held in *Frontiero,* and again in *Wiesenfeld,* and therefore hold again here, that such assumptions do not suffice to justify a gender-based discrimination in the distribution of employment-related benefits.

In Califano v. Westcott, 443 U.S. 76, 89 (1979), the Court invalidated yet another Social Security policy, this one granting Aid to Families and Dependent Children (AFDC) benefits to the children of unemployed fathers but not unemployed mothers. The Court reasoned that it was "part of the baggage of sexual stereotypes that presumes the father has the primary responsibility to provide a home and its essentials, while the mother is the center of home and family life." Wengler v. Druggists Mutual Insurance Company, 446 U.S. 142 (1980), struck down a Missouri law automatically entitling widows of men who died in work-related accidents to death benefits, while requiring widowers of women who perished in such accidents to prove that they were incapacitated or actually dependent on the wife's earnings. In Kirchberg v. Feenstra, 450 U.S. 455 (1981), the Justices unanimously invalidated a Louisiana statute granting a husband, as "head and master" of the family, the unilateral right to dispose of property jointly owned with his wife without her consent.

These cases represented a dramatic shift in the Court's understanding of the Equal Protection Clause. In the century before 1970, the Court understood differences in family roles as a legitimate reason for state policies that differentiated between the sexes, but, in this period, the Court was persuaded by advocates for the women's movement that such reasons for distinguishing between the sexes were a form of illegitimate stereotyping resembling race discrimination.

In invalidating laws based on the male breadwinner/female caregiver model, the Court never ruled that dependency or differentiation itself was a wrong or a harm. Rather, the Court ruled that government could not use sex-based laws to enforce dependency, differentiation, or other sex-stereotypical roles in marriage. For example, when the Court invalidated an Alabama statute requiring husbands but not wives to pay alimony upon divorce in Orr v. Orr, 440 U.S. 268, 279-280, 283 (1979), it asserted that the state could not employ gender-based rules in marriage to reinforce a traditional breadwinner-dependent model of marriage:

> Appellant views the Alabama alimony statutes as effectively announcing the State's preference for an allocation of family responsibilities under which the wife plays a dependent role, and as seeking for their objective the reinforcement of that model among the State's citizens. We agree, as he urges, that prior cases settle that this purpose cannot sustain the statutes. Stanton v. Stanton, 421 U.S. 7, 10 (1975), held that the "old notio[n]" that "generally it is the man's primary responsibility to provide a home and its essentials," can no longer justify a statute that discriminates on the basis of gender. "No longer is the female destined solely for the home and the rearing of the family, and only the male for the marketplace and the world of ideas." . . .
>
> Legislative classifications which distribute benefits and burdens on the basis of gender carry the inherent risk of reinforcing the stereotypes about the "proper place" of women and their need for special protection. . . . Thus, even statutes purportedly designed to compensate for and ameliorate the effects of past discrimination must be carefully tailored. Where, as here, the State's compensatory and ameliorative purposes are as well served by a gender-neutral classification as one that gender classifies and therefore carries with it the baggage of sexual stereotypes, the State cannot be permitted to classify on the basis of sex.

In its early sex discrimination cases, the Court repeatedly condemns "archaic and overbroad generalizations" and "stereotypes" about the "proper roles" of men and women in the family. What exactly is the harm that generalizations and stereotypes inflict?

Stereotypes, as scholars in the fields of law, sociology, and psychology have observed, reflect a common human tendency to make sense of the world through the imposition of categories.[56] Stereotyping involves both empirical generalizations

56. See Linda Hamilton Krieger, The Content of Our Categories: A Cognitive Bias Approach to Discrimination and Equal Opportunity, 47 Stan. L. Rev. 1161 (1995); Mahzarin Banaji and Anthony Greenwald, Implicit Stereotyping and Prejudice, in The Psychology of Prejudice: The Ontario Symposium 55 (M.P. Zanna & J.M. Olson eds., 1994); Frederick F. Schauer, Profiles, Probabilities, and Stereotypes (2003).

about how individuals behave, and normative prescriptions about how they should behave.[57]

It is useful to distinguish several distinct, though interlocking, kinds of harms that flow from stereotyping. People apprehend groups through generalizations about their members, a useful heuristic in making sense of the social world. But generalizations about groups may be inaccurate as an account of some or all group members. Thus, stereotypical reasoning, however helpful it may be in making sense of the social world, may also lead to cognitive error. These cognitive errors may be amplified, in practical reach and consequence, by prejudice. We are often concerned about stereotypes, not simply because they may reflect factual errors, but also because they reflect pejorative judgments about members of a group. Stepping back and considering stereotyping from a sociological standpoint, we can also see that stereotyping enforces prescriptive as well as descriptive judgments—judgments about social norms and the status roles of certain groups.[58] Of course, law ordinarily reflects and enforces social norms and status roles. Legal prescriptions of this kind will be experienced as a harm when the social norms and roles they enforce are contested, as racial roles were in the 1950s and 1960s, and as family roles were in the 1960s and 1970s.

In its sex discrimination decisions of the 1970s, the Supreme Court recognized several harmful effects of stereotyping. In striking down the "near-beer" law in *Craig* and other sex-differentiating provisions, the Court objected to sex-based laws as unfairly categorizing individuals on the basis of perceived group characteristics[59] and as unfairly denigrating groups. The 1970s cases emphasize that sex-based stereotypes inflict harm as they (1) perpetuate cognitive error, (2) express pejorative judgments, and (3) impose confining role prescriptions. Sex-differentiating laws, the Court recognized, "operate to perpetuate mythical or stereotyped assumptions about the proper roles and the relative capabilities of men and women that are unrelated to any inherent differences."[60] The Court also highlighted the relationship between sex stereotypes and the unequal distribution of political power, recognizing that "gender-based classifications too often have been inexcusably utilized to stereotype and stigmatize politically powerless segments of society."[61]

---

57. See Susan T. Fiske, Stereotyping, Prejudice, and Discrimination, in The Handbook of Social Psychology 357, 378 (Daniel T. Gilbert, Susan T. Fiske & Gardner Lindzey eds., 4th ed. 1998); Larry Alexander, What Makes Wrongful Discrimination Wrong? Biases, Preferences, Stereotypes, and Proxies, 141 U. Pa. L. Rev. 149, 157-190 (1992); David H. Gans, Note, Stereotyping and Difference: *Planned Parenthood v. Casey* and the Future of Sex Discrimination Law, 104 Yale. L.J. 1875, 1877 (1995).

58. Social psychologists theorizing stereotyping have tended to focus on the individual rather than group, and have been relatively inattentive to social structural accounts of stereotyping—tendencies that are now giving way to more interdisciplinary forms of analysis. See Fiske, Stereotyping, Prejudice, and Discrimination, supra n.57, at 392. For discussion of status-based hierarchies and equal protection law, see Jack M. Balkin, The Constitution of Status, 106 Yale L.J. 2313 (1997).

59. For an argument that this principle primarily drove the Court's 1970s jurisprudence, see Mary Anne Case, "The Very Stereotype the Law Condemns": Constitutional Sex Discrimination Law as a Question for Perfect Proxies, 85 Cornell L. Rev. 1447 (2000)..

60. Caban v. Mohammed, 441 U.S. 380, 398 (1979).

61. Kahn v. Shevin, 416 U.S. 351, 357 (1974).

Thus, in proscribing sex-based state action, the Court was concerned about much more than accuracy in governmental decisionmaking. The equal protection cases of the 1970s prohibited government from using sex categorization to reinforce traditional sex roles, with the aim of protecting both individuals and groups. The new doctrine of intermediate scrutiny protected individual freedom to deviate from status roles generally ascribed to a group, and eliminated forms of state action that subordinated groups by enforcing status roles on group members as a whole.

With the growth of this new body of equal protection law in the 1970s, courts began to invalidate many traditional forms of sex-based legislation. Protective labor legislation restricting women's conditions of employment had, in the first several decades of the twentieth century, survived court challenges in cases such as Muller v. Oregon and Goesaert v. Cleary, discussed supra, and remained in effect in many states as of the passage of the Civil Rights Act of 1964. However, these sex-based statutes often reflected and enforced stereotypes about women's capabilities, limiting their employment opportunities by excluding them from certain jobs, restricting their hours, regulating their wages, or barring them from lifting heavy objects. Lawsuits brought under Title VII invalidated some of these laws,[62] and the EEOC eventually promulgated implementing regulations making clear that protective labor laws that applied only to women discriminated on the basis of sex in violation of Title VII.[63] The Court also found such "protective" objectives to be invalid under the Equal Protection Clause, because they reflected stereotypic assumptions about women's relative capabilities. As Justice O'Connor wrote in Mississippi University for Women v. Hogan (1982), infra, "if the statutory objective is to exclude or 'protect' members of one gender because they are presumed to suffer from an inherent handicap or to be innately inferior, the objective itself is illegitimate." *Hogan*, 458 U.S. at 725.

And, as we have seen, the revolution in equal protection doctrine dramatically affected family law. In the years after *Frontiero*, courts and legislatures moved to eliminate sex distinctions in state and federal laws regulating the marriage relationship. After the Court struck down sex-based classifications in Social Security, welfare, alimony, and marital property laws, courts and legislatures revised laws governing custody, domestic violence, and other aspects of the marriage relationship, seeking to define rights and obligations of the spouses in formally gender-neutral terms.[64]

Making the law of marriage, which was once hierarchical, formally gender-neutral has not secured equality in marriage, given persisting differences in the family roles of most men and women.[65] But the law of marriage no longer expressly distinguishes between husbands and wives as it did for centuries.

---

62. See, e.g., Weeks v. Southern Bell, 408 F.2d 228 (5th Cir. 1969).

63. 29 C.F.R. §1604.1(b) (1970).

64. See, e.g., Martha F. Davis, Male Coverture: Law and the Illegitimate Family, 56 Rutgers L. Rev. 73, 78-79 (2003); Linda McClain, The Domain of Civic Virtue in a Good Society: Families, Schools, and Sex Equality, 69 Fordham L. Rev. 617 (2001); Reva B. Siegel, "The Rule of Love": Wife Beating as Prerogative and Privacy, 105 Yale L.J. 2117, 2190 (1996).

65. See Siegel, "The Rule of Love," supra n.64, at 2188-2196.

NOTE: ON SEX, GENDER, AND SEXUAL ORIENTATION

Many scholars in women's studies and related fields use the words "sex" and "gender" as terms of art. "Sex" designates biological differences between men and women—genitalia or chromosomes. "Gender" refers to the socially produced differences between the sexes in dress, grooming, speech patterns, and other forms of behavior. However, many if not most people often use the terms "sex" and "gender" interchangeably. Judges and practicing attorneys have similarly regarded them as synonyms. As a result, critics claim, we have inherited a sexual equality jurisprudence that is often ambiguous with respect to its key concepts.

Ironically, Justice Ruth Bader Ginsburg, who litigated important sex discrimination cases in the 1970s, is partly responsible for the analytic conflation of "sex" and "gender." As reported in one news account, Ginsburg[66]

> stopped talking about sex discrimination years ago. . . . [S]he explained that a secretary once told her, "I'm typing all these briefs and articles for you and the word sex, sex, sex is on every page. Don't you know those nine men [on the Supreme Court], they hear that word and their first association is not the way you want them to be thinking? Why don't you use the word 'gender'? It is a grammatical term and it will ward off distracting associations."

Mary Anne Case, among others, has called for the disaggregation of "gender" and "sex" as legal categories. According to Case, the conflation of the two categories, combined with a common tendency to confuse gender atypicality with homosexual orientation, imports into law a simplistic vision of "sex, gender, and orientation . . . as coming packaged together such that once one is identified, all the rest are determined": Human beings of the male sex are masculine and attracted to women, whereas human beings of the female sex are feminine and attracted to men. Moreover, Case points out, although women are discriminated against, there is also discrimination against femininity and all things coded feminine.

Thus, she points out, "feminists who wish to see feminine styles more generally valued, rather than gradually eliminated as they may be in an androgynous culture slanted toward the masculine," should also work to extend the protections of antidiscrimination law to effeminate men:[67]

> [I]t may be that certain behaviors are just like certain jobs—they will not be valued unless and until men can feel free to engage in them. So long as stereotypically feminine behavior, from wearing dresses and jewelry to speaking softly or in a high-pitched voice, to nurturing or raising children, is forced into a female ghetto, it may continue to be devalued. . . .
>
> It is my contention that, unfortunately, the world will not be safe for women in frilly pink dresses—they will not, for example, generally be as respected as either men or women in gray flannel suits—unless and until it is made safe for men in dresses as well.

---

66. Ernie Freda, Washington in Brief: Clinton's Old Underwear Full of Tax Holes, Atlanta J. & Constitution, Dec. 29, 1993, at A8.

67. Mary Anne Case, Disaggregating Gender from Sex and Sexual Orientation: The Effeminate Man in the Law and Feminist Jurisprudence, 105 Yale L.J. 1, 3, 7, 14 (1995).

Katherine Franke questions the conceptual coherence of sex/gender jurisprudence in a different way: In her view, "there is no principled way to distinguish sex from gender, and, concomitantly, sexual differentiation from sexual discrimination." However, the jurisprudential justification for less than heightened scrutiny of sex-based classifications is the presumption that, because of fundamental biological differences, "males and females are not similarly situated—they are in fact different kinds of beings." Yet by Franke's account, "[b]y accepting these biological differences, equality jurisprudence reifies as foundational *fact* that which is really an *effect* of normative gender ideology."

Through a series of examples, Franke argues that if it were not for gender ideology, our sexual (i.e., anatomical/physical) differences would not code as difference in the ways we currently imagine, or, in Franke's more evocative phrasing, it is "the roles, clothing, myths, and stereotypes that transform a vagina into a *she.*" Therefore, Franke argues, "biology is both a wrong and dangerous place to ground antidiscrimination law because it fails to account for the manner in which every sexual biological fact is meaningful only within a gendered frame of reference." In Franke's view, the targets of antidiscrimination law "should not be limited to the 'gross, stereotyped distinctions between the sexes' but should also include the social processes that construct and make coherent the categories male and female."[68]

Francisco Valdes argues that much confusion has been caused by the multiple conceptual linkages (and conflations) between sex, gender, and sexual orientation. Sex is conflated with gender when people assume that a person's sex (male or female) is also their gender (masculine or feminine). Gender is conflated with sexual orientation when it is assumed that "sissies" are gay and "tomboys" are lesbians, or conversely, that very masculine men and very feminine women are necessarily heterosexual. This conflation, says Valdes, is encouraged by the assumption that "sexual orientation serves as the sexual component of gender." Finally, sex is conflated with sexual orientation when people infer sexual orientation from the sex of a person's sexual partner: Same-sex coupling leads to an inference of homosexual orientation for both participants (even if the participants do not understand themselves to be homosexual), whereas different-sex coupling creates an inference of heterosexual orientation (as in the assumption that a man cannot be gay because he is married and has children).

Valdes argues that "there is no such thing as discrimination '*based*' solely or exclusively on sexual orientation." From his analysis of case law, Valdes concludes (like Mary Anne Case) that courts tend to interpret gender-inappropriate behavior as a sign of homosexuality, especially in men, which provides sex discrimination law with a "sexual orientation loophole": As long as it is generally legal to discriminate on the basis of sexual orientation, discrimination on the basis of gender atypicality is easy to justify as permissible discrimination against (suspected) homosexuals. According to Valdes, antidiscrimination law simply cannot redeem its promise so long as it conflates sex, gender, and sexual orientation.[69]

---

68. Katherine Franke, The Central Mistake of Sex Discrimination Law: The Disaggregation of Sex from Gender, 144 U. Pa. L. Rev. 1, 5 (1995).

69. Francisco Valdes, Queers, Sissies, Dykes and Tomboys: Deconstructing the Conflation of "Sex," "Gender," and "Sexual Orientation" in Euro-American Law and Culture, 83 Cal. L. Rev. 1, 16 (1995).

B. *Intermediate Scrutiny and the Race-Gender Analogy*

The race-gender analogy played a crucial role in the rise of sex discrimination doctrine. It guided the plurality's ruling in *Frontiero*, and it supplied the concept of stereotyping that courts now employ to evaluate challenges to sex-based state action under the Equal Protection Clause.

There are many contexts in which judgments about sex stereotyping seem to resemble judgments about race stereotyping. Consider, for example, the Court's decision to bar sex-based peremptory strikes. In J.E.B. v. Alabama ex rel. T.B., 511 U.S. 127 (1994), the Supreme Court extended the logic of Batson v. Kentucky, 476 U.S. 79 (1986)—which had banned prosecutorial use of peremptory challenges based on race—to gender discrimination. Accordingly, the Court held that the state's use of peremptory challenges based on gender was unconstitutional. The petitioner J.E.B. was the defendant in a paternity suit brought by Alabama on behalf of T.B., the mother of a minor child allegedly fathered by J.E.B. The state then used nine of its ten peremptory strikes to remove male jurors; petitioner used all but one of his strikes to remove female jurors. As a result, all the selected jurors were female. Justice Blackmun's majority opinion observed:[70]

> Respondent seems to assume that gross generalizations that would be deemed impermissible if made on the basis of race are somehow permissible when made on the basis of gender. . . . [A]ctive discrimination by litigants on the basis of gender during jury selection "invites cynicism respecting the jury's neutrality and its obligation to adhere to the law." . . . Striking individual jurors on the assumption that they hold particular views simply because of their gender is "practically a brand upon them, affixed by law, an assertion of their inferiority."

Justice O'Connor concurred, while expressing some misgivings:[71]

> We know that like race, gender matters. A plethora of studies make clear that in rape cases, for example, female jurors are somewhat more likely to vote to convict than male jurors. Moreover, though there have been no similarly definitive studies regarding, for example, sexual harassment, child custody, or spousal or child abuse, one need not be a sexist to share the intuition that in certain cases a person's gender and resulting life experience will be relevant to his or her view of the case. "Jurors are not expected to come into the jury box and leave behind all that their human experience has taught them." Individuals are not expected to ignore as jurors what they know as men—or women.
>
> Today's decision severely limits a litigant's ability to act on this intuition, for the import of our holding is that any correlation between a juror's gender and attitudes is irrelevant as a matter of constitutional law. But to say that gender makes no difference as a matter of law is not to say that gender makes no difference as a matter of fact. I previously

70. 511 U.S. at 139-142 (citing Strauder v. West Virginia, 100 U.S. 303 (1880)).

71. Id. at 148-149 (citing Beck v. Alabama, 447 U.S. 625 (1980); Batson v. Kentucky, 476 U.S. 79 (1986)).

have said with regard to *Batson*: "That the Court will not tolerate prosecutors' racially discriminatory use of the peremptory challenge, in effect, is a special rule of relevance, a statement about what this Nation stands for, rather than a statement of fact."

Chief Justice Rehnquist dissented, arguing:

> The two sexes differ biologically, and to a diminishing extent, in experience. It is not merely "stereotyping" to say that these differences may produce a difference in outlook which is brought to the jury room. Accordingly, the use of peremptory challenges on the basis of sex is generally not the sort of derogatory and invidious act which peremptory challenges directed at black jurors may be.

The race-gender analogy played a crucial role in the development of a body of equal protection law that limits government reliance on sex-based generalizations in many contexts. Equal protection law now bars most traditional gender-based regulation in the family, and prohibits gender-based regulation in most public institutions, such as the jury. Yet, the analogy is not always helpful in explaining the working of heightened scrutiny in the Court's sex discrimination cases. Does the Court's decision in *Brown* control sex-based segregation in education? At present, equal protection doctrine constrains the use of sex-based state action in education. Yet explicit forms of sex segregation in education are tolerated in ways that explicit forms of race segregation are not, even as the Court signals that sex-based state action in education is increasingly constitutionally suspect.

The Court addressed the permissibility of sex segregated education in United States v. Virginia—perhaps the Court's most important intermediate scrutiny case. The *Virginia Military Institute (VMI)* decision was authored by Justice Ginsburg, who has played a crucial role in the development of the sex discrimination line of cases, first as movement lawyer and now as judge. As you read the *VMI* case, you might reflect on how constitutional judgments about sex and race discrimination converge and diverge. If sex segregation in education is not "inherently" wrong, under what circumstances does sex segregation in education inflict constitutional harm? How, if at all, does the race analogy help answer this question? How, if at all, does the intermediate scrutiny test help answer this question? Does the Court modify the intermediate scrutiny framework in the course of applying it to the sex-based admissions practices challenged in *VMI*?

United States v. Virginia

[The VMI Case]
518 U.S. 515 (1996)

Justice GINSBURG delivered the opinion of the Court.

[In 1990, prompted by a complaint filed with the Attorney General by a female high school student seeking admission to the Virginia Military Institute (VMI), the United States sued the Commonwealth of Virginia and VMI, alleging that VMI's policy of admitting only men violated the Equal Protection Clause of the Fourteenth Amendment. VMI enrolls approximately 1,300 men as cadets. In the two years prior to the suit, VMI had received 347 inquiries from women seeking admission.]

I

Founded in 1839, VMI is today the sole single-sex school among Virginia's 15 public institutions of higher learning. VMI's distinctive mission is to produce "citizen-soldiers," men prepared for leadership in civilian life and in military service. VMI pursues this mission through pervasive training of a kind not available anywhere else in Virginia. Assigning prime place to character development, VMI uses an "adversative method" modeled on English public schools and once characteristic of military instruction. VMI constantly endeavors to instill physical and mental discipline in its cadets and impart to them a strong moral code. The school's graduates leave VMI with heightened comprehension of their capacity to deal with duress and stress, and a large sense of accomplishment for completing the hazardous course.

VMI has notably succeeded in its mission to produce leaders; among its alumni are military generals, Members of Congress, and business executives. The school's alumni overwhelmingly perceive that their VMI training helped them to realize their personal goals. VMI's endowment reflects the loyalty of its graduates; VMI has the largest per-student endowment of all public undergraduate institutions in the Nation.

Neither the goal of producing citizen-soldiers nor VMI's implementing methodology is inherently unsuitable to women. And the school's impressive record in producing leaders has made admission desirable to some women. Nevertheless, Virginia has elected to preserve exclusively for men the advantages and opportunities a VMI education affords.

II

A

In contrast to the federal service academies, institutions maintained "to prepare cadets for career service in the armed forces," VMI's program "is directed at preparation for both military and civilian life"; "[o]nly about 15% of VMI cadets enter career military service."

VMI produces its "citizen-soldiers" through "an adversative, or doubting, model of education" which features "[p]hysical rigor, mental stress, absolute equality of treatment, absence of privacy, minute regulation of behavior, and indoctrination in desirable values." As one Commandant of Cadets described it, the adversative method "dissects the young student," and makes him aware of his "limits and capabilities," so that he knows "how far he can go with his anger, . . . how much he can take under stress, . . . exactly what he can do when he is physically exhausted."

VMI cadets live in spartan barracks where surveillance is constant and privacy nonexistent; they wear uniforms, eat together in the mess hall, and regularly participate in drills. Entering students are incessantly exposed to the rat line, "an extreme form of the adversative model," comparable in intensity to Marine Corps boot camp. Tormenting and punishing, the rat line bonds new cadets to their fellow sufferers and, when they have completed the 7-month experience, to their former tormentors.

VMI's "adversative model" is further characterized by a hierarchical "class system" of privileges and responsibilities, a "dyke system" for assigning a senior class mentor to each entering class "rat," and a stringently enforced "honor code," which prescribes that a cadet "does not lie, cheat, steal nor tolerate those who do." VMI attracts some applicants because of its reputation as an extraordinarily challenging military school, and "because its alumni are exceptionally close to the school." "[W]omen have no opportunity anywhere to gain the benefits of [the system of education at VMI]."

B

The [District] court . . . recognized that, with recruitment, VMI could "achieve at least 10% female enrollment"—"a sufficient 'critical mass' to provide the female cadets with a positive educational experience" [and] that "some women are capable of all of the individual activities required of VMI cadets." In addition, experts agreed that if VMI admitted women, "the VMI ROTC experience would become a better training program from the perspective of the armed forces, because it would provide training in dealing with a mixed-gender army."

[The District Court nevertheless ruled in favor of VMI, arguing that single-sex education was justified because it added diversity to Virginia's uniformly coeducational system. Moreover, "VMI's unique method of instruction" added diversity. Although women were "denied a unique educational opportunity that is available only at VMI," VMI's "single-sex status would be lost, and some aspects of the [school's] distinctive method would be altered" if women were admitted. The school would have to make allowance "for personal privacy," "[p]hysical education requirements would have to be altered, at least for the women," and the adversative environment could not survive unmodified.

The Fourth Circuit Court of Appeals reversed, arguing that "[a] policy of diversity which aims to provide an array of educational opportunities, including single-gender institutions, must do more than favor one gender" and that "neither the goal of producing citizen soldiers nor VMI's implementing methodology is inherently unsuitable to women." However, it accepted the District Court's finding that physical training, limitations on privacy, and the adversative approach "would be materially affected by coeducation." It remanded the case asking the State of Virginia to choose among three options: Admit women to VMI, establish parallel institutions or programs for women, or abandon state support and leave VMI free to pursue its policies as a private institution.]

C

In response to the Fourth Circuit's ruling, Virginia proposed a parallel program for women: Virginia Women's Institute for Leadership (VWIL). The 4-year, state-sponsored undergraduate program would be located at Mary Baldwin College, a private liberal arts school for women, and would be open, initially, to about 25 to 30 students. Although VWIL would share VMI's mission—to produce "citizen-soldiers"—the VWIL program would differ, as does Mary Baldwin College, from VMI in academic offerings, methods of education, and financial resources.

The average combined SAT score of entrants at Mary Baldwin is about 100 points lower than the score for VMI freshmen. Mary Baldwin's faculty holds "significantly fewer Ph.D.'s than the faculty at VMI," and receives significantly lower salaries. While VMI offers degrees in liberal arts, the sciences, and engineering, Mary Baldwin, at the time of trial, offered only bachelor of arts degrees. A VWIL student seeking to earn an engineering degree could gain one, without public support, by attending Washington University in St. Louis, Missouri, for two years, paying the required private tuition.

[A] Task Force charged with designing the VWIL program . . . determined that a military model would be "wholly inappropriate" for VWIL. . . . In lieu of VMI's adversative method, the VWIL Task Force favored "a cooperative method which reinforces self-esteem." [S]tudents would take courses in leadership, complete an off-campus leadership externship, participate in community service projects, and assist in arranging a speaker series. . . .

D

[The district court approved Virginia's plan, holding that the two schools would "achieve substantially similar outcomes": "If VMI marches to the beat of a drum, then Mary Baldwin marches to the melody of a fife and when the march is over, both will have arrived at the same destination." The Court of Appeals affirmed.] . . .

IV

We note, once again, the core instruction of this Court's pathmarking decisions in J.E.B. v. Alabama ex rel. T.B., 511 U.S. 127 (1994), and Mississippi Univ. for Women, 458 U.S. [718 (1982)]: Parties who seek to defend gender-based government action must demonstrate an "exceedingly persuasive justification" for that action. . . .

Today's skeptical scrutiny of official action denying rights or opportunities based on sex responds to volumes of history. As a plurality of this Court acknowledged a generation ago, "our Nation has had a long and unfortunate history of sex discrimination." Frontiero v. Richardson, 411 U.S. 677 (1973). Through a century plus three decades and more of that history, women did not count among voters composing "We the People";[a] not until 1920 did women gain a constitutional right to the franchise. And for a half century thereafter, it remained the prevailing doctrine that government, both federal and state, could withhold from women opportunities accorded men so long as any "basis in reason" could be conceived for the discrimination.

In 1971, for the first time in our Nation's history, this Court ruled in favor of a woman who complained that her State had denied her the equal protection of its laws. Reed v. Reed, 404 U.S. 71 (1971). Since *Reed*, the Court has repeatedly

a. As Thomas Jefferson stated the view prevailing when the Constitution was new, "Were our State a pure democracy . . . there would yet be excluded from their deliberations . . . women, who, to prevent depravation of morals and ambiguity of issue, should not mix promiscuously in the public meetings of men."

recognized that neither federal nor state government acts compatibly with the equal protection principle when a law or official policy denies to women, simply because they are women, full citizenship stature—equal opportunity to aspire, achieve, participate in, and contribute to society based on their individual talents and capacities.

Without equating gender classifications, for all purposes, to classifications based on race or national origin, the Court, in post-*Reed* decisions, has carefully inspected official action that closes a door or denies opportunity to women (or to men). To summarize the Court's current directions for cases of official classification based on gender: Focusing on the differential treatment or denial of opportunity for which relief is sought, the reviewing court must determine whether the proffered justification is "exceedingly persuasive." The burden of justification is demanding and it rests entirely on the State. The State must show "at least that the [challenged] classification serves 'important governmental objectives and that the discriminatory means employed' are 'substantially related to the achievement of those objectives.'" The justification must be genuine, not hypothesized or invented post hoc in response to litigation. And it must not rely on overbroad generalizations about the different talents, capacities, or preferences of males and females.

The heightened review standard our precedent establishes does not make sex a proscribed classification. Supposed "inherent differences" are no longer accepted as a ground for race or national origin classifications. See Loving v. Virginia, 388 U.S. 1 (1967). Physical differences between men and women, however, are enduring: "[T]he two sexes are not fungible; a community made up exclusively of one [sex] is different from a community composed of both." Ballard v. United States, 329 U.S. 187 (1946).

"Inherent differences" between men and women, we have come to appreciate, remain cause for celebration, but not for denigration of the members of either sex or for artificial constraints on an individual's opportunity. Sex classifications may be used to compensate women "for particular economic disabilities [they have] suffered," to "promot[e] equal employment opportunity," to advance full development of the talent and capacities of our Nation's people.[b] But such classifications may not be used, as they once were, to create or perpetuate the legal, social, and economic inferiority of women.

[W]e conclude that Virginia has shown no "exceedingly persuasive justification" for excluding all women from the citizen-soldier training afforded by VMI. . . . Because the remedy proffered by Virginia—the Mary Baldwin VWIL

b. Several amici have urged that diversity in educational opportunities is an altogether appropriate governmental pursuit and that single-sex schools can contribute importantly to such diversity. Indeed, it is the mission of some single-sex schools "to dissipate, rather than perpetuate, traditional gender classifications." We do not question the State's prerogative evenhandedly to support diverse educational opportunities. We address specifically and only an educational opportunity recognized by the District Court and the Court of Appeals as "unique," an opportunity available only at Virginia's premier military institute, the State's sole single-sex public university or college. Cf. Mississippi Univ. for Women v. Hogan ("Mississippi maintains no other single-sex public university or college. Thus, we are not faced with the question of whether States can provide 'separate but equal' undergraduate institutions for males and females.").

program—does not cure the constitutional violation, i.e., it does not provide equal opportunity, we reverse the Fourth Circuit's final judgment in this case.

V

Virginia . . . asserts two justifications in defense of VMI's exclusion of women. First, the Commonwealth contends, "single-sex education provides important educational benefits," and the option of single-sex education contributes to "diversity in educational approaches." Second, the Commonwealth argues, "the unique VMI method of character development and leadership training," the school's adversative approach, would have to be modified were VMI to admit women. . . .

A

Single-sex education affords pedagogical benefits to at least some students, Virginia emphasizes, and that reality is uncontested in this litigation.[c]

Similarly, it is not disputed that diversity among public educational institutions can serve the public good. But Virginia has not shown that VMI was established, or has been maintained, with a view to diversifying, by its categorical exclusion of women, educational opportunities within the State. In cases of this genre, our precedent instructs that "benign" justifications proffered in defense of categorical exclusions will not be accepted automatically; a tenable justification must describe actual state purposes, not rationalizations for actions in fact differently grounded. . . .

Neither recent nor distant history bears out Virginia's alleged pursuit of diversity through single-sex educational options. In 1839, when the State established VMI, a range of educational opportunities for men and women was scarcely contemplated. Higher education at the time was considered dangerous for women;[d]

---

c. On this point, the dissent sees fire where there is no flame. "Both men and women can benefit from a single-sex education," the District Court recognized, although "the beneficial effects" of such education, . . . apparently "are stronger among women than among men." The United States does not challenge that recognition. Cf. C. Jencks & D. Riesman, The Academic Revolution 297-298 (1968):

> The pluralistic argument for preserving all-male colleges is uncomfortably similar to the pluralistic argument for preserving all-white colleges. . . . The all-male college would be relatively easy to defend if it emerged from a world in which women were established as fully equal to men. But it does not. It is therefore likely to be a witting or unwitting device for preserving tacit assumptions of male superiority—assumptions for which women must eventually pay.

d. Dr. Edward H. Clarke of Harvard Medical School, whose influential book, Sex in Education, went through 17 editions, was perhaps the most well-known speaker from the medical community opposing higher education for women. He maintained that the physiological effects of hard study and academic competition with boys would interfere with the development of girls' reproductive organs. [S]ee also H. Maudsley, Sex in Mind and in Education 17 (1874) ("It is not that girls have not ambition, nor that they fail generally to run the intellectual race [in coeducational settings], but it is asserted that they do it at a cost to their strength and health which entails life-long suffering, and even incapacitates them for the adequate performance of the natural functions of their sex."); C. Meigs, Females and Their Diseases 350 (1848) (after five or six weeks of "mental and educational discipline," a healthy woman would "lose . . . the habit of menstruation" and suffer numerous ills as a result of depriving her body for the sake of her mind).

reflecting widely held views about women's proper place, the Nation's first universities and colleges—for example, Harvard in Massachusetts, William and Mary in Virginia—admitted only men. VMI was not at all novel in this respect: In admitting no women, VMI followed the lead of the State's flagship school, the University of Virginia, founded in 1819.

"[N]o struggle for the admission of women to a state university," a historian has recounted, "was longer drawn out, or developed more bitterness, than that at the University of Virginia." . . . Familiar arguments were rehearsed. If women were admitted, it was feared, they "would encroach on the rights of men; there would be new problems of government, perhaps scandals; the old honor system would have to be changed; standards would be lowered to those of other coeducational schools; and the glorious reputation of the university, as a school for men, would be trailed in the dust."

Ultimately, in 1970, "the most prestigious institution of higher education in Virginia," the University of Virginia, introduced coeducation and, in 1972, began to admit women on an equal basis with men. . . .

Virginia describes the current absence of public single-sex higher education for women as "an historical anomaly." But the historical record indicates action more deliberate than anomalous: First, protection of women against higher education; next, schools for women far from equal in resources and stature to schools for men; finally, conversion of the separate schools to coeducation. The state legislature, prior to the advent of this controversy, had repealed "[a]ll Virginia statutes requiring individual institutions to admit only men or women." And in 1990, an official commission, "legislatively established to chart the future goals of higher education in Virginia," reaffirmed the policy "of affording broad access" while maintaining "autonomy and diversity." Significantly, the Commission reported:

> Because colleges and universities provide opportunities for students to develop values and learn from role models, it is extremely important that they deal with faculty, staff, and students without regard to sex, race, or ethnic origin.

This statement, the Court of Appeals observed, "is the only explicit one that we have found in the record in which the Commonwealth has expressed itself with respect to gender distinctions."

Our 1982 decision in *Mississippi Univ. for Women* prompted VMI to reexamine its male-only admission policy. . . . A Mission Study Committee, appointed by the VMI Board of Visitors, studied the problem from October 1983 until May 1986, and in that month counseled against "change of VMI status as a single-sex college." [W]e can hardly extract from that effort any state policy evenhandedly to advance diverse educational options. As the District Court observed, the Committee's analysis "primarily focuse[d] on anticipated difficulties in attracting females to VMI," and the report, overall, supplied "very little indication of how th[e] conclusion was reached."

In sum, we find no persuasive evidence in this record that VMI's male-only admission policy "is in furtherance of a state policy of 'diversity.'" No such policy, the Fourth Circuit observed, can be discerned from the movement of all other public colleges and universities in Virginia away from single-sex education. [It] also questioned "how one institution with autonomy, but with no authority over any other state institution, can give effect to a state policy of diversity among institutions." A purpose genuinely to advance an array of educational options . . . is not served by VMI's historic and constant plan—a plan to "affor[d] a unique educational benefit only to males." However "liberally" this plan serves the State's sons, it makes no provision whatever for her daughters. That is not equal protection.

B

Virginia next argues that VMI's adversative method of training provides educational benefits that cannot be made available, unmodified, to women. Alterations to accommodate women would necessarily be "radical," so "drastic," Virginia asserts, as to transform, indeed "destroy," VMI's program. Neither sex would be favored by the transformation, Virginia maintains: Men would be deprived of the unique opportunity currently available to them; women would not gain that opportunity because their participation would "eliminat[e] the very aspects of [the] program that distinguish [VMI] from . . . other institutions of higher education in Virginia."

[I]t is uncontested that women's admission would require accommodations, primarily in arranging housing assignments and physical training programs for female cadets. It is also undisputed, however, that "the VMI methodology could be used to educate women." The District Court even allowed that some women may prefer it to the methodology a women's college might pursue. "[S]ome women, at least, would want to attend [VMI] if they had the opportunity," the District Court recognized, and "some women," the expert testimony established, "are capable of all of the individual activities required of VMI cadets." The parties, furthermore, agree that "some women can meet the physical standards [VMI] now impose[s] on men." In sum, as the Court of Appeals stated, "neither the goal of producing citizen soldiers," VMI's raison d'être, "nor VMI's implementing methodology is inherently unsuitable to women."

In support of its initial judgment for Virginia . . . the District Court made "findings" on "gender-based developmental differences." These "findings" restate the opinions of Virginia's expert witnesses, opinions about typically male or typically female "tendencies." For example, "[m]ales tend to need an atmosphere of adversativeness," while "[f]emales tend to thrive in a cooperative atmosphere." "I'm not saying that some women don't do well under [the] adversative model," VMI's expert on educational institutions testified, "undoubtedly there are some [women] who do"; but educational experiences must be designed "around the rule," this expert maintained, and not "around the exception."

The United States does not challenge any expert witness estimation on average capacities or preferences of men and women. Instead, the United States emphasizes that time and again since this Court's turning point decision in Reed v. Reed, we have cautioned reviewing courts to take a "hard look" at generalizations or "tendencies" of the kind pressed by Virginia, and relied upon by the District Court. State actors controlling gates to opportunity, we have instructed, may not exclude qualified individuals based on "fixed notions concerning the roles and abilities of males and females." *Mississippi Univ. for Women*; see *J.E.B.*, 511 U.S., at 139, n.11 (equal protection principles, as applied to gender classifications, mean state actors may not rely on "overbroad" generalizations to make "judgments about people that are likely to . . . perpetuate historical patterns of discrimination").

It may be assumed . . . that most women would not choose VMI's adversative method. [I]t is also probable that "many men would not want to be educated in such an environment." . . . The issue, however, is not whether "women—or men—should be forced to attend VMI"; rather, the question is whether the State can constitutionally deny to women who have the will and capacity, the training and attendant opportunities that VMI uniquely affords.

The notion that admission of women would downgrade VMI's stature, destroy the adversative system and, with it, even the school,[e] is a judgment hardly proved, a prediction hardly different from other "self-fulfilling prophec[ies]," once routinely used to deny rights or opportunities. When women first sought admission to the bar and access to legal education, concerns of the same order were expressed. For example, in 1876, the Court of Common Pleas of Hennepin County, Minnesota, explained why women were thought ineligible for the practice of law. Women train and educate the young, the court said, which

> forbids that they shall bestow that time (early and late) and labor, so essential in attaining to the eminence to which the true lawyer should ever aspire. It cannot therefore be said that the opposition of courts to the admission of females to practice . . . is to any extent the outgrowth of . . . "old fogyism[.]" . . . [I]t arises rather from a comprehension of the magnitude of the responsibilities connected with the successful practice of law, and a desire to grade up the profession.

A like fear, according to a 1925 report, accounted for Columbia Law School's resistance to women's admission, although

> [t]he faculty . . . never maintained that women could not master legal learning. . . . No, its argument has been . . . more practical. If women were admitted to the Columbia Law School, [the faculty] said, then the choicer, more manly and redblooded graduates of our great universities would go to the Harvard Law School!

Medical faculties similarly resisted men and women as partners in the study of medicine. More recently, women seeking careers in policing encountered resistance based on fears that their presence would "undermine male solidarity," deprive male partners of adequate assistance, and lead to sexual misconduct. Field studies did not confirm these fears.

Women's successful entry into the federal military academies, and their participation in the Nation's military forces, indicate that Virginia's fears for the future of VMI may not be solidly grounded. The State's justification for excluding all women from "citizen-soldier" training for which some are qualified, in any event, cannot rank as "exceedingly persuasive," as we have explained and applied that standard.

Virginia and VMI trained their argument on "means" rather than "end," and thus misperceived our precedent. Single-sex education at VMI serves an "important governmental objective," they maintained, and exclusion of women is not only "substantially related," it is essential to that objective. By this notably circular

---

e. Forecasts of the same kind were made regarding admission of women to the federal military academies.

argument, the "straightforward" test *Mississippi Univ. for Women* described was bent and bowed.

The State's misunderstanding and, in turn, the District Court's, is apparent from VMI's mission: to produce "citizen-soldiers" individuals "imbued with love of learning, confident in the functions and attitudes of leadership, possessing a high sense of public service, advocates of the American democracy and free enterprise system, and ready . . . to defend their country in time of national peril."

Surely that goal is great enough to accommodate women, who today count as citizens in our American democracy equal in stature to men. Just as surely, the State's great goal is not substantially advanced by women's categorical exclusion, in total disregard of their individual merit, from the State's premier "citizen-soldier" corps.[f] Virginia, in sum, "has fallen far short of establishing the 'exceedingly persuasive justification,'" that must be the solid base for any gender-defined classification.

VI

A

. . . Having violated the Constitution's equal protection requirement, Virginia was obliged to show that its remedial proposal "directly address[ed] and relate[d] to" the violation, i.e., the equal protection denied to women ready, willing, and able to benefit from educational opportunities of the kind VMI offers. . . . VWIL affords women no opportunity to experience the rigorous military training for which VMI is famed. . . . Instead, the VWIL program "deemphasize[s]" military education, and uses a "cooperative method" of education "which reinforces self-esteem."

VWIL students participate in ROTC and a "largely ceremonial" Virginia Corps of Cadets, but Virginia deliberately did not make VWIL a military institute. The VWIL House is not a military-style residence and VWIL students need not live together throughout the 4-year program, eat meals together, or wear uniforms during the school day. VWIL students thus do not experience the "barracks" life "crucial to the VMI experience," the spartan living arrangements designed to foster an "egalitarian ethic." "[T]he most important aspects of the VMI educational experience occur in the barracks," the District Court found, yet Virginia deemed that core experience nonessential, indeed inappropriate, for training its female citizen-soldiers.

VWIL students receive their "leadership training" in seminars, externships, and speaker series, episodes and encounters lacking the "[p]hysical rigor, mental stress, . . . minute regulation of behavior, and indoctrination in desirable values" made hallmarks of VMI's citizen-soldier training. Kept away from the pressures, hazards, and psychological bonding characteristic of VMI's adversative training,

---

f. VMI has successfully managed another notable change. The school admitted its first African-American cadets in 1968. See The VMI Story 347-349 (students no longer sing "Dixie," salute the Confederate flag or the tomb of General Robert E. Lee at ceremonies and sports events). . . . VMI established a Program on "retention of black cadets" designed to offer academic and social-cultural support to "minority members of a dominantly white and tradition-oriented student body." The school maintains a "special recruitment program for blacks" which, the District Court found, "has had little, if any, effect on VMI's method of accomplishing its mission."

VWIL students will not know the "feeling of tremendous accomplishment" commonly experienced by VMI's successful cadets.

Virginia maintains that these methodological differences are "justified pedagogically," based on "important differences between men and women in learning and developmental needs," "psychological and sociological differences" Virginia describes as "real" and "not stereotypes." The Task Force charged with developing the leadership program for women, drawn from the staff and faculty at Mary Baldwin College, "determined that a military model and, especially VMI's adversative method, would be wholly inappropriate for educating and training most women." . . .

[G]eneralizations about "the way women are," estimates of what is appropriate for most women, no longer justify denying opportunity to women whose talent and capacity place them outside the average description. Notably, Virginia never asserted that VMI's method of education suits most men. It is also revealing that Virginia accounted for its failure to make the VWIL experience "the entirely militaristic experience of VMI" on the ground that VWIL "is planned for women who do not necessarily expect to pursue military careers." By that reasoning, VMI's "entirely militaristic" program would be inappropriate for men in general or as a group, for "[o]nly about 15% of VMI cadets enter career military service." . . .[g]

B

In myriad respects other than military training, VWIL does not qualify as VMI's equal. VWIL's student body, faculty, course offerings, and facilities hardly match VMI's. Nor can the VWIL graduate anticipate the benefits associated with VMI's 157-year history, the school's prestige, and its influential alumni network. . . . [T]he difference between the two schools' financial reserves is pronounced. Mary Baldwin's endowment, currently about $19 million, will gain an additional $35 million based on future commitments; VMI's current endowment, $131 million—the largest per-student endowment in the Nation—will gain $220 million.

The VWIL student does not graduate with the advantage of a VMI degree. Her diploma does not unite her with the legions of VMI "graduates [who] have distinguished themselves" in military and civilian life. . . . A VWIL graduate cannot assume that the "network of business owners, corporations, VMI graduates and non-graduate employers . . . interested in hiring VMI graduates," will be equally responsive to her search for employment. . . . Virginia's VWIL solution is reminiscent of the remedy Texas proposed 50 years ago, in response to a state trial court's 1946 ruling that, given the equal protection guarantee, African Americans could

---

g. Admitting women to VMI would undoubtedly require alterations necessary to afford members of each sex privacy from the other sex in living arrangements, and to adjust aspects of the physical training programs. Cf. note following 10 U.S.C. §4342 (academic and other standards for women admitted to the Military, Naval, and Air Force Academies "shall be the same as those required for male individuals, except for those minimum essential adjustments in such standards required because of physiological differences between male and female individuals"). Experience shows such adjustments are manageable. See U.S. Military Academy, A. Vitters, N. Kinzer, and J. Adams, Report of Admission of Women (Project Athena I-IV) (1977-1980) (4-year longitudinal study of the admission of women to West Point); Defense Advisory Committee on Women in the Services, Report on the Integration and Performance of Women at West Point 17-18 (1992).

not be denied a legal education at a state facility. See Sweatt v. Painter, 339 U.S. 629 (1950). Reluctant to admit African Americans to its flagship University of Texas Law School, the State set up a separate school for Herman Sweatt and other black law students. As originally opened, the new school had no independent faculty or library, and it lacked accreditation. . . .

More important than the tangible features, the Court emphasized, are "those qualities which are incapable of objective measurement but which make for greatness" in a school, including "reputation of the faculty, experience of the administration, position and influence of the alumni, standing in the community, traditions and prestige." Facing the marked differences reported in the *Sweatt* opinion, the Court unanimously ruled that Texas had not shown "substantial equality in the [separate] educational opportunities" the State offered. Accordingly, the Court held, the Equal Protection Clause required Texas to admit African Americans to the University of Texas Law School. In line with *Sweatt,* we rule here that Virginia has not shown substantial equality in the separate educational opportunities the State supports at VWIL and VMI.

VII

. . . A prime part of the history of our Constitution, historian Richard Morris recounted, is the story of the extension of constitutional rights and protections to people once ignored or excluded. VMI's story continued as our comprehension of "We the People" expanded. There is no reason to believe that the admission of women capable of all the activities required of VMI cadets would destroy the Institute rather than enhance its capacity to serve the "more perfect Union." . . .

Justice THOMAS took no part in the consideration or decision of this case.

Chief Justice REHNQUIST, concurring in judgment.

I

. . .

Had the State provided the kind of support for the private women's schools that it provides for VMI, this may have been a very different case. For in so doing, the State would have demonstrated that its interest in providing a single-sex education for men was to some measure matched by an interest in providing the same opportunity for women. . . .

I agree with the Court that [maintenance of the adversative method] does not serve an important governmental objective. . . . While considerable evidence shows that a single-sex education is pedagogically beneficial for some students, and hence a State may have a valid interest in promoting that methodology, there is no similar evidence in the record that an adversative method is pedagogically beneficial or is any more likely to produce character traits than other methodologies.

The Court defines the constitutional violation in this case as "the categorical exclusion of women from an extraordinary educational opportunity afforded to men." By defining the violation in this way, and by emphasizing that a remedy for a constitutional violation must place the victims of discrimination in "the position they would have occupied in the absence of [discrimination]," the Court necessarily implies that the only adequate remedy would be the admission of women to the all-male institution. . . . I would not define the violation in this way; it is not the "exclusion of women" that violates the Equal Protection Clause, but the maintenance of an all-men's school without providing any—much less a comparable—institution for women.

Accordingly, the remedy should not necessarily require either the admission of women to VMI, or the creation of a VMI clone for women. . . . [T]he State does not need to create two institutions with the same number of faculty PhD's, similar SAT scores, or comparable athletic fields. Nor would it necessarily require that the women's institution offer the same curriculum as the men's; one could be strong in computer science, the other could be strong in liberal arts. It would be a sufficient remedy, I think, if the two institutions offered the same quality of education and were of the same overall calibre. . . .

Justice SCALIA, dissenting.

Today the Court shuts down an institution that has served the people of the Commonwealth of Virginia with pride and distinction for over a century and a half. To achieve that desired result, it rejects (contrary to our established practice) the factual findings of two courts below, sweeps aside the precedents of this Court, and ignores the history of our people. As to facts: it explicitly rejects the finding that there exist "gender-based developmental differences" supporting Virginia's restriction of the "adversative" method to only a men's institution, and the finding that the all-male composition of the Virginia Military Institute (VMI) is essential to that institution's character. As to precedent: it drastically revises our established standards for reviewing sex-based classifications. And as to history: it counts for nothing the long tradition, enduring down to the present, of men's military colleges supported by both States and the Federal Government.

Much of the Court's opinion is devoted to deprecating the closed-mindedness of our forebears with regard to women's education, and even with regard to the treatment of women in areas that have nothing to do with education. Closed-minded they were—as every age is, including our own, with regard to matters it cannot guess, because it simply does not consider them debatable. The virtue of a democratic system with a First Amendment is that it readily enables the people, over time, to be persuaded that what they took for granted is not so, and to change their laws accordingly. That system is destroyed if the smug assurances of each age are removed from the democratic process and written into the Constitution. So to counterbalance the Court's criticism of our ancestors, let me say a word in their praise: they left us free to change. The same cannot be said of this most illiberal Court, which has embarked on a course of inscribing one after another of the current preferences of the society (and in some cases only the counter-majoritarian preferences of the society's law-trained elite) into our Basic Law. Today it enshrines the notion that no substantial educational value is to be served by an all-men's military academy—so that the decision by the people of Virginia to maintain such an institution denies equal protection to women who cannot attend that institution but can attend others. Since it is entirely clear that the Constitution of the United States—the old one—takes no sides in this educational debate, I dissent.

. . . [I]n my view the function of this Court is to preserve our society's values regarding (among other things) equal protection, not to revise them; to prevent backsliding from the degree of restriction the Constitution imposed upon democratic government, not to prescribe, on our own authority, progressively higher degrees. For that reason it is my view that, whatever abstract tests we may choose to devise, they cannot supersede — and indeed ought to be crafted so as to reflect — those constant and unbroken national traditions that embody the people's understanding of ambiguous constitutional texts. More specifically, it is my view that "when a practice not expressly prohibited by the text of the Bill of Rights bears the endorsement of a long tradition of open, widespread, and unchallenged use that dates back to the beginning of the Republic, we have no proper basis for striking it down." The same applies, mutatis mutandis, to a practice asserted to be in violation of the post–Civil War Fourteenth Amendment.

The all-male constitution of VMI comes squarely within such a governing tradition. Founded by the Commonwealth of Virginia in 1839 and continuously maintained by it since, VMI has always admitted only men. And in that regard it has not been unusual. For almost all of VMI's more than a century and a half of existence, its single-sex status reflected the uniform practice for government-supported military colleges. Another famous Southern institution, The Citadel, has existed as a state-funded school of South Carolina since 1842. And all the federal military colleges — West Point, the Naval Academy at Annapolis, and even the Air Force Academy, which was not established until 1954 — admitted only males for most of their history. Their admission of women in 1976 came not by court decree, but because the people, through their elected representatives, decreed a change. In other words, the tradition of having government-funded military schools for men is as well rooted in the traditions of this country as the tradition of sending only men into military combat. The people may decide to change the one tradition, like the other, through democratic processes; but the assertion that either tradition has been unconstitutional through the centuries is not law, but politics-smuggled-into-law.

And the same applies, more broadly, to single-sex education in general, which . . . is threatened by today's decision with the cut-off of all state and federal support. Government-run nonmilitary educational institutions for the two sexes have until very recently also been part of our national tradition. "[It is] [c]oeducation, historically, [that] is a novel educational theory. From grade school through high school, college, and graduate and professional training, much of the Nation's population during much of our history has been educated in sexually segregated classrooms." These traditions may of course be changed by the democratic decisions of the people, as they largely have been.

Today, however, change is forced upon Virginia, and reversion to single-sex education is prohibited nationwide, not by democratic processes but by order of this Court. Even while bemoaning the sorry, bygone days of "fixed notions" concerning women's education, the Court favors current notions so fixedly that it is willing to write them into the Constitution of the United States by application of custom-built "tests." This is not the interpretation of a Constitution, but the creation of one. . . .

[I]t is perfectly clear that, if the question of the applicable standard of review for sex-based classifications were to be regarded as an appropriate subject for reconsideration, the stronger argument would be not for elevating the standard to strict scrutiny, but for reducing it to rational-basis review. The latter certainly has a firmer foundation in our past jurisprudence: Whereas no majority of the Court has ever applied strict scrutiny in a case involving sex-based classifications, we routinely applied rational-basis review until the 1970s, see, e.g., Hoyt v. Florida, 368 U.S. 57 (1961); Goesaert v. Cleary, 335 U.S. 464 (1948). And of course normal, rational-basis review of sex-based classifications would be much more in accord with the genesis of heightened standards of judicial review, the famous footnote in United States v. Carolene Products Co., 304 U.S. 144, [152-153, n.4] (1938). . . .

It is hard to consider women a "discrete and insular minorit[y]" unable to employ the "political processes ordinarily to be relied upon," when they constitute a majority of the electorate. And the suggestion that they are incapable of exerting that political power smacks of the same paternalism that the Court so roundly condemns. Moreover, a long list of legislation proves the proposition false. See, e.g., Equal Pay Act of 1963; Title VII of the Civil Rights Act of 1964; Title IX of the Education Amendments of 1972; Women's Business Ownership Act of 1988; Violence Against Women Act of 1994. . . .

. . .

It is beyond question that Virginia has an important state interest in providing effective college education for its citizens. That single-sex instruction is an approach substantially related to that interest should be evident enough from the long and continuing history in this country of men's and women's colleges. But beyond that, as the Court of Appeals here stated: "That single-gender education at the college level is beneficial to both sexes is a fact established in this case." The evidence establishing that fact was overwhelming—indeed, "virtually uncontradicted." . . .

. . . As a theoretical matter, Virginia's educational interest would have been best served . . . by six different types of public colleges—an all-men's, an all-women's, and a coeducational college run in the "adversative method," and an all-men's, an all-women's, and a coeducational college run in the "traditional method." But as a practical matter, of course, Virginia's financial resources, like any State's, are not limitless, and the Commonwealth must select among the available options. Virginia thus has decided to fund, in addition to some 14 coeducational 4-year colleges, one college that is run as an all-male school on the adversative model: the Virginia Military Institute. [Moreover, while] there are "four all-female private [colleges] in Virginia," there is only "one private all-male college," which "indicates that the private sector is providing for th[e] [former] form of education to a much greater extent than it provides for all-male education." In these circumstances, Virginia's election to fund one public all-male institution and one on the adversative model—and to concentrate its resources in a single entity that serves both these interests in diversity—is substantially related to the State's important educational interests.

. . .

Under the constitutional principles announced and applied today, single-sex public education is unconstitutional. . . . [T]he rationale of today's decision is sweeping: for sex-based classifications, a redefinition of intermediate scrutiny that makes it indistinguishable from strict scrutiny. Indeed, the Court indicates that if any program restricted to one sex is "uniqu[e]," it must be opened to members of the opposite sex "who have the will and capacity" to participate in it. I suggest that the single-sex program that will not be capable of being characterized as "unique" is not only unique but nonexistent.[a]

In any event, regardless of whether the Court's rationale leaves some small amount of room for lawyers to argue, it ensures that single-sex public education is functionally dead. The costs of litigating the constitutionality of a single-sex education program, and the risks of ultimately losing that litigation, are simply too high to be embraced by public officials. . . . No state official in his right mind will buy such a high-cost, high-risk lawsuit by commencing a single-sex program. The enemies of single-sex education have won; by persuading only seven Justices (five would have been enough) that their view of the world is enshrined in the Constitution, they have effectively imposed that view on all 50 States. . . .

DISCUSSION

1. *Intermediate scrutiny evolving.* Nearly two decades after its decision in Craig v. Boren, supra, announcing the intermediate scrutiny framework for sex discrimination cases, the *VMI* Court explained the standard of review in considerably more detail. Writing for the Court, Justice Ginsburg observes that a "reviewing court must determine whether the [government's] proffered justification is 'exceedingly persuasive.' The burden of justification is demanding and it rests entirely on the State." She recites the intermediate standard of review (the state must show "that the [challenged] classification serves 'important governmental objectives and that the discriminatory means employed' are 'substantially related to the achievement of those objectives'") and then goes on to observe that the justification on which the government relies must be "genuine, not hypothesized or invented post hoc in response to litigation." Carrying forward the themes of its 1970s cases, the Court emphasizes that the government cannot justify sex-based state action in terms that "rely on overbroad generalizations about the different talents, capacities, or preferences of males and females." It then explains that the intermediate scrutiny framework will invalidate some forms of sex-based state action and not others, emphasizing that the Fourteenth Amendment proscribes sex-based state action that subordinates women:

> "Inherent differences" between men and women, we have come to appreciate, remain cause for celebration, but not for denigration of the members of either sex or for artificial constraints on an individual's opportunity. Sex classifications may be used to compensate women "for particular economic disabilities [they have] suffered," to "promot[e] equal employment opportunity," to advance full development of the talent and capacities of our Nation's people. But such classifications may not be used, as they once were, to create or perpetuate the legal, social, and economic inferiority of women.

How, if at all, does *VMI* change the intermediate scrutiny standard?

---

a. In this regard, I note that the Court—which I concede is under no obligation to do so—provides no example of a program that would pass muster under its reasoning today: not even, for example, a football or wrestling program. On the Court's theory, any woman ready, willing, and physically able to participate in such a program would, as a constitutional matter, be entitled to do so.

2. *Anticlassification versus antisubordination.* The anticlassification principle holds that government may not classify people overtly or surreptitiously on the basis of a forbidden category, for example, their race. The antisubordination principle holds that law may not aggravate or perpetuate the subordinate status of a specially disadvantaged group.[72] On what principle does the *VMI* opinion base its interpretation of the Equal Protection Clause—the anticlassification principle or the antisubordination principle? Note that *VMI* proscribes state action that classifies on the basis of sex—but only proscribes those sex-based policies that "denigrat[e] members of either sex" or impose "artificial constraints on an individual's opportunity" or "create or perpetuate the legal, social, and economic inferiority of women."

Is *VMI* properly read as proscribing sex-based state action that violates the antisubordination principle? If so, what forms of sex-based state action does it proscribe?

How might one determine whether a practice subordinates?[73] Subordination can occur through the creation of social meaning or the infliction of material disadvantage. Commentators observe that practices subordinate by enforcing the social understanding that "members of certain groups, like African Americans or women, are inferior to the members of other groups, like whites or men" or the social understanding that "members of certain groups are not part of the national or local community"—an understanding that "can injure the excluded people's sense of self and sense of belonging." In addition:[74]

> [W]riters in the anti-subordination tradition have . . . argued that practices, institutions, and activities can promote subordination by inflicting dignitary harms on the members of targeted groups. In this case, concern centers on practices that treat the members of disfavored classes as unworthy of equal respect and dignity and instead subject them to humiliation, stigmatization, denigration, and degradation.
>
> Finally, and most concretely, anti-subordination writers argue that practices, institutions, and activities can foster subordination by inflicting a wide variety of material harms on the members of targeted populations. Speaking generally, these writers have identified two, connected categories of material harm. The first . . . focuses on classic indicators of socioeconomic status and social welfare, explaining that practices cause subordinating material harm when they systematically leave the members of targeted groups with less wealth, less political power, less protection

---

72. Jack M. Balkin and Reva B. Siegel, The American Civil Rights Tradition: Anticlassification or Antisubordination?, 58 U. Miami L. Rev. 9 (2003).

73. See id. at 14-15 (observing that "the question of what practices or utterances or institutional arrangements might be subordinating involves interpretive judgments about social meanings, status, and the like, each of which is plainly contestable" as well as "a host of contestable value judgments . . . in determining what dignitary distinctions or distributive arrangements are unjust, and how the legal system should integrate the pursuit of antisubordination commitments with other social goals").

74. Jill Elaine Hasday, The Principle and Practice of Women's "Full Citizenship": A Case Study of Sex-Segregated Public Education, 101 Mich. L. Rev. 755, 775-777 (2002) (footnotes omitted).

from private or public violence, less education, less health, less life expectancy, less access to housing, and/or less leisure. The second focuses on control and autonomy, explaining that practices cause subordinating material harm when they systematically leave the members of targeted groups with less control or power over their own lives and more subject to the control and direction of another person or the state.

What guidance, if any, does the antisubordination principle supply in explaining the equal protection violation in United States v. Virginia, and in demonstrating how it is to be remedied?

a. What factors does the Court emphasize in declaring Virginia's single-sex school unconstitutional?

b. After the school admits women, can it take sex into account in matters of pedagogy or otherwise? Must it house men and women together? What does it mean to subject men and women "equally" to the adversative method? Can the school require men and women to do the same number of push-ups in daily exercises? Why or why not?

c. If administrators wish to run a single-sex school, how must they design their offering to conform with the *VMI* opinion? For one account, see Denise C. Morgan, Anti-Subordination Analysis After United States v. Virginia: Evaluating the Constitutionality of K-12 Single-Sex Public Schools, 1999 U. Chi. Legal F. 381 (1999).

d. Might principles for distinguishing permissible and impermissible sex-based state action in the education context be exported to the race discrimination context? See Serena Mayeri, Reconstructing the Race-Sex Analogy, 49 Wm. & Mary L. Rev. 1789 (2008) (exploring failed efforts to export distinction between "benign" and "invidious" classification, developed in sex equality jurisprudence, to the race context).

3. *The uses of history.* What role does historical evidence play in guiding judgments about VMI's policy? Justice Ginsburg's opinion spends a great deal of time describing the history of women's exclusion from educational institutions in the United States. She views this history as "negative precedent" that can guide the application of intermediate scrutiny. This history illustrates exclusionary forms of sex-based state action that the Court holds violate the Equal Protection Clause. Chief Justice Rehnquist thinks this discussion largely irrelevant; for him the question is what Virginia did after the Supreme Court's decision in Mississippi University for Women v. Hogan, infra, which suggested for the first time that there might be a constitutional problem with single-sex educational institutions. Rehnquist argues that until very recently, no one thought that it was a problem to exclude women from certain institutions. However, times have changed and so we must live according to today's conceptions of justice. Thus, he does not see Virginia's post-1982 decisions as necessarily related to or infected by its pre-1982 treatment of women. Justice Ginsburg disagrees.

Justice Scalia offers the basic principle that "when a practice not expressly prohibited by the text of the Bill of Rights bears the endorsement of a long tradition of open, widespread, and unchallenged use that dates back to the beginning of the Republic, we have no proper basis for striking it down," a principle that also applies "to a practice asserted to be in violation of the post–Civil War Fourteenth Amendment." Is Brown v. Board of Education consistent with this theory? Loving

v. Virginia? The entire corpus of the Court's sex equality jurisprudence, including, for example, the holding in Taylor v. Louisiana that women could not be excluded from juries?

For an analysis of how the history of sex segregation in education can inform application of *Virginia*'s framework, see Jill Elaine Hasday, The Principle and Practice of Women's "Full Citizenship": A Case Study of Sex-Segregated Public Education, 101 Mich. L. Rev. 755 (2002). For an account of how the *Virginia* opinion critically evaluates VMI's sex-based admissions policy by demonstrating its conformity with other repudiated past practices, see Deborah Widiss, Re-viewing the Past: The Use of the Past as Negative Precedent in United States v. Virginia, 108 Yale L.J. 237 (1998).

4. *Inter-branch dialogue on single-sex schools.* In October 2006, during the Bush presidency, the Department of Education amended Title IX[75] regulations to allow for the broader use of single-sex education in public schools. Whereas the previous guidelines only allowed school districts to provide single-sex schools if they offered a comparable single-sex school to students of the excluded sex, the amended regulations permit districts to offer single-sex schools as long as they offer a "substantially equal" coeducational school.[76] More significantly, the regulations allow nonvocational coed elementary or secondary schools to provide single-sex *classes* or educational activities as long as they meet one of two "important objective[s]": "to improve educational achievement" or "to meet the particular, identified educational needs" of students.[77] The regulations mandate that schools implement single-sex programs in an "evenhanded manner" and ensure that enrollment is "completely voluntary."[78] They also order schools to provide all other students with "a substantially equal coeducational class or extracurricular activity in the same subject or activity."[79] In addition, schools "may be required to provide a substantially equal single-sex class or extracurricular activity for students of the excluded sex."[80] When is single-sex education permissible under the Department of Education directive? Is the Bush policy consistent with the constitutional standards announced in *VMI*?

NOTE: INTERMEDIATE SCRUTINY AND SINGLE-SEX EDUCATION

Under what circumstances does *VMI* allow single-sex schools? Note the Court's claim that "[w]e do not question the State's prerogative evenhandedly to support diverse educational opportunities. We address specifically and only an educational opportunity recognized by the District Court and the Court of Appeals as 'unique,' an opportunity available only at Virginia's premier military institute, the

75. Title IX provides that "[n]o person in the United States shall, on the basis of sex, be excluded from participation in, be denied the benefits of, or be subjected to discrimination under any education program or activity receiving Federal financial assistance." 20 U.S.C.A. §1681.

76. 34 C.F.R. §106.34(c) (2006).

77. Id. §106.34(b)(1).

78. Id.

79. Id.

80. Id. §106.34(b)(2).

Commonwealth's sole single-sex public university or college. . . . Thus, we are not faced with the question of whether States can provide 'separate but equal' undergraduate institutions for males and females."

In *VMI*, Justice Ginsburg writes that the intermediate scrutiny framework will invalidate some forms of sex-based state action and not others, emphasizing that the Fourteenth Amendment proscribes sex-based state action that subordinates women:

> Sex classifications may be used to compensate women "for particular economic disabilities [they have] suffered," to "promot[e] equal employment opportunity," to advance full development of the talent and capacities of our Nation's people. But such classifications may not be used, as they once were, to create or perpetuate the legal, social, and economic inferiority of women.

When can sex-segregated education survive strict scrutiny? Does Ginsburg's footnote 7 (footnote b in the opinion supra) help answer this question? In this footnote, Ginsburg reserves the question of the legality of separate but equal institutions based on gender. However, she concludes that single-sex educational opportunities may be constitutional if they "dissipate, rather than perpetuate, traditional gender classifications." What types of single-sex education might satisfy this standard?

The following cases were all decided prior to *VMI*. Would the application of the *VMI* intermediate scrutiny test change the outcome? Should it?

1. *All-Female Nursing School.* In Mississippi University for Women v. Hogan, 458 U.S. 718 (1982), the Court decided whether a state statute that excluded males from enrolling in a state-supported professional nursing school violated equal protection. The respondent, Joe Hogan, an otherwise qualified individual, was denied admission to the school solely because of his sex. School officials informed Hogan that he was permitted to audit courses at MUW and participate fully in classes, but was prevented from enrolling in these courses for credit. Complaining "that he must travel to attend the state-supported nursing schools that concededly are available to him," Hogan contended that MUW's single-sex policy was unconstitutional. The majority reasoned as follows:

> The State's primary justification for maintaining the single-sex admissions policy of MUW's School of Nursing is that it compensates for discrimination against women and, therefore, constitutes educational affirmative action. As applied to the School of Nursing, we find the State's argument unpersuasive.
>
> In limited circumstances, a gender-based classification favoring one sex can be justified if it intentionally and directly assists members of the sex that is disproportionately burdened. However, we consistently have emphasized that "the mere recitation of a benign, compensatory purpose is not an automatic shield which protects against any inquiry into the actual purposes underlying a statutory scheme." Weinberger v. Wiesenfeld. . . . Mississippi has made no showing that women lacked opportunities to obtain training in the field of nursing or to attain positions of leadership in that field when the MUW School of Nursing opened its door

> or that women currently are deprived of such opportunities. In fact, in 1970, the year before the School of Nursing's first class enrolled, women earned 94 percent of the nursing baccalaureate degrees conferred in Mississippi and 98.6 percent of the degrees earned nationwide. . . . As one would expect, the labor force reflects the same predominance of women in nursing. When MUW's School of Nursing began operation, nearly 98 percent of all employed registered nurses were female.
>
> Rather than compensate for discriminatory barriers faced by women, MUW's policy of excluding males from admission to the School of Nursing tends to perpetuate the stereotyped view of nursing as an exclusively woman's job. By assuring that Mississippi allots more openings in its state-supported nursing schools to women than it does to men, MUW's admissions policy lends credibility to the old view that women, not men, should become nurses, and makes the assumption that nursing is a field for women a self-fulfilling prophecy. [A]lthough the State recited a "benign, compensatory purpose," it failed to establish that the alleged objective is the actual purpose underlying the discriminatory classification.
>
> [T]he State has [also] made no showing that the gender-based classification is substantially and directly related to its proposed compensatory objective. To the contrary, MUW's policy of permitting men to attend classes as auditors fatally undermines its claim that women, at least those in the School of Nursing, are adversely affected by the presence of men. . . .

Would "separate but equal" male-only and female-only schools satisfy the majority in *Hogan*? The majority in the *VMI* case?

Hogan argued that it was inconvenient for him to travel miles away to another nursing school when MUW was in Columbia, where he lived and worked, while similarly situated women working full time as nurses could attend MUW. What result if MUW were located across the street from a coed nursing school?

Chief Justice Burger, dissenting in *Hogan*, emphasized the narrowness of the majority's holding and suggested "that a State might well be justified in maintaining, for example, the option of an all-women's business school or liberal arts program." Justice Blackmun, in a separate dissent, also noted the purported narrowness of the Court's holding, but he expressed skepticism about preventing its "spillover" into the wider issue of sex-segregated education. Justice Powell could "see no principled way—in light of the Court's rationale—to reach a different result with respect to other MUW schools and departments." After the *VMI* case, what do you think the meaning of *Hogan* is?

2. *Boys and Girls High School.* In Vorcheimer v. School District of Philadelphia, 532 F.2d 880 (3d Cir. 1975), *aff'd by an equally divided Court,* 430 U.S. 703 (1977), a high-school girl argued for the right to attend Philadelphia's all-male academic high school, Central High School. *Vorcheimer* was decided after *Reed* and *Frontiero* but before Craig v. Boren. The majority held that maintaining separate facilities did not violate the Constitution:

> Academic high schools have high admission standards and offer only college preparatory courses. There are but two such schools in Philadelphia, and they accept students from the entire city rather than operating on a neighborhood basis. Central is restricted to males, and Girls High

> School, as the name implies, admits only females. . . . The Philadelphia school system does not have a co-ed academic school with similar scholastic requirements for admission. . . . The courses offered by the two schools are similar and of equal quality. The academic facilities are comparable, with the exception of those in the scientific field where Central's are superior. . . .
>
> [G]iven the objective of a quality education and a controverted, but respected theory that adolescents may study more effectively in single-sex schools, the policy of the school board here does bear a substantial relationship [to an important governmental interest].[81]

Judge Gibbon's dissenting opinion compared the majority's decision to Plessy v. Ferguson and argued:

> The Board [of Education] did not present sufficient evidence that coeducation has an adverse effect upon a student's academic achievement. Indeed the Board could not seriously assert that argument in view of its policy of assigning the vast majority of its students to coeducational schools. . . . Thus, the Board's single-sex policy reflects a choice among educational techniques but not necessarily one substantially related to its stated educational objectives. One of those objectives, in fact, is to provide "educational options to students and their parents." The implementation of the Board's policy excluding females from Central actually precludes achievement of this objective because there is no option of a coeducational academic senior high school.

Is *Vorcheimer* consistent with *Hogan*? With the *VMI* case?

3. *Race and Single-Sex Education.* Could the government use single-sex schooling to alleviate conditions associated with racial stereotyping and inequality? Would *VMI* allow for sex segregation in education in pursuit of these goals? Garrett v. Board of Education for the School District of the City of Detroit, 775 F. Supp. 1004 (E.D. Mich. 1991), examines single-sex education in a modern, urban setting. The public schools developed the academies, which allowed only boys to enroll, in order to mitigate what had been deemed as "the crisis facing African-American males manifested by high homicide, unemployment, and drop-out rates." Although the court deemed "the purpose for which the Academies came into being as an important one[,] . . . [t]he purpose, however, is insufficient to override the rights of females to equal opportunities." The court judged "dangerous . . . the prospect that should the male academies proceed and succeed, success would be equated with the absence of girls rather than any of the educational factors that more probably caused the outcome," recognizing the importance of the public perception of single-sex education.

---

81. The Third Circuit also referenced Williams v. McNair, 316 F. Supp. 134 (D.S.C. 1970), *aff'd*, 401 U.S. 951 (1971) (per curiam), which upheld, without opinion, a three-judge court's decision upholding the women-only admissions policy of Winthrop College in South Carolina. *Williams* was decided one year before *Reed*.

Do you think *Garrett* was rightly or wrongly decided? The *Garrett* litigation seems to have defused the movement for all-male urban public schools that was gaining in popularity across the nation; in its wake, several proposals for all-male schools were revised to provide for coed Afrocentric curricula.[82]

4. *Benefits of Single-Sex Education.* What are the benefits of single-sex education? In his dissenting opinion in Mississippi University for Women v. Hogan,[83] Justice Powell described the benefits that single-sex education can provide. Powell quoted comments by the president of Wellesley College explaining that "[t]he research we have clearly demonstrates that women's colleges produce a disproportionate number of women leaders and women in responsible positions in society."[84] In addition, Justice Powell's dissent in *Hogan* cited "[a] 10-year empirical study by the Cooperative Institutional Research Program of the American Council of Education and the University of California, Los Angeles . . . [which] has affirmed the distinctive benefits of single-sex colleges and universities. As summarized in A. Astin, Four Critical Years 232 (1977), the data established that

> [b]oth [male and female] single-sex colleges facilitate student involvement in several areas: academic, interaction with faculty, and verbal aggressiveness. . . . Men's and women's colleges also have a positive effect on intellectual self-esteem. Students at single-sex colleges are more satisfied than students at coeducational colleges with virtually all aspects of college life. . . . The only area where students are less satisfied is social life. . . .

As suggested by Powell's dissent in *Hogan*, and by the Third Circuit's opinion in *Vorcheimer*, some studies suggest that women may do better in single-sex educational institutions. There is also evidence to the contrary.[85] Nancy Levit sums up the arguments on both sides of the debate and acknowledges concerns that have yet to be addressed:[86]

---

82. Rosemary C. Salomone, Same, Different, Equal: Rethinking Single-Sex Schooling 131, 138 (2003). For a critical discussion of recent efforts to promote single-sex education in urban schools, see Verna L. Williams, Reform or Retrenchment? Single-Sex Education and the Construction of Race and Gender, 2004 Wis. L. Rev. 15. See also Rosemary C. Salomone, Rights and Wrongs in the Debate over Single-Sex Schooling, 93 B.U. L. Rev. 971 (2013) (proposing a context-based approach to single-sex schooling and presenting evidence that "single-sex schools may prove especially effective for minority students").

83. 458 U.S. 718 (1982).

84. Id. at 738 n.4.

85. For a sampling of the literature, see Nancy Levit, Separating Equals: Educational Research and the Long-Term Consequences of Sex Segregation, 67 Geo. Wash. L. Rev. 451 (1999); Cynthia Fuchs Epstein, The Myths and Justifications of Sex Segregation in Higher Education: VMI and the Citadel, 4 Duke J. Gender L. & Pol'y 101 (1997); Dianne Avery, Institutional Myths, Historical Narratives and Social Science Evidence: Reading the "Record" in the Virginia Military Institute Case, 5 S. Cal. Rev. L. & Women's Stud. 189 (1996); Kristin S. Caplice, The Case for Public Single-Sex Education, 18 Harv. J.L. & Pub. Pol'y 227 (1994); Karla Cooper-Boggs, Note, The Link Between Private and Public Single-Sex Colleges: Will Wellesley Stand or Fall with the Citadel?, 29 Ind. L. Rev. 131 (1995); Deborah Rhode, Association and Assimilation, 81 Nw. U. L. Rev. 106 (1986).

86. Nancy Levit, Separating Equals: Educational Research and the Long-Term Consequences of Sex Segregation, 67 Geo. Wash. L. Rev. 451, 452-455 (1999).

> Supporters argue that girls have been disadvantaged historically in education and presently in coeducational classrooms experience neglect, participate less, and suffer lowered self-esteem. The solution: a friendly, all-girl environment, away from the domination of boys, where girls can excel and become leaders. Although little empirical research supports it, some proponents also make the parallel argument that boys benefit from segregated schooling, free from the gonadal challenge of distracting girl classmates. For both sexes, the provision of a single-sex option offers a "diversity" of academic choices in the educational system. . . .
>
> Supporters assume that we can vest single-sex education with new social meaning. What they overlook, though, is the cultural significance that attaches to the relentless sex segregation in all other areas of life. . . .
>
> Although the educational research regarding the efficacy of single-sex schools is mixed at best, the social research is absolutely clear that separation on the basis of identity characteristics creates feelings of individual inadequacy and instills beliefs about group hierarchy. Government separation of equals sends the message that something is contaminative about the presence of the "opposite" sex.

There is academic debate about the benefits and harms of sex segregation in education. Should the constitutional question turn on this analysis? Are we more receptive to this kind of justification for single-sex education than for racially segregated schools? Why?

NOTE: AFFIRMATIVE ACTION AND INTERMEDIATE SCRUTINY

Does the *VMI* standard for sex discrimination govern the jurisprudence on affirmative action based on gender? The law in this area is unclear. Jason Skaggs explains:[87]

> The confusion associated with Virginia is exacerbated in the context of gender-based affirmative action, an issue which the Supreme Court has never examined under the Equal Protection Clause. This lack of direct Supreme Court guidance has forced the lower federal courts to look to other case law to determine how to evaluate gender-based affirmative action programs. The search has resulted in a circuit split on the proper level of scrutiny. Some courts analyze the programs under the intermediate scrutiny approach developed for examining gender classifications. Others employ the more demanding strict scrutiny standard of analysis found in the Court's precedents on race-based affirmative action. The fact that the Court has not developed precise requirements for each level of scrutiny only compounds the problem.

The Sixth Circuit applies strict scrutiny to affirmative action cases based on gender. See Brunet v. City of Columbus, 1 F.3d 390, 403-404 (6th Cir. 1993); Vogel

87. Jason M. Skaggs, Justifying Gender-Based Affirmative Action Under United States v. Virginia's "Exceedingly Persuasive Justification" Standard, 86 Cal. L. Rev. 1169, 1170-1171 (1998).

v. City of Cincinnati, 959 F.2d 594 (6th Cir. 1992); Long v. City of Saginaw, 911 F.2d 1192 (6th Cir. 1990); Conlin v. Blanchard, 890 F.2d 811 (6th Cir. 1989). Note that this position, taken literally, would mean that it would be easier to justify programs deliberately designed to discriminate against women than gender-conscious programs designed to combat sex discrimination against women.

The Third, Ninth, Tenth, and Eleventh Circuits all apply intermediate scrutiny to gender-based affirmative action policies. For example, in Contractors Association of Eastern Pennsylvania, Inc. v. City of Philadelphia, 6 F.3d 990 (3d Cir. 1993), the Third Circuit considered a City of Philadelphia ordinance creating preferences in city contracting for businesses owned by racial and ethnic minorities, women, and handicapped persons, applying the intermediate scrutiny standard. The ordinance set goals of 15 percent participation in city contracts for minority-owned businesses, 10 percent for women-owned businesses, and 2 percent for businesses owned by handicapped persons. The court reasoned that "[a]pplication of intermediate scrutiny to the Ordinance's gender preference . . . follows logically from *Croson*, which held municipal affirmative action programs benefiting racial minorities merit the same standard of review as that given other race-based classifications." For more cases in which intermediate scrutiny is applied to affirmative action based on gender, see Engineering Contractors Ass'n v. Metropolitan Dade County, 122 F.3d 895, 907-908 (11th Cir. 1997); Concrete Works, Inc. v. City & County of Denver, 36 F.3d 1513, 1519 (10th Cir. 1994); Ensley Branch, NAACP v. Seibels, 31 F.3d 1548 (11th Cir. 1994); Coral Constr. Co. v. King County, 941 F.2d 910, 930 (9th Cir. 1991). For recent commentary, see Rosalie Berger Levinson, Gender-Based Affirmative Action and Reverse Gender Bias: Beyond *Gratz, Parents Involved,* and *Ricci*, 34 Harv. J.L. & Gender 1 (2011).

C. *Intermediate Scrutiny and Claims of Sex Difference: Pregnancy as a Justification for Sex-Differentiated Treatment of Men and Women*

The Court has invalidated most laws that classify on the basis of sex challenged on equal protection grounds since the 1970s. But in a few cases, the Court has upheld the challenged regulation for reasons tied to the fact that men and women differ in their role in the reproduction of the species.

This section will focus on application of the intermediate scrutiny test in this small group of cases. It will focus in particular on a small group of cases *not involving pregnancy* in which the Court has pointed to reproductive differences between the sexes as justifying state action that classifies on the basis of sex.[88] As we will see, the laws in these cases do not regulate pregnancy; instead, one way or another, the laws regulate sex that occurs out of wedlock.

---

88. The group of cases considered here, which emphasize that differences in reproductive roles define the sexes, is especially difficult to reconcile the Court's decision in *Geduldig*, discussed infra, which reasons that state action directed at pregnant women does not necessarily classify on the basis of gender within the meaning of *Reed* or *Frontiero*.

In Michael M. v. Superior Court of Sonoma County, 450 U.S. 464 (1981), the Supreme Court examined California's statutory rape law, which defined unlawful sexual intercourse as "an act of sexual intercourse accomplished with a female not the wife of the perpetrator, where the female is under the age of 18 years." The petitioners claimed that since the law makes men alone liable for the crime, it was in violation of the Equal Protection Clause. Justice Rehnquist applied an extremely diluted version of the intermediate scrutiny test in a plurality opinion that credited claims about legislative purpose that were *not* advanced at the time of the statute's enactment:

> The justification for the [sex-based statutory rape law] offered by the State, and accepted by the Supreme Court of California, is that the legislature sought to prevent illegitimate teenage pregnancies. That finding, of course, is entitled to great deference. . . .
>
> We are satisfied not only that the prevention of illegitimate pregnancy is at least one of the "purposes" of the statute, but also that the State has a strong interest in preventing such pregnancy. At the risk of stating the obvious, teenage pregnancies, which have increased dramatically over the last two decades, have significant social, medical, and economic consequences for both the mother and her child, and the State. . . .
>
> We need not be medical doctors to discern that young men and young women are not similarly situated with respect to the problems and the risks of sexual intercourse. Only women may become pregnant, and they suffer disproportionately the profound physical, emotional, and psychological consequences of sexual activity. The statute at issue here protects women from sexual intercourse at an age when those consequences are particularly severe.
>
> The question thus boils down to whether a State may attack the problem of sexual intercourse and teenage pregnancy directly by prohibiting a male from having sexual intercourse with a minor female. We hold that such a statute is sufficiently related to the State's objectives to pass constitutional muster. . . .
>
> In upholding the California statute we also recognize that this is not a case where a statute is being challenged on the grounds that it "invidiously discriminates" against females. To the contrary, the statute places a burden on males which is not shared by females. But we find nothing to suggest that men, because of past discrimination or peculiar disadvantages, are in need of the special solicitude of the courts.

Justices Stewart and Blackmun concurred and Justice Stevens dissented from the opinion.

Critics of the plurality opinion in *Michael M.* have pointed out that sex-based statutory rape laws are not based on biology, but instead reflect conventional stereotypes about male and female roles. As the dissent emphasizes, the historic purpose of statutory rape laws was to preserve the chastity of young women before marriage, not to prevent teen pregnancy. Even Justice Rehnquist concedes: "Some legislators may have been concerned about preventing teenage pregnancies, others about protecting young females from physical injury or from the loss of 'chastity,' and still others about promoting various religious and moral attitudes towards premarital sex." If the purpose of the statutory rape law was to preserve the chastity of young women, rather than to prevent teen pregnancy, would that make a difference to constitutional analysis of the statute under *Craig*'s intermediate scrutiny standard? What about under *VMI*'s intermediate scrutiny standard? For more on statutory rape laws, see Rita Eidson, Comment, The Constitutionality of Statutory Rape Laws, 27 UCLA L. Rev. 757, 762 (1980); Kay L. Levine, No Penis, No Problem, 33 Fordham Urb. L.J. 357, 375-380 (2006).

In focusing on the reproductive consequences of statutory rape, the Court ignored other factors at issue. Catharine MacKinnon writes that in *Michael M.*[89]

> [the] fact that it is overwhelmingly girls who are sexually victimized by older males for reasons wholly unrelated to their capacity to become pregnant was completely obscured. The facts of social inequality, of sex aggravated by age, that could have supported particular legislative attention to the sexual assault of girls were not even considered. Underage girls form a credible disadvantaged group for equal protection purposes when the social facts of sexual assault are faced, facts which prominently feature one-sided sexual aggression by older males.

Are MacKinnon's justifications for sex-based statutory rape laws more compelling than those Rehnquist cites? Would they provide a compelling justification according to intermediate scrutiny analysis? Was the discussion of pregnancy a red herring for the real issues of gender inequality at play?

Is there any harm in removing gender classifications from laws that regulate gender-salient practices like rape or domestic violence?

Frances Olsen writes:[90]

> Statutory rape laws . . . pose a classic political dilemma for feminists. On one hand, they protect females; like laws against rape, incest, child molestation, and child marriage, statutory rape laws are a statement of social disapproval of certain forms of exploitation. To some extent they reduce abuse and victimization. On the other hand, statutory rape laws restrict the sexual activity of young women and reinforce the double standard of sexual morality. The laws both protect and undermine women's rights.

Most states now use sex-neutral language to describe both perpetrators and victims of the act of rape, and the federal government updated its definition of "forcible rape" in 2012 to include any gender of victim or perpetrator.[91] Nevertheless, there are a few cases involving equal protection challenges to statutes that define rape in terms of nonconsensual penetration of women by men. In almost all

---

89. Catharine A. MacKinnon, Reflections on Sex Equality Under Law, 100 Yale L.J. 1281, 1305-1306 (1991).

90. Frances Olsen, Statutory Rape: A Feminist Critique of Rights Analysis, 63 Tex. L. Rev. 387, 401-402, 412, 418-420, 426 (1984).

91. Press Release, U.S. Dep't of Just., Attorney General Eric Holder Announces Revisions to the Uniform Crime Report's Definition of Rape (Jan. 6, 2012), http://www.justice.gov/opa/pr/2012/January/12-ag-018.html.

cases, the statutes have been upheld.[92] In addition, almost all states no longer have gendered statutory rape laws, mostly as a result of legislative changes.[93] Nevertheless, *Michael M.* has never been explicitly overturned.

In *Michael M.* the statutory rape law provided that intercourse could not be punished as long as it was between a married couple, regardless of the female's age. The law upheld was therefore only punishing intercourse that occurred outside the bonds of marriage.

The Court has appealed to reproductive differences to justify applying a diluted form of intermediate scrutiny to other laws regulating sex outside of marriage. Consider the following case concerning the citizenship rights of persons born abroad and out of wedlock to American parents.

Tuan Anh Nguyen v. INS

533 U.S. 53 (2001)

[8 U.S.C. §1409(a) automatically grants American citizenship upon birth to a child born out of wedlock in a foreign country if born to an American mother. If American parent was the father, an out of wedlock child born in a foreign country does not become a citizen automatically. For the child to become a citizen, the father must establish paternity before the child turns 18, either through legitimation, a declaration of paternity under oath by the father, or a court order of paternity. In addition, "the father (unless deceased) [must] agree[] in writing to provide financial support for the person until the person reaches the age of 18 years."

Nguyen was born in Vietnam to an American father, Joseph Boulais, and a Vietnamese mother. When he was six years old he came to the United States to live with Boulais and became a permanent resident. When he was 22, Nguyen pleaded guilty to sexual assault on a minor. The INS began deportation proceedings. Nguyen defended on the grounds that he was a United States citizen, and his father established his paternity through DNA testing when Nguyen was 28 years old. Nguyen and his father argued that §1409(a) violates equal protection by providing different rules for attainment of citizenship by children born abroad and out of wedlock depending upon whether the one parent with American citizenship is the mother or the father. The Court considered a challenge to §1409(a) in Miller v. Albright, 523 U.S. 420 (1998), but was unable to agree on a single rationale.]

Justice KENNEDY delivered the opinion of the Court.

Congress' decision . . . is justified by two important governmental objectives. . . . The first . . . is the importance of assuring that a biological parent-child

---

92. See, e.g., Country v. Parratt, 684 F.2d 588 (8th Cir.), *cert. denied*, 459 U.S. 1043 (1982); People v. Salinas, 551 P.2d 703 (Colo. Sup. Ct. 1976) (en banc); State v. Witt, 245 N.W.2d 612 (Minn. 1976); Stewart v. State, 534 S.W.2d 875 (Ct. Crim. App. Tenn. 1976); State v. Kelly, 526 P.2d 720 (Ariz. 1974), *cert. denied*, 420 U.S. 935 (1975); State v. Ewald, 216 N.W.2d 213 (Wis. 1974); Brooks v. State, 330 A.2d 670 (Md. Ct. Spec. App. 1975). Contra, People v. Liberta, 64 N.Y.2d 152, 474 N.E.2d 567 (N.Y. 1984) (holding unconstitutional exemption of females for forcible rape of males).

93. Idaho is the only state that still has explicitly gendered statutory rape laws. See Idaho Code §18-6101.

relationship exists. In the case of the mother, the relation is verifiable from the birth itself. The mother's status is documented in most instances by the birth certificate or hospital records and the witnesses who attest to her having given birth. In the case of the father, the uncontestable fact is that he need not be present at the birth. If he is present, furthermore, that circumstance is not incontrovertible proof of fatherhood. . . . Section 1409(a)(4)'s provision of three options for a father seeking to establish paternity—legitimation, paternity oath, and court order of paternity—is designed to ensure an acceptable documentation of paternity.

Petitioners argue that [DNA testing] is sufficient to achieve the end of establishing paternity. . . . The Constitution, moreover, does not require that Congress elect one particular mechanism from among many possible methods of establishing paternity, even if that mechanism arguably might be the most scientifically advanced method. With respect to DNA testing, the expense, reliability, and availability of such testing in various parts of the world may have been of particular concern to Congress. . . . Given the proof of motherhood that is inherent in birth itself, it is unremarkable that Congress did not require the same affirmative steps of mothers.

[T]o require Congress to speak without reference to the gender of the parent with regard to its objective of ensuring a blood tie between parent and child would be to insist on a hollow neutrality. . . . Congress could have required both mothers and fathers to prove parenthood within 30 days or, for that matter, 18 years, of the child's birth. Given that the mother is always present at birth, but that the father need not be, the facially neutral rule would sometimes require fathers to take additional affirmative steps which would not be required of mothers, whose names will appear on the birth certificate as a result of their presence at the birth, and who will have the benefit of witnesses to the birth to call upon. . . . Here, the use of gender specific terms takes into account a biological difference between the parents.

The second important governmental interest . . . is . . . ensur[ing] that the child and the citizen parent have some demonstrated opportunity or potential to develop . . . real, everyday ties that provide a connection between child and citizen parent and, in turn, the United States. In the case of a citizen mother and a child born overseas, the opportunity for a meaningful relationship between citizen parent and child inheres in the very event of birth, an event so often critical to our constitutional and statutory understandings of citizenship. The mother knows that the child is in being and is hers and has an initial point of contact with him. There is at least an opportunity for mother and child to develop a real, meaningful relationship.

The same opportunity does not result from the event of birth, as a matter of biological inevitability, in the case of the unwed father. Given the 9-month interval between conception and birth, it is not always certain that a father will know that a child was conceived, nor is it always clear that even the mother will be sure of the father's identity. This fact takes on particular significance in the case of a child born overseas and out of wedlock. One concern in this context has always been with young people, men for the most part, who are on duty with the Armed Forces in foreign countries.

. . . The ease of travel and the willingness of Americans to visit foreign countries have resulted in numbers of trips abroad that must be of real concern when we contemplate the prospect of accepting petitioners' argument, which would mandate, contrary to Congress' wishes, citizenship by male parentage subject to no condition save the father's previous length of residence in this country. . . . Principles of equal protection do not require Congress to ignore this reality. To the contrary, these facts demonstrate the critical importance of the Government's interest in ensuring some opportunity for a tie between citizen father and foreign born child which is a reasonable substitute for the opportunity manifest between mother and child at the time of birth. Indeed, especially in light of the number of Americans who take short sojourns abroad, the prospect that a father might not even know of the conception is a realistic possibility. . . . [U]nlike the case of the mother, there is no assurance that the father and his biological child will ever meet. . . .

[Section] 1409 addresses an undeniable difference in the circumstance of the parents at the time a child is born. . . . [T]he difference does not result from some stereotype, defined as a frame of mind resulting from irrational or uncritical analysis. There is nothing irrational or improper in the recognition that at the moment of birth—a critical event in the statutory scheme and in the whole tradition of citizenship law—the mother's knowledge of the child and the fact of parenthood have been established in a way not guaranteed in the case of the unwed father. This is not a stereotype.

[T]he imposition of certain additional requirements upon an unwed father—substantially relate to [Congress's purposes]. . . . [I]t should be unsurprising that Congress decided to require that an opportunity for a parent-child relationship occur during the formative years of the child's minority. In furtherance of the desire to ensure some tie between this country and one who seeks citizenship, various other statutory provisions concerning citizenship and naturalization require some act linking the child to the United States to occur before the child reaches 18 years of age. . . .

To fail to acknowledge even our most basic biological differences—such as the fact that a mother must be present at birth but the father need not be—risks making the guarantee of equal protection superficial, and so disserving it. Mechanistic classification of all our differences as stereotypes would operate to obscure those misconceptions and prejudices that are real. The distinction embodied in the statutory scheme here at issue is not marked by misconception and prejudice, nor does it show disrespect for either class. The difference between men and women in relation to the birth process is a real one, and the principle of equal protection does not forbid Congress to address the problem at hand in a manner specific to each gender.

Justice SCALIA, with whom Justice THOMAS joins, concurring.

I remain of the view that the Court lacks power to provide relief of the sort requested in this suit—namely, conferral of citizenship on a basis other than that prescribed by Congress. [On] the merits of petitioners' equal protection claims[,] I join the opinion of the Court.

Justice O'CONNOR, with whom Justice SOUTER, Justice GINSBURG, and Justice BREYER join, dissenting.

. . . [T]he idea that a mother's presence at birth supplies adequate assurance of an opportunity to develop a relationship while a father's presence at birth does not would appear to rest only on an overbroad sex-based generalization. A mother may not have an opportunity for a relationship if the child is removed from his or her mother on account of alleged abuse or neglect, or if the child and mother are separated by tragedy, such as disaster or war, of the sort apparently present in this case. There is no reason, other than stereotype, to say that fathers who are present at birth lack an opportunity for a relationship on similar terms. The "physical differences between men and women," therefore do not justify §1409(a)(4)'s discrimination. . . .

. . . If Congress wishes to advance [the goal of "establishing . . . a real, practical relationship of considerable substance"], it could easily do so by employing a sex-neutral classification. . . . For example, Congress could require some degree of regular contact between the child and the citizen parent over a period of time.

The claim that §1409(a)(4) substantially relates to the achievement of the goal of a "real, practical relationship" thus finds support not in biological differences but instead in a stereotype—*i.e.*, "the generalization that mothers are significantly more likely than fathers . . . to develop caring relationships with their children." Such a claim relies on "the very stereotype the law condemns," "lends credibility" to the generalization, and helps to convert that "assumption" into "a self-fulfilling prophecy." Indeed, contrary to this stereotype, Boulais has reared Nguyen, while Nguyen apparently has lacked a relationship with his mother. . . .

[T]he majority [says that there is no stereotyping because] a "stereotype" is "defined as a frame of mind resulting from irrational or uncritical analysis." This Court has long recognized, however, that an impermissible stereotype may enjoy empirical support and thus be in a sense "rational." Indeed, the stereotypes that underlie a sex-based classification "may hold true for many, even most, individuals." But in numerous cases where a measure of truth has inhered in the generalization, "the Court has rejected official actions that classify unnecessarily and overbroadly by gender when more accurate and impartial functional lines can be drawn."

Nor do stereotypes consist only of those overbroad generalizations that the reviewing court considers to "show disrespect" for a class. Compare, e.g., *Craig*. The hallmark of a stereotypical sex-based classification under this Court's precedents is not whether the classification is insulting, but whether it "relie[s] upon the simplistic, outdated assumption that gender could be used as a 'proxy for other, more germane bases of classification.'" *Mississippi Univ. for Women*. . . .

Section 1409 was first enacted as §205 of the Nationality Act of 1940. [Its original rationale was that] "[u]nder American law the mother has a right to custody and control of such child as against the putative father, and is *bound* to maintain it as its *natural guardian*." Section 1409(a)(4) is thus paradigmatic of a historic regime that left women with responsibility, and freed men from responsibility, for nonmarital children. . . . [Today] our States' child custody and support laws no longer assume that mothers alone are "bound" to serve as "natural guardians" of nonmarital children. The majority, however, rather than confronting the stereotypical notion that mothers must care for these children and fathers may ignore them, quietly condones the "very stereotype the law condemns." . . . Indeed, the majority's discussion [of military personnel and overseas travel] may itself simply reflect the stereotype of male irresponsibility that is no more a basis for the validity of the classification than are stereotypes about the "traditional" behavior patterns of women.

DISCUSSION

1. *Extramarital sex.* In *Nguyen,* as in *Michael M.,* extramarital sex is a central issue in the case. The challenged statute only denies American citizenship to children born to an American father if the child is born out of wedlock. If the child was born to a non-American mother who was married to an American father, the statute would not apply. As the majority opinion acknowledges, a completely different statute (8 U.S.C. §1401(g)) governs the citizenship of children born abroad to married parents. How do the circumstances of conception and birth shape the Court's reasoning?

2. *Heightened scrutiny?* Is the standard of review applied in *Nguyen* more like that one the Court applied in United States v. Virginia or in *Michael M.*? The dissenting Justices in *Nguyen* argued that the majority actually applied a weaker standard of review than heightened scrutiny. They claimed that the majority "hypothesizes about the interest served by the statute and fails adequately to inquire into [its] actual purposes." Do you think that the real purpose of §1409 was to "ensur[e] some opportunity for a tie between [a] citizen father and foreign born child" during the child's minority years?

3. *Biological differences or sex-role expectations?* The majority argues that the biological fact that women must be present at birth while men need not makes it easier to establish who the mother is and increases the likelihood that the mother will form a lasting relationship with the child. Is the Court reasoning from biological facts only?

The implicit story behind §1409(a) and §1409(c) is that other people will know who the mother is and hold her responsible for the illegitimate child, and the mother herself will feel a responsibility to raise the child. Men, on the other hand, cannot be trusted (or expected) to take care of their illegitimate children. Note, however, that if a woman gives birth at home and then abandons the child, the child is a citizen if the mother meets the residency requirements of §1409(c). In this case, it was in fact the father, Joseph Boulais, who raised Nguyen, both in Vietnam and in the United States, and fought to keep him from being deported.

Why does the Court use biology as a shorthand for culture? One possibility is that the Court believes that maternal and paternal behaviors are "biological" in the sense of being hardwired. A second possibility is that the Court recognizes that different treatment of out-of-wedlock parenting by women and men is rooted in social roles of sufficient importance that the Court wishes to preserve these roles. The Court appeals to biological difference because, under equal protection law, biological difference supplies the most powerful justification for preserving role-differentiated treatment of men and women; equal protection doctrine assumes that regulation responsive to biological differences does not reflect stereotypes, but "real" differences. By characterizing the government's interest as predicated on biological differences (presence at the time and place of birth) the Court can justify upholding the statute with less judicial scrutiny.

Suppose the Court acknowledged that some cultural expectations about gendered behavior — like male irresponsibility with respect to illegitimate children — are sufficiently robust and have sufficiently important consequences that Congress must take them into account. Although §1409(a) and §1409(c) may actually reinforce gender stereotypes, one might argue, that is a risk worth taking. Put in those terms, is the result reasonable? How do we tell when the Court has properly struck this balance? Note that by couching the question in terms of biological difference, the Court can avoid the objection that it is engaged in a controversial, value-laden balancing. Do you think that if courts were more forthright, judges would be likely to reach more just results? Consider the reasoning of Judge Andrew Kleinfeld, offered in a dissenting opinion in a case raising a very similar issue. Judge Kleinfeld opined that Congress was well within its constitutional authority to pass a statute that would minimize the burdens created by "paternity and citizenship claims" asserted by "the women the [U.S.] soldiers left behind and their children." "This may not be pretty but it is a rational basis for a sex distinction." United States v. Ahumada-Aguilar, 189 F.3d 1121, 1129 (9th Cir. 1999) (Kleinfeld, J., dissenting).

4. *Do sex-differentiated parental rights and responsibilities reflect physical or traditional sex-role differences?* Section 1409 imposes a financial obligation on men who wish to obtain citizenship for their foreign-born nonmarital children. Section 1409(a)(3) requires that the father agree in writing to support the child until the age of 18. (Note that women are not required to provide any promise of financial support for the illegitimate child.) Kristin Collins argues that this requirement actually benefits fathers, who may avoid this burden by dissociating from their nonmarital children. At the same time, Collins argues, the law burdens mothers with full responsibility for caretaking.

A historical account locates this maternal obligation in coverture and citizenship law, which served to protect fathers from claims for property or support by nonmarital children:[94]

> [A]n expanded history of American citizenship transmission reveals that the problem with §1409 is not simply that it rests on stereotypes of caretaker mothers and uninterested ("fleeting") fathers. Rather, there is a more coercive aspect to the law: It assumes and perpetuates a legal rule that assigns full responsibility for nonmarital children to mothers, leaving similarly situated men free from the burdens of parenthood.

Is this the fundamental harm in *Nguyen*? Would a sex-neutral statute burden mothers in the same way?

5. *Sex, race and citizenship at the Nation's borders:* The not-so-implicit concern expressed in the majority opinion is that American men traveling around the globe may father large numbers of illegitimate children, leading to what the Court describes as "the difficult context of conferring citizenship on vast numbers of persons." Disentangle the considerations that might fuel this concern. What kinds of gender and racial stereotypes may be present? Which concerns does the Constitution allow Congress to take into consideration, and which are impermissible bases for restricting access to American citizenship? For a discussion of the role that race has played in the development and application of the gender-based citizenship statute at issue in *Nguyen*, see Kristin A. Collins, Illegitimate Borders: *Jus Sanguinis*

---

94. Kristin Collins, When Father's Rights Are Mothers' Duties: The Failure of Equal Protection in *Miller v. Albright*, 109 Yale L.J. 1669, 1681-1682 (2000).

Citizenship and the Legal Construction of Family, Race, and Nation, 123 Yale L.J. 2134 (2014), which argues that gender-asymmetrical citizenship laws were regularly used to deny the citizenship claims of non-white children of American fathers.

6. *Putative parenthood.* The Court has also addressed the issue of out-of-wedlock births in a group of cases involving the parental rights of unwed fathers of *citizen* children. The cases again involve extramarital relations—specifically whether government may consider sex in defining the rights of parents of children born out of wedlock. Appeal to reproductive differences between men and women is not as open, but often tacit, in this group of cases. For example, in Parham v. Hughes, 441 U.S. 347 (1979), a plurality of the Court upheld a Georgia statute prohibiting an unwed father, but not an unwed mother, from suing for a child's wrongful death unless the father had previously legitimated the child. The majority concluded that "it is clear that the Georgia statute does not invidiously discriminate against the appellant simply because he is of the male sex. The fact is that mothers and fathers of illegitimate children are not similarly situated. Under Georgia law, only a father can by voluntary unilateral action make an illegitimate child legitimate. Unlike the mother of an illegitimate child whose identity will rarely be in doubt, the identity of the father will frequently be unknown." The Supreme Court's position in this group of cases, decided several decades ago, is complex. See Stanley v. Illinois, 405 U.S. 645 (1972); Caban v. Mohammed, 441 U.S. 380 (1979); Lehr v. Robertson, 463 U.S. 248 (1983).

SESSIONS v. MORALES-SANTANA, 137 S. CT. 1678 (2017): [The Court distinguished *Nguyen* in Sessions v. Morales-Santana. At issue in that case was an additional requirement for unwed parents to transmit citizenship to their children born abroad—that the unwed parent had been physically present in the United States for a designated period of time. At the time of Morales-Santana's birth, Section 1401(a)(7) required ten years' physical presence in the United States prior to the child's birth, with at least five of those years after the parent turned 14. (The same rule applies when a child is born overseas and the parents are married, but only one parent is a U.S. citizen.)

Section 1409(c) created an exception for an unwed U.S.-citizen mother. Her citizenship can be transmitted to a child born abroad if she has lived continuously in the United States for just one year prior to the child's birth.

Respondent Luis Ramón Morales-Santana had lived in the United States since he was 13. His biological father, José Morales, moved to the Dominican Republic 20 days short of his 19th birthday, and therefore fell short of §1401(a)(7)'s requirement of five years' physical presence after age 14. Nevertheless, José lived with Luis's mother and eventually married her, accepted parental responsibility, and included Luis in his household. Years later Luis was threatened with deportation based on several criminal convictions. He argued that §1401(a)(7) discriminated on the basis of sex and that he should be considered a U.S. citizen.]

GINSBURG, J.:

Unlike the paternal-acknowledgment requirement at issue in *Nguyen* . . . , the physical-presence requirements now before us relate solely to the duration of the parent's prebirth residency in the United States, not to the parent's filial tie to the child. [Congress sought to ensure a connection between the child and the values of the United States.] As the Court of Appeals observed in this case, a man needs no more time in the United States than a woman "in order to have assimilated citizenship-related values to transmit to [his] child." . . .

[The government also argues that] [a]n unwed mother . . . is the child's only "legally recognized" parent at the time of childbirth. An unwed citizen father enters the scene later, as a second parent. A longer physical connection to the United States is warranted for the unwed father, the Government maintains, because of the "competing national influence" of the alien mother. . . . Congress, the Government suggests, designed the statute to bracket an unwed U.S.-citizen mother with a married couple in which both parents are U.S. citizens, and to align an unwed U.S.-citizen father with a married couple, one spouse a citizen, the other, an alien.

Underlying this apparent design is the assumption that the alien father of a nonmarital child born abroad to a U.S.-citizen mother will not accept parental responsibility. . . . Hardly gender neutral, that assumption conforms to the long-held view that unwed fathers care little about, indeed are strangers to, their children. Lump characterization of that kind, however, no longer passes equal protection inspection.

Accepting, arguendo, that Congress [sought to] . . . ensur[e] a connection between the foreign-born nonmarital child and the United States, the gender-based means scarcely serve the posited end. The scheme permits the transmission of citizenship to children who have no tie to the United States so long as their mother was a U.S. citizen continuously present in the United States for one year at any point in her life prior to the child's birth. The transmission holds even if the mother marries the child's alien father immediately after the child's birth and never returns with the child to the United States. At the same time, the legislation precludes citizenship transmission by a U.S.-citizen father who falls a few days short of meeting §1401(a)(7)'s longer physical-presence requirements, even if the father acknowledges paternity on the day of the child's birth and raises the child in the United States. One cannot see in this driven-by-gender scheme the close means-end fit required to survive heightened scrutiny.

[Justice Ginsburg also rejected the claim that the exception for unwed mothers would reduce the number of "stateless" children who had no citizenship at all. She pointed to expert studies suggesting that the risk of statelessness was greater for children of unmarried U.S. fathers.]

[Justice Ginsburg concluded, however, that] "this Court is not equipped to grant the relief Morales-Santana seeks, *i.e.*, extending to his father (and, derivatively, to him) the benefit of the one-year physical-presence term §1409(c) reserves for unwed mothers. . . . [W]hen the 'right invoked is that to equal treatment,' the appropriate remedy is a mandate of equal treatment, a result that can be accomplished by withdrawal of benefits from the favored class as well as by extension of benefits to the excluded class." . . . The choice between these outcomes is governed by the legislature's intent, as revealed by the statute at hand. . . . [Congress would have wanted to retain the longer physical presence requirement for both sexes because it wanted attachment to the United States and its values. Moreover,] if §1409(c)'s one-year dispensation were extended to unwed citizen fathers, would it not be irrational to retain the longer term when the U.S.-citizen parent is married? Disadvantageous treatment of marital children in comparison to nonmarital children is scarcely a purpose one can sensibly attribute to Congress. . . . Put to the choice, Congress, we believe, would have abrogated §1409(c)'s exception, preferring preservation of the general rule. . . . Going forward, Congress may address the issue and settle on a uniform prescription that neither favors nor disadvantages any person on the basis of gender. In the interim, as the Government suggests, §1401(a)(7)'s now-five-year requirement should apply, prospectively, to children born to unwed U.S.-citizen mothers.

[Justice Thomas joined by Justice Alito, concurred in the judgment in part: "Because respondent cannot obtain relief in any event, it is unnecessary for us to decide whether [§1401(a)(7) is] constitutional."]

DISCUSSION

1. *Did Morales-Santana win or lose his case?* The Court holds that the provisions challenged by Morales-Santana discriminate unconstitutionally based on sex, but then holds that the proper remedy is that both citizen mothers and fathers alike must satisfy the five-year rule. Because Morales-Santana's father fell short by 20 days, his son, the respondent in this case, is not a citizen. Why doesn't Justice Ginsburg "level up" instead of "leveling down"?

One consideration courts might take into account in deciding whether to level up or level down is to ask what the legislature would have done if it had not able to pursue the discriminatory policy. (To what extent should courts follow legislative intentions if they are tinged by unconstitutional motivations?) A second consideration is whether a proposed solution best achieves coherence and fairness in the larger statutory scheme. How important is it that in this case, leveling up would put unwed citizen fathers in a better position than married fathers? A third consideration is to take into account the area of law in which courts are intervening. Is it relevant that this is an immigration case, and that the Supreme Court might want to avoid interfering with Congress's decisions about who gets to be a U.S. citizen?

If the Court cannot give Morales-Santana the remedy he seeks, is the Court's entire discussion dicta, as Justice Thomas suggests? Or should it be relevant to how the Board of Immigration Appeals exercises prosecutorial discretion?[95]

2. *Discrimination against nonmarital fathers.* One of the most important consequences of *Morales-Santana* may be in family law outside of the immigration context. In another part of the opinion, Justice Ginsburg criticized "the obsolescing view that 'unwed fathers [are] invariably less qualified and entitled than mothers' to take responsibility for nonmarital children"; her argument suggests that family law doctrines that make overbroad and stereotypical generalizations about unwed fathers are constitutionally suspect.

3. *Sex discrimination and nationality.* Historically, immigration law proceeded on two tracks. Married couples were governed by coverture rules, under which the child's (and originally, the wife's) nationality was subsumed into the husband's. Children of unmarried couples, by contrast, were assigned the mother's nationality, based on assumptions about maternal closeness and paternal irresponsibility.

---

95. See Mark Tushnet, Did Morales-Santana (the Person) Win or Lose in the Supreme Court?, Balkinization, June 12, 2017, https://balkin.blogspot.com/2017/06/did-morales-santana-person-win-or-lose.html.

Gradually, Congress eliminated the discriminatory treatment of husbands and wives, but provisions treating men and women differently remained for unmarried couples. The Court upheld such a provision in Nguyen v. INS, but struck down a different one in *Morales-Santana.* Do you agree with Justice Ginsburg that *Nguyen* is distinguishable from *Morales-Santana*?

III. DISTINGUISHING SEX-BASED AND SEX-NEUTRAL POLICIES: EVOLVING PERSPECTIVES ON PREGNANCY

Intermediate scrutiny doctrine focuses equal protection review on the wrongs of classifying by sex. Heightened scrutiny applies only to those laws and practices that the Court recognizes as classifying on the basis of sex. Absent a showing that the government has classified on the basis of sex, plaintiffs must prove that the government has acted with discriminatory purpose to establish an equal protection violation. The case law opening this section sets forth a framework that governs both race and sex discrimination claims under the Equal Protection Clause.

Under this framework, it matters hugely whether laws are group-based or facially neutral. If a law is sex-based, it is presumptively unconstitutional and the burden is on the government to demonstrate its constitutionality. If a law is facially neutral, it is presumptively constitutional, and the burden is on the challenging party to demonstrate that the law is animated by an invidious purpose.

But is the distinction between sex-based and facially neutral laws always clear? We explore this question by examining the case of pregnancy. For decades, laws regulating pregnancy have been treated as facially neutral for equal protection purposes. But as the readings in this part show, in several constitutional and statutory contexts, regulation of pregnancy is understood to raise sex-equality concerns. There is evidence these views about the regulation of pregnancy have begun to shape equal protection law.

A. Criteria for Distinguishing Sex-Based and Sex-Neutral Policies

The most important "affirmative action" programs in American history have benefited military veterans, a group that until recently was virtually all male. Yet the Supreme Court does not recognize veterans' preference programs as classifying on the basis of sex. In Personnel Administrator of Massachusetts v. Feeney, 442 U.S. 256 (1979), the Supreme Court rejected an equal protection challenge to a veterans' preference program covering civil service jobs in the state of Massachusetts. In *Feeney,* the Supreme Court developed a two-part test to determine (1) whether government action classifies on the basis of sex, and if the government has not expressly classified on the basis of sex, and (2) whether government has nonetheless acted with a discriminatory purpose.

Personnel Administrator of Massachusetts v. Feeney

442 U.S. 256 (1979)

[Helen Feeney (née Buyo) attempted during World War II to enlist in the Woman's Auxiliary Army Corps. She remembered being told by a recruiting officer, "What's a nice girl like you want to go into service?" She was ultimately unable to enlist, though, because parental consent had to be given for any woman under 21, and Helen's mother refused to give such consent. (Women, of course, have never been subject to conscription.) Much later, in 1963, she was hired as a senior clerk stenographer by the Massachusetts Civil Defense Agency. She subsequently passed a number of open competitive civil service examinations for better jobs, but failed in her efforts because of a Massachusetts statute that gave an absolute preference to any veteran who had also passed the relevant tests. The statutory preference is available to "any person, male or female, including a nurse," who was honorably discharged from the United States Armed Forces after at least 90 days of active service, at least one day of which was during "wartime." In 1971, she took the civil service examination to become Assistant Secretary for the Massachusetts Board of Dental Examiners. Feeney received the second-highest score, but she was ranked sixth on the hiring list, behind five male veterans. The successful applicant had received a grade eight points lower than Feeney's.[96] As a matter of empirical fact, the preference operated overwhelmingly to the advantage of males. Feeney therefore sued, arguing that the absolute-preference formula served in effect to exclude women from the most desirable civil service jobs and, therefore, violated the Fourteenth Amendment. A three-judge court agreed, finding that, although the goals of the preference were legitimate and had not been enacted in order to discriminate against women, the exclusionary impact with regard to women was so severe as to require a more carefully tailored preference scheme.]

STEWART, J. . . .

When this litigation was commenced, then, over 98% of the veterans in Massachusetts were male; only 1.8% were female. And over one-quarter of the Massachusetts population were veterans. During the decade between 1963 and 1973 when the appellee was actively participating in the State's merit selection system, 47,005 new permanent appointments were made in the classified official service. Forty-three percent of those hired were women, and 57% were men. Of the women appointed, 1.8% were veterans, while 54% of the men had veteran status. A large unspecified percentage of the female appointees were serving in lower paying positions for which males traditionally had not applied. . . .

II

The sole question for decision on this appeal is whether Massachusetts, in granting an absolute lifetime preference to veterans, has discriminated against women in violation of the Equal Protection Clause of the Fourteenth Amendment.

---

96. See Linda K. Kerber, No Constitutional Right to Be Ladies: Women and the Obligations of Citizenship 220-222 (1998).

A

The equal protection guarantee of the Fourteenth Amendment does not take from the States all power of classification. Most laws classify, and many affect certain groups unevenly, even though the law itself treats them no differently from all other members of the class described by the law. When the basic classification is rationally based, uneven effects upon particular groups within a class are ordinarily of no constitutional concern. The calculus of effects, the manner in which a particular law reverberates in a society, is a legislative and not a judicial responsibility. In assessing an equal protection challenge, a court is called upon only to measure the basic validity of the legislative classification. When some other independent right is not at stake, see, e.g., Shapiro v. Thompson, 394 U.S. 618, and when there is no "reason to infer antipathy," Vance v. Bradley, 440 U.S. 93, 97, it is presumed that "even improvident decisions will eventually be rectified by the democratic process. . . ." Ibid.

Certain classifications, however, in themselves supply a reason to infer antipathy. Race is the paradigm. A racial classification, regardless of purported motivation, is presumptively invalid and can be upheld only upon an extraordinary justification. This rule applies as well to a classification that is ostensibly neutral but is an obvious pretext for racial discrimination. But, as was made clear in Washington v. Davis, 426 U.S. 229, and Arlington Heights v. Metropolitan Housing Dev. Corp., 429 U.S. 252, even if a neutral law has a disproportionately adverse effect upon a racial minority, it is unconstitutional under the Equal Protection Clause only if that impact can be traced to a discriminatory purpose.

Classifications based upon gender, not unlike those based upon race, have traditionally been the touchstone for pervasive and often subtle discrimination. This Court's recent cases teach that such classifications must bear a close and substantial relationship to important governmental objectives, Craig v. Boren, 429 U.S. 190, and are in many settings unconstitutional. Although public employment is not a constitutional right, Massachusetts Bd. of Retirement v. Murgia, supra, and the States have wide discretion in framing employee qualifications, see, e.g., New York City Transit Authority v. Beazer, supra, these precedents dictate that any state law overtly or covertly designed to prefer males over females in public employment would require an exceedingly persuasive justification to withstand a constitutional challenge under the Equal Protection Clause of the Fourteenth Amendment.

B

[*Davis* and *Arlington Heights*] recognize that when a neutral law has a disparate impact upon a group that has historically been the victim of discrimination, an unconstitutional purpose may still be at work. But those cases signaled no departure from the settled rule that the Fourteenth Amendment guarantees equal laws, not equal results. . . .

When a statute gender-neutral on its face is challenged on the ground that its effects upon women are disproportionately adverse, a twofold inquiry is thus appropriate. The first question is whether the statutory classification is indeed neutral in the sense that it is not gender based. If the classification itself, covert or overt, is not based upon gender, the second question is whether the adverse effect reflects invidious gender-based discrimination. In this second inquiry, impact provides an "important starting point," but purposeful discrimination is "the condition that offends the Constitution." . . .

III

A

The question whether ch. 31, §23, establishes a classification that is overtly or covertly based upon gender must first be considered. The appellee has conceded that ch. 31, §23, is neutral on its face. She has also acknowledged that state hiring preferences for veterans are not per se invalid, for she has limited her challenge to the absolute lifetime preference that Massachusetts provides to veterans. The District Court made two central findings that are relevant here: first, that ch. 31, §23, serves legitimate and worthy purposes; second, that the absolute preference was not established for the purpose of discriminating against women. The appellee has thus acknowledged and the District Court has thus found that the distinction between veterans and nonveterans drawn by ch. 31, §23, is not a pretext for gender discrimination. The appellee's concession and the District Court's finding are clearly correct.

If the impact of this statute could not be plausibly explained on a neutral ground, impact itself would signal that the real classification made by the law was in fact not neutral. But there can be but one answer to the question whether this veteran preference excludes significant numbers of women from preferred state jobs because they are women or because they are nonveterans. Apart from the fact that the definition of "veterans" in the statute has always been neutral as to gender and that Massachusetts has consistently defined veteran status in a way that has been inclusive of women who have served in the military, this is not a law that can plausibly be explained only as a gender-based classification. Indeed, it is not a law that can rationally be explained on that ground. . . . Too many men are [adversely] affected by ch. 31, §23, to permit the inference that the statute is but a pretext for preferring men over women.

Moreover, as the District Court implicitly found, the purposes of the statute provide the surest explanation for its impact. Just as there are cases in which impact alone can unmask an invidious classification, cf. Yick Wo v. Hopkins, 118 U.S. 356, there are others, in which—notwithstanding impact—the legitimate noninvidious purposes of a law cannot be missed. This is one. The distinction made by ch. 31, §23, is, as it seems to be, quite simply between veterans and nonveterans, not between men and women.

B

The dispositive question, then, is whether the appellee has shown that a gender-based discriminatory purpose has, at least in some measure, shaped the Massachusetts veterans' preference legislation. As did the District Court, she points to two basic factors which in her view distinguish ch. 31, §23, from the neutral rules at issue in the Washington v. Davis and *Arlington Heights* cases. The first is the nature of the preference, which is said to be demonstrably gender-biased in the sense that it favors a status reserved under federal military policy primarily to men. The second concerns the impact of the absolute lifetime preference upon the employment opportunities of women, an impact claimed to be too inevitable to have been unintended. The appellee contends that these factors, coupled with the fact that the preference itself has little if any relevance to actual job performance, more than suffice to prove the discriminatory intent required to establish a constitutional violation.

1

The contention that this veterans' preference is "inherently nonneutral" or "gender biased" presumes that the State, by favoring veterans, intentionally incorporated into its public employment policies the panoply of sex-based and assertedly discriminatory federal laws that have prevented all but a handful of women from becoming veterans. There are two serious difficulties with this argument. First, it is wholly at odds with the District Court's central finding that Massachusetts has not offered a preference to veterans for the purpose of discriminating against women. Second, it cannot be reconciled with the assumption made by both the appellee and the District Court that a more limited hiring preference for veterans could be sustained. Taken together, these difficulties are fatal.

To the extent that the status of veteran is one that few women have been enabled to achieve, every hiring preference for veterans, however modest or extreme, is inherently gender-biased. If Massachusetts by offering such a preference can be said intentionally to have incorporated into its state employment policies the historical gender-based federal military personnel practices, the degree of the preference would or should make no constitutional difference. Invidious discrimination does not become less so because the discrimination accomplished is of a lesser magnitude. Discriminatory intent is simply not amenable to calibration. It either is a factor that has influenced the legislative choice or it is not. The District Court's conclusion that the absolute veterans' preference was not originally enacted or subsequently reaffirmed for the purpose of giving an advantage to males as such necessarily compels the conclusion that the State intended nothing more than to prefer "veterans." Given this finding, simple logic suggests that an intent to exclude women from significant public jobs was not at work in this law. To reason that it was, by describing the preference as "inherently nonneutral" or "gender-biased," is merely to restate the fact of impact, not to answer the question of intent.

To be sure, this case is unusual in that it involves a law that by design is not neutral. The law overtly prefers veterans as such. As opposed to the written test at issue in *Davis,* it does not purport to define a job-related characteristic. To the contrary, it confers upon a specifically described group—perceived to be particularly deserving—a competitive headstart. But the District Court found, and the appellee has not disputed, that this legislative choice was legitimate. The basic distinction between veterans and nonveterans, having been found not gender-based, and the goals of the preference having been found worthy, ch. 31 must be analyzed as is any other neutral law that casts a greater burden upon women as a group than upon men as a group. The enlistment policies of the Armed Services may well have discriminated on the basis of sex. See Frontiero v. Richardson, 411 U.S. 677;

cf. Schlesinger v. Ballard, 419 U.S. 498. But the history of discrimination against women in the military is not on trial in this case.

2

The appellee's ultimate argument rests upon the presumption, common to the criminal and civil law, that a person intends the natural and foreseeable consequences of his voluntary actions. . . .

The decision to grant a preference to veterans was of course "intentional." So, necessarily, did an adverse impact upon nonveterans follow from that decision. And it cannot seriously be argued that the Legislature of Massachusetts could have been unaware that most veterans are men. It would thus be disingenuous to say that the adverse consequences of this legislation for women were unintended, in the sense that they were not volitional or in the sense that they were not foreseeable.

"Discriminatory purpose," however, implies more than intent as volition or intent as awareness of consequences. It implies that the decisionmaker, in this case a state legislature, selected or reaffirmed a particular course of action at least in part "because of," not merely "in spite of," its adverse effects upon an identifiable group. Yet nothing in the record demonstrates that this preference for veterans was originally devised or subsequently re-enacted because it would accomplish the collateral goal of keeping women in a stereotypic and predefined place in the Massachusetts Civil Service.

To the contrary, the statutory history shows that the benefit of the preference was consistently offered to "any person" who was a veteran. That benefit has been extended to women under a very broad statutory definition of the term veteran. . . . When the totality of legislative actions establishing and extending the Massachusetts veterans' preference are considered, the law remains what it purports to be: a preference for veterans of either sex over nonveterans of either sex, not for men over women.

STEVENS, J., joined by WHITE, J., concurring.

While I concur in the Court's opinion, I confess that I am not at all sure that there is any difference between the two questions posed. If a classification is not overtly based on gender, I am inclined to believe the question whether it is covertly gender-based is the same as the question whether its adverse effects reflect invidious gender-based discrimination. However the question is phrased, for me the answer is largely provided by the fact that the number of males disadvantaged by Massachusetts' veterans' preference (1,867,000) is sufficiently large — and sufficiently close to the number of disadvantaged females (2,954,000) — to refute the claim that the rule was intended to benefit males as a class over females as a class.

MARSHALL, J., joined by BRENNAN, J., dissenting.

Although acknowledging that in some circumstances, discriminatory intent may be inferred from the inevitable or foreseeable impact of a statute, the Court concludes that no such intent has been established here. I cannot agree. In my judgment, Massachusetts' choice of an absolute veterans' preference system evinces purposeful gender-based discrimination. And because the statutory scheme bears no substantial relationship to a legitimate governmental objective, it cannot withstand scrutiny under the Equal Protection Clause.

I

The District Court found that the "prime objective" of the Massachusetts veterans' preference statute, Mass. Gen. Laws Ann., ch. 31, §23, was to benefit individuals with prior military service. . . .

That a legislature seeks to advantage one group does not, as a matter of logic or of common sense, exclude the possibility that it also intends to disadvantage another. Individuals in general and lawmakers in particular frequently act for a variety of reasons. . . . [T]he critical constitutional inquiry is not whether an illicit consideration was the primary or but-for cause of a decision, but rather whether it had an appreciable role in shaping a given legislative enactment. Where there is "proof that a discriminatory purpose has been *a* motivating factor in the decision, . . . judicial deference is no longer justified." Arlington Heights v. Metropolitan Housing Dev. Corp.

Moreover, since reliable evidence of subjective intentions is seldom obtainable, resorting to inference based on objective factors is generally unavoidable. To discern the purposes underlying facially neutral policies, this Court has therefore considered the degree, inevitability, and foreseeability of any disproportionate impact as well as the alternatives reasonably available. In the instant case, the impact of the Massachusetts statute on women is undisputed. . . . Because less than 2% of the women in Massachusetts are veterans, the absolute preference formula has rendered desirable state civil service employment an almost exclusively male prerogative. As the District Court recognized, this consequence follows foreseeably, indeed inexorably, from the long history of policies severely limiting women's participation in the military. Although neutral in form, the statute is anything but neutral in application. . . . Where the foreseeable impact of a facially neutral policy is so disproportionate, the burden should rest on the State to establish that sex-based considerations played no part in the choice of the particular legislative scheme.

Clearly, that burden was not sustained here. The legislative history of the statute reflects the Commonwealth's patent appreciation of the impact the preference system would have on women, and an equally evident desire to mitigate that impact only with respect to certain traditionally female occupations. Until 1971, the statute and implementing civil service regulations exempted from operation of the preference any job requisitions "especially calling for women." In practice, this exemption, coupled with the absolute preference for veterans, has created a gender-based civil service hierarchy, with women occupying low-grade clerical secretarial jobs and men holding more responsible and remunerative positions.

Thus, for over 70 years, the Commonwealth has maintained, as an integral part of its veterans' preference system, an exemption relegating female civil service applicants to occupations traditionally filled by women. Such a statutory scheme both reflects and perpetuates precisely the kind of archaic assumptions about women's roles which we have previously held invalid. Particularly when viewed against the range of less discriminatory alternatives available to assist veterans,[a]

a. Only four States afford a preference comparable in scope to that of Massachusetts. Other States and the Federal Government grant point or tie-breaking preferences that do not foreclose opportunities for women.

Massachusetts' choice of a formula that so severely restricts public employment opportunities for women cannot reasonably be thought gender-neutral. . . .

II

To survive challenge under the Equal Protection Clause, statutes reflecting gender-based discrimination must be substantially related to the achievement of important governmental objectives. Appellants here advance three interests in support of the absolute preference system: (1) assisting veterans in their readjustment to civilian life; (2) encouraging military enlistment; and (3) rewarding those who have served their country. . . .

With respect to the first interest, facilitating veterans' transition to civilian status, the statute is plainly overinclusive. By conferring a permanent preference, the legislation allows veterans to invoke their advantage repeatedly, without regard to their date of discharge. . . . Nor is the Commonwealth's second asserted interest, encouraging military service, a plausible justification for this legislative scheme. In its original and subsequent re-enactments, the statute extended benefits retroactively to veterans who had served during a prior specified period. . . . Moreover, even if such influence could be presumed, the statute is still grossly overinclusive in that it bestows benefits on men drafted as well as those who volunteered.

Finally, the Commonwealth's third interest, rewarding veterans, does not "adequately justify the salient features" of this preference system. Where a particular statutory scheme visits substantial hardship on a class long subject to discrimination, the legislation cannot be sustained unless "carefully tuned to alternative considerations." Here, there are a wide variety of less discriminatory means by which Massachusetts could effect its compensatory purposes. For example, a point preference system, such as that maintained by many States and the Federal Government, or an absolute preference for a limited duration, would reward veterans without excluding all qualified women from upper level civil service positions. Apart from public employment, the Commonwealth can, and does, afford assistance to veterans in various ways, including tax abatements, educational subsidies, and special programs for needy veterans. Unlike these and similar benefits, the costs of which are distributed across the taxpaying public generally, the Massachusetts statute exacts a substantial price from a discrete group of individuals who have long been subject to employment discrimination, and who, "because of circumstances totally beyond their control, have [had] little if any chance of becoming members of the preferred class."

DISCUSSION

1. *Defining a sex-based classification.* When plaintiffs challenge a facially neutral statute with a disparate impact on women (or some other constitutionally protected group), *Feeney* suggests that a court must ask two kinds of questions to determine whether the challenged action violates the Equal Protection Clause. First, the court must determine whether the statute is facially neutral or whether it in fact classifies on the basis of sex. If the state has not classified on the basis of sex, then the court must determine whether the government has undertaken the challenged action

with a discriminatory purpose. Thus, after Washington v. Davis and *Feeney*, the question of whether state action classifies on the basis of race or sex matters tremendously. Presumptions of constitutionality depend on whether courts characterize regulatory practices as group-based or facially neutral.

What criteria should a court employ to determine whether a statute classifies on the basis of sex? Did the Court in *Feeney* employ the right criteria? As you read the ensuing cases in the chapter, you might ask whether the Court in *Feeney* employed criteria used consistently in other equal protection cases—for example, in analyzing the regulation of pregnancy and affirmative action. Is it possible to derive a standard for determining what counts as a gender-based classification that can be used consistently across all cases? Is it a problem if the characterization of practices as gender-based or gender-neutral depends instead on common-sense judgments about their legitimacy?[97]

Was the *Feeney* Court correct in deciding that the veterans' preference statute was a gender-neutral classification? Given that federal law regulates military service with reference to the gender of the applicant, doesn't the classification "veteran" incorporate by reference gender-based criteria? Under the majority's analysis, could a state limit the award of a veterans' preference or other social benefit to "all members of the armed forces who served in combat positions"? Should a court then review such a statute on the presumption that it is constitutional?

2. *Defining discriminatory purpose.* As we have seen, *Feeney* articulates a two-stage test for determining whether a facially neutral statute with a disparate impact on women discriminates on the basis of sex. First, the court must confirm that the statute does not in fact expressly classify on the basis of sex. If the court concludes that government has not expressly classified on the basis of sex, then the court must determine whether "the adverse effect reflects invidious gender-based discrimination"—a showing Washington v. Davis holds can only be satisfied by proof of "purposeful discrimination." *Feeney* then proceeds to define "discriminatory purpose" for the Washington v. Davis framework in terms that verge on malice: The plaintiff must show that the challenged action was undertaken "at least in part 'because of,' not merely 'in spite of' its adverse effects upon an identifiable group."

There are many forms of conscious, quasi-conscious, and unconscious bias that may lead government actors to adopt policies with adverse effects on protected groups. Why limit equal protection violations to cases where government undertook the challenged action at least in part because of its adverse effects on a

---

97. Some commentators have suggested that courts are not employing criteria consistently across cases in determining which practices "classify" within the meaning of *Davis* and *Feeney*. Intuitions about the legitimacy of the challenged practices may lead courts to characterize the practice as facially neutral rather than group-based. At times, social movement advocacy influences the characterization of practices. See, e.g., Balkin and Siegel, The American Civil Rights Tradition, supra, at 28; Richard A. Primus, Equal Protection and Disparate Impact: Round Three, 117 Harv. L. Rev. 493, 509 (2003); Reva B. Siegel, A Short History of Sexual Harassment, in Directions in Sexual Harassment Law 1, 11-18 (Catharine A. MacKinnon & Reva B. Siegel eds., 2003).

protected group? How often will plaintiffs be able to obtain evidence that government actors have adopted policies because of their adverse effects on particular groups?

Why did *Feeney* adopt such a narrow and exculpatory liability rule? Should the Court have adopted the foreseeability standard the dissent embraced? If so, should the same test apply in all cases in which government adopts a facially neutral law with a foreseeable disparate impact on an historically excluded group? Or should foreseeability matter only in those cases where gender was also part of the social meaning of the law—or where the law's gendered impact was especially acute?

What institutional considerations might have led the Supreme Court to the interpretation of the Equal Protection Clause it adopted in *Feeney*?[98] One possibility is that courts should defer to legislatures because legislatures, and not courts, are democratic institutions. But if so, the *Feeney* standard should not apply to *legislative* judgments about what equal protection requires. What should a conscientious legislator consider in deciding whether a proposed facially neutral law violates sex equality? (One way to consider this question is in the context of domestic violence and marital rape laws, discussed infra.)

3. *Challenging domestic violence and marital rape laws under* Feeney. *Feeney* greatly increases the burden on plaintiffs seeking to persuade a judge to enjoin enforcement of a law or policy on equal protection grounds. For example, *Feeney* has inhibited most equal protection challenges to domestic violence policies (policies that treat violence between intimates with greater deference than assault between strangers). Under what circumstances, if any, is a domestic violence policy of this kind sex-based within the meaning of *Feeney*? How does legislative drafting matter? What enforcement statistics, if any, would have a bearing on the question? Does the history or social meaning of the policy matter? If plaintiffs sought to challenge the domestic violence policy on the grounds that its adoption or enforcement reflected a sex-based discriminatory purpose, what would they have to show? What similar (or distinctive) challenges face plaintiffs challenging laws that treat rape in marriage differently than rape between unmarried persons?[99]

---

98. For an account of the institutional considerations that led the Supreme Court to require plaintiffs to prove discriminatory purpose within the narrow strictures of the *Feeney* framework, see Reva B. Siegel, The Supreme Court, 2012 Term—Foreword: Equality Divided, 127 Harv. L. Rev. 1, 9-23 (2013) (describing how the Burger Court crafted doctrines of discriminatory purpose to shift responsibility for redress of discrimination away from courts and toward representative government).

99. After decades of advocacy, legislatures have restricted, but not eliminated, immunities from criminal punishment in cases of domestic violence and marital rape. Federal courts enforcing guarantees of equal protection have played little role in prompting this change. For commentary on the modernization of these policies, having roots in the old marital status rules of the common law, see, e.g., Michelle J. Anderson, Marital Immunity, Intimate Relationships, and Improper Inferences: A New Law on Sexual Offenses, 54 Hastings L.J. 1465 (2003); Siegel, "The Rule of Love," supra; Jill Elaine Hasday, The Canon of Family Law, 57 Stan. L. Rev. 825, 837-841 (2004); Katherine E. Volovski, Crime and Punishment Law Chapter: Domestic Violence, 5 Geo. J. Gender & L. 175 (2004).

B. *Judicial and Legislative Perspectives on Pregnancy and Sex Equality: Alternative Understandings*

Are classifications on the basis of pregnancy or capacity to become pregnant—a capacity shared by most women and no men—classifications subject to intermediate scrutiny? Consider the different understandings expressed over time in American law.

1. Classifications on the Basis of Sex and Pregnancy

In its most prominently cited equal protection decision on pregnancy, the Court held that classifications on the basis of pregnancy are not always classifications on the basis of sex within the meaning of the Equal Protection Clause. In Geduldig v. Aiello, 417 U.S. 484 (1974), the Supreme Court reviewed an equal protection challenge to a state-run employment disability insurance program that covered work-related and non–work-related disabilities, but excluded disabilities associated with normal pregnancy. The Court upheld the regulation under a rational basis standard of review. Writing for the majority, Justice Stewart explained:

> . . . The State has a legitimate interest in maintaining the self-supporting nature of its insurance program. Similarly, it has an interest in distributing the available resources in such a way as to keep benefit payments at an adequate level for disabilities that are covered, rather than to cover all disabilities inadequately. Finally, California has a legitimate concern in maintaining the contribution rate at a level that will not unduly burden participating employees, particularly low-income employees who may be most in need of the disability insurance.
>
> These policies provide an objective and wholly noninvidious basis for the State's decision not to create a more comprehensive insurance program than it has. There is no evidence in the record that the selection of the risks insured by the program worked to discriminate against any definable group or class in terms of the aggregate risk protection derived by that group or class from the program.[a] There is no risk from which men

---

a. . . . [T]his case is thus a far cry from cases like Reed v. Reed and Frontiero v. Richardson, involving discrimination based upon gender as such. The California insurance program does not exclude anyone from benefit eligibility because of gender but merely removes one physical condition—pregnancy—from the list of compensable disabilities. While it is true that only women can become pregnant, it does not follow that every legislative classification concerning pregnancy is a sex-based classification like those considered in Reed and Frontiero. Normal pregnancy is an objectively identifiable physical condition with unique characteristics. Absent a showing that distinctions involving pregnancy are mere pretexts designed to effect an invidious discrimination against the members of one sex or the other, lawmakers are constitutionally free to include or exclude pregnancy from the coverage of legislation such as this on any reasonable basis, just as with respect to any other physical condition. The lack of identity between the excluded disability and gender as such under this insurance program becomes clear upon the most cursory analysis. The program divides potential recipients into two groups—pregnant women and nonpregnant persons. While the first group is exclusively female, the second includes members of both sexes. The fiscal and actuarial benefits of the program thus accrue to members of both sexes.

are protected and women are not. Likewise, there is no risk from which women are protected and men are not.

Justice Brennan in dissent, joined by Justices Douglas and Marshall, argued that different rules applied to men and women under California's policy. Men received full compensation for all disabilities—including those affecting only or primarily males—whereas women could not recover for pregnancy, a disability affecting only females. Brennan explained: "Such dissimilar treatment of men and women, on the basis of physical characteristics inextricably linked to one sex, inevitably constitutes sex discrimination." The dissent cited relevant EEOC guidelines, which stated pregnancy and childbirth-related disabilities should be treated as temporary disabilities for employment insurance and leave purposes and should be subject to same terms and conditions as other temporary disabilities.

DISCUSSION

1. *Classifications again.* Does the law in *Geduldig*—which affects all workers who are or may become pregnant—classify on the basis of sex? Or is it simply a facially neutral law whose impact is felt only by women? If a classification affects many Blacks and no whites, should it be subject to strict scrutiny? Revisit Brown v. City of Oneonta, 221 F.3d 329 (2d Cir. 1999), and related cases in Chapter 7. Are there general criteria for determining whether state action classifies on the basis of suspect criteria?

Are all facially neutral statutes equal—or might the case for characterizing the regulation in *Geduldig* as sex-based be stronger than in *Feeney*? Why or why not?

Should courts refuse to characterize laws regulating physical characteristics unique to one sex as "sex-based classifications" because, by definition, it is not possible to discriminate between the sexes in matters respecting that characteristic? (Does it matter that the insurance plan in *Geduldig* excluded pregnancy and covered conditions involving physiological characteristics unique to men?)

What factors do you think (1) might have, or (2) should have, played a role in the Court's decision in *Geduldig*? The belief that sex discrimination is not possible with respect to a real and defining physical difference between the sexes? The understanding that pregnancy is the gateway to new motherhood and is historically and symbolically associated with changes in women's labor force participation? The cost of including coverage for pregnancy in a state-run insurance program? For discussion of distributive dimensions of pregnancy discrimination questions, see, e.g., Deborah Dinner, The Costs of Reproduction: History and the Legal Construction of Sex Equality, 46 Harv. C.R.-C.L. L. Rev. 415 (2011).

2. *What exactly does* Geduldig *hold?* Does *Geduldig* hold that classification based on pregnancy is *never* sex discrimination, or can the opinion be interpreted more narrowly? In an often-cited footnote to the majority opinion, Justice Stewart explained:[100]

---

100. Geduldig v. Aiello, 417 U.S. 484, 497 n.20 (1974).

> While it is true that only women can become pregnant it does not follow that every legislative classification concerning pregnancy is a sex-based classification like those considered in *Reed, supra,* and *Frontiero, supra*. . . . Absent a showing that distinctions involving pregnancy are mere pretexts designed to effect an invidious discrimination against the members of one sex or the other, lawmakers are constitutionally free to include or exclude pregnancy from the coverage of legislation such as this on any reasonable basis, just as with respect to any other physical condition.

This passage "leaves open the possibility that some legislative classifications concerning pregnancy are sex-based classifications like those considered in *Reed* and *Frontiero*." Reva B. Siegel, "You've Come a Long Way, Baby": Rehnquist's New Approach to Pregnancy Discrimination in *Hibbs,* 58 Stan. L. Rev. 1871, 1891 (2006). Siegel points to Nevada Department of Human Resources v. Hibbs, 538 U.S. 721 (2003), infra, in which the Supreme Court held that legislation that classified on the basis of pregnancy was discriminatory because it reflected and reinforced impermissible stereotypes. When might legislation concerning pregnancy rest on stereotypical assumptions about male and female workers? What of the statute in *Geduldig*?

3. *Pregnancy discrimination under the Constitution and federal civil rights law.* As Justice Brennan's dissent points out, at the time of *Geduldig,* the Equal Employment Opportunity Commission interpreted the prohibition of sex discrimination under Title VII of the Civil Rights Act of 1964 to include pregnancy discrimination; it directed that employment benefits "shall be applied to disability due to pregnancy or childbirth on the same terms and conditions as they are applied to other temporary disabilities." In General Elec. Co. v. Gilbert, 429 U.S. 125 (1976), the Supreme Court rejected the EEOC's interpretation of Title VII[101] and instead applied *Geduldig*'s reasoning, concluding that an employer's decision to exclude pregnancy from a temporary disability benefits plan did not discriminate on the basis of sex within the meaning of Title VII.

In 1978, Congress responded to *Geduldig* and *Gilbert* by amending Title VII to prohibit discrimination "on the basis of pregnancy, childbirth, or related medical conditions." Pub. L. No. 95-555. Referring to Title VII's prohibition of discrimination "because of sex" or "on the basis of sex," the Pregnancy Discrimination Act of 1978 (PDA) provided that these terms "include, but are not limited to, because of or on the basis of pregnancy, childbirth, or related medical conditions; and women affected by pregnancy, childbirth, or related medical conditions shall be treated the same for all employment-related purposes, including receipt of benefits under fringe benefit programs, as other persons not so affected but similar in their ability or inability to work. . . ."[102]

Does Congress's decision to amend Title VII show that the Court was wrong in its decisions? Does it suggest, to the contrary, that the Court correctly left this complex social issue to the political process while protecting the core right of women to

101. The Supreme Court generally does not grant deference to EEOC interpretations and regulations. See, e.g., Melissa Hart, Skepticism and Expertise: The Supreme Court and the EEOC, 74 Fordham L. Rev. 1937 (2006).

102. 42 U.S.C. §2000e(k) (2000).

be free from discrimination? Does your answer to this question depend on (1) how likely Congress is to respond with something like the PDA, and (2) whether or not you see legal treatment of pregnancy as at the core of women's equal citizenship? For a history of efforts to redress work-family conflicts that explores how courts and Congress may diverge in the ways they enforce the equal protection of the laws, see Robert C. Post and Reva B. Siegel, Legislative Constitutionalism and Section Five Power: Policentric Interpretation of the Family and Medical Leave Act, 112 Yale L.J. 1943 (2003).

4. *Pregnancy classifications as sex classifications?* Over the decades the Court's understanding of sex-stereotyping has clearly evolved. Twenty years after *Geduldig*, in United States v. Virginia, 518 U.S. 515, 534 (1996), the Court discussed the regulation of pregnancy as an example of a sex-based classification subject to heightened equal protection scrutiny. The Court cited California Federal Savings and Loan Ass'n v. Guerra, 479 U.S. 272, 289 (1987), a decision arising under the Pregnancy Discrimination Act involving a state law mandating the reasonable accommodation of pregnant employees in its discussion of the heightened scrutiny framework.

In United States v. Virginia, the Court explained that sex classification's constitutionality depends on whether the classification is employed for a legitimate end (such as remedying past wrongs or promoting equal opportunity) or inflicts constitutional wrongs of the kind that sex classifications inflict when they are used "as they once were, to create or perpetuate the legal, social, and economic inferiority of women." United States v. Virginia, 518 U.S. 515, 534 (1996). The Court employed this historically informed antisubordination approach to evaluating the pregnancy accommodation statute in the Cal Fed case itself. See Reva B. Siegel, The Pregnant Citizen, from Suffrage to the Present, Geo. L.J. 19th Amend. Special Edition 167, 204-206 (2020).[103]

A few years later, in Nevada Department of Human Resources v. Hibbs, 538 U.S. 721, 736 (2003), Chief Justice Rehnquist held that Congress could enact the family leave provisions of the Family and Medical Leave Act to remedy and deter sex-stereotyping violations of equal protection involving women when they are "mothers or mothers-to-be" and never paused to mention Geduldig. Siegel, Pregnant Citizen, at 206-208 ("The Court's subsequent decisions in Virginia and Hibbs answer the question Geduldig raised; they demonstrate how regulation of pregnancy fits in the Court's equal protection cases. Geduldig understood judgments about pregnancy as judgments about the body, whereas Hibbs demonstrates that

103. Justice Ginsburg observed that

> Supposed "inherent differences" are no longer accepted as a ground for race or national origin classifications. . . . Physical differences between men and women, however, are enduring. . . . "Inherent differences" between men and women, we have come to appreciate, remain cause for celebration, but not for denigration of the members of either sex or for artificial constraints on an individual's opportunity. Sex classifications may be used to compensate women "for particular economic disabilities [they have] suffered," Califano v. Webster, 430 U.S. 313, 320 (1977) (per curiam), to "promot[e] equal employment opportunity," see California Fed. Sav. & Loan Assn. v. Guerra, 479 U. S. 272, 289 (1987), to advance full development of the talent and capacities of our Nation's people. But such classifications may not be used, as they once were, see *Goesaert*, 335 U.S., at 467, to create or perpetuate the legal, social, and economic inferiority of women.

judgments about pregnancy can be, and are also shaped by sex-role judgments, like other judgments about embodied persons.").

NOTE: ABORTION AND EQUAL PROTECTION

In 1973, Roe v. Wade recognized a right to privacy that protected a woman's decision whether to have an abortion (discussed infra, Chapter 9). A year later, in *Geduldig*, the Court held that a law denying disability benefits to pregnant women was not necessarily sex-based regulation within the meaning of the Equal Protection Clause. *Geduldig* is often read more broadly as declaring, categorically, that laws classifying on the basis of pregnancy do not classify on the basis of sex, and so are not subject to heightened scrutiny under the Fourteenth Amendment's Equal Protection Clause. Read in this way, *Geduldig* separated constitutional protections for the abortion right from the developing law of sex discrimination.

A split of this kind certainly was not inevitable. The second-wave feminist movement understood sex equality as a question rooted in the social organization of family life, and the advocates who litigated the first sex discrimination cases in the 1970s urged courts to treat the regulation of pregnancy as sex-based state action under the Fourteenth Amendment. The movement's constitutional lawyers argued that regulation of the pregnant woman was presumptively unconstitutional when it enforced stereotypes and sex-role prescriptions of the separate-spheres tradition. A number of federal courts began to adopt this reasoning. One of Ruth Bader Ginsburg's first equal-protection briefs in the Supreme Court involved a woman who faced an involuntary discharge from the Air Force because she was pregnant.[104] As Justice Ginsburg later noted, the *Struck* case was "an ideal case to argue the sex equality dimension of laws and regulations regarding pregnancy and childbirth."[105] (Ginsburg's brief in *Struck* has been neglected because the Court disposed of the case by remanding it to the Court of Appeals on mootness grounds and soon thereafter ruled that regulation directed at pregnant women was not the kind of "sex-based" state action that would trigger heightened scrutiny under equal protection principles.)

In this early period, women advanced sex-equality arguments for the abortion right in the streets and in a number of cases. Litigants challenging the constitutionality of Connecticut's anti-abortion law in 1972 explicitly invoked the First, Fourth, Fifth, Eighth, Ninth, Thirteenth, and Fourteenth Amendments. Striking down the law, Judge Edmund Lumbard emphasized sex equality themes, recognizing the "extraordinary ramifications" of motherhood for women, and noting that

---

104. See Brief for Petitioner, Struck v. Sec'y of Def., 409 U.S. 1071 (1972) (No. 72-178). Ginsburg's brief explains that "regulations applicable to pregnancy more onerous than regulations applicable to other temporary conditions discriminate invidiously on the basis of sex." For the story of the *Struck* case (with commentary by Justice Ginsburg), see Neil Siegel and Reva Siegel, Struck by Stereotype: Ruth Bader Ginsburg on Pregnancy Discrimination as Sex Discrimination, 59 Duke L.J. 771 (2010).

105. Ruth Bader Ginsburg, Remarks for the Celebration of 75 Years of Women's Enrollment at Columbia Law School, 102 Colum. L. Rev. 1441, 1447 (2002).

the "changed role of women in society and the changed attitudes toward them" required recognition of their right to make decisions about abortion.[106]

In the years after *Roe*, *Frontiero*, and *Craig*, Ruth Bader Ginsburg called on the Court to "take abortion, pregnancy, out-of-wedlock birth, and explicit gender-based differentials out of the separate cubbyholes in which they now rest, acknowledge the practical interrelationships, and treat these matters as part and parcel of a single, large, sex equality issue." Ruth Bader Ginsburg, Sex Equality and the Constitution, 52 Tul. L. Rev. 451, 462 (1978). Ginsburg explained:[107]

> Not only the sex discrimination cases, but the cases on contraception, abortion, and illegitimacy as well, present various faces of a single issue: the roles women are to play in society. Are women to have the opportunity to participate in full partnership with men in the nation's social, political, and economic life? This is a constitutional issue, . . . surely one of the most important in this final quarter of the twentieth century.

In years immediately after *Roe*, a largely male academy failed to register the sex equality claim regarding the right to reproductive freedom. In an influential critique of the *Roe* decision, John Hart Ely criticized the decision as a return to *Lochner*-type judging, in which judges impose their personal preferences into law.[108] Many writers were dismissive of the women's interests at stake; Joseph O'Meara, the Dean Emeritus at Notre Dame Law School, wrote, "Mr. Justice Blackmun seems unconscious of the fact that women want children. The few who don't, and those who don't want any more, need not become pregnant."[109]

Kenneth Karst was one of the first scholars to argue that abortion presented a question of women's equal citizenship.[110] By the early 1990s, as law schools began slowly to increase the number of tenured women faculty, a growing number of scholars began to speak of the abortion right as a sex equality right. For example, Laurence Tribe derided the "failure of . . . courts to frame the abortion controversy in terms of sexual equality."[111] Catharine MacKinnon challenged the idea that only similarly situated people must be treated equally, observing that this perspective pushes the issue of abortion "off the sex equality map."[112] Frances Olsen emphasized that anti-abortion laws "reinforce the subordination of women,"[113] and Sylvia

---

106. Abele v. Markle, 342 F. Supp. 800, 801-802 (D. Conn. 1972) (citing the Nineteenth Amendment, the pending Equal Rights Amendment, Title VII of the 1964 Civil Rights Act, Reed v. Reed, 404 U.S. 71 (1971), and Stanley v. Illinois, 405 U.S. 645 (1972)); Reva B. Siegel, *Roe*'s Roots: The Women's Rights Claims That Engendered *Roe*, 90 B.U. L. Rev. 1875, 1890-1893 (2010).

107. Ruth Bader Ginsburg, Sex Equality and the Constitution: The State of the Art, 4 Women's Rts. L. Rep. 143, 143 (1978).

108. John Hart Ely, The Wage of Crying Wolf: A Comment on *Roe v. Wade*, 82 Yale L.J. 920 (1973).

109. Joseph O'Meara, Abortion: The Court Decides a Non-Case, 1974 Sup. Ct. Rev. 337, 343 (1974).

110. Kenneth L. Karst, The Supreme Court 1976 Term Foreword: Equal Citizenship Under the Fourteenth Amendment, 91 Harv. L. Rev. 1 (1977).

111. Laurence H. Tribe, American Constitutional Law 1353 (1988).

112. MacKinnon, Reflections on Sex Equality Under Law, supra n.97, at 1297.

113. Frances Olsen, Unraveling Compromise, 103 Harv. L. Rev. 105, 120 (1989).

Law, calling for heightened scrutiny of laws governing reproduction, concluded, "Control of reproduction is the *sine qua non* of women's capacity to live as equal people."[114] Cass Sunstein advanced an anti-caste argument for reproductive rights based on an equality principle meant to "ensur[e] that women's sexuality and reproductive functions are not turned into something for the use and control of others."[115] A decade later, Jack Balkin turned Ely's critique of *Roe* on its head: He argued that the right to abortion was consistent with both the text and the original meaning of the Fourteenth Amendment because criminalization of abortion violated the principles against caste and class legislation.[116]

This new perception began to shape Supreme Court decisions. Equality values first began to find expression within substantive due process law. In overturning provisions of a Pennsylvania law that restricted women's access to abortions, Justice Blackmun described the fundamental liberty concerns at stake and noted their connection to equality: "A woman's right to make that choice freely is fundamental. Any other result, in our view, would protect inadequately a central part of the sphere of liberty that our law guarantees equally to all." Thornburgh v. Am. Coll. of Obstetricians & Gynecologists, 476 U.S. 747, 772 (1986). In Planned Parenthood v. Casey, Justice Kennedy reaffirmed a woman's constitutionally protected liberty interest in deciding whether to become a mother in terms deeply resonant with the sex equality cases the Court had decided in the years since *Roe*, explaining that the state could not impose "its own vision of the woman's role, however dominant that vision has been in the course of our history and our culture."[117]

Fifteen years later, Justice Ginsburg, writing for four Justices in dissent in *Carhart*, for the first time invoked equal protection case law as protecting women's reproductive liberties and gave full voice to the equality principles at the heart of the abortion right: "[L]egal challenges to undue restrictions on abortion procedures do not seek to vindicate some generalized notion of privacy; rather, they center on a woman's autonomy to determine her life's course, and thus to enjoy equal citizenship stature." 550 U.S. 124, 172 (2007).[118]

Chapter 9 discusses sex equality arguments for the abortion right in more detail, in the materials accompanying *Roe*.

---

114. Sylvia A. Law, Rethinking Sex and the Constitution, 132 U. Pa. L. Rev. 955, 1008-1009, 1028 (1984).

115. Cass Sunstein, Neutrality in Constitutional Law (With Special Reference to Pornography, Abortion, and Surrogacy), 92 Colum. L. Rev. 1, 15 (1992).

116. Jack M. Balkin, Abortion and Original Meaning, 24 Const. Comment. 291 (2007). See also Jack M. Balkin, Revised Opinion, in What *Roe* Should Have Said: The Nation's Top Legal Experts Rewrite America's Most Controversial Decision 31, 45 (Jack M. Balkin ed., 2005), arguing that abortion restrictions "reinforce women's subordinate status in society and therefore deny them equal citizenship."

117. 505 U.S. 833, 852 (1992). For further discussion of the equality reasoning in different passages of the *Casey* opinions, see Chapter 9 infra.

118. Justice Ginsburg's dissenting opinion in *Carhart* was also noteworthy for offering sex equality arguments in answer to the woman-protective anti-abortion arguments advanced in the majority opinion. See 550 U.S. 124, 183-186 (2007). For the distinction between fetal-protective and woman-protective anti-abortion arguments, see Chapter 9 infra.

2. Congress and the Court: Evolving Understandings of Pregnancy

The equal protection cases we have examined so far exhibit two apparently contradictory instincts in matters concerning pregnancy. Cases like *Geduldig* treat the regulation of pregnant women as a gender-neutral practice. Other equal protection cases, such as *Nguyen,* view reproductive physiology as the site of group-defining sex differences. Both approaches suggest that courts should defer to political judgments concerning pregnancy, either because judgments about pregnancy have nothing to do with sex discrimination, or because such judgments are by definition not invidious because they pertain to real physiological differences between the sexes. As Justice Kennedy observed in *Nguyen,* "[t]he difference between men and women in relation to the birth process is a real one, and the principle of equal protection does not forbid Congress to address the problem at hand in a manner specific to each gender."

But after decades of advocacy, there are other understandings of pregnancy discrimination in federal law. Since the 1960s, the women's movement has been pointing to the regulation of women's family roles as the paradigmatic site of sex discrimination. Movement lawyers made two key claims. They argued that it was stereotyping to treat all women as caregivers, where caregivers were assumed to be nonparticipants in civic life. The movement also argued that it was wrong to organize the socially essential work of caregiving so that those who performed it would actually be nonparticipants in civic life.

The movement had greater success in persuading the Court and nation of the merits of the first claim. Equal protection cases regularly prohibit government from discriminating against women on the assumption that all women are engaged in caregiving work. But what of women who are *in fact* engaged in the socially essential work of caregiving? The Court has been slow to recognize sex stereotyping in laws directed at women who are pregnant or to ask whether conflicts between caregiving and wage work might result from the same gender stereotypes that the Court's equal protection cases condemn.

There is, however, a body of federal law that (1) understands conflicts between family and market labor as arising out of traditional sex-role assumptions, and (2) seeks to alleviate such conflicts in order to promote the equal participation of caregivers in public life. In 1978, Congress amended Title VII of the 1964 Civil Rights Act to prohibit discrimination "on the basis of pregnancy, childbirth, or related medical conditions." 42 U.S.C. §2000e(k) (2000). In enacting the Pregnancy Discrimination Act (PDA), Congress made clear that Title VII's antidiscrimination protections applied to pregnant employees and affirmed an understanding of the workplace in which women were expected to combine employment and parenting. In 1993, Congress acted again to protect job security of caregivers at work by enacting the Family and Medical Leave Act (FMLA). 29 U.S.C. §§2601 et seq. (2000). The FMLA allows male[119] and female workers of many employers to take up to 12 weeks of unpaid leave to care for newborns, newly adopted children, and seriously

119. The FMLA provides unpaid leave to men and women because Congress feared that a gender-specific statute might result in discrimination against women. In addition, by providing unpaid leave for men the FMLA facilitates increased parity in caregiving responsibilities.

ill family members, or to recover from their own serious illness. Both statutes mitigate work family conflicts.

To enact the PDA and the FMLA, Congress drew upon two sources of authority: its power to regulate interstate commerce and its power under §5 of the Fourteenth Amendment to enforce the amendment's provisions by "appropriate legislation." Because the family leave provisions of the FMLA enforce the Fourteenth Amendment's Equal Protection Clause in ways the Court's equal protection cases do not, the family leave provisions were challenged as exceeding Congress's §5 powers. (For discussion of Congress's §5 powers, see Chapter 6.)

In upholding Congress's power to enact the family leave provisions of the FMLA, the Supreme Court offered an important statement of equal protection law. To demonstrate that Congress had §5 power to enact FMLA's family leave provisions, the Court explained how a statute providing caregivers unpaid leave enforced the Equal Protection Clause. In so doing, the Court described how work-family conflict, and many employer policies purporting to address it, reflect practices of gender stereotyping of a kind that the Court's equal protection cases condemn.

Handed down nearly 30 years after the Court's decision in *Geduldig*, *Hibbs* is an equal protection decision with a very different understanding of pregnancy in the workplace, one shaped by decades of litigation under the PDA. Pregnancy is not simply a real difference, outside the reach of gender stereotyping; instead, pregnancy is a central locus of gender stereotyping. As *Hibbs* explains, "'ideology about women's roles has in turn justified discrimination against women when they are mothers or mothers-to-be. . . .'"

Nevada Department of Human Resources v. Hibbs

538 U.S. 721 (2003)

Chief Justice Rehnquist delivered the opinion of the Court.

The Family and Medical Leave Act of 1993 (FMLA or Act) entitles eligible employees to take up to 12 work weeks of unpaid leave annually for any of several reasons, including the onset of a "serious health condition" in an employee's spouse, child, or parent. . . .

. . . Congress may, in the exercise of its §5 power, do more than simply proscribe conduct that we have held unconstitutional. "Congress' power 'to enforce' the Amendment includes the authority both to remedy and to deter violation of rights guaranteed thereunder by prohibiting a somewhat broader swath of conduct, including that which is not itself forbidden by the Amendment's text." In other words, Congress may enact so-called prophylactic legislation that proscribes facially constitutional conduct, in order to prevent and deter unconstitutional conduct.

. . . According to evidence that was before Congress when it enacted the FMLA, States continue to rely on invalid gender stereotypes in the employment context, specifically in the administration of leave benefits. Reliance on such stereotypes cannot justify the States' gender discrimination in this area. The long and extensive history of sex discrimination prompted us to hold that measures that differentiate on the basis of gender warrant heightened scrutiny; here, as in *Fitzpatrick*, the persistence of such unconstitutional discrimination by the States justifies Congress' passage of prophylactic §5 legislation.

As the FMLA's legislative record reflects, a 1990 Bureau of Labor Statistics (BLS) survey stated that 37 percent of surveyed private-sector employees were covered by maternity leave policies, while only 18 percent were covered by paternity leave policies. S. Rep. No. 103-3, pp. 14-15 (1993). . . . Thus, stereotype-based beliefs about the allocation of family duties remained firmly rooted, and employers' reliance on them in establishing discriminatory leave policies remained widespread.[a]

Congress also heard testimony that "[p]arental leave for fathers . . . is rare. Even . . . [w]here child-care leave policies do exist, men, *both in the public and private sectors*, receive notoriously discriminatory treatment in their requests for such leave." *Id.*, at 147 (Washington Council of Lawyers) (emphasis added). Many States offered women extended "maternity" leave that far exceeded the typical 4- to 8-week period of physical disability due to pregnancy and childbirth, but very few States granted men a parallel benefit: Fifteen States provided women up to one year of extended maternity leave, while only four provided men with the same. This and other differential leave policies were not attributable to any differential physical needs of men and women, but rather to the pervasive sex-role stereotype that caring for family members is women's work.[b]

. . .

The impact of the discrimination targeted by the FMLA is significant. Congress determined: "Historically, denial or curtailment of women's employment opportunities has been traceable directly to the pervasive presumption that women are mothers first, and workers second. This prevailing ideology about women's roles has in turn justified discrimination against women when they are mothers or mothers-to-be."

Stereotypes about women's domestic roles are reinforced by parallel stereotypes presuming a lack of domestic responsibilities for men. Because employers continued to regard the family as the woman's domain, they often denied men similar accommodations or discouraged them from taking leave. These mutually reinforcing stereotypes created a self-fulfilling cycle of discrimination that forced women to continue to assume the role of primary family caregiver, and fostered employers' stereotypical views about women's commitment to work and their value

---

a. While this and other material described leave policies in the private sector, a 50-state survey also before Congress demonstrated that "[t]he proportion and construction of leave policies available to public sector employees differs little from those offered private sector employees."

b. For example, state employers' collective-bargaining agreements often granted extended "maternity" leave of six months to a year to women only. . . .

Evidence pertaining to parenting leave is relevant here because state discrimination in the provision of both types of benefits is based on the same gender stereotype: that women's family duties trump those of the workplace. Justice Kennedy's dissent ignores this common foundation that, as Congress found, has historically produced discrimination in the hiring and promotion of women. Consideration of such evidence does not, as the dissent contends, expand our §5 inquiry to include "general genderbased stereotypes in employment." To the contrary, because parenting and family leave address very similar situations in which work and family responsibilities conflict, they implicate the same stereotypes.

as employees. Those perceptions, in turn, Congress reasoned, lead to subtle discrimination that may be difficult to detect on a case-by-case basis.

We believe that Congress' chosen remedy, the family-care leave provision of the FMLA, is "congruent and proportional to the targeted violation." Congress had already tried unsuccessfully to address this problem through Title VII and the amendment of Title VII by the Pregnancy Discrimination Act, 42 U.S.C. §2000e(k). Here, as in *Katzenbach,* Congress again confronted a "difficult and intractable problem," where previous legislative attempts had failed. Such problems may justify added prophylactic measures in response.

By creating an across-the-board, routine employment benefit for all eligible employees, Congress sought to ensure that family-care leave would no longer be stigmatized as an inordinate drain on the workplace caused by female employees, and that employers could not evade leave obligations simply by hiring men. By setting a minimum standard of family leave for all eligible employees, irrespective of gender, the FMLA attacks the formerly state-sanctioned stereotype that only women are responsible for family caregiving, thereby reducing employers' incentives to engage in discrimination by basing hiring and promotion decisions on stereotypes.

The dissent characterizes the FMLA as a "substantive entitlement program" rather than a remedial statute because it establishes a floor of 12 weeks' leave. In the dissent's view, in the face of evidence of gender-based discrimination by the States in the provision of leave benefits, Congress could do no more in exercising its §5 power than simply proscribe such discrimination. But this position cannot be squared with our recognition that Congress "is not confined to the enactment of legislation that merely parrots the precise wording of the Fourteenth Amendment," but may prohibit "a somewhat broader swath of conduct, including that which is not itself forbidden by the Amendment's text." . . .

Indeed, in light of the evidence before Congress, a statute mirroring Title VII, that simply mandated gender equality in the administration of leave benefits, would not have achieved Congress' remedial object. Such a law would allow States to provide for no family leave at all. Where "[t]wo-thirds of the nonprofessional caregivers for older, chronically ill, or disabled persons are working women," and state practices continue to reinforce the stereotype of women as caregivers, such a policy would exclude far more women than men from the workplace.

Unlike the statutes at issue in *City of Boerne, Kimel,* and *Garrett,* . . . the FMLA is narrowly targeted at the fault line between work and family—precisely where sex-based overgeneralization has been and remains strongest—and affects only one aspect of the employment relationship. . . .

For the above reasons, we conclude that §2612(a)(1)(C) is congruent and proportional to its remedial object, and can "be understood as responsive to, or designed to prevent, unconstitutional behavior."

The judgment of the Court of Appeals is therefore affirmed.

DISCUSSION

1. Hibbs, *equal protection, and sex stereotyping.* Was Congress enforcing the Equal Protection Clause as the Court has interpreted it when it enacted the

challenged provisions of the FMLA? How does *Hibbs* address this question? Robert Post observes:[120]

> *Hibbs* . . . offers an extraordinarily generous account of the constitutional harm of sex discrimination, which it locates in "firmly rooted" "stereotype-based beliefs about the allocation of family duties" that operate to the disadvantage of women in "situations in which work and family responsibilities conflict." *Hibbs* holds that in enacting the FMLA Congress properly sought "to adjust family leave policies in order to eliminate their reliance on and perpetuation of invalid stereotypes, and thereby dismantle persisting gender-based barriers to the hiring, retention, and promotion of women in the workplace." This conception of the relevant constitutional violation is quite distant from narrower formulations, which the Court tends to use in Section 1 litigation, and which associate the constitutional prohibition of sex discrimination either with explicit classifications based upon sex or with neutral government actions taken "'because of,' not merely 'in spite of,' [their] adverse effects upon" women.

Note that the FMLA can be understood as a remedy for disparate treatment in the provision of employment benefits (employers give early parenting leave to women and not men), and disparate treatment in hiring and promotion (employers avoid women believing that they will take family leave or have family conflicts). It might also rectify the disparate impact on women of workplace policies designed for workers without caregiving obligations. Which of these harms does the *Hibbs* Court treat as an injury of constitutional magnitude? Does *Hibbs* persuasively demonstrate how the FMLA remedies injuries recognized in the Court's earlier equal protection cases? How might *Hibbs* expand the concept of sex stereotyping that appears in the Court's earlier equal protection cases? For a reading of *Hibbs* as the first Supreme Court equal protection case to find that regulation of pregnant women rests on unconstitutional sex stereotypes, see Reva B. Siegel, "You've Come a Long Way, Baby": Rehnquist's New Approach to Pregnancy Discrimination in *Hibbs*, 58 Stan. L. Rev. 1871 (2006).

2. *Discrimination and accommodation.* Many scholars distinguish laws that prohibit simple discrimination ("differential treatment despite equality along 'relevant' dimensions") and laws that require accommodation ("demanding that the [employer] take particular affirmative steps to permit them to enjoy the relevant public accommodation or to work at the relevant job").[121] Mark Kelman sees important differences between discrimination and accommodation:[122]

> The plaintiff seeking accommodation does not claim to merit the treatment she asks for because she has the same relevant traits as the person who has received better treatment: She concedes that a business rationally

120. See Robert C. Post, The Supreme Court, 2002 Term—Foreword: Fashioning the Legal Constitution: Culture, Courts, and the Law, 117 Harv. L. Rev. 4, 17-18 (2003).

121. Mark Kelman, Market Discrimination and Groups, 53 Stan. L. Rev. 833, 840 (2001).

122. Id. at 843-844.

> differentiates workers or customers on the basis of the differential input costs associated with serving them. Instead, she argues that her "talent" is defined by her capacity to produce, and that her capacity to produce is measured by the output she can generate without using aids that benefit workers generally. . . . Because we must expend real resources to meet the demand for accommodation, we compare the value of expending the resources to meet the policy goals of accommodation with the value of expending the resources to meet other social policy aims.

By contrast, Christine Jolls questions whether there is a clear distinction between laws prohibiting discrimination and requiring accommodation. She points to ways in which familiar antidiscrimination mandates require employers to ignore potentially relevant differences and so impose costs on employers, like accommodation requirements:[123]

> [E]ven those aspects of antidiscrimination law that are not in fact accommodation requirements in the sense just described are similar to accommodation requirements in respects that have not previously been understood. The starting point for this argument—and this is a point that has been recognized previously—is the operation of antidiscrimination law when an employer's reluctance to employ members of a particular group stems from dislike of this group by customers or coworkers or from the employer's statistically accurate generalizations about group members. In these situations antidiscrimination law fairly obviously operates to require employers to incur undeniable financial costs associated with employing the disfavored group of employees—and thus in a real sense to "accommodate" these employees.

In what ways is the leave requirement of the FMLA distinct from or related to the prohibition on disparate treatment at the heart of the Court's equal protection cases?

3. *Economic rationality? Stereotypes concerning caregivers.* Many people assume that employer bias against caregivers reflects economically rational (self-interested) judgments. It may not. Joan Williams argues that many policies that disfavor caregivers in the workplace reflect bias against caregivers, rather than economically rational judgments.[124] A third possibility exists: Employers may fear that new mothers will prove unproductive, and endeavor to dismiss them before the feared circumstance materializes. As *Hibbs* recognizes, new mothers and mothers-to-be are subject to heightened sex stereotyping that exacerbates their already challenging task in negotiating the twin responsibilities of work and family.

In Back v. Hastings-on-Hudson Union Free School District, 365 F.3d 107 (2d Cir. 2004), Elena Back, a school psychologist, had received excellent employee evaluations until after she had her children, at which point (1) her evaluations began to

---

123. Christine Jolls, Antidiscrimination and Accommodation, 115 Harv. L. Rev. 642, 645 (2001).

124. Joan Williams and Nancy Segal, Beyond the Maternal Wall: Relief for Family Caregivers Who Are Discriminated Against on the Job, 26 Harv. Women's L.J. 77 (2003).

decline and (2) her supervisors made passing comments about her inability to work the number of hours required for her job when she had young children. Evaluating Back's claim that the school discriminated against her on the basis of sex, the Second Circuit addressed the kind of evidence plaintiffs could use to demonstrate that an employer had taken an adverse employment action based on gender stereotyping.[125]

> The instant case, however, foregrounds a crucial question: What constitutes a "gender-based stereotype"? *Price Waterhouse* suggested that this question must be answered in the particular context in which it arises, and without undue formulation. . . . [I]t takes no special training to discern stereotyping in the view that a woman cannot "be a good mother" and have a job that requires long hours, or in the statement that a mother who received tenure "would not show the same level of commitment [she] had shown because [she] had little ones at home." These are not the kind of "innocuous words" that we have previously held to be insufficient, as a matter of law, to provide evidence of discriminatory intent.

On remand the district court found that the plaintiff lacked sufficient evidence to sustain a §1983 claim for gender discrimination in violation of the Equal Protection Clause. What might constitute sufficient evidence of gender discrimination through stereotyping?

4. *The gender gap and the family.* While women may be closer to achieving parity with men in pay at the early stages of their career, the gap widens after they have children. Although overall women's mean wages rose between 1978 and 1994, mothers' wages not only started off lower than non-mothers' wages, but their wages also rose less (from $10.15 to $10.97) than women without children (from $11.11 to $12.15).[126] One recent study estimated a motherhood wage gap of about 15 percent per child.[127]

Gender differences manifest outside the wage context, as well. The family career gap affects men's and women's choices to have children and their ability to climb the career ladder while doing so. In law firms, for example, men are more likely to be married and more likely to have more children than women.[128] In academia, among those who have "early babies" (within five years of completion of the PhD), there is a 24 percent gap between men's and women's tenure achievement in the sciences, and a 20 percent gap in the social sciences and humanities.[129]

---

125. *Back*, 365 F.3d at 119-120; see also Lust v. Sealy, 277 F. Supp. 2d 973, 982 (W.D. Wis. 2003) (In a case where plaintiff's employer denied her promotion, explaining "You have kids," court ruled that "[d]enying a woman a promotion because of a stereotypical belief about her obligation to her family is discrimination because of sex.").

126. Jane Waldfogel, Understanding the Family Gap in Pay for Women with Children, 12 J. Econ. Persp. 137 (1998).

127. Deborah J. Anderson, Melissa Binder, and Kate Krause, The Motherhood Wage Penalty: Which Mothers Pay It and Why?, 92 Am. Econ. Rev. 354, 354 (2002).

128. Joni Hersch, The New Labor Market for Lawyers: Will Female Lawyers Still Earn Less?, 10 Cardozo Women's L.J. 1 (2003).

129. Mary Ann Mason and Marc Goulden, Do Babies Matter? The Effect of Family Formation on the Lifelong Careers of Academic Men and Women, http://www.aaup.org/publications/Academe/2002/02nd/02ndmas.htm.

A recent study found that mothers were evaluated differently in the workplace than non-mothers: "The competence ratings are approximately 10% lower for mothers than for nonmothers, and the commitment ratings are about 15% lower."[130] The study also found that the recommended starting salary for mothers was 7.4 percent less than that for non-mothers, and that mothers were rated as less promotable and were less likely to be recommended for management positions. In contrast, fathers often fared better than non-fathers in the same categories; they received higher commitment ratings, were allowed to be late to work more often than non-fathers, and were offered significantly higher salaries than non-fathers.[131]

How, if at all, are these data evidence of sex discrimination? Should society aspire to equalize the position of caregivers with others who do not engage in the work of caregiving? Is it fair to ask those who are not engaged in caring for children or other family members to subsidize the efforts of those who do?

5. *Frontiers beyond the FMLA*. The provisions of the FMLA, upheld in *Hibbs*, provide unpaid family leave to some employees. Yet pressures on many caregivers continue to inhibit their full participation in the workforce. For this reason, even after enactment of the FMLA, legislatures have continued to explore options to alleviate the burden on working parents. For example, in 2002, California became the first state to adopt a comprehensive *paid* family leave law. The statute provides workers with family responsibilities with up to six weeks of wage replacement benefits, paid for under the state's Temporary Disability Insurance (TDI) program. Cal. Unemp. Ins. Code §3301 (Deering 2004). In addition, a number of other states are experimenting with paid leave options paid for by TDI, unemployment insurance (UI), tax subsidies, or other funds. See Gillian Lester, A Defense of Paid Family Leave, 28 Harv. J.L. & Gender 1 (2005).

Many of these programs are specifically designed for low-income parents. One key federal program, the Child Care and Development Block Grant (CCDBG), provides eligible parents with assistance to pay for child care outside the home. With the CCDBG the government recognizes the importance of child care to the success of women in welfare-to-work programs. 45 C.F.R. §98.43 (2003). Some advocates, however, have argued that the state should provide parents with the option of caring for their children themselves. In response, a few states have varied their subsidy programs to provide eligible parents with child-care assistance to care for their own children at home. Minnesota, for example, implemented an "at-home infant care" program in 1997. Minn. Stat. §119B.035 (2000).

Should new federal or state legislation focus on providing working parents child care, or should they focus on securing family leave and other accommodations that would allow working parents more time to care for their own children? What different understandings do these two strategies reflect? What different groups might they benefit? Are there trade-offs?

---

130. Shelley J. Correll, Stephen Benard, and In Paik, Getting a Job: Is There a Motherhood Penalty?, 112 Am. J. Soc. 1297 (2007).

131. Id.

How, if at all, does the alleviation of work-family conflict concern the Constitution? Congress drew on its power to enforce the Fourteenth Amendment when it enacted the PDA and the FMLA. Do the state laws described above vindicate constitutional equality principles as well? Or are these statutes simply good (or bad) public policy, designed to strengthen the family and the economy, rather than to vindicate women's right to participate as equals in public life? What, if anything, is at stake in the way we characterize these initiatives? In what contexts might it matter?

6. *Coleman v. Court of Appeals of Maryland.* While the *Hibbs* Court held that the family-care provision of the FMLA was within Congress's §5 power to enact, the Court declared the FMLA's medical leave or "self-care" provision exceeded Congress's §5 power in Coleman v. Court of Appeals of Maryland, 132 S. Ct. 1327 (2012). The *Coleman* Court held that the medical leave provision of the FMLA—which permits an employee to take leave when the employee's own health condition interferes with work—was not congruent and proportional to an identified pattern of state sex discrimination. The majority noted: "[W]hat the family-care provisions have to support them, the self-care provision lacks, namely evidence of a pattern of state constitutional violations accompanied by a remedy drawn in narrow terms to address or prevent those violations." Thus, the Court determined that the self-care provision did not fall within Congress's §5 powers and states could not be sued for violations of the provision. In a vigorous dissent, Justice Ginsburg explained that the self-care provision was an essential component of the FMLA's purpose to combat gender discrimination in the workplace: "Self-care leave, I would hold, is a key part of Congress' endeavor to make it feasible for women to work and have families."

Justice Ginsburg's dissent in *Coleman* offers a lengthy account of the deliberations shaping the design of the FMLA. Ginsburg's dissent explains that the gender-neutral self-care and family leave provisions of the statute advanced Congress's goal of integrating work and family by means that would alleviate rather than exacerbate discrimination against women. The Act is premised on the understanding that (1) there are real conflicts between women's work and family roles and that (2) efforts to minimize these conflicts may intensify sex stereotyping in the workplace. Justice Ginsburg shows that Congress was concerned that a statute providing leave only for pregnancy would lead employers to avoid hiring women of childbearing age. To provide leave that would not exacerbate sex discrimination in hiring, Congress provided leave for men and women in gender-neutral form: The FMLA's "self-care" provisions allow both men and women to take employment leave for medical reasons. The provision provides female employees pregnancy-related leave, while "ward[ing] off the unconstitutional discrimination [Congress] believed would attend a pregnancy-only leave requirement."

Does Congress have power under the Fourteenth Amendment to redress and deter sex discrimination in this way? Why or why not? Given the Court's concerns about singling out groups for special treatment (see discussion of affirmative action in Chapter 6), why was the majority unsympathetic to the concerns shaping design of the self-care provisions of the FMLA?

IV. GENDER IN THE MILITARY: CONSTITUTIONAL CHANGE OUTSIDE THE COURTS

Core features of the military are organized on the basis of sex. Presumably, such sex classifications should be subject to constraint under the equal protection doctrine. Yet regulation of military life—like pregnancy—is an area where courts have historically been extremely deferential to the government's policy choices. For the most part, constitutional change in these areas has transpired outside the courts. In the armed services, constitutional change has been driven by the elected branches, military institutions, and social movement actors. Increased integration is, in part, a response to the pragmatic needs of a volunteer military. But these changes are also motivated by evolving understandings of gender equality and constitutional deliberation that occurs outside of the courts. As you read the chapter, consider which rationales—pragmatic or egalitarian—appear to drive which reforms.

A. A Brief History of Women in the Military: The Creation and Erosion of "Combat Exclusion" Rules[132]

Women have officially been excluded from military service throughout most of the nation's history. Nevertheless, women served in combat in the Revolutionary War and on both sides of the Civil War by passing as men, and women served as nurses during the Civil War, the Spanish American War, and World Wars I and II. By the end of World War II there were approximately 100,000 Women's Army Auxiliary Corps (WAC) members, 86,000 women in the Navy Women's Reserve (WAVES), 18,000 women Marines, and 11,000 members of the Air Force's female auxiliary, SPAR (for Semper Paratus, or "always ready"). Women were engaged in clerical jobs and also in repairing radio equipment, operating control towers, rigging parachutes, and serving as air navigators, aerophotographers, gunner instructors, and engine mechanics.

In 1948, Congress passed the Women's Armed Services Act, which was officially called an "Integration Act" but in fact did precisely the opposite. The Act gave the women's corps permanent military status but required that no more than 2 percent of each service could consist of women. It restricted the number of female officers, created separate promotion lists for women, severely restricted their opportunities for promotion, and set higher minimum ages for enlisted women than men.

The 1948 Act also for the first time specifically excluded women from combat. It authorized the Secretaries of each of the armed services to assign women to military duties, with the proviso that women could not be assigned to flight or ship duties when aircraft and naval vessels were engaged in "combat missions." The Army's exclusion of women from combat has been based on internal regulations

132. See Helen Hogan, Mixed Company (1981); Major General Jeanne Holm, USAF, Women in the Military: An Unfinished Revolution (1982); Judith Hicks Stiehm, Arms and the Enlisted Woman (1989).

that are justified as implementing congressional intention behind the statutory restrictions on the Navy and Air Force.[133]

By 1967, women began to serve in Vietnam, and their response under fire impressed members of the armed services. Approximately 7,500 women served in Vietnam, and many were decorated.

During the era of the ERA campaign, several government policy changes furthered women's integration into the military. In 1974, the age requirement for enlistment without parental consent became the same for men and women. In 1976, women were admitted to the Air Force Academy, the Naval Academy, and the Military Academy. In 1978, Congress amended the 1948 Integration Act to allow women to serve on additional types of noncombat ships, including repair ships, salvage ships, and rescue ships. In 1980, President Carter asked Congress to permit the registration of both men and women, at least in part based on an equality rationale, but Congress refused.

The need for large numbers of women recruits into volunteer service during the Persian Gulf War gave women additional opportunities to display their abilities in wartime and led to increased calls for modification of the combat exclusion rules. In 1991, Congress repealed the prohibition against women flying combat missions in the Air Force, Navy, and Marine Corps. Congress also established a new Commission on the Assignment of Women in the Armed Forces and authorized it to conduct tests of women in various combat positions and situations. The Commission's November 1992 report recommended retaining the direct ground combat exclusion for women. However, in November 1993, Congress repealed the naval combat ship exclusions.

In 1994, then-Secretary of Defense Les Aspin promulgated a direct ground combat exclusion rule (which remained in effect until 2013): "[S]ervice members are eligible to be assigned to all positions for which they are qualified, except that women shall be excluded from assignments to units below the brigade level whose primary mission is to engage in direct combat on the ground."[134] The services could also close positions to women if (1) the units and positions would be required to physically remain with direct ground combat units, (2) the cost of providing appropriate living arrangements for women would be prohibitive, (3) the units would be engaged in special operations forces' missions or

---

133. Congress has never defined the term "combat mission" in its statutory restrictions on the Navy and Air Force. As a result, each branch of the armed forces has its own interpretations of the jobs and missions women may participate in, which have changed over time as military doctrines and technologies have changed. Although each branch attempts to shield women from the risk of enemy fire or enemy capture, each branch assesses the risks differently, sometimes preventing women from serving even in certain noncombat positions.

134. Memorandum from the Secretary of Defense on the Direct Ground Combat Definition and Assignment Rule (Jan. 13, 1994). Brigades are ground combat units of about 3,000 to 5,000 soldiers whose primary mission is to engage and destroy enemy forces. They are comprised of battalions and form part of a division or corps. Although many positions in the armed services have secondary tasks related to direct ground combat, the combat rule focuses on the primary mission of the unit.

long-range reconnaissance, or (4) job-related physical requirements would exclude the vast majority of women.[135]

The war in Iraq dramatically increased gender integration of the military, a response to troop shortages and to changing modern warfare:[136]

> Historically, women's involvement in the military has surged in wartime. Today, that pattern is amplified by the all-volunteer U.S. military's growing share of women, which has steadily expanded in recent years to 15 percent of the active duty force.
>
> Moreover, in contrast to their roles in past wars, women are serving in a widening variety of Army ground units—from logistics to military police, military intelligence and civil affairs—where they routinely face the same risks as soldiers in all-male combat units such as infantry and armor. . . .
>
> At least as often as insurgents attack all-male infantry forces, they strike targets such as military supply convoys, checkpoints and camps where U.S. servicewomen are often present. As a result, hostile fire in Iraq has taken a proportionally larger toll on servicewomen than in any prior U.S. conflict, killing 35 and wounding 279.

As the military managed troop shortages in Iraq, it began to rely upon women in ways that eroded the combat exclusion. The Army began putting women in support units at the front lines of combat. The Army's Third Infantry Division included women in newly created "forward support companies" that provided "maintenance, food service, and other support services to infantry, armor, and Special Forces units" that engaged in combat.[137] In Iraq and Afghanistan, women flew combat aircraft; served on combat ships and on aircraft carriers; worked in support units as medics, engineers, and maintenance workers; and served in other dangerous jobs (as military police and on convoy duty). Army officials acknowledged that the changes would increasingly place women in combat situations. They claimed they were following federal law, which prohibited women from serving in units that engage in direct combat. But, as news reports noted at the time, "internal Army documents indicate the service is ignoring a 1994 regulation barring women from serving alongside units that conduct offensive operations," and Pentagon sources were reported to be considering repeal of the regulation.[138] As one report explained, these reforms provoked "a quiet, but highly charged debate within the Army over the role of women in the military. As a practical matter, the guerrilla tactics used against US troops during the occupation blurred the traditional lines between combat and support functions. . . ."[139]

---

135. For example, until recently, despite the lifting of the Navy combat ship exclusion, women could not serve on submarines, or on mine hunter, mine countermeasure, or coastal patrol ships. These ships were closed to women because of the cost of providing appropriate living arrangements.

136. Ann Scott Tyson, For Female GIs, Combat Is a Fact: Many Duties in Iraq Put Women at Risk Despite Restrictive Policy, Wash. Post, May 13, 2005, at A01.

137. Bryan Bender, U.S. Women Get Closer to Combat, Bos. Globe, Jan. 26, 2005, http://www.boston.com/news/nation/washington/articles/2005/01/26/us_women_get_closer_to/.

138. Id.

139. Id.

Although women assumed the risks of combat in modern warfare, however, they were precluded from much of the accompanying recognition and professional reward because of the official combat exclusion policy. Women often did not get credit for their combat experience, which is an important component of promotion to the most senior ranks.[140] This might explain why, as of February 2012, women accounted for 14 percent of the active-duty military, but only 7 percent of generals and admirals.[141] As one recent news article described, "women have been allowed to fight and die for their country, but not to hold assignments that are practically prerequisites for equality in promotion opportunities."[142] See also David S. Cloud, Pentagon to Ease Restrictions on Women in Combat, L.A. Times, Feb. 9, 2010 ("Many female soldiers already in effect serve in units that support frontline troops, but instead of being formally assigned to a battalion, they are 'attached' to the unit. That puts them close to combat but denies them the career advancement that male soldiers in combat receive. That has made it harder for women to rise to higher ranks, especially in the Army and Marines.").

B. The End of the Combat Exclusion?

On January 24, 2013, General Martin Dempsey, Chairman of the Joint Chiefs of Staff, and Defense Secretary Leon Panetta signed a memo rescinding the 1994 Direct Ground Combat Definition and Assignment Rule, effective immediately.[143] Under the new rules, units that are currently closed to women must be opened, consistent with guiding principles (described below) and after the development of gender-neutral performance standards. The policy change aims to ensure that those who are qualified for the military are able to participate. As Panetta explained, "I'm not talking about reducing the qualifications for the job—if they can meet the qualifications for the job, then they should have the right to serve, regardless of creed or color or gender or sexual orientation."[144] Military departments were directed to submit detailed implementation plans, and integration of women is to occur as expeditiously as possible and no later than January 1, 2016.

---

140. Lisa Daniel, American Foreign Press Services, Panel Says Rescind Policy on Women in Combat, U.S. Army (Mar. 8, 2011), http://www.army.mil/article/52934/.

141. Craig Whitlock, Pentagon to Ease Restrictions on Women in Some Combat Roles, Wash. Post, Feb. 9, 2012, http://www.washingtonpost.com/world/national-security/pentagon-to-ease-restrictions-on-women-in-some-combat-roles/2012/02/09/gIQAwnL41Q_story.html.

142. John H. Cushman, Jr., History of Women in Combat Still Being Written, Slowly, N.Y. Times, Feb. 9, 2012, http://www.nytimes.com/2012/02/10/us/history-of-women-in-combat-still-being-written-slowly.html.

143. Memorandum for Secretaries of the Military Departments Acting Under Secretary of Defense for Personnel and Readiness Chiefs of the Military Services (Jan. 24, 2013), available at http://www.defense.gov/news/WISRJointMemo.pdf.

144. Press Briefing by Secretary Panetta and General Dempsey from the Pentagon, News Transcript, U.S. Department of Defense (Jan. 24, 2013), available at http://www.defense.gov/transcripts/transcript.aspx?transcriptid=5183.

These changes are the capstone of years of debate and reflect the military's judgment about women's value to the service in recent conflicts.[145] Do you expect that at the end of the transition period, January 1, 2016, all positions in the military will be open to male and female service members? Should they be? Why or why not?

Although the combat ban has been rescinded, not all positions in the military will necessarily be open to women. Exceptions to the new rule are possible, although they must be "narrowly tailored" and require personal approval by the Chairman of the Joint Chiefs of Staff and Secretary of Defense. As a memorandum on the "Women in the Service Implementation Plan" from General Dempsey to Secretary Panetta describes, "[i]f we find that the assignment of women to a specific position or occupational specialty is in conflict with our stated principles, we will request an exception to policy."[146] The memorandum further explains:[147]

> To successfully integrate women into the remaining restricted occupational fields within our military, we must keep our guiding principles at the forefront. We are driven by:
>
> - Ensuring the success of our Nation's warfighting forces by preserving unit readiness, cohesion, and morale.
> - Ensuring all Service men and women are given the opportunity to succeed and are set up for success with viable career paths.
> - Retaining the trust and confidence of the American people to defend this Nation by promoting policies that maintain the best quality and most qualified people.
> - Validating occupational performance standards, both physical and mental, for all military occupational specialties (MOSs), specifically those that remain closed to women. Eligibility for training and development within designated occupational fields should consist of qualitative and quantifiable standards reflecting the knowledge, skills, and abilities necessary for each occupation. For occupational specialties

---

145. For sources debating justifications for the combat exclusion, see Kingsley R. Browne, The Report of the Military Leadership Diversity Commission: An Inadequate Basis for Lifting the Exclusion of Women from Direct Ground Combat, Wayne State University Law School Legal Studies Research Paper Series No. 2012-13 (2012) (arguing that the combat exclusion should be abolished only if doing so will not "degrade the military's capacity to perform its mission" and expressing concern that the Military Leadership Diversity Commission's focus on diversity precluded adequate assessment of the effect of integration on military effectiveness); Maia Goodell, Physical-Strength Rationales for De Jure Exclusion of Women from Military Combat Positions, 34 Seattle U. L. Rev. 17 (2010) (challenging physical strength rationales for the combat exclusion, citing stereotyping, differential training, trait selection, and task diffusion as problems with the theory); Kenneth L. Karst, The Pursuit of Manhood and the Desegregation of the Armed Forces, 38 UCLA L. Rev. 499, 500-501 (1991) (analyzing the exclusion and segregation of non-white men, women, and gays and lesbians in the military as "grounded in the symbolism of masculine power").

146. Memorandum from General Martin E. Dempsey on Women in the Service Implementation Plan to Secretary of Defense Leon Panetta (Jan. 9, 2013), available at: http://online.wsj.com/public/ resources/documents/DempseyLetter.pdf.

147. Id.

open to women, the occupational performance standards must be gender-neutral as required by Public Law 103-160, Section 542 (1993).

- Ensuring that a sufficient cadre of midgrade/senior women enlisted and officers are assigned to commands at the point of introduction to ensure success in the long run. This may require an adjustment to our recruiting efforts, assignment processes, and personnel policies. Assimilation of women into heretofore "closed units" will be informed by continual in-stride assessments and pilot efforts.

Do you believe that a full implementation of the policy abolishing the combat exclusion will result in gender integration of the military? If not, what further steps are required? What do you predict will be the rationale most commonly invoked to justify any remaining gender lines in military assignment policies?

Military leaders have expressed hope that ending the combat exclusion will improve cohesion and, perhaps, reduce military sexual harassment and assault. As General Dempsey explained:[148]

> We've had this ongoing issue with sexual harassment, sexual assault. . . . I believe it's because we've had separate classes of military personnel, at some level. Now, you know, it's far more complicated than that, but when you have one part of the population that is designated as warriors and another part that's designated as something else, I think that disparity begins to establish a psychology that in some cases led to that environment. I have to believe, the more we can treat people equally, the more likely they are to treat each other equally.

Despite the formal end of the combat exclusion and the ongoing gender integration of many military combat positions, however, the selective service has not yet changed its male-only conscription policy. What effect, if any, will elimination of the combat exclusion have on gender-based conscription policies?

C. Rostker *and the Constitutionality of Gender-Based Conscription*

For long periods of history, the nation met its military service needs through conscription in addition to voluntary service, as was the case most recently in the Vietnam War era. The nation's selective service laws required drafting men, but not women. Is a sex-based military draft a violation of equal protection? Against whom does it discriminate?

For most of the nation's history, sex-based conscription laws were viewed as natural.[149] But the 1970s, increasing numbers of men and women had begun to

---

148. Jennifer Steinhauer, Elite Units in U.S. Military to Admit Women, N.Y. Times, June 17, 2013, http://www.nytimes.com/2013/06/18/us/elite-units-in-us-military-to-admit-women.html.

149. See United States v. St. Clair, 291 F. Supp. 122 (D.S.D. 1968) (rejecting a sex discrimination challenge to the military draft because "[i]n providing for involuntary service for men and voluntary service for women, Congress followed the teachings of history that if a nation is to survive, men must provide the first line of defense while women keep the home fires burning").

question women's traditional exclusion from obligations of military service.[150] The question of whether the Equal Rights Amendment would subject women to military draft played a prominent role in debates over its ratification. In 1980, during the ERA debates and in response to the Soviet invasion of Afghanistan, President Carter asked Congress to amend the Military Selective Service Act in terms that would permit the registration of both men and women. President Carter emphasized sex equality justifications for the registration of women, explaining:[151]

> In every area of our national life, women are meeting the responsibilities of citizenship. That is as true of the military services as it is of the political arena or the economy of our Nation. Just as we are asking women to assume additional responsibilities, it is more urgent than ever that the women in America have full and equal rights under the Constitution. Equal obligations deserve equal rights.
>
> Congress refused, however, instead allocating funds only for the registration of men.

In Rostker v. Goldberg, 453 U.S. 57 (1981), the Supreme Court weighed in, and declared that the Constitution allowed Congress to require men but not women to register for the draft. Central to the Court's analysis was the explicit assumption that women would be excluded from combat. The Court further assumed, without ever discussing, the constitutionality of a sex-based combat exclusion.

In upholding Congress's decision to exclude women from registration under the Selective Service Act, Justice Rehnquist's majority opinion relied heavily on the fact that women were ineligible for combat. He observed that the Court traditionally accords Congress great deference in cases arising in "the context of Congress' authority over national defense and military affairs." Justice Rehnquist then found the exemption of women to be closely related to Congress's purpose in preparing a draft "*of combat troops*." Since women were ineligible for combat, Congress concluded there was no reason to require their registration for the draft. "The Constitution requires that Congress treat similarly situated persons similarly, not that it engage in gestures of superficial equality."

The majority pointed to floor debate and committee action concerning the role of women in the Armed Services to show that ". . . the decision to exempt women from registration was not the 'accidental by-product of a traditional way of thinking about women.' Califano v. Webster. . . . The issue was considered at great length, and Congress clearly expressed its purpose and intent." The majority quoted from the Senate Report:

---

150. Linda Kerber has argued that society regulates the social status of citizens by the ways it distributes responsibilities of citizenship (e.g., military or jury service) among them. See Linda K. Kerber, "A Constitutional Right to Be Treated Like . . . Ladies": Women, Civic Obligation, and Military Service, 1993 U. Chi. L. Sch. Roundtable 95, 97-98, 108-109, 115-124 (1993).

151. Jimmy Carter, Selective Service Revitalization: Statement on the Registration of Americans for the Draft (Feb. 8, 1980), available at http://www.presidency.ucsb.edu/ws/?pid=32906.

> The principle that women should not intentionally and routinely engage in combat is fundamental, and enjoys wide support among our people. It is universally supported by military leaders who have testified before the Committee. . . . Current law and policy exclude women from being assigned to combat in our military forces, and the Committee reaffirms this policy. . . . Men and women, because of the combat restrictions on women, are simply not similarly situated for purposes of a draft or registration for a draft.

The Court also addressed the issue that women might serve in noncombat positions "freeing men to go to the front." There was testimony that "in the event of a draft of 650,000 the military could absorb some 80,000 female inductees" in noncombat positions. The Court reasoned that this did not necessarily compel the registration of both men and women. Justice Rehnquist granted considerable deference to Congress:

> In the first place, assuming that a small number of women could be drafted for noncombat roles, Congress simply did not consider it worth the added burdens of including women in draft and registration plans. . . .
>
> Congress also concluded that whatever the need for women for noncombat roles during mobilization, whether 80,000 or less, it could be met by volunteers. . . .
>
> Most significantly, Congress determined that . . . [m]ilitary flexibility requires that a commander be able to move units or ships quickly. Units or ships not located at the front or not previously scheduled for the front nevertheless must be able to move into action if necessary. In peace and war, significant rotation of personnel is necessary. We should not divide the military into two groups—one in permanent combat and one in permanent support. Large numbers of non-combat positions must be available to which combat troops can return for duty before being redeployed.

Justice White, joined by Justice Brennan, dissented, stating that there was "some sense" to the notion that administrative burdens might be involved in registering all women for only some noncombat positions, but he insisted that "on the record before us, the number of women who could be used in the military without sacrificing combat-readiness is not at all small or insubstantial, and administrative convenience has not been sufficient justification for the kind of outright gender-based discrimination involved in registering and conscripting men but no women at all." Justice Powell pointed to military testimony in the record asserting that in a major military mobilization, 80,000 women could be deployed in the first six months.

Justice Marshall also dissented, joined by Justice Brennan, writing "there simply is no basis for concluding in this case that excluding women from registration is substantially related to the achievement of a concededly important governmental interest in maintaining an effective defense." He argued that the majority had focused upon the wrong issue:

> The relevant inquiry under the Craig v. Boren test is not whether a *gender-neutral* classification would substantially advance important governmental interests. Rather, the question is whether the gender-based

> classification is itself substantially related to the achievement of the asserted governmental interest. Thus, the Government's task in this case is to demonstrate that excluding women from registration substantially furthers the goal of preparing for a draft of combat troops. Or to put it another way, the Government must show that registering women would substantially impede its efforts to prepare for such a draft. Under our precedents, the Government cannot meet this burden without showing that a gender-neutral statute would be a less effective means of attaining this end.

Justice Marshall rejected the argument that there was "*no military need* to draft women," and he cited Defense Department estimates that in the event of a draft, "there will not be enough women volunteers to fill the positions for which women would be eligible. . . ." He maintained that "since the purpose of registration is to protect against unanticipated shortages of volunteers, it is difficult to see how excluding women from registration can be justified by conjectures about the expected number of female volunteers." While he accepted the importance of "military flexibility" posited by the majority, he denied that this warranted the exclusion of women from registration and the draft. Marshall argued that there was nothing in the Senate Report to suggest that "staffing even a limited number of noncombat positions with women would impede military flexibility."

DISCUSSION

1. *Diminishing authority of* Rostker? *Rostker* reasons that it is reasonable to exempt women from draft registration because women are ineligible for combat. Given the dramatic increase of women's role in the military and the formal elimination of the combat exclusion in the period since the Court's decision, does *Rostker* command the same authority? For an argument that the volunteer military's increased reliance on women undermines *Rostker*'s reasoning, see William A. Kamens, Comment, Selective Disservice: The Indefensible Discrimination of Draft Registration, 52 Am. U. L. Rev. 703 (2003); see also Linda Chavez, The First Generation of Draft Daughters?; If Women Can Fight, They Can Also Be Conscripted, Wash. Post, July 11, 1993, at C3.

A 2003 lawsuit filed in the U.S. District Court for the District of Massachusetts challenged the draft as violating equal protection, arguing that changed circumstances vitiated *Rostker's* reasoning. The court held that *Rostker* was still binding precedent and that the plaintiffs had not demonstrated that its factual underpinnings had eroded sufficiently to overrule it. See Schwartz v. Brodsky, 265 F. Supp. 2d 130 (D. Mass. 2003).

2. *Discrimination against whom?* Is the draft sex discrimination against men? What harms to men does the male-only draft inflict? Is the draft sex discrimination against women? What harms to women does the male-only draft inflict? Does the case for the male-only draft as sex discrimination against women depend on women being in all respects similarly situated with men for purposes of military service, including eligibility for combat?

3. *The draft and combat exclusion as sites of change.* Now that the executive branch has formally eliminated the combat exclusion, do you think courts will be

more or less likely to strike down sex-based restrictions on the draft? Are differences between the combat exclusion and the draft of continuing relevance here? Does preserving the voluntary character of women's participation in the military impede or advance change in the gendered organization of military life?

4. *Institutional considerations at stake in ending the combat exclusion and male-only draft.* Despite the end of the combat exclusion, the selective service is not yet changing its male-only conscription policy. Said Richard S. Flahavan, a Selective Service spokesman: "Until Congress and the president make a change, we will continue doing what we're doing."[152] Is Flahavan correct that the decision here requires Congress's ratification? At what point, if any, ought the Court step in to enforce the Fifth Amendment's equality guarantee?

5. *Constitutional change outside the courts.* In the last several decades, gender integration of the military has dramatically increased even though courts have not required these changes as a matter of equal protection law. Some of the changes the military has initiated in order to increase the pool of skilled volunteers available, especially during time of war. But the changes also reflect the efforts of advocates who are working to make the military a gender-equal institution.

Mary Fainsod Katzenstein describes how "everyday resistance and the politics of associationalism" allowed feminists to reshape institutions such as the armed forces from within. Change resulted from informal opposition to the status quo within the military by feminists and their supporters, as well as from the efforts of organizations in the military organized for the specific purpose of furthering the interests of women in the armed forces.[153]

Katzenstein describes the work of the Defense Advisory Committee on Women in the Services (DACOWITS), a committee of political appointees that provides counsel to the DOD on women's issues in the services. The Committee has been criticized by Phyllis Schlafly as the "feminist thought-control brigade of the U.S. military,"[154] and praised by historian Cynthia Enloe for persuading "the military of the connections between sexual harassment of military women and prostitution on foreign bases."[155] The Committee was a driving force in the movement to drop the cap on women's participation in the services, to appoint women to high positions in the military, including the courts of military appeals, and to provide abortions in military hospitals.[156] In the 1980s, it led efforts to combat sexual harassment against women in the armed forces. See also Linda Bird Francke, Ground Zero: The Gender Wars in the Military (1997).

---

152. Ernesto Londoño, Can Women Be Drafted? Selective Service Question Is Revived, Wash. Post, Jan. 26, 2013, http://www.washingtonpost.com/world/national-security/can-women-be-drafted-selective-service-question-is-revived/2013/01/26/414eeb18-6735-11e2-9e1b-07db1d2ccd5b_story.html.

153. Mary Fainsod Katzenstein, Feminism Within American Institutions: Unobtrusive Mobilization in the 1980s, 16 Signs: Journal of Women in Culture and Society 27, 27-54 (1990).

154. Id. at 48.

155. Id.

156. Id.

In short, formal and informal change agents are seeking equality for women in the military, and bringing about significant changes in their status. What is the relationship between this kind "unobtrusive mobilization inside institutions" and the Constitution? In what sense is DACOWITS forging *constitutional* change? What is at stake in characterizing its efforts in these terms—or in rejecting the characterization? Does mobilization within the military obviate the need for judicial intervention, or are courts still needed to remove legal barriers to entry that segregate women and restrict their access to many facets of military service?

What does this story of incremental change by informal change agents demonstrate about constitutional oversight of the military? Jill Hasday writes that the shift in public norms, the experience of women with successful military careers, and the total absence of judicial scrutiny "combine to make a strong case that Congress, the executive, and the military should assume a heightened responsibility to review and oversee military decisions about which positions are closed to women to ensure their rationality, freedom from bias, and consistency with constitutional norms of sex equality." Hasday, Fighting Women: The Military, Sex, and Extrajudicial Constitutional Change, 93 Minn. L. Rev. 96, 161 (2008). Do you agree? If persons outside the courts assume the responsibility of reviewing sex-based military policies, what role would be left to courts?

Is this an area where it is appropriate—or important—for persons in more than one institutional location to enforce constitutional norms? Why or why not? Is this because courts are ill suited to exercise authority in the military context? Or, are questions of race, sex, and sexual-orientation discrimination in the military an appropriate concern for judicial review as much as in any other location? If so, are there nonetheless context-sensitive ways in which courts might exercise judicial review to enable nonjudicial actors to enforce constitutional norms?

6. *Feminist objections to military service.* Although feminists' advocacy has been essential to the integration of the military, many feminists do not discuss issues of military service. The majority of those who discuss the question argue that gender differentiation in military service is unjust and harms women. But there are some feminists who are wary of compulsory military service for women, on the grounds that women should be opposed to militarism and violence. See Stephanie A. Levin, Women and Violence: Reflections on Ending the Combat Exclusion, 26 New Eng. L. Rev. 805 (1992); Ann Scales, Militarism, Male Dominance and Law: Feminist Jurisprudence as Oxymoron?, 12 Harv. Women's L.J. 25 (1989). Should women be permitted to opt for nonviolent national service alternatives to the military in time of war? If so, should men have the same options?

V. OTHER SUSPECT BASES OF CLASSIFICATION: THINKING OUTSIDE THE "TIERS OF SCRUTINY" MODEL

At this point in the course, you have learned about four types of classifications subject to heightened scrutiny: race, national origin, alienage, and gender. Although contemporary courses on constitutional law tend to teach these doctrines as fixed, in fact they have been quite mutable, and they were seriously contested during the 1970s and 1980s—the same period that the Second Reconstruction drew to a close and the modern conservative constitutional regime began.

The Court's debates over equal protection scrutiny during this crucial period are important because they prefigure contemporary debates over how courts should deal with discrimination based on sexual orientation and other categories. The key lesson of this history is that there is no single way of "doing" equal protection of the laws, and the current doctrines that one learns in law school courses stem from compromises among the various Justices in the 1970s and 1980s, compromises that may or may not make sense some 30 to 40 years later.

For a brief period in the late 1960s and early 1970s, the Court's jurisprudence featured a two-track model. In the 1960s, a decade after it held school segregation unconstitutional in *Brown*, the Court declared classification by race subject to strict scrutiny under the Equal Protection Clause. See Loving v. Virginia, 388 U.S. 1 (1967). Racial and national-origin classifications were subject to strict (and effectively fatal) scrutiny and *all* other classifications were subject to rational basis, which meant almost no scrutiny at all. As we saw in Chapter 7, classifications based on alienage were soon treated similarly to those of race, at least where state legislation was concerned. See In re Griffiths, 413 U.S. 717 (1973); Sugarman v. Dougall, 413 U.S. 634 (1973); Graham v. Richardson, 403 U.S. 365 (1971).

This understanding, however, quickly began to unravel as the Second Reconstruction and the sexual revolution proceeded. Starting with Reed v. Reed in 1971, the Court began to strike down classifications under the Equal Protection Clause based on gender, nominally under the rational basis test. A few years earlier, it had also begun to strike down classifications based on illegitimacy, also without stating that it was departing from rational basis. Weber v. Aetna Cas. & Sur. Co., 406 U.S. 164 (1972); Glona v. Am. Guarantee & Liability Ins. Co., 391 U.S. 73 (1968); Levy v. Louisiana, 301 U.S. 68 (1968).

Still other equal protection cases employed what we would today call heightened scrutiny under the guise of rational basis. In USDA v. Moreno, 413 U.S. 528 (1973), the Court struck down amendments to the Food Stamp Act that prohibited counting unrelated persons as part of a household for purposes of determining eligibility. The Court held that this classification was irrational, and implicitly concluded that the ban was probably based on congressional prejudice against cohabitation and communal lifestyles. *Moreno* would turn out to be a key decision in the creation of what is now called "rational basis with a bite": Courts sometimes strike down laws that they believe are based on malice or the bare desire to harm a politically unpopular group, whether or not the classification falls into a category generally subject to heightened scrutiny. Finally, in Eisenstadt v. Baird, 405 U.S. 438 (1972) (discussed in Chapter 9, infra), Justice Brennan's plurality opinion struck down a ban on contraceptive sales to unmarried persons, arguing that discrimination against unmarried persons with respect to the right of privacy violated equal protection.

Surveying some of these developments, Stanford law professor Gerald Gunther called them a "Newer Equal Protection." Gerald Gunther, Foreword: In Search of Evolving Doctrine on a Changing Court: A Model for a Newer Equal Protection, 86 Harv. L. Rev. 1 (1972). Gunther's article reflected a sense among some commentators that the two-track model had broken down and that the Justices were embarked on a period of experimentation in equal protection law.

During this period, some of the Justices, including most prominently Justices William Brennan and Thurgood Marshall, began arguing that the Court should recognize—and explicitly state—that its Equal Protection Clause decisions no longer matched the official (and toothless) test of Williamson v. Lee Optical and Ferguson v. Skrupa. Instead, the Court should adopt a "sliding-scale" approach to equal protection. Courts should view classifications in their social context, considering (1) the importance of the interests affected by a classification and (2) whether the group adversely affected by a classification faces some of the same difficulties faced by groups protected by strict scrutiny. In such cases, government classifications should receive a correspondingly greater level of scrutiny. This approach is spelled out in greatest detail in Justice Marshall's dissent in San Antonio Indep. Sch. Dist. v. Rodriguez, 411 U.S. 1 (1973), reprinted in Chapter 10, infra. (*Rodriguez* held that access to education was not a fundamental right and that poverty was not a suspect classification. Marshall, applying his sliding-scale approach, would have applied heightened scrutiny.)

Other Justices, especially Justice William Rehnquist, strongly resisted the new innovations in equal protection doctrine, arguing that they were inconsistent with judicial restraint and the New Deal settlement. See, e.g., his dissent in Trimble v. Gordon, 430 U.S. 762 (1977) (Rehnquist, J., dissenting) ("Without any antecedent constitutional mandate, we have created on the premises of the Equal Protection Clause a school for legislators, whereby opinions of this Court are written to instruct them in a better understanding of how to accomplish their ordinary legislative tasks."). Counseling judicial deference to democratic decisionmakers in interpreting equal protection guarantees, Justice Rehnquist sought narrowly to interpret the Court's race precedents and resisted any efforts to expand their protections to other groups. But as affirmative action cases began to reach the Court in the 1970s and 1980s, Justice Rehnquist and other conservatives advocated a more robust role for federal judges in equal protection cases. Conservatives sought to extend the Court's strict scrutiny precedents to affirmative action, while liberals sought to review affirmative action programs more deferentially, employing the newer forms of "intermediate" scrutiny.

At issue in this debate were fundamental questions concerning the role of federal courts in enforcing the Equal Protection Clause. On whose behalf and in respect of what concerns ought federal courts enforcing the Constitution's equality guarantees scrutinize the decisions of representative government? What forms of doctrine would appropriately balance the need for judicial oversight *and* judicial restraint?

The Court eventually reached a doctrinal compromise of sorts, largely at the insistence of its moderate or swing Justices, led by Lewis Powell and Byron White. These Justices shaped the course of equal protection law because their votes were crucial to form a majority in contested cases.

This compromise had four features. First, it rejected both the liberal "sliding-scale" approach of Marshall and Brennan, and the conservative two-track theory of Rehnquist, whereby race and national-origin classifications receive strict scrutiny and everything else is treated like Williamson v. Lee Optical. Second, the Court created a new intermediate level of scrutiny for sex classifications—and eventually for classifications based on illegitimacy.[157] Third, the Court refused to create any new suspect classes.[158]

Fourth, it eventually held in *Croson* and *Adarand* that all racial classifications were subject to strict scrutiny—at least officially; in practice, the *Bakke* and *Grutter* standard for reviewing college admissions programs designed to promote diversity was more forgiving.

These four features of the 1970s compromise on equal protection took over a decade to develop. They were not the product of a single theory of equality, but rather due to give-and-take among the various Justices who sat during this period. Nevertheless, by the time the federal courts began considering issues like sexual orientation in the 1990s and early 2000s, it was common to speak of key elements of this compromise as if they were part of a coherent and longstanding body of equal protection law. The period of experimentation appeared to be over, given that no new suspect (or quasi-suspect) classifications had been added since the 1970s. This strongly shaped the debate over sexual-orientation discrimination, as we shall see in the next chapter.

The emergence of an intermediate level of scrutiny required a new vocabulary to describe what the Court was doing. Accordingly, classifications subject to intermediate scrutiny are sometimes called "quasi-suspect." Cases involving strict and intermediate scrutiny are sometimes grouped together as involving "heightened scrutiny" to distinguish these tests from traditional rational basis. But even the creation of three tiers did not adequately describe the Court's doctrines. Building on the food stamp case, USDA v. Moreno, the Court eventually created yet another variant, called "rational basis with a bite," applying what was in effect heightened scrutiny, when judges believed that legislators had acted with animus, irrational prejudice, or malice. Whether officially or unofficially, tiers of scrutiny had proliferated.

---

157. The Court struggled over suspect status for classifications based on illegitimacy for some time. Mathews v. Lucas, 427 U.S. 495 (1976), denied that illegitimacy was a suspect classification, but in Trimble v. Gordon, 430 U.S. 762 (1977), the Court continued to apply higher scrutiny than the standard Williamson v. Lee Optical test. Justice Powell's opinion in *Trimble* noted that although "classifications based on illegitimacy fall in a 'realm of less than strictest scrutiny,' *Lucas* also establishes that the scrutiny 'is not a toothless one.'" See also Lalli v. Lalli, 439 U.S. 259 (1978) (plurality opinion) (Although "classifications based on illegitimacy are not subject to 'strict scrutiny,' they nevertheless are invalid under the Fourteenth Amendment if they are not substantially related to permissible state interests."). A decade later, Justice O'Connor's opinion in Clark v. Jeter, 486 U.S. 456 (1988), confirmed that classifications based on illegitimacy were subject to intermediate scrutiny.

158. In Massachusetts Board of Retirement v. Murgia, 427 U.S. 307 (1976), the Court held that age classifications were subject to ordinary rational basis scrutiny. This conclusion was reaffirmed in Vance v. Bradley, 440 U.S. 93 (1979). In New York City Transportation Authority v. Beazer, 440 U.S. 568 (1979), the Court held that classifications burdening persons receiving treatment for drug addiction were also subject to the ordinary rational basis test.

For a discussion of the internal deliberations of the Justices in *Murgia*, and their eventual rejection of the Marshall/Brennan sliding-scale approach, see Earl Maltz, The Burger Court and the Conflict over the Rational Basis Test: The Untold Story of Massachusetts Board of Retirement v. Murgia, 39 J. Sup. Ct. Hist. 264 (2014).

In the mid-1980s, the Court considered whether classifications based on disability should be subject to heightened scrutiny, adding a new member to the list of suspect or quasi-suspect classes. In response to this question, the Court, in effect, split the difference. While technically affirming the rational basis test, the Court held that the law was unconstitutional as applied, using "rational basis with a bite." The case produced an interesting debate among the Justices about whether the tiers of scrutiny model continued to make sense.

City of Cleburne, Texas v. Cleburne Living Center

473 U.S. 432 (1985)

[In July 1980, a four-bedroom house in Cleburne, Texas, was purchased for lease to the Cleburne Living Centers, Inc. (CLC), to serve as a group home for 13 mentally retarded men and women who would live there under the supervision of CLC staff members. CLC intended to comply with all applicable state and federal regulations. The city determined that a special use permit, required for the construction of "[h]ospitals for the insane or feeble-minded, or alcoholic[s] or drug addicts, or penal or correctional institutions," was required as well, on the basis of its classification of the home as a "hospital for the feeble-minded." CLC applied for a permit, which the city council denied by a vote of three to one. CLC then filed suit in the Federal District Court, which found that "[i]f the potential residents of the . . . home were not mentally retarded, but the home was the same in all other respects, its use would be permitted under the city's zoning ordinance." It further found that the city council's decision "was motivated primarily by the fact that the residents of the home would be persons who are mentally retarded." Nevertheless, the court held the ordinance and its application constitutional under the standard of minimal rationality, for it was rationally related to the city's legitimate interests in "the legal responsibility of CLC and its residents, . . . the safety and fears of residents in the adjoining neighborhood," and the number of people to be housed in the facility.

The Court of Appeals for the Fifth Circuit reversed, holding that mental retardation was a quasi-suspect classification triggering an intermediate-level standard of review, which the city could not pass. The city appealed.]

White, J., delivered the opinion of the Court. . . .

II

The Equal Protection Clause of the Fourteenth Amendment commands that no State shall "deny to any person within its jurisdiction the equal protection of the laws," which is essentially a direction that all persons similarly situated should be treated alike. Plyler v. Doe, 457 U.S. 202. Section 5 of the Amendment empowers Congress to enforce this mandate, but absent controlling congressional direction, the courts have themselves devised standards for determining the validity of state legislation or other official action that is challenged as denying equal protection. The general rule is that legislation is presumed to be valid and will be sustained if the classification drawn by the statute is rationally related to a legitimate state interest. . . . When social or economic legislation is at issue, the Equal Protection Clause allows the states wide latitude, and the Constitution presumes that even improvident decisions will eventually be rectified by the democratic processes.

The general rule gives way, however, when a statute classifies by race, alienage, or national origin. These factors are so seldom relevant to the achievement of any legitimate state interest that laws grounded in such considerations are deemed to reflect prejudice and antipathy—a view that those in the burdened class are not as worthy or deserving as others. For these reasons and because such discrimination is unlikely to be soon rectified by legislative means, these laws are subjected to strict scrutiny and will be sustained only if they are suitably tailored to serve a compelling state interest. . . .

Legislative classifications based on gender also call for a heightened standard of review. . . . Rather than resting on meaningful considerations, statutes distributing benefits and burdens between the sexes in different ways very likely reflect outmoded notions of the relative capabilities of men and women. A gender classification fails unless it is substantially related to a sufficiently important governmental interest. Because illegitimacy is beyond the individual's control and bears "no relation to the individual's ability to participate in and contribute to society," Mathews v. Lucas, 427 U.S. 495, 505 (1976), official discriminations resting on that characteristic are also subject to somewhat heightened review. Those restrictions "will survive equal protection scrutiny to the extent they are substantially related to a legitimate state interest." Mills v. Habluetzel, 456 U.S. 91, 99 (1982).

We have declined, however, to extend heightened review to differential treatment based on age:

> While the treatment of the aged in this Nation has not been wholly free of discrimination, such persons, unlike, say, those who have been discriminated against on the basis of race or national origin, have not experienced a "history of purposeful unequal treatment" or been subjected to unique disabilities on the basis of stereotyped characteristics not truly indicative of their abilities. Massachusetts Board of Retirement v. Murgia, 427 U.S. 307, 313 (1976).

The lesson of *Murgia* is that where individuals in the group affected by a law have distinguishing characteristics relevant to interests the state has the authority to implement, the courts have been very reluctant, as they should be in our federal system and with our respect for the separation of powers, to closely scrutinize legislative choices as to whether, how and to what extent those interests should be pursued. In such cases, the Equal Protection Clause requires only a rational means to serve a legitimate end.

III

Against this background, we conclude for several reasons that the Court of Appeals erred in holding mental retardation a quasi-suspect classification calling for a more exacting standard of judicial review than is normally accorded economic and social legislation. First, it is undeniable, and it is not argued otherwise here, that those who are mentally retarded have a reduced ability to cope with and function in the everyday world. Nor are they all cut from the same pattern: as the testimony in this record indicates, they range from those whose disability is not immediately evident to those who must be constantly cared for. They are thus different, immutably so, in relevant respects, and the states' interest in dealing with and providing for them is plainly a legitimate one.[a] How this large and diversified group is to be treated under the law is a difficult and often technical matter, very much a task for legislators guided by qualified professionals and not by the perhaps ill-informed opinions of the judiciary. Heightened scrutiny inevitably involves substantive judgments about legislative decisions, and we doubt that the predicate for such judicial oversight is present where the classification deals with mental retardation.

Second, the distinctive legislative response, both national and state, to the plight of those who are mentally retarded demonstrates not only that they have unique problems, but also that the lawmakers have been addressing their difficulties in a manner that belies a continuing antipathy or prejudice and a corresponding need for more intrusive oversight by the judiciary. [The Court then reviewed some recent protective legislation passed by both the federal and Texas governments.]

. . . It may be . . . that legislation designed to benefit, rather than disadvantage, the retarded would generally withstand examination under a test of heightened scrutiny. The relevant inquiry, however, is whether heightened scrutiny is constitutionally mandated in the first instance. Even assuming that many of these laws could be shown to be substantially related to an important governmental purpose, merely requiring the legislature to justify its efforts in these terms may lead it to refrain from acting at all. Much recent legislation intended to benefit the retarded also assumes the need for measures that might be perceived to disadvantage them. The [federal] Education of the Handicapped Act, for example, requires an "appropriate" education, not one that is equal in all respects to the education of non-retarded children. . . . Especially given the wide variation in the abilities and needs of the retarded themselves, governmental bodies must have a certain amount of flexibility and freedom from judicial oversight in shaping and limiting their remedial efforts.

Third, the legislative response, which could hardly have occurred and survived without public support, negates any claim that the mentally retarded are politically powerless in the sense that they have no ability to attract the attention of the lawmakers. Any minority can be said to be powerless to assert direct control over the legislature, but if that were a criterion for higher level scrutiny by the courts, much economic and social legislation would now be suspect. Fourth, if the large and amorphous class of the mentally retarded were deemed quasi-suspect, . . . it would be difficult to find a principled way to distinguish a variety of other groups who have perhaps immutable disabilities setting them off from others, who cannot

---

a. As Dean Ely has observed: "Surely one has to feel sorry for a person disabled by something he or she can't do anything about, but I'm not aware of any reason to suppose that elected officials are unusually unlikely to share that feeling. Moreover, classifications based on physical disability and intelligence are typically accepted as legitimate, even by judges and commentators who assert that immutability is relevant. The explanation, when one is given, is that those characteristics (unlike the one the commentator is trying to render suspect) are often relevant to legitimate purposes. At that point there's not much left of the immutability theory, is there?" J. Ely, Democracy and Distrust 150 (1980) (footnote omitted).

themselves mandate the desired legislative responses, and who can claim some degree of prejudice from at least part of the public at large. One need mention in this respect only the aging, the disabled, the mentally ill, and the infirm. We are reluctant to set out on that course, and we decline to do so. . . .

IV

We turn to the issue of the validity of the zoning ordinance insofar as it requires a special use permit for homes for the mentally retarded. We inquire first whether requiring a special use permit for the Featherston [Avenue] home in the circumstances here deprives respondents of the equal protection of the laws. If it does, there will be no occasion to decide whether the special use permit provision is facially invalid where the mentally retarded are involved. . . .

The constitutional issue is clearly posed. The city does not require a special use permit in an R-3 zone for apartment houses, multiple dwellings, boarding and lodging houses, fraternity or sorority houses, dormitories, apartment hotels, hospitals, sanitariums, nursing homes for convalescents or the aged (other than for the insane or feeble-minded or alcoholics or drug addicts), private clubs or fraternal orders, and other specified uses. It does, however, insist on a special permit for the Featherston home, and it does so, as the District Court found, because it would be a facility for the mentally retarded. May the city require the permit for this facility when other care and multiple dwelling facilities are freely permitted?

. . . Because in our view the record does not reveal any rational basis for believing that the Featherston home would pose any special threat to the city's legitimate interests, we affirm the judgment below insofar as it holds the ordinance invalid as applied in this case.

The District Court found that the City Council's insistence on the permit rested on several factors. First, the Council was concerned with the negative attitude of the majority of property owners located within 200 feet of the Featherston facility, as well as with the fears of elderly residents of the neighborhood. But mere negative attitudes, or fear, unsubstantiated by factors which are properly cognizable in a zoning proceeding, are not permissible bases for treating a home for the mentally retarded differently from apartment houses, multiple dwellings, and the like. . . . "Private biases may be outside the reach of the law, but the law cannot, directly or indirectly, give them effect." Palmore v. Sidoti.

Second, the Council had two objections to the location of the facility. It was concerned that the facility was across the street from a junior high school, and it feared that the students might harass the occupants of the Featherston home. But the school itself is attended by about 30 mentally retarded students, and denying a permit based on such vague, undifferentiated fears is again permitting some portion of the community to validate what would otherwise be an equal protection violation. The other objection to the home's location was that it was located on a "five hundred year flood plain." This concern with the possibility of a flood, however, can hardly be based on a distinction between the Featherston home and, for example, nursing homes, homes for convalescents or the aged, or sanitariums or hospitals, any of which could be located on the Featherston site without obtaining a special use permit. The same may be said of another concern of the Council—doubts about the legal responsibility for actions which the mentally retarded might take. . . .

Fourth, the Council was concerned with the size of the home and the number of people that would occupy it. . . . [But] there would be no restrictions on the number of people who could occupy this home as a boarding house, nursing home, family dwelling, fraternity house, or dormitory. . . . In the words of the Court of Appeals, "The City never justifies its apparent view that other people can live under such 'crowded' conditions when mentally retarded persons cannot."

In the courts below, the city also urged that the ordinance is aimed at avoiding concentration of population and at lessening congestion of the streets. These concerns obviously fail to explain why apartment houses, fraternity and sorority houses, hospitals and the like, may freely locate in the area without a permit. So, too, the expressed worry about fire hazards, the serenity of the neighborhood, and the avoidance of danger to other residents fail rationally to justify singling out a home such as 201 Featherston for the special use permit. . . .

The short of it is that requiring the permit in this case appears to us to rest on an irrational prejudice against the mentally retarded, including those who would occupy the Featherston facility and who would live under the closely supervised and highly regulated conditions expressly provided for by state and federal law.

The judgment of the Court of Appeals is affirmed insofar as it invalidates the zoning ordinance as applied to the Featherston home. . . .

Justice STEVENS, with whom THE CHIEF JUSTICE joins, concurring.

The Court of Appeals disposed of this case as if a critical question to be decided were which of three clearly defined standards of equal protection review should be applied to a legislative classification discriminating against the mentally retarded. In fact, our cases have not delineated three—or even one or two—such well-defined standards. Rather, our cases reflect a continuum of judgmental responses to differing classifications which have been explained in opinions by terms ranging from "strict scrutiny" at one extreme to "rational basis" at the other. I have never been persuaded that these so-called "standards" adequately explain the decisional process. Cases involving classifications based on alienage, illegal residency, illegitimacy, gender, age, or—as in this case—mental retardation, do not fit well into sharply defined classifications.

"I am inclined to believe that what has become known as the [tiered] analysis of equal protection claims does not describe a completely logical method of deciding cases, but rather is a method the Court has employed to explain decisions that actually apply a single standard in a reasonably consistent fashion." Craig v. Boren, 429 U.S. 190, 212 (1976) (Stevens, J., concurring). In my own approach to these cases, I have always asked myself whether I could find a "rational basis" for the classification at issue. The term "rational," of course, includes a requirement that an impartial lawmaker could logically believe that the classification would serve a legitimate public purpose that transcends the harm to the members of the disadvantaged class. Thus, the word "rational"—for me at least—includes elements of legitimacy and neutrality that must always characterize the performance of the sovereign's duty to govern impartially.

The rational-basis test, properly understood, adequately explains why a law that deprives a person of the right to vote because his skin has a different pigmentation than that of other voters violates the Equal Protection Clause. It would be utterly irrational to limit the franchise on the basis of height or weight; it is equally invalid to limit it on the basis of skin color. None of these attributes has any bearing at all on the citizen's willingness or ability to exercise that civil right. We do not need to apply a special standard, or to apply "strict scrutiny," or even "heightened scrutiny," to decide such cases.

In every equal protection case, we have to ask certain basic questions. What class is harmed by the legislation, and has it been subjected to a "tradition of disfavor" by our laws? What is the public purpose that is being served by the law? What is the characteristic of the disadvantaged class that justifies the disparate treatment? In most cases the answer to these questions will tell us whether the statute has a "rational basis." The answers will result in the virtually automatic invalidation of racial classifications and in the validation of most economic classifications, but they will provide differing results in cases involving classifications based on alienage, gender, or illegitimacy. But that is not because we apply an "intermediate standard of review" in these cases; rather it is because the characteristics of these groups are sometimes relevant and sometimes irrelevant to a valid public purpose, or, more specifically, to the purpose that the challenged laws purportedly intended to serve.

Every law that places the mentally retarded in a special class is not presumptively irrational. The differences between mentally retarded persons and those with greater mental capacity are obviously relevant to certain legislative decisions. An impartial lawmaker—indeed, even a member of a class of persons defined as mentally retarded—could rationally vote in favor of a law providing funds for special education and special treatment for the mentally retarded. A mentally retarded person could also recognize that he is a member of a class that might need special supervision in some situations, both to protect himself and to protect others. Restrictions on his right to drive cars or to operate hazardous equipment might well seem rational even though they deprived him of employment opportunities and the kind of freedom of travel enjoyed by other citizens. "That a civilized and decent society expects and approves such legislation indicates that governmental consideration of those differences in the vast majority of situations is not only legitimate but also desirable."

Even so, the Court of Appeals correctly observed that through ignorance and prejudice the mentally retarded "have been subjected to a history of unfair and often grotesque mistreatment." The discrimination against the mentally retarded that is at issue in this case is the city's decision to require an annual special use permit before property in an apartment house district may be used as a group home for persons who are mildly retarded. The record convinces me that this permit was required because of the irrational fears of neighboring property owners, rather than for the protection of the mentally retarded persons who would reside in respondent's home.

[I]n this Court, the city has argued that the discrimination was really motivated by a desire to protect the mentally retarded from the hazards presented by the neighborhood. Zoning ordinances are not usually justified on any such basis. . . . I find that justification wholly unconvincing. I cannot believe that a rational member of this disadvantaged class could ever approve of the discriminatory application of the city's ordinance in this case. Accordingly, I join the opinion of the Court.

MARSHALL, J., joined by BRENNAN and BLACKMUN, JJ., concurring in the judgment in part and dissenting in part.

. . . Cleburne's ordinance is invalidated only after being subjected to precisely the sort of probing inquiry associated with heightened scrutiny. . . . [H]owever labeled, the rational basis test invoked today is most assuredly not the rational basis test of *Williamson*. . . .

The Court, for example, concludes that legitimate concerns for fire hazards or the serenity of the neighborhood do not justify singling out respondents to bear the burdens of these concerns, for analogous permitted uses appear to pose similar threats. Yet under the traditional and most minimal version of the rational basis test, "reform may take one step at a time, addressing itself to the phase of the problem which seems most acute to the legislative mind." Williamson v. Lee Optical Co. The "record" is said not to support the ordinance's classifications, but under the traditional standard we do not sift through the record to determine whether policy decisions are squarely supported by a firm factual foundation. Finally, the Court further finds it "difficult to believe" that the retarded present different or special hazards than other groups. In normal circumstances, the burden is not on the legislature to convince the Court that the lines it has drawn are sensible. . . .

The refusal to acknowledge that something more than minimum rationality review is at work here is, in my view, unfortunate in at least two respects. The suggestion that the traditional rational basis test allows this sort of searching inquiry creates precedent for this Court and lower courts to subject economic and commercial classifications to similar and searching "ordinary" rational basis review—a small and regrettable step back toward the days of Lochner v. New York. Moreover, by failing to articulate the factors that justify today's "second order" rational basis review, the Court provides no principled foundation for determining when more searching inquiry is to be invoked.

II

I have long believed the level of scrutiny employed in equal protection cases should vary with "the constitutional and societal importance of the interest adversely affected and the recognized invidiousness of the basis upon which the particular classification is drawn." San Antonio Independent School District v. Rodriguez, 411 U.S. 1, 99 (1973) (dissenting). When a zoning ordinance works to exclude the retarded from all residential districts in a community, these two considerations require that the ordinance be convincingly justified as substantially furthering legitimate and important purposes.

First, the interest of the retarded in establishing group homes is substantial. . . . Excluding group homes deprives the retarded of much of what makes for human freedom and fulfillment—the ability to form bonds and take part in the life of a community.

Second, the mentally retarded have been subject to a "lengthy and tragic history," *Bakke*, of segregation and discrimination that can only be called grotesque. [In the early twentieth century, a] regime of state-mandated segregation and degradation . . . emerged that in its virulence and bigotry rivaled, and indeed paralleled, the worst excesses of Jim Crow. Massive custodial institutions were built to warehouse the retarded for life; the aim was to halt reproduction of the retarded and "nearly extinguish their race." Retarded children were categorically excluded from public schools, based on the false stereotype that all were ineducable and on the purported need to protect nonretarded children from them. State laws deemed the retarded "unfit for citizenship."

Segregation was accompanied by eugenic marriage and sterilization laws that extinguished for the retarded one of the "basic civil rights of man"—the right to marry and procreate. Marriages of the retarded were made, and in some states continue to be, not only voidable but also often a criminal offense. The purpose of such limitations, which frequently applied only to women of child-bearing age, was unabashedly eugenic: to prevent the retarded from propagating. To assure this end, 29 states enacted compulsory eugenic sterilization laws between 1907 and 1931.

Prejudice, once let loose, is not easily cabined. As of 1979, most states still categorically disqualified "idiots" from voting, without regard to individual capacity and with discretion to exclude left in the hands of low-level election officials. Not until Congress enacted the Education of the Handicapped Act were the "door[s] of public education" opened wide to handicapped children. But most important, lengthy and continuing isolation of the retarded has perpetuated the ignorance, irrational fears, and stereotyping that long have plagued them.

In light of the importance of the interest at stake and the history of discrimination the retarded have suffered, the Equal Protection Clause requires us to do more than review the distinctions drawn by Cleburne's zoning ordinance as if they appeared in a taxing statute or in economic or commercial legislation. . . .

III

In its effort to show that Cleburne's ordinance can be struck down under no "more exacting standard . . . than is normally accorded economic and social legislation," the Court offers several justifications as to why the retarded do not warrant heightened judicial solicitude. These justifications, however, find no support in our heightened scrutiny precedents and cannot withstand logical analysis.

The Court downplays the lengthy "history of purposeful unequal treatment" of the retarded by pointing to recent legislative action that is said to "beli[e] a continuing antipathy or prejudice." Building on this point, the Court similarly concludes that the retarded are not "politically powerless" and deserve no greater judicial protection than "any minority" that wins some political battles and loses others. The import of these conclusions, it seems, is that the only discrimination courts may remedy is the discrimination they alone are perspicacious enough to see. Once society begins to recognize certain practices as discriminatory, in part because previously stigmatized groups have mobilized politically to lift this stigma, the Court would refrain from approaching such practices with the added skepticism of heightened scrutiny.

Courts, however, do not sit or act in a social vacuum. Moral philosophers may debate whether certain inequalities are absolute wrongs, but history makes clear that constitutional principles of equality, like constitutional principles of liberty, property and due process, evolve over time; what once was a "natural" and "self-evident" ordering later comes to be seen as an artificial and invidious constraint on human potential and freedom. Compare Plessy v. Ferguson and Bradwell v. Illinois with Brown v. Board of Education and Reed v. Reed. Shifting cultural, political, and social patterns at times come to make past practices appear inconsistent with fundamental principles upon which American society rests, an inconsistency legally cognizable under the Equal Protection Clause. It is natural that evolving standards of equality come to be embodied in legislation. When that occurs, courts should look to the fact of such change as a source of guidance on evolving principles of equality. In [*Frontiero*], the Court reached this very conclusion when it extended heightened scrutiny to gender classifications and drew on parallel legislative developments to support that extension. . . .

Moreover, even when judicial action has catalyzed legislative change, that change certainly does not eviscerate the underlying constitutional principle. The Court, for example, has never suggested that race-based classifications became any less suspect once extensive legislation had been enacted on the subject.

For the retarded, just as for Negroes and women, much has changed in recent years, but much remains the same; out-dated statutes are still on the books, and irrational fears or ignorance, traceable to the prolonged social cultural isolation of the retarded, continue to stymie recognition of the dignity and individuality of retarded people. Heightened judicial scrutiny of action appearing to impose unnecessary barriers to the retarded is required in light of increasing recognition that such barriers are inconsistent with evolving principles of equality embedded in the Fourteenth Amendment.

The Court also offers a more general view of heightened scrutiny, a view focused primarily on when heightened scrutiny does not apply as opposed to when it does apply. Two principles appear central to the Court's theory. First, heightened scrutiny is said to be inapplicable where individuals in a group have distinguishing characteristics that legislatures properly may take into account in some circumstances. Heightened scrutiny is also purportedly inappropriate when many legislative classifications affecting the group are likely to be valid. . . . If the Court's first principle were sound, heightened scrutiny would have to await a day when people could be cut from a cookie mold. . . . Permissible distinctions between persons must bear a reasonable relationship to their relevant characteristics, and gender per se is almost never relevant. . . .

The Court's second assertion—that the standard of review must be fixed with reference to the number of classifications to which a characteristic would validly be relevant—is similarly flawed. Certainly the assertion is not a logical one; that a characteristic may be relevant under some or even many circumstances does not suggest any reason to presume it relevant under other circumstances where there is reason to suspect it is not. A sign that says "men only" looks very different on a bathroom door than a courthouse door.

Our heightened scrutiny precedents belie the claim that a characteristic must virtually always be irrelevant to warrant heightened scrutiny. . . . While *Frontiero* stated that gender "frequently" and "often" bears no relation to legitimate legislative aims, it did not deem gender an impermissible basis of state action in all circumstances. Indeed, the Court has upheld some gender-based classifications. . . . Potentially discriminatory classifications exist only where some constitutional basis can be found for presuming that equal rights are required. Discrimination, in the Fourteenth Amendment sense, connotes a substantive constitutional judgment that two individuals or groups are entitled to be treated equally with respect to some thing. With regard to economic and commercial matters, no basis for such a conclusion exists. . . . As a matter of substantive policy, therefore, government is free to move in any direction, or to change directions, in the economic and commercial sphere. . . . But the Fourteenth Amendment does prohibit other results under virtually all circumstances, such as castes created by law along racial or ethnic lines, and significantly constrains the range of permissible government choices where gender or illegitimacy, for example, are concerned. Where such constraints, derived from the Fourteenth Amendment, are present, and where history teaches they have systemically been ignored, a "more searching judicial inquiry" is required. United States v. Carolene Products Co.

That more searching inquiry, be it called heightened scrutiny or "second order" rational basis review, is a method of approaching certain classifications skeptically, with judgment suspended until the facts are in and the evidence considered. The government must establish that the classification is substantially related to important and legitimate objectives so that valid and sufficiently weighty policies actually justify the departure from equality. Heightened scrutiny does not allow courts to second guess reasoned legislative or professional judgments tailored to the unique needs of a group like the retarded, but it does seek to assure that the hostility or thoughtlessness with which there is reason to be concerned has not carried the day. . . .

As the history of discrimination against the retarded and its continuing legacy amply attest, the mentally retarded have been, and in some areas may still be, the targets of action the Equal Protection Clause condemns. With respect to a liberty so valued as the right to establish a home in the community, and so likely to be denied on the basis of irrational fears and outright hostility, heightened scrutiny is surely appropriate.

IV

In light of the scrutiny that should be applied here, Cleburne's ordinance sweeps too broadly to dispel the suspicion that it rests on a bare desire to treat the retarded as outsiders, pariahs who do not belong in the community. The Court, while disclaiming that special scrutiny is necessary or warranted, reaches the same conclusion. Rather than striking the ordinance down, however, the Court invalidates it merely as applied to respondents. I must dissent from the novel proposition that "the preferred course of adjudication" is to leave standing a legislative act resting on "irrational prejudice," thereby forcing individuals in the group discriminated against to continue to run the act's gauntlet.

. . . As a consequence, the Court's as applied remedy relegates future retarded applicants to the standardless discretion of low-level officials who have already shown an all too willing readiness to be captured by the "vague, undifferentiated fears" of ignorant or frightened residents.

Invalidating on its face the ordinance's special treatment of the "feeble-minded," in contrast, would place the responsibility for tailoring and updating Cleburne's unconstitutional ordinance where it belongs: with the legislative arm of the City of Cleburne. . . .

To my knowledge, the Court has never before treated an equal protection challenge to a statute on an as applied basis. When statutes rest on impermissibly overbroad generalizations, our cases have invalidated the presumption on its face. We do not instead leave to the courts the task of redrafting the statute through an ongoing and cumbersome process of "as applied" constitutional rulings. . . .

. . . When a presumption is unconstitutionally overbroad, the preferred course of adjudication is to strike it down.

DISCUSSION

1. The three opinions in *Cleburne* offer three different approaches to the problems created by the post-1970s doctrine of equal protection.

a. Justice White nominally adopts the three-tier 1970s compromise on equal protection, and he states that the mentally retarded are not a suspect class. Nevertheless, he holds for the plaintiffs by noting that the challenge is as-applied rather than facial, and that this case involves an "irrational prejudice" against the mentally retarded. (What is the evidentiary basis for his attribution of irrational prejudice?) White's finding of irrationality or animus is a version of what has come to be known as "rational basis with a bite." It allows White to apply heightened scrutiny without recognizing any new suspect classifications—a key feature of the 1970s compromise. As we shall see in Chapter 9, this approach is used again in a series of cases involving sexual-orientation discrimination.

b. Justice Stevens argues against using multiple tiers of scrutiny. He claims that courts should apply a single standard of scrutiny—or say nothing about scrutiny at all. Instead, judges should decide in every case whether legislative classifications are neutral, fair and reasonable, and untainted by prejudice or bias.

c. Justice Marshall, as he did throughout the 1970s, argues for a "sliding-scale" approach to equal protection. In every case, judges should take into account "the constitutional and societal importance of the interest adversely affected and the recognized invidiousness of the basis upon which the particular classification is drawn."

How does each approach negotiate (or disguise) controversial questions of value in applying equality norms? Which approach do you think is the best way to deal with questions of equal protection in the future? What criteria guide your selection of frameworks?

Note that the model of multiple tiers won out in the 1970s and 1980s because key swing Justices supported it. As we shall see in Chapter 9, in cases involving sexual orientation, Justice Anthony Kennedy was the swing Justice from the 1990s onward, and wrote the key opinions on gay rights. Therefore, the due process and equal protection doctrines in this area tend to reflect his views. His position has been closer to that of Justice Stevens—refusing to apply a particular level of scrutiny or not explicitly stating the level of scrutiny that applies.

2. Dean Martha Minow has argued that the majority and dissenting opinions in *Cleburne* rest on distinct visions of the status of "difference" under the Equal Protection Clause:[159]

---

159. Martha Minow, When Difference Has Its Home: Group Homes for the Mentally Retarded, Equal Protection and Legal Treatment of Difference, 22 Harv. C.R.-C.L. L. Rev. 111, 139-140 (1987).

> [B]eneath the debates [in *Cleburne*] over the proper fit between ends and means of legislative action and the proper level of scrutiny for reviewing legislative classifications lies a sharp division about the meaning of difference. On one side is the perhaps contentiously labeled "abnormal persons" view, a conception of real differences used to treat certain people as legally different. On the other side is the perhaps ambiguously designated "social relations" view, which emphasizes how differences acquire significance through social attributions, rather than the other way around; how we each have relationships even with those we think are different; and how "we" are as different from those we call different as they are different from us. The "abnormal persons" view makes differential treatment seem natural, unavoidable, and unproblematic; the social relations view makes differential treatment a problem of social choice and meaning, a problem for which all onlookers are responsible.

3. Note how Justice White describes Congress's power to enforce the Fourteenth Amendment in *Cleburne*. How does this account differ from the Court's recent §5 cases?

4. In Board of Trustees of Univ. of Alabama v. Garrett, 531 U.S. 356, 367-368 (2001), the Court described its holding in *Cleburne* in the following terms:

> [T]he result of *Cleburne* is that States are not required by the Fourteenth Amendment to make special accommodations for the disabled, so long as their actions toward such individuals are rational. They could quite hardheadedly—and perhaps hardheartedly—hold to job-qualification requirements which do not make allowance for the disabled. If special accommodations for the disabled are to be required, they have to come from positive law and not through the Equal Protection Clause.

a. Does this strike you as a fair account of the Court's reasoning in *Cleburne*? Can this reading of *Cleburne* be squared with the Court's decision to strike down the zoning ordinance?

b. Does this strike you as a fair account of Fourteenth Amendment case law more generally? Samuel Bagenstos objects that "[t]he assumption that discrimination on the basis of race or sex is never rational, and the related normative view that discrimination should be prohibited only when it is irrational, simply misdescribe the empirical and normative bases of antidiscrimination law." Samuel R. Bagenstos, The Supreme Court, The Americans With Disabilities Act, and Rational Discrimination, 55 Ala. L. Rev. 923, 925 (2004).

For other reflections on questions of accommodation and the antidiscrimination principle, see the discussion of *Hibbs*, supra. See also Samuel R. Bagenstos, "Rational Discrimination," Accommodation, and the Politics of (Disability) Civil Rights, 89 Va. L. Rev. 825 (2003); Samuel R. Bagenstos, The Future of Disability Law, 114 Yale L.J. 1 (2004); Christine Jolls, Antidiscrimination and Accommodation, 115 Harv. L. Rev. 642 (2001); Mark Kelman, Market Discrimination and Groups, 53 Stan. L. Rev. 833 (2001); Michael Ashley Stein, The Law and Economics of Disability Accommodations, 53 Duke L.J. 79 (2003); David A. Strauss, The Law and Economics of Racial Discrimination in Employment, 79 Geo. L.J. 1619 (1991); Richard A. Epstein, Forbidden Grounds: The Case Against Employment Discrimination Laws (1992).

NOTE: ACCOMMODATION AS A NORM—THE AMERICANS WITH DISABILITIES ACT OF 1990

In the summer of 1990, President Bush proudly signed the Americans with Disabilities Act, describing it as the most important step in civil rights since the Civil Rights Act of 1964. Section 102 provides:

> **(a)** General Rule. No covered entity shall discriminate against a qualified individual with a disability because of the disability of such individual in regard to . . . terms, conditions, and privileges of employment.
>
> **(b)** Construction. As used in subsection (a), the term "discriminate" includes—
>
> **(5)(A)** not making reasonable accommodations to the known physical or mental limitations of an otherwise qualified individual with a disability who is an applicant or employee, unless such covered entity can demonstrate that the accommodation would impose an undue hardship on the operation of the business of such covered entity.

Section 101 provides:

> **(9)** The term "reasonable accommodation" may include:
>
> **(A)** making existing facilities used by employees readily accessible to and useable by individuals with disabilities; and
>
> **(B)** job restructuring, part-time or modified work schedules, reassignment to a vacant position, acquisition or modification of equipment or devices, appropriate adjustment or modifications of examinations, training materials or policies, the provision of qualified readers or interpreters, and other similar accommodations for individuals with disabilities.
>
> **(10)** The term "undue hardship" means an action requiring significant difficulty or expense, when considered in the light of factors [including the nature and cost of the accommodation and the overall financial resources of the covered entity and the facility involved].

Many view the "reasonable accommodation" provision of the Americans with Disabilities Act of 1990 (ADA) as radically different from the antidiscrimination principle as it has been interpreted by courts construing the Equal Protection Clause, the Civil Rights Act of 1964, and other federal civil rights statutes. Others see closer affinities between the prohibition on discrimination and the requirement of reasonable accommodation. (See commentary following the *Hibbs* and *Cleburne* cases, supra.) In what respects are these approaches similar and different?

What values are at stake in this debate? Is there a reason for adopting a distinct approach in constitutional cases? In cases where courts are enforcing constitutional commitments?

CHAPTER 9

LIBERTY, EQUALITY, AND FUNDAMENTAL RIGHTS: THE CONSTITUTION, THE FAMILY, AND THE BODY

In this chapter, we examine a series of modern opinions in which the Court has protected rights at the intersection of liberty and equality. These fundamental rights are variously described in terms of dignity, privacy, procreational choice, sexual autonomy, marriage and family formation, intimate association, bodily integrity, and self-defense. Most but not all of these rights have their textual basis in guarantees of "liberty" in the Fourteenth Amendment and the Due Process Clause of the Fifth Amendment.

Two points of clarification are in order: First, these rights are sometimes called "implied fundamental rights" on the assumption that they are not explicitly stated in the Constitution. However, most constitutionally protected rights are interpretations of the Constitution's text and elaborated in doctrine, and are not explicitly stated in the Constitution. For example, many rights associated with the First Amendment—for example, the right of association—are not explicitly stated in the text of the amendment yet are not called "implied fundamental rights." Second, although many of the fundamental rights discussed in this chapter are derived from parts of Constitution's text that protect "liberty," the Court often guarantees "liberty" by appeal to values of dignity and equality, and vice versa. The Court's understanding of how values of liberty, dignity, and equality are implicated in the regulation of intimate relations has changed over the decades, and continues to evolve in our own day. This chapter discusses the popular debates that have shaped understandings of these rights and influenced the work of judges and lawyers in articulating them.

I. HISTORICAL ROOTS OF FUNDAMENTAL RIGHTS ADJUDICATION

Constitutional protection for decisions concerning family life rests, in part, on the early cases decided during the *Lochner* era. Although the post–New Deal Court repeatedly distanced itself from the economic due process decisions of the *Lochner* era, other cases concerning the rights of family formation were never overruled. Decades later, the Court would draw on the authority of these cases, as a debate about whether the criminal law should be used to regulate consensual sex became a debate about whether the Constitution's protections of liberty extended to matters of sexual and family life.

A. Doctrinal Antecedents

According to the nineteenth-century theory of the police power, the state had broad authority to promote the health, safety, and welfare of its citizens. Accordingly, during the *Lochner* era, the Court sometimes rejected constitutional claims to rights of bodily integrity, in deference to the states' police powers. In Jacobson v. Massachusetts, 197 U.S. 11 (1905), the Court upheld a compulsory smallpox vaccination scheme. Justice Harlan pointed out that "the police power of a state must be held to embrace, at least, such reasonable regulations established directly by legislative enactment as will protect the public health and the public safety. . . . Upon the principle of self-defense, of paramount necessity, a community has the right to protect itself against an epidemic of disease which threatens the safety of its members."

In Buck v. Bell, 274 U.S. 200 (1927), the state provided for the sterilization of institutionalized mentally disabled persons after a hearing at which, apparently, the issue of heritability could be contested. Petitioner Carrie Buck challenged not the procedure but the substantive provision itself. Justice Holmes described Buck as "a feeble minded white woman who was committed to the State Colony, . . . the daughter of a feeble minded mother in the same institution, and the mother of an illegitimate feeble minded child." Holmes then summarily dismissed the due process challenge with the comment that "three generations of imbeciles are enough." Comparing compulsory sterilization to compulsory vaccination and to the military draft, Holmes argued that "[w]e have seen more than once that the public welfare may call upon the best citizens for their lives. It would be strange if it could not call upon those who already sap the strength of the State for these lesser sacrifices, often not felt to be such by those concerned, in order to prevent our being swamped with incompetence. It is better for all the world, if instead of waiting to execute degenerate offspring for crime, or to let them starve for their imbecility, society can prevent those who are manifestly unfit from continuing their kind. The principle that sustains compulsory vaccination is broad enough to cover cutting the Fallopian tubes." To the equal protection claim that the sterilization law applied only to persons confined in state institutions and not to the multitudes outside, Holmes responded that "it is the usual last resort of constitutional arguments to point out shortcomings of this sort. But the answer is that the law does all that is needed when it does all that it can, indicates a policy, applies it to all within the lines, and seeks to bring within the lines all similarly situated so far and so fast as its means allow. Of course so far as the operations enable those who otherwise must be kept confined to be returned to the world, and thus open the asylum to others, the equality aimed at will be more nearly reached." Justice Butler dissented.

Nevertheless, not all such regulations were deemed within the state's police power. During the same period, the Court also intervened on several occasions to protect the interests of parents—and especially the head of the household—in making decisions concerning children. The language in two of the leading cases of the period, Meyer v. Nebraska, 262 U.S. 390 (1923), and Pierce v. Society of Sisters, 268 U.S. 510 (1925), suggests that the Court did not consider "economic" and "civil" liberties discrete areas of concern.

The petitioner in *Meyer* was an instructor in a parochial school, convicted under a state law prohibiting the teaching of a foreign language to any child not yet in the eighth grade. (The law in fact reflected the animosity against German-speaking German-Americans during World War I.) Over the dissents of Justices Holmes and Sutherland, the Court struck down the law, viewing it as an incursion on Meyer's right "to teach and the right of parents to engage him so to instruct their children." Justice McReynolds, writing for the Court, argued that "[t]he problem for our determination is whether the statute . . . unreasonably infringes the liberty guaranteed . . . by the Fourteenth Amendment":

> While this Court has not attempted to define with exactness the liberty thus guaranteed, the term has received much consideration and some of the included things have been definitely stated. Without doubt, it denotes not merely freedom from bodily restraint but also the right of the individual to contract, to engage in any of the common occupations of life, to acquire useful knowledge, to marry, establish a home and bring up children, to worship God according to the dictates of his own conscience, and generally to enjoy those privileges long recognized by common law as essential to the orderly pursuit of happiness by free men. The established doctrine is that this liberty may not be interfered with, under the guise of protecting the public interest, by legislative action which is arbitrary or without reasonable relation to some purpose within the competency of the State to effect. Determination by the legislature of what constitutes proper exercise of the police power is not final or conclusive but is subject to supervision by the courts. . . .

Pierce v. Society of Sisters and the consolidated case of Pierce v. Hill Military Academy were suits brought by parochial and private schools challenging an Oregon statute that required children to attend public schools. The Ku Klux Klan was a powerful force in local politics at the time and the law was a thinly disguised attempt at closing Catholic schools. Justice McReynolds wrote for a unanimous Court, invalidating the statute:

> Under the doctrine of Meyer v. Nebraska, we think it entirely plain that the Act of 1922 unreasonably interferes with the liberty of parents and guardians to direct the upbringing and education of children under their control. As often heretofore pointed out, rights guaranteed by the

> Constitution may not be abridged by legislation which has no reasonable relation to some purpose within the competency of the State. The fundamental theory of liberty upon which all governments in this Union repose excludes any general power of the State to standardize its children by forcing them to accept instruction from public teachers only. The child is not the mere creature of the State; those who nurture him and direct his destiny have the right, coupled with the high duty, to recognize and prepare him for additional obligations.

Note that in *Meyer* and *Pierce* the constitutional protection of liberty also vindicates equality interests (of German-Americans and Catholics, respectively). We will see the interaction of liberty and equality repeatedly in this chapter.

Although the Court retreated from constitutional protection of liberty of contract in 1937, it did not reverse *Meyer* or *Pierce*. During World War II, the Court incrementally added to constitutional protections for family life when it used the Equal Protection Clause to restrict the government's power to sterilize citizens as punishment for a crime. In Skinner v. Oklahoma, 316 U.S. 535 (1942), the Court struck down Oklahoma's Habitual Criminal Sterilization Act as a violation of the Equal Protection Clause. The Act required sterilization of a criminal offender upon a third conviction of a felony "involving moral turpitude." Several felonies, including embezzlement, were specifically exempted from serving as predicate offenses triggering the sterilization penalty. Skinner had been convicted over the course of a decade of three qualifying felonies—one chicken theft and two armed robberies—and was sentenced to sterilization. Justice Douglas wrote for the Court: "If we had here only a question as to the State's classification of crimes, such as embezzlement or larceny, no substantial federal question would be raised." Instead:

> We are dealing here with legislation which involves one of the basic civil rights of man. Marriage and procreation are fundamental to the very existence and survival of the race. The power to sterilize, if exercised, may have subtle, far-reaching and devastating effects. In evil or reckless hands it can cause races or types which are inimical to the dominant group to wither and disappear. There is no redemption for the individual whom the law touches. Any experiment which the State conducts is to his irreparable injury. He is forever deprived of a basic liberty. . . . [S]trict scrutiny of the classification which a State makes in a sterilization law is essential, lest unwittingly, or otherwise, invidious discriminations are made against groups or types of individuals in violation of the constitutional guaranty of just and equal laws. . . . When the law lays an unequal hand on those who have committed intrinsically the same quality of offense and sterilizes one and not the other, it has made as invidious a discrimination as if it had selected a particular race or nationality for oppressive treatment.

Justice Jackson added that "[t]here are limits to the extent to which a legislatively represented majority may conduct biological experiments at the expense of the dignity and personality and natural powers of a minority—even those who have been guilty of what the majority defines as crimes." Note that the Court avoided invoking notions of substantive due process, preferring to explain the result in terms of equal protection. Chief Justice Stone concurred in the judgment on the ground that the statute violated *procedural* due process. He argued that the defendant was not given a hearing "to discover whether his criminal tendencies are of an inheritable type." For Justice Douglas, however, such a hearing would not cure the constitutional problem.

Concerns of the World War II era plainly shaped *Skinner*. In the postwar period, the social sciences played a role in stirring law reform, prompting changes, first, in the criminal law, and ultimately, in constitutional law.

B. Popular and Philosophical Debate About the Criminalization of Sex

In the years after World War II, developments in the social sciences provoked increasing discussion of the role of the law, in particular criminal law, in the regulation of sexuality. In the United States, Alfred Kinsey challenged conventional understandings with his social scientific studies on human sexuality.[1] Kinsey's studies revealed that many more men and women than commonly believed engaged in same-sex experiences, adulterous sexual relations, and premarital sex. The empirical approach and neutral moral frame of scientific accounts of human sexuality implicitly supported less punitive laws.[2]

In the United Kingdom, the Wolfenden Commission, formally the Committee on Homosexual Offences and Prostitution, issued a report in 1957 that depicted human sexuality in the neutral and pragmatic terms, not unlike the Kinsey studies. The Commission reasoned that the law's function was to preserve public order and decency, and asserted that law should not interfere with what it termed "private" moral conduct except to prevent public harm. "There must remain a realm of private morality and immorality which is, in brief and crude terms, not the law's business."[3]

Distinguishing between sex in public and in private, the report recommended the decriminalization of "homosexual behavior between consenting adults in private," while recommending increased penalties for engaging in or facilitating prostitution, on the view that the latter were forms of consensual sex that caused public harm. The British Parliament implemented the recommendation on prostitution immediately, and ten years later, in 1967, decriminalized sodomy between males over the age of 21 and liberalized the law on abortion.[4]

Over this same period in the United States, the American Law Institute also proposed reforms in the regulation of sodomy and abortion, based on the goal

---

1. See Alfred C. Kinsey, Wardell B. Pomeroy, and Clyde E. Martin, Sexual Behavior in the Human Male (1948); Alfred C. Kinsey et al., Sexual Behavior in the Human Female (1953); William H. Masters and Virginia E. Johnson, Human Sexual Response (1966). For background, see David Allyn, Private Acts/Public Policy: Alfred Kinsey, The American Law Institute and the Privatization of American Sexual Morality, 30 J. Am. Stud. 405, 405, 410-413, 417 (1996).

2. Sexuality, Gender, and the Law 46-48 (William Eskridge, Jr. & Nan Hunter eds., 2d ed. 2003). See also William N. Eskridge, Jr., Dishonorable Passions: Sodomy Laws in America 1861-2003, at 114-117 (2008).

3. Wolfenden Report: Report of the Committee on Homosexual Offenses and Prostitution (Stein & Day 1963) (1957). See generally Jeffrey Weeks, Sex, Politics, and Society: The Regulation of Sexuality Since 1800, at 239-244 (1981) (discussing the Wolfenden Report's attempts to formulate distinctions between public and private).

4. Abortion Act, 1967, c. 87, §1 (Eng.); Sexual Offenses Act, 1967, c. 60, §1 (Eng.).

of decriminalizing "private" sexual activity between consenting adults.[5] State laws criminalizing such behavior were argued to be in need of revision because they were "ineffective, inhumane and thoroughly unscientific" given contemporary understandings of sex.[6] In 1952, drafting began on the Model Penal Code (MPC), which the American Law Institute adopted ten years later and which was used as a model in state reforms across the country.[7] The MPC, for example, was premised on the understanding that "no harm to the secular interest of the community is involved in atypical sex practice in private between consenting adult partners."[8]

While debates about the law's role in enforcing sexual morality initially played out as policy debates in the legislative arena, these debates plainly had constitutional dimensions. The Wolfenden Report's proposal to decriminalize traditional morals offenses prompted one of the most important jurisprudential debates of the latter half of the twentieth century: the Hart-Devlin debates on the relationship between law and morality.[9]

Lord Patrick Devlin argued that the use of the law to enforce morals norms (legal moralism) was essential for the protection not only of individuals, but of society, its values and way of life. He wrote that "[s]ociety is justified in taking the same steps to preserve its moral code as it does to preserve its government and other essential institutions."[10] Professor H.L.A. Hart, invoking J.S. Mill's "harm principle," argued that the proper use of law is restricted to the protection of individuals from harm. Legal enforcement of a moral code, he wrote, is unacceptable insofar as it interferes with individual liberty.[11] The harm principle carves out for individuals an area of freedom of action, securing the liberty necessary to debate and continuously reassess what they wished the moral code of their society to be.

The Wolfenden Report and the Hart-Devlin debates had resonance well beyond a small group of legal elites; they were widely known and discussed in legal circles during this period. Two prominent criminal law textbooks published in 1962 drew on and excerpted heavily from the report and debates to raise questions of the broader social meaning and values expressed by the criminal code.[12] The report and debates also made their way into law review articles of the era.[13]

---

5. See generally Allyn, Private Acts/Public Policy, supra n.1, at 424.

6. Herbert Wechsler, Challenge of a Model Penal Code, 65 Harv. L. Rev. 1103 (1952).

7. Anders Walker, American Oresteia: Herbert Wechsler, the Model Penal Code, and the Uses of Revenge, 2009 Wis. L. Rev. 1017, 1029-1051.

8. American Law Institute, Model Penal Code, §207.5 Sodomy and Related Offenses, Comment (Tentative Draft No. 4, 1955).

9. See generally Peter Cane, Taking Law Seriously: Starting Points of the Hart/Devlin Debate, 10 J. Ethics 21, 22 (2006).

10. Patrick Devlin, The Enforcement of Morals 13-14 (1965).

11. E.g., H.L.A. Hart, Law, Liberty, and Morality (1963).

12. Richard C. Donnelly, Joseph Goldstein, and Richard D. Schwartz, Criminal Law: Problems for Decision in the Promulgation, Invocation, and Administration of a Law of Crimes 188-199 (1962); Monrad G. Paulsen and Sanford H. Kadish, Criminal Law and Its Processes: Cases and Materials (1962).

13. See, e.g., Ronald Dworkin, Lord Devlin and the Enforcement of Morals, 75 Yale L.J. 986 (1966); Graham Hughes, Morals and the Criminal Law, 71 Yale L.J. 662 (1962).

Debates over the use of the criminal law to regulate sexuality often focused on the distinction between "private" and "public" sexuality.[14] But what made sexuality private and protected? And when was sex public and legitimately subject to regulation? Was private sexuality reserved for respectable acts between consenting adults? Was the domain of "private" sexual expression confined to traditional institutions of marriage and the family, to relations of love and intimacy, or to the bedroom, home, or other private physical space? Was sex of "public" concern similarly defined by the nature of the sexual act or where it took place? Need it be visible or within public view?

These debates on the proper role of criminal law in regulating sexual expression first assumed constitutional form in a case brought to challenge a Connecticut statute that criminalized the use of contraception, the most stringent in the nation.[15] In the United States, laws criminalizing contraception first appeared in the aftermath of the Civil War and rapidly spread across the nation. By the mid-twentieth century, many but not all states had repealed them. Interest in birth control spiked again with the introduction of oral birth control in the 1960s.[16] In 1965, the Supreme Court gave new energy to the debate with its decision in Griswold v. Connecticut, which considered whether the Constitution limited criminal restrictions on access to contraceptives.

II. CONTEMPORARY FUNDAMENTAL RIGHTS ADJUDICATION

A. The Contraception Case

Griswold v. Connecticut

381 U.S. 479 (1965)

Douglas, J.

Appellant Griswold is Executive Director of the Planned Parenthood League of Connecticut. Appellant Buxton is a licensed physician and a professor at the Yale Medical School who served as Medical Director for the League at its Center in New Haven—a center open and operating from November 1 to November 10, 1961, when appellants were arrested.

---

14. Harriet Pilpel, Sex vs. the Law, Harper's, Jan. 1965 ("My concern rather is with that large body of law which makes no distinction between private sins and public crimes, that body of law which is irrelevant and even damaging to our present day moral standards.").

15. For a recent account of the intellectual currents that helped shape challenges to laws criminalizing birth control, see Leigh Ann Wheeler, How Sex Became A Civil Liberty 93-119 (2013). For an insider's story of the *Griswold* litigation by one of the lead attorneys in the case, see Catherine G. Roraback, Griswold v. Connecticut: A Brief Case History, 16 Ohio Northern Univ. L. Rev. 395 (1989).

16. By 1964, more than 6.5 million married women (and untold numbers of unmarried women) in the United States used the birth control pill, then the most popular contraceptive. Elaine May, America and the Pill: A History of Promise, Peril, and Liberation 2 (2010).

They gave information, instruction, and medical advice to *married persons* as to the means of preventing conception. They examined the wife and prescribed the best contraceptive device or material for her use. Fees were usually charged, although some couples were serviced free.

The statutes whose constitutionality is involved in this appeal are §§53-32 and 54-196 of the General Statutes of Connecticut. The former provides: "Any person who uses any drug, medicinal article or instrument for the purpose of preventing conception shall be fined not less than fifty dollars or imprisoned not less than sixty days nor more than one year or be both fined and imprisoned."

Section 54-196 provides: "Any person who assists, abets, counsels, causes, hires or commands another to commit any offense may be prosecuted and punished as if he were the principal offender."

The appellants were found guilty as accessories and fined $100 each, against the claim that the accessory statute as so applied violated the Fourteenth Amendment.

[The Court held that appellants had standing to raise the constitutional rights of the married people with whom they had a professional relationship.]

Coming to the merits, we are met with a wide range of questions that implicate the Due Process Clause of the Fourteenth Amendment. Overtones of some arguments suggest that Lochner v. New York should be our guide. But we decline that invitation as we did in West Coast Hotel v. Parrish [and] Williamson v. Lee Optical Co. We do not sit as a super-legislature to determine the wisdom, need, and propriety of laws that touch economic problems, business affairs, or social conditions. This law, however, operates directly on an intimate relation of husband and wife and their physician's role in one aspect of that relation.

The association of people is not mentioned in the Constitution nor in the Bill of Rights. The right to educate a child in a school of the parents' choice—whether public or private or parochial—is also not mentioned. Nor is the right to study any particular subject or any foreign language. Yet the First Amendment has been construed to include certain of those rights.

By Pierce v. Society of Sisters the right to educate one's children as one chooses is made applicable to the States by the force of the First and Fourteenth Amendments. By Meyer v. Nebraska the same dignity is given the right to study the German language in a private school. In other words, the State may not consistently with the spirit of the First Amendment, contract the spectrum of available knowledge. The right of freedom of speech and press includes not only the right to utter or to print, but the right to distribute, the right to receive, the right to read and freedom of inquiry, freedom of thought, and freedom to teach—indeed the freedom of the entire university community. Without those peripheral rights the specific rights would be less secure. And so we reaffirm the principle of the *Pierce* and the *Meyer* cases.

In NAACP v. Alabama, 357 U.S. 449 (1958), we protected the "freedom to associate and privacy in one's associations," noting that freedom of association was a peripheral First Amendment right. Disclosure of membership lists of a constitutionally valid association, we held, was invalid, "as entailing the likelihood of a substantial restraint upon the exercise by petitioner's members of their right to freedom of association." In other words, the First Amendment has a penumbra where privacy is protected from governmental intrusion. In like context, we have protected forms of "association" that are not political in the customary sense but pertain to the social, legal, and economic benefit of the members. NAACP v. Button, 371 U.S. 415 (1963).[17] In Schware v. Board of Bar Examiners, 353 U.S. 232 (1957), we held it not permissible to bar a lawyer from practice, because he had once been a member of the Communist Party. . . .

Those cases involved more than the "right of assembly"—a right that extends to all irrespective of their race or ideology. The right of "association," like the right of belief is more than the right to attend a meeting; it includes the right to express one's attitudes or philosophies by membership in a group or by affiliation with it or by other lawful means. Association in that context is a form of expression of opinion; and while it is not expressly included in the First Amendment its existence is necessary in making the express guarantees fully meaningful.

The foregoing cases suggest that specific guarantees in the Bill of Rights have penumbras, formed by emanations from those guarantees that help give them life and substance. See Poe v. Ullman, 367 U.S. 497, 516-522 (1961) (dissenting opinion). Various guarantees create zones of privacy. The right of association contained in the penumbra of the First Amendment is one, as we have seen. The Third Amendment in its prohibition against the quartering of soldiers "in any house" in time of peace without the consent of the owner is another facet of that privacy. The Fourth Amendment explicitly affirms the "right of the people to be secure in their persons, houses, papers, and effects, against unreasonable searches and seizures." The Fifth Amendment in its Self-Incrimination Clause enables the citizen to create a zone of privacy which government may not force him to surrender to his detriment. The Ninth Amendment provides: "The enumeration in the Constitution, of certain rights, shall not be construed to deny or disparage others retained by the people." The Fourth and Fifth Amendments were described in Boyd v. United States, 116 U.S. 616 (1886), as protection against all governmental invasions "of the sanctity of a man's home and the privacies of life." We recently referred in Mapp v. Ohio, 367 U.S. 643 (1961), to the Fourth Amendment as creating a "right to privacy, no less important than any other right carefully and particularly reserved to the people." . . .

We have had many controversies over these penumbral rights of "privacy and repose." See, e.g., Skinner v. Oklahoma. These cases bear witness that the right of privacy which presses for recognition here is a legitimate one.

The present case, then, concerns a relationship lying within the zone of privacy created by several fundamental constitutional guarantees. And it concerns a law which, in forbidding the *use* of contraceptives rather than regulating their manufacture or sale, seeks to achieve its goals by means having a maximum destructive impact upon that relationship. Such a law cannot stand in light of the familiar principle, so often applied by this Court, that a "governmental purpose to control or prevent activities constitutionally subject to state regulation may not be achieved by

17. NAACP v. Button held that Virginia's prohibition of the solicitation of legal or professional business could not be employed to prevent the legal activities of the NAACP and NAACP Legal Defense and Educational Fund.

means which sweep unnecessarily broadly and thereby invade the area of protected freedoms." NAACP v. Alabama. Would we allow the police to search the sacred precincts of marital bedrooms for telltale signs of the use of contraceptives? The very idea is repulsive to the notions of privacy surrounding the marriage relationship.

We deal with a right of privacy older than the Bill of Rights—older than our political parties, older than our school system. Marriage is a coming together for better or for worse, hopefully enduring, and intimate to the degree of being sacred. It is an association that promotes a way of life, not causes; a harmony in living, not political faiths; a bilateral loyalty, not commercial or social projects. Yet it is an association for as noble a purpose as any involved in our prior decisions.

Reversed.

GOLDBERG, J., joined by WARREN, C.J., and BRENNAN, J., concurring.

I agree with the Court that Connecticut's birth-control law unconstitutionally intrudes upon the right of marital privacy, and I join in its opinion and judgment. Although I have not accepted the view that "due process" as used in the Fourteenth Amendment incorporates all of the first eight Amendments, I do agree that the concept of liberty protects those personal rights that are fundamental, and is not confined to the specific terms of the Bill of Rights. My conclusion that the concept of liberty is not so restricted and that it embraces the right of marital privacy though that right is not mentioned explicitly in the Constitution is supported . . . by the language and history of the Ninth Amendment. . . .

The Court stated many years ago that the Due Process Clause protects those liberties that are "so rooted in the traditions and conscience of our people as to be ranked as fundamental." Snyder v. Massachusetts, 291 U.S. 97, 105. . . . This Court, in a series of decisions, has held that the Fourteenth Amendment absorbs and applies to the States those specifics of the first eight amendments which express fundamental personal rights. The language and history of the Ninth Amendment reveal that the Framers of the Constitution believed that there are additional fundamental rights, protected from governmental infringement, which exist alongside those fundamental rights specifically mentioned in the first eight constitutional amendments.

The Ninth Amendment reads, "The enumeration in the Constitution, of certain rights, shall not be construed to deny or disparage others retained by the people." The Amendment is almost entirely the work of James Madison. It was introduced in Congress by him and passed the House and Senate with little or no debate and virtually no change in language. It was proffered to quiet expressed fears that a bill of specifically enumerated rights could not be sufficiently broad to cover all essential rights and that the specific mention of certain rights would be interpreted as a denial that others were protected.

In presenting the proposed Amendment, Madison said:

"It has been objected also against a bill of rights, that, by enumerating particular exceptions to the grant of power, it would disparage those rights which were not placed in that enumeration; and it might follow by implication, that those rights which were not singled out, were intended to be assigned into the hands of the General Government, and were consequently insecure. This is one of the most plausible arguments I have ever heard urged against the admission of a bill of rights into this system; but, I conceive, that it may be guarded against. I have attempted it, as gentlemen may see by turning to the last clause of the fourth resolution [the Ninth Amendment]." I Annals of Congress 439 (Gales and Seaton ed. 1834).

. . . [T]he Framers did not intend that the first eight amendments be construed to exhaust the basic and fundamental rights which the Constitution guaranteed to the people.

While this Court has had little occasion to interpret the Ninth Amendment, "[i]t cannot be presumed that any clause in the constitution is intended to be without effect." Marbury v. Madison. In interpreting the Constitution, "real effect should be given to all the words it uses." Myers v. United States, 272 U.S. 52, 151. . . . To hold that a right so basic and fundamental and so deep-rooted in our society as the right of privacy in marriage may be infringed because that right is not guaranteed in so many words by the first eight amendments to the Constitution is to ignore the Ninth Amendment and to give it no effect whatsoever. . . .

I do not mean to imply that the Ninth Amendment is applied against the States by the Fourteenth. Nor do I mean to state that the Ninth Amendment constitutes an independent source of rights protected from infringement by either the States or the Federal Government. Rather the Ninth Amendment simply lends strong support to the view that the "liberty" protected by the Fifth and Fourteenth Amendments from infringement by the Federal Government or the States is not restricted to rights specifically mentioned in the first eight amendments and an intent that the list of rights included there not be deemed exhaustive. As any student of this Court's opinions knows, this Court has held, often unanimously, that the Fifth and Fourteenth Amendments protect certain fundamental personal liberties from abridgment by the Federal Government or the States. See, e.g., Bolling v. Sharpe, 347 U.S. 497 [Fifth Amendment Due Process Clause guarantees equal protection by the federal government]; Aptheker v. Secretary of State, 378 U.S. 500 [Fifth Amendment guarantees right to travel]; Kent v. Dulles, 357 U.S. 116 [holding that "[t]he right to travel is a part of the 'liberty' of which the citizen cannot be deprived without due process of law under the Fifth Amendment"]; Cantwell v. Connecticut, 310 U.S. 296 [Fourteenth Amendment's Due Process Clause includes freedom of religion]; NAACP v. Alabama, 357 U.S. 449 [freedom of association]; Gideon v. Wainwright, 372 U.S. 335 [right to government subsidy for counsel]; New York Times Co. v. Sullivan, 376 U.S. 254 [constitutional privilege in defamation cases]. The Ninth Amendment simply shows the intent of the Constitution's authors that other fundamental personal rights should not be denied such protection or disparaged in any other way simply because they are not specifically listed in the first eight constitutional amendments. I do not see how this broadens the authority of the Court; rather it serves to support what this Court has been doing in protecting fundamental rights.

Nor am I turning somersaults with history in arguing that the Ninth Amendment is relevant in a case dealing with a State's infringement of a fundamental right. While the Ninth Amendment—and indeed the entire Bill of Rights—originally concerned restrictions upon federal power, the subsequently enacted Fourteenth Amendment prohibits the States as well from abridging fundamental personal liberties. And, the Ninth Amendment, in indicating that not all such liberties are specifically mentioned in the first eight amendments, is surely relevant in showing the existence of other fundamental personal rights, now protected from state, as well as federal, infringement. In sum, the Ninth Amendment simply lends strong support to the view that the "liberty" protected by the Fifth and Fourteenth Amendments from infringement by the Federal Government or the States is not restricted to rights specifically mentioned in the first eight amendments.

In determining which rights are fundamental, judges are not left at large to decide cases in light of their personal and private notions. Rather, they must look to the "traditions and [collective] conscience of our people" to determine whether a principle is "so rooted [there] . . . as to be ranked as fundamental." The inquiry is whether a right involved "is of such a character that it cannot be denied without violating those 'fundamental principles of liberty and justice which lie at the base of all our civil and political institutions.'" "Liberty" also "gains content from the emanations of . . . specific [constitutional] guarantees" and "from experience with the requirements of a free society."

I agree fully with the Court that, applying these tests, the right of privacy is a fundamental personal right, emanating "from the totality of the constitutional scheme under which we live." Mr. Justice Brandeis, dissenting in Olmstead v. United States, 277 U.S. 438, 478, comprehensively summarized the principles underlying the Constitution's guarantees of privacy: "The protection guaranteed by the [Fourth and Fifth] Amendments is much broader in scope. The makers of our Constitution undertook to secure conditions favorable to the pursuit of happiness. They recognized the significance of man's spiritual nature, of his feelings and of his intellect. They knew that only a part of the pain, pleasure and satisfactions of life are to be found in material things. They sought to protect Americans in their beliefs, their thoughts, their emotions and their sensations. They conferred, as against the Government, the right to be let alone—the most comprehensive of rights and the right most valued by civilized men."

The entire fabric of the Constitution and the purposes that clearly underlie its specific guarantees demonstrate that the rights to marital privacy and to marry and raise a family are of similar order and magnitude as the fundamental rights specifically protected.

Although the Constitution does not speak in so many words of the right of privacy in marriage, I cannot believe that it offers these fundamental rights no protection. The fact that no particular provision of the Constitution explicitly forbids the State from disrupting the traditional relation of the family—a relation as old and as fundamental as our entire civilization—surely does not show that the Government was meant to have the power to do so. . . .

The logic of the dissents would sanction federal or state legislation that seems to me even more plainly unconstitutional than the statute before us. Surely the Government, absent a showing of a compelling subordinating state interest, could not decree that all husbands and wives must be sterilized after two children have been born to them. Yet by their reasoning such an invasion of marital privacy would not be subject to constitutional challenge because, while it might be "silly," no provision of the Constitution specifically prevents the Government from curtailing the marital right to bear children and raise a family. While it may shock some of my Brethren that the Court today holds that the Constitution protects the right of marital privacy, in my view it is far more shocking to believe that the personal liberty guaranteed by the Constitution does not include protection against such totalitarian limitation of family size, which is at complete variance with our constitutional concepts. Yet, if upon a showing of a slender basis of rationality, a law outlawing voluntary birth control by married persons is valid, then, by the same reasoning, a law requiring compulsory birth control also would seem to be valid. In my view, however, both types of law would unjustifiably intrude upon rights of marital privacy which are constitutionally protected.

In a long series of cases this Court has held that where fundamental personal liberties are involved, they may not be abridged by the States simply on a showing that a regulatory statute has some rational relationship to the effectuation of a proper state purpose. "Where there is a significant encroachment upon personal liberty, the State may prevail only upon showing a subordinating interest which is compelling," Bates v. Little Rock, 361 U.S. 516 (1960). The law must be shown "necessary, and not merely rationally related, to the accomplishment of a permissible state policy." McLaughlin v. Florida, 379 U.S. 184 (1964).

Although the Connecticut birth-control law obviously encroaches upon a fundamental personal liberty, the State does not show that the law serves any "subordinating [state] interest which is compelling" or that it is "necessary . . . to the accomplishment of a permissible state policy." The State, at most, argues that there is some rational relation between this statute and what is admittedly a legitimate subject of state concern—the discouraging of extra-marital relations. It says that preventing the use of birth-control devices by married persons helps prevent the indulgence by some in such extra-marital relations. The rationality of this justification is dubious, particularly in light of the admitted widespread availability to all persons in the State of Connecticut, unmarried as well as married, of birth-control devices for the prevention of disease, as distinguished from the prevention of conception. But, in any event, it is clear that the state interest in safeguarding marital fidelity can be served by a more discriminately tailored statute, which does not, like the present one, sweep unnecessarily broadly, reaching far beyond the evil sought to be dealt with and intruding upon the privacy of all married couples. . . . The State of Connecticut does have statutes, the constitutionality of which is beyond doubt, which prohibit adultery and fornication. These statutes demonstrate that means for achieving the same basic purpose of protecting marital fidelity are available to Connecticut without the need to "invade the area of protected freedoms." . . .

Finally, it should be said of the Court's holding today that it in no way interferes with a State's proper regulation of sexual promiscuity or misconduct. As my Brother Harlan so well stated in his dissenting opinion in Poe v. Ullman:

> Adultery, homosexuality and the like are sexual intimacies which the State forbids . . . but the intimacy of husband and wife is necessarily an essential and accepted feature of the institution of marriage, an institution which the State not only must allow, but which always and in every age it has fostered and protected. It is one thing when the State exerts its power either to forbid extra-marital sexuality . . . or to say who may marry, but it is quite another when, having acknowledged a marriage and the intimacies inherent in it, it undertakes to regulate by means of the criminal law the details of that intimacy.

In sum, I believe that the right of privacy in the marital relation is fundamental and basic—a personal right "retained by the people" within the meaning of the Ninth Amendment. Connecticut cannot constitutionally abridge this fundamental right, which is protected by the Fourteenth Amendment from infringement by the States. I agree with the Court that petitioners' convictions must therefore be reversed. . . .

[Justice Harlan concurred in the judgment in *Griswold*, stating that "the proper constitutional inquiry in this case is whether this Connecticut statute infringes the Due Process Clause of the Fourteenth Amendment because the enactment violates basic values 'implicit in the concept of ordered liberty.' . . . For reasons stated at length in my dissenting opinion in Poe v. Ullman, 367 U.S. 497 (1961), I believe that it does." *Poe* was an earlier challenge to the Connecticut anti-contraception law, in which the Court dismissed the complainants' appeal on procedural grounds. In one of four dissenting opinions in *Poe*, Justice Harlan expressed his views on the merits:]

HARLAN, J., dissenting [in Poe v. Ullman]. . . .

Were due process merely a procedural safeguard it would fail to reach those situations where the deprivation of life, liberty or property was accomplished by legislation which by operating in the future could, given even the fairest possible procedure in application to individuals, nevertheless destroy the enjoyment of all three. Thus the guaranties of due process . . . have in this country "become bulwarks also against arbitrary legislation."

However, it is not the particular enumeration of rights in the first eight Amendments which spells out the reach of Fourteenth Amendment due process, but rather, as was suggested in another context long before the adoption of that Amendment, those concepts which are considered to embrace those rights "which are . . . *fundamental*; which belong . . . to the citizens of all free governments," Corfield v. Coryell, 4 Wash. C.C. 371, 380, for "the purposes [of securing] which men enter into society," Calder v. Bull, 3 Dall. 386, 388. . . .

Due process has not been reduced to any formula; its content cannot be determined by reference to any code. The best that can be said is that through the course of this Court's decisions it has represented the balance which our Nation, built upon postulates of respect for the liberty of the individual, has struck between that liberty and the demands of organized society. If the supplying of content to this Constitutional concept has of necessity been a rational process, it certainly has not been one where judges have felt free to roam where unguided speculation might take them. The balance of which I speak is the balance struck by this country, having regard to what history teaches are the traditions from which it developed as well as the traditions from which it broke. That tradition is a living thing. . . .

It is this outlook which has led the Court continuingly to perceive distinctions in the imperative character of Constitutional provisions, since that character must be discerned from a particular provision's larger context. And inasmuch as this context is one not of words, but of history and purposes, the full scope of the liberty guaranteed by the Due Process Clause cannot be found in or limited by the precise terms of the specific guarantees elsewhere provided in the Constitution. This "liberty" is not a series of isolated points pricked out in terms of the taking of property; the freedom of speech, press, and religion; the right to keep and bear arms; the freedom from unreasonable searches and seizures; and so on. It is a rational continuum which, broadly speaking, includes a freedom from all substantial arbitrary impositions and purposeless restraints, see Allgeyer v. Louisiana, 165 U.S. 578; Holden v. Hardy, 169 U.S. 366; Nebbia v. New York, 291 U.S. 502; Skinner v. Oklahoma, 316 U.S. 535, 544 (concurring opinion); Schware v. Board of Bar Examiners,

353 U.S. 232, and which also recognizes, what a reasonable and sensitive judgment must, that certain interests require particularly careful scrutiny of the state needs asserted to justify their abridgment. . . .

Precisely what is involved here is this: the state is asserting the right to enforce its moral judgments by intruding upon the most intimate details of the marital relation with the full power of the criminal law. Potentially, this could allow the deployment of all the incidental machinery of the criminal law, arrests, searches, and seizures; inevitably, it must mean at the very least the lodging of criminal charges, a public trial, and testimony as to the corpus delicti. Nor could any imaginable elaboration of presumptions, testimonial privileges, or other safeguards, alleviate the necessity for testimony as to the mode and manner of the married couples' sexual relations, or at least the opportunity for the accused to make denial of the charges. In sum, the statute allows the State to enquire into, prove, and punish married people for the private use of their marital intimacy.

. . . This enactment involves what, by common understanding throughout the English-speaking world, must be granted to be a most fundamental aspect of "liberty," the privacy of the home in its most basic sense, and it is this which requires that the statute be subjected to "strict scrutiny."

That aspect of liberty which embraces the concept of the privacy of the home receives explicit Constitutional protection at two places only. These are the Third Amendment, relating to the quartering of soldiers, and the Fourth Amendment, prohibiting unreasonable searches and seizures. While these Amendments reach only the Federal Government, this Court has held in the strongest terms . . . that the concept of "privacy" embodied in the Fourth Amendment is part of the "ordered liberty" assured against state action by the Fourteenth Amendment.

It is clear, of course, that this Connecticut statute does not invade the privacy of the home in the usual sense, since the invasion involved here may, and doubtless usually would, be accomplished without any physical intrusion whatever into the home. What the statute undertakes to do, however, is to create a crime which is grossly offensive to this privacy, while the Constitution refers only to methods of ferreting out substantive wrongs, and the procedure it requires presupposes that substantive offenses may be committed and sought out in the privacy of the home. But such an analysis forecloses any claim to Constitutional protection against this form of deprivation of privacy, only if due process in this respect is limited to what is explicitly provided in the Constitution, divorced from the rational purposes, historical roots, and subsequent developments of the relevant provisions. . . .

It would surely be an extreme instance of sacrificing substance to form were it to be held that the Constitutional principle of privacy against arbitrary official intrusion comprehends only physical invasions by the police. . . . [I]f the physical curtilage of the home is protected, it is surely as a result of solicitude to protect the privacies of the life within. Certainly the safeguarding of the home does not follow merely from the sanctity of property rights. The home derives its pre-eminence as the seat of family life. . . .

Of [the] whole "private realm of family life" it is difficult to imagine what is more private or more intimate than a husband and wife's marital relations. . . . [T]he intimacy of husband and wife is necessarily an essential and accepted feature of the institution of marriage, an institution which the State not only must allow, but which always and in every age it has fostered and protected. It is one thing when the State exerts its power either to forbid extramarital sexuality altogether, or to say who may marry, but it is quite another when, having acknowledged a marriage and the intimacies inherent in it, undertakes to regulate by means of the criminal law the details of that intimacy. . . .

Since, as it appears to me, the statute marks an abridgment of important fundamental liberties protected by the Fourteenth Amendment, it will not do to urge in justification of that abridgment simply that the statute is rationally related to the effectuation of a proper state purpose. A closer scrutiny and stronger justification than that are required. . . . To me the very circumstance that Connecticut has not chosen to press the enforcement of this statute against individual users, while it nevertheless persists in asserting its right to do so at any time—in effect a right to hold this statute as an imminent threat to the privacy of the households of the State—conduces to the inference either that it does not consider the policy of the statute a very important one, or that it does not regard the means it has chosen for its effectuation as appropriate or necessary.

But conclusive, in my view, is the utter novelty of this enactment. Although the Federal Government and many States have at one time or other had on their books statutes forbidding or regulating the distribution of contraceptives, none, so far as I can find, has made the *use* of contraceptives a crime. Indeed, a diligent search has revealed that no nation, including several which quite evidently share Connecticut's moral policy, has seen fit to effectuate that policy by the means presented here. . . .

WHITE, J., concurring [in *Griswold*].

In my view this Connecticut law as applied to married couples deprives them of "liberty" without due process of law, as that concept is used in the Fourteenth Amendment. I therefore concur in the judgment of the Court reversing these convictions under Connecticut's aiding and abetting statute. . . .

[T]his is not the first time this Court has had occasion to articulate that the liberty entitled to protection under the Fourteenth Amendment includes the right "to marry, establish a home and bring up children," Meyer v. Nebraska, and "the liberty . . . to direct the upbringing and education of children," Pierce v. Society of Sisters, and that these are among "the basic civil rights of man," Skinner v. Oklahoma. . . . These decisions affirm that there is a "realm of family life which the state cannot enter" without substantial justification. Prince v. Massachusetts, 321 U.S. 158 (1944). Surely the right invoked in this case, to be free of regulation of the intimacies of the marriage relationship, "come[s] to this Court with a momentum for respect lacking when appeal is made to liberties which derive merely from shifting economic arrangements." . . .

An examination of the justification offered, however, cannot be avoided by saying that the Connecticut anti-use statute invades a protected area of privacy and association or that it demeans the marriage relationship. The nature of the right invaded is pertinent, to be sure, for statutes regulating sensitive areas of liberty do, under the cases of this Court, require "strict scrutiny," Skinner v. Oklahoma, and "must be viewed in the light of less drastic means for achieving the same basic purpose." "Where there is a significant encroachment upon personal liberty, the State may prevail only upon showing a subordinating interest which is compelling." But such statutes, if reasonably necessary for the effectuation of a legitimate and substantial state interest, and not arbitrary or capricious in application, are not invalid under the Due Process Clause.

As I read the opinions of the Connecticut courts and the argument of Connecticut in this Court, the State claims but one justification for its anti-use statute. . . . [T]he statute is said to serve the State's policy against all forms of promiscuous or illicit sexual relationships, be they premarital or extramarital, concededly a permissible and legitimate legislative goal.

Without taking issue with the premise that the fear of conception operates as a deterrent to such relationships in addition to the criminal proscriptions Connecticut has against such conduct, I wholly fail to see how the ban on the use of contraceptives by married couples in any way reinforces the State's ban on illicit sexual relationships. Connecticut does not bar the importation or possession of contraceptive devices; they are not considered contraband material under state law, and their availability in that State is not seriously disputed. The only way Connecticut seeks to limit or control the availability of such devices is through its general aiding and abetting statute whose operation in this context has been quite obviously ineffective and whose most serious use has been against birth-control clinics rendering advice to married, rather than unmarried, persons. . . . Moreover, it would appear that the sale of contraceptives to prevent disease is plainly legal under Connecticut law.

In these circumstances one is rather hard pressed to explain how the ban on use by married persons in any way prevents use of such devices by persons engaging in illicit sexual relations and thereby contributes to the State's policy against such relationships. . . . At most the broad ban is of marginal utility to the declared objective. A statute limiting its prohibition on use to persons engaging in the prohibited relationship would serve the end posited by Connecticut in the same way, and with the same effectiveness, or ineffectiveness, as the broad anti-use statute under attack in this case. I find nothing in this record justifying the sweeping scope of this statute, with its telling effect on the freedoms of married persons, and therefore conclude that it deprives such persons of liberty without due process of law.

BLACK, J., joined by STEWART, J., dissenting. . . .

In order that there may be no room at all to doubt why I vote as I do, I feel constrained to add that the law is every bit as offensive to me as it is to my Brethren of the majority. . . . There is no single one of the graphic and eloquent strictures and criticisms fired at the policy of this Connecticut law either by the Court's opinion or by those of my concurring Brethren to which I cannot subscribe—except their conclusion that the evil qualities they see in the law make it unconstitutional. . . .

The Court talks about a constitutional "right of privacy" as though there is some constitutional provision or provisions forbidding any law ever to be passed which might abridge the "privacy" of individuals. But there is not. There are, of course, guarantees in certain specific constitutional provisions which are designed in part to protect privacy at certain times and places with respect to certain activities. Such, for example, is the Fourth Amendment's guarantee against "unreasonable searches and seizures." But I think it belittles that Amendment to talk about it as though it protects nothing but "privacy." . . .

One of the most effective ways of diluting or expanding a constitutionally guaranteed right is to substitute for the crucial word or words of a constitutional guarantee another word or words, more or less flexible and more or less restricted in meaning. . . . "Privacy" is a broad, abstract and ambiguous concept which can easily be shrunken in meaning but which can also, on the other hand, easily be interpreted as a constitutional ban against many things other than searches and seizures. . . . For these reasons I get nowhere in this case by talk about a constitutional "right of privacy" as an emanation from one or more constitutional provisions. I like my privacy as well as the next one, but I am nevertheless compelled to admit that government has a right to invade it unless prohibited by some specific constitutional provision. . . .

I discuss the due process and Ninth Amendment arguments together because on analysis they turn out to be the same thing—merely using different words to claim for this Court and the federal judiciary power to invalidate any legislative act which the judges find irrational, unreasonable or offensive. . . .

Of the cases on which my Brothers White and Goldberg rely so heavily, undoubtedly the reasoning of two of them supports their result here—as would that of a number of others which they do not bother to name, e.g., Lochner v. New York, Coppage v. Kansas, and Adkins v. Children's Hospital. The two they do cite and quote from, Meyer v. Nebraska and Pierce v. Society of Sisters, were both decided in opinions by Mr. Justice McReynolds which elaborated the same natural law due process philosophy found in Lochner v. New York, one of the cases on which he relied in *Meyer*, along with such other long-discredited decisions as, e.g., Adkins v. Children's Hospital. . . . Without expressing an opinion as to whether either of those cases reached a correct result in light of our later decisions applying the First Amendment to the States through the Fourteenth, I merely point out that the reasoning stated in *Meyer* and *Pierce* was the same natural law due process philosophy which many later opinions repudiated, and which I cannot accept. . . .

My Brother Goldberg has adopted the recent discovery that the Ninth Amendment as well as the Due Process Clause can be used by this Court as authority to strike down all state legislation which this Court thinks violates "fundamental principles of liberty and justice," or is contrary to the "traditions and [collective] conscience of our people." He also states, without proof satisfactory to me, that in making decisions on this basis judges will not consider "their personal and private notions." One may ask how they can avoid considering them. Our Court certainly has no machinery with which to take a Gallup Poll. And the scientific miracles of this age have not yet produced a gadget which the Court can use to determine what traditions are rooted in the "[collective] conscience of our people." Moreover, one would certainly have to look far beyond the language of the Ninth Amendment to find that the Framers vested in this Court any such awesome veto powers over lawmaking, either by the States or by the Congress. . . . That Amendment was passed not to broaden the powers of this Court or any other department of "the General Government," but, as every student of history knows, to assure the people that the Constitution in all its provisions was intended to limit the Federal Government to the powers granted expressly or by necessary implication. If any broad, unlimited power to hold laws unconstitutional because they offend what this Court conceives to be the "[collective] conscience of our people" is vested in this Court by the Ninth Amendment, the Fourteenth Amendment, or any other provision of the Constitution, it was not given by the Framers, but rather has been bestowed on the Court by the Court. This fact is perhaps responsible for the peculiar phenomenon that for a period of a century and a half no serious suggestion was ever made that the Ninth Amendment, enacted to protect state powers against federal invasion, could be used as a weapon of federal power to prevent state legislatures from passing laws they consider appropriate to govern local affairs. Use of any such broad, unbounded judicial authority would make of this Court's members a day-to-day constitutional convention.

[T]here is no provision of the Constitution which either expressly or impliedly vests power in this Court to sit as a supervisory agency over acts of duly constituted legislative bodies and set aside their laws because of the Court's belief that the legislative policies adopted are unreasonable, unwise, arbitrary, capricious or irrational. The adoption of such a loose, flexible, uncontrolled standard for holding laws unconstitutional, if ever it is finally achieved, will amount to a great unconstitutional shift of power to the courts which I believe and am constrained to say will be bad for the courts and worse for the country. . . .

I realize that many good and able men have eloquently spoken and written, sometimes in rhapsodical strains, about the duty of this Court to keep the Constitution in tune with the times. The idea is that the Constitution must be changed from time to time and that this Court is charged with a duty to make those changes. For myself, I must with all deference reject that philosophy. The Constitution makers knew the need for change and provided for it. Amendments suggested by the people's elected representatives can be submitted to the people or their selected agents for ratification. That method of change was good for our Fathers, and being somewhat old-fashioned I must add it is good enough for me. And so, I cannot rely on the Due Process Clause or the Ninth Amendment or any mysterious and uncertain natural law concept as a reason for striking down this state law. The Due Process Clause with an "arbitrary and capricious" or "shocking to the conscience" formula was liberally used by this Court to strike down economic legislation in the early decades of this century, threatening, many people thought, the tranquility and stability of the Nation. See, e.g., Lochner v. New York, 198 U.S. 45. That formula, based on subjective considerations of "natural justice," is no less dangerous when used to enforce this Court's views about personal rights than those about economic rights. I had thought that we had laid that formula, as a means for striking down state legislation, to rest once and for all in cases like West Coast Hotel Co. v. Parrish.

[M]y concurring Brethren . . . would reinstate the *Lochner, Coppage, Adkins, Burns* line of cases, cases from which this Court recoiled after the 1930's, and which had been I thought totally discredited until now. Apparently my Brethren have less quarrel with state economic regulations than former Justices of their persuasion had. But any limitation upon their using the natural law due process philosophy to strike down any state law, dealing with any activity whatever, will obviously be only self-imposed. . . . The late Judge Learned Hand, after emphasizing his view that judges should not use the due process formula suggested in the concurring opinions today or any other formula like it to invalidate legislation offensive to their "personal preferences," made the statement, with which I fully agree, that: "For myself it would be most irksome to be ruled by a bevy of Platonic Guardians, even if I knew how to choose them, which I assuredly do not." [Learned Hand, The Bill of Rights 70 (1958).] So far as I am concerned, Connecticut's law as applied here is not forbidden by any provision of the Federal Constitution as that Constitution was written, and I would therefore affirm.

STEWART, J., joined by BLACK, J., dissenting.

Since 1879 Connecticut has had on its books a law which forbids the use of contraceptives by anyone. I think this is an uncommonly silly law. . . . But we are not asked in this case to say whether we think this law is unwise, or even asinine. We are asked to hold that it violates the United States Constitution. And that I cannot do. . . .

As to the First, Third, Fourth, and Fifth Amendments, I can find nothing in any of them to invalidate this Connecticut law, even assuming that all those Amendments are fully applicable against the States. It has not even been argued that this is a law "respecting an establishment of religion, or prohibiting the free exercise thereof." And surely, unless the solemn process of constitutional adjudication is to descend to the level of a play on words, there is not involved here any abridgment of "the freedom of speech, or of the press; or the right of the people peaceably to assemble, and to petition the Government for a redress of grievances." No soldier has been quartered in any house. There has been no search, and no seizure. Nobody has been compelled to be a witness against himself.

The Court also quotes the Ninth Amendment, and my Brother Goldberg's concurring opinion relies heavily upon it. But to say that the Ninth Amendment has anything to do with this case is to turn somersaults with history. . . .

What provision of the Constitution, then, does make this state law invalid? The Court says it is the right of privacy "created by several fundamental constitutional guarantees." With all deference, I can find no such general right of privacy in the Bill of Rights, in any other part of the Constitution, or in any case ever before decided by this Court.

At the oral argument in this case we were told that the Connecticut l aw does not "conform to current community standards." But it is not the function of this Court to decide cases on the basis of community standards. We are here to decide cases "agreeably to the Constitution and laws of the United States." It is the essence of judicial duty to subordinate our own personal views, our own ideas of what legislation is wise and what is not. If, as I should surely hope, the law before us does not reflect the standards of the people of Connecticut, the people of Connecticut can freely exercise their true Ninth and Tenth Amendment rights to persuade their elected representatives to repeal it. That is the constitutional way to take this law off the books.

DISCUSSION

1. *Social context.* The Court had often protected liberty in the past, but *Griswold* speaks of a very different kind of liberty—sexual liberty. How is this liberty similar to and different from the kinds of liberty protected by *Meyer* and *Pierce*?

What developments best explain the shift in focus by 1965? Consider the history of debates over criminal law reform described above. The 1960s also heralded the beginning of the cultural transformations that we now call the sexual revolution. How do you think these cultural changes and legal debates might have influenced the development of constitutional law? Through what institutions and channels might this influence have occurred?

The Supreme Court described the challenge to Connecticut's law criminalizing the use of contraception as focused on the right of "privacy." But that was not how the argument was framed initially. The lawyers who challenged the ban on birth control first advanced a due process/liberty argument that emphasized the harms of abstinence in marriage, and the harms to women's health, only adding arguments about privacy later, especially after they were raised in dissent in the early rounds of litigation. See Catherine G. Roraback, Griswold v. Connecticut: A Brief Case History, 16 Ohio Northern Univ. L. Rev. 395, 399-401 (1989).

2. *Interpretive method.* The various opinions in *Griswold* prefigure many of the most common approaches to implied fundamental rights that we will discuss throughout this chapter.

a. *Textual implication.* The constitutional struggles of the *Lochner* era and the New Deal were still relatively recent history for the Justices in *Griswold,* and several of them—including Justices Black and Douglas—had played active roles in reshaping the post–New Deal approach to judicial review. Hence it is not surprising that William O. Douglas, a New Deal stalwart, tries to derive the right to privacy solely from the constitutional text.

Justice Douglas argues that the right of marital privacy is implied by textual commitments in various parts of the Bill of Rights. Douglas's use of "penumbras and emanations" is often mocked as a makeweight argument designed to avoid the accusation of "*Lochner*-ism." He lists, for example, the Third Amendment, which the Court had never applied to the states, and was hardly ever litigated.

Putting aside Douglas's actual argument in *Griswold,* however, the notion of implied or auxiliary rights makes some sense, and there are several examples elsewhere in constitutional doctrine. The right to travel between the states (recognized in Crandall v. Nevada) is inferred from constitutional structure, and the right of freedom of association is implied from the First Amendment rights of speech, press, assembly, and petition. If in McCulloch v. Maryland Chief Justice Marshall could imply powers auxiliary to or implied by the grant of federal enumerated powers, why couldn't later courts imply rights auxiliary to or implied by the enumeration of constitutional rights and liberties?

The problem with Douglas's textual implication argument lies elsewhere. What leads him to imply liberties from these rights but not others? Couldn't one as easily derive the *Lochner* era's conception of liberty of contract from the Contracts Clause, the Due Process Clause's protection of "liberty" and "property," and the Takings Clause?

b. *The open-ended nature of the constitutional text.* Justice Goldberg turns to the Ninth Amendment to show that the Constitution is textually committed to implied fundamental rights. The text is open ended, he argues, because the text says so explicitly. Couldn't one read the Ninth Amendment to say only that *federal power* does not extend to certain preexisting rights? If so, it would not be directly relevant to a state statute like Connecticut's.

A more plausible textual hook for unenumerated fundamental rights would be the Privileges or Immunities Clause, which actually says that "No State shall make or enforce any law which shall abridge the privileges or immunities of citizens of the United States." The "privileges or immunities of Citizens of the United States," in turn, would be those rights that are truly fundamental, whether or not explicitly enumerated. (Recall Senator Howard's speech introducing the Fourteenth Amendment in the Senate.) If the language of the Due Process Clause is ill fitted for protecting substantive liberties, one can hardly say this about the Privileges or Immunities Clause, which appears to have been designed for this very purpose.

The problem for the Court in *Griswold* was that *Slaughterhouse* and *Cruikshank* had long since closed that door. Even had the Court seriously considered reviving the Privileges or Immunities Clause, the Justices might have been concerned that this would re-open the door to constitutional protection of *Lochner*-style economic liberties. Hence the Justices have repeatedly sought to achieve the effective equivalent of a Privileges or Immunities Clause by other means.

Even if one accepts that the text is open ended, and that the Constitution protects implied fundamental rights, this does not demonstrate which rights they are. One needs additional forms of argument to show that a particular right is fundamental. (Should the clause be limited to those rights that were generally considered fundamental in 1868, for example?) To answer this question, Justice Goldberg primarily looks to tradition, an approach developed more fully in Justice Harlan's opinion.

c. *Tradition.* In his Poe v. Ullman dissent, Justice Harlan famously argues that the source of implied fundamental rights is tradition. There is considerable language in the Court's jurisprudence supporting such an approach. *Meyer* and *Pierce* themselves could be understood as appealing to longstanding traditions of respect for family autonomy. Another example is the Court's jurisprudence incorporating the Bill of Rights through the Due Process Clause—which is, after all, a version of substantive due process. The Court has argued that rights are incorporated against the states if they are "so rooted in the traditions and conscience of our people as to be ranked as fundamental." Snyder v. Massachusetts.

Appeals to tradition, however, are not particularly good ways to protect sexual freedoms, especially where community norms are conflicted about what kinds of practices deserve respect, and where even common sexual practices may not be openly sanctioned or approved. Justice Harlan attempts to navigate this difficulty by arguing that the proper inquiry is into "the balance struck by this country, having regard to what history teaches are the traditions from which it developed as well as the traditions from which it broke. That tradition is a living thing." How should courts decide what traditions the country still holds and what traditions the country has now abandoned? See Note: Tradition as a Source of Fundamental Rights, infra.

d. *Popular consensus and conventional morality—enforcing expectations about freedom held by ordinary Americans.* Related to tradition is a focus on contemporary beliefs about freedom. In enforcing constitutional protections for liberty, one might look at core beliefs about freedom—at what most Americans currently expect they have the right to do. The question is not what people think is officially "moral," i.e., praiseworthy, but what people assume they have the right to do without state interference whether or not others approve. Thus, if single people expect that they have the right to engage in sex outside of marriage, it does not matter that many people still regard this practice as immoral.

This model has various problems. How are mores to be measured? Won't such judgments be affected by implicit notions of class, elitism, race, ethnicity, or religion? Even if a practice is sufficiently widespread, why shouldn't states be able to bolster morality if they fear it is in decline? (Protecting the welfare and morals of the public was a traditional purpose of the states' police powers in the nineteenth century.)

At what point do we assert that a consensus for a fundamental liberty has been reached? Should the courts look to public opinion polls?

e. *State consensus — enforcing rights against "outlier" jurisdictions.* Another approach is to poll the various states to see if there is an emerging consensus that the right or interest deserves protection. Do most states protect the right or interest, either directly by statute or state constitutional provision, or indirectly, by not criminalizing or otherwise burdening the practice? If only a few states fail to protect the interest, a court might treat them as outliers and recognize a national standard. Thus, the consensus approach is a *nationalist* argument—it asserts that the American people as a whole now regard a right as one that either is protected or always should have been protected. For versions of this argument, see Akhil Reed Amar, America's Unwritten Constitution 133-136 (2012); Jack M. Balkin, Living Originalism 211-213 (2011).

Justice Harlan points at this approach in two places in his opinion in Poe v. Ullman. First, he cites Corfield v. Coryell, which defines fundamental rights as those "which belong . . . to the citizens of all free governments." This formula is clearly aspirational rather than descriptive, since obviously at least one state must not currently be protecting the right in question or there would be no appeal to the courts in the first place.

Second, Harlan notes that, as of 1961, Connecticut was the only state that criminalized the use of contraceptives. (He might also have pointed out that Connecticut's ban was rarely if ever enforced, and that the only reason it remained on the books was symbolic—the Catholic Church had repeatedly put pressure on Catholic legislators in the state not to vote to repeal the law.)

How should courts look to state practice to discover implied fundamental rights? *Griswold* seems an easy case because only one state banned or regulated the practice, and the statute was not enforced. But what if 15 states still ban or regulate the practice, and enforcement is merely intermittent? What if only ten states regulate the practice, but five of them have passed regulations in recent years—perhaps in response to social mobilization—so that the trend in these states seems to be moving towards less protection? For a discussion, see Justin Driver, Constitutional Outliers, 81 U. Chi. L. Rev. 929 (2014).

What if there are regional differences in public opinion or state practice? For example, suppose a right or interest is routinely protected on the East and West Coasts but not in the Deep South or the Mountain West? Is it fair, or consistent with federalism, for courts to impose the moral or political views of some parts of the nation on others? The flip side of an approach that imposes national values on localities is lack of respect for federalism and for local differences. As we have seen in previous chapters, this issue arises repeatedly in litigation under the Fourteenth Amendment.

f. *Popular deliberation.* Why should *decriminalization* of a practice justify courts in arguing that there should be *constitutional* protection for the practice? In the decade before *Griswold*, there were wide-ranging debates—both elite and popular—about whether the criminal law should be used to regulate sexual conduct between consenting adults. As we have seen, these debates, which unfolded in Great Britain and the United States, led to law reform movements for decriminalization of contraception, abortion, and sodomy. How might these debates have influenced constitutional conceptions of liberty? Should they have?

g. *Equality*. Another way of protecting implied fundamental rights is to base constitutional protection on the Equal Protection Clause. We have already seen this argument employed in Skinner v. Oklahoma. Several years after *Griswold*, Justice Brennan's 1971 decision in Eisenstadt v. Baird used equality to protect the right of unmarried persons to use contraceptives. Conversely, as we shall see in the abortion cases, courts may use liberty arguments to express considerations of equality or equal dignity. The Justices in *Griswold* did not base their arguments on sex equality, nor did they understand contraception in terms of women's rights. As noted in Chapter 8, the Court would not transform sex equality doctrine until the 1970s. Nevertheless, the litigators in *Griswold* thought about equality arguments and issues of women's rights and welfare in framing the case. See the discussion in note 4 infra on equality arguments in the context of the *Griswold* litigation—and beyond.

h. *Moral reasoning and moral philosophy*. None of the Justices in *Griswold* engages in sustained moral argument for the right of marital privacy; instead they tend to rely on appeals to precedent, consensus, or tradition. Nevertheless, the trend of the middle half of the twentieth century, as exemplified by the Hart-Devlin debate, and by later scholars like Ronald Dworkin, was to use philosophy to reason about the nature and scope of fundamental rights. Justice Black's dissent anticipates (and rejects) this approach, citing Justice Iredell in Calder v. Bull: "The ideas of natural justice are regulated by no fixed standard: the ablest and the purest men have differed upon the subject; and all that the Court could properly say, in such an event, would be, that the Legislature (possessed of an equal right of opinion) had passed an act which, in the opinion of the judges, was inconsistent with the abstract principles of natural justice." John Hart Ely put it more sardonically, imaging a Supreme Court opinion that read: "We like Rawls, you like Nozick. We win 6-3." John Hart Ely, Democracy and Distrust 58 (1980).

i. *Judicial restraint*. Just as the majority and concurrences in *Griswold* articulate familiar reasons for protecting implied fundamental rights, the dissents by Justices Black and Stewart show the most commonly offered reasons against recognizing such rights.

Both Stewart and Black argue that however well intentioned judges may be, it will be difficult if not impossible for judges to articulate a conception of constitutional fidelity in these cases. Instead, they argue, judges will end up imposing their own visions of the good on the public. In fact, will judges impose their own visions of the good or those of the segment of society in which they live?

Justice Goldberg's response is that without judicial protection of privacy, legislatures might impose compulsory sterilization on married couples, criminalize families with too many children, and so on. Although majoritarian norms will protect against some of these injustices, they will not protect against all, especially when actors deviate from conventional moral norms in a particular state or region, are members of minority communities, or are otherwise politically powerless.

What is Black and Stewart's best answer to such a parade of horribles? To the extent that the rights affected are actually deeply rooted in popular consensus, laws like this will not be passed very often, and if they are passed, there will be significant public pushback against them. Of course, this assumes that majorities actually shape policy on these questions. *Griswold* shows that a particularly powerful lobbying group or concentrated interest may prevent repeal of laws that majorities no longer support. Black and Stewart might respond that if a law seriously contravenes popular values, it will not be enforced and will in the long run be repealed.

A second reason to be concerned about a "parade of horribles" is that there may be significant differences on questions of morality and custom—especially with respect to sex and bodily autonomy—in some parts of the country. Therefore some local jurisdictions may pass laws that would seem deeply unjust to the rest of the country, and that abridge rights that most of the country would protect. But if so, Black and Stewart might respond, there really is no national consensus; the very existence of disagreement is an argument for federalism, or for respecting local differences.

3. *Privacy?* What is the nature of the "privacy" interest protected by *Griswold*? Is it concerned with the home? With control over very personal information? With the protection of the marital relationship (or of *any* intimate relationship)? A more general interest in autonomy? Which of these interests are implicit in the various opinions? Given the interests protected by *Griswold,* to what other activities or relations might the opinion arguably extend?

4. *Sex equality arguments for access to contraception. Griswold* concerned access to women's contraception, yet the Supreme Court did not characterize the case as about women's rights. The Court would not develop its sex equality jurisprudence until the early 1970s.

A number of pioneering women civil rights lawyers were involved in the strategy and litigation of *Griswold,* including Harriet Pilpel and Catherine Roraback. They understood a law banning contraception as threatening the welfare and standing of women. Women's equality figured in several different ways.

The first and perhaps most obvious concern was disparate treatment in Connecticut's enforcement of the ban. Connecticut banned the use of contraception, but allowed the sale of condoms as a means of preventing venereal disease and protecting men's health.[18] At the same time, the state banned the most effective forms of contraception used by women—which at that time were dispensed only by doctor's prescription—even when the ban posed a threat to women's health.[19] The state provided no exceptions in the enforcement of the law for women's health.[20]

Lawyers for the plaintiffs did not directly challenge Connecticut's disparate treatment of men's and women's access to contraception under the Equal Protection Clause. Nevertheless, they made due process/liberty arguments in previous litigation that pointed to this disparate treatment in a number of ways, foregrounding the law's harms to women's health. Advocates were especially concerned about the law's impact on poor women, who depended on clinics rather than private physicians for access to birth control.[21]

---

18. On the availability of condoms under the Connecticut statute, see Mary Dudziak, Just Say No: Birth Control in the Connecticut Supreme Court Before Griswold v. Connecticut, 75 Iowa L. Rev. 915, 927 (1990) ("[c]ondoms could be used to prevent venereal disease").

19. See Motion for Leave to File Brief for Planned Parent Federation of America, Griswold v. Connecticut, 1965 WL 115612, at *17-18 (reporting that Connecticut law was enforced against doctors prescribing diaphragms, birth control pills, and intrauterine devices).

20. See Tileston v. Ullman, 129 Conn. 84, 86 (1942) (holding that Connecticut laws criminalizing the use of devices to prevent contraception would be violated if a physician prescribed contraceptive drugs to a married woman for whom pregnancy would be life-threatening).

21. See Dudziak, Just Say No, supra n.18.

A second kind of equality argument emphasized the differential consequences for women of denying them control over when and whether to have children. In *Griswold,* an ACLU amicus brief challenged Connecticut's contraception ban directly under the Equal Protection Clause. The brief argued that denying women access to contraception violates both liberty and equality, implicating social, economic, and political dimensions of citizenship:

> In contemporary times, the liberty of "establishing a home" encompasses not only the right of parents to raise children, but includes the wife's right to order her childbearing according to her financial and emotional needs, her abilities, and her achievements. No citation of authority is required to support the fact that in addition to its economic consequences, the ability to regulate child-bearing has been a significant factor in the emancipation of married women. In this respect, effective means of contraception rank equally with the Nineteenth Amendment in enhancing the opportunities of women who wish to work in industry, business, the arts, and the professions. . . . Thus, the equal protection clause protects the class of women who wish to delay or regulate child-bearing effectively.[22]

Grounding reproductive rights in equality has two advantages. First, it connects these rights to the constitutional text—the Equal Protection Clause. Second, it connects these rights to the *Carolene Products* theory that the appropriate role of courts is to protect democracy and equal citizenship. See Douglas NeJaime and Reva Siegel, Answering the Lochner Objection: Reexamining Substantive Due Process and the Role of Courts in a Democracy, 96 N.Y.U. L. Rev. (forthcoming 2021).

We will see later on in this chapter that as the Court's privacy jurisprudence developed, it has increasingly incorporated equality ideas. For example, the Court has emphasized that it is not "for the State to insist . . . upon its own vision of the woman's role, however dominant that vision has been in the course of our history and our culture," and that "[t]he ability of women to participate equally in the economic and social life of the Nation has been facilitated by their ability to control their reproductive lives." Planned Parenthood of Southeastern Pennsylvania v. Casey, 505 U.S. 833, 852, 856 (1992).

The debate over the contraception coverage provisions of the Patient Protection and Affordable Care Act (ACA) featured several different kinds of equality claims about access to contraception. The legislative history of the ACA shows a concern with the "unique needs of women" in health care.[23] Different kinds of arguments appear in the legislative history and agency findings. First, contraception is part of women's health and excluding it imposes an extra expense on women. Second,

---

22. Motion for Leave to File Brief for the American Civil Liberties Union and the Connecticut Civil Liberties Union as Amici Curiae and Brief Amici Curiae, Griswold v. Connecticut, 1965 WL 115616, at *16. For a related claim, see Trubeck v. Ullman, 147 Conn. 633, 65 A.2d 158 (1960).

23. 155 Cong. Rec. S12, 265, 12,273 (daily ed. Dec. 3, 2009) (statement of Sen. Stabenow); 155 Cong. Rec. S12, 114 (daily ed. Dec. 2, 2009) (statement of Sen. Feinstein); 155 Cong. Rec. S12, 021, S12, 025 (daily ed. Dec. 1, 2009) (statement of Sen. Boxer); 155 Cong. Rec. S12, 265, S12, 271 (daily ed. Dec. 3, 2009) (statement of Sen. Franken).

depriving women of control over the timing and number of children greatly affects women's equal status in diverse social spheres, especially in the market economy:[24]

> This [coverage] disparity places women in the workforce at a disadvantage compared to their male co-workers. Researchers have shown that access to contraception improves the social and economic status of women. Contraceptive coverage, by reducing the number of unintended and potentially unhealthy pregnancies, furthers the goal of eliminating this disparity by allowing women to achieve equal status as healthy and productive members of the job force.

5. *Popular ratification of fundamental rights jurisprudence.* Judge Robert Bork famously criticized Griswold v. Connecticut as "an unprincipled decision, both in the way in which it derives a new constitutional right and in the way it defines that right or rather fails to define it. We are left with no idea of the sweep of the right of privacy and hence no notion of the cases to which it may or may not be applied in the future."[25] Judge Bork's confirmation hearings in 1987 precipitated a national debate about fundamental rights jurisprudence. Bork, of course, was an early advocate of originalism, and as such was a noted critic of the Court's sex discrimination and privacy decisions, including *Griswold* and Roe v. Wade. Bork's opponents, who recognized that Roe v. Wade was still controversial, focused instead on the fact that Bork even rejected the legitimacy of *Griswold.*[26] As Lackland Bloom explains:[27]

> There is no way to tell exactly how much Judge Bork's persistent attacks on *Griswold* contributed to his rejection by the Senate; however, it is fair to say that it was a significant factor. *Griswold* was a useful case for Judge Bork's opponents because its general right to privacy and its specific holding with respect to the use of contraceptives by married couples could be presented to the public at large in a comprehensible and appealing manner. The opposition portrayed Judge Bork as a threat to privacy; he could only defend himself by talking about confusing notions such as substantive due process, *Lochner*, neutral principles, and the Madisonian model. In retrospect, it became clear that Judge Bork may have spent too much of his career attacking the wrong case. . . . If the Bork hearings accomplished anything beyond the rejection of the Bork nomination itself, it was the enshrinement of Griswold v. Connecticut as "a fixed star in our constitutional" firmament, at least on its narrow facts.

Consider the following questions.

---

24. Group Health Plans and Health Insurance Issuers Relating to Coverage of Preventive Services Under the Patient Protection and Affordable Care Act, 77 Fed. Reg. 8725-01 (Feb. 15, 2012).

25. Robert Bork, Neutral Principles and Some First Amendment Problems, 47 Ind. L.J. 1, 9 (1971).

26. For a sample of the dialogue between Bork and Senate Judiciary Committee Chairman Joseph Biden on Bork's published criticisms of *Griswold,* see Nomination of Robert H. Bork to be Associate Justice of the Supreme Court of the United States, Hearings Before the Senate Committee on the Judiciary, 100th Cong. 1st Session (Part I), 86-93, 570-573 (1987).

27. Lackland H. Bloom, Twenty Fifth Anniversary of Griswold v. Connecticut and the Right to Privacy: The Legacy of *Griswold,* 16 Ohio N.U. L. Rev. 511, 542-543 (1989).

a. Do the Bork hearings confirm that the Court "got it right" in deciding *Griswold,* and accurately reflected the national ethos? Or, do the hearings instead suggest that the Court's fundamental rights jurisprudence helped shape the nation's understanding of its constitutional values? Are either of these appropriate roles for the Court?

b. How is it possible for confirmation hearings to alter a decision's authority as constitutional law? Constitutional change often occurs through the President's appointment of new Justices, see generally Jack M. Balkin and Sanford Levinson, Understanding the Constitutional Revolution, 87 Va. L. Rev. 1045 (2001); Bruce Ackerman, Transformative Appointments, 101 Harv. L. Rev. 1164 (1988); Brad Snyder, How the Conservatives Canonized Brown v. Board of Education, 52 Rutgers L. Rev. 383 (2000). Given increasing recognition of this fact by politicians, has the confirmation process become an important and exceptional moment in the making of constitutional law? Consider the extent to which the change in *Griswold*'s status is a special case of a more general dynamic in which the representative branches of government, the media, and the general public play a role in entrenching authoritative constitutional understandings.

NOTE: THE REACH OF *GRISWOLD*

Several of the *Griswold* opinions emphasize the unique importance of the marital relationship. Later cases both applied *Griswold* outside the marital setting and strengthened constitutional protection for the right to marry.

EISENSTADT v. BAIRD, 405 U.S. 438 (1972): [Appellee was convicted for distributing contraceptive foam to individuals, both married and unmarried, at a public meeting at Boston University. State law allowed "married persons [to] obtain contraceptives to prevent pregnancy, but only from doctors or druggists on prescription; . . . single persons may not obtain contraceptives from anyone to prevent pregnancy; and . . . married or single persons may obtain contraceptives from anyone to prevent, not pregnancy, but the spread of disease." The Court, through Justice Brennan, held that the conviction violated the Equal Protection Clause's rational basis test because the statutory distinctions between married and unmarried individuals did not rationally further a legitimate state interest, whether it be the preservation of health or the prevention of premarital sex. "It would be plainly unreasonable to assume that Massachusetts has prescribed pregnancy and the birth of an unwanted child as punishment for fornication, which is a misdemeanor under Massachusetts General Laws Ann. . . . Aside from the scheme of values that assumption would attribute to the State, it is abundantly clear that the effect of the ban on distribution of contraceptives to unmarried persons has at best a marginal relation to the proffered objective. . . . Even on the assumption that the fear of pregnancy operates as a deterrent to fornication, the Massachusetts statute is thus so riddled with exceptions that deterrence of premarital sex cannot reasonably be regarded as its aim." After quoting the lower court's opinion that prohibiting access to contraceptive devices might violate an individual's fundamental rights, the Court stated:] "We need not and do not, however, decide that important question in this case because, whatever the rights of the individual to access to contraceptives may be, the rights must be the same for the unmarried and the married alike."

"If under *Griswold* the distribution of contraceptives to married persons cannot be prohibited, a ban on distribution to unmarried persons would be equally impermissible. It is true that in *Griswold* the right of privacy in question inhered in the marital relationship. Yet the marital couple is not an independent entity with a mind and heart of its own, but an association of two individuals each with a separate intellectual and emotional makeup. If the right of privacy means anything, it is the right of the *individual*, married or single, to be free from unwarranted governmental intrusion into matters so fundamentally affecting a person as the decision whether to bear or beget a child."

Chief Justice Burger dissented, arguing that "I do not challenge Griswold v. Connecticut . . . despite its tenuous moorings to the text of the Constitution, but . . . [t]he Court was there confronted with a statute flatly prohibiting the use of contraceptives, not one regulating their distribution." Justices Powell and Rehnquist did not participate in the decision.

Five years later, in Carey v. Population Services International, 431 U.S. 678 (1977), the Court struck down a New York law prohibiting the sale of contraceptives to minors under 16, together with an ancillary provision (likely designed to enforce the age regulation) forbidding anyone other than a licensed pharmacist to sell even nonprescription contraceptives to persons of any age. With respect to the latter provision, Justice Brennan wrote for the Court that "*Griswold* may no longer be read as holding only that a State may not prohibit a married couple's use of contraceptives." Instead, "the teaching of *Griswold* is that the Constitution protects individual decisions in matters of childbearing from unjustified intrusion by the State. Restrictions on the distribution of contraceptives clearly burden the freedom to make such decisions." New York's limitation on the distribution of nonprescription contraceptives "clearly imposes a significant burden on the right of the individuals to use contraceptives if they choose to do so. . . ."

A section of Justice Brennan's opinion in *Carey* joined by Justices Stewart, Marshall, and Blackmun looked beyond the Constitution's protection for "decisions in matters of childbearing" and asked more searching questions about constitutional limitations on government's authority to regulate consensual sexual activity of adults, and even of minors. Id. at 694-695. Chief Justice Burger and Justice Rehnquist dissented.

Zablocki v. Redhail, 434 U.S. 374 (1978), struck down a Wisconsin statute that restricted the right to marry. The statute at issue in *Zablocki* conditioned marriage by a resident obligated to support a minor not in his custody upon a showing that support had been provided and that any covered children were not, nor were likely to become, public charges. Justice Marshall, citing various opinions in which the Court had found the right to marry to be fundamental, concluded that the Equal Protection Clause requires "critical examination of the state interests advanced" in support of a classification based on the exercise of that right. He rejected the state's asserted interest in counseling persons with child-support obligations before they incurred further obligations, noting that the statute neither required counseling nor automatically permitted marriage after counseling was completed. He also rejected Wisconsin's presentation of the law as a rational means of enforcing support obligations, noting that the state had other means for enforcing such obligations and that the statute was poorly suited to this goal. Justice Stewart, concurring in the judgment, would have invalidated the law under the due process rather than the Equal Protection Clause. Justice Powell, also concurring in the judgment, accepted the need for heightened scrutiny (a "fair and substantial relationship") under the Due Process and Equal Protection Clauses because the intrusion on the marriage decision was "contrary to deeply rooted traditions" and because it excluded indigents from a process in which the state exercised a monopoly.[28] Justice Rehnquist wrote a lone dissent.

Following *Griswold*, the Court also considered two cases challenging state zoning laws that regulated living arrangements.

In Village of Belle Terre v. Boraas, 416 U.S. 1 (1974), six unrelated college students challenged a local ordinance restricting land use to one-family dwellings, with "family" defined so as to exclude more than two unrelated people living together. Writing for the Court, Justice Douglas sustained the ordinance, noting that it involved no "fundamental" or "privacy" rights and that the state could use its zoning authority to safeguard "family values." Only Justice Marshall dissented on the merits.

Moore v. City of East Cleveland, 431 U.S. 494 (1977), distinguished *Belle Terre* to invalidate an ordinance that limited occupancy of a dwelling unit to members of a single family, where "family" was defined in terms of a nuclear rather than an extended family. Appellant, who lived in her home with her son and two grandsons—her son's son and his nephew—was convicted for failing to remove the nephew as an "illegal occupant." Justice Powell, writing for a plurality including Justices Brennan, Marshall, and Blackmun, contrasted *Belle Terre*'s impact on unrelated individuals with *East Cleveland*'s "slicing deeply into the family itself": "[W]hen the government intrudes on choices concerning family living arrangements, this Court must examine carefully the importance of the governmental interests advanced and the extent to which they are served by the challenged regulation." Justice Powell held that the Court's earlier decisions "establish that the Constitution protects the sanctity of the family precisely because the institution of the family is deeply rooted in this Nation's history and tradition," a protection that reaches even to extended families composed of "uncles, aunts, cousins, and especially grandparents sharing a household along with parents and children." He added that "the choice of relatives in this degree of kinship to live together may not lightly be denied by the State. . . . [T]he Constitution prevents East Cleveland from standardizing its children—and its adults—by forcing all to live in certain narrowly defined family patterns." He concluded that the city's proffered interests in preventing overcrowding, minimizing traffic and parking congestion, and avoiding burdening the school system were marginally served by the ordinance, but were outweighed by the appellant's constitutional interests.

---

28. See also Boddie v. Connecticut, 401 U.S. 371 (1971), Chapter 10, infra.

Justice Stevens concurred, viewing the ordinance as "a taking of property without due process and without just compensation," which cut "deeply into a fundamental right normally associated with the ownership of real property—that of an owner to decide who may reside on her property." Justice Stewart, joined by Justice Rehnquist, dissented:

> When the Court has found that the Fourteenth Amendment placed a substantive limitation on a State's power to regulate, it has been in those rare cases in which the personal interests at issue have been deemed "implicit in the concept of ordered liberty." The interest that the appellant may have in permanently sharing a single kitchen and a suite of contiguous rooms with some of her relatives simply does not rise to that level. To equate this interest with the fundamental decisions to marry and to bear and raise children is to extend the limited substantive contours of the Due Process Clause beyond recognition.

Justice White dissented in an opinion that questioned the validity of the notion of substantive due process and argued that judicial intervention "under the general rubric of the right to privacy" should be narrowly circumscribed. (Chief Justice Burger dissented on procedural grounds.)

NOTE: TRADITION AS A SOURCE OF FUNDAMENTAL RIGHTS

As noted in *Griswold*, courts attempting to justify the protection of implied fundamental rights have often turned to history and tradition. Thus, Justice Cardozo argued in Snyder v. Massachusetts, 291 U.S. 97 (1934), that the Due Process Clause protects those liberties "so rooted in the traditions and conscience of our people as to be ranked as fundamental."

There are two problems with this strategy. First, history and tradition are subject to multiple interpretations. Moreover, fundamental rights claims often contravene older mores and conventional practices. For this reason, Justice Harlan explained in Poe v. Ullman that courts should look to "the balance struck by this country, having regard to what history teaches are the traditions from which it developed as well as the traditions from which it broke."

Second, critics often appeal to history and tradition to deny the existence of fundamental rights to sexual autonomy or to restrict their constitutional protection.

The proper role of tradition in articulating rights is hotly debated on the Supreme Court. Although the debate focuses on interpretive method, what is at stake is the kind of practices the Constitution protects from governmental regulation. Two contrasting cases decided within six years of each other provide a useful example.

In Washington v. Glucksberg, 521 U.S. 702 (1997), the Court used tradition to reject claims of a fundamental right to assisted suicide. Chief Justice Rehnquist stated that "the Due Process Clause specially protects those fundamental rights and liberties which are, objectively, 'deeply rooted in this Nation's history and tradition,' [Moore v. City of East Cleveland] (plurality opinion) . . . and 'implicit in the concept of ordered liberty,' such that 'neither liberty nor justice would exist if they were sacrificed,' Palko v. Connecticut, 302 U.S. 319 (1937). . . . Our Nation's history, legal traditions, and practices thus provide the crucial 'guideposts for responsible decisionmaking,' that direct and restrain our exposition of the Due Process Clause. . . . This approach tends to rein in the subjective elements that are necessarily present in due process judicial review." There could be no substantive due process right to assisted suicide, the Court held, because there was "a consistent and almost universal tradition that has long rejected the asserted right [to choose the time and manner of one's death], and continues explicitly to reject it today, even for terminally ill, mentally competent adults."

The Court took a very different approach to tradition only six years later. In Lawrence v. Texas, 539 U.S. 558 (2003), the Court struck down Texas's criminal ban on same-sex sodomy. Texas asserted that there was "an established tradition of prosecuting acts because of their homosexual character," but the Court responded that "history and tradition are the starting point but not in all cases the ending point of the substantive due process inquiry." Recent history, the Court emphasized, had demonstrated that there was "an emerging awareness that liberty gives substantial protection to adult persons in deciding how to conduct their private lives in matters pertaining to sex." Quoting Justice Stevens's dissenting opinion in Bowers v. Hardwick, 478 U.S. 186 (1986), which *Lawrence* overruled, the Court asserted: "[T]he fact that the governing majority in a State has traditionally viewed a particular practice as immoral is not a sufficient reason for upholding a law prohibiting the practice; neither history nor tradition could save a law prohibiting miscegenation from constitutional attack."

How should courts establish that there is a tradition of protecting a claimed fundamental right? And what guides a court in concluding that activities traditionally proscribed or legally unprotected (like homosexuality) are now constitutionally protected? Does this represent a break with a tradition or a reinterpretation of it?

One way that courts respond to changing mores is to re-describe traditions at a higher level of generality so that the traditions now include activities that were customarily unprotected or condemned. Thus, one could generalize from the traditional protection of sex within heterosexual marriage to argue that there is a tradition of respect for sexual autonomy generally, which might include same-sex relations. Accordingly, Lawrence v. Texas argued that one should generalize from existing rights "to marriage, procreation, contraception, family relationships, child rearing, and education" to include the right of private consensual sexual relations between adults, and that the traditional disapproval of homosexuality should not be controlling: "Had those who drew and ratified the Due Process Clauses of the Fifth Amendment or the Fourteenth Amendment known the components of liberty in its manifold possibilities, they might have been more specific. They did not presume to have this insight. They knew times can blind us to certain truths and later generations can see that laws once thought necessary and proper in fact serve only to oppress. As the Constitution endures, persons in every generation can invoke its principles in their own search for greater freedom." Under what conditions is this sort of argument by analogy appropriate?

In contrast to *Lawrence, Glucksberg* used tradition to limit the expansion of unenumerated rights. It argued that due process analysis should be "carefully refined by concrete examples involving fundamental rights found to be deeply rooted in our legal tradition." It refused to argue that a traditional right to refuse unwanted medical treatment could be generalized into a more general right of bodily autonomy or "self sovereignty" that included a right to commit suicide.

Michael H. v. Gerald D., 491 U.S. 110 (1989), featured an extended debate among the members of the Court about the use of tradition, and, in particular, at what level of generality to describe tradition. *Michael H.* involved an attempt by the biological father of a child conceived in an adulterous relationship to establish paternity and visitation rights. The petitioner, Michael H., had an affair with Carole D. while she was still married to Gerald D. and had a child, Victoria. Gerald was listed as father on the birth certificate and always treated Victoria as his daughter. However, a blood test indicated with near certainty (a 98% probability) that Michael was Victoria's father. Carole and Michael intermittently lived together, and he presented Victoria to others as his daughter. In turn, Victoria apparently referred to him as "Daddy." After Carole and Victoria permanently returned to Gerald, Michael's attempts to visit Victoria were rebuffed. Michael H. then sought to establish his paternity and visitation rights in the California courts. Gerald argued that there were no triable issues of fact as to Victoria's paternity. He invoked Cal. Evid. Code §621, which provides that "the issue of a wife cohabiting with her husband, . . . is conclusively presumed to be a child of the marriage," unless within two years of the birth, paternity has been established in another man. Michael H. argued that this presumption was unconstitutional as a matter of substantive and procedural due process.

The Supreme Court rejected Michael H.'s claims. Justice Scalia's plurality opinion, writing for himself, Chief Justice Rehnquist, and Justices O'Connor and Kennedy, argued that there was a long history of protecting parental "relationships that develop within the unitary family." The "unitary family," Scalia, explained "is typified, of course, by the marital family, but also includes the household of unmarried parents and their children." However, Justice Scalia explained, there was no tradition of protecting the rights of biological fathers in Michael H.'s situation. The traditional concern of the common law was in avoiding declarations of illegitimacy, and in promoting the "peace and tranquility of States and families." . . . "We have found nothing in the older sources, nor in the older cases, addressing specifically the power of the natural father to assert parental rights over a child born into a woman's existing marriage with another man. . . . What counts is whether the States in fact award substantive parental rights to the natural father of a child conceived within and born into an extant marital union that wishes to embrace the child. We are not aware of a single case, old or new, that has done so. This is not the stuff of which fundamental rights qualifying as liberty interests are made."

Justice Brennan, joined by Justices Marshall and Blackmun, dissented:

> [The plurality] does not ask whether parenthood is an interest that historically has received our attention and protection; the answer to that question is too clear for dispute. Instead, the plurality asks whether the specific variety of parenthood under consideration—a natural father's relationship with a child whose mother is married to another man—has enjoyed such protection.
>
> If we had looked to tradition with such specificity in past cases, many a decision would have reached a different result. Surely the use of contraceptives by unmarried couples, Eisenstadt v. Baird, or even by

married couples, Griswold v. Connecticut; the freedom from corporal punishment in schools, Ingraham v. Wright, 430 U.S. 651 (1977); the freedom from an arbitrary transfer from a prison to a psychiatric institution, Vitek v. Jones, 445 U.S. 480 (1980); and even the right to raise one's natural but illegitimate children, Stanley v. Illinois[, 405 U.S. 645 (1972)], were not "interest[s] traditionally protected by our society," at the time of their consideration by this Court. . . . The plurality's interpretive method . . . ignores the good reasons for limiting the role of "tradition" in interpreting the Constitution's deliberately capacious language. In the plurality's constitutional universe, we may not take notice of the fact that the original reasons for the conclusive presumption of paternity are out of place in a world in which blood tests can prove virtually beyond a shadow of a doubt who sired a particular child and in which the fact of illegitimacy no longer plays the burdensome and stigmatizing role it once did. Nor, in the plurality's world, may we deny "tradition" its full scope by pointing out that the rationale for the conventional rule has changed over the years; . . . instead, our task is simply to identify a rule denying the asserted interest and not to ask whether the basis for that rule—which is the true reflection of the values undergirding it—has changed too often or too recently to call the rule embodying that rationale a "tradition." Moreover, by describing the decisive question as whether Michael and Victoria's interest is one that has been "traditionally protected by our society," rather than one that society traditionally has thought important (with or without protecting it), and by suggesting that our sole function is to "discern the society's views," the plurality acts as if the only purpose of the Due Process Clause is to confirm the importance of interests already protected by a majority of the States. . . .

In construing the Fourteenth Amendment to offer shelter only to those interests specifically protected by historical practice, moreover, the plurality ignores the kind of society in which our Constitution exists. We are not an assimilative, homogeneous society, but a facilitative, pluralistic one, in which we must be willing to abide someone else's unfamiliar or even repellant practice because the same tolerant impulse protects our own idiosyncrasies. Even if we can agree, therefore, that "family" and "parenthood" are part of the good life, it is absurd to assume that we can agree on the content of those terms and destructive to pretend that we do. In a community such as ours, "liberty" must include the freedom not to conform. The plurality today squashes this freedom by requiring specific approval from history before protecting anything in the name of liberty.

The document that the plurality construes today is unfamiliar to me. It is not the living charter that I have taken to be our Constitution; it is instead a stagnant, archaic, hidebound document steeped in the prejudices and superstitions of a time long past. This Constitution does not recognize that times change, does not see that sometimes a practice or rule outlives its foundations. I cannot accept an interpretive method that does such violence to the charter that I am bound by oath to uphold.

In a footnote joined only by Chief Justice Rehnquist, Justice Scalia responded:

> Justice Brennan criticizes our methodology in using historical traditions specifically relating to the rights of an adulterous natural father, rather than inquiring more generally "whether parenthood is an interest that historically has received our attention and protection." There seems to us no basis for the contention that this methodology is "nove[l]." For example, in Bowers v. Hardwick[, 478 U.S. 186 (1986), which upheld state sodomy laws], we noted that at the time the Fourteenth Amendment was ratified all but 5 of the 37 States had criminal sodomy laws, that all 50 of the States had such laws prior to 1961, and that 24 States and the District of Columbia continued to have them; and we concluded from that record, regarding that very specific aspect of sexual conduct, that "to claim that a right to engage in such conduct is 'deeply rooted in this Nation's history and tradition' or 'implicit in the concept of ordered liberty' is, at best, facetious." In *Roe* we spent about a fifth of our opinion negating the proposition that there was a longstanding tradition of laws proscribing abortion. We do not understand why, having rejected our focus upon the societal tradition regarding the natural father's rights vis-à-vis a child whose mother is married to another man, Justice Brennan would choose to focus instead upon "parenthood." Why should the relevant category not be even more general—perhaps "family relationships"; or "personal relationships"; or even "emotional attachments in general"?
>
> Though the dissent has no basis for the level of generality it would select, we do: We refer to the most specific level at which a relevant tradition protecting, or denying protection to, the asserted right can be identified. If, for example, there were no societal tradition, either way, regarding the rights of the natural father of a child adulterously conceived, we would have to consult, and (if possible) reason from, the traditions regarding natural fathers in general. But there is such a more specific tradition, and it unqualifiedly denies protection to such a parent.
>
> One would think that Justice Brennan would appreciate the value of consulting the most specific tradition available, since he acknowledges that "[e]ven if we can agree . . . that 'family' and 'parenthood' are part of the good life, it is absurd to assume that we can agree on the content of those terms and destructive to pretend that we do." Because such general traditions provide such imprecise guidance, they permit judges to dictate rather than discern the society's views. The need, if arbitrary decisionmaking is to be avoided, to adopt the most specific tradition as the point of reference—or at least to announce, as Justice Brennan declines to do, some other criterion for selecting among the innumerable relevant traditions that could be consulted—is well enough exemplified by the fact that in the present case Justice Brennan's opinion and Justice O'Connor's opinion, which disapprove this footnote, both appeal to tradition, but on the basis of the tradition they select reach opposite results. Although assuredly having the virtue (if it be that) of leaving judges free to decide as they think best when the unanticipated occurs, a rule of law that binds neither by text nor by any particular, identifiable tradition, is no rule of law at all.

Finally, we may note that this analysis is not inconsistent with the result in cases such as Griswold v. Connecticut or Eisenstadt v. Baird. None of those cases acknowledged a longstanding and still extant societal tradition withholding the very right pronounced to be the subject of a liberty interest and then rejected it. Justice Brennan must do so here. In this case, the existence of such a tradition, continuing to the present day, refutes any possible contention that the alleged right is "so rooted in the traditions and conscience of our people as to be ranked as fundamental," Snyder v. Massachusetts, or "implicit in the concept of ordered liberty," Palko v. Connecticut.

Jack M. Balkin, Tradition, Betrayal, and the Politics of Deconstruction

11 Cardozo L. Rev. 1623 (1990)

Justice Scalia's test of the most specific tradition [in Michael H. v. Gerald D.] . . . assumes that constitutionally protected liberties match or do not match existing traditions in an unproblematic way. For each asserted right there either is or is not a specific tradition associated with its protection. Yet there are many different ways of describing a liberty, and many different ways of characterizing a tradition. For example, we might point out that under his test, there has been no established tradition in California for protecting Justice Scalia's own rights to visit his children, since there is no tradition of affording protection to fathers who are children of Italian immigrants and who graduated from Ivy League law schools before 1965, were appointed to the United States Supreme Court by former governors of the state of California, and have more than two children but less than thirteen. Indeed, the question has hardly ever come up. . . .

To be sure, Justice Scalia has a plausible response. When Justice Scalia claims parental rights to his children, the liberty he claims is the parental right of fathers with respect to biological children born while the father was married to the child's mother. This has been traditionally protected. The rights of adulterous fathers, however, have not been traditionally protected.

But this answer reveals that Justice Scalia's theory is not simply a preference for narrower traditions over broader traditions. It rests upon an important metaphysical set of assumptions—that traditions or (more importantly) the absences of traditions, come in discrete units with discrete boundaries. To describe a tradition accurately is to respect the preexisting boundaries of the tradition. Similarly, to describe a liberty traditionally protected is to describe its actual contours. Thus, one cannot simply divide up traditions or liberties any way one wants. Like glass bottles, traditions and liberties come in premade sizes. One cannot cut them to fit, or else one will break the glass. Thus, there is a tradition of protecting marital privacy but not a tradition of protecting the marital privacy of a narrower class—for example, middle class persons, and certainly not a tradition of protecting the privacy of a broader class of persons that would include unmarried couples. Yet, under this logic, it is also historically clear that there is a tradition of protecting the marital right of privacy, but not a historical tradition of protecting married couples' right to purchase contraceptives. Griswold v. Connecticut is thus a potential embarrassment for Justice Scalia.

Moreover, Justice Scalia's vision of tradition assumes that traditions are not only discrete, but presumptively normatively correct. What is traditional is worthy of constitutional protection, and what is not traditional is not, whether it be marital privacy, the rights of married fathers to visit their children, sexual harassment in the workplace or racial segregation. This, too, is a potential source of embarrassment. . . . [I]f sexual harassment directed toward women in the workplace and respect for marital privacy are both traditions, but only one is worth protecting, how do we tell the difference? If back alley abortions are a tradition in response to the "traditional" prohibition on abortion in America, does this make abortion (in or out of a back alley) a tradition worth protecting and sustaining? In short, what normative status should be assigned to a set of values given the fact that many people have held these values at one point or another in our nation's history?

In his dissent in Poe v. Ullman, [Justice Harlan] spoke of the need for "regard to what history teaches are the traditions from which [this country] developed as well as the traditions from which it broke." [He] thus recognized, in a way that Justice Scalia appears not to, that the existence of a tradition may be a reason for rejecting it as controlling. Just as Learned Hand rejected the defense of custom in tort law on the ground that "a whole calling may have unduly lagged," so too the existing customs of the American people may not be appropriate for constitutional perpetuation. This is especially true, one might think, when they are impositions of values by a majority on a political, cultural, ethnic, religious, or ideological minority.

In fact, what is most troubling about Justice Scalia's call for respecting the most specific tradition available is that our most specific historical traditions may often be opposed to our more general commitments to liberty or equality. Curiously, then, different parts of the American tradition may conflict with each other. And indeed, this is one of the untidy facts of historical experience. The fourteenth amendment's abstract commitment to racial equality was accompanied by simultaneous acceptance of segregated public schools in the District of Columbia and acquiescence in antimiscegenation laws. The establishment clause and the principle of separation of church and state have coexisted with presidential proclamations of national days of prayer, official congressional chaplains, and national Christmas trees. Traditions do not exist as integrated wholes. They are a motley collection of principles and counterprinciples, standing for one thing when viewed narrowly and standing for another when viewed more generally. Tradition never speaks with one voice, although, to be sure, persons of particular predilections may hear only one. . . .

Nevertheless, a more realistic approach to tradition, along the lines of Justice Harlan, is cold comfort to Justice Scalia. It undermines the very reasons he has attempted to hew to tradition — [to avoid judges' engaging in] value-laden inquir[ies]. . . . To follow tradition because it reflects the values of the many is insufficient — one must also believe that these values are justified, or not so unjustified that they must be contradicted. Inquiry into tradition leads us back, in other words, to the basic problem of constitutionalism.

DISCUSSION

1. *Tradition and betrayal.* Balkin points out that the word "tradition" comes from the same root as the word "betrayal." The original word (*traditio*) meant to deliver or hand over.

> To respect tradition is also to betray in at least three senses. First, it is to forsake other alternatives for the future . . . to hinder and eliminate them in the name of social solidarity, propriety, order, or other goals. Tradition is always extradition. Second, to respect tradition is also to betray other existing and competing traditions, to submerge and extinguish them . . . just as in *Michael H.* Justice Scalia tried to write 1950s white middle class theories of the family into the Constitution—thus establishing the hegemony of Ozzie and Harriet, if you will. There are, of course, other traditions of family life in this country. There are traditions of extended families, of spousal separations, of common law marriage and unmarried cohabitation—but apparently they don't count, since we didn't see them on "I Love Lucy." Third, a tradition is often, in an uncanny way, a betrayal of itself. For Scalia's vision of the unitary family, as exemplified by television situation comedies of the 1950s, portrays a theory of the family that was hypocritical even in its own time since even what white middle class families in the 1950s said one should do and not do sexually was not in fact what they always did, as we all found out later on. To establish and enshrine a tradition is thus at the same time to establish a countertradition—a seamy underside consisting of what society also does and perhaps cannot help but do, but will not admit to doing. The overt, respectable tradition depends upon the forgetting of its submerged, less respectable opposite, even as it thrives and depends on its existence in unexpected ways. For example, in the television and movies of the 1950s, one sees Rock Hudson and other homosexual or bisexual males playing the parts of monogamous heterosexual males, and implicitly endorsing a heterosexual lifestyle. These roles served to support and define the very tradition of sexual practices of which Justice Scalia speaks. They furthered and reinforced a tradition of values that the persons playing these roles owed no fealty to—a tradition that . . . required of each of them a particular form of self-betrayal.

What follows from Balkin's analysis? Consider the following alternatives:

a. Appeals to tradition are not a check on majoritarianism, they are actually another form of majoritarianism and therefore deserve no special constitutional protection. In fact the language of tradition is just another way of legitimating disregard for unpopular practices or minority subcultures. This is particularly true if the tradition is articulated at a low level of generality. Is this an argument against appeals to tradition or an argument about the proper level of generality?

b. Appeals to tradition do not restrain judges from inserting their own values and preferences into the law. Different judges will see different things in the same tradition, or different traditions in the same history, and, in particular, they will tend to see their own values enshrined there. Moreover, because not all traditional practices are equally worthy of preservation, they will have different views about which practices are to be preserved and which are to be abandoned and broken away from. In what way do these features of constitutional arguments from tradition differ from other forms of constitutional argument?[29]

c. Appeals to tradition are not a value-free form of discourse or a method that discovers preexisting values in the Constitution. Rather, appeals to tradition are a way of arguing about conflicting values; they can be useful, but not if they become determinative tests. Simply toting up historical examples misses the unstable and internally conflicted nature of tradition. Is this an argument against the use of tradition or an argument against rigid and univocal assessments of tradition? Is that sort of rigidity and demand for clarity inevitable for lawyers, who want a rule that governs the case?

d. Appeals to tradition are actually appeals to contrasting narratives about the growth and development of the country and the meaning of its deepest commitments. Because one can always tell multiple stories about our nation's history, tradition can have no stable use in constitutional discourse. Is this true? Don't constitutional arguments continuously appeal to narratives (recall Marshall's story of American growth in *McCulloch*, or Ginsburg's narrative in the *VMI* case)? Are some narratives about the country simply more plausible than others? Plausible to whom?

2. *The nature of the right at stake in* Michael H. Do you agree with Justice Scalia that the fundamental right in question is that of an "[adulterous] natural father to assert parental rights over a child born into a woman's existing marriage with another man"? Or is it the right of "a parent to be heard before being deprived of any contact with his or her child" by the other parent? Is there a "neutral" or "principled" method of describing the right in question or determining the proper level of generality in construing previously recognized fundamental rights?

3. *Troxel v. Granville.* The Court addressed parental rights once again in Troxel v. Granville, 530 U.S. 57 (2000). Paternal grandparents sued the mother for visitation rights under a Washington statute that allowed "[a]ny person [to] petition the court for visitation rights at any time including, but not limited to, custody proceedings" based on "the best interest of the child." The trial court ordered visitation rights greater than the mother was willing to permit. Justice O'Connor, writing for a plurality that included Chief Justice Rehnquist, Justice Ginsburg, and Justice Breyer, held that, as applied to the facts of the case, the Washington statute violated the mother's "fundamental constitutional right to make decisions concerning the rearing of her own daughters" because "a parent's decision that visitation would not be in the child's best interest is accorded no deference. . . . Instead, the Washington statute places the best-interest determination solely in the hands of the judge." Justice Souter concurred in the judgment on the grounds that the statute was unconstitutional on its face. Justice Kennedy,

29. On the need for judges to define which traditions one has broken from, consider Rogers M. Smith, Civil Ideals: Conflicting Visions of Citizenship in U.S. History (1997), which documents the presence within American history of three distinctive and often conflicting traditions of American thought. In particular, Smith argues that there is a longstanding nativist tradition in American thought that has been used to justify anti-Black and anti-immigrant views, as well as the subordination of women.

dissenting, disagreed with the claim that "the application of the best interests of the child standard is always unconstitutional in third-party visitation cases" and would have remanded for further proceedings. Justice Stevens, dissenting, argued that "the Due Process Clause of the Fourteenth Amendment leaves room for States to consider the impact on a child of possibly arbitrary parental decisions that neither serve nor are motivated by the best interests of the child." Justice Scalia, dissenting, argued that *Meyer, Pierce,* and Wisconsin v. Yoder, 406 U.S. 205 (1972), were wrongly decided. "While I would not now overrule those earlier cases (that has not been urged), neither would I extend the theory upon which they rested to this new context." Justice Thomas, concurring in the judgment, stated that the case was controlled by *Pierce,* but noted "that neither party has argued that our substantive due process cases were wrongly decided and that the original understanding of the Due Process Clause precludes judicial enforcement of unenumerated rights under that constitutional provision."

Note that none of the Justices argued that the grandparents in this case—the Troxels—had *Meyer* and *Pierce* rights to have a say over the raising of their grandchildren. Why not? (Compare Moore v. City of East Cleveland.) What should be constitutionally necessary for a person to have such rights? Is it possible for more than one set of persons to have *Meyer* and *Pierce* rights? If so, how should the courts arbitrate between them?

III. REPRODUCTIVE RIGHTS AND ABORTION

A. The Decision in Roe v. Wade

Throughout this book, we have noted the complex interaction between Supreme Court decisions and social and political change. Supreme Court decisions about abortion provide yet another example.

At the founding, abortion was lawful. The common law allowed abortion in the early months of pregnancy, and states followed the common law until the mid-nineteenth century. By the post-Civil War period, however, many states had enacted laws criminalizing abortion and contraception.[30] But this law was erratically enforced. Some doctors liberally interpreted provisions allowing abortion to save a woman's life. Access to abortion was largely divided by socioeconomic class, leading a public health official to say that the difference between a legal abortion and an illegal one was "$300 and knowing the right person."[31] By the 1960s, public opinion about abortion had begun to shift, spurring first calls for law reform, and later calls for constitutional change.

---

30. See generally James C. Mohr, Abortion in America: The Origins and Evolution of National Policy, 1800-1900 (1978).

31. Mary Steichen Calderone [medical director of Planned Parenthood], Illegal Abortion as a Public Health Problem, 50 Am. J. Pub. Health 948, 959 (1960) (quoting a public health official). See also David J. Garrow, Abortion Before and After Roe v. Wade: An Historical Perspective, 62 Alb. L. Rev. 833, 834, 836, 837 (1999).

Several movements and interest groups argued for reforming abortion laws, on very different grounds.[32] The medical profession played an early role in advocating reform. Doctors sought freedom to practice medicine; many sought to eliminate criminal liability for acting in what they judged to be their patients' best interests. These doctors, and others in public health, blamed criminal abortion laws for unsafe abortions. They emphasized that the burdens of criminalization were unequally distributed by class. Criminalization of abortion affected all women of childbearing age; but poor women suffered in ways that wealthy women often did not. In this period, severely disabled children born to women who had been exposed to thalidomide and to the measles during pregnancy dramatized the importance of making abortion available even to women who sought to become mothers.[33]

As the public came increasingly to support medical arguments for reforming abortion laws, new advocates entered the debate, who offered very different justifications for reform or repeal. Environmentalists emphasized limits on natural resources as a reason for population control; population control supplied a new framework in which to talk about non-procreative sex as a public good. By the end of the 1960s, sexual liberation movements and a newly mobilizing women's movement pressed for the repeal of laws criminalizing abortion.

Feminists asserted that repeal of laws criminalizing abortion was a necessary step in securing women's full participation in economic and political life.[34] In feminist arguments for repeal, control over decisions concerning motherhood was the practical and symbolic site of empowerment for women. Betty Friedan, founding president of the National Organization for Women, was one of the first to voice this new perspective on abortion in 1969, and to express arguments for change as claiming a fundamental civil right:[35]

> . . . There are certain rights that have never been defined as rights, that are essential to equality for women, and they were not defined in the Constitution of this, or any country, when that Constitution was written only by men. The right of woman to control her reproductive process must be established as a basic and valuable human civil right not to be denied or abridged by the state.

---

32. See Jack M. Balkin, Roe v. Wade: An Engine of Controversy, in What Roe v. Wade Should Have Said: America's Top Legal Experts Rewrite America's Most Controversial Decision (Jack M. Balkin ed., 2005).

33. See Mark Graber, Rethinking Abortion: Equal Choice, the Constitution, and Reproductive Politics 41-64 (1996); Linda Greenhouse and Reva B. Siegel, Before (and After) Roe v. Wade: New Questions About Backlash, 120 Yale L.J. 2028, 2036-2038 (2011).

34. Greenhouse and Siegel, Before (and After) Roe v. Wade, supra n.33, at 2038-2041. For feminist arguments of the era, see Reva B. Siegel, Roe's Roots: The Women's Rights Claims That Engendered Roe, 90 B.U. L. Rev. 1875 (2010). For advocates invoking feminism as a reason for *opposing* abortion reform, see Mary Ziegler, Women's Rights on the Right: The History and Stakes of Modern Pro-Life Feminism, 28 Berkeley J. Gender L. & Just. 232 (2013).

35. Betty Friedan, President, Nat'l Org. for Women, Address at the First National Conference on Abortion Laws: Abortion: A Woman's Civil Right (Feb. 1969), reprinted in Before Roe v. Wade: Voices That Shaped the Abortion Debate Before the Supreme Court's Ruling 38, 39 (Linda Greenhouse & Reva B. Siegel eds., 2d ed. 2012).

These diverse calls for reform and repeal of criminal bans on abortion provoked opposition. Concerned that any dilution of the criminal prohibition on abortion—even passage of ALI reform statutes creating exceptions for health of the mother, rape, or fetal anomaly—was a threat to life, the Catholic Church began to provide national support to those seeking to prevent abortion reform as early as 1967.[36] By the early 1970s, a Catholic-led bloc of voters was strong enough to block reform in legislative contests around the country,[37] despite growing popular support for decriminalization of abortion.[38]

By the early 1970s, opposition to abortion began to flow from yet a new source, as the abortion issue became entangled in the competition of political parties for voters. During the 1972 election, strategists for the Republican Party who observed Catholic-led mobilization on abortion began to consider whether abortion could be used to recruit Catholics, who traditionally voted for Democrats, to the ranks of the Republican Party. Even though Republicans in this era were more inclined to support abortion reform than were Democrats, President Nixon began to incorporate anti-abortion appeals to Catholics into his reelection campaign. The campaign recognized other advantages in attacking abortion. As feminists mobilized for abortion rights, the Nixon campaign began to attack abortion as a more general symbol for threats to traditional values, associating abortion with permissive sexual norms,

---

36. Greenhouse and Siegel, Before (and After) Roe v. Wade, supra n.33, at 2047-2052.

37. By the early 1970s, "abortion had become a public and controversial enough concern that it had become increasingly difficult to pass legislative initiatives." Gene Burns, The Moral Veto: Framing Contraception, Abortion, and Cultural Pluralism in the United States 218 (2005). In the years immediately after decriminalization in New York, "public opinion polls showed better than 60 percent popular support for the 1970 law, but the intensity and commitment of abortion opponents had more than offset the majority sentiment." David J. Garrow, Liberty and Sexuality: The Right to Privacy and the Making of Roe v. Wade 546-547 (1994). For state contests, see David J. Garrow, Abortion Before and After Roe v. Wade: An Historical Perspective, 62 Alb. L. Rev. 833, 836-837, 840-841 (1999); Greenhouse and Siegel, Before (and After) Roe v. Wade, supra n.33, at 2078 n.175; Corinna Barrett Lain, Upside-Down Judicial Review, 101 Geo. L.J. 113, 139-141 (2012) (observing that "the state legislative stance on abortion in the early 1970s was more a testament to the power of an intensely committed right-to-life lobby than a reflection of majority will").

38. In June 1972, the Gallup Organization conducted a nationwide poll on attitudes toward abortion. George Gallup's syndicated article describing the poll results was published in the Washington Post on August 25, 1972, and was carried in other newspapers throughout the country. The results showed substantial majorities in all demographic categories, including Catholics, in favor of leaving the abortion decision up to a woman and her doctor. The Gallup poll reported that more Republicans than Democrats were in favor of liberalized abortion laws, an outcome that likely reflected the fact that most Catholics in 1972 identified themselves as Democrats; a majority of Catholics supported abortion reform, but by a closer margin than Protestants. Presumably, those Justices who were at home in Washington, or who read an American newspaper elsewhere, were aware of this poll. Clearly, Justice Blackmun was; a copy of the Washington Post article reporting the poll results was in his Roe v. Wade file. The following percentages of those surveyed agreed with the statement that "[t]he decision to have an abortion should be made solely by a woman and her physician": men (63%); women (64%); Protestants (65%); Catholics (56%); Republicans (68%); total (64%). George Gallup, Abortion Seen Up to Woman, Doctor (1972), reprinted in Greenhouse and Siegel, Before Roe v. Wade, supra n.35, at 207.

women's liberation, the youth movement, draft evasion, and drugs.[39] (The attack on abortion as a threat to traditional values anticipated the "pro-family" frame that the Republicans would employ later in the decade.)

Initially, arguments about how the regulation of abortion implicated values of life, liberty, and equality unfolded in legislative arenas. By the early 1970s, however, with popular support rising but opposition strong enough to block legislative change, advocates increasingly brought their claims to courts. Lawyers first raised constitutional challenges to abortion laws in defending doctors charged with exceeding the scope of their authority under criminal abortion bans.[40] But when legislative reform stalled in states such as Connecticut, lawyers brought constitutional cases challenging abortion laws on behalf of women as well as the doctors who worked with them. Feminist lawyers argued that the right to decide whether to bear a child raised issues of health, sex, family, and work fundamental to women's liberty and equality. Right-to-life advocates passionately defended laws criminalizing abortion as necessary to protect unborn life; in New York they challenged legislation decriminalizing abortion as unconstitutional.[41] Cases had been filed in many states by the time the Court heard constitutional arguments as part of Roe v. Wade.

Roe v. Wade

410 U.S. 113 (1973)

[An unmarried pregnant woman and others brought a class action challenging the constitutionality of the Texas criminal abortion laws, which prohibited procuring or attempting an abortion except for the purpose of saving the mother's life. A three-judge district court granted declaratory relief, holding that the statutes infringed plaintiff's rights protected by the Ninth Amendment.]

BLACKMUN, J.

I

The Texas statutes that concern us here . . . make it a crime to "procure an abortion," . . . or to attempt one, except with respect to "an abortion procured or attempted by medical advice for the purpose of saving the life of the mother." Similar statutes are in existence in a majority of the States. . . .

VI

"It is undisputed that at the common law, abortion performed *before* 'quickening'—the first recognizable movement of the fetus in utero, appearing usually from the 16th to the 18th week of pregnancy—was not an indictable

39. Greenhouse and Siegel, Before (and After) Roe v. Wade, supra n.33, at 2052-2058; Daniel K. Williams, The GOP's Abortion Strategy: Why Pro-Choice Republicans Became Pro-Life in the 1970s, 23 J. Pol. Hist. 513, 517-524 (2011).

40. See, e.g., United States v. Vuitch, 402 U.S. 62 (1971).

41. For documents from all sides of the conflict in New York and Connecticut, see Greenhouse and Siegel, Before Roe v. Wade, supra n.35, at 127-196.

offense." Coke and Blackstone wrote that abortion after quickening was a crime, and this view was uncritically adopted by American courts. But "[whether] abortion of a *quick* fetus was a felony at common law, or even a lesser crime" now appears "doubtful." Abortion was made a statutory crime in England in 1803. The first statute distinguished between abortion before and after quickening, with lighter penalties for the former, but later statutes dropped the distinction. The English Abortion Act of 1967 permits abortions when, inter alia, "the continuance of the pregnancy would involve risks to the . . . physical or mental health of the pregnant woman or any existing children of her family," taking account of her "actual or reasonably foreseen environment."

. . . In this country, the law in effect in all but a few States until mid-19th century was the pre-existing English common law. . . . In 1828, New York enacted legislation that, in two respects, was to serve as a model for early anti-abortion statutes. First, while barring destruction of an unquickened fetus as well as a quick fetus, it made the former only a misdemeanor, but the latter second-degree manslaughter. Second, it incorporated a concept of therapeutic abortion by providing that an abortion was excused if it "shall have been necessary to preserve the life of such mother, or shall have been advised by two physicians to be necessary for such purpose." By 1840, when Texas had received the common law, only eight American States had statutes dealing with abortion. It was not until after the War Between the States that legislation began generally to replace the common law. Most of these initial statutes dealt severely with abortion after quickening but were lenient with it before quickening. . . .

Gradually, in the middle and late 19th century the quickening distinction disappeared from the statutory law of most States and the degree of the offense and the penalties were increased. By the end of the 1950s, a large majority of the jurisdictions banned abortion, however and whenever performed, unless done to save or preserve the life of the mother. . . . In the past several years, however, a trend toward liberalization of abortion statute s has resulted in adoption, by about one-third of the States, of less stringent laws, most of them patterned after the ALI Model Penal Code, §230.3.[42]

It is thus apparent that at common law, at the time of the adoption of our Constitution, and throughout the major portion of the 19th century, abortion was viewed with less disfavor than under most American statutes currently in effect. Phrasing it another way, a woman enjoyed a substantially broader right to terminate a pregnancy than she does in most States today. At least with respect to the early stage of pregnancy, and very possibly without such a limitation, the opportunity to

---

42. Section 230.3 reads:

(1) *Unjustified Abortion.* A person who purposely and unjustifiably terminates the pregnancy of another otherwise than by a live birth commits a felony of the third degree or, where the pregnancy has continued beyond the twenty-sixth week, a felony of the second degree.
(2) *Justifiable Abortion.* A licensed physician is justified in terminating a pregnancy if he believes there is substantial risk that continuance of the pregnancy would gravely impair the physical or mental health of the mother or that the child would be born with grave physical or mental defect, or that the pregnancy resulted from rape, incest, or other felonious intercourse. All illicit intercourse with a girl below the age of 16 shall be deemed felonious for purposes of this subsection.

make this choice was present in this country well into the 19th century. Even later, the law continued for some time to treat less punitively an abortion procured in early pregnancy. . . .

[Finally, Justice Blackmun discusses the views of the American Medical Association, the American Public Health Association, and the American Bar Association: "The anti-abortion mood prevalent in this country in the late 19th century was shared by the medical profession. Indeed, the attitude of the profession may have played a significant role in the enactment of stringent criminal abortion legislation during the period." By 1970, however, an AMA committee noted that the profession was polarized and that there had been a remarkable shift of views "felt to be influenced 'by the rapid changes in state law and by the judicial decisions which tend to make abortion more freely available.' . . ." The AMA House of Delegates adopted statements emphasizing "'the best interests of the patient,' 'sound clinical judgment,' and 'informed patient consent,' in contrast to 'mere acquiescence to the patient's demand.'" In 1970 the Executive Board of the APHA adopted standards providing, inter alia, that "rapid and simple abortion referral must be readily available through state and local public health departments, medical societies, or other nonprofit organizations." And in 1972 the ABA House of Delegates approved the quite liberal Uniform Abortion Act.]

VII

Three reasons have been advanced to explain historically the enactment of criminal abortion laws in the 19th century and to justify their continued existence.

It has been argued occasionally that these laws were the product of a Victorian social concern to discourage illicit sexual conduct. Texas, however, does not advance this justification in the present case, and it appears that no court or commentator has taken the argument seriously. . . .

A second reason is concerned with abortion as a medical procedure. When most criminal abortion laws were first enacted, the procedure was a hazardous one for the woman. . . . Thus, it has been argued that a State's real concern in enacting a criminal abortion law was to protect the pregnant woman, that is, to restrain her from submitting to a procedure that placed her life in serious jeopardy.

Modern medical techniques have altered this situation. Appellants and various amici refer to medical data indicating that abortion in early pregnancy, that is, prior to the end of the first trimester, although not without its risk, is now relatively safe. Mortality rates for women undergoing early abortions, where the procedure is legal, appear to be as low as or lower than the rates for normal childbirth. Consequently, any interest of the State in protecting the woman from an inherently hazardous procedure, except when it would be equally dangerous for her to forgo it, has largely disappeared. Of course, important state interests in the area of health and medical standards do remain. The State has a legitimate interest in seeing to it that abortion, like any other medical procedure, is performed under circumstances that insure maximum safety for the patient. This interest obviously extends at least to the performing physician and his staff, to the facilities involved, to the availability of after-care, and to adequate provision for any complication or emergency that might arise. The prevalence of high mortality rates at illegal "abortion mills" strengthens, rather than weakens, the State's interest in regulating the conditions under which abortions are performed. Moreover, the risk to the woman increases as her pregnancy continues. Thus, the State retains a definite interest in protecting the woman's own health and safety when an abortion is proposed at a late stage of pregnancy.

The third reason is the State's interest—some phrase it in terms of duty—in protecting prenatal life. Some of the argument for this justification rests on the theory that a new human life is present from the moment of conception. The State's interest and general obligation to protect life then extends, it is argued, to prenatal life. Only when the life of the pregnant mother herself is at stake, balanced against the life she carries within her, should the interest of the embryo or fetus not prevail. Logically, of course, a legitimate state interest in this area need not stand or fall on acceptance or the belief that life begins at conception or at some other point prior to live birth. In assessing the State's interest, recognition may be given to the less rigid claim that as long as at least *potential* life is involved, the State may assert interests beyond the protection of the pregnant woman alone. . . .

It is with these interests, and the weight to be attached to them, that this case is concerned.

VIII

The Constitution does not explicitly mention any right of privacy. In a [long] line of decisions, however, . . . the Court has recognized that a right of personal privacy, or a guarantee of certain areas or zones of privacy, does exist under the Constitution. In varying contexts, the Court or individual Justices have, indeed, found at least the roots of that right in the First Amendment; in the penumbras of the Bill of Rights; in the Ninth Amendment; or in the concept of liberty guaranteed by the first section of the Fourteenth Amendment. These decisions make it clear that only personal rights that can be deemed "fundamental" or "implicit in the concept of ordered liberty," Palko v. Connecticut, are included in this guarantee of personal privacy. They also make it clear that the right has some extension to activities relating to marriage, Loving v. Virginia; procreation, Skinner v. Oklahoma; contraception, Eisenstadt v. Baird; family relationships, Prince v. Massachusetts; and child rearing and education, Pierce v. Society of Sisters, Meyer v. Nebraska.

This right of privacy, whether it be founded in the Fourteenth Amendment's concept of personal liberty and restrictions upon state action, as we feel it is, or, as the District Court determined, in the Ninth Amendment's reservation of rights to the people, is broad enough to encompass a woman's decision whether or not to terminate her pregnancy. The detriment that the State would impose upon the pregnant woman by denying this choice altogether is apparent. Specific and direct harm medically diagnosable even in early pregnancy may be involved. Maternity, or additional offspring, may force upon the woman a distressful life and future. Psychological harm may be imminent. Mental and physical health may be taxed by child care. There is also the distress, for all concerned, associated with the unwanted child; and there is the problem of bringing a child into a family already unable, psychologically and otherwise, to care for it. In other cases, as in this one, the additional difficulties and continuing stigma of unwed motherhood may be involved. All these are factors the woman and her responsible physician necessarily will consider in consultation.

On the basis of elements such as these, appellant and some amici argue that the woman's right is absolute and that she is entitled to terminate her pregnancy at whatever time, in whatever way, and for whatever reason she alone chooses. With this we do not agree. Appellant's arguments that Texas either has no valid interest at all in regulating the abortion decision, or no interest strong enough to support any limitation upon the woman's sole determination, is unpersuasive. The Court's decisions recognizing a right of privacy also acknowledge that some state regulation in areas protected by that right is appropriate. As noted above, a State may properly assert important interests in safeguarding health, in maintaining medical standards, and in protecting potential life. At some point in pregnancy, these respective interests become sufficiently compelling to sustain regulation of the factors that govern the abortion decision. The privacy right involved, therefore, cannot be said to be absolute. . . .

We, therefore, conclude that the right of personal privacy includes the abort ion decision, but that this right is not unqualified and must be considered against important state interests in regulation. . . .

Where certain "fundamental rights" are involved, the Court has held that regulation limiting these rights may be justified only by a "compelling state interest," . . . and that legislative enactments must be narrowly drawn to express only the legitimate state interests at stake. . . .

IX

. . . The appellee and certain amici argue that the fetus is a "person" within the language and meaning of the Fourteenth Amendment. In support of this, they outline at length and in detail the well-known facts of fetal development. If this suggestion of personhood is established, the appellant's case, of course, collapses, for the fetus' right to life is then guaranteed specifically by the Amendment. . . . [However, no case] holds that a fetus is a person within the meaning of the Fourteenth Amendment.

The Constitution does not define "person" in so many words. Section 1 of the Fourteenth Amendment contains three references to "person." The first, in defining "citizens," speaks of "persons born or naturalized in the United States." The word also appears both in the Due Process Clause and in the Equal Protection Clause. "Person" is used in other places in the Constitution. . . . But in nearly all these instances, the use of the word is such that it has application only postnatally. None indicates, with any assurance, that it has any possible prenatal application.[a]

All this, together with our observation, supra, that throughout the major portion of the 19th century prevailing legal abortion practices were far freer than they are today, persuades us that the word "person," as used in the Fourteenth Amendment, does not include the unborn. . . .

---

a When Texas urges that a fetus is entitled to Fourteenth Amendment protection as a person, it faces a dilemma. Neither in Texas nor in any other State are all abortions prohibited. Despite broad proscription, an exception always exists. The exception . . . for an abortion procured or attempted by medical advice for the purpose of saving the life of the mother, is typical. But if the fetus is a person who is not to be deprived of life without due process of law, and if the mother's condition is the sole determinant, does not the Texas exception appear to be out of line with the Amendment's command?

This conclusion, however, does not of itself fully answer the contentions raised by Texas . . . The pregnant woman cannot be isolated in her privacy. She carries an embryo and, later, a fetus, if one accepts the medical definitions of the developing young in the human uterus. The situation therefore is inherently different from marital intimacy, or bedroom possession of obscene material, or marriage, or procreation, or education, with which *Eisenstadt, Griswold, Stanley, Loving, Skinner, Pierce,* and *Meyer* were respectively concerned. As we have intimated above, it is reasonable and appropriate for a State to decide that at some point in time another interest, that of health of the mother or that of potential human life, becomes significantly involved. The woman's privacy is no longer sole and any right of privacy she possesses must be measured accordingly.

Texas urges that, apart from the Fourteenth Amendment, life begins at conception and is present throughout pregnancy, and that, therefore, the State has a compelling interest in protecting that life from and after conception. We need not resolve the difficult question of when life begins. When those trained in the respective disciplines of medicine, philosophy, and theology are unable to arrive at any consensus, the judiciary, at this point in the development of man's knowledge, is not in a position to speculate as to the answer. . . .

It should be sufficient to note briefly the wide divergence of thinking on this most sensitive and difficult question. . . . As we have noted, the common law found greater significance in quickening. Physicians and their scientific colleagues have regarded that event with less interest and have tended to focus either upon conception, upon live birth, or upon the interim point at which the fetus becomes "viable," that is, potentially able to live outside the mother's womb, albeit with artificial aid. Viability is usually placed at about seven months (28 weeks) but may occur earlier, even at 24 weeks. The Aristotelian theory of "mediate animation," that held sway throughout the Middle Ages and the Renaissance in Europe, continued to be official Roman Catholic dogma until the 19th century, despite opposition to this "ensoulment" theory from those in the Church who would recognize the existence of life from the moment of conception. The latter is now, of course, the official belief of the Catholic Church. As one of the briefs amicus discloses, this is a view strongly held by many non-Catholics as well, and by many physicians. Substantial problems for precise definition of this view are posed, however, by new embryological data that purport to indicate that conception is a "process" over time; rather than an event, and by new medical techniques such as menstrual extraction, the "morning-after" pill, implantation of embryos, artificial insemination, and even artificial wombs.

In areas other than criminal abortion, the law has been reluctant to endorse any theory that life, as we recognize it, begins before live birth or to accord legal rights to the unborn except in narrowly defined situations and except when the rights are contingent upon live birth. For example, the traditional rule of tort law denied recovery for prenatal injuries even though the child was born alive. That rule has been changed in almost every jurisdiction. In most States, recovery is said to be permitted only if the fetus was viable, or at least quick, when the injuries were sustained, though few courts have squarely so held. In a recent development, generally opposed by the commentators, some States permit the parents of a stillborn child to maintain an action for wrongful death because of prenatal injuries. Such an action, however, would appear to be one to vindicate the parents' interest and is thus consistent with the view that the fetus, at most, represents only the potentiality of life. Similarly, unborn children have been recognized as acquiring rights or interests by way of inheritance or other devolution of property, and have been represented by guardians ad litem. Perfection of the interests involved, again, has generally been contingent upon live birth. In short, the unborn have never been recognized in the law as persons in the whole sense.

X

In view of all this, we do not agree that, by adopting one theory of life, Texas may override the rights of the pregnant woman that are at stake. We repeat, however, that the State does have an important and legitimate interest in preserving and protecting the health of the pregnant woman, whether she be a resident of the State or a nonresident who seeks medical consultation and treatment there, and that it has still *another* important and legitimate interest in protecting the potentiality of human life. These interests are separate, and distinct. Each grows in substantiality as the woman approaches term and, at a point during pregnancy, each becomes "compelling."

With respect to the State's important and legitimate interest in the health of the mother, the "compelling" point, in the light of present medical knowledge, is at approximately the end of the first trimester. This is so because of the now established medical fact . . . that until the end of the first trimester mortality in abortion may be less than mortality in normal childbirth. It follows that, from and after this point, a State may regulate the abortion procedure to the extent that the regulation reasonably relates to the preservation and protection of maternal health. Examples of permissible state regulation in this area are requirements as to the qualifications of the person who is to perform the abortion; as to the licensure of that person; as to the facility in which the procedure is to be performed, that is, whether it must be a hospital or may be a clinic or some other place of less-than-hospital status; as to the licensing of the facility; and the like.

This means, on the other hand, that, for the period of pregnancy prior to this "compelling" point, the attending physician, in consultation with his patient, is free to determine, without regulation by the State, that, in his medical judgment, the patient's pregnancy should be terminated. If that decision is reached, the judgment may be effectuated by an abortion free of interference by the State.

With respect to the State's important and legitimate interest in potential life, the "compelling" point is at viability. This is so because the fetus then presumably has the capability of meaningful life outside the mother's womb. State regulation protective of fetal life after viability thus has both logical and biological justifications. If the State is interested in protecting fetal life after viability, it may go so far as to proscribe abortion during that period, except when it is necessary to preserve the life or health of the mother.

Measured against these standards, . . . the Texas Penal Code, in restricting legal abortions to those "procured or attempted by medical advice for the purpose of saving the life of the mother," sweeps too broadly. The statute makes no distinction between abortions performed early in pregnancy and those performed later, and it limits to a single reason, "saving" the mother's life, the legal justification for the procedure. The statute, therefore, cannot survive the constitutional attack made upon it here. . . .

XI

To summarize and to repeat:

1. A state criminal abortion statute of the current Texas type, that excepts from criminality only a *lifesaving* procedure on behalf of the mother, without regard to pregnancy stage and without recognition of the other interests involved, is violative of the Due Process Clause of the Fourteenth Amendment.

(a) For the stage prior to approximately the end of the first trimester, the abortion decision and its effectuation must be left to the medical judgment of the pregnant woman's attending physician.

(b) For the stage subsequent to approximately the end of the first trimester, the State, in promoting its interest in the health of the mother, may, if it chooses, regulate the abortion procedure in ways that are reasonably related to maternal health.

(c) For the stage subsequent to viability, the State in promoting its interest in the potentiality of human life may, if it chooses, regulate, and even proscribe, abortion except where it is necessary, in appropriate medical judgment, for the preservation of the life or health of the mother.

2. The State may define the term "physician" . . . to mean only a physician currently licensed by the State, and may proscribe any abortion by a person who is not a physician as so defined.

In Doe v. Bolton, . . . procedural requirements contained in one of the modern abortion statutes are considered. That opinion and this one, of course, are to be read together.[b]

This holding, we feel, is consistent with the relative weights of the respective interests involved, with the lessons and examples of medical and legal history, with the lenity of the common law, and with the demands of the profound problems of the present day. The decision leaves the State free to place increasing restrictions on abortion as the period of pregnancy lengthens, so long as those restrictions are tailored to the recognized state interests. The decision vindicated the right of the physician to administer medical treatment according to his professional judgment up to the points where important state interests provide compelling justifications for intervention. Up to those points, the abortion decision in all its aspects is inherently, and primarily, a medical decision, and basic responsibility for it must rest with the physician. . . .

---

b Neither in this opinion nor in Doe v. Bolton do we discuss the father's rights, if any exist in the constitutional context, in the abortion decision. No paternal right has been asserted in either of the cases, and the Texas and the Georgia statutes on their face take no cognizance of the father. We are aware that some statutes recognize the father under certain circumstances. North Carolina, for example, requires written permission for the abortion from the husband when the woman is a married minor, that is, when she is less than 18 years of age: if the woman is an unmarried minor, written permission from the parents is required. We need not now decide whether provisions of this kind are constitutional.

[Chief Justice Burger, concurring in the companion case of Doe v. Bolton, stated that "[p]lainly, the Court today rejects any claim that the Constitution requires abortions on demand." Justice Douglas and Stewart both wrote concurring opinions.]

REHNQUIST, J., dissenting. . . .

I have difficulty in concluding, as the Court does, that the right of "privacy" is involved in this case. . . . The Due Process Clause of the Fourteenth Amendment undoubtedly does place a limit, albeit a broad one, on legislative power to enact laws such as this. If the Texas statute were to prohibit an abortion even where the mother's life is in jeopardy, I have little doubt that such a statute would lack a rational relation to a valid state objective under the test stated in *Williamson [v. Lee Optical]*. But the Court's sweeping invalidation of any restrictions on abortion during the first trimester is impossible to justify under that standard, and the conscious weighing of competing factors that the Court's opinion apparently substitutes for the established test is far more appropriate to a legislative judgment than to a judicial one. . . .

While the Court's opinion quotes from the dissent of Mr. Justice Holmes in Lochner v. New York, the result it reaches is more closely attuned to the majority opinion of Mr. Justice Peckham in that case. As in *Lochner* and similar cases applying substantive due process standards to economic and social welfare legislation, the adoption of the compelling state interest standard will inevitably require this Court to examine the legislative policies and pass on the wisdom of these policies in the very process of deciding whether a particular state interest put forward may or may not be "compelling." The decision here to break pregnancy into three distinct terms and to outline the permissible restrictions the State may impose in each one, for example, partakes more of judicial legislation than it does of a determination of the intent of the drafters of the Fourteenth Amendment.

The fact that a majority of the States reflecting, after all, the majority sentiment in those States, have had restrictions on abortions for at least a century is a strong indication, it seems to me, that the asserted right to an abortion is not "so rooted in the traditions and conscience of our people as to be ranked as fundamental." . . .

There apparently was no question concerning the validity of [the Texas] or of any of the other state statutes when the Fourteenth Amendment was adopted. The only conclusion possible from this history is that the drafters did not intend to have the Fourteenth Amendment withdraw from the States the power to legislate with respect to this matter. . . .

WHITE, J., joined by REHNQUIST, J., dissenting [in Doe v. Bolton].

At the heart of the controversy in these cases are those recurring pregnancies that pose no danger whatsoever to the life or health of the mother but are, nevertheless, unwanted for any one or more of a variety of reasons—convenience, family planning, economics, dislike of children, the embarrassment of illegitimacy, etc. The common claim before us is that for any one of such reasons, or for no reason at all, and without asserting or claiming any threat to life or health, any woman is entitled to an abortion at her request if she is able to find a medical advisor willing to undertake the procedure. . . .

With all due respect, I dissent. I find nothing in the language or history of the Constitution to support the Court's judgment. The Court simply fashions and announces a new constitutional right for pregnant mothers and, with scarcely any reason or authority for its action, invests that right with sufficient substance to override most existing state abortion statutes. The upshot is that the people and the legislatures of the 50 States are constitutionally disentitled to weigh the relative importance of the continued existence and development of the fetus, on the one hand, against a spectrum of possible impacts on the mother, on the other hand. . . .

The Court apparently values the convenience of the pregnant mother more than the continued existence and development of the life or potential life that she carries. Whether or not I might agree with that marshaling of values, I can in no event join the Court's judgment because I find no constitutional warrant for imposing such an order of priorities on the people and legislatures of the States. In a sensitive area such as this, involving as it does issues over which reasonable men may easily and heatedly differ, I cannot accept the Court's exercise of its clear power of choice by interposing a constitutional barrier to state efforts to protect human life and by investing mothers and doctors with the constitutionally protected right to exterminate it. This issue, for the most part, should be left with the people and to the political processes the people have devised to govern their affairs. . . .

DOE v. BOLTON, 410 U.S. 179 (1973): *Doe*, the companion case to *Roe*, considered the constitutionality of Georgia's abortion reform statute, passed in 1968, and based on the Model Penal Code. The Court, in an opinion by Justice Blackmun, invalidated various procedural provisions of the Georgia abortion statute.

First, the Georgia statute required that all abortions, even in the earliest phases of pregnancy, be performed in hospitals as opposed to less expensive abortion clinics. The Court held this was invalid with respect to abortions performed in the first trimester.

Second, Georgia required that hospitals that performed abortions have special accreditation requirements separate from those for hospitals not specifically connected to abortion practice and not required for hospitals performing any other kind of surgery. Justice Blackmun struck this down on the grounds that "the State must show more than it has in order to prove that only the full resources of a licensed hospital, rather than those of some other appropriately licensed institution, satisfy these health interests."

Third, Georgia required prior permission of special hospital staff committees, as well as independent examinations by two other physicians; it did not apply these restrictions to any other surgical procedures. The Court rejected the staff committee requirement as "unduly restrictive of the patient's rights and needs that, at this point, have already been medically delineated and substantiated by her personal physician." It also struck down the independent examination requirement: "[N]o other voluntary medical or surgical procedure for which Georgia requires confirmation by two other physicians has been cited to us. If a physician is licensed by the State, he is recognized by the State as capable of exercising acceptable clinical judgment. If he fails in this, professional censure and deprivation of his license are available remedies. Required acquiescence by co-practitioners has no rational connection with a patient's needs and unduly infringes on the physician's right to practice."

Fourth, Georgia limited abortions to residents of the state. The Court held that this violated the Privileges and Immunities Clause, Const. Article IV, §2. "Just as [the Clause] protects persons who enter other States to ply their trade, so must it protect persons who enter Georgia seeking the medical services that are available there. A contrary holding would mean that a State could limit to its own residents the general medical care available within its borders."

DISCUSSION

1. *The trimester framework. Roe* reasoned that decisions concerning abortion were protected by the right to privacy. But the Court also recognized for the first time a government interest in protecting potential life. How does the trimester framework coordinate the relationship between the citizen's constitutional right and the state's regulatory interests?

2. *The right of privacy—family life and sexual freedom. Roe*'s argument draws upon previous cases recognizing a right of privacy: *Meyer, Pierce, Skinner, Griswold, Eisenstadt,* Loving v. Virginia (which recognized a fundamental right to marry), and Prince v. Massachusetts, 321 U.S. 158 (1944), which upheld a child labor law in the course of reaffirming the principle that there is a "private realm of family life which the state cannot enter." Is there a coherent conception of a right of privacy that explains the Court's decision in these cases? How would you describe this right? Is it the right to be free from state interference in family life? The right to decide whether and how to raise children?

Might these cases protect sexual freedom as well as family life? In Part VII of *Roe,* Justice Blackmun observes that nineteenth-century abortion laws may have been "the product of a Victorian social concern to discourage illicit sexual conduct" but "Texas . . . does not advance this justification in the present case, and it appears that no court or commentator has taken the argument seriously. . . ." Is the Court here suggesting that the state's interest in enforcing sexual morality is not a constitutionally sufficient reason to restrict a woman's decision whether to carry a pregnancy to term? Would that also mean that sexual expression is constitutionally protected? Under what circumstances? Justice Brennan reflected on this passage in *Roe* in a section of his opinion in *Carey,* supra, that commanded only four votes. Carey v. Population Services, 431 U.S. 678, 694-695 (1977) (discussing *Roe* and *Eisenstadt* and whether government can prescribe pregnancy, the birth of an unwanted child, or the dangers of an abortion "as punishment for fornication").

3. *Components of the right to abortion.*

a. *A dual right.* Consider the possibility that the right to abortion encompasses two different rights. The first is women's "right not to be forced by the state to sacrifice their lives or their health in order to bear children" (a right of bodily integrity). The second is women's "right to decide whether or not to become parents and take on the obligations of motherhood" (a right of decisional autonomy).[43] The first right protects the woman's interest in her body and against its instrumental

---

43. Jack M. Balkin, Judgment of the Court, in What Roe v. Wade Should Have Said, supra n.32, at 45; see also Jack M. Balkin, Abortion and Original Meaning, 24 Const. Comment. 291 (2007).

use by the state for reproductive purposes. The second guards against state interference in a woman's decision whether to assume the social, economic, and legal expectations, obligations, and dependencies that accompany parenthood. These consequences may be more severe for women than for men, as a disproportionate proportion of the responsibilities of childrearing continues to fall upon women. Parenthood may limit a woman's ability to participate fully in public life or to operate outside the traditional roles assigned to women, such that state restrictions on the woman's decision to bear a child constitute restrictions on the woman's present or future liberty. According to *Roe* (and later decisions) the first right to abortion—to protect one's life and health—continues throughout pregnancy, but the second right—to decide whether to become a parent—extends only to viability.

b. *Adoption?* To what extent does the availability of adoption redress interests protected by these rights? Is it sufficiently responsive to both? One? Neither?

4. *Liberty and equality.* Note that abortion restrictions are highly gendered in impact. Abortion restrictions may be gendered in impetus as well; they may reflect not only views about the unborn, but also judgments about women's proper role in society. For these reasons, constitutional objections to restrictions on abortion may sound in sex equality as well as liberty. See Section III.B, Abortion and the Equal Protection Clause, infra.

5. *The fetus as constitutional person. Roe* holds that fetuses are not persons within the meaning of the Fourteenth Amendment. It also holds that states do not have a compelling state interest in protection of potential human life from the moment of conception, but rather may only prevent abortions after the point of viability.

a. Consider Justice Blackmun's textual argument that the word "person" as used in the Fourteenth Amendment does not include the unborn. Could a fetus be a "person" for some legal purposes (due process, equal protection) but not others (the census, the privilege against self-incrimination)? What would be the legal consequences if fetuses were considered persons?[44] Would the fetus have procedural due process rights to a hearing before an abortion could be performed? Would the fetus have substantive due process rights not to be aborted? Would states be required to punish mothers and doctors for performing abortions the same as other persons who committed premeditated (i.e., first-degree) murder, so that if states made murder a crime they would be constitutionally required to outlaw all abortions? Note that, even before Roe v. Wade, no state treated abortion as equivalent, in all respects, with first-degree murder. Why do you think this is?

b. Justice Blackmun states that "[w]e need not resolve the difficult question of when life begins." Is this true? Doesn't the Court need to resolve that issue to some degree in order to hold that Texas's interest in potential life is not compelling from the moment of conception?

---

44. For an argument that the fetus has due process rights not to be aborted, see David Louisell, Abortion, The Practice of Medicine and the Due Process of Law, 16 UCLA L. Rev. 233 (1969). But see Donald Regan, Rewriting Roe v. Wade, 77 Mich. L. Rev. 1569 (1979), arguing that, even if the fetus is considered a person, general common law principles of good samaritanism would justify abortion in many contexts. See also Eileen L. McDonagh, Breaking the Abortion Deadlock: From Choice to Consent (1996) (arguing that a pregnant woman can assert rights of self-defense against a fetus/person threatening her bodily integrity).

In view of the fact that much of the opinion preceding Part X demonstrates the lack of a consensus regarding the medico-ethical issues of abortion, why shouldn't the first sentence of Part X have read as follows:

> In view of all this, we cannot conclude that the Constitution adopts one particular theory of life. Therefore we cannot conclude that the Ninth or Fourteenth Amendment prevents a state from determining that the unborn child's right to life attaches at any point after conception, or that the Constitution precludes a state from making whatever accommodation of the competing interests of the mother and her unborn child it believes appropriate.

c. What is the relation between the Court's holding on fetal personhood and the Court's holding recognizing that the state has an interest in protecting potential life which, over the course of pregnancy, grows sufficiently compelling that the state may constrain women's decisions about abortion?

6. *Preservation of potential life as a compelling state interest.* The Texas statute in *Roe* punished doctors who performed abortions but not the women who sought abortions. The statute also did not punish women who self-aborted. If the state has a compelling interest in the potentiality of human life, what justifies this underinclusiveness?

The Georgia abortion statute in Doe v. Bolton allowed abortions in cases of statutory or forcible rape. Why does the state have a compelling interest in preserving some fetuses (those conceived through consensual sex with women over the age of consent) but not others? Are fetuses conceived through rape or through sex with underage women less human or less deserving of state protection?

Might abortion laws with rape exceptions like Georgia's suggest that the state is less interested in protecting fetal life per se than in establishing women's responsibility for their sexual activity? Laws of this kind seem to be based on the notion that women should be able to end pregnancies they aren't responsible for, and they aren't responsible for their pregnancies when they are underage or have been forcibly raped. (If so, would this mean that women who have been coerced into sex by any means short of what a court would find to be rape are responsible for their pregnancies?)

Do laws that ban abortion with exceptions for rape, incest, fetal deformity, and risks to maternal health undermine a state's claim that it has a compelling interest in the protection of fetal life from the moment of conception that would overcome any fundamental right to abortion? Conversely, would a statute that treated abortion exactly the same as first-degree murder pass a test of strict scrutiny?

7. *Even-handed protection of potential life.* If a state wishes to assert a compelling interest in protecting potential life before birth, must it also protect life after birth, for example, by expenditures on social welfare programs? Even if the state would otherwise have no duty to support children after birth, does it assume this duty if it intervenes to prevent an act of contraception or an abortion? (See the discussion of affirmative rights and *DeShaney* in Chapter 10, infra.)

NOTE: DID *ROE* CAUSE THE ABORTION CONFLICT?

In 1985, (then) Judge Ruth Bader Ginsburg suggested that the Court's decision in *Roe* was unfortunate for the cause of abortion rights. Ruth Bader Ginsburg, Some Thoughts on Autonomy and Equality in Relation to Roe v. Wade,

63 N.C. L. Rev. 375, 376, 381-382 (1985). Contrasting the gender discrimination decisions (many of which she argued before the Supreme Court) with *Roe*, Judge Ginsburg noted:

> The Court's gender classification decisions overturning state and federal legislation, in the main, have not provoked large controversy; . . . Roe v. Wade on the other hand, became and remains a storm center. Roe v. Wade sparked public opposition and academic criticism, in part, I believe, because the Court ventured too far in the change it ordered and presented an incomplete justification for its action. . . .
>
> The sweep and detail of the opinion stimulated the mobilization of a right-to-life movement and an attendant reaction in Congress and state legislatures. In place of the trend "toward liberalization of abortion statutes" noted in *Roe*, legislatures adopted measures aimed at minimizing the impact of the 1973 rulings, including notification and consent requirements, prescriptions for the protection of fetal life, and bans on public expenditures for poor women's abortions.

Ginsburg also criticized the medical focus of the opinion and the trimester formula, arguing that the Court should have limited itself to the question whether complete criminalization of abortion was consistent with the Due Process Clause.

> If *Roe* had left off at that point and not adopted . . . a "medical approach," physicians might have been less pleased with the decision, but the legislative trend might have continued in the direction in which it was headed in the early 1970s. . . . Academic criticism of *Roe*, charging the Court with reading its own values into the due process clause, might have been less pointed had the Court placed the woman alone, rather than the woman tied to her physician, at the center of its attention.

Ginsburg linked "abortion prohibitions with discrimination against women," suggesting that *Roe*'s medicalized account of the abortion right was incomplete:

> It is not a sufficient answer to charge it all to women's anatomy—a natural, not manmade, phenomenon. Society, not anatomy, "places a greater stigma on unmarried women who become pregnant than on the men who father their children." Society expects, but nature does not command, that "women take the major responsibility . . . for child care" and that they will stay with their children, bearing nurture and support burdens alone, when fathers deny paternity or otherwise refuse to provide care or financial support for unwanted offspring.

Nevertheless, Ginsburg added:

> I do not pretend that, if the Court had added a distinct sex discrimination theme to its medically oriented opinion, the storm *Roe* generated would have been less furious.

Speaking seven years later, shortly before she was nominated to the Supreme Court, Judge Ginsburg added:

> [T]he Justices generally follow, they do not lead, changes taking place elsewhere in society. But without taking giant strides and thereby risking a backlash too forceful to contain, the Court, through constitutional adjudication, can reinforce or signal a green light for a social change. In most of the post-1970 gender-classification cases, unlike *Roe*, the Court functioned in just that way. It approved the direction of change through a temperate brand of decisionmaking, one that was not extravagant or divisive. *Roe*, on the other hand, halted a political process that was moving in a reform direction and thereby, I believe, prolonged divisiveness and deferred stable settlement of the issue.[45]

Justice Ginsburg suggested that had the Court issued a much narrower (and equality-themed) opinion, decriminalization of abortion might have occurred legislatively and without significant conflict. Her assumption that the liberalization of abortion law was proceeding legislatively and would have continued had the Court not intervened has been sharply criticized by a number of historians.[46] David Garrow points out that the key triggering event in the creation of a significant right-to-life movement was not the Court's decision in *Roe* but the passage of legislation legalizing abortion in New York State in 1970:[47]

> Prior to the 1970 victory in New York, pro-choice forces had encountered surprisingly little well-organized or outspokenly vocal opposition. The Roman Catholic Church's hierarchy had been relatively inactive on the issue prior to 1970, but the legalization of abortion in New York led to a very rapid mobilization of right-to-life opposition.

Garrow notes that the "fictionalized but nonetheless widely-accepted version of history" is that *Roe* mobilized pro-life forces and that without *Roe* "there supposedly would have been extensive but more gradual abortion law liberalization stemming from less shrill debates in countless state legislatures." This view, he contends, "is simply and utterly wrong":[48]

> Not only did the New York legalization energize right to life forces, [it] helped stimulate a very politically influential right to life upsurge all across the country, in state after state after state, throughout 1971 and 1972. During 1971 and 1972, pro-choice forces won no political victories, and New York activists were worried as to whether they could continue to protect their statute from legislative repeal. . . . In the two states that held 1972 popular vote referenda on abortion, pro-choice measures went down to heavy defeats, and in many others, legislators took the position that they could let the courts resolve the problem, that they did not need

---

45. Ruth Bader Ginsburg, Speaking in a Judicial Voice, 67 N.Y.U. L. Rev. 1185, 1208 (1992). For a more extensive version of the claim that *Roe* blunted liberalization of abortion laws, see Mary Ann Glendon, Abortion and Divorce in Western Law 42-46 (1987).

46. See n.37.

47. David J. Garrow, Abortion Before and After Roe v. Wade: An Historical Perspective, 62 Alb. L. Rev. 833, 836-837, 840-841 (1999).

48. Id. at 841.

> to go out on any political limbs by confronting the issue themselves. Thus, by November 1972, when Richard Nixon was overwhelmingly re-elected to the presidency after mounting a very explicitly anti-abortion general election campaign, prospects for making any sort of non-judicial headway with abortion law liberalization looked very bleak indeed. Pro-choice activists feared that more setbacks might be ahead.

In embracing an anti-abortion position, Nixon was shifting ground, deliberately cultivating a position designed to attract to the ranks of the Republican Party traditionally Democratic-voting Catholics and social conservatives. Republican strategists began experimenting with using abortion to recruit traditional Democratic voters before *Roe*, during the 1972 campaign. However, the strategy was not systematically deployed until the election of Ronald Reagan in 1980—when the Republican Party tied the "pro-life" cause to the "pro-family" movement that grew up in opposition to the Equal Rights Amendment, and when numbers of evangelical Protestants began for the first time to join Catholics in categorically opposing abortion.[49]

DISCUSSION

1. Even if Garrow is correct about the emergence of the right-to-life movement before *Roe*, would he necessarily deny that *Roe* further energized the right-to-life movement, gave it a highly visible national symbol on which to focus its energies, and allowed opposition to abortion rights to be combined with the rhetoric of majority rule and with the long rhetorical tradition of resistance to judicial oversight and judicial elitism? (In this respect, how is *Roe* like or unlike *Brown*, or other controversial judicial decisions protecting individual liberties?)

Does Justice Ginsburg maintain that a Court decision characterizing *Roe* as an equality right for women would have significantly blunted the right-to-life movement or opposition to abortion reform? Recall the conservative reaction to the Equal Rights Amendment discussed in Chapter 8. If *Roe* had been grounded in equality principles, what would have been the likely effect on American politics? Would the switch from liberty to equality have blunted conservative opposition to abortion rights, or exacerbated it? Note that federal courts would still have been overturning state and local abortion regulations. Do you think the political dynamic would have been similar to, or different from, the response to *Brown*?

2. Both the title of Justice Ginsburg's 1992 article (Speaking in a Judicial Voice) and her arguments in that article suggest that she believes that the political effects of Court decisions on legislative reform are appropriate considerations for judges who interpret the Constitution. Do you agree? Would it be permissible for a judge to state such considerations openly in an opinion?

3. Consider the fact that strategists used the abortion issue to shape the modern Republican and Democratic Parties in ways that helped Ronald Reagan gain the presidency and many other pro-life candidates gain political office. Would these developments have occurred without *Roe*? Should *any* of this matter to

---

49. Greenhouse and Siegel, Before (and After) Roe v. Wade, supra n.33, at 2076-2087; Williams, The GOP's Abortion Strategy, supra n.39, at 517-524.

constitutional interpretation? If backlash is attributable in part to judicial decisions, as well as to changes effectuated through legislation, should judges take this into account in deciding cases? How? Do concerns about backlash in *Roe* and in *Brown* present similar or different considerations? Why?

For further discussion of court- and politics-centered accounts of backlash, see the discussion of same-sex marriage, infra Section IV.C.

B. *Abortion and the Equal Protection Clause*

Roe is based on a fundamental rights analysis under the Due Process Clause, not the Equal Protection Clause. Given that abortion rights so clearly affect women, why didn't the Court approach the question in equality terms?

One reason, as noted previously, is that for many years the major proponents of abortion reform were the medical profession and public health groups. Nevertheless, by the late 1960s, a number of feminist advocates had begun to assert reproductive rights claims as equal rights claims. As Chapter 8 recounts, in 1970, on the half-century anniversary of the Nineteenth Amendment's ratification, the movement held a Strike for Equality that sought reform of the conditions in which women bore and raised children. In addition to the ratification of the Equal Rights Amendment (ERA), strike demands included equal education and employment opportunity, abortion rights, and publicly supported child care.

Before *Roe*, feminists seeking abortion rights spoke in the language of liberty and equality. Feminist litigators challenged discrimination against pregnant women as a violation of equal protection, and, invoking various clauses of the Constitution, drew on equality concepts to amplify *Griswold*-based challenges to abortion restrictions.[50]

But it was not easy to advance equality arguments for abortion rights in this period. *Griswold* was decided on privacy grounds, some years before the Court recognized the first sex discrimination claims under the Equal Protection Clause. And, at the time of *Roe*, the Court had handed down only one of its sex discrimination decisions, *Reed*. *Frontiero* was decided the same term as *Roe*. In this period, the women's movement argued that regulation of pregnant women's conduct that enforced sex-role stereotypes violated the Equal Protection Clause,[51] but the Court was not ready to accept the claim. As we have seen, the Court instead built out the equal protection sex discrimination framework in ways that made it difficult to advance claims of pregnancy discrimination, and difficult to express the sex equality argument for abortion rights.

In Chapter 8 we noted the effect of Geduldig v. Aiello, 417 U.S. 484 (1974), and Personnel Administrator of Massachusetts v. Feeney, 442 U.S. 256 (1979), in

---

50. Reva B. Siegel, *Roe*'s Roots: The Women's Rights Claims That Engendered *Roe*, 90 B.U. L. Rev. 1875 (2010); Linda Greenhouse and Reva B. Siegel, The Unfinished Story of Roe v. Wade in Reproductive Rights and Justice Stories 53 (Melissa Murray, Kate Shaw & Reva B. Siegel eds., 2019).

51. Neil Siegel and Reva B. Siegel, Pregnancy and Sex-Role Stereotyping, From *Struck* to *Carhart*, 70 Ohio St. L.J. 1095 (2009).

deflecting equal protection arguments for abortion rights. *Geduldig* holds that classifications based on pregnancy are not necessarily classifications based on sex. *Feeney* holds that facially neutral laws that have a disparate impact on women do not violate equal protection unless one can demonstrate that the decisionmaker acted because of, rather than in spite of, a desire to harm women. Together, *Geduldig* and *Feeney* make it much harder to argue that abortion regulations are sex-based classifications that work to the disadvantage of women.

Nevertheless, once the Court consolidated its major sex discrimination decisions under the Equal Protection Clause, growing numbers of scholars began to argue that the question of abortion rights was fundamentally an issue of sexual equality and therefore might more appropriately be analyzed under equal protection doctrine.[52] For example, Professor Sylvia Law argued:[53]

> The rhetoric of privacy, as opposed to equality, blunts our ability to focus on the fact that it is *women* who are oppressed when abortion is denied. A privacy right that demands that "the abortion decision . . . be left to the medical judgment of the pregnant woman's physician," gives doctors undue power by falsely casting the abortion decision as primarily a medical question. The rhetoric of privacy also reinforces a public/private dichotomy that is at the heart of the structures that perpetuate the powerlessness of women.

The equal protection argument for abortion rights is often based on antisubordination approaches of the kind discussed in Chapters 7 and 8.[54] (Scholars reasoning from this perspective have also been particularly critical of cases like *Geduldig* and *Feeney*.[55])

---

52. See, e.g., Kenneth Karst, Foreword: Equal Citizenship Under the Fourteenth Amendment, 91 Harv. L. Rev. 1 (1977). Professor Laurence Tribe has also recognized the equality implications of *Roe*: "To give society—especially a male-dominated society—the power to sentence women to childbearing against their will is to delegate to some a sweeping and unaccountable authority over the lives of others. Any such allocation of power operates to the serious detriment of women as a class . . . [and] burden[s] the participation of women as equals in society." Tribe, American Constitutional Law 1354 (2d ed. 1988). See also Jed Rubenfeld, The Right of Privacy, 102 Harv. L. Rev. 737, 782 (1989); Guido Calabresi, The Supreme Court, 1990 Term, Foreword: Antidiscrimination and Constitutional Accountability (What the Bork-Brennan Debate Ignores), 105 Harv. L. Rev. 80, 103-108 (1991); Cass R. Sunstein, The Partial Constitution 270-285 (1993). For an account tracing the rise of sex equality arguments for *Roe* in the late 1980s and early 1990s, in the period before the Court's decision in *Casey*, see Reva B. Siegel, Sex Equality Arguments for Reproductive Rights: Their Critical Basis and Evolving Constitutional Expression, 56 Emory L.J. 815, 828-829 (2007).

53. Sylvia A. Law, Rethinking Sex and the Constitution, 132 U. Pa. L. Rev. 955, 1020 (1984) (quoting Roe v. Wade).

54. See, e.g., Catharine A. MacKinnon, Toward a Feminist Theory of the State 189-194 (1989); Catharine A. MacKinnon, Reflections on Sex Equality Under the Law, 100 Yale L.J. 1281, 1308-1327 (1991).

55. See What Roe v. Wade Should Have Said, supra n.32, containing alternative versions of Roe v. Wade written by Jack M. Balkin, Reva Siegel, and Robin West, which argue for protecting abortion as an equality right.

The following excerpt, written by a constitutional scholar in the period before the Court's decision in *Casey*, draws on the nineteenth-century campaign to criminalize abortion to advance an equal protection argument grounded in social context—a context that is obscured whenever arguments about abortion focus on the physical but not social relations of reproduction.

Reva Siegel, Reasoning from the Body: A Historical Perspective on Abortion Regulation and Questions of Equal Protection

44 Stan. L. Rev. 261, 276-277, 350, 371-379 (1992)

Because *Roe* analyzes an exercise of state power from a medical, rather than a social, point of view, it authorizes state action against the pregnant woman on the basis of physiological criteria, requiring no inquiry into the state's reasons for acting against the pregnant woman, or the impact of its actions on her. Indeed, *Roe* analyzes the state's interest in potential life as a benign exercise of state power for the protection of the unborn, and not as a coercive exercise of state power against pregnant women, often reasoning as if the state's interest in protecting potential life scarcely pertained to the pregnant woman herself.

Abortion-restrictive regulation is sex-based regulation, the use of public power to force women to bear children. Yet, the Court has never described the state's interest in protecting potential life as an interest in forcing women to bear children. *Roe*'s physiological reasoning obscures that simple social fact. "[I]f one accepts the medical definitions of the developing young in the human uterus" as a sufficient, objective, and authoritative framework for evaluating the state's regulatory interest in abortion—as *Roe* did—state action compelling women to perform the work of motherhood can be justified without ever acknowledging that the state is enforcing a gender status role. In part, this is because analyzing abortion-restrictive regulation within physiological paradigms obscures its social logic, but also, and as importantly, it is because physiological reasons for regulating women's conduct are already laden with socio-political import: Facts about women's bodies have long served to justify regulation enforcing judgments about women's roles. . . .

Abortion-restrictive regulation is state action compelling pregnancy and motherhood, and this simple fact cannot be evaded by invoking nature or a woman's choices to explain the situation in which the pregnant woman subject to abortion restrictions finds herself. A pregnant woman seeking an abortion has the practical capacity to terminate a pregnancy, which she would exercise but for the community's decision to prevent or deter her. If the community successfully effectuates its will, it is the state, and not nature, which is responsible for causing her to continue the pregnancy. . . .

Hypothetically, a woman compelled to bear a child she does not want could give it up for adoption, abandon it, or pay someone to care for the child until maturity. In this society, however, these are not options that women avail themselves of with great frequency for the simple reason that few women are able to abandon a child born of their body. [A woman] is likely to experience intense familial and social pressure to raise a child she has borne. The pressure . . . will intensify dramatically if [women] are married and/or have other children, as current adoption placements illustrate. [W]hile discussions of abortion-restrictive regulation often assume that women who are forced to bear children can simply abandon them at will, the premise is wholly at odds with the norms of the society that would compel women to bear children. . . . Legislatures that enact restrictions on abortion understand this. They both desire and expect that most women will raise the child they are forced to bear, and in the vast majority of cases, women will.

Of course, a state can deny responsibility for imposing motherhood on women simply by emphasizing that the pregnant woman has chosen to raise the child that the state forced her to bear. Arguments about women's choices offer a familiar way to rationalize state action enforcing gender status roles. But, if one considers the powerful norms governing women's choices about whether to raise their children, it is clear that such formalistic arguments do not relieve the state of responsibility for dictating the pregnant woman's social fate.

[N]otwithstanding changing norms of family life, it remains the case that it is women who perform the vast majority of the labor necessary to make infants into adults. Mothers are expected to subordinate their personal interests to children in a way that men are not; most women give themselves over to the nurturance of life in a way that men do not—and face stigmatization, unlike men, if they will not. Consequently, a woman's identity, relations, and prospects are defined by becoming a parent in a way that a man's are not.

While this society celebrates the work of childcare, it continues to view the work of raising children as "women's work." Childcare remains status work, organized and valued in ways that limit the life prospects of those who perform it. Most prominently, childcare is uncompensated labor, traditionally performed under conditions of economic dependency; consequently, it remains a form of undercompensated labor for those who are paid to assist in the work. It is not merely the uncompensated character of childcare that betrays its peculiar social valuation. Those who devote their personal energies to raising children are likely to find their freedom to participate in so-called public sphere activities impaired for years on end, for the evident reason that most activities in the realms of education, employment, and politics are defined and structured as incommensurate with that work. Thus, a woman who becomes a parent will likely find that the energy she invests in childrearing will compromise her already constrained opportunities and impair her already unequal compensation in the work force—all the more so if she raises the child alone, whether by choice, divorce, or abandonment. Considered in cold dollar terms, it is the institution of motherhood that gives a gendered structure to the economics of family life, and a gendered face to poverty in the nation's life. . . . [W]hen the state enacts restrictions on abortion, it coerces women to perform the work of motherhood without altering the conditions that continue to make such work a principal cause of their secondary social status.

[S]tate action compelling motherhood injures women in predictable ways. Both the work of childbearing and the work of childrearing compromise women's opportunities in education and employment; neither the work of childbearing nor the work of childrearing produces any material compensation for women; most often the work of childbearing and the work of childrearing entangle women in relations of emotional and economic dependency—to men, extended family, or the state. None of these consequences is inherent in the physiology of reproduction; all are socially produced, reflecting communal designation of the work of mothering as "women's work." There is no other form of socially essential labor in this society similarly organized or valued: The more effort a woman personally invests in it, the more time she devotes to it, the more inexorably economically dependent she becomes. From this perspective, it is apparent that compelled pregnancy will injure women in context-dependent ways. It may be endured by women who have ordered their lives in conformity with traditional norms of motherhood, but it will profoundly threaten the material and psychic welfare of any woman whose life deviates from this traditional norm, whether by choice or socio-economic circumstance. When the state deprives women of choice in matters of motherhood, it deprives women of the ability to lead their lives with some rudimentary control over the sex-role constraints this society imposes on those who bear and rear children. It makes the social reality of women's lives more nearly conform with social stereotypes of women's lives. Considered from this perspective, choice in matters of motherhood implicates constitutional values of equality and liberty both.

Restrictions on abortion thus offend constitutional guarantees of equal protection, not simply because of the status-based injuries they inflict on women, but also because of the status-based attitudes about women they reflect. For centuries, this society has defined women as mothers and defined the work of motherhood as women's work. These are the assumptions which make it "reasonable" to force women to become mothers. Absent these deep-rooted assumptions about women, it is impossible to explain why this society insists that restrictions on abortion are intended to protect the unborn, and yet has never even considered taking action that would alleviate the burdens forced motherhood imposes on women.

Restrictions on abortion reflect the kind of bias that is at the root of the most invidious forms of stereotyping: a failure to consider, in a society always at risk of forgetting, that women are persons, too. It is a bias that manifests itself in this society's unreflective expectation that women should assume the burdens of bearing and rearing future generations, its tendency to denigrate the work of motherhood, and its readiness to castigate women who seek to avoid maternity as lacking in humanity, proof of which consists in a woman's failure perfectly to subordinate her energies, resources, and prospects to the task of making life—to a degree that men, employers, and the community as a whole most often will not.

DISCUSSION

1. *Sex equality arguments for abortion rights.* The sex equality argument asks whether abortion restrictions are shaped solely by the state's interest in protecting potential life, or whether they might also reflect constitutionally suspect judgments about women. (Does the state act consistently to protect potential life in contexts not involving women who resist motherhood? Does government vindicate its interest in protecting potential life by endeavoring to support those who bear and care for future generations? If not, might abortion restrictions reflect traditional sex-role stereotypes about sex, caregiving, or decisionmaking around motherhood?) The equality argument is also concerned about the gendered impact of abortion restrictions. The equality argument observes that abortion restrictions deprive women of control over the timing of motherhood and so predictably exacerbate the inequalities in educational, economic, and political life faced by those who

engage in childbearing and childrearing. The sex equality argument asks whether, before depriving women of control over the timing of motherhood, the state has taken steps to ameliorate the impact of compelled motherhood on women.

2. *Abortion regulation as status-enforcing state action.* Siegel argues that restrictions on abortion reflect and reinforce social norms and arrangements of the traditional family that presuppose that (female) caregivers are dependent on (male) breadwinners. Criminal abortion statutes may seem reasonable given traditional role assumptions concerning motherhood; but laws criminalizing abortion compel women to become mothers against their will under social arrangements that impose dependency and severe economic disadvantage on women who bear and rear children.

What role does liberty play in Siegel's story? If a legislature combined abortion restrictions with a general scheme of compensation to mothers, free childcare, and a comprehensive system of family leave provisions designed to reduce the economic costs of motherhood to women, would this satisfy constitutional concerns under Siegel's account?

3. *Giving practical effect to the antisubordination principle.* Siegel's account focuses on the subordination of women through abortion regulation. She argues that abortion-restrictive regulation is gender biased in impetus and impact. Under Siegel's account, what, if any, kinds of abortion restrictions would be permissible? At what point, and under what circumstances, would the state be able to claim that its interest in preserving unborn life would justify the additional coercive pressure on women to bear children? Could the state ban abortions in the third trimester? Would health measures that were asserted to be in the mother's interest be constitutional?

4. *Physiological naturalism.* Siegel criticizes the *Roe* decision for focusing exclusively on the woman's body and the developmental status of the fetus. She argues that talking in terms of fetal development and phrasing all constitutional analysis in morphological terms makes the social and economic consequences of motherhood invisible. Can you think of other examples of constitutional doctrines or arguments in which courts talk about a problem in terms that effectively disguise its social consequences? Note, moreover, that Siegel's argument is not merely a criticism of abortion restrictions, but of the ways the society views and treats those who bear and rear children. How might the opinion in *Roe* have been written to take these issues into account?

5. Geduldig *and* Feeney *(again).* Does Siegel's argument depend on overruling *Geduldig*? How might it be advanced, given the Court's reasoning in *Geduldig*? Siegel argues that the state interest in protecting potential life warrants closer scrutiny because, in the abortion context, it may be hard to distinguish from a state interest in forcing women to become mothers. Could the state respond that compelled childbearing may be an *effect* of abortion regulation because of the fact that the fetus is lodged inside the mother's body, but that it is not the *purpose* of the regulation, citing *Feeney*? Is viewing the fetus separate from the mother (and separate from effects on the mother) constitutionally permissible? To what extent can the state respond that the fetal presence inside the mother is due to some action to which the mother has consented or for which she is responsible? Do either of these rejoinders rely on judgments about women forbidden by the Equal Protection Clause?

6. How might the equality argument for protection of the abortion decision shape understanding of the liberty interests *Roe* protects?

7. *The history of abortion regulation.* Many state statutes restricting abortion date from the nineteenth century. At common law abortion prior to "quickening" of the fetus—the point at which a pregnant woman could perceive fetal movement, typically late in the fourth month or early in the fifth month of gestation—was not considered a crime or necessarily immoral. The new prohibitions arose from two different campaigns, one an anti-vice crusade against all forms of (and discussion of) contraception, and the second a crusade by the medical profession against abortion.[56] Like feminism itself, abortion was generally viewed by the medical profession as "a threat to social order and male authority."[57] Restricting abortions, doctors argued, "was necessary not only to protect the unborn, but also to ensure that women performed their obligations as wives and mothers and to preserve the ethnic character of the nation."[58] Protestant doctors feared that allowing abortions would result in Catholic immigrants producing more children.

Doctors reasoned "from the body," as well as from women's roles. Doctors opposed to abortion argued that the embryo was a separate form of human life from the moment of conception, wholly distinct from the woman's body, and that quickening was an irrelevant event. Women, on this view, were merely the passive instrumentalities of nature's inherent purposes. Second, doctors argued that the purpose of marital sexuality was procreation and that attempts to prevent procreation were physiologically inappropriate and unhealthy for women's bodies, or, in the words of one prominent advocate, a "physiological sin." Finally, the doctors' campaign argued that wives who shirked their natural duty of bearing and rearing children were selfish and self-indulgent, neglecting their natural maternal duty. Doctors argued that women wanted abortions simply to avoid the inconvenience of pregnancy, the labor and expense of raising children, and interference with their pleasure, their pursuit of fashion, and other trivial feminine pursuits.

Although the doctors' campaign often associated demands for abortion with the women's rights movement, the feminist movement during this period did not strongly support abortion rights, and, indeed, most feminists actively opposed abortion. The feminist concern with "voluntary motherhood" during this period was less a concern with abortion rights and more a concern with the right not to be forced into sexual relations by their husbands and to have children against their will. Rather than blaming women's selfishness for abortion, as

---

56. On the history of the nineteenth-century campaigns against abortion, see Linda Gordon, Woman's Body, Woman's Right: A Social History of Birth Control in America (1976); Kristin Luker, Abortion and the Politics of Motherhood (1984); James C. Mohr, Abortion in America: The Origins and Evolution of National Policy, 1800-1900 (1978); Reva Siegel, Reasoning from the Body: A Historical Perspective on Abortion Regulation and Questions of Equal Protection, 44 Stan. L. Rev. 261 (1992); Carroll Smith-Rosenberg, Disorderly Conduct: Visions of Gender in Victorian America 217-244 (1985).

57. Smith-Rosenberg, Disorderly Conduct, supra, at 235-236.

58. Siegel, Reasoning from the Body, supra, at 266.

the medical profession did, feminists explained (and sometimes even condoned) abortion as something women were driven to by marital rape or the pressures of motherhood.[59]

What relevance, if any, should this history have in assessing the due process or equal protection claims for abortion rights? Recall the discussion in the Note on Tradition as a Source of Fundamental Rights, supra. From the founding to the middle of the nineteenth century, states followed the common law tradition of protecting abortion decisions prior to quickening, but then adopted legislation that broke with this tradition, at least in cases where doctors were unwilling to warrant that an abortion was necessary to save a woman's life. One might argue that if there is something deeply rooted in our nation's traditions, it is the tradition of using expectations about gender and marriage to force women to become mothers against their will, and justifying this policy through discourses about women's natural proclivities or obligations. Is this a tradition worthy of constitutional protection?

Much of the history of abortion regulation in the nineteenth century seems grounded in stereotypes and judgments that would be considered constitutionally impermissible today under the Equal Protection Clause. Does this history undermine present justifications for restrictions on abortion? Consider the following "genealogical argument": Current opposition to abortion is descended from impermissible premises about women and motherhood in the nineteenth century, just as the antimiscegenation statute in Loving v. Virginia was descended from impermissible views about whites and Blacks. Have you seen this sort of argument before? (Recall, e.g., Justice Ginsburg's opinion in the *VMI* case.) What more would be required to create a successful version of such a genealogical argument? What evidence would be necessary to rebut such an argument?

C. *Decisions After* Roe

Roe has proved to be one of the most controversial and bitterly contested Supreme Court decisions of the last half-century. A series of fragmented decisions sometimes expanded *Roe*'s holding, while at other times allowed state regulation

---

59. The stark differences between the two groups' attitudes toward abortion is summed up in their contrasting uses of the term "legalized prostitution":

> Woman's rights advocates insisted that marriage was no better than legalized prostitution if a wife's consent to marital sex was inferred from the marital contract itself, or if marital sex was treated as a reciprocal obligation flowing from the fact of marital support. By contrast, doctors argued that marriage was a relation of legalized prostitution so long as man's natural sexual urge was allowed expression in marriage without reproductive consequence. Thus, while feminists used the critique of marriage as "legalized prostitution" to argue that wives should control decisions respecting reproduction, physicians used the same metaphor to justify depriving women of control over decisions respecting reproduction. In feminist usage, the critique of marriage as "legalized prostitution" identified a range of social reasons why a wife would seek to avoid maternity; in medical usage, the critique of marriage as "legalized prostitution" condemned the very aspiration to avoid maternity as an expression of unnatural egoism or immoral license.

Siegel, Reasoning from the Body, supra n.56, at 309-310.

of at least certain aspects of the abortion decision. As is true of many subject areas raised throughout this casebook, we make no pretense of offering a full overview of this extremely complex topic.

We mention only some representative decisions before turning to the most extensive reconsideration of *Roe* in the 1992 *Casey* case.

1. *State funding and use of state facilities.* In Maher v. Roe, 432 U.S. 464 (1977), the Supreme Court upheld a Connecticut state regulation that limited state Medicaid benefits for first-trimester abortions to those that are "medically necessary," a term defined to include psychiatric necessity. Writing for the majority, Justice Powell explained that "[t]his case involves no discrimination against a suspect class. . . . [T]his Court has never held that financial need alone identifies a suspect class for purposes of equal protection analysis." Turning to fundamental rights doctrine, Powell explained that "the right [to abortion] protects the woman from unduly burdensome interference with her freedom to decide whether to terminate her pregnancy. It implies no limitation on the authority of a State to make a value judgment favoring childbirth over abortion, and to implement that judgment by the allocation of public funds."

Powell argued that "[t]he Connecticut regulation places no obstacles—absolute or otherwise—in the pregnant woman's path to an abortion. An indigent woman who desires an abortion suffers no disadvantage as a consequence of Connecticut's decision to fund childbirth; she continues as before to be dependent on private sources for the service she desires. The State may have made childbirth a more attractive alternative, thereby influencing the woman's decision, but it has imposed no restriction on access to abortions that was not already there. The indigency that may make it difficult—and in some cases, perhaps, impossible—for some women to have abortions is neither created nor in any way affected by the Connecticut regulation." The regulation passed rational basis test: "The State unquestionably has a 'strong and legitimate interest in encouraging normal childbirth,' an interest honored over the centuries." The regulation rationally furthered that interest because "[t]he subsidizing of costs incident to childbirth is a rational means of encouraging childbirth."

Justice Brennan, joined by Justices Marshall and Blackmun, dissented: "As a practical matter, many indigent women will feel they have no choice but to carry their pregnancies to term because the State will pay for the associated medical services, even though they would have chosen to have abortions if the State had also provided funds for that procedure, or indeed if the State had provided funds for neither procedure. This disparity in funding by the State clearly operates to coerce indigent pregnant women to bear children they would not otherwise choose to have, and just as clearly, this coercion can only operate upon the poor, who are uniquely the victims of this form of financial pressure."

Justice Brennan compared the situation to other fundamental rights cases involving speech and religious freedom: "The Connecticut scheme cannot be distinguished from other grants and withholdings of financial benefits that we have held unconstitutionally burdened a fundamental right. Sherbert v. Verner[, 374 U.S. 398 (1963),] struck down a South Carolina statute that denied unemployment compensation to a woman who for religious reasons could not work on Saturday, but that would have provided such compensation if her unemployment had stemmed from a number of other nonreligious causes. Even though there was no proof of indigency in that case, *Sherbert* held that 'the pressure upon her to forgo [her religious] practice [was] unmistakable,' and therefore held that the effect was the same as a fine imposed for Saturday worship." In fact, Justice Brennan argued, "the case for application of the principle actually is stronger than in *Verner* since appellees are all indigents and therefore even more vulnerable to the financial pressures imposed by the Connecticut regulation."

Do you agree with Justice Powell that no suspect class is involved in *Maher*? How much of the logic of *Maher* depends on Geduldig v. Aiello?

Powell argues that the state leaves an indigent woman no worse off by withholding funding for abortions while funding childbirth. Is it constitutionally permissible to subject poor women to forms of coercion to which women of means are not subject?

In Harris v. McCrae, the Court, by a 5-4 majority, upheld the Hyde Amendment to the Medicaid program established in Title XIX of the Social Security Act. The Hyde Amendment prohibits the use of federal funds "to perform abortions except where the life of the mother would be endangered if the fetus were carried to term; or except for such medical procedures necessary for the victims of rape or incest. . . ." Whereas *Maher* only dealt with nontherapeutic abortions, *Harris* involved a ban on funding of abortions necessary to the mother's health in situations where her life is not threatened.

Justice Stewart concluded that *Maher* was controlling: "[I]t simply does not follow that a woman's freedom of choice carries with it a constitutional entitlement to the financial resources to avail herself of the full range of protected choices. . . . Although Congress has opted to subsidize medically necessary services generally, but not certain medically necessary abortions, the fact remains that the Hyde Amendment leaves an indigent woman with at least the same range of choice in deciding whether to obtain a medically necessary abortion as she would have had if Congress had chosen to subsidize no health care costs at all."

Justice Brennan, joined by Justices Marshall and Blackmun, dissented for essentially the reasons given in his dissent in *Maher*. Justice Marshall wrote a separate dissent arguing that this case was distinguishable from *Maher* because it involved medically necessary abortions: One might justify Maher on the grounds that "Medicaid funds were available only for medically necessary procedures. Thus the plaintiffs were seeking benefits which were not available to others similarly situated." But in this case respondents "are protesting their exclusion from a benefit that is available to all others similarly situated. This, it need hardly be said, is a crucial difference for equal protection purposes."

The Court has relied on *Maher* and *Harris* in dealing with policies prohibiting abortions in public hospitals even when the woman seeks no other state aid and is willing to pay the full cost of the hospital services. Thus, in Poelker v. Doe, 432 U.S. 519 (1977), the Court sustained St. Louis's policy of refusing to permit abortions in public hospitals unless there was a threat of great physiological injury or death. "For the reasons stated in *Maher*, the Constitution does not forbid a State or city, pursuant to democratic processes, from expressing a preference for normal childbirth."

The Court returned to the issue in Webster v. Reproductive Health Services, 492 U.S. 490 (1989), where Missouri law made it "unlawful for any public facility to be used for the purpose of performing or assisting an abortion not necessary to save the life of the mother." Chief Justice Rehnquist wrote: "Missouri's refusal to allow . . . abortions in public hospitals leaves a pregnant woman with the same choices as if the State had chosen not to operate any public hospitals at all." It did not matter whether "all of the public facility's costs in providing abortion services are recouped when the patient pays. . . . Nothing in the Constitution requires States to enter or remain in the business of performing abortions. Nor, as appellees suggest, do private physicians and their patients have some kind of constitutional right of access to public facilities for the performance of abortions. Indeed, if the State does recoup all of its costs in performing abortions, and no state subsidy, direct or indirect, is available, it is difficult to see how any procreational choice is burdened by the State's ban on the use of its facilities or employees for performing abortions." In a footnote, Chief Justice Rehnquist explained that "A different analysis might apply if a particular State had socialized medicine and all of its hospitals and physicians were publicly funded. This case might also be different if the State barred doctors who performed abortions in private facilities from the use of public facilities for any purpose."

2. *Spousal consent.* In Planned Parenthood of Central Missouri v. Danforth, 428 U.S. 52 (1976), the Court considered a Missouri requirement that a husband give "prior written consent" to the decision of his wife to seek an abortion during the first 12 weeks of pregnancy, unless the abortion is necessary to preserve the mother's life. The Court concluded that "since the State cannot regulate or proscribe abortion during the first stage, . . . the State cannot delegate authority to any particular person, even the spouse, to prevent abortion during that same period." Justice Blackmun recognized "the deep and proper concern and interest that a devoted and protective husband has in his wife's pregnancy and in the growth and development of the fetus she is carrying," and thought that "ideally, the decision to terminate a pregnancy should be one concurred in by both the wife and her husband." But he thought it unlikely that the marital relationship would be enhanced by giving the husband a veto power exercisable for any reason whatsoever or for no reason at all and concluded that "[i]nasmuch as it is the woman who physically bears the child and who is the more directly and immediately affected by the pregnancy, as between the two, the balance weighs in her favor." Dissenting on this issue, Justice White, joined by Chief Justice Burger and Justice Rehnquist, wrote:

> A father's interest in having a child—perhaps his only child—may be unmatched by any other interest in his life. . . . In describing the nature of a mother's interest in terminating a pregnancy, the Court in Roe v. Wade mentioned only the post-birth burdens of rearing a child, and rejected a rule based on her interest in controlling her own body during pregnancy. Missouri has a law which prevents a woman from putting a child up for adoption over her husband's objection. This law represents a judgment by the State that the mother's interest in avoiding the burdens of child rearing do not outweigh or snuff out the father's interest in participating in bringing up his own child. That law is plainly valid, but no more so than §3(3) of the Act now before us, resting as it does on precisely the same judgment.

3. *Parental consent.* In another portion of *Danforth,* the Court invalidated a Missouri statute prohibiting an unmarried woman under the age of 18 from obtaining an abortion without the written consent of a parent or person in loco parentis

unless a licensed physician certified that the abortion was necessary to preserve the life of the mother. Subsequently, in Bellotti v. Baird, 432 U.S. 622 (1979) (*Bellotti II*), the Court struck down a Massachusetts statute prohibiting an unmarried minor from obtaining an abortion unless both parents consent or the minor obtains a court order "for good cause shown." Justice Powell argued that

> every minor must have the opportunity [to] go directly to a court without first consulting or notifying her parents. If she satisfies the court that she is mature and well enough informed to make intelligently the abortion decision on her own, the court must authorize her to act without parental consultation or consent. If she fails to satisfy the court that she is competent to make this decision independently, she must be permitted to show that an abortion nevertheless would be in her best interests.

Justice Powell added that a court may ask itself whether her best interests would be served by parental consultation, "[b]ut this is the full extent to which parental involvement may be required." The Court subsequently upheld a parental consent provision in Planned Parenthood Association of Kansas City v. Ashcroft, 462 U.S. 476 (1983), which contained an "alternative procedure" that was considered consistent with the test Justice Powell announced in *Bellotti II*. Justice O'Connor argued that the statute "imposes no undue burden on any right that a minor may have to undergo an abortion."

4. *Parental notification.* In Hodgson v. Minnesota, 457 U.S. 417 (1990), and Ohio v. Akron Center for Reproductive Health, 457 U.S. 502 (1990) (*Akron II*), the Court considered parental-notification requirements for a minor to gain access to an abortion. In *Hodgson*, the Court invalidated a provision of a Minnesota statute that prohibited performance of an abortion on a woman under the age of 18 unless 48 hours has elapsed since both parents were notified. The notification provision applied even if the minor's parents had never been married, were divorced, or were otherwise not living with one another or the child. Justice Stevens, joined in part by Justices Brennan, Marshall, Blackmun, and O'Connor, held that the two-parent notification scheme by itself was unconstitutional. The Court emphasized trial testimony that parents of minors seeking abortions were often divorced or separated, and that requiring notice of both parents could provoke violence from family members, particularly fathers. The trial court also found that "many minors in Minnesota 'live in fear of violence by family members' and 'are, in fact, victims of rape, incest, neglect, and violence.'" At the same time, Justice O'Connor's opinion held that a two-parent notification rule would be constitutional if combined with a "judicial bypass procedure"—whereby a pregnant minor could obtain a court order for an abortion without notifying her parents. The Minnesota statute in *Hodgson* provided for a judicial bypass if the statute would otherwise be held unconstitutional. Because four other Justices (Kennedy, Rehnquist, White, and Scalia) believed that a two-parent notification provision was reasonable and therefore constitutional, the effect of O'Connor's position was that Minnesota's two-parent notification law was upheld with a judicial bypass.

Justice Marshall dissented from this holding. "[M]any women will carry the fetus to term rather than notify a parent. Other women may decide to inform a parent but then confront parental pressure or abuse so severe as to obstruct the abortion. For these women, the judge's refusal to authorize an abortion effectively constitutes an absolute veto." Justice Marshall noted that the trial court found that seeking a judicial order imposed "significant burdens on minors," including long delays, traveling long distances to obtain an order, absences from home and school, and "emotional trauma" for young women.

The *Akron* case involved a statute that prohibited any person from performing an abortion on an unmarried, unemancipated minor without giving notice to one parent at least 24 hours in advance. Notice would not be required if the minor obtained a court order approving the abortion, or if the minor and another relative filed an affidavit stating that the minor feared physical, sexual, or severe emotional abuse from the parent. Finally, the minor could also bypass notice by filing a complaint showing that notice was not in her best interest or that she had sufficient maturity and information to make an intelligent decision without notice, or that one of her parents had engaged in a pattern of physical, sexual, or emotional abuse. The Court upheld these provisions in an opinion by Justice Kennedy, which stated that whether or not bypass procedures were constitutionally required, the ones in this statute were adequate.

Together, *Hodgson* and *Akron* created a complicated mass of contrasting positions among the Justices. In his opinion in *Hodgson*, Justice Scalia dissented "from this enterprise of devising an Abortion Code, and from the illusion that we have authority to do so." In her concurring opinion in *Hodgson*, Justice O'Connor agreed with the Court's statement that "[a] woman's decision to beget or to bear a child is a component of her liberty that is protected by the Due Process Clause of the Fourteenth Amendment to the Constitution." She also noted that, after *Roe*, minors could be treated differently from adults. She then restated her previously expressed view that "[i]f the particular regulation does not 'unduly burde[n]' the fundamental right, . . . then our evaluation of that regulation is limited to our determination that the regulation rationally relates to a legitimate state purpose." Applying this standard, she concluded that the Minnesota statute imposed an undue burden, by requiring, for example, a minor to notify even an abusive parent of her pregnancy.

5. *The constitutional politics of abortion in the decades preceding* Casey. Larger trends in American politics greatly affected the development of constitutional doctrine in all of these areas.[60] During the 1970s, the two major political parties were not strongly identified with the issue and Justices appointed by both Democrats and Republicans supported the decision and opposed it. In fact, in 1976, the Democratic candidate, Jimmy Carter, an evangelical Christian, was more pro-life than his opponent Gerald Ford. Nevertheless, the abortion conflict offered political opportunities. Architects of the New Right used the conflict to forge an unprecedented alliance between Protestant and Catholic conservatives in the hopes of fracturing the New Deal alliance and capturing the energies and votes of Christian conservatives for the Republican Party. Ronald Reagan, who had almost won the Republican nomination in 1976, welcomed evangelical and fundamentalist Christian

60. This discussion note is drawn (with some minor editing) from Jack M. Balkin, Roe v. Wade: An Engine of Controversy, in What Roe v. Wade Should Have Said, supra n.32, at 12-15. For an account of the Republican Party's efforts to use abortion to court Democratic voters, see Williams, The GOP's Abortion Strategy, supra n.39.

voters into the Republican Party and actively courted pro-life leaders. In the 1980 election, many evangelicals and fundamentalist Christians moved squarely into the Republican camp, and became an important part of the party's base of support. The Republican Party became primarily a pro-life party, with some moderates still favoring abortion rights, and the more liberal Democratic Party became largely pro-choice. In 1980, the Republican Party platform, for the first time, included a call for "a constitutional amendment to restore protection of the right to life for unborn children."[61]

Once in office Reagan set out to nominate judges who would roll back liberal judicial decisions and promote his favored constitutional values, which included opposition to abortion. (We have seen the effects of his appointment strategy in the area of federalism in Chapter 6.) Not entirely coincidentally, the 1984 Republican Party platform "applaud[ed] President Reagan's fine record of judicial appointments, and . . . reaffirm[ed] [the party's] support for the appointment of judges at all levels of the judiciary who respect traditional family values and the sanctity of innocent human life."[62] Reagan's first three Supreme Court appointments, Sandra Day O'Connor, William Rehnquist (elevated to Chief Justice to replace Warren Burger), and Antonin Scalia, were all critics of *Roe*. By the beginning of 1987, the Supreme Court was generally believed to have five strong supporters of *Roe* and four equally strong critics. When Justice Lewis Powell announced his retirement in January 1987, President Reagan nominated D.C. Circuit Judge Robert Bork, an outspoken opponent of *Roe*. Reagan seemed poised to accelerate the entrenchment of his constitutional principles in the Supreme Court and secure a crucial fifth vote to overturn Roe v. Wade.

The Bork nomination produced a national controversy, and ultimately the Senate failed to confirm him. Pro-choice groups, which had often relied heavily on the courts to protect abortion rights, mobilized to help defeat the nomination.[63]

After Reagan's next nominee, D.C. Circuit Judge Douglas Ginsburg, withdrew his name after his marijuana use was discovered, Reagan nominated Anthony Kennedy, a conservative circuit judge from California who was nevertheless widely regarded as more moderate than Bork.

In hindsight, the failure of the Bork nomination marked an important turning point in the constitutional struggles over abortion, because pro-choice forces showed that they could mobilize effectively and demonstrated that pro-life politicians might pay more heavily than they had previously believed if they tried to overturn *Roe* through judicial appointments. Nevertheless, by 1987, President Reagan had succeeded in appointing three Justices to the Supreme Court who were widely regarded to be critics of *Roe* to join the two original dissenters in the opinion. The appointments now seemed to threaten the decision itself.

---

61. See Barbara Hinkson Craig and David M. O'Brien, Abortion and American Politics 166-168 (1993) (reprinting Republican and Democratic Party platform planks on abortion from 1980-1992).

62. Id.

63. For a history, see Ethan Bronner, Battle for Justice: How the Bork Nomination Shook America (1989).

The next test of *Roe*'s continued vitality came in 1989 in Webster v. Reproductive Health Services, 492 U.S. 490 (1989). A Missouri statute prohibited the use of public employees and facilities to perform or assist abortions that were not necessary to save the mother's life, and made it unlawful to use public funds, employees, or facilities to "encourag[e] or counsel[]" a woman to have an abortion not necessary to save her life. The statute also required that physicians determine whether a fetus is viable before performing an abortion where physicians had reason to believe the fetus is more than 20 weeks old. Finally, the preamble to the legislation declared that "[t]he life of each human being begins at conception," and that "unborn children have protectable interests in life, health, and well-being."

The Court upheld all of the statute's restrictions but was unable to agree on a rationale. Chief Justice Rehnquist's plurality opinion, joined by Justices White and Kennedy, stated that it was not necessary to overturn *Roe*'s constitutional prohibition on criminalization of abortions to decide the case but that *Roe*'s trimester framework should be jettisoned. Rehnquist stated that abortion was not a fundamental right; hence restrictions on abortion need only pass the rational basis test. Justice O'Connor, concurring in the result, argued that it was unnecessary to reject *Roe*'s trimester framework to uphold the Missouri law; the challenged provisions were consistent with her interpretation of the Court's previous decisions, and none of the provisions imposed an undue burden on the right to abortion. Justice Scalia, also concurring in the judgment, argued that *Roe* should be overturned immediately, and directly criticized Justice O'Connor for failing to provide the fifth vote.

The result in *Webster* left *Roe* in legal limbo, and it was widely assumed that it was only a matter of time before it would be officially overruled. This energized pro-choice forces; they successfully supported a number of pro-choice candidates who won state and local elections. Matters were further complicated when two of the Court's most liberal Justices, William Brennan and Thurgood Marshall, left the Court due to failing health. This brought the abortion issue front and center in subsequent confirmation hearings. Brennan resigned in July 1990 and was replaced by David Souter, whose views on abortion were unknown even to President George H.W. Bush, who had nominated him. Justice Marshall announced his retirement in June 1991. He was replaced by Clarence Thomas, an African-American judge on the D.C. Circuit and former head of the Equal Employment Opportunity Commission (EEOC). Although Thomas was widely believed to be hostile to *Roe*, Thomas stated at his confirmation hearings that he had never "debated" Roe v. Wade, did not "recollect ever commenting on it," could not "recall saying" whether it was properly decided or not, and had no "personal opinion" about it.[64] Matters were thrown into an uproar when Thomas was accused of sexual harassment by a former employee at the EEOC, Anita Hill. After weeks of controversy, Thomas was finally confirmed by a 52-48 vote, the narrowest margin in Supreme Court history.

Once Thomas took his seat on the Supreme Court in 1991 it seemed that there were finally enough votes to overturn Roe v. Wade. Of the seven Justices who had voted with the majority in *Roe*, only Blackmun, the author of *Roe*, remained

---

64. See Nomination of Judge Clarence Thomas to be Associate Justice of the Supreme Court of the United States: Hearings Before the Comm. on the Judiciary, United States Senate, 102d Cong., 1st Sess. pt. 1, 222-223 (1991).

on the Court. Brennan, Marshall, Stewart, Douglas, Burger, and Powell were gone, replaced by Souter, Thomas, O'Connor, Stevens, Scalia, and Kennedy, all appointed by Republican Presidents, and all but Stevens appointed after the Republican Party had become a pro-life party.

O'Connor's opinion in *Hodgson* seemed to assume that *Roe* remained good law, although she now reinterpreted the abortion right in terms of the "undue burden" test she had introduced in her dissent in a 1983 decision, Akron v. Akron Center for Reproductive Health, 462 U.S. 416, 462-466 (1983) (*Akron I*). The question was what a Court staffed with the new Justices would do once the question of overturning *Roe* was presented again. When the Court finally spoke on the issue, the views of these new Justices—and Justice O'Connor herself—proved crucial.

Planned Parenthood of Southeastern Pennsylvania v. Casey

505 U.S. 833 (1992)

Justice O'CONNOR, Justice KENNEDY, and Justice SOUTER announced the judgment of the Court and delivered the opinion of the Court with respect to Parts I, II, III, V-A, V-C, and VI, an opinion with respect to Part V-E, in which Justice Stevens joins, and an opinion with respect to Parts IV, V-B, and V-D.

I

Liberty finds no refuge in a jurisprudence of doubt. . . .

At issue in these cases are five provisions of the Pennsylvania Abortion Control Act of 1982 as amended in 1988 and 1989. . . . The Act requires that a woman seeking an abortion give her informed consent prior to the abortion procedure, and specifies that she be provided with certain information at least 24 hours before the abortion is performed. For a minor to obtain an abortion, the Act requires the informed consent of one of her parents, but provides for a judicial bypass option if the minor does not wish to or cannot obtain a parent's consent. Another provision of the Act requires that, unless certain exceptions apply, a married woman seeking an abortion must sign a statement indicating that she has notified her husband of her intended abortion. The Act exempts compliance with these three requirements in the event of a "medical emergency." . . . In addition to the above provisions regulating the performance of abortions, the Act imposes certain reporting requirements on facilities that provide abortion services.

. . . After considering the fundamental constitutional questions resolved by *Roe*, principles of institutional integrity, and the rule of stare decisis, we are led to conclude this: the essential holding of Roe v. Wade should be retained and once again reaffirmed.

. . . *Roe*'s essential holding, the holding we reaffirm, has three parts. First is a recognition of the right of the woman to choose to have an abortion before viability and to obtain it without undue interference from the State. Before viability, the State's interests are not strong enough to support a prohibition of abortion or the imposition of a substantial obstacle to the woman's effective right to elect the procedure. Second is a confirmation of the State's power to restrict abortions after fetal viability, if the law contains exceptions for pregnancies which endanger a woman's life or health. And third is the principle that the State has legitimate interests from the outset of the pregnancy in protecting the health of the woman and the life of the fetus that may become a child. These principles do not contradict one another; and we adhere to each.

II

Constitutional protection of the woman's decision to terminate her pregnancy derives from the Due Process Clause of the Fourteenth Amendment. . . . Although a literal reading of the Clause might suggest that it governs only the procedures by which a State may deprive persons of liberty, for at least 105 years, at least since Mugler v. Kansas, 123 U.S. 623, 660-61 (1887), the Clause has been understood to contain a substantive component as well, one "barring certain government actions regardless of the fairness of the procedures used to implement them." . . .

It is tempting, as a means of curbing the discretion of federal judges, to suppose that liberty encompasses no more than those rights already guaranteed to the individual against federal interference by the express provisions of the first eight amendments to the Constitution. But of course this Court has never accepted that view.

It is also tempting, for the same reason, to suppose that the Due Process Clause protects only those practices, defined at the most specific level, that were protected against government interference by other rules of law when the Fourteenth Amendment was ratified. See Michael H. v. Gerald D., (opinion of Scalia, J.). But such a view would be inconsistent with our law. It is a promise of the Constitution that there is a realm of personal liberty which the government may not enter. We have vindicated this principle before. Marriage is mentioned nowhere in the Bill of Rights and interracial marriage was illegal in most States in the 19th century, but the Court was no doubt correct in finding it to be an aspect of liberty protected against state interference by the substantive component of the Due Process Clause in Loving v. Virginia. [N]either the Bill of Rights nor the specific practices of States at the time of the adoption of the Fourteenth Amendment marks the outer limits of the substantive sphere of liberty which the Fourteenth Amendment protects. See U.S. Const., Amend. 9.

The inescapable fact is that adjudication of substantive due process claims may call upon the Court in interpreting the Constitution to exercise that same capacity which by tradition courts always have exercised: reasoned judgment. Its boundaries are not susceptible to expression as a simple rule. . . .

Our law affords constitutional protection to personal decisions relating to marriage, procreation, contraception, family relationships, child rearing, and education. *Carey.* Our cases recognize the right of the *individual,* married or single, to be free from unwarranted governmental intrusion into matters so fundamentally affecting a person as the decision whether to bear or beget a child. *Eisenstadt.* (emphasis in original). Our precedents "have respected the private realm of family life which the state cannot enter." Prince v. Massachusetts, 321 U.S. 158, 166 (1944). These matters, involving the most intimate and personal choices a person may make in a lifetime, choices central to personal dignity and autonomy, are central to the liberty protected by the Fourteenth Amendment. At the heart of liberty is the right to define one's own concept of existence, of meaning, of the universe, and of the mystery of human life. Beliefs about these matters could not define the attributes of personhood were they formed under compulsion of the State.

[A]bortion is a unique act. It is an act fraught with consequences for others: for the woman who must live with the implications of her decision; for the persons who perform and assist in the procedure; for the spouse, family, and society which must confront the knowledge that these procedures exist, procedures some deem nothing short of an act of violence against innocent human life; and, depending on one's beliefs, for the life or potential life that is aborted. . . . The mother who carries a child to full term is subject to anxieties, to physical constraints, to pain that only she must bear. That these sacrifices have from the beginning of the human race been endured by woman with a pride that ennobles her in the eyes of others and gives to the infant a bond of love cannot alone be grounds for the State to insist she make the sacrifice. Her suffering is too intimate and personal for the State to insist, without more, upon its own vision of the woman's role, however dominant that vision has been in the course of our history and our culture. The destiny of the woman must be shaped to a large extent on her own conception of her spiritual imperatives and her place in society.

It should be recognized, moreover, that in some critical respects the abortion decision is of the same character as the decision to use contraception, to which Griswold v. Connecticut, Eisenstadt v. Baird, and Carey v. Population Services International, afford constitutional protection. We have no doubt as to the correctness of those decisions. They support the reasoning in *Roe* relating to the woman's liberty because they involve personal decisions concerning not only the meaning of procreation but also human responsibility and respect for it. . . .

[T]he reservations any of us may have in reaffirming the central holding of *Roe* are outweighed by the explication of individual liberty we have given combined with the force of stare decisis. We turn now to that doctrine.

III

[I]t is common wisdom that the rule of stare decisis is not an "inexorable command," and certainly it is not such in every constitutional case. Rather, when this Court reexamines a prior holding, its judgment is customarily informed by a series of prudential and pragmatic considerations. . . . So in this case we may inquire whether *Roe*'s central rule has been found unworkable; whether the rule's limitation on state power could be removed without serious inequity to those who have relied upon it or significant damage to the stability of the society governed by the rule in question; whether the law's growth in the intervening years has left *Roe*'s central rule a doctrinal anachronism discounted by society; and whether *Roe*'s premises of fact have so far changed in the ensuing two decades as to render its central holding somehow irrelevant or unjustifiable in dealing with the issue it addressed.

1

Although *Roe* has engendered opposition, it has in no sense proven "unworkable". . . . While *Roe* has, of course, required judicial assessment of state laws . . . and although the need for such review will remain as a consequence of today's decision, the required determinations fall within judicial competence.

2

The inquiry into reliance counts the cost of a rule's repudiation as it would fall on those who have relied reasonably on the rule's continued application. . . . [F]or two decades of economic and social developments, people have organized intimate relationships and made choices that define their views of themselves and their places in society, in reliance on the availability of abortion in the event that contraception should fail. The ability of women to participate equally in the economic and social life of the Nation has been facilitated by their ability to control their reproductive lives. The Constitution serves human values, and while the effect of reliance on *Roe* cannot be exactly measured, neither can the certain cost of overruling *Roe* for people who have ordered their thinking and living around that case be dismissed.

3

No evolution of legal principle has left *Roe*'s doctrinal footings weaker than they were in 1973. No development of constitutional law since the case was decided has implicitly or explicitly left *Roe* behind as a mere survivor of obsolete constitutional thinking. . . .

Roe . . . may be seen not only as an exemplar of [the liberty protected by] *Griswold* . . . but as a rule (whether or not mistaken) of personal autonomy and bodily integrity, with doctrinal affinity to cases recognizing limits on governmental power to mandate medical treatment or to bar its rejection. If so, our cases since *Roe* accord with *Roe*'s view that a State's interest in the protection of life falls short of justifying any plenary override of individual liberty claims. Cruzan v. Director, Missouri Dept. of Health, 497 U.S. 261, 278 (1990). . . . Nor will courts building upon *Roe* be likely to hand down erroneous decisions as a consequence. Even on the assumption that the central holding of *Roe* was in error, that error would go only to the strength of the state interest in fetal protection, not to the recognition afforded by the Constitution to the woman's liberty. . . .

The soundness of this prong of the *Roe* analysis is apparent from a consideration of the alternative. If indeed the woman's interest in deciding whether to bear and beget a child had not been recognized as in *Roe*, the State might as readily restrict a woman's right to choose to carry a pregnancy to term as to terminate it, to further asserted state interests in population control, or eugenics, for example. Yet *Roe* has been sensibly relied upon to counter any such suggestions. E.g., Arnold v. Board of Education of Escambia County, Ala., 880 F.2d 305, 311 (CA11 1989) (relying upon *Roe* and concluding that government officials violate the Constitution by coercing a minor to have an abortion); Avery v. County of Burke, 660 F.2d 111, 115 (CA4 1981) (county agency inducing teenage girl to undergo unwanted sterilization on the basis of misrepresentation that she had sickle cell trait). . . .

4

[T]ime has overtaken some of *Roe*'s factual assumptions: advances in maternal health care allow for abortions safe to the mother later in pregnancy than was true in 1973, and advances in neonatal care have advanced viability to a point somewhat earlier. But these facts . . . have no bearing on the validity of *Roe*'s central holding, that viability marks the earliest point at which the State's interest in fetal life is constitutionally adequate to justify a legislative ban on nontherapeutic abortions. The soundness or unsoundness of that constitutional judgment in no sense turns on whether viability occurs at approximately 28 weeks, as was usual at the time of *Roe*, at 23 to 24 weeks, as it sometimes does today, or at some moment even slightly earlier in pregnancy, as it may if fetal respiratory capacity can somehow be enhanced in the future. . . .

B

In a less significant case, stare decisis analysis could, and would, stop at the point we have reached. But the sustained and widespread debate *Roe* has provoked calls for some comparison between that case and others of comparable dimension that have responded to national controversies and taken on the impress of the controversies addressed. . . .

The first example is that line of cases identified with Lochner v. New York. . . . West Coast Hotel Co. v. Parrish, 300 U.S. 379 (1937), signalled the demise of *Lochner* by overruling *Adkins*. [Following the Great Depression] the lesson . . . seemed unmistakable to most people by 1937, that the interpretation of contractual freedom protected in *Adkins* rested on fundamentally false factual assumptions about the capacity of a relatively unregulated market to satisfy minimal levels of human welfare. As Justice Jackson wrote of the constitutional crisis of 1937 shortly before he came on the bench, "The older world of laissez-faire was recognized everywhere outside the Court to be dead." R. Jackson, The Struggle for Judicial Supremacy 85 (1941). The facts upon which the earlier case had premised a constitutional resolution of social controversy had proved to be untrue, and history's demonstration of their untruth not only justified but required the new choice of constitutional principle that *West Coast Hotel* announced. . . .

[A] second comparison [is] the separate-but-equal rule [of] Plessy v. Ferguson. . . . The Court in *Brown* . . . observ[ed] that whatever may have been the understanding in *Plessy*'s time of the power of segregation to stigmatize those who were segregated with a "badge of inferiority," it was clear by 1954 that legally sanctioned segregation had just such an effect, to the point that racially separate public educational facilities were deemed inherently unequal. Society's understanding of the facts upon which a constitutional ruling was sought in 1954 was thus fundamentally different from the basis claimed for the decision in 1896. While we think *Plessy* was wrong the day it was decided, we must also recognize that the *Plessy* Court's explanation for its decision was so clearly at odds with the facts apparent to the Court in 1954 that the decision to reexamine *Plessy* was on this ground alone not only justified but required.

West Coast Hotel and *Brown* each rested on facts, or an understanding of facts, changed from those which furnished the claimed justifications for the earlier constitutional resolutions. Each case was comprehensible as the Court's response to facts that the country could understand, or had come to understand already, but which the Court of an earlier day, as its own declarations disclosed, had not been able to perceive. . . . In constitutional adjudication as elsewhere in life, changed circumstances may impose new obligations, and the thoughtful part of the Nation could accept each decision to overrule a prior case as a response to the Court's constitutional duty.

. . . Because neither the factual underpinnings of *Roe*'s central holding nor our understanding of it has changed (and because no other indication of weakened precedent has been shown) the Court could not pretend to be reexamining the prior law with any justification beyond a present doctrinal disposition to come out differently from the Court of 1973. To overrule prior law for no other reason than that would run counter to the view repeated in our cases, that a decision to overrule should rest on some special reason over and above the belief that a prior case was wrongly decided. . . .

C

[O]verruling *Roe*'s central holding would not only reach an unjustifiable result under principles of stare decisis, but would seriously weaken the Court's capacity to exercise the judicial power and to function as the Supreme Court of a Nation dedicated to the rule of law. . . .

The Court's power lies . . . in its legitimacy, a product of substance and perception that shows itself in the people's acceptance of the Judiciary as fit to determine what the Nation's law means and to declare what it demands. . . . The Court must take care to speak and act in ways that allow people to accept its decisions on the terms the Court claims for them, as grounded truly in principle, not as compromises with social and political pressures having, as such, no bearing on the principled choices that the Court is obliged to make. Thus, the Court's legitimacy depends on making legally principled decisions under circumstances in which their principled character is sufficiently plausible to be accepted by the Nation.

[T]he country can accept some correction of error without necessarily questioning the legitimacy of the Court.

In two circumstances, however, the Court would almost certainly fail to receive the benefit of the doubt in overruling prior cases. [F]irst . . . [too] frequent overruling would overtax the country's belief in the Court's good faith. . . .

[Second, when] the Court decides a case in such a way as to resolve the sort of intensely divisive controversy reflected in *Roe* and those rare, comparable cases, its decision has a dimension that the resolution of the normal case does not carry. It is the dimension present whenever the Court's interpretation of the Constitution calls the contending sides of a national controversy to end their national division by accepting a common mandate rooted in the Constitution.

The Court is not asked to do this very often, having thus addressed the Nation only twice in our lifetime, in the decisions of *Brown* and *Roe*. But when the Court does act in this way, its decision requires an equally rare precedential force to counter the inevitable efforts to overturn it and to thwart its implementation. . . . [O]nly the most convincing justification under accepted standards of precedent could suffice to demonstrate that a later decision overruling the first was anything but a surrender to political pressure, and an unjustified repudiation of the principle on which the Court staked its authority in the first instance. So to overrule under fire in the absence of the most compelling reason to reexamine a watershed decision would subvert the Court's legitimacy beyond any serious question. . . .

It is true that diminished legitimacy may be restored, but only slowly. . . . Like the character of an individual, the legitimacy of the Court must be earned over time. So, indeed, must be the character of a Nation of people who aspire to live according to the rule of law. Their belief in themselves as such a people is not readily separable from their understanding of the Court invested with the authority to decide their constitutional cases and speak before all others for their constitutional ideals. If the Court's legitimacy should be undermined, then, so would the country be in its very ability to see itself through its constitutional ideals. The Court's concern with legitimacy is not for the sake of the Court but for the sake of the Nation to which it is responsible. . . .

A decision to overrule *Roe*'s essential holding under the existing circumstances would address error, if error there was, at the cost of both profound and unnecessary damage to the Court's legitimacy, and to the Nation's commitment to the rule of law. It is therefore imperative to adhere to the essence of *Roe*'s original decision, and we do so today.

IV

. . . We conclude that the basic decision in *Roe* was based on a constitutional analysis which we cannot now repudiate. The woman's liberty is not so unlimited, however, that from the outset the State cannot show its concern for the life of the unborn, and at a later point in fetal development the State's interest in life has sufficient force so that the right of the woman to terminate the pregnancy can be restricted.

That brings us, of course, to the point where much criticism has been directed at *Roe*, a criticism that always inheres when the Court draws a specific rule from what in the Constitution is but a general standard. . . . Liberty must not be extinguished for want of a line that is clear. . . .

We conclude the line should be drawn at viability, so that before that time the woman has a right to choose to terminate her pregnancy. We adhere to this principle for two reasons. First, as we have said, is the doctrine of stare decisis. . . . Although we must overrule those parts of *Thornburgh* and *Akron I* which, in our view, are inconsistent with *Roe*'s statement that the State has a legitimate interest in promoting the life or potential life of the unborn, the central premise of those cases represents an unbroken commitment by this Court to the essential holding of *Roe*. [T]he second reason is that the concept of viability, as we noted in *Roe*, is the time at which there is a realistic possibility of maintaining and nourishing a life outside the womb, so that the independent existence of the second life can in reason and all fairness be the object of state protection that now overrides the rights of the woman. Consistent with other constitutional norms, legislatures may draw lines which appear arbitrary without the necessity of offering a justification. But courts may not. We must justify the lines we draw. And there is no line other than viability which is more workable. . . . The viability line also has, as a practical matter, an element of fairness. In some broad sense it might be said that a woman who fails to act before viability has consented to the State's intervention on behalf of the developing child. The woman's right to terminate her pregnancy before viability is the most central principle of Roe v. Wade. It is a rule of law and a component of liberty we cannot renounce.

On the other side of the equation is the interest of the State in the protection of potential life. [T]he weight to be given this state interest, not the strength of the woman's interest, was the difficult question faced in *Roe*. We do not need to say whether each of us, had we been Members of the Court when the valuation of the State interest came before it as an original matter, would have concluded, as the *Roe* Court did, that its weight is insufficient to justify a ban on abortions prior to viability even when it is subject to certain exceptions. [Y]et it must be remembered that Roe v. Wade speaks with clarity in establishing not only the woman's liberty but also the State's "important and legitimate interest in potential life." That portion of the decision in *Roe* has been given too little acknowledgement and implementation by the Court in its subsequent cases. Those cases decided that any regulation touching upon the abortion decision must survive strict scrutiny, to be sustained only if drawn in narrow terms to further a compelling state interest. Not all of the cases decided under that formulation can be reconciled with the holding in *Roe* itself that the State has legitimate interests in the health of the woman and in protecting the potential life within her. In resolving this tension, we choose to rely upon *Roe*, as against the later cases.

. . . The trimester framework [established by *Roe*] no doubt was erected to ensure that the woman's right to choose not become so subordinate to the State's interest in promoting fetal life that her choice exists in theory but not in fact. We do not agree, however, that the trimester approach is necessary to accomplish this objective. . . .

Though the woman has a right to choose to terminate or continue her pregnancy before viability, it does not at all follow that the State is prohibited from taking steps to ensure that this choice is thoughtful and informed. Even in the earliest stages of pregnancy, the State may enact rules and regulations designed to encourage her to know that there are philosophic and social arguments of great weight that can be brought to bear in favor of continuing the pregnancy to full term and that there are procedures and institutions to allow adoption of unwanted children as well as a certain degree of state assistance if the mother chooses to raise the child herself.

"[T]he Constitution does not forbid a State or city, pursuant to democratic processes, from expressing a preference for normal childbirth." Webster v. Reproductive Health Services, 492 U.S., at 511. . . .

We reject the trimester framework, which we do not consider to be part of the essential holding of *Roe*. Measures aimed at ensuring that a woman's choice contemplates the consequences for the fetus do not necessarily interfere with the right recognized in *Roe*, although those measures have been found to be inconsistent with the rigid trimester framework announced in that case. A logical reading of the central holding in *Roe* itself, and a necessary reconciliation of the liberty of the woman and the interest of the State in promoting prenatal life, require, in our view, that we abandon the trimester framework as a rigid prohibition on all previability regulation aimed at the protection of fetal life. The trimester framework suffers from these basic flaws: in its formulation it misconceives the nature of the pregnant woman's interest; and in practice it undervalues the State's interest in potential life, as recognized in *Roe*.

[N]ot every law which makes a right more difficult to exercise is, ipso facto, an infringement of that right. . . . We have held that not every ballot access limitation amounts to an infringement of the right to vote. Rather, the States are granted substantial flexibility in establishing the framework within which voters choose the candidates for whom they wish to vote.

The abortion right is similar. Numerous forms of state regulation might have the incidental effect of increasing the cost or decreasing the availability of medical care, whether for abortion or any other medical procedure. The fact that a law which serves a valid purpose, one not designed to strike at the right itself, has the incidental effect of making it more difficult or more expensive to procure an abortion cannot be enough to invalidate it. Only where state regulation imposes an undue burden on a woman's ability to make this decision does the power of the State reach into the heart of the liberty protected by the Due Process Clause. . . .

[I]t is an overstatement to describe [the abortion right] as a right to decide whether to have an abortion "without interference from the State." All abortion regulations interfere to some degree with a woman's ability to decide whether to terminate her pregnancy. . . . Not all governmental intrusion is of necessity unwarranted; and that brings us to the other basic flaw in the trimester framework: even in *Roe*'s terms, in practice it undervalues the State's interest in the potential life within the woman. . . . The trimester framework . . . does not fulfill *Roe*'s own promise that the State has an interest in protecting fetal life or potential life. . . . [Because] there is a substantial state interest in potential life throughout pregnancy . . . not all regulations must be deemed unwarranted. Not all burdens on the right to decide whether to terminate a pregnancy will be undue. In our view, the undue burden standard is the appropriate means of reconciling the State's interest with the woman's constitutionally protected liberty. . . .

A finding of an undue burden is a shorthand for the conclusion that a state regulation has the purpose or effect of placing a substantial obstacle in the path of a woman seeking an abortion of a nonviable fetus. A statute with this purpose is invalid because the means chosen by the State to further the interest in potential life must be calculated to inform the woman's free choice, not hinder it. And a statute which, while furthering the interest in potential life or some other valid state interest, has the effect of placing a substantial obstacle in the path of a woman's choice cannot be considered a permissible means of serving its legitimate ends. . . .

[W]hat is at stake is the woman's right to make the ultimate decision, not a right to be insulated from all others in doing so. Regulations which do no more than create a structural mechanism by which the State, or the parent or guardian of a minor, may express profound respect for the life of the unborn are permitted, if they are not a substantial obstacle to the woman's exercise of the right to choose. Unless it has that effect on her right of choice, a state measure designed to persuade her to choose childbirth over abortion will be upheld if reasonably related to that goal. Regulations designed to foster the health of a woman seeking an abortion are valid if they do not constitute an undue burden.

[W]e give this summary:

(a) To protect the central right recognized by Roe v. Wade while at the same time accommodating the State's profound interest in potential life, we will employ the undue burden analysis as explained in this opinion. An undue burden exists, and therefore a provision of law is invalid, if its purpose or effect is to place a substantial obstacle in the path of a woman seeking an abortion before the fetus attains viability.

(b) We reject the rigid trimester framework of Roe v. Wade. To promote the State's profound interest in potential life, throughout pregnancy the State may take measures to ensure that the woman's choice is informed, and measures designed to advance this interest will not be invalidated as long as their purpose is to persuade the woman to choose childbirth over abortion. These measures must not be an undue burden on the right.

(c) As with any medical procedure, the State may enact regulations to further the health or safety of a woman seeking an abortion. Unnecessary health regulations that have the purpose or effect of presenting a substantial obstacle to a woman seeking an abortion impose an undue burden on the right.

(d) Our adoption of the undue burden analysis does not disturb the central holding of Roe v. Wade, and we reaffirm that holding. Regardless of whether exceptions are made for particular circumstances, a State may not prohibit any woman from making the ultimate decision to terminate her pregnancy before viability.

(e) We also reaffirm *Roe*'s holding that "subsequent to viability, the State in promoting its interest in the potentiality of human life may, if it chooses, regulate, and even proscribe, abortion except where it is necessary, in appropriate medical judgment, for the preservation of the life or health of the mother."

V

A

Because it is central to the operation of various other requirements, we begin with the [Pennsylvania] statute's definition of medical emergency. Under the statute, a medical emergency is "[t]hat condition which, on the basis of the physician's good faith clinical judgment, so complicates the medical condition of a pregnant woman as to necessitate the immediate abortion of her pregnancy to avert her death or for which a delay will create serious risk of substantial and irreversible impairment of a major bodily function."

Petitioners argue that the definition is too narrow, contending that it forecloses the possibility of an immediate abortion despite some significant health risks. If the contention were correct, we would be required to invalidate the restrictive operation of the provision, for the essential holding of *Roe* forbids a State from interfering with a woman's choice to undergo an abortion procedure if continuing her pregnancy would constitute a threat to her health.

. . . [The Court of Appeals stated that it] "read the medical emergency exception as intended by the Pennsylvania legislature to assure that compliance with its abortion regulations would not in any way pose a significant threat to the life or health of a woman." . . . We . . . conclude that, as construed by the Court of Appeals, the medical emergency definition imposes no undue burden on a woman's abortion right.

B

We next consider the informed consent requirement. Except in a medical emergency, the statute requires that at least 24 hours before performing an abortion a physician inform the woman of the nature of the procedure, the health risks of the abortion and of childbirth, and the "probable gestational age of the unborn child." The physician or a qualified nonphysician must inform the woman of the availability of printed materials published by the State describing the fetus and providing information about medical assistance for childbirth, information about child support from the father, and a list of agencies which provide adoption and other services as alternatives to abortion. An abortion may not be performed unless the woman certifies in writing that she has been informed of the availability of these printed materials and has been provided them if she chooses to view them.

To the extent *Akron I* and *Thornburgh* find a constitutional violation when the government requires, as it does here, the giving of truthful, nonmisleading information about the nature of the procedure, the attendant health risks and those of childbirth, and the "probable gestational age" of the fetus, those cases go too far, are inconsistent with *Roe*'s acknowledgment of an important interest in potential life, and are overruled. . . . In attempting to ensure that a woman apprehend the full consequences of her decision, the State furthers the legitimate purpose of reducing the risk that a woman may elect an abortion, only to discover later, with devastating psychological consequences, that her decision was not fully informed. If the information the State requires to be made available to the woman is truthful and not misleading, the requirement may be permissible.

We also see no reason why the State may not require doctors to inform a woman seeking an abortion of the availability of materials relating to the consequences to the fetus, even when those consequences have no direct relation to her health. . . . We would think it constitutional for the State to require that in order for there to be informed consent to a kidney transplant operation the recipient must be supplied with information about risks to the donor as well as risks to himself or herself. . . . [I]t is worth noting that the statute now before us does not require a physician to comply with the informed consent provisions "if he or she can demonstrate by a preponderance of the evidence, that he or she reasonably believed that furnishing the information would have resulted in a severely adverse effect on the physical or mental health of the patient." In this respect, the statute does not prevent the physician from exercising his or her medical judgment. . . .

All that is left of petitioners' argument is an asserted First Amendment right of a physician not to provide information about the risks of abortion, and childbirth, in a manner mandated by the State. To be sure, the physician's First Amendment rights not to speak are implicated, but only as part of the practice of medicine, subject to reasonable licensing and regulation by the State. We see no constitutional infirmity in the requirement that the physician provide the information mandated by the State here. . . .

Pennsylvania's 24-hour waiting period between the provision of the information deemed necessary to informed consent and the performance of an abortion [is not unconstitutional] under the undue burden standard. . . . The idea that important decisions will be more informed and deliberate if they follow some period of reflection does not strike us as unreasonable, particularly where the statute directs that important information become part of the background of the decision. The statute, as construed by the Court of Appeals, permits avoidance of the waiting period in the event of a medical emergency and the record evidence shows that in the vast majority of cases, a 24-hour delay does not create any appreciable health risk. In theory, at least, the waiting period is a reasonable measure to implement the State's interest in protecting the life of the unborn, a measure that does not amount to an undue burden.

Whether the mandatory 24-hour waiting period is nonetheless invalid because in practice it is a substantial obstacle to a woman's choice to terminate her pregnancy is a closer question. The findings of fact by the District Court indicate that because of the distances many women must travel to reach an abortion provider, the practical effect will often be a delay of much more than a day because the waiting period requires that a woman seeking an abortion make at least two visits to the doctor. The District Court also found that in many instances this will increase the exposure of women seeking abortions to "the harassment and hostility of anti-abortion protestors demonstrating outside a clinic." As a result, the District Court found that for those women who have the fewest financial resources, those who must travel long distances, and those who have difficulty explaining their whereabouts to husbands, employers, or others, the 24-hour waiting period will be "particularly burdensome."

These findings are troubling in some respects, but they do not demonstrate that the waiting period constitutes an undue burden. . . . [U]nder the undue burden standard a State is permitted to enact persuasive measures which favor childbirth over abortion, even if those measures do not further a health interest. And while the waiting period does limit a physician's discretion, that is not, standing alone, a reason to invalidate it. In light of the construction given the statute's definition of medical emergency by the Court of Appeals, and the District Court's findings, we cannot say that the waiting period imposes a real health risk.

We also disagree with the District Court's conclusion that the "particularly burdensome" effects of the waiting period on some women require its invalidation. A particular burden is not of necessity a substantial obstacle. Whether a burden falls on a particular group is a distinct inquiry from whether it is a substantial obstacle even as to the women in that group. And the District Court did not conclude that the waiting period is such an obstacle even for the women who are most burdened by it. Hence, on the record before us, and in the context of this facial challenge, we are not convinced that the 24-hour waiting period constitutes an undue burden.

We are left with the argument that the various aspects of the informed consent requirement are unconstitutional because they place barriers in the way of abortion on demand. Even the broadest reading of *Roe*, however, has not suggested that there is a constitutional right to abortion on demand. Rather, the right protected by *Roe* is a right to decide to terminate a pregnancy free of undue interference by the State. Because the informed consent requirement facilitates the wise exercise of that right it cannot be classified as an interference with the right *Roe* protects. The informed consent requirement is not an undue burden on that right.

C

Section 3209 of Pennsylvania's abortion law provides, except in cases of medical emergency, that no physician shall perform an abortion on a married woman without receiving a signed statement from the woman that she has notified her spouse that she is about to undergo an abortion. The woman has the option of providing an alternative signed statement certifying that her husband is not the man who impregnated her; that her husband could not be located; that the pregnancy is the result of spousal sexual assault which she has reported; or that the woman believes that notifying her husband will cause him or someone else to inflict bodily injury upon her. A physician who performs an abortion on a married woman without receiving the appropriate signed statement will have his or her license revoked, and is liable to the husband for damages.

[The joint opinion summarizes the district court's findings of fact about the statute's effects.] [The district court found that] [t]he vast majority of women consult their husbands prior to deciding to terminate their pregnancy [but] [s]tudies reveal that family violence occurs in two million families in the United States. This figure, however, is a conservative one that substantially understates (because battering is usually not reported until it reaches life-threatening proportions) the actual number of families affected by domestic violence. In fact, researchers estimate that one of every two women will be battered at some time in their life. . . .

Women of all class levels, educational backgrounds, and racial, ethnic and religious groups are battered. . . . Battering can often involve a substantial amount of sexual abuse, including marital rape and sexual mutilation. . . . In a domestic abuse situation, it is common for the battering husband to also abuse the children in an attempt to coerce the wife. . . .

[The district court found that the statute's "bodily injury" exception was inadequate because it] could not be invoked by a married woman whose husband, if notified, would, in her reasonable belief, threaten to (a) publicize her intent to have an abortion to family, friends or acquaintances; (b) retaliate against her in future child custody or divorce proceedings; (c) inflict psychological intimidation or emotional harm upon her, her children or other persons; (d) inflict bodily harm on other persons such as children, family members or other loved ones; or (e) use his control over finances to deprive of necessary monies for herself or her children. . . .

Mere notification of pregnancy is frequently a flashpoint for battering and violence within the family. The number of battering incidents is high during the pregnancy and often the worst abuse can be associated with pregnancy. . . . The battering husband may deny parentage and use the pregnancy as an excuse for abuse. . . .

Secrecy typically shrouds abusive families. Family members are instructed not to tell anyone, especially police or doctors, about the abuse and violence. Battering husbands often threaten their wives or her children with further abuse if she tells an outsider of the violence and tells her that nobody will believe her. A battered woman, therefore, is highly unlikely to disclose the violence against her for fear of retaliation by the abuser. . . . Even when confronted directly by medical personnel or other helping professionals, battered women often will not admit to the battering because they have not admitted to themselves that they are battered. . . .

Marital rape is rarely discussed with others or reported to law enforcement authorities, and of those reported only a few are prosecuted. . . . It is common for battered women to have sexual intercourse with their husbands to avoid being battered. While this type of coercive sexual activity would be spousal sexual assault as defined by the Act, many women may not consider it to be so and others would fear disbelief. . . . The marital rape exception to section 3209 cannot be claimed by women who are victims of coercive sexual behavior other than penetration. The 90-day reporting requirement of the spousal sexual assault statute further narrows the class of sexually abused wives who can claim the exception, since many of these women may be psychologically unable to discuss or report the rape for several years after the incident. . . .

[In sum, the district court found that] [b]ecause of the nature of the battering relationship, battered women are unlikely to avail themselves of the exceptions to section 3209 of the Act, regardless of whether the section applies to them.

These findings are supported by studies of domestic violence. . . . [T]here are millions of women in this country who are the victims of regular physical and psychological abuse at the hands of their husbands. Should these women become pregnant, they may have very good reasons for not wishing to inform their husbands of their decision to obtain an abortion. . . . And many women who are pregnant as a result of sexual assaults by their husbands will be unable to avail themselves of the exception for spousal sexual assault, §3209(b)(3), because the exception requires that the woman have notified law enforcement authorities within 90 days of the assault, and her husband will be notified of her report once an investigation begins. If anything in this field is certain, it is that victims of spousal sexual assault are extremely reluctant to report the abuse to the government; hence, a great many spousal rape victims will not be exempt from the notification requirement imposed by §3209.

The spousal notification requirement is thus likely to prevent a significant number of women from obtaining an abortion. It does not merely make abortions a little more difficult or expensive to obtain; for many women, it will impose a substantial obstacle. We must not blind ourselves to the fact that the significant number of women who fear for their safety and the safety of their children are likely to be deterred from procuring an abortion as surely as if the Commonwealth had outlawed abortion in all cases.

Respondents attempt to avoid the conclusion that §3209 is invalid by pointing out that . . . the effects of §3209 are felt by only one percent of the women who obtain abortions. [However,] [t]he analysis does not end with the one percent of women upon whom the statute operates; it begins there. Legislation is measured for consistency with the Constitution by its impact on those whose conduct it affects. For example, we would not say that a law which requires a newspaper to print a candidate's reply to an unfavorable editorial is valid on its face because most newspapers would adopt the policy even absent the law. See Miami Herald Publishing Co. v. Tornillo, 418 U.S. 241 (1974). The proper focus of constitutional inquiry is the group for whom the law is a restriction, not the group for whom the law is irrelevant.

. . . The unfortunate yet persisting conditions we document above will mean that in a large fraction of the cases in which §3209 is relevant, it will operate as a substantial obstacle to a woman's choice to undergo an abortion. It is an undue burden, and therefore invalid.

This conclusion is in no way inconsistent with our decisions upholding parental notification or consent requirements. Those enactments, and our judgment that they are constitutional, are based on the quite reasonable assumption that minors will benefit from consultation with their parents and that children will often not realize that their parents have their best interests at heart. We cannot adopt a parallel assumption about adult women.

. . . It is an inescapable biological fact that state regulation with respect to the child a woman is carrying will have a far greater impact on the mother's liberty than on the father's. The effect of state regulation on a woman's protected liberty is doubly deserving of scrutiny in such a case, as the State has touched not only upon the private sphere of the family but upon the very bodily integrity of the pregnant woman. The Court has held that "when the wife and the husband disagree on this decision, the view of only one of the two marriage partners can prevail. Inasmuch as it is the woman who physically bears the child and who is the more directly and immediately affected by the pregnancy, as between the two, the balance weighs in her favor." *Danforth.* This conclusion rests upon the basic nature of marriage and the nature of our Constitution: "The marital couple is not an independent entity with a mind and heart of its own, but an association of two individuals each with a separate intellectual and emotional makeup. . . . The Constitution protects individuals, men and women alike, from unjustified state interference, even when that interference is enacted into law for the benefit of their spouses."

There was a time, not so long ago, when a different understanding of the family and of the Constitution prevailed. In Bradwell v. State, 83 U.S. (16 Wall.) 130 (1872), three Members of this Court reaffirmed the common-law principle that "a woman had no legal existence separate from her husband, who was regarded as her head and representative in the social state; and, notwithstanding some recent modifications of this civil status, many of the special rules of law flowing from and dependent upon this cardinal principle still exist in full force in most States." Id. at 141 (Bradley, J., joined by Swayne and Field, JJ., concurring in judgment). Only one generation has passed since this Court observed that "woman is still regarded as the center of home and family life," with attendant "special responsibilities" that precluded full and independent legal status under the Constitution. Hoyt v. Florida, 368 U.S. 57 (1961). These views, of course, are no longer consistent with our understanding of the family, the individual, or the Constitution.

In keeping with our rejection of the common-law understanding of a woman's role within the family, the Court held in *Danforth* that the Constitution does not permit a State to require a married woman to obtain her husband's consent before undergoing an abortion. The principles that guided the Court in *Danforth* should be our guides today. For the great many women who are victims of abuse inflicted by their husbands, or whose children are the victims of such abuse, a spousal notice requirement enables the husband to wield an effective veto over his wife's decision. Whether the prospect of notification itself deters such women from seeking abortions, or whether the husband, through physical force or psychological pressure or economic coercion, prevents his wife from obtaining an abortion until it is too late, the notice requirement will often be tantamount to the veto found unconstitutional in *Danforth.* The women most affected by this law—those who most reasonably fear the consequences of notifying their husbands that they are pregnant—are in the gravest danger.

The husband's interest in the life of the child his wife is carrying does not permit the State to empower him with this troubling degree of authority over his wife. The contrary view leads to consequences reminiscent of the common law. A husband has no enforceable right to require a wife to advise him before she exercises her personal choices. If a husband's interest in the potential life of the child outweighs a wife's liberty, the State could require a married woman to notify her husband before she uses a postfertilization contraceptive. Perhaps next in line would be a statute requiring pregnant married women to notify their husbands before engaging in conduct causing risks to the fetus. After all, if the husband's interest in the fetus' safety is a sufficient predicate for state regulation, the State could reasonably conclude that pregnant wives should notify their husbands before drinking alcohol or smoking. Perhaps married women should notify their husbands before using contraceptives or before undergoing any type of surgery that may have complications affecting the husband's interest in his wife's reproductive organs. And if a husband's interest justifies notice in any of these cases, one might reasonably argue that it justifies exactly what the *Danforth* Court held it did not justify—a requirement of the husband's consent as well. A State may not give to a man the kind of dominion over his wife that parents exercise over their children. Section 3209 embodies a view of marriage consonant with the common-law status of married women but repugnant to our present understanding of marriage and of the nature of the rights secured by the Constitution. Women do not lose their constitutionally protected liberty when they marry. The Constitution protects all individuals, male or female, married or unmarried, from the abuse of governmental power, even where that power is employed for the supposed benefit of a member of the individual's family. These considerations confirm our conclusion that §3209 is invalid.

D

We next consider the parental consent provision. Except in a medical emergency, an unemancipated young woman under 18 may not obtain an abortion unless she and one of her parents (or guardian) provides informed consent as defined above. If neither a parent nor a guardian provides consent, a court may authorize the performance of an abortion upon a determination that the young woman is mature and capable of giving informed consent and has in fact given her informed consent, or that an abortion would be in her best interests.

We have been over most of this ground before. Our cases establish, and we reaffirm today, that a State may require a minor seeking an abortion to obtain the consent of a parent or guardian, provided that there is an adequate judicial bypass procedure. . . . [I]n our view, the one-parent consent requirement and judicial bypass procedure are constitutional. . . .

E

Under the recordkeeping and reporting requirements of the statute, every facility which performs abortions is required to file a report stating its name and address as well as the name and address of any related entity, such as a controlling or subsidiary organization. In the case of state-funded institutions, the information becomes public. . . .

In *Danforth*, we held that recordkeeping and reporting provisions "that are reasonably directed to the preservation of maternal health and that properly respect a patient's confidentiality and privacy are permissible." We think that under this standard, all the provisions at issue here except that relating to spousal notice are constitutional. Although they do not relate to the State's interest in informing the woman's choice, they do relate to health. The collection of information with respect to actual patients is a vital element of medical research, and so it cannot be said that the requirements serve no purpose other than to make abortions more difficult. Nor do we find that the requirements impose a substantial obstacle to a woman's choice. At most they might increase the cost of some abortions by a slight amount. While at some point increased cost could become a substantial obstacle, there is no such showing on the record before us.

Subsection (12) of the reporting provision requires the reporting of, among other things, a married woman's "reason for failure to provide notice" to her husband. This provision in effect requires women, as a condition of obtaining an abortion, to provide the Commonwealth with the precise information we have already recognized that many women have pressing reasons not to reveal. Like the spousal notice requirement itself, this provision places an undue burden on a woman's choice, and must be invalidated for that reason.

Justice STEVENS, concurring in part and dissenting in part. . . .

II

[T]he interest in protecting potential life is not grounded in the Constitution. It is, instead, an indirect interest in . . . minimizing . . . offense [to people opposed to abortion]. The State may also have a broader interest in expanding the population.

[Sections] 3205(a)(2)(i)-(iii) are unconstitutional. Those sections require a physician or counselor to provide the woman with a range of materials clearly designed to persuade her to choose not to undergo the abortion. While the State is free to produce and disseminate such material, the State may not inject such information into the woman's deliberations just as she is weighing such an important choice. However, §§3205(a)(1)(i) and (iii) . . . are constitutional. Those sections, which require the physician to inform a woman of the nature and risks of the abortion procedure and the medical risks of carrying to term, are neutral requirements comparable to those imposed in other medical procedures. Those sections indicate no effort by the State to influence the woman's choice in any way. If anything, such requirements enhance, rather than skew, the woman's decisionmaking.

III

The 24-hour waiting period required by §§3205(a)(1)-(2) of the Pennsylvania statute . . . arguably furthers the State's interests in two ways, neither of which is constitutionally permissible.

[If] the 24-hour delay is justified by the mere fact that it is likely to reduce the number of abortions . . . such an argument would justify any form of coercion that placed an obstacle in the woman's path. The State cannot further its interests by simply wearing down the ability of the pregnant woman to exercise her constitutional right.

[I]t can more reasonably be argued that the 24-hour delay furthers the State's interest in ensuring that the woman's decision is informed and thoughtful. But there is no evidence that the mandated delay benefits women or that it is necessary to enable the physician to convey any relevant information to the patient. The mandatory delay thus appears to rest on outmoded and unacceptable assumptions about the decisionmaking capacity of women. While there are well-established and consistently maintained reasons for the State to view with skepticism the ability of minors to make decisions, none of those reasons applies to an adult woman's decisionmaking ability. . . .

In the alternative, the delay requirement may be premised on the belief that the decision to terminate a pregnancy is presumptively wrong. This premise is illegitimate. . . . No person undertakes such a decision lightly—and States may not presume that a woman has failed to reflect adequately merely because her conclusion differs from the State's preference. . . . Part of the constitutional liberty to choose is the equal dignity to which each of us is entitled. A woman who decides to terminate her pregnancy is entitled to the same respect as a woman who decides to carry the fetus to term. The mandatory waiting period denies women that equal respect.

IV

In my opinion, a correct application of the "undue burden" standard leads to the same conclusion concerning the constitutionality of these requirements. A state-imposed burden on the exercise of a constitutional right is measured both by its effects and by its character: A burden may be "undue" either because the burden is too severe or because it lacks a legitimate, rational justification.

The 24-hour delay requirement fails both parts of this test. The findings of the District Court establish the severity of the burden that the 24-hour delay imposes on many pregnant women. Yet even in those cases in which the delay is not especially onerous, it is, in my opinion, "undue" because there is no evidence that such a delay serves a useful and legitimate purpose. As indicated above, there is no legitimate reason to require a woman who has agonized over her decision to leave the clinic or hospital and return again another day. While a general requirement that a physician notify her patients about the risks of a proposed medical procedure is appropriate, a rigid requirement that all patients wait 24 hours or (what is true in practice) much longer to evaluate the significance of information that is either common knowledge or irrelevant is an irrational and, therefore, "undue" burden.

The counseling provisions are similarly infirm. Whenever government commands private citizens to speak or to listen, careful review of the justification for that command is particularly appropriate. In this case, the Pennsylvania statute directs that counselors provide women seeking abortions with information concerning alternatives to abortion, the availability of medical assistance benefits, and the possibility of child-support payments. The statute requires that this information be given to all women seeking abortions, including those for whom such information is clearly useless, such as those who are married, those who have undergone the procedure in the past and are fully aware of the options, and those who are fully convinced that abortion is their only reasonable option. Moreover, the statute requires physicians to inform all of their patients of "the probable gestational age of the unborn child." This information is of little decisional value in most cases, because 90% of all abortions are performed during the first trimester when fetal age has less relevance than when the fetus nears viability. . . . Accordingly, while I disagree with Parts IV, V-B, and V-D of the joint opinion, I join the remainder of the Court's opinion.

Justice Blackmun, concurring in part, concurring in the judgment in part, and dissenting in part.

I join parts I, II, III, V-A, V-C, and VI of the joint opinion of Justices O'Connor, Kennedy, and Souter, ante.

[R]estrictive abortion laws force women to endure physical invasions far more substantial than those this Court has held to violate the constitutional principle of bodily integrity in other contexts. . . . Further, [such restrictions] deprive[] a woman of the right to make her own decision about reproduction and family planning. . . . The decision to terminate or continue a pregnancy has no less an impact on a woman's life than decisions about contraception or marriage. Because motherhood has a dramatic impact on a woman's educational prospects, employment opportunities, and self-determination, restrictive abortion laws deprive her of basic control over her life. For these reasons, "the decision whether or not to beget or bear a child" lies at "the very heart of this cluster of constitutionally protected choices."

A State's restrictions on a woman's right to terminate her pregnancy also implicate constitutional guarantees of gender equality. State restrictions on abortion compel women to continue pregnancies they otherwise might terminate. By restricting the right to terminate pregnancies, the State conscripts women's bodies into its service, forcing women to continue their pregnancies, suffer the pains of childbirth, and in most instances, provide years of maternal care. The State does not compensate women for their services; instead, it assumes that they owe this duty as a matter of course. This assumption—that women can simply be forced to accept the "natural" status and incidents of motherhood—appears to rest upon a conception of women's role that has triggered the protection of the Equal Protection Clause. The joint opinion recognizes that these assumptions about women's place in society "are no longer consistent with our understanding of the family, the individual, or the Constitution." . . .

Application of the strict scrutiny standard results in the invalidation of all the challenged provisions. Indeed, as this Court has invalidated virtually identical provisions in prior cases, stare decisis requires that we again strike them down.

Chief Justice Rehnquist, with whom Justice White, Justice Scalia, and Justice Thomas join, concurring in the judgment in part and dissenting in part.

The joint opinion, following its newly-minted variation on stare decisis, retains the outer shell of Roe v. Wade, but beats a wholesale retreat from the substance of that case. We believe that *Roe* was wrongly decided, and that it can and should be overruled consistently with our traditional approach to stare decisis in constitutional cases. We would . . . uphold the challenged provisions of the Pennsylvania statute in their entirety.

I

Unlike marriage, procreation and contraception, abortion "involves the purposeful termination of potential life." The abortion decision must therefore "be recognized as sui generis, different in kind from the others that the Court has protected under the rubric of personal or family privacy and autonomy." One cannot ignore the fact that a woman is not isolated in her pregnancy, and that the decision to abort necessarily involves the destruction of a fetus. . . .

Nor do the historical traditions of the American people support the view that the right to terminate one's pregnancy is "fundamental." The common law which we inherited from England made abortion after "quickening" an offense.

At the time of the adoption of the Fourteenth Amendment, statutory prohibitions or restrictions on abortion were commonplace; in 1868, at least 28 of the then-37 States and 8 Territories had statutes banning or limiting abortion. By the turn of the century virtually every State had a law prohibiting or restricting abortion on its books. By the middle of the present century, a liberalization trend had set in. But 21 of the restrictive abortion laws in effect in 1868 were still in effect in 1973 when *Roe* was decided, and an overwhelming majority of the States prohibited abortion unless necessary to preserve the life or health of the mother. On this record, it can scarcely be said that any deeply rooted tradition of relatively unrestricted abortion in our history supported the classification of the right to abortion as "fundamental" under the Due Process Clause of the Fourteenth Amendment.

We think, therefore, both in view of this history and of our decided cases dealing with substantive liberty under the Due Process Clause, that the Court was mistaken in *Roe* when it classified a woman's decision to terminate her pregnancy as a "fundamental right" that could be abridged only in a manner which withstood "strict scrutiny." . . .

II

[The] joint opinion [cannot] bring itself to say that *Roe* was correct as an original matter. . . . Instead, . . . the opinion . . . contains an elaborate discussion of stare decisis. This discussion of the principle of stare decisis appears to be almost entirely dicta, because the joint opinion does not apply that principle in dealing with *Roe*. *Roe* decided that a woman had a fundamental right to an abortion. The joint opinion rejects that view. *Roe* decided that abortion regulations were to be subjected to "strict scrutiny" and could be justified only in the light of "compelling state interests." The joint opinion rejects that view. *Roe* analyzed abortion regulation under a rigid trimester framework, a framework which has guided this Court's decisionmaking for 19 years. The joint opinion rejects that framework. . . . Whatever the "central holding" of *Roe* that is left after the joint opinion finishes dissecting it is surely not the result of that principle. . . .

The joint opinion . . . points to the reliance interests involved in this context in its effort to explain why precedent must be followed for precedent's sake. . . . But . . . any traditional notion of reliance is not applicable here. The Court today cuts back on the protection afforded by *Roe*, and no one claims that this action defeats any reliance interest in the disavowed trimester framework. . . . The joint opinion. . . . surmise[s] that the availability of abortion since *Roe* has led to "two decades of economic and social developments" that would be undercut if the error of *Roe* were recognized. The joint opinion's assertion of this fact is undeveloped and totally conclusory. . . . Surely it is dubious to suggest that women have reached their "places in society" in reliance upon *Roe*, rather than as a result of their determination to obtain higher education and compete with men in the job market, and of society's increasing recognition of their ability to fill positions that were previously thought to be reserved only for men.

[T]he joint opinion's argument is based solely on generalized assertions about the national psyche, on a belief that the people of this country have grown accustomed to the *Roe* decision over the last 19 years and have "ordered their thinking and living around" it. As an initial matter, one might inquire how the joint opinion can view the "central holding" of *Roe* as so deeply rooted in our constitutional culture, when it so casually uproots and disposes of that same decision's trimester framework. Furthermore, at various points in the past, the same could have been said about this Court's erroneous decisions that the Constitution allowed "separate but equal" treatment of minorities, see Plessy v. Ferguson, or that "liberty" under the Due Process Clause protected "freedom of contract." See Lochner v. New York. . . . [T]he simple fact that a generation or more had grown used to these major decisions did not prevent the Court from correcting its errors in those cases, nor should it prevent us from correctly interpreting the Constitution here.

Apparently realizing that conventional stare decisis principles do not support its position, the joint opinion advances a belief that retaining a portion of *Roe* is necessary to protect the "legitimacy" of this Court. Because the Court must take care to render decisions "grounded truly in principle," and not simply as political and social compromises, the joint opinion properly declares it to be this Court's duty to ignore the public criticism and protest that may arise as a result of a decision. . . .

But the joint opinion goes on to state that when the Court "resolve[s] the sort of intensely divisive controversy reflected in *Roe* and those rare, comparable cases," its decision is exempt from reconsideration under established principles of stare decisis in constitutional cases. This is so, the joint opinion contends, because in those "intensely divisive" cases the Court has "call[ed] the contending sides of a national controversy to end their national division by accepting a common mandate rooted in the Constitution," and must therefore take special care not to be perceived as "surrender[ing] to political pressure" and continued opposition. This is a truly novel principle, one which is contrary to both the Court's historical practice and to the Court's traditional willingness to tolerate criticism of its opinions. Under this principle, when the Court has ruled on a divisive issue, it is apparently prevented from overruling that decision for the sole reason that it was incorrect, unless opposition to the original decision has died away.

The first difficulty with this principle lies in its assumption that cases which are "intensely divisive" can be readily distinguished from those that are not. . . . In addition, because the Court's duty is to ignore public opinion and criticism on issues that come before it, its members are in perhaps the worst position to judge whether a decision divides the Nation deeply enough to justify such uncommon protection. Although many of the Court's decisions divide the populace to a large degree, we have not previously on that account shied away from applying normal rules of stare decisis when urged to reconsider earlier decisions. Over the past 21 years, for example, the Court has overruled in whole or in part 34 of its previous constitutional decisions.

The joint opinion picks out and discusses two prior Court rulings [*Plessy* and *Lochner*], that it believes are of the "intensely divisive" variety, and concludes that they are of comparable dimension to *Roe*. It appears to us very odd indeed that the joint opinion chooses as benchmarks two cases in which the Court chose not to adhere to erroneous constitutional precedent, but instead enhanced its stature by acknowledging and correcting its error, apparently in violation of the joint opinion's "legitimacy" principle. . . . There is no reason to think that either *Plessy* or *Lochner* produced the sort of public protest when they were decided that *Roe* did. There were undoubtedly large segments of the bench and bar who agreed with the dissenting views in those cases, but surely that cannot be what the Court means when it uses the term "intensely divisive," or many other cases would have to be added to the list. In terms of public protest, however, *Roe*, so far as we know, was unique. But just as the Court should not respond to that sort of protest by retreating from the decision simply to allay the concerns of the protesters, it should likewise not respond by determining to adhere to the decision at all costs lest it seem to be retreating under fire. Public protests should not alter the normal application of stare decisis, lest perfectly lawful protest activity be penalized by the Court itself.

Taking the joint opinion on its own terms, we doubt that its distinction between *Roe*, on the one hand, and *Plessy* and *Lochner*, on the other, withstands analysis. The joint opinion acknowledges that the Court improved its stature by overruling *Plessy* in *Brown* on a deeply divisive issue. And our decision in *West Coast Hotel*, which overruled Adkins v. Children's Hospital and *Lochner*, was rendered at a time when Congress was considering President Franklin Roosevelt's proposal to "reorganize" this Court and enable him to name six additional Justices in the event that any member of the Court over the age of 70 did not elect to retire. It is difficult to imagine a situation in which the Court would face more intense opposition to a prior ruling than it did at that time, and, under the general principle proclaimed in the joint opinion, the Court seemingly should have responded to this opposition by stubbornly refusing to reexamine the *Lochner* rationale, lest it lose legitimacy by appearing to "overrule under fire."

The joint opinion agrees that the Court's stature would have been seriously damaged if in *Brown* and *West Coast Hotel* it had dug in its heels and refused to apply normal principles of stare decisis to the earlier decisions. But the opinion contends that the Court was entitled to overrule *Plessy* and *Lochner* in those cases, despite the existence of opposition to the original decisions, only because both the Nation and the Court had learned new lessons in the interim. This is at best a feebly supported, post hoc rationalization for those decisions.

For example, the opinion asserts that the Court could justifiably overrule its decision in *Lochner* only because the Depression had convinced "most people" that constitutional protection of contractual freedom contributed to an economy that failed to protect the welfare of all. Surely the joint opinion does not mean to suggest that people saw this Court's failure to uphold minimum wage statutes as the cause of the Great Depression! In any event, the *Lochner* Court did not base its rule upon the policy judgment that an unregulated market was fundamental to a stable economy; it simply believed, erroneously, that "liberty" under the Due Process Clause protected the "right to make a contract." Nor is it the case that the people of this Nation only discovered the dangers of extreme laissez faire economics because of the Depression. State laws regulating maximum hours and minimum wages were in existence well before that time. . . .

The joint opinion also agrees that the Court acted properly in rejecting the doctrine of "separate but equal" in *Brown*. In fact, the opinion lauds *Brown* in comparing it to *Roe*. This is strange, in that under the opinion's "legitimacy" principle the Court would seemingly have been forced to adhere to its erroneous decision in *Plessy* because of its "intensely divisive" character. To us, adherence to *Roe* today under the guise of "legitimacy" would seem to resemble more closely adherence to *Plessy* on the same ground. The joint opinion concludes that . . . repudiation [of *Plessy*] was justified only because of newly discovered evidence that segregation had the effect of treating one race as inferior to another. But it can hardly be argued that this was not urged upon those who decided *Plessy*. . . . The Court in *Brown* simply recognized, as Justice Harlan had recognized beforehand, that the Fourteenth Amendment does not permit racial segregation. The rule of *Brown* is not tied to popular opinion about the evils of segregation; it is a judgment that the Equal Protection Clause does not permit racial segregation, no matter whether the public might come to believe that it is beneficial. . . .

. . . The Judicial Branch derives its legitimacy, not from following public opinion, but from deciding by its best lights whether legislative enactments of the popular branches of Government comport with the Constitution. The doctrine of stare decisis is an adjunct of this duty, and should be no more subject to the vagaries of public opinion than is the basic judicial task.

[I]n assuming that the Court is perceived as "surrender[ing] to political pressure" when it overrules a controversial decision, the joint opinion forgets that there are two sides to any controversy. The joint opinion asserts that, in order to protect its legitimacy, the Court must refrain from overruling a controversial decision lest it be viewed as favoring those who oppose the decision. But a decision to adhere to prior precedent is subject to the same criticism, for in such a case one can easily argue that the Court is responding to those who have demonstrated in favor of the original decision. The decision in *Roe* has engendered large demonstrations, including repeated marches on this Court and on Congress, both in opposition to and in support of that opinion. A decision either way on *Roe* can therefore be perceived as favoring one group or the other. . . .

The end result of the joint opinion's paeans of praise for legitimacy is the enunciation of a brand new standard for evaluating state regulation of a woman's right to abortion—the "undue burden" standard. [T]his standard is based even more on a judge's subjective determinations than was the trimester framework, [it] will do nothing to prevent "judges from roaming at large in the constitutional field" guided only by their personal views. Because the undue burden standard is plucked from nowhere, the question of what is a "substantial obstacle" to abortion will undoubtedly engender a variety of conflicting views. For example, in the very matter before us now, the authors of the joint opinion would uphold Pennsylvania's 24-hour waiting period, concluding that a "particular burden" on some women is not a substantial obstacle. But the authors would at the same time strike down Pennsylvania's spousal notice provision, after finding that in a "large fraction" of cases the provision will be a substantial obstacle. . . .

Furthermore, while striking down the spousal notice regulation, the joint opinion would uphold a parental consent restriction that certainly places very substantial obstacles in the path of a minor's abortion choice. The joint opinion is forthright in admitting that it draws this distinction based on a policy judgment that parents will have the best interests of their children at heart, while the same is not necessarily true of husbands as to their wives. This may or may not be a correct judgment, but it is quintessentially a legislative one. . . . Despite the efforts of the joint opinion, the undue burden standard presents nothing more workable than the trimester framework which it discards today. Under the guise of the Constitution, this Court will still impart its own preferences on the States in the form of a complex abortion code. . . .

We have stated above our belief that the Constitution does not subject state abortion regulations to heightened scrutiny. . . . A woman's interest in having an abortion is a form of liberty protected by the Due Process Clause, but States may regulate abortion procedures in ways rationally related to a legitimate state interest. . . .

[Requiring physicians to provide information about] "[t]he risks associated with an abortion and the availability of assistance that might make the alternative of normal childbirth more attractive than it might otherwise appear" . . . is rationally related to the State's interest in assuring that a woman's consent to an abortion be a fully informed decision. [I]n providing time for reflection and reconsideration, the waiting period helps ensure that a woman's decision to abort is a well-considered one, and reasonably furthers the State's legitimate interest in maternal health and in the unborn life of the fetus. . . . [T]he spousal notification requirement also rationally furthers . . . legitimate state interests. First, a husband's interests in procreation within marriage and in the potential life of his unborn child are certainly substantial ones. [B]y providing that a husband will usually know of his spouse's intent to have an abortion, the provision makes it more likely that the husband will participate in deciding the fate of his unborn child, a possibility that might otherwise have been denied him. This participation might in some cases result in a decision to proceed with the pregnancy.

[The] State also has a legitimate interest in promoting "the integrity of the marital relationship." [I]n our view, the spousal notice requirement is a rational attempt by the State to improve truthful communication between spouses and encourage collaborative decisionmaking, and thereby fosters marital integrity. . . .

[W]e therefore would hold that each of the challenged provisions of the Pennsylvania statute is consistent with the Constitution. It bears emphasis that our conclusion in this regard does not carry with it any necessary approval of these regulations. Our task is, as always, to decide only whether the challenged provisions of a law comport with the United States Constitution. If, as we believe, these do, their wisdom as a matter of public policy is for the people of Pennsylvania to decide.

Justice SCALIA, with whom THE CHIEF JUSTICE, Justice WHITE, and Justice THOMAS join, concurring in the judgment in part and dissenting in part.

[T]he issue in this case [is] not whether the power of a woman to abort her unborn child is a "liberty" in the absolute sense; or even whether it is a liberty of great importance to many women. Of course it is both. The issue is whether it is a liberty protected by the Constitution of the United States. I am sure it is not. I reach that conclusion [for] the same reason I reach the conclusion that bigamy is not constitutionally protected—because of two simple facts: (1) the Constitution says absolutely nothing about it, and (2) the longstanding traditions of American society have permitted it to be legally proscribed.[a]

---

a. The Court's suggestion that adherence to tradition would require us to uphold laws against interracial marriage is entirely wrong. Any tradition in that case was contradicted by a text—an Equal Protection Clause that explicitly establishes racial equality as a constitutional value. The enterprise launched in *Roe,* by contrast, sought to establish—in the teeth of a clear, contrary tradition—a value found nowhere in the constitutional text. There is, of course, no comparable tradition barring recognition of a "liberty interest" in carrying one's child to term free from state efforts to kill it. . . .

The Court destroys the proposition, evidently meant to represent my position, that "liberty" includes "only those practices, defined at the most specific level, that were protected against government interference by other rules of law when the Fourteenth Amendment was ratified." That is not, however, what [my plurality opinion in] *Michael H.* says; it merely observes that, in defining "liberty," we may not disregard a specific, "relevant tradition protecting, or denying protection to, the asserted right." But the Court does not wish to be fettered by any such limitations on its preferences. The Court's statement that it is "tempting" to acknowledge the authoritativeness of tradition in order to "cur[b] the discretion of federal judges," is of course rhetoric rather than reality; no government official is "tempted" to place restraints upon his own freedom of action, which is why Lord Acton did not say "Power tends to purify." The Court's temptation is in the quite opposite and more natural direction—towards systematically eliminating checks upon its own power; and it succumbs.

. . . [A]pplying the rational basis test, I would uphold the Pennsylvania statute in its entirety. I must, however, respond to a few of the more outrageous arguments in today's opinion, which it is beyond human nature to leave unanswered. . . .

[A]fter more than 19 years of effort by some of the brightest (and most determined) legal minds in the country, after more than 10 cases upholding abortion rights in this Court, and after dozens upon dozens of amicus briefs submitted in this and other cases, the best the Court can do to explain how it is that the word "liberty" must be thought to include the right to destroy human fetuses is to rattle off a collection of adjectives that simply decorate a value judgment and conceal a political choice. The right to abort, we are told, inheres in "liberty" because it is among "a person's most basic decisions"; it involves a "most intimate and personal choic[e]"; it is "central to personal dignity and autonomy"; it "originate[s] within the zone of conscience and belief"; it is "too intimate and personal" for state interference; it reflects "intimate views" of a "deep, personal character"; it involves "intimate relationships," and notions of "personal autonomy and bodily integrity"; and it concerns a particularly "important decisio[n]." But it is obvious to anyone applying "reasoned judgment" that the same adjectives can be applied to many forms of conduct that this Court . . . has held are not entitled to constitutional protection—because, like abortion, they are forms of conduct that have long been criminalized in American society. Those adjectives might be applied, for example, to homosexual sodomy, polygamy, adult incest, and suicide, all of which are equally "intimate" and "deep[ly] personal" decisions involving "personal autonomy and bodily integrity," and all of which can constitutionally be proscribed because it is our unquestionable constitutional tradition that they are proscribable. It is not reasoned judgment that supports the Court's decision; only personal predilection. . . .

The "undue burden" standard is not at all the generally applicable principle the joint opinion pretends it to be; rather, it is a unique concept created specially for this case, to preserve some judicial foothold in this ill-gotten territory. . . . And "viability" is no longer the "arbitrary" dividing line previously decried by Justice O'Connor in *Akron I*; the Court now announces that "the attainment of viability may continue to serve as the critical fact." It is difficult to maintain the illusion that we are interpreting a Constitution rather than inventing one, when we amend its provisions so breezily.

[W]hat is remarkable about the joint opinion's fact-intensive analysis is that it does not result in any measurable clarification of the "undue burden" standard. Rather, the approach of the joint opinion is, for the most part, simply to highlight certain facts in the record that apparently strike the three Justices as particularly significant in establishing (or refuting) the existence of an undue burden; after describing these facts, the opinion then simply announces that the provision either does or does not impose a "substantial obstacle" or an "undue burden." . . . The inherently standardless nature of this inquiry invites the district judge to give effect to his personal preferences about abortion. By finding and relying upon the right facts, he can invalidate, it would seem, almost any abortion restriction that strikes him as "undue"—subject, of course, to the possibility of being reversed by a Circuit Court or Supreme Court that is as unconstrained in reviewing his decision as he was in making it.

To the extent I can discern any meaningful content in the "undue burden" standard as applied in the joint opinion, it appears to be that a State may not regulate abortion in such a way as to reduce significantly its incidence. . . . [D]espite flowery rhetoric about the State's "substantial" and "profound" interest in "potential human life," and criticism of *Roe* for undervaluing that interest, the joint opinion permits the State to pursue that interest only so long as it is not too successful. . . . Reason finds no refuge in this jurisprudence of confusion. . . .

The Court's description of the place of *Roe* in the social history of the United States is unrecognizable. Not only did *Roe* not, as the Court suggests, resolve the deeply divisive issue of abortion; it did more than anything else to nourish it, by elevating it to the national level where it is infinitely more difficult to resolve. National politics were not plagued by abortion protests, national abortion lobbying, or abortion marches on Congress, before Roe v. Wade was decided. Profound disagreement existed among our citizens over the issue—as it does over other issues, such as the death penalty—but that disagreement was being worked out at the state level. As with many other issues, the division of sentiment within each State was not as closely balanced as it was among the population of the Nation as a whole, meaning not only that more people would be satisfied with the results of state-by-state resolution, but also that those results would be more stable. Pre-*Roe*, moreover, political compromise was possible.

Roe's mandate for abortion-on-demand destroyed the compromises of the past, rendered compromise impossible for the future, and required the entire issue to be resolved uniformly, at the national level. At the same time, *Roe* created a vast new class of abortion consumers and abortion proponents by eliminating the moral opprobrium that had attached to the act. ("If the Constitution guarantees abort ion, how can it be bad?"—not an accurate line of thought, but a natural one.) Many favor all of those developments, and it is not for me to say that they are wrong. But to portray *Roe* as the statesmanlike "settlement" of a divisive issue, a jurisprudential Peace of Westphalia that is worth preserving, is nothing less than Orwellian. *Roe* fanned into life an issue that has inflamed our national politics in general, and has obscured with its smoke the selection of Justices to this Court in particular, ever since. . . .

. . . I cannot agree with, indeed I am appalled by, the Court's suggestion that the decision whether to stand by an erroneous constitutional decision must be strongly influenced—against overruling, no less—by the substantial and continuing public opposition the decision has generated. The Court's judgment that any other course would "subvert the Court's legitimacy" must be another consequence of reading the error-filled history book that described the deeply divided country brought together by *Roe.* In my history book, the Court was covered with dishonor and deprived of legitimacy by Dred Scott v. Sandford, 19 How. 393 (1857), an erroneous (and widely opposed) opinion that it did not abandon, rather than by West Coast Hotel Co. v. Parrish, which produced the famous "switch in time" from the Court's erroneous (and widely opposed) constitutional opposition to the social measures of the New Deal. . . .

In truth, I am as distressed as the Court is . . . about the "political pressure" directed to the Court: the marches, the mail, the protests aimed at inducing us to change our opinions. How upsetting it is, that so many of our citizens (good people, not lawless ones, on both sides of this abortion issue, and on various sides of other issues as well) think that we Justices should properly take into account their views, as though we were engaged not in ascertaining an objective law but in determining some kind of social consensus. The Court would profit, I think, from giving less attention to the fact of this distressing phenomenon, and more attention to the cause of it. That cause permeates today's opinion: a new mode of constitutional adjudication that relies not upon text and traditional practice to determine the law, but upon what the Court calls "reasoned judgment," which turns out to be nothing but philosophical predilection and moral intuition. . . .

What makes all this relevant to the bothersome application of "political pressure" against the Court are the twin facts that the American people love democracy and the American people are not fools. As long as this Court thought (and the people thought) that we Justices were doing essentially lawyers' work up here—reading text and discerning our society's traditional understanding of that text—the public pretty much left us alone. Texts and traditions are facts to study, not convictions to demonstrate about. But if . . . our pronouncement of constitutional law rests primarily on value judgments, then a free and intelligent people's attitude towards us can be expected to be (ought to be) quite different. The people know that their value judgments are quite as good as those taught in any law school—maybe better. If, indeed, the "liberties" protected by the Constitution are, as the Court says, undefined and unbounded, then the people should demonstrate, to protest that we do not implement their values instead of ours. Not only that, but confirmation hearings for new Justices should deteriorate into question-and-answer sessions in which Senators go through a list of their constituents' most favored and most disfavored alleged constitutional rights, and seek the nominee's commitment to support or oppose them. Value judgments, after all, should be voted on, not dictated; and if our Constitution has somehow accidently committed them to the Supreme Court, at least we can have a sort of plebiscite each time a new nominee to that body is put forward. . . .

[T]here is a poignant aspect to today's opinion. Its length, and what might be called its epic tone, suggest that its authors believe they are bringing to an end a troublesome era in the history of our Nation and of our Court. "It is the dimension" of authority, they say, to "cal[l] the contending sides of national controversy to end their national division by accepting a common mandate rooted in the Constitution."

There comes vividly to mind a portrait by Emanuel Leutze that hangs in the Harvard Law School: Roger Brooke Taney, painted in 1859, the 82d year of his life, the 24th of his Chief Justiceship, the second after his opinion in *Dred Scott.* He is all in black, sitting in a shadowed red armchair, left hand resting upon a pad of paper in his lap, right hand hanging limply, almost lifelessly, beside the inner arm of the chair. He sits facing the viewer, and staring straight out. There seems to be on his face, and in his deep-set eyes, an expression of profound sadness and disillusionment. Perhaps he always looked that way, even when dwelling upon the happiest of thoughts. But those of us who know how the lustre of his great Chief Justiceship came to be eclipsed by *Dred Scott* cannot help believing that he had that case—its already apparent consequences for the Court, and its soon-to-be-played-out consequences for the Nation—burning on his mind. I expect that two years earlier he, too, had thought himself "call[ing] the contending sides of national controversy to end their national division by accepting a common mandate rooted in the Constitution." It is no more realistic for us in this case, than it was for him in that, to think that an issue of the sort they both involved—an issue involving life and death, freedom and subjugation—can be "speedily and finally settled" by the Supreme Court, as President James Buchanan in his inaugural address said the issue of slavery in the territories would be. Quite to the contrary, by foreclosing all democratic outlet for the deep passions this issue arouses, by banishing the issue from the political forum that gives all participants, even the losers, the satisfaction of a fair hearing and an honest fight, by continuing the imposition of a rigid national rule instead of allowing for regional differences, the Court merely prolongs and intensifies the anguish.

We should get out of this area, where we have no right to be, and where we do neither ourselves nor the country any good by remaining.

DISCUSSION

1. *Stare decisis.* If the Joint Opinion were willing to state that the Court rightly decided *Roe* in 1973, would the section on stare decisis have been necessary? After all, the arguments for stare decisis matter most in cases that the Court thinks were wrongly decided originally but that should nevertheless not be overruled for a variety of prudential reasons. Is *Roe* such a case?

What is the principle of stare decisis articulated by *Casey*? What standard does the Joint Opinion set forth for determining whether to stand by the Court's prior judgment? Do you find the criteria, and their application in this case, persuasive?

2. *The Court's role.* The Joint Opinion suggests that it would be inappropriate for the Court to overturn *Roe* because a consensus has not formed that it is wrong, and the Court would appear to be buckling in the face of political pressure.

a. If a consensus did form that *Roe* was incorrectly decided, and the Court responded to it, why would this not also be buckling in the face of political pressure? Is the Court saying that overwhelming public sentiment against an opinion isn't political pressure or that when a consensus has formed it will no longer appear particularly partisan to follow it? In what sense, then, is the Court a countermajoritarian institution?

b. The Joint Opinion also argues that

> [t]he Court must take care to speak and act in ways that allow people to accept its decisions on the terms the Court claims for them, as grounded truly in principle, not as compromises with social and political pressures having, as such, no bearing on the principled choices that the Court is obliged to make. Thus, the Court's legitimacy depends on making legally principled decisions under circumstances in which their principled character is sufficiently plausible to be accepted by the Nation.

Is this argument itself an argument from principle?

c. Even if *Casey* does not overrule *Roe*, it significantly revises *Roe* in ways that appear responsive to the concerns of *Roe*'s critics. For example, *Casey* abolishes the trimester framework, and it allows restrictions on abortion for the purpose of protecting unborn life in the period *before* viability, so long as the burden on exercise of the pregnant woman's right to choice is not "undue." In revising *Roe* in these ways, why isn't the Court doing what the Joint Opinion said the Court should not do?

Are there good reasons for the Court to interpret the Constitution in ways that are responsive to public opinion? On balance, is it a good or bad thing that the plurality's opinion in *Casey* is more in dialogue with the claims of the pro-choice and pro-life movements than *Roe* itself had been?

3. Casey *and women's equality*. Note how the Joint Opinion begins to reason from equality-based concerns about women—in ways the Court in *Roe* did not. For example, in the section on stare decisis the Joint Opinion states, as a reason to stand by *Roe*, that "[t]he ability of women to participate equally in the economic and social life of the Nation has been facilitated by their ability to control their reproductive lives." The authors of the Joint Opinion draw on the core values of the sex discrimination cases when the Justices explain the core values vindicated by the abortion right: A pregnant woman's "suffering is too intimate and personal for the State to insist, without more, upon its own vision of the woman's role, however dominant that vision has been in the course of our history and our culture. The destiny of the woman must be shaped to a large extent on her own conception of her spiritual imperatives and her place in society." Finally, the Joint Opinion explains why the spousal notice provision imposes an undue burden on a woman's abortion decision by comparing the restriction on abortion to the common law of coverture, a body of gender status law that gave husbands absolute dominion over their wives. Note also Justice Blackmun's concurrence, which emphasizes that abortion restrictions are unconstitutional on both liberty *and* equality grounds: Justice Blackmun argues that the "assumption—that women can simply be forced to accept the 'natural' status and incidents of motherhood—appears to rest on a conception of women's role that has triggered the protection of the Equal Protection Clause."

Note that the Joint Opinion invokes equality values to explain how the Due Process Clause protects liberty. Can you formulate an equal protection argument for abortion rights based on the opinions in *Casey*? Can this argument avoid the problems created by *Geduldig* and *Feeney*?[65] What is the disadvantage of protecting equality indirectly through the Due Process Clause rather than directly through the Equal Protection Clause?

---

65. For discussion of the equality argument in *Casey*, see Neil Siegel and Reva B. Siegel, Equality Arguments for Abortion Rights, 60 UCLA L. Rev. Disc. 160 (2013).

4. Casey *and the right to life.* Note how the Joint Opinion responds to claims of the right-to-life movement in ways that *Roe* did not, allowing state regulation of abortion to protect potential life at *any* point during pregnancy (and not only at viability), so long as such regulation does not impose an undue burden on women's decision whether to carry a pregnancy to term. *Casey* further holds that states may express their preference for unborn life and attempt to persuade women not to have abortions as long as the government provides women with information that is "truthful and not misleading" and in forms that do not impose an undue burden on her decision. The question then becomes, what is an undue burden, within the meaning of *Casey*?

5. *Undue burden.* The test that emerges from the *Casey* opinion is that the states may not place an "undue burden" on the woman's right to choose to abort. It defines this as "a state regulation [that] has the purpose or effect of placing a substantial obstacle in the path of a woman seeking an abortion of a nonviable fetus." The Court draws an opposition between statutes that are "calculated to inform the woman's free choice," and those that "hinder it." This allows abortion opponents an opportunity to persuade, but not coerce, a pregnant woman to forgo exercising her right to have an abortion. Why does the Court think that the 24-hour waiting period is in the former category rather than the latter?

Is the Court's application of the undue burden test with respect to the 24-hour waiting period consistent with its application of the test with respect to the spousal notification provision? In both cases the district court found that the provisions at issue would hinder women from obtaining abortions. Why did the Court decide that only the spousal consent provision was an undue burden? Note that although only some women would be deterred by the 24-hour waiting period, the same is also true of the spousal notification provision. Is the difference that the spousal notification provision reminded the Court too much of the old model of coverture, whereby the husband exercised control over a woman's decisions, whereas the 24-hour waiting period appeared to ensure that women deliberated about their decisions? (This might suggest that sex equality values guide application of the undue burden test, even though the test makes no mention of them.)

Why is paternalism by a state less troublesome from the standpoint of the Due Process Clause than paternalism by a husband? Are there are other social values or meanings that a 24-hour waiting period might serve?

6. *Undue burden, "truthful, nonmisleading," and "informed consent."* Observe that the statute the Joint Opinion upholds requires a physician to "inform the woman of the nature of the procedure, the health risks of the abortion and of childbirth, and the 'probable gestational age of the unborn child.'" The woman must also be advised of the availability of materials addressing other matters potentially germane to a woman's decision. In so holding, *Casey* breaks with prior opinions holding that the state could not interfere with the privacy of the patient-physician relationship, or the woman's informed choice between abortion or childbirth. Justice Blackmun, writing in *Thornburgh,* wrote that "[s]tates are not free, under the guise of protecting maternal health or potential life, to intimidate women into continuing pregnancies" or "to deter a woman from making a decision that, with her physician, is hers to make." Thornburgh v. American College of Obstetricians and Gynecologists, 476 U.S. 747, 759 (1986).

Overruling in part portions of these decisions, *Casey* held that the State's interest in potential life justifies regulations designed to ensure that "a woman apprehend the full consequences of her decision," so long as the state provides "truthful, nonmisleading information." But *Casey* contains an important qualification: Laws must be designed to "inform the woman's free choice, not to hinder it." *Casey*, in other words, allows the states to vindicate their interest in protecting potential life through dissuasive counseling—as prior case law did not. However, *Casey* still requires the state to vindicate its interests in protecting potential life in ways that respect the woman's decisional autonomy. For examples of dissuasive counseling regulation that mandate communications reaching far beyond the particular law the Court upheld in *Casey*, see Note: Absolute and Incremental Restrictions on Abortion, infra.

7. *Probing the meaning of "undue burden."* Abortion restrictions have changed substantially in the two decades since the Court decided *Casey*. Which of the new restrictions are unconstitutional under the *Casey* framework? To recall, *Casey* explains that "a finding of an undue burden is a shorthand for the conclusion that a state regulation has the purpose or effect of placing a substantial obstacle in the path of a woman seeking an abortion of a nonviable fetus." It warns that "a statute with this purpose is invalid because the means chosen by the State to further the interest in potential life must be calculated to inform the woman's free choice, not hinder it." But it explains that "a statute which, while furthering the interest in potential life or some other valid state interest, has the effect of placing a substantial obstacle in the path of a woman's choice cannot be considered a permissible means of serving its legitimate ends. . . ." Which of the following abortion regulations amount to "undue burdens" on the abortion right?

a. Suppose that a state enacts a law requiring providers to tell a woman that she

(1) may view an ultrasound image of her pregnancy before an abortion;
(2) must view an ultrasound image of her pregnancy and hear a description of the image before an abortion.

Is the distinction between permitting an ultrasound viewing significant in determining whether government has imposed an undue burden? Some ultrasounds—transvaginal ultrasounds—involve bodily intrusions. How does this affect the determination of undue burden? What factors are relevant?

b. Suppose that a state enacts a law telling abortion clinics that they must comply with highly specific building codes, asserted to promote health, but that may not be applicable to other businesses or medical services (this is an example of a TRAP law, or a "targeted regulation of abortion providers"). Suppose further that the governor of the state goes on television saying that the purpose of the law is to eliminate abortion in that state. For instance, in signing a Mississippi bill into law, Governor Phil Bryant observed:[66]

66. Transcript, The Rachel Maddow Show, Sept. 28, 2012, available at http://www.msnbc.msn.com/id/49241861/ns/msnbc-rachel_maddow_show/t/rachel-maddow-show-friday-september-th/.UIdX gmnuXuo. The Mississippi law and Governor Bryant's signing statement was also discussed on NPR. See Kathy Lohr, Mississippi Law Could Force Women's Clinic to Close, May 3, 2013, http://www.npr.org/2013/05/03/180755052/miss-law-could-force-womens-clinic-to-close.

> GOV. PHIL BRYANT (R), MISSISSIPPI: I think it's historic that today you see the first step in a movement I believe to do what we campaigned on, to say we're going to try to end abortion in Mississippi. We're going to try to continue to work to try to end abortion in Mississippi and this is an historic day to begin that process.

If Mississippi's law were challenged under *Casey*, what questions would arise?

c. Suppose that a state enacts a law that only implicates a particular *method* of abortion, such as medication used to induce abortion within the first nine weeks of pregnancy.[67] For instance, consider a health measure that requires the medication only be prescribed according to the protocol approved by the FDA when the drug was first introduced, even though this is no longer the regimen considered by physicians to be the appropriate standard of care.[68] If this requires physicians to dispense the drug at dosages they no longer consider safe, effectively preventing the drug from being offered at all, is this an undue burden under *Casey*?[69] At what point, if any, do restrictions on methods of abortion constitute an undue burden on the right itself? Would these considerations change if the state enacted a law that regulated late-term abortion methods instead of methods used earliest in pregnancy, when there is the lowest risk of complication?

For a survey of the many forms of abortion regulations enacted in the two decades since *Casey*, see Note: Absolute and Incremental Restrictions on Abortion, infra. Each form of regulation requires separate evaluation under *Casey*'s undue burden framework.

D. Abortion Restrictions After Casey

GONZALES v. CARHART [*CARHART II*], 550 U.S. 124 (2007): [In Stenberg v. Carhart (*Carhart I*), 530 U.S. 914 (2000), the Court, in a 5-4 decision, invalidated a Nebraska statute criminalizing the performance of "partial-birth abortions" except where necessary to save the life of the mother. The Court held that the law was unconstitutional in part because it lacked an exception for the health of the mother.

Following the decision in Stenberg v. Carhart, Congress passed the Partial-Birth Abortion Act of 2003. The federal Partial-Birth Abortion Act defines "partial-birth abortion," in §1531(b)(1), as a procedure in which the doctor: "(A) deliberately and

---

67. For a discussion of medical abortion, see Note: Absolute and Incremental Restrictions on Abortion, infra.

68. See, e.g., Ohio Rev. Code Ann. §2919.123 (West); 63 Okla. Stat. §1-729a.

69. For an example of such claims in response to Oklahoma's medical abortion law, see Declaration of Marilyn Eldridge in Support of Plaintiffs' Motion for Summary Judgment, at 6 ¶21, Cline v. Oklahoma Coalition for Reproductive Justice, 2013 WL 1450985 (2013) ("[W]e might not be able to comply with the Act without harm to our patients, and so we would be forced to stop providing medication abortions entirely. For example, if the Act were interpreted to mean that we could only provide medication abortions according to the protocol described in the Mifeprex FPL, we would probably stop providing medication abortions because our physicians think that the Mifeprex FPL protocol for medication abortions does not meet the standards of care.").

intentionally vaginally delivers a living fetus until, in the case of a head-first presentation, the entire fetal head is outside the [mother's] body . . . , or, in the case of breech presentation, any part of the fetal trunk past the navel is outside the [mother's] body . . . , for the purpose of performing an overt act that the person knows will kill the partially delivered living fetus"; and "(B) performs the overt act, other than completion of delivery, that kills the fetus."

In the usual second-trimester procedure, "dilation and evacuation" (D & E), the doctor dilates the cervix and then inserts surgical instruments into the uterus and maneuvers them to grab the fetus and pull it back through the cervix and vagina. The fetus is usually ripped apart as it is removed, and the doctor may take 10 to 15 passes to remove it in its entirety.

The federal act bans a variation of the standard D & E, called intact D & E, or "dilation and extraction" (D & X), which is usually performed in the second and third trimesters of pregnancy. To perform an intact D & E abortion, a doctor extracts the fetus intact or largely intact with only a few passes, pulling out its entire body instead of ripping it apart. In order to allow the head to pass through the cervix, the doctor typically pierces or crushes the skull.

Congress found that, despite the district court's findings in Stenberg v. Carhart (which were accepted by the Supreme Court in that case), there was a moral, medical, and ethical consensus that partial-birth abortion is a gruesome and inhumane procedure that is never medically necessary and should be prohibited. The Act contains an exception that allows D & X abortions for situations where the mother's life is endangered, but it contains no exception for cases in which the mother's health would be endangered by using another method of abortion. Physicians challenged the Act on the ground that it imposed an undue burden on a woman's right to choose a second-trimester abortion, that the crime defined by the statute was unduly vague, and that it contained no health exception. The Court upheld the statute 5-4.]

Justice KENNEDY delivered the opinion of the Court.

. . . The Act expresses respect for the dignity of human life. . . . Congress was concerned, furthermore, with the effects on the medical community and on its reputation caused by the practice of partial-birth abortion . . . [because] "[p]artial-birth abortion . . . confuses the medical, legal, and ethical duties of physicians to preserve and promote life, as the physician acts directly against the physical life of a child, whom he or she had just delivered, all but the head, out of the womb, in order to end that life." There can be no doubt the government "has an interest in protecting the integrity and ethics of the medical profession." Washington v. Glucksberg. Under our precedents it is clear the State has a significant role to play in regulating the medical profession.

[T]he government may use its voice and its regulatory authority to show its profound respect for the life within the woman. . . . [*Casey*'s] premise, that the State, from the inception of the pregnancy, maintains its own regulatory interest in protecting the life of the fetus that may become a child, cannot be set at naught by interpreting *Casey*'s requirement of a health exception so it becomes tantamount to allowing a doctor to choose the abortion method he or she might prefer. . . . Congress could . . . conclude that the type of abortion proscribed by the Act requires specific regulation because it implicates additional ethical and moral concerns that justify a special prohibition. Congress determined that the abortion methods it proscribed had a "disturbing similarity to the killing of a newborn infant," and thus it was concerned with "draw[ing] a bright line that clearly distinguishes abortion and infanticide." The Court has in the past confirmed the validity of drawing boundaries to prevent certain practices that extinguish life and are close to actions that are condemned. *Glucksberg* found reasonable the State's "fear that permitting assisted suicide will start it down the path to voluntary and perhaps even involuntary euthanasia."

Respect for human life finds an ultimate expression in the bond of love the mother has for her child. The Act recognizes this reality as well. Whether to have an abortion requires a difficult and painful moral decision. While we find no reliable data to measure the phenomenon, it seems unexceptionable to conclude some women come to regret their choice to abort the infant life they once created and sustained. See Brief for Sandra Cano et al. as *Amici Curiae* in No. 05-380, pp. 22-24. Severe depression and loss of esteem can follow

In a decision so fraught with emotional consequence some doctors may prefer not to disclose precise details of the means that will be used, confining themselves to the required statement of risks the procedure entails. . . . It is, however, precisely this lack of information concerning the way in which the fetus will be killed that is of legitimate concern to the State. The State has an interest in ensuring so grave a choice is well informed. It is self-evident that a mother who comes to regret her choice to abort must struggle with grief more anguished and sorrow more profound when she learns, only after the event, what she once did not know: that she allowed a doctor to pierce the skull and vacuum the fast-developing brain of her unborn child, a child assuming the human form.

It is a reasonable inference that a necessary effect of the regulation and the knowledge it conveys will be to encourage some women to carry the infant to full term, thus reducing the absolute number of late-term abortions. The medical profession, furthermore, may find different and less shocking methods to abort the fetus in the second trimester, thereby accommodating legislative demand. The State's interest in respect for life is advanced by the dialogue that better informs the political and legal systems, the medical profession, expectant mothers, and society as a whole of the consequences that follow from a decision to elect a late-term abortion. . . .

[T]he prohibition in the Act would be unconstitutional . . . if it "subject[ed] [women] to significant health risks." Ayotte v. Planned Parenthood of Northern New Eng., 546 U.S. 320, 328 (2006). . . . [But this] has been a contested factual question. The evidence presented in the trial courts and before Congress demonstrates both sides have medical support for their position . . . The Court has given state and federal legislatures wide discretion to pass legislation in areas where there is medical and scientific uncertainty. . . .

[A]lternatives are available to the prohibited procedure. As we have noted, the Act does not proscribe D & E. . . . [T]he Act allows, among other means, a commonly used and generally accepted method, so it does not construct a substantial obstacle to the abortion right.

[T]he Attorney General urges us to uphold the Act on the basis of the congressional findings alone [that state that D & X is never medically necessary]. Although we review congressional factfinding under a deferential standard, we do not in the circumstances here place dispositive weight on Congress' findings. The Court retains an independent constitutional duty to review factual findings where constitutional rights are at stake. . . . The evidence presented in the District Courts contradicts [Congress's] conclusion. Uncritical deference to Congress' factual findings in these cases is inappropriate.

On the other hand, relying on the Court's opinion in *Stenberg*, respondents contend that an abortion regulation must contain a health exception "if 'substantial medical authority supports the proposition that banning a particular procedure could endanger women's health.'" [This approach] would strike down legitimate abortion regulations, like the present one, if some part of the medical community were disinclined to follow the proscription. This is too exacting a standard. . . . The Act is not invalid on its face where there is uncertainty over whether the barred procedure is ever necessary to preserve a woman's health, given the availability of other abortion procedures that are considered to be safe alternatives. . . .

[T]he proper means to consider [health] exceptions is by as-applied challenge. . . . This is the proper manner to protect the health of the woman if it can be shown that in discrete and well-defined instances a particular condition has or is likely to occur in which the procedure prohibited by the Act must be used. In an as-applied challenge the nature of the medical risk can be better quantified and balanced than in a facial attack. . . .

[Justice Thomas, joined by Justice Scalia, concurred: "I write separately to reiterate my view that the Court's abortion jurisprudence, including *Casey* and Roe v. Wade, has no basis in the Constitution. I also note that whether the Act constitutes a permissible exercise of Congress' power under the Commerce Clause is not before the Court."]

Justice GINSBURG, with whom Justice STEVENS, Justice SOUTER, and Justice BREYER join, dissenting.

[T]oday's decision is alarming. It refuses to take *Casey* and *Stenberg* seriously. It tolerates, indeed applauds, federal intervention to ban nationwide a procedure found necessary and proper in certain cases by the American College of Obstetricians and Gynecologists (ACOG). It blurs the line, firmly drawn in *Casey*, between previability and postviability abortions. And, for the first time since *Roe*, the Court blesses a prohibition with no exception safeguarding a woman's health. . . .

[T]he Court has consistently required that laws regulating abortion, at any stage of pregnancy and in all cases, safeguard a woman's health. . . . In *Stenberg*, we expressly held that a statute banning intact D & E was unconstitutional in part because it lacked a health exception. We noted that there existed a "division of medical opinion" about the relative safety of intact D & E, but we made clear that as long as "substantial medical authority supports the proposition that banning a particular abortion procedure could endanger women's health," a health exception is required. . . . Thus, we reasoned, division in medical opinion "at most means uncertainty, a factor that signals the presence of risk, not its absence." "[A] statute that altogether forbids [intact D & E] . . . consequently must contain a health exception."

[M]any of the Act's recitations are incorrect. . . . Congress claimed there was a medical consensus that the banned procedure is never necessary. . . . But the evidence "very clearly demonstrate[d] the opposite." Similarly, Congress found that "[t]here is no credible medical evidence that partial-birth abortions are safe or are safer than other abortion procedures." But the congressional record includes letters from numerous individual physicians stating that pregnant women's health would be jeopardized under the Act, as well as statements from nine professional associations, including ACOG, the American Public Health Association, and the California Medical Association, attesting that intact D & E carries meaningful safety advantages over other methods. No comparable medical groups supported the ban. In fact, "all of the government's own witnesses disagreed with many of the specific congressional findings." . . . The trial courts concluded, in contrast to Congress' findings, that "significant medical authority supports the proposition that in some circumstances, [intact D & E] is the safest procedure." . . . Today's opinion supplies no reason to reject those findings. Nevertheless, despite the District Courts' appraisal of the weight of the evidence, and in undisguised conflict with *Stenberg*, the Court asserts that the Partial-Birth Abortion Ban Act can survive "when . . . medical uncertainty persists." This assertion is bewildering. . . .

[T]oday's ruling, the Court declares, advances "a premise central to [*Casey*'s] conclusion"—i.e., the Government's "legitimate and substantial interest in preserving and promoting fetal life." But the Act scarcely furthers that interest: The law saves not a single fetus from destruction, for it targets only a *method* of performing abortion. And surely the statute was not designed to protect the lives or health of pregnant women. In short, the Court upholds a law that, while doing nothing to "preserv[e] . . . fetal life," bars a woman from choosing intact D & E although her doctor "reasonably believes [that procedure] will best protect [her]." . . . Nonintact D & E could equally be characterized as "brutal," involving as it does "tear[ing] [a fetus] apart" and "ripp[ing] off" its limbs. "[T]he notion that either of these two equally gruesome procedures . . . is more akin to infanticide than the other, or that the State furthers any legitimate interest by banning one but not the other, is simply irrational."

[T]he Court invokes an antiabortion shibboleth for which it concededly has no reliable evidence: Women who have abortions come to regret their choices, and consequently suffer from "[s]evere depression and loss of esteem."[a] Because of women's fragile emotional state and because of the "bond of love the mother has for her child," the Court worries, doctors may withhold information about the

---

a. The Court is surely correct that, for most women, abortion is a painfully difficult decision. But "neither the weight of the scientific evidence to date nor the observable reality of 33 years of legal abortion in the United States comports with the idea that having an abortion is any more dangerous to a woman's long-term mental health than delivering and parenting a child that she did not intend to have. . . ." Cohen, Abortion and Mental Health: Myths and Realities, 9 Guttmacher Policy Rev. 8 (2006); see generally Bazelon, Is There a Post-Abortion Syndrome? N.Y. Times Magazine, Jan. 21, 2007, p. 40. See also, e.g., American Psychological Association, APA Briefing Paper on the Impact of Abortion (2005) (rejecting theory of a postabortion syndrome and stating that "[a]ccess to legal abortion to terminate an unwanted pregnancy is vital to safeguard both the physical and mental health of women"). [Justice Ginsburg cites a series of medical studies to the same effect.]

nature of the intact D & E procedure.[b] The solution the Court approves, then, is *not* to require doctors to inform women, accurately and adequately, of the different procedures and their attendant risks. Instead, the Court deprives women of the right to make an autonomous choice, even at the expense of their safety.

This way of thinking reflects ancient notions about women's place in the family and under the Constitution—ideas that have long since been discredited. Compare, e.g., Muller v. Oregon; Bradwell v. [Illinois] (Bradley, J., concurring) ("Man is, or should be, woman's protector and defender. The natural and proper timidity and delicacy which belongs to the female sex evidently unfits it for many of the occupations of civil life. . . . The paramount destiny and mission of woman are to fulfil[l] the noble and benign offices of wife and mother."), with United States v. Virginia; Califano v. Goldfarb, 430 U.S. 199 (1977) (gender-based Social Security classification rejected because it rested on "archaic and overbroad generalizations" "such as assumptions as to [women's] dependency" (internal quotation marks omitted)).

Though today's majority may regard women's feelings on the matter as "self-evident," this Court has repeatedly confirmed that "[t]he destiny of the woman must be shaped . . . on her own conception of her spiritual imperatives and her place in society." *Casey*.

DISCUSSION

1. *The emerging equal protection argument on a divided Court.* In Gonzales v. Carhart, Justice Ginsburg's dissent—joined by three other Justices—also emphasizes the equality rationale foregrounded in *Casey*. Invoking intertwined liberty and equality interests, Justice Ginsburg explained that "legal challenges to undue restrictions on abortion procedures do not seek to vindicate some generalized notion of privacy; rather, they center on a woman's autonomy to determine her life's course, and thus to enjoy equal citizenship stature." Going even further than *Casey*, Justice Ginsburg expressly cites key equal protection sex discrimination cases, United States v. Virginia, 518 U.S. 515 (1996), and Califano v. Goldfarb, 430 U.S. 199 (1977), to argue that the Court's deprivation of women's right to make an autonomous choice "reflects ancient notions about women's place in the family and under the Constitution—ideas that have long since been discredited."[70]

---

b. Notwithstanding the "bond of love" women often have with their children, not all pregnancies, this Court has recognized, are wanted, or even the product of consensual activ ity. See *Casey*, 505 U.S., at 891, 112 S. Ct. 2791 ("[O]n an average day in the United States, nearly 11,000 women are severely assaulted by their male partners. Many of these incidents involve sexual assault."). See also Glander, Moore, Michielutte, & Parsons, The Prevalence of Domestic Violence Among Women Seeking Abortion, 91 Obstetrics & Gynecology 1002 (1998); Holmes, Resnick, Kilpatrick, & Best, Rape-Related Pregnancy; Estimates and Descriptive Characteristics from a National Sample of Women, 175 Am. J. Obstetrics & Gynecology 320 (Aug. 1996).

70. For discussion of different forms of equality argument in *Casey* and *Carhart*, see Neil Siegel and Reva B. Siegel, Equality Arguments for Abortion Rights, 60 UCLA L. Rev. Disc. 160 (2013).

2. *Fetal-protective versus woman-protective arguments against abortion; "postabortion syndrome."* The Partial-Birth Abortion Ban Act focused on the minority of abortions performed late in pregnancy, with the goal of cultivating concern about protecting unborn life. Although the decision upholding the federal statute will affect the procedure employed in abortions performed for only a few hundred women a year, another aspect of Gonzales v. Carhart may prove far more important. Justice Kennedy's opinion expresses concern about protecting women as well as the unborn. In a brief passage of the decision, Justice Kennedy suggests that the state might prevent women from having a particular abortion procedure because they may regret it later on:

> It is self-evident that a mother who comes to regret her choice to abort must struggle with grief more anguished and sorrow more profound when she learns, only after the event, what she once did not know: that she allowed a doctor to pierce the skull and vacuum the fast-developing brain of her unborn child, a child assuming the human form.

Can this be described as respecting a woman's choice or is it a thinly disguised form of paternalism? Could states prohibit other abortion procedures—or indeed all abortions—on the grounds that some percentage of women will later regret their choices?

In the middle of his argument for why the state may protect women from abortions they may later regret, Justice Kennedy cites an amicus brief by Sandra Cano—the original Mary Doe in Doe v. Bolton—who is now a pro-life advocate. He refers obliquely to the theory of "postabortion syndrome" (PAS), in which having an abortion can later cause women "[s]evere depression and loss of self esteem." Justice Kennedy states that "[w]hile we find no reliable data to measure the phenomenon, it seems unexceptionable to conclude some women come to regret their choice to abort the infant life they once created and sustained." Justice Ginsburg's dissent, citing numerous medical studies, objected that Justice Kennedy had relied on studies lacking social scientific credibility.

Justice Kennedy's appeal to woman-protective reasons for restricting abortion disconnected to a new class of pro-life arguments for abortion regulation. Early pro-life arguments focused on the fetus and fetal development. By the 1990s, pro-life advocates increasingly focused on the argument that abortion hurts women because of women's natural propensities for bearing and bonding with children. These new woman-protective arguments against abortion seek to turn the rhetoric of "choice" against the pro-choice movement; they argue that women do not freely choose abortion. Pro-life advocates argue either that women are misled by abortion providers who do not explain to them what they are actually doing to their unborn children, or that women do not fully understand the risks to their physical and mental health that abortion poses. Abortion restrictions are thus necessary to prevent women from making choices that are not really theirs. See Reva B. Siegel, The New Politics of Abortion: An Equality Analysis of Women-Protective Abortion Restrictions, 2007 Ill. L. Rev. 991. Justice Ginsburg's dissent in *Carhart* challenged the majority's use of woman-protective rhetoric, pointing out the sex stereotyping inherent in the majority's analysis.

Are statutes that limit access to abortion based on woman-protective reasoning vulnerable to an equal protection challenge, as Justice Ginsburg's dissent suggests? Consider two possible theories. The first is that statutes motivated by these concerns embody stereotypical views about women's true nature and their natural bond of affection for their unborn children: Women will naturally choose to have children whenever they become pregnant unless they are misinformed or coerced. The second is that women-protective arguments embody stereotypical views about women's reasoning capacities, and particularly about their reasoning about reproductive issues: Women do not have the independence and judgment necessary to make responsible decisions about abortion and hence need protection from unscrupulous abortion doctors. Are these unconstitutional purposes under the 1970s sex equality decisions? Under *Feeney*? Under *Hibbs*?

3. *"Informed consent" and the protection of women.* Consider South Dakota's 2005 dissuasive counseling statute. The legislative findings accompanying the bill state that "all abortions . . . terminate the life of a whole, separate, unique, living human being," and "that there is an existing relationship between a pregnant woman and her unborn child during the entire period of gestation." "[P]rocedures terminating the life of an unbor n child impose risks to the life and health of the pregnant woman. . . . [A] woman seeking to terminate the life of her unborn child may be subject to pressures which can cause an emotional crisis, undue reliance on the advice of others, clouded judgment, and a willingness to violate conscience to avoid those pressures." "[P]regnant women contemplating the termination of their right to their relationship with their unborn children . . . are faced with making a profound decision most often under stress and pressures from circumstances and from other persons. [T]here exists a need for special protection of the rights of such pregnant women, and . . . the State of South Dakota has a compelling interest in providing such protection." S.D. Codified Laws §§34-23A-1.2 to 1.5. (2006).

The statute requires doctors to explain in detail the various risks of undergoing abortions, but not the risks of carrying a pregnancy to term. According to the statute, "voluntary and informed consent" to abortion requires that "in addition to any other information that must be disclosed under the common law doctrine, the physician provides th[e] pregnant woman with . . . a statement in writing" including "the following information":[71]

> . . . **(b)** That the abortion will terminate the life of a whole, separate, unique, living human being;
>
> **(c)** That the pregnant woman has an existing relationship with that unborn human being and that the relationship enjoys protection under the United States Constitution and under the laws of South Dakota;
>
> **(d)** That by having an abortion, her existing relationship and her existing constitutional rights with regards to that relationship will be terminated;
>
> **(e)** A description of all known medical risks of the procedure and statistically significant risk factors to which the pregnant woman would be subjected, including:
>
> **(i)** Depression and related psychological distress;
>
> **(ii)** Increased risk of suicide ideation and suicide;
>
> **(iii)** A statement setting forth an accurate rate of deaths due to abortions, including all deaths in which the abortion procedure was a substantial contributing factor;

71. S.D. Codified Laws §34-23A-10.1(b)-(e) (2006).

> **(iv)** All other known medical risks to the physical health of the woman, including the risk of infection, hemorrhage, danger to subsequent pregnancies, and infertility. . . .

The statute defines a "human being" "as an individual living member of the species of Homo sapiens, including the unborn human being during the entire embryonic and fetal ages from fertilization to full gestation." Id. §34-23A-1. The South Dakota statute tries to combat misinformation and pressure that might lead women to choose abortions but not misinformation and pressure that might lead them to continue their pregnancies. The reason is that the state seeks to provide informed consent only where this might move women in the direction of its preferred moral choice, that women not have abortions. Moreover, section (b) suggests that state believes informed consent requires that doctors provide women with moral truths about the nature of the fetus.

Can dissuasive counseling statutes in the abortion context avoid making some kinds of moral judgments or stating what the legislature regards as moral truths? If not, what kinds of moral judgments and statements may they properly make and not make? Is this statute consistent with women's rights under *Casey*?

4. *Dissuasive counseling requirements and postabortion syndrome: What is "medical uncertainty"?* Section (e)(i) and (e)(ii) of the South Dakota dissuasive counseling statute require, in effect, that women be informed about the dangers of the controversial phenomenon of "postabortion syndrome." Suppose that there is a consensus among the medical, psychiatric, and psychological communities that the disclosures in (e)(i) and (e)(ii) of the South Dakota informed statute are not in fact "statistically significant" risks of abortion, because "[t]he best studies available on psychological responses to unwanted pregnancy terminated by abortion in the United States suggest that severe negative reactions are rare, and they parallel those following other normal life stresses." N.E. Adler et al., Psychological Factors in Abortion: A Review, American Psychologist, 1194-1204, 1202 (Oct. 1992). Therefore, according to these authorities, stating that the risks are significant is false and misleading. Nevertheless, advocates of postabortion syndrome argue that these effects are quite frequent, and offer their own more recent studies to support it. Does the statute violate *Casey*? Does it violate the First Amendment rights of either doctors or their patients? See Robert Post, Informed Consent to Abortion: A First Amendment Analysis of Compelled Physician Speech, 2007 U. Ill. L. Rev. 939, 961-963.

NOTE: ABSOLUTE AND INCREMENTAL RESTRICTIONS ON ABORTION

The battle between supporters and opponents of abortion rights has played out across hundreds of legal challenges across the country. This Note surveys the different legislative forms that statutes opposing abortion rights have taken since *Roe*, *Casey*, and *Carhart*. In broad strokes, some aim at "absolute" prohibitions on abortion, while many others impose "incremental" restrictions on the right. Consider as you read which of these restrictions would survive *Casey*'s "undue burden" and "truthful and not misleading" analysis. Under *Casey* (understood with attention to *Carhart*), which of these restrictions are unconstitutional in purpose or impact?

1. Absolute Restrictions

Abortion bans with exception for maternal death only. The anti-abortion movement initially sought the wholesale overturning of *Roe* through a Human Life Amendment (HLA), which would have defined "persons" with constitutional rights to include "unborn offspring at every stage of their biological developments." The HLA contained only a limited exception for "reasonable medical certainty that . . . the pregnancy will cause the death of the mother."

More than 330 human life amendments have been introduced in Congress since 1973, and all have failed. No state has yet passed a "personhood" amendment, but many continue to try. The reach of the "personhood" proposals is contested, with some said to ban not only abortion, but also forms of contraception and assisted reproduction.

Abortion bans with limited exceptions. Some states passed laws permitting abortions only in cases necessary to save the woman's life, in cases of grave fetal impairment, or in cases of rape or incest. Circuit courts have rejected these as direct attacks on *Roe,* but some states, including South Dakota, have continued to try to enact them.

Abortion bans before viability. Roe and *Casey* permit states to ban abortions after the fetus becomes viable. Recently, several states have banned abortion, with a limited exception for medical emergencies, from 20 weeks, earlier than the commonly accepted understanding of viability. Alternatively, some states are trying to challenge the viability framework by arguing that other markers, like a heartbeat or the fetus's ability to feel pain, supply the appropriate framework for restricting abortion. In 2012, the Mississippi legislature considered, but did not pass, a bill that would have required a transvaginal ultrasound and banned abortion if a fetal heartbeat was detectable.[72]

2. The Incremental Approach

Many anti-abortion advocates criticized the absolutist approach, particularly after repeated defeats of HLAs in the 1980s, and turned to strategies to reverse *Roe* incrementally.[73] Proponents argue that incrementalist measures, which restrict access to abortions without banning the procedure, can change beliefs as well as practices, and ultimately could encourage the Court to "modify and narrow *Roe* and succeeding cases," as the Court suggested it might in Reproductive Health Services v. Webster, 492 U.S. 490, 521 (1989).

---

72. H.B. 1196, 2012 Leg. Reg. Sess. (Miss. 2012), available at http://billstatus.ls.state.ms.us/2012/pdf/history/HB/HB1196.xml.

73. Victor G. Rosenblum and T.J. Marzen, Strategies for Reversing Roe v. Wade Through the Courts, in Abortion and the Constitution: Reversing Roe v. Wade Through the Courts (Edward R. Grant, Dennis J. Horan & Paige C. Cunningham eds., 1987). For a more recent statement of the incrementalist position, see Memorandum from James Bopp Jr. and Richard E. Coleson on Pro-Life Strategy Issues 3, 6 (Aug. 7, 2007), available at http://operationrescue.org/pdfs/Bopp%20Memo%20re%20State %20HLA.pdf.

Incrementalist restrictions probe the limits of *Casey*'s "undue burden" standard, under which a state may regulate abortion to express a "profound interest in prenatal life," to "persuade [a woman] to choose childbirth over abortion," or to "further the health and safety of a woman seeking an abortion," so long as the "purpose or effect" of the statute is not to "place a substantial obstacle in the path of a woman seeking an abortion" before viability. Any communications with a woman making a decision about abortion must be "truthful" and "not misleading." Under *Casey*, "incidental effects" of increasing the cost or decreasing the availability of abortions do not render the regulations unconstitutional.

But *Casey* left open questions. When are burdens "undue"? When are obstacles "substantial"? How should courts evaluate a law's purpose and effect? The federal courts have considered these questions in legal challenges to a range of abortion regulations intended to make it more difficult for women to obtain abortions.

Spousal and parental notification. As noted in the previous discussion of decisions between *Roe* and *Casey*, states have passed various regulations mandating that women notify or obtain consent from relatives before obtaining an abortion. Early cases tended to be more protective of women's rights. In Planned Parenthood of Central Missouri v. Danforth, 428 U.S. 52 (1976), the Court struck down a requirement that a woman obtain prior written consent from her husband before the procedure unless the abortion was necessary to save her life, holding that "since the State cannot regulate or proscribe abortion during the first stage . . . the State cannot delegate authority to any particular person . . . to prevent abortion during the same period." 428 U.S. at 69. In Bellotti v. Baird, 443 U.S. 622 (1979) (*Bellotti II*), the Court struck down a state parental consent requirement, holding that minors must have the opportunity to go directly to a court without consulting or notifying their parents. Courts could ask whether the minor's best interest would be served by parental consultation, the majority wrote, "[b]ut this is the full extent to which parental involvement may be required." 443 U.S. at 648. However, as *Casey* itself suggests, in later cases the Court has upheld state requirements for parental *notification*, distinguishing them from earlier cases requiring parental consent.[74]

Mandatory waiting periods and two-trip requirements. These regulations are designed to encourage women seeking abortions to delay the decision, and to consider information designed to dissuade women from following through with the procedure. In practical terms, waiting periods often mean that women must make two trips to a health facility to obtain an abortion. *Casey* upheld a 24-hour waiting period, holding that the two-trip burden did not constitute a "substantial obstacle" for the "large fraction of cases in which [the provision] is relevant," but noted that different facts might produce a "substantial obstacle." States are now passing laws establishing waiting periods of up to 72 hours.[75] Critics argue

---

74. See, e.g., Planned Parenthood Association of Kansas City v. Ashcroft, 462 U.S. 476 (1983) (upholding a parental consent provision that contained an "alternative procedure" considered consistent with *Bellotti II*); Ohio v. Akron Center for Reproductive Health, 497 U.S. 502 (1990).

75. See, e.g., H.B. 1217, 86th Leg. Assemb. Sess. (S.D. 2011) (enacted).

that mandatory waiting periods interact with practical constraints on travel to create substantial obstacles for women who are in abusive relationships, are impoverished, live in rural areas, live in states with few clinics, or cannot easily take time away from work.[76]

"Informed consent" and dissuasive counseling requirements. As we have seen, under *Casey* the government may provide "truthful, nonmisleading information" that might dissuade women from ending a pregnancy, so long as the law is designed to "inform the woman's free choice, not to hinder it." *Casey*, in other words, requires government to vindicate its interest in protecting potential life in ways that respect the women's decisional autonomy.

But courts have proven quite deferential to the state's interest in providing dissuasive counseling to protect potential life. South Dakota's mandatory information law, discussed previously in the context of Gonzales v. Carhart, has been the subject of extensive litigation. It requires doctors to inform women seeking abortions, in writing, that "the abortion will terminate the life of a whole, separate, unique, living human being"; that "the pregnant woman has an existing relationship with that unborn human being" protected by the Constitution and South Dakota law; and that "by having an abortion, her existing relationship and her existing constitutional rights with regards to that relationship will be terminated," in addition to conveying the "medical" information noted above. The Eighth Circuit upheld this disclosure against *Casey* ("truthful and not misleading") and First Amendment (compelled speech) challenges.[77] The law has since been replicated in North Dakota, Missouri, and Kansas.[78] The Eighth Circuit has also upheld against *Casey* challenge a South Dakota law linking abortion to an increased risk of suicidal ideation and suicide.[79] (See discussion after *Casey* and *Carhart.*)

Ultrasound laws. Many states require that doctors providing abortions offer women the opportunity to view an ultrasound and hear the image described to them before doctors certify women's "informed consent" to the procedure;

---

76. Courts considering whether such restrictions pose an "undue burden" must consider (1) whether the law imposes enough of a burden to be substantial; (2) what qualifies as a "large fraction of [affected] cases"; and (3) how to define the relevant group affected by the law. Much may depend on the answer to the latter question. What if the relevant group, in a given case, were understood not as "all women seeking abortions" but as "all women in abusive relationships seeking abortions"?

77. Planned Parenthood of Minnesota v. Rounds, 653 F.3d 662 (8th Cir. 2011) (holding that provision requiring doctors to advise a woman seeking an abortion that "the abortion will terminate the life of a whole, separate, unique, living human being" was not a facial violation of doctors' First Amendment rights).

78. N.D. Cent. Code §14-02.1-02 (2009); Mo. Rev. Stat. §188.039 (2010); Kan. Stat. Ann. §65-6709 (2011).

79. See Planned Parenthood of Minnesota, North Dakota & South Dakota v. Rounds, 686 F.3d 889, 899, 904 (8th Cir. 2012) (en banc) (holding that the statute's mandated suicide advisory is "truthful" and that "the disclosure of the observed correlation as an 'increased risk' is not unconstitutionally misleading or irrelevant under *Casey* and *Gonzales*").

some states now *require* doctors to show women the image.[80] The Fifth Circuit has upheld a law that required a physician providing an abortion to "perform and display a sonogram of the fetus, make audible the heart auscultation of the fetus for the woman to hear, and explain to her the results of each procedure and to wait 24 hours, in most cases, between these disclosures and performing the abortion. . . . A woman may decline to view the images or hear the heartbeat . . . but she may decline to receive an explanation for the sonogram images only on certification that her pregnancy falls into one of three statutory exceptions" reasoning that the required disclosures were "the epitome of truthful, non-misleading information."[81]

Regulation of providers. Some states have instituted elaborate regulations on abortion providers sometimes called TRAP ("targeted regulation of abortion providers") laws. Some of these laws regulate the layout or content of a clinic's physical plant, for example, by establishing exacting standards for clinics' type of flooring, lighting, and hand washing stations. Others require physicians to consent to warrantless inspections of their offices or impose additional licensure and practice requirements, like requirements that facilities be licensed as ambulatory surgical centers or that physicians have hospital privileges. Although these regulations appear incremental in form, they may often operate to close a high percentage of a state's clinics. The Court addressed some of these issues in its 2016 decision in Whole Woman's Health v. Hellerstedt, infra.

Restrictions on method. The Partial-Birth Abortion Ban Act at issue in *Carhart* did not regulate whether a woman could have an abortion, but rather restricted a particular method of performing an abortion. Since *Carhart,* the most prominent restrictions on method have targeted medical abortions. Medical abortion is the

---

80. See State Policies in Brief: Requirements for Ultrasound, Guttmacher Institute 1 (Dec. 1, 2012), available at http://www.guttmacher.org/statecenter/spibs/spib_RFU.pdf (explaining that two states mandate that abortion providers perform ultrasounds and show and describe the images (although the woman can look away from the image and, under certain circumstances, decline to listen to the description); six states require that abortion providers perform ultrasounds and offer the woman the opportunity to view the image; nine states require that a woman have the opportunity to view the ultrasound image if her provider performs an ultrasound as part of the abortion preparation; and five states require that a woman have the opportunity to view an ultrasound image). See La. Rev. Stat. Ann. §40:1299.35.2(D) (explaining that, except in cases of medical emergency, abortion "is voluntary and informed only if an obstetric ultrasound is performed" including "simultaneously display[ing] the screen which depicts the active ultrasound images so that the pregnant woman may view them; and mak[ing] audible the fetal heartbeat" as well as "provid[ing] a simultaneous and objectively accurate oral explanation of what the ultrasound is depicting"); Tex. Health & Safety Code Ann. §171.012 (West) (requiring, for "voluntary and informed" abortion, that a doctor provide a sonogram, "display[] the sonogram images in a quality consistent with current medical practice in a manner that the pregnant woman may view them," give "a verbal explanation of the results of the sonogram images," and "make audible the heart auscultation for the pregnant woman to hear").

81. Texas Medical Providers Performing Abortion Services v. Lakey, 667 F.3d 570, 573, 578 (5th Cir. 2012).

use of medication to induce an abortion within the first nine weeks of pregnancy.[82] Medical abortions make up approximately 25 percent of abortions performed at eight weeks or less.[83]

Medical abortion offers several benefits over surgical abortion: It is less invasive, offers increased privacy, and is safer for women with certain conditions.[84] Moreover, medical abortion has the potential of increasing abortion access. Because the procedure is nonsurgical, mid-level practitioners can administer the pill at nonsurgical facilities in rural areas. However, many states require by law that physicians perform abortions, and extend this requirement to include medical abortions.[85] Some facilities use telemedicine as an alternative; through telemedicine, a woman can visit a clinic without a physician on staff, and a live video feed allows a remote physician to counsel the woman and dispense the medication.[86] Some states have again responded to restrict this access and require a physician and patient to be in the same room when the pill is administered.[87] Other regulations require the drug to be prescribed according to the protocol approved by the FDA in 2000 when the pill was first introduced.[88] Not only do physicians and scientists no longer regard this protocol to be the appropriate standard of care, potentially prohibiting them from offering the medication at

---

82. Irving M. Spitz, Mimi Zieman, and Sandy J. Falk, Mifepristone for the Medical Termination of Pregnancy, UpToDate (last updated Nov. 9, 2010), available at http://www.uptodate.com/contents/mifepristone-for-the-medical-termination-of-pregnancy.

83. Karen Pazol et al., Abortion Surveillance—United States, 2009, Centers for Disease Control and Prevention (Nov. 23, 2012), available at http://www.cdc.gov/mmwr/pdf/ss/ss6108.pdf.

84. Declaration of Daniel A. Grossman in Support of Plaintiffs' Motion for Summary Judgment at 9 ¶34, Cline v. Oklahoma Coalition for Reproductive Justice, 2013 WL 1450985 (2013).

85. State Policies in Brief: Medication Abortion, Guttmacher Inst., (Oct. 1, 2013), available at http://www.guttmacher.org/statecenter/spibs/spib_MA.pdf [hereinafter "State Policies in Brief"].

86. Planned Parenthood of the Heartland in Iowa instituted such a regime beginning in 2008. See, e.g., Daniel Grossman et al., Changes in Service Delivery Patterns After Introduction of Telemedicine Provision of Medical Abortion in Iowa, 103 Am. J. Pub. Health 73 (2013). Several studies have analyzed the effectiveness of Iowa's program. After controlling for several variables, one study found that after the introduction of telemedicine in Iowa, women "had a 51 percent greater likelihood of having a medical abortion" and were 46 percent more likely to have "an abortion at or before 13 weeks' gestation." Id. at 74. The same study found that abortion access increased for women in more remote parts of the state, although there was a relatively small reduction in the distance women traveled. Id. Overall, women "were significantly more likely to have a medical abortion and to have a first-trimester abortion, and women in more rural areas of the state were more likely to access abortion care, especially early medical abortion." Kate Grindlay et al., Women's and Providers' Experiences with Medical Abortion Provided Through Telemedicine: A Qualitative Study, 23 Women's Health Issues 117, 117 (2013). The Iowa Board of Medicine has since prohibited telemedicine, and Iowa Planned Parenthood has initiated litigation.

87. See State Policies in Brief, supra n.85, at 2.

88. See, e.g., 63 Okla. Stat. §1-729a; State Policies in Brief, supra n.85.

all,[89] but such regulations also triple the medication's cost, shorten the timeframe during pregnancy when the medication may be prescribed, and require women to make additional clinic visits.[90] Courts have differed in their assessment of whether these effects constitute an undue burden.[91] Which effects, if any, do you think satisfy the effects prong of *Casey*, and why?

Bans on public funding or insurance coverage. Before *Casey*, the Court upheld state restrictions on Medicaid funding for abortions,[92] and the federal Hyde Amendment, which restricts federal Medicaid funding for abortions.[93] The Court concluded that such restrictions did not interfere with a woman's due process liberty rights under *Roe* because "the financial constraints that restrict an indigent woman's ability to enjoy the full range of constitutionally protected freedom of choice are the product not of governmental restrictions on access to abortions, but rather of her indigency."[94]

In addition, some states prohibit private health insurance plans from providing coverage for abortion, and permit coverage only through a separate optional rider. Others prohibit any plans offered on a state health insurance exchange from providing abortion coverage, even through purchase of a separate, optional rider using private funds. With the passage of federal health care legislation, the debate over financing of abortion has taken new form.

NOTE: HEALTH REGULATIONS AFTER *CASEY*

When a government restricts access to abortion not to protect *unborn life*, but to protect *women's health*, how should courts apply *Casey*'s undue burden standard? Although *Casey* primarily concerned fetal protection measures, it did consider regulations of abortion premised on women's health. It held that the undue burden test applied to these regulations as well, and it explained that "[u]nnecessary health regulations that have the purpose or effect of presenting a substantial obstacle to a woman seeking an abortion impose an undue burden on the right."

On one account, unnecessary health regulations are laws "singling out abortion for onerous regulation not applied to other medical procedures of similar

---

89. See Declaration of Marilyn Eldridge in Support of Plaintiffs' Motion for Summary Judgment, at 6 ¶21, Cline v. Oklahoma Coalition for Reproductive Justice, 2013 WL 1450985 (2013).

90. Declaration of Daniel A. Grossman in Support of Plaintiffs' Motion for Summary Judgment, at 7 ¶¶26-28, Cline v. Oklahoma Coalition for Reproductive Justice, 2013 WL 1450985 (2013). American College of Obstetricians and Gynecologists Practice Bulletin No. 67: Medical Management of Abortion, 106 Obstet. Gynecol. 871, 2 (2005).

91. Compare Oklahoma Coalition for Reproductive Justice v. Cline, 2011 WL 7463407 (Okla. Dist. Dec. 2, 2011), with Planned Parenthood of Greater Texas Surgical Health Servs. v. Abbott, 1:13-CV-862-LY, 2013 WL 5781583 (W.D. Tex. Oct. 28, 2013).

92. Maher v. Roe, 432 U.S. 464 (1977).

93. Harris v. McRae, 448 U.S. 297 (1980).

94. Id. at 316. Note, however, that several states have been ordered to provide public funding for abortions, in certain circumstances, under their state constitutions.

risk."[95] Hence courts should look to whether the government burdens abortion procedures with regulations, but not other procedures of equal or greater risk to women's health.

Opponents of abortion rights instead focused on the decision in Gonzales v. Carhart, where the Court appeared more deferential to Congress. They interpreted *Carhart* to mean that when there was genuine medical uncertainty or scientific dispute, Congress could decide what it believed best protected women's health, and courts should generally defer to Congress's judgment. The difficulty with this reading was that *Carhart* also held that "[t]he Court retains an independent constitutional duty to review factual findings where constitutional rights are at stake. . . . Uncritical deference to Congress' factual findings in these cases is inappropriate."

Pro-life groups took Gonzales v. Carhart as a sign that state legislatures could pass new regulations of abortion clinics officially premised on protecting women's health, but that also constricted women's access to abortion. Because many abortion clinics could not afford to meet the new regulatory standards in state abortion laws, some or all of them would close their doors. Slowly but surely, abortion opponents hoped to limit access to abortion in substantial parts of the country by imposing successive sets of health regulations on abortion providers. Pro-life advocates argued that, even if there was a dispute about the health benefits of the new regulations, under *Gonzales*, courts should defer to legislative judgments if they were rationally related to women's health and if women could still obtain abortions in the state.

This incrementalist approach eventually led to an ambitious gambit by the State of Texas, which sought to close most clinics in the state.

WHOLE WOMAN'S HEALTH v. HELLERSTEDT, 136 S. Ct. 2292 (2016): *Whole Woman's Health* was a challenge to two key provisions in a Texas abortion regulation, H.B. 2. The first, the "admitting-privileges requirement," required any "physician performing or inducing an abortion" to "have active admitting privileges at a hospital that . . . is located not further than 30 miles from the location at which the abortion is performed or induced." The second provision, the "surgical-center requirement," provided that "the minimum standards for an abortion facility must be equivalent to the minimum standards adopted under [the Texas Health and Safety Code section] for ambulatory surgical centers."

The District Court found that H.B. 2 had a severe impact on the availability of abortions in the State of Texas. The admitting-privileges requirement led to the number of facilities in the state providing abortions dropping in half, from about 40 to about 20. The number of women of reproductive age living more than 50 miles from a clinic doubled, the number living more than 100 miles away increased by 150 percent, the number living more than 150 miles away by more than 350 percent, and the number living more than 200 miles away by about 2,800 percent. The district court also found that if the surgical-center provision took effect, the number of facilities would drop to seven or eight in the entire state; facilities would remain only in five metropolitan areas and those remaining facilities would see a significant increase in patient traffic.

---

95. Linda Greenhouse and Reva B. Siegel, *Casey* and the Clinic Closings: When "Protecting Health" Obstructs Choice, 125 Yale. L. J. 1428, 1442 (2016). For an account of TRAP laws (targeted regulation of abortion providers) and their role in closing clinics, see id. at 1444-1449.

The district court also found that before H.B. 2's passage, abortion was an extremely safe procedure with very low rates of complications and virtually no deaths; it was also safer than many more common procedures not subject to the same level of regulation; and that the cost of compliance with the surgical-center requirement would most likely exceed $1.5 million to $3 million per clinic.

The Supreme Court held H.B. 2 unconstitutional under *Casey*. Justice Breyer, writing for five Justices, began with *Casey*'s statement that there is "an 'undue burden' on a woman's right to decide to have an abortion . . . if the '*purpose or effect*' of the provision '*is to place a substantial obstacle* in the path of a woman seeking an abortion before the fetus attains viability.' (Emphasis added.) The [*Casey*] plurality added that '[u]nnecessary health regulations that have the purpose or effect of presenting a substantial obstacle to a woman seeking an abortion impose an undue burden on the right.'"

"*Casey* . . . requires that courts consider the burdens a law imposes on abortion access together with the benefits those laws confer. . . . [Although] we must review legislative 'factfinding under a deferential standard,' . . . we must not "place dispositive weight" on those 'findings.' . . . [T]he 'Court retains an independent constitutional duty to review factual findings where constitutional rights are at stake.'" *Gonzales*. In articulating this test, the Court criticized the Fifth Circuit for assuming that ordinary rational basis review would apply to health regulations that burdened women's access to abortion. It was "wrong to equate the judicial review applicable to the regulation of a constitutionally protected personal liberty with the less strict review applicable where, for example, economic legislation is at issue."

Justice Breyer applied this test to the admitting privileges requirement: "The purpose of the admitting-privileges requirement is to help ensure that women have easy access to a hospital should complications arise during an abortion procedure. But the District Court found that it brought about no such health-related benefit. [It] found that '[t]he great weight of evidence demonstrates that, before the act's passage, abortion in Texas was extremely safe with particularly low rates of serious complications and virtually no deaths occurring on account of the procedure.' Thus, there was no significant health-related problem that the new law helped to cure." Yet "[a]t the same time, the record evidence indicates that the admitting-privileges requirement places a 'substantial obstacle in the path of a woman's choice.'" The record indicated that "[t]he admitting-privileges requirement does not serve any relevant credentialing function," while it "led to the closure of half of Texas' clinics, or thereabouts. Those closures meant fewer doctors, longer waiting times, and increased crowding."

Justice Breyer then turned to the surgical-center requirement: "Prior to enactment of the new requirement, Texas law required abortion facilities to meet a host of health and safety requirements. . . . policed by random and announced inspections, at least annually, as well as administrative penalties, injunctions, civil penalties, and criminal penalties for certain violations. H.B. 2 added the requirement that an 'abortion facility' meet the 'minimum standards . . . for ambulatory surgical centers' under Texas law." But the District Court found that the surgical center requirement "does not benefit patients and is not necessary." "[R]isks are not appreciably lowered for patients who undergo abortions at ambulatory surgical centers as compared to nonsurgical-center facilities," and "women 'will not obtain better care or experience more frequent positive outcomes at an ambulatory surgical center as compared to a previously licensed facility.'" "[A]bortions taking place in an abortion facility are safe — indeed, safer than numerous procedures that take place outside hospitals and to which Texas does not apply its surgical-center requirements." And "[m]any of the building standards mandated by the act and its implementing rules have such a tangential relationship to patient safety in the context of abortion as to be nearly arbitrary." Moreover, "in the face of no threat to women's health, Texas seeks to force women to travel long distances to get abortions in crammed-to-capacity superfacilities. Patients seeking these services are less likely to get the kind of individualized attention, serious conversation, and emotional support that doctors at less taxed facilities may have offered. Healthcare facilities and medical professionals are not fungible commodities. Surgical centers attempting to accommodate sudden, vastly increased demand . . . may find that quality of care declines."

At the same time, Justice Breyer explained, "the surgical-center requirement places a substantial obstacle in the path of women seeking an abortion. The parties stipulated that the requirement would further reduce the number of abortion facilities available to seven or eight facilities" in the entire state which would not be adequate to meet the needs of the state's women. "[T]he surgical-center requirement, like the admitting-privileges requirement, provides few, if any, health benefits for women, poses a substantial obstacle to women seeking abortions, and constitutes an 'undue burden' on their constitutional right to do so."

Justice Ginsburg concurred. "In truth, 'complications from an abortion are both rare and rarely dangerous.' . . . Many medical procedures, including childbirth, are far more dangerous to patients, yet are not subject to ambulatory-surgical-center or hospital admitting-privileges requirements. . . . Given those realities, it is beyond rational belief that H.B. 2 could genuinely protect the health of women, and certain that the law 'would simply make it more difficult for them to obtain abortions.' When a State severely limits access to safe and legal procedures, women in desperate circumstances may resort to unlicensed rogue practitioners, *faute de mieux*, at great risk to their health and safety. So long as this Court adheres to *Roe* and *Casey*, Targeted Regulation of Abortion Providers laws like H.B. 2 that 'do little or nothing for health, but rather strew impediments to abortion,' cannot survive judicial inspection."

Justice Thomas dissented: "[T]oday's opinion tells the courts that, when the law's justifications are medically uncertain, they need not defer to the legislature, and must instead assess medical justifications for abortion restrictions by scrutinizing the record themselves. Finally, even if a law imposes no 'substantial obstacle' to women's access to abortions, the law now must have more than a 'reasonabl[e] relat[ion] to . . . a legitimate state interest.' These precepts are nowhere to be found in *Casey* or its successors, and transform the undue-burden test to something much more akin to strict scrutiny. . . ."

Justice Alito, joined by Chief Justice Roberts and Justice Gorsuch, also dissented: "While there can be no doubt that H.B. 2 caused some clinics to cease operation, the absence of proof regarding the reasons for particular closures is a problem."

DISCUSSION

1. *Considering both costs and benefits. Whole Woman's Health* reads *Casey*'s "undue burden" standard to consider *both* the degree of health protection an abortion regulation actually affords as well as the practical effects of the regulation on women's access to abortion. Perhaps a burden on women's access to abortion might be justified by a regulation that seriously improved women's health, but a different regulation might be "undue" if it imposed a similar burden but the health benefits were minor or nonexistent. The less plausible the health benefits, the more likely it is that the burden is "undue." Where the legislation does not improve women's health at all, burdens on the ability of women to obtain abortion are likely to be unconstitutional, as Justice Ginsburg argues in her concurrence.

The dissenting Justices—and the Fifth Circuit in the litigation below—read *Gonzales* to require a different test. The Fifth Circuit held that the question whether a health-justified restriction on abortion provided benefits to women's health was subject to rational basis review. The question of health benefits, and the evidence for them, was for democratic determination, the circuit reasoned, and it held that the district court was prohibited from scrutinizing the factual basis of the state's claims. So long as the legislature had any reason to believe that a law advanced health to any degree, judges were obliged to defer to the legislature's reasoning. It was therefore inappropriate, for example, for the lower court to inquire into whether the ambulatory surgical center provision would actually improve women's health and safety. Then, assuming that the health regulation passed rational basis scrutiny, the court would inquire into whether it imposed an undue burden on women's ability to obtain abortions.

However, as *Whole Woman's Health* explains, *Casey* and *Gonzales* did not actually employ rational basis review. Rather, it was the *dissenting* judges in *Casey* who argued for rational basis review. Justice Breyer therefore argued that judges must scrutinize the factual record to determine whether laws impose an undue burden on women's right to decide whether to carry a pregnancy to term.

2. Whole Woman's Health *and judicial review of medical justifications.* In order to decide whether the health benefits of the state's regulation are sufficiently substantial, *Whole Woman's Health* held that courts should not simply defer to legislative assertions, but must engage in their own independent factfinding. Too deferential a standard of review would have allowed determined state legislatures gradually to eliminate most access to abortion within their borders.

Linda Greenhouse and Reva Siegel argue that courts must scrutinize the facts supporting health-justified restrictions on abortion because of basic assumptions in *Casey*:

> *Casey* gave states more latitude to protect potential life but only so long as states employed means that respect women's dignity: "[T]he means chosen by the State to further the interest in potential life must be calculated to inform the woman's free choice, not hinder it" and cannot impose an "undue burden" on the abortion decision. These values at *Casey*'s core should guide review of health-justified restrictions on abortion. When states single out abortion for burdensome health regulations, courts must confirm that the laws actually serve health-related ends and do not

instead provide a backdoor way of protecting potential life. Scrutinizing the facts that justify laws targeting abortion for onerous health restrictions thus . . . ensures that legislatures do not employ health restrictions on abortion to protect unborn life by unconstitutional means. Preserving the distinction between abortion restrictions that protect women's health and abortion restrictions that protect unborn life secures constitutional protection for women's dignity.[96]

3. *The elephant in the room—unconstitutional purpose. Casey*'s undue burden test actually has two prongs. State abortion regulations are unconstitutional if they have *either* the purpose *or* the effect of placing a substantial obstacle in the path of a woman seeking abortion of a fetus before viability. Nevertheless, Justice Breyer's opinion focuses only on the effect of Texas's law and says nothing about its likely purpose. Yet it would not be at all surprising if—indeed, it is fairly likely that—then-Texas Governor Rick Perry and many state legislators supported H.B. 2 because they wanted to reduce the number of abortions in Texas, if not eliminate abortion completely. In fact, during litigation the law's supporters talked candidly about their interest in protecting unborn life, as well as women's health.[97] Texas Governor Greg Abbott objected to the Supreme Court's decision in just these terms: "The decision erodes states' lawmaking authority to safeguard the health and safety of women, and subjects more innocent life to being lost." He added that "Texas' goal is to protect innocent life, while ensuring the highest health and safety standards for women."[98]

Moreover, Targeted Regulation of Abortion Provider (TRAP) laws like H.B. 2 were developed by pro-life organizations as part of their long-term strategy to protect unborn life and eventually outlaw abortion in the United States. Although Texas politicians repeatedly asserted that their goal was to protect women's health from the harms of abortion, it does not take very much imagination to conclude that this was not the only—or even the central—purpose of laws like H.B. 2.

Why do you think Justice Breyer said nothing about the likely purposes behind H.B. 2? First, *Whole Woman's Health* is the first Supreme Court case in a quarter-century to strike down an abortion law—and it called into question the constitutionality of many other state laws. It is possible that the members of the *Whole Woman's Health* majority wanted to write in a nonaccusatory fashion. It might not be a good idea to accuse state legislatures of acting in bad faith, especially if the Court wants their cooperation in the future. (Compare Earl Warren's opinion in Brown v. Board of Education, through which he hoped to induce acceptance by Southern states.)

---

96. Greenhouse and Siegel, *Casey* and the Clinic Closings, supra n.95, at 1432.

97. Reva Siegel and Linda Greenhouse, When "Protecting Health" Obstructs Choice, SCOTUSBlog, Jan. 5, 2016, at http://www.scotusblog.com/2016/01/symposium-when-protecting-health-obstructs-choice/ (quoting state officials' statements that their goals were protection of unborn life and closing abortion clinics in Texas). For many other examples, see Greenhouse and Siegel, *Casey* and the Clinic Closings, supra n.95, at 1432.

98. Jess Bravin, Supreme Court Rejects Texas Abortion Law as "Undue Burden," Wall St. J., June 27, 2016, http://www.wsj.com/articles/supreme-court-voids-texas-abortion-regulations-1467036610.

Second, it is difficult to prove unconstitutional intention by multimember legislatures without significant direct evidence of unlawful purpose. On the other hand, the Supreme Court apparently has had no difficulty in holding that Colorado voters acted with animus in Romer v. Evans, or that Congress demeaned gay couples in United States v. Windsor. (In fact, the same Justices were in the majority in *Whole Woman's Health* and *Windsor.*) Why do you think that the majority saw the issue of gay rights differently from the issue of abortion?

Third, Justice Breyer's fact-based approach tends to make purpose inquiries superfluous. If one can show that TRAP laws like H.B. 2 don't really promote women's health, it's a fair inference that they were passed for other reasons—i.e., to make it difficult for women to get abortions. But once one has proved the effect prong of *Casey*, there's no need to go on to infer purpose and argue for the other prong of the test.

This is one way of reading Justice Ginsburg's brief concurrence. She points out that "it is beyond rational belief that H.B. 2 could genuinely protect the health of women, and certain that the law 'would simply make it more difficult for them to obtain abortions.'" If it is "beyond rational belief" that Texas was protecting women's health, the inference as to purpose is obvious.

4. *The fate of* Whole Woman's Health. At the time it was decided, *Whole Woman's Health* appeared to significantly change the legal landscape for TRAP laws. In 2018, however, Justice Kennedy retired and was replaced by Justice Kavanaugh. This meant that only four Justices were on record as committed to protecting abortion rights. (Justice Barrett replaced Justice Ginsburg in 2020, further shrinking the number of these Justices to three.). In 2020, the Court limited *Whole Woman's Health* without overruling it.

JUNE MEDICAL SERVICES L.L.C. v. RUSSO, 140 S. Ct. 2103 (2020): Louisiana passed a TRAP statute that was "almost word-for-word identical" to the Texas admitting-privileges law struck down in *Whole Woman's Health.* Justice Breyer, writing for himself and Justices Ginsburg, Sotomayor, and Kagan, held that the statute was unconstitutional. He relied, as he had in *Whole Woman's Health,* on findings by the district court about the law's likely effects on women seeking abortions.

Chief Justice Roberts, concurring in the judgment, provided the fifth vote to overturn the law: "The legal doctrine of *stare decisis* requires us, absent special circumstances, to treat like cases alike. The Louisiana law imposes a burden on access to abortion just as severe as that imposed by the Texas law, for the same reasons. Therefore Louisiana's law cannot stand under our precedents."

Chief Justice Roberts, however, rejected the balancing test of *Whole Woman's Health.* He argued that the only relevant question is whether a law imposed a substantial obstacle to women seeking abortions:

> The plurality repeats [language from *Whole Woman's Health* that says] that the undue burden standard requires courts "to weigh the law's asserted benefits against the burdens it imposes on abortion access." Read in isolation from *Casey,* such an inquiry could invite a grand "balancing test in which unweighted factors mysteriously are weighed." Under such tests, "equality of treatment is . . . impossible to achieve; predictability is destroyed; judicial arbitrariness is facilitated; judicial courage is impaired."

In this context, courts applying a balancing test would be asked in essence to weigh the State's interests in "protecting the potentiality of human life" and the health of the woman, on the one hand, against the woman's liberty interest in defining her "own concept of existence, of meaning, of the universe, and of the mystery of human life" on the other. *Casey*. There is no plausible sense in which anyone, let alone this Court, could objectively assign weight to such imponderable values and no meaningful way to compare them if there were. Attempting to do so would be like "judging whether a particular line is longer than a particular rock is heavy," Pretending that we could pull that off would require us to act as legislators, not judges, and would result in nothing other than an "unanalyzed exercise of judicial will" in the guise of a "neutral utilitarian calculus."

Nothing about *Casey* suggested that a weighing of costs and benefits of an abortion regulation was a job for the courts. On the contrary, we have explained that the "traditional rule" that "state and federal legislatures [have] wide discretion to pass legislation in areas where there is medical and scientific uncertainty" is "consistent with *Casey*." *Gonzales v. Carhart*. Casey instead focuses on the existence of a substantial obstacle, the sort of inquiry familiar to judges across a variety of contexts. . . . To be sure, [*Casey*] at times discussed the benefits of the regulations, including when it distinguished spousal notification from parental consent. But in the context of *Casey*'s governing standard, these benefits were not placed on a scale opposite the law's burdens. Rather, *Casey* discussed benefits in considering the threshold requirement that the State have a "legitimate purpose" and that the law be "reasonably related to that goal." So long as that showing is made, the only question for a court is whether a law has the "effect of placing a substantial obstacle in the path of a woman seeking an abortion of a nonviable fetus." . . .

Under principles of *stare decisis*, I agree with the plurality that the determination in *Whole Woman's Health* that Texas's law imposed a substantial obstacle requires the same determination about Louisiana's law. Under those same principles, I would adhere to the holding of Casey, requiring a substantial obstacle before striking down an abortion regulation. . . .

Justice Thomas dissented on the ground that abortion providers should not have standing to raise the constitutional claims of pregnant women who seek abortions. Justices Alito, joined by Justices Gorsuch and Kavanaugh, dissented on the ground that abortion providers lacked standing and could not fairly represent the interests of women, and also on the ground that there was insufficient evidence that Louisiana's law created a substantial obstacle to women seeking abortions. Justice Gorsuch and Justice Kavanagh also dissented separately.

DISCUSSION

1. *Stare decisis or chipping away?* In *June Medical* , the Fifth Circuit appeared to defy the Court's 2016 decision in *Whole Woman's Health*, upholding a Louisiana TRAP law that was essentially the same as the Texas law struck down four years previously. When the Supreme Court took the case following Justice Kennedy's

retirement, it was the first time that there was a majority of clearly pro-life Justices in many years.

The Court could have weakened *Casey* in several ways. It could have rejected the idea that the Louisiana statute burdens women's abilities to get an abortion, because it was possible that some doctors could meet the statute's requirements. This approach was taken by several of the dissenters, who cast doubt on the lower court's factual findings.

Another approach, promoted by Justice Thomas and Justice Alito, was to alter the doctrines of standing, and hold that abortion providers do not have standing to raise the Due Process claims of pregnant women seeking abortions. Justice Alito argued that where Louisiana justified its regulation in terms of protecting women's health, pregnant women and abortion providers had an inherent conflict of interest: Abortion providers might sacrifice women's health for lower regulation and higher profits. And although "[s]ome may not see the conflict in this case because they are convinced that the admitting privileges requirement does nothing to promote safety and is really just a ploy . . . an abortion provider's ability to assert the rights of women when it challenges ostensible safety regulations should not turn on the merits of its claim." The effect of eliminating third-party standing would be to make it harder to challenge abortion laws. Why do you think that would be?

What actually happened was that Chief Justice Roberts, who dissented in *Whole Woman's Health,* joined the Court's liberals to strike down the law on *stare decisis* grounds. But in the process, he wrote a limiting concurrence that significantly altered the balancing test of *Whole Woman's Health.* He argued that Casey does not permit the balancing of costs and benefits. Its only concern is whether there is an undue burden, i.e., "the purpose or effect of placing a substantial obstacle in the path of a woman seeking an abortion of a nonviable fetus." Roberts argues that courts must decide this question in isolation from the presence or absence of a challenged law's benefits for women's health.

The result of Roberts's test is that if a law that restricts access to abortion claims to serve women's health—whether or not it actually does so—judges should uphold the law unless they find that the law imposes a substantial obstacle to obtaining an abortion. This test will make it easier for judges who doubt that TRAP laws inhibit women's access to abortion to uphold these laws. The dissenters in this case, for example, do not believe that the admitting privileges requirements really will stop doctors from performing abortions, and Justice Alito suggests the doctors are not really trying to meet the state's requirements.

On the other hand, Roberts's test has a strange consequence, as Justice Gorsuch points out: If law places a substantial obstacle in the way of women seeking abortion, it should be struck down even if it genuinely advances women's health: "[I]t seems possible that even the most compelling and narrowly tailored medical regulation would have to fail if it placed a substantial obstacle in the way of abortion access." This result is inconsistent both with Casey and *Whole Woman's Health.* Hence Gorsuch argues that although Roberts makes much of the need to follow precedent, Roberts is actually rejecting previous precedent.

To be sure, it is unlikely that future courts will hold that regulations that actually advance women's health create an undue burden. Instead, they will argue that the burden the regulation imposes is not "substantial." Thus, after *June Medical,* judges and Justices will continue to balance costs and benefits—they will simply not say so openly. And they will likely do this hidden balancing in ways that conform to their basic views about the importance—or the illegitimacy—of constitutional rights to abortion.

2. *Pro-woman or pro-life?* Notice the confusion of state interests in *Whole Woman's Health* and *June Medical.* On the face of it, the TRAP laws seem to be about protecting women's health, but barely concealed is an interest in protecting unborn life. Should states be permitted to regulate women's health care in order to protect unborn life?

Note that running together women's health and fetal health raises issues of sex equality, because it assumes that the real interests of women do not significantly diverge from the health of fetuses. Advocates who developed the TRAP law strategy promoted "pro-woman, pro-life" laws in response to *Casey*. In the words of Dorinda Bordlee, staff counsel for Americans United for Life, who would play an important role in *June Medical*: "What we have realized is that the woman and the child have a sacred bond that should not be divided. What's good for the child is good for the mother."[99] See also Reva B. Siegel, Why Restrict Abortion? Expanding the Frame on *June Medical,* 2020 Sup. Ct. Rev. __ (forthcoming 2021), https://papers.ssrn.com/sol3/papers.cfm?abstract_id=3799645 (explaining that health-justified restrictions on abortion can reflect and enforce sex-stereotypes with health consequences for the most vulnerable women).

3. *Pro-choice and Pro-life.* In Louisiana and other states, a pro-woman, pro-life strategy might mean supporting laws that pushed women into motherhood while declining to enact laws that provide for the health of pregnant women and the children they might bear. For an argument along these lines, see Reva B. Siegel, ProChoiceLife: Asking Who Protects Life and How—and Why It Matters In Law and Politics, 93 Ind. L.J. 207, 207 (2018):

> Government can protect new life in many ways. It can restrict a woman's access to abortion, help a woman avoid an unwanted pregnancy, or help a pregnant woman bear a healthy child. If we expand the frame and analyze restrictions on abortion as one of many ways government can protect new life, we observe facts that escape notice when we debate abortion in isolation. Jurisdictions that support abortion rights may protect new life in ways that jurisdictions that restrict abortion rights will not. One jurisdiction may protect new life by means that respect women's autonomy, while another protects new life by means that restrict women's autonomy.

IV. SEXUALITY AND SEXUAL ORIENTATION

The late 1950s witnessed growing discussion about whether the criminal law should be used to regulate sex between consenting adults. This discussion was prompted by Alfred Kinsey's research documenting the prevalence of

---

99. Barry Yeoman, The Quiet War on Abortion, Mother Jones, Sept./Oct. 2001, https://www.motherjones.com/politics/2001/09/quiet-war-abortion (quoting Dorinda Bordlee, staff counsel for Americans United for Life.)

homosexual experience,[100] Britain's Wolfenden Report[101] recommending the decriminalization of "private" homosexual conduct, the debate between H.L.A. Hart and Lord Devlin,[102] and shifting cultural norms on both sides of the Atlantic. In the United States, state law reform and revisions to the Model Penal Code reflected these evolving social understandings.[103] The dialogue initially took place not in a constitutional register, but rather in the language of public policy. Over time, policy debate about criminalizing consensual sex between adults grew into constitutional claims about the justice and legitimacy of criminalizing consensual sex between adults.

The Supreme Court's 1965 decision in Griswold v. Connecticut striking down a law that criminalized contraception offered a natural vehicle for this conversation. In the period immediately following *Griswold*, as lawyers debated the underlying principle and practical reach of the decision, a number of commentators argued that constitutional protections for "privacy" protected consensual sex. Many in the legal academy assumed that protection for same-sex sexual relations would follow naturally from the privacy line of cases, and, in this period, were more likely to link *Griswold* to the decriminalization of sodomy than of abortion.[104] Those who thought that consensual sex between adults was a fundamental liberty deserving constitutional protection often appealed to John Stuart Mill's principle that "the only legitimate reason for state coercion is to prevent harm to others."[105]

What changed in this period were the beliefs guiding the harm principle's application. Many came to believe that non-procreative sex—even out of wedlock—was not necessarily harmful, and might enable valuable forms of expression and relationship. This new understanding emerged out of cultural transformations of the era popularly termed the "sexual revolution." But it was also the work of particular movements, among them the gay rights movement.

A. *Sexual Orientation: Liberty and Equality*

The movement for gay rights—like the abolitionist movement, the women's suffrage movement, the civil rights movement, and the second wave of feminism that began in the 1960s—employed legal and political strategies to make

---

100. Alfred C. Kinsey et al., Sexual Behavior in the Human Female (1953); Alfred C. Kinsey et al., Sexual Behavior in the Human Male (1948).

101. Committee on Homosexual Offences and Prostitution, Report of the Committee on Homosexual Offences and Prostitution ("The Wolfenden Report") (1957).

102. Patrick Devlin, The Enforcement of Morals (1965); H.L.A. Hart, The Morality of the Criminal Law (1965); H.L.A. Hart, Law, Liberty, and Morality (1963). See Section I.B, supra.

103. See discussion in Eskridge, Dishonorable Passions, supra n.2, at 121-127 (2008).

104. See Timothy C. Grey, Eros, Civilization and the Burger Court, 43 Law & Contemp. Probs. 83, 99 (1979) (noting in the Appendix that of 41 law review articles and student notes published in the 14 years after *Griswold*, 38 pieces argued that a "principled reading of the privacy cases would bring the sexual relations of consenting adults within the protection of the constitutional right of privacy").

105. Id. at 84-85.

its claims audible and persuasive in public debate, and to change social and legal norms.[106]

In 1969, only a few years after *Griswold*, growing claims for gay rights exploded into public view when New York police raided the Stonewall Inn bar in Greenwich Village. Stonewall's patrons rioted, demonstrating against decades of police abuse of gays and lesbians with another round of protests the following night. The Stonewall riots led to the formation of political organizations representing gay and lesbian interests and public demonstrations affirming homosexual identity.[107] The nascent movement was initially based primarily in cities such as San Francisco and New York that had nurtured the sexual revolution of the 1960s, and it remained constrained by the reticence of many gays and lesbians to risk personal and professional backlash by publicly aligning with these early activists. As the gay and lesbian rights movement, the civil rights movement, and the second-wave feminist movement challenged traditional family norms, they provoked countermobilization.

By the late 1970s, a debate emerged between those seeking respect for nontraditional families—including female-headed, same-sex, and gender-egalitarian households—and those demanding respect for the traditional family with breadwinner/caregiver gender roles. Claiming to be "pro-family," conservatives asked law to respect the traditional family as superior to all others, while progressives asked law to respect nontraditional family forms as having equal dignity.[108]

In 1977, the struggle gained national attention when Anita Bryant, a former beauty pageant winner and popular American singer, successfully led a fight to repeal a Dade County, Florida ordinance that protected gay rights. Bryant's highly publicized "Save Our Children" campaign against the ordinance was supported by Jerry Falwell and other leaders of growing group of religious conservatives beginning to experiment with entering politics.[109]

---

106. See, e.g., Linda Hirshman, Victory: The Triumphant Gay Revolution: How a Despised Minority Pushed Back, Beat Death, Found Love, and Changed America for Everyone (2012); William B. Rubenstein, Divided We Litigate: Addressing Disputes Among Group Members and Lawyers in Civil Rights Campaigns, 106 Yale L.J. 1623 (1997); Andrew M. Jacobs, The Rhetorical Construction of Rights: The Case of the Gay Rights Movement 1969-1991, 72 Neb. L. Rev. 723 (1993); Patricia A. Cain, Litigating for Lesbian and Gay Rights: A Legal History, 79 Va. L. Rev. 1551 (1993).

107. In 1968, Frank Kameny, inspired by Stokely Carmichael's creation of the phrase "Black Is Beautiful" created the slogan "Gay Is Good" for the gay civil rights movement. See GLBTQ, Kameny, Frank (1925-2011), available at http://www.glbtq.com/sciences/kameny_f.html. Toby Marotta, The Politics of Homosexuality 71-99 (1981), gives a detailed account of the Stonewall riots. See also Martin Duberman, Stonewall (1993).

108. See, e.g., Leo Ribuffo, Family Policy Past as Prologue: Jimmy Carter, the White House Conference on Families, and the Mobilization of the New Christian Right, 23 Rev. Pol'y Res. 325 (2006).

109. See generally Fred Fejes, Gay Rights and Moral Panic: The Origins of America's Debate on Homosexuality (2008) (arguing that the Dade County campaigns produced the first major national debates about the sexual counterrevolution and spurred gays and lesbians to articulate a minority identity with identifiable civil rights goals).

1. The Court's First Ruling on Laws Criminalizing Sodomy

Opposition to gay rights escalated with the outbreak of the AIDS epidemic in the early 1980s, which both heightened the visibility of gays and also stoked new forms of prejudice against them.[110] With little initially known about the disease and its causes, some took the disease's high prevalence among gay men to be a sign that homosexuality itself was pathological. Criminal prohibitions against sodomy took on a new meaning, as many began to assert that such laws were not only morally appropriate but also a public health necessity.[111] This forced gay rights advocates to defend their positions in terms of public policy: They argued that criminalizing sodomy did not contribute to the fight against AIDS and could actually adversely affect treatment of infected individuals and inhibit scientific efforts to find a cure for the disease.[112]

The election of President Ronald Reagan, who campaigned on a "pro-family" platform, provided conservatives an opportunity to block recognition of gay rights claims. President Reagan refused to mention AIDS in a public speech for years after the first reported case. He also prohibited his Surgeon General from discussing the disease, until pressure from groups like the Gay Men's Health Crisis (GMHC) and the AIDS Coalition to Unleash Power (ACT UP) led the government to begin acknowledging the existence and needs of the gay community.[113] The urgency of the AIDS crisis encouraged gays and lesbians who had not previously participated in gay rights activism to join the movement, and many remained involved in political activism even after the initial crisis abated.[114]

It was in this context that a closely divided Supreme Court first addressed a constitutional challenge to a state sodomy law in the mid-1980s. The Justices' opinions provided competing accounts of the character, scope, and centrality of the Constitution's protection for privacy—and of the role of the judiciary in vindicating that right.

---

110. For an overview of the unique moment of "gay liberation" bounded by the civil rights movements of the 1960s and the outbreak of the AIDS crisis in the early 1980s, see generally John D'Emilio, Sexual Politics, Sexual Communities: The Making of a Homosexual Minority in the United States, 1940-1970 (2d ed. 1998).

111. Ellen Ann Andersen, Out of the Closets and into the Courts: Legal Opportunity Structure and Gay Rights Liberation 112 (2006).

112. See Brief of Amici Curiae American Psychological Association and American Public Health Association in Support of Respondents, Bowers v. Hardwick, 478 U.S. 186 (1986) (No. 85-140), 1986 WL 720445.

113. See generally Randy Shilts, And the Band Played On: Politics, People and the AIDS Epidemic (1988).

114. See generally Dennis Altman, Legitimation Through Disaster: AIDS and the Gay Movement, in AIDS: The Burdens of History (Elizabeth Fee & Daniel M. Fox eds., 1988); In Changing Times: Gay Men and Lesbians Encounter HIV/AIDS (Martin P. Levine et al. eds., 1997); Howard Lune, Urban Action Networks: HIV/AIDS and Community Organizing in New York City (2006).

Bowers v. Hardwick

478 U.S. 186 (1986)

Justice WHITE delivered the opinion of the Court.

[On the morning of August 3, 1982, Officer K.R. Torick entered Michael Hardwick's house in Atlanta, Georgia, to serve him with an arrest warrant for failing to appear in court for drinking in public. Torick later claimed in his official report that when he arrived to serve the arrest warrant, one of Michael's housemates answered the door and admitted the officer. "The roommate told me [he] didn't know if Hardwick was home but said I could come in to look for him. While walking down the hallway inside the house, I saw a bedroom door partially open."[115]

Torick entered the bedroom and found Hardwick engaged in oral sex with a male companion. Torick arrested the men for violating the Georgia sodomy statute. After a preliminary hearing, the District Attorney decided not to present the matter to the grand jury unless further evidence developed.

Respondent [Hardwick] then brought suit in federal district court, challenging the constitutionality of the statute insofar as it criminalized consensual sodomy. A married couple, John and Mary Doe, also challenged the statute but were dismissed for lack of standing because there was no danger that they would be prosecuted. In a footnote, Justice White asserted that "[t]he only claim properly before the Court, therefore, is Hardwick's challenge to the Georgia statute as applied to consensual homosexual sodomy. We express no opinion on the constitutionality of the Georgia statute as applied to other acts of sodomy."]

The issue presented is whether the Federal Constitution confers a fundamental right upon homosexuals to engage in sodomy and hence invalidates the laws of the many States that still make such conduct illegal and have done so for a very long time. . . .

We first register our disagreement with the Court of Appeals and with respondent that the Court's prior cases have construed the Constitution to confer a right of privacy that extends to homosexual sodomy and for all intents and purposes have decided this case. The reach of this line of cases was sketched in Carey v. Population Services International. Pierce v. Society of Sisters and Meyer v. Nebraska were described as dealing with child rearing and education; Prince v. Massachusetts, 321 U.S. 158 (1944), with family relationships; Skinner v. Oklahoma ex rel. Williamson, with procreation; Loving v. Virginia, with marriage; Griswold v. Connecticut and Eisenstadt v. Baird, with contraception; and Roe v. Wade, with abortion. The latter three cases were interpreted as construing the Due Process Clause of the Fourteenth Amendment to confer a fundamental individual right to decide whether or not to beget or bear a child. . . .

---

115. Peter Irons, The Courage of Their Convictions 381 (1989). The statutory provision at issue, Ga. Code Ann. §16-6-2 (1984) reads as follows:

> (a) A person commits the offense of sodomy when he performs or submits to any sexual act involving the sex organs of one person and the mouth or anus of another. . . .
> (b) A person convicted of the offense of sodomy shall be punished by imprisonment for not less than one nor more than 20 years. . . .

[W]e think it evident that none of the rights announced in those cases bears any resemblance to the claimed constitutional right of homosexuals to engage in acts of sodomy that is asserted in this case. No connection between family, marriage, or procreation on the one hand and homosexual activity on the other has been demonstrated.

. . . Moreover, any claim that these cases nevertheless stand for the proposition that any kind of private sexual conduct between consenting adults is constitutionally insulated from state proscription is unsupportable. Indeed, the Court's opinion in *Carey* twice asserted that the privacy right, which the *Griswold* line of cases found to be one of the protections provided by the Due Process Clause, did not reach so far. . . .

Precedent aside, however, respondent would have us announce . . . a fundamental right to engage in homosexual sodomy. This we are quite unwilling to do. . . . Striving to assure itself and the public that announcing rights not readily identifiable in the Constitution's text involves much more than the imposition of the Justices' own choice of values on the States and the Federal Government, the Court has sought to identify the nature of the rights qualifying for heightened judicial protection. In Palko v. Connecticut, 302 U.S. 319, 325, 326 (1937), it was said that this category includes those fundamental liberties that are "implicit in the concept of ordered liberty," such that "neither liberty nor justice would exist if [they] were sacrificed." A different description of fundamental liberties appeared in Moore v. East Cleveland, 431 U.S. 494, 503 (1977) (opinion of Powell, J.), where they are characterized as those liberties that are "deeply rooted in this Nation's history and tradition."

It is obvious to us that neither of these formulations would extend a fundamental right to homosexuals to engage in acts of consensual sodomy. Proscriptions against that conduct have ancient roots. Sodomy was a criminal offense at common law and was forbidden by the laws of the original thirteen States when they ratified the Bill of Rights. In 1868, when the Fourteenth Amendment was ratified, all but 5 of the 37 States in the Union had criminal sodomy laws. In fact, until 1961, all 50 States outlawed sodomy, and today, 24 States and the District of Columbia continue to provide criminal penalties for sodomy performed in private and between consenting adults. Against this background, to claim that a right to engage in such conduct is "deeply rooted in this Nation's history and tradition" or "implicit in the concept of ordered liberty" is, at best, facetious.

Nor are we inclined to take a more expansive view of our authority to discover new fundamental rights imbedded in the Due Process Clause. The Court is most vulnerable and comes nearest to illegitimacy when it deals with judge-made constitutional law having little or no cognizable roots in the language or design of the Constitution. [T]his was painfully demonstrated by the face-off between the Executive and the Court in the 1930s which resulted in the repudiation of much of the substantive gloss that the Court had placed on the Due Process Clause of the Fifth and Fourteenth Amendments. There should be, therefore, great resistance to expand the substantive reach of those Clauses, particularly if it requires redefining the category of rights deemed to be fundamental. Otherwise, the Judiciary necessarily takes to itself further authority to govern the country without express constitutional authority. . . . The claimed right pressed on us today falls far short of overcoming this resistance.

Respondent, however, asserts that the result should be different where the homosexual conduct occurs in the privacy of the home. . . . [I]f respondent's submission is limited to the voluntary sexual conduct between consenting adults, it would be difficult, except by fiat, to limit the claimed right to homosexual conduct while leaving exposed to prosecution adultery, incest, and other sexual crimes even though they are committed in the home. We are unwilling to start down that road.

Even if the conduct at issue here is not a fundamental right, respondent asserts that there must be a rational basis for the law and that there is none in this case other than the presumed belief of a majority of the electorate in Georgia that homosexual sodomy is immoral and unacceptable. This is said to be an inadequate rationale to support the law. The law, however, is constantly based on notions of morality, and if all laws representing essentially moral choices are to be invalidated under the Due Process Clause, the courts will be very busy indeed. Even respondent makes no such claim, but insists that majority sentiments about the morality of homosexuality should be declared inadequate. We do not agree, and are unpersuaded that the sodomy laws of some 25 States should be invalidated on this basis.[a]

BURGER, C.J., concurring.

I join the Court's opinion, but I write separately to underscore my view that in constitutional terms there is no such thing as a fundamental right to commit homosexual sodomy.

As the Court notes, the proscriptions against sodomy have very "ancient roots." . . . To hold that the act of homosexual sodomy is somehow protected as a fundamental right would be to cast aside millennia of moral teaching. . . .

POWELL, J., concurring.

I join the opinion of the Court. I agree with the Court that there is no fundamental right—i.e., no substantive right under the Due Process Clause—such as that claimed by respondent. . . . This is not to suggest, however, that respondent may not be protected by the Eighth Amendment of the Constitution. The Georgia statute at issue in this case . . . authorizes a court to imprison a person for up to 20 years for a single private, consensual act of sodomy. In my view, a prison sentence for such conduct—certainly a sentence of long duration—would create a serious Eighth Amendment issue. . . .

BLACKMUN, J., joined by BRENNAN, MARSHALL, and STEVENS, JJ., dissenting.

This case is no more about "a fundamental right to engage in homosexual sodomy," as the Court purports to declare, than Stanley v. Georgia was about a fundamental right to watch obscene movies, or Katz v. United States, 389 U.S. 347 (1967) [holding a warrantless wiretap of a public telephone prohibited by the Fourth Amendment], was about a fundamental right to place interstate bets from a telephone booth. Rather, this case is about "the most comprehensive of rights and the right most valued by civilized men," namely, "the right to be let alone." Olmstead v. United States, 277 U.S. 438, 478 (1928) (Brandeis, J., dissenting). The statute at

---

a. Respondent does not defend the judgment below based on the Ninth Amendment, the Equal Protection Clause or the Eighth Amendment.

issue denies individuals the right to decide for themselves whether to engage in particular forms of private, consensual sexual activity. The Court concludes that [the statute] is valid essentially because "the laws of . . . many States . . . still make such conduct illegal and have done so for a very long time." . . . Like Justice Holmes, I believe that "[i]t is revolting to have no better reason for a rule of law than that so it was laid down in the time of Henry IV. It is still more revolting if the grounds upon which it was laid down have vanished long since, and the rule simply persists from blind imitation of the past." Holmes, The Path of the Law, 10 Harv. L. Rev. 457, 469 (1897). I believe we must analyze respondent's claim in the light of the values that underlie the constitutional right to privacy. . . .

I

[T]he Court's almost obsessive focus on homosexual activity is particularly hard to justify in light of the broad language Georgia has used. . . . Georgia has provided that "(a) person commits the offense of sodomy when he performs or submits to any sexual act involving the sex organs of one person and the mouth or anus of another." Ga. Code Ann. §16-6-2(a). The sex or status of the persons who engage in the act is irrelevant as a matter of state law. In fact, to the extent I can discern a legislative purpose for Georgia's 1968 enactment of §16-6-2, that purpose seems to have been to broaden the coverage of the law to reach heterosexual as well as homosexual activity. . . . I therefore see no basis for the Court's decision to treat this case as an "as applied" challenge to §16-6-2 or for Georgia's attempt, both in its brief and at oral argument, to defend §16-6-2 solely on the grounds that it prohibits homosexual activity. . . . [Hardwick's] claim that §16-6-2 involves an unconstitutional intrusion into his privacy and his right of intimate association does not depend in any way on his sexual orientation. . . .

While it is true that [earlier] cases may be characterized by their connection to protection of the family, the Court's conclusion that they extend no further than this . . . "close[s] [its] eyes to the basic reasons why certain rights associated with the family have been accorded shelter under the Fourteenth Amendment's Due Process Clause." We protect those rights not because they contribute, in some direct and material way, to the general public welfare, but because they form so central a part of an individual's life. . . .

[W]e protect the decision whether to marry precisely because marriage "is an association that promotes a way of life, not causes; a harmony in living, not political faiths; a bilateral loyalty, not commercial or social projects." *Griswold.* We protect the decision whether to have a child because parenthood alters so dramatically an individual's self-definition, not because of demographic considerations or the Bible's command to be fruitful and multiply. And we protect the family because it contributes so powerfully to the happiness of individuals, not because of a preference for stereotypical households. . . .

Only the most willful blindness could obscure the fact that sexual intimacy is "a sensitive, key relationship of human existence, central to family life, community welfare, and the development of human personality." The fact that individuals define themselves in a significant way through their intimate sexual relationships with others suggests, in a Nation as diverse as ours, that there may be many "right" ways of conducting those relationships, and that much of the richness of a relationship will come from the freedom an individual has to choose the form and nature of these intensely personal bonds. . . .

The Court claims that its decision today merely refuses to recognize a fundamental right to engage in homosexual sodomy; what the Court really has refused to recognize is the fundamental interest all individuals have in controlling the nature of their intimate associations with others. . . .

The Court's failure to comprehend the magnitude of the liberty interests at stake in this case leads it to slight the question whether petitioner, on behalf of the State, has justified Georgia's infringement on these interests. . . . [P]etitioner asserts that the acts made criminal by the statute may have serious adverse consequences for "the general public health and welfare," such as spreading communicable diseases or fostering other criminal activity. . . . Nothing in the record before the Court provides any justification for finding the activity forbidden by 16-6-2 to be physically dangerous, either to the persons engaged in it or to others.

Although I do not think it necessary to decide today issues that are not even remotely before us, it does seem to me that a court could find simple, analytically sound distinctions between certain private, consensual sexual conduct, on the one hand, and adultery and incest (the only two vaguely specific "sexual crimes" to which the majority points), on the other. For example, marriage, in addition to its spiritual aspects, is a civil contract that entitles the contracting parties to a variety of governmentally provided benefits. A State might define the contractual commitment necessary to become eligible for these benefits to include a commitment of fidelity and then punish individuals for breaching that contract. Moreover, a State might conclude that adultery is likely to injure third persons, in particular, spouses and children of persons who engage in extramarital affairs. With respect to incest, a court might well agree with respondent that the nature of familial relationships renders true consent to incestuous activity sufficiently problematical that a blanket prohibition of such activity is warranted. [relocated footnote—EDS.]

The core of petitioner's defense of §16-6-2, however, is that respondent and others who engage in the conduct prohibited by §16-6-2 interfere with Georgia's exercise of the "right of the Nation and of the States to maintain a decent society." . . . I cannot agree that either the length of time a majority has held its convictions or the passions with which it defends them can withdraw legislation from this Court's scrutiny. See, e.g., Loving v. Virginia, 388 U.S. 1 (1967) [invalidating state antimiscegenation law]. It is precisely because the issue raised by this case touches the heart of what makes individuals what they are that we should be especially sensitive to the rights of those whose choices upset the majority.

The assertion that "traditional Judaeo-Christian values proscribe" the conduct involved cannot provide an adequate justification for §16-6-2. . . . The legitimacy of secular legislation depends instead on whether the State can advance some justification for its law beyond its conformity to religious doctrine. Thus, far from buttressing his case, [Bowers's] invocation of Leviticus, Romans, St. Thomas Aquinas, and sodomy's heretical status during the Middle Ages undermines his suggestion that §16-6-2 represents a legitimate use of secular coercive power. A State can no more punish private behavior because of religious intolerance than it can punish such behavior because of racial animus. . . .

Nor can §16-6-2 be justified as a "morally neutral" exercise of Georgia's power to "protect the public environment." Certainly, some private behavior can affect the fabric of society as a whole. . . . [But petitioner] and the Court fail to see the difference between laws that protect public sensibilities and those that enforce private morality. Statutes banning public sexual activity are entirely consistent with protecting the individual's liberty interest in decisions concerning sexual relations: the same recognition that those decisions are intensely private which justifies protecting them from governmental interference can justify protecting individuals from unwilling exposure to the sexual activities of others. But the mere fact that intimate behavior may be punished when it takes place in public cannot dictate how States can regulate intimate behavior that occurs in intimate places. . . .

STEVENS, J., joined by BRENNAN and MARSHALL, JJ., dissenting.

Like the statute that is challenged in this case, the rationale of the Court's opinion applies equally to the prohibited conduct regardless of whether the parties who engage in it are married or unmarried, or are of the same or different sexes. Sodomy was condemned as an odious and sinful type of behavior during the formative period of the common law. That condemnation was equally damning for heterosexual and homosexual sodomy. Moreover, it provided no special exemption for married couples. The license to cohabit and to produce legitimate offspring simply did not include any permission to engage in sexual conduct that was considered a "crime against nature." The history of the Georgia statute before us clearly reveals this traditional prohibition of heterosexual, as well as homosexual, sodomy. . . .

Our prior cases make two propositions abundantly clear. First, the fact that the governing majority in a State has traditionally viewed a particular practice as immoral is not a sufficient reason for upholding a law prohibiting the practice; neither history nor tradition could save a law prohibiting miscegenation from constitutional attack. Second, individual decisions by married persons, concerning the intimacies of their physical relationship, even when not intended to produce offspring, are a form of "liberty" protected by the Due Process Clause of the Fourteenth Amendment. Moreover, this protection extends to intimate choices by unmarried as well as married persons. . . . [O]ur prior cases . . . establish that a State may not prohibit sodomy within "the sacred precincts of marital bedrooms," *Griswold*, or, indeed, between unmarried heterosexual adults. *Eisenstadt*. In all events, it is perfectly clear that the State of Georgia may not totally prohibit the conduct proscribed by §16-6-2 of the Georgia Criminal Code.

If the Georgia statute cannot be enforced as it is written—if the conduct it seeks to prohibit is a protected form of liberty for the vast majority of Georgia's citizens—the State must assume the burden of justifying a selective application of its law. Either the persons to whom Georgia seeks to apply its statute do not have the same interest in "liberty" that others have, or there must be a reason why the State may be permitted to apply a generally applicable law to certain persons that it does not apply to others.

The first possibility is plainly unacceptable. Although the meaning of the principle that "all men are created equal" is not always clear, it surely must mean that every free citizen has the same interest in "liberty" that the members of the majority share. From the standpoint of the individual, the homosexual and the heterosexual have the same interest in deciding how he will live his own life, and, more narrowly, how he will conduct himself in his personal and voluntary associations with his companions. State intrusion into the private conduct of either is equally burdensome.

The second possibility is similarly unacceptable. A policy of selective application must be supported by a neutral and legitimate interest—something more substantial than a habitual dislike for, or ignorance about, the disfavored group. Neither the State nor the Court has identified any such interest in this case. The Court has posited as a justification for the Georgia statute "the presumed belief of a majority of the electorate in Georgia that homosexual sodomy is immoral and unacceptable." But the Georgia electorate has expressed no such belief—instead, its representatives enacted a law that presumably reflects the belief that all sodomy is immoral and unacceptable. . . . [T]he Georgia statute does not single out homosexuals as a separate class meriting special disfavored treatment. . . . Georgia's prohibition on private, consensual sodomy has not been enforced for decades. The record of nonenforcement, in this case and in the last several decades, belies the Attorney General's representations about the importance of the State's selective application of its generally applicable law. . . .

DISCUSSION

1. *The impact of unenforced sodomy laws.* At the time *Bowers* was decided, approximately half of the states and the District of Columbia still criminalized same-sex sodomy, but the practice was rarely prosecuted. While criminal prosecutions of private adult consensual sexual conduct were infrequent, the judicial decisions upholding sodomy laws had far-reaching effects on the ways the law treated gays and lesbians.[116] *Bowers* was soon interpreted as bearing on equal protection claims. In 1987, the Court of Appeals for the District of Columbia rejected a claim that discrimination by the FBI against gay job applicants violated the Equal Protection Clause. "If the [Supreme] Court was unwilling to object to state laws that criminalize the behavior that defines the class," the court explained, "it is hardly open to a lower court to conclude that state sponsored discrimination against the class is invidious. After all, there can hardly be more palpable discrimination against a class than making the conduct that defines the class criminal." Padula v. Webster, 822 F.2d 97, 103 (D.C. Cir. 1987).

Courts also pointed to laws criminalizing sodomy in deciding custody disputes. In 1998, for example, the Supreme Court of Alabama upheld a divorce judgment that granted custody to the father of the two minor children and placed severe restrictions on their lesbian mother's visitation rights. The court noted that "the conduct inherent in lesbianism [was] illegal in Alabama," and that the mother was therefore "continually engaging in conduct that violates the criminal law of this state." Ex parte D.W.W., 717 So. 2d 793, 796 (Ala. 1998). To expose her children to that "lifestyle, one that is illegal under the laws of this state and immoral in the eyes of most of its citizens, could greatly traumatize them." Id.

---

116. See Christopher R. Leslie, Creating Criminals: The Injuries Inflicted by "Unenforced" Sodomy Laws, 35 Harv. C.R.-C.L. L. Rev. 103, 113-168 (2000) (arguing that even unenforced sodomy laws symbolically brand gays and lesbians as criminals; harm their mental and emotional development; encourage anti-gay violence; enable police harassment; and license discrimination against gays and lesbians in employment, custody, immigration, and other domains).

2. *The "ancient roots" of the prohibition against homosexual sodomy.* Many scholars have pointed out that Justice White's and Chief Justice Burger's historical claims about longstanding moral condemnation of homosexual sodomy "oversimplif[y] and distort[] a complex historical record." Anne B. Goldstein, History, Homosexuality, and Political Values: Searching for the Hidden Determinants of Bowers v. Hardwick, 97 Yale L.J. 1073, 1086-1089 (1988). In the ancient world, sexual acts between males were both tolerated and condemned. (Plato's Symposium, of course, is a celebration not just of love but of same-sex love.[117]) The Roman Empire permitted some marriages between men until at least 342 A.D.[118] During the early Middle Ages, both church and state openly tolerated same-sex practices between men.[119]

Moreover, as Michel Foucault famously argued, the status-based, as opposed to the conduct-based, conception of homosexuality is a relatively recent development, dating only to the late nineteenth century.[120] Before that era's "perverse implantation" of conduct into status, homosexuality was understood as a kind of behavior, rather than a core attribute of the self.[121] Even the terms on which *Bowers*'s Michael Hardwick was convicted were modern; oral sex, the act of which he was convicted, was not even classified as "sodomy" until the late nineteenth and early twentieth centuries.[122] Prohibitions on sexual conduct tended to concern which parts of the body were touched rather than the sex of the parties. "Before the 1870s illicit sexual acts between men were not seen as fundamentally different from, or necessarily worse than, illicit acts between a man or a woman." Goldstein, 97 Yale L.J. at 1088. In 1817, English courts held that oral sex was not sodomy under the common law and its statutory complements; by legal definition sodomy was limited to anal sex.[123] In 1885, Parliament created a new crime of "gross indecency" to cover oral sex,[124] and most American jurisdictions adopted similar laws between 1885 and 1930.[125]

3. *The dissent: Concepts of privacy.* There are at least four different concepts of privacy: locational (or zonal) privacy protects what one does in a particular space; relational privacy protects a relationship, such as marriage, from state interference; decisional privacy protects the right to make important choices (including intimate ones) and decide on a course of action free from state sanction; informational privacy concerns the right to control the flow of information about one's self.[126]

---

117. Plato, The Symposium (R.E. Allen trans., 1993).

118. See the discussion in William N. Eskridge, The Case for Same-Sex Marriage 22-27 (1996).

119. See generally John Boswell, Christianity, Social Tolerance, and Homosexuality (1980).

120. 1 Michel Foucault, The History of Sexuality: An Introduction 43 (Robert Hurley trans., Vintage Books 1990) (1976) ("The sodomite had been a temporary aberration; the homosexual was now a species.").

121. Id. at 36-50.

122. Eskridge, Dishonorable Passions, supra n.2, at 387-407 (2008).

123. See Rex v. Jacobs, Russ. & Ry. 331 (1817).

124. William N. Eskridge, Jr., Gaylaw: Challenging the Apartheid of the Closet 158 (1999).

125. Id. at 24-25.

126. Cf. Kendall Thomas, Beyond the Privacy Principle, 92 Colum. L. Rev. 1431-1443, 1448 (1992) (distinguishing between zonal, relational, and decisional privacy).

The privacy cases may well shift among different forms of privacy. Which forms of privacy are involved in *Griswold*'s protection of the "sacred precincts of marital bedrooms"? In *Eisenstadt*'s protection of decisions "so fundamentally affecting a person as the decision whether to bear or beget a child"? Which are involved in *Bowers*? Are the cases appealing to one or several forms of privacy? Is this ambiguity a strength of the cases, or a weakness?

Does the concept of privacy inevitably reinforce the power of the closet? On one view, a right of privacy gives gays and lesbians the right to have same-sex relationships as long as they exist behind closed doors. It is not clear, however, that the right to privacy is a right to freedom from state regulation only for conduct that remains hidden from public view. What exactly is the scope of the right to privacy on which Justice Blackmun's dissent rests?

4. *Justice Powell's opinion and the closet.* As John Jeffries explains, Justice Lewis Powell originally voted to join four other Justices to strike down the law in *Bowers*, but later changed his mind and wrote a concurrence to what became the majority opinion as a result of his switch. See John C. Jeffries, Jr., Justice Lewis F. Powell, Jr. 511-530 (1994). At the time Powell cast his decisive vote, he explained to one of his clerks that he had never met a homosexual. (Note that by 1986 Powell had been not only a Supreme Court Justice but a former president of the ABA and a public figure for many decades.) In fact, as Jeffries reports, the clerk he was addressing was gay, like many of Powell's prior clerks, but Powell was not aware of it.[127]

Many scholars argue that the social pressures to stay in the closet are one reason why gays and lesbians are particularly disadvantaged in the political process. See Kenji Yoshino, Suspect Symbols: The Literary Argument for Heightened Scrutiny for Gays, 96 Colum. L. Rev. 1753, 1793-1816 (1996). Today, it would be difficult for a Justice to plausibly claim never to have met a gay person or lesbian; but the politics of the closet might still play a role in shaping impressions about who is in same-sex relations and might conceal the costs of conducting those relationships in hidden (or public but unequal) terms.

After his retirement from the Court, Justice Powell was quoted as saying that he regretted his concurrence in *Bowers*.[128] He did not, however, attach much importance to the decision.[129]

---

127. As Jeffries tells the story:

> Uncharacteristically, [just before oral argument] Powell had still not decided how he would vote. In great distress, the clerk debated whether to tell Powell of his sexual orientation. Perhaps if Powell could put a familiar face to these incomprehensible urges, they would seem less bizarre and threatening. He came to the edge of an outright declaration but ultimately drew back, settling for a "very emotional" speech urging Powell to support sexual freedom as a fundamental right. "The right to love the person of my choice," he argued, "would be far more important to me than the right to vote in elections." "That may be," Powell answered, "but that doesn't mean it's in the Constitution."

Id. at 1520-1521. What do you think the clerk should have done?

128. Ruth Marcus, Powell Regrets Backing Sodomy Law, Wash. Post, Oct. 26, 1990, at A3.

129. Id. "That case was not a major case," he explained, "and one of the reasons I voted the way I did was the case was a frivolous case" brought "just to see what the court would do." Powell considered the case "part of [his] past and not very important."

2. Bowers *Blunted, But Not Reversed*

The decade after *Bowers* was one of mixed accomplishment for supporters of gay rights and for their opponents. In the wake of *Bowers,* President Reagan endorsed conservative critiques of the Court's privacy jurisprudence by nominating Robert Bork to the Supreme Court. Judge Bork was long known for his criticism of the Court's privacy holdings, and, more recently, for his suggestion that lower courts were not obliged to adhere to them.[130] After confirmation hearings in which Judge Bork maintained, under skeptical questioning, that the Constitution did not protect a general right to privacy,[131] the Senate voted to reject Bork's nomination, ultimately confirming instead the more moderate Anthony Kennedy.

Supporters of the Court's privacy jurisprudence, including those in the gay rights community, had organized in opposition to Judge Bork's confirmation. At the same time, gay rights advocates turned mobilization for improved medical care, spurred by the AIDS crisis, into mobilization for a broader array of social and political rights. By the end of the 1980s, these efforts had produced notable gains: Local governments in several states passed or amended ordinances to prohibit discrimination on the basis of sexual orientation in employment, housing, and government services.[132]

Yet these gains provoked increasingly organized opposition. President Clinton assumed office in 1992 with open support from the gay community. The executive branch prepared to recognize civil rights for gay Americans across domains, but encountered stiff resistance from the ranks of both parties.

After the Joint Chiefs of Staff condemned the Administration's plan for integration of gay service members, President Clinton accepted "Don't Ask, Don't Tell," a political compromise permitting gays and lesbians to serve in the military so long as their sexual orientation remained undisclosed. The Employment Non-Discrimination Act, which would have prohibited employment discrimination on the basis of sexual orientation, repeatedly failed to secure the votes needed for passage.[133]

---

130. See Dronenburg v. Zech, 741 F.2d 1388, 1391 (D.C. Cir. 1984) (holding that the Navy's policy of mandatory discharge for homosexual conduct did not violate constitutional rights to privacy or equal protection). In *Dronenburg,* Bork authored an opinion for a panel including then-Judge Antonin Scalia, arguing that the Supreme Court's privacy holdings lacked an "explanatory principle."

131. See Excerpts from Questioning of Judge Bork by Senate Committee Chairman, N.Y. Times, Sept. 16, 1987 (printing exchange between Senator Biden and Judge Bork on the right to privacy, including Bork's statement that "the right of privacy, as defined or undefined by Justice Douglas, was a free-floating right that was not derived in a principled fashion from constitutional materials").

132. Vicki Torres, Gay Events Timeline, 1970-1999, Sexual Orientation Issues in the News, http://www.usc.edu/schools/annenberg/asc/projects/soin/enhancingCurricula/timeline.html (noting that, by 1992, gay rights legislation had been passed in California, Connecticut, Hawaii, Massachusetts, New Jersey, Vermont, and Wisconsin).

133. See Jerome Hunt, The History of the Employment Non-Discrimination Act, The Center for American Progress, July 19, 2011, http://www.americanprogress.org/issues/2011/07/enda_history.html; Congressional Record, 103rd Congress, 2d Sess., 140 Cong. Rec. E1311; Vol. 140, No. 81 (June 23, 1994).

Instead, Congress passed, and Clinton signed, the Defense of Marriage Act, which limited marriage to a union between a man and a woman.[134]

In several states, conservative ballot initiatives to roll back antidiscrimination statutes and ordinances passed by wide margins.[135] In Colorado, voters amended the state constitution to prohibit sexual orientation discrimination claims. After the amendment ("Amendment 2") was enjoined by the Colorado Supreme Court on equal protection grounds, Governor Roy Romer petitioned the United States Supreme Court.

Romer v. Evans

517 U.S. 620 (1996)

Justice KENNEDY delivered the opinion of the Court.

[In 1992, Colorado voters adopted "Amendment 2" by statewide referendum. The drive for Amendment 2 came after several Colorado municipalities—including Aspen, Boulder, and the City and County of Denver—passed ordinances banning discrimination based on sexual orientation in housing, employment, education, public accommodations, health and welfare services, and other transactions and activities. Amendment 2 provided:

> No Protected Status Based on Homosexual, Lesbian, or Bisexual Orientation.
>
> Neither the State of Colorado, through any of its branches or departments, nor any of its agencies, political subdivisions, municipalities or school districts, shall enact, adopt or enforce any statute, regulation, ordinance or policy whereby homosexual, lesbian or bisexual orientation, conduct, practices or relationships shall constitute or otherwise be the basis of or entitle any person or class of persons to have or claim any minority status, quota preferences, protected status or claim of discrimination. This Section of the Constitution shall be in all respects self executing.]

I

One century ago, the first Justice Harlan admonished this Court that the Constitution "neither knows nor tolerates classes among citizens." Plessy v. Ferguson, 163 U.S. 537, 559 (1896) (dissenting opinion). Unheeded then, those words now are understood to state a commitment to the law's neutrality where the rights of persons are at stake. The Equal Protection Clause enforces this principle and today requires us to hold invalid a provision of Colorado's Constitution. . . .

---

134. See Pub. L. No. 104-199, §3(a), Sept. 21, 1996, 110 Stat. 2419, codified at 1 U.S.C.A. §7 (1996). Clinton recorded his ambivalence in a signing statement broadly condemning discrimination against gay and lesbian people. See Statement of President Bill Clinton (Sept. 20, 1996), available at http://www.cs.cmu.edu/afs/cs/user/scotts/ftp/wpaf2mc/clinton.html.

135. See Amy L. Stone, Gay Rights at the Ballot Box 18-31, 63-89 (2012) (describing mobilization around anti-gay initiatives and referenda from 1988 to 1996, including campaigns around Ballot Measure 9 in Oregon and Amendment 2 in Colorado in November 1992).

Amendment 2 . . . does more than repeal or rescind [local municipal antidiscrimination] provisions. It prohibits all legislative, executive or judicial action at any level of state or local government designed to protect the named class, a class we shall refer to as homosexual persons or gays and lesbians. . . .

[Although the Colorado Supreme Court held that Amendment 2] infringed the fundamental right of gays and lesbians to participate in the political process, [we] affirm the judgment . . . on a [different] rationale.

II

The State's principal argument in defense of Amendment 2 is that it puts gays and lesbians in the same position as all other persons. So, the State says, the measure does no more than deny homosexuals special rights. This reading of the amendment's language is implausible. . . . Homosexuals, by state decree, are put in a solitary class with respect to transactions and relations in both the private and governmental spheres. The amendment withdraws from homosexuals, but no others, specific legal protection from the injuries caused by discrimination, and it forbids reinstatement of these laws and policies. . . .

Amendment 2 bars homosexuals from securing protection against [discrimination in] public[] accommodations[.] [I]n addition, [it] nullifies specific legal protections for this targeted class in all transactions in housing, sale of real estate, insurance, health and welfare services, private education, and employment. . . .

Amendment 2 also operates to repeal and forbid all laws or policies providing specific protection for gays or lesbians from discrimination by every level of Colorado government [including discrimination by state employers and state colleges]. . . .

Amendment 2's reach may not be limited to specific laws passed for the benefit of gays and lesbians. [It may deprive] gays and lesbians even of the protection of general laws and policies that prohibit arbitrary discrimination in governmental and private settings. . . . At some point in the systematic administration of these laws, an official must determine whether homosexuality is an arbitrary and thus forbidden basis for decision. Yet a decision to that effect would itself amount to a policy prohibiting discrimination on the basis of homosexuality [in violation of] Amendment 2. . . .

[E]ven if, as we doubt, homosexuals could find some safe harbor in laws of general application, we cannot accept the view that Amendment 2's prohibition on specific legal protections does no more than deprive homosexuals of special rights. To the contrary, the amendment imposes a special disability upon those persons alone. Homosexuals are forbidden the safeguards that others enjoy or may seek without constraint. They can obtain specific protection against discrimination only by enlisting the citizenry of Colorado to amend the state constitution or perhaps, on the State's view, by trying to pass helpful laws of general applicability. This is so no matter how local or discrete the harm, no matter how public and widespread the injury. We find nothing special in the protections Amendment 2 withholds. These are protections taken for granted by most people either because they already have them or do not need them; these are protections against exclusion from an almost limitless number of transactions and endeavors that constitute ordinary civic life in a free society. . . .

Amendment 2 fails, indeed defies, [the] conventional inquiry [into whether a law burdens a fundamental right or a suspect class]. First, the amendment has the peculiar property of imposing a broad and undifferentiated disability on a single named group, an exceptional and, as we shall explain, invalid form of legislation. Second, its sheer breadth is so discontinuous with the reasons offered for it that the amendment seems inexplicable by anything but animus toward the class that it affects; it lacks a rational relationship to legitimate state interests. . . .

By requiring that [a] classification bear a rational relationship to an independent and legitimate legislative end, we ensure that classifications are not drawn for the purpose of disadvantaging the group burdened by the law.

Amendment 2 confounds this normal process of judicial review. It is at once too narrow and too broad. It identifies persons by a single trait and then denies them protection across the board. The resulting disqualification of a class of persons from the right to seek specific protection from the law is unprecedented in our jurisprudence. . . .

It is not within our constitutional tradition to enact laws of this sort. Central both to the idea of the rule of law and to our own Constitution's guarantee of equal protection is the principle that government and each of its parts remain open on impartial terms to all who seek its assistance. . . . Respect for this principle explains why laws singling out a certain class of citizens for disfavored legal status or general hardships are rare. A law declaring that in general it shall be more difficult for one group of citizens than for all others to seek aid from the government is itself a denial of equal protection of the laws in the most literal sense. . . .

[L]aws of the kind now before us raise the inevitable inference that the disadvantage imposed is born of animosity toward the class of persons affected. "[I]f the constitutional conception of 'equal protection of the laws' means anything, it must at the very least mean that a bare . . . desire to harm a politically unpopular group cannot constitute a legitimate governmental interest." Department of Agriculture v. Moreno, 413 U.S. 528 (1973). Even laws enacted for broad and ambitious purposes often can be explained by reference to legitimate public policies which justify the incidental disadvantages they impose on certain persons. Amendment 2, however, in making a general announcement that gays and lesbians shall not have any particular protections from the law, inflicts on them immediate, continuing, and real injuries that outrun and belie any legitimate justifications that may be claimed for it. We conclude that, in addition to the far-reaching deficiencies of Amendment 2 that we have noted, the principles it offends, in another sense, are conventional and venerable; a law must bear a rational relationship to a legitimate governmental purpose, and Amendment 2 does not.

The primary rationale the State offers for Amendment 2 is respect for other citizens' freedom of association, and in particular the liberties of landlords or employers who have personal or religious objections to homosexuality. Colorado also cites its interest in conserving resources to fight discrimination against other groups. The breadth of the Amendment is so far removed from these particular justifications that we find it impossible to credit them. We cannot say that Amendment 2 is directed to any identifiable legitimate purpose or discrete objective. It is a status-based enactment divorced from any factual context from which we could discern a relationship to legitimate state interests; it is a classification of persons undertaken for its own sake, something the Equal Protection Clause does not permit. "[C]lass legislation . . . [is] obnoxious to the prohibitions of the Fourteenth Amendment. . . ." Civil Rights Cases, 109 U.S. at 24.

We must conclude that Amendment 2 classifies homosexuals not to further a proper legislative end but to make them unequal to everyone else. This Colorado cannot do. A State cannot so deem a class of persons a stranger to its laws. Amendment 2 violates the Equal Protection Clause, and the judgment of the Supreme Court of Colorado is affirmed.

It is so ordered.

Justice SCALIA, with whom THE CHIEF JUSTICE and Justice THOMAS join, dissenting.

The Court has mistaken a Kulturkampf for a fit of spite. The constitutional amendment before us here is not the manifestation of a "bare . . . desire to harm" homosexuals, but is rather a modest attempt by seemingly tolerant Coloradans to preserve traditional sexual mores against the efforts of a politically powerful minority to revise those mores through use of the laws. . . .

In holding that homosexuality cannot be singled out for disfavorable treatment, the Court contradicts a decision, unchallenged here, pronounced only 10 years ago, see Bowers v. Hardwick, 478 U.S. 186 (1986), and places the prestige of this institution behind the proposition that opposition to homosexuality is as reprehensible as racial or religious bias. Whether it is or not is precisely the cultural debate that gave rise to the Colorado constitutional amendment (and to the preferential laws against which the amendment was directed). Since the Constitution of the United States says nothing about this subject, it is left to be resolved by normal democratic means, including the democratic adoption of provisions in state constitutions. This Court has no business imposing upon all Americans the resolution favored by the elite class from which the Members of this institution are selected, pronouncing that "animosity" toward homosexuality is evil. I vigorously dissent.

. . . The clear import of the Colorado court's conclusion [is] that "general laws and policies that prohibit arbitrary discrimination" would continue to prohibit discrimination on the basis of homosexual conduct as well. This analysis . . . lays to rest such horribles . . . as the prospect that assaults upon homosexuals could not be prosecuted. The amendment prohibits special treatment of homosexuals, and nothing more. It would not affect, for example, a requirement of state law that pensions be paid to all retiring state employees with a certain length of service; homosexual employees, as well as others, would be entitled to that benefit. But it would prevent the State or any municipality from making death-benefit payments to the "life partner" of a homosexual when it does not make such payments to the long-time roommate of a nonhomosexual employee. Or again, it does not affect the requirement of the State's general insurance laws that customers be afforded coverage without discrimination unrelated to anticipated risk. Thus, homosexuals could not be denied coverage, or charged a greater premium, with respect to auto collision insurance; but neither the State nor any municipality could require that distinctive health insurance risks associated with homosexuality (if there are any) be ignored. . . .

[But] there was a legitimate rational basis for . . . the prohibition of special protection for homosexuals. . . . If it is constitutionally permissible for a State to make homosexual conduct criminal, [under *Bowers*] surely it is constitutionally permissible for a State to enact other laws merely disfavoring homosexual conduct. . . . And a fortiori it is constitutionally permissible for a State to adopt a provision not even disfavoring homosexual conduct, but merely prohibiting all levels of state government from bestowing special protections upon homosexual conduct. . . .

[A]ssuming that, in Amendment 2, a person of homosexual "orientation" is someone who does not engage in homosexual conduct but merely has a tendency or desire to do so, *Bowers* still suffices to establish a rational basis for the provision. If it is rational to criminalize the conduct, surely it is rational to deny special favor and protection to those with a self-avowed tendency or desire to engage in the conduct. Indeed, where criminal sanctions are not involved, homosexual "orientation" is an acceptable stand-in for homosexual conduct. . . . Amendment 2 is not constitutionally invalid simply because it could have been drawn more precisely so as to withdraw special antidiscrimination protections only from those of homosexual "orientation" who actually engage in homosexual conduct. . . .

The Court's opinion contains grim, disapproving hints that Coloradans have been guilty of "animus" or "animosity" toward homosexuality, as though that has been established as unAmerican. Of course it is our moral heritage that one should not hate any human being or class of human beings. But I had thought that one could consider certain conduct reprehensible—murder, for example, or polygamy, or cruelty to animals—and could exhibit even "animus" toward such conduct. Surely that is the only sort of "animus" at issue here: moral disapproval of homosexual conduct, the same sort of moral disapproval that produced the centuries-old criminal laws that we held constitutional in *Bowers*. The Colorado amendment does not, to speak entirely precisely, prohibit giving favored status to people who are homosexuals; they can be favored for many reasons—for example, because they are senior citizens or members of racial minorities. But it prohibits giving them favored status because of their homosexual conduct—that is, it prohibits favored status for homosexuality.

. . . Colorado not only is one of the 25 States that have repealed their antisodomy laws, but was among the first to do so [in 1971]. But the society that eliminates criminal punishment for homosexual acts does not necessarily abandon the view that homosexuality is morally wrong and socially harmful; often, abolition simply reflects the view that enforcement of such criminal laws involves unseemly intrusion into the intimate lives of citizens.

There is a problem, however, which arises when criminal sanction of homosexuality is eliminated but moral and social disapprobation of homosexuality is meant to be retained[; it] occasionally bubbles to the surface of the news, in heated political disputes over such matters as the introduction into local schools of books teaching that homosexuality is an optional and fully acceptable "alternate life style." . . . [B]ecause those who engage in homosexual conduct tend to reside in disproportionate numbers in certain communities, and of course care about homosexual-rights issues much more ardently than the public at large, they possess political power much greater than their numbers, both locally and statewide. Quite understandably, they devote this political power to achieving not merely a grudging social toleration, but full social acceptance, of homosexuality.

By the time Coloradans were asked to vote on Amendment 2, . . . [t]hree Colorado cities—Aspen, Boulder, and Denver—had enacted ordinances that listed "sexual orientation" as an impermissible ground for discrimination, equating the moral disapproval of homosexual conduct with racial and religious bigotry[, and] the Governor of Colorado had signed an executive order [requiring nondiscrimination on the basis of sexual orientation]. I do not mean to be critical of these legislative successes; homosexuals are as entitled to use the legal system for reinforcement of their moral sentiments as are the rest of society. But they are subject to being countered by lawful, democratic countermeasures as well.

Amendment 2 . . . sought to counter both the geographic concentration and the disproportionate political power of homosexuals by (1) resolving the controversy at the statewide level, and (2) making the election a single-issue contest for both sides. . . .

The constitutions of the States of Arizona, Idaho, New Mexico, Oklahoma, and Utah to this day contain provisions stating that polygamy is "forever prohibited." Polygamists, and those who have a polygamous "orientation," have been "singled out" by these provisions for much more severe treatment than merely denial of favored status; and that treatment can only be changed by achieving amendment of the state constitutions. The Court's disposition today suggests that these provisions are unconstitutional, and that polygamy must be permitted in these States on a state-legislated, or perhaps even local-option, basis—unless, of course, polygamists for some reason have fewer constitutional rights than homosexuals.

. . . I think it no business of the courts (as opposed to the political branches) to take sides in this culture war.

But the Court today has done so, not only by inventing a novel and extravagant constitutional doctrine to take the victory away from traditional forces, but even by verbally disparaging as bigotry adherence to traditional attitudes. To suggest, for example, that this constitutional amendment springs from nothing more than "'a bare . . . desire to harm a politically unpopular group,'" is nothing short of insulting. (It is also nothing short of preposterous to call "politically unpopular" a group which enjoys enormous influence in American media and politics, and which, as the trial court here noted, though composing no more than 4% of the population had the support of 46% of the voters on Amendment 2.)

When the Court takes sides in the culture wars, it tends to be with the knights rather than the villains—and more specifically with the Templars, reflecting the views and values of the lawyer class from which the Court's Members are drawn. How that class feels about homosexuality will be evident to anyone who wishes to interview job applicants at virtually any of the Nation's law schools. The interviewer may refuse to offer a job because the applicant is a Republican; because he is an adulterer; because he went to the wrong prep school or belongs to the wrong country club; because he eats snails; because he is a womanizer; because she wears real-animal fur; or even because he hates the Chicago Cubs. But if the interviewer should wish not to be an associate or partner of an applicant because he disapproves of the applicant's homosexuality, then he will have violated the pledge which the Association of American Law Schools requires all its member-schools to exact from job interviewers: "assurance of the employer's willingness" to hire homosexuals. This law-school view of what "prejudices" must be stamped out may be contrasted with the more plebeian attitudes that apparently still prevail in the United States Congress, which has been unresponsive to repeated attempts to extend to homosexuals the protections of federal civil rights laws, and which took the pains to exclude them specifically from the Americans With Disabilities Act of 1990.

Today's opinion has no foundation in American constitutional law, and barely pretends to. The people of Colorado have adopted an entirely reasonable provision which does not even disfavor homosexuals in any substantive sense, but merely denies them preferential treatment. Amendment 2 is designed to prevent piecemeal deterioration of the sexual morality favored by a majority of Coloradans, and is not only an appropriate means to that legitimate end, but a means that Americans have employed before. Striking it down is an act, not of judicial judgment, but of political will. I dissent.

DISCUSSION

1. *Amendment 2 as "class legislation."* Although Justice Scalia suggests that the Court's decision in *Romer* is unprecedented, its logic does bear interesting similarities to at least some of the concerns of the framers of the Fourteenth Amendment.[136] Influenced by Jacksonianism and free soil theories, the framers of the Fourteenth Amendment were opposed to "class legislation" that denied equal privileges and protections to certain groups and treated them as social inferiors. When the Jacksonians spoke of "class legislation," they were more likely to be worried about special privileges for the rich and wealthy (like monopolies and corporate charters) that posed the danger of creating a new nobility or social elite. By the end of the Civil War, however, the framers of the Fourteenth Amendment understood the concept as involving the converse phenomenon: legislation that denigrated or demeaned a group of persons and held them as less equal than others.[137]

In his proposed joint resolution for drafting the Fourteenth Amendment, for example, Charles Sumner invoked the Jacksonian heritage when he claimed that the proposed Fourteenth Amendment should abolish "oligarchy, aristocracy, caste, or monopoly with particular privileges and powers."[138] Sumner spoke of monopoly and caste in the same breath, equating legislation that singles out groups for special treatment with legislation that demeans and stigmatizes groups as social inferiors. Likewise, Senator Howard, the floor manager of the Fourteenth Amendment, offered an expanded interpretation of the Jacksonian principle. He argued that

---

136. This discussion is drawn from Jack M. Balkin, The Constitution of Status, 106 Yale L.J. 2313 (1997).

137. On the transformation of the Jacksonian idea of class legislation, see Eric Foner, Free Soil, Free Labor, Free Men 90-91 (1970); Mark G. Yudof, Equal Protection, Class Legislation, and Sex Discrimination: One Small Cheer for Mr. Herbert Spencer's Social Statics, 88 Mich. L. Rev. 1366, 1376-1379 (1990).

138. Cong. Globe, 39th Cong. (1st Sess.) 674 (1866). The joint resolution failed, but the debate affected the final language of the amendment. See Andrew Kull, The Color-Blind Constitution 74-75 (1992); see also Adamson v. California, 332 U.S. 46, 51 n.8 (1947) (quoting Sumner's resolution as evidence of the meaning of the Fourteenth Amendment).

the amendment's goal was to "abolis[h] all class legislation . . . and [do] away with the injustice of subjecting one caste of persons to a code not applicable to another." Cong. Globe, 39th Cong. (1st Sess.) 2766 (1866).

From a modern standpoint, the notion of "class legislation" seems puzzling because all legislation divides groups into classes. Hence, modern constitutional law looks to whether a suspect classification is invoked or a fundamental right is abridged. However, the Fourteenth Amendment was enacted long before courts adopted the language of scrutiny. The concept of "class legislation" makes particular sense in terms of social meaning; the question is whether the legislation treats a group as a whole as a sort of lower caste or social inferior. Did Colorado's Amendment 2 do this? Do Justice Scalia's remarks about the purpose of showing public disapproval for homosexuals and homosexuality shed any light on this question? Note that under the terms of Amendment 2, discrimination against *heterosexuals* could still be banned by any political subdivision in the State of Colorado. Does the fact that the amendment directed itself at a class (sexual orientation minorities) rather than at a classification (sexual orientation) make the "class legislation" argument stronger?[139]

2. Romer *and the rational basis test.* Although *Romer* nominally uses the rational basis test, Justice Kennedy's opinion has elements that suggest a higher level of scrutiny. Consider the following explanations:

a. *Irrational burdens.* One understanding of why Amendment 2 failed rational basis review is that Amendment 2 did not preserve equal rights for gays and lesbians but instead created special and irrational burdens on gays and lesbians. Consider the following interpretation of Amendment 2: Under Amendment 2, police officers and other administrative officials would be free to discriminate against homosexuals and bisexuals at will, and other government agencies would be powerless to remedy this treatment if the stated reason for discrimination was that the person was homosexual or bisexual. Thus, if firefighters wait to put out fires in the houses of homosexuals until the houses are completely destroyed, police officers fail to arrest gay bashers, or county clerks refuse to process parade permits for homosexuals because these persons are homosexual, they cannot be penalized because they acted out of anti-gay bias. Nor can any state agency create any policy that would prevent the exercise of anti-gay bias. There could only be a remedy if there were a general requirement of prosecuting all assaults, answering all fires promptly, and issuing parade permits on a first-come, first-served basis. Do you agree that this is the legal effect of Amendment 2? If it is, does it violate the rational basis test?

b. *Animus.* Another way of understanding why Amendment 2 failed rational basis review concerns the motivations of those who enacted it: The opinion speaks of "animus," "animosity," and "'a bare . . . desire to harm a politically unpopular group.'" From what evidence does the Court draw inferences about the motives of the persons who voted for Amendment 2? Is the evidence the Court considers

---

139. Along similar lines, Akhil Amar has argued that Amendment 2 was an unconstitutional bill of attainder. See Akhil Reed Amar, Attainder and Amendment 2: *Romer*'s Rightness, 95 Mich. L. Rev. 203, 218 (1996). Amar argues that the Bill of Attainder Clauses are designed to prevent governments from singling out and punishing identifiable social groups because of who they are.

sufficient, in your view, to sustain a judgment about Amendment 2's constitutionality? Would the Court's ruling in *Romer* call into constitutional question the enactment of a sodomy law? A law barring an openly gay person from teaching in an elementary school classroom? A law barring same-sex marriage? Why or why not? Why does the Court emphasize that the reach of Amendment 2 is "unprecedented"? What do these examples reveal about the meaning of "animus"? Might the kinds of judgments that courts would conclude reflect anti-gay "animus" have changed in the years since the Court's decision in *Romer*?

c. *Keeping your options open.* Yet another way of reading *Romer* is that the Court is implicitly departing from the approach the Court has taken in cases like Williamson v. Lee Optical or *Railway Express* although it still uses the term "rational basis" to describe its work. On this view, *Romer* belongs to a small group of cases like *Cleburne* or *Reed.* The Court presumes that unconstitutional prejudice is behind most legislation that draws certain kinds of classifications, but it is not willing—or not *yet* willing—to recognize the affected group as a suspect class. Recall Reed v. Reed, the 1971 sex discrimination case that struck down an Idaho statute favoring men over women as executors of estates.[140] While *Reed* only applied rational basis review, it was soon followed by Frontiero v. Richardson in 1973 and Craig v. Boren in 1976, which ultimately established intermediate scrutiny for gender classifications. On this view, *Romer* applied rational basis review but left open the opportunity for the Court to ultimately protect the rights of gays and lesbians, either through the Equal Protection or Due Process Clauses.

While in the years after *Romer* the Court would not move with similar speed to declare classifications on the basis of sexual orientation suspect, it would soon overrule *Bowers*—a case about which the *Romer* majority is conspicuously silent. What do you think explains the majority's silence about *Bowers*?

3. *The dissent: The Court and culture wars.* Justice Scalia sees the controversy over Amendment 2 as a cultural struggle, or *Kulturkampf.* In his view, the Court confused a battle over whose vision of morality should prevail with "a fit of spite," i.e., invidious motivation. He argues that the Constitution has nothing to say about such cultural struggles, and that such struggles should be left to the political process. Do you agree? Consider the fact that virtually every successful social movement for equality in the United States has involved a similar struggle over status and respect. Is Scalia saying that the Court should refuse to take sides in battles by social movements for equality until the battle is over? What would this entail in the case of the civil rights movement? The women's movement? Was there a "neutral" position in a case like Brown v. Board of Education? Is Justice Scalia's view that the Court should defer to political processes in ongoing cultural struggles consistent with his position in affirmative action cases like *Adarand* and *Croson*? In gun rights cases like District of Columbia v. Heller?

Consider the tone of Justice Scalia's dissent. Is he attempting to remain studiously neutral in the culture wars, or is he alerting critics of the Court's decision of the need to mobilize?

4. *Amendment 2 and status competition.* One way of understanding Amendment 2 is as an attempt by its proponents to preserve the superior moral meaning of heterosexuality over homosexuality at a time when public sympathies and attitudes about

140. Reed v. Reed, 404 U.S. 71 (1971).

homosexuality are undergoing change. In other words, Amendment 2 was an example of *status competition*, in which social groups fight over the comparative social approval, respect, and esteem of their respective identities and distinctive styles of life. Status competition can be especially bitter because contending groups perceive status as a zero-sum good. Increased respect for lower-status groups means a corresponding loss of respect for higher-status groups because their identity has been constructed around their greater prestige and the greater propriety of their ways of living:[141]

> Protecting homosexuals from discrimination is understood as a sign of increased social status [that] occurs at the expense of heterosexuals. From the perspective of the older baseline of social meanings, it appears that homosexuals are being given something new that is being taken away from heterosexuals. They are being given increased honor, respect, and esteem, hence "special treatment." . . . Every change in the semiotic status quo, no matter how unfair the previous baseline of social meanings, may be seen as sending the message of favoritism and special treatment.

3. Bowers *Reversed*

By 2000, the nation's views about criminalizing sexual relations between same-sex adults had significantly changed. A number of state supreme courts had invalidated state sodomy statutes,[142] and by the early 2000s, only 14 states still had sodomy laws in place.[143] In 1999, a Gallup Poll found for the first time that a majority of Americans believed that homosexual relations between consenting adults should be legal.[144] By 2003, nearly 90 percent of those polled believed that homosexuals should have equal rights in employment.[145]

With "pro-family" organizing strong at the national party level, conservatives continued to block federal legislation reflecting these changes, yet gay rights groups were increasingly successful in their state-level efforts to secure partnership recognition, protections from discrimination, and inclusion in hate crimes laws.[146]

Gay rights activists made public education a first step in law reform, whether through legislation or litigation.[147] The Human Rights Campaign (HRC)

---

141. Balkin, The Constitution of Status, supra n.136, at 2336.

142. After a lengthy period in the years after *Bowers* when no state repealed its sodomy laws, the Kentucky Supreme Court struck down the state's sodomy law under the state constitution in 1992. Kentucky v. Wasson, 842 S.W.2d 487 (Ky. 1992). The Georgia Supreme Court invalidated the law at issue in *Bowers* under the state constitution in 1998. Powell v. State, 510 S.E.2d 18 (Ga. 1998).

143. Andersen, Out of the Closets and into the Courts, supra n.111, at 60.

144. Gay and Lesbian Rights, Gallup, http://www.gallup.com/poll/1651/gay-lesbian-rights.aspx. The number would rise to 60 percent by 2003.

145. Id.

146. For discussions of related advances at the federal and state levels, see Mathew S. Nosanchuk, The Endurance Test: Executive Power and the Civil Rights of LGBT Americans, 5 Alb. Gov't L. Rev. 440, 452-456 (2012). For discussions of successful state-level campaigns in the years preceding *Lawrence*, see Stone, Gay Rights at the Ballot Box, supra n.135, at 91-127.

147. See, e.g., William N. Eskridge, Jr., Equality Practice: Civil Unions and the Future of Gay Rights (2001).

promoted National Coming Out Day, believing that as more Americans knew LGBT people personally, their perceptions of them would change.[148] The Gay and Lesbian Alliance Against Defamation (GLAAD) criticized stereotypical reporting and worked with broadcasters to improve representations in the media.[149] Hollywood offered positive portraits of gays and lesbians, first with *Ellen*, and later with *Will & Grace*, the first sitcom to portray a gay male lead on U.S. broadcast television.

Gay rights groups worked with corporate and religious leaders, accelerating the development of nondiscrimination policies, benefit schemes, and partnership recognition in the workplace.[150] By 1996, Jewish and Unitarian leadership groups had called for same-sex couples to have access to civil marriage, and same-sex relationships were increasingly recognized in Europe, with the Netherlands and Belgium legalizing same-sex marriage in 2001 and 2003.[151]

Yet these gains in cultural visibility and political influence prompted opposition. During the Administration of President George W. Bush, conservative and religious blocs in Congress resisted change at the federal level. And throughout this period, courts routinely invoked *Bowers* to justify the differential treatment or exclusion of LGBT persons, in cases addressing issues from adoption to employment to military service. Courts reasoned that if gays and lesbians regularly engaged in criminalizable behavior, they could be treated differently under the law.[152] With a gap widening between national public opinion and federal legislative and judicial responses, the Court once again agreed to hear a challenge to the constitutionality of sodomy laws.

Lawrence v. Texas

539 U.S. 558 (2003)

Justice KENNEDY delivered the opinion of the Court.

Liberty protects the person from unwarranted government intrusions into a dwelling or other private places. In our tradition the State is not omnipresent in the home. And there are other spheres of our lives and existence, outside the home, where the State should not be a dominant presence. Freedom extends

148. Human Rights Campaign, The History of Coming Out, http://www.hrc.org/resources/entry/the-history-of-coming-out.

149. See Gay and Lesbian Alliance Against Defamation, Accomplishments—2003, http://www.glaad.org/files/2003Accomplishments.pdf; Gay and Lesbian Alliance Against Defamation, Accomplishments—2002, http://www.glaad.org/files/2*ccomplishments.pdf (describing the organization's work around the time of Lawrence v. Texas).

150. The HRC began publishing its Corporate Equality Index in 2002. See Human Rights Campaign Foundation, Corporate Equality Index 2012, 3 (2011).

151. Dutch Legalize Gay Marriage, BBC, Sept. 12, 2000, http://news.bbc.co.uk/2/hi/europe/1253754.stm; Gareth Harding, Belgium Legalizes Gay Marriage, UPI, Jan. 31, 2003, http://www.upi.com/Business_News/Security-Industry/2003/01/31/Belgium-legalizes-gay-marriage/UPI-46741044012415.

152. See Leslie, Creating Criminals, supra n.116.

beyond spatial bounds. Liberty presumes an autonomy of self that includes freedom of thought, belief, expression, and certain intimate conduct. The instant case involves liberty of the person both in its spatial and more transcendent dimensions.

I

The question before the Court is the validity of a Texas statute making it a crime for two persons of the same sex to engage in certain intimate sexual conduct.

In Houston, Texas, officers of the Harris County Police Department were dispatched to a private residence in response to a reported weapons disturbance. They entered an apartment where one of the petitioners, John Geddes Lawrence, resided. The right of the police to enter does not seem to have been questioned. The officers observed Lawrence and another man, Tyron Garner, engaging in a sexual act. The two petitioners were arrested, held in custody overnight, and charged and convicted before a Justice of the Peace.

The complaints described their crime as "deviate sexual intercourse, namely anal sex, with a member of the same sex (man)." The applicable state law is Tex. Penal Code Ann. §21.06(a) (2003). It provides: "A person commits an offense if he engages in deviate sexual intercourse with another individual of the same sex." The statute defines "[d]eviate sexual intercourse" as follows:

> (A) any contact between any part of the genitals of one person and the mouth or anus of another person; or
> (B) the penetration of the genitals or the anus of another person with an object. §21.01(1).

The petitioners . . . challenged the statute as a violation of the Equal Protection Clause of the Fourteenth Amendment and of a like provision of the Texas Constitution. Those contentions were rejected. The petitioners, having entered a plea of *nolo contendere,* were each fined $200 and assessed court costs of $141.25. App. to Pet. for Cert. 107a-110a. . . . The petitioners were adults at the time of the alleged offense. Their conduct was in private and consensual.

II

We conclude the case should be resolved by determining whether the petitioners were free as adults to engage in the private conduct in the exercise of their liberty under the Due Process Clause of the Fourteenth Amendment to the Constitution. For this inquiry we deem it necessary to reconsider the Court's holding in *Bowers.* . . .

In *Griswold* the Court invalidated a state law prohibiting the use of drugs or devices of contraception and counseling or aiding and abetting the use of contraceptives. The Court described the protected interest as a right to privacy and placed emphasis on the marriage relation and the protected space of the marital bedroom.

After *Griswold* it was established that the right to make certain decisions regarding sexual conduct extends beyond the marital relationship. In Eisenstadt v. Baird, 405 U.S. 438 (1972), the Court invalidated a law prohibiting the distribution of contraceptives to unmarried persons. The case was decided under the

Equal Protection Clause; but with respect to unmarried persons, the Court went on to state the fundamental proposition that the law impaired the exercise of their personal rights. It quoted from the statement of the Court of Appeals finding the law to be in conflict with fundamental human rights, and it followed with this statement of its own: "It is true that in *Griswold* the right of privacy in question inhered in the marital relationship. . . . If the right of privacy means anything, it is the right of the *individual*, married or single, to be free from unwarranted governmental intrusion into matters so fundamentally affecting a person as the decision whether to bear or beget a child."

The opinions in *Griswold* and *Eisenstadt* were part of the background for the decision in Roe v. Wade. *Roe* recognized the right of a woman to make certain fundamental decisions affecting her destiny and confirmed once more that the protection of liberty under the Due Process Clause has a substantive dimension of fundamental significance in defining the rights of the person.

In Carey v. Population Services Int'l, 431 U.S. 678 (1977), the Court confronted a New York law forbidding sale or distribution of contraceptive devices to persons under 16 years of age. Although there was no single opinion for the Court, the law was invalidated. Both *Eisenstadt* and *Carey*, as well as the holding and rationale in *Roe*, confirmed that the reasoning of *Griswold* could not be confined to the protection of rights of married adults. This was the state of the law with respect to some of the most relevant cases when the Court considered Bowers v. Hardwick.

The facts in *Bowers* had some similarities to the instant case. A police officer, whose right to enter seems not to have been in question, observed Hardwick, in his own bedroom, engaging in intimate sexual conduct with another adult male. The conduct was in violation of a Georgia statute making it a criminal offense to engage in sodomy. One difference between the two cases is that the Georgia statute prohibited the conduct whether or not the participants were of the same sex, while the Texas statute, as we have seen, applies only to participants of the same sex. Hardwick was not prosecuted, but he brought an action in federal court to declare the state statute invalid. He alleged he was a practicing homosexual and that the criminal prohibition violated rights guaranteed to him by the Constitution. The Court, in an opinion by Justice White, sustained the Georgia law. . . .

The Court began its substantive discussion in *Bowers* as follows: "The issue presented is whether the Federal Constitution confers a fundamental right upon homosexuals to engage in sodomy and hence invalidates the laws of the many States that still make such conduct illegal and have done so for a very long time." That statement, we now conclude, discloses the Court's own failure to appreciate the extent of the liberty at stake. To say that the issue in *Bowers* was simply the right to engage in certain sexual conduct demeans the claim the individual put forward, just as it would demean a married couple were it to be said marriage is simply about the right to have sexual intercourse. The laws involved in *Bowers* and here are, to be sure, statutes that purport to do no more than prohibit a particular sexual act. Their penalties and purposes, though, have more far-reaching consequences, touching upon the most private human conduct, sexual behavior, and in the most private of places, the home. The statutes do seek to control a personal relationship that, whether or not entitled to formal recognition in the law, is within the liberty of persons to choose without being punished as criminals.

This, as a general rule, should counsel against attempts by the State, or a court, to define the meaning of the relationship or to set its boundaries absent injury to a person or abuse of an institution the law protects. It suffices for us to acknowledge that adults may choose to enter upon this relationship in the confines of their homes and their own private lives and still retain their dignity as free persons. When sexuality finds overt expression in intimate conduct with another person, the conduct can be but one element in a personal bond that is more enduring. The liberty protected by the Constitution allows homosexual persons the right to make this choice.

Having misapprehended the claim of liberty there presented to it, and thus stating the claim to be whether there is a fundamental right to engage in consensual sodomy, the *Bowers* Court said: "Proscriptions against that conduct have ancient roots." In academic writings, and in many of the scholarly *amicus* briefs filed to assist the Court in this case, there are fundamental criticisms of the historical premises relied upon by the majority and concurring opinions in *Bowers*. We need not enter this debate in the attempt to reach a definitive historical judgment, but the following considerations counsel against adopting the definitive conclusions upon which *Bowers* placed such reliance.

At the outset it should be noted that there is no longstanding history in this country of laws directed at homosexual conduct as a distinct matter. Beginning in colonial times there were prohibitions of sodomy derived from the English criminal laws passed in the first instance by the Reformation Parliament of 1533. The English prohibition was understood to include relations between men and women as well as relations between men and men. Nineteenth-century commentators similarly read American sodomy, buggery, and crime-against-nature statutes as criminalizing certain relations between men and women and between men and men. The absence of legal prohibitions focusing on homosexual conduct may be explained in part by noting that according to some scholars the concept of the homosexual as a distinct category of person did not emerge until the late 19th century. Thus early American sodomy laws were not directed at homosexuals as such but instead sought to prohibit nonprocreative sexual activity more generally. This does not suggest approval of homosexual conduct. It does tend to show that this particular form of conduct was not thought of as a separate category from like conduct between heterosexual persons.

Laws prohibiting sodomy do not seem to have been enforced against consenting adults acting in private. A substantial number of sodomy prosecutions and convictions for which there are surviving records were for predatory acts against those who could not or did not consent, as in the case of a minor or the victim of an assault. As to these, one purpose for the prohibitions was to ensure there would be no lack of coverage if a predator committed a sexual assault that did not constitute rape as defined by the criminal law. . . . Instead of targeting relations between consenting adults in private, 19th-century sodomy prosecutions typically involved relations between men and minor girls or minor boys, relations between adults involving force, relations between adults implicating disparity in status, or relations between men and animals.

To the extent that there were any prosecutions for the acts in question, 19th-century evidence rules imposed a burden that would make a conviction more difficult to obtain even taking into account the problems always inherent in prosecuting consensual acts committed in private. Under then-prevailing standards, a man could not be convicted of sodomy based upon testimony of a consenting partner, because the partner was considered an accomplice. A partner's testimony, however, was admissible if he or she had not consented to the act or was a minor, and therefore incapable of consent. The rule may explain in part the infrequency of these prosecutions. In all events that infrequency makes it difficult to say that society approved of a rigorous and systematic punishment of the consensual acts committed in private and by adults. The longstanding criminal prohibition of homosexual sodomy upon which the *Bowers* decision placed such reliance is as consistent with a general condemnation of nonprocreative sex as it is with an established tradition of prosecuting acts because of their homosexual character.

The policy of punishing consenting adults for private acts was not much discussed in the early legal literature. We can infer that one reason for this was the very private nature of the conduct. Despite the absence of prosecutions, there may have been periods in which there was public criticism of homosexuals as such and an insistence that the criminal laws be enforced to discourage their practices. But far from possessing "ancient roots," American laws targeting same-sex couples did not develop until the last third of the 20th century. The reported decisions concerning the prosecution of consensual, homosexual sodomy between adults for the years 1880-1995 are not always clear in the details, but a significant number involved conduct in a public place.

It was not until the 1970's that any State singled out same-sex relations for criminal prosecution, and only nine States have done so. Post-*Bowers* even some of these States did not adhere to the policy of suppressing homosexual conduct. Over the course of the last decades, States with same-sex prohibitions have moved toward abolishing them.

In summary, the historical grounds relied upon in *Bowers* are more complex than the majority opinion and the concurring opinion by Chief Justice Burger indicate. Their historical premises are not without doubt and, at the very least, are overstated.

It must be acknowledged, of course, that the Court in *Bowers* was making the broader point that for centuries there have been powerful voices to condemn homosexual conduct as immoral. The condemnation has been shaped by religious beliefs, conceptions of right and acceptable behavior, and respect for the traditional family. For many persons these are not trivial concerns but profound and deep convictions accepted as ethical and moral principles to which they aspire and which thus determine the course of their lives. These considerations do not answer the question before us, however. The issue is whether the majority may use the power of the State to enforce these views on the whole society through operation of the criminal law. "Our obligation is to define the liberty of all, not to mandate our own moral code." Planned Parenthood of Southeastern Pa. v. Casey, 505 U.S. 833, 850 (1992).

Chief Justice Burger joined the opinion for the Court in *Bowers* and further explained his views as follows: "Decisions of individuals relating to homosexual conduct have been subject to state intervention throughout the history of Western civilization. Condemnation of those practices is firmly rooted in Judeo-Christian moral and ethical standards." As with Justice White's assumptions about history, scholarship casts some doubt on the sweeping nature of the statement by Chief Justice Burger as it pertains to private homosexual conduct between consenting adults. In all events we think that our laws and traditions in the past half century are of most relevance here. These references show an emerging awareness that liberty gives substantial protection to adult persons in deciding how to conduct their private lives in matters pertaining to sex. "[H]istory and tradition are the starting point but not in all cases the ending point of the substantive due process inquiry."

This emerging recognition should have been apparent when *Bowers* was decided. In 1955 the American Law Institute promulgated the Model Penal Code and made clear that it did not recommend or provide for "criminal penalties for consensual sexual relations conducted in private." ALI, Model Penal Code §213.2, Comment 2, p. 372 (1980). It justified its decision on three grounds: (1) The prohibitions undermined respect for the law by penalizing conduct many people engaged in; (2) the statutes regulated private conduct not harmful to others; and (3) the laws were arbitrarily enforced and thus invited the danger of blackmail. ALI, Model Penal Code, Commentary 277-280 (Tent. Draft No. 4, 1955). In 1961 Illinois changed its laws to conform to the Model Penal Code. Other States soon followed.

In *Bowers* the Court referred to the fact that before 1961 all 50 States had outlawed sodomy, and that at the time of the Court's decision 24 States and the District of Columbia had sodomy laws. Justice Powell pointed out that these prohibitions often were being ignored, however. Georgia, for instance, had not sought to enforce its law for decades.

The sweeping references by Chief Justice Burger to the history of Western civilization and to Judeo-Christian moral and ethical standards did not take account of other authorities pointing in an opposite direction. A committee advising the British Parliament recommended in 1957 repeal of laws punishing homosexual conduct. Parliament enacted the substance of those recommendations 10 years later.

Of even more importance, almost five years before *Bowers* was decided the European Court of Human Rights . . . held that the laws proscribing [consensual homosexual] conduct were invalid under the European Convention on Human Rights. Dudgeon v. United Kingdom, 45 Eur. Ct. H.R. (1981). Authoritative in all countries that are members of the Council of Europe (21 nations then, 45 nations now), the decision is at odds with the premise in *Bowers* that the claim put forward was insubstantial in our Western civilization.

In our own constitutional system the deficiencies in *Bowers* became even more apparent in the years following its announcement. The 25 States with laws prohibiting the relevant conduct referenced in the *Bowers* decision are reduced now to 13, of which 4 enforce their laws only against homosexual conduct. In those States where sodomy is still proscribed, whether for same-sex or heterosexual conduct, there is a pattern of nonenforcement with respect to consenting adults acting in private. The State of Texas admitted in 1994 that as of that date it had not prosecuted anyone under those circumstances.

Two principal cases decided after *Bowers* cast its holding into even more doubt. In Planned Parenthood of Southeastern Pa. v. Casey, the Court reaffirmed the substantive force of the liberty protected by the Due Process Clause. The *Casey* decision again confirmed that our laws and tradition afford constitutional protection to personal decisions relating to marriage, procreation, contraception, family relationships, child rearing, and education. In explaining the respect the Constitution demands for the autonomy of the person in making these choices, we stated as follows:

> These matters, involving the most intimate and personal choices a person may make in a lifetime, choices central to personal dignity and autonomy, are central to the liberty protected by the Fourteenth Amendment. At the heart of liberty is the right to define one's own concept of existence, of meaning, of the universe, and of the mystery of human life. Beliefs about these matters could not define the attributes of personhood were they formed under compulsion of the State.

Persons in a homosexual relationship may seek autonomy for these purposes, just as heterosexual persons do. The decision in *Bowers* would deny them this right. . . .

Romer v. Evans . . . invalidated an amendment to Colorado's constitution which named as a solitary class persons who were homosexuals, lesbians, or bisexual either by "orientation, conduct, practices or relationships," and deprived them of protection under state antidiscrimination laws. We concluded that the provision was "born of animosity toward the class of persons affected" and further that it had no rational relation to a legitimate governmental purpose.

[C]ounsel for the petitioners and some *amici* contend that *Romer* provides the basis for declaring the Texas statute invalid under the Equal Protection Clause. That is a tenable argument, but we conclude the instant case requires us to address whether *Bowers* itself has continuing validity. Were we to hold the statute invalid under the Equal Protection Clause some might question whether a prohibition would be valid if drawn differently, say, to prohibit the conduct both between same-sex and different-sex participants.

Equality of treatment and the due process right to demand respect for conduct protected by the substantive guarantee of liberty are linked in important respects, and a decision on the latter point advances both interests. If protected conduct is made criminal and the law which does so remains unexamined for its substantive validity, its stigma might remain even if it were not enforceable as drawn for equal protection reasons. When homosexual conduct is made criminal by the law of the State, that declaration in and of itself is an invitation to subject homosexual persons to discrimination both in the public and in the private spheres. The central holding of *Bowers* has been brought in question by this case, and it should be addressed. Its continuance as precedent demeans the lives of homosexual persons.

The stigma this criminal statute imposes, moreover, is not trivial. The offense, to be sure, is but a class C misdemeanor, a minor offense in the Texas legal system. Still, it remains a criminal offense with all that imports for the dignity of the persons charged. The petitioners will bear on their record the history of their criminal convictions. Just this Term we rejected various challenges to state laws requiring the registration of sex offenders. We are advised that if Texas convicted an adult for private, consensual homosexual conduct under the statute here in question the convicted person would come within the registration laws of at least four States were he or she to be subject to their jurisdiction. This underscores the consequential nature of the punishment and the state-sponsored condemnation attendant to the criminal prohibition. Furthermore, the Texas criminal conviction carries with it the other collateral consequences always following a conviction, such as notations on job application forms, to mention but one example.

The foundations of *Bowers* have sustained serious erosion from our recent decisions in *Casey* and *Romer.* When our precedent has been thus weakened, criticism from other sources is of greater significance. In the United States criticism of *Bowers* has been substantial and continuing, disapproving of its reasoning in all respects, not just as to its historical assumptions. The courts of five different States have declined to follow it in interpreting provisions in their own state constitutions parallel to the Due Process Clause of the Fourteenth Amendment.

To the extent *Bowers* relied on values we share with a wider civilization, it should be noted that the reasoning and holding in *Bowers* have been rejected elsewhere. The European Court of Human Rights has followed not *Bowers* but its own decision in Dudgeon v. United Kingdom. Other nations, too, have taken action consistent with an affirmation of the protected right of homosexual adults to engage in intimate, consensual conduct. The right the petitioners seek in this case has been accepted as an integral part of human freedom in many other countries. There has been no showing that in this country the governmental interest in circumscribing personal choice is somehow more legitimate or urgent.

The doctrine of *stare decisis* is essential to the respect accorded to the judgments of the Court and to the stability of the law. It is not, however, an inexorable command. In *Casey* we noted that when a Court is asked to overrule a precedent recognizing a constitutional liberty interest, individual or societal reliance on the existence of that liberty cautions with particular strength against reversing course. The holding in *Bowers*, however, has not induced detrimental reliance comparable to some instances where recognized individual rights are involved. Indeed, there has been no individual or societal reliance on *Bowers* of the sort that could counsel against overturning its holding once there are compelling reasons to do so. *Bowers* itself causes uncertainty, for the precedents before and after its issuance contradict its central holding.

The rationale of *Bowers* does not withstand careful analysis. In his dissenting opinion in *Bowers* Justice Stevens came to these conclusions:

> Our prior cases make two propositions abundantly clear. First, the fact that the governing majority in a State has traditionally viewed a particular practice as immoral is not a sufficient reason for upholding a law prohibiting the practice; neither history nor tradition could save a law prohibiting miscegenation from constitutional attack. Second, individual decisions by married persons, concerning the intimacies of their physical relationship, even when not intended to produce offspring, are a form of "liberty" protected by the Due Process Clause of the Fourteenth Amendment. Moreover, this protection extends to intimate choices by unmarried as well as married persons.

Justice Stevens' analysis, in our view, should have been controlling in *Bowers* and should control here.

Bowers was not correct when it was decided, and it is not correct today. It ought not to remain binding precedent. Bowers v. Hardwick should be and now is overruled.

The present case does not involve minors. It does not involve persons who might be injured or coerced or who are situated in relationships where consent might not easily be refused. It does not involve public conduct or prostitution. It does not involve whether the government must give formal recognition to any relationship that homosexual persons seek to enter. The case does involve two adults who, with full and mutual consent from each other, engaged in sexual practices common to a homosexual lifestyle. The petitioners are entitled to respect for their private lives. The State cannot demean their existence or control their destiny by making their private sexual conduct a crime. Their right to liberty under the Due Process Clause gives them the full right to engage in their conduct without intervention of the government. "It is a promise of the Constitution that there is a realm of personal liberty which the government may not enter." *Casey.* The Texas statute furthers no legitimate state interest which can justify its intrusion into the personal and private life of the individual.

Had those who drew and ratified the Due Process Clauses of the Fifth Amendment or the Fourteenth Amendment known the components of liberty in its manifold possibilities, they might have been more specific. They did not presume to have this insight. They knew times can blind us to certain truths and later generations can see that laws once thought necessary and proper in fact serve only to oppress. As the Constitution endures, persons in every generation can invoke its principles in their own search for greater freedom.

The judgment of the Court of Appeals for the Texas Fourteenth District is reversed, and the case is remanded for further proceedings not inconsistent with this opinion.

It is so ordered.

Justice O'CONNOR, concurring in the judgment.

The Court today overrules Bowers v. Hardwick, 478 U.S. 186 (1986). I joined *Bowers,* and do not join the Court in overruling it. Nevertheless, I agree with the Court that Texas' statute banning same-sex sodomy is unconstitutional. Rather than relying on the substantive component of the Fourteenth Amendment's Due Process Clause, as the Court does, I base my conclusion on the Fourteenth Amendment's Equal Protection Clause. . . .

We have consistently held, however, that some objectives, such as "a bare . . . desire to harm a politically unpopular group," are not legitimate state interests. When a law exhibits such a desire to harm a politically unpopular group, we have applied a more searching form of rational basis review to strike down such laws under the Equal Protection Clause, [especially] where, as here, the challenged legislation inhibits personal relationships. In Department of Agriculture v. Moreno, for example, we held that a law preventing those households containing an individual unrelated to any other member of the household from receiving food stamps violated equal protection because the purpose of the law was to "discriminate against hippies." . . . In Eisenstadt v. Baird, we refused to sanction a law that discriminated between married and unmarried persons by prohibiting the distribution of contraceptives to single persons. Likewise, in Cleburne v. Cleburne Living Center, supra, we held that it was irrational for a State to require a home for the mentally disabled to obtain a special use permit when other residences—like fraternity houses and apartment buildings—did not have to obtain such a permit.

And in Romer v. Evans, we disallowed a state statute that "impos[ed] a broad and undifferentiated disability on a single named group"—specifically, homosexuals. The dissent apparently agrees that if these cases have *stare decisis* effect, Texas' sodomy law would not pass scrutiny under the Equal Protection Clause, regardless of the type of rational basis review that we apply.

[Texas] treats the same conduct differently based solely on the participants. Those harmed by this law are people who have a same-sex sexual orientation and thus are more likely to engage in behavior prohibited by §21.06. . . . The Texas statute makes homosexuals unequal in the eyes of the law by making particular conduct—and only that conduct—subject to criminal sanction. [Although] prosecutions . . . are rare, [t]his case shows, however, that [they] *do* occur. And while the penalty imposed on petitioners in this case was relatively minor, the consequences of conviction are not. [P]etitioners' convictions, if upheld, would disqualify them from or restrict their ability to engage in a variety of professions, including medicine, athletic training, and interior design. Indeed, were petitioners to move to one of four States, their convictions would require them to register as sex offenders to local law enforcement. . . . Texas' sodomy law brands all homosexuals as criminals, thereby making it more difficult for homosexuals to be treated in the same manner as everyone else. Indeed, Texas itself has previously acknowledged the collateral effects of the law, stipulating in a prior challenge to this action that the law "legally sanctions discrimination against [homosexuals] in a variety of ways unrelated to the criminal law," including in the areas of "employment, family issues, and housing." . . .

This case raises a different issue than *Bowers*: whether, under the Equal Protection Clause, moral disapproval is a legitimate state interest to justify by itself a statute that bans homosexual sodomy, but not heterosexual sodomy. It is not. Moral disapproval of this group, like a bare desire to harm the group, is an interest that is insufficient to satisfy rational basis review under the Equal Protection Clause. Indeed, we have never held that moral disapproval, without any other asserted state interest, is a sufficient rationale under the Equal Protection Clause to justify a law that discriminates among groups of persons.

Moral disapproval of a group cannot be a legitimate governmental interest under the Equal Protection Clause because legal classifications must not be "drawn for the purpose of disadvantaging the group burdened by the law." Texas' invocation of moral disapproval as a legitimate state interest proves nothing more than Texas' desire to criminalize homosexual sodomy. But the Equal Protection Clause prevents a State from creating "a classification of persons undertaken for its own sake." And because Texas so rarely enforces its sodomy law as applied to private, consensual acts, the law serves more as a statement of dislike and disapproval against homosexuals than as a tool to stop criminal behavior. The Texas sodomy law "raise[s] the inevitable inference that the disadvantage imposed is born of animosity toward the class of persons affected."

[T]he State maintains that the law discriminates only against homosexual conduct. While it is true that the law applies only to conduct, the conduct targeted by this law is conduct that is closely correlated with being homosexual. Under such circumstances, Texas' sodomy law is targeted at more than conduct. It is instead directed toward gay persons as a class. . . . When a State makes homosexual conduct criminal, and not "deviate sexual intercourse" committed by persons of different sexes, "that declaration in and of itself is an invitation to subject homosexual persons to discrimination both in the public and in the private spheres." . . .

In Romer v. Evans, we refused to sanction a law that singled out homosexuals "for disfavored legal status." The same is true here. The Equal Protection Clause "neither knows nor tolerates classes among citizens." Id. at 623 (quoting *Plessy*).

A State can of course assign certain consequences to a violation of its criminal law. But the State cannot single out one identifiable class of citizens for punishment that does not apply to everyone else, with moral disapproval as the only asserted state interest for the law. The Texas sodomy statute subjects homosexuals to "a lifelong penalty and stigma. A legislative classification that threatens the creation of an underclass . . . cannot be reconciled with" the Equal Protection Clause. Plyler v. Doe (Powell, J., concurring).

Whether a sodomy law that is neutral both in effect and application would violate the substantive component of the Due Process Clause is an issue that need not be decided today. I am confident, however, that so long as the Equal Protection Clause requires a sodomy law to apply equally to the private consensual conduct of homosexuals and heterosexuals alike, such a law would not long stand in our democratic society. In the words of Justice Jackson:

> The framers of the Constitution knew, and we should not forget today, that there is no more effective practical guaranty against arbitrary and unreasonable government than to require that the principles of law which officials would impose upon a minority be imposed generally. Conversely, nothing opens the door to arbitrary action so effectively as to allow those officials to pick and choose only a few to whom they will apply legislation and thus to escape the political retribution that might be visited upon them if larger numbers were affected. Railway Express Agency, Inc. v. New York, 336 U.S. 106, 112-113 (1949) (concurring opinion).

That this law as applied to private, consensual conduct is unconstitutional under the Equal Protection Clause does not mean that other laws distinguishing between heterosexuals and homosexuals would similarly fail under rational basis review. Texas cannot assert any legitimate state interest here, such as national security or preserving the traditional institution of marriage. Unlike the moral disapproval of same-sex relations—the asserted state interest in this case—other reasons exist to promote the institution of marriage beyond mere moral disapproval of an excluded group.

A law branding one class of persons as criminal solely based on the State's moral disapproval of that class and the conduct associated with that class runs contrary to the values of the Constitution and the Equal Protection Clause, under any standard of review. I therefore concur in the Court's judgment that Texas' sodomy law banning "deviate sexual intercourse" between consenting adults of the same sex, but not between consenting adults of different sexes, is unconstitutional.

Justice SCALIA, with whom THE CHIEF JUSTICE and Justice THOMAS join, dissenting.

Most of . . . today's opinion has no relevance to its actual holding—that the Texas statute "furthers no legitimate state interest which can justify" its application to petitioners under rational-basis review. Though there is discussion of "fundamental proposition[s]," and "fundamental decisions," nowhere does the Court's opinion declare that homosexual sodomy is a "fundamental right" under the Due Process Clause; nor does it subject the Texas law to the standard of review that would be appropriate (strict scrutiny) if homosexual sodomy *were* a "fundamental right." Thus, while overruling the *outcome* of *Bowers*, the Court leaves strangely untouched its central legal conclusion: "[R]espondent would have us announce . . . a fundamental right to engage in homosexual sodomy. This we are quite unwilling to do." Instead the Court simply describes petitioners' conduct as "an exercise of their liberty"—which it undoubtedly is—and proceeds to apply an unheard-of form of rational-basis review that will have far-reaching implications beyond this case.

I

I begin with the Court's surprising readiness to reconsider a decision rendered a mere 17 years ago in Bowers v. Hardwick. I do not myself believe in rigid adherence to *stare decisis* in constitutional cases; but I do believe that we should be consistent rather than manipulative in invoking the doctrine. Today's opinions in support of reversal do not bother to distinguish—or indeed, even bother to mention—the paean to *stare decisis* coauthored by three Members of today's majority in Planned Parenthood v. Casey. . . . Today, . . . the widespread opposition to *Bowers*, a decision resolving an issue as "intensely divisive" as the issue in *Roe*, is offered as a reason in favor of *overruling* it. Gone, too, is any "enquiry" (of the sort conducted in *Casey*) into whether the decision sought to be overruled has "proven 'unworkable.'"

Today's approach to *stare decisis* invites us to overrule an erroneously decided precedent (including an "intensely divisive" decision) *if:* (1) its foundations have been "eroded" by subsequent decisions; (2) it has been subject to "substantial and continuing" criticism; and (3) it has not induced "individual or societal reliance" that counsels against overturning. The problem is that *Roe* itself—which today's majority surely has no disposition to overrule—satisfies these conditions to at least the same degree as *Bowers*. . . .

(1) [I] do not quarrel with the Court's claim that Romer v. Evans "eroded" the "foundations" of *Bowers*' rational-basis holding. But *Roe* and *Casey* have been equally "eroded" by Washington v. Glucksberg, which held that *only* fundamental rights which are "deeply rooted in this Nation's history and tradition" qualify for anything other than rational basis scrutiny under the doctrine of "substantive due process." *Roe* and *Casey*, of course, subjected the restriction of abortion to heightened scrutiny without even attempting to establish that the freedom to abort *was* rooted in this Nation's tradition.

(2) *Bowers*, the Court says, has been subject to "substantial and continuing [criticism], disapproving of its reasoning in all respects, not just as to its historical assumptions." . . . Of course, *Roe* too (and by extension *Casey*) had been (and still is) subject to unrelenting criticism, including criticism from the two commentators cited by the Court today.

(3) That leaves, to distinguish the rock-solid, unamendable disposition of *Roe* from the readily overrulable *Bowers*, only the third factor. "[T]here has been," the Court says, "no individual or societal reliance on *Bowers* of the sort that could counsel against overturning its holding. . . ." It seems to me that the "societal reliance" on the principles confirmed in *Bowers* and discarded today has been overwhelming. Countless judicial decisions and legislative enactments have relied on the

ancient proposition that a governing majority's belief that certain sexual behavior is "immoral and unacceptable" constitutes a rational basis for regulation. . . . State laws against bigamy, same-sex marriage, adult incest, prostitution, masturbation, adultery, fornication, bestiality, and obscenity are likewise sustainable only in light of *Bowers*' validation of laws based on moral choices. Every single one of these laws is called into question by today's decision; the Court makes no effort to cabin the scope of its decision to exclude them from its holding. See ante (noting "an emerging awareness that liberty gives substantial protection to adult persons in deciding how to conduct their private lives *in matters pertaining to sex*" (emphasis added)). The impossibility of distinguishing homosexuality from other traditional "morals" offenses is precisely why *Bowers* rejected the rational-basis challenge. "The law," it said, "is constantly based on notions of morality, and if all laws representing essentially moral choices are to be invalidated under the Due Process Clause, the courts will be very busy indeed."

What a massive disruption of the current social order, therefore, the overruling of *Bowers* entails. Not so the overruling of *Roe*, which would simply have restored the regime that existed for centuries before 1973, in which the permissibility of and restrictions upon abortion were determined legislatively State by State. . . . To tell the truth, it does not surprise me, and should surprise no one, that the Court has chosen today to revise the standards of *stare decisis* set forth in *Casey*. It has thereby exposed *Casey*'s extraordinary deference to precedent for the result-oriented expedient that it is.

II

[Texas] Penal Code Ann. §21.06(a) (2003) undoubtedly imposes constraints on liberty. So do laws prohibiting prostitution, recreational use of heroin, and, for that matter, working more than 60 hours per week in a bakery. But there is no right to "liberty" under the Due Process Clause, though today's opinion repeatedly makes that claim. The Fourteenth Amendment *expressly allows* States to deprive their citizens of "liberty," *so long as "due process of law" is provided*: "No state shall . . . deprive any person of life, liberty, or property, *without due process of law*." Amdt. 14 (emphasis added).

Our opinions applying the doctrine known as "substantive due process" hold that the Due Process Clause prohibits States from infringing *fundamental* liberty interests, unless the infringement is narrowly tailored to serve a compelling state interest. Washington v. Glucksberg. We have held repeatedly, in cases the Court today does not overrule, that *only* fundamental rights qualify for this so-called "heightened scrutiny" protection—that is, rights which are "deeply rooted in this Nation's history and tradition." . . . All other liberty interests may be abridged or abrogated pursuant to a validly enacted state law if that law is rationally related to a legitimate state interest. . . .

III

The Court's description of "the state of the law" at the time of *Bowers* only confirms that *Bowers* was right. The Court points to Griswold v. Connecticut. But that case *expressly disclaimed* any reliance on the doctrine of "substantive due process," and grounded the so-called "right to privacy" in penumbras of constitutional provisions *other than* the Due Process Clause. Eisenstadt v. Baird likewise had nothing to do with "substantive due process"; it invalidated a Massachusetts law prohibiting the distribution of contraceptives to unmarried persons solely on the basis of the Equal Protection Clause. Of course *Eisenstadt* contains well-known dictum relating to the "right to privacy," but this referred to the right recognized in *Griswold*—a right penumbral to the *specific* guarantees in the Bill of Rights, and not a "substantive due process" right.

Roe v. Wade recognized that the right to abort an unborn child was a "fundamental right" protected by the Due Process Clause. The *Roe* Court, however, made no attempt to establish that this right was "deeply rooted in this Nation's history and tradition." . . . We have since rejected *Roe*'s holding that regulations of abortion must be narrowly tailored to serve a compelling state interest, see Planned Parenthood v. Casey, and thus, by logical implication, *Roe*'s holding that the right to abort an unborn child is a "fundamental right."

After discussing the history of antisodomy laws, the Court proclaims that, "it should be noted that there is no longstanding history in this country of laws directed at homosexual conduct as a distinct matter." This observation in no way casts into doubt the "definitive [historical] conclusion," on which *Bowers* relied: that our Nation has a longstanding history of laws prohibiting *sodomy in general*—regardless of whether it was performed by same-sex or opposite-sex couples. . . .

It is (as *Bowers* recognized) entirely irrelevant whether the laws in our long national tradition criminalizing homosexual sodomy were "directed at homosexual conduct as a distinct matter." Whether homosexual sodomy was prohibited by a law targeted at same-sex sexual relations or by a more general law prohibiting both homosexual and heterosexual sodomy, the only relevant point is that it *was* criminalized—which suffices to establish that homosexual sodomy is not a right "deeply rooted in our Nation's history and tradition." The Court today agrees that homosexual sodomy was criminalized and thus does not dispute the facts on which *Bowers actually* relied.

Next the Court makes the claim, again unsupported by any citations, that "[l]aws prohibiting sodomy do not seem to have been enforced against consenting adults acting in private." The key qualifier here is "acting in private"—since the Court admits that sodomy laws *were* enforced against consenting adults (although the Court contends that prosecutions were "infrequent"). I do not know what "acting in private" means; surely consensual sodomy, like heterosexual intercourse, is rarely performed on stage. If all the Court means by "acting in private" is "on private premises, with the doors closed and windows covered," it is entirely unsurprising that evidence of enforcement would be hard to come by. (Imagine the circumstances that would enable a search warrant to be obtained for a residence on the ground that there was probable cause to believe that consensual sodomy was then and there occurring.) Surely that lack of evidence would not sustain the proposition that consensual sodomy on private premises with the doors closed and windows covered was regarded as a "fundamental right," even though all other consensual sodomy was criminalized. There are 203 prosecutions for consensual, adult homosexual sodomy reported in the West Reporting system and official state reporters from the years 1880-1995. There are also records of 20 sodomy prosecutions and 4 executions during the colonial period. *Bowers*' conclusion that homosexual sodomy is not a fundamental right "deeply rooted in this Nation's history and tradition" is utterly unassailable.

Realizing that fact, the Court instead says: "[W]e think that our laws and traditions in the past half century are of most relevance here. These references show *an emerging awareness* that liberty gives substantial protection to adult persons in deciding how to conduct their private lives *in matters pertaining to sex.*" Apart from the fact that such an "emerging awareness" does not establish a "fundamental right," the statement is factually false. States continue to prosecute all sorts of crimes by adults "in matters pertaining to sex": prostitution, adult incest, adultery, obscenity, and child pornography. Sodomy laws, too, have been enforced "in the past half century," in which there have been 134 reported cases involving prosecutions for consensual, adult, homosexual sodomy. In relying, for evidence of an "emerging recognition," upon the American Law Institute's 1955 recommendation not to criminalize "consensual sexual relations conducted in private," the Court ignores the fact that this recommendation was "a point of resistance in most of the states that considered adopting the Model Penal Code."

In any event, an "emerging awareness" is by definition not "deeply rooted in this Nation's history and tradition[s]," as we have said "fundamental right" status requires. Constitutional entitlements do not spring into existence because some States choose to lessen or eliminate criminal sanctions on certain behavior. Much less do they spring into existence, as the Court seems to believe, because *foreign nations* decriminalize conduct. . . . The Court's discussion of these foreign views (ignoring, of course, the many countries that have retained criminal prohibitions on sodomy) is therefore meaningless dicta. Dangerous dicta, however, since "this Court . . . should not impose foreign moods, fads, or fashions on Americans." Foster v. Florida, 537 U.S. 990, n. (2002) (Thomas, J., concurring in denial of certiorari).

IV

[T]he Texas statute undeniably seeks to further the belief of its citizens that certain forms of sexual behavior are "immoral and unacceptable"—the same interest furthered by criminal laws against fornication, bigamy, adultery, adult incest, bestiality, and obscenity. *Bowers* held that this *was* a legitimate state interest. The Court today reaches the opposite conclusion. The Texas statute, it says, "furthers *no legitimate state interest* which can justify its intrusion into the personal and private life of the individual" (emphasis added). The Court embraces instead Justice Stevens' declaration in his *Bowers* dissent, that "the fact that the governing majority in a State has traditionally viewed a particular practice as immoral is not a sufficient reason for upholding a law prohibiting the practice." This effectively decrees the end of all morals legislation. If, as the Court asserts, the promotion of majoritarian sexual morality is not even a *legitimate* state interest, none of the above-mentioned laws can survive rational-basis review.

V

Finally, I turn to petitioners' equal-protection challenge. . . . On its face §21.06(a) applies equally to all persons. Men and women, heterosexuals and homosexuals, are all subject to its prohibition of deviate sexual intercourse with someone of the same sex. To be sure, §21.06 does distinguish between the sexes insofar as concerns the partner with whom the sexual acts are performed: men can violate the law only with other men, and women only with other women. But this cannot itself be a denial of equal protection, since it is precisely the same distinction regarding partner that is drawn in state laws prohibiting marriage with someone of the same sex while permitting marriage with someone of the opposite sex.

Loving v. Virginia [does not apply]; we correctly applied heightened scrutiny . . . because the Virginia statute was "designed to maintain White Supremacy." A racially discriminatory purpose is always sufficient to subject a law to strict scrutiny, even a facially neutral law that makes no mention of race. See Washington v. Davis. No purpose to discriminate against men or women as a class can be gleaned from the Texas law, so rational-basis review applies. That review is readily satisfied here by the same rational basis that satisfied it in *Bowers*—society's belief that certain forms of sexual behavior are "immoral and unacceptable." This is the same justification that supports many other laws regulating sexual behavior that make a distinction based upon the identity of the partner—for example, laws against adultery, fornication, and adult incest, and laws refusing to recognize homosexual marriage.

Justice O'Connor argues that . . . "Texas' sodomy law is targeted at more than conduct. It is instead directed toward gay persons as a class." Of course the same could be said of any law. A law against public nudity targets "the conduct that is closely correlated with being a nudist," and hence "is targeted at more than conduct"; it is "directed toward nudists as a class." But be that as it may, even if the Texas law *does* deny equal protection to "homosexuals as a class," that denial *still* does not need to be justified by anything more than a rational basis, which our cases show is satisfied by the enforcement of traditional notions of sexual morality.

[T]he [rational basis] cases [Justice O'Connor] cites . . . reach their conclusions only after finding . . . that no conceivable legitimate state interest supports the classification at issue. [She argues] that laws exhibiting "a . . . desire to harm a politically unpopular group," are invalid *even though* there may be a conceivable rational basis to support them. This reasoning leaves on pretty shaky grounds state laws limiting marriage to opposite-sex couples. Justice O'Connor seeks to preserve them by the conclusory statement that "preserving the traditional institution of marriage" is a legitimate state interest. But "preserving the traditional institution of marriage" is just a kinder way of describing the State's *moral disapproval* of same-sex couples. Texas' interest in §21.06 could be recast in similarly euphemistic terms: "preserving the traditional sexual mores of our society." In the jurisprudence Justice O'Connor has seemingly created, judges can validate laws by characterizing them as "preserving the traditions of society" (good); or invalidate them by characterizing them as "expressing moral disapproval" (bad).

* * *

Today's opinion is the product of a Court, which is the product of a law-profession culture, that has largely signed on to the so-called homosexual agenda, by which I mean the agenda promoted by some homosexual activists directed at eliminating the moral opprobrium that has traditionally attached to homosexual conduct. . . .

One of the most revealing statements in today's opinion is the Court's grim warning that the criminalization of homosexual conduct is "an invitation to subject homosexual persons to discrimination both in the public and in the private spheres." It is clear from this that the Court has taken sides in the culture war, departing from its role of assuring, as neutral observer, that the democratic rules of engagement are observed. Many Americans do not want persons who openly engage in homosexual conduct as partners in their business, as scoutmasters for their children, as teachers in their children's schools, or as boarders in their home. They view this as protecting themselves and their families from a lifestyle that they believe to be immoral and destructive. The Court views it as "discrimination" which it is the function of our judgments to deter. So imbued is the Court with the law profession's anti-anti-homosexual culture, that it is seemingly unaware that the attitudes of that culture are not obviously "mainstream"; that in most States what the Court calls "discrimination" against those who engage in homosexual acts is perfectly legal; that proposals to ban such "discrimination" under Title VII have repeatedly been rejected by Congress; that in some cases such "discrimination" is *mandated* by federal statute, see 10 U.S.C. §654(b)(1) (mandating discharge from the armed forces of any service member who engages in or intends to engage in homosexual acts); and that in some cases such "discrimination" is a constitutional right, see Boy Scouts of America v. Dale, 530 U.S. 640 (2000).

Let me be clear that I have nothing against homosexuals, or any other group, promoting their agenda through normal democratic means. Social perceptions of sexual and other morality change over time, and every group has the right to persuade its fellow citizens that its view of such matters is the best. That homosexuals have achieved some success in that enterprise is attested to by the fact that Texas is one of the few remaining States that criminalize private, consensual homosexual acts. But persuading one's fellow citizens is one thing, and imposing one's views in absence of democratic majority will is something else. I would no more *require* a State to criminalize homosexual acts—or, for that matter, display *any* moral disapprobation of them—than I would *forbid* it to do so. What Texas has chosen to do is well within the range of traditional democratic action, and its hand should not be stayed through the invention of a brand-new "constitutional right" by a Court that is impatient of democratic change. It is indeed true that "later generations can see that laws once thought necessary and proper in fact serve only to oppress"; and when that happens, later generations can repeal those laws. But it is the premise of our system that those judgments are to be made by the people, and not imposed by a governing caste that knows best.

One of the benefits of leaving regulation of this matter to the people rather than to the courts is that the people, unlike judges, need not carry things to their logical conclusion. The people may feel that their disapprobation of homosexual conduct is strong enough to disallow homosexual marriage, but not strong enough to criminalize private homosexual acts—and may legislate accordingly. The Court today pretends that it possesses a similar freedom of action, so that we need not fear judicial imposition of homosexual marriage, as has recently occurred in Canada. At the end of its opinion—after having laid waste the foundations of our rational-basis jurisprudence—the Court says that the present case "does not involve whether the government must give formal recognition to any relationship that homosexual persons seek to enter." Do not believe it. More illuminating than this bald, unreasoned disclaimer is the progression of thought displayed by an earlier passage in the Court's opinion, which notes the constitutional protections afforded to "personal decisions relating to *marriage*, procreation, contraception, family relationships, child rearing, and education," and then declares that "[p]ersons in a homosexual relationship may seek autonomy for these purposes, just as heterosexual persons do" (emphasis added). Today's opinion dismantles the structure of constitutional law that has permitted a distinction to be made between heterosexual and homosexual unions, insofar as formal recognition in marriage is concerned. If moral disapprobation of homosexual conduct is "no legitimate state interest" for purposes of proscribing that conduct; and if, as the Court coos (casting aside all pretense of neutrality), "[w]hen sexuality finds overt expression in intimate conduct with another person, the conduct can be but one element in a personal bond that is more enduring"; what justification could there possibly be for denying the benefits of marriage to homosexual couples exercising "[t]he liberty protected by the Constitution"? Surely not the encouragement of procreation, since the sterile and the elderly are allowed to marry. This case "does not involve" the issue of homosexual marriage only if one entertains the belief that principle and logic have nothing to do with the decisions of this Court. Many will hope that, as the Court comfortingly assures us, this is so.

The matters appropriate for this Court's resolution are only three: Texas' prohibition of sodomy neither infringes a "fundamental right" (which the Court does not dispute), nor is unsupported by a rational relation to what the Constitution considers a legitimate state interest, nor denies the equal protection of the laws. I dissent.

Justice THOMAS, dissenting.

I join Justice Scalia's dissenting opinion. I write separately to note that the law before the Court today "is . . . uncommonly silly." Griswold v. Connecticut, 381 U.S. 479, 527 (1965) (Stewart, J., dissenting). If I were a member of the Texas Legislature, I would vote to repeal it. Punishing someone for expressing his sexual preference through noncommercial consensual conduct with another adult does not appear to be a worthy way to expend valuable law enforcement resources.

Notwithstanding this, I recognize that as a member of this Court I am not empowered to help petitioners and others similarly situated. My duty, rather, is to "decide cases 'agreeably to the Constitution and laws of the United States.'" And, just like Justice Stewart, I "can find [neither in the Bill of Rights nor any other part of the Constitution a] general right of privacy," or as the Court terms it today, the "liberty of the person both in its spatial and more transcendent dimensions."

DISCUSSION

1. *"Liberty" versus "privacy."* In *Lawrence*, the majority rules on substantive due process grounds, seemingly offering a more robust understanding of the interest at stake. Justice Kennedy consistently uses the word "liberty," rather than "privacy," to describe the constitutional interest. Indeed, the word "privacy" appears outside of a quotation only once in the majority opinion, and even then it is used only to describe the holding of *Griswold*.

What explains this shift in language? Does the word "liberty" ground *Lawrence*'s holding more firmly in the text of the Fourteenth Amendment or better suggest the proper scope of the right at stake? Recall the earlier discussion of zonal, relational, decisional, and informational dimensions of privacy. Which, if any, does *Lawrence* protect?

2. *Does* Lawrence *recognize a fundamental right?* Justice Scalia argues that the majority does not specifically state that there is a fundamental right to same-sex conduct and that *Lawrence* is a rational basis decision. *Lawrence* is ambiguous on precisely this point. Justice Kennedy never uses the word "fundamental" to refer to the right in question; moreover, he argues that "[t]he Texas statute furthers no legitimate state interest which can justify its intrusion into the personal and private life of the individual," which sounds like the test of rational basis. Does this mean that the Court will now apply heightened scrutiny, whether we call it undue burden or "rational basis with a bite," to certain nonfundamental rights? Under this theory, *Lawrence* is the due process/liberty analogue to equal protection cases like *Cleburne* (discussed in Chapter 8), Romer v. Evans (discussed supra) and Plyler v. Doe (discussed in Chapter 10). If that is the case, how do courts identify those specially protected nonfundamental rights, and how do they distinguish them from fundamental rights on the one hand and from nonfundamental rights to which ordinary rational basis applies on the other?

At the same time, Justice Kennedy does not rule out the notion that *Lawrence* involved a fundamental right. For example, he argues that *Eisenstadt, Carey,* and *Roe* each extended the rights of intimate association and decisional privacy protected by *Griswold* beyond married adults. He then argues that homosexuals have similar rights to form intimate associations, which are more than mere sexual conduct. Finally, he endorses the reasoning of a portion of Justice Stevens's dissent in *Bowers.* All of this might suggest that *Lawrence* holds that the right to form same-sex intimate relations is part of a fundamental right of sexual privacy along with the rights protected in *Griswold, Carey,* and *Eisenstadt.* Not surprisingly, the lower courts have divided in the ways they characterize the Court's holding in *Lawrence.*

3. *What right does* Lawrence *recognize?* Assume for the moment that *Lawrence* does recognize a fundamental or quasi-fundamental right to engage in sexual relations. What is the principled basis of the right, and how far does that right extend?

After the Court overturned *Bowers,* does the Constitution permit criminalization of consensual sex between adults? The language of *Lawrence* broadly suggests that government should not interfere with individuals' private lives unless a "legitimate state interest . . . can justify its intrusion," *Lawrence,* 539 U.S. at 578, and "the fact that the governing majority . . . has traditionally viewed a particular practice as immoral is not sufficient reason for upholding a law prohibiting the practice." Id. at 588 (citing *Bowers,* 478 U.S. at 216 (Stevens, J., dissenting)). Nonetheless, lower courts have refused in nearly all cases to interpret *Lawrence* to extend to prosecutions for polygamy, incest, masturbation, adultery, bestiality, and other sex-related crimes.[153] Lower courts cite the *Lawrence* Court's qualification that

153. See generally J. Kelly Strader, *Lawrence*'s Criminal Law, 16 Berkeley J. Crim. L. 41 (2011). But see Brown v. Buhman, 947 F. Supp. 2d 1170 (D. Utah 2013) (construing *Lawrence* as bearing on the constitutionality of a law prohibiting bigamy enforced against practitioners of plural marriage).

"[t]he present case does not involve minors[,] . . . persons who might be injured or coerced or who are situated in relationships where consent might not easily be refused[, or] . . . public conduct or prostitution" to suggest that *Lawrence*'s apparently broad holding is in fact more limited.[154]

In the wake of *Lawrence,* should states still be able to criminalize polygamy or incest? In his dissent in *Bowers,* Justice Blackmun suggested that constitutional protection for intimate sexual relations need not extend to other sexual practices like adultery and incest because the latter practices arguably harmed third parties or did not allow for true consent. Are there distinct and weightier state interests in prohibiting adultery and incest than in prohibiting same-sex sexual relations? Is social acceptance key to the constitutional status of laws criminalizing sexual practices? If so, could *Bowers* have been rightly decided in 1986, when homosexuality was less acceptable to the American public, but wrongly decided in 2003?

4. *What precisely does* Lawrence *protect?* Does *Lawrence* protect only the same-sex intimate relations at issue in the case? Or does *Lawrence* protect all sexual expression between consenting adults? Alternatively, is *Lawrence* limited to a middle ground, prohibiting only some criminal and civil law restrictions—for example, those that impair the equal citizenship of gays and lesbians?

5. *What kind of sexual relations does* Lawrence *privilege, if any?* Justice Kennedy's opinion has been noted for its rhetoric about same-sex intimacy, including that it "involves liberty of the person both in its spatial and in its more transcendent dimensions." While the opinion specifically disclaims any holding that the case requires recognition of same-sex relationships, the majority nonetheless situates *Lawrence* as part of a line of cases involving the unique sanctity of marriage, conception, and child rearing rather than rulings on obscenity and the privacy of the home.

Yet, Dale Carpenter reports that the men at the heart of the *Lawrence* litigation were not in a relationship at the time, and may not have had sex; Lawrence was in a long-term partnership with another man, and Garner was involved with Robert Eubanks, who called the police with a false report of a weapons disturbance on the night they were arrested. Both denied being engaged in sexual activity on the night of the arrest, and the two officers who made the arrest disagree about what they saw that night. Dale Carpenter, Flagrant Conduct: The Story of Lawrence v. Texas 61-74 (2012). Does knowing that the relationship between Lawrence and Garner was brief—or that they may not have had sex at all—affect how you understand the logic of the opinion, or is knowledge of the facts irrelevant to what the majority in *Lawrence* actually protects? Is *Lawrence* about sex, or is it about the dignity of same-sex relationships? What is at stake in these different perspectives on the decision?

Katherine Franke argues that *Lawrence* "both echoes and reinforces a pull toward domesticity in current gay and lesbian organizing." Katherine Franke, The Domesticated Liberty of Lawrence v. Texas, 104 Colum. L. Rev. 1399, 1400 (2004). Others have argued that *Lawrence* opens up same-sex relationships to greater scrutiny, as LGBT people find that their relationships—just like heterosexual relationships—have become part of a system of state regulation. See, e.g., Nan

---

154. Id. at 57 (citing *Lawrence,* 539 U.S. at 578).

Hunter, Sexual Orientation and the Paradox of Heightened Scrutiny, 102 Mich. L. Rev. 1528 (2004). Have developments after *Lawrence* borne out these initial predictions?

The role that the law should play in recognizing and regulating sex and romantic relationships is a point of tension even within LGBT communities. Those who support assimilation to the mainstream argue that access to marriage, adoption, and military service will mark the successful conclusion of the gay rights movement. See, e.g., Andrew Sullivan, Virtually Normal: An Argument About Homosexuality (1995). Others worry that marriage is erasing a broader vision of sexual liberation and alternative kinship arrangements that queer people have creatively pioneered. See, e.g., Nancy D. Polikoff, Beyond (Straight and Gay) Marriage: Valuing All Families Under the Law (2009). For a history that explores the ways the institution of marriage shaped claims for legal recognition of nonmarital relationships, see Doug NeJaime, "Before Marriage: The Unexplored History of Nonmarital Recognition and its Relationship to Marriage," 102 Cal. L. Rev. 87 (2014).

6. *What are the standards used to overturn precedent in* Lawrence*? Lawrence* reflects a well-known tendency of the Court: The Court declares a legal prohibition or practice unconstitutional when many states have already repealed or greatly limited it. In 1960, for example, every state had an anti-sodomy law.[155] By the time of the decision in *Lawrence*, these statutes had been repealed or overturned in 36 states.[156] In *Lawrence*, the Court eliminated sodomy laws in the remaining 14 jurisdictions, where the laws were generally not directly enforced (although frequently used to justify differential treatment in civil law settings).

How might these considerations fit into the Court's inquiry when overturning precedents? In *Casey*, the Joint Opinion outlined four "prudential and pragmatic considerations" that the Court should take into account in deciding whether to overrule a precedent: (1) workability, (2) reliance, (3) change in surrounding doctrines, and (4) changes in facts or changes in the perception of facts.[157] This section of the *Casey* Joint Opinion commanded five votes. Does *Lawrence* adhere to these standards? If not, did *Lawrence* overrule or supersede the theory of stare decisis in *Casey*?

7. *Why does Kennedy cite foreign law, and when is this appropriate?* Note that the majority opinion cites the European Court of Human Rights opinion in Dudgeon v. United Kingdom, 45 Eur. Ct. H.R. (1981). Does Kennedy regard the case as authoritative precedent, as persuasive authority (like a state supreme court decision construing a related provision in the state's own constitution), or merely as evidence of changing views in the West about the morality of homosexuality responsive to certain claims asserted by the majority opinion in *Bowers*?

Recall Justice Harlan's justification of looking to the evolving traditions of the American people in Poe v. Ullman.[158] If substantive due process decisions are justified with reference to the evolving norms of Americans, why are the decisions of foreign courts relevant? At the time that *Lawrence* was decided, nearly 80 countries criminalized homosexuality, and there were fewer jurisdictions that recognized same-sex marriage than there were countries that imposed the death penalty for homosexuality.[159] Is it relevant that a wide range of countries throughout the world continue to regard homosexuality as sinful or immoral? What assumptions must a court make in deciding which foreign sources should count as persuasive, either as offering a plausible set of arguments about human rights or merely as evidence of changing norms among "civilized" nations?

NOTE: LIBERTY, EQUALITY, AND *LAWRENCE*

Like Planned Parenthood of Southeastern Pennsylvania v. Casey, *Lawrence* interprets the Due Process Clause in a decision that weaves together appeals to liberty and equality. The Court invokes concerns about dignity, respect, denigration, discrimination, and status throughout *Lawrence*. For example, Justice Kennedy writes that "[w]hen homosexual conduct is made criminal by the law of the State, that declaration in and of itself is an invitation to subject homosexual persons to discrimination both in the public and in the private spheres."[160] He goes on to argue that *Bowers*'s "continuance as precedent demeans the lives of homosexual persons."[161] At another point, Kennedy asserts that "petitioners are entitled to respect for their private lives. The State cannot demean their existence or control their destiny by making their private sexual conduct a crime."[162] He observes that the criminal statute imposes a "stigma" that is "not trivial" in that it is "a criminal offense with all that imports for the dignity of the persons charged."[163] *Lawrence* is thus a substantive due process opinion that is shaped by many of the same concerns that animate equal protection law. Indeed, Justice Kennedy's opinion observes: "Equality of treatment and the due process right to demand respect for conduct protected by the substantive guarantee of liberty are linked in important respects, and a decision on the latter point advances both interests."[164]

1. Liberty and/or Equality?

The *Lawrence* decision opened a new chapter in a continuing debate about the interaction between substantive due process and equal protection. After *Bowers*, gays and lesbians brought several unsuccessful cases arguing that sexual orientation

155. See Eskridge, Gaylaw, supra n.124, at 387-407 (appendix of state sodomy laws).

156. Id.

157. Planned Parenthood v. Casey, 505 U.S. 833, 854-855 (1992).

158. Poe v. Ullman, 367 U.S. 497, 542 (1961) ("Due process has not been reduced to any formula; its content cannot be determined by reference to any code. The best that can be said is that through the course of this Court's decisions it has represented the balance which our Nation, built upon postulates of respect for the liberty of the individual, has struck between that liberty and the demands of organized society. . . . The balance of which I speak is the balance struck by this country, having regard to what history teaches are the traditions from which it developed as well as the traditions from which it broke. That tradition is a living thing.").

159. As of 2009, 80 countries criminalized same-sex sexual relations and in 5 countries same-sex sexual activity was punishable by death. Daniel Ottosson, State-sponsored Homophobia: A World Survey of Laws Prohibiting Same Sex Activity Between Consenting Adults, Report by the International Lesbian, Gay, Bisexual, Trans and Intersex Association, 48-49 (2009). At the time *Lawrence* was decided, three countries allowed same-sex couples to jointly adopt children and a fourth country allowed a same-sex second parent to adopt children. Id. at 53-54.

160. Lawrence v. Texas, 539 U.S. 558, 575 (2003).

161. Id. at 575.

162. Id. at 578.

163. Id. at 575.

164. Id.

discrimination violated the Equal Protection Clause. The courts repeatedly dismissed these claims, reasoning that if it was constitutional under the Due Process Clause to criminalize private homosexual conduct, it was constitutional under the Equal Protection Clause for government to discriminate against those who engaged in private homosexual conduct.[165] The premise of those post-*Bowers* decisions was that the meaning of the Due Process and Equal Protection Clauses was closely connected.

Cass Sunstein sought to distinguish *Bowers* and limit its reach by arguing that the protections of due process and equal protection were fundamentally distinct. Sunstein proposed that the Due Process Clause is backward-looking while the Equal Protection Clause is forward-looking.[166] While the Due Process Clause "is closely associated with . . . the view that the role of the Court is to protect against ill-considered or short-term departures from time-honored practices,"[167] the Equal Protection Clause "is a self-conscious repudiation of history and tradition as defining constitutional principles."[168] The Equal Protection Clause is thus much better suited for dismantling sexual orientation discrimination than a liberty-based due process approach since "opposition to homosexuality has deep historical roots."[169] Because Sunstein read *Lawrence* as a due process decision, he disagreed with the majority's approach. He would have preferred O'Connor's use of the Equal Protection Clause to invalidate, as irrational, the ban on homosexual but not heterosexual sodomy.[170]

In response, Laurence Tribe objected that the Supreme Court has not hewn to such rigidly demarcated roles for the Due Process Clause and Equal Protection Clause: "*Lawrence*, more than any other decision in the Supreme Court's history, both presupposed and advanced an explicitly equality-based and relationally situated theory of substantive liberty. The 'liberty' of which the Court spoke was as much about equal dignity and respect as it was about freedom of action—more so, in fact."[171]

Kenji Yoshino also notes that the Court has long used the Due Process Clause to further equality concerns (i.e., for racial minorities) and the Equal Protection Clause to protect liberties (i.e., the right to vote).[172] *Lawrence*, he argues, makes sense as an attempt to quiet "pluralism anxiety."[173] By emphasizing that the right in question belonged to all people, the Court elevated the case from a "group-based equality case about gays" to "a universal liberty case about the right of all consenting

---

165. See, e.g., High Tech Gays v. Defense Indus. Sec. Clearance Office, 895 F.2d 563 (9th Cir. 1990) ("[I]f there is no fundamental right to engage in homosexual sodomy under the Due Process Clause of the Fifth Amendment, see *Hardwick*, 478 U.S. at 194, it would be incongruous to expand the reach of equal protection to find a fundamental right of homosexual conduct under the equal protection component of the Due Process Clause of the Fifth Amendment.").

166. Cass R. Sunstein, Sexual Orientation and the Constitution: A Note on the Relationship Between Due Process and Equal Protection, 55 U. Chi. L. Rev. 1161 (1988).

167. Id. at 1178.

168. Id. at 1168.

169. Cass R. Sunstein, Homosexuality and the Constitution, 70 Ind. L.J. 1, 3 (1994).

170. Cass R. Sunstein, What Did *Lawrence* Hold? Of Autonomy, Desuetude, Sexuality, and Marriage, 55 Sup. Ct. Rev. 27, 31-32 (2003).

171. Laurence H. Tribe, Lawrence v. Texas: The "Fundamental Right" That Dare Not Speak Its Name, 117 Harv. L. Rev. 1893, 1898 (2004).

172. Kenji Yoshino, The New Equal Protection, 124 Harv. L. Rev. 747, 749-750 (2011).

173. Id. at 778.

adults to engage in sexual intimacy."[174] That "liberty . . . frames the right at a high enough level of generality that opposite-sex couples are urged to imagine a world in which they were denied the right. In contrast, equal protection claims tend to stress distinctions among us, even as they ask us to overcome those distinctions."[175]

Pam Karlan has argued that the simplest explanation for the Court's reticence is that the Court was concerned about the potential reach of an equal protection decision.[176] Whereas liberty interests can be analyzed individually, case by case, equality holdings are not so easily cabined. The "suspect classification" framework of equal protection scrutiny is "far more binary" than fundamental rights/due process-based strict scrutiny: "[E]ither a group is entitled to heightened scrutiny across the board or it isn't."[177] By skirting the equal protection issue, the Court could more easily dodge the marriage question.[178]

2. *Liberty versus Equality: A Queer Perspective*

Basing *Lawrence* on liberty rather than equality is attractive to those who would prefer to shift constitutional protection away from status and toward conduct. The concern is that an equality holding would follow a "civil rights paradigm"; it would ascribe to all group members a common group identity (i.e., "gay"), analogous to the common identity ascribed to "Blacks" or "women." By contrast, advocates of a queer perspective might contend that the law should vindicate the rights of all persons to conduct their sexual lives as they see fit. Under this view, a liberty approach is preferable to an equality approach because it doesn't presuppose fixed or normalized identities or risk reifying them in law. Is it clear that reification of a person's identity occurs only with equality claims? Are there other independent legal or political reasons for relying on equality?

3. *Dignity in* Lawrence

The *Lawrence* opinion is also striking for its attention to the dignity of gay and lesbian persons, and for the ways dignity connects the opinion's appeal to liberty and equality values. In the first few paragraphs of the opinion, Justice Kennedy expressly repudiates the *Bowers* Court's characterization of the liberty at stake as "a fundamental right to engage in homosexual sodomy":[179]

> To say that the issue in *Bowers* was simply the right to engage in certain sexual conduct demeans the claim the individual put forward, just as it would demean a married couple were it said that marriage is just about the right to have sexual intercourse. . . . It suffices for us to acknowledge

---

174. Id. at 778.

175. Id. at 794.

176. Pamela S. Karlan, Foreword: Loving *Lawrence*, 102 Mich. L. Rev. 1447, 1459 (2004).

177. Id. at 1459-1460.

178. Karlan and Justice O'Connor in her concurrence both observe that even if the Court had relied on the Equal Protection Clause, it could have still avoided the suspect/quasi-suspect class question since the Texas statute failed even rational review. *Lawrence*, 539 U.S. at 585; Karlan, Foreword: Loving *Lawrence*, supra n.176, at 1460-1461.

179. *Lawrence*, 539 U.S. at 567.

> that adults may choose to enter upon this relationship in the confines of their homes and their own private lives and still retain their dignity as free persons. When sexuality finds overt expression in intimate conduct with another person, the conduct can be but one element in a personal bond that is more enduring. The liberty protected by the Constitution allows homosexual persons the right to make this choice.

Later, Kennedy links dignity to autonomy and self-definition, quoting *Casey*, noting that "the most intimate and personal choices a person may make in a lifetime, choices central to personal dignity and autonomy, are central to the liberty protected by the Fourteenth Amendment."[180]

What does "dignity" mean? Sometimes dignity means liberty, sometimes it means equality, and sometimes it means the value of life itself. A striking feature of dignity claims is that agonists on both sides of the gay rights debate (and the abortion debate) appeal to dignity.[181] In fact, the meaning of "dignity" as a legal concept is shaped through debates over laws regulating sexuality.

Courts outside the United States have often focused on dignity. In 1998, the Constitutional Court of South Africa invalidated South Africa's apartheid-era sodomy ban, declaring that "[t]he prohibition of unfair discrimination in the Constitution provides a bulwark against invasions which impair human dignity or which affect people adversely in a comparably serious manner."[182] In these and other cases, dignity has provided a primary lens through which courts interpreted guarantees of privacy, liberty, and equality.

B. *Sexual Orientation: Equal Protection and Heightened Scrutiny*

The Supreme Court has not yet decided whether to accord classifications based on sexual orientation heightened scrutiny in equal protection cases, but lower courts have considered the issue. Most circuits have ruled that laws classifying on the basis of sexual orientation are not subject to heightened scrutiny. The majority of circuit courts came to this conclusion before *Lawrence* overruled *Bowers* in 2003 and predicated their reasoning on *Bowers*'s holding that criminalization of same-sex sexual relations was not unconstitutional under the Due Process Clause.[183] The circuits addressing the equal protection question after *Lawrence*

---

180. Id. at 574 (quoting *Casey*, 505 U.S. at 851).

181. See, e.g., Reva B. Siegel, Dignity and Sexuality: Claims on Dignity in Transnational Debates over Abortion and Same-Sex Marriage, 10 ICON 355 (2012); Reva B. Siegel, Dignity and the Politics of Protection: Abortion Restrictions Under *Casey/Carhart*, 117 Yale L.J. 1694 (2008). See also Tribe, Lawrence v. Texas: The "Fundamental Right" That Dare Not Speak Its Name, supra n.171; Yoshino, The New Equal Protection, supra n.172.

182. National Coalition for Gay and Lesbian Equality and Another v. Minister of Justice and Others (CCT11/98) [1998] ZACC 15; 1999 (1) SA 6; 1998 (12) BCLR 1517 (9 October 1998).

183. Seven circuits held before *Lawrence* that classifications based on sexual orientation were not entitled to heightened scrutiny. The reasoning of the Seventh Circuit in Ben-Shalom v. Marsh is representative: "If homosexual conduct may constitutionally be criminalized, then homosexuals do not constitute a suspect or quasi-suspect class entitled to greater than

relied on the Supreme Court's failure in its decisions to identify gays and lesbians as a suspect class.[184] In *Romer*, as we have seen, the Supreme Court struck down Colorado's Amendment 2 employing what would appear to be some form of "heightened" rational basis review, without declaring classifications on the basis of orientation suspect.

But, in the years after *Romer* and *Lawrence*, signals of change continued to mount: in indices of public opinion; in judicial decisions invalidating restrictions on the right to marry (discussed in Section IV.C, infra); in the election of a President more responsive to gay civil rights claims; and in congressional repeal of restrictions on the right of gays and lesbians openly to serve in the military.[185]

One of the more striking signals of change occurred in 2011, when President Obama's Department of Justice concluded that the correct standard of review for sexual orientation discrimination had changed. As a consequence, the Department of Justice could no longer enforce the Defense of Marriage Act (DOMA), which limited marriage to a union between a man and a woman.[186] This aspect of DOMA was held unconstitutional on other grounds in United States v. Windsor, 570 U.S. 744 (2013), discussed infra. In February 2011, Attorney General Eric Holder sent a letter to congressional leaders to offer the executive branch's official constitutional position:

Letter from the Attorney General to Congress on Litigation Involving the Defense of Marriage Act

(February 23, 2011)[187]

After careful consideration . . . the President of the United States has made the determination that Section 3 of the Defense of Marriage Act ("DOMA"), 1 U.S.C. §7, as applied to same-sex couples who are legally married under state law, violates the equal protection component of the Fifth Amendment. . . .

Previously, the Administration has defended Section 3 in jurisdictions where circuit courts have already held that classifications based on sexual orientation are subject to rational basis review, and it has advanced arguments to defend DOMA Section 3

---

rational basis scrutiny for equal protection purposes. The Constitution, in light of *Hardwick*, cannot otherwise be rationally applied, lest an unjustified and indefensible inconsistency result." Ben-Shalom v. Marsh, 881 F.2d 454, 464-465 (7th Cir. 1989); see also High Tech Gays v. Defense Indus. Sec. Clearance Office, 895 F.2d 563, 574 (9th Cir. 1990).

184. Cook v. Gates, 528 F.3d 42, 61 (1st Cir. 2008); Citizens for Equal Protection v. Bruning, 455 F.3d 859, 866-867 (8th Cir. 2006); Johnson v. Johnson, 385 F.3d 503, 532 (5th Cir. 2004); Lofton v. Sec'y of Dept. of Children and Family Serv., 385 F.3d 804, 818 (11th Cir. 2004).

185. See Pub. L. No. 111-321, §2(f)(1)(A), Dec. 22, 2011, 124 Stat. 3516 (repealing "Don't Ask, Don't Tell").

186. See Pub. L. No. 104-199, §3(a), Sept. 21, 1996, 110 Stat. 2419, codified at 1 U.S.C.A. §7 (1996). DOMA provides, in relevant part, that "the word 'marriage' means only a legal union between one man and one woman as husband and wife, and the word 'spouse' refers only to a person of the opposite sex who is a husband or a wife." Id.

187. Letter from Eric H. Holder, Jr., Attorney Gen. of the U.S., to Rep. John A. Boehner, Speaker, U.S. House of Representatives (Feb. 23, 2011) (footnotes and citations omitted), available at http://www.justice.gov/opa/pr/2011/February/11-ag-223.html.

under the binding standard that has applied in those cases. []These new lawsuits, by contrast, will require the Department to take an affirmative position on the level of scrutiny that should be applied to DOMA Section 3 in a circuit without binding precedent on the issue. . . .

STANDARD OF REVIEW

The Supreme Court has yet to rule on the appropriate level of scrutiny for classifications based on sexual orientation. It has, however, rendered a number of decisions that set forth the criteria that should inform this and any other judgment as to whether heightened scrutiny applies: (1) whether the group in question has suffered a history of discrimination; (2) whether individuals "exhibit obvious, immutable, or distinguishing characteristics that define them as a discrete group"; (3) whether the group is a minority or is politically powerless; and (4) whether the characteristics distinguishing the group have little relation to legitimate policy objectives or to an individual's "ability to perform or contribute to society." . . .

Each of these factors counsels in favor of being suspicious of classifications based on sexual orientation. First and most importantly, there is, regrettably, a significant history of purposeful discrimination against gay and lesbian people, by governmental as well as private entities, based on prejudice and stereotypes that continue to have ramifications today. . . .

Second, while sexual orientation carries no visible badge, a growing scientific consensus accepts that sexual orientation is a characteristic that is immutable, see Richard A. Posner, Sex and Reason 101 (1992); it is undoubtedly unfair to require sexual orientation to be hidden from view to avoid discrimination, see Don't Ask, Don't Tell Repeal Act of 2010. . . .

Third, the adoption of laws like those at issue in Romer v. Evans, 517 U.S. 620 (1996), and *Lawrence*, the longstanding ban on gays and lesbians in the military, and the absence of federal protection for employment discrimination on the basis of sexual orientation show the group to have limited political power and "ability to attract the [favorable] attention of the lawmakers." . . . And while . . . the political process is not closed *entirely* to gay and lesbian people, that is not the standard by which the Court has judged "political powerlessness." Indeed, when the Court ruled that gender-based classifications were subject to heightened scrutiny, women already had won major political victories such as the Nineteenth Amendment (right to vote) and protection under Title VII (employment discrimination).

Finally, . . . [r]ecent evolutions in legislation . . . , in community practices and attitudes, in case law . . . and in social science regarding sexual orientation all make clear that sexual orientation is not a characteristic that generally bears on legitimate policy objectives. . . .

To be sure, there is substantial circuit court authority applying rational basis review to sexual-orientation classifications. . . . Many of them [offer] a line of reasoning that does not survive the overruling of *Bowers*. . . . Others rely on claims regarding "procreational responsibility" that the Department has disavowed already in litigation as unreasonable, or claims regarding the immutability of sexual orientation that we do not believe can be reconciled with more recent social science understandings. And none engages in an examination of all the factors that the Supreme Court has identified as relevant to a decision about the appropriate level of scrutiny.

Finally, many of the more recent decisions have relied on the fact that the Supreme Court has not recognized that gays and lesbians constitute a suspect class or the fact that the Court has applied rational basis review in its most recent decisions addressing classifications based on sexual orientation, *Lawrence* and *Romer*. But neither of those decisions reached, let alone resolved, the level of scrutiny issue because in both the Court concluded that the laws could not even survive the more deferential rational basis standard.

APPLICATION TO SECTION 3 OF DOMA

In reviewing a legislative classification under heightened scrutiny, the government must establish that the classification is "substantially related to an important government objective . . . [and] a tenable justification must describe actual state purposes, not rationalizations for actions in fact differently grounded." . . . In other words, under heightened scrutiny, the United States cannot defend Section 3 by advancing hypothetical rationales, independent of the legislative record, as it has done in circuits where precedent mandates application of rational basis review. Instead, the United States can defend Section 3 only by invoking Congress' actual justifications for the law.

Moreover, the legislative record underlying DOMA's passage . . . contains numerous expressions reflecting moral disapproval of gays and lesbians and their intimate and family relationships—precisely the kind of stereotype-based thinking and animus the Equal Protection Clause is designed to guard against. . . .

APPLICATION TO SECOND CIRCUIT CASES

[T]he President has concluded that given a number of factors, including a documented history of discrimination, classifications based on sexual orientation should be subject to a heightened standard of scrutiny. The President has also concluded that Section 3 of DOMA, as applied to legally married same-sex couples, fails to meet that standard and is therefore unconstitutional. Given that conclusion, the President has instructed the Department not to defend the statute in Windsor [v. United States] and Pedersen [v. Office of Personnel Management], now pending in the Southern District of New York and the District of Connecticut. . . .

Notwithstanding this determination, the President has informed me that Section 3 will continue to be enforced by the Executive Branch . . . consistent with the Executive's obligation to take care that the laws be faithfully executed, unless and until Congress repeals Section 3 or the judicial branch renders a definitive verdict against the law's constitutionality. This course of action respects the actions of the prior Congress that enacted DOMA, and it recognizes the judiciary as the final arbiter of the constitutional claims raised.

[T]he Department has a longstanding practice of defending the constitutionality of duly-enacted statutes if reasonable arguments can be made in their defense, a practice that accords the respect appropriately due to a coequal branch of government.

However, the Department in the past has declined to defend statutes despite the availability of professionally responsible arguments, in part because the Department does not consider every plausible argument to be a "reasonable" one. . . . This is the rare case where the proper course is to forgo the defense of this statute. . . . I will instruct the Department's lawyers to immediately inform the district courts in *Windsor* and *Pedersen* of the Executive Branch's view that heightened scrutiny is the appropriate standard of review.[188] . . . [I]n the event those courts determine that the applicable standard is rational basis, the Department will state that, consistent with the position it has taken in prior cases, a reasonable argument for Section 3's constitutionality may be proffered under that permissive standard. Our attorneys will also notify the courts of our interest in providing Congress a full and fair opportunity to participate in the litigation in those cases. . . .

Sincerely yours,
Eric H. Holder, Attorney General

DISCUSSION

1. *Executive power to decline to defend statutes.* Holder's letter reads like a judicial opinion. What is the role of the executive branch and the Department of Justice in interpreting the Constitution? Article II requires the President to "take Care that the Laws be faithfully executed," yet it also instructs the President to pledge to "preserve, protect and defend" the Constitution.[189] In discharging this responsibility, should the President simply endeavor to follow judicial decisions? In what circumstances, if any, should the President exercise independent judgment? Recall the criteria offered in Acting Solicitor General Walter Dellinger's letter, "Presidential Authority to Decline to Execute Unconstitutional Statutes," reprinted in Chapter 1.

Attorneys General and Solicitors General have only rarely invoked their authority not to defend a law that they, or the President, believe to be unconstitutional. In 1996, the Clinton Administration declined to defend a provision in a defense authorization bill that required the dismissal of all HIV-positive military personnel, arguing that the President, as Commander-in-Chief, was in a better position to understand the impact of the law on the military and therefore to question the rational basis of the congressional enactment.[190]

In 1989, the George H.W. Bush Administration declined to defend an affirmative action program of the Federal Communications Commission on the grounds that it "could not withstand the exacting scrutiny required by the Constitution,"[191] a decision that may be the closest analogue to Holder's letter. The Supreme Court later upheld the program.[192]

---

188. Notwithstanding the arguments of government lawyers following Holder's letter, the district courts in both cases found DOMA unconstitutional under rational basis review. See Windsor v. United States, 833 F. Supp. 2d 394 (S.D.N.Y. 2012); Pedersen v. Office of Personnel Mgmt., 881 F. Supp. 2d 294 (D. Conn. 2012).

189. U.S. Const., Art. II, §1, cl. 8; Art. II, §3.

190. See Ann Devroy, Clinton Administration Won't Defend HIV Law, Wash. Post, Feb. 10, 1996, at A4.

191. Brief for the United States as Amicus Curiae Supporting Petitioner, No. 89-453, Metro Broadcasting, Inc. v. FCC, 497 U.S. 547 (1990), 1989 WL 1126975.

192. Metro Broadcasting, Inc. v. FCC, 497 U.S. 547 (1990).

Are decisions by presidential administrations not to defend statutes they believe to be violations of equal protection appropriate? Desirable? Consider Professor Daniel Meltzer's argument:[193]

> [T]he question of whether the executive should enforce and defend these statutes is not the broad one of whether the president is a constitutional interpreter—for he must be—or whether he acts lawlessly when his constitutional views diverge from those of the courts—for he does not. Instead, the question is one of judgment—of the desirability, in view of an extant and reasonably stable set of institutional practices and expectations, of the president's determining in a particular case that he will not enforce or defend a statute that is constitutionally dubious but that nonetheless can plausibly be defended.

What is the precise nature of the stability Meltzer mentions? When are concerns about institutional stability implicated? And how should the President weigh this concern against concerns about enforcing a law the President believes to be unconstitutional?

Given all this, what can be said in favor of Holder's decision to enforce but not to defend DOMA? What are the institutional costs of this decision?

2. Do letters like Holder's necessarily pose a threat to courts, or might they help guide and legitimate judicial judgments? Note that support by the executive branch on a controversial constitutional question may give courts greater confidence about the political support that their decision might receive within the government.

Consider that after Holder's letter, one of two remaining circuits that had not yet determined the appropriate standard of review for sexual orientation classifications held that such classifications were subject to heightened scrutiny and ruled that DOMA was unconstitutional on that basis. Windsor v. United States, 699 F.3d 169 (2d Cir.), *aff'd in part on other grounds*, 570 U.S. 744 (2013).[194]

3. *Factors identifying a suspect class.* Holder found that classifications based on sexual orientation should be subject to heightened scrutiny because gays and lesbians meet the following four factors: "(1) . . . the group in question has suffered a history of discrimination; (2) . . . individuals 'exhibit obvious, immutable, or distinguishing characteristics that define them as a discrete group'; (3) . . . the group is a minority or is politically powerless; and (4) . . . the characteristics distinguishing the group have little relation to legitimate policy objectives or to an individual's 'ability to perform or contribute to society.'"

Are you persuaded that Holder has captured all of the factors that the Court set forth in *Frontiero* and in *Cleburne*? Are the appropriate factors satisfied in this case? Note in particular Holder's understanding of the requirement of political powerlessness. How does he conclude that gays and lesbians lack sufficient political power given the events of the past two decades? Doesn't the very fact of the Attorney General's memo—signaling that the President strongly supports gay rights—suggest that gays and lesbians are *no longer* politically powerless?

---

193. Daniel J. Meltzer, Executive Defense of Congressional Acts, 61 Duke L.J. 1183, 1208-1209 (2012).

194. For an account of responses to the Holder letter in the lower courts in the period leading up to *Windsor*, see Katie Eyer, Lower Court Popular Constitutionalism, 123 Yale L.J. Online 197 (2013).

Consider Jack Balkin's response: "[L]egal elites . . . usually respond to 'disadvantaged' groups only after a social movement has demanded a response. Ironically then, a [minority] group must display some degree of political power—whether at the ballot box or in the streets—before it can be considered 'politically powerless' and hence deserving of legal protection." Jack M. Balkin, The Constitution of Status, 106 Yale L.J. 2313, 2340 (1997); see also Jack M. Balkin, What *Brown* Teaches Us About Constitutional Theory, 90 U. Va. L. Rev. 1537, 1152 (2004) ("In general, courts will protect minorities only after minorities have shown a fair degree of clout in the political process. If they are truly politically powerless, courts may not even recognize their grievances; and if they have just enough influence to get on the political radar screen, courts will usually dismiss their claims with a wave of the hand."). This helps explain why the Supreme Court did not begin to protect gay rights until the middle of the 1990s, after almost 30 years of post-Stonewall mobilization.

If, paradoxically, a group must actually display some degree of political power to even be regarded as "politically powerless," what work is the "political powerlessness" test actually doing? Is it a proxy for other concerns?

Some courts have questioned whether gays and lesbians can meet the relevant factors. See, e.g., High Tech Gays v. Defense Industry Security Clearance Office, 895 F.2d 563, 573 (9th Cir. 1990) (finding that homosexuality "is not an immutable characteristic; it is behavioral," and gays and lesbians are not politically powerless because "legislatures have addressed and continue to address the discrimination [they] suffer[]"), *overruled in* SmithKline Beecham Corp. v. Abbott Laboratories, 740 F.3d 471, 480-484 (9th Cir. 2014); Sevick v. Sandoval, 911 F. Supp. 2d 996, 1013 (D. Nev. 2012) ("Only where a discrete minority group's political power is so weak and ineffective as to make attempts to succeed democratically utterly futile is it even arguably appropriate for a court to remove relevant issues from the democratic process, except where a constitutional prohibition clearly removes the issue from legislative control, in which case a court's intervention is mandated by democratic constitutional principles.").

Is it necessary for a group to satisfy all of the factors in order to be considered a suspect class? Do you think that these are the factors that *should* govern whether a group constitutes a suspect class?

C. *Same-Sex Marriage*

Over the last several decades, as the nation has debated the right of same-sex couples to marry, the conflict has played out across different branches of state and federal government.[195] State decisions have influenced the development of federal law;[196] and, at important junctures, federal law has shaped the development of state law.

---

195. For an account that examines the efforts of same-sex couples to marry in the years before *Baehr*, see George Chauncey, Why Marriage?: The History Shaping Today's Debate over Gay Equality 89-136 (2005).

196. State courts can enrich the "interpretive enterprise" of federal constitutional law—particularly when federal courts have become entrenched in a single view of the possibilities of law—because state and federal courts operate under different institutional constraints, including different judicial tenure regimes. See Paul W. Kahn, Interpretation and Authority in State Constitutionalism, 106 Harv. L. Rev. 1147, 1155-1156 (1993).

In 1993, the Hawaii Supreme Court ruled in Baehr v. Lewin that a state law restricting marriage to a union of a man and a woman was a form of sex discrimination that likely violated the equal rights amendment to the Hawaii constitution.[197] Voters quickly responded by amending the state constitution to give the Hawaii legislature authority to define who could marry. The U.S. Congress, concerned that Hawaii would legalize same-sex marriage and that other states would be compelled to recognize those marriages, responded with the Defense of Marriage Act (DOMA), which defined marriage for purposes of federal law as being between one man and one woman, and ensured that no state could impose its definition of marriage on another.[198] Many state legislatures passed "mini-DOMAs" that refused to recognize same-sex marriage in their states.[199] Backlash to *Baehr* was likely on the minds of the Vermont Supreme Court six years later when the court held that restricting marriage to male and female couples violated the state constitution—yet ruled that the legislature could remedy this wrong by offering same-sex couples either the right to marry or the right to enter a civil union that provided benefits equivalent to marriage.[200]

Soon after the Vermont decision—and just months after the Supreme Court struck down a law banning same-sex sodomy in *Lawrence*—the Supreme Judicial Court of Massachusetts recognized the right of same-sex couples to marry under the state's constitution. In Goodridge v. Dept. of Public Health, the Massachusetts Supreme Judicial Court invoked *Lawrence* and held that the Due Process and Equal Protection Clauses of the Massachusetts Constitution required the state to provide same-sex couples access to marriage.[201]

While many courts rejected the state constitutional claims of same-sex couples seeking to marry,[202] those courts that did recognize state constitutional claims for same-sex marriage in the immediate aftermath of *Lawrence* invoked the federal decision in the course of interpreting their state constitutions, often reasoning on

---

197. The sex discrimination argument for same-sex marriage was not uncommon in early marriage litigation, and was central to the rationale of *Baehr*. See Andrew Koppelman, Why Discrimination Against Lesbians and Gay Men Is Sex Discrimination, 69 N.Y.U. L. Rev. 197 (1994); see also Mary Anne Case, What Feminists Have to Lose in Same-Sex Marriage Litigation, 57 UCLA L. Rev. 1199 (2010); Cary Franklin, The Anti-Stereotyping Principle in Constitutional Sex Discrimination Law, N.Y.U. L. Rev. 85, 163-172 (2010).

198. Section 2 of DOMA allows states to decline to give effect to recognized same-sex relationships that are treated as marriages under the laws of another state, as well as any rights or claims arising from such a relationship. See 28 U.S.C.A. §1738C.

199. After *Baehr*, "mini-DOMAs" passed in 28 states, Sarah B. Fandry, Comment, The Goals of Marriage and Divorce in Missouri: The State's Interest in Regulating Marriage, Privatizing Dependence, and Allowing Same-Sex Divorce, 32 St. Louis U. Pub. L. Rev. 447, 470 (2013), and Alaska enacted the first constitutional amendment banning same-sex marriage, see Alaska Const. art. I, §25, all between 1995 and 1998.

200. Baker v. State, 170 Vt. 194, 744 A.2d 864 (1999).

201. Goodridge v. Dept. of Pub. Health, 440 Mass. 309, 342, 798 N.E.2d 941, 968 (2003).

202. See, e.g., Conaway v. Deane, 932 A.2d 571 (Md. 2007); Hernandez v. Robles, 855 N.E.2d 1 (N.Y. 2006); Andersen v. King Cty., 138 P.3d 963 (Wash. 2006); Frandsen v. Cty. of Brevard, 828 So. 2d 386 (Fla. 2002); Morrison v. Sadler, 821 N.E.2d 15 (Ind. Ct. App. 2005); Standhardt v. Superior Court ex rel. County of Maricopa, 77 P.3d 451 (Ariz. Ct. App. 2003).

the ground of equality as well as liberty. Connecticut and Iowa courts both invoked *Lawrence* for the proposition that gay and lesbian persons had suffered sustained discrimination that justified applying heightened scrutiny under state constitutional law.[203]

These early decisions recognizing the right of same-sex couples to marry met with fierce opposition. Opponents of same-sex marriage were concerned that the decisions might influence the law in other states and in the federal courts. President George W. Bush responded to *Goodridge* by endorsing a Federal Marriage Amendment that would have defined marriage as between a man and a woman under the U.S. Constitution. Although the drive to amend the federal Constitution failed, opponents of same-sex marriage consistently prevailed at the state level. In addition to statutory prohibitions, constitutional amendments banning same-sex marriage passed in 23 states in 2004-2006 alone.[204]

The most high-profile, expensive campaign occurred in California. After the California Supreme Court held that same-sex couples had a right to marry under the state constitution,[205] same-sex marriage opponents placed Proposition 8 on the California ballot, and waged a statewide campaign that warned of the effects that same-sex marriage might have on children.[206] Proposition 8 was ultimately approved by a small margin of voters, overturning the state supreme court and redefining marriage as between a man and a woman. Supporters of same-sex marriage then challenged Proposition 8 in the federal courts, arguing that revocation of the right to marry in California violated the federal Constitution. After a lengthy trial that directly grappled with some of the most contentious factual disputes in the same-sex marriage debate, the District Court declared Proposition 8 unconstitutional on federal substantive due process and equal protection grounds.[207]

As conflict raged, the public increasingly came to support same-sex marriage. Polls estimate that support for same-sex marriage increased two percentage points each year after 2004, and that public support surpassed public opposition in late 2010.[208] By 2012, David Blankenhorn, an expert witness called by the proponents of Proposition 8, announced that he no longer opposed marriage equality.[209] In early May 2012, Vice President Biden and President Obama announced support

---

203. Kerrigan v. Comm'r of Pub. Health, 289 Conn. 135, 178-179, 957 A.2d 407, 433-434 (2008); Varnum v. Brien, 763 N.W.2d 862, 889 (Iowa 2009).

204. See State Laws Prohibiting Recognition of Same-Sex Relationship, National Gay & Lesbian Task Force, May 15, 2013, available at http://www.ngltf.org/downloads/reports/issue_maps/samesex_relationships_5_15_13.pdf.

205. In re Marriage Cases, 43 Cal. 4th 757, 183 P.3d 384 (2008).

206. As historian George Chauncey noted in subsequent testimony, the anxiety and rhetoric of the Yes on 8 campaign bore striking resemblances to the Save Our Children campaign waged by Anita Bryant decades earlier.

207. Perry v. Schwarzenegger, 704 F. Supp. 2d 921, 991-1003 (N.D. Cal. 2010).

208. Nate Silver, How Opinion on Same-Sex Marriage Is Changing, and What It Means, Five Thirty Eight Blog, N.Y. Times, Mar. 26, 2013, available at http://fivethirtyeight.blogs.nytimes.com/2013/03/26/how-opinion-on-same-sex-marriage-is-changing-and-what-it-means.

209. See David Blankenhorn, How My View on Gay Marriage Changed, N.Y. Times, June 22, 2012.

for marriage equality.[210] In November 2012, marriage advocates won a clean sweep in the marriage initiatives on various state ballots, preserving marriage legislation in Maryland and Washington that had been stalled by referenda, passing marriage by popular referendum for the first time in Maine, and rejecting an anti-same-sex marriage amendment in Minnesota. In the months that followed, Minnesota, Delaware, and Rhode Island all passed laws authorizing same-sex marriage.[211]

In the two decades since the Hawaii court announced that restrictions on same-sex marriage were presumptively unconstitutional, arguments for and against same-sex marriage had evolved dramatically. The argument that defining marriage as a union of a man and a woman was sex discrimination—the basis of the *Baehr* decision[212]—was rapidly pushed aside in favor of the view that traditional marriage discriminated on the basis of orientation.[213] Increasingly, liberty arguments gave way to equality arguments.[214]

Changes in the arguments for preserving traditional marriage in this period were even more dramatic. With growing public support for marriage recognition, opponents no longer openly denigrated same-sex relationships in public settings as they once had, and instead began to employ more gay-respecting constitutional arguments.[215] For example, opponents of same-sex marriage argued that heterosexual couples were prone to accidental procreation in ways that same-sex couples were not, and so required the incentives of traditional marriage to marry and raise

---

210. Michael Barbaro, A Scramble as Biden Backs Same-Sex Marriage, N.Y. Times, May 6, 2012; Jackie Calmes and Peter Baker, Obama Says Same-Sex Marriage Should Be Legal, N.Y. Times, May 9, 2012.

211. Monica Davey, Minnesota Clears Way for Same-Sex Marriage, N.Y. Times, May 13, 2013.

212. Baehr v. Lewin, 852 P.2d 44, 60-61 (Haw. 1993).

213. For early examples of the sex discrimination argument, see Baehr v. Lewin, 852 P.2d 44 (Haw. 1993); Brause v. Bureau of Vital Statistics, 3AN-95-6562 CI, 1998 WL 88743 (Alaska Super. Ct. 1998); Baker v. State, 744 A.2d 864, 889-897 (Vt. 1999) (Johnson, J., concurring) ("A woman is denied the right to marry another woman because her would-be partner is a woman, not because one or both are lesbians. Similarly, a man is denied the right to marry another man because his would-be partner is a man, not because one or both are gay. Thus, an individual's right to marry a person of the same sex is prohibited solely on the basis of sex, not on the basis of sexual orientation."). For an example of how this argument's force has abated, see In re Marriage Cases, 43 Cal. 4th 757, 834 (2008) ("By contrast, past judicial decisions, in California and elsewhere, virtually uniformly hold that a statute or policy that treats men and women equally but that accords differential treatment either to a couple based upon whether it consists of persons of the same sex rather than opposite sexes, or to an individual based upon whether he or she generally is sexually attracted to persons of the same gender rather than the opposite gender, is more accurately characterized as involving differential treatment on the basis of *sexual orientation* rather than an instance of *sex discrimination*, and properly should be analyzed on the *former* ground.").

214. But see Perry v. Schwarzenegger, 704 F. Supp. 2d 921 (N.D. Cal. 2010) (holding Proposition 8 unconstitutional on substantive due process and equal protection grounds).

215. See Reva B. Siegel, Foreword: Equality Divided, 127 Harv. L. Rev. 1, 83 (2013) (describing the evolving justifications for excluding same-sex couples from marriage as "a process of 'preservation-through-transformation'").

children inside wedlock.[216] Others advanced religious and natural law arguments asserting that procreation was the purpose of marriage.[217] A related line of argument emphasized the importance of preserving gender role differentiation in marriage.[218] Many insisted that the marriage debate required democratic resolution; judicial intervention would be tantamount to dismissing the moral views of some as bigotry.[219]

Disapproval of the kind voiced in *Bowers* and the floor debates over DOMA did not disappear from the record, however, and what it meant to oppose same-sex marriage became a central point of disagreement for the Court.

UNITED STATES v. WINDSOR, 570 U.S. 744 (2013): The Supreme Court struck down §3 of the 1996 Defense of Marriage Act (DOMA), which amended the Dictionary Act—a law providing rules of construction for over 1,000 federal laws and the whole realm of federal regulations—to define "marriage" and "spouse" as excluding same-sex partners. The respondent, Edith Windsor, had married Thea Spyer in Ontario, Canada, in 2007; they lived in New York, which recognizes same-sex marriages. After Spyer died in 2009, she left her entire estate to Windsor. The federal government refused to give Windsor the federal estate tax exemption for surviving spouses, and charged her $363,053 in taxes.

---

216. For an example, see Hernandez v. Robles, 855 N.E.2d 1, 7 (N.Y. 2006) (observing that same-sex couples "do not become parents as a result of accident or impulse" whereas persons in different-sex relations do, so that "promoting stability in opposite-sex relationships will help children more. This is one reason why the Legislature could rationally offer the benefits of marriage to opposite-sex couples only.").

217. See, e.g., United States v. Windsor, 133 S. Ct. 2675, 2718 (2013) (Alito, J., dissenting) (describing "the 'traditional' or 'conjugal' view, [which] sees marriage as an intrinsically opposite-sex institution. . . . [Proponents] argue that marriage is essentially the solemnizing of a comprehensive, exclusive, permanent union that is intrinsically ordered to producing new life, even if it does not always do so") (citing Sherif Girgis, Ryan T. Anderson, and Robert P. George, What Is Marriage? Man and Woman: A Defense 23-28 (2012)).

218. See Allan C. Carlson and Paul T. Mero, The Natural Family: A Manifesto (2005), available at http://www.familymanifesto.net/fmDocs/FamilyManifesto.pdf ("We affirm that the complementarity of the sexes is a source of strength. Men and women exhibit profound biological and psychological differences. When united in marriage, though, the whole becomes greater than the sum of the parts."); see also Jessica Feinberg, Exposing the Traditional Marriage Agenda, 7 Nw. J.L. & Soc. Pol'y 301, 319-321 (2012) (citing examples from Maggie Gallagher, Focus on the Family, Liberty Counsel, and others); Ten Arguments from Social Science Against Same-Sex "Marriage," Focus on the Family, http://web.archive.org/web/20090623032905/http://frc.org/get.cfm?i=IF04G01 (last visited July 5, 2011) (advancing the "science-based" claim that children benefit physically and psychologically from different-sex parents).

219. For example, Paul Clement, the attorney defending the constitutionality of DOMA in *Windsor*, stated in oral argument: "That's what the democratic process requires. You have to persuade somebody you're right. You don't label them a bigot. You don't label them as motivated by animus. You persuade them you are right. That's going on across the country." Transcript of Oral Argument at 112-113, *Windsor*, 570 U.S. 744 (No. 12-307). For a more thorough discussion of the use of and objections to the bigotry argument, see Siegel, Foreword: Equality Divided, supra n.215, at 78-80.

Justice Kennedy, writing for five Justices, held that §3 of DOMA violated the Fifth Amendment's Due Process Clause: "'[T]he states, at the time of the adoption of the Constitution, possessed full power over the subject of marriage and divorce . . . [and] the Constitution delegated no authority to the Government of the United States on the subject of marriage and divorce.' . . . Consistent with this allocation of authority, the Federal Government, through our history, has deferred to state-law policy decisions with respect to domestic relations. . . . Against this background DOMA rejects the long-established precept that the incidents, benefits, and obligations of marriage are uniform for all married couples within each State, though they may vary, subject to constitutional guarantees, from one State to the next.

"[New York] State's decision to give [same-sex couples] the right to marry conferred upon them a dignity and status of immense import. When the State used its historic and essential authority to define the marital relation in this way, its role and its power in making the decision enhanced the recognition, dignity, and protection of the class in their own community. DOMA, because of its reach and extent, departs from this history and tradition of reliance on state law to define marriage. . . .

"DOMA seeks to injure the very class New York seeks to protect. By doing so it violates basic due process and equal protection principles applicable to the Federal Government. *Bolling*. The Constitution's guarantee of equality 'must at the very least mean that a bare congressional desire to harm a politically unpopular group cannot' justify disparate treatment of that group. Department of Agriculture v. Moreno, 413 U.S. 528 (1973). . . . DOMA's unusual deviation from the usual tradition of recognizing and accepting state definitions of marriage here operates to deprive same-sex couples of the benefits and responsibilities that come with the federal recognition of their marriages. This is strong evidence of a law having the purpose and effect of disapproval of that class. The avowed purpose and practical effect of the law here in question are to impose a disadvantage, a separate status, and so a stigma upon all who enter into same-sex marriages made lawful by the unquestioned authority of the States.

"The history of DOMA's enactment and its own text demonstrate that interference with the equal dignity of same-sex marriages, a dignity conferred by the States in the exercise of their sovereign power, was more than an incidental effect of the federal statute. It was its essence. . . . When New York adopted a law to permit same-sex marriage, it sought to eliminate inequality; but DOMA frustrates that objective through a system-wide enactment with no identified connection to any particular area of federal law. DOMA writes inequality into the entire United States Code. . . . Among the over 1,000 statutes and numerous federal regulations that DOMA controls are laws pertaining to Social Security, housing, taxes, criminal sanctions, copyright, and veterans' benefits.

"DOMA's principal effect is to identify a subset of state-sanctioned marriages and make them unequal. The principal purpose is to impose inequality, not for other reasons like governmental efficiency. . . . By creating two contradictory marriage regimes within the same State, DOMA forces same-sex couples to live as married for the purpose of state law but unmarried for the purpose of federal law, thus diminishing the stability and predictability of basic personal relations the State has found it proper to acknowledge and protect. . . . This places same-sex couples in an unstable position of being in a second-tier marriage. The differentiation demeans the couple, whose moral and sexual choices the Constitution protects, see *Lawrence*, and whose relationship the State has sought to dignify. And it humiliates tens of thousands of children now being raised by same-sex couples. The law in question makes it even more difficult for the children to understand the integrity and closeness of their own family and its concord with other families in their community and in their daily lives.

"DOMA singles out a class of persons deemed by a State entitled to recognition and protection to enhance their own liberty. It imposes a disability on the class by refusing to acknowledge a status the State finds to be dignified and proper. DOMA instructs all federal officials, and indeed all persons with whom same-sex couples interact, including their own children, that their marriage is less worthy than the marriages of others. The federal statute is invalid, for no legitimate purpose overcomes the purpose and effect to disparage and to injure those whom the State, by its marriage laws, sought to protect in personhood and dignity. By seeking to displace this protection and treating those persons as living in marriages less respected than others, the federal statute is in violation of the Fifth Amendment. This opinion and its holding are confined to those lawful marriages."

Chief Justice Roberts dissented: "At least without some more convincing evidence that the Act's principal purpose was to codify malice, and that it furthered *no* legitimate government interests, I would not tar the political branches with the brush of bigotry. . . . [W]hile I disagree with the result to which the majority's analysis leads it in this case, I think it more important to point out that its analysis leads no further. The Court does not have before it, and the logic of its opinion does not decide, the distinct question whether the States, in the exercise of their 'historic and essential authority to define the marital relation,' may continue to utilize the traditional definition of marriage. . . . The dominant theme of the majority opinion is that the Federal Government's intrusion into an area 'central to state domestic relations law applicable to its residents and citizens' is sufficiently 'unusual' to set off alarm bells. I think the majority goes off course, as I have said, but it is undeniable that its judgment is based on federalism."

Justice Scalia, joined by Justice Thomas, also dissented: "I do not mean to suggest disagreement with The Chief Justice's view . . . that lower federal courts and state courts can distinguish today's case when the issue before them is state denial of marital status to same-sex couples. . . . State and lower federal courts should take the Court at its word and distinguish away.

"In my opinion, however, the view that *this* Court will take of state prohibition of same-sex marriage is indicated beyond mistaking by today's opinion. . . . [T]he real rationale of today's opinion, whatever disappearing trail of its legalistic argle-bargle one chooses to follow, is that DOMA is motivated by '"bare . . . desire to harm"' couples in same-sex marriages. How easy it is, indeed how inevitable, to reach the same conclusion with regard to state laws denying same-sex couples marital status. . . . As far as this Court is concerned, no one should be fooled; it is just a matter of listening and waiting for the other shoe."

"By formally declaring anyone opposed to same-sex marriage an enemy of human decency, the majority arms well every challenger to a state law restricting marriage to its traditional definition. Henceforth those challengers will lead with this Court's declaration that there is 'no legitimate purpose' served by such a law, and will claim that the traditional definition has 'the purpose and effect to disparage and to injure' the 'personhood and dignity' of same-sex couples. The majority's limiting assurance will be meaningless in the face of language like that, as the majority well knows. That is why the language is there."

Justice Alito, joined by Justice Thomas, also dissented: "At present, no one—including social scientists, philosophers, and historians—can predict with any certainty what the long-term ramifications of widespread acceptance of same-sex marriage will be. And judges are certainly not equipped to make such an assessment. . . . [I]f the Constitution contained a provision guaranteeing the right to marry a person of the same sex, it would be our duty to enforce that right. But the Constitution simply does not speak to the issue of same-sex marriage. In our system of government, ultimate sovereignty rests with the people, and the people have the right to control their own destiny. Any change on a question so fundamental should be made by the people through their elected officials."

DISCUSSION

1. *The "bare . . . desire to harm a politically unpopular group."* Kennedy treats the case as falling within the rule that "'a bare congressional desire to harm a politically unpopular group cannot' justify disparate treatment of that group." How does Kennedy know that DOMA, passed by a congressional majority that included many liberal Democrats and signed by a liberal Democratic President, Bill Clinton, was based on a bare desire to harm a politically unpopular group? Could somebody have voted for DOMA in 1996 without such a view about homosexuals? Couldn't one argue, with Justice Alito, that Congress enacted DOMA to protect a centuries-old institution from an innovation that, in 1996, seemed particularly radical and dangerous and might have uncertain consequences? Why doesn't the argument that Congress wanted to wait and see what developed provide a rational (and nonmalicious) basis for DOMA? Is it because the majority does not believe that this is the real basis for DOMA? If so, that might suggest that, whatever the opinion says, the Court is applying some form of heightened scrutiny.

2. *What is animus?* The "bare . . . desire to harm a politically unpopular group" test employed in *Windsor* is only one of many understandings of "animus" that courts and commentators have identified.[220] Other versions include hate, moral disapproval, deliberate indifference, and the imposition of a class-wide disability or status distinction. Are these motivations equivalent? What kind of "animus" makes DOMA unconstitutional in *Windsor*? Consider the following:

a. *Voter animus.* Consider that some liberal Democrats in Congress, and probably President Clinton himself, may have supported the bill not because they had any hatred or disdain against homosexuals, but because they feared that if they opposed DOMA, they would create an excellent wedge issue for Republicans in the 1996 election. How, if at all, should this affect Justice Kennedy's analysis? Is the idea that politicians who fear the discriminatory animus of others somehow transfer that unconstitutional animus to the legislation they vote for?

---

220. See Susannah W. Pollvogt, *Windsor*, Animus, and the Future of Marriage Equality, 113 Colum. L. Rev. Sidebar 204, 216 (arraying in chart form the different models of animus that appear in across the case law).

b. *Lack of reflection, lack of respect.* Responding to a question from Chief Justice Roberts about whether the 84 senators who voted for DOMA and the President who signed it were "motivated by animus," the Solicitor General stated: "[I]t may well not have been animus or hostility. It may well have been what Garrett described as the simple want of careful reflection or an instinctive response to a class of people or a group of people who we perceive as alien or other. But whatever the explanation, whether it's animus, whether it's that—more subtle, more unthinking, more reflective [sic: unreflective or reactive?] kind of discrimination, Section 3 is discrimination."[221]

c. *Social meaning.* Is *Windsor* making a claim about the actual *psychology* of members of Congress, as well as President Clinton, who signed the bill? Or is *Windsor* making a judgment about the *social meaning* of DOMA to the public at large or to the citizens whose lives it affects? If "animus" means only a state of mind akin to hostility, why does Kennedy emphasize the structure and effects of DOMA on same-sex couples and their children?

d. *Moral disapproval.* Elsewhere in *Windsor,* Justice Kennedy cites statements in the legislative history expressing "moral disapproval" of homosexuality, suggesting that moral disapproval is a mark of animus. Is moral disapproval of homosexuality or same-sex marriage the same as a desire to hurt gay people?

Is there more than one version of animus at work in Justice Kennedy's opinion? The reach of equal protection law will change depending on the theory of animus the Court adopts. What institutional considerations counsel the adoption of one view over the other?

3. *We're not bigots.* Justices Scalia and Alito emphasize that it is perfectly reasonable to oppose same-sex marriage without being mean-spirited or bigoted, or without seeking to harm or humiliate homosexuals and their children. Justice Scalia argues that the effect of the majority opinion in *Windsor* is to "adjudg[e] those who oppose [same-sex marriage as] *hostes humani generis,* enemies of the human race." Do you agree? Did Romer v. Evans effectively adjudge the voters of the state of Colorado as bigoted?

4. *Taking the long view.* Compare the current state of the constitutional debate over gay rights and same-sex marriage with the constitutional debate over racial equality and gender equality. What do you think of people who defended Jim Crow and "separate but equal" before *Brown* and the civil rights revolution, or people who believed, before the 1970s, that the Constitution does not guarantee women equality? Is it fair to view opponents of gay rights in the same way? Is the situation different? Or is this a judgment that can only be made in retrospect?

5. *Consequences of the animus doctrine.* What are the consequences of conflating or equating moral disapproval and animus or otherwise attributing opposition to same-sex marriage to animosity toward gay people? Does this conflation help further the cause of gay rights by stigmatizing opponents? Might the animus approach further estrange sides of the dispute by posing one side as the enemy of the other?[222] If you accept the argument that DOMA, and laws limiting marriage to straight couples more generally, reflect animus toward gay people, does this affect

---

221. Transcript of Oral Argument at 91, Windsor, 570 U.S. 744 (No. 12-307).

222. See Steven D. Smith, The Jurisprudence of Denigration, 48 U.C. Davis L. Rev. 675 (2014).

your view about whether opponents of same-sex marriage should be entitled to religious or conscience-based exemptions from antidiscrimination laws?

William Eskridge has criticized Kennedy for lobbing a "gratuitous" "insult" at DOMA's backers "because the Court could readily have reached the same result in another, far more persuasive manner: by candidly adopting heightened scrutiny and invalidating section 3 on that basis."[223] Do you agree that applying heightened scrutiny would be a less divisive way for a court to adjudicate sexual orientation and marriage cases?

6. *Hollingsworth v. Perry and the California litigation.* Decided the same day as *Windsor*, Hollingsworth v. Perry, 570 U.S. 693 (2013), was an appeal from a successful constitutional challenge to California's Proposition 8, which overturned a court decision legalizing same-sex marriage and amended the state constitution to define marriage as a union between a man and a woman. Respondents hoped that the Court would use the opportunity to expand same-sex marriage nationwide. Chief Justice Roberts, writing for Justices Scalia, Ginsburg, Breyer, and Kagan, held that the proponents of Proposition 8 did not have standing to appeal the district court's order declaring Proposition 8 unconstitutional. The effect was to legalize same-sex marriage only in California but the Court expressed no opinion on the merits. Justice Kennedy, joined by Justices Thomas, Alito, and Sotomayor, dissented.

7. Windsor*'s aftermath.* Following the Supreme Court's decision in *Windsor*, many lower federal courts around the country considered constitutional challenges to state bans on same-sex marriage. In almost every case the lower courts upheld the challenges and required that states allow same-sex couples to marry. The rationales for upholding the right to same-sex marriage varied among the different courts. Some relied on a due process right to marry, others on different versions of equal protection doctrine, including rational basis and heightened scrutiny. None of these decisions, however, treated *Windsor* as primarily a case about federalism and the scope of Congress's power to interfere with state marriage laws. Rather, these courts took *Windsor* as a signal that the law of same-sex marriage had changed. The Supreme Court, in turn, denied certiorari in all of the decisions upholding the right of same-sex couples to marry. The effect of denying certiorari was that, by 2015, same-sex marriage was legal in 37 states and the District of Columbia.[224]

Finally, the Sixth Circuit Court of Appeals rejected a constitutional challenge brought by same-sex couples, creating a split among the federal circuits. The Supreme Court granted certiorari to resolve the issue.

Obergefell v. Hodges

135 S. Ct. 2584 (2015)

[Michigan, Kentucky, Ohio, and Tennessee defined marriage as a union between one man and one woman. The petitioners, 14 same-sex couples and two men whose same-sex partners are deceased, challenged the state laws, arguing

---

223. Daniel O. Conkle, Evolving Values, Animus, and Same-Sex Marriage, 89 Ind. L.J. 27, 40 (2014).

224. The Changing Landscape of Same-Sex marriage, Wash. Post, June 26, 2015, http://www.washingtonpost.com/wp-srv/special/politics/same-sex-marriage/.

that the Fourteenth Amendment gave them the right to marry or the right to have to have same-sex marriages lawfully performed in another state given full recognition.]

Justice KENNEDY delivered the opinion of the Court.

The Constitution promises liberty to all within its reach, a liberty that includes certain specific rights that allow persons, within a lawful realm, to define and express their identity. The petitioners in these cases seek to find that liberty by marrying someone of the same sex and having their marriages deemed lawful on the same terms and conditions as marriages between persons of the opposite sex. . . .

II

A

[T]he centrality of marriage to the human condition makes it unsurprising that the institution has existed for millennia and across civilizations. Since the dawn of history, marriage has transformed strangers into relatives, binding families and societies together. Confucius taught that marriage lies at the foundation of government. This wisdom was echoed centuries later and half a world away by Cicero, who wrote, "The first bond of society is marriage; next, children; and then the family." There are untold references to the beauty of marriage in religious and philosophical texts spanning time, cultures, and faiths, as well as in art and literature in all their forms. It is fair and necessary to say these references were based on the understanding that marriage is a union between two persons of the opposite sex.

That history is the beginning of these cases. The respondents say it should be the end as well. To them, it would demean a timeless institution if the concept and lawful status of marriage were extended to two persons of the same sex. Marriage, in their view, is by its nature a gender-differentiated union of man and woman. This view long has been held—and continues to be held—in good faith by reasonable and sincere people here and throughout the world.

The petitioners acknowledge this history but contend that these cases cannot end there. Were their intent to demean the revered idea and reality of marriage, the petitioners' claims would be of a different order. But that is neither their purpose nor their submission. To the contrary, it is the enduring importance of marriage that underlies the petitioners' contentions. This, they say, is their whole point. Far from seeking to devalue marriage, the petitioners seek it for themselves because of their respect—and need—for its privileges and responsibilities. And their immutable nature dictates that same-sex marriage is their only real path to this profound commitment.

Recounting the circumstances of three of these cases illustrates the urgency of the petitioners' cause from their perspective. Petitioner James Obergefell, a plaintiff in the Ohio case, met John Arthur over two decades ago. They fell in love and started a life together, establishing a lasting, committed relation. In 2011, however, Arthur was diagnosed with amyotrophic lateral sclerosis, or ALS. This debilitating disease is progressive, with no known cure. Two years ago, Obergefell and Arthur decided to commit to one another, resolving to marry before Arthur died. To fulfill their mutual promise, they traveled from Ohio to Maryland, where same-sex marriage was legal. It was difficult for Arthur to move, and so the couple were wed inside a medical transport plane as it remained on the tarmac in Baltimore. Three months later, Arthur died. Ohio law does not permit Obergefell to be listed as the surviving spouse on Arthur's death certificate. By statute, they must remain strangers even in death, a state-imposed separation Obergefell deems "hurtful for the rest of time." He brought suit to be shown as the surviving spouse on Arthur's death certificate.

April DeBoer and Jayne Rowse are co-plaintiffs in the case from Michigan. They celebrated a commitment ceremony to honor their permanent relation in 2007. They both work as nurses, DeBoer in a neonatal unit and Rowse in an emergency unit. In 2009, DeBoer and Rowse fostered and then adopted a baby boy. Later that same year, they welcomed another son into their family. The new baby, born prematurely and abandoned by his biological mother, required around-the-clock care. The next year, a baby girl with special needs joined their family. Michigan, however, permits only opposite-sex married couples or single individuals to adopt, so each child can have only one woman as his or her legal parent. If an emergency were to arise, schools and hospitals may treat the three children as if they had only one parent. And, were tragedy to befall either DeBoer or Rowse, the other would have no legal rights over the children she had not been permitted to adopt. This couple seeks relief from the continuing uncertainty their unmarried status creates in their lives.

Army Reserve Sergeant First Class Ijpe DeKoe and his partner Thomas Kostura, co-plaintiffs in the Tennessee case, fell in love. In 2011, DeKoe received orders to deploy to Afghanistan. Before leaving, he and Kostura married in New York. A week later, DeKoe began his deployment, which lasted for almost a year. When he returned, the two settled in Tennessee, where DeKoe works full-time for the Army Reserve. Their lawful marriage is stripped from them whenever they reside in Tennessee, returning and disappearing as they travel across state lines. DeKoe, who served this Nation to preserve the freedom the Constitution protects, must endure a substantial burden.

The cases now before the Court involve other petitioners as well, each with their own experiences. Their stories reveal that they seek not to denigrate marriage but rather to live their lives, or honor their spouses' memory, joined by its bond.

B

The ancient origins of marriage confirm its centrality, but it has not stood in isolation from developments in law and society. The history of marriage is one of both continuity and change. That institution—even as confined to opposite-sex relations—has evolved over time.

For example, marriage was once viewed as an arrangement by the couple's parents based on political, religious, and financial concerns; but by the time of the Nation's founding it was understood to be a voluntary contract between a man and a woman. See N. Cott, Public Vows: A History of Marriage and the Nation 9-17 (2000); S. Coontz, Marriage, A History 15-16 (2005). As the role and status of women changed, the institution further evolved. Under the centuries-old doctrine of coverture, a married man and woman were treated by the State as a single, male-dominated legal entity. See 1 W. Blackstone, Commentaries on the Laws of England 430 (1765). As women gained legal, political, and property rights, and as society began to understand that women have their own equal dignity, the law of coverture was abandoned. These and other developments in the institution of marriage over the past centuries were not mere superficial changes. Rather, they worked deep transformations in its structure, affecting aspects of marriage long viewed by many as essential.

These new insights have strengthened, not weakened, the institution of marriage. Indeed, changed understandings of marriage are characteristic of a Nation where new dimensions of freedom become apparent to new generations, often through perspectives that begin in pleas or protests and then are considered in the political sphere and the judicial process.

This dynamic can be seen in the Nation's experiences with the rights of gays and lesbians. Until the mid-20th century, same-sex intimacy long had been condemned as immoral by the state itself in most Western nations, a belief often embodied in the criminal law. For this reason, among others, many persons did not deem homosexuals to have dignity in their own distinct identity. A truthful declaration by same-sex couples of what was in their hearts had to remain unspoken. Even when a greater awareness of the humanity and integrity of homosexual persons came in the period after World War II, the argument that gays and lesbians had a just claim to dignity was in conflict with both law and widespread social conventions. Same-sex intimacy remained a crime in many States. Gays and lesbians were prohibited from most government employment, barred from military service, excluded under immigration laws, targeted by police, and burdened in their rights to associate.

For much of the 20th century, moreover, homosexuality was treated as an illness. When the American Psychiatric Association published the first Diagnostic and Statistical Manual of Mental Disorders in 1952, homosexuality was classified as a mental disorder, a position adhered to until 1973. Only in more recent years have psychiatrists and others recognized that sexual orientation is both a normal expression of human sexuality and immutable.

In the late 20th century, following substantial cultural and political developments, same-sex couples began to lead more open and public lives and to establish families. This development was followed by a quite extensive discussion of the issue in both governmental and private sectors and by a shift in public attitudes toward greater tolerance. As a result, questions about the rights of gays and lesbians soon reached the courts, where the issue could be discussed in the formal discourse of the law. [Justice Kennedy recites the history of prior case law including *Bowers, Romer,* and *Lawrence*; the Hawaii same-sex marriage litigation; and the passage of DOMA in 1996.] In 2003, the Supreme Judicial Court of Massachusetts held the State's Constitution guaranteed same-sex couples the right to marry. After that ruling, some additional States granted marriage rights to same-sex couples, either through judicial or legislative processes. . . .

Two Terms ago, in United States v. Windsor, 570 U.S. __ (2013), this Court invalidated DOMA to the extent it barred the Federal Government from treating same-sex marriages as valid even when they were lawful in the State where they were licensed. DOMA, the Court held, impermissibly disparaged those same-sex couples "who wanted to affirm their commitment to one another before their children, their family, their friends, and their community."

Numerous cases about same-sex marriage have reached the United States Courts of Appeals in recent years. . . . In accordance with the judicial duty to base their decisions on principled reasons and neutral discussions, without scornful or disparaging commentary, courts have written a substantial body of law considering all sides of these issues. That case law helps to explain and formulate the underlying principles this Court now must consider. With the exception of the opinion here under review and one other [from the Eighth Circuit decided in 2006], the Courts of Appeals have held that excluding same-sex couples from marriage violates the Constitution. There also have been many thoughtful District Court decisions addressing same-sex marriage—and most of them, too, have concluded same-sex couples must be allowed to marry. In addition the highest courts of many States have contributed to this ongoing dialogue in decisions interpreting their own State Constitutions.

After years of litigation, legislation, referenda, and the discussions that attended these public acts, the States are now divided on the issue of same-sex marriage.

III

[T]he identification and protection of fundamental rights is an enduring part of the judicial duty to interpret the Constitution. That responsibility, however, "has not been reduced to any formula." Poe v. Ullman, 367 U.S. 497, 542 (1961) (Harlan, J., dissenting). Rather, it requires courts to exercise reasoned judgment in identifying interests of the person so fundamental that the State must accord them its respect. That process is guided by many of the same considerations relevant to analysis of other constitutional provisions that set forth broad principles rather than specific requirements. History and tradition guide and discipline this inquiry but do not set its outer boundaries. See *Lawrence*. That method respects our history and learns from it without allowing the past alone to rule the present.

The nature of injustice is that we may not always see it in our own times. The generations that wrote and ratified the Bill of Rights and the Fourteenth Amendment did not presume to know the extent of freedom in all of its dimensions, and so they entrusted to future generations a charter protecting the right of all persons to enjoy liberty as we learn its meaning. When new insight reveals discord between the Constitution's central protections and a received legal stricture, a claim to liberty must be addressed.

Applying these established tenets, the Court has long held the right to marry is protected by the Constitution. In Loving v. Virginia, 388 U.S. 1 (1967), which invalidated bans on interracial unions, a unanimous Court held marriage is "one of the vital personal rights essential to the orderly pursuit of happiness by free men." The Court reaffirmed that holding in Zablocki v. Redhail, 434 U.S. 374 (1978), which held the right to marry was burdened by a law prohibiting fathers who were behind on child support from marrying. The Court again applied this principle in Turner v. Safley, 482 U.S. 78 (1987), which held the right to marry was abridged by regulations limiting the privilege of prison inmates to marry. Over time and in other contexts, the Court has reiterated that the right to marry is fundamental under the Due Process Clause. See, *e.g.*, M.L.B. v. S.L.J., 519 U.S. 102 (1996); Cleveland Bd. of Ed. v. LaFleur, 414 U.S. 632 (1974); *Griswold*; Skinner v. Oklahoma ex rel. Williamson, 316 U.S. 535 (1942); Meyer v. Nebraska, 262 U.S. 390 (1923).

It cannot be denied that this Court's cases describing the right to marry presumed a relationship involving opposite-sex partners. The Court, like many institutions, has made assumptions defined by the world and time of which it is a part.

This was evident in Baker v. Nelson, 409 U.S. 810 [(1972)], a one-line summary decision issued in 1972, holding the exclusion of same-sex couples from marriage did not present a substantial federal question.

Still, there are other, more instructive precedents. This Court's cases have expressed constitutional principles of broader reach. In defining the right to marry these cases have identified essential attributes of that right based in history, tradition, and other constitutional liberties inherent in this intimate bond. See, *e.g.*, *Lawrence*; *Turner*; *Zablocki*; *Loving*; *Griswold*. And in assessing whether the force and rationale of its cases apply to same-sex couples, the Court must respect the basic reasons why the right to marry has been long protected. See, *e.g.*, *Eisenstadt*; *Poe* (Harlan, J., dissenting).

This analysis compels the conclusion that same-sex couples may exercise the right to marry. The four principles and traditions to be discussed demonstrate that the reasons marriage is fundamental under the Constitution apply with equal force to same-sex couples.

A first premise of the Court's relevant precedents is that the right to personal choice regarding marriage is inherent in the concept of individual autonomy. This abiding connection between marriage and liberty is why *Loving* invalidated interracial marriage bans under the Due Process Clause. Like choices concerning contraception, family relationships, procreation, and childrearing, all of which are protected by the Constitution, decisions concerning marriage are among the most intimate that an individual can make. See *Lawrence*. Indeed, the Court has noted it would be contradictory "to recognize a right of privacy with respect to other matters of family life and not with respect to the decision to enter the relationship that is the foundation of the family in our society." *Zablocki*.

Choices about marriage shape an individual's destiny. As the Supreme Judicial Court of Massachusetts has explained, because "it fulfils yearnings for security, safe haven, and connection that express our common humanity, civil marriage is an esteemed institution, and the decision whether and whom to marry is among life's momentous acts of self-definition." *Goodridge*.

The nature of marriage is that, through its enduring bond, two persons together can find other freedoms, such as expression, intimacy, and spirituality. This is true for all persons, whatever their sexual orientation. See *Windsor*. There is dignity in the bond between two men or two women who seek to marry and in their autonomy to make such profound choices. Cf. *Loving* ("[T]he freedom to marry, or not marry, a person of another race resides with the individual and cannot be infringed by the State").

A second principle in this Court's jurisprudence is that the right to marry is fundamental because it supports a two-person union unlike any other in its importance to the committed individuals. This point was central to Griswold v. Connecticut, which held the Constitution protects the right of married couples to use contraception. Suggesting that marriage is a right "older than the Bill of Rights," *Griswold* described marriage this way:

> "Marriage is a coming together for better or for worse, hopefully enduring, and intimate to the degree of being sacred. It is an association that promotes a way of life, not causes; a harmony in living, not political faiths; a bilateral loyalty, not commercial or social projects. Yet it is an association for as noble a purpose as any involved in our prior decisions."

And in *Turner*, the Court again acknowledged the intimate association protected by this right, holding prisoners could not be denied the right to marry because their committed relationships satisfied the basic reasons why marriage is a fundamental right. The right to marry thus dignifies couples who "wish to define themselves by their commitment to each other." *Windsor*. Marriage responds to the universal fear that a lonely person might call out only to find no one there. It offers the hope of companionship and understanding and assurance that while both still live there will be someone to care for the other.

As this Court held in *Lawrence*, same-sex couples have the same right as opposite-sex couples to enjoy intimate association. *Lawrence* invalidated laws that made same-sex intimacy a criminal act. And it acknowledged that "[w]hen sexuality finds overt expression in intimate conduct with another person, the conduct can be but one element in a personal bond that is more enduring." But while *Lawrence* confirmed a dimension of freedom that allows individuals to engage in intimate association without criminal liability, it does not follow that freedom stops there. Outlaw to outcast may be a step forward, but it does not achieve the full promise of liberty.

A third basis for protecting the right to marry is that it safeguards children and families and thus draws meaning from related rights of childrearing, procreation, and education. See Pierce v. Society of Sisters, 268 U.S. 510 (1925); *Meyer*. The Court has recognized these connections by describing the varied rights as a unified whole: "[T]he right to 'marry, establish a home and bring up children' is a central part of the liberty protected by the Due Process Clause." *Zablocki* (quoting *Meyer*). Under the laws of the several States, some of marriage's protections for children and families are material. But marriage also confers more profound benefits. By giving recognition and legal structure to their parents' relationship, marriage allows children "to understand the integrity and closeness of their own family and its concord with other families in their community and in their daily lives." *Windsor*. Marriage also affords the permanency and stability important to children's best interests.

As all parties agree, many same-sex couples provide loving and nurturing homes to their children, whether biological or adopted. And hundreds of thousands of children are presently being raised by such couples. Most States have allowed gays and lesbians to adopt, either as individuals or as couples, and many adopted and foster children have same-sex parents. This provides powerful confirmation from the law itself that gays and lesbians can create loving, supportive families.

Excluding same-sex couples from marriage thus conflicts with a central premise of the right to marry. Without the recognition, stability, and predictability marriage offers, their children suffer the stigma of knowing their families are somehow lesser. They also suffer the significant material costs of being raised by unmarried parents, relegated through no fault of their own to a more difficult and uncertain family life. The marriage laws at issue here thus harm and humiliate the children of same-sex couples. See *Windsor*.

That is not to say the right to marry is less meaningful for those who do not or cannot have children. An ability, desire, or promise to procreate is not and has not been a prerequisite for a valid marriage in any State. In light of precedent protecting the right of a married couple not to procreate, it cannot be said the Court or the States have conditioned the right to marry on the capacity or commitment to procreate. The constitutional marriage right has many aspects, of which childbearing is only one.

Fourth and finally, this Court's cases and the Nation's traditions make clear that marriage is a keystone of our social order. Alexis de Tocqueville recognized this truth on his travels through the United States almost two centuries ago:

> "There is certainly no country in the world where the tie of marriage is so much respected as in America . . . [W]hen the American retires from the turmoil of public life to the bosom of his family, he finds in it the image of order and of peace. . . . [H]e afterwards carries [that image] with him into public affairs." 1 Democracy in America 309.

In Maynard v. Hill, 125 U.S. 190 (1888), the Court echoed de Tocqueville, explaining that marriage is "the foundation of the family and of society, without which there would be neither civilization nor progress." Marriage, the *Maynard* Court said, has long been "'a great public institution, giving character to our whole civil polity.'" This idea has been reiterated even as the institution has evolved in substantial ways over time, superseding rules related to parental consent, gender, and race once thought by many to be essential.

For that reason, just as a couple vows to support each other, so does society pledge to support the couple, offering symbolic recognition and material benefits to protect and nourish the union. Indeed, while the States are in general free to vary the benefits they confer on all married couples, they have throughout our history made marriage the basis for an expanding list of governmental rights, benefits, and responsibilities. These aspects of marital status include: taxation; inheritance and property rights; rules of intestate succession; spousal privilege in the law of evidence; hospital access; medical decisionmaking authority; adoption rights; the rights and benefits of survivors; birth and death certificates; professional ethics rules; campaign finance restrictions; workers' compensation benefits; health insurance; and child custody, support, and visitation rules. Valid marriage under state law is also a significant status for over a thousand provisions of federal law. See *Windsor.* The States have contributed to the fundamental character of the marriage right by placing that institution at the center of so many facets of the legal and social order.

There is no difference between same- and opposite-sex couples with respect to this principle. Yet by virtue of their exclusion from that institution, same-sex couples are denied the constellation of benefits that the States have linked to marriage. This harm results in more than just material burdens. Same-sex couples are consigned to an instability many opposite-sex couples would deem intolerable in their own lives. As the State itself makes marriage all the more precious by the significance it attaches to it, exclusion from that status has the effect of teaching that gays and lesbians are unequal in important respects. It demeans gays and lesbians for the State to lock them out of a central institution of the Nation's society. Same-sex couples, too, may aspire to the transcendent purposes of marriage and seek fulfillment in its highest meaning.

The limitation of marriage to opposite-sex couples may long have seemed natural and just, but its inconsistency with the central meaning of the fundamental right to marry is now manifest. With that knowledge must come the recognition that laws excluding same-sex couples from the marriage right impose stigma and injury of the kind prohibited by our basic charter.

Objecting that this does not reflect an appropriate framing of the issue, the respondents refer to Washington v. Glucksberg, 521 U.S. 702 (1997), which called for a "'careful description'" of fundamental rights. They assert the petitioners do not seek to exercise the right to marry but rather a new and nonexistent "right to same-sex marriage." *Glucksberg* did insist that liberty under the Due Process Clause must be defined in a most circumscribed manner, with central reference to specific historical practices. Yet while that approach may have been appropriate for the asserted right there involved (physician-assisted suicide), it is inconsistent with the approach this Court has used in discussing other fundamental rights, including marriage and intimacy. *Loving* did not ask about a "right to interracial marriage"; *Turner* did not ask about a "right of inmates to marry"; and *Zablocki* did not ask about a "right of fathers with unpaid child support duties to marry." Rather, each case inquired about the right to marry in its comprehensive sense, asking if there was a sufficient justification for excluding the relevant class from the right.

That principle applies here. If rights were defined by who exercised them in the past, then received practices could serve as their own continued justification and new groups could not invoke rights once denied. This Court has rejected that approach, both with respect to the right to marry and the rights of gays and lesbians. See *Loving*; *Lawrence*.

The right to marry is fundamental as a matter of history and tradition, but rights come not from ancient sources alone. They rise, too, from a better informed understanding of how constitutional imperatives define a liberty that remains urgent in our own era. Many who deem same-sex marriage to be wrong reach that conclusion based on decent and honorable religious or philosophical premises, and neither they nor their beliefs are disparaged here. But when that sincere, personal opposition becomes enacted law and public policy, the necessary consequence is to put the imprimatur of the State itself on an exclusion that soon demeans or stigmatizes those whose own liberty is then denied. Under the Constitution, same-sex couples seek in marriage the same legal treatment as opposite-sex couples, and it would disparage their choices and diminish their personhood to deny them this right.

The right of same-sex couples to marry that is part of the liberty promised by the Fourteenth Amendment is derived, too, from that Amendment's guarantee of the equal protection of the laws. The Due Process Clause and the Equal Protection Clause are connected in a profound way, though they set forth independent principles. Rights implicit in liberty and rights secured by equal protection may rest on different precepts and are not always co-extensive, yet in some instances each may be instructive as to the meaning and reach of the other. In any particular case one Clause may be thought to capture the essence of the right in a more accurate and comprehensive way, even as the two Clauses may converge in the identification and definition of the right. This interrelation of the two principles furthers our understanding of what freedom is and must become.

The Court's cases touching upon the right to marry reflect this dynamic. In *Loving* the Court invalidated a prohibition on interracial marriage under both the Equal Protection Clause and the Due Process Clause. The Court first declared the prohibition invalid because of its unequal treatment of interracial couples. It stated: "There can be no doubt that restricting the freedom to marry solely because of racial classifications violates the central meaning of the Equal Protection Clause." With this link to equal protection the Court proceeded to hold the prohibition offended central precepts of liberty: "To deny this fundamental freedom on so unsupportable a basis as the racial classifications embodied in these statutes, classifications so directly subversive of the principle of equality at the heart of the Fourteenth Amendment, is surely to deprive all the State's citizens of liberty without due process of law." The reasons why marriage is a fundamental right became more clear and compelling from a full awareness and understanding of the hurt that resulted from laws barring interracial unions.

The synergy between the two protections is illustrated further in *Zablocki*. There the Court invoked the Equal Protection Clause as its basis for invalidating the challenged law, which, as already noted, barred fathers who were behind on child-support payments from marrying without judicial approval. The equal protection analysis depended in central part on the Court's holding that the law burdened a right "of fundamental importance." It was the essential nature of the marriage right, discussed at length in *Zablocki*, that made apparent the law's incompatibility with requirements of equality. Each concept—liberty and equal protection—leads to a stronger understanding of the other.

Indeed, in interpreting the Equal Protection Clause, the Court has recognized that new insights and societal understandings can reveal unjustified inequality within our most fundamental institutions that once passed unnoticed and unchallenged. To take but one period, this occurred with respect to marriage in the 1970's and 1980's. Notwithstanding the gradual erosion of the doctrine of coverture, invidious sex-based classifications in marriage remained common through the mid-20th century. These classifications denied the equal dignity of men and women. One State's law, for example, provided in 1971 that "the husband is the head of the family and the wife is subject to him; her legal civil existence is merged in the husband, except so far as the law recognizes her separately, either for her own protection, or for her benefit." Ga. Code Ann. §53-501 (1935). Responding to a new awareness, the Court invoked equal protection principles to invalidate laws imposing sex-based inequality on marriage. See, *e.g.*, Kirchberg v. Feenstra, 450 U.S. 455 (1981); Wengler v. Druggists Mut. Ins. Co., 446 U.S. 142 (1980); Califano v. Westcott, 443 U.S. 76 (1979); Orr v. Orr, 440 U.S. 268 (1979); Califano v. Goldfarb, 430 U.S. 199 (1977) (plurality opinion); Weinberger v. Wiesenfeld, 420 U.S. 636 (1975); Frontiero v. Richardson, 411 U.S. 677 (1973). Like *Loving* and *Zablocki*, these precedents show the Equal Protection Clause can help to identify and correct inequalities in the institution of marriage, vindicating precepts of liberty and equality under the Constitution.

Other cases confirm this relation between liberty and equality. In M.L.B. v. S.L.J., the Court invalidated under due process and equal protection principles a statute requiring indigent mothers to pay a fee in order to appeal the termination of their parental rights. In Eisenstadt v. Baird, the Court invoked both principles to invalidate a prohibition on the distribution of contraceptives to unmarried persons but not married persons. And in Skinner v. Oklahoma ex rel. Williamson, the Court invalidated under both principles a law that allowed sterilization of habitual criminals.

In *Lawrence* the Court acknowledged the interlocking nature of these constitutional safeguards in the context of the legal treatment of gays and lesbians. Although *Lawrence* elaborated its holding under the Due Process Clause, it acknowledged, and sought to remedy, the continuing inequality that resulted from laws making intimacy in the lives of gays and lesbians a crime against the State. *Lawrence* therefore drew upon principles of liberty and equality to define and protect the rights of gays and lesbians, holding the State "cannot demean their existence or control their destiny by making their private sexual conduct a crime."

This dynamic also applies to same-sex marriage. It is now clear that the challenged laws burden the liberty of same-sex couples, and it must be further acknowledged that they abridge central precepts of equality. Here the marriage laws enforced by the respondents are in essence unequal: same-sex couples are denied all the benefits afforded to opposite-sex couples and are barred from exercising a fundamental right. Especially against a long history of disapproval of their relationships, this denial to same-sex couples of the right to marry works a grave and continuing harm. The imposition of this disability on gays and lesbians serves to disrespect and subordinate them. And the Equal Protection Clause, like the Due Process Clause, prohibits this unjustified infringement of the fundamental right to marry. See, *e.g., Zablocki*; *Skinner*.

These considerations lead to the conclusion that the right to marry is a fundamental right inherent in the liberty of the person, and under the Due Process and Equal Protection Clauses of the Fourteenth Amendment couples of the same-sex may not be deprived of that right and that liberty. The Court now holds that same-sex couples may exercise the fundamental right to marry. No longer may this liberty be denied to them. Baker v. Nelson must be and now is overruled, and the State laws challenged by Petitioners in these cases are now held invalid to the extent they exclude same-sex couples from civil marriage on the same terms and conditions as opposite-sex couples.

IV

There may be an initial inclination in these cases to proceed with caution—to await further legislation, litigation, and debate. The respondents warn there has been insufficient democratic discourse before deciding an issue so basic as the definition of marriage. In its ruling on the cases now before this Court, the majority opinion for the Court of Appeals made a cogent argument that it would be appropriate for the respondents' States to await further public discussion and political measures before licensing same-sex marriages.

Yet there has been far more deliberation than this argument acknowledges. There have been referenda, legislative debates, and grassroots campaigns, as well as countless studies, papers, books, and other popular and scholarly writings. There has been extensive litigation in state and federal courts. Judicial opinions addressing the issue have been informed by the contentions of parties and counsel, which, in turn, reflect the more general, societal discussion of same-sex marriage and its meaning that has occurred over the past decades. As more than 100 *amici* make clear in their filings, many of the central institutions in American life—state and local governments, the military, large and small businesses, labor unions, religious organizations, law enforcement, civic groups, professional organizations, and universities—have devoted substantial attention to the question. This has led to an enhanced understanding of the issue—an understanding reflected in the arguments now presented for resolution as a matter of constitutional law.

Of course, the Constitution contemplates that democracy is the appropriate process for change, so long as that process does not abridge fundamental rights. Last Term, a plurality of this Court reaffirmed the importance of the democratic principle in Schuette v. BAMN, 572 U.S. __ (2014), noting the "right of citizens to debate so they can learn and decide and then, through the political process, act in concert to try to shape the course of their own times." Indeed, it is most often through democracy that liberty is preserved and protected in our lives. But as *Schuette* also said, "[t]he freedom secured by the Constitution consists, in one of its essential dimensions, of the right of the individual not to be injured by the unlawful exercise of governmental power." Thus, when the rights of persons are violated, "the Constitution requires redress by the courts," notwithstanding the more general value of democratic decisionmaking. This holds true even when protecting individual rights affects issues of the utmost importance and sensitivity.

The dynamic of our constitutional system is that individuals need not await legislative action before asserting a fundamental right. The Nation's courts are open to injured individuals who come to them to vindicate their own direct, personal stake in our basic charter. An individual can invoke a right to constitutional protection when he or she is harmed, even if the broader public disagrees and even if the legislature refuses to act. The idea of the Constitution "was to withdraw certain subjects from the vicissitudes of political controversy, to place them beyond the reach of majorities and officials and to establish them as legal principles to be applied by the courts." West Virginia Bd. of Ed. v. Barnette, 319 U.S. 624 (1943). This is why "fundamental rights may not be submitted to a vote; they depend on the outcome of no elections." *Ibid.* It is of no moment whether advocates of same-sex marriage now enjoy or lack momentum in the democratic process. The issue before the Court here is the legal question whether the Constitution protects the right of same-sex couples to marry.

This is not the first time the Court has been asked to adopt a cautious approach to recognizing and protecting fundamental rights. In *Bowers*, a bare majority upheld a law criminalizing same-sex intimacy. That approach might have been viewed as a cautious endorsement of the democratic process, which had only just begun to consider the rights of gays and lesbians. Yet, in effect, *Bowers* upheld state action that denied gays and lesbians a fundamental right and caused them pain and humiliation. As evidenced by the dissents in that case, the facts and principles necessary to a correct holding were known to the *Bowers* Court. That is why *Lawrence* held *Bowers* was "not correct when it was decided." Although *Bowers* was eventually repudiated in *Lawrence*, men and women were harmed in the interim, and the substantial effects of these injuries no doubt lingered long after *Bowers* was overruled. Dignitary wounds cannot always be healed with the stroke of a pen.

A ruling against same-sex couples would have the same effect—and, like *Bowers*, would be unjustified under the Fourteenth Amendment. The petitioners' stories make clear the urgency of the issue they present to the Court. James Obergefell now asks whether Ohio can erase his marriage to John Arthur for all time. April DeBoer and Jayne Rowse now ask whether Michigan may continue to deny them the certainty and stability all mothers desire to protect their children, and for them and their children the childhood years will pass all too soon. Ijpe DeKoe and Thomas Kostura now ask whether Tennessee can deny to one who has served this Nation the basic dignity of recognizing his New York marriage. Properly presented with the petitioners' cases, the Court has a duty to address these claims and answer these questions.

Indeed, faced with a disagreement among the Courts of Appeals—a disagreement that caused impermissible geographic variation in the meaning of federal law—the Court granted review to determine whether same-sex couples may exercise the right to marry. Were the Court to uphold the challenged laws as constitutional, it would teach the Nation that these laws are in accord with our society's most basic compact. Were the Court to stay its hand to allow slower, case-by-case determination of the required availability of specific public benefits to same-sex couples, it still would deny gays and lesbians many rights and responsibilities intertwined with marriage.

The respondents also argue allowing same-sex couples to wed will harm marriage as an institution by leading to fewer opposite-sex marriages. This may occur, the respondents contend, because licensing same-sex marriage severs the connection between natural procreation and marriage. That argument, however, rests on a counterintuitive view of opposite-sex couple's decisionmaking processes regarding marriage and parenthood. Decisions about whether to marry and raise children are based on many personal, romantic, and practical considerations; and it is unrealistic to conclude that an opposite-sex couple would choose not to marry simply because same-sex couples may do so. See Kitchen v. Herbert, 755 F.3d 1193, 1223 (C.A.10 2014) ("[I]t is wholly illogical to believe that state recognition of the love and commitment between same-sex couples will alter the most intimate and personal decisions of opposite-sex couples"). The respondents have not shown a foundation for the conclusion that allowing same-sex marriage will cause the harmful outcomes they describe. Indeed, with respect to this asserted basis for excluding same-sex couples from the right to marry, it is appropriate to observe these cases involve only the rights of two consenting adults whose marriages would pose no risk of harm to themselves or third parties.

Finally, it must be emphasized that religions, and those who adhere to religious doctrines, may continue to advocate with utmost, sincere conviction that, by divine precepts, same-sex marriage should not be condoned. The First Amendment ensures that religious organizations and persons are given proper protection as they seek to teach the principles that are so fulfilling and so central to their lives and faiths, and to their own deep aspirations to continue the family structure they have long revered. The same is true of those who oppose same-sex marriage for other reasons. In turn, those who believe allowing same-sex marriage is proper or indeed essential, whether as a matter of religious conviction or secular belief, may engage those who disagree with their view in an open and searching debate. The Constitution, however, does not permit the State to bar same-sex couples from marriage on the same terms as accorded to couples of the opposite sex.

V

. . . The Court, in this decision, holds same-sex couples may exercise the fundamental right to marry in all States. It follows that the Court also must hold—and it now does hold—that there is no lawful basis for a State to refuse to recognize a lawful same-sex marriage performed in another State on the ground of its same-sex character.

* * *

No union is more profound than marriage, for it embodies the highest ideals of love, fidelity, devotion, sacrifice, and family. In forming a marital union, two people become something greater than once they were. As some of the petitioners in these cases demonstrate, marriage embodies a love that may endure even past death. It would misunderstand these men and women to say they disrespect the idea of marriage. Their plea is that they do respect it, respect it so deeply that they seek to find its fulfillment for themselves. Their hope is not to be condemned to live in loneliness, excluded from one of civilization's oldest institutions. They ask for equal dignity in the eyes of the law. The Constitution grants them that right.

Chief Justice ROBERTS, with whom Justice SCALIA and Justice THOMAS join, dissenting.

The majority's decision is an act of will, not legal judgment. The right it announces has no basis in the Constitution or this Court's precedent. The majority expressly disclaims judicial "caution" and omits even a pretense of humility, openly relying on its desire to remake society according to its own "new insight" into the "nature of injustice." As a result, the Court invalidates the marriage laws of more than half the States and orders the transformation of a social institution that has formed the basis of human society for millennia, for the Kalahari Bushmen and the Han Chinese, the Carthaginians and the Aztecs. Just who do we think we are?

It can be tempting for judges to confuse our own preferences with the requirements of the law. But as this Court has been reminded throughout our history, the Constitution "is made for people of fundamentally differing views." Lochner v. New York, 198 U.S. 45 (1905) (Holmes, J., dissenting). Accordingly, "courts are not concerned with the wisdom or policy of legislation." *Id.*, at 69 (Harlan, J., dissenting). The majority today neglects that restrained conception of the judicial role. It seizes for itself a question the Constitution leaves to the people, at a time when the people are engaged in a vibrant debate on that question. And it answers that question based not on neutral principles of constitutional law, but on its own "understanding of what freedom is and must become." I have no choice but to dissent.

Understand well what this dissent is about: It is not about whether, in my judgment, the institution of marriage should be changed to include same-sex couples. It is instead about whether, in our democratic republic, that decision should rest with the people acting through their elected representatives, or with five lawyers who happen to hold commissions authorizing them to resolve legal disputes according to law. The Constitution leaves no doubt about the answer. . . .

The majority purports to identify four "principles and traditions" in this Court's due process precedents that support a fundamental right for same-sex couples to marry. In reality, however, the majority's approach has no basis in principle or tradition, except for the unprincipled tradition of judicial policymaking that characterized discredited decisions such as Lochner v. New York. Stripped of its shiny rhetorical gloss, the majority's argument is that the Due Process Clause gives same-sex couples a fundamental right to marry because it will be good for them and for society. If I were a legislator, I would certainly consider that view as a matter of social policy. But as a judge, I find the majority's position indefensible as a matter of constitutional law. . . .

Rejecting *Lochner* does not require disavowing the doctrine of implied fundamental rights, and this Court has not done so. But to avoid repeating *Lochner*'s error of converting personal preferences into constitutional mandates, our modern substantive due process cases have stressed the need for "judicial self-restraint." Our precedents have required that implied fundamental rights be "objectively, deeply rooted in this Nation's history and tradition," and "implicit in the concept of ordered liberty, such that neither liberty nor justice would exist if they were sacrificed." *Glucksberg*. . . .

[T]he "right to marry" cases stand for the important but limited proposition that particular restrictions on access to marriage *as traditionally defined* violate due process. These precedents say nothing at all about a right to make a State change its definition of marriage, which is the right petitioners actually seek here. Neither petitioners nor the majority cites a single case or other legal source providing any basis for such a constitutional right. None exists, and that is enough to foreclose their claim.

It is striking how much of the majority's reasoning would apply with equal force to the claim of a fundamental right to plural marriage. If "[t]here is dignity in the bond between two men or two women who seek to marry and in their autonomy to make such profound choices," why would there be any less dignity in the bond between three people who, in exercising their autonomy, seek to make the profound choice to marry? If a same-sex couple has the constitutional right to marry because their children would otherwise "suffer the stigma of knowing their families are somehow lesser," why wouldn't the same reasoning apply to a family of three or more persons raising children? If not having the opportunity to marry "serves to disrespect and subordinate" gay and lesbian couples, why wouldn't the same "imposition of this disability," serve to disrespect and subordinate people who find fulfillment in polyamorous relationships?

I do not mean to equate marriage between same-sex couples with plural marriages in all respects. There may well be relevant differences that compel different legal analysis. But if there are, petitioners have not pointed to any. When asked about a plural marital union at oral argument, petitioners asserted that a State "doesn't have such an institution." But that is exactly the point: the States at issue here do not have an institution of same-sex marriage, either.

Near the end of its opinion, the majority offers perhaps the clearest insight into its decision. Expanding marriage to include same-sex couples, the majority insists, would "pose no risk of harm to themselves or third parties." This argument again echoes *Lochner*, which relied on its assessment that "we think that a law like the one before us involves neither the safety, the morals nor the welfare of the public, and that the interest of the public is not in the slightest degree affected by such an act."

Then and now, this assertion of the "harm principle" sounds more in philosophy than law. The elevation of the fullest individual self-realization over the constraints that society has expressed in law may or may not be attractive moral philosophy. But a Justice's commission does not confer any special moral, philosophical, or social insight sufficient to justify imposing those perceptions on fellow citizens under the pretense of "due process." There is indeed a process due the people on issues of this sort—the democratic process. Respecting that understanding requires the Court to be guided by law, not any particular school of social thought. As Judge Henry Friendly once put it, echoing Justice Holmes's dissent in *Lochner*, the Fourteenth Amendment does not enact John Stuart Mill's On Liberty any more than it enacts Herbert Spencer's Social Statics. And it certainly does not enact any one concept of marriage.

The majority's understanding of due process lays out a tantalizing vision of the future for Members of this Court: If an unvarying social institution enduring over all of recorded history cannot inhibit judicial policymaking, what can? But this approach is dangerous for the rule of law. The purpose of insisting that implied fundamental rights have roots in the history and tradition of our people is to ensure that when unelected judges strike down democratically enacted laws, they do so based on something more than their own beliefs. The Court today not only overlooks our country's entire history and tradition but actively repudiates it, preferring to live only in the heady days of the here and now. I agree with the majority that the "nature of injustice is that we may not always see it in our own times." As petitioners put it, "times can blind." But to blind yourself to history is both prideful and unwise. "The past is never dead. It's not even past." W. Faulkner, Requiem for a Nun 92 (1951). . . .

The legitimacy of this Court ultimately rests "upon the respect accorded to its judgments." That respect flows from the perception—and reality—that we exercise humility and restraint in deciding cases according to the Constitution and law. The role of the Court envisioned by the majority today, however, is anything but humble or restrained. Over and over, the majority exalts the role of the judiciary in delivering social change. In the majority's telling, it is the courts, not the people, who are responsible for making "new dimensions of freedom . . . apparent to new generations," for providing "formal discourse" on social issues, and for ensuring "neutral discussions, without scornful or disparaging commentary."

Nowhere is the majority's extravagant conception of judicial supremacy more evident than in its description—and dismissal—of the public debate regarding same-sex marriage. Yes, the majority concedes, on one side are thousands of years of human history in every society known to have populated the planet. But on the other side, there has been "extensive litigation," "many thoughtful District Court decisions," "countless studies, papers, books, and other popular and scholarly writings," and "more than 100" *amicus* briefs in these cases alone. What would be the point of allowing the democratic process to go on? It is high time for the Court to decide the meaning of marriage, based on five lawyers' "better informed understanding" of "a liberty that remains urgent in our own era." The answer is surely there in one of those *amicus* briefs or studies. . . .

The Court's accumulation of power does not occur in a vacuum. It comes at the expense of the people. And they know it. Here and abroad, people are in the midst of a serious and thoughtful public debate on the issue of same-sex marriage. They see voters carefully considering same-sex marriage, casting ballots in favor or opposed, and sometimes changing their minds. They see political leaders similarly reexamining their positions, and either reversing course or explaining adherence to old convictions confirmed anew. They see governments and businesses modifying policies and practices with respect to same-sex couples, and participating actively in the civic discourse. They see countries overseas democratically accepting profound social change, or declining to do so. This deliberative process is making people take seriously questions that they may not have even regarded as questions before.

When decisions are reached through democratic means, some people will inevitably be disappointed with the results. But those whose views do not prevail at least know that they have had their say, and accordingly are—in the tradition of our political culture—reconciled to the result of a fair and honest debate. In addition, they can gear up to raise the issue later, hoping to persuade enough on the winning side to think again. "That is exactly how our system of government is supposed to work."

But today the Court puts a stop to all that. By deciding this question under the Constitution, the Court removes it from the realm of democratic decision. There will be consequences to shutting down the political process on an issue of such profound public significance. Closing debate tends to close minds. People denied a voice are less likely to accept the ruling of a court on an issue that does not seem to be the sort of thing courts usually decide. As a thoughtful commentator observed about another issue, "The political process was moving . . . , not swiftly enough for advocates of quick, complete change, but majoritarian institutions were listening and acting. Heavy-handed judicial intervention was difficult to justify and appears to have provoked, not resolved, conflict." Ginsburg, Some Thoughts on Autonomy and Equality in Relation to Roe v. Wade, 63 N.C. L. Rev. 375, 385-386 (1985) (footnote omitted). Indeed, however heartened the proponents of same-sex marriage might be on this day, it is worth acknowledging what they have lost, and lost forever: the opportunity to win the true acceptance that comes from persuading their fellow citizens of the justice of their cause. And they lose this just when the winds of change were freshening at their backs. . . .

Hard questions arise when people of faith exercise religion in ways that may be seen to conflict with the new right to same-sex marriage—when, for example, a religious college provides married student housing only to opposite-sex married couples, or a religious adoption agency declines to place children with same-sex married couples. Indeed, the Solicitor General candidly acknowledged that the tax exemptions of some religious institutions would be in question if they opposed same-sex marriage. There is little doubt that these and similar questions will soon be before this Court. Unfortunately, people of faith can take no comfort in the treatment they receive from the majority today.

Perhaps the most discouraging aspect of today's decision is the extent to which the majority feels compelled to sully those on the other side of the debate. The majority offers a cursory assurance that it does not intend to disparage people who, as a matter of conscience, cannot accept same-sex marriage. That disclaimer is hard to square with the very next sentence, in which the majority explains that "the necessary consequence" of laws codifying the traditional definition of marriage is to "demea[n] or stigmatiz[e]" same-sex couples. The majority reiterates such characterizations over and over. By the majority's account, Americans who did nothing more than follow the understanding of marriage that has existed for our entire history—in particular, the tens of millions of people who voted to reaffirm their States' enduring definition of marriage—have acted to "lock . . . out," "disparage," "disrespect and subordinate," and inflict "[d]ignitary wounds" upon their gay and lesbian neighbors. These apparent assaults on the character of fairminded people will have an effect, in society and in court. Moreover, they are entirely gratuitous. It is one thing for the majority to conclude that the Constitution protects a right to same-sex marriage; it is something else to portray everyone who does not share the majority's "better informed understanding" as bigoted.

In the face of all this, a much different view of the Court's role is possible. That view is more modest and restrained. It is more skeptical that the legal abilities of judges also reflect insight into moral and philosophical issues. It is more sensitive to the fact that judges are unelected and unaccountable, and that the legitimacy of their power depends on confining it to the exercise of legal judgment. It is more attuned to the lessons of history, and what it has meant for the country and Court when Justices have exceeded their proper bounds. And it is less pretentious than to suppose that while people around the world have viewed an institution in a particular way for thousands of years, the present generation and the present Court are the ones chosen to burst the bonds of that history and tradition.

* * *

If you are among the many Americans—of whatever sexual orientation—who favor expanding same-sex marriage, by all means celebrate today's decision. Celebrate the achievement of a desired goal. Celebrate the opportunity for a new expression of commitment to a partner. Celebrate the availability of new benefits. But do not celebrate the Constitution. It had nothing to do with it.

I respectfully dissent.

Justice SCALIA, with whom Justice THOMAS joins, dissenting.

I join The Chief Justice's opinion in full. I write separately to call attention to this Court's threat to American democracy.

The substance of today's decree is not of immense personal importance to me. The law can recognize as marriage whatever sexual attachments and living arrangements it wishes, and can accord them favorable civil consequences, from tax treatment to rights of inheritance. . . . [I]t is not of special importance to me what the law says about marriage. It is of overwhelming importance, however, who it is that rules me. Today's decree says that my Ruler, and the Ruler of 320 million Americans coast-to-coast, is a majority of the nine lawyers on the Supreme Court. . . . This practice of constitutional revision by an unelected committee of nine, always accompanied (as it is today) by extravagant praise of liberty, robs the People of the most important liberty they asserted in the Declaration of Independence and won in the Revolution of 1776: the freedom to govern themselves.

The Constitution places some constraints on self-rule—constraints adopted *by the People themselves* when they ratified the Constitution and its Amendments. . . . These cases ask us to decide whether the Fourteenth Amendment contains a limitation that requires the States to license and recognize marriages between two people of the same sex. Does it remove *that* issue from the political process?

Of course not. It would be surprising to find a prescription regarding marriage in the Federal Constitution since, as the author of today's opinion reminded us only two years ago (in an opinion joined by the same Justices who join him today): "[R]egulation of domestic relations is an area that has long been regarded as a virtually exclusive province of the States." [and] "[T]he Federal Government, through our history, has deferred to state-law policy decisions with respect to domestic relations." [*Windsor.*]

But we need not speculate. When the Fourteenth Amendment was ratified in 1868, every State limited marriage to one man and one woman, and no one doubted the constitutionality of doing so. That resolves these cases. When it comes to determining the meaning of a vague constitutional provision—such as "due process of law" or "equal protection of the laws"—it is unquestionable that the People who ratified that provision did not understand it to prohibit a practice that remained both universal and uncontroversial in the years after ratification. We have no basis for striking down a practice that is not expressly prohibited by the Fourteenth Amendment's text, and that bears the endorsement of a long tradition of open, widespread, and unchallenged use dating back to the Amendment's ratification. Since there is no doubt whatever that the People never decided to prohibit the limitation of marriage to opposite-sex couples, the public debate over same-sex marriage must be allowed to continue.

Justice THOMAS, with whom Justice SCALIA joins, dissenting.

The Court's decision today is at odds not only with the Constitution, but with the principles upon which our Nation was built. Since well before 1787, liberty has been understood as freedom from government action, not entitlement to government benefits. The Framers created our Constitution to preserve that understanding of liberty. Yet the majority invokes our Constitution in the name of a "liberty" that the Framers would not have recognized, to the detriment of the liberty they sought to protect. Along the way, it rejects the idea—captured in our Declaration of Independence—that human dignity is innate and suggests instead that it comes from the Government. This distortion of our Constitution not only ignores the text, it inverts the relationship between the individual and the state in our Republic. I cannot agree with it. . . .

Even if the doctrine of substantive due process were somehow defensible—it is not—petitioners still would not have a claim. To invoke the protection of the Due Process Clause at all—whether under a theory of "substantive" or "procedural" due process—a party must first identify a deprivation of "life, liberty, or property." The majority claims these state laws deprive petitioners of "liberty," but the concept of "liberty" it conjures up bears no resemblance to any plausible meaning of that word as it is used in the Due Process Clauses.

As used in the Due Process Clauses, "liberty" most likely refers to "the power of locomotion, of changing situation, or removing one's person to whatsoever place one's own inclination may direct; without imprisonment or restraint, unless by due course of law." 1 W. Blackstone, Commentaries on the Laws of England 130 (1769) (Blackstone). . . . The Framers drew heavily upon Blackstone's formulation, adopting provisions in early State Constitutions that replicated Magna Carta's language, but were modified to refer specifically to "life, liberty, or property." State decisions interpreting these provisions between the founding and the ratification of the Fourteenth Amendment almost uniformly construed the word "liberty" to refer only to freedom from physical restraint. . . . [Given this history], it is hard to see how the "liberty" protected by the [Fifth Amendment's Due Process] Clause could be interpreted to include anything broader than freedom from physical restraint. If the Fifth Amendment uses "liberty" in this narrow sense, then the Fourteenth Amendment likely does as well. . . .

Even assuming that the "liberty" in those Clauses encompasses something more than freedom from physical restraint, it would not include the types of rights claimed by the majority. In the American legal tradition, liberty has long been understood as individual freedom *from* governmental action, not as a right *to* a particular governmental entitlement.

Whether we define "liberty" as locomotion or freedom from governmental action more broadly, petitioners have in no way been deprived of it. . . .

Instead, the States have refused to grant them governmental entitlements. Petitioners claim that as a matter of "liberty," they are entitled to access privileges and benefits that exist solely *because of* the government. They want, for example, to receive the State's *imprimatur* on their marriages — on state issued marriage licenses, death certificates, or other official forms. And they want to receive various monetary benefits, including reduced inheritance taxes upon the death of a spouse, compensation if a spouse dies as a result of a work-related injury, or loss of consortium damages in tort suits. But receiving governmental recognition and benefits has nothing to do with any understanding of "liberty" that the Framers would have recognized.

To the extent that the Framers would have recognized a natural right to marriage that fell within the broader definition of liberty, it would not have included a right to governmental recognition and benefits. Instead, it would have included a right to engage in the very same activities that petitioners have been left free to engage in — making vows, holding religious ceremonies celebrating those vows, raising children, and otherwise enjoying the society of one's spouse — without governmental interference. At the founding, such conduct was understood to predate government, not to flow from it. . . . Petitioners misunderstand the institution of marriage when they say that it would "mean little" absent governmental recognition. . . .

Perhaps recognizing that these cases do not actually involve liberty as it has been understood, the majority goes to great lengths to assert that its decision will advance the "dignity" of same-sex couples. The flaw in that reasoning, of course, is that the Constitution contains no "dignity" Clause, and even if it did, the government would be incapable of bestowing dignity.

Human dignity has long been understood in this country to be innate. . . . The corollary of that principle is that human dignity cannot be taken away by the government. Slaves did not lose their dignity (any more than they lost their humanity) because the government allowed them to be enslaved. Those held in internment camps did not lose their dignity because the government confined them. And those denied governmental benefits certainly do not lose their dignity because the government denies them those benefits. The government cannot bestow dignity, and it cannot take it away. . . .

Justice ALITO, with whom Justice SCALIA and Justice THOMAS join, dissenting.

[N]oting that marriage is a fundamental right, the majority argues that a State has no valid reason for denying that right to same-sex couples. This reasoning is dependent upon a particular understanding of the purpose of civil marriage. [T]he Court['s] argument is that the fundamental purpose of marriage is to promote the well-being of those who choose to marry. Marriage provides emotional fulfillment and the promise of support in times of need. And by benefiting persons who choose to wed, marriage indirectly benefits society because persons who live in stable, fulfilling, and supportive relationships make better citizens. . . . This understanding of the States' reasons for recognizing marriage enables the majority to argue that same-sex marriage serves the States' objectives in the same way as opposite-sex marriage.

This understanding of marriage, which focuses almost entirely on the happiness of persons who choose to marry, is shared by many people today, but it is not the traditional one. For millennia, marriage was inextricably linked to the one thing that only an opposite-sex couple can do: procreate. . . . [T]he States defend . . . [this] traditional understanding of marriage. . . . Their basic argument is that States formalize and promote marriage, unlike other fulfilling human relationships, in order to encourage potentially procreative conduct to take place within a lasting unit that has long been thought to provide the best atmosphere for raising children. They thus argue that there are reasonable secular grounds for restricting marriage to opposite-sex couples.

If this traditional understanding of the purpose of marriage does not ring true to all ears today, that is probably because the tie between marriage and procreation has frayed. Today, for instance, more than 40% of all children in this country are born to unmarried women. This development undoubtedly is both a cause and a result of changes in our society's understanding of marriage.

While, for many, the attributes of marriage in 21st-century America have changed, those States that do not want to recognize same-sex marriage have not yet given up on the traditional understanding. They worry that by officially abandoning the older understanding, they may contribute to marriage's further decay. It is far beyond the outer reaches of this Court's authority to say that a State may not adhere to the understanding of marriage that has long prevailed, not just in this country and others with similar cultural roots, but also in a great variety of countries and cultures all around the globe.

As I wrote in *Windsor*:

> "The family is an ancient and universal human institution. Family structure reflects the characteristics of a civilization, and changes in family structure and in the popular understanding of marriage and the family can have profound effects. Past changes in the understanding of marriage—for example, the gradual ascendance of the idea that romantic love is a prerequisite to marriage—have had far-reaching consequences. But the process by which such consequences come about is complex, involving the interaction of numerous factors, and tends to occur over an extended period of time.
>
> "We can expect something similar to take place if same-sex marriage becomes widely accepted. The long-term consequences of this change are not now known and are unlikely to be ascertainable for some time to come. There are those who think that allowing same-sex marriage will seriously undermine the institution of marriage. Others think that recognition of same-sex marriage will fortify a now-shaky institution.
>
> "At present, no one—including social scientists, philosophers, and historians—can predict with any certainty what the long-term ramifications of widespread acceptance of same-sex marriage will be. And judges are certainly not equipped to make such an assessment. The Members of this Court have the authority and the responsibility to interpret and apply the Constitution. Thus, if the Constitution contained a provision guaranteeing the right to marry a person of the same sex, it would be our duty to enforce that right. But the Constitution simply does not speak to the issue

> of same-sex marriage. In our system of government, ultimate sovereignty rests with the people, and the people have the right to control their own destiny. Any change on a question so fundamental should be made by the people through their elected officials."

. . . Today's decision usurps the constitutional right of the people to decide whether to keep or alter the traditional understanding of marriage. The decision will also have other important consequences.

It will be used to vilify Americans who are unwilling to assent to the new orthodoxy. In the course of its opinion, the majority compares traditional marriage laws to laws that denied equal treatment for African-Americans and women. The implications of this analogy will be exploited by those who are determined to stamp out every vestige of dissent.

Perhaps recognizing how its reasoning may be used, the majority attempts, toward the end of its opinion, to reassure those who oppose same-sex marriage that their rights of conscience will be protected. We will soon see whether this proves to be true. I assume that those who cling to old beliefs will be able to whisper their thoughts in the recesses of their homes, but if they repeat those views in public, they will risk being labeled as bigots and treated as such by governments, employers, and schools.

The system of federalism established by our Constitution provides a way for people with different beliefs to live together in a single nation. If the issue of same-sex marriage had been left to the people of the States, it is likely that some States would recognize same-sex marriage and others would not. It is also possible that some States would tie recognition to protection for conscience rights. The majority today makes that impossible. By imposing its own views on the entire country, the majority facilitates the marginalization of the many Americans who have traditional ideas. Recalling the harsh treatment of gays and lesbians in the past, some may think that turnabout is fair play. But if that sentiment prevails, the Nation will experience bitter and lasting wounds.

DISCUSSION

1. Obergefell *and fundamental rights.* Obergefell v. Hodges holds that the fundamental right to marriage protected by the Due Process Clause extends to same-sex couples. Lawrence v. Texas was ambiguous on whether the liberty interest in same-sex relations was fundamental. By contrast, *Obergefell* clearly states that gays and lesbians enjoy a fundamental right to marry. Does this now clarify that *Lawrence* is also a case about fundamental rights? If gays and lesbians enjoy a fundamental right to marry, do they also enjoy a fundamental right to sexual relations, or is this right limited only to married couples?

2. *Tradition! Obergefell* is an extended essay on tradition, but the majority and the dissent have very different ways of articulating what constitutionally protected tradition is and how we determine its contours.

Justice Kennedy argues that constitutionally protected traditions are those that are consistent with the underlying reasons why a social tradition is valuable to us today. "[I]n assessing whether the force and rationale of its cases apply to same-sex couples, the Court must respect the basic reasons why the right to marry has been long protected." Accordingly, he recites four features of marriage that make it valuable to us today and then argues that same-sex marriage applies to all of them. His opinion assumes that tradition—or at the very least, constitutionally protected tradition—is something that present generations can reason about and rationally extend or alter. Kennedy's recitation of how the couples in the case met, fell in love, married, lived, and raised children in *Obergefell* is more than an attempt to tug at our heartstrings. He also wants to show that the reason we sympathize with these couples and their plight is the same reason we sympathize with the hardships and sacrifices of married couples generally.

Roberts, Scalia, and especially Alito identify constitutionally protected traditions with longstanding social practices. They view tradition as the accumulated wisdom of previous generations. Therefore we should not disturb the judgments of previous generations because we are very likely to make a mistake. Present generations are likely to view the world from a very narrow perspective—our own lifetimes—and therefore if we try to make significant changes based on contemporary judgments and reasons, we are likely to produce unintended and undesirable consequences, as well as destroy institutions of long standing.

These different conceptions of tradition presume contrasting views about human knowledge and moral growth. Kennedy regards the evolution of tradition as beneficially shaped by increases in knowledge and understanding. Repeatedly he speaks of "new awareness," "new insight," or "enhanced understanding" of new facts and moral truths that result from deliberation and political interaction. These new insights and understandings should properly be incorporated into the constitutional tradition, altering what the tradition means for us today.

The dissenters, by contrast, do not think that present generations are necessarily getting any wiser, even if their values may have changed. At one point in his dissent, Chief Justice Roberts, almost in exasperation, exclaims, "Just who do we think we are?"

Kennedy emphasizes that traditional practices change over time and are always changing. Hence he offers a history of changing conceptions of marriage—from arranged marriages to marriage for love to the gradual decline of coverture rules to the emergence of companionate marriage between equals. Roberts and Alito, by contrast, emphasize that core features of the institution of marriage have not changed for centuries, and can be found in almost all civilizations, ancient and modern. (Note Chief Justice Roberts's reference to "the Kalahari Bushmen and the Han Chinese, the Carthaginians and the Aztecs.") The changes that Kennedy describes are not central to the core of the tradition, while the union of one man and one woman is central.

It is tempting to identify the dissenters with Edmund Burke, who famously criticized the French Revolution, and to view Kennedy as opposed to Burkeanism. Certainly the dissenters would like to brand Kennedy as a revolutionary or Jacobin, heedlessly destroying a valued institution at the center of society. But Kennedy's use of tradition is also Burkean in its own way. In particular Kennedy emphasizes change through respect for tradition that results from discussion and lived experience—as opposed to change that occurs through violence and revolutionary upheaval. Kennedy emphasizes the natural evolution and growth of previous commitments through debate, contestation, and social practice. Our commitments evolve as they we apply them to changed factual circumstances and our wisdom grows through encountering those changed circumstances in practical terms. We can have greater confidence in our judgments achieved in this way because, unlike previous generations, we have the benefit of their experience, while they do not have the benefit of ours.

3. *Bye, Bye,* Glucksberg. Justice Kennedy's opinion in *Obergefell* unceremoniously overrules the reasoning if not the specific results in Washington v. Glucksberg, without saying so directly. In order to reject a constitutional right to assisted suicide, *Glucksberg* offered a very narrow test of when courts could recognize new implied fundamental rights. (See the discussion in the Note on Tradition as a Source of Fundamental Rights, supra.) The Chief Justice well understands this: "It is revealing that the majority's position requires it to effectively overrule *Glucksberg,* the leading modern case setting the bounds of substantive due process."

Obergefell makes clear, however, that *Glucksberg* has never really been "the leading modern case on substantive due process" and implied fundamental rights. Rather, *Glucksberg* has been especially attractive to *critics* of implied fundamental rights because it seems to limit implied fundamental rights to practices that, when described very concretely, have a very long history of protection. Taken seriously, almost none of the Court's key substantive due process decisions would meet *Glucksberg*'s test. That is why critics of implied fundamental rights tend to like it.

Indeed, Chief Justice Rehnquist—no fan of implied fundamental rights himself—wrote *Glucksberg* in 1997 precisely to lay down a marker so that federal judges would stop trying to imply fundamental rights. Unfortunately for Rehnquist, he didn't succeed. The Court hasn't taken *Glucksberg* very seriously since it was decided. Not in *Lawrence,* not in *Windsor,* and certainly not in *Obergefell.*

Another way of putting this is that the debate between Justice Brennan and Justice Scalia in Michael H. v. Gerald D. is over, and Justice Brennan won. In *Michael H.,* Justice Scalia (joined by Chief Justice Rehnquist) argued that traditions of liberty should be construed as narrowly as possible—"the most specific level at which a relevant tradition protecting, or denying protection to, the asserted right can be identified." Justice Brennan argued that constitutional traditions of liberty should be construed abstractly and broadly, so that some existing practices might actually be inconsistent with our traditions properly understood in their best light. At the time, Scalia's theory had real difficulties accounting for the Court's jurisprudence up to that point; it wasn't really consistent with *Eisenstadt,* much less *Roe.* But that was fine with Scalia—he didn't want to extend these decisions any further.

Compare Justice Brennan's and Justice Kennedy's view of tradition with that of the second Justice Harlan, who famously wrote of "the balance struck by this country, having regard to what history teaches are the traditions from which it developed as well as the traditions from which it broke. That tradition is a living thing." Justice Harlan emphasized that sometimes following tradition means rejecting some traditional practices or assumptions that we now believe are no longer consistent with our traditions considered in their best light. Our traditions are living because they change over time, for example, by becoming more inclusive. Justice Harlan argued that sometimes the best way to read our traditions is as evolving, and therefore as rejecting some previous practices that we previously regarded as part of our traditions. In like fashion, Justice Kennedy argued that the best way to understand our traditions of marriage is as evolving—we have gradually been moving toward a view of marriage as a bond of commitment between two equals, which is as compatible with same-sex marriage as it is with opposite-sex marriage. Kennedy argues that when our traditions of liberty are considered in their best light, same-sex marriage is fully consistent with those traditions, rather than opposed to them.

4. *Polygamy.* The Chief Justice points out that Justice Kennedy's due process arguments don't adequately distinguish same-sex marriage from polygamy: "[The majority] offers no reason at all why the two-person element of the core definition of marriage may be preserved while the man-woman element may not. Indeed, from the standpoint of history and tradition, a leap from opposite-sex marriage to same-sex marriage is much greater than one from a two-person union to plural unions, which have deep roots in some cultures around the world. If the majority is willing to take the big leap, it is hard to see how it can say no to the shorter one." Chief Justice Roberts also argues that each of the four reasons for protecting the right to marry "would apply with equal force to the claim of a fundamental right to plural marriage."

If *Obergefell* had been decided on traditional equal protection grounds, the issue would not arise in the same way. The Court might point out that limiting marriage to two persons of either sex does not discriminate on the basis of either sex or sexual orientation.

Does Kennedy have a good response to Chief Justice Roberts? Does polygamy present a realistic possibility of social problems that same-sex marriage does not? Judge Richard Posner argues that in traditional polygamous societies, wealthy and powerful men tend to collect multiple wives, and this makes it more difficult for other men to find partners.[225] Of course, analogies to how polygamy operates in traditional societies may or may not tell us much; we don't yet know how polygamy will work in modern society—whether, for example, powerful women would also collect many husbands, whether adults would form families of roughly equal men and women, and whether members of polygamous families would be more equal than in traditional societies.

At this point in history, do you expect the Supreme Court to extend constitutional protection to plural marriage? Given the current state of American politics and culture, why might the Court extend marriage to same-sex couples but not recognize plural marriage? Are any of these reasons discussed in the opinion?

5. *Equality in* Obergefell. In Obergefell v. Hodges, Justice Kennedy holds that bans on same-sex marriage also violate the Equal Protection Clause. However, his equal protection analysis does not discuss the standard doctrinal tiers of scrutiny. He does not hold that restricting marriage to opposite-sex couples violates sex equality, as some *amici* proposed. He does not hold that sexual orientation is a suspect classification, as the Obama Administration urged the Court to do. He does not suggest that limiting marriage to opposite-sex couples involves unconstitutional animus, as he did in *Windsor*; nor does he say that the ban fails "rational basis with a bite," because it is premised on irrational prejudice.

---

225. See Richard A. Posner, The Chief Justice's Gay Marriage Dissent Is Heartless, Slate, June 27, 2015, at http://www.slate.com/articles/news_and_politics/the_breakfast_table/features/2015/scotus_ roundup/supreme_court_gay_marriage_john_roberts_dissent_in_obergefell_is_heartless.single.html.

At the very end of the opinion Kennedy includes language that suggests that the exclusion of gay couples would violate even the ordinary rational basis standard, because the states' justification—that keeping gays from marrying will encourage straights to marry—makes no sense: "[I]t is unrealistic to conclude that an opposite-sex couple would choose not to marry simply because same-sex couples may do so." Yet Kennedy does not argue that the exclusion violates rational basis.

Even so, Kennedy's argument for treating same-sex marriage as part of the fundamental right to marry has many significant equality ideas. He states that "[t]here is no difference between same- and opposite-sex couples with respect to" marriage's usefulness in grounding the social order. He argues that excluding same-sex couples "teaches that gays and lesbians are unequal in important respects." and that "[i]t demeans gays and lesbians for the State to lock them out of a central institution of the Nation's society." He adds that "laws excluding same-sex couples from the marriage right impose stigma and injury of the kind prohibited by our basic charter."

As in Lawrence v. Texas, the language of stigma and demeaning sounds in civil equality and the antisubordination principle. Indeed, later in the opinion, Kennedy says: "[T]he challenged laws abridge central precepts of equality. . . . [They are] essentially unequal: same-sex couples are denied all the benefits afforded to opposite-sex couples and are barred from exercising a fundamental right. Especially against a long history of disapproval of their relationships, this denial . . . works a grave and continuing harm. The imposition of this disability on gays and lesbians serves to disrespect and subordinate them. And the Equal Protection Clause, like the Due Process Clause, prohibits this unjustified infringement of the fundamental right to marry."

This sounds very much like an antisubordination rationale. Moreover, together with other parts of the opinion, Kennedy seems to be carefully laying the groundwork for arguing that gays and lesbians have suffered a long history of discrimination, and that they are excluded from important opportunities for reasons that have nothing to do with their contribution to society. (In fact, at one point, Kennedy even suggests that sexual orientation is akin to an immutable characteristic, arguing that the "immutable nature [of same-sex couples] dictates that same-sex marriage is their only real path to this profound commitment [of marriage].") If one added that gays and lesbians are a minority without significant representation in "the Nation's decision-making councils," one would have a pretty good argument for treating sexual orientation as a suspect classification. (This was the Obama Administration's argument as amicus curiae.) Nevertheless, having set up virtually all of the elements for this conclusion, Kennedy does not reach it.

Instead, Kennedy's equal protection argument emphasizes that equality and liberty are two sides of a coin—that they are two different perspectives on a problem that shine light on each other: "Each concept—liberty and equality—leads to a stronger understanding of the other." Hence selective denials of fundamental rights deny equal dignity. Accordingly, Justice Kennedy, in a very interesting passage, reinterprets the sex equality cases of the 1970s as protecting the equal dignity of men and women in the right to marry.

Kennedy's account of equality is perhaps closest to two ideas in previous jurisprudence. The first is in *Casey* and in Justice Ginsburg's dissent in Gonzales v. Carhart. Both opinions are officially about the liberty protected by the Due Process

Clause, but both argue that women's interest in reproductive liberty is tied to their equal status as citizens. One could read *Obergefell*—together with *Lawrence*—as drawing on and expanding these ideas of liberty as equal citizenship status (although, interestingly, the abortion cases are never mentioned in the majority opinion).

The second idea comes from Skinner v. Oklahoma and from some of the Warren Court's decisions on the rights of the poor, especially Harper v. Virginia Board of Elections (discussed in Chapter Ten, infra). This is the "fundamental rights" strand of equal protection doctrine. The government violates equal protection when it discriminates against or selectively burdens the exercise of a fundamental right or interest. One could also read *Obergefell* as part of this line of cases. Because marriage is a fundamental right (or more correctly, a *fundamental interest*, as discussed below), the state cannot deny the right to marry arbitrarily to a group of citizens without a compelling interest. Here the state does not even have a reasonable justification, so, a fortiori, the discrimination is unconstitutional.

6. *The doctrine and the dissents.* If Justice Kennedy generally avoids analyzing the case in terms of black-letter levels-of-scrutiny doctrine, so do the dissents. None of the dissents directly explain why the state governments' asserted justification for denying same-sex couples the right to marry passes the rational basis test. As noted above, the states' justification is fairly weak. The reason is that, after *Lawrence* and *Windsor*, the states could not argue that the laws were designed to enforce religious or moral objections to homosexual behavior, or that they reflected anxiety and fears about homosexuality. What arguments can you find in the dissents for why the state laws would nevertheless pass rational basis?

7. Lochner, *I say,* Lochner*!* Note the Chief Justice's invocation of *Lochner*. What does *Lochner* stand for in his opinion? The Chief Justice believes that courts should not make up new constitutional rights out of whole cloth; he denounces the idea of five unelected lawyers undermining democracy and imposing their own ideological convictions on the rest of the country. Are these sentiments consistent with the Chief Justice's majority opinion in Shelby County v. Holder, which announces a new doctrine of "equal sovereignty of the states," and which strikes down key parts of an important civil rights statute passed by overwhelming majorities in Congress? At oral argument in *Shelby County* Justice Scalia suggested that the very fact that the Voting Rights Act was passed by such overwhelming margins was a reason that the courts needed to strike it down.

Is *Obergefell* different than *Shelby County* because the latter involved structure rather than rights? What then, of the fact that all four dissenters joined Justice Kennedy's opinion in Citizens United v. Federal Election Commission, 558 U.S. 310 (2010)? How do we tell when judges have committed the sin of *Lochner*?

8. *They'll never take our dignity.* In dissent, Justice Thomas objects to the majority's argument that limiting marriage to opposite-sex couples denies same-sex couples their dignity. He notes that the term "dignity" does not appear in the Constitution. He argues that dignity is innate and that no man-made institution can take away this dignity. Even the inherent dignity of slaves, he argues, could not be taken away by the vicious institution of slavery. Thomas's argument is that natural rights and human dignity preexist the state and therefore it is wrong to assume that the state could or should bestow dignity on anyone.

Does this argument adequately engage with the majority? Of course, Kennedy might respond, Thomas is correct that human dignity is innate and cannot be taken away by the state. That is precisely why the Constitution values it. Rather, the issue is government actions that deny *appropriate respect* for human dignity. When the state fails to accord people the equal concern and respect that they deserve, this violates the Equal Protection Clause of the Constitution. Properly *recognizing* and *respecting* dignity is not the same thing as *creating* dignity or being the *source* of dignity.

9. *Fundamental rights and fundamental interests.* Another way of stating Kennedy's argument is that the state has an obligation to respect and recognize the inherent dignity of the people who live within its borders. The state fails to do this when it arbitrarily denies the rights and benefits of marriage to a class of its citizens without adequate public justification. Although the state may not have to provide those rights and benefits in the first place, once it has given them out, it may not make arbitrary distinctions in who receives them.

This restatement, however, suggests an important point. It may be better to call marriage a *fundamental interest* than a *fundamental right.* The difference is that the state does not have to provide a fundamental interest at all, but once it does, it must bestow and protect it equally among the members of the political community. Instead of having a bundle of rights called "marriage," for example, the state could simply allow private marriage ceremonies and enforce civil contracts between couples. Nevertheless, once the state creates a bundle of legal rights and calls it "marriage," it cannot arbitrarily limit who enjoys that bundle of rights.

10. *Why did Justice Kennedy not use standard equal protection law?* As noted above, Justice Kennedy avoided the standard language of equal protection scrutiny. There are many possible reasons for this. First, as a libertarian, Kennedy may simply be more comfortable talking about liberty. Second, Kennedy might not want to take on all of the legal consequences of creating a new suspect classification—the first since the 1970s—without more consideration about the consequences for legal doctrine in a host of different areas. Third, Kennedy may not be particularly enamored of the formalism of existing equal protection categories, which in many cases tend to obscure the real issues at stake.

Fourth, employing heightened scrutiny under the Equal Protection Clause has its own problems. A threshold question is whether the statutes involved in the marriage cases classify on the basis of *sex* or *sexual orientation.* If the latter, does limiting marriage to one man and one woman constitute *facial discrimination* on the basis of sexual orientation, or does it merely have a *disparate impact* on sexual orientation minorities? If the latter, could the plaintiffs prove discriminatory purpose within the meaning of *Feeney*—that is, could they show that all of the states' laws were enacted *because of,* not *in spite of,* the effect on gays and lesbians? Potentially, all of these problems could be surmounted—for example, Kennedy could have just employed a sex equality argument. But each of the alternatives would raise difficulties that he might have wanted to avoid.

Fifth, Kennedy might have decided against using the "rational basis with a bite" or "animus" lines of cases because he did not think that he could easily show that *all* of the state laws defining marriage in terms of opposite-sex couples were passed because of malice or irrational prejudice against gays and lesbians. Some of these laws were quite old. If he declared that all of them were based in animus, he would be declaring all of the people who voted for them had bad intentions or were prejudiced, or both. Instead, he simply states that whatever their motivations, the laws they produced had the effect of demeaning and subordinating gays and lesbians. Is this an important difference?

Although Kennedy's opinion has a lot of equality ideas in it, it does not offer a very clear account of how doctrine should develop. That may be deliberate. But it will mean that the lower courts will have to spend a lot of time puzzling out how best to apply Kennedy's arguments to a host of other issues, including, for example, state discrimination in adoption, family formation, employment, housing, and education.

11. *Religious liberty as the next battleground in the culture wars.* Just as *Obergefell* leaves open questions of discrimination based on sexual orientation, it does not resolve how courts will balance the dignitary interests and rights to equal treatment of gays and lesbians against claims of religious freedom by opponents of gay rights. Culture war issues have changed in recent years in anticipation of increasing protection for gay rights and same-sex marriage. Disputes about homosexuality and reproductive rights are increasingly being reframed as questions of religious liberty. Opponents of same-sex marriage, abortion, and contraception argue that they have a right not to cooperate or be complicit with what they regard as sinful conduct. See Douglas NeJaime and Reva B. Siegel, Conscience Wars: Complicity-Based Conscience Claims in Religion and Politics, 124 Yale L.J. 2516 (2015). Chief Justice Roberts's dissent notes some of the potential conflicts between same-sex marriage and religious belief and practice that may arise in the future.

As noted in Chapter 6, in 1990, the Supreme Court, in an opinion by Justice Scalia, severely limited the ability of religious minorities to object to laws of general application that burden the exercise of their religion. Employment Division v. Smith, 494 U.S. 872 (1990). In response, Congress passed the Religious Freedom Restoration Act (RFRA), which, after the decision in City of Boerne v. Flores (discussed in Chapter Six, supra), binds only the federal government. Nevertheless, many states have passed their own versions of RFRA. Interpretation and application of federal and state versions of RFRA will likely be a key site of disputes about whether religious objectors may refuse to do business with same-sex couples or with gays and lesbians more generally.

12. Obergefell, *Democratic Constitutionalism, and Judicial Review.* All of the dissenters in *Obergefell* criticize the majority for preempting the decisions of state legislatures across the country and prematurely ending the debate on same-sex marriage. Justice Kennedy offers two different kinds of responses, which, at first glance, seem in some tension with each other. On the one hand, quoting Justice Jackson in West Virginia Bd. of Ed. v. Barnette, 319 U.S. 624 (1943), he argues that "fundamental rights may not be submitted to a vote; they depend on the outcome of no elections." The relevant question is not how much public support there is for same-sex marriage, but whether the right is fundamental. For this reason, Kennedy explains, the Court was wrong in Bowers v. Hardwick and should have begun to protect gay rights in 1986, if not earlier.

Elsewhere in the opinion, however, Kennedy reasons quite differently. He argues that "changed understandings of marriage are characteristic of a Nation where new dimensions of freedom become apparent to new generations, often through perspectives that begin in pleas or protests and then are considered in the political sphere and the judicial process." He then spends several paragraphs summarizing the long fight for gay equality, describing numerous interactions between judicial decisions, the political process, and civil society. In an appendix to the decision he lists all of the state courts and lower federal courts that have passed on the question of same-sex marriage. And immediately before he quotes Justice Jackson in *Barnette,* he spends several paragraphs emphasizing the amount of public deliberation over same-sex marriage: "There have been referenda, legislative debates, and grassroots campaigns, as well as countless studies, papers, books, and other popular and scholarly writings, [as well as] extensive litigation in state and federal courts." All of this, he explains, "has led to an enhanced understanding of the issue—an understanding refined in the arguments now presented for resolution as a matter of constitutional law."

In these parts of the opinion, Justice Kennedy is describing what Robert Post and Reva Siegel have called "democratic constitutionalism"—the process by which continual interactions between civil society actors, political actors, and judges shape the constitutional ideas and judgements of the time. Robert C. Post and Reva Siegel, *Roe* Rage: Democratic Constitutionalism and Backlash, 42 Harv. C.R.-C.L. L. Rev. 373 (2007).

Justice Kennedy bases his constitutional arguments on "changed understandings," and "new awareness" of the rights of women, gays and lesbians—but those changed understandings and that new awareness did not occur only in the mind of Tony Kennedy. Rather, mechanisms of social influence, which operate in politics, law, and culture, changed many Americans' minds about liberty and equality. These mechanisms of social influence moved arguments about same-sex marriage from "off-the-wall" to "on-the-wall." Interactions between culture, law, and politics continually reshape constitutional common sense, thus enabling judges like Kennedy to reach the conclusions that they reach. Judges, as part of the culture, absorb the results of this process of cultural debate by osmosis. For that reason, judges need not and should not consult public opinion polls or statistical measures of public will in order to recognize that the practical meanings of liberty and equality, judgements about what is just and unjust, and the felt sense of what is reasonable and unreasonable have changed.

The process of social influence is "democratic" in the sense that it is interactive and participatory on multiple levels, but it is not "democratic" in the sense that judges are responding directly to elections and the wishes of either politicians or public opinion. Indeed, when Justices make decisions like *Obergefell,* there is often significant public support for what they do, but there is also usually some substantial segment of public opinion that strongly disagrees—and there are usually politicians who view the Court's decisions as an opportunity to mobilize against the Court.

13. Obergefell *and democratic legitimacy.* Post and Siegel offer their model of democratic constitutionalism only as a descriptive account of constitutional change. Jack Balkin argues that this model explains how the processes of living constitutionalism enjoy long-term democratic legitimacy. See Jack M. Balkin, Living Originalism (2011). One can only speak of legitimacy from a long-term perspective because at any point in time there is unlikely to be a one-to-one correspondence between the public's views about the Constitution on any particular subject and the views of the federal judiciary. For every *Obergefell,* there is a *Citizens United,* or vice versa, depending on one's substantive views. The point, rather, is that by processes of social influence, the decisions of the federal judiciary stay connected to long-term shifts in public views about constitutional values.

According to Balkin's account, the contemporary democratic legitimacy of the Constitution comes from two sources. First, legitimacy comes from the basic framework—the original meaning of the constitutional text and its choice of rules, standards, and principles. Second, the Constitution's contemporary legitimacy comes from constitutional constructions that are built on the basic framework—which include judicial precedents.

The democratic legitimacy of the basic framework derives from acts of adoption and subsequent amendment by We the People. The democratic legitimacy of constitutional constructions built on the framework comes from the processes of democratic constitutionalism (or living constitutionalism). These help ensure that constitutional constructions are connected to long-term shifts in the public's constitutional values. Both sources produce the Constitution's contemporary democratic legitimacy, and both are important to maintaining that legitimacy.

The four dissenters in *Obergefell* strongly object to the majority's confirmation of a sea change in American attitudes about same-sex marriage. The irony is that the dissenters' presence on the Supreme Court, and their conservative jurisprudence, are also the result of the same processes of democratic constitutionalism, albeit working in a different direction. The conservative mobilizations of the 1980s and afterwards led to judicial appointments, political protests, and litigation campaigns. These features of democratic constitutionalism on the right brought conservative constitutional values into ascendance and are reflected in many of the judicial precedents appearing in this casebook.

14. *Pavan v. Smith: What are the rights of married couples under* Obergefell*?* In Pavan v. Smith, 137 S. Ct. 2075 (2017) (per curiam), the Supreme Court summarily reversed a decision by the Arkansas Supreme Court that denied same-sex couples the right to have both spouses' names placed on a birth certificate. The Arkansas Supreme Court argued that the State had an interest in using birth certificates to record biological parentage, and this justified leaving the nonbiological parent of the same-sex couple off of the birth certificate.

The U.S. Supreme Court noted, however, that Arkansas law did not actually seem to promote that interest. Instead, its birth certificate law seemed to promote an interest in marital stability and reducing the number of illegitimate births. For example, Arkansas, like many states, had codified the common law presumption that a woman's husband is the father of a child born during marriage, even if he is not the biological father, and that "[i]f the mother was married at the time of either conception or birth, . . . the name of [her] husband shall be entered on the certificate as the father of the child." Similarly, Arkansas, like many other states, provides that if a married couple uses a sperm donor, and the husband consents to the use of artificial insemination, the husband, and not the sperm donor, will be listed on the birth certificate as the father, and the child "shall be deemed the legitimate natural child of the woman and the woman's husband."

The Court explained:

> Arkansas has thus chosen to make its birth certificates more than a mere marker of biological relationships: The State uses those certificates to give married parents a form of legal recognition that is not available to unmarried parents. Having made that choice, Arkansas may not, consistent with *Obergefell*, deny married same-sex couples that recognition. . . .

> *Obergefell* proscribes such disparate treatment. As we explained there, a State may not "exclude same-sex couples from civil marriage on the same terms and conditions as opposite-sex couples." Indeed, in listing those terms and conditions—the "rights, benefits, and responsibilities" to which same-sex couples, no less than opposite-sex couples, must have access—we expressly identified "birth and death certificates." That was no accident: Several of the plaintiffs in *Obergefell* challenged a State's refusal to recognize their same-sex spouses on their children's birth certificates. In considering those challenges, we held the relevant state laws unconstitutional to the extent they treated same-sex couples differently from opposite-sex couples. That holding applies with equal force to [Arkansas's birth certificate law].

Justice Gorsuch dissented, joined by Justices Thomas and Alito: "nothing in *Obergefell* indicates that a birth registration regime based on biology, one no doubt with many analogues across the country and throughout history, offends the Constitution."

Bostock v. Clayton County, Georgia

140 S. Ct. 1731 (2020)

[In *Bostock*, the Supreme Court held 6-3 that Title VII of the 1964 Civil Rights Act, which prohibits employment discrimination "because of [an] individual's . . . sex," 42 U.S.C. §2000e-2(a)(1), also prohibits discrimination based on sexual orientation and transgender status.]

Justice GORSUCH delivered the opinion of the Court.

Today, we must decide whether an employer can fire someone simply for being homosexual or transgender. The answer is clear. An employer who fires an individual for being homosexual or transgender fires that person for traits or actions it would not have questioned in members of a different sex. Sex plays a necessary and undisguisable role in the decision, exactly what Title VII forbids. . . .

We must determine the ordinary public meaning of Title VII's command that it is "unlawful . . . for an employer to fail or refuse to hire or to discharge any individual, or otherwise to discriminate against any individual with respect to his compensation, terms, conditions, or privileges of employment, because of such individual's race, color, religion, sex, or national origin." § 2000e-2(a)(1). . . .

Appealing to roughly contemporaneous dictionaries, the employers say that, as used here, the term "sex" in 1964 referred to "status as either male or female [as] determined by reproductive biology." The employees counter by submitting that, even in 1964, the term bore a broader scope, capturing more than anatomy and reaching at least some norms concerning gender identity and sexual orientation. But because nothing in our approach to these cases turns on the outcome of the parties' debate, and because the employees concede the point for argument's sake, we proceed on the assumption that "sex" signified what the employers suggest, referring only to biological distinctions between male and female. . . .

[T]he statute prohibits employers from taking certain actions "because of" sex. . . . [T]his means that Title VII's "because of" test incorporates the "'simple'" and "traditional" standard of but-for causation. . . . [T]he adoption of the traditional but-for causation standard means a defendant cannot avoid liability just by citing some *other* factor that contributed to its challenged employment decision. So long as the plaintiff 's sex was one but-for cause of that decision, that is enough to trigger the law.

No doubt, Congress could have taken a more parsimonious approach. . . . [I]t could have added "solely" to indicate that actions taken "because of" the confluence of multiple factors do not violate the law. Or it could have written "primarily because of" to indicate that the prohibited factor had to be the main cause of the defendant's challenged employment decision. But none of this is the law we have. . . .

[B]y virtue of the word *otherwise*, the employers suggest, Title VII concerns itself not with every discharge, only with those discharges that involve discrimination. . . . What did "discriminate" mean in 1964? As it turns out, it meant then roughly what it means today: "To make a difference in treatment or favor (of one as compared with others)." Webster's New International Dictionary 745 (2d ed. 1954). To "discriminate against" a person, then, would seem to mean treating that individual worse than others who are similarly situated. . . .

At first glance, another interpretation might seem possible. Discrimination sometimes involves "the act, practice, or an instance of discriminating categorically rather than individually." On that understanding, the statute would require us to consider the employer's treatment of groups rather than individuals, to see how a policy affects one sex as a whole versus the other as a whole. . . . Maybe the law concerns itself simply with ensuring that employers don't treat women generally less favorably than they do men. So how can we tell which sense, individual or group, "discriminate" carries in Title VII?

The statute answers that question directly. It tells us three times—including immediately after the words "discriminate against"—that our focus should be on individuals, not groups: Employers may not "fail or refuse to hire or . . . discharge any *individual*, or otherwise . . . discriminate against any *individual* with respect to his compensation, terms, conditions, or privileges of employment, because of such *individual's* . . . sex." § 2000e-2(a)(1) (emphasis added). . . . Here, again, Congress could have written the law differently. It might have said that "it shall be an unlawful employment practice to prefer one sex to the other in hiring, firing, or the terms or conditions of employment." It might have said that there should be no "sex discrimination," perhaps implying a focus on differential treatment between the two sexes as groups. More narrowly still, it could have forbidden only "sexist policies" against women as a class. But, once again, that is not the law we have.

The consequences of the law's focus on individuals rather than groups are anything but academic. Suppose an employer fires a woman for refusing his sexual advances. It's no defense for the employer to note that, while he treated that individual woman worse than he would have treated a man, he gives preferential treatment to female employees overall. The employer is liable for treating *this* woman worse in part because of her sex. Nor is it a defense for an employer to say it discriminates against both men and women because of sex. This statute works to protect individuals of both sexes from discrimination, and does so equally. So an employer who fires a woman, Hannah, because she is insufficiently feminine and also fires a man, Bob, for being insufficiently masculine may treat men and women as groups more or less equally. But in *both* cases the employer fires an individual in part because of sex. Instead of avoiding Title VII exposure, this employer doubles it. . . .

An individual's homosexuality or transgender status is not relevant to employment decisions. That's because it is impossible to discriminate against a person for being homosexual or transgender without discriminating against that individual based on sex. Consider, for example, an employer with two employees, both of whom are attracted to men. The two individuals are, to the employer's mind, materially identical in all respects, except that one is a man and the other a woman. If the employer fires the male employee for no reason other than the fact he is attracted to men, the employer discriminates against him for traits or actions it tolerates in his female colleague. Put differently, the employer intentionally singles out an employee to fire based in part on the employee's sex, and the affected employee's sex is a but-for cause of his discharge. Or take an employer who fires a transgender person who was identified as a male at birth but who now identifies as a female. If the employer retains an otherwise identical employee who was identified as female at birth, the employer intentionally penalizes a person identified as male at birth for traits or actions that it tolerates in an employee identified as female at birth. Again, the individual employee's sex plays an unmistakable and impermissible role in the discharge decision. . . .

Nor does it matter that, when an employer treats one employee worse because of that individual's sex, other factors may contribute to the decision. Consider an employer with a policy of firing any woman he discovers to be a Yankees fan. Carrying out that rule because an employee is a woman *and* a fan of the Yankees is a firing "because of sex" if the employer would have tolerated the same allegiance in a male employee. Likewise here. When an employer fires an employee because she is homosexual or transgender, two causal factors may be in play—*both* the individual's sex *and* something else (the sex to which the individual is attracted or with which the individual identifies). But Title VII doesn't care. If an employer would not have discharged an employee but for that individual's sex, the statute's causation standard is met, and liability may attach.

Reframing the additional causes in today's cases as additional intentions can do no more to insulate the employers from liability. Intentionally burning down a neighbor's house is arson, even if the perpetrator's ultimate intention (or motivation) is only to improve the view. No less, intentional discrimination based on sex violates Title VII, even if it is intended only as a means to achieving the employer's ultimate goal of discriminating against homosexual or transgender employees. There is simply no escaping the role intent plays here: Just as sex is necessarily a but-for *cause* when an employer discriminates against homosexual or transgender employees, an employer who discriminates on these grounds inescapably *intends* to rely on sex in its decisionmaking. Imagine an employer who has a policy of firing any employee known to be homosexual. The employer hosts an office holiday party and invites employees to bring their spouses. A model employee arrives and introduces a manager to Susan, the employee's wife. Will that employee be fired? If the policy works as the employer intends, the answer depends entirely on whether the model employee is a man or a woman. To be sure, that employer's ultimate goal might be to discriminate on the basis of sexual orientation. But to achieve that purpose the employer must, along the way, intentionally treat an employee worse based in part on that individual's sex.

An employer musters no better a defense by responding that it is equally happy to fire male and female employees who are homosexual or transgender. Title VII liability is not limited to employers who, through the sum of all of their employment actions, treat the class of men differently than the class of women. Instead, the law makes each instance of discriminating against an individual employee because of that individual's sex an independent violation of Title VII. So just as an employer who fires both Hannah and Bob for failing to fulfill traditional sex stereotypes doubles rather than eliminates Title VII liability, an employer who fires both Hannah and Bob for being gay or transgender does the same. . . .

[I]t's irrelevant what an employer might call its discriminatory practice, how others might label it, or what else might motivate it. . . . When an employer fires an employee for being homosexual or transgender, it necessarily and intentionally discriminates against that individual in part because of sex. And that is all Title VII has ever demanded to establish liability.

[T]he plaintiff 's sex need not be the sole or primary cause of the employer's adverse action. . . . [I]t has no significance here if another factor—such as the sex the plaintiff is attracted to or presents as—might also be at work, or even play a more important role in the employer's decision.

Finally, an employer cannot escape liability by demonstrating that it treats males and females comparably as groups. . . . [A]n employer who intentionally fires an individual homosexual or transgender employee in part because of that individual's sex violates the law even if the employer is willing to subject all male and female homosexual or transgender employees to the same rule. . . .

[T]he employers turn to Title VII's list of protected characteristics—race, color, religion, sex, and national origin. Because homosexuality and transgender status can't be found on that list and because they are conceptually distinct from sex, the employers reason, they are implicitly excluded from Title VII's reach. Put another way, if Congress had wanted to address these matters in Title VII, it would have referenced them specifically. . . .

We agree that homosexuality and transgender status are distinct concepts from sex. But, as we've seen, discrimination based on homosexuality or transgender status necessarily entails discrimination based on sex; the first cannot happen without the second. . . . [W]hen Congress chooses not to include any exceptions to a broad rule, courts apply the broad rule. And that is exactly how this Court has always approached Title VII. "Sexual harassment" is conceptually distinct from sex discrimination, but it can fall within Title VII's sweep. . . .

Since 1964, [the employers] observe, Congress has considered several proposals to add sexual orientation to Title VII's list of protected characteristics, but no such amendment has become law. Meanwhile, Congress has enacted other statutes addressing other topics that do discuss sexual orientation. This postenactment legislative history, they urge, should tell us something.

But what? There's no authoritative evidence explaining why later Congresses adopted other laws referencing sexual orientation but didn't amend this one. Maybe some in the later legislatures understood the impact Title VII's broad language already promised for cases like ours and didn't think a revision needed.

Maybe others knew about its impact but hoped no one else would notice. Maybe still others, occupied by other concerns, didn't consider the issue at all. All we can know for certain is that speculation about why a later Congress declined to adopt new legislation offers a "particularly dangerous" basis on which to rest an interpretation of an existing law a different and earlier Congress did adopt. *Sullivan v. Finkelstein*, 496 U.S. 617, 632 (1990) (Scalia, J., concurring) ("Arguments based on subsequent legislative history . . . should not be taken seriously, not even in a footnote"). . . .

[T]he employers . . . contend that few in 1964 would have expected Title VII to apply to discrimination against homosexual and transgender persons. . . . This Court has explained many times over many years that, when the meaning of the statute's terms is plain, our job is at an end. The people are entitled to rely on the law as written, without fearing that courts might disregard its plain terms based on some extratextual consideration. Of course, some Members of this Court have consulted legislative history when interpreting *ambiguous* statutory language. But that has no bearing here. "Legislative history, for those who take it into account, is meant to clear up ambiguity, not create it." And as we have seen, no ambiguity exists about how Title VII's terms apply to the facts before us. To be sure, the statute's application in these cases reaches "beyond the principal evil" legislators may have intended or expected to address. But "'the fact that [a statute] has been applied in situations not expressly anticipated by Congress'" does not demonstrate ambiguity; instead, it simply "'demonstrates [the] breadth'" of a legislative command. And "it is ultimately the provisions of" those legislative commands "rather than the principal concerns of our legislators by which we are governed."

Still, while legislative history can never defeat unambiguous statutory text, historical sources can be useful for a different purpose: Because the law's ordinary meaning at the time of enactment usually governs, we must be sensitive to the possibility a statutory term that means one thing today or in one context might have meant something else at the time of its adoption or might mean something different in another context. And we must be attuned to the possibility that a statutory phrase ordinarily bears a different meaning than the terms do when viewed individually or literally. To ferret out such shifts in linguistic usage or subtle distinctions between literal and ordinary meaning, this Court has sometimes consulted the understandings of the law's drafters as some (not always conclusive) evidence. . . .

Rather than suggesting that the statutory language bears some other *meaning*, the employers and dissents merely suggest that, because few in 1964 expected today's *result*, we should not dare to admit that it follows ineluctably from the statutory text. . . . The employers assert that "no one" in 1964 or for some time after would have anticipated today's result. . . . But to refuse enforcement just because . . . the parties before us happened to be unpopular at the time of the law's passage, would not only require us to abandon our role as interpreters of statutes; it would tilt the scales of justice in favor of the strong or popular and neglect the promise that all persons are entitled to the benefit of the law's terms.

The employer's position also proves too much. If we applied Title VII's plain text only to applications some (yet-to-be-determined) group expected in 1964, we'd have more than a little law to overturn. . . . [M]any, maybe most, applications of Title VII's sex provision were "unanticipated" at the time of the law's adoption. In fact, many now-obvious applications met with heated opposition early on, even among those tasked with enforcing the law. In the years immediately following Title VII's passage, the EEOC officially opined that listing men's positions and women's positions separately in job postings was simply helpful rather than discriminatory. Some courts held that Title VII did not prevent an employer from firing an employee for refusing his sexual advances. And courts held that a policy against hiring mothers but not fathers of young children wasn't discrimination because of sex.

Over time, though, the breadth of the statutory language proved too difficult to deny. By the end of the 1960s, the EEOC reversed its stance on sex-segregated job advertising. In 1971, this Court held that treating women with children differently from men with children violated Title VII. And by the late 1970s, courts began to recognize that sexual harassment can sometimes amount to sex discrimination. While to the modern eye each of these examples may seem "plainly [to] constitut[e] discrimination because of biological sex," all were hotly contested for years following Title VII's enactment. And as with the discrimination we consider today, many federal judges long accepted interpretations of Title VII that excluded these situations. Would the employers have us undo every one of these unexpected applications too? . . .

[T]he employers fear that complying with Title VII's requirement in cases like ours may require some employers to violate their religious convictions. We are also deeply concerned with preserving the promise of the free exercise of religion enshrined in our Constitution; that guarantee lies at the heart of our pluralistic society. But worries about how Title VII may intersect with religious liberties are nothing new; they even predate the statute's passage. As a result of its deliberations in adopting the law, Congress included an express statutory exception for religious organizations. § 2000e-1(a). This Court has also recognized that the First Amendment can bar the application of employment discrimination laws "to claims concerning the employment relationship between a religious institution and its ministers." *Hosanna-Tabor Evangelical Lutheran Church and School v. EEOC*, 565 U.S. 171, 188 (2012). And Congress has gone a step further yet in the Religious Freedom Restoration Act of 1993 (RFRA), 107 Stat. 1488, codified at 42 U.S.C. § 2000bb *et seq.* That statute prohibits the federal government from substantially burdening a person's exercise of religion unless it demonstrates that doing so both furthers a compelling governmental interest and represents the least restrictive means of furthering that interest. § 2000bb-1. Because RFRA operates as a kind of super statute, displacing the normal operation of other federal laws, it might supersede Title VII's commands in appropriate cases. See § 2000bb-3.

But how these doctrines protecting religious liberty interact with Title VII are questions for future cases too. . . . [W]hile other employers in other cases may raise free exercise arguments that merit careful consideration, none of the employers before us today represent in this Court that compliance with Title VII will infringe their own religious liberties in any way. . . .

Ours is a society of written laws. Judges are not free to overlook plain statutory commands on the strength of nothing more than suppositions about intentions or guesswork about expectations. In Title VII, Congress adopted broad language making it illegal for an employer to rely on an employee's sex when deciding to fire that employee. We do not hesitate to recognize today a necessary consequence of that legislative choice: An employer who fires an individual merely for being gay or transgender defies the law. . . .

Justice ALITO, with whom Justice THOMAS joins, dissenting.

There is only one word for what the Court has done today: legislation. The document that the Court releases is in the form of a judicial opinion interpreting a statute, but that is deceptive. . . . For the past 45 years, bills have been introduced in Congress to add "sexual orientation" to the list [of categories protected by Title VIII], and in recent years, bills have included "gender identity" as well. But to date, none has passed both Houses. . . . Usurping the constitutional authority of the other branches, the Court has essentially taken [currently proposed legislation] on employment discrimination and issued it under the guise of statutory interpretation. A more brazen abuse of our authority to interpret statutes is hard to recall.

The Court tries to convince readers that it is merely enforcing the terms of the statute, but that is preposterous. Even as understood today, the concept of discrimination because of "sex" is different from discrimination because of "sexual orientation" or "gender identity." And in any event, our duty is to interpret statutory terms to "mean what they conveyed to reasonable people *at the time they were written.*" A. Scalia & B. Garner, Reading Law: The Interpretation of Legal Texts 16 (2012) (emphasis added). If every single living American had been surveyed in 1964, it would have been hard to find any who thought that discrimination because of sex meant discrimination because of sexual orientation—not to mention gender identity, a concept that was essentially unknown at the time.

The Court attempts to pass off its decision as the inevitable product of the textualist school of statutory interpretation championed by our late colleague Justice Scalia, but no one should be fooled. The Court's opinion is like a pirate ship. It sails under a textualist flag, but what it actually represents is a theory of statutory interpretation that Justice Scalia excoriated—the theory that courts should "update" old statutes so that they better reflect the current values of society. If the Court finds it appropriate to adopt this theory, it should own up to what it is doing.

Many will applaud today's decision because they agree on policy grounds with the Court's updating of Title VII. But the question in these cases is not whether discrimination because of sexual orientation or gender identity *should be* outlawed. The question is *whether Congress did that in 1964.* It indisputably did not.

[I]t should be perfectly clear that Title VII does not reach discrimination because of sexual orientation or gender identity. If "sex" in Title VII means biologically male or female, then discrimination because of sex means discrimination because the person in question is biologically male or biologically female, not because that person is sexually attracted to members of the same sex or identifies as a member of a particular gender. . . .

The Court observes that a Title VII plaintiff need not show that "sex" was the sole or primary motive for a challenged employment decision or its sole or primary cause. . . . and that Title VII protects individual rights, not group rights.

All that is true, but so what? [T]he question we must decide comes down to this: if an individual employee or applicant for employment shows that his or her sexual orientation or gender identity was a "motivating factor" in a hiring or discharge decision, for example, is that enough to establish that the employer discriminated "because of . . . sex"? Or, to put the same question in different terms, if an employer takes an employment action solely because of the sexual orientation or gender identity of an employee or applicant, has that employer necessarily discriminated because of biological sex?

The answers to those questions must be no, unless discrimination because of sexual orientation or gender identity inherently constitutes discrimination because of sex. The Court attempts to prove that point, and it argues, not merely that the terms of Title VII *can* be interpreted that way but that they *cannot reasonably be interpreted any other way*. According to the Court, the text is unambiguous.

The arrogance of this argument is breathtaking. [T]here is not a shred of evidence that any Member of Congress interpreted the statutory text that way when Title VII was enacted. . . . [U]ntil 2017, every single Court of Appeals to consider the question interpreted Title VII's prohibition against sex discrimination to mean discrimination on the basis of biological sex. And for good measure, the Court's conclusion that Title VII unambiguously reaches discrimination on the basis of sexual orientation and gender identity necessarily means that the EEOC failed to see the obvious for the first 48 years after Title VII became law. Day in and day out, the Commission enforced Title VII but did not grasp what discrimination "because of . . . sex" unambiguously means.

The Court's argument is not only arrogant, it is wrong. It fails on its own terms. "Sex," "sexual orientation," and "gender identity" are different concepts, as the Court concedes. And neither "sexual orientation" nor "gender identity" is tied to either of the two biological sexes. Both men and women may be attracted to members of the opposite sex, members of the same sex, or members of both sexes. And individuals who are born with the genes and organs of either biological sex may identify with a different gender. . . .

Contrary to the Court's contention, discrimination because of sexual orientation or gender identity does not in and of itself entail discrimination because of sex. We can see this because it is quite possible for an employer to discriminate on those grounds without taking the sex of an individual applicant or employee into account. An employer can have a policy that says: "We do not hire gays, lesbians, or transgender individuals." And an employer can implement this policy without paying any attention to or even knowing the biological sex of gay, lesbian, and transgender applicants. In fact, at the time of the enactment of Title VII, the United States military had a blanket policy of refusing to enlist gays or lesbians, and under this policy for years thereafter, applicants for enlistment were required to complete a form that asked whether they were "homosexual."

At oral argument, the attorney representing the employees, a prominent professor of constitutional law, was asked if there would be discrimination because of sex if an employer with a blanket policy against hiring gays, lesbians, and transgender individuals implemented that policy without knowing the biological sex of any job applicants. Her candid answer was that this would "not" be sex discrimination. And she was right.

The attorney's concession was necessary, but it is fatal to the Court's interpretation, for if an employer discriminates against individual applicants or employees without even knowing whether they are male or female, it is impossible to argue that the employer intentionally discriminated because of sex. An employer cannot intentionally discriminate on the basis of a characteristic of which the employer has no knowledge. . . . [A] disparate treatment case requires proof of intent—*i.e.*, that the employee's sex motivated the firing. In short, what this example shows is that discrimination because of sexual orientation or gender identity does not inherently or necessarily entail discrimination because of sex, and for that reason, the Court's chief argument collapses. . . .

For most 21st-century Americans, it is painful to be reminded of the way our society once treated gays and lesbians, but any honest effort to understand what the terms of Title VII were understood to mean when enacted must take into account the societal norms of that time. And the plain truth is that in 1964 homosexuality was thought to be a mental disorder, and homosexual conduct was regarded as morally culpable and worthy of punishment. . . .

Society's treatment of homosexuality and homosexual conduct was consistent with this understanding. Sodomy was a crime in every State but Illinois, see W. Eskridge, Dishonorable Passions 387-407 (2008), and in the District of Columbia, a law enacted by Congress made sodomy a felony punishable by imprisonment for up to 10 years and permitted the indefinite civil commitment of "sexual psychopath[s]." . . .

To its credit, our society has now come to recognize the injustice of past practices, and this recognition provides the impetus to "update" Title VII. But that is not our job. Our duty is to understand what the terms of Title VII were understood to mean when enacted, and in doing so, we must take into account the societal norms of that time.

Justice KAVANAUGH, dissenting.

Like many cases in this Court, this case boils down to one fundamental question: Who decides? . . . The question here is whether Title VII should be expanded to prohibit employment discrimination because of sexual orientation. Under the Constitution's separation of powers, the responsibility to amend Title VII belongs to Congress and the President in the legislative process, not to this Court. . . .

For the sake of argument, I will assume that firing someone because of their sexual orientation may, as a very literal matter, entail making a distinction based on sex. But to prevail in this case with their literalist approach, the plaintiffs must *also* establish one of two other points. The plaintiffs must establish that courts, when interpreting a statute, adhere to literal meaning rather than ordinary meaning. Or alternatively, the plaintiffs must establish that the ordinary meaning of "discriminate because of sex"—not just the literal meaning—encompasses sexual orientation discrimination. The plaintiffs fall short on both counts.

[C]ourts must follow ordinary meaning, not literal meaning. And courts must adhere to the ordinary meaning of phrases, not just the meaning of the words in a phrase . . . for two main reasons: rule of law and democratic accountability. A society governed by the rule of law must have laws that are known and understandable to the citizenry. . . . Both the rule of law and democratic accountability badly suffer when a court adopts a hidden or obscure interpretation of the law, and not its ordinary meaning. . . .

[T]he question in this case boils down to the ordinary meaning of the phrase "discriminate because of sex." Does the ordinary meaning of that phrase encompass discrimination because of sexual orientation? The answer is plainly no.

On occasion, it can be difficult for judges to assess ordinary meaning. Not here. Both common parlance and common legal usage treat sex discrimination and sexual orientation discrimination as two distinct categories of discrimination—back in 1964 and still today. . . .

Consider the employer who has four employees but must fire two of them for financial reasons. Suppose the four employees are a straight man, a straight woman, a gay man, and a lesbian. The employer with animosity against women (animosity based on sex) will fire the two women. The employer with animosity against gays (animosity based on sexual orientation) will fire the gay man and the lesbian. Those are two distinct harms caused by two distinct biases that have two different outcomes. To treat one as a form of the other—as the majority opinion does—misapprehends common language, human psychology, and real life.

It also rewrites history. Seneca Falls was not Stonewall. The women's rights movement was not (and is not) the gay rights movement, although many people obviously support or participate in both. So to think that sexual orientation discrimination is just a form of sex discrimination is not just a mistake of language and psychology, but also a mistake of history and sociology.

Importantly, an overwhelming body of federal law reflects and reinforces the ordinary meaning and demonstrates that sexual orientation discrimination is distinct from, and not a form of, sex discrimination. Since enacting Title VII in 1964, Congress has never treated sexual orientation discrimination the same as, or as a form of, sex discrimination. Instead, Congress has consistently treated sex discrimination and sexual orientation discrimination as legally distinct categories of discrimination.

Many federal statutes prohibit sex discrimination, and many federal statutes also prohibit sexual orientation discrimination. But those sexual orientation statutes expressly prohibit sexual orientation discrimination in addition to expressly prohibiting sex discrimination. *Every single one.* To this day, Congress has never defined sex discrimination to encompass sexual orientation discrimination. Instead, when Congress wants to prohibit sexual orientation discrimination in addition to sex discrimination, Congress explicitly refers to sexual orientation discrimination.

That longstanding and widespread congressional practice matters. When interpreting statutes, as the Court has often said, we "usually presume differences in language" convey "differences in meaning." When Congress chooses distinct phrases to accomplish distinct purposes, and does so over and over again for decades, we may not lightly toss aside all of Congress's careful handiwork. . . .

I have the greatest, and unyielding, respect for my colleagues and for their good faith. But when this Court usurps the role of Congress, as it does today, the public understandably becomes confused about who the policymakers really are in our system of separated powers, and inevitably becomes cynical about the oft-repeated aspiration that judges base their decisions on law rather than on personal preference. The best way for judges to demonstrate that we are deciding cases based on the ordinary meaning of the law is to walk the walk, even in the hard cases when we might prefer a different policy outcome.

In judicially rewriting Title VII, the Court today cashiers an ongoing legislative process, at a time when a new law to prohibit sexual orientation discrimination was probably close at hand. . . .

Instead of a hard-earned victory won through the democratic process, today's victory is brought about by judicial dictate—judges latching on to a novel form of living literalism to rewrite ordinary meaning and remake American law. Under the Constitution and laws of the United States, this Court is the wrong body to change American law in that way. The Court's ruling "comes at a great cost to representative self-government." And the implications of this Court's usurpation of the legislative process will likely reverberate in unpredictable ways for years to come.

Notwithstanding my concern about the Court's transgression of the Constitution's separation of powers, it is appropriate to acknowledge the important victory achieved today by gay and lesbian Americans. Millions of gay and lesbian Americans have worked hard for many decades to achieve equal treatment in fact and in law. They have exhibited extraordinary vision, tenacity, and grit—battling often steep odds in the legislative and judicial arenas, not to mention in their daily lives. They have advanced powerful policy arguments and can take pride in today's result. Under the Constitution's separation of powers, however, I believe that it was Congress's role, not this Court's, to amend Title VII. I therefore must respectfully dissent from the Court's judgment.

DISCUSSION

1. *The interaction of statutory and constitutional law.* This casebook concerns constitutional law, not legislation. However, we regularly pay attention to the relationship between the development of constitutional norms and key statutes, such as the Civil Rights Act of 1964. As noted in the casebook, federal courts interpreted Title VII and the Equal Protection Clause together until Washington v. Davis in 1976. It is therefore worth asking what effect the Court's interpretation of Title VII in *Bostock* will have on the Court's equal protection jurisprudence.

There are two reasons this might happen. The first is external to legal doctrine: The general acceptance of equality rights for LGBTQ people in federal and state statutes might encourage the Court to recognize discrimination against sexual orientation minorities as a new suspect classification. The Court has not recognized a new suspect classification since the 1970s. However, during this period, the growth of statutory protections for sex equality led the Justices to their 1970s sex equality jurisprudence.

The second reason is internal to legal doctrine: Justice Gorsuch adopts an argument about the connection between sex discrimination and discrimination against gays and against transgender people that might easily be adapted to the Court's sex equality jurisprudence.

There are, of course, differences between the text of Title VII and the language of the Equal Protection Clause. Title VII speaks of "discriminat[ion]" against "individuals" "because of" "sex." The Equal Protection Clause uses none of these words. However, equal protection jurisprudence, as it has developed since the 1970s, focuses on discrimination, emphasizes that the protection of individuals and not groups is its central concern, and recognizes sex as a quasi-suspect classification.

Finally, the argument made by the dissenters—that we should be bound by what the adopters of a law believed would be its effect—plays little role in sex equality jurisprudence. Were the Justices to argue that the adopters of the Fourteenth Amendment did not expect that it would protect gays or transgender people, they would have to deal with the problem that the same adopters did not think that the new amendment would protect equality (at least in our modern sense) for married women either.

2. *Discrimination "on the basis of" sex.* What do you make of Justice Gorsuch's argument that one cannot discriminate on the basis of sexual orientation or transgender status without discriminating on the basis of sex? Suppose an employer

announces that he will not hire any homosexual or transgender people, sight unseen. Does this policy discriminate on the basis of sex, since presumably it applies to men and women alike?

Pointing to the text, Justice Gorsuch's responds that the policy discriminates against each affected *individual*—because for each individual, they could have been hired if their birth sex were the opposite. Thus, women who are sexually attracted to women could have been hired if they were men sexually attracted to women. Those born as women who now identify as men could have been hired if they were born as men and now identify as men. Do you agree with this argument?

Justice Gorsuch essentially adopts Andrew Koppelman's argument, made 25 years ago, that discrimination against gays and lesbians is sex discrimination, pure and simple. See Andrew Koppelman, Why Discrimination Against Lesbians and Gay Men Is Sex Discrimination, 69 N.Y.U. L. Rev. 197 (1994). An alternative view is that sexual orientation discrimination relies on similar mechanisms as sex discrimination—punishing those who do not conform to traditional gender roles and stereotypes—but is not the same thing.

3. *Bisexual erasure.* Does Gorsuch's argument work for bisexuals? Suppose an employer argues that gays, lesbians, and straights are perfectly fine, but not people attracted to both sexes. Does the employer discriminate against each individual bisexual applicant on the basis of their sex? Presumably if the applicants were of the opposite sex, they would still be bisexual. What, if anything, does this example tell us about using sex discrimination law to prevent discrimination against sexual orientation minorities? Cf. Kenji Yoshino, The Epistemic Contract of Bisexual Erasure, 52 Stan. L. Rev. 353 (2000) (arguing that both gays and straights have reasons to forget about the existence of bisexuals in anti-discrimination law).

4. *Statutory versus constitutional interpretation—institutional considerations.* If Justice Gorsuch—and Chief Justice Roberts, who joined his opinion—are willing to accept that sexual orientation discrimination is sex discrimination in interpreting a statute like Title VII, should they also accept it in interpreting the Equal Protection Clause? If they accept it as a constitutional matter, then a constitutional right to marriage equality becomes an easy case.

Note that Chief Justice Roberts dissented vigorously in Obergefell v. Hodges, arguing that the issue should have been left to the democratic process. Would he argue that interpreting Title VII is one thing, because Congress can change the statute if it does not like the Court's interpretation, but that interpreting the Constitution is a very different matter? Do you agree?

5. *Textualism and/or originalism.* The conservative Justices debate the role of "textualism" in statutory interpretation, each claiming the mantle of Justice Scalia, who championed this approach. Essentially, textualism in statutory interpretation argues that in interpreting a statute, the text is the primary consideration. Conversely, legislative history—in the sense of the intentions of the statute's adopters—should play no role, and cannot counteract the meaning of the text. Instead, interpreters should use various canons of construction to clarify the text where it is ambiguous or unclear.

As the opinions of Justices Gorsuch, Alito, and Kavanaugh make clear, there are many different ways to be a textualist. In the hands of Alito and Kavanaugh, textualism starts to look very much like an inquiry into the understandings of the adopters, although both insist that they are only interested in the original meaning of the words of the statute in 1964. Gorsuch argues that their textualism is precisely the sort of inquiry into the adopters' expectations that Justice Scalia foreswore. They respond that Gorsuch's textualism has been cut loose from the adopters' meanings to reach radical results, with Alito even comparing it to a pirate ship flying under a false flag.

One can make a similar point about the different ways of doing originalism. Whereas textualism argues that the central concern of interpretation should be the text, originalism argues that interpretation should be bound by what has been fixed at the time of adoption, whether that thing is original intentions, original understanding, or original meaning. According to the most widely adopted version of originalism these days, original public meaning originalism, constitutional interpreters should be bound by the meaning the text had to the public at the time of adoption, but not the secret intentions of any of its drafters or adopters.

In theory, original public meaning originalism could reach very liberal results, including constitutional protections for LGBTQ people. That is because the original public meaning of "equal protection of the laws" is the same today as it was in 1868 when the Fourteenth Amendment was adopted. See Jack M. Balkin, Living Originalism (2011). The proper question is whether today's laws give LGBTQ people the "equal protection of the laws." If they do not, then it does not matter that most people in 1868 would likely have disagreed.

In practice, however, conservative originalists tend to focus on how lawyers would have construed the text at the time of adoption. This focus on original legal meaning generally produces results that resemble what the adopting generation would have expected the text to do. Justice Thomas's opinions offer many examples of this approach.

Justice Gorsuch's opinion in *Bostock* has led to a reassessment of whether the conservative legal movement's embrace of textualism and originalism continues to make sense if it is going to produce such unexpected results. For examples of this debate, see Senator Josh Hawley, Was It All for This? The Failure of the Conservative Legal Movement, Public Discourse, June 16, 2020, https://www.thepublicdiscourse.com/2020/06/65043/; Jesse Merriam, Legal Conservatism after *Bostock*, Law and Liberty, June 29, 2020, https://lawliberty.org/legal-conservatism-after-bostock/.

MASTERPIECE CAKESHOP v. COLORADO CIVIL RIGHTS COMMISSION, 138 S. Ct. 1719 (2018): The owner of Masterpiece Cakeshop, Jack Philips, refused to bake a custom wedding cake for a gay couple planning their wedding, although he was willing to sell them goods already prepared. The Colorado Civil Rights Commission fined him for violating the state's public accommodation law, which prohibits discrimination on the basis of sexual orientation. Philips sued in federal court. He argued that baking a custom wedding cake was artistic expression, and he had a free speech right not to be compelled to say things he did not believe. He also argued that the fine violated his religious liberty.

The Supreme Court, in a narrow 7-2 decision by Justice Kennedy, sent the case back to the Colorado Civil Rights Commission for further proceedings. Kennedy argued that there was evidence that some of the members of the Commission had been motivated by anti-religious bias, and argued that Philips was entitled to a hearing that was not so tainted. Justice Ginsburg and Justice Sotomayor dissented.

Fulton v. City of Philadelphia

141 S. Ct. 1868 (2021)

[Philadelphia's foster care system relies on cooperation between the City and private foster care agencies. The City enters standard annual contracts with the agencies to place children with foster families. One of the responsibilities of the agencies is certifying prospective foster families under state statutory criteria.

For over 50 years, petitioner Catholic Social Services (CSS) had contracted with the City to provide foster care services. Because CSS believes that certification of prospective foster families is an endorsement of their relationships, it will not certify same-sex couples or unmarried couples—regardless of their sexual orientation. Other private foster agencies in Philadelphia will certify same-sex couples, and no same-sex couple has sought certification from CSS.

Following an investigation of CSS's practices, the City told CSS that unless CSS agreed to certify same-sex couples the City would no longer refer children to the agency or enter a full foster care contract with it in the future. The City explained that the refusal of CSS to certify same-sex married couples violated both a non-discrimination provision in the agency's contract with the City as well as the non-discrimination requirements of the citywide Fair Practices Ordinance. CSS and three affiliated foster parents filed suit seeking to enjoin the City's referral freeze on the grounds that the City's actions violated the Free Exercise and Free Speech Clauses of the First Amendment.]

Chief Justice ROBERTS delivered the opinion of the Court.

[Under Employment Division, Department of Human Resources of Oregon v. Smith, 494 U.S. 872 (1990)], laws incidentally burdening religion are ordinarily not subject to strict scrutiny under the Free Exercise Clause so long as they are neutral and generally applicable. CSS urges us to overrule *Smith*, and the concurrences in the judgment argue in favor of doing so. But we need not revisit that decision here. This case falls outside Smith because the City has burdened the religious exercise of CSS through policies that do not meet the requirement of being neutral and generally applicable. See Church of Lukumi Babalu Aye, Inc. v. Hialeah, 508 U.S. 520 (1993). . . .

A law is not generally applicable if it "invite[s]" the government to consider the particular reasons for a person's conduct by providing " 'a mechanism for individualized exemptions.' " *Smith.* For example, in Sherbert v. Verner, 374 U.S. 398 (1963), a Seventh-day Adventist was fired because she would not work on Saturdays. Unable to find a job that would allow her to keep the Sabbath as her faith required, she applied for unemployment benefits. The State denied her application under a law prohibiting eligibility to claimants who had "failed, without good cause . . . to accept available suitable work." We held that the denial infringed her free exercise rights and could be justified only by a compelling interest.

Smith later explained that the unemployment benefits law in *Sherbert* was not generally applicable because the "good cause" standard permitted the government to grant exemptions based on the circumstances underlying each application. Smith went on to hold that "where the State has in place a system of individual exemptions, it may not refuse to extend that system to cases of 'religious hardship' without compelling reason."

A law also lacks general applicability if it prohibits religious conduct while permitting secular conduct that undermines the government's asserted interests in a similar way. In Church of Lukumi Babalu Aye, Inc. v. Hialeah, for instance, the City of Hialeah adopted several ordinances prohibiting animal sacrifice, a practice of the Santeria faith. The City claimed that the ordinances were necessary in part to protect public health, which was "threatened by the disposal of animal carcasses in open public places." But the ordinances did not regulate hunters' disposal of their kills or improper garbage disposal by restaurants, both of which posed a similar hazard. The Court concluded that this and other forms of underinclusiveness meant that the ordinances were not generally applicable. . . .

[S]ection 3.21 of [the City's] standard foster care contract . . . specifies in pertinent part: "Rejection of Referral. Provider shall not reject a child or family including, but not limited to, . . . prospective foster or adoptive parents, for Services based upon . . . their . . . sexual orientation . . . unless an exception is granted by the Commissioner or the Commissioner's designee, in his/her sole discretion." . . .

Like the good cause provision in *Sherbert*, section 3.21 incorporates a system of individual exemptions, made available in this case at the "sole discretion" of the Commissioner. The City has made clear that the Commissioner "has no intention of granting an exception" to CSS. But the City "may not refuse to extend that [exemption] system to cases of 'religious hardship' without compelling reason." *Smith.*

The City and intervenor-respondents . . . argue that governments should enjoy greater leeway under the Free Exercise Clause when setting rules for contractors than when regulating the general public. . . . We have never suggested that the government may discriminate against religion when acting in its managerial role. And *Smith* itself drew support for the neutral and generally applicable standard from cases involving internal government affairs. . . . The City and intervenor-respondents accordingly ask only that courts apply a more deferential approach in determining whether a policy is neutral and generally applicable in the contracting context. We find no need to resolve that narrow issue in this case. No matter the level of deference we extend to the City, the inclusion of a formal system of entirely discretionary exceptions in section 3.21 renders the contractual non-discrimination requirement not generally applicable. . . .

[T]he City and intervenor-respondents contend that the availability of exceptions under section 3.21 is irrelevant because the Commissioner has never granted one. That misapprehends the issue. The creation of a formal mechanism for granting exceptions renders a policy not generally applicable, regardless whether any exceptions have been given, because it "invite[s]" the government to decide which reasons for not complying with the policy are worthy of solicitude — here, at the Commissioner's "sole discretion." . . .

The City contends that foster care agencies are public accommodations [under a city ordinance that bans discrimination on the basis of sexual orientation and marital status] and therefore forbidden from discriminating on the basis of sexual orientation when certifying foster parents. . . . [But] foster care agencies do not act as public accommodations in performing certifications. [Under Pennsylvania law] a public accommodation must "provide a benefit to the general public allowing individual members of the general public to avail themselves of that benefit if they so desire."

Certification as a foster parent, by contrast, is not readily accessible to the public. It involves a customized and selective assessment that bears little resemblance to staying in a hotel, eating at a restaurant, or riding a bus. The process takes three to six months. Applicants must pass background checks and a medical exam. Foster agencies are required to conduct an intensive home study during which they evaluate, among other things, applicants' "mental and emotional adjustment," "community ties with family, friends, and neighbors," and "[e]xisting family relationships, attitudes and expectations regarding the applicant's own children and parent/child relationships." Such inquiries would raise eyebrows at the local bus station. And agencies understandably approach this sensitive process from different angles. As the City itself explains to prospective foster parents, "[e]ach agency has slightly different requirements, specialties, and training programs." All of this confirms that the one-size-fits-all public accommodations model is a poor match for the foster care system. . . .

The City asserts that its non-discrimination policies serve three compelling interests: maximizing the number of foster parents, protecting the City from liability, and ensuring equal treatment of prospective foster parents and foster children. . . . Rather than rely on "broadly formulated interests," courts must "scrutinize[ ] the asserted harm of granting specific exemptions to particular religious claimants." The question, then, is not whether the City has a compelling interest in enforcing its non-discrimination policies generally, but whether it has such an interest in denying an exception to CSS.

Once properly narrowed, the City's asserted interests are insufficient. Maximizing the number of foster families and minimizing liability are important goals, but the City fails to show that granting CSS an exception will put those goals at risk. If anything, including CSS in the program seems likely to increase, not reduce, the number of available foster parents. As for liability, the City offers only speculation that it might be sued over CSS's certification practices. Such speculation is insufficient to satisfy strict scrutiny, particularly because the authority to certify foster families is delegated to agencies by the State, not the City.

That leaves the interest of the City in the equal treatment of prospective foster parents and foster children. We do not doubt that this interest is a weighty one, for "[o]ur society has come to the recognition that gay persons and gay couples cannot be treated as social outcasts or as inferior in dignity and worth." On the facts of this case, however, this interest cannot justify denying CSS an exception for its religious exercise. The creation of a system of exceptions under the contract undermines the City's contention that its non-discrimination policies can brook no departures. See *Lukumi.* The City offers no compelling reason why it has a particular interest in denying an exception to CSS while making them available to others. . . .

CSS seeks only an accommodation that will allow it to continue serving the children of Philadelphia in a manner consistent with its religious beliefs; it does not seek to impose those beliefs on anyone else. The refusal of Philadelphia to contract with CSS for the provision of foster care services unless it agrees to certify same-sex couples as foster parents cannot survive strict scrutiny, and violates the First Amendment.

Justice BARRETT, with whom Justice KAVANAUGH joins, and with whom Justice BREYER joins as to all but the first paragraph, concurring.

In . . . *Smith*, this Court held that a neutral and generally applicable law typically does not violate the Free Exercise Clause—no matter how severely that law burdens religious exercise. . . . I find the historical record more silent than supportive on the question whether the founding generation understood the First Amendment to require religious exemptions from generally applicable laws in at least some circumstances. In my view, the textual and structural arguments against *Smith* are more compelling. As a matter of text and structure, it is difficult to see why the Free Exercise Clause—lone among the First Amendment freedoms—offers nothing more than protection from discrimination.

Yet what should replace *Smith*? The prevailing assumption seems to be that strict scrutiny would apply whenever a neutral and generally applicable law burdens religious exercise. But I am skeptical about swapping *Smith*'s categorical antidiscrimination approach for an equally categorical strict scrutiny regime, particularly when this Court's resolution of conflicts between generally applicable laws and other First Amendment rights—like speech and assembly—has been much more nuanced. There would be a number of issues to work through if *Smith* were overruled. To name a few: Should entities like Catholic Social Services—which is an arm of the Catholic Church—be treated differently than individuals? Should there be a distinction between indirect and direct burdens on religious exercise? What forms of scrutiny should apply? And if the answer is strict scrutiny, would pre-*Smith* cases rejecting free exercise challenges to garden-variety laws come out the same way?

We need not wrestle with these questions in this case, though, because the same standard applies regardless whether *Smith* stays or goes. A longstanding tenet of our free exercise jurisprudence—one that both pre-dates and survives *Smith*—is that a law burdening religious exercise must satisfy strict scrutiny if it gives government officials discretion to grant individualized exemptions. . . . As the Court's opinion today explains, the government contract at issue provides for individualized exemptions from its nondiscrimination rule, thus triggering strict scrutiny. And all nine Justices agree that the City cannot satisfy strict scrutiny. I therefore see no reason to decide in this case whether *Smith* should be overruled, much less what should replace it. I join the Court's opinion in full.

Justice ALITO, with whom Justice THOMAS and Justice GORSUCH join, concurring in the judgment.

This case presents an important constitutional question that urgently calls out for review: whether this Court's governing interpretation of a bedrock constitutional right, the right to the free exercise of religion, is fundamentally wrong and should be corrected. . . .

If *Smith* is overruled, what legal standard should be applied in this case? The answer that comes most readily to mind is the standard that *Smith* replaced: A law that imposes a substantial burden on religious exercise can be sustained only if it is narrowly tailored to serve a compelling government interest.

Whether this test should be rephrased or supplemented with specific rules is a question that need not be resolved here because Philadelphia's ouster of CSS from foster care work simply does not further any interest that can properly be protected in this case. As noted, CSS's policy has not hindered any same-sex couples from becoming foster parents, and there is no threat that it will do so in the future.

CSS's policy has only one effect: It expresses the idea that same-sex couples should not be foster parents because only a man and a woman should marry. Many people today find this idea not only objectionable but hurtful. Nevertheless, protecting against this form of harm is not an interest that can justify the abridgment of First Amendment rights.

We have covered this ground repeatedly in free speech cases. In an open, pluralistic, self-governing society, the expression of an idea cannot be suppressed simply because some find it offensive, insulting, or even wounding. . . . The same fundamental principle applies to religious practices that give offense. The preservation of religious freedom depends on that principle. Many core religious beliefs are perceived as hateful by members of other religions or nonbelievers. Proclaiming that there is only one God is offensive to polytheists, and saying that there are many gods is anathema to Jews, Christians, and Muslims. Declaring that Jesus was the Son of God is offensive to Judaism and Islam, and stating that Jesus was not the Son of God is insulting to Christian belief. Expressing a belief in God is nonsense to atheists, but denying the existence of God or proclaiming that religion has been a plague is infuriating to those for whom religion is all-important.

Suppressing speech—or religious practice—simply because it expresses an idea that some find hurtful is a zero-sum game. While CSS's ideas about marriage are likely to be objectionable to same-sex couples, lumping those who hold traditional beliefs about marriage together with racial bigots is insulting to those who retain such beliefs. In Obergefell v. Hodges, the majority made a commitment. It refused to equate traditional beliefs about marriage, which it termed "decent and honorable," with racism, which is neither. And it promised that "religions, and those who adhere to religious doctrines, may continue to advocate with utmost, sincere conviction that, by divine precepts, same-sex marriage should not be condoned." An open society can keep that promise while still respecting the "dignity," "worth," and fundamental equality of all members of the community. *Masterpiece Cakeshop.*

Justice GORSUCH, with whom Justice THOMAS and Justice ALITO join, concurring in the judgment.

Had we followed the path Justice Alito outlines—holding that the City's rules cannot avoid strict scrutiny even if they qualify as neutral and generally applicable—this case would end today. Instead, the majority's course guarantees that this litigation is only getting started. As the final arbiter of state law, the Pennsylvania Supreme Court can effectively overrule the majority's reading of the Commonwealth's public accommodations law. The City can revise its FPO to make even plainer still that its law does encompass foster services. Or with a flick of a pen, municipal lawyers may rewrite the City's contract to close the § 3.21 loophole.

Once any of that happens, CSS will find itself back where it started. . . . those who cannot afford such endless litigation under *Smith*'s regime have been and will continue to be forced to forfeit religious freedom that the Constitution protects. . . . We hardly need to "wrestle" today with every conceivable question that might follow from recognizing *Smith* was wrong. . . . Rather than adhere to *Smith* until we settle on some "grand unified theory" of the Free Exercise Clause for all future cases until the end of time, the Court should overrule it now, set us back on the correct course, and address each case as it comes.

What possible benefit does the majority see in its studious indecision about *Smith* when the costs are so many? The particular appeal before us arises at the intersection of public accommodations laws and the First Amendment; it involves same-sex couples and the Catholic Church. Perhaps our colleagues believe today's circuitous path will at least steer the Court around the controversial subject matter and avoid "picking a side." But refusing to give CSS the benefit of what we know to be the correct interpretation of the Constitution is picking a side. *Smith* committed a constitutional error. Only we can fix it. Dodging the question today guarantees it will recur tomorrow. These cases will keep coming until the Court musters the fortitude to supply an answer. Respectfully, it should have done so today.

DISCUSSION

1. *The fate of* Smith. As Justice Alito explains, from the 1960s to the 1990 decision in *Smith,* the basic rule was that "[a] law that imposes a substantial burden on religious exercise can be sustained only if it is narrowly tailored to serve a compelling government interest." In practice, however, the Court did not actually apply "strict scrutiny" very strictly in cases involving religious liberty. Instead, the Court engaged in a balancing test and in some cases petitioners lost even though their religious exercise was burdened. (Justice Barrett mentions the "pre-*Smith* cases rejecting free exercise challenges to garden-variety laws" in her concurrence.)

In *Fulton,* the Supreme Court majority sought to avoid deciding whether to overrule *Smith,* in part because doing so would lead fairly directly to the questions of (1) the appropriate standard of review and (2) whether the Free Exercise Clause trumps public accommodations laws that protect LGBTQ people from discrimination. How would Justices Alito, Thomas, and Gorsuch answer these questions? Note Alito's implicit comparison of restrictions on free exercise to content-based restrictions on speech. Are there any important differences between the two situations? For example, when a hotel turns away a same-sex couple in violation of a public accommodations statute, is the hotel merely expressing a message disfavored by the government? Free exercise cases turn out to be most difficult to decide when exemptions from generally applicable laws concentrate their effects on innocent third parties.

2. *Strict scrutiny versus individualized exemptions versus most-favored-nation.* The majority in *Fulton* employs a doctrine derived from Sherbert v. Verner (and *Smith*) to decide the case narrowly: Laws are not "generally applicable" and thus subject to strict scrutiny if they allow "government to consider the particular reasons for a person's conduct by providing 'a mechanism for individualized exemptions.'"

This "individualized exemptions" test is narrower than another test that came out of the Court's encounter with COVID-19 restrictions in the states. The Court decided a series of cases in which religious plaintiffs sought injunctive relief from state and local COVID restrictions. The Court decided these petitions on an expedited basis without holding full briefing and oral argument. Tandon v. Newsom, 141 S. Ct. 129 (2021) (per curiam); Roman Catholic Diocese of Brooklyn v. Cuomo, 141 S. Ct. 63, 67-68 (2020) (per curiam). In *Tandon* and *Cuomo,* the Court upheld the injunctions. A third case, South Bay United Pentecostal Church v. Newsom, 141 S. Ct. 716 (2020), which allowed the COVID regulations to remain in place, was decided before Justice Ginsburg was replaced by Justice Barrett.

In *Tandon* and *Cuomo*, a majority of the Court advanced a more capacious theory of Free Exercise Clause, sometimes called the "most favored nation" doctrine. The Court outlined the basic elements in *Tandon*:

> First, government regulations are not neutral and generally applicable, and therefore trigger strict scrutiny under the Free Exercise Clause, whenever they treat *any* comparable secular activity more favorably than religious exercise. It is no answer that a State treats some comparable secular businesses or other activities as poorly as or even less favorably than the religious exercise at issue.
>
> Second, whether two activities are comparable for purposes of the Free Exercise Clause must be judged against the asserted government interest that justifies the regulation at issue. Comparability is concerned with the risks various activities pose, not the reasons why people gather.
>
> Third, the government has the burden to establish that the challenged law satisfies strict scrutiny. [In the context of COVID regulations that limit both religious gatherings and secular activities], it must do more than assert that certain risk factors "are always present in worship, or always absent from the other secular activities" the government may allow. Instead, narrow tailoring requires the government to show that measures less restrictive of the First Amendment activity could not address its interest in reducing the spread of COVID. Where the government permits other activities to proceed with precautions, it must show that the religious exercise at issue is more dangerous than those activities even when the same precautions are applied. Otherwise, precautions that suffice for other activities suffice for religious exercise too.
>
> Fourth, even if the government withdraws or modifies a COVID restriction in the course of litigation, that does not necessarily moot the case. And so long as a case is not moot, litigants otherwise entitled to emergency injunctive relief remain entitled to such relief where the applicants "remain under a constant threat" that government officials will use their power to reinstate the challenged restrictions.

The individualized exemptions rule employed in *Fulton* looks to whether the state has discretion to create individualized exemptions that might disfavor religion. As Chief Justice Roberts explains, it is irrelevant whether the state has actually granted any exemptions. The issue is unreviewable discretion: whether state officials can "decide which reasons for not complying with the policy are worthy of solicitude." The concern is that discretion may allow implicit discrimination against, or lack of appropriate concern for, religious liberty.

By contrast, the "most-favored-nation" theory asks whether a statute has any comparable secular exemptions. The principle here is if the state thinks that some value requires an exemption for some secular activity, religious activity should be treated at least as well. The way to protect religious freedom, in other words, is to ensure that no secular value gets treated better.

One issue raised by the most-favored-nation theory is that most statutes have exceptions and exemptions. "If a law with even a few secular exceptions isn't neutral and generally applicable, then not many laws are. Exceptions grease the wheels for legislation; legislators often exempt their friends and contributors, and they exempt interest groups that might be strong enough to block passage of the bill." Douglas Laycock, The Broader Implications of *Masterpiece Cakeshop*, 2019 BYU L. Rev. 167, 173 (2019).

This concern has special relevance for antidiscrimination laws and public accommodations laws. Under the most-favored-nation theory, any secular exemption from an antidiscrimination or public accommodation statute might trigger strict scrutiny under the Free Exercise Clause. To be sure, the test requires that the exempted secular activity must be "comparable" to religious activity. But judges have considerable leeway in deciding what secular activities are comparable to religious activities. For example in *Cuomo*, the majority thought it was clearly discriminatory to treat church services differently than "a grocery store, pet store, or big-box store down the street." The dissenters, by contrast, argued that these situations were not comparable, because "people neither congregate in large groups nor remain in close proximity for extended periods" in the secular spaces. *Cuomo* (Sotomayor, J., dissenting). The dissenters believed that the appropriate comparison was "secular gatherings, including lectures, concerts, movie showings, spectator sports, and theatrical performances, where large groups of people gather in close proximity for extended periods of time," and which were subject to the same restrictions as religious services.

D. Backlash and Social Movements

In the wake of the decisions in *Baehr* and *Goodridge*, the judiciary's role in securing rights for same-sex couples became the subject of intense political controversy. Concern about the role of courts spiked again in the lead-up to the Court's decisions in *Windsor* and *Perry* when opponents, and even many supporters of marriage equality, counseled the Court against recognizing a right to marry nationwide.[226] The concern repeated again and again was that a judicial decision protecting the constitutional rights of same-sex couples would spark "backlash."

Concerns about backlash perennially surface in debates about abortion and same-sex marriage, but the concerns at issue are not always clear. One way of understanding backlash is that it is a healthy part of political contestation, which occurs when groups mobilize against an outcome that they oppose. When used in relation to court rulings, however, commentators often invoke concerns specifically associated with courts, evoking a special kind of dysfunctional and virulent politics that results from (unwise or precipitous) judicial intervention on behalf of minority rights.

Response to the first decisions recognizing the rights of same-sex couples to marry initially provoked some scholars to warn that judicial intervention would be counterproductive. In recent years, several have revised and qualified these claims.[227]

---

226. For supporters, see, e.g., David Cole, Deciding Not to Decide Gay Marriage, N.Y. Times, Mar. 25, 2013; Kerry Eleveld, The Supreme Court's Middle Option: A Nine-State Solution, The Advocate, Mar. 22, 2013.

227. See, e.g., Michael J. Klarman, From the Closet to the Altar: Courts, Backlash, and the Struggle for Same-Sex Marriage (2012); William Eskridge, Backlash Politics: How Constitutional Litigation Has Advanced Marriage Equality in the United States, 93 B.U. L. Rev. 275 (2013).

1. The Judicial Backlash Thesis

Professor Michael Klarman has argued: "Court rulings such as *Brown* and *Goodridge* produce political backlashes for three principal reasons: They raise the salience of an issue, they incite anger over 'outside interference' or 'judicial activism,' and they alter the order in which social change would otherwise have occurred."[228]

Klarman sees the judiciary as especially likely to generate backlash, and therefore is critical of activists who seek swift judicial remedies rather than patiently working for success in popular or legislative campaigns. Gerald Rosenberg extended this view to the litigation campaign for same-sex marriage. In the second edition of *The Hollow Hope*, released in 2008, a new section on same-sex marriage faulted advocates for falling into the same trap as the litigators in Brown v. Board of Education and Roe v. Wade. Rosenberg argued that litigating marriage was not worth its costs, which included significant collateral damage to campaigns for same-sex marriage, gay rights, and liberal candidates and causes more broadly.[229]

2. Skeptics of the Judicial Backlash Thesis

Many scholars read the historical record differently and question whether this judicial backlash narrative is borne out in fact. They argue that we should see popular response to judicial decisions in larger context, as a normal part of politics—not reflecting judicial repression of politics, but rather as a dynamic of conflict that occurs whether change happens in courts, legislatures, and popular referenda. We can understand such contests not as examples of political dysfunction, but rather as a practice of popular constitutionalism, in which citizens form constitutional meanings through mobilization and countermobilization.[230] Courts are not necessarily the central actors in the mobilization/countermobilization dynamic. For example, although many people often point to Roe v. Wade as the prime example of backlash against the judiciary, the escalating conflict over abortion actually began in state legislatures well before the Court ruled; so too did the Republican Party's efforts to use the abortion issue to recruit Catholic voters from their historic association with

---

228. Michael J. Klarman, *Brown* and *Lawrence* (and *Goodridge*), 104 Mich. L. Rev. 431, 473 (2005). But see Klarman, From the Closet to the Altar, supra n.227 (offering a more temperate account of the backlash phenomenon).

229. Gerald N. Rosenberg, The Hollow Hope: Can Courts Bring About Social Change? 339-341 (1991). But see Laura Beth Nielsen, Social Movements, Social Process: A Response to Gerald Rosenberg, 42 J. Marshall L. Rev. 671, 673 (2009) (accusing backlash theorists of ignoring how marriage equality advocates have "employed all the strategies of traditional civil rights movements including violence, direct action, community organizing, political strategies, education, and . . . parades").

230. See Reva Siegel, Constitutional Culture, Social Movement Conflict and Constitutional Change: The Case of the De Facto ERA, 94 Cal. L. Rev. 1323 (2006); Robert Post and Reva Siegel, *Roe* Rage: Democratic Constitutionalism and Backlash, 42 Harv. C.R.-C.L. L. Rev. 373 (2007); Reva B. Siegel, Community in Conflict: Same-Sex Marriage and Backlash, 64 UCLA L. Rev. 1728 (2017).

the Democratic Party.[231] Litigation is by no means the only cause of constitutional conflict. Constitutional conflict unfolds in contests over legislation, referenda, and Article V amendments; in political strategies for reshaping coalitions and realigning political parties; and in the conduct of presidential elections and other political campaigns.

Many scholars have questioned whether judicial decisions upholding rights to same-sex marriage have a special propensity to ignite counterproductive forms of backlash. In the marriage context, Scott Lemieux observes that legislative and popular campaigns have fared at least as badly as litigation. When the political branches have taken action to secure rights for same-sex couples, their efforts met with similarly stiff resistance.[232]

Moreover, a number of scholars have argued that conflict—i.e., backlash—has positive as well as negative effects, and is an integral part of political change. For example, some scholars have shown how even losses in marriage litigation had quite valuable results for the marriage equality movement. Thomas Keck has argued that court decisions often work in dialogue with legislative reform to produce change. Judicial decisions can raise popular expectations, provoke mobilization, remove barriers to change, alter the agenda of lawmakers, and recast less sweeping reform legislation as a welcome compromise.[233]

To the skeptics, concerns about backlash to judicial decisions are not necessarily mistaken—both court decisions and legislation may prompt countermobilization. Rather, the costs of litigation need to be evaluated in light of the potential benefits across a wide range of social contexts, and there is no reason to assume that costs and benefits will be the same in all cases. Jane Schacter is skeptical that general principles explain or predict backlash. She points out that Perez v. Sharp, 32 Cal. 2d 711 (1948), the first judicial decision legalizing interracial marriage, did not trigger backlash despite fitting all three of Klarman's criteria: increased salience, anger over outside influence and judicial activism, and alteration of the order of social reform. She argues that judicial backlash can only be understood in the context of political backlash more generally, and that backlash itself should be treated as a heterogeneous concept.[234]

---

231. See Note: Did *Roe* Cause the Abortion Conflict?, supra; Linda Greenhouse and Reva Siegel, Before (and After) Roe v. Wade: New Questions About Backlash, 120 Yale L.J. 2028 (2011).

232. See Scott Lemieux, The Myth of Judicial Backlash, Am. Prospect, Nov. 11, 2009, http://prospect.org/article/myth-judicial-backlash-0; see also Scott Cummings and Douglas NeJaime, Lawyering for Marriage Equality, 57 UCLA L. Rev. 1235 (2010).

233. Thomas Keck, Beyond Backlash: Assessing the Impact of Judicial Decisions on LGBT Rights, 43 Law & Soc'y Rev. 151, 160 (2009). See also Mary Ziegler, The Terms of the Debate: Litigation, Argumentative Strategies, and Coalitions in the Same-Sex Marriage Struggle, 39 Fla. St. U. L. Rev. 467, 469 (2012). Scholars have continued to enrich this account of the constructive effects of constitutional conflict over marriage equality in the lead-up to the Court's decisions in *Windsor* and *Perry*, and in the decisions' aftermath. See Eskridge, Backlash Politics, supra n.227; Siegel, Foreword: Equality Divided, supra n.215, at 74-85.

234. Jane Schacter, Courts and the Politics of Backlash: Marriage Equality Litigation, Then and Now, 82 S. Cal. L. Rev. 1153 (2009); see also Jane Schacter, Sexual Orientation, Social Change, and the Courts, 54 Drake L. Rev. 861 (2006).

The social science studies on backlash are still comparatively recent, and scholars are still debating its effects. This leads to a further consideration. If backlash is such a complicated social phenomenon, there is no reason to believe that judges—who are not social scientists—will be especially good at guessing when backlash will occur, how great it will be, and whether it will ultimately have good or bad consequences, given a particular judge's constitutional commitments. Nevertheless, judges seem to act prudentially even when they do so largely as a matter of guesswork. Given this uncertainty, and based on the materials you have read thus far in this course, to what extent *should* judges consider that their decisions might cause backlash when deciding a case? Given their role as judges, what prudential factors should they take into account?

NOTE: THE RIGHT TO DIE AND OTHER IMPLIED FUNDAMENTAL RIGHTS

1. *The right to die.* In Cruzan v. Director, Missouri Dept. of Health, 497 U.S. 261 (1990), Nancy Beth Cruzan had been severely injured in an automobile accident and was in a persistent vegetative state, with "virtually no chance of recovering her cognitive faculties." The Court considered whether Cruzan had a constitutional right to require the hospital to withdraw life-sustaining treatment at her parents' request. Writing for the majority, Chief Justice Rehnquist explained that "the common law doctrine of informed consent is viewed as generally encompassing the right of a competent individual to refuse medical treatment," and stated that "[t]he principle that a competent person has a constitutionally protected liberty interest in refusing unwanted medical treatment may be inferred from our prior decisions." Therefore, "for purposes of this case, we assume that the United States Constitution would grant a competent person a constitutionally protected right to refuse lifesaving hydration and nutrition." The Court concluded, however, that Missouri could require clear and convincing evidence of an incompetent patient's wishes concerning the withdrawal of life-sustaining treatment. Because her parents lacked such evidence, and Cruzan had not signed a living will, the Court turned down her parents' request for relief. Justice Brennan dissented, joined by Justices Marshall and Blackmun. Justice Stevens also dissented.

2. *The right to assisted suicide.* In Washington v. Glucksberg, 521 U.S. 702 (1997), the Court rejected the claim that Washington's prohibition against "caus[ing]" or "aid[ing]" a suicide violated the Due Process Clause. Chief Justice Rehnquist, writing for the majority, explained that "[o]ur established method of substantive-due-process analysis has two primary features." First, "we have regularly observed that the Due Process Clause specially protects those fundamental rights and liberties which are, objectively, 'deeply rooted in this Nation's history and tradition' and 'implicit in the concept of ordered liberty.'" Second, "we have required in substantive-due-process cases a 'careful description' of the asserted fundamental liberty interest. Our Nation's history, legal traditions, and practices thus provide the crucial 'guideposts for responsible decisionmaking' that direct and restrain our exposition of the Due Process Clause."

Chief Justice Rehnquist argued that there was "a consistent and almost universal tradition that has long rejected the asserted right" to commit suicide, "and continues explicitly to reject it today, even for terminally ill, mentally competent adults.

To hold for respondents, we would have to reverse centuries of legal doctrine and practice, and strike down the considered policy choice of almost every State."

The Chief Justice distinguished *Cruzan*: "[The] right assumed in *Cruzan* . . . was not simply deduced from abstract concepts of personal autonomy. Given the common-law rule that forced medication was a battery, and the long legal tradition protecting the decision to refuse unwanted medical treatment, our assumption was entirely consistent with this Nation's history and constitutional traditions. The decision to commit suicide with the assistance of another may be just as personal and profound as the decision to refuse unwanted medical treatment, but it has never enjoyed similar legal protection. Indeed, the two acts are widely and reasonably regarded as quite distinct."

The Chief Justice concluded: "The history of the law's treatment of assisted suicide in this country has been and continues to be one of the rejection of nearly all efforts to permit it. That being the case, our decisions lead us to conclude that the asserted 'right' to assistance in committing suicide is not a fundamental liberty interest protected by the Due Process Clause."

In addition, Washington's statute passed the rational basis test, as it was rationally related to a number of state interests. The State had an interest in the preservation of human life, "an interest in protecting the integrity and ethics of the medical profession;" . . . "an interest in protecting vulnerable groups—including the poor, the elderly, and disabled persons—from abuse, neglect, and mistakes"; and an interest in "protecting disabled and terminally ill people from prejudice, negative and inaccurate stereotypes, and 'societal indifference.'" Finally, "the State may fear that permitting assisted suicide will start it down the path to voluntary and perhaps even involuntary euthanasia. . . . [D]espite the existence of various reporting procedures, euthanasia in the Netherlands has not been limited to competent, terminally ill adults who are enduring physical suffering, and that regulation of the practice may not have prevented abuses in cases involving vulnerable persons, including severely disabled neonates and elderly persons suffering from dementia."

In the companion case of Vacco v. Quill, 521 U.S. 793 (1997), the Court considered an equal protection challenge to New York's law prohibiting assisted suicide. Plaintiffs asserted the irrationality of New York's distinction between persons who wish to refuse or withdraw from lifesaving treatment and persons who wish assistance in committing suicide by receiving drugs that would hasten death.

Writing for the Court, Chief Justice Rehnquist rejected the claim: "[W]e think the distinction between assisting suicide and withdrawing life-sustaining treatment, a distinction widely recognized and endorsed in the medical profession and in our legal traditions, is both important and logical; it is certainly rational."

This distinction "comports with fundamental legal principles of causation and intent. First, when a patient refuses life-sustaining medical treatment, he dies from an underlying fatal disease or pathology; but if a patient ingests lethal medication prescribed by a physician, he is killed by that medication. . . . The law has long used actors' intent or purpose to distinguish between two acts that may have the same result. Put differently, the law distinguishes actions taken 'because of' a given end from actions taken 'in spite of' their unintended but foreseen consequences."

Chief Justice Rehnquist explained that the distinction could also be justified by many of the same reasons given in *Glucksberg*: "prohibiting intentional killing and preserving life; preventing suicide; maintaining physicians' role as their patients' healers; protecting vulnerable people from indifference, prejudice, and psychological and financial pressure to end their lives; and avoiding a possible slide towards euthanasia. . . . These valid and important public interests easily satisfy the constitutional requirement that a legislative classification bear a rational relation to some legitimate end."

Five other Justices wrote or signed opinions applying to the two cases. Several of the Justices pointed out that the Court did not need to reach the question whether there was a right to die in cases of patients suffering extreme pain in the last days of their lives, because, as Justice O'Connor pointed out, "[t]here is no dispute that dying patients in Washington and New York can obtain palliative care, even when doing so would hasten their deaths."

Justice Stevens added that

> [t]he illusory character of any differences in intent or causation is confirmed by the fact that the American Medical Association unequivocally endorses the practice of terminal sedation—the administration of sufficient dosages of pain-killing medication to terminally ill patients to protect them from excruciating pain even when it is clear that the time of death will be advanced. The purpose of terminal sedation is to ease the suffering of the patient and comply with her wishes, and the actual cause of death is the administration of heavy doses of lethal sedatives. This same intent and causation may exist when a doctor complies with a patient's request for lethal medication to hasten her death. Thus, although the differences the majority notes in causation and intent between terminating life-support and assisting in suicide support the Court's rejection of the respondents' facial challenge, these distinctions may be inapplicable to particular terminally ill patients and their doctors.

3. *Control over your body and civil commitment.* In Kansas v. Crane, 534 U.S. 407 (2002), the Supreme Court upheld a substantive due process challenge to the Kansas Sexually Violent Predatory Act, which establishes procedures for the civil commitment of persons who, due to a "mental abnormality" or a "personality disorder," are likely to engage in "predatory acts of sexual violence." Crane was a previously convicted sex offender who, according to at least one of the State's psychiatric witnesses, suffers from both exhibitionism and antisocial personality disorder. After a jury trial, the Kansas District Court ordered Crane's civil commitment.

The Court previously rejected a challenge to the statute in Kansas v. Hendricks, 521 U.S. 346 (1997), a case involving a pedophile. *Hendricks* distinguished criminal punishment from civil commitment, and held that substantive due process is satisfied if a civil commitment statute requires proof of dangerousness along with proof of some additional factor, such as a "mental illness" or "mental abnormality." In *Crane*, the question was what degree of dangerousness caused by the mental abnormality had to be shown. The Court argued that the state need not prove that the person committed by the state completely lacks the ability to control his or her behavior: "[I]n cases where lack of control is at issue, 'inability to control behavior' will not be demonstrable with mathematical precision. It is enough to say that there must be proof of serious difficulty in controlling behavior. And this, when viewed in light of such features of the case as the nature of the psychiatric diagnosis, and the severity of the mental abnormality itself, must be sufficient to distinguish the dangerous sexual offender whose serious mental illness, abnormality, or disorder subjects him to civil commitment from the dangerous but typical recidivist convicted in an ordinary criminal case." Without a showing of serious difficulty in controlling behavior, however, substantive due process prevented civil commitment. Justice Scalia, joined by Justice Thomas, would have applied a more relaxed standard. For them it would be sufficient "that the person previously convicted of one of the enumerated sexual offenses is suffering from a mental abnormality or personality disorder, and . . . that this condition renders him likely to commit future acts of sexual violence."

4. *Punitive damages:* Lochner *redux?* Is there any clear way to delimit the group of substantive due process rights? Consider what would seem to be a very different set of issues: punitive damage awards in tort suits. Despite the Supreme Court's general rejection of substantive due process challenges to economic regulation after 1937, the Court—contemporaneously with its debates over abortion, gay rights, and assisted suicide—has held that the Due Process Clause imposes substantive limits on the size of punitive damage awards. In Browning-Ferris Industries v. Kelco Disposal, Inc., 492 U.S. 257 (1989), the Court held that the Eighth Amendment's excessive fines clause did not limit punitive damages in ordinary civil litigation between private parties. Two years later, however, in Pacific Mutual Life Insurance Company v. Haslip, 499 U.S. 1 (1991), the Court held that the Due Process Clause did limit punitive damage awards both procedurally and substantively. Procedurally, juries had to be properly instructed on the purposes for punitive damage awards and the proper methods of assessing them. In Honda Motor Co. v. Oberg, 512 U.S. 415 (1994), the Court invoked these procedural limits to punitive damages when it struck down, under the Due Process Clause, an amendment to the Oregon Constitution that prohibits judicial review of the amount of punitive damages awarded by a jury "unless the court can affirmatively say there is no evidence to support the verdict." In addition, as a substantive matter, the Court held in BMW of North America, Inc. v. Gore, 517 U.S. 559 (1996), that the actual awards themselves had to be reasonable and not disproportionate or "grossly excessive."

These doctrines inevitably led the Court into assessing what constituted a grossly excessive verdict. Compare *Gore* (striking down a $2 million punitive damages award that accompanied a $4,000 compensatory damages award) with TXO Production Corp. v. Alliance Resources Corp., 509 U.S. 443 (1993) (upholding a $10 million award that accompanied a $19,000 compensatory damages award).

In State Farm Mutual Automobile Insurance Co. v. Campbell, 538 U.S. 408 (2003), the Court, in an opinion by Justice Kennedy, struck down a $145 million punitive damage award arising out of an insurer's bad faith refusal to settle a claim, where the plaintiffs had been awarded $1 million in compensatory damages. Justice Kennedy explained that "courts must ensure that the measure of punishment is both reasonable and proportionate to the amount of harm to the plaintiff and to the general damages recovered." This means that "single-digit multipliers are more likely to comport with due process, while still achieving the State's goals of deterrence and retribution" than much larger ratios between punitive and compensatory damages. In addition, Justice Kennedy's opinion suggested, "[w]hen compensatory damages are substantial, then a lesser ratio, perhaps only equal to compensatory damages, can reach the outermost limit of the due process guarantee."

Finally, the Court held that a punitive damage award cannot be used to punish a defendant's entire pattern of conduct when some of the conduct occurred within the state and some outside of it: "A State cannot punish a defendant for conduct that may have been lawful where it occurred, . . . [n]or, as a general rule, does a State have a legitimate concern in imposing punitive damages to punish a defendant for unlawful acts committed outside of the State's jurisdiction." Justices Scalia and Thomas dissented on the grounds that the Constitution imposes no substantive limits on punitive damage awards. Justice Ginsburg also dissented: "I remain of the view that this Court has no warrant to reform state law governing awards of punitive damages."

V. THE CONSTITUTIONAL RIGHT OF SELF-DEFENSE

District of Columbia v. Heller

554 U.S. 570 (2008)

Justice Scalia delivered the opinion of the Court.

We consider whether a District of Columbia prohibition on the possession of usable handguns in the home violates the Second Amendment to the Constitution.

I

The District of Columbia generally prohibits the possession of handguns. It is a crime to carry an unregistered firearm, and the registration of handguns is prohibited. See D.C. Code §§7-2501.01(12), 7-2502.01(a), 7-2502.02(a)(4) (2001). Wholly apart from that prohibition, no person may carry a handgun without a license, but the chief of police may issue licenses for 1-year periods. See §§22-4504(a), 22-4506. District of Columbia law also requires residents to keep their lawfully owned firearms, such as registered long guns, unloaded and dissembled or bound by a trigger lock or similar device unless they are located in a place of business or are being used for lawful recreational activities. See §7-2507.02.

Respondent Dick Heller is a D.C. special police officer authorized to carry a handgun while on duty at the Federal Judicial Center. He applied for a registration certificate for a handgun that he wished to keep at home, but the District refused. He thereafter filed a lawsuit in the Federal District Court for the District of Columbia seeking, on Second Amendment grounds, to enjoin the city from enforcing the bar on the registration of handguns, the licensing requirement insofar as it prohibits the carrying of a firearm in the home without a license, and the trigger-lock requirement insofar as it prohibits the use of functional firearms within the home. . . .

II

. . .

A

The Second Amendment provides: "A well regulated Militia, being necessary to the security of a free State, the right of the people to keep and bear Arms, shall not be infringed." In interpreting this text, we are guided by the principle that "[t]he Constitution was written to be understood by the voters; its words and phrases were used in their normal and ordinary as distinguished from technical meaning. Normal meaning may of course include an idiomatic meaning, but it excludes secret or technical meanings that would not have been known to ordinary citizens in the founding generation." . . .

The Second Amendment is naturally divided into two parts: its prefatory clause and its operative clause. . . . The former does not limit the latter grammatically, but rather announces a purpose. The Amendment could be rephrased, "Because a well regulated Militia is necessary to the security of a free State, the right of the people to keep and bear Arms shall not be infringed." . . .

Logic demands that there be a link between the stated purpose and the command. . . . But apart from [its] clarifying function, a prefatory clause does not limit or expand the scope of the operative clause. Therefore, while we will begin our textual analysis with the operative clause, we will return to the prefatory clause to ensure that our reading of the operative clause is consistent with the announced purpose.

1. OPERATIVE CLAUSE

a. "Right of the People." The first salient feature of the operative clause is that it codifies a "right of the people." The unamended Constitution and the Bill of Rights use the phrase "right of the people" two other times, in the First Amendment's Assembly-and-Petition Clause and in the Fourth Amendment's Search-and-Seizure Clause. The Ninth Amendment uses very similar terminology ("The enumeration in the Constitution, of certain rights, shall not be construed to deny or disparage others retained by the people"). All three of these instances unambiguously refer to individual rights, not "collective" rights, or rights that may be exercised only through participation in some corporate body. Three provisions of the Constitution refer to "the people" in a context other than "rights"—the famous preamble ("We the people"), §2 of Article I (providing that "the people" will choose members of the House), and the Tenth Amendment (providing that those powers not given the Federal Government remain with "the States" or "the people"). Those provisions arguably refer to "the people" acting collectively—but they deal with the exercise or reservation of powers, not rights. Nowhere else in the Constitution does a "right" attributed to "the people" refer to anything other than an individual right. What is more, in all six other provisions of the Constitution that mention "the people," the term unambiguously refers to all members of the political community, not an unspecified subset. . . . This contrasts markedly with the phrase "the militia" in the prefatory clause. As we will describe below, the "militia" in colonial America consisted of a subset of "the people"—those who were male, able bodied, and within a certain age range. Reading the Second Amendment as protecting only the right to "keep and bear Arms" in an organized militia therefore fits poorly with the operative clause's description of the holder of that right as "the people."

We start therefore with a strong presumption that the Second Amendment right is exercised individually and belongs to all Americans.

b. "Keep and bear Arms." . . . The 18th-century meaning [of "Arms"] is no different from the meaning today. The 1773 edition of Samuel Johnson's dictionary defined "arms" as "weapons of offence, or armour of defence." . . . The term was applied, then as now, to weapons that were not specifically designed for military use and were not employed in a military capacity. . . . Although one founding-era thesaurus limited "arms" (as opposed to "weapons") to "instruments of offence *generally* made use of in war," even that source stated that all firearms constituted "arms." . . .

Some have made the argument, bordering on the frivolous, that only those arms in existence in the 18th century are protected by the Second Amendment. We do not interpret constitutional rights that way. Just as the First Amendment protects modern forms of communications, and the Fourth Amendment applies to modern forms of search, the Second Amendment extends, prima facie, to all instruments that constitute bearable arms, even those that were not in existence at the time of the founding.

We turn to the phrases "keep arms" and "bear arms." . . . No party has apprised us of an idiomatic meaning of "keep Arms." Thus, the most natural reading of "keep Arms" in the Second Amendment is to "have weapons." . . . Petitioners point to militia laws of the founding period that required militia members to "keep" arms in connection with militia service, and they conclude from this that the phrase "keep Arms" has a militia-related connotation. This is rather like saying that, since there are many statutes that authorize aggrieved employees to "file complaints" with federal agencies, the phrase "file complaints" has an employment-related connotation. "Keep arms" was simply a common way of referring to possessing arms, for militiamen *and everyone else.*

At the time of the founding, as now, to "bear" meant to "carry." When used with "arms," however, the term has a meaning that refers to carrying for a particular purpose—confrontation. . . . Although the phrase implies that the carrying of the weapon is for the purpose of "offensive or defensive action," it in no way connotes participation in a structured military organization.

From our review of founding-era sources, we conclude that this natural meaning was also the meaning that "bear arms" had in the 18th century. In numerous instances, "bear arms" was unambiguously used to refer to the carrying of weapons outside of an organized militia. The most prominent examples are those most relevant to the Second Amendment: Nine state constitutional provisions written in the 18th century or the first two decades of the 19th, which enshrined a right of citizens to "bear arms in defense of themselves and the state" or "bear arms in defense of himself and the state." It is clear from those formulations that "bear arms" did not refer only to carrying a weapon in an organized military unit. . . .

The phrase "bear Arms" also had at the time of the founding an idiomatic meaning that was significantly different from its natural meaning: "to serve as a soldier, do military service, fight" or "to wage war." But it *unequivocally* bore that idiomatic meaning only when followed by the preposition "against," which was in turn followed by the target of the hostilities. (That is how, for example, our Declaration of Independence §28, used the phrase: "He has constrained our fellow Citizens taken Captive on the high Seas to bear Arms against their Country. . . .") . . .

Petitioners justify their limitation of "bear arms" to the military context by pointing out the unremarkable fact that it was often used in that context—the same mistake they made with respect to "keep arms." It is especially unremarkable that the phrase was often used in a military context in the federal legal sources (such as records of congressional debate) that have been the focus of petitioners' inquiry. Those sources would have had little occasion to use it *except* in discussions about the standing army and the militia. And the phrases used primarily in those military discussions include not only "bear arms" but also "carry arms," "possess arms," and "have arms"—though no one thinks that those *other* phrases also had special military meanings. . . .

Justice Stevens places great weight on James Madison's inclusion of a conscientious-objector clause in his original draft of the Second Amendment: "but no person religiously scrupulous of bearing arms, shall be compelled to render military service in person." He argues that this clause establishes that the drafters of the Second Amendment intended "bear Arms" to refer only to military service. It is always perilous to derive the meaning of an adopted provision from another provision deleted in the drafting process. In any case, what Justice Stevens would conclude from the deleted provision does not follow. It was not meant to exempt from military service those who objected to going to war but had no scruples about personal gunfights. Quakers opposed the use of arms not just for militia service, but for any violent purpose whatsoever. . . . Thus, the most natural interpretation of Madison's deleted text is that those opposed to carrying weapons for potential violent confrontation would not be "compelled to render military service," in which such carrying would be required. . . .

c. Meaning of the Operative Clause. Putting all of these textual elements together, we find that they guarantee the individual right to possess and carry weapons in case of confrontation. This meaning is strongly confirmed by the historical background of the Second Amendment. We look to this because it has always been widely understood that the Second Amendment, like the First and Fourth Amendments, codified a *pre-existing* right. The very text of the Second Amendment implicitly recognizes the pre-existence of the right and declares only that it "shall not be infringed." . . .

Between the Restoration and the Glorious Revolution, the Stuart Kings Charles II and James II succeeded in using select militias loyal to them to suppress political dissidents, in part by disarming their opponents. Under the auspices of the 1671 Game Act, for example, the Catholic James II had ordered general disarmaments of regions home to his Protestant enemies. These experiences caused Englishmen to be extremely wary of concentrated military forces run by the state and to be jealous of their arms. They accordingly obtained an assurance from William and Mary, in the Declaration of Right (which was codified as the English Bill of Rights), that Protestants would never be disarmed: "That the subjects which are Protestants may have arms for their defense suitable to their conditions and as allowed by law." 1 W. & M., c. 2, §7, in 3 Eng. Stat. at Large 441 (1689). This right has long been understood to be the predecessor to our Second Amendment. It was clearly an individual right, having nothing whatever to do with service in a militia. To be sure, it was an individual right not available to the whole population, given that it was restricted to Protestants, and like all written English rights it was held only against the Crown, not Parliament. But it was secured to them as individuals, according to "libertarian political principles," not as members of a fighting force.

By the time of the founding, the right to have arms had become fundamental for English subjects. Blackstone, whose works, we have said, "constituted the preeminent authority on English law for the founding generation," cited the arms provision of the Bill of Rights as one of the fundamental rights of Englishmen. His description of it cannot possibly be thought to tie it to militia or military service. It was, he said, "the natural right of resistance and self-preservation," and "the right of having and using arms for self-preservation and defence." . . . Thus, the right secured in 1689 as a result of the Stuarts' abuses was by the time of the founding understood to be an individual right protecting against both public and private violence.

And, of course, what the Stuarts had tried to do to their political enemies, George III had tried to do to the colonists. In the tumultuous decades of the 1760's and 1770's, the Crown began to disarm the inhabitants of the most rebellious areas. That provoked polemical reactions by Americans invoking their rights as Englishmen to keep arms. A New York article of April 1769 said that "[i]t is a natural right which the people have reserved to themselves, confirmed by the Bill of Rights, to keep arms for their own defence." They understood the right to enable individuals to defend themselves. As the most important early American edition of Blackstone's Commentaries (by the law professor and former Antifederalist St. George Tucker) made clear in the notes to the description of the arms right, Americans understood the "right of self-preservation" as permitting a citizen to "repe[l] force by force" when "the intervention of society in his behalf, may be too late to prevent an injury."

There seems to us no doubt, on the basis of both text and history, that the Second Amendment conferred an individual right to keep and bear arms. Of course the right was not unlimited, just as the First Amendment's right of free speech was not. Thus, we do not read the Second Amendment to protect the right of citizens to carry arms for *any sort* of confrontation, just as we do not read the First Amendment to protect the right of citizens to speak for *any purpose.* Before turning to limitations upon the individual right, however, we must determine whether the prefatory clause of the Second Amendment comports with our interpretation of the operative clause.

2. PREFATORY CLAUSE

The prefatory clause reads: "A well regulated Militia, being necessary to the security of a free State. . . ."

a. "Well-Regulated Militia." In United States v. Miller, 307 U.S. 174 (1939), we explained that "the Militia comprised all males physically capable of acting in concert for the common defense." . . . Petitioners take a seemingly narrower view of the militia, stating that "[m]ilitias are the state and congressionally-regulated military forces described in the Militia Clauses (art. I, §8, cls.15-16)." Although we agree with petitioners' interpretive assumption that "militia" means the same thing in Article I and the Second Amendment, we believe that petitioners identify the wrong thing, namely, the organized militia. Unlike armies and navies, which Congress is given the power to create ("to raise . . . Armies"; "to provide . . . a Navy," Art. I, §8, cls. 12-13), the militia is assumed by Article I already to be *in existence.* Congress is given the power to "provide for calling forth the militia," §8, cl. 15; and the power not to create, but to "organiz[e]" it . . . connoting a body already in existence, *ibid.*, cl. 16. This is fully consistent with the ordinary definition of the militia as all able-bodied men. From that pool, Congress has plenary power to organize the units that will make up an effective fighting force. That is what Congress did in the first militia Act, which specified that "each and every free able-bodied white male citizen of the respective states, resident therein, who is or shall be of the age of eighteen years, and under the age of forty-five years (except as is herein after excepted) shall severally and respectively be enrolled in the militia." Act of May 8, 1792, 1 Stat. 271. To be sure, Congress need not conscript every able-bodied man into the militia, because nothing in Article I suggests that in exercising its power to organize, discipline, and arm the militia, Congress must focus upon the entire body. Although the militia consists of all able-bodied men, the federally organized militia may consist of a subset of them.

Finally, the adjective "well-regulated" implies nothing more than the imposition of proper discipline and training.

b. Security of a Free State. The phrase "security of a free state" meant "security of a free polity," not security of each of the several States. . . . The presence of the term "foreign state" in Article I and Article III shows that the word "state" did not have a single meaning in the Constitution.

There are many reasons why the militia was thought to be "necessary to the security of a free state." First, of course, it is useful in repelling invasions and suppressing insurrections. Second, it renders large standing armies unnecessary—an argument that Alexander Hamilton made in favor of federal control over the militia. The Federalist No. 29 (A. Hamilton). Third, when the able-bodied men of a nation are trained in arms and organized, they are better able to resist tyranny.

3. RELATIONSHIP BETWEEN PREFATORY CLAUSE AND OPERATIVE CLAUSE

We reach the question, then: Does the preface fit with an operative clause that creates an individual right to keep and bear arms? It fits perfectly, once one knows the history that the founding generation knew and that we have described above. That history showed that the way tyrants had eliminated a militia consisting of all the able-bodied men was not by banning the militia but simply by taking away the people's arms, enabling a select militia or standing army to suppress political opponents. This is what had occurred in England that prompted codification of the right to have arms in the English Bill of Rights.

The debate with respect to the right to keep and bear arms, as with other guarantees in the Bill of Rights, was not over whether it was desirable (all agreed that it was) but over whether it needed to be codified in the Constitution. During the 1788 ratification debates, the fear that the federal government would disarm the people in order to impose rule through a standing army or select militia was pervasive in Antifederalist rhetoric. Federalists responded that because Congress was given no power to abridge the ancient right of individuals to keep and bear arms, such a force could never oppress the people. It was understood across the political spectrum that the right helped to secure the ideal of a citizen militia, which might be necessary to oppose an oppressive military force if the constitutional order broke down.

It is therefore entirely sensible that the Second Amendment's prefatory clause announces the purpose for which the right was codified: to prevent elimination of the militia. The prefatory clause does not suggest that preserving the militia was the only reason Americans valued the ancient right; most undoubtedly thought it even more important for self-defense and hunting. But the threat that the new

Federal Government would destroy the citizens' militia by taking away their arms was the reason that right—unlike some other English rights—was codified in a written Constitution. Justice Breyer's assertion that individual self-defense is merely a "subsidiary interest" of the right to keep and bear arms, is profoundly mistaken. He bases that assertion solely upon the prologue—but that can only show that self-defense had little to do with the right's *codification*; it was the *central component* of the right itself.

Besides ignoring the historical reality that the Second Amendment was not intended to lay down a "novel principl[e]" but rather codified a right "inherited from our English ancestors," petitioners' interpretation does not even achieve the narrower purpose that prompted codification of the right. If, as they believe, the Second Amendment right is no more than the right to keep and use weapons as a member of an organized militia—if, that is, the *organized* militia is the sole institutional beneficiary of the Second Amendment's guarantee—it does not assure the existence of a "citizens' militia" as a safeguard against tyranny. For Congress retains plenary authority to organize the militia, which must include the authority to say who will belong to the organiz ed force. That is why the first Militia Act's requirement that only whites enroll caused States to amend their militia laws to exclude free blacks. Thus, if petitioners are correct, the Second Amendment protects citizens' right to use a gun in an organization from which Congress has plenary authority to exclude them. It guarantees a select militia of the sort the Stuart kings found useful, but not the people's militia that was the concern of the founding generation.

B

Our interpretation is confirmed by analogous arms-bearing rights in state constitutions that preceded and immediately followed adoption of the Second Amendment. Four States adopted analogues to the Federal Second Amendment in the period between independence and the ratification of the Bill of Rights. Two of them—Pennsylvania and Vermont—clearly adopted individual rights unconnected to militia service. Pennsylvania's Declaration of Rights of 1776 said: "That the people have a right to bear arms *for the defence of themselves*, and the state. . . ." In 1777, Vermont adopted the identical provision, except for inconsequential differences in punctuation and capitalization.

North Carolina also codified a right to bear arms in 1776: "That the people have a right to bear arms, for the defence of the State. . . ." This could plausibly be read to support only a right to bear arms in a militia—but that is a peculiar way to make the point in a constitution that elsewhere repeatedly mentions the militia explicitly. Many colonial statutes required individual arms-bearing for public-safety reasons—such as the 1770 Georgia law that "for the security and *defence of this province* from internal dangers and insurrections" required those men who qualified for militia duty individually "to carry fire arms" to places of public worship. That broad public-safety understanding was the connotation given to the North Carolina right by that State's Supreme Court in 1843.

The 1780 Massachusetts Constitution presented another variation on the theme: "The people have a right to keep and to bear arms for the common defence. . . ." Once again, if one gives narrow meaning to the phrase "common defence" this can be thought to limit the right to the bearing of arms in a state-organized military force. But once again the State's highest court thought otherwise [in 1825].

We therefore believe that the most likely reading of all four of these pre-Second Amendment state constitutional provisions is that they secured an individual right to bear arms for defensive purposes. . . .

Between 1789 and 1820, nine States adopted Second Amendment analogues. Four of them—Kentucky, Ohio, Indiana, and Missouri—referred to the right of the people to "bear arms in defence of themselves and the State." Another three States—Mississippi, Connecticut, and Alabama—used the even more individualistic phrasing that each citizen has the "right to bear arms in defence of himself and the State." Finally, two States—Tennessee and Maine—used the "common defence" language of Massachusetts. That of the nine state constitutional protections for the right to bear arms enacted immediately after 1789 at least seven unequivocally protected an individual citizen's right to self-defense is strong evidence that that is how the founding generation conceived of the right. And with one possible exception . . . 19th-century courts and commentators interpreted these state constitutional provisions to protect an individual right to use arms for self-defense.

The historical narrative that petitioners must endorse would thus treat the Federal Second Amendment as an odd outlier, protecting a right unknown in state constitutions or at English common law, based on little more than an overreading of the prefatory clause.

C

Justice Stevens relies on the drafting history of the Second Amendment—the various proposals in the state conventions and the debates in Congress. It is dubious to rely on such history to interpret a text that was widely understood to codify a pre-existing right, rather than to fashion a new one. But even assuming that this legislative history is relevant, Justice Stevens flatly misreads the historical record.

It is true, as Justice Stevens says, that there was concern that the Federal Government would abolish the institution of the state militia. That concern found expression, however, *not* in the various Second Amendment precursors proposed in the State conventions, but in separate structural provisions that would have given the States concurrent and seemingly non-preemptible authority to organize, discipline, and arm the militia when the Federal Government failed to do so. The Second Amendment precursors, by contrast, referred to the individual English right already codified in two (and probably four) State constitutions. The Federalist-dominated first Congress chose to reject virtually all major structural revisions favored by the Antifederalists, including the proposed militia amendments. Rather, it adopted primarily the popular and uncontroversial (though, in the Federalists' view, unnecessary) individual-rights amendments. The Second Amendment right, protecting only individuals' liberty to keep and carry arms, did nothing to assuage Antifederalists' concerns about federal control of the militia. . . .

Justice Stevens' view . . . relies on the proposition, unsupported by any evidence, that different people of the founding period had vastly different conceptions of the right to keep and bear arms. That simply does not comport with our longstanding view that the Bill of Rights codified venerable, widely understood liberties.

D

We now address how the Second Amendment was interpreted from immediately after its ratification through the end of the 19th century. Before proceeding, however, we take issue with Justice Stevens' equating of these sources with postenactment legislative history, a comparison that betrays a fundamental misunderstanding of a court's interpretive task. "Legislative history," of course, refers to the pre-enactment statements of those who drafted or voted for a law; it is considered persuasive by some, not because they reflect the general understanding of the disputed terms, but because the legislators who heard or read those statements presumably voted with that understanding. "Postenactment legislative history," a deprecatory contradiction in terms, refers to statements of those who drafted or voted for the law that are made after its enactment and hence could have had no effect on the congressional vote. It most certainly does not refer to the examination of a variety of legal and other sources to determine *the public understanding* of a legal text in the period after its enactment or ratification. That sort of inquiry is a critical tool of constitutional interpretation.

[V]irtually all interpreters of the Second Amendment in the century after its enactment interpreted the amendment as we do. . . . Antislavery advocates routinely invoked the right to bear arms for self-defense. . . . In his famous Senate speech about the 1856 "Bleeding Kansas" conflict, Charles Sumner proclaimed:

> "The rifle has ever been the companion of the pioneer and, under God, his tutelary protector against the red man and the beast of the forest. Never was this efficient weapon more needed in just self-defence, than now in Kansas, and at least one article in our National Constitution must be blotted out, before the complete right to it can in any way be impeached. And yet such is the madness of the hour, that, in defiance of the solemn guarantee, embodied in the Amendments to the Constitution, that 'the right of the people to keep and bear arms shall not be infringed,' the people of Kansas have been arraigned for keeping and bearing them, and the Senator from South Carolina has had the face to say openly, on this floor, that they should be disarmed—of course, that the fanatics of Slavery, his allies and constituents, may meet no impediment." The Crime Against Kansas, May 19-20, 1856, in American Speeches: Political Oratory from the Revolution to the Civil War 553, 606-607 (2006).

[T]he 19th-century cases that interpreted the Second Amendment universally support an individual right unconnected to militia service. . . . Many early 19th-century state cases indicated that the Second Amendment right to bear arms was an individual right unconnected to militia service, though subject to certain restrictions. . . . In the aftermath of the Civil War, there was an outpouring of discussion of the Second Amendment in Congress and in public discourse, as people debated whether and how to secure constitutional rights for newly free slaves. Since those discussions took place 75 years after the ratification of the Second Amendment, they do not provide as much insight into its original meaning as earlier sources. Yet those born and educated in the early 19th century faced a widespread effort to limit arms ownership by a large number of citizens; their understanding of the origins and continuing significance of the Amendment is instructive.

Blacks were routinely disarmed by Southern States after the Civil War. Those who opposed these injustices frequently stated that they infringed blacks' constitutional right to keep and bear arms. Needless to say, the claim was not that blacks were being prohibited from carrying arms in an organized state militia. . . . Congress enacted the Freedmen's Bureau Act on July 16, 1866. Section 14 stated: "[T]he right . . . to have full and equal benefit of all laws and proceedings concerning personal liberty, personal security, and the acquisition, enjoyment, and disposition of estate, real and personal, including the constitutional right to bear arms, shall be secured to and enjoyed by all the citizens . . . without respect to race or color, or previous condition of slavery. . . ." 14 Stat. 176-177. The understanding that the Second Amendment gave freed blacks the right to keep and bear arms was reflected in congressional discussion of the bill. . . . Similar discussion attended the passage of the Civil Rights Act of 1871 and the Fourteenth Amendment. . . . It was plainly the understanding in the post-Civil War Congress that the Second Amendment protected an individual right to use arms for self-defense. . . .

Every late-19th-century legal scholar that we have read interpreted the Second Amendment to secure an individual right unconnected with militia service. The most famous was the judge and professor Thomas Cooley, who wrote a massively popular 1868 Treatise on Constitutional Limitations. . . . Cooley understood the right not as connected to militia service, but as securing the militia by ensuring a populace familiar with arms. . . . All other post-Civil War 19th-century sources we have found concurred with Cooley. . . .

E

We now ask whether any of our precedents forecloses the conclusions we have reached about the meaning of the Second Amendment. . . . Justice Stevens places overwhelming reliance upon this Court's decision in United States v. Miller, 307 U.S. 174 (1939). . . . *Miller* . . . upheld against a Second Amendment challenge two men's federal convictions for transporting an unregistered short-barreled shotgun in interstate commerce, in violation of the National Firearms Act. It is entirely clear that the Court's basis for saying that the Second Amendment did not apply was *not* that the defendants were "bear[ing] arms" not "for . . . military purposes" but for "nonmilitary use." Rather, it was that the *type of weapon at issue* was not eligible for Second Amendment protection: "In the absence of any evidence tending to show that the possession or use of a [short-barreled shotgun] at this time has some reasonable relationship to the preservation or efficiency of a well regulated militia, we cannot say that the Second Amendment guarantees the right to keep and bear *such an instrument*" (emphasis added). "Certainly," the Court continued, "it is not within judicial notice that this weapon is any part of the ordinary military equipment or that its use could contribute to the common defense." . . . This holding is not only consistent with, but positively suggests, that the Second Amendment confers an individual right to keep and bear arms (though only arms that "have some reasonable relationship to the preservation or efficiency of a well regulated militia"). Had the Court believed that the Second Amendment protects only those serving in the militia, it would have been odd to examine the character of the weapon rather than simply note that the two crooks were not militiamen. . . . It is particularly wrongheaded to read *Miller* for more than what it said, because the case did not even purport to be a thorough examination of the Second Amendment. . . . The respondent made no appearance in the case, neither filing a brief nor appearing at oral argument; the Court heard from no one but the Government (reason enough, one would think, not to make that case the beginning and the end of this Court's consideration of the Second Amendment). . . .

We may as well consider at this point (for we will have to consider eventually) *what* types of weapons *Miller* permits. Read in isolation, *Miller*'s phrase "part of ordinary military equipment" could mean that only those weapons useful in warfare are protected. That would be a startling reading of the opinion, since it would mean that the National Firearms Act's restrictions on machineguns (not challenged in *Miller*) might be unconstitutional, machineguns being useful in warfare in 1939. We think that *Miller*'s "ordinary military equipment" language must be read in tandem with what comes after: "[O]rdinarily when called for [militia] service [able-bodied] men were expected to appear bearing arms supplied by themselves and of the kind in common use at the time." The traditional militia was formed from a pool of men bringing arms "in common use at the time" for lawful purposes like self-defense. In the colonial and revolutionary war era, [small-arms] weapons used by militiamen and weapons used in defense of person and home were one and the same. Indeed, that is precisely the way in which the Second Amendment's operative clause furthers the purpose announced in its preface. We therefore read *Miller* to say only that the Second Amendment does not protect those weapons not typically possessed by law-abiding citizens for lawful purposes, such as short-barreled shotguns. That accords with the historical understanding of the scope of the right. . . .

We conclude that nothing in our precedents forecloses our adoption of the original understanding of the Second Amendment. It should be unsurprising that such a significant matter has been for so long judicially unresolved. For most of our history, the Bill of Rights was not thought applicable to the States, and the Federal Government did not significantly regulate the possession of firearms by law-abiding citizens. Other provisions of the Bill of Rights have similarly remained unilluminated for lengthy periods. This Court first held a law to violate the First Amendment's guarantee of freedom of speech in 1931, almost 150 years after the Amendment was ratified, and it was not until after World War II that we held a law invalid under the Establishment Clause. Even a question as basic as the scope of proscribable libel was not addressed by this Court until 1964, nearly two centuries after the founding. See New York Times Co. v. Sullivan, 376 U.S. 254 (1964). It is demonstrably not true that, as Justice Stevens claims, "for most of our history, the invalidity of Second-Amendment-based objections to firearms regulations has been well settled and uncontroversial." For most of our history the question did not present itself.

III

Like most rights, the right secured by the Second Amendment is not unlimited. From Blackstone through the 19th-century cases, commentators and courts routinely explained that the right was not a right to keep and carry any weapon whatsoever in any manner whatsoever and for whatever purpose. For example, the majority of the 19th-century courts to consider the question held that prohibitions on carrying concealed weapons were lawful under the Second Amendment or state analogues. Although we do not undertake an exhaustive historical analysis today of the full scope of the Second Amendment, nothing in our opinion should be taken to cast doubt on longstanding prohibitions on the possession of firearms by felons and the mentally ill, or laws forbidding the carrying of firearms in sensitive places such as schools and government buildings, or laws imposing conditions and qualifications on the commercial sale of arms.

We also recognize another important limitation on the right to keep and carry arms. *Miller* said, as we have explained, that the sorts of weapons protected were those "in common use at the time." We think that limitation is fairly supported by the historical tradition of prohibiting the carrying of "dangerous and unusual weapons."

It may be objected that if weapons that are most useful in military service — M-16 rifles and the like — may be banned, then the Second Amendment right is completely detached from the prefatory clause. But as we have said, the conception of the militia at the time of the Second Amendment's ratification was the body of all citizens capable of military service, who would bring the sorts of lawful weapons that they possessed at home to militia duty. It may well be true today that a militia, to be as effective as militias in the 18th century, would require sophisticated arms that are highly unusual in society at large. Indeed, it may be true that no amount of small arms could be useful against modern-day bombers and tanks. But the fact that modern developments have limited the degree of fit between the prefatory clause and the protected right cannot change our interpretation of the right.

IV

We turn finally to the law at issue here. As we have said, the law totally bans handgun possession in the home. It also requires that any lawful firearm in the home be disassembled or bound by a trigger lock at all times, rendering it inoperable.

[T]he inherent right of self-defense has been central to the Second Amendment right. The handgun ban amounts to a prohibition of an entire class of "arms" that is overwhelmingly chosen by American society for that lawful purpose. The prohibition extends, moreover, to the home, where the need for defense of self, family, and property is most acute. Under any of the standards of scrutiny that we have applied to enumerated constitutional rights, banning from the home "the most preferred firearm in the nation to 'keep' and use for protection of one's home and family," would fail constitutional muster.

Few laws in the history of our Nation have come close to the severe restriction of the District's handgun ban. . . . It is no answer to say, as petitioners do, that it is permissible to ban the possession of handguns so long as the possession of other firearms (*i.e.*, long guns) is allowed. It is enough to note, as we have observed, that the American people have considered the handgun to be the quintessential self-defense weapon. There are many reasons that a citizen may prefer a handgun for home defense: It is easier to store in a location that is readily accessible in an emergency; it cannot easily be redirected or wrestled away by an attacker; it is easier to use for those without the upper-body strength to lift and aim a long gun; it can be pointed at a burglar with one hand while the other hand dials the police.

Whatever the reason, handguns are the most popular weapon chosen by Americans for self-defense in the home, and a complete prohibition of their use is invalid.

We must also address the District's requirement (as applied to respondent's handgun) that firearms in the home be rendered and kept inoperable at all times. This makes it impossible for citizens to use them for the core lawful purpose of self-defense and is hence unconstitutional. . . .

Respondent conceded at oral argument that he does not "have a problem with . . . licensing" and that the District's law is permissible so long as it is "not enforced in an arbitrary and capricious manner." We therefore assume that petitioners' issuance of a license will satisfy respondent's prayer for relief and do not address the licensing requirement. . . .

Justice Breyer . . . criticizes us for declining to establish a level of scrutiny for evaluating Second Amendment restrictions. He proposes, explicitly at least, none of the traditionally expressed levels (strict scrutiny, intermediate scrutiny, rational basis), but rather a judge-empowering "interest-balancing inquiry" that "asks whether the statute burdens a protected interest in a way or to an extent that is out of proportion to the statute's salutary effects upon other important governmental interests." After an exhaustive discussion of the arguments for and against gun control, Justice Breyer arrives at his interest-balanced answer: because handgun violence is a problem, because the law is limited to an urban area, and because there were somewhat similar restrictions in the founding period (a false proposition that we have already discussed), the interest-balancing inquiry results in the constitutionality of the handgun ban. QED.

We know of no other enumerated constitutional right whose core protection has been subjected to a freestanding "interest-balancing" approach. The very enumeration of the right takes out of the hands of government—even the Third Branch of Government—the power to decide on a case-by-case basis whether the right is *really worth* insisting upon. A constitutional guarantee subject to future judges' assessments of its usefulness is no constitutional guarantee at all. Constitutional rights are enshrined with the scope they were understood to have when the people adopted them, whether or not future legislatures or (yes) even future judges think that scope too broad. We would not apply an "interest-balancing" approach to the prohibition of a peaceful neo-Nazi march through Skokie. The First Amendment contains the freedom-of-speech guarantee that the people ratified, which included exceptions for obscenity, libel, and disclosure of state secrets, but not for the expression of extremely unpopular and wrong-headed views. The Second Amendment is no different. Like the First, it is the very *product* of an interest-balancing by the people—which Justice Breyer would now conduct for them anew. And whatever else it leaves to future evaluation, it surely elevates above all other interests the right of law-abiding, responsible citizens to use arms in defense of hearth and home.

Justice Breyer chides us for leaving so many applications of the right to keep and bear arms in doubt, and for not providing extensive historical justification for those regulations of the right that we describe as permissible. But since this case represents this Court's first in-depth examination of the Second Amendment, one should not expect it to clarify the entire field. . . . In sum, we hold that the District's ban on handgun possession in the home violates the Second Amendment, as does its prohibition against rendering any lawful firearm in the home operable for the purpose of immediate self-defense. Assuming that Heller is not disqualified from the exercise of Second Amendment rights, the District must permit him to register his handgun and must issue him a license to carry it in the home.

We are aware of the problem of handgun violence in this country, and we take seriously the concerns raised by the many *amici* who believe that prohibition of handgun ownership is a solution. The Constitution leaves the District of Columbia a variety of tools for combating that problem, including some measures regulating handguns. But the enshrinement of constitutional rights necessarily takes certain policy choices off the table. These include the absolute prohibition of handguns held and used for self-defense in the home. Undoubtedly some think that the Second Amendment is outmoded in a society where our standing army is the pride of our Nation, where well-trained police forces provide personal security, and where gun violence is a serious problem. That is perhaps debatable, but what is not debatable is that it is not the role of this Court to pronounce the Second Amendment extinct.

. . .

Justice STEVENS, with whom Justice SOUTER, Justice GINSBURG, and Justice BREYER join, dissenting.

The question presented by this case is not whether the Second Amendment protects a "collective right" or an "individual right." Surely it protects a right that can be enforced by individuals. But a conclusion that the Second Amendment protects an individual right does not tell us anything about the scope of that right.

Guns are used to hunt, for self-defense, to commit crimes, for sporting activities, and to perform military duties. The Second Amendment plainly does not protect the right to use a gun to rob a bank; it is equally clear that it *does* encompass the right to use weapons for certain military purposes. Whether it also protects the right to possess and use guns for nonmilitary purposes like hunting and personal self-defense is the question presented by this case. The text of the Amendment, its history, and our decision in United States v. Miller, 307 U.S. 174 (1939), provide a clear answer to that question.

The Second Amendment was adopted to protect the right of the people of each of the several States to maintain a well-regulated militia. It was a response to concerns raised during the ratification of the Constitution that the power of Congress to disarm the state militias and create a national standing army posed an intolerable threat to the sovereignty of the several States. Neither the text of the Amendment nor the arguments advanced by its proponents evidenced the slightest interest in limiting any legislature's authority to regulate private civilian uses of firearms. Specifically, there is no indication that the Framers of the Amendment intended to enshrine the common-law right of self-defense in the Constitution.

In 1934, Congress enacted the National Firearms Act, the first major federal firearms law. Upholding a conviction under that Act, this Court held that, "[i]n the absence of any evidence tending to show that possession or use of a 'shotgun having a barrel of less than eighteen inches in length' at this time has some reasonable relationship to the preservation or efficiency of a well regulated militia, we cannot say that the Second Amendment guarantees the right to keep and bear such an instrument." *Miller*. The view of the Amendment we took in *Miller*—that it protects the right to keep and bear arms for certain military purposes, but that it does not curtail the Legislature's power to regulate the nonmilitary use and ownership of weapons—is both the most natural reading of the Amendment's text and the interpretation most faithful to the history of its adoption.

Since our decision in *Miller*, hundreds of judges have relied on the view of the Amendment we endorsed there; we ourselves affirmed it in 1980. See Lewis v. United States, 445 U.S. 55, 65-66, n.8 (1980). No new evidence has surfaced since 1980 supporting the view that the Amendment was intended to curtail the power of Congress to regulate civilian use or misuse of weapons. Indeed, a review of the drafting history of the Amendment demonstrates that its Framers *rejected* proposals that would have broadened its coverage to include such uses.

The opinion the Court announces today fails to identify any new evidence supporting the view that the Amendment was intended to limit the power of Congress to regulate civilian uses of weapons. . . .

Even if the textual and historical arguments on both sides of the issue were evenly balanced, respect for the well-settled views of all of our predecessors on this Court, and for the rule of law itself would prevent most jurists from endorsing such a dramatic upheaval in the law. . . .

I

[T]he preamble to the Second Amendment ["A well regulated Militia, being necessary to the security of a free State"] makes three important points. It identifies the preservation of the militia as the Amendment's purpose; it explains that the militia is necessary to the security of a free State; and it recognizes that the militia must be "well regulated." In all three respects it is comparable to provisions in several State Declarations of Rights that were adopted roughly contemporaneously with the Declaration of Independence. Those state provisions highlight the importance members of the founding generation attached to the maintenance of state militias; they also underscore the profound fear shared by many in that era of the dangers posed by standing armies. While the need for state militias has not been a matter of significant public interest for almost two centuries, that fact should not obscure the contemporary concerns that animated the Framers.

The parallels between the Second Amendment and these state declarations, and the Second Amendment's omission of any statement of purpose related to the right to use firearms for hunting or personal self-defense, is especially striking in light of the fact that the Declarations of Rights of Pennsylvania and Vermont *did* expressly protect such civilian uses at the time. Article XIII of Pennsylvania's 1776 Declaration of Rights announced that "the people have a right to bear arms for the defence *of themselves* and the state" (emphasis added); §43 of the Declaration assured that "the inhabitants of this state shall have the liberty to fowl and hunt in seasonable times on the lands they hold, and on all other lands therein not inclosed," *id.*, at 274. And Article XV of the 1777 Vermont Declaration of Rights guaranteed "[t]hat the people have a right to bear arms for the defence *of themselves* and the State" (emphasis added). The contrast between those two declarations and the Second Amendment reinforces the clear statement of purpose announced in the Amendment's preamble. It confirms that the Framers' single-minded focus in crafting the constitutional guarantee "to keep and bear arms" was on military uses of firearms, which they viewed in the context of service in state militias.

The preamble thus both sets forth the object of the Amendment and informs the meaning of the remainder of its text. Such text should not be treated as mere surplusage, for "[i]t cannot be presumed that any clause in the constitution is intended to be without effect." Marbury v. Madison, 1 Cranch 137, 174 (1803).

[W]hile the Court makes the novel suggestion that it need only find some "logical connection" between the preamble and the operative provision, it does acknowledge that a prefatory clause may resolve an ambiguity in the text. Without identifying any language in the text that even mentions civilian uses of firearms, the Court proceeds to "find" its preferred reading in what is at best an ambiguous text, and then concludes that its reading is not foreclosed by the preamble. Perhaps the Court's approach to the text is acceptable advocacy, but it is surely an unusual approach for judges to follow. . . .

The centerpiece of the Court's textual argument is its insistence that the words "the people" as used in the Second Amendment must have the same meaning, and protect the same class of individuals, as when they are used in the First and Fourth Amendments. According to the Court, in all three provisions—as well as the Constitution's preamble, section 2 of Article I, and the Tenth Amendment—the term unambiguously refers to all members of the political community, not an unspecified subset. But the Court *itself* reads the Second Amendment to protect a "subset" significantly narrower than the class of persons protected by the First and Fourth Amendments; when it finally drills down on the substantive meaning of the Second Amendment, the Court limits the protected class to "law-abiding, responsible citizens." But the class of persons protected by the First and Fourth Amendments is *not* so limited; for even felons (and presumably irresponsible citizens as well) may invoke the protections of those constitutional provisions. The Court offers no way to harmonize its conflicting pronouncements.

The Court also overlooks the significance of the way the Framers used the phrase "the people" in these constitutional provisions. In the First Amendment, no words define the class of individuals entitled to speak, to publish, or to worship; in that Amendment it is only the right peaceably to assemble, and to petition the Government for a redress of grievances, that is described as a right of "the people." These rights contemplate collective action. While the right peaceably to assemble protects the individual rights of those persons participating in the assembly, its concern is with action engaged in by members of a group, rather than any single individual. Likewise, although the act of petitioning the Government is a right that can be exercised by individuals, it is primarily collective in nature. For if they are to be effective, petitions must involve groups of individuals acting in concert.

Similarly, the words "the people" in the Second Amendment refer back to the object announced in the Amendment's preamble. They remind us that it is the collective action of individuals having a duty to serve in the militia that the text directly protects and, perhaps more importantly, that the ultimate purpose of the Amendment was to protect the States' share of the divided sovereignty created by the Constitution.

As used in the Fourth Amendment, "the people" describes the class of persons protected from unreasonable searches and seizures by Government officials. It is true that the Fourth Amendment describes a right that need not be exercised in any collective sense. But that observation does not settle the meaning of the phrase "the people" when used in the Second Amendment. For, as we have seen, the phrase means something quite different in the Petition and Assembly Clauses of the First Amendment. Although the abstract definition of the phrase "the people" could carry the same meaning in the Second Amendment as in the Fourth Amendment, the preamble of the Second Amendment suggests that the uses of the phrase in the First and Second Amendments are the same in referring to a collective activity. By way of contrast, the Fourth Amendment describes a right *against* governmental interference rather than an affirmative right *to* engage in protected conduct, and so refers to a right to protect a purely individual interest. As used in the Second Amendment, the words "the people" do not enlarge the right to keep and bear arms to encompass use or ownership of weapons outside the context of service in a well-regulated militia.

[The words "To keep and bear Arms"] describe a unitary right: to possess arms if needed for military purposes and to use them in conjunction with military activities. [T]he Court does not read that phrase to create a right to possess arms for "lawful, private purposes." Instead, the Court limits the Amendment's protection to the right "to possess and carry weapons in case of confrontation." No party or *amicus* urged this interpretation; the Court appears to have fashioned it out of whole cloth. But . . . the Amendment's text *does* justify a different limitation: the "right to keep and bear arms" protects only a right to possess and use firearms in connection with service in a state-organized militia.

The term "bear arms" is a familiar idiom; when used unadorned by any additional words, its meaning is "to serve as a soldier, do military service, fight." It is derived from the Latin *arma ferre*, which, translated literally, means "to bear [*ferre*] war equipment [*arma*]." . . . Had the Framers wished to expand the meaning of the phrase "bear arms" to encompass civilian possession and use, they could have done so by the addition of phrases such as "for the defense of themselves," as was done in the Pennsylvania and Vermont Declarations of Rights. The *unmodified* use of "bear arms," by contrast, refers most naturally to a military purpose, as evidenced by its use in literally dozens of contemporary texts. The absence of any reference to civilian uses of weapons tailors the text of the Amendment to the purpose identified in its preamble. But when discussing these words, the Court simply ignores the preamble.

[T]he Amendment's use of the term "keep" in no way contradicts the military meaning conveyed by the phrase "bear arms" and the Amendment's preamble. To the contrary, a number of state militia laws in effect at the time of the Second Amendment's drafting used the term "keep" to describe the requirement that militia members store their arms at their homes, ready to be used for service when necessary. The Virginia military law, for example, ordered that "every one of the said officers, non-commissioned officers, and privates, shall constantly *keep* the aforesaid arms, accoutrements, and ammunition, ready to be produced whenever called for by his commanding officer." Act for Regulating and Disciplining the Militia, 1785 Va. Acts ch. 1, §3, p. 2 (emphasis added). "[K]eep and bear arms" thus perfectly describes the responsibilities of a framing-era militia member.

This reading is confirmed by the fact that the clause protects only one right, rather than two. It does not describe a right "to keep arms" and a separate right "to bear arms." Rather, the single right that it does describe is both a duty and a right to have arms available and ready for military service, and to use them for military purposes when necessary. Different language surely would have been used to protect nonmilitary use and possession of weapons from regulation if such an intent had played any role in the drafting of the Amendment.

* * *

When each word in the text is given full effect, the Amendment is most naturally read to secure to the people a right to use and possess arms in conjunction with service in a well-regulated militia. So far as appears, no more than that was contemplated by its drafters or is encompassed within its terms. Even if the meaning of the text were genuinely susceptible to more than one interpretation, the burden would remain on those advocating a departure from the purpose identified in the preamble and from settled law to come forward with persuasive new arguments or evidence. The textual analysis offered by respondent and embraced by the Court falls far short of sustaining that heavy burden. . . . Indeed, not a word in the constitutional text even arguably supports the Court's overwrought and novel description of the Second Amendment as "elevat[ing] above all other interests" the right of law-abiding, responsible citizens to use arms in defense of hearth and home.

II

The proper allocation of military power in the new Nation was an issue of central concern for the Framers. The compromises they ultimately reached, reflected in Article I's Militia Clauses and the Second Amendment, represent quintessential examples of the Framers' "splitting the atom of sovereignty."

Two themes relevant to our current interpretive task ran through the debates on the original Constitution. On the one hand, there was a widespread fear that a national standing Army posed an intolerable threat to individual liberty and to the sovereignty of the separate States. . . . On the other hand, the Framers recognized the dangers inherent in relying on inadequately trained militia members "as the primary means of providing for the common defense"; during the Revolutionary War, "[t]his force, though armed, was largely untrained, and its deficiencies were the subject of bitter complaint." In order to respond to those twin concerns, a compromise was reached: Congress would be authorized to raise and support a national Army and Navy, and also to organize, arm, discipline, and provide for the calling forth of "the Militia." U.S. Const., Art. I, §8, cls. 12-16. The President, at the same time, was empowered as the "Commander in Chief of the Army and Navy of the United States, and of the Militia of the several States, when called into the actual Service of the United States." Art. II, §2. But, with respect to the militia, a significant reservation was made to the States: Although Congress would have the power to call forth, organize, arm, and discipline the militia, as well as to govern "such Part of them as may be employed in the Service of the United States," the States respectively would retain the right to appoint the officers and to train the militia in accordance with the discipline prescribed by Congress. Art. I, §8, cl. 16.

But the original Constitution's retention of the militia and its creation of divided authority over that body did not prove sufficient to allay fears about the dangers posed by a standing army. For it was perceived by some that Article I contained a significant gap: While it empowered Congress to organize, arm, and discipline the militia, it did not prevent Congress from providing for the militia's *dis*armament. As George Mason argued during the debates in Virginia on the ratification of the original Constitution:

> "The militia may be here destroyed by that method which has been practiced in other parts of the world before; that is, by rendering them useless—by disarming them. Under various pretences, Congress may neglect to provide for arming and disciplining the militia; and the state governments cannot do it, for Congress has the exclusive right to arm them."

This sentiment was echoed at a number of state ratification conventions; indeed, it was one of the primary objections to the original Constitution voiced by its opponents. The Anti-Federalists were ultimately unsuccessful in persuading state ratification conventions to condition their approval of the Constitution upon the eventual inclusion of any particular amendment. But a number of States did propose to the first Federal Congress amendments reflecting a desire to ensure that the institution of the militia would remain protected under the new Government. The proposed amendments sent by the States of Virginia, North Carolina, and New York focused on the importance of preserving the state militias and reiterated the dangers posed by standing armies. New Hampshire sent a proposal that differed significantly from the others; while also invoking the dangers of a standing army, it suggested that the Constitution should more broadly protect the use and possession of weapons, without tying such a guarantee expressly to the maintenance of the militia. The States of Maryland, Pennsylvania, and Massachusetts sent no relevant proposed amendments to Congress, but in each of those States a minority of the delegates advocated related amendments. While the Maryland minority proposals were exclusively concerned with standing armies and conscientious objectors, the unsuccessful proposals in both Massachusetts and Pennsylvania would have protected a more broadly worded right, less clearly tied to service in a state militia. Faced with all of these options, it is telling that James Madison chose to craft the Second Amendment as he did. . . .

Madison, charged with the task of assembling the proposals for amendments sent by the ratifying States, was the principal draftsman of the Second Amendment. He had before him, or at the very least would have been aware of, all of these proposed formulations. In addition, Madison had been a member, some years earlier, of the committee tasked with drafting the Virginia Declaration of Rights. That committee considered a proposal by Thomas Jefferson that would have included within the Virginia Declaration the following language: "No freeman shall ever be debarred the use of arms [within his own lands or tenements]." But the committee rejected that language, adopting instead the provision drafted by George Mason[, which focused on defense of the state, civilian control of the military and avoidance of standing armies in time of peace].

With all of these sources upon which to draw, it is strikingly significant that Madison's first draft omitted any mention of nonmilitary use or possession of weapons. Rather, his original draft repeated the essence of the two proposed amendments sent by Virginia, combining the substance of the two provisions succinctly into one, which read: "The right of the people to keep and bear arms shall not be infringed; a well armed, and well regulated militia being the best security of a free country; but no person religiously scrupulous of bearing arms, shall be compelled to render military service in person."

Madison's decision to model the Second Amendment on the distinctly military Virginia proposal is therefore revealing, since it is clear that he considered and rejected formulations that would have unambiguously protected civilian uses of firearms. When Madison prepared his first draft, and when that draft was debated and modified, it is reasonable to assume that all participants in the drafting process were fully aware of the other formulations that would have protected civilian use and possession of weapons and that their choice to craft the Amendment as they did represented a rejection of those alternative formulations.

Madison's initial inclusion of an exemption for conscientious objectors sheds revelatory light on the purpose of the Amendment. It confirms an intent to describe a duty as well as a right, and it unequivocally identifies the military character of both. The objections voiced to the conscientious-objector clause only confirm the central meaning of the text. Although records of the debate in the Senate, which is where the conscientious-objector clause was removed, do not survive, the arguments raised in the House illuminate the perceived problems with the clause: Specifically, there was concern that Congress "can declare who are those religiously scrupulous, and prevent them from bearing arms." The ultimate removal of the clause, therefore, only serves to confirm the purpose of the Amendment—to protect against congressional disarmament, by whatever means, of the States' militias.

The Court also contends that because "Quakers opposed the use of arms not just for militia service, but for any violent purpose whatsoever," the inclusion of a conscientious-objector clause in the original draft of the Amendment does not support the conclusion that the phrase "bear arms" was military in meaning. But that claim cannot be squared with the record. [B]oth Virginia and North Carolina included the following language: "That any person religiously scrupulous of bearing arms ought to be exempted, upon payment of an equivalent *to employ another to bear arms in his stead*" (emphasis added). There is no plausible argument that the use of "bear arms" in those provisions was not unequivocally and exclusively military: The State simply does not compel its citizens to carry arms for the purpose of private "confrontation," or for self-defense.

The history of the adoption of the Amendment thus describes an overriding concern about the potential threat to state sovereignty that a federal standing army would pose, and a desire to protect the States' militias as the means by which to guard against that danger. But state militias could not effectively check the prospect of a federal standing army so long as Congress retained the power to disarm them, and so a guarantee against such disarmament was needed. As we explained in *Miller*: "With obvious purpose to assure the continuation and render possible the effectiveness of such forces the declaration and guarantee of the Second Amendment were made. It must be interpreted and applied with that end in view." The evidence plainly refutes the claim that the Amendment was motivated by the Framers' fears that Congress might act to regulate any civilian uses of weapons. And even if the historical record were genuinely ambiguous, the burden would remain on the parties advocating a change in the law to introduce facts or arguments "'newly ascertained'"; the Court is unable to identify any such facts or arguments.

III

Although it gives short shrift to the drafting history of the Second Amendment, the Court dwells at length on four other sources: the 17th-century English Bill of Rights; Blackstone's Commentaries on the Laws of England; postenactment commentary on the Second Amendment; and post-Civil War legislative history. All of these sources shed only indirect light on the question before us, and in any event offer little support for the Court's conclusion. . . .

The Court suggests that by the post-Civil War period, the Second Amendment was understood to secure a right to firearm use and ownership for purely private purposes like personal self-defense. While it is true that some of the legislative history on which the Court relies supports that contention, such sources are entitled to limited, if any, weight. All of the statements the Court cites were made long after the framing of the Amendment and cannot possibly supply any insight into the intent of the Framers; and all were made during pitched political debates, so that they are better characterized as advocacy than good-faith attempts at constitutional interpretation. . . .

IV

The brilliance of the debates that resulted in the Second Amendment faded into oblivion during the ensuing years, for the concerns about Article I's Militia Clauses that generated such pitched debate during the ratification process and led to the adoption of the Second Amendment were short lived.

In 1792, the year after the Amendment was ratified, Congress passed a statute that purported to establish "an Uniform Militia throughout the United States." 1 Stat. 271. The statute commanded every able-bodied white male citizen between the ages of 18 and 45 to be enrolled therein and to "provide himself with a good musket or firelock" and other specified weaponry. The statute is significant, for it confirmed the way those in the founding generation viewed firearm ownership: as a duty linked to military service. The statute they enacted, however, "was virtually ignored for more than a century," and was finally repealed in 1901. . . . In 1901 the President revitalized the militia by creating "'the National Guard of the several States'"; meanwhile, the dominant understanding of the Second Amendment's inapplicability to private gun ownership continued well into the 20th century. The first two federal laws directly restricting civilian use and possession of firearms—the 1927 Act prohibiting mail delivery of "pistols, revolvers, and other firearms capable of being concealed on the person," and the 1934 Act prohibiting the possession of sawed-off shotguns and machine guns—were enacted over minor Second Amendment objections dismissed by the vast majority of the legislators who participated in the debates. Members of Congress clashed over the wisdom and efficacy of such laws as crime-control measures. But since the statutes did not infringe upon the military use or possession of weapons, for most legislators they did not even raise the specter of possible conflict with the Second Amendment.

Thus, for most of our history, the invalidity of Second-Amendment-based objections to firearms regulations has been well settled and uncontroversial. Indeed, the Second Amendment was not even mentioned in either full House of Congress during the legislative proceedings that led to the passage of the 1934 Act.

Yet enforcement of that law produced the judicial decision that confirmed the status of the Amendment as limited in reach to military usage. After reviewing many of the same sources that are discussed at greater length by the Court today, the *Miller* Court unanimously concluded that the Second Amendment did not apply to the possession of a firearm that did not have "some reasonable relationship to the preservation or efficiency of a well regulated militia."

The key to that decision did not, as the Court belatedly suggests, turn on the difference between muskets and sawed-off shotguns; it turned, rather, on the basic difference between the military and nonmilitary use and possession of guns. Indeed, if the Second Amendment were not limited in its coverage to military uses of weapons, why should the Court in *Miller* have suggested that some weapons but not others were eligible for Second Amendment protection? If use for self-defense were the relevant standard, why did the Court not inquire into the suitability of a particular weapon for self-defense purposes? . . .

V

The Court concludes its opinion by declaring that it is not the proper role of this Court to change the meaning of rights "enshrine[d]" in the Constitution. But the right the Court announces was not "enshrined" in the Second Amendment by the Framers; it is the product of today's law-changing decision. The majority's exegesis has utterly failed to establish that as a matter of text or history, "the right of law-abiding, responsible citizens to use arms in defense of hearth and home" is "elevate[d] above all other interests" by the Second Amendment.

Until today, it has been understood that legislatures may regulate the civilian use and misuse of firearms so long as they do not interfere with the preservation of a well-regulated militia. The Court's announcement of a new constitutional right to own and use firearms for private purposes upsets that settled understanding, but leaves for future cases the formidable task of defining the scope of permissible regulations. Today judicial craftsmen have confidently asserted that a policy choice that denies a "law-abiding, responsible citize[n]" the right to keep and use weapons in the home for self-defense is "off the table." Given the presumption that most citizens are law abiding, and the reality that the need to defend oneself may suddenly arise in a host of locations outside the home, I fear that the District's policy choice may well be just the first of an unknown number of dominoes to be knocked off the table.

I do not know whether today's decision will increase the labor of federal judges to the "breaking point" envisioned by Justice Cardozo, but it will surely give rise to a far more active judicial role in making vitally important national policy decisions than was envisioned at any time in the 18th, 19th, or 20th centuries.

The Court properly disclaims any interest in evaluating the wisdom of the specific policy choice challenged in this case, but it fails to pay heed to a far more important policy choice—the choice made by the Framers themselves. The Court would have us believe that over 200 years ago, the Framers made a choice to limit the tools available to elected officials wishing to regulate civilian uses of weapons, and to authorize this Court to use the common-law process of case-by-case judicial lawmaking to define the contours of acceptable gun control policy. Absent compelling evidence that is nowhere to be found in the Court's opinion, I could not possibly conclude that the Framers made such a choice.

For these reasons, I respectfully dissent.

Justice BREYER, with whom Justice STEVENS, Justice SOUTER, and Justice GINSBURG join, dissenting.

I agree with Justice Stevens [that the Second Amendment protects militia-related, not self-defense-related, interests], and I join his opinion. [But] the District's law is consistent with the Second Amendment even if that Amendment is interpreted as protecting a wholly separate interest in individual self-defense. That is so because the District's regulation, which focuses upon the presence of handguns in high-crime urban areas, represents a permissible legislative response to a serious, indeed life-threatening, problem. . . .

[W]hat kind of constitutional standard should the court use? . . . The majority is wrong when it says that the District's law is unconstitutional "[u]nder any of the standards of scrutiny that we have applied to enumerated constitutional rights." . . . It certainly would not be unconstitutional under, for example, a "rational basis" standard. . . . The law at issue here, which in part seeks to prevent gun-related accidents, at least bears a "rational relationship" to that "legitimate" life-saving objective. . . .

Respondent proposes that the Court adopt a "strict scrutiny" test, which would require reviewing with care each gun law to determine whether it is "narrowly tailored to achieve a compelling governmental interest." But the majority implicitly, and appropriately, rejects that suggestion by broadly approving a set of laws—prohibitions on concealed weapons, forfeiture by criminals of the Second Amendment right, prohibitions on firearms in certain locales, and governmental regulation of commercial firearm sales—whose constitutionality under a strict scrutiny standard would be far from clear. . . .

I would simply adopt such an interest-balancing inquiry explicitly. [R]eview of gun-control regulation is not a context in which a court should effectively presume either constitutionality (as in rational-basis review) or unconstitutionality (as in strict scrutiny). Rather, "where a law significantly implicates competing constitutionally protected interests in complex ways," the Court generally asks whether the statute burdens a protected interest in a way or to an extent that is out of proportion to the statute's salutary effects upon other important governmental interests. Any answer would take account both of the statute's effects upon the competing interests and the existence of any clearly superior less restrictive alternative. Contrary to the majority's unsupported suggestion that this sort of "proportionality" approach is unprecedented, the Court has applied it in various constitutional contexts, including election-law cases, speech cases, and due process cases.

In applying this kind of standard the Court normally defers to a legislature's empirical judgment in matters where a legislature is likely to have greater expertise and greater institutional factfinding capacity. Nonetheless, a court, not a legislature, must make the ultimate constitutional conclusion, exercising its "independent judicial judgment" in light of the whole record to determine whether a law exceeds constitutional boundaries. . . . [State] [c]ourts that *do* have experience in [construing analogous provisions in state constitutions] have uniformly taken an approach that treats empirically-based legislative judgment with a degree of deference. See Winkler, Scrutinizing the Second Amendment, 105 Mich. L. Rev. 683 (2007) (describing hundreds of gun-law decisions issued in the last half-century by Supreme Courts in 42 States, which courts with "surprisingly little variation," have adopted a standard more deferential than strict scrutiny). . . .

[T]he District law is tailored to the life-threatening problems it attempts to address. The law concerns one class of weapons, handguns, leaving residents free to possess shotguns and rifles, along with ammunition. The area that falls within its scope is totally urban. That urban area suffers from a serious handgun-fatality problem. The District's law directly aims at that compelling problem. And there is no less restrictive way to achieve the problem-related benefits that it seeks.

[T]he self-defense interest in maintaining loaded handguns in the home to shoot intruders is not the *primary* interest, but at most a subsidiary interest, that the Second Amendment seeks to serve. The Second Amendment's language, while speaking of a "Militia," says nothing of "self-defense." As Justice Stevens points out, the Second Amendment's drafting history shows that the language reflects the Framers' primary, if not exclusive, objective. And the majority itself says that "the threat that the new Federal Government would destroy the citizens' militia by taking away their arms was *the* reason that right . . . was codified in a written Constitution." (emphasis added). The *way* in which the Amendment's operative clause seeks to promote that interest—by protecting a right "to keep and bear Arms"—may *in fact* help further an interest in self-defense. But a factual connection falls far short of a primary objective. The Amendment itself tells us that militia preservation was first and foremost in the Framers' minds.

Further, any self-defense interest at the time of the Framing could not have focused exclusively upon urban-crime related dangers. Two hundred years ago, most Americans, many living on the frontier, would likely have thought of self-defense primarily in terms of outbreaks of fighting with Indian tribes, rebellions such as Shays' Rebellion, marauders, and crime-related dangers to travelers on the roads, on footpaths, or along waterways. Insofar as the Framers focused at all on the tiny fraction of the population living in large cities, they would have been aware that these city dwellers were subject to firearm restrictions that their rural counterparts were not. They are unlikely then to have thought of a right to keep loaded handguns in homes to confront intruders in urban settings as *central.* And the subsequent development of modern urban police departments, by diminishing the need to keep loaded guns nearby in case of intruders, would have moved any such right even further away from the heart of the amendment's more basic protective ends. . . .

The majority derides my approach as "judge-empowering." I take this criticism seriously, but I do not think it accurate. . . . [T]he very nature of the approach—requiring careful identification of the relevant interests and evaluating the law's effect upon them—limits the judge's choices; and the method's necessary transparency lays bare the judge's reasoning for all to see and to criticize. The majority's methodology is, in my view, substantially less transparent than mine. At a minimum, I find it difficult to understand the reasoning that seems to underlie certain conclusions that it reaches.

[It is not] at all clear to me how the majority decides *which* loaded "arms" a homeowner may keep. The majority says that that Amendment protects those weapons "typically possessed by law-abiding citizens for lawful purposes." This definition conveniently excludes machineguns, but permits handguns, which the majority describes as "the most popular weapon chosen by Americans for self-defense in the home." But what sense does this approach make? According to the majority's reasoning, if Congress and the States lift restrictions on the possession and use of machineguns, and people buy machineguns to protect their homes, the Court will have to reverse course and find that the Second Amendment *does*, in fact, protect the individual self-defense-related right to possess a machinegun. On the majority's reasoning, if tomorrow someone invents a particularly useful, highly dangerous self-defense weapon, Congress and the States had better ban it immediately, for once it becomes popular Congress will no longer possess the constitutional authority to do so. In essence, the majority determines what regulations are permissible by looking to see what existing regulations permit. There is no basis for believing that the Framers intended such circular reasoning.

I am similarly puzzled by the majority's list, in Part III of its opinion, of provisions that in its view would survive Second Amendment scrutiny. These consist of (1) "prohibitions on carrying concealed weapons"; (2) "prohibitions on the possession of firearms by felons"; (3) "prohibitions on the possession of firearms by . . . the mentally ill"; (4) "laws forbidding the carrying of firearms in sensitive places such as schools and government buildings"; and (5) government "conditions and qualifications" attached "to the commercial sale of arms." Why these? Is it that similar restrictions existed in the late 18th century? The majority fails to cite any colonial analogues. And even were it possible to find analogous colonial laws in respect to all these restrictions, why should these colonial laws count, while the Boston loaded-gun restriction (along with the other laws I have identified) apparently does not count?

At the same time the majority ignores a more important question: Given the purposes for which the Framers enacted the Second Amendment, how should it be applied to modern-day circumstances that they could not have anticipated? Assume, for argument's sake, that the Framers did intend the Amendment to offer a degree of self-defense protection. Does that mean that the Framers also intended to guarantee a right to possess a loaded gun near swimming pools, parks, and playgrounds? That they would not have cared about the children who might pick up a loaded gun on their parents' bedside table? That they (who certainly showed concern for the risk of fire) would have lacked concern for the risk of accidental deaths or suicides that readily accessible loaded handguns in urban areas might bring? Unless we believe that they intended future generations to ignore such matters, answering questions such as the questions in this case requires judgment—judicial judgment exercised within a framework for constitutional analysis that guides that judgment and which makes its exercise transparent. One cannot answer those questions by combining inconclusive historical research with judicial *ipse dixit*. . . .

McDONALD v. CITY OF CHICAGO, 561 U.S. 742 (2010): Two years after *Heller*, the Supreme Court held, 5-4, that the right of self-defense recognized in *Heller* was incorporated against the States through the Fourteenth Amendment. There was no majority opinion. Justice Alito, speaking for Chief Justice Roberts and Justices Scalia and Kennedy, argued that the right of self-defense was "deeply rooted in this Nation's history and tradition," Washington v. Glucksberg, and therefore was incorporated against the states under the Due Process Clause. First, *Heller* had established that the right was recognized as fundamental at the founding. Second, surveying the history of Reconstruction, Alito argued that "it is clear that the Framers and ratifiers of the Fourteenth Amendment counted the right to keep and bear arms among those fundamental rights necessary to our system of ordered liberty."

Respondents argued against incorporation on the ground that "the Second Amendment differs from all of the other provisions of the Bill of Rights because it concerns the right to possess a deadly implement and thus has implications for public safety . . . and there is intense disagreement on the question whether the private possession of guns in the home increases or decreases gun deaths and injuries." Alito responded: "The right to keep and bear arms . . . is not the only constitutional right that has controversial public safety implications. All of the constitutional provisions that impose restrictions on law enforcement and on the prosecution of crimes fall into the same category."

Alito also rejected arguments that "in order to respect federalism and allow useful state experimentation, a federal constitutional right should not be fully binding on the States." The same argument, he pointed out, "was made repeatedly and eloquently by Members of this Court [such as the second Justice Harlan] who rejected the concept of incorporation and urged retention of the two-track approach to incorporation. . . . Under our precedents, if a Bill of Rights guarantee is fundamental from an American perspective, then, unless stare decisis counsels otherwise, that guarantee is fully binding on the States and thus limits (but by no means eliminates) their ability to devise solutions to social problems that suit local needs and values."

Justice Scalia concurring, explained that "[d]espite my misgivings about Substantive Due Process as an original matter, I have acquiesced in the Court's incorporation of certain guarantees in the Bill of Rights 'because it is both long established and narrowly limited.' This case does not require me to reconsider that view, since straightforward application of settled doctrine suffices to decide it. . . ."

Justice Thomas concurred in the judgment. He rejected the Court's use of the Due Process Clause to protect (and incorporate) fundamental rights, arguing that it is "a legal fiction. The notion that a constitutional provision that guarantees only 'process' before a person is deprived of life, liberty, or property could define the substance of those rights strains credulity for even the most casual user of words. Moreover, this fiction is a particularly dangerous one. The one theme that links the Court's substantive due process precedents together is their lack of a guiding principle to distinguish 'fundamental' rights that warrant protection from nonfundamental rights that do not." Instead, Thomas argued, "the right to keep and bear arms is a privilege of American citizenship that applies to the States through the Fourteenth Amendment's Privileges or Immunities Clause." Pointing to the history of Reconstruction, Thomas argued that ordinary citizens at the time of adoption of the Fourteenth Amendment would have understood the Privileges or Immunities Clause to protect the right to keep and bear arms, noting that "the most widely publicized statements by the legislators who voted on §1 . . . point unambiguously toward the conclusion that the Privileges or Immunities Clause enforces at least those fundamental rights enumerated in the Constitution against the States, including the Second Amendment right to keep and bear arms." Justice Thomas therefore argued that the Court should distinguish the Slaughterhouse Cases (because it concerned unenumerated rights) and overrule United States v. Cruikshank: "*Cruikshank* squarely held that the right to keep and bear arms was not a privilege of American citizenship, thereby overturning the convictions of militia members responsible for the brutal Colfax Massacre. *Cruikshank* is not a precedent entitled to any respect."

By contrast, Justice Alito's plurality opinion rejected McDonald's argument for reviving the Privileges or Immunities Clause and overturning or modifying the Slaughterhouse Cases: "For many decades, the question of the rights protected by the Fourteenth Amendment against state infringement has been analyzed under the Due Process Clause of that Amendment and not under the Privileges or Immunities Clause. We therefore decline to disturb the *Slaughter-House* holding."

Justice Stevens dissented, arguing that "[t]he rights protected against state infringement by the Fourteenth Amendment's Due Process Clause need not be identical in shape or scope to the rights protected against Federal Government infringement by the various provisions of the Bill of Rights. . . . Elementary considerations of constitutional text and structure suggest there may be legitimate reasons to hold state governments to different standards than the Federal Government in certain areas. . . . [W]e have never accepted a 'total incorporation' theory of the Fourteenth Amendment."

Justice Breyer, joined by Justices Ginsburg and Sotomayor, also dissented: "I can find nothing in the Second Amendment's text, history, or underlying rationale that could warrant characterizing it as 'fundamental' insofar as it seeks to protect the keeping and bearing of arms for private self-defense purposes. Nor can I find any justification for interpreting the Constitution as transferring ultimate regulatory authority over the private uses of firearms from democratically elected legislatures to courts or from the States to the Federal Government. I therefore conclude that the Fourteenth Amendment does not 'incorporate' the Second Amendment's right 'to keep and bear Arms.'"

DISCUSSION

1. *Textualism and purposivism.* Note carefully Justice Scalia's methods for interpreting the Second Amendment in *Heller*. He delays discussing the so-called prefatory clause of the Second Amendment until after parsing what he calls the "operative clause," which mentions the right to keep and bear arms. From the "operative clause" he derives an individual right to "possess and carry weapons in case of confrontation." Why does he proceed in this way?

Justice Scalia notes that the Second Amendment is equivalent to the statement that "Because a well regulated Militia is necessary to the security of a free State, the right of the people to keep and bear Arms shall not be infringed." He argues that "apart from [its] clarifying function, a prefatory clause does not limit or expand the scope of the operative clause." Why should this be? Suppose someone says, "Because I need someone to drive my parents around, you may use my car." Does this give permission to use the car other than as a chauffeur? Does it give permission to use the car if the parents move out of state or to a different country? Suppose the Constitution had said, "Freedom of discussion on public issues being necessary to a free state, Congress shall not abridge the right of free speech." Should this have affected what kinds of speech (e.g., music, painting, pornography, advertisements) are protected and unprotected?

With the Second Amendment, compare the Progress Clause of Article I, §8, cl. 8, which gives Congress the power "[t]o promote the progress of science and useful arts, by securing for limited times to authors and inventors the exclusive right to their respective writings and discoveries." The structure of the Progress Clause is somewhat different than the structure of the Second Amendment: The first clause offers a grant of power (to promote progress) that is limited by the second clause as to the means (granting exclusive rights for limited times). Conversely, the power to grant exclusive rights that appears in the second clause is glossed by the purpose (promoting progress) stated in the first clause.

2. *Dueling theories.* Justice Scalia argues that the Second Amendment was placed in the Constitution because of "the threat that the new Federal Government would destroy the citizens' militia by taking away their arms" and that the purpose of the citizen's militia, in turn, was "to oppose an oppressive military force if the constitutional order broke down." The common law right to keep and bear arms for self-defense and for hunting, Scalia argues, was codified in order to prevent such disarmament.

Justice Stevens, by contrast, argues that the common law right was not constitutionalized, at least at this point in history. Instead, the Second Amendment guaranteed "the right of the people of each of the several States to maintain a well-regulated militia" so as to prevent the federal government from disarming state militias. Under Stevens's theory, what rights, if any, do individual Americans have under the Second Amendment? Presumably, they have the right to the military use of weapons in state militias. But if the state no longer has a militia, or if the state excludes people from its organized militia, is there any remaining individual right? Under Stevens's account, do citizens have the right to form their own militias outside of state control?

In fact, Scalia argues that a major flaw with Stevens's theory is that it allows states (and the federal government) to disarm their citizens by closing down the militia or excluding most people from it. Does this mean that under Scalia's account, citizens have the right to form militias free from federal or state control or supervision? Such militias might be formed not only for mutual self-defense but also to ensure that federal and state law enforcement do not oppress the people or violate the Constitution as members of these militias understand it. Suppose the government considers such private armies (which we assume employ nothing other than weapons permitted to ordinary citizens) a danger to public safety. May it disband them as long as it allows citizens to retain ordinary weapons for self-defense? Cf. Presser v. Illinois, 116 U.S. 252 (1886) (upholding a law banning private militias, but holding that the Second Amendment did not apply to the states). Suppose that the government proves that a group of citizens has formed a paramilitary organization designed to deter what the group regards as the potential for future government tyranny. May the government disarm those people? May it convict them of violating a ban on paramilitary organizations and then disarm them on the grounds that they are felons?

The history and the text of the Second Amendment focus on citizen militias because the Second Amendment was drafted in the context of a larger ideology of civic republicanism: Citizens had duties to work together to promote the public good. Participating in citizen militias to resist or deter tyranny or invasion was one of the common duties of members of the community. See Sanford Levinson, The Embarrassing Second Amendment, 99 Yale L.J. 637 (1989). Thus, the right to keep and bear arms at the founding was not a purely individualist or liberal right to be free from state interference, in the way we often think of rights today. Rather, it was a right that arose from a common political obligation and a common duty to fellow citizens and to the Republic.

This distinction is important in understanding the historical record debated by the Justices in *Heller*. While the right to bear arms together with one's fellow citizens to prevent tyranny is a *civic republican* conception of the right, the right to bear arms in self-defense is a *liberal individualist* conception. The latter is more of a privilege of individuals than a duty to fellow citizens or to the nation.

The need to preserve state militias to counteract federal tyranny, insurrection, and foreign invasion is a civic republican idea. So too is the preservation of an unorganized militia that could arise spontaneously to fight a tyrannical federal government, tyrannical state government, anti-republican insurrection, or foreign invasion. Citizens would band together, either organized by states, or spontaneously, to protect each other and the republic from invaders or tyrants.

3. *A vestigial right?* Does Scalia interpret the Second Amendment as protecting a liberal individualist or a civic republican conception of the right to bear arms? Might his opinion do both?

Scalia argues that in order to enable the militia to battle tyranny, the citizenry must have the sort of arms they would ordinarily use in self-defense of the home. In the 1790s, weapons commonly used in combat and weapons commonly used for self-defense overlapped considerably. They do no longer. As Scalia notes, a citizenry armed with handguns might be no match for today's heavy weaponry. Yet *Heller* holds that the citizenry does not have a right to keep and use the kind of military-style weapons that citizens could use to resist a tyrannical government today.

Nevertheless, Scalia argues that the right to bear arms in defense of self and home endures even if it no longer effectively serves the original purpose for which it was codified in the Constitution—defending the people against tyranny. In this way he downplays the Second Amendment's civic republican purposes. What justifies this move? To what extent is it consistent with originalism? With the amendment's opening clause?

Justice Scalia argues that originalism takes account of technological change, citing cases involving the First and Fourth Amendments as examples. But generally speaking, in such cases, courts try to *preserve* the practical effect of a constitutional right in light of new technology. For example, one might extend free speech rights to Internet technologies because that is where most people speak these days; one might extend Fourth Amendment protections to state use of electronic wiretaps and global positioning systems in order to preserve people's privacy in the face of increasing government technological prowess. Why does Scalia treat the Second Amendment differently?

4. *Which tyranny?* Scalia's historical account puts the best possible face on a tension inherent in the 1791 Constitution that was implicit in the possibility of unorganized militias. On the one hand, the militia had the right to keep and bear arms to prevent tyranny, including a tyrannical federal government (or state government, in the case of state constitutions). On the other hand, the federal government had the obligation to put down insurrections and invasions (see the Guarantee Clause of Article IV), and it had the right to organize and take over state militias for this purpose. See the Militia Clauses, Article I, §8, cl. 15 and 16.

This balance of powers did not decide which group—the "insurrectionists" or the "government"—was the problem and which was the solution. The government might be tyrannical, or it might be a republican government defending against a mob or a *putsch*. The (unorganized) militia exercising its Second Amendment rights might be rising up against a tyrannical government, or it might be a force threatening republican government. *Heller* resolves this problem largely by ignoring it; it reads the Second Amendment as guaranteeing the right to bear arms for self-defense, but not the right to possess "dangerous" weapons.

Consider a civic republican reading of *Heller*'s exclusion of "dangerous" weapons from constitutional protection. Civic republicanism requires cooperation and mutual support. Some weapons, such as nuclear bombs, tanks, or machine guns, don't require many people to cooperate to inflict enormous damage. Other weapons, such as swords and muskets, can inflict much less damage individually, and require people to band together to resist oppression. Under a civic republican reading, handguns and shotguns might be "republican" and are constitutionally protected while machine guns might be "anti-republican" and may be proscribed. Does *Heller* contemplate this distinction or a different one that is unrelated to civic republican ideology?

Does Scalia's reading of the individual right to keep and bear arms allow government to criminalize caches of arms that might someday be used to resist an oppressive government? *Heller* assumes that licensing requirements are constitutional. Do citizens have a constitutional right to stockpile as many weapons as they like, subject to obtaining a license for each one?

Suppose citizens stockpile weapons and engage in military exercises to resist government tyranny. Does *Heller* allow governments to prosecute these citizens for criminal conspiracy to commit insurrection or terrorism? What if the basis of the charge of conspiracy is that the citizens are stockpiling weapons, presumably in order to allow them to resist future tyranny or invasion?

5. *The uses of history, originalism, and the living Constitution.* Both Justices Scalia and Stevens state their historical conclusions confidently, asserting that the historical record is clear. As is often the case with attempts to recapture the past, however, the same facts can often be interpreted in more than one way, a point made abundantly clear by juxtaposing Scalia's and Stevens's equally self-assured claims about identical texts and events.

Justice Scalia's argument is that the Second Amendment codified the English common law right to use weapons for self-defense. There is some evidence for this position, but the historical record is mixed and can be read in several different ways. Different views about the nature of the right to keep and bear arms circulated during the founding period, which is hardly surprising given that it was one of the most intellectually lively periods in American political thought. On the ambiguities of the amendment's adoption history, see Mark V. Tushnet, Out of Range: Why the Constitution Can't End the Battle over Guns (2007); Saul Cornell, A Well-Regulated Militia: The Founding Fathers and the Origins of Gun Control in America (2006); Sanford Levinson, Guns and the Constitution, A Complex Relationship, 36 Reviews in American History 1-14 (2008) (reviewing Tushnet and Cornell).

On the other hand, as Scalia notes, there is fairly strong evidence that during the nineteenth century people believed that the Second Amendment guaranteed a right to use arms in self-defense, and the evidence grows stronger as the century proceeds. By the time of the Civil War, it was widely assumed that the common law right to keep and bear arms for self-defense was a fundamental constitutional right, whether it was protected by the Privileges and Immunities Clause of Article IV, the Second Amendment, or the Ninth Amendment.

Justice Scalia reads the nineteenth-century history not as evidence of evolving views about basic rights, but as evidence of the common understandings of 1791. Scalia does this because his originalist theory of interpretation commits him to focus on the understandings of late eighteenth-century Americans. The danger, of course, is that his use of history is anachronistic. (While the understanding of the right may have evolved from a civic republican emphasis in the eighteenth century to a more liberal individualist conception in the nineteenth, Justice Scalia may be reading the later understanding back into the earlier period.)

Scalia scoffs at "the proposition, unsupported by any evidence, that different people of the founding period had vastly different conceptions of the right to keep and bear arms. That simply does not comport with our longstanding view that the Bill of Rights codified venerable, widely understood liberties." But surely it is likely that people disagreed about the meaning of the right to bear arms in 1791 just as they disagree about basic rights today.

Do the historical sources that Court surveys show the degree of historical certainty and consensus that Scalia seems to assume? One potential problem is that if we assume that more than one view of the right to keep and bear arms was circulating at the founding, present-day judges must pick one reading as more faithful than the others. Would doing this pose any problems for originalism's conception of the judicial role, or with the democratic legitimacy of judicial review? In your view, does originalism provide significantly more determinacy than other methods for discovering and articulating fundamental rights?

A far more plausible reading of the history is that views about the purposes of the amendment were in flux at the founding and changed over the course of a century, and that by the time of Reconstruction, it was widely accepted that the right to self-defense was a constitutional liberty identified with the Second Amendment. Even if there was no consensus about whether the English common law right was constitutionalized in 1791, such a consensus had developed by Reconstruction. Hence the framers of the Fourteenth Amendment believed that the right to use arms in self-defense was one of the "Privileges or Immunities of Citizens of the United States" protected by the Fourteenth Amendment. (For example, see Senator Jacob Howard's Speech introducing the Fourteenth Amendment before the Senate in May 1866, reprinted in Chapter 4.)

Given this evidence, could a court read the text of the Second Amendment consistent with these nineteenth-century views, and particularly those widely held at the time of the Fourteenth Amendment? This would not be a necessary implication of the original meaning of the Second Amendment. Rather, it would be a constitutional *construction* of the original meaning that became commonplace in the nineteenth century. The original meaning of the text can easily bear this construction and, so the argument would go, we should accept it today, especially because it was assumed in the debates leading up to the ratification of the Fourteenth Amendment.

This reading of history, however, would require a "living Constitution" approach. It would maintain that a later generation's views on the scope of the Second Amendment can be accepted as part of the Constitution as long as those views are consistent with the original meaning of the words of the text. Why does the majority not adopt this model of interpretation? Equally important, why doesn't Justice Stevens's dissent?

What are the problems with accepting the nineteenth century's construction of the Second Amendment as the best interpretation? Does it commit us to accept nineteenth-century assumptions about the scope of other parts of the Bill of Rights, or, for that matter, the Fourteenth Amendment?

6. *Living constitutionalism and the role of social movements.* Justice Stevens makes much of the fact that for the better part of a century, courts had assumed that the Second Amendment did not guarantee an individual right to use guns for self-defense. Indeed, this was the conventional wisdom for many years. In 1991, for example, retired Chief Justice Warren Burger, a conservative Republican, insisted that the individual rights view of the Second Amendment was "one of the greatest pieces of fraud—I repeat the word 'fraud'—on the American public by special interest groups that I have ever seen in my lifetime." Burger cast particular scorn on the efforts of the National Rifle Association (NRA) and other groups—which he pejoratively labeled "special interest groups"—to convince Americans otherwise. As we have seen elsewhere in this course, in the context of social movements like the women's movement and the gay rights movement, sustained political and social mobilization can persuade people to change their minds about what is "off the wall" and "on the wall" concerning legal and constitutional claims. For a history of how the work of social movements eventually led to the decision in *Heller,* see Reva B. Siegel, Dead or Alive: Originalism as Popular Constitutionalism in *Heller,* 122 Harv. L. Rev. 191, 201-246 (2008).

Siegel's history of the gun rights movement suggests that popular understandings of the importance of the right to bear arms are of recent vintage. The modern movement for gun rights arose in reaction to increased political mobilization for stricter gun control laws, particularly after passage of the 1968 Crime Control Act, which Congress enacted following the assassinations of Martin Luther King, Jr. and Robert F. Kennedy. Beginning in the 1970s, the NRA began national lobbying efforts to oppose gun control legislation, arguing that gun control laws violated Second Amendment rights and that the conventional wisdom about the Constitution was incorrect. The gun rights movement gained influence within the Republican Party, as gun rights became one of many interconnected issues in the culture wars. Movement conservatives who used originalism to attack liberal judicial decisions also turned to originalism to defend Second Amendment rights. See, e.g., The Right to Keep and Bear Arms: Report of the Subcommittee on the Constitution of the Committee on the Judiciary, 1 S. 97th Cong., 2d Sess. (1982).

As conservatives gained increasing political influence during the last part of the twentieth century, the NRA's constitutional position gained increasing public support, and convinced members of a newer generation of conservative legal elites. In 1994, the Republicans took control of both Houses of Congress by making a key campaign issue of their opposition to recent gun control laws passed by a Democratic-controlled Congress. See Nicholas J. Johnson, A Second Amendment Moment: The Constitutional Politics of Gun Control, 71 Brook. L. Rev. 715 (2005). In May 2002, Attorney General John Ashcroft announced the Bush Justice Department's official position that the Second Amendment protected an individual right to use arms in self-defense.

As we have seen in Brown v. Board of Education and other cases, the Supreme Court tends to respond, in the long run, to the views of the dominant political coalition as well as to public opinion. The agendas of legal scholarship also tend to shift in response to political changes. An outpouring of new legal and historical scholarship began debating the individual rights interpretation in the 1990s and 2000s, and the third edition of Professor Laurence Tribe's treatise, American Constitutional Law, published in 2000, argued—in contrast to the two previous editions—that the Second Amendment protected an individual right. See Laurence H. Tribe, American Constitutional Law §5-11, 901-902 n.221 (3d ed. 2000).

In this sense, the result in *Heller* was not entirely surprising. As in Brown v. Board of Education, the 1970s sex equality cases, and Lawrence v. Texas, the Supreme Court has kept its interpretation of the Constitution in line with changing public values. Another name for this phenomenon is living constitutionalism.

The irony, of course, is that the arguments for modifying constitutional doctrine to reflect evolving public views were all phrased in the language of fidelity to original meaning. However, this may represent the ordinary role of orginalist argument. The best way for social movements to persuade others that their views are correct is to show how they follow ineluctably from the nation's deepest commitments. Appeals to the framers and the Constitution's original meaning are one way, although not the only way, to do that.

7. *A democratic constitutionalism argument for* Heller *and* McDonald. Suppose that as a result of the mobilizations described by Siegel, a substantial majority of the American public has coalesced behind the basic notion that the right to bear arms in self-defense is fundamental. Should courts interpret the Second Amendment to recognize that right, regardless of adoption history? Put differently, if you think that judges should protect contraceptive rights and gay rights because contemporary Americans believe these rights are fundamental, should judges treat gun rights any differently?

This account of *Heller* assumes a very different theory of the democratic legitimacy of judicial review than the one offered in Scalia's opinion. The implicit theory in *Heller* is that judges are simply bound by the original meaning and original understanding of the Constitution. That meaning is clear: It protects an individual right to use arms in self-defense. Therefore it is the duty of judges to enforce that meaning. But if we understand *Heller* as reflecting beliefs about the Second Amendment that emerged from contemporary debates among the general public and legal elites, we can see that the legitimacy of judicial review draws strength from both the past *and* the present—because it reflects how present-day Americans understand and value the achievements and commitments of their forebears. (That said, the regulation of firearms remains highly contested in American life, and there may not be a common view about the meaning of our constitutional commitments; the views of the judiciary about this fundamental right may be just as contested as any other.)

The first theory views the judges' role as faithfully following an ancient law of the framers as they would have understood and applied it. It asserts (or at least must assert) that the text is clear and there can be no other reasonable construction. The second views the judges' role as interpreting text and history in light of contemporary social values. Why are the opinions in *Heller* written according to the first theory rather than the second?

8. *Judicial scrutiny under the Second Amendment.* Justice Breyer suggests that Second Amendment rights should be determined according to a balancing test, roughly akin to the intermediate scrutiny employed in the sex equality cases and in First Amendment cases involving regulations of time, place, and manner. He notes

that state courts with analogous constitutional provisions have, by and large, used a balancing or intermediate scrutiny approach. For a review of the state cases, see Adam Winkler, Scrutinizing the Second Amendment, 105 Mich. L. Rev. 683 (2007). The majority, although striking down parts of the D.C. ordinance, leaves open the question of the appropriate level of scrutiny for a future case. However, it seems to reject Breyer's approach. Is this because it rejects the idea of applying intermediate scrutiny or merely Breyer's application of it?

Consider Breyer's argument that the empirical studies on gun control laws point in different directions; given this uncertainty, courts should defer to legislatures about the best way to balance home owners' rights and public safety. Compare Breyer's views with the Court's application of the "undue burden" test in abortion cases, in particular *Casey* and Gonzales v. Carhart. Could the majority respond that the D.C. ban on handguns is a complete ban of a commonly used weapon rather than merely a regulation of handgun use? Does the Second Amendment prohibit complete bans on any weapons that are currently in common use? Does it allow the government to prevent new weapons from becoming commonly used?

9. *Applying* Heller *and* McDonald*: The two-step test.* Since *Heller* and *McDonald*, many federal courts of appeals have adopted a "two-step" test for gun regulations.[235] First, as a threshold question, courts have asked whether the regulated conduct has historically fallen within the scope of the Second Amendment; or conversely, whether the conduct has historically been subject to regulation or prohibition. If so, then the Second Amendment does not apply at all.

The first step is motivated by several ideas. To begin with, in *Heller* itself, Justice Scalia asserted that only some kinds of weapons—those commonly used by law-abiding individuals for self-defense—were protected by the Second Amendment; the use of others was outside the amendment's scope. *Heller* also stated that "[n]othing in our opinion should be taken to cast doubt on longstanding prohibitions on the possession of firearms by felons and the mentally ill, or laws forbidding the carrying of firearms in sensitive places such as schools and government buildings, or laws imposing conditions and qualifications on the commercial sale of arms," and that this list of "presumptively lawful regulatory measures" was illustrative, not exhaustive. Justice Alito's opinion in *McDonald* repeated *Heller*'s "assurances" about these exceptions. In addition, courts have drawn an analogy to the First Amendment, which has historically excluded categories like obscenity, fraud, and incitement from the class of protected speech.

Courts applying the first prong generally engage in a historical inquiry: They ask whether regulations of the same kind as the one at issue were historically accepted or commonplace. Not surprisingly, there are often several ways to assess the history and its relationship to present-day regulations. Nevertheless, if the court concludes that regulations of the kind at issue were historically accepted, the Second Amendment does not apply at all.

---

235. See, e.g., NRA of Am. v. Bureau of Alcohol, 700 F.3d 185, 194 (5th Cir. 2012); United States v. Greeno, 679 F.3d 510 (6th Cir. 2012); Heller v. Dist. of Columbia, 670 F.3d 1244 (D.C. Cir. 2011) (*Heller II*); Ezell v. City of Chicago, 651 F.3d 684 (7th Cir. 2011); United States v. Chester, 628 F.3d 673 (4th Cir. 2010); United States v. Reese, 627 F.3d 792 (10th Cir. 2010); United States v. Marzzarella, 614 F.3d 85 (3d Cir. 2010).

If the historical evidence is inconclusive or suggests that the regulated activity is not categorically unprotected, the courts then go on to the second part of the two-step test. They apply heightened scrutiny to the regulation, assessing the importance of the government's justifications and how well they are furthered by the regulation in question. Different circuits have adopted slightly different formulations of the test. See, e.g., NRA of America v. BATF, 700 F.3d 185, 205 (5th Cir. 2012) ("A law that burdens the core of the Second Amendment guarantee—for example, 'the right of law-abiding, responsible citizens to use arms in defense of hearth and home,' *Heller*—would trigger strict scrutiny, while a less severe law would be proportionately easier to justify. The latter, 'intermediate' standard of scrutiny requires the government to show a reasonable fit between the law and an important government objective.").

The two-step test requires courts to make a number of judgment calls, both about how broadly or narrowly to construe historical precedents, and about judicial scrutiny of government regulation. In theory, therefore, the test might lead to a fairly significant restriction on gun regulations. Nevertheless, the practical effect of the two-step test, at least in the first several years after *Heller* and *McDonald*, is that relatively few gun regulations have been struck down. Why do you think this is so?

10. *What kind of self-defense?* Justice Scalia reads the Second Amendment to protect the common law right of self-defense. What precisely is this right? Does it protect only the right to keep firearms in the home for self-defense, or does it also include the right to keep them on one's person outside the home, for example, when one travels in dangerous neighborhoods? Does *Heller* protect the right to use weapons other than firearms for self-defense in the home? For example, are laws banning the possession of switchblades within the home constitutional under *Heller*? Does it protect the right to possess these weapons outside the home? See Moore v. Madigan, 702 F.3d 993 (7th Cir. 2012) (extending the logic of *Heller* outside the home and holding that Illinois statute that generally prohibits carrying of ready-to-use guns outside the home violated the Second Amendment); National Rifle Ass'n of America, Inc. v. McCraw, 719 F.3d 338 (5th Cir. 2013) (upholding Texas statute that prevented 18- to 20-year-olds from carrying handguns in public).

Does *Heller* protect the right of self-defense per se, whether with or without a firearm? Does it mean, for example, that states must, as a constitutional matter, have a doctrine of self-defense in their criminal and tort laws? If there is a constitutional right of self-defense, is it limited only to situations where a person is directly attacked by another? For example, would the constitutional right of self-defense extend to the use of drugs and surgeries that patients reasonably believe are necessary for their survival? See Eugene Volokh, Medical Self-Defense, Prohibited Experimental Therapies, and Payment for Organs, 120 Harv. L. Rev. 1813 (2007) (discussing possible rights of self-defense under the Due Process Clause); Abigail Alliance for Better Access to Developmental Drugs v. von Eschenbach, 495 F.3d 695 (D.C. Cir. 2007) (en banc), *cert. denied*, 552 U.S. 1159 (2008) (holding that terminally ill patients have no fundamental right under the Due Process Clause to obtain potentially life-saving medications still undergoing testing required by the Food and Drug Administration). Would the constitutional guarantee of self-defense protect the right of women to have abortions to save their lives? Compare the guarantee of abortions to save the mother's life in Roe v. Wade. Or does *Heller* merely hold that people have a right to keep weapons in their homes for purposes of self-defense where such weapons are of the sort commonly available and that might be used in a state militia, if the state had such a militia?

11. *Incorporation.* The result in McDonald v. City of Chicago was widely expected following the 2008 decision in *Heller.* One remarkable feature of the opinion is how fairly standard arguments made in the past by conservative judges against incorporation and broad readings of the Bill of Rights have become the arguments of liberal judges and vice versa. Justice Stevens argues (as the second Justice Harlan did before him) that the provisions of the Bill of Rights need not apply fully to the states. Justices Stevens and Breyer make standard arguments for judicial restraint and emphasize the inability of judges to fully consider the consequences of new rights; both emphasize that courts should not attempt to intervene in difficult and contested social controversies, and both make standard arguments for respecting states' rights and for the ability of states to experiment with forms of regulation best attuned to local conditions. Justice Alito, on the other hand, emphasizes that constitutional rights must be respected whether or not they may make law enforcement more difficult or even put lives at risk. (Compare Justice Alito's willingness to sacrifice public safety to ensure constitutional liberty with the arguments of the conservative Justices in *Boumediene* a few years previously.) Justice Scalia, for his part, argues that stare decisis must trump originalist considerations.

12. *Deeply rooted in our nation's traditions.* While Justice Thomas's concurrence is strongly originalist, Justice Alito's plurality opinion offers an interesting mix of modalities. Justice Alito's approach is not strictly originalist, because he employs the Due Process Clause to incorporate the Second Amendment. On the other hand, he asks whether people in 1791 and 1868 considered the right to keep arms in the home for self-defense to be fundamental, which resembles an originalist inquiry into understandings at the time of the founding and Reconstruction. But if the test is one of tradition, then Justice Alito should be concerned about a continuous regard for the right up to the present day. Why does he not focus more on respect for this right during the twentieth century?

13. *No privileges or immunities for you.* Justice Thomas is the only Justice willing to take seriously the original design of the Fourteenth Amendment. He argues that the Privileges or Immunities Clause was the primary vehicle for protecting substantive rights, not the Due Process Clause. The other eight Justices reject this idea, including Justice Scalia, the Court's other originalist judge. Why is this? One possibility is that the Justices do not know what would happen if the Court used the Privileges or Immunities Clause. Some Justices might fear that implied fundamental rights (like the rights recognized in *Lawrence* and *Casey*) would no longer be protected. Other Justices might fear, to the contrary, that moving to a clause that seems on its face to protect substantive rights would give judges greater discretion to protect new implied fundamental rights. Still other Justices might fear that reviving the Privileges or Immunities Clause would revive *Lochner*-style rights. And still others might fear that this would require incorporating the entire Bill of Rights, including the Seventh Amendment civil jury right and the Fifth Amendment right to grand jury indictments.

Given what you know about the path of doctrinal development in the United States Supreme Court in American history, how realistic are these fears? Is there any reason to think that a Justice who believes there is a right to abortion under the Due Process Clause would believe that such a right is not protected by the Privileges or Immunities Clause? Conversely, is there any reason to think that a Justice who does not think that abortion is a fundamental right under the Due Process Clause would conclude that it is protected as a privilege or immunity? Is there any reason to believe that a shift to the Privileges or Immunities Clause would cause a majority of the Justices (or even Justice Thomas) to reconsider Lochner v. New York? If constitutional protection of such rights came back into fashion, it is far more likely that it would be because of large-scale changes in American politics than because of a change in the relevant constitutional language.

Would a shift in focus to the Privileges or Immunities Clause require any significant changes in doctrine? One possibility concerns the rights of noncitizens. The Due Process Clause protects persons as well as citizens. Therefore, the Court would have to use the Due Process and Equal Protection Clauses together to explain why noncitizens enjoy the same fundamental rights as citizens. However, this result is consistent with the views of the Reconstruction-era framers. See Akhil Amar, The Bill of Rights: Creation and Reconstruction 172-174 (1998). Another possibility is that the Court would be required to incorporate the remaining individual rights mentioned in the Bill of Rights, including the Third Amendment and the Fifth Amendment's guarantee of grand jury indictments. It is unclear, however, whether the Seventh Amendment right to civil juries is such an individual right or is rather a structural *Erie*-like provision, requiring federal courts to provide litigants the same right to trial by jury they would receive in the state in which the federal court sits. See id. at 275-276.

14. *The effect of a national standard. McDonald* imposes a national standard on gun control measures. What effect will this have? Consider the following analysis:[236]

> The big difference between applying a constitutional right only against the federal government and applying it against state and local governments is that there are many more state and local regulations of firearms than federal regulations, and these regulations occur in many different varieties. This increases the number of possible constitutional claims, and it also increases the opportunities for litigation. It does not, however, guarantee that Second Amendment rights will become too robust over time.
>
> We can guess what is likely to happen from the way that courts have protected other federal constitutional rights against states and local governments in the past. Federal judicial protection of fundamental rights tends to converge toward the preferences of the national political coalition, which includes executive branch and law enforcement officials. Federal courts tend to strike down mostly laws in outlier jurisdictions that are markedly different from the norm. That is what happened in the District of Columbia, and will likely happen in Chicago. More than 40 states already recognize an individual right to bear arms under their own constitutions. By and large, they have upheld most gun control laws under a loose standard of reasonableness. The federal courts will probably follow suit.
>
> Gun control advocates are concerned that a single federal rule for gun rights will leave urban areas defenseless. Ironically, however, a national standard that lumps cities and rural areas together is far more likely to

236. Jack M. Balkin, Creating a National Norm, N.Y. Times, June 28, 2010, at http://roomfordebate.blogs.nytimes.com/2010/06/28/what-bolstering-gun-rights-will-mean/jack.

> produce moderation than radical change. That is because many more people live in metropolitan than in rural areas, and in the long run their preferences will shape the national political coalition.

In a footnote in his dissenting opinion in *McDonald*, Justice Stevens argues that incorporation means that "federal courts will face a profound pressure to reconcile [a single national] standard with the diverse interests of the States and their long history of regulating in this sensitive area. . . . [F]ederal courts will have little choice but to fix a highly flexible standard of review if they are to avoid leaving federalism and the separation of powers—not to mention gun policy—in shambles."

Do you agree with Balkin's analysis? With Stevens's? Consider that another lesson of political science studies is that rights protections will tend to expand if there are well-funded and continuous litigation campaigns assisted by other forms of grassroots political organization. See generally Charles R. Epp, The Rights Revolution: Lawyers, Activists, and Supreme Courts in Comparative Perspective (1998). Why won't a sustained litigation campaign by conservative public interest organizations and by interest groups such as the National Rifle Association lead to increasingly stronger gun rights?

Chapter 10

The Constitution in the Modern Welfare State

The welfare state is a way of governing in which the state attempts to reshape the power of markets and reduce economic insecurity through expenditures, tax policy, licenses, and social programs. For example, the state may provide supplements to income; offer tax breaks or subsidies to promote private activity; help individuals and families deal with sickness, old age, or unemployment; and provide or subsidize important goods and services like insurance, housing, health care, employment, education, and legal services.[1]

The welfare state both alters and helps to constitute modern capitalism. As Neil Gilbert explains:[2]

> Capitalism encourages competition and risk-taking behavior. Although success in the economic marketplace is often well rewarded, misfortune and failure can lead to harsh consequences. There are few market mechanisms to mitigate the consequences of accident, illness, age, and vicissitudes of industrial society. And these mechanisms, such as private insurance, provide the most protection to those who are relatively well off and least in need of it. The welfare state operates through a social market that provides a sort of communal safety net for the casualties of a market economy.

Although the welfare state is often identified with benefits to the poor, there is no reason to believe that government programs will only distribute income and benefits from the well-off to the less well-off. The least well-off may often also be the least well organized politically, and the middle class may draw far greater attention from politicians. Moreover, focused interest groups and economically powerful organizations and persons may be far better equipped to organize, to

---

1. See, e.g., Asa Briggs' definition in The Welfare State in Historical Perspective, quoted in Evelyn Z. Brodkin and Dennis Young, Making Sense of Privatization: What Can We Learn from Economic and Policy Analysis?, in Privatization and the Welfare State 140 (Kamerman & Kahn eds., 1989).

2. Neil Gilbert, Capitalism and the Welfare State 4-5 (1983). See also Amy Gutmann, ed., Democracy and the Welfare State (1988).

lobby, and to make political contributions, and thus better able to persuade politicians to alter taxing, spending, licensing, and entitlement programs to benefit their interests.

Objections to federal welfare and expenditure programs, and disputes about whom they really benefit, have a long history in American politics, often combining political and constitutional arguments. Recall the Jeffersonian Republicans' early objections to disaster relief, Jacksonian objections to federal internal improvements and the Second Bank of the United States, President Cleveland's objections to federal relief programs, and objections to New Deal programs such as the National Industrial Recovery Act and Social Security.

At no point did American government adopt a posture of pure laissez-faire; regulation, occupational licensing, and subsidies for developing industries had existed since at least the eighteenth century.[3] And, as we have seen in earlier chapters, Congress was often more than willing to pass "disaster relief" legislation that, almost by definition, involves redistribution of resources to those rendered "have-nots" by the force of disaster, whether from cities burning down or the flooding of great rivers. Still, the magnitude of state intervention in the lives of individuals and enterprises increased enormously in the twentieth century, especially in the decades that followed the New Deal. These changes in the reach of government power were accompanied by shifts in a number of fundamental constitutional concepts.

I. DOES THE CONSTITUTION AFFIRMATIVELY GUARANTEE ANY WELFARE RIGHTS?

Following the New Deal, mainstream political thought no longer denies that the state has the constitutional power to operate redistributive programs; rather, the debate usually turns on whether Congress has made unconstitutional distinctions in deciding who shall (or shall not) receive federally funded largesse. A further question is whether the Constitution *requires* the state to subsidize or supply any goods or services to individuals who cannot afford to purchase them through the market.[4] During the 1950s and 1960s, the federal courts began to consider this question.

A. The Rights of Indigents in the Criminal Justice System

The first cases concerned the rights of indigents in the criminal justice system. Griffin v. Illinois, 351 U.S. 12 (1956), held that a state must provide a trial transcript or its equivalent to an indigent criminal defendant appealing his conviction based on trial errors, notwithstanding the state's general practice of conditioning appeals

---

3. See, e.g., William J. Novak, The People's Welfare: Law and Regulation in Nineteenth-Century America (1996).

4. See, e.g., Sotorios Barber, Welfare and the Constitution (2003).

on appellants' furnishing transcripts at their own expense. Justice Black, writing for a plurality that included Chief Justice Warren and Justices Douglas and Clark, emphasized that

> [our] constitutional guaranties of due process and equal protection both call for procedures in criminal trials which allow no invidious discriminations between persons and different groups of persons. . . .
>
> In criminal trials a State can no more discriminate on account of poverty than on account of religion, race, or color. Plainly the ability to pay costs in advance bears no rational relationship to a defendant's guilt or innocence and could not be used as an excuse to deprive a defendant of a fair trial. . . .
>
> It is true that a State is not required by the Federal Constitution to provide appellate courts or a right to appellate review at all. . . . But that is not to say that a State that does grant appellate review can do so in a way that discriminates against some convicted defendants on account of their poverty. Appellate review has now become an integral part of the Illinois trial system for finally adjudicating the guilt or innocence of a defendant. Consequently at all stages of the proceedings the Due Process and Equal Protection Clauses protect persons like petitioners from invidious discriminations. . . .
>
> Destitute defendants must be afforded as adequate appellate review as defendants who have money enough to buy transcripts.

Four Justices dissented. With respect to the petitioner's equal protection claim, Justice Harlan argued that "[a]ll that Illinois has done is to fail to alleviate the consequences of differences in economic circumstances that exist wholly apart from any state action. . . . The real issue in this case is not whether Illinois has discriminated [against the poor] but whether it has a duty to discriminate [in favor of the poor]." With respect to the due process claim, Justice Harlan argued that the state's practice was not arbitrary and did not deprive petitioner of a right "implicit in the concept of ordered liberty."[5]

---

5. A number of later decisions elaborated the circumstances under which indigent convicted criminals would be entitled to free transcripts. See, e.g., Lane v. Brown, 372 U.S. 477 (1963) (indigent must be afforded free transcript of a postconviction hearing where filing of the transcript in the reviewing court was necessary to confer appellate jurisdiction); Long v. District Court, 385 U.S. 192 (1966) (free transcript required on appeal from denial of postconviction relief even if its filing is not jurisdictional); Roberts v. LaVallee, 389 U.S. 40 (1967) (entitlement to transcript of testimony of a major witness for the state at the preliminary hearing in order to aid prisoner in applying for postconviction relief).

The most recent transcript case is M.L.B. v. S.L.J., 519 U.S. 102 (1996), in which a sharply divided Court, through Justice Ginsburg, ruled invalid Mississippi's requirement that a parent wishing to appeal a termination-of-parental-rights order must pay in advance—in this case $2,352.36—for the preparation of the trial record. M.L.B.'s appeal was dismissed because of her inability to provide the record. The Court, relying substantially on *Griffin*, held that "Mississippi may not deny M.L.B., because of her poverty, appellate review of the sufficiency of the evidence on which the trial court found her unfit to remain a parent." Justice Ginsburg emphasized the "fundamental" importance of the state's decision to terminate

In Gideon v. Wainwright, 372 U.S. 335 (1963), a unanimous Court held that the Constitution required that counsel be provided to all felony defendants at trial if they do not have the resources to hire private counsel. The Sixth Amendment states that "[i]n all criminal prosecutions, the accused shall enjoy the right . . . to have the Assistance of Counsel for his defence." Although for many years this was interpreted to mean only that the state could not deprive a criminal defendant of the right to representation by retained counsel, in the 1930s the Court began holding that under certain circumstances, especially where there was a possibility of capital punishment, a criminal defendant who lacked the resources to retain a lawyer had the right to state-financed representation. See, e.g., Powell v. Alabama, 287 U.S. 45 (1932). Justice Black's majority opinion in *Gideon* made no real reference to the history or even the specific text of the Sixth Amendment. Instead he emphasized that "in our adversary system of criminal justice, any person haled into court, who is too poor to hire a lawyer, cannot be assured a fair trial unless counsel is provided for him. . . . That government hires lawyers to prosecute and defendants who have the money hire lawyers to defend are the strongest indications of the widespread belief that lawyers in criminal courts are necessities, not luxuries. The right of one charged with a crime to counsel may not be deemed fundamental and essential to fair trial in some countries, but it is in ours. . . ."

On the same day as it decided *Gideon*, a divided Court in Douglas v. California, 372 U.S. 353 (1963), invalidated California's procedure regulating the appointment of counsel for indigent defendants appealing criminal convictions. Under state procedure, the appellate court first made "an independent investigation of the record" in order to "determine whether it would be of advantage to the defendant or helpful to the appellate court to have counsel appointed." Appellants who retained private counsel were not required to submit to this prior scrutiny. In petitioner's case, the appellate court had concluded, based on the record, that "no good whatever could be served by appointment of counsel." Justice Douglas wrote that this violated the Equal Protection Clause by drawing "an unconstitutional line . . . between rich and poor."

---

the parental relationship. "The countervailing government interest . . . is financial. . . . But in the tightly circumscribed category of parental status termination cases, appeals are few, and not likely to impose an undue burden on the State." Justice Ginsburg thus dismissed the objection that the Court would "open floodgates if we do not rigidly restrict *Griffin* to cases typed 'criminal'" because of the special nature of parental status termination decrees, which set them apart "even from other domestic relations matters such as divorce, paternity, and child custody." Justice Kennedy concurred. Justice Thomas, joined by Chief Justice Rehnquist and Justice Scalia, dissented, calling for the overruling of *Griffin* or, in the alternative, limiting it rigorously to criminal cases. "[I]f all that is required to trigger the right to a free appellate transcript is that the interest at stake appear to us to be as fundamental as the interest of a convicted misdemeanant, several kinds of civil suits involving interests that seem fundamental enough leap to mind. Will the Court, for example, now extend the right to a free transcript to an indigent seeking to appeal the outcome of a paternity suit? To those who wish to appeal custody determinations? How about persons against whom divorce decrees are entered? Civil suits that arise out of challenges to zoning ordinances with an impact on families? Why not foreclosure actions—or at least foreclosure actions seeking to oust persons from their homes of many years?"

> [T]he discrimination is not between "possibly good and obviously bad cases," but between cases where the rich man can require the court to listen to argument of counsel before deciding on the merits, but a poor man cannot. There is lacking that equality demanded by the Fourteenth Amendment where the rich man, who appeals as of right, enjoys the benefit of counsel's examination into the record, research of the law, and marshalling of arguments on his behalf, while the indigent, already burdened by a preliminary determination that his case is without merit, is forced to shift for himself.

Again Justice Harlan dissented and insisted on distinguishing between due process and equal protection analysis. He suggested that if the holding were justified on equal protection grounds, rather than a conception of minimal requirements under the Due Process Clause, then "the requirement of counsel on appeal is the right to the most skilled advocate who is theoretically at the call of the defendant of means."[6]

B. The Creation of Fundamental Interests Under the Equal Protection Clause

In 1966, the Court developed these doctrines beyond the context of the criminal justice system. It created a new doctrinal structure that protected certain "fundamental interests" through the Equal Protection Clause.

HARPER v. VIRGINIA BD. OF ELECTIONS, 383 U.S. 663 (1966): [The Court struck down a $1.50 annual poll tax levied by Virginia on all persons over 21, enforced by disfranchising those who did not pay. The Twenty-Fourth Amendment had invalidated poll taxes for federal elections in 1964; *Harper* concerned the constitutionality of poll taxes for state elections.]

DOUGLAS, J.:

[W]hile the right to vote in federal elections is conferred by Art. I, 2, of the Constitution, the right to vote in state elections is nowhere expressly mentioned. . . . We do not stop to canvass the relation between voting and [First Amendment rights of] political expression. For it is enough to say that once the franchise is granted to the electorate, lines may not be drawn which are inconsistent with the Equal Protection Clause of the Fourteenth Amendment. [In] Lassiter v. Northampton Election Board, 360 U.S. 45, [we upheld] a state literacy test . . . warning that the

---

6. See also Justice Harlan's concurring opinion in Williams v. Illinois, 399 U.S. 235 (1970), which invalidated an Illinois statute that required convicts unable to pay their fines or court costs to "work off" their obligations by remaining in jail at an imputed rate of $5 per day, even if this would result in incarceration for a term longer than the maximum statutory term. "If equal protection implications of the Court's opinion were to be fully realized," he wrote, "it would require that the consequences of punishment be comparable for all individuals," which he presumably assumed would be, if not fanciful, then at least not constitutionally required.

result would be different if a literacy test, fair on its face, were used to discriminate against a class. [U]nlike a poll tax, the "ability to read and write . . . has some relation to standards designed to promote intelligent use of the ballot."

We conclude that a State violates the Equal Protection Clause of the Fourteenth Amendment whenever it makes the affluence of the voter or payment of any fee an electoral standard. Voter qualifications have no relation to wealth nor to paying or not paying this or any other tax. Our cases demonstrate that the Equal Protection Clause of the Fourteenth Amendment restrains the States from fixing voter qualifications which invidiously discriminate. . . . Thus without questioning the power of a State to impose reasonable residence restrictions on the availability of the ballot we held in Carrington v. Rash, 380 U.S. 89, that a State may not deny the opportunity to vote to a bona fide resident merely because he is a member of the armed services. . . . Previously we had said that neither homesite nor occupation "affords a permissible basis for distinguishing between qualified voters within the State." Gray v. Sanders, 372 U.S. 368. We think the same must be true of requirements of wealth or affluence or payment of a fee.

Long ago in Yick Wo v. Hopkins, 118 U.S. 356 (1886), the Court referred to "the political franchise of voting" as a "fundamental political right, because preservative of all rights." Recently in Reynolds v. Sims, 377 U.S. 533 (1964), we said, "Undoubtedly, the right of suffrage is a fundamental matter in a free and democratic society. Especially since the right to exercise the franchise in a free and unimpaired manner is preservative of other basic civil and political rights, any alleged infringement of the right of citizens to vote must be carefully and meticulously scrutinized." . . .

We say the same whether the citizen, otherwise qualified to vote, has $1.50 in his pocket or nothing at all, pays the fee or fails to pay it. The principle that denies the State the right to dilute a citizen's vote on account of his economic status or other such factors by analogy bars a system which excludes those unable to pay a fee to vote or who fail to pay.

It is argued that a State may exact fees from citizens for many different kinds of licenses; that if it can demand from all an equal fee for a driver's license, it can demand from all an equal poll tax for voting. But we must remember that the interest of the State, when it comes to voting, is limited to the power to fix qualifications. Wealth, like race, creed, or color, is not germane to one's ability to participate intelligently in the electoral process. Lines drawn on the basis of wealth or property, like those of race, are traditionally disfavored. See Edwards v. California, 314 U.S. 160 (Jackson, J., concurring); Griffin v. Illinois; Douglas v. California. To introduce wealth or payment of a fee as a measure of a voter's qualifications is to introduce a capricious or irrelevant factor. The degree of the discrimination is irrelevant. In this context—that is, as a condition of obtaining a ballot—the requirement of fee paying causes an "invidious" discrimination (Skinner v. Oklahoma) that runs afoul of the Equal Protection Clause. . . .

We agree, of course, with Mr. Justice Holmes that the Due Process Clause of the Fourteenth Amendment "does not enact Mr. Herbert Spencer's Social Statics" (Lochner v. New York). Likewise, the Equal Protection Clause is not shackled to the political theory of a particular era. In determining what lines are unconstitutionally discriminatory, we have never been confined to historic notions of equality, any more than we have restricted due process to a fixed catalogue of what was at a given time deemed to be the limits of fundamental rights. Notions of what constitutes equal treatment for purposes of the Equal Protection Clause do change. This Court in 1896 held that laws providing for separate public facilities for white and Negro citizens did not deprive the latter of the equal protection and treatment that the Fourteenth Amendment commands. Plessy v. Ferguson. Seven of the eight Justices then sitting subscribed to the Court's opinion, thus joining in expressions of what constituted unequal and discriminatory treatment that sound strange to a contemporary ear. When, in 1954—more than a half-century later—we repudiated the "separate-but-equal" doctrine of Plessy as respects public education we stated: "In approaching this problem, we cannot turn the clock back to 1868 when the Amendment was adopted, or even to 1896 when Plessy v. Ferguson was written." Brown v. Board of Education.

In a recent searching re-examination of the Equal Protection Clause, we held, as already noted, that "the opportunity for equal participation by all voters in the election of state legislators" is required. Reynolds v. Sims. We decline to qualify that principle by sustaining this poll tax. Our conclusion, like that in Reynolds v. Sims, is founded not on what we think governmental policy should be, but on what the Equal Protection Clause requires.

We have long been mindful that where fundamental rights and liberties are asserted under the Equal Protection Clause, classifications which might invade or restrain them must be closely scrutinized and carefully confined. See, e.g., Skinner v. Oklahoma; Reynolds v. Sims; Carrington v. Rash.

Those principles apply here. For to repeat, wealth or fee paying has, in our view, no relation to voting qualifications; the right to vote is too precious, too fundamental to be so burdened or conditioned.

Black, J., dissenting:

[T]he Court's decision is to no extent based on a finding that the Virginia law as written or as applied is being used as a device or mechanism to deny Negro citizens of Virginia the right to vote on account of their color. . . . The mere fact that a law results in treating some groups differently from others does not, of course, automatically amount to a violation of the Equal Protection Clause. To bar a State from drawing any distinctions in the application of its laws would practically paralyze the regulatory power of legislative bodies. . . . All voting laws treat some persons differently from others in some respects. Some bar a person from voting who is under 21 years of age; others bar those under 18. Some bar convicted felons or the insane, and some have attached a freehold or other property qualification for voting. [T]his Court has refused to use the general language of the Equal Protection Clause as though it provided a handy instrument to strike down state laws which the Court feels are based on bad governmental policy. The equal protection cases carefully analyzed boil down to the principle that distinctions drawn and even discriminations imposed by state laws do not violate the Equal Protection Clause so long as these distinctions and discriminations are not "irrational," "irrelevant," "unreasonable," "arbitrary," or "invidious." [U]nder a proper interpretation of the Equal Protection Clause States are to have the broadest kind of leeway in areas where they have a general constitutional competence to act. State poll tax legislation can "reasonably," "rationally" and without an "invidious" or evil purpose to injure anyone be found to rest on a number of state policies including (1) the State's desire to collect its revenue, and (2) its belief that voters who pay a poll tax will be interested in furthering the State's welfare when they vote. Certainly it is rational to believe that people may be more likely to pay taxes if payment is a prerequisite to voting. . . . Property qualifications existed in the Colonies and were continued by many States after the Constitution was adopted. . . .

[T]he Court seems to be using the old "natural-law-due-process formula" to justify striking down state laws as violations of the Equal Protection Clause. I have heretofore had many occasions to express my strong belief that there is no constitutional support whatever for this Court to use the Due Process Clause as though it provided a blank check to alter the meaning of the Constitution as written so as to add to it substantive constitutional changes which a majority of the Court at any given time believes are needed to meet present-day problems. Nor is there in my opinion any more constitutional support for this Court to use the Equal Protection Clause, as it has today, to write into the Constitution its notions of what it thinks is good governmental policy. . . .

The Court's justification for consulting its own notions rather than following the original meaning of the Constitution, as I would, apparently is based on the belief of the majority of the Court that for this Court to be bound by the original meaning of the Constitution is an intolerable and debilitating evil; that our Constitution should not be "shackled to the political theory of a particular era," and that to save the country from the original Constitution the Court must have constant power to renew it and keep it abreast of this Court's more enlightened theories of what is best for our society. It seems to me that this is an attack not only on the great value of our Constitution itself but also on the concept of a written constitution which is to survive through the years as originally written unless changed through the amendment process which the Framers wisely provided. Moreover, when a "political theory" embodied in our Constitution becomes outdated, it seems to me that a majority of the nine members of this Court are not only without constitutional power but are far less qualified to choose a new constitutional political theory than the people of this country proceeding in the manner provided by Article V. . . . [Moreover,] Congress has the power under section 5 [of the Fourteenth Amendment] to pass legislation to abolish the poll tax in order to protect the citizens of this country if it believes that the poll tax is being used as a device to deny voters equal protection of the laws.

HARLAN, J., joined by STEWART, J., dissenting:

Property and poll-tax qualifications, very simply, are not in accord with current egalitarian notions of how a modern democracy should be organized. It is of course entirely fitting that legislatures should modify the law to reflect such changes in popular attitudes. However, it is all wrong, in my view, for the Court to adopt the political doctrines popularly accepted at a particular moment of our history and to declare all others to be irrational and invidious, barring them from the range of choice by reasonably minded people acting through the political process. It was not too long ago that Mr. Justice Holmes felt impelled to remind the Court that the Due Process Clause of the Fourteenth Amendment does not enact the laissez-faire theory of society, Lochner v. New York. The times have changed, and perhaps it is appropriate to observe that neither does the Equal Protection Clause of that Amendment rigidly impose upon America an ideology of unrestrained egalitarianism.

DISCUSSION

1. *The right to vote as a fundamental interest. Harper* struck down the poll tax even as applied to persons who could clearly afford it, because, in effect, the state was charging the citizen in order to engage in a "fundamental" aspect of citizenship, voting. Do voter identification laws constitute a poll tax because they effectively charge citizens a user fee to vote? What if the state fully subsidizes the voter identification card?

2. *Shapiro v. Thompson and the right to travel.* The Court extended the "fundamental rights" wing of equal protection doctrine in Shapiro v. Thompson, 394 U.S. 618 (1969), holding that states could not deny welfare benefits to persons who had resided in the state less than a year. It held that this policy invidiously discriminated on the basis of the exercise of the fundamental right to travel. These "right to travel" cases are considered in more detail in Section V infra.

3. *Fundamental rights versus fundamental interests.* Note carefully Justice Douglas's statement that "once the franchise is granted to the electorate, lines may not be drawn which are inconsistent with the Equal Protection Clause of the Fourteenth Amendment." His argument is that although the state does not have to extend the right to vote generally, once it does so it may not invidiously discriminate in how it provides the right. We might call such a guarantee a "fundamental interest" as opposed to a "fundamental right" like speech or the right to travel that the state must guarantee to all of its citizens. Compare Chief Justice Warren's argument in Brown v. Board of Education: "In these days, it is doubtful that any child may reasonably be expected to succeed in life if he is denied the opportunity of an education. Such an opportunity, where the state has undertaken to provide it, is a right which must be made available to all on equal terms."

Why might it make sense for courts to label welfare state obligations like education as "fundamental interests" rather than "fundamental rights"? One reason is that this formula leaves up to legislatures the ultimate decision whether or not to provide the right (or the welfare benefit) at all if it proves too costly to offer it on an equal footing.

NOTE: PROTECTING THE POOR THROUGH THE FOURTEENTH AMENDMENT

The language of Justice Douglas's opinion in *Harper*, plus the earlier criminal procedure cases, led Harvard professor Frank Michelman, who had clerked for Justice Brennan, to write one of the most widely discussed articles of the 1960s, titled, fittingly enough, "On Protecting the Poor Through the Fourteenth Amendment." There he argued that the Constitution guaranteed some level of "minimum protection" against the effects of poverty.[7] Professor Michelman started from the premise that a pricing system is both constitutional and desirable: "We usually regard it as both the fairest and most efficient arrangement to require each consumer to pay

---

7. See On Protecting the Poor Through the Fourteenth Amendment, 83 Harv. L. Rev. 7 (1969). For a response, see Ralph Winter, Poverty, Economic Equality, and the Equal Protection Clause, 1972 Sup. Ct. Rev. 41.

the full market price of what he consumes, limiting his consumption to what his income permits." However, he notes that *Harper* held that a state may not charge a user fee for access to certain rights or privileges (in that case, access to the ballot). He placed *Harper* and other cases within the context of the ideas of political philosopher John Rawls and argued that even within a market economy that tolerates a measure of income and resource inequality, persons are both morally and constitutionally entitled to "minimum protection against economic hazard":

> As applied to economic hazards, a claim to "minimum protection" would mean that persons are entitled to have certain wants satisfied—certain existing needs filled—by government, free of any direct charge over and above the obligation to pay general taxes. . . .
>
> [It might be argued] that justice is satisfied as long as the prevailing social and economic institutions afford everyone a fair opportunity to derive an income sufficient over time to provide for whatever needs are considered "basic." [But] the argument of minimum protection as applied to specific needs and occasions . . . depend[s] on the proposition that justice requires more than a fair opportunity to realize an income which can cover these needs or insure against them—requires . . . absolute assurance that they will be met when and as felt, free of any remote[a] contingencies pertaining to effort, thrift or foresight.
>
> We might take our clue from Professor Rawls' idea of "justice as fairness." Rawls grants that social institutions and practices may be just, even though they produce unequal incomes and accumulations. Yet for an unequal system to be just, it must be the case that a rational person, hypothetically ignorant of what particular place in society awaits him, would find the inequalities acceptable. . . .
>
> The identity of "just wants" would then be determined according to a judgment arrived at through the following process of reasoning. Assume that a man has no idea what his social and economic station in a predominantly competitive society is to be and that he fully recognizes the role of income incentives and free markets in maximizing social productivity. Will he nevertheless wish to have each person insured against the risk that certain needs will remain unfulfilled as and when they accrue—and what specific risks of that sort, if any, will he say should be insured against?[b] Might he, for example, say that insofar as the society provides

---

a. "Remote" is intended to save the possibility that a person might deliberately and effectively waive his claims by informed and proximate choice. Such choice could, conceivably, assume a variety of forms—monastic vows, perhaps, or deliberate waste of publicly provided food or shelter.

b. Here we may briefly note some possible reasons for insisting on such assurances, over and above insistence on a system of economic rewards and transfers which would tend generally to assure each household head of an income adequate to his household's important needs. Assurances may be desired against the risk that one—or the family head upon whom one is dependent—will not measure up to generally reasonable minimum standards of active participation in the economy, or against the risk that a generally fair system of judging the quality of one's participation, or the extenuating force of one's disabilities, will in a particular case miscarry.

> for "democratic" political participation through such means as voting and standing for office, access to these activities should never be blocked by economic vicissitude? Or that persons must at all times be assured of effective access to some impartial and remedially competent forum for the peaceful settlement of bona fide legal disputes? Or that everyone at all times must be assured of facilities for a modicum of privacy, intimacy, confidentiality, self-expression? Or that each child must be guaranteed the means of developing his competence, self-knowledge, and tastes for living? . . .
>
> If the relevant insight concerning payment requirements must be given a doctrinal form of statement, the appropriate construction would seem to be something like: "It is no justification for deprivation of a fundamental right (i.e., involuntary nonfulfillment of a just want) that the deprivation results from a general practice of requiring persons to pay for what they get." Such a construction focuses the inquiry on the crucial variable—the nature and quality of the deprivation—and thereby avoids the distractions, false stirring of hopes, and tunneling of vision which results from a rhetorical emphasis on acts of "discrimination" that consist of nothing more than charging a price.

Michelman indicates that the notion of "minimum protection" is more readily assimilated to the Due Process Clause than to the Equal Protection Clause, for it focuses not on relative but on absolute deprivation: "'Minimum protection' radar scans, not for inequalities, but for instances in which persons have important needs or interests which they are prevented from satisfying because of traits or predicaments not adopted by free and proximate choice." But there are reasons why a court might choose to clothe a minimum protection decision "in the verbiage of inequality and discrimination." The language of the Due Process Clause requires that the state act to deprive a person of property, something not textually mandated by the Equal Protection Clause. Moreover, an equal protection standard provides some guidance as to how much protection must be furnished by looking to the benefits enjoyed by others in society. Finally,

> it must be noted that while the idea of "just wants" or "severe deprivations" expresses an ethical precept distinct from that of "equality," detecting a failure to provide the required minimum may nonetheless depend

---

More generally, assurance may be desired against the chance that the sincerest attempts to devise and maintain a generally fair system of rewards and transfers will nevertheless leave some persons on some occasions desperately unprovisioned. Most generally, flat assurances concerning just wants may upon reflection seem a desirable way of simplifying (and thus cheapening) the continuing task of adjustment of the reward/transfer system, either because this method obviates any need to place a dollar value from time to time on the whole catalogue of just wants (a composite we may call the just minimum) or because it assures society that transferred purchasing power will not be dissipated on other wants, leaving just wants unfulfilled and, accordingly, an unsatisfied claim still outstanding. The latter point, I suspect, will eventually turn out to be the key to the argument. It provides a reason why persons in a just system would agree to receive their guaranteed minimum in kind rather than in cash.

> in part upon the detection of inequalities; and elimination or reduction of inequality may be entailed in rectifying such a failure, insofar as the just minimum is understood to be a function (in part) of the existing maximum. Such an understanding could grow out of a residue of indissoluble interpenetration of the felt evils of relative deprivation and poignant hardship. Thus if the extent of society's obligation to tax itself for support of the needy depends in part upon its overall level of affluence, widening inequalities become increasingly suggestive of failure to furnish the just minimum. Or again, insofar as the components of the required (or "a decent") minimum are affected by what others have—by prevailing tastes and expectations, or by emulation—then extremity of inequality is suggestive. Standing on quite different ground is the relevance of what others have when the want in question is deemed specially significant—as education, for example, might be—because of its importance for success in competitive activities.

Several of the Court's cases during the Warren Court and early Burger Court years could be viewed as roughly consistent with Michelman's approach. In addition to the criminal procedure cases discussed earlier, another example was Boddie v. Connecticut, 401 U.S. 371 (1971). *Boddie* invalidated Connecticut's requirement, as applied to an indigent person, that one must pay a filing fee of $45 and an average of $15 for service of process in order to commence divorce proceedings.

Justice Harlan, writing for the majority, treated the case as raising due process (rather than equal protection) issues. In particular, he emphasized that *only* the state can grant a divorce, so that exclusion of the indigent from judicial process because of an inability to pay the requisite fees has the consequence of depriving them of something that only the state can provide. Moreover, wrote Justice Harlan, "[r]ecognition of this theoretical framework illuminates the precise issue presented in this case. As this Court on more than one occasion has recognized, marriage involves interests of basic importance in our society. See, e.g., Loving v. Virginia, 388 U.S. 1 (1967).... It is not surprising, then, that the States have seen fit to oversee many aspects of that institution. Without a prior judicial imprimatur, individuals may freely enter into and rescind commercial contracts, for example, but we are unaware of any jurisdiction where private citizens may . . . divorce and mutually liberate themselves from the constraints of legal obligations that go with marriage, and more fundamentally the prohibition against remarriage, without invoking the State's judicial machinery."

Justice Harlan concluded that "the State's refusal to admit these appellants to its courts, the sole means in Connecticut for obtaining a divorce, must be regarded as the equivalent of denying them an opportunity to be heard upon their claimed right to a dissolution of their marriages, and, in the absence of a sufficient countervailing justification for the State's action, a denial of due process."

Justice Douglas wrote a concurring opinion objecting to the reliance on the Due Process Clause and suggesting instead that the Equal Protection Clause, though "not definable with mathematical precision," offered the better rationale. "Here the invidious discrimination is based on one of the guidelines: poverty. An invidious discrimination based on poverty is adequate for this case."

> Justice Brennan also concurred only in the judgment, rejecting the Court's opinion insofar as today's holding is made to depend upon the factor that only the State can grant a divorce and that an indigent would be locked into a marriage if unable to pay the fees required to obtain a divorce. A State has an ultimate monopoly of all judicial process and attendant enforcement machinery. As a practical matter, if disputes cannot be successfully settled between the parties, the court system is usually "the only forum effectively empowered to settle their disputes. . . ." I see no constitutional distinction between appellants' attempt to enforce this state statutory right and an attempt to vindicate any other right arising under federal or state law. . . .
>
> The question that the Court treats exclusively as one of due process inevitably implicates considerations of both due process and equal protection. . . . The rationale of *Griffin* covers the present case. Courts are the central dispute-settling institutions in our society. They are bound to do equal justice under law, to rich and poor alike. They fail to perform their function in accordance with the Equal Protection Clause if they shut their doors to indigent plaintiffs altogether. Where money determines not merely "the kind of trial a man gets," but whether he gets into court at all, the great principle of equal protection becomes a mockery. . . .

Justice Black dissented, arguing that *Griffin* and its progeny were limited to criminal cases. In civil cases, "the government is not usually involved as a party, and there is no deprivation of life, liberty, or property as punishment for crime. Our Federal Constitution, therefore, does not place such private disputes on the same high level as it places criminal trials and punishment."

C. Minimum Needs Rejected

Despite the Court's decisions in *Boddie* and the right to travel case, Shapiro v. Thompson, 394 U.S. 618 (1969), the Court rejected the idea that the Constitution requires states to provide minimum levels of assistance in a series of cases.

DANDRIDGE v. WILLIAMS, 397 U.S. 471 (1970): [The year following Professor Michelman's article, the Court in *Dandridge* upheld a provision of Maryland's program of Aid to Families with Dependent Children that limited the monthly grant to any one family to $250, regardless of its size or computed need. Justice Stewart explained that "[l]ike every other State in the Union, Maryland participates in the Federal Aid to Families With Dependent Children, which originated with the Social Security Act of 1935 [and was repealed in the 1996 welfare legislation passed by Congress and signed by President Clinton]. Under this jointly financed program, a State computes the so-called 'standard of need' of each eligible family unit within its borders. Some States provide that every family shall receive grants sufficient to meet fully the determined standard of need. Other States provide that each family unit shall receive a percentage of the determined need. Still others provide grants to most families in full accord with the ascertained standard of need, but impose an upper limit on the total amount of money any one family unit may receive. Maryland, through administrative adoption of a 'maximum grant regulation,' has followed this last course."

As a result, individual members of a large family received less per capita than the members of smaller families, and less per capita than the state itself recognized as the minimum required for subsistence. (One might note, though, that some states had chosen to fund everyone at below-minimum levels.) The Court upheld this scheme, 5-4.]

STEWART, J.:

[A] State . . . may not, of course, impose a regime of invidious discrimination in violation of the Equal Protection Clause of the Fourteenth Amendment. Maryland says that its maximum grant regulation is wholly free of any invidiously discriminatory purpose or effect, and that the regulation is rationally supportable on at least four entirely valid grounds. The regulation can be clearly justified, Maryland argues, in terms of legitimate state interests in encouraging gainful employment, in maintaining an equitable balance in economic status as between welfare families and those supported by a wage-earner, in providing incentives for family planning, and in allocating available public funds in such a way as fully to meet the needs of the largest possible number of families. The District Court . . . nonetheless held that the regulation "is invalid on its face for overreaching,"—that it violates the Equal Protection Clause "(b)ecause it cuts too broad a swath on an indiscriminate basis as applied to the entire group of AFDC eligibles to which it purports to apply. . . ."

If this were a case involving government action claimed to violate the First Amendment guarantee of free speech, a finding of "overreaching" would be significant and might be crucial. . . . But the concept of "overreaching" has no place in this case. For here we deal with state regulation in the social and economic field, not affecting freedoms guaranteed by the Bill of Rights, and claimed to violate the Fourteenth Amendment only because the regulation results in some disparity in grants of welfare payments to the largest AFDC families. For this Court to approve the invalidation of state economic or social regulation as "overreaching" would be far too reminiscent of an era when the Court thought the Fourteenth Amendment gave it power to strike down state laws "because they may be unwise, improvident, or out of harmony with a particular school of thought." Williamson v. Lee Optical. That era long ago passed into history. Ferguson v. Skrupa.

In the area of economics and social welfare, . . . [a] statutory discrimination will not be set aside if any state of facts reasonably may be conceived to justify it.

To be sure, the cases cited, and many others enunciating this fundamental standard under the Equal Protection Clause, have in the main involved state regulation of business or industry. The administration of public welfare assistance, by contrast, involves the most basic economic needs of impoverished human beings. We recognize the dramatically real factual differences between [those] cases and this one, but we can find no basis for applying a different constitutional standard. . . .

Under this long-established meaning of the Equal Protection Clause, it is clear that the Maryland maximum grant regulation is constitutionally valid. We need not explore all the reasons that the State advances in justification of the regulation. It is enough that a solid foundation for the regulation can be found in the State's legitimate interest in encouraging employment and in avoiding discrimination between welfare families and the families of the working poor. . . . [B]y keying the maximum family AFDC grants to the minimum wage a steadily employed head of a household receives, the State maintains some semblance of an equitable balance between families on welfare and those supported by an employed breadwinner.

It is true that in some AFDC families there may be no person who is employable. It is also true that with respect to AFDC families whose determined standard of need is below the regulatory maximum, and who therefore receive grants equal to the determined standard, the employment incentive is absent. But the Equal Protection Clause does not require that a State must choose between attacking every aspect of a problem or not attacking the problem at all. It is enough that the State's action be rationally based and free from invidious discrimination. The regulation before us meets that test.

[Justice Douglas dissented on statutory grounds.]

MARSHALL, J., joined by BRENNAN, J., dissenting:

[T]he Court[] emasculat[es] . . . the Equal Protection Clause as a constitutional principle applicable to the area of social welfare administration. . . .

[T]he only distinction between those children with respect to whom assistance is granted and those children who are denied such assistance is the size of the family into which the child permits himself to be born. The class of individuals with respect to whom payments are actually made (the first four or five eligible dependent children in a family), is grossly underinclusive in terms of the class that the AFDC program was designed to assist, namely, all needy dependent children. Such underinclusiveness manifests "a prima facie violation of the equal protection requirement of reasonable classification," compelling the State to come forward with a persuasive justification for the classification.

The Court never undertakes to inquire for such a justification; rather it avoids the task by focusing upon the abstract dichotomy between two different approaches to equal protection problems that have been utilized by this Court. . . .

This case simply defies easy characterization in terms of [the "rational basis" versus "strict scrutiny" tests]. The cases relied on by the Court, in which a "mere rationality" test was actually used, e.g., Williamson v. Lee Optical, are most accurately described as involving the application of equal protection reasoning to the regulation of business interests. The extremes to which the Court has gone in dreaming up rational bases for state regulation in the area may in many instances be ascribed to a healthy revulsion from the Court's earlier excesses in using the Constitution to protect interests that have more than enough power to protect themselves in the legislative halls. This case, involving the literally vital interests of a powerless minority—poor families without breadwinners—is far removed from the area of business regulation, as the Court concedes. Why then is the standard used in those cases imposed here? We are told no more than that this case falls in "the area of economics and social welfare," with the implication that from there the answer is obvious.

In my view, equal protection analysis of this case is not appreciably advanced by the a priori definition of a "right," fundamental or otherwise. Rather, concentration must be placed upon the character of the classification in question, the relative importance to individuals in the class discriminated against of the governmental benefits that they do not receive, and the asserted state interests in support of the classification. . . .

[Justice Marshall examines the asserted state rationales:]

. . . Vital to the employment-incentive basis found by the Court to sustain the regulation is, of course, the supposition that an appreciable number of AFDC recipients are in fact employable. For it is perfectly obvious that limitations upon assistance cannot reasonably operate as a work incentive with regard to those who cannot work or who cannot be expected to work. . . . The State's position is . . . that the State may deprive certain needy children of assistance to which they would otherwise be entitled in order to provide an arguable work incentive for their parents. But the State may not wield its economic whip in this fashion when the effect is to cause a deprivation to needy dependent children in order to correct an arguable fault of their parents.

Even if the invitation of the State to focus upon the heads of AFDC families is accepted, the minimum rationality of the maximum grant regulation is hard to discern. The District Court found that of Maryland's more than 32,000 AFDC families, only about 116 could be classified as having employable members, and, of these, the number to which the maximum grant regulation was applicable is not disclosed by the record. . . . Thus . . . the total number of "employable" mothers is but a fraction of the total number of AFDC mothers. Furthermore, the record is silent as to what proportion of large families subject to the maximum have "employable" mothers. Indeed, one must assume that the presence of the mother in the homes can be less easily dispensed with in the case of large families, particularly where small children are involved and alternative provisions for their care are accordingly more difficult to arrange. In short, not only has the State failed to establish that there is a substantial or even a significant proportion of AFDC heads of households as to whom the maximum grant regulation arguably serves as a viable and logical work incentive, but it is also indisputable that the regulation at best is drastically overinclusive since it applies with equal vigor to a very substantial number of persons who like appellees are completely disabled from working.

Finally, it should be noted that, to the extent there is a legitimate state interest in encouraging heads of AFDC households to find employment, application of the maximum grant regulation is also grossly underinclusive because it singles out and affects only large families. No reason is suggested why this particular group should be carved out for the purpose of having unusually harsh "work incentives" imposed upon them. Not only has the State selected for special treatment a small group from among similarly situated families, but it has done so on a basis—family size—that bears no relation to the evil that the State claims the regulation was designed to correct. There is simply no indication whatever that heads of large families, as opposed to heads of small families, are particularly prone to refuse to seek or to maintain employment. . . .

In the final analysis, Maryland has set up an AFDC program structured to calculate and pay the minimum standard of need to dependent children. Having set up that program, however, the State denies some of those needy children the minimum subsistence standard of living, and it does so on the wholly arbitrary basis that they happen to be members of large families. One need not speculate too far on the actual reason for the regulation, for in the early stages of this litigation the State virtually conceded that it set out to limit the total cost of the program along the path of least resistance. . . .

[I]t cannot suffice merely to invoke the spectre of the past and to recite from . . . Williamson v. Lee Optical to decide the case. Appellees are not a gas company or an optical dispenser; they are needy dependent children and families who are discriminated against by the State. The basis of that discrimination—the classification of individuals into large and small families—is too arbitrary and too unconnected to the asserted rationale, the impact on those discriminated against—the denial of even a subsistence existence—too great, and the supposed interests served too contrived and attenuated to meet the requirements of the Constitution. In my view Maryland's maximum grant regulation is invalid under the Equal Protection Clause of the Fourteenth Amendment.

In Lindsey v. Normet, 405 U.S. 56 (1972), the Court rejected the claim that the "need for decent shelter" rose to the level of a fundamental interest that would call for heightened scrutiny of a summary "forcible entry and wrongful detainer" procedure for the eviction of tenants after alleged nonpayment of rent. Justice White, writing for the Court, stated:

> We do not denigrate the importance of decent, safe, and sanitary housing. But the Constitution does not provide judicial remedies for every social and economic ill. We are unable to perceive in that document any constitutional guarantee of access to dwellings of a particular quality. . . . Absent constitutional mandate, the assurance of adequate housing and the definition of landlord-tenant relationships are legislative, not judicial, functions.

As to criminal defendants, the Court also appeared to pull back from its earlier, more egalitarian, vision. Thus, in Ross v. Moffit, 417 U.S. 600 (1974), it declined to interpret *Gideon* as requiring the appointment of counsel for indigents seeking discretionary review in the Supreme Court. And in Murray v. Giarratano, 492 U.S. 1 (1989), the Court ruled against inmates of Virginia's death row who claimed a right to appointed counsel to challenge their convictions in collateral proceedings. Chief Justice Rehnquist, writing for a plurality including Justices White, O'Connor, and Scalia, found the case controlled by Pennsylvania v. Finley, 481 U.S. 551 (1987), which held that the Sixth Amendment does not require states to provide counsel in postconviction proceedings generally. In a concurring opinion, Justice O'Connor emphasized that "[a] postconviction proceeding is not part of the criminal process itself, but is instead a civil action designed to overturn a presumptively valid criminal judgment." Justice Stevens, in a dissent joined by Justices Brennan, Marshall, and Blackmun, argued that "even if it is permissible to leave an ordinary prisoner to his own resources in collateral proceedings, it is fundamentally unfair to require an indigent death row inmate to initiate collateral relief without counsel's guiding hand." He noted the presence of "significant evidence that in capital cases what is ordinarily considered direct review does not sufficiently safeguard against miscarriages of justice" to warrant the traditional presumption of finality. Thus, whereas "[f]ederal habeas courts granted relief in only 0.25% to 7% of noncapital cases in recent years, in striking contrast, the success rate in capital cases ranged from 60% to 70%. Such a high incidence of uncorrected error [at the ordinary appellate stage] demonstrates that the meaningful appellate review necessary in a capital case extends beyond the direct appellate process."

In Fuller v. Oregon, 417 U.S. 40 (1974), the Court held that a state may recoup legal expenses paid on behalf of a convicted defendant to the extent that he becomes able to repay and that it may condition a solvent defendant's probation on repayment. Against Fuller's argument that "a defendant's knowledge that he may remain under an obligation to repay the expenses incurred in providing him legal representation might impel him to decline the services of an appointed attorney and thus 'chill' his constitutional right to counsel," Justice Stewart responded:

> We live in a society where the distribution of legal assistance, like the distribution of all goods and services, is generally regulated by the dynamics of private enterprise. A defendant in a criminal case who is just above the line separating the indigent from the nonindigent must borrow money, sell off his meager assets, or call upon his family or friends in order to hire a lawyer. We cannot say that the Constitution requires that those only slightly poorer must remain forever immune from any obligation to shoulder the expenses of their legal defense, even when they are able to pay without hardship. . . .

Justice Marshall, joined by Justice Brennan, explicitly reserved judgment on the issue of "chilling effect" but dissented based on the state's different treatment of indigent criminal defendants and other judgment debtors.[8]

Almost a decade later, in Ake v. Oklahoma, 470 U.S. 68 (1985), the Court held that, in certain circumstances, a state must provide an indigent defendant with access to psychiatric assistance to make out a defense of insanity. In this case, the defendant Ake was sentenced to death, after his request for psychiatric evaluation at the state's expense was denied, for first-degree murder due to aggravating circumstances. With only Justice Rehnquist dissenting, the majority concluded that the denial of psychiatric assistance to Ake violated his due process rights to a fair trial.[9]

Finally, with regard to filing fees in civil cases, the Court firmly limited the reach of *Boddie* two years later in United States v. Kras, 409 U.S. 434 (1973), which reviewed a decision granting a motion by an indigent petitioner in bankruptcy seeking a waiver of the usual $50 fees, which cover a portion of the referee's, trustee's, and clerk's costs. Justice Harry Blackmun, who wrote the opinion for the Court, emphasized that "[t]he appellants in *Boddie*, on the one hand, and Robert Kras, on the other, stand in materially different postures." First, Blackmun noted the different level of importance of the two relevant interests. The marital relationship and its potential dissolution involved interests of "fundamental importance . . . under our Constitution." By contrast, wrote Blackmun, "Kras' alleged interest in the elimination of his debt burden, and in obtaining his desired new start in life, although important and so recognized by the enactment of the Bankruptcy Act, does not rise

---

8. James v. Strange, 407 U.S. 128 (1972), struck down a Kansas statute providing for the recoupment of all state expenditures for indigent defendants and depriving them of almost all of the usual exemptions and restrictions (e.g., limitations on wage garnishment, exemptions of personal clothing and food) afforded civil judgment debtors. The Court held that the Equal Protection Clause required "more even treatment of indigent criminal defendants with other classes of indigents for self-sufficiency and self-respect." Rinaldi v. Yeager, 384 U.S. 305 (1966), struck down a New Jersey statute that required unsuccessful appellants confined to prisons to repay the state for the costs of transcripts, but did not exact repayment from defendants receiving suspended sentences, placed on probation, or penalized only by a fine.

9. See also M.L.B. v. S.L.J., 519 U.S. 102 (1996).

to the same constitutional level. . . . We see no fundamental interest that is gained or lost depending on the availability of a discharge in bankruptcy. . . ."

A second variable concerned the degree of the government's monopoly over the relevant relief. "In contrast with divorce, bankruptcy is not the only method available to a debtor for the adjustment of his legal relationship with his creditors. . . . However unrealistic the remedy may be in a particular situation, a debtor, in theory, and often in actuality, may adjust his debts by negotiated agreement with his creditors."

Thus, Blackmun concluded, "There is no constitutional right to obtain a discharge of one's debts in bankruptcy," and "[t]he rational basis for the fee requirement is readily apparent." Moreover, he suggested,

> [i]f the $50 filing fees are paid in installments over six months as General Order No. 35(4) permits on a proper showing, the required average weekly payment is $1.92. If the payment period is extended for the additional three months as the Order permits, the average weekly payment is lowered to $1.28. This is a sum less than the payments Kras makes on his couch of negligible value in storage, and less than the price of a movie and little more than the cost of a pack or two of cigarettes. . . .[10]

Justice Stewart, joined by Douglas, Brennan, and Marshall, dissented: "The violation of due process seems to me [as] clear in the present case [as in *Boddie*]." In particular, he rejected the majority's view that the state enjoyed less of a monopoly in *Kras* than in *Boddie*:

> . . . [T]he debtor, like the married plaintiffs in *Boddie*, originally entered into his contract freely and voluntarily. But it is the government nevertheless that continues to enforce that obligation, and under our "legal system" that debt is effective only because the judicial machinery is there to collect it. The bankrupt is bankrupt precisely for the reason that the State stands ready to exact all of his debts through garnishment, attachment, and the panoply of other creditor remedies. The appellee can be pursued and harassed by his creditors since they hold his legally enforceable debts.
>
> And in the unique situation of the indigent bankrupt, the government provides the only effective means of his ever being free of these

---

10. Justice Marshall, who joined Justice Stewart's dissent, wrote separately to take the majority to task for its concluding comment:

> It may be easy for some people to think that weekly savings of less than $2 are no burden. But no one who has had close contact with poor people can fail to understand how close to the margin of survival many of them are. A sudden illness, for example, may destroy whatever savings they may have accumulated, and by eliminating a sense of security may destroy the incentive to save in the future. A pack or two of cigarettes may be, for them, not a routine purchase but a luxury indulged in only rarely. The desperately poor almost never go to see a movie, which the majority seems to believe is an almost weekly activity. They have more important things to do with what little money they have—like attempting to provide some comforts for a gravely ill child, as Kras must do.
>
> It is perfectly proper for judges to disagree about what the Constitution requires. But it is disgraceful for an interpretation of the Constitution to be premised upon unfounded assumptions about how people live. . . .

government-imposed obligations. As in *Boddie*, there are no "recognized, effective alternatives." While the creditors of a bankrupt with assets might well desire to reach a compromise settlement, that possibility is foreclosed to the truly indigent bankrupt. With no funds and not even a sufficient prospect of income to be able to promise the payment of a $50 fee in weekly installments of $1.28, the assetless bankrupt has absolutely nothing to offer his creditors. And his creditors have nothing to gain by allowing him to escape or reduce his debts; their only hope is that eventually he might make enough income for them to attach. Unless the government provides him access to the bankruptcy court, Kras will remain in the totally hopeless situation he now finds himself. The government has thus truly preempted the only means for the indigent bankrupt to get out from under a lifetime burden of debt. . . .

The Court today holds that Congress may say that some of the poor are too poor even to go bankrupt. I cannot agree.[11]

DISCUSSION

1. As of 2014, the minimum filing fee for personal bankruptcies is $246, for filings under Chapter 12. The cost of the far more popular Chapters 7 or 13 is, respectively, $306 or $281.[12] Even if filing fees were waived, one might well wonder about the capacity of indigent laypersons to navigate the legal shoals of the bankruptcy process. If you disagree with *Kras*, would you argue as well that the Constitution requires state-subsidized lawyers to help such people?

2. Reread very carefully Justice Stewart's dissent. Is it not true that *all* property rights have legal force if and only if the government puts its power behind the wishes of the property "owner" (as against the person who would otherwise like to use the good in question)? Can't one say that the poor are poor only because the government will put them in jail if they try to make use of resources that are not recognized as belonging to them? Many of the cases in this chapter are unwilling to ascribe claimants' poverty to decisions of the state. Does Justice Stewart's dissent, if taken fully seriously, allow that response? (For further discussion of the state-action problem in the context of the modern welfare state, see Note: State Action in the Age of the Welfare State, supra.)

---

11. See also Ortwein v. Schwab, 410 U.S. 656 (1973), where the Court summarily upheld Oregon's $25 appellate court filing fee as applied to appeals by indigents from administrative decisions reducing welfare payments. "The purpose of the filing fee, as with the bankruptcy fees in *Kras*, is apparent. The Oregon court system incurs operating costs, and the fee produces some small revenue to assist in offsetting those expenses. . . . Appellants do not contend that the fee is disproportionate or that it is not an effective means to accomplish the State's goal. The requirement of rationality is met." Moreover, the Court noted, "[t]hese appellants have had hearings . . . , not conditioned on payments of any fee, through which appellants have been able to seek redress. . . . Under the facts of this case, appellants were not denied due process." Justices Douglas, Stewart, Brennan, and Marshall dissented.

12. $50 in 1973 is the equivalent, after inflation, of approximately $265 in 2014.

In hindsight, the shift in the Court's personnel in the late 1960s and early 1970s proved crucial to the direction of doctrine. By the middle 1970s, the four Nixon appointees to the Supreme Court collectively signaled that they would put an end to the Court's experiment with securing affirmative welfare rights under the Constitution. The definitive statement came in a case litigating the right to one of the most important benefits provided by government, education.

D. *The Right to Education*

Recall that the Supreme Court in Brown v. Board of Education said:

> Today, education is the very foundation of good citizenship . . . , a principal instrument in awakening the child to cultural values, in preparing him for later professional training, and in helping him to adjust normally to his environment. In these days, it is doubtful that any child may reasonably be expected to succeed in life if he is denied the opportunity of an education. Such an opportunity, where the state has undertaken to provide it, is a right which must be made available to all on equal terms.

In retrospect, *Brown* seems to have rested far less on the special status of education than on the illegitimacy of the criterion (i.e., race) on which the state separated children attending its public schools. Is education nonetheless so important or special an interest as to call for heightened scrutiny of nonracial laws that allocate educational benefits differentially? Is it so important, indeed, that the Constitution should require the state to provide at least a minimal level of education to everyone within its jurisdiction?

1. "Equal Provision" of Public Education

San Antonio Independent School District v. Rodriguez

411 U.S. 1 (1973)

[Texas public school systems are financed through a combination of local property taxes and state funds. The state-funded "foundation program" tends to equalize disparities among district tax bases, but district expenditures nevertheless depend heavily on local property wealth. For example, in the 1967-1968 school year, the Edgewood Independent School District in San Antonio had an assessed property value per pupil of $5,960. By taxing itself at a rate of 1 percent and after paying its required share into the state program, it was able to raise $26 per pupil. State subventions brought its per pupil expenditure to $356. The Alamo Heights Independent School District, also located in San Antonio, had a tax base of $49,000 per pupil, and raised $333 locally by taxing itself at only .85 percent. State subventions brought its per pupil expenditure to $594. As Justice White noted in his dissent, "In order to equal the highest yield in any other Bexar County district, Alamo Heights would be required to tax at the rate of 68 cents per $100 of assessed valuation. Edgewood would be required to tax at the prohibitive rate of $5.76 per $100. But state law places a $1.50 per $100 ceiling on the maintenance tax rate, a limit that would surely be reached long before Edgewood attained an equal yield. Edgewood is thus precluded in law, as well as in fact, from achieving a yield even close to that of some other districts."

Appellees, the parents of children attending the Edgewood schools, brought this suit to invalidate the state school financing scheme on the ground that it violated the Equal Protection Clause of the Fourteenth Amendment. On the state's appeal from the district court's judgment for appellees, the Supreme Court reversed.]

POWELL, J. . . .

I

. . . We must decide, first, whether the Texas system of financing public education operates to the disadvantage of some suspect class or impinges upon a fundamental right explicitly or implicitly protected by the Constitution, thereby requiring strict judicial scrutiny. If so, the judgment of the District Court should be affirmed. If not, the Texas scheme must still be examined to determine whether it rationally furthers some legitimate, articulated state purpose and therefore does not constitute an invidious discrimination in violation of the Equal Protection Clause of the Fourteenth Amendment.

II

. . . In concluding that strict judicial scrutiny was required [the District Court] relied on decisions dealing with the rights of indigents to equal treatment in the criminal trial and appellate processes, and on cases disapproving wealth restrictions on the right to vote. Those cases, the District Court concluded, established wealth as a suspect classification. Finding that the local property tax system discriminated on the basis of wealth, it regarded those precedents as controlling. It then reasoned, based on decisions of this Court affirming the undeniable importance of education, that there is a fundamental right to education and that, absent some compelling state justification, the Texas system could not stand.

We are unable to agree that this case, which in significant aspects is sui generis, may be so neatly fitted into the conventional mosaic of constitutional analysis under the Equal Protection Clause. Indeed, for the several reasons that follow, we find neither the suspect-classification nor the fundamental-interest analysis persuasive.

A

. . . [Justice Powell first held that no suspect class was involved in the case.] The Texas system of school financing might be regarded as discriminating (1) against "poor" persons whose incomes fall below some identifiable level of poverty or who might be characterized as functionally "indigent," or (2) against those who are relatively poorer than others, or (3) against all those who, irrespective of their personal incomes, happen to reside in relatively poorer school districts. . . .

[In the Court's previous cases involving discrimination against the poor,] the class discriminated against . . . shared two distinguishing characteristics: because of their impecunity they were completely unable to pay for some desired benefit, and as a consequence, they sustained an absolute deprivation of a meaningful opportunity to enjoy that benefit. . . .

[But] appellees have made no effort to demonstrate that [Texas's system for financing schools] operates to the peculiar disadvantage of any class fairly definable as indigent, or as composed of persons whose incomes are beneath any designated poverty level. Indeed, there is reason to believe that the poorest families are not necessarily clustered in the poorest property districts. . . . [Moreover,] . . . lack of personal resources has not occasioned an absolute deprivation of the desired benefit. The argument here is . . . that the children in districts having relatively low assessable property values . . . are receiving a poorer quality education than that available to children in districts having more assessable wealth. Apart from the unsettled and disputed question whether the quality of education may be determined by the amount of money expended for it,[a] a sufficient answer to appellees' argument is that, at least where wealth is involved, the Equal Protection Clause does not require absolute equality or precisely equal advantages. . . .[b]

[The second approach is] a theory of relative or comparative discrimination based on family income. . . . the poorer the family the lower the dollar amount of education received by the family's children. . . . [Appellees failed to prove this, however, and even if they could show it, their] comparative-discrimination theory would still face serious unanswered questions, including whether a bare positive correlation or some higher degree of correlation is necessary to provide a basis for concluding that the financing system is designed to operate to the peculiar disadvantage of the comparatively poor, and whether a class of this size and diversity could ever claim the special protection accorded "suspect" classes.

[The third approach is] district wealth discrimination. [A]ppellees' suit asks this Court to extend its most exacting scrutiny to review a system that allegedly discriminates against a large, diverse, and amorphous class, unified only by the common factor of residence in districts that happen to have less taxable wealth than other districts. The system of alleged discrimination and the class it defines have none of the traditional indicia of suspectness: the class is not saddled with such disabilities, or subjected to such a history of purposeful unequal treatment, or relegated to such a position of political powerlessness as to command extraordinary protection from the majoritarian political process.

We thus conclude that the Texas system does not operate to the peculiar disadvantage of any suspect class. [A]ppellees have not relied solely on this contention.

---

a. Each of appellees' possible theories of wealth discrimination is founded on the assumption that the quality of education varies directly with the amount of funds expended on it and that, therefore, the difference in quality between two schools can be determined simplistically by looking at the difference in per pupil expenditures. This is a matter of considerable dispute among educators and commentators. . . .

b. An educational financing system might be hypothesized, however, in which the analogy to the wealth discrimination cases would be considerably closer. If elementary and secondary education were made available by the State only to those able to pay a tuition assessed against each pupil, there would be a clearly defined class of "poor" people—definable in terms of their inability to pay the prescribed sum—who would be absolutely precluded from receiving an education. That case would present a far more compelling set of circumstances for judicial assistance than the case before us today. . . .

They also assert that the State's system impermissibly interferes with the exercise of a "fundamental" right. . . .

B

In Brown v. Board of Education a unanimous Court recognized that "education is perhaps the most important function of state and local governments." . . . But the importance of a service performed by the State does not determine whether it must be regarded as fundamental for purposes of examination under the Equal Protection Clause. . . .

The lesson of [Lindsey v. Normet; Dandridge v. Williams; Jefferson v. Hackney, 406 U.S. 535 (1972); and Richardson v. Belcher, 404 U.S. 78 (1971),] in addressing the question now before the Court is plain. It is not the province of this Court to create substantive constitutional rights in the name of guaranteeing equal protection of the laws. Thus, the key to discovering whether education is "fundamental" is not to be found in comparisons of the relative societal significance of education as opposed to subsistence or housing. Nor is it to be found by weighing whether education is as important as the right to travel. Rather, the answer lies in assessing whether there is a right to education explicitly or implicitly guaranteed by the Constitution. Eisenstadt v. Baird, 405 U.S. 438 (1972); Dunn v. Blumstein;[c] Police Dept. of Chicago v. Mosley, 408 U.S. 92 (1972);[d] Skinner v. Oklahoma, 316 U.S. 535 (1942).[e]

Education, of course, is not among the rights afforded explicit protection under our Federal Constitution. Nor do we find any basis for saying it is implicitly so protected. . . . [Appellees argue] that education is distinguishable from other services and benefits provided by the State because it bears a peculiarly close relationship to other rights and liberties accorded protection under the Constitution. . . . [Education] is essential to the effective exercise of First Amendment freedoms and to intelligent utilization of the right to vote. . . . [A]ppellees urge that the right to speak is meaningless unless the speaker is capable of articulating his thoughts intelligently and persuasively. The "marketplace of ideas" is an empty forum for those lacking basic communicative tools. . . . A similar line of reasoning is pursued with

---

c. *Dunn* fully canvasses this Court's voting rights cases and explains that "this Court has made clear that a citizen has a *constitutionally protected right* to participate in elections on an equal basis with other citizens in the jurisdiction." Id. at 336 (emphasis supplied). The constitutional underpinnings of the right to equal treatment in the voting process can no longer be doubted even though, as the Court noted in Harper v. Virginia Bd. of Elections, . . . "the right to vote in state elections is nowhere expressly mentioned." . . .

d. In *Mosley*, the Court struck down a Chicago antipicketing ordinance that exempted labor picketing from its prohibitions. The ordinance was held invalid under the Equal Protection Clause after subjecting it to careful scrutiny and finding that the ordinance was not narrowly drawn. The stricter standard of review was appropriately applied since the ordinance was one "affecting First Amendment interests." . . .

e. Skinner applied the standard of close scrutiny to a state law permitting forced sterilization of "habitual criminals." Implicit in the Court's opinion is the recognition that the right of procreation is among the rights of personal privacy protected under the Constitution. See Roe v. Wade.

respect to the right to vote.[f] Exercise of the franchise, it is contended, cannot be divorced from the educational foundation of the voter.

We need not dispute any of these propositions. . . . Yet we have never presumed to possess either the ability or the authority to guarantee to the citizenry the most effective speech or the most informed electoral choice. . . .

Whatever merit appellees' argument might have if a State's financing system occasioned an absolute denial of educational opportunities to any of its children, that argument provides no basis for finding an interference with fundamental rights where only relative differences in spending levels are involved and where—as is true in the present case—no charge fairly could be made that the system fails to provide each child with an opportunity to acquire the basic minimal skills necessary for the enjoyment of the rights of speech and of full participation in the political process.

Furthermore, the logical limitations on appellees' nexus theory are difficult to perceive. How, for instance, is education to be distinguished from the significant personal interests in the basics of decent food and shelter? Empirical examination might well buttress an assumption that the ill-fed, ill-clothed, and ill-housed are among the most ineffective participants in the political process, and that they derive the least enjoyment from the benefits of the First Amendment. If so, appellees' thesis would cast serious doubt on the authority of Dandridge v. Williams and Lindsey v. Normet.

. . . [W]e find this a particularly inappropriate case in which to subject state action to strict judicial scrutiny. . . . Each of our prior cases involved legislation which "deprived," "infringed," or "interfered" with the free exercise of some such fundamental personal right or liberty. See Skinner v. Oklahoma; Shapiro v. Thompson; Dunn v. Blumstein. Every step leading to the establishment of the system Texas utilizes today—including the decisions permitting localities to tax and expend locally, and creating and continuously expanding state aid—was implemented in an effort to extend public education and to improve its quality. Of course, every reform that benefits some more than others may be criticized for what it fails to accomplish. But we think it plain that, in substance, the thrust of the Texas system is affirmative and reformatory and, therefore, should be scrutinized under judicial principles sensitive to the nature of the State's efforts and to the rights reserved to the States under the Constitution.

C

We [apply] . . . the traditional standard of review, which requires only that the State's system be shown to bear some rational relationship to legitimate state purposes. . . .

While assuring a basic education for every child in the State, [the Texas system of school finance] permits and encourages a large measure of participation in and

---

f. Since the right to vote, per se, is not a constitutionally protected right, we assume that appellees' references to that right are simply shorthand references to the protected right, implicit in our constitutional system, to participate in state elections on an equal basis with other qualified voters whenever the State has adopted an elective process for determining who will represent any segment of the State's population. See n.[c] supra.

control of each district's schools at the local level. In an era that has witnessed a consistent trend toward centralization of the functions of government, local sharing of responsibility for public education has survived. . . . In part, local control means . . . the freedom to devote more money to the education of one's children. Equally important, however, is the opportunity it offers for participation in the decisionmaking process that determines how those local tax dollars will be spent. Each locality is free to tailor local programs to local needs. Pluralism also affords some opportunity for experimentation, innovation, and a healthy competition for educational excellence. . . .

Appellees suggest that local control could be preserved and promoted under other financing systems that resulted in more equality in educational expenditures. While it is no doubt true that reliance on local property taxation for school revenues provides less freedom of choice with respect to expenditures for some districts than for others, the existence of "some inequality" in the manner in which the State's rationale is achieved is not alone a sufficient basis for striking down the entire system. . . .

Nor must the financing system fail because, as appellees suggest, other methods of satisfying the State's interest, which occasion "less drastic" disparities in expenditures, might be conceived. Only where state action impinges on the exercise of fundamental constitutional rights or liberties must it be found to have chosen the last restrictive alternative. . . . The people of Texas may be justified in believing that other systems of school financing, which place more of the financial responsibility in the hands of the State, will result in a comparable lessening of desired local autonomy. . . .

Appellees further urge that the Texas system is unconstitutionally arbitrary because it allows the availability of local taxable resources to turn on "happenstance." They see no justification for a system that allows, as they contend, the quality of education to fluctuate on the basis of the fortuitous positioning of the boundary lines of political subdivisions and the location of valuable commercial and industrial property. But any scheme of local taxation—indeed the very existence of identifiable local governmental units—requires the establishment of jurisdictional boundaries that are inevitably arbitrary. It is equally inevitable that some localities are going to be blessed with more taxable assets than others.[g] Nor is local wealth a static quantity. Changes in the level of taxable wealth within any district may result from any number of events, some of which local residents can and do influence. For instance, commercial and industrial enterprises may be encouraged to locate within a district by various actions—public and private.

Moreover, if local taxation for local expenditures were an unconstitutional method of providing for education then it might be an equally impermissible means of providing other necessary services customarily financed largely from local property taxes, including local police and fire protection, public health and hospitals, and public utility facilities of various kinds. . . .

In sum, to the extent that the Texas system of school financing results in unequal expenditures between children who happen to reside in different districts,

---

g. This Court has never doubted the propriety of maintaining political subdivisions within the States and has never found in the Equal Protection Clause any per se rule of "territorial uniformity." . . .

we cannot say that such disparities are the product of a system that is so irrational as to be invidiously discriminatory. . . .

[A concurring opinion by Justice Stewart is omitted.]

WHITE, J., joined by DOUGLAS and BRENNAN, JJ., dissenting. . . .

I cannot disagree with the proposition that local control and local decisionmaking play an important part in our democratic system of government. . . . The difficulty with the Texas system . . . is that it provides a meaningful option to [wealthy districts like] Alamo Heights . . . but almost none to Edgewood and those other districts with a low per-pupil real estate tax base. In these latter districts, no matter how desirous parents are of supporting their schools with greater revenues, it is impossible to do so through the use of the real estate property tax. In these districts, the Texas system utterly fails to extend a realistic choice to parents because the property tax, which is the only revenue-raising mechanism extended to school districts, is practically and legally unavailable. . . .

The Equal Protection Clause permits discriminations between classes but requires that the classification bear some rational relationship to a permissible object sought to be attained by the statute. It is not enough that the Texas system before us seeks to achieve the valid, rational purpose of maximizing local initiative; the means chosen by the State must also be rationally related to the end sought to be achieved. . . . If the State aims at maximizing local initiative and local choice . . . it utterly fails in achieving its purpose in districts with property tax bases so low that there is little if any opportunity for interested parents, rich or poor, to augment school district revenues. Requiring the State to establish only that unequal treatment is in furtherance of a permissible goal, without also requiring the State to show that the means chosen to effectuate that goal are rationally related to its achievement, makes equal protection analysis no more than an empty gesture. In my view, the parents and children in Edgewood, and in like districts, suffer from an invidious discrimination violative of the Equal Protection Clause. . . .

MARSHALL, J., joined by DOUGLAS, J., dissenting. . . .

II

The Court apparently seeks to establish today that equal protection cases fall into one of two neat categories which dictate the appropriate standard of review—strict scrutiny or mere rationality. But this Court's decisions in the field of equal protection defy such easy categorization. A principled reading of what this Court has done reveals that it has applied a spectrum of standards in reviewing discrimination allegedly violative of the Equal Protection Clause. This spectrum clearly comprehends variations in the degree of care with which the Court will scrutinize particular classifications, depending, I believe, on the constitutional and societal importance of the interest adversely affected and the recognized invidiousness of the basis upon which the particular classification is drawn. . . .

I therefore cannot accept the majority's labored efforts to demonstrate that fundamental interests, which call for strict scrutiny of the challenged classification, encompass only established rights which we are somehow bound to recognize from the text of the Constitution itself. To be sure, some interests which the Court has deemed to be fundamental for purposes of equal protection analysis are themselves constitutionally protected rights. . . . See Police Dept. of Chicago v. Mosley . . . ; Shapiro v. Thompson. . . . But it will not do to suggest that the "answer" to whether an interest is fundamental for purposes of equal protection analysis is always determined by whether that interest "is a right . . . explicitly or implicitly guaranteed by the Constitution."[a] . . .

I would like to know where the Constitution guarantees the right to procreate, Skinner v. Oklahoma, or the right to vote in state elections, e.g., [Harper v. Virginia Bd. of Elections,] or the right to an appeal from a criminal conviction, e.g., Griffin v. Illinois. These are instances in which, due to the importance of the interests at stake, the Court has displayed a strong concern with the existence of discriminatory state treatment. But the Court has never said or indicated that these are interests which independently enjoy full-blown constitutional protection.

Thus, in Buck v. Bell, 247 U.S. 200 (1927), the Court refused to recognize a substantive constitutional guarantee of the right to procreate. Nevertheless, in Skinner v. Oklahoma, . . . the Court, without impugning the continuing validity of Buck v. Bell, held that "strict scrutiny" of state discrimination affecting procreation "is essential," for "[m]arriage and procreation are fundamental to the very existence and survival of the race." . . .

Similarly, . . . "this Court has made clear that a citizen has a *constitutionally protected right* to participate in elections *on an equal basis with other citizens in the jurisdiction*." Dunn v. Blumstein (emphasis added). The final source of such protection from inequality in the provision of the state franchise is, of course, the Equal Protection Clause. Yet it is clear that whatever degree of importance has been attached to the state electoral process when unequally distributed, the right to vote in state elections has itself never been accorded the stature of an independent constitutional guarantee.[b] . . .

Finally, it is likewise "true that a State is not required by the Federal Constitution to provide appellate courts or a right to appellate review at all." Griffin v. Illinois. Nevertheless, discrimination adversely affecting access to an appellate process which a State has chosen to provide has been considered to require close judicial scrutiny. See, e.g., Griffin v. Illinois; Douglas v. California.[c]

---

a. Indeed, the Court's theory would render the established concept of fundamental interests in the context of equal protection analysis superfluous, for the substantive constitutional right itself requires that this Court strictly scrutinize any asserted state interest for restricting or denying access to any particular guaranteed right. . . .

b. It is interesting that in its effort to reconcile the state voting rights cases with its theory of fundamentality the majority can muster nothing more than the contention that "[t]he constitutional underpinnings of the *right to equal treatment in the voting process* can no longer be doubted. . . ." (emphasis added). If, by this, the Court intends to recognize a substantive constitutional "right to equal treatment in the voting process" independent of the Equal Protection Clause, the source of such a right is certainly a mystery to me.

c. It is true that *Griffin* and *Douglas* also involved discrimination against indigents, that is, wealth discrimination. But, as the majority points out, the Court has never deemed wealth discrimination alone to be sufficient to require strict judicial scrutiny; rather, such review of wealth classifications has been applied only where the discrimination affects an important individual interest, see, e.g., Harper v. Virginia Bd. of Elections. Thus, I believe *Griffin* and *Douglas* can only be understood as premised on a recognition of the fundamental importance of the criminal appellate process.

The majority is, of course, correct when it suggests that the process of determining which interests are fundamental is a difficult one. But I do not think the problem is insurmountable. And I certainly do not accept the view that the process need necessarily degenerate into an unprincipled, subjective "picking-and-choosing" between various interests or that it must involve this Court in creating "substantive constitutional rights in the name of guaranteeing equal protection of the laws." Although not all fundamental interests are constitutionally guaranteed, the determination of which interests are fundamental should be firmly rooted in the text of the Constitution. The task in every case should be to determine the extent to which constitutionally guaranteed rights are dependent on interests not mentioned in the Constitution. As the nexus between the specific constitutional guarantee and the nonconstitutional interest draws closer, the nonconstitutional interest becomes more fundamental and the degree of judicial scrutiny applied when the interest is infringed on a discriminatory basis must be adjusted accordingly. Thus, it cannot be denied that interests such as procreation, the exercise of the state franchise, and access to criminal appellate processes are not fully guaranteed to the citizen by our Constitution. But these interests have nonetheless been afforded special judicial consideration in the face of discrimination because they are, to some extent, interrelated with constitutional guarantees. Procreation is now understood to be important because of its interaction with the established constitutional right of privacy. The exercise of the state franchise is closely tied to basic civil and political rights inherent in the First Amendment. And access to criminal appellate processes enhances the integrity of the range of rights implicit in the Fourteenth Amendment guarantee of due process of law. Only if we closely protect the related interests from state discrimination do we ultimately ensure the integrity of the constitutional guarantee itself. This is the real lesson that must be taken from our previous decisions involving interests deemed to be fundamental. . . .

B

It is true that this Court has never deemed the provision of free public education to be required by the Constitution. . . . Nevertheless, the fundamental importance of education is amply indicated by the prior decisions of this Court, by the unique status accorded public education by our society, and by the close relationship between education and some of our most basic constitutional values. . . . In large measure, the explanation for the special importance attached to education must rest . . . on the facts that "some degree of education is necessary to prepare citizens to participate effectively and intelligently in our open political system . . . ," and that "education prepares individuals to be self-reliant and self-sufficient participants in society." Both facets of this observation are suggestive of the substantial relationship which education bears to guarantees of our Constitution.

Education directly affects the ability of a child to exercise his First Amendment interests, both as a source and as a receiver of information and ideas, whatever interests he may pursue in life. . . . Education may instill the interest and provide the tools necessary for political discourse and debate. . . . But of most immediate and direct concern must be the demonstrated effect of education on the exercise of the franchise by the electorate. . . . Data from the Presidential Election of 1968 clearly demonstrates a direct relationship between participation in the electoral process and level of educational attainment; and, as this Court recognized in Gaston County v. United States, 395 U.S. 284, 296 (1969), the quality of education offered may influence a child's decision to "enter or remain in school." It is this very sort of intimate relationship between a particular personal interest and specific constitutional guarantees that has heretofore caused the Court to attach special significance, for purposes of equal protection analysis, to individual interests such as procreation and the exercise of the state franchise.[d]

While ultimately disputing little of this, the majority seeks refuge in the fact that the Court has "never presumed to possess either the ability or the authority to guarantee to the citizenry the most effective speech or the most informed electoral choice." . . . This serves only to blur what is in fact at stake. With due respect, the issue is neither provision of the most effective speech nor of the most informed vote. Appellees do not now seek the best education Texas might provide. They do seek, however, an end to state discrimination resulting from the unequal distribution of taxable district property wealth that directly impairs the ability of some districts to provide the same educational opportunity that other districts can provide with the same or even substantially less tax effort. The issue is, in other words, one of discrimination that affects the quality of the education which Texas has chosen to provide its children; and, the precise question here is what importance should attach to education for purposes of equal protection analysis of that discrimination. . . .

C

The District Court found that in discriminating between Texas schoolchildren on the basis of the amount of taxable property wealth located in the district in which they live, the Texas financing scheme created a form of wealth discrimination. . . . The majority, however, considers any wealth classification in this case to lack certain essential characteristics which it contends are common to the instances of wealth discrimination that this Court has heretofore recognized. We are told that in every prior case involving a wealth classification, the members of the disadvantaged class have "shared two distinguishing characteristics: because of their

---

d. I believe that the close nexus between education and our established constitutional values with respect to freedom of speech and participation in the political process makes this a different case from our prior decisions concerning discrimination affecting public welfare, see, e.g., Dandridge v. Williams, and housing, see, e.g., Lindsey v. Normet. There can be no question that, as the majority suggests, constitutional rights may be less meaningful for someone without enough to eat or without decent housing. But the crucial difference lies in the closeness of the relationship. Whatever the severity of the impact of insufficient food or inadequate housing on a person's life, they have never been considered to bear the same direct and immediate relationship to constitutional concerns for free speech and for our political processes as education has long been recognized to bear. Perhaps, the best evidence of this fact is the unique status which has been accorded public education as the single public service nearly unanimously guaranteed in the constitutions of our States. . . . Education, in terms of constitutional values, is much more analogous, in my judgment, to the right to vote in state elections than to public welfare or public housing. Indeed, it is not without significance that we have long recognized education as an essential step in providing the disadvantaged with the tools necessary to achieve economic self-sufficiency.

impecunity they were completely unable to pay for some desired benefit, and as a consequence, they sustained an absolute deprivation of a meaningful opportunity to enjoy that benefit." . . . I cannot agree. . . .

Under the first part of the theory announced by the majority, the disadvantaged class in *Harper*, in terms of a wealth analysis, should have consisted only of those too poor to afford the $1.50 necessary to vote. But the *Harper* Court did not see it that way. In its view, the Equal Protection Clause "bars a system which excludes [from the franchise] those unable to pay a fee to vote or who fail to pay." So far as the Court was concerned, the "degree of the discrimination [was] irrelevant." Thus, the Court struck down the poll tax in toto; it did not order merely that those too poor to pay the tax be exempted; complete impecunity clearly was not determinative of the limits of the disadvantaged class, nor was it essential to make an equal protection claim. . . .

[In Griffin v. Illinois and Douglas v. California] the right of appeal itself was not absolutely denied to those too poor to pay; but because of the cost of a transcript and of counsel, the appeal was a substantially less meaningful right for the poor than for the rich.[e] It was on these terms that the Court found a denial of equal protection, and those terms clearly encompassed degrees of discrimination on the basis of wealth which do not amount to outright denial of the affected right or interest.

This is not to say that the form of wealth classification in this case does not differ significantly from those recognized in the previous decisions of this Court. Our prior cases have dealt essentially with discrimination on the basis of personal wealth. Here, by contrast, the children of the disadvantaged Texas school districts are being discriminated against not necessarily because of their personal wealth or the wealth of their families, but because of the taxable property wealth of the residents of the district in which they happen to live. The appropriate question, then, is whether the same degree of judicial solicitude and scrutiny that has previously been afforded wealth classifications is warranted here.

As the Court points out, no previous decision has deemed the presence of just a wealth classification to be sufficient basis to call forth rigorous judicial scrutiny of allegedly discriminatory state action. . . . That wealth classifications alone have not necessarily been considered to bear the same high degree of suspectness as have classifications based on, for instance, race or alienage may be explainable on a number of grounds. The "poor" may not be seen as politically powerless as certain discrete and insular minority groups. Personal poverty may entail much the same social stigma as is historically attached to certain racial or ethnic groups. But personal poverty is not a permanent disability; its shackles may be escaped. Perhaps most importantly, though, personal wealth may not necessarily share the general irrelevance as a basis for legislative action that race or nationality is recognized to have. While the "poor" have frequently been a legally disadvantaged group, it

---

e. This does not mean that the Court has demanded precise equality in the treatment of the indigent and the person of means in the criminal process. We have never suggested, for instance, that the Equal Protection Clause requires the best lawyer money can buy for the indigent. We are hardly equipped with the objective standards which such a judgment would require. But we have pursued the goal of substantial equality of treatment in the face of clear disparities in the nature of the appellate process afforded rich versus poor. . . .

cannot be ignored that social legislation must frequently take cognizance of the economic status of our citizens. Thus, we have generally gauged the invidiousness of wealth classifications with an awareness of the importance of the interests being affected and the relevance of personal wealth to those interests. See *Harper*.

When evaluated with these considerations in mind, it seems to me that discrimination on the basis of group wealth in this case likewise calls for careful judicial scrutiny. First, it must be recognized that while local district wealth may serve other interests, it bears no relationship whatsoever to the interest of Texas school children in the educational opportunity afforded them by the State of Texas. Given the importance of that interest, we must be particularly sensitive to the invidious characteristics of any form of discrimination that is not clearly intended to serve it, as opposed to some other distinct state interest. Discrimination on the basis of group wealth may not, to be sure, reflect the social stigma frequently attached to personal poverty. Nevertheless, insofar as group wealth discrimination involves wealth over which the disadvantaged individual has no significant control,[f] it represents in fact a more serious basis of discrimination than does personal wealth. For such discrimination is no reflection of the individual's characteristics or his abilities. And thus—particularly in the context of a disadvantaged class composed of children—we have previously treated discrimination on a basis which the individual cannot control as constitutionally disfavored. Cf. Weber v. Aetna Casualty & Surety Co., 406 U.S. 164 (1972); Levy v. Louisiana, 391 U.S. 68 (1968). . . .

Nor can we ignore the extent to which, in contrast to our prior decisions, the State is responsible for the wealth discrimination in this instance. *Griffin, Douglas, Williams, Tate,* and our other prior cases have dealt with discrimination on the basis of indigency which was attributable to the operation of the private sector. But we have no such simple de facto wealth discrimination here. The means for financing public education in Texas are selected and specified by the State. It is the State that has created local school districts, and tied educational funding to the local property tax and thereby to local district wealth. At the same time, governmentally imposed land use controls have undoubtedly encouraged and rigidified natural trends in the allocation of particular areas for residential or commercial use, and thus determined each district's amount of taxable property wealth. In short, this case, in contrast to the Court's previous wealth discrimination decision, can only be seen as "unusual in the extent to which governmental action is the cause of the wealth classifications."

In the final analysis, then, the invidious characteristics of the group wealth classification present in this case merely serve to emphasize the need for careful judicial scrutiny of the State's justifications for the resulting interdistrict discrimination in the educational opportunity afforded to the schoolchildren of Texas.

D

The nature of our inquiry into the justifications for state discrimination is essentially the same in all equal protection cases: We must consider the

---

f. True, a family may move to escape a property-poor school district, assuming it has the means to do so. But such a view would itself raise a serious constitutional question concerning an impermissible burdening of the right to travel, or, more precisely, the concomitant right to remain where one is. Cf. Shapiro v. Thompson.

substantiality of the state interests sought to be served, and we must scrutinize the reasonableness of the means by which the State has sought to advance its interests. Differences in the application of this test are, in my view, a function of the constitutional importance of the interests at stake and the invidiousness of the particular classification. In terms of the asserted state interests, the Court has indicated that it will require, for instance, a "compelling" or a "substantial" or "important" state interest to justify discrimination affecting individual interests of constitutional significance. Whatever the differences, if any, in these descriptions of the character of the state interest necessary to sustain such discrimination, basic to each is, I believe, a concern with the legitimacy and the reality of the asserted state interests. Thus, when interests of constitutional importance are at stake, the Court does not stand ready to credit the State's classification with any conceivable legitimate purpose, but demands a clear showing that there are legitimate state interests which the classification was in fact intended to serve. Beyond the question of the adequacy of the State's purpose for the classification, the Court traditionally has become increasingly sensitive to the means by which a State chooses to act as its action affects more directly interests of constitutional significance. Thus, by now, "less restrictive alternatives" analysis is firmly established in equal protection jurisprudence. It seems to me that the range of choice we are willing to accord the State in selecting the means by which it will act, and the care with which we scrutinize the effectiveness of the means which the State selects, also must reflect the constitutional importance of the interest affected and the invidiousness of the particular classification. Here both the nature of the interest and the classification dictate close judicial scrutiny of the purposes which Texas seeks to serve with its present educational financing scheme and of the means it has selected to serve that purpose.

The only justification offered by appellants to sustain the discrimination in educational opportunity caused by the Texas financing scheme is local educational control. . . .

At the outset, I do not question that local control of public education, as an abstract matter, constitutes a very substantial state interest. . . . Consequently, true state dedication to local control would present, I think, a substantial justification to weigh against simply interdistrict variations in the treatment of a State's school children. But I need not now decide how I might ultimately strike the balance were we confronted with a situation where the State's sincere concern for local control inevitably produced educational inequality. For on this record, it is apparent that the State's purported concern with local control is offered primarily as an excuse rather than as a justification for interdistrict inequality.

In Texas, statewide laws regulate in fact the most minute details of local public education. . . . [But] even if we accept Texas' general dedication to local control in educational matters, it is difficult to find any evidence of such dedication with respect to fiscal matters. . . . If Texas had a system truly dedicated to local fiscal control, one would expect the quality of the educational opportunity provided in each district to vary with the decision of the voters in that district as to the level of sacrifice they wish to make for public education. In fact, the Texas scheme produces precisely the opposite result. Local school districts cannot choose to have the best education in the State by imposing the highest tax rate. Instead, the quality of the educational opportunity offered by any particular district is largely determined by the amount of taxable property located in the district—a factor over which local voters can exercise no control. . . .

In my judgment, any substantial degree of scrutiny of the operation of the Texas financing scheme reveals that the State has selected means wholly inappropriate to secure its purported interest in assuring its school districts local fiscal control.[g] At the same time, appellees have pointed out a variety of alternative financing schemes which may serve the State's purported interest in local control as well as, if not better than, the present scheme without the current impairment of the educational opportunity of vast numbers of Texas schoolchildren. I see no need, however, to explore the practical or constitutional merits of those suggested alternatives at this time for, whatever their positive or negative features, experience with the present financing scheme impugns any suggestion that it constitutes a serious effort to provide local fiscal control. . . .[h]

[A dissenting opinion by Justice Brennan is omitted.]

---

g. My Brother White, in concluding that the Texas financing scheme runs afoul of the Equal Protection Clause, likewise finds on analysis that the means chosen by Texas—local property taxation dependent upon local taxable wealth—is completely unsuited in its present form to the achievement of the asserted goal of providing local fiscal control. Although my Brother White purports to reach this result by application of that lenient standard of mere rationality traditionally applied in the context of commercial interests, it seems to me that the care with which he scrutinizes the practical effectiveness of the present local property tax as a device for affording local fiscal control reflects the application of a more stringent standard of review, a standard which at the least is influenced by the constitutional significance of the process of public education.

h. [E]ven centralized financing would not deprive local school districts of what has been considered to be the essence of local educational control. . . . Central financing would leave in local hands the entire gamut of local educational policymaking—teachers, curriculum, school sites, the whole process of allocating resources among alternative educational objectives. [Local fiscal control could be achieved under] the theory of district power equalization put forth by Professors Coons, Clune and Sugarman in their seminal work, Private Wealth and Public Education 201-242 (1970). Such a scheme would truly reflect a dedication to local fiscal control. Under their system, each school district would receive a fixed amount of revenue per pupil for any particular level of tax effort regardless of the level of local property tax base. Appellants criticize this scheme on the rather extraordinary ground that it would encourage poorer districts to overtax themselves in order to obtain substantial revenues for education. But under the present discriminatory scheme, it is the poor districts that are already taxing themselves at the highest rates, yet are receiving the lowest returns.

District wealth reapportionment is yet another alternative which would accomplish directly essentially what district power equalization would seek to do artificially. Appellants claim that the calculations concerning state property required by such a scheme would be impossible as a practical matter. Yet Texas is already making far more complex annual calculations—involving not only local property values but also local income and other economic factors—in conjunction with the Local Fund Assignment portion of the Minimum Foundation School Program. . . . [Another] possibility would be to remove commercial, industrial, and mineral property from local tax rolls, to tax this property on a statewide basis, and to return the resulting revenues to the local districts in a fashion that would compensate for remaining variations in the local tax bases. None of these particular alternatives are necessarily constitutionally compelled: rather, they indicate the breadth of choice which would remain to the State if the present interdistrict disparities were eliminated.

DISCUSSION

1. *Comparative constitutional kinship.* Rank the following interests in terms of the firmness of their grounding in the text, structure, and original history of the Constitution: interstate mobility (protected in *Crandall* and *Shapiro*), privacy (protected in *Griswold* and Roe v. Wade), the franchise (protected in *Harper*), subsistence (denied protection in Dandridge v. Williams and Lindsey v. Normet), and education (denied protection in *Rodriguez*). Is Justice Powell persuasive that the Court has not picked and chosen among possible interests both in the creation of constitutional "rights" (e.g., privacy) and "fundamental interests" (e.g., political participation)? How persuasive is Justice Marshall's argument that education deserves special constitutional treatment because of its relationships with speech and the franchise? Assuming that some regulations concerning education do affect these interests, cf. Pierce v. Society of Sisters and Meyer v. Nebraska, supra, does the Texas school finance scheme affect them in a significant or in a constitutionally germane manner?

2. *The standard of judicial review and the substantive requirements of the Equal Protection Clause.* In *Dandridge* and *Rodriguez,* Justice Marshall criticizes the Court for its binary or "two-tier"[13] approach to equal protection adjudication, under which a classification is subjected either to minimal or to very demanding scrutiny. He proposes, instead, a variable standard determined by the nature of the classifying trait and the interests affected. What are the rationales for the Court's and Justice Marshall's approaches?

In a portion of *Rodriguez* not quoted above, Justice Powell asserts: "[I]f the degree of judicial scrutiny of state legislation fluctuated depending on the majority's view of the importance of the interest affected, we would have gone 'far toward making this Court a super-legislature.' We would, indeed, then be assuming a legislative role and one for which the Court lacks both authority and competence." Do *Dandridge* and *Rodriguez* reflect the Court's substantive position that the Equal Protection Clause demands nothing more than "minimum rationality" in the allocation of welfare and educational benefits or only an institutional reluctance to second-guess the legislature's application of a more demanding standard? What rationales support the two positions? Should we demand of legislators that they apply the imperatives of the Equal Protection Clause to their own decisions even in the absence of judicial monitoring?

3. *A "due process" minimum?* Does footnote b of Justice Powell's opinion suggest that the state can neither withdraw entirely from the educational marketplace nor bar children from public schools because of their or their families' inability to pay?[14]

---

13. See Gerald Gunther, In Search of Evolving Doctrine on a Changing Court: A Model for a Newer Equal Protection, 86 Harv. L. Rev. 1 (1972).

14. By "public schools" we are referring to elementary and secondary schools. It is clear that public universities exclude qualified students because of their inability to pay the costs of their education, and this is not, at least currently, thought to present a constitutional problem.

2. Is There a Right to Some Minimal Provision of Educational Resources?

Plyler v. Doe

457 U.S. 202 (1982)

[In 1975, the Texas legislature revised its education laws (1) to withhold from local school districts any state funds to pay for the education of children not "legally admitted" into the United States; and (2) to authorize local school districts to deny enrollment to such children. A class action was filed challenging the Texas legislation.]

BRENNAN, J. . . .

II

[Justice Brennan held that children of illegal aliens were "persons within [Texas's] jurisdiction" for purposes of the Fourteenth Amendment and that the Equal Protection Clause applied to them.]

III

. . .

A

Sheer incapability or lax enforcement of the laws barring entry into this country, coupled with the failure to establish an effective bar to the employment of undocumented aliens, has resulted in the creation of a substantial "shadow population" of illegal migrants—numbering in the millions—within our borders. This situation raises the specter of a permanent caste of undocumented resident aliens, encouraged by some to remain here as a source of cheap labor, but nevertheless denied the benefits that our society makes available to citizens and lawful residents. The existence of such an underclass presents most difficult problems for a Nation that prides itself on adherence to the principles of equality under law.

The children who are plaintiffs in these cases are special members of this underclass. Persuasive arguments support the view that a State may withhold its beneficence from those whose very presence within the United States is the product of their own unlawful conduct. These arguments do not apply with the same force to classifications imposing disabilities on the minor children of such illegal entrants. At the least, those who elect to enter our territory by stealth and in violation of our law should be prepared to bear the consequences, including, but not limited to, deportation. But the children of those illegal entrants are not comparably situated. Their "parents have the ability to conform their conduct to societal norms," and presumably the ability to remove themselves from the State's jurisdiction; but the children who are plaintiffs in these cases "can affect neither their parents' conduct nor their own status." Trimble v. Gordon, 430 U.S. 762, 770 (1977). Even if the State found it expedient to control the conduct of adults by acting against their children, legislation directing the onus of a parent's misconduct against his children does not comport with fundamental conceptions of justice. . . .

Public education is not a "right" granted to individuals by the Constitution. *Rodriguez*. But neither is it merely some governmental "benefit" indistinguishable from other forms of social welfare legislation. Both the importance of education in maintaining our basic institutions, and the lasting impact of its deprivation on the life of the child, mark the distinction. The "American people have always regarded education and the acquisition of knowledge as matters of supreme importance." Meyer v. Nebraska, 262 U.S. 390, 400 (1923). We have recognized "the public school as a most vital civic institution for the preservation of a democratic system of government" and as the primary vehicle for transmitting "the values on which our society rests." As noted early in our history, "some degree of education is necessary to prepare citizens to participate effectively and intelligently in our open political system if we are to preserve freedom and independence." And the historic "perceptions of the public schools as inculcating fundamental values necessary to the maintenance of a democratic political system have been confirmed by the observations of social scientists." In addition, education provides the basic tools by which individuals might lead economically productive lives to the benefit of us all. In sum, education has a fundamental role in maintaining the fabric of our society. We cannot ignore the significant social costs borne by our Nation when select groups are denied the means to absorb the values and skills upon which our social order rests.

In addition to the pivotal role of education in sustaining our political and cultural heritage, denial of education to some isolated group of children poses an affront to one of the goals of the Equal Protection Clause: the abolition of governmental barriers presenting unreasonable obstacles to advancement on the basis of individual merit. Paradoxically, by depriving the children of any disfavored group of an education, we foreclose the means by which that group might raise the level of esteem in which it is held by the majority. But more directly, "education prepares individuals to be self-reliant and self-sufficient participants in society." Illiteracy is an enduring disability. The inability to read and write will handicap the individual deprived of a basic education each and every day of his life. The inestimable toll of that deprivation on the social, economic, intellectual, and psychological well-being of the individual, and the obstacle it poses to individual achievement, makes it most difficult to reconcile the cost or the principle of a status-based denial of basic education within the framework of equality embodied in the Equal Protection Clause. . . .

B

These well-settled principles allow us to determine the proper level of deference to be afforded §21.031. Undocumented aliens cannot be treated as a suspect class because their presence in this country in violation of federal law is not a "constitutional irrelevancy." Nor is education a fundamental right; a State need not justify by compelling necessity every variation in the manner in which education is provided to its population. See *Rodriguez*. But more is involved in this case than the abstract question whether §21.031 discriminates against a suspect class, or whether education is a fundamental right. Section 21.031 imposes a lifetime hardship on a discrete class of children not accountable for their disabling status. The stigma of illiteracy will mark them for the rest of their lives. By denying these children a basic education, we deny them the ability to live within the structure of our civic institutions, and foreclose any realistic possibility that they will contribute in even the smallest way to the progress of our Nation. In determining the rationality of §21.031, we may appropriately take into account its costs to the Nation and to the innocent children who are its victims. In light of these countervailing costs, the discrimination contained in §21.031 can hardly be considered rational unless it furthers some substantial goal of the State.

IV

Appellants argue that the classification at issue furthers interests in the "preservation of the state's limited resources for the education of its lawful residents." Of course, a concern for the preservation of resources standing alone can hardly justify the classification used in allocating those resources. The State must do more than justify its classification with a concise expression of an intention to discriminate. Apart from the asserted state prerogative to act against undocumented children solely on the basis of their undocumented status—an asserted prerogative that carries only minimal force in the circumstances of this case—we discern three colorable state interests that might support §21.031.

First, appellants appear to suggest that the State may seek to protect the State from an influx of illegal immigrants. While a State might have an interest in mitigating the potentially harsh economic effects of sudden shifts in population, §21.031 hardly offers an effective method of dealing with an urgent demographic or economic problem. There is no evidence in the record suggesting that illegal entrants impose any significant burden on the State's economy. To the contrary, the available evidence suggests that illegal aliens under utilize public services, while contributing their labor to the local economy and tax money to the State fisc. The dominant incentive for illegal entry into the State of Texas is the availability of employment; few if any illegal immigrants come to this country, or presumably to the State of Texas, in order to avail themselves of a free education. Thus, even making the doubtful assumption that the net impact of illegal aliens on the economy of the State is negative, we think it clear that "[c]harging tuition to undocumented children constitutes a ludicrously ineffectual attempt to stem the tide of illegal immigration," at least when compared with the alternative of prohibiting the employment of illegal aliens.

Second, while it is apparent that a state may "not . . . reduce expenditures for education by barring [some arbitrarily chosen class of] children from its schools," appellants suggest that undocumented children are appropriately singled out for exclusion because of the special burdens they impose on the State's ability to provide high quality public education in the State. As the District Court noted, the State failed to offer any "credible supporting evidence that a proportionately small diminution of the funds spent on each child [which might result from devoting some State funds to the education of the excluded group] will have a grave impact on the quality of education." And, after reviewing the State's school financing mechanism, the District Court concluded that barring undocumented children from local schools would not necessarily improve the quality of education provided in these schools. Of course, even if improvement in the quality of education were a likely result of barring some number of children from the schools of the State, the State must support its selection of this group as the appropriate target for exclusion. In terms of educational cost and need, however, undocumented children are "basically indistinguishable" from legally resident alien children.

Finally, appellants suggest that undocumented children are appropriately singled out because their unlawful presence within the United States renders them less likely than other children to remain within the boundaries of the State, and to put their education to productive social or political use within the State. Even assuming that such an interest is legitimate, it is an interest that is most difficult to quantify. The State has no assurance that any child, citizen or not, will employ the education provided by the State within the confines of the State's borders. In any event, the record is clear that many of the undocumented children disabled by this classification will remain in this country indefinitely, and that some will become lawful residents or citizens of the United States. It is difficult to understand precisely what the State hopes to achieve by promoting the creation and perpetuation of a subclass of illiterates within our boundaries, surely adding to the problems and costs of unemployment, welfare, and crime. It is thus clear that whatever savings might be achieved by denying these children an education, they are wholly insubstantial in light of the costs involved to these children, the State, and the Nation.

V

If the state is to deny a discrete group of innocent children the free public education that it offers to other children residing within its borders, that denial must be justified by a showing that it furthers some substantial state interest. No such showing was made here.

[Concurring opinions by Justices Blackmun and Powell have been omitted.]

BURGER, C.J., with whom WHITE, REHNQUIST, and O'CONNOR, JJ., join dissenting.

The dispositive issue in these cases, simply put, is whether, for purposes of allocating its finite resources, a State has a legitimate reason to differentiate between persons who are lawfully within the State and those who are unlawfully there. The distinction the State of Texas has drawn—based not only upon its own legitimate interests but on classifications established by the federal government in its immigration laws and policies—is not unconstitutional.

A

The Court acknowledges that except in those cases when state classifications disadvantage a "suspect class" or impinge upon a "fundamental right," the Equal Protection Clause permits a State "substantial latitude" in distinguishing between different groups of persons. Moreover, the Court expressly—and correctly—rejects any suggestion that illegal aliens are a suspect class, or that education is a fundamental right. Yet by patching together bits and pieces of what might be termed quasi-suspect-class and quasi-fundamental-rights analysis, the Court spins out a theory custom-tailored to the facts of these cases. In the end, we are told little more than that the level of scrutiny employed to strike down the Texas law applies only when illegal alien children are deprived of a public education. If ever a court was guilty of an unabashedly result-oriented approach, this case is a prime example.

1

The Court first suggests that these illegal alien children, although not a suspect class, are entitled to special solicitude under the Equal Protection Clause because they lack "control" over or "responsibility" for their unlawful entry into this country. Similarly, the Court appears to take the position that §21.031 is presumptively "irrational" because it has the effect of imposing "penalties" on "innocent" children. However, the Equal Protection Clause does not preclude legislators from classifying among persons on the basis of factors and characteristics over which individuals may be said to lack "control." Indeed, in some circumstances persons generally, and children in particular, may have little control over or responsibility for such things as their ill-health, need for public assistance, or place of residence. Yet a state legislature is not barred from considering, for example, relevant differences between the mentally healthy and the mentally ill, or between the residents of different counties, simply because these may be factors unrelated to individual choice or to any "wrongdoing." The Equal Protection Clause protects against arbitrary and irrational classifications, and against invidious discrimination stemming from prejudice and hostility; it is not an all-encompassing "equalizer" designed to eradicate every distinction for which persons are not "responsible."

The Court does not presume to suggest that appellees' purported lack of culpability for their illegal status prevents them from being deported or otherwise "penalized" under federal law. Yet would deportation be any less a "penalty" than denial of privileges provided to legal residents? Illegality of presence in the United States does not—and need not—depend on some amorphous concept of "guilt" or "innocence" concerning an alien's entry. Similarly, a State's use of federal immigration status as a basis for legislative classification is not necessarily rendered suspect for its failure to take such factors into account.

The Court's analogy to cases involving discrimination against illegitimate children is grossly misleading. The State has not thrust any disabilities upon appellees due to their "status of birth." Cf. Weber v. Aetna Casualty & Surety Co., 406 U.S. 164, 176 (1972). Rather, appellees' status is predicated upon the circumstances of their concededly illegal presence in this country, and is a direct result of Congress' obviously valid exercise of its "broad constitutional powers" in the field of immigration and naturalization. U.S. Const., Art. I, §8, cl. 4. This Court has recognized that in allocating governmental benefits to a given class of aliens, one "may take into account the character of the relationship between the alien and this country." Mathews v. Diaz. When that "relationship" is a federally-prohibited one, there can, of course, be no presumption that a State has a constitutional duty to include illegal aliens among the recipients of its governmental benefits.

2

The second strand of the Court's analysis rests on the premise that, although public education is not a constitutionally-guaranteed right, "neither is it merely some governmental 'benefit' indistinguishable from other forms of social welfare legislation." Whatever meaning or relevance this opaque observation might have in some or other contexts, it simply has no bearing on the issues at hand. Indeed, it is never made clear what the Court's opinion means on this score. The importance of education is beyond dispute. Yet we have held repeatedly that the importance of a governmental service does not elevate it to the status of a "fundamental right" for purposes of equal protection analysis. In *Rodriguez*, supra, Justice Powell, speaking for the Court, expressly rejected the proposition that state laws dealing with public education are subject to special scrutiny under the Equal Protection Clause. Moreover, the Court points to no meaningful way to distinguish between education and other governmental benefits in this context. Is the Court suggesting that education is more "fundamental" than food, shelter, or medical care? . . .

B

Once it is conceded—as the Court does—that illegal aliens are not a suspect class, and that education is not a fundamental right, our inquiry should focus on and be limited to whether the legislative classification at issue bears a rational relationship to a legitimate state purpose.

The State contends primarily that §21.031 serves to prevent undue depletion of its limited revenues available for education, and to preserve the fiscal integrity of the State's school financing system against an ever-increasing flood of illegal aliens—aliens over whose entry or continued presence it has no control. Of course such fiscal concerns alone could not justify discrimination against a group of persons. Yet I assume no member of this Court would argue that prudent conservation of finite state revenues is per se an illegitimate goal. Indeed, the numerous classifications this Court has sustained in social welfare legislation were invariably related to the limited amount of revenues available to spend on any given program or set of programs. See, e.g., Jefferson v. Hackney, 406 U.S. 535, 549-51 (1972); Dandridge v. Williams. The significant question here is whether the requirement of tuition from illegal aliens who attend the public schools—as well as from residents of other States, for example—is a rational and reasonable means of furthering the State's legitimate fiscal ends.

Without laboring what will undoubtedly seem obvious to many, it simply is not "irrational" for a State to conclude that it does not have the same responsibility to provide benefits for persons whose very presence in the State and this country is illegal as it does to provide for persons lawfully present. By definition, illegal aliens have no right whatever to be here, and the State may reasonably, and constitutionally, elect not to provide them with governmental services at the expense of those who are lawfully in the State. In DeCanas v. Bica, 424 U.S. 351, 357 (1976), we held that a State may protect its "fiscal interests and lawfully resident labor force from the deleterious effects on its economy resulting from the employment of illegal aliens." And only recently this Court made clear that a State has a legitimate interest in protecting and preserving the quality of its schools and "the right of its own *bona fide* residents to attend such institutions on a preferential tuition basis." Vlandis v. Kline, 412 U.S. 441, 452-453 (1973) (emphasis added). The Court has failed to offer even a plausible explanation why illegality of residence in this country is not a factor that may legitimately bear upon the bona fides of state residence and entitlement to the benefits of lawful residence.

DISCUSSION

1. What is the value of education? Both Marshall's dissenting opinion in *Rodriguez* and Brennan's opinion in *Plyler* assume that education is an extremely important, indeed constitutionally protected, interest. What is it about education that makes it so important, however? Consider two possibilities:

a. Some education is necessary in order to make one a functioning citizen of a republican political order; i.e., one must know how to read and to analyze political arguments. It is also a good idea to have a sense of the history of the American nation and an appreciation of American culture in order to become a functioning member of that order. This vision is captured by Amy Gutmann's comment that "[a] democratic state . . . must take the steps that it can to avoid those inequalities in educational attainment that deprive children of an intellectual ability adequate to enable them to participate in the democratic political processes that socially structure individual choices."[15]

b. An education is important because it provides the knowledge and skill base with which to get a job and support oneself in a market-oriented society. From this perspective, the most important courses are not, say, American history, literature, or civics, but, rather, computer science and statistics. Ideally, a student should take both kinds of courses, but if choices have to made with regard to funding, required courses, and the like, they should always be made in terms of what will best prepare a student for gainful appointment (and thus to minimize the probability that the students will later turn out to make claims for public assistance).

Which of these two visions seems to feature in the Marshall and Brennan opinions? Is one more entrenched in the Constitution than the other?

NOTE: ON THE ENFORCEABILITY OF "POSITIVE RIGHTS"

One might object to constitutional rights to minimum levels of assistance on the grounds that they are contrary to the constitutional text or to existing precedents. Professor Frank Cross argues that the best case against judicial recognition of positive rights "does not rest upon moral philosophy [or doctrinal analysis] but relies upon a pragmatic understanding of the operation of government, particularly the judicial system."[16]

> [There are] two significant problems with relying on the courts to enforce positive rights and to promote the interests of the poor. The first problem involves the economics of rights enforcement. . . . The second problem is the politics of rights enforcement. While we espouse an independent judiciary in this nation, the reality is that courts are loathe to displease the elected branches or to tread upon their constitutional turf. An order requiring those branches to fund and to offer economic assistance to the poor is the sort of action that the judiciary is unlikely to make or to enforce.

---

15. Amy Gutmann, Public Education in a Democracy, in Democracy and the Welfare State 112 (Gutmann ed., 1988). See also Amy Gutmann, Democratic Education (2d ed. 1998).

16. Frank Cross, The Error of Positive Rights, 48 UCLA L. Rev. 857 (2001).

> . . . Rights enforcement requires resources. The mere introduction of a positive right into the Constitution may not have much effect unless and until it is fleshed out through litigation. The ability to litigate "depends on ample purses and effective mobilization of legal services, which vary greatly among different classes, groups, and sections of the country." Poor individuals and, to a degree, groups representing the poor may lack the resources to advance effectively the right. . . .
>
> Research supports doubts about the ability of the poor to advance their interests in court. . . . Poor individuals clearly are the least successful litigants before the Court, which bodes ill for their ability to achieve positive rights. . . . [P]ositive rights cases will pit poor individuals against the government. When poor individuals are matched against the federal government in litigation . . . , their prospects of success are minimal.
>
> . . . To some, positive rights are a "horror," because their enforcement raises the spectre of "the courts running everything—raising taxes and deciding how the money should be spent." [But] both the critics and the proponents often misconceive the likely consequences of positive rights recognition, namely that positive rights would not be aggressively enforced.
>
> It is futile to rely on the judiciary to provide basic welfare for the disadvantaged, if the political branches are unwilling to do so. . . . The interaction of the judiciary with the political branches makes the courts reluctant to countermand aggressively the preferences of the legislature and the executive. They may fear that the cooperation of those branches could "be jeopardized by excessively controversial or far-reaching policy decisions." . . .

Although Cross's principal argument is that "recognition of positive rights is likely to be practically trivial, if not meaningless," he also suggests that the consequences of "aggressive enforcement" of positive rights "are highly uncertain. Indeed, there is a high probability that judicial involvement will only make things worse for the beneficiaries of the positive rights," largely because of the complexity of required judgments and the lack of any particular reason to believe that judges will be skilled in making such judgments.

> Suppose an impoverished plaintiff appears before the Court and demands his or her right to government support. How would the Court decide if the individual were impoverished enough to qualify to invoke the right? Should it be an absolute or a relative standard? At what quantitative level should the standard be set? If the plaintiff qualifies under that standard, should the Court enter an order simply directing that this individual (and presumably all others similarly situated) be paid a certain amount of cash monthly or should in-kind services (such as food stamps or housing vouchers) be ordered? Should assistance be nationally uniform or geographically variable? Might the Court consider defenses to the government's constitutional obligations? What if the federal budget were strapped, and a court order would necessitate higher taxes or that money be taken from other programs, such as defense or environmental protection? Would alternative uses of the money be relevant? Could the Court consider the

> possibility that the plaintiff bore some responsibility for his impoverished status? What if he had gambled away a considerable sum of money? What if he had lost his job due to misfeasance? All of these questions are potentially answerable, but they illustrate the complexity of enforcing a positive right. . . . Given these complexities, it is unclear that the judiciary is the best branch for making wise decisions about positive rights. . . .

Cross also notes that there is no guarantee that the judges entrusted with enforcing positive rights will be sympathetic to these rights as ways of improving the condition of the poor.

> Conservative Justices are unlikely to take positive rights to minimal subsistence and interpret them to compel greater government redistribution of income to the poor. . . . [In fact] [a]n activist conservative Court might use that positive right of minimal substance to dismantle the very programs that advocates of positive rights seek to expand. . . .
>
> Ultimately, a defense of positive rights can only come down to a comparative institutional analysis of courts and other branches of government. Because courts could actually make the problem worse, they are not merely a backstop to legislative protection. For positive constitutional rights to make sense, the advocates have to explain why courts would do a better job of providing minimally adequate welfare support than would the legislative and executive branches. The historical record does not offer much support for this position. The Court has been "indifferen[t] to economic inequality" in society. . . .
>
> While one can certainly argue with the sufficiency of prevailing levels of statutory assistance to the poor, the various government entitlement programs in 1996 did provide $700 billion in assistance to various groups deemed deserving. Between 1965 and 1990, social security funding rose from $17 billion to $250 billion, medicare and medicaid spending grew from zero to $150 billion, and programs such as food stamps and AFDC grew from $3 billion to $40 billion. . . .
>
> Proponents of positive rights might still complain that the record of statutory assistance to the poor is insufficient. Perhaps so, but the real issue regarding positive rights is one of institutional comparison. The legislative and executive branches have done a lot more for the poor than have the courts.

DISCUSSION

1. *Polycentric problems.* Are there significant differences in judicial enforcement of positive rights and negative rights? Consider the following argument:[17]

> Generally speaking, it is easier for courts to supervise the regulatory state—the state's creation of crimes, administrative regulations, civil fines

17. Jack M. Balkin, What *Brown* Teaches Us About Constitutional Theory, 90 Va. L. Rev. 1537, 1568-1569 (2004).

and penalties, and civil causes of action — than to supervise the welfare state. Supervising the regulatory state is easier because fewer variables are involved and enforcement generally runs through the courts. Thus courts can protect constitutional rights simply by striking down laws that they believe violate the Constitution and refusing to enforce them thereafter.

Imposing constitutional requirements on the welfare state is usually considerably more difficult, particularly if courts require government officials to spend money to achieve a certain goal such as equal educational opportunity, adequate housing, or minimum levels of subsistence. Achieving these goals requires many complicated tradeoffs. It is often difficult to define or prove when a particular affirmative goal has been met. Government compliance may be hard to monitor, and government officials may have many different ways of dragging their heels and evading a court's constitutional demands. Often different groups of government actors with different political agendas may have to cooperate over long periods of time to make genuine progress, and securing their continuing collective cooperation may prove quite difficult. Reforms may require significant expenditures that cut into the government's budget and drain money away from other valuable government projects and services. Government officials may be unwilling or unable to raise additional revenues and may plead that they lack the funds necessary to carry out the reforms.

Is this distinction necessarily clear-cut? Consider, for example, that the right to vote, the right against self-incrimination and coerced confessions, the right against custodial mistreatment and/or torture, and the Establishment Clause's prohibitions on school prayer also may require the cooperation of public officials; indeed these constitutional norms may be effectively unenforceable without cooperation from the political branches. In addition, many negative rights, for example, the right to use public forums for speech, and the right to vote, are actually positive rights to the extent that they require governments to spend money to make them possible. Finally, consider the extent to which almost every negative liberty requires some expenditure of money or cooperation by political officials to be effectively vindicated. Does this suggest that the distinctions between positive and negative liberties are matters of degree rather than kind? Even if so, does it demonstrate that they are equally enforceable by courts?

2. *Statutory versus constitutional entitlements.* Professor Cross notes that statutes often contain positive entitlements. Thus, he notes that "[t]here is an indisputable statutory right to receive payments under the Earned Income Tax Credit, for example, assuming one meets the statutory conditions and at least until its statutory authority is revoked." If so, what distinguishes the ability of courts to enforce statutory versus constitutional entitlements, at least if one's concerns are principally those set out by Cross?

3. *Aspirational provisions and underenforced constitutional norms.* Suppose one is persuaded by Cross's argument that one ought not to look to judges to enforce positive rights. Nevertheless, one might still argue that the Constitution should be interpreted or amended to include such rights as "aspirations" to goad legislators and executives as to their "constitutional duties" to help the poor, even if that duty is not in fact subject to judicial enforcement in the absence of statutory

entitlements. Professor Larry Sager famously suggested that judicial protections for the poor were part of the underenforced norms of the Due Process and Equal Protection Clauses, which it was the job of legislatures to enforce.[18] And several constitutions, including those of Ireland and India, have social rights provisions that operate only as aspirations—or directives to legislators—insofar as they explicitly prohibit judicial enforcement of these provisions. What are the strengths and weaknesses of such an approach? Does it depend on whether legislatures take their constitutional obligations seriously? Does it let legislatures off the hook too easily, or, to the contrary, does it give them incentives to reason and talk directly about constitutional values when they consider the questions of poverty and social welfare?

Professor Cass Sunstein has suggested the passage of a "Second Bill of Rights" of the following form:[19]

> Section 1. Every citizen has the right to a good education.
> Section 2. Every citizen has the right to adequate protection in the event of extreme need stemming from illness, accident, old age, or unemployment.
> Section 3. Every citizen has the right of access to adequate food, shelter, clothing, and health care.
> Section 4. Every citizen has the right to a chance at remunerative employment.
> Section 5. Every citizen has the right to freedom from unfair competition and domination by monopolies at home or abroad.
> Section 6. Congress and state governments must take reasonable legislative and other measures, within available resources, to achieve the realization of these rights.

Such an amendment would serve, Sunstein argues, as at least a "constitutive commitment" binding upon legislators who, after all, take an oath of constitutional fidelity, even if one concludes, as may be suggested by Section 6, that there should be little or no judicial enforcement.

Would you support the passage of an amendment of this sort, knowing it to be aspirational? Would it alter the way that courts and legislatures approached other constitutional provisions? Would this be a good or a bad thing?

4. The South African constitution is probably the most notable example in the world today of a constitution with ostensibly strong guarantees of positive rights that are judicially enforceable. Consider only the following sections from that constitution:

> 26. (1) Everyone has the right to have access to adequate housing.
>
> (2) The state must take reasonable legislative and other measures, within its available resources, to achieve the progressive realisation of this right. . . .

---

18. Lawrence Gene Sager, Fair Measure: The Legal Status of Underenforced Constitutional Norms, 91 Harv. L. Rev. 1212 (1978). See also Charles L. Black, Jr., Further Reflections on the Constitutional Justice of Livelihood, 86 Colum. L. Rev. 1103 (1986) (arguing that Congress has constitutional duty to provide for "the common defence" and "promote the general welfare").

19. Cass R. Sunstein, The Second Bill of Rights, FDR's Unfinished Revolution and Why We Need It More Than Ever 183 (2004).

27. (1) Everyone has the right to have access to—

a. health care services, including reproductive health care;

b. sufficient food and water; and

c. social security, including, if they are unable to support themselves and their dependents, appropriate social assistance.

(2) The state must take reasonable legislative and other measures, within its available resources, to achieve the progressive realisation of each of these rights.

(3) No one may be refused emergency medical treatment.

28. (1) Every child has the right—

c. . . . to basic nutrition, shelter, basic health care services, and social services. . . .

29. (1) Everyone has the right—

a. to a basic education, including adult basic education; and

b. to further education, which the state must take reasonable measures to make progressively available and accessible. . . .

One might wonder how the now 20-year history of implementation of the South African constitution accords with Cross's deep skepticism about positive rights. An interesting example is Government of the Republic of South Africa v. Grootboom, 11 BCLA 1169 (CC) (2000), a case brought under section 26, in which plaintiffs invoked the right to housing. The Constitutional Court held that the government had indeed been derelict in its constitutional duties, but held that the appropriate remedy was simply that the government had an obligation to "establish a coherent public housing programme directed towards the progressive realisation of the right of access to adequate housing within the State's available means." The South African Constitutional Court did not hold that the government would have to provide a "minimum core" level of housing, nor did it require that any specific amount be appropriated for housing in the government's budget. It simply stated that "a reasonable part of the national housing budget [must] be devoted to [providing housing to those in desperate need], but the precise allocation is for national government to decide in the first instance." As a result of this holding, the actual plaintiffs in *Grootboom* received no specific remedy addressing their individual lack of adequate housing. Might courts play a useful role in forcing certain issues on the legislative agenda even if, as a matter of prudence, they decline to order specific remedies?[20]

One need not necessarily look abroad, however, for useful information about the judicial enforcement of positive rights. As a matter of fact, all of the 50 state constitutions guarantee at least some provision of public education. Emily Zackin has emphasized that it is simply a mistake to identify the "American constitutional tradition" only with so-called negative rights. As Professor Zackin conclusively demonstrates,[21] *all* American states include at least *some* positive rights, the most

---

20. For a discussion, see Cass R. Sunstein, Social and Economic Rights: Lessons from South Africa, 11 Forum Constitutionnel 123-132 (2000/2001).

21. Emily Zackin, Looking for Rights in All the Wrong Places: Why State Constitutions Contain America's Positive Rights (2013).

important by far involving rights to be provided some kind of education by the state. There is nothing particularly "new" about such rights. The 1780 Massachusetts constitution, drafted largely by John Adams and still in operation, included the following provision:

> Wisdom and knowledge, as well as virtue, diffused generally among the body of the people, being necessary for the preservation of their rights and liberties; and as these depend on spreading the opportunities and advantages of education in the various parts of the country, and among the different orders of the people, it shall be the duty of legislatures and magistrates, in all future periods of this commonwealth, to cherish the interests of literature and the sciences, and all seminaries of them; especially the university at Cambridge, public schools and grammar schools in the towns; to encourage private societies and public institutions, rewards and immunities, for the promotion of agriculture, arts, sciences, commerce, trades, manufactures, and a natural history of the country; to countenance and inculcate the principles of humanity and general benevolence, public and private charity, industry and frugality, honesty and punctuality in their dealings; sincerity, good humor, and all social affections, and generous sentiments, among the people.

Thus, as a practical matter, San Antonio Board of Education v. Rodriguez has turned out to be less important than expected, because proponents of educational equality could pursue claims under their respective state constitutions, often with quite dramatic results.[22] There is also an extensive literature about the ways that the states, acting as "laboratories of experimentation," could devise various ways of funding or otherwise carrying out their duties to provide public education.[23] Thus, to understand the right of education in the United States, one must play close attention to the panoply of state cases interpreting state constitutions. This is especially true of Texas itself, where the *Rodriguez* litigation was originally brought. Extensive litigation carried on over the quarter-century has led to significant intervention by the Texas Supreme Court, based on the Texas constitution, and responsive legislation passed by the Texas legislature.[24]

The Supreme Court's decision in *Rodriguez* was, however, important for three reasons. First, one of the most important issues in education lawsuits is sources of equitable funding. In many states, education is funded by local property taxes, a

---

22. See, e.g., Sanford Levinson, Courts as Participants in "Dialogue": A View from American States, 59 Kan. L. Rev. 791 (2011). See also Jeffrey S. Sutton, San Antonio Independent School District v. Rodriguez and Its Aftermath, 94 Va. L. Rev. 1963 (2008).

23. See, e.g. Scott R. Bauries, State Constitutions and Individual Rights: Conceptual Convergence in School Finance Litigation, 18 Geo. Mason L. Rev. 301 (2011); Douglas S. Reed, On Equal Terms: The Constitutional Politics of Educational Opportunity (2001); Michael Paris, Framing Equal Opportunity: Law and the Politics of School Finance Reform (2010); Michael A. Rebell, Courts and Kids: Pursuing Educational Equity Through the State Courts (2009).

24. See, e.g., Richard Shragger, San Antonio v. Rodriguez and the Legal Geography of School Finance Reform, in Civil Rights Stories 85 (Myriam E. Gilles & Risa L. Goluboff eds., 2008).

structural choice that often preserves or enhances inequality of funding. In proposing constitutional remedies, state courts are often limited because they cannot alter the funding requirements set forth in state constitutions; but federal courts imposing federal constitutional duties can. By way of comparison, in reapportionment cases, federal courts were able to require significant restructuring of state representational schemes—including the reorganization of state senates. Second, *Rodriguez* was important because it prevented the development of a common set of constitutional norms for educational equity. This might be a good or a bad thing, depending on your views about the advantages of local experimentation. Third, *Rodriguez* was important because it seemed to shut the door on further experimentation with constitutional welfare rights generally, even outside of the context of education policy.

E. Does the State Have a "Duty to Rescue"?

DeShaney v. Winnebago County Department of Social Services

489 U.S. 189 (1989)

[Joshua DeShaney, born in 1979, had been placed in the custody of his father, Randy, following the divorce of Joshua's parents. In January 1982, the Winnebago (Wisconsin) County Department of Social Services (DSS) was notified by Joshua's stepmother, who at the time sought a divorce from Randy, that Randy had abused Joshua. The DSS interviewed Randy, who denied the accusations. In January 1983, Joshua was admitted to a hospital; his multiple bruises and abrasions led the examining physician to notify the DSS of potential child abuse. At the insistence of the DSS, a Wisconsin juvenile court placed Joshua in the temporary custody of the hospital. A "Child Protection Team" then considered Joshua's situation and decided that there was insufficient evidence of abuse to justify retaining custody over Joshua. It did, however, recommend, among other things, that Randy receive counseling. A month later Joshua was again taken to a hospital emergency room with "suspicious" injuries, but the DSS caseworker decided that there was no cause for further action. Over the next six months the caseworker made monthly visits to the DeShaney home, during which "she observed a number of suspicious injuries on Joshua's head." "The caseworker dutifully recorded . . . her continuing suspicion that someone in the DeShaney household was physically abusing Joshua, but she did nothing more." In November 1983, Joshua was treated yet again for injuries believed to be the result of child abuse. "On the caseworker's next two visits to the DeShaney home, she was told that Joshua was too ill to see her. Still DSS took no action."

Five months later, in March 1984, "Randy DeShaney beat . . . Joshua so severely that he fell into a life-threatening coma." He "did not die, but he suffered brain damage so severe that he is expected to spend the rest of his life confined to an institution for the profoundly retarded." Randy was subsequently tried and convicted of child abuse.

Joshua, through his mother, claimed that the DSS had deprived him of his Fourteenth Amendment rights to liberty by its failure to protect him "against a risk of violence at his father's hands of which they knew or should have known."]

Rehnquist, C.J. . . .

[P]etitioners do not claim that the State denied Joshua protection without according him appropriate procedural safeguards, but that it was categorically obligated to protect him in these circumstances.

But nothing in the language of the Due Process Clause itself requires the State to protect the life, liberty, and property of its citizens against invasion by private actors. The Clause is phrased as a limitation on the State's power to act, not as a guarantee of certain minimal levels of safety and security. . . . Its purpose was to protect the people from the State, not to ensure that the State protected them from each other. The Framers were content to leave the extent of governmental obligation in the latter area to the democratic political processes.

Consistent with these principles, our cases have recognized that the Due Process Clauses generally confer no affirmative right to governmental aid, even where such aid may be necessary to secure life, liberty, or property interests of which the government itself may not deprive the individual. See, e.g., Harris v. McRae, 448 U.S. 297 (1980) (no obligation to fund abortions or other medical services) (discussing Due Process Clause of Fifth Amendment); Lindsey v. Normet (no obligation to provide adequate housing) (discussing Due Process Clause of Fourteenth Amendment); see also Youngsberg v. Romeo, 457 U.S. 307, 317 (1982) ("As a general matter, a State is under no constitutional duty to provide substantive services for those within its border"). As we said in Harris v. McRae, "[a]lthough the liberty protected by the Due Process Clause affords protection against unwarranted government interference, . . . it does not confer an entitlement to such [governmental aid] as may be necessary to realize all the advantages of that freedom." If the Due Process Clause does not require the State to provide its citizens with particular protective services, it follows that the State cannot be held liable under the Clause for injuries that could have been averted had it chosen to provide them.[a] As a general matter, then, we conclude that a State's failure to protect an individual against private violence simply does not constitute a violation of the Due Process Clause.

[The Court also rejected the argument that the State had in effect created a "special relationship" with Joshua through such services as the DSS did in fact provide. It distinguished earlier cases that had found the State obligated to provide certain services to incarcerated prisoners or involuntarily committed mental patients on the ground that] they stand only for the proposition that when the State takes a person into its custody and holds him there against his will, the Constitution imposes upon it a corresponding duty to assume some responsibility for his safety and general well-being. The rationale for this principle is simple enough: when the State by the affirmative exercise of its power so restrains an individual's liberty that it renders him unable to care for himself, and at the same time fails to provide for his basic human needs—e.g., food, clothing, shelter, medical care, and reasonable safety—it transgresses the substantive limits on state action set by the Eighth Amendment and the Due Process Clause. See Estelle v. Gamble, 429 U.S. 97 (1976); Youngberg v. Romeo. The affirmative duty to protect arises not from the

---

a. The State may not, of course, selectively deny its protective services to certain disfavored minorities without violating the Equal Protection Clause. But no such argument has been made here.

State's knowledge of the individual's predicament or from its expressions of intent to help him, but from the limitation which it has imposed on his freedom to act on his own behalf. In the substantive due process analysis, it is the State's affirmative act of restraining the individual's freedom to act on his own behalf—through incarceration, institutionalization, or other similar restraint of personal liberty—which is the "deprivation of liberty" triggering the protections of the Due Process Clause, not its failure to act to protect his liberty interests against harms inflicted by other means.

The *Estelle-Youngberg* analysis simply has no applicability in the present case. Petitioners concede that the harms Joshua suffered did not occur while he was in the State's custody, but while he was in the custody of his natural father, who was in no sense a state actor. While the State may have been aware of the dangers that Joshua faced in the free world, it played no part in their creation, nor did it do anything to render him any more vulnerable to them. That the State once took temporary custody of Joshua does not alter the analysis, for when it returned him to his father's custody, it placed him in no worse position than that in which he would have been had it not acted at all; the State does not become the permanent guarantor of an individual's safety by having once offered him shelter. Under these circumstances, the State had no constitutional duty to protect Joshua. . . .

BRENNAN, J., joined by MARSHALL and BLACKMUN, JJ., dissenting.

. . . It may well be . . . that the Due Process Clause as construed by our prior cases creates no general right to basic government services. That, however, is not the question presented here. . . .

The Court's baseline is the absence of positive rights in the Constitution and a concomitant suspicion of any claim that seems to depend on such rights. From this perspective, the DeShaneys' claim is first and foremost about inaction (the failure, here, of respondents to take steps to protect Joshua), and only tangentially about action (the establishment of a state program specifically designed to help children like Joshua). And from this perspective, holding these Wisconsin officials liable—where the only difference between this case and one involving a general claim to protective services is Wisconsin's establishment and operation of a program to protect children—would seem to punish an effort that we should seek to promote.

I would begin from the opposite direction. I would focus first on the action that Wisconsin has taken with respect to Joshua and children like him, rather than on the action that the State failed to take. Such a method is not new to this Court. Both *Estelle* and *Youngberg* began by emphasizing that the States had confined J.W. Gamble to prison and Nicholas Romeo to a psychiatric hospital. This initial action rendered these people helpless to help themselves or to seek help from persons unconnected to the government. Cases from the lower courts also recognize that a State's actions can be decisive in assessing the constitutional significance of subsequent inaction. . . .

Because of the Court's initial fixation on the general principle that the Constitution does not establish positive rights, it is unable to appreciate our recognition in *Estelle* and *Youngberg* that this principle does not hold true in all circumstances. . . . In addition, the Court's exclusive attention to State-imposed restraints of "the individual's freedom to act on his own behalf" suggests that it was the State that rendered

Romeo unable to care for himself, whereas in fact—with an I.Q. of between 8 and 10, and the mental capacity of an 18-month-old child—he had been quite incapable of taking care of himself long before the State stepped into his life. Thus, the fact of hospitalization was critical in *Youngberg* not because it rendered Romeo helpless to help himself, but because it separated him from other sources of aid that, we held, the State was obligated to replace. Unlike the Court, therefore, I am unable to see in *Youngberg* a neat and decisive divide between action and inaction.

. . . Thus, I would read *Youngberg* and *Estelle* to stand for the much more generous proposition that, if a State cuts off private sources of aid and then refuses aid itself, it cannot wash its hands of the harm that results from its inaction. . . .

[After discussing the complex structure established by Wisconsin in regard to child abuse, Justice Brennan wrote:] In these circumstances, a private person, or even a person working in a government agency other than DSS, would doubtless feel that her job was done as soon as she had reported her suspicions of child abuse to DSS. Through its child-welfare program, in other words, the State of Wisconsin has relieved ordinary citizens and governmental bodies other than the Department of any sense of obligation to do anything more than report their suspicions of child abuse to DSS. If DSS ignores or dismisses these suspicions, no one will step in to fill the gap. . . . Conceivably, then, children like Joshua are made worse off by the existence of this program when the persons and entities charged with carrying it out fail to do their jobs.

It simply belies reality, therefore, to contend that the State "stood by and did nothing" with respect to Joshua. Through its child-protection program, the State actively intervened in Joshua's life and, by virtue of this intervention, acquired ever more certain knowledge that Joshua was in grave danger. . . .

My disagreement with the Court arises from its failure to see that inaction can be every bit as abusive of power as action, that oppression can result when a State undertakes a vital duty and then ignores it. Today's opinion construes the Due Process Clause to permit a State to displace private sources of protection and then, at the critical moment, to shrug its shoulders and turn away from the harm that it has promised to try to prevent. Because I cannot agree that our Constitution is indifferent to such indifference, I respectfully dissent.

Blackmun, J., dissenting:

. . . The Court fails to recognize [the state's "fundamental duty to aid the boy" once it "learned of the severe danger to which he was exposed"] because it attempts to draw a sharp and rigid line between action and inaction. But such formalistic reasoning has no place in the interpretation of the broad and stirring Clauses of the Fourteenth Amendment. Indeed, I submit that these Clauses were designed, at least in part, to undo the formalistic legal reasoning that infected antebellum jurisprudence, which the late Professor Robert Cover analyzed so effectively in his significant work entitled Justice Accused (1975). Like the antebellum judges who denied relief to fugitive slaves, the Court today claims that its decision, however harsh, is compelled by existing legal doctrine. On the contrary, the question presented by this case is an open one, and our Fourteenth Amendment precedents may be read more broadly or narrowly depending upon how one chooses to read them. Faced with the choice, I would adopt a "sympathetic" reading, one which comports with dictates of fundamental justice and recognizes that compassion need not be exiled from the province of judging. Cf. A. Stone, Law, Psychiatry, and Morality 262 (1984) ("We will make mistakes if we go forward, but doing nothing can be the worst mistake. What is required of us is moral ambition. Until our composite sketch becomes a true portrait of humanity we must live with our uncertainty; we will grope, we will struggle, and our compassion may be our only guide and comfort").

Poor Joshua! Victim of repeated attacks by an irresponsible, bullying, cowardly, and intemperate father, and abandoned by respondents who placed him in a dangerous predicament and who knew or learned what was going on, and yet did essentially nothing except, as the Court revealingly observes, "dutifully recorded these incidents in [their] files." It is a sad commentary upon American life, and constitutional principles—so full of late of patriotic fervor and proud proclamations about "liberty and justice for all"—that this child, Joshua DeShaney, now is assigned to live out the remainder of his life profoundly retarded. Joshua and his mother, as petitioners here, deserve—but now are denied by this Court—the opportunity to have the facts of their case considered in the light of the constitutional protection that §42 U.S.C. 1983 is meant to provide.

DISCUSSION

1. If states are required to rescue Joshua from child abuse at the hands of his father, are they also required to provide needy children with health care and nutrition, since lack of each also threatens children with irreparable harm? How should Justice Brennan answer this question?

2. Consider the following provisions from the Universal Declaration of Human Rights, adopted by the General Assembly of the United Nations on December 10, 1948:[25]

> Article 23
>
> 1. Everyone has the right to work, to free choice of employment, [and] to just and favourable conditions of work. . . .
>
> 3. Everyone who works has the right to just and favourable remuneration ensuring for himself and his family an existence worthy of human dignity, and supplemented, if necessary, by other means of social protection. . . .
>
> Article 25
>
> 1. Everyone has the right to a standard of living adequate for the health and wellbeing of himself and of his family, including food, clothing, housing and medical care and necessary social services, and the right to security in the event of unemployment, sickness, disability, widowhood, old age or other lack of livelihood in circumstances beyond his control.
>
> 2. Motherhood and childhood are entitled to special care and assistance. All children, whether born in or out of wedlock, shall enjoy the same social protection.

---

25. See Human Rights: A Compilation of International Instruments 1-3 (1983).

> Article 26
> Everyone has the right to education. . . .

Many modern constitutions emulate the aspirations and language of the UDHR. Especially notable in this regard is the South African Constitution of 1994:

> Section 28 Children
> (1) Every child has the right—
> . . . (b) to family care or parental care, or to appropriate alternative care when removed from the family environment;
> (c) to basic nutrition, shelter, basic health care services and social services;
> (d) to be protected from maltreatment, neglect, abuse or degradation;
> (e) to be protected from exploitative labour practices. . . .

Article 29 adds the right to a "basic education."

The Iraqi Constitution of 2005 includes as part of Article 29 "B. The State guarantees the protection of motherhood, childhood and old age and shall care for children and youth and provides them with the appropriate conditions to further their talents and abilities."

If such provisions were part of our Constitution, would they compel a ruling in Joshua's favor?

3. Justice Blackmun's "poor Joshua" opinion has become famous (or notorious) for its invocation of "compassion" as a standard for interpreting the Constitution. And recall the earlier discussion, Chapter 2, supra, of Robert Cover's model of judging within the context of cases involving slavery. To what degree should judges rely on their compassion for the plaintiffs (or for defendants) in deciding what the Constitution means?

4. Castle Rock. In Castle Rock v. Gonzales, 545 U.S. 748 (2005), Jessica Gonzales had obtained a restraining order against her husband in May 1999, which commanded him not to "molest or disturb the peace of [respondent] or of any child," and to remain at least 100 yards from the family home at all times. Violation of the order constituted a criminal offense. The form served on Gonzales included a "Notice to Law Enforcement Officials," which read in part:

> YOU SHALL USE EVERY REASONABLE MEANS TO ENFORCE THIS RESTRAINING ORDER. YOU SHALL ARREST, OR, IF AN ARREST WOULD BE IMPRACTICAL UNDER THE CIRCUMSTANCES, SEEK A WARRANT FOR THE ARREST OF THE RESTRAINED PERSON WHEN YOU HAVE INFORMATION AMOUNTING TO PROBABLE CAUSE THAT THE RESTRAINED PERSON HAS VIOLATED OR ATTEMPTED TO VIOLATE ANY PROVISION OF THIS ORDER AND THE RESTRAINED PERSON HAS BEEN PROPERLY SERVED WITH A COPY OF THIS ORDER OR HAS RECEIVED ACTUAL NOTICE OF THE EXISTENCE OF THIS ORDER.

Her husband took their three daughters without warning. Ms. Gonzales called the Castle Rock Police Department and showed them a copy of the restraining order, requesting that it be enforced and that her children be returned to her immediately. The officers repeatedly rebuffed her entreaties for help. At approximately 3:20 A.M., the respondent's husband arrived at the police station and opened fire with a semiautomatic handgun he had purchased earlier that evening. Police shot back, killing him. Inside the cab of his pickup truck, they found the bodies of all three daughters, whom he had already murdered.

Gonzales sued, alleging that the town violated the Due Process Clause because its police department had "an official policy or custom of failing to respond properly to complaints of restraining order violations" and "tolerate[d] the nonenforcement of restraining orders by its police officers." The complaint also alleged that the town's actions "were taken either willfully, recklessly or with such gross negligence as to indicate wanton disregard and deliberate indifference to" respondent's civil rights.

The Court, in a 5-4 opinion, held that Gonzales did not state a claim under the Due Process Clause. Justice Scalia argued that she had no "property interest [or other entitlement] in police enforcement of the restraining order against her husband." "Our cases recognize that a benefit is not a protected entitlement if government officials may grant or deny it in their discretion." Justice Scalia noted that the preprinted notice to law-enforcement personnel that appeared on the back of the order appeared to make it mandatory for police officers to enforce restraining orders and to either arrest or seek a warrant for the arrest of a restrained person. But he argued that the language should not be taken literally: "We do not believe that these provisions of Colorado law truly made enforcement of restraining orders *mandatory*. Whatever mandatory language might exist as to arresting those who violate a restraining order, '[a] well established tradition of police discretion has long coexisted with apparently mandatory arrest statutes.' . . . [A] true mandate of police action would require some stronger indication from the Colorado Legislature than 'shall use every reasonable means to enforce a restraining order' (or even 'shall arrest . . . or . . . seek a warrant'). . . . The practical necessity for discretion is particularly apparent in a case such as this one, where the suspected violator is not actually present and his whereabouts are unknown. . . .

"[I]t is by no means clear that an individual entitlement to enforcement of a restraining order could constitute a 'property' interest for purposes of the Due Process Clause. Such a right would not, of course, resemble any traditional conception of property. . . . [T]he right to have a restraining order enforced does not 'have some ascertainable monetary value'. . . . Perhaps most radically, the alleged property interest here arises *incidentally*, not out of some new species of government benefit or service, but out of a function that government actors have always performed—to wit, arresting people who they have probable cause to believe have committed a criminal offense.

". . . We conclude, therefore, that respondent did not, for purposes of the Due Process Clause, have a property interest in police enforcement of the restraining order against her husband. It is accordingly unnecessary to address the Court of Appeals' determination that the town's custom or policy prevented the police from giving her due process when they deprived her of that alleged interest. . . . [T]he benefit that a third party may receive from having someone else arrested for a crime generally does not trigger protections under the Due Process Clause, neither in its procedural nor in its 'substantive' manifestations. This result reflects our continuing reluctance to treat the Fourteenth Amendment as 'a font of tort law,' but it does not mean States are powerless to provide victims with personally enforceable remedies. . . ."

Justice Souter concurred, joined by Justice Breyer.

Justice Stevens, joined by Justice Ginsburg, dissented: "Police enforcement of a restraining order is a government service that is no less concrete and no less valuable than other government services, such as education. . . . In this case, Colorado law *guaranteed* the provision of a certain service, in certain defined circumstances, to a certain class of beneficiaries, and respondent reasonably relied on that guarantee. . . . Surely, if respondent had contracted with a private security firm to provide her and her daughters with protection from her husband, it would be apparent that she possessed a property interest in such a contract. Here, Colorado undertook a comparable obligation, and respondent—with restraining order in hand—justifiably relied on that undertaking. Respondent's claim of entitlement to this promised service is no less legitimate than the other claims our cases have upheld, and no less concrete than a hypothetical agreement with a private firm. The fact that [respondent's claim of entitlement] is based on a statutory enactment and a judicial order entered for her special protection, rather than on a formal contract, does not provide a principled basis for refusing to consider it 'property' worthy of constitutional protection."

NOTE: STATE ACTION IN THE AGE OF THE WELFARE STATE

One might paraphrase Chief Justice Rehnquist's analysis in *DeShaney* as follows: The Constitution prohibits the state from depriving individuals, without due process of law, of whatever preexisting rights to life, liberty, or property they might have; but it does not require the State to provide anyone with resources, save for such "special circumstances" as where it confines individuals in a way that prevents them from being responsible for their own welfare. That is, "state action" must be present. Justice Brennan in effect found such state action in the consequences for others of the existence of the Wisconsin child welfare agency. Thus, he suggests, the state agency's intervention in situations like Joshua's may obviate others' concern for his welfare that would otherwise exist.

Moreover, we saw the suggestion, intended or not, in Justice Stewart's dissenting opinion in *Kras*, that one's economic status is in fact a function of state action insofar as it is the state's passage of laws criminalizing theft or requiring the repayment of debts that accounts for the level of one's resources in the world. (Compare Shelley v. Kraemer, 334 U.S. 1 (1948), in which the Court held that state judicial enforcement of racially restrictive covenants violated the Fourteenth Amendment.) Not surprisingly, the modern welfare state has brought with it a spate of state-action cases especially insofar as that state includes, very often, the payment or reimbursement for services provided to individuals covered by welfare programs. Under what circumstances does the receipt of such funds bind a putatively private entity to constitutional constraints? In Rendell-Baker v. Kohn, 457 U.S. 830 (1982), teachers employed by a private school claimed that its director violated the Due Process Clause when he dismissed them without a hearing. Ninety percent of the school's funds came from the state's payment of tuition for students referred to the school by local school boards or from other state and federal agencies. Similarly, in Blum

v. Yaretsky, 457 U.S. 991 (1982), a patient in a New York nursing home funded under Medicaid complained about the procedures by which he was determined to require a lower level of medical services than he desired. The Supreme Court refused to find state action in either case.

In *Rendell-Baker*, Chief Justice Burger, for a six-Justice majority, rejected the argument that the level of dependence on state funds subjected the school to the First and Fourteenth Amendments. "The school, like the nursing homes [in *Blum*,] is not fundamentally different from many private corporations whose business depends primarily on contracts to build roads, bridges, dams, ships, or submarines for the government. Acts of such private contractors do not become acts of their government by reason of their significant or even total engagement in performing public contracts." The Court went on to cite Polk County v. Dodson, 454 U.S. 312 (1981), which had declined to hold that a state public defender's activities vis-à-vis her client implicated the state. Justice Marshall, joined by Justice Brennan, dissented.

The Justices' lineup was identical in *Blum*; they focused here on the private decisionmakers' independence from state coercion: "[O]ur precedents indicate that a State normally can be held responsible for a private decision only when it has exercised coercive power or has provided such significant encouragement, either overt or covert, that the choice must in law be deemed to be that of the State." Although New York did require physicians to classify patients based on a computed "score" of their need for services, the physicians retained the ultimate judgment to authorize nursing home care even if the patient had a "low score": "These decisions ultimately turn on medical judgments made by private parties according to professional standards that are not established by the State."

The Court addressed similar issues in American Manufacturers Mutual Insurance Company v. Sullivan, 526 U.S. 40 (1999), which involved the administration of Pennsylvania's system of workers' compensation. Generally speaking, once a work-related injury is claimed to have occurred, the employer or its insurer is obligated to pay for all "reasonable" and "necessary" medical treatment within 30 days of receiving a bill. In 1993, Pennsylvania amended its system to create a "utilization review" procedure by which the reasonableness and necessity of an employee's medical treatment, whether past, ongoing, or prospective, could be reviewed prior to payment. Should an insurer wish to dispute "the reasonableness or necessity of the treatment provided," it may, within 30 days, request utilization review by filing with the Pennsylvania Workers' Compensation Bureau a notice to that effect.

The only function of the Bureau is to determine whether the form is "properly completed—i.e., that all information required by the form is provided." Once the request has been properly filed, the insurer is allowed to withhold payments to health care providers for the particular services being challenged. In the meantime, the Bureau notifies the relevant parties that utilization review has been requested and forwards the request to a randomly selected "utilization review organization" (URO), a private organization composed of health care providers who are "licensed in the same profession and hav[e] the same or similar specialty as that of the provider of the treatment under review." The URO determines "whether the treatment under review is reasonable or necessary for the medical condition of the employee" in light of "generally accepted treatment protocols." A number of affected employees and organizations representing them claimed that the procedures denied them due process of law. The first question, of course, was whether the relevant organizations implicated the state sufficiently to trigger any constitutional guarantees. Chief Justice Rehnquist, writing for a unanimous Court (on this point), held that no such state action was present:

> [I]n cases involving extensive state regulation of private activity, we have consistently held that "[t]he mere fact that a business is subject to state regulation does not by itself convert its action into that of the State for purposes of the Fourteenth Amendment." Faithful application of the state-action requirement in these cases ensures that the prerogative of regulating private business remains with the States and the representative branches, not the courts. Thus, the private insurers in this case will not be held to constitutional standards unless "there is a sufficiently close nexus between the State and the challenged action of the regulated entity so that the latter may be fairly treated as that of the State itself." Whether such a "close nexus" exists, our cases state, depends on whether the State "has exercised coercive power or has provided such significant encouragement, either overt or covert, that the choice must in law be deemed to be that of the State." Action taken by private entities with the mere approval or acquiescence of the State is not state action.
>
> Here, respondents do not assert that the decision to invoke utilization review should be attributed to the State because the State compels or is directly involved in that decision. Obviously the State is not so involved. It authorizes, but does not require, insurers to withhold payments for disputed medical treatment. The decision to withhold payment, like the decision to transfer Medicaid patients to a lower level of care in *Blum*, is made by concededly private parties, and "turns on . . . judgments made by private parties" without "standards . . . established by the State." Respondents do assert, however, that the decision to withhold payment to providers may be fairly attributable to the State because the State has "authorized" and "encouraged" it. Respondents' primary argument in this regard is that, in amending the Act to provide for utilization review and to grant insurers an option they previously did not have, the State purposely "encouraged" insurers to withhold payments for disputed medical treatment. This argument reads too much into the State's reform, and in any event cannot be squared with our cases.
>
> We do not doubt that the State's decision to provide insurers the option of deferring payment for unnecessary and unreasonable treatment pending review can in some sense be seen as encouraging them to do just that. But, as petitioners note, this kind of subtle encouragement is no more significant than that which inheres in the State's creation or modification of any legal remedy. . . .
>
> The State's decision to allow insurers to withhold payments pending review can just as easily be seen as state inaction, or more accurately, a legislative decision not to intervene in a dispute between an insurer and an employee over whether a particular treatment is reasonable and necessary. Before the 1993 amendments, Pennsylvania restricted the ability of an insurer (after liability had been established, of course) to defer workers'

compensation medical benefits, including payment for unreasonable and unnecessary treatment, beyond 30 days of receipt of the bill. The 1993 amendments, in effect, restored to insurers the narrow option, historically exercised by employers and insurers before the adoption of Pennsylvania's workers' compensation law, to defer payment of a bill until it is substantiated. The most that can be said of the statutory scheme, therefore, is that whereas it previously prohibited insurers from withholding payment for disputed medical services, it no longer does so. Such permission of a private choice cannot support a finding of state action. . . .

Nor does the State's role in creating, supervising, and setting standards for the URO process differ in any meaningful sense from the creation and administration of any forum for resolving disputes. While the decision of a URO, like that of any judicial official, may properly be considered state action, a private party's mere use of the State's dispute resolution machinery, without the "overt, significant assistance of state officials," cannot. The State, in the course of administering a many-faceted remedial system, has shifted one facet from favoring the employees to favoring the employer. This sort of decision occurs regularly in legislative review of such systems. But it cannot be said that such a change "encourages" or "authorizes" the insurer's actions as those terms are used in our state-action jurisprudence.

We also reject the notion, relied upon by the Court of Appeals, that the challenged decisions are state action because insurers must first obtain "authorization" or "permission" from the Bureau before withholding payment. . . . [T]he Bureau's participation is limited to requiring insurers to file "a form prescribed by the Bureau," processing the request for technical compliance, and then forwarding the matter to a URO and informing the parties that utilization review has been requested. In *Blum*, we rejected the notion that the State, "by requiring completion of a form," is responsible for the private party's decision. The additional "paper shuffling" performed by the Bureau here in response to an insurers' request does not alter that conclusion.

Respondents next contend that state action is present because the State has delegated to insurers "powers traditionally exclusively reserved to the State." Their argument here is twofold. Relying on West v. Atkins, 487 U.S. 42 (1988), respondents first argue that workers' compensation benefits are state-mandated "public benefits," and that the State has delegated the provision of these "public benefits" to private insurers. They also contend that the State has delegated to insurers the traditionally exclusive government function of determining whether and under what circumstances an injured worker's medical benefits may be suspended. The Court of Appeals apparently agreed on both points, stating that insurers "providing public benefits which honor State entitlements . . . become an arm of the State, fulfilling a uniquely governmental obligation," and that "[t]he right to invoke the supersedeas, or to stop payments, is a power that traditionally was held in the hands of the State."

We think neither argument has merit. *West* is readily distinguishable: there the State was constitutionally obligated to provide medical treatment to injured inmates, and the delegation of that traditionally exclusive

> public function to a private physician gave rise to a finding of state action. Here, on the other hand, nothing in Pennsylvania's constitution or statutory scheme obligates the State to provide either medical treatment or workers' compensation benefits to injured workers. Instead, the State's workers' compensation law imposes that obligation on employers. . . .

Even if one believes that state action doctrine is, as Charles Black once said, "a conceptual disaster area," it is clear that the Court remains strongly committed to the concept and that, as a practical matter, it seems unwilling to find state action where the government makes use of private agencies to administer its welfare programs.

II. THE PROCEDURAL DUE PROCESS PROTECTION OF ENTITLEMENTS AND OTHER NONTRADITIONAL PROPERTY AND LIBERTY INTERESTS: THE BASIC DOCTRINE [ONLINE]

III. THE WELFARE STATE AND BURDENS ON INTERSTATE MOBILITY [ONLINE]

IV. CONDITIONING SPENDING IN THE WELFARE STATE—THE PROBLEM OF UNCONSTITUTIONAL CONDITIONS [ONLINE]

Table of Justices

Year	President	Chief (1)	2	3	4	5	6	7	8	9
1789	George Washington (1789-1797)	John Jay (1789-1795)	John Rutledge (1789-1791)	William Cushing (1789-1810)	James Wilson (1789-1798)	John Blair (1789-1795)				
1790							James Iredell (1790-1799)			
•			Thomas Johnson (1791-1793)							
•										
•			William Paterson (1793-1806)							
•										
1795		John Rutledge (1795)								
•		Oliver Ellsworth (1796-1800)				Samuel Chase (1796-1811)				
•	John Adams (1797-1801)									
•					Bushrod Washington (1798-1829)					
•							Alfred Moore (1799-1804)			
1800										

Year	President	Chief (1)	2	3	4	5	6	7	8	9
•	Thomas Jefferson (1801-1809)	John Marshall (1801-1835) (appointed by Adams)								
•										
•										
•							William Johnson (1804-1834)			
1805										
•			H. Brockholst Livingston (1806-1823)							
•								Thomas Todd (1807-1826)		
•										
•	James Madison (1809-1817)									
1810										
•				Joseph Story (1811-1845)		Gabriel Duvall (1811-1835)				
•										
•										
•										
1815										

Year	President	Chief (1)	2	3	4	5	6	7	8	9
•										
•	James Monroe (1817-1825)									
•										
•										
1820										
•										
•										
•			Smith Thompson (1823-1843)							
•										
1825	John Quincy Adams (1825-1829)									
•								Robert Trimble (1826-1828)		
•										
•										
•	Andrew Jackson (1829-1837)							John McLean (1829-1861)		
1830					Henry Baldwin (1830-1844)					
•										
•										

Year	President	Chief (1)	2	3	4	5	6	7	8	9
•										
•										
1835							James M. Wayne (1835-1867)			
•		Roger B. Taney (1836-1864)			Philip P. Barbour (1836-1841)					
•	Martin Van Buren (1837-1841)								John Catron (1837-1865)	John McKinley (1837-1852)
•										
•										
1840										
•	William Henry Harrison (1841) John Tyler (1841-1845)					Peter V. Daniel (1841-1860) (appointed by Van Buren)				
•										
•										
•										
1845	James K. Polk (1845-1849)		Samuel Nelson (1845-1872) (appointed by Tyler)	Levi Woodbury (1845-1851)						
•					Robert C. Grier (1846-1870)					

Year	President	Chief (1)	2	3	4	5	6	7	8	9
•										
•										
•	Zachary Taylor (1849-1850)									
1850	Millard Fillmore (1850-1853)									
•				Benjamin R. Curtis (1851-1857)						
•										
•	Franklin Pierce (1853-1857)									John A. Campbell (1853-1861)
•										
1855										
•										
•	James Buchanan (1857-1861)									
•				Nathan Clifford (1858-1881)						
•										
1860										
•	Abraham Lincoln (1861-1865)									

Year	President	Chief (1)	2	3	4	5	6	7	8	9
•						Samuel F. Miller (1862-1890)		Noah H. Swayne (1862-1881)		David Davis (1862-1877)
•									Stephen J. Field[1] (1863-1897) (held tenth seat)	
•		Salmon P. Chase (1864-1873)								
1865	Andrew Johnson (1865-1869)									
•[2]										
•										
•										
•	Ulysses S. Grant (1869-1877)									
1870					William Strong (1870-1880)	Joseph P. Bradley (1870-1892)				
•										
•			Ward Hunt (1872-1882)							
•										

1. Congress established a tenth seat in 1863, to which Stephen J. Field was appointed.

2. Congress reduced the size of the Court to six justices in 1866. As a result, the seats of Justices Catron and Wayne remained unfilled after their deaths in 1865 and 1867. Congress restored the Court to nine seats in 1869.

Year	President	Chief (1)	2	3	4	5	6	7	8	9
•		Morrison Waite (1874-1888)								
1875										
•										
•	Rutherford B. Hayes (1877-1881)									John Marshall Harlan (1877-1911)
•										
•										
1880					William B. Woods (1880-1887)					
•	James A. Garfield (1881) Chester A. Arthur (1881-1885)			Horace Gray (1881-1902) (appointed by Arthur)				Stanley Matthews (1881-1889) (appointed by Garfield)		
•			Samuel Blatchford (1882-1893)							
•										
•										
1885	Grover Cleveland (1885-1889)									
•										
•										
•		Melville W. Fuller (1888-1910)			Lucius Q.C. Lamar (1888-1893)					

Year	President	Chief (1)	2	3	4	5	6	7	8	9
•	Benjamin Harrison (1889-1893)							David J. Brewer (1889-1910)		
1890						Henry B. Brown (1890-1906)				
•										
•							George Shiras (1892-1903)			
•	Grover Cleveland (1893-1897)				Howell E. Jackson (1893-1895) (appointed by Harrison)					
•			Edward D. White (1894-1910)							
1895					Rufus W. Peckham (1895-1909)					
•										
•	William McKinley (1897-1901)									
•									Joseph McKenna (1898-1925)	
•										
1900										
•	Theodore Roosevelt (1901-1909)									

Year	President	Chief (1)	2	3	4	5	6	7	8	9
•				Oliver Wendell Holmes (1902-1932)						
•							William R. Day (1903-1922)			
•										
1905										
•						William H. Moody (1906-1910)				
•										
•	William Howard Taft (1909-1913)				Horace H. Lurton (1909-1914)					
1910		Edward D. White (1910-1921)	Willis Van Devanter (1910-1937)			Joseph R. Lamar (1910-1916)		Charles E. Hughes (1910-1916)		
•										
•										Mahlon Pitney (1912-1922)
•	Woodrow Wilson (1913-1921)									
•					James C. McReynolds (1914-1941)					
1915										

Year	President	Chief (1)	2	3	4	5	6	7	8	9
•						Louis D. Brandeis (1916-1939)		John H. Clarke (1916-1922)		
•										
•										
•										
1920										
•	Warren G. Harding (1921-1923)	William Howard Taft (1921-1930)								
•							Pierce Butler (1922-1939)	George Sutherland (1922-1938)		
•	Calvin Coolidge (1923-1929)									Edward T. Sanford (1923-1930) (appointed by Harding)
•										
1925									Harlan F. Stone (1925-1941)	
•										
•										
•										
•	Herbert Hoover (1929-1933)									

Year	President	Chief (1)	2	3	4	5	6	7	8	9
1930		Charles E. Hughes (1930-1941)								Owen J. Roberts (1930-1945)
•										
•				Benjamin N. Cardozo (1932-1938)						
•	Franklin D. Roosevelt (1933-1945)									
•										
1935										
•										
•			Hugo L. Black (1937-1971)							
•								Stanley F. Reed (1938-1957)		
•				Felix Frankfurter (1939-1962)		William O. Douglas (1939-1975)				
1940							Frank Murphy (1940-1949)			
•		Harlan F. Stone (1941-1946)			James F. Byrnes (1941-1942)				Robert H. Jackson (1941-1954)	
•										

Year	President	Chief (1)	2	3	4	5	6	7	8	9
•					Wiley B. Rutledge (1943-1949)					
•										
1945	Harry S. Truman (1945-1953)									Harold H. Burton (1945-1958)
•		Fred M. Vinson (1946-1953)								
•										
•										
•					Sherman Minton (1949-1956)		Tom C. Clark (1949-1967)			
1950	Dwight D. Eisenhower (1953-1961)									
•										
•										
•		Earl Warren (1953-1969)								
•										
1955									John Marshall Harlan (1955-1971)	
•					William J. Brennan, Jr. (1956-1990)					

Year	President	Chief (1)	2	3	4	5	6	7	8	9
•								Charles E. Whittaker (1957-1962)		
•										Potter Stewart (1958-1981)
•										
1960										
•	John F. Kennedy (1961-1963)									
•				Arthur J. Goldberg (1962-1965)				Byron R. White (1962-1993)		
•	Lyndon B. Johnson (1963-1969)									
•										
1965				Abe Fortas (1965-1969)						
•										
•							Thurgood Marshall (1967-1991)			
•										
•	Richard M. Nixon (1969-1974)	Warren E. Burger (1969-1986)								
1970				Harry A. Blackmun (1970-1994)						

Year	President	Chief (1)	2	3	4	5	6	7	8	9
•										
•			Lewis F. Powell, Jr. (1972-1987)						William H. Rehnquist (1972-1986)	
•										
•	Gerald Ford (1974-1977)									
1975						John Paul Stevens (1975-2010)				
•										
•	Jimmy Carter (1977-1981)									
•										
•										
1980										
•	Ronald Reagan (1981-1989)									Sandra Day O'Connor (1981-2006)
•										
•										
•										
1985										
•		William H. Rehnquist (1986-2005)							Antonin Scalia (1986-2016)	
•										

Year	President	Chief (1)	2	3	4	5	6	7	8	9
•			Anthony M. Kennedy (1988-2018)							
•	George H.W. Bush (1989-1993)									
1990					David H. Souter (1990-2009)					
•							Clarence Thomas (1991-)			
•										
•	William J. Clinton (1993-2001)							Ruth Bader Ginsburg (1993-2020)		
•				Stephen G. Breyer (1994-)						
1995										
•										
•										
•										
•										
•										
2000										
•	George W. Bush (2001-2009)									

Year	President	Chief (1)	2	3	4	5	6	7	8	9
•										
•										
•										
2005		John G. Roberts (2005-)								
•										Samuel A. Alito, Jr. (2006-)
•										
•										
•	Barack Obama (2009-2017)				Sonia Sotomayor (2009-)					
2010						Elena Kagan (2010-)				
•										
•										
•										
•										
•										
2015	Donald J. Trump (2017-2021)								Neil M. Gorsuch (2017-)	

Year	President	Chief (1)	2	3	4	5	6	7	8	9
• • • • •			Brett Kavanaugh (2018-)							
2020								Amy Coney Barrett (2020-)		

Table of Cases

Principal cases are indicated by italics.

Page numbers in bold type refer to electronic-only materials online.

D

I

J

Q

R

Page numbers in bold type refer to electronic-only materials online.

G

H

I

O

S